THE NEW
ENGLISH BIBLE

THE BIBLE

A NEW ENGLISH TRANSLATION

Directed by Representatives of

THE BAPTIST UNION OF GREAT BRITAIN AND IRELAND

THE CHURCH OF ENGLAND

THE CHURCH OF SCOTLAND

THE COUNCIL OF CHURCHES FOR WALES

THE IRISH COUNCIL OF CHURCHES

THE LONDON YEARLY MEETING OF
THE SOCIETY OF FRIENDS

THE METHODIST CHURCH OF GREAT BRITAIN

THE ROMAN CATHOLIC CHURCH IN
ENGLAND AND WALES

THE ROMAN CATHOLIC CHURCH IN IRELAND

THE ROMAN CATHOLIC CHURCH
IN SCOTLAND

THE UNITED REFORMED CHURCH

THE BRITISH AND FOREIGN BIBLE SOCIETY

THE NATIONAL BIBLE SOCIETY OF SCOTLAND

THE NEW ENGLISH BIBLE

NEW YORK
OXFORD UNIVERSITY PRESS

The New Testament
First edition 1961
Second edition 1970
Corrected Impression 1972

The Old Testament
First published 1970
Corrected Impression 1972

Library of Congress Catalogue Card Number: 61-16025

PRINTED IN THE UNITED STATES OF AMERICA

PREFACE

TO THE NEW ENGLISH BIBLE

IN MAY 1946 the General Assembly of the Church of Scotland received an overture from the Presbytery of Stirling and Dunblane, where it had been initiated by the Reverend G. S. Hendry, recommending that a translation of the Bible be made in the language of the present day, inasmuch as the language of the Authorized Version, already archaic when it was made, had now become even more definitely archaic and less generally understood. The General Assembly resolved to make an approach to other Churches, and, as a result, delegates of the Church of England, the Church of Scotland, and the Methodist, Baptist, and Congregational Churches met in conference in October. They recommended that the work should be undertaken; that a completely new translation should be made, rather than a revision, such as had earlier been contemplated by the University Presses of Oxford and Cambridge; and that the translators should be free to employ a contemporary idiom rather than reproduce the traditional 'biblical' English.

In January 1947 a second conference, held like the first in the Central Hall, Westminster, included representatives of the University Presses. At the request of this conference, the Churches named above appointed representatives to form the Joint Committee on the New Translation of the Bible. This Committee met for the first time in July of the same year. By January 1948, when its third meeting was held, invitations to be represented had been sent to the Presbyterian Church of England, the Society of Friends, the Churches in Wales, the Churches in Ireland, the British and Foreign Bible Society, and the National Bible Society of Scotland: these invitations were accepted. At a much later stage the hierarchies of the Roman Catholic Church in England and Scotland accepted an invitation to appoint representatives, and these attended as observers.

The Joint Committee provided for the actual work of translation from the original tongues by appointing three panels, to deal, respectively, with the Old Testament, the Apocrypha, and the New Testament. Their members were scholars drawn from various British universities, whom the Committee believed to be representative of competent biblical scholarship at the present time. Apprehending, however, that sound scholarship does not necessarily carry with it a delicate sense of English style, the Committee appointed a fourth panel, of trusted literary advisers, to whom all the work of the translating panels was to be submitted for scrutiny. It should be said that denominational considerations played no part in the appointment of the panels.

The Joint Committee issued general directions to the panels, in pursuance of the aims which the enterprise had in view. The translating panels adopted the following procedure. An individual was invited to submit a draft translation of a particular book, or group of books. Normally he would be a member of the panel concerned. Very occasionally a draft translation was invited from a scholar outside the panel, who was known to have worked specially on the book in question. The draft was circulated in typescript to members of the panel for their consideration. They then met together and discussed the draft round a table, verse by verse, sentence by sentence. Each member brought his view about the meaning of the original to the judgement of his fellows, and discussion went on until they reached a common mind. There are passages where, in the present state of our knowledge, no one could say with certainty which of two (or even more) possible meanings is intended. In such cases, after careful discussion, alternative meanings have been recorded in footnotes, but only where they seemed of sufficient importance. There is probably no member of a panel who has not found himself obliged to give up, perhaps with lingering regret, a cherished view about the meaning of this or that difficult passage, but in the end the panel accepted corporate responsibility for the interpretation set forth in the translation adopted.

The resultant draft was now remitted to the panel of literary advisers. They scrutinized it, once again, verse by verse, sentence by sentence, and took pains to secure, as best they could, the tone and level of language appropriate to the different kinds of writing to be found in the Bible, whether narrative, familiar discourse, argument, law, rhetoric or poetry. The translation thus amended was returned to the translating panel, who examined it to make sure that the meaning intended had not been in any way misunderstood. Passages of peculiar difficulty might on occasion pass repeatedly between the panels. The final form of the version was reached by agreement between the translators concerned and the literary advisers. It was then ready for submission to the Joint Committee.

Since January 1948 the Joint Committee has met regularly twice a year in the Jerusalem Chamber, Westminster Abbey, with four exceptions during 1954-5 when the Langham Room in the precincts of the Abbey was kindly made available. At these meetings the Committee has received reports on the progress of the work from the Conveners of the four panels, and its members have had in their hands typescripts of the books so far translated and revised. They have made such comments and given such advice or decisions as they judged to be necessary, and from time to time they have met members of the panels in conference.

Of the original members of the panels most have happily been able to stay with the work all through, though some have been lost, through death or otherwise, and their places have been filled by fresh appointments.

The Committee has warmly appreciated the courteous hospitality of the Dean of Westminster and of the Trustees of the Central Hall. We owe a great debt to the support and the experienced counsel of the University Presses of Oxford and Cambridge. We recognize gratefully the service rendered to the enterprise by the Reverend Dr. G. S. Hendry and the Reverend Professor J. K. S. Reid, who have successively held the office of Secretary to the Committee. To those who have borne special responsibility, as Chairmen of the Joint Committee, we owe more than could readily be told. Dr. J. W. Hunkin, Bishop of Truro, our first Chairman, brought to the work an exuberant vigour and initiative without which the formidable project might hardly have got off the ground at all. On his lamented death in 1950 he was succeeded by Dr. A. T. P. Williams, then Bishop of Durham and subsequently Bishop of Winchester, who for eighteen years guided our enterprise with judicious wisdom, tact, and benign firmness, but who to our sorrow died when the end of the task was in sight. To both of these we would put on record the gratitude of the Committee and of all engaged in the enterprise.

If we embarked on mentioning the names of those who have served on the various committees and panels, the list would be a long one; and if we mentioned some and not others, the selection would be an invidious one. There are, nevertheless, three names the omission of which would be utterly wrong. As Vice-Chairman and Director, Dr. C. H. Dodd has from start to finish given outstanding leadership and guidance to the project, bringing to the work scholarship, sensitivity, and an ever watchful eye. Professor Sir Godfrey Driver, Joint Director since 1965, has also brought to the work a wealth of knowledge and wisdom; to his enthusiasm, tenacity of purpose, and unflagging devotion the whole enterprise is greatly indebted. Professor W. D. McHardy, Deputy Director since 1968, has made an invaluable contribution particularly, but by no means exclusively, in the sphere of the Apocrypha. It is right that the names of these three scholars should always be associated with The New English Bible. Our debt to them is incalculably great.

DONALD EBOR:
Chairman of the Joint Committee

CONTENTS

CONTENTS

THE NEW TESTAMENT

x

CONTENTS

CONTENTS

THE
OLD TESTAMENT

INTRODUCTION
TO THE OLD TESTAMENT

THE OLD TESTAMENT as here translated consists of a body of literature spread over a period extending from the twelfth to the second century B.C.; this literature is written in classical Hebrew, except some brief portions which are in Aramaic, a cognate or sister language (Ezra 4. 8—6. 18 and 7. 12-26, Jeremiah 10. 11, Daniel 2. 4—7. 28). No manuscripts of the Old Testament from the earlier part of this period have been preserved; indeed much of it must have been handed down by oral tradition from generation to generation. The impetus to collect, edit and make copies of the national literature may well have come from the disaster of 587/6 B.C., when the Babylonians captured and burnt Jerusalem and carried off many of its inhabitants into exile.

The earliest known Hebrew manuscripts containing any parts of the Old Testament are among the Scrolls (commonly called the Dead Sea Scrolls) found in caves at Qumran near the north-western end of the Dead Sea; they may be dated in the last two centuries B.C., though some may be a little earlier and others somewhat later. They include two copies of Isaiah, one complete and another badly damaged, a commentary containing most of the text of the first two chapters of Habakkuk, and fragments of every other Old Testament book, except Esther. The text which they present is to a large extent identical with that in our Hebrew Bibles.

In the second century A.D. or even earlier the Rabbis, the Jewish religious leaders, compiled a text from such manuscripts as had survived the destruction of Jerusalem in A.D. 70, and on this basis was established the traditional or Massoretic text, so called from the Hebrew word *massorah* 'tradition'. This text incorporated the mistakes of generations of copyists, and, in spite of the care bestowed on it, many errors of later copyists also found their way into it. The earliest surviving manuscripts of this text date from the ninth to eleventh centuries A.D.; and it is this text, as printed in R. Kittel's *Biblia Hebraica* (3rd edition, 1937), which has been used for the present translation.

The traditional text was originally written only in consonants, but in order to preserve what they regarded as the correct pronunciation of the words the Rabbis added vowel-signs to the text. Of the various systems of vowel-signs which were devised, that developed at Tiberias in the fifth to sixth centuries A.D. ultimately prevailed and is still used in our printed Bibles. The vowels are here represented by means of strokes and dots added to the consonantal text, and this method of vocalization made it possible for the Rabbis to indicate variant readings which they preferred, without meddling with the consonants: they put in the margin of their manuscript the consonants of the reading which they wished to adopt and added the vowel-signs of this reading to the consonants in the text which they were rejecting. The reader knew that he was to pronounce the consonants in the margin with the vowels in the text.

One variation of this convention is of special importance, inasmuch as it affects the divine name. This personal proper name, written with the consonants *YHWH*, was considered too sacred to be uttered; so the vowels for the words 'my Lord' or 'God' were added to the consonants *YHWH*, and the reader was warned by these vowels that he must substitute other consonants. This change having to be made so frequently, the Rabbis did not consider it necessary to put the consonants of the new reading in the margin. In course of time the true pronunciation of the divine name, probably *Yahweh*, passed into oblivion, and *YHWH* was read with the intruded vowels, the vowels of an entirely different word, namely 'my Lord' or 'God'. In late medieval times this mispronunciation became current as *Jehova*, and it was taken over as *Jehovah* by the Reformers in Protestant Bibles. The present translators have retained this incorrect but customary form in the text of passages where the name is explained with a note on its pronunciation (e.g. Exodus 3. 15) and in four place-names of which it forms a constituent element; elsewhere they have followed ancient translators in substituting 'LORD' or 'GOD', printed as here in capital letters, for the Hebrew name.

So much for the text of the Hebrew Old Testament as it lies before us; but it is certain that this does not always represent what was originally written. The translator must often go behind the traditional text to discover the writer's meaning. For this purpose he may have recourse first to the Scrolls; but these cover only a very small part of the Old Testament writings. Secondly he may have recourse to the Samaritan Pentateuch, which, though extant only in late manuscripts, the earliest being dated about the eleventh century A.D., may be somewhat earlier than the Scrolls and represents the text of the five books of the Law (Genesis to Deuteronomy) which the Samaritans took with them when they seceded from Judaism. It differs from the traditional Hebrew text in a considerable number of small and mostly unimportant points.

For further help the translator may turn to the ancient versions. Of these the earliest is the Old Testament in Greek, designed to meet the needs of Greek-speaking Jews in Egypt in the third and second centuries B.C. According to tradition the Pentateuch was translated by seventy-two elders, six from each of the twelve tribes of Israel, and so the Greek version of the Old Testament came to be called the Septuagint, from the Latin *septuaginta* 'seventy'. Clearly it is the work of a number of translators of unequal skill; their rendering is now literal, now paraphrastic, and now interpretative. Not infrequently it contains absurd mistranslations. Yet it is valuable for the recovery of the original Hebrew, because it is based on an underlying Hebrew text older than the Massoretic, and it often preserves the correct reading in passages where our Hebrew manuscripts are manifestly in error, or the true interpretation where this has been obscured in the traditional text. Its defects, however, were patent, and early in the

Christian era several scholars, Aquila, Symmachus and Theodotion, tried to improve on it; other scholars produced fresh recensions of it, among which the text associated with the name of Lucian is commonly included.

The Greek-speaking Christians adopted the Septuagint as their Scriptures, but with the spread of Christianity across the Mediterranean world there arose in time the need for a Latin translation. This, the Old Latin version, made from the Septuagint by unknown translators, was so unsatisfactory that towards the end of the fourth century Jerome produced a new translation. In the books with which we are here concerned he worked directly from the Hebrew text, and he had the help of Jewish scholars. His translation is idiomatic and forceful, and is specially helpful in recovering the form and sense of the Hebrew text. Jerome's new version is commonly called the Vulgate; it may be noted, however, that the Vulgate Psalter is not his translation from the Hebrew but an earlier revision he had made of the Old Latin Psalms.

As the knowledge of Hebrew died out among the Jews, the reading of the Scriptures in the synagogue had to be followed by a translation of the passages into Aramaic, the language which had supplanted Hebrew. Such renderings, known as Targums (Aramaic *targum*, 'translation'), tended to become traditional and stereotyped and finally were written down. Some of them contain pre-Christian material. There are Targums to every book of the Old Testament except Daniel, Ezra, and Nehemiah, but only one, on the Pentateuch, is a straightforward translation.

Between the first and third centuries A.D. a Syriac translation, known as the Peshitta (i.e. 'simple') Version, was made; some parts of it are more literal than others, and, though it agrees in the main with the Hebrew text, it bears traces of the influence of the Septuagint. Other versions in various languages appeared between the third and thirteenth centuries A.D., but they are of little value for the recovery and interpretation of the Hebrew text.

In spite of this wealth of ancient versions, and even when the earliest known form of the text has been established, many obscurities still remain in the Hebrew Scriptures. The classical Hebrew vocabulary as known today is small, with the consequence that the meaning of an unusually large number of words is uncertain or unknown. In such cases recourse may be had to the cognate languages. Already medieval scholars had begun to use the Arabic language for this purpose, and in later centuries Syriac and Ethiopic also were used. In more recent times scholars have had access to the vast literature in Babylonian, Assyrian, and kindred dialects which has been preserved on cuneiform tablets. Archaeology, too, has at times been helpful in clearing up an obscurity in the Hebrew text. But in the last resort, the translator may have to arrive at the sense of a word from the context alone, or he may even have to emend what is demonstrably faulty; such corrections of the text, except when only the vowels are affected, are recorded in the notes of the present translation.

The paragraphs in this translation are a modified form of those in the Authorized and Revised Versions, and the present translators have added brought together if a common refrain or other evidence shows that they have been wrongly separated; such changes are recorded in the notes.

The headings of the Psalms, consisting partly of musical instructions, of which the meanings have mostly been lost, and partly of historical notices, deduced (sometimes incorrectly) from the individual Psalms, have been omitted; they are almost certainly not original. On the other hand, the designations of the speakers in the Song of Songs, though absent from the Hebrew text, have been introduced, with occasional corrections, from two manuscripts of the Septuagint.

A major difficulty in translating the Old Testament lies in the difference of time and place. Palestine differs greatly from the Western world in its physical aspects, in its plants, birds and beasts, its arts and crafts, as it did also in its social, administrative and religious, institutions, so that no English words exist to represent much about which the Old Testament speaks. The modern translator then must be content to use paraphrase or even to transliterate certain Hebrew words. The present translators have transliterated the Hebrew words for technical terms, where verbal exactness has seemed essential, while in other passages they have allowed themselves a paraphrase to bring out the general sense, where no technical problem requiring particularization is involved; but they have adopted such devices as rarely as possible.

Finally, the translators have endeavoured to avoid anachronisms and expressions reminiscent of foreign idioms. They have tried to keep their language as close to current usage as possible, while avoiding words and phrases likely soon to become obsolete. They have made every effort not only to make sense but also to offer renderings that will meet the needs of readers with no special knowledge of the background of the Old Testament.

G. R. D.

GUIDE TO THE NOTES

The footnotes in this edition of the Old Testament serve (*a*) to give cross-references to parallel passages, chiefly in the historical books, (*b*) to indicate where verses or parts of verses have been transposed, (*c*) to give the meaning of proper names where it appears to be reflected in the context, (*d*) to give an alternative interpretation where the Hebrew is capable of such, and (*e*) to indicate places where the translators have adopted what seemed to them the most probable correction of the text where the Hebrew and the ancient versions cannot be convincingly translated as they stand.

Unless otherwise indicated by its wording, a note refers to the single word against which the reference is placed.

ABBREVIATIONS, ETC.

I. GENERAL

Aram.	Aramaic (text or word)
ch(s).	chapter(s)
cp.	compare
Heb.	Hebrew (text or word)
mng.	meaning
MS(S).	manuscript(s)
om.	omit(s)
or	indicating an alternative interpretation
poss.	possible
prob.	probable
rdg.	reading
Sept.	Septuagint (Greek version of the Old Testament)

[. . .]	In the text itself square brackets are used to indicate words that are probably late additions to the Hebrew text.

II. BOOKS OF THE OLD TESTAMENT

Gen.	Genesis	*Eccles.*	Ecclesiastes
Exod.	Exodus	*S. of S.*	Song of Songs
Lev.	Leviticus	*Isa.*	Isaiah
Num.	Numbers	*Jer.*	Jeremiah
Deut.	Deuteronomy	*Lam.*	Lamentations
Josh.	Joshua	*Ezek.*	Ezekiel
Judg.	Judges	*Dan.*	Daniel
Ruth	Ruth	*Hos.*	Hosea
1 Sam.	1 Samuel	*Joel*	Joel
2 Sam.	2 Samuel	*Amos*	Amos
1 Kgs.	1 Kings	*Obad.*	Obadiah
2 Kgs.	2 Kings	*Jonah*	Jonah
1 Chr.	1 Chronicles	*Mic.*	Micah
2 Chr.	2 Chronicles	*Nahum*	Nahum
Ezra	Ezra	*Hab.*	Habakkuk
Neh.	Nehemiah	*Zeph.*	Zephaniah
Esther	Esther	*Hag.*	Haggai
Job	Job	*Zech.*	Zechariah
Ps(s).	Psalm(s)	*Mal.*	Malachi
Prov.	Proverbs		

MARGINAL NUMBERS

THE conventional verse divisions in the Old Testament are based on those in Hebrew manuscripts. Nevertheless any system of division into numbered verses is foreign to the spirit of this translation, which is intended to convey the meaning in natural English—the prose in paragraphs, the poetic passages in lines corresponding to the structure of the Hebrew.

For purposes of reference, and of comparison with other translations, verse numbers are placed in the margin opposite the line in which the first word belonging to the verse in question appears. Sometimes, however, successive verses are combined in a continuous translation, so that the precise point where a new verse begins cannot be fixed; in these cases the verse numbers, joined by a hyphen, are placed at the point where the passage begins.

GENESIS

The creation of the world

IN THE BEGINNING OF CREATION, when God made 1
heaven and earth,*a* the earth was without form and void, with darkness 2
over the face of the abyss, and a mighty wind that swept*b* over the
surface of the waters. God said, 'Let there be light', and there was light; 3
and God saw that the light was good, and he separated light from darkness. 4
He called the light day, and the darkness night. So evening came, and 5
morning came, the first day.

God said, 'Let there be a vault between the waters, to separate water 6
from water.' So God made the vault, and separated the water under the 7
vault from the water above it, and so it was; and God called the vault 8
heaven. Evening came, and morning came, a second day.

God said, 'Let the waters under heaven be gathered into one place, so 9
that dry land may appear'; and so it was. God called the dry land earth, 10
and the gathering of the waters he called seas; and God saw that it was
good. Then God said, 'Let the earth produce fresh growth, let there be 11
on the earth plants bearing seed, fruit-trees bearing fruit each with seed
according to its kind.' So it was; the earth yielded fresh growth, plants 12
bearing seed according to their kind and trees bearing fruit each with seed
according to its kind; and God saw that it was good. Evening came, and 13
morning came, a third day.

God said, 'Let there be lights in the vault of heaven to separate day from 14
night, and let them serve as signs both for festivals and for seasons and
years. Let them also shine in the vault of heaven to give light on earth.' So 15
it was; God made the two great lights, the greater to govern the day and 16
the lesser to govern the night; and with them he made the stars. God put 17
these lights in the vault of heaven to give light on earth, to govern day and 18
night, and to separate light from darkness; and God saw that it was good.
Evening came, and morning came, a fourth day.   19

God said, 'Let the waters teem with countless living creatures, and let 20
birds fly above the earth across the vault of heaven.' God then created the 21
great sea-monsters and all living creatures that move and swarm in the
waters, according to their kind, and every kind of bird; and God saw that
it was good. So he blessed them and said, 'Be fruitful and increase, fill the 22
waters of the seas; and let the birds increase on land.' Evening came, and 23
morning came, a fifth day.

God said, 'Let the earth bring forth living creatures, according to their 24
kind: cattle, reptiles, and wild animals, all according to their kind.' So it
was; God made wild animals, cattle, and all reptiles, each according to its 25

a Or In the beginning God created heaven and earth.   *b Or* and the spirit
of God hovering.

I

26 kind; and he saw that it was good. Then God said, 'Let us make man in our image and likeness to rule the fish in the sea, the birds of heaven, the cattle, all wild animals on earth, and all reptiles that crawl upon the earth.'
27 So God created man in his own image; in the image of God he created
28 him; male and female he created them. God blessed them and said to them, 'Be fruitful and increase, fill the earth and subdue it, rule over the fish in the sea, the birds of heaven, and every living thing that moves upon
29 the earth.' God also said, 'I give you all plants that bear seed everywhere on earth, and every tree bearing fruit which yields seed: they shall be yours
30 for food. All green plants I give for food to the wild animals, to all the birds of heaven, and to all reptiles on earth, every living creature.' So it was;
31 and God saw all that he had made, and it was very good. Evening came, and morning came, a sixth day.
2 Thus heaven and earth were completed with all their mighty throng.
2 On the sixth day God completed all the work he had been doing, and on
3 the seventh day he ceased from all his work. God blessed the seventh day and made it holy, because on that day he ceased from all the work he had set himself to do.
4 This is the story of the making of heaven and earth when they were created.

The beginnings of history

5 WHEN THE LORD GOD MADE EARTH AND HEAVEN, there was neither shrub nor plant growing wild upon the earth, because the LORD God had sent no rain on the earth; nor was there any man to till the ground.
6 A flood*a* used to rise out of the earth and water all the surface of the ground.
7 Then the LORD God formed a man*b* from the dust of the ground*c* and breathed into his nostrils the breath of life. Thus the man became a living
8 creature. Then the LORD God planted a garden in Eden away to the east,
9 and there he put the man whom he had formed. The LORD God made trees spring from the ground, all trees pleasant to look at and good for food; and in the middle of the garden he set the tree of life and the tree of the knowledge of good and evil.
10 There was a river flowing from Eden to water the garden, and when it
11 left the garden it branched into four streams. The name of the first is Pishon; that is the river which encircles all the land of Havilah, where the
12 gold*d* is. The gold*d* of that land is good; bdellium*e* and cornelians are also
13 to be found there. The name of the second river is Gihon; this is the one
14 which encircles all the land of Cush. The name of the third is Tigris; this is the river which runs east of Asshur. The fourth river is the Euphrates.
15 The LORD God took the man and put him in the garden of Eden to till
16 it and care for it. He told the man, 'You may eat from every tree in the
17 garden, but not from the tree of the knowledge of good and evil; for on the
18 day that you eat from it, you will certainly die.' Then the LORD God said,

a Or mist.   *b* Heb. adam.   *c* Heb. adamah.   *d* Or frankincense.
e Or gum resin.

'It is not good for the man to be alone. I will provide a partner for him.'
So God formed out of the ground all the wild animals and all the birds of 19
heaven. He brought them to the man to see what he would call them, and
whatever the man called each living creature, that was its name. Thus the 20
man gave names to all cattle, to the birds of heaven, and to every wild
animal; but for the man himself no partner had yet been found. And so 21
the LORD God put the man into a trance, and while he slept, he took one
of his ribs and closed the flesh over the place. The LORD God then built 22
up the rib, which he had taken out of the man, into a woman. He brought
her to the man, and the man said: 23

> 'Now this, at last—
> bone from my bones,
> flesh from my flesh!—
> this shall be called woman,*a*
> for from man *b* was this taken.'

That is why a man leaves his father and mother and is united to his wife, 24
and the two become one flesh. Now they were both naked, the man and his 25
wife, but they had no feeling of shame towards one another.

THE SERPENT WAS MORE CRAFTY than any wild creature that the LORD 3
God had made. He said to the woman, 'Is it true that God has forbidden
you to eat from any tree in the garden?' The woman answered the serpent, 2
'We may eat the fruit of any tree in the garden, except for the tree in the 3
middle of the garden; God has forbidden us either to eat or to touch the
fruit of that; if we do, we shall die.' The serpent said, 'Of course you will 4
not die. God knows that as soon as you eat it, your eyes will be opened and 5
you will be like gods*c* knowing both good and evil.' When the woman saw 6
that the fruit of the tree was good to eat, and that it was pleasing to the eye
and tempting to contemplate, she took some and ate it. She also gave her
husband some and he ate it. Then the eyes of both of them were opened 7
and they discovered that they were naked; so they stitched fig-leaves
together and made themselves loincloths.
   The man and his wife heard the sound of the LORD God walking in the 8
garden at the time of the evening breeze and hid from the LORD God
among the trees of the garden. But the LORD God called to the man and 9
said to him, 'Where are you?' He replied, 'I heard the sound as you were 10
walking in the garden, and I was afraid because I was naked, and I hid myself.' God answered, 'Who told you that you were naked? Have you eaten 11
from the tree which I forbade you?' The man said, 'The woman you gave 12
me for a companion, she gave me fruit from the tree and I ate it.' Then 13
the LORD God said to the woman, 'What is this that you have done?' The
woman said, 'The serpent tricked me, and I ate.' Then the LORD God said 14
to the serpent:

> 'Because you have done this you are accursed
> more than all cattle and all wild creatures.

---

a Heb. ishshah.   *b Heb.* ish.   *c Or* God.

3

> On your belly you shall crawl, and dust you shall eat
> all the days of your life.
15   I will put enmity between you and the woman,
> between your brood and hers.
> They shall strike at your head,
> and you shall strike at their heel.'

16 To the woman he said:

> 'I will increase your labour and your groaning,
> and in labour you shall bear children.
> You shall be eager *a* for your husband,
> and he shall be your master.'

17 And to the man he said:

> 'Because you have listened to your wife
> and have eaten from the tree which I forbade you,
> accursed shall be the ground on your account.
> With labour you shall win your food from it
> all the days of your life.
18   It will grow thorns and thistles for you,
> none but wild plants for you to eat.
19   You shall gain your bread by the sweat of your brow
> until you return to the ground;
> for from it you were taken.
> Dust you are, to dust you shall return.'

20   The man called his wife Eve *b* because she was the mother of all who live.
21 The LORD God made tunics of skins for Adam and his wife and clothed
22 them. He said, 'The man has become like one of us, knowing good and
evil; what if he now reaches out his hand and takes fruit from the tree of
23 life also, eats it and lives for ever?' So the LORD God drove him out of the
24 garden of Eden to till the ground from which he had been taken. He cast
him out, and to the east of the garden of Eden he stationed the cherubim
and a sword whirling and flashing to guard the way to the tree of life.

4   The man lay with his wife Eve, and she conceived and gave birth to Cain.
She said, 'With the help of the LORD I have brought a man into being.'
2 Afterwards she had another child, his brother Abel. Abel was a shepherd
3 and Cain a tiller of the soil. The day came when Cain brought some of the
4 produce of the soil as a gift to the LORD; and Abel brought some of the
first-born of his flock, the fat portions of them. *c* The LORD received Abel
5 and his gift with favour; but Cain and his gift he did not receive. Cain was
6 very angry and his face fell. Then the LORD said to Cain, 'Why are you so
angry and cast down?

7   If you do well, you are accepted; *d*
> if not, sin is a demon crouching at the door.
> It shall be eager for you, and you will be mastered by it.' *e*

---

a Or feel an urge.   *b* That is Life.   *c* Or some of the first-born, that is the suck-
lings, of his flock.   *d* Or you hold your head up.   *e* Or but you must master it.

4

Cain said to his brother Abel, 'Let us go into the open country.' While 8
they were there, Cain attacked his brother Abel and murdered him. Then 9
the LORD said to Cain, 'Where is your brother Abel?' Cain answered, 'I
do not know. Am I my brother's keeper?' The LORD said, 'What have you 10
done? Hark! your brother's blood that has been shed is crying out to me
from the ground. Now you are accursed, and banished from*a* the ground 11
which has opened its mouth wide to receive your brother's blood, which
you have shed. When you till the ground, it will no longer yield you its 12
wealth. You shall be a vagrant and a wanderer on earth.' Cain said to the 13
LORD, 'My punishment is heavier than I can bear; thou hast driven me 14
today from the ground, and I must hide myself from thy presence. I shall
be a vagrant and a wanderer on earth, and anyone who meets me can kill
me.' The LORD answered him, 'No: if anyone kills Cain, Cain shall be 15
avenged sevenfold.' So the LORD put a mark on Cain, in order that anyone
meeting him should not kill him. Then Cain went out from the LORD's 16
presence and settled in the land of Nod*b c* to the east of Eden.

Then Cain lay with his wife; and she conceived and bore Enoch. Cain 17
was then building a city, which he named Enoch after his son. Enoch begot 18
Irad; Irad begot Mehujael; Mehujael begot Methushael; Methushael
begot Lamech.

Lamech married two wives, one named Adah and the other Zillah. Adah 19 20
bore Jabal who was the ancestor of herdsmen who live in tents; and his 21
brother's name was Jubal; he was the ancestor of those who play the harp
and pipe. Zillah, the other wife, bore Tubal-cain, the master of all copper- 22
smiths and blacksmiths, and Tubal-cain's sister was Naamah. Lamech said 23
to his wives:

> 'Adah and Zillah, listen to me;
> wives of Lamech, mark what I say:
> I kill a man for wounding me,
> a young man for a blow.
> Cain may be avenged seven times,
> but Lamech seventy-seven.'   24

Adam lay with his wife again. She bore a son, and named him Seth,*d* 'for', 25
she said, 'God has granted me another son in place of Abel, because Cain
killed him.' Seth too had a son, whom he named Enosh. At that time men 26
began to invoke the LORD*e* by name.

THIS IS THE RECORD of the descendants of Adam. On the day when 5
God created man he made him in the likeness of God. He created them 2
male and female, and on the day when he created them, he blessed them
and called them man.

Adam was one hundred and thirty years old when he begot a son in his 3
likeness and image, and named him Seth. After the birth of Seth he lived 4

---

a and banished from: *or* more than (*cp. 3. 17*).   *b* *That is* Wandering.   *c* and
settled ... Nod: *or* and he lived as a wanderer in the land.   *d* *That is* Granted.
e *This represents the Hebrew consonants* YHWH, *probably pronounced* Yahweh, *but
traditionally read as* Jehovah.

5 eight hundred years, and had other sons and daughters. He lived nine hundred and thirty years, and then he died.

6 7 Seth was one hundred and five years old when he begot Enosh. After the birth of Enosh he lived eight hundred and seven years, and had other 8 sons and daughters. He lived nine hundred and twelve years, and then he died.

9ª 10 Enosh was ninety years old when he begot Kenan. After the birth of Kenan he lived eight hundred and fifteen years, and had other sons and 11 daughters. He lived nine hundred and five years, and then he died.

12 13 Kenan was seventy years old when he begot Mahalalel. After the birth of Mahalalel he lived eight hundred and forty years, and had other sons 14 and daughters. He lived nine hundred and ten years, and then he died.

15 16 Mahalalel was sixty-five years old when he begot Jared. After the birth of Jared he lived eight hundred and thirty years, and had other sons and 17 daughters. He lived eight hundred and ninety-five years, and then he died.

18 Jared was one hundred and sixty-two years old when he begot Enoch. 19 After the birth of Enoch he lived eight hundred years, and had other sons 20 and daughters. He lived nine hundred and sixty-two years, and then he died.

21 22 Enoch was sixty-five years old when he begot Methuselah. After the birth of Methuselah, Enoch walked with God for three hundred years, and 23 had other sons and daughters. He lived three hundred and sixty-five years. 24 Having walked with God, Enoch was seen no more, because God had taken him away.

25 Methuselah was one hundred and eighty-seven years old when he begot 26 Lamech. After the birth of Lamech he lived for seven hundred and eighty- 27 two years, and had other sons and daughters. He lived nine hundred and sixty-nine years, and then he died.

28 Lamech was one hundred and eighty-two years old when he begot a son. 29 He named him Noah, saying, 'This boy will bring us relief from our work, and from the hard labour that has come upon us because of the LORD's 30 curse upon the ground.' After the birth of Noah, he lived for five hundred 31 and ninety-five years, and had other sons and daughters. Lamech lived 32 seven hundred and seventy-seven years, and then he died. Noah was five hundred years old when he begot Shem, Ham and Japheth.

The flood and the tower of Babel

6 WHEN MANKIND BEGAN TO INCREASE and to spread all over the 2 earth and daughters were born to them, the sons of the gods saw that the daughters of men were beautiful; so they took for themselves such 3 women as they chose. But the LORD said, 'My life-giving spirit shall not remain in man for ever; he for his part is mortal flesh: he shall live for a hundred and twenty years.'

4 In those days,ᵇ when the sons of the gods had intercourse with the

---

ª *Verses 9–32 : cp. 1 Chr. 1. 2–4.*   ᵇ *Prob. rdg.; Heb. adds and also afterwards* (*cp. Num. 13. 33*).

6

daughters of men and got children by them, the Nephilim[a] were on earth. They were the heroes of old, men of renown.

When the LORD saw that man had done much evil on earth and that his 5 thoughts and inclinations were always evil, he was sorry that he had made 6 man on earth, and he was grieved at heart. He said, 'This race of men whom 7 I have created, I will wipe them off the face of the earth—man and beast, reptiles and birds. I am sorry that I ever made them.' But Noah had won 8 the LORD's favour.

This is the story of Noah. Noah was a righteous man, the one blameless 9 man of his time; he walked with God. He had three sons, Shem, Ham and 10 Japheth. Now God saw that the whole world was corrupt[b] and full of 11 violence. In his sight the world had become corrupted, for all men had 12 lived corrupt lives on earth. God said to Noah, 'The loathsomeness[c] of all 13 mankind has become plain to me, for through them the earth is full of violence. I intend to destroy them, and the earth with them. Make yourself 14 an ark with ribs of cypress; cover it with reeds and coat it inside and out with pitch. This is to be its plan: the length of the ark shall be three hundred 15 cubits, its breadth fifty cubits, and its height thirty cubits. You shall make 16 a roof for the ark, giving it a fall of one cubit when complete; and put a door in the side of the ark, and build three decks, upper, middle, and lower. I intend to bring the waters of the flood over the earth to destroy every 17 human being under heaven that has the spirit of life; everything on earth shall perish. But with you I will make a covenant, and you shall go into the 18 ark, you and your sons, your wife and your sons' wives with you. And you 19 shall bring living creatures of every kind into the ark to keep them alive with you, two of each kind, a male and a female; two of every kind of bird, 20 beast, and reptile, shall come to you to be kept alive. See that you take and 21 store every kind of food that can be eaten; this shall be food for you and for them.' Exactly as God had commanded him, so Noah did. 22

The LORD said to Noah, 'Go into the ark, you and all your household; 7 for I have seen that you alone are righteous before me in this generation. Take with you seven pairs, male and female, of all beasts that are ritually 2 clean, and one pair, male and female, of all beasts that are not clean; also 3 seven pairs, male and female, of every bird—to ensure that life continues on earth. In seven days' time I will send rain over the earth for forty days 4 and forty nights, and I will wipe off the face of the earth every living thing that I have made.' Noah did all that the LORD had commanded him. He 5 6 was six hundred years old when the waters of the flood came upon the earth.

And so, to escape the waters of the flood, Noah went into the ark with 7 his sons, his wife, and his sons' wives. And into the ark with Noah went one 8–9 pair, male and female, of all beasts, clean and unclean, of birds and of everything that crawls on the ground, two by two, as God had commanded. Towards the end of seven days the waters of the flood came upon the earth. 10 In the year when Noah was six hundred years old, on the seventeenth day 11 of the second month, on that very day, all the springs of the great abyss broke through, the windows of the sky were opened, and rain fell on the 12 earth for forty days and forty nights. On that very day Noah entered the 13

[a] *Or* giants.　　　[b] *Or* ripe for destruction.　　　[c] *Or* end.

7

ark with his sons, Shem, Ham and Japheth, his own wife, and his three
14 sons' wives. Wild animals of every kind, cattle of every kind, reptiles of
15 every kind that move upon the ground, and birds of every kind—all came
16 to Noah in the ark, two by two of all creatures that had life in them. Those
which came were one male and one female of all living things; they came
in as God had commanded Noah, and the LORD closed the door on him.
17 The flood continued upon the earth for forty days, and the waters swelled
18 and lifted up the ark so that it rose high above the ground. They swelled
and increased over the earth, and the ark floated on the surface of the waters.
19 More and more the waters increased over the earth until they covered all
20 the high mountains everywhere under heaven. The waters increased and
21 the mountains were covered to a depth of fifteen cubits. Every living creature that moves on earth perished, birds, cattle, wild animals, all reptiles,
22 and all mankind. Everything died that had the breath of life in its nostrils,
23 everything on dry land. God wiped out every living thing that existed on
earth, man and beast, reptile and bird; they were all wiped out over the
whole earth, and only Noah and his company in the ark survived.
24   When the waters had increased over the earth for a hundred and fifty
8 days, God thought of Noah and all the wild animals and the cattle with him
in the ark, and he made a wind pass over the earth, and the waters began
2 to subside. The springs of the abyss were stopped up, and so were the
3 windows of the sky; the downpour from the skies was checked. The water
gradually receded from the earth, and by the end of a hundred and fifty
4 days it had disappeared. On the seventeenth day of the seventh month the
5 ark grounded on a mountain in Ararat. The water continued to recede
until the tenth month, and on the first day of the tenth month the tops of
the mountains could be seen.
6   After forty days Noah opened the trap-door that he had made in the
7 ark, and released a raven to see whether the water had subsided, but the
bird continued flying to and fro until the water on the earth had dried up.
8 Noah waited for seven days,[a] and then he released a dove from the ark to
9 see whether the water on the earth had subsided further. But the dove
found no place where she could settle, and so she came back to him in the
ark, because there was water over the whole surface of the earth. Noah
10 stretched out his hand, caught her and took her into the ark. He waited
11 another seven days and again released the dove from the ark. She came
back to him towards evening with a newly plucked olive leaf in her beak.
Then Noah knew for certain that the water on the earth had subsided still
12 further. He waited yet another seven days and released the dove, but she
13 never came back. And so it came about that, on the first day of the first
month of his six hundred and first year, the water had dried up on the
earth, and Noah removed the hatch and looked out of the ark. The surface
of the ground was dry.
14   By the twenty-seventh day of the second month the whole earth was dry.
15 16 And God said to Noah, 'Come out of the ark, you and your wife, your sons
17 and their wives. Bring out every living creature that is with you, live things
of every kind, bird and beast and every reptile that moves on the ground,

        [a] Noah . . . days: *prob. rdg., cp. verse 10; Heb. om.*

and let them swarm over the earth and be fruitful and increase there.' So 18
Noah came out with his sons, his wife, and his sons' wives. Every wild 19
animal, all cattle, every bird, and every reptile that moves on the ground,
came out of the ark by families. Then Noah built an altar to the Lord. He 20
took ritually clean beasts and birds of every kind, and offered whole-
offerings on the altar. When the Lord smelt the soothing odour, he said 21
within himself, 'Never again will I curse the ground because of man, however evil his inclinations may be from his youth upwards. I will never again
kill every living creature, as I have just done.

> While the earth lasts 22
> seedtime and harvest, cold and heat,
> summer and winter, day and night,
> shall never cease.'

GOD BLESSED NOAH and his sons and said to them, 'Be fruitful and in- **9**
crease, and fill the earth. The fear and dread of you shall fall upon all wild 2
animals on earth, on all birds of heaven, on everything that moves upon
the ground and all fish in the sea; they are given into your hands. Every 3
creature that lives and moves shall be food for you; I give you them all, as
once I gave you all green plants. But you must not eat the flesh with the 4
life, which is the blood, still in it. And further, for your life-blood I will 5
demand satisfaction; from every animal I will require it, and from a man
also I will require satisfaction for the death of his fellow-man.

> He that sheds the blood of a man, 6
> for that man his blood shall be shed;
> for in the image of God
> has God made man.

But you must be fruitful and increase, swarm throughout the earth and 7
rule*a* over it.'

   God spoke to Noah and to his sons with him: 'I now make my covenant 8 9
with you and with your descendants after you, and with every living crea- 10
ture that is with you, all birds and cattle, all the wild animals with you on
earth, all that have come out of the ark. I will make my covenant with you: 11
never again shall all living creatures be destroyed by the waters of the flood,
never again shall there be a flood to lay waste the earth.'

   God said, 'This is the sign of the covenant which I establish between 12
myself and you and every living creature with you, to endless generations:

> My bow I set in the cloud, 13
> sign of the covenant
> between myself and earth.
> When I cloud the sky over the earth, 14
> the bow shall be seen in the cloud.

Then will I remember the covenant which I have made between myself 15
and you and living things of every kind. Never again shall the waters become
a flood to destroy all living creatures. The bow shall be in the cloud; when 16

    a Prob. rdg., cp. 1. 28; Heb. increase.

I see it, it will remind me of the everlasting covenant between God and
17 living things on earth of every kind.' God said to Noah, 'This is the sign
of the covenant which I make between myself and all that lives on earth.'
18   The sons of Noah who came out of the ark were Shem, Ham and Japheth;
19 Ham was the father of Canaan. These three were the sons of Noah, and
their descendants spread over the whole earth.
20 21   Noah, a man of the soil, began the planting of vineyards. He drank some
22 of the wine, became drunk and lay naked inside his tent. When Ham,
father of Canaan, saw his father naked, he told his two brothers outside.
23 So Shem and Japheth took a cloak, put it on their shoulders and walked
backwards, and so covered their father's naked body; their faces were
24 turned the other way, so that they did not see their father naked. When
Noah woke from his drunken sleep, he learnt what his youngest son had
25 done to him, and said:

> 'Cursed be Canaan,
>   slave of slaves
>   shall he be to his brothers.'

26 And he continued:

> 'Bless, O Lord,
>   the tents of Shem; *a*
>   may Canaan be his slave.
27   May God extend *b* Japheth's bounds,
>   let him dwell in the tents of Shem,
>   may Canaan be their slave.'

28 29 After the flood Noah lived for three hundred and fifty years, and he was
nine hundred and fifty years old when he died.
10   These are the descendants of the sons of Noah, Shem, Ham and Japheth,
the sons born to them after the flood.
2 *c*   The sons of Japheth: Gomer, Magog, Madai, Javan, *d* Tubal, Meshech
3 4 and Tiras. The sons of Gomer: Ashkenaz, Riphath and Togarmah. The
5 sons of Javan: Elishah, Tarshish, Kittim *e* and Rodanim. From these the
peoples of the coasts and islands separated into their own countries, each
with their own language, family by family, nation by nation.
6 *f* 7   The sons of Ham: Cush, Mizraim, *g* Put and Canaan. The sons of
Cush: Seba, Havilah, Sabtah, Raamah and Sabtecha. The sons of Raamah:
8 Sheba and Dedan. Cush was the father of Nimrod, who began to show
9 himself a man of might on earth; and he was a mighty hunter before the
Lord, as the saying goes, 'Like Nimrod, a mighty hunter before the Lord.'
10 His kingdom in the beginning consisted of Babel, Erech, and Accad, all
11 of them in the land of Shinar. From that land he migrated to Asshur and
12 built Nineveh, Rehoboth-Ir, Calah, and Resen, a great city between
13 *h* Nineveh and Calah. From Mizraim sprang the Lydians, Anamites,

---

a Bless ... Shem: *prob. rdg.; Heb.* Blessed is the Lord the God of Shem.   *b* *Heb.*
japht.   *c* *Verses 2–4: cp. 1 Chr. 1. 5–7.*   *d* *Or* Greece.   *e* *Or*
Tarshish of the Kittians.   *f* *Verses 6–8: cp. 1 Chr. 1. 8–10.*   *g* *Or* Egypt.
h *Verses 13–18: cp. 1 Chr. 1. 11–16.*

Lehabites, Naphtuhites, Pathrusites, Casluhites, and the Caphtorites, from 14 whom the Philistines were descended.

Canaan was the father of Sidon, who was his eldest son, and Heth,*a* 15 the Jebusites, the Amorites, the Girgashites, the Hivites, the Arkites, the 16 17 Sinites, the Arvadites, the Zemarites, and the Hamathites. Later the 18 Canaanites spread, and then the Canaanite border ran from Sidon towards 19 Gerar all the way to Gaza; then all the way to Sodom and Gomorrah, Admah and Zeboyim as far as Lasha. These were the sons of Ham, by 20 families and languages with their countries and nations.

Sons were born also to Shem, elder brother of Japheth, the ancestor of 21 all the sons of Eber. The sons of Shem: Elam, Asshur, Arphaxad, Lud*b* 22*c* and Aram. The sons of Aram: Uz, Hul, Gether and Mash. Arphaxad was 23 24 the father of Shelah, and Shelah the father of Eber. Eber had two sons: one 25 was named Peleg,*d* because in his time the earth was divided; and his brother's name was Joktan. Joktan was the father of Almodad, Sheleph, 26 Hazarmoth, Jerah, Hadoram, Uzal, Diklah, Obal, Abimael, Sheba, 27 28 Ophir, Havilah and Jobab. All these were sons of Joktan. They lived in 29 30 the eastern hill-country, from Mesha all the way to Sephar. These were the 31 sons of Shem, by families and languages with their countries and nations.

These were the families of the sons of Noah according to their genea- 32 logies, nation by nation; and from them came the separate nations on earth after the flood.

ONCE UPON A TIME all the world spoke a single language and used the **11** same*e* words. As men journeyed in the east, they came upon a plain in the 2 land of Shinar and settled there. They said to one another, 'Come, let us 3 make bricks and bake them hard'; they used bricks for stone and bitumen for mortar. 'Come,' they said, 'let us build ourselves a city and a tower with 4 its top in the heavens, and make a name for ourselves; or we shall be dis- persed all over the earth.' Then the LORD came down to see the city and 5 tower which mortal men had built, and he said, 'Here they are, one people 6 with a single language, and now they have started to do this; henceforward nothing they have a mind to do will be beyond their reach. Come, let us 7 go down there and confuse their speech, so that they will not understand what they say to one another.' So the LORD dispersed them from there all 8 over the earth, and they left off building the city. That is why it is called 9 Babel,*f* because the LORD there made a babble of the language of all the world; from that place the LORD scattered men all over the face of the earth.

This is the table of the descendants of Shem. Shem was a hundred 10*g* years old when he begot Arphaxad, two years after the flood. After the 11 birth of Arphaxad he lived five hundred years, and had other sons and daughters. Arphaxad was thirty-five years old when he begot Shelah. After 12 13 the birth of Shelah he lived four hundred and three years, and had other sons and daughters.

---

a Or the Hittites. *b Or* the Lydians. *c Verses 22–29: cp. 1 Chr. 1. 17–23.*
d That is Division. *e Or* used few. *f That is* Babylon. *g Verses* *10–26: cp. 1 Chr. 1. 24–27.*

14 15   Shelah was thirty years old when he begot Eber. After the birth of Eber he lived four hundred and three years, and had other sons and daughters.

16 17   Eber was thirty-four years old when he begot Peleg. After the birth of Peleg he lived four hundred and thirty years, and had other sons and daughters.

18 19   Peleg was thirty years old when he begot Reu. After the birth of Reu he lived two hundred and nine years, and had other sons and daughters.

20 21   Reu was thirty-two years old when he begot Serug. After the birth of Serug he lived two hundred and seven years, and had other sons and daughters.

22 23   Serug was thirty years old when he begot Nahor. After the birth of Nahor he lived two hundred years, and had other sons and daughters.

24 25   Nahor was twenty-nine years old when he begot Terah. After the birth of Terah he lived a hundred and nineteen years, and had other sons and daughters.

26   Terah was seventy years old when he begot Abram, Nahor and Haran.

27   This is the table of the descendants of Terah. Terah was the father of

28 Abram, Nahor and Haran. Haran was the father of Lot. Haran died in the

29 presence of his father in the land of his birth, Ur of the Chaldees. Abram and Nahor married wives; Abram's wife was called Sarai, and Nahor's Milcah. She was Haran's daughter; and he was also the father of Milcah

30 31 and of Iscah. Sarai was barren; she had no child. Terah took his son Abram, his grandson Lot the son of Haran, and his daughter-in-law Sarai Abram's wife, and they set out from Ur of the Chaldees for the land of Canaan. But

32 when they reached Harran, they settled there. Terah was two hundred and five years old when he died in Harran.

Abraham and Isaac

12 T HE LORD SAID TO ABRAM, 'Leave your own country, your kinsmen,
2   and your father's house, and go to a country that I will show you. I will make you into a great nation, I will bless you and make your name so great that it shall be used in blessings:

3   Those that bless you I will bless,
                    those that curse you, I will execrate.
                    All the families on earth
                    will pray to be blessed as you are blessed.'

4 And so Abram set out as the LORD had bidden him, and Lot went with him.

5 Abram was seventy-five years old when he left Harran. He took his wife Sarai, his nephew Lot, all the property they had collected, and all the dependants they had acquired in Harran, and they started on their journey

6 to Canaan. When they arrived, Abram passed through the country to the sanctuary at Shechem, the terebinth-tree of Moreh. At that time the

7 Canaanites lived in this land. There the LORD appeared to Abram and said, 'I give this land to your descendants.' So Abram built an altar there to the

8 LORD who had appeared to him. Thence he went on to the hill-country

east of Bethel and pitched his tent between Bethel on the west and Ai on the
east. There he built an altar to the LORD and invoked the LORD by name.
Thus Abram journeyed by stages towards the Negeb.   9
   There came a famine in the land, so severe that Abram went down to   10
Egypt to live there for a while. When he was approaching Egypt, he said   11
to his wife Sarai, 'I know very well that you are a beautiful woman, and   12
that when the Egyptians see you, they will say, "She is his wife"; then
they will kill me but let you live. Tell them that you are my sister, so that   13
all may go well with me because of you and my life may be spared on your
account.' When Abram arrived in Egypt, the Egyptians saw that she was   14
indeed very beautiful. Pharaoh's courtiers saw her and praised her to   15
Pharaoh, and she was taken into Pharaoh's household. He treated Abram   16
well because of her, and Abram came to possess sheep and cattle and asses,
male and female slaves, she-asses, and camels. But the LORD struck   17
Pharaoh and his household with grave diseases on account of Abram's wife
Sarai. Pharaoh summoned Abram and said to him, 'Why have you treated   18
me like this? Why did you not tell me that she is your wife? Why did you   19
say that she was your sister, so that I took her as a wife? Here she is: take
her and be gone.' Then Pharaoh gave his men orders, and they sent Abram   20
away with his wife and all that he had.
   Abram went up from Egypt into the Negeb, he and his wife and all that **13**
he had, and Lot went with him. Abram was now very rich in cattle and in   2
silver and gold. From the Negeb he journeyed by stages to Bethel, to the   3
place between Bethel and Ai where he had pitched his tent in the beginning,
where he had set up an altar on the first occasion and had invoked the LORD   4
by name. Now Lot was travelling with Abram, and he too possessed sheep   5
and cattle and tents. The land could not support them both together; for   6
their livestock were so numerous that they could not settle in the same
district, and there were quarrels between Abram's herdsmen and Lot's.   7
The Canaanites and the Perizzites were then living in the land. So Abram   8
said to Lot, 'Let there be no quarrelling between us, between my herdsmen
and yours; for we are close kinsmen. The whole country is there in front   9
of you; let us part company. If you go left, I will go right; if you go right,
I will go left.' Lot looked up and saw how well-watered the whole Plain of   10
the Jordan was; all the way to Zoar it was like the Garden of the LORD, like
the land of Egypt. This was before the LORD had destroyed Sodom and
Gomorrah. So Lot chose all the Plain of the Jordan and took the road on   11
the east side. Thus they parted company. Abram settled in the land of   12
Canaan; but Lot settled among the cities of the Plain and pitched his tents
near Sodom. Now the men of Sodom were wicked, great sinners against   13
the LORD.
   After Lot and Abram had parted, the LORD said to Abram, 'Raise your   14
eyes and look into the distance from the place where you are, north and
south, east and west. All the land you can see I will give to you and to your   15
descendants for ever. I will make your descendants countless as the dust   16
of the earth; if anyone could count the dust upon the ground, then he
could count your descendants. Now go through the length and breadth   17
of the land, for I give it to you.' So Abram moved his tent and settled   18

by the terebinths of Mamre at Hebron; and there he built an altar to the
LORD.

14 IT WAS IN THE TIME OF AMRAPHEL king of Shinar, Arioch king of
2 Ellasar, Kedorlaomer king of Elam, and Tidal king of Goyim. They went
to war against Bera king of Sodom, Birsha king of Gomorrah, Shinab king
of Admah, Shemeber king of Zeboyim, and the king of Bela, that is Zoar.
3 These kings joined forces in the valley of Siddim, which is now the Dead
4 Sea. They had been subject to Kedorlaomer for twelve years, but in the
5 thirteenth year they rebelled. Then in the fourteenth year Kedorlaomer
and his confederate kings came and defeated the Rephaim in Ashteroth-
6 karnaim, the Zuzim in Ham, the Emim in Shaveh-kiriathaim, and the
Horites in the hill-country from Seir *a* as far as El-paran on the edge of the
7 wilderness. On their way back they came to En-mishpat, which is now
Kadesh, and laid waste all the country of the Amalekites and also that of
8 the Amorites who lived in Hazazon-tamar. Then the kings of Sodom,
Gomorrah, Admah, Zeboyim, and Bela, which is now Zoar, marched out
9 and drew up their forces against them in the valley of Siddim, against
Kedorlaomer king of Elam, Tidal king of Goyim, Amraphel king of Shinar,
10 and Arioch king of Ellasar, four kings against five. Now the valley of Siddim was full of bitumen pits; and when the kings of Sodom and Gomorrah
11 fled, they fell into them, but the rest escaped to the hill-country. The four
kings captured all the flocks and herds of Sodom and Gomorrah and all
12 their provisions, and went away. They also carried off Lot, Abram's
13 nephew, who was living in Sodom, and with him his flocks and herds. But
a fugitive came and told Abram the Hebrew, who at that time was dwelling
by the terebinths of Mamre the Amorite. This Mamre was the brother of
14 Eshcol and Aner, who were allies of Abram. When Abram heard that his
kinsman had been taken prisoner, he mustered his retainers, men born in
his household, three hundred and eighteen of them, and pursued as far as
15 Dan. Abram and his followers surrounded the enemy by night, attacked
16 them and pursued them as far as Hobah, north of Damascus; he then
brought back all the flocks and herds and also his kinsman Lot with his
17 flocks and herds, together with the women and the other captives. On his
return from this defeat of Kedorlaomer and his confederate kings, the king
of Sodom came out to meet him in the valley of Shaveh, which is now the
King's Valley.
18   Then Melchizedek king of Salem brought food and wine. He was priest
19 of God Most High, and he pronounced this blessing on Abram:

> 'Blessed be Abram
> by God Most High,
>   creator *b* of heaven and earth.
20   And blessed be God Most High,
>   who has delivered your enemies into your power.'

Abram gave him a tithe of all the booty.
21   The king of Sodom said to Abram, 'Give me the people, and you can

---

a Prob. rdg.; Heb. in their hill-country, Seir.   *b Or* owner.

take the property'; but Abram said to the king of Sodom, 'I lift my hand   22
and swear by the LORD, God Most High, creator of heaven and earth: not   23
a thread or a shoe-string will I accept of anything that is yours. You shall
never say, "I made Abram rich." I will accept nothing but what the young   24
men have eaten and the share of the men who went with me. Aner, Eshcol,
and Mamre shall have their share.'

AFTER THIS the word of the LORD came to Abram in a vision. He said,   15
'Do not be afraid, Abram, I am giving you a very great reward.'*a* Abram   2
replied, 'Lord GOD, what canst thou give me? I have no standing among
men, for the heir to my household is Eliezer of Damascus.' Abram con-   3
tinued, 'Thou hast given me no children, and so my heir must be a slave
born in my house.' Then came the word of the LORD to him: 'This man   4
shall not be your heir; your heir shall be a child of your own body.' He took   5
Abram outside and said, 'Look up into the sky, and count the stars if you
can. So many', he said, 'shall your descendants be.'

Abram put his faith in the LORD, and the LORD counted that faith to him   6
as righteousness; he said to him, 'I am the LORD who brought you out from   7
Ur of the Chaldees to give you this land to occupy.' Abram said, 'O Lord   8
GOD, how can I be sure that I shall occupy it?' The LORD answered, 'Bring   9
me a heifer three years old, a she-goat three years old, a ram three years old,
a turtle-dove, and a fledgling.' He brought him all these, halved the animals   10
down the middle and placed each piece opposite its corresponding piece,
but he did not halve the birds. When the birds of prey swooped down on   11
the carcasses, Abram scared them away. Then, as the sun was going down,   12
a trance came over Abram and great fear came upon him. The LORD said   13
to Abram, 'Know this for certain, that your descendants will be aliens
living in a land that is not theirs; they will be slaves, and will be held in
oppression there for four hundred years. But I will punish that nation   14
whose slaves they are, and after that they shall come out with great possessions. You yourself shall join your fathers in peace and be buried in a good   15
old age; and the fourth generation shall return here, for the Amorites will   16
not be ripe for punishment till then.' The sun went down and it was dusk,   17
and there appeared a smoking brazier and a flaming torch passing between
the divided pieces. That very day the LORD made a covenant with Abram,   18
and he said, 'To your descendants I give this land from the River of Egypt
to the Great River, the river Euphrates, the territory of the Kenites,   19
Kenizzites, Kadmonites, Hittites, Perizzites, Rephaim, Amorites, Canaan-   20 21
ites, Girgashites, Hivites, and Jebusites.'

Abram's wife Sarai had borne him no children. Now she had an Egyptian   16
slave-girl whose name was Hagar, and she said to Abram, 'You see that   2
the LORD has not allowed me to bear a child. Take my slave-girl; perhaps
I shall found a family through her.' Abram agreed to what his wife said;
so Sarai, Abram's wife, brought her slave-girl, Hagar the Egyptian,   3
and gave her to her husband Abram as a wife.*b* When this happened
Abram had been in Canaan for ten years.   He lay with Hagar and she   4

a   I am giving . . . reward: *or* I am your shield, your very great reward.
b   *Or* concubine.

conceived; and when she knew that she was with child, she despised her
5 mistress. Sarai said to Abram, 'I have been wronged and you must answer
for it. It was I who gave my slave-girl into your arms, but since she has
known that she is with child, she has despised me. May the LORD see justice
6 done between you and me.' Abram replied to Sarai, 'Your slave-girl is in
your hands; deal with her as you will.' So Sarai ill-treated her and she ran
away.

7   The angel of the LORD found her by a spring of water in the wilderness
8 on the way to Shur, and he said, 'Hagar, Sarai's slave-girl, where have you
come from and where are you going?' She answered, 'I am running away
9 from Sarai my mistress.' The angel of the LORD said to her, 'Go back to
10 your mistress and submit to her ill-treatment.' The angel also said, 'I will
11 make your descendants too many to be counted.' And the angel of the LORD
said to her:

'You are with child and will bear a son.
You shall name him Ishmael,*a*
because the LORD has heard of your ill-treatment.
12   He shall be a man like the wild ass,
his hand against every man
and every man's hand against him;
and he shall live at odds with*b* all his kinsmen.'

13 She called the LORD who was speaking to her by the name El-Roi,*c* for
14 she said, 'Have I indeed seen God and still live*d* after that vision?' That is
why men call the well Beer-lahai-roi;*e* it lies between Kadesh and Bered.
15 Hagar bore Abram a son, and he named the child she bore him Ishmael.
16 Abram was eighty-six years old when Hagar bore Ishmael.

17   When Abram was ninety-nine years old, the LORD appeared to him and
2 said, 'I am God Almighty. Live always in my presence and be perfect, so
that I may set my covenant between myself and you and multiply your
3 descendants.' Abram threw himself down on his face, and God spoke with
4 him and said, 'I make this covenant, and I make it with you: you shall be
5 the father of a host of nations. Your name shall no longer be Abram,*f* your
6 name shall be Abraham,*g* for I make you father of a host of nations. I will
make you exceedingly fruitful; I will make nations out of you, and kings
7 shall spring from you. I will fulfil my covenant between myself and you
and your descendants after you, generation after generation, an everlasting
8 covenant, to be your God, yours and your descendants' after you. As an
everlasting possession I will give you and your descendants after you the
land in which you now are aliens, all the land of Canaan, and I will be God
to your descendants.'

9   God said to Abraham, 'For your part, you must keep my covenant, you
10 and your descendants after you, generation by generation. This is how
you shall keep my covenant between myself and you and your descend-
11 ants after you: circumcise yourselves, every male among you. You shall

a That is God heard.   *b Or* live to the east of . . .   *c That is* God of a vision.
d God and still live: *prob. rdg.; Heb.* hither.   *e That is* the Well of the Living
One of Vision.   *f That is* High Father.   *g That is* Father of a Multitude.

circumcise the flesh of your foreskin, and it shall be the sign of the covenant between us. Every male among you in every generation shall be circum- 12 cised on the eighth day, both those born in your house and any foreigner, not of your blood but bought with your money. Circumcise both those 13 born in your house and those bought with your money; thus shall my covenant be marked in your flesh as an everlasting covenant. Every 14 uncircumcised male, everyone who has not had the flesh of his foreskin circumcised, shall be cut off from the kin of his father. He has broken my covenant.'

God said to Abraham, 'As for Sarai your wife; you shall call her not 15 Sarai,*a* but Sarah.*b* I will bless her and give you a son by her. I will bless 16 her and she shall be the mother of nations; the kings of many people shall spring from her.' Abraham threw himself down on his face; he laughed 17 and said to himself, 'Can a son be born to a man who is a hundred years old? Can Sarah bear a son when she is ninety?' He said to God, 'If only 18 Ishmael might live under thy special care!' But God replied, 'No. Your 19 wife Sarah shall bear you a son, and you shall call him Isaac.*c* With him I will fulfil my covenant, an everlasting covenant with his descendants after him. I have heard your prayer for Ishmael. I have blessed him and will 20 make him fruitful. I will multiply his descendants; he shall be father of twelve princes, and I will raise a great nation from him. But my covenant 21 I will fulfil with Isaac, whom Sarah will bear to you at this season next year.' When he had finished talking with Abraham, God ascended and left him. 22

Then Abraham took Ishmael his son, everyone who had been born in 23 his household and everyone bought with money, every male in his household, and he circumcised them that very same day in the flesh of their foreskins as God had told him to do. Abraham was ninety-nine years old when 24 he circumcised the flesh of his foreskin. Ishmael was thirteen years old 25 when he was circumcised in the flesh of his foreskin. Both Abraham and 26 Ishmael were circumcised on the same day, and all the men of his house- 27 hold, born in the house or bought with money from foreigners, were circumcised with him.

THE LORD APPEARED TO ABRAHAM by the terebinths of Mamre. As **18** Abraham was sitting at the opening of his tent in the heat of the day, he 2 looked up and saw three men standing in front of him. When he saw them, he ran from the opening of his tent to meet them and bowed low to the ground. 'Sirs,' he said, 'if I have deserved your favour, do not pass by my 3 humble self without a visit. Let me send for some water so that you may 4 wash your feet and rest under a tree; and let me fetch a little food so that 5 you may refresh yourselves. Afterwards you may continue the journey which has brought you my way.' They said, 'Do by all means as you say.' So Abraham hurried into the tent to Sarah and said, 'Take three measures 6 of flour quickly, knead it and make some cakes.' Then Abraham ran to the 7 cattle, chose a fine tender calf and gave it to a servant, who hurriedly prepared it. He took curds and milk and the calf he had prepared, set it before 8 them, and waited on them himself under the tree while they ate. They 9

a That is Mockery.   *b That is* Princess.   *c That is* He laughed.

10 asked him where Sarah his wife was, and he said, 'There, in the tent.' The stranger said, 'About this time next year I will be sure to come back to you, and Sarah your wife shall have a son.' Now Sarah was listening at the open-
11 ing of the tent, and he was close beside it. Both Abraham and Sarah had
12 grown very old, and Sarah was past the age of child-bearing. So Sarah laughed to herself and said, 'I am past bearing children now that I am out
13 of my time, and my husband is old.' The LORD said to Abraham, 'Why
14 did Sarah laugh and say, "Shall I indeed bear a child when I am old?" Is anything impossible for the LORD? In due season I will come back to you,
15 about this time next year, and Sarah shall have a son.' Sarah lied because she was frightened, and denied that she had laughed; but he said, 'Yes, you did laugh.'

16 The men set out and looked down towards Sodom, and Abraham went
17 with them to start them on their way. The LORD thought to himself, 'Shall
18 I conceal from Abraham what I intend to do? He will become a great and powerful nation, and all nations on earth will pray to be blessed as he is
19 blessed. I have taken care of him on purpose that he may charge his sons and family after him to conform to the way of the LORD and to do what is
20 right and just; thus I shall fulfil all that I have promised for him.' So the LORD said, 'There is a great outcry over Sodom and Gomorrah; their sin
21 is very grave. I must go down and see whether their deeds warrant the out-
22 cry which has reached me. I am resolved to know the truth.' When the men turned and went towards Sodom, Abraham remained standing before
23 the LORD. Abraham drew near him and said, 'Wilt thou really sweep away
24 good and bad together? Suppose there are fifty good men in the city; wilt thou really sweep it away, and not pardon the place because of the fifty
25 good men? Far be it from thee to do this—to kill good and bad together; for then the good would suffer with the bad. Far be it from thee. Shall not
26 the judge of all the earth do what is just?' The LORD said, 'If I find in the city of Sodom fifty good men, I will pardon the whole place for their sake.'
27 Abraham replied, 'May I presume to speak to the Lord, dust and ashes
28 that I am: suppose there are five short of the fifty good men? Wilt thou destroy the whole city for a mere five men?' He said, 'If I find forty-five
29 there I will not destroy it.' Abraham spoke again, 'Suppose forty can be
30 found there?'; and he said, 'For the sake of the forty I will not do it.' Then Abraham said, 'Please do not be angry, O Lord, if I speak again: suppose thirty can be found there?' He answered, 'If I find thirty there I will not
31 do it.' Abraham continued, 'May I presume to speak to the Lord: suppose twenty can be found there?' He replied, 'For the sake of the twenty I will
32 not destroy it.' Abraham said, 'I pray thee not to be angry, O Lord, if I speak just once more: suppose ten can be found there?' He said, 'For the
33 sake of the ten I will not destroy it.' When the LORD had finished talking with Abraham, he left him, and Abraham returned home.

19 The two angels came to Sodom in the evening, and Lot was sitting in the gateway of the city. When he saw them he rose to meet them and bowed
2 low with his face to the ground. He said, 'I pray you, sirs, turn aside to my humble home, spend the night there and wash your feet; you can rise early and continue your journey.' 'No,' they answered, 'we will spend the night

in the street.' But Lot was so insistent that they did turn aside and enter ₃
his house. He prepared a meal for them, baking unleavened cakes, and they
ate them. Before they lay down to sleep, the men of Sodom, both young ₄
and old, surrounded the house—everyone without exception. They called ₅
to Lot and asked him where the men were who had entered his house that
night. 'Bring them out', they shouted, 'so that we can have intercourse with
them.'

Lot went out into the doorway to them, closed the door behind him and ₆ ₇
said, 'No, my friends, do not be so wicked. Look, I have two daughters, ₈
both virgins; let me bring them out to you, and you can do what you like
with them; but do not touch these men, because they have come under the
shelter of my roof.' They said, 'Out of our way! This man has come and ₉
settled here as an alien, and does he now take it upon himself to judge us?
We will treat you worse than them.' They crowded in on the man Lot and
pressed close to smash in the door. But the two men inside reached out, ₁₀
pulled Lot in, and closed the door. Then they struck the men in the door- ₁₁
way with blindness, both small and great, so that they could not find the
door.

The two men said to Lot, 'Have you anyone else here, sons-in-law, sons, ₁₂
or daughters, or any who belong to you in the city? Get them out of this
place, because we are going to destroy it. The outcry against it has been so ₁₃
great that the LORD has sent us to destroy it.' So Lot went out and spoke ₁₄
to his intended sons-in-law.ᵃ He said, 'Be quick and leave this place; the
LORD is going to destroy the city.' But they did not take him seriously.

As soon as it was dawn, the angels urged Lot to go, saying, 'Be quick, ₁₅
take your wife and your two daughters who are here, or you will be swept
away when the city is punished.' When he lingered, they took him by the ₁₆
hand, with his wife and his daughters, and, because the LORD had spared
him, led him on until he was outside the city. When they had brought them ₁₇
out, they said, 'Flee for your lives; do not look back and do not stop anywhere in the Plain. Flee to the hills or you will be swept away.' Lot replied, ₁₈
'No, sirs. You have shown your servant favour and you have added to your ₁₉
unfailing care for me by saving my life, but I cannot escape to the hills; I
shall be overtaken by the disaster, and die. Look, here is a town, only a ₂₀
small place, near enough for me to reach quickly. Let me escape to it—it
is very small—and save my life.' He said to him, 'I grant your request: I ₂₁
will not overthrow this town you speak of. But flee there quickly, because ₂₂
I can do nothing until you are there.' That is why the place was called
Zoar.ᵇ The sun had risen over the land as Lot entered Zoar; and then the ₂₃ ₂₄
LORD rained down fire and brimstone from the skies on Sodom and Gomorrah. He overthrew those cities and destroyed all the Plain, with everyone ₂₅
living there and everything growing in the ground. But Lot's wife, behind ₂₆
him, looked back, and she turned into a pillar of salt.

Next morning Abraham rose early and went to the place where he had ₂₇
stood in the presence of the LORD. He looked down towards Sodom and ₂₈
Gomorrah and all the wide extent of the Plain, and there he saw thick smoke
rising high from the earth like the smoke of a lime-kiln. Thus, when God ₂₉

ᵃ *Or* his sons-in-law, who had married his daughters.   ᵇ *That is* Small.

destroyed the cities of the Plain, he thought of Abraham and rescued Lot from the disaster, the overthrow of the cities where he had been living.

30 Lot went up from Zoar and settled in the hill-country with his two daughters, because he was afraid to stay in Zoar; he lived with his two 31 daughters in a cave. The elder daughter said to the younger, 'Our father is old and there is not a man in the country to come to us in the usual way. 32 Come now, let us make our father drink wine and then lie with him and in 33 this way keep the family alive through our father.' So that night they gave him wine to drink, and the elder daughter came and lay with him, and he 34 did not know when she lay down and when she got up. Next day the elder said to the younger, 'Last night I lay with my father. Let us give him wine to drink again tonight; then you go in and lie with him. So we shall keep 35 the family alive through our father.' So they gave their father wine to drink again that night, and the younger daughter went and lay with him, and he 36 did not know, when she lay down and when she got up. In this way both 37 Lot's daughters came to be with child by their father. The elder daughter bore a son and called him Moab; he was the ancestor of the present Moab-38 ites. The younger also bore a son, whom she called Ben-ammi; he was the ancestor of the present Ammonites.

20 ABRAHAM JOURNEYED BY STAGES from there into the Negeb, and 2 settled between Kadesh and Shur, living as an alien in Gerar. He said that Sarah his wife was his sister, and Abimelech king of Gerar sent and took 3 her. But God came to Abimelech in a dream by night and said, 'You shall die because of this woman whom you have taken. She is a married woman.' 4 Now Abimelech had not gone near her; and he said, 'Lord, wilt thou des-5 troy an innocent people? Did he not tell me himself that she was his sister, and she herself said that he was her brother. It was with a clear conscience 6 and in all innocence that I did this.' God said to him in the dream, 'Yes: I know that you acted with a clear conscience. Moreover, it was I who held you back from committing a sin against me: that is why I did not let you 7 touch her. Send back the man's wife now; he is a prophet, and he will intercede on your behalf, and you shall live. But if you do not send her back, 8 I tell you that you are doomed to die, you and all that is yours.' So Abi-melech rose early in the morning, summoned all his servants and told them 9 the whole story; the men were terrified. Abimelech then summoned Abraham and said to him, 'Why have you treated us like this? What harm have I done to you that you should bring this great sin on me and my king-10 dom? You have done a thing that ought not to be done.' And he asked 11 Abraham, 'What was your purpose in doing this?' Abraham answered, 'I said to myself, There can be no fear of God in this place, and they will kill 12 me for the sake of my wife. She is in fact my sister, she is my father's 13 daughter though not by the same mother; and she became my wife. When God set me wandering from my father's house, I said to her, "There is a duty towards me which you must loyally fulfil: wherever we go, you must 14 say that I am your brother."' Then Abimelech took sheep and cattle, and male and female slaves, gave them to Abraham, and returned his wife 15 Sarah to him. Abimelech said, 'My country lies before you; settle wherever

you please.' To Sarah he said, 'I have given your brother a thousand pieces 16
of silver, so that your own people may turn a blind eye on it all, and you will
be completely vindicated.' Then Abraham interceded with God, and God 17
healed Abimelech, his wife, and his slave-girls, and they bore children; for 18
the LORD had made every woman in Abimelech's household barren on
account of Abraham's wife Sarah.

The LORD showed favour to Sarah as he had promised, and made good **21**
what he had said about her. She conceived and bore a son to Abraham for 2
his old age, at the time which God had appointed. The son whom Sarah 3
bore to him, Abraham named Isaac.*a* When Isaac was eight days old 4
Abraham circumcised him, as God had commanded. Abraham was a 5
hundred years old when his son Isaac was born. Sarah said, 'God has given 6
me good reason to laugh, and everybody who hears will laugh with me.'
She said, 'Whoever would have told Abraham that Sarah would suckle 7
children? Yet I have borne him a son for his old age.' The boy grew and 8
was weaned, and on the day of his weaning Abraham gave a feast. Sarah 9
saw the son whom Hagar the Egyptian had borne to Abraham laughing at
him, and she said to Abraham, 'Drive out this slave-girl and her son; I 10
will not have this slave-girl's son sharing the inheritance with my son
Isaac.' Abraham was vexed at this on his son Ishmael's account, but God 11 12
said to him, 'Do not be vexed on account of the boy and the slave-girl. Do
what Sarah says, because you shall have descendants through Isaac. I will 13
make a great nation of the slave-girl's son too, because he is your own
child.'

Abraham rose early in the morning, took some food and a waterskin full 14
of water and gave it to Hagar; he set the child on her shoulder and sent her
away, and she went and wandered in the wilderness of Beersheba. When 15
the water in the skin was finished, she thrust the child under a bush, and 16
went and sat down some way off, about two bowshots away, for she said,
'How can I watch the child die?' So she sat some way off, weeping bitterly.
God heard the child crying, and the *b* angel of God called from heaven to 17
Hagar, 'What is the matter, Hagar? Do not be afraid: God has heard the
child crying where you laid him. Get to your feet, lift the child up and hold 18
him in your arms, because I will make of him a great nation.' Then God 19
opened her eyes and she saw a well full of water; she went to it, filled her
waterskin and gave the child a drink. God was with the child, and he grew 20-21
up and lived in the wilderness of Paran. He became an archer, and his
mother found him a wife from Egypt.

Now about that time Abimelech, with Phicol the commander of his army, 22
addressed Abraham in these terms: 'God is with you in all that you do. Now 23
swear an oath to me in the name of God, that you will not break faith with
me, my offspring, or my descendants. As I have kept faith with you, so
shall you keep faith with me and with the country where you have come to
live as an alien.' Abraham said, 'I swear.' It happened that Abraham had a 24 25
complaint against Abimelech about a well which Abimelech's men had
seized. Abimelech said, 'I do not know who did this. You never told me, 26
and I have heard nothing about it till now.' So Abraham took sheep and 27

a That is He laughed.   *b   Or* an.

cattle and gave them to Abimelech; and the two of them made a pact.
28 29 Abraham set seven ewe-lambs apart, and when Abimelech asked him why
30 he had set these lambs apart, he said, 'Accept these from me in token that
31 I dug this well.' Therefore that place was called Beersheba,*a* because there
32 the two of them swore an oath. When they had made the pact at Beersheba,
Abimelech and Phicol the commander of his army returned at once to the
33 country of the Philistines, and Abraham planted a strip of ground*b* at
34 Beersheba. There he invoked the LORD, the everlasting God, by name, and
he lived as an alien in the country of the Philistines for many a year.

22 THE TIME CAME when God put Abraham to the test. 'Abraham', he
2 called, and Abraham replied, 'Here I am.' God said, 'Take your son Isaac,
your only son, whom you love, and go to the land of Moriah. There you
3 shall offer him as a sacrifice on one of the hills which I will show you.' So
Abraham rose early in the morning and saddled his ass, and he took with
him two of his men and his son Isaac; and he split the firewood for the sacri-
4 fice, and set out for the place of which God had spoken. On the third day
5 Abraham looked up and saw the place in the distance. He said to his men,
'Stay here with the ass while I and the boy go over there; and when we have
6 worshipped we will come back to you.' So Abraham took the wood for the
sacrifice and laid it on his son Isaac's shoulder; he himself carried the fire
7 and the knife, and the two of them went on together. Isaac said to Abraham,
'Father', and he answered, 'What is it, my son?' Isaac said, 'Here are the
8 fire and the wood, but where is the young beast for the sacrifice?' Abraham
answered, 'God will provide himself with a young beast for a sacrifice, my
9 son.' And the two of them went on together and came to the place of which
God had spoken. There Abraham built an altar and arranged the wood.
10 He bound his son Isaac and laid him on the altar on top of the wood. Then
11 he stretched out his hand and took the knife to kill his son; but the angel of
the LORD called to him from heaven, 'Abraham, Abraham.' He answered,
12 'Here I am.' The angel of the LORD said, 'Do not raise your hand against
the boy; do not touch him. Now I know that you are a God-fearing man.
13 You have not withheld from me your son, your only son.' Abraham looked
up, and there he saw a ram caught by its horns in a thicket. So he went and
14 took the ram and offered it as a sacrifice instead of his son. Abraham named
that place Jehovah-jireh;*c* and to this day the saying is: 'In the mountain of
15 the LORD it was provided.' Then the angel of the LORD called from heaven
16 a second time to Abraham, 'This is the word of the LORD: By my own self
I swear: inasmuch as you have done this and have not withheld your son,
17 your only son, I will bless you abundantly and greatly multiply your descendants until they are as numerous as the stars in the sky and the grains of
sand on the sea-shore. Your descendants shall possess the cities of their
18 enemies. All nations on earth shall pray to be blessed as your descendants
are blessed, and this because you have obeyed me.'
19   Abraham went back to his men, and together they returned to Beersheba;
and there Abraham remained.

a That is Well of Seven *and* Well of an Oath.   *b Or* planted a tamarisk.
c That is the LORD will provide.

After this Abraham was told, 'Milcah has borne sons to your brother 20
Nahor: Uz his first-born, then his brother Buz, and Kemuel father of 21
Aram, and Kesed, Hazo, Pildash, Jidlaph and Bethuel; and a daughter, 22 23
Rebecca, has been born to Bethuel.' These eight Milcah bore to Abraham's
brother Nahor. His concubine, whose name was Reumah, also bore him 24
sons: Tebah, Gaham, Tahash and Maacah.

Sarah lived for a hundred and twenty-seven years, and died in Kiriath- **23** 1 2
arba, which is Hebron, in Canaan. Abraham went in to mourn over Sarah
and to weep for her. At last he rose and left the presence of the dead. He 3
said to the Hittites, 'I am an alien and a settler among you. Give me land 4
enough for a burial-place, so that I can give my dead proper burial.' The 5
Hittites answered Abraham, 'Do, pray, listen to what we have to say, sir. 6
You are a mighty prince among us. Bury your dead in the best grave we
have. There is not one of us who will deny you his grave or hinder you from
burying your dead.' Abraham stood up and then bowed low to the Hittites, 7
the people of that country. He said to them, 'If you are willing to let me 8
give my dead proper burial, then listen to me and speak for me to Ephron
son of Zohar, asking him to give me the cave that belongs to him at Mach- 9
pelah, at the far end of his land. Let him give it to me for the full price, so
that I may take possession of it as a burial-place within your territory.'
Ephron the Hittite was sitting with the others, and he gave Abraham this 10
answer in the hearing of everyone as they came into the city gate: 'No, sir; 11
hear what I have to say. I will make you a gift of the land and I will also give
you the cave which is on it. In the presence of all my kinsmen I give it to
you; so bury your dead.' Abraham bowed low before the people of the 12
country and said to Ephron in their hearing, 'If you really mean it—but do 13
listen to me! I give you the price of the land: take it and I will bury my dead
there.' And Ephron answered, 'Do listen to me, sir: the land is worth four 14 15
hundred shekels of silver. But what is that between you and me? There
you may bury your dead.' Abraham came to an agreement with him and 16
weighed out the amount that Ephron had named in the hearing of the
Hittites, four hundred shekels of the standard recognized by merchants.
Thus the plot of land belonging to Ephron at Machpelah to the east of 17
Mamre, the plot, the cave that is on it, every tree on the plot, within the
whole area, became the legal possession of Abraham, in the presence of all 18
the Hittites as they came into the city gate. After this Abraham buried his 19
wife Sarah in the cave on the plot of land at Machpelah to the east of Mamre,
which is Hebron, in Canaan. Thus the plot and the cave on it became 20
Abraham's possession as a burial-place, by purchase from the Hittites.

BY THIS TIME Abraham had become a very old man, and the LORD had **24**
blessed him in all that he did. Abraham said to his servant, who had been 2
long in his service and was in charge of all his possessions, 'Put your hand
under my thigh: I want you to swear by the LORD, the God of heaven and 3
earth, that you will not take a wife for my son from the women of the
Canaanites in whose land I dwell; you must go to my own country and to 4
my own kindred to find a wife for my son Isaac.' The servant said to him, 5
'What if the woman is unwilling to come with me to this country? Must I

6 in that event take your son back to the land from which you came?' Abra-
7 ham said to him, 'On no account are you to take my son back there. The
Lord the God of heaven who took me from my father's house and the land
of my birth, the Lord who swore to me that he would give this land to my
descendants—he will send his angel before you, and from there you shall
8 take a wife for my son. If the woman is unwilling to come with you, then
you will be released from your oath to me; but you must not take my son
9 back there.' So the servant put his hand under his master Abraham's thigh
and swore an oath in those terms.

10   The servant took ten camels from his master's herds, and also all kinds
of gifts from his master; he set out for Aram-naharaim*a* and arrived at the
11 city where Nahor lived. Towards evening, the time when the women come
out to draw water, he made the camels kneel down by the well outside the
12 city. He said, 'O Lord God of my master Abraham, give me good fortune
13 this day; keep faith with my master Abraham. Here I stand by the spring,
14 and the women of the city are coming out to draw water. Let it be like this:
I shall say to a girl, "Please lower your jar so that I may drink"; and if she
answers, "Drink, and I will water your camels also", that will be the girl
whom thou dost intend for thy servant Isaac. In this way I shall know that
thou hast kept faith with my master.'

15   Before he had finished praying silently, he saw Rebecca coming out with
her water-jug on her shoulder. She was the daughter of Bethuel son of
16 Milcah, the wife of Abraham's brother Nahor. The girl was very beautiful,
a virgin, who had had no intercourse with a man. She went down to the
17 spring, filled her jar and came up again. Abraham's servant hurried to
18 meet her and said, 'Give me a sip of water from your jar.' 'Drink, sir', she
answered, and at once lowered her jar on to her hand to let him drink.
19 When she had finished giving him a drink, she said, 'Now I will draw water
20 for your camels until they have had enough.' So she quickly emptied her
jar into the water-trough, hurried again to the well to draw water and
21 watered all the camels. The man was watching quietly to see whether or not
22 the Lord had made his journey successful. When the camels had finished
drinking, the man took a gold nose-ring weighing half a shekel, and two
23 bracelets for her wrists weighing ten shekels, also of gold, and said, 'Tell
me, please, whose daughter you are. Is there room in your father's house for
24 us to spend the night?' She answered, 'I am the daughter of Bethuel, the
25 son of Nahor and Milcah; and we have plenty of straw and fodder and also
26 room for you to spend the night.' So the man bowed down and prostrated
27 himself to the Lord. He said, 'Blessed be the Lord the God of my master
Abraham, who has not failed to keep faith and truth with my master; for
I have been guided by the Lord to the house of my master's kinsman.'

28   The girl ran to her mother's house and told them what had happened.
29-30 Now Rebecca had a brother named Laban; and, when he saw the nose-
ring, and also the bracelets on his sister's wrists, and heard his sister
Rebecca tell what the man had said to her, he ran out to the man at the
spring. When he came to him and found him still standing there by the
31 camels, he said, 'Come in, sir, whom the Lord has blessed. Why stay

a That is Aram of Two Rivers.

outside? I have prepared the house, and there is room for the camels.' So 32
he brought the man into the house, unloaded the camels and provided straw
and fodder for them, and water for him and all his men to wash their feet.
Food was set before him, but he said, 'I will not eat until I have delivered 33
my message.' Laban said, 'Let us hear it.' He answered, 'I am the servant 34
of Abraham. The LORD has greatly blessed my master, and he has become a 35
man of power. The LORD has given him flocks and herds, silver and gold,
male and female slaves, camels and asses. My master's wife Sarah in her 36
old age bore him a son, to whom he has given all that he has. So my master 37
made me swear an oath, saying, "You shall not take a wife for my son from
the women of the Canaanites in whose land I dwell; but you shall go to my 38
father's house and to my family to find a wife for him." So I said to my 39
master, "What if the woman will not come with me?" He answered, "The 40
LORD, in whose presence I have lived, will send his angel with you and will
make your journey successful. You shall take a wife for my son from my
family and from my father's house; then you shall be released from the 41
charge I have laid upon you. But if, when you come to my family, they will
not give her to you, you shall still be released from the charge." So I came 42
to the spring today, and I said, "O LORD God of my master Abraham, if
thou wilt make my journey successful, let it be like this. Here I stand by 43
the spring. When a young woman comes out to draw water, I shall say to
her, 'Give me a little water to drink from your jar.' If she answers, 'Yes, 44
do drink, and I will draw water for your camels as well', she is the woman
whom the LORD intends for my master's son." Before I had finished pray- 45
ing silently, I saw Rebecca coming out with her water-jar on her shoulder.
She went down to the spring and drew some water, and I said to her,
"Please give me a drink." She quickly lowered her jar from her shoulder 46
and said, "Drink; and I will water your camels as well." So I drank, and
she also gave my camels water. I asked her whose daughter she was, and 47
she said, "I am the daughter of Bethuel, the son of Nahor and Milcah."
Then I put the ring in her nose and the bracelets on her wrists, and I 48
bowed low and prostrated myself before the LORD. I blessed the LORD the
God of my master Abraham, who had led me by the right road to take my
master's niece for his son. Now tell me if you will keep faith and truth with 49
my master. If not, say so, and I will turn elsewhere.'
    Laban and Bethuel answered, 'This is from the LORD; we can say no- 50
thing for or against. Here is Rebecca herself; take her and go. She shall be 51
the wife of your master's son, as the LORD has decreed.' When Abraham's 52
servant heard what they said, he prostrated himself on the ground before
the LORD. Then he brought out gold and silver ornaments, and robes, and 53
gave them to Rebecca, and he gave costly gifts to her brother and her
mother. He and his men then ate and drank and spent the night there. 54
When they rose in the morning, he said, 'Give me leave to go back to my
master.' Her brother and her mother said, 'Let the girl stay with us for a 55
few days, say ten days, and then she shall go.' But he said to them, 'Do not 56
detain me, for the LORD has granted me success. Give me leave to return
to my master.' They said, 'Let us call the girl and see what she says.' They 57 58
called Rebecca and asked her if she would go with the man, and she said,

59 'Yes, I will go.' So they let their sister Rebecca and her nurse go with
60 Abraham's servant and his men. They blessed Rebecca and said to her:

> 'You are our sister, may you be the mother of myriads;
> may your sons possess the cities of their enemies.'

61 Then Rebecca and her companions mounted their camels at once and
followed the man. So the servant took Rebecca and went his way.
62 Isaac meanwhile had moved on as far as Beer-lahai-roi and was living in
63 the Negeb. One evening when he had gone out into the open country hoping
64 to meet them,*a* he looked up and saw camels approaching. When Rebecca
65 raised her eyes and saw Isaac, she slipped hastily from her camel, saying to
the servant, 'Who is that man walking across the open towards us?' The
servant answered, 'It is my master.' So she took her veil and covered her-
66 67 self. The servant related to Isaac all that had happened. Isaac conducted
her into the tent*b* and took her as his wife. So she became his wife, and he
loved her and was consoled for the death of his mother.

25 1*c* 2 ABRAHAM MARRIED ANOTHER WIFE, whose name was Keturah. She
3 bore him Zimran, Jokshan, Medan, Midian, Ishbak and Shuah. Jokshan
became the father of Sheba and Dedan. The sons of Dedan were Asshurim,
4 Letushim and Leummim, and the sons of Midian were Ephah, Epher,
Enoch, Abida and Eldaah. All these were descendants of Keturah.
5 6 Abraham had given all that he had to Isaac; and he had already in his
lifetime given presents to the sons of his concubines, and had sent them
7 away eastwards, to a land of the east, out of his son Isaac's way. Abraham
8 had lived for a hundred and seventy-five years when he breathed his last.
He died at a good old age, after a very long life, and was gathered to his
9 father's kin. His sons, Isaac and Ishmael, buried him in the cave at Mach-
10 pelah, on the land of Ephron son of Zohar the Hittite, east of Mamre, the
plot which Abraham had bought from the Hittites. There Abraham was
11 buried with his wife Sarah. After the death of Abraham, God blessed his
son Isaac, who settled close by Beer-lahai-roi.
12 This is the table of the descendants of Abraham's son Ishmael, whom
13*d* Hagar the Egyptian, Sarah's slave-girl, bore to him. These are the names
of the sons of Ishmael named in order of their birth: Nebaioth, Ishmael's
14 15 eldest son, then Kedar, Adbeel, Mibsam, Mishma, Dumah, Massa, Hadad,
16 Teman, Jetur, Naphish and Kedemah. These are the sons of Ishmael,
after whom their hamlets and encampments were named, twelve princes
17 according to their tribal groups. Ishmael had lived for a hundred and thirty-
seven years when he breathed his last. So he died and was gathered to his
18 father's kin. Ishmael's sons inhabited the land from Havilah to Shur, which
is east of Egypt on the way to Asshur, having settled to the east of his
brothers.

19 THIS IS THE TABLE of the descendants of Abraham's son Isaac. Isaac's
20 father was Abraham. When Isaac was forty years old he married Rebecca

---

a hoping . . . them: *or* to relieve himself.   *b* *Prob. rdg.*; *Heb. adds* Sarah his mother.
c *Verses 1-4: cp. 1 Chr. 1. 32, 33.*   *d* *Verses 13-16: cp. 1 Chr. 1. 29-31.*

the daughter of Bethuel the Aramaean from Paddan-aram and the sister
of Laban the Aramaean. Isaac appealed to the LORD on behalf of his wife   21
because she was barren; the LORD yielded to his entreaty, and Rebecca
conceived. The children pressed hard on each other in her womb, and she   22
said, 'If this is how it is with me, what does it mean?' So she went to seek
guidance of the LORD. The LORD said to her: 23

> 'Two nations in your womb,
> two peoples, going their own ways from birth!
> One shall be stronger than the other;
> the older shall be servant to the younger.'

When her time had come, there were indeed twins in her womb. The first   24 25
came out red, hairy all over like a hair-cloak, and they named him Esau.*a*
Immediately afterwards his brother was born with his hand grasping   26
Esau's heel, and they called him Jacob.*b* Isaac was sixty years old when
they were born. The boys grew up; and Esau became skilful in hunting,   27
a man of the open plains, but Jacob led a settled life and stayed among the
tents. Isaac favoured Esau because he kept him supplied with venison, but 28
Rebecca favoured Jacob. One day Jacob prepared a broth and when Esau   29
came in from the country, exhausted, he said to Jacob, 'I am exhausted;   30
let me swallow some of that red broth': this is why he was called Edom.*c*
Jacob said, 'Not till you sell me your rights as the first-born.' Esau replied, 31 32
'I am at death's door; what use is my birthright to me?' Jacob said, 'Not 33
till you swear!'; so he swore an oath and sold his birthright to Jacob. Then 34
Jacob gave Esau bread and the lentil broth, and he ate and drank and went
away without more ado. Thus Esau showed how little he valued his birthright.

There came a famine in the land—not the earlier famine in Abraham's   **26**
time—and Isaac went to Abimelech the Philistine king at Gerar. The   2
LORD appeared to Isaac and said, 'Do not go down to Egypt, but stay in
this country as I bid you. Stay in this country and I will be with you and 3
bless you, for to you and to your descendants I will give all these lands.
Thus shall I fulfil the oath which I swore to your father Abraham. I will   4
make your descendants as many as the stars in the sky; I will give them all
these lands, and all the nations of the earth will pray to be blessed as they
are blessed—all because Abraham obeyed me and kept my charge, my   5
commandments, my statutes, and my laws.' So Isaac lived in Gerar.   6
When the men of the place asked him about his wife, he told them that   7
she was his sister; he was afraid to say that Rebecca was his wife, in case
they killed him because of her; for she was very beautiful. When they had 8
been there for some considerable time, Abimelech the Philistine king
looked down from his window and saw Isaac and his wife Rebecca laughing
together. He summoned Isaac and said, 'So she is your wife, is she? What   9
made you say she was your sister?' Isaac answered, 'I thought I should be
killed because of her.' Abimelech said, 'Why have you treated us like this? 10
One of the people might easily have gone to bed with your wife, and then
you would have made us liable to retribution.' So Abimelech warned all   11

a That is Covering.   *b That is* He caught by the heel.   *c That is* Red.

the people, threatening that whoever touched this man or his wife would be put to death.

12 Isaac sowed seed in that land, and that year he reaped a hundredfold,
13 and the LORD blessed him. He became more and more powerful, until he
14 was very powerful indeed. He had flocks and herds and many slaves, so
15 that the Philistines were envious of him. They had stopped up all the wells dug by the slaves in the days of Isaac's father Abraham, and filled them with
18 earth. Isaac dug them again, all those wells dug in his father Abraham's time, and stopped up by the Philistines after his death, and he called them by the names which his father had given them.

16 Then Abimelech said to him, 'Go away from here; you are too strong for
17 us.' So Isaac left that place and encamped in the valley of Gerar, and stayed
19*a* there. Then Isaac's slaves dug in the valley and found a spring of running
20 water, but the shepherds of Gerar quarrelled with Isaac's shepherds, claiming the water as theirs. He called the well Esek,*b* because they made diffi-
21 culties for him. His men then dug another well, but the others quarrelled
22 with him over that also, so he called it Sitnah.*c* He moved on from there and dug another well, but there was no quarrel over that one, so he called it Rehoboth,*d* saying, 'Now the LORD has given us plenty of room and we shall be fruitful in the land.'

23 24 Isaac went up country from there to Beersheba. That same night the LORD appeared to him there and said, 'I am the God of your father Abraham. Fear nothing, for I am with you. I will bless you and give you many
25 descendants for the sake of Abraham my servant.' So Isaac built an altar there and invoked the LORD by name. Then he pitched his tent there, and
26 there also his slaves dug a well. Abimelech came to him from Gerar with
27 Ahuzzath his friend and Phicol the commander of his army. Isaac said to them, 'Why have you come here? You hate me and you sent me away.'
28 They answered, 'We have seen plainly that the LORD is with you, so we thought, "Let the two of us put each other to the oath and make a treaty
29 that will bind us." We have not attacked you, we have done you nothing but good, and we let you go away peaceably. Swear that you will do us no
30 harm, now that the LORD has blessed you.' So Isaac gave a feast and they
31 ate and drank. They rose early in the morning and exchanged oaths. Then
32 Isaac bade them farewell, and they parted from him in peace. The same day Isaac's slaves came and told him about a well that they had dug: 'We have
33 found water', they said. He named the well Shibah.*e* This is why the city is called Beersheba*f* to this day.

34 When Esau was forty years old he married Judith daughter of Beeri
35 the Hittite, and Basemath daughter of Elon the Hittite; this was a bitter grief to Isaac and Rebecca.

a Verse 18 transposed to follow 15.   *b That is* Difficulty.   *c That is* Enmity.
d That is Plenty of room.   *e That is* Oath.   *f That is* Well of an Oath.

Jacob and Esau

WHEN ISAAC GREW OLD and his eyes became so dim that he could **27** not see, he called his elder son Esau and said to him, 'My son', and he answered, 'Here I am.' Isaac said, 'Listen now: I am old and I do not **2** know when I may die. Take your hunting gear, your quiver and your bow, **3** and go out into the country and get me some venison. Then make me a **4** savoury dish of the kind I like, and bring it to me to eat so that I may give you my blessing before I die.' Now Rebecca was listening as Isaac talked **5** to his son Esau. When Esau went off into the country to find some venison and bring it home, she said to her son Jacob, 'I heard your father talking to **6** your brother Esau, and he said, "Bring me some venison and make it into **7** a savoury dish so that I may eat it and bless you in the presence of the LORD before I die." Listen to me, my son, and do what I tell you. Go to the flock **8 9** and pick me out two fine young kids, and I will make them into a savoury dish for your father, of the kind he likes. Then take them in to your father, **10** and he will eat them so that he may bless you before he dies.' Jacob said **11** to his mother Rebecca, 'But my brother Esau is a hairy man, and my skin is smooth. Suppose my father feels me, he will know I am tricking him and **12** I shall bring a curse upon myself instead of a blessing.' His mother answered **13** him, 'Let the curse fall on me, my son, but do as I say; go and bring me the kids.' So Jacob fetched them and brought them to his mother, who made **14** them into a savoury dish of the kind that his father liked. Then Rebecca **15** took her elder son's clothes, Esau's best clothes which she kept by her in the house, and put them on her younger son Jacob. She put the goatskins **16** on his hands and on the smooth nape of his neck; and she handed her **17** son Jacob the savoury dish and the bread she had made. He came to his **18** father and said, 'Father.' He answered, 'Yes, my son; who are you?' Jacob **19** answered his father, 'I am Esau, your elder son. I have done as you told me. Come, sit up and eat some of my venison, so that you may give me your blessing.' Isaac said to his son, 'What is this that you found so quickly?', **20** and Jacob answered, 'It is what the LORD your God put in my way.' Isaac **21** then said to Jacob, 'Come close and let me feel you, my son, to see whether you are really my son Esau.' When Jacob came close to his father, Isaac **22** felt him and said, 'The voice is Jacob's voice, but the hands are the hands of Esau.' He did not recognize him because his hands were hairy like **23** Esau's, and that is why he blessed him. He said, 'Are you really my son **24** Esau?', and he answered, 'Yes.' Then Isaac said, 'Bring me some of your **25** venison to eat, my son, so that I may give you my blessing.' Then Jacob brought it to him, and he ate it; he brought wine also, and he drank it. Then his father Isaac said to him, 'Come near, my son, and kiss me.' So **26 27** he came near and kissed him, and when Isaac smelt the smell of his clothes, he blessed him and said:

> 'Ah! The smell of my son is like the smell of open country
>   blessed by the LORD.
> God give you dew from heaven **28**
>   and the richness of the earth,
> corn and new wine in plenty!

29   Peoples shall serve you,
             nations bow down to you.
                Be lord over your brothers;
             may your mother's sons bow down to you.
             A curse upon those who curse you;
             a blessing on those who bless you!'

30   Isaac finished blessing Jacob; and Jacob had scarcely left his father
31 Isaac's presence, when his brother Esau came in from his hunting. He too
   made a savoury dish and brought it to his father. He said, 'Come, father,
32 and eat some of my venison, so that you may give me your blessing.' His
   father Isaac said, 'Who are you?' He said, 'I am Esau, your elder son.'
33 Then Isaac became greatly agitated*a* and said, 'Then who was it that
   hunted and brought me venison? I ate it all before you came in and I
34 blessed him, and the blessing will stand.' When Esau heard what his father
35 said, he gave a loud and bitter cry and said, 'Bless me too, father.' But
   Isaac said, 'Your brother came treacherously and took away your blessing.'
36 Esau said, 'He is rightly called Jacob.*b* This is the second time he has supplanted me. He took away my right as the first-born and now he has taken
37 away my blessing. Have you kept back any blessing for me?' Isaac answered,
   'I have made him lord over you, and I have given him all his brothers as
   slaves. I have bestowed upon him corn and new wine for his sustenance.
38 What is there left that I can do for you, my son?' Esau asked his father,
   'Had you then only one blessing, father? Bless me too, my father.' And
39 Esau cried bitterly. Then his father Isaac answered:

             'Your dwelling shall be far from the richness of the earth,
                far from the dew of heaven above.
40   By your sword shall you live,
                and you shall serve your brother;
             but the time will come when you grow restive
                and break off his yoke from your neck.'

41   Esau bore a grudge against Jacob because of the blessing which his father
   had given him, and he said to himself, 'The time of mourning for my father
42 will soon be here; then I will kill my brother Jacob.' When Rebecca was
43 told what her elder son Esau was saying, she called her younger son Jacob,
44 and she said to him, 'Esau your brother is threatening to kill you. Now, my
45 son, listen to me. Slip away at once to my brother Laban in Harran. Stay
   with him for a while until your brother's anger cools. When it has subsided
   and he forgets what you have done to him, I will send and fetch you back.
   Why should I lose you both in one day?'

46   Rebecca said to Isaac, 'I am weary to death of Hittite women! If Jacob
   marries a Hittite woman like those who live here, my life will not be worth
28 living.' Isaac called Jacob, blessed him and gave him instructions. He said,
 2 'You must not marry one of these women of Canaan. Go at once to the
   house of Bethuel, your mother's father, in Paddan-aram, and there find
 3 a wife, one of the daughters of Laban, your mother's brother. God Almighty

---

a Or incensed.   *b* That is He supplanted.

bless you, make you fruitful and increase your descendants until they
become a host of nations. May he bestow on you and your offspring the 4
blessing of Abraham, and may you thus possess the country where you are
now living, the land which God gave to Abraham!' So Isaac sent Jacob 5
away, and he went to Paddan-aram to Laban, son of Bethuel the Aramaean,
and brother to Rebecca the mother of Jacob and Esau. Esau discovered 6
that Isaac had given Jacob his blessing and had sent him away to Paddan-
aram to find a wife there; and that when he blessed him he had forbidden
him to marry a woman of Canaan, and that Jacob had obeyed his father 7
and mother and gone to Paddan-aram. Then Esau, seeing that his father 8
disliked the women of Canaan, went to Ishmael, and, in addition to his 9
other wives, he married Mahalath sister of Nebaioth and daughter of
Abraham's son Ishmael.

Jacob set out from Beersheba and went on his way towards Harran. He 10 11
came to a certain place and stopped there for the night, because the sun
had set; and, taking one of the stones there, he made it a pillow for his head
and lay down to sleep. He dreamt that he saw a ladder, which rested on the 12
ground with its top reaching to heaven, and angels of God were going up
and down upon it. The LORD was standing beside him[a] and said, 'I am the 13
LORD, the God of your father Abraham and the God of Isaac. This land on
which you are lying I will give to you and your descendants. They shall be 14
countless as the dust upon the earth, and you shall spread far and wide, to
north and south, to east and west. All the families of the earth shall pray to
be blessed as you and your descendants are blessed. I will be with you, and 15
I will protect you wherever you go and will bring you back to this land; for
I will not leave you until I have done all that I have promised.' Jacob woke 16
from his sleep and said, 'Truly the LORD is in this place, and I did not
know it.' Then he was afraid and said, 'How fearsome is this place! This is 17
no other than the house of God, this is the gate of heaven.' Jacob rose early 18
in the morning, took the stone on which he had laid his head, set it up as a
sacred pillar and poured oil on the top of it. He named that place Beth- 19
El;[b] but the earlier name of the city was Luz.

Thereupon Jacob made this vow: 'If God will be with me, if he will 20
protect me on my journey and give me food to eat and clothes to wear, and 21
I come back safely to my father's house, then the LORD shall be my God,
and this stone which I have set up as a sacred pillar shall be a house of God. 22
And of all that thou givest me, I will without fail allot a tenth part to thee.'

JACOB CONTINUED HIS JOURNEY and came to the land of the eastern 29
tribes. There he saw a well in the open country and three flocks of sheep 2
lying beside it, because the flocks were watered from that well. Over its
mouth was a huge stone, and all the herdsmen used to gather there and roll 3
it off the mouth of the well and water the flocks; then they would put it
back in its place over the well. Jacob said to them, 'Where are you from, 4
my friends?' 'We are from Harran', they replied. He asked them if they 5
knew Laban the grandson of Nahor. They answered, 'Yes, we do.' 'Is he 6
well?' Jacob asked; and they answered, 'Yes, he is well, and here is his

_____
    [a] *Or* on it *or* by it.   [b] *That is* House of God.

31

7 daughter Rachel coming with the flock.' Jacob said, 'The sun is still high, and the time for folding the sheep has not yet come. Water the flocks and
8 then go and graze them.' But they replied, 'We cannot, until all the herdsmen have gathered together and the stone is rolled away from the mouth of
9 the well; then we can water our flocks.' While he was talking to them,
10 Rachel came up with her father's flock, for she was a shepherdess. When Jacob saw Rachel, the daughter of Laban his mother's brother, with Laban's flock, he stepped forward, rolled the stone off the mouth of the
11 well and watered Laban's sheep. He kissed Rachel, and was moved to
12 tears. He told her that he was her father's kinsman and Rebecca's son; so
13 she ran and told her father. When Laban heard the news of his sister's son Jacob, he ran to meet him, embraced him, kissed him warmly and welcomed
14 him to his home. Jacob told Laban everything, and Laban said, 'Yes, you are my own flesh and blood.' So Jacob stayed with him for a whole month.
15 Laban said to Jacob, 'Why should you work for me for nothing simply
16 because you are my kinsman? Tell me what your wages ought to be.' Now Laban had two daughters: the elder was called Leah, and the younger
17 18 Rachel. Leah was dull-eyed, but Rachel was graceful and beautiful. Jacob had fallen in love with Rachel and he said, 'I will work seven years for your
19 younger daughter Rachel.' Laban replied, 'It is better that I should give her
20 to you than to anyone else; stay with me.' So Jacob worked seven years for
21 Rachel, and they seemed like a few days because he loved her. Then Jacob said to Laban, 'I have served my time. Give me my wife so that we may
22 sleep together.' So Laban gathered all the men of the place together and
23 gave a feast. In the evening he took his daughter Leah and brought her to
24 Jacob, and Jacob slept with her. At the same time Laban gave his slave-
25 girl Zilpah to his daughter Leah. But when morning came, Jacob saw that it was Leah and said to Laban, 'What have you done to me? Did I not work
26 for Rachel? Why have you deceived me?' Laban answered, 'In our country
27 it is not right to give the younger sister in marriage before the elder. Go through with the seven days' feast for the elder, and the younger shall be
28 given you in return for a further seven years' work.' Jacob agreed, and completed the seven days for Leah.
29 Then Laban gave Jacob his daughter Rachel as wife; and he gave his
30 slave-girl Bilhah to serve his daughter Rachel. Jacob slept with Rachel also; he loved her rather than Leah, and he worked for Laban for a further seven
31 years. When the LORD saw that Leah was not loved, he granted her a child;
32 but Rachel was childless. Leah conceived and bore a son; and she called him Reuben,*a* for she said, 'The LORD has seen my humiliation; now my
33 husband will love me.' Again she conceived and bore a son and said, 'The LORD, hearing that I am not loved, has given me this child also'; and she
34 called him Simeon.*b* She conceived again and bore a son; and she said, 'Now that I have borne him three sons my husband and I will surely be
35 united.' So she called him Levi.*c* Once more she conceived and bore a son; and she said, 'Now I will praise the LORD'; therefore she named him Judah.*d* Then for a while she bore no more children.

a That is See, a son.   *b That is* Hearing.   *c That is* Union.
d That is Praise.

When Rachel found that she bore Jacob no children, she became jealous **30**
of her sister and said to Jacob, 'Give me sons, or I shall die.' Jacob said 2
angrily to Rachel, 'Can I take the place of God, who has denied you children?' She said, 'Here is my slave-girl Bilhah. Lie with her, so that she may 3
bear sons to be laid upon my knees, and through her I too may build up a
family.' So she gave him her slave-girl Bilhah as a wife, and Jacob lay with 4
her. Bilhah conceived and bore Jacob a son. Then Rachel said, 'God has 5 6
given judgement for me; he has indeed heard me and given me a son', so
she named him Dan.*a* Rachel's slave-girl Bilhah again conceived and bore 7
Jacob another son. Rachel said, 'I have played a fine trick on my sister, 8
and it has succeeded'; so she named him Naphtali.*b* When Leah found 9
that she was bearing no more children, she took her slave-girl Zilpah and
gave her to Jacob as a wife, and Zilpah bore Jacob a son. Leah said, 'Good 10 11
fortune has come', and she named him Gad.*c* Zilpah, Leah's slave-girl, 12
bore Jacob another son, and Leah said, 'Happiness has come, for young 13
women will call me happy.' So she named him Asher.*d*

In the time of wheat-harvest Reuben went out and found some man- 14
drakes in the open country and brought them to his mother Leah. Then
Rachel asked Leah for some of her son's mandrakes, but Leah said, 'Is it 15
so small a thing to have taken away my husband, that you should take my
son's mandrakes as well?' But Rachel said, 'Very well, let him sleep with
you tonight in exchange for your son's mandrakes.' So when Jacob came 16
in from the country in the evening, Leah went out to meet him and said,
'You are to sleep with me tonight; I have hired you with my son's mandrakes.' That night he slept with her, and God heard Leah's prayer, and 17
she conceived and bore a fifth son. Leah said, 'God has rewarded me, 18
because I gave my slave-girl to my husband.' So she named him Issachar.*e*
Leah again conceived and bore a sixth son. She said, 'God has endowed 19 20
me with a noble dowry. Now my husband will treat me in princely style,
because I have borne him six sons.' So she named him Zebulun.*f* Later 21
she bore a daughter and named her Dinah. Then God thought of Rachel; 22
he heard her prayer and gave her a child; so she conceived and bore a 23
son and said, 'God has taken away my humiliation.' She named him 24
Joseph,*g* saying, 'May the LORD add another son!'

When Rachel had given birth to Joseph, Jacob said to Laban, 'Let me 25
go, for I wish to return to my own home and country. Give me my wives 26
and my children for whom I have served you, and I will go; for you know
what service I have done for you.' Laban said to him, 'Let me have my say, 27
if you please. I have become prosperous and the LORD has blessed me for
your sake. So now tell me what I owe you in wages, and I will give it you.' 28
Jacob answered, 'You must know how I have served you, and how your 29
herds have prospered under my care. You had only a few when I came, but 30
now they have increased beyond measure, and the LORD brought blessings
to you wherever I went. But is it not time for me to provide for my family?'
Laban said, 'Then what shall I give you?', but Jacob answered, 'Give me 31

---

a That is He has given judgement.　　　*b That is* Trickery.　　　*c That is* Good
Fortune.　　*d That is* Happy.　　*e That is* Reward.　　*f That is* Prince.
g The name may mean either He takes away *or* May he add.

nothing; I will mind your flocks *a* as before, if you will do what I suggest.

32 Today I will go over your flocks and pick out from them every black lamb, and all the brindled and the spotted goats, and they shall be my wages.

33 This is a fair offer, and it will be to my own disadvantage later on, when we come to settling my wages: every goat amongst mine that is not spotted or

34 brindled and every lamb that is not black will have been stolen.' Laban

35 said, 'Agreed; let it be as you have said.' But that day he removed the he-goats that were striped and brindled and all the spotted and brindled she-goats, all that had any white on them, and every ram that was black, and

36 he handed them over to his own sons. Then he put a distance of three days' journey between himself and Jacob, while Jacob was left tending those of

37 Laban's flocks that remained. Thereupon Jacob took fresh rods of white poplar, almond, and plane tree, and peeled off strips of bark, exposing the

38 white of the rods. Then he fixed the peeled rods upright in the troughs at the watering-places where the flocks came to drink; they faced the she-

39 goats that were on heat when they came to drink. They felt a longing for the rods and they gave birth to young that were striped and spotted and

40 brindled. As for the rams, Jacob divided them, and let the ewes run only with such of the rams in Laban's flock as were striped and black; and thus he bred separate flocks for himself, which he did not add to Laban's sheep.

41 As for the goats, whenever the more vigorous were on heat, he put the rods

42 in front of them at the troughs so that they would long for the rods; he did not put them there for the weaker goats. Thus the weaker came to be

43 Laban's and the stronger Jacob's. So Jacob increased in wealth more and more until he possessed great flocks, male and female slaves, camels, and asses.

31 JACOB LEARNT that Laban's sons were saying, 'Jacob has taken every-thing that was our father's, and all his wealth has come from our father's

2 property.' He also noticed that Laban was not so well disposed to him as

3 he had once been. Then the LORD said to Jacob, 'Go back to the land of

4 your fathers and to your kindred. I will be with you.' So Jacob sent to

5 fetch Rachel and Leah to his flocks out in the country and said to them, 'I see that your father is not as well disposed to me as once he was; yet the

6 God of my father has been with me. You know how I have served your

7 father to the best of my power, but he has cheated me and changed my

8 wages ten times over. Yet God did not let him do me any harm. If Laban said, "The spotted ones shall be your wages", then all the flock bore spotted young; and if he said, "The striped ones shall be your wages", then all the

9 flock bore striped young. God has taken away your father's property and

10 has given it to me. In the season when the flocks were on heat, I had a dream: I looked up and saw that the he-goats mounting the flock were striped and

11 spotted and dappled. The angel of God said to me in my dream, "Jacob",

12 and I replied, "Here I am", and he said, "Look up and see: all the he-goats mounting the flock are striped and spotted and dappled. I have seen

13 all that Laban is doing to you. I am the God who appeared to you at Bethel where you anointed a sacred pillar and where you made your vow. Now

a *Prob. rdg.; Heb. adds* I will watch.

leave this country at once and return to the land of your birth."' Rachel 14
and Leah answered him, 'We no longer have any part or lot in our father's
house. Does he not look on us as foreigners, now that he has sold us and 15
spent on himself the whole of the money paid for us? But all the wealth 16
which God has saved from our father's clutches is ours and our children's.
Now do everything that God has said.' Jacob at once set his sons and his 17
wives on camels, and drove off all the herds and livestock which he had 18
acquired in Paddan-aram, to go to his father Isaac in Canaan.

When Laban the Aramaean had gone to shear his sheep, Rachel stole 19
her father's household gods, and Jacob deceived Laban, keeping his 20
departure secret. So Jacob ran away with all that he had, crossed the River 21
and made for the hill-country of Gilead. Three days later, when Laban 22
heard that Jacob had run away, he took his kinsmen with him, pursued 23
Jacob for seven days and caught up with him in the hill-country of Gilead.
But God came to Laban in a dream by night and said to him, 'Be careful 24
to say nothing to Jacob, either good or bad.'

When Laban overtook him, Jacob had pitched his tent in the hill- 25
country of Gilead, and Laban pitched his in the company of his kinsmen in
the same hill-country. Laban said to Jacob, 'What have you done? You 26
have deceived me and carried off my daughters as though they were captives taken in war. Why did you slip away secretly without telling me? I 27
would have set you on your way with songs and the music of tambourines
and harps. You did not even let me kiss my daughters and their children. 28
In this you were at fault. It is in my power to do you an injury, but yester- 29
day the God of your father spoke to me; he told me to be careful to say
nothing to you, either good or bad. I know that you went away because 30
you were homesick and pining for your father's house, but why did you
steal my gods?'

Jacob answered, 'I was afraid; I thought you would take your daughters 31
from me by force. Whoever is found in possession of your gods shall die 32
for it. Let our kinsmen here be witnesses: point out anything I have that
is yours, and take it back.' Jacob did not know that Rachel had stolen the
gods. So Laban went into Jacob's tent and Leah's tent and that of the two 33
slave-girls, but he found nothing. When he came out of Leah's tent he
went into Rachel's. Now she had taken the household gods and put them 34
in the camel-bag and was sitting on them. Laban went through everything
in the tent and found nothing. Rachel said to her father, 'Do not take it 35
amiss, sir, that I cannot rise in your presence: the common lot of woman
is upon me.' So for all his search Laban did not find his household gods.

Jacob was angry, and he expostulated with Laban, exclaiming, 'What 36
have I done wrong? What is my offence, that you have come after me in hot
pursuit and gone through all my possessions? Have you found anything 37
belonging to your household? If so, set it here in front of my kinsmen and
yours, and let them judge between the two of us. In all the twenty years 38
I have been with you, your ewes and she-goats have never miscarried; I
have not eaten the rams of your flocks; I have never brought to you the 39
body of any animal mangled by wild beasts, but I bore the loss myself; you
claimed compensation from me for anything stolen by day or by night.

40 This was the way of it: by day the heat consumed me and the frost by night,
41 and sleep deserted me. For twenty years I have been in your household. I
worked for you fourteen years to win your two daughters and six years for
42 your flocks, and you changed my wages ten times over. If the God of my
father, the God of Abraham and the Fear of Isaac, had not been with me,
you would have sent me away empty-handed. But God saw my labour and
my hardships, and last night he rebuked you.'

43　　Laban answered Jacob, 'The daughters are my daughters, the children
are my children, the flocks are my flocks; all that you see is mine. But as
for my daughters, what can I do today about them and the children they
44 have borne? Come now, we will make an agreement, you and I, and let it
45 stand as a witness between us.' So Jacob chose a great stone and set it up-
46 right as a sacred pillar. Then he told his kinsmen to gather stones, and they
took them and built a cairn, and there beside the cairn they ate together.
47 48 Laban called it Jegar-sahadutha,*a* and Jacob called it Gal-ed.*b* Laban said,
'This cairn is witness today between you and me.' For this reason it was
49 named Gal-ed; it was also named Mizpah,*c* for Laban said, 'May the LORD
50 watch between you and me, when we are parted from each other's sight. If
you ill-treat my daughters or take other wives beside them when no one is
51 there to see, then God be witness between us.' Laban said further to Jacob,
52 'Here is this cairn, and here the pillar which I have set up between us. This
cairn is witness and the pillar is witness: I for my part will not pass beyond
this cairn to your side, and you for your part shall not pass beyond this
53 cairn and this pillar to my side to do an injury, otherwise the God of Abraham and the God of Nahor will judge between us.' And Jacob swore this
54 oath in the name of the Fear of Isaac his father. He slaughtered an animal
for sacrifice, there in the hill-country, and summoned his kinsmen to the
feast. So they ate together and spent the night there.

55　　Laban rose early in the morning, kissed his daughters and their child-
32 ren, blessed them and went home again. Then Jacob continued his journey
2 and was met by angels of God. When he saw them, Jacob said, 'This is the
company of God', and he called that place Mahanaim.*d*

3　　Jacob sent messengers on ahead to his brother Esau to the district of Seir
4 in the Edomite country, and this is what he told them to say to Esau, 'My
lord, your servant Jacob says, I have been living with Laban and have
5 stayed there till now. I have oxen, asses, and sheep, and male and female
slaves, and I have sent to tell you this, my lord, so that I may win your
6 favour.' The messengers returned to Jacob and said, 'We met your brother
7 Esau already on the way to meet you with four hundred men.' Jacob, much
afraid and distressed, divided the people with him, as well as the sheep,
8 cattle, and camels, into two companies, thinking that, if Esau should come
9 upon one company and destroy it, the other company would survive. Jacob
said, 'O God of my father Abraham, God of my father Isaac, O LORD at
whose bidding I came back to my own country and to my kindred, and
10 who didst promise me prosperity, I am not worthy of all the true and steadfast love which thou hast shown to me thy servant. When I crossed the

---

a *Aramaic for* Cairn of Witness.　　　*b* *Hebrew for* Cairn of Witness.
c *That is* Watch-tower.　　*d* *That is* Two Companies.

Jordan, I had nothing but the staff in my hand; now I have two companies.
Save me, I pray, from my brother Esau, for I am afraid that he may come 11
and destroy me, sparing neither mother nor child. But thou didst say, I will 12
prosper you and will make your descendants like the sand of the sea, which
is beyond all counting.'

Jacob spent that night there; and as a present for his brother Esau he 13
chose from the herds he had with him two hundred she-goats, twenty he- 14
goats, two hundred ewes and twenty rams, thirty milch-camels with their 15
young, forty cows and ten young bulls, twenty she-asses and ten he-asses.
He put each herd separately into the care of a servant and said to each, 'Go 16
on ahead of me, and leave gaps between the herds.' Then he gave these 17
instructions to the first: 'When my brother Esau meets you and asks you
to whom you belong and where you are going and who owns these beasts
you are driving, you are to say, "They belong to your servant Jacob; he 18
sends them as a present to my lord Esau, and he is behind us."' He gave 19
the same instructions to the second, to the third, and all the drovers, telling
them to say the same thing to Esau when they met him. And they were to 20
add, 'Your servant Jacob is behind us'; for he thought, 'I will appease him
with the present that I have sent on ahead, and afterwards, when I come
into his presence, he will perhaps receive me kindly.' So Jacob's present 21
went on ahead of him, but he himself spent that night at Mahaneh.

During the night Jacob rose, took his two wives, his two slave-girls, and 22
his eleven sons, and crossed the ford of Jabbok. He took them and sent 23
them across the gorge with all that he had. So Jacob was left alone, and a 24
man wrestled with him there till[a] daybreak. When the man saw that he 25
could not throw Jacob, he struck him in the hollow of his thigh, so that
Jacob's hip was dislocated as they wrestled. The man said, 'Let me go, 26
for day is breaking', but Jacob replied, 'I will not let you go unless you bless
me.' He said to Jacob, 'What is your name?', and he answered, 'Jacob.' 27
The man said, 'Your name shall no longer be Jacob, but Israel,[b] because 28
you strove with God and with men, and prevailed.' Jacob said, 'Tell me, 29
I pray, your name.' He replied, 'Why do you ask my name?', but he gave
him his blessing there. Jacob called the place Peniel,[c] 'because', he said, 30
'I have seen God face to face and my life is spared.' The sun rose as Jacob 31
passed through Penuel, limping because of his hip. This is why the Israel- 32
ites to this day do not eat the sinew of the nerve that runs in the hollow of
the thigh; for the man had struck Jacob on that nerve in the hollow of the
thigh.

Jacob raised his eyes and saw Esau coming towards him with four 33
hundred men; so he divided the children between Leah and Rachel and
the two slave-girls. He put the slave-girls with their children in front, Leah 2
with her children next, and Rachel with Joseph last. He then went on 3
ahead of them, bowing low to the ground seven times as he approached his
brother. Esau ran to meet him and embraced him; he threw his arms round 4
him and kissed him, and they wept. When Esau looked up and saw the 5
women and children, he said, 'Who are these with you?' Jacob replied,
'The children whom God has graciously given to your servant.' The 6

[a] *Or* at.   [b] *That is* God strove.   [c] *That is* Face of God (*elsewhere* Penuel).

7 slave-girls came near, each with her children, and they bowed low. Then Leah with her children came near and bowed low, and afterwards Joseph
8 and Rachel came near and bowed low also. Esau said, 'What was all that company of yours that I met?' And he answered, 'It was meant to win favour
9 with you, my lord.' Esau answered, 'I have more than enough. Keep what
10 is yours, my brother.' But Jacob said, 'On no account: if I have won your favour, then, I pray, accept this gift from me; for, you see, I come into your
11 presence as into that of a god, and you receive me favourably. Accept this gift which I bring you; for God has been gracious to me, and I have all I want.' So he urged him, and he accepted it.
12 13   Then Esau said, 'Let us set out, and I will go at your pace.' But Jacob answered him, 'You must know, my lord, that the children are small; the flocks and herds are suckling their young and I am concerned for them, and
14 if the men overdrive them for a single day, all my beasts will die. I beg you, my lord, to go on ahead, and I will go by easy stages at the pace of the children and of the livestock that I am driving, until I come to my lord in Seir.'
15 Esau said, 'Let me detail some of my own men to escort you', but he replied,
16 'Why should my lord be so kind to me?' That day Esau turned back towards
17 Seir, but Jacob set out for Succoth; and there he built himself a house and made shelters for his cattle. Therefore he named that place Succoth.[a]
18   On his journey from Paddan-aram, Jacob came safely to the city of
19 Shechem in Canaan and pitched his tent to the east of it. The strip of country where he had pitched his tent he bought from the sons of Hamor
20 father of Shechem for a hundred sheep.[b] There he set up an altar and called it El-Elohey-Israel.[c]

34 DINAH, THE DAUGHTER WHOM LEAH HAD BORNE to Jacob, went out
2 to visit the women of the country, and Shechem, son of Hamor the Hivite the local prince, saw her; he took her, lay with her and dishonoured her.
3 But he remained true to Jacob's daughter Dinah; he loved the girl and
4 comforted her. So Shechem said to his father Hamor, 'Get me this girl for
5 a wife.' When Jacob heard that Shechem had violated his daughter Dinah, his sons were with the herds in the open country, so he said nothing until
6 they came home. Meanwhile Shechem's father Hamor came out to Jacob
7 to discuss it with him. When Jacob's sons came in from the country and heard, they were grieved and angry, because in lying with Jacob's daughter he had done what the Israelites held to be an outrage, an intolerable thing.
8 Hamor appealed to them in these terms: 'My son Shechem is in love with
9 this girl; I beg you to let him have her as his wife. Let us ally ourselves in marriage; you shall give us your daughters, and you shall take ours in
10 exchange. You must settle among us. The country is open to you; make
11 your home in it, move about freely and acquire land of your own.' And Shechem said to the girl's father and brothers, 'I am eager to win your
12 favour and I will give whatever you ask. Fix the bride-price and the gift as high as you like, and I will give whatever you ask; but you must give me the girl in marriage.'

[a] *That is* Shelters.   [b] *Or* pieces of money (*cp. Josh.* 24. 32; *Job* 42. 11).
[c] *That is* God the God of Israel.

Jacob's sons gave a dishonest reply to Shechem and his father Hamor, 13
laying a trap for them because Shechem had violated their sister Dinah:
'We cannot do this,' they said; 'we cannot give our sister to a man who is 14
uncircumcised; for we look on that as a disgrace. There is one condition 15
on which we will consent: if you will follow our example and have every
male among you circumcised, we will give you our daughters and take 16
yours for ourselves. Then we can live among you, and we shall all become
one people. But if you refuse to listen to us and be circumcised, we will 17
take the girl and go away.' Their proposal pleased Hamor and his son 18
Shechem; and the young man, who was held in respect above anyone in 19
his father's house, did not hesitate to do what they had said, because his
heart was taken by Jacob's daughter.

So Hamor and Shechem went back to the city gate and addressed their 20
fellow-citizens: 'These men are friendly to us; let them live in our country 21
and move freely in it. The land has room enough for them. Let us marry
their daughters and give them ours. But these men will agree to live with 22
us and become one people on this one condition only: every male among
us must be circumcised as they have been. Will not their herds, their live- 23
stock, and all their chattels then be ours? We need only consent to their
condition, and then they are free to live with us.' All the able-bodied men 24
agreed with Hamor and Shechem, and every single one of them was circumcised, every able-bodied male. Then two days later, while they were still 25
in great pain, Jacob's two sons Simeon and Levi, full brothers to Dinah,
armed themselves with swords, boldly entered the city and killed every
male. They cut down Hamor and his son Shechem and took Dinah from 26
Shechem's house and went off with her. Then Jacob's other sons came in 27
over the dead bodies and plundered the city, to avenge their sister's dishonour. They seized flocks, cattle, asses, and everything, both inside the 28
city and outside in the open country; they also carried off all their posses- 29
sions, their dependants, and their women, and plundered everything in
the houses.

Jacob said to Simeon and Levi, 'You have brought trouble on me, you 30
have made my name stink among the people of the country, the Canaanites
and the Perizzites. My numbers are few; if they muster against me and
attack me, I shall be destroyed, I and my household with me.' They 31
answered, 'Is our sister to be treated as a common whore?'

GOD SAID TO JACOB, 'Go up to Bethel and settle there; build an altar 35
there to the God who appeared to you when you were running away from
your brother Esau.' So Jacob said to his household and to all who were 2
with him, 'Rid yourselves of the foreign gods which you have among you,
purify yourselves, and see your clothes are mended.*a* We are going to 3
Bethel, so that I can set up an altar there to the God who answered me in
the day of my distress, and who has been with me all the way that I have
come.' So they handed over to Jacob all the foreign gods in their posses- 4
sion and the rings from their ears, and he buried them under the terebinth-
tree near Shechem. Then they set out, and the cities round about were 5

---

a Or change your clothes.

panic-stricken, and the inhabitants dared not pursue the sons of Jacob.

6 Jacob and all the people with him came to Luz, that is Bethel, in Canaan.

7 There he built an altar, and he called the place El-bethel, because it was there that God had revealed himself to him when he was running away from

8 his brother. Rebecca's nurse Deborah died and was buried under the oak below Bethel, and he named it Allon-bakuth. [a]

9 God appeared again to Jacob when he came back from Paddan-aram and

10 blessed him. God said to him:

> 'Jacob is your name,
> but your name shall no longer be Jacob:
> Israel shall be your name.'

11 So he named him Israel. And God said to him:

> 'I am God Almighty.
> Be fruitful and increase as a nation;
> a host of nations shall come from you,
> and kings shall spring from your body.

12 The land which I gave to Abraham and Isaac I give to you;
> and to your descendants after you I give this land.'

13 14 God then left him, and Jacob erected a sacred pillar in the place where God had spoken with him, a pillar of stone, and he offered a drink-offering over

15 it and poured oil on it. Jacob called the place where God had spoken with him Bethel.

16 They set out from Bethel, and when there was still some distance to go

17 to Ephrathah, Rachel was in labour and her pains were severe. While her pains were upon her, the midwife said, 'Do not be afraid, this is another

18 son for you.' Then with her last breath, as she was dying, she named him

19 Ben-oni, [b] but his father called him Benjamin. [c] So Rachel died and was

20 buried by the side of the road to Ephrathah, that is Bethlehem. Jacob set up a sacred pillar over her grave; it is known to this day as the Pillar of

21 Rachel's Grave. Then Israel journeyed on and pitched his tent on the other

22 side of Migdal-eder. While Israel was living in that district, Reuben went and lay with his father's concubine Bilhah, and Israel came to hear of it.

23 The sons of Jacob were twelve. The sons of Leah: Jacob's first-born

24 Reuben, then Simeon, Levi, Judah, Issachar and Zebulun. The sons of

25 Rachel: Joseph and Benjamin. The sons of Rachel's slave-girl Bilhah: Dan

26 and Naphtali. The sons of Leah's slave-girl Zilpah: Gad and Asher. These

27 were Jacob's sons, born to him in Paddan-aram. Jacob came to his father Isaac at Mamre by Kiriath-arba, that is Hebron, where Abraham and Isaac

28 had dwelt. Isaac had lived for a hundred and eighty years when he breathed

29 his last. He died and was gathered to his father's kin at a very great age, and his sons Esau and Jacob buried him.

36 1 2 THIS IS THE TABLE of the descendants of Esau: that is Edom. Esau took Canaanite women in marriage, Adah daughter of Elon the Hittite and

---

[a] *That is* Oak of Weeping.   [b] *That is* Son of my ill luck.   [c] *That is* Son of good luck *or* Son of the right hand.

Oholibamah daughter of Anah son of Zibeon the Horite,*a* and Basemath, 3
Ishmael's daughter, sister of Nebaioth.

Adah bore Eliphaz to Esau; Basemath bore Reuel, and Oholibamah bore 4*b* 5
Jeush, Jalam and Korah. These were Esau's sons, born to him in Canaan.
Esau took his wives, his sons and daughters and everyone in his household, 6
his herds, his cattle, and all the chattels that he had acquired in Canaan,
and went to the district of Seir out of the way of his brother Jacob, because 7
they had so much stock that they could not live together; the land where
they were staying could not support them because of their herds. So 8
Esau lived in the hill-country of Seir. Esau is Edom.

This is the table of the descendants of Esau father of the Edomites in 9
the hill-country of Seir.

These are the names of the sons of Esau: Eliphaz was the son of Esau's 10
wife Adah. Reuel was the son of Esau's wife Basemath. The sons of Eliphaz 11
were Teman, Omar, Zepho, Gatam and Kenaz. Timna was concubine to 12
Esau's son Eliphaz, and she bore Amalek to him. These are the descendants of Esau's wife Adah. These are the sons of Reuel: Nahath, Zerah, 13
Shammah and Mizzah. These were the descendants of Esau's wife Basemath. These were the sons of Esau's wife Oholibamah daughter of Anah 14
son of Zibeon. She bore him Jeush, Jalam and Korah.

These are the chiefs descended from Esau. The sons of Esau's eldest 15
son Eliphaz: chief Teman, chief Omar, chief Zepho, chief Kenaz, chief 16
Korah, chief Gatam, chief Amalek. These are the chiefs descended from
Eliphaz in Edom. These are the descendants of Adah.

These are the sons of Esau's son Reuel: chief Nahath, chief Zerah, chief 17
Shammah, chief Mizzah. These are the chiefs descended from Reuel in
Edom. These are the descendants of Esau's wife Basemath.

These are the sons of Esau's wife Oholibamah: chief Jeush, chief Jalam, 18
chief Korah. These are the chiefs born to Oholibamah daughter of Anah
wife of Esau.

These are the sons of Esau, that is Edom, and these are their chiefs. 19

These are the sons of Seir the Horite, the original inhabitants of the 20*c*
land: Lotan, Shobal, Zibeon, Anah, Dishon, Ezer and Dishan. These are 21
the chiefs of the Horites, the sons of Seir in Edom. The sons of Lotan were 22
Hori and Hemam, and Lotan had a sister named Timna.

These are the sons of Shobal: Alvan, Manahath, Ebal, Shepho and 23
Onam.

These are the sons of Zibeon: Aiah and Anah. This is the Anah who 24
found some mules in the wilderness while he was tending the asses of his
father Zibeon. These are the children of Anah: Dishon and Oholibamah 25
daughter of Anah.

These are the children of Dishon: Hemdan, Eshban, Ithran and Cheran. 26
These are the sons of Ezer: Bilhan, Zavan and Akan. These are the sons 27 28
of Dishan: Uz and Aran.

These are the chiefs descended from the Horites: chief Lotan, chief 29
Shobal, chief Zibeon, chief Anah, chief Dishon, chief Ezer, chief Dishan. 30

---

a *Prob. rdg. (cp. verses 20, 21); Heb.* Hivite.   *b* *Verses 4, 5, 9–13: cp. 1 Chr. 1. 35–37.*
c *Verses 20–28: cp. 1 Chr. 1. 38–42.*

These are the chiefs that were descended from the Horites according to
their clans in the district of Seir.

31[a]   These are the kings who ruled over Edom before there were kings in
32 Israel: Bela son of Beor became king in Edom, and his city was named
33 Dinhabah; when he died, he was succeeded by Jobab son of Zerah of
34 35 Bozrah. When Jobab died, he was succeeded by Husham of Teman. When
Husham died, he was succeeded by Hadad son of Bedad, who defeated
36 Midian in Moabite country. His city was named Avith. When Hadad died,
37 he was succeeded by Samlah of Masrekah. When Samlah died, he was
38 succeeded by Saul of Rehoboth on the River. When Saul died, he was suc-
39 ceeded by Baal-hanan son of Akbor. When Baal-hanan died, he was
succeeded by Hadar.[b] His city was named Pau; his wife's name was
Mehetabel daughter of Matred a woman of Me-zahab.[c]

40   These are the names of the chiefs descended from Esau, according to
their families, their places, by name: chief Timna, chief Alvah, chief
41 42 Jetheth, chief Oholibamah, chief Elah, chief Pinon, chief Kenaz, chief
43 Teman, chief Mibzar, chief Magdiel, and chief Iram: all chiefs of Edom
according to their settlements in the land which they possessed. (Esau is
the father of the Edomites.)

Joseph in Egypt

37   So JACOB LIVED IN CANAAN, the country in which his father had
2   settled. And this is the story of the descendants of Jacob.
When Joseph was a boy of seventeen, he used to accompany his brothers,
the sons of Bilhah and Zilpah, his father's wives, when they were in charge
3 of the flock; and he brought their father a bad report of them. Now Israel
loved Joseph more than any other of his sons, because he was a child of his
4 old age, and he made him a long, sleeved robe. When his brothers saw that
their father loved him more than any of them, they hated him and could
not say a kind word to him.
5   Joseph had a dream; and when he told it to his brothers, they hated him
6 7 still more. He said to them, 'Listen to this dream I have had. We were in
the field binding sheaves, and my sheaf rose on end and stood upright, and
8 your sheaves gathered round and bowed low before my sheaf.' His brothers
answered him, 'Do you think you will one day be a king and lord it over us?'
9 and they hated him still more because of his dreams and what he said. He
had another dream, which he told to his father and his brothers. He said,
'Listen: I have had another dream. The sun and moon and eleven stars
10 were bowing down to me.' When he told it to his father and his brothers,
his father took him to task: 'What is this dream of yours?' he said. 'Must
we come and bow low to the ground before you, I and your mother and
11 your brothers?' His brothers were jealous of him, but his father did not
forget.
12 13   Joseph's brothers went to mind their father's flocks in Shechem. Israel

---

[a] *Verses 31–43: cp. 1 Chr. 1. 43–54.*   [b] *Or Hadad; cp. 1 Chr. 1. 50.*
[c] *Or daughter of Mezahab.*

said to him, 'Your brothers are minding the flocks in Shechem; come, I
will send you to them', and he said, 'I am ready.' He said to him, 'Go and 14
see if all is well with your brothers and the sheep, and bring me back word.'
So he sent off Joseph from the vale of Hebron and he came to Shechem. A 15
man met him wandering in the open country and asked him what he was
looking for. He replied, 'I am looking for my brothers. Tell me, please, 16
where they are minding the flocks.' The man said, 'They have gone away 17
from here; I heard them speak of going to Dothan.' So Joseph followed his
brothers and he found them in Dothan. They saw him in the distance, and 18
before he reached them, they plotted to kill him. They said to each other, 19
'Here comes that dreamer. Now is our chance; let us kill him and throw him 20
into one of these pits and say that a wild beast has devoured him. Then we
shall see what will come of his dreams.' When Reuben heard, he came to 21
his rescue, urging them not to take his life. 'Let us have no bloodshed', he 22
said. 'Throw him into this pit in the wilderness, but do him no bodily harm.'
He meant to save him from them so as to restore him to his father. When 23
Joseph came up to his brothers, they stripped him of the long, sleeved robe
which he was wearing, took him and threw him into the pit. The pit was 24
empty and had no water in it.

Then they sat down to eat some food and, looking up, they saw an 25
Ishmaelite caravan coming in from Gilead on the way down to Egypt, with
camels carrying gum tragacanth and balm and myrrh. Judah said to his 26
brothers, 'What shall we gain by killing our brother and concealing his
death? Why not sell him to the Ishmaelites? Let us do him no harm, for 27
he is our brother, our own flesh and blood'; and his brothers agreed with
him. Meanwhile some Midianite merchants passed by and drew Joseph 28
up out of the pit. They sold him for twenty pieces of silver to the Ishmaelites, and they brought Joseph to Egypt. When Reuben went back to the 29
pit, Joseph was not there. He rent his clothes and went back to his brothers 30
and said, 'The boy is not there. Where can I go?'

Joseph's brothers took his robe, killed a goat and dipped it in the goat's 31
blood. Then they tore the robe, the long, sleeved robe, brought it to their 32
father and said, 'Look what we have found. Do you recognize it? Is this
your son's robe or not?' Jacob did recognize it, and he replied, 'It is my 33
son's robe. A wild beast has devoured him. Joseph has been torn to pieces.'
Jacob rent his clothes, put on sackcloth and mourned his son for a long 34
time. His sons and daughters all tried to comfort him, but he refused to be 35
comforted. He said, 'I will go to my grave mourning for my son.' Thus
Joseph's father wept for him. Meanwhile the Midianites had sold Joseph 36
in Egypt to Potiphar, one of Pharaoh's eunuchs, the captain of the guard. *a*

ABOUT THAT TIME JUDAH LEFT HIS BROTHERS and went south and 38
pitched his tent in company with an Adullamite named Hirah. There he 2
saw Bathshua the daughter of a Canaanite and married her. He slept with
her, and she conceived and bore a son, whom she called Er. She conceived 3 4
again and bore a son whom she called Onan. Once more she conceived and 5
bore a son whom she called Shelah, and she ceased to bear children *b* when

---

a Or executioner.   *b* ceased . . . children: or was at Kezib.

6 she had given birth to him. Judah found a wife for his eldest son Er; her
7 name was Tamar. But Judah's eldest son Er was wicked in the LORD's
8 sight, and the LORD took his life. Then Judah told Onan to sleep with his
   brother's wife, to do his duty as the husband's brother and raise up issue
9 for his brother. But Onan knew that the issue would not be his; so whenever
   he slept with his brother's wife, he spilled his seed on the ground so as not
10 to raise up issue for his brother. What he did was wicked in the LORD's
11 sight, and the LORD took his life. Judah said to his daughter-in-law Tamar,
   'Remain as a widow in your father's house until my son Shelah grows up';
   for he was afraid that he too would die like his brothers. So Tamar went
   and stayed in her father's house.

12   Time passed, and Judah's wife Bathshua died. When he had finished
   mourning, he and his friend Hirah the Adullamite went up to Timnath at
13 sheep-shearing. When Tamar was told that her father-in-law was on his
14 way to shear his sheep at Timnath, she took off her widow's weeds, veiled
   her face, perfumed herself and sat where the road forks in two directions
   on the way to Timnath. She did this because she knew that Shelah had
15 grown up and she had not been given to him as a wife. When Judah saw
16 her, he thought she was a prostitute, although she had veiled her face. He
   turned to her where she sat by the roadside and said, 'Let me lie with you',
   not knowing that she was his daughter-in-law. She said 'What will you
17 give me to lie with me?' He answered, 'I will send you a kid from my flock',
18 but she said, 'Will you give me a pledge until you send it?' He asked what
   pledge he should give her, and she replied, 'Your seal and its cord, and the
   staff which you hold in your hand.' So he gave them to her and lay with her,
19 and she conceived. She then rose and went home, took off her veil and
20 resumed her widow's weeds. Judah sent the kid by his friend the Adullamite in order to recover the pledge from the woman, but he could not find
21 her. He asked the men of that place, 'Where is that temple-prostitute, the
   one who was sitting where the road forks?', but they answered, 'There is
22 no temple-prostitute here.' So he went back to Judah and told him that he
   had not found her and that the men of the place had said there was no such
23 prostitute there. Judah said, 'Let her keep my pledge, or we shall get a
24 bad name. I did send a kid, but you could not find her.' About three months
   later Judah was told that his daughter-in-law Tamar had behaved like a
   common prostitute and through her wanton conduct was with child. Judah
25 said, 'Bring her out so that she may be burnt.' But when she was brought
   out, she sent to her father-in-law and said, 'The father of my child is the
   man to whom these things belong. See if you recognize whose they are,
26 the engraving on the seal, the pattern of the cord, and the staff.' Judah
   recognized them and said, 'She is more in the right than I am, because I
   did not give her to my son Shelah.' He did not have intercourse with her
27 28 again. When her time was come, there were twins in her womb, and while
   she was in labour one of them put out a hand. The midwife took a scarlet
   thread and fastened it round the wrist, saying, 'This one appeared first.'
29 No sooner had he drawn back his hand, than his brother came out and the
   midwife said, 'What! you have broken out first!' So he was named Perez. [a]

   [a] *That is* Breaking out.

Soon afterwards his brother was born with the scarlet thread on his wrist, 30
and he was named Zerah.[a]

WHEN JOSEPH WAS TAKEN DOWN TO EGYPT, he was bought by Poti- **39**
phar, one of Pharaoh's eunuchs, the captain of the guard, an Egyptian.
Potiphar bought him from the Ishmaelites who had brought him there.
The LORD was with Joseph and he prospered. He lived in the house of his 2
Egyptian master, who saw that the LORD was with him and was giving him 3
success in all that he undertook. Thus Joseph found favour with his master, 4
and he became his personal servant. Indeed, his master put him in charge of
his household and entrusted him with all that he had. From the time that 5
he put him in charge of his household and all his property, the LORD
blessed the Egyptian's household for Joseph's sake. The blessing of the
LORD was on all that was his in house and field. He left everything he 6
possessed in Joseph's care, and concerned himself with nothing but the
food he ate.

Now Joseph was handsome and good-looking, and a time came when his 7
master's wife took notice of him and said, 'Come and lie with me.' But he 8
refused and said to her, 'Think of my master. He does not know as much as
I do about his own house, and he has entrusted me with all he has. He has 9
given me authority in this house second only to his own, and has withheld
nothing from me except you, because you are his wife. How can I do anything so wicked, and sin against God?' She kept asking Joseph day after 10
day, but he refused to lie with her and be in her company. One day he came 11
into the house as usual to do his work, when none of the men of the household were there indoors. She caught him by his cloak, saying, 'Come and 12
lie with me', but he left the cloak in her hands and ran out of the house.
When she saw that he had left his cloak in her hands and had run out of the 13
house, she called out to the men of the household, 'Look at this! My 14
husband has brought in a Hebrew to make a mockery of us. He came in
here to lie with me, but I gave a loud scream. When he heard me scream and 15
call out, he left his cloak in my hand and ran off.' She kept his cloak with 16
her until his master came home, and then she repeated her tale. She said, 17
'That Hebrew slave whom you brought in to make a mockery of me, has
been here with me. But when I screamed for help and called out, he left 18
his cloak in my hands and ran off.' When Joseph's master heard his wife's 19
story of what his slave had done to her, he was furious. He took Joseph and 20
put him in the Round Tower, where the king's prisoners were kept;
and there he stayed in the Round Tower. But the LORD was with Joseph 21
and kept faith with him, so that he won the favour of the governor of the
Round Tower. He put Joseph in charge of all the prisoners in the tower and 22
of all their work. He ceased to concern himself with anything entrusted to 23
Joseph, because the LORD was with Joseph and gave him success in everything.

It happened later that the king's butler and his baker offended their **40**
master the king of Egypt. Pharaoh was angry with these two eunuchs, the 2
chief butler and the chief baker, and he put them in custody in the house of 3

[a] *That is* Redness.

45

the captain of the guard, in the Round Tower where Joseph was imprisoned.
4 The captain of the guard appointed Joseph as their attendant, and he
5 waited on them. One night, when they had been in prison for some time,
they both had dreams, each needing its own interpretation—the king of
Egypt's butler and his baker who were imprisoned in the Round Tower.
6 When Joseph came to them in the morning, he saw that they looked
7 dejected. So he asked these eunuchs, who were in custody with him in his
8 master's house, why they were so downcast that day. They replied, 'We
have each had a dream and there is no one to interpret it for us.' Joseph
said to them, 'Does not interpretation belong to God? Tell me your
9 dreams.' So the chief butler told Joseph his dream: 'In my dream', he said,
10 'there was a vine in front of me. On the vine there were three branches,
and as soon as it budded, it blossomed and its clusters ripened into grapes.
11 Now I had Pharaoh's cup in my hand, and I plucked the grapes, crushed
12 them into Pharaoh's cup and put the cup into Pharaoh's hand.' Joseph said
to him, 'This is the interpretation. The three branches are three days:
13 within three days Pharaoh will raise you and restore you to your post, and
then you will put the cup into Pharaoh's hand as you used to do when you
14 were his butler. But when things go well with you, if you think of me, keep
faith with me and bring my case to Pharaoh's notice and help me to get out
15 of this house. By force I was carried off*a* from the land of the Hebrews,
and I have done nothing here to deserve being put in this dungeon.'
16   When the chief baker saw that Joseph had given a favourable interpretation, he said to him, 'I too had a dream, and in my dream there were
17 three baskets of white bread on my head. In the top basket there was every
kind of food which the baker prepares for Pharaoh, and the birds were
18 eating out of the top basket on my head.' Joseph answered, 'This is the
19 interpretation. The three baskets are three days: within three days Pharaoh
will raise you and hang you up on a tree, and the birds of the air will eat
your flesh.'
20   The third day was Pharaoh's birthday and he gave a feast for all his
servants. He raised the chief butler and the chief baker in the presence of
21 his court. He restored the chief butler to his post, and the butler put the
22 cup into Pharaoh's hand; but he hanged the chief baker. All went as
23 Joseph had said in interpreting the dreams for them. Even so the chief
butler did not remember Joseph, but forgot him.

41   Nearly two years later Pharaoh had a dream: he was standing by the
2 Nile, and there came up from the river seven cows, sleek and fat, and they
3 grazed on the reeds. After them seven other cows came up from the river,
4 gaunt and lean, and stood on the river-bank beside the first cows. The cows
that were gaunt and lean devoured the cows that were sleek and fat. Then
5 Pharaoh woke up. He fell asleep again and had a second dream: he saw
6 seven ears of corn, full and ripe, growing on one stalk. Growing up after
7 them were seven other ears, thin and shrivelled by the east wind. The thin
ears swallowed up the ears that were full and ripe. Then Pharaoh woke up
8 and knew that it was a dream. When morning came, Pharaoh was troubled
in mind; so he summoned all the magicians and sages of Egypt. He told

a Or stolen.

them his dreams, but there was no one who could interpret them for him. Then Pharaoh's chief butler spoke up and said, 'It is time for me to recall 9 my faults. Once Pharaoh was angry with his servants, and he imprisoned 10 me and the chief baker in the house of the captain of the guard. One night 11 we both had dreams, each needing its own interpretation. We had with us 12 a young Hebrew, a slave of the captain of the guard, and we told him our dreams and he interpreted them for us, giving each man's dream its own interpretation. Each dream came true as it had been interpreted to us: I 13 was restored to my position, and he was hanged.'

Pharaoh thereupon sent for Joseph, and they hurriedly brought him out 14 of the dungeon. He shaved and changed his clothes, and came in to Pharaoh. Pharaoh said to him, 'I have had a dream, and no one can interpret it to 15 me. I have heard it said that you can understand and interpret dreams.' Joseph answered, 'Not I, but God, will answer for Pharaoh's welfare.' 16 Then Pharaoh said to Joseph, 'In my dream I was standing on the bank of 17 the Nile, and there came up from the river seven cows, fat and sleek, and 18 they grazed on the reeds. After them seven other cows came up that were 19 poor, very gaunt and lean; I have never seen such gaunt creatures in all Egypt. These lean, gaunt cows devoured the first cows, the fat ones. They 20 21 were swallowed up, but no one could have guessed that they were in the bellies of the others, which looked as gaunt as before. Then I woke up. After I had fallen asleep again, I saw in a dream seven ears of corn, full and 22 ripe, growing on one stalk. Growing up after them were seven other ears, 23 shrivelled, thin, and blighted by the east wind. The thin ears swallowed up 24 the seven ripe ears. When I told all this to the magicians, no one could explain it to me.'

Joseph said to Pharaoh, 'Pharaoh's dreams are one dream. God has 25 told Pharaoh what he is going to do. The seven good cows are seven years, 26 and the seven good ears of corn are seven years. It is all one dream. The 27 seven lean and gaunt cows that came up after them are seven years, and the empty ears of corn blighted by the east wind will be seven years of famine. It is as I have said to Pharaoh: God has let Pharaoh see what he is 28 going to do. There are to be seven years of great plenty throughout the 29 land. After them will come seven years of famine; all the years of plenty in 30 Egypt will be forgotten, and the famine will ruin the country. The good 31 years will not be remembered in the land because of the famine that follows; for it will be very severe. The doubling of Pharaoh's dream means 32 that God is already resolved to do this, and he will very soon put it into effect. Pharaoh should now look for a shrewd and intelligent man, and 33 put him in charge of the country. This is what Pharaoh should do: 34 appoint controllers over the land, and take one fifth of the produce of Egypt during the seven years of plenty. They should collect all this food 35 produced in the good years that are coming and put the corn under Pharaoh's control in store in the cities, and keep it under guard. This food 36 will be a reserve for the country against the seven years of famine which will come upon Egypt. Thus the country will not be devastated by the famine.'

The plan pleased Pharaoh and all his courtiers, and he said to them, 'Can 37 38

39 we find a man like this man, one who has the spirit of a god*a* in him?' He
said to Joseph, 'Since a god*b* has made all this known to you, there is no
40 one so shrewd and intelligent as you. You shall be in charge of my household, and all my people will depend on your every word. Only my royal
41 throne shall make me greater than you.' Pharaoh said to Joseph, 'I hereby
42 give you authority over the whole land of Egypt.' He took off his signet-ring
and put it on Joseph's finger, he had him dressed in fine linen, and hung a
43 gold chain round his neck. He mounted him in his viceroy's chariot and
men cried 'Make way!' before him. Thus Pharaoh made him ruler over all
44 Egypt and said to him, 'I am the Pharaoh. Without your consent no man
45 shall lift hand or foot throughout Egypt.' Pharaoh named him Zaphenath-
paneah, and he gave him as wife Asenath the daughter of Potiphera priest
of On. And Joseph's authority extended over the whole of Egypt.

46 Joseph was thirty years old when he entered the service of Pharaoh king
of Egypt. When he took his leave of the king, he made a tour of inspection
47 through the country. During the seven years of plenty there were abundant
48 harvests, and Joseph gathered all the food produced in Egypt during those
years and stored it in the cities, putting in each the food from the surround-
49 ing country. He stored the grain in huge quantities; it was like the sand of
the sea, so much that he stopped measuring: it was beyond all measure.

50 Before the years of famine came, two sons were born to Joseph by
51 Asenath the daughter of Potiphera priest of On. He named the elder
Manasseh,*c* 'for', he said, 'God has caused me to forget all my troubles and
52 my father's family.' He named the second Ephraim,*d* 'for', he said, 'God
53 has made me fruitful in the land of my hardships.' When the seven years
54 of plenty in Egypt came to an end, seven years of famine began, as Joseph
had foretold. There was famine in every country, but throughout Egypt
55 there was bread. So when the famine spread through all Egypt, the people
appealed to Pharaoh for bread, and he ordered them to go to Joseph and do
56 as he told them. In every region there was famine, and Joseph opened all
the granaries and sold corn to the Egyptians, for the famine was severe.
57 The whole world came to Egypt to buy corn from Joseph, so severe was
the famine everywhere.

42 WHEN JACOB SAW that there was corn in Egypt, he said to his sons, 'Why
2 do you stand staring at each other? I have heard that there is corn in Egypt.
Go down and buy some so that we may keep ourselves alive and not starve.'
3 So Joseph's brothers, ten of them, went down to buy grain from Egypt,
4 but Jacob did not let Joseph's brother Benjamin go with them, for fear that
he might come to harm.
5 So the sons of Israel came down with everyone else to buy corn, because
6 of the famine in Canaan. Now Joseph was governor of all Egypt, and it was
he who sold the corn to all the people of the land. Joseph's brothers came
7 and bowed to the ground before him, and when he saw his brothers, he
recognized them but pretended not to know them and spoke harshly to
them. 'Where do you come from?' he asked. 'From Canaan,' they answered,
8 'to buy food.' Although Joseph had recognized his brothers, they did not

a Or of God. *b* Or God. *c* That is Causing to forget. *d* That is Fruit.

recognize him. He remembered also the dreams he had had about them; 9
so he said to them, 'You are spies; you have come to spy out the weak
points in our defences.' They answered, 'No, sir: your servants have come 10
to buy food. We are all sons of one man. Your humble servants are honest 11
men, we are not spies.' 'No,' he insisted, 'it is to spy out our weaknesses that 12
you have come.' They answered him, 'Sir, there are twelve of us, all 13
brothers, sons of one man in Canaan. The youngest is still with our father,
and one has disappeared.' But Joseph said again to them, 'No, as I said 14
before, you are spies. This is how you shall be put to the proof: unless your 15
youngest brother comes here, by the life of Pharaoh, you shall not leave
this place. Send one of your number to bring your brother; the rest will 16
be kept in prison. Thus your story will be tested, and we shall see whether
you are telling the truth. If not, then, by the life of Pharaoh, you must be
spies.' So he kept them in prison for three days. 17
    On the third day Joseph said to the brothers, 'Do what I say and your 18
lives will be spared; for I am a God-fearing man: if you are honest men, 19
your brother there shall be kept in prison, and the rest of you shall take
corn for your hungry households and bring your youngest brother to me; 20
thus your words will be proved true, and you will not die.' *a*
    They said to one another, 'No doubt we deserve to be punished because 21
of our brother, whose suffering we saw; for when he pleaded with us we
refused to listen. That is why these sufferings have come upon us.' But 22
Reuben said, 'Did I not tell you not to do the boy a wrong? But you would
not listen, and his blood is on our heads, and we must pay.' They did not 23
know that Joseph understood, because he had used an interpreter. Joseph 24
turned away from them and wept. Then, turning back, he played a trick
on them. First he took Simeon and bound him before their eyes; then he 25
gave orders to fill their bags with grain, to return each man's silver, putting
it in his sack, and to give them supplies for the journey. All this was done;
and they loaded the corn on to their asses and went away. When they 26 27
stopped for the night, one of them opened his sack to give fodder to his ass,
and there he saw his silver at the top of the pack. He said to his brothers, 'My 28
silver has been returned to me, and here it is in my pack.' Bewildered and
trembling, they said to each other, 'What is this that God has done to us?'
    When they came to their father Jacob in Canaan, they told him all that 29
had happened to them. They said, 'The man who is lord of the country 30
spoke harshly to us and made out that we were spies. We said to him, "We 31
are honest men, we are not spies. There are twelve of us, all brothers, sons 32
of one father. One has disappeared, and the youngest is with our father in
Canaan." This man, the lord of the country, said to us, "This is how I shall 33
find out if you are honest men. Leave one of your brothers with me, take
food for your hungry households and go. Bring your youngest brother to 34
me, and I shall know that you are not spies, but honest men. Then I will
restore your brother to you, and you can move about the country freely."'
But on emptying their sacks, each of them found his silver inside, and when 35
they and their father saw the bundles of silver, they were afraid. Their 36
father Jacob said to them, 'You have robbed me of my children. Joseph has

a Prob. rdg.; Heb. adds and they did so.

49

disappeared; Simeon has disappeared; and now you are taking Benjamin.
37 Everything is against me.' Reuben said to his father, 'You may kill both
my sons if I do not bring him back to you. Put him in my charge, and I
38 shall bring him back.' But Jacob said, 'My son shall not go with you, for
his brother is dead and he alone is left. If he comes to any harm on the
journey, you will bring down my grey hairs in sorrow to the grave.'

43 1 2   The famine was still severe in the country. When they had used up the
corn they had brought from Egypt, their father said to them, 'Go back
3 and buy a little more corn for us to eat.' But Judah replied, 'The man
plainly warned us that we must not go into his presence unless our brother
4 was with us. If you let our brother go with us, we will go down and buy
5 food for you. But if you will not let him, we will not go; for the man said
to us, "You shall not come into my presence, unless your brother is with
6 you."' Israel said, 'Why have you treated me so badly? Why did you tell
7 the man that you had yet another brother?' They answered, 'He questioned
us closely about ourselves and our family: "Is your father still alive?" he
asked, "Have you a brother?", and we answered his questions. How could
we possibly know that he would tell us to bring our brother to Egypt?'
8 Judah said to his father Israel, 'Send the boy with me; then we can start at
once. By doing this we shall save our lives, ours, yours, and our dependants',
9 and none of us will starve. I will go surety for him and you may hold me
responsible. If I do not bring him back and restore him to you, you shall
10 hold me guilty all my life. If we had not wasted all this time, by now we
could have gone back twice over.'

11   Their father Israel said to them, 'If it must be so, then do this: take in
your baggage, as a gift for the man, some of the produce for which our
country is famous: a little balsam, a little honey, gum tragacanth, myrrh,
12 pistachio nuts, and almonds. Take double the amount of silver and restore
13 what was returned to you in your packs; perhaps it was a mistake. Take
14 your brother with you and go straight back to the man. May God Almighty
make him kindly disposed to you, and may he send back the one whom you
left behind, and Benjamin too. As for me, if I am bereaved, then I am
15 bereaved.' So they took the gift and double the amount of silver, and with
Benjamin they started at once for Egypt, where they presented themselves
to Joseph.

16   When Joseph saw Benjamin with them, he said to his steward, 'Bring
these men indoors, kill a beast and make dinner ready, for they will eat
17 with me at noon.' He did as Joseph told him and brought the men into the
18 house. When they came in they were afraid, for they thought, 'We have
been brought in here because of that affair of the silver which was replaced
in our packs the first time. He means to trump up some charge against us
19 and victimize us, seize our asses and make us his slaves.' So they approached
20 Joseph's steward and spoke to him at the door of the house. They said,
21 'Please listen, my lord. After our first visit to buy food, when we reached
the place where we were to spend the night, we opened our packs and each
of us found his silver in full weight at the top of his pack. We have brought
22 it back with us, and have added other silver to buy food. We do not know
23 who put the silver in our packs.' He answered, 'Set your minds at rest; do

not be afraid. It was your God, the God of your father, who hid treasure for you in your packs. I did receive the silver.' Then he brought Simeon out to them.

The steward brought them into Joseph's house and gave them water to 24 wash their feet, and provided fodder for their asses. They had their gifts 25 ready when Joseph arrived at noon, for they had heard that they were to eat there. When Joseph came into the house, they presented him with the 26 gifts which they had brought, bowing to the ground before him. He asked 27 them how they were and said, 'Is your father well, the old man of whom you spoke? Is he still alive?' They answered, 'Yes, my lord, our father is still 28 alive and well.' And they bowed low and prostrated themselves. Joseph 29 looked and saw his own mother's son, his brother Benjamin, and asked, 'Is this your youngest brother, of whom you told me?', and to Benjamin he said, 'May God be gracious to you, my son!' Joseph was overcome; his 30 feelings for his brother mastered him, and he was near to tears. So he went into the inner room and wept. Then he washed his face and came out; and, 31 holding back his feelings, he ordered the meal to be served. They served 32 him by himself, and the brothers by themselves, and the Egyptians who were at dinner were also served separately; for Egyptians hold it an abomination to eat with Hebrews. The brothers were seated in his presence, the 33 eldest first according to his age and so on down to the youngest: they looked at one another in astonishment. Joseph sent them each a portion from what 34 was before him, but Benjamin's was five times larger than any of the other portions. Thus they drank with him and all grew merry.

Joseph gave his steward this order: 'Fill the men's packs with as much **44** food as they can carry and put each man's silver at the top of his pack. And 2 put my goblet, my silver goblet, at the top of the youngest brother's pack with the silver for the corn.' He did as Joseph said. At daybreak the brothers 3 were allowed to take their asses and go on their journey; but before they 4 had gone very far from the city, Joseph said to his steward, 'Go after those men at once, and when you catch up with them, say, "Why have you repaid good with evil? Why have you stolen the silver goblet? It is the one from 5 which my lord drinks, and which he uses for divination. You have done a wicked thing."' When he caught up with them, he repeated all this to 6 them, but they replied, 'My lord, how can you say such things? No, sir, 7 God forbid that we should do any such thing! You remember the silver we 8 found at the top of our packs? We brought it back to you from Canaan. Why should we steal silver or gold from your master's house? If any one 9 of us is found with the goblet, he shall die; and, what is more, my lord, we will all become your slaves.' He said, 'Very well, then; I accept what you 10 say. The man in whose possession it is found shall be my slave, but the rest of you shall go free.' Each man quickly lowered his pack to the ground 11 and opened it. The steward searched them, beginning with the eldest and 12 finishing with the youngest, and the goblet was found in Benjamin's pack.

At this they rent their clothes; then each man loaded his ass and they 13 returned to the city. Joseph was still in the house when Judah and his 14 brothers came in. They threw themselves on the ground before him, and 15 Joseph said, 'What have you done? You might have known that a man like

16 myself would practise divination.' Judah said, 'What shall we say, my lord? What can we say to prove our innocence? God has found out our sin. Here we are, my lord, ready to be made your slaves, we ourselves as well as

17 the one who was found with the goblet.' Joseph answered, 'God forbid that I should do such a thing! The one who was found with the goblet shall become my slave, but the rest of you can go home to your father in peace.'

18 Then Judah went up to him and said, 'Please listen, my lord. Let me say a word to your lordship, I beg. Do not be angry with me, for you

19 are as great as Pharaoh. You, my lord, asked us whether we had a father or

20 a brother. We answered, "We have an aged father, and he has a young son born in his old age; this boy's full brother is dead and he alone is left of

21 his mother's children, he alone, and his father loves him." Your lordship

22 answered, "Bring him down to me so that I may set eyes on him." We told you, my lord, that the boy could not leave his father, and that his father

23 would die if he left him. But you answered, "Unless your youngest brother

24 comes here with you, you shall not enter my presence again." We went back

25 to your servant our father, and told him what your lordship had said. When

26 our father told us to go and buy food, we answered, "We cannot go down; for without our youngest brother we cannot enter the man's presence; but

27 if our brother is with us, we will go." Our father, my lord, then said to us,

28 "You know that my wife bore me two sons. One left me, and I said, 'He

29 must have been torn to pieces.' I have not seen him to this day. If you take this one from me as well, and he comes to any harm, then you will bring

30 down my grey hairs in trouble to the grave." Now, my lord, when I return to my father without the boy—and remember, his life is bound up with

31 the boy's—what will happen is this: he will see that the boy is not with us and will die, and your servants will have brought down our father's grey

32 hairs in sorrow to the grave. Indeed, my lord, it was I who went surety for the boy to my father. I said, "If I do not bring him back to you, then you

33 shall hold me guilty all my life." Now, my lord, let me remain in place of

34 the boy as your lordship's slave, and let him go with his brothers. How can I return to my father without the boy? I could not bear to see the misery which my father would suffer.'

45 Joseph could no longer control his feelings in front of his attendants, and he called out, 'Let everyone leave my presence.' So there was nobody

2 present when Joseph made himself known to his brothers, but so loudly did he weep that the Egyptians and Pharaoh's household heard him.

3 Joseph said to his brothers, 'I am Joseph; can my father be still alive?' His brothers were so dumbfounded at finding themselves face to face with

4 Joseph that they could not answer. Then Joseph said to his brothers, 'Come closer', and so they came close. He said, 'I am your brother Joseph whom

5 you sold into Egypt. Now do not be distressed or take it amiss that you sold me into slavery here; it was God who sent me ahead of you to save

6 men's lives. For there have now been two years of famine in the country, and there will be another five years with neither ploughing nor harvest.

7 God sent me ahead of you to ensure that you will have descendants on

8 earth, and to preserve you all, a great band of survivors. So it was not you

who sent me here, but God, and he has made me a father *a* to Pharaoh, and lord over all his household and ruler of all Egypt. Make haste and go back 9 to my father and give him this message from his son Joseph: "God has made me lord of all Egypt. Come down to me; do not delay. You shall live 10 in the land of Goshen and be near me, you, your sons and your grandsons, your flocks and herds and all that you have. I will take care of you there, 11 you and your household and all that you have, and see that you are not reduced to poverty; there are still five years of famine to come." You can 12 see for yourselves, and so can my brother Benjamin, that it is Joseph himself who is speaking to you. Tell my father of all the honour which I enjoy 13 in Egypt, tell him all you have seen, and make haste to bring him down here.' Then he threw his arms round his brother Benjamin and wept, and Ben- 14 jamin too embraced him weeping. He kissed all his brothers and wept over 15 them, and afterwards his brothers talked with him.

When the report that Joseph's brothers had come reached Pharaoh's 16 house, he and all his courtiers were pleased. Pharaoh said to Joseph, 'Say 17 to your brothers: "This is what you are to do. Load your beasts and go to Canaan. Fetch your father and your households and bring them to me. I 18 will give you the best that there is in Egypt, and you shall enjoy the fat of the land." You shall also tell them: "Take wagons from Egypt for your 19 dependants and your wives and fetch your father and come. Have no 20 regrets at leaving your possessions, for all the best that there is in Egypt is yours."' The sons of Israel did as they were told, and Joseph gave them 21 wagons, according to Pharaoh's orders, and food for the journey. He pro- 22 vided each of them with a change of clothing, but to Benjamin he gave three hundred pieces of silver and five changes of clothing. Moreover he sent 23 his father ten asses carrying the best that there was in Egypt, and ten she-asses loaded with grain, bread, and provisions for his journey. So he dis- 24 missed his brothers, telling them not to quarrel among themselves on the road, and they set out. Thus they went up from Egypt and came to their 25 father Jacob in Canaan. There they gave him the news that Joseph was still 26 alive and that he was ruler of all Egypt. He was stunned and could not believe it, but they told him all that Joseph had said; and when he saw the 27 wagons which Joseph had sent to take him away, his spirit revived. Israel 28 said, 'It is enough. Joseph my son is still alive; I will go and see him before I die.'

So ISRAEL SET OUT with all that he had and came to Beersheba where he **46** offered sacrifices to the God of his father Isaac. God said to Israel in a 2 vision by night, 'Jacob, Jacob', and he answered, 'I am here.' God said, 'I 3 am God, the God of your father. Do not be afraid to go down to Egypt, for there I will make you a great nation. I will go down with you to Egypt, 4 and I myself will bring you back again without fail; and Joseph shall close your eyes.' So Jacob set out from Beersheba. Israel's sons conveyed their 5 father Jacob, their dependants, and their wives in the wagons which Pharaoh had sent to carry them. They took the herds and the stock 6 which they had acquired in Canaan and came to Egypt, Jacob and all his

---

a *Or* counsellor.

7 descendants with him, his sons and their sons, his daughters and his sons' daughters: he brought all his descendants to Egypt.

8*a* These are the names of the Israelites who entered Egypt: Jacob and
9 his sons, as follows: Reuben, Jacob's eldest son. The sons of Reuben:
10 Enoch, Pallu, Hezron and Carmi. The sons of Simeon: Jemuel, Jamin, Ohad, Jachin, Zohar, and Saul, who was the son of a Canaanite woman.
11 12 The sons of Levi: Gershon, Kohath and Merari. The sons of Judah: Er, Onan, Shelah, Perez and Zerah; of these Er and Onan died in Canaan.
13 The sons of Perez were Hezron and Hamul. The sons of Issachar: Tola,
14 Pua, Iob and Shimron. The sons of Zebulun: Sered, Elon and Jahleel.
15 These are the sons of Leah whom she bore to Jacob in Paddan-aram, and there was also his daughter Dinah. His sons and daughters numbered thirty-three in all.

16 The sons of Gad: Ziphion, Haggi, Shuni, Ezbon, Eri, Arodi and Areli.
17 The sons of Asher: Imnah, Ishvah, Ishvi, Beriah, and their sister Serah.
18 The sons of Beriah: Heber and Malchiel. These are the descendants of Zilpah whom Laban gave to his daughter Leah; sixteen in all, born to Jacob.

19 20 The sons of Jacob's wife Rachel: Joseph and Benjamin. Manasseh and Ephraim were born to Joseph in Egypt. Asenath daughter of Potiphera
21 priest of On bore them to him. The sons of Benjamin: Bela, Becher and Ashbel; and the sons of Bela: Gera, Naaman, Ehi, Rosh, Muppim, Huppim
22 and Ard. These are the descendants of Rachel; fourteen in all, born to Jacob.

23 24 The son*b* of Dan: Hushim. The sons of Naphtali: Jahzeel, Guni, Jezer
25 and Shillem. These are the descendants of Bilhah whom Laban gave to his daughter Rachel; seven in all, born to Jacob.

26 The persons belonging to Jacob who came to Egypt, all his direct
27 descendants, not counting the wives of his sons, were sixty-six in all. Two sons were born to Joseph in Egypt. Thus the house of Jacob numbered seventy when it entered Egypt.

28 Judah was sent ahead that he might appear before Joseph in Goshen,
29 and so they entered Goshen. Joseph had his chariot made ready and went up to meet his father Israel in Goshen. When they met, he threw his arms
30 round him and wept, and embraced him for a long time, weeping. Israel said to Joseph, 'I have seen your face again, and you are still alive. Now I
31 am ready to die.' Joseph said to his brothers and to his father's household, 'I will go and tell Pharaoh; I will say to him, "My brothers and my father's
32 household who were in Canaan have come to me."' Now his brothers were shepherds, men with their own flocks and herds, and they had brought
33 them with them, their flocks and herds and all that they possessed. So Joseph said, 'When Pharaoh summons you and asks you what your
34 occupation is, you must say, "My lord, we have been herdsmen all our lives, as our fathers were before us." You must say this if you are to settle in the land of Goshen, because all shepherds are an abomination to the Egyptians.'

a Verses 8–25: cp. Exod. 6. 14–16; Num. 26. 5–50; 1 Chr. 4. 1, 24; 5. 3; 6. 1; 7. 1, 6, 13, 30; 8. 1–5.   *b* Prob. rdg.; Heb. sons.

Joseph came and told Pharaoh, 'My father and my brothers have arrived **47** from Canaan, with their flocks and their cattle and all that they have, and they are now in Goshen.' Then he chose five of his brothers and presented 2 them to Pharaoh, who asked them what their occupation was, and they 3 answered, 'My lord, we are shepherds, we and our fathers before us, and 4 we have come to stay in this land; for there is no pasture in Canaan for our sheep, because the famine there is so severe. We beg you, my lord, to let us settle now in Goshen.' Pharaoh said to Joseph, 'So your father and your 5 brothers have come to you. The land of Egypt is yours; settle them in the 6 best part of it. Let them live in Goshen, and if you know of any capable men among them, make them chief herdsmen over my cattle.'

Then Joseph brought his father in and presented him to Pharaoh, and 7 Jacob gave Pharaoh his blessing. Pharaoh asked Jacob his age, and he 8 9 answered, 'The years of my earthly sojourn are one hundred and thirty; hard years they have been and few, not equal to the years that my fathers lived in their time.' Jacob then blessed Pharaoh and went out from his 10 presence. So Joseph settled his father and his brothers, and gave them 11 lands in Egypt, in the best part of the country, in the district of Rameses, as Pharaoh had ordered. He supported his father, his brothers, and all his 12 father's household with all the food they needed.

There was no bread in the whole country, so very severe was the famine, 13 and Egypt and Canaan were laid low by it. Joseph collected all the silver in 14 Egypt and Canaan in return for the corn which the people bought, and deposited it in Pharaoh's treasury. When all the silver in Egypt and Canaan 15 had been used up, the Egyptians came to Joseph and said, 'Give us bread, or we shall die before your eyes. Our silver is all spent.' Joseph said, 'If your 16 silver is spent, give me your herds and I will give you bread in return.' So 17 they brought their herds to Joseph, who gave them bread in exchange for their horses, their flocks of sheep and herds of cattle, and their asses. He maintained them that year with bread in exchange for their herds. The year 18 came to an end, and the following year they came to him again and said, 'My lord, we cannot conceal it from you: our silver is all gone and our herds of cattle are yours. Nothing is left for your lordship but our bodies and our lands. Why should we perish before your eyes, we and our land as well? 19 Take us and our land in payment for bread, and we and our land alike will be in bondage to Pharaoh. Give us seed-corn to keep us alive, or we shall die and our land will become desert.' So Joseph bought all the land in 20 Egypt for Pharaoh, because the Egyptians sold all their fields, so severe was the famine; the land became Pharaoh's. As for the people, Pharaoh 21 set them to work as slaves from one end of the territory of Egypt to the other. But Joseph did not buy the land which belonged to the priests; they 22 had a fixed allowance from Pharaoh and lived on this, so that they had no need to sell their land.

Joseph said to the people, 'Listen; I have today bought you and your 23 land for Pharaoh. Here is seed-corn for you. Sow the land, and give one 24 fifth of the crop to Pharaoh. Four fifths shall be yours to provide seed for your fields and food for yourselves, your households, and your dependants.' The people said, 'You have saved our lives. If it please your lordship, we 25

26 will be Pharaoh's slaves.' Joseph established it as a law in Egypt that one fifth should belong to Pharaoh, and this is still in force. It was only the priests' land that did not pass into Pharaoh's hands.

27   Thus Israel settled in Egypt, in Goshen; there they acquired land, and
28 were fruitful and increased greatly. Jacob stayed in Egypt for seventeen
29 years and lived to be a hundred and forty-seven years old. When the time of his death drew near, he summoned his son Joseph and said to him, 'If I may now claim this favour from you, put your hand under my thigh and swear by the LORD that you will deal loyally and truly with me and not bury
30 me in Egypt. When I die like my forefathers, you shall carry me from Egypt
31 and bury me in their grave.' He answered, 'I will do as you say'; but Jacob said, 'Swear it.' So he swore the oath, and Israel sank down over the end of the bed.

48   The time came when Joseph was told that his father was ill, so he took
2 with him his two sons, Manasseh and Ephraim. Jacob heard that his son Joseph was coming to him, and he summoned his strength and sat up on
3 the bed. Jacob said to Joseph, 'God Almighty appeared to me at Luz in
4 Canaan and blessed me. He said to me, "I will make you fruitful and increase your descendants until they become a host of nations. I will give this
5 land to your descendants after you as a perpetual possession." Now, your two sons, who were born to you in Egypt before I came here, shall be counted as my sons; Ephraim and Manasseh shall be mine as Reuben and
6 Simeon are. Any children born to you after them shall be counted as yours, but in respect of their tribal territory they shall be reckoned under their
7 elder brothers' names. As I was coming from Paddan-aram I was bereaved of Rachel your mother on the way, in Canaan, whilst there was still some distance to go to Ephrath, and I buried her there by the road to Ephrath, that is Bethlehem.'

8 9   When Israel saw Joseph's sons, he said, 'Who are these?' Joseph replied to his father, 'They are my sons whom God has given me here.' Israel said,
10 'Bring them to me, I beg you, so that I may take them on my knees.'[a] Now Israel's eyes were dim with age, and he could not see; so Joseph brought
11 the boys close to his father, and he kissed them and embraced them. He said to Joseph, 'I had not expected to see your face again, and now God has
12 granted me to see your sons also.' Joseph took them from his father's knees
13 and bowed to the ground. Then he took the two of them, Ephraim on his right at Israel's left and Manasseh on his left at Israel's right, and brought
14 them close to him. Israel stretched out his right hand and laid it on Ephraim's head, although he was the younger, and, crossing his hands,
15 laid his left hand on Manasseh's head; but Manasseh was the elder. He blessed Joseph and said:

> 'The God in whose presence my forefathers lived,
>   my forefathers Abraham and Isaac,
> the God who has been my shepherd all my life until this day,
16   the angel who ransomed me from all misfortune,
>   may he bless these boys;

---

a *Or* may bless them.

they shall be called by my name,
and by that of my forefathers, Abraham and Isaac;
may they grow into a great people on earth.'

When Joseph saw that his father was laying his right hand on Ephraim's 17
head, he was displeased; so he took hold of his father's hand to move it
from Ephraim's head to Manasseh's. He said, 'That is not right, my father. 18
This is the elder; lay your right hand on his head.' But his father refused; 19
he said, 'I know, my son, I know. He too shall become a people; he too
shall become great, but his younger brother shall be greater than he, and
his descendants shall be a whole nation in themselves.' That day he blessed 20
them and said:

'When a blessing is pronounced in Israel,
men shall use your names and say,
God make you like Ephraim and Manasseh',

thus setting Ephraim before Manasseh. Then Israel said to Joseph, 'I am 21
dying. God will be with you and will bring you back to the land of your
fathers. I give you one ridge of land more than your brothers: I took it from 22
the Amorites with my sword and my bow.'

JACOB SUMMONED HIS SONS and said, 'Come near, and I will tell you 49
what will happen to you in days to come.

Gather round me and listen, you sons of Jacob; 2
listen to Israel your father.
Reuben, you are my first-born, 3
my strength and the first fruit of my vigour,
excelling in pride, excelling in might,
turbulent as a flood, you shall not excel; 4
because you climbed into your father's bed;
then you defiled his concubine's couch.
Simeon and Levi are brothers, 5
their spades became weapons of violence.
My soul shall not enter their council, 6
my heart shall not join their company;
for in their anger they killed men,
wantonly they hamstrung oxen.
A curse be on their anger because it was fierce; 7
a curse on their wrath because it was ruthless!
I will scatter them in Jacob,
I will disperse them in Israel.
Judah, your brothers shall praise you, 8
your hand is on the neck of your enemies.
Your father's sons shall do you homage.
Judah, you lion's whelp, 9
you have returned from the kill, my son,
and crouch and stretch like a lion;
and, like a lion,[a] who dare rouse you?

[a] *Or* lioness.

57

10
    The sceptre shall not pass from Judah,
    nor the staff from his descendants,
    so long as tribute is brought to him
    and the obedience of the nations is his.

11
    To the vine he tethers his ass,
    and the colt of his ass to the red vine;
    he washes his cloak in wine,
    his robes in the blood of grapes.

12
    Darker than wine are his eyes,
    his teeth whiter than milk.

13
Zebulun dwells by the sea-shore,
    his shore is a haven for ships,
    and his frontier rests on Sidon.

14
Issachar, a gelded ass
    lying down in the cattle-pens,

15
    saw that a settled home was good
    and that the land was pleasant,
    so he bent his back to the burden
    and submitted to perpetual forced labour.

16
Dan—how insignificant his people,
    lowly as any tribe in Israel! [a]

17
    Let Dan be a viper on the road,
    a horned snake on the path,
    who bites the horse's fetlock
    so that the rider tumbles backwards.

18
    For thy salvation I wait in hope, O Lord.

19
Gad is raided by raiders,
    and he raids them from the rear.

20
Asher shall have rich food as daily fare,
    and provide dishes fit for a king.

21
Naphtali is a spreading terebinth
    putting forth lovely boughs.

22
Joseph is a fruitful tree [b] by a spring
    with branches climbing over the wall.

23
    The archers savagely attacked him,
    they shot at him and pressed him hard,

24
    but their bow was splintered by the Eternal
    and the sinews of their arms were torn apart
    by the power of the Strong One of Jacob,
    by the name of the Shepherd [c] of Israel,

25
    by the God of your father—so may he help you,
    by God Almighty—so may he bless you
    with the blessings of heaven above,
    the blessings of the deep that lurks below.

---

[a] *Or* Dan shall judge his people as one of the tribes of Israel.   [b] *Or a fruitful ben-tree.*   [c] *Prob. rdg.; Heb. adds* stone.

The blessings of breast and womb
and the blessings of your father are stronger   26
than the blessings of the everlasting pools *a*
and the bounty of the eternal hills.
They shall be on the head of Joseph,
on the brow of the prince among *b* his brothers.
Benjamin is a ravening wolf: 27
in the morning he devours the prey,
in the evening he snatches a share of the spoil.'

These, then, are the twelve tribes of Israel, and this is what their father 28
Jacob said to them, when he blessed them each in turn. He gave them 29
his last charge and said, 'I shall soon be gathered to my father's kin;
bury me with my forefathers in the cave on the plot of land which
belonged to Ephron the Hittite, that is the cave on the plot of land at 30
Machpelah east of Mamre in Canaan, the field which Abraham bought
from Ephron the Hittite for a burial-place. There Abraham was buried 31
with his wife Sarah; there Isaac and his wife Rebecca were buried; and
there I buried Leah. The land and the cave on it were bought from the 32
Hittites.' When Jacob had finished giving his last charge to his sons, he 33
drew his feet up on to the bed, breathed his last, and was gathered to his
father's kin.

Then Joseph threw himself upon his father, weeping and kissing his **50**
face. He ordered the physicians in his service to embalm his father Israel, 2
and they did so, finishing the task in forty days, which was the usual time 3
for embalming. The Egyptians mourned him for seventy days; and then, 4
when the days of mourning for Israel were over, Joseph approached members of Pharaoh's household and said, 'If I can count on your goodwill,
then speak for me to Pharaoh; tell him that my father made me take an oath, 5
saying, "I am dying. Bury me in the grave that I bought *c* for myself in
Canaan." Ask him to let me go up and bury my father, and afterwards I
will return.' Pharaoh answered, 'Go and bury your father, as he has made 6
you swear to do.' So Joseph went to bury his father, accompanied by all 7
Pharaoh's courtiers, the elders of his household, and all the elders of Egypt,
together with all Joseph's own household, his brothers, and his father's 8
household; only their dependants, with the flocks and herds, were left in
Goshen. He took with him chariots and horsemen; they were a very great 9
company. When they came to the threshing-floor of Atad beside the river 10
Jordan, they raised a loud and bitter lament; and there Joseph observed
seven days' mourning for his father. When the Canaanites who lived there 11
saw this mourning at the threshing-floor of Atad, they said, 'How bitterly
the Egyptians are mourning!'; accordingly they named the place beside the
Jordan Abel-mizraim. *d*

Thus Jacob's sons did what he had told them to do. They took him to 12 13
Canaan and buried him in the cave on the plot of land at Machpelah, the
land which Abraham had bought as a burial-place from Ephron the Hittite,

a Or hills.   *b* the prince among: *or* the one cursed by.   *c Or* dug.
d That is Mourning (*or* Meadow) of Egypt.

14   to the east of Mamre. Then, after he had buried his father, Joseph returned
     to Egypt with his brothers and all who had gone up with him.
15   When their father was dead Joseph's brothers were afraid and said,
     'What if Joseph should bear a grudge against us and pay us out for all the
16   harm that we did to him?' They therefore approached Joseph with these
17   words: 'In his last words to us before he died, your father gave us this mes-
     sage for you: "I ask you to forgive your brothers' crime and wickedness;
     I know they did you harm." So now forgive our crime, we beg; for we are
     servants of your father's God.' When they said this to him, Joseph wept.
18   His brothers also wept*a* and prostrated themselves before him; they said,
19   'You see, we are your slaves.' But Joseph said to them, 'Do not be afraid.
20   Am I in the place of God? You meant to do me harm; but God meant to
     bring good out of it by preserving the lives of many people, as we see today.
21   Do not be afraid. I will provide for you and your dependants.' Thus he
     comforted them and set their minds at rest.
22   Joseph remained in Egypt, he and his father's household. He lived there
23   to be a hundred and ten years old and saw Ephraim's children to the third
     generation; he also recognized as his the children of Manasseh's son
24   Machir. He said to his brothers, 'I am dying; but God will not fail to come
     to your aid and take you from here to the land which he promised on oath
25   to Abraham, Isaac and Jacob.' He made the sons of Israel take an oath,
     saying, 'When God thus comes to your aid, you must take my bones with
26   you from here.' So Joseph died at the age of a hundred and ten. He was
     embalmed and laid in a coffin in Egypt.

EXODUS

Israel enslaved in Egypt

1   THESE ARE THE NAMES of the Israelites who entered Egypt
2   with Jacob, each with his household: Reuben, Simeon, Levi and
3 4 Judah; Issachar, Zebulun and Benjamin; Dan and Naphtali, Gad
5   and Asher. There were seventy of them all told, all direct descendants of
     Jacob. Joseph was already in Egypt.
6   In course of time Joseph died, he and all his brothers and that whole
7   generation. Now the Israelites were fruitful and prolific; they increased in
     numbers and became very powerful,*b* so that the country was overrun by
8   them. Then a new king ascended the throne of Egypt, one who knew
9   nothing of Joseph. He said to his people, 'These Israelites have become
10   too many and too strong for us. We must take precautions to see that they
     do not increase any further; or we shall find that, if war breaks out, they
     will join the enemy and fight against us, and they will become masters of
11   the country.' So they were made to work in gangs with officers set over

----

a *Prob. rdg.; Heb.* came.   *b* *Or* numerous.

them, to break their spirit with heavy labour. This is how Pharaoh's store-
cities, Pithom and Rameses, were built. But the more harshly they were 12
treated, the more their numbers increased beyond all bounds, until the
Egyptians came to loathe the sight of them. So they treated their Israelite 13
slaves with ruthless severity, and made life bitter for them with cruel 14
servitude, setting them to work on clay and brick-making, and all sorts of
work in the fields. In short they made ruthless use of them as slaves in every
kind of hard labour.

Then the king of Egypt spoke to the Hebrew midwives, whose names 15
were Shiphrah and Puah. 'When you are attending the Hebrew women in 16
childbirth,' he told them, 'watch as the child is delivered and if it is a boy,
kill him; if it is a girl, let her live.' But they were God-fearing women. They 17
did not do what the king of Egypt had told them to do, but let the boys live.
So he summoned those Hebrew midwives and asked them why they had 18
done this and let the boys live. They told Pharaoh that Hebrew women 19
were not like Egyptian women. When they were in labour they gave birth
before the midwife could get to them. So God made the midwives prosper, 20
and the people increased in numbers and in strength. God gave the mid- 21
wives homes and families of their own, because they feared him. Pharaoh 22
then ordered all his people to throw every new-born Hebrew boy into the
Nile, but to let the girls live.

A descendant of Levi married a Levite woman who conceived and bore **2** 1 2
a son. When she saw what a fine child he was, she hid him for three months,
but she could conceal him no longer. So she got a rush basket for him, made 3
it watertight with clay and tar, laid him in it, and put it among the reeds
by the bank of the Nile. The child's sister took her stand at a distance to see 4
what would happen to him. Pharaoh's daughter came down to bathe in the 5
river, while her ladies-in-waiting walked along the bank. She noticed the
basket among the reeds and sent her slave-girl for it. She took it from her
and when she opened it, she saw the child. It was crying, and she was filled 6
with pity for it. 'Why,' she said, 'it is a little Hebrew boy.' Thereupon the 7
sister said to Pharaoh's daughter, 'Shall I go and fetch one of the Hebrew
women as a wet-nurse to suckle the child for you?' Pharaoh's daughter told 8
her to go; so the girl went and called the baby's mother. Then Pharaoh's 9
daughter said to her, 'Here is the child, suckle him for me, and I will pay
you for it myself.' So the woman took the child and suckled him. When the 10
child was old enough, she brought him to Pharaoh's daughter, who adopted
him and called him Moses,*a* 'because', she said, 'I drew*b* him out of the
water.'

ONE DAY WHEN MOSES WAS GROWN UP, he went out to his own kins- 11
men and saw them at their heavy labour. He saw an Egyptian strike one
of his fellow-Hebrews. He looked this way and that, and, seeing there was 12
no one about, he struck the Egyptian down and hid his body in the sand.
When he went out next day, two Hebrews were fighting together. He asked 13
the man who was in the wrong, 'Why are you striking him?' 'Who set you 14
up as an officer and judge over us?' the man replied. 'Do you mean to

---

a Heb. Mosheh.   *b Heb. verb* mashah.

murder me as you murdered the Egyptian?' Moses was alarmed. 'The
15 thing must have become known', he said to himself. When Pharaoh heard
of it, he tried to put Moses to death, but Moses made good his escape and
settled in the land of Midian.
16   Now the priest of Midian had seven daughters. One day as Moses sat
by a well, they came to draw water and filled the troughs to water their
17 father's sheep. Some shepherds came and drove them away; but Moses
18 got up, took the girls' part and watered their sheep himself. When the girls
came back to their father Reuel, he asked, 'How is it that you are back so
19 quickly today?' 'An Egyptian rescued us from the shepherds,' they
answered; 'and he even drew the water for us and watered the sheep.'
20 'But where is he then?' he said to his daughters. 'Why did you leave him
21 behind? Go and invite him to eat with us.' So it came about that Moses
agreed to live with the man, and he gave Moses his daughter Zipporah in
22 marriage. She bore him a son, and Moses called him Gershom, 'because',
he said, 'I have become an alien*a* living in a foreign land.'

23 YEARS PASSED, and the king of Egypt died, but the Israelites still groaned
in slavery. They cried out, and their appeal for rescue from their slavery
24 rose up to God. He heard their groaning, and remembered his covenant
25 with Abraham, Isaac and Jacob; he saw the plight of Israel, and he took
heed of it.
3   Moses was minding the flock of his father-in-law Jethro, priest of Midian.
He led the flock along the side of the wilderness and came to Horeb, the
2 mountain of God. There the angel of the LORD appeared to him in the
flame of a burning bush. Moses noticed that, although the bush was on
3 fire, it was not being burnt up; so he said to himself, 'I must go across to
4 see this wonderful sight. Why does not the bush burn away?' When the
LORD saw that Moses had turned aside to look, he called to him out of the
5 bush, 'Moses, Moses.' And Moses answered, 'Yes, I am here.' God said,
'Come no nearer; take off your sandals; the place where you are standing
6 is holy ground.' Then he said, 'I am the God of your forefathers, the God
of Abraham, the God of Isaac, the God of Jacob.' Moses covered his face,
for he was afraid to gaze on God.
7   The LORD said, 'I have indeed seen the misery of my people in Egypt.
I have heard their outcry against their slave-masters. I have taken heed of
8 their sufferings, and have come down to rescue them from the power of
Egypt, and to bring them up out of that country into a fine, broad land; it is
a land flowing with milk and honey, the home of Canaanites, Hittites,
9 Amorites, Perizzites, Hivites, and Jebusites. The outcry of the Israelites
has now reached me; yes, I have seen the brutality of the Egyptians towards
10 them. Come now; I will send you to Pharaoh and you shall bring my people
11 Israel out of Egypt.' 'But who am I,' Moses said to God, 'that I should go
12 to Pharaoh, and that I should bring the Israelites out of Egypt?' God
answered, 'I am*b* with you. This shall be the proof that it is I who have sent
you: when you have brought the people out of Egypt, you shall all worship
God here on this mountain.'

a *Heb*. ger.   *b* *Or* I will be; *Heb*. ehyeh.

Then Moses said to God, 'If I go to the Israelites and tell them that the 13
God of their forefathers has sent me to them, and they ask me his name,
what shall I say?' God answered, 'I AM; that is who I am.*a* Tell them that 14
I AM has sent you to them.' And God said further, 'You must tell the 15
Israelites this, that it is JEHOVAH *b* the God of their forefathers, the God of
Abraham, the God of Isaac, the God of Jacob, who has sent you to them.
This is my name for ever; this is my title in every generation. Go and 16
assemble the elders of Israel and tell them that JEHOVAH the God of their
forefathers, the God of Abraham, Isaac and Jacob, has appeared to you
and has said, "I have indeed turned my eyes towards you; I have marked
all that has been done to you in Egypt, and I am resolved to bring you up 17
out of your misery in Egypt, into the country of the Canaanites, Hittites,
Amorites, Perizzites, Hivites, and Jebusites, a land flowing with milk and
honey." They will listen to you, and then you and the elders of Israel must 18
go to the king of Egypt. Tell him, "It has happened that the LORD the
God of the Hebrews met us. So now give us leave to go a three days' journey into the wilderness to offer sacrifice to the LORD our God." I know well 19
that the king of Egypt will not give you leave unless he is compelled. I shall 20
then stretch out my hand and assail the Egyptians with all the miracles I
shall work among them. After that he will send you away. Further, I will 21
bring this people into such favour with the Egyptians that, when you go,
you will not go empty-handed. Every woman shall ask her neighbour or 22
any woman who lives in her house for jewellery of silver and gold and for
clothing. Load your sons and daughters with them, and plunder Egypt.'

Moses answered, 'But they will never believe me or listen to me; they **4**
will say, "The LORD did not appear to you."' The LORD said, 'What have 2
you there in your hand?' 'A staff', Moses answered. The LORD said, 'Throw 3
it on the ground.' Moses threw it down and it turned into a snake. He ran
away from it, but the LORD said, 'Put your hand out and seize it by the tail.' 4
He did so and gripped it firmly, and it turned back into a staff in his hand.
'This is to convince the people that the LORD the God of their forefathers, 5
the God of Abraham, the God of Isaac, the God of Jacob, has appeared to
you.' Then the LORD said, 'Put your hand inside the fold of your cloak.' 6
He did so, and when he drew it out the skin was diseased, white as snow.
The LORD said, 'Put it back again', and he did so. When he drew it out this 7
time it was as healthy as the rest of his body. 'Now,' said the LORD, 'if they 8
do not believe you and do not accept the evidence of the first sign, they
may accept the evidence of the second. But if they are not convinced even 9
by these two signs, and will not accept what you say, then fetch some water
from the Nile and pour it out on the dry ground, and the water you take
from the Nile will turn to blood on the ground.'

But Moses said, 'O LORD, I have never been a man of ready speech, 10
never in my life, not even now that thou hast spoken to me; I am slow and
hesitant of speech.' The LORD said to him, 'Who is it that gives man speech? 11
Who makes him dumb or deaf? Who makes him clear-sighted or blind?
Is it not I, the LORD? Go now; I will help your speech and tell you what to 12

a I AM . . . I am: *or* I will be what I will be.   *b* *The Hebrew consonants are* YHWH,
probably pronounced Yahweh, *but traditionally read* Jehovah.

13 14 say.' But Moses still protested, 'No, Lord, send whom thou wilt.' At this the LORD grew angry with Moses and said, 'Have you not a brother, Aaron the Levite? He, I know, will do all the speaking. He is already on
15 his way out to meet you, and he will be glad indeed to see you. You shall speak to him and put the words in his mouth; I will help both of you to
16 speak and tell you both what to do. He will do all the speaking to the people for you, he will be the mouthpiece, and you will be the god he speaks for.
17 But take this staff, for with it you are to work the signs.'
18 At length Moses went back to Jethro his father-in-law and said, 'Let me return to my kinsfolk in Egypt and see if they are still alive.' Jethro told him to go and wished him well.

19 THE LORD SPOKE TO MOSES in Midian and said to him, 'Go back to
20 Egypt, for all those who wished to kill you are dead.' So Moses took his wife and children, mounted them on an ass and set out for Egypt with the
21 staff of God in his hand. The LORD said to Moses, 'While you are on your way back to Egypt, keep in mind all the portents I have given you power to show. You shall display these before Pharaoh, but I will make him
22 obstinate and he will not let the people go. Then tell Pharaoh that these are
23 the words of the LORD: "Israel is my first-born son. I have told you to let my son go, so that he may worship me. You have refused to let him go, so I will kill your first-born son." '

24 During the journey, while they were encamped for the night, the LORD
25 met Moses, meaning to kill him, but Zipporah picked up a sharp flint, cut off her son's foreskin, and touched him with it, saying, 'You are my blood-
26 bridegroom.' So the LORD let Moses alone. Then she said,*a* 'Blood-bride-groom by circumcision.'

27 Meanwhile the LORD had ordered Aaron to go and meet Moses in the wilderness. Aaron went and met him at the mountain of God, and he kissed
28 him. Then Moses told Aaron everything, the words the LORD had sent him
29 to say and the signs he had commanded him to perform. Moses and Aaron
30 went and assembled all the elders of Israel. Aaron told them everything that the LORD had said to Moses; he performed the signs before the people,
31 and they were convinced. They heard that the LORD had shown his concern for the Israelites and seen their misery; and they bowed themselves to the ground in worship.

5 After this, Moses and Aaron came to Pharaoh and said, 'These are the words of the LORD the God of Israel: "Let my people go so that they may
2 keep my pilgrim-feast in the wilderness." ' 'Who is the LORD,' asked Pharaoh, 'that I should obey him and let Israel go? I care nothing for the
3 LORD: and I tell you I will not let Israel go.' They replied, 'It has happened that the God of the Hebrews met us. So let us go three days' journey into the wilderness to offer sacrifice to the LORD our God, or else he will
4 attack us with pestilence or sword.' But the king of Egypt said, 'Moses and Aaron, what do you mean by distracting the people from their work? Back
5 to your labours! Your people already outnumber the native Egyptians; yet you would have them stop working!'

a Or Therefore women say.

64

That very day Pharaoh ordered the people's overseers and their foremen 6
not to supply the people with the straw used in making bricks, as they had 7
done hitherto. 'Let them go and collect their own straw, but see that they 8
produce the same tally of bricks as before. On no account reduce it. They
are a lazy people, and that is why they are clamouring to go and offer
sacrifice to their god. Keep the men hard at work; let them attend to that 9
and take no notice of a pack of lies.' The overseers and foremen went out 10
and said to the people, 'Pharaoh's orders are that no more straw is to be
supplied. Go and get it for yourselves wherever you can find it; but there 11
will be no reduction in your daily task.' So the people scattered all over 12
Egypt to gather stubble for straw, while the overseers kept urging them on, 13
bidding them complete, day after day, the same quantity as when straw was
supplied. Then the Israelite foremen were flogged because they were held 14
responsible by Pharaoh's overseers, who asked them, 'Why did you not
complete the usual number of bricks yesterday or today?' So the foremen 15
came and appealed to Pharaoh: 'Why do you treat your servants like this?'
they said. 'We are given no straw, yet they keep on telling us to make 16
bricks. Here are we being flogged, but it is your people's fault.' But 17
Pharaoh replied, 'You are lazy, you are lazy. That is why you talk about
going to offer sacrifice to the LORD. Now go; get on with your work. You 18
will be given no straw, but you must produce the tally of bricks.' When they 19
were told that they must not let the daily tally of bricks fall short, the Israelite foremen saw that they were in trouble. As they came out from Pharaoh's 20
presence they found Moses and Aaron waiting to meet them, and said, 'May 21
this bring the LORD's judgement down upon you: you have made us stink
in the nostrils of Pharaoh and his subjects; you have put a sword in their
hands to kill us.'

Moses went back to the LORD, and said, 'Why, O Lord, hast thou brought 22
misfortune on this people? And why didst thou ever send me? Since I first 23
went to Pharaoh to speak in thy name he has heaped misfortune on thy
people, and thou hast done nothing at all to rescue them.' The LORD 6
answered, 'Now you shall see what I will do to Pharaoh. In the end Pharaoh
will let them go with a strong hand, nay, will drive them from his country
with an outstretched arm.'

God spoke to Moses and said, 'I am the LORD. I appeared to Abraham, 2 3
Isaac, and Jacob as God Almighty. But I did not let myself be known to
them by my name JEHOVAH.*a* Moreover, I made a covenant with them to 4
give them Canaan, the land where they settled for a time as foreigners. And 5
now I have heard the groaning of the Israelites, enslaved by the Egyptians,
and I have called my covenant to mind. Say therefore to the Israelites, "I 6
am the LORD. I will release you from your labours in Egypt. I will rescue
you from slavery there. I will redeem you with arm outstretched and with
mighty acts of judgement. I will adopt you as my people, and I will become 7
your God. You shall know that I, the LORD, am your God, the God who
releases you from your labours in Egypt. I will lead you to the land which I 8
swore with uplifted hand to give to Abraham, to Isaac and to Jacob. I will
give it you for your possession. I am the LORD."'

a See note on 3. 15.

65

9 Moses repeated these words to the Israelites, but they did not listen to him; they had become impatient because of their cruel slavery.

10 11 Then the LORD spoke to Moses and said, 'Go and tell Pharaoh king of
12 Egypt to set the Israelites free to leave his country.' Moses made answer in the presence of the LORD, 'If the Israelites do not listen to me, how will Pharaoh listen to such a halting speaker as I am?'

13 Thus the LORD spoke to Moses and Aaron and gave them their commission to the Israelites and to Pharaoh, namely that they should bring the Israelites out of Egypt.

14*a* THESE WERE THE HEADS of fathers' families:
Sons of Reuben, Israel's eldest son: Enoch, Pallu, Hezron and Carmi; these were the families of Reuben.

15 Sons of Simeon: Jemuel, Jamin, Ohad, Jachin, Zohar, and Saul, who was the son of a Canaanite woman; these were the families of Simeon.

16 These were the names of the sons of Levi in order of seniority: Gershon, Kohath and Merari. Levi lived to be a hundred and thirty-seven.

17 Sons of Gershon, family by family: Libni and Shimei.

18 Sons of Kohath: Amram, Izhar, Hebron and Uzziel. Kohath lived to be a hundred and thirty-three.

19 Sons of Merari: Mahli and Mushi.

20 These were the families of Levi in order of seniority. Amram married his father's sister Jochebed, and she bore him Aaron and Moses. Amram lived to be a hundred and thirty-seven.

21 Sons of Izhar: Korah, Nepheg and Zichri.

22 Sons of Uzziel: Mishael, Elzaphan and Sithri.

23 Aaron married Elisheba, who was the daughter of Amminadab and the sister of Nahshon, and she bore him Nadab, Abihu, Eleazar and Ithamar.

24 Sons of Korah: Assir, Elkanah and Abiasaph; these were the Korahite families.

25 Eleazar son of Aaron married one of the daughters of Putiel, and she bore him Phinehas. These were the heads of the Levite families, family by family.

26 It was this Aaron, together with Moses, to whom the LORD said, 'Bring
27 the Israelites out of Egypt, mustered in their tribal hosts.' These were the men who told Pharaoh king of Egypt to let the Israelites leave Egypt. It was this same Moses and Aaron.

28 29 WHEN THE LORD SPOKE TO MOSES in Egypt he said, 'I am the LORD.
30 Tell Pharaoh king of Egypt all that I say to you.' Moses made answer in the presence of the LORD, 'I am a halting speaker; how will Pharaoh listen to
7 me?' The LORD answered Moses, 'See now, I have made you like a god for
2 Pharaoh, with your brother Aaron as your spokesman. You must tell your brother Aaron all I bid you say, and he will tell Pharaoh, and Pharaoh will
3 let the Israelites go out of his country; but I will make him stubborn. Then will I show sign after sign and portent after portent in the land of Egypt.
4 But Pharaoh will not listen to you, so I will assert my power in Egypt, and

a Verses 14–16: cp. Gen. 46. 8–11; Num. 26. 5, 6, 12, 13.

with mighty acts of judgement I will bring my people, the Israelites, out
of Egypt in their tribal hosts. When I put forth my power against the 5
Egyptians and bring the Israelites out from them, then Egypt will know
that I am the LORD.' So Moses and Aaron did exactly as the LORD had 6
commanded. At the time when they spoke to Pharaoh, Moses was eighty 7
years old and Aaron eighty-three.

The LORD said to Moses and Aaron, 'If Pharaoh demands some portent 8 9
from you, then you, Moses, must say to Aaron, "Take your staff and throw
it down in front of Pharaoh, and it will turn into a serpent."' When Moses 10
and Aaron came to Pharaoh, they did as the LORD had told them. Aaron
threw down his staff in front of Pharaoh and his courtiers, and it turned into
a serpent. At this, Pharaoh summoned the wise men and the sorcerers, and 11
the Egyptian magicians too did the same thing by their spells. Every man 12
threw his staff down, and each staff turned into a serpent; but Aaron's
staff swallowed up theirs. Pharaoh, however, was obstinate; as the LORD 13
had foretold, he would not listen to Moses and Aaron.

Then the LORD said to Moses, 'Pharaoh is obdurate: he has refused to set 14
the people free. Go to him in the morning on his way out to the river. Stand 15
and wait on the bank of the Nile to meet him, and take with you the staff
that turned into a snake. Say this to him: "The LORD the God of the 16
Hebrews sent me to bid you let his people go in order to worship him in the
wilderness. So far you have not listened to his words; so now the LORD 17
says, 'By this you shall know that I am the LORD.' With this rod that I have
in my hand, I shall now strike the water in the Nile and it will be changed
into blood. The fish will die and the river will stink, and the Egyptians will 18
be unable to drink water from the Nile."' The LORD then told Moses to 19
say to Aaron, 'Take your staff and stretch your hand out over the waters of
Egypt, its rivers and its streams, and over every pool and cistern, to turn
them into blood. There shall be blood throughout the whole of Egypt,
blood even in their wooden bowls and jars of stone.' So Moses and Aaron 20
did as the LORD had commanded. He lifted up his staff and struck the
water of the Nile in the sight of Pharaoh and his courtiers, and all the water
was changed into blood. The fish died and the river stank, and the Egyp- 21
tians could not drink water from the Nile. There was blood everywhere in
Egypt. But the Egyptian magicians did the same thing by their spells; and 22
still Pharaoh remained obstinate, as the LORD had foretold, and did not
listen to Moses and Aaron. He turned away, went into his house and dis- 23
missed the matter from his mind. Then the Egyptians all dug for drinking 24
water round about the river, because they could not drink from the waters
of the Nile itself. This lasted for seven days from the time when the LORD 25
struck the Nile.

The LORD then told Moses to go into Pharaoh's presence and say to him, 8
'These are the words of the LORD: "Let my people go in order to worship
me. If you refuse to let them go, I will plague the whole of your territory 2
with frogs. The Nile shall swarm with them. They shall come up from 3
the river into your house, into your bedroom and on to your bed, into
the houses of your courtiers and your people, into your ovens and your
kneading-troughs. The frogs shall clamber over you, your people, and your 4

5 courtiers."' Then the LORD told Moses to say to Aaron, 'Take your staff in your hand and stretch it out over the rivers, streams, and pools, to bring
6 up frogs upon the land of Egypt.' So Aaron stretched out his hand over the
7 waters of Egypt, and the frogs came up and covered all the land. The magicians did the same thing by their spells: they too brought up frogs
8 upon the land of Egypt. Then Pharaoh summoned Moses and Aaron. 'Pray to the LORD', he said, 'to take the frogs away from me and my people, and
9 I will let the people go to sacrifice to the LORD.' Moses said, 'Of your royal favour, appoint a time when I may intercede for you and your courtiers and people, so that you and your houses may be rid of the frogs, and none
10 be left except in the Nile.' 'Tomorrow', Pharaoh said. 'It shall be as you say,' replied Moses, 'so that you may know there is no one like our God,
11 the LORD. The frogs shall depart from you, from your houses, your
12 courtiers, and your people: none shall be left except in the Nile.' Moses and Aaron left Pharaoh's presence, and Moses appealed to the LORD to remove
13 the frogs which he had brought on Pharaoh. The LORD did as Moses had asked, and in house and courtyard and in the open the frogs all perished.
14 15 They piled them into countless heaps and the land stank; but when Pharaoh found that he was given relief he became obdurate; as the LORD had foretold, he did not listen to Moses and Aaron.

16 The LORD then told Moses to say to Aaron, 'Stretch out your staff and strike the dust on the ground, and it will turn into maggots throughout the
17 land of Egypt', and they obeyed. Aaron stretched out his staff and struck the dust, and it turned into maggots on man and beast. All the dust turned
18 into maggots throughout the land of Egypt. The magicians tried to produce maggots in the same way by their spells, but they failed. The maggots were
19 everywhere, on man and beast. 'It is the finger of God', said the magicians to Pharaoh, but Pharaoh remained obstinate; as the LORD had foretold, he did not listen to them.

20 The LORD told Moses to rise early in the morning and stand in Pharaoh's path as he went out to the river and to say to him, 'These are the words of
21 the LORD: "Let my people go in order to worship me. If you do not let my people go, I will send swarms of flies upon you, your courtiers, your people, and your houses. The houses of the Egyptians shall be filled with
22 the swarms and so shall all the land they live in, but on that day I will make an exception of Goshen, the land where my people live: there shall be no swarms there. Thus you shall know that I, the LORD, am here in the land.
23 I will make a distinction between my people and yours. Tomorrow this
24 sign shall appear."' The LORD did this; dense swarms of flies infested Pharaoh's house and those of his courtiers; throughout Egypt the land was
25 threatened with ruin by the swarms. Pharaoh summoned Moses and Aaron
26 and said to them, 'Go and sacrifice to your God, but in this country.' 'That we cannot do,' replied Moses, 'because the victim we shall sacrifice to the LORD our God is an abomination to the Egyptians. If the Egyptians see us
27 offer such an animal, will they not stone us to death? We must go a three days' journey into the wilderness to sacrifice to the LORD our God, as he
28 commands us.' 'I will let you go,' said Pharaoh, 'and you shall sacrifice to your God in the wilderness; only do not go far. Now intercede for me.'

Moses answered, 'As soon as I leave you I will intercede with the LORD. 29
Tomorrow the swarms will depart from Pharaoh, his courtiers, and his
people. Only let not Pharaoh trifle any more with the people by preventing
them from going to sacrifice to the LORD.' Then Moses left Pharaoh and 30
interceded with the LORD. The LORD did as Moses had said; he removed 31
the swarms from Pharaoh, his courtiers, and his people; not one was left.
But once again Pharaoh became obdurate and did not let the people go.   32

The LORD said to Moses, 'Go into Pharaoh's presence and say to him, 9
"These are the words of the LORD the God of the Hebrews: 'Let my people
go in order to worship me.' If you refuse to let them go and still keep 2
your hold on them, the LORD will strike your grazing herds, your horses 3
and asses, your camels, cattle, and sheep with a terrible pestilence. But 4
the LORD will make a distinction between Israel's herds and those of the
Egyptians. Of all that belong to Israel not a single one shall die." ' The 5
LORD fixed a time and said, 'Tomorrow I will do this throughout the land.'
The next day the LORD struck. All the herds of Egypt died, but from the 6
herds of the Israelites not one single beast died. Pharaoh inquired and was 7
told that not a beast from the herds of Israel had died; and yet he remained
obdurate and did not let the people go.

The LORD said to Moses and Aaron, 'Take handfuls of soot from a kiln. 8
Moses shall toss it into the air in Pharaoh's sight, and it will turn into a fine 9
dust over the whole of Egypt. All over Egypt it will become festering boils
on man and beast.' They took the soot from the kiln and stood before 10
Pharaoh. Moses tossed it into the air and it produced festering boils on
man and beast. The magicians were no match for Moses because of the 11
boils, which attacked them and all the Egyptians. But the LORD made 12
Pharaoh obstinate; as the LORD had foretold to Moses, he did not listen to
Moses and Aaron.

The LORD then told Moses to rise early in the morning, present himself 13
before Pharaoh, and say to him, 'These are the words of the LORD the God
of the Hebrews: "Let my people go in order to worship me. This time I 14
will strike home with all my plagues against you, your courtiers, and your
people, so that you may know that there is none like me in all the earth. By 15
now I could have stretched out my hand, and struck you and your people
with pestilence, and you would have vanished from the earth. I have let 16
you live only to show you my power and to spread my fame throughout the
land. Since you still obstruct my people and will not let them go, tomorrow 17 18
at this time I will send a violent hailstorm, such as has never been in Egypt
from its first beginnings until now. Send now and bring your herds under 19
cover, and everything you have out in the open field. If anything, whether
man or beast, which happens to be in the open, is not brought in, the hail
will fall on it, and it will die." ' Those of Pharaoh's subjects who feared the 20
word of the LORD hurried their slaves and cattle into their houses. But those 21
who did not take to heart the word of the LORD left their slaves and cattle
in the open.

The LORD said to Moses, 'Stretch out your hand towards the sky to 22
bring down hail on the whole land of Egypt, on man and beast and every
growing thing throughout the land.' Moses stretched out his staff towards 23

the sky, and the LORD sent thunder and hail, with fire flashing down to the
24 ground. The LORD rained down hail on the land of Egypt, hail and fiery
flashes through the hail, so heavy that there had been nothing like it in all
25 Egypt from the time that Egypt became a nation. Throughout Egypt the
hail struck everything in the fields, both man and beast; it beat down every
26 growing thing and shattered every tree. Only in the land of Goshen, where
the Israelites lived, was there no hail.
27   Pharaoh sent and summoned Moses and Aaron. 'This time I have
sinned,' he said; 'the LORD is in the right; I and my people are in the wrong.
28 Intercede with the LORD, for we can bear no more of this thunder and hail.
29 I will let you go; you need wait no longer.' Moses said, 'When I leave the
city I will spread out my hands in prayer to the LORD. The thunder shall
cease, and there shall be no more hail, so that you may know that the earth
30 is the LORD's. But you and your subjects—I know that you do not yet fear
31 the LORD God.' (The flax and barley were destroyed because the barley was
32 in the ear and the flax in bud, but the wheat and spelt were not destroyed
33 because they come later.) Moses left Pharaoh's presence, went out of the
city and lifted up his hands to the LORD in prayer: the thunder and hail
34 ceased, and no more rain fell. When Pharaoh saw that the downpour, the
hail, and the thunder had ceased, he sinned again, he and his courtiers, and
35 became obdurate. So Pharaoh remained obstinate; as the LORD had foretold through Moses, he did not let the people go.
10   Then the LORD said to Moses, 'Go into Pharaoh's presence. I have made
him and his courtiers obdurate, so that I may show these my signs among
2 them, and so that you can tell your children and grandchildren the story:
how I made sport of the Egyptians, and what signs I showed among them.
3 Thus you will know that I am the LORD.' Moses and Aaron went in to
Pharaoh and said to him, 'These are the words of the LORD the God of the
Hebrews: "How long will you refuse to humble yourself before me? Let
4 my people go in order to worship me. If you refuse to let my people go,
5 tomorrow I will bring locusts into your country. They shall cover the face
of the land so that it cannot be seen. They shall eat up the last remnant left
you by the hail. They shall devour every tree that grows in your country-
6 side. Your houses and your courtiers' houses, every house in Egypt, shall
be full of them; your fathers never saw the like nor their fathers before
them; such a thing has not happened from their time until now." ' He turned
7 and left Pharaoh's presence. Pharaoh's courtiers said to him, 'How long
must we be caught in this man's toils? Let their menfolk go and worship
8 the LORD their God. Do you not know by now that Egypt is ruined?' So
Moses and Aaron were brought back to Pharaoh, and he said to them, 'You
9 may go and worship the LORD your God; but who exactly is to go?' 'All,'
said Moses, 'young and old, boys and girls, sheep and cattle; for we have
10 to keep the LORD's pilgrim-feast.' Pharaoh replied, 'Very well then; take
your dependants with you when you go; and the LORD be with you. But
11 beware, there is trouble in store for you. No, your menfolk may go and
worship the LORD, for that is all you asked.' So they were driven out from
Pharaoh's presence.
12   Then the LORD said to Moses, 'Stretch out your hand over Egypt so

that the locusts may come and invade the land and devour all the vegetation
in it, everything the hail has left.' Moses stretched out his staff over the   13
land of Egypt, and the LORD sent a wind roaring in from the east all that
day and all that night. When morning came, the east wind had brought the
locusts. They invaded the whole land of Egypt, and settled on all its terri-   14
tory in swarms so dense that the like of them had never been seen before,
nor ever will be again. They covered the surface of the whole land till it   15
was black with them. They devoured all the vegetation and all the fruit of
the trees that the hail had spared. There was no green left on tree or plant
throughout all Egypt. Pharaoh hastily summoned Moses and Aaron. 'I   16
have sinned against the LORD your God and against you', he said. 'Forgive   17
my sin, I pray, just this once. Intercede with the LORD your God and beg
him only to remove this deadly plague from me.' Moses left Pharaoh and   18
interceded with the LORD. The LORD changed the wind into a westerly gale,   19
which carried the locusts away and swept them into the Red Sea.*a* There
was not a single locust left in all the territory of Egypt. But the LORD made 20
Pharaoh obstinate, and he did not let the Israelites go.

Then the LORD said to Moses, 'Stretch out your hand towards the sky so   21
that there may be darkness over the land of Egypt, darkness that can be
felt.' Moses stretched out his hand towards the sky, and it became pitch   22
dark throughout the land of Egypt for three days. Men could not see one   23
another; for three days no one stirred from where he was. But there was no
darkness wherever the Israelites lived. Pharaoh summoned Moses. 'Go',   24
he said, 'and worship the LORD. Your dependants may go with you; but
your flocks and herds must be left with us.' But Moses said, 'No, you must   25
yourself supply us with animals for sacrifice and whole-offering to the
LORD our God; and our own flocks must go with us too—not a hoof must   26
be left behind. We may need animals from our own flocks to worship the
LORD our God; we ourselves cannot tell until we are there how we are to
worship the LORD.' The LORD made Pharaoh obstinate, and he refused to   27
let them go. 'Out! Pester me no more!' he said to Moses. 'Take care you do   28
not see my face again, for on the day you do, you die.' 'You are right,' said   29
Moses; 'I shall never see your face again.'

Then the LORD said to Moses, 'One last plague I will bring upon Pharaoh **11**
and Egypt. After that he will let you go; he will send you packing, as a man
dismisses a rejected bride. Let the people be told that men and women alike   2
should ask their neighbours for jewellery of silver and gold.' The LORD   3
made the Egyptians well-disposed towards them, and, moreover, Moses
was a very great man in Egypt in the eyes of Pharaoh's courtiers and of
the people.

Moses then said, 'These are the words of the LORD: "At midnight I will   4
go out among the Egyptians. Every first-born creature in the land of   5
Egypt shall die: the first-born of Pharaoh who sits on his throne, the first-
born of the slave-girl at the handmill, and all the first-born of the cattle.
All Egypt will send up a great cry of anguish, a cry the like of which has   6
never been heard before, nor ever will be again. But among all Israel not   7
a dog's tongue shall be so much as scratched, no man or beast be hurt."

a Or the Sea of Reeds.

8   Thus you shall know that the LORD does make a distinction between Egypt and Israel. Then all these courtiers of yours will come down to me, prostrate themselves and cry, "Go away, you and all the people who follow at your heels." After that I will go away.' Then Moses left Pharaoh's presence hot with anger.

9   The LORD said to Moses, 'Pharaoh will not listen to you; I will therefore
10 show still more portents in the land of Egypt.' All these portents had Moses and Aaron shown in the presence of Pharaoh, and yet the LORD made him obstinate, and he did not let the Israelites leave the country.

The institution of the Passover

12 1 2 THE LORD SAID TO MOSES and Aaron in Egypt: This month is for you
3   the first of months; you shall make it the first month of the year. Speak to the whole community of Israel and say to them: On the tenth day of this month let each man take a lamb or a kid for his family, one for each
4 household, but if a household is too small for one lamb or one kid, then the man and his nearest neighbour may take one between them. They shall share the cost, taking into account both the number of persons and the
5 amount each of them eats. Your lamb or kid must be without blemish, a
6 yearling male. You may take equally a sheep or a goat. You must have it in safe keeping until the fourteenth day of this month, and then all the assembled community of Israel shall slaughter the victim between dusk
7 and dark. They must take some of the blood and smear it on the two door-
8 posts and on the lintel of every house in which they eat the lamb. On that night they shall eat the flesh roast on the fire; they shall eat it with un-
9 leavened cakes and bitter herbs. You are not to eat any of it raw or even
10 boiled in water, but roasted, head, shins, and entrails. You shall not leave any of it till morning; if anything is left over until morning, it must be destroyed by fire.

11   This is the way in which you must eat it: you shall have your belt fastened, your sandals on your feet and your staff in your hand, and you must eat in
12 urgent haste. It is the LORD's Passover. On that night I shall pass through the land of Egypt and kill every first-born of man and beast. Thus will I
13 execute judgement, I the LORD, against all the gods of Egypt. And as for you, the blood will be a sign on the houses in which you are: when I see the blood I will pass over*a* you; the mortal blow shall not touch you, when I strike the land of Egypt.

14   You shall keep this day as a day of remembrance, and make it a pilgrim-feast, a festival of the LORD; you shall keep it generation after generation as
15 a rule for all time. For seven days you shall eat unleavened cakes. On the very first day you shall rid your houses of leaven; from the first day to the
16 seventh anyone who eats leavened bread shall be outlawed from Israel. On the first day there shall be a sacred assembly and on the seventh day there shall be a sacred assembly: on these days no work shall be done, except what must be done to provide food for everyone; and that will be allowed.

a Or stand guard over.

You shall observe these commandments because this was the very day on 17
which I brought you out of Egypt in your tribal hosts. You shall observe
this day from generation to generation as a rule for all time.

You shall eat unleavened cakes in the first month from the evening which 18
begins the fourteenth day until the evening which begins the twenty-first
day. For seven days no leaven may be found in your houses, for anyone who 19
eats anything fermented shall be outlawed from the community of Israel,
be he foreigner or native. You must eat nothing fermented. Wherever you 20
live you must eat your cakes unleavened.

Moses summoned all the elders of Israel and said to them, 'Go at once 21
and get sheep for your families and slaughter the Passover. Then take a 22
bunch of marjoram,*a* dip it in the blood in the basin*b* and smear some blood
from the basin*c* on the lintel and the two door-posts. Nobody may go out
through the door of his house till morning. The LORD will go through 23
Egypt and strike it, but when he sees the blood on the lintel and the two
door-posts, he will pass over that door and will not let the destroyer enter
your houses to strike you. You shall keep this as a rule for you and your 24
children for all time. When you enter the land which the LORD will give 25
you as he promised, you shall observe this rite. Then, when your children 26
ask you, "What is the meaning of this rite?" you shall say, "It is the LORD's 27
Passover, for he passed over the houses of the Israelites in Egypt when he
struck the Egyptians but spared our houses."' The people bowed down
and prostrated themselves.

The Israelites went and did all that the LORD had commanded Moses and 28
Aaron; and by midnight the LORD had struck down every first-born in 29
Egypt, from the first-born of Pharaoh on his throne to the first-born of the
captive in the dungeon, and the first-born of cattle. Before night was over 30
Pharaoh rose, he and all his courtiers and all the Egyptians, and a great
cry of anguish went up, because not a house in Egypt was without its dead.
Pharaoh summoned Moses and Aaron while it was still night and said, 31
'Up with you! Be off, and leave my people, you and your Israelites. Go and
worship the LORD, as you ask; take your sheep and cattle, and go; and ask 32
God's blessing on me also.' The Egyptians urged on the people and hurried 33
them out of the country, 'or else', they said, 'we shall all be dead.' The 34
people picked up their dough before it was leavened, wrapped their
kneading-troughs in their cloaks, and slung them on their shoulders.
Meanwhile the Israelites had done as Moses had told them, asking the 35
Egyptians for jewellery of silver and gold and for clothing. As the LORD 36
had made the Egyptians well-disposed towards them, they let them have
what they asked; in this way they plundered the Egyptians.

The exodus from Egypt

THE ISRAELITES SET OUT from Rameses on the way to Succoth, about 37
six hundred thousand men on foot, not counting dependants. And with 38
them too went a large company of every kind, and cattle in great numbers,

a Or hyssop.　　　*b Or* on the threshold.　　　*c Or* from the threshold.

39 both flocks and herds. The dough they had brought from Egypt they baked into unleavened cakes, because there was no leaven; for they had been driven out of Egypt and allowed no time even to get food ready for themselves.

40 The Israelites had been settled in Egypt for four hundred and thirty
41 years. At the end of four hundred and thirty years, on this very day, all the
42 tribes of the LORD came out of Egypt. This was a night of vigil as the LORD waited to bring them out of Egypt. It is the LORD's night; all Israelites keep their vigil generation after generation.

43 The LORD said to Moses and Aaron: These are the rules for the Passover.
44 No foreigner may partake of it; any bought slave may eat it if you have
45 46 circumcised him; no stranger or hired man may eat it. Each lamb must be eaten inside the one house, and you must not take any of the flesh outside
47 the house. You must not break a single bone of it. The whole community
48 of Israel shall keep this feast. If there are aliens living with you and they are to keep the Passover to the LORD, every male of them must be circumcised, and then he can take part; he shall rank as native-born. No one who
49 is uncircumcised may eat of it. The same law shall apply both to the native-born and to the alien who is living among you.

50 The Israelites did all that the LORD had commanded Moses and Aaron;
51 and on this very day the LORD brought the Israelites out of Egypt mustered in their tribal hosts.

13 1 2 The LORD spoke to Moses and said, 'Every first-born, the first birth of every womb among the Israelites, you must dedicate to me, both man and beast; it is mine.'

3 Then Moses said to the people, 'Remember this day, the day on which you have come out of Egypt, the land of slavery, because the LORD by the strength of his hand has brought you out. No leaven may be eaten this day,
4 5 for today, in the month of Abib, is the day of your exodus; and when the LORD has brought you into the country of the Canaanites, Hittites, Amorites, Hivites, and Jebusites, the land which he swore to your forefathers to give you, a land flowing with milk and honey, then you must observe
6 this rite in this same month. For seven days you shall eat unleavened cakes,
7 and on the seventh day there shall be a pilgrim-feast of the LORD. Only unleavened cakes shall be eaten during the seven days; nothing fermented
8 and no leaven shall be seen throughout your territory. On that day you shall tell your son, "This commemorates what the LORD did for me when
9 I came out of Egypt." You shall have the record of it as a sign upon your hand, and upon your forehead as a reminder, to make sure that the law of the LORD is always on your lips, because the LORD with a strong hand
10 brought you out of Egypt. This is a rule, and you shall keep it at the appointed time from year to year.

11 'When the LORD has brought you into the land of the Canaanites as he
12 swore to you and to your forefathers, and given it to you, you shall surrender to the LORD the first birth of every womb; and of all first-born offspring of your cattle the males belong to the LORD. Every first-born male
13 ass you may redeem with a kid or lamb, but if you do not redeem it, you must break its neck. Every first-born among your sons you must redeem.

When in time to come your son asks you what this means, you shall say to 14
him, "By the strength of his hand the LORD brought us out of Egypt, out
of the land of slavery. When Pharaoh proved stubborn and refused to let 15
us go, the LORD killed all the first-born in Egypt both man and beast. That
is why I sacrifice to the LORD the first birth of every womb if it is a male and
redeem every first-born of my sons. You shall have the record of it as a sign 16
upon your hand, and upon your forehead as a phylactery, because by the
strength of his hand the LORD brought us out of Egypt."'

NOW WHEN PHARAOH LET THE PEOPLE GO, God did not guide them 17
by the road towards the Philistines, although that was the shortest; for he
said, 'The people may change their minds when they see war before them,
and turn back to Egypt.' So God made them go round by way of the wilder- 18
ness towards the Red Sea; and the fifth generation of Israelites departed
from Egypt.

Moses took the bones of Joseph with him, because Joseph had exacted 19
an oath from the Israelites: 'Some day', he said, 'God will show his care
for you, and then, as you go, you must take my bones with you.'

They set out from Succoth and encamped at Etham on the edge of the 20
wilderness. And all the time the LORD went before them, by day a pillar 21
of cloud to guide them on their journey, by night a pillar of fire to give them
light, so that they could travel night and day. The pillar of cloud never left 22
its place in front of the people by day, nor the pillar of fire by night.

The LORD spoke to Moses and said, 'Speak to the Israelites: they are to **14** 1 2
turn back and encamp before Pi-hahiroth,*ᵃ* between Migdol and the sea
to the east of Baal-zephon; your camp shall be opposite, by the sea.
Pharaoh will then think that the Israelites are finding themselves in difficult 3
country, and are hemmed in by the wilderness. I will make Pharaoh ob- 4
stinate, and he will pursue them, so that I may win glory for myself at the
expense of Pharaoh and all his army; and the Egyptians shall know that I
am the LORD.' The Israelites did as they were bidden.

When the king of Egypt was told that the Israelites had slipped away, 5
he and his courtiers changed their minds completely, and said, 'What have
we done? We have let our Israelite slaves go free!' So Pharaoh put horses 6
to his chariot, and took his troops with him. He took six hundred picked 7
chariots and all the other chariots of Egypt, with a commander in each.
Then Pharaoh king of Egypt, made obstinate by the LORD, pursued the 8
Israelites as they marched defiantly away. The Egyptians, all Pharaoh's 9
chariots and horses, cavalry and infantry, pursued them and overtook
them encamped beside the sea by Pi-hahiroth to the east of Baal-zephon.
Pharaoh was almost upon them when the Israelites looked up and saw the 10
Egyptians close behind. In their terror they clamoured to the LORD for
help and said to Moses, 'Were there no graves in Egypt, that you should 11
have brought us here to die in the wilderness? See what you have done to
us by bringing us out of Egypt! Is not this just what we meant when we 12
said in Egypt, "Leave us alone; let us be slaves to the Egyptians"? We

ᵃ Or where the desert tracks begin.

would rather be slaves to the Egyptians than die here in the wilderness.'
13 'Have no fear,' Moses answered; 'stand firm and see the deliverance that
the LORD will bring you this day; for as sure as you see the Egyptians now,
14 you will never see them again. The LORD will fight for you; so hold your
peace.'

15 The LORD said to Moses, 'What is the meaning of this clamour? Tell the
16 Israelites to strike camp. And you shall raise high your staff, stretch out
your hand over the sea and cleave it in two, so that the Israelites can pass
17 through the sea on dry ground. For my part I will make the Egyptians
obstinate and they will come after you; thus will I win glory for myself at
the expense of Pharaoh and his army, chariots and cavalry all together.
18 The Egyptians will know that I am the LORD when I win glory for myself
at the expense of their Pharaoh, his chariots and cavalry.'

19 The angel of God, who had kept in front of the Israelites, moved away
to the rear. The pillar of cloud moved from the front and took its place
20 behind them and so came between the Egyptians and the Israelites. And
the cloud brought on darkness and early nightfall, so that contact was lost
throughout the night.

21 Then Moses stretched out his hand over the sea, and the LORD drove
the sea away all night with a strong east wind and turned the sea-bed into
22 dry land. The waters were torn apart, and the Israelites went through the
sea on the dry ground, while the waters made a wall for them to right and
23 to left. The Egyptians went in pursuit of them far into the sea, all Pharaoh's
24 horse, his chariots, and his cavalry. In the morning watch the LORD looked
down on the Egyptian army through the pillar of fire and cloud, and he
25 threw them into a panic. He clogged their chariot wheels and made them
lumber along heavily, so that the Egyptians said, 'It is the LORD fighting
26 for Israel against Egypt; let us flee.' Then the LORD said to Moses, 'Stretch
out your hand over the sea, and let the water flow back over the Egyptians,
27 their chariots and their cavalry.' So Moses stretched out his hand over the
sea, and at daybreak the water returned to its accustomed place; but the
Egyptians were in flight as it advanced, and the LORD swept them out into
28 the sea. The water flowed back and covered all Pharaoh's army, the chariots
and the cavalry, which had pressed the pursuit into the sea. Not one man
29 was left alive. Meanwhile the Israelites had passed along the dry ground
through the sea, with the water making a wall for them to right and to
30 left. That day the LORD saved Israel from the power of Egypt, and the
31 Israelites saw the Egyptians lying dead on the sea-shore. When Israel
saw the great power which the LORD had put forth against Egypt, all the
people feared the LORD, and they put their faith in him and in Moses his
servant.

15 Then Moses and the Israelites sang this song to the LORD:

I will sing to the LORD, for he has risen up in triumph;
the horse and his rider he has hurled into the sea.
2   The LORD is my refuge and my defence,
he has shown himself my deliverer.
He is my God, and I will glorify him;
he is my father's God, and I will exalt him.

The LORD is a warrior: the LORD is his name.   3
The chariots of Pharaoh and his army   4
he has cast into the sea;
the flower of his officers
are engulfed in the Red Sea.
The watery abyss has covered them,   5
they sank into the depths like a stone.
Thy right hand, O LORD, is majestic in strength: 6
thy right hand, O LORD, shattered the enemy.
    In the fullness of thy triumph   7
    thou didst cast the rebels down:
    thou didst let loose thy fury;
    it consumed them like chaff.
At the blast of thy anger the sea piled up: 8
    the waters stood up like a bank:
    out at sea the great deep congealed.
The enemy said, 'I will pursue, I will overtake;   9
    I will divide the spoil,
    I will glut my appetite upon them;
    I will draw my sword,
    I will rid myself of them.'
Thou didst blow with thy blast; the sea covered them.   10
They sank like lead in the swelling waves.
    Who is like thee, O LORD, among the gods[a]?   11
    Who is like thee, majestic in holiness,
worthy of awe and praise, who workest wonders?
    Thou didst stretch out thy right hand,   12
    earth engulfed them.
In thy constant love thou hast led the people   13
    whom thou didst ransom:
thou hast guided them by thy strength
    to thy holy dwelling-place.
    Nations heard and trembled;   14
agony seized the dwellers in Philistia.
    Then the chieftains of Edom were dismayed,   15
    trembling seized the leaders of Moab,
all the inhabitants of Canaan were in turmoil;
    terror and dread fell upon them: 16
through the might of thy arm they stayed stone-still,
    while thy people passed, O LORD,
while the people whom thou madest thy own[b] passed by.
Thou broughtest them in and didst plant them   17
    in the mount that is thy possession,
    the dwelling-place, O LORD, of thy own making,
the sanctuary, O LORD, which thy own hands prepared.
    The LORD shall reign for ever and for ever.   18

    [a] *Or* in might.   [b] madest thy own: *or* didst create.

19   For Pharaoh's horse, both chariots and cavalry, went into the sea, and
the LORD brought back the waters over them, but Israel had passed through
20 the sea on dry ground. And Miriam the prophetess, Aaron's sister, took
up her tambourine, and all the women followed her, dancing to the sound
21 of tambourines; and Miriam sang them this refrain:

> Sing to the LORD, for he has risen up in triumph;
> the horse and his rider he has hurled into the sea.

22 MOSES LED ISRAEL FROM THE RED SEA out into the wilderness of Shur.
For three days they travelled through the wilderness without finding water.
23 They came to Marah, but could not drink the Marah water because it was
24 bitter; that is why the place was called Marah. The people complained to
25 Moses and asked, 'What are we to drink?' Moses cried to the LORD, and
the LORD showed him a log which he threw into the water, and then the
water became sweet.

It was there that the LORD laid down a precept and rule of life; there he
26 put them to the test. He said, 'If only you will obey the LORD your God, if
you will do what is right in his eyes, if you will listen to his commands and
keep all his statutes, then I will never bring upon you any of the sufferings
which I brought on the Egyptians; for I the LORD am your healer.'
27 They came to Elim, where there were twelve springs and seventy palm-
trees, and there they encamped beside the water.

16   The whole community of the Israelites set out from Elim and came into
the wilderness of Sin, which lies between Elim and Sinai. This was on the
fifteenth day of the second month after they had left Egypt.
2 3 The Israelites complained to Moses and Aaron in the wilderness and
said, 'If only we had died at the LORD's hand in Egypt, where we sat round
the fleshpots and had plenty of bread to eat! But you have brought us out
4 into this wilderness to let this whole assembly starve to death.' The LORD
said to Moses, 'I will rain down bread from heaven for you. Each day the
people shall go out and gather a day's supply, so that I can put them to
5 the test and see whether they will follow my instructions or not. But on the
sixth day, when they prepare what they bring in, it shall be twice as much
6 as they have gathered on other days.' Moses and Aaron then said to all the
Israelites, 'In the evening you will know that it was the LORD who brought
7 you out of Egypt, and in the morning you will see the glory of the LORD,
because he has heeded your complaints against him; it is not against us
8 that you bring your complaints; we are nothing.' 'You shall know this',
Moses said, 'when the LORD, in answer to your complaints, gives you flesh
to eat in the evening, and in the morning bread in plenty. What are we?
It is against the LORD that you bring your complaints, and not against us.'
9 Moses told Aaron to say to the whole community of Israel, 'Come into
10 the presence of the LORD, for he has heeded your complaints.' While Aaron
was speaking to the community of the Israelites, they looked towards the
wilderness, and there was the glory of the LORD appearing in the cloud.
11 12 The LORD spoke to Moses and said, 'I have heard the complaints of the
Israelites. Say to them, "Between dusk and dark you will have flesh to eat

and in the morning bread in plenty. You shall know that I the LORD am
your God." '

That evening a flock of quails flew in and settled all over the camp, and   13
in the morning a fall of dew lay all around it. When the dew was gone, there   14
in the wilderness, fine flakes appeared, fine as hoar-frost on the ground.
When the Israelites saw it, they said to one another, 'What is that?', *a* be-   15
cause they did not know what it was. Moses said to them, 'That is the bread
which the LORD has given you to eat. This is the command the LORD has   16
given: "Each of you is to gather as much as he can eat: let every man take
an omer a head for every person in his tent." ' The Israelites did this, and   17
they gathered, some more, some less, but when they measured it by the   18
omer, those who had gathered more had not too much, and those who had
gathered less had not too little. Each had just as much as he could eat.
Moses said, 'No one may keep any of it till morning.' Some, however, did   19 20
not listen to Moses; they kept part of it till morning, and it became full of
maggots and stank, and Moses was angry with them. Each morning every   21
man gathered as much as he could eat, and when the sun grew hot, it melted
away. On the sixth day they gathered twice as much food, two omers each.   22
All the chiefs of the community came and told Moses. 'This', he answered,   23
'is what the LORD has said: "Tomorrow is a day of sacred rest, a sabbath
holy to the LORD." So bake what you want to bake now, and boil what you
want to boil; put aside what remains over and keep it safe till morning.'
So they put it aside till morning as Moses had commanded, and it did not   24
stink, nor did maggots appear in it. 'Eat it today,' said Moses, 'because today   25
is a sabbath of the LORD. Today you will find none outside. For six days   26
you may gather it, but on the seventh day, the sabbath, there will be none.'

Some of the people did go out to gather it on the seventh day, but they   27
found none. The LORD said to Moses, 'How long will you refuse to obey   28
my commands and instructions? The LORD has given you the sabbath,   29
and so he gives you two days' food every sixth day. Let each man stay
where he is; no one may stir from his home on the seventh day.' And the   30
people kept the sabbath on the seventh day.

Israel called the food manna; it was white, like coriander seed, and it   31
tasted like a wafer made with honey.

'This', said Moses, 'is the command which the LORD has given: "Take   32
a full omer of it to be kept for future generations, so that they may see the
bread with which I fed you in the wilderness when I brought you out of
Egypt." ' So Moses said to Aaron, 'Take a jar and fill it with an omer of   33
manna, and store it in the presence of the LORD to be kept for future generations.' Aaron did as the LORD had commanded Moses, and stored it before   34
the Testimony for safe keeping. The Israelites ate the manna for forty   35
years until they came to a land where they could settle; they ate it until
they came to the border of Canaan. (An omer is one tenth of an ephah.)   36

The whole community of Israel set out from the wilderness of Sin and   **17**
travelled by stages as the LORD told them. They encamped at Rephidim,
where there was no water for the people to drink, and a dispute arose between them and Moses. When they said, 'Give us water to drink', Moses   2

a *Heb.* man-hu (*cp. verse 31*).

said, 'Why do you dispute with me? Why do you challenge the LORD?'
3 There the people became so thirsty that they raised an outcry against
Moses: 'Why have you brought us out of Egypt with our children and our
4 herds to let us all die of thirst?' Moses cried to the LORD, 'What shall I do
5 with these people? In a moment they will be stoning me.' The LORD
answered, 'Go forward ahead of the people; take with you some of the
6 elders of Israel and the staff with which you struck the Nile, and go. You
will find me waiting for you there, by a rock in Horeb. Strike the rock;
water will pour out of it, and the people shall drink.' Moses did this in the
7 sight of the elders of Israel. He named the place Massah*a* and Meribah,*b*
because the Israelites had disputed with him and challenged the LORD
with their question, 'Is the LORD in our midst or not?'

8 9   The Amalekites came and attacked Israel at Rephidim. Moses said to
Joshua, 'Pick your men, and march out tomorrow to fight for us against
Amalek; and I will take my stand on the hill-top with the staff of God in
10 my hand.' Joshua carried out his orders and fought against Amalek while
11 Moses, Aaron and Hur climbed to the top of the hill. Whenever Moses
raised his hands Israel had the advantage, and when he lowered his hands
12 Amalek had the advantage. But when his arms grew heavy they took a
stone and put it under him and, as he sat, Aaron and Hur held up his hands,
13 one on each side, so that his hands remained steady till sunset. Thus Joshua
defeated Amalek and put its people to the sword.

14   The LORD said to Moses, 'Record this in writing, and tell it to Joshua
in these words: "I am resolved to blot out all memory of Amalek from
15 16 under heaven."' Moses built an altar, and named it Jehovah-nissi and said,
'My oath upon it: the LORD is at war with Amalek generation after generation.'

18 JETHRO PRIEST OF MIDIAN, father-in-law of Moses, heard all that God
had done for Moses and Israel his people, and how the LORD had brought
2 Israel out of Egypt. When Moses had dismissed his wife Zipporah, Jethro
3 his father-in-law had received her and her two sons. The name of the one
was Gershom, 'for', said Moses, 'I have become an alien*c* living in a
4 foreign land'; the other's name was Eliezer,*d* 'for', he said, 'the God of
my father was my help and saved me from Pharaoh's sword.'

5   Jethro, Moses' father-in-law, now came to him with his sons and his
wife, to the wilderness where he was encamped at the mountain of God.
6 Moses was told, 'Here is Jethro, your father-in-law, coming to you with
7 your wife and her two sons.' Moses went out to meet his father-in-law,
bowed low to him and kissed him, and they greeted one another. When
8 they came into the tent Moses told him all that the LORD had done to
Pharaoh and to Egypt for Israel's sake, and about all their hardships on the
9 journey, and how the LORD had saved them. Jethro rejoiced at all the good
10-11 the LORD had done for Israel in saving them from the power of Egypt. He
said, 'Blessed be the LORD who has saved you from the power of Egypt and
of Pharaoh. Now I know that the LORD is the greatest of all gods, because

a *That is* Challenge.   b *That is* Dispute.   c *Cp. 2. 22.*
d *That is* God my help.

he has delivered the people from the power of the Egyptians who dealt so arrogantly with them.' Jethro, Moses' father-in-law, brought a whole-offering and sacrifices for God; and Aaron and all the elders of Israel came and shared the meal with Jethro in the presence of God.   12

The next day Moses took his seat to settle disputes among the people,   13
and they were standing round him from morning till evening. When   14
Jethro saw all that he was doing for the people, he said, 'What are you doing for all these people? Why do you sit alone with all of them standing round you from morning till evening?' 'The people come to me', Moses   15
answered, 'to seek God's guidance. Whenever there is a dispute among   16
them, they come to me, and I decide between man and man. I declare the statutes and laws of God.' But his father-in-law said to Moses, 'This is not   17
the best way to do it. You will only wear yourself out and wear out all the   18
people who are here. The task is too heavy for you; you cannot do it by yourself. Now listen to me: take my advice, and God be with you. It is for   19
you to be the people's representative before God, and bring their disputes to him. You must instruct them in the statutes and laws, and teach them   20
how they must behave and what they must do. But you must yourself   21
search for capable, God-fearing men among all the people, honest and incorruptible men, and appoint them over the people as officers over units of a thousand, of a hundred, of fifty or of ten. They shall sit as a permanent   22
court for the people; they must refer difficult cases to you but decide simple cases themselves. In this way your burden will be lightened, and they will share it with you. If you do this, God will give you strength, and you will   23
be able to go on. And, moreover, this whole people will here and now regain peace and harmony.' Moses listened to his father-in-law and did all he had   24
suggested. He chose capable men from all Israel and appointed them   25
leaders of the people, officers over units of a thousand, of a hundred, of fifty or of ten. They sat as a permanent court, bringing the difficult cases   26
to Moses but deciding simple cases themselves. Moses set his father-in-law   27
on his way, and he went back to his own country.

Israel at Mount Sinai

IN THE THIRD MONTH after Israel had left Egypt,[a] they came to the   19
wilderness of Sinai. They set out from Rephidim and entered the wilder-   2
ness of Sinai, where they encamped, pitching their tents opposite the mountain. Moses went up the mountain of God, and the LORD called to   3
him from the mountain and said, 'Speak thus to the house of Jacob, and tell this to the sons of Israel: You have seen with your own eyes what I   4
did to Egypt, and how I have carried you on eagles' wings and brought you here to me. If only you will now listen to me and keep my covenant, then   5
out of all peoples you shall become my special possession; for the whole earth is mine. You shall be my kingdom of priests, my holy nation. These   6
are the words you shall speak to the Israelites.'

[a] *Prob. rdg.; Heb. adds* on this day.

7 Moses came and summoned the elders of the people and set before them
8 all these commands which the LORD had laid upon him. The people all
answered together, 'Whatever the LORD has said we will do.' Moses brought
9 this answer back to the LORD. The LORD said to Moses, 'I am now coming
to you in a thick cloud, so that I may speak to you in the hearing of the
people, and their faith in you may never fail.' Moses told the LORD what
10 the people had said, and the LORD said to him, 'Go to the people and hal-
11 low them today and tomorrow and make them wash their clothes. They
must be ready by the third day, because on the third day the LORD will
12 descend upon Mount Sinai in the sight of all the people. You must put
barriers round the mountain and say, "Take care not to go up the mountain
or even to touch the edge of it." Any man who touches the mountain must
13 be put to death. No hand shall touch him;*a* he shall be stoned or shot dead:*b*
neither man nor beast may live. But when the ram's horn sounds, they
14 may go up the mountain.' Moses came down from the mountain to the
15 people. He hallowed them and they washed their clothes. He said to the
16 people, 'Be ready by the third day; do not go near a woman.' On the third
day, when morning came, there were peals of thunder and flashes of
lightning, dense cloud on the mountain and a loud trumpet blast; the
people in the camp were all terrified.
17 Moses brought the people out from the camp to meet God, and they
18 took their stand at the foot of the mountain. Mount Sinai was all smoking
because the LORD had come down upon it in fire; the smoke went up like
19 the smoke of a kiln; all the people were terrified, and the sound of the
trumpet grew ever louder. Whenever Moses spoke, God answered him in
20 a peal of thunder.*c* The LORD came down upon the top of Mount Sinai
21 and summoned Moses to the mountain-top, and Moses went up. The LORD
said to Moses, 'Go down; warn the people solemnly that they must not
force their way through to the LORD to see him, or many of them will perish.
22 Even the priests, who have access to the LORD, must hallow themselves,
23 for fear that the LORD may break out against them.' Moses answered the
LORD, 'The people cannot come up Mount Sinai, because thou thyself
didst solemnly warn us to set a barrier to the mountain and so to keep it
24 holy.' The LORD therefore said to him, 'Go down; then come up and bring
Aaron with you, but let neither priests nor people force their way up to the
25 LORD, for fear that he may break out against them.' So Moses went down
to the people and spoke to them.

20 God spoke, and these were his words:
2 I am the LORD your God who brought you out of Egypt, out of the land
of slavery.
3 You shall have no other god*d* to set against me.
4 You shall not make a carved image for yourself nor the likeness of anything in the heavens above, or on the earth below, or in the waters under the
earth.
5 You shall not bow down to them or worship*e* them; for I, the LORD your
God, am a jealous god. I punish the children for the sins of the fathers to

---

a Or it.   *b* Or hurled to his death.   *c* in . . . thunder: *or* by voice.
d Or gods.   *e* Or or be led to worship.

the third and fourth generations of those who hate me. But I keep faith 6
with thousands, with*a* those who love me and keep my commandments.

You shall not make wrong use of the name of the LORD your God; the 7
LORD will not leave unpunished the man who misuses his name.

Remember to keep the sabbath day holy. You have six days to labour and 8 9
do all your work. But the seventh day is a sabbath of the LORD your God; 10
that day you shall not do any work, you, your son or your daughter, your
slave or your slave-girl, your cattle or the alien within your gates; for in 11
six days the LORD made heaven and earth, the sea, and all that is in them,
and on the seventh day he rested. Therefore the LORD blessed the sabbath
day and declared it holy.

Honour your father and your mother, that you may live long in the land 12
which the LORD your God is giving you.

You shall not commit murder. 13

You shall not commit adultery. 14

You shall not steal. 15

You shall not give false evidence against your neighbour. 16

You shall not covet your neighbour's house; you shall not covet your 17
neighbour's wife, his slave, his slave-girl, his ox, his ass, or anything that
belongs to him.

When all the people saw how it thundered and the lightning flashed, 18
when they heard the trumpet sound and saw the mountain smoking, they
trembled and stood at a distance. 'Speak to us yourself,' they said to Moses, 19
'and we will listen; but if God speaks to us we shall die.' Moses answered, 20
'Do not be afraid. God has come only to test you, so that the fear of him
may remain with you and keep you from sin.' So the people stood at a 21
distance, while Moses approached the dark cloud where God was.

THE LORD SAID TO MOSES, Say this to the Israelites: You know now 22
that I have spoken to you from heaven. You shall not make gods of silver 23
to be worshipped as well as me, nor shall you make yourselves gods of gold.
You shall make an altar of earth for me, and you shall sacrifice on it both 24
your whole-offerings and your shared-offerings, your sheep and your
cattle. Wherever I cause my name to be invoked, I will come to you and
bless you. If you make an altar of stones for me, you must not build it of 25
hewn stones, for if you use a chisel on it, you will profane it. You must 26
not mount up to my altar by steps, in case your private parts be exposed
on it.

These are the laws you shall set before them: **21**

When you buy a Hebrew slave, he shall be your slave for six years, but 2
in the seventh year he shall go free and pay nothing.

If he comes to you alone, he shall go away alone; but if he is married, 3
his wife shall go away with him.

If his master gives him a wife, and she bears him sons or daughters, the 4
woman and her children shall belong to her master, and the man shall go
away alone. But if the slave should say, 'I love my master, my wife, and 5
my children; I will not go free', then his master shall bring him to God: 6

a with . . . with: *or* for a thousand generations with . . .

he shall bring him to the door or the door-post, and his master shall pierce his ear with an awl, and the man shall be his slave for life.

7 When a man sells his daughter into slavery, she shall not go free as a
8 male slave may. If her master has not had intercourse with her and she does not please him, he shall let her be ransomed. He has treated her
9 unfairly and therefore has no right to sell her to strangers. If he assigns her
10 to his son, he shall allow her the rights of a daughter. If he takes another woman, he shall not deprive the first of meat, clothes, and conjugal rights.
11 If he does not provide her with these three things, she shall go free without any payment.

12 13 Whoever strikes another man and kills him shall be put to death. But if he did not act with intent, but they met by act of God, the slayer may
14 flee to a place which I will appoint for you. But if a man has the presumption to kill another by treachery, you shall take him even from my altar to be put to death.

15 Whoever strikes his father or mother shall be put to death.

16 Whoever kidnaps a man shall be put to death, whether he has sold him, or the man is found in his possession.

17 Whoever reviles his father or mother shall be put to death.

18 When men quarrel and one hits another with a stone or with a spade,*a*
19 and the man is not killed but takes to his bed; if he recovers so as to walk about outside with a stick, then the one who struck him has no liability, except that he shall pay for loss of time and shall see that he is cured.

20 When a man strikes his slave or his slave-girl with a stick and the slave
21 dies on the spot, he must be punished. But he shall not be punished if the slave survives for one day or two, because he is worth money to his master.

22 When, in the course of a brawl, a man knocks against a pregnant woman so that she has a miscarriage but suffers no further hurt, then the offender must pay whatever fine the woman's husband demands after assessment.

23 24 Wherever hurt is done, you shall give life for life, eye for eye, tooth for
25 tooth, hand for hand, foot for foot, burn for burn, bruise for bruise, wound for wound.

26 When a man strikes his slave or slave-girl in the eye and destroys it, he
27 shall let the slave go free in compensation for the eye. When he knocks out the tooth of a slave or a slave-girl, he shall let the slave go free in compensation for the tooth.

28 When an ox gores a man or a woman to death, the ox shall be stoned, and its flesh may not be eaten; the owner of the ox shall be free from liability.
29 If, however, the ox has for some time past been a vicious animal, and the owner has been duly warned but has not kept it under control, and the ox kills a man or a woman, then the ox shall be stoned, and the owner shall
30 be put to death as well. If, however, the penalty is commuted for a money payment, he shall pay in redemption of his life whatever is imposed upon
31 32 him. If the ox gores a son or a daughter, the same rule shall apply. If the ox gores a slave or slave-girl, its owner shall pay thirty shekels of silver to their master, and the ox shall be stoned.

33 When a man removes the cover of a well*b* or digs a well*b* and leaves it

a Or fist.   *b Or* cistern.

84

uncovered, then if an ox or an ass falls into it, the owner of the well shall 34
make good the loss. He shall repay the owner of the beast in silver, and the
dead beast shall be his.

When one man's ox butts another's and kills it, they shall sell the live 35
ox, share the price and also share the dead beast. But if it is known that the 36
ox has for some time past been vicious and the owner has not kept it under
control, he shall make good the loss, ox for ox, but the dead beast is his.

When a man steals an ox or a sheep and slaughters or sells it, he shall repay 22
five beasts for the ox and four sheep for the sheep. He shall pay in full; 2-4*a*
if he has no means, he shall be sold to pay for the theft. But if the animal
is found alive in his possession, be it ox, ass, or sheep, he shall repay two.

If a burglar is caught in the act and is fatally injured, it is not murder;
but if he breaks in after sunrise and is fatally injured, then it is murder.

When a man burns off a field or a vineyard and lets the fire spread so that 5
it burns another man's field,*b* he shall make restitution from his own field
according to the yield expected; and if the whole field is laid waste, he
shall make restitution from the best part of his own field or vineyard.

When a fire starts and spreads to a heap of brushwood, so that sheaves, 6
or standing corn, or a whole field is destroyed, he who started the fire shall
make full restitution.

When one man gives another silver or chattels for safe keeping, and they 7
are stolen from that man's house, the thief, if he is found, shall restore
twofold. But if the thief is not found, the owner of the house shall appear 8
before God, to make a declaration that he has not touched his neighbour's
property. In every case of law-breaking involving an ox, an ass, or a sheep, 9
a cloak, or any lost property which may be claimed, each party shall bring
his case before God; he whom God declares to be in the wrong shall restore
twofold to his neighbour.

When a man gives an ass, an ox, a sheep or any beast into his neighbour's 10
keeping, and it dies or is injured or is carried off, there being no witness,
the neighbour shall swear by the LORD that he has not touched the man's 11
property. The owner shall accept this, and no restitution shall be made.
If it has been stolen from him, he shall make restitution to the owner. If 12 13
it has been mauled by a wild beast, he shall bring it in as evidence; he shall
not make restitution for what has been mauled.

When a man borrows a beast from his neighbour and it is injured or dies 14
while its owner is not with it, the borrower shall make full restitution; but 15
if the owner is with it, the borrower shall not make restitution. If it was
hired, only the hire shall be due.

When a man seduces a virgin who is not yet betrothed, he shall pay the 16
bride-price for her to be his wife. If her father refuses to give her to him, 17
the seducer shall pay in silver a sum equal to the bride-price for virgins.

You shall not allow a witch to live. 18

Whoever has unnatural connection with a beast shall be put to death. 19

Whoever sacrifices to any god but the LORD shall be put to death under 20
solemn ban.

---

a Verses 2-4 rearranged thus: 3b, 4, 2, 3a.   *b Or When a man uses his field or
vineyard for grazing, and lets his beast loose, and it feeds in another man's field.*

21   You shall not wrong an alien, or be hard upon him; you were yourselves
22 23 aliens in Egypt. You shall not ill-treat any widow or fatherless child. If
24 you do, be sure that I will listen if they appeal to me; my anger will be
roused and I will kill you with the sword; your own wives shall become
widows and your children fatherless.

25   If you advance money to any poor man amongst my people, you shall
not act like a money-lender: you must not exact interest in advance from
him.

26   If you take your neighbour's cloak in pawn, you shall return it to him
27 by sunset, because it is his only covering. It is the cloak in which he wraps
his body; in what else can he sleep? If he appeals to me, I will listen, for
I am full of compassion.

28   You shall not revile God, nor curse a chief of your own people.

29   You shall not hold back the first of your harvest, whether corn or wine.

30 You shall give me your first-born sons. You shall do the same with your
oxen and your sheep. They shall stay with the mother for seven days; on
the eighth day you shall give them to me.

31   You shall be holy to me: you shall not eat the flesh of anything in the
open country killed by beasts, but you shall throw it to the dogs.

23   You shall not spread a baseless rumour. You shall not make common
cause with a wicked man by giving malicious evidence.

2   You shall not be led into wrongdoing by the majority, nor, when you
give evidence in a lawsuit, shall you side with the majority to pervert
3 justice; nor shall you favour the poor man in his suit.

4   When you come upon your enemy's ox or ass straying, you shall take it
5 back to him. When you see the ass of someone who hates you lying helpless under its load, however unwilling you may be to help it, you must
give him a hand with it.

6 7   You shall not deprive the poor man of justice in his suit. Avoid all lies,
and do not cause the death of the innocent and the guiltless; for I the LORD
8 will never acquit the guilty. You shall not accept a bribe, for bribery makes
the discerning man blind and the just man give a crooked answer.

9   You shall not oppress the alien, for you know how it feels to be an alien;
you were aliens yourselves in Egypt.

10 11   For six years you may sow your land and gather its produce; but in the
seventh year you shall let it lie fallow and leave it alone. It shall provide
food for the poor of your people, and what they leave the wild animals
may eat. You shall do likewise with your vineyard and your olive-grove.

12   For six days you may do your work, but on the seventh day you shall
abstain from work, so that your ox and your ass may rest, and your home-
born slave and the alien may refresh themselves.

13   Be attentive to every word of mine. You shall not invoke other gods:
your lips shall not speak their names.

14 15   Three times a year you shall keep a pilgrim-feast to me. You shall celebrate the pilgrim-feast of Unleavened Bread for seven days; you shall eat
unleavened cakes as I have commanded you, at the appointed time in the
month of Abib, for in that month you came out of Egypt.

16   No one shall come into my presence empty-handed. You shall celebrate

the pilgrim-feast of Harvest, with the firstfruits of your work in sowing the
land, and the pilgrim-feast of Ingathering at the end*ᵃ* of the year, when you
bring in the fruits of all your work on the land. These three times a year 17
shall all your males come into the presence of the Lord GOD.

 You shall not offer the blood of my sacrifice at the same time as anything 18
leavened.

 The fat of my festal offering shall not remain overnight till morning.

 You shall bring the choicest firstfruits of your soil to the house of the 19
LORD your God.

 You shall not boil a kid in its mother's milk.

 And now I send an angel before you to guard you on your way and to 20
bring you to the place I have prepared. Take heed of him and listen to his 21
voice. Do not defy him; he will not pardon your rebelliousness, for my
authority rests in him. If you will only listen to his voice and do all I tell 22
you, then I will be an enemy to your enemies, and I will harass those who
harass you. My angel will go before you and bring you to the Amorites, 23
the Hittites, the Perizzites, the Canaanites, the Hivites, and the Jebusites,
and I will make an end of them. You are not to bow down to their gods, nor 24
worship them, nor observe their rites, but you shall tear down all their
images and smash their sacred pillars. Worship the LORD your God, and 25
he will bless your bread and your water. I will take away all sickness out
of your midst. None shall miscarry or be barren in your land. I will grant 26
you a full span of life.

 I will send my terror before you and throw into confusion all the peoples 27
whom you find in your path. I will make all your enemies turn their backs.
I will spread panic before you to drive out in front of you the Hivites, the 28
Canaanites and the Hittites. I will not drive them out all in one year, or the 29
land would become waste and the wild beasts too many for you. I will drive 30
them out little by little until your numbers have grown enough to take
possession of the whole country. I will establish your frontiers from the 31
Red Sea to the sea of the Philistines, and from the wilderness to the River.
I will give the inhabitants of the country into your power, and you shall
drive them out before you. You shall make no covenant with them and their 32
gods. They shall not stay in your land for fear they make you sin against 33
me; for then you would worship their gods, and in this way you would be
ensnared.

THEN HE SAID TO MOSES, 'Come up to the LORD, you and Aaron, **24**
Nadab and Abihu, and seventy of the elders of Israel. While you are still
at a distance, you are to bow down; and then Moses shall approach the 2
LORD by himself, but not the others. The people may not go up with him
at all.'

 Moses came and told the people all the words of the LORD, all his laws. 3
The whole people answered with one voice and said, 'We will do all that
the LORD has told us.' Moses wrote down all the words of the LORD. He 4
rose early in the morning and built an altar at the foot of the mountain, and
put up twelve sacred pillars, one for each of the twelve tribes of Israel. He 5

    ᵃ Or beginning.

then sent the young men of Israel and they sacrificed bulls to the LORD
6 as whole-offerings and shared-offerings. Moses took half the blood and put
7 it in basins and the other half he flung against[a] the altar. Then he took the
book of the covenant and read it aloud for all the people to hear. They said,
8 'We will obey, and do all that the LORD has said.' Moses then took the blood
and flung it over the people, saying, 'This is the blood of the covenant which
the LORD has made with you on the terms of this book.'

9 Moses went up with Aaron, Nadab and Abihu, and seventy of the elders
10 of Israel, and they saw[b] the God of Israel. Under his feet there was, as it
11 were, a pavement of sapphire,[c] clear blue as the very heavens; but the
LORD did not stretch out his hand towards the leaders of Israel. They
12 stayed there before God;[d] they ate and they drank. The LORD said to
Moses, 'Come up to me on the mountain, stay there and let me give you
the tablets of stone, the law and the commandment, which I have written
13 down that you may teach them.' Moses arose with Joshua his assistant and
14 went up the mountain of God; he said to the elders, 'Wait for us here until
we come back to you. You have Aaron and Hur; if anyone has a dispute,
15 let him go to them.' So Moses went up the mountain and a cloud covered
16 it. The glory of the LORD rested upon Mount Sinai, and the cloud covered
the mountain for six days; on the seventh day he called to Moses out of
17 the cloud. The glory of the LORD looked to the Israelites like a devouring
18 fire on the mountain-top. Moses entered the cloud and went up the
mountain; there he stayed forty days and forty nights.

25 1 2 THE LORD SPOKE TO MOSES AND SAID: Tell the Israelites to set aside
a contribution for me; you shall accept whatever contribution each
3 man shall freely offer. This is what you shall accept: gold, silver, copper;
4 5 violet, purple, and scarlet yarn; fine linen and goats' hair; tanned rams'
6 skins, porpoise[e]-hides, and acacia-wood; oil for the lamp, balsam for the
7 anointing oil and for the fragrant incense; cornelian and other stones ready
8 for setting in the ephod and the breast-piece.[f] Make me a sanctuary, and
9 I will dwell among them. Make it exactly according to the design I show
you, the design for the Tabernacle and for all its furniture. This is how you
must make it:

10 Make an Ark, a chest of acacia-wood, two and a half cubits long, one
11 cubit and a half wide, and one cubit and a half high. Overlay it with pure
12 gold both inside and out, and put a band of gold all round it. Cast four gold
13 rings for it, and fasten them to its four feet, two rings on each side. Make
14 poles of acacia-wood and plate them with gold, and insert the poles in the
15 rings at the sides of the Ark to lift it. The poles shall remain in the rings of
16 the Ark and never be removed. Put into the Ark the Tokens of the Cove-
17 nant,[g] which I shall give you. Make a cover of pure gold, two and a half
18 cubits long and one cubit and a half wide. Make two gold cherubim of
19 beaten work at the ends of the cover, one at each end; make each cherub of

---

a Or upon.   *b Or* they were afraid of . . .   *c Or* lapis lazuli.   *d Or* They
saw God; and . . .   *e Strictly* sea-cow.   *f Or* pouch.   *g* Tokens of the
Covenant: *or* Testimony.

one piece with the cover. They shall be made with wings outspread and 20
pointing upwards, and shall screen the cover with their wings. They shall
be face to face, looking inwards over the cover. Put the cover above the 21
Ark, and put into the Ark the Tokens that I shall give you. It is there that 22
I shall meet you, and from above the cover, between the two cherubim
over the Ark of the Tokens, I shall deliver to you all my commands for the
Israelites.

Make a table of acacia-wood, two cubits long, one cubit wide, and one 23
cubit and a half high. Overlay it with pure gold, and put a band of gold all 24
round it. Make a rim round it a hand's breadth wide, and a gold band round 25
the rim. Make four gold rings for the table, and put the rings at the four 26
corners by the legs. The rings, which are to receive the poles for carrying 27
the table, must be adjacent to the rim. Make the poles of acacia-wood and 28
plate them with gold; they are to be used for carrying the table. Make its 29
dishes and saucers, and its flagons and bowls from which drink-offerings
may be poured: make them of pure gold. Put the Bread of the Presence*a* on 30
the table, to be always before me.

Make a lamp-stand of pure gold. The lamp-stand, stem and branches, 31
shall be of beaten work, its cups, both calyxes and petals, shall be of one
piece with it. There are to be six branches springing from its sides; three 32
branches of the lamp-stand shall spring from the one side and three
branches from the other side. There shall be three cups shaped like almond 33
blossoms, with calyx and petals, on the first branch, three cups shaped like
almond blossoms, with calyx and petals, on the next branch, and similarly
for all six branches springing from the lamp-stand. On the main stem of the 34
lamp-stand there are to be four cups shaped like almond blossoms, with
calyx and petals, and there shall be calyxes of one piece with it under the 35
six branches which spring from the lamp-stand, a single calyx under each
pair of branches. The calyxes and the branches are to be of one piece with 36
it, all a single piece of beaten work of pure gold. Make seven lamps for this 37
and mount them to shed light over the space in front of it. Its tongs and 38
firepans shall be of pure gold. The lamp-stand and all these fittings shall 39
be made from one talent of pure gold. See that you work to the design which 40
you were shown on the mountain.

Make the Tabernacle of ten hangings of finely woven linen, and violet, **26**
purple, and scarlet yarn, with cherubim worked on them, all made by a
seamster. The length of each hanging shall be twenty-eight cubits and the 2
breadth four cubits; all are to be of the same size. Five of the hangings shall 3
be joined together, and similarly the other five. Make violet loops along the 4
edge of the last hanging in each set, fifty for each set; they must be opposite 5
one another. Make fifty gold fasteners, join the hangings one to another 6
with them, and the Tabernacle will be a single whole.

Make hangings of goats' hair, eleven in all, to form a tent over the 7
Tabernacle; each hanging is to be thirty cubits long and four wide; all 8
eleven are to be of the same size. Join five of the hangings together, and 9
similarly the other six; then fold the sixth hanging double at the front of
the tent. Make fifty loops on the edge of the last hanging in the first set and 10

a Or Shewbread.

11 make fifty loops on the joining edge of the second set. Make fifty bronze *a*
fasteners, insert them into the loops and join up the tent to make it a single
12 whole. The additional length of the tent hanging *b* is to fall over the back
13 of the Tabernacle. On each side there will be an additional cubit in the
length of the tent hangings; this shall fall over the two sides of the Taber-
14 nacle to cover it. Make for the tent a cover of tanned rams' skins and an
outer covering of porpoise-hides.
15 16   Make for the Tabernacle planks of acacia-wood as uprights, each plank
17 ten cubits long and a cubit and a half wide, and two tenons for each plank
joined to each other. You shall do the same for all the planks of the Taber-
18 nacle. Arrange the planks thus: twenty planks for the south side, facing
19 southwards, with forty silver sockets under them, two sockets under each
20 plank for its two tenons; and for the second or northern side of the Taber-
21 22 nacle, twenty planks, with forty silver sockets, two under each plank. Make
23 six planks for the far end of the Tabernacle on the west. Make two planks
24 for the corners of the Tabernacle at the far end; at the bottom they shall be
alike, and at the top, both alike, they shall fit into a single ring. Do the same
25 for both of them; they shall be for the two corners. There shall be eight
planks with their silver sockets, sixteen sockets in all, two sockets under
each plank severally.
26   Make bars of acacia-wood: five for the planks on the one side of the
27 Tabernacle, five for the planks on the other side and five for the planks on
28 the far end of the Tabernacle on the west. The middle bar is to run along
29 from end to end half-way up the planks. Overlay the planks with gold, make
30 rings of gold on them to hold the bars, and plate the bars with gold. Set up
the Tabernacle according to the design you were shown on the mountain.
31   Make a Veil of finely woven linen and violet, purple, and scarlet yarn,
32 with cherubim worked on it, all made by a seamster. Fasten it with hooks
of gold to four posts of acacia-wood overlaid with gold, standing in four
33 silver sockets. Hang the Veil below the fasteners and bring the Ark of the
Tokens inside the Veil. Thus the Veil will make a clear separation for you
34 between the Holy Place and the Holy of Holies. Place the cover over the
35 Ark of the Tokens in the Holy of Holies. Put the table outside the Veil and
the lamp-stand at the south side of the Tabernacle, opposite the table which
36 you shall put at the north side. For the entrance of the tent make a screen
37 of finely woven linen, embroidered with violet, purple, and scarlet. Make
five posts of acacia-wood for the screen and overlay them with gold; make
golden hooks for them and cast five bronze sockets for them.
27   Make the altar of acacia-wood; it shall be square, five cubits long by
2 five cubits broad and three cubits high. Let its horns at the four corners be
3 of one piece with it, and overlay it with bronze. Make for it pots to take away
the fat and the ashes, with shovels, tossing bowls, forks, and firepans, all
4 of bronze. Make a grating for it of bronze network, and fit four bronze rings
5 on the network at its four corners. Put it below the ledge of the altar, so that
6 the network comes half-way up the altar. Make poles of acacia-wood for
7 the altar and overlay them with bronze. They shall be inserted in the rings

---

a Or copper *and so throughout the description of the Tabernacle.*   *b* Prob. rdg.; Heb.
adds half the hanging which remains over.

at both sides of the altar to carry it. Leave the altar a hollow shell. As you 8
were shown on the mountain, so shall it be made.

Make the court of the Tabernacle. For the one side, the south side facing 9
southwards, the court shall have hangings of finely woven linen a hundred
cubits long, with twenty posts and twenty sockets of bronze; the hooks and 10
bands on the posts shall be of silver. Similarly all along the north side there 11
shall be hangings a hundred cubits long, with twenty posts and twenty
sockets of bronze; the hooks and bands on the posts shall be of silver. For 12
the breadth of the court, on the west side, there shall be hangings fifty
cubits long, with ten posts and ten sockets. On the east side, towards the 13
sunrise, which was fifty cubits, hangings shall extend fifteen cubits from 14
one corner, with three posts and three sockets, and hangings shall extend 15
fifteen cubits from the other corner, with three posts and three sockets. At 16
the gateway of the court, there shall be a screen twenty cubits long of finely
woven linen embroidered with violet, purple, and scarlet, with four posts
and four sockets. The posts all round the court shall have bands of silver, 17
with hooks of silver, and sockets of bronze. The length of the court shall be 18
a hundred cubits, and the breadth fifty, and the height five cubits, with
finely woven linen and bronze sockets throughout. All the equipment 19
needed for serving the Tabernacle, all its pegs and those of the court, shall
be of bronze.

You yourself are to command the Israelites to bring you pure oil of 20
pounded olives ready for the regular mounting of the lamp. In the Tent 21
of the Presence[a] outside the Veil that hides the Tokens, Aaron and his
sons shall keep the lamp in trim from dusk to dawn before the LORD.
This is a rule binding on their descendants among the Israelites for
all time.

You yourself are to summon to your presence your brother Aaron and **28**
his sons out of all the Israelites to serve as my priests: Aaron and his sons
Nadab and Abihu, Eleazar and Ithamar. For your brother Aaron make 2
sacred vestments, to give him dignity and grandeur. Tell all the craftsmen 3
whom I have endowed with skill to make the vestments for the consecration of Aaron as my priest. These are the vestments they shall make: a 4
breast-piece, an ephod, a mantle, a chequered tunic, a turban, and a sash.
They shall make sacred vestments for Aaron your brother and his sons to
wear when they serve as my priests, using gold; violet, purple, and scarlet 5
yarn; and fine linen.

The ephod shall be made of gold, and with violet, purple, and scarlet 6
yarn, and with finely woven linen worked by a seamster. It shall have two 7
shoulder-pieces joined back and front. The waist-band on it shall be of 8
the same workmanship and material as the fabric of the ephod, and shall
be of gold, with violet, purple, and scarlet yarn, and finely woven linen.
You shall take two cornelians and engrave on them the names of the sons 9
of Israel: six of their names on the one stone, and the six other names on 10
the second, all in order of seniority. With the skill of a craftsman, a seal- 11
cutter, you shall engrave the two stones with the names of the sons of
Israel; you shall set them in gold rosettes, and fasten them on the shoulders 12

     [a] *Or* Tent of Meeting.

of the ephod, as reminders of the sons of Israel. Aaron shall bear their names on his two shoulders as a reminder before the LORD.

13 14 Make gold rosettes and two chains of pure gold worked into the form of 15 ropes, and fix them on the rosettes. Make the breast-piece of judgement; it shall be made, like the ephod, by a seamster in gold, with violet, purple, 16 and scarlet yarn, and finely woven linen. It shall be a square folded, a span 17 long and a span wide. Set in it four rows of precious stones: the first row, 18 sardin, chrysolite and green felspar; the second row, purple garnet, lapis 19 20 lazuli and jade; the third row, turquoise, agate and jasper; the fourth row, 21 topaz, cornelian and green jasper, all set in gold rosettes. The stones shall correspond to the twelve sons of Israel name by name; each stone shall bear the name of one of the twelve tribes engraved as on a seal.

22 23 Make for the breast-piece chains of pure gold worked into a rope. Make two gold rings, and fix them on the two upper corners of the breast-piece. 24 Fasten the two gold ropes to the two rings at those corners of the breast- 25 piece, and the other ends of the ropes to the two rosettes, thus binding the 26 breast-piece to the shoulder-pieces on the front of the ephod. Make two gold rings and put them at the two lower corners of the breast-piece on the 27 inner side next to the ephod. Make two gold rings and fix them on the two shoulder-pieces of the ephod, low down in front, along its seam above the 28 waist-band of the ephod. Then the breast-piece shall be bound by its rings to the rings of the ephod with violet braid, just above the waist-band of the ephod, so that the breast-piece will not be detached from the ephod. 29 Thus, when Aaron enters the Holy Place, he shall carry over his heart in the breast-piece of judgement the names of the sons of Israel, as a constant reminder before the LORD.

30 Finally, put the Urim and the Thummim into the breast-piece of judge- ment, and they will be over Aaron's heart when he enters the presence of the LORD. So shall Aaron bear these symbols of judgement upon the sons of Israel over his heart constantly before the LORD.

31 32 Make the mantle of the ephod a single piece of violet stuff. There shall be a hole for the head in the middle of it. All round the hole there shall be a 33 hem of woven work, with an oversewn edge, so that it cannot be torn. All round its skirts make pomegranates of violet, purple, and scarlet stuff, with 34 golden bells between them, a golden bell and a pomegranate alternately the 35 whole way round the skirts of the mantle. Aaron shall wear it when he ministers, and the sound of it shall be heard when he enters the Holy Place before the LORD and when he comes out; and so he shall not die.

36 Make a rosette of pure gold and engrave on it as on a seal, 'Holy to the 37 LORD'.ᵃ Fasten it on a violet braid and set it on the very front of the turban. 38 It shall be on Aaron's forehead; he has to bear the blame for shortcomings in the rites with which the Israelites offer their sacred gifts, and the rosette shall be always on his forehead so that they may be acceptable to the LORD.

39 Make the chequered tunic and the turban of fine linen, but the sash of 40 embroidered work. For Aaron's sons make tunics and sashes; and make tall 41 head-dresses to give them dignity and grandeur. With these invest your brother Aaron and his sons, anoint them, install them and consecrate

ᵃ *as* ... LORD: *or* 'JEHOVAH' *as on a seal in sacred characters.*

them; so shall they serve me as priests. Make for them linen drawers 42
reaching to the thighs to cover their private parts; and Aaron and his sons 43
shall wear them when they enter the Tent of the Presence or approach the
altar to minister in the Holy Place. Thus they will not incur guilt and die.
This is a rule binding on him and his descendants for all time.

In consecrating them to be my priests this is the rite to be observed. Take **29**
a young bull and two rams without blemish. Take unleavened loaves, un- 2
leavened cakes mixed with oil, and unleavened wafers smeared with oil,
all made of wheaten flour; put them in a single basket and bring them in it. 3
Bring also the bull and the two rams. Bring Aaron and his sons to the 4
entrance of the Tent of the Presence, and wash them with water. Take the 5
vestments and invest Aaron with the tunic, the mantle of the ephod,
the ephod itself and the breast-piece, and fasten the ephod to him with its
waist-band. Set the turban on his head, and the symbol of holy dedication 6
on the turban. Take the anointing oil, pour it on his head and anoint him. 7
Then bring his sons forward, invest them with tunics, gird them with the 8 9
sashes and tie their tall head-dresses on them. They shall hold the priesthood by a rule binding for all time.

Next you shall install Aaron and his sons. Bring the bull to the front of the 10
Tent of the Presence, and they shall lay their hands on its head. Slaughter 11
the bull before the LORD at the entrance to the Tent of the Presence. Take 12
some of its blood, and put it with your finger on the horns of the altar. Pour
all the rest of it at the base of the altar. Then take the fat covering the entrails, 13
the long lobe of the liver, and the two kidneys with the fat upon them, and
burn it on the altar; but the flesh of the bull, and its skin and offal, you shall 14
destroy by fire outside the camp. It is a sin-offering.

Take one of the rams, and Aaron and his sons shall lay their hands on its 15
head. Then slaughter it, take its blood and fling it against the sides of the 16
altar. Cut the ram up; wash its entrails and its shins, lay them with the 17
pieces and the head, and burn the whole ram on the altar: it is a whole- 18
offering to the LORD; it is a soothing odour, a food-offering to the LORD.

Take the second ram, and let Aaron and his sons lay their hands on its 19
head. Then slaughter it, take some of its blood, and put it on the lobes of 20
the right ears of Aaron and his sons, and on their right thumbs and big toes.
Fling the rest of the blood against the sides of the altar. Take some of the 21
blood which is on the altar and some of the anointing oil, and sprinkle it on
Aaron and his vestments, and on his sons and their vestments. So shall he
and his vestments, and his sons and their vestments become holy. Take the 22
fat from the ram, the fat-tail, the fat covering the entrails, the long lobe of
the liver, the two kidneys with the fat upon them, and the right leg: for it is
a ram of installation. Take also one round loaf of bread, one cake cooked 23
with oil, and one wafer from the basket of unleavened bread that is before
the LORD. Set all these on the hands of Aaron and of his sons and present 24
them as a special gift before the LORD. Then take them out of their hands, 25
and burn them on the altar with the whole-offering for a soothing odour to
the LORD: it is a food-offering to the LORD. Take the breast of Aaron's ram 26
of installation, present it as a special gift before the LORD, and it shall be
your perquisite.

27 Hallow the breast of the special gift and the leg of the contribution, that which is presented and that which is set aside from the ram of installation,
28 that which is for Aaron and that which is for his sons; and they shall belong to Aaron and his sons, by a rule binding for all time, as a gift from the Israelites, for it is a contribution, set aside from their shared-offerings, their contribution to the LORD.
29 Aaron's sacred vestments shall be kept for the anointing and installation
30 of his sons after him. The priest appointed in his stead from among his sons, the one who enters*a* the Tent of the Presence to minister in the Holy Place, shall wear them for seven days.
31 32 Take the ram of installation, and boil its flesh in a sacred place; Aaron and his sons shall eat the ram's flesh and the bread left in the basket, at the
33 entrance to the Tent of the Presence. They shall eat the things with which expiation was made at their installation and their consecration. No un-
34 qualified person may eat them, for they are holy. If any of the flesh of the installation, or any of the bread, is left over till morning, you shall destroy it by fire; it shall not be eaten, for it is holy.
35 Do this with Aaron and his sons as I have commanded you, spending seven days over their installation.
36 Offer a bull daily, a sin-offering as expiation for sin; offer the sin-offering on the altar when you make expiation for it, and consecrate it by
37 anointing. For seven days you shall make expiation for the altar, and consecrate it, and it shall be most holy. Whatever touches the altar shall be forfeit as sacred.
38 This is what you shall offer on the altar: two yearling rams regularly
39 every day. You shall offer the one ram at dawn, and the second between
40 dusk and dark, a tenth of an ephah of flour mixed with a quarter of a hin of pure oil of pounded olives, and a drink-offering of a quarter of a hin of wine
41 for the first ram. You shall offer the second ram between dusk and dark, and with it the same grain-offering and drink-offering as at dawn, for a
42 soothing odour: it is a food-offering to the LORD, a regular whole-offering in every generation; you shall make the offering at the entrance to the Tent
43 of the Presence before the LORD, where I meet you and speak to you. I shall meet the Israelites there, and the place will be hallowed by my glory.
44 I shall hallow the Tent of the Presence and the altar; and Aaron and his
45 sons I shall consecrate to serve me as priests. I shall dwell in the midst of
46 the Israelites, I shall become their God, and by my dwelling among them they will know that I am the LORD their God who brought them out of Egypt. I am the LORD their God.

30 1 2 Make an altar on which to burn incense; make it of acacia-wood. It shall be square, a cubit long by a cubit broad and two cubits high; the horns of
3 one piece with it. Overlay it with pure gold, the top, the sides all round, and
4 the horns; and put round it a band of gold. Make pairs of gold rings for it; put them under the band at the two corners on both sides to receive the
5 poles by which it is to be carried. Make the poles of acacia-wood and over-
6 lay them with gold. Put it before the Veil in front of the Ark of the Tokens
7 where I will meet you. On it Aaron shall burn fragrant incense; every

---

a Or when he enters.

morning when he tends the lamps he shall burn the incense, and when he 8
mounts the lamps between dusk and dark, he shall burn the incense; so
there shall be a regular burning of incense before the LORD for all time.
You shall not offer on it any unauthorized incense, nor any whole-offering 9
or grain-offering; and you shall not pour a drink-offering over it. Aaron 10
shall make expiation with blood on its horns once a year; with blood from
the sin-offering of the yearly Expiation[a] he shall do this for all time. It is
most holy to the LORD.

The LORD spoke to Moses and said: When you number the Israelites 11 12
for the purpose of registration, each man shall give a ransom for his life
to the LORD, to avert plague among them during the registration. As each 13
man crosses over to those already counted he shall give half a shekel by the
sacred standard (twenty gerahs to the shekel) as a contribution to the LORD.
Everyone from twenty years old and upwards who has crossed over to those 14
already counted shall give a contribution to the LORD. The rich man shall 15
give no more than the half-shekel, and the poor man shall give no less, when
you give the contribution to the LORD to make expiation for your lives. The 16
money received from the Israelites for expiation you shall apply to the
service of the Tent of the Presence. The expiation for your lives shall be a
reminder of the Israelites to the LORD.

The LORD spoke to Moses and said: Make a bronze basin for ablution 17 18
with its stand of bronze; put it between the Tent of the Presence and the
altar, and fill it with water with which Aaron and his sons shall wash their 19
hands and feet. When they enter the Tent of the Presence they shall wash 20
with water, lest they die. So also when they approach the altar to minister,
to burn a food-offering to the LORD, they shall wash their hands and 21
feet, lest they die. It shall be a rule for all time binding on him and his
descendants in every generation.

The LORD spoke to Moses and said: You yourself shall take spices as 22 23
follows: five hundred shekels of sticks of myrrh, half that amount (two
hundred and fifty shekels) of fragrant cinnamon, two hundred and fifty
shekels of aromatic cane, five hundred shekels of cassia by the sacred 24
standard, and a hin of olive oil. From these prepare sacred anointing oil, 25
a perfume compounded by the perfumer's art. This shall be the sacred
anointing oil. Anoint with it the Tent of the Presence and the Ark of the 26
Tokens, the table and all its vessels, the lamp-stand and its fittings, the 27
altar of incense, the altar of whole-offering and all its vessels, the basin and 28
its stand. You shall consecrate them, and they shall be most holy; whatever 29
touches them shall be forfeit as sacred. Anoint Aaron and his sons, and 30
consecrate them to be my priests. Speak to the Israelites and say: This shall 31
be the holy anointing oil for my service in every generation. It shall not be 32
used for anointing the human body, and you must not prepare any oil like
it after the same prescription. It is holy, and you shall treat it as holy.
The man who compounds perfume like it, or who puts any of it on any 33
unqualified person, shall be cut off from his father's kin.

The LORD said to Moses, Take fragrant spices: gum resin,[b] aromatic 34
shell, galbanum; add pure frankincense to the spices in equal proportions.

---

[a] *Or* Atonement.   [b] *Or* mastic.

35 Make it into incense, perfume made by the perfumer's craft, salted and
36 pure, a holy thing. Pound some of it into fine powder, and put it in front of
the Tokens in the Tent of the Presence, where I shall meet you; you shall
37 treat it as most holy. The incense prepared according to this prescription
you shall not make for your own use. You shall treat it as holy to the LORD.
38 The man who makes any like it for his own pleasure shall be cut off from
his father's kin.

31 1 2 THE LORD SPOKE TO MOSES AND SAID, Mark this: I have specially
3 chosen Bezalel son of Uri, son of Hur, of the tribe of Judah. I have filled him
with divine spirit, making him skilful and ingenious, expert in every craft,
4 5 and a master of design, whether in gold, silver, copper, or cutting stones
6 to be set, or carving wood, for workmanship of every kind. Further, I have
appointed Aholiab*a* son of Ahisamach of the tribe of Dan to help him, and
I have endowed every skilled craftsman with the skill which he has. They
7 shall make everything that I have commanded you: the Tent of the Presence, the Ark for the Tokens, the cover over it, and all the furnishings of
8 the tent; the table and its vessels, the pure lamp-stand and all its fittings,
9 the altar of incense, the altar of whole-offering and all its vessels, the basin
10 and its stand; the stitched vestments, that is the sacred vestments for
Aaron the priest and the vestments for his sons when they minister as
11 priests, the anointing oil and the fragrant incense for the Holy Place. They
shall carry out all I have commanded you.
12 13   The LORD spoke to Moses and said, Speak to the Israelites, you yourself,
and say to them: Above all you shall observe my sabbaths, for the sabbath
is a sign between me and you in every generation that you may know that
14 I am the LORD who hallows you. You shall keep the sabbath, because it is
a holy day for you. If anyone profanes it he must be put to death. Anyone
15 who does work on it shall be cut off from his father's kin. Work may be
done on six days, but on the seventh day there is a sabbath of sacred rest,
holy to the LORD. Whoever does work on the sabbath day must be put to
16 death. The Israelites shall keep the sabbath, they shall keep it in every
17 generation as a covenant for ever. It is a sign for ever between me and the
Israelites, for in six days the LORD made the heavens and the earth, but on
the seventh day he ceased work and refreshed himself.
18   When he had finished speaking with Moses on Mount Sinai, the LORD
gave him the two tablets of the Tokens, tablets of stone written with the
finger of God.

32 WHEN THE PEOPLE SAW that Moses was so long in coming down from
the mountain, they confronted Aaron and said to him, 'Come, make us
gods to go ahead of us. As for this fellow Moses, who brought us up from
2 Egypt, we do not know what has become of him.' Aaron answered them,
'Strip the gold rings from the ears of your wives and daughters, and bring
3 them to me.' So all the people stripped themselves of their gold earrings
4 and brought them to Aaron. He took them out of their hands, cast the
metal in a mould, and made it into the image of a bull-calf. 'These', he

a Or Oholiab.

said, 'are your gods, O Israel, that brought you up from Egypt.' Then Aaron 5
was afraid and built an altar in front of it and issued this proclamation,
'Tomorrow there is to be a pilgrim-feast to the LORD.' Next day the people 6
rose early, offered whole-offerings, and brought shared-offerings. After this
they sat down to eat and drink and then gave themselves up to revelry.
But the LORD said to Moses, 'Go down at once, for your people, the people 7
you brought up from Egypt, have done a disgraceful thing; so quickly have 8
they turned aside from the way I commanded them. They have made
themselves an image of a bull-calf, they have prostrated themselves before
it, sacrificed to it and said, "These are your gods, O Israel, that brought
you up from Egypt."' So the LORD said to Moses, 'I have considered this 9
people, and I see that they are a stubborn people. Now, let me alone to vent 10
my anger upon them, so that I may put an end to them and make a great
nation spring from you.' But Moses set himself to placate the LORD his 11
God: 'O LORD,' he said, 'why shouldst thou vent thy anger upon thy
people, whom thou didst bring out of Egypt with great power and a strong
hand? Why let the Egyptians say, "So he meant evil when he took them 12
out, to kill them in the mountains and wipe them off the face of the earth"?
Turn from thy anger, and think better of the evil thou dost intend against
thy people. Remember Abraham, Isaac and Israel, thy servants, to whom 13
thou didst swear by thy own self: "I will make your posterity countless as
the stars in the sky, and all this land, of which I have spoken, I will give to
them, and they shall possess it for ever."' So the LORD relented, and spared 14
his people the evil with which he had threatened them.

Moses turned and went down the mountain with the two tablets of the 15
Tokens in his hands, inscribed on both sides; on the front and on the back
they were inscribed. The tablets were the handiwork of God, and the 16
writing was God's writing, engraved on the tablets. Joshua, hearing the 17
uproar the people were making, said to Moses, 'Listen! There is fighting
in the camp.' Moses replied,   18

> 'This is not the clamour of warriors,
> nor the clamour of a defeated people;
> it is the sound of singing that I hear.'

As he approached the camp, Moses saw the bull-calf and the dancing, and 19
he was angry; he flung the tablets down, and they were shattered to pieces
at the foot of the mountain. Then he took the calf they had made and burnt 20
it; he ground it to powder, sprinkled it on water, and made the Israelites
drink it. He demanded of Aaron, 'What did this people do to you that you 21
should have brought such great guilt upon them?' Aaron replied, 'Do not 22
be angry, sir. The people were deeply troubled; that you well know. And 23
they said to me, "Make us gods to go ahead of us, because, as for this fellow
Moses, who brought us up from Egypt, we do not know what has become
of him." So I said to them, "Those of you who have any gold, strip it off." 24
They gave it me, I threw it in the fire, and out came this bull-calf.' Moses 25
saw that the people were out of control and that Aaron had laid them open
to the secret malice of their enemies. He took his place at the gate of the 26
camp and said, 'Who is on the LORD's side? Come here to me'; and the

27 Levites all rallied to him. He said to them, 'These are the words of the LORD the God of Israel: "Arm yourselves, each of you, with his sword. Go through the camp from gate to gate and back again. Each of you kill his
28 brother, his friend, his neighbour." ' The Levites obeyed, and about three
29 thousand of the people died that day. Moses then said, 'Today you have consecrated yourselves to the LORD completely, because you have turned each against his own son and his own brother and so have this day brought a blessing upon yourselves.'

30   The next day Moses said to the people, 'You have committed a great sin. I shall now go up to the LORD; perhaps I may be able to secure pardon for
31 your sin.' So Moses returned to the LORD and said, 'O hear me! This people has committed a great sin: they have made themselves gods of gold.
32 If thou wilt forgive them, forgive. But if not, blot out my name, I pray,
33 from thy book which thou hast written.' The LORD answered Moses, 'It is the man who has sinned against me that I will blot out from my book.
34 But go now, lead the people to the place which I have told you of. My angel shall go ahead of you, but a day will come when I shall punish them
35 for their sin.' And the LORD smote the people for worshipping the bull-calf which Aaron had made.

33   THE LORD SPOKE TO MOSES: 'Come, go up from here, you and the people you have brought up from Egypt, to the land which I swore to Abraham,
2 Isaac, and Jacob that I would give to their posterity. I will send an angel ahead of you, and will drive out the Canaanites, the Amorites and the
3 Hittites and the Perizzites, the Hivites and the Jebusites. I will bring you to a land flowing with milk and honey, but I will not journey in your company, for fear that I annihilate you on the way; for you are a stubborn
4 people.' When the people heard this harsh sentence they went about like
5 mourners, and no man put on his ornaments. The LORD said to Moses, 'Tell the Israelites, "You are a stubborn people: at any moment, if I journey in your company, I may annihilate you. Put away your ornaments
6 now, and I will determine what to do to you." ' And so the Israelites stripped off their ornaments, and wore them no more from Mount Horeb onwards.

7   Moses used to take a[a] tent and pitch it at a distance outside the camp. He called it the Tent of the Presence, and everyone who sought the LORD
8 would go out to the Tent of the Presence outside the camp. Whenever Moses went out to the tent, all the people would rise and stand, each at the entrance to his tent, and follow Moses with their eyes until he entered the
9 tent. When Moses entered it, the pillar of cloud came down, and stayed at
10 the entrance to the tent while the LORD spoke with Moses. As soon as the people saw the pillar of cloud standing at the entrance to the tent, they
11 would all prostrate themselves, every man at the entrance to his tent. The LORD would speak with Moses face to face, as one man speaks to another. Then Moses would return to the camp, but his young assistant, Joshua son of Nun, never moved from inside the tent.

12   Moses said to the LORD, 'Thou bidst me lead this people up, but thou hast not told me whom thou wilt send with me. Thou hast said to me, "I

                 a Or the.

know you by name, and, further, you have found favour with me." If I 13
have indeed won thy favour, then teach me to know thy way, so that I can
know thee and continue in favour with thee, for this nation is thy own
people.' The LORD answered, 'I will go with you in person and set your 14
mind at rest.' Moses said to him, 'Indeed if thou dost not go in person, do 15
not send us up from here; for how can it ever be known that I and thy people 16
have found favour with thee, except by thy going with us? So shall we be
distinct, I and thy people, from all the peoples on earth.' The LORD said 17
to Moses, 'I will do this thing that you have asked, because you have found
favour with me, and I know you by name.'

And Moses prayed, 'Show me thy glory.' The LORD answered, 'I will 18 19
make all my goodness*ᵃ* pass before you, and I will pronounce in your
hearing the Name JEHOVAH.*ᵇ* I will be gracious to whom I will be gracious,
and I will have compassion on whom I will have compassion.' But he added, 20
'My face you cannot see, for no mortal man may see me and live.' The LORD 21
said, 'Here is a place beside me. Take your stand on the rock and when my 22
glory passes by, I will put you in a crevice of the rock and cover you with
my hand until I have passed by. Then I will take away my hand, and you 23
shall see my back, but my face shall not be seen.'

The LORD said to Moses, 'Cut two stone tablets like the first, and I will **34**
write on the tablets the words which were on the first tablets, which you
broke in pieces. Be ready by morning. Then in the morning go up Mount 2
Sinai; stand and wait for me there on the top. No man shall go up with you, 3
no man shall even be seen anywhere on the mountain, nor shall flocks or
herds graze within sight of that mountain.' So Moses cut two stone tablets 4
like the first, and he rose early in the morning and went up Mount Sinai
as the LORD had commanded him, taking the two stone tablets in his hands.
And the LORD came down in the cloud and took his place beside him and 5
pronounced the Name JEHOVAH. Then the LORD passed in front of him 6
and called aloud, 'JEHOVAH, the LORD, a god compassionate and gracious,
long-suffering, ever constant and true, maintaining constancy to thou- 7
sands, forgiving iniquity, rebellion, and sin, and not sweeping the guilty
clean away; but one who punishes sons and grandsons to the third and
fourth generation for the iniquity of their fathers!' Moses made haste, 8
bowed to the ground and prostrated himself. He said, 'If I have indeed won 9
thy favour, O Lord, then may the Lord go in our company. However stubborn a people they are, forgive our iniquity and our sin and take us as thy
own possession.'

The LORD said, Here and now I make a covenant. In full view of all 10
your people I will do such miracles as have never been performed in all
the world or in any nation. All the surrounding peoples shall see the work
of the LORD, for fearful is that which I will do for you.*ᶜ* Observe all I com- 11
mand you this day; and I for my part will drive out before you the Amorites
and the Canaanites and the Hittites and the Perizzites and the Hivites and
the Jebusites. Be careful not to make a covenant with the natives of the land 12
against which you are going, or they will prove a snare in your midst. No: 13

ᵃ Or character.   *ᵇ See note on 3. 15.*   *ᶜ* for fearful . . . for you: *or* (for he is to
be feared) which I will do for you.

you shall demolish their altars, smash their sacred pillars and cut down their
14 sacred poles. You shall not prostrate yourselves to any other god. For the
15 LORD's name is the Jealous God, and a jealous god he is. Be careful not to
make a covenant with the natives of the land, or, when they go wantonly
after their gods and sacrifice to them, you may be invited, any one of you,
16 to partake of their sacrifices, and marry your sons to their daughters, and
when their daughters go wantonly after their gods, they may lead your sons
astray too.

17 You shall not make yourselves gods of cast metal.

18 You shall observe the pilgrim-feast of Unleavened Bread: for seven days,
as I have commanded you, you shall eat unleavened cakes at the appointed
time, in the month of Abib, because in the month of Abib you went out
from Egypt.

19 Every first birth of the womb belongs to me, and the males of all your
20 herds, both cattle and sheep. You may buy back the first birth of an ass by
giving a sheep instead, but if you do not buy it, you must break its neck.
You shall buy back all the first-born of your sons, and no one shall come
into my presence empty-handed.

21 For six days you shall work, but on the seventh day you shall cease work;
even at ploughing time and harvest you shall cease work.

22 You shall observe the pilgrim-feast of Weeks, the firstfruits of the wheat
23 harvest, and the pilgrim-feast of Ingathering at the turn of the year. Three
times a year all your males shall come into the presence of the Lord, the
24 LORD the God of Israel; for after I have driven out the nations before you
and extended your frontiers, there will be no danger from covetous neighbours when you go up these three times to enter the presence of the LORD
your God.

25 You shall not offer the blood of my sacrifice at the same time as anything
leavened, nor shall any portion of the victim of the pilgrim-feast of Passover remain overnight till morning.

26 You shall bring the choicest firstfruits of your soil to the house of the
LORD your God.

You shall not boil a kid in its mother's milk.

27 The LORD said to Moses, 'Write these words down, because the cove-
28 nant I make with you and with Israel is in these words.' So Moses stayed
there with the LORD forty days and forty nights, neither eating nor drinking,
and wrote down the words of the covenant, the Ten Words,*a* on the tablets.

29 At length Moses came down from Mount Sinai with the two stone tablets
of the Tokens in his hands, and when he descended, he did not know that
the skin of his face shone because he had been speaking with the LORD.
30 When Aaron and the Israelites saw how the skin of Moses' face shone, they
31 were afraid to approach him. He called out to them, and Aaron and all the
32 chiefs in the congregation turned towards him. Moses spoke to them, and
afterwards all the Israelites drew near. He gave them all the commands
with which the LORD had charged him on Mount Sinai, and finished what
33 he had to say.

34 Then Moses put a veil over his face, and whenever he went in before the

a Or Ten Commandments.

LORD to speak with him, he removed the veil until he came out. Then he would go out and tell the Israelites all the commands he had received. Whenever the skin of Moses' face shone in the sight of the Israelites, he 35 would put the veil back over his face until he went in again to speak with the LORD.

M OSES CALLED THE WHOLE COMMUNITY of Israelites together and **35** thus addressed them: These are the LORD's commands to you: On 2 six days you may work, but the seventh you are to keep as a sabbath of sacred rest, holy to the LORD. Whoever works on that day shall be put to death. You are not even to light your fire at home on the sabbath day. 3
These words Moses spoke to all the community of Israelites: This is the 4 command the LORD has given: Each of you set aside a contribution to the 5 LORD. Let all who wish, bring a contribution to the LORD: gold, silver, copper; violet, purple, and scarlet yarn; fine linen and goats' hair; tanned 6 7 rams' skins, porpoise-hides, and acacia-wood; oil for the lamp, perfume for 8 the anointing oil and for the fragrant incense; cornelians and other stones 9 ready for setting in the ephod and the breast-piece. Let every craftsman 10 among you come and make everything the LORD has commanded. The 11 Tabernacle, its tent and covering, fasteners, planks, bars, posts, and sockets, the Ark and its poles, the cover and the Veil of the screen, the table, 12 13 its poles, and all its vessels, and the Bread of the Presence, the lamp- 14 stand for the light, its fittings, lamps and the lamp oil; the altar of incense 15 and its poles, the anointing oil, the fragrant incense, and the screen for the entrance of the Tabernacle, the altar of whole-offering, its bronze grating, 16 poles, and all appurtenances, the basin and its stand; the hangings of the 17 court, its posts and sockets, and the screen for the gateway of the court; the pegs of the Tabernacle and court and their cords, the stitched vest- 18 19 ments for ministering in the Holy Place, that is the sacred vestments for Aaron the priest and the vestments for his sons when they minister as priests.
The whole community of the Israelites went out from Moses' presence, 20 and everyone who was so minded brought of his own free will a contribu- 21 tion to the LORD for the making of the Tent of the Presence and all its service, and for the sacred vestments. Men and women alike came and 22 freely brought clasps, earrings, finger-rings, and pendants, gold ornaments of every kind, every one of them presenting a special gift of gold to the LORD. And every man brought what he possessed of violet, purple, and 23 scarlet yarn, fine linen and goats' hair, tanned rams' skins and porpoise-hides. Every man, setting aside a contribution of silver or copper, brought 24 it as a contribution to the LORD, and all who had acacia-wood suitable for any part of the work brought it. Every woman with the skill spun and 25 brought the violet, purple, and scarlet yarn, and fine linen. All the women 26 whose skill moved them spun the goats' hair. The chiefs brought cornelians 27 and other stones ready for setting in the ephod and the breast-piece, the 28 perfume and oil for the light, for the anointing oil, and for the fragrant incense. Every Israelite man and woman who was minded to bring offerings 29

to the LORD for all the work which he had commanded through Moses did so freely.

30 Moses said to the Israelites, 'Mark this: the LORD has specially chosen
31 Bezalel son of Uri, son of Hur, of the tribe of Judah. He has filled him with
32 divine spirit, making him skilful and ingenious, expert in every craft, and
33 a master of design, whether in gold, silver, and copper, or cutting precious
34 stones for setting, or carving wood, in every kind of design. He has inspired
    both him and Aholiab son of Ahisamach of the tribe of Dan to instruct
35 workers and designers of every kind, engravers, seamsters, embroiderers
    in violet, purple, and scarlet yarn and fine linen, and weavers, fully endow-
36 ing them with skill to execute all kinds of work. Bezalel and Aholiab shall
    work exactly as the LORD has commanded, and so also shall every craftsman
    whom the LORD has made skilful and ingenious in these matters, to know
    how to execute every kind of work for the service of the sanctuary.'

2   Moses summoned Bezalel, Aholiab, and every craftsman to whom the
    LORD had given skill and who was willing, to come forward and set to work.
3   They received from Moses every contribution which the Israelites had
    brought for the work of the service of the sanctuary, but the people still
4   brought freewill offerings morning after morning, so that the craftsmen at
    work on the sanctuary left what they were doing, every one of them, and
5   came to Moses and said, 'The people are bringing much more than we
6   need for doing the work which the LORD has commanded.' So Moses sent
    word round the camp that no man or woman should prepare anything more
    as a contribution for the sanctuary. So the people stopped bringing gifts;
7   what was there already was more than enough for all the work they had to do.

8   Then all the craftsmen among the workers made the Tabernacle of ten
    hangings of finely woven linen, and violet, purple, and scarlet yarn, with
9   cherubim worked on them, all made by a seamster. The length of each
    hanging was twenty-eight cubits and the breadth four cubits, all of the
10 same size. They joined five of the hangings together, and similarly the other
11 five. They made violet loops on the outer edge of the one set of hangings
12 and they did the same for the outer edge of the other set of hangings. They
    made fifty loops for each hanging; they made also fifty loops for the end
13 hanging in the second set, the loops being opposite each other. They made
    fifty gold fasteners, with which they joined the hangings one to another,
    and the Tabernacle became a single whole.
14 They made hangings of goats' hair, eleven in all, to form a tent over the
15 Tabernacle; each hanging was thirty cubits long and four cubits wide, all
16 eleven of the same size. They joined five of the hangings together, and
17 similarly the other six. They made fifty loops on the edge of the outer
    hanging in the first set and fifty loops on the joining edge of the second set,
18 and fifty bronze fasteners to join up the tent and make it a single whole.
19 They made for the tent a cover of tanned rams' skins and an outer covering
    of porpoise-hides.
20 21 They made for the Tabernacle planks of acacia-wood as uprights, each
22 plank ten cubits long and a cubit and a half wide, and two tenons for each
    plank joined to each other. They did the same for all the planks of the
23 Tabernacle. They arranged the planks thus: twenty planks for the south

side, facing southwards, with forty silver sockets under them, two sockets 24
under each plank for its two tenons; and for the second or northern side 25
of the Tabernacle twenty planks with forty silver sockets, two under each 26
plank. They made six planks for the far end of the Tabernacle on the west. 27
They made two planks for the corners of the Tabernacle at the far end; at 28 29
the bottom they were alike, and at the top, both alike, they fitted into a
single ring. They did the same for both of them at the two corners. There 30
were eight planks with their silver sockets, sixteen sockets in all, two sockets
under each plank.

They made bars of acacia-wood: five for the planks on the one side of 31
the Tabernacle, five bars for the planks on the second side of the Taber- 32
nacle, and five bars for the planks on the far end of the Tabernacle on the
west. They made the middle bar to run along from end to end half-way up 33
the frames. They overlaid the frames with gold, made rings of gold on them 34
to hold the bars and plated the bars with gold.

They made the Veil of finely woven linen and violet, purple, and scarlet 35
yarn, with cherubim worked on it, all made by a seamster. And they made 36
for it four posts of acacia-wood overlaid with gold, with gold hooks, and
cast four silver sockets for them. For the entrance of the tent a screen of 37
finely woven linen was made, embroidered with violet, purple, and scarlet,
and five posts of acacia-wood with their hooks. They overlaid the tops of 38
the posts and the bands round them with gold; the five sockets for them
were of bronze.

Bezalel then made the Ark, a chest of acacia-wood, two and a half cubits **37**
long, one cubit and a half wide, and one cubit and a half high. He overlaid 2
it with pure gold, both inside and out, and put a band of gold all round it.
He cast four gold rings to be on its four feet, two rings on each side of it. 3
He made poles of acacia-wood and plated them with gold, and inserted the 4 5
poles in the rings at the sides of the Ark to lift it. He made a cover of pure 6
gold, two and a half cubits long and one cubit and a half wide. He made 7
two gold cherubim of beaten work at the ends of the cover, one at each end; 8
he made each cherub of one piece with the cover. They had wings outspread 9
and pointing upwards, screening the cover with their wings; they stood
face to face, looking inwards over the cover.

He made the table of acacia-wood, two cubits long, one cubit wide, and 10
one cubit and a half high. He overlaid it with pure gold and put a band of 11
gold all round it. He made a rim round it a hand's breadth wide, and a gold 12
band round the rim. He cast four gold rings for it, and put the rings at the 13
four corners by the four legs. The rings, which were to receive the poles 14
for carrying the table, were close to the rim. These carrying-poles he made 15
of acacia-wood and plated them with gold. He made the vessels for the 16
table, its dishes and saucers, and its flagons and bowls from which drink-
offerings were to be poured; he made them of pure gold.

He made the lamp-stand of pure gold. The lamp-stand, stem, and 17
branches, were of beaten work, its cups, both calyxes and petals, were of
one piece with it. There were six branches springing from its sides; three 18
branches of the lamp-stand sprang from one side and three branches from
the other side. There were three cups shaped like almond blossoms, with 19

calyx and petals, on the first branch, three cups shaped like almond blossoms, with calyx and petals, on the next branch, and similarly for all six
20 branches springing from the lamp-stand. On the main stem of the lamp-
stand there were four cups shaped like almond blossoms, with calyx and
21 petals, and there were calyxes of one piece with it under the six branches
which sprang from the lamp-stand, a single calyx under each pair of
22 branches. The calyxes and the branches were of one piece with it, all a
23 single piece of beaten work of pure gold. He made its seven lamps, its tongs
24 and firepans of pure gold. The lamp-stand and all these fittings were made
from one talent of pure gold.

25   He made the altar of incense of acacia-wood, square, a cubit long by a
26 cubit broad and two cubits high, the horns of one piece with it. He overlaid it with pure gold, the top, the sides all round, and the horns, and he
27 put round it a band of gold. He made pairs of gold rings for it; he put them
under the band at the two corners on both sides to receive the poles by
28 which it was to be carried. He made the poles of acacia-wood and overlaid
them with gold.

29   He prepared the sacred anointing oil and the fragrant incense, pure,
compounded by the perfumer's art.

38   He made the altar of whole-offering of acacia-wood, square, five cubits
2 long by five cubits broad and three cubits high. Its horns at the four corners
3 were of one piece with it, and he overlaid it with bronze. He made all the
vessels for the altar, its pots, shovels, tossing bowls, forks, and firepans,
4 all of bronze. He made for the altar a grating of bronze network under the
5 ledge, coming half-way up. He cast four rings for the four corners of the
6 bronze grating to receive the poles, and he made the poles of acacia-wood
7 and overlaid them with bronze. He inserted the poles in the rings at the
sides of the altar to carry it. He left the altar a hollow shell.

8   The basin and its stand of bronze he made out of the bronze mirrors of
the women who were on duty at the entrance to the Tent of the Presence.

9   He made the court. For the south side facing southwards the hangings
10 of the court were of finely woven linen a hundred cubits long, with twenty
posts and twenty sockets of bronze; the hooks and bands on the posts were
11 of silver. Along the north side there were hangings of a hundred cubits,
with twenty posts and twenty sockets of bronze; the hooks and bands on
12 the posts were of silver. On the west side there were hangings fifty cubits
long, with ten posts and ten sockets; the hooks and bands on the posts were
13 14-15 of silver. On the east side, towards the sunrise, fifty cubits, there were
hangings on either side of the gateway of the court; they extended fifteen
cubits to one corner, with their three posts and their three sockets, and
fifteen cubits to the second corner, with their three posts and their three
16 sockets. The hangings of the court all round were of finely woven linen.
17 The sockets for the posts were of bronze, the hooks and bands on the posts
of silver, the tops of them overlaid with silver, and all the posts of the court
18 were bound with silver. The screen at the gateway of the court was of finely
woven linen, embroidered with violet, purple, and scarlet, twenty cubits
19 long and five cubits high to correspond to the hangings of the court, with
four posts and four sockets of bronze, their hooks of silver, and the tops of

them and their bands overlaid with silver. All the pegs for the Tabernacle 20
and those for the court were of bronze.

These were the appointments of the Tabernacle, that is the Tabernacle 21
of the Tokens which was assigned by Moses to the charge of the Levites
under Ithamar son of Aaron the priest. Bezalel son of Uri, son of Hur, of 22
the tribe of Judah made everything the LORD had commanded Moses. He 23
was assisted by Aholiab son of Ahisamach of the tribe of Dan, an engraver,
a seamster, and an embroiderer in fine linen with violet, purple, and scarlet
yarn.

The gold of the special gift used for the work of the sanctuary amounted 24
in all to twenty-nine talents seven hundred and thirty shekels, by the sacred
standard. The silver contributed by the community when registered was 25
one hundred talents one thousand seven hundred and seventy-five shekels,
by the sacred standard.

This amounted to a beka a head, that is half a shekel by the sacred 26
standard, for every man from twenty years old and upwards, who had been
registered, a total of six hundred and three thousand five hundred and fifty
men. The hundred talents of silver were for casting the sockets for the 27
sanctuary and for the Veil, a hundred sockets to a hundred talents, a talent
to a socket. With the one thousand seven hundred and seventy-five shekels 28
he made hooks for the posts, overlaid the tops of the posts and put bands
round them. The bronze of the special gift came to seventy talents two 29
thousand four hundred shekels; with this he made sockets for the entrance 30
to the Tent of the Presence, the bronze altar and its bronze grating, all the
vessels for the altar, the sockets all round the court, the sockets for the posts 31
at the gateway of the court, all the pegs for the Tabernacle, and the pegs all
round the court.

They used violet, purple, and scarlet yarn in making the stitched vest- **39**
ments for ministering in the sanctuary and in making the sacred vestments
for Aaron, as the LORD had commanded Moses.

They made the ephod of gold, with violet, purple, and scarlet yarn, and 2
finely woven linen. The gold was beaten into thin plates, cut and twisted 3
into braid to be worked in by a seamster with the violet, purple, and scarlet
yarn, and fine linen. They made shoulder-pieces for it, joined back and 4
front. The waist-band on it was of the same workmanship and material as 5
the fabric of the ephod; it was gold, with violet, purple, and scarlet yarn,
and finely woven linen, as the LORD commanded Moses.

They prepared the cornelians, fixed in gold rosettes, engraved by the 6
art of a seal-cutter with the names of the sons of Israel, and fastened them 7
on the shoulders of the ephod as reminders of the sons of Israel, as the LORD
had commanded Moses.

They made the breast-piece; it was worked like the ephod by a seamster, 8
in gold, with violet, purple, and scarlet yarn, and finely woven linen. They 9
made the breast-piece square, folded, a span long and a span wide. They 10
set in it four rows of precious stones: the first row, sardin, chrysolite and
green felspar; the second row, purple garnet, lapis lazuli and jade; the 11 12
third row, turquoise, agate and jasper; the fourth row, topaz, cornelian and 13
green jasper, all set in gold rosettes. The stones corresponded to the twelve 14

sons of Israel, name by name, each bearing the name of one of the twelve
15 tribes engraved as on a seal. They made for the breast-piece twisted cords
16 of pure gold worked into a rope. They made two gold rosettes and two
gold rings, and they fixed the two rings on the two corners of the breast-
17 piece. They fastened the two gold ropes to the two rings at those corners
18 of the breast-piece, and the other ends of the two ropes to the two rosettes,
19 thus binding them to the shoulder-pieces on the front of the ephod. They
made two gold rings and put them at the two corners of the breast-piece on
20 the inner side next to the ephod. They made two gold rings and fixed them
on the two shoulder-pieces of the ephod, low down and in front, close to its
21 seam above the waist-band on the ephod. They bound the breast-piece by
its rings to the rings of the ephod with a violet braid, just above the waist-
band on the ephod, so that the breast-piece would not become detached
22 from the ephod; so the Lord had commanded Moses. They made the
23 mantle of the ephod a single piece of woven violet stuff, with a hole in the
middle of it which had a hem round it, with an oversewn edge so that it
24 could not be torn. All round its skirts they made pomegranates of violet,
25 purple, and scarlet stuff, and finely woven linen. They made bells of pure
gold and put them all round the skirts of the mantle between the pome-
26 granates, a bell and a pomegranate alternately the whole way round the
skirts of the mantle, to be worn when ministering, as the Lord commanded
Moses.
27   They made the tunics of fine linen, woven work, for Aaron and his sons,
28 the turban of fine linen, the tall head-dresses and their bands all of fine
29 linen, the drawers of finely woven linen, and the sash of finely woven linen,
embroidered in violet, purple, and scarlet, as the Lord had commanded
Moses.
30   They made a rosette of pure gold as the symbol of their holy dedication
31 and inscribed on it as the engraving on a seal, 'Holy to the Lord',[a] and
they fastened on it a violet braid to fix it on the turban at the top, as the
Lord had commanded Moses.
32   Thus all the work of the Tabernacle of the Tent of the Presence was
completed, and the Israelites did everything exactly as the Lord had com-
33 manded Moses. They brought the Tabernacle to Moses, the tent and all
34 its furnishings, its fasteners, planks, bars, posts and sockets, the covering
of tanned rams' skins and the outer covering of porpoise-hides, the Veil of
35 36 the screen, the Ark of the Tokens and its poles, the cover, the table and its
37 vessels, and the Bread of the Presence, the pure lamp-stand with its lamps
38 in a row and all its fittings, and the lamp oil, the gold altar, the anointing
39 oil, the fragrant incense, and the screen at the entrance of the tent, the
bronze altar, the bronze grating attached to it, its poles and all its furnish-
40 ings, the basin and its stand, the hangings of the court, its posts and sockets,
the screen for the gateway of the court, its cords and pegs, and all the equip-
41 ment for the service of the Tabernacle for the Tent of the Presence, the
stitched vestments for ministering in the sanctuary, that is the sacred
vestments for Aaron the priest and the vestments for his sons when they
42 minister as priests. As the Lord had commanded Moses, so the Israelites

[a] on it . . . Lord: *or* 'Jehovah' on it in sacred characters as engraved on a seal.

carried out the whole work. Moses inspected all the work, and saw that 43
they had carried it out according to the command of the LORD; and he
blessed them.

THE LORD SPOKE TO MOSES AND SAID: On the first day of the first **40** 1 2
month you shall set up the Tabernacle, the Tent of the Presence. You 3
shall put the Ark of the Tokens in it and screen the Ark with the Veil. You 4
shall bring in the table and lay it; then you shall bring in the lamp-stand
and mount its lamps. You shall then set the gold altar of incense in front 5
of the Ark of the Tokens and put the screen of the entrance of the Tabernacle in place. You shall put the altar of whole-offering in front of the 6
entrance of the Tabernacle, the Tent of the Presence. You shall put the 7
basin between the Tent of the Presence and the altar and put water in it.
You shall set up the court all round and put in place the screen of the gate- 8
way of the court. You shall take the anointing oil and anoint the Taber- 9
nacle and everything in it; thus you shall consecrate it and all its furnishings,
and it shall be holy. You shall anoint the altar of whole-offering and all its 10
vessels; thus shall you consecrate it, and it shall be most holy. You shall 11
anoint the basin and its stand and consecrate it. You shall bring Aaron 12
and his sons to the entrance of the Tent of the Presence and wash them with
the water. Then you shall clothe Aaron with the sacred vestments, anoint 13
him and consecrate him; so shall he be my priest. You shall then bring 14
forward his sons, clothe them in tunics, anoint them as you anointed their 15
father, and they shall be my priests. Their anointing shall inaugurate a
hereditary priesthood for all time.

Exactly as the LORD had commanded him, so Moses did. In the first 16 17
month of the second year, on the first day of that month, the Tabernacle
was set up.

Moses set up the Tabernacle. He put the sockets in place, inserted the 18
planks, fixed the crossbars and set up the posts. He spread the tent over 19
the Tabernacle and fixed the covering of the tent above it, as the LORD
had commanded him. He took the Tokens and put them in the Ark, in- 20
serted the poles in the Ark, and put the cover over the top of the Ark. He 21
brought the Ark into the Tabernacle, set up the Veil of the screen and so
screened the Ark of the Tokens, as the LORD had commanded him. He put 22
the table in the Tent of the Presence on the north side of the Tabernacle
outside the Veil and arranged bread on it before the LORD, as the LORD 23
had commanded him. He set the lamp-stand in the Tent of the Presence 24
opposite the table at the south side of the Tabernacle and mounted the 25
lamps before the LORD, as the LORD had commanded him. He set up the 26
gold altar in the Tent of the Presence in front of the Veil and burnt fra- 27
grant incense on it, as the LORD had commanded him. He set up the screen 28
at the entrance of the Tabernacle, fixed the altar of whole-offering at the 29
entrance of the Tabernacle, the Tent of the Presence, and offered on it
whole-offerings and grain-offerings, as the LORD had commanded him.
He set up the basin between the Tent of the Presence and the altar and 30
put water there for washing, and Moses and Aaron and his sons used to 31
wash their hands and feet when they entered the Tent of the Presence or 32

33 approached the altar, as the LORD had commanded Moses. He set up the court all round the Tabernacle and the altar, and put a screen at the gateway of the court.

34 Thus Moses completed the work, and the cloud covered the Tent of the
35 Presence, and the glory of the LORD filled the Tabernacle. Moses was unable to enter the Tent of the Presence, because the cloud had settled on it
36 and the glory of the LORD filled the Tabernacle. At every stage of their journey, when the cloud lifted from the Tabernacle, the Israelites broke
37 camp; but if the cloud did not lift from the Tabernacle, they did not break
38 camp until the day it lifted. For the cloud of the LORD hovered over the Tabernacle by day, and there was fire in the cloud by night, and the Israelites could see it at every stage of their journey.

LEVITICUS

Laws concerning offerings and sacrifices

1 THE LORD SUMMONED MOSES and spoke to him from
2 the Tent of the Presence, and said, Say this to the Israelites: When any man among you presents an animal as an offering to the LORD, the offering may be presented either from the herd or from the flock.

3 If his offering is a whole-offering from the cattle, he shall present a male without blemish; he shall present it at the entrance to the Tent of the
4 Presence before the LORD so as to secure acceptance for himself. He shall lay his hand on the head of the victim and it will be accepted on his behalf [a]
5 to make expiation for him. He shall slaughter the bull before the LORD, and the Aaronite priests shall present the blood and fling it against the altar
6 all round at the entrance of the Tent of the Presence. He shall then flay
7 the victim and cut it up. The sons of Aaron the priest shall kindle a fire
8 on the altar and arrange wood on the fire. The Aaronite priests shall arrange the pieces, including the head and the suet, on the wood on the altar-
9 fire, the entrails and shins shall be washed in water, and the priest shall burn it all on the altar as a whole-offering, a food-offering of soothing odour to the LORD.

10 If the man's whole-offering is from the flock, either from the rams or
11 from the goats, he shall present a male without blemish. He shall slaughter it before the LORD at the north side of the altar, and the Aaronite priests
12 shall fling the blood against the altar all round. He shall cut it up, and the priest shall arrange the pieces, together with the head and the suet, on the
13 wood on the altar-fire, the entrails and shins shall be washed in water, and the priest shall present and burn it all on the altar: it is a whole-offering, a food-offering of soothing odour to the LORD.

14 If a man's offering to the LORD is a whole-offering of birds, he shall

a Or by him (the LORD).

present turtle-doves or young pigeons as his offering. The priest shall 15
present it at the altar, and shall wrench off the head and burn it on the altar;
and the blood shall be drained out against the side of the altar. He shall 16
take away the crop and its contents in one piece, and throw it to the east
side of the altar where the ashes are. He shall tear it by its wings without 17
severing them completely, and shall burn it on the altar, on top of the wood
of the altar-fire: it is a whole-offering, a food-offering of soothing odour to
the LORD.

When any person presents a grain-offering to the LORD, his offering 2
shall be of flour. He shall pour oil on it and add frankincense to it. He shall 2
bring it to the Aaronite priests, one of whom shall scoop up a handful of
the flour and oil with all the frankincense. The priest shall burn this as a
token on the altar, a food-offering of soothing odour to the LORD. The 3
remainder of the grain-offering belongs to Aaron and his sons: it is most
sacred, it is taken from the food-offerings of the LORD.

When you present as a grain-offering something baked in an oven, it 4
shall consist of unleavened cakes of flour mixed with oil and unleavened
wafers smeared with oil. If your offering is a grain-offering cooked on a 5
griddle, it shall be an unleavened cake of flour mixed with oil. Crumble it 6
in pieces and pour oil on it. This is a grain-offering.

If your offering is a grain-offering cooked in a pan, it shall be made of 7
flour with oil. Bring an offering made up in this way to the LORD and 8
present it to the priest, who shall bring it to the altar; then he shall set aside 9
part of the grain-offering as a token and burn it on the altar, a food-offering
of soothing odour to the LORD. The remainder of the grain-offering belongs 10
to Aaron and his sons: it is most sacred, it is taken from the food-offerings
of the LORD.

No grain-offering which you present to the LORD shall be made of any- 11
thing that ferments; you shall not burn any leaven or any honey as a food-
offering to the LORD. As for your offering of firstfruits, you shall present 12
them to the LORD, but they shall not be offered up at the altar as a soothing
odour. Every offering of yours which is a grain-offering shall be salted; 13
you shall not fail to put the salt of your covenant with God on your grain-
offering. Salt shall accompany all offerings.

If you present to the LORD a grain-offering of first-ripe grain, you must 14
present fresh corn roasted, crushed meal from fully ripened corn. You 15
shall add oil to it and put frankincense upon it. This is a grain-offering.
The priest shall burn as its token some of the crushed meal, some of the 16
oil, and all the frankincense as a food-offering to the LORD.

If a man's offering is a shared-offering from the cattle, male or female, 3
he shall present it without blemish before the LORD. He shall lay his hand 2
on the head of the victim and slaughter it at the entrance to the Tent of the
Presence. The Aaronite priests shall fling the blood against the altar all
round. One of them shall present part of the shared-offering as a food- 3
offering to the LORD: he shall remove the fat covering the entrails and
all the fat upon the entrails, the two kidneys with the fat on them be- 4
side the haunches, and the long lobe of the liver with the kidneys. The 5
Aaronites shall burn it on the altar on top of the whole-offering which

is upon the wood on the fire, a food-offering of soothing odour to the LORD.

6   If a man's offering as a shared-offering to the LORD is from the flock,
7 male or female, he shall present it without blemish. If he is presenting a
8 ram as his offering, he shall present it before the LORD, lay his hand on the
head of the victim and slaughter it in front of the Tent of the Presence. The
9 Aaronites shall then fling its blood against the altar all round. He shall
present part of the shared-offering as a food-offering to the LORD; he
shall remove its fat, the entire fat-tail cut off close by the spine, the fat
10 covering the entrails and all the fat upon the entrails, the two kidneys
with the fat on them beside the haunches, and the long lobe of the liver
11 with the kidneys. The priest shall burn it at the altar, as food offered to the
LORD.

12 13   If the man's offering is a goat, he shall present it before the LORD, lay
his hand on its head and slaughter it in front of the Tent of the Presence.
14 The Aaronites shall then fling its blood against the altar all round. He shall
present part of the victim as a food-offering to the LORD; he shall remove
15 the fat covering the entrails and all the fat upon the entrails, the two kidneys
with the fat on them beside the haunches, and the long lobe of the liver
16 with the kidneys. The priest shall burn this at the altar, as a food-offering
17 of soothing odour. All fat belongs to the LORD. This is a rule for all time
from generation to generation wherever you live: you shall not eat any fat
or any blood.

4 1 2   THE LORD SPOKE TO MOSES and said, Say this to the Israelites: These
are the rules for any man who inadvertently transgresses any of the commandments of the LORD and does anything prohibited by them:

3   If the anointed priest sins so as to bring guilt on the people, for the sin
he has committed he shall present to the LORD a young bull without blem-
4 ish as a sin-offering. He shall bring the bull to the entrance of the Tent of
the Presence before the LORD, lay his hand on its head and slaughter it
5 before the LORD. The anointed priest shall then take some of its blood and
6 bring it to the Tent of the Presence. He shall dip his finger in the blood and
sprinkle some of the blood in front of the sacred Veil seven times before
7 the LORD. The priest shall then put some of the blood before the LORD in
the Tent of the Presence on the horns of the altar where fragrant incense
is burnt, and he shall pour the rest of the bull's blood at the base of the altar
8 of whole-offering at the entrance of the Tent of the Presence. He shall set
aside all the fat from the bull of the sin-offering; he shall set aside the fat
9 covering the entrails and all the fat upon the entrails, the two kidneys with
the fat on them beside the haunches, and the long lobe of the liver with the
10 kidneys. It shall be set aside as the fat from the ox at the shared-offering is
set aside. The priest shall burn the pieces of fat on the altar of whole-
11 offering. But the skin of the bull and all its flesh, including head and shins,
12 its entrails and offal, the whole of it, he shall take away outside the camp
to a place ritually clean, where the ash-heap is, and destroy it on a wood-
fire on top of the ash-heap.

13   If the whole community of Israel sins inadvertently and the matter is

not known to the assembly, if they do what is forbidden in any commandment of the Lord and so incur guilt, then, when the sin they have committed is notified to them, the assembly shall present a young bull as a sin-offering and shall bring it in front of the Tent of the Presence. The elders of the community shall lay their hands on the victim's head before the Lord, and it shall be slaughtered before the Lord. The anointed priest shall then bring some of the blood to the Tent of the Presence, dip his finger in it and sprinkle it in front of the Veil seven times before the Lord. He shall put some of the blood on the horns of the altar before the Lord in the Tent of the Presence and pour all the rest at the base of the altar of whole-offering at the entrance of the Tent of the Presence. He shall then set aside all the fat from the bull and burn it on the altar. He shall deal with this bull as he deals with the bull of the sin-offering, and in this way the priest shall make expiation for their guilt and they shall be forgiven. He shall take the bull outside the camp and burn it as the other bull was burnt. This is a sin-offering for the assembly.

When a man of standing sins by doing inadvertently what is forbidden in any commandment of the Lord his God, thereby incurring guilt, and the sin he has committed is made known to him, he shall bring as his offering a he-goat without blemish. He shall lay his hand on the goat's head and shall slaughter it before the Lord in the place where the whole-offering is slaughtered. It is a sin-offering. The priest shall then take some of the blood of the victim with his finger and put it on the horns of the altar of whole-offering. He shall pour out the rest of the blood at the base of the altar of whole-offering. He shall burn all the fat at the altar in the same way as the fat of the shared-offering. Thus the priest shall make expiation for that man's sin, and it shall be forgiven him.

If any person among the common people sins inadvertently and does what is forbidden in any commandment of the Lord, thereby incurring guilt, and the sin he has committed is made known to him, he shall bring as his offering for the sin which he has committed a she-goat without blemish. He shall lay his hand on the head of the victim and slaughter it in the place where the whole-offering is slaughtered. The priest shall then take some of its blood with his finger and put it on the horns of the altar of whole-offering. All the rest of the blood he shall pour at the base of the altar. He shall remove all its fat as the fat of the shared-offering is removed, and the priest shall burn it on the altar as a soothing odour to the Lord. So the priest shall make expiation for that person's guilt, and it shall be forgiven him.

If the man brings a sheep as his offering for sin, it shall be a ewe without blemish. He shall lay his hand on the head of the victim and slaughter it as a sin-offering in the place where the whole-offering is slaughtered. The priest shall then take some of the blood of the victim with his finger and put it on the horns of the altar of whole-offering. All the rest of the blood he shall pour out at the base of the altar. He shall remove all the fat, as the fat of the sheep is removed from the shared-offering. The priest shall burn the pieces of fat at the altar on top of the food-offerings to the Lord, and shall make expiation for the sin that the man has committed, and it shall be forgiven him.

5 IF A PERSON HEARS a solemn adjuration to give evidence as a witness to something he has seen or heard and does not declare what he knows, he commits a sin and must accept responsibility.

2 If a person touches anything unclean, such as the dead body of an un-
3 clean animal, whether wild or domestic, or of an unclean reptile, or if he touches anything unclean in a man, whatever that uncleanness may be, and
4 it is concealed by him although he is aware of it, he shall incur guilt. Or if a person rashly utters an oath to do something evil or good, in any matter in which such a man may swear a rash oath, and it is concealed by him
5 although he is aware of it, he shall in either case incur guilt. Whenever a man incurs guilt in any of these cases and confesses how he has sinned
6 therein, he shall bring to the LORD, as his penalty for the sin that he has committed, a female of the flock, either a ewe or a she-goat, as a sin-offering, and the priest shall make expiation for him on account of his sin which he has committed, and he shall be pardoned.

7 But if he cannot afford as much as a young animal, he shall bring to the LORD for the sin he has committed two turtle-doves or two young pigeons,
8 one for a sin-offering and the other for a whole-offering. He shall bring them to the priest, and present first the one intended for the sin-offering.
9 He shall wrench its head back without severing it. He shall sprinkle some of the blood of the victim against the side of the altar, and what is left of the blood shall be drained out at the base of the altar: it is a sin-offering.
10 He shall deal with the second bird as a whole-offering according to custom, and the priest shall make expiation for the sin the man has committed, and it shall be forgiven him.
11 If the man cannot afford two turtle-doves or two young pigeons, for his sin he shall bring as his offering a tenth of an ephah of flour, as a sin-offering. He shall add no oil to it nor put frankincense on it, because it is a sin-
12 offering. He shall bring it to the priest, who shall scoop up a handful from it as a token and burn it on the altar on the food-offerings to the LORD: it
13 is a sin-offering. The priest shall make expiation for the sin the man has committed in any one of these cases, and it shall be forgiven him. The remainder belongs to the priest, as with the grain-offering.
14 15 The LORD spoke to Moses and said: When any person commits an offence by inadvertently defaulting in dues sacred to the LORD, he shall bring as his guilt-offering to the LORD a ram without blemish from the flock, the value to be determined by you in silver shekels according to the
16 sacred standard, for a guilt-offering; he shall make good his default in sacred dues, adding one fifth. He shall give it to the priest, who shall make expiation for his sin with the ram of the guilt-offering, and it shall be forgiven him.
17 If and when any person sins unwittingly and does what is forbidden by any commandment of the LORD, thereby incurring guilt, he must accept
18 responsibility. He shall bring to the priest as a guilt-offering a ram without blemish from the flock, valued by you, and the priest shall make expiation for the error into which he has unwittingly fallen, and it shall be forgiven
19 him. It is a guilt-offering; he has been guilty of an offence against the LORD.
6 1 2 The LORD spoke to Moses and said: When any person sins and commits

a grievous fault against the LORD, whether he lies to a fellow-countryman about a deposit or contract, or a theft, or wrongs him by extortion, or finds 3 lost property and then lies about it, and swears a false oath in regard to any sin of this sort that he commits—if he does this, thereby incurring guilt, 4 he shall restore what he has stolen or gained by extortion, or the deposit left with him or the lost property which he found, or anything at all con- 5 cerning which he swore a false oath. He shall make full restitution, adding one fifth to it, and give it back to the aggrieved party on the day when he offers his guilt-offering. He shall bring to the LORD as his guilt-offering a 6 ram without blemish from the flock, valued by you, as a guilt-offering. The 7 priest shall make expiation for his guilt before the LORD, and he shall be forgiven for any act which has brought guilt upon him.

THE LORD SPOKE TO MOSES and said, Give this command to Aaron and 8 9 his sons: This is the law of the whole-offering. The whole-offering shall remain on the altar-hearth all night till morning, and the altar-fire shall be kept burning there. Then the priest, having donned his linen robe and put 10 on linen drawers to cover himself, shall remove the ashes to which the fire reduces the whole-offering on the altar and put them beside the altar. He 11 shall then change into other garments and take the ashes outside the camp to a ritually clean place. The fire shall be kept burning on the altar; it shall 12 never go out. Every morning the priest shall have fresh wood burning thereon, arrange the whole-offering on it, and on top burn the fat from the shared-offerings. Fire shall always be kept burning on the altar; it shall not 13 go out.

This is the law of the grain-offering. The Aaronites shall present it before 14 the LORD in front of the altar. The priest shall set aside a handful of the 15 flour from it, with the oil of the grain-offering, and all the frankincense on it. He shall burn this token of it on the altar as a soothing odour to the LORD. The remainder Aaron and his sons shall eat. It shall be eaten in the 16 form of unleavened cakes and in a holy place. They shall eat it in the court of the Tent of the Presence. It shall not be baked with leaven. I have 17 allotted this to them as their share of my food-offerings. Like the sin-offering and the guilt-offering, it is most sacred. Any male descendant of 18 Aaron may eat it, as a due from the food-offerings to the LORD, for genera-tion after generation for all time. Whatever touches them is to be forfeit as sacred.

The LORD spoke to Moses and said: This is the offering which Aaron 19 20 and his sons shall present to the LORD: *a* one tenth of an ephah of flour, the usual grain-offering, half of it in the morning and half in the evening. It 21 shall be cooked with oil on a griddle; you shall bring it well-mixed, and so present it crumbled in small pieces as a grain-offering, a soothing odour to the LORD. The anointed priest in the line of Aaron shall offer it. This is a 22 rule binding for all time. It shall be burnt in sacrifice to the LORD as a complete offering. Every grain-offering of a priest shall be a complete 23 offering; it shall not be eaten.

The LORD spoke to Moses and said, Speak to Aaron and his sons in these 24 25

a Prob. rdg.; Heb. adds on the day when he is anointed.

words: This is the law of the sin-offering. The sin-offering shall be slaughtered before the LORD in the place where the whole-offering is slaughtered;
26 it is most sacred. The priest who officiates shall eat of the flesh; it shall be
27 eaten in a sacred place, in the court of the Tent of the Presence. Whatever
touches its flesh is to be forfeit as sacred. If any of the blood is splashed on
28 a garment, that shall be washed in a sacred place. An earthenware vessel
in which the sin-offering is boiled shall be smashed. If it has been boiled
29 in a copper vessel, that shall be scoured and rinsed with water. Any male
30 of priestly family may eat of this offering; it is most sacred. If, however,
part of the blood is brought to the Tent of the Presence to make expiation
in the holy place, the sin-offering shall not be eaten; it shall be destroyed
by fire.

7 1 2   This is the law of the guilt-offering: it is most sacred. The guilt-offering
shall be slaughtered in the place where the whole-offering is slaughtered,
3 and its blood shall be flung against the altar all round. The priest shall set
aside and present all the fat from it: the fat-tail and the fat covering the
4 entrails, the two kidneys with the fat on them beside the haunches, and
5 the long lobe of the liver with the kidneys. The priest shall burn these pieces
6 on the altar as a food-offering to the LORD; it is a guilt-offering. Any male
of priestly family may eat it. It shall be eaten in a sacred place; it is most
7 sacred. There is one law for both sin-offering and guilt-offering: they shall
8 belong to the priest who performs the rite of expiation. The skin of any
9 man's whole-offering shall belong to the priest who presents it. Every
grain-offering baked in an oven and everything that is cooked in a pan or
10 on a griddle shall belong to the priest who presents it. Every grain-offering,
whether mixed with oil or dry, shall be shared equally among all the
Aaronites.

11 12   This is the law of the shared-offering presented to the LORD. If a man
presents it as a thank-offering, then, in addition to the thank-offering, he
shall present unleavened cakes mixed with oil, wafers of unleavened flour
13 smeared with oil, and well-mixed flour and flat cakes mixed with oil. He
shall present flat cakes of leavened bread in addition to his shared thank-
14 offering. One part of every offering he shall present as a contribution for
the LORD: it shall belong to the priest who flings the blood of the shared-
15 offering against the altar. The flesh shall be eaten on the day of its presenta-
tion; none of it shall be put aside till morning.

16   If a man's sacrifice is a votive offering or a freewill offering, it may be
17 eaten on the day it is presented or on the next day. Any flesh left over on
18 the third day shall be destroyed by fire. If any flesh of his shared-offering
is eaten on the third day, the man who has presented it shall not be accepted.
It will not be counted to his credit, it shall be reckoned as tainted and the
19 person who eats any of it shall accept responsibility. No flesh which comes
into contact with anything unclean shall be eaten; it shall be destroyed by
fire.

20   The flesh may be eaten by anyone who is clean, but the person who,
while unclean, eats flesh from a shared-offering presented to the LORD
21 shall be cut off from his father's kin. When any person is contaminated by
contact with anything unclean, be it man, beast, or reptile, and then eats

any of the flesh from the shared-offerings presented to the LORD, that person shall be cut off from his father's kin.

The LORD spoke to Moses and said, Speak to the Israelites in these words: 22 23 You shall not eat the fat of any ox, sheep, or goat. The fat of an animal that 24 has died a natural death or has been mauled by wild beasts may be put to any other use, but you shall not eat it. Every man who eats fat from a beast 25 of which he has presented any part as a food-offering to the LORD shall be cut off from his father's kin.

You shall eat none of the blood, whether of bird or of beast, wherever you 26 may live. Every person who eats any of the blood shall be cut off from his 27 father's kin.

The LORD spoke to Moses and said, Speak to the Israelites in these 28 29 words: Whoever comes to present a shared-offering shall set aside part of it as an offering to the LORD. With his own hands he shall bring the food- 30 offerings to the LORD. He shall also bring the fat together with the breast which is to be presented as a special gift before the LORD; the priest shall 31 burn the fat on the altar, but the breast shall belong to Aaron and his descendants. You shall give the right hind-leg of your shared-offerings as 32 a contribution for the priest; it shall be the perquisite of the Aaronite who 33 presents the blood and the fat of the shared-offering. I have taken from the 34 Israelites the breast of the special gift and the leg of the contribution made out of the shared-offerings, and have given them as a due from the Israelites to Aaron the priest and his descendants for all time. This is the portion 35 prescribed for Aaron and his descendants out of the LORD's food-offerings, appointed on the day when they were presented as priests to the LORD; and on the day when they were anointed, the LORD commanded that these 36 prescribed portions should be given to them by the Israelites. This is a rule binding on their descendants for all time.

This, then, is the law of the whole-offering, the grain-offering, the sin- 37 offering, the guilt-offering, the installation-offerings, and the shared-offerings, with which the LORD charged Moses on Mount Sinai on the day 38 when he commanded the Israelites to present their offerings to the LORD in the wilderness of Sinai.

The hallowing and installation of the priests

THE LORD SPOKE TO MOSES and said, 'Take Aaron and his sons with 8 1 2 him, the vestments, the anointing oil, the ox for a sin-offering, the two rams, and the basket of unleavened cakes, and assemble all the community 3 at the entrance to the Tent of the Presence.' Moses did as the LORD had 4 commanded him, and the community assembled at the entrance to the Tent of the Presence. He told the community that this was what the LORD 5 had commanded. He presented Aaron and his sons and washed them in 6 water. He invested Aaron with the tunic, girded him with the sash, robed 7 him with the mantle, put the ephod on him, tied it with its waist-band and fastened the ephod to him with the band. He put the breast-piece*a* on him 8

a Or pouch.

9 and set the Urim and Thummim in it. He then put the turban upon his head and set the gold rosette as a symbol of holy dedication on the front of
10 the turban, as the LORD had commanded him. Moses then took the anointing oil, anointed the Tabernacle and all that was within it and consecrated
11 them. He sprinkled some of the oil seven times on the altar, anointing the
12 altar, all its vessels, the basin and its stand, to consecrate them. He poured
13 some of the anointing oil on Aaron's head and so consecrated him. Moses then brought the sons of Aaron forward, invested them with tunics, girded them with sashes and tied their tall head-dresses on them, as the LORD had commanded him.

14 He then brought up the ox for the sin-offering; Aaron and his sons laid
15 their hands on its head, and he slaughtered it. Moses took some of the blood and put it with his finger on the horns round the altar. Thus he purified the altar, and when he had poured out the rest of the blood at the base of the
16 altar, he consecrated it by making expiation for it. He took all the fat upon the entrails, the long lobe of the liver, and the two kidneys with their fat,
17 and burnt them on the altar, but the ox, its skin, its flesh, and its offal, he destroyed by fire outside the camp, as the LORD had commanded him.

18 Moses then brought forward the ram of the whole-offering; Aaron and
19 his sons laid their hands on the ram's head, and he slaughtered it. Moses
20 flung its blood against the altar all round. He cut the ram up and burnt
21 the head, the pieces, and the suet. He washed the entrails and the shins in water and burnt the whole on the altar. This was a whole-offering, a food-offering of soothing odour to the LORD, as the LORD had commanded Moses.

22 Moses then brought forward the second ram, the ram for the installation
23 of priests. Aaron and his sons laid their hands upon its head, and he slaughtered it. Moses took some of its blood and put it on the lobe of Aaron's right ear, on his right thumb, and on the big toe of his right foot.
24 He then brought forward the sons of Aaron, put some of the blood on the lobes of their right ears, on their right thumbs, and on the big toes of their
25 right feet. He flung the rest of the blood against the altar all round; he took the fat, the fat-tail, the fat covering the entrails, the long lobe of the
26 liver, the two kidneys with their fat, and the right leg. Then from the basket of unleavened cakes before the LORD he took one unleavened cake, one cake of bread made with oil, and one wafer, and laid them on the fatty
27 parts and the right leg. He put the whole on the hands of Aaron and of his
28 sons, and he presented it as a special gift before the LORD. He took it from their hands and burnt it on the altar on top of the whole-offering. This was an installation-offering, it was a food-offering of soothing odour to the LORD.

29 Moses then took the breast and presented it as a special gift before the LORD; it was his portion of the ram of installation, as the LORD had com-
30 manded him. He took some of the anointing oil and some of the blood on the altar and sprinkled it on Aaron and his vestments, and on his sons and their vestments with him. Thus he consecrated Aaron and his vestments, and with him his sons and their vestments.

31 Moses said to Aaron and his sons, 'Boil the flesh of the ram at the entrance to the Tent of the Presence, and eat it there, together with the bread in the

installation-basket, in accordance with the command: "Aaron and his sons shall eat it." The remainder of the flesh and bread you shall destroy by fire. 32 You shall not leave the entrance to the Tent of the Presence for seven days, 33 until the day which completes the period of your installation, for it lasts seven days. What was done this day followed the LORD's command to 34 make expiation for you. You shall stay at the entrance to the Tent of the 35 Presence day and night for seven days, keeping vigil to the LORD, so that you do not die, for so I was commanded.'

Aaron and his sons did everything that the LORD had commanded 36 through Moses.

On the eighth day Moses summoned Aaron and his sons and the **9** Israelite elders. He said to Aaron, 'Take for yourself a bull-calf for a sin- 2 offering and a ram for a whole-offering, both without blemish, and present them before the LORD. Then bid the Israelites take a he-goat for a sin- 3 offering, a calf and a lamb, both yearlings without blemish, for a whole-offering, and a bull and a ram for shared-offerings to be sacrificed before the 4 LORD, together with a grain-offering mixed with oil. This day the LORD will appear to you.'

They brought what Moses had commanded to the front of the Tent of 5 the Presence, and all the community approached and stood before the LORD. Moses said, 'This is what the LORD has commanded you to do, so 6 that the glory of the LORD may appear to you. Come near to the altar,' he 7 said to Aaron; 'prepare your sin-offering and your whole-offering and make expiation for yourself and for your household. Then prepare the offering of the people and make expiation for them, as the LORD has commanded.'

So Aaron came near to the altar and slaughtered the calf, which was his 8 sin-offering. The sons of Aaron presented the blood to him, and he dipped 9 his finger in the blood and put it on the horns of the altar. The rest of the blood he poured out at the base of the altar. Part of the sin-offering, the 10 fat, the kidneys, and the long lobe of the liver, he burnt on the altar as the LORD had commanded Moses, but the flesh and the skin he destroyed 11 by fire outside the camp. Then he slaughtered the whole-offering; his sons 12 handed him the blood, and he flung it against the altar all round. They 13 handed him the pieces of the whole-offering and the head, and he burnt them on the altar. He washed the entrails and the shins and burnt them 14 on the altar, on top of the whole-offering.

He then brought forward the offering of the people. He took the he-goat, 15 the people's sin-offering, slaughtered it and performed the rite of the sin-offering as he had previously done for himself. He presented the whole- 16 offering and prepared it in the manner prescribed. He brought forward the 17 grain-offering, took a handful of it and burnt it on the altar, in addition to the morning whole-offering. He slaughtered the bull and the ram, the 18 shared-offerings of the people. His sons handed him the blood, and he flung it against the altar all round. But the fatty parts of the bull, the fat- 19 tail of the ram, the fat covering the entrails, and the two kidneys with the fat upon them, and the long lobe of the liver, all this fat they first put on 20 the breasts of the animals and then burnt it on the altar. Aaron presented 21

the breasts and the right leg as a special gift before the LORD, as Moses
had commanded.

22 Then Aaron lifted up his hands towards the people and pronounced the
blessing over them. He came down from performing the rites of the sin-
23 offering, the whole-offering, and the shared-offerings. Moses and Aaron
entered the Tent of the Presence, and when they came out, they blessed the
24 people, and the glory of the LORD appeared to all the people. Fire came out
from before the LORD and consumed the whole-offering and the fatty parts
on the altar. All the people saw, and they shouted and fell on their faces.

10 NOW NADAB AND ABIHU, sons of Aaron, took their firepans, put fire in
them, threw incense on the fire and presented before the LORD illicit fire
2 which he had not commanded. Fire came out from before the LORD and
3 destroyed them; and so they died in the presence of the LORD. Then Moses
said to Aaron, 'This is what the LORD meant when he said: Among those
who approach me, I must be treated as holy; in the presence of all the
4 people I must be given honour.' Aaron was dumbfounded. Moses sent for
Mishael and Elzaphan, the sons of Aaron's uncle Uzziel, and said to them,
'Come and carry your cousins outside the camp away from the holy place.'
5 They came and carried them away in their tunics outside the camp, as
6 Moses had told them. Moses then said to Aaron and to his sons Eleazar and
Ithamar, 'You shall not leave your hair dishevelled or tear your clothes in
mourning, lest you die and the LORD be angry with the whole community.
Your kinsmen, all the house of Israel, shall weep for the destruction by fire
7 which the LORD has kindled. You shall not leave the entrance to the Tent
of the Presence lest you die, because the LORD's anointing oil is on you.'
They did as Moses had said.

8 9 THE LORD SPOKE TO AARON and said: You and your sons with you
shall not drink wine or strong drink when you are to enter the Tent of the
Presence, lest you die. This is a rule binding on your descendants for all
10 time, to make a distinction between sacred and profane, between clean and
11 unclean, and to teach the Israelites all the decrees which the LORD has
spoken to them through Moses.

12 Moses said to Aaron and his surviving sons Eleazar and Ithamar, 'Take
what is left over of the grain-offering out of the food-offerings of the LORD,
13 and eat it without leaven beside the altar; it is most sacred. You shall eat
it in a sacred place; it is your due and that of your sons out of the LORD's
14 food-offerings, for so I was commanded. You shall eat the breast of the
special gift and the leg of the contribution in a clean place, you and your
sons and daughters; for they have been given to you and your children as
15 your due out of the shared-offerings of the Israelites. The leg of the contribution and the breast of the special gift shall be brought, along with the
food-offerings of fat, to be presented as a special gift before the LORD, and
it shall belong to you and your children together, a due for all time; for
so the LORD has commanded.'

16 Moses made searching inquiry about the goat of the sin-offering and
found that it had been burnt. He was angry with Eleazar and Ithamar,

Aaron's surviving sons, and said, 'Why did you not eat the sin-offering in 17
the sacred place? It is most sacred. It was given to you to take away the
guilt of the community by making expiation for them before the LORD. If 18
the blood is not brought within the sacred precincts, you shall eat the sin-
offering there as I was commanded.' But Aaron replied to Moses, 'See, 19
they have today presented their sin-offering and their whole-offering before
the LORD, and this is what has befallen me; if I eat a sin-offering today, will
it be right in the eyes of the LORD?' When Moses heard this, he deemed it 20
right.

Laws of purification and atonement

THE LORD SPOKE TO MOSES and Aaron and said, Speak to the Israel- 11 1 2
ites in these words: Of all animals on land these are the creatures you
may eat: you may eat any animal which has a parted foot or a cloven hoof 3
and also chews the cud; those which have only a cloven hoof or only chew 4
the cud you may not eat. These are: the camel, because it chews the cud
but has not a cloven hoof; you shall regard it as unclean; the rock-badger,*a* 5
because it chews the cud but has not a parted foot; you shall regard it as
unclean; the hare, because it chews the cud but has not a parted foot; you 6
shall regard it as unclean; the pig, because it has a parted foot and a cloven 7
hoof but does not chew the cud; you shall regard it as unclean. You shall 8
not eat their flesh or even touch their dead bodies; you shall regard them
as unclean.

Of creatures that live in water these you may eat: all those that have fins 9
and scales, whether in salt water or fresh; but all that have neither fins nor 10
scales, whether in salt or fresh water, including both small creatures in
shoals and larger creatures, you shall regard as vermin. They shall be 11
vermin to you; you shall not eat their flesh, and their dead bodies you shall
treat as those of vermin. Every creature in the water that has neither fins 12
nor scales shall be vermin to you.

These are the birds you shall regard as vermin, and for this reason they 13
shall not be eaten: the griffon-vulture,*b* the black vulture, and the bearded
vulture;*c* the kite and every kind of falcon; every kind of crow,*d* the desert- 14 15 16
owl, the short-eared owl, the long-eared owl, and every kind of hawk; the 17
tawny owl, the fisher-owl, and the screech-owl; the little owl, the horned 18
owl, the osprey, the stork,*e* every kind of cormorant, the hoopoe, and 19
the bat.

All teeming winged creatures that go on four legs shall be vermin to you, 20
except those which have legs jointed above their feet for leaping on the 21
ground. Of these you may eat every kind of great locust, every kind of long- 22
headed locust, every kind of green locust, and every kind of desert locust.
Every other teeming winged creature that has four legs you shall regard as 23
vermin; you would make yourselves unclean with them: whoever*f* touches 24
their dead bodies shall be unclean till evening. Whoever picks up their 25
dead bodies shall wash his clothes but remain unclean till evening.

---

a Or rock-rabbit.   *b Or* eagle.   *c Or* ossifrage.   *d Or* raven.
e Or heron.   *f Or* whatever.

26   You shall regard as unclean every animal which has a parted foot but
has not a cloven hoof and does not chew the cud: whoever[a] touches them
27 shall be unclean. You shall regard as unclean all four-footed wild animals
that go on flat paws; whoever[a] touches their dead bodies shall be unclean
28 till evening. Whoever takes up their dead bodies shall wash his clothes but
remain unclean till evening. You shall regard them as unclean.

29   You shall regard these as unclean among creatures that teem on the
ground: the mole-rat,[b] the jerboa, and every kind of thorn-tailed lizard;
30 the gecko, the sand-gecko, the wall-gecko, the great lizard, and the
31 chameleon. You shall regard these as unclean among teeming creatures;
whoever[a] touches them when they are dead shall be unclean till evening.
32 Anything on which any of them falls when they are dead shall be unclean,
any article of wood or garment or skin or sacking, any article in regular use;
it shall be plunged into water but shall remain unclean till evening, when it
33 shall be clean. If any of these falls into an earthenware vessel, its contents
34 shall be unclean and it shall be smashed. Any food on which water from
such a vessel is poured shall be unclean, and any drink in such a vessel shall
35 be unclean. Anything on which the dead body of such a creature falls shall
be unclean; an oven or a stove shall be broken, for they are unclean and you
36 shall treat them as such; but a spring or a cistern where water collects shall
remain clean, though whatever[c] touches the dead body shall be unclean.
37 When any of their dead bodies falls on seed intended for sowing, it remains
38 clean; but if the seed has been soaked in water and any dead body falls on
it, you shall treat it as unclean.

39   When any animal allowed as food dies, all that touch the carcass shall be
40 unclean till evening. Whoever eats any of the carcass shall wash his clothes
but remain unclean till evening; whoever takes up the carcass shall wash
41 his clothes and be unclean till evening. All creatures that teem on the ground
42 are vermin; they shall not be eaten. All creatures that teem on the ground,
crawl on their bellies, go on all fours or have many legs, you shall not eat,
43 because they are vermin which contaminate. You shall not contaminate
yourselves through any teeming creature. You shall not defile yourselves
44 with them and make yourselves unclean by them. For I am the LORD your
God; you shall make yourselves holy and keep yourselves holy, because I
am holy. You shall not defile yourselves with any teeming creature that
45 creeps on the ground. I am the LORD who brought you up from Egypt to
become your God. You shall keep yourselves holy, because I am holy.

46   This, then, is the law concerning beast and bird, every living creature
that swims in the water and every living creature that teems on the land.
47 It is to make a distinction between the unclean and the clean, between
living creatures that may be eaten and living creatures that may not be
eaten.

12 2   The LORD spoke to Moses and said, Speak to the Israelites in these
words: When a woman conceives and bears a male child, she shall be unclean for seven days, as in the period of her impurity through menstruation.
3 On the eighth day, the child shall have the flesh of his foreskin circumcised.
4 The woman shall wait for thirty-three days because her blood requires

        [a] *Or* whatever.   [b] *Or* weasel.   [c] *Or* whoever.

purification; she shall touch nothing that is holy, and shall not enter the sanctuary till her days of purification are completed. If she bears a female 5 child, she shall be unclean for fourteen days as for her menstruation and shall wait for sixty-six days because her blood requires purification. When 6 her days of purification are completed for a son or a daughter, she shall bring a yearling ram for a whole-offering and a young pigeon or a turtle-dove for a sin-offering to the priest at the entrance to the Tent of the Presence. He shall present it before the LORD and make expiation for her, 7 and she shall be clean from the issue of her blood. This is the law for the woman who bears a child, whether male or female. If she cannot afford a 8 ram, she shall bring two turtle-doves or two young pigeons, one for a whole-offering and the other for a sin-offering. The priest shall make expiation for her and she shall be clean.

The LORD spoke to Moses and Aaron and said: When any man has a **13** 1 2 discoloration on the skin of his body, a pustule or inflammation, and it may develop into the sores of a malignant skin-disease, he shall be brought to the priest, either to Aaron or to one of his sons. The priest shall examine the 3 sore on the skin; if the hairs on the sore have turned white and it appears to be deeper than the skin, it shall be considered the sore of a malignant skin-disease, and the priest, after examination, shall pronounce him ritually unclean. But if the inflammation on his skin is white and seems no deeper 4 than the skin, and the hairs have not turned white, the priest shall isolate the affected person for seven days. If, when he examines him on the seventh 5 day, the sore remains as it was and has not spread in the skin, he shall keep him in isolation for another seven days. When the priest examines him again 6 on the seventh day, if the sore has faded and has not spread in the skin, the priest shall pronounce him ritually clean. It is only a scab; the man shall wash his clothes and so be clean. But if the scab spreads on the skin after 7 he has been to the priest to be pronounced ritually clean, the man shall show himself a second time to the priest. The priest shall examine him 8 again, and if it continues to spread, he shall pronounce him ritually unclean; it is a malignant skin-disease.

When anyone has the sores of a malignant skin-disease, he shall be 9 brought to the priest, and the priest shall examine him. If there is a white 10 mark on the skin, turning the hairs white, and an ulceration appears in the mark, it is a chronic skin-disease on the body, and the priest shall pronounce 11 him ritually unclean; there is no need for isolation because he is unclean already. If the skin-disease breaks out and covers the affected person from 12 head to foot as far as the priest can see, the priest shall examine him, and if 13 he finds the condition spread all over the body, he shall pronounce him ritually clean. It has all gone white; he is clean. But from the moment when 14 raw flesh appears, the man shall be considered unclean. When the priest 15 sees it, he shall pronounce him unclean. Raw flesh is to be considered unclean; it is a malignant skin-disease. On the other hand, when the raw 16 flesh heals and turns white, the man shall go to the priest, who shall examine 17 him, and if the sores have gone white, he shall pronounce him clean. He is ritually clean.

When a fester appears on the skin and heals up, but is followed by a 18 19

white mark or reddish-white inflammation on the site of the fester, the man
20 shall show himself to the priest. The priest shall examine him; if it seems
to be beneath the skin and the hairs have turned white, the priest shall
pronounce him ritually unclean. It is a malignant skin-disease which has
21 broken out on the site of the fester. But if the priest on examination finds
that it has no white hairs, is not beneath the skin and has faded, he shall
22 isolate him for seven days. If the affection has spread at all in the skin, then
the priest shall pronounce him unclean; for it is a malignant skin-disease.
23 But if the inflammation is no worse and has not spread, it is only the scar
of the fester, and the priest shall pronounce him ritually clean.

24   Again, in the case of a burn on the skin, if the raw spot left by the burn
25 becomes a reddish-white or white inflammation, the priest shall examine
it. If the hairs on the inflammation have turned white and it is deeper than
the skin, it is a malignant skin-disease which has broken out at the site of
the burn. The priest shall pronounce the man ritually unclean; it is a
26 malignant skin-disease. But if the priest on examination finds that there is
no white hair on the inflammation and it is not beneath the skin and has
27 faded, he shall keep him in isolation for seven days. When the priest
examines him on the seventh day, if the inflammation has spread at all in
the skin, the priest shall pronounce him unclean; it is a malignant skin-
28 disease. But if the inflammation is no worse, has not spread and has faded,
it is only a mark from the burn. The priest shall pronounce him ritually
clean because it is the scar of the burn.

29 30   When a man, or woman, has a sore on the head or chin, the priest shall
examine it; and if it seems deeper than the skin and the hair is yellow and
sparse, the priest shall pronounce him ritually unclean; it is a scurf, a
31 malignant skin-disease of the head or chin. But when the priest sees the
sore, if it appears to be no deeper than the skin and yet there is no yellow
hair on the place, the priest shall isolate the affected person for seven days.
32 He shall examine the sore on the seventh day: if the scurf has not spread
and there are no yellow hairs on it and it seems no deeper than the skin,
33 the man shall get himself shaved except for the scurfy part, and the priest
34 shall keep him in isolation for another seven days. The priest shall examine
it again on the seventh day, and if the scurf has not spread on the skin and
appears to be no deeper than the skin, the priest shall pronounce him clean.
35 The man shall wash his clothes and so be ritually clean. But if the scurf
36 spreads at all in the skin after the man has been pronounced clean, the priest
shall examine him again. If it has spread in the skin, the priest need not even
37 look for yellow hair; the man is unclean. If, however, the scurf remains as
it was but black hair has begun to grow on it, it has healed. The man is
ritually clean and the priest shall pronounce him so.

38   When a man, or woman, has inflamed patches on the skin and they are
39 white, the priest shall examine them. If they are white and fading, it is
dull-white leprosy that has broken out on the skin. The man is ritually
clean.

40   When a man's hair falls out from his head, he is bald behind but not
41 ritually unclean. If the hair falls out from the front of the scalp, he is
42 bald on the forehead but clean. But if on the bald patch behind or on the

forehead there is a reddish-white sore, it is a malignant skin-disease
breaking out on those parts. The priest shall examine him, and if the   43
discoloured sore on the bald patch behind or on the forehead is reddish-
white, similar in appearance to a malignant skin-disease on the body, the man   44
is suffering from such a disease; he is ritually unclean and the priest must
not fail to pronounce him so. The symptoms are in this case on his head.

One who suffers from a malignant skin-disease shall wear his clothes   45
torn, leave his hair dishevelled, conceal his upper lip, and cry, 'Unclean,
unclean.' So long as the sore persists, he shall be considered ritually unclean.   46
The man is unclean: he shall live apart and must stay outside the settlement.

When there is a stain of mould, whether in a garment of wool or linen,   47
or in the warp or weft of linen or wool, or in a skin or anything made of   48
skin; if the stain is greenish or reddish in the garment or skin, or in the   49
warp or weft, or in anything made of skin, it is a stain of mould which must
be shown to the priest. The priest shall examine it and put the stained   50
material aside for seven days. On the seventh day he shall examine it again.   51
If the stain has spread in the garment, warp, weft, or skin, whatever the
use of the skin, the stain is a rotting mould: it is ritually unclean. He shall   52
burn the garment or the warp or weft, whether wool or linen, or anything
of skin which is stained; because it is a rotting mould, it must be destroyed by fire. But if the priest sees that the stain has not spread in the   53
garment, warp or weft, or anything made of skin, he shall give orders for   54
the stained material to be washed, and then he shall put it aside for another
seven days. After it has been washed the priest shall examine the stain; if   55
it has not changed its appearance, although it has not spread, it is unclean
and you shall destroy it by fire, whether the rot is on the right side or the
wrong. If the priest examines it and finds the stain faded after being washed,   56
he shall tear it out of the garment, skin, warp, or weft. If, however, the stain   57
reappears in the garment, warp or weft, or in anything of skin, it is breaking
out afresh and you shall destroy by fire whatever is stained. If you wash the   58
garment, warp, weft, or anything of skin and the stain disappears, it shall be
washed a second time and then it shall be ritually clean.

This is the law concerning stain of mould in a garment of wool or linen,   59
in warp or weft, or in anything made of skin; by it they shall be pronounced
clean or unclean.

THE LORD SPOKE TO MOSES and said: This is the law concerning a man   **14** 1 2
suffering from a malignant skin-disease. On the day when he is to be
cleansed he shall be brought to the priest. The priest shall go outside the   3
camp and examine him. If the man is healed of his disease, then the priest   4
shall order two clean small birds to be brought alive for the man who is to
be cleansed, together with cedar-wood, scarlet thread, and marjoram.*a* He   5
shall order one of the birds to be killed over an earthenware bowl containing fresh water. He shall then take the living bird and the cedar-wood,   6
scarlet thread, and marjoram and dip them and the living bird in the blood
of the bird that has been killed over the fresh water. He shall sprinkle the   7
blood seven times on the man who is to be cleansed from his skin-disease

                              a Or hyssop.

and so cleanse him; the living bird he shall release to fly away over the open
8 country. The man to be cleansed shall wash his clothes, shave off all his
hair, bathe in water and so be ritually clean. He may then enter the camp
9 but must stay outside his tent for seven days. On the seventh day he shall
shave off all the hair on his head, his beard, and his eyebrows, and then
shave the rest of his hair, wash his clothes and bathe in water; then he shall
be ritually clean.

10   On the eighth day he shall bring two yearling rams and one yearling
ewe, all three without blemish, a grain-offering of three tenths of an ephah
11 of flour mixed with oil, and one log of oil. The officiating priest shall place
the man to be cleansed and his offerings before the LORD at the entrance
12 to the Tent of the Presence. He shall then take one of the rams and offer it
with the log of oil as a guilt-offering, presenting them as a special gift
13 before the LORD. The ram shall be slaughtered where the sin-offerings
and the whole-offerings are slaughtered, within the sacred precincts,
because the guilt-offering, like the sin-offering, belongs to the priest. It is
14 most sacred. The priest shall then take some of the blood of the guilt-
offering and put it on the lobe of the right ear of the man to be cleansed, and
15 on his right thumb and the big toe of his right foot. He shall next take the
16 log of oil and pour some of it on the palm of his own left hand, dip his right
forefinger into the oil on his left palm and sprinkle some of it with his
17 finger seven times before the LORD. He shall then put some of the oil
remaining on his palm on the lobe of the right ear of the man to be cleansed,
on his right thumb and on the big toe of his right foot, on top of the blood
18 of the guilt-offering. The remainder of the oil on the priest's palm shall be
put upon the head of the man to be cleansed, and thus the priest shall make
19 expiation for him before the LORD. The priest shall then perform the sin-
offering and make expiation for the uncleanness of the man who is to be
20 cleansed. After this he shall slaughter the whole-offering and offer it and
the grain-offering on the altar. Thus the priest shall make expiation for him,
and then he shall be clean.

21   If the man is poor and cannot afford these offerings, he shall bring one
young ram as a guilt-offering to be a special gift making expiation for him,
and a grain-offering of a tenth of an ephah of flour mixed with oil, and a log
22 of oil, also two turtle-doves or two young pigeons, whichever he can afford,
23 one for a sin-offering and the other for a whole-offering. He shall bring
them to the priest for his cleansing on the eighth day, at the entrance to the
24 Tent of the Presence before the LORD. The priest shall take the ram for the
guilt-offering and the log of oil, and shall present them as a special gift
25 before the LORD. The ram for the guilt-offering shall then be slaughtered,
and the priest shall take some of the blood of the guilt-offering, and put it
on the lobe of the right ear of the man to be cleansed and on his right thumb
26 and on the big toe of his right foot. He shall pour some of the oil on the
27 palm of his own left hand and sprinkle some of it with his right forefinger
28 seven times before the LORD. He shall then put some of the oil remaining on
his palm on the lobe of the right ear of the man to be cleansed, and on his
right thumb and on the big toe of his right foot exactly where the blood of
29 the guilt-offering was put. The remainder of the oil on the priest's palm

shall be put upon the head of the man to be cleansed to make expiation for
him before the LORD. Of the birds which the man has been able to afford, 30
turtle-doves or young pigeons, whichever it may be, the priest shall deal 31
with one as a sin-offering and with the other as a whole-offering and shall
make the grain-offering with them. Thus the priest shall make expiation
before the LORD for the man who is to be cleansed. This is the law for the 32
man with a malignant skin-disease who cannot afford the regular offering
for his cleansing.

The LORD spoke to Moses and Aaron and said: When you have entered 33 34
the land of Canaan which I give you to occupy, if I inflict a fungous infection upon a house in the land you have occupied, its owner shall come and 35
report to the priest that there appears to him to be a patch of infection in
his house. The priest shall order the house to be cleared before he goes in 36
to examine the infection, or everything in it will become unclean. After this
the priest shall go in to inspect the house. If on inspection he finds the 37
patch on the walls consists of greenish or reddish depressions, apparently
going deeper than the surface, he shall go out of the house and, standing 38
at the entrance, shall put it in quarantine for seven days. On the seventh 39
day he shall come back and inspect the house, and if the patch has spread
in the walls, he shall order the infected stones to be pulled out and thrown 40
away outside the city in an unclean place. He shall then have the house 41
scraped inside throughout, and all the daub[a] they have scraped off shall
be tipped outside the city in an unclean place. They shall take fresh stones 42
to replace the others and replaster the house with fresh daub.

If the infection reappears in the house and spreads after the stones have 43
been pulled out and the house scraped and redaubed, the priest shall come 44
and inspect it. If the infection has spread in the house, it is a corrosive
growth; the house is unclean. The house shall be demolished, stones, 45
timber, and daub, and it shall all be taken away outside the city to an unclean place. Anyone who has entered the house during the time it has been 46
in quarantine shall be unclean till evening. Anyone who has slept or eaten 47
a meal in the house shall wash his clothes. But if, when the priest goes 48
into the house and inspects it, he finds that the infection has not spread
after the redaubing, then he shall pronounce the house ritually clean, because
the infection has been cured.

In order to rid the house of impurity, he shall take two small birds, cedar- 49
wood, scarlet thread, and marjoram. He shall kill one of the birds over an 50
earthenware bowl containing fresh water. He shall then take the cedar- 51
wood, marjoram, and scarlet thread, together with the living bird, dip
them in the blood of the bird that has been killed and in the fresh water,
and sprinkle the house seven times. Thus he shall purify the house, using 52
the blood of the bird, the fresh water, the living bird, the cedar-wood, the
marjoram, and the scarlet thread. He shall set the living bird free outside 53
the city to fly away over the open country, and make expiation for the house;
and then it shall be clean.

This is the law for all malignant skin-diseases, and for scurf, for mould 54 55
in clothes and fungus in houses, for a discoloration of the skin, scab, and 56

[a] *Or* mud.

57 inflammation, to declare when these are pronounced unclean and when clean. This is the law for skin-disease, mould, and fungus.

15 1 2 THE LORD SPOKE TO MOSES and Aaron and said, Speak to the Israel-ites and say to them: When any man has a discharge from his body, the
3 discharge is ritually unclean. This is the law concerning the uncleanness due to his discharge whether it continues or has been stopped; in either case he is unclean.

4 Every bed on which the man with a discharge lies down shall be ritually
5 unclean, and everything on which he sits shall be unclean. Any man who touches the bed shall wash his clothes, bathe in water and remain unclean
6 till evening. Whoever sits on anything on which the man with a discharge has sat shall wash his clothes, bathe in water and remain unclean till even-
7 ing. Whoever touches the body of the man with a discharge shall wash his
8 clothes, bathe in water and remain unclean till evening. If the man spits on one who is ritually clean, the latter shall wash his clothes, bathe in water
9 and remain unclean till evening. Everything on which the man sits when
10 riding shall be unclean. Whoever touches anything that has been under him shall be unclean till evening, and whoever handles such things shall
11 wash his clothes, bathe in water and remain unclean till evening. Anyone whom the man with a discharge touches without having rinsed his hands in water shall wash his clothes, bathe in water and remain unclean till
12 evening. Any earthenware bowl touched by the man shall be smashed, and every wooden bowl shall be rinsed with water.

13 When the man is cleansed from his discharge, he shall reckon seven days to his cleansing, wash his clothes, bathe his body in fresh water and be
14 ritually clean. On the eighth day he shall obtain two turtle-doves or two young pigeons and, coming before the LORD at the entrance to the Tent of
15 the Presence, shall give them to the priest. The priest shall deal with one as a sin-offering and the other as a whole-offering, and shall make for him before the LORD the expiation required by the discharge.

16 When a man has emitted semen, he shall bathe his whole body in water
17 and be unclean till evening. Every piece of clothing or skin on which there
18 is any semen shall be washed and remain unclean till evening. This applies also to the woman with whom a man has had intercourse; they shall both bathe themselves in water and remain unclean till evening.

19 When a woman has a discharge of blood, her impurity shall last for
20 seven days; anyone who touches her shall be unclean till evening. Every-
21 thing on which she lies or sits during her impurity shall be unclean. Any-one who touches her bed shall wash his clothes, bathe in water and remain
22 unclean till evening. Whoever touches anything on which she sits shall
23 wash his clothes, bathe in water and remain unclean till evening. If he is on the bed or seat where she is sitting, by touching it he shall become un-
24 clean till evening. If a man goes so far as to have intercourse with her and any of her discharge gets on to him, then he shall be unclean for seven days, and every bed on which he lies down shall be unclean.

25 When a woman has a prolonged discharge of blood not at the time of her menstruation, or when her discharge continues beyond the period of

menstruation, her impurity shall last all the time of her discharge; she shall be unclean as during the period of her menstruation. Any bed on which she 26 lies during the time of her discharge shall be like that which she used during menstruation, and everything on which she sits shall be unclean as in her menstrual uncleanness. Every person who touches them shall be unclean; 27 he shall wash his clothes, bathe in water and remain unclean till evening. If she is cleansed from her discharge, she shall reckon seven days and after 28 that she shall be ritually clean. On the eighth day she shall obtain two 29 turtle-doves or two young pigeons and bring them to the priest at the entrance to the Tent of the Presence. The priest shall deal with one as a 30 sin-offering and with the other as a whole-offering, and make for her before the LORD the expiation required by her unclean discharge.

In this way you shall warn the Israelites against uncleanness, in order 31 that they may not bring uncleanness upon the Tabernacle where I dwell among them, and so die.

This is the law for the man who has a discharge, or who has an emission 32 of semen and is thereby unclean, and for the woman who is suffering her 33 menstruation—for everyone, male or female, who has a discharge, and for the man who has intercourse with a woman who is unclean.

THE LORD SPOKE TO MOSES after the death of Aaron's two sons, who **16** died when they offered illicit fire before the LORD. He said to him: Tell 2 your brother Aaron that he must not enter the sanctuary within the Veil, in front of the cover over the Ark, except at the appointed time, on pain of death; for I appear in the cloud above the cover. When Aaron enters the 3 sanctuary, this is what he shall do. He shall bring a young bull for a sin-offering and a ram for a whole-offering. He shall wear a sacred linen tunic 4 and linen drawers to cover himself, and he shall put a linen sash round his waist and wind a linen turban round his head; all these are sacred vestments, and he shall bathe in water before putting them on. He shall take 5 from the community of the Israelites two he-goats for a sin-offering and a ram for a whole-offering. He shall present the bull as a sin-offering and 6 make expiation for himself and his household. Then he shall take the two 7 he-goats and set them before the LORD at the entrance to the Tent of the Presence. He shall cast lots over the two goats, one to be for the LORD and 8 the other for the Precipice.*a* He shall present the goat on which the lot 9 for the LORD has fallen and deal with it as a sin-offering; but the goat on 10 which the lot for the Precipice has fallen shall be made to stand alive before the LORD, for expiation to be made over it before it is driven away into the wilderness to the Precipice.

Aaron shall present his bull as a sin-offering, making expiation for him- 11 self and his household, and then slaughter the bull as a sin-offering. He 12 shall take a firepan full of glowing embers from the altar before the LORD, and two handfuls of powdered fragrant incense, and bring them within the Veil. He shall put the incense on the fire before the LORD, and the 13 cloud of incense will hide the cover over the Tokens so that he shall not die. He shall take some of the bull's blood and sprinkle it with his finger 14

a Or for Azazel.

both on the surface of the cover, eastwards, and seven times in front of the cover.

15 He shall then slaughter the people's goat as a sin-offering, bring its blood within the Veil and do with its blood as he did with the bull's blood,
16 sprinkling it on the cover and in front of it. He shall make for the sanctuary the expiation required by the ritual uncleanness of the Israelites and their acts of rebellion, that is by all their sins; and he shall do the same for the Tent of the Presence, which dwells among them in the midst of all their
17 uncleanness. No other man shall be within the Tent of the Presence from the time when he enters the sanctuary to make expiation until he comes out, and he shall make expiation for himself, his household, and the whole assembly of Israel.

18 He shall then come out to the altar which is before the LORD and make expiation for it. He shall take some of the bull's blood and some of the
19 goat's blood and put it all over the horns of the altar; he shall sprinkle some of the blood on the altar with his finger seven times. So he shall purify it from all the uncleanness of the Israelites and hallow it.

20 When Aaron has finished making expiation for the sanctuary, for the Tent of the Presence, and for the altar, he shall bring forward the live goat.
21 He shall lay both his hands on its head and confess over it all the iniquities of the Israelites and all their acts of rebellion, that is all their sins; he shall lay them on the head of the goat and send it away into the wilderness in
22 charge of a man who is waiting ready. The goat shall carry all their iniquities upon itself into some barren waste and the man shall let it go, there in the wilderness.

23 Aaron shall then enter the Tent of the Presence, take off the linen clothes which he had put on when he entered the sanctuary, and leave them there.
24 He shall bathe in water in a consecrated place and put on his vestments; then he shall go out and perform his own whole-offering and that of the
25 people, thus making expiation for himself and for the people. He shall
26 burn the fat of the sin-offering upon the altar. The man who drove the goat away to the Precipice shall wash his clothes and bathe in water,
27 and not till then may he enter the camp. The two sin-offerings, the bull and the goat, the blood of which was brought within the Veil to make expiation in the sanctuary, shall be taken outside the camp and
28 destroyed by fire—skin, flesh, and offal. The man who burns them shall wash his clothes and bathe in water, and not till then may he enter the camp.

29 This shall become a rule binding on you for all time. On the tenth day of the seventh month you shall mortify yourselves; you shall do no work,
30 whether native Israelite or alien settler, because on this day expiation shall be made on your behalf to cleanse you, and so make you clean before the
31 LORD from all your sins. This is a sabbath of sacred rest for you, and you
32 shall mortify yourselves; it is a rule binding for all time. Expiation shall be made by the priest duly anointed and installed to serve in succession to his
33 father; he shall put on the sacred linen clothes and shall make expiation for the holy sanctuary, the Tent of the Presence, and the altar, on behalf of the
34 priests and the whole assembly of the people. This shall become a rule

binding on you for all time, to make for the Israelites once a year the expiation required by all their sins.

And Moses carried out the LORD's commands.

The law of holiness

THE LORD SPOKE TO MOSES and said, Speak to Aaron, his sons, and **17** 1 2
all the Israelites in these words: This is what the LORD has commanded.
Any Israelite who slaughters an ox, a sheep, or a goat, either inside or 3
outside the camp, and does not bring it to the entrance of the Tent of the 4
Presence to present it as an offering to the LORD before the Tabernacle of
the LORD shall be held guilty of bloodshed: that man has shed blood and
shall be cut off from his people. The purpose is that the Israelites should 5
bring to the LORD the animals which they slaughter in the open country;
they shall bring them to the priest at the entrance to the Tent of the
Presence and sacrifice them as shared-offerings to the LORD. The priest 6
shall fling the blood against the altar of the LORD at the entrance to the
Tent of the Presence, and burn the fat as a soothing odour to the LORD.
They shall no longer sacrifice their slaughtered beasts to the demons*a* whom 7
they wantonly follow. This shall be a rule binding on them and their
descendants for all time.

You shall say to them: Any Israelite or alien settled in Israel who offers 8
a whole-offering or a sacrifice and does not bring it to the entrance of the 9
Tent of the Presence to sacrifice it to the LORD shall be cut off from his
father's kin.

If any Israelite or alien settled in Israel eats any blood, I will set my face 10
against the eater and cut him off from his people, because the life of a 11
creature is the blood, and I appoint it to make expiation on the altar for
yourselves: it is the blood, that is the life, that makes expiation. Therefore 12
I have told the Israelites that neither you, nor any alien settled among you,
shall eat blood.

Any Israelite or alien settled in Israel who hunts beasts or birds that may 13
lawfully be eaten shall drain out the blood and cover it with earth, because 14
the life of every living creature is the blood, and I have forbidden the
Israelites to eat the blood of any creature, because the life of every creature
is its blood: every man who eats it shall be cut off.

Every person, native or alien, who eats that which has died a natural 15
death or has been mauled by wild beasts shall wash his clothes and
bathe in water, and remain ritually unclean till evening; then he shall be
clean. If he does not wash his clothes and bathe his body, he must accept 16
responsibility.

THE LORD SPOKE TO MOSES and said, Speak to the Israelites in these **18** 1 2
words: I am the LORD your God. You shall not do as they do in Egypt 3
where you once dwelt, nor shall you do as they do in the land of Canaan to
which I am bringing you; you shall not conform to their institutions. You 4

a Or satyrs.

129

must keep my laws and conform to my institutions without fail: I am the
5 LORD your God. You shall observe my institutions and my laws: the man
who keeps them shall have life through them. I am the LORD.
6   No man shall approach a blood-relation for intercourse. I am the LORD.
7 You shall not bring shame on your father by intercourse with your mother:
8 she is your mother; you shall not bring shame upon her. You shall not have
intercourse with your father's wife: that is to bring shame upon your father.
9 You shall not have intercourse with your sister, your father's daughter, or
your mother's daughter, whether brought up in the family or in another
10 home; you shall not bring shame upon them. You shall not have intercourse with your son's daughter or your daughter's daughter: that is to
11 bring shame upon yourself. You shall not have intercourse with a daughter
of your father's wife, begotten by your father: she is your sister, and you
12 shall not bring shame upon her. You shall not have intercourse with your
13 father's sister: she is a blood-relation of your father. You shall not have
intercourse with your mother's sister: she is a blood-relation of your
14 mother. You shall not bring shame upon your father's brother by approach-
15 ing his wife: she is your aunt. You shall not have intercourse with your
daughter-in-law: she is your son's wife; you shall not bring shame upon her.
16 You shall not have intercourse with your brother's wife: that is to bring
17 shame upon him. You shall not have intercourse with both a woman and her
daughter, nor shall you take her son's daughter or her daughter's daughter to
have intercourse with them: they are her blood-relations, and such conduct
18 is lewdness. You shall not take a woman who is your wife's sister to make her
a rival-wife, and to have intercourse with her during her sister's lifetime.
19   You shall not approach a woman to have intercourse with her during
20 her period of menstruation. You shall not have sexual intercourse with the
wife of your fellow-countryman and so make yourself unclean with her.
21 You shall not surrender any of your children to Molech and thus profane
22 the name of your God: I am the LORD. You shall not lie with a man as with
23 a woman: that is an abomination. You shall not have sexual intercourse
with any beast to make yourself unclean with it, nor shall a woman submit
24 herself to intercourse with a beast: that is a violation of nature. You shall
not make yourselves unclean in any of these ways; for in these ways the
heathen, whom I am driving out before you, made themselves unclean.
25 This is how the land became unclean, and I punished it for its iniquity so
26 that it spewed out its inhabitants. You, unlike them, shall keep my laws
and my rules: none of you, whether natives or aliens settled among you,
27 shall do any of these abominable things. The people who were there before
28 you did these abominable things and the land became unclean. So the land
29 will not spew you out for making it unclean as it spewed them out; for
anyone who does any of these abominable things shall be cut off from his
30 people. Observe my charge, therefore, and follow none of the abominable
institutions customary before your time; do not make yourselves unclean
with them. I am the LORD your God.

19 1 2   THE LORD SPOKE TO MOSES and said, Speak to all the community of
the Israelites in these words: You shall be holy, because I, the LORD your

God, am holy. You shall revere, every man of you, his mother and his ₃
father. You shall keep my sabbaths. I am the LORD your God. Do not ₄
resort to idols; you shall not make gods of cast metal for yourselves. I am
the LORD your God.

When you sacrifice a shared-offering to the LORD, you shall slaughter it ₅
so as to win acceptance for yourselves. It must be eaten on the day of your ₆
sacrifice or the next day. Whatever is left over till the third day shall be
destroyed by fire; it is tainted, and if any of it is eaten on the third day, it ₇
will not be acceptable. He who eats it must accept responsibility, because ₈
he has profaned the holy-gift to the LORD: that person shall be cut off from
his father's kin.

When you reap the harvest of your land, you shall not reap right into the ₉
edges of your field; neither shall you glean the loose ears of your crop; you ₁₀
shall not completely strip your vineyard nor glean the fallen grapes. You
shall leave them for the poor and the alien. I am the LORD your God.

You shall not steal; you shall not cheat or deceive a fellow-countryman. ₁₁
You shall not swear in my name with intent to deceive and thus profane ₁₂
the name of your God. I am the LORD. You shall not oppress your neigh- ₁₃
bour, nor rob him. You shall not keep back a hired man's wages till next
morning. You shall not treat the deaf with contempt, nor put an obstruc- ₁₄
tion in the way of the blind. You shall fear your God. I am the LORD.

You shall not pervert justice, either by favouring the poor or by sub- ₁₅
servience to the great. You shall judge your fellow-countryman with strict
justice. You shall not go about spreading slander among your father's kin, ₁₆
nor take sides against your neighbour on a capital charge. I am the LORD.
You shall not nurse hatred against your brother. You shall reprove your ₁₇
fellow-countryman frankly and so you will have no share in his guilt.[a] You ₁₈
shall not seek revenge, or cherish anger towards your kinsfolk; you shall
love your neighbour as a man like yourself. I am the LORD.

You shall keep my rules. You shall not allow two different kinds of beast ₁₉
to mate together. You shall not plant your field with two kinds of seed.
You shall not put on a garment woven with two kinds of yarn.

When a man has intercourse with a slave-girl who has been assigned to ₂₀
another man and neither ransomed nor given her freedom, inquiry shall be
made. They shall not be put to death, because she has not been freed. The ₂₁
man shall bring his guilt-offering, a ram, to the LORD to the entrance of
the Tent of the Presence, and with it the priest shall make expiation for him ₂₂
before the LORD for his sin, and he shall be forgiven the sin he has committed.

When you enter the land, and plant any kind of tree for food, you shall ₂₃
treat it as bearing forbidden fruit. For three years it shall be forbidden and
may not be eaten. In the fourth year all its fruit shall be a holy-gift to the ₂₄
LORD, and this releases it for use. In the fifth year you may eat its fruit, and ₂₅
thus the yield it gives you shall be increased. I am the LORD your God.

You shall not eat meat with the blood in it. You shall not practise ₂₆
divination or soothsaying. You shall not round off your hair from side to ₂₇
side, and you shall not shave the edge of your beards. You shall not gash ₂₈

[a] *Or* and for that you will incur no blame.

yourselves in mourning for the dead; you shall not tattoo yourselves. I am the LORD.

29 30 Do not prostitute your daughter and so make her a whore; thus the land shall not play the prostitute and be full of lewdness. You shall keep my sabbaths, and revere my sanctuary. I am the LORD.

31 Do not resort to ghosts and spirits, nor make yourselves unclean by seeking them out. I am the LORD your God.

32 You shall rise in the presence of grey hairs, give honour to the aged, and fear your God. I am the LORD.

33 34 When an alien settles with you in your land, you shall not oppress him. He shall be treated as a native born among you, and you shall love him as a man like yourself, because you were aliens in Egypt. I am the LORD your God.

35 36 37 You shall not pervert justice in measurement of length, weight, or quantity. You shall have true scales, true weights, true measures dry and liquid. I am the LORD your God who brought you out of Egypt. You shall observe all my rules and laws and carry them out. I am the LORD.

20 1 2 The LORD spoke to Moses and said, Say to the Israelites: Any Israelite or alien settled in Israel who gives any of his children to Molech shall be 3 put to death: the common people shall stone him. I, for my part, set my face against that man and cut him off from his people, because he has given a child of his to Molech, thus making my sanctuary unclean and profaning 4 my holy name. If the common people connive at it when a man has given 5 a child of his to Molech and do not put him to death, I will set my face against man and family, and both him and all who follow him in his wanton following after Molech,^a I will cut off from their people.

6 I will set my face against the man who wantonly resorts to ghosts and 7 spirits, and I will cut that person off from his people. Hallow yourselves 8 and be holy, because I the LORD your God am holy. You shall keep my rules and obey them: I am the LORD who hallows you.

9 When any man reviles his father and his mother, he shall be put to death. He has reviled his father and his mother; his blood shall be on his own head. 10 If a man commits adultery with his neighbour's wife, both adulterer and 11 adulteress shall be put to death. The man who has intercourse with his father's wife has brought shame on his father. They shall both be put to 12 death; their blood shall be on their own heads. If a man has intercourse with his daughter-in-law, they shall both be put to death. Their deed is a 13 violation of nature; their blood shall be on their own heads. If a man has intercourse with a man as with a woman, they both commit an abomination. 14 They shall be put to death; their blood shall be on their own heads. If a man takes both a woman and her mother, that is lewdness. Both he and they 15 shall be burnt; thus there shall be no lewdness in your midst. A man who has sexual intercourse with any beast shall be put to death, and you shall 16 kill the beast. If a woman approaches any animal to have intercourse with it, you shall kill both woman and beast. They shall be put to death; their 17 blood shall be on their own heads. If a man takes his sister, his father's daughter or his mother's daughter, and they see one another naked, it is a scandalous disgrace. They shall be cut off in the presence of their people.

^a *Or* in his lusting after human sacrifice.

The man has had intercourse with his sister and he shall accept responsibility. If a man lies with a woman during her monthly period and brings 18 shame upon her, he has exposed her discharge and she has uncovered the source of her discharge; they shall both be cut off from their people. You 19 shall not have intercourse with your mother's sister or your father's sister: it is the exposure of a blood-relation. They shall accept responsibility. A 20 man who has intercourse with his uncle's wife has brought shame upon his uncle. They shall accept responsibility for their sin and shall be proscribed and put to death. If a man takes his brother's wife, it is impurity. He has 21 brought shame upon his brother; they shall be proscribed.

You shall keep all my rules and my laws and carry them out, that the 22 land into which I am bringing you to live may not spew you out. You shall 23 not conform to the institutions of the nations whom I am driving out before you: they did all these things and I abhorred them, and I told you 24 that you should occupy their land, and I would give you possession of it, a land flowing with milk and honey. I am the LORD your God: I have made a clear separation between you and the nations, and you shall make a clear 25 separation between clean beasts and unclean beasts and between unclean and clean birds. You shall not make yourselves vile through beast or bird or anything that creeps on the ground, for I have made a clear separation between them and you, declaring them unclean. You shall be holy to me, 26 because I the LORD am holy. I have made a clear separation between you and the heathen, that you may belong to me. Any man or woman among 27 you who calls up ghosts or spirits shall be put to death. The people shall stone them; their blood shall be on their own heads.

THE LORD SAID TO MOSES, Say to the priests, the sons of Aaron: A **21** priest shall not render himself unclean for the death of any of his kin except for a near blood-relation, that is for mother, father, son, daughter, 2 brother, or full sister who is unmarried and a virgin; nor shall he make 3 4 himself unclean for any married woman *a* among his father's kin, and so profane himself.

Priests shall not make bald patches on their heads as a sign of mourning, 5 nor cut the edges of their beards, nor gash their bodies. They shall be holy 6 to their God, and they shall not profane the name of their God, because they present the food-offerings of the LORD, the food of their God, and they shall be holy. A priest shall not marry a prostitute or a girl who has 7 lost her virginity, nor shall he marry a woman divorced from her husband; for he is holy to his God. You shall keep him holy because he presents the 8 food of your God; you shall regard him as holy because I the LORD, I who hallow them, am holy. When a priest's daughter profanes herself by becom- 9 ing a prostitute, she profanes her father. She shall be burnt to death.

The high priest, the one among his fellows who has had the anointing 10 oil poured on his head and has been consecrated to wear the vestments, shall neither leave his hair dishevelled nor tear his clothes. He shall not 11 enter the place where any man's dead body lies; not even for his father or his mother shall he render himself unclean. He shall not go out of the 12

a for any married woman: *prob. rdg.; Heb.* husband.

sanctuary for fear that he dishonour the sanctuary of his God, because the consecration of the anointing oil of his God is upon him. I am the LORD.

13 14 He shall marry a woman who is still a virgin. He shall not marry a widow, a divorced woman, a woman who has lost her virginity, or a prostitute, but
15 only a virgin from his father's kin; he shall not dishonour his descendants among his father's kin, for I am the LORD who hallows him.

16 17 The LORD spoke to Moses and said, Speak to Aaron in these words: No man among your descendants for all time who has any physical defect shall
18 come and present the food of his God. No man with a defect shall come,
19 whether a blind man, a lame man, a man stunted or overgrown, a man
20 deformed in foot or hand, or with mis-shapen brows or a film over his eye or a discharge from it, a man who has a scab or eruption or has had a testicle
21 ruptured. No descendant of Aaron the priest who has any defect in his body shall approach to present the food-offerings of the LORD; because
22 he has a defect he shall not approach to present the food of his God. He may eat the bread of God both from the holy-gifts and from the holiest
23 of holy-gifts, but he shall not come up to the Veil nor approach the altar, because he has a defect in his body. Thus he shall not profane my sanctuaries, because I am the LORD who hallows them.

24 Thus did Moses speak to Aaron and his sons and to all the Israelites.

22 1 2 The LORD spoke to Moses and said, Tell Aaron and his sons that they must be careful in the handling of the holy-gifts of the Israelites which they
3 hallow to me, lest they profane my holy name. I am the LORD. Say to them: Any man of your descent for all time who while unclean approaches the holy-gifts which the Israelites hallow to the LORD shall be cut off from my
4 presence. I am the LORD. No man descended from Aaron who suffers from a malignant skin-disease, or has a discharge, shall eat of the holy-gifts until he is cleansed. A man who touches anything which makes him unclean
5 or who has an emission of semen, a man who touches any vermin which
6 makes him unclean or any human being who makes him unclean: any person who touches such a thing shall be unclean till sunset and unless he
7 washes his body shall not eat of the holy-gifts. When the sun goes down, he shall be clean, and after that he may eat from the holy-gifts, because they
8 are his food. He shall not eat an animal that has died a natural death or has been mauled by wild beasts, thereby making himself unclean. I am the
9 LORD. The priests shall observe my charge, lest they make themselves guilty and die for profaning my name. I am the LORD who hallows them.
10 No unqualified person may eat any holy-gift; nor may a stranger lodging
11 with a priest or a hired man eat a holy-gift. A slave bought by a priest with his own money may do so, and slaves born in his household may also share
12 his food. When a priest's daughter marries an unqualified person, she shall
13 not eat any of the contributions of holy-gifts; but if she is widowed or divorced and is childless and comes back to her father's house as in her childhood, she shall share her father's food. No unqualified person may eat any of it.
14 When a man inadvertently eats a holy-gift, he shall make good the holy-
15 gift to the priest, adding a fifth to its value. The priests shall not profane
16 the holy-gifts of the Israelites which they set aside for the LORD; they shall

not let men eat their holy-gifts and so incur guilt and its penalty, because I am the LORD who hallows them.

The LORD spoke to Moses and said, Speak to Aaron and his sons and 17 18 to all the Israelites in these words: When any man of the house of Israel or any alien in Israel presents, whether in fulfilment of a vow or for a freewill offering, such an offering as is presented to the LORD for a whole-offering so as to win acceptance for yourselves, it shall be a male without 19 defect, of cattle, sheep, or goats. You shall not present anything which is 20 defective, because it will not be acceptable on your behalf. When a man 21 presents a shared-offering to the LORD, whether cattle or sheep, to fulfil a special*a* vow or as a freewill offering, if it is to be acceptable it must be perfect; there shall be no defect in it. You shall present to the LORD nothing 22 blind, disabled, mutilated, with running sore, scab, or eruption, nor set any such creature on the altar as a food-offering to the LORD. If a bull or a 23 sheep is overgrown or stunted, you may make of it a freewill offering, but it will not be acceptable in fulfilment of a vow. If its testicles have been 24 crushed or bruised, torn or cut, you shall not present it to the LORD; this is forbidden in your land.

You shall not procure any such creature from a foreigner and present it 25 as food for your God. Their deformity is inherent in them, a permanent defect, and they will not be acceptable on your behalf.

The LORD spoke to Moses and said: When a calf, a lamb, or a kid is born, 26 27 it must not be taken from its mother for seven days. From the eighth day onwards it will be acceptable when offered as a food-offering to the LORD. You shall not slaughter a cow or sheep at the same time as its young. When 28 29 you make a thank-offering to the LORD, you shall sacrifice it so as to win acceptance for yourselves; it shall be eaten that same day, and none be left 30 till morning. I am the LORD.

You shall observe my commandments and perform them. I am the LORD. 31 You shall not profane my holy name; I will be hallowed among the Israel- 32 ites. I am the LORD who hallows you, who brought you out of Egypt to 33 become your God. I am the LORD.

THE LORD SPOKE TO MOSES AND SAID, Speak to the Israelites in these 23 1 2 words: These are the appointed seasons of the LORD, and you shall pro-claim them as sacred assemblies; these are my appointed seasons. On six 3 days work may be done, but every seventh day is a sabbath of sacred rest, a day of sacred assembly, on which you shall do no work. Wherever you live, it is the LORD's sabbath.

These are the appointed seasons of the LORD, the sacred assemblies 4 which you shall proclaim in their appointed order. In the first month on 5 the fourteenth day between dusk and dark is the LORD's Passover. On the 6 fifteenth day of this month begins the LORD's pilgrim-feast of Unleavened Bread; for seven days you shall eat unleavened cakes. On the first day there 7 shall be a sacred assembly; you shall not do your daily work. For seven 8 days you shall present your food-offerings to the LORD. On the seventh day also there shall be a sacred assembly; you shall not do your daily work.

a fulfil a special: *or* discharge a . . .

9 10   The LORD spoke to Moses and said, Speak to the Israelites in these
words: When you enter the land which I give you, and you reap its harvest,
11 you shall bring the first sheaf of your harvest to the priest. He shall present
the sheaf as a special gift before the LORD on *a* the day after the sabbath, so
12 as to gain acceptance for yourselves. On the day you present the sheaf, you
13 shall prepare a perfect yearling ram for a whole-offering to the LORD, with
the proper grain-offering, two tenths of an ephah of flour mixed with oil,
as a food-offering to the LORD, of soothing odour, and also with the proper
14 drink-offering, a quarter of a hin of wine. You shall eat neither bread, nor
grain, parched or fully ripened, during that day, the day on which you bring
your God his offering; this is a rule binding on your descendants for all
time wherever you live.

15   From the day after the sabbath, the day on which you bring your sheaf
16 as a special gift, you shall count seven full weeks. The day after the seventh
sabbath will make fifty days, and then you shall present to the LORD a
17 grain-offering from the new crop. You shall bring from your homes two
loaves as a special gift; they shall contain two tenths of an ephah of flour
18 and shall be baked with leaven. They are the LORD's firstfruits. In addition
to the bread you shall present seven perfect yearling sheep, one young bull,
and two rams. They shall be a whole-offering to the LORD with the proper
grain-offering and the proper drink-offering, a food-offering of soothing
19 odour to the LORD. You shall also prepare one he-goat for a sin-offering
20 and two yearling sheep for a shared-offering, and the priest shall present
them in addition to the bread of the firstfruits as a special gift before the
21 LORD. They shall be a holy-gift to the LORD for the priest. On that same day
you shall proclaim a sacred assembly for yourselves; you shall not do your
daily work. This is a rule binding on your descendants for all time wherever
you live.

22   When you reap the harvest in your land, you shall not reap right into the
edges of your field, neither shall you glean the fallen ears. You shall leave
them for the poor and for the alien. I am the LORD your God.

23 24   The LORD spoke to Moses and said, Speak to the Israelites in these words:
In the seventh month you shall keep the first day as a sacred rest, a day of
25 remembrance and acclamation, a day of sacred assembly. You shall not
do your daily work; you shall present a food-offering to the LORD.

26 27   The LORD spoke to Moses and said: Further, the tenth day of this
seventh month is the Day of Atonement. There shall be a sacred assembly;
28 you shall mortify yourselves and present a food-offering to the LORD. On
that same day you shall do no work because it is a day of expiation, to make
29 expiation for you before the LORD your God. Therefore every person who
does not mortify himself on that day shall be cut off from his father's kin.
30 31 I will extirpate any person who does any work on that day. You shall do
no work; it is a rule binding on your descendants for all time wherever you
32 live. It is for you a sabbath of sacred rest, and you shall mortify yourselves.
From the evening of the ninth day to the following evening you shall keep
your sabbath-rest.

33 34   The LORD spoke to Moses and said, Speak to the Israelites in these

a Or from.

words: On the fifteenth day of this seventh month the LORD's pilgrim-feast of Tabernacles*ᵃ* begins, and it lasts for seven days. On the first day 35
there shall be a sacred assembly; you shall not do your daily work. For 36
seven days you shall present a food-offering to the LORD; and on the eighth
day there shall be a sacred assembly, and you shall present a food-offering
to the LORD. It is the closing ceremony; you shall not do your daily work.

These are the appointed seasons of the LORD which you shall proclaim 37
as sacred assemblies for presenting food-offerings to the LORD, whole-offerings and grain-offerings, shared-offerings and drink-offerings, each
on its day, besides the LORD's sabbaths and all your gifts, your vows, and 38
your freewill offerings to the LORD.

Further, from the fifteenth day of the seventh month, when the harvest 39
has been gathered, you shall keep the LORD's pilgrim-feast for seven days.
The first day is a sacred rest and so is the eighth day. On the first day you 40
shall take the fruit of citrus-trees, palm fronds, and leafy branches, and
willows *ᵇ* from the riverside, and you shall rejoice before the LORD your
God for seven days. You shall keep this as a pilgrim-feast in the LORD's 41
honour for seven days every year. It is a rule binding for all time on your
descendants; in the seventh month you shall hold this pilgrim-feast. You 42
shall live in arbours for seven days, all who are native Israelites, so that 43
your descendants may be reminded how I made the Israelites live in
arbours when I brought them out of Egypt. I am the LORD your God.

Thus Moses announced to the Israelites the appointed seasons of the 44
LORD.

THE LORD SPOKE TO MOSES and said: Command the Israelites to take **24** 1 2
pure oil of pounded olives ready for the regular mounting of the lamp
outside the Veil of the Tokens in the Tent of the Presence. Aaron shall 3
keep the lamp in trim regularly from dusk to dawn before the LORD: this
is a rule binding on your descendants for all time. The lamps on the lamp- 4
stand, ritually clean, shall be regularly kept in trim by him before the LORD.

You shall take flour and bake it into twelve loaves, two tenths of an ephah 5
to each. You shall arrange them in two rows, six to a row on the table, 6
ritually clean, before the LORD. You shall sprinkle pure frankincense on 7
the rows, and this shall be a token of the bread, offered to the LORD as a
food-offering. Sabbath after sabbath he shall arrange it regularly before 8
the LORD as a gift from the Israelites. This is a covenant for ever; it is the 9
privilege of Aaron and his sons, and they shall eat the bread in a holy place,
because it is the holiest of holy-gifts. It is his due out of the food-offerings
of the LORD for all time.

Now there was in the Israelite camp a man whose mother was an Israel- 10–11
ite and his father an Egyptian; his mother's name was Shelomith daughter
of Dibri of the tribe of Dan; and he went out and became involved in a
brawl with an Israelite of pure descent. He uttered the Holy Name in
blasphemy, so they brought him to Moses; and they kept him in custody 12
until the LORD's will should be clearly made known to them.

The LORD spoke to Moses and said, Take the man who blasphemed out 13 14

ᵃ Or Booths *or* Arbours.   *ᵇ Or* poplars.

of the camp. Everyone who heard him shall put a hand[a] on his head, and
15 then all the community shall stone him to death. You shall say to the
Israelites: When any man whatever blasphemes his God, he shall accept
16 responsibility for his sin. Whoever utters the Name of the LORD shall be
put to death: all the community shall stone him; alien or native, if he utters
the Name, he shall be put to death.

17 When one man strikes another and kills him, he shall be put to death.
18 Whoever strikes a beast and kills it shall make restitution, life for life.
19 When one man injures and disfigures his fellow-countryman, it shall be
20 done to him as he has done; fracture for fracture, eye for eye, tooth for
tooth; the injury and disfigurement that he has inflicted upon another
shall in turn be inflicted upon him.

21 Whoever strikes a beast and kills it shall make restitution, but whoever
22 strikes a man and kills him shall be put to death. You shall have one penalty
for alien and native alike. For I am the LORD your God.

23 Thus did Moses speak to the Israelites, and they took the man who
blasphemed out of the camp and stoned him to death. The Israelites did
as the LORD had commanded Moses.

25 1 2 THE LORD SPOKE TO MOSES on Mount Sinai and said, Speak to the
Israelites in these words: When you enter the land which I give you, the
3 land shall keep sabbaths to the LORD. For six years you may sow your
4 fields and for six years prune your vineyards and gather the harvest, but
in the seventh year the land shall keep a sabbath of sacred rest, a sabbath
5 to the LORD. You shall not sow your field nor prune your vineyard. You
shall not harvest the crop that grows from fallen grain, nor gather in the
grapes from the unpruned vines. It shall be a year of sacred rest for the
6 land. Yet what the land itself produces in the sabbath year shall be food
for you, for your male and female slaves, for your hired man, and for the
7 stranger lodging under your roof, for your cattle and for the wild animals
in your country. Everything it produces may be used for food.

8 You shall count seven sabbaths of years, that is seven times seven years,
9 forty-nine years, and in the seventh month on the tenth day of the month,
on the Day of Atonement, you shall send the ram's horn round. You shall
10 send it through all your land to sound a blast, and so you shall hallow the
fiftieth year and proclaim liberation in the land for all its inhabitants. You
shall make this your year of jubilee. Every man of you shall return to his
11 patrimony, every man to his family. The fiftieth year shall be your jubilee.
You shall not sow, and you shall not harvest the self-sown crop, nor shall
12 you gather in the grapes from the unpruned vines, because it is a jubilee,
to be kept holy by you. You shall eat the produce direct from the land.

13 In this year of jubilee you shall return, every one of you, to his patri-
14 mony. When you sell or buy land amongst yourselves, neither party shall
15 drive a hard bargain. You shall pay your fellow-countryman according to
the number of years since the jubilee, and he shall sell to you according
16 to the number of annual crops. The more years there are to run, the higher
the price, the fewer the years, the lower, because he is selling you a series

[a] *Or* their hands.

of crops. You must not victimize one another, but you shall fear your God, 17
because I am the LORD your God. Observe my statutes, keep my judgements 18
and carry them out; and you shall live in the land in security. The land 19
shall yield its harvest; you shall eat your fill and live there secure. If you 20
ask what you are to eat during the seventh year, seeing that you will neither
sow nor gather the harvest, I will ordain my blessing for you in the sixth 21
year and the land shall produce a crop to carry over three years. When you 22
sow in the eighth year, you will still be eating from the earlier crop; you
shall eat the old until the new crop is gathered in the ninth year.

No land shall be sold outright, because the land is mine, and you are 23
coming into it as aliens and settlers. Throughout the whole land of your 24
patrimony, you shall allow land which has been sold to be redeemed.

When one of you is reduced to poverty and sells part of his patrimony, 25
his next-of-kin who has the duty of redemption shall come and redeem
what his kinsman has sold. When a man has no such next-of-kin and him- 26
self becomes able to afford its redemption, he shall take into account the 27
years since the sale and pay the purchaser the balance up to the jubilee.
Then he may return to his patrimony. But if the man cannot afford to buy 28
back the property, it shall remain in the hands of the purchaser till the year
of jubilee. It shall then revert to the original owner, and he shall return to
his patrimony.

When a man sells a dwelling-house in a walled town, he shall retain the 29
right of redemption till the end of the year of the sale; for a time he shall
have the right of redemption. If it is not redeemed before a full year is out, 30
the house in the walled town shall vest in perpetuity in the buyer and his
descendants; it shall not revert at the jubilee. Houses in unwalled hamlets 31
shall be treated as property in the open country: the right of redemption
shall hold good, and in any case the house shall revert at the jubilee.
Levites shall have the perpetual right to redeem houses of their own patri- 32
mony in towns belonging to them. If one of the Levites does not redeem his 33
house in such a town, then it shall still revert to him at the jubilee, because
the houses in Levite towns are their patrimony in Israel. The common land 34
surrounding their towns shall not be sold, because it is their property in
perpetuity.

When your brother-Israelite is reduced to poverty and cannot support 35
himself in the community, you shall assist him as you would an alien or a
stranger, and he shall live with you. You shall not charge him interest on 36
a loan, either by deducting it in advance from the capital sum, or by adding
it on repayment. You shall fear your God, and your brother shall live with
you; you shall not deduct interest when advancing him money nor add 37
interest to the payment due for food supplied on credit. I am the LORD 38
your God who brought you out of Egypt to give you the land of Canaan
and to become your God.

When your brother is reduced to poverty and sells himself to you, you 39
shall not use him to work for you as a slave. His status shall be that of a 40
hired man or a stranger lodging with you; he shall work for you until the
year of jubilee. He shall then leave your service, with his children, and go 41
back to his family and to his ancestral property: because they are my slaves 42

43 whom I brought out of Egypt, they shall not be sold as slaves are sold. You
shall not drive him with ruthless severity, but you shall fear your God.
44 Such slaves as you have, male or female, shall come from the nations round
45 about you; from them you may buy slaves. You may also buy the children
of those who have settled and lodge with you and such of their family as
46 are born in the land. These may become your property, and you may leave
them to your sons after you; you may use them as slaves permanently. But
your fellow-Israelites you shall not drive with ruthless severity.

47 When an alien or a stranger living with you becomes rich, and your
brother becomes poor and sells himself to the alien or stranger or to a
48 member of some alien family, he shall have the right of redemption after
49 he has sold himself. One of his brothers may redeem him, or his uncle, his
cousin, or any blood-relation of his family, or, if he can afford it, he may
50 redeem himself. He and his purchaser together shall reckon from the year
when he sold himself to the year of jubilee, and the price shall be adjusted
to the number of years. His period of service with his owner shall be
51 reckoned at the rate of a hired man. If there are still many years to run to
the year of jubilee, he must repay for his redemption a proportionate
52 amount of the sum for which he sold himself; if there are few, he shall
53 reckon and repay accordingly. He shall have the status of a labourer hired
from year to year, and you shall not let him be driven with ruthless severity
54 by his owner. If the man is not redeemed in the intervening years, he and
55 his children shall be released in the year of jubilee; for it is to me that the
Israelites are slaves, my slaves whom I brought out of Egypt. I am the
LORD your God.

26 YOU SHALL NOT MAKE IDOLS for yourselves; you shall not erect a carved
image or a sacred pillar; you shall not put a figured stone on your land to
2 prostrate yourselves upon, because I am the LORD your God. You shall
keep my sabbaths and revere my sanctuary. I am the LORD.

3 If you conform to my statutes, if you observe my commandments and
4 carry them out, I will give you rain at the proper time; the land shall yield
5 its produce and the trees of the country-side their fruit. Threshing shall
last till vintage and vintage till sowing; you shall eat your fill and live
6 secure in your land. I will give peace in the land, and you shall lie down to
sleep with no one to terrify you. I will rid your land of dangerous beasts
7 and it shall not be ravaged by war. You shall put your enemies to flight and
8 they shall fall in battle before you. Five of you shall pursue a hundred and
a hundred of you ten thousand; so shall your enemies fall in battle before
9 you. I will look upon you with favour, I will make you fruitful and increase
10 your numbers: I will give my covenant with you its full effect. Your old
harvest shall last you in store until you have to clear out the old to make
11 room for the new. I will establish my Tabernacle among you and will not
12 spurn you. I will walk to and fro among you; I will become your God and
13 you shall become my people. I am the LORD your God who brought you
out of Egypt and let you be their slaves no longer; I broke the bars of your
yoke and enabled you to walk upright.
14 But if you do not listen to me, if you fail to keep all these commandments

of mine, if you reject my statutes, if you spurn my judgements, and do not 15
obey all my commandments, but break my covenant, then be sure that this 16
is what I will do: I will bring upon you sudden terror, wasting disease,
recurrent fever, and plagues that dim the sight and cause the appetite to
fail. You shall sow your seed to no purpose, for your enemies shall eat the
crop. I will set my face against you, and you shall be routed by your enemies. 17
Those that hate you shall hound you on until you run when there is no
pursuit.

If after all this you do not listen to me, I will go on to punish you seven 18
times over for your sins. I will break down your stubborn pride. I will make 19
the sky above you like iron and the earth beneath you like bronze. Your 20
strength shall be spent in vain; your land shall not yield its produce nor the
trees of the land their fruit.

If you still defy me and refuse to listen, I will multiply your calamities 21
seven times, as your sins deserve. I will send wild beasts among you; they 22
shall tear your children from you, destroy your cattle and bring your numbers low; and your roads shall be deserted. If after all this you have not 23
learnt discipline but still defy me, I in turn will defy you and scourge you 24
seven times over for your sins. I will bring war in vengeance upon you, 25
vengeance irrevocable under covenant; you shall be herded into your
cities, I will send pestilence among you, and you shall be given over to the
enemy. I will cut short your daily bread until ten women can bake your 26
bread in a single oven; they shall dole it out by weight, and though you eat,
you shall not be satisfied.

If in spite of this you do not listen to me and still defy me, I will defy 27 28
you in anger, and I myself will punish you seven times over for your sins.
Instead of meat you shall eat your sons and your daughters. I will destroy 29 30
your hill-shrines and demolish your incense-altars. I will pile your rotting
carcasses on the rotting logs*a* that were your idols, and I will spurn you.
I will make your cities desolate and destroy your sanctuaries; the soothing 31
odour of your offerings I will not accept. I will destroy your land, and the 32
enemies who occupy it shall be appalled. I will scatter you among the 33
heathen, and I will pursue you with the naked sword; your land shall be
desolate and your cities heaps of rubble. Then, all the time that it lies 34
desolate, while you are in exile in the land of your enemies, your land shall
enjoy its sabbaths to the full. All the time of its desolation it shall have the 35
sabbath rest which it did not have when you lived there. And I will make 36
those of you who are left in the land of your enemies so ridden with fear
that, when a leaf flutters behind them in the wind, they shall run as if it
were the sword behind them; they shall fall with no one in pursuit. Though 37
no one pursues them they shall stumble over one another, as if the sword
were behind them, and there shall be no stand made against the enemy.
You shall meet your end among the heathen, and your enemies' land shall 38
swallow you up. Those who are left shall pine away in an enemy land under 39
their own iniquities; and with their fathers' iniquities upon them too, they
shall pine away as they did.

But though they confess their iniquity, their own and their fathers', 40

a rotting logs: *or* effigies.

41 their treachery, and even their defiance of me, I will defy them in my turn
and carry them off into their enemies' land. Yet if then their stubborn
42 spirit is broken and they accept their punishment in full, I will remember
my covenant with Jacob and my covenant with Isaac, yes, and my covenant
43 with Abraham, and I will remember the land. The land shall be rid of its
people and enjoy in full its sabbaths while it lies desolate, and they shall
pay in full the penalty because they rejected my judgements and spurned
44 my statutes. Yet even then, in their enemies' land, I shall not have rejected
nor spurned them, bringing them to an end and so breaking my covenant
45 with them, because I am the LORD their God. I will remember on their
behalf the covenant with the men of former times whom I brought out of
Egypt in full sight of all the nations, that I might be their God. I am the
LORD.
46   These are the statutes, the judgements, and the laws which the LORD
established between himself and the Israelites on Mount Sinai through
Moses.

27 1 2 THE LORD SPOKE TO MOSES and said, Speak to the Israelites in these
words: When a man makes a special*a* vow to the LORD which requires
3 your valuation of living persons, a male between twenty and sixty years old
shall be valued at fifty silver shekels, that is shekels by the sacred standard.
4 5 If it is a female, she shall be valued at thirty shekels. If the person is between
five years old and twenty, the valuation shall be twenty shekels for a male
6 and ten for a female. If the person is between a month and five years old,
7 the valuation shall be five shekels for a male and three for a female. If the
person is over sixty and a male, the valuation shall be fifteen shekels, but
8 if a female, ten shekels. If the man is too poor to pay the amount of your
valuation, the person shall be set before the priest, and the priest shall
value him according to the sum which the man who makes the vow can
afford: the priest shall make the valuation.
9   If the vow concerns a beast such as may be offered as an offering to the
10 LORD, then every gift shall be holy to the LORD. He shall not change it for
another, or substitute good for bad or bad for good. But if a substitution is
in fact made of one beast for another, then both the original beast and its
11 substitute shall be holy to the LORD. If the vow concerns any unclean beast
such as may not be offered as an offering to the LORD, then the animal shall
12 be brought before the priest, and he shall value it whether good or bad. The
13 priest's valuation shall be decisive; in case of redemption the payment shall
be increased by one fifth.
14   When a man dedicates his house as holy to the LORD, the priest shall
value it whether good or bad, and the priest's valuation shall be decisive.
15 If the donor redeems his house, he shall pay the amount of the valuation
increased by one fifth, and the house shall be his.
16   If a man dedicates to the LORD part of his ancestral land, you shall value
it according to the amount of seed-corn it can carry, at the rate of fifty
17 shekels of silver for a homer of barley seed. If he dedicates his land from
18 the year of jubilee, it shall stand at your valuation; but if he dedicates it

———————
a makes a special: *or* discharges a . . .

after the year of jubilee, the priest shall estimate the price in silver according to the number of years remaining till the next year of jubilee, and this shall be deducted from your valuation. If the man who dedicates his field 19 should redeem it, he shall pay the amount of your valuation in silver, increased by one fifth, and it shall be his. If he does not redeem it but sells 20 the land to another man, it shall no longer be redeemable; when the land 21 reverts at the year of jubilee, it shall be like land that has been devoted, holy to the LORD. It shall belong to the priest as his patrimony.

If a man dedicates to the LORD land which he has bought, land which 22 is not part of his ancestral land, the priest shall estimate the amount of 23 the value for the period until the year of jubilee, and the man shall give the amount fixed as at that day; it is holy to the LORD. At the year of jubilee the 24 land shall revert to the man from whom he bought it, whose patrimony it is. Every valuation you make shall be made by the sacred standard (twenty 25 gerahs to the shekel).

Notwithstanding, no man may dedicate to the LORD the first-born of a 26 beast which in any case has to be offered as a first-born, whether an ox or a sheep. It is the LORD's. If it is any unclean beast, he may redeem it at 27 your valuation and shall add one fifth; but if it is not redeemed, it shall be sold at your valuation. Notwithstanding, nothing which a man devotes to 28 the LORD irredeemably from his own property, whether man or beast or ancestral land, may be sold or redeemed. Everything so devoted is most holy to the LORD. No human being thus devoted may be redeemed, but he 29 shall be put to death.

Every tithe on land, whether from grain or from the fruit of a tree, 30 belongs to the LORD; it is holy to the LORD. If a man wishes to redeem any 31 of his tithe, he shall pay its value increased by one fifth. Every tenth creature 32 that passes under the counting rod shall be holy to the LORD; this applies to all tithes of cattle and sheep. There shall be no inquiry whether it is good 33 or bad, and no substitution. If any ·substitution is made, then both the tithe-animal and its substitute shall be forfeit as holy; it shall not be redeemed.

These are the commandments which the LORD gave Moses for the 34 Israelites on Mount Sinai.

NUMBERS

Israel in the wilderness of Sinai

1 ON THE FIRST DAY OF THE SECOND MONTH in
the second year after the Israelites came out of Egypt, the LORD
spoke to Moses at the Tent of the Presence in the wilderness of
2 Sinai in these words: 'Number the whole community of Israel by families
3 in the father's line, recording the name of every male person aged twenty
years and upwards fit for military service. You and Aaron are to make a
4 detailed list of them by their tribal hosts, and you shall have to assist you
5 one head of family from each tribe. These are their names:

    of Reuben, Elizur son of Shedeur;
6   of Simeon, Shelumiel son of Zurishaddai;
7   of Judah, Nahshon son of Amminadab;
8   of Issachar, Nethaneel son of Zuar;
9   of Zebulun, Eliab son of Helon;
10   of Joseph: of Ephraim, Elishama son of Ammihud;
              of Manasseh, Gamaliel son of Pedahzur;
11   of Benjamin, Abidan son of Gideoni;
12   of Dan, Ahiezer son of Ammishaddai;
13   of Asher, Pagiel son of Ocran;
14   of Gad, Eliasaph son of Reuel;
15   of Naphtali, Ahira son of Enan.'

16 These were the conveners of the whole community, chiefs of their fathers'
17 tribes and heads of Israelite clans. So Moses and Aaron took these men who
18 had been indicated by name. They summoned the whole community on
the first day of the second month, and they registered their descent by
families in the father's line, recording every male person aged twenty years
19 and upwards, as the LORD had told Moses to do. Thus it was that he drew
up the detailed lists in the wilderness of Sinai:
20   The tribal list of Reuben, Israel's eldest son, by families in the father's
line, with the name of every male person aged twenty years and upwards
21 fit for service, the number in the list of the tribe of Reuben being forty-six
thousand five hundred.
22   The tribal list of Simeon, by families in the father's line, with the name
23 of every male person aged twenty years and upwards fit for service, the
number in the list of the tribe of Simeon being fifty-nine thousand three
hundred.
24   The tribal list of Gad, by families in the father's line, with the names
25 of all men aged twenty years and upwards fit for service, the number
in the list of the tribe of Gad being forty-five thousand six hundred and
fifty.

The tribal list of Judah, by families in the father's line, with the names of 26
all men aged twenty years and upwards fit for service, the number in the 27
list of the tribe of Judah being seventy-four thousand six hundred.

The tribal list of Issachar, by families in the father's line, with the names 28
of all men aged twenty years and upwards fit for service, the number in 29
the list of the tribe of Issachar being fifty-four thousand four hundred.

The tribal list of Zebulun, by families in the father's line, with the names 30
of all men aged twenty years and upwards fit for service, the number in the 31
list of the tribe of Zebulun being fifty-seven thousand four hundred.

The tribal lists of Joseph: that of Ephraim, by families in the father's 32
line, with the names of all men aged twenty years and upwards fit for
service, the number in the list of the tribe of Ephraim being forty thousand 33
five hundred; that of Manasseh, by families in the father's line, with the 34
names of all men aged twenty years and upwards fit for service, the num- 35
ber in the list of the tribe of Manasseh being thirty-two thousand two
hundred.

The tribal list of Benjamin, by families in the father's line, with the 36
names of all men aged twenty years and upwards fit for service, the number 37
in the list of the tribe of Benjamin being thirty-five thousand four hundred.

The tribal list of Dan, by families in the father's line, with the names of 38
all men aged twenty years and upwards fit for service, the number in the 39
list of the tribe of Dan being sixty-two thousand seven hundred.

The tribal list of Asher, by families in the father's line, with the names 40
of all men aged twenty years and upwards fit for service, the number in the 41
list of the tribe of Asher being forty-one thousand five hundred.

The tribal list of Naphtali, by families in the father's line, with the names 42
of all men aged twenty years and upwards fit for service, the number in the 43
list of the tribe of Naphtali being fifty-three thousand four hundred.

These were the numbers recorded in the detailed lists by Moses and 44
Aaron and the twelve chiefs of Israel, each representing one tribe and being
the head of a family. The total number of Israelites aged twenty years and 45
upwards fit for service, recorded in the lists of fathers' families, was six 46
hundred and three thousand five hundred and fifty. A list of the Levites 47
by their fathers' families was not made.

The Lord spoke to Moses and said, 'You shall not record the total 48 49
number of the Levites or make a detailed list of them among the Israelites.
You shall put the Levites in charge of the Tabernacle of the Tokens, with 50
its equipment and everything in it. They shall carry the Tabernacle and
all its equipment; they alone shall be its attendants and shall pitch their
tents round it. The Levites shall take the Tabernacle down when it is due 51
to move and shall put it up when it halts; any unqualified person who
comes near it shall be put to death. All other Israelites shall pitch their 52
tents, each tribal host in its proper camp and under its own standard. But 53
the Levites shall encamp round the Tabernacle of the Tokens, so that
divine wrath may not follow the whole community of Israel; the Tabernacle of the Tokens shall be in their keeping.'

The Israelites did exactly as the Lord had told Moses to do. 54

The Lord spoke to Moses and Aaron and said, 'The Israelites shall **2** 1 2 encamp each under his own standard by the emblems of his father's family; they shall pitch their tents round the Tent of the Presence, facing it.

3 'In front of it, on the east, the division of Judah shall be stationed under the standard of its camp by tribal hosts. The chief of Judah shall be Nahshon
4 son of Amminadab. His host, with its members as detailed, numbers
5 seventy-four thousand six hundred men. Next to Judah the tribe of
6 Issachar shall be stationed. Its chief shall be Nethaneel son of Zuar; his host, with its members as detailed, numbers fifty-four thousand four
7 hundred. Then the tribe of Zebulun: its chief shall be Eliab son of Helon;
8 his host, with its members as detailed, numbers fifty-seven thousand four
9 hundred. The number listed in the camp of Judah, by hosts, is one hundred and eighty-six thousand four hundred. They shall be the first to march.

10 'To the south the division of Reuben shall be stationed under the standard of its camp by tribal hosts. The chief of Reuben shall be Elizur son
11 of Shedeur; his host, with its members as detailed, numbers forty-six
12 thousand five hundred. Next to him the tribe of Simeon shall be stationed.
13 Its chief shall be Shelumiel son of Zurishaddai; his host, with its members
14 as detailed, numbers fifty-nine thousand three hundred. Then the tribe
15 of Gad: its chief shall be Eliasaph son of Reuel; his host, with its members
16 as detailed, numbers forty-five thousand six hundred and fifty. The number listed in the camp of Reuben, by hosts, is one hundred and fifty-one thousand four hundred and fifty. They shall be the second to march.

17 'When the Tent of the Presence moves, the camp of the Levites shall keep its station in the centre of the other camps; they shall all move in the order of their encamping, each man in his proper place under his standard.

18 'To the west the division of Ephraim shall be stationed under the standard of its camp by tribal hosts. The chief of Ephraim shall be Elishama
19 son of Ammihud; his host, with its members as detailed, numbers
20 forty thousand five hundred. Next to him the tribe of Manasseh shall be
21 stationed. Its chief shall be Gamaliel son of Pedahzur; his host, with its
22 members as detailed, numbers thirty-two thousand two hundred. Then
23 the tribe of Benjamin: its chief shall be Abidan son of Gideoni; his host, with its members as detailed, numbers thirty-five thousand four hundred.
24 The number listed in the camp of Ephraim, by hosts, is one hundred and eight thousand one hundred. They shall be the third to march.

25 'To the north the division of Dan shall be stationed under the standard of its camp by tribal hosts. The chief of Dan shall be Ahiezer son of
26 Ammishaddai; his host, with its members as detailed, numbers sixty-two
27 thousand seven hundred. Next to him the tribe of Asher shall be stationed.
28 Its chief shall be Pagiel son of Ocran; his host, with its members as detailed,
29 numbers forty-one thousand five hundred. Then the tribe of Naphtali: its
30 chief shall be Ahira son of Enan; his host, with its members as detailed,
31 numbers fifty-three thousand four hundred. The number listed in the camp of Dan is a hundred and fifty-seven thousand six hundred. They shall march, under their standards, last.'

32 These were the Israelites listed by their fathers' families. The total number in the camp, recorded by tribal hosts, was six hundred and three thousand five hundred and fifty.

The Levites were not included in the detailed lists with their fellow-Israelites, for so the LORD had commanded Moses. The Israelites did exactly as the LORD had commanded Moses, pitching and breaking camp standard by standard, each man according to his family in his father's line. 33 34

THESE WERE THE DESCENDANTS OF AARON and Moses at the time when the LORD spoke to Moses on Mount Sinai. The names of the sons of Aaron were Nadab the eldest, Abihu, Eleazar and Ithamar. These were the names of Aaron's sons, the anointed priests who had been installed in the priestly office. Nadab and Abihu fell dead before the LORD because they had presented illicit fire before the LORD in the wilderness of Sinai. They left no sons; Eleazar and Ithamar continued to perform the priestly office in their father's presence. 3 2 3 4

The LORD spoke to Moses and said, 'Bring forward the tribe of Levi and appoint them to serve Aaron the priest and to minister to him. They shall be in attendance on him and on the whole community before the Tent of the Presence, undertaking the service of the Tabernacle. They shall be in charge of all the equipment in the Tent of the Presence, and be in attendance on the Israelites, undertaking the service of the Tabernacle. You shall assign the Levites to Aaron and his sons as especially dedicated to him out of all the Israelites. To Aaron and his line you shall commit the priestly office and they shall perform its duties; any unqualified person who intrudes upon it shall be put to death.' 5 6 7 8 9 10

The LORD spoke to Moses and said, 'I take the Levites for myself out of all the Israelites as a substitute for the eldest male child of every woman; the Levites shall be mine. For every eldest child, if a boy, became mine when I destroyed all the eldest sons in Egypt. So I have consecrated to myself all the first-born in Israel, both man and beast. They shall be mine. I am the LORD.' 11 12 13

The LORD spoke to Moses in the wilderness of Sinai and said, 'Make a detailed list of all the Levites by their families in the father's line, every male from the age of one month and upwards.' 14 15

Moses made a detailed list of them in accordance with the command given him by the LORD. Now these were the names of the sons of Levi: 16 17

Gershon, Kohath and Merari.

Descendants of Gershon, by families: Libni and Shimei. 18

Descendants of Kohath, by families: Amram, Izhar, Hebron and Uzziel. 19

Descendants of Merari, by families: Mahli and Mushi. 20

These were the families of Levi, by fathers' families:

Gershon: the family of Libni and the family of Shimei. These were the families of Gershon, and the number of males in their list as detailed, from the age of one month and upwards, was seven thousand five hundred. The families of Gershon were stationed on the west, behind the Tabernacle. Their chief was Eliasaph son of Lael, and in the service of the Tent of the Presence they were in charge of the Tabernacle and its coverings, of the screen at the entrance to the Tent of the Presence, the hangings of the court, 21 22 23 24 25 26 the screen at the entrance to the court all round the Tabernacle and the altar, and of all else needed for its maintenance.

27 28 29 Kohath: the family of Amram, the family of Izhar, the family of Hebron, the family of Uzziel. These were the families of Kohath, and the number of males, from the age of one month and upwards, was eight thousand six hundred. They were the guardians of the holy things. The families of Kohath were stationed on the south, at the side of the Tabernacle. 30 31 Their chief was Elizaphan son of Uzziel; they were in charge of the Ark, the table, the lamp-stands and the altars, together with the sacred vessels used in their service, and the screen with everything needed for its 32 maintenance. The chief over all the chiefs of the Levites was Eleazar son of Aaron the priest, who was appointed overseer of those in charge of the sanctuary.

33 34 35 Merari: the family of Mahli, the family of Mushi. These were the families of Merari, and the number of males in their list as detailed from the age of one month and upwards was six thousand two hundred. Their chief was Zuriel son of Abihail; they were stationed on the north, at the 36 side of the Tabernacle. The Merarites were in charge of the planks, bars, posts, and sockets of the Tabernacle, together with its vessels and all the 37 equipment needed for its maintenance, the posts, sockets, pegs, and cords of the surrounding court.

38 In front of the Tabernacle on the east, Moses was stationed, with Aaron and his sons, in front of the Tent of the Presence eastwards. They were in charge of the sanctuary on behalf of the Israelites; any unqualified person who came near would be put to death.

39 The number of Levites recorded by Moses on the detailed list by families at the command of the LORD was twenty-two thousand males aged one month and upwards.

40 The LORD said to Moses, 'Make a detailed list of all the male first-born in Israel aged one month and upwards, and count the number of persons. 41 You shall reserve the Levites for me—I am the LORD—in substitution for the eldest sons of the Israelites, and in the same way the Levites' cattle in 42 substitution for the first-born cattle of the Israelites.' As the LORD had told 43 him to do, Moses made a list of all the eldest sons of the Israelites, and the total number of first-born males recorded by name in the register, aged one month and upwards, was twenty-two thousand two hundred and seventy-three.

44 45 The LORD spoke to Moses and said, 'Take the Levites as a substitute for all the eldest sons in Israel and the cattle of the Levites as a substitute 46 for their cattle. The Levites shall be mine. I am the LORD. The eldest sons in Israel will outnumber the Levites by two hundred and seventy-three. 47 This remainder must be ransomed, and you shall accept five shekels for each of them, taking the sacred shekel and reckoning twenty gerahs to the 48 shekel; you shall give the money with which they are ransomed to Aaron and his sons.'

49 Moses took the money paid as ransom for those who remained over when 50 the substitution of Levites was complete. The amount received was one thousand three hundred and sixty-five shekels of silver by the sacred

standard. In accordance with what the LORD had said, he gave the money 51
to Aaron and his sons, doing what the LORD had told him to do.

The LORD spoke to Moses and Aaron and said, 'Among the Levites, **4** 1 2
make a count of the descendants of Kohath between the ages of thirty and 3
fifty, by families in the father's line, comprising everyone who comes to
take duty in the service of the Tent of the Presence.

'This is the service to be rendered by the Kohathites in the Tent of the 4
Presence; it is most sacred. When the camp is due to move, Aaron and his 5
sons shall come and take down the Veil of the screen and cover the Ark of
the Tokens with it; over this they shall put a covering of porpoise-hide *a* 6
and over that again a violet cloth all of one piece; they shall then put its
poles in place. Over the Table of the Presence they shall spread a violet 7
cloth and lay on it the dishes, saucers, and flagons, and the bowls for drink-
offerings; the Bread regularly presented shall also lie upon it; then they 8
shall spread over them a scarlet cloth and over that a covering of porpoise-
hide, and put the poles in place. They shall take a violet cloth and cover 9
the lamp-stand, its lamps, tongs, firepans, and all the containers for the
oil used in its service; they shall put it with all its equipment in a sheet of 10
porpoise-hide slung from a pole. Over the gold altar they shall spread a 11
violet cloth, cover it with a porpoise-hide covering, and put its poles in
place. They shall take all the articles used for the service of the sanctuary, 12
put them on a violet cloth, cover them with a porpoise-hide covering, and
sling them from a pole. They shall clear the altar of the fat and ashes, spread 13
a purple cloth over it, and then lay on it all the equipment used in its service, 14
the firepans, forks, shovels, tossing-bowls, and all the equipment of the
altar, spread a covering of porpoise-hide over it and put the poles in place.
Once Aaron and his sons have finished covering the sanctuary and all the 15
sacred equipment, when the camp is due to move, the Kohathites shall
come to carry it; they must not touch it on pain of death. All these things
are the load to be carried by the Kohathites, the things connected with the
Tent of the Presence. Eleazar son of Aaron the priest shall have charge of 16
the lamp-oil, the fragrant incense, the regular grain-offering, and the
anointing oil, with the general oversight of the whole Tabernacle and its
contents, the sanctuary and its equipment.'

The LORD spoke to Moses and Aaron and said, 'You must not let the 17 18
families of Kohath be extirpated, and lost to the tribe of Levi. If they are 19
to live and not die when they approach the most holy things, this is what
you must do: Aaron and his sons shall come and set each man to his
appointed task and to his load, and the Kohathites themselves shall not 20
enter to cast even a passing glance on the sanctuary, on pain of death.'

The LORD spoke to Moses and said, 'Number the Gershonites by 21 22
families in the father's line. Make a detailed list of all those between the 23
ages of thirty and fifty who come on duty to perform service in the Tent
of the Presence.

'This is the service to be rendered by the Gershonite families, comprising 24
their general duty and their loads. They shall carry the hangings of the 25
Tabernacle, the Tent of the Presence, its covering, that is the covering of

---

a *Strictly* hide of sea-cow.

26 porpoise-hide which is over it, the screen at the entrance to the Tent of the Presence, the hangings of the court, the screen at the entrance to the court surrounding the Tabernacle and the altar, their cords and all the equipment for their service; and they shall perform all the tasks connected

27 with them. These are the acts of service they shall render. All the service of the Gershonites, their loads and their other duties, shall be directed by Aaron and his sons; you shall assign them the loads for which they shall be

28 responsible. This is the service assigned to the Gershonite families in connection with the Tent of the Presence; Ithamar son of Aaron shall be in charge of them.

29 'You shall make a detailed list of the Merarites by families in the father's
30 line, all those between the ages of thirty and fifty, who come on duty to perform service in the Tent of the Presence.

31 'These are the loads for which they shall be responsible in virtue of their service in the Tent of the Presence: the planks of the Tabernacle with its

32 bars, posts, and sockets, the posts of the surrounding court with their sockets, pegs, and cords, and all that is needed for the maintenance of them; you shall assign to each man by name the load for which he is responsible.

33 These are the duties of the Merarite families in virtue of their service in the Tent of the Presence. Ithamar son of Aaron the priest shall be in charge of them.'

34 Moses and Aaron and the chiefs of the community made a detailed list
35 of the Kohathites by families in the father's line, taking all between the ages of thirty and fifty who came on duty to perform service in the Tent

36 of the Presence. The number recorded by families in the detailed lists was
37 two thousand seven hundred and fifty. This was the total number in the detailed lists of the Kohathite families who did duty in the Tent of the Presence; they were recorded by Moses and Aaron as the LORD had told them to do through Moses.

38-39 The Gershonites between the ages of thirty and fifty, who came on duty for service in the Tent of the Presence, were recorded in detailed lists by
40 families in the father's line. Their number, by families in the father's line,
41 was two thousand six hundred and thirty. This was the total recorded in the lists of the Gershonite families who came on duty in the Tent of the Presence, and were recorded by Moses and Aaron as the LORD had told them to do.

42-43 The families of Merari, between the ages of thirty and fifty, who came on duty to perform service in the Tent of the Presence, were recorded
44 in detailed lists by families in the father's line. Their number by families
45 was three thousand two hundred. These were recorded in the Merarite families by Moses and Aaron as the LORD had told them to do through Moses.

46 Thus Moses and Aaron and the chiefs of Israel made a detailed list of all
47 the Levites by families in the father's line, between the ages of thirty and fifty years; these were all who came to perform their various duties and

48 carry their loads in the service of the Tent of the Presence. Their number
49 was eight thousand five hundred and eighty. They were recorded one by one by Moses at the command of the LORD, according to their

general duty and the loads they carried.^a For so the LORD had told Moses to do.

THE LORD SPOKE TO MOSES and said: Command the Israelites to expel **5** 1 2 from the camp everyone who suffers from a malignant skin-disease or a discharge, and everyone ritually unclean from contact with a corpse. You 3 shall put them outside the camp, both male and female, so that they will not defile your camps in which I dwell among you. The Israelites did this: 4 they put them outside the camp. As the LORD had said when he spoke to Moses, so the Israelites did.

The LORD spoke to Moses and said, Say to the Israelites: When anyone, 5 6 man or woman, wrongs another and thereby breaks faith with the LORD, that person has incurred guilt which demands reparation. He shall confess 7 the sin he has committed, make restitution in full with the addition of one fifth, and give it to the man to whom compensation is due. If there is no 8 next-of-kin to whom compensation can be paid, the compensation payable in that case shall be the LORD's, for the use of the priest, in addition to the ram of expiation with which the priest makes expiation for him.

Every contribution made by way of holy-gift which the Israelites bring 9 to the priest shall be the priest's. The priest shall have the holy-gifts which 10 a man gives; whatever is given to him shall be his.

The LORD spoke to Moses and said, Speak to the Israelites in these 11 12 words: When a married woman goes astray, is unfaithful to her husband, and has sexual intercourse with another man, and this happens without 13 the husband's knowledge, and the crime is undetected, because, though she has been defiled, there is no direct evidence against her and she was not caught in the act, but when in such a case a fit of jealousy comes over 14 the husband which causes him to suspect his wife, she being in fact defiled; or when, on the other hand, a fit of jealousy comes over a husband which causes him to suspect his wife, when she is not in fact defiled; then in either 15 case, the husband shall bring his wife to the priest together with the pre-scribed offering for her, a tenth of an ephah of barley meal. He shall not pour oil on it nor put frankincense on it, because it is a grain-offering for jealousy, a grain-offering of protestation conveying an imputation of guilt. The priest shall bring her forward and set her before the LORD. He shall 16 17 take clean^b water in an earthenware vessel, and shall take dust from the floor of the Tabernacle and add it to the water. He shall set the woman 18 before the LORD, uncover her head, and place the grain-offering of pro-testation in her hands; it is a grain-offering for jealousy. The priest shall hold in his own hand the water of contention which brings out the truth. He shall then put the woman on oath and say to her, 'If no man has had 19 intercourse with you, if you have not gone astray and let yourself become defiled while owing obedience to your husband, then may your innocence be established by the water of contention which brings out the truth. But 20 if, while owing him obedience, you have gone astray and let yourself become defiled, if any man other than your husband has had intercourse with you' (the priest shall here put the woman on oath with an adjuration, 21

<hr>

^a *Prob. rdg.; Heb. adds* and his registered ones.   ^b *Or* holy.

and shall continue), 'may the LORD make an example of you among your
people in adjurations and in swearing of oaths by bringing upon you mis-
22 carriage and untimely birth; and this water that brings out the truth shall
enter your body, bringing upon you miscarriage and untimely birth.' The
23 woman shall respond, 'Amen, Amen.' The priest shall write these curses
24 on a scroll and wash them off into the water of contention; he shall make
the woman drink the water that brings out the truth, and the water shall
25 enter her body. The priest shall take the grain-offering for jealousy from
the woman's hand, present it as a special gift before the LORD, and offer it
26 at the altar. He shall take a handful from the grain-offering by way of token,
and burn it at the altar; after this he shall make the woman drink the water.
27 If she has let herself become defiled and has been unfaithful to her husband,
then when the priest makes her drink the water that brings out the truth
and the water has entered her body, she will suffer a miscarriage or untimely birth, and her name will become an example in adjuration among
28 her kin. But if the woman has not let herself become defiled and is pure,
then her innocence is established and she will bear her child.

29 Such is the law for cases of jealousy, where a woman, owing obedience
30 to her husband, goes astray and lets herself become defiled, or where a fit
of jealousy comes over a man which causes him to suspect his wife. He
shall set her before the LORD, and the priest shall deal with her as this law
31 prescribes. No guilt will attach to the husband, but the woman shall bear
the penalty of her guilt.

6 1 2 The LORD spoke to Moses and said, Speak to the Israelites in these
words: When anyone, man or woman, makes a special[a] vow dedicating
3 himself to the LORD as a Nazirite,[b] he shall abstain from wine and strong
drink. These he shall not drink, nor anything made from the juice of grapes;
4 nor shall he eat grapes, fresh or dried. During the whole term of his vow
he shall eat nothing that comes from the vine, nothing whatever, shoot or
5 berry. During the whole term of his vow no razor shall touch his head; he
shall let his hair grow long and plait it until he has completed the term of
6 his dedication: he shall keep himself holy to the LORD. During the whole
7 term of his vow he shall not go near a corpse, not even when his father or
mother, brother or sister, dies; he shall not make himself ritually unclean
8 for them, because the Nazirite vow to his God is on his head. He shall keep
himself holy to the LORD during the whole term of his Nazirite vow.

9 If someone suddenly falls dead by his side touching him and thereby
making his hair, which has been dedicated, ritually unclean, he shall shave
10 his head seven days later, on the day appointed for his ritual cleansing. On
the eighth day he shall bring two turtle-doves or two young pigeons to the
11 priest at the entrance to the Tent of the Presence. The priest shall offer one
as a sin-offering and the other as a whole-offering and shall make expiation
for him for the sin he has incurred through contact with the dead body;
12 and he shall consecrate his head afresh on that day. The man shall re-
dedicate himself to the LORD for the term of his vow and bring a yearling
ram as a guilt-offering. The previous period shall not be reckoned, because
the hair which he dedicated became unclean.

[a] makes a special: *or* performs a . . .   [b] *That is* separated one *or* dedicated one.

The law for the Nazirite, when the term of his dedication is completed, 13
shall be this. He shall be brought to the entrance to the Tent of the Presence
and shall present his offering to the LORD: one yearling ram without blemish 14
as a whole-offering, one yearling ewe without blemish as a sin-offering, one
ram without blemish as a shared-offering, and a basket of cakes made of 15
flour mixed with oil, and of wafers smeared with oil, both unleavened,
together with the proper grain-offerings and drink-offerings. The priest 16
shall present all these before the LORD and offer the man's sin-offering
and whole-offering; the ram he shall offer as a shared-offering to the 17
LORD, together with the basket of unleavened cakes and the proper grain-
offering and drink-offering. The Nazirite shall shave his head at the 18
entrance to the Tent of the Presence, take the hair which had been dedicated
and put it on the fire where the shared-offering is burning. The priest shall 19
take the shoulder of the ram, after boiling it, and take also one unleavened
cake from the basket and one unleavened wafer, and put them on the palms
of the Nazirite's hands, his hair which had been dedicated having been
shaved. The priest shall then present them as a special gift before the LORD; 20
these, together with the breast of the special gift and the leg of the contribution, are holy and belong to the priest. When this has been done, the
Nazirite is again free to drink wine.

Such is the law for the Nazirite who has made his vow. Such is the 21
offering he must make to the LORD for his dedication, apart from anything
else that he can afford. He must carry out his vow in full according to the
law governing his dedication.

The LORD spoke to Moses and said, Speak to Aaron and his sons in these 22 23
words: These are the words with which you shall bless the Israelites:

> The LORD bless you and watch over you; 24
> the LORD make his face shine upon*a* you 25
>   and be gracious to you;
> the LORD look kindly on you and give you peace. 26

They shall pronounce my name over the Israelites, and I will bless them. 27

ON THE DAY THAT MOSES COMPLETED the setting up of the Taber- 7
nacle, he anointed and consecrated it; he also anointed and consecrated
its equipment, and the altar and its vessels. The chief men of Israel, heads 2
of families—that is the chiefs of the tribes, who had assisted in preparing
the detailed lists—came forward and brought their offering before the 3
LORD, six covered wagons and twelve oxen, one wagon from every two
chiefs and from each one an ox.*b* These they brought forward before the
Tabernacle; and the LORD spoke to Moses and said, 'Accept these from 4 5
them: they shall be used for the service of the Tent of the Presence. Assign
them to the Levites as their several duties require.'

So Moses accepted the wagons and oxen and assigned them to the 6
Levites. He gave two wagons and four oxen to the Gershonites as required 7
for their service; four wagons and eight oxen to the Merarites as required 8
for their service, in charge of Ithamar the son of Aaron the priest. He gave 9

---

a Or to.   *b* Or a bull.

none to the Kohathites because the service laid upon them was that of the holy things: these they had to carry themselves on their shoulders.

10 When the altar was anointed, the chiefs brought their gift for its dedica-
11 tion and presented their offering before it. The LORD said to Moses, 'Let the chiefs present their offering for the dedication of the altar one by one, on consecutive days.'

12 The chief who presented his offering on the first day was Nahshon son
13 of Amminadab of the tribe of Judah. His offering was one silver dish weigh-ing a hundred and thirty shekels by the sacred standard and one silver tossing-bowl weighing seventy, both full of flour mixed with oil as a grain-
14 15 offering; one saucer weighing ten gold shekels, full of incense; one young
16 bull, one full-grown ram, and one yearling ram, as a whole-offering; one
17 he-goat as a sin-offering; and two bulls, five full-grown rams, five he-goats, and five yearling rams, as a shared-offering. This was the offering of Nahshon son of Amminadab.

18 On the second day Nethaneel son of Zuar, chief of Issachar, brought his
19 offering. He brought one silver dish weighing a hundred and thirty shekels by the sacred standard and one silver tossing-bowl weighing seventy, both
20 full of flour mixed with oil as a grain-offering; one saucer weighing ten
21 gold shekels, full of incense; one young bull, one full-grown ram, and one
22 23 yearling ram, as a whole-offering; one he-goat as a sin-offering; and two bulls, five full-grown rams, five he-goats, and five yearling rams, as a shared-offering. This was the offering of Nethaneel son of Zuar.

24 On the third day the chief of the Zebulunites, Eliab son of Helon, came.
25 His offering was one silver dish weighing a hundred and thirty shekels by the sacred standard and one silver tossing-bowl weighing seventy, both full
26 of flour mixed with oil as a grain-offering; one saucer weighing ten gold
27 shekels, full of incense; one young bull, one full-grown ram, and one year-
28 29 ling ram, as a whole-offering; one he-goat as a sin-offering; and two bulls, five full-grown rams, five he-goats, and five yearling rams, as a shared-offering. This was the offering of Eliab son of Helon.

30 On the fourth day the chief of the Reubenites, Elizur son of Shedeur,
31 came. His offering was one silver dish weighing a hundred and thirty shekels by the sacred standard and one silver tossing-bowl weighing
32 seventy, both full of flour mixed with oil as a grain-offering; one saucer
33 weighing ten gold shekels, full of incense; one young bull, one full-grown
34 ram, and one yearling ram, as a whole-offering; one he-goat as a sin-offer-
35 ing; and two bulls, five full-grown rams, five he-goats, and five yearling rams, as a shared-offering. This was the offering of Elizur son of Shedeur.

36 On the fifth day the chief of the Simeonites, Shelumiel son of Zurishad-
37 dai, came. His offering was one silver dish weighing a hundred and thirty shekels by the sacred standard and one silver tossing-bowl weighing
38 seventy, both full of flour mixed with oil as a grain-offering; one saucer
39 weighing ten gold shekels, full of incense; one young bull, one full-grown
40 ram, and one yearling ram, as a whole-offering; one he-goat as a sin-
41 offering; and two bulls, five full-grown rams, five he-goats, and five year-ling rams, as a shared-offering. This was the offering of Shelumiel son of Zurishaddai.

On the sixth day the chief of the Gadites, Eliasaph son of Reuel, came. 42
His offering was one silver dish weighing a hundred and thirty shekels by 43
the sacred standard and one silver tossing-bowl weighing seventy, both
full of flour mixed with oil as a grain-offering; one saucer weighing ten 44
gold shekels, full of incense; one young bull, one full-grown ram, and one 45
yearling ram, as a whole-offering; one he-goat as a sin-offering; and two 46 47
bulls, five full-grown rams, five he-goats, and five yearling rams, as a
shared-offering. This was the offering of Eliasaph son of Reuel.

On the seventh day the chief of the Ephraimites, Elishama son of 48
Ammihud, came. His offering was one silver dish weighing a hundred and 49
thirty shekels by the sacred standard and one silver tossing-bowl weighing
seventy, both full of flour mixed with oil as a grain-offering; one saucer 50
weighing ten gold shekels, full of incense; one young bull, one full-grown 51
ram, and one yearling ram, as a whole-offering; one he-goat as a sin- 52
offering; and two bulls, five full-grown rams, five he-goats, and five year- 53
ling rams, as a shared-offering. This was the offering of Elishama son of
Ammihud.

On the eighth day the chief of the Manassites, Gamaliel son of Pedahzur, 54
came. His offering was one silver dish weighing a hundred and thirty 55
shekels by the sacred standard and one silver tossing-bowl weighing
seventy, both full of flour mixed with oil as a grain-offering; one saucer 56
weighing ten gold shekels, full of incense; one young bull, one full-grown 57
ram, and one yearling ram, as a whole-offering; one he-goat as a sin-offering; 58
and two bulls, five full-grown rams, five he-goats, and five yearling rams, 59
as a shared-offering. This was the offering of Gamaliel son of Pedahzur.

On the ninth day the chief of the Benjamites, Abidan son of Gideoni, 60
came. His offering was one silver dish weighing a hundred and thirty 61
shekels by the sacred standard and one silver tossing-bowl weighing
seventy, both full of flour mixed with oil as a grain-offering; one saucer 62
weighing ten gold shekels, full of incense; one young bull, one full-grown 63
ram, and one yearling ram, as a whole-offering; one he-goat as a sin- 64
offering; and two bulls, five full-grown rams, five he-goats, and five year- 65
ling rams, as a shared-offering. This was the offering of Abidan son of
Gideoni.

On the tenth day the chief of the Danites, Ahiezer son of Ammishaddai, 66
came. His offering was one silver dish weighing a hundred and thirty 67
shekels by the sacred standard and one silver tossing-bowl weighing
seventy, both full of flour mixed with oil as a grain-offering; one saucer 68
weighing ten gold shekels, full of incense; one young bull, one full-grown 69
ram, and one yearling ram, as a whole-offering; one he-goat as a sin- 70
offering; and two bulls, five full-grown rams, five he-goats, and five year- 71
ling rams, as a shared-offering. This was the offering of Ahiezer son of
Ammishaddai.

On the eleventh day the chief of the Asherites, Pagiel son of Ocran, came. 72
His offering was one silver dish weighing a hundred and thirty shekels by 73
the sacred standard and one silver tossing-bowl weighing seventy, both
full of flour mixed with oil as a grain-offering; one saucer weighing ten 74
gold shekels, full of incense; one young bull, one full-grown ram, and one 75

76 77 yearling ram, as a whole-offering; one he-goat as a sin-offering; and two bulls, five full-grown rams, five he-goats, and five yearling rams, as a shared-offering. This was the offering of Pagiel son of Ocran.

78 On the twelfth day the chief of the Naphtalites, Ahira son of Enan, came.
79 His offering was one silver dish weighing a hundred and thirty shekels by the sacred standard and one silver tossing-bowl weighing seventy, both
80 full of flour mixed with oil as a grain-offering; one saucer weighing ten
81 gold shekels, full of incense; one young bull, one full-grown ram, and one
82 83 yearling ram, as a whole-offering; one he-goat as a sin-offering; and two bulls, five full-grown rams, five he-goats, and five yearling rams, as a shared-offering. This was the offering of Ahira son of Enan.

84 This was the gift from the chiefs of Israel for the dedication of the altar when it was anointed: twelve silver dishes, twelve silver tossing-bowls, and
85 twelve golden saucers; each silver dish weighed a hundred and thirty shekels, each silver tossing-bowl seventy shekels. The total weight of the silver vessels was two thousand four hundred shekels by the sacred stan-
86 dard. There were twelve golden saucers full of incense, ten shekels each by the sacred standard: the total weight of the gold of the saucers was a
87 hundred and twenty shekels. The number of beasts for the whole-offering was twelve bulls, twelve full-grown rams, and twelve yearling rams, with the prescribed grain-offerings, and twelve he-goats for the sin-offering.
88 The number of beasts for the shared-offering was twenty-four bulls, sixty full-grown rams, sixty he-goats, and sixty yearling rams. This was the gift
89 for the dedication of the altar when it was anointed. And when Moses entered the Tent of the Presence to speak with God, he heard the Voice speaking from above the cover over the Ark of the Tokens from between the two cherubim: the Voice spoke to him.

8 1 2 The LORD spoke to Moses and said, 'Speak to Aaron in these words: "When you mount the seven lamps, see that they shed their light forwards
3 in front of the lamp-stand." ' Aaron did this: he mounted the lamps, so as to shed light forwards in front of the lamp-stand, as the LORD had in-
4 structed Moses. The lamp-stand was made of beaten-work in gold, as well as the stem and the petals. Moses made it to match the pattern which the LORD had shown him.

5 6 The LORD spoke to Moses and said: Take the Levites apart from the
7 rest of the Israelites and cleanse them ritually. This is what you shall do to cleanse them. Sprinkle lustral water over them; they shall then shave
8 their whole bodies, wash their clothes, and so be cleansed. Next, they shall take a young bull as a whole-offering [a] with its prescribed grain-offering, flour mixed with oil; and you shall take a second young bull as a sin-
9 offering. Bring the Levites before the Tent of the Presence and call the
10 whole community of Israelites together. Bring the Levites before the LORD,
11 and let the Israelites lay their hands on their heads. Aaron shall present the Levites before the LORD as a special gift from the Israelites, and they shall
12 be dedicated to the service of the LORD. The Levites shall lay their hands on the heads of the bulls; one bull shall be offered as a sin-offering and the other as a whole-offering to the LORD, to make expiation for the Levites.

[a] as a whole-offering: *prob. rdg.; Heb. om.*

Then you shall set the Levites before Aaron and his sons, presenting them 13
to the LORD as a special gift. You shall thus separate the Levites from the 14
rest of the Israelites, and they shall be mine.

After this, the Levites shall enter the Tent of the Presence to serve in it, 15
ritually cleansed and presented as a special gift; for they are given and 16
dedicated to me, out of all the Israelites. I have accepted them as mine in
place of all that comes first from the womb, every first child among the
Israelites; for every first-born male creature, man or beast, among the 17
Israelites is mine. On the day when I struck down every first-born creature
in Egypt, I hallowed all the first-born of the Israelites to myself, and I 18
have accepted the Levites in their place. I have given the Levites to Aaron 19
and his sons, dedicated among the Israelites to perform the service of the
Israelites in the Tent of the Presence and to make expiation for them, and
then no calamity will befall them when they come close to the sanctuary.

Moses and Aaron and the whole community of Israelites carried out all 20
the commands the LORD had given to Moses for the dedication of the
Levites. The Levites purified themselves of sin and washed their clothes, 21
and Aaron presented them as a special gift before the LORD and made
expiation for them, to cleanse them. Then at last they went in to perform 22
their service in the Tent of the Presence, before Aaron and his sons. Thus
the commands the LORD had given to Moses concerning the Levites were
all carried out.

The LORD spoke to Moses and said: Touching the Levites: they shall 23 24
begin their active work in the service of the Tent of the Presence at the
age of twenty-five. At the age of fifty a Levite shall retire from regular 25
service and shall serve no longer. He may continue to assist his colleagues 26
in attendance in the Tent of the Presence but shall perform no regular
service. This is how you shall arrange the attendance of the Levites.

In the first month of the second year after they came out of Egypt, the 9
LORD spoke to Moses in the wilderness of Sinai and said, 'Let the Israel- 2
ites prepare the Passover at the time appointed for it. This shall be between 3
dusk and dark on the fourteenth day of this month, and you shall keep it
at this appointed time, observing every rule and custom proper to it.' So 4
Moses told the Israelites to prepare the Passover, and they prepared it on 5
the fourteenth day of the first month, between dusk and dark, in the
wilderness of Sinai. The Israelites did exactly as the LORD had instructed
Moses.

It happened that some men were ritually unclean through contact with 6
a corpse and so could not keep the Passover on the right day. They came
before Moses and Aaron that same day and said, 'We are unclean through 7
contact with a corpse. Must we therefore be debarred from presenting the
LORD's offering at its appointed time with the rest of the Israelites?' Moses 8
answered, 'Wait, and let me hear what commands the LORD has for you.'

The LORD spoke to Moses and said, Tell the Israelites: If any one of 9 10
you or of your descendants is ritually unclean through contact with a
corpse, or if he is away on a long journey, he shall keep a Passover to the
LORD none the less. But in that case he shall prepare the victim in the 11
second month, between dusk and dark on the fourteenth day. It shall be

12 eaten with unleavened cakes and bitter herbs; nothing shall be left over
till morning, and no bone of it shall be broken. The Passover shall be kept
13 exactly as the law prescribes. The man who, being ritually clean and
not absent on a journey, neglects to keep the Passover, shall be cut off
from his father's kin, because he has not presented the LORD's offering at
its appointed time. That man shall accept responsibility for his sin.
14 When an alien is settled among you, he also shall keep the Passover to
the LORD, observing every rule and custom proper to it. The same law is
binding on you all, alien and native alike.

The journey from Sinai to Edom

15 ON THE DAY WHEN THEY SET UP THE TABERNACLE, that is the Tent
of the Tokens, cloud covered it, and in the evening a brightness like
16 fire appeared over it till morning. So it continued: the cloud covered it by
17 day and a brightness like fire by night. Whenever the cloud lifted from
the tent, the Israelites struck camp, and at the place where the cloud
18 settled, there they pitched their camp. At the command of the LORD they
struck camp, and at the command of the LORD they encamped again, and
19 continued in camp as long as the cloud rested over the Tabernacle. When
the cloud stayed long over the Tabernacle, the Israelites remained in
20 attendance on the LORD and did not move on; and it was the same when
the cloud continued over the Tabernacle only a few days: at the command
of the LORD they remained in camp, and at the command of the LORD they
21 struck camp. There were also times when the cloud continued only from
evening till morning, and in the morning, when the cloud lifted, they moved
on. Whether by day or by night, they moved as soon as the cloud lifted.
22 Whether it was for a day or two, for a month or a year, whenever the cloud
stayed long over the Tabernacle, the Israelites remained where they were
23 and did not move on; they did so only when the cloud lifted. At the command of the LORD they encamped, and at his command they struck camp.
At the LORD's command, given through Moses, they remained in attendance on the LORD.

10 1 2 The LORD spoke to Moses and said: Make two trumpets of beaten silver
and use them for summoning the community and for breaking camp.
3 When both are sounded, the whole community shall muster before you
4 at the entrance to the Tent of the Presence. If a single trumpet is sounded,
5 the chiefs who are heads of the Israelite clans shall muster. When you give
the signal for a shout, those encamped on the east side are to move off.
6 When the signal is given for a second shout those encamped to the south
7 are to move off. A signal to shout is the signal to move off. When you con-
8 vene the assembly, you shall sound a trumpet but not raise a shout. This
sounding of the trumpets is the duty of the Aaronite priests and shall be a
rule binding for all time on your descendants.
9 When you go into battle against an invader and you are hard pressed
by him, you shall raise a cheer when the trumpets sound, and this will
serve as a reminder of you before the LORD your God and you will be

delivered from your enemies. On your festal days and at your appointed 10
seasons and on the first day of every month, you shall sound the trumpets
over your whole-offerings and your shared-offerings, and the trumpets
shall be a reminder on your behalf before the LORD your God. I am the
LORD your God.

In the second year, on the twentieth day of the second month, the cloud 11
lifted from the Tabernacle of the Tokens, and the Israelites moved by 12
stages from the wilderness of Sinai, until the cloud came to rest in the
wilderness of Paran. The first time that they broke camp at the command 13
of the LORD given through Moses, the standard of the division of Judah 14
moved off first with its tribal hosts: the host of Judah under Nahshon son
of Amminadab, the host of Issachar under Nethaneel son of Zuar, and the 15 16
host of Zebulun under Eliab son of Helon. Then the Tabernacle was taken 17
down, and its bearers, the sons of Gershon and Merari, moved off.

Secondly, the standard of the division of Reuben moved off with its 18
tribal hosts: the host of Reuben under Elizur son of Shedeur, the host of 19
Simeon under Shelumiel son of Zurishaddai, and the host of Gad under 20
Eliasaph son of Reuel. The Kohathites, the bearers of the holy things, 21
moved off next, and on their arrival found the Tabernacle set up.

Thirdly, the standard of the division of Ephraim moved off with its 22
tribal hosts: the host of Ephraim under Elishama son of Ammihud, the 23
host of Manasseh under Gamaliel son of Pedahzur, and the host of Ben- 24
jamin under Abidan son of Gideoni.

Lastly, the standard of the division of Dan, the rearguard of all the 25
divisions, moved off with its tribal hosts: the host of Dan under Ahiezer
son of Ammishaddai, the host of Asher under Pagiel son of Ocran, and the 26 27
host of Naphtali under Ahira son of Enan.

This was the order of march for the Israelites, mustered in their hosts, 28
and in this order they broke camp.

And Moses said to Hobab son of Reuel the Midianite, his brother-in- 29
law, 'We are setting out for the place which the LORD promised to give us.
Come with us, and we will deal generously with you, for the LORD has
given an assurance of good fortune for Israel.' But he replied, 'No, I will 30
not; I would rather go to my own country and my own people.' Moses 31
said, 'Do not desert us, I beg you; for you know where we ought to camp
in the wilderness, and you will be our guide. If you will go with us, then 32
all the good fortune with which the LORD favours us we will share
with you.'

Then they moved off from the mountain of the LORD and journeyed for 33
three days, and the Ark of the Covenant of the LORD kept a day's journey
ahead of them to find them a place to rest. The cloud of the LORD hung 34
over them by day when they moved camp. Whenever the Ark began to 35
move, Moses said,

'Up, LORD, and may thy enemies be scattered
and those that hate thee flee before thee.'

When it halted, he said, 36

'Rest, LORD of the countless thousands of Israel.'

11 There came a time when the people complained to the Lord of their hardships. When he heard, he became angry and fire from the Lord broke
2 out among them, and was raging at one end of the camp, when the people appealed to Moses. He interceded with the Lord, and the fire died down.
3 Then they named that place Taberah,[a] because the fire of the Lord had burned among them there.

4 Now there was a mixed company of strangers who had joined the Israelites. These people began to be greedy for better things, and the Israelites themselves wept once again and cried, 'Will no one give us meat?
5 Think of it! In Egypt we had fish for the asking, cucumbers and water-
6 melons, leeks and onions and garlic. Now our throats are parched; there
7 is nothing wherever we look except this manna.' (The manna looked like
8 coriander seed, the colour of gum resin. The people went about collecting it, ground it up in hand-mills or pounded it in mortars, then boiled it in
9 the pot and made it into cakes. It tasted like butter-cakes. When dew fell on
10 the camp at night, the manna fell with it.) Moses heard the people wailing, all of them in their families at the opening of their tents. Then the Lord
11 became very angry, and Moses was troubled. He said to the Lord, 'Why hast thou brought trouble on thy servant? How have I displeased the Lord
12 that I am burdened with the care of this whole people? Am I their mother? Have I brought them into the world, and am I called upon to carry them in my bosom, like a nurse with her babies, to the land promised by thee on
13 oath to their fathers? Where am I to find meat to give them all? They
14 pester me with their wailing and their "Give us meat to eat." This whole
15 people is a burden too heavy for me; I cannot carry it alone. If that is thy purpose for me, then kill me outright. But if I have won thy favour, let me suffer this trouble at thy hands [b] no longer.'

16 The Lord answered Moses, 'Assemble seventy elders from Israel, men known to you as elders and officers in the community; bring them to me at
17 the Tent of the Presence, and there let them take their stand with you. I will come down and speak with you there. I will take back part of that same spirit which has been conferred on you and confer it on them, and they will share with you the burden of taking care for the people; then you will
18 not have to bear it alone. And to the people you shall say this: "Hallow yourselves in readiness for tomorrow; you shall have meat to eat. You wailed in the Lord's hearing; you said, 'Will no one give us meat? In Egypt we lived well.' The Lord will give you meat and you shall eat it.
19 20 Not for one day only, nor for two days, nor five, nor ten, nor twenty, but for a whole month you shall eat it until it comes out at your nostrils and makes you sick; because you have rejected the Lord who dwells in your midst, wailing in his presence and saying, 'Why did we ever come out of Egypt?' " '

21 Moses replied, 'Here am I with six hundred thousand men on the march around me, and thou dost promise them meat to eat for a whole month.
22 How can the sheep and oxen be slaughtered that would be enough for them?
23 If all the fish in the sea could be caught, would they be enough?' The Lord

---

[a] *That is* Burning. [b] this trouble ... hands: *prob. original rdg., altered in Heb.* to my trouble.

said to Moses, 'Is there a limit to the power of the Lord? You will see this very day whether or not my words come true.'

Moses came out and told the people what the Lord had said. He assem- 24 bled seventy men from the elders of the people and stationed them round the Tent. Then the Lord descended in the cloud and spoke to him. He 25 took back part of that same spirit which he had conferred on Moses and conferred it on the seventy elders; as the spirit alighted on them, they fell into a prophetic ecstasy, for the first and only time.

Now two men named Eldad and Medad, who had been enrolled with the 26 seventy, were left behind in the camp. But, though they had not gone out to the Tent, the spirit alighted on them none the less, and they fell into an ecstasy there in the camp. A young man ran and told Moses that Eldad and 27 Medad were in an ecstasy in the camp, whereupon Joshua son of Nun, who 28 had served with Moses since he was a boy, broke in, 'My lord Moses, stop them!' But Moses said to him, 'Are you jealous on my account? I wish that 29 all the Lord's people were prophets and that the Lord would confer his spirit on them all!' And Moses rejoined the camp with the elders of Israel. 30

Then a wind from the Lord sprang up; it drove quails in from the west, 31 and they were flying all round the camp for the distance of a day's journey, three feet above the ground. The people were busy gathering quails all 32 that day, all night, and all next day, and even the man who got least gathered ten homers. They spread them out to dry all about the camp. But the meat 33 was scarcely between their teeth, and they had not so much as bitten it, when the Lord's anger broke out against the people and he struck them with a deadly plague. That place was called Kibroth-hattaavah[a] because 34 there they buried the people who had been greedy for meat.

From Kibroth-hattaavah the Israelites went on to Hazeroth, and while 35 they were at Hazeroth, Miriam and Aaron began to speak against Moses. **12** They blamed him for his Cushite wife (for he had married a Cushite woman), and they said, 'Is Moses the only one with[b] whom the Lord has 2 spoken? Has he not spoken with[b] us as well?' Moses was in fact a man of 3 great humility, the most humble man on earth. But the Lord heard them and suddenly he said to Moses, Aaron and Miriam, 'Go out all three of 4 you to the Tent of the Presence.' So the three went out, and the Lord 5 descended in a pillar of cloud; he stood at the entrance to the tent and summoned Aaron and Miriam. The two of them went forward, and he said, 6

'Listen to my words.
If he[c] were your prophet and nothing more,
I would make myself known to him in a vision,
I would speak with him in a dream.
But my servant Moses is not such a prophet;   7
he alone is faithful[d] of all my household.
    With him I speak face to face,   8
    openly and not in riddles.
    He shall see the very form of the Lord.
How do you dare speak against my servant Moses?'

[a] *That is* the Graves of Greed.   [b] *Or* by.   [c] *Prob. rdg.; Heb.* the Lord.
[d] *Or* to be trusted.

9 Thus the anger of the Lord was roused against them, and he left them;
10 and as the cloud moved from the tent, there was Miriam, her skin diseased and white as snow. Aaron turned towards her and saw her skin diseased.
11 Then he said to Moses, 'Pray, my lord, do not make us pay the penalty of
12 sin, foolish and wicked though we have been. Let her not be like something still-born, whose flesh is half eaten away when it comes from the womb.'
13 14 So Moses cried, 'Not this, O Lord! Heal her, I pray.' The Lord replied, 'Suppose her father had spat in her face, would she not have to remain in disgrace for seven days? Let her be kept for seven days in confinement
15 outside the camp and then be brought back.' So Miriam was kept outside for seven days, and the people did not strike camp until she was brought
16 back. After this they set out from Hazeroth and pitched camp in the wilderness of Paran.

13 1 2 THE LORD SPOKE TO MOSES and said, 'Send men out to explore the land of Canaan which I am giving to the Israelites; from each of their fathers'
3 tribes send one man, and let him be a man of high rank.' So Moses sent them from the wilderness of Paran at the command of the Lord, all of
4 them leading men among the Israelites. These were their names:

  from the tribe of Reuben, Shammua son of Zaccur;
5 from the tribe of Simeon, Shaphat son of Hori;
6 from the tribe of Judah, Caleb son of Jephunneh;
7 from the tribe of Issachar, Igal son of Joseph;
8 from the tribe of Ephraim, Hoshea son of Nun;
9 from the tribe of Benjamin, Palti son of Raphu;
10 from the tribe of Zebulun, Gaddiel son of Sodi;
11 from the tribe of Joseph (that is from the tribe of Manasseh), Gaddi son of Susi;
12 from the tribe of Dan, Ammiel son of Gemalli;
13 from the tribe of Asher, Sethur son of Michael;
14 from the tribe of Naphtali, Nahbi son of Vophsi;
15 from the tribe of Gad, Geuel son of Machi.

16 These are the names of the men whom Moses sent to explore the land. But Moses called the son of Nun Joshua, not Hoshea.
17 When Moses sent them to explore the land of Canaan, he said to them,
18 'Make your way up by the Negeb, and go on into the hill-country. See what the land is like, and whether the people who live there are strong or
19 weak, few or many. See whether it is easy or difficult country in which they live, and whether the cities in which they live are weakly defended or
20 well fortified; is the land fertile or barren, and does it grow trees or not? Go boldly in and take some of its fruit.' It was the season when the first grapes were ripe.
21 They went up and explored the country from the wilderness of Zin as
22 far as Rehob by Lebo-hamath. They went up by the Negeb and came to Hebron, where Ahiman, Sheshai and Talmai, the descendants of Anak,[a]
23 were living. (Hebron was built seven years before Zoan in Egypt.) They

---

[a] descendants of Anak: *or* tall men.

came to the gorge of Eshcol,[a] and there they cut a branch with a single
bunch of grapes, and they carried it on a pole two at a time; they also
picked pomegranates and figs. It was from the bunch of grapes which the 24
Israelites cut there that that place was named the gorge of Eshcol. After 25
forty days they returned from exploring the country, and came back to 26
Moses and Aaron and the whole community of Israelites at Kadesh in the
wilderness of Paran. They made their report to them and to the whole
community, and showed them the fruit of the country. And this was the 27
story they told Moses: 'We made our way into the land to which you sent
us. It is flowing with milk and honey, and here is the fruit it grows; but its 28
inhabitants are sturdy, and the cities are very strongly fortified; indeed,
we saw there the descendants of Anak. We also saw the Amalekites who 29
live in the Negeb, Hittites, Jebusites, and Amorites who live in the hill-
country, and the Canaanites who live by the sea and along the Jordan.'

Then Caleb called for silence before Moses and said, 'Let us go up at 30
once and occupy the country; we are well able to conquer it.' But the men 31
who had gone with him said, 'No, we cannot attack these people; they are
stronger than we are.' Thus their report to the Israelites about the land 32
which they had explored was discouraging: 'The country we explored',
they said, 'will swallow up any who go to live in it. All the people we saw
there are men of gigantic size. When we set eyes on the Nephilim[b] (the 33
sons of Anak[c] belong to the Nephilim) we felt no bigger than grasshoppers;
and that is how we looked to them.'

Then the whole Israelite community cried out in dismay; all night long **14**
they wept. One and all they made complaints against Moses and Aaron: 'If 2
only we had died in Egypt or in the wilderness!' they said. 'Far happier if
we had! Why should the LORD bring us to this land, to die in battle and 3
leave our wives and our dependants to become the spoils of war? To go
back to Egypt would be better than this.' And they began to talk of choos- 4
ing someone to lead them back.

Then Moses and Aaron flung themselves on the ground before the 5
assembled community of the Israelites, and two of those who had explored 6
the land, Joshua son of Nun and Caleb son of Jephunneh, rent their clothes
and addressed the whole community: 'The country we penetrated and 7
explored', they said, 'is very good land indeed. If the LORD is pleased with 8
us, he will bring us into this land which flows with milk and honey, and
give it to us. But you must not rebel against the LORD. You need not fear 9
the people of the land; for there we shall find food. They have lost the
protection that they had: the LORD is with us. You have nothing to fear
from them.' But by way of answer the assembled Israelites threatened to 10
stone them, when suddenly the glory of the LORD appeared to them all in
the Tent of the Presence.

Then the LORD said to Moses, 'How much longer will this people treat 11
me with contempt? How much longer will they refuse to trust me in spite
of all the signs I have shown among them? I will strike them with pestilence. 12
I will deny them their heritage, and you and your descendants I will make
into a nation greater and more numerous than they.' But Moses answered 13

[a] Eshcol: *that is* Bunch of Grapes.   [b] *Or* giants.   [c] sons of Anak: *or* tall men.

the LORD, 'What if the Egyptians hear of it? It was thou who didst bring
14 this people out of Egypt by thy strength. What if they tell the inhabitants
of this land? They too have heard of thee, LORD, that thou art with this
people, and art seen face to face, that thy cloud stays over them, and thou
goest before them in a pillar of cloud by day and in a pillar of fire by night.
15 If then thou dost put them all to death at one blow, the nations who have
16 heard these tales of thee will say, "The LORD could not bring this people
into the land which he promised them by oath; and so he destroyed them
in the wilderness."

17   'Now let the LORD's might be shown in its greatness, true to thy pro-
18 clamation of thyself—"The LORD, long-suffering, ever constant, who for-
gives iniquity and rebellion, and punishes sons to the third and fourth
generation for the iniquity of their fathers, though he does not sweep them
19 clean away." Thou hast borne with this people from Egypt all the way here;
forgive their iniquity, I beseech thee, as befits thy great and constant love.'

20 21   The LORD said, 'Your prayer is answered; I pardon them. But as I live,
22-23 in very truth the glory of the LORD shall fill the earth. Not one of all those
who have seen my glory and the signs which I wrought in Egypt and in the
wilderness shall see the country which I promised on oath to their fathers.
Ten times they have challenged me and not obeyed my voice. None of
24-25 those who have flouted me shall see this land. But my servant Caleb showed
a different spirit: he followed me with his whole heart. Because of this, I
will bring him into the land in which he has already set foot, the territory
of the Amalekites and the Canaanites who dwell in the Vale, and put his
descendants in possession of it. Tomorrow you must turn back and set
out for the wilderness by way of the Red Sea.' *a*

26 27   The LORD spoke to Moses and Aaron and said, 'How long must I tolerate *b* the complaints of this wicked community? I have heard the Israelites
28 making complaints against me. Tell them that this is the very word of the
LORD: As I live, I will bring home to you the words I have heard you utter.
29 Here in this wilderness your bones shall lie, every man of you on the
register from twenty years old and upwards, because you have made these
30 complaints against me. Not one of you shall enter the land which I swore
with uplifted hand should be your home, except only Caleb son of Jephun-
31 neh and Joshua son of Nun. As for your dependants, those dependants who,
you said, would become the spoils of war, I will bring them in to the land
32 you have rejected, and they shall enjoy it. But as for the rest of you, your
33 bones shall lie in this wilderness; your sons shall be wanderers in the
wilderness forty years, paying the penalty of your wanton disloyalty till
34 the last man of you dies there. Forty days you spent exploring the country,
and forty years you shall spend—a year for each day—paying the penalty
35 of your iniquities. You shall know what it means to have me against you. *c* I,
the LORD, have spoken. This I swear to do to all this wicked community
who have combined against me. There shall be an end of them here in this
36 wilderness; here they shall die.' But the men whom Moses had sent to
explore the land, and who came back and by their report set all the com-
37 munity complaining against him, died of the plague before the LORD; they

a Or the Sea of Reeds.   *b* must I tolerate: *prob. rdg.; Heb.* for.   *c* Or to thwart me.

died of the plague because they had made a bad report. Of those who went 38
to explore the land, Joshua son of Nun and Caleb son of Jephunneh alone
remained alive.

When Moses reported the LORD's words to all the Israelites, the people 39
were plunged in grief. They set out early next morning and made for the 40
heights of the hill-country, saying, 'Look, we are on our way up to the
place the LORD spoke of. We admit that we have been wrong.' But Moses 41
replied, 'Must you persist in disobeying the LORD's command? No good
will come of this. Go no further; you will not have the LORD with you, and 42
your enemies will defeat you. For in front of you are the Amalekites and 43
Canaanites, and you will die by the sword, because you have ceased to
follow the LORD, and he will no longer be with you.' But they went reck- 44
lessly on their way towards the heights of the hill-country, though neither
the Ark of the Covenant of the LORD nor Moses moved with them out of
the camp; and the Amalekites and Canaanites from those hills came down 45
and fell upon them, and crushed them at Hormah.

THE LORD SPOKE TO MOSES and said, Speak to the Israelites in these **15** 1 2
words: When you enter the land where you are to live, the land I am giving
you, you will make food-offerings to the LORD; they may be whole-offer- 3
ings or any sacrifice made in fulfilment of a special*ᵃ* vow or by way of freewill offering or at one of the appointed seasons. When you thus make an
offering of soothing odour from herd or flock to the LORD, the man who 4
offers, in presenting it, shall add a grain-offering of a tenth of an ephah of
flour mixed with a quarter of a hin of oil. You shall also add to the whole- 5
offering or shared-offering a quarter of a hin of wine as a drink-offering
with each lamb sacrificed.

If the animal is a ram, the grain-offering shall be two tenths of an ephah 6
of flour mixed with a third of a hin of oil, and the wine for the drink- 7
offering shall be a third of a hin; in this way you will make an offering of
soothing odour to the LORD.

When you offer to the LORD a young bull, whether as a whole-offering 8
or as a sacrifice to fulfil a special*ᵇ* vow, or as a shared-offering, you shall 9
add a grain-offering of three tenths of an ephah of flour mixed with half
a hin of oil, and for the drink-offering, half a hin of wine; the whole will 10
thus be a food-offering of soothing odour to the LORD. This is what must 11
be done in each case, for every bull or ram, lamb or kid, whatever the 12
number of each that you offer. Every native Israelite shall observe these 13
rules in each case when he offers a food-offering of soothing odour to the
LORD.

When an alien residing with you or permanently settled among you 14
offers a food-offering of soothing odour to the LORD, he shall do as you do.
There is one and the same rule for you and for the resident alien, a rule 15
binding for all time on your descendants; you and the alien are alike before
the LORD. There shall be one law and one custom for you and for the alien 16
residing with you.

     ᵃ in fulfilment of a special: *or* to discharge a . . .
     ᵇ fulfil a special: *or* discharge a . . .

17 18   The LORD spoke to Moses and said, Speak to the Israelites in these words:
19   After you have entered the land into which I am bringing you, whenever you eat the bread of the country, you shall set aside a contribution for the
20   LORD. You shall set aside a cake made of your first kneading of dough, as
21   you set aside the contribution from the threshing-floor. You must give a contribution to the LORD from your first kneading of dough; this rule is binding on your descendants.

22   When through inadvertence you omit to carry out any of these com-
23   mands which the LORD gave to Moses—any command whatever that the LORD gave you through Moses on that first day and thereafter and made
24   binding on your descendants—if it be done inadvertently, unnoticed by the community, then the whole community shall offer one young bull as a whole-offering, a soothing odour to the LORD, with its proper grain-offering and drink-offering according to custom; and they shall add one
25   he-goat as a sin-offering. The priest shall make expiation for the whole community of Israelites, and they shall be forgiven. The omission was inadvertent; and they have brought their offering, a food-offering to the LORD; they have made their sin-offering before the LORD for their in-
26   advertence; the whole community of Israelites and the aliens residing among you shall be forgiven. The inadvertence was shared by the whole people.

27   If any individual sins inadvertently, he shall present a yearling she-goat
28   as a sin-offering, and the priest shall make expiation before the LORD for
29   the said individual, and he shall be forgiven. For anyone who sins inadvertently, there shall be one law for all, whether native Israelite or
30   resident alien. But the person who sins presumptuously, native or alien,
31   insults the LORD. He shall be cut off from his people, because he has brought the word of the LORD into contempt and violated his command. That person shall be wholly cut off; the guilt shall be on his head alone.

32   During the time that the Israelites were in the wilderness, a man was
33   found gathering sticks on the sabbath day. Those who had caught him in
34   the act brought him to Moses and Aaron and all the community, and they kept him in custody, because it was not clearly known what was to be done
35   with him. The LORD said to Moses, 'The man must be put to death; he
36   must be stoned by all the community outside the camp.' So they took him outside the camp and all stoned him to death, as the LORD had commanded Moses.

37 38   The LORD spoke to Moses and said, Speak to the Israelites in these words: You must make tassels like flowers on the corners of your garments, you and your children's children. Into this tassel you shall work a violet
39   thread, and whenever you see this in the tassel, you shall remember all the LORD's commands and obey them, and not go your own wanton ways,
40   led astray by your own eyes and hearts. This token is to ensure that you remember all my commands and obey them, and keep yourselves holy, consecrated to your God.
41   I am the LORD your God who brought you out of Egypt to become your God. I am the LORD your God.

Now KORAH SON OF IZHAR, son of Kohath, son of Levi, with the Reuben- **16**
ites Dathan and Abiram sons of Eliab and On son of Peleth, challenged the **2**
authority of Moses. With them in their revolt were two hundred and fifty
Israelites, all men of rank in the community, conveners of assembly and
men of good standing. They confronted Moses and Aaron and said to them, **3**
'You take too much upon yourselves. Every member of the community is
holy and the LORD is among them all. Why do you set yourselves up above
the assembly of the LORD?' When Moses heard this, he prostrated himself, **4**
and he said to Korah and all his company, 'Tomorrow morning the LORD **5**
shall declare who is his, who is holy and may present offerings to him. The
man whom the LORD chooses shall present them. This is what you must **6**
do, you, Korah, and all your company: you must take censers and put fire **7**
in them, and then place incense on them before the LORD tomorrow. The
man whom the LORD then chooses is the man who is holy. You take too
much upon yourselves, you sons of Levi.'

Moses said to Korah, 'Now listen, you sons of Levi. Is it not enough for **8 9**
you that the God of Israel has set you apart from the community of Israel,
bringing you near him to maintain the service of the Tabernacle of the
LORD and to stand before the community as their ministers? He has **10**
brought you near him and your brother Levites with you; now you seek
the priesthood as well. That is why you and all your company have com- **11**
bined together against the LORD. What is Aaron that you should make these
complaints against him?'

Moses sent to fetch Dathan and Abiram sons of Eliab, but they answered, **12**
'We are not coming. Is it a small thing that you have brought us away from **13**
a land flowing with milk and honey to let us die in the wilderness? Must
you also set yourself up as prince over us? What is more, you have not **14**
brought us into a land flowing with milk and honey, nor have you given us
fields and vineyards to inherit. Do you think you can hoodwink men like
us? We are not coming.' This answer made Moses very angry, and he said **15**
to the LORD, 'Take no notice of their murmuring. I have not taken from
them so much as a single ass; I have done no wrong to any of them.'

Moses said to Korah, 'Present yourselves before the LORD tomorrow, **16**
you and all your company, you and they and Aaron. Each man of you is to **17**
take his censer and put incense on it. Then you shall present them before
the LORD with their two hundred and fifty censers, and you and Aaron
shall also bring your censers.' So each man took his censer and put fire in **18**
it and placed incense on it; Moses and Aaron took their stand at the entrance
to the Tent of the Presence, and Korah gathered his whole company **19**
together and faced them at the entrance to the Tent of the Presence.

Then the glory of the LORD appeared to the whole community. And the **20**
LORD spoke to Moses and Aaron and said, 'Stand apart from this company, **21**
so that I may make an end of them in a single instant.' But they prostrated **22**
themselves and said, 'O God, God of the spirits of all mankind, if one man
sins, wilt thou be angry with the whole community?' But the LORD said **23**
to Moses, 'Tell them to stand back from the dwellings of Korah, Dathan **24**
and Abiram.'

So Moses rose and went to Dathan and Abiram, and the elders of Israel **25**

26 followed him. He said to the whole community, 'Stand well away from the
tents of these wicked men; touch nothing of theirs, or you will be swept
27 away because of all their sins.' So they moved away from the places occupied by Korah, Dathan and Abiram. Now Dathan and Abiram, holding
themselves erect, had come out to the entrance of their tents with their
28 wives, their sons, and their dependants. Then Moses said, 'This shall prove
to you that it is the LORD who sent me to do all these things, and it was not
29 my own heart that prompted me. If these men die a natural death and share
30 the common fate of man, then the LORD has not sent me; but if the LORD
makes a great chasm, and the ground opens its mouth and swallows them
and all that is theirs, and they go down alive to Sheol, then you will know
that these men have held the LORD in contempt.'

31 32   Hardly had Moses spoken when the ground beneath them split; the
earth opened its mouth and swallowed them and their homes—all the
33 followers of Korah and all their property. They went down alive into Sheol
with all that they had; the earth closed over them, and they vanished from
34 the assembly. At their cries all the Israelites round them fled, shouting,
35 'Look to yourselves! the earth will swallow us up.' Meanwhile fire had come
out from the LORD and burnt up the two hundred and fifty men who were
presenting the incense.

36 37   Then the LORD spoke to Moses and said, 'Bid Eleazar son of Aaron the
priest set aside the censers from the burnt remains, and scatter the fire
38 from them far and wide, because they are holy. And the censers of these
men who sinned at the cost of their lives you shall make into beaten plates
to cover the altar; they are holy, because they have been presented before
39 the LORD. Let them be a sign to the Israelites.' So Eleazar the priest took
the bronze*a* censers which the victims of the fire had presented, and they
40 were beaten into plates to make a covering for the altar, as a reminder to the
Israelites that no person unqualified, not descended from Aaron, should
come forward to burn incense before the LORD, or his fate would be that of
Korah and his company. All this was done as the LORD commanded
Eleazar through Moses.

41   Next day all the community of the Israelites raised complaints against
Moses and Aaron and taxed them with causing the death of some of the
42 LORD's people. As they gathered against Moses and Aaron, they turned
towards the Tent of the Presence and saw that the cloud covered it, and
43 the glory of the LORD appeared. Moses and Aaron came to the front of the
44 Tent of the Presence, and the LORD spoke to Moses and Aaron and said,
45 'Stand well clear of this community, so that in a single instant I may make
46 an end of them.' Then they prostrated themselves, and Moses said to
Aaron, 'Take your censer, put fire from the altar in it, set incense on it, and
go with it quickly to the assembled community to make expiation for them.
Wrath has gone forth already from the presence of the LORD. The plague
47 has begun.' So Aaron took his censer, as Moses had said, ran into the midst
of the assembly and found that the plague had begun among the people.
48 He put incense on the censer and made expiation for the people, stand-
49 ing between the dead and the living, and the plague stopped. Fourteen

a Or copper.

thousand seven hundred died of it, in addition to those who had died for
the offence of Korah. When Aaron came back to Moses at the entrance to 50
the Tent of the Presence, the plague had stopped.

The LORD spoke to Moses and said, 'Speak to the Israelites and tell **17** 1 2
them to give you a staff for each tribe, one from every tribal chief, twelve in
all, and write each man's name on his staff. On Levi's staff write the name 3
of Aaron, for there shall be one staff for each head of a tribe. You shall put 4
them all in the Tent of the Presence before the Tokens, where I meet you,
and the staff of the man I choose shall sprout. I will rid myself of the com- 5
plaints of these Israelites, who keep on complaining against you.'

Moses thereupon spoke to the Israelites, and each of their chiefs handed 6
him a staff, each of them one for his tribe, twelve in all, and Aaron's staff
among them. Moses put them before the LORD in the Tent of the Tokens, 7
and next day when he entered the tent, he found that Aaron's staff, the 8
staff for the tribe of Levi, had sprouted. Indeed, it had sprouted, blossomed, and produced ripe almonds. Moses then brought out the staffs 9
from before the LORD and showed them to all the Israelites; they saw for
themselves, and each man took his own staff. The LORD said to Moses, 10
'Put back Aaron's staff in front of the Tokens to be kept as a warning to all
rebels, so that you may rid me once and for all of their complaints, and then
they shall not die.' Moses did this; as the LORD had commanded him, so 11
he did.

The Israelites said to Moses, 'This is the end of us! We perish, one and 12
all! Every single person who goes near the Tabernacle of the LORD dies. 13
Is this to be our final end?'

THE LORD SAID TO AARON: You and your sons, together with the **18**
members of your father's tribe, shall be fully answerable for the sanctuary.
You and your sons alone shall be answerable for your priestly office; but 2
you shall admit your kinsmen of Levi, your father's tribe, to be attached
to you and assist you while you and your sons are before the Tent of the
Tokens. They shall be in attendance on you and fulfil all the duties of the 3
Tent, but shall not go near the holy vessels and the altar, or they will die
and you with them. They shall be attached to you and be responsible for 4
the maintenance of the Tent of the Presence in every detail; no unqualified
person shall come near you. You yourselves shall be responsible for the 5
sanctuary and the altar, so that wrath may no more fall on the Israelites.
I have myself taken the Levites your kinsmen out of all the Israelites as a 6
gift for you, given to the LORD for the maintenance of the Tent of the
Presence. But only you and your sons may fulfil the duties of your priestly 7
office that concern the altar or lie within the Veil. This duty is yours; I
bestow on you this gift of priestly service. The unqualified person who
intrudes on it shall be put to death.

The LORD said to Aaron: I, the LORD, commit to your control the con- 8
tributions made to me, that is all the holy-gifts of the Israelites. I give them
to you and to your sons for your allotted portion due to you in perpetuity.
Out of the most holy gifts kept back from the altar-fire this part shall 9
belong to you: every offering, whether grain-offering, sin-offering, or

guilt-offering, rendered to me as a most holy gift, belongs to you and to
10   your sons. You shall eat it as befits most holy gifts; every male may eat it.
You shall regard it as holy.
11   This also is yours: the contribution from all such of their gifts as are
presented as special gifts by the Israelites. I give them to you and to your
sons and daughters with you as a due in perpetuity. Every person in your
household who is ritually clean may eat them.
12   I give you all the choicest of the oil, the choicest of the new wine and the
13   corn, the firstfruits which are given to the LORD. The first-ripe fruits of all
produce in the land which are brought to the LORD shall be yours. Everyone in your household who is clean may eat them.
14   Everything in Israel which has been devoted to God shall be yours.
15   All the first-born of man or beast which are brought to the LORD shall
be yours. Notwithstanding, you must accept payment in redemption of
16   any first-born of man and of unclean beasts: at the end of one month you
shall redeem it at the fixed price of five shekels of silver by the sacred
17   standard (twenty gerahs to the shekel). You must not, however, allow the
redemption of the first-born of a cow, sheep, or goat; they are holy. You
shall fling their blood against the altar and burn their fat in sacrifice as a
18   food-offering of soothing odour to the LORD; their flesh shall be yours, as
are the breast of the special gift and the right leg.
19   All the contributions from holy-gifts, which the Israelites set aside for
the LORD, I give to you and to your sons and daughters with you as a due
in perpetuity. This is a perpetual covenant of salt before the LORD with you
and your descendants also.
20   The LORD said to Aaron: You shall have no patrimony in the land of
Israel, no holding among them; I am your holding in Israel, I am your
patrimony.
21   To the Levites I give every tithe in Israel to be their patrimony, in
return for the service they render in maintaining the Tent of the Presence.
22   In order that the Israelites may not henceforth approach the Tent and thus
23   incur the penalty of death, the Levites alone shall perform the service of
the Tent, and they shall accept the full responsibility for it. This rule is
binding on your descendants for all time. They shall have no patrimony
24   among the Israelites, because I give them as their patrimony the tithe which
the Israelites set aside as a contribution to the LORD. Therefore I say to
them: You shall have no patrimony among the Israelites.
25 26   The LORD spoke to Moses and said, Speak to the Levites in these words:
When you receive from the Israelites the tithe which I give you from them
as your patrimony, you shall set aside from it the contribution to the LORD,
27   a tithe of the tithe. Your contribution shall count for you as if it were corn
28   from the threshing-floor and juice from the vat. In this way you too shall
set aside the contribution due to the LORD out of all tithes which you
receive from the Israelites and shall give the LORD's contribution to Aaron
29   the priest. Out of all the gifts you receive you shall set aside the contribution due to the LORD; and the gift which you hallow*a* must be taken from
the choicest of them.

a you hallow: *prob. rdg.; Heb. obscure.*

You shall say to the Levites: When you have set aside the choicest part 30
of your portion, the remainder shall count for you as the produce of the
threshing-floor and the winepress, and you may eat it anywhere, you and 31
your households. It is your payment for service in the Tent of the Presence.
When you have set aside its choicest part, you will incur no penalty in 32
respect of it, and you will not be profaning the holy-gifts of the Israelites;
so you will not die.

THE LORD SPOKE TO MOSES and Aaron and said: This is a law and a 19 1 2
statute which the LORD has ordained. Tell the Israelites to bring you a red
cow without blemish or defect, which has never borne the yoke. You shall 3
give it to Eleazar the priest, and it shall be taken outside the camp and
slaughtered*a* to the east of it. Eleazar the priest shall take some of the blood 4
on his finger and sprinkle it seven times towards the front of the Tent of
the Presence. The cow shall be burnt in his sight, skin, flesh, and blood, 5
together with the offal. The priest shall then take cedar-wood, marjoram, 6
and scarlet thread, and throw them into the heart of the fire in which the
cow is burning. He shall wash his clothes and bathe his body in water; 7
after which he may enter the camp, but he remains ritually unclean till
sunset. The man who burnt the cow shall wash his clothes and bathe 8
his body in water, but he also remains unclean till sunset. Then a man 9
who is clean shall collect the ashes of the cow and deposit them outside
the camp in a clean place. They shall be reserved for use by the Israelite
community in the water of ritual purification; for the cow is a sin-offering.
The man who collected the ashes of the cow shall wash his clothes, but he 10
remains unclean till sunset. This rule shall be binding for all time on the
Israelites and on the alien who is living with them.

Whoever touches a corpse shall be ritually unclean for seven days. He 11 12
shall get himself purified with the water of ritual purification on the third
day and on the seventh day, and then he shall be clean. If he is not purified
both on the third day and on the seventh, he shall not be clean. Everyone 13
who touches a corpse, that is the body of a man who has died, and does not
purify himself, defiles the Tabernacle of the LORD. That person shall be
cut off from Israel. The water of purification has not been flung over him;
he remains unclean, and his impurity is still upon him.

When a man dies in a tent, this is the law: everyone who goes into the 14
tent and everyone who was inside the tent shall be ritually unclean for seven
days, and every open vessel which has no covering tied over it shall also 15
be unclean. In the open, anyone who touches a man killed with a weapon 16
or one who has died naturally, or who touches a human bone or a grave,
shall be unclean for seven days. For such uncleanness, they shall take some 17
of the ash from the burnt mass of the sin-offering and add fresh water to
it in a vessel. Then a man who is clean shall take marjoram, dip it in the 18
water, and sprinkle the tent with all the vessels in it and all the people who
were there, or the man who has touched a human bone, a corpse (whether
the man was killed or died naturally), or a grave. The man who is clean 19
shall sprinkle the unclean man on the third day and on the seventh; on the

a Or he shall take it outside the camp and slaughter it . . .

seventh day he shall purify him; then the man shall wash his clothes and
20 bathe in water, and at sunset he shall be clean. If a man who is unclean
does not get himself purified, that person shall be cut off from the assembly,
because he has defiled the sanctuary of the LORD. The water of purification
21 has not been flung over him: he is unclean. This rule shall be binding on
you for all time. The man who sprinkles the water of purification shall also
wash his clothes, and whoever touches the water shall be unclean till sun-
22 set. Whatever the unclean man touches shall be unclean, and any person
who touches that shall be unclean till sunset.

20 IN THE FIRST MONTH the whole community of Israel reached the wilderness of Zin and stayed some time at Kadesh; there Miriam died and was
buried.
2   There was no water for the community; so they gathered against Moses
3 and Aaron. The people disputed with Moses and said, 'If only we had
4 perished when our brothers perished in the presence of the LORD! Why
have you brought the assembly of the LORD into this wilderness for us and
5 our beasts to die here? Why did you fetch us up from Egypt to bring us to
this vile place, where nothing will grow, neither corn nor figs, vines nor
6 pomegranates? There is not even any water to drink.' Moses and Aaron
came forward in front of the assembly to the entrance of the Tent of the
Presence. There they fell prostrate, and the glory of the LORD appeared
to them.
7 8   The LORD spoke to Moses and said, 'Take a *a* staff, and then with Aaron
your brother assemble all the community, and, in front of them all, speak
to the rock and it will yield its water. Thus you will produce water for the
9 community out of the rock, for them and their beasts to drink.' Moses left
10 the presence of the LORD with the staff, as he had commanded him. Then
he and Aaron gathered the assembly together in front of the rock, and he
said to them, 'Listen to me, you rebels. Must we get water out of this rock
11 for you?' Moses raised his hand and struck the rock twice with his staff.
12 Water gushed out in abundance and they all drank, men and beasts. But
the LORD said to Moses and Aaron, 'You did not trust me so far as to uphold my holiness in the sight of the Israelites; therefore you shall not lead
13 this assembly into the land which I promised to give them.' Such were the
waters of Meribah,*b* where the people disputed with the LORD and through
which his holiness was upheld.

The approach to the promised land

14 FROM KADESH MOSES SENT ENVOYS to the king of Edom: 'This is a
message from your brother Israel. You know all the hardships we have
15 encountered, how our fathers went down to Egypt, and we lived there for
16 many years. The Egyptians ill-treated us and our fathers before us, and
we cried to the LORD for help. He listened to us and sent an angel, and he
brought us out of Egypt; and now we are here at Kadesh, a town on your

a Or the.   *b* *That is* Dispute.

frontier. Grant us passage through your country. We will not trespass on 17
field or vineyard, or drink from your wells. We will keep to the king's highway; we will not turn off to right or left until we have crossed your territory.' But the Edomites answered, 'You shall not cross our land. If you 18
do, we will march out and attack you in force.' The Israelites said, 'But we 19
will keep to the main road. If we and our flocks drink your water, we will
pay you for it; we will simply cross your land on foot.' But the Edomites 20
said, 'No, you shall not', and took the field against them with a large army
in full strength. Thus the Edomites refused to allow Israel to cross their 21
frontier, and Israel went a different way to avoid a conflict.

The whole community of Israel set out from Kadesh and came to Mount 22
Hor. At Mount Hor, near the frontier of Edom, the LORD said to Moses 23
and Aaron, 'Aaron shall be gathered to his father's kin. He shall not enter 24
the land which I promised to give the Israelites, because over the waters
of Meribah you rebelled against my command. Take Aaron and his son 25
Eleazar, and go up Mount Hor. Strip Aaron of his robes and invest Eleazar 26
his son with them, for Aaron shall be taken from you: he shall die there.'
Moses did as the LORD had commanded him: they went up Mount Hor 27
in sight of the whole community, and Moses stripped Aaron of his robes 28
and invested his son Eleazar with them. There Aaron died on the mountain-
top, and Moses and Eleazar came down from the mountain. So the whole 29
community saw that Aaron had died, and all Israel mourned him for thirty
days.

When the Canaanite king of Arad who lived in the Negeb heard that **21**
the Israelites were coming by way of Atharim, he attacked them and took
some of them prisoners. Israel thereupon made a vow to the LORD and 2
said, 'If thou wilt deliver this people into my power, I will destroy their
cities.' The LORD listened to Israel and delivered the Canaanites into their 3
power. Israel destroyed them and their cities and called the place Hormah. *ᵃ*

Then they left Mount Hor by way of the Red Sea to march round the 4
flank of Edom. But on the way they grew impatient and spoke against God 5
and Moses. 'Why have you brought us up from Egypt', they said, 'to die
in the desert where there is neither food nor water? We are heartily sick
of this miserable fare.' Then the LORD sent poisonous snakes among the 6
people, and they bit the Israelites so that many of them died. The people 7
came to Moses and said, 'We sinned when we spoke against the LORD and
you. Plead with the LORD to rid us of the snakes.' Moses therefore pleaded
with the LORD for the people; and the LORD told Moses to make a serpent *ᵇ* 8
of bronze and erect it as a standard, so that anyone who had been bitten
could look at it and recover. So Moses made a bronze serpent and erected 9
it as a standard, so that when a snake had bitten a man, he could look at
the bronze serpent and recover.

The Israelites went on and encamped at Oboth. They moved on from 10 11
Oboth and encamped at Iye-abarim in the wilderness on the eastern
frontier of Moab. From there they moved and encamped by the gorge of 12
the Zared. They moved on from the Zared and encamped by the farther 13
side of the Arnon in the wilderness which extends into Amorite territory,

ᵃ That is Destruction.   *ᵇ Or* snake.

for the Arnon was the Moabite frontier; it lies between Moab and the
14 Amorites. That is why the Book of the Wars of the LORD speaks of Vaheb[a]
in Suphah and the gorges:

15   Arnon and the watershed of the gorges
             that falls away towards the dwellings at Ar
             and slopes towards the frontier of Moab.

16 From there they moved on to Beer:[b] this is the water-hole where the LORD
17 said to Moses, 'Gather the people together and I will give them water.' It
was then that Israel sang this song:

             Well up, spring water! Greet it with song,
18   the spring unearthed by the princes,
             laid open by the leaders of the people
                 with sceptre and with mace,
                 a gift from the wilderness.

19 And they proceeded from Beer[c] to Nahaliel, and from Nahaliel to Bamoth;
20 then from Bamoth to the valley in the Moabite country below the summit
of Pisgah overlooking the desert.

21 22   Then Israel sent envoys to the Amorite king Sihon and said, 'Grant us
passage through your country. We will not trespass on field or vineyard,
nor will we drink from your wells. We will travel by the king's highway till
23 we have crossed your territory.' But Sihon would not grant Israel passage
through his territory; he mustered all his people and came out against
Israel in the wilderness. He advanced as far as Jahaz and attacked Israel,
24 but Israel put them to the sword, giving no quarter, and occupied their
land from the Arnon to the Jabbok, the territory of the Ammonites, where
25 the country became difficult. So Israel took all these Amorite cities and
26 settled in them, that is in Heshbon and all its dependent villages. Heshbon
was the capital of the Amorite king Sihon, who had fought against the
former king of Moab and taken from him all his territory as far as the Arnon.
27 Therefore the bards say:

             Come to Heshbon, come!
           Let us see the city of Sihon rebuilt and restored!
28   For fire blazed out from Heshbon,
             and flames from Sihon's city.
             It devoured Ar of Moab,
             and swept the high ground at Arnon head.

29   Woe to you, Moab;
             it is the end of you, you people of Kemosh.
             He has made his sons fugitives
           and his daughters the prisoners of Sihon the Amorite king.
30   From Heshbon to Dibon their very embers are burnt out
                 and they are extinct,
             while the fire spreads onward to Medeba.

31 Thus Israel occupied the territory of the Amorites.

---

[a] *Name meaning* Watershed.   [b] *Name meaning* Water-hole.   [c] *Prob. rdg.;*
Heb. from a gift.

Moses then sent men to explore Jazer; the Israelites captured it together 32
with its dependent villages and drove out the Amorites living there. Then 33
they turned and advanced along the road to Bashan. Og king of Bashan,
with all his people, took the field against them at Edrei. The LORD said to 34
Moses, 'Do not be afraid of him. I have delivered him into your hands, with
all his people and his land. Deal with him as you dealt with Sihon the
Amorite king who lived in Heshbon.' So they put him to the sword with his 35
sons and all his people, until there was no survivor left, and they occupied
his land.

Israel in the plains of Moab

THE ISRAELITES WENT FORWARD and encamped in the lowlands of 22
Moab on the farther side of the Jordan from Jericho.
Balak son of Zippor saw what Israel had done to the Amorites, and 2 3
Moab was in terror of the people because there were so many of them. The
Moabites were sick with fear at the sight of them; and they said to the 4
elders of Midian, 'This horde will soon lick up everything round us as a
bull crops the spring grass.' Balak son of Zippor was at that time king of
Moab. He sent a deputation to summon Balaam son of Beor, who was at 5
Pethor by the Euphrates in the land of the Amavites, with this message,
'Look, an entire nation has come out of Egypt; they cover the face of the
country and are settling at my very door. Come at once and lay a curse on 6
them, because they are too many for me; then I may be able to defeat them
and drive them from the country. I know that those whom you bless are
blessed, and those whom you curse are cursed.'
The elders of Moab and Midian took the fees for augury with them, and 7
they came to Balaam and told him what Balak had said. 'Spend this night 8
here,' he said, 'and I will give you whatever answer the LORD gives to me.'
So the Moabite chiefs stayed with Balaam. God came to Balaam and asked 9
him, 'Who are these men with you?' Balaam replied, 'Balak son of Zippor 10
king of Moab has sent them to me and he says, "Look, a people newly come 11
out of Egypt is covering the face of the country. Come at once and denounce
them for me; then I may be able to fight them and drive them away."' God 12
said to Balaam, 'You are not to go with them or curse the people, because
they are to be blessed.'*a* So Balaam rose in the morning and said to Balak's 13
chiefs, 'Go back to your own country; the LORD has refused to let me go
with you.' Then the Moabite chiefs took their leave and went back to Balak, 14
and told him that Balaam had refused to come with them; whereupon 15
Balak sent a second and larger embassy of higher rank than the first. They 16
came to Balaam and told him, 'This is the message from Balak son of
Zippor: "Let nothing stand in the way of your coming. I will confer great 17
honour upon you; I will do whatever you ask me. But you must come and
denounce this people for me."' Balaam gave this answer to Balak's mes- 18
sengers: 'Even if Balak were to give me all the silver and gold in his house,
I could not disobey the command of the LORD my God in anything, small

a Or are blessed.

19 or great. But stay here for this night, as the others did, that I may learn
20 what more the LORD has to say to me.' During the night God came to
Balaam and said to him, 'If these men have come to summon you, then
21 rise and go with them, but do only what I tell you.' So in the morning
Balaam rose, saddled his ass and went with the Moabite chiefs.

22   But God was angry because Balaam was going, and as he came riding on
his ass, accompanied by his two servants, the angel of the LORD took his
23 stand in the road to bar his way. When the ass saw the angel standing in the
road with his sword drawn, she turned off the road into the fields, and
24 Balaam beat the ass to bring her back on to the road. Then the angel of the
LORD stood where the road ran through a hollow, with fenced vineyards
25 on either side. The ass saw the angel and, crushing herself against the wall,
26 crushed Balaam's foot against it, and he beat her again. The angel of the
LORD moved on further and stood in a narrow place where there was no
27 room to turn either to right or left. When the ass saw the angel, she lay
down under Balaam. At that Balaam lost his temper and beat the ass with
28 his stick. The LORD then made the ass speak, and she said to Balaam, 'What
29 have I done? This is the third time you have beaten me.' Balaam answered
the ass, 'You have been making a fool of me. If I had had a sword here, I
30 should have killed you on the spot.' But the ass answered, 'Am I not still
the ass which you have ridden all your life? Have I ever taken such a liberty
31 with you before?' He said, 'No.' Then the LORD opened Balaam's eyes:
he saw the angel of the LORD standing in the road with his sword drawn,
32 and he bowed down and fell flat on his face before him. The angel said to
him, 'What do you mean by beating your ass three times like this? I came
33 out to bar your way but you made straight for me, and three times your ass
saw me and turned aside. If she had not turned aside, I should by now have
34 killed you and spared her.' Balaam replied to the angel of the LORD, 'I have
done wrong. I did not know that you stood in the road confronting me.
35 But now, if my journey displeases you, I am ready to go back.' The angel
of the LORD said to Balaam, 'Go on with these men; but say only what I
tell you.' So Balaam went on with Balak's chiefs.

36   When Balak heard that Balaam was coming, he came out to meet him as
37 far as Ar of Moab by the Arnon on his frontier. Balak said to Balaam, 'Did
I not send time and again to summon you? Why did you not come? Did
38 you think that I could not do you honour?' Balaam replied, 'I have come,
as you see. But now that I am here, what power have I of myself to say
anything? Whatever the word God puts into my mouth, that is what I
39 40 will say.' So Balaam went with Balak till they came to Kiriath-huzoth, and
Balak slaughtered cattle and sheep and sent them to Balaam and to the
chiefs who were with him.

41   In the morning Balak took Balaam and led him up to the Heights of
23 Baal, from where he could see the full extent of the Israelite host. Then
Balaam said to Balak, 'Build me here seven altars and prepare for me seven
2 bulls and seven rams.' Balak did as he asked and offered a bull and a ram
3-4 on each altar. Then he said to him, 'I have prepared the seven altars, and
I have offered the bull and the ram on each altar.' Balaam said to Balak,
'Take your stand beside your sacrifice, and let me go off by myself. It may

happen that the LORD will meet me. Whatever he reveals to me, I will tell
you.' So he went forthwith, and God met him. The LORD put words into   5
Balaam's mouth and said, 'Go back to Balak, and speak as I tell you.' So   6
he went back, and found Balak standing by his sacrifice, and with him all
the Moabite chiefs. And Balaam uttered his oracle: 7

> From Aram,[a] from the mountains of the east,
> Balak king of Moab has brought me:
> 'Come, lay a curse for me on Jacob,
> come, execrate Israel.'
> How can I denounce whom God has not denounced?   8
> How can I execrate whom the LORD has not execrated?
> From the rocky heights I see them,   9
> I watch them from the rounded hills.
> I see a people that dwells alone,
> that has not made itself one with the nations.
> Who can count the host [b] of Jacob   10
> or number the hordes[c] of Israel?
> Let me die as men die who are righteous,
> grant that my end may be as theirs!

Then Balak said to Balaam, 'What is this you have done? I sent for you   11
to denounce my enemies, and what you have done is to bless them.' But   12
he replied, 'Must I not keep to the words that the LORD puts into my
mouth?'

Balak then said to him, 'Come with me now to another place from which   13
you will see them, though not the full extent of them; you will not see them
all. Denounce them for me from there.' So he took him to the Field of the   14
Watchers[d] on the summit of Pisgah, where he built seven altars and offered
a bull and a ram on each altar. Balaam said to Balak, 'Take your stand beside   15
your sacrifice, and I will meet God over there.' The LORD met Balaam and   16
put words into his mouth, and said, 'Go back to Balak, and speak as I tell
you.' So he went back, and found him standing beside his sacrifice, with   17
the Moabite chiefs. Balak asked what the LORD had said, and Balaam   18
uttered his oracle:

> Up, Balak, and listen:
> hear what I am charged to say, son of Zippor.
> God is not a mortal that he should lie,   19
> not a man that he should change his mind.[e]
> Has he not spoken, and will he not make it good?
> What he has proclaimed, he will surely fulfil.
> I have received command to bless;   20
> I will bless and I cannot gainsay it.
> He has discovered no iniquity in Jacob   21
> and has seen no mischief in Israel.[f]

---

[a] *Or* Syria.   [b] *Or* dust.   [c] *Or* quarter *or* sands.
[d] *Or* Field of Zophim.   [e] *Or* feel regret.   [f] *Or* None can discover
calamity in Jacob nor see trouble in Israel.

> The LORD their God is with them,
> acclaimed among them as king. *a*

22 What its curving horns are to the wild ox,
> God is to them, who brought them out of Egypt.

23 Surely there is no divination in *b* Jacob,
> and no augury in *b* Israel;
> now is the time to say of Jacob
> and of Israel, 'See what God has wrought!'

24 Behold a people rearing up like a lioness,
> rampant like a lion;
> he will not couch till he devours the prey
> and drinks the blood of the slain.

25 Then Balak said to Balaam, 'You will not denounce them; then at least do not
26 bless them'; and he answered, 'Did I not warn you that I must do all the
27 LORD tells me?' Balak replied, 'Come, let me take you to another place; per-
28 haps God will be pleased to let you denounce them for me from there.' So he
29 took Balaam to the summit of Peor overlooking Jeshimon, and Balaam told
him to build seven altars for him there and prepare seven bulls and seven rams.
30 Balak did as Balaam had said, and he offered a bull and a ram on each altar.
24 But now that Balaam knew that the LORD wished him to bless Israel, he
did not go and resort to divination as before. He turned towards the desert;
2 and as he looked, he saw Israel encamped tribe by tribe. The spirit of God
3 came upon him, and he uttered his oracle:

> The very word of Balaam son of Beor,
> the very word of the man whose sight is clear,

4 the very word of him who hears the words of God,
> who with staring eyes sees in a trance
> the vision from the Almighty:

5 how goodly are your tents, O Jacob,
> your dwelling-places, Israel,

6 like long rows of palms,
> like gardens by a river,
> like lign-aloes planted by the LORD,
> like cedars beside the water!

7 The water in his vessels shall overflow,
> and his seed shall be like great waters
> so that his king may be taller than Agag,
> and his kingdom lifted high.

8 What its curving horns are to the wild ox,
> God is to him, who brought him out of Egypt;
> he shall devour his adversaries the nations,
> crunch their bones, and smash their limbs in pieces.

9 When he reclines he couches like a lion,
> like a lioness, and no one dares rouse him.
> Blessed be they that bless you,
> and they that curse you be accursed!

a *Or* royal care is bestowed on them.   *b* *Or* against.

At that Balak was very angry with Balaam, beat his hands together and 10
said, 'I summoned you to denounce my enemies, and three times you have
persisted in blessing them. Off with you to your own place! I promised to 11
confer great honour upon you, but now the LORD has kept this honour from
you.' Balaam answered, 'But I told your own messengers whom you sent: 12
"If Balak gives me all the silver and gold in his house, I cannot disobey the 13
command of the LORD by doing anything of my own will, good or bad.
What the LORD speaks to me, that is what I will say." Now I am going to 14
my own people; but first, I will warn you what this people will do to yours
in the days to come.' So he uttered his oracle: 15

> The very word of Balaam son of Beor,
> the very word of the man whose sight is clear,
> the very word of him who hears the words of God, 16
> who shares the knowledge of the Most High,
> who with staring eyes sees in a trance
> the vision from the Almighty:
>   I see him, but not now; 17
> I behold him, but not near:
> a star shall come forth out of Jacob,
> a comet arise from Israel.
> He shall smite the squadrons*a* of Moab,
> and beat down all the sons of strife.
> Edom shall be his by conquest 18
> and Seir, his enemy, shall be his.
> Israel shall do valiant deeds;
> Jacob shall trample them down, 19
> the last survivor from Ar shall he destroy.

He saw Amalek and uttered his oracle: 20

> First of all the nations was Amalek,
> but his end shall be utter destruction.

He saw the Kenites and uttered his oracle: 21

> Your refuge, though it seems secure,
> your nest, though set on the mountain crag,
> is doomed to burning, O Cain. 22
> How long must you dwell there in my sight?

He uttered his oracle: 23

> Ah, who are these assembling in the north,
> invaders from the region of Kittim? 24
> They will lay waste Assyria; they will lay Eber waste:
> he too shall perish utterly.

Then Balaam arose and returned home, and Balak also went on his way. 25

WHEN THE ISRAELITES WERE IN SHITTIM, the people began to have 25
intercourse with Moabite women, who invited them to the sacrifices 2
offered to their gods; and they ate the sacrificial food and prostrated

a *Or* heads.

179

3 themselves before the gods of Moab. The Israelites joined in the worship
4 of the Baal of Peor, and the LORD was angry with them. He said to Moses,
'Take all the leaders of the people and hurl them down to their death before
the LORD in the full light of day, that the fury of his anger may turn away
5 from Israel.' So Moses said to the judges of Israel, 'Put to death, each one
of you, those of his tribe who have joined in the worship of the Baal of Peor.'

6   One of the Israelites brought a Midianite woman into his family in open
defiance of Moses and all the community of Israel, while they were weep-
7 ing by the entrance of the Tent of the Presence. Phinehas son of Eleazar,
son of Aaron the priest, saw him. He stepped out from the crowd and took
8 up a spear, and he went into the inner room after the Israelite and trans-
fixed the two of them, the Israelite and the woman, pinning them together.
9 Thus the plague which had attacked the Israelites was brought to a stop;
but twenty-four thousand had already died.

10 11   The LORD spoke to Moses and said, 'Phinehas son of Eleazar, son of
Aaron the priest, has turned my wrath away from the Israelites; he displayed among them the same jealous anger that moved me, and therefore
12 in my jealousy I did not exterminate the Israelites. Tell him that I hereby
13 grant him my covenant of security of tenure. He and his descendants after
him shall enjoy the priesthood under a covenant for all time, because he
14 showed his zeal for his God and made expiation for the Israelites.' The
name of the Israelite struck down with the Midianite woman was Zimri
15 son of Salu, a chief in a Simeonite family, and the Midianite woman's
name was Cozbi daughter of Zur, who was the head of a group of fathers'
families in Midian.

16 17–18   The LORD spoke to Moses and said, 'Make the Midianites suffer as they
made you suffer with their crafty tricks, and strike them down; their
craftiness was your undoing at Peor and in the affair of Cozbi their sister,
the daughter of a Midianite chief, who was struck down at the time of the
plague that followed Peor.'

19 26 1   AFTER THE PLAGUE the LORD said to Moses and Eleazar the priest, son
2 of Aaron, 'Number the whole community of Israel by fathers' families,
recording everyone in Israel aged twenty years and upwards fit for military
3 service.' Moses and Eleazar collected them in the lowlands of Moab by
4 the Jordan near Jericho,*a* all who were twenty years of age and upwards,
as the LORD had commanded Moses.

These were the Israelites who came out of Egypt:
5*b*   Reubenites (Reuben was Israel's eldest son): Enoch, the Enochite
6 family; Pallu, the Palluite family; Hezron, the Hezronite family; Carmi,
7 the Carmite family. These were the Reubenite families; the number in
8 their detailed list was forty-three thousand seven hundred and thirty. Son
9 of Pallu: Eliab. Sons of Eliab: Nemuel, Dathan and Abiram. These were
the same Dathan and Abiram, conveners of the community, who defied
Moses and Aaron and joined the company of Korah in defying the LORD.
10 Then the earth opened its mouth and swallowed them up with Korah, and

a Prob. rdg.; Heb. adds saying.   *b Verses 5–50: cp. Gen. 46. 8–25; Exod. 6. 14, 15;
1 Chr. chs. 4–8.*

so their company died, while fire burnt up the two hundred and fifty men, and they became a warning sign. The Korahites, however, did not die. 11

Simeonites, by their families: Nemuel, the Nemuelite family; Jamin, 12 the Jaminite family; Jachin, the Jachinite family; Zerah, the Zarhite 13 family; Saul, the Saulite family. These were the Simeonite families; the 14 number in their detailed list was twenty-two thousand two hundred.

Gadites, by their families: Zephon, the Zephonite family; Haggi, the 15 Haggite family; Shuni, the Shunite family; Ozni, the Oznite family; Eri, 16 the Erite family; Arod, the Arodite family; Areli, the Arelite family. These 17 18 were the Gadite families; the number in their detailed list was forty thousand five hundred.

The sons of Judah were Er, Onan, Shelah, Perez and Zerah; Er and 19 Onan died in Canaan. Judahites, by their families: Shelah, the Shelanite 20 family; Perez, the Perezite family; Zerah, the Zarhite family. Perezites: 21 Hezron, the Hezronite family; Hamul, the Hamulite family. These were 22 the families of Judah; the number in their detailed list was seventy-six thousand five hundred.

Issacharites, by their families: Tola, the Tolaite family; Pua, the Puite 23 family; Jashub, the Jashubite family; Shimron, the Shimronite family. 24 These were the families of Issachar; the number in their detailed list was 25 sixty-four thousand three hundred.

Zebulunites, by their families: Sered, the Sardite family; Elon, the 26 Elonite family; Jahleel, the Jahleelite family. These were the Zebulun- 27 ite families; the number in their detailed list was sixty thousand five hundred.

Josephites, by their families: Manasseh and Ephraim. Manassites: 28 29 Machir, the Machirite family. Machir was the father of Gilead: Gilead, the Gileadite family. Gileadites: Jeezer, the Jeezerite family; Helek, the 30 Helekite family; Asriel, the Asrielite family; Shechem, the Shechemite 31 family; Shemida, the Shemidaite family; Hepher, the Hepherite family. 32 Zelophehad son of Hepher had no sons, only daughters; their names were 33 Mahlah, Noah, Hoglah, Milcah and Tirzah. These were the families of 34 Manasseh; the number in their detailed list was fifty-two thousand seven hundred.

Ephraimites, by their families: Shuthelah, the Shuthalhite family; 35 Becher, the Bachrite family; Tahan, the Tahanite family. Shuthalhites: 36 Eran, the Eranite family. These were the Ephraimite families; the number 37 in their detailed list was thirty-two thousand five hundred. These were the Josephites, by families.

Benjamites, by their families: Bela, the Belaite family; Ashbel, the 38 Ashbelite family; Ahiram, the Ahiramite family; Shupham, the Shupham- 39 ite family; Hupham, the Huphamite family. Belaites: Ard and Naaman. 40 Ard, the Ardite family; Naaman, the Naamite family. These were the 41 Benjamite families; the number in their detailed list was forty-five thousand six hundred.

Danites, by their families: Shuham, the Shuhamite family. These were 42 the families of Dan by their families; the number in the detailed list of the 43 Shuhamite family was sixty-four thousand four hundred.

44 Asherites, by their families: Imna, the Imnite family; Ishvi, the Ishvite
45 family; Beriah, the Beriite family. Beriite families: Heber, the Heberite
46 family; Malchiel, the Malchielite family. The daughter of Asher was named
47 Serah. These were the Asherite families; the number in their detailed list
was fifty-three thousand four hundred.

48 Naphtalites, by their families: Jahzeel, the Jahzeelite family; Guni, the
49 Gunite family; Jezer, the Jezerite family; Shillem, the Shillemite family.
50 These were the Naphtalite families by their families; the number in their
detailed list was forty-five thousand four hundred.

51 The total in the Israelite lists was six hundred and one thousand seven
hundred and thirty.

52 53 The LORD spoke to Moses and said, 'The land shall be apportioned
54 among these tribes according to the number of names recorded. To the
larger group you shall give a larger property and to the smaller a smaller;
a property shall be given to each in proportion to its size as shown in the
55 detailed lists. The land, however, shall be apportioned by lot; the lots shall
56 be cast for the properties by families in the father's line. Properties shall
be apportioned by lot between the larger families and the smaller.'

57 The detailed lists of Levi, by families: Gershon, the Gershonite family;
Kohath, the Kohathite family; Merari, the Merarite family.

58 These were the families of Levi: the Libnite, Hebronite, Mahlite,
Mushite, and Korahite families.

59 Kohath was the father of Amram; Amram's wife was named Jochebed
daughter of Levi, born to him in Egypt. She bore to Amram Aaron, Moses,
60 and their sister Miriam. Aaron's sons were Nadab, Abihu, Eleazar and
61 Ithamar. Nadab and Abihu died because they presented illicit fire before
the LORD.

62 In the detailed lists of Levi the number of males, aged one month and
upwards, was twenty-three thousand. They were recorded separately from
the other Israelites because no property was allotted to them among the
Israelites.

63 These were the detailed lists prepared by Moses and Eleazar the priest
when they numbered the Israelites in the lowlands of Moab by the Jordan
64 near Jericho. Among them there was not a single one of the Israelites whom
65 Moses and Aaron the priest had recorded in the wilderness of Sinai; for
the LORD had said they should all die in the wilderness. None of them was
still living except Caleb son of Jephunneh and Joshua son of Nun.

27 A claim was presented by the daughters of Zelophehad son of Hepher,
son of Gilead, son of Machir, son of Manasseh, son of Joseph. Their
2 names were Mahlah, Noah, Hoglah, Milcah and Tirzah. They appeared
at the entrance of the Tent of the Presence before Moses, Eleazar the priest,
3 the chiefs, and all the community, and spoke as follows: 'Our father died
in the wilderness. He was not among the company of Korah which combined together against the LORD; he died for his own sin and left no sons.
4 Is it right that, because he had no son, our father's name should disappear
from his family? Give us our property on the same footing as our father's
brothers.'

5 6 So Moses brought their case before the LORD, and the LORD spoke to

Moses and said, 'The claim of the daughters of Zelophehad is good. You 7
must allow them to inherit on the same footing as their father's brothers.
Let their father's patrimony pass to them. Then say this to the Israelites: 8
"When a man dies leaving no son, his patrimony shall pass to his daughter.
If he has no daughter, you shall give it to his brothers. If he has no brothers, 9 10
you shall give it to his father's brothers. If his father had no brothers, then 11
you shall give possession to the nearest survivor in his family, and he shall
inherit. This shall be a legal precedent for the Israelites, as the LORD has
commanded Moses."'

The LORD said to Moses, 'Go up this mountain, Mount Abarim, and 12
look out over the land which I have given to the Israelites. Then, when 13
you have looked out over it, you shall be gathered to your father's kin like
your brother Aaron; for you and Aaron disobeyed my command when the 14
community disputed with me in the wilderness of Zin: you did not uphold
my holiness before them at the waters.' These were the waters of Meribah-
by-Kadesh in the wilderness of Zin.

Then Moses said, 'Let the LORD, the God of the spirits of all mankind, 15 16
appoint a man over the community to go out and come in at their head, to 17
lead them out and bring them home, so that the community of the LORD
may not be like sheep without a shepherd.' The LORD answered Moses, 18
'Take Joshua son of Nun, a man endowed with spirit; lay your hand on
him and set him before Eleazar the priest and all the community. Give him 19
his commission in their presence, and delegate some of your authority to 20
him, so that all the community of the Israelites may obey him. He must 21
appear before Eleazar the priest, who will obtain a decision for him by
consulting the Urim before the LORD; at his word they shall go out and
shall come home, both Joshua and the whole community of the Israelites.'

Moses did as the LORD had commanded him. He took Joshua, presented 22
him to Eleazar the priest and the whole community, laid his hands on him 23
and gave him his commission, as the LORD had instructed him.

THE LORD SPOKE TO MOSES and said, Give this command to the Israel- **28** 1 2
ites: See that you present my offerings, the food for the food-offering of
soothing odour, to me at the appointed time.

Tell them: This is the food-offering which you shall present to the 3
LORD: the regular daily whole-offering of two yearling rams without
blemish. One you shall sacrifice in the morning and the second between 4
dusk and dark. The grain-offering shall be a tenth of an ephah of flour 5
mixed with a quarter of a hin of oil of pounded olives. (This was the regular 6
whole-offering made at Mount Sinai, a soothing odour, a food-offering to
the LORD.) The wine for the proper drink-offering shall be a quarter of a 7
hin to each ram; you are to pour out this strong drink in the holy place as
an offering to the LORD. You shall sacrifice the second ram between dusk 8
and dark, with the same grain-offering as at the morning sacrifice and with
the proper drink-offering; it is a food-offering of soothing odour to the
LORD.

For the sabbath day: two yearling rams without blemish, a grain- 9
offering of two tenths of an ephah of flour mixed with oil, and the proper

10 drink-offering. This whole-offering, presented every sabbath, is in addition to the regular whole-offering and the proper drink-offering.

11 On the first day of every month you shall present a whole-offering to the LORD, consisting of two young bulls, one ram and seven yearling rams
12 without blemish. The grain-offering shall be three tenths of flour mixed with oil for each bull, two tenths of flour mixed with oil for the full-grown
13 ram, and one tenth of flour mixed with oil for each young ram. This is a
14 whole-offering, a food-offering of soothing odour to the LORD. The proper drink-offering shall be half a hin of wine for each bull, a third for the full-grown ram and a quarter for each young ram. This is the whole-offering
15 to be made, month by month, throughout the year. Further, one he-goat shall be sacrificed as a sin-offering to the LORD, in addition to the regular whole-offering and the proper drink-offering.

16 The Passover of the LORD shall be held on the fourteenth day of the
17 first month, and on the fifteenth day there shall be a pilgrim-feast; for seven
18 days you must eat only unleavened cakes. On the first day there shall be a
19 sacred assembly; you shall not do your daily work. As a food-offering, a whole-offering to the LORD, you shall present two young bulls, one ram,
20 and seven yearling rams, all without blemish. You shall offer the proper grain-offerings of flour mixed with oil, three tenths for each bull, two
21 22 tenths for the ram, and one tenth for each of the seven young rams; and as
23 a sin-offering, one he-goat to make expiation for you. All these you shall offer in addition to the morning whole-offering, which is the regular
24 sacrifice. You shall repeat this daily till the seventh day, presenting food as a food-offering of soothing odour to the LORD, in addition to the regu-
25 lar whole-offering and the proper drink-offering. On the seventh day there shall be a sacred assembly; you shall not do your daily work.

26 On the day of Firstfruits, when you bring to the LORD your grain-offering from the new crop at your Feast of Weeks, there shall be a sacred
27 assembly; you shall not do your daily work. You shall bring a whole-offering as a soothing odour to the LORD: two young bulls, one full-grown
28 ram, and seven yearling rams. The proper grain-offering shall be of flour
29 mixed with oil, three tenths for each bull, two tenths for the one ram, and
30 a tenth for each of the seven young rams, and there shall be one he-
31 goat as a sin-offering to make expiation for you; they shall all be without blemish. All these you shall offer in addition to the regular whole-offering with the proper grain-offering and drink-offering.

29 On the first day of the seventh month there shall be a sacred assembly;
2 you shall not do your daily work. It shall be a day of acclamation. You shall sacrifice a whole-offering as a soothing odour to the LORD: one young
3 bull, one full-grown ram, and seven yearling rams, without blemish. Their proper grain-offering shall be of flour mixed with oil, three tenths for the
4 bull, two tenths for the one ram, and one tenth for each of the seven young
5 rams, and there shall be one he-goat as a sin-offering to make expiation for
6 you. This is in addition to the monthly whole-offering and the regular whole-offering with their proper grain-offerings and drink-offerings according to custom; it is a food-offering of soothing odour to the LORD.
7 On the tenth day of this seventh month there shall be a sacred assembly,

and you shall mortify yourselves; you shall not do any work. You shall 8
bring a whole-offering to the LORD as a soothing odour: one young bull,
one full-grown ram, and seven yearling rams; they shall all be without
blemish. The proper grain-offering shall be of flour mixed with oil, three 9
tenths for the bull, two tenths for the one ram, and one tenth for each of the 10
seven young rams, and there shall be one he-goat as a sin-offering, in addi- 11
tion to the expiatory sin-offering and the regular whole-offering, with the
proper grain-offering and drink-offering.

On the fifteenth day of the seventh month there shall be a sacred assem- 12
bly. You shall not do your daily work, but shall keep a pilgrim-feast to the
LORD for seven days. As a whole-offering, a food-offering of soothing 13
odour to the LORD, you shall bring thirteen young bulls, two full-grown
rams, and fourteen yearling rams; they shall all be without blemish. The 14
proper grain-offering shall be of flour mixed with oil, three tenths for each
of the thirteen bulls, two tenths for each of the two rams, and one tenth for 15
each of the fourteen young rams, and there shall be one he-goat as a sin- 16
offering, in addition to the regular whole-offering with the proper grain-
offering and drink-offering.

On the second day: twelve young bulls, two full-grown rams, and four- 17
teen yearling rams, without blemish, together with the proper grain- 18
offerings and drink-offerings for bulls, full-grown rams, and young rams,
as prescribed according to their number, and there shall be one he-goat 19
as a sin-offering, in addition to the regular whole-offering with the proper
grain-offering and drink-offering.

On the third day: eleven bulls, two full-grown rams, and fourteen 20
yearling rams, without blemish, together with the proper grain-offerings 21
and drink-offerings for bulls, full-grown rams, and young rams, as prescribed according to their number, and there shall be one he-goat as a 22
sin-offering, in addition to the regular whole-offering, with the proper
grain-offering and drink-offering.

On the fourth day: ten bulls, two full-grown rams, and fourteen yearling 23
rams, without blemish, together with the proper grain-offerings and drink- 24
offerings for bulls, full-grown rams, and young rams, as prescribed according to their number, and there shall be one he-goat as a sin-offering, in 25
addition to the regular whole-offering with the proper grain-offering and
drink-offering.

On the fifth day: nine bulls, two full-grown rams, and fourteen yearling 26
rams, without blemish, together with the proper grain-offerings and drink- 27
offerings for bulls, full-grown rams, and young rams, as prescribed according to their number, and there shall be one he-goat as a sin-offering, in 28
addition to the regular whole-offering with the proper grain-offering and
drink-offering.

On the sixth day: eight bulls, two full-grown rams, and fourteen yearling 29
rams, without blemish, together with the proper grain-offerings and drink- 30
offerings for bulls, full-grown rams, and young rams, as prescribed according to their number, and there shall be one he-goat as a sin-offering, in 31
addition to the regular whole-offering with the proper grain-offering and
drink-offering.

32 On the seventh day: seven bulls, two full-grown rams, and fourteen
33 yearling rams, without blemish, together with the proper grain-offerings
and drink-offerings for bulls, full-grown rams, and young rams, as pre-
34 scribed according to their number, and there shall be one he-goat as a
sin-offering, in addition to the regular whole-offering with the proper
grain-offering and drink-offering.

35 The eighth day you shall keep as a closing ceremony; you shall not do
36 your daily work. As a whole-offering, a food-offering of soothing odour to
the LORD, you shall bring one bull, one full-grown ram, and seven yearling
37 rams, without blemish, together with the proper grain-offerings and drink-
offerings for bulls, full-grown rams, and young rams, as prescribed accord-
38 ing to their number, and there shall be one he-goat as a sin-offering, in
addition to the regular whole-offering with the proper grain-offering and
drink-offering.

39 These are the sacrifices which you shall offer to the LORD at the appointed seasons, in addition to the votive offerings, the freewill offerings,
the whole-offerings, the grain-offerings, the drink-offerings, and the
shared-offerings.

40 Moses told the Israelites exactly what the LORD had commanded
him.

30 THEN MOSES SPOKE to the heads of the Israelite tribes and said, This is
2 the LORD's command: When a man makes a vow to the LORD or swears
an oath and so puts himself under a binding obligation, he must not break
3 his word. Every word he has spoken, he must make good. When a woman,
still young and living in her father's house, makes a vow to the LORD or
4 puts herself under a binding obligation, if her father hears of it and keeps
5 silence, then any such vow or obligation shall be valid. But if her father
disallows it when he hears of it, none of her vows or obligations shall be
6 valid; the LORD will absolve her, because her father has disallowed it. If
the woman is married when she is under a vow or a binding obligation
7 rashly uttered, then if her husband hears of it and keeps silence when he
hears, her vow or obligation by which she has bound herself shall be valid.
8 If, however, her husband disallows it when he hears of it and repudiates
the vow which she has taken upon herself or the rash utterance with which
9 she has bound herself, then the LORD will absolve her. Every vow by which
10 a widow or a divorced woman has bound herself shall be valid. But if it is
in her husband's house that a woman makes a vow or puts herself under a
11 binding obligation by an oath, and her husband, hearing of it, keeps silence
and does not disallow it, then every vow and obligation under which she
12 has put herself shall be valid; but if her husband clearly repudiates them
when he hears of them, then nothing that she has uttered, whether vow or
obligation, shall be valid. Her husband has repudiated them, and the LORD
will absolve her.

13 The husband can confirm or repudiate any vow or oath by which a
14 woman binds herself to mortification. If he maintains silence day after day,
he thereby confirms every vow or obligation under which she has put herself: he confirms them, because he kept silence at the time when he heard

them. If he repudiates them some time after he has heard them, he shall be   15
responsible for her default.

Such are the decrees which the LORD gave to Moses concerning a husband   16
and his wife and a father and his daughter, still young and living in her
father's house.

THE LORD SPOKE TO MOSES and said, 'You are to exact vengeance for   31 1 2
Israel on the Midianites and then you will be gathered to your father's kin.'

Then Moses spoke to the people in these words: 'Let some men among   3
you be drafted for active service. They shall fall upon Midian and exact
vengeance in the LORD's name. You shall send out a thousand men from   4
each of the tribes of Israel.' So the men were called up from the clans of   5
Israel, a thousand from each tribe, twelve thousand in all, drafted for active
service. Moses sent out this force, a thousand from each tribe, with   6
Phinehas son of Eleazar the priest, who was in charge of the holy vessels
and of the trumpets to give the signal for the battle-cry. They made war   7
on Midian as the LORD had commanded Moses, and slew all the men. In   8
addition to those slain in battle they killed the kings of Midian—Evi,
Rekem, Zur, Hur, and Reba, the five kings of Midian—and they put to
death also Balaam son of Beor. The Israelites took captive the Midianite   9
women and their dependants, and carried off all their beasts, their flocks,
and their property. They burnt all their cities, in which they had settled,   10
and all their encampments. They took all the spoil and plunder, both   11
man and beast, and brought them—captives, plunder, and spoil—to Moses   12
and Eleazar the priest and to all the community of the Israelites, to the
camp in the lowlands of Moab by the Jordan at Jericho.

Moses and Eleazar the priest and all the leaders of the community went   13
to meet them outside the camp. Moses spoke angrily to the officers of the   14
army, the commanders of units of a thousand and of a hundred, who were
returning from the campaign: 'Have you spared all the women?' he said.   15
'Remember, it was they who, on Balaam's departure, set about seducing   16
the Israelites into disloyalty to the LORD that day at Peor, so that the
plague struck the community of the LORD. Now kill every male dependant,   17
and kill every woman who has had intercourse with a man, but spare for   18
yourselves every woman among them who has not had intercourse. You   19
yourselves, every one of you who has taken life and every one who has
touched the dead, must remain outside the camp for seven days. Purify
yourselves and your captives on the third day and on the seventh day, and   20
purify also every piece of clothing, every article made of skin, everything
woven of goat's hair, and everything made of wood.'

Eleazar the priest said to the soldiers returning from battle, 'This is a   21
law and statute which the LORD has ordained through Moses. Anything   22-23
which will stand fire, whether gold, silver, copper, iron, tin, or lead, you
shall pass through fire and then it will be clean. Other things shall be
purified by the water of ritual purification; whatever cannot stand fire shall
be passed through the water. On the seventh day you shall wash your   24
clothes, and then be clean; after this you may re-enter the camp.'

The LORD spoke to Moses and said, 'Count all that has been captured,   25 26

man or beast, you and Eleazar the priest and the heads of families in the
27 community, and divide it equally between the fighting men who went on
28 the campaign and the whole community. You shall levy a tax for the LORD:
from the combatants it shall be one out of every five hundred, whether
29 men, cattle, asses, or sheep, to be taken out of their share and given to
30 Eleazar the priest as a contribution for the LORD. Out of the share of the
Israelites it shall be one out of every fifty taken, whether man or beast,
cattle, asses, or sheep, to be given to the Levites who are in charge of the
LORD's Tabernacle.'

31   Moses and Eleazar the priest did as the LORD had commanded Moses.
32 These were the spoils, over and above the plunder taken by the fighting
33 men: six hundred and seventy-five thousand sheep, seventy-two thousand
34 35 cattle, sixty-one thousand asses; and of persons, thirty-two thousand girls
who had had no intercourse with a man.

36   The half-share of those who took part in the campaign was thus three
37 hundred and thirty-seven thousand five hundred sheep, the tax for the
38 LORD from these being six hundred and seventy-five; thirty-six thousand
39 cattle, the tax being seventy-two; thirty thousand five hundred asses, the
40 tax being sixty-one; and sixteen thousand persons, the tax being thirty-
41 two. Moses gave Eleazar the priest the tax levied for the LORD, as the LORD
had commanded him.

42-43   The share of the community, being the half-share for the Israelites
which Moses divided off from that of the combatants, was three hundred
44 and thirty-seven thousand five hundred sheep, thirty-six thousand cattle,
45 46 47 thirty thousand five hundred asses, and sixteen thousand persons. Moses
took one out of every fifty, whether man or beast, from the half-share of the
Israelites, and gave it to the Levites who were in charge of the LORD's
Tabernacle, as the LORD had commanded him.

48   Then the officers who had commanded the forces on the campaign, the
49 commanders of units of a thousand and of a hundred, came to Moses and
said to him, 'Sir, we have checked the roll of the fighting men who were
50 under our command, and not one of them is missing. So we have brought
the gold ornaments, the armlets, bracelets, finger-rings, earrings, and
pendants that each man has found, to offer them before the LORD as a
ransom for our lives.'

51   Moses and Eleazar the priest received this gold from the commanders
52 of units of a thousand and of a hundred, all of it craftsman's work, and the
gold thus levied as a contribution to the LORD weighed sixteen thousand
53 seven hundred and fifty shekels; for every man in the army had taken
54 plunder. So Moses and Eleazar the priest received the gold from the commanders of units of a thousand and of a hundred, and brought it to the
Tent of the Presence that the LORD might remember Israel.

32   Now the Reubenites and the Gadites had large and very numerous
flocks, and when they saw that the land of Jazer and Gilead was good
2 grazing country, they came and said to Moses and Eleazar the priest and
3 to the leaders of the community, 'Ataroth, Dibon, Jazer, Nimrah, Heshbon,
4 Elealeh, Sebam, Nebo, and Beon, the region which the LORD has subdued
before the advance of the Israelite community, is grazing country, and our

flocks are our livelihood. If', they said, 'we have found favour with you, 5
sir, then let this country be given to us as our possession, and do not make
us cross the Jordan.' Moses replied to the Gadites and the Reubenites, 6
'Are your kinsmen to go into battle while you stay here? How dare you dis- 7
courage the Israelites from crossing over to the land which the LORD has
given them? This is what your fathers did when I sent them out from 8
Kadesh-barnea to view the land. They went up as far as the gorge of 9
Eshcol and viewed the land, and on their return so discouraged the Israelites that they would not enter the land which the LORD had given them.
The LORD became angry that day, and he solemnly swore: "Because they 10 11
have not followed me with their whole heart, none of the men who came
out of Egypt, from twenty years old and upwards, shall see the land which
I promised on oath to Abraham, Isaac and Jacob." This meant all except 12
Caleb son of Jephunneh the Kenizzite and Joshua son of Nun, who followed the LORD with their whole heart. The LORD became angry with 13
Israel, and he made them wander in the wilderness for forty years until
that whole generation was dead which had done what was wrong in his
eyes. And now you are following in your fathers' footsteps, a fresh brood 14
of sinful men to fire the LORD's anger once more against Israel; for if you 15
refuse to follow him, he will again abandon this whole people in the wilderness and you will be the cause of their destruction.'

Presently they came forward with this offer: 'We will build folds for our 16
sheep here and towns for our dependants. Then we can be drafted as a 17
fighting force to go at the head of the Israelites until we have brought them
to the lands that will be theirs. Meanwhile our dependants can live in the
walled towns, safe from the people of the country. We will not return 18
until every Israelite is settled in possession of his patrimony; we will claim 19
no share of the land with them over the Jordan and beyond, because our
patrimony has already been allotted to us east of the Jordan.' Moses 20
answered, 'If you stand by your promise, if in the presence of the LORD
you are drafted for battle, and the whole draft crosses the Jordan in front of 21
the LORD and remains there until the LORD has driven out his enemies, and 22
the land falls before him, then you may come back and be quit of your
obligation to the LORD and to Israel; and this land shall be your possession
in the sight of the LORD. But I warn you, if you fail to do all this, you will 23
have sinned against the LORD, and your sin will find you out. So build 24
towns for your dependants and folds for your sheep; but carry out your
promise.'

The Gadites and Reubenites answered Moses, 'Sir, we are your servants 25
and will do as you command. Our dependants and wives, our flocks and 26
all our beasts shall remain here in the cities of Gilead; but we, all who have 27
been drafted for active service with the LORD, will cross the river and fight,
according to your command.'

Accordingly Moses gave these instructions to Eleazar the priest and 28
Joshua son of Nun and to the heads of the families in the Israelite tribes:
'If the Gadites and Reubenites, all who have been drafted for battle before 29
the LORD, cross the Jordan with you, and if the land falls into your hands,
then you shall give them Gilead for their possession. But if, thus drafted, 30

they fail to cross with you, then they shall acquire land alongside you in
31 Canaan.' The Gadites and Reubenites said in response, 'Sir, the LORD
32 has spoken, and we will obey. Once we have been drafted, we will cross
over before the LORD into Canaan; then we shall have our patrimony here
beyond the Jordan.'

33 So to the Gadites, the Reubenites, and half the tribe of Manasseh son
of Joseph, Moses gave the kingdoms of Sihon king of the Amorites and
Og king of Bashan, the whole land with its towns and the country round
34 35 them. The Gadites built Dibon, Ataroth, Aroer, Atroth-shophan, Jazer,
36 Jogbehah, Beth-nimrah, and Beth-haran, all of them walled towns with
37 folds for their sheep. The Reubenites built Heshbon, Elealeh, Kiriathaim,
38 Nebo, Baal-meon (whose name was changed), and Sibmah; these were the
39 names they gave to the towns they built. The sons of Machir son of Manas-
40 seh invaded Gilead, took it and drove out the Amorite inhabitants; Moses
then assigned Gilead to Machir son of Manasseh, and he made his home
41 there. Jair son of Manasseh attacked and took the tent-villages of Ham *a*
42 and called them Havvoth-jair. *b* Nobah attacked and took Kenath and its
villages and gave it his own name, Nobah.

33 THESE ARE THE STAGES in the journey of the Israelites, when they were
2 led by Moses and Aaron in their tribal hosts out of Egypt. Moses recorded
their starting-points stage by stage as the LORD commanded him. These
are their stages from one starting-point to the next:
3 The Israelites left Rameses on the fifteenth day of the first month, the
day after the Passover; they marched out defiantly in full view of all the
4 Egyptians, while the Egyptians were burying all the first-born struck down
by the LORD as a judgement on their gods.
5 The Israelites left Rameses and encamped at Succoth.
6 They left Succoth and encamped at Etham on the edge of the wilderness.
7 They left Etham, turned back near Pi-hahiroth *c* on the east of Baal-
zephon, and encamped before Migdol.
8 They left Pi-hahiroth, passed through the Sea into the wilderness,
marched for three days through the wilderness of Etham, and encamped
at Marah.
9 They left Marah and came to Elim, where there were twelve springs of
water and seventy palm-trees, and encamped there.
10 They left Elim and encamped by the Red Sea.
11 They left the Red Sea and encamped in the wilderness of Sin.
12 They left the wilderness of Sin and encamped at Dophkah.
13 They left Dophkah and encamped at Alush.
14 They left Alush and encamped at Rephidim, where there was no water
for the people to drink.
15 They left Rephidim and encamped in the wilderness of Sinai.
16 They left the wilderness of Sinai and encamped at Kibroth-hattaavah.
17 They left Kibroth-hattaavah and encamped at Hazeroth.
18 They left Hazeroth and encamped at Rithmah.

---

a *Prob. rdg.; Heb.* their tent-villages.   *b* *That is* Tent-villages of Jair.
c *See* Exod. 14. 2.

They left Rithmah and encamped at Rimmon-parez.   19
They left Rimmon-parez and encamped at Libnah.   20
They left Libnah and encamped at Rissah.   21
They left Rissah and encamped at Kehelathah.   22
They left Kehelathah and encamped at Mount Shapher.   23
They left Mount Shapher and encamped at Haradah.   24
They left Haradah and encamped at Makheloth.   25
They left Makheloth and encamped at Tahath.   26
They left Tahath and encamped at Tarah.   27
They left Tarah and encamped at Mithcah.   28
They left Mithcah and encamped at Hashmonah.   29
They left Hashmonah and encamped at Moseroth.   30
They left Moseroth and encamped at Bene-jaakan.   31
They left Bene-jaakan and encamped at Hor-haggidgad.   32
They left Hor-haggidgad and encamped at Jotbathah.   33
They left Jotbathah and encamped at Ebronah.*a*   34
They left Ebronah and encamped at Ezion-geber.   35
They left Ezion-geber and encamped in the wilderness of Zin, that is of   36
Kadesh.

They left Kadesh and encamped on Mount Hor on the frontier of Edom.   37
Aaron the priest went up Mount Hor at the command of the LORD and   38
there he died, on the first day of the fifth month in the fortieth year after
the Israelites came out of Egypt; he was a hundred and twenty-three years 39
old when he died there.

The Canaanite king of Arad, who lived in the Canaanite Negeb, heard   40
that the Israelites were coming.

They left Mount Hor and encamped at Zalmonah.   41
They left Zalmonah and encamped at Punon.   42
They left Punon and encamped at Oboth.   43
They left Oboth and encamped at Iye-abarim on the frontier of Moab.   44
They left Iyim and encamped at Dibon-gad.   45
They left Dibon-gad and encamped at Almon-diblathaim.   46
They left Almon-diblathaim and encamped in the mountains of Abarim   47
east of Nebo.

They left the mountains of Abarim and encamped in the lowlands of   48
Moab by the Jordan near Jericho. Their camp beside the Jordan extended   49
from Beth-jeshimoth to Abel-shittim in the lowlands of Moab. In the   50
lowlands of Moab by the Jordan near Jericho the LORD spoke to Moses and
said, Speak to the Israelites in these words: You will soon be crossing the 51
Jordan to enter Canaan. You must drive out all its inhabitants as you   52
advance, destroy all their carved figures and their images of cast metal,
and lay their hill-shrines in ruins. You must take possession of the land 53
and settle there, for to you I have given the land to occupy. You must divide 54
it by lot among your families, each taking its own territory, the large family
a large territory and the small family a small. It shall be assigned to them
according to the fall of the lot, each tribe and family taking its own territory.
If you do not drive out the inhabitants of the land as you advance, any   55

a Or Abronah.

191

56 whom you leave in possession will become like a barbed hook in your eye and a thorn in your side. They shall continually dispute your possession of the land, and what I meant to do to them I will do to you.

34 1 2 The LORD spoke to Moses and said, Give these instructions to the Israelites: Soon you will be entering Canaan. This is the land assigned to you as a perpetual patrimony, the land of Canaan thus defined by its
3 frontiers. Your southern border shall start from the wilderness of Zin, where it marches with Edom, and run southwards from the end of the
4 Dead Sea on its eastern side. It shall then turn from the south up the ascent of Akrabbim and pass by Zin, and its southern limit shall be Kadesh-
5 barnea. It shall proceed by Hazar-addar to Azmon and from Azmon turn
6 towards the Torrent of Egypt, and its limit shall be the sea. Your western frontier shall be the Great Sea and the seaboard; this shall be your frontier
7 to the west. This shall be your northern frontier: you shall draw a line from
8 the Great Sea to Mount Hor and from Mount Hor to Lebo-hamath, and
9 the limit of the frontier shall be Zedad. From there it shall run to Ziphron, and its limit shall be Hazar-enan; this shall be your frontier to the north.
10 11 To the east you shall draw a line from Hazar-enan to Shepham; it shall run down from Shepham to Riblah east of Ain, continuing until it strikes the
12 ridge east of the sea of Kinnereth. The frontier shall then run down to the Jordan and its limit shall be the Dead Sea. The land defined by these frontiers shall be your land.

13 Moses gave these instructions to the Israelites: This is the land which you shall assign by lot, each taking your own territory; it is the land which
14 the LORD has ordered to be given to nine tribes and a half tribe. For the Reubenites, the Gadites, and the half tribe of Manasseh have already
15 occupied their territories, family by family. These two and a half tribes have received their territory here beyond the Jordan, east of Jericho, towards the sunrise.

16 17 The LORD spoke to Moses and said, These are the men who shall assign
18 the land for you: Eleazar the priest and Joshua son of Nun. You shall also
19 take one chief from each tribe to assign the land. These are their names:
    from the tribe of Judah: Caleb son of Jephunneh;
20   from the tribe of Simeon: Samuel son of Ammihud;
21   from the tribe of Benjamin: Elidad son of Kislon;
22   from the tribe of Dan: the chief Bukki son of Jogli;
23   from the Josephites: from Manasseh, the chief Hanniel son of Ephod;
24 and from Ephraim, the chief Kemuel son of Shiphtan;
25   from Zebulun: the chief Elizaphan son of Parnach;
26   from Issachar: the chief Paltiel son of Azzan;
27   from Asher: the chief Ahihud son of Shelomi;
28   from Naphtali: the chief Pedahel son of Ammihud.
29 These were the men whom the LORD appointed to assign the territories in the land of Canaan.

35 THE LORD SPOKE TO MOSES in the lowlands of Moab by the Jordan near
2 Jericho and said: Tell the Israelites to set aside towns in their patrimony as homes for the Levites, and give them also the common land surrounding

the towns. They shall live in the towns, and keep their beasts, their herds, 3
and all their livestock on the common land. The land of the towns which 4
you give the Levites shall extend from the centre of the town outwards for
a thousand cubits in each direction. Starting from the town the eastern 5
boundary shall measure two thousand cubits, the southern two thousand,
the western two thousand, and the northern two thousand, with the town
in the centre. They shall have this as the common land adjoining their
towns.

When you give the Levites their towns, six of them shall be cities of 6
refuge, in which the homicide may take sanctuary; and you shall give them
forty-two other towns. The total number of towns to be given to the 7
Levites, each with its common land, is forty-eight. When you set aside 8
these towns out of the territory of the Israelites, you shall allot more from
the larger tribe and less from the smaller; each tribe shall give towns to the
Levites in proportion to the patrimony assigned to it.

The LORD spoke to Moses and said, Speak to the Israelites in these 9 10
words: You are crossing the Jordan to the land of Canaan. You shall 11
designate certain cities to be places of refuge, in which the homicide who
has killed a man by accident may take sanctuary. These cities shall be 12
places of refuge from the vengeance of the dead man's next-of-kin, so
that the homicide shall not be put to death without standing his trial before
the community. The cities appointed as places of refuge shall be six in 13
number, three east of the Jordan and three in Canaan. These six cities 14 15
shall be places of refuge, so that any man who has taken life inadvertently,
whether he be Israelite, resident alien, or temporary settler, may take
sanctuary in one of them.

If the man strikes his victim with anything made of iron and he dies, 16
then he is a murderer: the murderer must be put to death. If a man has a 17
stone in his hand capable of causing death and strikes another man and he
dies, he is a murderer: the murderer must be put to death. If a man has a 18
wooden thing in his hand capable of causing death, and strikes another man
and he dies, he is a murderer: the murderer must be put to death. The dead 19
man's next-of-kin shall put the murderer to death; he shall put him to death
because he had attacked his victim. If the homicide sets upon a man openly 20
of malice aforethought or aims a missile at him of set purpose and he dies,
or if in enmity he falls upon him with his bare hands and he dies, then the 21
assailant must be put to death; he is a murderer. His next-of-kin shall put
the murderer to death because he had attacked his victim.

If he attacks a man on the spur of the moment, not being his enemy, or 22
hurls a missile at him not of set purpose, or if without looking he throws a 23
stone capable of causing death and it hits a man, then if the man dies,
provided he was not the man's enemy and was not harming him of set
purpose, the community shall judge between the striker and the next-of- 24
kin according to these rules. The community shall protect the homicide 25
from the vengeance of the kinsman and take him back to the city of refuge
where he had taken sanctuary. He must stay there till the death of the duly
anointed high priest. If the homicide ever goes beyond the boundaries of 26
the city where he has taken sanctuary, and the next-of-kin finds him outside 27

28 and kills him, then the next-of-kin shall not be guilty of murder. The homicide must remain in the city of refuge till the death of the high priest;
29 after the death of the high priest he may go back to his property. These shall be legal precedents for you for all time wherever you live.
30   The homicide shall be put to death as a murderer only on the testimony of witnesses; the testimony of a single witness shall not be enough to bring
31 him to his death. You shall not accept payment for the life of a homicide
32 guilty of a capital offence; he must be put to death. You shall not accept a payment from a man who has taken sanctuary in a city of refuge, allowing
33 him to go back before the death of the high priest and live at large. You shall not defile your land by bloodshed. Blood defiles the land, and expiation cannot be made on behalf of the land for blood shed on it except by the
34 blood of the man that shed it. You shall not make the land which you inhabit unclean, the land in which I dwell; for I, the LORD, dwell among the Israelites.

36 THE HEADS OF THE FATHERS' FAMILIES OF GILEAD son of Machir, son of Manasseh, one of the families of the sons of Joseph, approached Moses and the chiefs, heads of families in Israel, and addressed them.
2 'Sir,' they said, 'the LORD commanded you to distribute the land by lot to the Israelites, and you were also commanded to give the patrimony of our
3 brother Zelophehad to his daughters. Now if any of them shall be married to a husband from another Israelite tribe, her patrimony will be lost to the patrimony of our fathers and be added to that of the tribe into which she is
4 married, and so part of our allotted patrimony will be lost. Then, when the jubilee year comes round in Israel, her patrimony would be added to the patrimony of the tribe into which she is married, and it would be permanently lost to the patrimony of our fathers' tribe.'
5   So Moses, instructed by the LORD, gave the Israelites this ruling: 'The
6 tribe of the sons of Joseph is right. This is the LORD's command for the daughters of Zelophehad: They may marry whom they please, but only
7 within a family of their father's tribe. No patrimony in Israel shall pass from
8 tribe to tribe, but every Israelite shall retain his father's patrimony. Any woman of an Israelite tribe who is an heiress may marry a man from any family in her father's tribe. Thus the Israelites shall retain each one the
9 patrimony of his forefathers. No patrimony shall pass from one tribe to another, but every tribe in Israel shall retain its own patrimony.'
10   The daughters of Zelophehad acted in accordance with the LORD's
11 command to Moses; Mahlah, Tirzah, Hoglah, Milcah and Noah, the
12 daughters of Zelophehad, married sons of their father's brothers. They married within the families of the sons of Manasseh son of Joseph, and their patrimony remained with the tribe of their father's family.
13   These are the commandments and the decrees which the LORD issued to the Israelites through Moses in the lowlands of Moab by the Jordan near Jericho.

DEUTERONOMY

Primary charge of Moses to the people

THESE ARE THE WORDS THAT MOSES SPOKE to all 1
Israel in Transjordan, in the wilderness, that is to say in the Arabah
opposite Suph, between Paran on the one side and Tophel, Laban,
Hazeroth, and Dizahab on the other. (The journey from Horeb through the 2
hill-country of Seir to Kadesh-barnea takes eleven days.)

On the first day of the eleventh month of the fortieth year, after the 3-4
defeat of Sihon king of the Amorites who ruled in Heshbon, and the defeat
at Edrei of Og king of Bashan who ruled in Ashtaroth, Moses repeated to
the Israelites all the commands that the LORD had given him for them. It 5
was in Transjordan, in Moab, that Moses resolved to promulgate this law.
These were his words: The LORD our God spoke to us at Horeb and said, 6
'You have stayed on this mountain long enough; go now, make for the 7
hill-country of the Amorites, and pass on to all their neighbours in the
Arabah, in the hill-country, in the Shephelah, in the Negeb, and on
the coast, in short, all Canaan and the Lebanon as far as the great river, the
Euphrates. I have laid the land open before you; go in and occupy it, 8
the land which the LORD swore to give to your forefathers Abraham, Isaac
and Jacob, and to their descendants after them.'

At that time I said to you, 'You are a burden too heavy for me to carry 9
unaided. The LORD your God has increased you so that today you are as 10
numerous as the stars in the sky. May the LORD the God of your fathers 11
increase your number a thousand times and may he bless you as he promised. How can I bear unaided the heavy burden you are to me, and put 12
up with your complaints? Choose men of wisdom, understanding, and 13
repute for each of your tribes, and I will set them in authority over you.'
Your answer was, 'What you have told us to do is right.' So I took men of 14 15
wisdom and repute and set them in authority over you, some as commanders
over units of a thousand, of a hundred, of fifty or of ten, and others as
officers, for each of your tribes. And at that time I gave your judges this 16
command: 'You are to hear the cases that arise among your kinsmen and
judge fairly between man and man, whether fellow-countryman or resident
alien. You must be impartial and listen to high and low alike: have no fear 17
of man, for judgement belongs to God. If any case is too difficult for you,
bring it before me and I will hear it.' At the same time I instructed you in 18
all these duties.

Then we set out from Horeb, in obedience to the orders of the LORD 19
our God, and marched through that vast and terrible wilderness, as you
found it to be, on the way to the hill-country of the Amorites; and so we
came to Kadesh-barnea. Then I said to you, 'You have reached the 20

21 hill-country of the Amorites which the LORD our God is giving us. The LORD your God has indeed now laid the land open before you. Go forward and occupy it in fulfilment of the promise which the LORD the God of your 22 fathers made you; do not be discouraged or afraid.' But you all came to me and said, 'Let us send men ahead to spy out the country and report back 23 to us about the route we should take and the cities we shall find.' I approved 24 this plan and picked twelve of you, one from each tribe. They set out and made their way up into the hill-country as far as the gorge of Eshcol, 25 which they explored. They took samples of the fruit of the country and brought them back to us, and made their report: 'It is a rich land that the LORD our God is giving us.'

26 But you refused to go up and rebelled against the command of the LORD 27 your God. You muttered treason in your tents and said, 'It was because the LORD hated us that he brought us out of Egypt to hand us over to the 28 Amorites to be wiped out. What shall we find up there? Our kinsmen have discouraged us by their report of a people bigger and taller than we are, and of great cities with fortifications towering to the sky. And they told us they saw there the descendants of the Anakim.'[a]

29 Then I said to you, 'You must not dread them nor be afraid of them. 30 The LORD your God who goes at your head will fight for you and he will 31 do again what you saw him do for you in Egypt and in the wilderness. You saw there how the LORD your God carried you all the way to this place, 32 as a father carries his son.' In spite of this you did not trust the LORD your 33 God, who went ahead on the journey to find a place for your camp. He went in fire by night to show you the way you should take, and in a cloud by day.

34 When the LORD heard your complaints, he was indignant and solemnly 35 swore: 'Not one of these men, this wicked generation, shall see the rich 36 land which I swore to give your forefathers, except Caleb son of Jephunneh. He shall see it, and to him and his descendants I will give the land on which 37 he has set foot, because he followed the LORD with his whole heart.' On your account the LORD was angry with me also and said, 'You yourself 38 shall never enter it, but Joshua son of Nun, who is in attendance on you, shall enter it. Encourage him, for he shall put Israel in possession of that 39 land. Your dependants who, you thought, would become spoils of war, and your children who do not yet know good and evil, they shall enter; 40 I will give it to them, and they shall occupy it. You must turn back and set out for the wilderness by way of the Red Sea.'[b]

41 You answered me, 'We have sinned against the LORD; we will now go up and attack just as the LORD our God commanded us.' And each of you fastened on his weapons, thinking it an easy thing to invade the hill- 42 country. But the LORD said to me, 'Tell them not to go up and not to fight; 43 for I will not be with them, and their enemies will defeat them.' And I told you this, but you did not listen; you rebelled against the LORD's command 44 and defiantly went up to the hill-country. The Amorites living in the hills came out against you and like bees they chased you; they crushed you at 45 Hormah in Seir. Then you came back and wept before the LORD, but he

[a] *the descendants ... Anakim: or the tall men.*   [b] *Or the Sea of Reeds.*

would not hear you or listen to you. That is why you remained in Kadesh 46
as long as you did.

So we turned and set out for the wilderness by way of the Red Sea as 2
the LORD had told me we must do, and we spent many days marching
round the hill-country of Seir. Then the LORD said to me, 'You have been 2 3
long enough marching round these hills; turn towards the north. And give 4
the people this charge: "You are about to go through the territory of your
kinsmen the descendants of Esau who live in Seir. Although they are
afraid of you, be on your guard and do not provoke them; for I shall not 5
give you any of their land, not so much as a foot's-breadth: I have given
the hill-country of Seir to Esau as a possession. You may purchase food 6
from them for silver, and eat it, and you may buy*a* water to drink." ' The 7
LORD your God has blessed you in everything you have undertaken; he
has watched your journey through this great wilderness; these forty years
the LORD your God has been with you and you have gone short of nothing.
So we went on past our kinsmen, the descendants of Esau who live in Seir, 8
and along the road of the Arabah which comes from Elath and Ezion-
geber, and we turned and followed the road to the wilderness of Moab.
There the LORD said to me, 'Do not harass the Moabites nor provoke them 9
to battle, for I will not give you any of their land as a possession. I have
given Ar to the descendants of Lot as a possession.' (The Emim once lived 10
there—a great and numerous people, as tall as the Anakim. The Rephaim 11
also were reckoned as Anakim; but the Moabites called them Emim. The 12
Horites lived in Seir at one time, but the descendants of Esau occupied their
territory: they destroyed them as they advanced and then settled in the land
instead of them, just as Israel did in their own territory which the LORD
gave them.) 'Come now, cross the gorge of the Zared.' So we went across. 13
The journey from Kadesh-barnea to the crossing of the Zared took us 14
thirty-eight years, until the whole generation of fighting men had passed
away as the LORD had sworn that they would. The LORD's hand was raised 15
against them, and he rooted them out of the camp to the last man.

When the last of the fighting men among the people had died, the LORD 16 17
spoke to me, 'Today', he said, 'you are to cross by Ar*b* which lies on the 18
frontier of Moab, and when you reach the territory of the Ammonites, you 19
must not harass them or provoke them to battle, for I will not give you any
Ammonite land as a possession; I have assigned it to the descendants of
Lot.' (This also is reckoned as the territory of the Rephaim, who lived there 20
at one time; but the Ammonites called them Zamzummim. They were a 21
great and numerous people, as tall as the Anakim, but the LORD destroyed
them as the Ammonites advanced and occupied their territory instead of
them, just as he had done for the descendants of Esau who lived in Seir. As 22
they advanced, he destroyed the Horites so that they occupied their territory and took possession instead of them: so it is to this day. It was 23
Caphtorites from Caphtor who destroyed the Avvim who lived in the
hamlets near Gaza, and settled in the land instead of them.) 'Come, set out 24
on your journey and cross the gorge of the Arnon, for I have put Sihon the
Amorite, king of Heshbon, and his territory into your hands. Begin to

a Or dig for.   *b* by Ar: or the gully.

25 occupy it and provoke him to battle. Today I will begin to put the fear and dread of you upon all the peoples under heaven; if they so much as hear a rumour of you, they will quake and tremble before you.'

26 Then I sent messengers from the wilderness of Kedemoth to Sihon king
27 of Heshbon with these peaceful overtures: 'Grant us passage through your country by the highway: we will keep to the highway, trespassing neither
28 to right nor to left, and we will pay you the full price for the food we eat
29 and the water we drink. The descendants of Esau who live in Seir granted us passage, and so did the Moabites who live in Ar. We will simply pass through your land on foot, until we cross the Jordan to the land which
30 the LORD our God is giving us.' But Sihon king of Heshbon refused to grant us passage; for the LORD your God had made him stubborn and obstinate, in order that he and his land might become subject to you, as it
31 still is. So the LORD said to me, 'Come, I have begun to deliver Sihon and
32 his territory into your hands. Begin now to occupy his land.' Then Sihon
33 with all his people came out to meet us in battle at Jahaz, and the LORD our God delivered him into our hands; we killed him with his sons and all
34 his people. We captured all his cities at that time and put to death everyone
35 in the cities, men, women, and dependants; we left no survivor. We took
36 the cattle as booty and plundered the cities we captured. From Aroer on the edge of the gorge of the Arnon and the level land of the gorge, as far as Gilead, no city walls were too lofty for us; the LORD our God laid them all
37 open to us. But you avoided the territory of the Ammonites, both the parts along the gorge of the Jabbok and their cities in the hills, thus fulfilling all that the LORD our God had commanded.

3 Next we turned and advanced along the road to Bashan. Og king of
2 Bashan, with all his people, came out against us at Edrei. The LORD said to me, 'Do not be afraid of him, for I have delivered him into your hands, with all his people and his land. Deal with him as you dealt with Sihon the
3 king of the Amorites who lived in Heshbon.' So the LORD our God also delivered Og king of Bashan into our hands, with all his people. We
4 slaughtered them and left no survivor, and at the same time we captured all his cities; there was not a single town that we did not take from them. In all we took sixty cities, the whole region of Argob, the kingdom of Og
5 in Bashan; all these were fortified cities with high walls, gates, and bars,
6 apart from a great many open settlements. Thus we put to death all the men, women, and dependants in every city, as we did to Sihon king of
7 Heshbon. All the cattle and the spoil from the cities we took as booty for ourselves.

8 At that time we took from these two Amorite kings in Transjordan the
9 territory that runs from the gorge of the Arnon to Mount Hermon (the
10 mountain that the Sidonians call Sirion and the Amorites Senir), all the cities of the tableland, and the whole of Gilead and Bashan as far as
11 Salcah and Edrei, cities in the kingdom of Og in Bashan. (Only Og king of Bashan remained as the sole survivor of the Rephaim. His sarcophagus of basalt*a* was nearly fourteen feet long and six feet wide, and it may still be seen in the Ammonite city of Rabbah.)

a Or iron.

At that time, when we occupied this territory, I assigned to the Reuben- 12
ites and Gadites the land beyond Aroer on the gorge of the Arnon and half
the hill-country of Gilead with its towns. The rest of Gilead and the whole 13
of Bashan the kingdom of Og, all the region of Argob, I assigned to half
the tribe of Manasseh. (All Bashan used to be called the land of the
Rephaim. Jair son of Manasseh took all the region of Argob as far as the 14
Geshurite and Maacathite border. There are tent-villages in Bashan still
called by his name, Havvoth-jair.*a*) To Machir I assigned Gilead, and to 15 16
the Reubenites and the Gadites I assigned land from Gilead to the gorge of
the Arnon, that is to the middle of the gorge; and its territory ran *bc* to the
gorge of the Jabbok, the Ammonite frontier, and included the Arabah, 17
with the Jordan and adjacent land, from Kinnereth to the Sea of the
Arabah, that is the Dead Sea, below the watershed of Pisgah on the east.
At that time I gave you this command: 'The LORD your God has given 18
you this land to occupy; let all your fighting men be drafted and cross at
the head of their fellow-Israelites. Only your wives and dependants and 19
your livestock—I know you have much livestock—shall stay in the towns
I have given you. This you shall do until the LORD gives your kinsmen 20
security as he has given it to you, and until they too occupy the land which
the LORD your God is giving them on the other side of the Jordan; then you
may return to the possession which I have given you, every man to his own.'

At that time also I gave Joshua this charge: 'You have seen with your 21
own eyes all that the LORD your God has done to these two kings; he will
do the same to all the kingdoms into which you will cross over. Do not be 22
afraid of them, for the LORD your God himself will fight for you.'

At that same time I pleaded with the LORD, 'O Lord GOD, thou hast 23 24
begun to show to thy servant thy greatness and thy strong hand: what god
is there in heaven or on earth who can match thy works and mighty deeds?
Let me cross over and see that rich land which lies beyond the Jordan, and 25
the fine hill-country and the Lebanon.' But because of you the LORD 26
brushed me aside and would not listen. 'Enough!' he answered. 'Say no
more about this. Go to the top of Pisgah and look west and north, south and 27
east; look well at what you see, for you shall not cross this river Jordan.
Give Joshua his commission, encourage him and strengthen him; for he 28
will lead this people across, and he will put them in possession of the land
you see before you.'

So we remained in the valley opposite Beth-peor. 29

NOW, ISRAEL, LISTEN to the statutes and laws which I am teaching you, 4
and obey them; then you will live, and go in and occupy the land which
the LORD the God of your fathers is giving you. You must not add any- 2
thing to my charge, nor take anything away from it. You must carry out all
the commandments of the LORD your God which I lay upon you.

You saw with your own eyes what the LORD did at Baal-peor; the LORD 3
your God destroyed among you every man who went over to the Baal of

---

a *That is* Tent-villages of Jair.   *b* that is ... ran: *or* including the bed of the gorge
and the adjacent strip of land ...   *c* and its territory ran: *prob. rdg.; Heb.* and
territory and ...

4 5 Peor, but you who held fast to the LORD your God are all alive today. I
have taught you statutes and laws, as the LORD my God commanded me;
6 these you must duly keep when you enter the land and occupy it. You
must observe them carefully, and thereby you will display your wisdom
and understanding to other peoples. When they hear about these statutes,
they will say, 'What a wise and understanding people this great nation is!'
7 What great nation has a god*a* close at hand as the LORD our God is close to
8 us whenever we call to him? What great nation is there whose statutes and
9 laws are just, as is all this law which I am setting before you today? But
take good care: be on the watch not to forget the things that you have seen
with your own eyes, and do not let them pass from your minds as long as
10 you live, but teach them to your sons and to your sons' sons. You must
never forget that day when you stood before the LORD your God at Horeb,
and the LORD said to me, 'Assemble the people before me; I will make
them hear my words and they shall learn to fear me all their lives on earth,
11 and they shall teach their sons to do so.' Then you came near and stood at
the foot of the mountain. The mountain was ablaze with fire to the very
12 skies: there was darkness, cloud, and thick mist. When the LORD spoke to
you from the fire you heard a voice speaking, but you saw no figure; there
13 was only a voice. He announced the terms of his covenant to you, bidding
you observe the Ten Words,*b* and he wrote them on two tablets of stone.
14 At that time the LORD charged me to teach you statutes and laws which you
should observe in the land into which you are passing to occupy it.

15 On the day when the LORD spoke to you out of the fire on Horeb, you
16 saw no figure of any kind; so take good care not to fall into the degrading
practice of making figures carved in relief, in the form of a man or a woman,
17 18 or of any animal on earth or bird that flies in the air, or of any reptile on the
19 ground or fish in the waters under the earth. Nor must you raise your eyes
to the heavens and look up to the sun, the moon, and the stars, all the host
of heaven, and be led on to bow down to them and worship them; the LORD
your God assigned these for the worship of*c* the various peoples under
20 heaven. But you are the people whom the LORD brought out of Egypt,
from the smelting-furnace, and took for his own possession, as you are
21 to this day. The LORD was angry with me on your account and swore that
I should not cross the Jordan nor enter the rich land which the LORD your
22 God is giving you for your possession. I shall die in this country; I shall
not cross the Jordan, but you are about to cross and occupy that rich land.
23 Be careful not to forget the covenant which the LORD your God made with
you, and do not make yourselves a carved figure of anything which the
24 LORD your God has forbidden. For the LORD your God is a devouring fire,
a jealous god.

25 When you have children and grandchildren and grow old in the land,
if you then fall into the degrading practice of making any kind of carved
figure, doing what is wrong in the eyes of the LORD your God and provok-
26 ing him to anger, I summon heaven and earth to witness against you this
day: you will soon vanish from the land which you are to occupy after

a Or gods.   *b* Or Ten Commandments.   *c* assigned . . . worship of: or
created these for.

crossing the Jordan. You will not live long in it; you will be swept away. The LORD will disperse you among the peoples, and you will be left few in 27 number among the nations to which the LORD will lead you. There you 28 will worship gods made by human hands out of wood and stone, gods that can neither see nor hear, neither eat nor smell. But if from there you seek 29 the LORD your God, you will find him, if indeed you search with all your heart and soul. When you are in distress and all these things come upon 30 you, you will in days to come turn back to the LORD your God and obey him. The LORD your God is a merciful god; he will never fail you nor 31 destroy you, nor will he forget the covenant guaranteed by oath with your forefathers.

Search into days gone by, long before your time, beginning at the day 32 when God created man on earth; search from one end of heaven to the other, and ask if any deed as mighty as this has been seen or heard. Did 33 any people ever hear the voice of God speaking out of the fire, as you heard it, and remain alive? Or did ever a god attempt to come and take a 34 nation for himself away from another nation, with a challenge, and with signs, portents, and wars, with a strong hand and an outstretched arm, and with great deeds of terror, as the LORD your God did for you in Egypt in the sight of you all? You have had sure proof that the LORD is God; 35 there is no other. From heaven he let you hear his voice for your instruction, 36 and on earth he let you see his great fire, and out of the fire you heard his words. Because he loved your fathers and chose their children after them, 37 he in his own person brought you out of Egypt by his great strength, so 38 that he might drive out before you nations greater and more powerful than you and bring you in to give you their land in possession as it is today. This 39 day, then, be sure and take to heart that the LORD is God in heaven above and on earth below; there is no other. You shall keep his statutes and his 40 commandments which I give you today; then all will be well with you and with your children after you, and you will live long in the land which the LORD your God is giving you for all time.

Then Moses set apart three cities in the east, in Transjordan, to be places 41 42 of refuge for the homicide who kills a man without intent, with no previous enmity between them. If he takes sanctuary in one of these cities his life shall be safe. The cities were: Bezer-in-the-Wilderness on the tableland 43 for the Reubenites, Ramoth in Gilead for the Gadites, and Golan in Bashan for the Manassites.

This is the law which Moses laid down for the Israelites. These are the 44 45 precepts, the statutes, and the laws which Moses proclaimed to the Israelites, when they came out of Egypt and were in Transjordan in the valley 46 opposite Beth-peor in the land of Sihon king of the Amorites who lived in Heshbon. Moses and the Israelites had defeated him when they came out of Egypt and had occupied his territory and the territory of Og king of 47 Bashan, the two Amorite kings in the east, in Transjordan. The territory 48 ran from Aroer on the gorge of the Arnon to Mount Sirion, that is Hermon; and all the Arabah on the east, in Transjordan, as far as the Sea of the Arabah 49 below the watershed of Pisgah.

Moses summoned all Israel and said to them: Listen, O Israel, to the 5

statutes and the laws which I proclaim in your hearing today. Learn them
2 and be careful to observe them. The LORD our God made a covenant with
3 us at Horeb. It was not with our forefathers that the LORD made this cove-
4 nant, but with us, all of us who are alive and are here this day. The LORD
5 spoke with you face to face on the mountain out of the fire. I stood between
the LORD and you at that time to report the words of the LORD; for you were
afraid of the fire and did not go up the mountain. And the LORD said:

6   I am the LORD your God who brought you out of Egypt, out of the land
of slavery.

7   You shall have no other god*a* to set against me.

8   You shall not make a carved image for yourself nor the likeness of anything in the heavens above, or on the earth below, or in the waters under
the earth.

9   You shall not bow down to them or worship*b* them; for I, the LORD your
God, am a jealous god. I punish the children for the sins of the fathers to
10 the third and fourth generations of those who hate me. But I keep faith
with thousands, with*c* those who love me and keep my commandments.

11   You shall not make wrong use of the name of the LORD your God; the
LORD will not leave unpunished the man who misuses his name.

12   Keep the sabbath day holy as the LORD your God commanded you.
13 14 You have six days to labour and do all your work. But the seventh day is a
sabbath of the LORD your God; that day you shall not do any work, neither
you, your son or your daughter, your slave or your slave-girl, your ox,
your ass, or any of your cattle, nor the alien within your gates, so that your
15 slaves and slave-girls may rest as you do. Remember that you were slaves
in Egypt and the LORD your God brought you out with a strong hand and
an outstretched arm, and for that reason the LORD your God commanded
you to keep the sabbath day.

16   Honour your father and your mother, as the LORD your God commanded
you, so that you may live long, and that it may be well with you in the land
which the LORD your God is giving you.

17   You shall not commit murder.

18   You shall not commit adultery.

19   You shall not steal.

20   You shall not give false evidence against your neighbour.

21   You shall not covet your neighbour's wife; you shall not set your heart
on your neighbour's house, his land, his slave, his slave-girl, his ox, his
ass, or on anything that belongs to him.

22   These Commandments the LORD spoke in a great voice to your whole
assembly on the mountain out of the fire, the cloud, and the thick mist;
then he said no more. He wrote them on two tablets of stone and gave them
23 to me. When you heard the voice out of the darkness, while the mountain
was ablaze with fire, all the heads of your tribes and the elders came to me
24 and said, 'The LORD our God has shown us his glory and his greatness,
and we have heard his voice out of the fire: today we have seen that God
25 may speak with men and they may still live. Why should we now risk

a Or gods.   *b* Or or be led to worship . . .   *c* with . . . with: or for a
thousand generations with . . .

death? for this great fire will devour us. If we hear the voice of the LORD
our God again, we shall die. Is there any mortal man who has heard the 26
voice of the living God speaking out of the fire, as we have, and has lived?
You shall go near and listen to all that the LORD our God says, and report 27
to us all that the LORD our God has said to you; we will listen and obey.'

When the LORD heard these words which you spoke to me, he said, 'I 28
have heard what this people has said to you; every word they have spoken
is right. Would that they always had such a heart to fear me and to observe 29
all my commandments, so that all might be well with them and their
children for ever! Go, and tell them to return to their tents, but you your- 30 31
self stand here beside me, and I will set forth to you all the commandments,
the statutes and laws which you shall teach them to observe in the land
which I am giving them to occupy.'

You shall be careful to do as the LORD your God has commanded you; 32
do not turn from it to right or to left. You must conform to all the LORD 33
your God commands you, if you would live and prosper and remain long
in the land you are to occupy.

These are the commandments, statutes, and laws which the LORD your 6
God commanded me to teach you to observe in the land into which you
are passing to occupy it, a land flowing with milk and honey, so that you 2
may fear the LORD your God and keep all his statutes and commandments
which I am giving you, both you, your sons, and your descendants all your
lives, and so that you may live long. If you listen, O Israel, and are careful 3
to observe them, you will prosper and increase greatly as the LORD the
God of your fathers promised you.

Hear, O Israel, the LORD[a] is our God, one LORD, and you must love the 4 5
LORD your God with all your heart and soul and strength. These com- 6
mandments which I give you this day are to be kept in your heart; you 7
shall repeat them to your sons, and speak of them indoors and out of doors,
when you lie down and when you rise. Bind them as a sign on the hand and 8
wear them as a phylactery on the forehead; write them up on the door- 9
posts of your houses and on your gates.

The LORD your God will bring you into the land which he swore to your 10
forefathers Abraham, Isaac and Jacob that he would give you, a land of
great and fine cities which you did not build, houses full of good things 11
which you did not provide, rock-hewn cisterns which you did not hew,
and vineyards and olive-groves which you did not plant. When you eat
your fill there, be careful not to forget the LORD who brought you out of 12
Egypt, out of the land of slavery. You shall fear the LORD your God, serve 13
him alone and take your oaths in his name. You must not follow other gods, 14
gods of the nations that are around you; if you do, the LORD your God who 15
is in your midst will be angry with you, and he will sweep you away off the
face of the earth, for the LORD your God is a jealous god.

You must not challenge the LORD your God as you challenged him at 16
Massah.[b] You must diligently keep the commandments of the LORD your 17
God as well as the precepts and statutes which he gave you. You must do 18
what is right and good in the LORD's eyes so that all may go well with you,

[a] *See note on Exod.* 3. 15.   [b] *That is* Challenge.

19 and you may enter and occupy the rich land which the LORD promised by oath to your forefathers; then you shall drive out all your enemies before you, as the LORD promised.

20 When your son asks you in time to come, 'What is the meaning of the
21 precepts, statutes, and laws which the LORD our God gave you?', you shall say to him, 'We were Pharaoh's slaves in Egypt, and the LORD brought us
22 out of Egypt with his strong hand, sending great disasters, signs, and portents against the Egyptians and against Pharaoh and all his family, as we
23 saw for ourselves. But he led us out from there to bring us into the land and
24 give it to us as he had promised to our forefathers. The LORD commanded us to observe all these statutes and to fear the LORD our God; it will be for
25 our own good at all times, and he will continue to preserve our lives. It will be counted to our credit if we keep all these commandments in the sight of the LORD our God, as he has bidden us.'

7 WHEN THE LORD YOUR GOD BRINGS YOU into the land which you are entering to occupy and drives out many nations before you—Hittites, Girgashites, Amorites, Canaanites, Perizzites, Hivites, and Jebusites,
2 seven nations more numerous and powerful than you—when the LORD your God delivers them into your power and you defeat them, you must put them to death. You must not make a treaty with them or spare them.
3 You must not intermarry with them, neither giving your daughters to
4 their sons nor taking their daughters for your sons; if you do, they will draw your sons away from the LORD[a] and make them worship other gods.
5 Then the LORD will be angry with you and will quickly destroy you. But this is what you must do to them: pull down their altars, break their sacred
6 pillars, hack down their sacred poles and destroy their idols by fire, for you are a people holy to the LORD your God; the LORD your God chose you out of all nations on earth to be his special possession.

7 It was not because you were more numerous than any other nation that the LORD cared for you and chose you, for you were the smallest of all
8 nations; it was because the LORD loved you and stood by his oath to your forefathers, that he brought you out with his strong hand and redeemed you from the land of slavery, from the power of Pharaoh king of Egypt.
9 Know then that the LORD your God is God, the faithful God; with those who love him and keep his commandments he keeps covenant and faith
10 for a thousand generations, but those who defy him and show their hatred for him he repays with destruction: he will not be slow to requite any who so hate him.

11 You are to observe these commandments, statutes, and laws which I give you this day, and keep them.

12 If you listen to these laws and are careful to observe them, then the LORD your God will observe the sworn covenant he made with your forefathers
13 and will keep faith with you. He will love you, bless you and cause you to increase. He will bless the fruit of your body and the fruit of your land, your corn and new wine and oil, the offspring of your herds, and of your lamb-
14 ing flocks, in the land which he swore to your forefathers to give you. You

a Prob. rdg.; Heb. me.

shall be blessed above every other nation; neither among your people nor among your cattle shall there be impotent male or barren female. The LORD 15 will take away all sickness from you; he will not bring upon you any of the foul diseases of Egypt which you know so well, but will bring them upon all your enemies. You shall devour all the nations which the LORD your 16 God is giving over to you. Spare none of them, and do not worship their gods; that is the snare which awaits you.

You may say to yourselves, 'These nations outnumber us, how can we 17 drive them out?' But you need have no fear of them; only remember what 18 the LORD your God did to Pharaoh and to the whole of Egypt, the great 19 challenge which you yourselves witnessed, the signs and portents, the strong hand and the outstretched arm by which the LORD your God brought you out. He will deal thus with all the nations of whom you are afraid. He 20 will also spread panic among them until all who are left or have gone into hiding perish before you. Be in no dread of them, for the LORD your God 21 is in your midst, a great and terrible god. He will drive out these nations 22 before you little by little. You will not be able to exterminate them quickly, for fear the wild beasts become too numerous for you. The LORD your God 23 will deliver these nations over to you and will throw them into great panic in the hour of their destruction. He will put their kings into your hands, 24 and you shall wipe out their name from under heaven. When you destroy them, no man will be able to withstand you. Their idols you shall destroy 25 by fire; you must not covet the silver and gold on them and take it for yourselves, or you will be ensnared by it; for these things are abominable to the LORD your God. You must not introduce any abominable idol 26 into your houses and thus bring yourselves under solemn ban along with it. You shall hold it loathsome and abominable, for it is forbidden under the ban.

You must carefully observe everything that I command you this day so 8 that you may live and increase and may enter and occupy the land which the LORD promised to your forefathers upon oath. You must remember all 2 that road by which the LORD your God has led you these forty years in the wilderness to humble you, to test you and to discover whether or no it was in your heart to keep his commandments. He humbled you and made you 3 hungry; then he fed you on manna which neither you nor your fathers had known before, to teach you that man cannot live on bread alone but lives by every word that comes from the mouth of the LORD. The clothes on 4 your backs did not wear out nor did your feet swell all these forty years. Take this lesson to heart: that the LORD your God was disciplining you as 5 a father disciplines his son; and keep the commandments of the LORD your 6 God, conforming to his ways and fearing him. For the LORD your God is 7 bringing you to a rich land, a land of streams, of springs and underground waters gushing out in hill and valley, a land of wheat and barley, of vines, 8 fig-trees, and pomegranates, a land of olives, oil, and honey. It is a land 9 where you will never live in poverty nor want for anything, a land whose stones are iron-ore and from whose hills you will dig copper. You will have 10 plenty to eat and will bless the LORD your God for the rich land that he has given you.

11 Take care not to forget the LORD your God and do not fail to keep his
12 commandments, laws, and statutes which I give you this day. When you
13 have plenty to eat and live in fine houses of your own building, when your
     herds and flocks increase, and your silver and gold and all your possessions
14 increase too, do not become proud and forget the LORD your God who
15 brought you out of Egypt, out of the land of slavery; he led you through the
     vast and terrible wilderness infested with poisonous snakes and scorpions,
     a thirsty, waterless land, where he caused water to flow from the hard rock;
16 he fed you in the wilderness on manna which your fathers did not know, to
17 humble you and test you, and in the end to make you prosper. Nor must
     you say to yourselves, 'My own strength and energy have gained me this
18 wealth', but remember the LORD your God; it is he that gives you strength
     to become prosperous, so fulfilling the covenant guaranteed by oath with
     your forefathers, as he is doing now.

19 If you forget the LORD your God and adhere to other gods, worshipping
     them and bowing down to them, I give you a solemn warning this day that
20 you will certainly be destroyed. You will be destroyed because of your dis-
     obedience to the LORD your God, as surely as were the nations whom the
     LORD destroyed at your coming.

9   Listen, O Israel; this day you will cross the Jordan to occupy the
     territory of nations greater and more powerful than you, and great cities
2   with walls towering to the sky. They are great and tall people, the descend-
     ants of the Anakim, of whom you know, for you have heard it said, 'Who
3   can withstand the sons of Anak?' Know then this day that it is the LORD
     your God himself who goes at your head as a devouring fire; he will subdue
     them and destroy them at your approach; you shall drive them out and
     overwhelm them, as he promised you.

4   When the LORD your God drives them out before you, do not say to
     yourselves, 'It is because of my own merit that the LORD has brought me in
5   to occupy this land.' It is not because of your merit or your integrity that
     you are entering their land to occupy it; it is because of the wickedness of
     these nations that the LORD your God is driving them out before you, and
     to fulfil the promise which the LORD made to your forefathers, Abraham,
     Isaac and Jacob.

6   Know then that it is not because of any merit of yours that the LORD
     your God is giving you this rich land to occupy; indeed, you are a stubborn
7   people. Remember and never forget, how you angered the LORD your God
     in the wilderness: from the day when you left Egypt until you came to this
8   place you have defied the LORD. In Horeb you roused the LORD's anger,
9   and the LORD in his wrath was on the point of destroying you. When I
     went up the mountain to receive the tablets of stone, the tablets of the
     covenant which the LORD made with you, I remained on the mountain
10 forty days and forty nights without food or drink. Then the LORD gave me
     the two tablets of stone written with the finger of God, and upon them
     were all the words the LORD spoke to you out of the fire, upon the mountain
11 on the day of the assembly. At the end of forty days and forty nights the
12 LORD gave me the two tablets of stone, the tablets of the covenant, and said
     to me, 'Make haste down from the mountain because your people whom

you brought out of Egypt have done a disgraceful thing. They have already turned aside from the way which I told them to follow and have cast for themselves an image of metal.'

Then the LORD said to me, 'I have considered this people and I find 13 them a stubborn people. Let me be, and I will destroy them and blot out 14 their name from under heaven; and of you alone I will make a nation more powerful and numerous than they.' So I turned and went down the moun- 15 tain, and it was ablaze; and I had the two tablets of the covenant in my hands. When I saw that you had sinned against the LORD your God and 16 had cast for yourselves an image of a bull-calf, and had already turned aside from the way the LORD had told you to follow, I took the two tablets 17 and flung them down and shattered them in the sight of you all. Then once 18 again I lay prostrate before the LORD, forty days and forty nights without food or drink, on account of all the sins that you had committed, and because you had done what was wrong in the eyes of the LORD and provoked him to anger. I dreaded the LORD's anger and his wrath which threatened 19 to destroy you; and once again the LORD listened to me. The LORD was 20 greatly incensed with Aaron also and would have killed him; so I prayed for him as well at that same time. I took the calf, that sinful thing that you 21 had made, and burnt it and pounded it, grinding it until it was as fine as dust; then I flung its dust into the torrent that flowed down the mountain. You also roused the LORD's anger at Taberah, and at Massah, and at 22 Kibroth-hattaavah. Again, when the LORD sent you from Kadesh-barnea 23 with orders to advance and occupy the land which he was giving you, you defied the LORD your God and did not trust him or obey him. You were 24 defiant from the day that the LORD first knew you. Forty days and forty 25 nights I lay prostrate before the LORD because he had threatened to destroy you, and I prayed to the LORD and said, 'O Lord GOD, do not destroy thy 26 people, thy own possession, whom thou didst redeem by thy great power and bring out of Egypt by thy strong hand. Remember thy servants, 27 Abraham, Isaac and Jacob, and overlook the stubbornness of this people, their wickedness and their sin; otherwise the people in the land out of 28 which thou didst lead us will say, "It is because the LORD was not able to bring them into the land which he promised them and because he hated them, that he has led them out to kill them in the wilderness." But they are 29 thy people, thy own possession, whom thou didst bring out by thy great strength and by thy outstretched arm.'

AT THAT TIME THE LORD SAID to me, 'Cut two tablets of stone like the **10** first, and make also a wooden chest, an Ark. Come to me on the mountain, and I will write on the tablets the words that were on the first tablets which 2 you broke in pieces, and you shall put them into the Ark.' So I made the 3 Ark of acacia-wood and cut two tablets of stone like the first, and went up the mountain taking the tablets with me. Then in the same writing as 4 before, the LORD wrote down the Ten Words[a] which he had spoken to you out of the fire, upon the mountain on the day of the assembly, and the LORD gave them to me. I turned and came down the mountain, and I put 5

[a] *Or* Ten Commandments.

the tablets in the Ark that I had made, as the LORD had commanded me, and there they have remained ever since.

6*a* (The Israelites journeyed by stages from Beeroth-bene-jaakan to Moserah. There Aaron died and was buried; and his son Eleazar succeeded him in
7 the priesthood. From there they came to Gudgodah and from Gudgodah
8 to Jotbathah, a land of many ravines. At that time the LORD set apart the tribe of Levi to carry the Ark of the Covenant of the LORD, to attend on the LORD and minister to him, and to give the blessing in his name, as they
9 have done to this day. That is why the Levites have no holding or patrimony with their kinsmen; the LORD is their patrimony, as he promised them.)

10 I stayed on the mountain forty days and forty nights, as I did before, and once again the LORD listened to me; he consented not to destroy you.
11 The LORD said to me, 'Set out now at the head of the people so that they may enter and occupy the land which I swore to give to their forefathers.'

12 What then, O Israel, does the LORD your God ask of you? Only to fear the LORD your God, to conform to all his ways, to love him and to serve
13 him with all your heart and soul. This you will do by keeping the commandments of the LORD and his statutes which I give you this day for your good.
14 To the LORD your God belong heaven itself, the highest heaven, the earth
15 and everything in it; yet the LORD cared for your forefathers in his love for them and chose their descendants after them. Out of all nations you were
16 his chosen people as you are this day. So now you must circumcise the
17 foreskin of your hearts and not be stubborn any more, for the LORD your God is God of gods and Lord of lords, the great, mighty, and terrible God.
18 He is no respecter of persons and is not to be bribed; he secures justice for widows and orphans, and loves the alien who lives among you, giving
19 him food and clothing. You too must love the alien, for you once lived as
20 aliens in Egypt. You must fear the LORD your God, serve him, hold fast
21 to him and take your oaths in his name. He is your praise, your God who has done for you these great and terrible things which you have seen with
22 your own eyes. When your forefathers went down into Egypt they were only seventy strong, but now the LORD your God has made you countless as the stars in the sky.

11 You shall love the LORD your God and keep for all time the charge he
2 laid upon you, the statutes, the laws, and the commandments. This day you know the discipline of the LORD, though your children who have neither known nor experienced it do not; you know his greatness, his
3 strong hand and outstretched arm, the signs he worked and his acts in
4 Egypt against Pharaoh the king and his country, and all that he did to the Egyptian army, its horses and chariots, when he caused the waters of the Red Sea to flow over them as they pursued you. In this way the LORD
5 destroyed them, and so things remain to this day. You know what he did
6 for you in the wilderness as you journeyed to this place, and what he did to Dathan and Abiram sons of Eliab, son of Reuben, when the earth opened its mouth and swallowed them in the sight of all Israel, together with their

a Verses 6, 7: cp. Num. 33. 31, 32.

households and their tents and every living thing in their company. With 7
your own eyes you have seen the mighty work that the LORD did.

You shall observe all that I command you this day, so that you may have 8
strength to enter and occupy the land into which you are crossing, and so 9
that you may live long in the land which the LORD swore to your forefathers
to give them and their descendants, a land flowing with milk and honey.
The land which you are entering to occupy is not like the land of Egypt 10
from which you have come, where, after sowing your seed, you irrigated it
by foot like a vegetable garden. But the land into which you are crossing 11
to occupy is a land of mountains and valleys watered by the rain of heaven.
It is a land which the LORD your God tends*a* and on which his eye rests 12
from year's end to year's end. If you pay heed to the commandments which 13
I give you this day, and love the LORD your God and serve him with all
your heart and soul, then I will send rain for your land in season, both 14
autumn and spring rains, and you will gather your corn and new wine and
oil, and I will provide pasture in the fields for your cattle: you shall eat 15
your fill. Take good care not to be led astray in your hearts nor to turn 16
aside and serve other gods and prostrate yourselves to them, or the LORD 17
will become angry with you: he will shut up the skies and there will be no
rain, your ground will not yield its harvest, and you will soon vanish from
the rich land which the LORD is giving you. You shall take these words of 18
mine to heart and keep them in mind; you shall bind them as a sign on the
hand and wear them as a phylactery on the forehead. Teach them to your 19
children, and speak of them indoors and out of doors, when you lie down
and when you rise. Write them up on the door-posts of your houses and 20
on your gates. Then you will live long, you and your children, in the land 21
which the LORD swore to your forefathers to give them, for as long as the
heavens are above the earth.

If you diligently keep all these commandments that I now charge you 22
to observe, by loving the LORD your God, by conforming to his ways and
by holding fast to him, the LORD will drive out all these nations before you 23
and you shall occupy the territory of nations greater and more powerful
than you. Every place where you set the soles of your feet shall be yours. 24
Your borders shall run from the wilderness to*b* the Lebanon and from the
River, the river Euphrates, to the western sea. No man will be able to 25
withstand you; the LORD your God will put the fear and dread of you upon
the whole land on which you set foot, as he promised you. Understand that 26
this day I offer you the choice of a blessing and a curse. The blessing will 27
come if you listen to the commandments of the LORD your God which I
give you this day, and the curse if you do not listen to the commandments 28
of the LORD your God but turn aside from the way that I command you
this day and follow other gods whom you do not know.

When the LORD your God brings you into the land which you are enter- 29
ing to occupy, there on Mount Gerizim you shall pronounce the blessing
and on Mount Ebal the curse. (These mountains are on the other side of 30
the Jordan, close to Gilgal beside the terebinth of Moreh, beyond the road

a which . . . tends: *or* whose soil the LORD your God has made firm.
b *Prob. rdg.; Heb.* and.

to the west which lies in the territory of the Canaanites of the Arabah.)
31 You are about to cross the Jordan to enter and occupy the land which the
32 LORD your God is giving you; you shall occupy it and settle in it, and you
shall be careful to observe all the statutes and laws which I set before you
this day.

God's laws delivered by Moses

12 THESE ARE THE STATUTES AND LAWS that you shall be careful to
observe in the land which the LORD the God of your fathers is giving
2 you to occupy as long as you live on earth. You shall demolish all the
sanctuaries where the nations whose place you are taking worship their
3 gods, on mountain-tops and hills and under every spreading tree. You shall
pull down their altars and break their sacred pillars, burn their sacred poles
and hack down the idols of their gods and thus blot out the name of them
from that place.
4   You shall not follow such practices in the worship of the LORD your God,
5 but you shall resort to the place which the LORD your God will choose out
of all your tribes to receive his Name that it may dwell there. There you
6 shall come and bring your whole-offerings and sacrifices, your tithes and
contributions, your vows and freewill offerings, and the first-born of your
7 herds and flocks. There you shall eat before the LORD your God; so you
shall find joy in whatever you undertake, you and your families, because
the LORD your God has blessed you.
8   You shall not act as we act here today, each of us doing what he pleases,
9 for till now you have not reached the place of rest, the patrimony which
10 the LORD your God is giving you. You shall cross the Jordan and settle in
the land which the LORD your God allots you as your patrimony; he will
grant you peace from all your enemies on every side, and you will live in
11 security. Then you shall bring everything that I command you to the place
which the LORD your God will choose as a dwelling for his Name—your
whole-offerings and sacrifices, your tithes and contributions, and all the
12 choice gifts that you have vowed to the LORD. You shall rejoice before the
LORD your God with your sons and daughters, your male and female
slaves, and the Levites who live in your settlements because they have no
holding or patrimony among you.
13 See that you do not offer your whole-offerings in any place at random,
14 but offer them only at the place which the LORD will choose in one of your
15 tribes, and there you must do all I command you. On the other hand, you
may freely kill for food in all your settlements, as the LORD your God blesses
you. Clean and unclean alike may eat it, as they would eat the meat of
16 gazelle or buck. But on no account must you eat the blood; pour it out on
17 the ground like water. In all your settlements you may not eat any of the
tithe of your corn and new wine and oil, or any of the first-born of your
cattle and sheep, or any of the gifts that you vow, or any of your freewill
18 offerings and contributions; but you shall eat it before the LORD your God
in the place that the LORD your God will choose—you, your sons and

daughters, your male and female slaves, and the Levites in your settlements; so you shall find joy before the LORD your God in all that you
undertake. Be careful not to neglect the Levites in your land as long as   19
you live.

When the LORD your God extends your boundaries, as he has promised   20
you, and you say to yourselves, 'I would like to eat meat', because you have
a craving for it, then you may freely eat it. If the place that the LORD your   21
God will choose to receive his Name is far away, then you may slaughter
a beast from the herds or flocks which the LORD has given you and freely
eat it in your own settlements as I command you. You may eat it as you   22
would the meat of gazelle or buck; both clean and unclean alike may eat it.
But you must strictly refrain from eating the blood, because the blood is   23
the life; you must not eat the life with the flesh. You must not eat it, you   24
must pour it out on the ground like water. If you do not eat it, all will be   25
well with you and your children after you; for you will be doing what is
right in the eyes of the LORD. But such holy-gifts as you may have and the   26
gifts you have vowed, you must bring to the place which the LORD will
choose. You must present your whole-offerings, both the flesh and the   27
blood, on the altar of the LORD your God; but of your shared-offerings
you shall eat the flesh, while the blood is to be poured on the altar of the
LORD your God. See that you listen and do all that I command you, and   28
then it will go well with you and your children after you for ever; for you
will be doing what is good and right in the eyes of the LORD your God.

When the LORD your God exterminates, as you advance, the nations   29
whose country you are entering to occupy, you shall take their place and
settle in their land. After they have been destroyed, take care that you are   30
not ensnared into their ways. Do not inquire about their gods and say,
'How do these nations worship their gods? I too will do the same.' You   31
must not do for the LORD your God what they do, for all that they do for
their gods is hateful and abominable to the LORD. As sacrifices for their
gods they even burn their sons and their daughters.

See that you observe everything I command you: you must not add   32
anything to it, nor take anything away from it.

When a prophet or dreamer appears among you and offers you a sign   **13**
or a portent and calls on you to follow other gods whom you have not known   2
and worship them, even if the sign or portent should come true, do not   3
listen to the words of that prophet or that dreamer. God is testing you
through him to discover whether you love the LORD your God with all
your heart and soul. You must follow the LORD your God and fear him;   4
you must keep his commandments and obey him, serve him and hold fast
to him. That prophet or that dreamer shall be put to death, for he has   5
preached rebellion against the LORD your God who brought you out of
Egypt and redeemed you from that land of slavery; he has tried to lead you
astray from the path which the LORD your God commanded you to take.
You must rid yourselves of this wickedness.

If your brother, your father's son or your mother's son, or your son or   6
daughter, or the wife of your bosom or your dearest friend should entice
you secretly to go and worship other gods—gods whom neither you nor

7 your fathers have known, gods of the people round about you, near or far,
8 at one end of the land or the other—then you shall not consent or listen.
9 You shall have no pity on him, you shall not spare him nor shield him, you shall put him to death; your own hand shall be the first to be raised against
10 him and then all the people shall follow. You shall stone him to death, because he tried to lead you astray from the LORD your God who brought
11 you out of Egypt, out of the land of slavery. All Israel shall hear of it and be afraid; never again will anything as wicked as this be done among you.
12-13 When you hear that miscreants have appeared in any of the cities which the LORD your God is giving you to occupy, and have led its inhabitants astray by calling on them to serve other gods whom you have not known,
14 then you shall investigate the matter carefully. If, after diligent examination, the report proves to be true and it is shown that this abominable thing has
15 been done among you, you shall put the inhabitants of that city to the sword; you shall lay the city under solemn ban together with everything
16 in it. You shall gather all its goods into the square and burn both city and goods as a complete offering to the LORD your God; and it shall remain a
17 mound of ruins, never to be rebuilt. Let nothing out of all that has been laid under the ban be found in your possession, so that the LORD may turn from his anger and show you compassion; and in his compassion he will
18 increase you as he swore to your forefathers, provided that you obey the LORD your God and keep all his commandments which I give you this day, doing only what is right in the eyes of the LORD your God.

14 YOU ARE THE SONS OF THE LORD your God: you shall not gash your-
2 selves nor shave your forelocks in mourning for the dead. You are a people holy to the LORD your God, and the LORD has chosen you out of all peoples on earth to be his special possession.

3 4 You shall not eat any abominable thing. These are the animals you may
5 eat: ox, sheep, goat, buck, gazelle, roebuck, wild-goat, white-rumped deer,
6 long-horned antelope, and rock-goat. You may eat any animal which has
7 a parted foot or a cloven hoof and also chews the cud; those which only chew the cud or only have a parted or cloven hoof you may not eat. These are: the camel, the hare, and the rock-badger,*a* because they chew the cud
8 but do not have cloven hoofs; you shall regard them as unclean; and the pig, because it has a cloven hoof but does not chew the cud, you shall regard as unclean. You shall not eat their flesh or even touch their dead
9 carcasses. Of creatures that live in water you may eat all those that have
10 fins and scales, but you may not eat any that have neither fins nor scales;
11 12 you shall regard them as unclean. You may eat all clean birds. These are the birds you may not eat: the griffon-vulture,*b* the black vulture, the
13 14 bearded vulture,*c* the kite, every kind of falcon, every kind of crow,*d*
15 the desert-owl, the short-eared owl, the long-eared owl, every kind of
16 17 hawk, the tawny owl, the screech-owl, the little owl, the horned owl, the
18 osprey, the fisher-owl, the stork,*e* every kind of cormorant, the hoopoe, and the bat.

a Or rock-rabbit.   *b* Or eagle.   *c* Or ossifrage.   *d* Or raven.
e Or heron.

All teeming winged creatures you shall regard as unclean; they may not 19
be eaten. You may eat every clean insect. 20

You shall not eat anything that has died a natural death. You shall give 21
it to the aliens who live in your settlements, and they may eat it, or you may
sell it to a foreigner; for you are a people holy to the LORD your God.

You shall not boil a kid in its mother's milk.

Year by year you shall set aside a tithe of all the produce of your seed, 22
of everything that grows on the land. You shall eat it in the presence of the 23
LORD your God in the place which he will choose as a dwelling for his
Name—the tithe of your corn and new wine and oil, and the first-born of
your cattle and sheep, so that for all time you may learn to fear the LORD
your God. When the LORD your God has blessed you with prosperity, and 24
the place which he will choose to receive his Name is far from you and the
journey too great for you to be able to carry your tithe, then you may 25
exchange it for silver. You shall tie up the silver and take it with you to the
place which the LORD your God will choose. There you shall spend it as 26
you will on cattle or sheep, wine or strong drink, or whatever you desire;
you shall consume it there with rejoicing, both you and your family, in the
presence of the LORD your God. You must not neglect the Levites who live 27
in your settlements; for they have no holding or patrimony among you.

At the end of every third year you shall bring out all the tithe of your 28
produce for that year and leave it in your settlements so that the Levites, 29
who have no holding or patrimony among you, and the aliens, orphans,
and widows in your settlements may come and eat their fill. If you do this
the LORD your God will bless you in everything to which you set your hand.

At the end of every seventh year you shall make a remission of debts. **15**
This is how the remission shall be made: everyone who holds a pledge shall 2
remit the pledge of anyone indebted to him. He shall not press a fellow-
countryman for repayment, for the LORD's year of remission has been
declared.[a] You may press foreigners; but if it is a fellow-countryman that 3
holds anything of yours, you must remit all claim upon it. There will 4-5
never be any poor among you if only you obey the LORD your God by carefully keeping these commandments which I lay upon you this day; for
the LORD your God will bless you with great prosperity in the land which
he is giving you to occupy as your patrimony. When the LORD your God 6
blesses you, as he promised, you will lend to men of many nations, but you
yourselves will not borrow; you will rule many nations, but they will not
rule you.

When one of your fellow-countrymen in any of your settlements in the 7
land which the LORD your God is giving you becomes poor, do not be
hard-hearted or close-fisted with your countryman in his need. Be open- 8
handed towards him and lend him on pledge as much as he needs. See that 9
you do not harbour iniquitous thoughts when you find that the seventh
year, the year of remission, is near, and look askance at your needy countryman and give him nothing. If you do, he will appeal to the LORD against
you, and you will be found guilty of sin. Give freely to him and do not 10
begrudge him your bounty, because it is for this very bounty that the LORD

a Or has come.

11 your God will bless you in everything that you do or undertake. The poor will always be with you in the land, and for that reason I command you to be open-handed with your countrymen, both poor and distressed, in your own land.

12 When a fellow-Hebrew, man or woman, sells himself to you as a slave, he shall serve you for six years and in the seventh year you shall set him 13 14 free. But when you set him free, do not let him go empty-handed. Give to him lavishly from your flock, from your threshing-floor and your wine-press. Be generous to him, because the LORD your God has blessed you. 18 Do not take it amiss when you have to set him free, for his six years' service to you has been worth twice *a* the wage of a hired man. Then the LORD your 15 God will bless you in everything you do. Remember that you were slaves in Egypt and the LORD your God redeemed you; that is why I am giving you this command today.

16 If, however, a slave is content to be with you and says, 'I will not leave 17 you, I love you and your family', then you shall take an awl and pierce through his ear to the door, and he will be your slave for life. You shall treat a slave-girl in the same way.

19*b* You shall dedicate to the LORD your God every male first-born of your herds and flocks. You shall not plough with the first-born of your cattle, 20 nor shall you shear the first-born of your sheep. Year by year you and your family shall eat them in the presence of the LORD your God, in the place 21 which the LORD will choose. If any animal is defective, if it is lame or blind, or has any other serious defect, you must not sacrifice it to the LORD your 22 God. Eat it in your settlements; both clean and unclean alike may eat it as 23 they would the meat of gazelle or buck. But you must not eat the blood; pour it out on the ground like water.

16 OBSERVE THE MONTH OF ABIB and keep the Passover to the LORD your God, for it was in that month that the LORD your God brought you out 2 of Egypt by night. You shall slaughter a lamb, a kid, or a calf as a Passover victim to the LORD your God in the place which he will choose as a dwelling 3 for his Name. You shall eat nothing leavened with it. For seven days you shall eat unleavened cakes, the bread of affliction. In urgent haste you came out of Egypt, and thus as long as you live you shall commemorate the day 4 of your coming out of Egypt. No leaven shall be seen in all your territory for seven days, nor shall any of the flesh which you have slaughtered in the 5 evening of the first day remain overnight till morning. You may not slaughter the Passover victim in any of the settlements which the LORD 6 your God is giving you, but only in the place which he will choose as a dwelling for his Name; you shall slaughter the Passover victim in the 7 evening as the sun goes down, the time of your coming out of Egypt. You shall boil it and eat it in the place which the LORD your God will choose, 8 and then next morning you shall turn and go to your tents. For six days you shall eat unleavened cakes, and on the seventh day there shall be a closing ceremony in honour of the LORD your God; you shall do no work. 9 Seven weeks shall be counted: start counting the seven weeks from the

a worth twice: *or* equivalent to.   *b* *Verse 18 transposed to follow verse 14.*

time when the sickle is put to the standing corn; then you shall keep the 10
pilgrim-feast of Weeks to the LORD your God and offer a freewill offering
in proportion to the blessing that the LORD your God has given you. You 11
shall rejoice before the LORD your God, with your sons and daughters,
your male and female slaves, the Levites who live in your settlements, and
the aliens, orphans, and widows among you. You shall rejoice in the place
which the LORD your God will choose as a dwelling for his Name and 12
remember that you were slaves in Egypt. You shall keep and observe all
these statutes.

You shall keep the pilgrim-feast of Tabernacles*a* for seven days, when 13
you bring in the produce from your threshing-floor and winepress. You 14
shall rejoice in your feast, with your sons and daughters, your male and
female slaves, the Levites, aliens, orphans, and widows who live in your
settlements. For seven days you shall keep this feast to the LORD your God 15
in the place which he will choose, when the LORD your God gives you his
blessing in all your harvest and in all your work; you shall keep the feast
with joy.

Three times a year all your males shall come into the presence of the 16
LORD your God in the place which he will choose: at the pilgrim-feasts of
Unleavened Bread, of Weeks, and of Tabernacles. No one shall come into
the presence of the LORD empty-handed. Each of you shall bring such a 17
gift as he can in proportion to the blessing which the LORD your God has
given you.

You shall appoint for yourselves judges and officers, tribe by tribe, in 18
every settlement which the LORD your God is giving you, and they shall
dispense true justice to the people. You shall not pervert the course of 19
justice or show favour, nor shall you accept a bribe; for bribery makes the
wise man blind and the just man give a crooked answer. Justice, and justice 20
alone, you shall pursue, so that you may live and occupy the land which
the LORD your God is giving you.

You shall not plant any kind of tree as a sacred pole beside the altar of 21
the LORD your God which you shall build. You shall not set up a sacred 22
pillar, for the LORD your God hates them.

You shall not sacrifice to the LORD your God a bull or sheep that has any **17**
defect or serious blemish, for that would be abominable to the LORD your
God.

If so be that, in any one of the settlements which the LORD your God is 2
giving you, a man or woman is found among you who does what is wrong
in the eyes of the LORD your God, by breaking his covenant and going to 3
worship other gods and prostrating himself before them or before the sun
and moon and all the host of heaven—a thing that I have forbidden—then, 4
if it is reported to you or you hear of it, make thorough inquiry. If the report
proves to be true, and it is shown that this abominable thing has been done
in Israel, then bring the man or woman who has done this wicked deed to 5
the city gate and stone him to death. Sentence of death shall be carried 6
out on the testimony of two or of three witnesses: no one shall be put to
death on the testimony of a single witness. The first stones shall be thrown 7

a Or Booths *or* Arbours.

by the witnesses and then all the people shall follow; thus you shall rid yourselves of this wickedness.

8 When the issue in any lawsuit is beyond your competence, whether it be a case of blood against blood, plea against plea, or blow against blow, that is disputed in your courts, then go up without delay to the place which the

9 LORD your God will choose. There you must go to the levitical priests or to the judge then in office; seek their guidance, and they will pronounce the

10 sentence. You shall act on the pronouncement which they make from the place which the LORD will choose. See that you carry out all their instruc-

11 tions. Act on the instruction which they give you, or on the precedent that they cite; do not swerve from what they tell you, either to right or to left.

12 Anyone who presumes to reject the decision either of the priest who ministers there to the LORD your God, or of the judge, shall die; thus you

13 will rid Israel of wickedness. Then all the people will hear of it and be afraid, and will never again show such presumption.

14 When you come into the land which the LORD your God is giving you, and occupy it and settle in it, and you then say, 'Let us appoint over us a

15 king, as all the surrounding nations do', you shall appoint as king the man whom the LORD your God will choose. You shall appoint over you a man of your own race; you must not appoint a foreigner, one who is not of your

16 own race. He shall not acquire many horses, nor, to add to his horses, shall he cause the people to go back to Egypt, for this is what the LORD said to

17 you, 'You shall never go back that way.' He shall not acquire many wives and so be led astray; nor shall he acquire great quantities of silver and gold

18 for himself. When he has ascended the throne of the kingdom, he shall make a copy of this law in a book at the dictation of the levitical priests.

19 He shall keep it by him and read from it all his life, so that he may learn to fear the LORD his God and keep all the words of this law and observe

20 these statutes. In this way he shall not become prouder than his fellow-countrymen, nor shall he turn from these commandments to right or to left; then he and his sons will reign long over his kingdom in Israel.

18 The levitical priests, the whole tribe of Levi, shall have no holding or patrimony in Israel; they shall eat the food-offerings of the LORD, their

2 patrimony. They shall have no patrimony among their fellow-countrymen; the LORD is their patrimony, as he promised them.

3 This shall be the customary due of the priests from those of the people who offer sacrifice, whether a bull or a sheep: the shoulders, the cheeks,

4 and the stomach shall be given to the priest. You shall give him also the firstfruits of your corn and new wine and oil, and the first fleeces at the

5 shearing of your flocks. For it was he whom the LORD your God chose from all your tribes to attend on the LORD and to minister in the name of the LORD, both he and his sons for all time.

6 When a Levite comes from any settlement in Israel where he may be lodging to the place which the LORD will choose, if he comes in the eager-

7 ness of his heart and ministers in the name of the LORD his God, like all

8 his fellow-Levites who attend on the LORD there, he shall have an equal share of food with them, besides what he may inherit from his father's family.

When you come into the land which the LORD your God is giving you,   9
do not learn to imitate the abominable customs of those other nations. Let   10
no one be found among you who makes his son or daughter pass through
fire, no augur or soothsayer or diviner or sorcerer, no one who casts spells   11
or traffics with ghosts and spirits, and no necromancer. Those who do   12
these things are abominable to the LORD, and it is because of these abominable practices that the LORD your God is driving them out before you. You   13
shall be whole-hearted in your service of the LORD your God.

These nations whose place you are taking listen to soothsayers and   14
augurs, but the LORD your God does not permit you to do this. The LORD   15
your God will raise up a prophet from among you like myself, and you
shall listen to him. All this follows from your request to the LORD your   16
God on Horeb on the day of the assembly. There you said, 'Let us not hear
again the voice of the LORD our God, nor see this great fire again, or we
shall die.' Then the LORD said to me, 'What they have said is right. I will   17 18
raise up for them a prophet like you, one of their own race, and I will put
my words into his mouth. He shall convey all my commands to them, and   19
if anyone does not listen to the words which he will speak in my name I will
require satisfaction from him. But the prophet who presumes to utter in   20
my name what I have not commanded him or who speaks in the name of
other gods—that prophet shall die.' If you ask yourselves, 'How shall we   21
recognize a word that the LORD has not uttered?', this is the answer: When   22
the word spoken by the prophet in the name of the LORD is not fulfilled
and does not come true, it is not a word spoken by the LORD. The prophet
has spoken presumptuously; do not hold him *a* in awe.

WHEN THE LORD YOUR GOD EXTERMINATES the nations whose land **19**
he is giving you, and you take their place and settle in their cities and
houses, you shall set apart three cities in the land which he is giving you   2
to occupy. Divide into three districts the territory which the LORD your   3
God is giving you as patrimony, and determine where each city shall lie.
These shall be places in which homicides may take sanctuary.

This is the kind of homicide who may take sanctuary there and save his   4
life: the man who strikes another without intent and with no previous
enmity between them; for instance, the man who goes into a wood with   5
his mate to fell trees, and, when cutting a tree, he relaxes his grip on the
axe,*b* the head glances off the tree, hits the other man and kills him. The
homicide may take sanctuary in any one of these cities, and his life shall be
safe. Otherwise, when the dead man's next-of-kin who had the duty of   6
vengeance pursued him in the heat of passion, he might overtake him if
the distance were great, and take his life, although the homicide was not
liable to the death-penalty because there had been no previous enmity on
his part. That is why I command you to set apart three cities.   7

If the LORD your God extends your boundaries, as he swore to your fore-   8
fathers, and gives you the whole land which he promised to them, because   9
you keep all the commandments that I am laying down today and carry
them out by loving the LORD your God and by conforming to his ways for

    a Or it.   *b* when . . . axe: *or* as he swings the axe to cut a tree.

10 all time, then you shall add three more cities of refuge to these three. Let no innocent blood be shed in the land which the LORD your God is giving you as your patrimony, or blood-guilt will fall on you.

11 When one man is the enemy of another, and he lies in wait for him, attacks him and strikes him a blow so that he dies, and then takes sanctuary

12 in one of these cities, the elders of his own city shall send to fetch him; they

13 shall hand him over to the next-of-kin, and he shall die. You shall show him no mercy, but shall rid Israel of the guilt of innocent blood; then all will be well with you.

14 Do not move your neighbour's boundary stone, fixed by the men of former times in the patrimony which you shall occupy in the land the LORD your God gives you for your possession.

15 A single witness may not give evidence against a man in the matter of any crime or sin which he commits: a charge must be established on the evidence of two or of three witnesses.

16 When a malicious witness comes forward to give false evidence against

17 a man, and the two disputants stand before the LORD, before the priests

18 and the judges then in office, if, after careful examination by the judges, he be proved to be a false witness giving false evidence against his fellow,

19 you shall treat him as he intended to treat his fellow, and thus rid your-

20 selves of this wickedness. The rest of the people when they hear of it will be afraid: never again will anything as wicked as this be done among you.

21 You shall show no mercy: life for life, eye for eye, tooth for tooth, hand for hand, foot for foot.

20 WHEN YOU TAKE THE FIELD against an enemy and are faced by horses and chariots and an army greater than yours, do not be afraid of them; for the LORD your God, who brought you out of Egypt, will be with you.

2 When you are about to join battle, the priest shall come forward and

3 address the army in these words: 'Hear, O Israel, this day you are joining battle with the enemy; do not lose heart, or be afraid, or give way to panic

4 in face of them; for the LORD your God will go with you to fight your

5 enemy for you and give you the victory.' Then the officers shall address the army in these words: 'Any man who has built a new house and has not dedicated it shall go back to his house; or he may die in battle and another

6 man dedicate it. Any man who has planted a vineyard and has not begun to use it shall go back home; or he may die in battle and another man use

7 it. Any man who has pledged himself to take a woman in marriage and has not taken her shall go back home; or he may die in battle and another man

8 take her.' The officers shall further address the army: 'Any man who is afraid and has lost heart shall go back home; or his comrades will be dis-

9 couraged as he is.' When these officers have finished addressing the army, commanders shall be appointed to lead it.

10 11 When you advance on a city to attack it, make an offer of peace. If the city accepts the offer and opens its gates to you, then all the people in it

12 shall be put to forced labour and shall serve you. If it does not make peace

13 with you but offers battle, you shall besiege it, and the LORD your God will

14 deliver it into your hands. You shall put all its males to the sword, but you

may take the women, the dependants, and the cattle for yourselves, and plunder everything else in the city. You may enjoy the use of the spoil of your enemies which the LORD your God gives you. That is what you shall 15 do to cities at a great distance, as opposed to those which belong to nations near at hand. In the cities of these nations whose land the LORD your God 16 is giving you as a patrimony, you shall not leave any creature alive. You 17 shall annihilate them—Hittites, Amorites, Canaanites, Perizzites, Hivites, Jebusites—as the LORD your God commanded you, so that they may not 18 teach you to imitate all the abominable things that they have done for their gods and so cause you to sin against the LORD your God.

When you are at war, and lay siege to a city for a long time in order to 19 take it, do not destroy its trees by taking the axe to them, for they provide you with food; you shall not cut them down. The trees of the field are not men that you should besiege them. But you may destroy or cut down any 20 trees that you know do not yield food, and use them in siege-works against the city that is at war with you, until it falls.

When a dead body is found lying in open country, in the land which the **21** LORD your God is giving you to occupy, and it is not known who struck the blow, your elders and your judges shall come out and measure the 2 distance to the surrounding towns to find which is nearest. The elders of 3 that town shall take a heifer that has never been mated*a* or worn a yoke, and bring it down to a ravine where there is a stream that never runs dry 4 and the ground is never tilled or sown, and there in the ravine they shall break its neck. The priests, the sons of Levi, shall then come forward; for 5 the LORD your God has chosen them to minister to him and to bless in the name of the LORD, and their voice shall be decisive in all cases of dispute and assault. Then all the elders of the town nearest to the dead body shall 6 wash their hands over the heifer whose neck has been broken in the ravine. They shall solemnly declare: 'Our hands did not shed this blood, nor did 7 we witness the bloodshed. Accept expiation, O LORD, for thy people 8 Israel whom thou hast redeemed, and do not let the guilt of innocent blood rest upon thy people Israel: let this bloodshed be expiated on their behalf.' Thus, by doing what is right in the eyes of the LORD, you shall rid yourselves 9 of the guilt of innocent blood.

When you wage war against your enemy and the LORD your God 10 delivers them into your hands and you take some of them captive, then if 11 you see a comely woman among the captives and take a liking to her, you may marry her. You shall bring her into your house, where she shall shave 12 her head, pare her nails, and discard the clothes which she had when 13 captured. Then she shall stay in your house and mourn for her father and mother for a full month. After that you may have intercourse with her; you shall be her husband and she your wife. But if you no longer find her 14 pleasing, let her go free. You must not sell her, nor treat her harshly, since you have had your will with her.

When a man has two wives, one loved and the other unloved, if they 15 both bear him sons, and the son of the unloved wife is the elder, then, when 16 the day comes for him to divide his property among his sons, he shall not

a Prob. rdg.; Heb. put to work.

treat the son of the loved wife as his first-born in contempt of his true first-
17 born, the son of the unloved wife. He shall recognize the rights of his first-
born, the son of the unloved wife, and give him a double share of all that
he possesses; for he was the firstfruits of his manhood, and the right of
the first-born is his.

18   When a man has a son who is disobedient and out of control, and will
not obey his father or his mother, or pay attention when they punish
19 him, then his father and mother shall take hold of him and bring him out
20 to the elders of the town, at the town gate. They shall say to the elders of
the town, 'This son of ours is disobedient and out of control; he will not
21 obey us, he is a wastrel and a drunkard.' Then all the men of the town shall
stone him to death, and you will thereby rid yourselves of this wickedness.
All Israel will hear of it and be afraid.

22   When a man is convicted of a capital offence and is put to death, you
23 shall hang him on a gibbet; but his body shall not remain on the gibbet
overnight; you shall bury it on the same day, for a hanged man is offensive[a]
in the sight of God. You shall not pollute the land which the LORD your
God is giving you as your patrimony.

22 WHEN YOU SEE A FELLOW-COUNTRYMAN'S OX or sheep straying, do
2 not ignore it but take it back to him. If the owner is not a near neighbour
and you do not know who he is, take the animal into your own house and
3 keep it with you until he claims it, and then give it back to him. Do the same
with his ass or his cloak or anything else that your fellow-countryman has
lost, if you find it. You may not ignore it.

4   When you see your fellow-countryman's ass or ox lying on the road, do
not ignore it; you must help him to lift it to its feet again.

5   No woman shall wear an article of man's clothing, nor shall a man put
on woman's dress; for those who do these things are abominable to the
LORD your God.

6   When you come across a bird's nest by the road, in a tree or on the
ground, with fledglings or eggs in it and the mother-bird on the nest, do
7 not take both mother and young. Let the mother-bird go free, and take
only the young; then you will prosper and live long.

8   When you build a new house, put a parapet along the roof, or you will
bring the guilt of bloodshed on your house if anyone should fall from it.

9   You shall not sow your vineyard with a second crop, or the full yield
will be forfeit, both the yield of the seed you sow and the fruit of the vineyard.

10   You shall not plough with an ox and an ass yoked together.

11   You shall not wear clothes woven with two kinds of yarn, wool and flax
together.

12   You shall make twisted tassels on the four corners of your cloaks which
you wrap round you.

13   When a man takes a wife and after having intercourse with her turns
14 against her and brings trumped-up charges against her, giving her a bad
name and saying, 'I took this woman and slept with her and did not find

[a] *Or* accursed.

proof of virginity in her', then the girl's father and mother shall take the 15
proof of her virginity to the elders of the town, at the town gate. The girl's 16
father shall say to the elders, 'I gave my daughter in marriage to this man,
and he has turned against her. He has trumped up a charge and said, "I 17
have not found proofs of virginity in your daughter." Here are the proofs.'
They shall then spread the garment before the elders of the town. The 18
elders shall take the man and punish him: they shall fine him a hundred 19
pieces of silver because he has given a bad name to a virgin of Israel, and
hand them to the girl's father. She shall be his wife: he is not free to divorce
her all his life long. If, on the other hand, the accusation is true and no 20
proof of the girl's virginity is found, then they shall bring her out to the 21
door of her father's house and the men of her town shall stone her to death.
She has committed an outrage in Israel by playing the prostitute in her
father's house: you shall rid yourselves of this wickedness.

When a man is discovered lying with a married woman, they shall both 22
die, the woman as well as the man who lay with her: you shall rid Israel
of this wickedness.

When a virgin is pledged in marriage to a man and another man comes 23
upon her in the town and lies with her, you shall bring both of them out to 24
the gate of that town and stone them to death; the girl because, although in
the town, she did not cry for help, and the man because he dishonoured
another man's wife: you shall rid yourselves of this wickedness. If the man 25
comes upon such a girl in the country and rapes her, then the man alone
shall die because he lay with her. You shall do nothing to the girl, she has 26
done nothing worthy of death: this deed is like that of a man who attacks
another and murders him, for the man came upon her in the country and, 27
though the girl cried for help, there was no one to rescue her.

When a man comes upon a virgin who is not pledged in marriage and 28
forces her to lie with him, and they are discovered, then the man who lies 29
with her shall give the girl's father fifty pieces of silver, and she shall be
his wife because he has dishonoured her. He is not free to divorce her all
his life long.

A man shall not take his father's wife: he shall not bring shame on his 30
father.

No man whose testicles have been crushed or whose organ has been **23**
severed shall become a member of the assembly of the LORD.

No descendant of an irregular union, even down to the tenth generation, 2
shall become a member of the assembly of the LORD.

No Ammonite or Moabite, even down to the tenth generation, shall 3
become a member of the assembly of the LORD. They shall never become
members of the assembly of the LORD, because they did not meet you with 4
food and water on your way out of Egypt, and because they hired Balaam
son of Beor from Pethor in Aram-naharaim[a] to revile you. The LORD 5
your God refused to listen to Balaam and turned his denunciation into a
blessing, because the LORD your God loved you. You shall never seek their 6
welfare or their good all your life long.

You shall not regard an Edomite as an abomination, for he is your own 7

[a]   *That is* Aram of Two Rivers.

8 kin; nor an Egyptian, for you were aliens in his land. The third generation of children born to them may become members of the assembly of the LORD.

9 When you are encamped against an enemy, you shall be careful to avoid
10 any foulness. When one of your number is unclean because of an emission of seed at night, he must go outside the camp; he may not come within it.
11 Towards evening he shall wash himself in water, and at sunset he may come
12 back into the camp. You shall have a sign outside the camp showing where
13 you can withdraw. With your equipment you will have a trowel, and when you squat outside, you shall scrape a hole with it and then turn and cover
14 your excrement. For the LORD your God goes about in your camp, to keep you safe and to hand over your enemies as you advance, and your camp must be kept holy for fear that he should see something indecent and go with you no further.

15 You shall not surrender to his master a slave who has taken refuge with
16 you. Let him stay with you anywhere he chooses in any one of your settlements, wherever suits him best; you shall not force him.

17 No Israelite woman shall become a temple-prostitute, and no Israelite man shall prostitute himself in this way.

18 You shall not allow a common prostitute's fee, or the pay of a male prostitute, to be brought into the house of the LORD your God in fulfilment of any vow, for both of them are abominable to the LORD your God.

19 You shall not charge interest on anything you lend to a fellow-countryman, money or food or anything else on which interest can be
20 charged. You may charge interest on a loan to a foreigner but not on a loan to a fellow-countryman, for then the LORD your God will bless you in all you undertake in the land which you are entering to occupy.

21 When you make a vow to the LORD your God, do not put off its fulfilment; otherwise the LORD your God will require satisfaction of you and you will
22 be guilty of sin. If you choose not to make a vow, you will not be guilty of
23 sin; but if you voluntarily make a vow to the LORD your God, mind what you say and do what you have promised.

24 When you go into another man's vineyard, you may eat as many grapes as you wish to satisfy your hunger, but you may not put any into your basket.

25 When you go into another man's standing corn, you may pluck ears to rub in your hands, but you may not put a sickle to his standing corn.

24 When a man has married a wife, but she does not win his favour because he finds something shameful in her, and he writes her a note of divorce,
2 gives it to her and dismisses her; and suppose after leaving his house she
3 goes off to become the wife of another man, and this next husband turns against her and writes her a note of divorce which he gives her and dis-
4 misses her, or dies after making her his wife—then in that case her first husband who dismissed her is not free to take her back to be his wife again after she has become for him unclean. This is abominable to the LORD; you must not bring sin upon the land which the LORD your God is giving you as your patrimony.

5 When a man is newly married, he shall not be liable for military service

or any other public duty. He shall remain at home exempt from service for one year and enjoy the wife he has taken.

No man shall take millstones, or even the upper one alone, in pledge; 6 that would be taking a life in pledge.

When a man is found to have kidnapped a fellow-countryman, an Israel- 7 ite, and to have treated him harshly and sold him, he shall die: you shall rid yourselves of this wickedness.

Be careful how you act in all cases of malignant skin-disease; be careful 8 to observe all that the levitical priests tell you; I gave them my commands which you must obey. Remember what the LORD your God did to Miriam, 9 on your way out of Egypt.

When you make a loan to another man, do not enter his house to take a 10 pledge from him. Wait outside, and the man whose creditor you are shall 11 bring the pledge out to you. If he is a poor man, you shall not sleep in the 12 cloak he has pledged. Give it back to him at sunset so that he may sleep in 13 it and bless you; then it will be counted to your credit in the sight of the LORD your God.

You shall not keep back the wages of a man who is poor and needy, 14 whether a fellow-countryman or an alien living in your country in one of your settlements. Pay him his wages on the same day before sunset, for 15 he is poor and his heart is set on them: he may appeal to the LORD against you, and you will be guilty of sin.

Fathers shall not be put to death for their children, nor children for 16 their fathers; a man shall be put to death only for his own sin.

You shall not deprive aliens and orphans of justice nor take a widow's 17 cloak in pledge. Remember that you were slaves in Egypt and the LORD 18 your God redeemed you from there; that is why I command you to do this.

When you reap the harvest in your field and forget a swathe, do not go 19 back to pick it up; it shall be left for the alien, the orphan, and the widow, in order that the LORD your God may bless you in all that you undertake.

When you beat your olive-trees, do not strip them afterwards; what is 20 left shall be for the alien, the orphan, and the widow.

When you gather the grapes from your vineyard, do not glean after- 21 wards; what is left shall be for the alien, the orphan, and the widow. Remember that you were slaves in Egypt; that is why I command you to 22 do this.

When two men go to law and present themselves for judgement, the **25** judges shall try the case; they shall acquit the innocent and condemn the guilty. If the guilty man is sentenced to be flogged, the judge shall cause him 2 to lie down and be beaten in his presence; the number of strokes shall correspond to the gravity of the offence. They may give him forty strokes, 3 but not more; otherwise, if they go further and exceed this number, your fellow-countryman will have been publicly degraded.

You shall not muzzle an ox while it is treading out the corn. 4

When brothers live together and one of them dies without leaving a son, 5 his widow shall not marry outside the family. Her husband's brother shall have intercourse with her; he shall take her in marriage and do his duty by her as her husband's brother. The first son she bears shall perpetuate the 6

7 dead brother's name so that it may not be blotted out from Israel. But if the man is unwilling to take his brother's wife, she shall go to the elders at the town gate and say, 'My husband's brother refuses to perpetuate his
8 brother's name in Israel; he will not do his duty by me.' At this the elders of the town shall summon him and reason with him. If he still stands his
9 ground and says, 'I will not take her', his brother's widow shall go up to him in the presence of the elders; she shall pull his sandal off his foot and spit in his face and declare: 'Thus we requite the man who will not build
10 up his brother's family.' His family shall be known in Israel as the House of the Unsandalled Man.

11 When two men are fighting and the wife of one of them comes near to drag her husband clear of his opponent, if she puts out her hand and
12 catches hold of the man's genitals, you shall cut off her hand and show her no mercy.

13 You shall not have unequal weights in your bag, one heavy, the other
14 light. You shall not have unequal measures in your house, one large, the
15 other small. You shall have true and correct weights and true and correct measures, so that you may live long in the land which the LORD your God
16 is giving you. All who commit these offences, all who deal dishonestly, are abominable to the LORD.

17 Remember what the Amalekites did to you on your way out of Egypt,
18 how they met you on the road when you were faint and weary and cut off your rear, which was lagging behind exhausted: they showed no fear of
19 God. When the LORD your God gives you peace from your enemies on every side, in the land which he is giving you to occupy as your patrimony, you shall not fail to blot out the memory of the Amalekites from under heaven.

26 WHEN YOU COME INTO THE LAND which the LORD your God is giving
2 you to occupy as your patrimony and settle in it, you shall take the first-fruits of all the produce of the soil, which you gather in from the land which the LORD your God is giving you, and put them in a basket. Then you shall go to the place which the LORD your God will choose as a dwelling for his
3 Name and come to the priest, whoever he shall be in those days. You shall say to him, 'I declare this day to the LORD your God that I have entered
4 the land which the LORD swore to our forefathers to give us.' The priest shall take the basket from your hand and set it down before the altar of the
5 LORD your God. Then you shall solemnly recite before the LORD your God: 'My father was a homeless *a* Aramaean who went down to Egypt with a small company and lived there until they became a great, powerful, and
6 numerous nation. But the Egyptians ill-treated us, humiliated us and im-
7 posed cruel slavery upon us. Then we cried to the LORD the God of our fathers for help, and he listened to us and saw our humiliation, our hard-
8 ship and distress; and so the LORD brought us out of Egypt with a strong hand and outstretched arm, with terrifying deeds, and with signs and
9 portents. He brought us to this place and gave us this land, a land flowing
10 with milk and honey. And now I have brought the firstfruits of the soil

a Or wandering.

which thou, O LORD, hast given me.' You shall then set the basket before the LORD your God and bow down in worship before him. You shall all rejoice, you and the Levites and the aliens living among you, for all the good things which the LORD your God has given to you and to your family. 11

When you have finished taking a tithe of your produce in the third year, 12 the tithe-year, you shall give it to the Levites and to the aliens, the orphans, and the widows. They shall eat it in your settlements and be well fed. Then 13 you shall declare before the LORD your God: 'I have rid my house of the tithe that was holy to thee and given it to the Levites, to the aliens, the orphans, and the widows, according to all the commandments which thou didst lay upon me. I have not broken or forgotten any of thy commandments. I have not eaten any of the tithe while in mourning, nor have I rid 14 myself of it for unclean purposes, nor offered any of it to *a* the dead. I have obeyed the LORD my God: I have done all that thou didst command me. Look down from heaven, thy holy dwelling-place, and bless thy people 15 Israel and the ground which thou hast given to us as thou didst swear to our forefathers, a land flowing with milk and honey.'

This day the LORD your God commands you to keep these statutes and 16 laws: be careful to observe them with all your heart and soul. You have 17 recognized the LORD this day as your God; you are to conform to his ways, to keep his statutes, his commandments, and his laws, and to obey him. The LORD has recognized you this day as his special possession, as he 18 promised you, and to keep his commandments; he will raise you high 19 above all the nations which he has made, to bring him praise and fame and glory, and to be a people holy to the LORD your God, according to his promise.

Concluding charge of Moses to the people

MOSES, WITH THE ELDERS OF ISRAEL, gave the people this charge: 27 'Keep all the commandments that I lay upon you this day. On the 2 day that you cross the Jordan to the land which the LORD your God is giving you, you shall set up great stones and plaster them over. You shall 3 inscribe on them all the words of this law, when you have crossed over to enter the land which the LORD your God is giving you, a land flowing with milk and honey, as the LORD the God of your fathers promised you. When 4 you have crossed the Jordan you shall set up these stones on Mount Ebal, as I command you this day, and cover them with plaster. You shall build 5 an altar there to the LORD your God: it shall be an altar of stones on which you shall use no tool of iron. You shall build the altar of the LORD your 6 God with blocks of undressed stone, and you shall offer whole-offerings upon it to the LORD your God. You shall slaughter shared-offerings and 7 eat them there, and rejoice before the LORD your God. You shall inscribe 8 on the stones all the words of this law, engraving them with care.'

Moses and the levitical priests spoke to all Israel, 'Be silent, Israel, and 9 listen; this day you have become a people belonging to the LORD your God.

a Or for.

10 Obey the LORD your God, and observe his commandments and statutes which I lay upon you this day.'

11 12 That day Moses gave the people this command: 'Those who shall stand for the blessing of the people on Mount Gerizim when you have crossed the Jordan are these: Simeon, Levi, Judah, Issachar, Joseph, and Benjamin.

13 Those who shall stand on Mount Ebal for the curse are these: Reuben, Gad, Asher, Zebulun, Dan, and Naphtali.'

14 The Levites, in the hearing of all Israel, shall intone these words:

15 'A curse upon the man who carves an idol or casts an image, anything abominable to the LORD that craftsmen make, and sets it up in secret': the people shall all respond and say, 'Amen.'

16 'A curse upon him who slights his father or his mother': the people shall all say, 'Amen.'

17 'A curse upon him who moves his neighbour's boundary stone': the people shall all say, 'Amen.'

18 'A curse upon him who misdirects a blind man': the people shall all say, 'Amen.'

19 'A curse upon him who withholds justice from the alien, the orphan, and the widow': the people shall all say, 'Amen.'

20 'A curse upon him who lies with his father's wife, for he brings shame upon his father': the people shall all say, 'Amen.'

21 'A curse upon him who lies with any animal': the people shall all say, 'Amen.'

22 'A curse upon him who lies with his sister, his father's daughter or his mother's daughter': the people shall all say, 'Amen.'

23 'A curse upon him who lies with his wife's mother': the people shall all say, 'Amen.'

24 'A curse upon him who strikes another man in secret': the people shall all say, 'Amen.'

25 'A curse upon him who takes reward to kill a man with whom he has no feud': the people shall all say, 'Amen.'

26 'A curse upon any man who does not fulfil this law by doing all that it prescribes': the people shall all say, 'Amen.'

28 IF YOU WILL OBEY THE LORD your God by diligently observing all his commandments which I lay upon you this day, then the LORD your
2 God will raise you high above all nations of the earth, and all these blessings shall come to you and light upon you, because you obey the LORD your God:

3 A blessing on you in the city; a blessing on you in the country.

4 A blessing on the fruit of your body, the fruit of your land and of your cattle, the offspring of your herds and of your lambing flocks.

5 A blessing on your basket and your kneading-trough.

6 A blessing on you as you come in; and a blessing on you as you go out.

7 May the LORD deliver up the enemies who attack you and let them be put to rout before you. Though they come out against you by one way, they shall flee before you by seven ways.

8 May the LORD grant you a blessing in your granaries and in all your

labours; may the LORD your God bless you in the land which he is giving you.

The LORD will set you up as his own holy people, as he swore to you, if you keep the commandments of the LORD your God and conform to his ways. Then all people on earth shall see that the LORD has named you as his very own, and they shall go in fear of you. The LORD will make you prosper greatly in the fruit of your body and of your cattle, and in the fruit of the ground in the land which he swore to your forefathers to give you. May the LORD open the heavens for you, his rich treasure house, to give rain upon your land at the proper time and bless everything to which you turn your hand. You shall lend to many nations, but you shall not borrow; the LORD will make you the head and not the tail: you shall be always at the top and never at the bottom, when you listen to the commandments of the LORD your God, which I give you this day to keep and to fulfil. You shall turn neither to the right nor to the left from all the things which I command you this day nor shall you follow after and worship other gods.

BUT IF YOU DO NOT OBEY the LORD your God by diligently observing all his commandments and statutes which I lay upon you this day, then all these maledictions shall come to you and light upon you:

A curse upon you in the city; a curse upon you in the country.

A curse upon your basket and your kneading-trough.

A curse upon the fruit of your body, the fruit of your land, the offspring of your herds and of your lambing flocks.

A curse upon you as you come in; and a curse upon you as you go out.

May the LORD send upon you starvation, burning thirst, and dysentery,*a* whatever you are about, until you are destroyed and quickly perish for your evil doings, because you have forsaken me.

May the LORD cause pestilence to haunt you until he has exterminated you out of the land which you are entering to occupy; may the LORD afflict you with wasting disease and recurrent fever, ague and eruptions; with drought, black blight and red; and may these plague you until you perish. May the skies above you be bronze, and the earth beneath you iron. May the LORD turn the rain upon your country into fine sand, and may dust come down upon you from the sky until you are blotted out.

May the LORD put you to rout before the enemy. Though you go out against them by one way, you shall flee before them by seven ways. May you be repugnant to all the kingdoms on earth. May your bodies become food for the birds of the air and the wild beasts, with no man to scare them away.

May the LORD strike you with Egyptian boils and with tumours, scabs, and itches, for which you will find no cure. May the LORD strike you with madness, blindness, and bewilderment; so that you will grope about in broad daylight, just as a blind man gropes in darkness, and you will fail to find your way. You will also be oppressed and robbed, day in, day out, with no one to save you. A woman will be pledged to you, but another shall ravish her; you will build a house but not live in it; you will plant a

a Or cursing, confusion, and rebuke.

31 vineyard but not enjoy its fruit. Your ox will be slaughtered before your eyes, but you will not eat any of it; and before your eyes your ass will be stolen and will not come back to you; your sheep will be given to the enemy,
32 and there will be no one to recover them. Your sons and daughters will be given to another people while you look on; your eyes will strain after them
33 all day long, and you will be powerless. A nation whom you do not know shall eat the fruit of your land and all your toil, and your lot will be nothing
34 35 but brutal oppression. The sights you see will drive you mad. May the LORD strike you on knee and leg with malignant boils for which you will find no cure; they will spread from the sole of your foot to the crown of
36 your head. May the LORD give you up, you and the king whom you have appointed, to a nation whom neither you nor your fathers have known, and
37 there you will worship other gods, gods of wood and stone. You will become a horror, a byword, and an object-lesson to all the peoples amongst whom the LORD disperses you.

38 You will carry out seed for your fields in plenty, but you will harvest
39 little; for the locusts will devour it. You will plant vineyards and cultivate them, but you will not drink the wine or gather the grapes; for the grub
40 will eat them. You will have olive-trees all over your territory, but you will
41 not anoint yourselves with their oil; for your olives will drop off. You will bear sons and daughters, but they will not remain yours because they will be
42 taken into captivity. All your trees and the fruit of the ground will be
43 infested with the mole-cricket. The alien who lives with you will raise
44 himself higher and higher, and you will sink lower and lower. He will lend to you but you will not lend to him: he will be the head and you the tail.
45 All these maledictions will come upon you; they will pursue you and overtake you until you are destroyed because you did not obey the LORD your God by keeping the commandments and statutes which he gave you.
46 They shall be a sign and a portent to you and your descendants for ever,
47 because you did not serve the LORD your God with joy and with a glad
48 heart for all your blessings. Then in hunger and thirst, in nakedness and extreme want, you shall serve your enemies whom the LORD will send against you, and they will put a yoke of iron on your neck when they have
49 subdued you. May the LORD raise against you a nation from afar, from the other end of the earth, who will swoop upon you like a vulture, a nation
50 whose language you will not understand, a nation of grim aspect with no
51 reverence for age and no pity for the young. They will devour the young of your cattle and the fruit of your land, when you have been subdued. They will leave you neither corn, nor new wine nor oil, neither the off-spring of your herds nor of your lambing flocks, until you are annihilated.
52 They will besiege you in all your cities until they bring down your lofty impregnable walls, those city walls throughout your land in which you trust. They will besiege you within all your cities, throughout the land
53 which the LORD your God has given you. Then you will eat your own children, the flesh of your sons and daughters whom the LORD your God has given you, because of the dire straits to which you will be reduced
54 when your enemy besieges you. The pampered, delicate man will not share with his brother, or the wife of his bosom, or his own remaining children,

any of the meat which he is eating, the flesh of his own children. He is left 55
with nothing else because of the dire straits to which you will be reduced
when your enemy besieges you within your cities. The pampered, delicate 56
woman, the woman who has never even tried to put a foot to the ground,
so delicate and pampered she is, will not share with her own husband or
her son or her daughter the afterbirth which she expels, or any boy or girl 57
that she may bear. She will herself eat them secretly in her extreme want,
because of the dire straits to which you will be reduced when your enemy
besieges you within your cities.

If you do not observe and fulfil all the law written down in this book, if 58
you do not revere this honoured and dreaded name, this name 'the LORD *a*
your God', then the LORD will strike you and your descendants with 59
unimaginable plagues, malignant and persistent, and with sickness,
persistent and severe. He will bring upon you once again all the diseases of 60
Egypt which you dread, and they will cling to you. The LORD will bring 61
upon you sickness and plague of every kind not written down in this book
of the law, until you are destroyed. Then you who were countless as the 62
stars in the sky will be left few in number, because you did not obey the
LORD your God. Just as the LORD took delight in you, prospering and 63
increasing you, so now it will be his delight to destroy and exterminate you,
and you will be uprooted from the land which you are entering to occupy.
The LORD will scatter you among all peoples from one end of the earth to 64
the other, and there you will worship other gods whom neither you have
known nor your forefathers, gods of wood and stone. Among those nations 65
you will find no peace, no rest for the sole of your foot. Then the LORD
will give you an unquiet mind, dim eyes, and failing appetite. Your life 66
will hang continually in suspense, fear will beset you night and day, and
you will find no security all your life long. Every morning you will say, 67
'Would God it were evening!', and every evening, 'Would God it were
morning!', for the fear that lives in your heart and the sights that you see.
The LORD will bring you sorrowing back to Egypt by that very road of 68
which I said to you, 'You shall not see that road again'; and there you will
offer to sell yourselves to your enemies as slaves and slave-girls, but there
will be no buyer.

These are the words of the covenant which the LORD commanded Moses **29**
to make with the Israelites in Moab, in addition to the covenant which he
made with them on Horeb.

MOSES SUMMONED ALL THE ISRAELITES and said to them: 'You 2
have seen with your own eyes all that the LORD did in Egypt to Pharaoh,
to all his servants, and to the whole land, the great challenge which you 3
yourselves witnessed, those great signs and portents, but to this day the 4
LORD has not given you a mind to learn, or eyes to see, or ears to hear. I 5
led you for forty years in the wilderness; your clothes did not wear out on
you, nor did your sandals wear out and fall off your feet; you ate no bread 6
and drank no wine or strong drink, in order that you might learn that I am
the LORD your God. You came to this place where Sihon king of Heshbon 7

a See note on Exod. 3. 15.

8 and Og king of Bashan came to attack us, and we defeated them. We took their land and gave it as patrimony to the Reubenites, the Gadites, and
9 half the tribe of Manasseh. You shall observe the provisions of this covenant and keep them so that you may be successful in all you do.

10 'You all stand here today before the LORD your God, tribal chiefs,
11 elders, and officers, all the men of Israel, with your dependants, your wives, the aliens who live in your camp—all of them, from those who chop
12 wood to those who draw water—and you are ready to accept the oath and enter into the covenant which the LORD your God is making with you
13 today. The covenant is to constitute you his people this day, and he will be your God, as he promised you and as he swore to your forefathers,
14 Abraham, Isaac and Jacob. It is not with you alone that I am making this
15 covenant and this oath, but with all those who stand here with us today before the LORD our God and also with those who are not here with us
16 today. For you know how we lived in Egypt and how we and you, as we
17 passed through the nations, saw their loathsome idols and the false gods
18 they had, the gods of wood and stone, of silver and gold. If there should be among you a man or woman, family or tribe, who is moved today to turn from the LORD our God and to go worshipping the gods of those nations— if there is among you such a root from which springs gall and wormwood,
19 then when he hears the terms of this oath, he may inwardly flatter himself and think, "All will be well with me even if I follow the promptings of my
20 stubborn heart"; but this will bring everything to ruin. The LORD will not be willing to forgive him; for then his anger and resentment will overwhelm this man, and the denunciations prescribed in this book will fall heavily
21 on him, and the LORD will blot out his name from under heaven. The LORD will single him out from all the tribes of Israel for disaster to fall upon him, according to the oath required by the covenant and prescribed in this book of the law.

22 'The next generation, your sons who follow you and the foreigners who come from distant countries, will see the plagues of this land and the
23 ulcers which the LORD has brought upon its people, the whole land burnt up with brimstone and salt, so that it cannot be sown, or yield herb or green plant. It will be as desolate as were Sodom and Gomorrah, Admah and
24 Zeboyim, when the LORD overthrew them in his anger and rage. Then they, and all the nations with them, will ask, "Why has the LORD so afflicted this land? Why has there been this great outburst of wrath?"
25 The answer will be: "Because they forsook the covenant of the LORD the God of their fathers which he made with them when he brought them out
26 of Egypt. They began to worship other gods and to bow down to them, gods whom they had not known and whom the LORD had not assigned to
27 them. The anger of the LORD was roused against that land, so that he
28 brought upon it all the maledictions written in this book. The LORD uprooted them from their soil in anger, in wrath and great fury, and banished them to another land, where they are to this day."

29 'There are things hidden, and they belong to the LORD our God, but what is revealed belongs to us and our children for ever; it is for us to observe all that is prescribed in this law.

'When these things have befallen you, the blessing and the curse of **30**
which I have offered you the choice, if you and your sons take them to heart
there in all the countries to which the LORD your God has banished you,
if you turn back to him and obey him heart and soul in all that I command   2
you this day, then the LORD your God will show you compassion and   3
restore your fortunes. He will gather you again from all the countries to
which he has scattered you. Even though he were to banish you to the four   4
corners of the world, the LORD your God will gather you from there, from
there he will fetch you home. The LORD your God will bring you into the   5
land which your forefathers occupied, and you will occupy it again; then
he will bring you prosperity and make you more numerous than your forefathers were. The LORD your God will circumcise *a* your hearts and the   6
hearts of your descendants, so that you will love him with all your heart
and soul and you will live. Then the LORD your God will turn all these   7
denunciations against your enemies and the foes who persecute you. You   8
will then again obey the LORD and keep all his commandments which I
give you this day. The LORD your God will make you more than prosperous   9-10
in all that you do, in the fruit of your body and of your cattle and in the
fruits of the earth; for, when you obey the LORD your God by keeping his
commandments and statutes, as they are written in this book of the law,
and when you turn back to the LORD your God with all your heart and soul,
he will again rejoice over you and be good to you, as he rejoiced over your
forefathers.

'The commandment that I lay on you this day is not too difficult for you,   11
it is not too remote. It is not in heaven, that you should say, "Who will go   12
up to heaven for us to fetch it and tell it to us, so that we can keep it?"
Nor is it beyond the sea, that you should say, "Who will cross the sea for   13
us to fetch it and tell it to us, so that we can keep it?" It is a thing very   14
near to you, upon your lips and in your heart ready to be kept.

'Today I offer you the choice of life and good, or death and evil. If you   15 16
obey the commandments of the LORD your God which I give you this day,
by loving the LORD your God, by conforming to his ways and by keeping
his commandments, statutes, and laws, then you will live and increase, and
the LORD your God will bless you in the land which you are entering to
occupy. But if your heart turns away and you do not listen and you are led   17
on to bow down to other gods and worship them, I tell you this day that   18
you will perish; you will not live long in the land which you will enter to
occupy after crossing the Jordan. I summon heaven and earth to witness   19
against you this day: I offer you the choice of life or death, blessing or
curse. Choose life and then you and your descendants will live; love the   20
LORD your God, obey him and hold fast to him: that is life for you and
length of days in the land which the LORD swore to give to your forefathers,
Abraham, Isaac and Jacob.'

Moses finished speaking these words to all Israel, and then he said, 'I   **31** 1 2
am now a hundred and twenty years old, and I can no longer move about
as I please; and the LORD has told me that I may not cross the Jordan. The   3
LORD your God will cross over at your head and destroy these nations before

a Or incline.

your advance, and you shall occupy their lands; and, as he directed, Joshua
4 will lead you across. The LORD will do to these nations as he did to Sihon
and Og, kings of the Amorites, and to their lands; he will destroy them.
5 The LORD will deliver them into your power, and you shall do to them as I
6 commanded you. Be strong, be resolute; you must not dread them or be
afraid, for the LORD your God himself goes with you; he will not fail you
or forsake you.'

7 Moses summoned Joshua and said to him in the presence of all Israel,
'Be strong, be resolute; for it is you who are to lead this people into the
land which the LORD swore to give their forefathers, and you are to bring
8 them into possession of it. The LORD himself goes at your head; he will
be with you; he will not fail you or forsake you. Do not be discouraged or
afraid.'

9 Moses wrote down this law and gave it to the priests, the sons of Levi,
who carried the Ark of the Covenant of the LORD, and to all the elders of
10 Israel. Moses gave them this command: 'At the end of every seven years,
at the appointed time for the year of remission, at the pilgrim-feast of
11 Tabernacles, when all Israel comes to enter the presence of the LORD your
God in the place which he will choose, you shall read this law publicly in
12 the hearing of all Israel. Assemble the people, men, women, and dependants,
together with the aliens who live in your settlements, so that they may listen,
and learn to fear the LORD your God and observe all these laws with care.
13 Their children, too, who do not know them, shall hear them, and learn to
fear the LORD your God all their lives in the land which you will occupy
after crossing the Jordan.'

Joshua appointed successor to Moses

14 THE LORD SAID TO MOSES, 'The time of your death is drawing near;
call Joshua, and then come and stand in the Tent of the Presence so
that I may give him his commission.' So Moses and Joshua went and took
15 their stand in the Tent of the Presence; and the LORD appeared in the tent
in a pillar of cloud, and the pillar of cloud stood at the entrance of the tent.
16 The LORD said to Moses, 'You are about to die like your forefathers,
and this people, when they come into the land and live among foreigners,
will go wantonly after their gods; they will abandon me and break the
17 covenant which I have made with them. Then my anger will be roused
against them, and I will abandon them and hide my face from them. They
will be an easy prey, and many terrible disasters will come upon them.
They will say on that day, "These disasters have come because our God is
18 not among us." On that day I will hide my face because of all the evil they
have done in turning to other gods.
19 'Now write down this rule of life[a] and teach it to the Israelites; make
20 them repeat it, so that it may be on record against them. When I have
brought them into the land which I swore to give to their forefathers, a
land flowing with milk and honey, and they have plenty to eat and grow

a rule of life: *or* song.

fat, they will turn to other gods and worship them, they will spurn me
and break my covenant; and many calamities and disasters will follow. 21
Then this rule of life will confront them as a record, for it will not be
forgotten by their descendants. For even before I bring them into the
land which I swore to give them, I know which way their thoughts incline
already.'

That day Moses wrote down this rule of life and taught it to the Israelites. 22
The Lord*a* gave Joshua son of Nun his commission in these words: 'Be 23
strong, be resolute; for you shall bring the Israelites into the land which
I swore to give them, and I will be with you.'

When Moses had finished writing down these laws in a book, from begin- 24
ning to end, he gave this command to the Levites who carried the Ark of 25
the Covenant of the Lord: 'Take this book of the law and put it beside the 26
Ark of the Covenant of the Lord your God to be a witness against you. For 27
I know how defiant and stubborn you are; even during my lifetime you
have defied the Lord; how much more, then, will you do so when I am
dead? Assemble all the elders of your tribes and your officers; I will say 28
all these things in their hearing and will summon heaven and earth to
witness against them. For I know that after my death you will take 29
to degrading practices and turn aside from the way which I told you to
follow, and in days to come disaster will come upon you, because you are
doing what is wrong in the eyes of the Lord and so provoking him to
anger.'

Two historical poems

MOSES RECITED THIS SONG from beginning to end in the hearing 30
of the whole assembly of Israel:

Give ear to what I say, O heavens,　　　　　　　　　　　**32**
　earth, listen to my words;
my teaching shall fall like drops of rain,　　　　　　　　　2
my words shall distil like dew,
like fine rain upon the grass
and like the showers on young plants.

When I call aloud the name of the Lord,*b*　　　　　　　3
you shall respond, 'Great is our God,
the creator*c* whose work is perfect,　　　　　　　　　　4
and all his ways are just,
a faithful god, who does no wrong,
righteous and true is He!'

Perverse and crooked generation　　　　　　　　　　　5
whose faults have proved you no children of his,
is this how you repay the Lord,　　　　　　　　　　　　6
you brutish and stupid people?

a Prob. rdg.; Heb. He.　　　*b Or the name* JEHOVAH.　　　*c Or* rock.

Is he not your father who formed you?
Did he not make you and establish you?

7 Remember the days of old,
think of the generations long ago;
ask your father to recount it
and your elders to tell you the tale.

8 When the Most High parcelled out the nations,
when he dispersed all mankind,
he laid down the boundaries of every people
according to the number of the sons of God;

9 but the LORD's share was his own people,
Jacob was his allotted portion.

10 He found him in a desert land,
in a waste and howling void.
He protected and trained him,
he guarded him as the apple of his eye,

11 as an eagle watches over its nest,
hovers above its young,
spreads its pinions and takes them up,
and carries them upon its wings.

12 The LORD alone led him,
no alien god at his side.

13 He made him ride on the heights of the earth
and fed him on the harvest of the fields;
he satisfied him with honey from the crags
and oil from the flinty rock,

14 curds from the cattle, milk from the ewes,
the fat of lambs' kidneys,
of rams, the breed of Bashan, and of goats,
with the finest flour of wheat;
and he drank wine from the blood of the grape.

15 Jacob ate and was well fed,
Jeshurun grew fat and unruly,*a*
he grew fat, he grew bloated and sleek.
He forsook God who made him
and dishonoured the Rock of his salvation.

16 They roused his jealousy with foreign gods
and provoked him with abominable practices.

17 They sacrificed to foreign demons that are no gods,
gods who were strangers to them;
they took up with new gods from their neighbours,
gods whom your fathers did not acknowledge.

18 You forsook the creator *b* who begot you
and cared nothing for God who brought you to birth.

19 The LORD saw and spurned them;
his own sons and daughters provoked him.

a Or and kicked. *b Or* rock.

'I will hide my face from them,' he said;   20
'let me see what their end will be,
for they are a mutinous generation,
sons who are not to be trusted.
They roused my jealousy with a god of no account,   21
with their false gods they provoked me;
so I will rouse their jealousy with a people of no account,
with a brutish nation I will provoke them.
For fire is kindled by my anger,   22
it burns to the depths of Sheol;
it devours earth and its harvest
and sets fire to the very roots of the mountains.
I will heap on them one disaster after another,   23
I will use up all my arrows on them:
pangs of hunger, ravages of plague,   24
and bitter pestilence.
I will harry them with the fangs of wild beasts
and the poison of creatures that crawl in the dust.
The sword will make orphans in the streets   25
and widows in their own homes;
it will take toll of young man and maid,
of babes in arms and old men.
I had resolved to strike them down   26
and to destroy all memory of them,
but I feared that I should be provoked by their foes,   27
that their enemies would take the credit
and say, "It was not the LORD,
it was we who raised the hand that did this."'

They are a nation that lacks good counsel,   28
devoid of understanding.
If only they had the wisdom to understand this   29
and give thought to their end!
How could one man pursue a thousand of them,   30
how could two put ten thousand to flight,
if their Rock had not sold them to their enemies,
if the LORD had not handed them over?
For the enemy have no Rock like ours,   31
in themselves they are mere fools.
Their vines are vines of Sodom,   32
grown on the terraces of Gomorrah;
their grapes are poisonous,
the clusters bitter to the taste.
Their wine is the venom of serpents,   33
the cruel poison of asps;
all this I have in reserve,   34
sealed up in my storehouses
till the day of punishment and vengeance,   35

till the moment when they slip and fall;
for the day of their downfall is near,
their doom is fast approaching.

36 The LORD will give his people justice
and have compassion on his servants;
for he will see that their strength is gone:
alone, or defended by his clan, no one is left.

37 He will say, 'Where are your gods,
the rock in which you sought shelter,
38 the gods who ate the fat of your sacrifices
and drank the wine of your drink-offerings?
Let them rise to help you!
Let them give you shelter!
39 See now that I, I am He,
and there is no god beside me:
I put to death and I keep alive,
I wound and I heal;
there is no rescue from my grasp.
40 I lift my hand to heaven
and swear: As I live for ever,
41 when I have whetted my flashing sword,
when I have set my hand to judgement,
then I will punish my adversaries
and take vengeance on my enemies.
42 I will make my arrows drunk with blood,
my sword shall devour flesh,
blood of slain and captives,
the heads of the enemy princes.'
43 Rejoice with him, you heavens,
bow down, all you gods, before him;
for he will avenge the blood of his sons
and take vengeance on his adversaries;
he will punish those who hate him
and make expiation for his people's land.

44 This is the song that Moses came and recited in the hearing of the people, he and Joshua son of Nun.

45 46 Moses finished speaking to all Israel, and then he said, 'Take to heart all these warnings which I solemnly give you this day: command your
47 children to be careful to observe all the words of this law. For you they are no empty words; they are your very life, and by them you shall live long in the land which you are to occupy after crossing the Jordan.'

48 49 That same day the LORD spoke to Moses and said, 'Go up this mount Abarim, Mount Nebo in Moab, to the east of Jericho, and look out over the land of Canaan that I am giving to the Israelites for their possession.
50 On this mountain you shall die and be gathered to your father's kin, just as Aaron your brother died on Mount Hor and was gathered to his father's
51 kin. This is because both of you were unfaithful to me at the waters of

Meribah-by-Kadesh in the wilderness of Zin, when you did not uphold my holiness among the Israelites. You shall see the land from a distance 52 but you may not enter the land I am giving to the Israelites.'

THIS IS THE BLESSING that Moses the man of God pronounced upon 33 the Israelites before his death:

> The LORD came from Sinai 2
> and shone forth from Seir.
> He showed himself from Mount Paran,
> and with him were myriads of holy ones *a*
> streaming along at his right hand.
> > Truly he loves his people 3
> > and blesses his saints.*b*
> > They sit at his feet
> > and receive his instruction,
> > the law which Moses laid upon us,
> as a possession for the assembly of Jacob. 4
> Then a king arose*c* in Jeshurun, 5
> when the chiefs of the people were assembled
> together with all the tribes of Israel.

Of Reuben he said: *d* 6

> May Reuben live and not die out,
> but may he be few in number.

And of Judah he said this: 7

> Hear, O LORD, the cry of Judah
> and join him to his people,
> thou whose hands fight for him,
> who art his helper against his foes.

Of Levi he said: 8

> Thou didst give thy Thummim to Levi,
> thy Urim to thy loyal servant
> whom thou didst prove at Massah,
> for whom thou didst plead at the waters of Meribah,
> who said of his parents, I do not know them, 9
> who did not acknowledge his brothers,
> nor recognize his children.
> They observe thy word
> and keep thy covenant;
> they teach thy precepts to Jacob, 10
> thy law to Israel.
> They offer thee the smoke of sacrifice
> and offerings on thy altar.

a and with . . . holy ones: *prob. rdg.; Heb.* and he came from myriads of holiness.
b Or holy ones.   *c Or* Then there was a king . . .   *d* Of Reuben he said:
prob. rdg.; Heb. om.

11   Bless all his powers,^a O Lord,
            and accept the work of his hands.
            Strike his adversaries hip and thigh,
            and may his enemies rise no more.

12   Of Benjamin he said:

            The Lord's beloved dwells in security,
            the High God^b shields him all the day long,
            and he dwells under his protection.

13   Of Joseph he said:

            The Lord's blessing is on his land
            with precious fruit watered from heaven above
            and from the deep that lurks below,
14   with precious fruit ripened by the sun,
            precious fruit, the produce of the months,
15   with all good things from the ancient mountains,
            the precious fruit of the everlasting hills,
16   the precious fruits of earth and all its store,
            by the favour of him who dwells in the burning bush.
            This shall rest^c upon the head of Joseph,
            on the brow of him who was prince among^d his brothers.
17   In majesty he shall be like a first-born ox,
            his horns those of a wild ox
            with which he will gore nations
            and drive^e them to the ends of earth.
            Such will be the myriads of Ephraim,
            and such the thousands of Manasseh.

18   Of Zebulun he said:

            Rejoice, Zebulun, when you sally forth,
            rejoice in your tents, Issachar.
19   They shall summon nations to the mountain,
            there they will offer true sacrifices,
            for they shall suck the abundance of the seas
            and draw out^f the hidden wealth of the sand.

20   Of Gad he said:

            Blessed be Gad, in his wide domain;
            he couches like a lion
            tearing an arm or a scalp.
21   He chose the best for himself,
            for to him was allotted a ruler's portion,
            when the chiefs of the people were assembled together.
            He did what the Lord deemed right,
            observing his ordinances for Israel.

---

^a Or skill.   ^b the High God: *prob. rdg.; Heb.* upon him.   ^c *Prob. rdg., cp. Gen.*
49. 26; Heb. has an unintelligible form.   ^d him . . . among: *or* the one cursed by.
^e and drive: *prob. rdg.; Heb.* together.   ^f draw out: *prob. rdg.; Heb. obscure.*

Of Dan he said: 22

> Dan is a lion's cub
> springing out from Bashan.

Of Naphtali he said: 23

> Naphtali is richly favoured
> and full of the blessings of the LORD;
> his patrimony stretches to the sea and southward.

Of Asher he said: 24

> Asher is most blest of sons,
> may he be the favourite among*ᵃ* his brothers
> and bathe his feet in oil.
> May your bolts be of iron and bronze,   25
> and your strength last as long as you live.
>
> There is none like the God of Jeshurun   26
> who rides the heavens to your help,
> riding the clouds in his glory,
> who humbled the gods of old   27
> and subdued*ᵇ* the ancient powers;
> who drove out the enemy before you
> and gave the word to destroy.
> Israel lives in security,   28
> the tribes of Jacob by themselves,
> in a land of corn and wine*ᶜ*
> where the skies drip with dew.
> Happy are you, people of Israel, peerless, set free;   29
> the LORD is the shield that guards you,
> the Blessed One is your glorious sword.
> Your enemies come cringing to you,
> and you shall trample their bodies under foot.

The death of Moses

THEN MOSES WENT UP from the lowlands of Moab to Mount Nebo, **34** to the top of Pisgah, eastwards from Jericho, and the LORD showed him the whole land: Gilead as far as Dan; the whole of Naphtali; the 2 territory of Ephraim and Manasseh, and all Judah as far as the western sea; the Negeb and the Plain; the valley of Jericho, the Vale of Palm Trees, 3 as far as Zoar. The LORD said to him, 'This is the land which I swore to 4 Abraham, Isaac and Jacob that I would give to their descendants. I have let you see it with your own eyes, but you shall not cross over into it.'

There in the land of Moab Moses the servant of the LORD died, as the 5 LORD had said. He was buried in a valley in Moab opposite Beth-peor, but 6 to this day no one knows his burial-place. Moses was a hundred and twenty 7

ᵃ Or of.   *ᵇ Prob. rdg.; Heb. under.*   *ᶜ Or new wine.*

years old when he died; his sight was not dimmed nor had his vigour failed.
8 The Israelites wept for Moses in the lowlands of Moab for thirty days;
9 then the time of mourning for Moses was ended. And Joshua son of Nun was filled with the spirit of wisdom, for Moses had laid his hands on him, and the Israelites listened to him and did what the LORD had commanded Moses.

10 There has never yet risen in Israel a prophet like Moses, whom the LORD
11 knew face to face: remember all the signs and portents which the LORD sent him to show in Egypt to Pharaoh and all his servants and the whole
12 land; remember the strong hand of Moses and the terrible deeds which he did in the sight of all Israel.

THE BOOK OF

JOSHUA

Israel's entry into the promised land

AFTER THE DEATH OF MOSES the servant of the LORD, 1
the LORD said to Joshua son of Nun, his assistant, 'My servant 2
Moses is dead; now it is for you to cross the Jordan, you and this
whole people of Israel, to the land which I am giving them. Every place 3
where you set foot is yours: I have given it to you, as I promised Moses.
From the desert and the Lebanon to the great river, the river Euphrates, and 4
across all the Hittite country westwards to the Great Sea,^a all this shall be
your land. No one will ever be able to stand against you: as I was with 5
Moses, so will I be with you; I will not fail you or forsake you. Be strong, 6
be resolute; it is you who are to put this people in possession of the land
which I swore to give to their fathers. Only be strong and resolute; observe 7
diligently all the law which my servant Moses has given you. You must
not turn from it to right or left, if you would prosper wherever you go.
This book of the law must ever be on your lips; you must keep it in mind 8
day and night so that you may diligently observe all that is written in it.
Then you will prosper and be successful in all that you do. This is my 9
command: be strong, be resolute; do not be fearful or dismayed, for the
LORD your God is with you wherever you go.' Then Joshua told the officers 10
to pass through the camp and give this order to the people: 'Get food ready 11
to take with you; for within three days you will be crossing the Jordan to
occupy the country which the LORD your God is giving you to possess.'
To the Reubenites, the Gadites, and the half tribe of Manasseh, Joshua 12
said, 'Remember the command which Moses the servant of the LORD 13
gave you when he said, "The LORD your God will grant you security here
and will give you this territory." Your wives and dependants and your 14
herds may stay east of the Jordan in the territory which Moses has given
you, but for yourselves, all the warriors among you must cross over as a
fighting force at the head of your kinsmen. You must help them, until the 15
LORD grants them security like you and they too take possession of the land
which the LORD your God is giving them. You may then return to the land
which is your own possession, the territory which Moses the servant of
the LORD has given you east of the Jordan.' They answered Joshua, 'What- 16
ever you tell us, we will do; wherever you send us, we will go. As we obeyed 17
Moses, so will we obey you; and may the LORD your God be with you as he
was with Moses! Whoever rebels against your authority, and fails to carry 18
out all your orders, shall be put to death. Only be strong and resolute.'

^a Or the Mediterranean Sea.

2 Joshua son of Nun sent two spies out from Shittim secretly with orders to reconnoitre the country. The two men came to Jericho and went to the
2 house of a prostitute named Rahab, and spent the night there. It was reported to the king of Jericho that some Israelites had arrived that night
3 to explore the country. So the king sent to Rahab and said, 'Bring out the men who have come to you and are now in your house; they are here to
4 explore the whole country.' The woman, who had taken the two men and hidden them,*a* replied, 'Yes, the men did come to me, but I did not know
5 where they came from; and when it was time to shut the gate at nightfall, they had gone. I do not know where they were going, but if you hurry after
6 them, you will catch them up.' In fact, she had taken them up on to the roof and concealed them among the stalks of flax which she had laid out
7 there in rows. The messengers went in pursuit of them down the road to the fords of the Jordan, and the gate was closed as soon as they had gone
8 out. The men had not yet settled down, when Rahab came up to them on
9 the roof and said to them, 'I know that the LORD has given this land to you, that terror of you has descended upon us all, and that because of you the
10 whole country is panic-stricken. For we have heard how the LORD dried up the water of the Red Sea *b* before you when you came out of Egypt, and what you did to Sihon and Og, the two Amorite kings beyond the Jordan,
11 whom you put to death. When we heard this, our courage failed us; your coming has left no spirit in any of us; for the LORD your God is God in
12 heaven above and on earth below. Swear to me now by the LORD that you will keep faith with my family, as I have kept faith with you. Give me a
13 token of good faith; promise that you will spare the lives of my father and mother, my brothers and sisters and all who belong to them, and save us
14 from death.' The men replied, 'Our lives for yours, so long as you do not betray our business. When the LORD gives us the country, we will deal
15 honestly and faithfully by you.' She then let them down through an opening
16 by a rope; for the house where she lived was on an angle of the wall. 'Take to the hills,' she said, 'or the pursuers will come upon you. Hide yourselves
17 there for three days until they come back, and then go on your way.' The men warned her that they would be released from the oath she had made
18 them take unless she did what they told her. 'When we enter the land,' they said, 'you must fasten this strand of scarlet cord in the opening through which you have lowered us, and get everybody together here in the house,
19 your father and mother, your brothers and all your family. If anybody goes out of doors into the street, his blood shall be on his own head; we shall be quit of the oath. But if a hand is laid on anyone who stays indoors with you,
20 his blood shall be on our heads. Remember too that, if you betray our
21 business, then we shall be quit of the oath you have made us take.' She replied, 'It shall be as you say', and sent them away. They set off, and she
22 fastened the strand of scarlet cord in the opening. The men made their way into the hills and stayed there three days until the pursuers returned. They
23 had searched all along the road, but had not found them. *c* The two men

---

a Prob. rdg.; Heb. him.   *b Or* the Sea of Reeds.   *c* three days . . . found them: *or* three days while the pursuers scoured the land and searched all along the road, but did not find them.

then turned and came down from the hills, crossed the river and returned
to Joshua son of Nun. They told him all that had happened to them and   24
said to him, 'The LORD has put the whole country into our hands, and now
all its people are panic-stricken at our approach.'

Joshua rose early in the morning, and he and all the Israelites set out   **3**
from Shittim and came to the Jordan, where they encamped before crossing
the river. At the end of three days the officers passed through the camp,   2
and gave this order to the people: 'When you see the Ark of the Covenant   3
of the LORD your God being carried forward by the levitical priests, then
you too shall leave your positions and set out. Follow it, but do not go   4
close to it; keep some distance behind, about a thousand yards. This will
show you the way you are to go, for you have not travelled this way before.'
Joshua then said to the people, 'Hallow yourselves, for tomorrow the LORD   5
will do a great miracle among you.' To the priests he said, 'Lift up the Ark 6
of the Covenant and pass in front of the people.' So they lifted up the Ark
of the Covenant and went in front of the people. Then the LORD said to   7
Joshua, 'Today I will begin to make you stand high in the eyes of all
Israel, and they shall know that I will be with you as I was with Moses.
Give orders to the priests who carry the Ark of the Covenant, and tell them 8
that when they come to the edge of the waters of the Jordan, they are to
take their stand in the river.'

Then Joshua said to the Israelites, 'Come here and listen to the words   9
of the LORD your God. By this you shall know that the living God is among   10
you and that he will drive out before you the Canaanites, the Hittites, the
Hivites, the Perizzites, the Girgashites, the Amorites, and the Jebusites:
the Ark of the Covenant of the LORD,[a] the lord of all the earth, is to cross 11
the Jordan at your head. Choose twelve men from the tribes of Israel, one   12
man from each tribe. When the priests carrying the Ark of the LORD, the   13
lord of all the earth, set foot in the waters of the Jordan, then the waters of
the Jordan will be cut off; the water coming down from upstream will
stand piled up like a bank.' So the people set out from their tents to cross 14
the Jordan, with the priests in front of them carrying the Ark of the Covenant. Now the Jordan is in full flood in all its reaches throughout the time 15
of harvest. When the priests reached the Jordan and dipped their feet in
the water at the edge, the water coming down from upstream was brought   16
to a standstill; it piled up like a bank for a long way back, as far as Adam,
a town near Zarethan. The waters coming down to the Sea of the Arabah,
the Dead Sea, were completely cut off, and the people crossed over opposite
Jericho. The priests carrying the Ark of the Covenant of the LORD stood   17
firm on the dry bed in the middle of the Jordan; and all Israel passed over
on dry ground until the whole nation had crossed the river.

WHEN THE WHOLE NATION HAD FINISHED CROSSING the Jordan,   **4**
the LORD said to Joshua, 'Take twelve men from the people, one from each   2
tribe, and order them to lift up twelve stones from this place, out of the   3
middle of the Jordan, where the feet of the priests stood firm. They are to
carry them across and set them down in the camp where you spend the

[a] of the LORD: *prob. rdg., cp. verse 17; Heb. om.*

4 night.' Joshua summoned the twelve men whom he had chosen out of the
5 Israelites, one man from each tribe, and said to them, 'Cross over in front
   of the Ark of the LORD your God as far as the middle of the Jordan, and let
   each of you take a stone and hoist it on his shoulder, one for each of the
6 tribes of Israel. These stones are to stand as a memorial among you; and
7 in days to come, when your children ask you what these stones mean, you
   shall tell them how the waters of the Jordan were cut off before the Ark of
   the Covenant of the LORD when it crossed the Jordan. Thus these stones
8 will always be a reminder to the Israelites.' The Israelites did as Joshua had
   commanded: they lifted up twelve stones from the middle of the Jordan,
   as the LORD had instructed Joshua, one for each of the tribes of Israel,
   carried them across to the camp and set them down there.

9   Joshua set up twelve stones in the middle of the Jordan at the place
   where the priests stood who carried the Ark of the Covenant, and there
10 they are to this day. The priests carrying the Ark remained standing in the
   middle of the Jordan until every command which the LORD had told Joshua
   to give to the people was fulfilled, and the people had made good speed
11 across. When all the people had finished crossing, then the Ark of the LORD
12 crossed, and the priests with it.*[a]* At the head of the Israelites, there crossed
   over the Reubenites, the Gadites, and the half tribe of Manasseh, as a
13 fighting force, as Moses had told them to do; about forty thousand strong,
   drafted for active service, they crossed over to the lowlands of Jericho in
   the presence of the LORD to do battle.

14   That day the LORD made Joshua stand very high in the eyes of all Israel,
   and the people revered him, as they had revered Moses all his life.

15 16   The LORD said to Joshua, 'Command the priests carrying the Ark of the
17 Tokens to come up from the Jordan.' So Joshua commanded the priests
18 to come up from the Jordan; and when the priests carrying the Ark of the
   Covenant of the LORD came up from the river-bed, they had no sooner set
   foot on dry land than the waters of the Jordan came back to their place and
19 filled up all its reaches as before. On the tenth day of the first month the
   people came up out of the Jordan and camped in Gilgal in the district east
20 of Jericho, and there Joshua set up the twelve stones which they had taken
21 from the Jordan. He said to the Israelites, 'In days to come, when your
22 descendants ask their fathers what these stones mean, you shall explain
23 that the Jordan was dry when Israel crossed over, and that the LORD your
   God dried up the waters of the Jordan in front of you until you had gone
   across, just as the LORD your God did at the Red Sea when he dried it up
24 for us until we had crossed. Thus all people on earth will know how strong
   is the hand of the LORD; and thus they will stand in awe of the LORD your
   God for ever.'

5   When all the Amorite kings to the west of the Jordan and all the Canaanite kings by the sea-coast heard that the LORD had dried up the waters before
   the advance of the Israelites until they had crossed, their courage melted
   away and there was no more spirit left in them for fear of the Israelites.

2   At that time the LORD said to Joshua, 'Make knives of flint, seat yourself,
3 and make Israel a circumcised people again.' Joshua thereupon made knives

---

[a] Prob. rdg.; Heb. adds before the people.

of flint and circumcised the Israelites at Gibeath-haaraloth.^a This is why 4
Joshua circumcised them: all the males who came out of Egypt, all the
fighting men, had died in the wilderness on the journey from Egypt. The 5
people who came out of Egypt had all been circumcised, but not those who
had been born in the wilderness during the journey. For the Israelites 6
travelled in the wilderness for forty years, until the whole nation, all the
fighting men among them, had passed away, all who came out of Egypt
and had disobeyed the voice of the LORD. The LORD swore that he would
not allow any of these to see the land which he had sworn to their fathers
to give us, a land flowing with milk and honey. So it was their sons, whom 7
he had raised up in their place, that Joshua circumcised; they were uncircumcised because they had not been circumcised on the journey. When 8
the circumcision of the whole nation was complete, they stayed where they
were in camp until they had recovered. The LORD then said to Joshua, 9
'Today I have rolled away from you the reproaches of the Egyptians.'
Therefore the place is called Gilgal^b to this very day.

The Israelites encamped in Gilgal, and at sunset on the fourteenth day 10
of the month they kept the Passover in the lowlands of Jericho. On the day 11
after the Passover, they ate their unleavened cakes and parched grain, and
that day it was the produce of the country. It was from that day, when they 12
first ate the produce of the country, that the manna ceased. The Israelites
received no more manna; and that year they ate what had grown in the
land of Canaan.

When Joshua came near Jericho he looked up and saw a man standing in 13
front of him with a drawn sword in his hand. Joshua went up to him and
said, 'Are you for us or for our enemies?' And the man said to him, 'I am 14
here as captain of the army of the LORD.' Joshua fell down before him, face
to the ground, and said, 'What have you to say to your servant, my lord?'
The captain of the LORD's army said to him, 'Take off your sandals; the 15
place where you are standing is holy'; and Joshua did so.

JERICHO WAS BOLTED AND BARRED against the Israelites; no one went **6**
out, no one came in. The LORD said to Joshua, 'Look, I have delivered 2
Jericho and her king^c into your hands. You shall march round the city with 3
all your fighting men, making the circuit of it once, for six days running.
Seven priests shall go in front of the Ark carrying seven trumpets made 4
from rams' horns. On the seventh day you shall march round the city
seven times and the priests shall blow their trumpets. At the blast of the 5
rams' horns, when you hear the trumpet sound, the whole army shall raise
a great shout; the wall of the city will collapse and the army shall advance,
every man straight ahead.' So Joshua son of Nun summoned the priests 6
and gave them their orders: 'Take up the Ark of the Covenant; let seven
priests with seven trumpets of ram's horn go in front of the Ark of the
LORD.' Then he said to the army, 'March on and make the circuit of the 7
city, and let the men drafted from the two and a half tribes go in front of
the Ark of the LORD.' When Joshua had spoken to the army, the seven 8

^a *That is* the Hill of Foreskins.   ^b *That is* Rolling Stones.   ^c *Prob. rdg.;*
Heb. *adds* the fighting men.

priests carrying the seven trumpets of ram's horn before the LORD passed
on and blew the trumpets, with the Ark of the Covenant of the LORD
9 following them. The drafted men marched in front of the priests who blew
the trumpets, and the rearguard followed the Ark, the trumpets sounding
10 as they marched. But Joshua ordered the army not to shout, or to raise their
voices or utter a word, till the day came when he would tell them to shout;
11 then they were to give a loud shout. Thus he caused the Ark of the LORD
to go round the city, making the circuit of it once, and then they went back
12 to the camp and spent the night there. Joshua rose early in the morning and
13 the priests took up the Ark of the LORD. The seven priests carrying the
seven trumpets of ram's horn went marching in front of the Ark of the
LORD, blowing the trumpets as they went, with the drafted men in front
of them and the rearguard following the Ark of the LORD, the trumpets
14 sounding as they marched. They marched round the city once on the
15 second day and returned to the camp; this they did for six days. But on the
seventh day they rose at dawn and marched seven times round the city in
the same way; that was the only day on which they marched round seven
16 times. The seventh time the priests blew the trumpets and Joshua said to
17 the army, 'Shout! The LORD has given you the city. The city shall be under
solemn ban: everything in it belongs to the LORD. No one is to be spared
except the prostitute Rahab and everyone who is with her in the house,
18 because she hid the men whom we sent. And you must beware of coveting
anything that is forbidden under the ban; you must take none of it for
yourselves; this would put the Israelite camp itself under the ban and
19 bring trouble on it. All the silver and gold, all the vessels of copper and iron,
shall be holy; they belong to the LORD and they must go into the LORD's
20 treasury.' So they blew the trumpets, and when the army heard the
trumpet sound, they raised a great shout, and down fell the walls. The
21 army advanced on the city, every man straight ahead, and took it. Under
the ban they destroyed everything in the city; they put everyone to
the sword, men and women, young and old, and also cattle, sheep, and
asses.

22   But the two men who had been sent out as spies were told by Joshua to
go into the prostitute's house and bring out her and all who belonged to
23 her, as they had sworn to do. So the young men went and brought out
Rahab, her father and mother, her brothers and all who belonged to her.
They brought out the whole family and left them outside the Israelite
24 camp. They then set fire to the city and everything in it, except that they
deposited the silver and gold and the vessels of copper and iron in the
25 treasury of the LORD's house. Thus Joshua spared the lives of Rahab the
prostitute, her household and all who belonged to her, because she had
hidden the men whom Joshua had sent to Jericho as spies; she and her
26 family settled permanently among the Israelites. It was then that Joshua
laid this curse on Jericho:

> May the LORD's curse light on the man who comes forward
>   to rebuild this city of Jericho:
> the laying of its foundations shall cost him his eldest son,
> the setting up of its gates shall cost him his youngest.

Thus the LORD was with Joshua, and his fame spread throughout the 27 country.

But the Israelites defied the ban: Achan son of Carmi, son of Zabdi, son 7 of Zerah, of the tribe of Judah, took some of the forbidden things, and the LORD was angry with the Israelites.

Joshua sent men from Jericho with orders to go up to Ai, near Beth- 2 aven, east of Bethel, and see how the land lay; so the men went up and explored Ai. They returned to Joshua and reported that there was no need 3 for the whole army to move: 'Let some two or three thousand men go forward to attack Ai. Do not make the whole army toil up there; the popula- tion is small.' And so about three thousand men went up, but they turned 4 tail before the men of Ai, who killed some thirty-six of them; they chased 5 them all the way from the gate to the Quarries*a* and killed them on the pass. At this the courage of the people melted and flowed away like water. Joshua and the elders of Israel rent their clothes and flung themselves face 6 downwards to the ground; they lay before the Ark of the LORD till evening and threw dust on their heads. Joshua said, 'Alas, O Lord GOD, why didst 7 thou bring this people across the Jordan only to hand us over to the Amorites to be destroyed? If only we had been content to settle on the other side of the Jordan! I beseech thee, O Lord; what can I say, now that 8 Israel has been routed by the enemy? When the Canaanites and all the 9 natives of the country hear of this, they will come swarming around us and wipe us off the face of the earth. What wilt thou do then for the honour of thy great name?'

The LORD said to Joshua, 'Stand up; why lie prostrate on your face? 10 Israel has sinned: they have broken the covenant which I laid upon them, 11 by taking forbidden things for themselves. They have stolen them, and concealed it by mingling them with their own possessions. That is why the 12 Israelites cannot stand against their enemies: they are put to flight because they have brought themselves under the ban. Unless they destroy every single thing among them that is forbidden under the ban, I will be with them no longer. Stand up; you must hallow the people; tell them they must 13 hallow themselves for tomorrow. Tell them, These are the words of the LORD the God of Israel: You have forbidden things among you, Israel; you cannot stand against your enemies until you have rid yourselves of them. In the morning come forward tribe by tribe, and the tribe which the 14 LORD chooses shall come forward clan by clan; the clan which the LORD chooses shall come forward family by family; and the family which the LORD chooses shall come forward man by man. The man who is chosen as 15 the harbourer of forbidden things shall be burnt, he and all that is his, because he has broken the covenant of the LORD and committed outrage in Israel.' Early in the morning Joshua rose and brought Israel forward tribe 16 by tribe, and the tribe of Judah was chosen. He brought forward the clans 17 of Judah, and the clan of Zerah was chosen; then the clan of Zerah family by family, and the family of Zabdi was chosen. He brought that family 18 forward man by man, and Achan son of Carmi, son of Zabdi, son of Zerah, of the tribe of Judah, was chosen. Then Joshua said to Achan, 'My 19

a Or to Shebarim.

son, give honour to the LORD the God of Israel and make your confession
20 to him: tell me what you have done, hide nothing from me.' Achan answered
Joshua, 'I confess, I have sinned against the LORD the God of Israel. This
21 is what I did: among the booty I caught sight of a fine mantle from Shinar,
two hundred shekels of silver, and a bar of gold weighing fifty shekels. I
coveted them and I took them. You will find them hidden in the ground
22 inside my tent, with the silver underneath.' So Joshua sent messengers,
who ran to the tent, and there was the stuff *a* hidden in the tent with the
23 silver underneath. They took the things from the tent, brought them to
24 Joshua and all the Israelites, and spread them out before the LORD. Then
Joshua took Achan son of Zerah, with the silver, the mantle, and the bar
of gold, together with his sons and daughters, his oxen, his asses, and his
sheep, his tent, and everything he had, and he and all Israel brought them
25 up to the Vale of Achor.*b* Joshua said, 'What trouble you have brought on
us! Now the LORD will bring trouble on you.' Then all the Israelites stoned
26 him to death; and they raised a great pile of stones over him, which remains
to this day. So the LORD's anger was abated. That is why to this day that
place is called the Vale of Achor.

8 THE LORD SAID TO JOSHUA, 'Do not be fearful or dismayed; take the
whole army and attack Ai. I deliver the king of Ai into your hands, him
2 and his people, his city and his country. Deal with Ai and her king as you
dealt with Jericho and her king; but you may keep for yourselves the cattle
and any other spoil that you may take. Set an ambush for the city to the
3 west of it.' So Joshua and all the army prepared for the assault on Ai. He
4 chose thirty thousand fighting men and dispatched them by night, with
these orders: 'Lie in ambush to the west of the city, not far from it, and all
5 of you hold yourselves in readiness. I myself will approach the city with
the rest of the army, and when the enemy come out to meet us as they did
6 last time, we shall take to flight before them. Then they will come out and
pursue us until we have drawn them away from the city, thinking that we
7 have taken to flight as we did last time. While we are in flight, come out
from your ambush and occupy the city; the LORD your God will deliver it
8 into your hands. When you have taken it, set it on fire. Thus you will do
9 what the LORD commands. These are your orders.' So Joshua sent them
off, and they went to the place of ambush and waited between Bethel and
Ai to the west of Ai, while Joshua spent the night with the army.
10 Early in the morning Joshua rose, mustered the army and marched
11 against Ai, he himself and the elders of Israel at its head. All the armed
forces with him marched on until they came within sight of the city. They
12 encamped north of Ai, with the valley between them and the city; but
Joshua took some five thousand men and set them in ambush between
14 Bethel and Ai to the west of the city. *c* When the king of Ai saw them, he
and the citizens rose with all speed that morning and marched out to do
battle against Israel; he did not know that there was an ambush set for him

---

a Or the mantle.   *b* That is Trouble.   *c* So Sept.; Heb. adds (13) So the
army pitched camp to the north of the city, and the rearguard to the west, while Joshua
went that night into the valley.

to the west of the city. Joshua and all the Israelites made as if they were 15
routed by them and fled towards the wilderness, and all the people in the 16
city were called out in pursuit. So they pursued Joshua and were drawn
away from the city. Not a man was left in Ai; they had all gone out 17
in pursuit of the Israelites and during the pursuit had left the city
undefended.

Then the LORD said to Joshua, 'Point towards Ai with the dagger you 18
are holding, for I will deliver the city into your hands.' So Joshua pointed
with his dagger towards Ai. At his signal, the men in ambush rose quickly 19
from their places and, entering the city at a run, took it and promptly set fire
to it. The men of Ai looked back and saw the smoke from the city already 20
going up to the sky; they were powerless to make their escape in any direction, and the Israelites who had feigned flight towards the wilderness turned
on their pursuers. For when Joshua and all the Israelites saw that the 21
ambush had seized the city and that smoke was already going up from it,
they turned and fell upon the men of Ai. Those who had come out to meet 22
the Israelites were now hemmed in with Israelites on both sides of them,
and the Israelites cut them down until there was not a single survivor, nor
had any escaped. The king of Ai was taken alive and brought to Joshua. 23
When the Israelites had cut down to the last man all the citizens of Ai who 24
were in the open country or in the wilderness to which they had pursued
them, and the massacre was complete, they all turned back to Ai and put it
to the sword. The number who were killed that day, men and women, was 25
twelve thousand, the whole population of Ai. Joshua held out his dagger 26
and did not draw back his hand until he had put to death all who lived in
Ai; but the Israelites kept for themselves the cattle and any other spoil that 27
they took, following the word of the LORD spoken to Joshua. So Joshua 28
burnt Ai to the ground, and left it the desolate ruined mound it remains to
this day. He hanged the king of Ai on a tree and left him there till sunset; 29
and when the sun had set, he gave the order and they cut him down and
flung down his body at the entrance of the city gate. Over the body they
raised a great pile of stones, which is there to this day.

At that time Joshua built an altar to the LORD the God of Israel on Mount 30
Ebal. The altar was of blocks of undressed stone on which no tool of iron 31
had been used, following the commands given to the Israelites by Moses the
servant of the LORD, as is described in the book of the law of Moses. At the
altar they offered whole-offerings to the LORD, and slaughtered shared-
offerings. There in the presence of the Israelites he engraved on blocks *a* of 32
stone a copy of the law of Moses. And all Israel, elders, officers, and judges, 33
took their stand on either side of the Ark, facing the levitical priests who
carried the Ark of the Covenant of the LORD—all Israel, native and alien
alike. Half of them stood facing Mount Gerizim and half facing Mount
Ebal, to fulfil the command of Moses the servant of the LORD that the
blessing should be pronounced first. Then Joshua recited the whole of the 34
blessing and the cursing word by word, as they are written in the book of
the law. There was not a single word of all that Moses had commanded 35
which he did not read aloud before the whole congregation of Israel,

a Or on the blocks.

including the women and dependants and the aliens resident in their company.

9 When the news of these happenings reached all the kings west of the Jordan, in the hill-country, the Shephelah, and all the coast of the Great Sea running up to the Lebanon, the kings of the Hittites, Amorites, 2 Canaanites, Perizzites, Hivites, and Jebusites agreed to join forces and fight against Joshua and Israel.

3 When the inhabitants of Gibeon heard how Joshua had dealt with 4 Jericho and Ai, they adopted a ruse of their own. They went and disguised themselves, with old sacking for their asses, old wine-skins split and 5 mended, old and patched sandals for their feet, old clothing to wear, and by 6 way of provisions nothing but dry and mouldy bread. They came to Joshua in the camp at Gilgal and said to him and the Israelites, 'We have come from 7 a distant country to ask you now to grant us a treaty.' The Israelites said to the Hivites, 'But maybe you live in our neighbourhood: if so, how can we 8 grant you a treaty?' They said to Joshua, 'We are your slaves.' Joshua asked 9 them who they were and where they came from. 'Sir,' they replied, 'our country is very far away, and we have come because of the renown of the LORD your God. We have heard of his fame, of all that he did to Egypt, 10 and to the two Amorite kings east of the Jordan, Sihon king of Heshbon 11 and Og king of Bashan who lived at Ashtaroth. Our elders and all the people of our country told us to take provisions for the journey and come 12 to meet you, and say, "We are your slaves; please grant us a treaty." Look at our bread; it was hot from the oven when we packed it at home on the 13 day we came away. Now it is dry and mouldy. Look at the wine-skins; they were new when we filled them, and now they are all split; look at our clothes 14 and our sandals, worn out by the long journey.' The chief men of the community accepted some of their provisions, and did not at first seek guidance 15 from the LORD. So Joshua received them peaceably and granted them a treaty, promising to spare their lives, and the chiefs pledged their faith to them on oath.

16 Within three days of granting them the treaty, the Israelites learnt that 17 they were in fact neighbours and lived near by. So the Israelites set out and on the third day they reached their cities; these were Gibeon, Kephirah, 18 Beeroth, and Kiriath-jearim. The Israelites did not slaughter them, because of the oath which the chief men of the community had sworn to them by the LORD the God of Israel, but the people were all indignant with their 19 chiefs. The chiefs all replied to the assembled people, 'But we swore an oath to them by the LORD the God of Israel; we cannot touch them now. 20 What we will do is this: we will spare their lives so that the oath which we 21 swore to them may bring no harm upon us. But though their lives must be spared, they shall be set to chop wood and draw water for the com-22 munity.' The people agreed to do as their chiefs had said. Joshua summoned the Gibeonites and said, 'Why did you play this trick on us? You told us 23 that you live a long way off, when you are near neighbours. There is a curse upon you for this: for all time you shall provide us with slaves, to 24 chop wood and draw water for the house of my God.' They answered Joshua, 'We were told, sir, that the LORD your God had commanded Moses

his servant to give you the whole country and to exterminate all its inhabitants; so because of you we were in terror of our lives, and that is why we did this. We are in your power: do with us whatever you think right and 25 proper.' What he did was this: he saved them from death at the hands of 26 the Israelites, and they did not kill them; but thenceforward he set them to 27 chop wood and draw water for the community and for the altar of the LORD. And to this day they do it at the place which the LORD chose.

When Adoni-zedek king of Jerusalem heard that Joshua had captured 10 Ai and destroyed it (for Joshua had dealt with Ai and her king as he had dealt with Jericho and her king), and that the inhabitants of Gibeon had made their peace with Israel and were living among them, he was greatly 2 alarmed; for Gibeon was a large place, like a royal city: it was larger than Ai, and its men were all good fighters. So Adoni-zedek king of Jerusalem 3 sent to Hoham king of Hebron, Piram king of Jarmuth, Japhia king of Lachish, and Debir king of Eglon, and said, 'Come up and help me, and 4 we will attack the Gibeonites, because they have made their peace with Joshua and the Israelites.' So the five Amorite kings, the kings of Jerusalem, 5 Hebron, Jarmuth, Lachish, and Eglon, joined forces and advanced to take up their positions for the attack on Gibeon. But the men of Gibeon sent 6 this message to Joshua in the camp at Gilgal: 'We are your slaves, do not abandon us, come quickly to our relief. All the Amorite kings in the hill-country have joined forces against us; come and help us.' So Joshua went 7 up from Gilgal with all his forces and all his fighting men. The LORD said 8 to Joshua, 'Do not be afraid of them; I have delivered them into your hands, and not a man will be able to stand against you.' Joshua came upon them 9 suddenly, after marching all night from Gilgal. The LORD threw them into 10 confusion before the Israelites, and Joshua defeated them utterly in Gibeon; he pursued them down the pass of Beth-horon and kept up the slaughter as far as Azekah and Makkedah. As they were fleeing from Israel down the 11 pass, the LORD hurled great hailstones at them out of the sky all the way to Azekah: more died from the hailstones than the Israelites slew by the sword.

On that day when the LORD delivered the Amorites into the hands of 12 Israel, Joshua spoke with the LORD, and he said in the presence of Israel:

> Stand still, O Sun, in Gibeon;
> stand, Moon, in the Vale of Aijalon.

So the sun stood still and the moon halted until a nation had taken vengeance 13 on its enemies, as indeed is written in the Book of Jashar.[a] The sun stayed in mid heaven and made no haste to set for almost a whole day. Never 14 before or since has there been such a day as this day on which the LORD listened to the voice of a man; for the LORD fought for Israel. So Joshua 15 and all the Israelites returned to the camp at Gilgal.

The five kings fled and hid themselves in a cave at Makkedah, and 16 17 Joshua was told that they had been found hidden in this cave. Joshua 18 replied, 'Roll some great stones to the mouth of the cave and post men there to keep watch over the kings. But you must not stay; keep up the 19

_____
[a] *Or* the Book of the Upright.

pursuit, attack your enemies from the rear and do not let them reach their
20 cities; the LORD your God has delivered them into your hands.' When
Joshua and the Israelites had finished the work of slaughter and all had
been put to the sword—except a few survivors who escaped and entered
21 the fortified cities—the whole army rejoined Joshua at Makkedah in peace;
not a man of the Israelites suffered so much as a scratch on his tongue.
22 Then Joshua said, 'Open the mouth of the cave, and bring me out those
23 five kings.' They did so; they brought the five kings out of the cave, the
24 kings of Jerusalem, Hebron, Jarmuth, Lachish, and Eglon. When they
had brought them to Joshua, he summoned all the Israelites and said to
the commanders of the troops who had served with him, 'Come forward
and put your feet on the necks of these kings.' So they came forward and
25 put their feet on their necks. Joshua said to them, 'Do not be fearful or
dismayed; be strong and resolute; for the LORD will do this to every enemy
26 you fight against.' And he struck down the kings and slew them; then he
hung their bodies on five trees, where they remained hanging till evening.
27 At sunset, on Joshua's orders they took them down from the trees and
threw them into the cave in which they had hidden; they piled great stones
against its mouth, and there the stones are to this day. *a*

28 On that same day, Joshua captured Makkedah and put both king and
people to the sword, destroying both them and every living thing in the
city. He left no survivor, and he dealt with the king of Makkedah as he
29 had dealt with the king of Jericho. Then Joshua and all the Israelites
30 marched on from Makkedah to Libnah and attacked it. The LORD delivered the city and its king to the Israelites, and they put its people and
every living thing in it to the sword; they left no survivor there, and dealt
31 with its king as they had dealt with the king of Jericho. From Libnah
Joshua and all the Israelites marched on to Lachish, took up their positions
32 and attacked it. The LORD delivered Lachish into their hands; they took
it on the second day and put every living thing in it to the sword, as they
had done at Libnah.

33 Meanwhile Horam king of Gezer had advanced to the relief of Lachish;
but Joshua struck them down, both king and people, and not a man of
34 them survived. Then Joshua and all the Israelites marched on from Lachish
35 to Eglon, took up their positions and attacked it; that same day they captured it and put its inhabitants to the sword, destroying every living thing
36 in it as they had done at Lachish. From Eglon Joshua and all the Israelites
37 advanced to Hebron and attacked it. They captured it and put its king to
the sword together with every living thing in it and in all its villages; as at
38 Eglon, he left no survivor, destroying it and every living thing in it. Then
Joshua and all the Israelites wheeled round towards Debir and attacked it.
39 They captured the city with its king, and all its villages, put them to the
sword and destroyed every living thing; they left no survivor. They dealt
with Debir and its king as they had dealt with Hebron and with Libnah
and its king.

40 So Joshua massacred the population of the whole region—the hill-
country, the Negeb, the Shephelah, the watersheds—and all their kings.

a and there . . . day: *or* on this very day.

He left no survivor, destroying everything that drew breath, as the LORD
the God of Israel had commanded. Joshua carried the slaughter from 41
Kadesh-barnea to Gaza, over the whole land of Goshen and as far as
Gibeon. All these kings he captured at the same time, and their country 42
with them, for the LORD the God of Israel fought for Israel. And Joshua 43
returned with all the Israelites to the camp at Gilgal.

When Jabin king of Hazor heard of all this, he sent to Jobab king of 11
Madon, to the kings of Shimron and Akshaph, to the northern kings in the 2
hill-country, in the Arabah opposite Kinnereth, in the Shephelah, and in
the district of Dor on the west, the Canaanites to the east and the west, the 3
Amorites, Hittites, Perizzites, and Jebusites in the hill-country, and the
Hivites below Hermon in the land of Mizpah. They took the field with all 4
their forces, a great horde countless as the grains of sand on the sea-shore,
among them a great number of horses and chariots. All these kings made 5
common cause, and came and encamped at the waters of Merom to fight
against Israel. The LORD said to Joshua, 'Do not be afraid of them, for at 6
this time tomorrow I shall deliver them to Israel all dead men; you shall
hamstring their horses and burn their chariots.' So Joshua and his army 7
surprised them by the waters of Merom and fell upon them. The LORD 8
delivered them into the hands of Israel; they struck them down and pursued
them as far as Greater Sidon, Misrephoth on the west, and the Vale of
Mizpah on the east. They struck them down until not a man was left alive.
Joshua dealt with them as the LORD had commanded: he hamstrung their 9
horses and burnt their chariots.

At this point Joshua turned his forces against Hazor, formerly the head 10
of all these kingdoms. He captured the city and put its king to death with
the sword. They killed every living thing in it and wiped them all out; they 11
spared nothing that drew breath, and Hazor itself they destroyed by fire.
So Joshua captured these kings and their cities and put them to the sword, 12
destroying them all, as Moses the servant of the LORD had commanded.
The cities whose ruined mounds are still standing were not burnt by the 13
Israelites; it was Hazor alone that Joshua burnt. The Israelites plundered 14
all these cities and kept for themselves the cattle and any other spoil they
took; but they put every living soul to the sword until they had destroyed
every one; they did not leave alive any one that drew breath. The LORD 15
laid his commands on his servant Moses, and Moses laid these same commands on Joshua, and Joshua carried them out. Not one of the commands
laid on Moses by the LORD did he leave unfulfilled.

And so Joshua took the whole country, the hill-country, all the Negeb, 16
all the land of Goshen, the Shephelah, the Arabah, and the Israelite hill-
country with the adjoining lowlands. His conquests extended from the 17
bare mountain which leads up to Seir as far as Baal-gad in the Vale of
Lebanon under Mount Hermon. He took prisoner all their kings, struck
them down and put them to death. It was a long war that he fought 18
against all these kingdoms. Except for the Hivites who lived in Gibeon, 19
not one of their cities came to terms with the Israelites; all were taken
by storm. It was the LORD's purpose that they should offer an obstin- 20
ate resistance to the Israelites in battle, and that thus they should be

annihilated without mercy and utterly destroyed,*a* as the LORD had commanded Moses.

21 It was then that Joshua proceeded to wipe out the Anakim from the
hill-country, from Hebron, Debir, Anab, all the hill-country of Judah and
22 all the hill-country of Israel, destroying both them and their cities. No
Anakim were left in the land taken by the Israelites; they survived only in
Gaza, Gath, and Ashdod.

23 Thus Joshua took the whole country, fulfilling all the commands that
the LORD had laid on Moses; he assigned it as Israel's patrimony, allotting
to each tribe its share; and the land was at peace.

12 These are the names of the kings of the land whom the Israelites slew,
and whose territory they occupied beyond the Jordan towards the sunrise
from the gorge of the Arnon as far as Mount Hermon and all the Arabah
2 on the east. Sihon the Amorite king who lived in Heshbon: his rule extended from Aroer, which is on the edge of the gorge of the Arnon, along
the middle of the gorge and over half Gilead as far as the gorge of the Jabbok,
3 the Ammonite frontier; along the Arabah as far as the eastern side of the
Sea of Kinnereth and as far as the eastern side of the Sea of the Arabah,
the Dead Sea, by the road to Beth-jeshimoth and from Teman under the
4 watershed of Pisgah. Og king of Bashan, one of the survivors of the Reph-
5 aim, who lived in Ashtaroth and Edrei: he ruled over Mount Hermon,
Salcah, all Bashan as far as the Geshurite and Maacathite borders, and half
6 Gilead as far as the boundary of Sihon king of Heshbon. Moses the servant
of the LORD put them to death, he and the Israelites, and he gave their land
to the Reubenites, the Gadites, and half the tribe of Manasseh, as their
possession.

7 These are the names of the kings whom Joshua and the Israelites put to
death beyond the Jordan to the west, from Baal-gad in the Vale of Lebanon
as far as the bare mountain that leads up to Seir. Joshua gave their land to
the Israelite tribes to be their possession according to their allotted shares,
8 in the hill-country, the Shephelah, the Arabah, the watersheds, the wilderness, and the Negeb; lands of the Hittites, Amorites, Canaanites, Perizzites,
9 Hivites, and Jebusites. The king of Jericho; the king of Ai which is beside
10 11 Bethel; the king of Jerusalem; the king of Hebron; the king of Jarmuth;
12 13 the king of Lachish; the king of Eglon; the king of Gezer; the king of
14 15 Debir; the king of Geder; the king of Hormah; the king of Arad; the king
16 of Libnah; the king of Adullam; the king of Makkedah; the king of Bethel;
17 18 the king of Tappuah; the king of Hepher; the king of Aphek; the king of
19 20 Aphek*b*-in-Sharon; the king of Madon; the king of Hazor; the king
21 of Shimron-meron; the king of Akshaph; the king of Taanach; the king
22 23 of Megiddo; the king of Kedesh; the king of Jokneam-in-Carmel; the
24 king of Dor in the district of Dor; the king of Gaiam-in-Galilee; the king of
Tirzah: thirty-one kings in all, one of each town.

a offer . . . destroyed: *or* obstinately engage the Israelites in battle so that they should
annihilate them without mercy, only that he might destroy them . . .   *b* of Aphek:
prob. rdg.; Heb. om.

The division of the land among the tribes

BY THIS TIME JOSHUA HAD BECOME VERY OLD, and the LORD said **13** to him, 'You are now a very old man, and much of the country remains to be occupied. The country which remains is this: all the districts of the **2** Philistines and all the Geshurite country (this is reckoned as Canaanite **3** territory from Shihor to the east of Egypt as far north as Ekron; and it belongs to the five lords of the Philistines, those of Gaza, Ashdod, Ashkelon, Gath, and Ekron); all the districts of the Avvim on the south; all the **4** Canaanite country from the low-lying land which belongs to the Sidonians as far as Aphek, the Amorite frontier; the land of the Gebalites and all the **5** Lebanon to the east from Baal-gad under Mount Hermon as far as Lebo-hamath. I will drive out in favour of the Israelites all the inhabitants of the **6** hill-country from the Lebanon as far as Misrephoth on the west, and all the Sidonians. In the mean time you are to allot all this to the Israelites for their patrimony, as I have commanded you. Distribute this land now to the **7** nine tribes and half the tribe of Manasseh for their patrimony.' For half **8** the tribe of Manasseh and *a* with them the Reubenites and the Gadites had each taken their patrimony which Moses gave them east of the Jordan, as Moses the servant of the LORD had ordained. It started from Aroer **9** which is by the edge of the gorge of the Arnon, and the level land half-way along the gorge, and included all the tableland from Medeba as far as Dibon; all the cities of Sihon, the Amorite king who ruled in Heshbon, as **10** far as the Ammonite frontier; and it also included Gilead and the Geshurite **11** and Maacathite territory, and all Mount Hermon and the whole of Bashan as far as Salcah, all the kingdom of Og which he ruled from both Ashtaroth **12** and Edrei in Bashan. He was a survivor of the remnant of the Rephaim, but Moses put them both to death and occupied their lands. But the **13** Israelites did not drive out the Geshurites and the Maacathites; the Geshurites and the Maacathites live among the Israelites to this day. The tribe of Levi, however, received no patrimony; the LORD the God of **14** Israel is their patrimony, as he promised them.

So Moses allotted territory to the tribe of the Reubenites family by **15** family. Their territory started from Aroer which is by the edge of the gorge **16** of the Arnon, and the level land half-way along the gorge, and included all the tableland as far as Medeba; Heshbon and all its cities on the tableland, **17** Dibon, Bamoth-baal, Beth-baal-meon, Jahaz, Kedemoth, Mephaath, **18** Kiriathaim, Sibmah, Zereth-shahar on the hill in the Vale, Beth-peor, the **19 20** watershed of Pisgah, and Beth-jeshimoth, all the cities of the tableland, all **21** the kingdom of Sihon the Amorite king who ruled in Heshbon, whom Moses put to death together with the princes of Midian, Evi, Rekem, Zur, Hur, and Reba, the vassals of Sihon who dwelt in the country. Balaam son **22** of Beor, who practised augury, was among those whom the Israelites put to the sword. The boundary of the Reubenites was the Jordan and the **23** adjacent land: this is the patrimony of the Reubenites family by family, both the cities and their hamlets.

Moses allotted territory to the Gadites family by family. Their territory **24 25**

a For half . . . Manasseh and: *prob. rdg.; Heb. om.*

255

was Jazer, all the cities of Gilead and half the Ammonite country as far as
26 Aroer which is east of Rabbah. It reached from Heshbon as far as Ramoth-
mizpeh and Betonim, and from Mahanaim as far as the boundary of Lo-
27 debar; it included in the valley Beth-haram, Beth-nimrah, Succoth, and
Zaphon, the rest of the kingdom of Sihon king of Heshbon. The boundary
was the Jordan and the adjacent land as far as the end of the Sea of Kinnereth
28 east of the Jordan. This is the patrimony of the Gadites family by family,
both the cities and their hamlets.
29   Moses allotted territory to the half tribe of Manasseh: it was for half the
30 tribe of the Manassites family by family. Their territory ran from Mahanaim and included all Bashan, all the kingdom of Og king of Bashan and all
31 Havvoth-jair in Bashan—sixty cities. Half Gilead, and Ashtaroth and
Edrei the royal cities of Og in Bashan, belong to the sons of Machir son of
Manasseh on behalf of half the Machirites family by family.
32   These are the territories which Moses allotted to the tribes as their
33 patrimonies in the lowlands of Moab east of the Jordan. But to the tribe of
Levi he gave no patrimony: the LORD the God of Israel is their patrimony,
as he promised them.

14   Now follow the possessions which the Israelites acquired in the land of
Canaan, as Eleazar the priest, Joshua son of Nun, and the heads of the
2 families of the Israelite tribes allotted them. They were assigned by lot,
following the LORD's command given through Moses, to the nine and a
3 half tribes. To two and a half tribes Moses had given patrimonies beyond
4 the Jordan; but he gave none to the Levites as he did to the others. The
tribe of Joseph formed the two tribes of Manasseh and Ephraim. The
Levites were given no share in the land, only cities to dwell in, with their
5 common land for flocks and herds. So the Israelites, following the LORD's
command given to Moses, assigned the land.
6   Now the tribe of Judah had come to Joshua in Gilgal, and Caleb son of
Jephunneh the Kenizzite said to him, 'You remember what the LORD said
7 to Moses the man of God concerning you and me at Kadesh-barnea. I was
forty years old when Moses the servant of the LORD sent me from there to
8 explore the land, and I brought back an honest report. The others who went
with me discouraged the people, but I loyally carried out the purpose of
9 the LORD my God. Moses swore an oath that day and said, "The land on
which you have set foot shall be your patrimony and your sons' after you
as a possession for ever; for you have loyally carried out the purpose of the
10 LORD my God." Well, the LORD has spared my life as he promised; it is
now forty-five years since he made this promise to Moses, at the time when
Israel was journeying in the wilderness. Today I am eighty-five years old.
11 I am still as strong as I was on the day when Moses sent me out; I am as fit
12 now for war as I was then and am ready to take the field again. Give me
today this hill-country which the LORD then promised me. You heard on
that day that the Anakim were there and their cities were large and well
fortified. Perhaps the LORD will be with me and I shall dispossess them as
13 he promised.' Joshua blessed Caleb and gave him Hebron for his patri-
14 mony, and that is why Hebron remains to this day in the patrimony of
Caleb son of Jephunneh the Kenizzite. It is because he loyally carried out

the purpose of the LORD the God of Israel. Formerly the name of Hebron 15
was Kiriath-arba. This Arba was the chief man of the Anakim. And the
land was at peace.

This is the territory allotted to the tribe of the sons of Judah family by 15
family. It started from the Edomite frontier at the wilderness of Zin and
ran as far as the Negeb at its southern end, and it had a common border 2
with the Negeb at the end of the Dead Sea, where an inlet of water bends
towards the Negeb. It continued from the south by the ascent of Akrabbim, 3
passed by Zin, went up from the south of Kadesh-barnea, passed by Hezron,
went on to Addar and turned round to Karka. It then passed along to 4
Azmon, reached the Torrent of Egypt, and its limit was the sea. This was
their southern boundary.

The eastern boundary is the Dead Sea as far as the mouth of the Jordan 5
and the adjacent land northwards from the inlet of the sea, at the mouth of
the Jordan. The boundary goes up to Beth-hoglah; it passes north of 6
Beth-arabah and thence to the stone of Bohan son of Reuben, thence to 7
Debir from the Vale of Achor, and then turns north to the districts *a* in
front of the ascent of Adummim south of the gorge. The boundary then
passes the waters of En-shemesh and the limit there is En-rogel. It then 8
goes up by the Valley of Ben-hinnom to the southern slope of the Jebusites
(that is Jerusalem). Thence it goes up to the top of the hill which faces the
Valley of Hinnom on the west; this is at the northern end of the Vale of
Rephaim. The boundary then bends round from the top of the hill to the 9
spring of the waters of Nephtoah, runs round to the cities of Mount
Ephron and round to Baalah, that is Kiriath-jearim. It then continues 10
westwards from Baalah to Mount Seir, passes on to the north side of the
slope of Mount Jearim, that is Kesalon, down to Beth-shemesh and on to
Timnah. The boundary then goes north to the slope of Ekron, bends round 11
to Shikkeron, crosses to Mount Baalah and reaches Jabneel; its limit is the
sea. The western boundary is the Great Sea and the land adjacent. This is 12
the whole circuit of the boundary of the tribe of Judah family by family.

Caleb son of Jephunneh received his share of the land within the tribe 13
of Judah as the LORD had said to Joshua. It was Kiriath-arba, that is
Hebron. This Arba was the ancestor of the Anakim. Caleb drove out the 14
three Anakim: these were Sheshai, Ahiman and Talmai, descendants of
Anak. From there he attacked the inhabitants of Debir; the name of Debir 15
was formerly Kiriath-sepher. Caleb announced that whoever should 16
attack Kiriath-sepher and capture it would receive his daughter Achsah in
marriage. Othniel, son of Caleb's brother Kenaz, captured it, and Caleb 17
gave him his daughter Achsah. When she came to him, he incited her to 18
ask her father for a piece of land. As she sat on the ass, she made a noise, and
Caleb asked her, 'What did you mean by that?' She replied, 'I want a 19
favour from you. You have put me in this dry Negeb; you must give me
pools of water as well.' So Caleb gave her the upper pool and the lower pool.

This is the patrimony of the tribe of the sons of Judah family by family. 20
These are the cities belonging to the tribe of Judah, the full count. By the 21
Edomite frontier in the Negeb: Kabzeel, Eder, Jagur, Kinah, Dimonah, 22

a Prob. rdg., cp. 18. 17; Heb. to Gilgal.

23 24 25   Ararah,*ᵃ* Kedesh, Hazor, Ithnan, Ziph, Telem, Bealoth, Hazor-hadattah,
26 27   Kerioth-hezron, Amam, Shema, Moladah, Hazar-gaddah, Heshmon,
28 29   Beth-pelet, Hazar-shual, Beersheba and its villages, Baalah, Iyim, Ezem,
30 31 32   Eltolad, Kesil, Hormah, Ziklag, Madmannah, Sansannah, Lebaoth, Shilhim, Ain, and Rimmon: in all, twenty-nine cities with their hamlets.

33 34   In the Shephelah: Eshtaol, Zorah, Ashnah, Zanoah, En-gannim,
35 36   Tappuah, Enam, Jarmuth, Adullam, Socoh, Azekah, Shaaraim, Adithaim, Gederah, namely both parts of Gederah: fourteen cities with their hamlets.

37 38 39   Zenan, Hadashah, Migdal-gad, Dilan, Mizpeh, Joktheel, Lachish, Boz-
40 41   kath, Eglon, Cabbon, Lahmas, Kithlish, Gederoth, Beth-dagon, Naamah,
42   and Makkedah: sixteen cities with their hamlets. Libnah, Ether, Ashan,
43 44   Jiphtah, Ashnah, Nezib, Keilah, Achzib, and Mareshah: nine cities with
45 46   their hamlets. Ekron, with its villages and hamlets, and from Ekron west-
47   wards, all the cities near Ashdod and their hamlets. Ashdod with its villages and hamlets, Gaza with its villages and hamlets as far as the Torrent of Egypt and the Great Sea and the land adjacent.

48 49   In the hill-country: Shamir, Jattir, Socoh, Dannah, Kiriath-sannah,
50 51   that is Debir, Anab, Eshtemoh, Anim, Goshen, Holon, and Giloh: eleven
52 53   cities in all with their hamlets. Arab, Dumah, Eshan, Janim, Beth-
54   tappuah, Aphek,*ᵇ* Humtah, Kiriath-arba, that is Hebron, and Zior: nine
55 56   cities in all with their hamlets. Maon, Carmel, Ziph, Juttah, Jezreel,
57   Jokdeam, Zanoah, Cain, Gibeah, and Timnah: ten cities in all with their
58 59   hamlets. Halhul, Beth-zur, Gedor, Maarath, Beth-anoth, and Eltekon: six cities in all with their hamlets. Tekoa, Ephrathah, that is Bethlehem, Peor, Etam, Culom, Tatam, Sores, Carem, Gallim, Baither, and Manach:
60   eleven cities in all with their hamlets. Kiriath-baal, that is Kiriath-jearim, and Rabbah: two cities with their hamlets.

61 62   In the wilderness: Beth-arabah, Middin, Secacah, Nibshan, Ir-melach, and En-gedi: six cities with their hamlets.

63   At Jerusalem, the men of Judah were unable to drive out the Jebusites who lived there, and to this day Jebusites and men of Judah live together in Jerusalem.

16   This is the lot that fell to the sons of Joseph: the boundary runs from the Jordan at Jericho, east of the waters of Jericho by the wilderness, and goes
2   up from Jericho into the hill-country to Bethel. It runs on from Bethel to
3   Luz and crosses the Archite border at Ataroth.*ᶜ* Westwards it descends to the boundary of the Japhletites as far as the boundary of Lower Beth-
4   horon and Gezer; its limit is the sea. Here Manasseh and Ephraim the sons of Joseph received their patrimony.

5   This was the boundary of the Ephraimites family by family: their
6   eastern boundary ran from Ataroth-addar up to Upper Beth-horon. It continued westwards to Michmethath on the north, going round by the
7   east of Taanath-shiloh and passing by it on the east of Janoah. It descends from Janoah to Ataroth and Naarath, touches Jericho and continues to the
8   Jordan, and from Tappuah it goes westwards by the gorge of Kanah; and its limit is the sea. This is the patrimony of the tribe of Ephraim family by

ᵃ Prob. rdg.; Heb. Adadah.   *ᵇ Or Aphekah.*   *ᶜ Ataroth-addar in 16. 5; 18. 13.*

family. There were also cities reserved for the Ephraimites within the 9
patrimony of the Manassites, each of these cities with its hamlets. They 10
did not however drive out the Canaanites who dwelt in Gezer; the Canaanites have lived among the Ephraimites to the present day but have been
subject to forced labour in perpetuity.

This is the territory allotted to the tribe of Manasseh, Joseph's eldest 17
son. Machir was Manasseh's eldest son and father of Gilead, a fighting
man; Gilead and Bashan were allotted to him.

The rest of the Manassites family by family were the sons of Abiezer, 2
the sons of Helek, the sons of Asriel, the sons of Shechem, the sons of
Hepher, and the sons of Shemida; these were the male offspring of Manasseh son of Joseph family by family.

Zelophehad son of Hepher, son of Gilead, son of Machir, son of Manas- 3
seh, had no sons but only daughters: their names were Mahlah, Noah,
Hoglah, Milcah and Tirzah. They presented themselves before Eleazar 4
the priest and Joshua son of Nun, and before the chiefs, and they said, 'The
LORD commanded Moses to allow us to inherit on the same footing as our
kinsmen.' They were therefore given a patrimony on the same footing as
their father's brothers according to the commandment of the LORD.

There fell to Manasseh's lot ten shares, apart from the country of Gilead 5
and Bashan beyond the Jordan, because Manasseh's daughters had re- 6
ceived a patrimony on the same footing as his sons. The country of Gilead
belonged to the rest of Manasseh's sons. The boundary of Manasseh 7
reached from Asher as far as Michmethath, which is to the east of Shechem,
and thence southwards towards Jashub by *a* En-tappuah. The territory of 8
Tappuah belonged to Manasseh, but Tappuah itself was on the border of
Manasseh and belonged to Ephraim. The boundary then followed the 9
gorge of Kanah to the south of the gorge (these cities *b* belong to Ephraim,
although they lie among the cities of Manasseh), the boundary of Manasseh
being on the north of the gorge; its limit was the sea. The southern side 10
belonged to Ephraim and the northern to Manasseh, and their boundary
was the sea. They marched with Asher on the north and Issachar on the
east. But in Issachar and Asher, Manasseh possessed Beth-shean and its 11
villages, Ibleam and its villages, the inhabitants of Dor and its villages, the
inhabitants of En-dor and its villages, the inhabitants of Taanach and its
villages, and the inhabitants of Megiddo and its villages. (The third is the
district of Dor.*c*) The Manassites were unable to occupy these cities; 12
the Canaanites maintained their hold on that part of the country. When 13
the Israelites grew stronger, they put the Canaanites to forced labour, but
they did not drive them out.

The sons of Joseph appealed to Joshua and said, 'Why have you given 14
us only one lot and one share as our patrimony? We are a numerous people;
so far the LORD has blessed us.' Joshua replied, 'If you are so numerous, 15
go up into the forest in the territory of the Perizzites and the Rephaim and
clear it for yourselves. You are their near neighbours *d* in the hill-country

---

a Jashub by: *prob. rdg.; Heb.* the inhabitants of.   *b* these cities: *prob. rdg.;*
Heb. obscure.   *c* The third . . . Dor: *prob. rdg.; Heb.* The three districts.   *d* You
are . . . neighbours: *prob. rdg.; Heb. obscure.*

16 of Ephraim.' The sons of Joseph said, 'The hill-country is not enough for us; besides, all the Canaanites have chariots of iron, those who inhabit the valley beside Beth-shean and its villages and also those in the Vale of

17 Jezreel.' Joshua replied to the tribes of Joseph, that is Ephraim and Manasseh: 'You are a numerous people with great resources. You shall not have

18 one lot only. The hill-country is yours. It is forest land; clear it and it shall be yours to its furthest limits. The Canaanites may be powerful and equipped with chariots of iron, but you will be able to drive them out.'

18 THE WHOLE COMMUNITY OF THE ISRAELITES met together at Shiloh and established the Tent of the Presence there. The country now lay sub-

2 dued at their feet, but there remained seven tribes among the Israelites who had not yet taken possession of the patrimonies which would fall to

3 them. Joshua therefore said to them, 'How much longer will you neglect to take possession of the land which the LORD the God of your fathers has

4 given you? Appoint three men from each tribe whom I may send out to travel through the whole country. They shall make a register showing the

5 patrimony suitable for each tribe, and come back to me, and then it can be shared out among you in seven portions. Judah shall retain his boundary

6 in the south, and the house of Joseph their boundary in the north. You shall register the land in seven portions, bring the lists here, and I will cast

7 lots for you in the presence of the LORD our God. Levi has no share among you, because his share is the priesthood of the LORD; and Gad, Reuben, and the half tribe of Manasseh have each taken possession of their patrimony east of the Jordan, which Moses the servant of the LORD gave them.'

8 So the men set out on their journeys. Joshua ordered the emissaries to survey the country: 'Go through the whole country,' he said, 'survey it and return to me, and I will cast lots for you here before the LORD in

9 Shiloh.' So the men went and passed through the country; they registered it on a scroll, city by city, in seven portions, and came to Joshua in the

10 camp at Shiloh. Joshua cast lots for them in Shiloh before the LORD, and distributed the land there to the Israelites in their proper shares.

11 This is the lot which fell to the tribe of the Benjamites family by family. The territory allotted to them lay between the territory of Judah and

12 Joseph. Their boundary at its northern corner starts from the Jordan; it goes up the slope on the north side of Jericho, continuing westwards into

13 the hill-country, and its limit there is the wilderness of Beth-aven. From there it runs on to Luz, to the southern slope of Luz, that is Bethel, and down to Ataroth-addar over the hill-country south of Lower Beth-horon.

14 The boundary then bends round at the west corner southwards from the hill-country above Beth-horon, and its limit is Kiriath-baal, that is

15 Kiriath-jearim, a city of Judah. This is the western side. The southern side starts from the edge of Kiriath-jearim and ends *a* at the spring of the

16 waters of Nephtoah. It goes down to the edge of the hill to the east of the Valley of Ben-hinnom, north of the Vale of Rephaim, down the Valley of

17 Hinnom, to the southern slope of the Jebusites and so to En-rogel. It then bends round north and comes out at En-shemesh, goes on to the districts

a Prob. rdg.; Heb. adds westwards and ends . . .

in front of the ascent of Adummim and thence down to the Stone of
Bohan son of Reuben. It passes to the northern side of the slope facing the 18
Arabah and goes down to the Arabah, passing the northern slope of Beth- 19
hoglah, and its limit is the northern inlet of the Dead Sea, at the southern
mouth of the Jordan. This forms the southern boundary. The Jordan is 20
the boundary on the east side. This is the patrimony of the Benjamites, the
complete circuit of their boundaries family by family.

The cities belonging to the tribe of the Benjamites family by family are: 21
Jericho, Beth-hoglah, Emek-keziz, Beth-arabah, Zemaraim, Bethel, 22
Avvim, Parah, Ophrah, Kephar-ammoni, Ophni, and Geba: twelve cities 23 24
in all with their hamlets. Gibeon, Ramah, Beeroth, Mizpah, Kephirah, 25 26
Mozah, Rekem, Irpeel, Taralah, Zela, Eleph, Jebus, that is Jerusalem, 27 28
Gibeah, and Kiriath-jearim: fourteen cities in all with their hamlets. This
is the patrimony of the Benjamites family by family.

The second lot cast was for Simeon, the tribe of the Simeonites family **19**
by family. Their patrimony was included in that of Judah. For their patri- 2
mony they had Beersheba,[a] Moladah, Hazar-shual, Balah, Ezem, Eltolad, 3 4
Bethul, Hormah, Ziklag, Beth-marcaboth, Hazar-susah, Beth-lebaoth, 5 6
and Sharuhen: in all, thirteen cities and their hamlets. They had Ain, 7
Rimmon, Ether, and Ashan: four cities and their hamlets, all the hamlets 8
round these cities as far as Baalath-beer, Ramath-negeb. This was the
patrimony of the tribe of Simeon family by family. The patrimony of the 9
Simeonites was part of the land allotted to the men of Judah, because their
share was larger than they needed. The Simeonites therefore had their
patrimony within the territory of Judah.

The third lot fell to the Zebulunites family by family. The boundary of 10
their patrimony extended to Shadud.[b] Their boundary went up westwards 11
as far as Maralah and touched Dabbesheth and the gorge east of Jokneam.
It turned back from Shadud eastwards towards the sunrise up to the border 12
of Kisloth-tabor, on to Daberath and up to Japhia. From there it crossed 13
eastwards towards the sunrise to Gath-hepher, to Ittah-kazin, out to
Rimmon, and bent round[c] to Neah. The northern boundary went round 14
to Hannathon, and its limits were the Valley of Jiphtah-el, Kattath, 15
Nahalal, Shimron, Idalah, and Bethlehem: twelve cities in all with their
hamlets. These cities and their hamlets were the patrimony of Zebulun 16
family by family.

The fourth lot cast was for the sons of Issachar family by family. Their 17 18
boundary included Jezreel, Kesulloth, Shunem, Hapharaim, Shion, 19
Anaharath, Rabbith, Kishion, Ebez, Remeth, En-gannim, En-haddah, 20 21
and Beth-pazzez. The boundary touched Tabor, Shahazumah, and Beth- 22
shemesh, and its limit was the Jordan: sixteen cities with their hamlets.
This was the patrimony of the tribe of the sons of Issachar family by family, 23
both cities and hamlets.

The fifth lot cast was for the tribe of the Asherites family by family. 24
Their boundary included Helkath, Hali, Beten, Akshaph, Alammelech, 25 26
Amad, and Mishal; it touched Carmel on the west and the swamp of

[a] *Prob. rdg., cp. 1 Chr. 4. 28; Heb. adds and Sheba.*   [b] *Prob. rdg.; Heb. Sarid*
(similarly in verse 12).   [c] *and bent round: prob. rdg.; Heb. which stretched.*

27 Libnath. It then turned back towards the east to Beth-dagon, touched
Zebulun and the Valley of Jiphtah-el on the north at Beth-emek and Neiel,
28 and reached Cabul on its northern side, and Abdon, Rehob, Hammon, and
29 Kanah as far as Greater Sidon. The boundary turned at Ramah, going as
far as the fortress city of Tyre, and then back again to Hosah, and its limits
30 to the west were Mehalbeh, Achzib, Acco,*a* Aphek, and Rehob: twenty-
31 two cities in all with their hamlets. This was the patrimony of the tribe of
Asher family by family, these cities and their hamlets.

32 33   The sixth lot cast was for the sons of Naphtali family by family. Their
boundary started from Heleph and from Elon-bezaanannim and ran past
Adami-nekeb and Jabneel as far as Lakkum, and its limit was the Jordan.
34 The boundary turned back westwards to Aznoth-tabor and from there on
to Hukok. It touched Zebulun on the south, Asher on the west, and the
35 low-lying land by the Jordan on the east. Their fortified cities were Ziddim,
36 37 Zer, Hammath, Rakkath, Kinnereth, Adamah, Ramah, Hazor, Kedesh,
38 Edrei, En-hazor, Iron, Migdal-el, Horem, Beth-anath, and Beth-shemesh:
39 nineteen cities with their hamlets. This was the patrimony of the tribe of
Naphtali family by family, both cities and hamlets.

40   The seventh lot cast was for the tribe of the sons of Dan family by
41 family. The boundary of their patrimony was Zorah, Eshtaol, Ir-shemesh,
42 43 44 Shaalabbin, Aijalon, Jithlah, Elon, Timnah, Ekron, Eltekeh, Gibbethon,
45 46 Baalath, Jehud, Bene-berak, Gath-rimmon; and on the west Jarkon was
47 the boundary opposite Joppa. But the Danites, when they lost this territory,
marched against Leshem, attacked it and captured it. They put its people
to the sword, occupied it and settled in it; and they renamed the place Dan
48 after their ancestor Dan. This was the patrimony of the tribe of the sons
of Dan family by family, these cities and their hamlets.

49   So the Israelites finished allocating the land and marking out its frontiers; and they gave Joshua son of Nun a patrimony within their territory.
50 They followed the commands of the LORD and gave him the city for which
he asked, Timnath-serah in the hill-country of Ephraim, and he rebuilt
the city and settled in it.

51   These are the patrimonies which Eleazar the priest and Joshua son of
Nun and the heads of families assigned by lot to the Israelite tribes at
Shiloh before the LORD at the entrance of the Tent of the Presence. Thus
they completed the distribution of the land.

20 1 2   THE LORD SPOKE TO JOSHUA and commanded him to say this to the
Israelites: 'You must now appoint your cities of refuge, of which I spoke
3 to you through Moses. They are to be places where the homicide, the man
who kills another inadvertently without intent, may take sanctuary. You
shall single them out as cities of refuge from the vengeance of the dead
4 man's next-of-kin. When a man takes sanctuary in one of these cities, he
shall halt at the entrance of the city gate and state his case in the hearing of
the elders of that city; if they admit him into the city, they shall grant him
5 a place where he may live as one of themselves. When the next-of-kin
comes in pursuit, they shall not surrender him: he struck down his fellow

a Mehalbeh . . . Acco: *prob. rdg.; Heb.* from the district of Achzib and Ummah.

without intent and had not previously been at enmity with him. The 6
homicide may stay in that city until he stands trial before the community.
On the death of the ruling high priest, he may return to the city and home
from which he has fled.' They dedicated Kedesh in Galilee in the hill- 7
country of Naphtali, Shechem in the hill-country of Ephraim, and Kiriath-
arba, that is Hebron, in the hill-country of Judah. Across the Jordan 8
eastwards from Jericho they appointed these cities: from the tribe of
Reuben, Bezer-in-the-wilderness on the tableland, from the tribe of Gad,
Ramoth in Gilead, and from the tribe of Manasseh, Golan in Bashan. These 9
were the appointed cities where any Israelite or any alien residing among
them might take sanctuary. They were intended for any man who killed
another inadvertently, to ensure that no one should die at the hand of the
next-of-kin until he had stood his trial before the community.

The heads of the Levite families approached Eleazar the priest and 21
Joshua son of Nun and the heads of the families of the tribes of Israel.
They came before them at Shiloh in the land of Canaan and said, 'The 2
LORD gave his command through Moses that we were to receive cities to
live in, together with the common land belonging to them for our cattle.'
The Israelites therefore gave part of their patrimony to the Levites, the 3
following cities with their common land, according to the command of the
LORD.

This is the territory allotted to the Kohathite family: those Levites who 4
were descended from Aaron the priest received thirteen cities chosen by
lot from the tribes of Judah, Simeon, and Benjamin; the rest of the Kohath- 5
ites were allotted family by family *a* ten cities from the tribes of Ephraim,
Dan, and half Manasseh.

The Gershonites were allotted family by family thirteen cities from the 6
tribes of Issachar, Asher, Naphtali, and the half tribe of Manasseh in
Bashan.

The Merarites were allotted family by family twelve cities from the 7
tribes of Reuben, Gad, and Zebulun.

So the Israelites gave the Levites these cities with their common land, 8
allocating them by lot as the LORD had commanded through Moses.

The Israelites designated the following cities out of the tribes of Judah 9
and Simeon for those sons of Aaron who were of the Kohathite families of 10
the Levites, because their lot came out first. They gave them Kiriath-arba 11
(Arba was the father of Anak), that is Hebron, in the hill-country of Judah,
and the common land round it, but they gave the open country near the 12
city, and its hamlets, to Caleb son of Jephunneh as his patrimony.

To the sons of Aaron the priest they gave Hebron, a city of refuge for 13*b*
the homicide, Libnah, Jattir, Eshtemoa, Holon, Debir, Ashan, *c* Juttah, 14 15 16
and Beth-shemesh, each with its common land: nine cities from these two
tribes. They also gave cities from the tribe of Benjamin, Gibeon, Geba, 17
Anathoth, and Almon, each with its common land: four cities. The number 18 19
of the cities with their common land given to the sons of Aaron the priest
was thirteen.

a family by family: *prob. rdg.*; *Heb.* from the families (*similarly in verse 6*).   *b Verses*
13–39: *cp. I Chr. 6. 57–81.*   *c Prob. rdg., cp. I Chr. 6. 59; Heb. Ain.*

20,21 The cities which the rest of the Kohathite families of the Levites received by lot were from the tribe of Ephraim. They gave them Shechem, a city of refuge for the homicide, in the hill-country of Ephraim, Gezer,
22,23 Kibzaim, and Beth-horon, each with its common land: four cities. From
24 the tribe of Dan, they gave them Eltekeh, Gibbethon, Aijalon, and Gath-
25 rimmon, each with its common land: four cities. From the half tribe of Manasseh, they gave them Taanach and Gath-rimmon, each with its
26 common land: two cities. The number of the cities belonging to the rest of the Kohathite families with their common land was ten.

27 The Gershonite families of the Levites received, out of the share of the half tribe of Manasseh, Golan in Bashan, a city of refuge for the homicide,
28 and Be-ashtaroth,*a* each with its common land: two cities. From the tribe
29 of Issachar they received Kishon, Daberah, Jarmuth, and En-gannim,
30 each with its common land: four cities. From the tribe of Asher they
31 received Mishal, Abdon, Helkath, and Rehob, each with its common land:
32 four cities. From the tribe of Naphtali they received Kedesh in Galilee, a city of refuge for the homicide, Hammoth-dor, and Kartan, each with its
33 common land: three cities. The number of the cities of the Gershonite families with their common land was thirteen.

34 From the tribe of Zebulun the rest of the Merarite families of the Levites
35 received Jokneam, Kartah, Rimmon,*b* and Nahalal, each with its common
36 land: four cities. East of the Jordan at Jericho, from the tribe of Reuben they were given Bezer-in-the-wilderness on the tableland, a city of refuge
37 for the homicide, Jahaz, Kedemoth, and Mephaath, each with its common
38 land: four cities. From the tribe of Gad they received Ramoth in Gilead,
39 a city of refuge for the homicide, Mahanaim, Heshbon, and Jazer, each
40 with its common land: four cities in all. Twelve cities in all fell by lot to the rest of the Merarite families of the Levites.

41 The cities of the Levites within the Israelite patrimonies numbered
42 forty-eight in all, with their common land. Each city had its common land round it, and it was the same for all of them.

43 Thus the LORD gave Israel all the land which he had sworn to give to
44 their forefathers; they occupied it and settled in it. The LORD gave them security on every side as he had sworn to their forefathers. Of all their enemies not a man could withstand them; the LORD delivered all their
45 enemies into their hands. Not a word of the LORD's promises to the house of Israel went unfulfilled; they all came true.

22 AT THAT TIME JOSHUA SUMMONED THE REUBENITES, the Gadites,
2 and the half tribe of Manasseh, and said to them, 'You have observed all the commands of Moses the servant of the LORD, and you have obeyed me
3 in all the commands that I too have laid upon you. All this time you have not deserted your brothers; up to this day you have diligently observed
4 the charge laid on you by the LORD your God. And now that the LORD your God has given your brothers security as he promised them, you may turn now and go to your homes in your own land, the land which Moses

a Prob. rdg.; Heb. Be-ashtarah.   *b Prob. rdg., cp. 19. 13; 1 Chr. 6. 77; Heb.* Dimnah.

the servant of the LORD gave you east of the Jordan. But take good care to 5
keep the commands and the law which Moses the servant of the LORD
gave you: to love the LORD your God; to conform to his ways; to observe
his commandments; to hold fast to him; to serve him with your whole
heart and soul.' Joshua blessed them and dismissed them; and they went 6
to their homes. He sent them home with his blessing, and with these words: 7–8
'Go to your homes richly laden, with great herds, with silver and gold,
copper and iron, and with large stores of clothing. See that you share with
your kinsmen the spoil you have taken from your enemies.'

Moses had given territory to one half of the tribe of Manasseh in Bashan,
and Joshua gave territory to the other half west of the Jordan among their
kinsmen.

So the Reubenites, the Gadites, and the half tribe of Manasseh left the 9
rest of the Israelites and went from Shiloh in Canaan on their way into
Gilead, the land which belonged to them according to the decree of the
LORD given through Moses. When these tribes came to Geliloth by the 10
Jordan,[a] they built a great altar there by the river for all to see. The Israel- 11
ites heard that the Reubenites, the Gadites, and the half tribe of Manasseh
had built the altar facing the land of Canaan, at Geliloth by the Jordan
opposite the Israelite side. When the news reached them, all the com- 12
munity of the Israelites assembled at Shiloh to advance against them with
a display of force. At the same time the Israelites sent Phinehas son of 13
Eleazar the priest into the land of Gilead, to the Reubenites, the Gadites,
and the half tribe of Manasseh, and ten leading men with him, one from 14
each of the tribes of Israel, each of them the head of a household among the
clans of Israel. They came to the Reubenites, the Gadites, and the half 15
tribe of Manasseh in the land of Gilead, and remonstrated with them in
these words: 'We speak for the whole community of the LORD. What is 16
this treachery you have committed against the God of Israel? Are you
ceasing to follow the LORD and building your own altar this day in defiance
of the LORD? Remember our offence at Peor, for which a plague fell upon 17
the community of the LORD; to this day we have not been purified from it.
Was that offence so slight that you dare cease to follow the LORD today? 18
If you defy the LORD today, then tomorrow he will be angry with the whole
community of Israel. If the land you have taken is unclean, then cross over 19
to the LORD's own land, where the Tabernacle of the LORD now rests, and
take a share of it with us; but do not defy the LORD and involve us in your
defiance by building an altar of your own apart from the altar of the LORD
our God. Remember the treachery of Achan son of Zerah, who defied the 20
ban and the whole community of Israel suffered for it. He was not the only
one who paid for that sin with his life.'

Then the Reubenites, the Gadites, and the half tribe of Manasseh 21
remonstrated with the heads of the clans of Israel: 'The LORD the God of 22
gods, the LORD the God of gods, he knows, and Israel must know: if this
had been an act of defiance or treachery against the LORD, you could not
save us today. If we had built ourselves an altar meaning to forsake the 23
LORD, or had offered whole-offerings and grain-offerings upon it, or had

          [a] *Prob. rdg.; Heb. adds* which was in Canaan.

presented shared-offerings, the LORD himself would exact punishment.
24 The truth is that we have done this for fear that the day may come when
your sons will say to ours, "What have you to do with the LORD, the God
25 of Israel? The LORD put the Jordan as a boundary between our sons and
your sons. You have no share in the LORD, you men of Reuben and Gad."
26 Thus your sons will prevent our sons from going in awe of the LORD. So
we resolved to set ourselves to build an altar, not for whole-offerings and
27 sacrifices, but as a witness between us and you, and between our descendants after us. Thus we shall be able to do service before the LORD, as we do
now, with our whole-offerings, our sacrifices, and our shared-offerings;
and your sons will never be able to say to our sons that they have no
28 share in the LORD. And we thought, if ever they do say this to us and our
descendants, we will point to this copy of the altar of the LORD which we
have made, not for whole-offerings and not for sacrifices, but as a witness
29 between us and you. God forbid that we should defy the LORD and forsake
him this day by building another altar for whole-offerings, grain-offerings,
and sacrifices, in addition to the altar of the LORD our God which stands in
front of his Tabernacle.'
30 When Phinehas the priest and the leaders of the community, the heads
of the Israelite clans, who were with him, heard what the Reubenites, the
31 Gadites, and the Manassites said, they were satisfied. Phinehas son of
Eleazar the priest said to the Reubenites, Gadites, and Manassites, 'We
know now that the LORD is in our midst today; you have not acted treacherously against the LORD, and thus you have preserved all Israel from punish-
32 ment at his hand.' Then Phinehas son of Eleazar the priest and the leaders
left the Reubenites and the Gadites in Gilead and reported to the Israelites
33 in Canaan. The Israelites were satisfied, and they blessed God and thought
34 no more of attacking Reuben and Gad and ravaging their land. The
Reubenites and Gadites said, 'The altar is a witness between us that the
LORD is God', and they named it 'Witness'.

Joshua's farewell and death

23 A LONG TIME HAD PASSED since the LORD had given Israel security
from all the enemies who surrounded them, and Joshua was now a
2 very old man. He summoned all Israel, their elders and heads of families,
their judges and officers, and said to them, 'I have become a very old man.
3 You have seen for yourselves all that the LORD our God has done to these
peoples for your sake; it was the LORD God himself who fought for you.
4 I have allotted you your patrimony tribe by tribe, the land of all the peoples
that I have wiped out and of all these that remain between the Jordan and
5 the Great Sea which lies towards the setting sun. The LORD your God himself drove them out for your sake; he drove them out to make room for
you, and you occupied their land, as the LORD your God had promised
6 you. Be resolute therefore: observe and perform everything written in the
7 book of the law of Moses, without swerving to right or to left. You must
not associate with the peoples that are left among you; you must not call

upon their gods by name, nor ^a swear by them nor prostrate yourselves in
worship before them. You must hold fast to the LORD your God as you 8
have done down to this day. For your sake the LORD has driven out great 9
and mighty nations; to this day not a man of them has withstood you. One 10
of you can put to flight a thousand, because the LORD your God fights for
you, as he promised. Be on your guard then, love the LORD your God, for ^b 11 12
if you do turn away and attach yourselves to the peoples that still remain
among you, and intermarry with them and associate with them and they
with you, then be sure that the LORD will not continue to drive those 13
peoples out to make room for you. They will be snares to entrap you,
whips for your backs and barbed hooks in your eyes, until you vanish from
the good land which the LORD your God has given you. And now I am going 14
the way of all mankind. You know in your heart of hearts that nothing
that the LORD your God has promised you has failed to come true, every
word of it. But the same LORD God who has kept his word to you to such 15
good effect can equally bring every kind of evil on you, until he has rooted
you out from this good land which he has given you. If you break the cove- 16
nant which the LORD your God has prescribed and prostrate yourselves in
worship before other gods, then the LORD will be angry with you and you
will quickly vanish from the good land he has given you.'

Joshua assembled all the tribes of Israel at Shechem. He summoned the **24**
elders of Israel, the heads of families, the judges and officers; and they
presented themselves before God. Joshua then said this to all the people: 2
'This is the word of the LORD the God of Israel: "Long ago your forefathers, Terah and his sons Abraham and Nahor, lived beside the Euphrates, and they worshipped other gods. I took your father Abraham from 3
beside the Euphrates and led him through the length and breadth of Canaan.
I gave him many descendants: I gave him Isaac, and to Isaac I gave Jacob 4
and Esau. I put Esau in possession of the hill-country of Seir, but Jacob
and his sons went down to Egypt. I sent Moses and Aaron, and I struck 5
the Egyptians with plagues—you know well what I did among them—and
after that I brought you out; I brought your fathers out of Egypt and you 6
came to the Red Sea. The Egyptians sent their chariots and cavalry to
pursue your fathers to the sea. But when they appealed to the LORD, he 7
put a screen of darkness between you and the Egyptians, and brought the
sea down on them and it covered them; you saw for yourselves what I did
to Egypt. For a long time you lived in the wilderness. Then I brought you 8
into the land of the Amorites who lived east of the Jordan; they fought
against you, but I delivered them into your hands; you took possession of
their country and I destroyed them for your sake. The king of Moab, Balak 9
son of Zippor, took the field against Israel. He sent for Balaam son of Beor
to lay a curse on you, but I would not listen to him. Instead of that he 10
blessed you; and so I saved you from the power of Balak. Then you crossed 11
the Jordan and came to Jericho. The citizens of Jericho fought against you, ^c

---

^a you must not call . . . nor: *or* the name of their gods shall not be your boast, nor must
you . . .   ^b Be on . . . for: *or* Take very good care to love the LORD your God,
but . . .   ^c *Prob. rdg.; Heb. adds* Amorites, Perizzites, Canaanites, Hittites,
Girgashites, Hivites, and Jebusites.

12 but I delivered them into your hands. I spread panic before you, and it was this, not your sword or your bow, that drove out the two kings of the
13 Amorites. I gave you land on which you had not laboured, cities which you had never built; you have lived in those cities and you eat the produce of vineyards and olive-groves which you did not plant."

14 'Hold the LORD in awe then, and worship him in loyalty and truth. Banish the gods whom your fathers worshipped beside the Euphrates and
15 in Egypt, and worship the LORD. But if it does not please you to worship the LORD, choose here and now whom you will worship: the gods whom your forefathers worshipped beside the Euphrates, or the gods of the Amorites in whose land you are living. But I and my family, we will
16 worship the LORD.' The people answered, 'God forbid that we should for-
17 sake the LORD to worship other gods, for it was the LORD our God who brought us and our fathers up from Egypt, that land of slavery; it was he who displayed those great signs before our eyes and guarded us on all our
18 wanderings among the many peoples through whose lands we passed. The LORD drove out before us the Amorites and all the peoples who lived in
19 that country. We too will worship the LORD; he is our God.' Joshua answered the people, 'You cannot worship the LORD. He is a holy god, a
20 jealous god, and he will not forgive your rebellion and your sins. If you forsake the LORD and worship foreign gods, he will turn and bring adversity upon you and, although he once brought you prosperity, he will make
21 an end of you.' The people said to Joshua, 'No; we will worship the LORD.'
22 He said to them, 'You are witnesses against yourselves that you have chosen the LORD and will worship him.' 'Yes,' they answered, 'we are witnesses.'
23 He said to them, 'Then here and now banish the foreign gods that are
24 among you, and turn your hearts to the LORD the God of Israel.' The people said to Joshua, 'The LORD our God we will worship and his voice
25 we will obey.' So Joshua made a covenant that day with*ᵃ* the people; he
26 drew up a statute and an ordinance for them in Shechem and wrote its terms in the book of the law of God. He took a great stone and set it up there under
27 the terebinth *ᵇ* in the sanctuary of the LORD, and said to all the people, 'This stone is a witness against us; for it has heard all the words which the LORD has spoken to us. If you renounce your God, it shall be a witness against
28 you.' Then Joshua dismissed the people, each man to his patrimony.

29   After these things, Joshua son of Nun the servant of the LORD died; he
30 was a hundred and ten years old. They buried him within the border of his own patrimony in Timnath-serah in the hill-country of Ephraim to the
31 north of Mount Gaash. Israel served the LORD during the lifetime of Joshua and of the elders who outlived him and who well knew all that the LORD had done for Israel.

32   The bones of Joseph, which the Israelites had brought up from Egypt, were buried in Shechem, in the plot of land which Jacob had bought from the sons of Hamor father of Shechem for a hundred sheep; *ᶜ* and they passed
33 into the patrimony of the house of Joseph. Eleazar son of Aaron died and was buried in the hill which had been given to Phinehas his son in the hill-country of Ephraim.

        ᵃ Or for.   *ᵇ Or pole.*   *ᶜ Or pieces of money (cp. Gen. 33. 19; Job 42. 11).*

THE BOOK OF
JUDGES

The conquest of Canaan completed

AFTER THE DEATH OF JOSHUA the Israelites inquired of 1
the LORD which tribe should attack the Canaanites first. The LORD 2
answered, 'Judah shall attack. I hereby deliver the country into
his power.' Judah said to his brother Simeon, 'Go forward with me into 3
my allotted territory, and let us do battle with the Canaanites; then I in
turn will go with you into your territory.' So Simeon went with him; then 4
Judah advanced to the attack, and the LORD delivered the Canaanites and
Perizzites into their hands. They slaughtered ten thousand of them at
Bezek. There they came upon Adoni-bezek, engaged him in battle and 5
defeated the Canaanites and Perizzites. Adoni-bezek fled, but they pursued 6
him, took him prisoner and cut off his thumbs and his great toes. Adoni- 7
bezek said, 'I once had seventy kings whose thumbs and great toes were cut
off picking up the scraps from under my table. What I have done God has
done to me.' He was brought to Jerusalem and died there.

The men of Judah made an assault on Jerusalem and captured it, put its 8
people to the sword and set fire to the city. Then they turned south to 9
fight the Canaanites of the hill-country, the Negeb, and the Shephelah.
Judah attacked the Canaanites in Hebron, formerly called Kiriath-arba, 10
and defeated Sheshai, Ahiman and Talmai. From there they marched 11
against the inhabitants of Debir, formerly called Kiriath-sepher. Caleb 12
said, 'Whoever attacks Kiriath-sepher and captures it, to him I will give
my daughter Achsah in marriage.' Othniel, son of Caleb's younger 13
brother Kenaz, captured it, and Caleb gave him his daughter Achsah.
When she came to him, he incited her to ask her father for a piece of land. 14
As she sat on the ass, she made a noise, and Caleb said, 'What did you mean
by that?' She replied, 'I want to ask a favour of you. You have put me in 15
this dry Negeb; you must give me pools of water as well.' So Caleb gave
her the upper pool and the lower pool.

The descendants of Moses' father-in-law, the Kenite, went up with the 16
men of Judah from the Vale of Palm Trees to the wilderness of Judah
which is in the Negeb of Arad and settled among the Amalekites. Judah 17
then accompanied his brother Simeon, attacked the Canaanites in Zephath
and destroyed it; hence the city was called Hormah.*a* Judah took Gaza, 18
Ashkelon, and Ekron, and the territory of each. The LORD was with Judah 19
and they occupied the hill-country, but they could not drive out the inhabitants of the Vale because they had chariots of iron. Hebron was given 20

---

a That is Destruction.

to Caleb as Moses had directed, and he drove out the three sons of Anak.
21 But the Benjamites did not drive out the Jebusites of Jerusalem; and the Jebusites have lived on in Jerusalem with the Benjamites till the present day.
22 23 The tribes of Joseph attacked Bethel, and the LORD was with them. They
24 sent spies to Bethel, formerly called Luz. These spies saw a man coming out of the city and said to him, 'Show us how to enter the city, and we will
25 see that you come to no harm.' So he showed them how to enter, and they
26 put the city to the sword, but let the man and his family go free. He went into Hittite country, built a city and named it Luz, which is still its name today.
27 Manasseh did not drive out the inhabitants of Beth-shean with its villages, nor of Taanach, Dor, Ibleam, and Megiddo, with the villages of
28 each of them; the Canaanites held their ground in that region. Later, when Israel became strong, they put them to forced labour, but they never completely drove them out.
29 Ephraim did not drive out the Canaanites who lived in Gezer, but the Canaanites lived among them there.
30 Zebulun did not drive out the inhabitants of Kitron and Nahalol, but the Canaanites lived among them and were put to forced labour.
31 Asher did not drive out the inhabitants of Acco and Sidon, of Ahlab,
32 Achzib, Helbah, Aphik and Rehob. Thus the Asherites lived among the Canaanite inhabitants and did not drive them out.
33 Naphtali did not drive out the inhabitants of Beth-shemesh and of Beth-anath, but lived among the Canaanite inhabitants and put the inhabitants of Beth-shemesh and Beth-anath to forced labour.
34 The Amorites pressed the Danites back into the hill-country and did
35 not allow them to come down into the Vale. The Amorites held their ground in Mount Heres and in Aijalon and Shaalbim, but the tribes of Joseph increased their pressure on them until they reduced them to forced labour.
36 The boundary of the Edomites ran from the ascent of Akrabbim, upwards from Sela.
2 The angel of the LORD came up from Gilgal to Bokim, and said, 'I brought*a* you up out of Egypt and into the country which I vowed I would give to your forefathers. I said, I will never break my covenant with you,
2 and you in turn must make no covenant with the inhabitants of the country; you must pull down their altars. But you did not obey me, and look what
3 you have done! So I said, I will not drive them out before you; they will
4 decoy you, and their gods will shut you fast in the trap.' When the angel of
5 the LORD said this to the Israelites, they all wept and wailed, and so the place was called Bokim;*b* and they offered sacrifices there to the LORD.

a Prob. rdg.; Heb. I will bring.   *b That is* Weepers.

Israel under the judges

JOSHUA DISMISSED THE PEOPLE, and the Israelites went off to occupy 6
the country, each man to his allotted portion. As long as Joshua was 7
alive and the elders who survived him—everyone, that is, who had witnessed the whole great work which the LORD had done for Israel—the
people worshipped the LORD. At the age of a hundred and ten Joshua son of 8
Nun, the servant of the LORD, died, and they buried him within the border 9
of his own property in Timnath-heres north of Mount Gaash in the hill-
country of Ephraim. Of that whole generation, all were gathered to their 10
forefathers, and another generation followed who did not acknowledge the
LORD and did not know what he had done for Israel. Then the Israelites 11
did what was wrong in the eyes of the LORD, and worshipped the Baalim. *a*
They forsook the LORD, their fathers' God who had brought them out of 12
Egypt, and went after other gods, gods of the races among whom they
lived; they bowed down before them and provoked the LORD to anger;
they forsook the LORD and worshipped the Baal and the Ashtaroth. *b* The 13 14
LORD in his anger made them the prey of bands of raiders and plunderers;
he sold them to their enemies all around them, and they could no longer
make a stand. Every time they went out to battle the LORD brought 15
disaster upon them, as he had said when he gave them his solemn warning, and they were in dire straits.

The LORD set judges over them, who rescued them from the marauding 16
bands. Yet they did not listen even to these judges, but turned wantonly 17
to worship other gods and bowed down before them; all too soon they
abandoned the path of obedience to the LORD's commands which their
forefathers had followed. They did not obey the LORD. Whenever the LORD 18
set up a judge over them, he was with that judge, and kept them safe from
their enemies so long as he lived. The LORD would relent as often as he
heard them groaning under oppression and ill-treatment. But as soon as 19
the judge was dead, they would relapse into deeper corruption than their
forefathers and give their allegiance to other gods, worshipping them and
bowing down before them. They gave up none of their evil practices and
their wilful ways. And the LORD was angry with Israel and said, 'This 20
nation has broken the covenant which I laid upon their forefathers and
has not obeyed me, and now, of all the nations which Joshua left at his 21
death, I will not drive out to make room for them one single man. By their 22
means I will test Israel, to see whether or not they will keep strictly to the
way of the LORD as their forefathers did.' So the LORD left those nations 23
alone and made no haste to drive them out or give them into Joshua's
hands.

These are the nations which the LORD left as a means of testing all the **3**
Israelites who had not taken part in the battles for Canaan, his purpose 2
being to teach succeeding generations of Israel, or those at least who had
not learnt in former times, how to make war. These were: the five lords of 3
the Philistines, all the Canaanites, the Sidonians, and the Hivites who
lived in Mount Lebanon from Mount Baal-hermon as far as Lebo-hamath.

a The Baalim *were Canaanite deities.*   *b* The Ashtaroth *were Canaanite deities.*

4 His purpose also was to test whether the Israelites would obey the com-
5 mands which the LORD had given to their forefathers through Moses. Thus
the Israelites lived among the Canaanites, the Hittites, the Amorites, the
6 Perizzites, the Hivites, and the Jebusites. They took their daughters in
marriage and gave their own daughters to their sons; and they worshipped
their gods.

7 The Israelites did what was wrong in the eyes of the LORD; they forgot
8 the LORD their God and worshipped the Baalim and the Asheroth.[a] The
LORD was angry with Israel and he sold them to Cushan-rishathaim, king
9 of Aram-naharaim,[b] who kept them in subjection for eight years. Then
the Israelites cried to the LORD for help and he raised up a man to deliver
them, Othniel son of Caleb's younger brother Kenaz, and he set them
10 free. The spirit of the LORD came upon him and he became judge over
Israel. He took the field, and the LORD delivered Cushan-rishathaim king
11 of Aram into his hands; Othniel was too strong for him. Thus the land was
at peace for forty years until Othniel son of Kenaz died.

12 Once again the Israelites did what was wrong in the eyes of the LORD,
13 and because of this he roused Eglon king of Moab against Israel. Eglon
mustered the Ammonites and the Amalekites, advanced to attack Israel
14 and took possession of the Vale of Palm Trees. The Israelites were subject
15 to Eglon king of Moab for eighteen years. When they cried to the LORD
for help, he raised up a man to deliver them, Ehud son of Gera the Benjamite, who was left-handed. The Israelites sent him to pay their tribute
16 to Eglon king of Moab. Ehud made himself a two-edged sword, only
fifteen inches long, which he fastened on his right side under his clothes,
17 and he brought the tribute to Eglon king of Moab. Eglon was a very fat
18 man. When Ehud had finished presenting the tribute, he sent on the men
19 who had carried it, and he himself turned back from the Carved Stones at
Gilgal. 'My lord king,' he said, 'I have a word for you in private.' Eglon
20 called for silence and dismissed all his attendants. Ehud then came up to
him as he sat in the roof-chamber of his summer palace and said, 'I have
21 a word from God for you.' So Eglon rose from his seat, and Ehud reached
with his left hand, drew the sword from his right side and drove it into his
22 belly. The hilt went in after the blade and the fat closed over the blade;
23 he did not draw the sword out but left it protruding behind. Ehud went
24 out to the porch, shut the doors on him and fastened them. When he had
gone away, Eglon's servants came and, finding the doors fastened, they
said, 'He must be relieving himself in the closet of his summer palace.'
25 They waited until they were ashamed to delay any longer, and still he did
not open the doors of the roof-chamber. So they took the key and opened
26 the doors; and there was their master lying on the floor dead. While they
had been waiting, Ehud made his escape; he passed the Carved Stones and
27 escaped to Seirah. When he arrived there, he sounded the trumpet in the
hill-country of Ephraim, and the Israelites came down from the hills with
28 him at their head. He said to them, 'Follow me, for the LORD has delivered
your enemy the Moabites into your hands.' Down they came after him,
and they seized the fords of the Jordan against the Moabites and allowed

---

[a] *Plural of* Asherah, *the name of a Canaanite goddess.*   [b] *That is* Aram of Two Rivers.

no man to cross. They killed that day some ten thousand Moabites, all of 29
them men of substance and all fighting men; not one escaped. Thus Moab 30
on that day became subject to Israel, and the land was at peace for eighty
years.

After Ehud there was Shamgar of Beth-anath.*ᵃ* He killed six hundred 31
Philistines with an ox-goad, and he too delivered Israel.

After Ehud's death the Israelites once again did what was wrong in the **4**
eyes of the LORD, so he sold them to Jabin the Canaanite king, who ruled 2
in Hazor. The commander of his forces was Sisera, who lived in Harosheth-
of-the-Gentiles. The Israelites cried to the LORD for help, because Sisera 3
had nine hundred chariots of iron and had oppressed Israel harshly for
twenty years. At that time Deborah wife of Lappidoth,*ᵇ* a prophetess, was 4
judge in Israel. It was her custom to sit beneath the Palm-tree of Deborah 5
between Ramah and Bethel in the hill-country of Ephraim, and the
Israelites went up to her for justice. She sent for Barak son of Abinoam 6
from Kedesh in Naphtali and said to him, 'These are the commands of
the LORD the God of Israel: "Go and draw ten thousand men from Naphtali
and Zebulun and bring them with you to Mount Tabor, and I will draw 7
Sisera, Jabin's commander, to the Torrent of Kishon with his chariots and
all his rabble, and there I will deliver them into your hands."' Barak 8
answered her, 'If you go with me, I will go; but if you will not go, neither
will I.' 'Certainly I will go with you,' she said, 'but this venture will bring 9
you no glory, because the LORD will leave Sisera to fall into the hands of a
woman.' So Deborah rose and went with Barak to Kedesh. Barak sum- 10
moned Zebulun and Naphtali to Kedesh and marched up with ten thousand men, and Deborah went with him.

Now Heber the Kenite had parted company with the Kenites, the 11
descendants of Hobab, Moses' brother-in-law, and he had pitched his
tent at Elon-bezaanannim near Kedesh.

Word was brought to Sisera that Barak son of Abinoam had gone up to 12
Mount Tabor; so he summoned all his chariots, nine hundred chariots of 13
iron, and his troops, from Harosheth-of-the-Gentiles to the Torrent of
Kishon. Then Deborah said to Barak, 'Up! This day the LORD gives 14
Sisera into your hands. Already the LORD has gone out to battle before
you.' So Barak came charging down from Mount Tabor with ten thousand
men at his back. The LORD put Sisera to rout with all his chariots and his 15
army before Barak's onslaught; but Sisera himself dismounted from his
chariot and fled on foot. Barak pursued the chariots and the army as far 16
as Harosheth, and the whole army was put to the sword and perished; not
a man was left alive. Meanwhile Sisera fled on foot to the tent of Jael wife 17
of Heber the Kenite, because Jabin king of Hazor and the household of
Heber the Kenite were at peace. Jael came out to meet Sisera and said to 18
him, 'Come in here, my lord, come in; do not be afraid.' So he went into
the tent, and she covered him with a rug. He said to her, 'Give me some 19
water to drink; I am thirsty.' She opened a skin full of milk, gave him a
drink and covered him up again. He said to her, 'Stand at the tent door, 20
and if anybody comes and asks if someone is here, say No.' But Jael, 21

ᵃ of Beth-anath: *or* son of Anath.　　　　*ᵇ* wife of Lappidoth: *or* a spirited woman.

Heber's wife, took a tent-peg, picked up a hammer, crept up to him, and
drove the peg into his skull as he lay sound asleep. His brains oozed out
22 on the ground, his limbs twitched, and he died. When Barak came up in
pursuit of Sisera, Jael went out to meet him and said to him, 'Come, I will
show you the man you are looking for.' He went in with her, and there
23 was Sisera lying dead with the tent-peg in his skull. That day God gave
24 victory to the Israelites over Jabin king of Canaan, and they pressed
home their attacks upon that king of Canaan until they had made an end
of him.

5   That day Deborah and Barak son of Abinoam sang this song:

2   For the leaders, the leaders[a] in Israel,
            for the people who answered the call,
            bless ye the LORD.

3   Hear me, you kings; princes, give ear;
            I will sing, I will sing to the LORD.
            I will raise a psalm to the LORD the God of Israel.

4   O LORD, at thy setting forth from Seir,
            when thou camest marching out of the plains of Edom,
            earth trembled; heaven quaked;
            the clouds streamed down in torrents.

5   Mountains shook in fear before the LORD, the lord of Sinai,
            before the LORD, the God of Israel.

6   In the days of Shamgar of Beth-anath,[b]
            in the days of Jael, caravans plied no longer;
            men who had followed the high roads
            went round by devious paths.

7   Champions there were none,
            none left in Israel,
            until I,[c] Deborah, arose,
            arose, a mother in Israel.

8   They chose new gods,
            they consorted with demons.[d]
            Not a shield, not a lance was to be seen
            in the forty thousand of Israel.

9   Be proud at heart, you marshals of Israel;
            you among the people that answered the call,
            bless ye the LORD.

10   You that ride your tawny she-asses,
            that sit on saddle-cloths,
            and you that take the road afoot,
                ponder this well.

11   Hark, the sound of the players striking up
            in the places where the women draw water!
            It is the victories of the LORD that they commemorate there,
            his triumphs as the champion of Israel.

---

[a] *Or* For those who had flowing locks.   [b] of Beth-anath: *or* son of Anath.
[c] *Or* you.   [d] *Or* satyrs.

Down to the gates came the LORD's people:
  'Rouse, rouse yourself, Deborah,   12
  rouse yourself, lead out the host.
  Up, Barak! Take prisoners in plenty,
  son of Abinoam.'
Then down marched the column*a* and its chieftains,   13
the people of the LORD marched down*b* like warriors.
The men of Ephraim showed a brave front in the vale,   14
crying, 'With you, Benjamin! Your clansmen are here!'
From Machir down came the marshals,
from Zebulun the bearers of the musterer's staff.
Issachar joined with Deborah in the uprising,*c*   15
Issachar stood by Barak;
down into the valley they rushed.
But Reuben, he was split into factions,
great were their heart-searchings.
What made you linger by the cattle-pens   16
to listen to the shrill calling of the shepherds?*d*
Gilead stayed beyond Jordan;   17
and Dan, why did he tarry by the ships?
Asher lingered by the sea-shore,
by its creeks he stayed.
The people of Zebulun risked their very lives,   18
so did Naphtali on the heights of the battlefield.

Kings came, they fought;   19
then fought the kings of Canaan
at Taanach by the waters of Megiddo;
no plunder of silver did they take.
The stars fought from heaven,   20
the stars in their courses fought against Sisera.
The Torrent of Kishon swept him away,   21
the Torrent barred his flight, the Torrent of Kishon;
  march on in might, my soul!
Then hammered the hooves of his horses,   22
his chargers galloped, galloped away.
A curse on Meroz, said the angel of the LORD;   23
a curse, a curse on its inhabitants,
because they brought no help to the LORD,
no help to the LORD and the fighting men.
Blest above women be Jael,   24
the wife of Heber the Kenite;
blest above all women in the tents.
He asked for water: she gave him milk,   25
she offered him curds in a bowl fit for a chieftain.

---

a *Prob. rdg.; Heb.* survivor.   *b* *Prob. rdg.; Heb. adds* to me.   *c* in the uprising:
prob. rdg.; Heb. my officers.   *d* *Prob. rdg.; Heb. adds* Reuben was split into factions,
great were their heart-searchings.

26   She stretched out her hand for the tent-peg,
      her right hand to hammer the weary.
      With the hammer she struck Sisera, she crushed his head;
      she struck and his brains ebbed out.

27   At her feet he sank down, he fell, he lay;
      at her feet he sank down and fell.
      Where he sank down, there he fell, done to death.

28   The mother of Sisera peered through the lattice,
      through the window she peered and shrilly cried,
      'Why are his chariots so long coming?
      Why is the clatter of his chariots so long delayed?'

29   The wisest of her princesses answered her,
      yes, she found her own answer:

30   'They must be finding spoil, taking their shares,
      a wench to each man, two wenches,
      booty of dyed stuffs for Sisera,
      booty of dyed stuffs,
      dyed stuff, and striped, two lengths of striped stuff—
      to grace the victor's neck.'

31   So perish all thine enemies, O LORD;
      but let all who love thee be like the sun rising in strength.

The land was at peace for forty years.

6 THE ISRAELITES DID WHAT WAS WRONG in the eyes of the LORD and
2 he delivered them into the hands of Midian for seven years. The Midianites were too strong for Israel, and the Israelites were forced to find them-
3 selves hollow places in the mountains, and caves and strongholds. If the
Israelites had sown their seed, the Midianites and the Amalekites and other
4 eastern tribes would come up and attack Israel. They then pitched their
camps in the country and destroyed the crops as far as the outskirts of
5 Gaza, leaving nothing to support life in Israel, sheep or ox or ass. They
came up with their herds and their tents, like a swarm of locusts; they and
their camels were past counting. They had come into the land for its
6 growing crop,[a] and so the Israelites were brought to destitution by the
7 Midianites, and they cried to the LORD for help. When the Israelites cried
8 to the LORD because of what they had suffered from the Midianites, he
sent them a prophet who said to them, 'These are the words of the LORD
9 the God of Israel: I brought you up from Egypt, that land of slavery. I
delivered you from the Egyptians and from all your oppressors. I drove
10 them out before you and gave you their lands. I said to you, "I am the
LORD your God: do not stand in awe of the gods of the Amorites in whose
country you are settling." But you did not listen to me.'
11   Now the angel of the LORD came and sat under the terebinth at Ophrah
which belonged to Joash the Abiezrite. His son Gideon was threshing
wheat in the winepress, so that he might get it away quickly from the

_____
a for its growing crop: *or* and laid it waste.

Midianites. The angel of the LORD showed himself to Gideon and said, 12
'You are a brave man, and the LORD is with you.' Gideon said, 'But pray, 13
my lord, if the LORD really is with us, why has all this happened to us?
What has become of all those wonderful deeds of his, of which we have
heard from our fathers, when they told us how the LORD brought us out
of Egypt? But now the LORD has cast us off and delivered us into the
power of the Midianites.' The LORD turned to him and said, 'Go and use 14
this strength of yours to free Israel from the power of the Midianites. It
is I that send you.' Gideon said, 'Pray, my lord, how can I save Israel? 15
Look at my clan: it is the weakest in Manasseh, and I am the least in my
father's family.' The LORD answered, 'I will be with you, and you shall lay 16
low all Midian as one man.' He replied, 'If I stand so well with you, give 17
me a sign that it is you who speak to me. Please do not leave this place until 18
I come with my gift and lay it before you.' He answered, 'I will stay until
you come back.' So Gideon went in, prepared a kid and made an ephah of 19
flour into unleavened cakes. He put the meat in a basket, poured the broth
into a pot and brought it out to him under the terebinth. As he approached,
the angel of God said to him, 'Take the meat and the cakes, and put them 20
here on the rock and pour out the broth', and he did so. Then the angel of 21
the LORD reached out the staff in his hand and touched the meat and the
cakes with the tip of it. Fire sprang up from the rock and consumed the
meat and the cakes; and the angel of the LORD was no more to be seen.
Then Gideon knew that it was the angel of the LORD and said, 'Alas, Lord 22
GOD! Then it is true: I have seen the angel of the LORD face to face.' But 23
the LORD said to him, 'Peace be with you; do not be afraid, you shall not
die.' So Gideon built an altar there to the LORD and named it Jehovah- 24
shalom.*a* It stands to this day at Ophrah-of-the-Abiezrites.

That night the LORD said to Gideon, 'Take a young bull of your father's, 25
the yearling bull,*b* tear down the altar of Baal which belongs to your father
and cut down the sacred pole which stands beside*c* it. Then build an altar 26
of the proper pattern*d* to the LORD your God on the top of this earthwork;*e*
take the yearling bull and offer it as a whole-offering with the wood of the
sacred pole that you cut down.' So Gideon took ten of his servants and did 27
as the LORD had told him. He was afraid of his father's family and his
fellow-citizens, and so he did it by night, and not by day. When the citizens 28
rose early in the morning, they found the altar of Baal overturned and the
sacred pole which had stood beside it cut down and the yearling bull
offered up as a whole-offering on the altar which he had built. They asked 29
each other who had done it, and, after searching inquiries, were told that
it was Gideon son of Joash. So the citizens said to Joash, 'Bring out your 30
son. He has overturned the altar of Baal and cut down the sacred pole
beside it, and he must die.' But as they crowded round him Joash retorted, 31
'Are you pleading Baal's cause then? Do you think that it is for you to save
him? Whoever pleads his cause shall be put to death at dawn. If Baal is a
god, and someone has torn down his altar, let him take up his own cause.'

a That is the LORD is peace.   *b* the yearling bull: *prob. rdg.; Heb.* the second bull,
seven years old.   *c Or* on.   *d* of . . . pattern: *or* with the stones in rows.
e Or stronghold *or* refuge.

32 That day Joash named Gideon Jerubbaal,[a] saying, 'Let Baal plead his cause against this man, for he has torn down his altar.'

33 All the Midianites, the Amalekites, and the eastern tribes joined forces,
34 crossed the river and camped in the Vale of Jezreel. Then the spirit of the LORD took possession of Gideon; he sounded the trumpet and the Abi-
35 ezrites were called out to follow him. He sent messengers all through Manas-seh; and they too were called out. He sent messengers to Asher, Zebulun,
36 and Naphtali, and they came up to meet the others. Gideon said to God, 'If
37 thou wilt deliver Israel through me as thou hast promised—now, look, I am putting a fleece of wool on the threshing-floor. If there is dew only on the fleece and all the ground is dry, then I shall be sure that thou wilt
38 deliver Israel through me, as thou hast promised.' And that is what hap-pened. He rose early next day and wrung out the fleece, and he squeezed
39 enough dew from it to fill a bowl with water. Gideon then said to God, 'Do not be angry with me, but give me leave to speak once again. Let me, I pray thee, make one more test with the fleece. This time let the fleece
40 alone be dry, and all the ground be covered with dew.' God let it be so that night: the fleece alone was dry, and on all the ground there was dew.

7 Jerubbaal, that is Gideon, and all the people with him rose early and pitched camp at En-harod;[b] the Midianite camp was in the vale to the
2 north of the hill of Moreh. The LORD said to Gideon, 'The people with you are more than I need to deliver Midian into their hands: Israel will claim the glory for themselves and say that it is their own strength that has given
3 them the victory. Now make a proclamation for all the people to hear, that anyone who is scared or frightened is to leave Mount Galud[c] at once and go back home.' Twenty-two thousand of them went, and ten thousand
4 were left. The LORD then said to Gideon, 'There are still too many. Bring them down to the water, and I will separate them for you there. When I say to you, "This man shall go with you", he shall go; and if I say, "This
5 man shall not go with you", he shall not go.' So Gideon brought the people down to the water and the LORD said to him, 'Make every man who laps the water with his tongue like a dog stand on one side, and on the other
6 every man who goes down on his knees and drinks.' The number of those who lapped was three hundred, and all the rest went down on their knees
7 to drink, putting their hands to their mouths. The LORD said to Gideon, 'With the three hundred men who lapped I will save you and deliver
8 Midian into your hands, and all the rest may go home.' So Gideon sent all these Israelites home, but he kept the three hundred, and they took with them the jars[d] and the trumpets which the people had. The Midianite camp was below him in the vale.

9 That night the LORD said to him, 'Go down at once and attack the camp,
10 for I have delivered it into your hands. If you are afraid to do so, then go
11 down first with your servant Purah and listen to what they are saying. That will give you courage to go down and attack the camp.' So he and his servant Purah went down to the part of the camp where the fighting men
12 lay. Now the Midianites, the Amalekites, and the eastern tribes were so

---

[a] *That is* Let Baal plead.   [b] *That is* Spring of Fright.   [c] *Prob. rdg.; Heb.* Mount Gilead.   [d] *Prob. rdg.; Heb.* provisions.

many that they lay there in the valley like a swarm of locusts; there was no
counting their camels; in number they were like grains of sand on the sea-
shore. When Gideon came close, there was a man telling his companion a 13
dream. He said, 'I dreamt that I saw a hard, stale barley-cake rolling over
and over through the Midianite camp; it came to a tent, hit it*a* and turned
it upside down, and the tent collapsed.' The other answered, 'Depend upon 14
it, this is the sword of Gideon son of Joash the Israelite. God has delivered
Midian and the whole army into his hands.' When Gideon heard the story 15
of the dream and its interpretation, he prostrated himself. Then he went
back to the Israelite camp and said, 'Up! The LORD has delivered the camp
of the Midianites into your hands.' He divided the three hundred men into 16
three companies, and gave every man a trumpet and an empty jar with a
torch inside it. Then he said to them, 'Watch me: when I come to the 17
edge of the camp, do exactly as I do. When I and my men blow our trum- 18
pets, you too all round the camp will blow your trumpets, and shout, "For
the LORD and for Gideon!"'

Gideon and the hundred men who were with him reached the outskirts 19
of the camp at the beginning of the middle watch; the sentries had just
been posted. They blew their trumpets and smashed their jars. The three 20
companies all blew their trumpets and smashed their jars, then grasped
the torches in their left hands and the trumpets in their right, and shouted,
'A sword for the LORD and for Gideon!' Every man stood where he was, 21
all round the camp, and the whole camp leapt up in a panic and fled. The 22
three hundred blew their trumpets, and throughout the camp the LORD
set every man against his neighbour. The army fled as far as Beth-shittah
in Zererah, as far as the ridge of Abel-meholah by Tabbath. The Israelites 23
from Naphtali and Asher and all Manasseh were called out and they
pursued the Midianites. Gideon sent men through all the hill-country of 24
Ephraim with this message: 'Come down and cut off the Midianites. Hold
the fords of the Jordan against them as far as Beth-barah.' So all the
Ephraimites were called out and they held the fords of the Jordan as far
as Beth-barah. They captured the two Midianite princes, Oreb and Zeeb. 25
Oreb they killed at the Rock of Oreb, and Zeeb by the Winepress of Zeeb,
and they kept up the pursuit of the Midianites; afterwards they brought
the heads of Oreb and Zeeb across the Jordan to Gideon.

The men of Ephraim said to Gideon, 'Why have you treated us like 8
this? Why did you not summon us when you went to fight Midian?'; and
they reproached him violently. But he said to them, 'What have I done 2
compared with you? Are not Ephraim's gleanings better than the whole
vintage of Abiezer? God has delivered Oreb and Zeeb, the princes of 3
Midian, into your hands. What have I done compared with you?' At these
words of his, their anger died down.

Gideon came to the Jordan, and he and his three hundred men crossed 4
over to continue the pursuit, weary though they were. He said to the men 5
of Succoth, 'Will you give these men of mine some bread, for they are
weary, and I am pursuing Zebah and Zalmunna, the kings of Midian?'
But the chief men of Succoth replied, 'Are Zebah and Zalmunna already 6

a Prob. rdg.; Heb. adds and it fell.

7 in your hands, that we should give your army bread?' Gideon said, 'For that, when the LORD delivers Zebah and Zalmunna into my hands, I will
8 thresh your bodies with desert thorns and briars.' He went on from there to Penuel and made the same request; the men of Penuel answered like
9 the men of Succoth. He said to the men of Penuel, 'When I return safely, I will pull down your castle.'

10 Zebah and Zalmunna were in Karkor with their army of fifteen thousand men. These were all that remained of the whole host of the eastern tribes;
11 a hundred and twenty thousand armed men had fallen in battle Gideon advanced along the track used by the tent-dwellers east of Nobah and Jogbehah, and his attack caught the army when they were off their guard.
12 Zebah and Zalmunna fled; but he went in pursuit of these Midianite kings and captured them both; and their whole army melted away.

13 As Gideon son of Joash was returning from the battle by the Ascent of
14 Heres, he caught a young man from Succoth. He questioned him, and one by one he numbered off the names of the rulers of Succoth and its elders,
15 seventy-seven in all. Gideon then came to the men of Succoth and said, 'Here are Zebah and Zalmunna, about whom you taunted me. "Are Zebah and Zalmunna", you said, "already in your hands, that we should give
16 your weary men bread?"' Then he took the elders of the city and he dis-
17 ciplined those men of Succoth with desert thorns and briars. He also pulled
18 down the castle of Penuel and put the men of the city to death. Then he said to Zebah and Zalmunna, 'What of the men you killed in Tabor?' They answered, 'They were like you, every one had the look of a king's
19 son.' 'They were my brothers,' he said, 'my mother's sons. I swear by the
20 LORD, if you had let them live I would not have killed you'; and he said to his eldest son Jether, 'Up with you, and kill them.' But he was still only a
21 lad, and did not draw his sword, because he was afraid. So Zebah and Zalmunna said, 'Rise up yourself and dispatch us, for you have a man's strength.' So Gideon rose and killed them both, and he took the crescents from the necks of their camels.

22 After this the Israelites said to Gideon, 'You have saved us from the Midianites; now you be our ruler, you and your son and your grandson.'
23 Gideon replied, 'I will not rule over you, nor shall my son; the LORD will
24 rule over you.' Then he said, 'I have a request to make: will every one of you give me the earrings from his booty?'—for the enemy wore golden
25 earrings, being Ishmaelites. They said, 'Of course, we will give them.' So a cloak was spread out and every man threw on to it the golden earrings
26 from his booty. The earrings for which he asked weighed seventeen hundred shekels of gold; this was in addition to the crescents and pendants and the purple cloaks worn by the Midianite kings, not counting the chains on the
27 necks of their camels. Gideon made it into an ephod and he set it up in his own city of Ophrah. All the Israelites turned wantonly to its worship, and it became a trap to catch Gideon and his household.

28 Thus the Midianites were subdued by the Israelites; they could no longer hold up their heads. For forty years the land was at peace, all the
29 lifetime of Gideon, that is Jerubbaal son of Joash; and he retired to his
30 own home. Gideon had seventy sons, his own offspring, for he had many

wives. He had a concubine who lived in Shechem, and she also bore him 31
a son, whom he named Abimelech. Gideon son of Joash died at a ripe old 32
age and was buried in his father's grave at Ophrah-of-the-Abiezrites.
After his death, the Israelites again went wantonly to the worship of the 33
Baalim and made Baal-berith their god. They forgot the LORD their God 34
who had delivered them from their enemies on every side, and did not 35
show to the family of Jerubbaal, that is Gideon, the loyalty that was due to
them for all the good he had done for Israel.

ABIMELECH SON OF JERUBBAAL went to Shechem to his mother's 9
brothers, and spoke with them and with all the clan of his mother's family.
'I beg you,' he said, 'whisper a word in the ears of the chief citizens of 2
Shechem. Ask them which is better for them: that seventy men, all the
sons of Jerubbaal, should rule over them, or one man. Tell them to remember that I am their own flesh and blood.' So his mother's brothers 3
repeated all this to each of them on his behalf; and they were moved to
come over to Abimelech's side, because, as they said, he was their brother.
They gave him seventy pieces of silver from the temple of Baal-berith, and 4
with these he hired idle and reckless men, who followed him. He came to 5
his father's house in Ophrah and butchered his seventy brothers, the sons
of Jerubbaal, on a single stone block, all but Jotham the youngest, who
survived because he had hidden himself. Then all the citizens of Shechem 6
and all Beth-millo came together and made Abimelech king beside the old
propped-up terebinth at Shechem.

When this was reported to Jotham, he went and stood on the summit of 7
Mount Gerizim. He cried at the top of his voice: 'Listen to me, you
citizens of Shechem, and may God listen to you:

'Once upon a time the trees came to anoint a king, and they said to the 8
olive-tree: Be king over us. But the olive-tree answered: What, leave my 9
rich oil by which gods and men are honoured, to come and hold sway over
the trees?

'So the trees said to the fig-tree: Then will you come and be king over 10
us? But the fig-tree answered: What, leave my good fruit and all its sweet- 11
ness, to come and hold sway over the trees?

'So the trees said to the vine: Then will you come and be king over us? 12
But the vine answered: What, leave my new wine which gladdens gods and 13
men, to come and hold sway over the trees?

'Then all the trees said to the thorn-bush: Will you then be king over 14
us? And the thorn said to the trees: If you really mean to anoint me as your 15
king, then come under the protection of my shadow; if not, fire shall come
out of the thorn and burn up the cedars of Lebanon.'

Then Jotham said, 'Now, have you acted fairly and honestly in making 16
Abimelech king? Have you done the right thing by Jerubbaal and his
household? Have you given my father his due—who fought for you, and 17
threw himself into the forefront of the battle and delivered you from the
Midianites? Today you have risen against my father's family, butchered 18
his seventy sons on a single stone block, and made Abimelech, the son of
his slave-girl, king over the citizens of Shechem because he is your brother.

19 In this day's work have you acted fairly and honestly by Jerubbaal and his
20 family? If so, I wish you joy in Abimelech and wish him joy in you! If not,
    may fire come out of Abimelech and burn up the citizens of Shechem and
    all Beth-millo; may fire also come out from the citizens of Shechem and
21 Beth-millo and burn up Abimelech.' After which Jotham slipped away
    and made his escape; he came to Beer, and there he settled out of reach of
    his brother Abimelech.

22 23   After Abimelech had been prince over Israel for three years, God sent
    an evil spirit to make a breach between Abimelech and the citizens of
24 Shechem, and they played him false. This was done on purpose, so that
    the violent murder of the seventy sons of Jerubbaal might recoil on their
    brother Abimelech who did the murder and on the citizens of Shechem
25 who encouraged him to do it. The citizens of Shechem set men to lie in
    wait for him on the hill-tops, but they robbed all who passed that way, and
    so the news reached Abimelech.

26   Now Gaal son of Ebed came with his kinsmen to Shechem, and the
27 citizens of Shechem transferred their allegiance to him. They went out
    into the country-side, picked the early grapes in their vineyards, trod them
    in the winepress and held festival. They went into the temple of their god,
28 where they ate and drank and reviled Abimelech. 'Who is Abimelech,' said
    Gaal son of Ebed, 'and who are the Shechemites, that we should be his
    subjects? Have not this son of Jerubbaal and his lieutenant Zebul been
    subjects of the men of Hamor the father of Shechem? Why indeed should
29 we be subject to him? If only this people were in my charge I should know
    how to get rid of Abimelech! I would say to him, "Get your men together,
30 and come out and fight."' When Zebul the governor of the city heard what
31 Gaal son of Ebed said, he was very angry. He resorted to a ruse and sent
    messengers to Abimelech to say, 'Gaal son of Ebed and his kinsmen have
32 come to Shechem and are turning the city against you. Get up now in the
    night, you and the people with you, and lie in wait in the open country.
33 Then be up in the morning at sunrise, and advance rapidly against the city.
    When he and his people come out, do to him what the situation demands.'
34 So Abimelech and his people rose in the night, and lay in wait to attack
35 Shechem, in four companies. Gaal son of Ebed came out and stood in the
    entrance of the city gate, and Abimelech and his people rose from their
36 hiding-place. Gaal saw them and said to Zebul, 'There are people coming
    down from the tops of the hills', but Zebul replied, 'What you see is the
37 shadow of the hills, looking like men.' Once more Gaal said, 'There are
    people coming down from the central ridge of the hills, and one company
38 is coming along the road of the Soothsayers' Terebinth.' Then Zebul said
    to him, 'Where are your brave words now? You said, "Who is Abimelech
    that we should be subject to him?" Are not these the people you despised?
39 Go out and fight him.' Gaal led the citizens of Shechem out and attacked
40 Abimelech, but Abimelech routed him and he fled. The ground was
41 strewn with corpses all the way to the entrance of the gate. Abimelech
    established himself in Arumah, and Zebul drove away Gaal and his kins-
    men and allowed them no place in Shechem.

42   Next day the people came out into the open, and this was reported to

Abimelech. He on his side took his supporters, divided them into three 43
companies and lay in wait in the open country; and when he saw the people
coming out of the city, he rose and attacked them. Abimelech and the 44
company with him advanced rapidly and took up position at the entrance
of the city gate, while the other two companies advanced against all those
who were in the open and struck them down. Abimelech kept up the attack 45
on the city all that day and captured it; he killed the people in it, pulled the
city down and sowed the site with salt. When the occupants of the castle 46
of Shechem heard of this, they went into the great hall *a* of the temple of
El-berith. It was reported to Abimelech that all the occupants of the castle 47
of Shechem had collected together. So he and his people went up Mount 48
Zalmon carrying axes; there he cut brushwood, and took it and hoisted it
on his shoulder. He said to his men, 'You see what I am doing; be quick
and do the same.' So each man cut brushwood; then they followed Abi- 49
melech and laid the brushwood against the hall, and burnt it over their
heads. Thus all the occupants of the castle of Shechem died, about a
thousand men and women.

Abimelech then went to Thebez, besieged it and took it. There was a 50 51
strong castle in the middle of the city, and all the citizens, men and women,
took refuge there. They shut themselves in and went on to the roof.
Abimelech came up to the castle and attacked it. As he approached the 52
entrance to the castle to set fire to it, a woman threw a millstone down on 53
his head and fractured his skull. He called hurriedly to his young armour- 54
bearer and said, 'Draw your sword and dispatch me, or men will say of me:
A woman killed him.' So the young man ran him through and he died.
When the Israelites saw that Abimelech was dead, they all went back to 55
their homes. It was thus that God requited the crime which Abimelech 56
had committed against his father by the murder of his seventy brothers,
and brought all the wickedness of the men of Shechem on their own heads. 57
The curse of Jotham son of Jerubbaal came home to them.

After Abimelech, Tola son of Pua, son of Dodo, a man of Issachar who **10**
lived in Shamir in the hill-country of Ephraim, came in his turn to deliver
Israel. He was judge over Israel for twenty-three years, and when he died 2
he was buried in Shamir.

After him came Jair the Gileadite; he was judge over Israel for twenty- 3
two years. He had thirty sons, who rode thirty asses; they had thirty towns 4
in the land of Gilead, which to this day are called Havvoth-jair. *b* When 5
Jair died, he was buried in Kamon.

Once more the Israelites did what was wrong in the eyes of the LORD, 6
worshipping the Baalim and the Ashtaroth, the deities of Aram and of
Sidon and of Moab, of the Ammonites and of the Philistines. They forsook
the LORD and did not worship him. The LORD was angry with Israel, and 7
he sold them to the Philistines and the Ammonites, who *c* for eighteen 8
years harassed and oppressed the Israelites who lived beyond the Jordan
in the Amorite country in Gilead. Then the Ammonites crossed the Jordan 9
to attack Judah, Benjamin, and Ephraim, so that Israel was in great distress. The Israelites cried to the LORD for help and said, 'We have sinned 10

a Or vault.   b That is Tent-villages of Jair.   c Prob. rdg.; Heb. adds in that year.

11 against thee; we have forsaken our God and worshipped the Baalim.' And
the LORD said to the Israelites, 'The Egyptians, the Amorites, the Ammon-
12 ites, the Philistines; the Sidonians too and the Amalekites and the Midianites—all these oppressed you and you cried to me for help; and did not I
13 deliver you? But you forsook me and worshipped other gods; therefore I
14 will deliver you no more. Go and cry for help to the gods you have chosen,
15 and let them save you in the day of your distress.' But the Israelites said
to the LORD, 'We have sinned. Deal with us as thou wilt; only save us this
16 day, we implore thee.' They banished the foreign gods and worshipped the
LORD; and he could endure no longer to see the plight of Israel.

17   Then the Ammonites were called to arms, and they encamped in Gilead,
18 while the Israelites assembled and encamped in Mizpah. The people of
Gilead and their chief men said to one another, 'If any man will strike the
first blow at the Ammonites, he shall be lord over the inhabitants of Gilead.'

11   Jephthah the Gileadite was a great warrior; he was the son of Gilead by
2 a prostitute. But Gilead had a wife who bore him several sons, and when
they grew up they drove Jephthah away; they said to him, 'You have no
3 inheritance in our father's house; you are another woman's son.' So
Jephthah, to escape his brothers, went away and settled in the land of Tob,
and swept up a number of idle men who followed him.

4 5   The time came when the Ammonites made war on Israel, and when the
fighting began, the elders of Gilead went to fetch Jephthah from the land
6 of Tob. They said to him, 'Come and be our commander so that we can
7 fight the Ammonites.' But Jephthah said to the elders of Gilead, 'You drove
me from my father's house in hatred. Why come to me now when you are
8 in trouble?' 'It is because of that', they replied, 'that we have turned to you
now. Come with us and fight the Ammonites, and become lord over all the
9 inhabitants of Gilead.' Jephthah said to them, 'If you ask me back to fight
the Ammonites and if the LORD delivers them into my hands, then I will
10 be your lord.' The elders of Gilead said again to Jephthah, 'We swear by
the LORD, who shall be witness between us, that we will do what you say.'
11 Jephthah then went with the elders of Gilead, and the people made him
their lord and commander. And at Mizpah, in the presence of the LORD,
Jephthah repeated all that he had said.

12   Jephthah sent a mission to the king of Ammon to ask what quarrel he
13 had with them that made him invade their country. The king gave Jephthah's men this answer: 'When the Israelites came up from Egypt, they
took our land from the Arnon as far as the Jabbok and the Jordan. Give us
14 back these lands in peace.' Jephthah sent a second mission to the king of
15 Ammon, and they said, 'This is Jephthah's answer: Israel did not take
16 either the Moabite country or the Ammonite country. When they came up
from Egypt, the Israelites passed through the wilderness to the Red Sea*a*
17 and came to Kadesh. They then sent envoys to the king of Edom asking
him to grant them passage through his country, but the king of Edom would
not hear of it. They sent also to the king of Moab, but he was not willing;
18 so Israel remained in Kadesh. They then passed through the wilderness,
skirting Edom and Moab, and kept to the east of Moab. They encamped

a Or the Sea of Reeds.

beside the Arnon, but they did not enter Moabite territory, because the
Arnon is the frontier of Moab. Israel then sent envoys to the king of the 19
Amorites, Sihon king of Heshbon, asking him to give them free passage
through his country to their destination. But Sihon would not grant Israel 20
free passage through his territory; he mustered all his people, encamped
in Jahaz and fought Israel. But the LORD the God of Israel delivered Sihon 21
and all his people into the hands of Israel; they defeated them and occupied
all the territory of the Amorites in that region. They took all the Amorite 22
territory from the Arnon to the Jabbok and from the wilderness to the
Jordan. The LORD the God of Israel drove out the Amorites for the benefit 23
of his people Israel. And do you now propose to take their place? It is for 24
you to possess whatever Kemosh your god gives you; and all that the LORD
our God gave us as we advanced is ours. For that matter, are you any better 25
than Balak son of Zippor, king of Moab? Did he ever quarrel with Israel or
attack them? For three hundred years Israelites have lived in Heshbon and 26
its dependent villages, in Aroer and its villages, and in all the towns by the
Arnon. Why did you not oust *a* them during all that time? We have done you 27
no wrong; it is you who are doing us wrong by attacking us. The LORD who
is judge will judge this day between the Israelites and the Ammonites.'
But the king of the Ammonites would not listen to the message which 28
Jephthah had sent him.

Then the spirit of the LORD came upon Jephthah and he passed through 29
Gilead and Manasseh, by Mizpeh of Gilead, and from Mizpeh over to the
Ammonites. Jephthah made this vow to the LORD: 'If thou wilt deliver the 30
Ammonites into my hands, then the first creature that comes out of the door 31
of my house to meet me when I return from them in peace shall be the
LORD's; I will offer that as a whole-offering.' So Jephthah crossed over to 32
attack the Ammonites, and the LORD delivered them into his hands. He 33
routed them with great slaughter all the way from Aroer to Minnith, taking
twenty towns, and as far as Abel-keramim. Thus Israel crushed Ammon.
But when Jephthah came to his house in Mizpah, who should come out to 34
meet him with tambourines and dances but his daughter, and she his only
child; he had no other, neither son nor daughter. When he saw her, he rent 35
his clothes and said, 'Alas, my daughter, you have broken my heart, such
trouble you have brought upon me. I have made a vow to the LORD and I
cannot go back.' She replied, 'Father, you have made a vow to the LORD; 36
do to me what you have solemnly vowed, since the LORD has avenged you
on the Ammonites, your enemies. But, father, grant me this one favour. 37
For two months let me be, that I may roam *b* the hills with my companions
and mourn that I must die a virgin.' 'Go', he said, and he let her depart for 38
two months. She went with her companions and mourned her virginity on
the hills. At the end of two months she came back to her father, and he 39
fulfilled the vow he had made; she died a virgin. It became a tradition that 40
the daughters of Israel should go year by year and commemorate the fate
of Jephthah's daughter, four days in every year.

The Ephraimites mustered their forces and crossed over to Zaphon. **12**
They said to Jephthah, 'Why did you march against the Ammonites and

a Or recover.   *b Or* that I may go down country to . . .

not summon us to go with you? We will burn your house over your head.'
2 Jephthah answered, 'I and my people had a feud with the Ammonites, and had I appealed to you for help, you would not have saved us*a* from them.
3 When I saw that we were not to look for help from you, I took my life in my hands and marched against the Ammonites, and the LORD delivered
4 them into my power. Why then do you attack me today?' Jephthah then mustered all the men of Gilead and fought Ephraim, and the Gileadites
5 defeated them. The Gileadites seized the fords of the Jordan and held them against Ephraim. When any Ephraimite who had escaped begged leave to cross, the men of Gilead asked him, 'Are you an Ephraimite?',
6 and if he said, 'No', they would retort, 'Say Shibboleth.' He would say 'Sibboleth', and because he could not pronounce the word properly, they seized him and killed him at the fords of the Jordan. At that time forty-two thousand men of Ephraim lost their lives.

7 Jephthah was judge over Israel for six years; when he died he was
8 buried in his own city in Gilead. After him Ibzan of Bethlehem was judge
9 over Israel. He had thirty sons and thirty daughters. He gave away the thirty daughters in marriage and brought in thirty girls for his sons. He
10 was judge over Israel for seven years, and when he died he was buried in Bethlehem.
11 After him Elon the Zebulunite was judge over Israel for ten years.
12 13 When he died, he was buried in Aijalon in the land of Zebulun. Next
14 Abdon son of Hillel the Pirathonite was judge over Israel. He had forty sons and thirty grandsons, who rode each on his own ass. He was judge
15 over Israel for eight years; and when he died he was buried in Pirathon in the land of Ephraim on the hill of the Amalekite.

Israel oppressed by the Philistines

13 ONCE MORE THE ISRAELITES DID WHAT WAS WRONG in the eyes of the LORD, and he delivered them into the hands of the Philistines for forty years.
2 There was a man from Zorah of the tribe of Dan whose name was
3 Manoah and whose wife was barren and childless. The angel of the LORD appeared to her and said, 'You are barren and have no child, but you shall
4 conceive and give birth to a son. Now you must do as I say: be careful to
5 drink no wine or strong drink, and to eat no forbidden food; you will conceive and give birth to a son, and no razor shall touch his head, for the boy is to be a Nazirite consecrated to God from the day of his birth. He will strike the first blow to deliver Israel from the power of the Philistines.'
6 The woman went and told her husband; she said to him, 'A man of God came to me; his appearance was that of an*b* angel of God, most terrible to
7 see. I did not ask him where he came from nor did he tell me his name. He said to me, "You shall conceive and give birth to a son. From this time onwards drink no wine or strong drink and eat no forbidden food, for the

---

a and had I . . . saved us: *or* I did appeal to you for help, but you would not save us . . .
b *Or* the.

boy is to be a Nazirite consecrated to God from his birth to the day of his
death."' Manoah prayed to the LORD, 'If it please thee, O LORD, let the 8
man of God whom thou didst send come again to tell us what we are to do
with the boy who is to be born.' God heard Manoah's prayer, and the angel 9
of God came again to the woman, who was sitting in the fields; her husband
was not with her. The woman ran quickly and said to him, 'The man who 10
came to me the other day has appeared to me again.' Manoah went with 11
her at once and approached the man and said, 'Was it you who talked with
my wife?' He said, 'Yes, it was I.' 'Now when your words come true,' 12
Manoah said, 'what kind of boy will he be and what will he do?' The angel 13
of the LORD answered him, 'Your wife must be careful to do all that I told
her: she must not taste anything that comes from the vine. She must 14
drink no wine or strong drink, and she must eat no forbidden food. She
must do what I say.' Manoah said to the angel of the LORD, 'May we urge 15
you to stay? Let us prepare a kid for you.' The angel of the LORD replied, 16
'Though you urge me to stay, I will not eat your food; but prepare a whole-
offering if you will, and offer that to the LORD.' Manoah did not perceive
that he was the angel of the LORD and said to him, 'What is your name? 17
For we shall want to honour you when your words come true.' The angel 18
of the LORD said to him, 'How can you ask my name? It is a name of
wonder.' Manoah took a kid with the proper grain-offering, and offered it 19
on the rock to the LORD, to him whose works are full of wonder. And while
Manoah and his wife were watching, the flame went up from the altar 20
towards heaven, and the angel of the LORD went up in the flame; and seeing
this, Manoah and his wife fell on their faces. The angel of the LORD did 21
not appear again to Manoah and his wife; and Manoah knew that he was
the angel of the LORD. He said to his wife, 'We are doomed to die, we have 22
seen God',*a* but she replied, 'If the LORD had wanted to kill us, he would 23
not have accepted a whole-offering and a grain-offering at our hands; he
would not now have let us see and hear all this.' The woman gave birth to 24-25
a son and named him Samson. The boy grew up in Mahaneh-dan between
Zorah and Eshtaol, and the LORD blessed him, and the spirit of the LORD
began to drive him hard.

Samson went down to Timnath, and there he saw a woman, one of the **14**
Philistines. When he came back, he told his father and mother that he had 2
seen a Philistine woman in Timnath and asked them to get her for him as
his wife. His father and mother said to him, 'Is there no woman among 3
your cousins or in all our own people? Must you go and marry one of the
uncircumcised Philistines?' But Samson said to his father, 'Get her for
me, because she pleases me.' His father and mother did not know that the 4
LORD was at work in this, seeking an opportunity against the Philistines,
who at that time were masters of Israel.

Samson*b* went down to Timnath and, when he reached the vineyards 5
there, a young lion came at him growling. The spirit of the LORD suddenly 6
seized him and, having no weapon in his hand, he tore the lion in pieces as
if it were a kid. He did not tell his parents what he had done. Then he went 7
down and spoke to the woman, and she pleased him. After a time he went 8

a Or a god.   b Prob. rdg.; Heb. adds and his father and mother.

9 down again to take her to wife; he turned aside to look at the carcass of the lion, and he saw a swarm of bees in it, and honey. He scraped the honey into his hands and went on, eating as he went. When he came to his father and mother, he gave them some and they ate it; but he did not tell them that

10 he had scraped the honey out of the lion's carcass. His father went down to see the woman, and Samson gave a feast there as the custom of young men

11 was. When the people saw him, they brought thirty young men to be his

12 escort. Samson said to them, 'Let me ask you a riddle. If you can guess it during the seven days of the feast, I will give you thirty lengths of linen and

13 thirty changes of clothing; but if you cannot guess the answer, then you shall give me thirty lengths of linen and thirty changes of clothing.' 'Tell

14 us your riddle,' they said; 'let us hear it.' So he said to them:

> Out of the eater came something to eat;
> out of the strong came something sweet.

15 At the end of three days they had failed to guess the riddle. On the fourth day they said to Samson's wife, 'Coax your husband and make him tell you the riddle, or we shall burn you and your father's house. Did you

16 invite us here to beggar us?' So Samson's wife wept over him and said, 'You do not love me, you only hate me. You have asked my kinsfolk a riddle and you have not told it to me.' He said to her, 'I have not told it

17 even to my father and mother; and am I to tell you?' But she wept over him every day until the seven feast days were ended, and on the seventh day, because she pestered him, he told her, and she told the riddle to her

18 kinsfolk. So that same day the men of the city said to Samson before he entered the bridal chamber: [a]

> What is sweeter than honey?
> What is stronger than a lion?

and he replied, 'If you had not ploughed with my heifer, you would not

19 have found out my riddle.' Then the spirit of the LORD suddenly seized him. He went down to Ashkelon and there he killed thirty men, took their belts and gave their clothes to the men who had answered his riddle; but

20 he was very angry and went off to his father's house. And Samson's wife was given in marriage to the friend who had been his groomsman.

15 After a while, during the time of wheat harvest, Samson went to visit his wife, taking a kid as a present for her. He said, 'I am going to my wife

2 in our bridal chamber', but her father would not let him in. He said, 'I was sure that you hated her, so I gave her in marriage to your groomsman. Her

3 young sister is better than she—take her instead.' But Samson said, 'This time I will settle my score with the Philistines; I will do them some real

4 harm.' So he went and caught three hundred jackals and got some torches; he tied the jackals tail to tail and fastened a torch between each pair of tails.

5 He then set the torches alight and turned the jackals loose in the standing corn of the Philistines. He burnt up standing corn and stooks as well,

6 vineyards and olive groves. The Philistines said, 'Who has done this?' They were told that it was Samson, because the Timnite, his father-in-law, had

---

[a] he entered ... chamber: *prob. rdg.; Heb.* the sun went down.

288

taken his wife and given her to his groomsman. So the Philistines came and
burnt her and her father. Samson said, 'If you do things like this, I swear 7
I will be revenged upon you before I have done.' He smote them hip and 8
thigh with great slaughter; and after that he went down to live in a cave in
the Rock of Etam.

The Philistines came up and pitched camp in Judah, and overran Lehi. 9
The men of Judah said, 'Why have you attacked us?' They answered, 'We 10
have come to take Samson prisoner and serve him as he served us.' So 11
three thousand men from Judah went down to the cave in the Rock of
Etam. They said to Samson, 'Surely you know that the Philistines are our
masters? Now see what you have brought upon us.' He answered, 'I only
served them as they had served me.' They said to him, 'We have come down 12
to bind you and hand you over to the Philistines.' 'Then you must swear
to me', he said, 'that you will not set upon me yourselves.' They answered, 13
'No; we will only bind you and hand you over to them, we will not kill you.'
So they bound him with two new ropes and brought him up from the cave
in the Rock. He came to Lehi, and when they met him, the Philistines 14
shouted in triumph; but the spirit of the LORD suddenly seized him, the
ropes on his arms became like burnt tow and his bonds melted away. He 15
found the jaw-bone of an ass, all raw, and picked it up and slew a thousand
men. He made this saying: 16

> With the jaw-bone of an ass*a* I have flayed them like asses;*b*
> with the jaw-bone of an ass I have slain a thousand men.

When he had said his say, he threw away the jaw-bone; and he called that 17
place Ramath-lehi.*c* He began to feel very thirsty and cried aloud to the 18
LORD, 'Thou hast let me, thy servant, win this great victory, and must I
now die of thirst and fall into the hands of the uncircumcised?' God split 19
open the Hollow of Lehi and water came out of it. Samson drank, his
strength returned and he revived. This is why the spring in Lehi is called
En-hakkore*d* to this day.

Samson was judge over Israel for twenty years in the days of the 20
Philistines.

Samson went to Gaza, and there he saw a prostitute and went in to **16**
spend the night with her. The people of Gaza heard that Samson had come, 2
and they surrounded him and lay in wait for him all that night at the city
gate. During the night, however, they took no action, saying to themselves,
'When day breaks we shall kill him.' Samson lay in bed till midnight; and 3
when midnight came he rose, seized hold of the doors of the city gate and
the two posts, pulled them out, bar and all, hoisted them on to his shoulders
and carried them to the top of the hill east of Hebron.

After this Samson fell in love with a woman named Delilah, who lived 4
in the valley of Sorek. The lords of the Philistines went up country to see 5
her and said, 'Coax him and find out what gives him his great strength,
and how we can master him, bind him and so hold him captive; then we

---

a ass: *Heb.* hamor.   *b* I have . . . asses: *or* I have reddened them blood-red, *or* I
have heaped them in heaps; *Heb.* hamor himmartim.   *c* *That is* Jaw-bone Hill.
d *That is* the Crier's Spring.

6 will each give you eleven hundred pieces of silver.' So Delilah said to Samson, 'Tell me what gives you your great strength, and how you can be
7 bound and held captive.' Samson replied, 'If they bind me with seven fresh bowstrings not yet dry, then I shall become as weak as any other man.'
8 So the lords of the Philistines brought her seven fresh bowstrings not yet
9 dry, and she bound him with them. She had men already hidden in the inner room, and she cried, 'The Philistines are upon you, Samson!' But he snapped the bowstrings as a strand of tow snaps when it feels the fire,
10 and his strength was not tamed. Delilah said to Samson, 'I see you have made a fool of me and told me lies. Tell me this time how you can be
11 bound.' He said to her, 'If you bind me tightly with new ropes that have
12 never been used, then I shall become as weak as any other man.' So Delilah took new ropes and bound him with them. Then she cried, 'The Philistines are upon you, Samson!', while the men waited hidden in the
13 inner room. He snapped the ropes off his arms like pack-thread. Delilah said to him, 'You are still making a fool of me and have told me lies. Tell me: how can you be bound?' He said, 'Take the seven loose locks of my hair and weave them into the warp, and then drive them tight with the beater; and I shall become as weak as any other man.' So she lulled him to
14 sleep, wove the seven loose locks of his hair into the warp, and drove them tight with the beater, and cried, 'The Philistines are upon you, Samson!'
15 He woke from sleep and pulled away the warp and the loom with it.*ᵃ* She said to him, 'How can you say you love me when you do not confide in me? This is the third time you have made a fool of me and have not told me
16 what gives you your great strength.' She so pestered him with these words
17 day after day, pressing him hard and wearying him to death, that he told her his secret. 'No razor has touched my head,' he said, 'because I am a Nazirite, consecrated to God from the day of my birth. If my head were shaved, then my strength would leave me, and I should become as weak as
18 any other man.' Delilah saw that he had told her his secret; so she sent to the lords of the Philistines and said, 'Come up at once, he has told me his secret.' So the lords of the Philistines came up and brought the money
19 with them. She lulled him to sleep on her knees, summoned a man and he shaved the seven locks of his hair for her. She began to take him captive
20 and his strength left him. Then she cried, 'The Philistines are upon you, Samson!' He woke from his sleep and said, 'I will go out as usual and shake
21 myself'; he did not know that the Lᴏʀᴅ had left him. The Philistines seized him, gouged out his eyes and brought him down to Gaza. There they bound him with fetters of bronze, and he was set to grinding corn in
22 the prison. But his hair, after it had been shaved, began to grow again.
23   The lords of the Philistines assembled together to offer a great sacrifice to their god Dagon and to rejoice before him. They said, 'Our god has
24 delivered Samson our enemy into our hands.' The people, when they saw him, praised their god, chanting:

> Our god has delivered our enemy into our hands,
> the scourge of our land who piled it with our dead.

ᵃ the warp . . . with it: *prob. rdg.; Heb. adds an unintelligible word.*

When they grew merry, they said, 'Call Samson, and let him fight to make 25
sport for us.' So they summoned Samson from prison and he made sport
before them all. They stood him between the pillars, and Samson said to 26
the boy who held his hand, 'Put me where I can feel the pillars which support the temple, so that I may lean against them.' The temple was full of 27
men and women, and all the lords of the Philistines were there, and there
were about three thousand men and women on the roof watching Samson
as he fought. Samson called on the LORD and said, 'Remember me, O 28
Lord GOD, remember me: give me strength only this once, O God, and let
me at one stroke be avenged on the Philistines for my two eyes.' He put 29
his arms round the two central pillars which supported the temple, his
right arm round one and his left round the other, and braced himself and 30
said, 'Let me die with the Philistines.' Then Samson leaned forward with
all his might, and the temple fell on the lords and on all the people who were
in it. So the dead whom he killed at his death were more than those he had
killed in his life. His brothers and all his father's family came down, carried 31
him up to the grave of his father Manoah between Zorah and Eshtaol and
buried him there. He had been judge over Israel for twenty years.

Years of lawlessness

THERE WAS ONCE A MAN NAMED MICAH from the hill-country of 17
Ephraim. He said to his mother, 'You remember the eleven hundred 2
pieces of silver which were taken from you, and how you called down a
curse on the thief in my hearing? I have the money; I took it and now I
will give it back to you.'*a* His mother said, 'May the LORD bless you, my
son.' So he gave the eleven hundred pieces of silver back to his mother, 3
and she said, 'I now solemnly dedicate this money of mine to the LORD for
the benefit of my son, to make a carved idol and a cast image.' He returned 4
the money to his mother, and she took two hundred pieces of silver and
handed them to a silversmith, who made them into an idol and an image,
which stood in Micah's house.

This man Micah had a shrine, and he made an ephod and teraphim*b* 5
and installed one of his sons to be his priest. In those days there was no 6
king in Israel and every man did what was right in his own eyes. Now 7
there was a young man from Bethlehem in Judah, from the clan of Judah,
a Levite named Ben-gershom.*c* He had left the city of Bethlehem to go 8
and find somewhere to live. On his way he came to Micah's house in the
hill-country of Ephraim. Micah said to him, 'Where have you come from?' 9
He replied, 'I am a Levite from Bethlehem in Judah, and I am looking for
somewhere to live.' Micah said to him, 'Stay with me and be priest and 10
father to me. I will give you ten pieces of silver a year, and provide you with
food and clothes.' The Levite agreed to stay with the man and was treated 11
as one of his own sons. Micah installed the Levite, and the young man 12
became his priest and a member of his household. Micah said, 'Now I 13

a and now . . . you: *transposed from verse 3.*   *b* Or household gods.   *c* named
Ben-gershom: *prob. rdg., cp. 18. 30; Heb. he lodged there.*

know that the LORD will make me prosper, because I have a Levite for my priest.'

18 In those days there was no king in Israel and the tribe of the Danites was looking for territory to occupy, because they had not so far come into 2 possession of the territory allotted to them among the tribes of Israel. The Danites therefore sent out five fighting men of their clan from Zorah and Eshtaol to prospect, with instructions to go and explore the land. They came to Micah's house in the hill-country of Ephraim and spent the night 3 there. While they were there, they recognized the speech of the young Levite; they turned there and then and said to him, 'Who brought you 4 here? What are you doing? What is your business here?' He said, 'This is 5 all Micah's doing: he has hired me and I have become his priest.' They said to him, 'Then inquire of God on our behalf whether our mission will 6 be successful.' The priest replied, 'Go in peace. Your mission is in the 7 LORD's hands.' The five men went on their way and came to Laish. There they found the inhabitants living a carefree life, in the same way as the Sidonians, a quiet, carefree folk, with no hereditary king to keep the country under his thumb.[a] They were a long way from the Sidonians, and 8 had no contact with the Aramaeans. So the five men went back to Zorah 9 and Eshtaol, and when their kinsmen asked their news, they said, 'Come and attack them. It is an excellent country that we have seen. Will you hang back and do nothing about it? Start off now and take possession of the land. 10 When you get there, you will find a people living a carefree life in a wide expanse of open country. God has delivered it into your hands, a place where there is no lack of anything on earth.'

11 And so six hundred armed men from the clan of the Danites set out from 12 Zorah and Eshtaol. They went up country and encamped in Kiriath-jearim in Judah: this is why that place to this day is called Mahaneh-dan;[b] 13 it lies west of Kiriath-jearim. From there they passed on to the hill-country 14 of Ephraim and came to Micah's house. The five men who had been to explore the country round Laish spoke up and said to their kinsmen, 'Do you know that in one of these houses there are now an ephod and teraphim, 15 an idol and an image? Now consider what you had best do.' So they turned 16 aside to Micah's house and greeted him. The six hundred armed Danites 17 took their stand at the entrance of the gate, and the five men who had gone to explore the country went indoors to take the idol and the image, ephod and teraphim, while the priest was standing at the entrance with the six 18 hundred armed men. The five men entered Micah's house and took the idol and the image, ephod and teraphim.[c] The priest asked them what they 19 were doing, but they said to him, 'Be quiet; not a word. Come with us and be our priest and father. Which is better, to be priest in the household of 20 one man or to be priest to a whole tribe and clan in Israel?' This pleased the priest; so he took the ephod and teraphim, the idol and the image, and 21 joined the company. They turned and went off, putting the dependants, 22 the herds, and the valuables in front. The Danites had gone some distance

---

[a] with no . . . thumb: *prob. rdg.*; *Heb.* and none humiliating anything in the land with inherited authority.   [b] *That is* the Camp of Dan.   [c] *Prob. rdg.*; *Heb.* the idol of the ephod, and teraphim and image.

from Micah's house, when his neighbours were called out in pursuit and
caught up with them. They shouted after them, and the Danites turned 23
round and said to Micah, 'What is the matter with you? Why have you
come after us?' He said, 'You have taken my gods which I made for myself, 24
you have taken the priest, and you have gone off and left me nothing. How
dare you say, "What is the matter with you?"' The Danites said to him, 25
'Do not shout at us. We are desperate men and if we fall upon you it will
be the death of yourself and your family.' With that the Danites went on 26
their way and Micah, seeing that they were too strong for him, turned and
went home.

Thus they carried off the priest and the things Micah had made for 27
himself, and attacked Laish, whose people were quiet and carefree. They
put them to the sword and set fire to their city. There was no one to save 28
them, for the city was a long way from Sidon and they had no contact with
the Aramaeans,*a* although the city was in the vale near Beth-rehob. They
rebuilt the city and settled in it, naming it Dan after the name of their fore- 29
father Dan, a son of Israel; but its original name was Laish. The Danites 30
set up the idol, and Jonathan son of Gershom, son of Moses, and his sons
were priests to the tribe of Dan until the people went into exile. (They set 31
up for themselves the idol which Micah had made, and it was there as long
as the house of God was at Shiloh.)

IN THOSE DAYS when no king ruled in Israel, a Levite was living in the **19**
heart of the hill-country of Ephraim. He had taken himself a concubine
from Bethlehem in Judah. In a fit of anger she had left him and had gone 2
to her father's house in Bethlehem in Judah. When she had been there four
months, her husband set out after her with his servant and two asses to 3
appeal to her and bring her back. She brought him in to the house of her
father, who welcomed him when he saw him. His father-in-law, the girl's 4
father, pressed him and he stayed with him three days, and they were well
entertained during their visit. On the fourth day, they rose early in the 5
morning, and he prepared to leave, but the girl's father said to his son-in-
law, 'Have something to eat first, before you go.' So the two of them sat 6
down and ate and drank together. The girl's father said to the man, 'Why
not spend the night and enjoy yourself?' When he rose to go, his father-in- 7
law urged him to stay, and again he stayed for the night. He rose early in 8
the morning on the fifth day to depart, but the girl's father said, 'Have
something to eat first.' So they lingered till late afternoon, eating and
drinking together. Then the man stood up to go with his concubine and 9
servant, but his father-in-law said, 'See how the day wears on towards
sunset. Spend the night here and enjoy yourself, and then rise early tomorrow and set out for home.' But the man would not stay the night; he 10
rose and left. He had reached a point opposite Jebus, that is Jerusalem,
with his two laden asses and his concubine, and when they were close to 11
Jebus, the weather grew wild and stormy, and the young man said to his
master, 'Come now, let us turn into this Jebusite town and spend the night
there.' But his master said to him, 'No, not into a strange town where the 12

a Prob. rdg., cp. verse 7; Heb. men.

293

13 people are not Israelites; let us go on to Gibeah. Come, we will go and find
14 some other place, and spend the night in Gibeah or Ramah.' So they went
on until sunset overtook them; they were then near Gibeah which belongs
15 to Benjamin. They turned in to spend the night there, and went and sat
down in the open street of the town; but nobody took them into his house
for the night.

16 Meanwhile an old man was coming home in the evening from his work
in the fields. He was from the hill-country of Ephraim, but he lived in
17 Gibeah, where the people were Benjamites. He looked up, saw the traveller in the open street of the town, and asked him where he was going and
18 where he came from. He answered, 'We are travelling from Bethlehem in
Judah to the heart of the hill-country of Ephraim. I come from there; I
have been to Bethlehem in Judah and I am going home, but nobody has
19 taken me into his house. I have straw and provender for the asses, food and
wine for myself, the girl, and the young man; we have all we need, sir.'
20 The old man said, 'You are welcome, I will supply all your wants; you
21 must not spend the night in the street.' So he took him inside and provided
22 fodder for the asses; they washed their feet, and ate and drank. While they
were enjoying themselves, some of the worst scoundrels in the town surrounded the house, hurling themselves against the door and shouting to
the old man who owned the house, 'Bring out the man who has gone into
23 your house, for us to have intercourse with him.' The owner of the house
went outside to them and said, 'No, my friends, do nothing so wicked. This
24 man is my guest; do not commit this outrage. Here is my daughter, a
virgin;*a* let me bring her*b* out to you. Rape her*b* and do to her*b* what you
25 please; but you shall not commit such an outrage against this man.' But
the men refused to listen to him, so the Levite took hold of his concubine
and thrust her outside for them. They assaulted her and abused her all
26 night till the morning, and when dawn broke, they let her go. The girl
came at daybreak and fell down at the entrance of the man's house where
27 her master was, and lay there until it was light. Her master rose in the
morning and opened the door of the house to set out on his journey, and
there was his concubine lying at the door with her hands on the threshold.
28 He said to her, 'Get up and let us be off'; but there was no answer. So he
29 lifted her on to his ass and set off for home. When he arrived there, he
picked up a knife, and he took hold of his concubine and cut her up limb
by limb into twelve pieces; and he sent them through the length and
30 breadth of Israel. He told the men he sent with them to say to every
Israelite, 'Has the like of this happened or been seen from the time the
Israelites came up from Egypt till today? Consider this among yourselves
and speak your minds.' So everyone who saw them said, 'No such thing
has ever happened or been seen before.'

20 All the Israelites, the whole community from Dan to Beersheba and out
of Gilead also, left their homes as one man and assembled before the LORD
2 at Mizpah. The leaders of the people and all the tribes of Israel presented
themselves in the general assembly of the people of God, four hundred
3 thousand foot-soldiers armed with swords; and the Benjamites heard that

a Prob. rdg.; Heb. adds and his concubine.   *b Prob. rdg.; Heb.* them.

the Israelites had gone up to Mizpah. The Israelites asked how this wicked
thing had come about, and the Levite, to whom the murdered woman 4
belonged, answered, 'I and my concubine came to Gibeah in Benjamin to
spend the night there. The citizens of Gibeah rose against me that night 5
and surrounded the house where I was, intending to kill me; and they raped
my concubine and she died. I took her and cut her in pieces, and sent them 6
through the length and breadth of Israel, because of the filthy outrage they
had committed in Israel. Now it is for you, the whole of Israel, to say here 7
and now what you think ought to be done.' All the people rose to their feet 8
as one man and said, 'Not one of us shall go back to his tent, not one shall
return home. This is what we will now do to Gibeah. We will draw lots for 9
the attack: and we will take ten men out of every hundred in all the tribes 10
of Israel, a hundred out of every thousand, and a thousand out of every
ten thousand, to collect provisions from the people for those who have taken
the field against Gibeah in Benjamin to avenge the outrage committed in
Israel.' Thus all the Israelites to a man were massed against the town. 11

The tribes of Israel sent men all through the tribe of Benjamin saying, 12
'What is this wicked thing which has happened in your midst? Hand over 13
to us those scoundrels in Gibeah, and we will put them to death and purge
Israel of this wickedness.' But the Benjamites refused to listen to their
fellow-Israelites. They flocked from their cities to Gibeah to go to war with 14
the Israelites, and that day they mustered out of their cities twenty-six 15
thousand men armed with swords. There were also seven hundred picked
men from Gibeah, left-handed men, who could sling a stone and not miss 16
by a hair's breadth. The Israelites, without Benjamin, numbered four 17
hundred thousand men armed with swords, every one a fighting man. The 18
Israelites at once moved on to Bethel, and there they sought an oracle from
God, asking, 'Which of us shall attack Benjamin first?', and the LORD's
answer was, 'Judah shall attack first.' So the Israelites set out at dawn and 19
encamped opposite Gibeah. They advanced to do battle with Benjamin 20
and drew up their forces before the town. The Benjamites made a sally 21
from Gibeah and left twenty-two thousand of Israel dead on the field that
day. The Israelites went up to Bethel,*a* lamented before the LORD until 23*b*
evening and inquired whether they should again attack their brother
Benjamin. The LORD said, 'Yes, attack him.' Then the Israelites took fresh 22
courage and again formed up on the same ground as the first day. So the 24
second day they advanced against the Benjamites, who sallied out from 25
Gibeah to meet them and laid another eighteen thousand armed men low.
The Israelites, the whole people, went back to Bethel, where they sat before 26
the LORD lamenting and fasting until evening, and they offered whole-
offerings and shared-offerings before the LORD. In those days the Ark of 27
the Covenant of God was there, and Phinehas son of Eleazar, son of 28
Aaron, served before the LORD.*c* The Israelites inquired of the LORD and
said, 'Shall we again march out to battle against Benjamin our brother or
shall we desist?' The LORD answered, 'Attack him: tomorrow I will deliver
him into your hands.' Israel then posted men in ambush all round Gibeah. 29

a to Bethel: *prob. rdg., cp. verses 18, 26; Heb. om.*   *b Verses 22 and 23 transposed.*
c Or before the Ark.

30 On the third day the Israelites advanced against the Benjamites and
31 drew up their forces at Gibeah as they had before; and the Benjamites
sallied out to meet the army. They were drawn away from the town and
began the attack as before by killing a few Israelites, about thirty,[a] on the
highways which led across open country, one to Bethel and the other to
32 Gibeah. They thought they were defeating them once again, but the
Israelites had planned a retreat to draw them away from the town out on to
33 the highways. Meanwhile the main body of Israelites left their positions
and re-formed in Baal-tamar, while those in ambush, ten thousand picked
men all told, burst out from their position in the neighbourhood of Gibeah
34 and came in on the east of the town. There was soon heavy fighting; yet
35 the Benjamites did not suspect the disaster that was threatening them. So
the LORD put Benjamin to flight before Israel, and on that day the Israelites
killed twenty-five thousand one hundred Benjamites, all armed men.
36 The men of Benjamin now saw that they had been defeated, for all that
the Israelites, trusting in the ambush which they had set by Gibeah, had
37 given way before them. The men in ambush made a sudden dash on
Gibeah, fell on the town from all sides and put all the inhabitants to the
38 sword. The agreed signal between the Israelites and those in ambush[b] was
39 to be a column of smoke sent up from the town. The Israelites then faced
about in the battle; and Benjamin began to cut down the Israelites, killing
about thirty of them,[c] in the belief that they were defeating them as they
40 had done in the first encounter. As the column of smoke began to go up
from the town, the Benjamites looked back and thought the whole town
41 was going up in flames. When the Israelites faced about, the Benjamites
42 saw that disaster had overtaken them and were seized with panic. They
turned and fled before the Israelites in the direction of the wilderness, but
the fighting caught up with them and soon those from the town were
43 among them, cutting them down. They hemmed in the Benjamites, pursuing them without respite,[d] and overtook them at a point to the east of
44 Gibeah. Eighteen thousand of the Benjamites fell, all of them fighting
45 men. The survivors turned and fled into the wilderness towards the Rock
of Rimmon. The Israelites picked off the stragglers on the roads, five thousand of them, and chased them until they had cut down and killed two
46 thousand more. Twenty-five thousand armed men of Benjamin fell in battle
47 that day, all fighting men. The six hundred who survived turned and fled
into the wilderness as far as the Rock of Rimmon, and there they remained
48 for four months. The Israelites then turned back to deal with the Benjamites, and put to the sword the people in the towns and the cattle, every
creature that they found; they also set fire to every town within their reach.
21 In Mizpah the Israelites had bound themselves by oath that none of
2 them would marry his daughter to a Benjamite. The people now came to
Bethel and remained there in God's presence till sunset, raising their voices
3 in loud lamentation. They said, 'O LORD God of Israel, why has it happened
4 in Israel that one tribe should this day be lost to Israel?' Next day the

---

[a] *Or* about thirty wounded men.   [b] *Prob. rdg.; Heb. adds an unintelligible word.*
[c] to cut . . . them: *or* to kill about thirty wounded men among the Israelites.   [d] without
respite: *or* from Nohah.

people rose early, built an altar there and offered whole-offerings and shared-offerings. At that the Israelites asked themselves whether among all 5 the tribes of Israel there was anyone who did not go up to the assembly before the LORD; for under the terms of the great oath anyone who had not gone up to the LORD at Mizpah was to be put to death. And the Israelites 6 felt remorse over their brother Benjamin, because, as they said, 'This day Israel has lost one whole tribe.' So they asked, 'What shall we do for wives 7 for those who are left? We have sworn to the LORD not to give any of our daughters to them in marriage. Is there anyone in all the tribes of Israel 8 who did not go up to the LORD at Mizpah?' Now it happened that no one from Jabesh-gilead had come to the camp for the assembly; so when they 9 held a roll-call of the people, they found that no inhabitant of Jabesh-gilead was present. Thereupon the community sent off twelve thousand 10 fighting men with orders to go and put the inhabitants of Jabesh-gilead to the sword, men, women, and dependants. 'This is what you shall do,' they 11 said: 'put to death every male person, and every woman who has had intercourse with a man, but spare any who are virgins.' This they did. Among 12 the inhabitants of Jabesh-gilead they found four hundred young women who were virgins and had not had intercourse with a man, and they brought them to the camp at Shiloh in Canaan. Then the whole community sent 13 messengers to the Benjamites at the Rock of Rimmon to parley with them, and peace was proclaimed. At this the Benjamites came back, and were 14 given those of the women of Jabesh-gilead who had been spared; but these were not enough.

The people were still full of remorse over Benjamin because the LORD 15 had made this gap in the tribes of Israel, and the elders of the community 16 said, 'What shall we do for wives for the rest? All the women in Benjamin have been massacred.' They said, 'Heirs there must be for the remnant 17 of Benjamin who have escaped! Then Israel will not see one of its tribes blotted out. We cannot give them our own daughters in marriage because 18 we have sworn that there shall be a curse on the man who gives a wife to a Benjamite.' Then they bethought themselves of the pilgrimage in honour 19 of the LORD, made every year to Shiloh, the place which lies to the north of Bethel, on the east side of the highway from Bethel to Shechem and to the south of Lebonah. They said to the Benjamites, 'Go and hide in the vine- 20 yards and keep watch. When the girls of Shiloh come out to dance, sally 21 out of the vineyards, and each of you seize one of them for his wife; then make your way home to the land of Benjamin. Then, if their fathers or 22 brothers come and complain to you, say to them, "Let us keep them with your approval, for none of us has captured a wife in battle. Had you offered them to us, the guilt would be yours."'

All this the Benjamites did. They carried off as many wives as they 23 needed, snatching them as they danced; then they went their way and returned to their patrimony, rebuilt their cities and settled in them. The 24 Israelites also dispersed by tribes and families, and every man went back to his own patrimony.

In those days there was no king in Israel and every man did what was 25 right in his own eyes.

RUTH

Naomi and Ruth

1 LONG AGO, IN THE TIME OF THE JUDGES, there was a famine in the land, and a man from Bethlehem in Judah went to
2 live in the Moabite country with his wife and his two sons. The man's name was Elimelech, his wife's name was Naomi, and the names of his two sons Mahlon and Chilion. They were Ephrathites from Bethlehem in Judah. They arrived in the Moabite country and there they stayed.
3 Elimelech Naomi's husband died, so that she was left with her two sons.
4 These sons married Moabite women, one of whom was called Orpah and
5 the other Ruth. They had lived there about ten years, when both Mahlon and Chilion died, so that the woman was bereaved of her two sons as well
6 as of her husband. Thereupon she set out with her two daughters-in-law to return home, because she had heard while still in the Moabite country
7 that the LORD had cared for his people and given them food. So with her two daughters-in-law she left the place where she had been living, and took
8 the road home to Judah. Then Naomi said to her two daughters-in-law, 'Go back, both of you, to your mothers' homes. May the LORD keep faith
9 with you, as you have kept faith with the dead and with me; and may he grant each of you security in the home of a new husband.' She kissed them
10 and they wept aloud. Then they said to her, 'We will return with you to
11 your own people.' But Naomi said, 'Go back, my daughters. Why should you go with me? Am I likely to bear any more sons to be husbands for you?
12 Go back, my daughters, go. I am too old to marry again. But even if I could say that I had hope of a child, if I were to marry this night and if I were to
13 bear sons, would you then wait until they grew up? Would you then refrain from marrying? No, no, my daughters, my lot is more bitter than yours,
14 because the LORD has been against me.' At this they wept again. Then Orpah kissed her mother-in-law and returned to her people, but Ruth clung to her.
15 'You see,' said Naomi, 'your sister-in-law has gone back to her people
16 and her gods;ª go back with her.' 'Do not urge me to go back and desert you', Ruth answered. 'Where you go, I will go, and where you stay, I will
17 stay. Your people shall be my people, and your God my God. Where you die, I will die, and there I will be buried. I swear a solemn oath before the
18 LORD your God: nothing but *b* death shall divide us.' When Naomi saw
19 that Ruth was determined to go with her, she said no more, and the two of them went on until they came to Bethlehem. When they arrived in Bethlehem, the whole town was in great excitement about them, and the
20 women said, 'Can this be Naomi?' 'Do not call me Naomi,'ᶜ she said, 'call

---

ª *Or* god.   *b* I swear . . . nothing but: *or* The LORD your God do so to me and more if . . .   ᶜ *That is* Pleasure.

me Mara,*a* for it is a bitter lot that the Almighty has sent me. I went away   21
full, and the LORD has brought me back empty. Why do you call me Naomi?
The LORD has pronounced against me; the Almighty has brought disaster
on me.' This is how Naomi's daughter-in-law, Ruth the Moabitess,   22
returned with her from the Moabite country. The barley harvest was
beginning when they arrived in Bethlehem.

Ruth and Boaz

N OW NAOMI HAD A KINSMAN on her husband's side, a well-to-do   2
man of the family of Elimelech; his name was Boaz. Ruth the   2
Moabitess said to Naomi, 'May I go out to the cornfields and glean behind
anyone who will grant me that favour?' 'Yes, go, my daughter', she replied.
So Ruth went gleaning in the fields behind the reapers. As it happened,   3
she was in that strip of the fields which belonged to Boaz of Elimelech's
family, and there was Boaz coming out from Bethlehem. He greeted the   4
reapers, saying, 'The LORD be with you'; and they replied, 'The LORD
bless you.' Then he asked his servant in charge of the reapers, 'Whose girl   5
is this?' 'She is a Moabite girl', the servant answered, 'who has just come   6
back with Naomi from the Moabite country. She asked if she might glean   7
and gather among the swathes behind the reapers. She came and has been
on her feet with hardly a moment's rest *b* from daybreak till now.' Then   8
Boaz said to Ruth, 'Listen to me, my daughter: do not go and glean in any
other field, and do not look any further, but keep close to my girls. Watch   9
where the men reap, and follow the gleaners; I have given them orders not
to molest you. If you are thirsty, go and drink from the jars the men have
filled.' She fell prostrate before him and said, 'Why are you so kind as to   10
take notice of me when I am only a foreigner?' Boaz answered, 'They have   11
told me all that you have done for your mother-in-law since your husband's
death, how you left your father and mother and the land of your birth, and
came to a people you did not know before. The LORD reward your deed;   12
may the LORD the God of Israel, under whose wings you have come to
take refuge, give you all that you deserve.' 'Indeed, sir,' she said, 'you have   13
eased my mind and spoken kindly to me; may I ask you as a favour not to
treat me only as one of your slave-girls?' *c* When meal-time came round,   14
Boaz said to her, 'Come here and have something to eat, and dip your
bread into the sour wine.' So she sat beside the reapers, and he passed her
some roasted grain. She ate all she wanted and still had some left over.
When she got up to glean, Boaz gave the men orders. 'She', he said, 'may   15
glean even among the sheaves; do not scold her. Or you may even pull out   16
some corn from the bundles and leave it for her to glean, without reproving
her.'

So Ruth gleaned in the field till evening, and when she beat out what she   17
had gleaned, it came to about a bushel of barley. She took it up and went   18
into the town, and her mother-in-law saw how much she had gleaned.

a That is Bitter.   *b Prob. rdg.; Heb. adds* in the house.   *c* may I . . . slave-
girls?: *or* if you please, treat me as one of your slave-girls.

Then Ruth brought out what she had saved from her meal and gave it to
19 her. Her mother-in-law asked her, 'Where did you glean today? Which
way did you go? Blessings on the man who kindly took notice of you.' So
she told her mother-in-law whom she had been working with. 'The man
20 with whom I worked today', she said, 'is called Boaz.' 'Blessings on him
from the LORD', said Naomi. 'The LORD has kept faith with the living and
21 the dead. For this man is related to us and is our next-of-kin.' 'And what
is more,' said Ruth the Moabitess, 'he told me to stay close to his men until
22 they had finished all his harvest.' 'It is best for you, my daughter,' Naomi
answered, 'to go out with his girls; let no one catch you in another field.'
23 So she kept close to his girls, gleaning with them till the end of both barley
and wheat harvests; but she lived with her mother-in-law.

3   One day Ruth's mother-in-law Naomi said to her, 'My daughter, I want
2 to see you happily settled. Now there is our kinsman Boaz; you were with
3 his girls. Tonight he is winnowing barley at his threshing-floor. Wash and
anoint yourself, put on your cloak and go down to the threshing-floor, but
do not make yourself known to the man until he has finished eating and
4 drinking. But when he lies down, take note of the place where he lies.
Then go in, turn back the covering at his feet and lie down. He will tell
5 6 you what to do.' 'I will do whatever you tell me', Ruth answered. So she
went down to the threshing-floor and did exactly as her mother-in-law
7 had told her. When Boaz had eaten and drunk, he felt at peace with the
world and went to lie down at the far end of the heap of grain. She came in
8 quietly, turned back the covering at his feet and lay down. About midnight
something disturbed the man as he slept; he turned over and, lo and behold,
9 there was a woman lying at his feet. 'Who are you?' he asked. 'I am your
servant, Ruth', she replied. 'Now spread your skirt over your servant,
10 because you are my next-of-kin.' He said, 'The LORD has blessed you, my
daughter. This last proof of your loyalty is greater than the first; you have
11 not sought after any young man, rich or poor. Set your mind at rest, my
daughter. I will do whatever you ask; for, as the whole neighbourhood
12 knows, you are a capable woman. Are you sure that I am the next-of-kin?
13 There is a kinsman even closer than I. Spend the night here and then in
the morning, if he is willing to act as your next-of-kin, well and good; but
if he is not willing, I will do so; I swear it by the LORD. Now lie down till
14 morning.' So she lay at his feet till morning, but rose before one man could
recognize another; and he said, 'It must not be known that a woman has
15 been to the threshing-floor.' Then he said, 'Bring me the cloak you have
on, and hold it out.' So she held it out, and he put in six measures of barley
16 and lifted it on her back, and she went to the town. When she came to her
mother-in-law, Naomi asked, 'How did things go with you, my daughter?'
17 Ruth told her all that the man had done for her. 'He gave me these six measures of barley,' she said; 'he would not let me come home to my mother-in-
18 law empty-handed.' Naomi answered, 'Wait, my daughter, until you see
what will come of it. He will not rest until he has settled the matter today.'

4   Now Boaz had gone up to the city gate, and was sitting there; and, after
a time, the next-of-kin of whom he had spoken passed by. 'Here,' he cried,
2 calling him by name, 'come and sit down.' He came and sat down. Then

Boaz stopped ten elders of the town, and asked them to sit there, and they did so. Then he said to the next-of-kin, 'You will remember the strip of 3 field that belonged to our brother Elimelech. Naomi has returned from the Moabite country and is selling it. I promised to open the matter with 4 you, to ask you to acquire it in the presence of those who sit here, in the presence of the elders of my people. If you are going to do your duty as next-of-kin, then do so, but if not, someone must do it. So tell me, and then I shall know; for I come after you as next-of-kin.' He answered, 'I will act as next-of-kin.' Then Boaz said, 'On the day when you acquire the field 5 from Naomi, you also acquire Ruth the Moabitess, the dead man's wife, so as to perpetuate the name of the dead man with his patrimony.' There- 6 upon the next-of-kin said, 'I cannot act myself, for I should risk losing my own patrimony. You must therefore do my duty as next-of-kin. I cannot act.'

Now in those old days, when property was redeemed or exchanged, it 7 was the custom for a man to pull off his sandal and give it to the other party. This was the form of attestation in Israel. So the next-of-kin said to 8 Boaz, 'Acquire it for yourself', and pulled off his sandal. Then Boaz 9 declared to the elders and all the people, 'You are witnesses today that I have acquired from Naomi all that belonged to Elimelech and all that belonged to Mahlon and Chilion; and, further, that I have myself acquired 10 Ruth the Moabitess, wife of Mahlon, to be my wife, to perpetuate the name of the deceased with his patrimony, so that his name may not be missing among his kindred and at the gate of his native place. You are witnesses this day.' Then the elders and all who were at the gate said, 'We are wit- 11 nesses. May the LORD make this woman, who has come to your home, like Rachel and Leah, the two who built up the house of Israel. May you do great things in Ephrathah and keep a name alive in Bethlehem. May your 12 house be like the house of Perez, whom Tamar bore to Judah, through the offspring the LORD will give you by this girl.'

So Boaz took Ruth and made her his wife. When they came together, 13 the LORD caused her to conceive and she bore Boaz a son. Then the women 14 said to Naomi, 'Blessed be the LORD today, for he has not left you without a next-of-kin. May the dead man's name be kept alive in Israel. The child 15 will give you new life and cherish you in your old age; for your daughter-in-law who loves you, who has proved better to you than seven sons, has borne him.' Naomi took the child and laid him in her lap and became his 16 nurse. Her neighbours gave him a name: 'Naomi has a son,' they said; 'we 17 will call him Obed.' He was the father of Jesse, the father of David.

THIS IS THE GENEALOGY OF PEREZ: Perez was the father of Hezron, 18 Hezron of Ram, Ram of Amminadab, Amminadab of Nahshon, Nahshon of 19 20 Salmon, Salmon of Boaz, Boaz of Obed, Obed of Jesse, and Jesse of David. 21 22

THE FIRST BOOK OF
SAMUEL

The birth and call of Samuel

1 THERE WAS A MAN FROM RAMATHAIM, a Zuphite
from the hill-country of Ephraim, named Elkanah son of Jeroham,
2 son of Elihu, son of Tohu, son of Zuph an Ephraimite; and he had
two wives named Hannah and Peninnah. Peninnah had children, but
3 Hannah was childless. This man used to go up from his own town every
year to worship and to offer sacrifice to the LORD of Hosts in Shiloh. There
4 Eli's two sons, Hophni and Phinehas, were priests of the LORD. On the
day when Elkanah sacrificed, he gave several shares of the meat to his wife
5 Peninnah with all her sons and daughters; but, although he loved Hannah,
he gave her only one share, because the LORD had not granted her children.
6 Further, Hannah's rival used to torment her and humiliate her because
7 she had no children. Year after year this happened when they went up to
the house of the LORD; her rival used to torment her. Once when she was
8 in tears and would not eat, her husband Elkanah said to her, 'Hannah, why
are you crying and eating nothing? Why are you so miserable? Am I not
9-10 more to you than ten sons?' After they had finished eating and drinking
at the sacrifice at Shiloh, Hannah rose in deep distress, and stood before
the LORD and prayed to him, weeping bitterly. Meanwhile Eli the priest
11 was sitting on his seat beside the door of the temple of the LORD. Hannah
made a vow in these words: 'O LORD of Hosts, if thou wilt deign to take
notice of my trouble and remember me, if thou wilt not forget me but
grant me offspring, then I will give the child to the LORD for his whole life,
12 and no razor shall ever touch his head.' For a long time she went on praying
13 before the LORD, while Eli watched her lips. Hannah was praying silently;
but, although her voice could not be heard, her lips were moving and Eli
14 took her for a drunken woman. He said to her, 'Enough of this drunken
15 behaviour! Go away till the wine has worn off.' 'No, sir,' she answered,
'I am a sober person, I have drunk no wine or strong drink, and I have
16 been pouring out my heart before the LORD. Do not think me so degraded,
sir; all this time I have been speaking out of the fullness of my grief and
17 misery.' 'Go in peace,' said Eli, 'and may the God of Israel answer the
18 prayer you have made to him.' Hannah said, 'May I be worthy of your
kindness.' And she went away and took something to eat, no longer down-
19 cast. Next morning they were up early and, after prostrating themselves
before the LORD, returned to their own home at Ramah. Elkanah had
20 intercourse with his wife Hannah, and the LORD remembered her. She
conceived, and in due time bore a son, whom she named Samuel, 'because',
she said, 'I asked the LORD for him.'

Elkanah, with his whole household, went up to make the annual sacrifice 21
to the LORD and to redeem his vow. Hannah did not go with them, but said 22
to her husband, 'When the child is weaned I will come up with him to
enter the presence of the LORD, and he shall*a* stay there always.' Her 23
husband Elkanah said to her, 'Do what you think best; stay at home until
you have weaned him. Only, may the LORD indeed see your vow fulfilled.'
So the woman stayed and nursed her son until she had weaned him; and 24
when she had weaned him, she took him up with her. She took also a bull
three years old, an ephah of meal, and a flagon of wine, and she brought
him, child as he was, into the house of the LORD at Shiloh. They slaughtered 25
the bull, and brought the boy to Eli. Hannah said to him, 'Sir, as sure as 26
you live, I am the woman who stood near you here praying to the LORD.
It was this boy that I prayed for and the LORD has given me what I asked. 27
What I asked I have received; and now I lend him to the LORD; for his 28
whole life he is lent to the LORD.' And they prostrated themselves there
before the LORD.

Then Hannah offered this prayer: **2**

> My heart rejoices in the LORD,
> in the LORD I now hold my head high;
> my mouth is full of derision of my foes,
> exultant because thou hast saved me.
>
>> There is none except thee,   2
>> none so holy as the LORD,
>> no rock like our God.
>
> Cease your proud boasting,   3
> let no word of arrogance pass your lips;
> for the LORD is a god of all knowledge:
> he governs all that men do.
>
> Strong men stand in mute*b* dismay   4
> but those who faltered put on new strength.
> Those who had plenty sell themselves for a crust,   5
> and the hungry grow strong again.
> The barren woman has seven children,
> and the mother of many sons is left to languish.
>
> The LORD kills and he gives life,   6
> he sends down to Sheol, he can bring the dead up again.
> The LORD makes a man poor, he makes him rich,   7
> he brings down and he raises up.
> He lifts the weak out of the dust   8
> and raises the poor from the dunghill;
> to give them a place among the great,
> to set them in seats of honour.
>
> For the foundations of the earth are the LORD's,
> he has built the world upon them.

---

a come up . . . he shall: *or* bring him up, and he shall come into the presence of the LORD
and . . .   *b* in mute: *prob. rdg.; Heb. obscure.*

9 He will guard the footsteps of his saints,
while the wicked sink into silence and gloom;
not by mere strength shall a man prevail.

10 Those that stand against the LORD will be terrified
when the High God*a* thunders out of heaven.
The LORD is judge even to the ends of the earth,
he will give strength to his king
and raise high the head of his anointed prince.

11 Then Elkanah went to Ramah with his household, but the boy remained behind in the service of the LORD under Eli the priest.

12 13 Now Eli's sons were scoundrels and had no regard for the LORD. The custom of the priests in their dealings with the people was this: when a man offered a sacrifice, the priest's servant would come while the flesh
14 was stewing and would thrust a three-pronged fork into the cauldron or pan or kettle or pot; and the priest would take whatever the fork brought out. This should have been their practice whenever Israelites came to
15 sacrifice at Shiloh; but now under Eli's sons, even before the fat was burnt, the priest's servant came and said to the man who was sacrificing, 'Give me meat to roast for the priest; he will not accept what has been already stewed,
16 only raw meat.' And if the man answered 'Let them burn the fat first, and then take what you want', he said, 'No, give it to me now, or I will take it
17 by force.' The young men's sin was very great in the LORD's sight; for they brought the LORD's sacrifice into general contempt.

18 Samuel continued in the service of the LORD, a mere boy with a linen
19 ephod fastened round him. Every year his mother made him a little cloak and took it to him when she went up with her husband to offer the annual
20 sacrifice. Eli would give his blessing to Elkanah and his wife and say, 'The LORD grant you children by this woman in place of the one for which you asked him.'*b* Then they went home again.

21 The LORD showed his care for Hannah, and she conceived and gave birth to three sons and two daughters; meanwhile the boy Samuel grew up in the presence of the LORD.

22 Eli, now a very old man, had heard how his sons were treating all the Israelites, and how they lay with the women who were serving at the
23 entrance to the Tent of the Presence. So he said to them, 'Why do you do
24 such things? I hear from all the people how wickedly you behave. Have done with it, my sons; for it is no good report that I hear spreading among
25 the LORD's people. If a man sins against another man, God will intervene; but if a man sins against the LORD, who can intercede for him?' For all this, they did not listen to their father's rebuke, for the LORD meant that they
26 should die. But the young Samuel, as he grew up, commended himself to the LORD and to men.

27 Now a man of God came to Eli and said, 'This is the word of the LORD: You know that I revealed myself to your forefather when he and his family
28 were in Egypt in slavery in the house of Pharaoh. You know that I chose

a the High God: *prob. rdg.; Heb.* upon him.   *b* for which . . . him: *or* which you lent him.

him from all the tribes of Israel to be my priest, to mount the steps of my
altar, to burn sacrifices and to carry*a* the ephod before me; and that I
assigned all the food-offerings of the Israelites to your family. Why then 29
do you show disrespect for my sacrifices and the offerings which I have
ordained? What makes you resent them? Why do you honour your sons
more than me by letting them batten on the choicest offerings of my
people Israel? The LORD's word was, "I promise that your house and your 30
father's house shall serve before me for all time"; but now his word is,
"I will have no such thing: I will honour those who honour me, and those
who despise me shall meet with contempt. The time is coming when I will 31
lop off every limb of your own and of your father's family, so that no man
in your house shall come to old age. You will even resent*b* the prosperity I 32
give to Israel; never again shall there be an old man in your house. If I 33
allow any to survive to serve my altar, his eyes will grow dim and his
appetite fail, his issue will be weaklings and die off. The fate of your two 34
sons shall be a sign to you: Hophni and Phinehas shall both die on the same
day. I will appoint for myself a priest who will be faithful, who will do 35
what I have in my mind and in my heart. I will establish his family to
serve in perpetual succession before my anointed king. Any of your family 36
that still live will come and bow humbly before him to beg a fee, a piece of
silver and a loaf, and will ask for a turn of priestly duty to earn a crust of
bread."'

So the child Samuel was in the LORD's service under his master Eli. Now **3**
in those days the word of the LORD was seldom heard, and no vision was 2
granted. But one night Eli, whose eyes were dim and his sight failing, was 2
lying down in his usual place, while Samuel slept in the temple of the LORD 3
where the Ark of God was. Before the lamp of God had gone out, the LORD 4
called him, and Samuel answered, 'Here I am', and ran to Eli saying, 'You 5
called me: here I am.' 'No, I did not call you,' said Eli; 'lie down again.'
So he went and lay down. The LORD called Samuel again, and he got up 6
and went to Eli. 'Here I am,' he said; 'surely you called me.' 'I did not call,
my son,' he answered; 'lie down again.' Now Samuel had not yet come to 7
know the LORD, and the word of the LORD had not been disclosed to him.
When the LORD called him for the third time, he again went to Eli and said, 8
'Here I am; you did call me.' Then Eli understood that it was the LORD
calling the child; he told Samuel to go and lie down and said, 'If he calls 9
again, say, "Speak, LORD; thy servant hears thee."' So Samuel went and
lay down in his place.

The LORD came and stood there, and called, 'Samuel, Samuel', as before. 10
Samuel answered, 'Speak; thy servant hears thee.' The LORD said, 'Soon 11
I shall do something in Israel which will ring in the ears of all who hear it.
When that day comes I will make good every word I have spoken against 12
Eli and his family from beginning to end. You are to*c* tell him that my 13
judgement on his house shall stand for ever because*d* he knew of his sons'
blasphemies against God*e* and did not rebuke them. Therefore I have 14

---

a Or wear.   *b* You . . . resent: *prob. rdg.; Heb. obscure.*   *c Prob. rdg.; Heb.*
I will.   *d* because: *prob. rdg.; Heb.* in guilt.   *e* against God: *prob. original
reading, altered in Heb. to* to them.

sworn to the family of Eli that their abuse of sacrifices and offerings shall never be expiated.'

15 Samuel lay down till morning and then opened the doors of the house
16 of the LORD, but he was afraid to tell Eli about the vision. Eli called
17 Samuel: 'Samuel, my son', he said; and he answered, 'Here I am.' Eli asked, 'What did the LORD say to you? Do not hide it from me. God forgive
18 you if you hide one word of all that he said to you.' Then Samuel told him everything and hid nothing. Eli said, 'The LORD must do what is good in his eyes.'

19 As Samuel grew up, the LORD was with him, and none of his words
20 went unfulfilled. From Dan to Beersheba, all Israel recognized that
21 Samuel was confirmed as a prophet of the LORD. So the LORD continued to appear in Shiloh, because he had revealed himself there to Samuel.[a]

The struggle with the Philistines

4 SO SAMUEL'S WORD HAD AUTHORITY throughout Israel. And the time came when the Philistines mustered for battle against Israel, and the Israelites went out to meet them. The Israelites encamped at Eben-
2 ezer and the Philistines at Aphek. The Philistines drew up their lines facing the Israelites, and when they joined battle the Israelites were routed
3 by the Philistines, who killed about four thousand men on the field. When the army got back to the camp, the elders of Israel asked, 'Why did the LORD let us be routed today by the Philistines? Let us fetch the Ark of the Covenant of the LORD from Shiloh to go with us and deliver us from the
4 power of our enemies.' So the people sent to Shiloh and fetched the Ark of the Covenant of the LORD of Hosts, who is enthroned upon the cherubim;
5 Eli's two sons, Hophni and Phinehas, were there with the Ark. When the Ark came into the camp all the Israelites greeted it with a great shout, and
6 the earth rang with the shouting. The Philistines heard the noise and asked, 'What is this great shouting in the camp of the Hebrews?' When
7 they knew that the Ark of the LORD had come into the camp, they were afraid and cried, 'A god has come into the camp. We are lost! No such
8 thing has ever happened before. We are utterly lost! Who can deliver us from the power of these mighty gods? These are the very gods who broke
9 the Egyptians and crushed them in the wilderness. Courage, Philistines, and act like men, or you will become slaves to the Hebrews as they were
10 yours. Be men, and fight!' The Philistines then gave battle, and the Israelites were defeated and fled to their homes. It was a great defeat, and thirty
11 thousand Israelite foot-soldiers perished. The Ark of God was taken, and Eli's two sons, Hophni and Phinehas, were killed.
12 A Benjamite ran from the battlefield and reached Shiloh on the same
13 day, his clothes rent and dust on his head. When he arrived Eli was sitting on a seat by the road to Mizpah, for he was deeply troubled about the Ark of God. The man entered the city with his news, and all the people cried
14 out in horror. When Eli heard it, he asked, 'What does this uproar mean?'

[a] *Prob. rdg.; Heb. adds* according to the word of the LORD.

The man hurried to Eli and told him. Eli was ninety-eight years old and 15
sat staring with sightless eyes; so the man said to him, 'I am the man who 16
has just arrived from the battle; this very day I have escaped from the field.'
Eli asked, 'What is the news, my son?' The runner answered, 'The 17
Israelites have fled from the Philistines; utter panic has struck the army;
your two sons, Hophni and Phinehas, are killed, and the Ark of God is
taken.' At the mention of the Ark of God, Eli fell backwards from his seat 18
by the gate and broke his neck, for he was old and heavy. So he died; he
had been judge over Israel for forty years. His daughter-in-law, the wife 19
of Phinehas, was with child and near her time, and when she heard of the
capture of the Ark and the deaths of her father-in-law and her husband,
her labour suddenly began and she crouched down and was delivered.
As she lay dying, the women who attended her said, 'Do not be afraid; 20
you have a son.' But she did not answer or heed what they said. Then they 21
named the boy Ichabod,*a* saying, 'Glory has departed from Israel' (in
allusion to the capture of the Ark of God and the death of her father-in-
law and her husband); 'Glory has departed from Israel,' they said, 'because 22
the Ark of God is taken.'

After the Philistines had captured the Ark of God, they brought it 5
from Eben-ezer to Ashdod; and there they carried it into the temple of 2
Dagon and set it beside Dagon himself. When the people of Ashdod rose 3
next morning, there was Dagon fallen face downwards before the Ark of
the LORD; so they took him and put him back in his place. Next morning 4
when they rose, Dagon had again fallen face downwards before the Ark
of the LORD, with his head and his two hands lying broken off beside his
platform; only Dagon's body remained on it. This is why from that day 5
to this the priests of Dagon and all who enter the temple of Dagon at Ashdod
do not set foot upon Dagon's platform.

Then the LORD laid a heavy hand upon the people of Ashdod; he threw 6
them into distress and plagued them with tumours, and their territory
swarmed with rats.*b* There was death and destruction all through the city.
When the men of Ashdod saw this, they said, 'The Ark of the God of 7
Israel shall not stay here, for he has laid a heavy hand upon us and upon
Dagon our god.' So they sent and called all the Philistine princes together 8
to ask what should be done with the Ark. They said, 'Let the Ark of the
God of Israel be taken across to Gath.' They took it there, and after its 9
arrival the hand of the LORD caused great havoc in the city; he plagued
everybody, high and low alike, with the tumours which broke out. Then 10
they sent the Ark of God on to Ekron. When the Ark reached Ekron, the
people cried, 'They have brought the Ark of the God of Israel over to us,
to kill us and our families.' So they summoned all the Philistine princes and 11
said, 'Send the Ark of the God of Israel away; let it go back to its own place,
or it will be the death of us all.' There was death and destruction all through
the city; for the hand of God lay heavy upon it. Even those who did not die 12
were plagued with tumours; the cry of the city went up to heaven.

When the Ark of the LORD had been in their territory for seven months, 6
the Philistines summoned the priests and soothsayers and asked, 'What 2

a That is No-glory.   *b Or* mice.

shall we do with the Ark of the LORD? Tell us how we ought to send it
3 back to its own place.' They answered, 'If you send the Ark of the God of
Israel back, do not let it go without a gift, but send it back with a gift for
him by way of indemnity; then you will be healed and restored to favour;
4 there is no reason why his hand should not be lifted from you.' When they
were asked, 'What gift shall we send back to him?', they answered, 'Send
five tumours modelled in gold and five gold rats, one for each of the
Philistine princes, for the same plague afflicted all of you and your princes.
5 Make models of your tumours and of the rats which are ravaging the land,
and give honour to the God of Israel; perhaps he will relax the pressure of
6 his hand on you, on your god, and on your land. Why should you be stubborn like Pharaoh and the Egyptians? Remember how this god made
7 sport of them until they let Israel go. Now make a new wagon ready with
two milch-cows which have never been yoked; harness the cows to the
wagon, and take their calves from them and drive them back to their stalls.
8 Then take the Ark of the LORD and put it on the wagon, place in a casket,
beside it, the gold offerings that you are sending to him as an indemnity,
9 and let it go where it will. Watch it: if it goes up towards its own territory
to Beth-shemesh, then it is the LORD who has done us this great injury;
but if not, then we shall know that his hand has not touched us, but we
have been the victims of chance.'

10   The men did this. They took two milch-cows and harnessed them to a
11 wagon, shutting up their calves in the stall, and they placed the Ark of the
LORD on the wagon together with the casket, the gold rats, and the models
12 of their haemorrhoids. Then the cows went straight in the direction of
Beth-shemesh; they kept to the same road, lowing as they went and turning
neither right nor left, while the Philistine princes followed them as far as
13 the territory of Beth-shemesh. Now the people of Beth-shemesh were
harvesting their wheat in the Vale, and when they looked up and saw the
14 Ark they rejoiced at the sight of it. The wagon came to the farm of Joshua
of Beth-shemesh and halted there. Close by stood a great stone; so they
chopped up the wood of the wagon and offered the cows as a whole-
15 offering to the LORD. Then the Levites lifted down the Ark of the LORD
and the casket containing the gold offerings, and laid them on the great
stone; and the men of Beth-shemesh offered whole-offerings and shared-
16 offerings that day to the LORD. The five princes of the Philistines watched
all this, and returned to Ekron the same day.

17   These golden haemorrhoids which the Philistines sent back as a gift of
indemnity to the LORD were for Ashdod, Gaza, Ashkelon, Gath, and
18 Ekron, one for each city. The gold rats were for all the towns of the Philistines governed by the five princes, both fortified towns and open settlements. The great stone where they deposited the Ark of the LORD stands
witness on the farm of Joshua of Beth-shemesh to this very day.

19   But the sons of Jeconiah did not rejoice with the rest of the men of
Beth-shemesh when they welcomed the Ark of the LORD, and he struck
down seventy of them. The people mourned because the LORD had struck
20 them so heavy a blow, and the men of Beth-shemesh said, 'No one is safe
in the presence of the LORD, this holy God. To whom can we send it, to

be rid of him?' So they sent this message to the inhabitants of Kiriath- 21
jearim: 'The Philistines have returned the Ark of the LORD; come down
and take charge of it.' Then the men of Kiriath-jearim came and took the 7
Ark of the LORD away; they brought it into the house of Abinadab on the
hill and consecrated his son Eleazar as its custodian.

Samuel judge over Israel

SO FOR A LONG WHILE the Ark was housed in Kiriath-jearim; and 2
after some time, twenty years later, there was a movement throughout
Israel to follow the LORD. So Samuel addressed these words to the whole 3
nation: 'If your return to the LORD is whole-hearted, banish the foreign
gods and the Ashtaroth from your shrines; turn to the LORD with heart
and mind, and worship him alone, and he will deliver you from the Philistines.' The Israelites then banished the Baalim and the Ashtaroth, and 4
worshipped the LORD alone.

Samuel summoned all Israel to an assembly at Mizpah, so that he might 5
intercede with the LORD for them. When they had assembled there, they 6
drew water and poured it out before the LORD and fasted all day, confessing
that they had sinned against the LORD. It was at Mizpah that Samuel acted
as judge over Israel.

When the Philistines heard that the Israelites had assembled at Mizpah, 7
their princes marched against them. The Israelites heard that the Philistines were advancing, and they were afraid. They said to Samuel, 'Do 8
not cease to pray for us to the LORD our God to save us from the power of
the Philistines.' Thereupon Samuel took a sucking lamb, offered it up 9
complete as a whole-offering and prayed aloud to the LORD on behalf of
Israel; and the LORD answered his prayer. As Samuel was offering the 10
sacrifice and the Philistines were advancing to battle with the Israelites,
the LORD thundered loud and long over the Philistines and threw them into
confusion. They fled in panic before the Israelites, who set out from Mizpah 11
in pursuit and kept up the slaughter of the Philistines till they reached a
point below Beth-car. There Samuel took a stone and set it up as a monu- 12
ment between Mizpah and Jeshanah,[a] naming it Eben-ezer,[b] 'for to this
point', he said, 'the LORD has helped us.' Thus the Philistines were sub- 13
dued and no longer encroached on the territory of Israel; and the hand
of the LORD was against them as long as Samuel lived. The cities they had 14
captured were restored to Israel, and from Ekron to Gath the borderland
was freed from their control. Between Israel and the Amorites peace was
maintained. Samuel acted as judge in Israel as long as he lived, and every 15 16
year went on circuit to Bethel and Gilgal and Mizpah; he dispensed justice
at all these places, returning always to Ramah. That was his home and 17
the place from which he governed Israel, and there he built an altar to
the LORD.

[a] *Prob. rdg. (cp. 2 Chr. 13. 19); Heb.* the tooth.   [b] *That is* Stone of Help.

Saul anointed king

8 WHEN SAMUEL GREW OLD, he appointed his sons to be judges in
2 Israel. The eldest son was named Joel and the second Abiah; they
3 acted as judges in Beersheba. His sons did not follow in their father's
footsteps but were intent on their own profit, taking bribes and perverting
4 the course of justice. So all the elders of Israel met, and came to Samuel
5 at Ramah and said to him, 'You are now old and your sons do not follow
6 in your footsteps; appoint us a king to govern us, like other nations.' But
their request for a king to govern them displeased Samuel, and he prayed
7 to the LORD. The LORD answered Samuel, 'Listen to the people and all
that they are saying; they have not rejected you, it is I whom they have
8 rejected, I whom they will not have to be their king. They are now doing
to you just what they have done to me since I brought them up from Egypt:
9 they have forsaken me and worshipped other gods. Hear what they have
to say now, but give them a solemn warning and tell them what sort of king
10 will govern them.' Samuel told the people who were asking him for a king
11 all that the LORD had said to him. 'This will be the sort of king who will
govern you', he said. 'He will take your sons and make them serve in his
chariots and with his cavalry, and will make them run before his chariot.
12 Some he will appoint officers over units of a thousand and units of fifty.
Others will plough his fields and reap his harvest; others again will make
13 weapons of war and equipment for mounted troops. He will take your
14 daughters for perfumers, cooks, and confectioners, and will seize the best
of your cornfields, vineyards, and olive-yards, and give them to his lackeys.
15 He will take a tenth of your grain and your vintage to give to his eunuchs
16 and lackeys. Your slaves, both men and women, and the best of your cattle
17 and your asses he will seize and put to his own use. He will take a tenth of
18 your flocks, and you yourselves will become his slaves. When that day
comes, you will cry out against the king whom you have chosen; but it
19 will be too late, the LORD will not answer you.' The people refused to listen
20 to Samuel; 'No,' they said, 'we will have a king over us; then we shall be
like other nations, with a king to govern us, to lead us out to war and fight
21 our battles.' So Samuel, when he had heard what the people said, told the
22 LORD; and he answered, 'Take them at their word and appoint them a
king.' Samuel then dismissed all the men of Israel to their homes.

9 There was a man from the district of Benjamin, whose name was Kish
son of Abiel, son of Zeror, son of Bechorath, son of Aphiah a Benjamite.
2 He was a man of substance, and had a son named Saul, a young man in
his prime; there was no better man among the Israelites than he. He was
a head taller than any of his fellows.
3 One day some asses belonging to Saul's father Kish had strayed, so he
said to his son Saul, 'Take one of the servants with you, and go and look
4 for the asses.' They crossed the hill-country of Ephraim and went through
the district of Shalisha but did not find them; they passed through the
district of Shaalim but they were not there; they passed through the
5 district of Benjamin but again did not find them. When they had entered
the district of Zuph, Saul said to the servant with him, 'Come, we ought to

turn back, or my father will stop thinking about the asses and begin to
worry about us.' The servant answered, 'There is a man of God in the city 6
here, who has a great reputation, because everything he says comes true.
Suppose we go there; he may tell us something about this errand of ours.'
Saul said, 'If we do go, what shall we offer him? There is no food left in 7
our packs and we have no present for the man of God, nothing at all.' The 8
servant answered him again, 'Wait! I have here a quarter-shekel of silver.
I can give that to the man, to tell us what we should do.' Saul said, 'Good! 10*a*
let us go to him.' So they went to the city where the man of God was. (In 9
days gone by in Israel, when a man wished to consult God, he would say,
'Let us go to the seer.' For what is nowadays called a prophet used to be
called a seer.) As they were going up the hill to the city they met some girls 11
coming out to draw water and asked, 'Shall we find the seer there?' 'Yes,' 12
they said, 'the seer is ahead of you now; he has just *b* arrived in the city
because there is a feast at the hill-shrine today. As you enter the city you 13
will meet him before he goes up to the shrine to eat; the people will not
start until he comes, for he has to bless the sacrifice before the company
can eat. Go up now, and you will find him at once.' So they went up to the 14
city, and just as they were going in, there was Samuel coming towards them
on his way up to the shrine.

Now the day before Saul came, the LORD had disclosed his intention to 15
Samuel in these words: 'At this same time tomorrow I will send you a man 16
from the land of Benjamin. Anoint him prince over my people Israel, and
then he shall deliver my people from the Philistines. I have seen the
sufferings of my people and their cry has reached my ears.' The moment 17
Saul appeared the LORD said to Samuel, 'Here is the man of whom I
spoke to you. This man shall rule my people.' Saul came up to Samuel in 18
the gateway and said, 'Would you tell me where the seer lives?' Samuel 19
replied, 'I am the seer. Go on ahead of me to the hill-shrine and you shall
eat with me today; in the morning I will set you on your way, after telling
you what you have on your mind. Trouble yourself no more about the 20
asses lost three days ago, for they have been found. But what is it that all
Israel is wanting? It is you and your ancestral house.' 'But I am a Benjamite,' 21
said Saul, 'from the smallest of the tribes of Israel, and my family is the
least important of all the families of the tribe of Benjamin. Why do you
say this to me?' Samuel then brought Saul and his servant into the dining- 22
hall and gave them a place at the head of the company, which numbered
about thirty. Then he said to the cook, 'Bring the portion that I gave you 23
and told you to put on one side.' So the cook took up the whole haunch 24
and leg and put it before Saul; and Samuel said, 'Here is the portion of
meat *c* kept for you. Eat it: it has been reserved for you at this feast to
which I have invited the people.' So Saul dined with Samuel that day, and 25
when they came down from the hill-shrine to the city a bed was spread on
the roof for Saul, and he stayed there that night. At dawn Samuel called 26
to Saul on the roof, 'Get up, and I will set you on your way.' When Saul

a *Verses 9 and 10 transposed.*   *b* the seer . . . just: *prob. rdg.; Heb.* he is ahead of
you, hurry now, for he has today . . .   *c* the portion of meat: *prob. rdg.; Heb.* what
is left over.

27 rose, he and Samuel went out together into the street. As they came to the end of the town, Samuel said to Saul, 'Tell the boy to go on.' He did so, and then Samuel said, 'Stay here a moment, and I will tell you the word of God.'

10 Samuel took a flask of oil and poured it over Saul's head, and he kissed him and said, 'The LORD anoints you prince over his people Israel; you shall rule the people of the LORD and deliver them from the enemies round about them. You shall have a sign that the LORD has anointed you prince 2 to govern his inheritance: when you leave me today, you will meet two men by the tomb of Rachel at Zelzah in the territory of Benjamin. They will tell you that the asses you are looking for have been found and that your father is concerned for them no longer; he is anxious about you and says 3 again and again, "What shall I do about my son?" From there go across country as far as the terebinth of Tabor, where three men going up to Bethel to worship God will meet you. One of them will be carrying three 4 kids, the second three loaves, and the third a flagon of wine. They will greet you and will offer you two loaves, which you will accept from them. 5 Then when you reach the Hill of God, where the Philistine governor *a* resides, you will meet a company of prophets coming down from the hill-shrine, led by lute, harp, fife, and drum, and filled with prophetic rapture. 6 Then the spirit of the LORD will suddenly take possession of you, and you 7 too will be rapt like a prophet and become another man. When these signs 8 happen, do whatever the occasion demands; God will be with you. You shall go down to Gilgal ahead of me, and I will come to you to sacrifice whole-offerings and shared-offerings. Wait seven days until I join you; 9 then I will tell you what to do.' As Saul turned to leave Samuel, God gave 10 him a new heart. On that same day all these signs happened. When they reached the Hill there was a company of prophets coming to meet him, and the spirit of God suddenly took possession of him, so that he too was filled 11 with prophetic rapture. When people who had known him previously saw that he was rapt like the prophets, they said to one another, 'What can 12 have happened to the son of Kish? Is Saul also among the prophets?' One of the men of that place said, 'And whose sons are they?' Hence the pro- 13 verb, 'Is Saul also among the prophets?' When the prophetic rapture had 14 passed, he went home. *b* Saul's uncle said to him and the boy, 'Where have you been?' Saul answered, 'To look for the asses, and when we could not 15 find them, we went to Samuel.' His uncle said, 'Tell me what Samuel said.' 16 'He told us that the asses had been found', said Saul; but he did not repeat what Samuel had said about his being king.

17 Meanwhile Samuel summoned the Israelites to the LORD at Mizpah 18 and said to the people, 'This is the word of the LORD the God of Israel: I brought Israel up from Egypt; I delivered you from the Egyptians and 19 from all the kingdoms that oppressed you; but today you have rejected your God who saved you from all your misery and distress; you have said, "No, set up a king over us." Now therefore take up your positions before 20 the LORD tribe by tribe and clan by clan.' Samuel then presented all the 21 tribes of Israel, and Benjamin was picked by lot. Then he presented the

---

a Or garrison.   *b* *Prob. rdg.; Heb.* to the hill-shrine.

tribe of Benjamin, family by family, and the family of Matri was picked. Then he presented the family of Matri, man by man, and Saul son of Kish was picked; but when they looked for him he could not be found. They 22 went on to ask the LORD, 'Will the man be coming back?' The LORD answered, 'There he is, hiding among the baggage.' So someone ran and 23 fetched him out, and as he took his stand among the people, he was a head taller than anyone else. Samuel said to the people, 'Look at the man whom 24 the LORD has chosen; there is no one like him in this whole nation.' They all acclaimed him, shouting, 'Long live the king!' Samuel then explained 25 to the people the nature of a king, and made a written record of it on a scroll which he deposited before the LORD; he then dismissed them to their homes. Saul too went home to Gibeah, and with him went some fighting 26 men whose hearts God had moved. But there were scoundrels who said, 27 'How can this fellow deliver us?' They thought nothing of him and brought him no gifts.

About a month later Nahash the Ammonite attacked and besieged 11 Jabesh-gilead. The men of Jabesh said to Nahash, 'Come to terms with us and we will be your subjects.' Nahash answered them, 'On one con- 2 dition only will I come to terms with you: that I gouge out your right eyes and bring disgrace on Israel.' The elders of Jabesh-gilead then said, 'Give 3 us seven days' respite to send messengers throughout Israel and then, if no one relieves us, we will surrender to you.' When the messengers came 4 to Gibeah, where Saul lived, and delivered their message, all the people broke into lamentation. Saul was just coming from the field driving in the 5 oxen, and asked why the people were lamenting; and they repeated what the men of Jabesh had said. When Saul heard this, the spirit of God 6 suddenly seized him. In his anger he took a pair of oxen and cut them in 7 pieces, and sent messengers with the pieces all through Israel to proclaim that the same would be done to the oxen of any man who did not follow Saul and Samuel into battle. The fear of the LORD fell upon the people and they came out, to a man. Saul mustered them in Bezek; there were three 8 hundred thousand men from Israel and thirty thousand from Judah. He said to the men who brought the message, 'Tell the men of Jabesh- 9 gilead, "Victory will be yours tomorrow by the time the sun is hot."' The men of Jabesh heard what the messengers reported and took heart; and 10 they said to Nahash, 'Tomorrow we will surrender to you, and then you may deal with us as you think fit.' Next day Saul drew up his men in three 11 columns; they forced their way right into the enemy camp during the morning watch and massacred the Ammonites while the day grew hot, after which the survivors scattered until no two men were left together.

Then the people said to Samuel, 'Who said that Saul should not reign 12 over us? Hand the men over to us to be put to death.' But Saul said, 'No 13 man shall be put to death on a day when the LORD has won such a victory in Israel.' Samuel said to the people, 'Let us now go to Gilgal and there 14 renew our allegiance to the kingdom.' So they all went to Gilgal and 15 invested Saul there as king in the presence of the LORD, sacrificing shared-offerings before the LORD; and Saul and all the Israelites celebrated the occasion with great joy.

12 Then samuel thus addressed the assembled Israelites: 'I have
2 listened to your request and installed a king to rule over you. And the king
is now your leader, while I am old and white-haired and my sons are with
3 you; but I have been your leader ever since I was a child. Here I am. Lay
your complaints against me in the presence of the Lord and of his anointed
king. Whose ox have I taken, whose ass have I taken? Whom have I
wronged, whom have I oppressed? From whom have I taken a bribe, to
4 turn a blind eye? Tell me, and I will make restitution.' They answered,
'You have not wronged us, you have not oppressed us; you have not taken
5 anything from any man.' Samuel then said to them, 'This day the Lord
is witness among you, his anointed king is witness, that you have found
6 my hands empty.' They said, 'He is witness.' Samuel said to the people,
'Yes, the Lord is witness, the Lord who gave you Moses and Aaron and
7 brought your fathers out of Egypt. Now stand up, and here in the presence
of the Lord I will put the case against you and recite all the victories which
8 he has won for you and for your fathers. After Jacob and his sons had come
down to Egypt and the Egyptians had made them suffer, your fathers cried
to the Lord for help, and he sent Moses and Aaron, who brought them out
9 of Egypt and settled them in this place. But they forgot the Lord their
God, and he abandoned them to Sisera, commander-in-chief of Jabin
king of Hazor, to the Philistines, and to the king of Moab, and they had to
10 fight against them. Then your fathers cried to the Lord for help: "We
have sinned, we have forsaken the Lord and we have worshipped the
Baalim and the Ashtaroth. But now, if thou wilt deliver us from our
11 enemies, we will worship thee." So the Lord sent Jerubbaal and Barak,
Jephthah and Samson, and delivered you from your enemies on every
side; and you lived in peace and quiet.

12 'Then, when you saw Nahash king of the Ammonites coming against
you, although the Lord your God was your king, you said to me, "No, let
13 us have a king to rule over us." Now, here is the king you asked for; you
14 chose him, and the Lord has set a king over you. If you will revere the Lord
and give true and loyal service, if you do not rebel against his commands,
and if you and the king who reigns over you are faithful to the Lord your
15 God, well and good; but if you do not obey the Lord, and if you rebel
against his commands, then he will set his face against you and against
your king.

16 'Stand still, and see the great wonder which the Lord will do before your
17 eyes. It is now wheat harvest; when I call upon the Lord and he sends
thunder and rain, you will see and know how wicked it was in the Lord's
18 eyes for you to ask for a king.' So Samuel called upon the Lord and he
sent thunder and rain that day; and all the people were in great fear of the
19 Lord and of Samuel. They said to Samuel, 'Pray for us your servants to
the Lord your God, to save us from death; for we have added to all our
20 other sins the great wickedness of asking for a king.' Samuel said to the
people, 'Do not be afraid; although you have been so wicked, do not give
21 up the worship of the Lord, but serve him with all your heart. Give up
the worship of false gods which can neither help nor save, because they
22 are false. For his name's sake the Lord will not cast you off, because he

has resolved to make you his own people. As for me, God forbid that I 23
should sin against the LORD and cease to pray for you. I will show you what
is right and good: to revere the LORD and worship him faithfully with all 24
your heart. Consider what great things he has done for you; but if you per- 25
sist in wickedness, you shall be swept away, you and your king.'

Saul was fifty years*a* old when he became king, and he reigned over 13
Israel for twenty-two *b* years. He picked three thousand men from Israel, 2
two thousand to be with him in Michmash and the hill-country of Bethel
and a thousand to be with Jonathan in Gibeah of Benjamin; and he sent
the rest of the people home.

Jonathan killed the Philistine governor*c* in Geba, and the news spread 3
among the Philistines that the Hebrews were in revolt.*d* Saul sounded
the trumpet all through the land; and when the Israelites all heard that 4
Saul had killed a Philistine governor and that the name of Israel stank
among the Philistines, they answered the call to arms and came to join
Saul at Gilgal.*e* The Philistines mustered to attack Israel; they had thirty 5
thousand chariots and six thousand horse, with infantry as countless as
sand on the sea-shore. They went up and camped at Michmash, to the east
of Beth-aven. The Israelites found themselves in sore straits, for the army 6
was hard pressed, so they hid themselves in caves and holes and among the
rocks, in pits and cisterns. Some of them crossed the Jordan into the 7
district of Gad and Gilead, but Saul remained at Gilgal, and all the people
at his back were in alarm.*f* He waited seven days for his meeting with 8
Samuel, but Samuel did not come to Gilgal; so the people began to drift
away from Saul. He said therefore, 'Bring me the whole-offering and the 9
shared-offerings', and he offered up the whole-offering. Saul had just 10
finished the sacrifice, when Samuel arrived, and he went out to greet him.
Samuel said, 'What have you done?', and Saul answered, 'I saw that the 11
people were drifting away from me, and you yourself had not come as
you had promised, and the Philistines were assembling at Michmash; and 12
I thought, "The Philistines will now move against me at Gilgal, and I
have not placated the LORD"; so I felt compelled to make the whole-
offering myself.' Samuel said to Saul, 'You have behaved foolishly. You 13
have not kept the command laid on you by the LORD your God; if you had,
he would have established your dynasty over Israel for all time. But now 14
your line will not endure; the LORD will seek a man after his own heart, and
will appoint him prince over his people, because you have not kept the
LORD's command.'

Samuel left Gilgal without more ado and went on his way. The rest of 15
the people followed Saul, as he moved from Gilgal towards the enemy.
At Gibeah of Benjamin he mustered the people who were with him; they
were about six hundred men. Saul and his son Jonathan and the men they 16
had with them took up their quarters in Gibeah of Benjamin, while the
Philistines were encamped in Michmash. Raiding parties went out from 17

a fifty years: *prob. rdg.; Heb.* a year.   *b Prob. rdg.; Heb.* two.   *c Or* garrison.
d that . . . revolt: *prob. rdg.; Heb. has* saying, Let the Hebrews hear *after* through the
land.   *e* they answered . . . Gilgal: *or* they were summoned to follow Saul to Gilgal.
f but Saul . . . in alarm: *or* but Saul was still at Gilgal, and all the army joined him there.

the Philistine camp in three directions. One party turned towards Ophrah
18 in the district of Shual, another towards Beth-horon, and the third towards
the range of hills overlooking the valley of Zeboim and the wilderness
beyond.

19 No blacksmith was to be found in the whole of Israel, for the Philistines
were determined to prevent the Hebrews from making swords and spears.
20 The Israelites had to go down to the Philistines for their ploughshares,
21 mattocks, axes, and sickles to be sharpened. The charge was two-thirds of
a shekel for ploughshares and mattocks, and one-third of a shekel for
22 sharpening the axes and setting the goads.*a* So when war broke out none
of the followers of Saul and Jonathan had either sword or spear; only Saul
and Jonathan carried arms.

23 Now the Philistines had posted a force to hold the pass of Michmash;
14 and one day Saul's son Jonathan said to his armour-bearer, 'Come, let us
go over to the Philistine post beyond that ridge'; but he did not tell his
2 father. Saul, at the time, had his tent under the pomegranate-tree at
Migron on the outskirts of Gibeah; and he had about six hundred men
3 with him. The ephod was carried by Ahijah son of Ahitub, Ichabod's
brother, son of Phinehas son of Eli, the priest of the LORD at Shiloh.
4 Nobody knew that Jonathan had gone. On either side of the pass through
which Jonathan tried to make his way over to the Philistine post stood two
5 sharp columns of rock, called Bozez*b* and Seneh; *c* one of them was on the
north towards Michmash, and the other on the south towards Geba.
6 Jonathan said to his armour-bearer, 'Now we will visit the post of those
uncircumcised rascals. Perhaps the LORD will take a hand in it, and if he
will, nothing can stop him. He can bring us safe through, whether we are
7 few or many.' The young man answered, 'Do what you will, go forward;
8 I am with you whatever you do.' 'Good!' said Jonathan, 'we will cross over
9 and let them see us. If they say, "Stay where you are till we come to you",
10 then we will stay where we are and not go up to them. But if they say,
"Come up to us", we will go up; this will be the sign that the LORD has put
11 them into our power.' So they showed themselves to the Philistines, and
the Philistines said, 'Look! Hebrews coming out of the holes where they
12 have been hiding!' And they called across to Jonathan and the young man,
'Come up to us; we have something to show you.' Jonathan said to the
young man, 'Come on, the LORD has put them into the power of Israel.'
13 Jonathan climbed up on hands and feet, and the young man followed him.
The Philistines fell in front of Jonathan, and the young man, coming
14 behind him, dispatched them. In that first attack Jonathan and his armour-
bearer killed about twenty of them, like men cutting a furrow across a
15 half-acre field. Terror spread through the army in the field and through
the whole people; the men at the post and the raiding parties were terrified;
the very earth quaked, and there was panic.

16 Saul's men on the watch in Gibeah of Benjamin saw the mob of Philis-
17 tines surging to and fro in confusion; so he ordered the people to call the
roll and find out who was missing; and they called the roll and found that

a one-third . . . the goads: *prob. rdg.; Heb. obscure.*   *b* *That is Shining.*   *c* *That
is* Bramble-bush.

Jonathan and his armour-bearer were absent. Saul said to Ahijah, 'Bring 18
forward the ephod', for it was he who carried the ephod at that time before
Israel. But while Saul was still speaking, the confusion in the Philistine 19
camp was increasing more and more, and he said to the priest, 'Hold your
hand.' Then Saul and all his men with shouting made for the battlefield, 20
where they found the enemy fighting one another in complete disorder.
The Hebrews who up to now had been under the Philistines, and had been 21
with them in camp, changed sides and joined the Israelites under Saul and
Jonathan. All the Israelites in hiding in the hill-country of Ephraim heard 22
that the Philistines were in flight, and they also joined in and set off in hot
pursuit. The LORD delivered Israel that day, and the fighting passed on 23
beyond Beth-aven.

Now the Israelites on that day had been driven to exhaustion. Saul had 24
adjured the people in these words: 'A curse be on the man who eats any
food before nightfall until I have taken vengeance on my enemies.' So no
one ate any food. Now there was honeycomb^a in the country-side; but 25 26
when his men came upon it, dripping with honey though it was, not one
of them put his hand to his mouth for fear of the oath. But Jonathan had 27
not heard his father lay this solemn prohibition on the people, and he
stretched out the stick that was in his hand, dipped the end of it in the
honeycomb, put it to his mouth and was refreshed. One of the people said 28
to him, 'Your father solemnly forbade this; he said, "A curse on the man
who eats food today!"' Now the men were faint with hunger. Jonathan 29
said, 'My father has done the people nothing but harm; see how I am
refreshed by this mere taste of honey. How much better if the people had 30
eaten today whatever they took from their enemies by way of spoil! Then
there would indeed have been a great slaughter of Philistines.'

They defeated the Philistines that day, and pursued them from Mich- 31
mash to Aijalon. But the people were so faint with hunger that they turned 32
to plunder and seized sheep, cattle, and bullocks; they slaughtered them
on the bare ground, and ate the meat with the blood in it. Someone told 33
Saul that the people were sinning against the LORD by eating their meat with
the blood in it. 'This is treason!' cried Saul. 'Roll a great stone here at
once.' He then said, 'Go about among the people and tell them to bring 34
their oxen and sheep, and let each man slaughter his here and eat it; and
so they will not sin against the LORD by eating meat with the blood in it.'
So as night fell each man came, driving his own ox, and slaughtered it
there. Thus Saul came to build an altar to the LORD, and this was the first 35
altar to the LORD that Saul built.

Saul said, 'Let us go down and make a night attack on the Philistines 36
and harry them till daylight; we will not spare a man of them.' The people
answered, 'Do what you think best', but the priest said, 'Let us first consult
God.' So Saul inquired of God, 'Shall I pursue the Philistines? Wilt 37
thou put them into Israel's power?'; but this time he received no answer.
So he said, 'Let all the leaders of the people come forward and let us find 38
out where the sin lies this day. As the LORD lives, the deliverer of Israel, 39

---

^a *Now . . . honeycomb: prob. rdg.; Heb.* All the land went into the forest, and there was
honey.

even if it lies in my son Jonathan, he shall die.' Not a soul answered him.
40 Then he said to the Israelites, 'All of you stand on one side, and I and my
son Jonathan will stand on the other.' The people answered, 'Do what you
41 think best.' Saul said to the LORD the God of Israel, 'Why hast thou not
answered thy servant today? If this guilt lie in me or in my son Jonathan,
O LORD God of Israel, let the lot be Urim; if it lie in thy people Israel,
let it be Thummim.' Jonathan and Saul were taken, and the people were
42 cleared. Then Saul said, 'Cast lots between me and my son Jonathan';
43 and Jonathan was taken. Saul said to Jonathan, 'Tell me what you have
done.' Jonathan told him, 'True, I did taste a little honey on the tip of my
44 stick. Here I am; I am ready to die.' Then Saul swore a great oath that
45 Jonathan should die. But the people said to Saul, 'Shall Jonathan die,
Jonathan who has won this great victory in Israel? God forbid! As the
LORD lives, not a hair of his head shall fall to the ground, for he has been
at work with God today.' So the people ransomed Jonathan and he did not
46 die. Saul broke off the pursuit of the Philistines because they had made their
way home.

47 When Saul had made his throne secure in Israel, he fought against his
enemies on every side, the Moabites, the Ammonites, the Edomites, the
king of Zobah, and the Philistines; and wherever he turned he was success-
48 ful.*a* He displayed his strength by defeating the Amalekites and freeing
Israel from hostile raids.

49 Saul's sons were: Jonathan, Ishyo and Malchishua. These were the
50 names of his two daughters: Merab the elder and Michal the younger. His
wife was Ahinoam daughter of Ahimaaz, and his commander-in-chief
51 was Abner son of his uncle Ner; Kish, Saul's father, and Ner, Abner's
father, were sons*b* of Abiel.

52 There was bitter warfare with the Philistines throughout Saul's lifetime;
any strong man and any brave man that he found he took into his own
service.

15 Samuel said to Saul, 'The LORD sent me to anoint you king over his
2 people Israel. Now listen to the voice of the LORD. This is the very word of
the LORD of Hosts: "I am resolved to punish the Amalekites for what they
3 did to Israel, how they attacked them on their way up from Egypt." Go
now and fall upon the Amalekites and destroy them, and put their property
under ban. Spare no one; put them all to death, men and women, children
4 and babes in arms, herds and flocks, camels and asses.' Thereupon Saul
called out the levy and mustered them in Telaim. There were two hundred
5 thousand foot-soldiers and another ten thousand from Judah.*c* He came
6 to the Amalekite city and halted for a time in the gorge. Meanwhile he sent
word to the Kenites to leave the Amalekites and come down, 'or', he said,
'I shall destroy you as well as them; but you were friendly to Israel when
7 they came up from Egypt.' So the Kenites left the Amalekites. Then Saul
cut the Amalekites to pieces, all the way from Havilah to Shur on the borders
8 of Egypt. Agag the king of the Amalekites he took alive, but he destroyed
9 all the people, putting them to the sword. Saul and his army spared Agag

a Or he found ample provision.   *b Prob. rdg.; Heb.* son.   *c Prob. rdg.; Heb.*
ten thousand with the men of Judah.

and the best of the sheep and cattle, the fat beasts and the lambs and everything worth keeping; they were unwilling to destroy them, but anything
that was useless and of no value they destroyed.

Then the word of the LORD came to Samuel: 'I repent of having made   10 11
Saul king, for he has turned his back on me and has not obeyed my commands.' Samuel was angry; all night he cried aloud to the LORD. Early   12
next morning he went to meet Saul, but was told that he had gone to
Carmel; Saul had set up a monument for himself there, and had then
turned and gone down to Gilgal. There Samuel found him, and Saul   13
greeted him with the words, 'The LORD's blessing upon you! I have
obeyed the LORD's commands.' But Samuel said, 'What then is this bleat-   14
ing of sheep in my ears? Why do I hear the lowing of cattle?' Saul answered,   15
'The people have taken them from the Amalekites. These are what they
spared, the best of the sheep and cattle, to sacrifice to the LORD your God.
The rest we completely destroyed.' Samuel said to Saul, 'Let be, and I will   16
tell you what the LORD said to me last night.' 'Tell me', said Saul. So   17
Samuel went on, 'Time was when you thought little of yourself, but now
you are head of the tribes of Israel, and the LORD has anointed you king
over Israel. The LORD sent you with strict instructions to destroy that   18
wicked nation, the Amalekites; you were to fight against them until you
had wiped them out. Why then did you not obey the LORD? Why did you   19
pounce upon the spoil and do what was wrong in the eyes of the LORD?'
Saul answered Samuel, 'But I did obey the LORD; I went where the LORD   20
sent me, and I have brought back Agag king of the Amalekites. The rest
of them I destroyed. Out of the spoil the people took sheep and oxen, the   21
choicest of the animals laid under ban, to sacrifice to the LORD your God
at Gilgal.' Samuel then said: 22

> Does the LORD desire offerings and sacrifices
>   as he desires obedience?
> Obedience is better than sacrifice,
>   and to listen to him than the fat of rams.
> Defiance of him is sinful as witchcraft,   23
>   yielding to men*a* as evil as*b* idolatry.*c*
> Because you have rejected the word of the LORD,
>   the LORD has rejected you as king.

Saul said to Samuel, 'I have sinned. I have ignored the LORD's com-   24
mand and your orders: I was afraid of the people and deferred to them.
But now forgive my sin, I implore you, and come back with me, and I will   25
make my submission before the LORD.' Samuel answered, 'I will not come   26
back with you; you have rejected the word of the LORD and therefore the
LORD has rejected you as king over Israel.' He turned to go, but Saul caught   27
the edge of his cloak and it tore. And Samuel said to him, 'The LORD has   28
torn the kingdom of Israel from your hand today and will give it to another,
a better man than you. God who is the Splendour of Israel does not deceive   29
or change his mind; he is not a man that he should change his mind.' Saul   30

a yielding to men: *or* arrogance *or* obstinacy.   *b* as evil as: *prob. rdg.; Heb.* evil
and . . .   *c* *Or* household gods; *Heb.* teraphim.

said, 'I have sinned; but honour me this once before the elders of my people and before Israel and come back with me, and I will make my submission
31 to the LORD your God.' So Samuel went back with Saul, and Saul made
32 his submission to the LORD. Then Samuel said, 'Bring Agag king of the Amalekites.' So Agag came to him with faltering step and said, 'Surely the
33 bitterness of death has passed.' Samuel said, 'Your sword has made women childless, and your mother of all women shall be childless too.' Then Samuel hewed Agag in pieces before the LORD at Gilgal.
34 35 Saul went to his own home at Gibeah, and Samuel went to Ramah; and he never saw Saul again to his dying day, but he mourned for him, because the LORD had repented of having made him king over Israel.

Saul and David

16 THE LORD SAID TO SAMUEL, 'How long will you mourn for Saul because I have rejected him as king over Israel? Fill your horn with oil and take it with you; I am sending you to Jesse of Bethlehem; for I
2 have chosen myself a king among his sons.' Samuel answered, 'How can I go? Saul will hear of it and kill me.' 'Take a heifer with you,' said the
3 LORD; 'say you have come to offer a sacrifice to the LORD, and invite Jesse to the sacrifice; then I will let you know what you must do. You shall
4 anoint for me the man whom I show you.' Samuel did as the LORD had told him, and went to Bethlehem. The elders of the city came in haste to
5 meet him, saying, 'Why have you come? Is all well?' 'All is well,' said Samuel; 'I have come to sacrifice to the LORD. Hallow yourselves and come with me to the sacrifice.' He himself hallowed Jesse and his sons and
6 invited them to the sacrifice also. They came, and when Samuel saw Eliab
7 he thought, 'Here, before the LORD, is his anointed king.' But the LORD said to him, 'Take no account of it if he is handsome and tall; I reject him. The LORD does not see as man sees; men judge by appearances but the
8 LORD judges by the heart.' Then Jesse called Abinadab and made him pass before Samuel, but he said, 'No, the LORD has not chosen this one.'
9 Then he presented Shammah, and Samuel said, 'Nor has the LORD chosen
10 him.' Seven of his sons Jesse presented to Samuel, but he said, 'The LORD
11 has not chosen any of these.' Then Samuel asked, 'Are these all?' Jesse answered, 'There is still the youngest, but he is looking after the sheep.' Samuel said to Jesse, 'Send and fetch him; we will not sit down until he
12 comes.' So he sent and fetched him. He was handsome, with ruddy cheeks and bright eyes.[a] The LORD said, 'Rise and anoint him: this is the man.'
13 Samuel took the horn of oil and anointed him in the presence of his brothers. Then the spirit of the LORD came upon David and was with him from that day onwards. And Samuel set out on his way back to Ramah.
14 The spirit of the LORD had forsaken Saul, and at times an evil spirit
15 from the LORD would seize him suddenly. His servants said to him, 'You
16 see, sir, how an evil spirit from God seizes you; why do you not command your servants here to go and find some man who can play the harp?—then,

[a] *and bright eyes: prob. rdg.; Heb. obscure.*

when an evil spirit from God comes on you, he can play and you will
recover.' Saul said to his servants, 'Find me a man who can play well and 17
bring him to me.' One of his attendants said, 'I have seen a son of Jesse of 18
Bethlehem who can play; he is a brave man and a good fighter, wise in
speech and handsome, and the LORD is with him.' Saul therefore sent 19
messengers to Jesse and asked him to send him his son David, who was
with the sheep. Jesse took a homer of bread, a skin of wine, and a kid, and 20
sent them to Saul by his son David. David came to Saul and entered his 21
service; and Saul loved him dearly, and he became his armour-bearer. So 22
Saul sent word to Jesse: 'Let David stay in my service, for I am pleased
with him.' And whenever a spirit from God came upon Saul, David would 23
take his harp and play on it, so that Saul found relief; he recovered and the
evil spirit left him alone.

The Philistines collected their forces for war and massed at Socoh in 17
Judah; they camped between Socoh and Azekah at Ephes-dammim. Saul 2
and the Israelites also massed, and camped in the Vale of Elah. They drew
up their lines facing the Philistines, the Philistines occupying a position 3
on one hill and the Israelites on another, with a valley between them. A 4
champion came out from the Philistine camp, a man named Goliath, from
Gath; he was over nine feet in height. He had a bronze helmet on his head, 5
and he wore plate-armour of bronze, weighing five thousand shekels. On 6
his legs were bronze greaves, and one of his weapons was a dagger of bronze.
The shaft of his spear was like a weaver's beam, and its head, which was 7
of iron, weighed six hundred shekels; and his shield-bearer marched
ahead of him. The champion stood and shouted to the ranks of Israel, 8
'Why do you come out to do battle, you slaves of Saul? I am the Philistine
champion; choose your man to meet me. If he can kill me in fair fight, we 9
will become your slaves; but if I prove too strong for him and kill him, you
shall be our slaves and serve us. Here and now I defy the ranks of Israel. 10
Give me a man,' said the Philistine, 'and we will fight it out.' When Saul 11
and the Israelites heard what the Philistine said, they were shaken and
dismayed.

David was the son of an Ephrathite*a* called Jesse, who had eight sons. 12
By Saul's time he had become a feeble old man, and his three eldest sons 13
had followed Saul to the war. The eldest was called Eliab, the next Abinadab, and the third Shammah; David was the youngest. The three eldest 14
followed Saul, while David used to go to Saul's camp and back to Bethlehem 15
to mind his father's flocks.

Morning and evening for forty days the Philistine came forward and 16
took up his position. Then one day Jesse said to his son David, 'Take your 17
brothers an ephah of this parched grain and these ten loaves of bread, and
run with them to the camp. These ten cream-cheeses are for you to take 18
to the commanding officer. See if your brothers are well and bring back
some token from them.' Saul and the brothers and all the Israelites were 19
in the Vale of Elah, fighting the Philistines. Early next morning David 20
left someone in charge of the sheep, set out on his errand and went as
Jesse had told him. He reached the lines just as the army was going out to

---

a Prob. rdg.; Heb. adds Is this the man from Bethlehem in Judah?

21 take up position and was raising the war-cry. The Israelites and the
22 Philistines drew up their ranks opposite each other. David left his things
   in charge of the quartermaster, ran to the line and went up to his brothers
23 to greet them. While he was talking to them the Philistine champion,
   Goliath, came out from the Philistine ranks and issued his challenge in the
24 same words as before; and David heard him. When the Israelites saw the
25 man they ran from him in fear. 'Look at this man who comes out day after
   day to defy Israel', they said. 'The king is to give a rich reward to the man
   who kills him; he will give him his daughter in marriage too and will
26 exempt his family from service due in Israel.' Then David turned to his
   neighbours and said, 'What is to be done for the man who kills this Philistine and wipes out our disgrace? And who is he, an uncircumcised Philis-
27 tine, to defy the army of the living God?' The people told him how the
28 matter stood and what was to be done for the man who killed him. His
   elder brother Eliab overheard David talking with the men and grew angry.
   'What are you doing here?' he asked. 'And who have you left to look after
   those few sheep in the wilderness? I know you, you impudent young
29 rascal; you have only come to see the fighting.' David answered, 'What
30 have I done now? I only asked a question.' And he turned away from him
   to someone else and repeated his question, but everybody gave him the
   same answer.

31   What David had said was overheard and reported to Saul, who sent for
32 him. David said to him, 'Do not lose heart, sir. I will go and fight this
33 Philistine.' Saul answered, 'You cannot go and fight with this Philistine;
34 you are only a lad, and he has been a fighting man all his life.' David said
   to Saul, 'Sir, I am my father's shepherd; when a lion or bear comes and
35 carries off a sheep from the flock, I go after it and attack it and rescue the
   victim from its jaws. Then if it turns on me, I seize it by the beard and batter
36 it to death. Lions I have killed and bears, and this uncircumcised Philistine will fare no better than they; he has defied the army of the living God.
37 The LORD who saved me from the lion and the bear will save me from this
38 Philistine.' 'Go then,' said Saul; 'and the LORD will be with you.' He put
   his own tunic on David, placed a bronze helmet on his head and gave him
39 a coat of mail to wear; he then fastened his sword on David over his tunic.
   But David hesitated, because he had not tried them, and said to Saul, 'I
   cannot go with these, because I have not tried them.' So he took them off.
40 Then he picked up his stick, chose five smooth stones from the brook and
   put them in a shepherd's bag which served as his pouch. He walked out to
   meet the Philistine with his sling in his hand.
41   The Philistine came on towards David, with his shield-bearer marching
42 ahead; and he looked David up and down and had nothing but contempt
43 for this handsome lad with his ruddy cheeks and bright eyes.[a] He said to
   David, 'Am I a dog that you come out against me with sticks?' And he
44 swore at him in the name of his god. 'Come on,' he said, 'and I will give
45 your flesh to the birds and the beasts.' David answered, 'You have come
   against me with sword and spear and dagger, but I have come against you
   in the name of the LORD of Hosts, the God of the army of Israel which you

[a] handsome . . . bright eyes: *prob. rdg.; Heb. obscure.*

have defied. The LORD will put you into my power this day; I will kill you   46
and cut your head off and leave your carcass and the carcasses of the
Philistines to the birds and the wild beasts; all the world shall know that
there is a God in Israel. All those who are gathered here shall see that the   47
LORD saves neither by sword nor spear; the battle is the LORD's, and he
will put you all into our power.'

When the Philistine began moving towards him again, David ran quickly   48
to engage him. He put his hand into his bag, took out a stone, slung it, and   49
struck the Philistine on the forehead. The stone sank into his forehead, and
he fell flat on his face on the ground. So David proved the victor with his   50
sling and stone; he struck Goliath down and gave him a mortal wound,
though he had no sword. Then he ran to the Philistine and stood over him,   51
and grasping his sword, he drew it out of the scabbard, dispatched him and
cut off his head. The Philistines, when they saw that their hero was dead,
turned and ran. The men of Israel and Judah at once raised the war-cry   52
and hotly pursued them all the way to Gath and even to the gates of Ekron.
The road that runs to Shaaraim, Gath, and Ekron was strewn with their
dead. On their return from the pursuit of the Philistines, the Israelites   53
plundered their camp. David took Goliath's head and carried it to Jerusa-   54
lem, leaving his weapons in his tent.

Saul had said to Abner his commander-in-chief, when he saw David   55
going out against the Philistine, 'That boy there, Abner, whose son is he?'
'By your life, your majesty,' said Abner, 'I do not know.' The king said   56
to Abner, 'Go and find out whose son the lad is.' When David came back   57
after killing the Philistine, Abner took him and presented him to Saul
with the Philistine's head still in his hand. Saul asked him, 'Whose son   58
are you, young man?', and David answered, 'I am the son of your servant
Jesse of Bethlehem.'

That same day, when Saul had finished talking with David, he kept him   **18** 1-2
and would not let him return any more to his father's house, for he saw that
Jonathan had given his heart to David and had grown to love him as
himself. So Jonathan and David made a solemn compact because each   3
loved the other as dearly as himself. And Jonathan stripped off the cloak   4
he was wearing and his tunic, and gave them to David, together with his
sword, his bow, and his belt. David succeeded so well in every venture on   5
which Saul sent him that he was given a command in the army, and his
promotion pleased the ordinary people, and even pleased Saul's officers.

At the home-coming of the army when David returned from the   6
slaughter of the Philistines, the women came out from all the cities of
Israel to look on, and the dancers came out to meet King Saul with tambourines, singing, and dancing. The women as they made merry sang to   7
one another:

> Saul made havoc among thousands
> but David among tens of thousands.

Saul was furious, and the words rankled. He said, 'They have given David   8
tens of thousands and me only thousands; what more can they do but
make him king?' From that day forward Saul kept a jealous eye on David.   9

10 Next day an evil spirit from God seized upon Saul; he fell into a frenzy*ᵃ* in the house, and David played the harp to him as he had before. Saul had
11 his spear in his hand, and he hurled it at David, meaning to pin him to the
12 wall; but twice David swerved aside. After this Saul was afraid of David,
13 because he saw that the LORD had forsaken him and was with David. He therefore removed David from his household and appointed him to the
14 command of a thousand men. David led his men into action, and succeeded
15 in everything that he undertook, because the LORD was with him. When
16 Saul saw how successful he was, he was more afraid of him than ever; all Israel and Judah loved him because he took the field at their head.

17 Saul said to David, 'Here is my elder daughter Merab; I will give her to you in marriage, but in return you must serve me valiantly and fight the LORD's battles.' For Saul meant David to meet his end at the hands of the
18 Philistines and not himself. David answered Saul, 'Who am I and what are my father's people, my kinsfolk, in Israel, that I should become the
19 king's son-in-law?' However, when the time came for Saul's daughter Merab to be married to David, she had already been given to Adriel of
20 Meholah. But Michal, Saul's other daughter, fell in love with David, and
21 when Saul was told of this, he saw that it suited his plans. He said to himself, 'I will give her to him; let her be the bait that lures him to his death at the hands of the Philistines.' So Saul proposed a second time to make
22 David his son-in-law, and ordered his courtiers to say to David privately, 'The king is well disposed to you and you are dear to us all; now is the time
23 for you to marry into the king's family.' When Saul's people spoke in this way to David, he said to them, 'Do you think that marrying the king's daughter is a matter of so little consequence that a poor man of no con-
24 sequence, like myself, can do it?' Saul's courtiers reported what David
25 had said, and he replied, 'Tell David this: all the king wants as the bride-price is the foreskins of a hundred Philistines, by way of vengeance on his enemies.' Saul was counting on David's death at the hands of the Philis-
26 tines. The courtiers told David what Saul had said, and marriage with the king's daughter on these terms pleased him well. Before the appointed
27 time, David went out with his men and slew two hundred Philistines; he brought their foreskins and counted them out to the king in order to be accepted as his son-in-law. So Saul married his daughter Michal to David.
28 He saw clearly that the LORD was with David, and knew that Michal his
29 daughter had fallen in love with him; and so he grew more and more afraid of David and was his enemy for the rest of his life.

30 The Philistine officers used to come out to offer single combat; and whenever they did, David had more success against them than all the rest of Saul's men, and he won a great name for himself.

19 SAUL SPOKE TO JONATHAN his son and all his household about killing
2 David. But Jonathan was devoted to David and told him that his father Saul was looking for an opportunity to kill him. 'Be on your guard to-
3 morrow morning,' he said; 'conceal yourself, and remain in hiding. Then I will come out and join my father in the open country where you are and

ᵃ *Or* fell into prophetic rapture.

speak to him about you, and if I discover anything I will tell you.' Jonathan 4
spoke up for David to his father Saul and said to him, 'Sir, do not wrong
your servant David; he has not wronged you; his conduct towards you has
been beyond reproach. Did he not take his life in his hands when he killed 5
the Philistine, and the LORD won a great victory for Israel? You saw it, you
shared in the rejoicing; why should you wrong an innocent man and put
David to death without cause?' Saul listened to Jonathan and swore 6
solemnly by the LORD that David should not be put to death. So Jonathan 7
called David and told him all this; then he brought him to Saul, and he
was in attendance on the king as before.

War broke out again, and David attacked the Philistines and dealt them 8
such a blow that they ran before him.

An evil spirit from the LORD came upon Saul as he was sitting in the 9
house with his spear in his hand; and David was playing the harp. Saul 10
tried to pin David to the wall with the spear, but he avoided the king's
thrust so that Saul drove the spear into the wall. David escaped and got
safely away. That night Saul sent servants to keep watch on David's house, 11
intending to kill him in the morning, but David's wife Michal warned him
to get away that night, 'or tomorrow', she said, 'you will be a dead man.'
She let David down through a window and he slipped away and escaped. 12
Michal took their household gods and put them on the bed; at its head she 13
laid a goat's-hair rug and covered it all with a cloak. When the men arrived 14
to arrest David she told them he was ill. Saul sent them back to see David 15
for themselves. 'Bring him to me, bed and all,' he said, 'and I will kill him.'
When they came, there were the household gods on the bed and the goat's- 16
hair rug at its head. Then Saul said to Michal, 'Why have you played this 17
trick on me and let my enemy get safe away?' And Michal answered, 'He
said to me, "Help me to escape or I will kill you." '

Meanwhile David made good his escape and came to Samuel at Ramah, 18
and told him how Saul had treated him. Then he and Samuel went to
Naioth and stayed there. Saul was told that David was there, and he sent 19 20
a party of men to seize him. When they saw the company of prophets in
rapture, with Samuel standing at their head, the spirit of God came upon
them and they fell into prophetic rapture. When this was reported to Saul 21
he sent another party. These also fell into a rapture, and when he sent more
men a third time, they did the same. Saul himself then set out for Ramah 22
and came to the great cistern in Secu. He asked where Samuel and David
were and was told that they were at Naioth in Ramah. On his way there the 23
spirit of God came upon him too and he went on, in a rapture as he went,
till he came to Naioth in Ramah. There he too stripped off his clothes and 24
like the rest fell into a rapture before Samuel and lay down naked all that
day and all that night. That is why men say, 'Is Saul also among the
prophets?'

Then David made his escape from Naioth in Ramah and came to **20**
Jonathan. 'What have I done?' he asked. 'What is my offence? What does
your father think I have done wrong, that he seeks my life?' Jonathan 2
answered him, 'God forbid! There is no thought of putting you to death.
I am sure my father will not do anything whatever without telling me. Why

3   should my father hide such a thing from me? I cannot believe it!' David
    said, 'I am ready to swear to it: your father has said to himself, "Jonathan
    must not know this or he will resent it", because he knows that you have a
    high regard for me. As the LORD lives, your life upon it, there is only a step
4   between me and death.' Jonathan said to David, 'What do you want me to
5   do for you?' David answered, 'It is new moon tomorrow, and I ought to
    dine with the king. Let me go and lie hidden in the fields until the third
6   evening. If your father happens to miss me, then say, "David asked me for
    leave to pay a rapid visit to his home in Bethlehem, for it is the annual
7   sacrifice there for the whole family." If he says, "Well and good", that will
    be a good sign for me; but if he flies into a rage, you will know that he is set
8   on doing me wrong. My lord, keep faith with me; for you and I have entered
    into a solemn compact before the LORD. Kill me yourself if I am guilty.
9   Why let me fall into your father's hands?' 'God forbid!' cried Jonathan.
10 'If I find my father set on doing you wrong I will tell you.' David answered
11 Jonathan, 'How will you let me know if he answers harshly?' Jonathan said,
12 'Come with me into the fields.' So they went together into the fields, and
    Jonathan said to David, 'I promise you, David, in the sight of the LORD
    the God of Israel, this time tomorrow I will sound my father for the third
13 time and, if he is well disposed to you, I will send and let you know. If my
    father means mischief, the LORD do the same to me and more, if I do not
    let you know and get you safely away. The LORD be with you as he has been
14 with my father! I know that as long as I live you will show me faithful
15 friendship, as the LORD requires; and if I should die, you will continue
    loyal to my family for ever. When the LORD rids the earth of all David's
16 enemies, may the LORD call him to account if he and his house are no longer
17 my friends.' Jonathan pledged himself afresh to David because of his love
18 for him, for he loved him as himself. Then he said to him, 'Tomorrow is
19 the new moon, and you will be missed when your place is empty. So go
    down at nightfall for the third time to the place where you hid on the
20 evening of the feast and stay by the mound there. Then I will shoot three
21 arrows towards it, as though I were aiming at a mark. Then I will send my
    boy to find the arrows. If I say to him, "Look, the arrows are on this side
    of you, pick them up", then you can come out of hiding. You will be quite
22 safe, I swear it; for there will be nothing amiss. But if I say to the lad,
    "Look, the arrows are on the other side of you, further on", then the LORD
23 has said that you must go; the LORD stand witness between us for ever to
    the pledges we have exchanged.'

24   So David hid in the fields. The new moon came, the dinner was prepared,
25 and the king sat down to eat. Saul took his customary seat by the wall, and
    Abner sat beside him; Jonathan too was present, but David's place was
26 empty. That day Saul said nothing, for he thought that David was absent
27 by some chance, perhaps because he was ritually unclean. But on the second
    day, the day after the new moon, David's place was still empty, and Saul
    said to his son Jonathan, 'Why has not the son of Jesse come to the feast,
28 either yesterday or today?' Jonathan answered Saul, 'David asked permis-
29 sion to go to Bethlehem. He asked my leave and said, "Our family is hold-
    ing a sacrifice in the town and my brother himself has ordered me to be

there. Now, if you have any regard for me, let me slip away to see my brothers." That is why he has not come to dine with the king.' Saul was 30 angry with Jonathan, 'You son of a crooked and unfaithful mother! You have made friends with the son of Jesse only to bring shame on yourself and dishonour on your mother; I see how it will be. As long as Jesse's son 31 remains alive on earth, neither you nor your crown will be safe. Send at once and fetch him; he deserves to die.' Jonathan answered his father, 32 'Deserves to die! Why? What has he done?' At that, Saul picked up his 33 spear and threatened to kill him; and he knew that his father was bent on David's death. Jonathan left the table in a rage and ate nothing on the 34 second day of the festival; for he was indignant on David's behalf because his father had humiliated him.

Next morning, Jonathan went out into the fields to meet David at the 35 appointed time, taking a young boy with him. He said to the boy, 'Run and 36 find the arrows; I am going to shoot.' The boy ran on, and he shot the arrows over his head. When the boy reached the place where Jonathan's 37 arrows had fallen, Jonathan called out after him, 'Look, the arrows are beyond you. Hurry! No time to lose! Make haste!' The boy gathered up 38 the arrows and brought them to his master; but only Jonathan and David 39 knew what this meant; the boy knew nothing. Jonathan handed his weapons 40 to the boy and told him to take them back to the city. When the boy had 41 gone, David got up from behind the mound and bowed humbly three times. Then they kissed one another and shed tears together, until David's grief was even greater than Jonathan's. Jonathan said to David, 'Go in 42 safety; we have pledged each other in the name of the LORD who is witness for ever between you and me and between your descendants and mine.'

David went off at once, while Jonathan returned to the city. David made **21** his way to the priest Ahimelech at Nob, who hurried out to meet him and said, 'Why have you come alone and no one with you?' David answered 2 Ahimelech, 'I am under orders from the king: I was to let no one know about the mission on which he was sending me or what these orders were. When I took leave of my men I told them to meet me in such and such a place. Now, what have you got by you? Let me have five loaves, or as many 3 as you can find.' The priest answered David, 'I have no ordinary bread 4 available. There is only the sacred bread; but have the young men kept themselves from women?' David answered the priest, 'Women have been 5 denied us hitherto, when I have been on campaign, even an ordinary campaign, and the young men's bodies have remained holy; and how much more will they be holy today?' So, as there was no other bread there, the 6 priest gave him the sacred bread, the Bread of the Presence, which had just been taken from the presence of the LORD to be replaced by freshly baked bread on the day that the old was removed. One of Saul's servants 7 happened to be there that day, detained before the LORD; his name was Doeg the Edomite, and he was the strongest of all Saul's herdsmen. David 8 said to Ahimelech, 'Have you a spear or sword here at hand? I have no sword or other weapon with me, because the king's business was urgent.' The priest answered, 'There is the sword of Goliath the Philistine whom 9 you slew in the Vale of Elah; it is wrapped up in a cloak behind the ephod.

If you wish to take that, take it; there is no other weapon here.' David said, 'There is no sword like it; give it to me.'

10 That day, David went on his way, eluding Saul, and came to Achish
11 king of Gath. The servants of Achish said to him, 'Surely this is David, the king of his country, the man of whom they sang as they danced:

> Saul made havoc among thousands
> but David among tens of thousands.'

12 These words were not lost on David, and he became very much afraid of
13 Achish king of Gath. So he altered his behaviour in public and acted like a lunatic in front of them all, scrabbling on the double doors of the city gate
14 and dribbling down his beard. Achish said to his servants, 'The man is
15 mad! Why bring him to me? Am I short of madmen that you bring this one to plague me? Must I have this fellow in my house?'

22 DAVID MADE HIS ESCAPE and went from there to the cave of Adullam. When his brothers and all his family heard that he was there, they joined
2 him. Men in any kind of distress or in debt or with a grievance gathered round him, about four hundred in number, and he became their chief.
3 From there David went to Mizpeh in Moab and said to the king of Moab, 'Let my father and mother come and take shelter with you until I know
4 what God will do for me.' So he left them at the court of the king of Moab, and they stayed there as long as David was in his stronghold.
5 The prophet Gad said to David, 'You must not stay in your stronghold;
6 go at once into Judah.' So David went as far as the forest of Hareth. News that David and his men had been seen reached Saul while he was in Gibeah, sitting under the tamarisk-tree on the hill-top with his spear in
7 his hand and all his retainers standing about him. He said to them, 'Listen to me, you Benjamites: do you expect the son of Jesse to give you all fields and vineyards, or make you all officers over units of a thousand and a
8 hundred? Is that why you have all conspired against me? Not one of you told me when my son made a compact with the son of Jesse; none of you spared a thought for me or told me that my son had set my own servant against me, who is lying in wait for me now.'
9 Then Doeg the Edomite, who was standing with the servants of Saul, spoke: 'I saw the son of Jesse coming to Nob, to Ahimelech son of Ahitub.
10 Ahimelech consulted the LORD on his behalf, then gave him food and
11 handed over to him the sword of Goliath the Philistine.' The king sent for Ahimelech the priest and his family, who were priests at Nob, and they
12 all came into his presence. Saul said, 'Now listen, you son of Ahitub', and
13 the man answered, 'Yes, my lord?' Then Saul said to him, 'Why have you and the son of Jesse plotted against me? You gave him food and the sword too, and consulted God on his behalf; and now he has risen against me and
14 is at this moment lying in wait for me.' 'And who among all your servants', answered Ahimelech, 'is like David, a man to be trusted, the king's son-in-law, appointed to your staff and holding an honourable place in your
15 household? Have I on this occasion done something profane in consulting God on his behalf? God forbid! I trust that my lord the king will not accuse

me or my family; for I know nothing whatever about it.' But the king said, 16
'Ahimelech, you must die, you and all your family.' He then turned to the 17
bodyguard attending him and said, 'Go and kill the priests of the LORD;
for they are in league with David, and, though they knew that he was a
fugitive, they did not tell me.' The king's men, however, were unwilling
to raise a hand against the priests of the LORD. The king therefore said to 18
Doeg the Edomite, 'You, Doeg, go and fall upon the priests'; so Doeg went
and fell upon the priests, killing that day with his own hand eighty-five
men who could carry the ephod. He put to the sword every living thing in 19
Nob, the city of priests: men and women, children and babes in arms, oxen,
asses, and sheep. One son of Ahimelech named Abiathar made his escape 20
and joined David. He told David how Saul had killed the priests of the 21
LORD. Then David said to him, 'When Doeg the Edomite was there that 22
day, I knew that he would inform Saul. I have gambled with the lives of all
your father's family. Stay here with me, have no fear; he who seeks your 23
life seeks mine, and you will be safe with me.'

The Philistines were fighting against Keilah and plundering the **23**
threshing-floors; and when David heard this, he consulted the LORD and 2
asked whether he should go and attack the Philistines. The LORD answered,
'Go, attack them, and relieve Keilah.' But David's men said to him, 'As 3
we are now, we have enough to fear from Judah. How much worse if we
challenge the Philistine forces at Keilah!' David consulted the LORD once 4
again and the LORD answered him, 'Go to Keilah; I will give the Philistines into your hands.' So David and his men went to Keilah and fought 5
the Philistines; they carried off their cattle, inflicted a heavy defeat on them
and relieved the inhabitants. Abiathar son of Ahimelech made good his 6
escape and joined David at Keilah, bringing the ephod with him. Saul was 7
told that David had entered Keilah, and he said, 'God has put him into
my hands; for he has walked into a trap by entering a walled town with
gates and bars.' He called out the levy to march on Keilah and besiege David 8
and his men. When David learnt how Saul planned his undoing, he told 9
Abiathar the priest to bring the ephod, and then he prayed, 'O LORD God 10
of Israel, I thy servant have heard news that Saul intends to come to Keilah
and destroy the city because of me. Will the citizens of Keilah surrender me 11
to him? Will Saul come as I have heard? O LORD God of Israel, I pray
thee, tell thy servant.' The LORD answered, 'He will come.' Then David 12
asked, 'Will the citizens of Keilah surrender me and my men to Saul?',
and the LORD answered, 'They will.' Then David left Keilah at once with 13
his men, who numbered about six hundred, and moved about from place
to place. When the news reached Saul that David had escaped from Keilah,
he made no further move.

While David was living in the fastnesses of the wilderness of Ziph, in 14
the hill-country, Saul searched for him day after day, but God did not put
him into his power. David well knew that Saul had come out to seek his 15
life; and while he was at Horesh in the wilderness of Ziph, Saul's son 16
Jonathan came to him there and gave him fresh courage in God's name:
'Do not be afraid,' he said; 'my father's hand shall not touch you. You will 17
become king of Israel and I shall hold rank after you; and my father knows

18 it.' The two of them made a solemn compact before the LORD; then David
19 remained in Horesh and Jonathan went home. While Saul was at Gibeah
the Ziphites brought him this news: 'David, we hear, is in hiding among
us in the fastnesses of Horesh on the hill of Hachilah, south of Jeshimon.
20 Come down, your majesty, come whenever you will, and we are able to
21 surrender him to you.' Saul said, 'The LORD has indeed blessed you; you
22 have saved me a world of trouble. Go now and make further inquiry, and
find out exactly where he is and who saw him there. They tell me that he
23 by himself is crafty enough to outwit me. Find out which of his hiding-
places he is using; then come back to me at such and such a place, and I
will go along with you. So long as he stays in this country, I will hunt him
24 down, if I have to go through all the clans of Judah one by one.' They set
out for Ziph without delay, ahead of Saul; David and his men were in the
25 wilderness of Maon in the Arabah to the south of Jeshimon. Saul set off
with his men to look for him; but David got wind of it and went down to a
refuge in the rocks, and there he stayed in the wilderness of Maon. Hearing
26 of this, Saul went into the wilderness after him; he was on one side of the
hill, David and his men on the other. While David and his men were
trying desperately to get away and Saul and his followers were closing in
27 for the capture, a runner brought a message to Saul: 'Come at once! the
28 Philistines are harrying the land.' So Saul called off the pursuit and turned
back to face the Philistines. This is why that place is called the Dividing
29 Rock. David went up from there and lived in the fastnesses of En-gedi.
24   When Saul returned from the pursuit of the Philistines, he learnt that
2 David was in the wilderness of En-gedi. So he took three thousand men
picked from the whole of Israel and went in search of David and his men
3 to the east of the Rocks of the Wild Goats. There beside the road were
some sheepfolds, and near by was a cave, at the far end of which David and
his men were sitting concealed. Saul came to the cave and went in to relieve
4-7*a* himself. His men said to David, 'The day has come: the LORD has put your
enemy into your hands, as he promised he would, and you may do what you
please with him.' David said to his men, 'God forbid that I should harm
my master, the LORD's anointed, or lift a finger against him; he is the LORD's
anointed.' So David reproved his men severely and would not let them
attack Saul. He himself got up stealthily and cut off a piece of Saul's cloak;
but when he had cut it off, his conscience smote him. Saul rose, left the
8 cave and went on his way; whereupon David also came out of the cave and
called after Saul, 'My lord the king!' When Saul looked round, David
9 prostrated himself in obeisance and said to him, 'Why do you listen when
10 they say that David is out to do you harm? Today you can see for yourself
that the LORD put you into my power in the cave; I had a mind to kill you,
but no, I spared your life and said, "I cannot lift a finger against my master,
11 for he is the LORD's anointed." Look, my dear lord, look at this piece of
your cloak in my hand. I cut it off, but I did not kill you; this will show you
that I have no thought of violence or treachery against you, and that I have
12 done you no wrong; yet you are resolved to take my life. May the LORD
judge between us! but though he may take vengeance on you for my sake,

a Verses 4–7 are re-arranged thus: 4a, 6, 7a, 4b, 5, 7b.

I will never lift my hand against you; "One wrong begets another", as   13
the old saying goes, yet I will never lift my hand against you. Who has the   14
king of Israel come out against? What are you pursuing? A dead dog, a
mere flea. The LORD will be judge and decide between us; let him look into   15
my cause, he will plead for me and will acquit me.'

When David had finished speaking, Saul said, 'Is that you, David my   16
son?', and he wept. Then he said, 'The right is on your side, not mine;   17
you have treated me so well, I have treated you so badly. Your goodness to   18
me this day has passed all bounds: the LORD put me at your mercy but you
did not kill me. Not often does a man find his enemy and let him go safely   19
on his way; so may the LORD reward you well for what you have done for
me today! I know now for certain that you will become king, and that the   20
kingdom of Israel will flourish under your rule. Swear to me by the LORD   21
then that you will not exterminate my descendants and blot out my name
from my father's house.' David swore an oath to Saul; and Saul went back   22
to his home, while David and his men went up to their fastness.

SAMUEL DIED, and all Israel came together to mourn for him, and he   **25**
was buried in his house in Ramah. Afterwards David went down to the
wilderness of Paran.

There was a man at Carmel in Maon, who had great influence and owned   2
three thousand sheep and a thousand goats; and he was shearing his flocks
in Carmel. His name was Nabal and his wife's name Abigail; she was a   3
beautiful and intelligent woman, but her husband, a Calebite, was surly
and mean. David heard in the wilderness that Nabal was shearing his   4
flocks, and sent ten of his men, saying to them, 'Go up to Carmel, find   5
Nabal and give him my greetings. You are to say, "All good wishes for the   6
year ahead! Prosperity to yourself, your household, and all that is yours!
I hear that you are shearing. Your shepherds have been with us lately and   7
we did not molest them; nothing of theirs was missing all the time they
were in Carmel. Ask your own people and they will tell you. Receive my   8
men kindly, for this is an auspicious day with us, and give what you can to
David your son and your servant."' David's servants came and delivered   9
this message to Nabal in David's name. When they paused, Nabal answered,   10
'Who is David? Who is this son of Jesse? In these days every slave who
breaks away from his master sets himself up as a chief.*a* Am I to take my   11
food and my wine and the meat I have provided for my shearers and give
it to men who come from I know not where?' David's men turned and   12
made their way back to him and told him all this. He said to his men,   13
'Buckle on your swords, all of you.' So they buckled on their swords and
followed David, four hundred of them, while two hundred stayed behind
with the baggage.

One of the young men said to Abigail, Nabal's wife, 'David sent mes-   14
sengers from the wilderness to ask our master politely for a present, and
he flew out*b* at them. The men have been very good to us and have not   15
molested us, nor did we miss anything all the time we were going about

---

a *Or* In these days there are many slaves who break away from their master.
b flew out: *or* screamed.

16 with them in the open country. They were as good as a wall round us, night
17 and day, while we were minding the flocks. Think carefully what you had
better do, for it is certain ruin for our master and his whole family; he is
18 such a good-for-nothing that it is no good talking to him.' So Abigail
hastily collected two hundred loaves and two skins of wine, five sheep
ready dressed, five measures of parched grain, a hundred bunches of
19 raisins, and two hundred cakes of dried figs, and loaded them on asses, but
told her husband nothing about it. Then she said to her servants, 'Go on
20 ahead, I will follow you.' As she made her way on her ass, hidden by the
hill, there were David and his men coming down towards her, and she met
21 them. David had said, 'It was a waste of time to protect this fellow's property in the wilderness so well that nothing of his was missing. He has
22 repaid me evil for good.' David swore a great oath: 'God do the same to
me and more if I leave him a single mother's son alive by morning!'

23   When Abigail saw David she dismounted in haste and prostrated herself
24 before him, bowing low to the ground at his feet, and said, 'Let me take
the blame, my lord, but allow me, your humble servant, to speak out and
25 let my lord give me a hearing. How can you take any notice of this good-
for-nothing? He is just what his name Nabal means: "Churl" is his name,
and churlish his behaviour. I did not myself, sir, see the men you sent.
26 And now, sir, the LORD has restrained you from bloodshed and from giving
vent to your anger. As the LORD lives, your life upon it, your enemies and
27 all who want to see you ruined will be like Nabal. Here is the present which
I, your humble servant, have brought; give it to the young men under
28 your command. Forgive me, my lord, if I am presuming; for the LORD
will establish your family for ever, because you have fought his wars. No
29 calamity shall overtake you as long as you live. If any man sets out to pursue
you and take your life, the LORD your God will wrap your life up and put
it with his own treasure, but the lives of your enemies he will hurl away like
30 stones from a sling. When the LORD has made good all his promises to you,
31 and has made you ruler of Israel, there will be no reason why you should
stumble or your courage falter because you have shed innocent blood or
given way to your anger. Then when the LORD makes all you do prosper,
32 you will remember me, your servant.' David said to Abigail, 'Blessed is
33 the LORD the God of Israel who has sent you today to meet me. A blessing
on your good sense, a blessing on you because you have saved me today
34 from the guilt of bloodshed and from giving way to my anger. For I swear
by the life of the LORD the God of Israel who has kept me from doing you
wrong: if you had not come at once to meet me, not a man of Nabal's
household, not a single mother's son, would have been left alive by morn-
35 ing.' Then David took from her what she had brought him and said, 'Go
home in peace, I have listened to you and I grant your request.'

36   On her return she found Nabal holding a banquet in his house, a banquet
fit for a king. He grew merry and became very drunk, so drunk that his wife
37 said nothing to him, trivial or serious, till daybreak. In the morning, when
the wine had worn off, she told him everything, and he had a seizure and
38 lay there like a stone. Ten days later the LORD struck him again and he
39 died. When David heard that Nabal was dead he said, 'Blessed be the LORD,

who has himself punished Nabal for his insult, and has kept me his servant from doing wrong. The LORD has made Nabal's wrongdoing recoil on his own head.' David then sent to make proposals that Abigail should become his wife. And his servants came to Abigail at Carmel and said to her, 'David 40 has sent us to fetch you to be his wife.' She rose and prostrated herself with 41 her face to the ground, and said, 'I am his slave to command, I would wash the feet of my lord's servants.' So Abigail made her preparations with all 42 speed and, with her five maids in attendance, accompanied by David's messengers, rode away on an ass; and she became David's wife. David had 43 also married Ahinoam of Jezreel; both these women became his wives. Saul meanwhile had given his daughter Michal, David's wife, to Palti son 44 of Laish from Gallim.

THE ZIPHITES CAME TO SAUL at Gibeah to report that David was in **26** hiding on the hill of Hachilah overlooking Jeshimon. Saul went down at 2 once to the wilderness of Ziph, taking with him three thousand picked men, to search for David there. He encamped beside the road on the hill 3 of Hachilah overlooking Jeshimon, while David was still in the wilderness. As soon as David knew that Saul had come to the wilderness in pursuit of him, he sent out scouts and found that Saul had reached such and such a 4 place. Without delay, he went to the place where Saul had pitched his 5 camp and observed where Saul and Abner son of Ner, the commander-in-chief, were lying. Saul lay within the lines with his troops encamped in a circle round him. David turned to Ahimelech the Hittite and Abishai son 6 of Zeruiah, Joab's brother, and said, 'Who will venture with me into the camp, to go to Saul?' Abishai answered, 'I will.' David and Abishai 7 entered the camp at night and found Saul lying asleep within the lines with his spear thrust into the ground by his head. Abner and the army were lying all round him. Abishai said to David, 'God has put your enemy into 8 your power today; let me strike him and pin him to the ground with one thrust of the spear; I shall not have to strike twice.' David said to him, 'Do 9 him no harm; who has ever lifted a finger against the LORD's anointed and gone unpunished? As the LORD lives,' went on David, 'the LORD will 10 strike him down; either his time will come and he will die, or he will go down to battle and meet his end. God forbid that I should lift a finger 11 against the LORD's anointed! But now let us take the spear which is by his head, and the water-jar, and go.' So David took the spear and the water- 12 jar from beside Saul's head and they went. The whole camp was asleep; no one saw him, no one knew anything, no one even woke up. A heavy sleep sent by the LORD had fallen on them.

Then David crossed over to the other side and stood on the top of a hill 13 a long way off; there was no little distance between them. David shouted 14 across to the army and hailed Abner, 'Answer me, Abner!' He answered, 'Who are you to shout to the king?' David said to Abner, 'Do you call 15 yourself a man? Is there anyone like you in Israel? Why, then, did you not keep watch over your lord the king, when someone came to harm your lord the king? This was not well done. As the LORD lives, you deserve to die, all 16 of you, because you have not kept watch over your master the LORD's anointed. Look! Where are the king's spear and the water-jar that were by his head?'

17 Saul recognized David's voice and said, 'Is that you, David my son?'
18 'Yes, sir, it is', said David. 'Why must your majesty pursue me? What have
19 I done? What mischief am I plotting? Listen, my lord, to what I have to say. If it is the LORD who has set you against me, may an offering be acceptable to him; but if it is men, a curse on them in the LORD's name; for they have ousted me today from my share in the LORD's inheritance and
20 have banished me to serve other gods! Do not let my blood be shed on foreign soil, far from the presence of the LORD, just because the king of Israel came out to look for a flea, as one might hunt a partridge over the
21 hills.' Saul answered, 'I have done wrong; come back, David my son. You have held my life precious this day, and I will never harm you again. I have
22 been a fool, I have been sadly in the wrong.' David answered, 'Here is the
23 king's spear; let one of your men come across and fetch it. The LORD who rewards uprightness and loyalty will reward the man into whose power he put you today, when I refused to lift a finger against the LORD's anointed.
24 As I held your life precious today, so may the LORD hold mine precious and
25 deliver me from every distress.' Then Saul said to David, 'A blessing is on you, David my son. You will do great things and be victorious.' So David went on his way and Saul returned home.

27 David thought, 'One of these days I shall be killed by Saul. The best thing for me to do will be to escape into Philistine territory; then Saul will lose all further hope of finding me anywhere in Israel, search as he may, and
2 I shall escape his clutches.' So David and his six hundred men crossed the
3 frontier forthwith to Achish son of Maoch king of Gath. David settled in Gath with Achish, taking with him his men and their families and his two
4 wives, Ahinoam of Jezreel and Abigail of Carmel, Nabal's widow. Saul was told that David had escaped to Gath, and he gave up the search.
5 David said to Achish, 'If I stand well in your opinion, grant me a place in one of your country towns where I may settle. Why should I remain in the
6 royal city with your majesty?' Achish granted him Ziklag on that day: that is why Ziklag still belongs to the kings of Judah.

7 8 David spent a year and four months in Philistine country. He and his men would sally out and raid the Geshurites, the Gizrites, and the Amalekites, for it was they who inhabited the country from Telaim[a] all the way
9 to Shur and Egypt. When David raided the country he left no one alive, man or woman; he took flocks and herds, asses and camels, and clothes too,
10 and then came back again to Achish. When Achish asked, 'Where was your raid today?', David would answer, 'The Negeb of Judah' or 'The Negeb
11 of the Jerahmeelites' or 'The Negeb of the Kenites'. Neither man nor woman did David bring back alive to Gath, for fear that they should denounce him and his men for what they had done. This was his practice
12 as long as he remained with the Philistines. Achish trusted David, thinking that he had won such a bad name among his own people the Israelites that he would remain his subject all his life.

a from Telaim: *prob. rdg.; Heb.* from of old.

Saul and his sons killed

IN THOSE DAYS THE PHILISTINES MUSTERED their army for an attack **28** on Israel. Achish said to David, 'You know that you and your men must take the field with me.' David answered Achish, 'Good, you will 2 learn what your servant can do.' And Achish said to David, 'I will make you my bodyguard for life.'

By this time Samuel was dead, and all Israel had mourned for him and 3 buried him in Ramah, his own city; and Saul had banished from the land all who trafficked with ghosts and spirits. The Philistines mustered and 4 encamped at Shunem, and Saul gathered all the Israelites and encamped on Gilboa; and when Saul saw the Philistine force, fear struck him to the 5 heart. He inquired of the LORD, but the LORD did not answer him, whether 6 by dreams or by Urim or by prophets. So he said to his servants, 'Find me a 7 woman who has a familiar spirit, and I will go and inquire through her.' His servants told him that there was such a woman at En-dor. Saul put on 8 different clothes and went in disguise with two of his men. He came to the woman by night and said, 'Tell me my fortunes by consulting the dead, and call up the man I name to you.' But the woman answered, 'Surely you 9 know what Saul has done, how he has made away with those who call up ghosts and spirits; why do you press me to do what will lead to my death?' Saul swore her an oath: 'As the LORD lives, no harm shall come to you for 10 this.' The woman asked whom she should call up, and Saul answered, 11 'Samuel.' When the woman saw Samuel appear, she shrieked and said to 12 Saul, 'Why have you deceived me? You are Saul!' The king said to her, 13 'Do not be afraid. What do you see?' The woman answered, 'I see a ghostly form coming up from the earth.' 'What is it like?' he asked; she answered, 14 'Like an old man coming up, wrapped in a cloak.' Then Saul knew it was Samuel, and he bowed low with his face to the ground, and prostrated himself. Samuel said to Saul, 'Why have you disturbed me and brought 15 me up?' Saul answered, 'I am in great trouble; the Philistines are pressing me and God has turned away; he no longer answers me through prophets or through dreams, and I have summoned you to tell me what I should do.' Samuel said, 'Why do you ask me, now that the LORD has turned from you 16 and become your adversary? He has done what he foretold through me. 17 He has torn the kingdom from your hand and given it to another man, to David. You have not obeyed the LORD, or executed the judgement of his 18 fury against the Amalekites; that is why he has done this to you today. For the same reason the LORD will let your people Israel fall into the hands 19 of the Philistines and, what is more, tomorrow you and your sons shall be with me. Yes, indeed, the LORD will give the Israelite army into the hands of the Philistines.' Saul was overcome and fell his full length to the ground, 20 terrified by Samuel's words. He had no strength left, for he had eaten nothing all day and all night.

The woman went to Saul and saw that he was much disturbed, and she 21 said to him, 'I listened to what you said and I risked my life to obey you. Now listen to me: let me set before you a little food to give you strength for 22 your journey.' But he refused to eat anything. When his servants joined the 23

335

woman in pressing him, he yielded, rose from the ground and sat on the
24 couch. The woman had a fatted calf at home, which she quickly slaughtered.
25 She took some meal, kneaded it and baked unleavened cakes, which she
set before Saul and his servants. They ate the food and departed that same
night.

29 The Philistines mustered all their troops at Aphek, while the Israelites
2 encamped at En-harod[a] in Jezreel. The Philistine princes were advancing
with their troops in units of a hundred and a thousand; David and his men
3 were in the rear of the column with Achish. The Philistine commanders
asked, 'Why are those Hebrews there?' Achish answered, 'This is David,
the servant of Saul king of Israel who has been with me now for a year or
more. I have had no fault to find in him ever since he came over to me.'
4 The Philistine commanders were indignant and said to Achish, 'Send the
man back to the town which you allotted to him. He shall not fight side by
side with us, or he may turn traitor in the battle. What better way to buy
5 his master's favour, than at the price of our lives? This is that David of
whom they sang, as they danced:

> Saul made havoc among thousands
> but David among tens of thousands.'

6 Achish summoned David and said to him, 'As the LORD lives, you are
an upright man and your service with my troops has well satisfied me. I
have had no fault to find with you ever since you joined me, but the other
7 princes are not willing to accept you. Now go home in peace, and you will
8 then be doing nothing that they can regard as wrong.' David protested,
'What have I done, or what fault have you found in me from the day I
first entered your service till now, that I should not come and fight against
9 the enemies of my lord the king?' Achish answered David, 'I agree that
you have been as true to me as an angel of God, but the Philistine com-
10 manders insist that you shall not fight alongside them. Now rise early in
the morning with those of your lord's subjects who have followed you, and
go to the town which I allotted to you; harbour no evil thoughts, for I am
11 well satisfied with you. Rise early and start as soon as it is light.' So David
and his men rose early to start that morning on their way back to the land
of the Philistines, while the Philistines went on to Jezreel.

30 On the third day David and his men reached Ziklag. Now the Amalekites
2 had made a raid into the Negeb, attacked Ziklag and set fire to it; they had
carried off all the women, high and low, without putting one of them to
3 death. These they drove with them and continued their march. When
David and his men approached the town, they found it destroyed by fire,
4 and their wives, their sons, and their daughters carried off. David and the
5 people with him wept aloud until they could weep no more. David's two
wives, Ahinoam of Jezreel and Abigail widow of Nabal of Carmel, were
6 among the captives. David was in a desperate position because the people,
embittered by the loss of their sons and daughters, threatened to stone him.
7 So David sought strength in the LORD his God. He told Abiathar the priest,
son of Ahimelech, to bring the ephod. When Abiathar had brought the

---

[a] *Prob. rdg.; Heb.* at the spring.

ephod, David inquired of the LORD, 'Shall I pursue these raiders? and 8
shall I overtake them?' The answer came, 'Pursue them: you will overtake
them and rescue everyone.' So David and his six hundred men set out and 9
reached the ravine of Besor.*a* Two hundred of them who were too weary to 10
cross the ravine stayed behind, and David with four hundred pressed on
in pursuit.

In the open country they came across an Egyptian and took him to 11
David. They gave him food to eat and water to drink, also a lump of dried 12
figs and two bunches of raisins. When he had eaten these he revived; for
he had had nothing to eat or drink for three days and nights. David asked 13
him, 'Whose slave are you? and where have you come from?' 'I am an
Egyptian boy,' he answered, 'the slave of an Amalekite, but my master left
me behind because I fell ill three days ago. We had raided the Negeb of the 14
Kerethites, part of Judah, and the Negeb of Caleb; we also set fire to
Ziklag.' David asked, 'Can you guide me to this band?' 'Swear to me by 15
God', he answered, 'that you will not put me to death or hand me back to
my master, and I will guide you to them.' So he led him down, and there 16
they were scattered everywhere, eating and drinking and celebrating the
capture of the great mass of spoil taken from Philistine and Judaean
territory.

David attacked from dawn till dusk and continued till next day; only 17
four hundred young men mounted on camels made good their escape.
David rescued all those whom the Amalekites had taken, including his 18
two wives. No one was missing, high or low, sons or daughters, and none 19
of the spoil, nor anything they had taken for themselves: David recovered
everything. They took all the flocks and herds, drove the cattle before 20
him*b* and said, 'This is David's spoil.' When David returned to the two 21
hundred men who had been too weak to follow him and whom he had left
behind at the ravine of Besor, they came forward to meet him and his men.
David greeted them all, inquiring how things were with them. But some 22
of those who had gone with David, worthless men and scoundrels, broke
in and said, 'These men did not go with us; we will not allot them any of
the spoil that we have retrieved, except that each of them may take his own
wife and children and then go.' 'That you shall never do,' said David, 23
'considering what the LORD has given us, and how he has kept us safe and
given the raiding party into our hands. Who could agree with what you 24
propose? Those who stayed with the stores shall have the same share as
those who went into battle. They shall share and share alike.' From 25
that time onwards, this has been the established custom in Israel down to
this day.

When David reached Ziklag, he sent some of the spoil to the elders of 26
Judah and to his friends, with this message: 'This is a present for you out
of the spoil taken from the LORD's enemies.' He sent to those in Bethuel, 27
in Ramoth-negeb, in Jattir, in Ararah,*c* in Siphmoth, in Eshtemoa, in 28 29
Rachal, in the cities of the Jerahmeelites, in the cities of the Kenites, in 30

---

a *Prob. rdg.; Heb. adds* those who were left over remained.   *b* They took ... before
him: *prob. rdg.; Heb.* David took all the flocks and herds; they drove before that cattle.
c *Prob. rdg.; Heb.* Aroer.

31 Hormah, in Borashan, in Athak, in Hebron, and in all the places over which he and his men had ranged.

31 1ª   The Philistines fought a battle against Israel, and the men of Israel were
2   routed, leaving their dead on Mount Gilboa. The Philistines hotly pursued Saul and his sons and killed the three sons, Jonathan, Abinadab and
3   Malchishua. The battle went hard for Saul, for some archers came upon
4   him and he was wounded in the belly by the archers. So he said to his armour-bearer, 'Draw your sword and run me through, so that these uncircumcised brutes may not come and taunt me and make sport of me.' But the armour-bearer refused, he dared not; whereupon Saul took his
5   own sword and fell on it. When the armour-bearer saw that Saul was dead,
6   he too fell on his sword and died with him. Thus they all died together on that day, Saul, his three sons, and his armour-bearer, as well as his men.
7   And all the Israelites in the district of the Vale and of the Jordan, when they saw that the other Israelites had fled and that Saul and his sons had perished, fled likewise, abandoning their cities, and the Philistines went in and occupied them.
8   Next day, when the Philistines came to strip the slain, they found Saul
9   and his three sons lying dead on Mount Gilboa. They cut off his head and stripped him of his weapons; then they sent messengers through the length and breadth of their land to take the good news to idols and people
10   alike. They deposited his armour in the temple of Ashtoreth and nailed his
11   body on the wall of Beth-shan. When the inhabitants of Jabesh-gilead
12   heard what the Philistines had done to Saul, the bravest of them journeyed together all night long and recovered the bodies of Saul and his sons from the wall of Beth-shan; they brought them back to Jabesh and anointed
13   them there with spices. Then they took their bones and buried them under the tamarisk-tree in Jabesh, and fasted for seven days.

THE SECOND BOOK OF
SAMUEL

David's rule at Hebron

1   WHEN DAVID RETURNED from his victory over the
2   Amalekites, he spent two days in Ziklag. And on the third day after Saul's death a man came from the army with his clothes rent and dust on his head. When he came into David's presence he fell to
3   the ground in obeisance, and David asked him where he had come from.
4   He answered, 'I have escaped from the army of Israel.' And David said to him, 'What news? Tell me.' 'The army has been driven from the field,' he answered, 'and many have fallen in battle. Saul and Jonathan his son
5   are dead.' David said to the young man who brought the news, 'How do

ª *Verses 1–13: cp. 1 Chr. 10. 1–12.*

338

you know that Saul and Jonathan are dead?' The man answered, 'It so   6
happened that I was on Mount Gilboa and saw Saul leaning on his spear
with the chariots and horsemen closing in upon him. He turned round and,   7
seeing me, called to me. I said, "What is it, sir?" He asked who I was, and   8
I said, "An Amalekite." Then he said to me, "Come and stand over me   9
and dispatch me. I still live, but the throes of death have seized me." So I   10
stood over him and gave him the death-blow; for I knew that, broken as
he was, he could not live. Then I took the crown from his head and the
armlet from his arm, and I have brought them here to you, sir.' At that   11
David caught at his clothes and rent them, and so did all the men with him.
They beat their breasts and wept, because Saul and Jonathan his son and   12
the people of the LORD, the house of Israel, had fallen in battle; and they
fasted till evening. David said to the young man who brought the news,   13
'Where do you come from?', and he answered, 'I am the son of an alien,
an Amalekite.' 'How is it', said David, 'that you were not afraid to raise your   14
hand to slay the LORD's anointed?' And he summoned one of his own   15
young men and ordered him to fall upon the man. So the young man struck
him down and killed him; and David said, 'Your blood be on your own   16
head; for out of your own mouth you condemned yourself when you said,
"I killed the LORD's anointed."'

David made this lament over Saul and Jonathan his son; and he ordered   17 18
that this dirge over them should be taught to the people of Judah. It was
written down and may be found in the Book of Jashar: *a*

O prince of Israel, laid low in death!   19
How are the men of war fallen!

Tell it not in Gath,   20
proclaim it not in the streets of Ashkelon,
lest the Philistine women rejoice,
lest the daughters of the uncircumcised exult.

Hills of Gilboa, let no dew or rain fall on you,   21
no showers on the uplands *b* !
For there the shields of the warriors lie tarnished,
and the shield of Saul, no longer bright with oil.
The bow of Jonathan never held back   22
from the breast of the foeman, from the blood of the slain;
the sword of Saul never returned
empty to the scabbard.

Delightful and dearly loved were Saul and Jonathan;   23
in life, in death, they were not parted.
They were swifter than eagles,
stronger than lions.

Weep for Saul, O daughters of Israel!   24
who clothed you in scarlet and rich embroideries,
who spangled your dress with jewels of gold.

a Or the Book of the Upright.   *b* showers on the uplands: *prob. rdg.; Heb.* fields
of offerings.

25 How are the men of war fallen, fallen on the field!
    O Jonathan, laid low in death!
26 I grieve for you, Jonathan my brother;
    dear and delightful you were to me;
    your love for me was wonderful,
    surpassing the love of women.

27 Fallen, fallen are the men of war;
    and their armour left on the field.

2 After this David inquired of the LORD, 'Shall I go up into one of the cities of Judah?' The LORD answered, 'Go.' David asked, 'To which city?', 2 and the answer came, 'To Hebron.' So David went to Hebron with his two wives, Ahinoam of Jezreel and Abigail widow of Nabal of Carmel. 3 David also brought the men who had joined him, with their families, and 4 they settled in the city *a* of Hebron. The men of Judah came, and there they anointed David king over the house of Judah.

Word came to David that the men of Jabesh-gilead had buried Saul, 5 and he sent them this message: 'The LORD bless you because you kept 6 faith with Saul your lord and buried him. For this may the LORD keep faith and truth with you, and I for my part will show you favour too, because 7 you have done this. Be strong, be valiant, now that Saul your lord is dead, and the people of Judah have anointed me to be king over them.'

8 Meanwhile Saul's commander-in-chief, Abner son of Ner, had taken 9 Saul's son Ishbosheth, brought him across the Jordan to Mahanaim, and made him king over Gilead, the Asherites, Jezreel, Ephraim, and Benjamin, 10 and all Israel. Ishbosheth was forty years old when he became king over Israel, and he reigned two years. The tribe of Judah, however, followed 11 David. David's rule over Judah in Hebron lasted seven years and a half.

12 Abner son of Ner, with the troops of Saul's son Ishbosheth, marched 13 out from Mahanaim to Gibeon, and Joab son of Zeruiah marched out with David's troops from Hebron. They met at the pool of Gibeon and took up their positions one on one side of the pool and the other on the other side. 14 Abner said to Joab, 'Let the young men come forward and join in single 15 combat before us.' Joab answered, 'Yes, let them.' So they came up, one by one, and took their places, twelve for Benjamin and for Ishbosheth and 16 twelve from David's men. Each man seized his opponent by the head and thrust his sword into his side; and thus they fell together. That is why that place, which lies in Gibeon, was called the Field of Blades.

17 There ensued a fierce battle that day, and Abner and the men of Israel 18 were defeated by David's troops. All three sons of Zeruiah were there, Joab, Abishai and Asahel. Asahel, who was swift as a gazelle on the plains, 19 ran straight after Abner, swerving neither to right nor left in his pursuit. 20 Abner turned and asked, 'Is it you, Asahel?' Asahel answered, 'It is.' 21 Abner said, 'Turn aside to right or left, tackle one of the young men and win his belt for yourself.' But Asahel would not abandon the pursuit. 22 Abner again urged him to give it up. 'Why should I kill you?' he said. 'How 23 could I look Joab your brother in the face?' When he still refused to turn

a Prob. rdg.; Heb. cities.

aside, Abner struck him in the belly with a back-thrust of his spear *a* so that the spear came out behind him, and he fell dead in his tracks. All who came to the place where Asahel lay dead stopped there. But Joab and Ab- 24 ishai kept up the pursuit of Abner, until, at sunset, they reached the hill of Ammah, opposite Giah on the road leading to the pastures of Gibeon.

The Benjamites rallied to Abner and, forming themselves into a single 25 company, took up their stand on the top of the hill of Ammah.*b* Abner 26 called to Joab, 'Must the slaughter go on for ever? Can you not see that it will be all the more bitter in the end? Will you never recall the people from the pursuit of their kinsmen?' Joab answered, 'As God lives, if you had 27 not spoken, the people would not have given up the pursuit till morning.' Then Joab sounded the trumpet, and all the people abandoned the pursuit 28 of the men of Israel and the fighting ceased. Abner and his men moved 29 along the Arabah all that night, crossed the Jordan and went on all the morning till they reached Mahanaim. When Joab returned from the 30 pursuit of Abner, he assembled his troops and found that, besides Asahel, nineteen of David's men were missing. David's forces had routed the Ben- 31 jamites and the followers of Abner, killing three hundred and sixty of them. They took up Asahel and buried him in his father's tomb at Bethlehem. 32 Joab and his men marched all night, and as day broke they reached Hebron.

THE WAR BETWEEN THE HOUSES of Saul and David was long drawn **3** out, David growing steadily stronger while the house of Saul became weaker and weaker.

Sons were born to David at Hebron. His eldest was Amnon, whose 2 *c* mother was Ahinoam of Jezreel; his second Chileab, whose mother was 3 Abigail widow of Nabal of Carmel; the third Absalom, whose mother was Maacah daughter of Talmai king of Geshur; the fourth Adonijah, 4 whose mother was Haggith; the fifth Shephatiah, whose mother was Abital; and the sixth Ithream, whose mother was David's wife Eglah. 5 These were all born to David at Hebron.

As the war between the houses of Saul and David went on, Abner made 6 his position gradually stronger in the house of Saul. Now Saul had had 7 a concubine named Rizpah daughter of Aiah. Ishbosheth asked Abner, 'Why have you slept with my father's concubine?' Abner was very angry 8 at this and exclaimed, 'Am I a baboon in the pay of Judah? Up to now I have been loyal to the house of your father Saul, to his brothers and friends, and I have not betrayed you into David's hands; yet you choose this moment to charge me with disloyalty over this woman. But now, so help me 9 God, I will do all I can to bring about what the LORD swore to do for David: I will set to work to bring down the house of Saul and to put David on the 10 throne over Israel and Judah from Dan to Beersheba.' Ishbosheth could 11 not say another word; he was too much afraid of Abner. Then Abner, seek- 12 ing to make friends where he could, instead of going to David himself sent envoys with this message: 'Let us come to terms, and I will do all I can to bring the whole of Israel over to you.' David sent answer: 'Good, I will 13

---

a a back-thrust of his spear: *prob. rdg.; Heb. obscure.*   *b* the hill of Ammah: *prob. rdg., cp. verse 24; Heb. a single hill.*   *c* *Verses 2–5: cp. 1 Chr. 3. 1–4.*

come to terms with you, but on this one condition, that you do not come into
14 my presence without bringing Saul's daughter Michal to me.' David also
sent messengers to Saul's son Ishbosheth with the demand: 'Hand over
to me my wife Michal to whom I was betrothed at the price of a hundred
15 Philistine foreskins.' Thereupon Ishbosheth sent and took her away from
16 her husband, Paltiel son of Laish. Paltiel followed her as far as Bahurim,
weeping all the way, until Abner ordered him to go back home, and he went.
17 Abner now approached the elders of Israel and said, 'For some time
18 past you have wanted David for your king; now is the time to act, for this
is the word of the LORD about David: "By the hand of my servant David
I will deliver my people Israel from the Philistines and from all their
19 enemies."' Abner spoke also to the Benjamites and then went on to report
to David at Hebron all that the Israelites and the Benjamites had agreed.
20 When Abner was admitted to David's presence, there were twenty men
21 with him and David gave a feast for them all. Then Abner said to David,
'I shall now go and bring the whole of Israel over to your majesty, and they
shall make a covenant with you. Then you will be king over a realm after
your own heart.' David dismissed Abner, granting him safe conduct.
22 David's men and Joab returned from a raid bringing a great deal of
plunder with them, and by this time Abner, after his dismissal, was no
23 longer with David in Hebron. So when Joab and his raiding party arrived,
they were greeted with the news that Abner son of Ner had been with the
24 king and had departed under safe conduct. Joab went in to the king and
said, 'What have you done? Here you have had Abner with you. How
25 could you let him go? He has got clean away! You know Abner son of Ner:
he came meaning to deceive you, to learn all about your movements and
26 to find out what you are doing.' When he left David's presence, Joab sent
messengers after Abner and they brought him back from the Pool of Sirah;
27 but David knew nothing of all this. On Abner's return to Hebron, Joab
drew him aside in the gateway, as though to speak privately with him, and
there, in revenge for his brother Asahel, he stabbed him in the belly, and he
28 died. When David heard the news he said, 'I and my realm are for ever
29 innocent in the sight of the LORD of the blood of Abner son of Ner. May it
recoil upon the head of Joab and upon all his family! May the house of
Joab never be free from running sore or foul disease, nor lack a son fit
30 only to ply the distaff or doomed to die by the sword or beg his bread!' So
Joab and Abishai his brother slew Abner because he had killed their brother
31 Asahel in battle at Gibeon. Then David ordered Joab and all the people
with him to rend their clothes, put on sackcloth and beat their breasts for
32 Abner, and the king himself walked behind the bier. They buried Abner
in Hebron and the king wept aloud at the tomb, while all the people wept
33 with him. The king made this lament for Abner:

> Must Abner die so base a death?
34 > Your hands were not bound,
> your feet not thrust into fetters;
> you fell as one who falls at a ruffian's hands.

And the people wept for him again.

They came to persuade David to eat something; but it was still day and 35
he swore, 'So help me God! I will not touch food of any kind before sunset.'
The people took note of this and approved; indeed, everything the king 36
did pleased them. Everyone throughout Israel knew on that day that the 37
king had had no hand in the murder of Abner son of Ner. The king said 38
to his servants, 'Do you not know that a warrior, a great man, has fallen
this day in Israel? King though I am, I feel weak and powerless in face of 39
these ruthless sons of Zeruiah; they are too much for me; the LORD will
requite the wrongdoer as he deserves.'

When Saul's son Ishbosheth heard that Abner had been killed in Hebron, **4**
his courage failed him and all Israel was dismayed. Now Ishbosheth had*a* 2
two officers, who were captains of raiding parties, and whose names were
Baanah and Rechab; they were Benjamites, sons of Rimmon of Beeroth,
Beeroth being reckoned part of Benjamin; but the Beerothites had fled to 3
Gittaim, where they have lived ever since.

(Saul's son Jonathan had a son lame in both feet. He was five years old 4
when word of the death of Saul and Jonathan came from Jezreel. His nurse
had picked him up and fled, but in her hurry to get away he fell and was
crippled. His name was Mephibosheth.)

Rechab and Baanah, the sons of Rimmon of Beeroth, came to the house 5
of Ishbosheth in the heat of the day and went in, while he was taking his
midday rest. Now the door-keeper had been sifting wheat, but she had 6
grown drowsy and fallen asleep, so Rechab and his brother Baanah crept in,
found their way to the room where he was asleep on the bed, and struck 7
him dead. They cut off his head and took it with them, and, making their
way along the Arabah all night, came to Hebron. They brought Ish- 8
bosheth's head to David at Hebron and said to the king, 'Here is the head
of Ishbosheth son of Saul, your enemy, who sought your life. The LORD
has avenged your majesty today on Saul and on his family.' David answered 9
Rechab and his brother Baanah, the sons of Rimmon of Beeroth, with an
oath: 'As the LORD lives, who has rescued me from all my troubles! I 10
seized the man who brought me word that Saul was dead and thought it
good news; I killed him in Ziklag, and that was how I rewarded him for
his news. How much more when ruffians have killed an innocent man on 11
his bed in his own house? Am I not to take vengeance on you now for the
blood you have shed, and rid the earth of you?' David gave the word, and 12
the young men killed them; they cut off their hands and feet and hung
them up beside the pool in Hebron, but the head of Ishbosheth they took
and buried in Abner's tomb at Hebron.

David king in Jerusalem

NOW ALL THE TRIBES OF ISRAEL came to David at Hebron and said **5** 1*b*
to him, 'We are your own flesh and blood. In the past, while Saul was 2
still king over us, you led the forces of Israel to war and you brought them
home again. And the LORD said to you, "You shall be shepherd of my

a had: *prob. rdg.; Heb. om.*   *b* *Verses 1-3, 6-10: cp. 1 Chr. 11. 1-9.*

3 people Israel; you shall be their prince." ' All the elders of Israel came to the king at Hebron; there David made a covenant with them before the
4 LORD, and they anointed David king over Israel. David came to the throne
5 at the age of thirty and reigned for forty years. In Hebron he had ruled over Judah for seven years and a half, and for thirty-three years he reigned in Jerusalem over Israel and Judah together.

6 The king and his men went to Jerusalem to attack the Jebusites, whose land it was. The Jebusites said to David, 'Never shall you come in here; not till you have disposed of the blind and the lame', meaning that David
7 should never come in. None the less David did capture the stronghold of
8 Zion, and it is now known as the City of David. David said on that day, 'Everyone who would kill a Jebusite, let him use his grappling-iron to reach the lame and the blind, David's bitter enemies.' That is why they say, 'No blind or lame man shall come into the LORD's house.'

9 David took up his residence in the stronghold and called it the City of David. He built the city *a* round it, starting at the Millo and working
10 inwards. So David steadily grew stronger, for the LORD the God of Hosts was with him.

11 *b* Hiram king of Tyre sent an embassy to David; he sent cedar logs, and
12 with them carpenters and stonemasons, who built David a house. David knew by now that the LORD had confirmed him as king over Israel and had made his royal power stand higher for the sake of his people Israel.

13 After he had moved from Hebron he took more concubines and wives
14 *c* from Jerusalem; and more sons and daughters were born to him. These are the names of the children born to him in Jerusalem: Shammua,
15 16 Shobab, Nathan, Solomon, Ibhar, Elishua, Nepheg, Japhia, Elishama, Eliada and Eliphelet.

17 When the Philistines learnt that David had been anointed king over Israel, they came up in force to seek him out. David, hearing of this, took
18 refuge in the stronghold. The Philistines had come and overrun the Vale
19 of Rephaim. So David inquired of the LORD, 'If I attack the Philistines, wilt thou deliver them into my hands?' And the LORD answered, 'Go, I
20 will deliver the Philistines into your hands.' So he went up and attacked them at Baal-perazim and defeated them there. 'The LORD has broken through my enemies' lines,' David said, 'as a river breaks its banks.' That
21 is why the place was named Baal-perazim. *d* The Philistines left their idols behind them there, and David and his men carried them off.

22 The Philistines made another attack and overran the Vale of Rephaim.
23 David inquired of the LORD, who said, 'Do not attack now but wheel round
24 and take them in the rear opposite the aspens. As soon as you hear a rustling sound in the tree-tops, then act at once; for the LORD will have gone out
25 before you to defeat the Philistine army.' David did as the LORD had commanded, and drove the Philistines in flight all the way from Geba to Gezer.

6 After that David again summoned the picked men of Israel, thirty

a the city: *prob. rdg., cp. 1 Chr. 11. 8; Heb. om.*   *b* *Verses 11–25: cp. 1 Chr. 14. 1–16.*   *c* *Verses 14–16: cp. 1 Chr. 3. 5–8; 14. 4–7.*   *d* *That is* Baal of Break-through.

thousand in all, and went with the whole army to Baalath-judah *a* to fetch   2 *b*
the Ark of God which bears the name of the LORD of Hosts, who is enthroned upon the cherubim. They mounted the Ark of God on a new cart   3
and conveyed it from the house of Abinadab on the hill, with Uzzah and
Ahio, sons of Abinadab, guiding the cart. They took it with the Ark of God   4
upon it from Abinadab's house on the hill, with Ahio walking in front.
David and all Israel danced for joy before the LORD without restraint to the   5
sound of singing, *c* of harps and lutes, of tambourines and castanets and
cymbals. But when they came to a certain threshing-floor, the oxen   6
stumbled, and Uzzah reached out to the Ark of God and took hold of it.
The LORD was angry with Uzzah and struck him down there for his rash   7
act. So he died there beside the Ark of God. David was vexed because the   8
LORD's anger had broken out upon Uzzah, and he called the place Perez-
uzzah, *d* the name it still bears. David was afraid of the LORD that day and   9
said, 'How can I harbour the Ark of the LORD after this?' He felt he could   10
not take the Ark of the LORD with him to the City of David, but turned
aside and carried it to the house of Obed-edom the Gittite. Thus the Ark   11
of the LORD remained at Obed-edom's house for three months, and the
LORD blessed Obed-edom and all his family.

When they told David that the LORD had blessed Obed-edom's family   12 *e*
and all that was his because of the Ark of God, he went and brought up
the Ark of God from the house of Obed-edom to the City of David with
much rejoicing. When the bearers of the Ark of the LORD had gone six   13
steps he sacrificed an ox and a buffalo. David, wearing a linen ephod,   14
danced without restraint before the LORD. He and all the Israelites brought   15
up the Ark of the LORD with shouting and blowing of trumpets. But as the   16
Ark of the LORD was entering the City of David, Saul's daughter Michal
looked down through a window and saw King David leaping and capering
before the LORD, and she despised him in her heart. When they had brought   17
in the Ark of the LORD, they put it in its place inside the tent that David had
pitched for it, and David offered whole-offerings and shared-offerings
before the LORD. After David had completed these sacrifices, he blessed the   18
people in the name of the LORD of Hosts and gave food to all the people, a flat   19
loaf of bread, a portion of meat, and a cake of raisins, to every man and woman
in the whole gathering of the Israelites. Then all the people went home.
When David returned to greet his household, Michal, Saul's daughter,   20
came out to meet him and said, 'What a glorious day for the king of Israel,
when he exposed his person in the sight of his servants' slave-girls like any
empty-headed fool!' David answered Michal, 'But it was done in the   21
presence of the LORD, who chose me instead of your father and his family
and appointed me prince over Israel, the people of the LORD. Before the
LORD I will dance for joy, yes, and I will earn yet more disgrace and lower   22
myself still more in your eyes. But those girls of whom you speak, they will
honour me for it.' Michal, Saul's daughter, had no child to her dying day.   23

---

a to Baalath-judah: *prob. rdg., cp. 1 Chr. 13. 6; Heb.* from the lords of Judah.   *b Verses*
2–11 : cp. 1 Chr. 13. 6–14.   *c* without . . . singing: *prob. rdg., cp. 1 Chr. 13.*
8; Heb. to the beating of batons.   *d That is* Outbreak on Uzzah.   *e Verses*
12–19 : cp. 1 Chr. 15. 25—16. 3.

7 1[a] As soon as the king was established in his house and the LORD had given
2 him security from his enemies on all sides, he said to Nathan the prophet,
'Here I live in a house of cedar, while the Ark of God is housed in curtains.'
3 Nathan answered the king, 'Very well, do whatever you have in mind, for
4 the LORD is with you.' But that night the word of the LORD came to Nathan:
5 'Go and say to David my servant, "This is the word of the LORD: Are you
6 the man to build me a house to dwell in? Down to this day I have never
dwelt in a house since I brought Israel up from Egypt; I made my journey
7 in a tent and a tabernacle. Wherever I journeyed with Israel, did I ever ask
any of the judges [b] whom I appointed shepherds of my people Israel why
8 they had not built me a house of cedar?" Then say this to my servant David:
"This is the word of the LORD of Hosts: I took you from the pastures, and
9 from following the sheep, to be prince over my people Israel. I have been
with you wherever you have gone, and have destroyed all the enemies in
your path. I will make you a great name among the great ones of the earth.
10 I will assign a place for my people Israel; there I will plant them, and they
shall dwell in their own land. They shall be disturbed no more, never again
11 shall wicked men oppress them as they did in the past, ever since the time
when I appointed judges over Israel my people; and I will give you peace
from all your enemies. The LORD has told you that he would build up your
12 royal house. When your life ends and you rest with your forefathers, I
will set up one of your family, one of your own children, to succeed you
13 and I will establish his kingdom. It is he shall build a house in honour of
14 my name, and I will establish his royal throne for ever. I will be his father,
and he shall be my son. When he does wrong, I will punish him as any
15 father might, and not spare the rod. My love will never be withdrawn from
16 him as I withdrew it from Saul, whom I removed from your path. Your
family shall be established and your kingdom shall stand for all time in my
sight, and your throne shall be established for ever."'

17 Nathan recounted to David all that had been said to him and all that
18 had been revealed. Then King David went into the presence of the LORD
and took his place there and said, 'What am I, Lord GOD, and what is my
19 family, that thou hast brought me thus far? It was a small thing in thy
sight to have planned for thy servant's house in days long past. But such,
20 O Lord GOD, is the lot of a man embarked on a high career. [c] And now
what more can I say? for well thou knowest thy servant David, O Lord
21 GOD. Thou hast made good thy word; it was thy purpose to spread thy
22 servant's fame, and so thou hast raised me to this greatness. Great indeed
art thou, O Lord GOD; we have never heard of one like thee; there is no
23 god but thee. And thy people Israel, to whom can they be compared? Is
there any other nation on earth whom thou, O God, hast set out to redeem
from slavery to be thy people? Any other for whom thou hast done great
and terrible things to win fame for thyself? Any other whom thou hast
redeemed for thyself from Egypt by driving out other nations and their
24 gods to make way for them? Thou hast established thy people Israel as
25 thy own for ever, and thou, O LORD, hast become their God. But now,

---

[a] *Verses 1–29: cp. 1 Chr. 17. 1–27.*   [b] *Prob. rdg., cp. 1 Chr. 17. 6; Heb. tribes.*
[c] *embarked on a high career: prob. rdg., cp. 1 Chr. 17. 17; Heb. om.*

LORD God, perform what thou hast promised for thy servant and his house, and for all time; make good what thou hast said. May thy fame be 26 great for evermore and let men say, "The LORD of Hosts is God over Israel." So shall the house of thy servant David be established before thee. O LORD 27 of Hosts, God of Israel, thou hast shown me thy purpose, in saying to thy servant, "I will build up your house"; and therefore I have made bold to offer this prayer to thee. Thou, O Lord GOD, art God; thou hast made these 28 noble promises to thy servant, and thy promises come true; be pleased now 29 to bless thy servant's house that it may continue always before thee; thou, O Lord GOD, hast promised, and thy blessing shall rest upon thy servant's house for evermore.'

After this David defeated the Philistines and conquered them, and took 8 1 *a* from them Metheg-ha-ammah. He defeated the Moabites, and he made 2 them lie along the ground and measured them off with a length of cord; for every two lengths that were to be put to death one full length was spared. The Moabites became subject to him and paid him tribute. David also 3 defeated Hadadezer the Rehobite, king of Zobah, who was on his way to re-erect his monument of victory by *b* the river Euphrates. From him 4 David captured seventeen hundred horse and twenty thousand foot; he hamstrung all the chariot-horses, except a hundred which he retained. When the Aramaeans of Damascus came to the help of Hadadezer king of 5 Zobah, David destroyed twenty-two thousand of them, and established 6 garrisons among these Aramaeans; they became subject to him and paid him tribute. Thus the LORD gave David victory wherever he went. David 7 took the gold quivers borne by Hadadezer's servants and brought them to Jerusalem; and he also took a great quantity of bronze *c* from Hadadezer's 8 cities, Betah and Berothai.

When Toi king of Hamath heard that David had defeated the entire 9 army of Hadadezer, he sent his son Joram to King David to greet him and 10 to congratulate him on defeating Hadadezer in battle (for Hadadezer had been at war with Toi); and he brought with him vessels of silver, gold, and copper, which King David dedicated to the LORD. He dedicated 11 also the silver and gold taken from all the nations he had subdued, from 12 Edom and Moab, from the Ammonites, the Philistines, and Amalek, as well as part of the spoil taken from Hadadezer the Rehobite, king of Zobah.

David made a great name for himself by the slaughter of eighteen 13 thousand Edomites in the Valley of Salt, and on returning he stationed 14 garrisons throughout Edom, and all the Edomites were subject to him. Thus the LORD gave victory to David wherever he went.

David ruled over the whole of Israel and maintained law and justice 15 *d* among all his people. Joab son of Zeruiah was in command of the army; 16 Jehoshaphat son of Ahilud was secretary of state; Zadok and Abiathar son 17 of Ahimelech, son of Ahitub, *e* were priests; Seraiah was adjutant-general;

a *Verses 1–14: cp. 1 Chr. 18. 1–13.* *b* *re-erect ... victory by: or recover control of the crossings of ...* *c* *Or copper.* *d* *Verses 15–18: cp. 20. 23–26; 1 Kgs. 4. 2–6; 1 Chr. 18. 14–17.* *e* *and Abiathar ... Ahitub: prob. rdg., cp. 1 Sam. 22. 11, 20; 2 Sam. 20. 25; Heb. son of Ahitub and Ahimelech son of Abiathar.*

18 Benaiah son of Jehoiada commanded the Kerethite and Pelethite guards. David's sons were priests.

9 David asked, 'Is any member of Saul's family left, to whom I can show
2 true kindness for Jonathan's sake?' There was a servant of Saul's family named Ziba; and he was summoned to David. The king asked, 'Are you
3 Ziba?', and he answered, 'Your servant, sir.' So the king said, 'Is no member of Saul's family still alive to whom I may show the kindness that God requires?' 'Yes,' said Ziba, 'there is a son of Jonathan still alive; he is a
4 cripple, lame in both feet.' 'Where is he?' said the king, and Ziba answered, 'He is staying with Machir son of Ammiel in Lo-debar.'
5 So the king sent and fetched him from Lo-debar, from the house of
6 Machir son of Ammiel, and when Mephibosheth, son of Jonathan and Saul's grandson, entered David's presence, he prostrated himself and did obeisance. David said to him, 'Mephibosheth', and he answered, 'Your
7 servant, sir.' Then David said, 'Do not be afraid; I mean to show you kindness for your father Jonathan's sake, and I will give you back the whole estate of your grandfather Saul; you shall have a place for yourself at my
8 table.' So Mephibosheth prostrated himself again and said, 'Who am I
9 that you should spare a thought for a dead dog like me?' Then David summoned Saul's servant Ziba to his presence and said to him, 'I assign to your master's grandson all the property that belonged to Saul and his
10 family. You and your sons and your slaves must cultivate the land and bring in the harvest to provide for your master's household, but Mephibosheth your master's grandson shall have a place at my table.' This man
11 Ziba had fifteen sons and twenty slaves. Then Ziba answered the king, 'I will do all that your majesty commands.' So Mephibosheth took his
12 place in the royal household like one of the king's sons. He had a young son, named Mica; and the members of Ziba's household were all Mephi-
13 bosheth's servants, while Mephibosheth lived in Jerusalem and had his regular place at the king's table, crippled as he was in both feet.

10 1 [a] Some time afterwards the king of the Ammonites died and was succeeded
2 by his son Hanun. David said, 'I must keep up the same loyal friendship with Hanun son of Nahash as his father showed me', and he sent a mission to condole with him on the death of his father. But when David's envoys
3 entered the country of the Ammonites, the Ammonite princes said to Hanun their lord, 'Do you suppose David means to do honour to your father when he sends you his condolences? These men of his are spies
4 whom he has sent to find out how to overthrow the city.' So Hanun took David's servants, and he shaved off half their beards, cut off half their
5 garments up to the buttocks, and dismissed them. When David heard how they had been treated, he sent to meet them, for they were deeply humiliated, and ordered them to wait in Jericho and not to return until
6 their beards had grown again. The Ammonites knew that they had fallen into bad odour with David, so they hired the Aramaeans of Beth-rehob and of Zobah to come to their help with twenty thousand infantry; they also hired the king of Maacah with a thousand men, and twelve thousand men
7 from Tob. When David heard of it, he sent out Joab and all the fighting

[a] *Verses 1-19: cp. 1 Chr. 19. 1-19.*

men. The Ammonites came and took up their position at the entrance to the 8
city, while the Aramaeans of Zobah and of Rehob and the men of Tob
and Maacah took up theirs in the open country. When Joab saw that he was 9
threatened both front and rear, he detailed some picked Israelite troops
and drew them up facing the Aramaeans. The rest of his forces he put under 10
his brother Abishai, who took up a position facing the Ammonites. 'If 11
the Aramaeans prove too strong for me,' he said, 'you must come to my
relief; and if the Ammonites prove too strong for you, I will come to yours.
Courage! Let us fight bravely for our people and for the cities *a* of our God. 12
And the LORD's will be done.' But when Joab and his men came to close 13
quarters with the Aramaeans, they put them to flight; and when the 14
Ammonites saw them in flight, they too fled before Abishai and entered the
city. Then Joab returned from the battle against the Ammonites and came
to Jerusalem. The Aramaeans saw that they had been worsted by Israel; 15
but they rallied their forces, and Hadadezer sent to summon other Ara- 16
maeans from the Great Bend of the Euphrates, and they advanced to
Helam under Shobach, commander of Hadadezer's army. Their move- 17
ment was reported to David, who immediately mustered all the forces of
Israel, crossed the Jordan and advanced to meet them at Helam. There the
Aramaeans took up positions facing David and engaged him, but were put 18
to flight by Israel. David slew seven hundred Aramaeans in chariots and
forty thousand horsemen, mortally wounding Shobach, who died on the
field. When all the vassal kings of Hadadezer saw that they had been 19
worsted by Israel, they sued for peace and submitted to the Israelites. The
Aramaeans never dared help the Ammonites again.

AT THE TURN OF THE YEAR, when kings take the field, David sent Joab 11
out with his other officers and all the Israelite forces, and they ravaged
Ammon and laid siege to Rabbah, while David remained in Jerusalem.
One evening David got up from his couch and, as he walked about on the 2
roof of the palace, he saw from there a woman bathing, and she was very
beautiful. He sent to inquire who she was, and the answer came, 'It must 3
be Bathsheba daughter of Eliam and wife of Uriah the Hittite.' So he sent 4
messengers to fetch her, and when she came to him, he had intercourse with
her; though she was still being purified after her period, and then she went
home. She conceived, and sent word to David that she was pregnant. David 5 6
ordered Joab to send Uriah the Hittite to him. So Joab sent him to David,
and when he arrived, David asked him for news of Joab and the troops and 7
how the campaign was going; and then said to him, 'Go down to your house 8
and wash your feet after your journey.' As he left the palace, a present from
the king followed him. But Uriah did not return to his house; he lay down 9
by the palace gate with the king's slaves. David heard that Uriah had not 10
gone home, and said to him, 'You have had a long journey, why did you
not go home?' Uriah answered David, 'Israel and Judah are under canvas, *b* 11
and so is the Ark, and my lord Joab and your majesty's officers are camping
in the open; how can I go home to eat and drink and to sleep with my wife?
By your life, I cannot do this!' David then said to Uriah, 'Stay here another 12

a Or altars.   *b* under canvas: *or* at Succoth.

day, and tomorrow I will let you go.' So Uriah stayed in Jerusalem that
13 day. The next day David invited him to eat and drink with him and made
him drunk. But in the evening Uriah went out to lie down in his blanket [a]
among the king's slaves and did not go home.

14 The following morning David wrote a letter to Joab and sent Uriah with
15 it. He wrote in the letter, 'Put Uriah opposite the enemy where the fighting
16 is fiercest and then fall back, and leave him to meet his death.' Joab had
been watching the city, and he stationed Uriah at a point where he knew
17 they would put up a stout fight. The men of the city sallied out and engaged
Joab, and some of David's guards fell; Uriah the Hittite was also killed.
18 19 Joab sent David a dispatch with all the news of the battle and gave the
messenger these instructions: 'When you have finished your report to the
20 king, if he is angry and asks, "Why did you go so near the city during
the fight? You must have known there would be shooting from the wall.
21 Remember who killed Abimelech son of Jerubbesheth. It was a woman
who threw down an upper millstone on to him from the wall of Thebez
and killed him! Why did you go so near the wall?"—if he asks this, then
tell him, "Your servant Uriah the Hittite also is dead."'
22 So the messenger set out and, when he came to David, he made his report
as Joab had instructed. David was angry with Joab and said to the messenger, 'Why did you go so near the city during the fight? You must have
known you would be struck down from the wall. Remember who killed
Abimelech son of Jerubbesheth. Was it not a woman who threw down an
upper millstone on to him from the wall of Thebez and killed him? Why
23 did you go near the wall?' He answered, 'The enemy massed against us
and sallied out into the open; we pressed them back as far as the gateway.
24 There the archers shot down at us from the wall and some of your majesty's
25 men fell; and your servant Uriah the Hittite is dead.' David said to the
man, 'Give Joab this message: "Do not let this distress you—there is no
knowing where the sword will strike; press home your attack on the city,
and you will take it and raze it to the ground"; and tell him to take heart.'
26 When Uriah's wife heard that her husband was dead, she mourned for
27 him; and when the period of mourning was over, David sent for her and
brought her into his house. She became his wife and bore him a son. But
what David had done was wrong in the eyes of the LORD.

12 The LORD sent Nathan the prophet to David, and when he entered his
presence, he said to him, 'There were once two men in the same city, one
2 3 rich and the other poor. The rich man had large flocks and herds, but the
poor man had nothing of his own except one little ewe lamb. He reared
it himself, and it grew up in his home with his own sons. It ate from his
dish, drank from his cup and nestled in his arms; it was like a daughter to
4 him. One day a traveller came to the rich man's house, and he, too mean to
take something from his own flocks and herds to serve to his guest, took
5 the poor man's lamb and served up that.' David was very angry, and burst
6 out, 'As the LORD lives, the man who did this deserves to die! He shall pay
for the lamb four times over, because he has done this and shown no pity.'
7 Then Nathan said to David, 'You are the man. This is the word of the LORD

[a] *in his blanket: or* on his pallet.

the God of Israel to you: "I anointed you king over Israel, I rescued you
from the power of Saul, I gave you your master's daughter *a* and his wives 8
to be your own, I gave you the daughters of Israel and Judah; and, had this
not been enough, I would have added other favours as great. Why then 9
have you flouted the word of the LORD by doing what is wrong in my eyes?
You have struck down Uriah the Hittite with the sword; the man himself
you murdered by the sword of the Ammonites, and you have stolen his
wife. Now, therefore, since you have despised me and taken the wife of 10
Uriah the Hittite to be your own wife, your family shall never again have
rest from the sword." This is the word of the LORD: "I will bring trouble 11
upon you from within your own family; I will take your wives and give
them to another man before your eyes, and he will lie with them in broad
daylight. What you did was done in secret; but I will do this in the light of 12
day for all Israel to see." ' David said to Nathan, 'I have sinned against the 13
LORD.' Nathan answered him, 'The LORD has laid on another the consequences of your sin: you shall not die, but, because in this you have 14
shown your contempt for the LORD,*b* the boy that will be born to you shall
die.'

When Nathan had gone home, the LORD struck the boy whom Uriah's 15
wife had borne to David, and he was very ill. David prayed to God for 16
the child; he fasted and went in and spent the night fasting, lying on the
ground. The older men of his household tried to get him to rise from the 17
ground, but he refused and would eat no food with them. On the seventh 18
day the boy died, and David's servants were afraid to tell him. 'While the
boy was alive,' they said, 'we spoke to him, and he did not listen to us; how
can we now tell him that the boy is dead? He may do something desperate.'
But David saw his servants whispering among themselves and guessed 19
that the boy was dead. He asked, 'Is the boy dead?', and they answered,
'He is dead.' Then David rose from the ground, washed and anointed 20
himself, and put on fresh clothes; he entered the house of the LORD and
prostrated himself there. Then he went home, asked for food to be brought,
and when it was ready, he ate it. His servants asked him, 'What is this? 21
While the boy lived you fasted and wept for him, but now that he is dead
you rise up and eat.' He answered, 'While the boy was still alive I fasted 22
and wept, thinking, "It may be that the LORD will be gracious to me, and
the boy may live." But now that he is dead, why should I fast? Can I 23
bring him back again? I shall go to him; he will not come back to me.'
David consoled Bathsheba his wife; he went to her and had intercourse 24
with her, and she gave birth to a son and called him Solomon. And because
the LORD loved him, he sent word through Nathan the prophet that for 25
the LORD's sake he should be given the name Jedidiah. *c*

Joab attacked the Ammonite city of Rabbah and took the King's Pool. 26*d*
He sent messengers to David with this report: 'I have attacked Rabbah and 27
have taken the pool. You had better muster the rest of the army yourself, 28
besiege the city and take it; otherwise I shall take the city and the name to
be proclaimed over it will be mine.' David accordingly mustered his whole 29

a *Prob. rdg.; Heb.* house.   *b* the LORD: *prob. rdg.; Heb.* the enemies of the LORD.
c *That is* Beloved of the LORD.   *d* *Verses 26–31 : cp. 1 Chr. 20. 1–3.*

30 forces, marched to Rabbah, attacked it and took it. He took the crown from
the head of Milcom, which weighed a talent of gold and was set with a
precious stone, and this he placed on his own head. He also removed a
31 great quantity of booty from the city; he took its inhabitants and set them
to work with saws and other iron tools, sharp and toothed, and made them
work in the brick-kilns. David did this to all the cities of the Ammonites;
then he and all his people returned to Jerusalem.

Absalom's rebellion and other conflicts

13 NOW DAVID'S SON ABSALOM had a beautiful sister named Tamar,
2 and Amnon, another of David's sons, fell in love with her. Amnon was
so distressed that he fell sick with love for his half-sister; for he thought it
3 an impossible thing to approach her since she was a virgin. But he had a
friend named Jonadab, son of David's brother Shimeah, who was a very
4 shrewd man. He said to Amnon, 'Why are you so low-spirited morning
after morning, my lord? Will you not tell me?' So Amnon told him that
5 he was in love with Tamar, his brother Absalom's sister. Jonadab said to
him, 'Take to your bed and pretend to be ill. When your father comes to
visit you, say to him, "Please let my sister Tamar come and give me my
food. Let her prepare it in front of me, so that I may watch her and then
6 take it from her own hands."' So Amnon lay down and pretended to be
ill. When the king came to visit him, he said, 'Sir, let my sister Tamar come
and make a few cakes in front of me, and serve them to me with her own
7 hands.' So David sent a message to Tamar in the palace: 'Go to your
8 brother Amnon's quarters and prepare a meal for him.' Tamar came to
her brother and found him lying down; she took some dough and kneaded
9 it, made the cakes in front of him and baked them. Then she took the pan
and turned them out before him. But Amnon refused to eat and ordered
10 everyone out of the room. When they had all left, he said to Tamar, 'Bring
the food over to the recess so that I may eat from your own hands.' Tamar
took the cakes she had made and brought them to Amnon in the recess.
11 But when she offered them to him, he caught hold of her and said, 'Come
12 to bed with me, sister.' But she answered, 'No, brother, do not dishonour
13 me, we do not do such things in Israel; do not behave like a beast. Where
could I go and hide my disgrace?—and you would sink as low as any beast
in Israel. Why not speak to the king for me? He will not refuse you leave
14 to marry me.' He would not listen, but overpowered her, dishonoured her
and raped her.
15 Then Amnon was filled with utter hatred for her; his hatred was stronger
16 than the love he had felt, and he said to her, 'Get up and go.' She answered,
'No. It is wicked to send me away. This is harder to bear than all you have
17 done to me.' He would not listen to her, but summoned the boy who
attended him and said, 'Get rid of this woman, put her out and bolt the
18 door after her.' She had on a long, sleeved robe, the usual dress of unmarried princesses; and the boy turned her out and bolted the door.
19 Tamar threw ashes over her head, rent the long, sleeved robe that she was

wearing, put her hands on her head and went away, sobbing as she went. Her brother Absalom asked her, 'Has your brother Amnon been with you? 20 Keep this to yourself, he is your brother; do not take it to heart.' So Tamar remained in her brother Absalom's house, desolate. When King David 21 heard the whole story he was very angry; but he would not hurt Amnon because he was his eldest son and he loved him. Absalom did not speak a 22 single word to Amnon, friendly or unfriendly; he hated him for having dishonoured his sister Tamar.

Two years later Absalom invited all the king's sons to his sheep-shearing 23 at Baal-hazor, near Ephron. *a* He approached the king and said, 'Sir, I am 24 shearing; will your majesty and your servants come?' The king answered, 25 'No, my son, we must not all come and be a burden to you.' Absalom pressed him, but David was still unwilling to go and dismissed him with his blessing. But Absalom said, 'If you cannot, may my brother Amnon 26 come with us?' 'Why should he go with you?' the king asked; but Absalom 27 pressed him again, so he let Amnon and all the other princes go with him.

Then Absalom prepared a feast fit for a king. He gave his servants these 28 orders: 'Bide your time, and when Amnon is merry with wine I shall say to you, "Strike." Then kill Amnon. You have nothing to fear, these are my orders; be bold and resolute.' Absalom's servants did as he had told 29 them, whereupon all the king's sons mounted their mules in haste and set off for home.

While they were on their way, a rumour reached David that Absalom 30 had murdered all the royal princes and that not one was left alive. The king 31 stood up and rent his clothes and then threw himself on the ground; all his servants were standing round him with their clothes rent. Then 32 Jonadab, son of David's brother Shimeah, said, 'Your majesty must not think that they have killed all the young princes; only Amnon is dead; Absalom has looked black ever since Amnon ravished his sister Tamar. Your majesty must not pay attention to a mere rumour that all the princes 33 are dead; only Amnon is dead.'

Absalom made good his escape. Meanwhile the sentry looked up and 34 saw a crowd of people coming down the hill from the direction of Horonaim. *b* He came and reported to the king, 'I see men coming down the hill from Horonaim.' Then Jonadab said to the king, 'Here come the royal 35 princes, just as I said they would.' As he finished speaking, the princes 36 came in and broke into loud lamentations; the king and all his servants also wept bitterly.

But Absalom went to take refuge with Talmai son of Ammihur king of 37 Geshur; and for a long while the king mourned for Amnon. Absalom, 38 having escaped to Geshur, stayed there for three years; and David's heart 39 went out to him with longing, for he became reconciled to the death of Amnon.

Joab son of Zeruiah saw that the king's heart was set on Absalom, so he 14 1 2 sent to Tekoah and fetched a wise woman. He said to her, 'Pretend to be a mourner; put on mourning, go without anointing yourself, and behave like a bereaved woman who has been long in mourning. Then go to the 3

---

a *Prob. rdg.; Heb.* Ephraim.   *b* *Prob. rdg.; Heb.* from a road behind him.

king and repeat what I tell you.' He then told her exactly what she was to say.

4 When the woman from Tekoah came into the king's presence, she threw herself, face downwards, on the ground and did obeisance, and cried,
5 'Help, your majesty!' The king asked, 'What is it?' She answered, 'O sir,
6 I am a widow; my husband is dead. I had two sons; they came to blows out in the country where there was no one to part them, and one of them struck
7 the other and killed him. Now, sir, the kinsmen have risen against me and they all cry, "Hand over the man who has killed his brother, so that we can put him to death for taking his brother's life, and so cut off the succession." If they do this, they will stamp out my last live ember and leave my husband
8 no name and no descendant upon earth.' 'Go home,' said the king to the
9 woman, 'and I will settle your case.' But the woman continued, 'The guilt be on me, your majesty, and on my father's house; let the king and his
10 throne be blameless.' The king said, 'If anyone says anything more to you,
11 bring him to me and he shall never molest you again.' Then the woman went on, 'Let your majesty call upon the LORD your God, to prevent his kinsmen bound to vengeance from doing their worst and destroying my son.' The king swore, 'As the LORD lives, not a hair of your son's head shall fall to the ground.'

12 The woman then said, 'May I add one word more, your majesty?' 'Say
13 on', said the king. So she continued, 'How then could it enter your head to do this same wrong to God's people? Out of your own mouth, your majesty, you condemn yourself: you have refused to bring back the man
14 you have banished. We shall all die; we shall be like water that is spilt on the ground and lost; but God will spare the man who does not set himself
15 to keep the outlaw in banishment. I came to say this to your majesty because the people have threatened me. I thought, "If I can only speak to the
16 king, perhaps he will attend to my case; for he will listen, and he will save me from the man who is seeking to cut off me and my son together from
17 Israel, God's own possession." I thought too that the words of my lord the king would be a comfort to me; for your majesty is like the angel of God and can decide between right and wrong. The LORD your God be with
18 you!' Then the king said to the woman, 'Tell me no lies: I shall now ask you
19 a question.' 'Speak on, your majesty', she said. So he asked, 'Is the hand of Joab behind you in all this?' 'Your life upon it, sir!' she answered; 'when your majesty asks a question, there is no way round it, right or left. Yes, your servant Joab did prompt me; it was he who put the whole story
20 into my mouth. He did it to give a new turn to this affair. Your majesty is as wise as the angel of God and knows all that goes on in the land.'

21 The king said to Joab, 'You have my consent; go and fetch back the
22 young man Absalom.' Then Joab humbly prostrated himself, took leave of the king with a blessing and said, 'Now I know that I have found favour
23 with your majesty, because you have granted my humble petition.' Joab
24 went at once to Geshur and brought Absalom to Jerusalem, but the king said, 'Let him go to his own quarters; he shall not come into my presence.' So Absalom went to his own quarters and did not enter the king's presence.
25 No one in all Israel was so greatly admired for his beauty as Absalom;

he was without flaw from the crown of his head to the sole of his foot. His   26
hair, when he cut his hair (as he had to do every year, for he found it heavy),
weighed two hundred shekels by the royal standard. Three sons were born   27
to Absalom, and a daughter named Tamar, who was a very beautiful
woman.

Absalom remained in Jerusalem for two whole years without entering   28
the king's presence. He summoned Joab to send a message by him to the   29
king, but Joab refused to come; he sent for him a second time, but he still
refused. Then Absalom said to his servants, 'You know that Joab has a   30
field next to mine with barley growing in it; go and set fire to it.' So
Absalom's servants set fire to the field. Joab promptly came to Absalom   31
in his own quarters and said to him, 'Why have your servants set fire to my
field?' Absalom answered Joab, 'I had sent for you to come here, so that   32
I could ask you to give the king this message from me: "Why did I leave
Geshur? It would be better for me if I were still there. Let me now come
into your majesty's presence and, if I have done any wrong, put me to
death."' When Joab went to the king and told him, he summoned Absalom,   33
who came and prostrated himself humbly before the king; and he greeted
Absalom with a kiss.

AFTER THIS, ABSALOM PROVIDED himself with a chariot and horses   **15**
and an escort of fifty men. He made it a practice to rise early and stand   2
beside the road which runs through the city gate. He would hail every man
who had a case to bring before the king for judgement and would ask him
what city he came from. When he answered, 'I come, sir, from such and
such a tribe of Israel', Absalom would say to him, 'I can see that you have   3
a very good case, but you will get no hearing from the king.' And he would   4
add, 'If only I were appointed judge in the land, it would be my business
to see that everyone who brought a suit or a claim got justice from me.'
Whenever a man approached to prostrate himself, Absalom would stretch   5
out his hand, take hold of him and kiss him. By behaving like this to every   6
Israelite who sought the king's justice, Absalom stole the affections of the
Israelites.

At the end of four years, Absalom said to the king, 'May I have leave   7
now to go to Hebron to fulfil a vow there that I made to the LORD? For   8
when I lived in Geshur, in Aram, I made this vow: "If the LORD brings
me back to Jerusalem, I will become a worshipper of the LORD in Hebron."'
The king answered, 'Certainly you may go'; so he set off for Hebron at   9
once. Absalom sent runners through all the tribes of Israel with this   10
message: 'As soon as you hear the sound of the trumpet, then say, "Absalom
is king in Hebron."' Two hundred men accompanied Absalom from   11
Jerusalem; they were invited and went in all innocence, knowing nothing
of the affair. Absalom also sent to summon Ahithophel the Gilonite,   12
David's counsellor, from Giloh his city, where he was offering the customary sacrifices. The conspiracy gathered strength, and Absalom's supporters
increased in number.

When news reached David that the men of Israel had transferred their   13
allegiance to Absalom, he said to those who were with him in Jerusalem,   14

'We must get away at once; or there will be no escape from Absalom for any of us. Make haste, or else he will soon be upon us and bring disaster
15 on us, showing no mercy to anyone in the city.' The king's servants said to him, 'As your majesty thinks best; we are ready.'
16 When the king departed, all his household followed him except ten
17 concubines, whom he left in charge of the palace. At the Far House the
18 king and all the people who were with him halted. His own servants then stood *a* beside him, while the Kerethite and Pelethite guards and Ittai *b*
19 with the six hundred Gittites under him marched past the king. The king said to Ittai the Gittite, 'Are you here too? Why are you coming with us? Go back and stay with the new king, for you are a foreigner and, what is
20 more, an exile from your own country. You came only yesterday, and today must you be compelled to share my wanderings? I do not know where I am going. Go back home and take your countrymen with you; and may
21 the LORD ever be your steadfast friend.' Ittai swore to the king, 'As the LORD lives, your life upon it, wherever you may be, in life or in death, I,
22 your servant, will be there.' David said to Ittai, 'It is well, march on!' So Ittai the Gittite marched on with his whole company and all the depend-
23 ants who were with him. The whole country-side re-echoed with their weeping. And the king remained standing *c* while all the people crossed the gorge of the Kidron before him, by way of the olive-tree in the wilderness. *d*
24 Zadok also was there with all the Levites; they were carrying the Ark of the Covenant of God, which they set down beside Abiathar *e* until all
25 the people had passed out of the city. But the king said to Zadok, 'Take the Ark of God back to the city. If I find favour with the LORD, he will bring
26 me back and will let me see the Ark and its dwelling-place again. But if he says he does not want me, then here I am; let him do what he pleases
27 with me.' The king went on to say to Zadok the priest, 'Can you make good use of your eyes? You may safely go back to the city, you and Abiathar, *f* and take with you the two young men, Ahimaaz your son and Abiathar's
28 son Jonathan. Do not forget: I will linger at the Fords of the Wilderness
29 until you can send word to me.' Then Zadok and Abiathar took the Ark of God back to Jerusalem and stayed there.
30 David wept as he went up the slope of the Mount of Olives; he was bare-headed and went bare-foot. The people with him all had their heads un-
31 covered and wept as they went. David had been told that Ahithophel was among the conspirators with Absalom, and he prayed, 'Frustrate, O LORD, the counsel of Ahithophel.'
32 As David was approaching the top of the ridge where it was the custom to prostrate oneself to God, Hushai the Archite was there to meet him with
33 his tunic rent and earth on his head. David said to him, 'If you come with
34 me you will only be a hindrance; but you can help me to frustrate Ahitho-phel's plans if you go back to the city and say to Absalom, "I will be your majesty's servant; up to now I have been your father's servant, and now

---

a Prob. rdg.; *Heb.* passed.   *b* and Ittai: *prob. rdg.; Heb. om.*   *c* Prob. rdg.; *Heb.* passing.   *d* by way ... wilderness: *prob. rdg.; Heb. obscure.*   *e* beside Abiathar: *prob. rdg.; Heb.* and Abiathar went up.   *f* you and Abiathar: *prob. rdg.,* cp. *verse 29; Heb. om.*

I will be yours." You will have with you, as you know, the priests Zadok 35
and Abiathar; tell them everything that you hear in the king's household.
They have with them Zadok's son Ahimaaz and Abiathar's son Jonathan, 36
and through them you may pass on to me everything you hear.' So Hushai, 37
David's friend, came to the city as Absalom was entering Jerusalem.

When David had moved on a little from the top of the ridge, he was met 16
by Ziba the servant of Mephibosheth, who had with him a pair of asses
saddled and loaded with two hundred loaves, a hundred clusters of raisins,
a hundred bunches of summer fruit, and a flagon of wine. The king said 2
to him, 'What are you doing with these?' Ziba answered, 'The asses are
for the king's family to ride on, the bread and the summer fruit are for the
servants to eat, and the wine for anyone who becomes exhausted in the
wilderness.' The king asked, 'Where is your master's grandson?' 'He is 3
staying in Jerusalem,' said Ziba, 'for he thought that the Israelites might
now restore to him his grandfather's throne.' The king said to Ziba, 'You 4
shall have everything that belongs to Mephibosheth.' Ziba said, 'I am your
humble servant, sir; may I continue to stand well with you.'

As King David approached Bahurim, a man of Saul's family, whose 5
name was Shimei son of Gera, came out, cursing as he came. He showered 6
stones right and left on David and on all the king's servants and on everyone, soldiers and people alike. This is what Shimei said as he cursed him: 7
'Get out, get out, you scoundrel! you man of blood! The LORD has taken 8
vengeance on you for the blood of the house of Saul whose throne you stole,
and he has given the kingdom to your son Absalom. You murderer, see
how your crimes have overtaken you!'

Then Abishai son of Zeruiah said to the king, 'Why let this dead dog 9
curse your majesty? I will go across and knock off his head.' But the king 10
said, 'What has this to do with you, you sons of Zeruiah? If he curses and
if the LORD has told him to curse David, who can question it?' David said 11
to Abishai and to all his servants, 'If my son, my own son, is out to kill me,
who can wonder at this Benjamite? Let him be, let him curse; for the LORD
has told him to do it. But perhaps the LORD will mark my sufferings and 12
bestow a blessing on me in place of the curse laid on me this day.' David 13
and his men continued on their way, and Shimei moved along the ridge
of the hill parallel to David's path, cursing as he went and hurling stones
across the valley at him and kicking up the dust. When the king and all the 14
people with him reached the Jordan, they were worn out; and they refreshed
themselves there.

By now Absalom and all his Israelites had reached Jerusalem, and 15
Ahithophel with him. When Hushai the Archite, David's friend, met 16
Absalom he said to him, 'Long live the king! Long live the king!' But 17
Absalom retorted, 'Is this your loyalty to your friend? Why did you not go
with him?' Hushai answered Absalom, 'Because I mean to attach myself 18
to the man chosen by the LORD, by this people, and by all the men of Israel,
and with him I will remain. After all, whom ought I to serve? Should I not 19
serve the son? I will serve you as I have served your father.' Then Absalom 20
said to Ahithophel, 'Give us your advice: how shall we act?' Ahithophel 21
answered, 'Have intercourse with your father's concubines whom he left

in charge of the palace. Then all Israel will come to hear that you have given
great cause of offence to your father, and this will confirm the resolution
22 of your followers.' So they set up a tent for Absalom on the roof, and he
23 lay with his father's concubines in the sight of all Israel. In those days a
man would seek counsel of Ahithophel as readily as he might make an
inquiry of the word of God; that was how Ahithophel's counsel was
esteemed by David and Absalom.

17 Ahithophel said to Absalom, 'Let me pick twelve thousand men, and I
2 will pursue David tonight. I shall overtake him when he is tired and dis-
pirited; I will cut him off from his people and they will all scatter; and I
3 shall kill no one but the king. I will bring all the people over to you as a
bride is brought to her husband. It is only one man's life that you are seek-
4 ing; the rest of the people will be unharmed.' Absalom and all the elders
5 of Israel approved of Ahithophel's advice; but Absalom said, 'Summon
6 Hushai the Archite and let us hear what he too has to say.' Hushai came,
and Absalom told him all that Ahithophel had said and asked him, 'Shall
we do what he says? If not, say what you think.'

7 Hushai said to Absalom, 'For once the counsel that Ahithophel has given
8 is not good. You know', he went on, 'that your father and the men with him
are hardened warriors and savage as a bear in the wilds robbed of her cubs.
Your father is an old campaigner and will not spend the night with the
9 main body; even now he will be lying hidden in a pit or in some such place.
10 Then if any of your men are killed at the outset, anyone who hears the news
will say, "Disaster has overtaken the followers of Absalom." The courage
of the most resolute and lion-hearted will melt away, for all Israel knows
11 that your father is a man of war and has determined men with him. My
advice is this. Wait until the whole of Israel, from Dan to Beersheba, is
gathered about you, countless as grains of sand on the sea-shore, and then
12 you shall march with them in person. Then we shall come upon him somewhere, wherever he may be, and descend on him like dew falling on the
13 ground, and not a man of his family or of his followers will be left alive. If
he retreats into a city, all Israel will bring ropes to that city, and we will
14 drag it into a ravine until not a stone can be found on the site.' Absalom
and all the men of Israel said, 'Hushai the Archite gives us better advice
than Ahithophel.' It was the LORD's purpose to frustrate Ahithophel's
good advice and so bring disaster upon Absalom.

15 Hushai told Zadok and Abiathar the priests all the advice that Ahithophel
16 had given to Absalom and the elders of Israel, and also his own. 'Now send
quickly to David,' he said, 'and warn him not to spend the night at the
Fords of the Wilderness but to cross the river at once, before a blow can
17 be struck at the king and his followers.' Jonathan and Ahimaaz were
waiting at En-rogel, and a servant girl would go and tell them what happened and they would pass it on to King David; for they could not risk
18 being seen entering the city. But this time a lad saw them and told Absalom;
so the two of them hurried to the house of a man in Bahurim. He had a pit
19 in his courtyard, and they climbed down into it. The man's wife took a
covering, spread it over the mouth of the pit and strewed grain over it,
20 and no one was any the wiser. Absalom's servants came to the house and

358

asked the woman, 'Where are Ahimaaz and Jonathan?' She answered, 'They went beyond the pool.' The men searched but could not find them; so they went back to Jerusalem. When they had gone the two climbed out 21 of the pit and went off to report to King David and said, 'Over the water at once, make haste!', and they told him Ahithophel's plan against him. So 22 David and all his company began at once to cross the Jordan; by daybreak there was not one who had not reached the other bank.

When Ahithophel saw that his advice had not been taken he saddled his 23 ass, went straight home to his own city, gave his last instructions to his household, and hanged himself. So he died and was buried in his father's grave.

By the time that Absalom had crossed the Jordan with the Israelites, 24 David was already at Mahanaim. Absalom had appointed Amasa as 25 commander-in-chief instead of Joab; he was the son of a man named Ithra, an Ishmaelite, by Abigal daughter of Nahash and sister to Joab's mother Zeruiah. The Israelites and Absalom camped in the district of Gilead. 26 When David came to Mahanaim, he was met by Shobi son of Nahash 27 from the Ammonite town Rabbah, Machir son of Ammiel from Lo-debar, and Barzillai the Gileadite from Rogelim, bringing mattresses and blankets, 28 bowls and jugs.*a* They brought also wheat and barley, meal and parched grain, beans and lentils, honey and curds, sheep and fat cattle, and offered 29 them to David and his people to eat, knowing that the people must be hungry and thirsty and weary in the wilderness.

David mustered the people who were with him, and appointed officers **18** over units of a thousand and a hundred. Then he divided the army in three, 2 one division under the command of Joab, one under Joab's brother Abishai son of Zeruiah, and the third under Ittai the Gittite. The king announced to the army that he was coming out himself with them to battle. But they said, 'No, you must not come out; if we turn and run, no 3 one will take any notice, nor will they, even if half of us are killed; but you are worth ten thousand of us, and it would be better now for you to remain in the city in support.' 'I will do what you think best', answered the king; 4 and he then stood beside the gate, and the army marched past in their units of a thousand and a hundred. The king gave orders to Joab, Abishai, 5 and Ittai: 'Deal gently with the young man Absalom for my sake.' The whole army heard the king giving all his officers this order to spare Absalom.

The army took the field against the Israelites and the battle was fought 6 in the forest of Ephron.*b* There the Israelites were routed before the 7 onslaught of David's men; so great was the rout that twenty thousand men fell that day. The fighting spread over the whole country-side, and the 8 forest took toll of more people that day than the sword.

Now some of David's men caught sight of Absalom. He was riding a 9 mule and, as it passed beneath a great oak,*c* his head was caught in its boughs; he found himself in mid air and the mule went on from under him. One of the men who saw it went and told Joab, 'I saw Absalom hanging 10 from an oak.' While the man was telling him, Joab broke in, 'You saw him? 11

---

a bringing . . . jugs: *prob. rdg.; Heb.* a couch, bowls and a potter's vessel.   *b* *Prob. rdg.; Heb.* Ephraim.   *c* *Or* terebinth.

Why did you not strike him to the ground then and there? I would have
12 given you ten pieces of silver and a belt.' The man answered, 'If you were
to put in my hands a thousand pieces of silver, I would not lift a finger
against the king's son; for we all heard the king giving orders to you and
Abishai and Ittai that whoever finds himself near the young man Absalom
13 must take great care of him. If I had dealt him a treacherous blow, the king
14 would soon have known, and you would have kept well out of it.' 'That is a
lie!' said Joab. 'I will make a start and show you.'^a So he picked up three
stout sticks and drove them against Absalom's chest while he was held
15 fast in the tree and still alive. Then ten young men who were Joab's
16 armour-bearers closed in on Absalom, struck at him and killed him. Joab
sounded the trumpet, and the army came back from the pursuit of Israel
17 because he had called it off. They took Absalom's body and flung it into
a great pit in the forest, and raised over it a huge pile of stones. The Israelites
all fled to their homes.

18   The pillar in the King's Vale had been set up by Absalom in his lifetime,
for he said, 'I have no son to carry on my name.' He had named the pillar
after himself; and to this day it is called Absalom's Monument.

19   Ahimaaz son of Zadok said, 'Let me run and take the news to the king
20 that the LORD has avenged him and delivered him from his enemies.' But
Joab replied, 'This is no day for you to be the bearer of news. Another day
you may have news to carry, but not today, because the king's son is dead.'
21 Joab told a Cushite to go and report to the king what he had seen. The
22 Cushite bowed low before Joab and set off running. Ahimaaz pleaded again
with Joab, 'Come what may,' he said, 'let me run after the Cushite.' 'Why
should you, my son?' asked Joab. 'You will get no reward for your news.'
23 'Come what may,' he said, 'I will run.' 'Go, then', said Joab. So Ahimaaz
ran by the road through the Plain of the Jordan and outstripped the Cushite.

24   David was sitting between the two gates when the watchman went up
to the roof of the gatehouse by the wall and, looking out, saw a man running
25 alone. The watchman called to the king and told him. 'If he is alone,' said
26 the king, 'then he has news.' The man came nearer and nearer. Then the
watchman saw another man running. He called down to the gate-keeper
and said, 'Look, there is another man running alone.' The king said, 'He
27 too brings news.' The watchman said, 'I see by the way he runs that the
first runner is Ahimaaz son of Zadok.' The king said, 'He is a good fellow
28 and shall earn the reward for good news.' Ahimaaz called out to the king,
'All is well!' He bowed low before him and said, 'Blessed be the LORD
your God who has given into your hands the men who rebelled against
29 your majesty.' The king asked, 'Is all well with the young man Absalom?'
Ahimaaz answered, 'Sir, your servant Joab sent me,^b I saw a great com-
30 motion, but I did not know what had happened.' The king told him
31 to stand on one side; so he turned aside and stood there. Then the Cushite came in and said, 'Good news, your majesty! The LORD has avenged
32 you this day on all those who rebelled against you.' The king said to
the Cushite, 'Is all well with the young man Absalom?' The Cushite

^a I will . . . show you: *or* I can waste no more time on you like this.   ^b Sir . . . sent
me: *prob. rdg.; Heb.* At the sending of Joab the king's servant and your servant.

answered, 'May all the king's enemies and all rebels who would do you harm be as that young man is.' The king was deeply moved and went up 33 to the roof-chamber over the gate and wept, crying out as he went, 'O, my son! Absalom my son, my son Absalom! If only I had died instead of you! O Absalom, my son, my son.'

Joab was told that the king was weeping and mourning for Absalom; **19** and that day victory was turned to mourning for the whole army, because 2 they heard how the king grieved for his son; they stole into the city like 3 men ashamed to show their faces after a defeat in battle. The king hid his 4 face and cried aloud, 'My son Absalom; O Absalom, my son, my son.' But Joab came into the king's quarters and said to him, 'You have put to 5 shame this day all your servants, who have saved you and your sons and daughters, your wives and your concubines. You love those that hate you 6 and hate those that love you; you have made us feel, officers and men alike, that we are nothing to you; for it is plain that if Absalom were still alive and all of us dead, you would be content. Now go at once and give your 7 servants some encouragement; if you refuse, I swear by the LORD that not a man will stay with you tonight, and that would be a worse disaster than any you have suffered since your earliest days.' Then the king rose and took 8 his seat in the gate; and when the army was told that the king was sitting in the gate, they all appeared before him.

Various events of David's reign

MEANWHILE THE ISRAELITES had all scattered to their homes. Throughout all the tribes of Israel people were discussing it among 9 themselves and saying, 'The king has saved us from our enemies and freed us from the power of the Philistines, and now he has fled the country because of Absalom. But Absalom, whom we anointed king, has fallen in 10 battle; so now why have we no plans for bringing the king back?' What all Israel was saying came to the king's ears.[a] So he sent word to 11 Zadok and Abiathar the priests: 'Ask the elders of Judah why they should be the last to bring the king back to his palace. Tell them, "You are my 12 brothers, my flesh and my blood; why are you last to bring me back?" And 13 tell Amasa, "You are my own flesh and blood. You shall be my commander-in-chief, so help me God, for the rest of your life in place of Joab."' David's message won all hearts in Judah, and they sent to the king, urging 14 him to return with all his men.

So the king came back to the Jordan; and the men of Judah came to 15 Gilgal to meet him and escort him across the river. Shimei son of Gera the 16 Benjamite from Bahurim hastened down among the men of Judah to meet King David with a thousand men from Benjamin; Ziba was there too, the 17 servant of Saul's family, with his fifteen sons and twenty servants. They rushed into the Jordan under the king's eyes and crossed to and fro con- 18 veying his household in order to win his favour. Shimei son of Gera,

[a] What . . . ears: *prob. rdg.; Heb. has these words after* back to his palace *and adds* to his palace.

19   when he had crossed the river, fell down before the king and said to him,
'I beg your majesty not to remember how disgracefully your servant
behaved when your majesty left Jerusalem; do not hold it against me or take
20   it to heart. For I humbly acknowledge that I did wrong, and today I am
the first of all the house of Joseph to come down to meet your majesty.'
21   But Abishai son of Zeruiah objected, 'Ought not Shimei to be put to death
22   because he cursed the LORD's anointed prince?' David answered, 'What
right have you, you sons of Zeruiah, to oppose me today? Why should any
man be put to death this day in Israel? I know now that I am king of Israel.'
23   Then the king said to Shimei, 'You shall not die', and confirmed it with an
oath.

24   Saul's grandson Mephibosheth also went down to meet the king. He had
not dressed his feet, combed his beard or washed his clothes, from the day
25   the king went out until he returned victorious. When he came from Jerusalem to meet the king, David said to him, 'Why did you not go with me,
26   Mephibosheth?' He answered, 'Sir, my servant deceived me; I did intend
27   to harness my ass and ride with the king (for I am lame), but his stories set
your majesty against me. Your majesty is like the angel of God; you must
28   do what you think right. My father's whole family, one and all, deserved
to die at your majesty's hands, but you gave me, your servant, my place at
29   your table. What further favour can I expect of the king?' The king
answered, 'You have said enough. My decision is that you and Ziba are to
30   share the estate.' Mephibosheth said, 'Let him have it all, now that your
majesty has come home victorious.'

31   Barzillai the Gileadite too had come down from Rogelim, and he went
32   as far as the Jordan with the king to send him on his way. Now Barzillai
was very old, eighty years of age; it was he who had provided for the king
33   while he was at Mahanaim, for he was a man of high standing. The king
said to Barzillai, 'Cross over with me and I will provide for your old age in
34   my household in Jerusalem.' Barzillai answered, 'Your servant is far too
35   old to go up with your majesty to Jerusalem. I am already eighty; and I
cannot tell good from bad. I cannot taste what I eat or drink; I cannot hear
the voices of men and women singing. Why should I be a burden any
36   longer on your majesty? Your servant will attend the king for a short way
across the Jordan; and why should the king reward me so handsomely?
37   Let me go back and end my days in my own city near the grave of my father
and mother. Here is my son Kimham; let him cross over with your majesty,
38   and do for him what you think best.' The king answered, 'Kimham shall
cross with me and I will do for him whatever you think best; and I will do
for you whatever you ask.'

39   All the people crossed the Jordan while the king waited. The king then
kissed Barzillai and gave him his blessing. Barzillai went back to his own
40   home; the king crossed over to Gilgal, Kimham with him. All the people
of Judah escorted the king over the river, and so did half the people of
Israel.

41   The men of Israel came to the king in a body and said, 'Why should our
brothers of Judah have got possession of the king's person by joining King
David's own men and then escorting him and his household across the

Jordan?' The men of Judah replied, 'Because his majesty is our near kins- 42
man. Why should you resent it? Have we eaten at the king's expense? Have
we received any gifts?' The men of Israel answered, 'We have ten times 43
your interest in the king and, what is more, are senior to you; why do
you disparage us? Were we not the first to speak of bringing the king back?'
The men of Judah used language even fiercer than the men of Israel.

There happened to be a man there, a scoundrel named Sheba son of 20
Bichri, a man of Benjamin. He blew the trumpet and cried out:

> What share have we in David?
> We have no lot in the son of Jesse.
> Away to your homes, O Israel.

The men of Israel all left David, to follow Sheba son of Bichri, but the men 2
of Judah stood by their king and followed him from the Jordan to Jerusalem.

When David came home to Jerusalem he took the ten concubines whom 3
he had left in charge of the palace and put them under guard; he maintained
them but did not have intercourse with them. They were kept in confinement to the day of their death, widowed in the prime of life.

The king said to Amasa, 'Call up the men of Judah and appear before 4
me again in three days' time.' So Amasa went to call up the men of Judah, 5
but it took longer than the time fixed by the king. David said to Abishai, 6
'Sheba son of Bichri will give us more trouble than Absalom; take the
royal bodyguard and follow him closely. If he has occupied some fortified
cities, he may escape us.' Abishai was followed by Joab [a] with the Kerethite 7
and Pelethite guards and all the fighting men; they left Jerusalem in
pursuit of Sheba son of Bichri. When they reached the great stone in 8
Gibeon, Amasa came towards them. Joab was wearing his tunic and over
it a belt supporting a sword in its scabbard. He came forward, concealing
his treachery, and said to Amasa, 'I hope you are well, my brother', and with 9
his right hand he grasped Amasa's beard to kiss him. Amasa was not on his 10
guard against the sword in Joab's hand. Joab struck him with it in the
belly and his entrails poured out to the ground; he did not strike a second
blow, for Amasa was dead. Joab and his brother Abishai went on in pursuit of Sheba son of Bichri. One of Joab's young men stood over Amasa 11
and called out, 'Follow Joab, all who are for Joab and for David!' Amasa's 12
body lay soaked in blood in the middle of the road, and when the man
saw how all the people stopped, he rolled him off the road into the field
and threw a cloak over him; for everyone who came by saw the body
and stopped. When he had been dragged from the road, they all went on 13
after Joab in pursuit of Sheba son of Bichri.

Sheba passed through all the tribes of Israel until he came to Abel-beth- 14
maacah,[b] and all the clan of Bichri[c] rallied to him and followed him into
the city. Joab's forces came up and besieged him in Abel-beth-maacah, 15
raised a siege-ramp against it and began undermining the wall to bring it
down. Then a wise woman stood on the rampart[d] and called from the city, 16

---

[a] Abishai . . . Joab: *prob. rdg.; Heb.* Some men of Joab followed him.   [b] *Prob. rdg.,*
cp. verse 15; Heb. Abel and Beth-maacah.   [c] *Prob. rdg.; Heb.* Beri.   [d] stood . . .
rampart: *transposed from verse 15.*

17 'Listen, listen! Tell Joab to step forward and let me speak with him.' So he came forward and the woman said, 'Are you Joab?' He answered, 'I am.'
18 'Listen to what I have to say, sir', she went on, to which he replied, 'I am listening.' 'In the old days', she said, 'there was a saying, "Go to Abel for
19 the answer", and that settled the matter. My city is known to be one of the most peaceable and loyal *a* in Israel; she is like a watchful mother in Israel, and you are seeking to kill her. Would you destroy the LORD's own posses-
20 sion?' Joab answered, 'God forbid, far be it from me to ruin or destroy!
21 That is not our aim; but a man from the hill-country of Ephraim named Sheba son of Bichri has raised a revolt against King David; surrender this one man, and I will retire from the city.' The woman said to Joab, 'His
22 head shall be thrown to you over the wall.' Then the woman withdrew, and her wisdom won over the assembled people; they cut off Sheba's head and threw it to Joab. Then he sounded the trumpet and the whole army left the city and dispersed to their homes, while Joab went back to the king in Jerusalem.

23 *b*   Joab was in command of the army, *c* and Benaiah son of Jehoiada com-
24 manded the Kerethite and Pelethite guards. Adoram was in charge of the
25 forced levy, and Jehoshaphat son of Ahilud was secretary of state. Sheva
26 was adjutant-general, and Zadok and Abiathar were priests; Ira the Jairite was David's priest.

21 IN DAVID'S REIGN there was a famine that lasted year after year for three years. So David consulted the LORD, and he answered, 'Blood-guilt rests
2 on Saul and on his family because he put the Gibeonites to death.' (The Gibeonites were not of Israelite descent; they were a remnant of Amorite stock whom the Israelites had sworn that they would spare. Saul, however, had sought to exterminate them in his zeal for Israel and Judah.) King
3 David summoned the Gibeonites, therefore, and said to them, 'What can be done for you? How can I make expiation, so that you may have cause to
4 bless the LORD's own people?' The Gibeonites answered, 'Our feud with Saul and his family cannot be settled in silver and gold, and there is no one man in Israel whose death would content us.' 'Then what do you want me
5 to do for you?' asked David. They answered, 'Let us make an end of the man who caused our undoing and ruined us, so that he shall never again
6 have his place within the borders of Israel. Hand over to us seven of that man's sons, and we will hurl them down to their death before *d* the LORD in Gibeah of Saul, the LORD's chosen king.' The king agreed to hand them
7 over, but he spared Mephibosheth son of Jonathan, son of Saul, because of the oath that had been taken in the LORD's name by David and Saul's son
8 Jonathan. The king then took the two sons whom Rizpah daughter of Aiah had borne to Saul, Armoni and Mephibosheth, and the five sons whom Merab, Saul's daughter, had borne to Adriel son of Barzillai of Meholah.
9 He handed them over to the Gibeonites, and they flung them down from the mountain before the LORD; the seven of them fell together. They were

a My city . . . loyal: *prob. rdg.*; *Heb.* I am the requited ones of the loyal ones.
b *Verses 23–26: cp. 8. 16–18; 1 Kgs. 4. 2–6; 1 Chr. 18. 15–17.*   *c* *Prob. rdg.,*
cp. 8. 16; Heb. adds Israel.   *d* *Or* for.

364

put to death in the first days of harvest at the beginning of the barley harvest. Rizpah daughter of Aiah took sackcloth and spread it out as a bed for her- 10 self on the rock, from the beginning of harvest until the rains came and fell from heaven upon the bodies. She allowed no bird to set upon them by day nor any wild beast by night. When David was told what Rizpah 11 daughter of Aiah the concubine of Saul had done, he went and took the 12 bones of Saul and his son Jonathan from the citizens of Jabesh-gilead, who had stolen them from the public square at Beth-shan, where the Philistines had hung them on the day they defeated Saul at Gilboa. He removed the 13 bones of Saul and Jonathan from there and gathered up the bones of the men who had been hurled to death. They buried the bones of Saul and his 14 son Jonathan in the territory of Benjamin at Zela, in the grave of his father Kish. Everything was done as the king ordered, and thereafter the LORD was willing to accept prayers offered for the country.

Once again war broke out between the Philistines and Israel. David and 15 his men went down to the battle, but as he fought with the Philistines he fell exhausted. Then Benob, one of the race of the Rephaim, whose bronze 16 spear weighed three hundred shekels *a* and who wore a belt of honour, took David prisoner and was about to kill him. But Abishai son of Zeruiah came 17 to David's help, struck the Philistine down and killed him. Then David's officers took an oath that he should never again go out with them to war, for fear that the lamp of Israel might be extinguished.

Some time later war with the Philistines broke out again in Gob: it was 18 *b* then that Sibbechai of Hushah killed Saph, a descendant of the Rephaim. In another war with the Philistines in Gob, Elhanan son of Jair *c* of Bethle- 19 hem killed Goliath of Gath, whose spear had a shaft like a weaver's beam. In yet another war in Gath there appeared a giant with six fingers on each 20 hand and six toes on each foot, twenty-four in all. He too was descended from the Rephaim; and, when he defied Israel, Jonathan son of David's 21 brother Shimeai killed him. These four giants were the descendants of the 22 Rephaim in Gath, and they all fell at the hands of David and his men.

THESE ARE THE WORDS OF THE SONG David sang to the LORD on the 22 1 day when the LORD delivered him from the power of all his enemies and from the power of Saul:

> The LORD is my stronghold, my fortress and my champion, 2 *d*
> my God, my rock where I find safety; 3
> my shield, my mountain fastness, my strong tower,
> my refuge, my deliverer, who saves me from violence.
> I will call on the LORD to whom all praise is due, 4
> and I shall be delivered from my enemies.
> When the waves of death swept round me, 5
> and torrents of destruction overtook me,
> the bonds of Sheol tightened about me, 6
> the snares of death were set to catch me;

a shekels: *prob. rdg.; Heb.* weight.   *b Verses 18–22: cp. 1 Chr. 20. 4–7.*   *c* Jair: *prob. rdg., cp. 1 Chr. 20. 5; Heb.* Jaare-oregim.   *d Verses 2–51: cp. Ps. 18. 2–50.*

7   then in anguish of heart I cried to the LORD,
     I called for help to my God;
     he heard me from his temple,
     and my cry rang in his ears.

8   The earth heaved and quaked,
     heaven's foundations shook;
     they heaved, because he was angry.

9   Smoke rose from his nostrils,
     devouring fire came out of his mouth,
     glowing coals and searing heat.

10   He swept the skies aside as he descended,
     thick darkness lay under his feet.

11   He rode on a cherub, he flew through the air;
     he swooped*a* on the wings of the wind.

12   He curtained himself in darkness
     and made dense vapour his canopy.

13   Thick clouds came out of the radiance before him;
     glowing coals burned brightly.

14   The LORD thundered from the heavens
     and the voice of the Most High spoke out.

15   He loosed his arrows, he sped them far and wide,
     his lightning shafts, and sent them echoing.

16   The channels of the sea-bed were revealed,
     the foundations of earth laid bare
     at the LORD's rebuke,
     at the blast of the breath of his nostrils.

17   He reached down from the height and took me,
     he drew me out of mighty waters,

18   he rescued me from my enemies, strong as they were,
     from my foes when they grew too powerful for me.

19   They confronted me in the hour of my peril,
     but the LORD was my buttress.

20   He brought me out into an open place,
     he rescued me because he delighted in me.

21   The LORD rewarded me as my righteousness deserved;
     my hands were clean, and he requited me.

22   For I have followed the ways of the LORD
     and have not turned wickedly from my God;

23   all his laws are before my eyes,
     I have not failed to follow his decrees.

24   In his sight I was blameless
     and kept myself from wilful sin;

25   the LORD requited me as my righteousness deserved
     and my purity in his eyes.

26   With the loyal thou showest thyself loyal
     and with the blameless man blameless.

a Prob. rdg., cp. Ps. 18. 10; Heb. was seen.

With the savage man thou showest thyself savage,   27
and *ᵃ* tortuous with the perverse.
Thou deliverest humble folk,   28
thou lookest with contempt upon the proud.
Thou, Lord, art my lamp,   29
and the Lord will lighten my darkness.
With thy help I leap over a bank,   30
by God's aid I spring over a wall.

The way of God is perfect,   31
the Lord's word has stood the test;
he is the shield of all who take refuge in him.
What god is there but the Lord?   32
What rock but our God?—
the God who girds me *ᵇ* with strength   33
and makes my way blameless, *ᶜ*
who makes me swift as a hind   34
and sets me secure on the mountains;
who trains my hands for battle,   35
and my arms aim an arrow tipped with bronze.

Thou hast given me the shield of thy salvation,   36
in thy providence thou makest me great.
Thou givest me room for my steps,   37
my feet have not faltered.
I pursue my enemies and destroy them,   38
I do not return until I have made an end of them.
I make an end of them, I strike them down;   39
they rise no more, they fall beneath my feet.
Thou dost arm me with strength for the battle   40
and dost subdue my foes before me.
Thou settest *ᵈ* my foot on my enemies' necks,   41
and I bring to nothing those that hate me.
They cry out *ᵉ* and there is no one to help them,   42
they cry to the Lord and he does not answer.
I will pound them fine as dust on the ground,   43
like mud in the streets will I trample them. *ᶠ*
Thou dost deliver me from the clamour of the people,   44
and makest me master of the nations.
A people I never knew shall be my subjects.
Foreigners shall come cringing to me;   45
as soon as they hear tell of me, they shall obey me.
Foreigners shall be brought captive to me,   46
and come limping from their strongholds.

ᵃ With the savage . . . savage, and: *or* With the pure thou showest thyself pure, but . . .
ᵇ who girds me: *prob. rdg., cp. Ps. 18. 32; Heb.* my refuge *or* my strength.   *ᶜ* and
makes . . . blameless: *prob. rdg., cp. Ps. 18. 32; Heb. unintelligible.*   *ᵈ Prob. rdg.,*
cp. Ps. 18. 40; Heb. unintelligible.   *ᵉ* cry out: *prob. rdg., cp. Ps. 18. 41; Heb.* look.
ᶠ Prob. rdg., cp. Ps. 18. 42; Heb. adds will I stamp them down.

47 The LORD lives, blessed is my rock,
high above all is God my rock and safe refuge.

48 O God, who grantest me vengeance,
who dost subdue peoples under me,

49 who dost snatch me from my foes and set me over my enemies,
thou dost deliver me from violent men.

50 Therefore, LORD, I will praise thee among the nations
and sing psalms to thy name,

51 to one who gives his king great victories
and in all his acts keeps faith with his anointed king,
with David and his descendants for ever.

23 These are the last words of David:

The very word of David son of Jesse,
the very word of the man whom the High God raised up,
the anointed prince of the God of Jacob,
and the singer of Israel's psalms:

2 the spirit of the LORD has spoken through me,
and his word is on my lips.

3 The God of Israel spoke,
the Rock of Israel spoke of me:
'He who rules men in justice,
who rules in the fear of God,

4 is like the light of morning at sunrise,
a morning that is cloudless after rain
and makes the grass sparkle from the earth.'

5 Surely, surely my house is true to God;
for he has made a pact with me for all time,
its terms spelled out and faithfully kept,
my whole salvation, all my *a* delight.

6 But the ungodly put forth no shoots,
they are all like briars tossed aside;
none dare put out his hand to pick them up,

7 none touch them but *b* with tool of iron or of wood;
they are fit only for burning in the fire. *c*

8 *d* THESE ARE THE NAMES OF DAVID'S HEROES. First came Ishbosheth
the Hachmonite, *e* chief of the three; it was he who brandished his spear *f*
9 over eight hundred dead, all slain at one time. Next to him was Eleazar
son of Dodo the Ahohite, *g* one of the heroic three. He was with David
at Pas-dammim where the Philistines *h* had gathered for battle. When the

---

a *Prob. rdg.; Heb. om.* *b* but: *prob. rdg.; Heb.* he shall be filled. *c* *Prob. rdg.;*
Heb. adds in sitting. *d* *Verses 8–39: cp. I Chr. 11. 10–41.* *e* *Prob. rdg.; Heb.*
Josheb-basshebeth a Tahchemonite. *f* who . . . spear: *prob. rdg., cp. I Chr. 11. 11;*
Heb. unintelligible. *g* the Ahohite: *prob. rdg., cp. I Chr. 11. 12; Heb.* son of Ahohi.
h He was . . . Philistines: *prob. rdg., cp. I Chr. 11. 13; Heb.* With David when they
taunted them among the Philistines.

Israelites fell back, he stood his ground and rained blows on the Philistines 10
until, from sheer weariness, his hand stuck fast to his sword; and so the
LORD brought about a great victory that day. Afterwards the people rallied
behind him, but it was only to strip the dead. Next to him was Shammah son 11
of Agee a Hararite. The Philistines had gathered at Lehi, where there was a
field with a fine crop of lentils; and, when the Philistines put the people to
flight, he stood his ground in the field, saved it *a* and defeated them. So 12
the LORD again brought about a great victory.

Three of the thirty went down towards the beginning of harvest to join 13
David at the cave of Adullam, while a band of Philistines was encamped in
the Vale of Rephaim. At that time David was in the stronghold and a Philis- 14
tine garrison held Bethlehem. One day a longing came over David, and he 15
exclaimed, 'If only I could have a drink of water from the well *b* by the gate
of Bethlehem!' At this the heroic three made their way through the 16
Philistine lines and drew water from the well by the gate of Bethlehem and
brought it to David. But David refused to drink it; he poured it out to the
LORD and said, 'God forbid that I should do such a thing! Can I drink *c* 17
the blood of these men who risked their lives for it?' So he would not
drink it. Such were the exploits of the heroic three.

Abishai the brother of Joab son of Zeruiah was chief of the thirty. He 18
once brandished his spear over three hundred dead, and he was famous
among the thirty. Some think he even surpassed the rest of the thirty *d* in 19
reputation, and he became their captain, but he did not rival the three.
Benaiah son of Jehoiada, from Kabzeel, was a hero of many exploits. It 20
was he who smote the two champions of Moab, and who went down into
a pit and killed a lion on a snowy day. It was he who also killed the Egyptian, 21
a man of striking appearance armed with a spear: he went to meet him
with a club, snatched the spear out of the Egyptian's hand and killed him
with his own weapon. Such were the exploits of Benaiah son of Jehoiada, 22
famous among the heroic thirty. *d* He was more famous than the rest of the 23
thirty, but he did not rival the three. David appointed him to his household.

Asahel the brother of Joab was one of the thirty, and Elhanan son of 24
Dodo from Bethlehem; Shammah from Harod, and Elika from Harod; 25
Helez from Beth-pelet,*e* and Ira son of Ikkesh from Tekoa; Abiezer from 26 27
Anathoth, and Mebunnai from Hushah; Zalmon the Ahohite, and Maharai 28
from Netophah; Heled son of Baanah from Netophah, and Ittai son of 29
Ribai from Gibeah of Benjamin; Benaiah from Pirathon, and Hiddai 30
from the ravines of Gaash; Abi-albon from Beth-arabah, *f* and Azmoth 31
from Bahurim;*g* Eliahba from Shaalbon, and Hashem the Gizonite; 32
Jonathan son of *h* Shammah the Hararite, and Ahiam son of Sharar the 33
Hararite;*i* Eliphelet son of Ahasbai son of the Maacathite, and Eliam son 34
of Ahithophel the Gilonite; Hezrai from Carmel, and Paarai the Arbite; 35

a saved it: *or* cleared it of the Philistines.   *b* Or cistern.   *c* I drink: *prob. rdg.,*
cp. 1 Chr. 11. 19; Heb. om.   *d Prob. rdg.; Heb.* three.   *e Prob. rdg., cp. Josh. 15.*
27; Heb. from Pelet.   *f Prob. rdg., cp. Josh. 18. 22; Heb.* from Arabah.   *g Prob.*
rdg., cp. 1 Chr. 11. 33; Heb. from Barhum.   *h* Hashem ... son of: *prob. rdg., cp.*
1 Chr. 11. 34; Heb. the sons of Jashen, Jonathan.   *i Prob. rdg., cp. 1 Chr. 11. 35;*
Heb. Ararite.

36 37 Igal son of Nathan from Zobah, and Bani the Gadite; Zelek the Ammonite,
38 and Naharai from Beeroth, armour-bearer to Joab son of Zeruiah; Ira the
39 Ithrite, Gareb the Ithrite, and Uriah the Hittite: there were thirty-seven
in all.

24 1[a] ONCE AGAIN THE ISRAELITES felt the LORD's anger, when he incited
David against them and gave him orders that Israel and Judah should
2 be counted. So he instructed Joab and the officers of the army[b] with him
to go round all the tribes of Israel, from Dan to Beersheba, and make a
3 record of the people and report the number to him. Joab answered, 'Even
if the LORD your God should increase the people a hundredfold and your
majesty should live to see it, what pleasure would that give your majesty?'
4 But Joab and the officers were overruled by the king and they left his
5 presence in order to count the people. They crossed the Jordan and began
at Aroer and the level land of the gorge, proceeding towards Gad[c] and
6 Jazer. They came to Gilead and to the land of the Hittites, to Kadesh,
7 and then to Dan and Iyyon[d] and so round towards Sidon. They went as
far as the walled city of Tyre and all the towns of the Hivites and Canaan-
8 ites, and then went on to the Negeb of Judah at Beersheba. They covered
the whole country and arrived back at Jerusalem after nine months and
9 twenty days. Joab reported to the king the total number of people: the
number of able-bodied men, capable of bearing arms, was eight hundred
thousand in Israel and five hundred thousand in Judah.

10   After he had counted the people David's conscience smote him, and
he said to the LORD, 'I have done a very wicked thing: I pray thee, LORD,
11 remove thy servant's guilt, for I have been very foolish.' He rose next
morning, and meanwhile the command of the LORD had come to the
12 prophet Gad, David's seer, to go and speak to David: 'This is the word of
the LORD: I have three things in store for you; choose one and I will bring
13 it upon you.' So Gad came to David and repeated this to him and said, 'Is
it to be three years of famine in your land, or three months of flight with
the enemy at your heels, or three days of pestilence in your land? Consider
14 carefully what answer I am to take back to him who sent me.' Thereupon
David said to Gad, 'I am in a desperate plight; let us fall into the hands of
the LORD, for his mercy is great; and let me not fall into the hands of men.'
15 So the LORD sent a pestilence throughout Israel from morning till the hour
of dinner, and from Dan to Beersheba seventy thousand of the people died.
16 Then the angel stretched out his arm towards Jerusalem to destroy it; but
the LORD repented of the evil and said to the angel who was destroying the
people, 'Enough! Stay your hand.' At that moment the angel of the LORD
was standing by the threshing-floor of Araunah the Jebusite.
17   When David saw the angel who was striking down the people, he said to
the LORD, 'It is I who have done wrong, the sin is mine; but these poor
sheep, what have they done? Let thy hand fall upon me and upon my

---

[a] *Verses 1–25: cp. 1 Chr. 21. 1–27.*   [b] Joab ... army: *prob. rdg., cp. 1 Chr. 21. 2;
Heb.* Joab the officer of the army.   [c] began at ... Gad: *prob. rdg.; Heb.* encamped
in Aroer on the right of the level land of the gorge Gad.   [d] *Prob. rdg., cp. 1 Kgs. 15.
20; Heb.* Yaan.

family.' That same day Gad came to David and said to him, 'Go and set 18
up an altar to the LORD on the threshing-floor of Araunah the Jebusite.'
David did what Gad told him to do, and went up as the LORD had com- 19
manded. When Araunah looked down and saw the king and his servants 20
coming over towards him, he went out, prostrated himself low before the
king and said, 'Why has your majesty come to visit his servant?' David 21
answered, 'To buy the threshing-floor from you to build an altar to the
LORD, so that the plague which has attacked the people may be stopped.'
Araunah answered David, 'I beg your majesty to take it and sacrifice what 22
you think fit. I have here the oxen for a whole-offering, and their harness
and the threshing-sledges for the fuel.' Araunah *a* gave it all to the king 23
for his own use and said to him, 'May the LORD your God accept you.'
But the king said to Araunah, 'No, I will buy it from you; I will not offer 24
to the LORD my God whole-offerings that have cost me nothing.' So
David bought the threshing-floor and the oxen for fifty shekels of silver.
He built an altar to the LORD there and offered whole-offerings and shared- 25
offerings. Then the LORD yielded to his prayer for the land; and the plague
in Israel stopped.

a *Prob. rdg.; Heb. adds* the king.

THE FIRST BOOK OF
KINGS

The death of David and accession of Solomon

1
2
KING DAVID WAS NOW A VERY OLD MAN and, though they wrapped clothes round him, he could not keep warm. So his household said to him, 'Let us find a young virgin for your majesty, to attend you and take care of you; and let her lie in your bosom,
3 sir, and make you warm.' So they searched all over Israel for a beautiful maiden and found Abishag, a Shunammite, and brought her to the king.
4 She was a very beautiful girl, and she took care of the king and waited on him, but he had no intercourse with her.

5 Now Adonijah, whose mother was Haggith, was boasting that he was to be king; and he had already provided himself with chariots and horse-
6 men*a* and fifty outrunners. Never in his life had his father corrected him or asked why he behaved as he did. He was a very handsome man, too,
7 and was next in age to Absalom. He talked with Joab son of Zeruiah and
8 with Abiathar the priest, and they gave him their strong support; but Zadok the priest, Benaiah son of Jehoiada, Nathan the prophet, Shimei,
9 Rei, and David's bodyguard of heroes, did not take his side. Adonijah then held a sacrifice of sheep, oxen, and buffaloes at the stone Zoheleth beside En-rogel, and he invited all his royal brothers and all those
10 officers of the household who were of the tribe of Judah. But he did not invite Nathan the prophet, Benaiah and the bodyguard, or Solomon his brother.

11 Then Nathan said to Bathsheba, the mother of Solomon, 'Have you not heard that Adonijah son of Haggith has become king, all unknown to our
12 lord David? Now come, let me advise you what to do for your own safety
13 and for the safety of your son Solomon. Go in and see King David and say to him, "Did not your majesty swear to me, your servant, that my son Solomon should succeed you as king; that it was he who should sit on
14 your throne? Why then has Adonijah become king?" Then while you are still speaking there with the king, I will follow you in and tell the whole story.'

15 So Bathsheba went to the king in his private chamber; he was now very
16 old, and Abishag the Shunammite was waiting on him. Bathsheba bowed before the king and prostrated herself. 'What do you want?' said the king.
17 She answered, 'My lord, you swore to me your servant, by the LORD your God, that my son Solomon should succeed you as king, and that he should
18 sit on your throne. But now, here is Adonijah become king, all unknown to

a Or a chariot and horses.

your majesty. He has sacrificed great numbers of oxen, buffaloes, and ₁₉
sheep, and has invited to the feast all the king's sons, and Abiathar the
priest, and Joab the commander-in-chief, but he has not invited your
servant Solomon. And now, your majesty, all Israel is looking to you to ₂₀
announce who is to succeed you on the throne. Otherwise, when you, ₂₁
sir, rest with your forefathers, my son Solomon and I shall be treated as
criminals.' She was still speaking to the king when Nathan the prophet ₂₂
arrived. The king was told that Nathan was there; he came into the king's ₂₃
presence and prostrated himself with his face to the ground. 'My lord,' he ₂₄
said, 'your majesty must, I suppose, have declared that Adonijah should
succeed you and that he should sit on your throne. He has today gone ₂₅
down and sacrificed great numbers of oxen, buffaloes, and sheep, and has
invited to the feast all the king's sons, Joab the commander-in-chief, and
Abiathar the priest; and at this very moment they are eating and drinking
in his presence and shouting, "Long live King Adonijah!" But he has not ₂₆
invited me your servant, Zadok the priest, Benaiah son of Jehoiada, or
your servant Solomon. Has this been done by your majesty's authority, ₂₇
while we *a* your servants have not been told who should succeed you on
the throne?' Thereupon King David said, 'Call Bathsheba', and she came ₂₈
into the king's presence and stood before him. Then the king swore an oath ₂₉
to her: 'As the LORD lives, who has delivered me from all my troubles: I ₃₀
swore by the LORD the God of Israel that Solomon your son should succeed
me and that he should sit on my throne, and this day I give effect to my
oath.' Bathsheba bowed low to the king and prostrated herself; and she ₃₁
said, 'May my lord King David live for ever!'
    Then King David said, 'Call Zadok the priest, Nathan the prophet, and ₃₂
Benaiah son of Jehoiada.' They came into the king's presence and he gave ₃₃
them these orders: 'Take the officers of the household with you; mount
my son Solomon on the king's mule and escort him down to Gihon. There ₃₄
Zadok the priest and Nathan the prophet shall anoint him king over Israel.
Sound the trumpet and shout, "Long live King Solomon!" Then escort ₃₅
him home again, and he shall come and sit on my throne and reign in my
place; for he is the man that I have appointed prince over Israel and Judah.'
Benaiah son of Jehoiada answered the king, 'It shall be done. And may the ₃₆
LORD, the God of my lord the king, confirm it! As the LORD has been with ₃₇
your majesty, so may he be with Solomon; may he make his throne even
greater than the throne of my lord King David.' So Zadok the priest, ₃₈
Nathan the prophet, and Benaiah son of Jehoiada, together with the
Kerethite and Pelethite guards, went down and mounted Solomon on
King David's mule and escorted him to Gihon. Zadok the priest took the ₃₉
horn of oil from the Tent of the LORD and anointed Solomon; they sounded
the trumpet and all the people shouted, 'Long live King Solomon!' Then ₄₀
all the people escorted him home in procession, with great rejoicing and
playing of pipes, so that the very earth split with the noise.
    Adonijah and his guests had finished their banquet when the noise ₄₁
reached their ears. Joab, hearing the sound of the trumpet, exclaimed,

a Has this . . . while we: *or* If this has been done by your majesty's authority, then
we . . .

42 'What is all this uproar in the city? What has happened?' While he was
still speaking, Jonathan son of Abiathar the priest arrived. 'Come in', said
43 Adonijah. 'You are an honourable man and bring good news.' 'Far otherwise,' Jonathan replied; 'our lord King David has made Solomon king
44 and has sent with him Zadok the priest, Nathan the prophet, and Benaiah
son of Jehoiada, together with the Kerethite and Pelethite guards; they
45 have mounted him on the king's mule, and Zadok the priest and Nathan
the prophet have anointed him king at Gihon, and they have now escorted
him home rejoicing, and the city is in an uproar. That was the noise you
46 heard. More than that, Solomon has taken his seat on the royal throne.
47 Yes, and the officers of the household have been to greet our lord King
David with these words: "May your God make the name of Solomon your
son more famous than your own and his throne even greater than yours",
48 and the king bowed upon his couch. What is more, he said this: "Blessed
be the LORD the God of Israel who has set a successor on my throne this
49 day while I am still alive to see it."' Then Adonijah's guests all rose in
50 panic and scattered. Adonijah himself, in fear of Solomon, sprang up and
51 went to the altar and caught hold of its horns. Then a message was sent to
Solomon: 'Adonijah is afraid of King Solomon; he has taken hold of the
horns of the altar and has said, "Let King Solomon first swear to me that
52 he will not put his servant to the sword."' Solomon said, 'If he proves
himself a man of worth, not a hair of his head shall fall to the ground; but
53 if he is found to be troublesome, he shall die.' Then King Solomon sent
and had him brought down from the altar; he came in and prostrated
himself before the king, and Solomon ordered him home.

2 When the time of David's death drew near, he gave this last charge to
2 his son Solomon: 'I am going the way of all the earth. Be strong and show
3 yourself a man. Fulfil your duty to the LORD your God; conform to his
ways, observe his statutes and his commandments, his judgements and
his solemn precepts, as they are written in the law of Moses, so that you
4 may prosper in whatever you do and whichever way you turn, and that
the LORD may fulfil this promise that he made about me: "If your descendants take care to walk faithfully in my sight with all their heart and
with all their soul, you shall never lack a successor on the throne of Israel."
5 You know how Joab son of Zeruiah treated me and what he did to two
commanders-in-chief in Israel, Abner son of Ner and Amasa son of
Jether. He killed them both, breaking the peace by bloody acts of war; and
with that blood he stained the belt about my waist and the sandals on my
6 feet. Do as your wisdom prompts you, and do not let his grey hairs go
7 down to the grave in peace. Show constant friendship to the family of
Barzillai of Gilead; let them have their place at your table; they befriended
8 me when I was a fugitive from your brother Absalom. Do not forget
Shimei son of Gera, the Benjamite from Bahurim, who cursed me bitterly
the day I went to Mahanaim. True, he came down to meet me at the
9 Jordan, and I swore by the LORD that I would not put him to death. But
you do not need to let him go unpunished now; you are a wise man and
will know how to deal with him; bring down his grey hairs in blood to the
grave.'

So David rested with his forefathers and was buried in the city of David, 10
having reigned over Israel for forty years, seven in Hebron and thirty- 11
three in Jerusalem; and Solomon succeeded his father David as king and 12
was firmly established on the throne.

The reign of Solomon

THEN ADONIJAH SON OF HAGGITH came to Bathsheba, the mother 13
of Solomon. 'Do you come as a friend?' she asked. 'As a friend,' he
answered; 'I have something to say to you.' 'Tell me', she said. 'You 14 15
know', he went on, 'that the throne was mine and that all Israel was looking to me to be king; but I was passed over and the throne has gone to my
brother; it was his by the LORD's will. And now I have one request to make 16
of you; do not refuse me.' 'What is it?' she said. He answered, 'Will you 17
ask King Solomon (he will never refuse you) to give me Abishag the
Shunammite in marriage?' 'Very well,' said Bathsheba, 'I will speak for 18
you to the king.' So Bathsheba went in to King Solomon to speak for 19
Adonijah. The king rose to meet her and kissed her, and seated himself on
his throne. A throne was set for the king's mother and she sat at his right
hand. Then she said, 'I have one small request to make of you; do not 20
refuse me.' 'What is it, mother?' he replied; 'I will not refuse you.' 'It is 21
this, that Abishag the Shunammite should be given to your brother Adonijah in marriage.' At that Solomon answered his mother, 'Why do you 22
ask for Abishag the Shunammite as wife for Adonijah? you might as well
ask for the throne, for he is my elder brother and has both Abiathar the
priest and Joab son of Zeruiah on his side.' Then King Solomon swore 23
by the LORD: 'So help me God, Adonijah shall pay for this with his life.
As the LORD lives, who has established me and set me on the throne of 24
David my father and has founded a house for me as he promised, this
very day Adonijah shall be put to death!' Thereupon King Solomon 25
gave Benaiah son of Jehoiada his orders, and he struck him down and
he died.

Abiathar the priest was told by the king to go off to Anathoth to his own 26
estate. 'You deserve to die,' he said, 'but in spite of this day's work I shall
not put you to death, for you carried the Ark of the Lord GOD before my
father David, and you shared in all the hardships that he endured.' So 27
Solomon dismissed Abiathar from his office as priest of the LORD, and so
fulfilled the sentence that the LORD had pronounced against the house of
Eli in Shiloh.

News of all this reached Joab, and he fled to the Tent of the LORD and 28
caught hold of the horns of the altar; for he had sided with Adonijah,
though not with Absalom. When King Solomon learnt that Joab had fled 29
to the Tent of the LORD and that he was by the altar, he sent Benaiah son of
Jehoiada with orders to strike him down. Benaiah came to the Tent of the 30
LORD and ordered Joab in the king's name to come away; but he said, 'No;
I will die here.' Benaiah reported Joab's answer to the king, and the king 31
said, 'Let him have his way; strike him down and bury him, and so rid me

32 and my father's house of the guilt for the blood that he wantonly shed. The
LORD will hold him responsible for his own death, because he struck down
two innocent men who were better men than he, Abner son of Ner, commander of the army of Israel, and Amasa son of Jether, commander of the
army of Judah, and ran them through with the sword, without my father
33 David's knowledge. The guilt of their blood shall recoil on Joab and his
descendants for all time; but David and his descendants, his house and
34 his throne, will enjoy perpetual prosperity from the LORD.' So Benaiah
son of Jehoiada went up to the altar and struck Joab down and killed him,
35 and he was buried in his house on the edge of the wilderness. Thereafter
the king appointed Benaiah son of Jehoiada to command the army in his
place, and installed Zadok the priest in place of Abiathar.

36 Next the king sent for Shimei and said to him, 'Build yourself a house in
Jerusalem and stay there; you are not to leave the city for any other place.
37 If ever you leave it and cross the gorge of the Kidron, you shall die; make
38 no mistake about that. Your blood will be on your own head.' And Shimei
said to the king, 'I accept your sentence; I will do as your majesty com-
39 mands.' So for a long time Shimei remained in Jerusalem; but three years
later two of his slaves ran away to Achish son of Maacah, king of Gath.
40 When Shimei heard that his slaves were in Gath, he immediately saddled
his ass and went there to Achish in search of his slaves; he came to Gath
41 and returned with them. When King Solomon was told that Shimei had
42 gone from Jerusalem to Gath and back, he sent for him and said, 'Did I
not require you to swear by the LORD? Did I not give you this solemn
warning: "If ever you leave this city for any other place, you shall die;
make no mistake about it"? And you said, "I accept your sentence; I
43 obey." Why then have you not kept the oath which you swore by the LORD,
44 and the order which I gave you? Shimei, you know in your own heart all
the mischief you did to my father David; the LORD is now making that
45 mischief recoil on your own head. But King Solomon is blessed and the
46 throne of David will be secure before the LORD for all time.' The king then
gave orders to Benaiah son of Jehoiada, and he went out and struck Shimei
down; and he died. Thus Solomon's royal power was securely established.

3   Solomon allied himself to Pharaoh king of Egypt by marrying his
daughter. He brought her to the City of David, until he had finished
building his own house and the house of the LORD and the wall round
2 Jerusalem. The people however continued to sacrifice at the hill-shrines,
for till then no house had been built in honour of the name of the LORD.
3 Solomon himself loved the LORD, conforming to the precepts laid down
by his father David; but he too slaughtered and burnt sacrifices at the
hill-shrines.

4   Now King Solomon went to Gibeon to offer a sacrifice, for that was the
chief hill-shrine, and he used to offer a thousand whole-offerings on its
5[a] altar. There that night the LORD God appeared to him in a dream and said,
6 'What shall I give you? Tell me.' And Solomon answered, 'Thou didst
show great and constant love to thy servant David my father, because he

---

[a] *Verses 5–14: cp. 2 Chr. 1. 7–12.*

walked before thee in loyalty, righteousness, and integrity of heart; and
thou hast maintained this great and constant love towards him and hast
now given him a son to succeed him on the throne. Now, O LORD my God, 7
thou hast made thy servant king in place of my father David, though I am
a mere child, unskilled in leadership. And I am here in the midst of thy 8
people, the people of thy choice, too many to be numbered or counted.
Give thy servant, therefore, a heart with skill to listen, so that he may 9
govern thy people justly and distinguish good from evil. For who is equal
to the task of governing this great people of thine?' The Lord was well 10
pleased that Solomon had asked for this, and he said to him, 'Because you 11
have asked for this, and not for long life for yourself, or for wealth, or for
the lives of your enemies, but have asked for discernment in administering
justice, I grant your request; I give you a heart so wise and so understand- 12
ing that there has been none like you before your time nor will be after you.
I give you furthermore those things for which you did not ask, such wealth 13
and honour[a] as no king of your time can match. And if you conform to 14
my ways and observe my ordinances and commandments, as your father
David did, I will give you long life.' Then he awoke, and knew it was a 15
dream.

Solomon came to Jerusalem and stood before the Ark of the Covenant
of the Lord; there he sacrificed whole-offerings and brought shared-
offerings, and gave a feast to all his household.

Then there came into the king's presence two women who were pro- 16
stitutes and stood before him. The first said, 'My lord, this woman and I 17
share the same house, and I gave birth to a child when she was there with
me. On the third day after my baby was born she too gave birth to a child. 18
We were quite alone; no one else was with us in the house; only the two
of us were there. During the night this woman's child died because she 19
overlaid it, and she got up in the middle of the night, took my baby from 20
my side while I, your servant, was asleep, and laid it in her bosom, putting
her dead child in mine. When I got up in the morning to feed my baby, I 21
found him dead; but when I looked at him closely, I found that it was not
the child that I had borne.' The other woman broke in, 'No; the living 22
child is mine; yours is the dead one', while the first retorted, 'No; the dead
child is yours; mine is the living one.' So they went on arguing in the king's
presence. The king thought to himself, 'One of them says, "This is my 23
child, the living one; yours is the dead one." The other says, "No; it is your
child that is dead and mine that is alive." ' Then he said, 'Fetch me a sword.' 24
They brought in a sword and the king gave the order: 'Cut the living child 25
in two and give half to one and half to the other.' At this the woman who 26
was the mother of the living child, moved with love for her child, said to
the king, 'Oh! sir, let her have the baby; whatever you do, do not kill it.'
The other said, 'Let neither of us have it; cut it in two.' Thereupon the 27
king gave judgement: 'Give the living baby to the first woman; do not kill
it. She is its mother.' When Israel heard the judgement which the king had 28
given, they all stood in awe of him; for they saw that he had the wisdom of
God within him to administer justice.

[a] Or riches.

4 1 2[a] KING SOLOMON REIGNED OVER ISRAEL. His officers were as follows:

In charge of the calendar:[b] Azariah son of Zadok the priest.

3   Adjutant-general:[c] Ahijah son[d] of Shisha.
Secretary of state: Jehoshaphat son of Ahilud.

4   Commander of the army: Benaiah son of Jehoiada.
Priests: Zadok and Abiathar.

5   Superintendent of the regional governors: Azariah son of Nathan.
King's Friend: Zabud son of Nathan.

6   Comptroller of the household: Ahishar.
Superintendent of the forced levy: Adoniram son of Abda.

7   Solomon had twelve regional governors over Israel and they supplied
the food for the king and the royal household, each being responsible for
8 one month's provision in the year. These were their names:

Ben-hur in the hill-country of Ephraim.

9   Ben-dekar in Makaz, Shaalbim, Beth-shemesh, Elon, and Beth-hanan.

10   Ben-hesed in Aruboth; he had charge also of Socoh and all the land of
Hepher.

11   Ben-abinadab, who had married Solomon's daughter Taphath, in all
the district of Dor.

12   Baana son of Ahilud in Taanach and Megiddo, all Beth-shean as far as
Abel-meholah beside Zartanah, and from Beth-shean below Jezreel
as far as Jokmeam.

13   Ben-geber in Ramoth-gilead, including the tent-villages of Jair son of
Manasseh in Gilead and the region of Argob in Bashan, sixty large
walled cities with gate-bars of bronze.

14   Ahinadab son of Iddo in Mahanaim.

15   Ahimaaz in Naphtali; he also had married a daughter of Solomon,
Basmath.

16   Baanah son of Hushai in Asher and Aloth.

17   Jehoshaphat son of Paruah in Issachar.

18   Shimei son of Elah in Benjamin.

19   Geber son of Uri in Gilead, the land of Sihon king of the Amorites and
of Og king of Bashan.
In addition, one governor over all the governors[e] in the land.

20   The people of Judah and Israel were countless as the sands of the sea;
21 they ate and they drank, and enjoyed life. Solomon ruled over all the kingdoms from the river Euphrates to Philistia and as far as the frontier of
Egypt; they paid tribute and were subject to him all his life.

22   Solomon's provision for one day was thirty kor of flour and sixty kor
23 of meal, ten fat oxen and twenty oxen from the pastures and a hundred
24 sheep, as well as stags, gazelles, roebucks, and fattened fowl. For he was
paramount over all the land west of the Euphrates from Tiphsah to Gaza,
25 ruling all the kings west of the river; and he enjoyed peace on all sides. All

---

[a] *Verses 2–6*: cp. *2 Sam. 8. 16–18; 20. 23–26; 1 Chr. 18. 15–17.*   [b] *In . . . calendar: prob. rdg.; Heb. Elihoreph.*   [c] *Prob. rdg., cp. 1 Chr. 18. 16; Heb. Adjutants-general.*
[d] *Prob. rdg.; Heb. sons.*   [e] *over . . . governors: prob. rdg.; Heb. om.*

through his reign Judah and Israel continued at peace, every man under
his own vine and fig-tree, from Dan to Beersheba.

Solomon had forty thousand chariot-horses in his stables and twelve 26
thousand cavalry horses.

The regional governors, each for a month in turn, supplied provisions 27
for King Solomon and for all who came to his table; they never fell short
in their deliveries. They provided also barley and straw, each according to 28
his duty, for the horses and chariot-horses where it was required.

And God gave Solomon depth of wisdom and insight, and under- 29
standing as wide as the sand on the sea-shore, so that Solomon's wisdom 30
surpassed that of all the men of the east and of all Egypt. For he was wiser 31
than any man, wiser than Ethan the Ezrahite, and Heman, Kalcol, and
Darda, the sons of Mahol; his fame spread among all the surrounding
nations. He uttered three thousand proverbs, and his songs numbered a 32
thousand and five. He discoursed of trees, from the cedar of Lebanon down 33
to the marjoram that grows out of the wall, of beasts and birds, of reptiles
and fishes. Men of all races came to listen to the wisdom of Solomon, and 34
from all the kings of the earth who had heard of his wisdom he received
gifts.

WHEN HIRAM KING OF TYRE heard that Solomon had been anointed 5
king in his father's place, he sent envoys to him, because he had always
been a friend of David. Solomon sent this answer to Hiram: 'You know 2ª 3
that my father David could not build a house in honour of the name of the
LORD his God, because he was surrounded by armed nations until the
LORD made them subject to him. But now on every side the LORD my God 4
has given me peace; there is no one to oppose me, I fear no attack. So I 5
propose to build a house in honour of the name of the LORD my God,
following the promise given by the LORD to my father David: "Your son
whom I shall set on the throne in your place will build the house in
honour of my name." If therefore you will now give orders that cedars be 6
felled and brought from Lebanon, my men will work with yours, and I will
pay you for your men whatever sum you fix; for, as you know, we have none
so skilled at felling timber as your Sidonians.'

When Hiram received Solomon's message, he was greatly pleased and 7
said, 'Blessed be the LORD today who has given David a wise son to rule
over this great people.' And he sent this reply to Solomon: 'I have received 8
your message. In this matter of timber, both cedar and pine, I will do all
you wish. My men shall bring down the logs from Lebanon to the sea and 9
I will make them up into rafts to be floated to the place you appoint; I will
have them broken up there and you can remove them. You, on your part,
will meet my wishes if you provide the food for my household.' So Hiram 10
kept Solomon supplied with all the cedar and pine that he wanted, and 11
Solomon supplied Hiram with twenty thousand kor of wheat as food for
his household and twenty kor of oil of pounded olives; Solomon gave this
yearly to Hiram. (The LORD had given Solomon wisdom as he had 12
promised him; there was peace between Hiram and Solomon and they

ª Verses 2-11 : cp. 2 Chr. 2. 3-16.

379

13 concluded an alliance.) King Solomon raised a forced levy from the whole
14 of Israel amounting to thirty thousand men. He sent them to Lebanon in
monthly relays of ten thousand, so that the men spent one month in
Lebanon and two at home; Adoniram was superintendent of the whole
15 levy. Solomon had also seventy thousand hauliers and eighty thousand
16 quarrymen, apart from the three thousand three hundred foremen in
17 charge of the work who superintended the labourers. By the king's orders
they quarried huge, massive blocks for laying the foundation of the Lord's
18 house in hewn stone. Solomon's and Hiram's builders and the Gebalites
shaped the blocks and prepared both timber and stone for the building of
the house.

6 1ᵃ   It was in the four hundred and eightieth year after the Israelites had
come out of Egypt, in the fourth year of Solomon's reign over Israel, in
the second month of that year, the month of Ziv, that he began to build
the house of the Lord.

2   The house which King Solomon built for the Lord was sixty cubits
3 long by twenty cubits broad, and its height was thirty cubits. The vestibule
in front of the sanctuary was twenty cubits long, spanning the whole
breadth of the house, while it projected ten cubits in front of the house;
4 5 and he furnished the house with embrasures. Then he built a terrace
against its wall round both the sanctuary and the inner shrine. He made
6 arcades all round: the lowest arcade was five cubits in depth, the middle
six, and the highest seven; for he made rebates all round the outside of
the main wall so that the bearer beams might not be set into the walls.
7 In the building of the house, only blocks of undressed stone direct from
the quarry were used; no hammer or axe or any iron tool whatever was
heard in the house while it was being built.
8   The entrance to the lowest arcade was in the right-hand corner of the
house; there was access by a spiral stairway from that to the middle arcade,
9-10 and from the middle arcade to the highest. So he built the house and finished
it, having constructed the terrace five cubits high against the whole
building, braced the house with struts of cedar and roofed it with beams
and coffering of cedar.
11 12   Then the word of the Lord came to Solomon, saying, 'As for this house
which you are building, if you are obedient to my ordinances and conform
to my precepts and loyally observe all my commands, then I will fulfil my
13 promise to you, the promise I gave to your father David, and I will dwell
among the Israelites and never forsake my people Israel.'
14 15   So Solomon built the Lord's house and finished it. He lined the inner
walls of the house with cedar boards, covering the interior from floor to
16 rafters with wood; the floor he laid with boards of pine. In the innermost
part of the house he partitioned off a space of twenty cubits with cedar
boards from floor to rafters and made of it an inner shrine, to be the Most
17 18 Holy Place. The sanctuary in front of this was forty cubits long. The cedar
inside the house was carved with open flowers and gourds; all was cedar,
no stone was left visible.
19   He prepared an inner shrine in the furthest recesses of the house to

ᵃ Verses 1–3: cp. 2 Chr. 3. 2–4.

receive the Ark of the Covenant of the LORD. This inner shrine was twenty 20
cubits square and it stood twenty cubits high; he overlaid it with red gold
and made an altar of cedar. And Solomon overlaid the inside of the house 21
with red gold and drew a Veil*a* with golden chains across in front of the
inner shrine.*b* The whole house he overlaid with gold until it was all 22
covered; and the whole of the altar by the inner shrine he overlaid with gold.

In the inner shrine he made two cherubim of wild olive, each ten cubits 23*c*
high. Each wing of the cherubim was five cubits long, and from wing-tip 24
to wing-tip was ten cubits. Similarly the second cherub measured ten 25
cubits; the two cherubim were alike in size and shape, and each ten cubits 26
high. He put the cherubim within the shrine at the furthest recesses and 27
their wings were outspread, so that a wing of the one cherub touched the
wall on one side and a wing of the other touched the wall on the other side,
and their other wings met in the middle; and he overlaid the cherubim 28
with gold.

Round all the walls of the house he carved figures of cherubim, palm- 29
trees, and open flowers, both in the inner chamber and in the outer. The 30
floor of the house he overlaid with gold, both in the inner chamber and in
the outer. At the entrance to the inner shrine he made a double door of 31
wild olive; the pilasters and the *d* door-posts were pentagonal. The doors 32
were of wild olive, and he carved cherubim, palms, and open flowers on
them, overlaying them with gold and hammering the gold upon the
cherubim and the palms. Similarly for the doorway of the sanctuary he 33
made a square frame of wild olive and a double door of pine, each leaf 34
having two swivel-pins. On them he carved cherubim, palms, and open 35
flowers, overlaying them evenly with gold over the carving.

He built the inner court with three courses of dressed stone and one 36
course of lengths of cedar.

In the fourth year of Solomon's reign the foundation of the house of 37
the LORD was laid, in the month of Ziv; and in the eleventh year, in the 38
month of Bul, which is the eighth month, the house was finished in all its
details according to the specification. It had taken seven years to build.

Solomon had been engaged on his building for thirteen years by the 7
time he had finished it. He built the House of the Forest of Lebanon, a 2
hundred cubits long, fifty broad, and thirty high, constructed of four rows
of cedar columns, over which were laid lengths of cedar. It had a cedar roof, 3
extending over the beams, which rested on the columns, fifteen in each row;
and the number of the beams was forty-five. There were three rows of 4
window-frames, and the windows corresponded to each other at three
levels. All the doorways and the windows had square frames, and window 5
corresponded to window at three levels.

He made also the colonnade, fifty cubits long and thirty broad,*e* with 6
a cornice above.

He built the Hall of Judgement, the hall containing the throne where he 7
was to give judgement; this was panelled in cedar from floor to rafters.

a a Veil: *prob. rdg.; Heb. om. b Prob. rdg.; Heb. adds* and overlaid it with gold.
c Verses 23–28 : cp. 2 Chr. 3. 10–13. d and the: *prob. rdg.; Heb. om. e Prob.
rdg.; Heb. adds* and a colonnade and pillars in front of them.

8   His own house where he was to reside, in a court set back from the colonnade, and the house he made for Pharaoh's daughter whom he had married, were constructed like the hall.

9   All these were made of heavy blocks of stone, hewn to measure and trimmed with the saw on the inner and outer sides, from foundation to
10 coping and from the court of the house^a as far as the great court. At the base were heavy stones, massive blocks, some ten and some eight cubits
11 12 in size, and above were heavy stones dressed to measure, and cedar. The great court had three courses of dressed stone all around and a course of lengths of cedar; so had the inner court of the house of the LORD, and so had the vestibule of the house.

13 14   King Solomon fetched from Tyre Hiram, the son of a widow of the tribe of Naphtali. His father, a native of Tyre, had been a worker in bronze, and he himself was a man of great skill and ingenuity, versed in every kind of craftsmanship in bronze. Hiram came to King Solomon and executed all his works.

15^b   He cast in a mould the two bronze pillars. One stood eighteen cubits high and it took a cord twelve cubits long to go round it; it was hollow, and
16 the metal was four fingers thick.^c The second pillar was the same. He made two capitals of solid copper to set on the tops of the pillars, each capital five
17 cubits high. He made two bands of ornamental network, in festoons of chain-work, for the capitals on the tops of the pillars, a band of network
18 for each capital. Then he made pomegranates in two rows all round on top of the ornamental network of the one pillar; he did the same with the
19 other capital. (The capitals at the tops of the pillars in the vestibule were
20 shaped like lilies and were four cubits high.) Upon the capitals at the tops of the two pillars, immediately above the cushion, which was beyond the network upwards, were two hundred pomegranates in rows all round on
21 the two capitals.^d Then he erected the pillars at the vestibule of the sanctuary. When he had erected the pillar on the right side, he named it Jachin;^e
22 and when he had erected the one on the left side, he named it Boaz.^f On the tops of the pillars was lily-work. Thus the work of the pillars was finished.

23^g   He then made the Sea of cast metal; it was round in shape, the diameter from rim to rim being ten cubits; it stood five cubits high, and it took a line
24 thirty cubits long to go round it. All round the Sea on the outside under its rim, completely surrounding the thirty^h cubits of its circumference, were
25 two rows of gourds, cast in one piece with the Sea itself. It was mounted on twelve oxen, three facing north, three west, three south, and three east,
26 their hind quarters turned inwards; the Sea rested on top of them. Its thickness was a hand-breadth; its rim was made like that of a cup, shaped like the calyx of a lily; it held two thousand bath of water.

27   He also made the ten trolleys of bronze; each trolley was four cubits long,
28 four wide, and three high. This was the construction of the trolleys. They

^a *Prob. rdg., cp. verse 12; Heb.* from outside.   ^b *Verses 15-21: cp. 2 Chr. 3. 15-17.*
^c it was . . . thick: *prob. rdg., cp. Jer. 52. 21; Heb. om.*   ^d the two capitals: *prob. rdg.; Heb.* the second capital.   ^e *Or* Jachun, *meaning* It shall stand.   ^f *Or* Booz, *meaning* In strength.   ^g *Verses 23-26: cp. 2 Chr. 4. 2-5.*   ^h *Prob. rdg.; Heb.* ten.

had panels set in frames; on these panels were portrayed lions, oxen, and 29
cherubim, and similarly on the frames. Above and below the lions, oxen,
and cherubim*a* were fillets of hammered work of spiral design. Each 30
trolley had four bronze wheels with axles of bronze; it also had four
flanges and handles beneath the laver, and these handles were of cast
metal with a spiral design on their sides. The opening for the basin was set 31
within a crown which projected one cubit; the opening was round with
a level edge,*b* and it had decorations in relief. (The panels of the trolleys
were square, not round.) The four wheels were beneath the panels, and 32
the wheel-forks were made in one piece with the trolleys; the height of
each wheel was a cubit and a half. The wheels were constructed like those 33
of a chariot, their axles, hubs, spokes, and felloes being all of cast metal.
The four handles were at the four corners of each trolley, of one piece with 34
the trolley. At the top of the trolley there was a circular band half a cubit 35
high; the struts and panels on*c* the trolley were of one piece with it. On 36
the plates, that is on the panels,*d* he carved cherubim, lions, and palm-
trees, wherever there was a blank space, with spiral work all round it.
This is how the ten trolleys were made; all of them were cast alike, having 37
the same size and the same shape.

He then made ten bronze basins, each holding forty bath and measuring 38
four cubits; there was a basin for each of the ten trolleys. He put five 39
trolleys on the right side of the house and five on the left side; and he put
the Sea in the south-east corner of it.

Hiram made also the pots, the shovels, and the tossing-bowls. So he 40*e*
finished all the work which he had undertaken for King Solomon on the
house of the LORD: the two pillars; the two bowl-shaped capitals on the 41
tops of the pillars; the two ornamental networks to cover the two bowl-
shaped capitals on the tops of the pillars; the four hundred pomegranates 42
for the two networks, two rows of pomegranates for each network, to cover
the bowl-shaped capitals on the two pillars; the ten trolleys and the ten 43
basins on the trolleys; the one Sea and the twelve oxen which supported 44
it; the pots, the shovels, and the tossing-bowls—all these objects in the 45
house of the LORD which Hiram made for King Solomon being of bronze,
burnished work. In the Plain of the Jordan the king cast them, in the 46
foundry between Succoth and Zarethan.

Solomon put all these objects in their places; so great was the quantity 47
of bronze used in their making that the weight of it was beyond all reckoning. He made also all the furnishings for the house of the LORD: the golden 48
altar and the golden table upon which was set the Bread of the Presence;
the lamp-stands of red gold, five on the right side and five on the left side 49
of the inner shrine; the flowers, lamps, and tongs, of gold; the cups, 50
snuffers, tossing-bowls, saucers, and firepans, of red gold; and the panels
for the doors of the inner sanctuary, the Most Holy Place, and for the doors
of the house,*f* of gold.

When all the work which King Solomon did for the house of the LORD 51

---

a and cherubim: *prob. rdg.; Heb. om.*   *b* *Prob. rdg.; Heb. adds* a cubit and a half (*cp. verse 32*).   *c* *Prob. rdg.; Heb. adds* the head of.   *d* *Prob. rdg.; Heb. adds* its struts.
e *Verses 40–51: cp. 2 Chr. 4. 11–5. 1.*   *f* *Prob. rdg.; Heb. adds* for the temple.

was completed, he brought in the sacred treasures of his father David, the silver, the gold, and the vessels, and deposited them in the storehouses of the house of the LORD.

8 1^a THEN SOLOMON SUMMONED THE ELDERS of Israel, all the heads of the tribes who were chiefs of families in Israel, to assemble in Jerusalem, in order to bring up the Ark of the Covenant of the LORD from the City of
2 David, which is called Zion. All the men of Israel assembled in King Solomon's presence at the pilgrim-feast in the month Ethanim, the
3 seventh month. When the elders of Israel had all come, the priests took
4 the Ark of the LORD and carried it up with the Tent of the Presence and all the sacred furnishings of the Tent: it was the priests and the Levites
5 together who carried them up. King Solomon and the whole congregation of Israel, assembled with him before the Ark, sacrificed sheep and oxen
6 in numbers past counting or reckoning. Then the priests brought in the Ark of the Covenant of the LORD to its place, the inner shrine of the house,
7 the Most Holy Place, beneath the wings of the cherubim. The cherubim spread their wings over the place of the Ark; they formed a screen above
8 the Ark and its poles. The poles projected, and their ends could be seen from the Holy Place immediately in front of the inner shrine, but from
9 nowhere else outside; they are there to this day. There was nothing inside the Ark but the two tablets of stone which Moses had deposited there at Horeb, the tablets of the covenant which the LORD made with the Israelites when they left Egypt.

10 Then the priests came out of the Holy Place, since the cloud was filling
11 the house of the LORD, and they could not continue to minister because of
12^b it, for the glory of the LORD filled his house. And Solomon said:

> O LORD who hast set the sun in heaven,
>> but hast chosen to dwell in thick darkness,
13 > here have I built thee a lofty house,
>> a habitation for thee to occupy for ever.

14 And as they stood waiting, the king turned round and blessed all the
15 assembly of Israel in these words: 'Blessed be the LORD the God of Israel who spoke directly to my father David and has himself fulfilled his pro-
16 mise. For he said, "From the day when I brought my people Israel out of Egypt, I chose no city out of all the tribes of Israel where I should build a house for my Name to be there, but I chose David to be over my people
17 Israel." My father David had in mind to build a house in honour of the
18 name of the LORD the God of Israel, but the LORD said to him, "You purposed to build a house in honour of my name; and your purpose was
19 good. Nevertheless, you shall not build it; but the son who is to be born to
20 you, he shall build the house in honour of my name." The LORD has now fulfilled his promise: I have succeeded my father David and taken his place on the throne of Israel, as the LORD promised; and I have built the
21 house in honour of the name of the LORD the God of Israel. I have assigned

^a Verses 1–9: cp. 2 Chr. 5. 2–10.   *^b Verses 12–50: cp. 2 Chr. 6. 1–39.*

therein a place for the Ark containing the Covenant of the LORD, which he
made with our forefathers when he brought them out of Egypt.'

Then Solomon, standing in front of the altar of the LORD in the presence 22
of the whole assembly of Israel, spread out his hands towards heaven and
said, 'O LORD God of Israel, there is no god like thee in heaven above or 23
on earth beneath, keeping covenant with thy servants and showing them
constant love while they continue faithful to thee in heart and soul. Thou 24
hast kept thy promise to thy servant David my father; by thy deeds this
day thou hast fulfilled what thou didst say to him in words. Now therefore, 25
O LORD God of Israel, keep this promise of thine to thy servant David my
father: "You shall never want for a man appointed by me to sit on the
throne of Israel, if only your sons look to their ways and walk before me as
you have walked before me." And now, O God of Israel, let the words 26
which thou didst speak to thy servant David my father be confirmed.

'But can God indeed dwell on earth? Heaven itself, the highest heaven, 27
cannot contain thee; how much less this house that I have built! Yet 28
attend to the prayer and the supplication of thy servant, O LORD my God,
listen to the cry and the prayer which thy servant utters this day, that thine 29
eyes may ever be upon this house night and day, this place of which thou
didst say, "My Name shall be there"; so mayest thou hear thy servant
when he prays towards this place. Hear the supplication of thy servant and 30
of thy people Israel when they pray towards this place. Hear thou in heaven
thy dwelling and, when thou hearest, forgive.

'When a man wrongs his neighbour and he is adjured to take an oath, 31
and the adjuration is made before thy altar in this house, then do thou hear 32
in heaven and act: be thou thy servants' judge, condemning the guilty
man and bringing his deeds upon his own head, acquitting the innocent
and rewarding him as his innocence may deserve.

'When thy people Israel are defeated by an enemy because they have 33
sinned against thee, and they turn back to thee, confessing thy name and
making their prayer and supplication to thee in this house, do thou hear 34
in heaven; forgive the sin of thy people Israel and restore them to the land
which thou gavest to their forefathers.

'When the heavens are shut up and there is no rain because thy servant 35
and thy people Israel have sinned against thee, and when they pray towards this place, confessing thy name and forsaking their sin when they
feel thy punishment, do thou hear in heaven and forgive their sin; so mayest 36
thou teach them the good way which they should follow; and grant rain
to thy land which thou hast given to thy people as their own possession.

'If there is famine in the land, or pestilence, or black blight or red, or 37
locusts new-sloughed or fully grown; or if their enemies besiege them in
any of their cities; or if plague or sickness befall them, then hear the prayer 38
or supplication of every man among thy people Israel, as each one, prompted
by the remorse of his own heart, spreads out his hands towards this house:
hear it in heaven thy dwelling and forgive, and act. And, as thou knowest 39
a man's heart, reward him according to his deeds, for thou alone knowest
the hearts of all men; and so they will fear thee all their lives in the land 40
thou gavest to our forefathers.

41 'The foreigner too, the man who does not belong to thy people Israel,
42 but has come from a distant land because of thy fame (for men shall hear
of thy great fame and thy strong hand and arm outstretched), when he
43 comes and prays towards this house, hear in heaven thy dwelling and
respond to the call which the foreigner makes to thee, so that like thy
people Israel all peoples of the earth may know thy fame and fear thee, and
learn that this house which I have built bears thy name.

44 'When thy people go to war with an enemy, wherever thou dost send
them, when they pray to the LORD, turning towards this city which thou
hast chosen and towards this house which I have built in honour of thy
45 name, do thou in heaven hear their prayer and supplication, and grant
them justice.

46 'Should they sin against thee (and what man is free from sin?) and
shouldst thou in thy anger give them over to an enemy, who carries them
47 captive to his own land, far or near; if in the land of their captivity they
learn their lesson and make supplication again to thee in that land and say,
48 "We have sinned and acted perversely and wickedly", if they turn back to
thee with heart and soul in the land of their captors, and pray to thee,
turning towards their land which thou gavest to their forefathers and
towards this city which thou didst choose and this house which I have
49 built in honour of thy name; then in heaven thy dwelling do thou hear
50 their prayer and supplication, and grant them justice. Forgive thy people
their sins and transgressions against thee; put pity for them in their
51 captors' hearts. For they are thy possession, thy people whom thou didst
52 bring out of Egypt, from the smelting-furnace, and so thine eyes are ever
open to the entreaty of thy servant and of thy people Israel, and thou dost
53 hear whenever they call to thee. Thou thyself hast singled them out from
all the peoples of the earth to be thy possession; so thou didst promise
through thy servant Moses when thou didst bring our forefathers from
Egypt, O Lord GOD.'

54 When Solomon had finished this prayer and supplication to the LORD,
he rose from before the altar of the LORD, where he had been kneeling with
55 his hands spread out to heaven, stood up and in a loud voice blessed the
56 whole assembly of Israel: 'Blessed be the LORD who has given his people
Israel rest, as he promised: not one of the promises he made through his
57 servant Moses has failed. The LORD our God be with us as he was with
58 our forefathers; may he never leave us nor forsake us. May he turn our
hearts towards him, that we may conform to all his ways, observing his
commandments, statutes, and judgements, as he commanded our fore-
59 fathers. And may the words of my supplication to the LORD be with the
LORD our God day and night, that, as the need arises day by day, he may
60 grant justice to his servant and justice to his people Israel. So all the
61 peoples of the earth will know that the LORD is God, he and no other, and
you will be perfect in loyalty to the LORD our God as you are this day,
conforming to his statutes and observing his commandments.'

62 When the king and all Israel came to offer sacrifices before the LORD,
63 Solomon offered as shared-offerings to the LORD twenty-two thousand
oxen and a hundred and twenty thousand sheep; thus it was that the king

and the Israelites dedicated the house of the LORD. On that day also the 64ᵃ
king consecrated the centre of the court which lay in front ᵇ of the house of
the LORD; there he offered the whole-offering, the grain-offering, and the
fat portions of the shared-offerings, because the bronze altar which stood
before the LORD was too small to take them all, the whole-offering, the
grain-offering, and the fat portions of the shared-offerings.

So Solomon and all Israel with him, a great assembly from Lebo- 65
hamath to the Torrent of Egypt, celebrated the pilgrim-feast at that time
before the LORD our God for seven days. On the eighth day he dismissed 66
the people; and they blessed the king, and went home happy and glad at
heart for all the prosperity granted by the LORD to his servant David and
to his people Israel.

WHEN SOLOMON HAD FINISHED the house of the LORD and the royal 9 1ᶜ
palace and all the plans for building on which he had set his heart, the LORD 2
appeared to him a second time, as he had appeared to him at Gibeon. The 3
LORD said to him, 'I have heard the prayer and supplication which you
have offered me; I have consecrated this house which you have built, to
receive my Name for all time, and my eyes and my heart shall be fixed on
it for ever. And if you, on your part, live in my sight as your father David 4
lived, in integrity and uprightness, doing all I command you and observing
my statutes and my judgements, then I will establish your royal throne 5
over Israel for ever, as I promised your father David when I said, "You
shall never want for a man upon the throne of Israel." But if you or your 6
sons turn back from following me and do not observe my commandments
and my statutes which I have set before you, and if you go and serve other
gods and prostrate yourselves before them, then I will cut off Israel from 7
the land which I gave them; I will renounce this house which I have consecrated in honour of my name, and Israel shall become a byword and an
object lesson among all peoples. And this house will become a ruin; every 8
passer-by will be appalled and gasp at the sight of it; and they will ask,
"Why has the LORD so treated this land and this house?" The answer will 9
be, "Because they forsook the LORD their God, who brought their forefathers out of Egypt, and clung to other gods, prostrating themselves
before them and serving them; that is why the LORD has brought this great
evil on them." '

Solomon had taken twenty years to build the two houses, the house of 10ᵈ
the LORD and the royal palace. Hiram king of Tyre had supplied him with 11
all the timber, both cedar and pine, and all the gold, that he desired, and
King Solomon gave Hiram twenty cities in the land of Galilee. But when 12
Hiram went from Tyre to inspect the cities which Solomon had given him,
they did not satisfy him, and he said, 'What kind of cities are these you have 13
given me, my brother?' And so he called them the Land of Cabul,ᵉ the
name they still bear. Hiram sent a hundred and twenty talents of gold to 14
the king.

This is the record of the forced labour which King Solomon conscripted 15

ᵃ *Verses 64-66: cp. 2 Chr. 7. 7-10.*   ᵇ *Or to the east.*   ᶜ *Verses 1-9: cp. 2 Chr. 7.
11-22.*   ᵈ *Verses 10-28: cp. 2 Chr. 8. 1-18.*   ᵉ *That is* Sterile Land.

to build the house of the LORD, his own palace, the Millo, the wall of
16 Jerusalem, and Hazor, Megiddo, and Gezer. Gezer had been attacked and
captured by Pharaoh king of Egypt, who had burnt it to the ground, put
its Canaanite inhabitants to death, and given it as a marriage gift to his
17 daughter, Solomon's wife; and Solomon rebuilt it. He also built Lower
18 19 Beth-horon, Baalath, and Tamar in the wilderness, as well as all his store-
cities, and the towns where he quartered his chariots and horses; and he
carried out all his cherished plans for building in Jerusalem, in the Lebanon,
20 and throughout his whole dominion. All the survivors of the Amorites,
Hittites, Perizzites, Hivites, and Jebusites, who did not belong to Israel—
21 that is their descendants who survived in the land, wherever the Israelites
had been unable to annihilate them—were employed by Solomon on
22 perpetual forced labour, as they still are. But Solomon put none of the
Israelites to forced labour; they were his fighting men,*a* his captains and
23 lieutenants, and the commanders of his chariots and of his cavalry. The
number of officers in charge of the foremen over Solomon's work was five
hundred and fifty; these superintended the people engaged on the work.
24   Then Solomon brought Pharaoh's daughter up from the City of David
to her own house which he had built for her; later on he built the Millo.
25   Three times a year Solomon used to offer whole-offerings and shared-
offerings on the altar which he had built to the LORD, making smoke-
offerings before the LORD. So he completed the house.
26   King Solomon built a fleet of ships at Ezion-geber, near Eloth*b* on the
27 shore of the Red Sea,*c* in Edom. Hiram sent men of his own to serve with
28 the fleet, experienced seamen, to work with Solomon's men; and they went
to Ophir and brought back four hundred and twenty talents of gold, which
they delivered to King Solomon.

10 1*d* THE QUEEN OF SHEBA HEARD of Solomon's fame*e* and came to test him
2 with hard questions. She arrived in Jerusalem with a very large retinue,
camels laden with spices, gold in great quantity, and precious stones. When
3 she came to Solomon, she told him everything she had in her mind, and
Solomon answered all her questions; not one of them was too abstruse for
4 the king to answer. When the queen of Sheba saw all the wisdom of Sol-
5 omon, the house which he had built, the food on his table, the courtiers
sitting round him, and his attendants standing behind in their livery, his
cupbearers, and the whole-offerings which he used to offer in the house of
6 the LORD, there was no more spirit left in her. Then she said to the king,
'The report which I heard in my own country about you and your wisdom
7 was true, but I did not believe it until I came and saw for myself. Indeed
I was not told half of it; your wisdom and your prosperity go far beyond
8 the report which I had of them. Happy are your wives, happy these courtiers
9 of yours who wait on you every day and hear your wisdom! Blessed be the
LORD your God who has delighted in you and has set you on the throne of
Israel; because he loves Israel for ever, he has made you their king to

---

a Prob. rdg.; Heb. adds and his servants.   *b Or* Elath.   *c Or* the Sea of Reeds.
d Verses 1–25 : cp. 2 Chr. 9. 1–24.   *e Prob. rdg., cp. 2 Chr. 9. 1; Heb. adds* to the
name of the LORD.

maintain law and justice.' Then she gave the king a hundred and twenty   10
talents of gold, spices in great abundance, and precious stones. Never again
came such a quantity of spices as the queen of Sheba gave to King Solomon.

Besides all this, Hiram's fleet of ships, which had brought gold from   11
Ophir, brought in also from Ophir cargoes of almug wood and precious
stones. The king used the wood to make stools for the house of the LORD   12
and for the royal palace, as well as harps and lutes for the singers. No such
almug wood has ever been imported or even seen since that time.

And King Solomon gave the queen of Sheba all she desired, whatever   13
she asked, in addition to all that he gave her of his royal bounty. So she
departed and returned with her retinue to her own land.

Now the weight of gold which Solomon received yearly was six hundred   14
and sixty-six talents, in addition to the tolls levied by the customs officers   15
and profits on foreign trade, and the tribute of [a] the kings of Arabia and the
regional governors.

King Solomon made two hundred shields of beaten gold, and six hundred   16
shekels of gold went to the making of each one; he also made three hundred   17
bucklers of beaten gold, and three minas of gold went to the making of each
buckler. The king put these into the House of the Forest of Lebanon.

The king also made a great throne of ivory and overlaid it with fine gold.   18
Six steps led up to the throne; at the back of the throne there was the head   19
of a calf. There were arms on each side of the seat, with a lion standing beside each of them, and twelve lions stood on the six steps, one at either end   20
of each step. Nothing like it had ever been made for any monarch. All Sol-   21
omon's drinking vessels were of gold, and all the plate in the House of the
Forest of Lebanon was of red gold; no silver was used, for it was reckoned
of no value in the days of Solomon. The king had a fleet of merchantmen   22
at sea with Hiram's fleet; once every three years this fleet of merchantmen
came home, bringing gold and silver, ivory, apes and monkeys.

Thus King Solomon outdid all the kings of the earth in wealth and   23
wisdom, and all the world courted him, to hear the wisdom which God   24
had put in his heart. Each brought his gift with him, vessels of silver and   25
gold, garments, perfumes and spices, horses and mules, so much year by
year.

And Solomon got together many chariots and horses; he had fourteen   26 [b]
hundred chariots and twelve thousand horses, and he stabled some in the
chariot-towns and kept others at hand in Jerusalem. The king made silver   27
as common in Jerusalem as stones, and cedar as plentiful as sycomore-fig
in the Shephelah. Horses were imported from Egypt and Coa for Solomon;   28
the royal merchants obtained them from Coa by purchase. Chariots were   29
imported from Egypt for six hundred silver shekels each, and horses for a
hundred and fifty; in the same way the merchants obtained them for export
from all the kings of the Hittites and the kings of Aram.

King Solomon was a lover of women, and besides Pharaoh's daughter   **11**
he married many foreign women, Moabite, Ammonite, Edomite, Sidonian,
and Hittite, from the nations with whom the LORD had forbidden the   2

[a] and the tribute of: *prob. rdg.; Heb.* and all.   [b] *Verses 26–29: cp. 2 Chr. 1.*
14–17; 9. 25–28.

Israelites to intermarry, 'because', he said, 'they will entice you to serve
3 their gods.' But Solomon was devoted to them and loved them dearly. He
had seven hundred wives, who were princesses, and three hundred con-
4 cubines, and they turned his heart from the truth. When he grew old, his
wives turned his heart to follow other gods, and he did not remain wholly
5 loyal to the LORD his God as his father David had been. He followed
Ashtoreth, goddess of the Sidonians, and Milcom, the loathsome god of
6 the Ammonites. Thus Solomon did what was wrong in the eyes of the
7 LORD, and was not loyal to the LORD like his father David. He built a
hill-shrine for Kemosh, the loathsome god of Moab, on the height to the
east of Jerusalem, and for Molech, the loathsome god of the Ammonites.
8 Thus he did for the gods to which all his foreign wives burnt offerings and
9 made sacrifices. The LORD was angry with Solomon because his heart had
turned away from the LORD the God of Israel, who had appeared to him
10 twice and had strictly commanded him not to follow other gods; but he
11 disobeyed the LORD's command. The LORD therefore said to Solomon,
'Because you have done this and have not kept my covenant and my
statutes as I commanded you, I will tear the kingdom from you and give
12 it to your servant. Nevertheless, for the sake of your father David I will
13 not do this in your day; I will tear it out of your son's hand. Even so not
the whole kingdom; I will leave him one tribe for the sake of my servant
David and for the sake of Jerusalem, my chosen city.'

14   Then the LORD raised up an adversary for Solomon, Hadad the Edomite,
15 of the royal house of Edom. At the time when David reduced Edom, his
commander-in-chief Joab had destroyed every male in the country when
16 he went into it to bury the slain. He and the armies of Israel remained there
17 for six months, until he had destroyed every male in Edom. Then Hadad,
who was still a boy, fled the country with some of his father's Edomite
18 servants, intending to enter Egypt. They set out from Midian, made their
way to Paran and, taking some men from there, came to Pharaoh king of
Egypt, who assigned Hadad a house and maintenance and made him a
19 grant of land. Hadad found great favour with Pharaoh, who gave him in
20 marriage a sister of Queen Tahpenes his wife. She bore him his son
Genubath; Tahpenes weaned the child in Pharaoh's house, and he lived
21 there along with Pharaoh's children. When Hadad heard in Egypt that
David rested with his forefathers and that his commander-in-chief Joab
was also dead, he said to Pharaoh, 'Let me go so that I may return to my
22 own country.' 'What is it that you find wanting in my country', said
Pharaoh, 'that you want to go back to your own?' 'Nothing,' said Hadad,
25 'but do, pray, let me go.' He remained an adversary for Israel all through
Solomon's reign. This is the harm that Hadad caused: he maintained a
stranglehold on Israel and became king of Edom.

23   Then God raised up another adversary against Solomon, Rezon son of
24 Eliada, who had fled from his master Hadadezer king of Zobah. He gathered
men about him and became a captain of freebooters, who came to Damascus
and occupied it; he became king there.

26*a*   Jeroboam son of Nebat, one of Solomon's courtiers, an Ephrathite from

a Verse 25 transposed to follow verse 22.

Zeredah, whose widowed mother was named Zeruah, rebelled against the king. And this is the story of his rebellion. Solomon had built the Millo and 27 closed the breach in the wall of the city of his father David. Now this 28 Jeroboam was a man of great energy; and Solomon, seeing how the young man worked, had put him in charge of all the labour-gangs in the tribal district of Joseph. On one occasion Jeroboam had left Jerusalem, and the 29 prophet Ahijah from Shiloh met him on the road. The prophet was wrapped in a new cloak, and the two of them were alone in the open country. Then 30 Ahijah took hold of the new cloak he was wearing, tore it into twelve pieces and said to Jeroboam, 'Take ten pieces, for this is the word of the LORD 31 the God of Israel: "I am going to tear the kingdom from the hand of Solomon and give you ten tribes. But one tribe will remain his, for the sake 32 of my servant David and for the sake of Jerusalem, the city I have chosen out of all the tribes of Israel. I have done this because Solomon has for- 33 saken me; he has prostrated himself before Ashtoreth goddess of the Sidonians, Kemosh god of Moab, and Milcom god of the Ammonites, and has not conformed to my ways. He has not done what is right in my eyes or observed my statutes and judgements as David his father did. Nevertheless I will not take the whole kingdom from him, but will maintain 34 his rule as long as he lives, for the sake of my chosen servant David, who did observe my commandments and statutes. But I will take the kingdom, 35 that is the ten tribes, from his son and give it to you. One tribe I will give 36 to his son, that my servant David may always have a flame burning before me in Jerusalem, the city which I chose to receive my Name. But I will 37 appoint you to rule over all that you can desire, and to be king over Israel. If you pay heed to all my commands, if you conform to my ways and do 38 what is right in my eyes, observing my statutes and commandments as my servant David did, then I will be with you. I will establish your family for ever as I did for David; I will give Israel to you, and punish David's 39 descendants as they have deserved, but not for ever." '

After this Solomon sought to kill Jeroboam, but he fled to King Shishak 40 in Egypt and remained there till Solomon's death.

The other acts and events of Solomon's reign, and all his wisdom, are 41^a recorded in the annals of Solomon. The reign of King Solomon in Jerusalem 42 over the whole of Israel lasted forty years. Then he rested with his fore- 43 fathers and was buried in the city of David his father, and he was succeeded by his son Rehoboam.

The divided kingdom

R EHOBOAM WENT TO SHECHEM, for all Israel had gone there to make 12 1^b him king. When Jeroboam son of Nebat, who was still in Egypt, heard 2 of it, he remained there, having taken refuge there to escape King Solomon. They now recalled him, and he and all the assembly of Israel came to 3 Rehoboam and said, 'Your father laid a cruel yoke upon us; but if you will 4 now lighten the cruel slavery he imposed on us and the heavy yoke he laid

a Verses 41–43: cp. 2 Chr. 9. 29–31.   *b Verses 1–19: cp. 2 Chr. 10. 1–19.*

5 on us, we will serve you.' 'Give me three days,' he said, 'and come back
6 again.' So the people went away. King Rehoboam then consulted the
   elders who had been in attendance on his father Solomon while he lived:
7 'What answer do you advise me to give to this people?' And they said, 'If
   today you are willing to serve this people, show yourself their servant now
8 and speak kindly to them, and they will be your servants ever after.' But
   he rejected the advice which the elders gave him. He next consulted those
9 who had grown up with him, the young men in attendance, and asked
   them, 'What answer do you advise me to give to this people's request that
10 I should lighten the yoke which my father laid on them?' The young men
   replied, 'Give this answer to the people who say that your father made
   their yoke heavy and ask you to lighten it; tell them: "My little finger is
11 thicker than my father's loins. My father laid a heavy yoke on you; I will
   make it heavier. My father used the whip on you; but I will use the lash."'
12 Jeroboam and the people all came back to Rehoboam on the third day, as
13 the king had ordered. And the king gave them a harsh answer. He rejected
14 the advice which the elders had given him and spoke to the people as the
   young men had advised: 'My father made your yoke heavy; I will make it
15 heavier. My father used the whip on you; but I will use the lash.' So the
   king would not listen to the people; for the LORD had given this turn to the
   affair, in order that the word he had spoken by Ahijah of Shiloh to Jeroboam
   son of Nebat might be fulfilled.
16   When all Israel saw that the king would not listen to them, they answered:

> What share have we in David?
> We have no lot in the son of Jesse.
> Away to your homes, O Israel;
> now see to your own house, David.

17 So Israel went to their homes, and Rehoboam ruled over those Israelites
   who lived in the cities of Judah.
18   Then King Rehoboam sent out Adoram, the commander of the forced
   levies, but the Israelites stoned him to death; thereupon King Reho-
19 boam mounted his chariot in haste and fled to Jerusalem. From that day
   to this, the whole of Israel has been in rebellion against the house of
   David.
20   When the men of Israel heard that Jeroboam had returned, they sent
   and called him to the assembly and made him king over the whole of
   Israel. The tribe of Judah alone followed the house of David.
21*a* When Rehoboam reached Jerusalem, he assembled all the house of
   Judah, the tribe of Benjamin also, a hundred and eighty thousand chosen
22 warriors, to fight against the house of Israel and recover his kingdom. But
23 the word of God came to Shemaiah the man of God: 'Say to Rehoboam
   son of Solomon, king of Judah, and to the house of Judah and to Benjamin
24 and the rest of the people, "This is the word of the LORD: You shall not
   go up to make war on your kinsmen the Israelites. Return to your homes,
   for this is my will."' So they listened to the word of the LORD and returned
   home, as the LORD had told them.

a Verses 21–24: cp. 2 Chr. 11. 1–4.

THEN JEROBOAM REBUILT SHECHEM in the hill-country of Ephraim 25
and took up residence there; from there he went out and built Penuel. 'As 26
things now stand,' he said to himself, 'the kingdom will revert to the house
of David. If this people go up to sacrifice in the house of the LORD in 27
Jerusalem, it will revive their allegiance to their lord Rehoboam king of
Judah, and they will kill me and return to King Rehoboam.' After giving 28
thought to the matter he made two calves of gold and said to the people,
'It is too much trouble for you to go up to Jerusalem; here are your gods,
Israel, that brought you up from Egypt.' One he set up at Bethel and the 29
other he put at Dan, and this thing became a sin in Israel; the people went 30
to Bethel to worship the one, and all the way to Dan to worship the other.
He set up shrines on the hill-tops also and appointed priests from every 31
class of the people, who did not belong to the Levites. He instituted a 32
pilgrim-feast on the fifteenth day of the eighth month like that in Judah,
and he offered sacrifices upon the altar. This he did at Bethel, sacrificing
to the calves that he had made and compelling the priests of the hill-
shrines, which he had set up, to serve at Bethel. So he went up to the altar 33
that he had made at Bethel on the fifteenth day of the eighth month; there,
in a month of his own choosing, he instituted for the Israelites a pilgrim-
feast and himself went up to the altar to burn the sacrifice.

As Jeroboam stood by the altar to burn the sacrifice, a man of God from **13**
Judah, moved by the word of the LORD, appeared at Bethel. He inveighed 2
against the altar in the LORD's name, crying out, 'O altar, altar! This is the
word of the LORD: "Listen! A child shall be born to the house of David,
named Josiah. He will sacrifice upon you the priests of the hill-shrines
who make offerings upon you, and he will burn human bones upon you."'
He gave a sign the same day: 'This is the sign which the LORD has ordained: 3
This altar will be rent in pieces and the ashes upon it will be spilt.' When 4
King Jeroboam heard the sentence which the man of God pronounced
against the altar at Bethel, he pointed to him from the altar and said,
'Seize that man!' Immediately the hand which he had pointed at him
became paralysed, so that he could not draw it back. The altar too was rent 5
in pieces and the ashes were spilt, in fulfilment of the sign that the man of
God had given at the LORD's command. The king appealed to the man of 6
God to pacify the LORD his God and pray for him that his hand might be
restored. The man of God did as he asked; his hand was restored and
became as it had been before. Then the king said to the man of God, 'Come 7
home and take refreshment at my table, and let me give you a present.' But 8
the man of God answered, 'If you were to give me half your house, I would
not enter it with you: I will eat and drink nothing in this place, for the 9
LORD's command to me was to eat and drink nothing, and not to go back
by the way I came.' So he went back another way; he did not return by the 10
road he had taken to Bethel.

At that time there was an aged prophet living in Bethel. His sons came 11
and recounted to him all that the man of God had done in Bethel that day;
they also told their father what he had said to the king. Their father said to 12
them, 'Which road did he take?' They pointed out the road taken by the
man of God who had come from Judah. He said to his sons, 'Saddle an 13

14 ass for me.' They saddled the ass, and he mounted it and went after the man of God. He found him seated under a terebinth and said to him, 'Are you the man of God who came from Judah?' And he said, 'Yes, I am.'

15 16 'Come home and eat with me', said the prophet. 'I cannot go back with you or enter your house,' said the other; 'I can neither eat nor drink with

17 you in this place, for it was told me by the word of the LORD: "You shall eat and drink nothing there, nor shall you go back the way you came."'

18 And the old man said to him, 'I also am a prophet, as you are; and an angel commanded me by the word of the LORD to bring you home with me to

19 eat and drink with me.' He was lying; but the man of Judah went back

20 with him and ate and drank in his house. While they were still seated at table the word of the LORD came to the prophet who had brought him back,

21 and he cried out to the man of God from Judah, 'This is the word of the LORD: "You have defied the word of the LORD your God and have not

22 obeyed his command; you have come back to eat and to drink in the place where he forbade it; therefore your body shall not be laid in the grave of your forefathers."'

23 After they had eaten and drunk, he saddled an ass for the prophet whom

24 he had brought back. As he went on his way a lion met him and killed him, and his body was left lying in the road, with the ass and the lion both

25 standing beside it. Some passers-by saw the body lying in the road and the lion standing beside it, and they brought the news to the city where the old

26 prophet lived. When the prophet who had caused him to break his journey heard it, he said, 'It is the man of God who defied the word of the LORD. The LORD has given him to the lion, and it has broken his neck and killed

27 him in fulfilment of the word of the LORD.' He told his sons to saddle an

28 ass and, when they had saddled it, he set out and found the body lying in the road with the ass and the lion standing beside it; the lion had neither

29 devoured the body nor broken the back of the ass. Then the prophet lifted the body of the man of God, laid it on the ass and brought it back to his

30 own city to mourn over it and bury it. He laid the body in his own grave

31 and they mourned for him, saying, 'My brother, my brother!' After burying him, he said to his sons, 'When I die, bury me in the grave where the

32 man of God lies buried; lay my bones beside his; for the sentence which he pronounced at the LORD's command against the altar in Bethel and all the hill-shrines of Samaria shall be carried out.'

33 After this Jeroboam still did not abandon his evil ways but went on appointing priests for the hill-shrines from all classes of the people; any man who offered himself he would consecrate to be priest of a hill-shrine.

34 By doing this he brought guilt upon his own house and doomed it to utter destruction.

14 1 2 At that time Jeroboam's son Abijah fell ill, and Jeroboam said to his wife, 'Come now, disguise yourself so that people may not be able to recognize you as my wife, and go to Shiloh. Ahijah the prophet is there, the man who

3 said I was to be king over this people. Take with you ten loaves, some raisins, and a flask of syrup, and go to him; he will tell you what will happen to the

4 child.' Jeroboam's wife did so; she set off at once for Shiloh and came to Ahijah's house. Now Ahijah could not see, for his eyes were fixed in the

blindness of old age, and the LORD had said to him, 'The wife of Jeroboam 5
is on her way to consult you about her son, who is ill; you shall give her
such and such an answer.' When she came in, concealing who she was, and 6
Ahijah heard her footsteps at the door, he said, 'Come in, wife of Jeroboam.
Why conceal who you are? I have heavy news for you. Go and tell Jeroboam: 7
"This is the word of the LORD the God of Israel: I raised you out of the
people and appointed you prince over my people Israel; I tore away the 8
kingdom from the house of David and gave it to you; but you have not
been like my servant David, who kept my commands and followed me
with his whole heart, doing only what was right in my eyes. You have out- 9
done all your predecessors in wickedness; you have provoked me to anger
by making for yourself other gods and images of cast metal; and you have
turned your back on me. For this I will bring disaster on the house of 10
Jeroboam and I will destroy them all, every mother's son, whether still
under the protection of the family or not, and I will sweep away the house
of Jeroboam in Israel, as a man sweeps up dung until none is left. Those 11
of that house who die in the city shall be food for the dogs, and those
who die in the country shall be food for the birds. It is the word of the
LORD."

'You must go home now; the moment you set foot in the city, the child 12
will die. All Israel will mourn for him and bury him; he alone of all Jero- 13
boam's family will have proper burial, because in him alone could the LORD
the God of Israel find anything good. Then the LORD will set up a king 14
over Israel who shall put an end to the house of Jeroboam. This first; and
what next? The LORD will strike Israel, till it trembles like a reed in the 15
water; he will uproot its people from this good land which he gave to their
forefathers and scatter them beyond the Euphrates, because they have
made their sacred poles and provoked the LORD's anger. And he will 16
abandon Israel for the sins that Jeroboam has committed and has led
Israel to commit.' Jeroboam's wife went home at once to Tirzah and, as 17
she crossed the threshold of the house, the boy died. They buried him, and 18
all Israel mourned over him; and thus the word of the LORD was fulfilled
which he had spoken through his servant Ahijah the prophet.

The other events of Jeroboam's reign, in war and peace, are recorded in 19
the annals of the kings of Israel. He reigned twenty-two years; then he 20
rested with his forefathers and was succeeded by his son Nadab.

IN JUDAH REHOBOAM SON OF SOLOMON had become king. He was 21
forty-one years old when he came to the throne, and he reigned for seventeen years in Jerusalem, the city which the LORD had chosen out of all the
tribes of Israel to receive his Name. Rehoboam's mother was a woman of
Ammon called Naamah. Judah did what was wrong in the eyes of the LORD, 22
rousing his jealous indignation by the sins they committed, beyond anything that their forefathers had done. They erected hill-shrines, sacred 23
pillars, and sacred poles, on every high hill and under every spreading tree.
Worse still, all over the country there were male prostitutes attached to the 24
shrines, and the people adopted all the abominable practices of the nations
whom the LORD had dispossessed in favour of Israel.

25ᵃ   In the fifth year of Rehoboam's reign Shishak king of Egypt attacked
26 Jerusalem. He removed the treasures of the house of the LORD and of the
royal palace, and seized everything, including all the shields of gold that
27 Solomon had made. King Rehoboam replaced them with bronze shields
and entrusted them to the officers of the escort who guarded the entrance
28 of the royal palace. Whenever the king entered the house of the LORD,
the escort carried them; afterwards they returned them to the guard-
room.

29ᵇ   The other acts and events of Rehoboam's reign are recorded in the annals
30 of the kings of Judah. There was continual fighting between him and
31 Jeroboam. He rested with his forefathers and was buried with them in the
city of David. (His mother was a woman of Ammon, whose name was
Naamah.) He was succeeded by his son Abijam.

15   In the eighteenth year of the reign of Jeroboam son of Nebat, Abijam
2 became king of Judah. He reigned in Jerusalem for three years; his mother
3 was Maacah granddaughter of Abishalom. All the sins that his father had
committed before him he committed too, nor was he faithful to the LORD
4 his God as his ancestor David had been. But for David's sake the LORD
his God gave him a flame to burn in Jerusalem, by establishing his dynasty
5 and making Jerusalem secure, because David had done what was right in
the eyes of the LORD and had not disobeyed any of his commandments all
7 his life, except in the matter of Uriah the Hittite.ᶜ The other acts and
events of Abijam's reign are recorded in the annals of the kings of Judah.
8 There was fighting between Abijam and Jeroboam. And Abijam rested
with his forefathers and was buried in the city of David; and he was
succeeded by his son Asa.

9   In the twentieth year of Jeroboam king of Israel, Asa became king of
10 Judah. He reigned in Jerusalem for forty-one years; his grandmother was
11 Maacah granddaughter of Abishalom. Asa did what was right in the eyes
12 of the LORD, like his ancestor David. He expelled from the land the male
prostitutes attached to the shrines and did away with all the idols which
13ᵈ his predecessors had made. He even deprived his own grandmother
Maacah of her rank as queen mother because she had an obscene object
made for the worship of Asherah; Asa cut it down and burnt it in the gorge
14 of the Kidron. Although the hill-shrines were allowed to remain, Asa
15 himself remained faithful to the LORD all his life. He brought into the house
of the LORD all his father's votive offerings and his own, gold and silver
and sacred vessels.

16 17ᵉ   Asa was at war with Baasha king of Israel all through their reigns. Baasha
king of Israel invaded Judah and fortified Ramah to cut off all access to
18 Asa king of Judah. So Asa took all the gold and silver that remained in the
treasuries of the house of the LORD and of the royal palace, and sent his
servants with them to Ben-hadad son of Tabrimmon, son of Hezion, king
19 of Aram, whose capital was Damascus, with instructions to say, 'There is
an alliance between us, as there was between our fathers. I now send you

ᵃ *Verses 25–28: cp. 2 Chr. 12. 9–11.*   ᵇ *Verses 29–31: cp. 2 Chr. 12. 13–16.*   ᶜ *Prob. rdg.; Heb. adds* (6) There was war between Rehoboam and Jeroboam all his days (*cp. 14. 30).*   ᵈ *Verses 13–15: cp. 2 Chr. 15. 16–18.*   ᵉ *Verses 17–22: cp. 2 Chr. 16. 1–6.*

this present of silver and gold; break off your alliance with Baasha king of
Israel, so that he may abandon his campaign against me.' Ben-hadad 20
listened willingly to King Asa; he ordered the commanders of his armies
to move against the cities of Israel, and they attacked Iyyon, Dan, Abel-
beth-maacah, and that part of Kinnereth which marches with the land of
Naphtali. When Baasha heard of it, he stopped fortifying Ramah and fell 21
back on Tirzah. Then King Asa issued a proclamation requiring every 22
man in Judah to join in removing the stones of Ramah and the timbers
with which Baasha had fortified it; no one was exempted; and he used
them to fortify Geba of Benjamin and Mizpah.

All the other events of Asa's reign, his exploits and his achievements, 23*a*
and the cities he built, are recorded in the annals of the kings of Judah.
But in his old age his feet were crippled by disease. He rested with his 24
forefathers and was buried with them in the city of his ancestor David;
and he was succeeded by his son Jehoshaphat.

Nadab son of Jeroboam became king of Israel in the second year of Asa 25
king of Judah, and he reigned for two years. He did what was wrong in the 26
eyes of the LORD and followed in his father's footsteps, repeating the sin
which he had led Israel to commit. Baasha son of Ahijah, of the house of 27
Issachar, conspired against him and attacked him at Gibbethon, a Philistine city, which Nadab was besieging with all his forces. And Baasha slew 28
him and usurped the throne in the third year of Asa king of Judah. As soon 29
as he became king, he struck down all the family of Jeroboam, destroying
every living soul and leaving not one survivor. Thus the word of the LORD
was fulfilled which he spoke through his servant Ahijah the Shilonite. This 30
happened because of the sins of Jeroboam and the sins which he led Israel
to commit, and because he had provoked the anger of the LORD the God
of Israel. The other events of Nadab's reign and all his acts are recorded in 31
the annals of the kings of Israel. Asa was at war with Baasha king of Israel 32
all through their reigns.

In the third year of Asa king of Judah, Baasha son of Ahijah became king 33
of all Israel in Tirzah and reigned twenty-four years. He did what was 34
wrong in the eyes of the LORD and followed in Jeroboam's footsteps,
repeating the sin which he had led Israel to commit. Then the word of the **16**
LORD came to Jehu son of Hanani concerning Baasha: 'I raised you from 2
the dust and made you a prince over my people Israel, but you have
followed in the footsteps of Jeroboam and have led my people Israel into
sin, and have provoked me to anger with their sins. Therefore I will sweep 3
away Baasha and his house and will deal with it as I dealt with the house of
Jeroboam son of Nebat. Those of Baasha's family who die in the city shall 4
be food for the dogs, and those who die in the country shall be food for the
birds.' The other events of Baasha's reign, his achievements and his 5
exploits, are recorded in the annals of the kings of Israel. Baasha rested 6
with his forefathers and was buried in Tirzah; and he was succeeded by his
son Elah. Moreover the word of the LORD concerning Baasha and his 7
family came through the prophet Jehu son of Hanani, because of all the
wrong that he had done in the eyes of the LORD, thereby provoking his

a Verses 23, 24: cp. 2 Chr. 16. 11–14.

anger: because he had not only sinned like the house of Jeroboam, but had also brought destruction upon it.

8 In the twenty-sixth year of Asa king of Judah, Elah son of Baasha be-
9 came king of Israel and he reigned in Tirzah two years. Zimri, who was in his service commanding half the chariotry, plotted against him. The king was in Tirzah drinking himself drunk in the house of Arza, comptroller
10 of the household there, when Zimri broke in and attacked him, assassinated him and made himself king. This took place in the twenty-seventh
11 year of Asa king of Judah. As soon as he had become king and was enthroned, he struck down all the family of Baasha and left not a single
12 mother's son alive, kinsman or friend. He destroyed the whole family of Baasha, and thus fulfilled the word of the LORD concerning Baasha, spoken
13 through the prophet Jehu. This was what came of all the sins which Baasha and his son Elah had committed and the sins into which they had led Israel, provoking the anger of the LORD the God of Israel with their worth-
14 less idols. The other events and acts of Elah's reign are recorded in the annals of the kings of Israel.

15 In the twenty-seventh year of Asa king of Judah, Zimri reigned in Tirzah for seven days. At the time the army was investing the Philistine
16 city of Gibbethon. When the Israelite troops in the field heard of Zimri's conspiracy and the murder of the king, there and then in the camp they
17 made their commander Omri king of Israel by common consent. Then Omri and his whole force withdrew from Gibbethon and laid siege to
18 Tirzah. Zimri, as soon as he saw that the city had fallen, retreated to the keep of the royal palace, set the whole of it on fire over his head and so
19 perished. This was what came of the sin he had committed by doing what was wrong in the eyes of the LORD and following in the footsteps of Jero-
20 boam, repeating the sin into which he had led Israel. The other events of Zimri's reign, and his conspiracy, are recorded in the annals of the kings of Israel.

21 Thereafter the people of Israel were split into two factions: one supported Tibni son of Ginath, determined to make him king; the other
22 supported Omri. Omri's party proved the stronger; Tibni lost his life and Omri became king.

23 It was in the thirty-first year of Asa king of Judah that Omri became king
24 of Israel and he reigned twelve years, six of them in Tirzah. He bought the hill of Samaria from Shemer for two talents of silver and built a city on it
25 which he named Samaria after Shemer the owner of the hill. Omri did what was wrong in the eyes of the LORD; he outdid all his predecessors in
26 wickedness. He followed in the footsteps of Jeroboam son of Nebat, repeating the sins which he had led Israel to commit, so that they provoked
27 the anger of the LORD their God with their worthless idols. The other events of Omri's reign, and his exploits, are recorded in the annals of the
28 kings of Israel. So Omri rested with his forefathers and was buried in Samaria; and he was succeeded by his son Ahab.

Ahab and Elijah

AHAB SON OF OMRI BECAME KING of Israel in the thirty-eighth 29
year of Asa king of Judah, and he reigned over Israel in Samaria for
twenty-two years. He did more that was wrong in the eyes of the LORD than 30
all his predecessors. As if it were not enough for him to follow the sinful 31
ways of Jeroboam son of Nebat, he contracted a marriage with Jezebel
daughter of Ethbaal king of Sidon, and went and worshipped Baal; he
prostrated himself before him and erected an altar to him in the temple of 32
Baal which he built in Samaria. He also set up a sacred pole; indeed he did 33
more to provoke the anger of the LORD the God of Israel than all the kings
of Israel before him. In his days Hiel of Bethel rebuilt Jericho; laying its 34
foundations cost him his eldest son Abiram, and the setting up of its gates
cost him Segub his youngest son. Thus was fulfilled what the LORD had
spoken through Joshua son of Nun.

Elijah the Tishbite, of Tishbe in Gilead, said to Ahab, 'I swear by the **17**
life of the LORD the God of Israel, whose servant I am, that there shall be
neither dew nor rain these coming years unless I give the word.' Then the 2
word of the LORD came to him: 'Leave this place and turn eastwards; and 3
go into hiding in the ravine of Kerith east of the Jordan. You shall drink 4
from the stream, and I have commanded the ravens to feed you there.' He 5
did as the LORD had told him: he went and stayed in the ravine of Kerith
east of the Jordan, and the ravens brought him bread and meat morning 6
and evening, and he drank from the stream. After a while the stream dried 7
up, for there had been no rain in the land. Then the word of the LORD 8
came to him: 'Go now to Zarephath, a village of Sidon, and stay there; 9
I have commanded a widow there to feed you.' So he went off to Zarephath. 10
When he reached the entrance to the village, he saw a widow gathering
sticks, and he called to her and said, 'Please bring me a little water in a
pitcher to drink.' As she went to fetch it, he called after her, 'Bring me, 11
please, a piece of bread as well.' But she said, 'As the LORD your God lives, 12
I have no food to sustain me except a handful of flour in a jar and a little oil
in a flask. Here I am, gathering two or three sticks to go and cook something
for my son and myself before we die.' 'Never fear,' said Elijah; 'go and do 13
as you say; but first make me a small cake from what you have and bring it
out to me; and after that make something for your son and yourself. For 14
this is the word of the LORD the God of Israel: "The jar of flour shall not
give out nor the flask of oil fail, until the LORD sends rain on the land."'
She went and did as Elijah had said, and there was food for him and for 15
her and her family for a long time. The jar of flour did not give out nor did 16
the flask of oil fail, as the word of the LORD foretold through Elijah.

Afterwards the son of this woman, the mistress of the house, fell ill and 17
grew worse and worse, until at last his breathing ceased. Then she said to 18
Elijah, 'What made you interfere, you man of God? You came here to
bring my sins to light and kill my son!' 'Give me your son', he said. He 19
took the boy from her arms and carried him up to the roof-chamber where
his lodging was, and laid him on his own bed. Then he called out to the 20
LORD, 'O LORD my God, is this thy care for the widow with whom I lodge,

21 that thou hast been so cruel to her son?' Then he breathed deeply *a* upon the
child three times and called on the LORD, 'O LORD my God, let the breath of
22 life, I pray, return to the body of this child.' The LORD listened to Elijah's
cry, and the breath of life returned to the child's body, and he revived;
23 Elijah lifted him up and took him down from the roof into the house, gave
24 him to his mother and said, 'Look, your son is alive.' Then she said to
Elijah, 'Now I know for certain that you are a man of God and that the
word of the LORD on your lips is truth.'

18   Time went by, and in the third year the word of the LORD came to
Elijah: 'Go and show yourself to Ahab, and I will send rain upon the land.'
2 So he went to show himself to Ahab. At this time the famine in Samaria
3 was at its height, and Ahab summoned Obadiah, the comptroller of his
4 household, a devout worshipper of the LORD. When Jezebel massacred
the prophets of the LORD, he had taken a hundred of them and hidden
them in caves, fifty by fifty, giving them food and drink to keep them alive.
5 Ahab said to Obadiah, 'Let us go through the land, both of us, to every
spring and gully; if we can find enough grass we may keep the horses and
6 mules alive and lose none of our cattle.' They divided the land between
them for their survey, Ahab going one way by himself and Obadiah
another.
7   As Obadiah was on his way, Elijah met him. Obadiah recognized him and
8 fell prostrate before him and said, 'Can it be you, my lord Elijah?' 'Yes,'
9 he said, 'it is I; go and tell your master that Elijah is here.' 'What wrong
have I done?' said Obadiah. 'Why should you give me into Ahab's hands?
10 He will put me to death. As the LORD your God lives, there is no nation or
kingdom to which my master has not sent in search of you. If they said,
"He is not here", he made that kingdom or nation swear on oath that they
11 could not find you. Yet now you say, "Go and tell your master that Elijah
12 is here." What will happen? As soon as I leave you, the spirit of the LORD
will carry you away, who knows where? I shall go and tell Ahab, and when
he fails to find you, he will kill me. Yet I have been a worshipper of the
13 LORD from boyhood. Have you not been told, my lord, what I did when
Jezebel put the LORD's prophets to death, how I hid a hundred of them in
14 caves, fifty by fifty, and kept them alive with food and drink? And now you
15 say, "Go and tell your master that Elijah is here"! He will kill me.' Elijah
answered, 'As the LORD of Hosts lives, whose servant I am, I swear that I
16 will show myself to him this very day.' So Obadiah went to find Ahab and
gave him the message, and Ahab went to meet Elijah.
17   As soon as Ahab saw Elijah, he said to him, 'Is it you, you troubler of
18 Israel?' 'It is not I who have troubled Israel,' he replied, 'but you and
your father's family, by forsaking the commandments of the LORD and
19 following Baal. But now, send and summon all Israel to meet me on Mount
Carmel, and the four hundred and fifty prophets of Baal with them and the
four hundred prophets of the goddess Asherah, who are Jezebel's pen-
20 sioners.' So Ahab sent out to all the Israelites and assembled the prophets
21 on Mount Carmel. Elijah stepped forward and said to the people, 'How
long will you sit on the fence? If the LORD is God, follow him; but if Baal,

a Or stretched himself.

then follow him.' Not a word did they answer. Then Elijah said to the 22
people, 'I am the only prophet of the LORD still left, but there are four
hundred and fifty prophets of Baal. Bring two bulls; let them choose one 23
for themselves, cut it up and lay it on the wood without setting fire to it,
and I will prepare the other and lay it on the wood without setting fire to it.
You shall invoke your god by name and I will invoke the LORD by name; 24
and the god who answers by fire, he is God.' And all the people shouted
their approval.

Then Elijah said to the prophets of Baal, 'Choose one of the bulls and 25
offer it first, for there are more of you; invoke your god by name, but do
not set fire to the wood.' So they took the bull provided for them and 26
offered it, and they invoked Baal by name from morning until noon,
crying, 'Baal, Baal, answer us'; but there was no sound, no answer. They
danced wildly beside the altar they had set up. At midday Elijah mocked 27
them: 'Call louder, for he is a god; it may be he is deep in thought, or
engaged, or on a journey; or he may have gone to sleep and must be woken
up.' They cried still louder and, as was their custom, gashed themselves 28
with swords and spears until the blood ran. All afternoon they raved and 29
ranted till the hour of the regular sacrifice, but still there was no sound, no
answer, no sign of attention.

Then Elijah said to all the people, 'Come here to me.' They all came, 30
and he repaired the altar of the LORD which had been torn down. He took 31
twelve stones, one for each tribe of the sons of Jacob, the man named
Israel by the word of the LORD. With these stones he built an altar in the 32
name of the LORD; he dug a trench round it big enough to hold two
measures of seed; he arranged the wood, cut up the bull and laid it on the 33
wood. Then he said, 'Fill four jars with water and pour it on the whole- 34
offering and on the wood.' They did so, and he said, 'Do it again.' They did
it again, and he said, 'Do it a third time.' They did it a third time, and the 35
water ran all round the altar and even filled the trench. At the hour of the 36
regular sacrifice the prophet Elijah came forward and said, 'LORD God of
Abraham, of Isaac, and of Israel, let it be known today that thou art God
in Israel and that I am thy servant and have done all these things at thy
command. Answer me, O LORD, answer me and let this people know that 37
thou, LORD, art God and that it is thou that hast caused them to be back-
sliders.'*a* Then the fire of the LORD fell. It consumed the whole-offering, 38
the wood, the stones, and the earth, and licked up the water in the trench.
When all the people saw it, they fell prostrate and cried, 'The LORD is 39
God, the LORD is God.' Then Elijah said to them, 'Seize the prophets of 40
Baal; let not one of them escape.' They seized them, and Elijah took them
down to the Kishon and slaughtered them there in the valley.

Elijah said to Ahab, 'Go back now, eat and drink, for I hear the sound 41
of coming rain.' He did so, while Elijah himself climbed to the crest of 42
Carmel. There he crouched on the ground with his face between his
knees. He said to his servant, 'Go and look out to the west.' He went and 43
looked; 'There is nothing to see', he said. Seven times Elijah ordered him
back, and seven times he went. The seventh time he said, 'I see a cloud no 44

a Or thou that dost bring them back to their allegiance.

bigger than a man's hand, coming up from the west.' 'Now go', said
Elijah, 'and tell Ahab to harness his chariot and be off, or the rain will
45 stop him.' Meanwhile the sky had grown black with clouds, the wind rose,
and heavy rain began to fall. Ahab mounted his chariot and set off for
46 Jezreel; but the power of the LORD had come upon Elijah: he tucked up
his robe and ran before Ahab all the way to Jezreel.

19 Ahab told Jezebel all that Elijah had done and how he had put all the
2 prophets to death with the sword. Jezebel then sent a messenger to Elijah
to say, 'The gods do the same to me and more, unless by this time to-
3 morrow I have taken your life as you took theirs.' He was afraid and fled
for his life. When he reached Beersheba in Judah, he left his servant there
4 and himself went a day's journey into the wilderness. He came upon a
broom-bush, and sat down under it and prayed for death: 'It is enough,'
he said; 'now, LORD, take my life, for I am no better than my fathers before
5 me.' He lay down under the bush and, while he slept, an angel touched
6 him and said, 'Rise and eat.' He looked, and there at his head was a cake
baked on hot stones, and a pitcher of water. He ate and drank and lay down
7 again. The angel of the LORD came again and touched him a second time,
8 saying, 'Rise and eat; the journey is too much for you.' He rose and ate and
drank and, sustained by this food, he went on for forty days and forty
9 nights to Horeb, the mount of God. He entered a cave and there he spent
the night.

Suddenly the word of the LORD came to him: 'Why are you here,
10 Elijah?' 'Because of my great zeal for the LORD the God of Hosts', he said.
'The people of Israel have forsaken thy covenant, torn down thy altars
and put thy prophets to death with the sword. I alone am left, and they
11 seek to take my life.' The answer came: 'Go and stand on the mount before
the LORD.' For the LORD was passing by: a great and strong wind came
rending mountains and shattering rocks before him, but the LORD was not
in the wind; and after the wind there was an earthquake, but the LORD
12 was not in the earthquake; and after the earthquake fire, but the LORD
13 was not in the fire; and after the fire a low murmuring sound. When
Elijah heard it, he muffled his face in his cloak and went out and stood at
the entrance of the cave. Then there came a voice: 'Why are you here,
14 Elijah?' 'Because of my great zeal for the LORD the God of Hosts', he said.
'The people of Israel have forsaken thy covenant, torn down thy altars
and put thy prophets to death with the sword. I alone am left, and they
seek to take my life.'

15 The LORD said to him, 'Go back by way of the wilderness of Damascus,
16 enter the city and anoint Hazael to be king of Aram; anoint Jehu son[a] of
Nimshi to be king of Israel, and Elisha son of Shaphat of Abel-meholah
17 to be prophet in your place. Anyone who escapes the sword of Hazael Jehu
18 will slay, and anyone who escapes the sword of Jehu Elisha will slay. But
I will leave seven thousand in Israel, all who have not bent the knee to Baal,
all whose lips have not kissed him.'

19 Elijah departed and found Elisha son of Shaphat ploughing; there were
twelve pair of oxen ahead of him, and he himself was with the last of them.

[a] *Or* grandson (*cp. 2 Kgs. 9. 2*).

As Elijah passed, he threw his cloak over him, and Elisha, leaving his oxen, 20 ran after Elijah and said, 'Let me kiss my father and mother goodbye, and then I will follow you.' 'Go back,' he replied; 'what have I done to prevent you?' He followed him no further but went home, took his pair of oxen, 21 slaughtered them and burnt the wooden gear to cook the flesh, which he gave to the people to eat. Then he followed Elijah and became his disciple.

BEN-HADAD KING OF ARAM, having mustered all his forces, and taking **20** with him thirty-two kings with their horses and chariots, marched against Samaria to take it by siege or assault. He sent envoys into the city to Ahab 2 king of Israel to say, 'Hear what Ben-hadad says: Your silver and gold are 3 mine, your wives and your splendid sons are mine.'*a* The king of Israel 4 answered, 'As you say, my lord king, I am yours and all that I have.' The 5 envoys came again and said, 'Hear what Ben-hadad says: I demand that you hand over your silver and gold, your wives and your sons. This time 6 tomorrow I will send my servants to search your house and your subjects' houses and to take possession of everything you prize, and remove it.' The 7 king of Israel then summoned all the elders of the land and said, 'You see this? The man is plainly picking a quarrel; for I did not demur when he sent to claim my wives and my sons, my silver and gold.' All the elders and 8 all the people answered, 'Do not listen to him; you must not consent.' So 9 he gave this reply to Ben-hadad's envoys: 'Say to my lord the king: I accepted your majesty's demands on the first occasion; but what you now ask I cannot do.' The envoys went away and reported to their master, and 10 Ben-hadad sent back word: 'The gods do the same to me and more, if there is enough dust in Samaria to provide a handful for each of my men.' The 11 king of Israel made reply, 'Remind him of the saying: "The lame must not think himself a match for the nimble."' This message reached Ben- 12 hadad while he and the kings were drinking in their quarters. *b* At once he ordered his men to attack the city, and they did so.

Meanwhile a prophet had come to Ahab king of Israel and said to him, 13 'This is the word of the LORD: "You see this great rabble? Today I will give it into your hands and you shall know that I am the LORD."' 'Whom will 14 you use for that?' asked Ahab. 'The young men who serve the district officers', was the answer. 'Who will draw up the line of battle?' asked the king. 'You', said the prophet. Then Ahab called up these young men, two 15 hundred and thirty-two all told, and behind them the people of Israel, seven thousand in all. They went out at midday, while Ben-hadad and his 16 allies, those thirty-two kings, were drinking themselves drunk in their quarters.*b* The young men sallied out first, and word was sent to Ben- 17 hadad that a party had come out of Samaria. 'If they have come out for 18 peace,' he said, 'take them alive; if for battle, take them alive.'

So out of the city the young men went, and the army behind them; each 19 20 struck down his man, and the Aramaeans fled. The Israelites pursued them, but Ben-hadad king of Aram escaped on horseback with some of the cavalry. Then the king of Israel advanced and captured the horses and 21 chariots, inflicting a heavy defeat on the Aramaeans.

a Or are your wives and your sons any good to me? *b* in their quarters: or at Succoth.

22 Then the prophet came to the king of Israel and said to him, 'Build up
your forces; you know what you must do. At the turn of the year the king
23 of Aram will renew the attack.' But the king of Aram's ministers gave him
this advice: 'Their gods are gods of the hills; that is why they defeated us.
Let us fight them in the plain; and then we shall have the upper hand.
24 What you must do is to relieve the kings of their command and appoint
25 other officers in their place. Raise another army like the one you have lost.
Bring your cavalry and chariots up to their former strength, and then let
us fight them in the plain, and we shall have the upper hand.' He listened
to their advice and acted on it.

26 At the turn of the year Ben-hadad mustered the Aramaeans and advanced
27 to Aphek to attack Israel. The Israelites too were mustered and formed into
companies, and then went out to meet them and encamped opposite them.
They seemed no better than a pair of new-born kids, while the Aramaeans
28 covered the country-side. The man of God came to the king of Israel and
said, 'This is the word of the LORD: The Aramaeans may think that the
LORD is a god of the hills and not a god of the valleys; but I will give all this
great rabble into your hands and you shall know that I am the LORD.'

29 They lay in camp opposite one another for seven days; on the seventh
day battle was joined and the Israelites destroyed a hundred thousand of
30 the Aramaean infantry in one day. The survivors fled to Aphek, into the
citadel, and the city wall fell upon the twenty-seven thousand men who were
left. Ben-hadad took refuge in the citadel, retreating into an inner room;
31 and his attendants said to him, 'Listen; we have heard that the kings
of Israel are men to be trusted. Let us therefore put sackcloth round our
waists and wind rough cord round our heads and go out to the king of
32 Israel. It may be that he will spare your life.' So they fastened on the
sackcloth and the cord, and went to the king of Israel and said, 'Your
servant Ben-hadad pleads for his life.' 'My royal cousin,' he said, 'is he still
33 alive?' The men, taking the word for a favourable omen, caught it up at
once and said, 'Your cousin, yes, Ben-hadad.' 'Go and fetch him', he said.
34 Then Ben-hadad came out and Ahab invited him into his chariot. And
Ben-hadad said to him, 'I will restore the cities which my father took from
your father, and you may establish for yourself a trading quarter in
Damascus, as my father did in Samaria.' 'On these terms', said Ahab, 'I
will let you go.' So he granted him a treaty and let him go.

35 One of a company of prophets, at the command of the LORD, ordered a
36 certain man to strike him, but the man refused. 'Because you have not
obeyed the LORD,' said the prophet, 'when you leave me, a lion will attack
37 you.' When the man left, a lion did meet him and attacked him. The prophet fell in with another man and ordered him to strike him. He struck and
38 wounded him. Then the prophet went off, with a bandage over his eyes,
39 and thus disguised waited by the wayside for the king. As the king was
passing, he called out to him, 'Sir, I went into the thick of the battle, and a
soldier came over to me with a prisoner and said, "Take charge of this
fellow. If by any chance he gets away, your life shall be forfeit, or you shall
40 pay a talent of silver." As I was busy with one thing and another, sir, he
disappeared.' The king of Israel said to him, 'You deserve to die.' And he

said to the king of Israel,[a] 'You have passed sentence on yourself.' Then he   41
tore the bandage from his eyes, and the king of Israel saw that he was one
of the prophets. And he said to the king, 'This is the word of the LORD: 42
"Because you let that man go when I had put him under a ban, your life
shall be forefeit for his life, your people for his people."' The king of   43
Israel went home sullen and angry and entered Samaria.

NABOTH OF JEZREEL HAD A VINEYARD near the palace of Ahab king   **21**
of Samaria. One day Ahab made a proposal to Naboth: 'Your vineyard is   2
close to my palace; let me have it for a garden; I will give you a better
vineyard in exchange for it or, if you prefer, its value in silver.' But Naboth   3
answered, 'The LORD forbid that I should let you have land which has
always been in my family.' So Ahab went home sullen and angry because   4
Naboth would not let him have his ancestral land. He lay down on his bed,
covered his face and refused to eat. His wife Jezebel came in to him and   5
said, 'What makes you so sullen and why do you refuse to eat?' He told   6
her, 'I proposed to Naboth of Jezreel that he should let me have his vineyard at its value or, if he liked, in exchange for another; but he would not
let me have the vineyard.' 'Are you or are you not king in Israel?' said   7
Jezebel. 'Come, eat and take heart; I will make you a gift of the vineyard
of Naboth of Jezreel.' So she wrote a letter in Ahab's name, sealed it with   8
his seal and sent it to the elders and notables of Naboth's city, who sat in
council with him. She wrote: 'Proclaim a fast and give Naboth the seat of   9
honour among the people. And see that two scoundrels are seated opposite   10
him to charge him with cursing God and the king, then take him out and
stone him to death.' So the elders and notables of Naboth's city, who sat   11
with him in council, carried out the instructions Jezebel had sent them in
her letter: they proclaimed a fast and gave Naboth the seat of honour, and   12 13
these two scoundrels came in, sat opposite him and charged him publicly
with cursing God and the king. Then they took him outside the city and
stoned him, and sent word to Jezebel that Naboth had been stoned to   14
death.
     As soon as Jezebel heard that Naboth had been stoned and was dead,   15
she said to Ahab, 'Get up and take possession of the vineyard which Naboth
refused to sell you, for he is no longer alive; Naboth of Jezreel is dead.'
When Ahab heard that Naboth was dead, he got up and went to the vine-   16
yard to take possession. Then the word of the LORD came to Elijah the   17
Tishbite: 'Go down at once to Ahab king of Israel, who is in Samaria; you   18
will find him in Naboth's vineyard, where he has gone to take possession.
Say to him, "This is the word of the LORD: Have you killed your man, and   19
taken his land as well?" Say to him, "This is the word of the LORD: Where
dogs licked the blood of Naboth, there dogs shall lick your blood."' Ahab   20
said to Elijah, 'Have you found me, my enemy?' 'I have found you', he
said, 'because you have sold yourself to do what is wrong in the eyes of the
LORD. I will bring [b] disaster upon you; I will sweep you away and destroy   21
every mother's son of the house of Ahab in Israel, whether under protection

---

a You deserve ... Israel: *prob. rdg.; Heb. om.*   *b* he said, ... bring: *or* he said.
'Because you ... LORD, I am bringing ...

22 of the family or not. And I will deal with your house as I did with the house of Jeroboam son of Nebat and of Baasha son of Ahijah, because you have
23 provoked my anger and led Israel into sin.' And the LORD went on to say
24 of Jezebel, 'Jezebel shall be eaten by dogs by the rampart of Jezreel. Of the house of Ahab, those who die in the city shall be food for the dogs, and
25 those who die in the country shall be food for the birds.' (Never was a man who sold himself to do what is wrong in the LORD's eyes as Ahab did, and
26 all at the prompting of Jezebel his wife. He committed gross abominations in going after false gods, doing everything that the Amorites did, whom the
27 LORD had dispossessed in favour of Israel.) When Ahab heard this, he rent his clothes, put on sackcloth and fasted; he lay down in his sackcloth
28 and went about muttering to himself. Then the word of the LORD came to
29 Elijah the Tishbite: 'Have you seen how Ahab has humbled himself before me? Because he has thus humbled himself, I will not bring disaster upon his house in his own lifetime, but in his son's.'

22 FOR THREE YEARS THERE WAS NO WAR between the Aramaeans and
2ᵃ the Israelites, but in the third year Jehoshaphat king of Judah went down
3 to visit the king of Israel. The latter said to his courtiers, 'You know that Ramoth-gilead belongs to us, and yet we do nothing to recover it from the
4 king of Aram.' He said to Jehoshaphat, 'Will you join me in attacking Ramoth-gilead?' Jehoshaphat said to the king of Israel, 'What is mine is
5 yours: myself, my people, and my horses.' Then Jehoshaphat said to the
6 king of Israel, 'First let us seek counsel from the LORD.' The king of Israel assembled the prophets, some four hundred of them, and asked them, 'Shall I attack Ramoth-gilead or shall I refrain?' 'Attack,' they answered;
7 'the Lord will deliver it into your hands.' Jehoshaphat asked, 'Is there no other prophet of the LORD here through whom we may seek guidance?'
8 'There is one more', the king of Israel answered, 'through whom we may seek guidance of the LORD, but I hate the man, because he prophesies no good for me; never anything but evil. His name is Micaiah son of Imlah.' Jehoshaphat exclaimed, 'My lord king, let no such word pass your lips!'
9 So the king of Israel called one of his eunuchs and told him to fetch Micaiah son of Imlah with all speed.
10   The king of Israel and Jehoshaphat king of Judah were seated on their thrones, in shining armour, at the entrance to the gate of Samaria, and all
11 the prophets were prophesying before them. One of them, Zedekiah son of Kenaanah, made himself horns of iron and said, 'This is the word of the LORD: "With horns like these you shall gore the Aramaeans and make an
12 end of them."' In the same vein all the prophets prophesied, 'Attack Ramoth-gilead and win the day; the LORD will deliver it into your hands.'
13 The messenger sent to fetch Micaiah told him that the prophets had with one voice given the king a favourable answer. 'And mind you agree with
14 them', he added. 'As the LORD lives,' said Micaiah, 'I will say only what the LORD tells me to say.'
15   When Micaiah came into the king's presence, the king said to him, 'Micaiah, shall we attack Ramoth-gilead or shall we refrain?' 'Attack and

ᵃ *Verses 2–35 : cp. 2 Chr. 18. 2–34.*

win the day,' he said; 'the LORD will deliver it into your hands.' 'How 16
often must I adjure you', said the king, 'to tell me nothing but the truth
in the name of the LORD?' Then Micaiah said, 'I saw all Israel scattered on 17
the mountains, like sheep without a shepherd; and I heard the LORD say,
"They have no master, let them go home in peace."' The king of Israel 18
said to Jehoshaphat, 'Did I not tell you that he never prophesies good for
me, nothing but evil?' Micaiah went on, 'Listen now to the word of the 19
LORD. I saw the LORD seated on his throne, with all the host of heaven in
attendance on his right and on his left. The LORD said, "Who will entice 20
Ahab to attack and fall on*ᵃ* Ramoth-gilead?" One said one thing and one
said another; then a spirit came forward and stood before the LORD and 21
said, "I will entice him." "How?" said the LORD. "I will go out", he said, 22
"and be a lying spirit in the mouth of all his prophets." "You shall entice
him," said the LORD, "and you shall succeed; go and do it." You see, then, 23
how the LORD has put a lying spirit in the mouth of all these prophets of
yours, because he has decreed disaster for you.' Then Zedekiah son of 24
Kenaanah came up to Micaiah and struck him in the face: 'And how did
the spirit of the LORD pass from me to speak to you?' he said. Micaiah 25
answered, 'That you will find out on the day when you run into an inner
room to hide yourself.' Then the king of Israel ordered Micaiah to be 26
arrested and committed to the custody of Amon the governor of the city
and Joash the king's son.*ᵇ* 'Lock this fellow up', he said, 'and give him 27
prison diet of bread and water until I come home in safety.' Micaiah 28
retorted, 'If you do return in safety, the LORD has not spoken by me.'

So the king of Israel and Jehoshaphat king of Judah marched on Ramoth- 29
gilead, and the king of Israel said to Jehoshaphat, 'I will disguise myself 30
to go into battle, but you shall wear your royal robes.' So he went into
battle in disguise. Now the king of Aram had commanded the thirty-two 31
captains of his chariots not to engage all and sundry but the king of Israel
alone. When the captains saw Jehoshaphat, they thought he was the king 32
of Israel and turned to attack him. But Jehoshaphat cried out and, when the 33
captains saw that he was not the king of Israel, they broke off the attack on
him. But one man drew his bow at random and hit the king of Israel where 34
the breastplate joins the plates of the armour. So he said to his driver,
'Wheel round and take me out of the line; I am wounded.' When the day's 35
fighting reached its height, the king was facing the Aramaeans propped up
in his chariot, and the blood from his wound flowed down upon the floor
of the chariot; and in the evening he died. At sunset the herald went 36
through the ranks, crying, 'Every man to his city, every man to his country.'
Thus died the king. He was brought to Samaria and they buried him there. 37
The chariot was swilled out at the pool of Samaria, and the dogs licked up 38
the blood, and the prostitutes washed themselves in it, in fulfilment of the
word the LORD had spoken.

Now the other acts and events of Ahab's reign, the ivory house and all 39
the cities he built, are recorded in the annals of the kings of Israel. So 40
Ahab rested with his forefathers and was succeeded by his son Ahaziah.

Jehoshaphat son of Asa had become king of Judah in the fourth year of 41*ᶜ*

ᵃ Or at.   *ᵇ son: or deputy.*   *ᶜ Verses 41–43: cp. 2 Chr. 20. 31–33.*

42 Ahab king of Israel. He was thirty-five years old when he came to the throne, and he reigned in Jerusalem for twenty-five years; his mother was
43 Azubah daughter of Shilhi. He followed in the footsteps of Asa his father and did not swerve from them; he did what was right in the eyes of the LORD. But the hill-shrines were allowed to remain; the people continued
44 to slaughter and burn sacrifices there. Jehoshaphat remained at peace with
45 the king of Israel. The other events of Jehoshaphat's reign, his exploits
46 and his wars, are recorded in the annals of the kings of Judah. But he did away with such of the male prostitutes attached to the shrines as were still left over from the days of Asa his father.
47 48 There was no king in Edom, only*a* a viceroy of Jehoshaphat; he built merchantmen to sail to Ophir for gold, but they never made the journey
49 because they were wrecked at Ezion-geber. Ahaziah son of Ahab proposed to Jehoshaphat that his own men should go to sea with his; but Jehoshaphat would not consent.
50 Jehoshaphat rested with his forefathers and was buried with them in the city of David his father, and was succeeded by his son Joram.
51 Ahaziah son of Ahab became king of Israel in Samaria in the seventeenth year of Jehoshaphat king of Judah, and reigned over Israel for two years.
52 He did what was wrong in the eyes of the LORD, following in the footsteps of his father and mother and in those of Jeroboam son of Nebat, who had
53 led Israel into sin. He served Baal and worshipped him, and provoked the anger of the LORD the God of Israel, as his father had done.

THE SECOND BOOK OF
KINGS

Elisha and the end of the house of Ahab

1 AFTER AHAB'S DEATH Moab rebelled against Israel.
2 Ahaziah fell through a latticed window in his roof-chamber in Samaria and injured himself; he sent messengers to inquire of Baal-
3 zebub the god of Ekron whether he would recover from his illness. The angel of the LORD ordered Elijah the Tishbite to go and meet the messengers of the king of Samaria and say to them, 'Is there no god in Israel,
4 that you go to inquire of Baal-zebub the god of Ekron? This is the word of the LORD to your master: "You shall not rise from the bed where you are
5 lying; you will die."' Then Elijah departed. The messengers went back
6 to the king. When asked why they had returned, they answered that a man had come to meet them and had ordered them to return and say to the king who had sent them, 'This is the word of the LORD: "Is there no god in Israel, that you send to inquire of Baal-zebub the god of Ekron? In consequence, you shall not rise from the bed where you are lying; you will

a only: *prob. rdg.; Heb. om.*

die." ' The king asked them what kind of man it was who had met them and   7
said this. 'A hairy man', they answered, 'with a leather apron round his   8
waist.' 'It is Elijah the Tishbite', said the king.

Then the king sent a captain to him with his company of fifty. He went   9
up and found the prophet sitting on a hill-top and said to him, 'Man of
God, the king orders you to come down.' Elijah answered the captain, 'If   10
I am a man of God, may fire fall from heaven and consume you and your
company!' Fire fell from heaven and consumed the officer and his fifty
men. The king sent another captain of fifty with his company, and he went   11
up and said to the prophet, 'Man of God, this is the king's command: Come
down at once.' Elijah answered, 'If I am a man of God, may fire fall from   12
heaven and consume you and your company!' God's fire fell from heaven
and consumed the man and his company. The king sent the captain of a   13
third company with his fifty men, and this third captain went up the hill
to Elijah and knelt down before him and pleaded with him: 'Man of God,
consider me and these fifty servants of yours, and set some value on our
lives. Fire fell from heaven and consumed the other two captains of fifty   14
and their companies; but let my life have some value in your eyes.' The   15
angel of the LORD said to Elijah, 'Go down with him. Do not be afraid.'
So he rose and went down with him to the king, and he said, 'This is the   16
word of the LORD: "You have sent to inquire of Baal-zebub the god of
Ekron, and therefore you shall not rise from the bed where you are lying;
you will die." ' The word of the LORD which Elijah had spoken was ful-   17
filled, and Ahaziah died; and because he had no son, his brother Jehoram
succeeded him in the second year of Joram son of Jehoshaphat king of
Judah.

The other events of Ahaziah's reign are recorded in the annals of the   18
kings of Israel.

The time came when the LORD would take Elijah up to heaven in a   **2**
whirlwind. Elijah and Elisha left Gilgal, and Elijah said to Elisha, 'Stay   2
here; for the LORD has sent me to Bethel.' But Elisha said, 'As the LORD
lives, your life upon it, I will not leave you.' So they went down country
to Bethel. There a company of prophets came out to Elisha and said to   3
him, 'Do you know that the LORD is going to take your lord and master
from you today?' 'I do know,' he replied; 'say no more.' Then Elijah said   4
to him, 'Stay here, Elisha; for the LORD has sent me to Jericho.' But he
replied, 'As the LORD lives, your life upon it, I will not leave you.' So they
went to Jericho. There a company of prophets came up to Elisha and said   5
to him, 'Do you know that the LORD is going to take your lord and master
from you today?' 'I do know,' he said; 'say no more.' Then Elijah said to   6
him, 'Stay here; for the LORD has sent me to the Jordan.' The other
replied, 'As the LORD lives, your life upon it, I will not leave you.' So the
two of them went on.

Fifty of the prophets followed them, and stood watching from a distance   7
as the two of them stopped by the Jordan. Elijah took his cloak, rolled it up   8
and struck the water with it. The water divided to right and left, and they
both crossed over on dry ground. While they were crossing, Elijah said to   9
Elisha, 'Tell me what I can do for you before I am taken from you.' Elisha

10 said, 'Let me inherit a double share of your spirit.' 'You have asked a hard thing', said Elijah. 'If you see me taken from you, may your wish be
11 granted; if you do not, it shall not be granted.' They went on, talking as they went, and suddenly there appeared chariots of fire and horses of fire, which separated them one from the other, and Elijah was carried up in the
12 whirlwind to heaven. When Elisha saw it, he cried, 'My father, my father, the chariots and the horsemen of Israel!', and he saw him no more. Then
13 he took hold of his mantle and rent it in two, and he picked up the cloak which had fallen from Elijah, and came back and stood on the bank of the
14 Jordan. There he too struck the water with Elijah's cloak and said, 'Where is the LORD the God of Elijah?' When he struck the water, it was again
15 divided to right and left, and he crossed over. The prophets from Jericho, who were watching, saw him and said, 'The spirit of Elijah has settled on
16 Elisha.' So they came to meet him, and fell on their faces before him and said, 'Your servants have fifty stalwart men. Let them go and search for your master; perhaps the spirit of the LORD has lifted him up and cast him on some mountain or into some valley.' But he said, 'No, you must not
17 send them.' They pressed him, however, until he had not the heart to refuse. So they sent out the fifty men but, though they searched for three
18 days, they did not find him. When they came back to Elisha, who had remained at Jericho, he said to them, 'Did I not tell you not to go?'
19 The people of the city said to Elisha, 'You can see how pleasantly our city is situated, but the water is polluted and the country is troubled with
20 miscarriages.' He said, 'Fetch me a new bowl and put some salt in it.' When
21 they had fetched it, he went out to the spring and, throwing the salt into it, he said, 'This is the word of the LORD: "I purify this water. It shall cause
22 no more death or miscarriage."' The water has remained pure till this day, in fulfilment of Elisha's word.
23 He went up from there to Bethel and, as he was on his way, some small boys came out of the city and jeered at him, saying, 'Get along with you,
24 bald head, get along.' He turned round and looked at them and he cursed them in the name of the LORD; and two she-bears came out of a wood and
25 mauled forty-two of them. From there he went on to Mount Carmel, and thence back to Samaria.

3 In the eighteenth year of Jehoshaphat king of Judah, Jehoram son of Ahab became king of Israel in Samaria, and he reigned for twelve years.
2 He did what was wrong in the eyes of the LORD, though not as his father and his mother had done; he did remove the sacred pillar of the Baal
3 which his father had made. Yet he persisted in the sins into which Jeroboam son of Nebat had led Israel, and did not give them up.
4 Mesha king of Moab was a sheep-breeder, and he used to supply the king of Israel regularly with the wool of a hundred thousand lambs and a
5 hundred thousand rams. When Ahab died, the king of Moab rebelled
6 against the king of Israel. Then King Jehoram came from Samaria and
7 mustered all Israel. He also sent this message to Jehoshaphat king of Judah: 'The king of Moab has rebelled against me. Will you join me in attacking Moab?' 'I will,' he replied; 'what is mine is yours: myself, my
8 people, and my horses.' 'From which direction shall we attack?' Jehoram

asked. 'Through the wilderness of Edom', replied the other. So the king 9
of Israel set out with the king of Judah and the king of Edom. When they
had been seven days on the march, they had no water left for the army or
the pack-animals. Then the king of Israel said, 'Alas, the LORD has brought 10
together three kings, only to put us at the mercy of the Moabites.' But 11
Jehoshaphat said, 'Is there not a prophet of the LORD here through whom
we may seek guidance of the LORD?' One of the officers of the king of Israel
answered, 'Elisha son of Shaphat is here, the man who poured water on
Elijah's hands.' 'The word of the LORD is with him', said Jehoshaphat. So 12
the king of Israel and Jehoshaphat and the king of Edom went down to
Elisha. Elisha said to the king of Israel, 'Why do you come to me? Go to 13
the prophets of your father and your mother.' But the king of Israel said
to him, 'No; the LORD has called us three kings out to put us at the mercy of
the Moabites.' 'As the LORD of Hosts lives, whom I serve,' said Elisha, 'I 14
would not spare a look or a glance for you, if it were not for my regard for
Jehoshaphat king of Judah. But now, fetch me a minstrel.' They fetched a 15
minstrel, and while he was playing, the power of the LORD came upon
Elisha and he said, 'This is the word of the LORD: "Pools will form all over 16
this ravine." The LORD has decreed that you shall see neither wind nor 17
rain, yet this ravine shall be filled with water for you and your army and
your pack-animals to drink. But that is a mere trifle in the sight of the LORD; 18
what he will also do, is to put Moab at your mercy. You will raze to the 19
ground every fortified town and every noble city; you will cut down all
their fine trees; you will stop up all the springs of water; and you will spoil
every good piece of land by littering it with stones.' In the morning at the 20
hour of the regular sacrifice they saw water flowing in from the direction
of Edom, and the land was flooded.

Meanwhile all Moab had heard that the kings had come up to fight against 21
them, and every man, young and old, who could carry arms, was called out
and stationed on the frontier. When they got up next morning and the sun 22
had risen over the water, the Moabites saw the water in front of them red
like blood and cried out, 'It is blood. The kings must have quarrelled and 23
attacked one another. Now to the plunder, Moab!' When they came to the 24
Israelite camp, the Israelites turned out and attacked them and drove the
Moabites headlong in flight, and themselves entered the land of Moab,
destroying as they went. They razed the cities to the ground; they littered 25
every good piece of land with stones, each man casting one stone on to it;
they stopped up every spring of water; they cut down all their fine trees;
and they harried Moab until only in Kir-hareseth were any buildings left
standing, and even this city the slingers surrounded and attacked.

When the king of Moab saw that the war had gone against him, he took 26
seven hundred men with him, armed with swords, to cut a way through to
the king of Aram, but they failed in the attempt. Then he took his eldest 27
son, who would have succeeded him, and offered him as a whole-offering
upon the city wall. The Israelites were filled with such consternation at
this sight,*a* that they struck camp and returned to their own land.

The wife of a member of a company of prophets appealed to Elisha. **4**

a The Israelites . . . sight: *or* There was such great anger against the Israelites . . .

'My husband, your servant, has died', she said. 'You know that he was a man who feared the LORD; but a creditor has come to take away my two
2 boys as his slaves.' Elisha said to her, 'How can I help you? Tell me what you have in the house.' 'Nothing at all', she answered, 'except a flask of
3 oil.' 'Go out then', he said, 'and borrow vessels from all your neighbours;
4 get as many empty ones as you can. Then, when you come home, shut yourself in with your sons, pour from the flask into all these vessels and, as
5 they are filled, set them aside.' She left him and shut herself in with her
6 sons. As they brought her the vessels she filled them. When they were all full, she said to one of her sons, 'Bring me another.' 'There is not one left',
7 he said. Then the flow of oil ceased. She came out and told the man of God, and he said, 'Go and sell the oil and redeem your boys who are being taken as pledges,*a* and you and they can live on what is left.'

8   It happened once that Elisha went over to Shunem. There was a great lady there who pressed him to accept her hospitality, and so, whenever he
9 came that way, he stopped to take food there. One day she said to her husband, 'I know that this man who comes here regularly is a holy man of
10 God. Why not build up the wall to make him a little roof-chamber, and put in it a bed, a table, a seat, and a lamp, and let him stay there whenever
11 he comes to us?' Once when he arrived and went to this roof-chamber and
12 lay down to rest, he said to Gehazi, his servant, 'Call this Shunammite
13 woman.' He called her and, when she appeared before the prophet, he said to his servant, 'Say to her, "You have taken all this trouble for us. What can I do for you? Shall I speak for you to the king or to the commander-in-chief?"' But she replied, 'I am content where I am, among my
14 own people.' He said, 'Then what can be done for her?' Gehazi said,
15 'There is only this: she has no child and her husband is old.' 'Call her
16 back', Elisha said. When she was called, she appeared in the doorway, and he said, 'In due season, this time next year, you shall have a son in your arms.' But she said, 'No, no, my lord, you are a man of God and would not
17 lie to your servant.' Next year in due season the woman conceived and bore a son, as Elisha had foretold.

18   When the child was old enough, he went out one day to the reapers where
19 his father was. All of a sudden he cried out to his father, 'O my head, my
20 head!' His father told a servant to carry him to his mother. He brought him to his mother; the boy sat on her lap till midday, and then he died.
21 She went up and laid him on the bed of the man of God, shut the door and
22 went out. She called her husband and said, 'Send me one of the servants and a she-ass, I must go to the man of God as fast as I can, and come straight
23 back.' 'Why go to him today?' he asked. 'It is neither new moon nor
24 sabbath.'*b* 'Never mind that', she answered. When the ass was saddled, she said to her servant, 'Lead on and do not slacken pace unless I tell you.'
25 So she set out and came to the man of God on Mount Carmel. The man of God spied her in the distance and said to Gehazi, his servant, 'That is the
26 Shunammite woman coming. Run and meet her, and ask, "Is all well with you? Is all well with your husband? Is all well with the boy?"' She
27 answered, 'All is well.' When she reached the man of God on the hill, she

---

a redeem . . . pledges: *or* pay off your debt.   *b* *Or* full moon.

clutched his feet. Gehazi came forward to push her away, but the man of God said, 'Let her alone; she is in great distress, and the LORD has concealed it from me and not told me.' 'My lord,' she said, 'did I ask for a 28 son? Did I not beg you not to raise my hopes and then dash them?' Then 29 he turned to Gehazi: 'Hitch up your cloak; take my staff with you and run. If you meet anyone on the way, do not stop to greet him; if anyone greets you, do not answer him. Lay my staff on the boy's face.' But the mother 30 cried, 'As the LORD lives, your life upon it, I will not leave you.' So he got up and followed her. *a*

Gehazi went on ahead of them and laid the staff on the boy's face, but 31 there was no sound and no sign of life. So he went back to meet Elisha and told him that the boy had not roused. When Elisha entered the house, there 32 was the boy dead, on the bed where he had been laid. He went into the room, 33 shut the door on the two of them and prayed to the LORD. Then, getting 34 on to the bed, he lay upon the child, put his mouth to the child's mouth, his eyes to his eyes and his hands to his hands; and, as he pressed *b* upon him, the child's body grew warm. Elisha got up and walked once up and 35 down the room; then, getting on to the bed again, he pressed *b* upon him and breathed into him *c* seven times; and the boy opened his eyes. The 36 prophet summoned Gehazi and said, 'Call this Shunammite woman.' She answered his call and the prophet said, 'Take your child.' She came in and 37 fell prostrate before him. Then she took up her son and went out.

Elisha returned to Gilgal at a time when there was a famine in the land. 38 One day, when a group of prophets was sitting at his feet, he said to his servant, 'Set the big pot on the fire and prepare some broth for the company.' One of them went out into the fields to gather herbs and found a 39 wild vine, and filled the skirt of his garment with bitter-apples. *d* He came back and sliced them into the pot, not knowing what they were. They 40 poured it out for the men to eat, but, when they tasted it, they cried out, 'Man of God, there is death in the pot', and they could not eat it. The 41 prophet said, 'Fetch some meal.' He threw it into the pot and said, 'Now pour out for the men to eat.' This time there was no harm in the pot.

A man came from Baal-shalisha, bringing the man of God some of the 42 new season's bread, twenty barley loaves, and fresh ripe ears of corn. *e* Elisha said, 'Give this to the people to eat.' But his disciple protested, 'I 43 cannot set this before a hundred men.' Still he repeated, 'Give it to the people to eat; for this is the word of the LORD: "They will eat and there will be some left over."' So he set it before them, and they ate and left 44 some over, as the LORD had said.

NAAMAN, COMMANDER of the king of Aram's army, was a great man 5 highly esteemed by his master, because by his means the LORD had given victory to Aram; but he was a leper. *f* On one of their raids the Aramaeans 2 brought back as a captive from the land of Israel a little girl, who became a servant to Naaman's wife. She said to her mistress, 'If only my master 3

a Or went with her.   *b Prob. rdg.; Heb.* crouched.   *c* and breathed into him:
or and the boy sneezed.   *d Or* poisonous wild gourds.   *e* fresh . . . corn: *prob.*
rdg.; Heb. unintelligible.   *f* he was a leper: *or* his skin was diseased.

4 could meet the prophet who lives in Samaria, he would get rid of the
disease for him.' Naaman went in and reported to his master word for
5 word what the girl from the land of Israel had said. 'Very well, you may
go,' said the king of Aram, 'and I will send a letter to the king of Israel.'
So Naaman went, taking with him ten talents of silver, six thousand shekels
6 of gold, and ten changes of clothing. He delivered the letter to the king of
Israel, which read thus: 'This letter is to inform you that I am sending to
7 you my servant Naaman, and I beg you to rid him of his disease.' When
the king of Israel read the letter, he rent his clothes and said, 'Am I a god *a*
to kill and to make alive, that this fellow sends to me to cure a man of his
8 disease? Surely you must see that he is picking a quarrel with me.' When
Elisha, the man of God, heard how the king of Israel had rent his clothes,
he sent to him saying, 'Why did you rend your clothes? Let the man come
9 to me, and he will know that there is a prophet in Israel.' So Naaman came
with his horses and chariots and stood at the entrance to Elisha's house.
10 Elisha sent out a messenger to say to him, 'If you will go and wash seven
times in the Jordan, your flesh will be restored and you will be clean.'
11 Naaman was furious and went away, saying, 'I thought he would at least
have come out and stood, and invoked the LORD his God by name, waved
12 his hand over the place and so rid me of the disease. Are not Abana and
Pharpar, rivers of Damascus, better than all the waters of Israel? Can I
13 not wash in them and be clean?' So he turned and went off in a rage. But
his servants came up to him and said, 'If the prophet had bidden you do
something difficult, would you not do it? How much more then, if he tells
14 you to wash and be clean?' So he went down and dipped himself in the
Jordan seven times as the man of God had told him, and his flesh was
restored as a little child's, and he was clean.
15   Then he and his retinue went back to the man of God and stood before
him; and he said, 'Now I know that there is no god anywhere on earth
except in Israel. Will you accept a token of gratitude from your servant?'
16 'As the LORD lives, whom I serve,' said the prophet, 'I will accept nothing.'
17 He was pressed to accept, but he refused. 'Then if you will not,' said
Naaman, 'let me, sir, have two mules' load of earth. For I will no longer
18 offer whole-offering or sacrifice to any god but the LORD. In this one matter
only may the LORD pardon me: when my master goes to the temple of
Rimmon to worship, leaning on my arm, and I worship in the temple of
19 Rimmon when he worships there, for this let the LORD pardon me.' And
Elisha bade him farewell.
20   Naaman had gone only a short distance on his way, when Gehazi, the
servant of Elisha the man of God, said to himself, 'What? Has my master let
this Aramaean, Naaman, go scot-free, and not accepted what he brought?
21 As the LORD lives, I will run after him and get something from him.' So
Gehazi hurried after Naaman. When Naaman saw him running after him,
he jumped down from his chariot to meet him and said, 'Is anything
22 wrong?' 'Nothing,' said Gehazi, 'but my master sent me to say that two
young men of the company of prophets from the hill-country of Ephraim
have just arrived. Could you provide them with a talent of silver and two

a Or Am I God.

414

changes of clothing?' Naaman said, 'By all means; take two talents.' He   23
pressed[a] him to take them; so he tied up the two talents of silver in two
bags, and the two changes of clothing, and gave them to his two servants,
and they walked ahead carrying them. When Gehazi came to the citadel[b]   24
he took them from the two servants, deposited them in the house and dismissed the men; and they departed. When he went in and stood before   25
his master, Elisha said, 'Where have you been, Gehazi?' 'Nowhere', said
Gehazi. But he said to him, 'Was I not with you in spirit when the man   26
turned back from his chariot to meet you? Is it not true that you have the
money? You may buy gardens with it,[c][d] and olive-trees and vineyards,
sheep and oxen, slaves and slave-girls; but the disease of Naaman will   27
fasten on you and on your descendants for ever.' Gehazi left his presence,
his skin diseased, white as snow.

A COMPANY OF PROPHETS said to Elisha, 'You can see that this place   6
where our community is living, under you as its head, is too small for us.
Let us go to the Jordan and each fetch a log, and make ourselves a place to   2
live in.' The prophet agreed. Then one of them said, 'Please, sir, come with   3
us.' 'I will', he said, and he went with them. When they reached the   4
Jordan, they began cutting down trees; but it chanced that, as one man was   5
felling a trunk, the head of his axe flew off into the water. 'Oh, master!'
he exclaimed, 'it was a borrowed one.' 'Where did it fall?' asked the man   6
of God. When he was shown the place, he cut off a piece of wood and threw
it in and made the iron float. Then he said, 'There you are, lift it out.' So   7
he stretched out his hand and took it.

Once, when the king of Aram was making war on Israel, he held a con-   8
ference with his staff at which he said, 'I mean to attack in such and such a
direction.' But the man of God warned the king of Israel: 'Take care to   9
avoid this place, for the Aramaeans are going down that way.' So the king   10
of Israel sent to the place about which the man of God had given him this
warning; and the king took special precautions every time he found himself near that place. The king of Aram was greatly perturbed at this and,   11
summoning his staff, he said to them, 'Tell me, one of you, who has betrayed us to the king of Israel?' 'None of us, my lord king,' said one of his   12
staff; 'but Elisha, the prophet in Israel, tells the king of Israel the very
words you speak in your bedchamber.' 'Go and find out where he is,' said   13
the king, 'and I will send and seize him.' He was told that the prophet was
at Dothan, and he sent a strong force there with horses and chariots. They   14
came by night and surrounded the city.

When the disciple of the man of God rose early in the morning and went   15
out, he saw a force with horses and chariots surrounding the city. 'Oh,
master,' he said, 'which way are we to turn?' He answered, 'Do not be   16
afraid, for those who are on our side are more than those on theirs.' Then   17
Elisha offered this prayer: 'O LORD, open his eyes and let him see.' And
the LORD opened the young man's eyes, and he saw the hills covered with
horses and chariots of fire all round Elisha. As they came down towards   18

[a] *Prob. rdg.; Heb.* broke out on.   [b] *Or* hill.   [c] gardens with it: *prob. rdg.; Heb.*
garments.   [d] Is it not ... with it: *or* Was it a time to get the money and to get garments?

19 him, Elisha prayed to the LORD: 'Strike this host, I pray thee, with blindness'; and he struck them blind as Elisha had asked. Then Elisha said to them, 'You are on the wrong road; this is not the city. Follow me and I will lead you to the man you are looking for.' And he led them to Sama-
20 ria. As soon as they had entered Samaria, Elisha prayed, 'O LORD, open the eyes of these men and let them see again.' And he opened their eyes
21 and they saw that they were inside Samaria. When the king of Israel
22 saw them, he said to Elisha, 'My father, am I to destroy them?' 'No, you must not do that', he answered. 'You may destroy *a* those whom you have taken prisoner with your own sword and bow, but as for these men, give them food and water, and let them eat and drink, and then go back to their
23 master.' So he prepared a great feast for them, and they ate and drank and then went back to their master. And Aramaean raids on Israel ceased.

24 But later, Ben-hadad king of Aram called up his entire army and marched
25 to the siege of Samaria. The city was near starvation, and they besieged it so closely that a donkey's head was sold for eighty shekels of silver, and a
26 quarter of a kab of locust-beans for five shekels. One day, as the king of Israel was walking along the city wall, a woman called to him, 'Help, my
27 lord king!' He said, 'If the LORD will not bring you help, where can I find
28 any for you? From threshing-floor or from winepress? What is your trouble?' She replied, 'This woman said to me, "Give up your child for
29 us to eat today, and we will eat mine tomorrow." So we cooked my son and ate him; but when I said to her the next day, "Now give up your child
30 for us to eat", she had hidden him.' When he heard the woman's story, the king rent his clothes. He was walking along the wall at the time, and when the people looked, they saw that he had sackcloth underneath, next to his
31 skin. Then he said, 'The LORD do the same to me and more, if the head of Elisha son of Shaphat stays on his shoulders today.'
32 Elisha was sitting at home, the elders with him. The king had dispatched one of his retinue but, before the messenger arrived, Elisha said to the elders, 'See how this son of a murderer has sent to behead me! Take care, when the messenger comes, to shut the door and hold it fast against him.
33 Can you not hear his master following on his heels?' While he was still speaking, the king *b* arrived and said, 'Look at our plight! This is the
7 LORD's doing. Why should I wait any longer for him to help us?' But Elisha answered, 'Hear this word of the LORD: By this time tomorrow a shekel will buy a measure of flour or two measures of barley in the gateway
2 of Samaria.' Then the lieutenant on whose arm the king leaned said to the man of God, 'Even if the LORD were to open windows in the sky, such a thing could not happen!' He answered, 'You will see it with your own eyes, but none of it will you eat.'

3 At the city gate were four lepers. *c* They said to one another, 'Why
4 should we stay here and wait for death? If we say we will go into the city, there is famine there, and we shall die; if we say we will stay here, we shall die just the same. Well then, let us go to the camp of the Aramaeans and give ourselves up: if they spare us, we shall live; if they put us to death,

a Prob. rdg.; Heb. Would you destroy.   *b Prob. rdg.; Heb.* messenger.   *c Or men* suffering from skin-disease.

we can but die.' And so in the twilight they set out for the Aramaean camp; 5
but when they reached the outskirts, they found no one there; for the 6
Lord had caused the Aramaean army to hear a sound like that of chariots
and horses and of a great host, so that the word went round: 'The king of
Israel has hired the kings of the Hittites and the kings of Egypt to attack
us.' They had fled at once in the twilight, abandoning their tents, their 7
horses and asses, and leaving the camp as it stood, while they fled for their
lives. When the four men came to the outskirts of the camp, they went into 8
a tent and ate and drank and looted silver and gold and clothing, and made
off and hid them. Then they came back, went into another tent and rifled
it, and made off and hid the loot. Then they said to one another, 'What we 9
are doing is not right. This is a day of good news and we are keeping it to
ourselves. If we wait till morning, we shall be held to blame. We must go
now and give the news to the king's household.' So they came and called 10
to the watch at the city gate and described how they had gone to the
Aramaean camp and found not a single man in it and had heard no sound:
nothing but horses and asses tethered, and the tents left as they were. Then 11
the watch called out and gave the news to the king's household in the
palace. The king rose in the night and said to his staff, 'I will tell you what 12
the Aramaeans have done. They know that we are starving, and they have
left their camp to go and hide in the open country, expecting us to come
out, and then they can take us alive and enter the city.' One of his staff said, 13
'Send out a party of men with some of the horses that are left; if they live,
they will be as well off as all the other Israelites who are still left; if they
die,[a] they will be no worse off than all those who have already perished.
Let them go and see what has happened.' So they picked two mounted 14
men, and the king dispatched them in the track of the Aramaean army
with the order to go and find out what had happened. They followed as 15
far as the Jordan and found the whole road littered with clothing and
equipment which the Aramaeans had flung aside in their haste. The messengers returned and reported this to the king. Then the people went out 16
and plundered the Aramaean camp, and a measure of flour was sold for a
shekel and two measures of barley for a shekel, so that the word of the
LORD came true. Now the king had appointed the lieutenant on whose 17
arm he leaned to take charge of the gate, and the people trampled him to
death there, just as the man of God had foretold when the king visited him.
For when the man of God said to the king, 'By this time tomorrow a shekel 18
will buy two measures of barley or one measure of flour in the gateway of
Samaria', the lieutenant had answered, 'Even if the LORD were to open 19
windows in the sky, such a thing could not happen!' And the man of God
had said, 'You will see it with your own eyes, but none of it will you eat.'
And this is just what happened to him: the people trampled him to death 20
at the gate.

Elisha said to the woman whose son he had restored to life, 'Go away at **8**
once with your household and find lodging where you can, for the LORD
has decreed a seven years' famine and it has already come upon the land.'
The woman acted at once on the word of the man of God and went away 2

---

[a] *if they live . . . if they die: prob. rdg.; Heb. obscure.*

with her household; and she stayed in the Philistine country for seven years.
3 When she came back at the end of the seven years, she sought an audience
4 of the king to appeal for the return of her house and land. Now the king was
questioning Gehazi, the servant of the man of God, about all the great
5 things Elisha had done; and, as he was describing to the king how he had
brought the dead to life, the selfsame woman began appealing to the king
for her house and her land. 'My lord king,' said Gehazi, 'this is the very
6 woman, and this is her son whom Elisha brought to life.' The king asked
the woman about it, and she told him. Then he entrusted the case to a
eunuch and ordered him to restore all her property to her, with all the
revenues from her land from the time she left the country till that day.

7   Elisha came to Damascus, at a time when Ben-hadad king of Aram was
8 ill; and when he was told that the man of God had arrived, he bade Hazael
take a gift with him and go to the man of God and inquire of the LORD
9 through him whether he would recover from his illness. Hazael went,
taking with him as a gift all kinds of wares of Damascus, forty camel-
loads. When he came into the prophet's presence, he said, 'Your son Ben-
hadad king of Aram has sent me to you to ask whether he will recover from
10 his illness.' 'Go and tell him that he will recover,' he answered; 'but the
11 LORD has revealed to me that in fact he will die.' The man of God stood
there with set face like a man stunned, until he could bear it no longer;
12 then he wept. 'Why do you weep, my lord?' said Hazael. He answered,
'Because I know the harm you will do to the Israelites: you will set their
fortresses on fire and put their young men to the sword; you will dash their
13 children to the ground and you will rip open their pregnant women.' But
Hazael said, 'But I am a dog, a mere nobody; how can I do this great thing?'
Elisha answered, 'The LORD has revealed to me that you will be king of
14 Aram.' Hazael left Elisha and returned to his master, who asked him what
15 Elisha had said. 'He told me that you would recover', he replied. But the
next day he took a blanket and, after dipping it in water, laid it over the
king's face, and he died; and Hazael succeeded him.

16   In the fifth year of Jehoram son of Ahab king of Israel, Joram son of
17*a* Jehoshaphat king of Judah became king. He was thirty-two years old when
18 he came to the throne, and he reigned in Jerusalem for eight years. He
followed the practices of the kings of Israel as the house of Ahab had done,
for he had married Ahab's daughter; and he did what was wrong in the
19 eyes of the LORD. But for his servant David's sake the LORD was unwilling
to destroy Judah, since he had promised to give him and his sons a flame,
to burn for all time.

20   During his reign Edom revolted against Judah and set up its own king.
21 Joram crossed over to Zair with all his chariots. He and his chariot-
commanders set out by night, but they were surrounded by the Edomites
22 and defeated,*b* whereupon the people fled to their tents. So Edom has
remained independent of Judah to this day; Libnah also revolted at the
23 same time. The other acts and events of Joram's reign are recorded in
24 the annals of the kings of Judah. So Joram rested with his forefathers

---

a Verses 17–22: cp. 2 Chr. 21. 5–10.   *b and defeated: prob. rdg.; Heb. and he defeated Edom.*

and was buried with them in the city of David, and his son Ahaziah succeeded him.

In the twelfth year of Jehoram son of Ahab king of Israel, Ahaziah son 25[a] of Joram king of Judah became king. Ahaziah was twenty-two years old 26 when he came to the throne, and he reigned in Jerusalem for one year; his mother was Athaliah granddaughter of Omri king of Israel. He followed 27 the practices of the house of Ahab and did what was wrong in the eyes of the LORD like the house of Ahab, for he was connected with that house by marriage. He allied himself with Jehoram son of Ahab to fight against 28 Hazael king of Aram at Ramoth-gilead; but King Jehoram was wounded by the Aramaeans, and returned to Jezreel to recover from the wounds 29 which were inflicted on him at Ramoth in battle with Hazael king of Aram; and because of his illness Ahaziah son of Joram king of Judah went down to Jezreel to visit him.

ELISHA THE PROPHET SUMMONED one of the company of prophets 9 and said to him, 'Hitch up your cloak, take this flask of oil with you and go to Ramoth-gilead. When you arrive, you will find Jehu son of Jehosha- 2 phat, son of Nimshi; go in and call him aside from his fellow-officers, and lead him through to an inner room. Then take the flask and pour the oil 3 on his head and say, "This is the word of the LORD: I anoint you king over Israel"; then open the door and flee for your life.' So the young prophet 4 went to Ramoth-gilead. When he arrived, he found the officers sitting 5 together and said, 'Sir, I have a word for you.' 'For which of us?' asked Jehu. 'For you, sir', he said. He rose and went into the house, and the 6 prophet poured the oil on his head, saying, 'This is the word of the LORD the God of Israel: "I anoint you king over Israel, the people of the LORD. You shall strike down the house of Ahab your master, and I will take 7 vengeance on Jezebel for the blood of my servants the prophets and for the blood of all the LORD's servants. All the house of Ahab shall perish and I 8 will destroy every mother's son of his house in Israel, whether under the protection of the family or not. And I will make the house of Ahab like the 9 house of Jeroboam son of Nebat and the house of Baasha son of Ahijah. Jezebel shall be devoured by dogs in the plot of ground at Jezreel and 10 no one will bury her." ' Then he opened the door and fled. When Jehu 11 rejoined the king's officers, they said to him, 'Is all well? What did this crazy fellow want with you?' 'You know him and the way his thoughts run', he said. 'Nonsense!' they replied; 'tell us what happened.' 'I will tell 12 you exactly what he said: "This is the word of the LORD: I anoint you king over Israel." ' They snatched up their cloaks and spread them under him 13 on the stones[b] of the steps, and sounded the trumpet and shouted, 'Jehu is king.'

Then Jehu son of Jehoshaphat, son of Nimshi, laid his plans against 14 Jehoram, while Jehoram and the Israelites were defending Ramoth-gilead against Hazael king of Aram. King Jehoram had returned to Jezreel to 15 recover from the wounds inflicted on him by the Aramaeans when he fought against Hazael king of Aram. Jehu said to them, 'If you are on my side, see

[a] *Verses 25–29: cp. 2 Chr. 22. 1–6.*   [b] *Prob. rdg.; Heb. obscure.*

16 that no one escapes from the city to tell the news in Jezreel.' He mounted
his chariot and drove to Jezreel, for Jehoram was laid up there, and Ahaziah
king of Judah had gone down to visit him.

17 The watchman standing on the watch-tower in Jezreel saw Jehu and
his troop approaching and called out, 'I see a troop of men.' Then Jehoram
18 said, 'Fetch a horseman and send to find out if they come peaceably.' The
horseman went to meet him and said, 'The king asks, "Is it peace?"' Jehu
said, 'Peace? What is peace to you? Fall in behind me.' Thereupon the
messenger reported, 'The messenger has met them but he is not coming
19 back.' A second horseman was sent; when he met them, he also said, 'The
king asks, "Is it peace?"' 'Peace?' said Jehu. 'What is peace to you? Fall
20 in behind me.' Then the watchman reported, 'He has met them but he is
not coming back. The driving is like the driving of Jehu son[a] of Nimshi,
21 for he drives furiously.' 'Harness my chariot', said Jehoram. They harnessed it, and Jehoram king of Israel and Ahaziah king of Judah went out
each in his own chariot to meet Jehu, and met him by the plot of Naboth of
22 Jezreel. When Jehoram saw Jehu, he said, 'Is it peace, Jehu?' But he
replied, 'Do you call it peace while your mother Jezebel keeps up her
23 obscene idol-worship and monstrous sorceries?' Jehoram wheeled about
24 and fled, crying out to Ahaziah, 'Treachery, Ahaziah!' Jehu seized his
bow and shot Jehoram between the shoulders; the arrow pierced his heart
25 and he sank down in his chariot. Then Jehu said to Bidkar, his lieutenant,
'Pick him up and throw him into the plot of land belonging to Naboth of
Jezreel; remember how, when you and I were riding side by side behind
26 Ahab his father, the LORD pronounced this sentence against him: "It is
the very word of the LORD: as surely as I saw yesterday the blood of Naboth
and the blood of his sons, I will requite you in this plot." So pick him up
27 and throw him into it and thus fulfil the word of the LORD.' When Ahaziah
king of Judah saw this, he fled by the road to Beth-haggan. Jehu went after
him and said, 'Make sure of him too.' They shot him down in his chariot
on the road up the valley[b] near Ibleam, but he escaped to Megiddo and died
28 there. His servants conveyed his body to Jerusalem and buried him in his
tomb with his forefathers in the city of David.

29 In the eleventh year of Jehoram son of Ahab, Ahaziah became king over
Judah.

30 Jehu came to Jezreel. Now Jezebel had heard what had happened; she
had painted her eyes and dressed her hair, and she stood looking down from
31 a window. As Jehu entered the gate, she said, 'Is it peace, you Zimri, you
32 murderer of your master?' He looked up at the window and said, 'Who is
33 on my side, who?' Two or three eunuchs looked out, and he said, 'Throw
her down.' They threw her down, and some of her blood splashed on to
34 the wall and the horses, which trampled her underfoot. Then he went in
and ate and drank. 'See to this accursed woman', he said, 'and bury her;
35 for she is a king's daughter.' But when they went to bury her they found
36 nothing of her but the skull, the feet, and the palms of the hands; and they
went back and told him. Jehu said, 'It is the word of the LORD which his
servant Elijah the Tishbite spoke, when he said, "In the plot of ground at

---

[a] Or grandson (*cp. verse 2*).   [b] the valley: *prob. rdg.; Heb.* to Gur.

Jezreel the dogs shall devour the flesh of Jezebel, and Jezebel's corpse shall 37 lie like dung upon the ground in the plot at Jezreel so that no one will be able to say: This is Jezebel." '

Now seventy sons of Ahab were left in Samaria. Jehu therefore sent a **10** letter to Samaria, to the elders, the rulers of the city, and to the tutors of Ahab's children, in which he wrote: 'Now, when this letter reaches you, 2 since you have in your care your master's family as well as his chariots and horses, fortified cities and weapons, choose the best and the most suitable 3 of your master's family, set him on his father's throne, and fight for your master's house.' They were panic-stricken and said, 'The two kings could 4 not stand against him; what hope is there that we can?' Therefore the 5 comptroller of the household and the governor of the city, with the elders and the tutors, sent this message to Jehu: 'We are your servants. Whatever you tell us we will do; but we will not make anyone king. Do as you think fit.' Then he wrote them a second letter: 'If you are on my side and will 6 obey my orders, then bring the heads of your master's sons to me at Jezreel by this time tomorrow.' Now the royal princes, seventy in all, were with the nobles of the city who were bringing them up. When the letter 7 reached them, they took the royal princes and killed all seventy; they put their heads in baskets and sent them to Jehu in Jezreel. When the mes- 8 senger came to him and reported that they had brought the heads of the royal princes, he ordered them to be put in two heaps and left at the entrance of the city gate till morning. In the morning he went out, stood 9 there and said to all the people, 'You are fair judges. If I conspired against my master and killed him, who put all these to death? Be sure then that 10 every word which the LORD has spoken against the house of Ahab shall be fulfilled, and that the LORD has now done what he spoke through his servant Elijah.' So Jehu put to death all who were left of the house of Ahab 11 in Jezreel, as well as all his nobles, his close friends, and his priests, until he had left not one survivor.

Then he set out for Samaria, and on the way there, when he had reached 12 a shepherds' shelter,[a] he came upon the kinsmen of Ahaziah king of 13 Judah and said, 'Who are you?' 'We are kinsmen of Ahaziah,' they replied; 'and we have come down to greet the families of the king and of the queen mother.' 'Take them alive', he said. So they took them alive; then they 14 slew them and flung them into the pit that was there, forty-two of them; they did not leave a single survivor.

When he had left that place, he found Jehonadab son of Rechab coming 15 to meet him. He greeted him and said, 'Are you with me heart and soul, as I am with you?' 'I am', said Jehonadab. 'Then if you are,' said Jehu, 'give me your hand.' He gave him his hand and Jehu helped him up into his chariot. 'Come with me,' he said, 'and you will see my zeal for the LORD.' 16 So he took him with him in his chariot. When he came to Samaria, he put 17 to death all of Ahab's house who were left there and so blotted it out, in fulfilment of the word which the LORD had spoken to Elijah. Then Jehu 18 called all the people together and said to them, 'Ahab served the Baal a little; Jehu will serve him much. Now, summon all the prophets of Baal, 19

[a] *a shepherds' shelter: or* Beth-eker of the Shepherds.

all his ministers and priests; not one must be missing. For I am holding a great sacrifice to Baal, and no one who is missing from it shall live.' In this

20 way Jehu outwitted the ministers of Baal in order to destroy them. So

21 Jehu said, 'Let a sacred ceremony for Baal be held.' They did so, and Jehu himself sent word throughout Israel, and all the ministers of Baal came; there was not a man left who did not come. They went into the temple of

22 Baal and it was filled from end to end. Then he said to the person who had charge of the wardrobe, 'Bring out robes for all the ministers of Baal'; and

23 he brought them out. Then Jehu and Jehonadab son of Rechab went into the temple of Baal and said to the ministers of Baal, 'Look carefully and make sure that there are no servants of the LORD here with you, but only

24 the ministers of Baal.' Then they went in to offer sacrifices and whole-offerings. Now Jehu had stationed eighty men outside and said to them, 'I am putting these men in your charge, and any man who lets one escape

25 shall answer for it with his life.' When he had finished offering the whole-offering, Jehu ordered the guards and the lieutenants to go and cut them all down, and let not one of them escape; so they slew them without quarter. The escort and the lieutenants then rushed into the keep of the temple of

26 Baal and brought out the sacred pole[a] from the temple of Baal and burnt it;

27 and they pulled down the sacred pillar of the Baal and the temple itself and

28 made a privy of it—as it is today. Thus Jehu stamped out the worship of

29 Baal in Israel. He did not however abandon the sins of Jeroboam son of Nebat who led Israel into sin, but he maintained the worship of the golden calves of Bethel and Dan.

30 Then the LORD said to Jehu, 'You have done well what is right in my eyes and have done to the house of Ahab all that it was in my mind to do. Therefore your sons to the fourth generation shall sit on the throne of

31 Israel.' But Jehu was not careful to follow the law of the LORD the God of Israel with all his heart; he did not abandon the sins of Jeroboam who led Israel into sin.

32 In those days the LORD began to work havoc on Israel, and Hazael struck

33 at them in every corner of their territory eastwards from the Jordan: all the land of Gilead, Gad, Reuben, and Manasseh, from Aroer which is by the gorge of the Arnon, including Gilead and Bashan.

34 The other events of Jehu's reign, his achievements and his exploits, are

35 recorded in the annals of the kings of Israel. So Jehu rested with his fore-fathers and was buried in Samaria; and he was succeeded by his son

36 Jehoahaz. Jehu reigned over Israel in Samaria for twenty-eight years.

Kings of Israel and Judah

11 1[b] AS SOON AS ATHALIAH mother of Ahaziah saw that her son was dead,

2 she set out to destroy all the royal line. But Jehosheba daughter of King Joram, sister of Ahaziah, took Ahaziah's son Joash and stole him away from among the princes who were being murdered; she put[c] him

---

[a] *Prob. rdg.; Heb.* sacred pillars.   [b] *Verses 1–20: cp. 2 Chr. 22. 10—23. 21.*

[c] she put: *prob. rdg., cp. 2 Chr. 22. 11; Heb. om.*

and his nurse in a bedchamber where he was hidden from Athaliah and
was not put to death. He remained concealed with her in the house of the 3
LORD for six years, while Athaliah ruled the country. In the seventh year 4
Jehoiada sent for the captains of units of a hundred, both of the Carites
and of the guards, and he brought them into the house of the LORD; he
made an agreement with them and put them on their oath in the house of
the LORD, and showed them the king's son, and gave them the following 5
orders: 'One third of you who are on duty on the sabbath are to be on
guard in the palace; the rest of you are to be on special duty in the house of 6
the LORD, one third at the Sur Gate and the other third at the gate with*a*
the outrunners. Your two companies who are off duty on the sabbath shall 7
be on duty for the king in the house of the LORD. So you shall be on guard 8
round the king, each man with his arms at the ready, and anyone who
comes near the ranks is to be put to death; you must be with the king
wherever he goes.'

The captains carried out the orders of Jehoiada the priest to the letter. 9
Each took his men, both those who came on duty on the sabbath and those
who came off, and came to Jehoiada. The priest handed out to the captains 10
King David's spears and shields, which were in the house of the LORD.
Then the guards took up their stations, each man carrying his arms at the 11
ready, from corner to corner of the house to north and south,*b* surrounding
the king. Then he brought out the king's son, put the crown on his head, 12
handed him the warrant and anointed him king. The people clapped their
hands and shouted, 'Long live the king.' When Athaliah heard the noise 13
made by the guards and the people, she came into the house of the LORD
where the people were and found the king standing, as was the custom, 14
on the dais,*c* amidst outbursts of song and fanfares of trumpets in his
honour, and all the populace rejoicing and blowing trumpets. Then
Athaliah rent her clothes and cried, 'Treason! Treason!' Jehoiada the 15
priest gave orders to the captains in command of the troops: 'Bring her
outside the precincts and put to the sword anyone in attendance on her';
for the priest said, 'She shall not be put to death in the house of the LORD.'
So they laid hands on her and took her out by the entry for horses to the 16
royal palace, and there she was put to death.

Then Jehoiada made a covenant between the LORD and the king and 17
people that they should be the LORD's people, and also between the king
and the people. And all the people went into the temple of Baal and pulled 18
it down; they smashed to pieces its altars and images, and they slew Mattan
the priest of Baal before the altars. Then Jehoiada set a watch over the house
of the LORD; he took the captains of units of a hundred, the Carites and the 19
guards and all the people, and they escorted the king from the house of the
LORD through the Gate of the Guards to the royal palace, and seated him
on the royal throne. The whole people rejoiced and the city was tranquil. 20
That is how Athaliah was put to the sword in the royal palace.

Joash was seven years old when he became king. In the seventh year of 21*d* **12** 1
Jehu, Joash became king, and he reigned in Jerusalem for forty years; his

---

a *Or* behind.   *b* *Prob. rdg.; Heb. adds* of the altar and the house.   *c* *Or by the*
pillar.   *d* *11. 21—12. 15: cp. 2 Chr. 24. 1-14.*

423

2 mother was Zibiah of Beersheba. He did what was right in the eyes of the
3 LORD all his days, as Jehoiada the priest had taught him. The hill-shrines,
however, were allowed to remain; the people still continued to sacrifice
and make smoke-offerings there.

4 Then Joash ordered the priests to take all the silver brought as holy-
gifts into the house of the LORD, the silver for which each man was assessed,[a]
the silver for the persons assessed under his name, and any silver which
5 any man brought voluntarily to the house of the LORD. He ordered the
priests, also, each to make a contribution from his own funds, and to repair
6 the house wherever it was found necessary. But in the twenty-third year
of the reign of Joash the priests had still not carried out the repairs to the
7 house. King Joash summoned Jehoiada the priest and the other priests and
said to them, 'Why are you not repairing the house? Henceforth you need
8 not contribute from your own funds for the repair of the house.' So the
priests agreed neither to receive money from the people nor to undertake
9 the repairs of the house. Then Jehoiada the priest took a chest and bored a
hole in the lid and put it beside the altar on the right side going into the
house of the LORD, and the priests on duty at the entrance put in it all the
10 money brought into the house of the LORD. And whenever they saw that
the chest was well filled, the king's secretary and the high priest came and
melted down the silver found in the house of the LORD and weighed it.
11 When it had been checked, they gave the silver to the foremen over the
work in the house of the LORD and they paid the carpenters and the builders
12 working on the temple and the masons and the stone-cutters; they used it
also to buy timber and hewn stone for the repairs and for all other expenses
13 connected with them. They did not use the silver brought into the house
of the LORD to make silver cups, snuffers, tossing-bowls, trumpets, or
14 any gold or silver vessels; but they paid it to the workmen and used it for
15 the repairs. No account was demanded from the foremen to whom the
money was given for the payment of the workmen, for they were acting on
16 trust. Money from guilt-offerings and sin-offerings was not brought into
the house of the LORD: it belonged to the priests.

17 Then Hazael king of Aram came up and attacked Gath and took it; and
18 he moved on against Jerusalem. But Joash king of Judah took all the holy-
gifts that Jehoshaphat, Joram, and Ahaziah his forefathers, kings of Judah,
had dedicated, and his own holy-gifts, and all the gold that was found in
the treasuries of the house of the LORD and in the royal palace, and sent
them to Hazael king of Aram; and he withdrew from Jerusalem.

19 The other acts and events of the reign of Joash are recorded in the annals
20 [b] of the kings of Judah. His servants revolted against him and struck him
21 down in the house of Millo on the descent to Silla. It was his servants
Jozachar son of Shimeath and Jehozabad son of Shomer who struck the
fatal blow; and he was buried with his forefathers in the city of David. He
was succeeded by his son Amaziah.

13 In the twenty-third year of Joash son of Ahaziah king of Judah, Jehoahaz
son of Jehu became king over Israel in Samaria and he reigned seventeen

---

[a] *the silver . . . assessed: prob. rdg.; Heb. obscure.*   [b] *Verses 20, 21: cp. 2 Chr. 24.*
25–27.

years. He did what was wrong in the eyes of the LORD and continued the 2
sinful practices of Jeroboam son of Nebat who led Israel into sin, and did
not give them up. So the LORD was roused to anger against Israel and he 3
made them subject for some years to Hazael king of Aram and Ben-hadad
son of Hazael. Then Jehoahaz sought to placate the LORD, and the LORD 4
heard his prayer, for he saw how the king of Aram oppressed Israel. The 5
LORD appointed a deliverer for Israel, who rescued them from the power
of Aram, and the Israelites settled down again in their own homes. But 6
they did not give up the sinful practices of the house of Jeroboam who led
Israel into sin, but continued in them; the goddess Asherah[a] remained in
Samaria. Hazael had left Jehoahaz no armed force except fifty horsemen, 7
ten chariots, and ten thousand infantry; all the rest the king of Aram had
destroyed and made like dust under foot.

The other events of the reign of Jehoahaz, and all his achievements and 8
his exploits, are recorded in the annals of the kings of Israel. So Jehoahaz 9
rested with his forefathers and was buried in Samaria; and he was succeeded by his son Jehoash.

In the thirty-ninth year of Joash king of Judah, Jehoash son of Jehoahaz 10
became king over Israel in Samaria and reigned sixteen years. He did what 11
was wrong in the eyes of the LORD; he did not give up any of the sinful
practices of Jeroboam son of Nebat who led Israel into sin, but continued
in them. The other events of the reign of Jehoash, all his achievements, his 12
exploits and his war with Amaziah king of Judah, are recorded in the annals
of the kings of Israel. So Jehoash rested with his forefathers and was buried 13
in Samaria with the kings of Israel, and Jeroboam sat upon his throne.

Elisha fell ill and lay on his deathbed, and Jehoash king of Israel went 14
down to him and wept over him and said, 'My father! My father, the
chariots and the horsemen of Israel!' 'Take bow and arrows', said Elisha, 15
and he took bow and arrows. 'Put your hand to the bow', said the prophet. 16
He did so, and Elisha laid his hands on those of the king. Then he said, 17
'Open the window toward the east'; he opened it and Elisha told him to
shoot, and he shot. Then the prophet said, 'An arrow for the LORD's
victory, an arrow for victory over Aram! You will defeat Aram utterly at
Aphek'; and he added, 'Now take up your arrows.' When the king had 18
taken them, Elisha said, 'Strike the ground with them.' He struck three
times and stopped. The man of God was furious with him and said, 'You 19
should have struck five or six times; then you would have defeated Aram
utterly; as it is, you will strike Aram three times and no more.'

Then Elisha died and was buried. 20

Year by year Moabite raiders used to invade the land. Once some men 21
were burying a dead man when they caught sight of the raiders. They
threw the body into the grave of Elisha and made off; when the body
touched the prophet's bones, the man came to life and rose to his feet.

All through the reign of Jehoahaz, Hazael king of Aram oppressed Israel. 22
But the LORD was gracious and took pity on them; because of his covenant 23
with Abraham, Isaac, and Jacob, he looked on them with favour and was
unwilling to destroy them; nor has he even yet banished them from his

[a] the goddess Asherah: *or* the sacred pole.

24 sight. When Hazael king of Aram died and was succeeded by his son Ben-
25 hadad, Jehoash son of Jehoahaz recaptured the cities which Ben-hadad
    had taken in war from Jehoahaz his father; three times Jehoash defeated
    him and recovered the cities of Israel.

14 1[a]   In the second year of Jehoash son of Jehoahaz king of Israel, Amaziah
2   son of Joash king of Judah succeeded his father. He was twenty-five years
    old when he came to the throne, and he reigned in Jerusalem for twenty-
3   nine years; his mother was Jehoaddin of Jerusalem. He did what was right
    in the eyes of the LORD, yet not as his forefather David had done; he
4   followed his father Joash in everything. The hill-shrines were allowed to
5   remain; the people continued to slaughter and burn sacrifices there. When
    the royal power was firmly in his grasp, he put to death those of his servants
6   who had murdered the king his father; but he spared the murderers'
    children in obedience to the LORD's command written in the law of Moses:
    'Fathers shall not be put to death for their children, nor children for their
7   fathers; a man shall be put to death only for his own sin.' He defeated ten
    thousand Edomites in the Valley of Salt and captured Sela; he gave it the
    name Joktheel, which it still bears.

8[b]   Then Amaziah sent messengers to Jehoash son of Jehoahaz, son of
9   Jehu, king of Israel, to propose a meeting. But Jehoash king of Israel sent
    this answer to Amaziah king of Judah: 'A thistle in Lebanon sent to a
    cedar in Lebanon to say, "Give your daughter in marriage to my son." But
10 a wild beast in Lebanon, passing by, trampled on the thistle. You have
    defeated Edom, it is true; and it has gone to your head. Stay at home and
    enjoy your triumph. Why should you involve yourself in disaster and bring
    yourself to the ground, and Judah with you?'

11 But Amaziah would not listen; so Jehoash king of Israel marched out,
    and he and Amaziah king of Judah met one another at Beth-shemesh in
12 Judah. The men of Judah were routed by Israel and fled to their homes.
13 But Jehoash king of Israel captured Amaziah king of Judah, son of Joash,
    son of Ahaziah, at Beth-shemesh. He went to Jerusalem and broke down
    the city wall from the Gate of Ephraim to the Corner Gate, a distance of
14 four hundred cubits. He also took all the gold and silver and all the vessels
    found in the house of the LORD and in the treasuries of the royal palace,
    as well as hostages, and returned to Samaria.

15 The other events of the reign of Jehoash, and all his achievements, his
    exploits and his wars with Amaziah king of Judah, are recorded in the
16 annals of the kings of Israel. So Jehoash rested with his forefathers and
    was buried in Samaria with the kings of Israel; and he was succeeded by
    his son Jeroboam.

17[c]   Amaziah son of Joash, king of Judah, outlived Jehoash son of Jehoahaz,
18 king of Israel, by fifteen years. The other events of Amaziah's reign are
19 recorded in the annals of the kings of Judah. A conspiracy was formed
    against him in Jerusalem and he fled to Lachish; but they sent after him
20 to Lachish and put him to death there. Then his body was conveyed on
    horseback to Jerusalem, and there he was buried with his forefathers in the

---

a Verses 1–6: cp. 2 Chr. 25. 1–4.   *b Verses 8–14: cp. 2 Chr. 25. 17–24.*   *c Verses
17–22: cp. 2 Chr. 25. 25—26. 2.*

city of David. The people of Judah took Azariah, now sixteen years old, 21
and made him king in succession to his father Amaziah. It was he who 22
built Elath and restored it to Judah after the king rested with his forefathers.

In the fifteenth year of Amaziah son of Joash king of Judah, Jeroboam 23
son of Jehoash king of Israel became king in Samaria and reigned for
forty-one years. He did what was wrong in the eyes of the LORD; he did 24
not give up the sinful practices of Jeroboam son of Nebat who led Israel
into sin. He re-established the frontiers of Israel from Lebo-hamath to the 25
Sea of the Arabah, in fulfilment of the word of the LORD the God of Israel
spoken by his servant the prophet Jonah son of Amittai, of Gath-hepher.
For the LORD had seen how bitterly Israel had suffered; no one was safe, 26
whether under the protection of his family or not, and Israel was left
defenceless. But the LORD had made no threat to blot out the name of 27
Israel under heaven, and he saved them through Jeroboam son of Jehoash.
The other events of Jeroboam's reign, and all his achievements, his ex- 28
ploits, the wars he fought and how he recovered Damascus and Hamath
in Jaudi for*ᵃ* Israel, are recorded in the annals of the kings of Israel. So 29
Jeroboam rested with his forefathers the kings of Israel; and he was
succeeded by his son Zechariah.

In the twenty-seventh year of Jeroboam king of Israel, Azariah*ᵇ* son of **15**
Amaziah king of Judah became king. He was sixteen years old when he 2*ᶜ*
came to the throne, and he reigned in Jerusalem for fifty-two years; his
mother was Jecoliah of Jerusalem. He did what was right in the eyes of 3
the LORD, as Amaziah his father had done. But the hill-shrines were allowed 4
to remain; the people still continued to slaughter and burn sacrifices there.
The LORD struck the king with leprosy,*ᵈ* which he had till the day of his 5*ᵉ*
death; he was relieved of all duties and lived in his own house, while his
son Jotham was comptroller of the household and regent. The other acts 6
and events of Azariah's reign are recorded in the annals of the kings of
Judah. So he rested with his forefathers and was buried with them in the 7
city of David; and he was succeeded by his son Jotham.

In the thirty-eighth year of Azariah king of Judah, Zechariah son of 8
Jeroboam became king over Israel in Samaria and reigned six months. He 9
did what was wrong in the eyes of the LORD, as his forefathers had done;
he did not give up the sinful practices of Jeroboam son of Nebat who led
Israel into sin. Shallum son of Jabesh formed a conspiracy against him, 10
attacked him in Ibleam, killed him and usurped the throne. The other 11
events of Zechariah's reign are recorded in the annals of the kings of
Israel. Thus the word of the LORD spoken to Jehu was fulfilled: 'Your sons 12
to the fourth generation shall sit on the throne of Israel.'

Shallum son of Jabesh became king in the thirty-ninth year of Uzziah 13
king of Judah, and he reigned one full month in Samaria. Then Menahem 14
son of Gadi came up from Tirzah to Samaria, attacked Shallum son of
Jabesh there, killed him and usurped the throne. The other events of 15

ᵃ in Jaudi for: *prob. rdg.; Heb.* to Judah in.   *ᵇ* Uzziah *in verses 13, 30, 32, 34.*
ᶜ *Verses 2, 3 : cp.* 2 Chr. 26. 3, 4.   *ᵈ* *Or* a skin-disease.   *ᵉ* *Verses 5–7 : cp.*
2 Chr. 26. 21–23.

Shallum's reign and the conspiracy that he formed are recorded in the annals of the kings of Israel.

16 Then Menahem, starting out from Tirzah, destroyed Tappuah' and everything in it and ravaged its territory; he ravaged it because it had not opened its gates to him, and he ripped open all the pregnant women.

17 In the thirty-ninth year of Azariah king of Judah, Menahem son of Gadi
18 became king over Israel and he reigned in Samaria for ten years. He did what was wrong in the eyes of the LORD; he did not give up the sinful
19 practices of Jeroboam son of Nebat who led Israel into sin. In his days Pul king of Assyria invaded the country, and Menahem gave him a thousand talents of silver to obtain his help in strengthening his hold on the kingdom.
20 Menahem laid a levy on all the men of wealth in Israel, and each had to give the king of Assyria fifty silver shekels. Then the king of Assyria withdrew
21 without occupying the country. The other acts and events of Menahem's
22 reign are recorded in the annals of the kings of Israel. So Menahem rested with his forefathers; and he was succeeded by his son Pekahiah.

23 In the fiftieth year of Azariah king of Judah, Pekahiah son of Menahem
24 became king over Israel in Samaria and reigned for two years. He did what was wrong in the eyes of the LORD; he did not give up the sinful practices
25 of Jeroboam son of Nebat who led Israel into sin. Pekah son of Remaliah, his lieutenant, formed a conspiracy against him and, with the help of fifty Gileadites, attacked him in Samaria in the citadel of the royal palace,[a]
26 killed him and usurped the throne. The other acts and events of Pekahiah's reign are recorded in the annals of the kings of Israel.

27 In the fifty-second year of Azariah king of Judah, Pekah son of Remaliah
28 became king over Israel in Samaria and reigned for twenty years. He did what was wrong in the eyes of the LORD; he did not give up the sinful
29 practices of Jeroboam son of Nebat who led Israel into sin. In the days of Pekah king of Israel, Tiglath-pileser king of Assyria came and seized Iyyon, Abel-beth-maacah, Janoah, Kedesh, Hazor, Gilead, and Galilee,
30 with all the land of Naphtali, and deported the people to Assyria. Then Hoshea son of Elah formed a conspiracy against Pekah son of Remaliah, attacked him, killed him and usurped the throne in the twentieth year of
31 Jotham son of Uzziah. The other acts and events of Pekah's reign are recorded in the annals of the kings of Israel.

32 In the second year of Pekah son of Remaliah king of Israel, Jotham son
33b of Uzziah king of Judah became king. He was twenty-five years old when he came to the throne, and he reigned in Jerusalem for sixteen years; his
34 mother was Jerusha daughter of Zadok. He did what was right in the eyes
35 of the LORD, as his father Uzziah had done; but the hill-shrines were allowed to remain and the people continued to slaughter and burn sacrifices there. It was he who constructed the upper gate of the house of the LORD.
36 The other acts and events of Jotham's reign are recorded in the annals of
37 the kings of Judah. In those days the LORD began to make Rezin king of
38 Aram and Pekah son of Remaliah attack Judah. And Jotham rested with his forefathers and was buried with them in the city of David his forefather; and he was succeeded by his son Ahaz.

[a] *Prob. rdg.; Heb. adds* Argob and Arieh. [b] *Verses 33–35: cp. 2 Chr. 27. 1–3.*

Downfall of the northern kingdom

IN THE SEVENTEENTH YEAR OF PEKAH son of Remaliah, Ahaz son **16**
of Jotham king of Judah became king. Ahaz was twenty years old when **2** *a*
he came to the throne, and he reigned in Jerusalem for sixteen years. He
did not do what was right in the eyes of the LORD his God like his forefather David, but followed in the footsteps of the kings of Israel; he even **3**
passed his son through the fire, adopting the abominable practice of the
nations whom the LORD had dispossessed in favour of the Israelites. He **4**
slaughtered and burnt sacrifices at the hill-shrines and on the hill-tops and
under every spreading tree.

Then Rezin king of Aram and Pekah son of Remaliah king of Israel **5**
attacked Jerusalem and besieged Ahaz but could not bring him to battle.
At that time the king of Edom *b* recovered Elath and drove the Judaeans **6**
out of it; so the Edomites entered the city and have occupied it to this day.
Ahaz sent messengers to Tiglath-pileser king of Assyria to say, 'I am your **7**
servant and your son. Come and save me from the king of Aram and from
the king of Israel who are attacking me.' Ahaz took the silver and gold found **8**
in the house of the LORD and in the treasuries of the royal palace and sent
them to the king of Assyria as a bribe. The king of Assyria listened to him; **9**
he advanced on Damascus, captured it, deported its inhabitants to Kir
and put Rezin to death.

When King Ahaz went to meet Tiglath-pileser king of Assyria at **10**
Damascus, he saw there an altar of which he sent a sketch and a detailed
plan to Uriah the priest. Accordingly, Uriah built an altar, following all the **11**
instructions that the king had sent him from Damascus, and had it ready
against the king's return. When the king returned from Damascus, he saw **12**
the altar, approached it and mounted the steps; there he burnt his whole- **13**
offering and his grain-offering and poured out his drink-offering, and he
flung the blood of his shared-offerings against it. The bronze altar that was **14**
before the LORD he removed from the front of the house, from between this
altar and the house of the LORD, and put it on the north side of this altar.
Then King Ahaz gave these instructions to Uriah the priest: 'Burn on the **15**
great altar the morning whole-offering and the evening grain-offering, and
the king's whole-offering and his grain-offering, and the whole-offering of
all the people of the land, their grain-offering and their drink-offerings,
and fling against it all the blood of the sacrifices. But the bronze altar shall
be mine, to offer morning sacrifice.' Uriah the priest did all that the king **16**
told him. Then King Ahaz broke up the trolleys and removed the panels, **17**
and he took down the basin and the Sea of bronze from the oxen which
supported it and put it on a stone base. In the house of the LORD he **18**
turned round the structure they had erected for use on the sabbath, and
the outer gate for the king, to satisfy the king of Assyria. The other acts **19** *c*
and events of the reign of Ahaz are recorded in the annals of the kings of
Judah. So Ahaz rested with his forefathers and was buried with them in the **20**
city of David; and he was succeeded by his son Hezekiah.

a Verses 2–4: cp. 2 Chr. 28. 1–4. *b the king of Edom: prob. rdg.; Heb. Rezin king
of Aram.* *c Verses 19, 20: cp. 2 Chr. 28. 26, 27.*

17 In the twelfth year of Ahaz king of Judah, Hoshea son of Elah became
2 king over Israel in Samaria and reigned nine years. He did what was wrong
in the eyes of the LORD, but not as the previous kings of Israel had done.
3 Shalmaneser king of Assyria made war upon him and Hoshea became
4 tributary to him. But when the king of Assyria discovered that Hoshea was
being disloyal to him, sending messengers to the king of Egypt at So,[a] and
withholding the tribute which he had been paying year by year, the king of
5 Assyria arrested him and put him in prison. Then he invaded the whole
6 country and, reaching Samaria, besieged it for three years. In the ninth
year of Hoshea he captured Samaria and deported its people to Assyria and
settled them in Halah and on the Habor, the river of Gozan, and in the
cities of Media.

7 All this happened to the Israelites because they had sinned against the
LORD their God who brought them up from Egypt, from the rule of
8 Pharaoh king of Egypt; they paid homage to other gods and observed the
laws and customs of the nations whom the LORD had dispossessed before
9 them and uttered blasphemies against the LORD their God; they built hill-
shrines for themselves in all their settlements, from watch-tower to fortified
10 city, and set up sacred pillars and sacred poles on every high hill and under
11 every spreading tree, and burnt sacrifices at all the hill-shrines there, as
the nations did whom the LORD had displaced before them. By this wicked-
12 ness of theirs they provoked the LORD's anger. They worshipped idols, a
13 thing which the LORD had forbidden them to do. Still the LORD solemnly
charged Israel and Judah by every prophet and seer, saying, 'Give up your
evil ways; keep my commandments and statutes given in the law which I
enjoined on your forefathers and delivered to you through my servants the
14 prophets.' They would not listen, however, but were as stubborn and rebellious as their forefathers had been, who refused to put their trust in the
15 LORD their God; they rejected his statutes and the covenant which he had
made with their forefathers and the solemn warnings which he had given
to them; they followed worthless idols and became worthless themselves;
they imitated the nations round about them, a thing which the LORD had
16 forbidden them to do. Forsaking every commandment of the LORD their
God, they made themselves images of cast metal, two calves, and also a
sacred pole; they prostrated themselves to all the host of heaven and wor-
17 shipped the Baal, and they made their sons and daughters pass through
the fire. They practised augury and divination; they sold themselves to do
what was wrong in the eyes of the LORD and so provoked his anger.

18 Thus it was that the LORD was incensed against Israel and banished them
19 from his presence; only the tribe of Judah was left. Even Judah did not
keep the commandments of the LORD their God but followed the practices
20 adopted by Israel; so the LORD rejected the whole race of Israel and
punished them and gave them over to plunderers and finally flung them
21 out of his sight. When he tore Israel from the house of David, they made
Jeroboam son of Nebat king, who seduced Israel from their allegiance to
22 the LORD and led them into grave sin. The Israelites persisted in all the
23 sins that Jeroboam had committed and did not give them up, until finally

[a] *to the king of Egypt at So: prob. rdg.; Heb. to So king of Egypt.*

the LORD banished the Israelites from his presence, as he had threatened through his servants the prophets, and they were carried into exile from their own land to Assyria; and there they are to this day.

Then the king of Assyria brought people from Babylon, Cuthah, Avva, 24 Hamath, and Sepharvaim, and settled them in the cities of Samaria in place of the Israelites; so they occupied Samaria and lived in its cities. In 25 the early years of their settlement they did not pay homage to the LORD; and the LORD sent lions among them, and the lions preyed upon them. The king was told that the deported peoples whom he had settled in the 26 cities of Samaria did not know the established usage of the god of the country, and that he had sent lions among them which were preying upon them because they did not know this. The king of Assyria, therefore, gave 27 orders that one of the priests deported from Samaria should be sent back to live there and teach the people the usage of the god of the country. So 28 one of the deported priests came and lived at Bethel, and taught them how they should pay their homage to the LORD. But each of the nations made 29 its own god, and they set them up within[a] the hill-shrines which the Samaritans had made, each nation in its own settlements. Succoth-benoth 30 was worshipped by the men of Babylon, Nergal by the men of Cuth, Ashima by the men of Hamath, Nibhaz and Tartak by the Avvites; and the 31 Sepharvites burnt their children as offerings to Adrammelech and Anam-melech, the gods of Sepharvaim. While still paying homage to the LORD, 32 they appointed people from every class to act as priests of the hill-shrines and they resorted to them there. They paid homage to the LORD while at 33 the same time they served their own gods, according to the custom of the nations from which they had been carried into exile.

They keep up these old practices to this day; they do not pay homage to 34 the LORD, for they do not keep his[b] statutes and his[b] judgements, the law and commandment, which he enjoined upon the descendants of Jacob whom he named Israel. When the LORD made a covenant with them, he 35 gave them this commandment: 'You shall not pay homage to other gods or bow down to them or serve them or sacrifice to them, but you shall pay 36 homage to the LORD who brought you up from Egypt with great power and with outstretched arm; to him you shall bow down, to him you shall offer sacrifice. You shall faithfully keep the statutes, the judgements, the law, 37 and the commandments which he wrote for you, and you shall not pay homage to other gods. You shall not forget the covenant which I made 38 with you; you shall not pay homage to other gods. But to the LORD your 39 God you shall pay homage, and he will preserve you from all your enemies.' However, they would not listen but continued their former practices. 40 While these nations paid homage to the LORD they continued to serve their 41 images, and their children and their children's children have maintained the practice of their forefathers to this day.

IN THE THIRD YEAR OF HOSHEA son of Elah king of Israel, Hezekiah **18** 1[c] son of Ahaz king of Judah became king. He was twenty-five years old when 2 he came to the throne, and he reigned in Jerusalem for twenty-nine years;

---

[a] *Or* in niches at.   [b] *Prob. rdg.; Heb.* their.   [c] *Verses 1–3: cp. 2 Chr. 29. 1, 2.*

3 his mother was Abi daughter of Zechariah. He did what was right in the
4 eyes of the LORD, as David his forefather had done. It was he who suppressed the hill-shrines, smashed the sacred pillars, cut down every sacred pole and broke up the bronze serpent that Moses had made; for up to that time the Israelites had been burning sacrifices to it; they called it
5 Nehushtan. He put his trust in the LORD the God of Israel; there was nobody like him among all the kings of Judah who succeeded him or among
6 those who had gone before him. He remained loyal to the LORD and did not fail in his allegiance to him, and he kept the commandments which the
7 LORD had given to Moses. So the LORD was with him and he prospered in all that he undertook; he rebelled against the king of Assyria and was no
8 longer subject to him. He conquered the Philistine country as far as Gaza and its boundaries, alike the watch-tower and the fortified city.

9 In the fourth year of Hezekiah's reign (that was the seventh year of Hoshea son of Elah king of Israel) Shalmaneser king of Assyria made an
10 attack on Samaria, invested it and captured it after a siege of three years; it was in the sixth year of Hezekiah (the ninth year of Hoshea king of Israel)
11 that Samaria was captured. The king of Assyria deported the Israelites to Assyria and settled them in Halah and on the Habor, the river of Gozan,
12 and in the cities of Media, because they did not obey the LORD their God but violated his covenant and every commandment that Moses the servant of the LORD had given them; they would not listen and they would not obey.

13[a]   In the fourteenth year of the reign of Hezekiah, Sennacherib king of
14 Assyria attacked and took all the fortified cities of Judah. Hezekiah king of Judah sent a message to the king of Assyria at Lachish: 'I have done wrong; withdraw from my land, and I will pay any penalty you impose upon me.' So the king of Assyria laid on Hezekiah king of Judah a penalty
15 of three hundred talents of silver and thirty talents of gold; and Hezekiah gave him all the silver found in the house of the LORD and in the treasuries
16 of the royal palace. At that time Hezekiah broke up the doors of the temple of the LORD and the door-frames which he himself had plated, and gave them to the king of Assyria.

17   From Lachish the king of Assyria sent the commander-in-chief, the chief eunuch, and the chief officer[b] with a strong force to King Hezekiah at Jerusalem, and they went up and came to Jerusalem and halted by the conduit of the Upper Pool on the causeway which leads to the Fuller's
18 Field. When they called for the king, Eliakim son of Hilkiah, the comptroller of the household, came out to them, with Shebna the adjutant-general and
19 Joah son of Asaph, the secretary of state. The chief officer said to them, 'Tell Hezekiah that this is the message of the Great King, the king of
20 Assyria: "What ground have you for this confidence of yours? Do you think fine words can take the place of skill and numbers? On whom then
21 do you rely for support in your rebellion against me? On Egypt? Egypt is a splintered cane that will run into a man's hand and pierce it if he leans on it. That is what Pharaoh king of Egypt proves to all who rely on him.

---

a Verses 13–37 : cp. Isa. 36. 1–22; 2 Chr. 32. 1–19.   *b the commander-in-chief,*
the chief eunuch, and the chief officer: *or* Tartan, Rab-saris, and Rab-shakeh.

And if you tell me that you are relying on the LORD your God, is he not 22
the god whose hill-shrines and altars Hezekiah has suppressed, telling
Judah and Jerusalem that they must prostrate themselves before this altar
in Jerusalem?"

'Now, make a bargain with my master the king of Assyria: I will give 23
you two thousand horses if you can find riders for them. Will you reject 24
the authority of even the least of my master's servants and rely on Egypt
for chariots and horsemen? Do you think that I have come to attack this 25
place and destroy it without the consent of the LORD? No; the LORD
himself said to me, "Attack this land and destroy it."'

Eliakim son of Hilkiah, Shebna, and Joah said to the chief officer, 26
'Please speak to us in Aramaic, for we understand it; do not speak Hebrew
to us within earshot of the people on the city wall.' The chief officer 27
answered, 'Is it to your master and to you that my master has sent me to
say this? Is it not to the people sitting on the wall who, like you, will have
to eat their own dung and drink their own urine?' Then he stood and 28
shouted in Hebrew, 'Hear the message of the Great King, the king of
Assyria. These are the king's words: "Do not be taken in by Hezekiah. He 29
cannot save you from me. Do not let him persuade you to rely on the LORD, 30
and tell you that the LORD will save you and that this city will never be
surrendered to the king of Assyria." Do not listen to Hezekiah; these are 31
the words of the king of Assyria: "Make peace with me. Come out to me,
and then you shall each eat the fruit of his own vine and his own fig-tree,
and drink the water of his own cistern, until I come and take you to a land 32
like your own, a land of grain and new wine, of corn and vineyards, of olives,
fine oil, and honey—life for you all, instead of death. Do not listen to
Hezekiah; he will only mislead you by telling you that the LORD will save
you. Did the god of any of these nations save his land from the king of 33
Assyria? Where are the gods of Hamath and Arpad? Where are the gods of 34
Sepharvaim, Hena, and Ivvah? Where are the gods of Samaria? Did they
save Samaria from me? Among all the gods of the nations is there one who 35
saved his land from me? And how is the LORD to save Jerusalem?"'

The people were silent and answered not a word, for the king had given 36
orders that no one was to answer him. Eliakim son of Hilkiah, comptroller 37
of the household, Shebna the adjutant-general, and Joah son of Asaph,
secretary of state, came to Hezekiah with their clothes rent and reported
what the chief officer had said.

When King Hezekiah heard their report, he rent his clothes and wrapped **19** 1 *a*
himself in sackcloth, and went into the house of the LORD. He sent Eliakim 2
comptroller of the household, Shebna the adjutant-general, and the senior
priests, all covered in sackcloth, to the prophet Isaiah son of Amoz, to 3
give him this message from the king: 'This day is a day of trouble for us, a
day of reproof and contempt. We are like a woman who has no strength to
bear the child that is coming to the birth. It may be that the LORD your 4
God heard all the words of the chief officer whom his master the king of
Assyria sent to taunt the living God, and will confute what he, the LORD
your God, heard. Offer a prayer for those who still survive.' King Hezekiah's 5

a Verses 1–37 : cp. Isa. 37. 1–38; 2 Chr. 32. 20–22.

433

6 servants came to Isaiah, and he told them to say this to their master: 'This is the word of the LORD: "Do not be alarmed at what you heard when the
7 lackeys of the king of Assyria blasphemed me. I will put a spirit in him and he shall hear a rumour and withdraw to his own country; and there I will make him fall by the sword."'
8 So the chief officer withdrew. He heard that the king of Assyria had
9 left Lachish, and he found him attacking Libnah. But when the king learnt that Tirhakah king of Cush was on the way to make war on him, he sent
10 messengers again to Hezekiah king of Judah, to say to him, 'How can you be deluded by your god on whom you rely when he promises that Jerusalem
11 shall not fall into the hands of the king of Assyria? Surely you have heard what the kings of Assyria have done to all countries, exterminating their
12 people; can you then hope to escape? Did their gods save the nations which my forefathers destroyed, Gozan, Harran, Rezeph, and the people of Beth-
13 eden living in Telassar? Where are the kings of Hamath, of Arpad, and of Lahir, Sepharvaim, Hena, and Ivvah?'
14 Hezekiah took the letter from the messengers and read it; then he went
15 up into the house of the LORD, spread it out before the LORD and offered this prayer: 'O LORD God of Israel, enthroned on the cherubim, thou alone art God of all the kingdoms of the earth; thou hast made heaven and
16 earth. Turn thy ear to me, O LORD, and listen; open thine eyes, O LORD, and see; hear the message that Sennacherib has sent to taunt the living God.
17 It is true, O LORD, that the kings of Assyria have ravaged the nations and
18 their lands, that they have consigned their gods to the fire and destroyed them; for they were no gods but the work of men's hands, mere wood
19 and stone. But now, O LORD our God, save us from his power, so that all the kingdoms of the earth may know that thou, O LORD, alone art God.'
20 Isaiah son of Amoz sent to Hezekiah and said, 'This is the word of the LORD the God of Israel: I have heard your prayer to me concerning
21 Sennacherib king of Assyria. This is the word which the LORD has spoken concerning him:

> The virgin daughter of Zion disdains you,
>   she laughs you to scorn;
> the daughter of Jerusalem tosses her head
>   as you retreat.

22
> Whom have you taunted and blasphemed?
>   Against whom have you clamoured,
> casting haughty glances at the Holy One of Israel?

23
> You have sent your messengers to taunt the Lord,
>   and said:
> I have mounted my chariot and done mighty deeds:
> I have gone high up in the mountains,
>   into the recesses of Lebanon.
> I have cut down its tallest cedars,
>   the best of its pines,
> I have reached its farthest corners,
>   forest and meadow.

434

I have dug wells
and drunk the waters of a foreign land,
and with the soles of my feet I have dried up
all the streams of Egypt.   24

Have you not heard long ago?   25
I did it all.
In days gone by I planned it
and now I have brought it about,
making fortified cities tumble down
into heaps of rubble.*a*

Their citizens, shorn of strength,   26
disheartened and ashamed,
were but as plants in the field, as green herbs,
as grass on the roof-tops blasted before the east wind. *b*
I know your rising up*c* and your sitting down,   27
your going out and your coming in.
The frenzy of your rage against me*d* and your arrogance   28
have come to my ears.
I will put a ring in your nose
and a hook in your lips,
and I will take you back by the road
on which you have come.

This shall be the sign for you: this year you shall eat shed grain and in the   29
second year what is self-sown; but in the third year sow and reap, plant
vineyards and eat their fruit. The survivors left in Judah shall strike fresh   30
root under ground and yield fruit above ground, for a remnant shall come   31
out of Jerusalem and survivors from Mount Zion. The zeal of the Lord
will perform this.

'Therefore, this is the word of the Lord concerning the king of Assyria: 32

He shall not enter this city
nor shoot an arrow there,
he shall not advance against it with shield
nor cast up a siege-ramp against it.
By the way on which he came he shall go back;   33
this city he shall not enter.
This is the very word of the Lord.
I will shield this city to deliver it,   34
for my own sake and for the sake of my servant David.'

That night the angel of the Lord went out and struck down a hundred   35
and eighty-five thousand men in the Assyrian camp; when morning dawned,
they all lay dead. So Sennacherib king of Assyria broke camp, went back   36
to Nineveh and stayed there. One day, while he was worshipping in the   37
temple of his god Nisroch, Adrammelech and Sharezer his sons murdered

---

a heaps of rubble: *prob. rdg., cp. Isa. 37. 26; Heb. obscure.*   *b* the east wind: *prob.*
rdg., cp. Isa. 37. 27; Heb. it is mature.   *c* your rising up: *prob. rdg., cp. Isa. 37. 28;*
Heb. om.   *d Prob. rdg., cp. Isa. 37. 29; Heb. repeats* the frenzy of your rage against me.

him and escaped to the land of Ararat. He was succeeded by his son Esarhaddon.

20 1^a At this time Hezekiah fell dangerously ill and the prophet Isaiah son of Amoz came to him and said, 'This is the word of the LORD: Give your last instructions to your household, for you are a dying man and will not
2 recover.' Hezekiah turned his face to the wall and offered this prayer to
3 the LORD: 'O LORD, remember how I have lived before thee, faithful and loyal in thy service, always doing what was good in thine eyes.' And he
4 wept bitterly. But before Isaiah had left the citadel, the word of the LORD
5 came to him: 'Go back and say to Hezekiah, the prince of my people: "This is the word of the LORD the God of your father David: I have heard your prayer and seen your tears; I will heal you and on the third day you
6 shall go up to the house of the LORD. I will add fifteen years to your life and deliver you and this city from the king of Assyria, and I will protect
7 this city for my own sake and for my servant David's sake." ' Then Isaiah told them to apply a fig-plaster; so they made one and applied it to the
8 boil, and he recovered. Then Hezekiah asked Isaiah what sign the LORD would give him that he would be cured and would go up into the house of
9 the LORD on the third day. And Isaiah said, 'This shall be your sign from the LORD that he will do what he has promised; shall the shadow go for-
10 ward ten steps or back ten steps?' Hezekiah answered, 'It is an easy thing for the shadow to move forward ten steps; rather let it go back ten steps.'
11 Isaiah the prophet called to the LORD, and he made the shadow go back ten steps where it had advanced down the stairway of Ahaz.

12^b At this time Merodach-baladan son of Baladan king of Babylon sent envoys with a gift to Hezekiah; for he had heard that he had been ill.
13 Hezekiah welcomed them and showed them all his treasury, silver and gold, spices and fragrant oil, his armoury and everything to be found among his treasures; there was nothing in his house and in all his realm
14 that Hezekiah did not show them. Then the prophet Isaiah came to King Hezekiah and asked him, 'What did these men say and where have they come from?' 'They have come from a far-off country,' Hezekiah answered,
15 'from Babylon.' Then Isaiah asked, 'What did they see in your house?' 'They saw everything,' Hezekiah replied; 'there was nothing among my
16 treasures that I did not show them.' Then Isaiah said to Hezekiah, 'Hear
17 the word of the LORD: The time is coming, says the LORD, when everything in your house, and all that your forefathers have amassed till the present day,
18 will be carried away to Babylon; not a thing shall be left. And some of the sons who will be born to you, sons of your own begetting, shall be taken and
19 shall be made eunuchs in the palace of the king of Babylon.' Hezekiah answered, 'The word of the LORD which you have spoken is good'; thinking to himself that peace and security would last out his lifetime.

20 The other events of Hezekiah's reign, his exploits, and how he made the pool and the conduit and brought water into the city, are recorded in
21 the annals of the kings of Judah. So Hezekiah rested with his forefathers and was succeeded by his son Manasseh.

a Verses 1–11: cp. Isa. 38. 1–8, 21, 22.   *b Verses 12–19: cp. Isa. 39. 1–8.*

The last kings of Judah

MANASSEH WAS TWELVE YEARS OLD when he came to the throne, 21 1ᵃ
and he reigned in Jerusalem for fifty-five years; his mother was
Hephzi-bah. He did what was wrong in the eyes of the LORD, in following 2
the abominable practices of the nations which the LORD had dispossessed
in favour of the Israelites. He rebuilt the hill-shrines which his father 3
Hezekiah had destroyed, he erected altars to the Baal and made a sacred
pole as Ahab king of Israel had done, and prostrated himself before all the
host of heaven and worshipped them. He built altars in the house of the 4
LORD, that house of which the LORD had said, 'Jerusalem shall receive my
Name.' He built altars for all the host of heaven in the two courts of the 5
house of the LORD; he made his son pass through the fire, he practised sooth- 6
saying and divination, and dealt with ghosts and spirits. He did much
wrong in the eyes of the LORD and provoked his anger; and the image that 7
he had made of the goddess Asherah he put in the house, the place of which
the LORD had said to David and Solomon his son, 'This house and Jerusalem, which I chose out of all the tribes of Israel, shall receive my Name
for all time. I will not again make Israel outcasts from the land which I gave 8
to their forefathers, if only they will be careful to observe all my commands
and all the law that my servant Moses gave them.' But they did not obey, 9
and Manasseh misled them into wickedness far worse than that of the
nations which the LORD had exterminated in favour of the Israelites.

Then the LORD spoke through his servants the prophets: 'Because 10 11
Manasseh king of Judah has done these abominable things, outdoing the
Amorites before him in wickedness, and because he has led Judah into sin
with his idols, this is the word of the LORD the God of Israel: I will bring 12
disaster on Jerusalem and Judah, disaster which will ring in the ears of all
who hear of it. I will mark down every stone of Jerusalem with the plumb- 13
line of Samaria and the plummet of the house of Ahab; I will wipe away
Jerusalem as when a man wipes his plate and turns it upside down, and I 14
will cast off what is left of my people, my own possession, and hand them
over to their enemies. They shall be plundered and fall a prey to all
their enemies; for they have done what is wrong in my eyes and have 15
provoked my anger from the day their forefathers left Egypt up to the
present day. And this Manasseh shed so much innocent blood that he 16
filled Jerusalem full to the brim, not to mention the sin into which he led
Judah by doing what is wrong in my eyes.' The other events and acts of 17
Manasseh's reign, and the sin that he committed, are recorded in the
annals of the kings of Judah. So Manasseh rested with his forefathers and 18
was buried in the garden-tomb of his family, in the garden of Uzza; he
was succeeded by his son Amon.

Amon was twenty-two years old when he came to the throne, and he 19ᵇ
reigned in Jerusalem for two years; his mother was Meshullemeth daughter
of Haruz of Jotbah. He did what was wrong in the eyes of the LORD as his 20
father Manasseh had done. He followed in his father's footsteps and served 21
the idols that his father had served and prostrated himself before them. He 22

ᵃ *Verses 1–9: cp. 2 Chr. 33. 1–9.*   ᵇ *Verses 19–24: cp. 2 Chr. 33. 21–25.*

forsook the LORD the God of his fathers and did not conform to his ways.
23 King Amon's courtiers conspired against him and murdered him in his
24 house; but the people of the land killed all the conspirators and made his
25 son Josiah king in his place. The other events of Amon's reign are recorded
26 in the annals of the kings of Judah. He was buried in his grave in the garden
of Uzza; he was succeeded by his son Josiah.

22 1[a]   Josiah was eight years old when he came to the throne, and he reigned
in Jerusalem for thirty-one years; his mother was Jedidah daughter of
2 Adaiah of Bozkath. He did what was right in the eyes of the LORD; he
followed closely in the footsteps of his forefather David, swerving neither
right nor left.

3[b]   In the eighteenth year of his reign Josiah sent Shaphan son of Azaliah,
4 son of Meshullam, the adjutant-general, to the house of the LORD. 'Go to
the high priest Hilkiah,' he said, 'and tell him to melt down the silver that
has been brought into the house of the LORD, which those on duty at the
5 entrance have received from the people, and to hand it over to the foremen
in the house of the LORD, to pay the workmen who are carrying out repairs
6 in it, the carpenters, builders, and masons, and to purchase timber and
7 hewn stones for its repair. They are not to be asked to account for the
8 money that has been given them; they are acting on trust.' The high priest
Hilkiah told Shaphan the adjutant-general that he had discovered the book
of the law in the house of the LORD, and he gave it to him, and Shaphan
9 read it. Then Shaphan came to report to the king and told him that his
servants had melted down the silver in the house of the LORD and handed
10 it over to the foremen there. Then Shaphan the adjutant-general told the
king that the high priest Hilkiah had given him a book, and he read it out
11 in the king's presence. When the king heard what was in the book of the
12 law, he rent his clothes, and ordered the priest Hilkiah, Ahikam son of
Shaphan, Akbor son of Micaiah, Shaphan the adjutant-general, and
13 Asaiah the king's attendant, to go and seek guidance of the LORD for himself, for the people, and for all Judah, about what was written in this book
that had been discovered. 'Great is the wrath of the LORD', he said, 'that
has been kindled against us, because our forefathers did not obey the
commands in this book and do all that is laid upon us.'

14   So Hilkiah the priest, Ahikam, Akbor, Shaphan, and Asaiah went to
Huldah the prophetess, wife of Shallum son of Tikvah, son of Harhas, the
keeper of the wardrobe, and consulted her at her home in the second
15 quarter of Jerusalem. 'This is the word of the LORD the God of Israel,' she
16 answered: 'Say to the man who sent you to me, "This is the word of the
LORD: I am bringing disaster on this place and its inhabitants as foretold
17 in the book which the king of Judah has read, because they have forsaken
me and burnt sacrifices to other gods, provoking my anger with all the idols
they have made with their own hands; therefore, my wrath is kindled
18 against this place and will not be quenched." This is what you shall say to
the king of Judah who sent you to seek guidance of the LORD: "This is the
19 word of the LORD the God of Israel: You have listened to my words and
shown a willing heart, you humbled yourself before the LORD when you

[a] Verses 1, 2: cp. 2 Chr. 34. 1, 2.   [b] Verses 3–20: cp. 2 Chr. 34. 8–28.

heard me say that this place and its inhabitants would become objects of
loathing and scorn, you rent your clothes and wept before me. Because of
all this, I for my part have heard you. This is the very word of the LORD.
Therefore, I will gather you to your forefathers, and you will be gathered   20
to your grave in peace; you will not live to see all the disaster which I am
bringing upon this place."' So they brought back word to the king.

    Then the king sent and called all the elders of Judah and Jerusalem   **23** 1[a]
together, and went up to the house of the LORD; he took with him the men   2
of Judah and the inhabitants of Jerusalem, the priests and the prophets,
the whole population, high and low. There he read out to them all the book
of the covenant discovered in the house of the LORD; and then, standing   3
on the dais,[b] the king made a covenant before the LORD to obey him and
keep his commandments, his testimonies, and his statutes, with all his
heart and soul, and so fulfil the terms of the covenant written in this book.
And all the people pledged themselves to the covenant.

    Next, the king ordered the high priest Hilkiah, the deputy high priest,[c]   4
and those on duty at the entrance, to remove from the house of the LORD
all the objects made for Baal and Asherah and all the host of heaven; he
burnt these outside Jerusalem, in the open country by the Kidron, and
carried the ashes to Bethel. He suppressed the heathen priests whom the   5
kings of Judah had appointed to burn sacrifices at the hill-shrines in the
cities of Judah and in the neighbourhood of Jerusalem, as well as those who
burnt sacrifices to Baal, to the sun and moon and planets and all the host of
heaven. He took the symbol of Asherah[d] from the house of the LORD to   6
the gorge of the Kidron outside Jerusalem, burnt it there and pounded it
to dust, which was then scattered over the common burial-ground. He   7
also pulled down the houses of the male prostitutes attached to the house
of the LORD, where the women wove vestments in honour of Asherah.

    He brought in all the priests from the cities of Judah and desecrated the   8
hill-shrines where they had burnt sacrifices, from Geba to Beersheba, and
dismantled the hill-shrines of the demons[e] in front of the gate of Joshua,
the governor of the city, to the left of the city gate. These priests, however,   9
never came up to the altar of the LORD in Jerusalem but used to eat unleavened bread with the priests of their clan. He desecrated Topheth in the   10
Valley of Ben-hinnom, so that no one might make his son or daughter pass
through the fire in honour of Molech.[f] He destroyed the horses that the   11
kings of Judah had set up in honour of the sun at the entrance to the house
of the LORD, beside the room of Nathan-melek the eunuch in the colonnade, and he burnt the chariots of the sun. He pulled down the altars made   12
by the kings of Judah on the roof by the upper chamber of Ahaz and the
altars made by Manasseh in the two courts of the house of the LORD; he
pounded them to dust and threw it into the gorge of the Kidron. Also, on   13
the east of Jerusalem, to the south of the Mount of Olives, the king desecrated the hill-shrines which Solomon the king of Israel had built for
Ashtoreth the loathsome goddess of the Sidonians, and for Kemosh the

[a] *Verses 1–3: cp. 2 Chr. 34. 29–32.*   [b] *Or by the pillar.*   [c] *Prob. rdg.; Heb.* priests.
[d] symbol of Asherah: *or* sacred pole.   [e] *Or* satyrs.   [f] *in honour of Molech: or*
for an offering.

439

loathsome god of Moab, and for Milcom the abominable god of the Ammon-
14 ites; he broke down the sacred pillars and cut down the sacred poles and
filled the places where they had stood with human bones.

15 At Bethel he dismantled the altar by*a* the hill-shrine made by Jeroboam
son of Nebat who led Israel into sin, together with the hill-shrine itself;
he broke its stones in pieces, crushed them to dust and burnt the sacred
16 pole. When Josiah set eyes on the graves which were there on the hill, he
sent and took the bones from them and burnt them on the altar to desecrate
it, thus fulfilling the word of the LORD announced by the man of God
when Jeroboam stood by the altar at the feast. But when he caught sight
17 of the grave of the man of God who had foretold these things, he asked,
'What is that monument I see there?' The people of the city answered,
'The grave of the man of God who came from Judah and foretold all that
18 you have done to the altar at Bethel.' 'Leave it alone,' he said; 'let no one
disturb his bones.' So they spared his bones and also those of the prophet
19 who came from Samaria. Further, Josiah suppressed all the hill-shrines
in the cities of Samaria, which the kings of Israel had set up and thereby
provoked the LORD's anger, and he did to them what he had done at
20 Bethel. He slaughtered on the altars all the priests of the hill-shrines who
were there, and he burnt human bones upon them. Then he went back to
Jerusalem.

21 The king ordered all the people to keep the Passover to the LORD their
22 God, as this book of the covenant prescribed; no such Passover had been
kept either when the judges were ruling Israel or during the times of the
23 kings of Israel and Judah. But in the eighteenth year of Josiah's reign this
24 Passover was kept to the LORD in Jerusalem. Further, Josiah got rid of all
who called up ghosts and spirits, of all household gods and idols and all
the loathsome objects seen in the land of Judah and in Jerusalem, so that he
might fulfil the requirements of the law written in the book which the
25 priest Hilkiah had discovered in the house of the LORD. No king before
him had turned to the LORD as he did, with all his heart and soul and
strength, following the whole law of Moses; nor did any king like him
appear again.

26 Yet the LORD did not abate his fierce anger; it still burned against Judah
27 because of all the provocation which Manasseh had given him. 'Judah also
I will banish from my presence', he declared, 'as I banished Israel; and I
will cast off this city of Jerusalem which once I chose, and the house where
I promised that my Name should be.'

28 The other events and acts of Josiah's reign are recorded in the annals of
29 the kings of Judah. It was in his reign that Pharaoh Necho king of Egypt
set out for the river Euphrates to help the king of Assyria. King Josiah
went to meet him; and when they met at Megiddo, Pharaoh Necho slew
30*b* him. His attendants conveyed his body in a chariot from Megiddo to
Jerusalem and buried him in his own burial place. Then the people of the
land took Josiah's son Jehoahaz and anointed him king in place of his
father.

31 Jehoahaz was twenty-three years old when he came to the throne, and

a Prob. rdg.; Heb. om.   *b Verses 30–34: cp. 2 Chr. 36. 1–4.*

he reigned in Jerusalem for three months; his mother was Hamutal daughter of Jeremiah of Libnah. He did what was wrong in the eyes of the 32 LORD, as his forefathers had done. Pharaoh Necho removed him from the 33 throne*a* in Jerusalem, and imposed on the land a fine of a hundred talents of silver and one talent of gold. Pharaoh Necho made Josiah's son Eliakim 34 king in place of his father and changed his name to Jehoiakim. He took Jehoahaz and brought him to Egypt, where he died. Jehoiakim paid the 35 silver and gold to Pharaoh, taxing the country to meet Pharaoh's demands; he exacted it from the people, from every man according to his assessment, so that he could pay Pharaoh Necho.

Jehoiakim was twenty-five years old when he came to the throne, and 36 he reigned in Jerusalem for eleven years; his mother was Zebidah daughter of Pedaiah of Rumah. He did what was wrong in the eyes of the LORD, as 37 his forefathers had done. During his reign Nebuchadnezzar king of **24** Babylon took the field, and Jehoiakim became his vassal; but three years later he broke with him and revolted. The LORD launched against him 2 raiding-parties of Chaldaeans, Aramaeans, Moabites, and Ammonites, letting them range through Judah and ravage it, as the LORD had foretold through his servants the prophets. All this happened to Judah in fulfilment 3 of the LORD's purpose to banish them from his presence, because of all the sin that Manasseh had committed and because of the innocent blood 4 that he had shed; he had drenched Jerusalem with innocent blood, and the LORD would not forgive him. The other events and acts of Jehoiakim's 5 reign are recorded in the annals of the kings of Judah. He rested with his 6 forefathers, and was succeeded by his son Jehoiachin. The king of Egypt 7 did not leave his own land again, because the king of Babylon had stripped him of all his possessions, from the Torrent of Egypt to the river Euphrates.

Downfall of the southern kingdom

JEHOIACHIN WAS EIGHTEEN YEARS OLD when he came to the throne, 8*b* and he reigned in Jerusalem for three months; his mother was Nehushta daughter of Elnathan of Jerusalem. He did what was wrong in the eyes of 9 the LORD, as his father had done. At that time the troops of Nebuchad- 10 nezzar king of Babylon advanced on Jerusalem and besieged the city. Nebuchadnezzar arrived while his troops were besieging it, and Jehoiachin 11 12 king of Judah, his mother, his courtiers, his officers, and his eunuchs, all surrendered to the king of Babylon. The king of Babylon, now in the eighth year of his reign, took him prisoner; and, as the LORD had foretold, 13 he carried off all the treasures of the house of the LORD and of the royal palace and broke up all the vessels of gold which Solomon king of Israel had made for the temple of the LORD. He carried the people of Jerusalem 14 into exile, the officers and the fighting men, ten thousand in number, together with all the craftsmen and smiths; only the weakest class of people were left. He deported Jehoiachin to Babylon; he also took into exile from 15

a removed . . . throne: *prob. rdg., cp. 2 Chr. 36. 3; Heb.* bound him at Riblah in the land of Hamath when he was king . . .   *b* *Verses 8–17 : cp. 2 Chr. 36. 9, 10.*

Jerusalem to Babylon the king's mother and his wives, his eunuchs and
16 the foremost men of the land. He also deported to Babylon all the men of
substance, seven thousand in number, and a thousand craftsmen and
17 smiths, all of them able-bodied men and skilled armourers. He made
Mattaniah, uncle of Jehoiachin, king in his place and changed his name to
Zedekiah.

18[a] Zedekiah was twenty-one years old when he came to the throne, and he
reigned in Jerusalem for eleven years; his mother was Hamutal daughter
19 of Jeremiah of Libnah. He did what was wrong in the eyes of the LORD, as
20 Jehoiakim had done. Jerusalem and Judah so angered the LORD that in the
end he banished them from his sight; and Zedekiah rebelled against the
king of Babylon.

25 1[b] In the ninth year of his reign, in the tenth month, on the tenth day of the
month, Nebuchadnezzar king of Babylon advanced with all his army
against Jerusalem, invested it and erected watch-towers against it on every
2 3 side; the siege lasted till the eleventh year of King Zedekiah. In the fourth
month of that year,[c] on the ninth day of the month, when famine was
4 severe in the city and there was no food for the common people, the city
was thrown open. When Zedekiah king of Judah saw this,[d] he and all his
armed escort left the city and fled by night through the gate called Between
the Two Walls, near the king's garden. They escaped towards the Arabah,
5 although the Chaldaeans were surrounding the city. But the Chaldaean
army pursued the king and overtook him in the lowlands of Jericho; and
6 all his company was dispersed. The king was seized and brought before the
7 king of Babylon at Riblah, where he pleaded his case before him. Zedekiah's
sons were slain before his eyes; then his eyes were put out, and he was
brought to Babylon in fetters of bronze.

8 In the fifth month, on the seventh day of the month, in the nineteenth
year of Nebuchadnezzar king of Babylon, Nebuzaradan, captain of the
9 king's bodyguard, came to Jerusalem and set fire to the house of the LORD
and the royal palace; all the houses in the city, including the mansion of
10 Gedaliah,[e] were burnt down. The Chaldaean forces with the captain of
11 the guard pulled down the walls all round Jerusalem. Nebuzaradan captain
of the guard deported the rest of the people left in the city, those who had
12 deserted to the king of Babylon and any remaining artisans.[f] He left only
the weakest class of people to be vine-dressers and labourers.

13 The Chaldaeans broke up the pillars of bronze in the house of the LORD,
14 the trolleys, and the Sea of bronze, and took the metal to Babylon. They
took also the pots, shovels, snuffers, saucers, and all the vessels of bronze
15 used in the service of the temple. The captain of the guard took away the
precious metal, whether gold or silver, of which the firepans and the
16 tossing-bowls were made. The bronze of the two pillars, the one Sea, and
the trolleys, which Solomon had made for the house of the LORD, was

---

[a] 24. 18—25. 21: cp. Jer. 52. 1–27.   [b] Verses 1–12: cp. Jer. 39. 1–10; verses
1–17: cp. 2 Chr. 36. 17–20.   [c] In . . . year: prob. rdg., cp. Jer. 52. 6; Heb. om.
[d] When . . . this: prob. rdg., cp. Jer. 39. 4; Heb. om.   [e] Gedaliah: prob. rdg.;
Heb. a great man.   [f] any remaining artisans: prob. rdg., cp. Jer. 52. 15; Heb.
the remaining crowd.

beyond weighing. The one pillar was eighteen cubits high and its capital 17
was bronze; the capital was three cubits high, and a decoration of network
and pomegranates ran all round it, wholly of bronze. The other pillar,
with its network, was exactly like it.

The captain of the guard took Seraiah the chief priest and Zephaniah 18
the deputy chief priest and the three on duty at the entrance; he took also 19
from the city a eunuch who was in charge of the fighting men, five of those
with right of access to the king who were still in the city, the adjutant-
general*a* whose duty was to muster the people for war, and sixty men of
the people who were still there. These Nebuzaradan captain of the guard 20
brought to the king of Babylon at Riblah. There, in the land of Hamath, 21
the king of Babylon had them flogged and put to death. So Judah went into
exile from their own land.

Nebuchadnezzar king of Babylon appointed Gedaliah son of Ahikam, 22
son of Shaphan, governor over the few people whom he had left in Judah.
When the captains of the armed bands and their men heard that the king 23
of Babylon had appointed Gedaliah governor, they all came to him at
Mizpah: Ishmael son of Nethaniah, Johanan son of Kareah, Seraiah son
of Tanhumeth of Netophah, and Jaazaniah of Beth-maacah. Then Gedaliah 24
gave them and their men this assurance: 'Have no fear of the Chaldaean
officers. Settle down in the land and serve the king of Babylon; and then
all will be well with you.' But in the seventh month Ishmael son of Nethan- 25
iah, son of Elishama, who was a member of the royal house, came with ten
men and murdered Gedaliah and the Jews and Chaldaeans who were with
him at Mizpah. Thereupon all the people, high and low, and the captains 26
of the armed bands, fled to Egypt for fear of the Chaldaeans.

In the thirty-seventh year of the exile of Jehoiachin king of Judah, on 27*b*
the twenty-seventh day of the twelfth month, Evil-merodach*c* king of
Babylon in the year of his accession showed favour to Jehoiachin king
of Judah. He brought him out of prison, treated him kindly and gave him 28
a seat at table above the kings with him in Babylon. So Jehoiachin dis- 29
carded his prison clothes and lived as a pensioner of the king for the rest
of his life. For his maintenance, a regular daily allowance was given him 30
by the king as long as he lived.

a *Prob. rdg.; Heb. adds* commander-in-chief.   *b* *Verses 27–30: cp. Jer. 52. 31–34.*
c *Or* Ewil-marduk.

THE FIRST BOOK OF THE
CHRONICLES

Genealogies from Adam to Saul

1 2^a3 ADAM, SETH, ENOSH, Kenan, Mahalalel, Jared, Enoch, Methu-
4 selah, Lamech, Noah.
The sons of Noah: Shem, Ham and Japheth.
5^b The sons of Japheth: Gomer, Magog, Madai, Javan,^c Tubal, Meshech
6 7 and Tiras. The sons of Gomer: Ashkenaz, Diphath and Togarmah. The
sons of Javan: Elishah, Tarshish, Kittim^d and Rodanim.
8^e 9 The sons of Ham: Cush, Mizraim,^f Put and Canaan. The sons of Cush:
Seba, Havilah, Sabta, Raama and Sabtecha. The sons of Raama: Sheba
10 and Dedan. Cush was the father of Nimrod, who began to show himself a
11^g man of might on earth. From Mizraim sprang the Lydians, Anamites,
12 Lehabites, Naphtuhites, Pathrusites, Casluhites, and the Caphtorites,
from whom the Philistines were descended.
13 14 Canaan was the father of Sidon, who was his eldest son, and Heth,^h the
15 Jebusites, the Amorites, the Girgashites, the Hivites, the Arkites, the
16 Sinites, the Arvadites, the Zemarites, and the Hamathites.
17ⁱ The sons of Shem: Elam, Asshur, Arphaxad, Lud^j and Aram. The sons
18 of Aram: Uz, Hul, Gether and Mash. Arphaxad was the father of Shelah,
19 and Shelah the father of Eber. Eber had two sons: one was named Peleg,^k
because in his time the earth was divided, and his brother's name was
20 Joktan. Joktan was the father of Almodad, Sheleph, Hazarmoth, Jerah,
21 22 23 Hadoram, Uzal, Diklah, Ebal,^l Abimael, Sheba, Ophir, Havilah and
Jobab. All these were sons of Joktan.
24^m 25 26 The line of ⁿ Shem: Arphaxad, Shelah, Eber, Peleg, Reu, Serug, Nahor,
27 28 Terah, Abram, also known as Abraham, whose sons were Isaac and
Ishmael.
29° The sons of^p Ishmael in the order of their birth: Nebaioth the eldest,
30 then Kedar, Adbeel, Mibsam, Mishma, Dumah, Massa, Hadad, Teman,
31 Jetur, Naphish and Kedemah. These were Ishmael's sons.
32^q The sons of Keturah, Abraham's concubine: she bore him Zimran,
Jokshan, Medan, Midian, Ishbak and Shuah. The sons of Jokshan: Sheba
33 and Dedan. The sons of Midian: Ephah, Epher, Enoch, Abida and Eldaah.
All these were descendants of Keturah.

Abraham was the father of Isaac, and Isaac's sons were Esau and Israel. 34
The sons of Esau: Eliphaz, Reuel, Jeush, Jalam and Korah. The sons of 35ª 36
Eliphaz: Teman, Omar, Zephi, Gatam, Kenaz, Timna and Amalek. The 37
sons of Reuel: Nahath, Zerah, Shammah and Mizzah.

The sons of Seir: Lotan, Shobal, Zibeon, Anah, Dishon, Ezer and 38ᵇ
Dishan. The sons of Lotan: Hori and Homam; and Lotan had a sister 39
named Timna. The sons of Shobal: Alvan, Manahath, Ebal, Shephi and 40
Onam. The sons of Zibeon: Aiah and Anah. The sonᶜ of Anah: Dishon. 41
The sons of Dishon: Amram, Eshban, Ithran and Cheran. The sons of 42
Ezer: Bilhan, Zavan and Akan. The sons of Dishan: Uz and Aran.

These are the kings who ruled over Edom before there were kings in 43ᵈ
Israel: Bela son of Beor, whose city was named Dinhabah. When he died, 44
he was succeeded by Jobab son of Zerah of Bozrah. When Jobab died, he 45
was succeeded by Husham of Teman. When Husham died, he was suc- 46
ceeded by Hadad son of Bedad, who defeated Midian in Moabite country.
His city was named Avith. When Hadad died, he was succeeded by Samlah 47
of Masrekah. When Samlah died, he was succeeded by Saul of Rehoboth 48
on the River. When Saul died, he was succeeded by Baal-hanan son of 49
Akbor. When Baal-hanan died, he was succeeded by Hadad. His city was 50
named Pai; his wife's name was Mehetabel daughter of Matred a woman of
Me-zahab.ᵉ

After Hadad died the chiefs in Edom were: chief Timna, chief Aliah, 51
chief Jetheth, chief Oholibamah, chief Elah, chief Pinon, chief Kenaz, chief 52 53
Teman, chief Mibzar, chief Magdiel and chief Iram. These were the chiefs 54
of Edom.

These were the sons of Israel: Reuben, Simeon, Levi, Judah, Issachar, **2**
Zebulun, Dan, Joseph, Benjamin, Naphtali, Gad and Asher. 2

The sons of Judah: Er, Onan and Shelah; the mother of these three was 3
a Canaanite woman, Bathshua.ᶠ Er, Judah's eldest son, displeased the
LORD and the LORD slew him. Then Tamar, Judah's daughter-in-law, 4
bore him Perez and Zerah, making in all five sons of Judah. The sons of 5
Perez: Hezron and Hamul. The sons of Zerah: Zimri, Ethan, Heman, 6
Calcol and Darda, five in all. The son of Zimri: Carmi.ᵍ The son of Carmi: 7
Achar, who troubled Israel by his violation of the sacred ban. The son of 8
Ethan: Azariah. The sons of Hezron: Jerahmeel, Ram and Caleb. Ram 9 10
was the father of Amminadab, Amminadab father of Nahshon prince of
Judah. Nahshon was the father of Salma, Salma father of Boaz, Boaz 11 12
father of Obed, Obed father of Jesse. The eldest son of Jesse was Eliab, 13
the second Abinadab, the third Shimea, the fourth Nethaneel, the fifth 14
Raddai, the sixth Ozem, the seventh David; their sisters were Zeruiah 15 16
and Abigail. The sons of Zeruiah: Abishai, Joab and Asahel, three in all.
Abigail was the mother of Amasa; his father was Jether the Ishmaelite. 17

Caleb son of Hezron had Jerioth by Azubah his wife;ʰ these were her 18

ᵃ *Verses 35–37: cp. Gen. 36. 4, 5, 9–13.*   ᵇ *Verses 38–42: cp. Gen. 36. 20–28.*
ᶜ *Prob. rdg.; Heb.* sons; *the same correction is made in several other places in chs. 1–9.*
ᵈ *Verses 43–54: cp. Gen. 36. 31–43.*   ᵉ *Or* daughter of Mezahab.   ᶠ Bathshua: *or*
daughter of Shua.   ᵍ The son . . . Carmi: *prob. rdg. (cp. Josh. 7. 1, 18); Heb. om.*
ʰ his wife: *prob. rdg.; Heb.* a woman and.

445

19 sons: Jesher, Shobab and Ardon. When Azubah died, Caleb married
20 Ephrath, who bore him Hur. Hur was the father of Uri, and Uri father of
21 Bezalel. Later, Hezron, then sixty years of age, had intercourse with the
daughter of Machir father of Gilead, having married her, and she bore
22 Segub. Segub was the father of Jair, who had twenty-three cities in Gilead.
23 Geshur and Aram took from them Havvoth-jair, and Kenath and its
dependent villages, a total of sixty towns. All these were descendants of
24 Machir father of Gilead. After the death of Hezron, Caleb had intercourse
with Ephrathah and she bore him Ashhur the founder of Tekoa.

25 The sons of Jerahmeel eldest son of Hezron by *a* Ahijah were Ram the
26 eldest, Bunah, Oren and Ozem. Jerahmeel had another wife, whose name
27 was Atarah; she was the mother of Onam. The sons of Ram eldest son of
28 Jerahmeel: Maaz, Jamin and Eker. The sons of Onam: Shammai and Jada.
29 The sons of Shammai: Nadab and Abishur. The name of Abishur's wife
30 was Abihail; she bore him Ahban and Molid. The sons of Nadab: Seled
31 and Ephraim; Seled died without children. Ephraim's son was Ishi, Ishi's
32 son Sheshan, Sheshan's son Ahlai. The sons of Jada brother of Shammai:
33 Jether and Jonathan; Jether died without children. The sons of Jonathan:
Peleth and Zaza. These were the descendants of Jerahmeel.

34 Sheshan had daughters but no sons. He had an Egyptian servant named
35 Jarha; he gave his daughter in marriage to this Jarha, and she bore him
36 37 Attai. Attai was the father of Nathan, Nathan father of Zabad, Zabad
38 father of Ephlal, Ephlal father of Obed, Obed father of Jehu, Jehu father
39 40 of Azariah, Azariah father of Helez, Helez father of Elasah, Elasah father
41 of Sisamai, Sisamai father of Shallum, Shallum father of Jekamiah, and
Jekamiah father of Elishama.

42 The sons of Caleb brother of Jerahmeel: Mesha the eldest, founder of
43 Ziph, and *b* Mareshah founder of Hebron. The sons of Hebron: Korah,
44 Tappuah, Rekem and Shema. Shema was the father of Raham father of
45 Jorkoam, and Rekem was the father of Shammai. The son of Shammai was
46 Maon, and Maon was the founder of Beth-zur. Ephah, Caleb's concubine,
was the mother of Haran, Moza and Gazez; Haran was the father of Gazez.
47 The sons of Jahdai: Regem, Jotham, Geshan, Pelet, Ephah and Shaaph.
48 49 Maacah, Caleb's concubine, was the mother of Sheber and Tirhanah; she
bore also Shaaph founder of Madmannah, and Sheva founder of Machbe-
nah and Gibea. Caleb also had a daughter named Achsah.

50 The descendants of Caleb: the sons of Hur, the eldest son of Ephrathah:
51 Shobal the founder of Kiriath-jearim, Salma the founder of Bethlehem,
52 and Hareph the founder of Beth-gader. Shobal the founder of Kiriath-
jearim was the father of Reaiah *c* and the ancestor of half the Manahethites. *d*
53 The clans of Kiriath-jearim: Ithrites, Puhites, Shumathites, and
Mishraites, from whom were descended the Zareathites and the Eshtaulites.
54 The descendants of Salma: Bethlehem, the Netophathites, Ataroth,
Beth-joab, half the Manahethites, and the Zorites.
55 The clans of Sophrites *e* living at Jabez: Tirathites, Shimeathites, and

---

a by: *prob. rdg.; Heb. om.*   *b* *Prob. rdg.; Heb. adds* the sons of.   *c* *Prob. rdg.,*
cp. 4. 2; Heb. the seer.   *d* *Prob. rdg., cp. verse 54; Heb.* Menuhoth.   *e Or*
secretaries.

Suchathites. These were Kenites who were connected by marriage with the ancestor of the Rechabites.

These were the sons of David, born at Hebron: the eldest Amnon, **3** 1[a] whose mother was Ahinoam of Jezreel; the second Daniel, whose mother was Abigail of Carmel; the third Absalom, whose mother was Maacah 2 daughter of Talmai king of Geshur; the fourth Adonijah, whose mother was Haggith; the fifth Shephatiah, whose mother was Abital; the sixth 3 Ithream, whose mother was David's wife Eglah. These six were born at 4 Hebron, where David reigned seven years and six months. In Jerusalem he reigned thirty-three years, and there the following sons were born to 5[b] him: Shimea, Shobab, Nathan and Solomon; these four were sons of Bathsheba daughter of Ammiel. There were nine others: Ibhar, Elishama, 6 Eliphelet, Nogah, Nepheg, Japhia, Elishama, Eliada and Eliphelet. These 7 8 9 were all the sons of David, with their sister Tamar, in addition to his sons by concubines.

Solomon's son was Rehoboam, his son Abia, his son Asa, his son 10 Jehoshaphat, his son Joram, his son Ahaziah, his son Joash, his son Amazi- 11 12 ah, his son Azariah, his son Jotham, his son Ahaz, his son Hezekiah, his 13 son Manasseh, his son Amon, and his son Josiah. The sons of Josiah: the 14 15 eldest was Johanan, the second Jehoiakim, the third Zedekiah, the fourth Shallum. The sons of Jehoiakim: Jeconiah and Zedekiah. The sons of 16 17 Jeconiah, a prisoner:[c] Shealtiel, Malchiram, Pedaiah, Shenazzar, Jekami- 18 ah, Hoshama and Nedabiah. The sons of Pedaiah: Zerubbabel and 19 Shimei. The sons of Zerubbabel: Meshullam and Hananiah; they had a sister, Shelomith. There were five others: Hashubah, Ohel, Berechiah, 20 Hasadiah and Jushab-hesed. The sons of Hananiah: Pelatiah and Isaiah; 21 his son was Rephaiah, his son Arnan, his son Obadiah, his son Shecaniah. The sons of Shecaniah: Shemaiah,[d] Hattush, Igeal, Bariah, Neariah and 22 Shaphat, six in all. The sons of Neariah: Elioenai, Hezekiah and Azrikam, 23 three in all. The sons of Elioenai: Hodaiah, Eliashib, Pelaiah, Akkub, 24 Johanan, Dalaiah and Anani, seven in all.

The sons of Judah: Perez, Hezron, Carmi, Hur and Shobal. Reaiah son **4** 1 2 of Shobal was the father of Jahath, Jahath father of Ahumai and Lahad. These were the clans of the Zorathites.

The sons of Etam: Jezreel, Ishma, Idbash, Penuel the founder of Gedor, 3-4 and Ezer the founder of Hushah; they had a sister named Hazelelponi. These were the sons of Hur: Ephrathah the eldest, the founder of Bethlehem.

Ashhur the founder of Tekoa had two wives, Helah and Naarah. 5 Naarah bore him Ahuzam, Hepher, Temeni and Haahashtari.[e] These 6 were the sons of Naarah. The sons of Helah: Zereth, Jezoar, Ethnan and 7 Coz. Coz was the father of Anub and Zobebah and the clans of Aharhel 8 son of Harum.

Jabez ranked higher than his brothers; his mother called him Jabez 9 because, as she said, she had borne him in pain. Jabez called upon the God 10

---

[a] *Verses 1-4: cp. 2 Sam. 3. 2-5.*   [b] *Verses 5-8: cp. 14. 4-7; 2 Sam. 5. 14-16.*
[c] Jeconiah, a prisoner: *or* Jeconiah: Assir, ...   [d] *Prob. rdg.; Heb. adds* and the sons of Shemaiah.   [e] Temeni and Haahashtari: *or* the Temanite and the Ahashtarite.

of Israel and said, 'I pray thee, bless me and grant me wide territories. May thy hand be with me, and do me no harm, I pray thee, and let me be free from pain'; and God granted his petition.

11 Kelub brother of Shuah was the father of Mehir the father of Eshton.
12 Eshton was the father of Beth-rapha, Paseah, and Tehinnah father of Ir-nahash. These were the men of Rechah.
13 The sons of Kenaz: Othniel and Seraiah. The sons of Othniel: Hathath and Meonothai.
14 Meonothai was the father of Ophrah.
Seraiah was the father of Joab founder of Ge-harashim, *a* for they were craftsmen.
15 The sons of Caleb son of Jephunneh: Iru, Elah and Naam. The son of Elah: Kenaz.
16 The sons of Jehaleleel: Ziph and Ziphah, Tiria and Asareel.
17–18 The sons of Ezra: Jether, Mered, Epher and Jalon. These were the sons of Bithiah daughter of Pharaoh, whom Mered had married; she conceived and gave birth to *b* Miriam, Shammai and Ishbah founder of Eshtemoa. His Jewish wife was the mother of Jered founder of Gedor, Heber founder
19 of Soco, and Jekuthiel founder of Zanoah. The sons of his *c* wife Hodiah sister of Naham were Daliah father of Keilah the Garmite, and Eshtemoa the Maacathite.
20 The sons of Shimon: Amnon, Rinnah, Ben-hanan and Tilon.
The sons of Ishi: Zoheth and Ben-zoheth.
21 The sons of Shelah son of Judah: Er founder of Lecah, Laadah founder of Mareshah, the clans of the guild of linen-workers at Ashbea,
22 Jokim, the men of Kozeba, Joash, and Saraph who fell out with Moab
23 and came back to Bethlehem. *d* (The records are ancient.) They were the potters, and those who lived at Netaim and Gederah were there on the king's service.
24 25 The sons of Simeon: Nemuel, Jamin, Jarib, Zerah, Saul, his son Shal-
26 lum, his son Mibsam and his son Mishma. The sons of Mishma: his son
27 Hamuel, his son Zaccur and his son Shimei. Shimei had sixteen sons and six daughters, but others of his family had fewer children, and the clan as
28 a whole did not increase as much as the tribe of Judah. They lived at
29 30 Beersheba, Moladah, Hazar-shual, Bilhah, Ezem, Tolad, Bethuel,
31 Hormah, Ziklag, Beth-marcaboth, Hazar-susim, Beth-birei, and Shaaraim.
32 These were their cities until David came to the throne. Their settlements *e*
33 were Etam, Ain, Rimmon, Tochen, and Ashan, five cities in all. They had also hamlets round these cities as far as Baal. These were the places where they lived.
34 The names on their register were: Meshobab, Jamlech, Joshah son of
35 36 Amaziah, Joel, Jehu son of Josibiah, son of Seraiah, son of Asiel, Elioenai,
37 Jaakobah, Jeshohaiah, Asaiah, Adiel, Jesimiel, Benaiah, Ziza son of
38 Shiphi, son of Allon, son of Jedaiah, son of Shimri, son of Shemaiah, whose names are recorded as princes in their clans, and their families had greatly

---

a Or the Valley of Craftsmen.   *b* and gave birth to: *prob. rdg.; Heb. om.*   *c* his: *prob. rdg.; Heb. om.*   *d* and came ... Bethlehem: *prob. rdg.; Heb. unintelligible.*   *e* *Prob. rdg.; Heb.* hamlets.

increased. They then went from the approaches to Gedor east of the valley 39
in search of pasture for their flocks. They found rich and good pasture in a 40
wide stretch of open country where everything was quiet and peaceful;
before then it had been occupied by Hamites. During the reign of Hezekiah 41
king of Judah these whose names are written above came and destroyed
the tribes of Ham[a] and the Meunites whom they found there. They
annihilated them so that no trace of them has remained to this day; and
they occupied the land in their place, for there was pasture for their flocks.
Of their number five hundred Simeonites invaded the hill-country of Seir, 42
led by Pelatiah, Neariah, Rephaiah, and Uzziel, the sons of Ishi. They 43
destroyed all who were left of the surviving Amalekites; and they live there
still.

The sons of Reuben, the eldest of Israel's sons. (He was, in fact, the 5
first son born, but because he had committed incest with a wife of his
father's the rank of the eldest was transferred to the sons of Joseph,
Israel's son, who, however, could not be registered as the eldest son. Judah 2
held the leading place among his brothers because he fathered a ruler,
and the rank of the eldest was his, not[b] Joseph's.) The sons of Reuben, the 3
eldest of Israel's sons: Enoch, Pallu, Hezron and Carmi. The sons of Joel: 4
his son Shemaiah, his son Gog, his son Shimei, his son Micah, his son 5
Reaia, his son Baal, his son Beerah, whom Tiglath-pileser king of Assyria 6
carried away into exile; he was a prince of the Reubenites. His kinsmen, 7
family by family, as registered in their tribal lists: Jeiel the chief, Zechariah,
Bela son of Azaz, son of Shema, son of Joel. They lived in Aroer, and their 8
lands stretched as far as Nebo and Baal-meon. Eastwards they occupied 9
territory as far as the edge of the desert which stretches from the river
Euphrates, for they had large numbers of cattle in Gilead. During Saul's 10
reign they made war on the Hagarites, whom they conquered, occupying
their encampments over all the country east of Gilead.

Adjoining them were the Gadites, occupying the district of Bashan as 11
far as Salcah: Joel the chief; second in rank, Shapham; then Jaanai and 12
Shaphat in Bashan. Their fellow-tribesmen belonged to the families of 13
Michael, Meshullam, Sheba, Jorai, Jachan, Zia and Heber, seven in all.
These were the sons of Abihail son of Huri, son of Jaroah, son of Gilead, 14
son of Michael, son of Jeshishai, son of Jahdo, son of Buz. Ahi son of 15
Abdiel, son of Guni, was head of their family; they lived in Gilead, in 16
Bashan and its villages, in all the common land of Sharon as far as it
stretched. These registers were all compiled in the reigns of Jotham king 17
of Judah and Jeroboam king of Israel.

The sons of Reuben, Gad, and half the tribe of Manasseh: of their 18
fighting men armed with shield and sword, their archers and their
battle-trained soldiers, forty-four thousand seven hundred and sixty
were ready for active service. They made war on the Hagarites, Jetur, 19
Nephish, and Nodab. They were given help against them, for they cried 20
to their God for help in the battle, and because they trusted him he listened
to their prayer, and the Hagarites and all their allies surrendered to

[a] the tribes of Ham: *prob. rdg., cp. verse 40; Heb.* their tribes.   [b] his, not: *prob.
rdg.; Heb. om.*

21 them.ᵃ They drove off their cattle, fifty thousand camels, two hundred and fifty thousand sheep, and two thousand asses, and they took a hundred
22 thousand captives. Many had been killed, for the war was of God's making, and they occupied the land instead of them until the exile.
23 Half the tribe of Manasseh lived in the land from Bashan to Baalhermon, Senir, and Mount Hermon, and were numerous also in Lebanon.
24 The heads of their families were: Epher, Ishi, Eliel, Azriel, Jeremiah, Hodaviah, and Jahdiel, all men of ability and repute, heads of their
25 families. But they sinned against the God of their fathers, and turned wantonly to worship the gods of the peoples whom God had destroyed
26 before them. So the God of Israel stirred up Pul king of Assyria, that is Tiglath-pileser king of Assyria, and he carried into exile Reuben, Gad, and half the tribe of Manasseh. He took them to Halah, Habor, Hara, and the river Gozan, where they are to this day.

6 1 2 THE SONS OF LEVI: Gershon,ᵇ Kohath and Merari. The sons of Kohath:
3 Amram, Izhar, Hebron and Uzziel. The children of Amram: Aaron, Moses and Miriam. The sons of Aaron: Nadab, Abihu, Eleazar and
4ᶜ Ithamar. Eleazar was the father of Phinehas, Phinehas father of Abishua,
5 6 Abishua father of Bukki, Bukki father of Uzzi, Uzzi father of Zerahiah,
7 Zerahiah father of Meraioth, Meraioth father of Amariah, Amariah father
8 9 of Ahitub, Ahitub father of Zadok, Zadok father of Ahimaaz, Ahimaaz
10 father of Azariah, Azariah father of Johanan, and Johanan father of Azariah, the priest who officiated in the LORD's house which Solomon
11 built at Jerusalem. Azariah was the father of Amariah, Amariah father of
12 13 Ahitub, Ahitub father of Zadok, Zadok father of Shallum, Shallum father
14 of Hilkiah, Hilkiah father of Azariah, Azariah father of Seraiah, and
15 Seraiah father of Jehozadak. Jehozadak went into exile when the LORD sent Judah and Jerusalem into exile under Nebuchadnezzar.
16ᵈ 17 The sons of Levi: Gershom, Kohath and Merari. The sons of Gershom:
18 Libni and Shimei. The sons of Kohath: Amram, Izhar, Hebron and
19 Uzziel. The sons of Merari: Mahli and Mushi. The clans of Levi, family
20ᵉ 21 by family: Gershom: his son Libni, his son Jahath, his son Zimmah, his
22ᶠ son Joah, his son Iddo, his son Zerah, his son Jeaterai. The sons of Kohath:
23 his son Amminadab, his son Korah, his son Assir, his son Elkanah, his
24 son Ebiasaph, his son Assir, his son Tahath, his son Uriel, his son Uzziah,
25 26 his son Saul. The sons of Elkanah: Amasai and Ahimoth, his son Elkanah,
27 his son Zophai, his son Nahath, his son Eliab, his son Jeroham, his son
28 29 Elkanah. The sons of Samuel: Joel the eldest and Abiah the second. The sons of Merari: his son Mahli, his son Libni, his son Shimei, his son Uzza,
30 his son Shimea, his son Haggiah, his son Asaiah.
31 These are the men whom David appointed to take charge of the music
32 in the house of the LORD when the Ark should be deposited there. They

ᵃ They were . . . surrendered to them: *or* They attacked them boldly, and the Hagarites and all their allies surrendered to them, for they cried . . . to their prayer.   ᵇ Gershom *in verses 16 and 17.*   ᶜ *Verses 4–8: cp. verses 50–53.*   ᵈ *Verses 16–19: cp. Exod. 6. 16–19.*   ᵉ *Verses 20, 21: cp. verses 41–43.*   ᶠ *Verses 22–28: cp. verses 33–38.*

performed their musical duties before the Tent of the Presence until
Solomon built the house of the LORD in Jerusalem, and took their regular
turns of duty there. The following, with their descendants, took this duty. 33
Of the line of Kohath: Heman the musician, son of Joel, son of Samuel,
son of Elkanah, son of Jeroham, son of Eliel, son of Toah, son of Zuph, 34 35
son of Elkanah, son of Mahath, son of Amasai, son of Elkanah, son of 36
Joel, son of Azariah, son of Zephaniah, son of Tahath, son of Assir, son 37
of Ebiasaph, son of Korah, son of Izhar, son of Kohath, son of Levi, son of 38
Israel. Heman's colleague Asaph stood at his right hand. He was the son 39
of Berachiah, son of Shimea, son of Michael, son of Baaseiah, son of 40
Malchiah, son of Ethni, son of Zerah, son of Adaiah, son of Ethan, son of 41^a 42
Zimmah, son of Shimei, son of Jahath, son of Gershom, son of Levi. On 43 44
their left stood their colleague of the line of Merari: Ethan son of Kishi,
son of Abdi, son of Malluch, son of Hashabiah, son of Amaziah, son of 45
Hilkiah, son of Amzi, son of Bani, son of Shamer, son of Mahli, son of 46 47
Mushi, son of Merari, son of Levi. Their kinsmen the Levites were dedi- 48
cated to all the service of the Tabernacle, the house of God.

But it was Aaron and his descendants who burnt the sacrifices on the 49
altar of whole-offering and the altar of incense, in fulfilment of all the
duties connected with the most sacred gifts, and to make expiation for
Israel, exactly as Moses the servant of God had commanded. The sons of 50^b
Aaron: his son Eleazar, his son Phinehas, his son Abishua, his son Bukki, 51
his son Uzzi, his son Zerahiah, his son Meraioth, his son Amariah, his 52
son Ahitub, his son Zadok, his son Ahimaaz. 53

These are their settlements in encampments in the districts assigned to 54
the descendants of Aaron, to the clan of Kohath, for it was to them that
the lot had fallen: they gave them Hebron in Judah, with the common land 55
round it, but they assigned to Caleb son of Jephunneh the open country 56
belonging to the town and its hamlets. They gave to the sons of Aaron: 57^c
Hebron the city^d of refuge, Libnah, Jattir, Eshtemoa, Hilen, Debir, 58
Ashan, and Beth-shemesh, each with its common land. And from the tribe 59 60
of Benjamin: Geba, Alemeth, and Anathoth, each with its common land,
making thirteen cities in all by their clans.

They gave to the remaining clans of the sons of Kohath ten cities by lot 61
from the half tribe of Manasseh. To the sons of Gershom according to 62
their clans they gave thirteen cities from the tribes of Issachar, Asher,
Naphtali, and Manasseh in Bashan. To the sons of Merari according to 63
their clans they gave by lot twelve cities from the tribes of Reuben, Gad,
and Zebulun. Israel gave these cities, each with its common land, to the 64
Levites. (The cities mentioned above, from the tribes of Judah, Simeon, 65
and Benjamin, were assigned by lot.)

Some of the clans of Kohath had cities allotted^e to them. They gave 66 67
them the city^f of refuge, Shechem in the hill-country of Ephraim, Gezer,
Jokmeam, Beth-horon, Aijalon, and Gath-rimmon, each with its common 68 69

70 land. From the half tribe of Manasseh, Aner and Bileam, each with its common land, were given to the rest of the clans of Kohath.

71 To the sons of Gershom they gave from the half tribe of Manasseh:
72 Golan in Bashan, and Ashtaroth, each with its common land. From the
73 tribe of Issachar: Kedesh, Daberath, Ramoth, and Anem, each with its
74 75 common land. From the tribe of Asher: Mashal, Abdon, Hukok, and
76 Rehob, each with its common land. From the tribe of Naphtali: Kedesh in Galilee, Hammon, and Kiriathaim, each with its common land.

77 To the rest of the sons of Merari they gave from the tribe of Zebulun:
78 Rimmon and Tabor, each with its common land. On the east of Jordan, opposite Jericho, from the tribe of Reuben: Bezer-in-the-wilderness,
79 80 Jahzah, Kedemoth, and Mephaath, each with its common land. From the
81 tribe of Gad: Ramoth in Gilead, Mahanaim, Heshbon, and Jazer, each with its common land.

7 1*a* 2 The sons of Issachar: Tola, Pua, Jashub and Shimron, four. The sons of Tola: Uzzi, Rephaiah, Jeriel, Jahmai, Jibsam, and Samuel, all able men and heads of families by paternal descent from Tola according to their tribal lists; their number in David's time was twenty-two thousand six
3 hundred. The son of Uzzi: Izrahiah. The sons of Izrahiah: Michael,
4 Obadiah, Joel and Isshiah, making a total of five, all of them chiefs. In addition there were bands of fighting men recorded by families according to the tribal lists to the number of thirty-six thousand, for they had many
5 wives and children. Their fellow-tribesmen in all the clans of Issachar were able men, eighty-seven thousand; every one of them was registered.

6 7 The sons of Benjamin: Bela, Becher and Jediael, three. The sons of Bela: Ezbon, Uzzi, Uzziel, Jerimoth and Iri, five. They were heads of their families and able men; the number registered was twenty-two
8 thousand and thirty-four. The sons of Becher: Zemira, Joash, Eliezer, Elioenai, Omri, Jeremoth, Abiah, Anathoth and Alemeth; all these were
9 sons of Becher according to their tribal lists, heads of their families and able men; and the number registered was twenty thousand two hundred.
10 The son of Jediael: Bilhan. The sons of Bilhan: Jeush, Benjamin, Ehud,
11 Kenaanah, Zethan, Tarshish and Ahishahar. All these were descendants of Jediael, heads of*b* families and able men. The number was seventeen thousand two hundred men, fit for active service in war.
12 The sons of Dan:*c* Hushim and the sons of Aher.*d*
13 The sons of Naphtali: Jahziel, Guni, Jezer, Shallum. These were sons of Bilhah.
14*e* The sons of Manasseh,*f* born of his concubine, an Aramaean: Machir
15 father of Gilead. Machir married a woman whose name was*g* Maacah. The second son was named Zelophehad, and Zelophehad had daughters.
16 Maacah wife of Machir had a son whom she named Peresh. His brother's
17 name was Sheresh, and his sons were Ulam and Rakem. The son of Ulam:

---

a *Verses 1, 6, 13, 30 and 8. 1–5 : cp. Gen. 46. 13, 17, 21–24.*   *b* *Prob. rdg.; Heb. to the heads of.*   *c* *The sons of Dan: prob. rdg., cp. Gen. 46. 23; Heb. And Shuppim and Huppim, the sons of Ir.*   *d* *Or another.*   *e* *Verses 14–19 : cp. Num. 26. 29–33.*   *f* *Prob. rdg.; Heb. adds Asriel.*   *g* *whose name was: prob. rdg.; Heb. to Huppim and Shuppim, and his sister's name was . . .*

Bedan. These were the sons of Gilead son of Machir, son of Manasseh.
His sister Hammoleketh was the mother of Ishhod, Abiezer and Mahalah. 18
The sons of Shemida: Ahian, Shechem, Likhi and Aniam. 19

The sons of Ephraim: Shuthelah, his son Bered, his son Tahath, his 20
son Eladah, his son Tahath, his son Zabad, his son Shuthelah. Ephraim's 21
other sons Ezer and Elead were killed by the native Gittites when they
came down to lift their cattle. Their father Ephraim long mourned for 22
them, and his kinsmen came to comfort him. Then he had intercourse with 23
his wife; she conceived and had a son whom he named Beriah (because
disaster*a* had come on his family). He had a daughter named Sherah; she 24
built Lower and Upper Beth-horon and Uzzen-sherah. He also had a son 25
named Rephah; his son was Resheph, his son Telah, his son Tahan, his 26
son Laadan, his son Ammihud, his son Elishama, his son Nun, his son 27
Joshua.

Their lands and settlements were: Bethel and its dependent villages, to 28
the east Naaran, to the west Gezer, Shechem, and Gaza, with their villages.
In the possession of Manasseh were Beth-shean, Taanach, Megiddo, and 29
Dor, with their villages. In all of these lived the descendants of Joseph the
son of Israel.

The sons of Asher: Imnah, Ishvah, Ishvi and Beriah, together with their 30
sister Serah. The sons of Beriah: Heber and Malchiel father of Birzavith. 31
Heber was the father of Japhlet, Shomer, Hotham, and their sister Shua. 32
The sons of Japhlet: Pasach, Bimhal and Ashvath. These were the sons of 33
Japhlet. The sons of Shomer: Ahi, Rohgah, Jehubbah and Aram. The sons 34 35
of his brother Hotham:*b* Zophah, Imna, Shelesh and Amal. The sons of 36
Zophah: Suah, Harnepher, Shual, Beri, Imrah, Bezer, Hod, Shamma, 37
Shilshah, Ithran and Beera. The sons of Jether: Jephunneh, Pispah and 38
Ara. The sons of Ulla: Arah, Haniel and Rezia. All these were descendants 39 40
of Asher, heads of families, picked men of ability, leading princes. They
were enrolled among the fighting troops; the total number was twenty-six
thousand men.

The sons of Benjamin were: the eldest Bela, the second Ashbel, the third **8**
Aharah, the fourth Nohah and the fifth Rapha. The sons of Bela: Addar, 2 3
Gera father of Ehud,*c* Abishua, Naaman, Ahoah, Gera, Shephuphan and 4 5
Huram. These were the sons of Ehud, heads of families living in Geba, 6
who were removed to Manahath: Naaman, Ahiah, and Gera—he it was 7
who removed them. He was the father of Uzza and Ahihud. Shaharaim 8
had sons born to him in Moabite country, after putting away his wives
Mahasham and Baara. By his wife Hodesh he had Jobab, Zibia, Mesha, 9
Malcham, Jeuz, Shachia and Mirmah. These were his sons, heads of fami- 10
lies. By Mahasham he had had Abitub and Elpaal. The sons of Elpaal: 11 12
Eber, Misham, Shamed who built Ono and Lod with its villages, also Beriah 13
and Shema who were heads of families living in Aijalon, having expelled the
inhabitants of Gath. Ahio, Shashak, Jeremoth, Zebadiah, Arad, Ader, 14 15
Michael, Ispah, and Joha were sons of Beriah; Zebadiah, Meshullam, 16 17
Hezeki, Heber, Ishmerai, Jezliah, and Jobab were sons of Elpaal; Jakim, 18 19

---

a Heb. beraah.　　　*b Prob. rdg., cp. verse 32; Heb.* Helem.　　　*c* father of Ehud:
prob. rdg., cp. Judg. 3. 15; Heb. Abihud.

20 21 Zichri, Zabdi, Elienai, Zilthai, Eliel, Adaiah, Beraiah, and Shimrath were
22 23 24 sons of Shimei; Ishpan, Heber, Eliel, Abdon, Zichri, Hanan, Hananiah,
25 26 Elam, Antothiah, Iphedeiah, and Penuel were sons of Shashak; Sham-
27 sherai, Shehariah, Athaliah, Jaresiah, Eliah, and Zichri were sons of
28 Jeroham. These were enrolled in the tribal lists as heads of families, chiefs
living in Jerusalem.

29ᵃ   Jehiel founder of Gibeon lived at Gibeon; his wife's name was Maacah.
30 31 His eldest son was Abdon, followed by Zur, Kish, Baal, Nadab, Gedor,
32 Ahio, Zacher and Mikloth. Mikloth was the father of Shimeah; they lived
alongside their kinsmen in Jerusalem.

33   Ner was the father of Kish, Kish father of Saul, Saul father of Jonathan,
34 Malchishua, Abinadab and Eshbaal. Jonathan's son was Meribbaal, and
35 he was the father of Micah. The sons of Micah: Pithon, Melech, Tarea
36 and Ahaz. Ahaz was the father of Jehoaddah, Jehoaddah father of Alemeth,
37 Azmoth and Zimri. Zimri was the father of Moza, and Moza father of
38 Binea; his son was Raphah, his son Elasah, and his son Azel. Azel had six
sons, whose names were Azrikam, Bocheru, Ishmael, Sheariah, Obadiah
39 and Hanan. All these were sons of Azel. The sons of his brother Eshek:
40 the eldest Ulam, the second Jeush, the third Eliphelet. The sons of Ulam
were able men, archers, and had many sons and grandsons, a hundred and
fifty. All these were descendants of Benjamin.

The restored community

9   SO ALL ISRAEL WERE REGISTERED and recorded in the book of the
kings of Israel; but Judah for their sins were carried away to exile
2ᵇ in Babylon. The first to occupy their ancestral land in their cities were
3 lay Israelites, priests, Levites, and temple-servitors. Jerusalem was
occupied partly by Judahites, partly by Benjamites, and partly by men of
4 Ephraim and Manasseh. Judahites:ᶜ Uthai son of Ammihud, son of
Omri, son of Imri, son of Bani, a descendant of Perez son of Judah.
5 6 Shelanites: Asaiah the eldest and his sons. The sons of Zerah: Jeuel and
7 six hundred and ninety of their kinsmen. Benjamites: Sallu son of Meshul-
8 lam, son of Hodaviah, son of Hassenuah, Ibneiah son of Jeroham, Elah
son of Uzzi, son of Micri, Meshullam son of Shephatiah, son of Reuel, son
9 of Ibniah, and their recorded kinsmen numbering nine hundred and
fifty-six, all heads of families.

10 11   Priests: Jedaiah, Jehoiarib, Jachin, Azariah son of Hilkiah, son of
Meshullam, son of Zadok, son of Meraioth, son of Ahitub, the officer in
12 charge of the house of God, Adaiah son of Jeroham, son of Pashhur, son
of Malchiah, Maasai son of Adiel, son of Jahzerah, son of Meshullam, son
13 of Meshillemith, son of Immer, and their colleagues, heads of families
numbering one thousand seven hundred and sixty, men of substance and
fit for the work connected with the service of the house of God.

14   Levites: Shemaiah son of Hasshub, son of Azrikam, son of Hashabiah,

---

ᵃ *Verses 29–38: cp. 9. 35–44.*   ᵇ *Verses 2–22: cp. Neh. 11. 3–22.*   ᶜ *Prob. rdg.;
Heb. om.*

a descendant of Merari, Bakbakkar, Heresh, Galal, Mattaniah son of 15
Mica, son of Zichri, son of Asaph, Obadiah son of Shemaiah, son of Galal, 16
son of Jeduthun, and Berechiah son of Asa, son of Elkanah, who lived in
the hamlets of the Netophathites.

The door-keepers were Shallum, Akkub, Talmon, and Ahiman; their 17
brother Shallum was the chief. Until then they had all been door-keepers 18
in the quarters of the Levites at the king's gate, on the east. Shallum son 19
of Kore, son of Ebiasaph, son of Korah, and his kinsmen of the Korahite
family were responsible for service as guards of the thresholds of the
Tabernacle; their ancestors had performed the duty of guarding the
entrances to the camp of the LORD. Phinehas son of Eleazar had been their 20
overseer in the past—the LORD be with him! Zechariah son of Meshelemiah 21
was the door-keeper of the Tent of the Presence. Those picked to be door- 22
keepers numbered two hundred and twelve in all, registered in their
hamlets. David and Samuel the seer had installed them because they were
trustworthy. They and their sons had charge, by watches, of the gates of 23
the house, the tent-dwelling of the LORD. The door-keepers were to be on 24
four sides, east, west, north, and south. Their kinsmen from their hamlets 25
had to come on duty with them for seven days at a time in turn. The four 26
principal door-keepers were chosen for their trustworthiness; they were
Levites and had charge of the rooms and the stores in the house of God.
They always slept in the precincts of the house of God (for the watch was 27
their duty) and they had charge of the key for opening the gates every
morning. Some of them had charge of the vessels used in the service of the 28
temple, keeping count of them as they were brought in and taken out.
Some of them were detailed to take charge of the furniture and all the 29
sacred vessels, the flour, the wine, the oil, the incense, and the spices.

Some of the priests compounded the ointment for the spices. Mat- 30 31
tithiah the Levite, the eldest son of Shallum the Korahite, was in charge of
the preparation of the wafers because he was trustworthy. Some of their 32
Kohathite kinsmen were in charge of setting out the rows of the Bread of
the Presence every sabbath.

These, the musicians, heads of Levite families, were lodged in rooms 33
set apart for them, because they were liable for duty by day and by night.

These are the heads of Levite families, chiefs according to their tribal 34
lists, living in Jerusalem.

Jehiel founder of Gibeon lived at Gibeon; his wife's name was Maacah, 35[a]
and his sons were Abdon the eldest, Zur, Kish, Baal, Ner, Nadab, Gedor, 36 37
Ahio, Zechariah and Mikloth. Mikloth was the father of Shimeam; they 38
lived alongside their kinsmen in Jerusalem.[b] Ner was the father of Kish, 39
Kish father of Saul, Saul father of Jonathan, Malchishua, Abinadab and
Eshbaal. The son of Jonathan was Meribbaal, and Meribbaal was the 40
father of Micah. The sons of Micah: Pithon, Melech, Tahrea and Ahaz. 41
Ahaz was the father of Jarah, Jarah father of Alemeth, Azmoth, and Zimri; 42
Zimri father of Moza, and Moza father of Binea; his son was Rephaiah, his 43
son Elasah, his son Azel. Azel had six sons, whose names were Azrikam, Bo- 44
cheru, Ishmael, Sheariah, Obadiah and Hanan. These were the sons of Azel.

[a] *Verses 35–44: cp. 8. 29–38.*   [b] *Prob. rdg.; Heb. adds* with their kinsmen.

The death of Saul

10 1ª THE PHILISTINES FOUGHT A BATTLE against Israel, and the men
2 of Israel were routed, leaving their dead on Mount Gilboa. The
Philistines hotly pursued Saul and his sons and killed the three sons,
3 Jonathan, Abinadab and Malchishua. The battle went hard for Saul, for
4 some archers came upon him and he was wounded by them. So he said
to his armour-bearer, 'Draw your sword and run me through, so that these
uncircumcised brutes may not come and make sport of me.' But the
armour-bearer refused, he dared not; whereupon Saul took his own sword
5 and fell on it. When the armour-bearer saw that Saul was dead, he too fell
6 on his sword and died. Thus Saul died and his three sons; his whole house
7 perished at one and the same time. And all the Israelites in the Vale, when
they saw that their army had fled and that Saul and his sons had perished,
fled likewise, abandoning their cities, and the Philistines went in and
occupied them.
8   Next day, when the Philistines came to strip the slain, they found Saul
9 and his sons lying dead on Mount Gilboa. They stripped him, cut off his
head and took away his armour; then they sent messengers through the
length and breadth of their land to take the good news to idols and people
10 alike. They deposited his armour in the temple of their god,ᵇ and nailed
11 up his skull in the temple of Dagon. When the people of Jabesh-gilead
12 heard all that the Philistines had done to Saul, the bravest of them set out
together to recover the bodies of Saul and his sons; they brought them
back to Jabesh and buried their bones under the oak-tree there, and fasted
13 for seven days. Thus Saul paid with his life for his unfaithfulness: he had
disobeyed the word of the LORD and had resorted to ghosts for guidance.
14 He had not sought guidance of the LORD, who therefore destroyed him and
transferred the kingdom to David son of Jesse.

David king over Israel

11 1ᶜ THEN ALL ISRAEL ASSEMBLED at Hebron to wait upon David. 'We
2 are your own flesh and blood', they said. 'In the past, while Saul was
still king, you led the forces of Israel to war, and you brought them home
again. And the LORD your God said to you, "You shall be shepherd of my
3 people Israel, you shall be their prince."' All the elders of Israel came to
the king at Hebron; there David made a covenant with them before the
LORD, and they anointed David king over Israel, as the LORD had said
through the lips of Samuel.
4   Then David and all Israel went to Jerusalem (that is Jebus, where the
5 Jebusites, the inhabitants of the land, lived). The people of Jebus said to
David, 'Never shall you come in here'; none the less David did capture
6 the stronghold of Zion, and it is now known as the City of David. David
said, 'The first man to kill a Jebusite shall become a commander or an

---

ª *Verses 1–12: cp. 1 Sam. 31. 1–13.*   ᵇ *Or gods.*   ᶜ *Verses 1–9: cp. 2 Sam. 5. 1–3, 6–10.*

officer', and the first man to go up was Joab son of Zeruiah; so he was given the command.

David took up his residence in the stronghold: that is why they called it 7 the City of David. He built the city round it, starting at the Millo and 8 including its neighbourhood, while Joab reconstructed the rest of the city. So David steadily grew stronger, for the LORD of Hosts was with him. 9

Of David's heroes these were the chief, men who lent their full strength 10^a to his government and, with all Israel, joined in making him king; such was the LORD's decree for Israel. First came Jashoboam the Hachmonite, chief 11 of the three; he it was who brandished his spear over three hundred, all slain at one time. Next to him was Eleazar son of Dodo the Ahohite, one of 12 the heroic three. He was with David at Pas-dammim where the Philistines 13 had gathered for battle in a field carrying a good crop of barley; and when the people had fled from the Philistines he stood his ground in the field, 14 saved it^b and defeated them. So the LORD brought about a great victory.

Three of the thirty chiefs went down to the rock to join David at the 15 cave of Adullam, while the Philistines were encamped in the Vale of Rephaim. At that time David was in the stronghold, and a Philistine 16 garrison held Bethlehem. One day a longing came over David, and he 17 exclaimed, 'If only I could have a drink of water from the well^c by the gate of Bethlehem!' At this the three made their way through the Philistine 18 lines and drew water from the well by the gate of Bethlehem, and brought it to David. But David refused to drink it; he poured it out to the LORD and said, 'God forbid that I should do such a thing! Can I drink the blood 19 of these men? They have brought it at the risk of their lives.' So he would not drink it. Such were the exploits of the heroic three.

Abishai the brother of Joab was chief of the thirty. He once brandished 20 his spear over three hundred dead, and he was famous among the thirty. He held higher rank than the rest of the thirty and became their captain, 21 but he did not rival the three. Benaiah son of Jehoiada, from Kabzeel, was 22 a hero of many exploits. It was he who smote the two champions of Moab, and who went down into a pit and killed a lion on a snowy day. It was he 23 who also killed the Egyptian, a giant seven and a half feet high armed with a spear as big as the beam of a loom; he went to meet him with a club, snatched the spear out of the Egyptian's hand and killed him with his own weapon. Such were the exploits of Benaiah son of Jehoiada, famous among 24 the heroic thirty.^d He was more famous than the rest of the thirty, but did 25 not rival the three. David appointed him to his household.

These were his valiant heroes: Asahel the brother of Joab, and Elhanan 26 son of Dodo from Bethlehem; Shammoth from Harod,^e and Helez from 27 a place unknown; Ira son of Ikkesh from Tekoa, and Abiezer from Ana- 28 thoth; Sibbecai from Hushah, and Ilai the Ahohite; Maharai from Neto- 29 30 phah, and Heled son of Baanah from Netophah; Ithai son of Ribai from 31 Gibeah of Benjamin, and Benaiah from Pirathon; Hurai from the ravines 32 of Gaash, and Abiel from Beth-arabah; Azmoth from Bahurim, and 33

^a *Verses 10–41: cp. 2 Sam. 23. 8–39.*   ^b saved it: *or* cleared it of the Philistines.
^c *Or* cistern.   ^d *Prob. rdg.; Heb.* three.   ^e *Prob. rdg., cp. 2 Sam. 23. 25; Heb.* Haror.

457

34 Eliahba from Shaalbon; Hashem the Gizonite, and Jonathan son of Shage
35 the Hararite; Ahiam son of Sacar the Hararite, and Eliphal son of Ur;
36 37 Hepher from Mecherah, and Ahijah from a place unknown; Hezro from
38 Carmel, and Naarai son of Ezbai; Joel the brother of Nathan, and Mibhar
39 the son of Haggeri; Zelek the Ammonite, and Naharai from Beeroth,
40 armour-bearer to Joab son of Zeruiah; Ira the Ithrite, and Gareb the
41 42 Ithrite; Uriah the Hittite, and Zabad son of Ahlai. Adina son of Shiza the
43 Reubenite, a chief of the Reubenites, was over these thirty. Also Hanan
44 son of Maacah, and Joshaphat the Mithnite; Uzzia from Ashtaroth, Shama
45 and Jeiel the sons of Hotham from Aroer; Jediael son of Shimri, and Joha
46 his brother, the Tizite; Eliel the Mahavite, and Jeribai and Joshaviah sons
47 of Elnaam, and Ithmah the Moabite; Eliel, Obed, and Jasiel, from Zobah. *a*

12 These are the men who joined David at Ziklag while he was banned from
the presence of Saul son of Kish. They ranked among the warriors valiant
2 in battle. They carried bows and could sling stones or shoot arrows with
3 the left hand or the right; they were Benjamites, kinsmen of Saul. The
foremost were Ahiezer and Joash, the sons of Shemaah the Gibeathite;
Jeziel and Pelet, men of Beth-azmoth; Berachah and Jehu of Anathoth;
4 Ishmaiah the Gibeonite, a hero among the thirty and a chief among them;
5 Jeremiah, Jahaziel, Johanan, and Josabad of Gederah; Eluzai, Jerimoth,
6 Bealiah, Shemariah, and Shephatiah the Haruphite; Elkanah, Isshiah,
7 Azareel, Joezer, Jashobeam, the Korahites; and Joelah and Zebadiah sons
of Jeroham, of Gedor.

8 Some Gadites also joined David at the stronghold in the wilderness,
valiant men trained for war, who could handle the heavy shield and spear,
9 grim as lions and swift as gazelles on the hills. Ezer was their chief, Obadiah
10 the second, Eliab the third; Mishmannah the fourth and Jeremiah the
11 12 fifth; Attai the sixth and Eliel the seventh; Johanan the eighth and Elzabad
13 14 the ninth; Jeremiah the tenth and Machbanai the eleventh. These were
chiefs of the Gadites in the army, the least of them a match for a hundred,
15 the greatest a match for a thousand. These were the men who in the first
month crossed the Jordan, which was in full flood in all its reaches, and
wrought havoc in the valleys, east and west.

16 Some men of Benjamin and Judah came to David at the stronghold.
17 David went out to them and said, 'If you come as friends to help me, join
me and welcome; but if you come to betray me to my enemies, innocent
though I am of any crime of violence, may the God of our fathers see and
18 judge.' At that a spirit took possession of Amasai, the chief of the thirty,
and he said:

> We are on your side, David!
> We are with you, son of Jesse!
> Greetings, greetings to you
> and greetings to your ally!
> For your God is your ally.

So David welcomed them and attached them to the columns of his raiding
parties.

a from Zobah: *prob. rdg.; Heb. obscure.*

Some men of Manasseh had deserted to David when he went with the 19
Philistines to war against Saul, though he did not, in fact, fight on the side
of the Philistines. Their princes brusquely dismissed him, saying to
themselves that he would desert them for his master Saul, and that would
cost them their heads. The men of Manasseh who deserted to him when 20
he went to Ziklag were these: Adnah, Jozabad, Jediael, Michael, Jozabad,
Elihu, and Zilthai, each commanding his thousand in Manasseh. It was 21
they who stood valiantly by David against the raiders, for they were all
good fighters, and they were given commands in his forces. From day to 22
day men came in to help David, until he had gathered an immense army.

These are the numbers of the armed bands which joined David at 23
Hebron to transfer Saul's sovereignty to him, as the LORD had said: men 24
of Judah, bearing heavy shield and spear, six thousand eight hundred,
drafted for active service; of Simeon, fighting men drafted for active service, 25
seven thousand one hundred; of Levi, four thousand six hundred, together 26 27
with Jehoiada prince of the house of Aaron and three thousand seven hundred men, and Zadok a valiant fighter, with twenty-two officers of his own 28
clan; of Benjamin, Saul's kinsmen, three thousand, though most of them 29
had hitherto remained loyal to the house of Saul; of Ephraim, twenty 30
thousand eight hundred, fighting men, famous in their own clans; of the 31
half tribe of Manasseh, eighteen thousand, who had been nominated to
come and make David king; of Issachar, whose tribesmen were skilled in 32
reading the signs of the times to discover what course Israel should follow,
two hundred chiefs, with all their kinsmen under their command; of 33
Zebulun, fifty thousand troops well-drilled for battle, armed with every
kind of weapon, bold and single-minded; of Naphtali, a thousand officers 34
with thirty-seven thousand men bearing heavy shield and spear; of the 35
Danites, twenty-eight thousand six hundred well-drilled for battle; of 36
Asher, forty thousand troops well-drilled for battle; of the Reubenites and 37
the Gadites and the half tribe of Manasseh east of Jordan, a hundred and
twenty thousand, armed with every kind of weapon.

All these warriors, bold men in battle, came to Hebron, loyally deter- 38
mined to make David king over the whole of Israel; the rest of Israel, too,
had but one thought, to make him king. They spent three days there with 39
David, eating and drinking, for their kinsmen made provision for them.
Their neighbours also round about, as far away as Issachar, Zebulun, and 40
Naphtali, brought food on asses and camels, on mules and oxen, supplies
of meal, fig-cakes, raisin-cakes, wine and oil, oxen and sheep, in plenty;
for there was rejoicing in Israel.

DAVID CONSULTED THE OFFICERS over units of a thousand and a 13
hundred on every matter brought forward. Then he said to the whole 2
assembly of Israel, 'If you approve, and if the LORD our God opens a way,
let us *a* send to our kinsmen who have stayed behind, in all the districts of
Israel, and also to the priests and Levites in the cities where they have
common lands, bidding them join us. Let us fetch the Ark of our God, for 3

a and if . . . let us: *or* and if it is from the LORD our God, let us seize the opportunity
and . . .

4 while Saul lived we never resorted to it.' The whole assembly resolved to do this; the entire nation approved it.

5 So David assembled all Israel from the Shihor in Egypt to Lebo-hamath,
6*a* in order to fetch the Ark of God from Kiriath-jearim. Then David and all Israel went up to Baalah, to Kiriath-jearim, which belonged to Judah, to fetch the Ark of God, the LORD enthroned upon the cherubim, the Ark
7 which bore his name.*b* And they conveyed the Ark of God on a new cart
8 from the house of Abinadab, with Uzza and Ahio guiding the cart. David and all Israel danced for joy before God without restraint to the sound of singing, of harps and lutes, of tambourines, and cymbals and trumpets.
9 But when they came to the threshing-floor of Kidon, the oxen stumbled,
10 and Uzza put out his hand to hold the Ark. The LORD was angry with Uzza and struck him down because he had put out his hand to the Ark.
11 So he died there before God. David was vexed because the LORD's anger had broken out upon Uzza, and he called the place Perez-uzza,*c* the name
12 it still bears. David was afraid of God that day and said, 'How can I harbour
13 the Ark of God after this?' So he did not take the Ark with him into the City of David, but turned aside and carried it to the house of Obed-edom
14 the Gittite. Thus the Ark of God remained beside the house of Obed-edom, in its tent,*d* for three months, and the LORD blessed the family of Obed-edom and all that he had.

14 1*e* Hiram king of Tyre sent an embassy to David; he sent cedar logs, and
2 masons and carpenters with them to build him a house. David knew by now that the LORD had confirmed him as king over Israel and had made his royal power stand higher for the sake of his people Israel.

3 David married more wives in Jerusalem, and more sons and daughters
4*f* were born to him. These are the names of the children born to him in
5 Jerusalem: Shammua, Shobab, Nathan, Solomon, Ibhar, Elishua, Elpelet,
6 7 Nogah, Nepheg, Japhia, Elishama, Beeliada and Eliphelet.

8 When the Philistines learnt that David had been anointed king over the whole of Israel, they came up in force to seek him out. David, hearing of
9 this, went out to face them. Now the Philistines had come and raided the
10 Vale of Rephaim. So David inquired of God, 'If I attack the Philistines, wilt thou deliver them into my hands?' And the LORD answered, 'Go; I
11 will deliver them into your hands.' So he went up and attacked them at Baal-perazim and defeated them there. 'God has used me to break through my enemies' lines,' David said, 'as a river breaks its banks'; that is why the
12 place was named Baal-perazim.*g* The Philistines left their gods behind them there, and by David's orders these were burnt.

13 14 The Philistines made another raid on the Vale. Again David inquired of God, and God said to him, 'No, you must go up towards their rear; wheel round without making contact and*h* come upon them opposite the
15 aspens. Then, as soon as you hear a rustling sound in the tree-tops, you

---

a Verses 6–14: cp. 2 Sam. 6. 2–11.   *b which bore his name: prob. rdg.; Heb.*
obscure.   *c That is Outbreak on Uzza.*   *d Or in his tent.*   *e Verses 1–16:*
cp. 2 Sam. 5. 11–25.   *f Verses 4–7: cp. 3. 5–8.*   *g That is Baal of Break-through.*
h No . . . contact and: or Do not go up to the attack; withdraw from them and
then . . .

shall give battle, for God will have gone out before you to defeat the
Philistine army.' David did as God commanded, and they drove the 16
Philistine army in flight all the way from Gibeon to Gezer. So David's 17
fame spread through every land, and the LORD inspired all nations with
dread of him.

DAVID BUILT HIMSELF QUARTERS in the City of David, and prepared **15**
a place for the Ark of God and pitched a tent for it. Then he decreed that 2
only Levites should carry the Ark of God, since they had been chosen by
the LORD to carry it and to serve him *a* for ever. Next David assembled all 3
Israel at Jerusalem, to bring up the Ark of the LORD to the place he had
prepared for it. He gathered together the sons of Aaron and the Levites: 4
of the sons of Kohath, Uriel the chief with a hundred and twenty of his 5
kinsmen; of the sons of Merari, Asaiah the chief with two hundred and 6
twenty of his kinsmen; of the sons of Gershom, Joel the chief with a 7
hundred and thirty of his kinsmen; of the sons of Elizaphan, Shemaiah 8
the chief with two hundred of his kinsmen; of the sons of Hebron, Eliel the 9
chief with eighty of his kinsmen; of the sons of Uzziel, Amminadab the 10
chief with a hundred and twelve of his kinsmen. And David summoned 11
Zadok and Abiathar the priests, together with the Levites, Uriel, Asaiah,
Joel, Shemaiah, Eliel, and Amminadab, and said to them, 'You who are 12
heads of families of the Levites, hallow yourselves, you and your kinsmen,
and bring up the Ark of the LORD the God of Israel to the place which I
have prepared for it. It was because you were not present the first time, 13
that the LORD our God broke out upon us. For we had not sought his
guidance as we should have done.' So the priests and the Levites hallowed 14
themselves to bring up the Ark of the LORD the God of Israel, and the 15
Levites carried the Ark of God, bearing it on their shoulders with poles as
Moses had prescribed at the command of the LORD.

David also ordered the chiefs of the Levites to install as musicians those 16
of their kinsmen who were players skilled in making joyful music on their
instruments, lutes and harps and cymbals. So the Levites installed Heman 17
son of Joel and, from his kinsmen, Asaph son of Berechiah; and from their
kinsmen the Merarites, Ethan son of Kushaiah, together with their kins- 18
men of the second degree, Zechariah, Jaaziel, Shemiramoth, Jehiel, Unni,
Eliab, Benaiah, Maaseiah, Mattithiah, Eliphelehu, and Mikneiah, and the
door-keepers Obed-edom and Jeiel. They installed the musicians Heman, 19
Asaph, and Ethan to sound the cymbals of bronze; Zechariah, Jaaziel, 20
Shemiramoth, Jehiel, Unni, Eliab, Maaseiah, and Benaiah to play on
lutes; *b* Mattithiah, Eliphelehu, Mikneiah, Obed-edom, Jeiel, and Azaziah 21
to play on harps. *c* Kenaniah, officer of the Levites, was precentor in charge 22
of the music because of his proficiency. Berechiah and Elkanah were door- 23
keepers for the Ark, while the priests Shebaniah, Jehoshaphat, Nethaneel,
Amasai, Zechariah, Benaiah, and Eliezer sounded the trumpets before 24
the Ark of God; and Obed-edom and Jehiah also were door-keepers for
the Ark.

a Or it.   b Prob. rdg.; Heb. adds al alamoth, *possibly a musical term.   c Prob. rdg.;
Heb. adds* al hashsheminith lenasseah, *possibly musical terms.*

25^a Then David and the elders of Israel and the captains of units of a thousand went to bring up the Ark of the Covenant of the LORD with much
26 rejoicing from the house of Obed-edom. Because God had helped the Levites who carried the Ark of the Covenant of the LORD, they sacrificed seven bulls and seven rams.

27 Now David and all the Levites who carried the Ark, and the musicians, and Kenaniah the precentor,^b were arrayed in robes of fine linen; and
28 David had on a linen ephod. All Israel escorted the Ark of the Covenant of the LORD with shouts of acclamation, blowing on horns and trumpets,
29 clashing cymbals and playing on lutes and harps. But as the Ark of the Covenant of the LORD was entering the city of David, Saul's daughter Michal looked down through a window and saw King David dancing and making merry, and she despised him in her heart.

16 1^c When they had brought in the Ark of God, they put it inside the tent that David had pitched for it, and they offered whole-offerings and shared-
2 offerings before God. After David had completed these sacrifices, he
3 blessed the people in the name of the LORD and gave food, a loaf of bread, a portion of meat, and a cake of raisins, to each Israelite, man or woman.
4 He appointed certain Levites to serve before the Ark of the LORD, to repeat the Name, to confess and to praise the LORD the God of Israel.
5 Their leader was Asaph; second to him was Zechariah; then came Jaaziel,^d Shemiramoth, Jehiel, Mattithiah, Eliab, Benaiah, Obed-edom, and Jeiel,
6 with lutes and harps, Asaph, who sounded the cymbals; and Benaiah and Jahaziel the priests, who blew the trumpets before the Ark of the Covenant
7 of God continuously throughout that day. It was then that David first ordained the offering of thanks to the LORD by Asaph and his kinsmen:

8^e Give the LORD thanks and invoke him by name,
   make his deeds known in the world around.

9 Pay him honour with song and psalm
   and think upon all his wonders.

10 Exult in his hallowed name;
   let those who seek the LORD be joyful in heart.

11 Turn to the LORD, your strength,^f
   seek his presence always.

12 Remember the wonders that he has wrought,
   his portents and the judgements he has given,

13 O offspring of Israel his servants, O chosen sons of Jacob.

14 He is the LORD our God;
   his judgements fill the earth.

15 He called to mind his covenant from long ago,^g
   the promise he extended to a thousand generations—

16 the covenant made with Abraham,
   his oath given to Isaac,

---

^a *Verses 25–29: cp. 2 Sam. 6. 12–16.*   ^b the precentor: *prob. rdg.; Heb. obscure.*
^c *Verses 1–3: cp. 2 Sam. 6. 17–19.*   ^d *Prob. rdg., cp. 15. 18, 20; Heb.* Jeiel.
^e *Verses 8–22: cp. Ps. 105. 1–15.*   ^f your strength: *or the symbol of his strength;*
lit. and his strength.   ^g from long ago: *or for ever.*

the decree by which he bound himself for Jacob,   17
his everlasting covenant with Israel:
'I will give you the land of Canaan', he said,   18
    'to be your possession, your patrimony.'
    A small company it was,   19
few in number, strangers in that land,
roaming from nation to nation,   20
from one kingdom to another;
but he let no man ill-treat them,   21
for their sake he admonished kings:
    'Touch not my anointed servants,   22
    do my prophets no harm.'

Sing to the LORD, all men on earth,   23[a]
proclaim his triumph day by day.
Declare his glory among the nations,   24
    his marvellous deeds among all peoples.
Great is the LORD and worthy of all praise;   25
he is more to be feared than all gods.
For the gods of the nations are idols every one;   26
but the LORD made the heavens.
Majesty and splendour attend him,   27
might and joy are in his dwelling.

Ascribe to the LORD, you families of nations,   28
ascribe to the LORD glory and might;
    ascribe to the LORD the glory due to his name,   29
bring a gift and come before him.
    Bow down to the LORD in the splendour of holiness,[b]
    and dance in his honour, all men on earth.   30
    He has fixed the earth firm, immovable.
Let the heavens rejoice and the earth exult,   31
let men declare among the nations, 'The LORD is king.'
    Let the sea roar and all the creatures in it,   32
    let the fields exult and all that is in them;
    then let the trees of the forest shout for joy   33
    before the LORD when he comes to judge the earth.

It is good to give thanks to the LORD,   34[c]
    for his love endures for ever.
Cry, 'Deliver us, O God our saviour,   35[d]
gather us in and save us from the nations
    that we may give thanks to thy holy name
    and make thy praise our pride.'

Blessed be the LORD the God of Israel   36
    from everlasting to everlasting.

And all the people said 'Amen' and 'Praise the LORD.'

[a] *Verses 23–33: cp. Ps. 96. 1–13.*   [b] *Or in holy vestments.*   [c] *Verse 34:*
cp. Ps. 107. 1.   [d] *Verses 35, 36: cp. Ps. 106. 47, 48.*

37 David left Asaph and his kinsmen there before the Ark of the Covenant of the Lord, to perform regular service before the Ark as each day's duty
38 required; as door-keepers he left Obed-edom son of Jeduthun, and Hosah.
39 (Obed-edom and his kinsmen were sixty-eight in number.) He left Zadok the priest and his kinsmen the priests before the Tabernacle of the Lord
40 at the hill-shrine in Gibeon, to make offerings there to the Lord upon the altar of whole-offering regularly morning and evening, exactly as it is
41 written in the law enjoined by the Lord upon Israel. With them he left Heman and Jeduthun and the other men chosen and nominated to give
42 thanks to the Lord, 'for his love endures for ever.' They had trumpets and cymbals for the players, and the instruments used for sacred song. The sons of Jeduthun kept the gate.
43 So all the people went home, and David returned to greet his household.

17 1ᵃ As soon as David was established in his house, he said to Nathan the prophet, 'Here I live in a house of cedar, while the Ark of the Covenant
2 of the Lord is housed in curtains.' Nathan answered David, 'Do whatever
3 you have in mind, for God is with you.' But that night the word of God
4 came to Nathan: 'Go and say to David my servant, "This is the word of
5 the Lord: It is not you who shall build me a house to dwell in. Down to this day I have never dwelt in a house since I brought Israel up from
6 Egypt; I lived in a tent and a tabernacle.ᵇ Wherever I journeyed with Israel, did I ever ask any of the judges whom I appointed shepherds of my
7 people why they had not built me a house of cedar?" Then say this to my servant David: "This is the word of the Lord of Hosts: I took you from the pastures, and from following the sheep, to be prince over my people
8 Israel. I have been with you wherever you have gone, and have destroyed all the enemies in your path. I will make you as famous as the great ones
9 of the earth. I will assign a place for my people Israel; there I will plant them, and they shall dwell in their own land. They shall be disturbed no
10 more, never again shall wicked men wear them down as they did from the time when I first appointed judges over Israel my people, and I will subdue all your enemies. But I will make you great and the Lord shall build
11 up your royal house. When your life ends and you go to join your forefathers, I will set up one of your family, one of your own sons, to succeed
12 you, and I will establish his kingdom. It is he shall build me a house, and
13 I will establish his throne for all time. I will be his father, and he shall be my son. I will never withdraw my love from him as I withdrew it from your
14 predecessor. But I will give him a sure place in my house and kingdom for all time, and his throne shall be established for ever."'
15 Nathan recounted to David all that had been said to him and all that
16 had been revealed. Then King David went into the presence of the Lord and took his place there and said, 'What am I, Lord God, and what is my
17 family, that thou hast brought me thus far? It was a small thing in thy sight, O God, to have planned for thy servant's house in days long past, and now thou lookest upon me as a man already embarked on a high

---

ᵃ *Verses 1–27: cp. 2 Sam. 7. 1–29.*　　ᵇ I lived . . . tabernacle: *prob. rdg.; Heb.* I have been from tent to tent and from a tabernacle.

career, O LORD God. What more can David say to thee of the honour thou 18
hast done thy servant, well though thou knowest him? For the sake of thy 19
servant, LORD, and according to thy purpose, thou hast brought me to all
this greatness. O LORD, we have never heard of one like thee; there is no 20
god but thee. And thy people Israel, to whom can they be compared? Is 21
there any other nation on earth whom God has gone out to redeem from
slavery, to make them his people? Thou hast won a name for thyself by
great and terrible deeds, driving out nations before thy people whom thou
didst redeem from Egypt. Thou hast made thy people Israel thy own for 22
ever, and thou, O LORD, hast become their God. But now, LORD, let what 23
thou hast promised for thy servant and his house stand fast for all time;
make good what thou hast said. Let it stand fast, that thy fame may be 24
great for ever, and let men say, "The LORD of Hosts, the God of Israel, is
Israel's God." So shall the house of thy servant David be established before
thee. Thou, my God, hast shown me thy purpose to build up thy servant's 25
house; therefore I have been able to pray before thee. Thou, O LORD, art 26
God, and thou hast made these noble promises to thy servant; thou hast 27
been pleased to bless thy servant's house, that it may continue always
before thee; thou it is who hast blessed it, and it shall be blessed for
ever.'

After this David defeated the Philistines and conquered them, and took **18** 1[a]
from them Gath with its villages; he defeated the Moabites, and they 2
became subject to him and paid him tribute. He also defeated Hadadezer 3
king of Zobah-hamath, who was on his way to set up a monument of victory
by the river Euphrates. From him David captured a thousand chariots, 4
seven thousand horsemen and twenty thousand foot; he hamstrung all the
chariot-horses, except a hundred which he retained. When the Aramaeans 5
of Damascus came to the help of Hadadezer king of Zobah, David destroyed
twenty-two thousand of them, and established garrisons among these 6
Aramaeans; they became subject to him and paid him tribute. Thus the
LORD gave David victory wherever he went. David took the gold quivers 7
borne by Hadadezer's servants and brought them to Jerusalem. He also 8
took a great quantity of bronze[b] from Hadadezer's cities, Tibhath and
Kun; from this Solomon made the Sea of bronze,[b] the pillars, and the
bronze[b] vessels.

When Tou king of Hamath heard that David had defeated the entire 9
army of Hadadezer king of Zobah, he sent his son Hadoram to King David 10
to greet him and to congratulate him on defeating Hadadezer in battle (for
Hadadezer had been at war with Tou); and he brought with him vessels of
gold, silver, and copper, which King David dedicated to the LORD. He 11
dedicated also the silver and the gold which he had carried away from all
the other nations, from Edom and Moab, from the Ammonites and the
Philistines, and from Amalek.

Edom was defeated by Abishai son of Zeruiah, who destroyed eighteen 12
thousand of them in the Valley of Salt and stationed garrisons in the 13
country. All the Edomites now became subject to David. Thus the LORD
gave victory to David wherever he went.

[a] *Verses 1-13: cp. 2 Sam. 8. 1-14.*   [b] *Or* copper.

14 *a* David ruled over the whole of Israel and maintained law and justice
15 among all his people. Joab son of Zeruiah was in command of the army;
16 Jehoshaphat son of Ahilud was secretary of state; Zadok and Abiathar
son of Ahimelech, son of Ahitub, *b* were priests; Shavsha was adjutant-
17 general; Benaiah son of Jehoiada commanded the Kerethite and Pelethite
guards. The eldest sons of David were in attendance on the king.

19 1 *c* Some time afterwards Nahash king of the Ammonites died and was
2 succeeded by his son. David said, 'I must keep up the same loyal friendship with Hanun son of Nahash as his father showed me', and he sent a
mission to condole with him on the death of his father. But when David's
3 envoys entered the country of the Ammonites to condole with Hanun,
the Ammonite princes said to Hanun, 'Do you suppose David means to do
honour to your father when he sends you his condolences? These men of
his are spies whom he has sent to find out how to overthrow the country.'
4 So Hanun took David's servants, and he shaved them, cut off half their
5 garments up to the hips, and dismissed them. When David heard how they
had been treated, he sent to meet them, for they were deeply humiliated,
and ordered them to wait in Jericho and not to return until their beards
6 had grown again. The Ammonites knew that they had brought themselves
into bad odour with David, so Hanun and the Ammonites sent a thousand
talents of silver to hire chariots and horsemen from Aram-naharaim, *d*
7 Maacah, and Aram-zobah. *e* They hired thirty-two thousand chariots and
the king of Maacah and his people, who came and encamped before
Medeba, while the Ammonites came from their cities and mustered for
8 battle. When David heard of it, he sent out Joab and all the fighting men.
9 The Ammonites came and took up their position at the entrance to the
10 city, while the allied kings took up theirs in the open country. When Joab
saw that he was threatened both front and rear, he detailed some picked
11 Israelite troops and drew them up facing the Aramaeans. The rest of his
forces he put under his brother Abishai, who took up a position facing the
12 Ammonites. 'If the Aramaeans prove too strong for me,' he said, 'you must
come to my relief; and if the Ammonites prove too strong for you, I will
13 relieve you. Courage! Let us fight bravely for our people and for the cities *f*
14 of our God. And the LORD's will be done.' But when Joab and his men came
15 to close quarters with the Aramaeans, they put them to flight; and when the
Ammonites saw them in flight, they too fled before his brother Abishai and
16 entered the city. Then Joab came to Jerusalem. The Aramaeans saw that
they had been worsted by Israel, and they sent messengers to summon other
Aramaeans from the Great Bend of the Euphrates under Shophach, com-
17 mander of Hadadezer's army. Their movement was reported to David,
who immediately mustered all the forces of Israel, crossed the Jordan and
advanced against them and took up battle positions. The Aramaeans like-
18 wise took up positions facing David and engaged him, but were put to
flight by Israel. David slew seven thousand Aramaeans in chariots and

---

a *Verses 14–17: cp. 2 Sam. 8. 15–18; 20. 23–26; 1 Kgs. 4. 2–4.*   *b* and Abiathar . . .
Ahitub: *prob. rdg., cp. 2 Sam. 8. 17; Heb.* son of Ahitub and Abimelech son of Abiathar.
c *Verses 1–19: cp. 2 Sam. 10. 1–19.*   *d* *That is* Aram of Two Rivers.   *e* Maacah,
and Aram-zobah: *prob. rdg.; Heb.* Aram-maacah, and Zobah.   *f* *Or* altars.

forty thousand infantry, killing Shophach the commander of the army. When Hadadezer's men saw that they had been worsted by Israel, they 19 sued for peace and submitted to David. The Aramaeans were never again willing to give support to the Ammonites.

AT THE TURN OF THE YEAR, when kings take the field, Joab led the army 20 1*a* out and ravaged the Ammonite country. He came to Rabbah and laid siege to it, while David remained in Jerusalem; he reduced the city and razed it to the ground. David took the crown from the head of Milcom and found 2 that it weighed a talent of gold and was set with a precious stone, and this he placed on his own head. He also removed a great quantity of booty from the city; he took its inhabitants and set them to work with saws and other 3 iron tools, sharp and toothed. David did this to all the cities of the Ammonites; then he and all his people returned to Jerusalem.

· Some time later war with the Philistines broke out in Gezer; it was then 4*b* that Sibbechai of Hushah killed Sippai, a descendant of the Rephaim, and the Philistines were reduced to submission. In another war with the 5 Philistines, Elhanan son of Jair killed Lahmi brother of Goliath of Gath, whose spear had a shaft like a weaver's beam. In yet another war in Gath, 6 there appeared a giant with six fingers on each hand and six toes on each foot, twenty-four in all; he too was descended from the Rephaim, and, 7 when he defied Israel, Jonathan son of David's brother Shimea killed him. These giants were the descendants of the Rephaim in Gath, and they all 8 fell at the hands of David and his men.

NOW SATAN, SETTING HIMSELF AGAINST ISRAEL, incited David 21 1*c* to count the people. So he instructed Joab and his public officers to go 2 out and number Israel, from Beersheba to Dan, and to report the number to him. Joab answered, 'Even if the LORD should increase his people a 3 hundredfold, would not your majesty still be king and all the people your slaves? Why should your majesty want to do this? It will only bring guilt on Israel.' But Joab was overruled by the king; he set out and went up and 4 down the whole country. He then came to Jerusalem and reported to 5 David the numbers recorded: those capable of bearing arms were one million one hundred thousand in Israel, and four hundred and seventy thousand in Judah. Levi and Benjamin were not counted by Joab, so deep 6 was his repugnance against the king's order.

God was displeased with all this and proceeded to punish Israel. David 7 8 said to God, 'I have done a very wicked thing: I pray thee remove thy servant's guilt, for I have been very foolish.' And the LORD said to Gad, 9 David's seer, 'Go and tell David, "This is the word of the LORD: I have 10 three things to offer you; choose one of them and I will bring it upon you."' So Gad came to David and said to him, 'This is the word of the LORD: 11 "Make your choice: three years of famine, three months of harrying by your 12 foes and close pursuit by the sword of your enemy, or three days of the LORD's own sword, bringing pestilence throughout the country, and the

a *Verses 1-3 : cp. 2 Sam. 12. 26-31.*   *b* *Verses 4-7 : cp. 2 Sam. 21. 18-22.*
c *Verses 1-27 : cp. 2 Sam. 24. 1-25.*

LORD's angel working destruction in all the territory of Israel." Consider
13 now what answer I am to take back to him who sent me.' Thereupon David
said to Gad, 'I am in a desperate plight; let me fall into the hands of the
LORD, for his mercy is very great; and let me not fall into the hands of man.'
14 So the LORD sent a pestilence throughout Israel, and seventy thousand men
15 of Israel died. And God sent an angel to Jerusalem to destroy it; but, as he
was destroying it, the LORD saw and repented of the evil, and said to the
destroying angel at the moment when he was standing beside the threshing-
floor of Ornan the Jebusite, 'Enough! Stay your hand.'
16 When David looked up and saw the angel of the LORD standing between
earth and heaven, with his sword drawn in his hand and stretched out over
Jerusalem, he and the elders, clothed in sackcloth, fell prostrate to the
17 ground; and David said to God, 'It was I who gave the order to count the
people. It was I who sinned, I, the shepherd,*a* who did wrong. But these
poor sheep, what have they done? O LORD my God, let thy hand fall upon
me and upon my family, but check this plague on the people.'*b*
18 The angel of the LORD, speaking through the lips of Gad, commanded
David to go to the threshing-floor of Ornan the Jebusite and to set up there
19 an altar to the LORD. David went up as Gad had bidden him in the LORD's
20 name. Ornan's four sons who were with him hid themselves, but he was
21 busy threshing his wheat when he turned and saw the angel. As David
approached, Ornan looked up and, seeing the king, came out from the
22 threshing-floor and prostrated himself before him. David said to Ornan,
'Let me have the site of the threshing-floor that I may build on it an altar
to the LORD; sell it me at the full price, that the plague which has attacked
23 my people may be stopped.' Ornan answered David, 'Take it and let your
majesty do as he thinks fit; see, here are the oxen for whole-offerings, the
threshing-sledges for the fuel, and the wheat for the grain-offering; I give
24 you everything.' But King David said to Ornan, 'No, I will pay the full
price; I will not present to the LORD what is yours, or offer a whole-offering
25 which has cost me nothing.' So David gave Ornan six hundred shekels of
26 gold for the site, and built an altar to the LORD there; on this he offered
whole-offerings and shared-offerings, and called upon the LORD, who
answered him with fire falling from heaven on the altar of whole-offering.
27 Then, at the LORD's command, the angel sheathed his sword.
28 It was when David saw that the LORD had answered him at the threshing-
29 floor of Ornan the Jebusite that he offered sacrifice there. The tabernacle
of the LORD and the altar of whole-offering which Moses had made in the
30 wilderness were then at the hill-shrine in Gibeon; but David had been
unable to go there and seek God's guidance, so shocked and shaken was he
22 at the sight of the angel's sword. Then David said, 'This is to be the house
of the LORD God, and this is to be an altar of whole-offering for Israel.'

---

a I, the shepherd: *prob. rdg.; Heb.* doing wrong.   *b* check ... people: *prob. rdg.;*
Heb. among thy people, not for a plague.

468

The temple and its organization

DAVID NOW GAVE ORDERS to assemble the aliens resident in Israel, 2 and he set them as masons to dress hewn stones and to build the house of God. He laid in a great store of iron to make nails and clamps for the 3 doors, more bronze than could be weighed and cedar-wood without limit; 4 the men of Sidon and Tyre brought David an ample supply of cedar. David said, 'My son Solomon is a boy of tender years, and the house that 5 is to be built to the LORD must be exceedingly magnificent, renowned and celebrated in every land; therefore I must make preparations for it myself.' So David made abundant preparation before his death.

He sent for Solomon his son and charged him to build a house for the 6 LORD the God of Israel. 'Solomon, my son,' he said, 'I had intended to 7 build a house in honour of the name of the LORD my God; but the LORD 8 forbade me and said, "You have shed much blood in my sight and waged great wars; for this reason you shall not build a house in honour of my name. But you shall have a son who shall be a man of peace; I will give him 9^a peace from all his enemies on every side; his name shall be Solomon, 'Man of Peace', and I will grant peace and quiet to Israel in his days. He 10 shall build a house in honour of my name; he shall be my son and I will be a father to him, and I will establish the throne of his sovereignty over Israel for ever." Now, Solomon my son, the LORD be with you! May you 11 prosper and build the house of the LORD your God, as he promised you should. But may the LORD grant you wisdom and discretion, so that when 12 he gives you authority in Israel you may keep the law of the LORD your God. You will prosper only if you are careful to observe the decrees and 13 ordinances which the LORD enjoined upon Moses for Israel; be strong and resolute, neither faint-hearted nor dismayed.

'In spite of all my troubles, I have here ready for the house of the LORD 14 a hundred thousand talents of gold and a million talents of silver, with great quantities of bronze and iron, more than can be weighed; timber and stone, too, I have got ready; and you may add to them. Besides, you have 15 a large force of workmen, masons, sculptors, and carpenters, and countless men skilled in work of every kind, in gold and silver, bronze and iron. So 16 now to work, and the LORD be with you!'

David ordered all the officers of Israel to help Solomon his son: 'Is not 17 18 the LORD your God with you? Will he not give you peace on every side? For he has given the inhabitants of the land into my power, and they will be subject to the LORD and his people. Devote yourselves, therefore, heart 19 and soul, to seeking guidance of the LORD your God, and set about building his sanctuary, so that the Ark of the Covenant of the LORD and God's holy vessels may be brought into a house built in honour of his name.'

David was now an old man, weighed down with years, and he appointed **23** Solomon his son king over Israel. He gathered together all the officers of 2 Israel, the priests, and the Levites. The Levites were enrolled from the age 3 of thirty upwards, their males being thirty-eight thousand in all. Of these, 4 twenty-four thousand were to be responsible for the maintenance and

a Verse 9: cp. 1 Kgs. 5. 4.

service of the house of the LORD, six thousand to act as officers and magis-
5 trates, four thousand to be door-keepers, and four thousand to praise the
LORD on the musical instruments which David had made for the service
6 of praise. David organized them in divisions, called after Gershon, Kohath,
and Merari, the sons of Levi.

7 8   The sons of Gershon: Laadan and Shimei. The sons of Laadan: Jehiel
9 the chief, Zetham and Joel, three.[a] These were the heads of the families
10 grouped under Laadan. The sons of Shimei: Jahath, Ziza, Jeush and
11 Beriah, four. Jahath was the chief and Ziza the second, but Jeush and
Beriah, having few children, were reckoned for duty as a single family.

12 13   The sons of Kohath: Amram, Izhar, Hebron and Uzziel, four. The sons
of Amram: Aaron and Moses. Aaron was set apart, he and his sons in
perpetuity, to dedicate the most holy gifts,[b] to burn sacrifices before the
14 LORD, to serve him, and to give the blessing in his name for ever, but
15 the sons of Moses, the man of God, were to keep the name of Levite. The
16 sons of Moses: Gershom and Eliezer. The sons of Gershom: Shubael the
17 chief. The sons of Eliezer: Rehabiah the chief. Eliezer had no other sons,
18 but Rehabiah had very many. The sons of Izhar: Shelomoth the chief.
19 The sons of Hebron: Jeriah the chief, Amariah the second, Jahaziel the
20 third and Jekameam the fourth. The sons of Uzziel: Micah the chief and
Isshiah the second.

21   The sons of Merari: Mahli and Mushi. The sons of Mahli: Eleazar and
22 Kish. When Eleazar died, he left daughters but no sons, and their cousins,
23 the sons of Kish, married them. The sons of Mushi: Mahli, Eder and
Jeremoth, three.

24   Such were the Levites, grouped by families in the father's line whose
heads were entered in the detailed list; they performed duties in the
25 service of the house of the LORD, from the age of twenty upwards. For
David said, 'The LORD the God of Israel has given his people peace and
26 has made his abode in Jerusalem for ever. The Levites will no longer have
27 to carry the Tabernacle or any of the vessels for its service.' By these last
words of David the Levites were enrolled from the age of twenty upwards.
28 Their duty was to help the sons of Aaron in the service of the house of the
LORD: they were responsible for the care of the courts and the rooms, for
the cleansing of all holy things, and the general service of the house of God;
29 for the rows of the Bread of the Presence, the flour for the grain-offerings,
unleavened wafers, cakes baked on the griddle, and pastry, and for the
30 weights and measures. They were to be on duty continually before the
31 LORD every morning and evening, giving thanks and praise to him, and
at every offering of whole-offerings to the LORD, on sabbaths, new moons
32 and at the appointed seasons, according to their prescribed number. The
Levites were to have charge of the Tent of the Presence and of the sanctuary,
but the sons of Aaron their kinsmen were charged with the service of
worship in the house of the LORD.

24   The divisions of the sons of Aaron: his sons were Nadab and Abihu,
2 Eleazar and Ithamar. Nadab and Abihu died before their father, leaving

---

[a] *Prob. rdg.; Heb. adds* The sons of Shimei: Shelomith, Haziel and Haran, three.
[b] to dedicate ... gifts: *or* to be hallowed as most holy.

no sons; therefore Eleazar and Ithamar held the office of priest. David, 3
acting with Zadok of the sons of Eleazar and with Ahimelech of the sons
of Ithamar, organized them in divisions for the discharge of the duties of
their office. The male heads of families proved to be more numerous in the 4
line of Eleazar than in that of Ithamar, so that sixteen heads of families
were grouped under the line of Eleazar and eight under that of Ithamar.
He organized them by drawing lots among them, for there were sacred 5
officers[a] and officers of God in the line of Eleazar and in that of Ithamar.
Shemaiah the clerk, a Levite, son of Nethaneel, wrote down the names in 6
the presence of the king, the officers, Zadok the priest, and Ahimelech son
of Abiathar, and of the heads of the priestly and levitical families, one
priestly family being taken from the line of Eleazar and one from that of
Ithamar. The first lot fell to Jehoiarib, the second to Jedaiah, the third to 7 8
Harim, the fourth to Seorim, the fifth to Malchiah, the sixth to Mijamin, 9
the seventh to Hakkoz, the eighth to Abiah, the ninth to Jeshua, the tenth 10 11
to Shecaniah, the eleventh to Eliashib, the twelfth to Jakim, the thirteenth 12 13
to Huppah, the fourteenth to Jeshebeab, the fifteenth to Bilgah, the six- 14
teenth to Immer, the seventeenth to Hezir, the eighteenth to Aphses, the 15 16
nineteenth to Pethahiah, the twentieth to Jehezekel, the twenty-first to 17
Jachin, the twenty-second to Gamul, the twenty-third to Delaiah, and the 18
twenty-fourth to Maaziah. This was their order of duty for the discharge 19
of their service when they entered the house of the LORD, according to the
rule prescribed for them by their ancestor Aaron, who had received his
instructions from the LORD the God of Israel.

Of the remaining Levites: of the sons of Amram: Shubael. Of the sons 20
of Shubael: Jehdeiah. Of Rehabiah: Isshiah, the chief of Rehabiah's sons. 21
Of the line of Izhar: Shelomoth. Of the sons of Shelomoth: Jahath. The 22 23
sons of Hebron: Jeriah the chief, Amariah the second, Jahaziel the third
and Jekameam the fourth. The sons of Uzziel: Micah. Of the sons of 24
Micah: Shamir; Micah's brother: Isshiah. Of the sons of Isshiah: Zechari- 25
ah. The sons of Merari: Mahli and Mushi and also[b] Jaaziah his son. The 26 27
sons of Merari: of Jaaziah: Beno, Shoham, Zaccur and Ibri. Of Mahli: 28
Eleazar, who had no sons; of Kish: the sons of Kish: Jerahmeel; and the 29 30
sons of Mushi: Mahli, Eder and Jerimoth. These were the Levites by
families. These also, side by side with their kinsmen the sons of Aaron, 31
cast lots in the presence of King David, Zadok, Ahimelech, and the heads
of the priestly and levitical families, the senior and junior houses casting
lots side by side.

David and his chief officers assigned special duties to the sons of Asaph, **25**
of Heman, and of Jeduthun, leaders in inspired prophecy to the accompaniment of harps, lutes, and cymbals; the number of the men who performed this work in the temple was as follows. Of the sons of Asaph: 2
Zaccur, Joseph, Nethaniah and Asarelah; these were under Asaph, a
leader in inspired prophecy under the king. Of the sons of Jeduthun: 3
Gedaliah, Izri,[c] Isaiah, Shimei, Hashabiah, Mattithiah, these six under
their father Jeduthun, a leader in inspired prophecy to the accompaniment

[a] sacred officers: *or* officers of the sanctuary.   [b] and also: *prob. rdg.*; *Heb.* the sons of.
[c] *Prob. rdg., cp. verse 11*; *Heb.* Zeri.

4 of the harp, giving thanks and praise to the LORD. Of the sons of Heman: Bukkiah, Mattaniah, Uzziel, Shubael, Jerimoth, Hananiah, Hanani, Eliathah, Giddalti, Romamti-ezer, Joshbekashah, Mallothi, Hothir, and
5 Mahazioth; all these were sons of Heman the king's seer, given to him through the promises of God for his greater glory. God had given Heman
6 fourteen sons and three daughters, and they all served under their father for the singing in the house of the LORD; they took part in the service of the house of God, with cymbals, lutes, and harps, while Asaph, Jeduthun,
7 and Heman were under the king. Reckoned with their kinsmen, trained singers of the LORD, they brought the total number of skilled musicians up
8 to two hundred and eighty-eight. They cast lots for their duties, young and old, master-singer and apprentice side by side.

9 The first lot fell[a] to Joseph: he and his brothers and his sons, twelve. [b]
10 The second to Gedaliah: he and his brothers and his sons, twelve. The third
11 to Zaccur: his sons and his brothers, twelve. The fourth to Izri: his sons
12 and his brothers, twelve. The fifth to Nethaniah: his sons and his brothers,
13 14 twelve. The sixth to Bukkiah: his sons and his brothers, twelve. The
15 seventh to Asarelah: his sons and his brothers, twelve. The eighth to
16 Isaiah: his sons and his brothers, twelve. The ninth to Mattaniah: his sons
17 and his brothers, twelve. The tenth to Shimei: his sons and his brothers,
18 19 twelve. The eleventh to Azareel: his sons and his brothers, twelve. The
20 twelfth to Hashabiah: his sons and his brothers, twelve. The thirteenth
21 to Shubael: his sons and his brothers, twelve. The fourteenth to Mat-
22 tithiah: his sons and his brothers, twelve. The fifteenth to Jeremoth: his
23 sons and his brothers, twelve. The sixteenth to Hananiah: his sons and
24 his brothers, twelve. The seventeenth to Joshbekashah: his sons and his
25 brothers, twelve. The eighteenth to Hanani: his sons and his brothers,
26 twelve. The nineteenth to Mallothi: his sons and his brothers, twelve.
27 28 The twentieth to Eliathah: his sons and his brothers, twelve. The twenty-
29 first to Hothir: his sons and his brothers, twelve. The twenty-second to
30 Giddalti: his sons and his brothers, twelve. The twenty-third to Mahazioth:
31 his sons and his brothers, twelve. The twenty-fourth to Romamti-ezer: his sons and his brothers, twelve.

26   The divisions of the door-keepers: Korahites: Meshelemiah son of
2 Kore, son of Ebiasaph.[c] Sons of Meshelemiah: Zechariah the eldest,
3 Jediael the second, Zebediah the third, Jathniel the fourth, Elam the fifth,
4 Jehohanan the sixth, Elioenai the seventh. Sons of Obed-edom: Shemaiah the eldest, Jehozabad the second, Joah the third, Sacar the fourth, Neth-
5 aneel the fifth, Ammiel the sixth, Issachar the seventh, Peulthai the eighth
6 (for God had blessed him). Shemaiah, his son, was the father of sons who
7 had authority in their family, for they were men of great ability. Sons of Shemaiah: Othni, Rephael, Obed, Elzabad and his brothers Elihu and
8 Semachiah, men of ability. All these belonged to the family of Obed-edom; they, their sons and brothers, were men of ability, fit for service in the
9 temple; total: sixty-two. Sons and brothers of Meshelemiah, all men of abil-
10 ity, eighteen. Sons of Hosah, a Merarite: Shimri the chief (he was not the

[a] *Prob. rdg.; Heb. adds* to Asaph.   [b] he . . . twelve: *prob. rdg.; Heb. om.*   [c] son of Ebiasaph: *prob. rdg.; Heb.* from the sons of Asaph.

eldest, but his father had made him chief), Hilkiah the second, Tebaliah the 11 third, Zechariah the fourth. Total of Hosah's sons and brothers: thirteen.

The male heads of families constituted the divisions of the door-keepers; 12 their duty was to serve in the house of the LORD side by side with their kinsmen. Young and old, family by family, they cast lots for the gates. The 13 14 lot for the east gate fell to Shelemiah; then lots were cast for his son Zechariah, a prudent counsellor, and he was allotted the north gate. To 15 Obed-edom was allotted the south gate, and the gatehouse to his sons. Hosah*a* was allotted the west gate, together with the Shallecheth gate on 16 the ascending causeway. Guard corresponded to guard. Six Levites were 17 on duty daily on the east side, four on the north and four on the south, and two at each gatehouse; at the western colonnade there were four at the 18 causeway and two at the colonnade itself. These were the divisions of the 19 door-keepers, Korahites and Merarites.

Fellow-Levites were in charge of the stores of the house of God and of the 20 stores of sacred gifts. Of the children of Laadan, descendants of the Ger- 21 shonite line through Laadan, heads of families in the group of Laadan the Gershonite, Jehiel and*b* his brothers Zetham and Joel were in charge of the 22 stores of the house of the LORD. Of the families of Amram, Izhar, Hebron 23 and Uzziel, Shubael son of Gershom, son of Moses, was overseer of the 24 stores. The line of Eliezer his brother: his son Rehabiah, his son Isaiah, 25 his son Joram, his son Zichri, and his son Shelomoth. This Shelomoth and 26 his kinsmen were in charge of all the stores of the sacred gifts dedicated by David the king, the heads of families, the officers over units of a thousand and a hundred, and other officers of the army. They had dedicated some 27 of the spoils taken in the wars for the upkeep of the house of the LORD. Everything which Samuel the seer, Saul son of Kish, Abner son of Ner, 28 and Joab son of Zeruiah had dedicated, in short every sacred gift, was under the charge of Shelomoth and his kinsmen. Of the family of Izhar, 29 Kenaniah and his sons acted as clerks and magistrates in the secular affairs of Israel. Of the family of Hebron, Hashabiah and his kinsmen, men of 30 ability to the number of seventeen hundred, had the oversight of Israel west of the Jordan, both in the work of the LORD and in the service of the king. Also of the family of Hebron, Jeriah was the chief. (In the fortieth 31 year of David's reign search was made in the family histories of the Hebron- ites, and men of great ability were found among them at Jazer in Gilead.) His kinsmen, all men of ability, two thousand seven hundred of them, 32 heads of families, were charged by King David with the oversight of the Reubenites, the Gadites, and the half tribe of Manasseh, in religious and civil affairs alike.

THE NUMBER OF THE ISRAELITES—that is to say, of the heads of fami- **27** lies, the officers over units of a thousand and a hundred, and the clerks who had their share in the king's service in the various divisions which took monthly turns of duty throughout the year—was twenty-four thousand in each division.

a Hosah: *prob. rdg.; Heb.* Shuppim and Hosah.   *b* Jehiel and: *prob. rdg.; Heb.* Jehieli. The sons of Jehieli . . .

2 First, Jashobeam son of Zabdiel commanded the division for the first
3 month with twenty-four thousand in his division; a member of the house
4 of Perez, he was chief officer of the temple staff for the first month. Eleazar
   son of *a* Dodai the Ahohite commanded the division for the second month
5 with twenty-four thousand in his division. Third, Benaiah son of Jehoiada
   the chief priest, commander of the army, was the officer for the third month
6 with twenty-four thousand in his division (he was the Benaiah who was
   one of the thirty warriors and was a chief among the thirty); but his son
7 Ammizabad commanded his division. Fourth, Asahel, the brother of
   Joab, was the officer commanding for the fourth month with twenty-four
8 thousand in his division; and his successor was Zebediah his son. Fifth,
   Shamhuth the Zerahite *b* was the officer commanding for the fifth month
9 with twenty-four thousand in his division. Sixth, Ira son of Ikkesh, a man
   of Tekoa, was the officer commanding for the sixth month with twenty-
10 four thousand in his division. Seventh, Helez an Ephraimite, from a
   place unknown, was the officer commanding for the seventh month with
11 twenty-four thousand in his division. Eighth, Sibbecai the Hushathite,
   of the family of Zerah, was the officer commanding for the eighth month
12 with twenty-four thousand in his division. Ninth, Abiezer, from Anathoth
   in Benjamin, was the officer commanding for the ninth month with twenty-
13 four thousand in his division. Tenth, Maharai the Netophathite, of the
   family of Zerah, was the officer commanding for the tenth month with
14 twenty-four thousand in his division. Eleventh, Benaiah the Pirathonite,
   from Ephraim, was the officer commanding for the eleventh month with
15 twenty-four thousand in his division. Twelfth, Heldai the Netophathite,
   of the family of Othniel, was the officer commanding for the twelfth month
   with twenty-four thousand in his division.

16 The following were the principal officers in charge of the tribes of
   Israel: of Reuben, Eliezer son of Zichri; of Simeon, Shephatiah son of
17 18 Maacah; of Levi, Hashabiah son of Kemuel; of Aaron, Zadok; of Judah,
19 Elihu a kinsman of David; of Issachar, Omri son of Michael; of Zebulun,
20 Ishmaiah son of Obadiah; of Naphtali, Jerimoth son of Azriel; of Ephraim,
   Hoshea son of Azaziah; of the half tribe of Manasseh, Joel son of Pedaiah;
21 of the half of Manasseh in Gilead, Iddo son of Zechariah; of Benjamin,
22 Jaasiel son of Abner; of Dan, Azareel son of Jeroham. These were the
   officers in charge of the tribes of Israel.

23 David took no census of those under twenty years of age, for the LORD
   had promised to make the Israelites as many as the stars in the heavens.
24 Joab son of Zeruiah did begin to take a census but he did not finish it;
   this brought harm upon Israel, and the census was not entered in the
   chronicle of King David's reign.

25 Azmoth son of Adiel was in charge of the king's stores; Jonathan son of
   Uzziah was in charge of the stores in the country, in the cities, in the
26 villages and in the fortresses. Ezri son of Kelub had oversight of the workers
27 on the land; Shimei of Ramah was in charge of the vine-dressers, while
   Zabdi of Shephem had charge of the produce of the vineyards for the

---

a Eleazar son of: *prob. rdg., cp. 11. 12; Heb. om.*   *b* the Zerahite: *prob. rdg.; Heb.*
the Izrah.

wine-cellars. Baal-hanan the Gederite supervised the wild olives and the 28
sycomore-figs in the Shephelah; Joash was in charge of the oil-stores.
Shitrai of Sharon was in charge of the herds grazing in Sharon, Shaphat son 29
of Adlai of the herds in the vales. Obil the Ishmaelite was in charge of the 30
camels, Jehdeiah the Meronothite of the asses. Jaziz the Hagerite was in 31
charge of the flocks. All these were the officers in charge of King David's
possessions. David's favourite nephew Jonathan, a counsellor, a discreet 32
and learned man, and Jehiel the Hachmonite, were tutors to the king's sons.
Ahithophel was a king's counsellor; Hushai the Archite was the King's 33
Friend. Ahithophel was succeeded by Jehoiada son of Benaiah, and 34
Abiathar. Joab was commander of the army.

DAVID ASSEMBLED AT JERUSALEM all the officers of Israel, the officers 28
over the tribes, over the divisions engaged in the king's service, over the
units of a thousand and a hundred, and those in charge of all the property
and the cattle of the king and of his sons, as well as the eunuchs, the heroes
and all the men of ability. Then King David rose to his feet and said, 'Hear 2
me, kinsmen and people. I had in mind to build a house as a resting-place
for the Ark of the Covenant of the LORD which might serve as a footstool
for the feet of our God, and I made preparations to build it. But God said 3
to me, "You shall not build a house in honour of my name, for you have
been a fighting man and you have shed blood." Nevertheless, the LORD 4
the God of Israel chose me out of all my father's family to be king over
Israel in perpetuity; for it was Judah that he chose as ruling tribe, and, out
of the house of Judah, my father's family; and among my father's sons it
was I whom he was pleased to make king over all Israel. And out of all 5
my sons—for the LORD gave me many sons—he chose Solomon to sit
upon the throne of the LORD's sovereignty over Israel; and he said to me, 6
"It is Solomon your son who shall build my house and my courts, for I
have chosen him to be a son to me and I will be a father to him. I will 7
establish his sovereignty in perpetuity, if only he steadfastly obeys my
commandments and my laws as they are now obeyed." Now therefore, in 8
the presence of all Israel, the assembly of the LORD, and within the hearing
of our God, I bid you all study carefully the commandments of the LORD
your God, that you may possess this good land and hand it down as an
inheritance for all time to your children after you. And you, Solomon my 9
son, acknowledge your father's God and serve him with whole heart and
willing mind, for the LORD searches all hearts and discerns every invention
of men's thoughts. If you search for him, he will let you find him, but if you
forsake him, he will cast you off for ever. Remember, then, that the LORD 10
has chosen you to build a house for a sanctuary: be steadfast and do it.'

David gave Solomon his son the plan of the porch of the temple *a* and 11
its buildings, strong-rooms, roof-chambers and inner courts, and the
shrine of expiation;*b* also the plans of all he had in mind for the courts of 12
the house of the LORD and for all the rooms around it, for the stores of
God's house and for the stores of the sacred gifts, for the divisions of the 13

a of the temple: *prob. rdg.; Heb. om.*   *b* the shrine ... expiation: *or* the place for
the Ark with its cover.

priests and the Levites, for all the work connected with the service of the
14 house of the LORD and for all the vessels used in its service. He prescribed
the weight of gold for all the gold vessels *a* used in the various services, and
the weight of silver *b* for all the silver vessels used in the various services;
15 and the weight of gold for the gold lamp-stands and their lamps; and the
weight of silver for the silver lamp-stands, the weight required for each
16 lamp-stand and its lamps according to the use of each; and the weight of
gold for each of the tables for the rows of the Bread of the Presence, and
17 of silver for the silver tables. He prescribed also the weight of pure gold
for the forks, tossing-bowls and cups, the weight of gold for each of the
18 golden dishes and of silver *b* for each of the silver dishes; the weight also
of refined gold for the altar of incense, and of gold for the model of the
chariot, that is the cherubim with their wings outspread to screen the Ark
19 of the Covenant of the LORD. 'All this was drafted by the LORD's own hand,'
said David; 'my part was to consider the detailed working out of the plan.'
20   Then David said to Solomon his son, 'Be steadfast and resolute and do
it; be neither faint-hearted nor dismayed, for the LORD God, my God, will
be with you; he will neither fail you nor forsake you, until you have finished
21 all the work needed for the service of the house of the LORD. Here are the
divisions of the priests and the Levites, ready for all the service of the house
of God. In all the work you will have the help of every willing craftsman for
any task; and the officers and all the people will be entirely at your
command.'

29   King David then said to the whole assembly, 'My son Solomon is the
one chosen by God, Solomon alone, a boy of tender years; and this is a
2 great work, for it is a palace not for man but for the LORD God. Now to the
best of my strength I have made ready for the house of my God gold for
the gold work, silver for the silver, bronze for the bronze, iron for the iron,
and wood for the woodwork, together with cornelian and other gems for
setting, stones for mosaic work, precious stones of every sort, and marble
3 in plenty. Further, because I delight in the house of my God, I give my
own private store of gold and silver for the house of my God—over and
4 above all the store which I have collected for the sanctuary—namely three
thousand talents of gold, gold from Ophir, and seven thousand talents of
5 fine silver for overlaying the walls of the buildings, for providing gold for
the gold work, silver for the silver, and for any work to be done by skilled
craftsmen. Now who is willing to give with open hand to the LORD today?'
6   Then the heads of families, the officers administering the tribes of
Israel, the officers over units of a thousand and a hundred, and the officers
7 in charge of the king's service, responded willingly and gave for the work
of the house of God five thousand talents of gold, ten thousand darics,
ten thousand talents of silver, eighteen thousand talents of bronze, and a
8 hundred thousand talents of iron. Further, those who possessed precious
stones gave them to the treasury of the house of the LORD, into the charge
9 of Jehiel the Gershonite. The people rejoiced at this willing response,
because in the loyalty of their hearts they had given willingly to the LORD;
10 King David also was full of joy, and he blessed the LORD in the presence of

---

a for . . . vessels: *prob. rdg.; Heb.* for gold.   *b* of silver: *prob. rdg.; Heb. om.*

all the assembly and said, 'Blessed art thou, LORD God of our father Israel, from of old and for ever. Thine, O LORD, is the greatness, the power, the 11 glory, the splendour, and the majesty; for everything in heaven and on earth is thine;*ᵃ* thine, O LORD, is the sovereignty, and thou art exalted over all as head. Wealth and honour come from thee; thou rulest over all; 12 might and power are of thy disposing; thine it is to give power and strength to all. And now, we give thee thanks, our God, and praise thy glorious 13 name.

'But what am I, and what is my people, that we should be able to give 14 willingly like this? For everything comes from thee, and it is only of thy gifts that we give to thee. We are aliens before thee and settlers, as were all 15 our fathers; our days on earth are like a shadow, we have no abiding place. O LORD our God, from thee comes all this wealth that we have laid up to 16 build a house in honour of thy holy name, and everything is thine. I know, 17 O my God, that thou dost test the heart and that plain honesty pleases thee; with an honest heart I have given all these gifts willingly, and have rejoiced now to see thy people here present give willingly to thee. O LORD 18 God of Abraham, Isaac and Israel our fathers, maintain this purpose for ever in thy people's thoughts and direct their hearts toward thyself. Grant 19 that Solomon my son may loyally keep thy commandments, thy solemn charge, and thy statutes, that he may fulfil them all and build the palace for which I have prepared.'

Then, turning to the whole assembly, David said, 'Now bless the LORD 20 your God.' So all the assembly blessed the LORD the God of their fathers, bowing low and prostrating themselves before the LORD and the king. The 21 next day they sacrificed to the LORD and offered whole-offerings to him, a thousand oxen, a thousand rams, a thousand lambs, with the prescribed drink-offerings, and abundant sacrifices for all Israel. So they ate and drank 22 before the LORD that day with great rejoicing. They then appointed Solomon, David's son, king a second time and anointed him as the LORD's prince, and Zadok as priest. So Solomon sat on the LORD's throne as king 23 in place of his father David, and he prospered and all Israel obeyed him. All the officers and the warriors, as well as all the sons of King David, 24 swore fealty to King Solomon. The LORD made Solomon stand very high 25 in the eyes of all Israel, and bestowed upon him sovereignty such as no king in Israel had had before him.

David son of Jesse had ruled over the whole of Israel, and the length of 26 27 his reign over Israel was forty years; he ruled for seven years in Hebron, and for thirty-three in Jerusalem. He died in ripe old age, full of years, 28 wealth, and honour; and Solomon his son ruled in his place. The events 29 of King David's reign from first to last are recorded in the books of Samuel the seer, of Nathan the prophet, and of Gad the seer, with a full account 30 of his reign, his prowess, and of the times through which he and Israel and all the kingdoms of the world had passed.

ᵃ is thine: *prob. rdg.; Heb. om.*

THE SECOND BOOK OF THE
CHRONICLES

The reign of Solomon and dedication of the temple

1 KING SOLOMON, DAVID'S SON, strengthened his hold on the kingdom, for the LORD his God was with him and made him very great.

2 Solomon spoke to all Israel, to the officers over units of a thousand and of a hundred, the judges and all the leading men of Israel, the heads of
3 families; and he, together with all the assembled people, went to the hill-shrine at Gibeon; for the Tent of God's Presence, which Moses the
4 LORD's servant had made in the wilderness, was there. (But David had brought up the Ark of God from Kiriath-jearim to the place which he had
5 prepared for it, for he had pitched a tent for it in Jerusalem.) The altar of bronze also, which Bezalel son of Uri, son of Hur, had made, was there in front of the Tabernacle of the LORD; and Solomon and the assembly
6 resorted to it.*a* There Solomon went up to the altar of bronze before the LORD in the Tent of the Presence and offered on it a thousand whole-
7*b* offerings. That night God appeared to Solomon and said, 'What shall I
8 give you? Tell me.' Solomon answered, 'Thou didst show great and constant love to David my father and thou hast made me king in his place.
9 Now, O LORD God, let thy word to David my father be confirmed, for thou hast made me king over a people as numerous as the dust on the earth.
10 Give me now wisdom and knowledge, that I may lead this people; for who
11 is fit to govern this great people of thine?' God answered Solomon, 'Because this is what you desire, because you have not asked for wealth or possessions or honour *c* or the lives of your enemies or even long life for yourself, but have asked for wisdom and knowledge to govern my
12 people over whom I have made you king, wisdom and knowledge are given to you; I shall also give you wealth and possessions and honour *c* such as
13 no king has had before you and none shall have after you.' Then Solomon returned from the hill-shrine at Gibeon, from before the Tent of the Presence, to Jerusalem and ruled over Israel.

14*d* Solomon got together many chariots and horses; he had fourteen hundred chariots and twelve thousand horses, and he stabled some in the chariot-
15 towns and kept others at hand in Jerusalem. The king made silver and gold as common in Jerusalem as stones, and cedar as plentiful as sycomore-fig
16 in the Shephelah. Horses were imported from Egypt and Coa for Solomon;
17 the royal merchants obtained them from Coa by purchase. Chariots were

a resorted to it: *or* worshipped him. *b* *Verses 7–12: cp. 1 Kgs. 3. 5–14.*
c *Or* riches. *d* *Verses 14–17: cp. 9. 25–28; 1 Kgs. 10. 26–29.*

imported from Egypt for six hundred silver shekels each, and horses for a hundred and fifty; in the same way the merchants obtained them for export from all the kings of the Hittites and the kings of Aram.

Solomon resolved to build a house in honour of the name of the LORD, and a royal palace for himself. He engaged seventy thousand hauliers and eighty thousand quarrymen, and three thousand six hundred men to superintend them. Then Solomon sent this message to Huram king of Tyre: 'You were so good as to send my father David cedar-wood to build his royal residence. Now I am about to build a house in honour of the name of the LORD my God and to consecrate it to him, so that I may burn fragrant incense in it before him, and present the rows of the Bread of the Presence regularly, and whole-offerings morning and evening, on the sabbaths and the new moons and the appointed festivals of the LORD our God; for this is a duty laid upon Israel for ever. The house I am about to build will be a great house, because our God is greater than all gods. But who is able to build him a house when heaven itself, the highest heaven, cannot contain him? And who am I that I should build him a house, except that I may burn sacrifices before him? Send me then a skilled craftsman, a man able to work in gold and silver, copper *b* and iron, and in purple, crimson, and violet yarn, who is also an expert engraver and will work with my skilled workmen in Judah and in Jerusalem who were provided by David my father. Send me also cedar, pine, and algum timber from Lebanon, for I know that your men are expert at felling the trees of Lebanon; my men will work with yours to get an ample supply of timber ready for me, for the house which I shall build will be great and wonderful. I will supply provisions for your servants, the woodmen who fell the trees: twenty thousand kor of wheat and twenty thousand kor of barley, with twenty thousand bath of wine and twenty thousand bath of oil.'

Huram king of Tyre sent this answer by letter to Solomon: 'It is because of the love which the LORD has for his people that he has made you king over them.' The letter went on to say, 'Blessed is the LORD the God of Israel, maker of heaven and earth, who has given to King David a wise son, endowed with intelligence and understanding, to build a house for the LORD and a royal palace for himself. I now send you a skilful and experienced craftsman, master Huram. He is the son of a Danite woman, his father a Tyrian; he is an experienced worker in gold and silver, copper *b* and iron, stone and wood, as well as in purple, violet, and crimson yarn, and in fine linen; he is also a trained engraver who will be able to work with your own skilled craftsmen and those of my lord David your father, to any design submitted to him. Now then, let my lord send his servants the wheat and the barley, the oil and the wine, which he promised; we will fell all the timber in Lebanon that you need and float it as rafts to the roadstead at Joppa, and you will convey it from there up to Jerusalem.'

Solomon took a census of all the aliens resident in Israel, similar to the census which David his father had taken; these were found to be a hundred and fifty-three thousand six hundred. He made seventy thousand of them

a Verses 3–16: cp. 1 Kgs. 5. 2–11.   *b* Or bronze.

hauliers and eighty thousand quarrymen, and three thousand six hundred superintendents to make the people work.

3   Then Solomon began to build the house of the LORD in Jerusalem on Mount Moriah, where the LORD had appeared to his father David, on the site which David had prepared on the threshing-floor of Ornan the
2*a* Jebusite. He began to build in the second month of the fourth year of his
3   reign. These are the foundations which Solomon laid for building the house of God: the length, according to the old standard of measurement,
4   was sixty cubits and the breadth twenty. The vestibule in front of the house *b* was twenty cubits long, spanning the whole breadth of the house, and its
5   height was twenty; on the inside he overlaid it with pure gold. He panelled the large chamber with pine, covered it with fine gold and carved on it
6   palm-trees and chain-work. He adorned the house with precious stones for
7   decoration, and the gold he used was from Parvaim. He covered the whole house with gold, its rafters and frames, its walls and doors; and he carved cherubim on the walls.

8   He made the Most Holy Place twenty cubits long, corresponding to the breadth of the house, and twenty cubits broad. He covered it all with six
9   hundred talents of fine gold, and the weight of the nails was fifty shekels of gold. He also covered the upper chambers with gold.
10*c* In the Most Holy Place he carved two images of cherubim and overlaid
11   them with gold. The total span of the wings of the cherubim was twenty cubits. A wing of the one cherub extended five cubits to reach the wall of the house, while its other wing reached out five cubits to meet a wing of the
12   other cherub. Similarly, a wing of the second cherub extended five cubits to reach the other wall of the house, while its other wing met a wing of the
13   first cherub. The wings of these cherubim extended twenty cubits; they
14   stood with their feet on the ground, facing the outer chamber. He made the Veil of violet, purple, and crimson yarn, and fine linen, and embroidered cherubim on it.
15*d* In front of the house he erected two pillars eighteen cubits high, with an
16   architrave five cubits high on top of each. He made chain-work like a necklace *e* and set it round the tops of the pillars, and he carved a hundred
17   pomegranates and set them in the chain-work. He erected the two pillars in front of the temple, one on the right and one on the left; the one on the right he named Jachin *f* and the one on the left Boaz. *g*

4   He then made an altar of bronze, twenty cubits long, twenty cubits
2*h* broad, and ten cubits high. He also made the Sea of cast metal; it was round in shape, the diameter from rim to rim being ten cubits; it stood five cubits
3   high, and it took a line thirty cubits long to go round it. Under the Sea, on every side, completely surrounding the thirty *i* cubits of its circumference, were what looked like gourds, *j* two rows of them, cast in one piece
4   with the Sea itself. It was mounted on twelve oxen, three facing north,

---

a Verses 2-4: cp. 1 Kgs. 6. 1-3.   *b* house: *prob. rdg.; Heb.* length.   *c Verses 10-13: cp. 1 Kgs. 6. 23-28.*   *d Verses 15-17: cp. 1 Kgs. 7. 15-21.*   *e* necklace: *prob. rdg.; Heb.* obscure.   *f Or* Jachun, *meaning* It shall stand.   *g Or* Booz, *meaning* In strength.   *h Verses 2-5: cp. 1 Kgs. 7. 23-26.*   *i Prob. rdg.; Heb.* ten.   *j Prob. rdg., cp. 1 Kgs. 7. 24; Heb.* oxen.

three west, three south, and three east, their hind quarters turned inwards; the Sea rested on top of them. Its thickness was a hand-breadth; its rim 5 was made like that of a cup, shaped like the calyx of a lily; when full it held three thousand bath. He also made ten basins for washing, setting 6 five on the left side and five on the right; in these they rinsed everything used for the whole-offering. The Sea was made for the priests to wash in.

He made ten golden lamp-stands in the prescribed manner and set them 7 in the temple, five on the right side and five on the left. He also made ten 8 tables and placed them in the temple, five on the right and five on the left; and he made a hundred golden tossing-bowls. He made the court of the 9 priests and the great precinct and the doors for it, and overlaid the doors of both with copper; he put the Sea at the right side, at the south-east 10 corner of the temple.

Huram made the pots, the shovels, and the tossing-bowls. So he finished 11ᵃ the work which he had undertaken for King Solomon on the house of God. The two pillars; the two bowl-shaped capitals ᵇ on the tops of the pillars; 12 the two ornamental networks to cover the two bowl-shaped capitals on the tops of the pillars; the four hundred pomegranates for the two networks, 13 two rows of pomegranates for each network, to cover the two bowl-shaped capitals on the twoᶜ pillars; the tenᵈ trolleys and the tenᵈ basins on the 14 trolleys; the one Sea and the twelve oxen which supported it; the pots, the 15 16 shovels, and the tossing-bowlsᵉ—all these ᶠ objects master Huram made of bronze, burnished work for King Solomon for the house of the LORD. In the Plain of the Jordan the king cast them, in the foundry between 17 Succoth and Zeredah. Solomon made great quantities of all these objects; 18 the weight of the copperᵍ used was beyond reckoning.

Solomon made also all the furnishings for the house of God: the golden 19 altar, the tables upon which was set the Bread of the Presence, the lamp- 20 stands of red gold whose lamps burned before the inner shrine in the prescribed manner, the flowers and lamps and tongs of solid gold, 21 the snuffers, tossing-bowls, saucers, and firepans of red gold, and, at the 22 entrance to the house, the inner doors leading to the Most Holy Place and those leading to the sanctuary, of gold.

When all the work which Solomon did for the house of the LORD was 5 completed, he brought in the sacred treasures of his father David, the silver, the gold, and the vessels, and deposited them in the storehouses of the house of God.

THEN SOLOMON SUMMONED THE ELDERS of Israel, and all the heads 2ʰ of the tribes who were chiefs of families in Israel, to assemble in Jerusalem, in order to bring up the Ark of the Covenant of the LORD from the City of David, which is called Zion. All the men of Israel assembled in the king's 3

ᵃ *4. 11—5. 1: cp. 1 Kgs. 7. 40-51.*   ᵇ bowl-shaped capitals: *prob. rdg., cp. 1 Kgs. 7. 41; Heb.* the bowls and the capitals.   ᶜ two: *prob. rdg., cp. 1 Kgs. 7. 42; Heb.* surface of the.   ᵈ the ten: *prob. rdg., cp. 1 Kgs. 7. 43; Heb.* he made the . . . ᵉ tossing-bowls: *prob. rdg., cp. 1 Kgs. 7. 45; Heb.* forks.   ᶠ *Prob. rdg., cp. 1 Kgs. 7. 45; Heb.* their.   ᵍ *Or* bronze.   ʰ *Verses 2-10: cp. 1 Kgs. 8. 1-9.*

4 presence at the pilgrim-feast in the seventh month. When the elders of
5 Israel had all come, the Levites took the Ark and carried it up with the
Tent of the Presence and all the sacred furnishings of the Tent: it was the
6 priests and the Levites together who carried them up. King Solomon and
the whole congregation of Israel, assembled with him before the Ark, sacri-
7 ficed sheep and oxen in numbers past counting or reckoning. Then the
priests brought in the Ark of the Covenant of the LORD to its place,
the inner shrine of the house, the Most Holy Place, beneath the wings of
8 the cherubim. The cherubim spread their wings over the place of the Ark,
9 and formed a covering above the Ark and its poles. The poles projected,
and their ends could be seen from the Holy Place immediately in front of
the inner shrine, but from nowhere else outside; they are there to this day.
10 There was nothing inside the Ark but the two tablets which Moses had
put there at Horeb, the tablets of the covenant *a* which the LORD made with
the Israelites when they left Egypt.

11 Now when the priests came out of the Holy Place (for all the priests who
were present had hallowed themselves without keeping to their divisions),
12 all the levitical singers, Asaph, Heman, and Jeduthun, their sons and their
kinsmen, clothed in fine linen, stood with cymbals, lutes, and harps, to
the east of the altar, together with a hundred and twenty priests who blew
13 trumpets. Now the trumpeters and the singers joined in unison to sound
forth praise and thanksgiving to the LORD, and the song was raised with
trumpets, cymbals, and musical instruments, in praise of the LORD,
because 'that *b* is good, for his love endures for ever'; and the house was
14 filled with the cloud of the glory of the LORD. The priests could not continue to minister because of the cloud, for the glory of the LORD filled the
6 1*c* house of God. Then Solomon said:

> O LORD who hast chosen to dwell in thick darkness,
2 > here have I built thee a lofty house,
> a habitation for thee to occupy for ever.

3 And as they stood waiting, the king turned round and blessed all the
4 assembly of Israel in these words: 'Blessed be the LORD the God of Israel
who spoke directly to my father David and has himself fulfilled his promise.
5 For he said, "From the day when I brought my people out of Egypt, I
chose no city out of all the tribes of Israel where I should build a house for
my Name to be there, nor did I choose any man to be prince over my
6 people Israel. But I chose Jerusalem for my Name to be there, and I chose
7 David to be over my people Israel." My father David had in mind to build
8 a house in honour of the name of the LORD the God of Israel, but the LORD
said to him, "You purposed to build a house in honour of my name; and
9 your purpose was good. Nevertheless, you shall not build it; but the son
who is to be born to you, he shall build the house in honour of my name."
10 The LORD has now fulfilled his promise: I have succeeded my father
David and taken his place on the throne of Israel, as the LORD promised;
and I have built the house in honour of the name of the LORD the God of

---

a the tablets of the covenant: *prob. rdg., cp. 1 Kgs. 8. 9; Heb. om.*   *b* *Or he.*
c *Verses 1–39 : cp. 1 Kgs. 8. 12–50.*

Israel. I have installed there the Ark containing the covenant of the LORD 11
which he made with Israel.'

Then Solomon, standing in front of the altar of the LORD, in the presence 12
of the whole assembly of Israel, spread out his hands. He had made a 13
bronze^a platform, five cubits long, five cubits broad, and three cubits
high, and had placed it in the centre of the precinct. He mounted it and
knelt down in the presence of the assembly, and, spreading out his hands
towards heaven, he said, 'O LORD God of Israel, there is no god like thee in 14
heaven or on earth, keeping covenant with thy servants and showing them
constant love while they continue faithful to thee in heart and soul. Thou 15
hast kept thy promise to thy servant David my father; by thy deeds this
day thou hast fulfilled what thou didst say to him in words. Now, therefore, 16
O LORD God of Israel, keep this promise of thine to thy servant David my
father: "You shall never want for a man appointed by me to sit on the
throne of Israel, if only your sons look to their ways and conform to my
law, as you have done in my sight." And now, O LORD God of Israel, let 17
the word which thou didst speak to thy servant David be confirmed.

'But can God indeed dwell with man on the earth? Heaven itself, the 18
highest heaven, cannot contain thee; how much less this house that I have
built! Yet attend to the prayer and the supplication of thy servant, O LORD 19
my God; listen to the cry and the prayer which thy servant utters before
thee, that thine eyes may ever be upon this house day and night, this place 20
of which thou didst say, "It shall receive my Name"; so mayest thou hear
thy servant when he prays towards this place. Hear thou the supplications 21
of thy servant and of thy people Israel when they pray towards this place.
Hear from heaven thy dwelling and, when thou hearest, forgive.

'When a man wrongs his neighbour and he is adjured to take an oath, 22
and the adjuration is made before thy altar in this house, then do thou hear 23
from heaven and act: be thou thy servants' judge, requiting the guilty man
and bringing his deeds upon his own head, acquitting the innocent and
rewarding him as his innocence may deserve.

'When thy people Israel are defeated by an enemy because they have 24
sinned against thee, and they turn back to thee, confessing thy name and
making their prayer and supplication before thee in this house, do thou 25
hear from heaven; forgive the sin of thy people Israel and restore them to
the land which thou gavest to them and to their forefathers.

'When the heavens are shut up and there is no rain, because thy servant 26
and thy people Israel have sinned against thee, and when they pray towards
this place, confessing thy name and forsaking their sin when they feel thy
punishment, do thou hear in heaven and forgive their sin; so mayest thou 27
teach them the good way which they should follow, and grant rain to thy
land which thou hast given to thy people as their own possession.

'If there is famine in the land, or pestilence, or black blight or red, or 28
locusts new-sloughed or fully grown, or if their enemies besiege them in
any^b of their cities, or if plague or sickness befall them, then hear the 29
prayer or supplication of every man among thy people Israel, as each one,
prompted by his own suffering and misery, spreads out his hands towards

^a *Or* copper.   ^b in any: *prob. rdg.*; *Heb.* in the land.

483

30 this house; hear it from heaven thy dwelling and forgive. And, as thou
knowest a man's heart, reward him according to his deeds, for thou alone
31 knowest the hearts of all men; and so they will fear and obey thee all their
lives in the land thou gavest to our forefathers.

32 'The foreigner too, the man who does not belong to thy people Israel,
but has come from a distant land because of thy great fame and thy strong
hand and arm outstretched, when he comes and prays towards this house,
33 hear from heaven thy dwelling and respond to the call which the foreigner
makes to thee, so that like thy people Israel all peoples of the earth may
know thy fame and fear thee, and learn that this house which I have built
bears thy name.

34 'When thy people go to war with their enemies, wherever thou dost
send them, and they pray to thee, turning towards this city which thou hast
chosen and towards this house which I have built in honour of thy name,
35 do thou from heaven hear their prayer and supplication, and grant them
justice.

36 'Should they sin against thee (and what man is free from sin?) and
shouldst thou in thy anger give them over to an enemy, who carries them
37 captive to a land far or near; if in the land of their captivity they learn their
lesson and turn back and make supplication to thee in that land and say, "We
38 have sinned and acted perversely and wickedly", if they turn back to thee
with heart and soul in the land of their captivity to which they have been
taken, and pray, turning towards their land which thou gavest to their forefathers and towards this city which thou didst choose and this house which
39 I have built in honour of thy name; then from heaven thy dwelling do thou
hear their prayer and supplications and grant them justice. Forgive thy
40 people their sins against thee. Now, O my God, let thine eyes be open and
41 thy ears attentive to the prayer made in this place. Arise now, O LORD God,
and come to thy place of rest, thou and the Ark of thy might. Let thy
priests, O LORD God, be clothed with salvation and thy saints rejoice in
42 prosperity. O LORD God, reject not thy anointed prince; remember thy
servant David's loyal service.'[a]

7 When Solomon had finished this prayer, fire came down from heaven
and consumed the whole-offering and the sacrifices, while the glory of the
2 LORD filled the house. The priests were unable to enter the house of the
3 LORD because the glory of the LORD had filled it. All the Israelites were
watching as the fire came down with the glory of the LORD on the house,
and where they stood on the paved court they bowed low to the ground and
worshipped and gave thanks to the LORD, because 'that[b] is good, for his
love endures for ever.'

4 5 Then the king and all the people offered sacrifice before the LORD. King
Solomon offered a sacrifice of twenty-two thousand oxen and a hundred
and twenty thousand sheep; in this way the king and all the people dedi-
6 cated the house of God. The priests stood at their appointed posts; so too
the Levites with their musical instruments for the LORD's service, which
King David had made for giving thanks to the LORD—'for his love endures
for ever'—whenever he rendered praise with their help; opposite them,

[a] thy servant . . . service: *or* thy constant love for David thy servant.   [b] *Or* he.

the priests sounded their trumpets; and all the Israelites were standing there.

Then Solomon consecrated the centre of the court which lay in front*[a]* of the house of the LORD; there he offered the whole-offerings and the fat portions of the shared-offerings, because the bronze altar which he had made could not take the whole-offering, the grain-offering, and the fat portions. So Solomon and all Israel with him, a very great assembly from Lebo-hamath to the Torrent of Egypt, celebrated the pilgrim-feast at that time for seven days. On the eighth day they held a closing ceremony; for they had celebrated the dedication of the altar for seven days; the pilgrim-feast lasted seven days. On the twenty-third day of the seventh month he sent the people to their homes, happy and glad at heart for all the prosperity granted by the LORD to David and Solomon and to his people Israel.

When Solomon had finished the house of the LORD and the royal palace and had successfully carried out all that he had planned for the house of the LORD and the palace, the LORD appeared to him by night and said, 'I have heard your prayer and I have chosen this place to be my place of sacrifice. When I shut up the heavens and there is no rain, or command the locusts to consume the land, or send a pestilence against my people, if my people whom I have named my own submit and pray to me and seek me and turn back from their evil ways, I will hear from heaven and forgive their sins and heal their land. Now my eyes will be open and my ears attentive to the prayers which are made in this place. I have chosen and consecrated this house, that my Name may be there for all time and my eyes and my heart be fixed on it for ever. And if you, on your part, live in my sight as your father David lived, doing all I command you, and observing my statutes and my judgements, then I will establish your royal throne, as I promised by a covenant granted to your father David when I said, "You shall never want for a man to rule over Israel." But if you turn away and forsake my statutes and my commandments which I have set before you, and if you go and serve other gods and prostrate yourselves before them, then I will uproot you from my land which I gave you, I will reject this house which I have consecrated in honour of my name, and make it a byword and an object-lesson among all peoples. And this house will become a ruin; every passer-by will be appalled at the sight of it, and they will ask, "Why has the LORD so treated this land and this house?" The answer will be, "Because they forsook the LORD the God of their fathers, who brought them out of Egypt, and clung to other gods, prostrating themselves before them and serving them; that is why the LORD has brought this great evil on them."'

Solomon had taken twenty years to build the house of the LORD and his own palace, and he rebuilt the cities which Huram had given him and settled Israelites in them. He went to Hamath-zobah and seized it, and rebuilt Tadmor in the wilderness and all the store-cities which he had built in Hamath. He also built Upper Beth-horon and Lower Beth-horon as fortified cities with walls and barred gates, and Baalath, as well as all

[a] Or to the east.   *[b]* Verses 7–22: cp. 1 Kgs. 8. 64—9. 9.   *[c]* Verses 1–18: cp. 1 Kgs. 9. 10–28.

his store-cities, and all the towns where he quartered his chariots and horses; and he carried out all his cherished plans for building in Jerusalem,
7 in the Lebanon, and throughout his whole dominion. All the survivors of the Hittites, Amorites, Perizzites, Hivites, and Jebusites, who did not
8 belong to Israel—that is their descendants who survived in the land, wherever the Israelites had been unable to exterminate them—were
9 employed by Solomon on forced labour, as they still are. He put none of the Israelites to forced labour for his public works; they were his fighting men, his captains and lieutenants, and the commanders of his chariots
10 and of his cavalry. These were King Solomon's officers, two hundred and fifty of them, in charge of the foremen who superintended the people.

11 Solomon brought Pharaoh's daughter up from the City of David to the house he had built for her, for he said, 'No wife of mine shall live in the house of David king of Israel, because this place which the Ark of the LORD has entered is[a] holy.'

12 Then Solomon offered whole-offerings to the LORD on the altar which
13 he had built to the east of the vestibule, according to what was required for each day, making offerings according to the law of Moses for the sabbaths, the new moons, and the three annual appointed feasts—the pilgrim-feasts
14 of Unleavened Bread, of Weeks, and of Tabernacles.[b] Following the practice of his father David, he drew up the roster of service for the priests and that for the Levites for leading the praise and for waiting upon the priests, as each day required, and that for the door-keepers at each gate;
15 for such was the instruction which David the man of God had given. The instructions which David had given concerning the priests and the Levites and concerning the treasuries were not forgotten.

16 By this time all Solomon's work was achieved, from the foundation of the house of the LORD to its completion; the house of the LORD was
17 perfect. Then Solomon went to Ezion-geber and to Eloth on the coast of
18 Edom, and Huram sent ships under the command of his own officers and manned by crews of experienced seamen; and these, in company with Solomon's servants, went to Ophir and brought back four hundred and fifty talents of gold, which they delivered to King Solomon.

9 1[c] THE QUEEN OF SHEBA HEARD of Solomon's fame and came to test him with hard questions. She arrived in Jerusalem with a very large retinue, camels laden with spices, gold in abundance, and precious stones. When
2 she came to Solomon, she told him everything she had in her mind, and Solomon answered all her questions; not one of them was too abstruse for
3 him to answer. When the queen of Sheba saw the wisdom of Solomon, the
4 house which he had built, the food on his table, the courtiers sitting round him, his attendants and his cupbearers in their livery standing behind, and the stairs by which he went up to the house of the LORD, there was no
5 more spirit left in her. Then she said to the king, 'The report which I
6 heard in my own country about you and your wisdom was true, but I did not believe what they told me until I came and saw for myself. Indeed, I

a this place which . . . is: *prob. rdg.; Heb.* those which . . . are.   b Or Booths.
c Verses 1–24: cp. 1 Kgs. 10. 1–25.

was not told half of the greatness of your wisdom; you surpass the report
which I had of you. Happy are your wives, happy these courtiers of yours 7
who wait on you every day and hear your wisdom! Blessed be the LORD 8
your God who has delighted in you and has set you on his throne as his
king; because in his love your God has elected Israel to make it endure for
ever, he has made you king over it to maintain law and justice.' Then she 9
gave the king a hundred and twenty talents of gold, spices in great abundance, and precious stones. There had never been any spices to equal
those which the queen of Sheba gave to King Solomon.

Besides all this, the servants of Huram and of Solomon, who had 10
brought gold from Ophir, brought also cargoes of algum wood and precious
stones. The king used the wood to make stands for the house of the LORD 11
and for the royal palace, as well as harps and lutes for the singers. The
like of them had never before been seen in the land of Judah.

King Solomon gave the queen of Sheba all she desired, whatever she 12
asked, besides his gifts in return for *a* what she had brought him. Then she
departed and returned with her retinue to her own land.

Now the weight of gold which Solomon received yearly was six hundred 13
and sixty-six talents, in addition to the tolls levied on merchants and on 14
traders who imported goods; all the kings of Arabia and the regional
governors also *b* brought gold and silver to the king.

King Solomon made two hundred shields of beaten gold, and six hundred 15
shekels of gold went to the making of each one; he also made three hundred 16
bucklers of beaten gold, and three hundred shekels of gold went to the
making of each buckler. The king put these into the House of the Forest
of Lebanon.

The king also made a great throne of ivory and overlaid it with pure 17
gold. Six steps and a footstool for the throne were all encased in gold. 18
There were arms on each side of the seat, with a lion standing beside each
of them, and twelve lions stood on the six steps, one at either end of each 19
step. Nothing like it had ever been made for any monarch. All Solomon's 20
drinking vessels were of gold, and all the plate in the House of the Forest
of Lebanon was of red gold; silver was reckoned of no value in the days of
Solomon. The king had a fleet of ships plying to Tarshish with Huram's 21
men; once every three years this fleet of merchantmen came home,
bringing gold and silver, ivory, apes, and monkeys.

Thus King Solomon outdid all the kings of the earth in wealth and 22
wisdom, and all the kings of the earth courted him, to hear the wisdom 23
which God had put in his heart. Each brought his gift with him, vessels of 24
silver and gold, garments, perfumes and spices, horses and mules, so much
year by year.

Solomon had standing for four thousand horses and chariots, and twelve 25 *c*
thousand cavalry horses, and he stabled some in the chariot-towns and
kept others at hand in Jerusalem. He ruled over all the kings from the 26
Euphrates to the land of the Philistines and the border of Egypt. He made 27

---

a his gifts . . . for: *prob. rdg.; Heb. om.*   *b* all . . . also: *or* and on all the kings of
Arabia and the regional governors who . . .   *c* *Verses 25-28: cp. 1. 14-17; 1 Kgs. 10.
26-29.*

28 silver as common in Jerusalem as stones, and cedar as plentiful as sycamore-fig in the Shephelah. Horses were imported from Egypt and from all countries for Solomon.

29[a] The rest of the acts of Solomon's reign, from first to last, are recorded in the history of Nathan the prophet, in the prophecy of Ahijah of Shiloh, and in the visions of Iddo the seer concerning Jeroboam son of Nebat.

30 31 Solomon ruled in Jerusalem over the whole of Israel for forty years. Then he rested with his forefathers and was buried in the city of David his father, and he was succeeded by his son Rehoboam.

The kings of Judah from Rehoboam to Ahaz

10 1[b]   REHOBOAM WENT TO SHECHEM, for all Israel had gone there to make
2   him king. When Jeroboam son of Nebat heard of it in Egypt, where
3   he had taken refuge to escape Solomon, he returned from Egypt. They
4   now recalled him, and he and all Israel came to Rehoboam and said, 'Your father laid a cruel yoke upon us; but if you will now lighten the cruel slavery he imposed on us and the heavy yoke he laid on us, we will serve
5   you.' 'Give me three days,' he said, 'and come back again.' So the people
6   went away. King Rehoboam then consulted the elders who had been in attendance on his father Solomon while he lived: 'What answer do you
7   advise me to give to this people?' And they said, 'If you show yourself well-disposed to this people and gratify them by speaking kindly to them,
8   they will be your servants ever after.' But he rejected the advice which the elders gave him. He next consulted those who had grown up with him, the
9   young men in attendance, and asked them, 'What answer do you advise me to give to this people's request that I should lighten the yoke which my
10   father laid on them?' The young men replied, 'Give this answer to the people who say that your father made their yoke heavy and ask you to
11   lighten it; tell them: "My little finger is thicker than my father's loins. My father laid a heavy yoke on you; I will make it heavier. My father used the
12   whip on you; but I will use the lash."' Jeroboam and the people all came
13   back to Rehoboam on the third day, as the king had ordered. And the king gave them a harsh answer. He rejected the advice which the elders had given
14   him and spoke to the people as the young men had advised: 'My father made your yoke heavy; I will make it heavier. My father used the whip on
15   you; but I will use the lash.' So the king would not listen to the people; for the LORD had given this turn to the affair, in order that the word he had spoken by Ahijah of Shiloh to Jeroboam son of Nebat might be fulfilled.

16   When all Israel saw[c] that the king would not listen to them, they answered:

> What share have we in David?
> We have no lot in the son of Jesse.
> Away to your homes, O Israel;
> now see to your own house, David.

---

[a] *Verses 29–31: cp. 1 Kgs. 11. 41–43.*   [b] *Verses 1–19: cp. 1 Kgs. 12. 1–19.*   [c] saw: prob. rdg., cp. 1 Kgs. 12. 16; Heb. om.

So all Israel went to their homes, and Rehoboam ruled over those Israelites 17
who lived in the cities of Judah.

Then King Rehoboam sent out Hadoram, the commander of the forced 18
levies, but the Israelites stoned him to death; whereupon King Rehoboam
mounted his chariot in haste and fled to Jerusalem. From that day to this, 19
Israel has been in rebellion against the house of David.

When Rehoboam reached Jerusalem, he assembled the tribes of Judah 11 1[a]
and Benjamin, a hundred and eighty thousand chosen warriors, to fight
against Israel and recover his kingdom. But the word of the LORD came to 2
Shemaiah the man of God: 'Say to Rehoboam son of Solomon, king of 3
Judah, and to all the Israelites in Judah and Benjamin, "This is the word 4
of the LORD: You shall not go up to make war on your kinsmen. Return to
your homes, for this is my will."' So they listened to the word of the LORD
and abandoned their campaign against Jeroboam.

Rehoboam resided in Jerusalem and built up the defences of certain 5
cities in Judah. The cities in Judah and Benjamin which he fortified were 6
Bethlehem, Etam, Tekoa, Beth-zur, Soco, Adullam, Gath, Mareshah, 7 8
Ziph, Adoraim, Lachish, Azekah, Zorah, Aijalon, and Hebron. He 9 10 11
strengthened the fortifications of these fortified cities, and put governors
in them, as well as supplies of food, oil, and wine. Also he stored shields 12
and spears in every one of the cities, and strengthened their fortifications.
Thus he retained possession of Judah and Benjamin.

Now the priests and the Levites throughout the whole of Israel resorted 13
to Rehoboam from all their territories; for the Levites had left all their 14
common land and their own patrimony and had gone to Judah and Jerusalem, because Jeroboam and his successors rejected their services as
priests of the LORD, and he appointed his own priests for the hill-shrines, 15
for the demons,[b] and for the calves which he had made. Those, from all 16
the tribes of Israel, who were resolved to seek the LORD the God of Israel
followed the Levites to Jerusalem to sacrifice to the LORD the God of their
fathers. So they strengthened the kingdom of Judah and for three years 17
made Rehoboam son of Solomon secure, because he followed the example
of David and Solomon during that time.

Rehoboam married Mahalath, whose father was Jerimoth son of David 18
and whose mother was Abihail daughter of Eliab son of Jesse. His sons 19
by her were: Jeush, Shemariah and Zaham. Next he married Maacah 20
granddaughter of Absalom, who bore him Abijah, Attai, Ziza and Shelomith. Of all his wives and concubines, Rehoboam loved Maacah most; 21
he had in all eighteen wives and sixty concubines and became the father
of twenty-eight sons and sixty daughters. He appointed Abijah son of 22
Maacah chief among his brothers, making him crown prince and planning
to make him his successor on the throne. He showed discretion in detailing 23
his sons to take charge of all the fortified cities throughout the whole
territory of Judah and Benjamin; he also made generous provision for
them and procured them[c] wives.

When the kingdom of Rehoboam was on a firm footing and he became **12**

[a] *Verses 1-4: cp. 1 Kgs. 12. 21-24.*   [b] *Or satyrs.*   [c] *procured them: prob. rdg.;*
Heb. asked for a multitude of . . .

2 strong, he forsook the law of the LORD, he and all Israel with him. In the
fifth year of Rehoboam's reign, because of this disloyalty to the LORD,
3 Shishak king of Egypt attacked Jerusalem with twelve hundred chariots
and sixty thousand horsemen, and brought with him from Egypt an
4 innumerable following of Libyans, Sukkites, and Cushites.*[a]* He captured
5 the fortified cities of Judah and reached Jerusalem. Then Shemaiah the
prophet came to Rehoboam and the leading men of Judah, who had
assembled in Jerusalem before the advance of Shishak, and said to them,
'This is the word of the LORD: You have abandoned me; therefore I now
6 abandon you to Shishak.' The princes of Israel and the king submitted and
7 said, 'The LORD is just.' When the LORD saw that they had submitted,
there came from him this word to Shemaiah: 'Because they have submitted I will not destroy them, I will let them barely escape; my wrath
8 shall not be poured out on Jerusalem by means of Shishak, but they shall
become his servants; then they will know the difference between serving
9*[b]* me and serving the rulers of other countries.' Shishak king of Egypt in his
attack on Jerusalem removed the treasures of the house of the LORD and
of the royal palace. He seized everything, including the shields of gold that
10 Solomon had made. King Rehoboam replaced them with bronze shields
and entrusted them to the officers of the escort who guarded the entrance
11 of the royal palace. Whenever the king entered the house of the LORD, the
escort entered, carrying the shields; afterwards they returned them to the
12 guard-room. Because Rehoboam submitted, the LORD's wrath was
averted from him, and he was not utterly destroyed; Judah enjoyed
prosperity.
13*[c]* Thus King Rehoboam increased his power in Jerusalem. He was forty-
one years old when he came to the throne, and he reigned for seventeen
years in Jerusalem, the city which the LORD had chosen out of all the tribes
of Israel as the place to receive his Name. Rehoboam's mother was a
14 woman of Ammon called Naamah. He did what was wrong, he did not
15 make a practice of seeking guidance of the LORD. The events of Rehoboam's
reign, from first to last, are recorded in the histories of Shemaiah the
prophet and Iddo the seer.*[d]* There was continual fighting between
16 Rehoboam and Jeroboam. He rested with his forefathers and was buried
in the city of David; and he was succeeded by his son Abijah.

13 IN THE EIGHTEENTH YEAR of King Jeroboam's reign Abijah became
2 king of Judah. He reigned in Jerusalem for three years; his mother was
Maacah daughter of Uriel of Gibeah. There was fighting between Abijah
3 and Jeroboam. Abijah drew up his army of four hundred thousand picked
troops in order of battle, while Jeroboam formed up against him with
4 eight hundred thousand picked troops. Abijah took up position on the
slopes of Mount Zemaraim in the hill-country of Ephraim and called out,
5 'Hear me, Jeroboam and all Israel: Ought you not to know that the LORD
the God of Israel gave the kingship over Israel to David and his descend-
6 ants in perpetuity by a covenant of salt? Yet Jeroboam son of Nebat, the

---

[a] Or Nubians.   *[b]* Verses 9-11: cp. 1 Kgs. 14. 25-28.   *[c]* Verses 13-16: cp.
1 Kgs. 14. 29-31.   *[d]* Prob. rdg.; Heb. adds to be enrolled by genealogy.

servant of Solomon son of David, rose in rebellion against his lord, and ⁷ certain worthless scoundrels gathered round him, who stubbornly opposed Solomon's son Rehoboam when he was young and inexperienced, and he was no match for them. Now you propose to match yourselves against the ⁸ kingdom of the LORD as ruled by David's sons, you and your mob of supporters and the golden calves which Jeroboam has made to be your gods. Have you not dismissed from office the Aaronites, priests of the ⁹ LORD, and the Levites, and followed the practice of other lands in appointing priests? Now, if any man comes for consecration with an offering of a young bull and seven rams, you accept him as a priest to a god that is no god. But as for us, the LORD is our God and we have not forsaken him; we ¹⁰ have Aaronites as priests ministering to the LORD with the Levites, duly discharging their office. Morning and evening, these burn whole-offerings ¹¹ and fragrant incense to the LORD and offer the Bread of the Presence arranged in rows on a table ritually clean; they also kindle the lamps on the golden lamp-stand every evening. Thus we do indeed keep the charge of the LORD our God, whereas you have forsaken him. God is with us at ¹² our head, and his priests stand there with trumpets to signal the battle-cry against you. Men of Israel, do not fight the LORD the God of your fathers; you will have no success.'

Jeroboam sent a detachment of his troops to go round and lay an ambush ¹³ in the rear, so that his main body faced Judah while the ambush lay behind them. The men of Judah turned to find that they were engaged front and ¹⁴ rear. Then they cried to the LORD for help. The priests sounded their trumpets, and the men of Judah raised a shout, and when they did so, God ¹⁵ put Jeroboam and all Israel to rout before Abijah and Judah. The Israelites ¹⁶ fled before the men of Judah, and God delivered them into their power. So ¹⁷ Abijah and his men defeated them with very heavy losses, and five hundred thousand picked Israelites fell in the battle. After this, the Israelites were ¹⁸ reduced to submission, and Judah prevailed because they relied on the LORD the God of their fathers. Abijah followed up his victory over Jero- ¹⁹ boam and captured from him the cities of Bethel, Jeshanah, and Ephron, with their villages. Jeroboam did not regain his power during the days of ²⁰ Abijah; finally the LORD struck him down and he died.

But Abijah established his position; he married fourteen wives and ²¹ became the father of twenty-two sons and sixteen daughters. The other ²² events of Abijah's reign, both what he said and what he did, are recorded in the story of the prophet Iddo. Abijah rested with his forefathers and **14** was buried in the city of David; and he was succeeded on the throne by his son Asa. In his days the land was at peace for ten years.

Asa did what was good and right in the eyes of the LORD his God. He ²,³ suppressed the foreign altars and the hill-shrines, smashed the sacred pillars and hacked down the sacred poles, and ordered Judah to seek ⁴ guidance of the LORD the God of their fathers and to keep the law and the commandments. He also suppressed the hill-shrines and the incense- ⁵ altars in all the cities, and the kingdom was at peace under him. He built ⁶ fortified cities in Judah, for the land was at peace. He had no war to fight during those years, because the LORD had given him security. He said to ⁷ the men of Judah, 'Let us build these cities and fortify them, with walls round them, and towers and barred gates. The land still lies open before us. Because we have sought guidance of the LORD our God, he has sought us and given us security on every side.' So they built and prospered.

8 Asa had an army equipped with shields and spears; three hundred thousand men came from Judah, and two hundred and eighty thousand from Benjamin, shield-bearers and archers; all were valiant warriors. 9 Zerah the Cushite came out against them with an army a million strong 10 and three hundred chariots. When he reached Mareshah, Asa came out to meet him and they took up position in the valley of Zephathah at Mareshah. 11 Asa called upon the LORD his God and said, 'There is none like thee, O LORD, to help men, whether strong or weak; help us, O LORD our God, for on thee we rely and in thy name we have come out against this horde. 12 O LORD, thou art our God, how can man vie with thee?' So the LORD gave 13 Asa and Judah victory over the Cushites and they fled, and Asa and his men pursued them as far as Gerar. The Cushites broke before the LORD and his army, and many of them fell mortally wounded; and Judah carried 14 off great loads of spoil. They destroyed all the cities around Gerar, for the LORD had struck the people with panic; and they plundered the cities, 15 finding rich spoil in them all. They also killed the herdsmen and seized many sheep and camels, and then they returned to Jerusalem.

15 1 2 The spirit of God came upon Azariah son of Oded, and he went out to meet Asa and said to him, 'Hear me, Asa and all Judah and Benjamin. The LORD is with you when you are with him; if you look for him, he will let 3 himself be found; if you forsake him, he will forsake you. For a long time Israel was without the true God, without a priest to interpret the law and 4 without law. *a* But when, in their distress, they turned to the LORD the God 5 of Israel and sought him, he let himself be found by them. At those times there was no safety for people as they went about their business; the inhabitants of every land had their fill of trouble; there was ruin on every 6 side, nation at odds with nation, city with city, for God harassed them with 7 every kind of distress. But now you must be strong and not let your courage 8 fail; for your work will be rewarded.' When Asa heard these words, *b* he resolutely suppressed the loathsome idols in all Judah and Benjamin and in the cities which he had captured in the hill-country of Ephraim; and he repaired the altar of the LORD which stood before the vestibule of the 9 LORD's house. *c* Then he assembled all Judah and Benjamin and all who had come from Ephraim, Manasseh, and Simeon to reside among them; for great numbers had come over to him from Israel, when they saw that 10 the LORD his God was with him. So they assembled at Jerusalem in the 11 third month of the fifteenth year of Asa's reign, and that day they sacrificed to the LORD seven hundred oxen and seven thousand sheep from the spoil 12 which they had brought. And they entered into a covenant to seek guidance 13 of the LORD the God of their fathers with all their heart and soul; all who would not seek the LORD the God of Israel were to be put to death, young 14 and old, men and women alike. Then they bound themselves by an oath

a without law: *or* without the law.   *b* *Prob. rdg.; Heb. adds* and the prophecy, Oded the prophet.   *c* house: *prob. rdg.; Heb. om.*

to the LORD, with loud shouts of acclamation while trumpets and horns sounded; and all Judah rejoiced at the oath, because they had bound 15 themselves with all their heart and had sought him earnestly, and he had let himself be found by them. So the LORD gave them security on every side. King Asa also deprived Maacah his grandmother of her rank as 16^a queen mother because she had an obscene object made for the worship of Asherah; Asa cut it down, ground it to powder and burnt it in the gorge of the Kidron. Although the hill-shrines were allowed to remain in Israel, 17 Asa himself remained faithful all his life. He brought into the house of 18 God all his father's votive offerings and his own, gold and silver and sacred vessels. And there was no more war until the thirty-fifth year of Asa's 19 reign.

In the thirty-sixth year of the reign of Asa, Baasha king of Israel invaded **16** 1^b Judah and fortified Ramah to cut off all access to Asa king of Judah. So 2 Asa brought out silver and gold from the treasuries of the house of the LORD and the royal palace, and sent this request to Ben-hadad king of Aram, whose capital was Damascus: 'There is an alliance between us, as 3 there was between our fathers. I now send you herewith silver and gold; break off your alliance with Baasha king of Israel, so that he may abandon his campaign against me.' Ben-hadad listened willingly to King Asa 4 and ordered the commanders of his armies to move against the cities of Israel, and they attacked Iyyon, Dan, Abel-mayim, and all the store-cities of Naphtali. When Baasha heard of it, he ceased fortifying Ramah 5 and stopped all work on it. Then King Asa took with him all the men 6 of Judah and they carried away the stones of Ramah and the timbers with which Baasha had fortified it; and he used them to fortify Geba and Mizpah.

At that time the seer Hanani came to Asa king of Judah and said to him, 7 'Because you relied on the king of Aram and not on the LORD your God, the army of the king of Israel has escaped. The Cushites and the Libyans, 8 were they not a great army with a vast number of chariots and horsemen? Yet, because you relied on the LORD, he delivered them into your power. The eyes of the LORD range through the whole earth, to bring aid and 9 comfort to those whose hearts are loyal to him. You have acted foolishly in this affair; you will have wars from now on.' Asa was angry with the 10 seer and put him in the stocks; for these words of his had made the king very indignant. At the same time he treated some of the people with great brutality.

The events of Asa's reign, from first to last, are recorded in the annals 11^c of the kings of Judah and Israel. In the thirty-ninth year of his reign Asa 12 became gravely affected with gangrene in his feet; he did not seek guidance of the LORD but resorted to physicians. He rested with his forefathers, 13 in the forty-first year of his reign, and was buried in the tomb which he 14 had bought^d for himself in the city of David, being laid on a bier ^e which had been heaped with all kinds of spices skilfully compounded; and they kindled a great fire in his honour.

^a *Verses 16–18: cp. 1 Kgs. 15. 13–15.*   ^b *Verses 1–6: cp. 1 Kgs. 15. 17–22.*
^c *Verses 11–14: cp. 1 Kgs. 15. 23, 24.*   ^d *Or dug.*   ^e *Or in a niche.*

17 ASA WAS SUCCEEDED BY HIS SON JEHOSHAPHAT, who determined
2 to resist Israel by force. He posted troops in all the fortified cities of Judah
and stationed officers *a* throughout Judah and in the cities of Ephraim
3 which his father Asa had captured. The LORD was with Jehoshaphat, for
he followed the example his father had set in his early years and did not
4 resort to the Baalim; he sought guidance of the God of his father and
5 obeyed his commandments and did not follow the practices of Israel. So
the LORD established the kingdom under his rule, and all Judah brought
6 him gifts, and his wealth and fame *b* became very great. He took pride in
the service of the LORD; he also suppressed the hill-shrines and the sacred
poles in Judah.

7   In the third year of his reign he sent his officers, Ben-hayil, Obadiah,
8 Zechariah, Nethaneel, and Micaiah, to teach in the cities of Judah, together with the Levites, Shemaiah, Nethaniah, Zebadiah, Asahel, Shemiramoth, Jehonathan, Adonijah, Tobiah, and Tob-adonijah, *c* accompanied
9 by the priests Elishama and Jehoram. They taught in Judah, having with
them the book of the law of the LORD; they went round the cities of Judah,
teaching the people.

10   So the dread of the LORD fell upon all the rulers of the lands surrounding
11 Judah, and they did not make war on Jehoshaphat. Certain Philistines
brought a gift, a great quantity of silver, to Jehoshaphat; the Arabs too
brought him seven thousand seven hundred rams and seven thousand
12 seven hundred he-goats. Jehoshaphat became ever more powerful and
13 built fortresses and store-cities in Judah; and he had much work on hand
in the cities of Judah. He had regular, seasoned troops in Jerusalem,
14 enrolled according to their clans in this way: of Judah, the officers over
units of a thousand: Adnah the commander, together with three hundred
15 thousand seasoned troops; and next to him the commander Johanan, with
16 two hundred and eighty thousand; and next to him Amasiah son of
Zichri, who had volunteered for the service of the LORD, with two hundred
17 thousand seasoned troops; and of Benjamin: an experienced soldier
Eliada, with two hundred thousand men armed with bows and shields;
18 next to him Jehozabad, with a hundred and eighty thousand fully-armed
19 men. These were the men who served the king, apart from those whom
the king had posted in the fortified cities throughout Judah.

18   When Jehoshaphat had become very wealthy and famous, *d* he allied
2*e* himself with Ahab by marriage. Some years afterwards he went down to
visit Ahab in Samaria, and Ahab slaughtered many sheep and oxen for
3 him and his retinue, and incited him to attack Ramoth-gilead. What Ahab
king of Israel said to Jehoshaphat king of Judah was this: 'Will you join
me in attacking Ramoth-gilead?' And he answered, 'What is mine is yours,
4 myself and my people; I will join with you in the war.' Then Jehoshaphat
5 said to the king of Israel, 'First let us seek counsel from the LORD.' The
king of Israel assembled the prophets, some four hundred of them, and
asked them, 'Shall I attack Ramoth-gilead or shall I refrain?' 'Attack,'
6 they answered; 'God will deliver it into your hands.' Jehoshaphat asked,

a Or garrisons.   *b* Or riches.   *c* Prob. rdg.; Heb. adds the Levites.   *d* Or rich.
e Verses 2–34: cp. 1 Kgs. 22. 2–35.

'Is there no other prophet of the LORD here through whom we may seek
guidance?' 'There is one more', the king of Israel answered, 'through whom   7
we may seek guidance of the LORD, but I hate the man, because he never
prophesies any good for me; never anything but evil. His name is Micaiah
son of Imla.' Jehoshaphat exclaimed, 'My lord king, let no such word pass
your lips!' So the king of Israel called one of his eunuchs and told him to   8
fetch Micaiah son of Imla with all speed.

The king of Israel and Jehoshaphat king of Judah were seated on their   9
thrones, clothed in their royal robes and in shining armour, at the entrance
to the gate of Samaria, and all the prophets were prophesying before them.
One of them, Zedekiah son of Kenaanah, made himself horns of iron and   10
said, 'This is the word of the LORD: "With horns like these you shall gore
the Aramaeans and make an end of them."' In the same vein all the pro-   11
phets prophesied, 'Attack Ramoth-gilead and win the day; the LORD will
deliver it into your hands.' The messenger sent to fetch Micaiah told him   12
that the prophets had with one voice given the king a favourable answer.
'And mind you agree with them', he added. 'As the LORD lives,' said   13
Micaiah, 'I will say only what my God tells me to say.'

When Micaiah came into the king's presence, the king said to him,   14
'Micaiah, shall I attack Ramoth-gilead or shall I refrain?' 'Attack and win
the day,' he said, 'and it will fall into your hands.' 'How often must I   15
adjure you', said the king, 'to tell me nothing but the truth in the name of
the LORD?' Then Micaiah said, 'I saw all Israel scattered on the mountains,   16
like sheep without a shepherd; and I heard the LORD say, "They have no
master; let them go home in peace."' The king of Israel said to Jehoshaphat,   17
'Did I not tell you that he never prophesies good for me, nothing but evil?'
Micaiah went on, 'Listen now to the word of the LORD: I saw the LORD   18
seated on his throne, with all the host of heaven in attendance on his right
and on his left. The LORD said, "Who will entice Ahab to attack and fall on *a*   19
Ramoth-gilead?" One said one thing and one said another; then a spirit   20
came forward and stood before the LORD and said, "I will entice him."
"How?" said the LORD. "I will go out", he said, "and be a lying spirit in   21
the mouth of all his prophets." "You shall entice him," said the LORD,
"and you shall succeed; go and do it." You see, then, how the LORD has   22
put a lying spirit in the mouth of all these prophets of yours, because he
has decreed disaster for you.' Then Zedekiah son of Kenaanah came up to   23
Micaiah and struck him in the face: 'And how did the spirit of the LORD
pass from me to speak to you?' he said. Micaiah answered, 'That you will   24
find out on the day when you run into an inner room to hide yourself.'
Then the king of Israel ordered Micaiah to be arrested and committed to   25
the custody of Amon the governor of the city and Joash the king's son. *b*
'Lock this fellow up', he said, 'and give him prison diet of bread and water   26
until I come home in safety.' Micaiah retorted, 'If you do return in safety,   27
the LORD has not spoken by me.' *c*

So the king of Israel and Jehoshaphat king of Judah marched on Ramoth-   28
gilead, and the king of Israel said to Jehoshaphat, 'I will disguise myself   29

a Or at.   *b* son: or deputy.   *c* *Prob. rdg.; Heb. adds* and he said, 'Listen, peoples,
all together.'

to go into battle, but you shall wear your royal robes.' So he went into battle
30 in disguise. Now the king of Aram had commanded the captains of his
31 chariots not to engage all and sundry but the king of Israel alone. When
the captains saw Jehoshaphat, they thought he was the king of Israel and
wheeled to attack him. But Jehoshaphat cried out, and the LORD came to
32 his help; and God drew them away from him. When the captains saw that
33 he was not the king of Israel, they broke off the attack on him. But one
man drew his bow at random and hit the king of Israel where the breastplate joins the plates of the armour. So he said to his driver, 'Wheel round
34 and take me out of the line; I am wounded.' When the day's fighting reached
its height, the king of Israel was facing the Aramaeans, propped up in his
chariot; he remained so till evening, and at sunset he died.

19 As Jehoshaphat king of Judah returned in safety to his home in Jeru-
2 salem, Jehu son of Hanani, the seer, went out to meet him and said, 'Do
you take delight in helping the wicked and befriending the enemies of the
3 LORD? The LORD will make you suffer for this. Yet there is some good in
you, for you have swept away the sacred poles from the land and have made
a practice of seeking guidance of God.'

4   Jehoshaphat had his residence in Jerusalem, but he went out again
among his people from Beersheba to the hill-country of Ephraim and
5 brought them back to the LORD the God of their fathers. He appointed
judges throughout the land, one in each of the fortified cities of Judah,
6 and said to them, 'Be careful what you do; you are there as judges, to please
7 not man but the LORD, who is with you when you pass sentence. Let the
dread of the LORD be upon you, then; take care what you do, for the LORD
our God will not tolerate injustice, partiality, or bribery.'

8   In Jerusalem Jehoshaphat appointed some of the Levites and priests
and some heads of families by paternal descent in Israel to administer the
law of the LORD and to arbitrate in lawsuits among the inhabitants*a* of
9 the city, and he gave them these instructions: 'You must always act in the
10 fear of the LORD, faithfully and with singleness of mind. In every suit
which comes before you from your kinsmen, in whatever city they live,
whether cases of bloodshed or offences against the law or the commandments, against statutes or regulations, you shall warn them to commit no
offence against the LORD; otherwise you and your kinsmen will suffer for
11 it. If you act thus, you will be free of all offence. Your authority in all
matters which concern the LORD is Amariah the chief priest, and in those
which concern the king it is Zebediah son of Ishmael, the prince of the
house of Judah; the Levites are your officers. Be strong and resolute, and
may the LORD be on the side of the good!'

20 It happened some time afterwards that the Moabites, the Ammonites,
2 and some of the Meunites made war on Jehoshaphat. News was brought
to him that a great horde of them was attacking him from beyond the Dead
Sea, from Edom, and was already at Hazazon-tamar, which is En-gedi.
3 Jehoshaphat in his alarm resolved to seek guidance of the LORD and pro-
4 claimed a fast for all Judah. Judah gathered together to ask counsel of the
5 LORD; from every city of the land they came to consult him. Jehoshaphat

---

a in ... inhabitants: *prob. rdg.; Heb. obscure.*

stood up in the assembly of Judah and Jerusalem in the house of the LORD, in front of the New Court, and said, 'O LORD God of our fathers, art not 6 thou God in heaven? Thou rulest over all the kingdoms of the nations; in thy hand are strength and power, and there is none who can withstand thee. Didst not thou, O God our God, dispossess the inhabitants of this land 7 in favour of thy people Israel, and give it for ever to the descendants of Abraham thy friend? So they lived in it and have built a sanctuary in it in 8 honour of thy name and said, "Should evil come upon us, war or flood,*a* 9 pestilence or famine, we will stand before this house and before thee, for in this house is thy Name, and we will cry to thee in our distress and thou wilt hear and save." Thou didst not allow Israel, when they came out of 10 Egypt, to enter the land of the Ammonites, the Moabites, and the people of the hill-country of Seir, so they turned aside and left them alone and did not destroy them. Now see how these people repay us: they are coming 11 to drive us out of thy possession which thou didst give to us. Judge them, 12 O God our God, for we have no strength to face this great horde which is invading our land; we know not what we ought to do; we lift our eyes to thee.'

So all Judah stood there before the LORD, with their dependants, their 13 wives and their children. Then, in the midst of the assembly, the spirit of 14 the LORD came upon Jahaziel son of Zechariah, son of Benaiah, son of Jeiel, son of Mattaniah, a Levite of the line of Asaph, and he said, 'Attend, 15 all Judah, all inhabitants of Jerusalem, and King Jehoshaphat; this is the word of the LORD to you: "Have no fear; do not be dismayed by this great horde, for the battle is in God's hands, not yours. Go down to 16 meet them tomorrow; they will come up by the Ascent of Ziz. You will find them at the end of the valley, east of the wilderness of Jeruel. It 17 is not you who will fight this battle; stand firm and wait, and you will see the deliverance worked by the LORD: he is on your side, O Judah and Jerusalem. Do not fear or be dismayed; go out tomorrow to face them; for the LORD is on your side." ' Jehoshaphat bowed his face to the ground, and 18 all Judah and the inhabitants of Jerusalem fell down before the LORD to make obeisance to him. Then the Levites of the lines of Kohath and Korah 19 stood up and praised the LORD the God of Israel with a mighty shout.

So they rose early in the morning and went out to the wilderness of 20 Tekoa; and, as they were starting, Jehoshaphat took his stand and said, 'Hear me, O Judah and inhabitants of Jerusalem: hold firmly to your faith in the LORD your God and you will be upheld; have faith in his prophets and you will prosper.' After consulting with the people, he appointed 21 men to sing to the LORD and praise the splendour of his holiness*b* as they went before the armed troops, and they sang:

> Give thanks to the LORD,
> for his love endures for ever.

As soon as their loud shouts of praise were heard, the LORD deluded the 22 Ammonites and Moabites and the men of the hill-country of Seir, who

a *Prob. rdg.; Heb.* judgement.   *b* *Or* singers in sacred vestments to praise the LORD.

23 were invading Judah, and they were defeated. It turned out that the Ammonites and Moabites had taken up a position against the men of the hill-country of Seir, and set themselves to annihilate and destroy them; and when they had exterminated the men of Seir, they savagely attacked
24 one another. So when Judah came to the watch-tower in the wilderness and looked towards the enemy horde, there they were all lying dead upon
25 the ground; none had escaped. When Jehoshaphat and his men came to collect the booty, they found a large number of cattle, goods, clothing, and precious things, which they plundered until they could carry away no more. They spent three days collecting the booty, there was so much of it.
26 On the fourth day they assembled in the Valley of Berakah,*a* the name that
27 it bears to this day because they blessed the LORD there. Then all the men of Judah and Jerusalem, with Jehoshaphat at their head, returned home to the city in triumph; for the LORD had given them cause to triumph over
28 their enemies. They entered Jerusalem with lutes, harps, and trumpets
29 playing, and went into the house of the LORD. So the dread of God fell upon the rulers of every country, when they heard that the LORD had
30 fought against the enemies of Israel; and the realm of Jehoshaphat was at peace, God giving him security on all sides.

31*b*   Thus Jehoshaphat reigned over Judah. He was thirty-five years old when he came to the throne, and he reigned in Jerusalem for twenty-five
32 years; his mother was Azubah daughter of Shilhi. He followed in the footsteps of Asa his father and did not swerve from them; he did what was
33 right in the eyes of the LORD. But the hill-shrines were allowed to remain,
34 and the people did not set their hearts upon the God of their fathers. The other events of Jehoshaphat's reign, from first to last, are recorded in the history of Jehu son of Hanani, which is included in the annals of the kings of Israel.

35   Later Jehoshaphat king of Judah allied himself with Ahaziah king of
36 Israel; he did wrong in joining with him to build ships for trade with
37 Tarshish; these were built in Ezion-geber. But Eliezer son of Dodavahu of Mareshah denounced Jehoshaphat with this prophecy: 'Because you have joined with Ahaziah, the LORD will bring your work to nothing.' So the ships were wrecked and could not make the voyage to Tarshish.

21 JEHOSHAPHAT RESTED WITH HIS FOREFATHERS and was buried with
2 them in the city of David. He was succeeded by his son Joram, whose brothers were Azariah, Jehiel, Zechariah, Azariah, Michael, and Shephatiah, sons of Jehoshaphat. All of them were sons of Jehoshaphat king of
3 Judah, and their father gave them many gifts, silver and gold and other costly things, as well as fortified cities in Judah; but the kingship he gave to Joram because he was the eldest.

4   When Joram was firmly established on his father's throne, he put to
5*c* the sword all his brothers and also some of the princes of Israel. He was thirty-two years old when he came to the throne, and he reigned in Jeru-
6 salem for eight years. He followed the practices of the kings of Israel as

a That is Valley of Blessing.   *b* Verses 31–33: cp. 1 Kgs. 22. 41–43.   *c* Verses 5–10: cp. 2 Kgs. 8. 17–22.

the house of Ahab had done, for he had married Ahab's daughter; and he did what was wrong in the eyes of the LORD. But for the sake of the covenant 7 which he had made with David, the LORD was unwilling to destroy the house of David, since he had promised to give him and his sons a flame, to burn for all time.

During his reign Edom revolted against Judah and set up its own king. 8 Joram, with his commanders and all his chariots, advanced into Edom. 9 He and his chariot-commanders set out by night, but they were surrounded by the Edomites and defeated.[a] So Edom has remained independent of 10 Judah to this day. Libnah revolted against him at the same time, because he had forsaken the LORD the God of his fathers, and because he had built 11 hill-shrines in the hill-country of Judah and had seduced the inhabitants of Jerusalem into idolatrous practices and corrupted Judah.

A letter reached Joram from Elijah the prophet, which ran thus: 'This 12 is the word of the LORD the God of David your father: "You have not followed in the footsteps of Jehoshaphat your father and of Asa king of Judah, but have followed the kings of Israel and have seduced Judah and 13 the inhabitants of Jerusalem, as the house of Ahab did; and you have put to death your own brothers, sons of your father's house, men better than yourself. Because of all this, the LORD is about to strike a heavy blow at 14 your people, your children, your wives, and all your possessions, and you 15 yourself will suffer from a chronic disease of the bowels, until they prolapse and become severely ulcerated."' Then the LORD aroused against Joram 16 the anger of the Philistines and of the Arabs who live near the Cushites, and they invaded Judah and made their way right through it, carrying 17 off all the property which they found in the king's palace, as well as his sons and wives; not a son was left to him except the youngest, Jehoahaz. It was after all this that the LORD struck down the king with an incurable 18 disease of the bowels. It continued for some time, and towards the end of 19 the second year the disease caused his bowels to prolapse, and the painful ulceration brought on his death. But his people kindled no fire in his honour as they had done for his fathers. He was thirty-two years old when 20 he became king, and he reigned in Jerusalem for eight years. His passing went unsung, and he was buried in the city of David, but not in the burial-place of the kings.

Then the inhabitants of Jerusalem made Ahaziah, his youngest son, **22** 1[b] king in his place, for the raiders who had joined the Arabs in the campaign had killed all the elder sons. So Ahaziah son of Joram became king of Judah. He was forty-two years old when he came to the throne, and he 2 reigned in Jerusalem for one year; his mother was Athaliah granddaughter of Omri. He too followed the practices of the house of Ahab, for his mother 3 was his counsellor in wickedness. He did what was wrong in the eyes of the 4 LORD like the house of Ahab, for they had been his counsellors after his father's death, to his undoing. He followed their counsel also in the 5 alliance he made with Jehoram son of Ahab king of Israel, to fight against Hazael king of Aram at Ramoth-gilead. But Jehoram was wounded by the

---

[a] *and defeated*: prob. rdg.; Heb. *and he defeated them.*   [b] *Verses 1–6*: cp.
2 Kgs. 8. 25–29.

6 Aramaeans, and returned to Jezreel to recover from the wounds which were inflicted on him at Ramoth in battle with Hazael king of Aram.

7 Because of Jehoram's illness Ahaziah son of Joram king of Judah went down to Jezreel to visit him. It was God's will that the visit of Ahaziah to Jehoram should be the occasion of his downfall. During the visit he went

8 out with Jehoram to meet Jehu son of Nimshi, whom the LORD had anointed to bring the house of Ahab to an end. So it came about that Jehu, who was then at variance with the house of Ahab, found the officers of Judah and the kinsmen of Ahaziah who were his attendants, and killed

9 them. Then he searched out Ahaziah himself, and his men captured him in Samaria, where he had gone into hiding. They brought him to Jehu and put him to death; they gave him burial, for they said, 'He was a son of Jehoshaphat who sought the guidance of the LORD with his whole heart.' Then the house of Ahaziah had no one strong enough to rule.

10[a] As soon as Athaliah mother of Ahaziah saw that her son was dead, she

11 set out to extirpate the royal line of the house of Judah. But Jehosheba daughter of King Joram took Ahaziah's son Joash and stole him away from among the princes who were being murdered; she put him and his nurse in a bedchamber. Thus Jehosheba, daughter of King Joram and wife of Jehoiada the priest, because she was Ahaziah's sister, hid Joash from

12 Athaliah so that she did not put him to death. He remained concealed with them in the house of God for six years, while Athaliah ruled the country.

23 In the seventh year Jehoiada felt himself strong enough to make an agreement with Azariah son of Jeroham, Ishmael son of Jehohanan, Azariah son of Obed, Maaseiah son of Adaiah, and Elishaphat son of

2 Zichri, all captains of units of a hundred. They went all through Judah and gathered to Jerusalem the Levites from the cities of Judah and the heads

3 of clans in Israel, and they came to Jerusalem. All the assembly made a compact with the king in the house of God, and Jehoiada said to them, 'Here is the king's son! He shall be king, as the LORD promised that the

4 sons of David should be. This is what you must do: a third of you, priests and Levites, as you come on duty on the sabbath, are to be on guard at the

5 threshold gates, another third are to be in the royal palace, and another third are to be at the Foundation Gate, while all the people will be in the

6 courts of the house of the LORD. Let no one enter the house of the LORD except the priests and the attendant Levites; they may enter, for they are

7 holy, but all the people shall continue to keep the LORD's charge. The Levites shall mount guard round the king, each with his weapons at the ready; anyone who tries to enter the house is to be put to death. They shall stay with the king wherever he goes.'

8 The Levites and all Judah carried out the orders of Jehoiada the priest to the letter. Each captain took his men, both those who came on duty on the sabbath and those who came off, for Jehoiada the priest had not

9 released the outgoing divisions. And Jehoiada the priest handed out to the captains King David's spears, shields, and bucklers, which were in the

10 house of God; and he posted all the people, each man carrying his weapon

[a] *22. 10—23. 21: cp. 2 Kgs. 11. 1-20.*

at the ready, from corner to corner of the house to north and south,^{*a*} surrounding the king. Then they brought out the king's son, put the crown   11
on his head, handed him the warrant and proclaimed him king, and
Jehoiada and his sons anointed him; and a shout went up: 'Long live the
king.' When Athaliah heard the noise of the people as they ran about   12
cheering for the king, she came into the house of the LORD where the people
were and found the king standing on the dais^{*b*} at the entrance, amidst   13
outbursts of song and fanfares of trumpets in his honour; all the populace
were rejoicing and blowing trumpets, and singers with musical instruments were leading the celebrations. Athaliah rent her clothes and cried,
'Treason! Treason!' Jehoiada the priest gave orders to^{*c*} the captains in   14
command of the troops: 'Bring her outside the precincts and let anyone
in attendance on her be put to the sword'; for the priest said, 'Do not kill
her in the house of the LORD.' So they laid hands on her and took her to   15
the royal palace and killed her there at the passage to the Horse Gate.

Then Jehoiada made a covenant between the LORD^{*d*} and the whole   16
people and the king, that they should be the LORD's people. And all the   17
people went into the temple of Baal and pulled it down; they smashed its
altars and images, and they slew Mattan the priest of Baal before the altars.
Then Jehoiada committed the supervision of the house of the LORD to the   18
charge of the priests and the Levites whom David had allocated to the
house of the LORD, to offer whole-offerings to the LORD as prescribed in
the law of Moses, with the singing and rejoicing as handed down from
David. He stationed the door-keepers at the gates of the house of the LORD,   19
to prevent anyone entering who was in any way unclean. Then he took the   20
captains of units of a hundred, the nobles, and the governors of the people,
and all the people of the land, and they escorted the king from the house of
the LORD through the Upper Gate to the royal palace, and seated him on
the royal throne. The whole people rejoiced and the city was tranquil.   21
That is how Athaliah was put to the sword.

Joash was seven years old when he became king, and he reigned in   **24** 1^{*e*}
Jerusalem for forty years; his mother was Zibiah of Beersheba. He did   2
what was right in the eyes of the LORD as long as Jehoiada the priest was
alive. Jehoiada chose him two wives, and he had a family of sons and   3
daughters.

Some time after this, Joash decided to repair the house of the LORD. So   4 5
he assembled the priests and the Levites and said to them, 'Go through
the cities of Judah and collect the annual tax from all the Israelites for the
restoration of the house of your God, and do it quickly.' But the Levites
did not act quickly. The king then called for Jehoiada the chief priest and   6
said to him, 'Why have you not required the Levites to bring in from Judah
and Jerusalem the tax imposed by Moses the servant of the LORD and by
the assembly of Israel for the Tent of the Tokens?' For the wicked Athaliah   7
and her adherents had broken into the house of God and had devoted all

---

^{*a*} *Prob. rdg.; Heb. adds of the altar and the house.*   ^{*b*} *Prob. rdg., cp. 2 Kgs. 11. 14;*
Heb. by his pillar.   ^{*c*} *gave orders to: prob. rdg., cp. 2 Kgs. 11. 15; Heb. brought out.*
^{*d*} *the LORD: prob. rdg., cp. 2 Kgs. 11. 17; Heb. him.*   ^{*e*} *Verses 1–14: cp. 2 Kgs.*
11. 21—12. 15.

8 its holy things to the service of the Baalim. So the king ordered them to
9 make a chest and to put it outside the gate of the house of the LORD; and
proclamation was made throughout Judah and Jerusalem that the people
should bring to the LORD the tax imposed on Israel in the wilderness by
10 Moses the servant of God. And all the leaders and all the people gladly
11 brought their taxes and cast them into the chest until it was full. Whenever the chest was brought to the king's officers by the Levites and they
saw that it was well filled, the king's secretary and the chief priest's officer
would come to empty it, after which it was carried back to its place. This
12 they did daily, and they collected a great sum of money. The king and
Jehoiada gave it to those responsible for carrying out the work in the house
of the LORD, and they hired masons and carpenters to do the repairs, as
13 well as craftsmen in iron and copper *a* to restore the house. So the workmen
proceeded with their task and the new work progressed under their hands;
they restored the house of God according to its original design and
14 strengthened it. When they had finished, they brought what was left of
the money to the king and to Jehoiada, and it was made into vessels for the
house of the LORD, both for service and for sacrificing, saucers and other
vessels of gold and silver. While Jehoiada lived, whole-offerings were
offered in the house of the LORD continually.

15 Jehoiada, now old and weighed down with years, died at the age of a
16 hundred and thirty and was buried with the kings in the city of David,
because he had done good in Israel and served God and his house.

17 After the death of Jehoiada the leading men of Judah came and made
18 obeisance to the king. He listened to them, and they forsook the house of
the LORD the God of their fathers and worshipped sacred poles and idols.
19 And Judah and Jerusalem suffered for this wickedness. But the LORD sent
prophets to bring them back to himself, prophets who denounced them
20 and were not heeded. Then the spirit of God took possession of Zechariah
son of Jehoiada the priest, and he stood looking down on the people and
said to them, 'This is the word of God: "Why do you disobey the commands
of the LORD and court disaster? Because you have forsaken the LORD, he
21 has forsaken you."' But they made common cause against him, and on
orders from the king they stoned him to death in the court of the house of
22 the LORD. King Joash did not remember the loyalty of Zechariah's father
Jehoiada but killed his son, who said as he was dying, 'May the LORD see
this and exact the penalty.'

23 At the turn of the year an Aramaean army advanced against Joash; they
invaded Judah and Jerusalem and massacred all the officers, so that the
army ceased to exist, and sent all their spoil to the king of Damascus.
24 Although the Aramaeans had invaded with a small force, the LORD
delivered a very great army into their hands, because the people had forsaken the LORD the God of their fathers; and Joash suffered just punishment.

25*b* When the Aramaeans had withdrawn, leaving the king severely wounded,
his servants conspired against him to avenge the death of the son of
Jehoiada the priest; and they killed him on his bed. Thus he died and was

---

a Or bronze.   *b* *Verses 25-27: cp. 2 Kgs. 12. 20, 21.*

buried in the city of David, but not in the burial-place of the kings. The 26
conspirators were Zabad son of Shimeath an Ammonite woman and
Jehozabad son of Shimrith a Moabite woman. His children, the many 27
oracles about him, and his reconstruction of the house of God are all on
record in the story given in the annals of the kings. He was succeeded by
his son Amaziah.

AMAZIAH WAS TWENTY-FIVE YEARS OLD when he came to the throne, 25 1*a*
and he reigned in Jerusalem for twenty-nine years; his mother was
Jehoaddan of Jerusalem. He did what was right in the eyes of the LORD, 2
but not whole-heartedly. When the royal power was firmly in his grasp, 3
he put to death those of his servants who had murdered the king his father;
but he spared their children, in obedience to the LORD's command written 4
in the law of Moses: 'Fathers shall not die for their children, nor children
for their fathers; a man shall die only for his own sin.'

Then Amaziah assembled the men of Judah and drew them up by 5
families, all Judah and Benjamin as well, under officers over units of a
thousand and a hundred. He mustered those of twenty years old and
upwards and found their number to be three hundred thousand, all
picked troops ready for service, able to handle spear and shield. He also 6
hired a hundred thousand seasoned troops from Israel for a hundred talents
of silver. But a man of God came to him and said, 'My lord king, do not let 7
the Israelite army march with you; the LORD is not with Israel—all these
Ephraimites! For, if you make these people *b* your allies in the war, God will 8
overthrow you in battle; he has power to help or to overthrow.' Then Ama- 9
ziah said to the man of God, 'What am I to do about the hundred talents
which I have spent on the Israelite army?' The man of God answered, 'It
is in the LORD's power to give you much more than that.' So Amaziah 10
detached the troops which had come to him from Ephraim and sent them
home; that infuriated them against Judah and they went home in a rage.

Then Amaziah took heart and led his men to the Valley of Salt and there 11
killed ten thousand men of Seir. The men of Judah captured another ten 12
thousand men alive, brought them to the top of a cliff *c* and hurled them
over so that they were all dashed to pieces. Meanwhile the troops which 13
Amaziah had sent home without allowing them to take part in the battle
raided the cities of Judah from Samaria to Beth-horon, massacred three
thousand people in them and carried off quantities of booty.

After Amaziah had returned from the defeat of the Edomites, he brought 14
the gods of the people of Seir and, setting them up as his own gods, worshipped them and burnt sacrifices to them. The LORD was angry with 15
Amaziah for this and sent a prophet who said to him, 'Why have you resorted to gods who could not save their own people from you?' But while 16
he was speaking, the king said to him, 'Have we appointed you counsellor
to the king? Stop! Why risk your life?' The prophet did stop, but first he
said, 'I know that God has determined to destroy you because you have
done this and have not listened to my counsel.'

a Verses 1–4: cp. 2 Kgs. 14. 1–6.   *b* these people: *prob. rdg.; Heb. obscure.*
c a cliff: *or* Sela.

17[a] Then Amaziah king of Judah, after consultation, sent messengers to Jehoash son of Jehoahaz, son of Jehu, king of Israel, to propose a meeting.
18 But Jehoash king of Israel sent this answer to Amaziah king of Judah: 'A thistle in Lebanon sent to a cedar in Lebanon to say, "Give your daughter in marriage to my son." But a wild beast in Lebanon, passing by, trampled
19 on the thistle. You have defeated Edom, you say, but it has gone to your head. Enjoy your glory at home and stay there. Why should you involve yourself in disaster and bring yourself to the ground, and Judah with you?'
20 But Amaziah would not listen; and this was God's doing in order to give Judah into the power of Jehoash, because they had resorted to the gods of
21 Edom. So Jehoash king of Israel marched out, and he and Amaziah king
22 of Judah met one another at Beth-shemesh in Judah. The men of Judah
23 were routed by Israel and fled to their homes. But Jehoash king of Israel captured Amaziah king of Judah, son of Joash, son of Jehoahaz, at Beth-shemesh, and brought him to Jerusalem. There he broke down the city wall from the Gate of Ephraim to the Corner Gate, a distance of four
24 hundred cubits; he also took[b] all the gold and silver and all the vessels found in the house of God, in the care of Obed-edom, and the treasures of the royal palace, as well as hostages, and returned to Samaria.
25[c] Amaziah son of Joash, king of Judah, outlived Jehoash son of Jehoahaz,
26 king of Israel, by fifteen years. The other events of Amaziah's reign, from first to last, are recorded in the annals of the kings of Judah and Israel.
27 From the time when he turned away from the LORD, there was conspiracy against him in Jerusalem and he fled to Lachish; but they sent after him
28 to Lachish and put him to death there. Then his body was conveyed on horseback to Jerusalem, and there he was buried with his forefathers in the city of David.

26 All the people of Judah took Uzziah, now sixteen years old, and made
2 him king in succession to his father Amaziah. It was he who built Eloth and restored it to Judah after the king rested with his forefathers.
3[d] Uzziah was sixteen years old when he came to the throne, and he reigned in Jerusalem for fifty-two years; his mother was Jecoliah of Jerusalem.
4 He did what was right in the eyes of the LORD, as Amaziah his father had
5 done. He set himself to seek the guidance of God in the days of Zechariah, who instructed him in the fear of God; as long as he sought guidance of the LORD, God caused him to prosper.
6 He took the field against the Philistines and broke down the walls of Gath, Jabneh, and Ashdod; and he built cities in the territory of Ashdod
7 and among the Philistines. God aided him against them, against the Arabs
8 who lived in Gur-baal, and against the Meunites. The Ammonites brought gifts to Uzziah and his fame spread to the borders of Egypt, for he had
9 become very powerful. Besides, he built towers in Jerusalem at the Corner
10 Gate, at the Valley Gate, and at the escarpment, and fortified them. He built other towers in the wilderness and dug many cisterns, for he had large herds of cattle both in the Shephelah and in the plain. He also had

---

[a] *Verses 17–24: cp. 2 Kgs. 14. 8–14.*   [b] he also took: *prob. rdg., cp. 2 Kgs. 14. 14;* Heb. om.   [c] *25. 25—26. 2: cp. 2 Kgs. 14. 17–22.*   [d] *Verses 3, 4: cp. 2 Kgs. 15. 2, 3.*

farmers and vine-dressers in the hill-country and in the fertile lands, for he loved the soil.

Uzziah had an army of soldiers trained and ready for service, grouped   11
according to the census made by Jeiel the adjutant-general and Maaseiah
the clerk under the direction of Hananiah, one of the king's commanders.
The total number of heads of families which supplied seasoned warriors   12
was two thousand six hundred. Under their command was an army of   13
three hundred and seven thousand five hundred, a powerful fighting force
to aid the king against his enemies. Uzziah prepared for the whole army   14
shields, spears, helmets, coats of mail, bows, and*a* sling-stones. In Jeru-   15
salem he had machines designed by engineers for use upon towers and
bastions, made to discharge arrows and large stones. His fame spread far
and wide, for he was so wonderfully gifted that he became very powerful.

But when he grew powerful his pride led to his own undoing:*b* he   16
offended against the LORD his God by entering the temple of the LORD to
burn incense on the altar of incense. Azariah the priest and eighty others   17
of the LORD's priests, courageous men, went in after King Uzziah, con-   18
fronted him and said, 'It is not for you, Uzziah, to burn incense to the
LORD, but for the Aaronite priests who have been consecrated for that
office. Leave the sanctuary; for you have offended, and that will certainly
bring you no honour from the LORD God.' The king, who had a censer in   19
his hand ready to burn incense, was indignant; and because of his indignation at the priests, leprosy broke out on his forehead in the presence of the
priests, there in the house of the LORD, beside the altar of incense. When   20
Azariah the chief priest and the other priests looked towards him, they saw
that he had leprosy on his forehead and they hurried him out of the temple,
and indeed he himself hastened to leave, because the LORD had struck him
with the disease. And King Uzziah remained a leper till the day of his   21*c*
death; he lived in his own house as a leper, relieved of all duties and
excluded from the house of the LORD, while his son Jotham was comptroller
of the household and regent. The other events of Uzziah's reign, from first   22
to last, are recorded by the prophet Isaiah son of Amoz. So he rested with   23
his forefathers and was buried in a burial-ground, but not that of the kings;
for they said, 'He is a leper'; and he was succeeded by his son Jotham.

Jotham was twenty-five years old when he came to the throne, and he   **27** 1*d*
reigned in Jerusalem for sixteen years; his mother was Jerushah daughter
of Zadok. He did what was right in the eyes of the LORD, as his father   2
Uzziah had done, but unlike him he did not enter the temple of the LORD;
the people, however, continued their corrupt practices. He constructed   3
the upper gate of the house of the LORD and built extensively on the wall
at Ophel. He built cities in the hill-country of Judah, and forts and towers   4
on the wooded hills. He made war on the king of the Ammonites and   5
defeated him; and that year the Ammonites gave him a hundred talents of
silver, ten thousand kor of wheat and ten thousand of barley. They paid
him the same tribute in the second and third years. Jotham became very   6

a Prob. rdg.; Heb. adds for.   *b* his pride . . . undoing: *or* he became so proud that
he acted corruptly.   *c Verses 21–23: cp. 2 Kgs. 15. 5–7.*   *d Verses 1–3: cp.*
2 Kgs. 15. 33–35.

7 powerful because he maintained a steady course of obedience to the LORD
his God. The other events of Jotham's reign, all that he did in war and in
8 peace, are recorded in the annals of the kings of Israel and Judah. He was
twenty-five years old when he came to the throne, and he reigned in
9 Jerusalem for sixteen years. He rested with his forefathers and was buried
in the city of David; and he was succeeded by his son Ahaz.

28 1ᵃ AHAZ WAS TWENTY YEARS OLD when he came to the throne, and he
reigned in Jerusalem for sixteen years. He did not do what was right in the
2 eyes of the LORD like his forefather David, but followed in the footsteps of
3 the kings of Israel, and cast metal images for the Baalim. He also burnt
sacrifices in the Valley of Ben-hinnom; he even burnt his sons in the fire
according to the abominable practice of the nations whom the LORD had
4 dispossessed in favour of the Israelites. He slaughtered and burnt sacrifices
at the hill-shrines and on the hill-tops and under every spreading tree.

5 The LORD his God let him suffer at the hands of the king of Aram, and
the Aramaeans defeated him, took many captives and brought them to
Damascus; he was also made to suffer at the hands of the king of Israel,
6 who inflicted a severe defeat on him. This was Pekah son of Remaliah, who
killed in one day a hundred and twenty thousand men of Judah, seasoned
7 troops, because they had forsaken the LORD the God of their fathers. And
Zichri, an Ephraimite hero, killed Maaseiah the king's son ᵇ and Azrikam
the comptroller of the household and Elkanah the king's chief minister.
8 The Israelites took captive from their kinsmen two hundred thousand
women and children; they also took a large amount of booty and brought
it to Samaria.

9 A prophet of the LORD was there, Oded by name; he went out to meet
the army as it returned to Samaria and said to them, 'It is because the
LORD the God of your fathers is angry with Judah that he has given them
into your power; and you have massacred them in a rage that has towered
10 up to heaven. Now you propose to force the people of Judah and Jerusalem,
male and female, into slavery. Are not you also guilty men before the LORD
11 your God? Now, listen to me. Send back those you have taken captive from
12 your kinsmen, for the anger of the LORD is roused against you.' Next, some
Ephraimite chiefs, Azariah son of Jehohanan, Berechiah son of Meshillemoth, Hezekiahᶜ son of Shallum, and Amasa son of Hadlai, met those who
13 were returning from the war and said to them, 'You must not bring these
captives into our country; what you are proposing would make us guilty
before the LORD and add to our sins and transgressions. We are guilty
14 enough already, and there is fierce anger against Israel.' So the armed men
left the captives and the spoil with the officers and the assembled people.
15 The captives were put in charge of men nominated for this duty, who
found clothes from the spoil for all who were naked. They clothed them
and shod them, gave them food and drink, and anointed them; those who
were tottering from exhaustion they conveyed on the backs of asses, and
so brought them to their kinsmen in Jericho, in the Vale of Palm Trees.
Then they themselves returned to Samaria.

ᵃ *Verses 1–4: cp. 2 Kgs. 16. 2–4.*   ᵇ son: *or* deputy.   ᶜ *Or* Jehizkiah.

At that time King Ahaz sent to the king of Assyria for help. The Edom- 16 17
ites had invaded again and defeated Judah and taken away prisoners; and 18
the Philistines had raided the cities of the Shephelah and of the Negeb of
Judah and had captured Beth-shemesh, Aijalon, and Gederoth, as well as
Soco, Timnah, and Gimzo with their villages, and occupied them. The 19
LORD had reduced Judah to submission because of Ahaz king of Judah;
for his actions in Judah had been unbridled and he had been grossly unfaithful to the LORD. Then Tiglath-pileser king of Assyria marched against 20
him and, so far from assisting him, pressed him hard. Ahaz stripped the 21
house of the LORD, the king's palace and the houses of his officers, and gave
the plunder to the king of Assyria; but all to no purpose.

This King Ahaz, when hard pressed, became more and more unfaithful 22
to the LORD; he sacrificed to the gods of Damascus who had defeated him 23
and said, 'The gods of the kings of Aram helped them; I will sacrifice to
them so that they may help me.' But in fact they caused his downfall and
that of all Israel. Then Ahaz gathered together the vessels of the house of 24
God and broke them up, and shut the doors of the house of the LORD; he
made himself altars at every corner in Jerusalem, and at every single city 25
of Judah he made hill-shrines to burn sacrifices to other gods and provoked
the anger of the LORD the God of his fathers.

The other acts and all the events of his reign, from first to last, are 26*a*
recorded in the annals of the kings of Judah and Israel. So Ahaz rested with 27
his forefathers and was buried in the city of Jerusalem, but was not given
burial with the kings of Judah. He was succeeded by his son Hezekiah.

The kings of Judah from Hezekiah to the exile

HEZEKIAH WAS TWENTY-FIVE YEARS OLD when he came to the 29 1*b*
throne, and he reigned in Jerusalem for twenty-nine years; his
mother was Abijah daughter of Zechariah. He did what was right in the 2
eyes of the LORD, as David his forefather had done.

In the first year of his reign, in the first month, he opened the gates of 3
the house of the LORD and repaired them. He brought in the priests and 4
the Levites and gathered them together in the square on the east side, and 5
said to them, 'Levites, listen to me. Hallow yourselves now, hallow the
house of the LORD the God of your fathers, and remove the pollution from
the sanctuary. For our forefathers were unfaithful and did what was wrong 6
in the eyes of the LORD our God: they forsook him, they would have nothing
to do with his dwelling-place, they turned their backs on it. They shut the 7
doors of the porch and extinguished the lamps, they ceased to burn incense
and offer whole-offerings in the sanctuary to the God of Israel. Therefore 8
the anger of the LORD fell upon Judah and Jerusalem and he made them
repugnant, an object of horror and derision, as you see for yourselves.
Hence it is that our fathers have fallen by the sword, our sons and daughters 9
and our wives are in captivity. Now I intend that we should pledge our- 10
selves to the LORD the God of Israel, in order that his anger may be averted

a Verses 26, 27 : cp. 2 Kgs. 16. 19, 20.   *b Verses 1, 2 : cp. 2 Kgs. 18. 1–3.*

11 from us. So, my sons, let no time be lost; for the LORD has chosen you to serve him and to minister to him, to be his ministers and to burn sacrifices.'

12 Then the Levites set to work—Mahath son of Amasai and Joel son of Azariah of the family of Kohath; of the family of Merari, Kish son of Abdi and Azariah son of Jehalelel; of the family of Gershon, Joah son of Zim-

13 mah and Eden son of Joah; of the family of Elizaphan, Shimri and Jeiel;

14 of the family of Asaph, Zechariah and Mattaniah; of the family of Heman, Jehiel and Shimei; and of the family of Jeduthun, Shemaiah and Uzziel.

15 They assembled their kinsmen and hallowed themselves, and then went in, as the king had instructed them at the LORD's command, to purify the

16 house of the LORD. The priests went inside to purify the house of the LORD; they removed all the pollution which they found in the temple into the court of the house of the LORD, and the Levites took it from them and

17 carried it outside to the gorge of the Kidron. They began the rites on the first day of the first month, and on the eighth day they reached the porch; then for eight days they consecrated the house of the LORD, and on the

18 sixteenth day of the first month they finished. Then they went into the palace and said to King Hezekiah, 'We have purified the whole of the house of the LORD, the altar of whole-offering with all its vessels, and the table

19 for the Bread of the Presence arranged in rows with all its vessels; and we have put in order and consecrated all the vessels which King Ahaz cast aside during his reign, when he was unfaithful. They are now in place before the altar of the LORD.'

20 Then King Hezekiah rose early, assembled the officers of the city and

21 went up to the house of the LORD. They brought seven bulls, seven rams, and seven lambs for the whole-offering,*a* and seven he-goats as a sin-offering for the kingdom, for the sanctuary, and for Judah; these he com-

22 manded the priests of Aaron's line to offer on the altar of the LORD. So the bulls were slaughtered, and the priests took their blood and flung it against the altar; the rams were slaughtered, and their blood was flung against the altar; the lambs were slaughtered, and their blood was flung against

23 the altar. Then the he-goats for the sin-offering were brought before the

24 king and the assembly, who laid their hands on them; and the priests slaughtered them and used their blood as a sin-offering on the altar to make expiation for all Israel. For the king had commanded that the whole-offering and the sin-offering should be made for all Israel.

25 He posted the Levites in the house of the LORD with cymbals, lutes, and harps, according to the rule prescribed by David, by Gad the king's seer and Nathan the prophet; for this rule had come from the LORD through

26 his prophets. The Levites stood ready with the instruments of David, and

27 the priests with the trumpets. Hezekiah gave the order that the whole-offering should be offered on the altar. At the moment when the whole-offering began, the song to the LORD began too, with the trumpets, led by

28 the instruments of David king of Israel. The whole assembly prostrated themselves, the singers sang and the trumpeters sounded; all this con-

29 tinued until the whole-offering was complete. When the offering was

a for the whole-offering: *prob. rdg.; Heb. om.*

complete, the king and all his company bowed down and prostrated themselves. And King Hezekiah and his officers commanded the Levites to 30 praise the LORD in the words of David and of Asaph the seer. So they praised him most joyfully and bowed down and prostrated themselves.

Then Hezekiah said, 'You have now given to the LORD with open hands; 31 approach with your sacrifices and thank-offerings for the house of the LORD.' So the assembly brought sacrifices and thank-offerings; and every man of willing spirit brought whole-offerings. The number of whole- 32 offerings which the assembly brought was seventy bulls, a hundred rams, and two hundred lambs; all these made a whole-offering to the LORD. And 33 the consecrated offerings were six hundred bulls and three thousand sheep. But the priests were too few and could not flay all the whole-offerings; so 34 their colleagues the Levites helped them until the work was completed and all the priests had hallowed themselves—for the Levites had been more scrupulous than the priests in hallowing themselves. There were 35 indeed whole-offerings in abundance, besides the fat of the shared-offerings and the drink-offerings for the whole-offerings. In this way the service of the house of the LORD was restored; and Hezekiah and all the 36 people rejoiced over what God had done for the people and because it had come about so suddenly.

Then Hezekiah sent word to all Israel and Judah, and also wrote letters **30** to Ephraim and Manasseh, inviting them to come to the house of the LORD in Jerusalem to keep the Passover of the LORD the God of Israel. The king 2 and his officers and all the assembly in Jerusalem had agreed to keep the Passover in the second month, but they had not been able to keep it at that 3 time, because not enough priests had hallowed themselves and the people had not assembled in Jerusalem. The proposal was acceptable to the king 4 and the whole assembly. So they resolved to make a proclamation through- 5 out all Israel, from Beersheba to Dan, that the people should come to Jerusalem to keep the Passover of the LORD the God of Israel. Never before had so many kept it according to the prescribed form. Couriers went 6 throughout all Israel and Judah with letters from the king and his officers, proclaiming the royal command: 'Turn back, men of Israel, to the LORD the God of Abraham, Isaac, and Israel, so that he may turn back to those of you who escaped capture by the kings of Assyria. Do not be like your 7 forefathers and your kinsmen, who were unfaithful to the LORD the God of their fathers, so that he made them an object of horror, as you yourselves saw. Do not be stubborn as your forefathers were; submit yourselves to 8 the LORD and enter his sanctuary which he has sanctified for ever, and worship the LORD your God, so that his anger may be averted from you. For when you turn back to the LORD, your kinsmen and your children will 9 win compassion from their captors and return to this land. The LORD your God is gracious and compassionate, and he will not turn away from you if you turn back to him.'

So the couriers passed from city to city through the land of Ephraim and 10 Manasseh and as far as Zebulun, but they were treated with scorn and ridicule. However, a few men of Asher, Manasseh, and Zebulun submitted 11 and came to Jerusalem. Further, the hand of God moved the people in 12

Judah with one accord to carry out what the king and his officers had ordered at the LORD's command.

13 Many people, a very great assembly, came together in Jerusalem to
14 keep the pilgrim-feast of Unleavened Bread in the second month. They began by removing the altars in Jerusalem; they removed the altars for
15 burning sacrifices and threw them into the gorge of the Kidron. They killed the passover lamb on the fourteenth day of the second month; and the priests and the Levites were bitterly ashamed. They hallowed
16 themselves and brought whole-offerings to the house of the LORD. They took their accustomed places, according to the direction laid down for them in the law of Moses the man of God; the priests flung against the
17 altar the blood which they received from the Levites. But many in the assembly had not hallowed themselves; therefore the Levites had to kill the passover lamb for every one who was unclean, in order to hallow him
18 to the LORD. For a majority of the people, many from Ephraim, Manasseh, Issachar, and Zebulun, had not kept themselves ritually clean, and therefore kept the Passover irregularly. But Hezekiah prayed for them, saying,
19 'May the good LORD grant pardon to every one who makes a practice of seeking guidance of God, the LORD the God of his fathers, even if he has
20 not observed the rules for the purification of the sanctuary.' The LORD
21 heard Hezekiah and healed the people. And the Israelites who were present in Jerusalem kept the feast of Unleavened Bread for seven days with great rejoicing, and the Levites and the priests praised the LORD every day with
22 unrestrained fervour.[a] Hezekiah spoke encouragingly to all the Levites who had shown true understanding in the service of the LORD. So they spent the seven days of the festival sacrificing shared-offerings and making confession to[b] the LORD the God of their fathers.

23 Then the whole assembly agreed to keep the feast for another seven days;
24 so they kept it for another seven days with general rejoicing. For Hezekiah king of Judah set aside for the assembly a thousand bulls and seven thousand sheep, and his officers set aside for the assembly a thousand bulls and ten
25 thousand sheep; and priests hallowed themselves in great numbers. So the whole assembly of Judah, including the priests and the Levites, rejoiced, together with all the assembly which came out of Israel, and the
26 resident aliens from Israel and those who lived in Judah. There was great rejoicing in Jerusalem, the like of which had not been known there since
27 the days of Solomon son of David king of Israel. Then the priests and the Levites stood to bless the people; the LORD listened to their cry, and their prayer came to God's holy dwelling-place in heaven.

31 When this was over, all the Israelites present went out to the cities of Judah and smashed the sacred pillars, hacked down the sacred poles and broke up the hill-shrines and the altars throughout Judah and Benjamin, Ephraim and Manasseh, until they had made an end of them. That done, the Israelites returned, each to his own patrimony in his own city.

2 Then Hezekiah installed the priests and the Levites in office, division by division, allotting to each priest or Levite his own particular duty, for

[a] with unrestrained fervour: *prob. rdg.; Heb.* with powerful instruments.   [b] making confession to: *or* confessing.

whole-offerings or shared-offerings, to give thanks or to sing praise, or to serve in the gates of the several quarters in the LORD's house.

The king provided from his own resources, as the share due from him, 3 the whole-offerings for both morning and evening, and for sabbaths, new moons, and appointed seasons, as prescribed in the law of the LORD. He 4 ordered the people living in Jerusalem to provide the share due from the priests and the Levites, so that they might devote themselves entirely to the law of the LORD. As soon as the king's order was issued to the Israelites, 5 they gave generously from the firstfruits of their corn and new wine, oil and honey, all the produce of their land; they brought a full tithe of everything. The Israelites and the Judaeans living in the cities of Judah also 6 brought a tithe of cattle and sheep, and a tithe of all produce as offerings dedicated to the LORD their God, and they stacked the produce in heaps. They began to deposit the heaps in the third month and completed them 7 in the seventh. When Hezekiah and his officers came and saw the heaps, 8 they blessed the LORD and his people Israel. Hezekiah asked the priests 9 and the Levites about these heaps, and Azariah the chief priest, who was 10 of the line of Zadok, answered, 'From the time when the people began to bring their contribution into the house of the LORD, they have had enough to eat, enough and to spare; indeed, the LORD has so greatly blessed them that they have this great store left over.'

Then Hezekiah ordered store-rooms to be prepared in the house of the 11 LORD, and this was done; and the people honestly brought in their con- 12 tributions, the tithe, and their dedicated gifts. The overseer in charge of them was Conaniah the Levite, with Shimei his brother as his deputy; Jehiel, Azaziah, Nahath, Asahel, Jerimoth, Jozabad, Eliel, Ismachiah, 13 Mahath, and Benaiah were appointed by King Hezekiah and Azariah, the chief overseer of the house of God, to assist Conaniah and Shimei his brother. And Kore son of Imnah the Levite, keeper of the East Gate, was 14 in charge of the freewill offerings to God, to apportion the contributions made to the LORD and the most sacred offerings. Eden, Miniamin, Jeshua, 15 Shemaiah, Amariah, and Shecaniah in the priestly cities assisted him in the fair distribution of portions to their kinsmen, young and old*a* alike, by divisions. Irrespective of their registration, shares were distributed to 16 all males three years of age and upwards who entered the house of the LORD to take their daily part in the service, according to their divisions, as their office demanded. The priests were registered by families, the Levites from 17 twenty years of age and upwards by their offices in their divisions. They 18 were registered with all their dependants, their wives, their sons, and their daughters, the whole company of them, because in virtue of their per- manent standing they had to keep themselves duly hallowed. As for the 19 priests of Aaron's line in the common lands attached to their cities, in every city men were nominated to distribute portions to every male among the priests and to every one who was registered with the Levites.

Such was the action taken by Hezekiah throughout Judah; he did what 20 was good and right and loyal in the sight of the LORD his God. Whatever 21 he undertook in the service of the house of God and in obedience to the

a Or high and low.

law and the commandment to seek guidance of his God, he did with all his heart, and he prospered.

32 1ᵃ   After these events and this example of loyal conduct, Sennacherib king of Assyria invaded Judah and encamped against the fortified cities, believ-
2 ing that he could attach them to himself. When Hezekiah saw that he had
3 come and was determined to attack Jerusalem, he consulted his civil and military officers about blocking up the springs outside the city; and they
4 encouraged him. They gathered together a large number of people and blocked up all the springs and the stream which flowed through the land. 'Why', they said, 'should Assyrian kings come here and find plenty of
5 water?' Then the king acted boldly; he made good every breach in the city wall and erected towers on it; he built another wall outside it and strengthened the Millo of the city of David; he also collected a great
6 quantity of weapons and shields. He appointed military commanders over the people and assembled them in the square by the city gate and spoke
7 encouragingly to them in these words: 'Be strong; be brave. Do not let the king of Assyria or the rabble he has brought with him strike terror or
8 panic into your hearts. We have more on our side than he has. He has human strength; but we have the LORD our God to help us and to fight our battles.' So spoke Hezekiah king of Judah, and the people were buoyed up by his words.

9   After this, Sennacherib king of Assyria, while he and his high command were at Lachish, sent envoys to Jerusalem to deliver this message to
10 Hezekiah king of Judah and to all the Judaeans in Jerusalem: 'Sennacherib king of Assyria says, "What gives you confidence to stay in Jerusalem under
11 siege? Hezekiah is misleading you into risking death by famine or thirst where you are, when he tells you that the LORD your God will save you
12 from the grip of the Assyrian king. Was it not Hezekiah himself who suppressed the LORD's hill-shrines and altars and told the people of Judah and Jerusalem that they must prostrate themselves before one altar only and
13 burn sacrifices there? You know very well what I and my forefathers have done to all the peoples of the lands. Were the gods of these nations able to
14 save their lands from me? Not one of the gods of these nations, which my forefathers exterminated, was able to save his people from me. Much less
15 will your god save you! How, then, can Hezekiah deceive you or mislead you like this? How can you believe him, for no god of any nation or kingdom has been able to save his people from me or my forefathers? Much less will your gods save you!" '

16   The envoys of Sennacherib spoke still more against the LORD God and
17 against his servant Hezekiah. And the king himself wrote a letter to defy the LORD the God of Israel, in these terms: 'Just as the gods of other nations could not save their people from me, so the god of Hezekiah will
18 not save his people from me.' Then they shouted in Hebrew at the top of their voices at the people of Jerusalem on the wall, to strike them with fear
19 and terror, hoping thus to capture the city. They described the godᵇ of Jerusalem as being like the gods of the other peoples of the earth—things made by the hands of men.

ᵃ *Verses 1–19: cp. 2 Kgs. 18. 13–37; Isa. 36. 1–22.*   ᵇ *Or* gods.

In this plight King Hezekiah and the prophet Isaiah son of Amoz cried 20 *a*
to heaven in prayer. So the LORD sent an angel who cut down all the fighting 21
men, as well as the leaders and the commanders, in the camp of the king
of Assyria, so that he went home disgraced to his own land. When he
entered the temple of his god, certain of his own sons struck him down
with their swords.

Thus the LORD saved Hezekiah and the inhabitants of Jerusalem from 22
Sennacherib king of Assyria and all their enemies; and he gave them respite
on every side. Many people brought to Jerusalem offerings for the LORD 23
and costly gifts for Hezekiah king of Judah. From then on he was held in
high honour by all the nations.

About this time Hezekiah fell dangerously ill and prayed to the LORD; 24
the LORD said, 'I will heal you', *b* and granted him a sign. But, being a 25
proud man, he was not grateful for the good done to him, and Judah and
Jerusalem suffered for it. Then, proud as he was, Hezekiah submitted, 26
and the people of Jerusalem with him, and the LORD's anger did not fall
on them again in Hezekiah's time.

Hezekiah enjoyed great wealth and fame. *c* He built for himself treasuries 27
for silver and gold, precious stones and spices, shields and other costly
things; and barns for the harvests of corn, new wine, and oil; and stalls for 28
every kind of cattle, as well as sheepfolds. He amassed *d* a great many 29
flocks and herds; God had indeed given him vast riches. It was this same 30
Hezekiah who blocked the upper outflow of the waters of Gihon and
directed them downwards and westwards to the city of David. In fact,
Hezekiah was successful in everything he attempted, even in the affair of 31
the envoys sent by the king *e* of Babylon—the envoys who came to inquire
about the portent which had been seen in the land at the time when God
left him to himself, to test him and to discover all that was in his heart.

The other events of Hezekiah's reign, and his works of piety, are re- 32
corded in the vision of the prophet Isaiah son of Amoz and in the annals of
the kings of Judah and Israel. So Hezekiah rested with his forefathers and 33
was buried in the uppermost of the graves of David's sons; all Judah and
the people of Jerusalem paid him honour when he died, and he was
succeeded by his son Manasseh.

MANASSEH WAS TWELVE YEARS OLD when he came to the throne, and **33** 1 *f*
he reigned in Jerusalem for fifty-five years. He did what was wrong in the 2
eyes of the LORD, in following the abominable practices of the nations
which the LORD had dispossessed in favour of the Israelites. He rebuilt the 3
hill-shrines which his father Hezekiah had dismantled, he erected altars
to the Baalim and made sacred poles, he prostrated himself before all
the host of heaven and worshipped them. He built altars in the house of the 4
LORD, that house of which the LORD had said, 'In Jerusalem shall my Name
be for ever.' He built altars for all the host of heaven in the two courts of the 5
house of the LORD; he made his sons pass through the fire in the Valley 6

---

a Verses 20-22: cp. 2 Kgs. 19. 1-37; Isa. 37. 1-38.   *b I will heal you: prob. rdg.,*
cp. 2 Kgs. 20. 5; Heb. om.   *c Or riches.*   *d Prob. rdg.; Heb. adds cities.*
e Prob. rdg., cp. 2 Kgs. 20. 12; Heb. officers.   *f Verses 1-9: cp. 2 Kgs. 21. 1-9.*

of Ben-hinnom, he practised soothsaying, divination, and sorcery, and dealt with ghosts and spirits. He did much wrong in the eyes of the LORD

7 and provoked his anger; and the image that he had had carved in relief he put in the house of God, the place of which God had said to David and Solomon his son, 'This house and Jerusalem, which I chose out of all the

8 tribes of Israel, shall receive my Name for all time. I will not again displace Israel from the land which I assigned to their forefathers, if only they will be careful to observe all that I commanded them through Moses, all

9 the law, the statutes, and the rules.' But Manasseh misled Judah and the inhabitants of Jerusalem into wickedness far worse than that of the nations which the LORD had exterminated in favour of the Israelites.

10 The LORD spoke to Manasseh and to his people, but they paid no heed.

11 So the LORD brought against them the commanders of the army of the king of Assyria; they captured Manasseh with spiked weapons, and bound

12 him with fetters, and brought him to Babylon. In his distress he prayed to the LORD his God and sought to placate him, and made his humble sub-

13 mission before the God of his fathers. He prayed, and God accepted his petition and heard his supplication. He brought him back to Jerusalem and restored him to the throne; and thus Manasseh learnt that the LORD was God.

14 After this he built an outer wall for the city of David, west of Gihon in the gorge, and extended it to the entrance by the Fish Gate, enclosing Ophel; and he raised it to a great height. He also put military commanders

15 in all the fortified cities of Judah. He removed the foreign gods and the carved image from the house of the LORD and all the altars which he had built on the temple mount and in Jerusalem, and threw them out of the

16 city. Moreover, he repaired the altar of the LORD and sacrificed at it shared-offerings and thank-offerings, and commanded Judah to serve the LORD

17 the God of Israel. But the people still continued to sacrifice at the hill-shrines, though only to the LORD their God.

18 The rest of the acts of Manasseh, his prayer to his God, and the discourses of the seers who spoke to him in the name of the LORD the God of

19 Israel, are recorded in the chronicles of the kings of Israel. His prayer and the answer he received to it, and all his sin and unfaithfulness, and the places where he built hill-shrines and set up sacred poles and carved idols,

20 before he submitted, are recorded in the chronicles of the seers. So Manasseh rested with his forefathers and was buried in the garden-tomb of *a* his family; he was succeeded by his son Amon.

21*b* Amon was twenty-two years old when he came to the throne, and he

22 reigned in Jerusalem for two years. He did what was wrong in the eyes of the LORD as his father Manasseh had done. He sacrificed to all the images

23 that his father Manasseh had made, and worshipped them. He was not submissive before the LORD like his father Manasseh; his guilt was much

24 greater. His courtiers conspired against him and murdered him in his

25 house; but the people of the land killed all the conspirators and made his son Josiah king in his place.

a the garden-tomb of: *prob. rdg., cp. 2 Kgs. 21. 18; Heb. om.*   *b* *Verses 21–25:* *cp. 2 Kgs. 21. 19–24.*

JOSIAH WAS EIGHT YEARS OLD when he came to the throne, and he   34 1ᵃ
reigned in Jerusalem for thirty-one years. He did what was right in the   2
eyes of the LORD; he followed in the footsteps of his forefather David,
swerving neither right nor left. In the eighth year of his reign, when he was   3
still a boy, he began to seek guidance of the God of his forefather David;
and in the twelfth year he began to purge Judah and Jerusalem of the hill-
shrines and the sacred poles, and the carved idols and the images of metal.
He saw to it that the altars for the Baalim were destroyed and he hacked   4
down the incense-altars which stood above them; he broke in pieces the
sacred poles and the carved and metal images, grinding them to powder
and scattering it on the graves of those who had sacrificed to them. He also   5
burnt the bones of the priests on their altars and purged Judah and Jerusalem. In the cities of Manasseh, Ephraim, and Simeon, and as far as   6
Naphtali, he burnt down their houses wherever he found them; he de-   7
stroyed the altars and the sacred poles, ground the idols to powder, and
hacked down the incense-altars throughout the land of Israel. Then he
returned to Jerusalem.

In the eighteenth year of his reign, after he had purified the land and   8ᵇ
the house, he sent Shaphan son of Azaliah and Maaseiah the governor of
the city and Joah son of Joahaz the secretary of state to repair the house
of the LORD his God. They came to Hilkiah the high priest and gave him   9
the silver that had been brought to the house of God, the silver which the
Levites, on duty at the threshold, had gathered from Manasseh, Ephraim,
and all the rest of Israel, as well as from Judah and Benjamin and the
inhabitants of Jerusalem. It was then handed over to the foremen in   10
charge of the work in the house of the LORD, and these men, working in the
house, used it for repairing and strengthening the fabric; they gave it also   11
to the carpenters and builders to buy hewn stone, and timber for rafters
and beams, for the buildings which the kings of Judah had allowed to fall
into ruin. The men did their work honestly under the direction of Jahath   12-13
and Obadiah, Levites of the line of Merari, and Zechariah and Meshullam,
members of the family of Kohath. These also had control of the porters
and directed the workmen of every trade. The Levites were all skilled
musicians, and some of them were secretaries, clerks, or door-keepers.
When they fetched the silver which had been brought to the house of the   14
LORD, the priest Hilkiah discovered the book of the law of the LORD which
had been given through Moses. Then Hilkiah told Shaphan the adjutant-   15
general, 'I have discovered the book of the law in the house of the LORD.'
Hilkiah gave the book to Shaphan, and he brought it to the king and reported   16
to him: 'Your servants are doing all that was entrusted to them. They have   17
melted down the silver in the house of the LORD and have handed it over
to the foremen and the workmen.' Shaphan the adjutant-general also told   18
the king that the priest Hilkiah had given him a book; and he read it out
in the king's presence. When the king heard what was in the book of the   19
law, he rent his clothes, and ordered Hilkiah, Ahikam son of Shaphan,   20
Abdon son of Micah, Shaphan the adjutant-general, and Asaiah the king's
attendant, to go and seek guidance of the LORD, for himself and for all who   21

ᵃ *Verses 1, 2 : cp. 2 Kgs. 22. 1, 2.*   ᵇ *Verses 8–32 : cp. 2 Kgs. 22. 3—23. 3.*

still remained in Israel and Judah, about the contents of the book that had been discovered. 'Great is the wrath of the LORD,' he said, 'and it has been poured out upon us because our forefathers did not observe the command of the LORD and do all that is written in this book.'

22 So Hilkiah and those whom the king had instructed went to Huldah the prophetess, wife of Shallum son of Tikvah,*a* son of Hasrah, the keeper of the wardrobe, and consulted her at her home in the second quarter of

23 Jerusalem. 'This is the word of the LORD the God of Israel,' she answered:

24 'Say to the man who sent you to me, "This is the word of the LORD: I am bringing disaster on this place and its inhabitants, fulfilling all the imprecations recorded in the book which was read in the presence of the king of

25 Judah, because they have forsaken me and burnt sacrifices to other gods, provoking my anger with all the idols they have made with their own hands; therefore my wrath is poured out upon this place and will not be quenched."

26 This is what you shall say to the king of Judah who sent you to seek guidance of the LORD: "This is the word of the LORD the God of Israel: You

27 have listened to my words and shown a willing heart, you humbled yourself before God when you heard what I said about this place and its inhabitants; you humbled yourself and rent your clothes and wept before me. Because of all this,*b* I for my part have heard you. This is the very word

28 of the LORD. Therefore, I will gather you to your forefathers, and you will be gathered to your grave in peace; you will not live to see all the disaster which I am bringing upon this place and upon its inhabitants."' So they brought back word to the king.

29 Then the king sent and called all the elders of Judah and Jerusalem

30 together, and went up to the house of the LORD; he took with him all the men of Judah and the inhabitants of Jerusalem, the priests and the Levites, the whole population, high and low. There he read them the whole book

31 of the covenant discovered in the house of the LORD; and then, standing on the dais, the king made a covenant before the LORD to obey him and keep his commandments, his testimonies, and his statutes, with all his heart and soul, and so fulfil the terms of the covenant written in this book.

32 Then he swore an oath with all who were present in Jerusalem to keep the covenant.*c* Thereafter the inhabitants of Jerusalem did obey the covenant

33 of God, the God of their fathers. Josiah removed all abominable things from all the territories of the Israelites, so that everyone living in Israel might serve the LORD his God. As long as he lived they did not fail in their allegiance to the LORD the God of their fathers.

35 Josiah kept a Passover to the LORD in Jerusalem, and the passover lamb

2 was killed on the fourteenth day of the first month. He appointed the priests to their offices and encouraged them to perform the service of the

3 house of the LORD. He said to the Levites, the teachers of Israel, who were dedicated to the LORD, 'Put the holy Ark in the house which Solomon son of David king of Israel built; it is not to be carried about on your shoulders.

4 Now is the time to serve the LORD your God and his people Israel: prepare yourselves by families according to your divisions, following the written

a Prob. rdg., cp. 2 Kgs. 22. 14; Heb. Tokhath.   b Because of all this: prob. rdg.; Heb. om.   c to keep the covenant: prob. rdg., cp. 2 Kgs. 23. 3; Heb. and Benjamin.

instructions of David king of Israel and those of Solomon his son; and 5 stand in the Holy Place as representatives of the family groups of the lay people, your brothers, one division of Levites to each family group. Kill 6 the passover lamb and hallow yourselves and prepare for your brothers to fulfil the word of the LORD given through Moses.'

Josiah contributed on behalf of all the lay people present thirty thousand 7 small cattle, that is young rams and goats, for the Passover, in addition to three thousand bulls; all these were from the king's own resources. And 8 his officers contributed willingly for the people, the priests, and the Levites. Hilkiah, Zechariah, and Jehiel, the chief officers of the house of God, gave on behalf of the priests two thousand six hundred small cattle for the Passover, in addition to three hundred bulls. And Conaniah, Shemaiah 9 and Nethaneel his brothers, and Hashabiah, Jeiel, and Jozabad, the chiefs of the Levites, gave on behalf of the Levites for the Passover five thousand small cattle in addition to five hundred bulls.

When the service had been arranged, the priests stood in their places 10 and the Levites in their divisions, according to the king's command. They 11 killed the passover victim, and the priests flung the blood against the altar as the Levites flayed the animals. Then they removed the fat flesh,[a] which 12 they allocated to the people by groups of families for them to offer to the LORD, as prescribed in the book of Moses; and so with the bulls. They 13 cooked the passover victim over the fire according to custom, and boiled the holy offerings in pots, cauldrons, and pans, and served them quickly to all the people. After that they made the necessary preparations for 14 themselves and the priests, because the priests of Aaron's line were engaged till nightfall in offering whole-offerings and the fat portions; so the Levites made the necessary preparations for themselves and for the priests of Aaron's line. The singers, the sons of Asaph, were in their places according 15 to the rules laid down by David and by Asaph, Heman, and Jeduthun, the king's seers. The door-keepers stood, each at his gate; there was no need for them to leave their posts, because their kinsmen the Levites had made the preparations for them.

In this manner all the service of the LORD was arranged that day, to keep 16 the Passover and to offer whole-offerings on the altar of the LORD, according to the command of King Josiah. The people of Israel who were present 17 kept the Passover at that time and the pilgrim-feast of Unleavened Bread for seven days. No Passover like it had been kept in Israel since the days 18 of the prophet Samuel; none of the kings of Israel had ever kept such a Passover as Josiah kept, with the priests and Levites and all Judah and Israel who were present and the inhabitants of Jerusalem. In the eighteenth 19 year of Josiah's reign this Passover was kept.

After Josiah had thus organized all the service of the house, Necho 20 king of Egypt marched up to attack Carchemish on the Euphrates; and Josiah went out to confront him. But Necho sent envoys to him, saying, 21 'What do you want with me, king of Judah? I have no quarrel with you today, only with those with whom I am at war. God has purposed to speed me on my way, and God is on my side; do not stand in his way, or he will

---

[a] *fat flesh: or* whole-offering.

22 destroy you.' Josiah would not be deflected from his purpose but insisted
on fighting; he refused to listen to Necho's words spoken at God's com-
23 mand, and he sallied out to join battle in the vale of Megiddo. The archers
shot at him; he was severely wounded and told his bodyguard to carry him
24 off. They lifted him out of his chariot and carried him in his viceroy's
chariot to Jerusalem. There he died and was buried among the tombs of
25 his ancestors, and all Judah and Jerusalem mourned for him. Jeremiah
also made a lament for Josiah; and to this day the minstrels, both men and
women, commemorate Josiah in their lamentations. Such laments have
become traditional in Israel, and they are found in the written collections.
26 The other events of Josiah's reign, and his works of piety, all performed
27 in accordance with what is laid down in the law of the LORD, and his
acts, from first to last, are recorded in the annals of the kings of Israel and
Judah.

36 1[a] THE PEOPLE OF THE LAND took Josiah's son Jehoahaz and made him
2 king in place of his father in Jerusalem. He was twenty-three years old
when he came to the throne, and he reigned in Jerusalem for three months.
3 Then Necho king of Egypt deposed him and fined the country a hundred
4 talents of silver and one talent of gold, and made his brother Eliakim king
over Judah and Jerusalem in his place, changing his name to Jehoiakim;
5 he also carried away his brother Jehoahaz to Egypt. Jehoiakim was twenty-
five years old when he came to the throne, and he reigned in Jerusalem for
6 eleven years. He did what was wrong in the eyes of the LORD his God. So
Nebuchadnezzar king of Babylon marched against him and put him in
7 fetters and took him to Babylon. He also removed to Babylon some of the
vessels of the house of the LORD and put them into his own palace there.
8 The other events of Jehoiakim's reign, including the abominations he
committed, and everything of which he was held guilty, are recorded in
the annals of the kings of Israel and Judah. He was succeeded by his son
Jehoiachin.

9[b] Jehoiachin was eight years old when he came to the throne, and he
reigned in Jerusalem for three months and ten days. He did what was
10 wrong in the eyes of the LORD. At the turn of the year King Nebuchadnezzar
sent and brought him to Babylon, together with the choicest vessels of the
house of the LORD, and made his father's brother Zedekiah king over
Judah and Jerusalem.

11 Zedekiah was twenty-one years old when he came to the throne, and he
12 reigned in Jerusalem for eleven years. He did what was wrong in the eyes
of the LORD his God; he did not defer to the guidance of the prophet
13 Jeremiah, the spokesman of the LORD. He also rebelled against King
Nebuchadnezzar, who had laid on him a solemn oath of allegiance. He was
obstinate and stubborn and refused to return to the LORD the God of
14 Israel. All the chiefs of Judah and the priests and the people became more
and more unfaithful, following all the abominable practices of the other
nations; and they defiled the house of the LORD which he had hallowed in
15 Jerusalem. The LORD God of their fathers had warned them betimes

a Verses 1-4: cp. 2 Kgs. 23. 30-34.   b Verses 9, 10: cp. 2 Kgs. 24. 8-17.

through his messengers, for he took pity on his people and on his dwelling-place; but they never ceased to deride his messengers, scorn his words and **16** scoff at his prophets, until the anger of the LORD burst out against his people and could not be appeased. So he brought against them the king of **17**[a] the Chaldaeans, who put their young men to the sword in the sanctuary and spared neither young man nor maiden, neither the old nor the weak; God gave them all into his power. And he brought all the vessels of the **18** house of God, great and small, and the treasures of the house of the LORD and of the king and his officers—all these he brought to Babylon. And they **19** burnt down the house of God, razed the city wall of Jerusalem and burnt down all its stately mansions and all their precious possessions until everything was destroyed. Those who escaped the sword he took captive to **20** Babylon, and they became slaves to him and his sons until the sovereignty passed to the Persians, while the land of Israel ran the full term of its **21** sabbaths. All the time that it lay desolate it kept the sabbath rest, to complete seventy years in fulfilment of the word of the LORD by the prophet Jeremiah.

Now in the first year of Cyrus king of Persia, so that the word of the LORD **22**[b] spoken through Jeremiah might be fulfilled, the LORD stirred up the heart of Cyrus king of Persia; and he issued a proclamation throughout his kingdom, both by word of mouth and in writing, to this effect:

> This is the word of Cyrus king of Persia: The LORD the God of heaven **23** has given me all the kingdoms of the earth, and he himself has charged me to build him a house at Jerusalem in Judah. To every man of his people now among you I say, the LORD his God be[c] with him, and let him go up.

THE BOOK OF
EZRA

The return of the exiles to Jerusalem

NOW IN THE FIRST YEAR OF CYRUS king of Persia, **1** so that the word of the LORD spoken through Jeremiah might be fulfilled, the LORD stirred up the heart of Cyrus king of Persia; and he issued a proclamation throughout his kingdom, both by word of mouth and in writing, to this effect:

> This is the word of Cyrus king of Persia: The LORD the God of heaven **2** has given me all the kingdoms of the earth, and he himself has charged me to build him a house at Jerusalem in Judah. To every man of his **3**

[a] *Verses 17–20: cp. 2 Kgs. 25. 1–17.*   [b] *Verses 22, 23: cp. Ezra 1. 1–3.*
[c] be: *prob. rdg., cp. Ezra 1. 3; Heb. om.*

people now among you I say, God be with him, and let him go up to Jerusalem in Judah, and rebuild the house of the Lord the God of
4 Israel, the God whose city is Jerusalem. And every remaining Jew, wherever he may be living, may claim aid from his neighbours in that place, silver and gold, goods*a* and cattle, in addition to the voluntary offerings for the house of God in Jerusalem.

5 Thereupon the heads of families of Judah and Benjamin, and the priests and the Levites, answered the summons, all whom God had moved to go
6 up to rebuild the house of the Lord in Jerusalem. Their neighbours all assisted them with gifts of every kind, silver*b* and gold, goods*a* and cattle and valuable gifts in abundance,*c* in addition to any voluntary service.
7 Moreover, Cyrus king of Persia produced the vessels of the house of the Lord which Nebuchadnezzar had removed from Jerusalem and placed in
8 the temple of his god; and he handed them over into the charge of Mithredath the treasurer, who made an inventory of them for Sheshbazzar the
9 ruler of Judah. This was the list: thirty gold basins, a thousand silver basins,
10 twenty-nine vessels of various kinds, thirty golden bowls, four hundred
11 and ten silver bowls of various types, and a thousand other vessels. The vessels of gold and silver amounted in all to five thousand four hundred; and Sheshbazzar took them all up to Jerusalem, when the exiles were brought back from Babylon.

2 1*d*   Of the captives whom Nebuchadnezzar king of Babylon had taken into exile in Babylon, these were the people of the province who returned to
2 Jerusalem and Judah, each to his own city, led by Zerubbabel, Jeshua, *e* Nehemiah, Seraiah, Reelaiah, Mordecai, Bilshan, Mispar, Bigvai, Rehum and Baanah.

3 The roll of the men of the people of Israel: the family of Parosh, two
4 thousand one hundred and seventy-two; the family of Shephatiah, three
5 hundred and seventy-two; the family of Arah, seven hundred and seventy-
6 five; the family of Pahath-moab, namely the families of Jeshua and *f* Joab,
7 two thousand eight hundred and twelve; the family of Elam, one thousand
8 two hundred and fifty-four; the family of Zattu, nine hundred and forty-
9 10 five; the family of Zaccai, seven hundred and sixty; the family of Bani, six
11 hundred and forty-two; the family of Bebai, six hundred and twenty-three;
12 13 the family of Azgad, one thousand two hundred and twenty-two; the
14 family of Adonikam, six hundred and sixty-six; the family of Bigvai, two
15 thousand and fifty-six; the family of Adin, four hundred and fifty-four;
16 17 the family of Ater, namely that of Hezekiah, ninety-eight; the family of
18 Bezai, three hundred and twenty-three; the family of Jorah, one hundred
19 20 and twelve; the family of Hashum, two hundred and twenty-three; the
21 family of Gibbar, ninety-five. The men *g* of Bethlehem, one hundred and
22 23 twenty-three; the men of Netophah, fifty-six; the men of Anathoth, one
24 25 hundred and twenty-eight; the men of Beth-azmoth,*h* forty-two; the men

---

a Or pack-animals.   *b* with gifts . . . silver: *prob. rdg., cp. 1 Esdras 2. 9; Heb.* with vessels of silver.   *c* in abundance: *prob. rdg., cp. 1 Esdras 2. 9; Heb.* apart.
d Verses 1–70: cp. Neh. 7. 6–73.   *e* Or Joshua (cp. Hag. 1. 1).   *f* and: *prob. rdg., cp. Neh. 7. 11; Heb.* om.   *g* Prob. rdg., cp. Neh. 7. 26; Heb.* family.   *h* Prob. rdg., cp. Neh. 7. 28; Heb.* the family of Azmoth.

of Kiriath-jearim,^a Kephirah, and Beeroth, seven hundred and forty-
three; the men^b of Ramah and Geba, six hundred and twenty-one; the 26 27
men of Michmas, one hundred and twenty-two; the men of Bethel and Ai, 28
two hundred and twenty-three; the men^c of Nebo, fifty-two; the men of 29 30
Magbish, one hundred and fifty-six; the men of the other Elam, one 31
thousand two hundred and fifty-four; the men of Harim, three hundred 32
and twenty; the men of Lod, Hadid, and Ono, seven hundred and twenty- 33
five; the men of Jericho, three hundred and forty-five; the men of Senaah, 34 35
three thousand six hundred and thirty.

Priests: the family of Jedaiah, of the line of Jeshua, nine hundred and 36
seventy-three; the family of Immer, one thousand and fifty-two; the 37 38
family of Pashhur, one thousand two hundred and forty-seven; the family 39
of Harim, one thousand and seventeen.

Levites: the families of Jeshua and Kadmiel, of the line of Hodaviah, 40
seventy-four. Singers: the family of Asaph, one hundred and twenty-eight. 41
The guild of door-keepers: the family of Shallum, the family of Ater, the 42
family of Talmon, the family of Akkub, the family of Hatita, and the family
of Shobai, one hundred and thirty-nine in all.

Temple-servitors: the family of Ziha, the family of Hasupha, the family 43
of Tabbaoth, the family of Keros, the family of Siaha, the family of Padon, 44
the family of Lebanah, the family of Hagabah, the family of Akkub, the 45 46
family of Hagab, the family of Shamlai,^d the family of Hanan, the family 47
of Giddel, the family of Gahar, the family of Reaiah, the family of Rezin, 48
the family of Nekoda, the family of Gazzam, the family of Uzza, the family 49
of Paseah, the family of Besai, the family of Asnah, the family of the 50
Meunim,^e the family of the Nephusim,^f the family of Bakbuk, the family 51
of Hakupha, the family of Harhur, the family of Bazluth, the family of 52
Mehida, the family of Harsha, the family of Barkos, the family of Sisera, 53
the family of Temah, the family of Neziah, and the family of Hatipha. 54

Descendants of Solomon's servants: the family of Sotai, the family of 55
Hassophereth, the family of Peruda, the family of Jaalah, the family of 56
Darkon, the family of Giddel, the family of Shephatiah, the family of Hattil, 57
the family of Pochereth-hazzebaim, and the family of Ami.

The temple-servitors and the descendants of Solomon's servants 58
amounted to three hundred and ninety-two in all.

The following were those who returned from Tel-melah, Tel-harsha, 59
Kerub, Addan, and Immer, but could not establish their father's family
nor whether by descent they belonged to Israel: the family of Delaiah, the 60
family of Tobiah, and the family of Nekoda, six hundred and fifty-two.
Also of the priests: the family of Hobaiah, the family of Hakkoz, and the 61
family of Barzillai who had married a daughter of Barzillai the Gileadite
and went by his^g name. These searched for their names among those 62
enrolled in the genealogies, but they could not be found; they were disqualified for the priesthood as unclean, and the governor forbade them to 63

^a *Prob. rdg., cp. Neh. 7. 29; Heb.* the family of Kiriath-arim.   ^b *Prob. rdg.,
cp. Neh. 7. 30; Heb.* family.   ^c *Prob. rdg.; Heb.* family (*also in verses 30–35*).
^d *Or* Shalmai (*cp. Neh. 7. 48*).   ^e *Or* Meinim.   ^f *Or* Nephisim.   ^g *Prob. rdg.
cp. 1 Esdras 5. 38; Heb.* their.

521

partake of the most sacred food until there should be a priest able to consult the Urim and the Thummim.

64 The whole assembled people numbered forty-two thousand three
65 hundred and sixty, apart from their slaves, male and female, of whom there were seven thousand three hundred and thirty-seven; and they had two
66 hundred singers, men and women. Their horses numbered seven hundred
67 and thirty-six, their mules two hundred and forty-five, their camels four hundred and thirty-five, and their asses six thousand seven hundred and twenty.

68 When they came to the house of the LORD in Jerusalem, some of the heads of families volunteered to rebuild the house of God on its original
69 site. According to their resources they gave for the fabric fund a total of sixty-one thousand drachmas of gold, five thousand minas of silver, and one hundred priestly robes.

70 The priests, the Levites, and some of the people lived in Jerusalem and its suburbs;[a] the singers, the door-keepers, and temple-servitors,[b] and all other Israelites, lived in their own towns.

Worship restored and the temple rebuilt

3 WHEN THE SEVENTH MONTH CAME, the Israelites now being settled
2 in their towns, the people assembled as one man in Jerusalem. Then Jeshua son of Jozadak and his fellow-priests, and Zerubbabel son of Shealtiel and his kinsmen, set to work and built the altar of the God of Israel, in order to offer upon it whole-offerings as prescribed in the law of Moses
3 the man of God. They put the altar in place first, because they lived in fear of the foreign population; and they offered upon it whole-offerings
4 to the LORD, both morning and evening offerings. They kept the pilgrim-feast of Tabernacles[c] as ordained, and offered whole-offerings every day
5 in the number prescribed for each day, and, in addition to these, the regular whole-offerings and the offerings for sabbaths,[d] for new moons and for all the sacred seasons appointed by the LORD, and all voluntary offerings
6 brought to the LORD. The offering of whole-offerings began from the first day of the seventh month, although the foundation of the temple of the
7 LORD had not yet been laid. They gave money for the masons and carpenters, and food and drink and oil for the Sidonians and the Tyrians to fetch cedar-wood from the Lebanon to the roadstead at Joppa, by licence from Cyrus king of Persia.

8 In the second year after their return to the house of God in Jerusalem, and in the second month, Zerubbabel son of Shealtiel and Jeshua son of Jozadak started work, aided by all their fellow-Israelites, the priests and the Levites and all who had returned from captivity to Jerusalem. They appointed Levites from the age of twenty years and upwards to supervise
9 the work of the house of the LORD. Jeshua with his sons and his kinsmen,

---

[a] in Jerusalem and its suburbs: *prob. rdg.*, *cp. 1 Esdras 5. 46; Heb. om.*   [b] *Prob. rdg.; Heb. adds* in their towns.   [c] *Or* Booths.   [d] for sabbaths: *prob. rdg.*, *cp. 1 Esdras 5. 52; Heb. om.*

Kadmiel, Binnui, and Hodaviah,[a] together assumed control of those responsible for the work on the house of God.[b]

When the builders had laid the foundation of the temple of the LORD, 10 the priests in their robes took their places with their trumpets, and the Levites, the sons of Asaph, with their cymbals, to praise the LORD in the manner prescribed by David king of Israel; and they chanted praises and 11 thanksgiving to the LORD, singing, 'It is good to give thanks to the LORD,[c] for his love towards Israel endures for ever.' All the people raised a great shout of praise to the LORD because the foundation of the house of the LORD had been laid. But many of the priests and Levites and heads of 12 families, who were old enough to have seen the former house, wept and wailed aloud when they saw the foundation of this house laid, while many others shouted for joy at the top of their voice. The people could not dis- 13 tinguish the sound of the shout of joy from that of the weeping and wailing, so great was the shout which the people were raising, and the sound could be heard a long way off.

When the enemies of Judah and Benjamin heard that the returned exiles 4 were building a temple to the LORD the God of Israel, they approached 2 Zerubbabel and Jeshua[d] and the heads of families and said to them, 'Let us join you in building, for like you we seek your God, and we have been sacrificing to him ever since the days of Esarhaddon king of Assyria, who brought us here.' But Zerubbabel and Jeshua and the rest of the heads of 3 families in Israel said to them, 'The house which we are building for our God is no concern of yours. We alone will build it for the LORD the God of Israel, as his majesty Cyrus king of Persia commanded us.'

Then the people of the land caused the Jews to lose heart and made them 4 afraid to continue building; and in order to defeat their purpose they 5 bribed officials at court to act against them. This continued throughout the reign of Cyrus and into the reign of Darius king of Persia.

At the beginning of the reign of Ahasuerus, the people of the land 6 brought a charge in writing against the inhabitants of Judah and Jerusalem. And in the days of Artaxerxes king of Persia, with the agreement of 7 Mithredath, Tabeel and all his colleagues wrote to him; the letter was written in Aramaic and read aloud in Aramaic.

Rehum the high commissioner and Shimshai the secretary wrote a 8[e] letter to King Artaxerxes concerning Jerusalem in the following terms:

From Rehum the high commissioner, Shimshai the secretary, and all 9 their colleagues, the judges, the commissioners, the overseers, and chief officers, the men of Erech and Babylon, and the Elamites in Susa, and the 10 other peoples whom the great and renowned Asnappar[f] deported and settled in the city of Samaria and in the rest of the province of Beyond-Euphrates.

---

[a] Binnui, and Hodaviah: *prob. rdg.; Heb.* and his sons the family of Judah.   [b] *Prob. rdg.; Heb. adds* the family of Henadad, their family and their kinsmen the Levites.   [c] to give thanks to the LORD: *prob. rdg., cp. Ps. 106. 1; Heb. om.*   [d] and Jeshua: *prob. rdg., cp. 1 Esdras 5. 68; Heb. om.*   [e] *From 4. 8 to 6. 18 the text is in Aramaic.*   [f] *Or* Osnappar.

11 Here follows the text of their letter:

To King Artaxerxes from his servants, the men of the province of Beyond-Euphrates:

12 Be it known to Your Majesty that the Jews who left you and came to these parts have reached Jerusalem and are rebuilding that wicked and rebellious city; they have surveyed[a] the foundations and are completing

13 the walls. Be it known to Your Majesty that, if their city is rebuilt and the walls are completed, they will pay neither general levy, nor poll-tax,

14 nor land-tax, and in the end[b] they will harm the monarchy. Now, because we eat the king's salt and it is not right that we should witness the king's dishonour, therefore we have sent to inform Your Majesty,

15 in order that search may be made in the annals of your predecessors. You will discover by searching through the annals that this has been a rebellious city, harmful to the monarchy and its provinces, and that sedition has long been rife within its walls. That is why the city was laid waste.

16 We submit to Your Majesty that, if it is rebuilt and its walls are completed, the result will be that you will have no more footing in the province of Beyond-Euphrates.

17 The king sent this answer:

To Rehum the high commissioner, Shimshai the secretary, and all your colleagues resident in Samaria and in the rest of the province of

18 Beyond-Euphrates, greeting. The letter which you sent to me has now

19 been read clearly in my presence. I have given orders and search has been made, and it has been found that the city in question has a long history of revolt against the monarchy, and that rebellion and sedition

20 have been rife in it. Powerful kings have ruled in Jerusalem, exercising authority over the whole province of Beyond-Euphrates, and general

21 levy, poll-tax, and land-tax have been paid to them. Therefore, issue orders that these men must desist. This city is not to be rebuilt until a

22 decree to that effect is issued by me. See that you do not neglect your duty in this matter, lest more damage and harm be done to the monarchy.

23 When the text of the letter from King Artaxerxes was read before Rehum the high commissioner, Shimshai the secretary, and their colleagues, they

24 hurried to Jerusalem and forcibly compelled the Jews to stop work. From then onwards the work on the house of God in Jerusalem stopped; and it remained at a standstill till the second year of the reign of Darius king of Persia.

5 But the prophets Haggai[c] and Zechariah grandson of Iddo upbraided the Jews in Judah and Jerusalem, prophesying in the name of the God of

2 Israel. Then Zerubbabel son of Shealtiel and Jeshua son of Jozadak at once began to rebuild the house of God in Jerusalem, and the prophets of

3 God were with them and supported them. Tattenai, governor of the province of Beyond-Euphrates, Shethar-bozenai, and their colleagues promptly came to them and said, 'Who issued a decree permitting you to

4 rebuild this house and complete its furnishings?' They also asked them

---

[a] have surveyed: *prob. rdg.; Aram.* are surveying.   [b] in the end: *or* certainly.
[c] *Prob. rdg., cp. 1 Esdras 6. 1; Aram. adds* the prophet.

for the names of the men engaged in the building. But the elders of the 5
Jews were under God's watchful eye, and they were not prevented from
continuing the work, until such time as a report should reach Darius and
a royal letter should be received in answer.

Here follows the text of the letter sent by Tattenai, governor of the 6
province of Beyond-Euphrates, Shethar-bozenai, and his colleagues, the
inspectors in the province of Beyond-Euphrates, to King Darius. This is 7
the written report that they sent:

To King Darius, all greetings. Be it known to Your Majesty that we 8
went to the province of Judah and found the house of the great God
being rebuilt by the Jewish elders,*a* with massive stones and timbers
laid in the walls. The work was being done thoroughly and was making
good progress under their direction. We asked these elders who had 9
issued a decree for the rebuilding of this house and the completion of
the furnishings. We also asked them for their names, so that we might 10
make a list of the leaders for your information. This was their reply: 'We 11
are the servants of the God of heaven and earth, and we are rebuilding
the house originally built many years ago; a great king of Israel built it
and completed it. But because our forefathers provoked the anger of the 12
God of heaven, he put them into the power of Nebuchadnezzar the
Chaldaean, king of Babylon, who pulled down this house and carried
the people captive to Babylon. However, Cyrus king of Babylon in the 13
first year of his reign issued a decree that this house of God should be
rebuilt. Moreover, there were gold and silver vessels of the house of God, 14
which Nebuchadnezzar had taken from the temple in Jerusalem and put
in the temple in Babylon; and these King Cyrus took out of the temple
in Babylon. He gave them to a man named Sheshbazzar, whom he had
appointed governor, and said to him, "Take these vessels; go and restore 15
them to the temple in Jerusalem, and let the house of God there be
rebuilt on its original site." Then this Sheshbazzar came and laid the 16
foundation of the house of God in Jerusalem; and from that time until
now the rebuilding has continued, but it is not yet finished.' Now, there- 17
fore, if it please Your Majesty, let search be made in the royal archives
in Babylon, to discover whether a decree was issued by King Cyrus for
the rebuilding of this house of God in Jerusalem. Then let the king send
us his wishes in the matter.

Then King Darius issued an order, and search was made in the archives 6
where the treasures were deposited in Babylon. But it was in Ecbatana, 2
in the royal residence in the province of Media, that a scroll was found, on
which was written the following memorandum:

In the first year of King Cyrus, the king issued this decree concerning 3
the house of God in Jerusalem: Let the house be rebuilt as a place where
sacrifices are offered and fire-offerings brought. Its height shall be sixty
cubits and its breadth sixty cubits, with three courses of massive stones 4
and one*b* course of timber, the cost to be defrayed from the royal

---

a by . . . elders: *prob. rdg., cp. 1 Esdras 6. 8; Aram. om.*　　　　*b Prob. rdg., cp.*
1 Esdras 6. 25; Aram. a new.

5   treasury. Also the gold and silver vessels of the house of God, which
    Nebuchadnezzar took out of the temple in Jerusalem and brought to
    Babylon, shall be restored; they shall all be taken back to the temple in
    Jerusalem, and restored each to its place in the house of God.

6   Then King Darius issued this order:[a]

    Now, Tattenai, governor of the province of Beyond-Euphrates,
    Shethar-bozenai, and your colleagues, the inspectors in the province of
7   Beyond-Euphrates, you are to keep away from the place, and to leave
    the governor of the Jews and their elders free to rebuild this house of
8   God; let them rebuild it on its original site. I also issue an order pre-
    scribing what you are to do for these elders of the Jews, so that the said
    house of God may be rebuilt. Their expenses are to be defrayed in full
    from the royal funds accruing from the taxes of the province of Beyond-
9   Euphrates, so that the work may not be brought to a standstill. And let
    them have daily without fail whatever they want, young bulls, rams, or
    lambs as whole-offerings for the God of heaven, or wheat, salt, wine, or
10 oil, as the priests in Jerusalem demand, so that they may offer soothing
    sacrifices to the God of heaven, and pray for the life of the king and his
11 sons. Furthermore, I decree that, if any man tampers with this edict,
    a beam shall be pulled out of his house and he shall be fastened erect to
12 it and flogged; and, in addition, his house shall be forfeit.[b] And may the
    God who made that place a dwelling for his Name overthrow any king
    or people that shall presume to tamper with this edict or to destroy this
    house of God in Jerusalem. I Darius have issued a decree; it is to be
    carried out to the letter.

13 Then Tattenai, governor of the province of Beyond-Euphrates, Shethar-
    bozenai, and their colleagues carried out to the letter the instructions which
14 King Darius had sent them, and the elders of the Jews went on with the
    rebuilding. As a result of the prophecies of Haggai the prophet and
    Zechariah grandson of Iddo they had good success and finished the re-
    building as commanded by the God of Israel and according to the decrees
15 of Cyrus and Darius;[c] and the house was completed on the twenty-third[d]
    day of the month Adar, in the sixth year of King Darius.

16   Then the people of Israel, the priests and the Levites and all the other
    exiles who had returned, celebrated the dedication of the house of God
17 with great rejoicing. For its dedication they offered one hundred bulls,
    two hundred rams, and four hundred lambs, and as a sin-offering for all
    Israel twelve he-goats, corresponding to the number of the tribes of Israel.
18 And they re-established the priests in their groups and the Levites in their
    divisions for the service of God in Jerusalem, as prescribed in the book of
    Moses.

19   On the fourteenth day of the first month the exiles who had returned
20 kept the Passover. The priests and the Levites, one and all, had purified
    themselves; all of them were ritually clean, and they killed the passover

---

[a] *Then . . . order: prob. rdg., cp. 1 Esdras 6. 27; Aram. om.*   [b] *Or made into a
dunghill (mng. of Aram. word uncertain).*   [c] *Prob. rdg.; Aram. adds and Artaxerxes
king of Persia.*   [d] *Prob. rdg., cp. 1 Esdras 7. 5; Aram. third.*

lamb for all the exiles who had returned, for their fellow-priests and for
themselves. It was eaten by the Israelites who had come back from exile 21
and by all who had separated themselves from the peoples of the land and
their uncleanness and sought the LORD the God of Israel. And they kept 22
the pilgrim-feast of Unleavened Bread for seven days with rejoicing; for
the LORD had given them cause for joy by changing the disposition of the
king of Assyria towards them, so that he encouraged them in the work of
the house of God, the God of Israel.

Ezra's mission to Jerusalem

NOW AFTER THESE EVENTS, in the reign of Artaxerxes king of Persia, 7
there came up from Babylon one Ezra son of Seraiah, son of Azariah,
son of Hilkiah, son of Shallum, son of Zadok, son *a* of Ahitub, son of 2 3
Amariah, son of Azariah, son of Meraioth, son of Zerahiah, son of Uzzi, 4
son of Bukki, son of Abishua, son of Phinehas, son of Eleazar, son of Aaron 5
the chief priest. He was a scribe *b* learned in the law of Moses which the 6
LORD the God of Israel had given them; and the king granted him all that
he asked, for the hand of the LORD his God was upon him. In the seventh 7
year of King Artaxerxes, other Israelites, priests, Levites, singers, door-
keepers, and temple-servitors went up with him to Jerusalem; and they 8
reached Jerusalem in the fifth month, in the seventh year of the king. On 9
the first day of the first month Ezra fixed the day for departure from Babylon, and on the first day of the fifth month he arrived at Jerusalem, for the
gracious hand of his God was upon him. For Ezra had devoted himself to 10
the study and observance of the law of the LORD and to teaching statute and
ordinance in Israel.

This is a copy of the royal letter which King Artaxerxes had given to 11
Ezra the priest and scribe, a scribe versed in questions concerning the
commandments and the statutes of the LORD laid upon Israel:

Artaxerxes, king of kings, to Ezra the priest and scribe learned in the 12 *c*
law of the God of heaven:

This is my decision. I hereby issue a decree that any of the people of 13
Israel or of its priests or Levites in my kingdom who volunteer to go to
Jerusalem may go with you. You are sent by the king and his seven 14
counsellors to find out how things stand in Judah and Jerusalem with
regard to the law of your God with which you are entrusted. You are 15
also to convey the silver and gold which the king and his counsellors
have freely offered to the God of Israel whose dwelling is in Jerusalem,
together with any silver and gold that you may find throughout the 16
province of Babylon, and the voluntary offerings of the people and of the
priests which they freely offer for the house of their God in Jerusalem.
In pursuance of this decree you shall use the money solely for the 17
purchase of bulls, rams, and lambs, and the proper grain-offerings and
drink-offerings, to be offered on the altar in the house of your God in

a Or grandson.   *b* Or doctor of the law.   *c* The text of verses 12–26 is in
Aramaic.

18 Jerusalem. Further, should any silver and gold be left over, you and your
    colleagues may use it at your discretion according to the will of your
19 God. The vessels which have been given you for the service of the house
20 of your God you shall hand over to the God of Jerusalem; and if any-
    thing else should be required for the house of your God, which it may
    fall to you to provide, you may provide it out of the king's treasury.

21   And I, King Artaxerxes, issue an order to all treasurers in the province
    of Beyond-Euphrates that whatever is demanded of you by Ezra the
    priest, a scribe learned in the law of the God of heaven, is to be supplied
22 exactly, up to a hundred talents of silver, a hundred kor of wheat, a
    hundred bath of wine, a hundred bath of oil, and salt without reckoning.
23 Whatever is demanded by the God of heaven, let it be diligently carried
    out for the house of the God of heaven; otherwise wrath may fall upon
24 the realm of the king and his sons. We also make known to you that you
    have no authority to impose general levy, poll-tax, or land-tax on any of
    the priests, Levites, musicians, door-keepers, temple-servitors, or other
    servants of this house of God.

25   And you, Ezra, in accordance with the wisdom of your God with
    which you are entrusted, are to appoint arbitrators and judges to judge
    all your people in the province of Beyond-Euphrates, all who acknow-
    ledge the laws of your God;[a] and you and they are to instruct those who
26 do not acknowledge them. Whoever will not obey the law of your God
    and the law of the king, let judgement be rigorously executed upon him,
    be it death, banishment, confiscation of property, or imprisonment.

27   Then Ezra said,[b] 'Blessed be the LORD the God of our fathers who has
    prompted the king thus to add glory to the house of the LORD in Jerusalem,
28 and has made the king and his counsellors and all his high officers well
    disposed towards me!'
        So, knowing that the hand of the LORD my God was upon me, I took
    courage and assembled leading men out of Israel to go up with me.

8   These are the heads of families, as registered, family by family, of those
2   who went up with me from Babylon in the reign of King Artaxerxes: of
    the family of Phinehas, Gershom; of the family of Ithamar, Daniel; of the
3   family of David, Hattush son of[c] Shecaniah; of the family of Parosh,
4   Zechariah, and with him a hundred and fifty males in the register; of the
    family of Pahath-moab, Elihoenai son of Zerahiah, and with him two
5   hundred males; of the family of Zattu,[d] Shecaniah son of Jahaziel, and
6   with him three hundred males; of the family of Adin, Ebed son of Jonathan,
7   and with him fifty males; of the family of Elam, Isaiah son of Athaliah,
8   and with him seventy males; of the family of Shephatiah, Zebadiah son of
9   Michael, and with him eighty males; of the family of Joab, Obadiah son
10 of Jehiel, and with him two hundred and eighteen males; of the family of
    Bani,[e] Shelomith son of Josiphiah, and with him a hundred and sixty males;

[a] to judge . . . your God: *or* all of them versed in the laws of your God, to judge all the
people in the province of Beyond-Euphrates.   [b] Then Ezra said: *prob. rdg., cp.*
1 Esdras 8. 25; Heb. om.   [c] son of: *prob. rdg.; Heb.* of the family of.   [d] of Zattu:
prob. rdg., cp. 1 Esdras 8. 32; Heb. om.   [e] of Bani: *prob. rdg., cp. 1 Esdras 8. 36;*
Heb. om.

of the family of Bebai, Zechariah son of Bebai, and with him twenty-eight 11
males; of the family of Azgad, Johanan son of Hakkatan, and with him a hun- 12
dred and ten males. The last were the family of Adonikam, and these were 13
their names: Eliphelet, Jeiel, and Shemaiah, and with them sixty males;
and the family of Bigvai, Uthai and Zabbud, and with them seventy males. 14

I assembled them by the river which flows toward Ahava; and we en- 15
camped there three days. When I reviewed the people and the priests, I
found no Levite there. So I sent Eliezer, Ariel, Shemaiah, Elnathan, Jarib, 16
Elnathan, Nathan, Zechariah, and Meshullam, prominent men, and
Joiarib and Elnathan, men of discretion, with instructions to go to Iddo, 17
the chief man of the settlement at Casiphia; and I gave them a message for
him and his kinsmen, the temple-servitors there, asking for servitors for
the house of our God to be sent to us. And, because the gracious hand of 18
our God was upon us, they let us have Sherebiah, a man of discretion, of
the family of Mahli son of Levi, son of Israel, together with his sons and
kinsmen, eighteen men; also Hashabiah, together with Isaiah of the family 19
of Merari, his kinsmen and their sons, twenty men; besides two hundred 20
and twenty temple-servitors (this was an order instituted by David and his
officers to assist the Levites). These were all indicated by name.

Then I proclaimed a fast there by the river Ahava, so that we might 21
mortify ourselves before our God and ask from him a safe journey for ourselves, our dependants, and all our possessions. For I was ashamed to ask 22
the king for an escort of soldiers and horsemen to help us against enemies
on the way, because we had said to the king, 'The hand of our God is upon
all who seek him, working their good; but his fierce anger is on all who
forsake him.' So we fasted and asked our God for a safe journey, and he 23
answered our prayer.

Then I separated twelve of the chiefs of the priests, together with*[a]* 24
Sherebiah and Hashabiah and ten of their kinsmen, and handed over to 25
them the silver and gold and the vessels which had been set aside by the
king, his counsellors and his officers and all the Israelites who were present,
as their contribution to the house of our God. I handed over to them six 26
hundred and fifty talents of silver, a hundred silver vessels weighing two
talents, a hundred talents of gold, twenty golden bowls worth a thousand 27
drachmas, and two vessels of a fine red copper,*[b]* precious as gold. And I 28
said to the men, 'You are dedicated to the LORD, and the vessels too are
sacred; the silver and gold are a voluntary offering to the LORD the God of
your fathers. Watch over them and guard them, until you hand them over 29
in the presence of the chiefs of the priests and the Levites and the heads
of families of Israel in Jerusalem, in the rooms of the house of the LORD.'

So the priests and Levites received the consignment of silver and gold 30
and vessels, to be taken to the house of our God in Jerusalem; and on the 31
twelfth day of the first month we left the river Ahava bound for Jerusalem.
The hand of our God was upon us, and he saved us from enemy attack and
from ambush on the way. When we arrived at Jerusalem, we rested for 32
three days. And on the fourth day the silver and gold and the vessels were 33
deposited in the house of our God in the charge of Meremoth son of Uriah

[a] together with: *prob. rdg., cp. I Esdras 8. 54; Heb. om.*   *[b]* red copper: *or orichalc.*

the priest, who had with him Eleazar son of Phinehas, and they had with
them the Levites Jozabad son of Jeshua and Noadiah son of Binnui.
34 Everything was checked as it was handed over, and at the same time a
35 written record was made of the whole consignment. Then those who had
come home from captivity, the exiles who had returned, offered as whole-
offerings to the God of Israel twelve bulls for all Israel, ninety-six rams
and seventy-two*a* lambs, with twelve he-goats as a sin-offering; all these
36 were offered as a whole-offering to the LORD. They also delivered the king's
commission to the royal satraps and governors in the province of Beyond-
Euphrates; and these gave support to the people and the house of God.

9 When all this had been done, some of the leaders approached me and
said, 'The people of Israel, including priests and Levites, have not kept
themselves apart from the foreign population and from the abominable
practices of the Canaanites, the Hittites, the Perizzites, the Jebusites, the
2 Ammonites, the Moabites, the Egyptians, and the Amorites. They have
taken women of these nations as wives for themselves and their sons, so
that the holy race has become mixed with the foreign population; and the
3 leaders and magistrates have been the chief offenders.' When I heard this
news, I rent my robe and mantle, and tore my hair and my beard, and I sat
4 dumbfounded; and all who went in fear of the words of the God of Israel
rallied to me because of the offence of these exiles. I sat there dumbfounded
till the evening sacrifice.

5 Then, at the evening sacrifice, I rose from my humiliation and, in my
rent robe and mantle, I knelt down and spread out my hands to the LORD
6 my God and said, 'O my God, I am humiliated, I am ashamed to lift my
face to thee, my God; for we are sunk in our iniquities, and our guilt is so
7 great that it reaches high heaven. From the days of our fathers down to this
present day our guilt has been great. For our iniquities we, our kings, and
our priests have been subject to death, captivity, pillage, and shameful
humiliation at the hands of foreign kings, and such is our present plight.
8 But now, for a brief moment, the LORD our God has been gracious to us,
leaving us some survivors and giving us a foothold in his holy place. He
has brought light to our eyes again and given us some chance to renew our
9 lives in our slavery. For slaves we are; nevertheless, our God has not forsaken us in our slavery, but has made the kings of Persia so well disposed
towards us as to give us the means of renewal, so that we may repair
the house of our God and rebuild its ruins, and to give us a wall of defence
10 in*b* Judah and Jerusalem. Now, O our God, what are we to say after this?
11 For we have neglected the commands which thou gavest through thy
servants the prophets, when thou saidst, "The land which you are entering
and will possess is a polluted land, polluted by the foreign population with
their abominable practices, which have made it unclean from end to end.
12 Therefore, do not give your daughters in marriage to their sons, and do not
marry your sons to their daughters, and never seek their welfare or prosperity. Thus you will be strong and enjoy the good things of the land, and
13 pass it on to your children as an everlasting possession." Now, after all

---

a Prob. rdg., cp. 1 Esdras 8. 65; Heb. seventy-seven.   *b Or* thereby giving us a
wall of defence for . . .

that we have suffered for our evil deeds and for our great guilt—although
thou, our God, hast punished us less than our iniquities deserved and hast
allowed us to survive as now we do—shall we again disobey thy commands 14
and join in marriage with peoples who indulge in such abominable practices? Would not thy anger against us be unrelenting, until no remnant,
no survivor was left? O Lord God of Israel, thou art righteous; now as 15
before, we are only a remnant that has survived. Look upon us, guilty as
we are in thy sight; for because of our guilt none of us can stand in thy
presence.'

While Ezra was praying and making confession, prostrate in tears before **10**
the house of God, a very great crowd of Israelites assembled round him,
men, women, and children, and they all wept bitterly. Then Shecaniah son 2
of Jehiel, one of the family of Elam, spoke up and said to Ezra, 'We have
committed an offence against our God in marrying foreign wives, daughters
of the foreign population. But in spite of this, there is still hope for Israel.
Now, therefore, let us pledge ourselves to our God to dismiss all these 3
women and their brood, according to your advice, my lord, and the
advice of those who go in fear of the command of our God; and let us act as
the law prescribes. Up now, the task is yours, and we will support you. 4
Take courage and act.'

Ezra stood up and made the chiefs of the priests, the Levites, and all the 5
Israelites swear to do as had been said; and they took the oath. Then Ezra 6
left his place in front of the house of God and went to the room of Jehohanan
grandson of Eliashib and lodged[a] there; he neither ate bread nor drank
water, for he was mourning for the offence committed by the exiles who
had returned. Next, there was issued throughout Judah and Jerusalem a 7
proclamation that all the exiles should assemble in Jerusalem, and that if 8
anyone did not arrive within three days, it should be within the discretion
of the chief officers and the elders to confiscate all his property and to
exclude him from the community of the exiles. So all the men of Judah and 9
Benjamin assembled in Jerusalem within the three days; and on the twentieth day of the ninth month the people all sat in the forecourt of the house
of God, trembling with apprehension and shivering in the heavy rain.
Ezra the priest stood up and said, 'You have committed an offence in 10
marrying foreign wives and have added to Israel's guilt. Make your con- 11
fession now to the Lord the God of your fathers and do his will, and
separate yourselves from the foreign population and from your foreign
wives.' Then all the assembled people shouted in reply, 'Yes; we must do 12
what you say. But there is a great crowd of us here, and it is the rainy 13
season; we cannot go on standing out here in the open. Besides, this business will not be finished in one day or even two, because we have committed
so grave an offence in this matter. Let our leading men act for the whole 14
assembly, and let all in our cities who have married foreign women present
themselves at appointed times, each man with the elders and judges of his
own city, until God's anger against us on this account is averted.' Only 15
Jonathan son of Asahel and Jahzeiah son of Tikvah, supported by Meshullam and Shabbethai the Levite, opposed this.

[a] *Prob. rdg., cp. 1 Esdras 9. 2; Heb.* went.

16   So the exiles acted as agreed, and Ezra the priest selected [a] certain men, heads of households representing their families, all of them designated by name. They began their formal inquiry into the matter on the first day of

17 the tenth month, and by the first day of the first month they had finished their inquiry into all the marriages with foreign women.

18   Among the members of priestly families who had married foreign women were found Maaseiah, Eliezer, Jarib, and Gedaliah of the family of

19 Jeshua son of Jozadak and his brothers. They pledged themselves to dismiss their wives, and they brought a ram from the flock as a guilt-offering

20 21 for their sins. Of the family of Immer: Hanani and Zebadiah. Of the family

22 of Harim: Maaseiah, Elijah, Shemaiah, Jehiel and Uzziah. Of the family of Pashhur: Elioenai, Maaseiah, Ishmael, Nethaneel, Jozabad and Elasah.

23   Of the Levites: Jozabad, Shimei, Kelaiah (that is Kelita), Pethahiah,

24 Judah and Eliezer. Of the singers: Eliashib. Of the door-keepers: Shallum, Telem and Uri.

25   And of Israel: of the family of Parosh: Ramiah, Izziah, Malchiah,

26 Mijamin, Eleazar, Malchiah and Benaiah. Of the family of Elam: Mat-

27 taniah, Zechariah, Jehiel, Abdi, Jeremoth and Elijah. Of the family of

28 Zattu: Elioenai, Eliashib, Mattaniah, Jeremoth, Zabad and Aziza. Of the

29 family of Bebai: Jehohanan, Hananiah, Zabbai and Athlai. Of the family

30 of Bani: Meshullam, Malluch, Adaiah, Jashub, Sheal and Jeremoth. Of the family of Pahath-moab: Adna, Kelal, Benaiah, Maaseiah, Mattaniah,

31 Bezalel, Binnui and Manasseh. Of the family of Harim: Eliezer, Isshijah,

32 33 Malchiah, Shemaiah, Simeon, Benjamin, Malluch and Shemariah. Of the family of Hashum: Mattenai, Mattattah, Zabad, Eliphelet, Jeremai,

34 Manasseh and Shimei. Of the family of Bani: Maadai, Amram and Uel,

35 36 37 Benaiah, Bedeiah and Keluhi, Vaniah, Meremoth, Eliashib, Mattaniah,

38 39 Mattenai and Jaasau. Of the family of [b] Binnui: Shimei, Shelemiah,

40 41 Nathan and Adaiah, Maknadebai, Shashai and Sharai, Azareel, Shelemiah

42 43 and Shemariah, Shallum, Amariah and Joseph. Of the family of Nebo:

44 Jeiel, Mattithiah, Zabad, Zebina, Jaddai, Joel and Benaiah. All these had married foreign women, and they dismissed them, together with their children.[c]

[a] and Ezra the priest selected: *prob. rdg.*, *cp. 1 Esdras 9. 16*; *Heb. obscure.*   [b] Of the family of: *prob. rdg.*, *cp. 1 Esdras 9. 34*; *Heb. and Bani and.*   [c] and they ... children: *prob. rdg.*, *cp. 1 Esdras 9. 36*; *Heb. and some of them were women; and they had borne sons.*

THE BOOK OF

NEHEMIAH

Nehemiah's commission

T HE NARRATIVE OF NEHEMIAH son of Hacaliah. 1
In the month Kislev in the twentieth year, when I was in Susa
the capital city, it happened that one of my brothers, Hanani, arrived 2
with some others from Judah; and I asked them about Jerusalem and about
the Jews, the families still remaining of those who survived the captivity.
They told me that those still remaining in the province who had survived 3
the captivity were facing great trouble and reproach; the wall of Jerusalem
was broken down and the gates had been destroyed by fire. When I heard 4
this news, I sat down and wept; I mourned for some days, fasting and
praying to the God of heaven. This was my prayer: 'O LORD God of heaven, 5
O great and terrible God who faithfully keepest covenant with those who
love thee and observe thy commandments, let thy ear be attentive and 6
thine eyes open, to hear my humble prayer which I make to thee day and
night on behalf of thy servants the sons of Israel. I confess the sins which
we Israelites have all committed against thee, and of which I and my father's
house are also guilty. We have wronged thee and have not observed the 7
commandments, statutes, and rules which thou didst enjoin upon thy
servant Moses. Remember what thou didst impress upon him in these 8
words: "If you are unfaithful, I will disperse you among the nations; but 9
if you return to me and observe my commandments and fulfil them, I will
gather your children who have been scattered to the ends of the earth and
will bring them home to the place which I have chosen as a dwelling for my
Name." They are thy servants and thy people, whom thou hast redeemed 10
with thy great might and thy strong hand. O Lord, let thy ear be attentive 11
to my humble prayer, and to the prayer of thy servants who delight to
revere thy name. Grant me good success this day, and put it into this
man's heart to show me kindness.'

Now I was the king's cupbearer, and one day, in the month Nisan, in the 2
twentieth year of King Artaxerxes, when his wine was ready, I took it up
and handed it to the king, and as I stood before him I was feeling very
unhappy. He said to me, 'Why do you look so unhappy? You are not ill; 2
it can be nothing but unhappiness.' I was much afraid and answered, 'The 3
king will live for ever. But how can I help looking unhappy when the city
where my forefathers are buried lies waste and its gates are burnt?' 'What 4
are you asking of me?' said the king. I prayed to the God of heaven, and 5
then I answered, 'If it please your majesty, and if I enjoy your favour, I
beg you to send me to Judah, to the city where my forefathers are buried,
so that I may rebuild it.' The king, with the queen consort sitting beside 6

him, asked me, 'How long will the journey last, and when will you return?'
Then the king approved the request and let me go, and I told him how long
7 I should be. Then I said to the king, 'If it please your majesty, let letters be
given me for the governors in the province of Beyond-Euphrates with
8 orders to grant me all the help I need for my journey to Judah. Let me have
also a letter for Asaph, the keeper of your royal forests, instructing him to
supply me with timber to make beams for the gates of the citadel, which
adjoins the palace, and for the city wall, and for the palace which I shall
occupy.' The king granted my requests, for the gracious hand of my God
9 was upon me. I came in due course to the governors in the province of
Beyond-Euphrates and presented to them the king's letters; the king had
10 given me an escort of army officers with cavalry. But when Sanballat the
Horonite and the slave Tobiah, an Ammonite, heard this, they were much
vexed that someone should have come to promote the interests of the
Israelites.

The walls of Jerusalem rebuilt

11 12 WHEN I ARRIVED IN JERUSALEM, I waited three days. Then I set
out by night, taking a few men with me; but I told no one what my
God was prompting me to do for Jerusalem. I had no beast with me except
13 the one on which I myself rode. I went out by night through the Valley
Gate towards the Dragon Spring and the Dung Gate, and I inspected the
places where the walls of Jerusalem had been broken down and her gates
14 burnt. Then I passed on to the Fountain Gate and the King's Pool; but
15 there was no room for me to ride through. I went up the valley in the night
and inspected the city wall; then I re-entered the city by the Valley Gate.
16 So I arrived back without the magistrates knowing where I had been or
what I was doing. I had not yet told the Jews, the priests, the nobles, the
magistrates, or any of those who would be responsible for the work.
17 Then I said to them, 'You see our wretched plight. Jerusalem lies in
ruins, its gates destroyed by fire. Come, let us rebuild the wall of Jerusalem
18 and be rid of the reproach.' I told them how the gracious hand of my God
had been upon me and also what the king had said to me. They replied,
'Let us start the rebuilding.' So they set about the work vigorously and to
good purpose.
19 But when Sanballat the Horonite, Tobiah the Ammonite slave, and
Geshem the Arab heard of it, they jeered at us, asking contemptuously,
20 'What is this you are doing? Is this a rebellion against the king?' But I
answered them, 'The God of heaven will give us success. We, his servants,
are making a start with the rebuilding. You have no stake, or claim, or
traditional right in Jerusalem.'
3 Eliashib the high priest and his fellow-priests started work and rebuilt
the Sheep Gate. They laid its beams *a* and set its doors in place; they carried
the work as far as the Tower of the Hundred, as far as the Tower of Hananel,

---

a laid its beams: *prob. rdg.; Heb.* consecrated it.

534

and consecrated it. Next to Eliashib the men of Jericho worked; and next 2
to them Zaccur son of Imri.

The Fish Gate was built by the sons of Hassenaah; they laid its tie- 3
beams and set its doors in place with their bolts and bars. Next to them 4
Meremoth son of Uriah, son of Hakkoz, repaired his section; next to them
Meshullam son of Berechiah, son of Meshezabel; next to them Zadok son
of Baana did the repairs; and next again the men of Tekoa did the repairs, 5
but their nobles would not demean themselves to serve their governor.

The Jeshanah Gate*a* was repaired by Joiada son of Paseah and Meshul- 6
lam son of Besodeiah; they laid its tie-beams and set its doors in place with
their bolts and bars. Next to them Melatiah the Gibeonite and Jadon the 7
Meronothite, the men of Gibeon and Mizpah, did the repairs as far as the
seat of the governor of the province of Beyond-Euphrates. Next to them 8
Uzziel son of Harhaiah, a goldsmith, did the repairs, and next Hananiah,
a perfumer; they reconstructed Jerusalem as far as the Broad Wall. Next 9
to them Rephaiah son of Hur, ruler of half the district of Jerusalem, did
the repairs. Next to them Jedaiah son of Harumaph did the repairs opposite 10
his own house; and next Hattush son of Hashabniah. Malchiah son of 11
Harim and Hasshub son of Pahath-moab repaired a second section including the Tower of the Ovens.*b* Next to them Shallum son of Hallohesh, ruler 12
of half the district of Jerusalem, did the repairs with the help of his
daughters.

The Valley Gate was repaired by Hanun and the inhabitants of Zanoah; 13
they rebuilt it and set its doors in place with their bolts and bars, and they
repaired a thousand cubits of the wall as far as the Dung Gate. The Dung 14
Gate itself was repaired by Malchiah son of Rechab, ruler of the district
of Beth-hakkerem; he rebuilt*c* it and set its doors in place with their bolts
and bars. The Fountain Gate was repaired by Shallun son of Col-hozeh, 15
ruler of the district of Mizpah; he rebuilt*c* it and roofed it and set its doors
in place with their bolts and bars; and he built the wall of the Pool of
Shelah next to the king's garden and onwards as far as the steps leading
down from the City of David.

After him Nehemiah son of Azbuk, ruler of half the district of Beth-zur, 16
did the repairs as far as a point opposite the burial-place of David, as far
as the artificial pool and the House of the Heroes.*d* After him the Levites 17
did the repairs: Rehum son of Bani and next to him Hashabiah, ruler of
half the district of Keilah, did the repairs for his district. After him their 18
kinsmen did the repairs: Binnui son of Henadad, ruler of half the district
of Keilah; next to him Ezer son of Jeshua, ruler of Mizpah, repaired a 19
second section opposite the point at which the ascent meets the escarpment; after him Baruch son of Zabbai repaired a second section, from the 20
escarpment to the door of the house of Eliashib the high priest. After him 21
Meremoth son of Uriah, son of Hakkoz, repaired a second section, from
the door of the house of Eliashib to the end of the house of Eliashib.

After him the priests of the neighbourhood of Jerusalem did the repairs. 22
Next Benjamin and Hasshub did the repairs opposite their own house; 23

a The Jeshanah Gate: *or* The gate of the Old City.   *b Or* Furnaces.   *c Prob. rdg.;*
Heb. he will rebuild.   *d Or* and the barracks.

and next Azariah son of Maaseiah, son of Ananiah, did the repairs beside
24 his house. After him Binnui son of Henadad repaired a second section,
25 from the house of Azariah as far as the escarpment and the corner. Palal
son of Uzai worked opposite the escarpment and the upper tower which
projects from the king's house and belongs to the court of the guard. After
26 him Pedaiah son of Parosh*a* worked as far as a point on the east opposite
27 the Water Gate and the projecting tower. Next the men of Tekoa repaired
a second section, from a point opposite the great projecting tower as far as
the wall of Ophel.
28   Above the Horse Gate the priests did the repairs opposite their own
29 houses. After them Zadok son of Immer did the repairs opposite his own
house; after him Shemaiah son of Shecaniah, the keeper of the East Gate,
30 did the repairs. After him Hananiah son of Shelemiah and Hanun, sixth
son of Zalaph, repaired a second section. After him Meshullam son of
31 Berechiah did the repairs opposite his room. After him Malchiah, a goldsmith, did the repairs as far as the house of the temple-servitors and the
merchants, opposite the Mustering Gate, as far as the roof-chamber at
32 the corner. Between the roof-chamber at the corner and the Sheep Gate
the goldsmiths and merchants did the repairs.

4 WHEN SANBALLAT HEARD that we were rebuilding the wall, he was very
2 indignant; in his anger he jeered at the Jews and said in front of his companions and of the garrison in Samaria, 'What do these feeble Jews think
they are doing? Do they mean to reconstruct the place? Do they hope to
offer sacrifice and finish the work in a day? Can they make stones again out
3 of heaps of rubble, and burnt at that?' Tobiah the Ammonite, who was
beside him, said, 'Whatever it is they are building, if a fox climbs up their
stone walls, it will break them down.'
4   Hear us, our God, for they treat us with contempt. Turn back their
reproach upon their own heads and let them become objects of contempt
5 in a land of captivity. Do not condone their guilt or let their sin be struck
off the record, for they have openly provoked the builders.
6   We built up the wall until it was continuous all round up to half its
7 height; and the people worked with a will. But when Sanballat and Tobiah,
the Arabs and Ammonites and Ashdodites, heard that the new work on
the walls of Jerusalem had made progress and that the filling of the breaches
8 had begun, they were very angry; and they all banded together to come and
9 attack Jerusalem and to create confusion. So we prayed to our God, and
posted a guard day and night against them.
10   But the men of Judah said, 'The labourers' strength has failed, and there
is too much rubble; we shall never be able to rebuild the wall by ourselves.'
11 And our adversaries said, 'Before they know it or see anything, we shall be
12 upon them and kill them, and so put an end to the work.' When the Jews
who lived among them came in to the city, they warned us many times
that they would gather from every place where they lived to attack us,
13 and that they would station themselves on the lowest levels below the wall,
on patches of open ground. Accordingly I posted my people by families,

a *Prob. rdg.; Heb. adds* and the temple-servitors lodged on Ophel (*cp. 11. 21*).

armed with swords, spears, and bows. Then I surveyed the position 14
and at once addressed the nobles, the magistrates, and all the people.
'Do not be afraid of them', I said. 'Remember the Lord, great and terrible,
and fight for your brothers, your sons and daughters, your wives and
your homes.' Our enemies heard that everything was known to us, and 15
that God had frustrated their plans; and we all returned to our work on
the wall.

From that day forward half the men under me were engaged in the 16
actual building, while the other half stood by holding their spears, shields,
and bows, and wearing coats of mail; and officers supervised all the people
of Judah who were engaged on the wall. The porters carrying the loads had 17
one hand on the load and a weapon in the other. The builders had their 18
swords attached to their belts as they built; the trumpeter was beside me.
I addressed the nobles, the magistrates, and all the people: 'The work is 19
great and covers much ground', I said. 'We are isolated on the wall, each
man at some distance from his neighbour. Wherever the trumpet sounds, 20
rally to us there, and our God will fight for us.' So we continued with the 21
work, half the men holding the spears, from daybreak until the stars came
out. At the same time I had said to the people, 'Let every man and his 22
servant pass the night in Jerusalem, to act as a guard for us by night and a
working party by day.' So neither I nor my kinsmen nor the men under 23
me nor my bodyguard ever took off our clothes, each keeping his right hand
on*a* his weapon.

THERE CAME A TIME when the common people, both men and women, 5
raised a great outcry against their fellow-Jews. Some complained that they 2
were giving their sons and daughters as pledges*b* for food to keep themselves alive; others that they were mortgaging their fields, vineyards, and 3
houses to buy corn in the famine; others again that they were borrowing 4
money on their fields and vineyards to pay the king's tax. 'But', they said, 5
'our bodily needs are the same as other people's, our children are as good as
theirs; yet here we are, forcing our sons and daughters to become slaves.
Some of our daughters are already enslaved, and there is nothing we can
do, because our fields and vineyards now belong to others.' I was very 6
angry when I heard their outcry and the story they told. I mastered my 7
feelings and reasoned with the nobles and the magistrates. I said to them,
'You are holding your fellow-Jews as pledges for debt.' I rebuked them
severely and said, 'As far as we have been able, we have bought back our 8
fellow-Jews who had been sold to other nations; but you are now selling
your own fellow-countrymen, and they will have to be bought back by us!'
They were silent and had not a word to say. I went on, 'What you are doing 9
is wrong. You ought to live so much in the fear of God that you are above
reproach in the eyes of the nations who are our enemies. Speaking for 10
myself, I and my kinsmen and the men under me are advancing them money
and corn. Let us give up this taking of persons as pledges for debt. Give 11
back today to your debtors their fields and vineyards, their olive-groves

a keeping his right hand on: *prob. rdg.; Heb. obscure.*   *b* that they . . . as pledges:
prob. rdg.; Heb. that they, their sons and daughters were many.

12 and houses, as well as the income*a* in money, and in corn, new wine, and
oil.' 'We will give them back', they promised, 'and exact nothing more.
We will do what you say.' So, summoning the priests, I put the offenders

13 on oath to do as they had promised. Then I shook out the fold of my robe
and said, 'So may God shake out from his house and from his property
every man who does not fulfil this promise. May he be shaken out like this
and emptied!' And all the assembled people said 'Amen' and praised the
LORD. And they did as they had promised.

14 Moreover, from the time when I was appointed governor in the land of
Judah, from the twentieth to the thirty-second year of King Artaxerxes,
a period of twelve years, neither I nor my kinsmen drew the governor's

15 allowance of food. Former governors had laid a heavy burden on the
people, exacting from them a daily toll*b* of bread and wine to the value of
forty shekels of silver. Further, the men under them had tyrannized over

16 the people; but, for fear of God, I did not behave like this. I also put all my
energy into the work on this wall, and I acquired no land; and all my men

17 were gathered there for the work. Also I had as guests at my table a hundred
and fifty Jews, including the magistrates, as well as men who came to us

18 from the surrounding nations. The provision which had to be made each
day was an ox and six prime sheep; fowls also were prepared for me, and
every ten days skins of wine in abundance. Yet, in spite of all this, I did
not draw the governor's allowance, because the people were so heavily bur-

19 dened. Remember for my good, O God, all that I have done for this people.

6 When the news came to Sanballat, Tobiah, Geshem the Arab, and the
rest of our enemies, that I had rebuilt the wall and that not a single breach

2 remained in it, although I had not yet set up the doors in the gates, Sanballat
and Geshem sent me an invitation to come and confer with them at
Hakkephirim in the plain of Ono; this was a ruse on their part to do me

3 harm. So I sent messengers to them with this reply: 'I have important
work on my hands at the moment; I cannot come down. Why should the

4 work be brought to a standstill while I leave it and come down to you?' They
sent me a similar invitation four times, and each time I gave them the same

5 answer. On a fifth occasion Sanballat made a similar approach, but this

6 time his messenger came with an open letter. It ran as follows: 'It is
reported among the nations—and Gashmu*c* confirms it—that you and the
Jews are plotting rebellion, and it is for this reason that you are rebuilding

7 the wall, and—so the report goes—that you yourself want to be king. You
are also said to have put up prophets to proclaim in Jerusalem that Judah
has a king, meaning yourself. The king will certainly hear of this. So come

8 at once and let us talk the matter over.' Here is the reply I sent: 'No such
thing as you allege has taken place; you have made up the whole story.'

9 They were all trying to intimidate us, in the hope that we should then relax
our efforts and that the work would never be finished. So I applied myself
to it with greater energy.

10 One day I went to the house of Shemaiah son of Delaiah, son of Mehetabel, for he was confined to his house. He said, 'Let us meet in the house of

---

a *Prob. rdg.; Heb.* hundredth.　　　　　*b* a daily toll: *prob. rdg.; Heb. obscure.*
c Geshem *in 2. 19 and 6. 1, 2.*

God, within the sanctuary, and let us shut the doors, for they are coming
to kill you—they are coming to kill you by night.' But I said, 'Should a 11
man like me run away? And can a man like me go into the sanctuary and
survive*a*? I will not go in.' Then it dawned on me: God had not sent him. 12
His prophecy aimed at harming me, and Tobiah and Sanballat had bribed
him to utter it. He had been bribed to frighten me into compliance and into 13
committing sin; then they could give me a bad name and discredit me.
Remember Tobiah and Sanballat, O God, for what they have done, and 14
also the prophetess Noadiah and all the other prophets who have tried to
intimidate me.

On the twenty-fifth day of the month Elul the wall was finished; it had 15
taken fifty-two days. When our enemies heard of it, and all the surrounding 16
nations saw it,*b* they thought it a very wonderful achievement,*c* and they
recognized that this work had been accomplished by the help of our God.

All this time the nobles in Judah were sending many letters to Tobiah, 17
and receiving replies from him. For many in Judah were in league with 18
him, because he was a son-in-law of Shecaniah son of Arah, and his son
Jehohanan had married a daughter of Meshullam son of Berechiah. They 19
were always praising*d* him in my presence and repeating to him what I
said. Tobiah also wrote to me to intimidate me.

NOW WHEN THE WALL HAD BEEN REBUILT, and I had set the doors 7
in place and the gate-keepers*e* had been appointed, I gave the charge of 2
Jerusalem to my brother Hanani, and to Hananiah, the governor of the
citadel, for he was trustworthy and God-fearing above other men. And I 3
said to them, 'The entrances to Jerusalem are not to be left open during
the heat of the day; the gates must be kept shut and barred while the gate-
keepers are standing at ease. Appoint guards from among the inhabitants
of Jerusalem, some on sentry-duty and others posted in front of their own
homes.'

The city was large and spacious; there were few people in it and no 4
houses had yet been rebuilt. Then God prompted me to assemble the 5
nobles, the magistrates, and the people, to be enrolled family by family.
And I found the book of the genealogies of those who had been the first
to come back. This is what I found written in it: Of the captives whom 6*f*
Nebuchadnezzar king of Babylon had taken into exile, these are the people
of the province who have returned to Jerusalem and Judah, each to his
own town, led by Zerubbabel, Jeshua,*g* Nehemiah, Azariah, Raamiah, 7
Nahamani, Mordecai, Bilshan, Mispereth, Bigvai, Nehum and Baanah.

The roll of the men of the people of Israel: the family of Parosh, two 8
thousand one hundred and seventy-two; the family of Shephatiah, three 9
hundred and seventy-two; the family of Arah, six hundred and fifty-two; 10
the family of Pahath-moab, namely the families of Jeshua and Joab, two 11
thousand eight hundred and eighteen; the family of Elam, one thousand 12

---

a and survive: *or* to save his life.   *b* *Or* were afraid.   *c* they thought . . . achievement: *prob. rdg.; Heb.* they fell very much in their own eyes.   *d* *Or* repeating rumours
about . . .   *e* *Prob. rdg.; Heb. adds* the singers and the Levites.   *f* *Verses 6–73:
cp. Ezra 2. 1–70.*   *g* *Or* Joshua (*cp. Hag. 1. 1*).

13 two hundred and fifty-four; the family of Zattu, eight hundred and forty-
14 15 five; the family of Zaccai, seven hundred and sixty; the family of Binnui,
16 six hundred and forty-eight; the family of Bebai, six hundred and twenty-
17 eight; the family of Azgad, two thousand three hundred and twenty-two;
18 19 the family of Adonikam, six hundred and sixty-seven; the family of Bigvai,
20 two thousand and sixty-seven; the family of Adin, six hundred and fifty-
21 22 five; the family of Ater, namely that of Hezekiah, ninety-eight; the family
23 of Hashum, three hundred and twenty-eight; the family of Bezai, three
24 hundred and twenty-four; the family of Harif, one hundred and twelve;
25 26 the family of Gibeon, ninety-five. The men of Bethlehem and Netophah,
27 one hundred and eighty-eight; the men of Anathoth, one hundred and
28 29 twenty-eight; the men of Beth-azmoth, forty-two; the men of Kiriath-
30 jearim, Kephirah, and Beeroth, seven hundred and forty-three; the men
31 of Ramah and Geba, six hundred and twenty-one; the men of Michmas,
32 one hundred and twenty-two; the men of Bethel and Ai, one hundred and
33 34 twenty-three; the men of *a* Nebo, fifty-two; the men *b* of the other Elam,
35 one thousand two hundred and fifty-four; the men of Harim, three hundred
36 37 and twenty; the men of Jericho, three hundred and forty-five; the men of
38 Lod, Hadid, and Ono, seven hundred and twenty-one; the men of Senaah,
three thousand nine hundred and thirty.

39 Priests: the family of Jedaiah, of the line of Jeshua, nine hundred and
40 41 seventy-three; the family of Immer, one thousand and fifty-two; the
42 family of Pashhur, one thousand two hundred and forty-seven; the family
of Harim, one thousand and seventeen.

43 Levites: the families of Jeshua and *c* Kadmiel, of the line of Hodvah,
44 seventy-four. Singers: the family of Asaph, one hundred and forty-eight.
45 Door-keepers: the family of Shallum, the family of Ater, the family of
Talmon, the family of Akkub, the family of Hatita, and the family of
Shobai, one hundred and thirty-eight in all.

46 Temple-servitors: the family of Ziha, the family of Hasupha, the family
47 of Tabbaoth, the family of Keros, the family of Sia, the family of Padon,
48 49 the family of Lebanah, the family of Hagabah, the family of Shalmai, the
50 family of Hanan, the family of Giddel, the family of Gahar, the family of
51 Reaiah, the family of Rezin, the family of Nekoda, the family of Gazzam,
52 the family of Uzza, the family of Paseah, the family of Besai, the family of
53 the Meunim, the family of the Nephishesim, *d* the family of Bakbuk, the
54 family of Hakupha, the family of Harhur, the family of Bazlith, *e* the
55 family of Mehida, the family of Harsha, the family of Barkos, the family of
56 Sisera, the family of Temah, the family of Neziah, and the family of Hatipha.

57 Descendants of Solomon's servants: the family of Sotai, the family of
58 Sophereth, the family of Perida, the family of Jaalah, the family of Darkon,
59 the family of Giddel, the family of Shephatiah, the family of Hattil, the
family of Pochereth-hazzebaim, and the family of Amon.

60 The temple-servitors and the descendants of Solomon's servants
amounted to three hundred and ninety-two in all.

a Prob. rdg., cp. Ezra 2. 29.; Heb. adds the other.   *b* Prob. rdg.; Heb. family (*also
in verses 35–38*).   *c* and: prob. rdg., cp. Ezra 2. 40; Heb. to.   *d* Or Nephushesim.
e Or Bazluth (cp. Ezra 2. 52).

The following were those who returned from Tel-melah, Tel-harsha, 61
Kerub, Addon, and Immer, but could not establish their father's family
nor whether by descent they belonged to Israel: the family of Delaiah, the 62
family of Tobiah, the family of Nekoda, six hundred and forty-two. Also 63
of the priests: the family of Hobaiah, the family of Hakkoz, and the family
of Barzillai who had married a daughter of Barzillai the Gileadite and went
by his*a* name. These searched for their names among those enrolled in the 64
genealogies, but they could not be found; they were disqualified for the
priesthood as unclean, and the governor forbade them to partake of 65
the most sacred food until there should be a priest able to consult the Urim
and the Thummim.

The whole assembled people numbered forty-two thousand three 66
hundred and sixty, apart from their slaves, male and female, of whom there 67
were seven thousand three hundred and thirty-seven; and they had two
hundred and forty-five singers, men and women. Their horses numbered 68
seven hundred and thirty-six, their mules two hundred and forty-five,
their camels four hundred and thirty-five, and their asses six thousand seven 69
hundred and twenty.

Some of the heads of families gave contributions for the work. The 70
governor gave to the treasury a thousand drachmas of gold, fifty tossing-
bowls, and five hundred and thirty priestly robes. Some of the heads of 71
families gave for the fabric fund twenty thousand drachmas of gold and
two thousand two hundred minas of silver. What the rest of the people gave 72
was twenty thousand drachmas of gold, two thousand minas of silver, and
sixty-seven priestly robes.

The priests, the Levites, and some of the people lived in Jerusalem and 73
its suburbs;*b* the door-keepers, the singers, the temple-servitors, and all
other Israelites, lived in their own towns.

The law read by Ezra and the covenant renewed

WHEN THE SEVENTH MONTH CAME, and the Israelites were now
settled in their towns, the people assembled as one man in the 8
square in front of the Water Gate, and Ezra the scribe*c* was asked to bring
the book of the law of Moses, which the LORD had enjoined upon Israel.
On the first day of the seventh month, Ezra the priest brought the law 2
before the assembly, every man and woman, and all who were capable of
understanding what they heard.*d* He read from it, facing the square in 3
front of the Water Gate, from early morning till noon, in the presence of
the men and the women, and those who could understand;*e* all the people
listened attentively to the book of the law. Ezra the scribe stood on a wooden 4
platform made for the purpose,*f* and beside him stood Mattithiah, Shema,
Anaiah, Uriah, Hilkiah, and Maaseiah on his right hand; and on his left

---

a *Prob. rdg., cp. 1 Esdras 5. 38; Heb.* their.   *b* *in Jerusalem and its suburbs: prob.*
rdg., cp. 1 Esdras 5. 46; Heb. om.   *c* *Or* doctor of the law.   *d* were capable . . .
heard: *or* would teach them to understand.   *e* could understand: *or* were to
instruct.   *f* *Or* for the address.

Pedaiah, Mishael, Malchiah, Hashum, Hashbaddanah, Zechariah and
5 Meshullam. Ezra opened the book in the sight of all the people, for he was
6 standing above them; and when he opened it, they all stood. Ezra blessed
the LORD, the great God, and all the people raised their hands and answered,
'Amen, Amen'; and they bowed their heads and prostrated themselves
7 humbly before the LORD. Jeshua, Bani, Sherebiah, Jamin, Akkub, Shabbethai, Hodiah, Maaseiah, Kelita, Azariah, Jozabad, Hanan, Pelaiah,
the Levites,[a] expounded the law to the people while they remained in their
8 places. They read from the book of the law of God clearly, made its sense
plain and gave instruction in what was read.
9   Then Nehemiah the governor and Ezra the priest and scribe, and the
Levites who instructed the people, said to them all, 'This day is holy to
the LORD your God; do not mourn or weep.' For all the people had been
10 weeping while they listened to the words of the law. Then he said to them,
'You may go now; refresh yourselves with rich food and sweet drinks, and
send a share to all who cannot provide for themselves; for this day is holy
to our Lord. Let there be no sadness, for joy in the LORD is your strength.'
11 The Levites silenced the people, saying, 'Be quiet, for this day is holy;
12 let there be no sadness.' So all the people went away to eat and to drink, to
send shares to others and to celebrate the day with great rejoicing, because
they had understood what had been explained to them.
13   On the second day the heads of families of the whole people, with the
priests and the Levites, assembled before Ezra the scribe to study the law.
14 And they found written in the law that the LORD had given commandment
through Moses that the Israelites should live in arbours [b] during the feast
15 of the seventh month, and that they should make proclamation throughout
all their cities and in Jerusalem: 'Go out into the hills and fetch branches
of olive and wild olive, myrtle and palm, and other leafy boughs to make
16 arbours, as prescribed.' So the people went out and fetched them and made
arbours for themselves, each on his own roof, and in their courts and in the
courts of the house of God, and in the square at the Water Gate and the
17 square at the Ephraim Gate. And the whole community of those who had
returned from the captivity made arbours and lived in them, a thing that
the Israelites had not done from the days of Joshua son of Nun to that day;
18 and there was very great rejoicing. And day by day, from the first day to
the last, the book of the law of God was read. They kept the feast for seven
days, and on the eighth day there was a closing ceremony, according to
the rule.

9 ON THE TWENTY-FOURTH DAY of this month the Israelites assembled
2 for a fast, clothed in sackcloth and with earth on their heads. Those who
were of Israelite descent separated themselves from all the foreigners; they
took their places and confessed their sins and the iniquities of their fore-
3 fathers. Then they stood up in their places, and the book of the law of the
LORD their God was read for one fourth of the day, and for another fourth
4 they confessed and did obeisance to the LORD their God. Upon the steps
assigned to the Levites stood Jeshua, Bani, Kadmiel, Shebaniah, Bunni,

[a] *Prob. rdg.; Heb.* and the Levites.   [b] *Or* tabernacles *or* booths.

Sherebiah, Bani, and Kenani, and they cried aloud to the L ORD their God.
Then the Levites, Jeshua, Kadmiel, Bani, Hashabniah, Sherebiah, Hodiah,   5
Shebaniah, and Pethahiah, said, 'Stand up and bless the L ORD your God,
saying: From everlasting to everlasting thy glorious name is blessed *a* and
exalted above all blessing and praise. Thou alone art the L ORD; thou hast   6
made heaven, the highest heaven with all its host, the earth and all that is
on it, the seas and all that is in them. Thou preservest all of them, and the
host of heaven worships thee. Thou art the L ORD, the God who chose   7
Abram and brought him out of Ur of the Chaldees and named him
Abraham. Thou didst find him faithful to thee and didst make a covenant   8
with him to give to him and to his descendants the land of the Canaanites,
the Hittites, the Amorites, the Perizzites, the Jebusites, and the Girgashites; and thou didst fulfil thy promise, for thou art just.

'And thou didst see the misery of our forefathers in Egypt and didst hear   9
their cry for help at the Red Sea,*b* and didst work signs and portents   10
against Pharaoh, all his courtiers and all the people of his land, knowing
how arrogantly they treated our forefathers, and thou didst win for thyself
a name that lives on to this day. Thou didst tear the sea apart before them   11
so that they went through the middle of it on dry ground; but thou didst
cast their pursuers into the depths, like a stone cast into turbulent waters.
Thou didst guide them by a pillar of cloud in the day-time and by a pillar   12
of fire at night to give them light on the road by which they travelled. Thou   13
didst descend upon Mount Sinai and speak with them from heaven, and
give them right judgements and true laws, and statutes and commandments which were good, and thou didst make known to them thy holy   14
sabbath and give them commandments, statutes, and laws through thy
servant Moses. Thou gavest them bread from heaven to stay their hunger   15
and thou broughtest water out from a rock for them to quench their thirst,
and thou didst bid them enter and take possession of the land which thou
hadst solemnly sworn to give them. But they, our forefathers, were arro-   16
gant and stubborn, and disobeyed thy commandments. They refused to   17
obey and did not remember the miracles which thou didst accomplish
among them; they remained stubborn, and they appointed a man to lead
them back to slavery in Egypt. But thou art a forgiving god, gracious and
compassionate, long-suffering and ever constant, and thou didst not forsake them. Even when they made the image of a bull-calf in metal and said,   18
"This is your god who brought you up from Egypt", and were guilty of
great blasphemies, thou in thy great compassion didst not forsake them in   19
the wilderness. The pillar of cloud did not fail to guide them on their
journey by day nor the pillar of fire by night to give them light on the road
by which they travelled. Thou gavest thy good spirit to instruct them; thy   20
manna thou didst not withhold from them, and thou gavest them water to
quench their thirst. Forty years long thou didst sustain them in the wilder-   21
ness, and they lacked nothing; their clothes did not wear out and their feet
were not swollen.

'Thou gavest them kingdoms and peoples, allotting these to them as   22

a   thy glorious name is blessed: *prob. rdg.; Heb.* and let them bless thy glorious name.
b   *Or* the Sea of Reeds.

spoils of war. Thus they took possession of the land of Sihon king of
23 Heshbon and the land of Og king of Bashan. Thou didst multiply their
descendants so that they became countless as the stars in the sky, bringing
them into the land which thou didst promise to give to their forefathers
24 as their possession. When their descendants entered the land and took
possession of it, thou didst subdue before them the Canaanites who
inhabited it and gavest these, kings and peoples alike, into their hands to
25 do with them whatever they wished. They captured fortified cities and a
fertile land and took possession of houses full of all good things, rock-
hewn cisterns, vineyards, olive-trees, and fruit-trees in abundance; so
they ate and were satisfied and grew fat and found delight in thy great
26 goodness. But they were defiant and rebelled against thee; they turned
their backs on thy law and killed thy prophets, who solemnly warned them
27 to return to thee, and they were guilty of great blasphemies. Because of
this thou didst hand them over to their enemies who oppressed them. But
when, in the time of their oppression, they cried to thee for help, thou
heardest them from heaven and in thy great compassion didst send them
28 saviours to save them from their enemies. But when they had had a respite,
they once more did what was wrong in thine eyes; and thou didst abandon
them to their enemies who held them in subjection. But again they cried
to thee for help, and many times over thou heardest them from heaven and
29 in thy compassion didst save them. Thou didst solemnly warn them to
return to thy law, but they grew arrogant and did not heed thy commandments; they sinned against thy ordinances, which bring life to him who
keeps them. Stubbornly they turned away in mulish obstinacy and would
30 not obey. Many years thou wast patient with them and didst warn them by
thy spirit through thy prophets; but they would not listen. Therefore thou
31 didst hand them over to foreign peoples. Yet in thy great compassion thou
didst not make an end of them nor forsake them; for thou art a gracious and
compassionate god.
32 'Now therefore, our God, thou great and mighty and terrible God, who
faithfully keepest covenant, do not make light of the hardships that have
befallen us—our kings, our princes, our priests, our prophets, our forefathers, and all thy people—from the days of the kings of Assyria to this
33 day. In all that has befallen us thou hast been just, thou hast kept faith,
34 but we have done wrong. Our kings, our princes, our priests, and our forefathers did not keep thy law nor heed thy commandments and the warnings
35 which thou gavest them. Even under their own kings, while they were
enjoying the great prosperity which thou gavest them and the broad and
fertile land which thou didst bestow upon them, they did not serve thee;
36 they did not abandon their evil ways. Today we are slaves, slaves here in
the land which thou gavest to our forefathers so that they might eat its
37 fruits and enjoy its good things. All its produce now goes to the kings
whom thou hast set over us because of our sins. They have power over our
bodies, and they do as they please with our beasts, while we are in dire
distress.
38 'Because of all this we make a binding declaration in writing, and our
princes, our Levites, and our priests witness the sealing.

'Those who witness the sealing are Nehemiah the governor, son of **10** Hacaliah, Zedekiah, Seraiah, Azariah, Jeremiah, Pashhur, Amariah, 2 3 Malchiah, Hattush, Shebaniah, Malluch, Harim, Meremoth, Obadiah, 4 5 Daniel, Ginnethon, Baruch, Meshullam, Abiah, Mijamin, Maaziah, 6 7 8 Bilgai, Shemaiah; these are the priests. The Levites: Jeshua*a* son of 9 Azaniah, Binnui of the family of Henadad, Kadmiel; and their brethren, .10 Shebaniah, Hodiah,*b* Kelita, Pelaiah, Hanan, Mica, Rehob, Hashabiah, 11 Zaccur, Sherebiah, Shebaniah, Hodiah, Bani, Beninu. The chiefs of the 12 13 14 people: Parosh, Pahath-moab, Elam, Zattu, Bani, Bunni, Azgad, Bebai, 15 Adonijah, Bigvai, Adin, Ater, Hezekiah, Azzur, Hodiah, Hashum, Bezai, 16 17 18 Hariph, Anathoth, Nebai,*c* Magpiash, Meshullam, Hezir, Meshezabel, 19 20 21 Zadok, Jaddua, Pelatiah, Hanan, Anaiah, Hoshea, Hananiah, Hasshub, 22 23 Hallohesh, Pilha, Shobek, Rehum, Hashabnah, Maaseiah, Ahiah, Hanan, 24 25 26 Anan, Malluch, Harim, Baanah. 27

'The rest of the people, the priests, the Levites, the door-keepers, the 28 singers, the temple-servitors, with their wives, their sons, and their daughters, all who are capable of understanding, all who for the sake of the law of God have kept themselves apart from the foreign population, join 29 with the leading brethren,*d* when the oath is put to them, in swearing to obey God's law given by Moses the servant of God, and to observe and fulfil all the commandments of the LORD our Lord, his rules and his statutes.

'We will not give our daughters in marriage to the foreign population or 30 take their daughters for our sons. If on the sabbath these people bring in 31 merchandise, especially corn, for sale, we will not buy from them on the sabbath or on any holy day. We will forgo the crops of the seventh year and release every person still held as a pledge for debt.

'We hereby undertake the duty of giving yearly the third of a shekel for 32 the service of the house of our God, for the Bread of the Presence, the 33 regular grain-offering and whole-offering, the sabbaths, the new moons, the appointed seasons, the holy-gifts, and the sin-offerings to make expiation on behalf of Israel, and for all else that has to be done in the house of our God. We, the priests, the Levites, and the people, have cast lots for the 34 wood-offering, so that it may be brought into the house of our God by each family in turn, at appointed times, year by year, to burn upon the altar of the LORD our God, as prescribed in the law. We undertake to bring 35 the firstfruits of our land and the firstfruits of every fruit-tree, year by year, to the house of the LORD; also to bring to the house of our God, to the 36 priests who minister in the house of our God, the first-born of our sons and of our cattle, as prescribed in the law, and the first-born of our herds and of our flocks; and to bring to the priests the first kneading of our dough, 37 and the first of the fruit of every tree, of the new wine and of the oil, to the store-rooms in the house of our God; and to bring to the Levites the tithes from our land, for it is the Levites who collect the tithes in all our farming villages. The Aaronite priest shall be with the Levites when they collect 38 the tithes; and the Levites shall bring up one tenth of the tithes to the

---

a *Prob. rdg.; Heb.* and Jeshua.   *b* *Or, with Ezra 2. 40,* Hodaviah.   *c* *Or* Nobai.
d the leading brethren: *prob. rdg.; Heb.* their brethren, their leading men.

39 house of our God, to the appropriate rooms in the storehouse. For the
Israelites and the Levites shall bring the contribution of corn, new wine,
and oil to the rooms where the vessels of the sanctuary are kept, and where
the ministering priests, the door-keepers, and the singers are lodged. We
will not neglect the house of our God.'

11 THE LEADERS OF THE PEOPLE settled in Jerusalem; and the rest of the
people cast lots to bring one in every ten to live in Jerusalem, the holy city,
2 while the remaining nine lived in other towns. And the people were grateful to all those who volunteered to live in Jerusalem.

3   These are the chiefs of the province who lived in Jerusalem; but, in the
towns of Judah, other Israelites, priests, Levites, temple-servitors, and
descendants of Solomon's servants lived on their own property, in their
4 own towns. Some members of the tribes of Judah and Benjamin lived in
Jerusalem. Of Judah: Athaiah son of Uzziah, son of Zechariah, son of
6 Amariah, son of Shephatiah, son of Mahalalel of the family of Perez, all of
whose family, to the number of four hundred and sixty-eight men of sub-
5 stance, lived in Jerusalem; and Maaseiah son of Baruch, son of Col-hozeh,
son of Hazaiah, son of Adaiah, son of Joiarib, son of Zechariah of the
Shelanite family.

7   These were the Benjamites: Sallu son of Meshullam, son of Joed, son
of Pedaiah, son of Kolaiah, son of Maaseiah, son of Ithiel, son of Isaiah,
8 and his kinsmen Gabbai and Sallai, nine hundred and twenty-eight in all.
9 Joel son of Zichri was their overseer, and Judah son of Hassenuah was
second over the city.[a]

10 11   Of the priests: Jedaiah son of Joiarib, son of[b] Seraiah, son of Hilkiah,
son of Meshullam, son of Zadok, son of Meraioth, son of Ahitub, super-
12 visor of the house of God, and his[c] brethren responsible for the work in
the temple, eight hundred and twenty-two in all; and Adaiah son of
Jeroham, son of Pelaliah, son of Amzi, son of Zechariah, son of Pashhur,
13 son of Malchiah, and his brethren, heads of fathers' houses, two hundred
and forty-two in all; and Amasai[d] son of Azarel, son of Ahzai, son of
14 Meshillemoth, son of Immer, and his brethren, men of substance, a
hundred and twenty-eight in all; their overseer was Zabdiel son of
Haggedolim.

15   And of the Levites: Shemaiah son of Hasshub, son of Azrikam, son of
16 Hashabiah, son of Bunni; and Shabbethai and Jozabad of the chiefs of
the Levites, who had charge of the external business of the house of God;
17 and Mattaniah son of Micah, son of Zabdi, son of Asaph, who as precentor
led the prayer of thanksgiving, and Bakbukiah who held the second place
among his brethren; and Abda son of Shammua, son of Galal, son of
18 Jeduthun. The number of Levites in the holy city was two hundred and
eighty-four in all.

19   The gate-keepers who kept guard at the gates were Akkub, Talmon, and
20 their brethren, a hundred and seventy-two. The rest of the Israelites[e] were

---

[a] *second over the city: or* over the second quarter of the city.   [b] *son of: prob. rdg.;*
Heb. obscure.   [c] *Prob. rdg.; Heb. their.*   [d] *Prob. rdg.; Heb.* Amashsai.
[e] *Prob. rdg.; Heb. adds* the levitical priests.

in all the towns of Judah, each man on his own inherited property. But the ²¹ temple-servitors lodged on Ophel, and Ziha and Gishpa were in charge of them.

The overseer of the Levites in Jerusalem was Uzzi son of Bani, son of ²² Hashabiah, son of Mattaniah, son of Mica, of the family of Asaph the singers, for the supervision of the business of the house of God. For they ²³ were under the king's orders, and there was obligatory duty for the singers every day. Pethahiah son of Meshezabel, of the family of Zerah son of ²⁴ Judah, was the king's adviser on all matters affecting the people.

As for the hamlets with their surrounding fields: some of the men of ²⁵ Judah lived in Kiriath-arba and its villages, in Dibon and its villages, and in Jekabzeel and its hamlets, in Jeshua, Moladah, and Bethpelet, in Hazar- ²⁶ ²⁷ shual, and in Beersheba and its villages, in Ziklag and in Meconah and its ²⁸ villages, in Enrimmon, Zorah, and Jarmuth, in Zanoah, Adullam, and their ²⁹ ³⁰ hamlets, in Lachish and its fields and Azekah and its villages. Thus they occupied the country from Beersheba to the Valley of Hinnom.

The men of Benjamin lived in*ᵃ* Geba, Michmash, Aiah, and Bethel with ³¹ its villages, in Anathoth, Nob, and Ananiah, in Hazor, Ramah, and Git- ³² ³³ taim, in Hadid, Zeboim, and Neballat, in Lod, Ono, and*ᵇ* Ge-harashim.*ᶜ* ³⁴ ³⁵ And certain divisions of the Levites in Judah were attached to Benjamin. ³⁶

These are the priests and the Levites who came back with Zerubbabel **12** son of Shealtiel, and Jeshua:*ᵈ* Seraiah, Jeremiah, Ezra, Amariah, Malluch, ² Hattush, Shecaniah, Rehum, Meremoth, Iddo, Ginnethon, Abiah, ³ ⁴ Mijamin, Maadiah, Bilgah, Shemaiah, Joiarib, Jedaiah, Sallu, Amok, ⁵ ⁶ ⁷ Hilkiah, Jedaiah. These were the chiefs of the priests and of their brethren in the days of Jeshua.

And the Levites: Jeshua, Binnui, Kadmiel, Sherebiah, Judah, and Mat- ⁸ taniah, who with his brethren was in charge of the songs of thanksgiving. And Bakbukiah and Unni their brethren stood opposite them in the ⁹ service. And Jeshua was the father of Joiakim, Joiakim the father of ¹⁰ Eliashib, Eliashib of Joiada, Joiada the father of Jonathan, and Jonathan ¹¹ the father of Jaddua. And in the days of Joiakim the priests who were heads ¹² of families were: of Seraiah, Meraiah; of Jeremiah, Hananiah; of Ezra, ¹³ Meshullam; of Amariah, Jehohanan; of Malluch,*ᵉ* Jonathan; of Shebaniah, ¹⁴ Joseph; of Harim, Adna; of Meraioth, Helkai; of Iddo, Zechariah; of ¹⁵ ¹⁶ Ginnethon, Meshullam; of Abiah, Zichri; of Miniamin*ᶠ*; of Moadiah, ¹⁷ Piltai; of Bilgah, Shammua; of Shemaiah, Jehonathan; of Joiarib, Mat- ¹⁸ ¹⁹ tenai; of Jedaiah, Uzzi; of Sallu,*ᵍ* Kallai; of Amok, Eber; of Hilkiah, ²⁰ ²¹ Hashabiah; of Jedaiah, Nethaneel.

*ʰ*The heads of the priestly families*ⁱ* in the days of Eliashib, Joiada, ²² Johanan, and Jaddua were recorded down to the reign of Darius the Persian. The heads of the levitical families were recorded in the annals ²³ only down to the days of Johanan the grandson of Eliashib. And the chiefs ²⁴

ᵃ Prob. rdg.; Heb. from.   *ᵇ* and: *prob. rdg.; Heb. om.*   *ᶜ Or* and the Valley of Woods *or* and the Valley of Craftsmen.   *ᵈ Or* Joshua.   *ᵉ Prob. rdg.; Heb.* Malluchi, *or* Melichu.   *ᶠ A name is missing here.*   *ᵍ Prob. rdg., cp. verse 7; Heb.* Sallai. *ʰ Prob. rdg.; Heb. prefixes* The Levites.   *ⁱ* heads ... families: *prob. rdg.; Heb.* heads of the families and the priests.

of the Levites: Hashabiah, Sherebiah, Jeshua, Binnui,[a] Kadmiel, with their brethren in the other turn of duty, to praise and to give thanks, according to the commandment of David the man of God, turn by turn.

25 Mattaniah, Bakbukiah, Obadiah, Meshullam, Talmon, and Akkub were
26 gate-keepers standing guard at the gatehouses. This was the arrangement in the days of Joiakim son of Jeshua, son of Jozadak, and in the days of Nehemiah the governor and of Ezra the priest and scribe.

27 At the dedication of the wall of Jerusalem they sought out the Levites in all their settlements, and brought them to Jerusalem to celebrate the dedication with[b] rejoicing, with thanksgiving and song, to the accompani-
28 ment of cymbals, lutes, and harps. And the Levites,[c] the singers, were assembled from the district round Jerusalem and from the hamlets of the
29 Netophathites; also from Beth-gilgal and from the region of Geba and Beth-azmoth;[d] for the singers had built themselves hamlets in the neigh-
30 bourhood of Jerusalem. The priests and the Levites purified themselves;
31 and they purified the people, the gates, and the wall. Then I brought the leading men of Judah up on to the city wall, and appointed two great choirs to give thanks. One went in procession[e] to the right, going along the wall
32 to the Dung Gate; and after it went Hoshaiah with half the leading men of
33 34 Judah, and Azariah, Ezra, Meshullam, Judah, Benjamin, Shemaiah, and
35 Jeremiah; and certain of the priests with trumpets: Zechariah son of Jonathan, son of Shemaiah, son of Mattanaiah, son of Micaiah, son of
36 Zaccur, son of Asaph, and his kinsmen, Shemaiah, Azarel, Milalai, Gilalai, Maai, Nethaneel, Judah, and Hanani, with the musical instru-
37 ments of David the man of God; and Ezra the scribe led them. They went past the Fountain Gate and thence straight forward by the steps up to the City of David, by the ascent to the city wall, past the house of David, and
38 on to the Water Gate on the east. The other thanksgiving choir went to the left,[f] and I followed it with half the leading men of[g] the people, continuing
39 along the wall, past the Tower of the Ovens[h] to the Broad Wall, and past the Ephraim Gate, and over the Jeshanah Gate,[i] and over the Fish Gate, taking in the Tower of Hananel and the Tower of the Hundred, as far as
40 the Sheep Gate; and they halted at the Gate of the Guardhouse. So the two thanksgiving choirs took their place in the house of God, and I and
41 half the magistrates with me; and the priests Eliakim, Maaseiah, Miniamin,
42 Micaiah, Elioenai, Zechariah, and Hananiah, with trumpets; and Maaseiah, Shemaiah, Eleazar, Uzzi, Jehohanan, Malchiah, Elam, and Ezer. The
43 singers, led by Izrahiah, raised their voices. A great sacrifice was celebrated that day, and they all rejoiced because God had given them great cause for rejoicing; the women and children rejoiced with them. And the rejoicing in Jerusalem was heard a long way off.

44 On that day men were appointed to take charge of the store-rooms for the contributions, the firstfruits, and the tithes, to gather in the portions

---

[a] Jeshua, Binnui: *prob. rdg.; Heb.* and Jeshua son of.   [b] *Prob. rdg.; Heb.* and.
[c] the Levites: *prob. rdg.; Heb.* the sons of.   [d] Beth-azmoth: *prob. rdg., cp.* 7. 28;
Heb. Azmoth.   [e] One . . . procession: *prob. rdg.; Heb.* Processions.   [f] to the
left: *prob. rdg.; Heb.* to the front.   [g] the leading men of: *prob. rdg.; Heb. om.*
[h] *Or* Furnaces.   [i] the Jeshanah Gate: *or* the gate of the Old City.

required by the law for the priests and Levites according to the extent of the farmlands round the towns; for all Judah was full of rejoicing at the ministry of the priests and Levites. And they performed the service of their 45 God and the service of purification, as did the singers and the door-keepers, according to the rules laid down by David and his son Solomon. For it was 46 in the days of David that Asaph took the lead as chief of the singers and director*ᵃ* of praise and thanksgiving to God. And in the days of Zerubbabel 47 and of Nehemiah all Israel gave the portions for the singers and the door-keepers as each day required; and they set apart the portion for the Levites, and the Levites set apart the portion for the Aaronites.

Nehemiah's reforms

O N THAT DAY AT THE PUBLIC READING from the book of Moses, 13 it was found to be laid down that no Ammonite or Moabite should ever enter the assembly of God, because they did not meet the Israelites 2 with food and water but hired Balaam to curse them, though our God turned the curse into a blessing. When the people heard the law, they 3 separated from Israel all who were of mixed blood.

But before this, Eliashib the priest, who was appointed over the store- 4 rooms of the house of our God, and who was connected by marriage with Tobiah, had provided for his use a large room where formerly they had 5 kept the grain-offering, the incense, the temple vessels, the tithes of corn, new wine, and oil prescribed for the Levites, singers, and door-keepers, and the contributions for the priests. All this time I was not in Jerusalem 6 because, in the thirty-second year of Artaxerxes king of Babylon, I had gone to the king. Some time later, I asked permission from him and returned 7 to Jerusalem. There I discovered the wicked thing that Eliashib had done for Tobiah's sake in providing him with a room in the courts of the house of God. I was greatly displeased and threw all Tobiah's belongings out of 8 the room. Then I gave orders that the room should be purified, and that 9 the vessels of the house of God, with the grain-offering and incense, should be put back into it.

I also learnt that the Levites had not been given their portions; both they 10 and the singers, who were responsible for their respective duties, had made off to their farms. So I remonstrated with the magistrates and said, 'Why 11 is the house of God deserted?' And I recalled the men and restored them to their places. Then all Judah brought the tithes of corn, new wine, and 12 oil into the storehouses; and I put in charge of them Shelemiah the priest, 13 Zadok the accountant, and Pedaiah a Levite, with Hanan son of Zaccur, son of Mattaniah, as their assistant, for they were considered trustworthy men; their duty was the distribution of their shares to their brethren. Remember this, O God, to my credit, and do not wipe out of thy memory 14 the devotion which I have shown in the house of my God and in his service.

In those days I saw men in Judah treading winepresses on the sabbath, 15 collecting quantities of produce and piling it on asses—wine, grapes, figs,

ᵃ Prob. rdg.; Heb. song.

and every kind of load, which they brought into Jerusalem on the sabbath;
16 and I protested to them about selling food on that day. Tyrians living in
Jerusalem also brought in fish and all kinds of merchandise and sold them
17 on the sabbath to the people of Judah, even in Jerusalem. Then I complained to the nobles of Judah and said to them, 'How dare you profane
18 the sabbath in this wicked way? Is not this just what your fathers did, so
that our God has brought all this evil on us and on this city? Now you are
19 bringing more wrath upon Israel by profaning the sabbath.' When the
entrances to Jerusalem had been cleared in preparation for the sabbath, I
gave orders that the gates should be shut and not opened until after the
sabbath. And I appointed some of the men under me to have charge of the
20 gates so that no load might enter on the sabbath. Then on one or two
occasions the merchants and all kinds of traders camped just outside
21 Jerusalem, but I cautioned them. 'Why are you camping in front of the
city wall?' I asked. 'If you do it again, I will take action against you.' After
22 that they did not come on the sabbath again. And I commanded the
Levites who were to purify themselves and take up duty as guards at the
gates, to ensure that the sabbath was kept holy. Remember this also to my
credit, O God, and spare me in thy great love.

23   In those days also I saw that some Jews had married women from Ashdod,
24 Ammon, and Moab. Half their children spoke the language of Ashdod or
25 of the other peoples and could not speak the language of the Jews. I argued
with them and reviled them, I beat them and tore out their hair; and I
made them swear in the name of God: 'We will not marry our daughters
to their sons, or take any of their daughters in marriage for our sons or for
26 ourselves.' 'Was it not for such women', I said, 'that King Solomon of
Israel sinned? Among all the nations there was no king like him; he was
loved by his God, and God made him king over all Israel; nevertheless
27 even he was led by foreign women into sin. Are we then to follow your
example and commit this grave offence, breaking faith with our God by
marrying foreign women?'

28   Now one of the sons of Joiada son of Eliashib the high priest had married
a daughter of Sanballat the Horonite; therefore I drove him out of my
29 presence. Remember, O God, to their shame that they have defiled the
priesthood and the covenant of the priests *a* and the Levites.

30   Thus I purified them from everything foreign, and I made the Levites
31 and the priests resume the duties of their office; I also made provision for
the wood-offering, at appointed times, and for the firstfruits. Remember
me for my good, O God.

a Or priesthood.

ESTHER

Esther chosen as queen by the Persian king

THE EVENTS HERE RELATED happened in the days of 1 Ahasuerus, the Ahasuerus who ruled from India to Ethiopia, a hundred and twenty-seven provinces. At this time he sat on his royal 2 throne in Susa the capital city. In the third year of his reign he gave a 3 banquet for all his officers and his courtiers; and when his army of Persians and Medes, with his nobles and provincial governors, were in attendance, he displayed the wealth of his kingdom and the pomp and splendour of his 4 majesty for many days, a hundred and eighty in all. When these days were 5 over, the king gave a banquet for all the people present in Susa the capital city, both high and low; it was held in the garden court of the royal pavilion and lasted seven days. There were white curtains and violet hangings 6 fastened to silver rings with bands of fine linen and purple;*a* there were alabaster pillars and couches of gold and silver set on a mosaic pavement of malachite and alabaster, of mother-of-pearl and turquoise. Wine was 7 served in golden cups of various patterns: the king's wine flowed freely as befitted a king, and the law of the drinking was that there should be no 8 compulsion, for the king had laid it down that all the stewards of his palace should respect each man's wishes. In addition, Queen Vashti gave a 9 banquet for the women in the royal apartments of King Ahasuerus.

On the seventh day, when he was merry with wine, the king ordered 10 Mehuman, Biztha, Harbona, Bigtha, Abagtha, Zethar, and Carcas, the seven eunuchs who were in attendance on the king's person, to bring Queen 11 Vashti before him wearing her royal crown, in order to display her beauty to the people and the officers; for she was indeed a beautiful woman. But 12 Queen Vashti refused to come in answer to the royal command conveyed by the eunuchs. This greatly incensed the king, and he grew hot with anger.

Then the king conferred with his wise men versed in misdemeanours;*b* 13 for it was his royal custom to consult all who were versed in law and religion, those closest to him being Carshena, Shethar, Admatha, Tarshish, Meres, 14 Marsena, and Memucan, the seven princes of Persia and Media who had access to the king and held first place in the kingdom. He asked them, 15 'What does the law require to be done with Queen Vashti for disobeying the command of King Ahasuerus brought to her by the eunuchs?' Then 16 Memucan made answer before the king and the princes: 'Queen Vashti has done wrong, and not to the king alone, but also to all the officers and to all the peoples in all the provinces of King Ahasuerus. Every woman will 17 come to know what the queen has done, and this will make them treat their husbands with contempt; they will say, "King Ahasuerus ordered Queen

---

a bands . . . purple: *or* white and purple cords.   *b* *Or* times.

18 Vashti to be brought before him and she did not come." The great ladies of Persia and Media, who have heard of the queen's conduct, will tell all the king's officers about this day, and there will be endless disrespect and

19 insolence! If it please your majesty, let a royal decree go out from you and let it be inscribed in the laws of the Persians and Medes, never to be revoked, that Vashti shall not again appear before King Ahasuerus; and let the king give her place as queen to another woman who is more worthy

20 of it than she. Thus when this royal edict is heard through the length and breadth of the kingdom, all women will give honour to their husbands,

21 high and low alike.' Memucan's advice pleased the king and the princes,

22 and the king did as he had proposed. Letters were sent to all the royal provinces, to every province in its own script and to every people in their own language, in order that each man might be master in his own house and control all his own womenfolk.[a]

2   Later, when the anger of King Ahasuerus had died down, he remembered

2   Vashti and what she had done and what had been decreed against her. So the king's attendants said, 'Let beautiful young virgins be sought out for

3   your majesty; and let your majesty appoint commissioners in all the provinces of your kingdom to bring all these beautiful young virgins into the women's quarters in Susa the capital city. Let them be committed to the care of Hegai, the king's eunuch in charge of the women, and let cosmetics

4   be provided for them; and let the one who is most acceptable to the king become queen in place of Vashti.' This idea pleased the king and he acted on it.

5   Now there was in Susa the capital city a Jew named Mordecai son of

6   Jair, son of Shimei, son of Kish, a Benjamite; he had been carried into exile from Jerusalem among those whom Nebuchadnezzar king of Babylon

7   had carried away with Jeconiah king of Judah. He had a foster-child Hadassah, that is Esther, his uncle's daughter, who had neither father nor mother. She was a beautiful and charming girl, and after the death of her

8   father and mother Mordecai had adopted her as his own daughter. When the king's order and his edict were published, and many girls were brought to Susa the capital city to be committed to the care of Hegai, Esther too was taken to the king's palace to be entrusted to Hegai, who had charge

9   of the women. She attracted his notice and received his special favour: he readily provided her with her cosmetics and her allowance of food, and also with seven picked maids from the king's palace, and he gave her and her maids privileges in the women's quarters.

10 Esther had not disclosed her race or her family, because Mordecai had

11 forbidden her to do so. Every day Mordecai passed along by the forecourt of the women's quarters to learn how Esther was faring and what was happening to her.

12 The full period of preparation prescribed for the women was twelve months, six months with oil and myrrh and six months with perfumes and cosmetics. When the period was complete, each girl's turn came to go to

13 King Ahasuerus, and she was allowed to take with her whatever she asked,

14 when she went from the women's quarters to the king's palace. She went

[a] and control . . . womenfolk: *prob. rdg.; Heb.* and speak in his own language.

into the palace in the evening and returned in the morning to another part of the women's quarters, to be under the care of Shaashgaz, the king's eunuch in charge of the concubines. She did not again go to the king unless he expressed a wish for her; then she was summoned by name.

When the turn came for Esther, daughter of Abihail the uncle of 15 Mordecai her adoptive father, to go to the king, she asked for nothing to take with her except what was advised by Hegai, the king's eunuch in charge of the women; and Esther charmed all who saw her. When she was 16 taken to King Ahasuerus in the royal palace, in the seventh year of his reign, in the tenth month, that is the month Tebeth, the king loved her 17 more than any of his other women and treated her with greater favour and kindness than the rest of the virgins. He put a royal crown on her head and made her queen in place of Vashti. Then the king gave a great banquet for 18 all his officers and courtiers, a banquet in honour of Esther. He also proclaimed a holiday*a* throughout the provinces and distributed gifts worthy of a king.

Mordecai was in attendance at court; on his instructions Esther had 19 20 not disclosed her family or her race, she had done what Mordecai told her, as she did when she was his ward. One day when Mordecai was in attendance at court, Bigthan and Teresh, two of the king's eunuchs, keepers of 21 the threshold, who were disaffected, were plotting to lay hands on King Ahasuerus. This became known to Mordecai, who told Queen Esther; and 22 she told the king, mentioning Mordecai by name. The affair was investigated 23 and the report confirmed; the two men were hanged on the gallows. All this was recorded in the royal chronicle in the presence of the king.

Haman's plot against the Jews

AFTER THIS, KING AHASUERUS promoted Haman son of Hammedatha 3 the Agagite, advancing him and giving him precedence above all his fellow-officers. So the king's attendants at court all bowed down to Haman 2 and did obeisance, for so the king had commanded; but Mordecai did not bow down to him or do obeisance. Then the attendants at court said to 3 Mordecai, 'Why do you flout his majesty's command?' Day by day they 4 challenged him, but he refused to listen to them; so they informed Haman, in order to discover if Mordecai's refusal would be tolerated, for he had told them that he was a Jew. When Haman saw that Mordecai was not 5 bowing down to him or doing obeisance, he was infuriated. On learning 6 who Mordecai's people were, he scorned to lay hands on him alone, and looked for a way to destroy all the Jews throughout the whole kingdom of Ahasuerus, Mordecai and all his race.

In the twelfth year of King Ahasuerus, in the first month, Nisan, they 7 cast lots, Pur as it is called, in the presence of Haman, taking day by day and month by month, and the lot fell on the thirteenth day of the twelfth month,*b* the month Adar. Then Haman said to King Ahasuerus, 'There is 8

a Or an amnesty.   *b* and the lot . . . twelfth month: *prob. rdg., cp. verse 13; Heb.* the twelfth.

a certain people, dispersed among the many peoples in all the provinces of your kingdom, who keep themselves apart. Their laws are different from those of every other people; they do not keep your majesty's laws. It does
9 not befit your majesty to tolerate them. If it please your majesty, let an order be made in writing for their destruction; and I will pay ten thousand talents of silver to your majesty's officials, to be deposited in the royal
10 treasury.' So the king took the signet-ring from his hand and gave it to
11 Haman son of Hammedatha the Agagite, the enemy of the Jews; and he said to him, 'The money and the people are yours; deal with them as you wish.'

12   On the thirteenth day of the first month the king's secretaries were summoned and, in accordance with Haman's instructions, a writ was issued to the king's satraps and the governor of every province, and to the officers over each separate people: for each province in its own script and for each people in their own language. It was drawn up in the name of King
13 Ahasuerus and sealed with the king's signet. Thus letters were sent by courier to all the king's provinces with orders to destroy, slay, and exterminate all Jews, young and old, women and children, in one day, the thirteenth day of the twelfth month, the month Adar, and to plunder their
14 possessions. A copy of the writ was to be issued as a decree in every province and to be published to all the peoples, so that they might be ready for
15 that day. The couriers were dispatched post-haste at the king's command, and the decree was issued in Susa the capital city. The king and Haman sat down to drink; but the city of Susa was thrown into confusion.

4   When Mordecai learnt all that had been done, he rent his clothes, put on sackcloth and ashes, and went through the city crying loudly and bitterly.
2 He came within sight of the palace gate, because no one clothed with sack-
3 cloth was allowed to pass through the gate. In every province reached by the royal command and decree there was great mourning among the Jews, with fasting and weeping and beating of the breast. Most of them made
4 their beds of sackcloth and ashes. When Queen Esther's maids and eunuchs came and told her, she was distraught, and sent garments for Mordecai, so that they might take off the sackcloth and clothe him with them; but he
5 would not accept them. Then Esther summoned Hathach, one of the king's eunuchs who had been appointed to wait upon her, and ordered him to
6 find out from Mordecai what the trouble was and what it meant. Hathach
7 went to Mordecai in the city square in front of the palace gate, and Mordecai told him all that had happened to him and how much money Haman had offered to pay into the royal treasury for the destruction of the Jews.
8 He also gave him a copy of the writ for their destruction issued in Susa, so that he might show it to Esther and tell her about it, bidding her go to
9 the king to plead for his favour and entreat him for her people. Hathach
10 went and told Esther what Mordecai had said, and she sent him back with
11 this message: 'All the king's courtiers and the people of the provinces are aware that if any person, man or woman, enters the king's presence in the inner court unbidden, there is one law only: that person shall be put to death, unless the king stretches out to him the golden sceptre; then and then only shall he live. It is now thirty days since I myself was called to go

to the king.' But when they told Mordecai what Esther had said, he bade   12 13
them go back to her and say, 'Do not imagine that you alone of all the Jews
will escape because you are in the royal palace. If you remain silent at such   14
a time as this, relief and deliverance for the Jews will appear from another
quarter, but you and your father's family will perish. Who knows whether
it is not for such a time as this that you have come to royal estate?' Esther   15
gave them this answer to take back to Mordecai: 'Go and assemble all the   16
Jews to be found in Susa and fast for me; take neither food nor drink for
three days, night or day, and I and my maids will fast as you do. After that
I will go to the king, although it is against the law; and if I perish, I perish.'
So Mordecai went away and did exactly as Esther had bidden him.   17

On the third day Esther put on her royal robes and stood in the inner   5
court of the king's palace, facing the palace itself; the king was seated on
his royal throne in the palace, facing the entrance. When the king caught   2
sight of Queen Esther standing in the court, she won his favour and he
stretched out to her the golden sceptre which he was holding. Thereupon
Esther approached and touched the head of the sceptre. Then the king said   3
to her, 'What is it, Queen Esther? Whatever you ask of me, up to half my
kingdom, shall be given to you.' 'If it please your majesty,' said Esther,   4
'will you come today, sire, and Haman with you, to a banquet which I have
made ready for you?' The king gave orders that Haman should be fetched   5
quickly, so that Esther's wish might be fulfilled; and the king and Haman
went to the banquet which she had prepared. Over the wine the king said   6
to Esther, 'Whatever you ask of me shall be given to you. Whatever you
request of me, up to half my kingdom, it shall be done.' Esther said in   7
answer, 'What I ask and request of you is this. If I have won your majesty's   8
favour, and if it please you, sire, to give me what I ask and to grant my
request, will your majesty and Haman come tomorrow to the banquet
which I shall prepare for you both? Tomorrow I will do as your majesty
has said.'

So Haman went away that day in good spirits and well pleased with   9
himself. But when he saw Mordecai in attendance at court and how he did
not rise nor defer to him, he was filled with rage; but he kept control of   10
himself and went home. Then he sent for his friends and his wife Zeresh
and held forth to them about the splendour of his wealth and his many   11
sons, and how the king had promoted him and advanced him above the
other officers and courtiers. 'That is not all,' said Haman; 'Queen Esther   12
invited no one but myself to accompany the king to the banquet which she
had prepared; and she has invited me again tomorrow with the king. Yet   13
all this means nothing to me so long as I see that Jew Mordecai in attendance
at court.' Then his wife Zeresh and all his friends said to him, 'Let a gallows   14
seventy-five feet high be set up, and recommend to the king in the morning to have Mordecai hanged upon it. Then go with the king to the banquet
in good spirits.' Haman thought this an excellent plan, and he set up the
gallows.

Haman's downfall and Mordecai's triumph

6 **2** THAT NIGHT SLEEP ELUDED THE KING, so he ordered the chronicle of daily events to be brought; and it was read to him. Therein was recorded that Mordecai had given information about Bigthana and Teresh, the two royal eunuchs among the keepers of the threshold who had plotted to lay hands on King Ahasuerus. **3** Whereupon the king said, 'What honour or dignity has been conferred on Mordecai for this?' The king's courtiers who were in attendance told him that nothing had been done for Mordecai. **4** The king asked, 'Who is that in the court?' Now Haman had just entered the outer court of the palace to recommend to the king that Mordecai should **5** be hanged on the gallows which he had prepared for him. The king's servants answered, 'It is Haman standing there'; and the king bade him **6** enter. He came in, and the king said to him, 'What should be done for the man whom the king wishes to honour?' Haman said to himself, 'Whom **7** would the king wish to honour more than me?' And he said to the king, **8** 'For the man whom the king wishes to honour, let there be brought royal robes which the king himself wears, and a horse which the king rides, with **9** a royal crown upon its head. And let the robes and the horse be delivered to one of the king's most honourable officers, and let him attire the man whom the king wishes to honour and lead him mounted on the horse through the city square, calling out as he goes: "See what is done for the **10** man whom the king wishes to honour."' Then the king said to Haman, 'Fetch the robes and the horse at once, as you have said, and do all this for Mordecai the Jew who is in attendance at court. Leave nothing undone of **11** all that you have said.' So Haman took the robes and the horse, attired Mordecai, and led him mounted through the city square, calling out as he went: 'See what is done for the man whom the king wishes to honour.'

12 Then Mordecai returned to court and Haman hurried off home mourn- **13** ing, with head uncovered. He told his wife Zeresh and all his friends everything that had happened to him. And this was the reply of his friends and his wife Zeresh: 'If Mordecai, in face of whom your fortunes begin to fall, belongs to the Jewish race, you will not get the better of him; he will see your utter downfall.'

14 While they were still talking with Haman, the king's eunuchs arrived and hurried him away to the banquet which Esther had prepared.

7 1 2 So the king and Haman went to dine with Queen Esther. Again on that second day, over the wine, the king said, 'Whatever you ask of me will be given to you, Queen Esther. Whatever you request of me, up to half my **3** kingdom, it shall be done.' Queen Esther answered, 'If I have found favour with your majesty, and if it please your majesty, my request and petition is **4** that my own life and the lives of my people may be spared. For we have been sold, I and my people, to be destroyed, slain, and exterminated. If it had been a matter of selling us, men and women alike, into slavery, I should have kept silence; for then our plight would not be such as to injure the **5** king's interests.' Then King Ahasuerus said to Queen Esther, 'Who is he, **6** and where is he, who has presumed to do such a thing as this?' 'An adversary and an enemy,' said Esther, 'this wicked Haman.' At that Haman was

dumbfounded in the presence of the king and the queen. The king rose 7
from the banquet in a rage and went to the garden of the pavilion, while
Haman remained where he was, to plead for his life with Queen Esther;
for he saw that in the king's mind his fate was determined. When the king 8
returned from the garden to the banqueting hall, Haman had flung himself
across the couch on which Esther was reclining. The king exclaimed, 'Will
he even assault the queen here in my presence?' No sooner had the words
left the king's mouth than Haman hid his face in despair. [a] Then Harbona, 9
one of the eunuchs in attendance on the king, said, 'At Haman's house
stands the gallows, seventy-five feet high, which he himself has prepared
for Mordecai, who once served the king well.' 'Hang Haman on it', said
the king. So they hanged him on the gallows that he himself had prepared 10
for Mordecai. After that the king's rage abated.

On that day King Ahasuerus gave Queen Esther the house of Haman, 8
enemy of the Jews; and Mordecai came into the king's presence, for Esther
had told him how he was related to her. Then the king took off his signet- 2
ring, which he had taken back from Haman, and gave it to Mordecai. And
Esther put Mordecai in charge of Haman's house.

Once again Esther spoke before the king, falling at his feet in tears and 3
pleading with him to avert the calamity planned by Haman the Agagite
and to frustrate his plot against the Jews. The king stretched out the golden 4
sceptre to Esther, and she rose and stood before the king, and said, 'May 5
it please your majesty: if I have found favour with you, and if the proposal
seems right to your majesty and I have won your approval, let a writ be
issued to recall the letters which Haman son of Hammedatha the Agagite
wrote in pursuance of his plan to destroy the Jews in all the royal provinces.
For how can I bear to see the calamity which is coming upon my race? Or 6
how can I bear to see the destruction of my family?' Then King Ahasuerus 7
said to Queen Esther and to Mordecai the Jew, 'I have given Haman's house
to Esther, and he has been hanged on the gallows, because he threatened the
lives of the Jews. Now you shall issue a writ concerning the Jews in my 8
name, in whatever terms you think fit, and seal it with the royal signet; for
an order written in the name of the king and sealed with the royal signet
cannot be revoked.'

And so, on the twenty-third day of the third month, the month Sivan, 9
the king's secretaries were summoned; and a writ was issued to the Jews,
exactly as Mordecai directed, and to the satraps, the governors, and the
officers in the provinces from India to Ethiopia, a hundred and twenty-
seven provinces, for each province in its own script and for each people in
their own language, and also for the Jews in their own script and language.
The writ was drawn up in the name of King Ahasuerus and sealed with the 10
royal signet, and letters were sent by mounted couriers riding on horses
from the royal stables. By these letters the king granted permission to the 11
Jews in every city to unite and defend themselves, and to destroy, slay, and
exterminate the whole strength of any people or province which might
attack them, women and children too, and to plunder their possessions,
throughout all the provinces of King Ahasuerus, in one day, the thirteenth 12

[a] Haman . . . despair: *prob. rdg.*; *Heb.* they covered Haman's face.

13 day of the twelfth month, the month Adar. A copy of the writ was to be issued as a decree in every province and published to all peoples, and the Jews were to be ready for that day, the day of vengeance on their enemies.

14 So the couriers, mounted on their royal horses, were dispatched posthaste at the king's urgent command; and the decree was issued also in Susa the capital city.

15 Mordecai left the king's presence in royal robes of violet and white, wearing a great golden crown and a cloak of fine linen and purple, and all

16 the city of Susa shouted for joy. For the Jews there was light and joy,

17 gladness and honour. In every province and every city reached by the royal command and decree, there was joy and gladness for the Jews, feasting and holiday. And many of the peoples of the land professed themselves Jews, because fear of the Jews had seized them.

9 ON THE THIRTEENTH DAY of the twelfth month, the month Adar, the time came for the king's command and his edict to be carried out. The very day on which the enemies of the Jews had hoped to gain the upper hand over them was to become the day when the Jews should gain the upper

2 hand over those who hated them. On that day the Jews united in their cities in all the provinces of King Ahasuerus to fall upon those who had planned their ruin. No one could resist them, because fear of them had

3 seized all peoples. All the officers of the provinces, the satraps and the governors, and all the royal officials, aided the Jews, because fear of

4 Mordecai had seized them. Mordecai had become a great personage in the royal palace; his fame had spread throughout all the provinces as the power

5 of the man grew steadily greater. So the Jews put their enemies to the sword, with great slaughter and destruction; they worked their will on

6 those who hated them. In Susa, the capital city, the Jews killed five hundred

7 men and destroyed them; and they killed also Parshandatha, Dalphon and

8 9 Aspatha, Poratha, Adalia and Aridatha, Parmashta, Arisai, Aridai and

10 Vaizatha, the ten sons of Haman son of Hammedatha, the enemy of the Jews; but they did not touch the plunder.

11 That day when the number of those killed in Susa the capital city came to

12 the notice of the king, he said to Queen Esther, 'In Susa, the capital city, the Jews have killed and destroyed five hundred men and the ten sons of Haman. What have they done in the rest of the king's provinces? Whatever you ask further will be given to you; whatever more you seek shall be done.'

13 Esther answered him, 'If it please your majesty, let tomorrow be granted to the Jews in Susa to do according to the edict for today; and let the bodies

14 of Haman's ten sons be hung up on the gallows.' The king gave orders for this to be done; the edict was issued in Susa and Haman's ten sons were

15 hung up on the gallows. The Jews in Susa united again on the fourteenth day of the month Adar and killed three hundred men in Susa; but they did not touch the plunder.

16 The rest of the Jews in the king's provinces had united to defend themselves; they took vengeance on[a] their enemies by killing seventy-five thousand of those who hated them; but they did not touch the plunder.

a Prob. rdg.; Heb. got respite from.

This was on the thirteenth day of the month Adar, and they rested on the 17
fourteenth day and made that a day of feasting and joy. The Jews in Susa 18
had united on the thirteenth and fourteenth days of the month, and rested
on the fifteenth day and made that a day of feasting and joy. This is why 19
isolated Jews who live in remote villages keep the fourteenth day of the
month Adar in joy and feasting, as a holiday on which they send presents
of food to one another.

Then Mordecai set these things on record and sent letters to all the Jews 20
in all the provinces of King Ahasuerus, far and near, binding them to keep 21
the fourteenth and fifteenth days of the month Adar, year by year, as the 22
days on which the Jews obtained relief from their enemies and as the month
which was changed for them from sorrow into joy, from a time of mourning
to a holiday. They were to keep them as days of feasting and joy, days for
sending presents of food to one another and gifts to the poor.

So the Jews undertook to continue the practice that they had begun in 23
accordance with Mordecai's letter. This they did because Haman son of 24
Hammedatha the Agagite, the enemy of all the Jews, had plotted to destroy
the Jews and had cast lots, Pur as it is called, with intent to crush and
destroy them. But when the matter came before the king, he issued written 25
orders that the wicked plot which Haman had devised against the Jews
should recoil on his own head, and that he and his sons should be hanged on
the gallows. Therefore, these days were named Purim after the word Pur. 26
Accordingly, because of all that was written in this letter, because of all they
had seen and experienced in this affair, the Jews resolved and undertook, 27
on behalf of themselves, their descendants, and all who should join them,
that they would without fail keep these two days as a yearly festival in the
prescribed manner and at the appointed time; that these days should be re- 28
membered and kept, generation after generation, in every family, province,
and city, that the days of Purim should always be observed among the Jews,
and that the memory of them should never cease among their descendants.

Queen Esther daughter of Abihail gave full authority in writing to *a* 29
Mordecai the Jew, to confirm this second letter about Purim. Letters 30
wishing peace and security were sent to all the Jews in the hundred and
twenty-seven provinces of King Ahasuerus, making the observance of 31
these days of Purim at their appointed time binding on them, as Mordecai
the Jew *b* had prescribed. In the same way they had prescribed regulations
for fasts and lamentations for themselves and their descendants. The com- 32
mand of Esther confirmed these regulations for Purim, and the record is
preserved in writing.

King Ahasuerus imposed forced labour on the land and the coasts and **10**
islands. All the king's acts of authority and power, and the dignities which 2
he conferred on Mordecai, are written in the annals of the kings of Media
and Persia. For Mordecai the Jew was second only to King Ahasuerus; he 3
was a great man among the Jews and was popular with the mass of his
countrymen, for he sought the good of his people and promoted the welfare
of all their descendants. *c*

a Prob. rdg.; Heb. and.   *b Prob. rdg.; Heb. adds* and Queen Esther.   *c Or* and
was in friendly relations with all his race.

THE BOOK OF
JOB

Prologue

1 THERE LIVED IN THE LAND OF UZ a man of blameless
and upright life named Job, who feared God and set his face against
2 3 wrongdoing. He had seven sons and three daughters; and he owned
seven thousand sheep and three thousand camels, five hundred yoke of
oxen and five hundred asses, with a large number of slaves. Thus Job was
the greatest man in all the East.

4 Now his sons used to foregather and give, each in turn, a feast in his
own house; and they used to send and invite their three sisters to eat and
5 drink with them. Then, when a round of feasts was finished, Job sent for
his children and sanctified them, rising early in the morning and sacrificing
a whole-offering for each of them; for he thought that they might somehow
have sinned against God and committed blasphemy in their hearts. This
he always did.

6 The day came when the members of the court of heaven took their
places in the presence of the LORD, and Satan*a* was there among them.
7 The LORD asked him where he had been. 'Ranging over the earth', he said,
8 'from end to end.' Then the LORD asked Satan, 'Have you considered my
servant Job? You will find no one like him on earth, a man of blameless
and upright life, who fears God and sets his face against wrongdoing.'
9 Satan answered the LORD, 'Has not Job good reason to be God-fearing?
10 Have you not hedged him round on every side with your protection,
him and his family and all his possessions? Whatever he does you have
11 blessed, and his herds have increased beyond measure. But stretch out your
hand and touch all that he has, and then he will curse you to your face.'
12 Then the LORD said to Satan, 'So be it. All that he has is in your hands;
only Job himself you must not touch.' And Satan left the LORD's presence.

13 When the day came that Job's sons and daughters were eating and drink-
14 ing in the eldest brother's house, a messenger came running to Job and
15 said, 'The oxen were ploughing and the asses were grazing near them, when
the Sabaeans swooped down and carried them off, after putting the herds-
16 men to the sword; and I am the only one to escape and tell the tale.' While
he was still speaking, another messenger arrived and said, 'God's fire
flashed from heaven. It struck the sheep and the shepherds and burnt them
17 up; and I am the only one to escape and tell the tale.' While he was still
speaking, another arrived and said, 'The Chaldaeans, three bands of them,
have made a raid on the camels and carried them off, after putting the drivers

---

a Or the adversary.

to the sword; and I am the only one to escape and tell the tale.' While this 18
man was speaking, yet another arrived and said, 'Your sons and daughters
were eating and drinking in the eldest brother's house, when suddenly a 19
whirlwind swept across from the desert and struck the four corners of the
house, and it fell on the young people and killed them; and I am the only
one to escape and tell the tale.' At this Job stood up and rent his cloak; then 20
he shaved his head and fell prostrate on the ground, saying: 21

> Naked I came from the womb,
> naked I shall return whence I came.
> The LORD gives and the LORD takes away;
> blessed be the name of the LORD.

Throughout all this Job did not sin; he did not charge God with unreason. 22
    Once again the day came when the members of the court of heaven took 2
their places in the presence of the LORD, and Satan was there among them.
The LORD asked him where he had been. 'Ranging over the earth', he said, 2
'from end to end.' Then the LORD asked Satan, 'Have you considered my 3
servant Job? You will find no one like him on earth, a man of blameless and
upright life, who fears God and sets his face against wrongdoing. You
incited me to ruin him without a cause, but his integrity is still unshaken.'
Satan answered the LORD, 'Skin for skin! There is nothing the man will 4
grudge to save himself. But stretch out your hand and touch his bone and 5
his flesh, and see if he will not curse you to your face.'
    Then the LORD said to Satan, 'So be it. He is in your hands; but spare 6
his life.' And Satan left the LORD's presence, and he smote Job with running 7
sores from head to foot, so that he took a piece of a broken pot to scratch 8
himself as he sat among the ashes. Then his wife said to him, 'Are you still 9
unshaken in your integrity? Curse God and die!' But he answered, 'You 10
talk as any wicked fool of a woman might talk. If we accept good from God,
shall we not accept evil?' Throughout all this, Job did not utter one sinful
word.
    When Job's three friends, Eliphaz of Teman, Bildad of Shuah, and 11
Zophar of Naamah, heard of all these calamities which had overtaken him,
they left their homes and arranged to come and condole with him and
comfort him. But when they first saw him from a distance, they did not 12
recognize him; and they wept aloud, rent their cloaks and tossed dust into
the air over their heads. For seven days and seven nights they sat beside 13
him on the ground, and none of them said a word to him; for they saw that
his suffering was very great.

Job's complaint to God

After this Job broke silence and cursed the day of his birth: 3 1-2

> Perish the day when I was born 3
> and the night which said, 'A man is conceived'!
> May that day turn to darkness; may God above not look for it, 4
> nor light of dawn shine on it.

5   May blackness sully it, and murk and gloom,
    cloud smother that day, swift darkness eclipse its sun.
6   Blind darkness swallow up that night;
    count it not among the days of the year,
    reckon it not in the cycle of the months.
7   That night, may it be barren for ever,
    no cry of joy be heard in it.
8   Cursed be it by those whose magic binds even the monster of the deep,
    who are ready to tame Leviathan himself with spells.
9   May no star shine out in its twilight;
    may it wait for a dawn that never comes,
    nor ever see the eyelids of the morning,
10 because it did not shut the doors of the womb that bore me
    and keep trouble away from my sight.
11 Why was I not still-born,
    why did I not die when I came out of the womb?
12 Why was I ever laid on my mother's knees
    or put to suck at her breasts?
16 Why was I not hidden like an untimely birth,
    like an infant that has not lived to see the light?
13 For then I should be lying in the quiet grave,
    asleep in death, at rest,
14 with kings and their ministers
    who built themselves palaces,
15 with princes rich in gold
    who filled their houses with silver.
17 *a* There the wicked man chafes no more,
    there the tired labourer rests;
18 the captive too finds peace there
    and hears no taskmaster's voice;
19 high and low are there,
    even the slave, free from his master.

20 Why should the sufferer be born to see the light?
    Why is life given to men who find it so bitter?
21 They wait for death but it does not come,
    they seek it more eagerly than *b* hidden treasure.
22 They are glad when they reach the tomb,
    and when they come to the grave they exult.
23 Why should a man be born to wander blindly,
    hedged in by God on every side?
24 My sighing is all my food,
    and groans pour from me in a torrent.
25 Every terror that haunted me has caught up with me,
    and all that I feared has come upon me.
26 There is no peace of mind nor quiet for me;
    I chafe in torment and have no rest.

a Verse 16 transposed to follow verse 12.   *b Or seek it among . . .*

First cycle of speeches

Then Eliphaz the Temanite began: **4**

If one ventures to speak with you, will you lose patience? 2
For who could hold his tongue any longer?
Think how once you encouraged those who faltered, 3
how you braced feeble arms,
how a word from you upheld the stumblers 4
and put strength into weak knees.
But now that adversity comes upon you, you lose patience; 5
it touches you, and you are unmanned.
Is your religion no comfort to you? 6
Does your blameless life give you no hope?
For consider, what innocent man has ever perished? 7
Where have you seen the upright destroyed?
This I know, that those who plough mischief and sow trouble 8
reap as they have sown;
they perish at the blast of God 9
and are shrivelled by the breath of his nostrils.

The roar of the lion, the whimpering of his cubs, fall silent; 10
the teeth of the young lions are broken;
the lion perishes for lack of prey 11
and the whelps of the lioness are abandoned.

A word stole into my ears, 12
and they caught the whisper of it;
in the anxious visions of the night, 13
when a man sinks into deepest sleep,
terror seized me and shuddering; 14
the trembling of my body frightened me.
A wind brushed my face 15
and made the hairs bristle on my flesh;
and a figure stood there whose shape I could not discern, 16
an apparition loomed before me,
and I heard the sound of a low voice:
'Can mortal man be more righteous than God, 17
or the creature purer than his Maker?
If God mistrusts his own servants 18
and finds his messengers at fault,
how much more those that dwell in houses whose walls are clay, 19
whose foundations are dust,
which can be crushed like a bird's nest
or torn down between dawn and dark, 20
how much more shall such men perish outright and unheeded,
a die, without ever finding wisdom?' 21

a Prob. rdg.; transposing Their rich possessions are snatched from them to follow 5. 4.

5   Call if you will; is there any to answer you?
    To which of the holy ones will you turn?

2   The fool is destroyed by his own angry passions,
    and the end of childish resentment is death.

3   I have seen it for myself: a fool uprooted,
    his home in sudden ruin about him,[a]

4   his children past help,
    browbeaten in court with none to save them.

5   [b]Their rich possessions are snatched from them;
    what they have harvested others hungrily devour;
    the stronger man seizes it from the panniers,
    panting, thirsting for their wealth.

6   Mischief does not grow out of the soil
    nor trouble spring from the earth;

7   man is born to trouble,
    as surely as birds fly[c] upwards.

8   For my part, I would make my petition to God
    and lay my cause before him,

9   who does great and unsearchable things,
    marvels without number.

10 He gives rain to the earth
    and sends water on the fields;

11 he raises the lowly to the heights,
    the mourners are uplifted by victory;

12 he frustrates the plots of the crafty,
    and they win no success,

13 he traps the cunning in their craftiness,
    and the schemers' plans are thrown into confusion.

14 In the daylight they run into darkness,
    and grope at midday as though it were night.

15 He saves the destitute from their greed,
    and the needy from the grip of the strong;

16 so the poor hope again,
    and the unjust are sickened.

17 Happy the man whom God rebukes!
    therefore do not reject the discipline of the Almighty.

18 For, though he wounds, he will bind up;
    the hands that smite will heal.

19 You may meet disaster six times, and he will save you;
    seven times, and no harm shall touch you.

20 In time of famine he will save you from death,
    in battle from the sword.

21 You will be shielded from the lash of slander,[d]
    and when violence comes you need not fear.

---

[a] *ruin about him*: prob. rdg.; Heb. obscure.   [b] *Line transposed from 4. 21.*
[c] *Or* as sparks shoot.   [d] from . . . slander: *or* when slander is rife.

You will laugh at violence and starvation
and have no need to fear wild beasts;
for you have a covenant with the stones to spare your fields,
and the weeds have been constrained to leave you at peace.
You will know that all is well with your household,
you will look round your home and find nothing amiss;
you will know, too, that your descendants will be many
and your offspring like grass, thick upon the earth.
You will come in sturdy old age to the grave
as sheaves come in due season to the threshing-floor.

We have inquired into all this, and so it is;
this we have heard, and you may know it for the truth.

Then Job answered:

O that the grounds for my resentment might be weighed,
and my misfortunes set with them on the scales!
For they would outweigh the sands of the sea:
what wonder if my words are wild?*a*
The arrows of the Almighty find their mark in me,
and their poison soaks into my spirit;
God's onslaughts wear me away.
Does the wild ass bray when he has grass
or the ox low when he has fodder?
Can a man eat tasteless food unseasoned with salt,
or find any flavour in the juice of mallows?
Food that should nourish me sticks in my throat,
and my bowels rumble with an echoing sound.

O that I might have my request,
that God would grant what I hope for:
that he would be pleased to crush me,
to snatch me away with his hand and cut me off!
For that would bring me relief,
and in the face of unsparing anguish I would leap for joy.*b*
Have I the strength to wait?
What end have I to expect, that I should be patient?
Is my strength the strength of stone,
or is my flesh bronze?
Oh how shall I find help within myself?
The power to aid myself is put out of my reach.

Devotion is due from his friends
to one who despairs and loses faith in the Almighty;
but my brothers have been treacherous as a mountain stream,
like the channels of streams that run dry,

22
23
24
25
26

27

6
2

3

4

5

6

7

8

9

10

11

12

13

14

15

what . . . wild?: *or therefore words fail me.*   *b Prob. rdg.; Heb. adds* I have not
enied the words of the Holy One.

565

16   which turn dark with ice
     or are hidden with piled-up snow;
17   or they vanish the moment they are in spate,
     dwindle in the heat and are gone.
18   Then the caravans, winding hither and thither,
     go up into the wilderness and perish;[a]
19   the caravans of Tema look for their waters,
     travelling merchants of Sheba hope for them;
20   but they are disappointed, for all their confidence,
     they reach them only to be balked.
21   So treacherous have you now been to me:[b]
     you felt dismay and were afraid.
22   Did I ever say, 'Give me this or that;
     open your purses to save my life;
23   rescue me from my enemy;
     ransom me out of the hands of ruthless men'?

24   Tell me plainly, and I will listen in silence;
     show me where I have erred.
25   How harsh are the words of the upright man!
     What do the arguments of wise men[c] prove?
26   Do you mean to argue about words
     or to sift the utterance of a man past hope?
27   Would you assail an orphan[d]?
     Would you hurl yourselves on a friend?
28   So now, I beg you, turn and look at me:
     am I likely to lie to your faces?
29   Think again, let me have no more injustice;
     think again, for my integrity is in question.
30   Do I ever give voice to injustice?
     Does my sense not warn me when my words are wild?

7   Has not man hard service on earth,
     and are not his days like those of a hired labourer,
2   like those of a slave longing for the shade
     or a servant kept waiting for his wages?
3   So months of futility are my portion,
     troubled nights are my lot.
4   When I lie down, I think,
     'When will it be day that I may rise?'
     When the evening grows long and I lie down,
     I do nothing but toss till morning twilight.
5   My body is infested with worms,
     and scabs cover my skin.[e]
6   My days are swifter than a shuttle[f]
     and come to an end as the thread runs out.[g]

---

[a] *Or* and are lost.   [b] So ... to me: *prob. rdg.; Heb. obscure.*   [c] wise men:
prob. rdg.; Heb. unintelligible.   [d] *Or* a blameless man.   [e] *Prob. rdg.; Heb. adds it*
is cracked and discharging.   [f] *Or* a fleeting odour.   [g] as ... out: *or* without hope.

Remember, my life is but a breath of wind;   7
I shall never again see good days.
Thou wilt behold me no more with a seeing eye;   8
under thy very eyes I shall disappear.
As clouds break up and disperse,   9
so he that goes down to Sheol never comes back;
he never returns home again,   10
and his place will know him no more.^{*a*}

But I will not hold my peace;   11
I will speak out in the distress of my mind
and complain in the bitterness of my soul.
Am I the monster of the deep, am I the sea-serpent,   12
that thou settest a watch over me?
When I think that my bed will comfort me,   13
that sleep will relieve my complaining,
thou dost terrify me with dreams   14
and affright me with visions.
I would rather be choked outright;   15
I would prefer death to all my sufferings.
I am in despair, I would not go on living;   16
leave me alone, for my life is but a vapour.
What is man that thou makest much of him   17
and turnest thy thoughts towards him,
only to punish him morning by morning   18
or to test him every hour of the day?
Wilt thou not look away from me for an instant?   19
Wilt thou not let me be while I swallow my spittle?
If I have sinned, how do I injure thee,   20
thou watcher of the hearts of men?
Why hast thou made me thy butt,
and why have I become thy target?
Why dost thou not pardon my offence   21
and take away my guilt?
But now I shall lie down in the grave;
seek me, and I shall not be.

Then Bildad the Shuhite began: **8**

How long will you say such things,   2
the long-winded ramblings of an old man?
Does God pervert judgement?   3
Does the Almighty pervert justice?
Your sons sinned against him,   4
so he left them to be victims of their own iniquity.
If only you will seek God betimes   5
and plead for the favour of the Almighty,

^{*a*} *Or* and he will not be noticed any more in his place.

6   if you are innocent and upright,
    then indeed will he watch over you
    and see your just intent fulfilled.
7   Then, though your beginnings were humble,
    your end will be great.

8   Inquire now of older generations
    and consider the experience of their fathers;
9   for we ourselves are of yesterday and are transient;
    our days on earth are a shadow.
10 Will not they speak to you and teach you
    and pour out the wisdom of their hearts?
11 Can rushes grow where there is no marsh?
    Can reeds flourish without water?
12 While they are still in flower and not ready to cut, *a*
    they wither earlier than *b* any green plant.
13 Such is the fate of all who forget God;
    the godless man's life-thread breaks off;
14 his confidence is gossamer,
    and the ground of his trust a spider's web.
15 He leans against his house but it does not stand;
    he clutches at it but it does not hold firm.
16 His is the lush growth of a plant in the sun,
    pushing out shoots over the garden;
17 but its roots become entangled in a stony patch
    and run against a bed of rock.
18 Then someone uproots it from its place,
    which*c* disowns it and says, 'I have never known you.'
19 That is how its life withers away,
    and other plants spring up from the earth.

20 Be sure, God will not spurn the blameless man,
    nor will he grasp the hand of the wrongdoer.
21 He will yet fill your mouth with laughter,
    and shouts of joy will be on your lips;
22 your enemies shall be wrapped in confusion,
    and the tents of the wicked shall vanish away.

9 Then Job answered:

2   Indeed this I know for the truth,
    that no man can win his case against God.
3   If a man chooses to argue with him,
    God will not answer one question in a thousand.*d*
4   He is wise, he is powerful;
    what man has stubbornly resisted him and survived?

---

a and . . . cut: *or* they are surely cut.   *b* *Or* wither like . . .   *c* *Or* and.
d If a man . . . thousand: *or* If God is pleased to argue with him, man cannot answer one
question in a thousand.

It is God who moves mountains, giving them no rest,   5
turning them over in his wrath;
who makes the earth start from its place   6
so that its pillars are convulsed;
who commands the sun's orb not to rise   7
and shuts up the stars under his seal;
who by himself spread out the heavens   8
and trod on the sea-monster's back; *a*
who made Aldebaran and Orion,   9
the Pleiades and the circle of the southern stars;
who does great and unsearchable things,   10
marvels without number.

He passes by me, and I do not see him;   11
he moves on his way undiscerned by me;
if he hurries on, who can bring him back?   12
Who will ask him what he does?
God does not turn back his wrath;   13
the partisans of Rahab lie prostrate at his feet.
How much less can I answer him   14
or find words to dispute with him?
Though I am right, I get no answer,   15
though I plead with my accuser for mercy.
If I summoned him to court and he responded,   16
I do not believe that he would listen to my plea—
for he bears hard upon me for a trifle   17
and rains blows on me without cause;
he leaves me no respite to recover my breath   18
but fills me with bitter thoughts.
If the appeal is to force, see how strong he is;   19
if to justice, who can compel him to give me a hearing?
Though I am right, he condemns me out of my own mouth;   20
though I am blameless, he twists my words.
Blameless, I say; of myself   21
I reck nothing, I hold my life cheap.
But it is all one; therefore I say,   22
'He destroys blameless and wicked alike.'
When a sudden flood brings death,   23
he mocks the plight of the innocent.
The land is given over to the power of the wicked,   24
and the eyes of its judges are blindfold. *b*

My days have been swifter than a runner,   25
they have slipped away and seen no prosperity;
they have raced by like reed-built skiffs,   26
swift as vultures swooping on carrion.

---

a *Or* on the crests of the waves.   *b* *Prob. rdg.; Heb. adds* if not he, then who?

27   If I think, 'I will forget my griefs,
I will show a cheerful face and smile',

28   I tremble in every nerve;[a]
I know that thou wilt not hold me innocent.

29   If I am to be accounted guilty,
why do I labour in vain?

30   Though I wash myself with soap
or cleanse my hands with lye,

31   thou wilt thrust me into the mud
and my clothes will make me loathsome.

32   He is not a man as I am, that I can answer him
or that we can confront one another in court.

33   If only there were one to arbitrate between us
and impose his authority on us both,

34   so that God might take his rod from my back,
and terror of him might not come on me suddenly.

35   I would then speak without fear of him;
for I know I am not what I am thought to be.

10   I am sickened of life;
I will give free rein to my griefs,
I will speak out in bitterness of soul.

2   I will say to God, 'Do not condemn me,
but tell me the ground of thy complaint against me.

3   Dost thou find any advantage in oppression,
in spurning the fruit of all thy labour
and smiling on the policy of wicked men?

4   Hast thou eyes of flesh
or dost thou see as mortal man sees?

5   Are thy days as those of a mortal
or thy years as the life of a man,

6   that thou lookest for guilt in me
and dost seek in me for sin,

7   though thou knowest that I am guiltless
and have none to save me from thee?

8   'Thy hands gave me shape and made me;
and dost thou at once turn and destroy me?

9   Remember that thou didst knead me like clay;
and wouldst thou turn me back into dust?

10   Didst thou not pour me out like milk
and curdle me like cheese,

11   clothe me with skin and flesh
and knit me together with bones and sinews?

12   Thou hast given me life and continuing favour,
and thy providence has watched over my spirit.

[a] *Or* I am afraid of all that I must suffer.

Yet this was the secret purpose of thy heart,   13
and I know that this was thy intent:
that, if I sinned, thou wouldst be watching me   14
and wouldst not acquit me of my guilt.
If I indeed am wicked, the worse for me!   15
If I am righteous, even so I may lift up my head; *a*
if I am proud as a lion, thou dost hunt me down   16
and dost confront me again with marvellous power;
thou dost renew thy onslaught upon me,   17
and with mounting anger against me
bringest fresh forces to the attack.
Why didst thou bring me out of the womb?   18
O that I had ended there and no eye had seen me,
that I had been carried from the womb to the grave   19
and were as though I had not been born.
Is not my life short and fleeting?   20
Let me be, that I may be happy for a moment,
before I depart to a land of gloom,   21
a land of deep darkness, never to return,
a land of gathering shadows, of deepening darkness,   22
lit by no ray of light, *b* dark *c* upon dark.'

Then Zophar the Naamathite began: **11**

Should this spate of words not be answered?   2
Must a man of ready tongue be always right?
Is your endless talk to reduce men to silence?   3
Are you to talk nonsense and no one rebuke you?
You claim that your opinions are sound;   4
you say to God, 'I am spotless in thy sight.'
But if only he would speak   5
and open his lips to talk with you,
and expound to you the secrets of wisdom,   6
for wonderful are its effects!
[Know then that God exacts from you less than your sin deserves.]
Can you fathom the mystery of God,   7
can you fathom the perfection of the Almighty?
It is higher than heaven; you can do nothing.   8
It is deeper than Sheol; you can know nothing.
Its measure is longer than the earth   9
and broader than the sea.
If he passes by, he may keep secret his passing;   10
if he proclaims it, who can turn him back?
He surely knows which men are false,   11
and when he sees iniquity, does he not take note of it? *d*

a Prob. rdg.; Heb. adds filled with shame and steeped in my affliction.   *b* lit . . .
light: *or* a place of disorder.   *c Prob. rdg.; Heb. obscure.*   *d* does . . . of it?:
or he does not stand aloof.

12   Can a fool grow wise?
      can a wild ass's foal be born a man?

13   If only you had directed your heart rightly
      and spread out your hands to pray to him!

14   If you have wrongdoing in hand, thrust it away;
      let no iniquity make its home with you.

15   Then you could hold up your head without fault,
      a man of iron, knowing no fear.

16   Then you will forget your trouble;
      you will remember it only as flood-waters that have passed;

17   life will be lasting, bright as noonday,
      and darkness will be turned to morning.

18   You will be confident, because there is hope;
      sure of protection, you will lie down in confidence;[a]

19   great men will seek your favour.

20   Blindness will fall on the wicked;
      the ways of escape are closed to them,
      and their hope is despair.

12   Then Job answered:

2   No doubt you are perfect men[b]
      and absolute wisdom is yours!

3   But I have sense as well as you;
      in nothing do I fall short of you;
      what gifts indeed have you that others have not?

4   Yet I am a laughing-stock to my friend—
      a laughing-stock, though I am innocent and blameless,
      one that called upon God, and he answered.[c]

5   Prosperity and ease look down on misfortune,
      on the blow that fells the man who is already reeling,

6   while the marauders' tents are left undisturbed
      and those who provoke God live safe and sound. [d]

7   Go and ask the cattle,
      ask the birds of the air to inform you,

8   or tell the creatures that crawl to teach you,
      and the fishes of the sea to give you instruction.

9   Who cannot learn from all these
      that the LORD's own hand has done this?

11[e]   (Does not the ear test what is spoken
      as the palate savours food?

12   There is wisdom, remember, in age,
      and long life brings understanding.)

---

[a] *Prob. rdg.; Heb. adds* and you will lie down unafraid.
doubt you are people.   [c] *Or* and he afflicted me.
adds He brings it in full measure to whom he will (*cp. 21. 17*).
posed to follow verse 12.

[b] *Prob. rdg.; Heb.* No
[d] *Prob. rdg.; Heb.*
[e] *Verse 10 trans-*

In God's hand are the souls of all that live,   10
the spirits of all human kind.
Wisdom and might are his,   13
with him are firmness and understanding.
If he pulls down, there is no rebuilding;   14
if he imprisons, there is no release.
If he holds up the waters, there is drought;   15
if he lets them go, they turn the land upside down.
Strength and success belong to him,   16
deceived and deceiver are his to use.
He makes counsellors behave like idiots   17
and drives judges mad;
he looses the bonds imposed by kings   18
and removes the girdle of office from their waists;
he makes priests behave like idiots   19
and overthrows men long in office;
those who are trusted he strikes dumb,   20
he takes away the judgement of old men;
he heaps scorn on princes   21
and abates the arrogance of nobles.
He leads peoples astray and destroys them,   23[a]
he lays them low, and there they lie.
He takes away their wisdom from the rulers of the nations   24
and leaves them wandering in a pathless wilderness;
they grope in the darkness without light   25
and are left to wander like a drunkard.
He uncovers mysteries deep in obscurity   22
and into thick darkness he brings light.

All this I have seen with my own eyes,   **13**
with my own ears I have heard it, and understood it.
What you know, I also know;   2
in nothing do I fall short of you.
But for my part I would speak with the Almighty   3
and am ready to argue with God,
while you like fools are smearing truth with your falsehoods,   4
stitching a patchwork of lies, one and all.
Ah, if you would only be silent   5
and let silence be your wisdom!
Now listen to my arguments   6
and attend while I put my case.
Is it on God's behalf that you speak so wickedly,   7
or in his defence that you allege what is false?
Must you take God's part,   8
or put his case for him?
Will all be well when he examines you?   9
Will you quibble with him as you quibble with a man?

a Verse 22 transposed to follow verse 25.

10 He will most surely expose you
   if you take his part by falsely accusing me.
11 Will not God's majesty strike you with dread,
   and terror of him overwhelm you?
12 Your pompous talk is dust and ashes,
   your defences will crumble like clay.
13 Be silent, leave me to speak my mind,
   and let what may come upon me!
14 I will put my neck in the noose
   and take my life in my hands.
15 If he would slay me, I should not hesitate;
   I should still argue my cause to his face.
16 This at least assures my success,
   that no godless man may appear before him.
17 Listen then, listen to my words,
   and give a hearing to my exposition.
18 Be sure of this: once I have stated my case
   I know that I shall be acquitted.
19 Who is there that can argue so forcibly with me
   that he could reduce me straightway to silence and death?

20 Grant me these two conditions only,
   and then I will not hide myself out of thy sight:
21 take thy heavy hand clean away from me
   and let not the fear of thee strike me with dread.
22 Then summon me, and I will answer;
   or I will speak first, and do thou answer me.
23 How many iniquities and sins are laid to my charge?
   let me know my offences and my sin.
24 Why dost thou hide thy face
   and treat me as thy enemy?
25 Wilt thou chase a driven leaf,
   wilt thou pursue dry chaff,
26 prescribing punishment for me
   and making me heir to the iniquities of my youth,
27 putting my feet in the stocks[a]
   and setting a slave-mark on the arches of my feet?[b]

14 Man born of woman is short-lived and full of disquiet.
2 He blossoms like a flower and then he withers;
   he slips away like a shadow and does not stay;
   [c] he is like a wine-skin that perishes
   or a garment that moths have eaten.
3 Dost thou fix thine eyes on such a creature,
   and wilt thou bring him into court to confront thee?[d]

[a] *Prob. rdg.; Heb. adds* keeping a close watch on all I do.   [b] *Prob. rdg.; Heb. adds* verse 28, he is like . . . have eaten, *now transposed to follow 14. 2.*   [c] he is like . . . have eaten: *13. 28 transposed here.*   [d] *So one Heb. MS.; others add* (4) Who can produce pure out of unclean? No one.

The days of his life are determined,   5
and the number of his months is known to thee;
thou hast laid down a limit, which he cannot pass.
Look away from him therefore and leave him alone   6
counting the hours day by day like a hired labourer.

If a tree is cut down,   7
there is hope that it will sprout again
and fresh shoots will not fail.
Though its roots grow old in the earth,   8
and its stump is dying in the ground,
if it scents water it may break into bud   9
and make new growth like a young plant.
But a man dies, and he disappears;^{*a*}   10
man comes to his end, and where is he?
As the waters of a lake dwindle,   11
or as a river shrinks and runs dry,
so mortal man lies down, never to rise   12
until the very sky splits open.
If a man dies, can he live again? ^{*b*}
He shall never be roused from his sleep.
If only thou wouldst hide me in Sheol   13
and conceal me till thy anger turns aside,
if thou wouldst fix a limit for my time there, and then remember me!
^{*c*} Then I would not lose hope, however long my service,   14
waiting for my relief to come.
Thou wouldst summon me, and I would answer thee;   15
thou wouldst long to see the creature thou hast made.
But now thou dost count every step I take,   16
watching all my course.
Every offence of mine is stored in thy bag;   17
thou dost keep my iniquity under seal.
Yet as a falling mountain-side is swept away,   18
and a rock is dislodged from its place,
as water wears away stones,   19
and a rain-storm scours the soil from the land,
so thou hast wiped out the hope of frail man;
thou dost overpower him finally, and he is gone;   20
his face is changed, and he is banished from thy sight.
His flesh upon him becomes black,   22 ^{*d*}
and his life-blood dries up within him. ^{*e*}
His sons rise to honour, and he sees nothing of it;   21
they sink into obscurity, and he knows it not.

---

^{*a*} *Or* and is powerless.   ^{*b*} *Line transposed from beginning of verse 14.*   ^{*c*} *See note*
on verse 12.   ^{*d*} *Verses 21 and 22 transposed.*   ^{*e*} His flesh . . . within him: *or*
His own kin, maybe, regret him, and his slaves mourn his loss.

Second cycle of speeches

15 Then Eliphaz the Temanite answered:

2   Would a man of sense give vent to such foolish notions
    and answer with a bellyful of wind?

3   Would he bandy useless words
    and arguments so unprofitable?

4   Why! you even banish the fear of God from your mind,
    usurping the sole right to speak in his presence;

5   your iniquity dictates what you say,
    and deceit is the language of your choice.

6   You are condemned out of your own mouth, not by me;
    your own lips give evidence against you.

7   Were you born first of mankind?
    were you brought forth before the hills?

8   Do you listen in God's secret council
    or usurp all wisdom for yourself alone?

9   What do you know that we do not know?
    What insight have you that we do not share?

10   We have age and white hairs in our company,
    men older than your father.

11   Does not the consolation of God suffice you,
    a word whispered quietly in your ear?

12   What makes you so bold at heart,
    and why do your eyes flash,

13   that you vent your anger on God
    and pour out such a torrent of words?

14   What is frail man that he should be innocent,
    or any child of woman that he should be justified?

15   If God puts no trust in his holy ones,
    and the heavens are not innocent in his sight,

16   how much less so is man, who is loathsome and rotten
    and laps up evil like water!

17   I will tell you, if only you will listen,
    and I will describe what I have seen

18   [what has been handed down by wise men
    and was not concealed from them by their fathers;

19   to them alone the land was given,
    and no foreigner settled among them]:

20   the wicked are racked with anxiety all their days,
    the ruthless man for all the years in store for him.

21   The noise of the hunter's scare rings in his ears,
    and in time of peace the raider falls on him;

22   he cannot hope to escape from dark death;
    he is marked down for the sword;

he is flung out as food for vultures;   23
such a man knows that his destruction is certain.
Suddenly a black day comes upon him,   24
distress and anxiety overwhelm him
[like a king ready for battle];
for he has lifted his hand against God   25
and is pitting himself against the Almighty,
charging him head down,   26
with the full weight of his bossed shield.

Heavy though his jowl is and gross,   27
and though his sides bulge with fat,
the city where he lives will lie in ruins,   28
his house will be deserted;
it will soon become a heap of rubble.
He will no longer be rich, his wealth will not last,   29
and he will strike no root in the earth; *a*
scorching heat will shrivel his shoots,   30
and his blossom will be shaken off by the wind.
He deceives himself, trusting in his high rank,   31
for all his dealings will come to nothing.
His palm-trees will wither unseasonably,   32
and his branches will not spread;
he will be like a vine that sheds its unripe grapes,   33
like an olive-tree that drops its blossom.
For the godless, one and all, are barren,   34
and their homes, enriched by bribery, are destroyed by fire;
they conceive mischief and give birth to trouble,   35
and the child of their womb is deceit.

Then Job answered: **16**

I have heard such things often before,   2
you who make trouble, all of you, with every breath,
saying, 'Will this windbag never have done?   3
What makes him so stubborn in argument?'
If you and I were to change places,   4
I could talk like you;
how I could harangue you
and wag my head at you!
But no, I would speak words of encouragement,   5
and then my condolences would flow in streams.
If I speak, my pain is not eased;   6
if I am silent, it does not leave me.
Meanwhile, my friend wearies me with false sympathy;   7
they tear me to pieces, he and his *b* fellows.   8
He has come forward to give evidence against me;

a *Prob. rdg.; Heb. adds* he will not escape from darkness.   *b* *Prob. rdg.; Heb.* my.

the liar testifies against me to my face,
9   in his wrath he wears me down, his hatred is plain to see;
    he grinds his teeth at me.

    My enemies look daggers at me,
10 they bare their teeth to rend me,
    they slash my cheeks with knives;
    they are all in league against me.
11 God has left me at the mercy of malefactors
    and cast me into the clutches of wicked men.
12 I was at ease, but he set upon me and mauled me,
    seized me by the neck and worried me.
    He set me up as his target;
13 his arrows rained upon me from every side;
    pitiless, he cut deep into my vitals,
    he spilt my gall on the ground.
14 He made breach after breach in my defences;
    he fell upon me like a fighting man.

15 I stitched sackcloth together to cover my body
    and I buried my forelock in the dust;
16 my cheeks were flushed with weeping
    and dark shadows were round my eyes,
17 yet my hands were free from violence
    and my prayer was sincere.

18 O earth, cover not my blood
    and let my cry for justice find no rest!
19 For look! my witness is in heaven;
    there is one on high ready to answer for me.
20 My appeal will come before God,
    while my eyes turn again and again to him.
21 If only there were one to arbitrate between man and God,
    as between a man and his neighbour!
22 For there are but few years to come
    before I take the road from which I shall not return.

17 My mind is distraught, my days are numbered,
    and the grave is waiting for me.
2   Wherever I turn, men taunt me,
    and my day is darkened by their sneers.
3   Be thou my surety with thyself,
    for who else can pledge himself for me?
4   Thou wilt not let those men triumph,
    whose minds thou hast sunk in ignorance;
5   if such a man denounces his friends to their ruin,
    his sons' eyes shall grow dim.

6   I am held up as a byword in every land,
    a portent for all to see;

my eyes are dim with grief,   7
my limbs wasted to a shadow.
Honest men are bewildered at this,   8
and the innocent are indignant at my plight.
In spite of all, the righteous man maintains his course,   9
and he whose hands are clean grows strong again.

But come on, one and all, try again!   10
I shall not find a wise man among you.

My days die away like an echo;   11
my heart-strings^a are snapped.
Day is turned into night,   12
and morning ^b light is darkened before me.
If I measure Sheol for my house,   13
if I spread my couch in the darkness,
if I call the grave my father   14
and the worm my mother or my sister,
where, then, will my hope be,   15
and who will take account of my piety?
I cannot take them down to Sheol with me,   16
nor can they descend with me into the earth.

Then Bildad the Shuhite answered: **18**

How soon will you bridle ^c your tongue?   2
Do but think, and then we will talk.
What do you mean by treating us as cattle?   3
Are we nothing but brute beasts to you? ^d
Is the earth to be deserted to prove you right,   4
or the rocks to be moved from their place?

No, it is the wicked whose light is extinguished,   5
from whose fire no flame will rekindle;
the light fades in his tent,   6
and his lamp dies down and fails him.
In his iniquity his steps totter,   7
and his disobedience trips him up;
he rushes headlong into a net   8
and steps through the hurdle that covers a pit;
his heel is caught in a snare,   9
the noose grips him tight;
a cord lies hidden in the ground for him   10
and a trap in the path.
The terrors of death suddenly beset him   11
and make him piss over his feet.

^a *Prob. rdg.; Heb.* the desires of my heart.   ^b morning: *prob. rdg.; Heb.* near.
^c bridle: *prob. rdg.; Heb. unintelligible.*   ^d *Prob. rdg.; Heb. adds* rending himself
in his anger.

12   For all his vigour he is paralysed with fear;
       strong as he is, disaster awaits him.

13   Disease eats away his skin,
       Death's eldest child devours his limbs.

14   He is torn from the safety of his home,
       and Death's terrors escort him to their king. *a*

15   Magic herbs lie strewn about his tent,
       and his home is sprinkled with sulphur to protect it.

16   His roots beneath dry up,
       and above, his branches wither.

17   His memory vanishes from the face of the earth
       and he leaves no name in the world.

18   He is driven from light into darkness
       and banished from the land of the living.

19   He leaves no issue or offspring among his people,
       no survivor in his earthly home;

20   in the west men hear of his doom and are appalled;
       in the east they shudder with horror.

21   Such is the fate of the dwellings of evildoers,
       and of the homes of those who care nothing for God.

19   Then Job answered:

2   How long will you exhaust me
       and pulverize me with words?

3   Time and time again you have insulted me
       and shamelessly done me wrong.

4   If in fact I had erred,
       the error would still be mine.

5   But if indeed you lord it over me
       and try to justify the reproaches levelled at me,

6   I tell you, God himself has put me in the wrong,
       he has drawn the net round me.

7   If I cry 'Murder!' no one answers;
       if I appeal for help, I get no justice.

8   He has walled in my path so that I cannot break away,
       and he has hedged in the road before me.

9   He has stripped me of all honour
       and has taken the crown from my head.

10   On every side he beats me down and I am gone;
       he has pulled up my tent-rope *b* like a tree.

11   His anger is hot against me
       and he counts me his enemy.

12   His raiders gather in force *c*
       and encamp about my tent.

---

a *Or* and you conduct him to the king of terrors.   *b* *Or* he has uprooted my hope.
c *Prob. rdg.; Heb. adds* they raise an earthwork against me.

My brothers hold aloof from me,   13
my friends are utterly estranged from me;
my kinsmen and intimates fall away,   14-15
my retainers have forgotten me;
my slave-girls treat me as a stranger,
I have become an alien in their eyes.
I summon my slave, but he does not answer,   16
though I entreat him as a favour.
My breath is noisome to my wife,   17
and I stink in the nostrils of my own family.
Mere children despise me   18
and, when I rise, turn their backs on me;
my intimate companions loathe me,   19
and those whom I love have turned against me.
My bones stick out through my skin,*a*   20
and I gnaw my under-lip with my teeth.

Pity me, pity me, you that are my friends;   21
for the hand of God has touched me.
Why do you pursue me as God pursues me?   22
Have you not had your teeth in me long enough?
O that my words might be inscribed,   23
O that they might be engraved in an inscription,
cut with an iron tool and filled with lead   24
to be a witness*b* in hard rock!
But in my heart I know that my vindicator lives   25
and that he will rise last to speak in court;
and I shall discern my witness standing at my side*c*   26
and see my defending counsel, even God himself,
whom I shall see with my own eyes,   27
I myself and no other.

My heart failed me when you said,   28
'What a train of disaster he has brought on himself!
The root of the trouble lies in him.'
Beware of the sword that points at you,   29
the sword that sweeps away all iniquity;
then you will know that there is a judge.*d*

Then Zophar the Naamathite answered: **20**

My distress of mind forces me to reply,   2
and this is why*e* I hasten to speak:
I have heard arguments that are a reproach to me,   3
a spirit beyond my understanding gives me the answers.

---

a Prob. rdg.; Heb. adds and my flesh.   *b* to . . . witness: *or* for ever.   *c* my
witness . . . side: *prob. rdg.; Heb. unintelligible.*   *d Or* judgement.   *e* this is
why: *prob. rdg.; Heb. obscure.*

4   Surely you know that this has been so since time began,
    since man was first set on the earth:

5   the triumph of the wicked is short-lived,
    the glee of the godless lasts but a moment?

6   Though he stands high as heaven,
    and his head touches the clouds,

7   he will be swept utterly away like his own dung,
    and all that saw him will say, 'Where is he?'

8   He will fly away like a dream and be lost,
    driven off like a vision of the night;

9   the eye which glimpsed him shall do so no more
    and shall never again see him in his place.

11*a* The youth and strength which filled his bones
    shall lie with him in the dust.

10 His sons will pay court to the poor,
    and their*b* hands will give back his wealth.

12 Though evil tastes sweet in his mouth,
    and he savours it, rolling it round his tongue,

13 though he lingers over it and will not let it go,
    and holds it back on his palate,

14 yet his food turns in his stomach,
    changing to asps' venom within him.

15 He gulps down wealth, then vomits it up,
    or God makes him discharge it.

16 He sucks the poison of asps,
    and the tongue of the viper kills him.

17 Not for him to swill down rivers of cream*c*
    or torrents of honey and curds;

18 he must give back his gains without swallowing them,
    and spew up his profit undigested;

19 for he has hounded and harassed the poor,
    he has seized houses which he did not build.

20 Because his appetite gave him no rest,
    and he cannot escape his own desires,

21 nothing is left for him to eat,
    and so his well-being does not last;

22 with every need satisfied his troubles begin,
    and the full force of hardship strikes him.

23 God vents his anger upon him
    and rains on him cruel blows.

24 He is wounded by weapons of iron
    and pierced by a bronze-tipped arrow;

25 out at his back the point comes,
    the gleaming tip from his gall-bladder.

26 Darkness unrelieved awaits him,
    a fire that needs no fanning will consume him.

---

a *Verses 10 and 11 transposed.*   *b* *Prob. rdg.; Heb.* his.   *c* rivers of cream:
prob. rdg.; Heb. obscure.

[Woe betide any survivor in his tent!]
The heavens will lay bare his guilt,   27
and earth will rise up to condemn him.
A flood will sweep away his house,   28
rushing waters on the day of wrath.
Such is God's reward for the wicked man   29
and the lot appointed for the rebel*a* by God.

Then Job answered: **21**

Listen to me, do but listen,   2
and let that be the comfort you offer me.
Bear with me while I have my say;   3
when I have finished, you may mock.
May not I too voice*b* my thoughts?   4
Have not I as good cause to be impatient?
Look at my plight, and be aghast;   5
clap your hand to your mouth.
When I stop to think, I am filled with horror,   6
and my whole body is convulsed.

Why do the wicked enjoy long life,   7
hale in old age, and great and powerful?
They live to see their children settled,   8
their kinsfolk and descendants flourishing;
their families are secure and safe;   9
the rod of God's justice does not reach them.
Their bull mounts and fails not of its purpose;   10
their cow calves and does not miscarry.
Their children like lambs run out to play,   11
and their little ones skip and dance;
they rejoice with tambourine and harp   12
and make merry to the sound of the flute.
Their lives close in prosperity,   13
and they go down to Sheol in peace.
To God they say, 'Leave us alone;   14
we do not want to know your ways.
What is the Almighty that we should worship him,   15
or what should we gain by seeking his favour?'

Is not the prosperity of the wicked in their own hands?   16
Are not their purposes very different from God's*c*?
How often is the lamp of the wicked snuffed out,   17
and how often does their ruin come upon them?
How often does God in his anger deal out suffering,
bringing it in full measure to whom he will?*d*

---

a the rebel: *prob. rdg.; Heb.* his word.   *b* May . . . voice: *prob. rdg.; Heb. obscure.*
c God's: *prob. rdg.; Heb.* mine.   *d Line transposed from 12. 6.*

18   How often is that man like a wisp of straw before the wind,
       like chaff which the storm-wind whirls away?

19   You say, 'The trouble he has earned, God will keep for his
            sons';
       no, let him be paid for it in full and be punished.

20   Let his own eyes see damnation come upon him,
       and the wrath of the Almighty be the cup he drinks.

21   What joy shall he have in his children after him,
       if his very months and days are numbered?

22   Can any man teach God,
       God who judges even those in heaven above?

23   One man, I tell you, dies crowned with success,
       lapped in security and comfort,

24   his loins full of vigour
       and the marrow juicy in his bones;

25   another dies in bitterness of soul
       and never tastes prosperity;

26   side by side they are laid in earth,
       and worms are the shroud of both.

27   I know well what you are thinking
       and the arguments you are marshalling against me;

28   I know you will ask, 'Where is the great man's home now,
       what has become of the home of the wicked?'

29   Have you never questioned travellers?
       Can you not learn from the signs they offer,

30   that the wicked is spared when disaster comes
       and conveyed to safety before the day of wrath?

31   No one denounces his conduct to his face,
       no one requites him for what he has done.

32-33   When he is carried to the grave,
       all the world escorts him, before and behind;
       the dust of earth is sweet to him,
       and thousands keep watch at his tomb.

34   How futile, then, is the comfort you offer me!
       How false your answers ring!

Third cycle of speeches

22   Then Eliphaz the Temanite answered:

2   Can man be any benefit to God?
       Can even a wise man benefit him?

3   Is it an asset to the Almighty if you are righteous?
       Does he gain if your conduct is perfect?

Do not think that he reproves you because you are pious,   4
that on this count he brings you to trial.
No: it is because you are a very wicked man,   5
and your depravity passes all bounds.
Without due cause you take a brother in pledge,   6
you strip men of their clothes and leave them naked.
When a man is weary, you give him no water to drink   7
and you refuse bread to the hungry.
Is the earth, then, the preserve of the strong   8
and a domain for the favoured few?
Widows you have sent away empty-handed,   9
orphans you have struck defenceless.
No wonder that there are pitfalls in your path,   10
that scares are set to fill you with sudden fear.
The light is turned into darkness, and you cannot see;   11
the flood-waters cover you.
Surely God is at the zenith of the heavens   12
and looks down on all the stars, high as they are.
But you say, 'What does God know?   13
Can he see through thick darkness to judge?
His eyes cannot pierce the curtain of the clouds   14
as he walks to and fro on the vault of heaven.'
Consider the course of the wicked man,   15
the path the miscreant treads:
see how they are carried off before their time,   16
their very foundation flowing away like a river;
these men said to God, 'Leave us alone;   17
what can the Almighty do to us?'
Yet it was he that filled their houses with good things,   18
although their purposes and his were very different.
The righteous see their fate and exult,   19
the innocent make game of them;
for their riches are swept away,   20
and the profusion of their wealth is destroyed by fire.

Come to terms with God and you will prosper;   21
that is the way to mend your fortune.
Take instruction from his mouth   22
and store his words in your heart.
If you come back to the Almighty in true sincerity,   23
if you banish wrongdoing from your home,
if you treat your precious metal as dust *a*   24
and the gold of Ophir as stones from the river-bed,
then the Almighty himself will be your precious metal;   25
he will be your silver in double measure.
Then, with sure trust in *b* the Almighty,   26
you will raise your face to God;

a Prob. rdg.; Heb. if you put your precious metal on dust.   *b* with . . . in: *or* delighting in.

27   you will pray to him, and he will hear you,
      and you will have cause to fulfil your vows.
28   In all your designs you will succeed,
      and light will shine on your path;
29   but God brings down the pride of the haughty *a*
      and keeps safe the man of modest looks.
30   He will deliver the innocent, *b*
      and you will be delivered, because your hands are clean.

23 Then Job answered:

2   My thoughts today are resentful,
      for God's hand is heavy on me in my trouble.
3   If only I knew how to find him,
      how to enter his court,
4   I would state my case before him
      and set out my arguments in full;
5   then I should learn what answer he would give
      and find out what he had to say.
6   Would he exert his great power to browbeat me?
      No; God himself would never bring a charge against me.
7   There the upright are vindicated before him,
      and I shall win from my judge an absolute discharge.
8   If I go forward, *c* he is not there;
      if backward, *d* I cannot find him;
9   when I turn *e* left, *f* I do not descry him;
      I face right, *g* but I see him not.
10   But he knows me in action or at rest;
      when he tests me, I prove to be gold.
11   My feet have kept to the path he has set me,
      I have followed his way and not turned from it.
12   I do not ignore the commands that come from his lips,
      I have stored in my heart what he says.
13   He decides, *h* and who can turn him from his purpose?
      He does what his own heart desires.
14   What he determines, that he carries out;
      his mind is full of plans like these.
15   Therefore I am fearful of meeting him;
      when I think about him, *i* I am afraid;
16   it is God who makes me faint-hearted
      and the Almighty who fills me with fear,
17   yet I am not reduced to silence by the darkness
      nor *j* by the mystery which hides him.

---

a but . . . haughty: *prob. rdg.; Heb.* obscure.   *b Prob. rdg.; Heb.* the not innocent.
c Or east.   *d Or* west.   *e Prob. rdg.; Heb.* he turns.   *f Or* north.   *g Or* south.
h He decides: *prob. rdg.; Heb.* He in one.   *i* when . . . him: *or* I stand aloof.
j yet I am not . . . nor: *or* indeed I am . . . and . . .

^a The day of reckoning is no secret to the Almighty,   **24**
though those who know him have no hint of its date.
Wicked men move boundary-stones   2
and carry away flocks and their shepherds.
In the field they reap what is not theirs,   6^b
and filch the late grapes from the rich ^c man's vineyard.
They drive off the orphan's ass   3
and lead away the widow's ox with a rope.
They snatch the fatherless infant from the breast   9
and take the poor man's child in pledge.
They jostle the poor out of the way;   4
the destitute huddle together, hiding from them.
The poor rise early like the wild ass,   5
when it scours the wilderness for food;
but though they work till nightfall, ^d
their children go hungry. ^e
Naked and bare they pass the night;   7
in the cold they have nothing to cover them.
They are drenched by rain-storms from the hills   8
and hug the rock, their only shelter.
Naked and bare they go about their work,   10
and hungry they carry the sheaves;
they press the oil in the shade where two walls meet,   11
they tread the winepress but themselves go thirsty.
Far from the city, they groan like dying men,   12
and like wounded men they cry out;
but God pays no heed to their prayer.
Some there are who rebel against the light of day,   13
who know nothing of its ways
and do not linger in the paths of light.
The murderer rises before daylight   14
to kill some miserable wretch. ^f
The seducer watches eagerly for twilight,   15
thinking, 'No eye will catch sight of me.'
The thief prowls^g by night, ^h
his face covered with a mask,
and in the darkness breaks into houses   16
which he has marked down in the day.
One and all, ⁱ they are strangers to the daylight,
but dark night is morning to them;   17
and in the welter of night they are at home.
Such men are scum on the surface of the water;   18
their fields have a bad name throughout the land,
and no labourer will go near their vineyards.

19   As drought and heat make away with snow,
      so the waters of Sheol[a] make away with the sinner.
20   The womb forgets him, the worm sucks him dry;
      he will not be remembered ever after. [b]
21   He may have wronged the barren childless woman
      and been no help to the widow;
22   yet God in his strength carries off even the mighty;
      they may rise, but they have no firm hope of life.
23   He lulls them into security and confidence;
      but his eyes are fixed on their ways.
24   For a moment they rise to the heights, but are soon gone;
      iniquity is snapped like a stick. [c]
      They are laid low and wilt like a mallow-flower;
      they droop like an ear of corn on the stalk.
25   If this is not so, who will prove me wrong
      and make nonsense of my argument?

25 Then Bildad the Shuhite answered:

2   Authority and awe rest with him
      who has established peace in his realm on high.
3   His squadrons are without number;
      at whom will they not spring from ambush?
4   How then can a man be justified in God's sight,
      or one born of woman be innocent?
5   If the circling moon is found wanting,
      and the stars are not innocent in his eyes,
6   much more so man who is but a maggot,
      mortal man who is only a worm.

26 Then Job answered:

2   What help you have given to the man without resource,
      what deliverance you have brought to the powerless!
3   What counsel you offer to a man at his wit's end,
      what sound advice to the foolish!
4   Who has prompted you to say such things,
      and whose spirit is expressed in your speech?

5   In the underworld the shades writhe in fear,
      the waters and all that live in them are struck with terror. [d]
6   Sheol is laid bare,
      and Abaddon uncovered before him.
7   God spreads the canopy of the sky over chaos
      and suspends earth in the void.
8   He keeps the waters penned in dense cloud-masses,
      and the clouds do not burst open under their weight.

[a] snow . . . Sheol: *prob. rdg.; Heb.* snow-water, Sheol.   [b] *Prob. rdg.; Heb. here*
adds iniquity is snapped like a stick (*see note on verse 24*).   [c] *Line transposed from*
end of verse 20.   [d] are struck with terror: *prob. rdg.; Heb. om.*

He covers the face of the full moon,[a]   9
unrolling his clouds across it.
He has fixed the horizon on the surface of the waters   10
at the farthest limit of light and darkness.
The pillars of heaven quake   11
and are aghast at his rebuke.
With his strong arm he cleft the sea-monster,   12
and struck down the Rahab by his skill.
At his breath the skies are clear,   13
and his hand breaks the twisting [b] sea-serpent.
These are but the fringe of his power;   14
and how faint the whisper that we hear of him!
[Who could fathom the thunder of his might?]

Then Job resumed his discourse: **27**

I swear by God, who has denied me justice,   2
and by the Almighty, who has filled me with bitterness:
so long as there is any life left in me   3
and God's breath is in my nostrils,
no untrue word shall pass my lips   4
and my tongue shall utter no falsehood.
God forbid that I should allow you to be right;   5
till death, I will not abandon my claim to innocence.
I will maintain the rightness of my cause, I will never give up;   6
so long as I live, I will not change.

May my enemy meet the fate of the wicked,   7
and my antagonist the doom of the wrongdoer!
What hope has a godless man, when he is cut off, [c]   8
when God takes away his life?
Will God listen to his cry   9
when trouble overtakes him?
Will he trust himself to the Almighty   10
and call upon God at all times?

I will teach you what is in God's power,   11
I will not conceal the purpose of the Almighty.
If all of you have seen these things,   12
why then do you talk such empty nonsense?

This is the lot prescribed by God for the wicked,   13
and the ruthless man's reward from the Almighty.
He may have many sons, but they will fall by the sword,   14
and his offspring will go hungry;
the survivors will be brought to the grave by pestilence,   15
and no widows will weep for them.

---

[a] *Or* He overlays the surface of his throne.   [b] *Or* primeval.   [c] *Or* What
is a godless man's thread of life when it is cut . . .

16 He may heap up silver like dirt
  and get himself piles of clothes;
17 he may get them, but the righteous will wear them,
  and his silver will be shared among the innocent.
18 The house he builds is flimsy as a bird's nest
  or a shelter put up by a watchman.
19 He may lie down rich one day, but never again;
  he opens his eyes and all is gone.
20 Disaster overtakes him like a flood,
  and a storm snatches him away in the night;
21 the east wind lifts him up and he is gone;
  it whirls him far from home;
22 it flings itself on him without mercy,
  and he is battered and buffeted by its force;
23 it snaps its fingers at him
  and whistles over him wherever he may be.

God's unfathomable wisdom

28 There are mines for silver
  and places where men refine gold;
2 where iron is won from the earth
  and copper smelted from the ore;
3 the end of the seam lies in darkness,
  and it is followed to its farthest limit.[a]
4 Strangers cut the galleries;[b]
  they are forgotten as they drive forward far from men.[c]
5 While corn is springing from the earth above,
  what lies beneath is raked over like a fire,
6 and out of its rocks comes lapis lazuli,
  dusted with flecks of gold.
7 No bird of prey knows the way there,
  and the falcon's keen eye cannot descry it;
8 proud beasts do not set foot on it,
  and no serpent comes that way.
9 Man sets his hand to the granite rock
  and lays bare the roots of the mountains;
10 he cuts galleries in the rocks,
  and gems of every kind meet his eye;
11 he dams up the sources of the streams
  and brings the hidden riches of the earth to light.
12 But where can wisdom be found?
  And where is the source of understanding?
13 No man knows the way to it;
  it is not found in the land of living men.

[a] *Prob. rdg.; Heb. adds* stones of darkness and deep darkness. [b] Strangers . . . galleries:
prob. rdg.; Heb. obscure.   [c] *Prob. rdg.; Heb. adds* languishing without foothold.

The depths of ocean say, 'It is not in us',   14
and the sea says, 'It is not with me.'
Red gold cannot buy it,   15
nor can its price be weighed out in silver;
it cannot be set in the scales against gold of Ophir,   16
against precious cornelian or lapis lazuli;
gold and crystal are not to be matched with it,   17
no work in fine gold can be bartered for it;
black coral and alabaster are not worth mention,   18
and a parcel of wisdom fetches more than red coral;
topaz *ᵃ* from Ethiopia is not to be matched with it,   19
it cannot be set in the scales against pure gold.
Where then does wisdom come from,   20
and where is the source of understanding?
No creature on earth can see it,   21
and it is hidden from the birds of the air.
Destruction and death say,   22
'We know of it only by report.'
But God understands the way to it,   23
he alone knows its source;
for he can see to the ends of the earth   24
and he surveys everything under heaven.
When he made a counterpoise for the wind   25
and measured out the waters in proportion,
when he laid down a limit for the rain   26
and a path for the thunderstorm,
even then he saw wisdom and took stock of it,   27
he considered it and fathomed its very depths.
And he said to man: 28
    The fear of the Lord is wisdom,
    and to turn from evil is understanding.

Job's final survey of his case

Then Job resumed his discourse: **29**

    If I could only go back to the old days,   2
    to the time when God was watching over me,
    when his lamp shone above my head,   3
    and by its light I walked through the darkness!
    If I could be as in the days of my prime,   4
    when God protected my home,
    while the Almighty was still there at my side,   5
    and my servants stood round me,
    while my path flowed with milk,   6
    and the rocks streamed oil!

ᵃ Or chrysolite.

7 If I went through the gate out of the town
  to take my seat in the public square,

8 young men saw me and kept out of sight;
  old men rose to their feet,

9 men in authority broke off their talk
  and put their hands to their lips;

10 the voices of the nobles died away,
  and every man held his tongue.

21*ᵃ* They listened to me expectantly
  and waited in silence for my opinion.

22 When I had spoken, no one spoke again;
  my words fell gently on them;

23 they waited for them as for rain
  and drank them in like showers in spring.

24 When I smiled on them, they took heart;
  when my face lit up, they lost their gloomy looks.

25 I presided over them, planning their course,
  like a king encamped with his troops. *ᵇ*

11 Whoever heard of me spoke in my favour,
  and those who saw me bore witness to my merit,

12 how I saved the poor man when he called for help
  and the orphan who had no protector.

13 The man threatened with ruin blessed me,
  and I made the widow's heart sing for joy.

14 I put on righteousness as a garment and it clothed me;
  justice, like a cloak or a turban, wrapped me round.

15 I was eyes to the blind
  and feet to the lame;

16 I was a father to the needy,
  and I took up the stranger's cause.

17 I broke the fangs of the miscreant
  and rescued the prey from his teeth.

18 I thought, 'I shall die with my powers unimpaired
  and my days uncounted as the grains of sand, *ᶜ*

19 with my roots spreading out to the water
  and the dew lying on my branches,

20 with the bow always new in my grasp
  and the arrow ever ready to my hand.' *ᵈ*

30 But now I am laughed to scorn
  by men of a younger generation,
  men whose fathers I would have disdained
  to put with the dogs who kept my flock.

2 What use were their strong arms to me,
  since their sturdy vigour had wasted away?

ᵃ Verses 21–25 transposed to this point. *ᵇ Prob. rdg.; Heb. adds as when one* comforts mourners. *ᶜ Or as those of the phoenix.* *ᵈ Verses 21–25 transposed to follow verse 10.*

They gnawed roots^a in the desert,   3
gaunt with want and hunger,^b
they plucked saltwort and wormwood   4
and root of broom^c for their food.
Driven out from the society of men,^d   5
pursued like thieves with hue and cry,
they lived in gullies and ravines,   6
holes in the earth and rocky clefts;
they howled like beasts among the bushes,   7
huddled together beneath the scrub,
vile base-born wretches,   8
hounded from the haunts of men.
Now I have become the target of their taunts,   9
my name is a byword among them.
They loathe me, they shrink from me,   10
they dare to spit in my face.
They run wild and savage^e me;   11
at sight of me they throw off all restraint.
On my right flank they attack in a mob;^f   12
they raise their siege-ramps against me,
they tear down my crumbling defences to my undoing,   13
and scramble up against me unhindered;
they burst in through the gaping breach;   14
at the moment of the crash they come rolling in.
Terror upon terror overwhelms me,   15
it sweeps away my resolution like the wind,
and my hope of victory vanishes like a cloud.
So now my soul is in turmoil within me,   16
and misery has me daily in its grip.
By night pain pierces my very bones,   17
and there is ceaseless throbbing in my veins;
my garments are all bespattered with my phlegm,   18
which chokes me like the collar of a shirt.
God himself^g has flung me down in the mud,   19
no better than dust or ashes.

I call for thy help, but thou dost not answer;   20
I stand up to plead, but thou sittest aloof;
thou hast turned cruelly against me   21
and with thy strong hand pursuest me in hatred;
thou dost snatch me up and set me astride the wind,   22
and the tempest^h tosses me up and down.
I know that thou wilt hand me over to death,   23
to the place appointed for all mortal men.

---

^a roots: *prob. rdg.; Heb. om.*   ^b *Prob. rdg.; Heb. adds* yesterday waste and derelict land.   ^c root of broom: *probably* fungus on broom root.   ^d the society of men: *prob. rdg.; Heb. obscure.*   ^e They run . . . savage: *prob. rdg.; Heb.* He runs . . . savages.   ^f *Prob. rdg.; Heb. adds* they let loose my feet.   ^g God himself: *prob. rdg.; Heb. om.*   ^h the tempest: *prob. rdg.; Heb. unintelligible.*

24   Yet no beggar held out his hand
     but was relieved[a] by me in his distress.

25   Did I not weep for the man whose life was hard?
     Did not my heart grieve for the poor?

26   Evil has come though I expected good;
     I looked for light but there came darkness.

27   My bowels are in ferment and know no peace;
     days of misery stretch out before me.

28   I go about dejected and friendless;
     I rise in the assembly, only to appeal for help.

29   The wolf is now my brother,
     the owls of the desert have become my companions.

30   My blackened skin peels off,
     and my body is scorched by the heat.

31   My harp has been tuned for a dirge,
     my flute to the voice of those who weep.

31 2[b]   What is the lot prescribed by God above,
     the reward from the Almighty on high?

3   Is not ruin prescribed for the miscreant
     and calamity for the wrongdoer?

4   Yet does not God himself see my ways
     and count my every step?

5   I swear I have had no dealings with falsehood
     and have not embarked on a course of deceit.

1   I have come to terms with my eyes,
     never to take notice of a girl.

6   Let God weigh me in the scales of justice,
     and he will know that I am innocent!

7   If my steps have wandered from the way,
     if my heart has followed my eyes,
     or any dirt stuck to my hands,

8   may another eat what I sow,
     and may my crops be pulled up by the roots!

9   If my heart has been enticed by a woman
     or I have lain in wait at my neighbour's door,

10   may my wife be another man's slave,
     and may other men enjoy her.

11   [But that is a wicked act, an offence before the law;

12   it would be a consuming and destructive fire,
     raging [c] among my crops.]

13   If I have ever rejected the plea of my slave
     or of my slave-girl, when they brought their complaint to me,

14   what shall I do if God appears?
     What shall I answer if he intervenes?

15   Did not he who made me in the womb make them?

---

[a] was relieved: *prob. rdg.; Heb. unintelligible.*   [b] *Verse 1 transposed to follow verse 5.*
[c] *Prob. rdg.; Heb.* uprooting.

Did not the same God create us in the belly?
If I have withheld their needs from the poor   16
or let the widow's eye grow dim with tears,
if I have eaten my crust alone,   17
and the orphan has not shared it with me—
the orphan who from boyhood honoured me like a father,   18
whom I guided from the day of his*ª* birth—
if I have seen anyone perish for lack of clothing,   19
or a poor man with nothing to cover him,
if his body had no cause to bless me,   20
because he was not kept warm with a fleece from my flock,
if I have raised*ᵇ* my hand against the innocent,*ᶜ*   21
knowing that men would side with me in court,
then may my shoulder-blade be torn from my shoulder,   22
my arm be wrenched out of its socket!
But the terror of God was heavy upon me,*ᵈ*   23
and for fear of his majesty I could do none of these things.
If I have put my faith in gold   24
and my trust in the gold of Nubia,
if I have rejoiced in my great wealth   25
and in the increase of riches;
if I ever looked on the sun in splendour   26
or the moon moving in her glory,
and was led astray in my secret heart   27
and raised my hand in homage;
this would have been an offence before the law,   28
for I should have been unfaithful to God on high.
If my land has cried out in reproach at me,   38*ᵉ*
and its furrows have joined in weeping,
if I have eaten its produce without payment   39
and have disappointed my creditors,
may thistles spring up instead of wheat,   40
and weeds instead of barley!

Have I rejoiced at the ruin of the man that hated me   29
or been filled with malice when trouble overtook him,
even though I did not allow my tongue to sin   30
by demanding his life with a curse?
Have the men of my household never said,   31
'Let none of us speak ill of him!
No stranger has spent the night in the street'?   32
For I have kept open house for the traveller.
Have I ever concealed my misdeeds as men do,   33
keeping my guilt to myself,
because I feared the gossip of the town   34
or dreaded the scorn of my fellow-citizens?

ª Prob. rdg.; Heb. my.   *ᵇ Or waved.*   *ᶜ Or orphan.*   *ᵈ Prob. rdg.; Heb. A fear to-*
wards me is a disaster from God.   *ᵉ Verses 38-40 transposed (but see note c, page 596).*

35   Let me but call a witness in my defence!
       Let the Almighty state his case against me!
       If my accuser had written out his indictment,
       I would not keep silence and remain indoors.[a]
36   No! I would flaunt it on my shoulder
       and wear it like a crown on my head;
37   I would plead the whole record of my life
       and present that in court as my defence.[b]

Job's speeches are finished.[c]

Speeches of Elihu

32   So these three men gave up answering Job; for he continued to think him-
2   self righteous. Then Elihu son of Barakel the Buzite, of the family of Ram,
   grew angry; angry because Job had made himself out more righteous than
3   God,[d] and angry with the three friends because they had found no answer
4   to Job and had let God appear wrong.[e] Now Elihu had hung back while
5   they were talking with Job because they were older than he; but, when he
6   saw that the three had no answer, he could no longer contain his anger. So
   Elihu son of Barakel the Buzite began to speak:

       I am young in years,
       and you are old;
       that is why I held back and shrank
       from displaying my knowledge in front of you.
7   I said to myself, 'Let age speak,
       and length of years expound wisdom.'
8   But the spirit of God himself is in man,
       and the breath of the Almighty gives him understanding;
9   it is not only the old who are wise
       or the aged who understand what is right.
10   Therefore I say: Listen to me;
       I too will display my knowledge.
11   Look, I have been waiting upon your words,
       listening for the conclusions of your thoughts,
       while you sought for phrases;
12   I have been giving thought to your conclusions,
       but not one of you refutes Job or answers his arguments.
13   Take care then not to claim that you have found wisdom;
       God will rebut him, not man.
14   I will not string[f] words together like you[g]
       or answer him as you have done.

---

[a] *Line transposed from verse 34.*   [b] *Verses 38–40 transposed to follow verse 28 (but see note c).*   [c] *The last line of verse 40 retained here.*   [d] *Or had justified himself with God.*   [e] *Prob. original rdg., altered in Heb. to and had not proved Job wrong.* [f] *Prob. rdg.; Heb. He has not strung.*   [g] *Prob. rdg.; Heb. towards me.*

If these men are confounded and no longer answer,   15
if words fail them,
am I to wait because they do not speak,   16
because they stand there and no longer answer?
I, too, have a furrow to plough;   17
I will express my opinion;
for I am bursting with words,   18
a bellyful of wind gripes me.
My stomach is distended as if with wine,   19
bulging like a blacksmith's bellows;
I must speak to find relief,   20
I must open my mouth and answer;
I will show no favour to anyone,   21
I will flatter no one, God or man;*a*
for I cannot use flattering titles,   22
or my Maker would soon do away with me.

Come now, Job, listen to my words   **33**
and attend carefully to everything I say.
Look, I am ready to answer;   2
the words are on the tip of my tongue.
My heart assures me that I speak with knowledge,   3
and that my lips speak with sincerity.
For the spirit of God made me,   4
and the breath of the Almighty gave me life.
Answer me if you can,   5
marshal your arguments and confront me.
In God's sight*b* I am just what you are;   6
I too am only a handful of clay.
Fear of me need not abash you,   7
nor any pressure from me overawe you.
You have said your say and I heard you;   8
I have listened to the sound of your words:
'I am innocent', you said, 'and free from offence,   9
blameless and without guilt.
Yet God finds occasions to put me in the wrong   10
and counts me his enemy;
he puts my feet in the stocks   11
and keeps a close watch on all I do.'

Well, this is my answer: You are wrong.   12
God is greater than man;
why then plead your case with him?   13
for no one can answer his arguments.
Indeed, once God has spoken   14
he does not speak a second time to confirm it.

---

a *Prob. rdg.; Heb.* I will not flatter man.   *b* In God's sight: *or* In strength.

15   In dreams, in visions of the night,
            when deepest sleep falls upon men,

16   while they sleep on their beds, God makes them listen,
            and his correction strikes them with terror.

17   To turn a man from reckless conduct,
            to check the pride[a] of mortal man,

18   at the edge of the pit he holds him back alive
            and stops him from crossing the river of death.

19   Or again, man learns his lesson on a bed of pain,
            tormented by a ceaseless ague in his bones;

20   he turns from his food with loathing
            and has no relish for the choicest meats;

21   his flesh hangs loose upon him,
            his bones are loosened and out of joint,

22   his soul draws near to the pit,
            his life to the ministers of death.

23   Yet if an angel, one of thousands, stands by him,
            a mediator between him and God,
            to expound what he has done right
            and to secure mortal man his due;[b]

24   if he speaks in the man's favour and says, 'Reprieve him,
            let him not go down to the pit, I have the price of his release';

25   then that man will grow sturdier[c] than he was in youth,
            he will return to the days of his prime.

26   If he entreats God to show him favour,
            to let him see his face and shout for joy;[d]

27   if he declares before all men, 'I have sinned,
            turned right into wrong and thought nothing of it';

28   then he saves himself from going down to the pit,
            he lives and sees the light.

29   All these things God may do to a man,
            again and yet again,

30   bringing him back from the pit
            to enjoy the full light of life.

31   Listen, Job, and attend to me;
            be silent, and I myself will speak.

32   If you have any arguments, answer me;
            speak, and I would gladly find you proved right;

33   but if you have none, listen to me:
            keep silence, and I will teach you wisdom.

34   Then Elihu went on to say:

2   Mark my words, you wise men;
            you men of long experience, listen to me;

3   for the ear tests what is spoken
            as the palate savours food.

---

[a] *the pride: prob. rdg.; Heb. obscure.*   [b] *Line transposed from verse 26.*   [c] will
grow sturdier: *prob. rdg.; Heb. unintelligible.*   [d] *See note on verse 23.*

Let us then examine for ourselves what is right;   4
let us together establish the true good.
Job has said, 'I am innocent,   5
but God has deprived me of justice,
he has falsified my case;   6
my state is desperate, yet I have done no wrong.'
Was there ever a man like Job   7
with his thirst for irreverent talk,
choosing bad company to share his journeys,   8
a fellow-traveller with wicked men?
For he says that it brings a man no profit   9
to find favour with God.
But listen to me, you men of good sense.   10
    Far be it from God to do evil
    or the Almighty to play false!
For he pays a man according to his work   11
and sees that he gets what his conduct deserves.
The truth is, God does no wrong,   12
the Almighty does not pervert justice.
Who committed the earth to his keeping?   13
Who but he established the whole world?
If he were to turn his thoughts inwards   14
and recall his life-giving spirit,
all that lives would perish on the instant,   15
and man return again to dust.

Now Job, if you have the wit, consider this;   16
listen to the words I speak.
Can it be that a hater of justice holds the reins?   17
Do you disparage a sovereign whose rule is so fair,
who will say to a prince, 'You scoundrel',   18
and call his magnates blackguards to their faces;
who does not show special favour to those in office   19
and thinks no more of rich than of poor?
All alike are God's creatures,
who may die in a moment, in the middle of the night;   20
at his touch the rich are no more,
and the mighty vanish though no hand is laid on them.
His eyes are on the ways of men,   21
and he sees every step they take;
there is nowhere so dark, so deep in shadow,   22
that wrongdoers may hide from him.
Therefore he repudiates all that they do;   25
he turns on them in the night, and they are crushed.
There are no appointed days for men   23
to appear before God for judgement.
He holds no inquiry, but breaks the powerful   24
and sets up others in their place.

26 ^a For their crimes he strikes them down ^b
    and makes them disgorge their bloated wealth, ^c

27   because they have ceased to obey him
    and pay no heed to his ways.

28   Then the cry of the poor reaches his ears,
    and he hears the cry of the distressed.

29-30   [Even if he is silent, who can condemn him?
    If he looks away, who can find fault?
    What though he makes a godless man king
    over a stubborn nation and all its people?]

31   But suppose you were to say to God,
    'I have overstepped the mark; I will do no more ^d mischief.

32   Vile wretch that I am, be thou my guide;
    whatever wrong I have done, I will do wrong no more.'

33   Will he, at these words, condone your rejection of him?
    It is for you to decide, not me:
    but what can you answer?

34   Men of good sense will say,
    any intelligent hearer will tell me,

35   'Job talks with no knowledge,
    and there is no sense in what he says.

36   If only Job could be put to the test once and for all
    for answers that are meant to make mischief!

37   He is a sinner and a rebel as well ^e
    with his endless ranting against God.'

35 Then Elihu went on to say:

2   Do you think that this is a sound plea
    or maintain that you are in the right against God?—

3   if you say, 'What would be the advantage to me?
    how much should I gain from sinning?'

4   I will bring arguments myself against you,
    you and your three friends.

5   Look up at the sky and then consider,
    observe the rain-clouds towering above you.

6   How does it touch him if you have sinned?
    However many your misdeeds, what does it mean to him?

7   If you do right, what good do you bring him,
    or what does he gain from you?

8   Your wickedness touches only men, such as you are;
    the right that you do affects none but mortal man.

9   Men will cry out beneath the burdens of oppression
    and call for help against the power of the great;

---

^a *Verse 25 transposed to follow verse 22.*   ^b he strikes them down: *prob. rdg.; Heb. om.*
^c *Or and chastises them where people see.*   ^d more: *prob. rdg.; Heb. obscure.*
^e *Prob. rdg.; Heb. adds* between us it is enough.

but none of them asks, 'Where is God my Maker   10
who gives protection by night,
who grants us more knowledge than the beasts of the earth   11
and makes us wiser than the birds of the air?'
So, when they cry out, he does not answer,   12
because they are self-willed and proud.
All to no purpose! God does not listen,   13
the Almighty does not see.

The worse for you when you say, 'He does not see me'!   14
Humble yourself*a* in his presence and wait for his word.
But now, because God does not grow angry and punish   15
and because he lets folly pass unheeded,
Job gives vent to windy nonsense   16
and makes a parade of empty words.

Then Elihu went on to say: **36**

Be patient a little longer, and let me enlighten you;   2
there is still something more to be said on God's side.
I will search far and wide to support my conclusions,   3
as I defend the justice of my Maker.
There are no flaws in my reasoning;   4
before you stands one whose conclusions are sound.

God,*b* I say, repudiates the high and*c* mighty   5
and does not let the wicked prosper,   6
but allows the just claims of the poor and suffering;
he does not deprive the sufferer of his due.*d*   7
Look at kings on their thrones:
when God gives them sovereign power, they grow arrogant.
Next you may see them loaded with fetters,   8
held fast in captives' chains:
he denounces their conduct to them,   9
showing how insolence and tyranny was their offence;
his warnings sound in their ears   10
and summon them to turn back from their evil courses.
If they listen to him, they spend*e* their days in prosperity 11
and their years in comfort.
But, if they do not listen, they die, their lesson unlearnt, 12
and cross the river of death.
Proud men rage against him   13
and do not cry to him for help when caught in his toils;
so they die in their prime,   14
like male prostitutes,*f* worn out.*g*

---

a Humble yourself: *prob. rdg.; Heb.* Judge.   *b* *Prob. rdg.; Heb. adds* a mighty one
and not.   *c* and: *prob. rdg.; Heb. om.*   *d* deprive . . . due: *or* withdraw his
gaze from the righteous.   *e* *Prob. rdg.; Heb. adds* they end.   *f* *Cp. Deut. 23. 17.*
g worn out: *prob. rdg.; Heb. unintelligible.*

15   Those who suffer he rescues through suffering
      and teaches them by the discipline of affliction.

16   Beware, if you are tempted to exchange hardship for comfort, [a]
      for unlimited plenty spread before you, and a generous table;
17   if you eat your fill of a rich man's fare
      when you are occupied with the business of the law,
18   do not be led astray by lavish gifts of wine
      and do not let bribery warp your judgement.
19   Will that wealth of yours, however great, avail you,
      or all the resources of your high position?
21 [b]   Take care not to turn to mischief;
      for that is why you are tried by affliction.

20   Have no fear if in the breathless terrors of the night
      you see nations vanish where they stand.
22   God towers in majesty above us;
      who wields such sovereign power as he?
23   Who has prescribed his course for him?
      Who has said to him, 'Thou hast done wrong'?
24   Remember then to sing the praises of his work,
      as men have always sung them.
25   All men stand back from [c] him;
      the race of mortals look on from afar.
26   Consider; God is so great that we cannot know him;
      the number of his years is beyond reckoning.
27   He draws up drops of water from the sea [d]
      and distils rain from the mist he has made;
28   the rain-clouds pour down in torrents, [e]
      they descend in showers on mankind;
31   thus he sustains the nations
      and gives them food in plenty.
29   Can any man read the secret of the sailing clouds,
      spread like a carpet under [f] his pavilion?
30   See how he unrolls the mist across the waters,
      and its streamers [g] cover the sea.
32 [h]   He charges the thunderbolts with flame
      and launches them straight [i] at the mark;
33   in his anger he calls up the tempest,
      and the thunder is the herald of its coming. [j]

37   This too makes my heart beat wildly
      and start from its place.
2   Listen, listen to the thunder of God's voice
      and the rumbling of his utterance.

---

[a] *for comfort: prob. rdg.; Heb. om.*   [b] *Verses 20 and 21 transposed.*   [c] *Or gaze at.*
[d] *from the sea: prob. rdg.; Heb. om.*   [e] *in torrents: prob. rdg.; Heb. which.*   [f] *spread
... under: prob. rdg.; Heb. crashing noises.*   [g] *its streamers: prob. rdg.; Heb. the
roots of.*   [h] *Verse 31 transposed to follow verse 28.*   [i] *and ... straight: prob. rdg.; Heb.
and gives orders concerning it.*   [j] *in his anger ... coming: prob. rdg.; Heb. obscure.*

Under the vault of heaven he lets it roll,   3
and his lightning reaches the ends of the earth;
there follows a sound of roaring   4
as he thunders with the voice of majesty. *a*
God's voice is marvellous in its working; *b*   5
he does great deeds that pass our knowledge.
For he says to the snow, 'Fall to earth',   6
and to the rainstorms, 'Be fierce.'
And when his voice is heard,
the floods of rain pour down unchecked. *c*
He shuts every man fast indoors, *d*   7
and all men whom he has made must stand idle;
the beasts withdraw into their lairs   8
and take refuge in their dens.
The hurricane bursts from its prison,   9
and the rain-winds bring bitter cold;
at the breath of God the ice-sheet is formed,   10
and the wide waters are frozen hard as iron.
He gives the dense clouds their load of moisture,   11
and the clouds spread his mist abroad,
as they travel round in their courses,   12
steered by his guiding hand
to do his bidding
all over the habitable world. *e*

Listen, Job, to this argument;   14
stand still, and consider God's wonderful works.
Do you know how God assigns them their tasks,   15
how he sends light flashing from his clouds?
Do you know why the clouds hang poised overhead,   16
a wonderful work of his consummate skill,
sweating there in your stifling clothes,   17
when the earth lies sultry under the south wind?
Can you beat out the vault of the skies, as he does,   18
hard as a mirror of cast metal?
Teach us then what to say to him;   19
for all is dark, and we cannot marshal our thoughts.
Can any man dictate to God when he is *f* to speak?   20
or command him to make proclamation?
At one moment the light is not seen,   21
it is overcast with clouds and rain;
then the wind passes by and clears them away,
and a golden glow comes from the north. *g*   22

---

a *See note on verse 6.*   *b* *Prob. rdg.; Heb.* thundering.   *c* And when . . . unchecked:
prob. rdg.; some words in these lines transposed from verse 4.   *d* indoors: *prob. rdg.;*
Heb. obscure.   *e* *Prob. rdg.; Heb. adds* (13) whether he makes him attain the rod,
or his earth, or constant love.   *f* *Prob. rdg.; Heb.* I am.   *g* *Prob. rdg.; Heb. adds*
this refers to God, terrible in majesty.

23   But the Almighty we cannot find; his power is beyond our ken,
      and his righteousness not slow to do justice.
24   Therefore mortal men pay him reverence,
      and all who are wise look to him.

God's answer and Job's submission

38   Then the LORD answered Job out of the tempest:
2   Who is this whose ignorant words
      cloud my design in darkness?
3   Brace yourself and stand up like a man;
      I will ask questions, and you shall answer.
4   Where were you when I laid the earth's foundations?
      Tell me, if you know and understand.
5   Who settled its dimensions? Surely you should know.
      Who stretched his measuring-line over it?
6   On what do its supporting pillars rest?
      Who set its corner-stone in place,
7   when the morning stars sang together
      and all the sons of God shouted aloud?
8   Who watched over the birth of the sea, *a*
      when it burst in flood from the womb?—
9   when I wrapped it in a blanket of cloud
      and cradled it in fog,
10   when I established its bounds,
      fixing its doors and bars in place,
11   and said, 'Thus far shall you come and no farther,
      and here your surging waves shall halt.' *b*
12   In all your life have you ever called up the dawn
      or shown the morning its place?
13   Have you taught it to grasp the fringes of the earth
      and shake the Dog-star from its place;
14   to bring up the horizon in relief as clay under a seal,
      until all things stand out like the folds of a cloak,
15   when the light of the Dog-star is dimmed
      and the stars of the Navigator's Line go out one by one?
16   Have you descended to the springs of the sea
      or walked in the unfathomable deep?
17   Have the gates of death been revealed to you?
      Have you ever seen the door-keepers of the place of darkness?
18   Have you comprehended the vast expanse of the world?
      Come, tell me all this, if you know.
19   Which is the way to the home of light
      and where does darkness dwell?

a Who . . . sea: *prob. rdg.; Heb.* And he held back the sea with two doors.   *b Prob.*
rdg.; Heb. here one shall set on your surging waves.

And can you then take each to its appointed bound   20
and escort it on its homeward path?
Doubtless you know all this; for you were born already,   21
so long is the span of your life!

Have you visited the storehouse of the snow   22
or seen the arsenal where hail is stored,
which I have kept ready for the day of calamity,   23
for war and for the hour of battle?
By what paths is the heat spread abroad   24
or the east wind carried far and wide over the earth?
Who has cut channels for the downpour   25
and cleared a passage for the thunderstorm,
for rain to fall on land where no man lives   26
and on the deserted wilderness,
clothing lands waste and derelict with green   27
and making grass grow on thirsty ground *a*?
Has the rain a father?   28
Who sired the drops of dew?
Whose womb gave birth to the ice,   29
and who was the mother of the frost from heaven,
which lays a stony cover over the waters   30
and freezes the expanse of ocean?
Can you bind the cluster of the Pleiades   31
or loose Orion's belt?
Can you bring out the signs of the zodiac in their season   32
or guide Aldebaran and its train?
Did you proclaim the rules that govern the heavens,   33
or determine the laws of nature on earth?
Can you command the dense clouds   34
to cover you with their weight of waters?
If you bid lightning speed on its way,   35
will it say to you, 'I am ready'?
Who put wisdom in depths of darkness   36
and veiled understanding in secrecy *b*?
Who is wise enough to marshal the rain-clouds   37
and empty the cisterns of heaven,
when the dusty soil sets hard as iron,   38
and the clods of earth cling together?
Do you hunt her prey for the lioness   39
and satisfy the hunger of young lions,
as they crouch in the lair   40
or lie in wait in the covert?
Who provides the raven with its quarry   41
when its fledglings croak *c* for lack of food?

---

a thirsty ground: *prob. rdg.; Heb.* source.   *b* secrecy: *prob. rdg.; Heb. word unknown.*
c *Prob. rdg.; Heb. adds* they cry to God.

39 Do you know when the mountain-goats are born
or attend the wild doe when she is in labour?

2   Do you count the months that they carry their young
or know the time of their delivery,

3   when they crouch down to open their wombs
and bring their offspring to the birth,

4   when the fawns grow and thrive in the open forest,
and go forth and do not return?

5   Who has let the wild ass of Syria range at will
and given the wild ass of Arabia its freedom?—

6   whose home I have made in the wilderness
and its lair in the saltings;

7   it disdains the noise of the city
and is deaf to the driver's shouting;

8   it roams the hills as its pasture
and searches for anything green.

9   Does the wild ox consent to serve you,
does it spend the night in your stall?

10   Can you harness its strength ^{a} with ropes,
or will it harrow the furrows ^{a} after you?

11   Can you depend on it, strong as it is,
or leave your labour to it?

12   Do you trust it to come back
and bring home your grain to the threshing-floor?

13   The wings of the ostrich are stunted; ^{b}
^{c}her pinions and plumage are so scanty ^{d}

14   that she abandons her eggs to the ground,
letting them be kept warm by the sand.

15   She forgets that a foot may crush them,
or a wild beast trample on them;

16   she treats her chicks heartlessly as if they were not hers,
not caring if her labour is wasted

17   (for God has denied her wisdom
and left her without sense),

18   while like a cock she struts over the uplands,
scorning both horse and rider.

19   Did you give the horse his strength?
Did you clothe his neck with a mane?

20   Do you make him quiver like a locust's wings,
when his shrill neighing strikes terror?

21   He shows his mettle as he paws and prances;
he charges the armoured line with all his might.

22   He scorns alarms and knows no dismay;
he does not flinch before the sword.

---

^{a} *Prob. rdg.; Heb. transposes* strength *and* furrows.
Heb. unintelligible. ^{c} *Prob. rdg.; Heb. prefixes* if. ^{b} are stunted: *prob. rdg.;*
or stork. ^{d} *Prob. rdg.; Heb.* godly

The quiver rattles at his side,   23
the spear and sabre flash.
Trembling with eagerness, he devours the ground   24
and cannot be held in when he hears the horn;
at the blast of the horn he cries 'Aha!'   25
and from afar he scents the battle.*a*
Does your skill teach the hawk to use its pinions   26
and spread its wings towards the south?
Do you instruct the vulture to fly high   27
and build its nest aloft?
It dwells among the rocks and there it lodges;   28
its station is a crevice in the rock;
from there it searches for food,   29
keenly scanning the distance,
that its brood may be gorged with blood;   30
and where the slain are, there the vulture is.
Can you pull out the whale*b* with a gaff   **41** 1*c*
or can you slip a noose round its tongue?
Can you pass a cord through its nose   2
or put a hook through its jaw?
Will it plead with you for mercy   3
or beg its life with soft words?
Will it enter into an agreement with you   4
to become your slave for life?
Will you toy with it as with a bird   5
or keep it on a string like a song-bird for your maidens?
Do trading-partners haggle over it   6
or merchants share it out?

Then the Lord said to Job: **40**

Is it for a man who disputes with the Almighty to be stubborn?   2
Should he that argues with God answer back?

And Job answered the Lord: 3

What reply can I give thee, I who carry no weight?   4
I put my finger to my lips.
I have spoken once and now will not answer again;   5
twice have I spoken, and I will do so no more.

Then the Lord answered Job out of the tempest: 6

Brace yourself and stand up like a man;   7
I will ask questions, and you shall answer.
Dare you deny that I am just   8
or put me in the wrong that you may be right?

a Prob. rdg.; Heb. adds the thunder of the captains and the shouting.   *b Or* Leviathan.
c 41. 1–6 (in Heb. 40. 25–30) transposed to this point.

9   Have you an arm like God's arm,
    can you thunder with a voice like his?

10 Deck yourself out, if you can, in pride and dignity,
    array yourself in pomp and splendour;

11 unleash the fury of your wrath,
    look upon the proud man and humble him;

12 look upon every proud man and bring him low,
    throw down the wicked where they stand;

13 hide them in the dust together,
    and shroud them in an unknown grave.

14 Then I in my turn will acknowledge
    that your own right hand can save you.

15 Consider the chief of the beasts, the crocodile,*a*
    who devours cattle as if they were grass:*b*

16 what strength is in his loins!
    what power in the muscles of his belly!

17 His tail is rigid as*c* a cedar,
    the sinews of his flanks are closely knit,

18 his bones are tubes of bronze,
    and his limbs like bars of iron.

19 He is the chief of God's works,
    made to be a tyrant over his peers;*d*

20 for he takes*e* the cattle of the hills for his prey
    and in his jaws he crunches all wild beasts.

21 There under the thorny lotus he lies,
    hidden in the reeds and the marsh;

22 the lotus conceals him in its shadow,
    the poplars of the stream surround him.

23 If the river is in spate, he is not scared,
    he sprawls at his ease though the stream is in flood.

24 Can a man blind*f* his eyes and take him
    or pierce his nose with the teeth of a trap?

41 7*g* Can you fill his skin with harpoons
    or his head with fish-hooks?

8   If ever you lift your hand against him,
    think of the struggle that awaits you, and let be.

9   No, such a man is in desperate case,
    hurled headlong at the very sight of him.

10 How fierce he is when he is roused!
    Who is there to stand up to him?

11 Who has ever attacked him*h* unscathed?
    Not a man*i* under the wide heaven.

---

a chief . . . crocodile: *prob. rdg.; Heb.* beasts (behemoth) which I have made with you.
b cattle . . . grass: *prob. rdg.; Heb.* grass like cattle.   *c Or* He bends his tail like . . .
d Prob. rdg.; Heb. his sword.   *e Prob. rdg.; Heb.* they take.   *f* Can a man blind:
prob. rdg.; Heb. obscure.   *g Verses 1–6 transposed to follow 39. 30.*   *h Prob. rdg.;*
Heb. me.   *i Prob. rdg.; Heb.* He is mine.

I will not pass over in silence his limbs,   12
his prowess and the grace of his proportions.
Who has ever undone his outer garment   13
or penetrated his doublet of hide?
Who has ever opened the portals of his face?   14
for there is terror in his arching teeth.
His back *a* is row upon row of shields,   15
enclosed in a wall *b* of flints;
one presses so close on the other   16
that air cannot pass between them,
each so firmly clamped to its neighbour   17
that they hold and cannot spring apart.
His sneezing sends out sprays of light,   18
and his eyes gleam like the shimmer of dawn.
Firebrands shoot from his mouth,   19
and sparks come streaming out;
his nostrils pour forth smoke   20
like a cauldron on a fire blown to full heat.
His breath sets burning coals ablaze,   21
and flames flash from his mouth.
Strength is lodged in his neck,   22
and untiring energy dances ahead of him.
Close knit is his underbelly,   23
no pressure will make it yield.
His heart is firm as a rock,   24
firm as the nether millstone.
When he raises himself, strong men *c* take fright,   25
bewildered at the lashings of his tail.
Sword or spear, dagger or javelin,   26
if they touch him, they have no effect.
Iron he counts as straw,   27
and bronze as rotting wood.
No arrow can pierce him,   28
and for him sling-stones are turned into chaff;
to him a club is a mere reed,   29
and he laughs at the swish of the sabre.
Armoured beneath with jagged sherds,   30
he sprawls on the mud like a threshing-sledge.
He makes the deep water boil like a cauldron,   31
he whips up the lake like ointment in a mixing-bowl.
He leaves a shining trail behind him,   32
and the great river is like white hair in his wake.
He has no equal on earth;   33
for he is made quite without fear.
He looks down on all creatures, even the highest;   34
he is king over all proud beasts.

a Prob. rdg.; Heb. pride.   *b Prob. rdg.; Heb.* seal.   *c* strong men: *or* leaders *or* gods.

42 Then Job answered the LORD:

2 I know that thou canst do all things
   and that no purpose is beyond thee.
3 But I have spoken of great things which I have not understood,
   things too wonderful for me to know.[a]
5 I knew of thee then only by report,
   but now I see thee with my own eyes.
6 Therefore I melt away;[b]
   I repent in dust and ashes.

Epilogue

7 When the LORD had finished speaking to Job, he said to Eliphaz the Temanite, 'I am angry with you and your two friends, because you have not spoken
8 as you ought about me, as my servant Job has done. So now take seven bulls and seven rams, go to my servant Job and offer a whole-offering for yourselves, and he will intercede for you; I will surely show him favour by not being harsh with you because you have not spoken as you ought about me,
9 as he has done.' Then Eliphaz the Temanite and Bildad the Shuhite and Zophar the Naamathite went and carried out the LORD's command, and the LORD showed favour to Job when he had interceded for his friends.
10 So the LORD restored Job's fortunes and doubled all his possessions.
11 Then all Job's brothers and sisters and his former acquaintance came and feasted with him in his home, and they consoled and comforted him for all the misfortunes which the LORD had brought on him; and each of them
12 gave him a sheep[c] and a gold ring. Furthermore, the LORD blessed the end of Job's life more than the beginning; and he had fourteen thousand head of small cattle and six thousand camels, a thousand yoke of oxen and
13 14 as many she-asses. He had seven[d] sons and three daughters; and he named his eldest daughter Jemimah, the second Keziah and the third Keren-
15 happuch. There were no women in all the world so beautiful as Job's daughters; and their father gave them an inheritance with their brothers.
16 Thereafter Job lived another hundred and forty years, he saw his sons
17 and his grandsons to four generations, and died at a very great age.

[a] *Prob. rdg.; Heb. adds* (4) O listen, and let me speak; I will ask questions, and you shall answer.   [b] *Or* despise myself.   [c] *Or* piece of money.   [d] *Or* fourteen.

610

PSALMS

BOOK 1

1

Happy is the man   1
   who does not take the wicked for his guide
   nor walk the road that sinners tread
   nor take his seat among the scornful;
   the law of the LORD is his delight,   2
the law his meditation night and day.
     He is like a tree   3
   planted beside a watercourse,
   which yields its fruit in season
     and its leaf never withers:
   in all that he does he prospers.
Wicked men are not like this;   4
   they are like chaff driven by the wind.
So when judgement comes the wicked shall not stand firm,   5
nor shall sinners stand in the assembly of the righteous.
   The LORD watches over the way of the righteous,   6
     but the way of the wicked is doomed.

2

Why are the nations in turmoil?   1
Why do the peoples hatch their futile plots?
   The kings of the earth stand ready,   2
and the rulers conspire together
against the LORD and his anointed king.
'Let us break their fetters,' they cry,   3
'let us throw off their chains!'
The Lord who sits enthroned in heaven   4
   laughs them to scorn;
then he rebukes them in anger,   5
   he threatens them in his wrath.
Of me he says, 'I have enthroned my king   6
   on Zion my holy mountain.'
I will repeat the LORD's decree: 7
'You are my son,' he said;
   'this day I become your father.
Ask of me what you will: 8
I will give you nations as your inheritance,
the ends of the earth as your possession.

9   You shall break them with a rod of iron,
you shall shatter them like a clay pot.'

10   Be mindful then, you kings;
learn your lesson, rulers of the earth:

11–12   worship the LORD with reverence;
tremble, and kiss the king,[a]
lest the LORD be angry and you are struck down in mid course;
for his anger flares up in a moment.
Happy are all who find refuge in him.

3

1   LORD, how my enemies have multiplied!
Many rise up against me,

2   many there are who say of me,
'God will not bring him victory.'

3   But thou, LORD, art a shield to cover me:
thou art my glory, and thou dost raise my head high.

4   I cry aloud to the LORD,
and he answers me from his holy mountain.

5   I lie down and sleep,
and I wake again, for the LORD upholds me.

6   I will not fear the nations in their myriads
who set on me from all sides.

7   Rise up, LORD; save me, O my God.
Thou dost strike all my foes across the face
and breakest the teeth of the wicked.

8   Thine is the victory, O LORD,
and may[b] thy blessing rest upon thy people.

4

1   Answer me when I call, O God, maintainer of my right,
I was hard pressed, and thou didst set me at large;
be gracious to me now and hear my prayer.

2   Mortal men, how long will you pay me not honour but dishonour,
or set your heart on trifles and run after lies?

3   Know that the LORD has shown me[c] his marvellous love;
the LORD hears when I call to him.

4   However angry your hearts, do not do wrong;
though you lie abed resentful,[d] do not break silence:

5   pay your due of sacrifice, and trust in the LORD.

6   There are many who say, 'If only we might be prosperous again!
But the light of thy presence has fled from us, O LORD.'

[a] tremble . . . king: *prob. rdg.; lit.* tremble and kiss the mighty one; *Heb. obscure.*
[b] Thine . . . and may: *or* O LORD of salvation, may . . .   [c] *Prob. rdg.; Heb.* him.
[d] lie abed resentful: *prob. rdg.; Heb.* say on your beds.

Yet in my heart thou hast put more happiness 　　　　　　7
than they enjoyed when there was corn and wine in plenty.
Now I will lie down in peace, and sleep; 　　　　　　　　8
for thou alone, O LORD, makest me live unafraid.

5

Listen to my words, O LORD, 　　　　　　　　　　　　1
　　consider my inmost thoughts;
heed my cry for help, my king and my God. 　　　　　　2
In the morning, when I say my prayers, 　　　　　　　3
　　thou wilt hear me.
I set out my morning sacrifice[a]
　　and watch for thee, O LORD.
For thou art not a God who welcomes wickedness; 　　4
　　evil can be no guest of thine.[b]
　　There is no place for arrogance before thee; 　　　5
　　　　thou hatest evildoers,
　　　　thou makest an end of all liars. 　　　　　　6

The LORD detests traitors and men of blood.
But I, through thy great love, may come into thy house, 　7
and bow low toward thy holy temple in awe of thee.
　　Lead me, LORD, in thy righteousness, 　　　　　8
　　　　because my enemies are on the watch;
　　give me a straight path to follow.
　　There is no trusting what they say, 　　　　　　9
　　　　they are nothing but wind.
　　Their throats are an open[c] sepulchre;
　　smooth talk runs off their tongues.
　　Bring ruin on them, O God; 　　　　　　　　10
　　let them fall by their own devices.
　　Cast them out, after all their rebellions,
　　for they have defied thee.
　　But let all who take refuge in thee rejoice, 　　11
　　let them for ever break into shouts of joy;
　　shelter those who love thy name,
　　that they may exult in thee.
For thou, O LORD, wilt bless the righteous; 　　　　12
　　thou wilt hedge him round with favour as with a shield.

6

O LORD, do not condemn me in thy anger, 　　　　1
　　do not punish me in thy fury.
Be merciful to me, O LORD, for I am weak; 　　　　2
　　heal me, my very bones are shaken;

[a] *Or* plea. 　　[b] who welcomes . . . thine: *or* who protects a wicked man; an evil man cannot be thy guest. 　　[c] *Or* inscribed.

3   my soul quivers in dismay.
    And thou, O Lord—how long?
4   Come back, O Lord; set my soul free,
    deliver me for thy love's sake.
5   None talk of thee among the dead;
    who praises thee in Sheol?

6   I am wearied with groaning;
all night long my pillow is wet with tears,
I soak my bed with weeping.
7   Grief dims my eyes;
    they are worn out with all my woes.
8   Away from me, all you evildoers,
for the Lord has heard the sound of my weeping.
9   The Lord has heard my entreaty;
    the Lord will accept my prayer.
10   All my enemies shall be confounded and dismayed;
    they shall turn away in sudden confusion.

7

1   O Lord my God, in thee I find refuge;
    save me, rescue me from my pursuers,
2   before they tear at my throat like a lion
and carry me off beyond hope of rescue.
3   O Lord my God, if I have done any of these things—
    if I have stained my hands with guilt,
4   if I have repaid a friend evil for good
or set free an enemy who attacked me without cause,
5   may my adversary come after me and overtake me,
    trample my life to the ground
and lay my honour in the dust!

6   Arise, O Lord, in thy anger,
rouse thyself in wrath against my foes.
Awake, my God who hast ordered that justice be done;
7   let the peoples assemble around thee,
and take thou thy seat on high above them.
8   O Lord, thou who dost pass sentence on the nations,
O Lord, judge me as my righteousness deserves,
for I am clearly innocent.
9   Let wicked men do no more harm,
establish the reign of righteousness,[a]
thou who examinest both heart and mind,
    thou righteous God.

10   God, the High God, is my shield
    who saves men of honest heart.

[a] the reign of righteousness: *or* the cause of the righteous.

God is a just judge,   11
every day he requites the raging enemy.

He sharpens his sword,   12
strings his bow and makes it ready.
He has prepared his deadly shafts   13
and tipped his arrows with fire.
But the enemy is in labour with iniquity;   14
he conceives mischief, and his brood is lies.
He has made a pit and dug it deep,   15
and he himself shall fall into the hole that he has made.
His mischief shall recoil upon himself,   16
and his violence fall on his own head.

I will praise the LORD for his righteousness   17
and sing a psalm to the name of the LORD Most High.

8

O LORD our sovereign,   1
how glorious is thy name in all the earth!
Thy majesty is praised high as the heavens.
Out of the mouths of babes, of infants at the breast,   2
thou hast rebuked^a the mighty,
silencing enmity and vengeance to teach thy foes a lesson.
When I look up at thy heavens, the work of thy fingers,   3
the moon and the stars set in their place by thee,
what is man that thou shouldst remember him,   4
mortal man that thou shouldst care for him?
Yet thou hast made him little less than a god,   5
crowning him with glory and honour.
Thou makest him master over all thy creatures;   6
thou hast put everything under his feet:
all sheep and oxen, all the wild beasts,   7
the birds in the air and the fish in the sea,   8
and all that moves along the paths of ocean.
O LORD our sovereign,   9
how glorious is thy name in all the earth!

9-10

I will praise thee, O LORD, with all my heart,   1
I will tell the story of thy marvellous acts.
I will rejoice and exult in thee,   2
I will praise thy name in psalms, O thou Most High,
when my enemies turn back,   3
when they fall headlong and perish at thy appearing;

---

^a *Prob. rdg.; Heb.* founded.

4   for thou hast upheld my right and my cause,
      seated on thy throne, thou righteous judge.

5   Thou hast rebuked the nations and overwhelmed the ungodly,
      thou hast blotted out their name for all time.

6   The strongholds of the enemy are thrown down for evermore;
      thou hast laid their cities in ruins, all memory of them is lost.

7   The LORD thunders,[a] he sits enthroned for ever:
      he has set up his throne, his judgement-seat.

8   He it is who will judge the world with justice
      and try the cause of the peoples fairly.

9   So may the LORD be a tower of strength for the oppressed,
      a tower of strength in time of need,

10   that those who acknowledge thy name may trust in thee;
      for thou, LORD, dost not forsake those who seek thee.

11   Sing psalms to the LORD who dwells in Zion,
      proclaim his deeds among the nations.

12   For the Avenger of blood has remembered men's desire,
      and has not forgotten the cry of the poor.

13   Have pity on me, O LORD; look upon my affliction,
      thou who hast lifted me up[b] and caught me back from the gates of death,

14   that I may repeat all thy praise
      and exult at this deliverance in the gates of Zion's city.

15   The nations have plunged into a pit of their own making;
      their own feet are entangled in the net which they hid.

16   Now the LORD makes himself known. Justice is done:
      the wicked man is trapped in his own devices.

17   They rush blindly down to Sheol, the wicked,
      all the nations who are heedless of God.

18   But the poor shall not always be unheeded
      nor the hope of the destitute be always vain.

19   Arise, LORD, give man no chance to boast his strength;
      summon the nations before thee for judgement.

20   Strike them with fear, O LORD,
      let the nations know that they are but men.

10 Why stand so far off, LORD,
      hiding thyself in time of need?

2   The wicked man in his pride hunts down the poor:
      may his crafty schemes be his own undoing!

3   The wicked man is obsessed with his own desires,
      and in his greed gives wickedness his blessing;

4   arrogant as he is, he scorns the LORD
      and leaves no place for God in all his schemes.

5   His ways are always devious;
      thy judgements are beyond his grasp,[c]
      and he scoffs at all restraint.

---

[a] thunders: *prob. rdg.; Heb. unintelligible.*   [b] thou . . . me up: *prob. rdg.; Heb.* from those who hate me.   [c] beyond his grasp: *prob. rdg.; Heb.* on high before him.

He says to himself, 'I shall never be shaken;	6
no misfortune can check my course.' ^a	

He says to himself, 'I shall never be shaken; 6
no misfortune can check my course.' *a*

His mouth is full of lies and violence; 7
 mischief and trouble lurk under his tongue.

 He lies in ambush in the villages 8
 and murders innocent men by stealth.

 He is watching *b* intently for some poor wretch;
he seizes him and drags him away in his net; 9
he crouches stealthily, like a lion in its lair
 crouching to seize its victim;
 the good man *c* is struck down and sinks to the ground, 10
 and poor wretches fall into his toils.

He says to himself, 'God has forgotten; 11
he has hidden his face and has seen nothing.'

Arise, LORD, set *d* thy hand to the task; 12
 do not forget the poor, O God.

Why, O God, has the wicked man rejected thee 13
 and said to himself that thou dost not care?

Thou seest that mischief and trouble are his companions, 14
 thou takest the matter into thy own hands.

 The poor victim commits himself to thee;
fatherless, he finds in thee his helper.

 Break the power of wickedness and wrong; 15
 hunt out all wickedness until thou canst find no more.

The LORD is king for ever and ever; 16
 the nations have vanished from his land.

 Thou hast heard the lament of the humble, O LORD, 17
 and art attentive to their heart's desire,

 bringing justice to the orphan and the downtrodden 18
that fear may never drive men from their homes again.

11

In the LORD I have found my refuge; why do you say to me, 1
 'Flee to the mountains like a bird;

see how the wicked string their bows 2
 and fit the arrow to the string,

 to shoot down honest men out of the darkness'?

When foundations are undermined, what can the good man do? 3

 The LORD is in his holy temple, 4
 the LORD's throne is in heaven.

His eye is upon mankind, he takes their measure at a glance.

The LORD weighs just and unjust 5
 and hates with all his soul the lover of violence.

---

a my course: *prob. rdg.; Heb.* which. *b* *Prob. rdg.; Heb.* storing up. *c* the good
man: *prob. rdg.; Heb. om.* *d* *Or* who settest.

6   He shall rain down red-hot coals upon the wicked;
        brimstone and scorching winds shall be the cup they drink.

7   For the LORD is just and loves just dealing;
        his face is turned towards the upright man.

12

1   Help, LORD, for loyalty is no more;
        good faith between man and man is over.

2   One man lies to another:
        they talk with smooth lip and double heart.

3   May the LORD make an end of such smooth lips
        and the tongue that talks so boastfully!

4   They said, 'Our tongue can win the day.
        Words are our ally; who can master us?'

5   'For the ruin of the poor, for the groans of the needy,
        now I will arise,' says the LORD,
        'I will place him in the safety for which he longs.'

6   The words of the LORD are pure words:
        silver refined in a crucible,
        gold [a] seven times purified.

7   Do thou, LORD, protect us
        and guard us from a profligate and evil generation. [b]

8   The wicked flaunt themselves on every side,
        while profligacy stands high among mankind.

13

1   How long, O LORD, wilt thou quite forget me?
        How long wilt thou hide thy face from me?

2   How long must I suffer anguish in my soul,
        grief in my heart, day and night?
        How long shall my enemy lord it over me?

3   Look now and answer me, O LORD my God.
        Give light to my eyes lest I sleep the sleep of death,

4   lest my adversary say, 'I have overthrown him',
        and my enemies rejoice at my downfall.

5   But for my part I trust in thy true love.
        My heart shall rejoice, for thou hast set me free.

6   I will sing to the LORD, who has granted all my desire.

14

1 [c]   The impious fool says in his heart,
        'There is no God.'
        How vile men are, how depraved and loathsome;
        not one does anything good!

[a] gold: *prob. rdg.; Heb.* to the earth.   [b] a profligate and evil generation: *prob. rdg.;*
Heb. the generation which is for ever.   [c] *Verses 1-7 : cp. Ps. 53. 1-6.*

The Lord looks down from heaven
 on all mankind
to see if any act wisely,
 if any seek out God.   2
But all are disloyal, all are rotten to the core;   3
 not one does anything good,
 no, not even one.

 Shall they not rue it,   4
all evildoers who devour my people
 as men devour bread,
 and never call upon the Lord?
There they were in dire alarm;   5
for God was in the brotherhood of the godly.
 The resistance of their victim was too much for them,   6
 because the Lord was his refuge.
If only Israel's deliverance might come out of Zion!   7
 When the Lord restores his people's fortunes,
let Jacob rejoice, let Israel be glad.

15

O Lord, who may lodge in thy tabernacle?   1
Who may dwell on thy holy mountain?
The man of blameless life, who does what is right   2
and speaks the truth from his heart;
 who has no malice on his tongue,   3
who never wrongs a friend
and tells no tales against his neighbour;
the man who shows his scorn for the worthless   4
and honours all who fear the Lord;
who swears to his own hurt and does not retract;
who does not put his money out to usury   5
and takes no bribe against an innocent man.
He who does these things shall never be brought low.

16

Keep me, O God, for in thee have I found refuge.   1
 I have said to the Lord,   2
'Thou, Lord, art my felicity.'
The gods whom earth holds sacred are all worthless,   3
and cursed are all who make them their delight; [a]
those who run after them [b] find trouble without end.   4
 I will not offer them libations of blood
nor take their names upon my lips.
 Thou, Lord, my allotted portion, thou my cup,   5
 thou dost enlarge my boundaries:

---

[a] are all worthless . . . delight: *prob. rdg.; Heb. obscure.*   [b] after them: *prob. rdg.;*
Heb. obscure.

6   the lines fall for me in pleasant places,
       indeed I am well content with my inheritance.

7   I will bless the LORD who has given me counsel:
       in the night-time wisdom comes to me in my inward parts.

8   I have set the LORD continually before me:
       with him*ᵃ* at my right hand I cannot be shaken.

9   Therefore my heart exults
       and my spirit rejoices,
       my body too rests unafraid;

10   for thou wilt not abandon me to Sheol
       nor suffer thy faithful servant to see the pit.

11   Thou wilt show me the path of life;
       in thy presence is the fullness of joy,
       in thy right hand pleasures for evermore.

17

1   Hear, LORD, my plea for justice,
       give my cry a hearing,
       listen to my prayer,
       for it is innocent of all deceit.

2   Let judgement in my cause issue from thy lips,
       let thine eyes be fixed on justice.

3   Thou hast tested my heart and watched me all night long;
       thou hast assayed me and found in me no mind to evil.

4   I will not speak of the deeds of men;
       I have taken good note of all thy sayings.

5   I have not strayed from the course of duty;
       I have followed thy path and never stumbled.

6   I call upon thee, O God, for thou wilt answer me.
    Bend down thy ear to me, listen to my words.

7   Show me how marvellous thy true love can be,
       who with thy hand dost save
       all who seek sanctuary from their enemies.

8   Keep me like the apple of thine eye;
       hide me in the shadow of thy wings

9   from the wicked who obstruct me,
    from deadly foes who throng round me.

10   They have stifled all compassion;
       their mouths are full of pride;

11   they press me hard,*ᵇ* now they hem me in,
    on the watch to bring me to the ground.

12   The enemy is like a lion eager for prey,
       like a young lion crouching in ambush.

13   Arise, LORD, meet him face to face and bring him down.

ᵃ with him: *prob. rdg.; Heb. om.*   *ᵇ* they press me hard: *prob. rdg.; Heb.* our footsteps.

Save my life from the wicked;
  make an end of them*a* with thy sword.   14
With thy hand, O LORD, make an end of them; *a*
thrust them out of this world in the prime of their life,
gorged as they are with thy good things,
    blest with many sons
and leaving their children wealth in plenty.
But my plea is just: I shall see thy face,   15
  and be blest with a vision of thee when I awake.

18

I love thee, O LORD my strength.   1
The LORD is my stronghold, my fortress and my champion,   2*b*
my God, my rock where I find safety,
my shield, my mountain refuge, my strong tower.
I will call on the LORD to whom all praise is due,   3
and I shall be delivered from my enemies.
When the bonds of death held me fast,   4
destructive torrents overtook me,
the bonds of Sheol tightened round me,   5
the snares of death were set to catch me;
then in anguish of heart I cried to the LORD,   6
I called for help to my God;
he heard me from his temple,
and my cry reached his ears.
The earth heaved and quaked,   7
the foundations of the mountains shook;
they heaved, because he was angry.
Smoke rose from his nostrils,   8
devouring fire came out of his mouth,
glowing coals and searing heat.
He swept the skies aside as he descended,   9
thick darkness lay under his feet.
He rode on a cherub, he flew through the air;   10
he swooped on the wings of the wind.
He made darkness around him his hiding-place   11
and dense *c* vapour his canopy. *d*
Thick clouds came out of the radiance before him,   12
hailstones and glowing coals.
The LORD thundered from the heavens   13
and the voice of the Most High spoke out. *e*
He loosed his arrows, he sped them far and wide,   14
he shot forth lightning shafts and sent them echoing.

---

a make an end of them: *prob. rdg.; Heb. unintelligible.*   *b* *Verses 2–50: cp. 2 Sam.*
22. 2–51.   *c* *Prob. rdg., cp. 2 Sam. 22. 12; Heb.* dark.   *d* *Prob. rdg.;*
Heb. adds thick clouds.   *e* *Prob. rdg.; Heb. adds* hailstones and glowing coals.

15 The channels of the sea-bed were revealed,
    the foundations of earth laid bare
      at the LORD's rebuke,
    at the blast of the breath of his *a* nostrils.

16 He reached down from the height and took me,
    he drew me out of mighty waters,

17 he rescued me from my enemies, strong as they were,
    from my foes when they grew too powerful for me.

18 They confronted me in the hour of my peril,
    but the LORD was my buttress.

19 He brought me out into an open place,
    he rescued me because he delighted in me.

20 The LORD rewarded me as my righteousness deserved;
    my hands were clean, and he requited me.

21 For I have followed the ways of the LORD
    and have not turned wickedly from my God;

22 all his laws are before my eyes,
    I have not failed to follow his decrees.

23 In his sight I was blameless
    and kept myself from wilful sin;

24 the LORD requited me as my righteousness deserved
    and the purity of my life in his eyes.

25 With the loyal thou showest thyself loyal
    and with the blameless man blameless.

26 With the savage man thou showest thyself savage,
    and *b* tortuous with the perverse.

27 Thou deliverest humble folk,
    and bringest proud looks down to earth.

28 Thou, LORD, dost make my lamp burn bright,
    and my God will lighten my darkness.

29 With thy help I leap over a bank,
    by God's aid I spring over a wall.

30 The way of God is perfect,
    the LORD's word has stood the test;
    he is the shield of all who take refuge in him.

31 What god is there but the LORD?
    What rock but our God?—

32 the God who girds me with strength
    and makes my way blameless,

33 who makes me swift as a hind
    and sets me secure on the mountains;

34 who trains my hands for battle,
    and my arms aim an arrow tipped with bronze.

---

a *Prob. rdg.; Heb.* thy.   *b* With the savage . . . savage, and: *or* With the pure thou
showest thyself pure, but . . .

Thou hast given me the shield of thy salvation, 35
thy hand sustains me, thy providence makes me great.
Thou givest me room for my steps, 36
my feet have not faltered.
I pursue my enemies and overtake them, 37
I do not return until I have made an end of them.
I strike them down and they will never rise again; 38
they fall beneath my feet.
Thou dost arm me with strength for the battle 39
and dost subdue my foes before me.
Thou settest my foot on my enemies' necks, 40
and I bring to nothing those that hate me.
They cry out and there is no one to help them, 41
they cry to the LORD and he does not answer.
I will pound them fine as dust before the wind, 42
like mud in the streets will I trample them. *a*
Thou dost deliver me from the clamour of the people, 43
and makest me master of the nations.
A people I never knew shall be my subjects; 44
as soon as they hear tell of me, they shall obey me,
and foreigners shall come cringing to me.
Foreigners shall be brought captive to me, 45
and emerge from their strongholds.

The LORD lives, blessed is my rock, 46
high above all is God who saves me.

O God, who grantest me vengeance, 47
who layest nations prostrate at my feet,
who dost rescue me from my foes and set me over my enemies, 48
thou dost deliver me from violent men.
Therefore, LORD, I will praise thee among the nations 49
and sing psalms to thy name,
to one who gives his king great victories 50
and in all his acts keeps faith with his anointed king,
with David and his descendants for ever.

19

The heavens tell out the glory of God, 1
the vault of heaven reveals his handiwork.
One day speaks to another, 2
night with night shares its knowledge,
and this without speech or language 3
or sound of any voice.
Their music goes out through all the earth, 4
their words reach to the end of the world.

---

a *Prob. rdg., cp. 2 Sam. 22. 43; Heb.* will I empty them out.

In them a tent is fixed for the sun,
5   who comes out like a bridegroom from his wedding canopy,
rejoicing like a strong man to run his race.
6   His rising is at one end of the heavens,
his circuit touches their farthest ends;
and nothing is hidden from his heat.

7   The law of the LORD is perfect and revives the soul.
The LORD's instruction never fails,
and makes the simple wise.
8   The precepts of the LORD are right and rejoice the heart.
The commandment of the LORD shines clear
and gives light to the eyes.
9   The fear of the LORD is pure and abides for ever.
The LORD's decrees are true and righteous every one,
10 more to be desired than gold, pure gold in plenty,
sweeter than syrup or honey from the comb.
11 It is these that give thy servant warning,
and he who keeps them wins a great reward.

12   Who is aware of his unwitting sins?
Cleanse me of any secret fault.
13   Hold back thy servant also from sins of self-will,
lest they get the better of me.
Then I shall be blameless
and innocent of any great transgression.

14   May all that I say and think be acceptable to thee,
O LORD, my rock and my redeemer!

20

1   May the LORD answer you in the hour of trouble!
The name of Jacob's God be your tower of strength,
2   give you help from the sanctuary
and send you support from Zion!
3   May he remember all your offerings
and look with favour on your rich sacrifices,
4   give you your heart's desire
and grant success to all your plans!
5   Let us sing aloud in praise of your victory,
let us do homage to the name of our God!
The LORD grant all you ask!

6   Now I know
that the LORD has given victory to his anointed king:
he will answer him from his holy heaven
with the victorious might of his right hand.
7   Some boast of chariots and some of horses,
but our boast is the name of the LORD our God.

They totter and fall,   8
but we rise up and are full of courage.
O Lord, save the king,   9
    and answer us in the hour of our calling.

21

The king rejoices in thy might, O Lord: 1
    well may he exult in thy victory,
        for thou hast given him his heart's desire   2
            and hast not refused him what he asked.
    Thou dost welcome him with blessings and prosperity   3
    and set a crown of fine gold upon his head.
He asked of thee life, and thou didst give it him,   4
    length of days for ever and ever.
    Thy salvation has brought him great glory;   5
thou dost invest him with majesty and honour,
    for thou bestowest blessings on him for evermore   6
    and dost make him glad with joy in thy presence.
    The king puts his trust in the Lord;   7
        the loving care of the Most High holds him unshaken.

    Your hand shall reach all your enemies: 8
your right hand shall reach those who hate you;
    at your coming you shall plunge them into a fiery furnace;   9
    the Lord in his anger will strike them down,
        and fire shall consume them.
    It will exterminate their offspring from the earth   10
    and rid mankind of their posterity.
    For they have aimed wicked blows at you,   11
    they have plotted mischief but could not prevail;
    but you will catch them round the shoulders   12
    and will aim with your bow-strings at their faces.

    Be exalted, O Lord, in thy might;   13
    we will sing a psalm of praise to thy power.

22

My God, my God, why hast thou forsaken me   1
    and art so far from saving me, from heeding my groans?
O my God, I cry in the day-time but thou dost not answer,   2
    in the night I cry but get no respite.
And yet thou art enthroned in holiness,   3
    thou art he whose praises Israel sings.
In thee our fathers put their trust;   4
    they trusted, and thou didst rescue them.
Unto thee they cried and were delivered;   5
    in thee they trusted and were not put to shame.

6   But I am a worm, not a man,
           abused by all men, scorned by the people.

7   All who see me jeer at me,
       make mouths at me and wag their heads:

8   'He threw himself on the LORD for rescue;
            let the LORD deliver him, for he holds him dear!'

9   But thou art he who drew me from the womb,
           who laid me at my mother's breast.

10   Upon thee was I cast at birth;
       from my mother's womb thou hast been my God.

11   Be not far from me,
       for trouble is near, and I have no helper.

12   A herd of bulls surrounds me,
           great bulls of Bashan beset me.

13   Ravening and roaring lions
       open their mouths wide against me.

14   My strength drains away like water
           and all my bones are loose.
       My heart has turned to wax and melts within me.

15   My mouth[a] is dry as a potsherd,
           and my tongue sticks to my jaw;
           I am laid[b] low in the dust of death.

16   The huntsmen are all about me;
           a band of ruffians rings me round,
       and they have hacked off[c] my hands and my feet.

17   I tell my tale of misery,
       while they look on and gloat.

18   They share out my garments among them
       and cast lots for my clothes.

19   But do not remain so far away, O LORD;
       O my help, hasten to my aid.

20   Deliver my very self from the sword,
           my precious life from the axe.

21   Save me from the lion's mouth,
           my poor body[d] from the horns of the wild ox.

22   I will declare thy fame to my brethren;
           I will praise thee in the midst of the assembly.

23   Praise him, you who fear the LORD;
           all you sons of Jacob, do him honour;
       stand in awe of him, all sons of Israel.

24   For he has not scorned the downtrodden,
           nor shrunk in loathing from his plight,
       nor hidden his face from him,
       but gave heed to him when he cried out.

[a] *Prob. rdg.; Heb.* My strength.   [b] I am laid: *prob. rdg.; Heb.* thou wilt lay me.
[c] and they have hacked off: *prob. rdg.; Heb.* like a lion.   [d] my poor body: *prob. rdg.; Heb.* thou hast answered me.

Thou dost inspire my praise in the full assembly;   25
   and I will pay my vows before all who fear thee.
Let the humble eat and be satisfied.   26
Let those who seek the LORD praise him
   and be in good heart for ever.
Let all the ends of the earth remember and turn again to the   27
     LORD;
let all the families of the nations bow down before him.
   For kingly power belongs to the LORD,   28
   and dominion over the nations is his.
How can those buried in the earth do him homage,   29
   how can those who go down to the grave bow before him?
   But I shall live for his sake,
   my posterity*a* shall serve him.   30
This shall be told of the Lord to future generations;
   and they shall justify him,   31
     declaring to a people yet unborn
     that this was his doing.

23

The LORD is my shepherd; I shall want nothing.   1
   He makes me lie down in green pastures,   2
and leads me beside the waters of peace;
   he renews life within me,   3
and for his name's sake guides me in the right path.
   Even though I walk through a valley dark as death   4
   I fear no evil, for thou art with me,
thy staff and thy crook are my comfort.

Thou spreadest a table for me in the sight of my enemies;   5
   thou hast richly bathed my head with oil,
     and my cup runs over.
   Goodness and love unfailing, these will follow me   6
     all the days of my life,
     and I shall dwell in the house of the LORD
     my whole life long.

24

The earth is the LORD's and all that is in it,   1
   the world and those who dwell therein.
For it was he who founded it upon the seas   2
   and planted it firm upon the waters beneath.

Who may go up the mountain of the LORD?   3
And who may stand in his holy place?

    a But I . . . posterity: *prob. rdg.; Heb. obscure.*

4 He who has clean hands and a pure heart,
who has not set his mind on falsehood,
and has not committed perjury.

5 He shall receive a blessing from the LORD,
and justice from God his saviour.

6 Such is the fortune of those who seek him,
who seek the face of the God of Jacob.

7 Lift up your heads, you gates,
lift yourselves up, you everlasting doors,
that the king of glory may come in.

8 Who is the king of glory?
The LORD strong and mighty,
the LORD mighty in battle.

9 Lift up your heads, you gates,
lift them up, you everlasting doors,
that the king of glory may come in.

10 Who then is the king of glory?
The king of glory is the LORD of Hosts.

25

1 Unto thee, O LORD my God, I lift up my heart.

2 In thee I trust: do not put me to shame,
let not my enemies exult over me.

3 No man who hopes in thee is put to shame;
but shame comes to all who break faith without cause.

4 Make thy paths known to me, O LORD;
teach me thy ways.

5 Lead me in thy truth and teach me;
thou art God my saviour.
For thee I have waited all the day long,
for the coming of thy goodness, LORD. *a*

6 Remember, LORD, thy tender care and thy love unfailing,
shown from ages past.

7 Do not remember the sins and offences of my youth,
but remember me in thy unfailing love.

8 The LORD is good and upright;
therefore he teaches sinners the way they should go.

9 He guides the humble man in doing right,
he teaches the humble his ways.

10 All the ways of the LORD are loving and sure
to men who keep his covenant and his charge.

11 For the honour of thy name, O LORD,
forgive my wickedness, great as it is.

12 If there is any man who fears the LORD,
he shall be shown the path that he should choose;

a for the coming ... LORD: *transposed from end of verse 7.*

he shall enjoy lasting prosperity,   13
and his children after him shall inherit the land.
    The LORD confides his purposes to those who fear him,   14
    and his covenant is theirs to know.
My eyes are ever on the LORD,   15
who alone can free my feet from the net.

Turn to me and show me thy favour,   16
for I am lonely and oppressed.
    Relieve the sorrows of my heart   17
    and bring me out of my distress.
Look at my misery and my trouble   18
    and forgive me every sin.
Look at my enemies, see how many they are   19
    and how violent their hatred for me.
Defend me and deliver me,   20
do not put me to shame when I take refuge in thee.
Let integrity and uprightness protect me,   21
    for I have waited for thee, O LORD.
O God, redeem Israel from all his sorrows.   22

26

    Give me justice, O LORD,   1
for I have lived my life without reproach,
and put unfaltering trust in the LORD.
Test me, O LORD, and try me;   2
put my heart and mind to the proof.
For thy constant love is before my eyes,   3
    and I live in thy truth.
I have not sat among worthless men,   4
    nor do I mix with hypocrites;
    I hate the company of evildoers   5
    and will not sit among the ungodly.
I wash my hands in innocence   6
to join in procession round thy altar, O LORD,
singing of thy marvellous acts,   7
    recounting them all with thankful voice.
O LORD, I love the beauty of thy house,   8
    the place where thy glory dwells.
Do not sweep me away with sinners,   9
nor cast me out with men who thirst for blood,
    whose fingers are active in mischief,   10
and their hands are full of bribes.
But I live my life without reproach;   11
redeem me, O LORD, and show me thy favour.
When once my feet are planted on firm ground,   12
I will bless the LORD in the full assembly.

27

1   The LORD is my light and my salvation;
        whom should I fear?
    The LORD is the refuge of my life;
        of whom then should I go in dread?
2   When evildoers close in on me to devour me,
        it is my enemies, my assailants,
            who stumble and fall.
3   If an army should encamp against me,
        my heart would feel no fear;
    if armed men should fall upon me,
        even then I should be undismayed.
4   One thing I ask of the LORD,
        one thing I seek:
        that I may be constant in the house of the LORD
        all the days of my life,
        to gaze upon the beauty of the LORD
        and to seek him*a* in his temple.
5   For he will keep me safe beneath his roof
        in the day of misfortune;
    he will hide me under the cover of his tent;
        he will raise me beyond reach of distress.
6   Now I can raise my head high
        above the enemy all about me;
    so will I acclaim him with sacrifice before his tent
        and sing a psalm of praise to the LORD.

7   Hear, O LORD, when I call aloud;
        show me favour and answer me.
8   'Come,' my heart has said,
        'seek his face.'*b*
    I will seek thy face, O LORD;
9   do not hide it from me,
    nor in thy anger turn away thy servant,
        whose help thou hast been;
    do not cast me off or forsake me, O God my saviour.
10 Though my father and my mother forsake me,
        the LORD will take me into his care.
11-12 Teach me thy way, O LORD;
    do not give me up to the greed of my enemies;
    lead me by a level path
        to escape my watchful foes;
    liars stand up to give evidence against me,
        breathing malice.

---

a Or and to pay my morning worship.   *b* seek his face: *prob. rdg.; Heb.* seek ye
my face.

Well I know that I shall see the goodness of the LORD   13
  in the land of the living.

Wait for the LORD; be strong, take courage,   14
  and wait for the LORD.

28

To thee, O LORD, I call;   1
O my Rock, be not deaf to my cry,
  lest, if thou answer me with silence,
I become like those who go down to the abyss.
  Hear my cry for mercy   2
    when I call to thee for help,
  when I lift my hands to thy holy shrine.
Do not drag me away with the ungodly, with evildoers,   3
who speak civilly to neighbours, with malice in their hearts.
Reward them for their works, their evil deeds;   4
  reward them for what their hands have done;
  give them their deserts.
Because they pay no heed to the works of the LORD   5
  or to what his hands have done,
    may he tear them down and never build them up!

  Blessed be the LORD,   6
for he has heard my cry for mercy.
The LORD is my strength, my shield,   7
  in him my heart trusts;
so I am sustained, and my heart leaps for joy,
  and I praise him with my whole body. *a*
The LORD is strength to his people,   8
a safe refuge for his anointed king.

O save thy people and bless thy own,   9
  shepherd them, carry them for ever.

29

Ascribe to the LORD, you gods,   1
ascribe to the LORD glory and might.
  Ascribe to the LORD the glory due to his name;   2
  bow down to the LORD in the splendour of holiness. *b*
    The God of glory thunders: 3
    the voice of the LORD echoes over the waters,
    the LORD is over the mighty waters.
    The voice of the LORD is power.   4
    The voice of the LORD is majesty.

a with my whole body: *prob. rdg.; Heb.* from my song.   *b* the splendour of holiness: *or* holy vestments.

5   The voice of the LORD breaks the cedars,
          the LORD splinters the cedars of Lebanon.
6   He makes Lebanon skip like a calf,
          Sirion like a young wild ox.
7   The voice of the LORD makes flames of fire burst forth,
8   the voice of the LORD makes the wilderness writhe in travail;
          the LORD makes the wilderness of Kadesh writhe.
9   The voice of the LORD makes the hinds calve
            and brings kids early to birth;
     and in his temple all cry, 'Glory!'
10   The LORD is king above *a* the flood,
       the LORD has taken his royal seat as king for ever.
11   The LORD will give strength to his people;
       the LORD will bless his people with peace.

30

1   I will exalt thee, O LORD;
          thou hast lifted me up
      and hast not let my enemies make merry over me.
2   O LORD my God, I cried to thee and thou didst heal me.
3   O LORD, thou hast brought me up from Sheol
          and saved my life as I was sinking into the abyss. *b*
4   Sing a psalm to the LORD, all you his loyal servants,
          and give thanks to his holy name.
5   In his anger is disquiet, in his favour there is life.
        Tears may linger at nightfall,
          but joy comes in the morning.
6   Carefree as I was, I had said,
          'I can never be shaken.'
7   But, LORD, it was thy will to shake my mountain refuge;
      thou didst hide thy face, and I was struck with dismay.
8   I called unto thee, O LORD,
          and I pleaded with thee, Lord, for mercy:
9   'What profit in my death if I go down into the pit?
      Can the dust confess thee or proclaim thy truth?
10   Hear, O LORD, and be gracious to me;
        LORD, be my helper.'
11   Thou hast turned my laments into dancing;
      thou hast stripped off my sackcloth and clothed me with joy,
12   that my spirit may sing psalms to thee and never cease.
     I will confess thee for ever, O LORD my God.

---

a *Or* since.   *b* *and saved . . . abyss: or* and rescued me alive from among those
who go down to the abyss.

31

With thee, O Lord, I have sought shelter, 1
  let me never be put to shame.
  Deliver me in thy righteousness;
bow down and hear me, 2
  come quickly to my rescue;
be thou my rock of refuge,
  a stronghold to keep me safe.
Thou art to me both rock and stronghold; 3
  lead me and guide me for the honour of thy name.
Set me free from the net men have hidden for me; 4
  thou art my refuge,
  into thy keeping I commit my spirit. 5
Thou hast redeemed me, O Lord thou God of truth.
  Thou hatest all who worship useless idols, 6
but I put my trust in the Lord.
I will rejoice and be glad in thy unfailing love; 7
  for thou hast seen my affliction
  and hast cared for me in my distress.
Thou hast not abandoned me to the power of the enemy 8
but hast set me free to range at will.
Be gracious to me, O Lord, for I am in distress, 9
and my eyes are dimmed with grief. *a*
My life is worn away with sorrow 10
  and my years with sighing;
strong as I am, I stumble under my load of misery;
  there is disease in all my bones.
I have such enemies that all men scorn me; *b* 11
  my neighbours find me a burden,
  my friends shudder at me;
when they see me in the street they turn quickly away.
I am forgotten, like a dead man out of mind; 12
I have come to be like something lost.
For I hear many men whispering 13
  threats from every side,
in league against me as they are
and plotting to take my life.
But, Lord, I put my trust in thee; 14
  I say, 'Thou art my God.'
  My fortunes are in thy hand; 15
rescue me from my enemies and those who persecute me.
Make thy face shine upon thy servant; 16
  save me in thy unfailing love.
O Lord, do not put me to shame when I call upon thee; 17
let the wicked be ashamed, let them sink into Sheol.

---

a Prob. rdg.; Heb. adds my soul and my body.   *b* I have . . . scorn me: *or* I am scorned by all my enemies.

18   Strike dumb the lying lips
        which speak with contempt against the righteous
            in pride and arrogance.

19   How great is thy goodness,
            stored up for those who fear thee,
        made manifest before the eyes of men
            for all who turn to thee for shelter.

20   Thou wilt hide them under the cover of thy presence
            from men in league together;
            thou keepest them beneath thy roof,
            safe from contentious men.

21   Blessed be the LORD,
        who worked a miracle of unfailing love for me
            when I was in sore straits.*a*

22   In sudden alarm I said,
            'I am shut out from thy sight.'
        But thou didst hear my cry for mercy
            when I called to thee for help.

23   Love the LORD, all you his loyal servants.
        The LORD protects the faithful
            but pays the arrogant in full.

24   Be strong and take courage,
            all you whose hope is in the LORD.

32

1   Happy the man whose disobedience is forgiven,
            whose sin is put away!

2   Happy is a man when the LORD lays no guilt to his account,
            and in his spirit there is no deceit.

3   While I refused to speak, my body wasted away
            with moaning all day long.

4   For day and night
        thy hand was heavy upon me,
        the sap in me dried up as in summer drought.

5   Then I declared my sin, I did not conceal my guilt.
            I said, 'With sorrow I will confess
                my disobedience to the LORD';
            then thou didst remit the penalty of my sin.

6   So every faithful heart shall pray to thee
            in the hour of anxiety,*b* when great floods threaten.
            Thou art a refuge for me from distress
                so that it cannot touch me;*c*

---

a when . . . straits: *prob. rdg.; Heb.* like a city besieged.   *b* of anxiety: *prob. rdg.;*
Heb. unintelligible.   *c Prob. rdg.; Heb.* him.

thou dost guard me^a and enfold me in salvation   7
   beyond all reach of harm.^b

I will teach you, and guide you in the way you should go.   8
   I will keep you under my eye.
Do not behave like horse or mule, unreasoning creatures,   9
whose course must be checked with bit and bridle.
   Many are the torments of the ungodly;   10
but unfailing love enfolds him who trusts in the LORD.
Rejoice in the LORD and be glad, you righteous men,   11
   and sing aloud, all men of upright heart.

33

Shout for joy before the LORD, you who are righteous;   1
praise comes well from the upright.
Give thanks to the LORD on the harp;   2
sing him psalms to the ten-stringed lute.
Sing to him a new song;   3
strike up with all your art and shout in triumph.
   The word of the LORD holds true,   4
     and all his work endures.
The LORD loves righteousness and justice,   5
his love unfailing fills the earth.
The LORD's word made the heavens,   6
all the host of heaven was made at his command.
He gathered the sea like water in a goatskin;   7
he laid up the deep in his store-chambers.
Let the whole world fear the LORD   8
and all men on earth stand in awe of him.
For he spoke, and it was;   9
he commanded, and it stood firm.
The LORD brings the plans of nations to nothing;   10
   he frustrates the counsel of the peoples.
But the LORD's own plans shall stand for ever,   11
and his counsel endure for all generations.
Happy is the nation whose God is the LORD,   12
   the people he has chosen for his own possession.
The LORD looks out from heaven,   13
he sees the whole race of men;
he surveys from his dwelling-place   14
   all the inhabitants of earth.
It is he who fashions the hearts of all men alike,   15
who discerns all that they do.
A king is not saved by a great army,   16
nor a warrior delivered by great strength.

^a *Prob. rdg.; Heb. adds an unintelligible word.*   ^b beyond . . . harm: *transposed
from end of verse 9.*

17 A man cannot trust his horse to save him,
        nor can it deliver him for all its strength.
18 The LORD's eyes are turned towards those who fear him,
        towards those who hope for his unfailing love
19 to deliver them from death,
        to keep them alive in famine.
20 We have waited eagerly for the LORD;
        he is our help and our shield.
21   For in him our hearts are glad,
        because we have trusted in his holy name.
22 Let thy unfailing love, O LORD, rest upon us,
        as we have put our hope in thee.

34

1   I will bless the LORD continually;
        his praise shall be always on my lips.
2   In the LORD I will glory;
        the humble shall hear and be glad.
3   O glorify the LORD with me,
        and let us exalt his name together.
4   I sought the LORD's help and he answered me;
        he set me free from all my terrors.
5   Look towards him and shine with joy;
        no longer hang your heads in shame.
6   Here was a poor wretch who cried to the LORD;
        he heard him and saved him from all his troubles.
7   The angel of the LORD is on guard
        round those who fear him, and rescues them.
8   Taste, then, and see that the LORD is good.
        Happy the man who finds refuge in him!
9   Fear the LORD, all you his holy people;
        for those who fear him lack nothing.
10 Unbelievers suffer want and go hungry,
        but those who seek the LORD lack no good thing.
11 Come, my children, listen to me:
        I will teach you the fear of the LORD.
12 Which of you delights in life
        and desires a long life to enjoy all good things?
13 Then keep your tongue from evil
        and your lips from uttering lies;
14 turn from evil and do good,
        seek peace and pursue it.
15   The eyes of the LORD are upon the righteous,
        and his ears are open to their cries.
16 The LORD sets his face against evildoers
        to blot out their memory from the earth.

When men cry for help, the Lord hears them   17
and sets them free from all their troubles.
The Lord is close to those whose courage is broken   18
and he saves those whose spirit is crushed.
The good man's misfortunes may be many,   19
the Lord delivers him out of them all.
   He guards every bone of his body,   20
and not one of them is broken.
Their own misdeeds are death to the wicked,   21
   and those who hate the righteous are brought to ruin.

The Lord ransoms the lives of his servants,   22
and none who seek refuge in him are brought to ruin.

35

Strive, O Lord, with those who strive against me;   1
   fight against those who fight me.
Grasp shield and buckler,   2
   and rise up to help me.
Uncover the spear and bar the way   3
against my pursuers.
Let me hear thee declare,
   'I am your salvation.'
Shame and disgrace be on those who seek my life;   4
and may those who plan to hurt me retreat in dismay!
   May they be like chaff before the wind,   5
      driven by the angel of the Lord!
Let their way be dark and slippery   6
      as the angel of the Lord pursues them!
For unprovoked they have hidden a net[a] for me,   7
unprovoked they have dug a pit to trap me.
May destruction unforeseen come on him;   8
may the net which he hid catch him;
may he crash headlong into it!
Then I shall rejoice in the Lord   9
   and delight in his salvation.
   My very bones cry out,   10
   'Lord, who is like thee?—
thou saviour of the poor from those too strong for them,
the poor and wretched from those who prey on them.'
   Malicious witnesses step forward;   11
      they question me on matters of which I know nothing.
They return me evil for good,   12
   lying in wait[b] to take my life.
And yet when they were sick, I put on sackcloth,   13
   I mortified myself with fasting.

a Prob. rdg., transposing a pit *from this line to follow* have dug.   *b* lying in wait:
prob. rdg.; Heb. bereavement.

When my prayer came back unanswered,

14   I walked with head bowed in grief as if for a brother;
as one in sorrow for his mother I lay prostrate in mourning.

15   But when I stumbled, they crowded round rejoicing,
        they crowded about me;
    nameless ruffians*a* jeered at me
    and nothing would stop them.

16   When I slipped, brutes who would mock even a hunchback
    ground their teeth at me.

17   O Lord, how long wilt thou look on
    at those who hate me for no reason*b*?
    Rescue me out of their cruel grasp,
    save my precious life from the unbelievers.

18   Then I will praise thee before a great assembly,
    I will extol thee where many people meet.

19   Let no treacherous enemy gloat over me
    nor leer at me in triumph.*c*

20   No friendly greeting do they give
    to peaceable folk.
    They invent lie upon lie,

21   they open their mouths at me:
    'Hurrah!' they shout in their joy,
    feasting their eyes on me.

22   Thou hast seen all this, O LORD, do not keep silence;
    O Lord, be not far from me.

23   Awake, bestir thyself, to do me justice,
    to plead my cause, my Lord and my God.

24   Judge me, O LORD my God, as thou art true;
    do not let them gloat over me.

25   Do not let them say to themselves, 'Hurrah!
    We have swallowed him up at one gulp.'

26   Let them all be disgraced and dismayed
    who rejoice at my fall;
    let them be covered with shame and dishonour
    who glory over me.

27   But let all who would see me righted shout for joy,
    let them cry continually,
    'All glory to the LORD
    who would see his servant thrive!'

28   So shall I talk of thy justice
    and of thy praise all the day long.

36

1   Deep in his heart, sin whispers to the wicked man
    who cherishes no fear of God.

---

a nameless ruffians: *or* ruffians who give me no rest.   *b* *Line transposed from verse 19.*
c *See note on verse 17.*

For he flatters himself in his own opinion   2
and, when he is found out, he does not mend his ways. *a*
All that he says is mischievous and false;   3
he has turned his back on wisdom;
in his bed he plots how best to do mischief.   4
So set is he on his wrong courses
    that he rejects nothing evil.
But thy unfailing love, O Lord, reaches to heaven,   5
    thy faithfulness to the skies.
    Thy righteousness is like the lofty mountains,   6
thy judgements are like the great abyss;
O Lord, who savest man and beast,
    how precious is thy unfailing love!   7
Gods and men seek refuge in the shadow of thy wings.
    They are filled with the rich plenty of thy house,   8
    and thou givest them water from the flowing stream of thy
        delights;
    for with thee is the fountain of life,   9
and in thy light we are bathed with light.
Maintain thy love unfailing over those who know thee,   10
    and thy justice toward men of honest heart.
    Let not the foot of pride come near me,   11
    no wicked hand disturb me.
There they lie, the evildoers,   12
they are hurled down and cannot rise.

37

    Do not strive to outdo the evildoers   1
    or emulate those who do wrong.
    For like grass they soon wither,   2
    and fade like the green of spring.
Trust in the Lord and do good;   3
settle in the land and find safe pasture.
    Depend upon the Lord,   4
and he will grant you your heart's desire.
Commit your life to the Lord;   5
trust in him and he will act.
He will make your righteousness shine clear as the day   6
    and the justice of your cause like the sun at noon.
Wait quietly for the Lord, be patient till he comes;   7
    do not strive to outdo the successful
    nor envy him who gains his ends.
Be angry no more, have done with wrath;   8
    strive not to outdo in evildoing.
    For evildoers will be destroyed,   9
but they who hope in the Lord shall possess the land.

a he does ... ways: *prob. rdg.; Heb. unintelligible.*

10	A little while, and the wicked will be no more;
	look well, and you will find their place is empty.
11	But the humble shall possess the land
	and enjoy untold prosperity.
12	The wicked mutter against the righteous man
	and grind their teeth at the sight of him;
13	the Lord shall laugh at them,
	for he sees that their time is coming.
14	The wicked have drawn their swords
	and strung their bows
	to bring low the poor and needy
	and to slaughter honest men.
15	Their swords shall pierce their own hearts
	and their bows be broken.
16	Better is the little which the righteous has
	than the great wealth of the wicked.
17	For the strong arm of the wicked shall be broken,
	but the LORD upholds the righteous.
18	The LORD knows each day of the good man's life,
	and his inheritance shall last for ever.
19	When times are bad, he shall not be distressed,
	and in days of famine he shall have enough.
20	But the wicked shall perish,
	and their children shall beg their bread. *a*
	The enemies of the LORD, like fuel in a furnace, *b*
	are consumed in smoke.
21	The wicked man borrows and does not pay back,
	but the righteous is a generous giver.
22	All whom the LORD has blessed shall possess the land,
	and all who are cursed by him shall be destroyed.
23	It is the LORD who directs a man's steps,
	he holds him firm and watches over his path.
24	Though he may fall, he will not go headlong,
	for the LORD grasps him by the hand.
25	I have been young and am now grown old,
	and never have I seen a righteous man forsaken. *c*
26	Day in, day out, he lends generously,
	and his children become a blessing.
27	Turn from evil and do good,
	and live at peace for ever;
28	for the LORD is a lover of justice
	and will not forsake his loyal servants.
	The lawless are banished for ever
	and the children of the wicked destroyed.
29	The righteous shall possess the land
	and shall live there at peace for ever.

a Line transposed from verse 25.   *b* like . . . furnace: *prob. rdg.; Heb.* like the worth
of rams.   *c See note on verse 20.*

The righteous man utters words of wisdom   30
and justice is always on his lips.
   The law of his God is in his heart,   31
   his steps do not falter.
The wicked watch for the righteous man   32
   and seek to take his life;
   but the Lord will not leave him in their power   33
   nor let him be condemned before his judges.
Wait for the Lord and hold to his way;   34
   he will keep you*a* safe from wicked men*b*
and will raise you to be master of the land.
When the wicked are destroyed, you shall be there to see.
   I have watched a wicked man at his work,   35
   rank as a spreading tree in its native soil.
   I passed by one day, and he was gone;   36
   I searched for him, but he could not be found.
Now look at the good man, watch him who is honest,   37
   for the man of peace leaves descendants;
   but transgressors are wiped out one and all,   38
   and the descendants of the wicked are destroyed.
Deliverance for the righteous comes from the Lord,   39
   their refuge in time of trouble.
   The Lord will help them and deliver them;*c*   40
he will save them because they seek shelter with him.

38

O Lord, do not rebuke me in thy anger,   1
   nor punish me in thy wrath.
For thou hast aimed thy arrows*d* at me,   2
   and thy hand weighs heavy upon me.
Thy indignation has left no part of my body unscarred;   3
there is no health in my whole frame because of my sin.
For my iniquities have poured over my head;   4
they are a load heavier than I can bear.
My wounds fester and stink because of my folly.   5
I am bowed down and utterly prostrate.   6
All day long I go about as if in mourning,
   for my loins burn with fever,   7
   and there is no wholesome flesh in me.
All battered and benumbed,   8
   I groan aloud in my heart's longing.
O Lord, all my lament lies open before thee   9
and my sighing is no secret to thee.
My heart beats fast, my strength has ebbed away,   10
   and the light has gone out of my eyes.

a Prob. rdg.; Heb. them.   *b* he will ... wicked men: *transposed from verse 40.*
c See note on verse 34.   *d* thou ... arrows: *prob. rdg.; Heb.* thy arrows have come down.

11   My friends and my companions shun me in my sickness,
      and my kinsfolk keep far away.

12   Those who wish me dead defame me,
      those who mean to injure me spread cruel gossip
      and mutter slanders all day long.

13   But I am deaf, I do not listen;
      I am like a dumb man who cannot open his mouth.

14   I behave like a man who cannot hear
      and whose tongue offers no defence.

15   On thee, O Lord, I fix my hope;
    thou wilt answer, O Lord my God.

16   I said, 'Let them never rejoice over me
      who exult when my foot slips.'

17   I am indeed prone to stumble,
    and suffering is never far away.

18   I make no secret of my iniquity
      and am anxious at the thought of my sin.

19   But many are my enemies, all without cause, *a*
    and many those who hate me wrongfully.

20   Those who repay good with evil
    oppose me because my purpose is good.

21   But, Lord, do not thou forsake me;
    keep not far from me, my God.

22   Hasten to my help, O Lord my salvation.

39

1   I said: I will keep close watch over myself
      that all I say may be free from sin.
    I will keep a muzzle on my mouth,
      so long as wicked men confront me.

2   In dumb silence I held my peace.
    So my agony was quickened,

3   and my heart burned within me.
    My mind wandered as the fever grew,
      and I began to speak:

4   Lord, let me know my end
      and the number of my days;
    tell me how short my life must be.

5   I know thou hast made my days a mere span long,
    and my whole life is nothing in thy sight.
    Man, though he stands upright, is but a puff of wind,

6   he moves like a phantom;
    the riches *b* he piles up are no more than vapour,
    he does not know who will enjoy them.

7   And now, Lord, what do I wait for?
    My hope is in thee.

a all . . . cause: *prob. rdg.; Heb.* living.   *b* the riches: *prob. rdg.; Heb.* they murmur.

Deliver me from all who do me wrong,   8
   make me no longer the butt of fools.
I am dumb, I will not open my mouth,   9
   because it is thy doing.
Plague me no more;   10
I am exhausted by thy blows.
When thou dost rebuke a man to punish his sin,   11
   all his charm festers and drains away;
      indeed man is only a puff of wind.
Hear my prayer, O Lord;   12
   listen to my cry,
hold not thy peace at my tears;
for I find shelter with thee,
I am thy guest, as all my fathers were.
Frown on me no more and let me smile again,   13
before I go away and cease to be.

40

I waited, waited for the Lord,   1
he bent down to me and heard my cry.
He brought me up out of the muddy pit,   2
   out of the mire and the clay;
he set my feet on a rock
   and gave me a firm footing;
and on my lips he put a new song,   3
   a song of praise to our God.
Many when they see will be filled with awe
   and will learn to trust in the Lord:
   happy is the man   4
who makes the Lord his trust,
and does not look to brutal and treacherous men.
Great things thou hast done,   5
   O Lord my God;
thy wonderful purposes are all for our good;
   none can compare with thee;
I would proclaim them and speak of them,
   but they are more than I can tell.
If thou hadst desired sacrifice and offering   6
   thou wouldst have given me ears to hear.
If thou hadst asked for whole-offering and sin-offering
   I would have said, 'Here I am.'*a*   7
My desire is to do thy will, O God,   8
   and thy law is in my heart.
In the great assembly I have proclaimed what is right,   9
   I do not hold back my words,
      as thou knowest, O Lord.

a Prob. rdg.; Heb. adds in a scroll of a book it is prescribed for me.

10 I have not kept thy goodness hidden in my heart;
I have proclaimed thy faithfulness and saving power,
and not concealed thy unfailing love and truth
from the great assembly.

11 Thou, O LORD, dost not withhold
thy tender care from me;
thy unfailing love and truth for ever guard me.

12 For misfortunes beyond counting
press on me from all sides;
my iniquities have overtaken me,
and my sight fails;
they are more than the hairs of my head,
and my courage forsakes me.

13[a] Show me favour, O LORD, and save me;
hasten to help me, O LORD.

14 Let those who seek to take my life
be put to shame and dismayed one and all;
let all who love to hurt me shrink back disgraced;

15 let those who cry 'Hurrah!' at my downfall
be horrified at their reward of shame.

16 But let all those who seek thee
be jubilant and rejoice in thee;
and let those who long for thy saving help ever cry,
'All glory to the LORD!'

17 But I am poor and needy;
O Lord, think of me.[b]
Thou art my help and my salvation;
O my God, make no delay.

41

1 Happy the man who has a concern for the helpless!
The LORD will save him in time of trouble.

2 The LORD protects him and gives him life,
making him secure in the land;
the LORD never leaves him[c] to the greed of his enemies.

3 He nurses him on his sick-bed;
he turns his bed when he is ill.

4 But I said, 'LORD, be gracious to me;
heal me, for I have sinned against thee.'

5 'His case is desperate,' my enemies say;
'when will he die, and his line become extinct?'

6 All who visit me speak from an empty heart,
alert to gather bad news;
then they go out to spread it abroad.

---

[a] *Verses 13–17 : cp. Ps. 70. 1–5.*   [b] O Lord ... me: *prob. rdg.; Heb.* may the Lord
think of me.   [c] never leaves him: *prob. rdg.; Heb.* do thou not give him up ...

All who hate me whisper together about me   7
and love to make the worst of everything:
   'An evil spell is cast upon him;   8
he is laid on his bed, and will rise no more.'
Even the friend whom I trusted, who ate at my table, [a]   9
   exults over my misfortune.
O LORD, be gracious and restore me,   10
   that I may pay them out to the full. [b]
Then I shall know that thou delightest in me   11
   and that my enemy will not triumph over me.
But I am upheld by thee because of my innocence;   12
   thou keepest me for ever in thy sight.

   Blessed be the LORD, the God of Israel,   13
     from everlasting to everlasting.
        Amen, Amen.

BOOK 2

42-43

As a hind longs for the running streams,   1
so do I long for thee, O God.
With my whole being I thirst for God, the living God.   2
When shall I come to God and appear in his presence?
Day and night, tears are my food;   3
'Where is your God?' they ask me all day long.
As I pour out my soul in distress, I call to mind   4
how I marched in the ranks of the great to the house of God,
among exultant shouts of praise, the clamour of the pilgrims.
   How deep I am sunk in misery,   5
     groaning in my distress:
   yet I will wait for God;
   I will praise him continually,
     my deliverer, my God.
I am sunk in misery, therefore will I remember thee,   6
   though from the Hermons and the springs of Jordan,
     and from the hill of Mizar,
deep calls to deep in the roar of thy cataracts,   7
and all thy waves, all thy breakers, pass over me.
   The LORD makes his unfailing love shine forth [c]   8
     alike by day and night;
   his praise on my lips is a prayer
     to the God of my life.

[a] who . . . table: *or* slanders me.   [b] to the full: *transposed from end of verse 9.*
[c] makes . . . forth: *or* entrusts me to his unfailing love.

9 I will say to God my rock, 'Why hast thou forgotten me?'
   Why must I go like a mourner because my foes oppress me?
10 My enemies taunt me, jeering *a* at my misfortunes;
   'Where is your God?' they ask me all day long.
11   How deep I am sunk in misery,
         groaning in my distress:
         yet I will wait for God;
         I will praise him continually,
         my deliverer, my God.

43 Plead my cause and give me judgement against an impious race;
   save me from malignant men and liars, O God.
2 Thou, O God, art my refuge; why hast thou rejected me?
   Why must I go like a mourner because my foes oppress me?
3 Send forth thy light and thy truth to be my guide
   and lead me to thy holy hill, to thy tabernacle,
4 then shall I come to the altar of God, the God of my joy,
   and praise thee on the harp, O God, thou God of my delight.
5   How deep I am sunk in misery,
         groaning in my distress:
         yet I will wait for God;
         I will praise him continually,
         my deliverer, my God.

44

1   O God, we have heard for ourselves,
         our fathers have told us
   all the deeds which thou didst in their days,
2 all the work of thy hand in days of old.
   Thou didst plant them in the land and drive the nations out,
   thou didst make them strike root, breaking up the peoples;
3 it was not our fathers' swords won them the land,
   nor their arm that gave them the victory,
       but thy right hand and thy arm
         and the light of thy presence; such was thy favour to them.
4 Thou art my king and my God;
   at thy bidding Jacob is victorious.
5 By thy help we will throw back our enemies,
   in thy name we will trample down our adversaries.
6 I will not trust in my bow,
   nor will my sword win me the victory;
7 for thou dost deliver us from our foes
   and put all our enemies to shame.
8 In God have we gloried all day long,
   and we will praise thy name for ever.
9 But now thou hast rejected and humbled us
   and dost no longer lead our armies into battle.

a jeering: *prob. rdg.; Heb. obscure.*

Thou hast hurled us back before the enemy,   10
and our foes plunder us as they will.
Thou hast given us up to be butchered like sheep   11
    and hast scattered us among the nations.
Thou hast sold thy people for next to nothing   12
and had no profit from the sale.
Thou hast exposed us to the taunts of our neighbours,   13
to the mockery and contempt of all around.
Thou hast made us a byword among the nations,   14
    and the peoples shake their heads at us;
so my disgrace confronts me all day long,   15
and I am covered with shame
    at the shouts of those who taunt and abuse me   16
    as the enemy takes his revenge.
All this has befallen us, but we do not forget thee   17
    and have not betrayed thy covenant;
we have not gone back on our purpose,   18
nor have our feet strayed from thy path.
Yet thou hast crushed us as the sea-serpent was crushed   19
and covered us with the darkness of death.
If we had forgotten the name of our God   20
and spread our hands in prayer to any other,
would not God find this out,   21
for he knows the secrets of the heart?
Because of thee we are done to death all day long,   22
    and are treated as sheep for slaughter.
Bestir thyself, Lord; why dost thou sleep?   23
    Awake, do not reject us for ever.
Why dost thou hide thy face,   24
heedless of our misery and our sufferings?
For we sink down to the dust   25
and lie prone on the earth.
Arise and come to our help;   26
    for thy love's sake set us free.

45

My heart is stirred by a noble theme,   1
in a king's honour I utter the song I have made,
    and my tongue runs like the pen of an expert scribe.

    You surpass all mankind in beauty,   2
    your lips are moulded in grace,
so you are blessed by God for ever.
With your sword ready at your side, warrior king,   3
your limbs resplendent *a* in their royal armour,   4
    ride on to execute true sentence and just judgement.

---

a your limbs resplendent: *prob. rdg.; Heb.* and in your pomp prosper.

            Your right hand shall show you a scene of terror:
5   your sharp arrows flying, nations beneath your feet,
              the courage of the king's foes melting away! [a]

6   Your throne is like God's throne, eternal,
          your royal sceptre a sceptre of righteousness.
7   You have loved right and hated wrong;
          so God, your God, has anointed you
             above your fellows with oil, the token of joy.
8   Your robes are all fragrant with myrrh and powder of aloes,
             and the music of strings greets you
             from a palace panelled with ivory.
9   A princess takes her place among the noblest of your women,
          a royal lady at your side in gold of Ophir.

10   Listen, my daughter, hear my words
             and consider them:
          forget your own people and your father's house;
11   and, when the king desires your beauty,
             remember that he is your lord.
12   Do him obeisance, daughter of Tyre,
          and the richest in the land will court you with gifts.

13   In the palace honour awaits her; [b]
            she is a king's daughter,
14   arrayed in cloth-of-gold richly embroidered.
      Virgins shall follow her into the presence of the king;
          her companions shall be brought to her,
15   escorted with the noise of revels and rejoicing
            as they enter the king's palace.

16   You shall have sons, O king, in place of your forefathers
          and will make them rulers over all the land. [c]
17   I will declare your fame to all generations;
          therefore the nations will praise you for ever and ever.

46

1   God is our shelter and our refuge,
          a timely help in trouble;
2   so we are not afraid when the earth heaves
            and the mountains are hurled into the sea,
3   when its waters seethe in tumult
            and the mountains quake before his majesty.
4   There is a river whose streams gladden the city of God, [d]
          which the Most High has made his holy dwelling;

[a] the courage . . . away: *prob. rdg.; Heb. obscure.*   [b] honour awaits her: *prob. rdg.;*
Heb. all honoured.   [c] over all the land: *or* in all the earth.   [d] the city of God:
or a wondrous city.

God is in that city; she will not be overthrown,   5
  and he will help her at the break of day.
Nations are in tumult, kingdoms hurled down;   6
  when he thunders, the earth surges like the sea.
The LORD of Hosts is with us,   7
  the God of Jacob our high stronghold.

Come and see what the LORD has done,   8
  the devastation he has brought upon earth,
from end to end of the earth he stamps out war: 9
he breaks the bow, he snaps the spear
  and burns the shield in the fire.

Let be then: learn that I am God,   10
high over the nations, high above earth.
  The LORD of Hosts is with us,   11
  the God of Jacob our high stronghold.

47

Clap your hands, all you nations;   1
acclaim our God with shouts of joy.
How fearful is the LORD Most High,   2
great sovereign over all the earth!
He lays the nations prostrate beneath us,   3
  he lays peoples under our feet;
he chose our patrimony for us,   4
the pride of Jacob whom he loved.

God has gone up with shouts of acclamation,   5
  the LORD has gone up with a fanfare of trumpets.
Praise God,[a] praise him with psalms;   6
praise our king, praise him with psalms.
God is king of all the earth;   7
  sing psalms with all your art.
God reigns over the nations,   8
God is seated on his holy throne.
  The princes of the nations assemble   9
  with the families of Abraham's line;[b]
for the mighty ones of earth belong to God,
and he is raised above them all.

48

The LORD is great and worthy of our praise   1
  in the city of our God, upon his holy hill.

[a] Praise God: *or* Praise, you gods.   [b] the families of Abraham's line: *prob. rdg.;*
Heb. the God of Abraham.

2   Fair and lofty, the joy of the whole earth
            is Zion's hill, like the farthest reaches of the north, [a]
            the hill of the great King's city.
3   In her palaces God is known for a tower of strength.
4   See how the kings all gather round her,
            marching on in company.
5   They are struck with amazement when they see her,
            they are filled with alarm and panic;
6   they are seized with trembling,
            they toss in pain like a woman in labour,
7   like the ships of Tarshish
        when an east wind wrecks them.
8   All we had heard we saw with our own eyes
            in the city of the LORD of Hosts,
            in the city of our God,
            the city which God plants firm for evermore.
9   O God, we re-enact the story of thy true love
            within thy temple;
10   the praise thy name deserves, O God,
            is heard at earth's farthest bounds.
        Thy hand is charged with justice,
11   and the hill of Zion rejoices,
        Judah's daughter-cities exult
            in thy judgements.

12   Make the round of Zion in procession,
            count the number of her towers,
13   take good note of her ramparts,
            pass her palaces in review,
        that you may tell generations yet to come:
14   Such is God,
        our God for ever and ever;
            he shall be our guide eternally.

49

1   Hear this, all you nations;
        listen, all who inhabit this world,
2   all mankind, every living man,
        rich and poor alike;
3   for the words that I speak are wise,
            my thoughtful heart is full of understanding.

4   I will set my ear to catch the moral of the story
        and tell on the harp how I read the riddle;
5   why should I be afraid in evil times,
        beset by the wickedness of treacherous foes,

[a] *Or* of Zaphon.

who trust in their riches 6
and boast of their great wealth?
Alas! no man can ever ransom himself 7
nor pay God the price of that release;
his ransom would cost too much, 8
for ever beyond his power to pay,
the ransom that would let him live on always 9
and never see the pit of death.

But remember this:*a* wise men must die; 10
stupid men, brutish men, all perish.*b*
The grave is their eternal home, 11
their dwelling for all time to come;
they may give their own names to estates,
but they must leave their riches to others.*c*
For men are like oxen whose life cannot last, 12
they are like cattle whose time is short.
Such is the fate of foolish men 13
and of all who seek to please them:
like sheep they run headlong into Sheol, the land of 14
Death;
he is their shepherd and urges them on;
their flesh must rot away *d*
and their bodies be wasted by Sheol,
stripped of all honour.
But God will ransom my life, 15
he will take me from the power of Sheol.
Do not envy a man when he grows rich, 16
when the wealth of his family increases;
for he will take nothing when he dies, 17
and his wealth will not go with him.
Though in his lifetime he counts himself happy 18
and men praise him in his*e* prosperity,
he*f* will go to join the company of his forefathers 19
who will never again see the light.
For men are like oxen whose life cannot last, 20
they are like cattle whose time is short.

50

God, the LORD God, has spoken 1
and summoned the world from the rising to the setting sun.
God shines out from Zion, perfect in beauty. 2

a But remember this: *prob. rdg.; Heb.* But he will remember this. *b Line trans-posed from here to follow verse 11.* *c Line transposed from verse 10.* *d* and urges . . . rot away: *prob. rdg.; Heb. obscure.* *e* him . . . his: *prob. rdg.; Heb.* you . . . your. *f* he: *prob. rdg.; Heb.* you.

3   Our God is coming and will not keep silence:
    consuming fire runs before him
    and wreathes him closely round.^a

4   He summons heaven on high and earth
    to the judgement of his people:

5   'Gather to me my loyal servants,
    all who by sacrifice have made a covenant with me.'

6   The heavens proclaim his justice,
    for God himself is the judge.

7   Listen, my people, and I will speak;
    I will bear witness against you, O Israel:
    I am God, your God,

8   shall I not [b] find fault with your sacrifices,
    though[c] your offerings are before me always?

9   I need take no young bull from your house,
    no he-goat from your folds;

10   for all the beasts of the forest are mine
    and the cattle in thousands on my hills.

11   I know every bird on those hills,
    the teeming life of the fields is my care.

12   If I were hungry, I would not tell you,
    for the world and all that is in it are mine.

13   Shall I eat the flesh of your bulls
    or drink the blood of he-goats?

14   Offer to God the sacrifice of thanksgiving
    and pay your vows to the Most High.

15   If you call upon me in time of trouble,
    I will come to your rescue, and you shall honour me.

16   God's word to the wicked man is this:
    What right have you to recite my laws
    and make so free with the words of my covenant,

17   you who hate correction
    and turn your back when I am speaking?

18   If you meet a thief, you choose him as your friend;
    you make common cause with adulterers;

19   you charge your mouth with wickedness
    and harness your tongue to slander.

20   You are for ever talking against your brother,
    stabbing your own mother's son in the back.

21   All this you have done, and shall I keep silence?
    You thought that I was another like yourself,
    but point by point I will rebuke you to your face.

22   Think well on this, you who forget God,
    or I will tear you in pieces and no one shall save you.

---

[a] and wreathes him closely round: *or* and rages round him.   [b] *Or* I will not.
[c] *Or* for.

He who offers a sacrifice of thanksgiving   23
  does me due honour,
and to him who follows my way *a*
I will show the salvation of God.

51

Be gracious to me, O God, in thy true love;   1
in the fullness of thy mercy blot out my misdeeds.

Wash away all my guilt   2
  and cleanse me from my sin.
For well I know my misdeeds,   3
and my sins confront me all the day long.
Against thee, thee only, I have sinned   4
and done what displeases thee,
so that thou mayest be proved right in thy charge
  and just in passing sentence.

In iniquity I was brought to birth   5
and my mother conceived me in sin;
yet, though thou hast hidden the truth in darkness,   6
through this mystery thou dost teach me wisdom.
Take hyssop *b* and sprinkle me, that I may be clean;   7
wash me, that I may become whiter than snow;
let me hear the sounds of joy and gladness,   8
let the bones dance which thou hast broken.
Turn away thy face from my sins   9
  and blot out all my guilt.

Create a pure heart in me, O God,   10
  and give me a new and steadfast spirit;
    do not drive me from thy presence   11
or take thy holy spirit from me;
  revive in me the joy of thy deliverance   12
    and grant me a willing spirit to uphold me.

I will teach transgressors the ways that lead to thee,   13
and sinners shall return to thee again.
O LORD God, my deliverer, save me from bloodshed, *c*   14
and I will sing the praises of thy justice.
Open my lips, O Lord,   15
that my mouth may proclaim thy praise.
Thou hast no delight in sacrifice;   16
if I brought thee an offering, thou wouldst not accept it.
My sacrifice, O God, is a broken spirit;   17
a wounded heart, O God, thou wilt not despise.

---

a him who follows my way: *prob. rdg.; Heb.* him who puts a way.   *b Or* marjoram.
c Or from punishment by death.

18　Let it be thy pleasure to do good to Zion,
　　　to build anew the walls of Jerusalem.
19　Then only shalt thou delight in the appointed sacrifices; [a]
　　　then shall young bulls be offered on thy altar.

52

1–2　Why make your wickedness your boast, you man of might,
　　　forging wild lies all day against God's loyal servant?
　　　Your slanderous tongue is sharp as a razor.
3　　　You love evil and not good,
　　　　　falsehood, not speaking the truth;
4　cruel gossip you love and slanderous talk.
5　　　So may God [b] pull you down to the ground,
　　　　sweep you away, leave you ruined and homeless,
　　　　　uprooted from the land of the living.
6　　　The righteous will look on, awestruck,
　　　　and laugh at his plight:
7　　　　'This is the man', they say,
　　　　'who does not make God his refuge,
　　　but trusts in his great wealth
　　　　and takes refuge in wild lies.'
8　But I am like a spreading olive-tree in God's house;
　　for I trust in God's true love for ever and ever.
9　I will praise thee for ever for what thou hast done,
　　and glorify thy name among thy loyal servants;
　　　for that is good.

53

1 [c]　The impious fool says in his heart,
　　　　'There is no God.'
　　　How vile men are, how depraved and loathsome;
　　　　not one does anything good!
2　　　God looks down from heaven
　　　　on all mankind
　　　to see if any act wisely,
　　　　if any seek out God.
3　But all are unfaithful, all are rotten to the core;
　　　not one does anything good,
　　　　no, not even one.

4　　　Shall they not rue it,
　　　these evildoers who devour my people
　　　　as men devour bread,
　　　　and never call upon God?

[a] *Prob. rdg.; Heb. adds* a whole-offering and one wholly consumed.　[b] *Or* So God will.　[c] *Verses 1–6: cp. Ps. 14. 1–7.*

There they were in dire alarm   5
　　when God scattered them.
The crimes of the godless were frustrated; *a*
　　for God had rejected them.
If only Israel's deliverance might come out of Zion!   6
　　When God restores his people's fortunes,
let Jacob rejoice, let Israel be glad.

54

Save me, O God, by the power of thy name,   1
　　and vindicate me through thy might.
O God, hear my prayer,   2
　　listen to my supplication.
Insolent men rise to attack me,   3
ruthless men seek my life;
they give no thought to God.

But God is my helper,   4
　　the Lord the mainstay of my life.
May their own malice recoil on my watchful foes;   5
silence them by thy truth, O LORD.
I will offer thee a willing sacrifice   6
and praise thy name, for that is good;
God has rescued me from every trouble,   7
and I look on my enemies' downfall with delight.

55

Listen, O God, to my pleading,   1
do not hide thyself when I pray.
Hear me and answer,   2
　　for my cares give me no peace.
I am panic-stricken at the shouts of my enemies,   3
　　at the shrill clamour of the wicked;
for they heap trouble on me
　　and they revile me in their anger.
My heart is torn with anguish   4
and the terrors of death come upon me.
Fear and trembling overwhelm me   5
　　and I shudder from head to foot.
*b*Oh that I had the wings of a dove   6
　　to fly away and be at rest!
I should escape far away   7
　　and find a refuge in the wilderness;

---

a The crimes . . . frustrated: *prob. rdg.; Heb. obscure.*　　　　*b* *Prob. rdg.; Heb. prefixes*
And I said.

8   soon I should find myself a sanctuary
       from wind and storm,
9   from the blasts of calumny, O Lord,
       from my enemies' contentious tongues.
I have seen violence and strife in the city;
10   day and night they encircle it,
       all along its walls;
it is filled with trouble and mischief,
11   alive with rumour and scandal,
and its public square is never free
       from violence and spite.

12   It was no enemy that taunted me,
       or I should have avoided him;
no adversary that treated me with scorn,
       or I should have kept out of his way.
13   It was you, a man of my own sort,
       my comrade, my own dear friend,
14-15   with whom I kept pleasant company
       in the house of God.

       May death strike them,
and may they [a] perish in confusion,
may they go down alive into Sheol;
       for their homes are haunts of evil!

16   But I will call upon God;
       the LORD will save me.
17   Evening and morning and at noon
       I nurse my woes, and groan.
18   He has heard my cry, he rescued me
       and gave me back my peace,
when they beset me like archers, [b]
       massing against me,
19   like Ishmael and the desert tribes
       and those who dwell in the East,
who have no respect for an oath
       nor any fear of God.
20   Such men do violence to those at peace with them
       and break their promised word;
21   their speech is smoother than butter
       but their thoughts are of war;
their words are slippery as oil
       but sharp as drawn swords.

22   Commit your fortunes to the LORD,
       and he will sustain you;
he will never let the righteous be shaken.

---

[a] *Prob. rdg.; Heb.* we.   [b] when . . . archers: *prob. rdg.; Heb. obscure.*

Cast them, O God, into the pit of destruction;   23
   bloodthirsty and treacherous,
they shall not live out half their days;
but I will put my trust in thee.

56

Be gracious to me, O God, for the enemy persecute me,   1
   my assailants harass me all day long.
All the day long my watchful foes persecute me;   2
   countless are those who assail me.
Appear on high*a* in my day of fear;   3
I put my trust in thee.
With God to help me I will shout defiance,   4
in God I trust and shall not be afraid;
what can mortal men do to me?
All day long abuse of me is their only theme,   5
   all their thoughts are hostile.
In malice they are on the look-out, and watch for me,   6
   they dog my footsteps;
but, while they lie in wait for me,
it is they who will not *b* escape.   7
O God, in thy anger bring ruin on the nations.

Enter my lament in thy book,*c*   8
store every tear in thy flask. *d*
Then my enemies will turn back   9
   on the day when I call upon thee; *e*
for this I know, that God is on my side,
with God to help me I will shout defiance. *f*   10
In God I trust and shall not be afraid;   11
what can man do to me?
I have bound myself with vows to thee, O God,   12
and will redeem them with due thank-offerings;
for thou hast rescued me from death*g*   13
to walk in thy presence, in the light of life.

57

Be gracious to me, O God, be gracious;   1
for I have made thee my refuge.
I will take refuge in the shadow of thy wings
   until the storms are past.

---

a Appear on high: *prob. rdg.; Heb.* Height.   *b* it is . . . not: *prob. rdg.; Heb.* for
iniquity.   *c* Enter . . . book: *prob. rdg.; Heb.* obscure.   *d* *Prob. rdg.; Heb. adds*
is it not in thy book?   *e* Enter . . . thee: *or* Thou hast entered my lament in thy
book, my tears are put in thy flask. Then my enemies turned back, when I called upon thee.
f *Prob. rdg.; Heb. adds* With the LORD to help me I will shout defiance.   *g* *Prob.
rdg.; Heb. adds* is it not my feet from stumbling (*cp. Ps. 116. 8*).

2   I will call upon God Most High,
     on God who fulfils his purpose for me.

3   He will send his truth and his love that never fails,
     he will send from heaven and save me.
    God himself will frustrate my persecutors;

4   for I lie down among lions, man-eaters,
     whose teeth are spears and arrows
     and whose tongues are sharp swords.

5   Show thyself, O God, high above the heavens;
     let thy glory shine over all the earth.

6   Men have prepared a net to catch me as I walk,
     but I bow my head to escape from it;
    they have dug a pit in my path
     but have fallen into it themselves.

7[a]   My heart is steadfast, O God,
     my heart is steadfast.
    I will sing and raise a psalm;

8   awake, my spirit,
    awake, lute and harp,
     I will awake at dawn of day.[b]

9   I will confess thee, O Lord, among the peoples,
     among the nations I will raise a psalm to thee,

10   for thy unfailing love is wide as the heavens
     and thy truth reaches to the skies.

11   Show thyself, O God, high above the heavens;
     let thy glory shine over all the earth.

58

1   Answer, you rulers:[c] are your judgements just?
    Do you decide impartially between man and man?

2   Never! Your hearts devise all kinds of wickedness
    and survey the violence that you have done on earth.

3   Wicked men, from birth they have taken to devious ways;
    liars, no sooner born than they go astray,

4   venomous with the venom of serpents,
    of the deaf asp which stops its ears

5   and will not listen to the sound of the charmer,
    however skilful his spells may be.

6   O God, break the teeth in their mouths.
    Break, O Lord, the jaws of the unbelievers.[d]

---

[a] *Verses 7–11 : cp. Ps. 108. 1–5.*   [b] at dawn of day: *or* the dawn.   [c] *Or* you gods. [d] the jaws of the unbelievers: *or* the lions' fangs.

May they melt, may they vanish like water,   7
may they wither like trodden grass,^{*a*}
    like an abortive birth which melts away   8
    or a still-born child which never sees^{*b*} the sun!
All unawares, may they be rooted up like^{*c*} a thorn-bush,   9
    like weeds which a man angrily^{*d*} clears away!

The righteous shall rejoice that he has seen vengeance done   10
    and shall wash his feet in the blood of the wicked,
        and men shall say,   11
    'There is after all a reward for the righteous;
after all, there is a God that judges on earth.'

59

Rescue me from my enemies, O my God,   1
be my tower of strength against all who assail me,
    rescue me from these evildoers,   2
    deliver me from men of blood.
Savage men lie in wait for me,   3
they lie in ambush ready to attack me;
for no fault or guilt of mine, O Lord,
innocent as I am, they run to take post against me.   4-5
But thou, Lord God of Hosts, Israel's God,
    do thou bestir thyself at my call, and look:
awake, and punish all the nations.
Have no mercy on villains and traitors,
who run wild at nightfall like dogs,   6
snarling and prowling round the city,
wandering to and fro in search of food,   15^{*e*}
and howling if they are not satisfied.
From their mouths comes a stream of nonsense;   7
'But who will hear?' they murmur.
But thou, O Lord, dost laugh at them,   8
    and deride all the nations.
O my strength,^{*f*} to thee I turn in the night-watches;   9
for thou, O God, art my strong tower.
My God, in his true love, shall be my champion;   10
with God's help, I shall gloat over my watchful foes.
Wilt thou not kill them, lest my people forget?   11
Scatter them by thy might and bring them to ruin.
    Deliver them,^{*g*} O Lord, to be destroyed   12
    by their own sinful words;
let what they have spoken entrap them in their pride.

---

^{*a*} like trodden grass: *prob. rdg.; Heb. obscure.*   ^{*b*} sees: *prob. rdg.; Heb. they see.*
^{*c*} may they be rooted up like: *prob. rdg.; Heb. your pots.*   ^{*d*} angrily: *prob. rdg.;*
Heb. like anger.   ^{*e*} *Verse transposed.*   ^{*f*} *Or refuge.*   ^{*g*} Deliver them: *prob.*
rdg.; Heb. Our shield.

13
    Let them be cut off for their cursing and falsehood;
        bring them to an end in thy wrath,
        and they will be no more;
    then they will know that God is ruler in Jacob,
        even to earth's farthest limits. [a] [b]

16
    But I will sing of thy strength,
    and celebrate thy love when morning comes;
    for thou hast been my strong tower
    and a sure retreat in days of trouble.

17
    O thou my strength, I will raise a psalm to thee;
    for thou, O God, art my strong tower.

60

1
    O God, thou hast cast us off and broken us;
    thou hast been angry and rebuked us cruelly.

2
    Thou hast made the land quake and torn it open;
    it gives way and crumbles into pieces.

3
    Thou hast made thy people drunk with a bitter draught,
    thou hast given us wine that makes us stagger.

4
    But thou hast given a warning to those who fear thee,
        to make their escape before the sentence falls.

5 [c]
    Deliver those that are dear to thee;
    save them with thy right hand, and answer.

6
God has spoken from his sanctuary: [d]
    'I will go up now and measure out Shechem;
    I will divide the valley of Succoth into plots;

7
Gilead and Manasseh are mine;
Ephraim is my helmet, Judah my sceptre;

8
Moab is my wash-bowl, I fling my shoes at Edom;
    Philistia is the target of my anger.'

9
Who can bring me to the fortified city,
    who can guide me to Edom,

10
since thou, O God, hast abandoned us
    and goest not forth with our armies?

11
Grant us help against the enemy,
    for deliverance by man is a vain hope.

12
    With God's help we shall do valiantly,
    and God himself will tread our enemies under foot.

---

[a] *Prob. rdg.; Heb. adds* (14) who run wild at nightfall like dogs, snarling and prowling round the city (*cp. verse 6*).   [b] *Verse 15 transposed to follow verse 6.*   [c] *Verses 5–12: cp. Ps. 108. 6–13.*   [d] from his sanctuary: *or* in his holiness.

61

Hear my cry, O God, listen to my prayer.   1
From the end of the earth I call to thee with fainting heart;   2
    lift me up and set me upon a rock.
    For thou hast been my shelter,   3
        a tower for refuge from the enemy.
    In thy tent will I make my home for ever   4
        and find my shelter under the cover of thy wings.
For thou, O God, hast heard my vows   5
    and granted the wish *a* of all who revere thy name.

To the king's life add length of days,   6
    year upon year for many generations;
    may he dwell in God's presence for ever,   7
    may true and constant love preserve him.

So will I ever sing psalms in honour of thy name   8
    as I fulfil my vows day after day.

62

Truly my heart waits silently for God;   1
    my deliverance comes from him.
In truth he is my rock of deliverance,   2
    my tower of strength, so that I stand unshaken.
    How long will you assail a man with your threats, 3
    all battering on a leaning wall?
In truth men plan to topple him from his height,   4
    and stamp on the fallen stones. *b*
    With their lips they bless him, the hypocrites,
    but revile him in their hearts.
Truly my heart waits silently for God;   5
    my hope of deliverance comes from him.
In truth he is my rock of deliverance,   6
    my tower of strength, so that I am unshaken.
    My deliverance and my honour depend upon God,   7
    God who is my rock of refuge and my shelter.
Trust always in God, my people,   8
    pour out your hearts before him;
        God is our shelter.

    In very truth men are a puff of wind,   9
        all men are faithless;
    put them in the balance and they can only rise,
        all of them lighter than wind.

a *Prob. rdg.; Heb.* the inheritance.   *b* the fallen stones: *transposed from end of* verse 3.

10   Put no trust in extortion,
          do not be proud of stolen goods;
        though wealth breeds wealth, set not your heart on it.
11   One thing God has spoken,
          two things I have learnt:
        'Power belongs to God'
12   and 'True love, O Lord, is thine';
        thou dost requite a man for his deeds.

63

1   O God, thou art my God, I seek thee early
          with a heart that thirsts for thee
          and a body wasted with longing for thee,
        like a dry and thirsty land that has no water.
2   So longing, I come before thee in the sanctuary
          to look upon thy power and glory.
3   Thy true love is better than life;
          therefore I will sing thy praises.
4   And so I bless thee all my life
          and in thy name lift my hands in prayer.
5   I am satisfied as with a rich and sumptuous feast
          and wake the echoes with thy praise.
6   When I call thee to mind upon my bed
          and think on thee in the watches of the night,
7   remembering how thou hast been my help
           and that I am safe in the shadow of thy wings,
8   then I humbly follow thee with all my heart,
          and thy right hand is my support.

9   Those who seek my life, bent on evil,
           shall sink into the depths of the earth;
10   they shall be given over to the sword;
           they shall be carrion for jackals.

11   The king shall rejoice in God,
          and whoever swears by God's name shall exult;
        the voice of falsehood shall be silenced.

64

1   Hear me, O God, hear my lament;
          keep me safe from the threats of the enemy.
2   Hide me from the factions of the wicked,
           from the turbulent mob of evildoers,
3   who sharpen their tongues like swords
          and wing their cruel words like arrows, *a*
4   to shoot down the innocent from cover,
          shooting suddenly, themselves unseen.

a and wing . . . arrows: *prob. rdg.; Heb.* they tread their arrow a cruel word.

They boldly^a hide their snares,   5
    sure that none will see them;
they hatch their secret plans^b with skill and cunning,   6
with evil^c purpose and deep design.
    But God with his arrow shoots them down,   7
    and sudden is their overthrow.

    They may repeat their wicked tales,^d   8
but their mischievous tongues^e are their undoing.
All who see their fate take fright at it,
    every man is afraid;   9
    'This is God's work', they declare;
    they learn their lesson from what he has done.
The righteous rejoice and seek refuge in the LORD   10
    and all the upright exult.

65

We owe thee praise, O God, in Zion;   1–2
thou hearest prayer, vows shall be paid to thee.
All men shall lay their guilt before thee: 3
    our sins are too heavy for us;
    only thou canst blot them out.
Happy is the man of thy choice, whom thou dost bring 4
    to dwell in thy courts;
    let us enjoy the blessing of thy house,
    thy holy temple.
    By deeds of terror answer us with victory,   5
    O God of our deliverance,
in whom men trust from the ends of the earth
    and far-off seas;
    thou art girded with strength,   6
and by thy might dost fix the mountains in their place,
dost calm the rage of the seas and their raging waves. ^f 7
    The dwellers at the ends of the earth   8
    hold thy signs in awe;
thou makest morning and evening sing aloud in triumph.

Thou dost visit the earth and give it abundance,   9
    as often as thou dost enrich it
with the waters of heaven, brimming in their channels,
    providing rain^g for men.
    For this is thy provision for it,
watering its furrows, levelling its ridges,   10
softening it with showers and blessing its growth.

^a *See first note on verse 8.*   ^b their secret plans: *prob. rdg.; Heb. unintelligible.*
^c evil: *prob. rdg.; Heb.* man.   ^d They . . . tales: *transposed from after* boldly *in*
verse 5.   ^e their mischievous tongues: *prob. rdg.; Heb.* against them their tongues.
^f *Prob. rdg.; Heb. adds* and tumult of people.   ^g *Or* corn.

11 Thou dost crown the year with thy good gifts
    and the palm-trees drip with sweet juice;
12   the pastures in the wild are rich with blessing
    and the hills wreathed in happiness,
13   the meadows are clothed with sheep
    and the valleys mantled in corn,
        so that they shout, they break into song.

66

1   Acclaim our God, all men on earth;
2   let psalms declare the glory of his name,
        make glorious his praise.
3   Say unto God, 'How fearful are thy works!
    Thy foes cower before the greatness of thy strength.
4   All men on earth fall prostrate in thy presence,
    and sing to thee, sing psalms in honour of thy name.'
5   Come and see all that God has done,
        tremendous in his dealings with mankind.
6   He turned the waters into dry land
    so that his people passed through the sea on foot;
        there did we rejoice in him. *a*

7   He rules for ever by his power,
    his eye rests on the nations;
    let no rebel rise in defiance.

8   Bless our God, all nations;
        let his praise be heard far and near.
9   He set us in the land of the living;
    he keeps our feet from stumbling.
10   For thou, O God, hast put us to the proof
        and refined us iike silver.
11   Thou hast caught us in a net,
    thou hast bound our bodies fast;
12 thou hast let men ride over our heads.
    We went through fire and water,
        but thou hast brought us out into liberty.

13 I will bring sacrifices into thy temple
    and fulfil my vows to thee,
14 vows which I made with my own lips
    and swore with my own mouth when in distress.
15 I will offer thee fat beasts as sacrifices
        and burn rams as a savoury offering;
    I will make ready oxen and he-goats.

16 Come, listen, all who fear God,
    and I will tell you all that he has done for me;

---

a there ... him: *or* where we see this, we will rejoice in him.

I lifted up my voice in prayer,   17
    his high praise was on my lips.
If I had cherished evil thoughts,   18
    the Lord would not have heard me;
but in truth God has heard   19
    and given heed to my prayer.
    Blessed is God   20
who has not withdrawn his love and care from me.

67

God be gracious to us and bless us,   1
God make his face shine upon us,
that his ways may be known on earth   2
and his saving power among all the nations.
Let the peoples praise thee, O God;   3
let all peoples praise thee.
Let all nations rejoice and shout in triumph; 4
for thou dost judge the peoples with justice
and guidest the nations of the earth.
Let the peoples praise thee, O God;   5
let all peoples praise thee.
The earth has given its increase   6
and God, our God, will bless us.

      God grant us his blessing,   7
that all the ends of the earth may fear him.

68

God arises and his enemies are scattered;   1
    those who hate him flee before him,
    driven away like smoke in the wind;   2
    like wax melting at the fire,
    the wicked perish at the presence of God.
But the righteous are joyful, they exult before God, 3
    they are jubilant and shout for joy.

Sing the praises of God, raise a psalm to his name, 4
    extol him who rides over the desert plains. *a*
Be joyful *b* and exult before him,
    father of the fatherless, the widow's champion— 5
        God in his holy dwelling-place.
God gives the friendless a home   6
    and brings out the prisoner safe and sound;
but rebels must live in the scorching desert.

---

a over the desert plains: *or* on the plains.   *b* Be joyful: *prob. rdg.; Heb.* In the
Lord is his name.

7   O God, when thou didst go forth before thy people,
                marching across the wilderness,
8   earth trembled, the very heavens quaked
      before God the lord of Sinai, before God the God of Israel.

9   Of thy bounty, O God, thou dost refresh with rain
             thy own land in its weariness,
             the land which thou thyself didst provide,
10   where thy own people made their home,
     which thou, O God, in thy goodness providest for the poor.

11–13   The Lord proclaims good news: [a]
'Kings with their armies have fled headlong.'
O mighty host, will you linger among the sheepfolds
    while the women in your tents divide the spoil—
    an image of a dove, its wings sheathed in silver
    and its pinions in yellow gold—
14   while the Almighty scatters kings far and wide
      like snowflakes falling on Zalmon?

15   The hill of Bashan is a hill of God indeed,
          a hill of many peaks is Bashan's hill.
16   But, O hill of many peaks, why gaze in envy
    at the hill where the LORD delights to dwell,
   where the LORD himself will live for ever?
17   Twice ten thousand were God's chariots, thousands upon
               thousands,
    when the Lord came in holiness from Sinai. [b]
18   Thou didst go up to thy lofty home with captives in thy train,
      having received tribute from men;
   in the presence of the LORD God no rebel could live.

19   Blessed is the Lord:
          he carries us day by day,
           God our salvation.
20   Our God is a God who saves us,
    in the LORD God's hand lies escape from death. [c]
21   God himself will smite [d] the head of his enemies,
    those proud sinners with their flowing locks.
22   The Lord says, 'I will return from the Dragon, [e]
    I will return from the depths of the sea,
23   that you may dabble your feet in blood,
    while the tongues of your dogs are eager [f] for it.'

24   Thy procession, O God, comes into view,
          the procession of my God and King into the sanctuary:

---

[a] proclaims good news: *or* gives the word, women bearing good news.   [b] came . . .
from Sinai: *prob. rdg.; Heb. obscure.*   [c] in the LORD God's hand . . . death: *or*
death is expelled by the LORD God.   [d] will smite: *or* smites.   [e] the Dragon:
or Bashan.   [f] are eager: *prob. rdg.; Heb.* from enemies.

at its head the singers, next come minstrels,   25
girls among them playing on tambourines.
In the great concourse they bless God,   26
all Israel assembled^{*a*} bless the LORD.
There is the little tribe of Benjamin leading them,   27
there the company of Judah's princes,
the princes of Zebulun and of Naphtali.

O God, in virtue of thy power^{*b*}—   28
that godlike power which has acted for us—
command kings to bring gifts to thee   29
for the honour of thy temple in Jerusalem.
Rebuke those wild beasts of the reeds, that herd of bulls,   30
the bull-calf warriors of the nations;^{*c*}
scatter these nations which revel in war;
make them bring tribute from Egypt,   31
precious stones and silver from Pathros;^{*d*}
let Nubia stretch out^{*e*} her hands to God.

All you kingdoms of the world, sing praises to God,   32
sing psalms to the Lord,
to him who rides on the heavens, the ancient heavens.   33
Hark! he speaks in the mighty thunder.
Ascribe all might to God, Israel's High God,   34
Israel's pride and might throned in the skies.
Terrible is God as he comes from his sanctuary;   35
he is Israel's own God,
who gives to his people might and abundant power.

Blessed be God.

69

Save me, O God;   1
for the waters have risen up to my neck.
I sink in muddy depths and have no foothold;   2
I am swept into deep water, and the flood carries me away.
I am wearied with crying out, my throat is sore,   3
my eyes grow dim as I wait for God to help me.
Those who hate me without reason   4
are more than the hairs of my head;
they outnumber my hairs, those who accuse me falsely.
How can I give back what I have not stolen?
O God, thou knowest how foolish I am,   5
and my guilty deeds are not hidden from thee.

---

^{*a*} assembled: *prob. rdg.; Heb. obscure.*   ^{*b*} O God . . . power: *prob. rdg.; Heb.*
Your God your power.   ^{*c*} *See first note on verse 31.*   ^{*d*} precious . . . Pathros:
prob. rdg., transposed from verse 30 and slightly altered.   ^{*e*} stretch out: *prob. rdg.;*
Heb. obscure.

6   Let none of those who look to thee be shamed on my account,
        O Lord GOD of Hosts;
    let none who seek thee be humbled through my fault,
        O God of Israel.

7   For in thy service I have suffered reproach;
    I dare not show my face for shame.

8   I have become a stranger to my brothers,
        an alien to my own mother's sons;

9   bitter enemies of thy temple tear me in pieces; *a*
    those who reproach thee reproach me.

10   I have broken my spirit with fasting,
    only to lay myself open to many reproaches.

11   I have made sackcloth my clothing
    and have become a byword among them.

12   Those who sit by the town gate talk about me;
    drunkards sing songs about me in their cups.

13   But I lift up this prayer to thee, O LORD:
    accept me *b* now in thy great love,
    answer me with thy sure deliverance, O God.

14   Rescue me from the mire, do not let me sink;
    let me be rescued from the muddy depths, *c*

15   so that no flood may carry me away,
        no abyss swallow me up,
        no deep close over me.

16   Answer me, O LORD, in the goodness of thy unfailing love,
    turn towards me in thy great affection.

17   I am thy servant, do not hide thy face from me.
    Make haste to answer me, for I am in distress.

18   Come near to me and redeem me;
        ransom me, for I have many enemies.

19   Thou knowest what reproaches I bear,
    all my anguish is seen by thee.

20   Reproach has broken my heart,
    my shame and my dishonour *d* are past hope;
    I looked for consolation and received none,
        for comfort and did not find any.

21   They put poison in my food
    and gave me vinegar when I was thirsty.

22   May their own table be a snare to them
    and their sacred feasts lure them to their ruin;

23   may their eyes be darkened so that they do not see,
    let a continual ague shake their loins.

24   Pour out thine indignation upon them
        and let thy burning anger overtake them.

---

a bitter . . . pieces: *or* zeal for thy temple has eaten me up (*cp. John 2. 17*).   *b* *Prob. rdg.;*
Heb. acceptance.   *c* from . . . depths: *prob. rdg.; Heb.* from my haters and from the
depths.   *d* my shame and my dishonour: *transposed from after* reproaches *in verse 19*.

May their settlements be desolate,   25
and no one living in their tents;
for they pursue him whom thou hast struck down   26
and multiply the torments of those whom thou hast wounded.
Give them the punishment their sin deserves;^a   27
exclude them from thy righteous mercy;
let them be blotted out from the book of life   28
and not be enrolled among the righteous.

But by thy saving power, O God, lift me high   29
above my pain and my distress,
then I will praise God's name in song   30
and glorify him with thanksgiving;
that will please the LORD more than the offering of a bull,   31
a young bull with horn and cloven hoof.

See and rejoice, you humble folk,   32
take heart, you seekers after God;
for the LORD listens to the poor   33
and does not despise those bound to his service.
Let sky and earth praise him,   34
the seas and all that move in them,
for God will deliver Zion   35-36
and rebuild the cities of Judah.
His servants' children shall inherit them;
they shall dwell there in their own possession
and all who love his name shall live in them.

70

Show me favour,^b O God, and save me;   1^c
hasten to help me, O LORD.
Let all who seek my life be brought to shame and dismay,   2
let all who love to hurt me shrink back disgraced;
let those who cry 'Hurrah!' at my downfall   3
turn back at the shame they incur,
but let all who seek thee   4
be jubilant and rejoice in thee,
and let those who long for thy saving help ever cry,
'All glory to God!'

But I am poor and needy;   5
O God, hasten to my aid.
Thou art my help, my salvation;
O LORD, make no delay.

---

^a Give them . . . deserves: *or* Add punishment to punishment.   ^b Show me favour:
prob. rdg., cp. Ps. 40. 13; Heb. om.   ^c *Verses 1–5: cp. Ps. 40. 13–17.*

71

1   In thee, O LORD, I have taken refuge;
     never let me be put to shame.
2   As thou art righteous rescue me and save my life;
     hear me and set me free,
3   be a rock of refuge for me,
     where I may ever find safety at thy call;
          for thou art my towering crag and stronghold.
4   O God, keep my life safe from the wicked,
          from the clutches of unjust and cruel men.

5   Thou art my hope, O Lord,
     my trust, O LORD, since boyhood.
6   From birth I have leaned upon thee,
     my protector since I left[a] my mother's womb.[b]
7   To many I seem a solemn warning;
     but I have thee for my strong refuge.
8   My mouth shall be full of thy praises,
          I shall tell of thy splendour all day long.
9   Do not cast me off when old age comes,
          nor forsake me when my strength fails,
10   when my enemies' rancour bursts upon me[c]
     and those who watch me whisper together,
11   saying, 'God has forsaken him;
     after him! seize him; no one will rescue him.'
12   O God, do not stand aloof from me;
     O my God, hasten to my help.
13   Let all my traducers be shamed and dishonoured,
     let all who seek my hurt be covered with scorn.
14   But I will wait in continual hope,
     I will praise thee again and yet again;
15   all day long thy righteousness,
               thy saving acts, shall be upon my lips.
     Thou shalt ever be the theme of my praise,[d]
     although I have not the skill of a poet.
16   I will begin with a tale of great deeds, O Lord GOD,
     and sing of thy righteousness, thine alone.
17   O God, thou hast taught me from boyhood,
     all my life I have proclaimed thy marvellous works;
18   and now that I am old and my hairs are grey,
          forsake me not, O God,
     when I extol thy mighty arm to future generations,
19   thy power and righteousness, O God, to highest heaven;
          for thou hast done great things.
          Who is like thee, O God?

[a] my . . . left: *or who didst bring me out from.*   [b] *See note on verse 15.*
[c] enemies' . . . me: *prob. rdg.; Heb.* enemies say of me.   [d] *Line transposed from verse 6.*

Thou hast made me pass through bitter and deep distress,   20
    yet dost revive me once again
  and lift me again from earth's watery depths.
Restore me to honour, turn and comfort me,   21
    then I will praise thee on the lute   22
      for thy faithfulness, O God;
  I will sing psalms to thee with the harp,
    thou Holy One of Israel;
      songs of joy shall be on my lips;   23
I will sing thee psalms, because thou hast redeemed me.
All day long my tongue shall tell of thy righteousness;   24
  shame and disgrace await those who seek my hurt.

72

O God, endow the king with thy own justice,   1
  and give thy righteousness to a king's son,
  that he may judge thy people rightly   2
    and deal out justice to the poor and suffering.
May hills and mountains afford thy people   3
  peace and prosperity in righteousness.
    He shall give judgement for the suffering   4
    and help those of the people that are needy;
    he shall crush the oppressor.
    He shall live as long as the sun endures,   5
    long as the moon, age after age.
    He shall be like rain falling on early crops,   6
    like showers watering *a* the earth.
In his days righteousness shall flourish,   7
prosperity abound until the moon is no more.
May he hold sway from sea to sea,   8
from the River to the ends of the earth.
Ethiopians shall crouch low before him;   9
  his enemies shall lick the dust.
The kings of Tarshish and the islands shall bring gifts,   10
the kings of Sheba and Seba shall present their tribute,
  and all kings shall pay him homage,   11
    all nations shall serve him.
For he shall rescue the needy from their rich oppressors,   12
  the distressed who have no protector.
  May he have pity on the needy and the poor,   13
    deliver the poor from death;
  may he redeem them from oppression and violence   14
  and may their blood be precious in his eyes.

May the king live long   15
and receive gifts of gold *b* from Sheba;

---

a   like showers watering: *prob. rdg.; Heb. unintelligible.*   *b*   *Or* frankincense.

prayer be made for him continually,
  blessings be his all the day long.
16 May there be abundance of corn in the land,
     growing in plenty to the tops of the hills;
   may the crops flourish like Lebanon,
     and the sheaves *a* be numberless as blades of grass.
17 Long may the king's name endure,
     may it live for ever like the sun;
   so shall all peoples pray to be blessed as he was,
     all nations tell of his happiness.

18 Blessed be the LORD God, the God of Israel,
   who alone does marvellous things;
19 blessed be his glorious name for ever,
   and may his glory fill all the earth.
                    Amen, Amen.

20 Here end the prayers of David son of Jesse.

BOOK 3

73

1 How good God is to the upright! *b*
   How good to those who are pure in heart!

2 My feet had almost slipped,
     my foothold had all but given way,
3 because the boasts of sinners roused my envy
     when I saw how they prosper.
4 No pain, no suffering is theirs;
     they are sleek and sound in limb;
5 they are not plunged in trouble as other men are,
     nor do they suffer the torments of mortal men.
6 Therefore pride is their collar of jewels
     and violence the robe that wraps them round.
7 Their eyes gleam through folds of fat;
     while vain fancies pass through their minds.
8 Their talk is all sneers and malice;
     scornfully they spread their calumnies.
9 Their slanders reach up to heaven,
     while their tongues ply to and fro on earth.
10 And so my people follow their lead *c*
     and find nothing to blame in them, *d*
11 even though they say, 'What does God know?
     The Most High neither knows nor cares.'

---

a the sheaves: *prob. rdg.; Heb.* from a city.   *b* How . . . upright: *prob. rdg.; Heb.*
How good it is to Israel!   *c* their lead: *prob. rdg.; Heb.* hither.   *d* and find . . .
in them: *prob. rdg.; Heb.* obscure.

So wicked men talk, yet still they prosper,   12
  and rogues^a amass great wealth.

So it was all in vain that I kept my heart pure   13
  and washed my hands in innocence.
For all day long I suffer torment   14
  and am punished every morning.
Yet had I let myself talk on in this fashion,   15
I should have betrayed the family of God.
  So I set myself to think this out   16
  but I found it too hard for me,
  until I went into God's sacred courts;   17
    there I saw clearly what their end would be.

How often thou dost set them on slippery ground   18
  and drive them headlong into ruin!
Then in a moment how dreadful their end,   19
  cut off root and branch by death with all its terrors,
  like a dream when a man rouses himself, O Lord,   20
  like images in sleep which are dismissed on waking!

    When my heart was embittered   21
      I felt the pangs of envy,
  I would not understand, so brutish was I,   22
  I was a mere beast in thy sight, O God.
    Yet I am always with thee,   23
      thou holdest my right hand;
      thou dost guide me by thy counsel   24
      and afterwards wilt receive me with glory.
  Whom have I in heaven but thee?   25
  And having thee,^b I desire nothing else on earth.
  Though heart and body fail,   26
    yet God is my possession for ever.
  They who are far from thee are lost;   27
    thou dost destroy all who wantonly forsake thee.
  But my chief good is to be near thee, O God;   28
I have chosen thee, Lord GOD, to be my refuge.^c

74

Why hast thou cast us off, O God? Is it for ever?   1
Why art thou so stern, so angry with the sheep of thy flock?
    Remember the assembly of thy people,   2
      taken long since for thy own,^d
    and Mount Zion, which was thy home.

---

^a yet . . . rogues: *prob. rdg.; Heb.* those at ease for ever.
with thee.   ^c *Prob. rdg.; Heb. adds* to tell all thy works.
adds thou didst redeem the tribe of thy possession.

^b *Or* And compared
^d *Prob. rdg.; Heb.*

3   Now at last*a* restore what was ruined beyond repair,
     the wreck that the foe has made of thy sanctuary.

4   The shouts of thy enemies filled the holy place,*b*
         they planted their standards there as tokens of victory.
5   They brought it crashing down,*c*
             like woodmen plying their axes in the forest;
6   they ripped the carvings clean out,
             they smashed them with hatchet and pick.
7   They set fire to thy sanctuary,
             tore down and polluted the shrine sacred to thy name.
8   They said to themselves, 'We will sweep them away',
             and all over the land they burnt God's holy places.*d*

9   We cannot see what lies before us,*e* we have no prophet now;
         we have no one who knows how long this is to last.
10   How long, O God, will the enemy taunt thee?
         Will the adversary pour scorn on thy name for ever?
11   Why dost thou hold back thy hand,
             why keep thy right hand within thy bosom?

12   But thou, O God, thou king from of old,
             thou mighty conqueror all the world over,
13   by thy power thou didst cleave the sea-monster in two
         and break the sea-serpent's heads above the waters;
14   thou didst crush Leviathan's many heads
             and throw him to the sharks*f* for food.
15   Thou didst open channels for spring and torrent;
         thou didst dry up rivers never known to fail.
16   The day is thine, and the night is thine also,
         thou didst ordain the light of moon and sun;
17   thou hast fixed all the regions of the earth;
         summer and winter, thou didst create them both.

18   Remember, O LORD, the taunts of the enemy,
         the scorn a savage nation pours on thy name.
19   Cast not to the beasts the soul that confesses thee;
         forget not for ever the sufferings of thy servants.
20   Look upon thy creatures:*g* they are filled with hatred,
         and earth is the haunt of violence.
21   Let not the oppressed be shamed and turned away;
         let the poor and the downtrodden praise thy name.
22   Rise up, O God, maintain thy own cause;
             remember how brutal men taunt thee all day long.
23   Ignore no longer the cries of thy assailants,
             the mounting clamour of those who defy thee.

a Now at last: *prob. rdg.; Heb.* Thy steps.   *b* the holy place: *or* thy meeting place.
c They . . . down: *prob. rdg.; Heb. unintelligible.*   *d* holy places: *or* meeting places.
e what . . . us: *prob. rdg.; Heb.* our signs.   *f* to the sharks: *prob. rdg.; Heb.* to a
people, desert-dwellers.   *g* thy creatures: *prob. rdg.; Heb.* the covenant, because.

75

We give thee thanks, O God, we give thee thanks;   1
   thy name is brought very near to us
   in the story of thy wonderful deeds.

   I seize the appointed time   2
   and then I judge mankind with justice.
   When the earth rocks, with all who live on it,   3
   I make its pillars firm.
   To the boastful I say, 'Boast no more',   4
   and to the wicked, 'Do not toss your proud horns:
   toss not your horns against high heaven   5
   nor speak arrogantly against your Creator.'
   No power from the east nor from the west,   6
   no power from the wilderness, can raise a man up.
     For God is judge;   7
he puts one man down and raises up another.
   The LORD holds a cup in his hand,   8
and the wine foams in it, hot with spice;
he offers it to every man for drink,
and all the wicked on earth must drain it to the dregs.
   But I will glorify him for ever;   9
   I will sing praises to the God of Jacob.

   I will break off the horns of the wicked,   10
   but the horns of the righteous shall be lifted high.

76

   In Judah God is known,   1
   his name is great in Israel;
   his tent is pitched in Salem,
   in Zion his battle-quarters are set up.*a*   2
   He has broken the flashing arrows,   3
   shield and sword and weapons of war.

   Thou art terrible, O Lord, and mighty: 4
   men that lust for plunder stand aghast,   5
   the boldest swoon away,
   and the strongest cannot lift a hand.
     At thy rebuke, O God of Jacob,   6
   rider and horse fall senseless.
   Terrible art thou, O Lord;   7
   who can stand in thy presence when thou art angry?
   Thou didst give sentence out of heaven;   8
   the earth was afraid and kept silence.

a   are set up: *prob. rdg.; Heb.* thither (*at beginning of verse 3*).

9   O God, at thy rising^a in judgement
    to deliver all humble men on the earth,
10   for all her fury Edom shall confess thee,
    and the remnant left in Hamath shall dance in worship.

11 Make vows to the LORD your God, and pay them duly;
    let the peoples all around him bring their tribute; ^b
12   for he breaks the spirit of princes,
    he is the terror of the kings on earth.

77

1   I cried aloud to God,
   I cried to God, and he heard me.
2   In the day of my distress I sought the Lord,
   and by night I lifted^c my outspread hands in prayer.
   I lay sweating and nothing would cool me;
   I refused all comfort.
3   When I called God to mind, I groaned;
   as I lay thinking, darkness came over my spirit.
4   My eyelids were tightly closed;
   I was dazed and I could not speak.
5   My thoughts went back to times long past,
    I remembered forgotten years;
6   all night long I was in deep distress,
   as I lay thinking, my spirit was sunk in despair.

7   Will the Lord reject us for evermore
    and never again show favour?
8   Has his unfailing love now failed us utterly,
   must his promise time and again be unfulfilled?
9   Has God forgotten to be gracious,
   has he in anger withheld his mercies?
10   'Has his right hand', I said, 'lost its grasp?
    Does it hang powerless,^d the arm of the Most High?'

11 But then, O LORD, I call to mind thy deeds;^e
   I recall thy wonderful acts in times gone by.
12   I meditate upon thy works
    and muse on all that thou hast done.
13   O God, thy way is holy;
   what god is so great as our God?
14   Thou art the God who workest miracles;
   thou hast shown the nations thy power.

---

^a O God . . . rising: *prob. rdg.; Heb.* When God rises. ^b *Prob. rdg.; Heb. adds* for
the terror (*cp. verse 12*). ^c I lifted: *prob. rdg.; Heb. om.* ^d lost . . . powerless:
prob. rdg.; Heb. unintelligible. ^e *Prob. rdg.; Heb.* then I call to mind the deeds
of the LORD, for.

With thy strong arm thou didst redeem thy people,   15
    the sons of Jacob and Joseph.

The waters saw thee, O God,   16
    they saw thee and writhed in anguish;
    the ocean was troubled to its depths.
The clouds poured water, the skies thundered,   17
    thy arrows flashed hither and thither.
The sound of thy thunder was in the whirlwind,[a]   18
    thy lightnings lit up the world,
    earth shook and quaked.
Thy path was through the sea, thy way through mighty   19
    waters,
    and no man marked thy footsteps.
Thou didst guide thy people like a flock of sheep,   20
    under the hand of Moses and Aaron.

78

Mark my teaching, O my people,   1
    listen to the words I am to speak.
I will tell you a story with a meaning,   2
I will expound the riddle of things past,
things that we have heard and know,   3
and our fathers have repeated to us.
From their sons we will not hide   4
the praises of the LORD and his might
nor the wonderful acts he has performed;
then they shall repeat them to the next generation.
He laid on Jacob a solemn charge   5
and established a law in Israel,
which he commanded our fathers
    to teach their sons,
that it might be known to a future generation,   6
    to children yet unborn,
and these would repeat it to their sons in turn.
He charged them to put their trust in God,   7
to hold his great acts ever in mind
    and to keep all his commandments;
not to do as their fathers did,   8
a disobedient and rebellious race,
a generation with no firm purpose,
with hearts not fixed steadfastly on God.

The men of Ephraim, bowmen all and marksmen,   9
    turned and ran in the hour of battle.

       [a] Or in the chariot-wheels.

10 They had not kept God's covenant
    and had refused to live by his law;
11   they forgot all that he had done
    and the wonderful acts which he had shown them.

12 He did wonders in their fathers' sight
        in the land of Egypt, the country of Zoan:
13 he divided the sea and took them through it,
    making the water stand up like banks on either side.
14 He led them with a cloud by day
    and all night long with a glowing fire.
15 He cleft the rock in the wilderness
    and gave them water to drink, abundant as the sea;
16 he brought streams out of the cliff
    and made water run down like rivers.
17 But they sinned against him yet again:
    in the desert they defied the Most High,
18 they tried God's patience wilfully,
    demanding food to satisfy their hunger.
19 They vented their grievance against God and said,
    'Can God spread a table in the wilderness?'
20 When he struck a rock, water gushed out
    until the gullies overflowed;
    they said, 'Can he give bread as well,
    can he provide meat for his people?'
21 When he heard this, the LORD was filled with fury:
        fire raged against Jacob,
        anger blazed up against Israel,
22   because they put no trust in God
    and had no faith in his power to save.
23 Then he gave orders to the skies above
        and threw open heaven's doors,
24 he rained down manna for them to eat
    and gave them the grain of heaven.
25 So men ate the bread of angels;
    he sent them food to their heart's desire.
26 He let loose the east wind from heaven
    and drove the south wind by his power;
27 he rained meat like a dust-storm upon them,
    flying birds like the sand of the sea-shore,
28 which he made settle all over the camp
        round the tents where they lived.
29 So the people ate and were well filled,
    for he had given them what they craved.
30 Yet they did not abandon their complaints[a]
    even while the food was in their mouths.
31 Then the anger of God blazed up against them;

    [a] *Or* craving.

he spread death among their stoutest men
and brought the young men of Israel to the ground.

In spite of all, they persisted in their sin   32
and had no faith in his wonderful acts.
So in one moment he snuffed out their lives   33
    and ended their years in calamity.
When he struck them, they began to seek him,   34
they would turn and look eagerly for God;
they remembered that God was their Creator,   35
that God Most High was their deliverer.
    But still they beguiled him with words   36
and deceived him with fine speeches;
they were not loyal to him in their hearts   37
nor were they faithful to his covenant.
Yet he wiped out their guilt   38
and did not smother his own[a] natural affection;
often he restrained his wrath
and did not rouse his anger to its height.
He remembered that they were only mortal men,   39
who pass by like a wind and never return.

How often they rebelled against him in the wilderness   40
    and grieved him in the desert!
Again and again they tried God's patience   41
    and provoked the Holy One of Israel.
They did not remember his prowess   42
on the day when he saved them from the enemy,
how he set his signs in Egypt,   43
    his portents in the land of Zoan.
He turned their streams into blood,   44
and they could not drink the running water.
He sent swarms of flies which devoured them,   45
and frogs which brought devastation;
    he gave their harvest over to locusts   46
and their produce to the grubs;
he killed their vines with hailstones   47
    and their figs with torrents of rain;
he abandoned their cattle to the plague   48
    and their beasts to the arrows of pestilence.
He loosed upon them the violence of his anger,   49
wrath and enmity and rage,
launching those messengers of evil
to open a way for his fury.   50-51
He struck down all the first-born in Egypt,
the flower of their manhood in the tents of Ham,
not shielding their lives from death
but abandoning their bodies to the plague.

    [a] his own: *prob. rdg.; Heb. om.*

52 But he led out his own people like sheep
and guided them like a flock in the wilderness.

53 He led them in safety and they were not afraid,
and the sea closed over their enemies.

54 He brought them to his holy mountain,
the hill which his right hand had won;

55 he drove out nations before them,
he allotted their lands to Israel as a possession
and settled his tribes in their dwellings.

56 Yet they tried God's patience and rebelled against him;
they did not keep the commands of the Most High;

57 they were renegades, traitors like their fathers,
they changed, they went slack like a bow.

58 They provoked him to anger with their hill-shrines
and roused his jealousy with their carved images.

59 When God heard this, he put them out of mind
and utterly rejected Israel.

60 He forsook his home at Shiloh,
the tabernacle in which he dwelt among men;

61 he surrendered the symbol of his strength into captivity
and his pride into enemy hands;

62 he gave his people over to the sword
and put his own possession out of mind.

63 Fire devoured his young men,
and his maidens could raise no lament for them;

64 his priests fell by the sword,
and his widows could not weep.

65 Then the Lord awoke as a sleeper awakes,
like a warrior heated with wine;

66 he struck his foes in the back parts
and brought perpetual shame upon them.

67 He despised the clan of Joseph
and did not choose the tribe of Ephraim;

68 he chose the tribe of Judah
and Mount Zion which he loved;

69 he built his sanctuary high as the heavens,
founded like the earth to last for ever.

70 He chose David to be his servant
and took him from the sheepfolds;

71 he brought him from minding the ewes
to be the shepherd of his people Jacob; *a*

72 and he shepherded them in singleness of heart
and guided them with skilful hand.

a Prob. rdg.; Heb. adds and Israel his possession.

79

O God, the heathen have set foot in thy domain,   1
    defiled thy holy temple
and laid Jerusalem in ruins.
    They have thrown out the dead bodies of thy servants   2
       to feed the birds of the air;
    they have made thy loyal servants carrion for wild beasts.
Their blood is spilled all round Jerusalem like water,   3
    and there they lie unburied.
    We suffer the contempt of our neighbours,   4
    the gibes and mockery of all around us.

How long, O LORD, wilt thou be roused to such fury?   5
    Must thy jealousy rage like a fire?
Pour out thy wrath over nations which do not know thee   6
and over kingdoms which do not invoke thee by name;
see how they have devoured Jacob and laid waste his homesteads.   7
    Do not remember against us the guilt of past generations 8
    but let thy compassion come swiftly to meet us,
       we have been brought so low.

Help us, O God our saviour, for the honour of thy name;   9
    for thy name's sake deliver us and wipe out our sins.
Why should the nations ask, 'Where is their God?'   10
    Let thy vengeance for the bloody slaughter of thy servants
    fall on those nations before our very eyes.

Let the groaning of the captives reach thy presence   11
    and in thy great might set free death's prisoners.
As for the contempt our neighbours pour on thee, O Lord,   12
    turn it back sevenfold on their own heads.
    Then we thy people, the flock which thou dost shepherd, 13
    will give thee thanks for ever
and repeat thy praise to every generation.

80

Hear us, O shepherd of Israel,   1
who leadest Joseph like a flock of sheep.
    Show thyself, thou that art throned on the cherubim,
    to Ephraim and to Benjamin.   2
    Rouse thy victorious might from slumber,*a*
    come to our rescue.
    Restore us, O God,   3
and make thy face shine upon us that we may be saved.
    O LORD God of Hosts,   4
how long wilt thou resist thy people's prayer?

      a from slumber: *prob. rdg.*; *Heb.* and Manasseh.

5   Thou hast made sorrow their daily bread
       and tears of threefold grief their drink.

6   Thou hast humbled us before our neighbours,
       and our enemies mock us to their hearts' content.

7   O God of Hosts, restore us;
       make thy face shine upon us that we may be saved.

8   Thou didst bring a vine out of Egypt;
       thou didst drive out nations and plant it;

9   thou didst clear the ground before it,
    so that it made good roots and filled the land.

10   The mountains were covered with its shade,
       and its branches were like those of mighty cedars.

11   It put out boughs all the way to the Sea
       and its shoots as far as the River.

12   Why hast thou broken down the wall round it
    so that every passer-by can pluck its fruit?

13   The wild boar from the thickets gnaws it,
       and swarming insects from the fields feed on it.

14   O God of Hosts, once more look down from heaven,
       take thought for this vine and tend it,

15   this stock that thy right hand has planted. *a*

16   Let them that set fire to it or cut it down
       perish before thy angry face.

17   Let thy hand rest upon the man at thy right side,
       the man whom thou hast made strong for thy service.

18   We have not turned back from thee,
       so grant us new life, and we will invoke thee by name.

19   LORD God of Hosts, restore us;
       make thy face shine upon us that we may be saved.

81

1   Sing out in praise of God our refuge, *b*
       acclaim the God of Jacob.

2   Take pipe and tabor,
       take tuneful harp and lute.

3   Blow the horn for the new month,
       for the full moon on the day of our pilgrim-feast.

4   This is a law for Israel,
       an ordinance of the God of Jacob,

5   laid as a solemn charge on Joseph
       when he came out of Egypt. *c*

6   When I lifted the load from his shoulders,
       his hands let go the builder's basket.

---

a Prob. rdg.; Heb. adds and on the son whom thou hast made strong for thy service
(*cp. verse 17*).   *b Or* strength.   *c Prob. rdg.; Heb. adds* I hear an unfamiliar
language.

When you cried to me in distress, I rescued you;   7
   unseen, I answered you in thunder.
I tested you at the waters of Meribah,
   where I opened your mouths and filled them.*a*
I fed Israel*b* with the finest wheat-flour   16*c*
and satisfied him with honey from the rocks.
Listen, my people, while I give you a solemn charge—   8
do but listen to me, O Israel:
you shall have no strange god   9
nor bow down to any foreign god;
I am the LORD your God   10
   who brought you up from Egypt.*d*
But my people did not listen to my words   11
and Israel would have none of me;
   so I sent them off, stubborn as they were,   12
   to follow their own devices.

If my people would but listen to me,   13
if Israel would only conform to my ways,
I would soon bring their enemies to their knees   14
and lay a heavy hand upon their persecutors.
Let those who hate them*e* come cringing to them,   15
and meet with everlasting troubles.*f*

82

God takes his stand in the court of heaven   1
   to deliver judgement among the gods themselves.

How long will you judge unjustly   2
   and show favour to the wicked?
You ought to give judgement for the weak and the orphan,   3
   and see right done to the destitute and downtrodden,
you ought to rescue the weak and the poor,   4
   and save them from the clutches of wicked men.
   But you know nothing, you understand nothing,   5
   you walk in the dark
   while earth's foundations are giving way.
This is my sentence: Gods you may be,   6
   sons all of you of a high god,*g*
yet you shall die as men die;*h*   7
princes fall, every one of them, and so shall you.

Arise, O God, and judge the earth;   8
   for thou dost pass all nations through thy sieve.

---

a Line transposed from end of verse 10.   *b* I fed Israel: *prob. rdg.; Heb.* He fed him.
c Verse transposed.   *d See note on verse 7.*   *e* those . . . them: *prob. rdg.; Heb.*
those who hate the LORD.   *f Verse 16 transposed to follow verse 7.*   *g Or of the*
Most High.   *h Or as Adam died.*

83

1   Rest not, O God;
        O God, be neither silent nor still,
2   for thy enemies are making a tumult,
        and those that hate thee carry their heads high.
3   They devise cunning schemes against thy people
        and conspire against those thou hast made thy treasure:
4   'Come, away with them,' they cry,
            'let them be a nation no longer,
        let Israel's name be remembered no more.'
5   With one mind they have agreed together
        to make a league against thee:
6   the families of Edom, the Ishmaelites,
            Moabites and Hagarenes,
7   Gebal, Ammon and Amalek,
            Philistia and the citizens of Tyre,
8   Asshur too their ally,
        all of them lending aid to the descendants of Lot.
9   Deal with them as with Sisera,
        as with Jabin by the torrent of Kishon,
10   who fell vanquished as Midian*ᵃ* fell at En-harod,*ᵇ*
        and were spread on the battlefield like dung.
11   Make their princes like Oreb and Zeeb,
        make all their nobles like Zebah and Zalmunna;
12   for they said, 'We will seize for ourselves
        all the pastures of God's people.'
13   Scatter them, O God, like thistledown,
        like chaff before the wind.
14   Like fire raging through the forest
        or flames which blaze across the hills,
15   hunt them down with thy tempest,
        and dismay them with thy storm-wind.
16   Heap shame upon their heads, O Lord,
        until they confess the greatness of thy name.
17   Let them be abashed, and live in perpetual dismay;
        let them feel their shame and perish.
18   So let them learn that thou alone art Lord,
        God Most High over all the earth.

84

1   How dear is thy dwelling-place,
        thou Lord of Hosts!
2   I pine, I faint with longing
        for the courts of the Lord's temple;

ᵃ as Midian: *transposed from previous verse.*   *ᵇ* En-harod: *prob. rdg., cp. Judg. 7. 1;*
Heb. Endor.

my whole being cries out with joy
    to the living God.
Even the sparrow finds a home,   3
    and the swallow has her nest,
where she rears her brood beside thy altars,
    O LORD of Hosts, my King and my God.
Happy are those who dwell in thy house;   4
    they never cease from praising thee.
Happy the men whose refuge is in thee,   5
    whose hearts are set on the pilgrim ways*a*!
    As they pass through the thirsty valley   6
    they find water from a spring;
and the LORD provides even men who lose their way
    with pools to quench their thirst. *b*
So they pass on from outer wall to inner,   7
and the God of gods shows himself in Zion.

O LORD God of Hosts, hear my prayer;   8
    listen, O God of Jacob.
O God, look upon our lord the king   9
    and accept thy anointed prince with favour.

Better one day in thy courts   10
    than a thousand days at home;
better to linger by the threshold of God's house
    than to live in the dwellings of the wicked.
The LORD God is a battlement and a shield;   11
    grace and honour are his to give.
The LORD will hold back no good thing
    from those whose life is blameless.

    O LORD of Hosts,   12
happy the man who trusts in thee!

85

LORD, thou hast been gracious to thy land   1
    and turned the tide of Jacob's fortunes.
Thou hast forgiven the guilt of thy people   2
    and put away all their sins.
Thou hast taken back all thy anger   3
    and turned from thy bitter wrath.

    Turn back to us, O God our saviour,   4
and cancel thy displeasure.
Wilt thou be angry with us for ever?   5
Must thy wrath last for all generations?

---

a are set . . . ways: *or* high praises fill.   *b* they find . . . thirst: *prob. rdg.; Heb.*
obscure.

6   Wilt thou not give us new life
          that thy people may rejoice in thee?
7   O LORD, show us thy true love
          and grant us thy deliverance.

8   Let me hear the words of the LORD:
          are they not *a* words of peace,
             peace to his people and his loyal servants
             and to all who turn and trust in him?
9   Deliverance is near to those who worship him,
          so that glory may dwell in our land.
10   Love and fidelity have come together;
          justice and peace join hands.
11   Fidelity springs up from earth
          and justice looks down from heaven.
12   The LORD will add prosperity,
          and our land shall yield its harvest.
13   Justice shall go in front of him
          and the path before his feet shall be peace. *b*

86

1   Turn to me, LORD, and answer;
          I am downtrodden and poor.
2   Guard me, for I am constant and true;
      save thy servant who puts his trust in thee.
3   O Lord my God, *c* show me thy favour;
          I call to thee all day long.
4   Fill thy servant's heart with joy, O Lord,
      for I lift up my heart to thee.
5   Thou, O Lord, art kind and forgiving,
          full of true love for all who cry to thee.
6   Listen, O LORD, to my prayer
             and hear my pleading.
7   In the day of my distress I call on thee;
          for thou wilt answer me.

8   Among the gods not one is like thee, O Lord,
           no deeds are like thine.
9   All the nations thou hast made, O Lord, will come,
      will bow down before thee and honour thy name;
10   for thou art great, thy works are wonderful,
          thou alone art God.

11   Guide me, O LORD,
          that I may be true to thee and follow thy path;

a of the LORD: are they not: *prob. rdg.; Heb.* of God the LORD.   *b* and the path . . .
peace: *prob. rdg.; Heb.* so that he may put his feet to the way.   *c* my God: *transposed from previous verse.*

let me be one in heart
   with those who revere thy name.
I will praise thee, O Lord my God, with all my heart   12
   and honour thy name for ever.
   For thy true love stands high above me;   13
thou hast rescued my soul from the depths of Sheol.
O God, proud men attack me;   14
   a mob of ruffians seek my life
      and give no thought to thee.
Thou, Lord, art God, compassionate and gracious,   15
   forbearing, ever constant and true.
   Turn towards me and show me thy favour;   16
   grant thy slave protection
      and rescue thy slave-girl's son.
Give me proof of thy kindness;   17
   let those who hate thee see to their shame
that thou, O Lord, hast been my help and comfort.

87 ^a

The Lord loves the gates of Zion   1-2
   more than all the dwellings of Jacob;
   her^b foundations are laid upon holy hills,
and he has made her his home.^c   4-5
I will count Egypt and Babylon among my friends;
Philistine, Tyrian and Nubian shall be ^d there;
   and Zion shall be called a mother
   in whom men of every race are born.
   The Lord shall write against each in the roll of nations: 6
   'This one was born in her.'
Singers and dancers alike all chant^e your praises,   7
proclaiming glorious things of you, O city of God.   3

88

O Lord, my God, by day I call for help,^f   1
by night I cry aloud in thy presence.
Let my prayer come before thee,   2
   hear my loud lament;
   for I have had my fill of woes,   3
   and they have brought me to the threshold of Sheol.

---

^a *The text of this psalm is disordered, and several verses have been re-arranged.*   ^b *Prob.
rdg.; Heb.* his.   ^c his home: *prob. rdg.; Heb.* most high.   ^d *Prob. rdg.; Heb. adds*
this one was born (*cp. verse 6*).   ^e all chant: *prob. rdg.; Heb.* all my springs.
^f I call for help: *prob. rdg.; Heb.* my deliverance.

4   I am numbered with those who go down to the abyss
     and have become like a man beyond help,
5   like a man who lies dead *a*
         or the slain who sleep in the grave,
     whom thou rememberest no more
     because they are cut off from thy care.
6   Thou hast plunged me into the lowest abyss,
         in dark places, in the depths.
7   Thy wrath rises against me,
     thou hast turned on me the full force of thy anger. *b*
8   Thou hast taken all my friends far from me,
     and made me loathsome to them.
         I am in prison and cannot escape;
     my eyes are failing and dim with anguish.
9   I have called upon thee, O Lord, every day
     and spread out my hands in prayer to thee.

10   Dost thou work wonders for the dead?
         Shall their company rise up and praise thee?
11   Will they speak of thy faithful love in the grave,
             of thy sure help in the place of Destruction?
12   Will thy wonders be known in the dark,
             thy victories in the land of oblivion?

13   But, Lord, I cry to thee,
     my prayer comes before thee in the morning.
14   Why hast thou cast me off, O Lord,
     why dost thou hide thy face from me?
15   I have suffered from boyhood and come near to death;
     I have borne thy terrors, I cower beneath thy blows.
16   Thy burning fury has swept over me,
         thy onslaughts have put me to silence;
17   all the day long they surge round me like a flood,
     they engulf me in a moment.
18   Thou hast taken lover and friend far from me,
         and parted me from my companions.

89

1   I will sing the story of thy love, O Lord, for ever;
     I will proclaim thy faithfulness to all generations.
2   Thy true love is firm as the ancient earth, *c*
     thy faithfulness fixed as the heavens.
5 *d* The heavens praise thy wonders, O Lord,
         and the council of the holy ones exalts thy faithfulness.

---

a who lies dead: *prob. rdg.; Heb. obscure.*   *b* anger: *or* waves.   *c* Thy . . .
earth: *prob. rdg.; Heb.* Thou hast said for ever true love shall be made firm.   *d Verses
3 and 4 transposed to follow* servants *in verse 19.*

In the skies who is there like the Lord,   6
    who like the Lord in the court of heaven,
    like God who is dreaded among the assembled holy ones,   7
    great and terrible above all who stand about him?
O Lord God of Hosts, who is like thee?   8
Thy strength*a* and faithfulness, O Lord, surround thee.
    Thou rulest the surging sea,   9
    calming the turmoil*b* of its waves.
Thou didst crush the monster Rahab with a mortal blow   10
    and scatter thy enemies with thy strong arm.
Thine are the heavens, the earth is thine also;   11
the world with all that is in it is of thy foundation.
Thou didst create Zaphon and Amanus;*c*   12
Tabor and Hermon echo thy name.
    Strength of arm and valour are thine;   13
thy hand is mighty, thy right hand lifted high;
    thy throne is built upon righteousness and justice,   14
true love and faithfulness herald thy coming.

    Happy the people who have learnt to acclaim thee,   15
    who walk, O Lord, in the light of thy presence!
In thy name they shall rejoice all day long;   16
    thy righteousness shall lift them up.
Thou art thyself the strength in which they glory;   17
    through thy favour we hold our heads high.
    The Lord, he is our shield;   18
    the Holy One of Israel, he is our king.

Then didst thou announce in a vision   19
and declare to thy faithful servants:
    I have made a covenant with him I have chosen,   3
    I have sworn to my servant David:
'I will establish your posterity for ever,   4
I will make your throne endure for all generations.'
I have endowed a warrior with princely gifts,
so that the youth I have chosen towers over his people.
I have discovered David my servant;   20
    I have anointed him with my holy oil.
My hand shall be ready to help him   21
    and my arm to give him strength.
No enemy shall strike at him   22
    and no rebel bring him low;
I will shatter his foes before him   23
    and vanquish those who hate him.
My faithfulness and true love shall be with him   24
and through my name he shall hold his head high.

---

a Thy strength: *prob. rdg.; Heb. obscure.*   *b* turmoil: *prob. rdg.; Heb. obscure.*
c Amanus: *prob. rdg.; Heb.* right hand *or* south.

25	I will extend his rule over the Sea and his dominion as far as the River.
26	He will say to me, 'Thou art my father, my God, my rock and my safe refuge.'
27	And I will name him my first-born, highest among the kings of the earth.
28	I will maintain my love for him for ever and be faithful in my covenant with him.
29	I will establish his posterity for ever and his throne as long as the heavens endure.
30	If his sons forsake my law and do not conform to my judgements,
31	if they renounce my statutes and do not observe my commands,
32	I will punish their disobedience with the rod and their iniquity with lashes.
33	Yet I will not deprive him of my true love nor let my faithfulness prove false;
34	I will not renounce my covenant nor change my promised purpose.
35	I have sworn by my holiness once and for all, I will not break my word to David:
36	his posterity shall continue for ever, his throne before me like the sun;
37	it shall be sure for ever as the moon's return, faithful so long as the skies remain.*a*
38	Yet thou hast rejected thy anointed king, thou hast spurned him and raged against him,*b*
39	thou hast denounced the covenant with thy servant, defiled his crown and flung it to the ground.
40	Thou hast breached his walls and laid his fortresses in ruin;
41	all who pass by plunder him, and he suffers the taunts of his neighbours.
42	Thou hast increased the power of his enemies and brought joy to all his foes;
43	thou hast let his sharp sword be driven back and left him without help in the battle.
44	Thou hast put an end to his glorious rule*c* and hurled his throne to the ground;
45	thou hast cut short the days of his youth and vigour and covered him with shame.
46	How long, O Lord, wilt thou hide thyself from sight? How long must thy wrath blaze like fire?

a so long . . . remain: *prob. rdg.*; *Heb.* a witness in the skies.   *b* raged against him:
or put him out of mind.   *c* his glorious rule: *prob. rdg.*; *Heb.* from his purity.

Remember that I shall not live for ever; [a]	47
hast thou created man in vain?	
What man shall live and not see death	48
or save himself from the power of Sheol?	
Where are those former acts of thy love, O Lord,	49
those faithful promises given to David?	
Remember, O Lord, the taunts hurled at thy servant,	50
how I have borne in my heart the calumnies of the nations; [b]	
so have thy enemies taunted us, O LORD,	51
taunted the successors of thy anointed king.	

Blessed is the LORD for ever.	52
Amen, Amen.	

BOOK 4

90

Lord, thou hast been our refuge	1
from generation to generation.	
Before the mountains were brought forth,	2
or earth and world were born in travail,	
from age to age everlasting thou art God.	
Thou turnest man back into dust;	3
'Turn back,' thou sayest, 'you sons of men';	
for in thy sight a thousand years are as yesterday;	4
a night-watch passes, and thou hast cut them off;	5
they are like a dream at daybreak,	
they fade like grass which springs up[c] with the morning	6
but when evening comes is parched and withered.	
So we are brought to an end by thy anger	7
and silenced by thy wrath.	
Thou dost lay bare our iniquities before thee	8
and our lusts in the full light of thy presence.	
All our days go by under the shadow of thy wrath;	9
our years die away like a murmur.	
Seventy years is the span of our life,	10
eighty if our strength holds; [d]	
the hurrying years are labour and sorrow,	
so quickly they pass and are forgotten.	
Who feels the power of thy anger,	11
who feels thy wrath like those that fear thee?	
Teach us to order our days rightly,	12
that we may enter the gate of wisdom.	

[a] live for ever: *prob. rdg.*; *Heb. obscure.*   [b] the calumnies ... nations: *prob. rdg.*; *Heb.* all of many peoples.   [c] *Prob. rdg.*; *Heb. adds* and passes away.   [d] *Or* eighty at the most.

13   How long, O Lord?
Relent, and take pity on thy servants.

14   Satisfy us with thy love when morning breaks,
that we may sing for joy and be glad all our days.

15   Repay us days of gladness for our days of suffering,
for the years thou hast humbled us.

16   Show thy servants thy deeds
and their children thy majesty.

17   May all delightful things be ours, O Lord our God;
establish firmly all we do.

91

1   You that live in the shelter of the Most High
and lodge under the shadow of the Almighty,

2   who say, 'The Lord is my safe retreat,
my God the fastness in which I trust';

3   he himself will snatch you away
from fowler's snare or raging tempest.

4   He will cover you with his pinions,
and you shall find safety beneath his wings;

5   you shall not fear the hunters' trap by night
or the arrow that flies by day,

6   the pestilence that stalks in darkness
or the plague raging at noonday.

7   A thousand may fall at your side,
ten thousand close at hand,
but you it shall not touch;
his truth*a* will be your shield and your rampart. *b*

8   With your own eyes you shall see all this;
you shall watch the punishment of the wicked.

9   For you, the Lord is a*c* safe retreat;
you have made the Most High your refuge.

10   No disaster shall befall you,
no calamity shall come upon your home.

11   For he has charged his angels
to guard you wherever you go,

12   to lift you on their hands
for fear you should strike your foot against a stone.

13   You shall step on asp and cobra,
you shall tread safely on snake and serpent.

14   Because his love is set on me, I will deliver him;
I will lift him beyond danger, for he knows me by my name.

15   When he calls upon me, I will answer;
I will be with him in time of trouble;
I will rescue him and bring him to honour.

a Or his arm.   *b* his truth . . . rampart: *transposed from end of verse 4.*
c Prob. rdg.; Heb. my.

I will satisfy him with long life 16
to enjoy the fullness of my salvation.

92

O LORD, it is good to give thee thanks, 1
to sing psalms to thy name, O Most High,
to declare thy love in the morning 2
   and thy constancy every night,
      to the music of a ten-stringed lute, 3
      to the sounding chords of the harp.
Thy acts, O LORD, fill me with exultation; 4
   I shout in triumph at thy mighty deeds.
How great are thy deeds, O LORD! 5
How fathomless thy thoughts!

He who does not know this is a brute, 6
a fool is he who does not understand this:
that though the wicked grow like grass 7
and every evildoer prospers,
   they will be destroyed for ever.
While thou, LORD, dost reign on high eternally, 8
   thy foes will surely perish, 9
   all evildoers will be scattered.

I lift my head high, like a wild ox tossing its horn; 10
   I am anointed richly with oil.
   I gloat over all who speak ill of me, 11
I listen for the downfall of my cruel foes.
   The righteous flourish like a palm-tree, 12
   they grow tall as a cedar on Lebanon;
      planted as they are in the house of the LORD, 13
      they flourish in the courts of our God,
vigorous in old age like trees full of sap, 14
   luxuriant, wide-spreading,
eager to declare that the LORD is just, 15
the LORD my rock,*a* in whom there is no unrighteousness.

93

The LORD is king; he is clothed in majesty; 1
the LORD clothes himself with might and fastens on his belt of wrath.

Thou hast fixed the earth immovable and firm,
   thy throne firm from of old; 2
   from all eternity thou art God.
O LORD, the ocean lifts up, the ocean lifts up its clamour; 3
   the ocean lifts up*b* its pounding waves.

---

a Or creator. *b* the ocean lifts up: or let the ocean lift up.

4
> The Lord on high is mightier far
> than the noise of great waters,
> mightier than the breakers of the sea.

5
> Thy law stands firm, and holiness is the beauty of thy temple,
> while time shall last, O Lord.

94

1
> O Lord, thou God of vengeance,
> thou God of vengeance, show thyself.

2
> Rise up, judge of the earth;
> punish the arrogant as they deserve.

3
> How long shall the wicked, O Lord,
> how long shall the wicked exult?

4
> Evildoers are full of bluster,
> boasting and swaggering;

5
> they beat down thy people, O Lord,
> and oppress thy chosen nation;

6
> they murder the widow and the stranger
> and do the fatherless to death;

7
> they say, 'The Lord does not see,
> the God of Jacob pays no heed.'

8
> Pay heed yourselves, most brutish of the people;
> you fools, when will you be wise?

9
> Does he that planted the ear not hear,
> he that moulded the eye not see?

10
> Shall not he that instructs the nations correct them?
> The teacher of mankind, has he no[a] knowledge?

11
> The Lord knows the thoughts of man,
> that they are but a puff of wind.

12
> Happy the man whom thou dost instruct, O Lord,
> and teach out of thy law,

13
> giving him respite from adversity
> until a pit is dug for the wicked.

14
> The Lord will not abandon his people
> nor forsake his chosen nation;

15
> for righteousness still informs his judgement,[b]
> and all upright men follow it.

16
> Who is on my side against these sinful men?
> Who will stand up for me against these evildoers?

17
> If the Lord had not been my helper,
> I should soon have slept in the silent grave.

18
> When I felt that my foot was slipping,
> thy love, O Lord, held me up.

---

[a] no: *prob. rdg.; Heb.* om.   [b] for . . . judgement: *prob. rdg.; Heb.* for judgement will return as far as righteousness.

Anxious thoughts may fill my heart,   19
but thy presence is my joy and my consolation.
Shall sanctimonious calumny call thee partner,   20
or he that contrives a mischief under cover of law?
For they put the righteous on trial[a] for his life   21
and condemn to death innocent men.
But the LORD has been my strong tower,   22
and God my rock of refuge;
our God requites the wicked for their injustice,   23
the LORD puts them to silence for their misdeeds.

95

Come! Let us raise a joyful song to the LORD,   1
a shout of triumph to the Rock of our salvation.
Let us come into his presence with thanksgiving,   2
and sing him psalms of triumph.
For the LORD is a great God,   3
a great king over all gods;
the farthest places of the earth are in his hands,   4
and the folds of the hills are his;
the sea is his, he made it;   5
the dry land fashioned by his hands is his.
Come! Let us throw ourselves at his feet in homage,   6
let us kneel before the LORD who made us;
for he is our God,   7
we are his people, we the flock he shepherds.
You shall know[b] his power today
if you will listen to his voice.

Do not grow stubborn, as you were at Meribah,[c]   8
as at the time of Massah[d] in the wilderness,
when your forefathers challenged me,   9
tested me and saw for themselves all that I did.
For forty years I was indignant   10
with that generation, and I said:
They are a people whose hearts are astray,
and they will not discern my ways.
As I swore in my anger: 11
They shall never enter my rest.

96

Sing a new song to the LORD;   1[e]
sing to the LORD, all men on earth.

---

[a] they put . . . trial: *prob. rdg.; Heb.* they cut the righteous.   [b] You shall know: *prob. rdg.; Heb. om.*   [c] *That is* Dispute.   [d] *That is* Challenge.   [e] *Verses 1-13: cp. 1 Chr. 16. 23-33.*

2   Sing to the Lord and bless his name,
                      proclaim his triumph day by day.
3   Declare his glory among the nations,
                      his marvellous deeds among all peoples.
4   Great is the Lord and worthy of all praise;
                      he is more to be feared than all gods.
5   For the gods of the nations are idols every one;
                      but the Lord made the heavens.
6   Majesty and splendour attend him,
                      might and beauty are in his sanctuary.

7   Ascribe to the Lord, you families of nations,
              ascribe to the Lord glory and might;
8   ascribe to the Lord the glory due to his name,
              bring a gift and come into his courts.
9   Bow down to the Lord in the splendour of holiness, *a*
                      and dance in his honour, all men on earth.
10   Declare among the nations, 'The Lord is king.
                      He has fixed the earth firm, immovable;
                      he will judge the peoples justly.'
11   Let the heavens rejoice and the earth exult,
                      let the sea roar and all the creatures in it,
12   let the fields exult and all that is in them;
                      then let all the trees of the forest shout for joy
13   before the Lord when he comes to judge the earth.
                  He will judge the earth with righteousness
                      and the peoples in good faith.

97

1   The Lord is king, let the earth be glad,
                      let coasts and islands all rejoice.
2   Cloud and mist enfold him,
                        righteousness and justice
                      are the foundation of his throne.
3   Fire goes before him
                      and burns up his enemies all around.
4   The world is lit up beneath his lightning-flash;
                      the earth sees it and writhes in pain.
5   The mountains melt like wax as the Lord approaches,
                      the Lord of all the earth.
6   The heavens proclaim his righteousness,
                      and all peoples see his glory.
7   Let all who worship images, who vaunt their idols,
                      be put to shame;
                  bow down, all gods, *b* before him.

---

a the splendour of holiness: *or* holy vestments.   *b* bow . . . gods: *or* all gods bow down . . .

Zion heard and rejoiced, the cities of Judah were glad   8
    at thy judgements, O LORD.
For thou, LORD, art most high over all the earth,   9
    far exalted above all gods.

    The LORD loves *a* those who hate evil;   10
    he keeps his loyal servants safe
    and rescues them from the wicked.
    A harvest of light is sown for the righteous,   11
    and joy for all good men.
    You that are righteous, rejoice in the LORD   12
    and praise his holy name.

98

Sing a new song to the LORD,   1
    for he has done marvellous deeds;
his right hand and holy arm have won him victory.
    The LORD has made his victory known;   2
    he has displayed his righteousness to all the nations.
    He has remembered his constancy,   3
    his love for the house of Israel.
All the ends of the earth have seen
    the victory of our God.

    Acclaim the LORD, all men on earth,   4
    break into songs of joy, sing psalms.
    Sing psalms in the LORD's honour with the harp,   5
    with the harp and with the music of the psaltery.
    With trumpet and echoing horn   6
    acclaim the presence of the LORD our king.
    Let the sea roar and all its creatures,   7
    the world and those who dwell in it.
    Let the rivers clap their hands,   8
    let the hills sing aloud together
    before the LORD; for he comes   9
    to judge the earth.
    He will judge the world with righteousness
    and the peoples in justice.

99

The LORD is king, the peoples are perturbed;   1
he is throned on the cherubim, earth quivers.
    The LORD is great in Zion;   2
    he is exalted above all the peoples.

    a The LORD loves: *prob. rdg.; Heb.* Lovers of the LORD.

3   They extol his *a* name as great and terrible;
4   he is holy, he is mighty,
            a king who loves justice.

        Thou hast established justice and equity;
        thou hast dealt righteously in Jacob.
5   Exalt the LORD our God,
                bow down before his footstool;
                he is holy.

6   Moses and Aaron among his priests,
                and Samuel among those who call on his name,
        called to the LORD, and he answered.
7   He spoke to them in a pillar of cloud;
        they followed his teaching and kept the law he gave them.
8   Thou, O LORD our God, thou didst answer them;
        thou wast a God who forgave all their misdeeds
                and held them innocent.
9   Exalt the LORD our God,
                bow down towards his holy hill;
                for the LORD our God is holy.

100

1   Acclaim the LORD, all men on earth,
2   worship the LORD in gladness;
        enter his presence with songs of exultation.
3   Know that the LORD is God;
        he has made us and we are his own,
                his people, the flock which he shepherds.
4   Enter his gates with thanksgiving
                and his courts with praise.
            Give thanks to him and bless his name;
5   for the LORD is good and his love is everlasting,
                his constancy endures to all generations.

101

1   I sing of loyalty and justice;
            I will raise a psalm to thee, O LORD.*b*

2   I will follow a wise and blameless course,
                whatever may befall me.*c*
            I will go about my house in purity of heart.
3   I will set before myself no sordid aim;
            I will hate disloyalty, I will have none of it.

---

a *Prob. rdg.; Heb.* thy.   *b* I sing ... O LORD: *or* I will follow a course of justice
and loyalty; I will hold thee in awe, O LORD.   *c* whatever may befall me: *prob.
rdg.; Heb.* when comest thou to me?

I will reject all crooked thoughts;   4
    I will have no dealings with evil.
I will silence those who spread tales behind men's backs,   5
I will not sit at table with proud, pompous men,
I will choose the most loyal for my companions;   6
my servants shall be men whose lives are blameless.
No scandal-monger shall live in my household;   7
no liar shall set himself up where I can see him.
Morning after morning I will put all wicked men to silence 8
and will rid the LORD's city of all evildoers.

102

LORD, hear my prayer   1
    and let my cry for help reach thee.
Hide not thy face from me   2
    when I am in distress.
Listen to my prayer
    and, when I call, answer me soon;
for my days vanish like smoke,   3
    my body is burnt up as in an oven.
I am stricken, withered like grass;   4
    I cannot find the strength to eat.
Wasted away,*a* I groan aloud   5
    and my skin hangs on my bones.
I am like a desert-owl in the wilderness,   6
    an owl that lives among ruins.
Thin and meagre, I wail in solitude,   7
    like a bird that flutters on the roof-top.
My enemies insult me all the day long;   8
    mad with rage, they conspire against me.
I have eaten ashes for bread   9
    and mingled tears with my drink.
    In thy wrath and fury   10
        thou hast taken me up and flung me aside.
My days decline as the shadows lengthen,   11
    and like grass I wither away.

But thou, LORD, art enthroned for ever   12
    and thy fame shall be known to all generations.
Thou wilt arise and have mercy on Zion;   13
    for the time is come*b* to pity her.
    Her very stones are dear to thy servants,   14
        and even her dust moves them with pity.
Then shall the nations revere thy name, O LORD;   15
    and all the kings of the earth thy glory,

    a Wasted away: *transposed from previous verse.*
    b *Prob. rdg.; Heb. adds* season.

16   when the LORD builds up Zion again
            and shows himself in his glory.

17   He turns to hear the prayer of the destitute
            and does not scorn them when they pray.

18   This shall be written down for future generations,
            and a people yet unborn shall praise the LORD.

19   The LORD looks down from his sanctuary on high,
            from heaven he surveys the earth

20   to listen to the groaning of the prisoners
            and set free men under sentence of death;

21   so shall the LORD's name be on men's lips in Zion
            and his praise shall be told in Jerusalem,

22   when peoples are assembled together,
            peoples and kingdoms, to serve the LORD.

23   My strength is broken in mid course;

24   the time allotted me is short.
            Snatch me not away before half my days are done,
            for thy years last through all generations.

25   Long ago thou didst lay the foundations of the earth,
            and the heavens were thy handiwork.

26   They shall pass away, but thou endurest;
            like clothes they shall all grow old;
            thou shalt cast them off like a cloak,
            and they shall vanish;

27   but thou art the same and thy years shall have no end;

28   thy servants' children shall continue,
            and their posterity shall be established in thy presence.

103

1   Bless the LORD, my soul;
            my innermost heart, bless his holy name.

2   Bless the LORD, my soul,
            and forget none of his benefits.

3   He pardons all my guilt
            and heals all my suffering.

4   He rescues me from the pit of death
            and surrounds me with constant love,
            with tender affection;

5   he contents me with all good in the prime of life,
            and my youth is ever new like an eagle's.

6   The LORD is righteous in his acts;
            he brings justice to all who have been wronged.

7   He taught Moses to know his way
            and showed the Israelites what he could do.

8   The LORD is compassionate and gracious,
            long-suffering and for ever constant;

he will not always be the accuser   9
  or nurse his anger for all time.
He has not treated us as our sins deserve   10
or requited us for our misdeeds.
For as the heaven stands high above the earth,   11
so his strong love stands high over all who fear him.
    Far as east is from west,   12
so far has he put our offences away from us.
    As a father has compassion on his children,   13
so has the LORD compassion on all who fear him.
For he knows how we were made,   14
he knows full well that we are dust.

Man's days are like the grass;   15
he blossoms like the flowers of the field:
a wind passes over them, and they cease to be,   16
and their place knows them no more.
But the LORD's love never fails those who fear him;   17
  his righteousness never fails their sons and their grandsons
  who listen to his voice*a* and keep his covenant,   18
    who remember his commandments and obey them.

The LORD has established his throne in heaven,   19
  his kingly power over the whole world.
Bless the LORD, all his angels,   20
    creatures of might who do his bidding.
Bless the LORD, all his hosts,   21
    his ministers who serve his will.
Bless the LORD, all created things,   22
    in every place where he has dominion.

Bless the LORD, my soul.

104

Bless the LORD, my soul: 1
O LORD my God, thou art great indeed,
  clothed in majesty and splendour,
  and wrapped in a robe of light.   2
Thou hast spread out the heavens like a tent
and on their waters laid the beams of thy pavilion;   3
who takest the clouds for thy chariot,
  riding on the wings of the wind;
who makest the winds thy messengers   4
and flames of fire thy servants;
thou didst fix the earth on its foundation   5
so that it never can be shaken;

  a who listen to his voice: *transposed from end of verse 20.*

6	the deep overspread it like a cloak,
	and the waters lay above the mountains.
7	At thy rebuke they ran,
	at the sound of thy thunder they rushed away,
8	flowing over the hills,
	pouring down into the valleys
	to the place appointed for them.
9	Thou didst fix a boundary which they might not pass;
	they shall not return to cover the earth.
10	Thou dost make springs break out in the gullies,
	so that their water runs between the hills.
11	The wild beasts all drink from them,
	the wild asses quench their thirst;
12	the birds of the air nest on their banks
	and sing among the leaves.
13	From thy high pavilion thou dost water the hills;
	the earth is enriched by thy provision.
14	Thou makest grass grow for the cattle
	and green things for those who toil for man,
	bringing bread out of the earth
15	and wine to gladden men's hearts,
	oil to make their faces shine
	and bread to sustain their strength.
16	The trees of the LORD are green and leafy,
	the cedars of Lebanon which he planted;
17	the birds build their nests in them,
	the stork makes her home in their tops.*a*
18	High hills are the haunt of the mountain-goat,
	and boulders a refuge for the rock-badger.
19	Thou hast made the moon to measure the year
	and taught the sun where to set.
20	When thou makest darkness and it is night,
	all the beasts of the forest come forth;
21	the young lions roar for prey,
	seeking their food from God.
22	When thou makest the sun rise, they slink away
	and go to rest in their lairs;
23	but man comes out to his work
	and to his labours until evening.
24	Countless are the things thou hast made, O LORD.
	Thou hast made all by thy wisdom;
	and the earth is full of thy creatures,
25	beasts great and small.

a in their tops: *prob. rdg.*; *Heb.* the pine-trees.

Here is the great immeasurable sea,
   in which move creatures beyond number.
Here ships sail to and fro,   26
here is Leviathan whom thou hast made thy plaything.*a*

All of them look expectantly to thee   27
   to give them their food at the proper time;
what thou givest them they gather up;   28
   when thou openest thy hand, they eat their fill.
Then thou hidest thy face, and they are restless and troubled;   29
   when thou takest away their breath, they fail
[and they return to the dust from which they came];
but when thou breathest into them, they recover;   30
   thou givest new life to the earth.

May the glory of the LORD stand for ever   31
   and may he rejoice in his works!
When he looks at the earth, it quakes;   32
   when he touches the hills, they pour forth smoke.

I will sing to the LORD as long as I live,   33
   all my life I will sing psalms to my God.
May my meditation please the LORD,   34
   as I show my joy in him!
Away with all sinners from the earth   35
   and may the wicked be no more!

Bless the LORD, my soul.

   O praise the LORD.

105

Give the LORD thanks and invoke him by name,   1*b*
   make his deeds known in the world around.
Pay him honour with song and psalm   2
   and think upon all his wonders.
Exult in his hallowed name;   3
   let those who seek the LORD be joyful in heart.
Turn to the LORD, your strength,   4
   seek his presence always.
Remember the wonders that he has wrought,   5
   his portents and the judgements he has given,
O offspring of Abraham his servant, O chosen sons of Jacob.   6

He is the LORD our God;   7
   his judgements fill the earth.

a thy plaything: *or* that it may sport in it.   *b Verses 1–15 : cp. 1 Chr. 16. 8–22.*

8   He called to mind his covenant from long ago, ^a
     the promise he extended to a thousand generations—
9   the covenant made with Abraham,
         his oath given to Isaac,
10   the decree by which he bound himself for Jacob,
     his everlasting covenant with Israel:
11   'I will give you the land of Canaan', he said,
         'to be your possession, your patrimony.'
12   A small company it was,
     few in number, strangers in that land,
13   roaming from nation to nation,
     from one kingdom to another;
14   but he let no one ill-treat them,
     for their sake he admonished kings:
15   'Touch not my anointed servants,
         do my prophets no harm.'

16   He called down famine on the land
     and cut short their daily bread.
17   But he had sent on a man before them,
     Joseph, who was sold into slavery;
18   he was kept a prisoner with fetters on his feet
     and an iron collar clamped on his neck.
19   He was tested by the LORD's command
     until what he foretold came true.
20   Then the king sent and set him free,
         the ruler of nations released him;
21   he made him master of his household
         and ruler over all his possessions,
22   to correct his officers at will
         and teach his counsellors wisdom.
23   Then Israel too went down into Egypt
     and Jacob came to live in the land of Ham.
24   There God made his people very fruitful,
         he made them stronger than their enemies,
25   whose hearts he turned to hatred of his people
         and double-dealing with his servants.
26   He sent his servant Moses
     and Aaron whom he had chosen.
27   They were his mouthpiece to announce his signs,
         his portents in the land of Ham.
28   He sent darkness, and all was dark,
     but still they resisted his commands.
29   He turned their waters into blood
         and killed all their fish.
30   Their country swarmed with frogs,
         even their princes' inner chambers.

     ^a *from long ago: or* for ever.

At his command came swarms of flies   31
    and maggots the whole land through.
He changed their rain into hail   32
    and flashed fire over their country.
He blasted their vines and their fig-trees   33
    and splintered the trees throughout the land.
At his command came locusts,   34
    hoppers past all number,
they consumed every green thing in the land,   35
    consumed all the produce of the soil.
Then he struck down all the first-born in Egypt,   36
    the firstfruits of their manhood;
he led Israel out, laden with silver and gold,   37
    and among all their tribes no man fell.
The Egyptians were glad when they went,   38
    for fear of Israel had taken hold of them.
He spread a cloud as a screen,   39
    and fire to light up the night.
They asked, and he sent them quails,   40
    he gave them bread from heaven in plenty.
He opened a rock and water gushed out,   41
    a river flowing in a parched land;
    for he had remembered his solemn promise   42
      given to his servant Abraham.
So he led out his people rejoicing,   43
    his chosen ones in triumph.
He gave them the lands of heathen nations   44
and they took possession where others had toiled,
    so that they might keep his statutes   45
    and obey his laws.

    O praise the LORD.

106

    O praise the LORD.   1

It is good to give thanks to the LORD;
    for his love endures for ever.
Who will tell of the LORD's mighty acts   2
    and make his praises heard?
    Happy are they who act justly   3
    and do right at all times!
Remember me, LORD, when thou showest favour to thy people,   4
    look upon me when thou savest them,
    that I may see the prosperity of thy chosen,   5
rejoice in thy nation's joy and exult with thy own people.

We have sinned like our forefathers,   6
    we have erred and done wrong.

7   Our fathers in Egypt took no account of thy marvels,
         they did not remember thy many acts of faithful love,
         but in spite of all[a] they rebelled by the Red Sea.[b]
8   Yet the LORD delivered them for his name's sake
         and so made known his mighty power.
9   He rebuked the Red Sea and it dried up,
     he led his people through the deeps as through the wilderness.
10   So he delivered them from those who hated them,
         and claimed them back from the enemy's hand.
11   The waters closed over their adversaries,
     not one of them survived.
12   Then they believed his promises and sang praises to him.

13   But they quickly forgot all he had done
         and would not wait to hear his counsel;
14   their greed was insatiable in the wilderness,
         they tried God's patience in the desert.
15   He gave them what they asked
         but sent a wasting sickness among them.[c]

16   They were envious of Moses in the camp,
         and of Aaron, who was consecrated to the LORD.
17   The earth opened and swallowed Dathan,
         it closed over the company of Abiram;
18   fire raged through their company,
         the wicked perished in flames.

19   At Horeb they made a calf
         and bowed down to an image;
20   they exchanged their Glory[d]
     for the image of a bull that feeds on grass.
21   They forgot God their deliverer,
     who had done great deeds in Egypt,
22   marvels in the land of Ham,
         terrible things at the Red Sea.
23   So his purpose was to destroy them,
     but Moses, the man he had chosen,
     threw himself into the breach
     to turn back his wrath lest it destroy them.

24   They made light of the pleasant land,
         disbelieving his promise;
25   they muttered treason in their tents
     and would not obey the LORD.
26   So with uplifted hand he swore
     to strike them down in the wilderness,

a in spite of all: *prob. rdg.; Heb. obscure.*   b *Or* the Sea of Reeds.   c among
them: *or* in their throats.   d their Glory: *or* the glory of God (*cp. Jer. 2. 11;
Romans 1. 23*).

to scatter their descendants among the nations   27
    and disperse them throughout the world.

They joined in worshipping the Baal of Peor   28
    and ate meat sacrificed to lifeless gods.
    Their deeds provoked the LORD to anger,   29
and plague broke out amongst them;
but Phinehas stood up and interceded,   30
    so the plague was stopped.
This was counted to him as righteousness   31
throughout all generations for ever.

They roused the LORD to anger at the waters of Meribah,   32
and Moses suffered because of them;
    for they had embittered his spirit   33
    and he had spoken rashly.

They did not destroy the peoples round about,   34
as the LORD had commanded them to do,
    but they mingled with the nations,   35
    learning their ways;
    they worshipped their idols   36
and were ensnared by them.
    Their sons and their daughters   37
    they sacrificed to foreign demons;
they shed innocent blood,   38
    the blood of sons and daughters
    offered to the gods of Canaan,
and the land was polluted with blood.
Thus they defiled themselves by their conduct   39
and they followed their lusts and broke faith with God.
Then the LORD grew angry with his people   40
    and loathed them, his own chosen nation;
    so he gave them into the hands of the nations,   41
and they were ruled by their foes;
    their enemies oppressed them   42
    and made them subject to their power.
Many times he came to their rescue,   43
but they were disobedient and rebellious still.*a*
And yet, when he heard them wail and cry aloud,   44
    he looked with pity on their distress;
he called to mind his covenant with them   45
    and, in his boundless love, relented;
he roused compassion for them   46
    in the hearts of all their captors.

a Prob. rdg.; Heb. adds and were brought low by their guilt.

47   Deliver us, O LORD our God,
           and gather us in from among the nations
           that we may give thanks to thy holy name
           and make thy praise our pride.

48   Blessed be the LORD the God of Israel
           from everlasting to everlasting;
       and let all the people say 'Amen.'

           O praise the LORD.

BOOK 5

107

1   It is good to give thanks to the LORD,
           for his love endures for ever.
2   So let them say who were redeemed by the LORD,
           redeemed by him from the power of the enemy
3   and gathered out of every land,
       from east and west, from north and south.

4   Some lost their way in desert wastes;
           they found no road to a city to live in;
5   hungry and thirsty,
           their spirit sank within them.
6   So they cried to the LORD in their trouble,
           and he rescued them from their distress;
7   he led them by a straight and easy way
           until they came to a city to live in.
8   Let them thank the LORD for his enduring love
           and for the marvellous things he has done for men:
9   he has satisfied the thirsty
           and filled the hungry with good things.

10   Some sat in darkness, dark as death,
           prisoners bound fast in iron,
11   because they had rebelled against God's commands
           and flouted the purpose of the Most High.
12   Their spirit was subdued by hard labour;
           they stumbled and fell with none to help them.
13   So they cried to the LORD in their trouble,
           and he saved them from their distress;
14   he brought them out of darkness, dark as death,
           and broke their chains.
15   Let them thank the LORD for his enduring love
           and for the marvellous things he has done for men:

he has shattered doors of bronze, 16
    bars of iron he has snapped in two.

Some were fools, they took to rebellious ways, 17
    and for their transgression they suffered punishment.
They sickened at the sight of food 18
    and drew near to the very gates of death.
So they cried to the LORD in their trouble, 19
    and he saved them from their distress;
he sent his word to heal them 20
    and bring them alive out of the pit of death.*a*
Let them thank the LORD for his enduring love 21
    and for the marvellous things he has done for men.
Let them offer sacrifices of thanksgiving 22
    and recite his deeds with shouts of joy.

Others there are who go to sea in ships 23
    and make their living on the wide waters.
These men have seen the acts of the LORD 24
    and his marvellous doings in the deep.
At his command the storm-wind rose 25
    and lifted the waves high.
Carried up to heaven, plunged down to the depths, 26
    tossed to and fro in peril,
they reeled and staggered like drunken men, 27
    and their seamanship was all in vain.
So they cried to the LORD in their trouble, 28
    and he brought them out of their distress.
The storm sank to a murmur 29
    and the waves of the sea were stilled.
They were glad then that all was calm, 30
    as he guided them to the harbour they desired.
Let them thank the LORD for his enduring love 31
    and for the marvellous things he has done for men.
Let them exalt him in the assembly of the people 32
    and praise him in the council of the elders.

He turns rivers into desert 33
    and springs of water into thirsty ground;
he turns fruitful land into salt waste, 34
    because the men who dwell there are so wicked.
Desert he changes into standing pools, 35
    and parched land into springs of water.
There he gives the hungry a home, 36
    and they build themselves a city to live in;
they sow fields and plant vineyards 37
    and reap a fruitful harvest.

a alive . . . death: *prob. rdg.*; *Heb.* from their corruption.

38 He blesses them and their numbers increase,
  and he does not let their herds lose strength.

39 Tyrants^a lose their strength and are brought low
  in the grip of misfortune and sorrow;

40 he brings princes into contempt
  and leaves them wandering in a trackless waste.

41 But the poor man he lifts clear of his troubles
  and makes families increase like flocks of sheep.

42 The upright see it and are glad,
  while evildoers are filled with disgust.

43 Let the wise man lay these things to heart,
  and ponder the record of the LORD's enduring love.

108

1^b   My heart is steadfast, O God,
    my heart is steadfast.
  I will sing and raise a psalm;
    awake,^c my spirit,

2   awake, lute and harp,
    I will awake at dawn of day.^d

3   I will confess thee, O LORD, among the peoples,
    among the nations I will raise a psalm to thee;

4   for thy unfailing love is wider than the heavens
    and thy truth reaches to the skies.

5   Show thyself, O God, high above the heavens;
    let thy glory shine over all the earth.

6^e   Deliver those that are dear to thee;
    save with thy right hand and answer.

7   God has spoken from his sanctuary:^f
    'I will go up now and measure out Shechem;
    I will divide the valley of Succoth into plots;

8   Gilead and Manasseh are mine;
    Ephraim is my helmet, Judah my sceptre;

9   Moab is my wash-bowl, I fling my shoes at Edom;
    Philistia is the target of my anger.'

10   Who can bring me to the impregnable city,
    who can guide me to Edom,

11   since thou, O God, hast abandoned us
    and goest not forth with our armies?

12   Grant us help against the enemy,
    for deliverance by man is a vain hope.

13   With God's help we shall do valiantly,
    and God himself will tread our enemies under foot.

---

^a *Prob. rdg.; Heb. om.*   ^b *Verses 1–5: cp. Ps. 57. 7–11.*   ^c awake: *prob. rdg.;*
Heb. also.   ^d at dawn of day: *or* the dawn.   ^e *Verses 6–13: cp. Ps. 60. 5–12.*
^f from his sanctuary: *or* in his holiness.

109

O God of my praise, be silent no longer,   1
    for wicked men heap calumnies upon me.   2
They have lied to my face
    and ringed me round with words of hate.   3
They have attacked me without a cause^a
    and accused me though I have done nothing unseemly.^b   4
They have repaid me evil for good   5
    and hatred in return for my love.
They say, 'Put up some rascal to denounce him,   6
    an accuser to stand at his right side.'
But when judgement is given, that rascal will be exposed   7
    and his follies accounted a sin.
May his days be few;   8
    may his hoarded wealth^c fall to another!
May his children be fatherless,   9
    his wife a widow!
May his children be vagabonds and beggars,   10
    driven from their homes!
May the money-lender distrain on all his goods   11
    and strangers seize his earnings!
May none remain loyal to him,   12
    and none have mercy on his fatherless children!
May his line be doomed to extinction,   13
    may their name be wiped out within a generation!
May the sins of his forefathers be remembered   14
    and his mother's wickedness never be wiped out!
May they remain on record before the LORD,   15
    but may he extinguish their name from the earth!
For that man never set himself   16
    to be loyal to his friend
but persecuted the downtrodden and the poor
    and hounded the broken-hearted to their death.
Curses he loved: may the curse fall on him!   17
He took no pleasure in blessing: may no blessing be his!
He clothed himself in cursing like a garment: 18
may it seep into his body like water
    and into his bones like oil!
May it wrap him round like the clothes he puts on,   19
    like the belt which he wears every day!
May the LORD so requite my accusers   20
    and those who speak evil against me!

But thou, O Lord God,   21
    deal with me as befits thy honour;

---

^a *Prob. rdg.; Heb. adds* in return for my love.   ^b though . . . unseemly: *prob. rdg.;*
Heb. obscure.   ^c hoarded wealth: *or* charge, *cp. Acts 1. 20.*

	in the goodness of thy unfailing love deliver me,
22	for I am downtrodden and poor,
	and my heart within me is distracted.
23	I fade like a passing shadow,
	I am shaken off like a locust.
24	My knees are weak with fasting
	and my flesh wastes away, so meagre is my fare.
25	I have become the victim of their taunts;
	when they see me they toss their heads.
26	Help me, O LORD my God;
	save me, by thy unfailing love,
27	that men may know this is thy doing
	and thou alone, O LORD, hast done it.
28	They may curse, but thou dost bless;
	may my opponents be put to shame,
	but may thy servant rejoice!
29	May my accusers be clothed with dishonour,
	wrapped in their shame as in a cloak!
30	I will lift up my voice to extol the LORD,
	and before a great company I will praise him.
31	For he stands at the poor man's right side
	to save him from his adversaries. *a*

110

1	The LORD said to my lord,
	'You shall sit *b* at my right hand
	when *c* I make your enemies the footstool under your feet.'
2	When the LORD from Zion hands you the sceptre, the symbol of your power,
	march forth through the ranks of *d* your enemies.
3	At birth *e* you were endowed with princely gifts
	and *f* resplendent *g* in holiness.
	You have shone with the dew of youth since your mother bore you.
4	The LORD has sworn and will not change his purpose:
	'You are a priest for ever,
	in the succession of Melchizedek.'
5	The Lord at your right hand
	has broken kings in the day of his anger.
6	So the king in his majesty, *h* sovereign of a mighty land,
	will punish nations; *i*
7	he will drink from the torrent beside the path
	and therefore will hold his head high.

---

a Prob. rdg.; Heb. his judges.   *b* You shall sit: *or* Sit.   *c Or* until *or* while.
d Or reign in the midst of.   *e* At birth: *or* On the day of your power.   *f* you
were ... and: *or* your people offered themselves willingly; *mng. of Heb. uncertain.*   *g Or*
apparelled.   *h* So ... majesty: *poss. rdg.; Heb.* full of corpses, he crushed.
i So ... nations: *or* He shall punish the nations—heaps of corpses, broken heads—over
a wide expanse.

111

O praise the LORD.   1

With all my heart will I praise the LORD
in the company of good men, in the whole congregation.
Great are the doings of the LORD;   2
  all men study them for their delight.
His acts are full of majesty and splendour;   3
  righteousness is his for ever.
He has won a name by his marvellous deeds;   4
  the LORD is gracious and compassionate.
He gives food to those who fear him,   5
  he keeps his covenant always in mind.
He showed his people what his strength could do,   6
  bestowing on them the lands of other nations.
His works are truth and justice;   7
  his precepts all stand on firm foundations,
strongly based to endure for ever,   8
  their fabric goodness and truth.
He sent and redeemed his people;   9
he decreed that his covenant should always endure.
  Holy is his name, inspiring awe.
The fear of the LORD is the beginning *a* of wisdom,   10
and they who live by it grow in understanding.
  Praise will be his for ever.

112

O praise the LORD.   1

Happy is the man who fears the LORD
  and finds great joy in his commandments.
His descendants shall be the mightiest in the land,   2
  a blessed generation of good men.
His house shall be full of wealth and riches;   3
  righteousness shall be his for ever.
He is gracious, compassionate, good,   4
  a beacon in darkness for honest men.
It is right for a man to be gracious in his lending,   5
  to order his affairs with judgement.
Nothing shall ever shake him;   6
  his goodness shall be remembered for all time.
Bad news shall have no terrors for him,   7
  because his heart is steadfast, trusting in the LORD.
His confidence is strongly based, he will have no fear;   8
  and in the end he will gloat over his enemies.

a Or chief part.

713

9   He gives freely to the poor;
            righteousness shall be his for ever;
            in honour he carries his head high.
10   The wicked man shall see it with rising anger
            and grind his teeth in despair;
            the hopes of wicked men shall come to nothing.

113

1   O praise the LORD.

            Praise the LORD, you that are his servants,
               praise the name of the LORD.
2   Blessed be the name of the LORD
               now and evermore.
3   From the rising of the sun to its setting
               may the LORD's name be praised.
4   High is the LORD above all nations,
               his glory above the heavens.
5–6   There is none like the LORD our God
               in heaven or on earth,
            who sets his throne so high
               but deigns to look down so low;
7   who lifts the weak out of the dust
               and raises the poor from the dunghill,
8   giving them a place among princes,
               among the princes of his people;
9   who makes the woman in a childless house
               a happy mother of children. *a*

114

1   O praise the LORD. *b*

            When Israel came out of Egypt,
               Jacob from a people of outlandish speech,
2   Judah became his sanctuary,
               Israel his dominion.
3   The sea looked and ran away;
               Jordan turned back.
4   The mountains skipped like rams,
               the hills like young sheep.
5   What was it, sea? Why did you run?
               Jordan, why did you turn back?
6   Why, mountains, did you skip like rams,
               and you, hills, like young sheep?

a O praise the LORD *transposed to the beginning of Ps. 114.*   *b* *See note*
on Ps. 113. 9.

Dance, O earth, at the presence of the Lord,   7
    at the presence of the God of Jacob,
who turned the rock into a pool of water,   8
    the granite cliff into a fountain.

115

Not to us, O LORD, not to us,   1
    but to thy name ascribe the glory,
    for thy true love and for thy constancy.

Why do the nations ask,   2
    'Where then is their God?'
Our God is in high heaven;   3
    he does whatever pleases him.
Their idols are silver and gold,   4
    made by the hands of men.
They have mouths that cannot speak,   5
    and eyes that cannot see;
they have ears that cannot hear,   6
    nostrils, and cannot smell;
with their hands they cannot feel,   7
    with their feet they cannot walk,
    and no sound comes from their throats.
Their makers grow to be like them,   8
    and so do all who trust in them.

But Israel trusts in the LORD;   9
    he is their helper and their shield.
The house of Aaron trusts in the LORD;   10
    he is their helper and their shield.
Those who fear the LORD trust in the LORD;   11
    he is their helper and their shield.
The LORD remembers us, and he will bless us;   12
    he will bless the house of Israel,
    he will bless the house of Aaron.
The LORD will bless all who fear him,   13
    high and low alike.

May the LORD give you increase,   14
    both you and your sons.
You are blessed by the LORD,   15
    the LORD who made heaven and earth.
The heavens, they are the LORD's;   16
    the earth he has given to all mankind.
It is not the dead who praise the LORD,   17
    not those who go down into silence;

18   but we, the living, bless the LORD,
       now and for evermore.

     O praise the LORD.

116

1   I love the LORD, for he has heard me
       and listens to my prayer;
2   for he has given me a hearing
       whenever I have cried to him.
3   The cords of death bound me,
       Sheol held me in its grip.
     Anguish and torment held me fast;
4   so I invoked the LORD by name,
     'Deliver me, O LORD, I beseech thee;
       for I am thy slave.' *a*
5   Gracious is the LORD and righteous,
       our God is full of compassion.
6   The LORD preserves the simple-hearted;
       I was brought low and he saved me.
7   Be at rest once more, my heart,
       for the LORD has showered gifts upon you.
8   He has rescued me from death
       and my feet from stumbling.
9   I will walk in the presence of the LORD
       in the land of the living.

10   I was sure that I should be swept away,
       and my distress was bitter.
11   In panic I cried,
       'How faithless all men are!'
12   How can I repay the LORD
       for all his gifts to me?
13   I will take in my hands the cup of salvation
       and invoke the LORD by name.
14   I will pay my vows to the LORD
       in the presence of all his people.
15   A precious thing in the LORD's sight
       is the death of those who die faithful to him.
16   *b* I am thy slave, thy slave-girl's son;
       thou hast undone the bonds that bound me.
17   To thee will I bring a thank-offering
       and invoke the LORD by name.
18   I will pay my vows to the LORD
       in the presence of all his people,

a for . . . slave: *transposed from the beginning of verse 16; Heb. adds* O LORD.
b *Prob. rdg.; Heb. prefixes* For I am thy slave, O LORD; *see note on verse 4.*

in the courts of the Lord's house,   19
    in the midst of you, Jerusalem.

    O praise the Lord.

117

Praise the Lord, all nations,   1
    extol him, all you peoples;
for his love protecting us is strong,   2
    the Lord's constancy is everlasting.

    O praise the Lord.

118

It is good to give thanks to the Lord,   1
    for his love endures for ever.
Declare it, house of Israel: 2
    his love endures for ever.
Declare it, house of Aaron: 3
    his love endures for ever.
Declare it, you that fear the Lord: 4
    his love endures for ever.
When in my distress I called to the Lord,   5
    his answer was to set me free.
The Lord is on my side, I have no fear;   6
    what can man do to me?
The Lord is on my side, he is my helper,   7
    and I shall gloat over my enemies.
It is better to find refuge in the Lord   8
    than to trust in men.
It is better to find refuge in the Lord   9
    than to trust in princes.
All nations surround me,   10
    but in the Lord's name I will drive them away.
They surround me on this side and on that,   11
    but in the Lord's name I will drive them away.
They surround me like bees at the honey;   12
    they attack me, as fire attacks brushwood,
    but in the Lord's name I will drive them away.
They thrust hard against me so that I nearly fall;   13
    but the Lord has helped me.
The Lord is my refuge and defence,   14
    and he has become my deliverer.
Hark! Shouts of deliverance   15
    in the camp of the victors[a]!

       [a] Or righteous.

With his right hand the LORD does mighty deeds,
16   the right hand of the LORD raises up.
17 I shall not die but live
      to proclaim the works of the LORD.
18 The LORD did indeed chasten me,
      but he did not surrender me to Death.

19 Open to me the gates of victory; *a*
      I will enter by them and praise the LORD.
20 This is the gate of the LORD;
      the victors *b* shall make their entry through it.
21 I will praise thee, for thou hast answered me
      and hast become my deliverer.
22 The stone which the builders rejected
      has become the chief corner-stone.
23 This is the LORD's doing;
      it is marvellous in our eyes.
24 This is the day on which the LORD has acted: *c*
      let us exult and rejoice in it.
25 We pray thee, O LORD, deliver us;
      we pray thee, O LORD, send us prosperity.
26 Blessed in the name of the LORD are all who come;
      we bless you from the house of the LORD.
27 The LORD is God; he has given light to us,
      the ordered line of pilgrims by the horns of the altar.
28 Thou art my God and I will praise thee;
      my God, I will exalt thee.
29 It is good to give thanks to the LORD,
      for his love endures for ever.

119

1 Happy are they whose life is blameless,
      who conform to the law of the LORD.
2 Happy are they who obey his instruction,
      who set their heart on finding him;
3 who have done no wrong
      and have lived according to his will.
4 Thou, Lord, hast laid down thy precepts
      for men to keep them faithfully.
5 If only I might hold a steady course,
      keeping thy statutes!
6 I shall never be put to shame
      if I fix my eyes on thy commandments.
7 I will praise thee in sincerity of heart
      as I learn thy just decrees.

a   Or righteousness.   *b*   Or righteous.   *c*   Or which the LORD has made.

Thy statutes will I keep faithfully; 8
  O do not leave me forsaken.

How shall a young man steer an honest course? 9
  By holding to thy word.
With all my heart I strive to find thee; 10
  let me not stray from thy commandments.
I treasure thy promise in my heart, 11
  for fear that I might sin against thee.
Blessed art thou, O LORD; 12
  teach me thy statutes.
I say them over, one by one, 13
  the decrees that thou hast proclaimed.
I have found more joy along the path of thy instruction 14
  than in any kind of wealth.
I will meditate on thy precepts 15
  and keep thy paths ever before my eyes.
In thy statutes I find continual delight; 16
  I will not forget thy word.

Grant this to me, thy servant: let me live 17
  and, living, keep thy word.
Take the veil from my eyes, that I may see 18
  the marvels that spring from thy law.
I am but a stranger here on earth,[a] 19
  do not hide thy commandments from me.
My heart pines with longing 20
  day and night for thy decrees.
The proud have felt thy rebuke; 21
  cursed are those who turn from thy commandments.
Set me free from scorn and insult, 22
  for I have obeyed thy instruction.
The powers that be sit scheming together against me; 23
  but I, thy servant, will study thy statutes.
Thy instruction is my continual delight; 24
  I turn to it for counsel.

I lie prone in the dust; 25
  grant me life according to thy word.
I tell thee all I have done and thou dost answer me; 26
  teach me thy statutes.
Show me the way set out in thy precepts, 27
  and I will meditate on thy wonders.
I cannot rest for misery; 28
  renew my strength in accordance with thy word.
Keep falsehood far from me 29
  and grant me the grace of living by thy law.

[a] *Or* in the land.

30 I have chosen the path of truth
   and have set thy decrees before me.
31 I hold fast to thy instruction;
   O LORD, let me not be put to shame.
32 I will run the course set out in thy commandments,
   for they gladden my heart.

33 Teach me, O LORD, the way set out in thy statutes,
   and in keeping them I shall find my reward.
34 Give me the insight to obey thy law
   and to keep it with all my heart;
35 make me walk in the path of thy commandments,
   for that is my desire.
36 Dispose my heart toward thy instruction
   and not toward ill-gotten gains;
37 turn away my eyes from all that is vile,
   grant me life by thy word.
38 Fulfil thy promise for thy servant,
   the promise made to those who fear thee.
39 Turn away the censure which I dread,
   for thy decrees are good.
40 How I long for thy precepts!
   In thy righteousness grant me life.

41 Thy love never fails; let it light on me, O LORD,
   and thy deliverance, for that was thy promise;
42 then I shall have my answer to the man who taunts me,
   because I trust in thy word.
43 Rob me not of my power to speak the truth,
   for I put my hope in thy decrees.
44 I will heed thy law continually,
   for ever and ever;
45 I walk in freedom wherever I will,
   because I have studied thy precepts.
46 I will speak of thy instruction before kings
   and will not be ashamed;
47 in thy commandments I find continuing delight;
   I love them with all my heart.
48 I will welcome thy commandments *a*
   and will meditate on thy statutes.

49 Remember the word spoken to me, thy servant,
   on which thou hast taught me to fix my hope.
50 In time of trouble my consolation is this,
   that thy promise has given me life.
51 Proud men treat me with insolent scorn,
   but I do not swerve from thy law.

a Prob. rdg.; Heb. adds which I love.

I have cherished thy decrees all my life long,   52
    and in them I find consolation, O Lord.
Gusts of anger seize me as I think of evil men   53
    who forsake thy law.
Thy statutes are the theme of my song*a*   54
    wherever I make my home.
In the night I remember thy name, O Lord,   55
    and dwell upon thy law.
This is true of me,   56
    that I have kept thy precepts.

Thou, Lord, art all I have;   57
    I have promised to keep thy word.
With all my heart I have tried to please thee;   58
    fulfil thy promise and be gracious to me.
I have thought much about the course of my life   59
    and always turned back to thy instruction;
I have never delayed but always made haste   60
    to keep thy commandments.
Bands of evil men close round me,   61
    but I do not forget thy law.
At midnight I rise to give thee thanks   62
    for the justice of thy decrees.
I keep company with all who fear thee,   63
    with all who follow thy precepts.
The earth is full of thy never-failing love;   64
    O Lord, teach me thy statutes.

Thou hast shown thy servant much kindness,   65
    fulfilling thy word, O Lord.
Give me insight, give me knowledge,   66
    for I put my trust in thy commandments.
I went astray before I was punished;   67
    but now I pay heed to thy promise.
Thou art good and thou doest good;   68
    teach me thy statutes.
Proud men blacken my name with lies,   69
    yet I follow thy precepts with all my heart;
their hearts are thick and gross;   70
    but I continually delight in thy law.
How good it is for me to have been punished,   71
    to school me in thy statutes!
The law thou hast ordained means more to me   72
    than a fortune in gold and silver.

Thy hands moulded me and made me what I am;   73
    show me how I may learn thy commandments.

a the theme of my song: *or* wonderful to me.

74   Let all who fear thee be glad when they see me,
          because I hope for the fulfilment of thy word.
75   I know, O LORD, that thy decrees are just
          and even in punishing thou keepest faith with me.
76   Let thy never-failing love console me,
          as thou hast promised me, thy servant.
77   Extend thy compassion to me, that I may live;
          for thy law is my continual delight.
78   Put the proud to shame, for with their lies they wrong me;
          but I will meditate on thy precepts.
79   Let all who fear thee turn to me,
          all who cherish thy instruction.
80   Let me give my whole heart to thy statutes,
          so that I am not put to shame.

81   I long with all my heart for thy deliverance,
          hoping for the fulfilment of thy word;
82   my sight grows dim with looking for thy promise
          and still I cry, 'When wilt thou comfort me?'
83   Though I shrivel like a wine-skin in the smoke,
          I do not forget thy statutes.
84   How long has thy servant to wait
          for thee to fulfil thy decree against my persecutors?
85   Proud men who flout thy law
          spread tales about me.
86   Help me, for they hound me with their lies,
          but thy commandments all stand for ever.
87   They had almost swept me from the earth,
          but I did not forsake thy precepts;
88   grant me life, as thy love is unchanging,
          that I may follow all thy instruction.

89   Eternal is thy word, O LORD,
          planted firm in heaven.
90   Thy promise*a* endures for all time,
          stable as the earth which thou hast fixed.
91   This day, as ever, thy decrees stand fast;
          for all things serve thee.
92   If thy law had not been my continual delight,
          I should have perished in all my troubles;
93   never will I forget thy precepts,
          for through them thou hast given me life.
94   I am thine; O save me,
          for I have pondered thy precepts.
95   Evil men lie in wait to destroy me;
          but I will give thought to thy instruction.

a Prob. rdg.; Heb. Thy constancy.

I see that all things come to an end,   96
    but thy commandment has no limit.

O how I love thy law!   97
    It is my study all day long.
Thy commandments are mine for ever;   98
    through them I am wiser than my enemies.
I have more insight than all my teachers,   99
    for thy instruction is my study;
I have more wisdom than the old,   100
    because I have kept thy precepts.
I set no foot on any evil path   101
    in my obedience to thy word;
I do not swerve from thy decrees,   102
    for thou thyself hast been my teacher.
How sweet is thy promise in my mouth,   103
    sweeter on my tongue than honey!
From thy precepts I learn wisdom;   104
    therefore I hate the paths of falsehood.

Thy word is a lamp to guide my feet   105
    and a light on my path;
I have bound myself by oath and solemn vow   106
    to keep thy just decrees.
I am cruelly afflicted;   107
    O LORD, revive me and make good thy word.
Accept, O LORD, the willing tribute of my lips   108
    and teach me thy decrees.
Every day I take my life in my hands,   109
    yet I never forget thy law.
Evil men have set traps for me,   110
    but I do not stray from thy precepts.
Thy instruction is my everlasting inheritance;   111
    it is the joy of my heart.
I am resolved to fulfil thy statutes;   112
    they are a reward that never fails.

I hate men who are not single-minded,   113
    but I love thy law.
Thou art my shield and hiding-place;   114
    I hope for the fulfilment of thy word.
Go, you evildoers, and leave me to myself,   115
    that I may keep the commandments of my God.
Support me as thou hast promised, that I may live;   116
    do not disappoint my hope.
Sustain me, that I may see deliverance;   117
    so shall I always be occupied with thy statutes.
Thou dost reject those who stray from thy statutes,   118
    for their talk is all malice and lies.

119	In thy sight all the wicked on earth are scum;
	therefore I love thy instruction.
120	The dread of thee makes my flesh creep,
	and I stand in awe of thy decrees.
121	I have done what is just and right;
	thou wilt not abandon me to my oppressors.
122	Stand surety for the welfare of thy servant;
	let not the proud oppress me.ᵃ
123	My sight grows dim with looking for thy deliverance
	and waiting for thy righteous promise.
124	In all thy dealings with me, LORD, show thy true love
	and teach me thy statutes.
125	I am thy servant; give me insight
	to understand thy instruction.
126	It is time to act, O LORD;
	for men have broken thy law.
127	Truly I love thy commandments
	more than the finest gold.
128	It is by thy precepts that I find the right way;
	I hate the paths of falsehood.
129	Thy instruction is wonderful;
	therefore I gladly keep it.
130	Thy word is revealed, and all is light;
	it gives understanding even to the untaught.
131	I pant, I thirst,
	longing for thy commandments.
132	Turn to me and be gracious,
	as thou hast decreed for those who love thy name.
133	Make my step firm according to thy promise,
	and let no wrong have the mastery over me.
134	Set me free from man's oppression,
	that I may observe thy precepts.
135	Let thy face shine upon thy servant
	and teach me thy statutes.
136	My eyes stream with tears
	because men do not heed thy law.
137	How just thou art, O LORD!
	How straight and true are thy decrees!
138	How just is the instruction thou givest!
	It is fixed firm and sure.
139	I am speechless with resentment,
	for my enemies have forgotten thy words.
140	Thy promise has been tested through and through,
	and thy servant loves it.

ᵃ oppress me: *or* charge me falsely.

I may be despised and of little account, 141
  but I do not forget thy precepts.
Thy justice is an everlasting justice, 142
  and thy law is truth.
Though I am oppressed by trouble and anxiety, 143
  thy commandments are my continual delight.
Thy instruction is ever just; 144
  give me understanding that I may live.

I call with my whole heart; answer me, LORD. 145
  I will keep thy statutes.
I call to thee; O save me 146
  that I may heed thy instruction.
I rise before dawn and cry for help; 147
  I hope for the fulfilment of thy word.
Before the midnight watch also my eyes are open 148
  for meditation on thy promise.
Hear me, as thy love is unchanging, 149
  and give me life, O LORD, by thy decree.
My pursuers in their malice are close behind me, 150
  but they are far from thy law.
Yet thou art near, O LORD, 151
  and all thy commandments are true.
I have long known from thy instruction 152
  that thou hast given it eternal foundations.

See in what trouble I am and set me free, 153
  for I do not forget thy law.
Be thou my advocate and win release for me; 154
  true to thy promise, give me life.
Such deliverance is beyond the reach of wicked men, 155
  because they do not ponder thy statutes.
Great is thy compassion, O LORD; 156
  grant me life by thy decree.
Many are my persecutors and enemies, 157
  but I have not swerved from thy instruction.
I was cut to the quick when I saw traitors 158
  who had no regard for thy promise.
See how I love thy precepts, O LORD! 159
  Grant me life, as thy love is unchanging.
Thy word is founded in truth, 160
  and thy just decrees are everlasting.

The powers that be persecute me without cause, 161
  yet my heart thrills at thy word.
I am jubilant over thy promise, 162
  like a man carrying off much booty.
Falsehood I detest and loathe, 163
  but I love thy law.

164 Seven times a day I praise thee
    for the justice of thy decrees.

165 Peace is the reward of those who love thy law;
    no pitfalls beset their path.

166 I hope for thy deliverance, O Lord,
    and I fulfil thy commandments;

167 gladly I heed thy instruction
    and love it greatly.

168 I heed thy precepts and thy instruction,
    for all my life lies open before thee.

169 Let my cry of joy reach thee, O Lord;
    give me understanding of thy word.

170 Let my supplication reach thee;
    be true to thy promise and save me.

171 Let thy praise pour from my lips,
    because thou teachest me thy statutes;

172 let the music of thy promises be on my tongue,
    for thy commandments are justice itself.

173 Let thy hand be prompt to help me,
    for I have chosen thy precepts;

174 I long for thy deliverance, O Lord,
    and thy law is my continual delight.

175 Let me live and I will praise thee;
    let thy decrees be my support.

176 I have strayed like a lost sheep;
    come, search for thy servant,
    for I have not forgotten thy commandments.

120

1 I called to the Lord in my distress,
    and he answered me.

2 'O Lord,' I cried, 'save me from lying lips
    and from the tongue of slander.'

3 What has he in store for you, slanderous tongue?
    What more has he for you?

4 Nothing but a warrior's sharp arrows
    or red-hot charcoal.

5 Hard is my lot, exiled in Meshech,
dwelling by the tents of Kedar.

6 All the time that I dwelt
    among men who hated peace,

7 I sought peace; but whenever I spoke of it,
    they were for war.

121

If I lift up my eyes to the hills,   1
  where shall I find help?
Help comes only from the LORD,   2
  maker of heaven and earth.
How could he let your foot stumble?   3
  How could he, your guardian, sleep?
The guardian of Israel   4
  never slumbers, never sleeps.
The LORD is your guardian,   5
  your defence at your right hand;
the sun will not strike you by day   6
  nor the moon by night.
The LORD will guard you against all evil;   7
  he will guard you, body and soul.
The LORD will guard your going and your coming,   8
  now and for evermore.

122

I rejoiced when they said to me,   1
  'Let us go to the house of the LORD.'
Now we stand within your gates,   2
  O Jerusalem:
Jerusalem that is built to be a city   3
  where people come together in unity;
to which the tribes resort, the tribes of the LORD,   4
  to give thanks to the LORD himself,
  the bounden duty of Israel.
For in her are set the thrones of justice,   5
  the thrones of the house of David.
Pray for the peace of Jerusalem: 6
  'May those who love you prosper;
peace be within your ramparts   7
  and prosperity in your palaces.'
For the sake of these my brothers and my friends,   8
  I will say, 'Peace be within you.'
For the sake of the house of the LORD our God   9
  I will pray for your good.

123

I lift my eyes to thee   1
  whose throne is in heaven.
As the eyes of a slave follow his master's hand   2
  or the eyes of a slave-girl her mistress,
  so our eyes are turned to the LORD our God
  waiting for kindness from him.

3   Deal kindly with us, O Lord, deal kindly,
         for we have suffered insult enough;
4   too long have we had to suffer
         the insults of the wealthy,
         the scorn of proud men.

124

1   If the Lord had not been on our side,
         Israel may now say,
2   if the Lord had not been on our side
         when they assailed us,
3   they would have swallowed us alive
         when their anger was roused against us.
4   The waters would have carried us away
         and the torrent swept over us;
5   over us would have swept
         the seething waters.
6   Blessed be the Lord, who did not leave us
         to be the prey between their teeth.
7   We have escaped like a bird
         from the fowler's trap;
         the trap broke, and so we escaped.
8   Our help is in the name of the Lord,
         maker of heaven and earth.

125

1   Those who trust in the Lord are like Mount Zion,
     which cannot be shaken but stands fast for ever.
2   As the hills enfold Jerusalem,
     so the Lord enfolds his people, now and evermore.
3   The sceptre of wickedness shall surely find no home
         in the land allotted to the righteous,
     so that the righteous shall not set
         their hands to injustice.
4   Do good, O Lord, to those who are good
         and to those who are upright in heart.
5   But those who turn aside into crooked ways,
     may the Lord destroy them, as he destroys all evildoers!

     Peace be upon Israel!

126

1   When the Lord turned the tide of Zion's fortune,
     we were like men who had found new health.[a]

         [a] like . . . health: *or* like dreamers.

728

Our mouths were full of laughter   2
   and our tongues sang aloud for joy.
Then word went round among the nations,
   'The LORD has done great things for them.'
Great things indeed the LORD then did for us,   3
   and we rejoiced.

Turn once again our fortune, LORD,   4
   as streams return in the dry south.
Those who sow in tears   5
   shall reap with songs of joy.
A man may go out weeping,   6
   carrying his bag of seed;
but he will come back with songs of joy,
   carrying home his sheaves.

127

Unless the LORD builds the house,   1
   its builders will have toiled in vain.
Unless the LORD keeps watch over a city,
   in vain the watchman stands on guard.
In vain you rise up early   2
   and go late to rest,
toiling for the bread you eat;
   he supplies the need of those he loves.*a*
Sons are a gift from the LORD   3
   and children a reward from him.
Like arrows in the hand of a fighting man   4
   are the sons of a man's youth.
Happy is the man   5
   who has his quiver full of them;
such men shall not be put to shame
   when they confront their enemies in court.

128

Happy are all who fear the LORD,   1
   who live according to his will.
You shall eat the fruit of your own labours,   2
   you shall be happy and you shall prosper.
Your wife shall be like a fruitful vine   3
   in the heart of your house;
your sons shall be like olive-shoots
   round about your table.
This is the blessing in store for the man   4
   who fears the LORD.

    a Prob. rdg.; Heb. adds an unintelligible word.

5   May the LORD bless you from Zion;
         may you share the prosperity of Jerusalem
     all the days of your life,
6   and live to see your children's children!

     Peace be upon Israel!

129

1   Often since I was young have men attacked me—
         let Israel now say—
2   often since I was young have men attacked me,
         but never have they prevailed.
3   They scored my back with scourges,
         like ploughmen driving long furrows.
4   Yet the LORD in his justice
         has cut me loose from the bonds of the wicked.
5   Let all enemies of Zion
         be thrown back in shame;
6   let them be like grass growing on the roof,
         which withers before it can shoot,
7   which will never fill a mower's hand
         nor yield an armful for the harvester,
8   so that passers-by will never say to them,
         'The blessing of the LORD be upon you!
         We bless you in the name of the LORD.'

130

1   Out of the depths have I called to thee, O LORD;
2   Lord, hear my cry.
     Let thy ears be attentive
         to my plea for mercy.
3   If thou, LORD, shouldest keep account of sins,
         who, O Lord, could hold up his head?
4   But in thee is forgiveness,
         and therefore thou art revered.
5   I wait for the LORD with all my soul,
         I hope for the fulfilment of his word.
6   My soul waits*a* for the Lord
         more eagerly than watchmen for the morning.
     Like men who watch for the morning,
         O Israel, look for the LORD.
7   For in the LORD is love unfailing,
         and great is his power to set men free.
8   He alone will set Israel free
         from all their sins.

         a waits: *transposed from after* the LORD *in verse 5.*

730

131

O Lord, my heart is not proud,   1
    nor are my eyes haughty;
I do not busy myself with great matters
    or things too marvellous for me.
No; I submit myself, I account myself lowly,   2
    as a weaned child clinging to its mother.*a*
O Israel, look for the Lord   3
    now and evermore.

132

O Lord, remember David   1
    in the time of his adversity,
how he swore to the Lord   2
    and made a vow to the Mighty One of Jacob:
'I will not enter my house   3
    nor will I mount my bed,
I will not close my eyes in sleep   4
    or my eyelids in slumber,
until I find a sanctuary for the Lord,   5
    a dwelling for the Mighty One of Jacob.'
We heard of it in Ephrathah;   6
    we came upon it in the region of Jaar.
Let us enter his dwelling,   7
    let us fall in worship at his footstool.
Arise, O Lord, and come to thy resting-place,   8
    thou and the ark of thy power.
Let thy priests be clothed in righteousness   9
    and let thy loyal servants shout for joy.
For thy servant David's sake   10
    reject not thy anointed king.
The Lord swore to David   11
    an oath which he will not break:
'A prince of your own line
    will I set upon your throne.
If your sons keep my covenant   12
    and heed the teaching that I give them,
their sons in turn for all time
    shall sit upon your throne.'
For the Lord has chosen Zion   13
    and desired it for his home:
'This is my resting-place for ever;   14
    here will I make my home, for such is my desire.

---

    a   *Prob. rdg.; Heb. adds* as a weaned child clinging to me.

15   I will richly bless her destitute *a*
       and satisfy her needy with bread.
16   With salvation will I clothe her priests;
       her loyal servants shall shout for joy.
17   There will I renew the line of David's house
       and light a lamp for my anointed king;
18   his enemies will I clothe with shame,
       but on his head shall be a shining crown.'

133

1   How good it is and how pleasant
       for brothers to live *b* together!
2   It is fragrant as oil poured upon the head
       and falling over the beard,
    Aaron's beard, when the oil runs down
       over the collar of his vestments.
3   It is like the dew of Hermon falling
       upon the hills of Zion.
    There the LORD bestows his blessing,
       life for evermore.

134

1   Come, bless the LORD,
       all you servants of the LORD,
    who stand night after night
       in the house of the LORD.
2   Lift up your hands in the sanctuary
       and bless the LORD.
3   The LORD, maker of heaven and earth,
       bless you from Zion!

135

1   O praise the LORD.

    Praise the name of the LORD;
       praise him, you servants of the LORD,
2   who stand in the house of the LORD,
       in the temple courts of our God.
3   Praise the LORD, for that is good;
       honour his name with psalms, for that is pleasant.
4   The LORD has chosen Jacob to be his own
       and Israel as his special treasure.
5   I know that the LORD is great,
       that our Lord is above all gods.

a her destitute: *prob. rdg.; Heb.* her provisions.   *b Or* to worship.

Whatever the LORD pleases,   6
    that he does, in heaven and on earth,
    in the sea, in the depths of ocean.
He brings up the mist from the ends of the earth,   7
he opens rifts[a] for the rain,
and brings the wind out of his storehouses.
He struck down all the first-born in Egypt,   8
    both man and beast.
In Egypt he sent signs and portents   9
    against Pharaoh and all his subjects.
He struck down mighty nations   10
    and slew great kings,
Sihon king of the Amorites, Og the king of Bashan,   11
    and all the princes of Canaan,
and gave their land to Israel,   12
    to Israel his people as their patrimony.
O LORD, thy name endures for ever;   13
thy renown, O LORD, shall last for all generations.
The LORD will give his people justice   14
    and have compassion on his servants.
The gods of the nations are idols of silver and gold,   15
    made by the hands of men.
They have mouths that cannot speak   16
    and eyes that cannot see;
they have ears that do not hear,   17
    and there is no breath in their nostrils.[b]
Their makers grow like them,   18
    and so do all who trust in them.
O house of Israel, bless the LORD;   19
    O house of Aaron, bless the LORD.
O house of Levi, bless the LORD;   20
    you who fear the LORD, bless the LORD.
Blessed from Zion be the LORD   21
    who dwells in Jerusalem.

    O praise the LORD.

136

It is good to give thanks to the LORD,   1
    for his love endures for ever.
Give thanks to the God of gods;   2
    his love endures for ever.
Give thanks to the Lord of lords;   3
    his love endures for ever.
Alone he works great marvels;   4
    his love endures for ever.

[a] *Prob. rdg.; Heb.* lightnings.   [b] *Prob. rdg.; Heb.* mouths.

5	In wisdom he made the heavens;
	his love endures for ever.
6	He laid the earth upon the waters;
	his love endures for ever.
7	He made the great lights,
	his love endures for ever,
8	the sun to rule by day,
	his love endures for ever,
9	the moon and the stars to rule by night;
	his love endures for ever.
10	He struck down the first-born of the Egyptians,
	his love endures for ever,
11	and brought Israel from among them;
	his love endures for ever.
12	With strong hand and outstretched arm,
	his love endures for ever,
13	he divided the Red Sea in two,
	his love endures for ever,
14	and made Israel pass through it,
	his love endures for ever;
15	but Pharaoh and his host he swept into the sea;
	his love endures for ever.
16	He led his people through the wilderness;
	his love endures for ever.
17	He struck down great kings;
	his love endures for ever.
18	He slew mighty kings,
	his love endures for ever,
19	Sihon king of the Amorites,
	his love endures for ever,
20	and Og the king of Bashan;
	his love endures for ever.
21	He gave their land to Israel,
	his love endures for ever,
22	to Israel his servant as their patrimony;
	his love endures for ever.
23	He remembered us when we were cast down,
	his love endures for ever,
24	and rescued us from our enemies;
	his love endures for ever.
25	He gives food to all his creatures;
	his love endures for ever.
26	Give thanks to the God of heaven,
	for his love endures for ever.

137

By the rivers of Babylon we sat down and wept   1
    when we remembered Zion.
There on the willow-trees [a]   2
    we hung up our harps,
for there those who carried us off   3
    demanded music and singing,
and our captors called on us to be merry:
    'Sing us one of the songs of Zion.'
How could we sing the LORD's song   4
    in a foreign land?

If I forget you, O Jerusalem,   5
    let my right hand wither away;
let my tongue cling to the roof of my mouth   6
    if I do not remember you,
if I do not set Jerusalem
    above my highest joy.
Remember, O LORD, against the people of Edom   7
    the day of Jerusalem's fall,
when they said, 'Down with it, down with it,
    down to its very foundations!'
O Babylon, Babylon the destroyer,   8
    happy the man who repays you
    for all that you did to us!
Happy is he who shall seize your children   9
    and dash them against the rock.

138

I will praise thee, O LORD, with all my heart;   1
    boldly, O God, will I sing psalms to thee. [b]
I will bow down towards thy holy temple,   2
for thy love and faithfulness I will praise thy name;
for thou hast made thy promise wide as the heavens.
When I called to thee thou didst answer me   3
    and make me bold and valiant-hearted.
Let all the kings of the earth praise [c] thee, O LORD,   4
    when they hear the words thou hast spoken;
and let them sing of [d] the LORD's ways,   5
    for great is the glory of the LORD.
For the LORD, high as he is, cares for the lowly,   6
    and from afar he humbles the proud.
Though I walk among foes thou dost preserve my life,   7
    exerting thy power against the rage of my enemies,
    and with thy right hand thou savest me.

[a] *Or* poplars.   [b] boldly . . . thee: *or* I will sing psalms to thee before the gods.
[c] *Or* confess.   [d] *Or* walk in.

8   The LORD will accomplish his purpose for me.
          Thy true love, O LORD, endures for ever;
          leave not thy work unfinished.

139

1   LORD, thou hast examined me and knowest me.
2   Thou knowest all, whether I sit down or rise up;
          thou hast discerned my thoughts from afar.
3   Thou hast traced my journey and my resting places,
          and art familiar with all my paths.
4   For there is not a word on my tongue
          but thou, LORD, knowest them all.*a*
5   Thou hast kept close guard before me and behind
          and hast spread thy hand over me.
6   Such knowledge is beyond my understanding,
          so high that I cannot reach it.
7   Where can I escape from thy spirit?
          Where can I flee from thy presence?
8   If I climb up to heaven, thou art there;
          if I make my bed in Sheol, again I find thee.
9   If I take my flight to the frontiers of the morning
          or dwell at the limit of the western sea,
10   even there thy hand will meet me
          and thy right hand will hold me fast.
11   If I say, 'Surely darkness will steal over me,
          night will close around me',
12   darkness is no darkness for thee
          and night is luminous as day;
          to thee both dark and light are one.

13   Thou it was who didst fashion my inward parts;
          thou didst knit me together in my mother's womb.
14   I will praise thee, for thou dost fill me with awe;
          wonderful thou art, and wonderful thy works.
          Thou knowest me through and through:
15   my body is no mystery to thee,
          how I was secretly kneaded into shape
          and patterned in the depths of the earth.
16   Thou didst see my limbs unformed in the womb,
          and in thy book they are all recorded;
          day by day they were fashioned,
          not one of them was late in growing.*b*
17   How deep I find thy thoughts, O God,
          how inexhaustible their themes!

---

a For . . . them all: *or* If there is any offence on my tongue, thou, LORD, knowest it all.
b was late in growing: *prob. rdg.; Heb. om.*

Can I count them? They outnumber the grains of sand;   18
to finish the count, my years must equal thine.

O God, if only thou wouldst slay the wicked!   19
If those men of blood would but leave me in peace—
those who provoke thee with deliberate evil   20
    and rise in vicious rebellion against thee!
How I hate them, O Lord, that hate thee!   21
I am cut to the quick when they oppose thee;
I hate them with undying hatred;   22
    I hold them all my enemies.

Examine me, O God, and know my thoughts;   23
    test me, and understand my misgivings.
Watch lest I follow any path that grieves thee;   24
    guide me in the ancient*a* ways.

140

Rescue me, O Lord, from evil men;   1
    keep me safe from violent men,
whose heads are full of wicked schemes,   2
    who stir up contention day after day.
Their tongues are sharp as serpents' fangs;   3
    on their lips is spiders' poison.
Guard me, O Lord, from wicked men;   4
    keep me safe from violent men,
    who plan to thrust me out of the way.
Arrogant men set hidden traps for me,   5
    rogues spread their nets
    and lay snares for me along the path.
I said, 'O Lord, thou art my God;   6
    O Lord, hear my plea for mercy.
O Lord God, stronghold of my safety,   7
thou hast shielded my head in the day of battle.
Frustrate, O Lord, their designs against me;   8-9
    never let the wicked gain their purpose.
If any of those at my table rise against me,
    let their own conspiracies be their undoing.
Let burning coals be tipped upon them;   10
    let them be plunged into the miry depths,
    never to rise again.
Slander shall find no home in the land;   11
evil and violence shall be hounded to destruction.'

I know that the Lord will give their due to the needy   12
    and justice to the downtrodden.

a Or everlasting.

13   Righteous men will surely give thanks to thy name;
               the upright will worship in thy presence.

141

1   O Lord, I call to thee, come quickly to my aid;
               listen to my cry when I call to thee.

2   Let my prayer be like incense duly set before thee
               and my raised hands like the evening sacrifice.

3   Set a guard, O Lord, over my mouth;
               keep watch at the door of my lips.

4   Turn not my heart to sinful thoughts
               nor to any pursuit of evil courses.
            The evildoers appal me; [a]
               not for me the delights of their table.

5   I would rather be buffeted by the righteous
               and reproved by good men.
   My head shall not be anointed with the oil of wicked men,
               for that would make me a party to their crimes.

6   They shall founder on the rock of justice
               and shall learn how acceptable my words are.

7   Their bones shall be scattered at the mouth of Sheol,
               like splinters of wood or stone on the ground.

8   But my eyes are fixed on thee, O Lord God;
               thou art my refuge; leave me not unprotected.

9   Keep me from the trap which they have set for me,
               from the snares of evildoers.

10   Let the wicked fall into their own nets,
               whilst I pass in safety, all alone.

142

1   I cry aloud to the Lord;
               to the Lord I plead aloud for mercy.

2   I pour out my complaint before him
            and tell over my troubles in his presence.

3   When my spirit is faint within me,
               thou art there to watch over my steps.
            In the path that I should take
               they have hidden a snare.

4   I look to my right hand,
               I find no friend by my side;
            no way of escape is in sight,
               no one comes to rescue me.

5   I cry to thee, O Lord,
               and say, 'Thou art my refuge;

[a] *appal me: prob. rdg.; Heb. with men.*

thou art all I have
   in the land of the living.
Give me a hearing when I cry,   6
   for I am brought very low;
save me from my pursuers,
   for they are too strong for me.
Set me free from my prison,   7
   so that I may praise thy name.'
The righteous shall crown me with garlands,^a
   when thou givest me my due reward.

143

LORD, hear my prayer;   1
be true to thyself, and listen to my pleading;
   then in thy righteousness answer me.
Bring not thy servant to trial before thee;   2
against thee no man on earth can be right.
An enemy has hunted me down,   3
   has ground my living body under foot
and plunged me into darkness like a man long dead,
so that my spirit fails me   4
   and my heart is dazed with despair.
I dwell upon the years long past,   5
   upon the memory of all that thou hast done;
   the wonders of thy creation fill my mind.
To thee I lift my outspread hands,   6
   athirst for thee in a thirsty land.
LORD, make haste to answer,   7
   for my spirit faints.
Do not hide thy face from me
or I shall be like those who go down to the abyss.
In the morning let me know thy true love;   8
   I have put my trust in thee.
Show me the way that I must take;
   to thee I offer all my heart.
Deliver me, LORD, from my enemies,   9
   for with thee have I sought refuge.
Teach me to do thy will, for thou art my God;   10
in thy gracious kindness, show me the level road.
Keep me safe, O LORD, for the honour of thy name   11
and, as thou art just, release me from my distress.
In thy love for me, reduce my enemies to silence   12
and bring destruction on all who oppress me;
   for I am thy servant.

    ^a crown me with garlands: *or* crowd round me.

144

1   Blessed is the LORD, my rock,
        who trains my hands for war,
        my fingers for battle;
2   my help that never fails, my fortress,
        my strong tower and my refuge,
        my shield in which I trust,
        he who puts nations under my feet.

3   O LORD, what is man that thou carest for him?
    What is mankind? Why give a thought to them?
4   Man is no more than a puff of wind,
        his days a passing shadow.
5   If thou, LORD, but tilt the heavens, down they come;
        touch the mountains, and they smoke.
6   Shoot forth thy lightning flashes, far and wide,
        and send thy arrows whistling.
7   Stretch out thy hands from on high to rescue me
        and snatch me from great waters.*a*

9   I will sing a new song to thee, O God,
        psalms to the music of a ten-stringed lute.
10 O God who gavest victory to kings
        and deliverance to thy servant David,
    rescue me from the cruel sword;
11 snatch me from the power of foreign foes,
        whose every word is false
        and all their oaths are perjury.

12 Happy*b* are we whose sons in their early prime
        stand like tall towers,
        our daughters like sculptured pillars
        at the corners of a palace.
13 Our barns are full and furnish plentiful provision;
    our sheep bear lambs in thousands upon thousands;
14 the oxen in our fields are fat and sleek;
        there is no miscarriage or untimely birth,
        no cries of distress in our public places.
15 Happy are the people in such a case as ours;
    happy the people who have the LORD for their God.

145

1   I will extol thee, O God my king,
        and bless thy name for ever and ever.
2   Every day will I bless thee
        and praise thy name for ever and ever.

a Prob. rdg.; Heb. adds from the power of foreign foes, (8) whose every word is false and
all their oaths are perjury (*cp. verse 11*).   *b Prob. rdg.; Heb.* Who.

Great is the Lord and worthy of all praise;   3
   his greatness is unfathomable.
One generation shall commend thy works to another   4
   and set forth thy mighty deeds.
My theme shall be thy marvellous works,   5
   the glorious splendour of thy majesty.
Men shall declare thy mighty acts with awe   6
   and tell of thy great deeds.
They shall recite the story of thy abounding goodness   7
   and sing of thy righteousness with joy.

The Lord is gracious and compassionate,   8
   forbearing, and constant in his love.
The Lord is good to all men,   9
and his tender care rests upon all his creatures.

All thy creatures praise thee, Lord,   10
   and thy servants bless thee.
They talk of the glory of thy kingdom   11
   and tell of thy might,
they proclaim to their fellows how mighty are thy deeds,   12
   how glorious the majesty of thy kingdom.
Thy kingdom is an everlasting kingdom,   13
and thy dominion stands for all generations.

In all his promises the Lord keeps faith,   14
   he is unchanging in all his works;
the Lord holds up those who stumble
   and straightens backs which are bent.
The eyes of all are lifted to thee in hope,   15
and thou givest them their food when it is due;
with open and bountiful hand   16
thou givest what they desire[a] to every living creature.
The Lord is righteous in all his ways,   17
   unchanging in all that he does;
very near is the Lord to those who call to him,   18
   who call to him in singleness of heart.
He fulfils their desire if only they fear him;   19
   he hears their cry and saves them.
The Lord watches over all who love him   20
   but sends the wicked to their doom.
My tongue shall speak out the praises of the Lord,   21
   and all creatures shall bless his holy name
   for ever and ever.

[a] they desire: *or* thou wilt.

146

1   O praise the LORD.

Praise the LORD, my soul.
2   As long as I live I will praise the LORD;
        I will sing psalms to my God all my life long.
3   Put no faith in princes,
        in any man, who has no power to save.
4   He breathes his last breath,
         he returns to the dust;
and in that same hour all his thinking ends.

5   Happy the man whose helper is the God of Jacob,
        whose hopes are in the LORD his God,
6   maker of heaven and earth,
        the sea, and all that is in them;
who serves wrongdoers as he has sworn
7   and deals out justice to the oppressed.
The LORD feeds the hungry
        and sets the prisoner free.
8   The LORD restores sight to the blind
        and straightens backs which are bent;
the LORD loves the righteous
9   and watches over the stranger;
the LORD gives heart to the orphan and widow
but turns the course of the wicked to their ruin.
10   The LORD shall reign for ever,
        thy God, O Zion, for all generations.

O praise the LORD.

147

1   O praise the LORD.

How good it is to sing psalms to our God!
        How pleasant to praise him!
2   The LORD is rebuilding Jerusalem;
he gathers in the scattered sons of Israel.
3   It is he who heals the broken in spirit
        and binds up their wounds,
4   he who numbers the stars one by one
        and names them one and all.
5   Mighty is our Lord and great his power,
        and his wisdom beyond all telling.
6   The LORD gives new heart to the humble
        and brings evildoers down to the dust.
7   Sing to the LORD a song of thanksgiving,
        sing psalms to the harp in honour of our God.

He veils the sky in clouds   8
   and prepares rain for the earth;
he clothes the hills with grass
   and green plants for the use of man.
He gives the cattle their food   9
and the young ravens all that they gather.
The LORD sets no store by the strength of a horse   10
   and takes no pleasure in a runner's legs;
his pleasure is in those who fear him,   11
   who wait for his true love.

Sing to the LORD, Jerusalem;   12
   O Zion, praise your God,
for he has put new bars in your gates;   13
   he has blessed your children within them.
He has brought peace to your realm   14
   and given you fine wheat in plenty.
He sends his command to the ends of the earth,   15
   and his word runs swiftly.
He showers down snow, white as wool,   16
   and sprinkles hoar-frost thick as ashes;
crystals of ice he scatters like bread-crumbs;   17
he sends the cold, and the water stands frozen,
he utters his word, and the ice is melted;   18
   he blows with his wind and the waters flow.
To Jacob he makes his word known,   19
   his statutes and decrees to Israel;
he has not done this for any other nation,   20
   nor taught them his decrees.

   O praise the LORD.

148

   O praise the LORD.   1

Praise the LORD out of heaven;
   praise him in the heights.
Praise him, all his angels;   2
   praise him, all his host.
Praise him, sun and moon;   3
   praise him, all you shining stars;
praise him, heaven of heavens,   4
   and you waters above the heavens.
Let them all praise the name of the LORD,   5
for he spoke the word and they were created;
he established them for ever and ever   6
by an ordinance which shall never pass away.

7   Praise the LORD from the earth,
        you water-spouts and ocean depths;
8   fire and hail, snow and ice,
        gales of wind obeying his voice;
9   all mountains and hills;
        all fruit-trees and all cedars;
10   wild beasts and cattle,
        creeping things and winged birds;
11   kings and all earthly rulers,
        princes and judges over the whole earth;
12   young men and maidens,
        old men and young together.
13   Let all praise the name of the LORD,
        for his name is high above all others,
        and his majesty above earth and heaven;
14   he has exalted his people in the pride of power
    and crowned with praise his loyal servants,
        all Israel, the people nearest him.

    O praise the LORD.

149

1   O praise the LORD.

    Sing to the LORD a new song,
        sing his praise in the assembly of the faithful;
2   let Israel rejoice in his maker
    and the sons of Zion exult in their king.
3   Let them praise his name in the dance,
    and sing him psalms with tambourine and harp.
4   For the LORD accepts the service of his people;
    he crowns his humble folk with victory.
5   Let his faithful servants exult in triumph;
    let them shout for joy as they kneel before him.
6   Let the high praises of God be on their lips
        and a two-edged sword in their hand,
7   to wreak vengeance on the nations
        and to chastise the heathen;
8   to load their kings with chains
        and put their nobles in irons;
9   to execute the judgement decreed against them—
    this is the glory of all his faithful servants.

    O praise the LORD.

150

O praise the LORD.   1

O praise God in his holy place,
praise him in the vault of heaven, the vault of his power;
praise him for his mighty works,   2
   praise him for his immeasurable greatness.
Praise him with fanfares on the trumpet,   3
   praise him upon lute and harp;
praise him with tambourines and dancing,   4
   praise him with flute and strings;
praise him with the clash of cymbals,   5
   praise him with triumphant cymbals;
let everything that has breath praise the LORD!   6

O praise the LORD.

PROVERBS

Advice to the reader

1 The proverbs of Solomon son of David, king of Israel,
2   by which men will come to wisdom and instruction
    and will understand words that bring understanding,
3   and by which they will gain a well-instructed intelligence,
    righteousness, justice, and probity.
4   The simple will be endowed with shrewdness
    and the young with knowledge and prudence.
5   If the wise man listens, he will increase his learning,
    and the man of understanding will acquire skill
6   to understand proverbs and parables,
    the sayings of wise men and their riddles.

7   The fear of the LORD is the beginning[a] of knowledge,
    but fools scorn wisdom and discipline.

8   Attend, my son, to your father's instruction
    and do not reject the teaching of your mother;
9   for they are a garland of grace on your head
    and a chain of honour round your neck.

10 11 My son, bad men may tempt you[b] and say,
    'Come with us; let us lie in wait for someone's blood;
    let us waylay[c] an innocent man who has done us no harm.
12   Like Sheol we will swallow them alive;
    though blameless, they shall be like men who go down to the abyss.
13   We shall take rich treasure of every sort
    and fill our homes with booty;
14   throw in your lot with us,
    and we will have a common purse.'
15   My son, do not go along with them,
    keep clear of their ways;
16   they hasten hot-foot into crime,
    impatient to shed blood.

17   In vain is a net spread wide
    if any bird that flies can see it.

18   These men lie in wait for their own blood
    and waylay[c] no one but themselves.

[a] *Or* chief part.   [b] *Prob. rdg.; Heb. adds* do not come, *or, with some MSS.,* do not consent.   [c] *Prob. rdg.; Heb.* store up.

This is the fate*a* of men eager for ill-gotten gain: 19
  it robs those who get it of their lives.

Wisdom cries aloud in the open air,   20
  she raises her voice in public places;
she calls at the top of the busy street   21
  and proclaims at the open gates of the city:
'Simple fools, how long will you be content with your simplicity?*b*   22
If only you would respond to my reproof,   23
  I would give you my counsel
  and teach you my precepts.
But because you refused to listen when I called,   24
because no one attended when I stretched out my hand,
because you spurned all my advice   25
  and would have nothing to do with my reproof,
I in my turn will laugh at your doom   26
  and deride you when terror comes upon you,
when terror comes upon you like a hurricane   27
  and your doom descends like a whirlwind.*c*
Insolent men delight in their insolence;
  stupid men hate knowledge.*d*
When they call upon me, I will not answer them;   28
  when they search for me, they shall not find me.
Because they hate knowledge   29
  and have not chosen to fear the LORD,
because they have not accepted my counsel   30
  and have spurned all my reproof,
they shall eat the fruits of their behaviour   31
  and have a surfeit of their own devices;
for the simpleton turns a deaf ear and comes to grief,   32
  and the stupid are ruined by their own complacency.
But whoever listens to me shall live without a care,   33
  undisturbed by fear of misfortune.'

My son, if you take my words to heart   **2**
  and lay up my commands in your mind,
giving your attention to wisdom   2
  and your mind to understanding,
if you summon discernment to your aid   3
  and invoke understanding,
if you seek her out like silver   4
  and dig for her like buried treasure,
then you will understand the fear of the LORD   5
  and attain to the knowledge of God;
for the LORD bestows wisdom   6
  and teaches knowledge and understanding.

a This . . . fate: *prob. rdg.; Heb.* Such are the courses.   *b* *The rest of verse 22*
transposed to follow verse 27.   *c* *Prob. rdg.; Heb. adds* when anguish and distress
come upon you.   *d* Insolent . . . knowledge: *transposed from end of verse 22.*

7 Out of his store he endows the upright with ability
as a shield for those who live blameless lives;
8 for he guards the course of justice
and keeps watch over the way of his loyal servants.

9 Then you will understand what is right and just
and keep *a* only to the good man's path;
10 for wisdom will sink into your mind,
and knowledge will be your heart's delight.
11 Prudence will keep watch over you,
understanding will guard you,
12 it will save you from evil ways
and from men whose talk is subversive,
13 who forsake the honest course
to walk in ways of darkness,
14 who rejoice in doing evil
and exult in evil and subversive acts,
15 whose own ways are crooked,
whose tracks are devious.
16 It will save you from the adulteress,
from the loose woman with her seductive words,
17 who forsakes the teaching of her childhood
and has forgotten the covenant of her God;
18 for her path *b* runs downhill towards death,
and her course is set for the land of the dead.
19 No one who resorts to her *c* finds his way back
or regains the path to life.

20 See then that you follow the footsteps of good men
and keep to the course of the righteous;
21 for the upright shall dwell on earth
and blameless men remain there;
22 but the wicked shall be uprooted from it
and traitors weeded out.

3 My son, do not forget my teaching,
but guard my commands in your heart;
2 for long life and years in plenty
will they bring you, and prosperity as well.
3 Let your good faith and loyalty never fail,
but bind them about your neck.
4 Thus will you win favour and success
in the sight of God and man.

5 Put all your trust in the LORD
and do not rely on your own understanding.

---

a keep: *prob. rdg.; Heb.* uprightness.   *b Prob. rdg.; Heb.* house.   *c* resorts to
her: *or* takes to them.

Think of him in all your ways, 6
and he will smooth your path.
Do not think how wise you are, 7
but fear the LORD and turn from evil.
Let that be the medicine to keep you in health, 8
the liniment for your limbs.
Honour the LORD with your wealth 9
as the first charge on all your earnings;
then your granaries will be filled with corn *a* 10
and your vats bursting with new wine.
My son, do not spurn the LORD's correction 11
or take offence at his reproof;
for those whom he loves the LORD reproves, 12
and he punishes a favourite son.

Happy he who has found wisdom, 13
and the man who has acquired understanding;
for wisdom is more profitable than silver, 14
and the gain she brings is better than gold.
She is more precious than red coral, 15
and all your jewels are no match for her.
Long life is in her right hand, 16
in her left hand are riches and honour.
Her ways are pleasant ways 17
and all her paths lead to prosperity.
She is a staff of life to all who grasp her, 18
and those who hold her fast are safe.

In wisdom the LORD founded the earth 19
and by understanding he set the heavens in their place;
by his knowledge the depths burst forth 20
and the clouds dropped dew.

My son, keep watch over your ability and prudence, 21
do not let them slip from sight;
they shall be a charm hung about your neck 22
and an ornament on your breast.
Then you will go your way without a care, 23
and your feet will not stumble.
When you sit, you need have no fear; 24
when you lie down, your sleep will be pleasant.
Do not be afraid when fools are frightened 25
or when ruin comes upon the wicked;
for the LORD will be at your side, 26
and he will keep your feet clear of the trap.
Refuse no man any favour that you owe him 27
when it lies in your power to pay it.

a with corn: *or* to overflowing.

28   Do not say to your friend, 'Come back again;
      you shall have it tomorrow'—when you have it already.

29   Plot no evil against your friend,
      your unsuspecting neighbour.

30   Do not pick a quarrel with a man for no reason,
      if he has not done you a bad turn.

31   Do not emulate a lawless man,
      do not choose to follow his footsteps;

32   for one who is not straight is detestable to the Lord,
      but upright men are in God's confidence.

33   The Lord's curse rests on the house of the evildoer,
      while he blesses the home of the righteous.

34   Though God himself meets the arrogant with arrogance,
      yet he bestows his favour on the meek.[a]

35   Wise men are adorned with[b] honour,
      but the coat[c] on a fool's back is contempt.

4 Listen, my sons, to a father's instruction,
      consider attentively how to gain understanding;

2   for it is sound learning I give you;
      so do not forsake my teaching.

3   I too have been a father's son,
      tender in years, my mother's only child.

4   He taught me and said to me:
      Hold fast to my words with all your heart,
      keep my commands and you will have life.

5   Do not forget or turn a deaf ear to what I say.

7   The first thing[d] is to acquire wisdom;
      gain understanding though it cost you all you have.

6   Do not forsake her, and she will keep you safe;
      love her, and she will guard you;

8   cherish her, and she will lift you high;
      if only you embrace her, she will bring you to honour.

9   She will set a garland of grace on your head
      and bestow on you a crown of glory.

10   Listen, my son, take my words to heart,
      and the years of your life shall be multiplied.

11   I will guide you in the paths of wisdom
      and lead you in honest ways.

12   As you walk you will not slip,
      and, if you run, nothing will bring you down.

13   Cling to instruction and never let it go;
      observe it well, for it is your life.

14   Do not take to the course of the wicked
      or follow the way of evil men;

---

[a] *Or* wretched.   [b] are adorned with: *prob. rdg.; Heb.* shall inherit.   [c] the coat:
prob. rdg.; Heb. obscure.   [d] *Prob. rdg.; Heb. adds* wisdom.

do not set foot on it, but avoid it;   15
turn aside and go on your way.
For they cannot sleep unless they have done some wrong;   16
unless they have been someone's downfall they lose their sleep.
The bread they eat is the fruit of crime   17
and they drink wine got by violence.
The course of the righteous is like morning light,   18
growing brighter till it is broad day;
but the ways of the wicked are like darkness at night,   19
and they do not know what has been their downfall.

My son, attend to my speech,   20
pay heed to my words;
do not let them slip out of your mind,   21
keep them close in your heart;
for they are life to him who finds them,   22
and health to his whole body.
Guard your heart more than any treasure,   23
for it is the source of all life.
Keep your mouth from crooked speech   24
and your lips from deceitful talk.
Let your eyes look straight before you,   25
fix your gaze upon what lies ahead.
Look out for the path that your feet must take,   26
and your ways will be secure.
Swerve neither to right nor left,   27
and keep clear of every evil thing.

My son, attend to my wisdom   **5**
and listen to my good counsel,
so that you may observe proper prudence   2
and your speech be informed with knowledge.
For though the lips of an adulteress drip honey   3
and her tongue is smoother than oil,
yet in the end she is more bitter than wormwood,   4
and sharp as a two-edged sword.
Her feet go downwards on the path to death,   5
her course is set for Sheol.
She does not watch for the road that leads to life;   6
her course turns this way and that, and what does she care? *a*

Now, my son, listen to me   7
and do not ignore what I say:
keep well away from her   8
and do not go near the door of her house;
or you will lose your dignity in the eyes of others   9
and your honour before strangers;

a what . . . care?: *or* she is restless.

10   strangers will batten on your wealth,
      and your hard-won gains pass to another man's family.

11   The end will be that you will starve,
      you will shrink to mere skin and bones.

12   Then you will say, 'Why did I hate correction
      and set my heart against reproof?

13   I did not listen to the voice of my teachers
      or pay attention to my masters.

14   I soon earned[a] a bad name
      and was despised in the public assembly.'

15   Drink water from your own cistern
      and running water from your own spring;

16   do not let your[b] well overflow into the road,
      your runnels of water pour into the street;

17   let them be yours alone,
      not shared with strangers.

18   Let your fountain, the wife of your youth,
      be blessed, rejoice in her,

19   a lovely doe, a graceful hind, let her be your companion;
      you will at all times be bathed in her love,
      and her love will continually wrap you round.
      Wherever you turn, she will guide you;
      when you lie in bed, she will watch over you,
      and when you wake she will talk with you.[c]

20   Why, my son, are you wrapped up in the love of an adulteress?
      Why do you embrace a loose woman?

21   For a man's ways are always in the LORD's sight
      who watches for every path that he must take.

22   The wicked man is caught in his own iniquities
      and held fast in the toils of his own sin;

23   he will perish for want of discipline,
      wrapped in the shroud of his boundless folly.

6 My son, if you pledge yourself to another man
      and stand surety for a stranger,

2   if you are caught by your promise,
      trapped by some promise you have made,

3   do what I now tell you
      and save yourself, my son:
      when you fall into another man's power,
      bestir yourself, go and pester the man,

4   give yourself no rest,
      allow yourself no sleep.

5   Save yourself like a gazelle from the toils,
      like a bird from the grasp of the fowler.

---

[a] *Or* I almost earned.   [b] do not let your: *prob. rdg.; Heb.* shall your.
[c] Wherever . . . with you: *transposed from ch. 6 (verse 22).*

Go to the ant, you sluggard,   6
watch her ways and get wisdom.
She has no overseer,   7
no governor or ruler;
but in summer she prepares her store of food   8
and lays in her supplies at harvest.
How long, you sluggard, will you lie abed?   9
When will you rouse yourself from sleep?
A little sleep, a little slumber,   10
a little folding of the hands in rest,
and poverty will come upon you like a robber,   11
want like a ruffian.

A scoundrel, a mischievous man, is he   12
who prowls about with crooked talk—
    a wink of the eye,   13
    a touch with the foot,
    a sign with the fingers.
Subversion is the evil that he is plotting,   14
he stirs up quarrels all the time.
Down comes disaster suddenly upon him;   15
suddenly he is broken beyond all remedy.

Six things the LORD hates,   16
    seven things are detestable to him:
    a proud eye, a false tongue,   17
    hands that shed innocent blood,
    a heart that forges thoughts of mischief,   18
    and feet that run swiftly to do evil,
    a false witness telling a pack of lies,   19
    and one who stirs up quarrels between brothers.

My son, observe your father's commands   20
    and do not reject the teaching of your mother;
    wear them always next your heart   21
    and bind them close about your neck;
    for a command is a lamp, and teaching a light,   23[a]
    reproof and correction point the way of life,
    to keep you from the wife of another man,   24
    from the seductive tongue of the loose woman.
Do not desire her beauty in your heart   25
    or let her glance provoke you;
    for a prostitute can be had for the price of a loaf,   26
    but a married woman is out for bigger game.

Can a man kindle fire in his bosom   27
without burning his clothes?

---

[a] *Verse 22 transposed to follow* wrap you round *in 5. 19.*

753

28   If a man walks on hot coals,
    will his feet not be scorched?

29   So is he who sleeps with his neighbour's wife;
    no one can touch such a woman and go free.

30   Is not a thief contemptible when he steals
    to satisfy his appetite, even if he is hungry?

31   And, if he is caught, must he not pay seven times over
    and surrender all that his house contains?

32   So one who commits adultery is a senseless fool:
    he dishonours the woman and ruins himself;

33   he will get nothing but blows and contumely
    and will never live down the disgrace;

34   for a husband's anger is a jealous anger
    and in the day of vengeance he will show no mercy;

35   compensation will not buy his forgiveness; [a]
    no bribe, however large, will purchase his connivance.

7   My son, keep my words,
    store up my commands in your mind.

2   Keep my commands if you would live,
    and treasure my teaching as the apple of your eye.

3   Wear them like a ring on your finger;
    write them on the tablet of your memory.

4   Call Wisdom your sister,
    greet Understanding as a familiar friend;

5   then they will save you from the adulteress,
    from the loose woman with her seductive words.

6   I glanced [b] out of the window of my house,
    I looked down through the lattice,

7   and I saw among simple youths,
    there amongst the boys I noticed
    a lad, a foolish lad,

8   passing along the street, at the corner,
    stepping out in the direction of her house

9   at twilight, as the day faded,
    at dusk as the night grew dark;

10   suddenly a woman came to meet him,
    dressed like a prostitute, full of wiles,

11   flighty and inconstant,
    a woman never content to stay at home,

12   lying in wait at every corner,
    now in the street, now in the public squares.

13   She caught hold of him and kissed him;
    brazenly she accosted him and said,

14   'I have had a sacrifice, an offering, to make
    and I have paid my vows today;

[a] compensation . . . forgiveness: *prob. rdg.; Heb. obscure.*   [b] I glanced: *prob.*
rdg.; Heb. om.

that is why I have come out to meet you,   15
to watch for you and find you.
I have spread coverings on my bed   16
of coloured linen from Egypt.
I have sprinkled my bed with myrrh,   17
my clothes *a* with aloes and cassia.
Come! Let us drown ourselves in pleasure,   18
let us spend a whole night of love;
for the man of the house is away,   19
he has gone on a long journey,
he has taken a bag of silver with him;   20
until the moon is full he will not be home.'
Persuasively she led him on,   21
she pressed him with seductive words.
Like a simple fool he followed her,   22
like an ox on its way to the slaughter-house,
like an antelope bounding into the noose,
like a bird hurrying into the trap;   23
he did not know that he was risking his life
until the arrow pierced his vitals.

But now, my son, listen to me,   24
attend to what I say.
Do not let your heart entice you into her ways,   25
do not stray down her paths;
many has she pierced and laid low,   26
and her victims are without number.
Her house is the entrance to Sheol,   27
   which leads down to the halls of death.

Wisdom and folly contrasted

Hear how Wisdom lifts her voice   **8**
and Understanding cries out.
She stands at the cross-roads,   2
by the wayside, at the top of the hill;
beside the gate, at the entrance to the city,   3
at the entry by the open gate she calls aloud:
'Men, it is to you I call,   4
I appeal to every man:
understand, you simple fools, what it is to be shrewd;   5
you stupid people, understand what sense means.
Listen! For I will speak clearly,   6
you will have plain speech from me;
for I speak nothing but truth   7
and my lips detest wicked talk.

     a my clothes: *prob. rdg.; Heb. om.*

8   All that I say is right,
    not a word is twisted or crooked.
9   All is straightforward to him who can understand,
    all is plain to the man who has knowledge.
10 Accept instruction and not silver,
    knowledge rather than pure gold;
11 for wisdom is better than red coral,
    no jewels can match her.
12 I am Wisdom, I bestow shrewdness
    and show the way to knowledge and prudence.
13 ^aPride, presumption, evil courses,
    subversive talk, all these I hate.
14 I have force, I also have ability;
    understanding and power are mine.
15 Through me kings are sovereign
    and governors make just laws.
16 Through me princes act like princes,
    from me all rulers on earth derive their nobility.
17 Those who love me I love,
    those who search for me find me.
18 In my hands are riches and honour,
    boundless wealth and the rewards of virtue.
19 My harvest is better than gold, fine gold,
    and my revenue better than pure silver.
20 I follow the course of virtue,
    my path is the path of justice;
21 I endow with riches those who love me
        and I will fill their treasuries.

22 'The LORD created me the beginning of his works,
    before all else that he made, long ago.
23 Alone, I was fashioned in times long past,
    at the beginning, long before earth itself.
24 When there was yet no ocean I was born,
    no springs brimming with water.
25 Before the mountains were settled in their place,
    long before the hills I was born,
26 when as yet he had made neither land nor lake
    nor the first clod ^b of earth.
27 When he set the heavens in their place I was there,
    when he girdled the ocean with the horizon,
28 when he fixed the canopy of clouds overhead
    and set the springs of ocean firm in their place,
29 when he prescribed its limits for the sea ^c
    and knit together earth's foundations.

---

^a *Prob. rdg.; Heb. prefixes* The fear of the LORD is to hate evil.   ^b the first clod:
or the sum of the clods.   ^c *Prob. rdg.; Heb. adds* and the water shall not disobey
his command.

Then I was at his side each day,   30
his darling and delight,
playing in his presence continually,
playing on the earth, when he had finished it,   31
while my delight was in mankind.

'Now, my sons, listen to me,   32-33
listen to instruction and grow wise, do not reject it.
Happy is the man who keeps to my ways,
happy the man who listens to me,   34
watching daily at my threshold
with his eyes on the doorway;
for he who finds me finds life   35
and wins favour with the LORD,
while he who finds me not, hurts himself,   36
and all who hate me are in love with death.'

Wisdom has built her house,   **9**
she has hewn her seven pillars;
she has killed a beast and spiced her wine,   2
and she has spread her table.
She has sent out her maidens to proclaim   3
from the highest part of the town,
'Come in, you simpletons.'   4
She says also to the fool,
'Come, dine with me   5
and taste the wine that I have spiced.
Cease to be silly, and you will live,   6
you will grow in understanding.'

Correct an insolent man, and be sneered at for your pains;   7
    correct a bad man, and you will put yourself in the wrong.
Do not correct the insolent or they will hate you;   8
    correct a wise man, and he will be your friend.
Lecture a wise man, and he will grow wiser;   9
    teach a righteous man, and his learning will increase.

The first step to wisdom is the fear of the LORD,   10
    and knowledge of the Holy One is understanding;
for through me your days will be multiplied   11
    and years will be added to your life.
If you are wise, it will be to your own advantage;   12
    if you are haughty, you alone are to blame.
The Lady Stupidity is a flighty creature;   13
    the simpleton, she cares for nothing.
She sits at the door of her house,   14
on a seat in the highest part of the town,
to invite the passers-by indoors   15
as they hurry on their way:
'Come in, you simpletons', she says.   16

She says also to the fool,
17   'Stolen water is sweet
     and bread got by stealth tastes good.'
18   Little does he know that death lurks there,
     that her guests are in the depths of Sheol.

A collection of wise sayings

10   The proverbs of Solomon:

A wise son brings joy to his father;
a foolish son is his mother's bane.
2   Ill-gotten wealth brings no profit;
     uprightness is a safeguard against death.
3   The LORD does not let the righteous go hungry,[a]
     but he disappoints the cravings[b] of the wicked.
4   Idle hands make a man poor;
     busy hands grow rich.
5   A thoughtful son puts by in summer;
     a son who sleeps at harvest is a disgrace.
6   Blessings are showered on the righteous;
     the wicked are choked by their own violence.
7   The righteous are remembered in blessings;
     the name of the wicked turns rotten.
8   A wise man takes a command to heart;
     a foolish talker comes to grief.
9   A blameless life makes for security;
     crooked ways bring a man down.
10   To wink at a fault causes trouble;
     a frank rebuke leads to peace.
11   The words of good men are a fountain of life;
     the wicked are choked by their own violence.
12   Hate is always picking a quarrel,
     but love turns a blind eye to every fault.
13   The man of understanding has wisdom on his lips;
     a rod is in store for the back of the fool.
14   Wise men lay up knowledge;
     when a fool speaks, ruin is near.
15   A rich man's wealth is his strong city,
     but poverty is the undoing of the helpless.
16   The good man's labour is his livelihood;
     the wicked man's earnings bring him to a bad end.
17   Correction is the high road to life;
     neglect reproof and you miss the way.
18   There is no spite in a just man's talk;
     it is the stupid who are fluent with calumny.
19   When men talk too much, sin is never far away;

a Or be afraid.   *b* Or the clamour.

common sense holds its tongue.
A good man's tongue is pure silver;　　　20
the heart of the wicked is trash.
The lips of a good man teach many,　　　21
but fools perish for want of sense.
The blessing of the LORD brings riches　　　22
and he sends no sorrow with them.
Lewdness is sport for the stupid;　　　23
wisdom a delight to men of understanding.
The fears of the wicked will overtake them;　　　24
the desire of the righteous will be granted.
When the whirlwind has passed by, the wicked are gone;　　　25
the foundations of the righteous are eternal.
Like vinegar on the teeth or smoke in the eyes,　　　26
so is the lazy servant to his master.
The fear of the LORD brings length of days;　　　27
the years of the wicked are few.
The hope of the righteous blossoms;　　　28
the expectation of the wicked withers away.
The way of the LORD gives refuge to the honest man,　　　29
but dismays those who do evil.
The righteous man will never be shaken;　　　30
the wicked shall not remain on earth.
Wisdom flows from the mouth of the righteous;　　　31
the subversive tongue will be rooted out.
The righteous man can suit his words to the occasion;　　　32
the wicked know only subversive talk.

False scales are the LORD's abomination;　　　**11**
correct weights are dear to his heart.
When presumption comes in, in comes contempt,　　　2
but wisdom goes with sagacity.
Honesty is a guide to the upright,　　　3
but rogues are balked by their own perversity.
Wealth is worth nothing in the day of wrath,　　　4
but uprightness is a safeguard against death.
By uprightness the blameless keep their course,　　　5
but the wicked are brought down by their wickedness.
Uprightness saves the righteous,　　　6
but rogues are trapped in their own greed.
When a man dies, his thread of life ends,　　　7
and with it ends the hope of affluence.
A righteous man is rescued from disaster,　　　8
and the wicked man plunges into it.
By his words a godless man tries to ruin others,　　　9
but they are saved when the righteous plead for them.
A city rejoices in the prosperity of the righteous;　　　10
there is jubilation when the wicked perish.

11   By the blessing of the upright a city is built up;
     the words of the wicked tear it down.
12   A man without sense despises others,
     but a man of understanding holds his peace.
13   A gossip gives away secrets,
     but a trusty man keeps his own counsel.
14   For want of skilful strategy an army is lost;
     victory is the fruit of long planning.
15   Give a pledge for a stranger and know no peace;
     refuse to stand surety and be safe.
16   Grace in a woman wins honour,
     but she who hates virtue makes a home for dishonour.
     Be timid in business and come to beggary;
     be bold and make a fortune.
17   Loyalty brings its own reward;
     a cruel man makes trouble for his kin.
18   A wicked man earns a fallacious *a* profit;
     he who sows goodness reaps a sure reward. *b*
19   A man set on righteousness finds life,
     but the pursuit of evil leads to death.
20   The LORD detests the crooked heart,
     but honesty is dear to him.
21   Depend upon it: an evil man shall not escape punishment;
     the righteous and all their offspring shall go free.
22   Like a gold ring in a pig's snout
     is a beautiful woman without good sense.
23   The righteous desire only what is good;
     the hope of the wicked comes to nothing.
24   A man may spend freely and yet grow richer;
     another is sparing beyond measure, yet ends in poverty.
25   A generous man grows fat and prosperous,
     and he who refreshes others will himself be refreshed.
26   He who withholds his grain is cursed by the people,
     but he who sells his corn is blessed.
27   He who eagerly seeks what is good finds much favour,
     but if a man pursues evil it turns upon him.
28   Whoever relies on his wealth is riding for a fall,
     but the righteous flourish like the green leaf.
29   He who brings trouble on his family inherits the wind,
     and a fool becomes slave to a wise man.
30   The fruit of righteousness is a tree of life,
     but violence means the taking away of life.
31   If the righteous in the land get their deserts,
     how much more the wicked man and the sinner!

12   He who loves correction loves knowledge;
     he who hates reproof is a mere brute.

        a Or fraudulent.   *b* a sure reward: *or* the reward of honesty.

A good man earns favour from the LORD; 2
the schemer is condemned.
No man can establish himself by wickedness, 3
but good men have roots that cannot be dislodged.
A capable wife is her husband's crown; 4
one who disgraces him is like rot in his bones.
The purposes of the righteous are lawful; 5
the designs of the wicked are full of deceit.
The wicked are destroyed*a* by their own words; 6
the words of the good man are his salvation.
Once the wicked are down, that is the end of them, 7
but the good man's line continues.
A man is commended for his intelligence, 8
but a warped mind is despised.
It is better to be modest*b* and earn one's living 9
than to be conceited*c* and go hungry.
A righteous man cares for his beast, 10
but a wicked man is cruel at heart.
He who tills his land has enough to eat, 11
but to follow idle pursuits is foolishness.
The stronghold of the wicked crumbles like clay, *d* 12
but the righteous take lasting root.
The wicked man is trapped by his own falsehoods, 13
but the righteous comes safe through trouble.
One man wins success by his words; 14
another gets his due reward by the work of his hands.
A fool thinks that he is always right; 15
wise is the man who listens to advice.
A fool shows his ill humour at once; 16
a clever man slighted conceals his feelings.
An honest speaker comes out with the truth, 17
but the false witness is full of deceit.
Gossip can be sharp as a sword, 18
but the tongue of the wise heals.
Truth spoken stands firm for ever, 19
but lies live only for a moment.
Those who plot evil delude themselves, 20
but there is joy for those who seek the common good.
No mischief will befall the righteous, 21
but wicked men get their fill of adversity.
The LORD detests a liar 22
but delights in the honest man.
A clever man conceals his knowledge, 23
but a stupid man broadcasts his folly.
Diligence brings a man to power, 24
but laziness to forced labour.

a Prob. rdg.; Heb. are an ambush for blood.   *b Or* scorned.   *c Or* honoured.
d Prob. rdg.; Heb. A wicked man covets a stronghold of crumbling earth.

25 An anxious heart dispirits a man,
   and a kind word fills him with joy.
26 A righteous man recoils from evil,^a
   but the wicked take a path that leads them astray.
27 The lazy hunter puts up no game,
   but the industrious man reaps a rich harvest.^b
28 The way of honesty leads to life,
   but there is a well-worn path to death.

13 A wise man sees the reason for his father's correction;
   an arrogant man will not listen to rebuke.
2 A good man enjoys the fruit of righteousness,
   but violence is meat and drink for the treacherous.
3 He who minds his words preserves his life;
   he who talks too much comes to grief.
4 A lazy man is torn by appetite unsatisfied,
   but the diligent grow fat and prosperous.
5 The righteous hate falsehood;
   the doings of the wicked are foul and deceitful.
6 To do right is the protection of an honest man,
   but wickedness brings sinners to grief.^c
7 One man pretends to be rich, although he has nothing;
   another has great wealth but goes in rags.^d
8 A rich man must buy himself off,
   but a poor man is immune from threats.
9 The light of the righteous burns brightly;
   the embers of the wicked will be put out.
10 A brainless fool causes strife by his presumption;
   wisdom is found among friends in council.
11 Wealth quickly come by dwindles away,
   but if it comes little by little, it multiplies.
12 Hope deferred makes the heart sick;
   a wish come true is a staff of life.
13 To despise a word of advice is to ask for trouble;
   mind what you are told, and you will be rewarded.
14 A wise man's teaching is a fountain of life
   for one who would escape the snares of death.
15 Good intelligence wins favour,
   but treachery leads to disaster.
16 A clever man is wise and conceals everything,
   but the stupid parade their folly.
17 An evil messenger causes trouble,^e
   but a trusty envoy makes all go well again.
18 To refuse correction brings poverty and contempt;
   one who takes a reproof to heart comes to honour.

^a recoils from evil: *prob. rdg.; Heb.* let him spy out his friend.   ^b but ... harvest:
prob. rdg.; Heb. obscure.   ^c brings ... grief: *or* plays havoc with a man.
^d One man ... rags: *or* One man may grow rich though he has nothing; another may
grow poor though he has great wealth.   ^e causes trouble: *or* is unsuccessful.

Lust indulged sickens a man;[a]   19
stupid people loathe to mend their ways.
Walk with the wise and be wise;   20
mix with the stupid and be misled.
Ill fortune follows the sinner close behind,   21
but good rewards the righteous.
A good man leaves an inheritance to his descendants,   22
but the sinner's hoard passes to the righteous.
Untilled land might yield food enough for the poor,   23
but even that may be lost through injustice.
A father who spares the rod hates his son,   24
but one who loves him keeps him in order.
A righteous man eats his fill,   25
    but the wicked go hungry.

The wisest women build up their homes;   **14**
the foolish pull them down with their own hands.
A straightforward man fears the LORD;   2
the double-dealer scorns him.
The speech of a fool is a rod for his back;[b]   3
a wise man's words are his safeguard.
Where there are no oxen the barn is empty,   4
but the strength of a great ox ensures rich crops.
A truthful witness is no liar;   5
a false witness tells a pack of lies.
A conceited man seeks wisdom, yet finds none;   6
to one of understanding, knowledge comes easily.
Avoid a stupid man,   7
you will hear not a word of sense from him.
A clever man has the wit to find the right way;   8
the folly of stupid men misleads them.
A fool is too arrogant to make amends;   9
upright men know what reconciliation means.
The heart knows its own bitterness,   10
and a stranger has no part in its joy.
The house of the wicked will be torn down,   11
but the home of the upright flourishes.
A road may seem straightforward to a man,   12
yet may end as the way to death.
Even in laughter the heart may grieve,   13
and mirth may end in sorrow.
The renegade reaps the fruit of his conduct,   14
a good man the fruit of his own achievements.
A simple man believes every word he hears;   15
a clever man understands the need for proof.
A wise man is cautious and turns his back on evil;   16

---

[a] Lust . . . a man: *or* Desire fulfilled is pleasant to the appetite.   [b] his back: *prob. rdg.; Heb.* pride.

the stupid is heedless and falls headlong.

17 Impatience runs into folly;
distinction comes by careful thought. *a*

18 The simple wear the trappings of folly;
the clever are crowned with knowledge.

19 Evil men cringe before the good,
wicked men at the righteous man's door.

20 A poor man is odious even to his friend;
the rich have friends in plenty.

21 He who despises a hungry man does wrong,
but he who is generous to the poor is happy.

22 Do not those who intend evil go astray,
while those with good intentions are loyal and faithful?

23 The pains of toil bring gain,
but mere talk brings nothing but poverty.

24 Insight is the crown of the wise;
folly the chief ornament of the stupid.

25 A truthful witness saves life;
the false accuser utters nothing but lies.

26 A strong man who trusts in the fear of the LORD
will be a refuge for his sons.

27 The fear of the LORD is the fountain of life
for the man who would escape the snares of death.

28 Many subjects make a famous king;
with none to rule, a prince is ruined.

29 To be patient shows great understanding;
quick temper is the height of folly.

30 A tranquil mind puts flesh on a man,
but passion rots his bones.

31 He who oppresses *b* the poor insults his Maker;
he who is generous to the needy honours him.

32 An evil man is brought down by his wickedness;
the upright man is secure in his own honesty.

33 Wisdom is at home in a discerning mind,
but is ill at ease in the heart of a fool.

34 Righteousness raises a people to honour;
to do wrong is a disgrace to any nation.

35 A king shows favour to an intelligent servant,
but his displeasure strikes down those who fail him.

15 A soft answer turns away anger,
but a sharp word makes tempers hot.

2 A wise man's tongue spreads knowledge;
stupid men talk nonsense.

3 The eyes of the LORD are everywhere,
surveying evil and good men alike.

a distinction . . . thought: *prob. rdg.; Heb.* a man of careful thought is hated.
b *Or* slanders.

A soothing word is a staff of life,   4
but a mischievous tongue breaks the spirit.
A fool spurns his father's correction,   5
but to take a reproof to heart shows good sense.
In the righteous man's house there is ample wealth;   6
the gains of the wicked bring trouble.
The lips of a wise man promote knowledge;   7
the hearts of the stupid are dishonest.
The wicked man's sacrifice is abominable to the LORD;   8
the good man's prayer is his delight.
The conduct of the wicked is abominable to the LORD,   9
but he loves the seeker after righteousness.
A man who leaves the main road resents correction,   10
and he who hates reproof will die.
Sheol and Abaddon lie open before the LORD,   11
how much more the hearts of men!
The conceited man does not take kindly to reproof   12
and he will not consult the wise.
A merry heart makes a cheerful face;   13
heartache crushes the spirit.
A discerning mind seeks knowledge,   14
but the stupid man feeds on folly.
In the life of the downtrodden every day is wretched,   15
but to have a glad heart is a perpetual feast.
Better a pittance with the fear of the LORD   16
than great treasure and trouble in its train.
Better a dish of vegetables if love go with it   17
than a fat ox eaten in hatred.
Bad temper provokes a quarrel,   18
but patience heals discords.
The path of the sluggard is a tangle of weeds,   19
but the road of the diligent is a highway.
A wise son brings joy to his father;   20
a young fool despises his mother.
Folly may amuse the empty-headed;   21
a man of understanding makes straight for his goal.
Schemes lightly made come to nothing,   22
but with long planning they succeed.
A man may be pleased with his own retort;   23
how much better is a word in season!
For men of intelligence the path of life leads upwards   24
and keeps them clear of Sheol below.
The LORD pulls down the proud man's home   25
but fixes the widow's boundary-stones.
A bad man's thoughts are the LORD's abomination,   26
but the words of the pure are a delight. *a*

[a] the words . . . delight: *or* gracious words are pure.

27 A grasping man brings trouble on his family,
    but he who spurns a bribe will enjoy long life.
28 The righteous think before they answer;
    a bad man's ready tongue is full of mischief.
29 The LORD stands aloof from the wicked,
    he listens to the righteous man's prayer.
30 A bright look brings joy to the heart,
    and good news warms a man's marrow.
31 Whoever listens to wholesome reproof
    shall enjoy the society of the wise.
32 He who refuses correction is his own worst enemy,
    but he who listens to reproof learns sense.
33 The fear of the LORD is a training in wisdom,
    and the way to honour is humility.

16 A man may order his thoughts,
    but the LORD inspires the words he utters.
2 A man's whole conduct may be pure in his own eyes,
    but the LORD fixes a standard for the spirit of man.
3 Commit to the LORD all that you do,
    and your plans will be fulfilled.
4 The LORD has made each thing for its own end;
    he made even the wicked for a day of disaster.
5 Proud men, one and all, are abominable to the LORD;
    depend upon it: they will not escape punishment.
6 Guilt is wiped out by faith and loyalty,
    and the fear of the LORD makes men turn from evil.
7 When the LORD is pleased with a man and his ways,
    he makes even his enemies live at peace with him.
8 Better a pittance honestly earned
    than great gains ill gotten.
9 Man plans his journey by his own wit,
    but it is the LORD who guides his steps.
10 The king's mouth is an oracle,
    he cannot err when he passes sentence.
11 Scales *a* and balances *b* are the LORD's concern;
    all the weights in the bag are his business.
12 Wickedness is abhorrent to kings,
    for a throne rests firm on righteousness.
13 Honest speech is the desire of kings,
    they love a man who speaks the truth.
14 A king's anger is a messenger of death,
    and a wise man will appease it.
15 In the light of the king's countenance is life,
    his favour is like a rain-cloud in the spring.
16 How much better than gold it is to gain wisdom,
    and to gain discernment is better than pure silver.

a Or Pointer.   *b Prob. rdg.; Heb.* balances of justice.

To turn from evil is the highway of the upright;   17
watch your step and save your life.

Pride comes before disaster,   18
and arrogance before a fall.

Better sit humbly with those in need   19
than divide the spoil with the proud.

The shrewd man of business will succeed well,   20
but the happy man is he who trusts in the LORD.

The sensible man seeks advice from the wise,   21
he drinks it in and increases his knowledge. *a*

Intelligence is a fountain of life to its possessors,   22
but a fool is punished by his own folly.

The wise man's mind guides his speech,   23
and what his lips impart increases learning. *b*

Kind words are like dripping honey,   24
sweetness on the tongue and health for the body.

A road may seem straightforward to a man,   25
yet may end as the way to death.

The labourer's appetite is always plaguing him,   26
his hunger spurs him on.

A scoundrel repeats evil gossip;   27
it is like a scorching fire on his lips.

Disaffection stirs up quarrels,   28
and tale-bearing breaks up friendship.

A man of violence draws others on   29
and leads them into lawless ways.

The man who narrows his eyes is disaffected at heart,   30
and a close-lipped man is bent on mischief.

Grey hair is a crown of glory,   31
and it is won by a virtuous life.

Better be slow to anger than a fighter,   32
better govern one's temper than capture a city.

The lots may be cast into the lap,   33
but the issue depends wholly on the LORD.

Better a dry crust and concord with it   **17**
than a house full of feasting and strife.

A wise slave may give orders to a disappointing son   2
and share the inheritance with the brothers.

The melting-pot is for silver and the crucible for gold,   3
but it is the LORD who assays the hearts of men.

A rogue gives a ready ear to mischievous talk,   4
and a liar listens to slander.

A man who sneers at the poor insults his Maker,   5
and he who gloats over another's ruin will answer for it.

Grandchildren are the crown of old age,   6

---

a   he drinks . . . knowledge: *or* and he whose speech is persuasive increases learning.
b   and what . . . learning: *or* and increases the learning of his utterance.

     and sons are proud of their fathers.

7   Fine talk is out of place in a boor,
    how much more is falsehood in the noble!

8   He who offers a bribe finds it work like a charm,
    he prospers in all he undertakes.

9   He who conceals another's offence seeks his goodwill,
    but he who harps on something breaks up friendship.

10 A reproof is felt by a man of discernment
    more than a hundred blows by a stupid man.

11 An evil man is set only on disobedience,
    but a messenger without mercy will be sent against him.

12 Better face a she-bear robbed of her cubs
    than a stupid man in his folly.

13 If a man repays evil for good,
    evil will never quit his house.

14 Stealing water starts a quarrel;
    drop a dispute before you bare your teeth.

15 To acquit the wicked and condemn the righteous,
    both are abominable in the LORD's sight.

16 What use is money in the hands of a stupid man?
    Can he buy wisdom if he has no sense?

17 A friend is a loving companion at all times,
    and a brother is born to share troubles.

18 A man is without sense who gives a guarantee
    and surrenders himself to another as surety.

19 He who loves strife loves sin.
    He who builds a lofty entrance invites thieves.

20 A crooked heart will come to no good,
    and a mischievous tongue will end in disaster.

21 A stupid man is the bane of his parent,
    and his father has no joy in a boorish son.

22 A merry heart makes a cheerful countenance,
    but low spirits sap a man's strength.

23 A wicked man accepts a bribe under his cloak
    to pervert the course of justice.

24 Wisdom is never out of sight of a discerning man,
    but a stupid man's eyes are roving everywhere.

25 A stupid son exasperates his father
    and is a bitter sorrow to the mother who bore him.

26 Again, to punish the righteous is not good
    and it is wrong to inflict blows on men of noble mind.

27 Experience uses few words;
    discernment keeps a cool head.

28 Even a fool, if he holds his peace, is thought wise;
    keep your mouth shut and show your good sense.

18   The man who holds aloof seeks every pretext
    to bare his teeth in scorn at competent people.

The foolish have no interest in seeking to understand, 2
but prefer to display their wit.
When wickedness comes in, in comes contempt; 3
with loss of honour comes reproach.
The words of a man's mouth are a gushing torrent, 4
but deep is the water in the well of wisdom.*a*
It is not good to show favour to the wicked 5
or to deprive the righteous of justice.
When the stupid man talks, contention follows; 6
his words provoke blows.
The stupid man's tongue is his undoing; 7
his lips put his life in jeopardy.
A gossip's whispers are savoury morsels, 8
gulped down into the inner man.
Again, the lazy worker is own brother 9
to the man who enjoys destruction.
The name of the LORD is a tower of strength, 10
where the righteous may run for refuge.
A rich man's wealth is his strong city, 11
a towering wall, so he supposes.
Before disaster comes, a man is proud, 12
but the way to honour is humility.
To answer a question before you have heard it out 13
is both stupid and insulting.
A man's spirit may sustain him in sickness, 14
but if the spirit is wounded, who can mend it?
Knowledge comes to the discerning mind; 15
the wise ear listens to get knowledge.
A gift opens the door to the giver 16
and gains access to the great.
In a lawsuit the first speaker seems right, 17
until another steps forward and cross-questions him.
Cast lots, and settle a quarrel, 18
and so keep litigants apart.
A reluctant brother is more unyielding than a fortress, 19
and quarrels are stubborn as the bars of a castle.
A man may live by the fruit of his tongue, 20
his lips may earn him a livelihood.
The tongue has power of life and death; 21
make friends with it and enjoy its fruits.
Find a wife, and you find a good thing; 22
so you will earn the favour of the LORD.
The poor man speaks in a tone of entreaty, 23
and the rich man gives a harsh answer.
Some companions are good only for idle talk, 24
but a friend may stick closer than a brother.

a The words ... wisdom: *prob. rdg., inverting phrases.*

19 Better be poor and above reproach
than rich and crooked in speech.

2 Again, desire without knowledge is not good;
the man in a hurry misses the way.

3 A man's own folly wrecks his life,
and then he bears a grudge against the LORD.

4 Wealth makes many friends,
but a man without means loses the friend he has.

5 A false witness will not escape punishment,
and one who utters nothing but lies will not go free.

6 Many curry favour with the great;
a lavish giver has the world for his friend.

7 A poor man's brothers all dislike him,
how much more is he shunned by his friends!
Practice in evil makes the perfect scoundrel;
the man who talks too much meets his deserts.

8 To learn sense is true self-love;
cherish discernment and make sure of success.

9 A false witness will not escape punishment,
and one who utters nothing but lies will perish.

10 A fool at the helm is out of place,
how much worse a slave in command of men of rank!

11 To be patient shows intelligence;
to overlook faults is a man's glory.

12 A king's rage is like a lion's roar,
his favour like dew on the grass.

13 A stupid son is a calamity to his father;
a nagging wife is like water dripping endlessly.

14 Home and wealth may come down from ancestors,
but an intelligent wife is a gift from the LORD.

15 Laziness is the undoing of the worthless;
idlers must starve.

16 To keep the commandments keeps a man safe,
but scorning the way of the LORD brings death.

17 He who is generous to the poor lends to the LORD;
he will repay him in full measure.

18 Chastise your son while there is hope for him,
but be careful not to flog him to death.

19 A man's ill temper brings its own punishment;
try to save him, and you make matters worse.

20 Listen to advice and accept instruction,
and you will die a wise man.

21 A man's heart may be full of schemes,
but the LORD's purpose will prevail.

22 Greed is a disgrace to a man;
better be a poor man than a liar.

23 The fear of the LORD is life;
he who is full of it will rest untouched by evil.

The sluggard plunges his hand in the dish 24
but will not so much as lift it to his mouth.
Strike an arrogant man, and he resents it like a fool; 25
reprove an understanding man, and he understands what you mean.
He who talks his father down vexes his mother; 26
he is a son to bring shame and disgrace on them.
A son who ceases to accept correction 27
is sure to turn his back on the teachings of knowledge.
A rascally witness perverts justice, 28
and the talk of the wicked fosters mischief.
There is a rod in pickle for the arrogant, 29
and blows ready for the stupid man's back.

Wine is an insolent fellow, and strong drink makes an uproar; **20**
no one addicted to their company grows wise.
A king's threat is like a lion's roar; 2
one who ignores it is his own worst enemy.
To draw back from a dispute is honourable; 3
it is the fool who bares his teeth.
The sluggard who does not plough in autumn 4
goes begging at harvest and gets nothing.
Counsel in another's heart is like deep water, 5
but a discerning man will draw it up.
Many a man protests his loyalty, 6
but where will you find one to keep faith?
If a man leads a good and upright life, 7
happy are the sons who come after him!
A king seated on the judgement-throne 8
has an eye to sift all that is evil.
Who can say, 'I have a clear conscience; 9
I am purged from my sin'?
A double standard in weights and measures 10
is an abomination to the LORD.
Again, a young man is known by his actions, 11
whether his conduct is innocent or guilty.*a*
The ear that hears, the eye that sees, 12
the LORD made them both.
Love sleep, and you will end in poverty; 13
keep your eyes open, and you will eat your fill.
'A bad bargain!' says the buyer to the seller, 14
but off he goes to brag about it.
There is gold in plenty and coral too, 15
but a wise word is a rare jewel.
Take a man's garment when he pledges his word for a stranger 16
and hold that as a pledge for the unknown person.
Bread got by fraud tastes good, 17
but afterwards it fills the mouth with grit.

a Prob. rdg.; Heb. upright.

18 Care is the secret of good planning;
    wars are won by skilful strategy.
19 A gossip will betray secrets; *a*
    have nothing to do with a tattler.
20 If a man reviles father and mother,
    his lamp will go out when darkness comes.
21 If you begin by piling up property in haste,
    it will bring you no blessing in the end.
22 Do not think to repay evil for evil,
    wait for the LORD to deliver you.
23 A double standard in weights is an abomination to the LORD,
    and false scales are not good in his sight.
24 It is the LORD who directs a man's steps;
    how can mortal man understand the road he travels?
25 It is dangerous to dedicate a gift rashly
    or to make a vow and have second thoughts.
26 A wise king sifts out the wicked
    and turns back for them the wheel of fortune.
27 The LORD shines into a man's very soul,
    searching out his inmost being.
28 A king's guards are loyalty and good faith,
    his throne is upheld by righteousness.
29 The glory of young men is their strength,
    the dignity of old men their grey hairs.
30 A good beating purges the mind,
    and blows chasten the inmost being.

21 The king's heart is under the LORD's hand;
    like runnels of water, he turns it wherever he will.
2   A man may think that he is always right,
    but the LORD fixes a standard for the heart.
3   Do what is right and just;
    that is more pleasing to the LORD than sacrifice.
4   Haughty looks and a proud heart—
    these sins mark a wicked man.
5   Forethought and diligence are sure of profit;
    the man in a hurry is as sure of poverty.
6   He who makes a fortune by telling lies
    runs needlessly into the toils of death.
7   The wicked are caught up in their own violence,
    because they refuse to do what is just.
8   The criminal's conduct is tortuous;
    straight dealing is a sign of integrity.
9   Better to live in a corner of the house-top
    than have a nagging wife and a brawling household.
10 The wicked man is set on evil;
    he has no pity to spare for his friend.

a Or He who betrays secrets is a gossip.

The simple man is made wise when he sees the insolent punished, 11
and learns his lesson when the wise man prospers.
The just God *a* makes the wicked man's home childless; *b* 12
he overturns the wicked and ruins them.
If a man shuts his ears to the cry of the helpless, 13
he will cry for help himself and not be heard.
A gift in secret placates an angry man; 14
a bribe slipped under the cloak pacifies great wrath.
When justice is done, all good men rejoice, 15
but it brings ruin to evildoers.
A man who takes leave of common sense 16
comes to rest in the company of the dead.
Love pleasure and you will beg your bread; 17
a man who loves wine and oil will never grow rich.
The wicked man serves as a ransom for the righteous, 18
so does a traitor for the upright.
Better to live alone in the desert 19
than with a nagging and ill-tempered wife.
The wise man has his home full of fine and costly treasures; 20
the stupid man is a mere spendthrift.
Persevere in right conduct and loyalty 21
and you shall find life and honour.
A wise man climbs into a city full of armed men 22
and undermines its strength and its confidence.
Keep a guard over your lips and tongue 23
and keep yourself out of trouble.
The conceited man is haughty, his name is insolence; 24
conceit and impatience are in all he does.
The sluggard's cravings will be the death of him, 25
because his hands refuse to work;
all day long his cravings go unsatisfied, 26
while the righteous man gives without stint.
The wicked man's sacrifice is an abomination to the LORD; 27
how much more when he offers it with vileness at heart!
A lying witness will perish, 28
but he whose words ring true will leave children behind him.
A wicked man puts a bold face on it, 29
whereas the upright man secures his line of retreat.
Face to face with the LORD, 30
wisdom, understanding, counsel go for nothing.
A horse may be made ready for the day of battle, 31
but victory comes from the LORD.

A good name is more to be desired than great riches; **22**
esteem is better than silver or gold.
Rich and poor have this in common: 2

---

a Or The just man.   *b* makes . . . childless: *prob. rdg.*; *Heb.* considers the wicked
man's home.

the LORD made them both.

3   A shrewd man sees trouble coming and lies low;
     the simple walk into it and pay the penalty.

4   The fruit of humility is the fear of God
     with riches and honour and life.

5   The crooked man's path is set with snares and pitfalls;
     the cautious man will steer clear of them.

6   Start a boy on the right road,
     and even in old age he will not leave it.

7   The rich lord it over the poor;
     the borrower becomes the lender's slave.

8   The man who sows injustice reaps trouble,
     and the end of his work will be the rod. *a*

9   The kindly man will be blessed,
     for he shares his food with the poor.

10   Drive out the insolent man, and strife goes with him;
     if he sits on the bench, he makes a mockery of justice.

11   The LORD loves a sincere man;
     but you will make a king your friend with your fine phrases.

12   The LORD keeps watch over every claim at law,
     and overturns the scoundrel's case.

13   The sluggard protests, 'There's a lion outside;
     I shall get myself killed in the street.'

14   The words of an adulteress are like a deep pit;
     those whom the LORD has cursed will fall into it.

15   Folly is deep-rooted in the heart of a boy;
     a good beating will drive it right out of him.

16   Oppression of the poor may bring gain to a man,
     but giving to the rich leads only to penury.

Thirty wise sayings

17   The sayings of the wise:

     Pay heed and listen to my words,
     open your mind to the knowledge I impart;

18   to keep them in your heart will be a pleasure,
     and then you will always have them ready on your lips.

19   I would have you trust in the LORD
     and so I tell you these things this day for your own good.

20   Here I have written out for you thirty sayings,
     full of knowledge and wise advice,

21   to impart to you a knowledge of the truth,
     that you may take back a true report *b* to him who sent you.

22   Never rob a helpless man because he is helpless,
     nor ill-treat a poor wretch in court;

a the rod: *or* the threshing.   *b* *Prob. rdg.; Heb. adds* words of truth.

for the LORD will take up their cause   23
and rob him who robs them of their livelihood.

Never make friends with an angry man   24
nor keep company with a bad-tempered one;
be careful not to learn his ways,   25
or you will find yourself caught in a trap.

Never be one to give guarantees,   26
or to pledge yourself as surety for another;
for if you cannot pay, beware: 27
your bed will be taken from under you.

Do not move the ancient boundary-stone   28
which your forefathers set up.

You see a man skilful at his craft: 29
he will serve kings, he will not serve common men.

When you sit down to eat with a ruling prince,   **23**
be sure to keep your mind on what is before you,
and if you are a greedy man,   2
cut your throat first.
Do not be greedy for his dainties,   3
for they are not what they seem.
Do not slave to get wealth; *a*   4
be a sensible man, and give up.
Before you can look round, it will be gone;   5
it will surely grow wings
like an eagle, like a bird in the sky.
Do not go to dinner with a miser, *b*   6
do not be greedy for his dainties;
for they will stick in your *c* throat like a hair.   7
He will bid you eat and drink,
but his heart is not with you;
you will bring up the mouthful you have eaten,   8
and your winning words will have been wasted.

Hold your tongue in the hearing of a stupid man;   9
for he will despise your words of wisdom.
Do not move the ancient boundary-stone   10
or encroach on the land of orphans:
they have a powerful guardian   11
who will take up their cause against you.
Apply your mind to instruction   12
and open your ears to knowledge when it speaks.
Do not withhold discipline from a boy;   13
take the stick to him, and save him from death.
If you take the stick to him yourself,   14
you will preserve him from the jaws of death.

---

a to get wealth: *or* for an invitation to a feast.   *b* *Or* a man with an evil eye.
c *Prob. rdg.; Heb.* his.

15   My son, if you are wise at heart,
        my heart in its turn will be glad;
16   I shall rejoice with all my soul
        when you speak plain truth.

17   Do not try to emulate sinners;
        envy only those who fear the LORD day by day;
18   do this, and you may look forward to the future,
        and your thread of life will not be cut short.

19   Listen, my son, listen, and become wise;
        set your mind on the right course.
20   Do not keep company with drunkards
        or those who are greedy for the fleshpots;
21   for drink and greed will end in poverty,
        and drunken stupor goes in rags.

22   Listen to your father, who gave you life,
        and do not despise your mother when she is old.
23   Buy truth, never sell it;
        buy wisdom, instruction, and understanding.
24   A good man's father will rejoice
        and he who has a wise son will delight in him.
25   Give your father and your mother cause for delight,
        let her who bore you rejoice.

26   My son, mark my words,
        and accept my guidance with a will.
27   A prostitute is a deep pit,
        a loose woman a narrow well;
28   she lies in wait like a robber
        and betrays her husband with man after man.

29   Whose is the misery? whose the remorse?
        Whose are the quarrels and the anxiety?
        Who gets the bruises without knowing why?
        Whose eyes are bloodshot?
30   Those who linger late over their wine,
        those who are always trying some new spiced liquor.
31   Do not gulp down the wine, the strong red wine,
        when the droplets form on the side of the cup; *a*
32   in the end it will bite like a snake
        and sting like a cobra.
33   Then your eyes see strange sights,
        your wits and your speech are confused;
34   you become like a man tossing out at sea,
        like one who clings to *b* the top of the rigging;

---

a *Prob. rdg.; Heb. adds* it runs smoothly to and fro.   *b* clings to: *prob. rdg.;*
Heb. lies on.

you say, 'If it lays me flat, what do I care?   35
If it brings me to the ground, what of it?
As soon as I wake up,
I shall turn to it again.'

Do not emulate wicked men   **24**
or long to make friends with them;
for violence is all they think of,   2
and all they say means mischief.

Wisdom builds the house,   3
good judgement makes it secure,
knowledge furnishes the rooms   4
with all the precious and pleasant things that wealth can buy.

Wisdom prevails over strength,   5
knowledge over brute force;
for wars are won by skilful strategy,   6
and victory is the fruit of long planning.

Wisdom is too high for a fool;   7
he dare not open his mouth in court.

A man who is bent on mischief   8
gets a name for intrigue;
the intrigues of foolish men misfire,   9
and the insolent man is odious to his fellows.

If your strength fails on a lucky*a* day,   10
how helpless will you be on a day of disaster!

When you see a man being dragged to be killed, go to his rescue,   11
and save those being hurried away to their death.
If you say, 'But I do not know this man',   12
God, who fixes a standard for the heart, will take note.
God who watches you—be sure he will know;
he will requite every man for what he does.

Eat honey, my son, for it is good,   13
and the honeycomb so sweet upon the tongue.
Make wisdom too your own;   14
if you find it, you may look forward to the future,
and your thread of life will not be cut short.

Do not lie in wait like a felon at the good man's house,   15
or raid his farm.
Though the good man may fall seven times, he is soon up again,   16
but the rascal is brought down by misfortune.
Do not rejoice when your enemy falls,   17
do not gloat when he is brought down;

a lucky: *prob. rdg.; Heb. om.*

18   or the Lord will see and be displeased with you,
        and he will cease to be angry with him.

19   Do not vie with evildoers
        or emulate the wicked;
20   for wicked men have no future to look forward to;
        their embers will be put out.

21   My son, fear the Lord and grow rich,
        but have nothing to do with men of rank,
22   they will bring about disaster without warning;
        who knows what ruin such men may cause*a*?

23 More sayings of wise men:

        Partiality in dispensing justice is not good.
24   A judge who pronounces a guilty man innocent
        is cursed by all nations, all peoples execrate him;
25   but for those who convict the guilty all will go well,
        they will be blessed with prosperity.
26   A straightforward answer
        is as good as a kiss of friendship.

27   First put all in order out of doors
        and make everything ready on the land;
        then establish your house and home.

28   Do not be a witness against your neighbour without good reason
        nor misrepresent him in your evidence.
29   Do not say,
        'I will do to him what he has done to me;
        I will requite him for what he has done.'

30   I passed by the field of an idle man,
        by the vineyard of a man with no sense.
31   I looked, and it was all dried up,
        it was overgrown with thistles
        and covered with weeds,
        and the stones of its walls had been torn down.
32   I saw and I took good note,
        I considered and learnt the lesson:
33   a little sleep, a little slumber,
            a little folding of the hands in rest,
34   and poverty will come upon you like a robber,
            want like a ruffian.

        a they . . . cause: *or* they will come to sudden disaster; who knows what the ruin of such
        men will be.

Other collections of wise sayings

More proverbs of Solomon transcribed by the men of Hezekiah king of **25**
Judah:

The glory of God is to keep things hidden   2
but the glory of kings is to fathom them.
The heavens for height, the earth*a* for depth: 3
unfathomable is the heart of a king.
Rid silver of its impurities,   4
then it may go to*b* the silversmith;
rid the king's presence of wicked men,   5
and his throne will rest firmly on righteousness.
Do not put yourself forward in the king's presence   6
or take your place among the great;
for it is better that he should say to you, 'Come up here',   7
than move you down to make room for a nobleman.
Be in no hurry to tell everyone what you have seen,   8
or it will end in bitter reproaches from your friend.
Argue your own case with your neighbour,   9
but do not reveal another man's secrets,
or he will reproach you when he hears of it   10
and your indiscretion will then be beyond recall.
Like apples of gold set in silver filigree   11
is a word spoken in season.
Like a golden earring or a necklace of Nubian gold   12
is a wise man whose reproof finds attentive ears.
Like the coolness of snow in harvest   13
is a trusty messenger to those who send him.*c*
Like clouds and wind that bring no rain   14
is the man who boasts of gifts he never gives.
A prince may be persuaded by patience,   15
and a soft tongue may break down solid bone.*d*
If you find honey, eat only what you need,   16
too much of it will make you sick;
be sparing in visits to your neighbour's house,   17
if he sees too much of you, he will dislike you.
Like a club or a sword or a sharp arrow   18
is a false witness who denounces his friend.
Like a tooth decayed or a foot limping   19
is a traitor relied on in the day of trouble.
Like one who dresses*e* a wound with vinegar,   20
so is the sweetest of singers to the heavy-hearted.
If your enemy is hungry, give him bread to eat;   21
if he is thirsty, give him water to drink;

---

a *Or* the underworld.   *b* then it may go to: *or* and it will come out bright for.
c *Prob. rdg.; Heb. adds* refreshing his master.   *d* solid bone: *or* authority.
e *Prob. rdg.; Heb. adds* a garment on a cold day.

22   so you will heap glowing coals on his head,
      and the LORD will reward you.
23   As the north wind holds back the rain,
      so an angry glance holds back slander.
24   Better to live in a corner of the house-top
      than have a nagging wife and a brawling household.
25   Like cold water to the throat when it is dry
      is good news from a distant land.
26   Like a muddied spring or a tainted well
      is a righteous man who gives way to a wicked one.
27   A surfeit of honey is bad for a man,
      and the quest for honour is burdensome.
28   Like a city that has burst out of its confining walls [a]
      is a man who cannot control his temper.

26   Like snow in summer or rain at harvest,
         honour is unseasonable in a stupid man.
2   Like a fluttering sparrow or a darting swallow,
      groundless abuse gets nowhere.
3   The whip for a horse, the bridle for an ass,
      the rod for the back of a fool!
4   Do not answer a stupid man in the language of his folly,
      or you will grow like him;
5   answer a stupid man as his folly deserves,
      or he will think himself a wise man.
6   He who sends a fool on an errand
      cuts his own leg off and displays the stump.
7   A proverb in the mouth of stupid men
      dangles helpless as a lame man's legs.
8   Like one who gets the stone caught in his sling
      is he who bestows honour on a fool.
9   Like a thorn that pierces a drunkard's hand
      is a proverb in a stupid man's mouth.
10   Like an archer who shoots at any passer-by [b]
      is one who hires a stupid man or a drunkard.
11   Like a dog returning to its vomit
      is a stupid man who repeats his folly.
12   Do you see that man who thinks himself so wise?
      There is more hope for a fool than for him.
13   The sluggard protests, 'There is a lion [c] in the highway,
      a lion at large in the streets.'
14   A door turns on its hinges,
      a sluggard on his bed.
15   A sluggard plunges his hand in the dish
      but is too lazy to lift it to his mouth.
16   A sluggard is wiser in his own eyes

---

[a] *Or* that is breached and left unwalled.   [b] passer-by: *transposed from end of verse.*
[c] *Or* snake.

than seven men who answer sensibly.
Like a man who seizes a passing cur by the ears   17
is he who meddles in another's quarrel.
A man who deceives another   19 [a]
and then says, 'It was only a joke',
is like a madman shooting at random   18
his deadly darts and arrows.
For lack of fuel a fire dies down   20
and for want of a tale-bearer a quarrel subsides.
Like bellows for the coal and fuel for the fire   21
is a quarrelsome man for kindling strife.
A gossip's whispers are savoury morsels   22
gulped down into the inner man.
Glib speech that covers a spiteful heart   23
is like glaze spread on earthenware.
With his lips an enemy may speak you fair   24
but inwardly he harbours deceit;
when his words are gracious, do not trust him,   25
for seven abominations fill his heart;
he may cloak his enmity in dissimulation,   26
but his wickedness is shown up before the assembly.
If he digs a pit, he will fall into it;   27
if he rolls a stone, it will roll back upon him.
A lying tongue makes innocence seem guilty,   28
and smooth words conceal their sting.

Do not flatter yourself about tomorrow,   **27**
for you never know what a day will bring forth.
Let flattery come from a stranger, not from yourself,   2
from the lips of an outsider and not from your own.
Stone is a burden and sand a dead weight,   3
but to be vexed by a fool is more burdensome than either.
Wrath is cruel and anger is a deluge;   4
but who can stand up to jealousy?
Open reproof is better   5
than love concealed.
The blows a friend gives are well meant,   6
but the kisses of an enemy are perfidious.
A man full-fed refuses honey,   7
but even bitter food tastes sweet to a hungry man.
Like a bird that strays far from its nest   8
is a man far from his home.
Oil and perfume bring joy to the heart,   9
but cares torment a man's very soul.
Do not neglect your own friend or your father's; [b]   10
a neighbour at hand is better than a brother far away.

[a] *Verses 18 and 19 transposed.*   [b] *Prob. rdg.; Heb. adds* or how should you enter
your brother's house in the day of your ruin?

11 Be wise, my son, then you will bring joy to my heart,
and I shall be able to forestall my critics.

12 A shrewd man sees trouble coming and lies low;
the simple walk into it and pay the penalty.

13 Take a man's garment when he pledges his word for a stranger
and hold that as a pledge for the unknown person.

14 If one man greets another too heartily,
he may give great offence.

15 Endless dripping on a rainy day—
that is what a nagging wife is like.

16 As well try to control the wind as to control her!
As well try to pick up oil in one's fingers!

17 As iron sharpens iron,
so one man sharpens the wits of another.

18 He who guards the fig-tree will eat its fruit,
and he who watches his master's interests will come to honour.

19 As face answers face reflected in the water,
so one man's heart answers another's.

20 Sheol and Abaddon are insatiable;
a man's eyes too are never satisfied.

21 The melting-pot is for silver and the crucible for gold,
but praise is the test of character.

22 Pound a fool with pestle and mortar,[a]
his folly will never be knocked out of him.

23 Be careful to know your own sheep
and take good care of your flocks;

24 for possessions do not last for ever,
nor will a crown endure to endless generations.

25 The grass disappears, new shoots are seen
and the green growth on the hills is gathered in;

26 the lambs clothe you,
the he-goats are worth the price of a field,

27 while the goats' milk is enough for your food
and nourishment for your maidens.

28 The wicked man runs away with no one in pursuit,
but the righteous is like a young lion in repose.

2 It is the fault of a violent man that quarrels start,
but they are settled by a man of discernment.

3 A tyrant oppressing the poor
is like driving rain which ruins the crop.

4 The lawless praise wicked men;
the law-abiding contend with them.

5 Bad men do not know what justice is,
but those who seek the LORD know everything good.

6 Better be poor and above reproach
than rich and crooked.

a Prob. rdg.; Heb. adds with groats.

A discerning son observes the law,   7
but one who keeps riotous company wounds his father.

He who grows rich by lending at discount or at interest   8
is saving for another who will be generous to the poor.

If a man turns a deaf ear to the law,   9
even his prayers are an abomination.

He who tempts the upright into evil courses   10
will himself fall into the pit he has dug.

The honest shall inherit a fortune,
but the wicked shall inherit nothing.

The rich man may think himself wise,   11
but a poor man of discernment sees through him.

When the just are in power, there are great celebrations,*a*   12
but when the wicked come to the top, others are downtrodden.

Conceal your faults, and you will not prosper;   13
confess and give them up, and you will find mercy.

Happy the man who is scrupulous in conduct,   14
but he who hardens his heart falls into misfortune.

Like a starving lion or a thirsty bear   15
is a wicked man ruling a helpless people.

The man who is stupid and grasping will perish,   16
but he who hates ill-gotten gain will live long.

A man charged with bloodshed   17
will jump into a well to escape arrest.

Whoever leads an honest life will be safe,   18
but a rogue will fail, one way or another.

One who cultivates his land has plenty to eat;   19
idle pursuits lead to poverty.

A man of steady character will enjoy many blessings,   20
but one in a hurry to grow rich will not go unpunished.

To show favour is not good;   21
but men will do wrong for a mere crust of bread.

The miser *b* is in a hurry to grow rich,   22
never dreaming that want will overtake him.

Take a man to task and in the end win more thanks   23
than the man with a flattering tongue.

To rob your father or mother and say you do no wrong   24
is no better than wanton destruction.

A self-important *c* man provokes quarrels,   25
but he who trusts in the LORD grows fat and prosperous.

It is plain stupidity to trust in one's own wits,   26
but he who walks the path of wisdom will come safely through.

He who gives to the poor will never want,   27
but he who turns a blind eye gets nothing but curses.

When the wicked come to the top, others are pulled down; *d*   28
but, when they perish, the righteous come into power.

a Or there is great pageantry.   *b* Or The man with the evil eye.   *c* Or grasping.
d are pulled down: or hide themselves.

29 A man who is still stubborn after much reproof
will suddenly be broken past mending.

2 When the righteous are in power the people rejoice,
but they groan when the wicked hold office.

3 A lover of wisdom brings joy to his father,
but one who keeps company with harlots squanders his wealth.

4 By just government a king gives his country stability,
but by forced contributions he reduces it to ruin.

5 A man who flatters his neighbour
is spreading a net for his feet.

6 An evil man is ensnared by his sin, *a*
but a righteous man lives and flourishes.

7 The righteous man is concerned for the cause of the helpless,
but the wicked understand no such concern.

8 Arrogance can inflame a city,
but wisdom averts the people's anger.

9 If a wise man goes to law with a fool,
he will meet abuse or derision, but get no remedy.

10 Men who have tasted blood hate an honest man,
but the upright set much store by his life.

11 A stupid man gives free rein to his anger;
a wise man waits and lets it grow cool.

12 If a prince listens to falsehood,
all his servants will be wicked.

13 Poor man and oppressor have this in common:
what happiness each has comes from the LORD.

14 A king who steadfastly deals out justice to the weak
will be secure for ever on his throne.

15 Rod and reprimand impart wisdom,
but a boy who runs wild brings shame on his mother.

16 When the wicked are in power, sin is in power,
but the righteous will gloat over their downfall.

17 Correct your son, and he will be a comfort to you
and bring you delights of every kind.

18 Where there is no one in authority,*b* the people break loose,
but a guardian of the law keeps them on the straight path.

19 Mere words will not keep a slave in order;
he may understand, but he will not respond.

20 When you see someone over-eager to speak,*c*
there will be more hope for a fool than for him.

21 Pamper a slave from boyhood,
and in the end he will prove ungrateful.

22 A man prone to anger provokes a quarrel
and a hot-head is always doing wrong.

23 Pride will bring a man low;
a man lowly in spirit wins honour.

a An evil . . . sin: *or* When an evil man steps out a trap awaits him.　　*b* *Or* no vision.
c *Or* someone hasty in business.

He who goes shares with a thief is his own enemy:　　　　　24
he hears himself put on oath and dare not give evidence.
A man's fears will prove a snare to him,　　　　　　　　25
but he who trusts in the LORD has a high tower of refuge.
Many seek audience of a prince,　　　　　　　　　　26
but in every case the LORD decides.
The righteous cannot abide an unjust man,　　　　　27
nor the wicked a man whose conduct is upright.

Sayings of Agur son of Jakeh from Massa:[a]　　　　　**30**

This is the great man's very word: I am weary, O God,
I am weary and worn out;
I am a dumb brute, scarcely a man,　　　　　　　　2
without a man's powers of understanding;
I have not learnt wisdom　　　　　　　　　　　3
nor have I received knowledge from the Holy One.
Who has ever gone up to heaven and come down again?　　4
Who has cupped the wind in the hollow of his hands?
Who has bound up the waters in the fold of his garment?
Who has fixed the boundaries of the earth?
What is his name or his son's name, if you know it?

God's every promise has stood the test:　　　　　　5
he is a shield to all who seek refuge with him.
Add nothing to his words,　　　　　　　　　　6
or he will expose you for a liar.
Two things I ask of thee;　　　　　　　　　　7
do not withhold them from me before I die.
Put fraud and lying far from me;　　　　　　　　8
give me neither poverty nor wealth,
provide me only with the food I need.
If I have too much, I shall deny thee　　　　　　9
and say, 'Who is the LORD?'
If I am reduced to poverty, I shall steal
and blacken the name of my God.

Never disparage a slave to his master,　　　　　　10
or he will speak ill of you, and you will pay for it.

There is a sort of people who defame their fathers　　　11
and do not speak well of their own mothers;
a sort who are pure in their own eyes　　　　　　12
and yet are not cleansed of their filth;
a sort—how haughty are their looks,　　　　　　13
how disdainful their glances!
A sort whose teeth are swords,　　　　　　　　14
their jaws are set with knives,

[a] *from Massa: prob. rdg. (cp. 31. 1); Heb.* the oracle.

785

they eat the wretched out of the country
and the needy out of house and home. *a*

15   The leech has two daughters;
'Give', says one, and 'Give', says the other.

Three things there are which will never be satisfied,
four which never say, 'Enough!'
16   The grave and a barren womb,*b*
a land thirsty for water
and fire that never says, 'Enough!'

17   The eye that mocks a father or scorns a mother's old age *c*
will be plucked out by magpies
or eaten by the vulture's young.

18 Three things there are which are too wonderful for me,
four which I do not understand:
19 the way of a vulture in the sky,
the way of a serpent on the rock,
the way of a ship out at sea,
and the way of a man with a girl.

20 The way of an unfaithful wife is this:
she eats, then she wipes her mouth
and says, 'I have done no harm.'

21 At three things the earth shakes,
four things it cannot bear:
22 a slave turned king,
a churl gorging himself,
23 a woman unloved when she is married,
and a slave-girl displacing her mistress.

24 Four things there are which are smallest on earth
yet wise beyond the wisest:
25 ants, a people with no strength,
yet they prepare their store of food in the summer;
26 rock-badgers, a feeble folk,
yet they make their home among the rocks;
27 locusts, which have no king,
yet they all sally forth in detachments;
28 the lizard, which can be grasped in the hand,
yet is found in the palaces of kings.

29 Three things there are which are stately in their stride,
four which are stately as they move:
30 the lion, a hero among beasts,
which will not turn tail for anyone;

---

a house and home: *prob. rdg.; Heb.* man.   *b Or* a woman's desire.   *c* old age: *prob. rdg.; Heb. unintelligible.*

the strutting cock and the he-goat;   31
and a king going forth to lead his army. *ᵃ*

If you are churlish and arrogant   32
and fond of filthy talk, hold your tongue;
for wringing out the milk produces curd   33
and wringing the nose produces blood,
so provocation leads to strife.

Sayings of Lemuel king of Massa, which his mother taught him: **31**

What, O my son, what shall I say to you,   2
you, the child of my womb and answer to my prayers?
Do not give the vigour of your manhood to women   3
nor consort with those who make eyes at *ᵇ* kings.
It is not for kings, O Lemuel, not for kings to drink wine   4
nor for princes to crave strong drink;
if they drink, they will forget rights and customs   5
and twist the law against their wretched victims.
Give strong drink to the desperate   6
and wine to the embittered;
such men will drink and forget their poverty   7
and remember their trouble no longer.
Open your mouth and speak up for the dumb,   8
against the suit of any that oppose them;
open your mouth and pronounce just sentence   9
and give judgement for the wretched and the poor.

A capable wife

Who can find a capable wife?   10
Her worth is far beyond coral.
Her husband's whole trust is in her,   11
and children are not lacking.
She repays him with good, not evil,   12
all her life long.
She chooses wool and flax   13
and toils at her work.
Like a ship laden with merchandise,   14
she brings home food from far off.
She rises while it is still night   15
and sets meat before her household. *ᶜ*
After careful thought she buys a field   16
and plants a vineyard out of her earnings.

ᵃ going forth to lead his army: *prob. rdg.; Heb. unintelligible.*   *ᵇ* who make eyes
at: *prob. rdg.; Heb. unintelligible.*   *ᶜ Prob. rdg.; Heb. adds* and a prescribed portion
for her maidens.

17 She sets about her duties with vigour
    and braces herself for the work.
18 She sees that her business goes well,
    and never puts out her lamp at night.
19 She holds the distaff in her hand,
    and her fingers grasp the spindle.
20 She is open-handed to the wretched
    and generous to the poor.
21 She has no fear for her household when it snows,
    for they are wrapped in two cloaks.
22 She makes her own coverings,
    and clothing of fine linen and purple.
23 Her husband is well known in the city gate
    when he takes his seat with the elders of the land.
24 She weaves linen and sells it,
    and supplies merchants with their sashes.
25 She is clothed in dignity and power
    and can afford to laugh at tomorrow.
26 When she opens her mouth, it is to speak wisely,
    and loyalty is the theme of her teaching.
27 She keeps her eye on the doings of her household
    and does not eat the bread of idleness.
28 Her sons with one accord call her happy;
    her husband too, and he sings her praises:
29 'Many a woman shows how capable she is; *a*
    but you excel them all.'
30 Charm is a delusion and beauty fleeting;
    it is the God-fearing woman who is honoured.
31 Extol her for the fruit of all her toil,
    and let her labours bring her honour in the city gate.

ECCLESIASTES

The emptiness of all endeavour

1 THE WORDS OF THE SPEAKER, the son of David, king in
   Jerusalem.
2 Emptiness, emptiness, says the Speaker, emptiness, all is empty.
3 What does man gain from all his labour and his toil here under the sun?
4 Generations come and generations go, while the earth endures for ever.
5 The sun rises and the sun goes down; back it returns to its place *b* and
6 rises there again. The wind blows south, the wind blows north, round and
7 round it goes and returns full circle. All streams run into the sea, yet the

a Or Many daughters show how capable they are.   *b* back ... place: *prob. rdg.;*
Heb. to its place panting.

788

sea never overflows; back to the place from which the streams ran they return to run again.

All things are wearisome;[a] no man can speak of them all. Is not the eye 8 surfeited with seeing, and the ear sated with hearing? What has happened 9 will happen again, and what has been done will be done again, and there is nothing new under the sun. Is there anything of which one can say, 10 'Look, this is new'? No, it has already existed, long ago before our time. The men of old are not remembered, and those who follow will not be 11 remembered by those who follow them.

I, the Speaker, ruled as king over Israel in Jerusalem; and in wisdom I 12 13 applied my mind to study and explore all that is done under heaven. It is a sorry business that God has given men to busy themselves with. I have 14 seen all the deeds that are done here under the sun; they are all emptiness and chasing the wind. What is crooked cannot become straight; what is 15 not there cannot be counted. I said to myself, 'I have amassed great wisdom, 16 more than all my predecessors on the throne in Jerusalem; I have become familiar with wisdom and knowledge.' So I applied my mind to under- 17 stand wisdom and knowledge, madness and folly, and I came to see that this too is chasing the wind. For in much wisdom is much vexation, and 18 the more a man knows, the more he has to suffer.

I said to myself, 'Come, I will plunge into pleasures and enjoy myself'; **2** but this too was emptiness. Of laughter I said, 'It is madness!' And of 2 pleasure, 'What is the good of that?' So I sought to stimulate myself with 3 wine, in the hope of finding out what was good for men to do under heaven throughout the brief span of their lives. But my mind was guided by wisdom, not blinded by[b] folly.

I undertook great works; I built myself houses and planted vineyards; 4 I made myself gardens and parks and planted all kinds of fruit-trees in 5 them; I made myself pools of water to irrigate a grove of growing trees; 6 I bought slaves, male and female, and I had my home-born slaves as well; 7 I had possessions, more cattle and flocks than any of my predecessors in Jerusalem; I amassed silver and gold also, the treasure of kings and pro- 8 vinces; I acquired singers, men and women, and all that man delights in. [c] I was great, greater than all my predecessors in Jerusalem; and my wisdom 9 stood me in good stead. Whatever my eyes coveted, I refused them nothing, 10 nor did I deny myself any pleasure. Yes indeed, I got pleasure from all my labour, and for all my labour this was my reward. Then I turned and 11 reviewed all my handiwork, all my labour and toil, and I saw that everything was emptiness and chasing the wind, of no profit under the sun.

I set myself to look at wisdom and at madness and folly.[d] Then I per- 12 13 ceived that wisdom is more profitable than folly, as light is more profitable than darkness: the wise man has eyes in his head, but the fool walks in the 14 dark. Yet I saw also that one and the same fate overtakes them both. So I 15 said to myself, 'I too shall suffer the fate of the fool. To what purpose have I been wise? What [e] is the profit of it? Even this', I said to myself, 'is

16 emptiness. The wise man is remembered no longer than the fool, for, as the passing days multiply,[a] all will be forgotten. Alas, wise man and fool
17 die the same death!' So I came to hate life, since everything that was done here under the sun was a trouble to me; for all is emptiness and chasing the
18 wind. So I came to hate all my labour and toil here under the sun, since I should have to leave its fruits to my successor. What sort of a man will he
19 be who succeeds me, who inherits what others have acquired?[b] Who knows whether he will be a wise man or a fool? Yet he will be master of all the fruits of my labour and skill here under the sun. This too is emptiness.
20 Then I turned and gave myself up to despair, reflecting upon all my
21 labour and toil here under the sun. For anyone who toils with wisdom, knowledge, and skill must leave it all to a man who has spent no labour on
22 it. This too is emptiness and utterly wrong. What reward has a man for all
23 his labour, his scheming, and his toil here under the sun? All his life long his business is pain and vexation to him; even at night his mind knows no
24 rest. This too is emptiness. There is nothing better for a man to do than to eat and drink and enjoy himself in return for his labours. And yet I saw
25 that this comes from the hand of God. For without him who can enjoy his
26 food, or who can be anxious? God gives wisdom and knowledge and joy to the man who pleases him, while to the sinner is given the trouble of gathering and amassing wealth only to hand it over to someone else who pleases God. This too is emptiness and chasing the wind.

3 FOR EVERYTHING ITS SEASON, and for every activity under heaven its time:

2   a time to be born and a time to die;
            a time to plant and a time to uproot;
3   a time to kill and a time to heal;
            a time to pull down and a time to build up;
4   a time to weep and a time to laugh;
            a time for mourning and a time for dancing;
5   a time to scatter stones and a time to gather them;
            a time to embrace and a time to refrain from embracing;
6   a time to seek and a time to lose;
            a time to keep and a time to throw away;
7   a time to tear and a time to mend;
            a time for silence and a time for speech;
8   a time to love and a time to hate;
            a time for war and a time for peace.

9 10 What profit does one who works get from all his labour? I have seen
11 the business that God has given men to keep them busy. He has made everything to suit its time; moreover he has given men a sense of time past and future, but no comprehension of God's work from beginning to end.
12 I know that there is nothing good for man[c] except to be happy and live
13 the best life he can while he is alive. Moreover, that a man should eat and

---

a for ... multiply: *prob. rdg.; Heb.* because already.   *b* What sort ... acquired: *see note on verse 12.*   *c* for man: *prob. rdg., cp. 2. 24; Heb.* in them.

drink and enjoy himself, in return for all his labours, is a gift of God. I 14
know that whatever God does lasts for ever; to add to it or subtract from it
is impossible. And he has done it all in such a way that men must feel awe
in his presence. Whatever is has been already,[a] and whatever is to come has 15
been already, and God summons each event back in its turn. Moreover I 16
saw here under the sun that, where justice ought to be, there was wickedness, and where righteousness ought to be, there was wickedness. I said to 17
myself, 'God will judge the just man and the wicked equally; every activity
and [b] every purpose has its proper time.' I said to myself, 'In dealing with 18
men it is God's purpose[c] to test them and to see what they truly are.[d] For 19
man is a creature of chance and the beasts are creatures of chance, and one
mischance awaits them all: death comes to both alike. They all draw the
same breath. Men have no advantage over beasts; for everything is emptiness. All go to the same place: all came from the dust, and to the dust all 20
return. Who knows whether the spirit[e] of man goes upward or whether 21
the spirit[e] of the beast goes downward to the earth?' So I saw that there is 22
nothing better than that a man should enjoy his work, since that is his lot.
For who can bring him through to see what will happen next?

Again, I considered all the acts of oppression here under the sun; I saw 4
the tears of the oppressed, and I saw that there was no one to comfort them.
Strength was on the side of their oppressors, and there was no one to avenge
them. I counted the dead happy because they were dead, happier than the 2
living who are still in life. More fortunate than either I reckoned the man 3
yet unborn, who had not witnessed the wicked deeds done here under the
sun. I considered all toil and all achievement and saw that it comes from 4
rivalry between man and man. This too is emptiness and chasing the wind.
The fool folds his arms and wastes away. Better one hand full and peace of 5 6
mind, than both fists full and toil that is chasing the wind.

Here again, I saw emptiness under the sun: a lonely man without a 7 8
friend, without son or brother, toiling endlessly yet never satisfied with his
wealth—'For whom', he asks, 'am I toiling and denying myself the good
things of life?' This too is emptiness, a sorry business. Two are better 9
than one; they receive a good reward for their toil, because, if one falls, the 10
other[f] can help his companion up again; but alas for the man who falls
alone with no partner to help him up. And, if two lie side by side, they keep 11
each other warm; but how can one keep warm by himself? If a man is 12
alone, an assailant may overpower him, but two can resist; and a cord of
three strands is not quickly snapped.

Better a young man poor and wise than a king old and foolish who will 13
listen to advice no longer. A man who leaves prison may well come to be 14
king, though born a pauper in his future kingdom. But I have studied all 15
life here under the sun, and I saw his place taken by yet another young man,
and no limit set to the number of the subjects whose master he became. 16
And he in turn will be no hero to those who come after him. This too is
emptiness and chasing the wind.

[a] *Or* Whatever has been already is.   [b] *Prob. rdg.; Heb.* and upon.   [c] it is God's
purpose: *prob. rdg.; Heb. obscure.*   [d] *Prob. rdg.; Heb. adds* they to them.
[e] *Or* breath.   [f] if one falls, the other: *prob. rdg.; Heb. obscure.*

5 Go carefully when you visit the house of God. Better draw near in
2 obedience than offer the sacrifice of fools, who sin without a thought. Do
not rush into speech, let there be no hasty utterance in God's presence.
3 God is in heaven, you are on earth; so let your words be few. The sensible
man has much business on his hands; the fool talks and it is so much chatter.
4 When you make a vow to God, do not be slow to pay it, for he has no use for
5 fools; pay whatever you vow. Better not vow at all than vow and fail to pay.
6 Do not let your tongue lead you into sin, and then say before the angel of
God that it was a mistake; or God will be angry at your words, and all your
7 achievements will be brought to nothing.[a] You must fear God.
8 If you witness in some province the oppression of the poor and the
denial of right and justice, do not be surprised at what goes on, for every
official has a higher one set over him, and the highest[b] keeps watch over
9 them all. The best thing for a country is a king whose[c] own lands are well
tilled.
10 The man who loves money can never have enough, and the man who is
in love with great wealth enjoys no return from it. This too is emptiness.
11 When riches multiply, so do those who live off them; and what advantage
12 has the owner, except to look at them? Sweet is the sleep of the labourer
whether he eats little or much; but the rich man owns too much and cannot
13 sleep. There is a singular evil here under the sun which I have seen: a man
14 hoards wealth to his own hurt, and then that wealth is lost through an
15 unlucky venture, and the owner's son left with nothing. As he came from
the womb of mother earth, so must he return, naked as he came; all his
16 toil produces nothing which he can take away with him. This too is a
singular evil: exactly as he came, so shall he go, and what profit does he
17 get when his labour is all for the wind? What is more, all his days are overshadowed; gnawing anxiety and great vexation are his lot, sickness[d] and
18 resentment. What I have seen is this: that it is good and proper for a man
to eat and drink and enjoy himself in return for his labours here under the
19 sun, throughout the brief span of life which God has allotted him. Moreover, it is a gift of God that every man to whom he has granted wealth and
riches and the power to enjoy them should accept his lot and rejoice in his
20 labour. He will not dwell overmuch upon the passing years; for God fills
his[e] time with joy of heart.
6 Here is an evil under the sun which I have seen, and it weighs heavy
2 upon men. Consider the man to whom God grants wealth, riches, and substance,[f] and who lacks nothing that he has set his heart on: if God has not
given him the power to enjoy these things, but a stranger enjoys them
3 instead, that is emptiness and a grave disorder. A man may have a hundred
children and live a long life; but however many his days may be, if he does
not get satisfaction from the good things of life and in the end receives no
4 burial, then I maintain that the still-born child is in better case than he. Its
coming is an empty thing, it departs into darkness, and in darkness its

---

[a] *Prob. rdg.; Heb. adds* for in a multitude of dreams and empty things and many words.
[b] for every . . . the highest: *or* though every . . . over him, the Highest . . .   [c] whose:
prob. rdg.; Heb. for.   [d] sickness: *prob. rdg.; Heb.* and his sickness.   [e] his: *prob.
rdg.; Heb. om.*   [f] *Or* honour.

name is hidden; it has never seen the sun or known anything, ^a yet its state 5
is better than his. What if a man should live a thousand years twice over, 6
and never prosper? Do not both go to one place?

    The end of all man's toil is but to fill his belly, yet his appetite is never 7
satisfied. What advantage then in facing life has the wise man over the fool, 8
or the poor man for all his experience? It is better to be satisfied with what 9
is before your eyes than give rein to desire; this too is emptiness and chasing the wind. Whatever has already existed has been given a name, its 10
nature is known; a man cannot contend with what is stronger than he. The 11
more words one uses the greater is the emptiness of it all; and where is the
advantage to a man? For who can know what is good for a man in this life, 12
this brief span of empty existence through which he passes like a shadow?
Who can tell a man what is to happen next here under the sun?

Wisdom and folly compared

A GOOD NAME SMELLS SWEETER than the finest ointment, and the 7
day of death is better than the day of birth. Better to visit the house of 2
mourning than the house of feasting; for to be mourned is the lot of every
man, and the living should take this to heart. Grief is better than laughter: 3
a sad face may go with a cheerful heart. Wise men's thoughts are at home 4
in the house of mourning, but a fool's thoughts in the house of mirth. It is 5
better to listen to a wise man's rebuke than to the praise of fools. For the 6
laughter of a fool is like the crackling of thorns under a pot. This too is
emptiness. Slander drives a wise man crazy and breaks a strong man's ^b 7
spirit. Better the end of anything than its beginning; better patience than 8
pride. Do not be quick to show resentment; for resentment is nursed by 9
fools. Do not ask why the old days were better than these; for that is a 10
foolish question. Wisdom is better than possessions and an advantage to 11
all who see the sun. Better have wisdom behind you than money; wisdom 12
profits men by giving life to those who know her.

    Consider God's handiwork; who can straighten what he has made 13
crooked? When things go well, be glad; but when things go ill, consider 14
this: God has set the one alongside the other in such a way that no one can
find out what is to happen next. ^c In my empty existence I have seen it all, 15
from a righteous man perishing in his righteousness to a wicked man
growing old in his wickedness. Do not be over-righteous and do not be 16
over-wise. Why make yourself a laughing-stock? Do not be over-wicked 17
and do not be a fool. Why should you die before your time? It is good to 18
hold on to the one thing and not lose hold of the other; for a man who fears
God will succeed both ways. Wisdom makes the wise man stronger than 19
the ten rulers of a city. The world contains no man so righteous that he can 20
do right always and never do wrong. ^d Moreover, do not pay attention to 21
everything men say, or you may hear your servant disparage you; for you 22

^a *Or* it.   ^b strong man's: *prob. rdg.; Heb. obscure.*   ^c find out . . . next: *or*
hold him responsible.   ^d can do . . . wrong: *or* prospers without ever making
a mistake.

23 know very well how many times you yourself have disparaged others. All
this I have put to the test of wisdom. I said, 'I am resolved to be wise', but
24 wisdom was beyond my grasp—whatever has happened lies beyond our
grasp, deep down, deeper than man can fathom.

25   I went on to reflect, I set my mind *a* to inquire and search for wisdom and
for the reason in things, only to discover that it is folly to be wicked and
26 madness to act like a fool. The wiles of a woman I find mightier *b* than
death; her heart is a trap to catch you and her arms are fetters. The man
27 who is pleasing to God may escape her, but she will catch a sinner. 'See,'
says the Speaker, 'this is what I have found, reasoning things out one by
28 one, after searching long without success: I have found one man in a
thousand worth the name, but I have not found one woman among them
29 all. This alone I have found, that God, when he made man, made him
straightforward, but man invents endless subtleties of his own.'

8   Who is wise enough for all this? Who knows the meaning of anything?
2 Wisdom lights up a man's face, but grim looks make a man hated. *c* Do as
the king commands you, and if you have to swear by God, do not be
3 precipitate. Leave the king's presence and do not persist in a thing which
4 displeases him; he does what he chooses. For the king's word carries
5 authority. Who can question what he does? Whoever obeys a command
will come to no harm. A wise man knows in his heart the right time and
6 method for action. There is a time and a method for every enterprise,
7 although man is greatly troubled by ignorance of the future; who can tell
8 him what it will bring? It is not in man's power to restrain the wind, *d*
and no one has power over the day of death. In war no one can lay aside
9 his arms, no wealth will save its possessor. All this I have seen, having
applied my mind to everything done under the sun. There was a time when
10 one man had power over another and could make him suffer. It was then
that I saw wicked men approaching and even entering *e* the holy place;
and they went about the city priding themselves on having done right. This
11 too is emptiness. It is because sentence upon a wicked act is not promptly
12 carried out that men do evil so boldly. A sinner may do wrong *f* and live to
old age, yet I know that it will be well with those who fear God: their fear
13 of him ensures this, but it will not be well with a wicked man nor will he
14 live long; the man who does not fear God is a mere shadow. There is an
empty thing found on earth: when the just man gets what is due to the
unjust, and the unjust what is due to the just. I maintain that this too is
15 emptiness. So I commend enjoyment, since there is nothing good for a
man to do here under the sun but to eat and drink and enjoy himself; this
is all that will remain with him to reward his toil throughout the span of
16 life which God grants him here under the sun. I applied my mind to acquire
wisdom and to observe the business which goes on upon earth, when man
17 never closes an eye in sleep day or night; and always I perceived that God
has so ordered it that man should not be able to discover what is happening
here under the sun. However hard a man may try, he will not find out; the

a Prob. rdg.; Heb. adds to know and.   *b Or* more bitter.   *c* make . . . hated:
prob. rdg.; Heb. obscure.   *d Or* to retain the breath of life.   *e* approaching . . .
entering: *prob. rdg.; Heb. obscure.*   *f Prob. rdg.; Heb. adds an unintelligible word.*

wise man may think that he knows, but he will be unable to find the truth of it.

I applied my mind to all this, and I understood that the righteous and 9 the wise and all their doings are under God's control; but is it love or hatred? No man knows. Everything that confronts him, everything is empty, since 2 one and the same fate befalls every one, just and unjust alike, good and bad, clean and unclean, the man who offers sacrifice and the man who does not. Good man and sinner fare alike, the man who can take an oath and the man who dares not. This is what is wrong in all that is done here under the sun: 3 that one and the same fate befalls every man. The hearts of men are full of evil; madness fills their hearts all through their lives, and after that they go down to join the dead. But for a man who is counted among the living 4 there is still hope: remember, a live dog is better than a dead lion. True, 5 the living know that they will die; but the dead know nothing. There are no more rewards for them; they are utterly forgotten. For them love, hate, 6 ambition,*a* all are now over. Never again will they have any part in what is done here under the sun.

Go to it then, eat your food and enjoy it, and drink your wine with a 7 cheerful heart; for already God has accepted what you have done. Always 8 be dressed in white and never fail to anoint your head. Enjoy life with a 9 woman you love all the days of your allotted span here under the sun, empty as they are;*b* for that is your lot while you live and labour here under the sun. Whatever task lies to your hand, do it with all your might; because 10 in Sheol, for which you are bound, there is neither doing nor thinking, neither understanding nor wisdom. One more thing I have observed here 11 under the sun: speed does not win the race nor strength the battle. Bread does not belong to the wise, nor wealth to the intelligent, nor success to the skilful; time and chance govern all. Moreover, no man knows when his 12 hour will come; like fish caught in a net, like a bird taken in a snare, so men are trapped when bad times come suddenly.

This too is an example of wisdom as I have observed it here under the 13 sun, and notable I find it. There was a small town with few inhabitants, and 14 a great king came to attack it; he besieged it and constructed great siege-works against it. There was in it a poor wise man, and he alone might have 15 saved the town by his wisdom, but no one remembered that poor wise man. 'Surely', I said to myself, 'wisdom is better than strength.' But the poor 16 man's wisdom was despised, and his words went unheeded. A wise man 17 who speaks his mind calmly is more to be heeded than a commander shouting orders among fools. Wisdom is better than weapons of war, and 18 one mistake can undo many things done well.

Dead flies make the perfumer's sweet ointment turn rancid and ferment; **10** so can a little folly make wisdom lose its worth. The mind of the wise man 2 faces right, but the mind of the fool faces left. Even when he walks along 3 the road, the fool shows no sense and calls everyone else*c* a fool. If your 4 ruler breaks out in anger against you, do not resign your post; submission makes amends for great mistakes. There is an evil that I have observed 5

---

a Or passion.   *b Prob. rdg.; Heb. adds* all your days, empty as they are.
c calls everyone else: *or* tells everyone he is.

6 here under the sun, an error for which a ruler is responsible: the fool given
7 high office, but ^{a} the great and the rich in humble posts. I have seen slaves
8 on horseback and men of high rank going on foot like slaves. The man who
digs a pit may fall into it, and he who pulls down a wall may be bitten by a
9 snake. The man who quarries stones may strain himself, and the wood-
10 cutter runs a risk of injury. When the axe is blunt and has not first ^{b} been
sharpened, then one must use more force; the wise man has a better chance
11 of success. If a snake bites before it is charmed, the snake-charmer loses
his fee.
12   A wise man's words win him favour, but a fool's tongue is his undoing.
13 14 He begins by talking nonsense and ends in mischief run mad. The fool
talks on and on; but no man knows what is coming, and who can tell him
15 what will come after that? The fool wearies himself to death ^{c} with all his
labour, for he does not know the way to town.
16   Woe betide the land when a slave has become its king, and its princes
17 feast in the morning. Happy the land when its king is nobly born, and its
princes feast at the right time of day, with self-control, and not as drunkards.
18 If the owner is negligent the rafters collapse, and if he is idle the house
19 crumbles away. The table has its pleasures, and wine makes a cheerful
20 life; and money is behind it all. Do not speak ill of the king in your ease, or
of a rich man in your bedroom; for a bird may carry your voice, and a
winged messenger may repeat what you say.

11 1 2   Send your grain across the seas, and in time you will get a return. Divide
your merchandise among seven ventures, eight maybe, since you do not
3 know what disasters may occur on earth. ^{d} If the clouds are heavy with rain,
they will discharge it on the earth; whether a tree falls south or north, it
4 must lie as it falls. He who watches the wind will never sow, and he who
5 keeps an eye on the clouds will never reap. You do not know how a pregnant
woman comes to have a body and a living spirit in her womb; nor do you
6 know how God, the maker of all things, works. In the morning sow your
seed betimes, and do not stop work until evening, for you do not know
whether this or that sowing will be successful, or whether both alike will
do well.

Advice to a young man

7 THE LIGHT OF DAY IS SWEET, and pleasant to the eye is the sight
8 of the sun; if a man lives for many years, he should rejoice in all of
them. But let him remember that the days of darkness will be many.
9 Everything that is to come will be emptiness. Delight in your boyhood,
young man, make the most of the days of your youth; let your heart
and your eyes show you the way; but remember that for all these things
10 God will call you to account. Banish discontent from your mind, and
shake off the troubles of the body; boyhood and the prime of life are mere
emptiness.

^{a} but: *prob. rdg.; Heb. om.* ^{b} first: *prob. rdg.; Heb.* face. ^{c} fool . . . death:
prob. rdg.; Heb. obscure. ^{d} *Or on land.*

Remember your Creator in the days of your youth, before the time of **12**
trouble comes and the years draw near when you will say, 'I see no purpose
in them.'*ᵃ* Remember him before the sun and the light of day give place 2
to darkness, before the moon and the stars grow dim, and the clouds return
with the rain—when the guardians of the house tremble, and the strong 3
men stoop, when the women grinding the meal cease work because they
are few, and those who look through the windows look no longer, when 4
the street-doors are shut, when the noise of the mill is low, when the chirp-
ing of the sparrow grows faint *ᵇ* and the song-birds fall silent; *ᶜ* when men 5
are afraid of a steep place and the street is full of terrors, when the blossom
whitens on the almond-tree and the locust's paunch is swollen and caper-
buds have no more zest. For man goes to his everlasting home, and the
mourners go about the streets. Remember him before the silver cord is 6
snapped *ᵈ* and the golden bowl is broken, before the pitcher is shattered at
the spring and the wheel broken at the well, before the dust returns to the 7
earth as it began and the spirit *ᵉ* returns to God who gave it. Emptiness, 8
emptiness, says the Speaker, all is empty.

So the Speaker, in his wisdom, continued to teach the people what he 9
knew. He turned over many maxims in his mind and sought how best to
set them out. He chose his words to give pleasure, but what he wrote was 10
the honest truth. The sayings of the wise are sharp as goads, like nails 11
driven home; they lead the assembled people, for they come from one
shepherd. One further warning, my son: the use of books is endless, and 12
much study is wearisome.

This is the end of the matter: you have heard it all. Fear God and obey 13
his commands; there is no more to man than this. For God brings every- 14
thing we do to judgement, and every secret, whether good or bad.

THE SONG OF SONGS

Bride ᶠ

   I will sing the song of all songs to Solomon   1
    that he may *ᵍ* smother me with kisses.   2

   Your love is more fragrant than wine,
    fragrant is *ʰ* the scent of your perfume,   3
   and your name like perfume poured out; *ⁱ*
   for this the maidens love you.
   Take me with you, and we will run together;   4
    bring me into your chamber, O king.

ᵃ Or I have no pleasure in them.   *ᵇ* grows faint: *prob. rdg.; Heb. obscure.*
ᶜ Prob. rdg.; Heb. sink low.   *ᵈ* is snapped: *prob. rdg.; Heb. unintelligible.*
ᵉ Or breath. *ᶠ The Hebrew text implies, by its pronouns, different speakers, but does
not indicate them; they are given, however, in two MSS. of Sept.* *ᵍ* I will . . . that
he may: *or* The song of all songs which was Solomon's; may he . . . *ʰ Or* more
fragrant than. *ⁱ* poured out: *prob. rdg.; Heb. word uncertain.*

Companions

> Let us rejoice and be glad for you;
> let us praise your love more than wine,
>   and your caresses more than any song.

Bride

5 I am dark but lovely, daughters of Jerusalem,
       like the tents of Kedar
       or the tent-curtains of Shalmah.
6 Do not look down on me; a little dark I may be
       because I am scorched by the sun.
   My mother's sons were displeased with me,
   they sent me to watch over the vineyards;
   so I did not watch over my own vineyard.
7 Tell me, my true love,
       where you mind your flocks,
   where you rest them at midday,
   that I may not be left picking lice
       as I sit among your companions' herds.

Bridegroom

8 If you yourself do not know,
       O fairest of women,
   go, follow the tracks of the sheep
   and mind your kids by the shepherds' huts.

9 I would compare you, my dearest,
       to Pharaoh's chariot-horses.
10 Your cheeks are lovely between plaited tresses,
       your neck with its jewelled chains.

Companions

11 We will make you braided plaits of gold
       set with beads of silver.

Bride

12 While the king reclines on his couch,
   my spikenard gives forth its scent.
13 My beloved is for me a bunch of myrrh
       as he lies on my breast,
14 my beloved is for me a cluster of henna-blossom
       from the vineyards of En-gedi.

Bridegroom

15 How beautiful you are, my dearest,
       O how beautiful,
       your eyes are like doves!

Bride

How beautiful you are, O my love,
and how pleasant!   16

Bridegroom

Our couch is shaded with branches;
the beams of our house are of cedar,   17
our ceilings are all of fir.

Bride

I am an asphodel in Sharon,
a lily growing in the valley.   2

Bridegroom

No, a lily among thorns
is my dearest among girls.   2

Bride

Like an apricot-tree among the trees of the wood,
so is my beloved among boys.   3
To sit in its shadow was my delight,
and its fruit was sweet to my taste.
He took me into the wine-garden   4
and gave me loving glances.
He refreshed me with raisins, he revived me with apricots;   5
for I was faint with love.
His left arm was under my head, his right arm was round me.   6

Bridegroom

I charge you, daughters of Jerusalem,   7
by the spirits and the goddesses *a* of the field:
Do not rouse her, do not disturb my love
until she is ready. *b*

Bride

Hark! My beloved! Here he comes,   8
bounding over the mountains, leaping over the hills.
My beloved is like a gazelle   9
or a young wild goat:
there he stands outside our wall,
peeping in at the windows, glancing through the lattice.

My beloved answered, he said to me: 10
Rise up, my darling;
my fairest, come away.

---

a by ... goddesses: *or* by the gazelles and the hinds.   *b* until ... ready: *or* while
she is resting.

11 For now the winter is past,
the rains are over and gone;
12 the flowers appear in the country-side;
the time is coming when the birds will sing,
and the turtle-dove's cooing will be heard in our land;
13 when the green figs will ripen on the fig-trees
and the vines *a* give forth their fragrance.
Rise up, my darling;
my fairest, come away.

Bridegroom

14 My dove, that hides in holes in the cliffs
or in crannies on the high ledges,
let me see your face, let me hear your voice;
for your voice is pleasant, your face is lovely.

Companions

15 Catch for us the jackals, the little jackals,*b*
that spoil our vineyards, when the vines are in flower.

Bride

16 My beloved is mine and I am his;
he delights in the lilies.
17 While the day is cool and the shadows are dispersing,
turn, my beloved, and show yourself
a gazelle or a young wild goat
on the hills where cinnamon grows. *c*

3 Night after night on my bed
I have sought my true love;
I have sought him but not found him,
I have called him but he has not answered.
2 I said, 'I will rise and go the rounds of the city,
through the streets and the squares,
seeking my true love.'
I sought him but I did not find him,
I called him but he did not answer.
3 The watchmen, going the rounds of the city, met me,
and I asked, 'Have you seen my true love?'
4 Scarcely had I left them behind me
when I met my true love.
I seized him and would not let him go
until I had brought him to my mother's house,
to the room of her who conceived me.

---

a Prob. rdg.; Heb. adds blossom.   *b Or* fruit-bats.   *c* on . . . grows: *or* on the rugged hills *or* on the hills of Bether.

Bridegroom

> I charge you, daughters of Jerusalem,   5
> by the spirits and the goddesses *a* of the field:
> Do not rouse her, do not disturb my love
>   until she is ready. *b*

Companions

> What is this coming up from the wilderness   6
>   like a column of smoke
> from burning myrrh or frankincense,
> from all the powdered spices that merchants bring?
>   Look; it is Solomon carried in his litter;   7
> sixty of Israel's chosen warriors
>   are his escort,
>   all of them skilled swordsmen,   8
>   all trained to handle arms,
> each with his sword ready at his side
>   to ward off the demon of the night.

> The palanquin which King Solomon had made for himself
>   was of wood from Lebanon.
> Its poles he had made of silver,   10
>   its head-rest of gold;
>   its seat was of purple stuff,
> and its lining was of leather.

> Come out, daughters of Jerusalem;   11
> you daughters of Zion, come out and welcome King Solomon,
>   wearing the crown with which his mother has crowned him,
>   on his wedding day, on his day of joy.

Bridegroom

> How beautiful you are, my dearest, how beautiful!   **4**
> Your eyes behind your veil are like doves,
> your hair like a flock of goats streaming down Mount Gilead.
>   Your teeth are like a flock of ewes just shorn   2
>   which have come up fresh from the dipping;
> each ewe has twins and none has cast a lamb.
>   Your lips are like a scarlet thread,   3
>   and your words are delightful; *c*
> your parted lips behind your veil
>   are like a pomegranate cut open.
>   Your neck is like David's tower,   4
>   which is built with winding courses;
> a thousand bucklers hang upon it,
>   and all are warriors' shields.

---

a by . . . goddesses: *or* by the gazelles and the hinds.   *b* until . . . ready: *or* while she is resting.   *c* *Or* and your mouth is lovely.

5   Your two breasts are like two fawns,
                twin fawns of a gazelle. [a]

6   While the day is cool and the shadows are dispersing,
             I will go to the mountains of myrrh
             and to the hills of frankincense.

7   You are beautiful, my dearest,
              beautiful without a flaw.

8   Come from Lebanon, my bride;
             come with me from Lebanon.
        Hurry down from the top of Amana,
             from Senir's top and Hermon's,
             from the lions' lairs, and the hills the leopards haunt.

9   You have stolen my heart,[b] my sister,
             you have stolen it,[c] my bride,
             with one of your eyes, with one jewel of your necklace.

10   How beautiful are your breasts, my sister, my bride!
             Your love is more fragrant than wine,
             and your perfumes sweeter than any spices.

11   Your lips drop sweetness like the honeycomb, my bride,
             syrup and milk are under your tongue,
             and your dress has the scent of Lebanon.

13 [d]   Your two cheeks [e] are an orchard of pomegranates,
             an orchard full of rare fruits: [f]

14   spikenard and saffron, sweet-cane and cinnamon
             with every incense-bearing tree,
              myrrh and aloes
             with all the choicest spices.

12   My sister, my bride, is a garden close-locked,
           a garden close-locked, a fountain sealed.

Bride

15   The fountain in my garden [g] is a spring of running water
             pouring down from Lebanon.

16   Awake, north wind, and come, south wind;
     blow upon my garden that its perfumes may pour forth,
             that my beloved may come to his garden
             and enjoy its rare fruits.

Bridegroom

5   I have come to my garden, my sister and bride,
           and have plucked my myrrh with my spices;
           I have eaten my honey and my syrup,
           I have drunk my wine and my milk.

---

[a] *Prob. rdg.; Heb. adds* which delight in the lilies.   [b] stolen my heart: *or* put heart into me.   [c] stolen it: *or* put heart into me.   [d] *Verse 12 transposed to follow verse 14.*   [e] Your two cheeks: *prob. rdg.; Heb.* Your shoots.   [f] *Prob. rdg.; Heb. adds* henna with spikenard.   [g] my garden: *prob. rdg.; Heb.* gardens.

Eat, friends, and drink,
　　until you are drunk with love.

Bride

I sleep but my heart is awake.　　　　　　　　　　　2
　　Listen! My beloved is knocking:

'Open to me, my sister, my dearest,
　　my dove, my perfect one;
for my head is drenched with dew,
　　my locks with the moisture of the night.'

'I have stripped off my dress; must I put it on again?　3
I have washed my feet; must I soil them again?'

When my beloved slipped his hand through the latch-hole,　4
　　my bowels stirred within me.
When I arose to open for my beloved,　　　　　　　　5
　　my hands dripped with myrrh;
the liquid myrrh from my fingers
　　ran over the knobs of the bolt.
　　With my own hands I opened to my love,　　　　　6
　　but my love had turned away and gone by;
　　my heart sank when he turned his back.
　　I sought him but I did not find him,
　　I called him but he did not answer.
The watchmen, going the rounds of the city, met me;　7
　　they struck me and wounded me;
the watchmen on the walls took away my cloak.
　　I charge you, daughters of Jerusalem,　　　　　　8
if you find my beloved, will you not tell him *a*
　　that I am faint with love?

Companions

What is your beloved more than any other,　　　　　9
　　O fairest of women?
What is your beloved more than any other,
　　that you give us this charge?

Bride

My beloved is fair and ruddy,　　　　　　　　　　10
　　a paragon among ten thousand.
His head is gold, finest gold;　　　　　　　　　　11
　　his locks are like palm-fronds. *b*
His eyes are like doves beside brooks of water,　　　12
　　splashed by the milky water
　　　　as they sit where it is drawn.

---

a will you . . . him: *or* what will you tell him?　　　*b Prob. rdg.; Heb. adds* black as
the raven.

13	His cheeks are like beds of spices or chests full of perfumes;
	his lips are lilies, and drop liquid myrrh;
14	his hands are golden rods set in topaz;
	his belly a plaque of ivory overlaid with lapis lazuli.
15	His legs are pillars of marble in sockets of finest gold;
	his aspect is like Lebanon, noble as cedars.
16	His whispers are[a] sweetness itself, wholly desirable.
	Such is my beloved, such is my darling,
	daughters of Jerusalem.

Companions

6 Where has your beloved gone,
O fairest of women?
Which way did your beloved go,
that we may help you to seek him?

Bride

2 My beloved has gone down to his garden,
to the beds where balsam grows,
to delight in the garden[b] and to pick the lilies.
3 I am my beloved's, and my beloved is mine,
he who delights in the lilies.

Bridegroom

4 You are beautiful, my dearest, as Tirzah,
lovely as Jerusalem.[c]
5 Turn your eyes away from me;
they dazzle me.
Your hair is like a flock of goats streaming down Mount Gilead;
6 your teeth are like a flock of ewes come up fresh from the dipping,
each ewe has twins and none has cast a lamb.
7 Your parted lips behind your veil
are like a pomegranate cut open.
8 There may be sixty princesses,
eighty concubines, and young women past counting,
9 but there is one alone, my dove, my perfect one,
her mother's only child,
devoted to the mother who bore her;
young girls see her and call her happy,
princesses and concubines praise her.
10 Who is this that looks out like the dawn,
beautiful as the moon, bright as the sun,
majestic as the starry heavens?

11 I went down to a garden of nut-trees
to look at the rushes by the stream,

[a] *Or* His nature is. [b] *Prob. rdg.; Heb.* gardens. [c] *Prob. rdg.; Heb. adds*
majestic as the starry heavens (*see verse 10*).

to see if the vine had budded
  or the pomegranates were in flower.
  I did not know myself;   12
  she made me feel more than a prince
  reigning over the myriads *a* of his people.

Companions

  Come back, come back, Shulammite maiden,   13
  come back, that we may gaze upon you.

Bridegroom

  How you love to gaze on the Shulammite maiden,
    as she moves between the lines of dancers!

How beautiful are your sandalled feet, O prince's daughter!   **7**
  The curves of your thighs are like jewels,
    the work of a skilled craftsman.
    Your navel is a rounded goblet   2
    that never shall want for spiced wine.
    Your belly is a heap of wheat
    fenced in by lilies.
  Your two breasts are like two fawns,   3
    twin fawns of a gazelle.
  Your neck is like a tower of ivory.   4
  Your eyes are the pools in Heshbon,
    beside the gate of the crowded city. *b*
  Your nose is like towering Lebanon
    that looks towards Damascus.
  You carry your head like Carmel;   5
    the flowing hair on your head is lustrous black,
    your tresses are braided with ribbons.
    How beautiful, how entrancing you are,   6
    my loved one, daughter of delights!
  You are stately as a palm-tree,   7
    and your breasts are the clusters of dates.
  I said, 'I will climb up into the palm   8
    to grasp its fronds.'
May I find your breasts like clusters of grapes on the vine,
    the scent of your breath like apricots,
  and your whispers like spiced wine   9
  flowing smoothly to welcome my caresses,
  gliding down through lips and teeth.

Bride

  I am my beloved's, his longing is all for me.   10
  Come, my beloved, let us go out into the fields   11
    to lie among the henna-bushes;

  a Prob. rdg.; Heb. chariots.   *b Or the gate of Beth-rabbim.*

12   let us go early to the vineyards
and see if the vine has budded or its blossom opened,
      if the pomegranates are in flower.
      There will I give you my love,
13   when the mandrakes give their perfume,
      and all rare fruits are ready at our door,
      fruits new and old
      which I have in store for you, my love.

8   If only you were my own true brother
      that sucked my mother's breasts!
      Then, if I found you outside, I would kiss you,
      and no man would despise me.
2   I would lead you to the room of the mother who bore me,
bring you to her house for you to embrace me;[a]
      I would give you mulled wine to drink
      and the fresh juice of pomegranates,
3   your[b] left arm under my head and your[b] right arm round me.

Bridegroom

4   I charge you, daughters of Jerusalem:
      Do not rouse her, do not disturb my love
         until she is ready.[c]

Companions

5   Who is this coming up from the wilderness
         leaning on her beloved?

Bridegroom

           Under the apricot-trees I roused you,
      there where your mother was in labour with you,
      there where she who bore you was in labour.
6   Wear me as a seal upon your heart,
         as a seal upon your arm;
      for love is strong as death,
      passion cruel as the grave;
         it blazes up like blazing fire,
         fiercer than any flame.
7   Many waters cannot quench love,
         no flood can sweep it away;
      if a man were to offer for love
         the whole wealth of his house,
         it would be utterly scorned.

Companions

8   We have a little sister
      who has no breasts;

---

[a] *for you to embrace me: or* to teach me how to love you.   [b] *Prob. rdg.; Heb.* his.
[c] *until . . . ready: or* while she is resting.

> what shall we do for our sister
> when she is asked in marriage?
>> If she is a wall,   9
> we will build on it a silver parapet,
>> but [a] if she is a door,
> we will close it up with planks of cedar.

Bride

> I am a wall and my breasts are like towers;   10
> so in his eyes I am as one who brings contentment.
> Solomon has a vineyard at Baal-hamon;   11
>> he has let out his vineyard to guardians,
>> and each is to bring for its fruit
>>> a thousand pieces of silver.
>> But my vineyard is mine to give;   12
>> the thousand pieces are yours, O Solomon,
>> and the guardians of the fruit shall have two hundred.

Bridegroom

> My bride, you who sit in my garden,   13
> what is it that my friends [b] are listening to?
> Let me also hear your voice.

Bride

> Come into the open, my beloved,   14
> and show yourself like a gazelle or a young wild goat
> on the spice-bearing mountains.

[a] *Or* and.   [b] my garden ... friends: *prob. rdg.; Heb.* the gardens, friends.

THE BOOK OF THE PROPHET
ISAIAH

Judah arraigned

1 THE VISION RECEIVED BY ISAIAH son of Amoz concerning Judah and Jerusalem during the reigns of Uzziah, Jotham, Ahaz, and Hezekiah, kings of Judah.

2
　　Hark you heavens, and earth give ear,
　　　　for the LORD has spoken:
　　I have sons whom I reared and brought up,
　　　　but they have rebelled against me.

3
　　The ox knows its owner
　　　　and the ass its master's stall;
　　but Israel, my own people,
　　　　has no knowledge, no discernment.

4
　　O sinful nation, people loaded with iniquity,
　　race of evildoers, wanton destructive children
　　　　who have deserted the LORD,
　　　　　　spurned the Holy One of Israel
　　　　　　and turned your backs on him.

5
　　Where can you still be struck
　　　　if you will be disloyal still?
　　　　Your head is covered with sores,
　　　　　　your body diseased;

6
　　from head to foot there is not a sound spot in you—
　　nothing but bruises and weals and raw wounds
　　　　which have not felt compress or bandage
　　　　　　or soothing oil.

7
　　Your country is desolate, your cities lie in ashes.
　　Strangers devour your land before your eyes;
　　　　it is desolate as Sodom[a] in its overthrow.

8
　　　　Only Zion is left,
　　like a watchman's shelter in a vineyard,
　　a shed in a field of cucumbers,
　　　　a city well guarded.

9
　　If the LORD of Hosts had not left us a remnant,
　　　　we should soon have been like Sodom,
　　　　　　no better than Gomorrah.

---

[a] Sodom: prob. rdg.; Heb. strangers.

Hear the word of the LORD, you rulers of Sodom;   10
attend, you people of Gomorrah, to the instruction of our God:
   Your countless sacrifices, what are they to me?   11
     says the LORD.
   I am sated with whole-offerings of rams
     and the fat of buffaloes;
   I have no desire for the blood of bulls,
     of sheep and of he-goats.
   Whenever you come to enter my presence—   12-13
who asked you for this?
No more shall you trample my courts.
    The offer of your gifts is useless,
the reek of sacrifice is abhorrent to me.
New moons and sabbaths and assemblies,
sacred seasons and ceremonies, I cannot endure.
I cannot tolerate your new moons and your festivals;   14
   they have become a burden to me,
     and I can put up with them no longer.
    When you lift your hands outspread in prayer,   15
   I will hide my eyes from you.
   Though you offer countless prayers,
    I will not listen.
   There is blood on your hands;
    wash yourselves and be clean.   16
   Put away the evil of your deeds,
    away out of my sight.
Cease to do evil and learn to do right,   17
pursue justice and champion the oppressed;
give the orphan his rights, plead the widow's cause.

   Come now, let us argue it out,   18
    says the LORD.
   Though your sins are scarlet,
    they may become white as snow;
    though they are dyed crimson,
    they may yet be like wool.
   Obey with a will,   19
and you shall eat the best that earth yields;
    but, if you refuse and rebel,   20
    locust-beans shall be your only food.*a*
The LORD himself has spoken.

How the faithful city has played the whore,   21
once the home of justice where righteousness dwelt—
   but now murderers!
   Your silver has turned into base metal   22
   and your liquor is diluted with water.

a locust-beans . . . food: *or, with Scroll,* you shall be eaten by the sword.

23   Your very rulers are rebels, confederate with thieves;
          every man of them loves a bribe
             and itches for a gift;
             they do not give the orphan his rights,
         and the widow's cause never comes before them.

24   This therefore is the word of the Lord, the LORD of Hosts, the Mighty
One of Israel:

          Enough! I will secure a respite from my foes
             and take vengeance on my enemies.
25   Once again I will act against you
             to refine away your base metal as with potash
             and purge all your impurities;
26   I will again make your judges what once they were
             and your counsellors like those of old.
         Then at length you shall be called
             the home of righteousness, the faithful city.
27   Justice shall redeem Zion
              and righteousness her repentant people.
28   Rebels and sinners shall be broken together
             and those who forsake the LORD shall cease to be.
29   For the sacred oaks in which you delighted shall fail you,
           the garden-shrines of your fancy shall disappoint you.
30   You shall be like a terebinth whose leaves have withered,
           like a garden without water;
31   the strongest tree[a] shall become like tow,
          and what is made of it[b] shall go up in sparks,
         and the two shall burst into flames together
             with no one to quench them.

2   This is the word which Isaiah son of Amoz received in a vision concerning Judah and Jerusalem.

2[c]   In days to come
          the mountain of the LORD's house
       shall be set over all other mountains,
          lifted high above the hills.
       All the nations shall come streaming to it,
3   and many peoples shall come and say,
       'Come, let us climb up on to the mountain of the LORD,
         to the house of the God of Jacob,
          that he may teach us his ways
          and we may walk in his paths.'
       For instruction issues from Zion,
         and out of Jerusalem comes the word of the LORD;
4   he will be judge between nations,
       arbiter among many peoples.

---

        [a] *Or* the strong man.   [b] *Or* what he makes.
        [c] *Verses 2–4: cp. Mic. 4. 1–3.*

They shall beat their swords into mattocks
   and their spears into pruning-knives;[a]
nation shall not lift sword against nation
   nor ever again be trained for war.

   O people of Jacob, come,   5
   let us walk in the light of the LORD.
Thou hast abandoned thy people the house of Jacob;   6
   for they are crowded with traders[b]
and barbarians like the Philistines,
   and with the children of foreigners everywhere.
Their land is filled with silver and gold,   7
   and there is no end to their treasure;
their land is filled with horses,
   and there is no end to their chariots;
their land is filled with idols,   8
and they bow down to the work of their own hands,
to what their fingers have made.
Mankind shall be brought low,   9
all men shall be humbled;
and how can they raise themselves?[c]
Get you into the rocks and hide yourselves in the ground   10
from the dread of the LORD and the splendour of his majesty.
   Man's proud eyes shall be humbled,   11
     the loftiness of men brought low,
   and the LORD alone shall be exalted
     on that day.

   For the LORD of Hosts has a day of doom waiting   12
     for all that is proud and lofty,
     for all that is high and lifted up,
for all the cedars of Lebanon, lofty and high,   13
   and for all the oaks of Bashan,
for all lofty mountains and for all high hills,   14
for every high tower and for every sheer wall,   15
for all ships of Tarshish and all the dhows of Arabia.   16
   Then man's pride shall be brought low,   17
     and the loftiness of man shall be humbled,
   and the LORD alone shall be exalted
     on that day,
while the idols shall pass away utterly.   18
Get you into caves in the rocks   19
   and crevices in the ground
from the dread of the LORD and the splendour of his majesty,
   when he rises to inspire the earth with fear.
On that day a man shall fling away   20

---

[a] They shall beat . . . pruning-knives: *cp. Joel* 3. 9–12.   [b] *Or* hawkers.
[c] *Prob. rdg.; Heb.* and do not forgive them.

his idols of silver and his idols of gold
   which he has made for himself to worship;
he shall fling them to the dung-beetles and the bats,

21 and creep into clefts in the rocks and crannies in the cliffs
from the dread of the LORD and the splendour of his majesty,
   when he rises to inspire the earth with fear.

22 Have no more to do with man, for what is he worth?
   He is no more than the breath in his nostrils.

3   Be warned: the Lord, the LORD of Hosts,
   is stripping Jerusalem and Judah
     of every prop and stay,*a*

2   warrior and soldier,
judge and prophet, diviner and elder,

3   captains of companies and men of rank,
    counsellor, magician, and cunning enchanter.

4   Then I will appoint mere boys to be their captains,
   who shall govern as the fancy takes them;

5   the people shall deal harshly
each man with his fellow and with his neighbour;
   children shall break out against their elders,
    and nobodies against men of substance.

6   If a man takes hold of his brother in his father's house,
saying, 'You have a cloak, you shall be our chief;
   our stricken family shall be under you',

7   he will cry out that day and say,
    'I will not be your master;
   there is neither bread nor cloak in my house,
   and you shall not make me head of the clan.'

8   Jerusalem is stricken and Judah fallen
   because they have spoken and acted against the LORD,
    rebelling against the glance of his glorious eye.

9   The look on their faces testifies against them;
   like Sodom they proclaim their sins
    and do not conceal them.*b*
Woe upon them! they have earned their own disaster.

10   Happy*c* the righteous man! all goes well with him,
   for such men enjoy the fruit of their actions.

11   Woe betide the wicked! with him all goes ill,
   for he reaps the reward that he has earned.

12   Money-lenders strip my people bare,
   and usurers lord it over them.
   O my people! your guides lead you astray
    and confuse the path that you should take.

---

a Prob. rdg.; Heb. adds all stay of bread and all stay of water.   *b* like . . . them:
or and their sins, like those of Sodom, denounce them; they do not deny them.   *c Prob.*
rdg.; Heb. Say.

The LORD comes forward to argue his case   13
and stands to judge his people.
The LORD opens the indictment   14
against the elders of his people and their officers:
You have ravaged the vineyard,
    and the spoils of the poor are in your houses.
Is it nothing to you that you crush my people   15
    and grind the faces of the poor?
This is the very word of the Lord, the LORD of Hosts.

Then the LORD said: 16
Because the women of Zion hold themselves high
and walk with necks outstretched and wanton glances,
    moving with mincing gait
        and jingling feet,
the Lord will give the women of Zion bald heads,   17
the LORD will strip the hair from their foreheads.

In that day the Lord will take away all finery: anklets, discs, crescents,   18
pendants, bangles, coronets, head-bands, armlets, necklaces, lockets,   19 20
charms, signets, nose-rings, fine dresses, mantles, cloaks, flounced skirts, 21 22
scarves of gauze, kerchiefs of linen, turbans, and flowing veils.   23

So instead of perfume you shall have the stench of decay,   24
    and a rope in place of a girdle,
baldness instead of hair elegantly coiled,
a loin-cloth of sacking instead of a mantle,
    and branding instead of beauty.
Your men shall fall by the sword,   25
    and your warriors in battle;
then Zion's gates shall mourn and lament,   26
and she shall sit on the ground stripped bare.

Then on that day   **4**
seven women shall take hold of one man and say,
'We will eat our own bread and wear our own clothes
    if only we may be called by your name;
        take away our disgrace.'

On that day the plant that the LORD has grown   2
shall become glorious in its beauty,
and the fruit of the land shall be
    the pride and splendour
        of the survivors of Israel.

Then those who are left in Zion, who remain in Jerusalem, every one   3
enrolled in the book of life, shall be called holy. If the Lord washes away   4
the filth of the women of Zion and cleanses Jerusalem from the blood that
is in it by a spirit of judgement, a consuming spirit, then over every build-   5
ing on Mount Zion and on all her places of assembly the LORD will create
a cloud of smoke by day and a bright flame of fire by night; for glory shall

6 be spread over all as a covering and a canopy, a shade from the heat by
day, a refuge and a shelter from rain and tempest.

5
        I will sing for my beloved
           my love-song about his vineyard:
        My beloved had a vineyard
           high up on a fertile hill-side.

2
           He trenched it and cleared it of stones
           and planted it with red vines;
        he built a watch-tower in the middle
        and then hewed out a winepress in it.
        He looked for it to yield grapes,
           but it yielded wild grapes.

3
        Now, you who live in Jerusalem,
           and you men of Judah,
        judge between me and my vineyard.

4
        What more could have been done for my vineyard
        that I did not do in it?
      Why, when I looked for it to yield grapes,
        did it yield wild grapes?

5
        Now listen while I tell you
        what I will do to my vineyard:
      I will take away its fences and let it be burnt,
      I will break down its walls and let it be trampled underfoot,

6
           and so I will leave it derelict;
        it shall be neither pruned nor hoed,
        but shall grow thorns and briars.
           Then I will command the clouds
        to send no more rain upon it.

7
    The vineyard of the LORD of Hosts is Israel,
        and the men of Judah are the plant he cherished.
    He looked for justice and found it denied,
        for righteousness but heard cries of distress.

8
    Shame on you! you who add house to house
        and join field to field,
        until not an acre remains,
    and you are left to dwell alone in the land.

9
    The LORD of Hosts has sworn[a] in my hearing:
    Many houses shall go to ruin,
    fine large houses shall be uninhabited.

10
    Five acres of vineyard shall yield only a gallon,
    and ten bushels of seed return only a peck.

11
    Shame on you! you who rise early in the morning
        to go in pursuit of liquor
    and draw out the evening inflamed with wine,

12
        at whose feasts there are harp and lute,
        tabor and pipe and wine,

           [a] has sworn: *prob. rdg.; Heb. om.*

who have no eyes for the work of the LORD,
    and never see the things that he has done.
Therefore my people are dwindling away   13
    all unawares;
    the nobles are starving to death,
and the common folk die of thirst.
Therefore Sheol gapes with straining throat   14
    and has opened her measureless jaws:
    down go nobility and common people,
    their noisy bustling mob.*a*
Mankind is brought low, men are humbled,   15
    humbled are haughty looks.
But the LORD of Hosts sits high in judgement,   16
and by righteousness the holy God shows himself holy.
Young rams shall feed where fat bullocks once pastured,   17
and kids shall graze broad acres where cattle grew fat.*b*
Shame on you! you who drag wickedness along like a tethered sheep 18
    and sin like a heifer on a rope,
    who say, 'Let the LORD make haste,   19
    let him speed up his work for us to see it,
    let the purpose of the Holy One of Israel
    be soon fulfilled, so that we may know it.'
Shame on you! you who call evil good and good evil,   20
who turn darkness into light and light into darkness,
who make bitter sweet and sweet bitter.
    Shame on you! you who are wise in your own eyes   21
        and prudent in your own esteem.
Shame on you! you mighty topers, valiant mixers of drink,   22
    who for a bribe acquit the guilty   23
    and deny justice to those in the right.

So he will hoist a signal to a nation far away,   26*c*
    he will whistle to call them from the end of the earth;
    and see, they come, speedy and swift;
    none is weary, not one of them stumbles,   27
        not one slumbers or sleeps.
None has his belt loose about his waist
    or a broken thong to his sandals.
Their arrows are sharpened and their bows all strung,   28
    their horses' hooves flash like shooting stars,
    their chariot-wheels are like the whirlwind.
Their growling is the growling of a lioness,   29
    they growl like young lions,
which roar as they seize the prey
    and carry it beyond reach of rescue.

---

a nobility . . . mob: *or* nobility, common people and noisy mob, and are restless there.
b Young . . . grew fat: *prob. rdg.; Heb. unintelligible.*   *c Verses 24 and 25 transposed to follow 10. 4.*

30
> They shall roar over it on that day
>> like the roaring of the sea.
> If a man looks over the earth, behold, darkness closing in,
>> and the light darkened on the hill-tops*a* !

The call of Isaiah

6
2 I N THE YEAR OF KING UZZIAH'S DEATH I saw the Lord seated on a throne, high and exalted, and the skirt of his robe filled the temple. About him were attendant seraphim, and each had six wings; one pair covered

3 his face and one pair his feet, and one pair was spread in flight. They were calling ceaselessly to one another,

> Holy, holy, holy is the LORD of Hosts:
>> the whole earth is full of his glory.

4 And, as each one called, the threshold shook to its foundations, while the
5 house was filled with smoke. Then I cried,

> Woe is me! I am lost,
>> for I am a man of unclean lips
>> and I dwell among a people of unclean lips;
> yet with these eyes I have seen the King, the LORD of Hosts.

6 Then one of the seraphim flew to me carrying in his hand a glowing coal
7 which he had taken from the altar with a pair of tongs. He touched my mouth with it and said,

> See, this has touched your lips;
>> your iniquity is removed,
>> and your sin is wiped away.

8 Then I heard the Lord saying, Whom shall I send? Who will go for me?
9 And I answered, Here am I; send me. He said, Go and tell this people:

> You may listen and listen, but you will not understand.*b*
> You may look and look again, but you will never know.*c*
10 > This people's wits are dulled,
>> their ears are deafened and their eyes blinded,
>>> so that they cannot see with their eyes
>>> nor listen with their ears
>>> nor understand with their wits,
>> so that they may turn and be healed.

11 Then I asked, How long, O Lord? And he answered,

> Until cities fall in ruins and are deserted,
>> houses are left without people,
> and the land goes to ruin and lies waste,
12 >> until the LORD has sent all mankind far away,
>> and the whole country is one vast desolation.

a hill-tops: *or* clouds.   *b* *Or* but how will you understand?   *c* *Or* but how will you know?

Even if a tenth part of its people remain there,   13
they too will be exterminated
[like an oak or a terebinth,
a sacred pole thrown out from its place in a hill-shrine*a*].

Prophecies during the Syro-Ephraimite war

WHILE AHAZ SON OF JOTHAM and grandson of Uzziah was king of   7
Judah, Rezin king of Aram with Pekah son of Remaliah, king of
Israel, marched on Jerusalem, but could not force a battle. When the house   2
of David heard that the Aramaeans had come to terms with the Ephraimites,
king and people were shaken like forest trees in the wind. Then the LORD   3
said to Isaiah, Go out with your son Shear-jashub*b* to meet Ahaz at the
end of the conduit of the Upper Pool by the causeway leading to the Fuller's
Field, and say to him, Be on your guard, keep calm; do not be frightened   4
or unmanned by these two smouldering stumps of firewood, because Rezin
and his Aramaeans with Remaliah's son are burning with rage. The   5
Aramaeans with Ephraim and Remaliah's son have laid their plans against
you, saying, Let us invade Judah and break her spirit;*c* let us make her   6
join with us, and set the son of Tabeal on the throne. Therefore the Lord   7
GOD has said:

> This shall not happen now, and never shall,
> for all that the chief city of Aram is Damascus,   8
> and Rezin is the chief of Damascus;
> within sixty-five years
> Ephraim shall cease to be a nation,
> for all that Samaria is the chief city of Ephraim,   9
> and Remaliah's son the chief of Samaria.

Have firm faith, or you will not stand firm.

Once again the LORD spoke to Ahaz and said, Ask the LORD your God   10 11
for a sign, from lowest Sheol or from highest heaven. But Ahaz said, No,   12
I will not put the LORD to the test by asking for a sign. Then the answer   13
came: Listen, house of David. Are you not content to wear out men's
patience? Must you also wear out the patience of my God? Therefore the   14
Lord himself shall give you a sign: A young woman is with child, and she
will bear a son, and will*d* call him Immanuel.*e* By the time that he has learnt   15
to reject evil and choose good, he will be eating curds and honey;*f* before   16
that child has learnt to reject evil and choose good, desolation will come
upon the land before whose two kings you cower now. The LORD will bring   17
on you, your people, and your house, a time the like of which has not been
seen since Ephraim broke away from Judah.*g*

On that day the LORD will whistle for the fly from the distant streams of   18
Egypt and for the bee from Assyria. They shall all come and settle in the   19

---

a a sacred pole . . . hill-shrine: *prob. rdg.; Heb. obscure.*   *b* *That is* A remnant
shall return.   *c* *Or* and parley with her.   *d* *Or* you will.   *e* *That is* God
is with us.   *f* he will . . . honey: *or* curds and honey will be eaten.   *g* *Prob. rdg.;*
Heb. adds the king of Assyria.

precipitous ravines and in the clefts of the rock; camel-thorn and stink-
20 wood shall be black with them. On that day the Lord shall shave the head
and body with a razor hired on the banks of the Euphrates,[a] and it shall
21 remove the beard as well. On that day a man shall save alive a young cow
22 and two ewes; and he shall get so much milk that he eats curds; for all who
23 are left in the land shall eat curds and honey. On that day every place where
there used to be a thousand vines worth a thousand pieces of silver shall be
24 given over to thorns and briars. A man shall go there only to hunt with bow
25 and arrows, for thorns and briars cover the whole land; and no one who
fears thorns and briars shall set foot on any of those hills once worked with
the hoe. Oxen shall be turned loose on them, and sheep shall trample them.

8 The LORD said to me, Take a large tablet and write on it in common
2 writing,[b] Maher-shalal-hash-baz;[c] and fetch Uriah the priest and Zech-
3 ariah son of Jeberechiah for me as trustworthy witnesses. Then I lay with
the prophetess, and she conceived and bore a son; and the LORD said to
4 me, Call him Maher-shalal-hash-baz. Before the boy can say Father or
Mother, the wealth of Damascus and the spoils of Samaria shall be carried
off and presented to the king of Assyria.

5 Once again the LORD said to me:

6 Because this nation has rejected
the waters of Shiloah, which run so softly and gently,[d]
7 therefore the Lord will bring up against it
the strong, flooding waters of the Euphrates,
the king of Assyria and all his glory;
it shall run up all its channels
and overflow all its banks;
8 it shall sweep through Judah in a flood,
pouring over it and rising shoulder-high.
The whole expanse of the land shall be filled,
so wide he spreads his wings; for God is with us.[e]
9 Take note, you nations, and be dismayed.
Listen, all you distant parts of the earth:
you may arm yourselves but will be dismayed;
you may arm yourselves but will be dismayed.
10 Make your plans, but they will be foiled,
propose what you please, but it shall not stand;
for God is with us.[e]

11 These were the words of the LORD to me, for his hand was strong
upon me; and he warned me not to follow[f] the ways of this people:
12 You shall not say 'too hard' of everything that this people calls hard;
13 you shall neither dread nor fear that which they fear. It is the LORD of
Hosts whom you must count 'hard';[g] he it is whom you must fear and
14 dread. He shall become your 'hardship',[g] a boulder and a rock which

[a] *Prob. rdg.; Heb. adds* with the king of Assyria.   [b] in common writing: *or* with
an ordinary stylus.   [c] *That is* Speed-spoil-hasten-plunder.   [d] *Prob. rdg.; Heb.
adds* Rezin and the son of Remaliah.   [e] God is with us: *Heb.* Immanuel.
[f] *Or* and he turned me from following . . .   [g] 'hard' *and* 'hardship': *prob. rdg.;
Heb. unintelligible in this context.*

the two houses of Israel shall run against and over which they shall
stumble, a trap and a snare to those who live in Jerusalem; and many shall   15
stumble over them, many shall fall and be broken, many shall be snared
and caught.

> Fasten up the message,   16
>   seal the oracle with my teaching;*a*
>   and I will wait for the LORD   17
>   who hides his face from the house of Jacob;
>   I will watch for him.
> See, I and the sons whom the LORD has given me   18
>   are to be signs and portents in Israel,
> sent by the LORD of Hosts who dwells on Mount Zion.
>   But men will say to you,   19
>   'Seek guidance of ghosts and familiar spirits
>   who squeak and gibber;
>   a nation may surely seek guidance of its gods,
>   of the dead on behalf of the living,
>   for an oracle or a message?'   20
> They will surely say some such thing as this;
>   but what they say is futile.
> So despondency and fear will come over them,   21
>   and then, when they are afraid and fearful,
>   they will turn against their king and their gods.
> Then, whether they turn their gaze upwards or look down,   22
>   everywhere is distress and darkness inescapable,
>   constraint and gloom that cannot be avoided;
> for there is no escape for an oppressed people.   **9**

For, while the first invader has dealt lightly with the land of Zebulun
and the land of Naphtali, the second has dealt heavily with Galilee of the
Nations on the road beyond Jordan to the sea.

> The people who walked in darkness   2
>   have seen a great light:
>   light has dawned upon them,
>   dwellers in a land as dark as death.
> Thou hast increased their joy and*b* given them great gladness;   3
> they rejoice in thy presence as men rejoice at harvest,
> or as they are glad when they share out the spoil;
>   for thou hast shattered the yoke that burdened them,   4
>   the collar that lay heavy on their shoulders,
>   the driver's goad, as on the day of Midian's defeat.
>   All the boots of trampling soldiers   5
>   and the garments fouled with blood
> shall become a burning mass, fuel for fire.
>   For a boy has been born for us, a son given to us   6
>   to bear the symbol of dominion on his shoulder;

---

a *Or* among my disciples.   *b* their joy and: *prob. rdg.; Heb.* the nation, not.

and he shall be called
in purpose wonderful, in battle God-like,
Father for all time,[a] Prince of peace.

7   Great shall the dominion be,
and boundless the peace
bestowed on David's throne and on his kingdom,
to establish it and sustain it
with justice and righteousness
from now and for evermore.
The zeal of the LORD of Hosts shall do this.

Prophecies addressed to Israel

8   The Lord has sent forth his word against Jacob
and it shall fall on Israel;
9   all the people shall be humbled,
Ephraim and the dwellers in Samaria,
though in their pride and arrogance they say,
10   The bricks are fallen, but we will build in hewn stone;
the sycomores are hacked down,
but we will use cedars instead.
11   The LORD has raised their foes[b] high against them
and spurred on their enemies,
12   Aramaeans from the east and Philistines from the west,
and they have swallowed Israel in one mouthful.
For all this his anger has not turned back,
and his hand is stretched out still.
13   Yet the people did not come back to him who struck them,
or seek guidance of the LORD of Hosts;
14   therefore on one day the LORD cut off from Israel
head and tail, palm and reed.[c]
16   This people's guides have led them astray;
those who should have been guided are in confusion.
17   Therefore the Lord showed no mercy to their young men,
no tenderness to their orphans and widows;
all were godless and evildoers,
every one speaking profanity.
For all this his anger has not turned back,
and his hand is stretched out still.

18   Wicked men have been set ablaze like a fire
fed with briars and thorns,
kindled in the forest thickets;
they are wrapped in a murky pall of smoke.

---

[a] *Or* of a wide realm.   [b] their foes: *prob. rdg.; Heb.* the foes of Rezin.
[c] *Prob. rdg.; Heb. adds* (15) The aged and honoured are the head, and the prophet who
gives false instruction is the tail.

The land is scorched by the fury of the LORD of Hosts,   19
    and the people have become fuel for the fire.^a
On the right, one man eats his fill but yet is hungry;   20
    on the left, another devours but is not satisfied;
    each feeds on his own children's flesh,
    and neither spares his own brother.^b
    ^c For all this his anger has not turned back,   21
    and his hand is stretched out still.

Shame on you! you who make unjust laws   **10**
    and publish burdensome decrees,
    depriving the poor of justice,   2
    robbing the weakest of my people of their rights,
despoiling the widow and plundering the orphan.
    What will you do when called to account,   3
    when ruin from afar confronts you?
    To whom will you flee for help
    and where will you leave your children,
    so that they do not cower before the gaoler   4
        or fall by the executioner's hand?
    For all this his anger has not turned back,
    and his hand is stretched out still.

So, as tongues of fire lick up the stubble   [24^d]
    and the heat of the flame dies down,
    their root shall moulder away,
    and their shoots vanish like dust;
for they have spurned the instruction of the LORD of Hosts
and have rejected the word of the Holy One of Israel.
So the anger of the LORD is roused against his people,   [25^d]
he has stretched out his hand against them and struck them down;
        the mountains trembled,
    and their corpses lay like offal in the streets.
    For all this his anger has not turned back,
    and his hand is stretched out still.

The Assyrian! He is the rod that I wield in my anger,   5
    and the staff of my wrath is in his hand.^e
I send him against a godless nation,   6
    I bid him march against a people who rouse my wrath,
to spoil and plunder at will
    and trample them down like mud in the streets.
    But this man's purpose is lawless,   7
    lawless are the plans in his mind;

---

^a *See note on verse 20.*   ^b *and neither ... brother: transposed from end of verse 19.*
^c *Prob. rdg.; Heb. prefixes* Manasseh devours Ephraim, and Ephraim Manasseh; *together they are against Judah.*   ^d *These are verses 24 and 25 of ch. 5, transposed to this point.*   ^e *and ... hand: prob. rdg.; Heb. obscure.*

for his thought is only to destroy
and to wipe out nation after nation.
8 'Are not my officers all kings?' he says;
9 'see how Calno has suffered the fate of Carchemish.
Is not Hamath like Arpad, and Samaria like Damascus?
10 Before now I have found kingdoms full of idols,
with more images than Jerusalem and Samaria,
11 and now, what I have done to Samaria and her worthless gods,
I will do also to Jerusalem and her idols.'

12 When the Lord has finished all that he means to do on Mount Zion and
in Jerusalem, he will punish the king of Assyria for this fruit of his pride
13 and for his arrogance and vainglory, because he said:

By my own might I have acted
and in my own wisdom I have laid my schemes;
I have removed the frontiers of nations
and plundered their treasures,
like a bull I have trampled on their inhabitants.
14 My hand has found its way to the wealth of nations,
and, as a man takes the eggs from a deserted nest,
so have I taken every land;
not a wing fluttered,
not a beak gaped, no chirp was heard.

15 Shall the axe set itself up against the hewer,
or the saw claim mastery over the sawyer,
as if a stick were to brandish him who wields it,
or a staff of wood to wield one who is not wood?

16 Therefore the Lord, the LORD of Hosts, will send disease
on his sturdy frame, from head to toe,[a]
and within his flesh[b] a fever like fire shall burn.
17 The light of Israel shall become a fire
and his Holy One a flame,
which in one day shall burn up and consume
his thorns and his briars;
18 the glory of forest and meadow shall be destroyed
as when a man falls in a fit;
19 and the remnant of trees in the forest shall be so few
that a child may count them one by one.

20 On that day the remnant of Israel, the survivors of Jacob, shall cease to
lean on him that proved their destroyer, but shall loyally lean on the LORD,
the Holy One of Israel.

21 A remnant shall turn again, a remnant of Jacob,
to God their champion.

[a] from . . . toe: *transposed from verse 18.*   [b] within his flesh: *or* in his strong
body.

Your people, Israel, may be many as the sands of the sea,   22
    but only a remnant shall turn again,
  the instrument of final destruction,
    justice in full flood;^a — *rendered* justice in full flood;<i>a</i>

for the Lord, the LORD of Hosts, will bring final destruction   23
  upon all the earth.

Therefore these are the words of the Lord, the LORD of Hosts: My   24
people who live in Zion, you must not be afraid of the Assyrians, though
they beat you with their rod and lift their staff against you as the Egyptians
did; for soon, very soon, my anger will come to an end, and my wrath will   25
all be spent.[b] Then the LORD of Hosts will brandish his whip over them as   26
he did when he struck Midian at the Rock of Oreb, and will lift his staff
against the River as he did against Egypt.

On that day   27
  the burden they laid on your shoulder shall be removed
  and their yoke shall be broken from your neck.
An invader from Rimmon[c] has come to Aiath,   28
    has passed by Migron,
  and left his baggage-train at Michmash;
    he has passed by Maabarah   29
  and camped for the night at Geba.
Ramah is anxious, Gibeah of Saul is in panic.
  Raise a shrill cry, Bath-gallim;   30
hear it, Laish, and answer her, Anathoth:
'Madmenah is in flight; take refuge, people of Gebim.'   31
Today he is due to pitch his camp in Nob;   32
  he gives the signal to advance
against the mount of the daughter of Zion,
  the hill of Jerusalem.

Look, the Lord, the LORD of Hosts,   33
cleaves the trees with a flash of lightning,
the tallest are hewn down, the lofty laid low,
  the heart of the forest is felled with the axe,   34
  and Lebanon with its noble trees has fallen.
Then a shoot shall grow from the stock of Jesse,   **11**
  and a branch shall spring from his roots.
The spirit of the LORD shall rest upon him,   2
  a spirit of wisdom and understanding,
  a spirit of counsel[d] and power,
  a spirit of knowledge and the fear of the LORD.[e]
He shall not judge by what he sees   3
  nor decide by what he hears;

---

[a] the instrument . . . flood: *or* wasting with sickness, yet overflowing with righteousness.
[b] will . . . spent: *prob. rdg.; Heb. obscure.*   [c] and their yoke . . . Rimmon: *prob. rdg.; Heb.* and their yoke from upon your neck, and a yoke shall be broken because of oil. He . . .   [d] *Or* force.   [e] *Prob. rdg.; Heb. adds* and his delight shall be in the fear of the LORD.

4   he shall judge the poor with justice
         and defend the humble in the land with equity;
         his mouth shall be a rod to strike down the ruthless, [a]
         and with a word he shall slay the wicked.

5   Round his waist he shall wear the belt of justice,
         and good faith shall be the girdle round his body.

6   Then the wolf shall live with the sheep,
         and the leopard lie down with the kid;
    the calf and the young lion shall grow up together,
    and a little child shall lead them;

7   the cow and the bear shall be friends,
         and their young shall lie down together.
    The lion shall eat straw like cattle;

8   the infant shall play over the hole of the cobra,
    and the young child dance over the viper's nest.

9   They shall not hurt or destroy in all my holy mountain;
         for as the waters fill the sea,
    so shall the land be filled with the knowledge of the LORD.

10   On that day a scion from the root of Jesse
         shall be set up as a signal to the peoples;
         the nations shall rally to it,
         and its resting-place shall be glorious.

11   On that day the Lord will make his power more glorious by recovering
    the remnant of his people, those who are still left, from Assyria and Egypt,
    from Pathros, from Cush and Elam, from Shinar, Hamath and the islands
    of the sea.

12   Then he will raise a signal to the nations
         and gather together those driven out of Israel;
         he will assemble Judah's scattered people
         from the four corners of the earth.

13   Ephraim's jealousy shall vanish,
         and Judah's enmity shall be done away.
    Ephraim shall not be jealous of Judah,
    nor Judah the enemy of Ephraim.

14   They shall swoop down on the Philistine flank in the west
         and together they shall plunder the tribes of the east;
         Edom and Moab shall be within their grasp,
         and Ammon shall obey them.

15   The LORD will divide the tongue of the Egyptian sea
         and wave his hand over the River
         to bring a scorching wind;
         he shall split it into seven channels
         and let men go across dry-shod.

16   So there shall be a causeway for the remnant of his people,
         for the remnant rescued from Assyria,
    as there was for Israel when they came up out of Egypt.

         [a] *Prob. rdg.; Heb.* land.

824

You shall say on that day: **12**
    I will praise thee, O LORD,
      though thou hast been angry with me;
      thy anger has turned back,
      and thou hast comforted me.
God is indeed my deliverer. 2
    I am confident and unafraid;
for the LORD is my refuge and defence
    and has shown himself my deliverer.
And so you shall draw water with joy 3
    from the springs of deliverance.

You shall all say on that day: 4
Give thanks to the LORD and invoke him by name,
    make his deeds known in the world around;
    declare that his name is supreme.
Sing psalms to the LORD, for he has triumphed, 5
    and this must be made known in all the world.
Cry out, shout aloud, you that dwell in Zion, 6
for the Holy One of Israel is among you in majesty.

Prophecies relating to foreign nations

BABYLON: AN ORACLE which Isaiah son of Amoz received in a **13**
vision.

Raise the standard on a windy height, 2
roar out your summons,
    beckon with arm upraised to the advance,
    draw your swords, you nobles.
I have given my warriors their orders 3
and summoned my fighting men to launch my anger;
    they are eager for my triumph.
Hark, a tumult in the mountains, the sound of a vast multitude; 4
hark, the roar of kingdoms, of nations gathering!
The LORD of Hosts is mustering a host for war,
men from a far country, from beyond the horizon. 5
    It is the LORD with the weapons of his wrath
    coming to lay the whole land waste.
Howl, for the Day of the LORD is at hand; 6
it comes, a mighty blow from Almighty God.
Thereat shall every hand hang limp, 7
    every man's courage shall melt away,
    his stomach hollow with fear; 8
anguish shall grip them, like a woman in labour.
    One man shall look aghast at another,
    and their faces shall burn with shame.
    The Day of the LORD is coming indeed, 9
    that cruel day of wrath and fury,

to make the land a desolation
and exterminate its wicked people.

10   The stars of heaven in their constellations shall give no light,
the sun shall be darkened at its rising,
and the moon refuse to shine.

11   I will bring disaster upon the world
and their due punishment upon the wicked.
I will check the pride of the haughty
and bring low the arrogance of ruthless men.

12   I will make men scarcer than fine gold,
rarer than gold of Ophir.

13   Then the heavens shall shudder,[a]
and the earth shall be shaken from its place
at the fury of the LORD of Hosts, on the day of his anger.

14   Then, like a gazelle before the hunter
or a flock with no man to round it up,
each man will go back to his own people,
every one will flee to his own land.

15   All who are found will be stabbed,
all who are taken will fall by the sword;

16   their infants will be dashed to the ground before their eyes,
their houses rifled and their wives ravished.

17   I will stir up against them the Medes,
who care nothing for silver and are not tempted by gold,[b]

18   who have no pity on little children
and spare no mother's son;

19   and Babylon, fairest of kingdoms,
proud beauty of the Chaldaeans,
shall be like Sodom and Gomorrah
when God overthrew them.

20   Never again shall she be inhabited,
no man shall dwell in her through all the ages;
there no Arab shall pitch his tent,
no shepherds fold their flocks.

21   There marmots shall have their lairs,
and porcupines shall overrun her houses;
there desert owls shall dwell,
and there he-goats shall gambol;

22   jackals shall occupy her mansions,[c]
and wolves her gorgeous palaces.
Her time draws very near,
and her days have not long to run.

14   The LORD will show compassion for Jacob and will once again make
Israel his choice. He will settle them on their own soil, and strangers will
2   come to join them and attach themselves to Jacob. Many nations shall

---

[a] *Prob. rdg.; Heb.* Then I will make the heavens shudder.   [b] *Prob. rdg.; Heb.*
adds bows shall dash young men to the ground.   [c] *Prob. rdg.; Heb.* her widows.

escort Israel to her place, and she shall employ them as slaves and slave-
girls on the land of the LORD; she shall take her captors captive and rule
over her task-masters.

When the LORD gives you relief from your pain and your fears and from   3
the cruel slavery laid upon you, you will take up this song of derision over   4
the king of Babylon:

See how the oppressor has met his end and his frenzy ceased!
The LORD has broken the rod of the wicked,   5
   the sceptre of the ruler
     who struck down peoples in his rage   6
      with unerring blows,
   who crushed nations in anger
   and persecuted them unceasingly.
The whole world has rest and is at peace;   7
   it breaks into cries of joy.
The pines themselves and the cedars of Lebanon exult over you: 8
   Since you have been laid low, they say,
   no man comes up to fell us.

Sheol below was all astir   9
   to meet you at your coming;
she roused the ancient dead to meet you,
   all who had been leaders on earth;
   she made all who had been kings of the nations
   rise from their thrones.
One and all they greet you with these words: 10
So you too are weak as we are,
   and have become one of us!
Your pride and all the music of your lutes   11
   have been brought down to Sheol;*a*
maggots are the pallet beneath you,
   and worms your coverlet.

How you have fallen from heaven, bright morning star,   12
felled to the earth, sprawling helpless across the nations!
You thought in your own mind,   13
   I will scale the heavens;
I will set my throne high above the stars of God,
   I will sit on the mountain where the gods meet
   in the far recesses of the north.
I will rise high above the cloud-banks   14
   and make myself like the Most High.
Yet you shall be brought down to Sheol,   15
   to the depths of the abyss.
Those who see you will stare at you,   16
   they will look at you and ponder:

a Or Your pride has been brought down to Sheol to the crowding throng of your
dead.

Is this, they will say, the man who shook the earth,
    who made kingdoms quake,
17 who turned the world into a desert
    and laid its cities in ruins,
who never let his prisoners go free to their homes,
18   the kings of every land?
Now they lie all of them in honour,
    each in his last home.
19 But you have been flung out unburied,
    mere loathsome carrion,
a companion to the slain pierced by the sword
who have gone down to the stony abyss.
    And you, a corpse trampled underfoot,
20 shall not share burial with them,
for you have ruined your land and slaughtered your people.
Such a brood of evildoers shall never be seen again.
21 Make the shambles ready for his sons
    butchered for their fathers' sin;
they shall not rise up and possess the world
nor cover the face of the earth with cities.

22   I will rise against them, says the LORD of Hosts; I will destroy the name
of Babylon and what remains of her, her offspring and posterity, says the
23 LORD; I will make her a haunt of the bustard, a waste of fen, and sweep
her with the besom of destruction. This is the very word of the LORD of
Hosts.

24   The LORD of Hosts has sworn:
In very truth, as I planned, so shall it be;
    as I designed, so shall it fall out:
25 I will break the Assyrian in my own land
    and trample him underfoot upon my mountains;
his yoke shall be lifted from you,
    his burden taken from your shoulders.
26 This is the plan prepared for the whole earth,
this the hand stretched out over all the nations.
27   For the LORD of Hosts has prepared his plan:
    who shall frustrate it?
His is the hand stretched out, and who shall turn it back?

28   In the year that King Ahaz died this oracle came from God:

29   Let none of you rejoice, you Philistines,
    because the rod that chastised you is broken;
for a viper shall be born of a snake as a plant from the root,
    and its fruit shall be a flying serpent.
30 But the poor shall graze their flocks in my meadows,
    and the destitute shall lie down in peace;
but the offspring of your roots I will kill by starvation,
    and put the remnant of you to death.

Howl in the gate, cry for help in the city,　　　31
　　let all Philistia be in turmoil;
　　for a great enemy is coming from the north,
　　　　not a man straying from his ranks.
What answer is there for the envoys of the nation?　　　32
This, that the LORD has fixed Zion in her place,
　　and the afflicted among his people shall take refuge there.

Moab: an oracle.　　　**15**

On the night when Ar is sacked, Moab meets her doom;
on the night when Kir is sacked, Moab meets her doom.
The people of Dibon go up*a* to the hill-shrines to weep;　　　2
Moab howls over Nebo and over Medeba.
The hair is torn from every head, and every beard shaved off.
　　In the streets men go clothed with sackcloth,　　　3
　　　　they cry out on the roofs;
　　in the public squares every man howls,
　　　　weeping as he goes through them.
　　Heshbon and Elealeh cry for help,　　　4
　　　　their voices are heard as far as Jahaz.
　　Thus Moab's stoutest warriors become cowards,
　　　　and her courage ebbs away.
　　My heart cries out for Moab,　　　5
　　　　whose nobles have fled*b* as far as Zoar.*c*
On the ascent to Luhith men go up weeping;
on the road to Horonaim there are cries of 'Disaster!'
The waters of Nimrim are desolate indeed;　　　6
the grass is parched, the herbage dead,
　　　　not a green thing is left;
and so the people carry off across the gorge of the Arabim　　　7
　　　　their hard-earned wealth and all their savings.
The cry for help echoes round the frontiers of Moab,　　　8
their howling reaches Eglaim and Beer-elim.
　　The waters of Dimon already run with blood;　　　9
　　yet I have more troubles in store for Dimon,
　　　　for I have a vision*d* of the survivors of Moab,
　　　　of the remnant of Admah.
The rulers of the country send a present of lambs　　　**16**
　　　　from Sela in the wilderness
　　　　to the hill of the daughter of Zion;
the daughters of Moab at the fords of the Arnon　　　2
shall be like fluttering birds, like scattered nestlings.
'Take up our cause with all your might;　　　3
let your shadow shield us at high noon, dark as night.

---

a The people . . . go up: *prob. rdg.; Heb.* He has gone up to the house and Dibon.
b have fled: *prob. rdg.; Heb. om.*　　*c* *Prob. rdg.; Heb. adds* Eglath Shelishiya.
d I have a vision: *prob. rdg.; Heb.* a lion.

Shelter the homeless, do not betray the fugitive;
4   let the homeless people of Moab find refuge with you;
hide them from the despoiler.'

When extortion has done its work and the looting is over,
    when the heel of the oppressor has vanished from the land,
5   a throne shall be set up in mutual trust in David's tent,
    and on it there shall sit a true judge,
one who seeks justice and is swift to do right.

6   We have heard tell of Moab's pride, how great it is,
    we have heard of his pride, his overweening pride;
      his talk is full of lies.
7   For this all Moab shall howl;
    Moab shall howl indeed;
he *a* shall mourn for the prosperous farmers of Kir-hareseth,
    utterly ruined;
8   the orchards of Heshbon,
    the vines of Sibmah languish,
though their red grapes once laid low the lords of the nations,
    though they reached as far as Jazer
    and trailed out to the wilderness,
though their branches spread abroad and crossed the sea.
9   Therefore I will weep for Sibmah's vines as I weep for Jazer.
I will drench you with my tears, Heshbon and Elealeh;
    for over your summer-fruits and your harvest
    the shouts of the harvesters are ended.
10   Joy and gladness shall be banished from the meadows,
no more shall men shout and sing in the vineyards,
    no more shall they tread wine in the winepresses;
    I have silenced the shouting of the harvesters.
11   Therefore my heart throbs
    like a harp for Moab,
    and my very soul for Kir-hareseth. *b*
12   When Moab comes to worship
    and wearies himself at the hill-shrines,
    when he enters his sanctuary to pray,
    he will gain nothing.

13 14   These are the words which the Lord spoke long ago about Moab; and
now he says, In three years, as a hired labourer counts them off, the glory
of Moab shall become contemptible for all his vast numbers; a handful
shall be left and those of no account.

17   Damascus: an oracle.

Damascus shall be a city no longer,
    she shall be but a heap of ruins.

        a Prob. rdg.; Heb. you.   *b Prob. rdg.; Heb.* Kir-hares.

For ever desolate, flocks shall have her for their own,   2
    and lie there undisturbed.
No longer shall Ephraim boast a fortified city,   3
    or Damascus a kingdom;
the remnant of Aram and the glory of Israel, their fate is one.
This is the very word of the Lord of Hosts.

On that day Jacob's weight shall dwindle   4
    and the fat on his limbs waste away,
as when the harvester gathers up the standing corn   5
    and reaps the ears in armfuls,
or as when a man gleans the ears in the Vale of Rephaim,
    or as when one beats an olive-tree   6
    and only gleanings are left on it,
two or three berries on the top of a branch,
    four or five on the boughs of the fruiting tree.
This is the very word of the Lord the God of Israel.

On that day men shall look to their Maker and turn their eyes to the   7
Holy One of Israel; they shall not look to the altars made by their own   8
hands nor to anything that their fingers have made, sacred poles or incense-
altars.
On that day their strong cities shall be deserted like the cities of the   9
Hivites and the Amorites, which they abandoned when Israel came in;
all shall be desolate.

For you forgot the God who delivered you,   10
    and did not remember the rock, your stronghold.
Plant then, if you will, your gardens in honour of Adonis,
    strike your cuttings for a foreign god;
protect your gardens on the day you plant them,   11
    and next day make the seed sprout.
But the crop will be scorched when wasting disease comes
    in the day of incurable pain.

Listen! it is the thunder of many peoples,   12
they thunder with the thunder of the sea.
Listen! it is the roar of nations
roaring with the roar of mighty waters.
When he rebukes them, away they fly,   13
driven like chaff on the hills before the wind,
    like thistledown before the storm.
At evening all is confusion,   14
    and before morning they are gone.
Such is the fate of our plunderers,
    the lot of those who despoil us.

There is a land of sailing ships,   **18**
a land beyond the rivers of Cush
which sends its envoys by the Nile,   2
journeying on the waters in vessels of reed.

> Go, swift messengers,
>> go to a people tall and smooth-skinned,
>> to a people dreaded near and far,
>> a nation strong and proud,
>> whose land is scoured by rivers.

3   All you who dwell in the world, inhabitants of earth,
> shall see when the signal is hoisted on the mountains
>> and shall hear when the trumpet sounds.

4 These were the words of the LORD to me:

> From my dwelling-place I will look quietly down
>> when the heat shimmers in the summer sun,
>> when the dew is heavy at harvest time.

5   Before the vintage, when the budding is over
> and the flower ripens into a berry,
>> the shoots shall be cut down with knives,
>> the branches struck off and cleared away.

6   All shall be left to birds of prey on the hills
>> and to beasts of the earth;
>> in summer the birds shall make their home there,
> in winter every beast of the earth.

7   At that time tribute shall be brought to the LORD of Hosts from a people tall and smooth-skinned, dreaded near and far, a nation strong and proud, whose land is scoured by rivers. They shall bring it to Mount Zion, the place where men invoke the name of the LORD of Hosts.

19   Egypt: an oracle.

> See how the LORD comes riding swiftly upon a cloud,
>> he shall descend upon Egypt;
>> the idols of Egypt quail before him,
> Egypt's courage melts within her.

2   I will set Egyptian against Egyptian,
> and they shall fight one against another,
>> neighbour against neighbour,
> city against city and kingdom against kingdom.

3   Egypt's spirit shall sink within her,
>> and I will throw her counsels into confusion.
> They may resort to idols and oracle-mongers,
>> to ghosts and spirits,

4   but I will hand Egypt over to a hard master,
> and a cruel king shall rule over them.
> This is the very word of the Lord, the LORD of Hosts.

5   The waters of the Nile shall drain away,
> the river shall be parched and run dry;

6   its channels shall stink,
> the streams of Egypt shall be parched and dry up;
>> reeds and rushes shall wither away;

the lotus too beside the Nile *a*   7
and all that is sown along the Nile shall dry up,
    shall be blown away and vanish.
The fishermen shall groan and lament,   8
all who cast their hooks into the Nile
and those who spread nets on the water shall lose heart.
    The flax-dressers shall hang their heads,   9
    the women carding and the weavers shall grow pale,
    Egypt's spinners shall be downcast,   10
    and all her artisans sick at heart.

Fools that you are, you princes of Zoan!   11
Wisest of Pharaoh's counsellors you may be,
    but stupid counsellors you are.
    How can you say to Pharaoh,
'I am the heir of wise men and spring from ancient kings'?
    Where are your wise men, Pharaoh,   12
    to teach you and make known to you
what the LORD of Hosts has planned for Egypt?
Zoan's princes are fools, the princes of Noph are dupes;   13
    the chieftains of her clans have led Egypt astray.
The LORD has infused into them   14
        a spirit that warps their judgement;
    they make Egypt miss her way in all she does,
    as a drunkard will miss his footing as he vomits.
There shall be nothing in Egypt that any man can do,   15
head or tail, palm or rush.

When that day comes the Egyptians shall become weak as women; they   16
shall fear and tremble when they see the LORD of Hosts raise his hand
against them, as raise it he will. The land of Judah shall strike terror into   17
Egypt; its very name shall cause dismay, because of the plans that the LORD
of Hosts has laid against them.

When that day comes there shall be five cities in Egypt speaking the   18
language of Canaan and swearing allegiance to the LORD of Hosts, and one
of them shall be called the City of the Sun.*b*

When that day comes there shall be an altar to the LORD in the heart of   19
Egypt, and a sacred pillar set up for the LORD upon her frontier. It shall   20
stand as a token and a reminder to the LORD of Hosts in Egypt, so that
when they appeal to him against their oppressors, he may send a deliverer
to champion their cause, and he shall rescue them. The LORD will make   21
himself known to the Egyptians; on that day they shall acknowledge the
LORD and do him service with sacrifice and grain-offering, make vows to
him and pay them. The LORD will strike down Egypt, healing as he   22
strikes; then they will turn back to him and he will hear their prayers and
heal them.

When that day comes there shall be a highway between Egypt and   23

a Prob. rdg.; Heb. adds on the mouth of the Nile.   *b* the City of the Sun: *or*
Heliopolis.

Assyria; Assyrians shall come to Egypt and Egyptians to Assyria; then Egyptians shall worship with*a* Assyrians.

24 When that day comes Israel shall rank with Egypt and Assyria, those
25 three, and shall be a blessing in the centre of the world. So the LORD of Hosts will bless them: A blessing be upon Egypt my people, upon Assyria the work of my hands, and upon Israel my possession.

20 SARGON KING OF ASSYRIA SENT his commander-in-chief*b* to Ashdod,
2 and he took it by storm. At that time the LORD said to Isaiah son of Amoz, Come, strip the sackcloth from your waist and take your sandals off. He did
3 so, and went about naked and barefoot. The LORD said, My servant Isaiah has gone naked and barefoot for three years as a sign and a warning to
4 Egypt and Cush; just so shall the king of Assyria lead the captives of Egypt and the exiles of Cush naked and barefoot, their buttocks shame-
5 fully exposed, young and old alike. All men shall be dismayed, their hopes
6 in Cush and their pride in Egypt humbled. On that day those who dwell along this coast will say, So much for all our hopes on which we relied for help and deliverance from the king of Assyria; what escape have we now?

21   A wilderness: an oracle.

Rough weather, advancing like a storm in the south,
  coming from the wilderness, from a land of terror!
2   Grim is the vision shown to me:
  the traitor betrayed, the spoiler himself despoiled.
  Up, Elam; up, Medes, to the siege,
    no time for weariness!
3 At this my limbs writhe in anguish,
  I am gripped by pangs like a woman in labour.
  I am distraught past hearing, dazed past seeing,
4 my mind reels, sudden convulsions seize me.

  The cool twilight I longed for has become a terror:
5 the banquet is set out, the rugs are spread;
    they are eating and drinking—
  rise, princes, burnish your shields.
6 For these were the words of the Lord to me:
  Go, post a watchman to report what he sees.
7 He sees chariots, two-horsed chariots,
  riders on asses, riders on camels.
  He is alert, alert, always on the alert.
8   Then the look-out cried:
All day long I stand on the Lord's watch-tower
and night after night I keep my station.
9 See, there come men in a chariot, a two-horsed chariot.
    And a voice calls back:
  Fallen, fallen is Babylon,
and all the images of her gods lie shattered on the ground.

a Or shall be slaves to.   *b* Or sent Tartan.

O my people,   10
once trodden out and winnowed on the threshing-floor,
what I have heard from the LORD of Hosts,
from the God of Israel, I have told you.

Dumah: an oracle.   11

One calls to me from Seir:
Watchman, what is left of the night?
Watchman, what is left?
    The watchman answered: 12
Morning comes, and also night. *a*
Ask if you must; then come back again.

With the Arabs: an oracle.   13

You caravans of Dedan, that camp in the scrub with the Arabs,
    bring water to meet the thirsty.   14
You dwellers in Tema, meet the fugitives with food,
    for they flee from the sword, the sharp edge of the sword,   15
    from the bent bow, and from the press of battle.

For these are the words of the Lord to me: Within a year, as a hired 16
labourer counts off the years, all the glory of Kedar shall come to an end;
few shall be the bows left to the warriors of Kedar.   17
The LORD the God of Israel has spoken.

The Valley of Vision: *b* an oracle.   22

Tell me, what is amiss
that you have all climbed on to the roofs,
O city full of tumult, town in ferment   2
    and filled with uproar,
whose slain were not slain with the sword
    and did not die in battle?
Your commanders are all in flight,   3
huddled together out of bowshot;
all your stoutest warriors are huddled together,
    they have taken to their heels.
Then I said, Turn your eyes away from me;   4
    leave me to weep in misery.
Do not thrust consolation on me
    for the ruin of my own people.

For the Lord, the LORD of Hosts, has ordained a day of tumult, a day of 5
trampling and turmoil in the Valley of Vision, *b* rousing cries for help that
echo among the mountains.

Elam took up his quiver,   6
horses were harnessed to the chariots of Aram, *c*
Kir took the cover from his shield.

a and also night: *or* and the night is full spent.   *b* *Or* of Calamity.
c *Prob. rdg.; Heb.* man.

835

7   Your fairest valleys were overrun by chariots and horsemen,
            the gates were hard beset,
8   the heart of Judah's defence was laid open.

    On that day you looked to the weapons stored in the House of the Forest;
9 you filled all the many pools in the City of David, collecting water from
10 the Lower Pool.*a* Then you surveyed the houses in Jerusalem, tearing some
11 down to make the wall inaccessible, and between the two walls you made
a cistern for the Waters of the Old Pool;
          but you did not look to the Maker of it all
          or consider him who fashioned it long ago.
12   On that day the Lord, the LORD of Hosts,
          called for weeping and beating the breast,
          for shaving the head and putting on sackcloth;
13   but instead there was joy and merry-making,
        slaughtering of cattle and killing of sheep,
        eating of meat and drinking of wine, as you thought,
        Let us eat and drink; for tomorrow we die.

14   The LORD of Hosts has revealed himself to me; in my hearing he swore:
        Your wickedness shall never be purged
          until you die.
        This is the word of the Lord, the LORD of Hosts.

15 These were the words of the Lord, the LORD of Hosts:
        Go to this steward,
        to Shebna, comptroller of the household, and say:
16   What right, what business, have you here,
        that you have dug yourself a grave here,
        cutting out your grave on a height
        and carving yourself a resting-place in the rock?
17   The LORD will shake you out,
        shake you as a garment *b* is shaken out
        to rid it of lice;
18   then he will bundle you tightly and throw you
        like a ball into a great wide land.
        There you shall die,
        and there shall lie your chariot of honour,
        an object of contempt to your master's household.
19   I will remove you from office and drive you from your post.

20 21   On that day I will send for my servant Eliakim son of Hilkiah; I will
invest him with your robe, gird him with your sash; and hand over your
authority to him. He shall be a father to the inhabitants of Jerusalem and
22 the people of Judah. I will lay the key of the house of David on his shoulder;
what he opens no man shall shut, and what he shuts no man shall open.

   a you filled . . . Lower Pool: *or* you took note of the cracks, many as they were, in the wall
of the City of David, and you collected water from the Lower Pool.   *b Prob. rdg.;*
Heb. man.

He shall be a seat of honour for his father's family; I will fasten him firmly 23
in place like a peg. On him shall hang all the weight of the family, down to 24
the lowest dregs—all the little vessels, both bowls and pots. On that day, 25
says the LORD of Hosts, the peg which was firmly fastened in its place shall
be removed; it shall be hacked out and shall fall, and the load of things
hanging on it shall be destroyed. The LORD has spoken.

Tyre: an oracle. 23

The ships of Tarshish howl, for the harbour is sacked;
the port of entry from Kittim is swept away.
  The people of the sea-coast, the merchants of Sidon, wail, 2-3
  people whose agents cross the great waters,
    whose harvest*a* is the grain of the Shihor
    and their revenue the trade of nations.
Sidon, the sea-fortress,*b* cries in her disappointment,*c* 4
I no longer feel the anguish of labour or bear children;
I have no young sons to rear, no daughters to bring up.
  When the news is confirmed in Egypt 5
  her people sway in anguish at the fate of Tyre.
    Make your way to Tarshish, they say, 6
    howl, you who dwell by the sea-coast.
  Is this your busy city, ancient in story, 7
on whose voyages you were carried to settle far away?

Whose plan was this against Tyre, the city of battlements, 8
  whose merchants were princes
  and her traders the most honoured men on earth?
The LORD of Hosts planned it to prick every noble's pride 9
  and bring all the most honoured men on earth into contempt.
Take to the tillage of your fields, you people of Tarshish; 10
  for your market*d* is lost.
The LORD has stretched out his hand over the sea 11
  and shaken kingdoms,
he has given his command to destroy the marts of Canaan;
and he has said, You shall busy yourselves no more, 12
  you, the sorely oppressed virgin city of Sidon.
  Though you arise and cross over to Kittim,
  even there you shall find no rest.

Look at this land, the destined home of ships*e*! The Chaldaeans*f* 13
erected their*g* siege-towers, dismantled its palaces and laid it in ruins.

  Howl, you ships of Tarshish; 14
  for your haven is sacked.

---

a whose harvest: *prob. rdg.; Heb.* the harvest of the Nile.   *b* the sea-fortress:
prob. rdg.; Heb. the sea, sea-fortress, saying.   *c* in her disappointment: *prob.*
rdg.; Heb. be disappointed.   *d* *Prob. rdg.; Heb.* girdle.   *e* *Or* marmots.
f *Prob. rdg.; Heb. adds* this was the people; it was not Assyria.   *g* *Prob. rdg.;*
Heb. his.

15 From that day Tyre shall be forgotten for seventy years, the span of one king's life. At the end of the seventy years her plight shall be that of the harlot in the song:

16
    Take your harp, go round the city,
      poor forgotten harlot;
    touch the strings sweetly, sing all your songs,
      make men remember you again.

17 At the end of seventy years, the LORD will turn again to Tyre; she shall go
18 back to her old trade and hire herself out to every kingdom on earth. The profits of her trading will be dedicated to the LORD; they shall not be hoarded or stored up, but shall be given to those who worship the LORD, to purchase food in plenty and fine attire.

The LORD's judgement on the earth

24
    Beware, the LORD will empty the earth,
    split it open and turn it upside down,
      and scatter its inhabitants.

2
    Then it will be the same for priest and people,
    the same for master and slave, mistress and slave-girl,
      seller and buyer,
    borrower and lender, debtor and creditor.

3
    The earth is emptied clean away
      and stripped clean bare.
    For this is the word that the LORD has spoken.

4
    The earth dries up and withers,
      the whole world withers and grows sick;
      the earth's high places sicken,

5
    and earth itself is desecrated by the feet of those who live in it,
    because they have broken the laws, disobeyed the statutes
      and violated the eternal covenant.

6
    For this a curse has devoured the earth
      and its inhabitants stand aghast.
    For this those who inhabit the earth dwindle
    and only a few men are left.

7
    The new wine dries up, the vines sicken,
    and all the revellers turn to sorrow.

8
    Silent the merry beat of tambourines,
      hushed the shouts of revelry,
      the merry harp is silent.

9
    No one shall drink wine to the sound of song;
    the liquor will be bitter to the man who drinks it.

10
    The city of chaos is a broken city,
    every house barred, that no one may enter.

11
    Men call for wine in the streets;
      all revelry is darkened,
      and mirth is banished from the land.

Desolation alone is left in the city 12
and the gate is broken into pieces.
So shall it be in all the world, in every nation, 13
as when an olive-tree is beaten and stripped,
as when the vintage is ended.

Men raise their voices and cry aloud, 14
they shout in the west,[a] so great is the LORD's majesty.
Therefore let the LORD be glorified in the regions of the east, 15
and the name of the LORD the God of Israel
in the coasts and islands of the west.

From the ends of the earth we have heard them sing, 16
How lovely is righteousness!
But I thought, Villainy, villainy!
Woe to the traitors and their treachery!
Traitors double-dyed they are indeed!
The hunter's scare, the pit, and the trap 17
threaten all who dwell in the land;
if a man runs from the rattle of the scare 18
he will fall into the pit;
if he climbs out of the pit
he will be caught in the trap.
When the windows of heaven above are opened
and earth's foundations shake,
the earth is utterly shattered, 19
it is convulsed and reels wildly.
The earth reels to and fro like a drunken man 20
and sways like a watchman's shelter;
the sins of men weigh heavy upon it,
and it falls to rise no more.

On that day the LORD will punish 21
the host of heaven in heaven, and on earth the kings of the earth,
herded together, close packed like prisoners in a dungeon; 22
shut up in gaol, after a long time they shall be punished.
The moon shall grow pale and the sun hide its face in shame; 23
for the LORD of Hosts has become king
on Mount Zion and in Jerusalem,
and shows his glory before their elders.

The deliverance and ingathering of Judah

O LORD, thou art my God; 25
I will exalt thee and praise thy name;
for thou hast accomplished a wonderful purpose,
certain and sure, from of old.

[a] in the west: *or* more loudly than the sea.

2   For thou hast turned cities into heaps of ruin,
          and fortified towns into rubble;
          every mansion in the cities is swept away,
            never to be rebuilt.

3   For this a cruel nation holds thee in honour,
          the cities of ruthless nations fear thee.

4   Truly thou hast been a refuge to the poor,
          a refuge to the needy in his trouble,
     shelter from the tempest and shade from the heat.
        For the blast of the ruthless is like an icy storm

5   or a scorching drought;
          thou subduest the roar of the foe,[a]
          and the song of the ruthless dies away.

6   On this mountain the LORD of Hosts will prepare
          a banquet of rich fare for all the peoples,
          a banquet of wines well matured and richest fare,
          well-matured wines strained clear.

7   On this mountain the LORD will swallow up
          that veil that shrouds all the peoples,
          the pall thrown over all the nations;

8   he will swallow up death for ever.
        Then the Lord GOD will wipe away the tears
          from every face
     and remove the reproach of his people from the whole earth.
        The LORD has spoken.

9   On that day men will say,
          See, this is our God
        for whom we have waited to deliver us;
        this is the LORD for whom we have waited;
        let us rejoice and exult in his deliverance.

10   For the hand of the LORD will rest on this mountain,
          but Moab shall be trampled under his feet
          as straw is trampled into a midden.

11   In it Moab shall spread out his hands
          as a swimmer spreads his hands to swim,
     but he shall sink his pride with every stroke of his hands.

12   The LORD has thrown down the high defences of your walls,
          has levelled them to the earth
          and brought them down to the dust.

26   On that day this song shall be sung in Judah:
        We have a strong city
      whose walls and ramparts are our deliverance.

2   Open the gates to let a righteous nation in,
          a nation that keeps faith.

[a] *Prob. rdg.; Heb. adds* heat in the shadow of a cloud.

Thou dost keep in peace men of constant mind,   3
    in peace because they trust in thee.
   Trust in the LORD for ever;   4
   for the LORD himself is an everlasting rock.
He has brought low all who dwell high in a towering city;   5
    he levels it to the ground and lays it in the dust,
that the oppressed and the poor may tread it underfoot.   6
   The path of the righteous is level,   7
and thou markest out the right way for the upright.
We too look to the path prescribed in thy laws, O LORD;   8
    thy name and thy memory are our heart's desire.
   With all my heart I long for thee in the night,   9
   I seek thee eagerly when dawn breaks;
   for, when thy laws prevail in the land,
   the inhabitants of the world learn justice.
The wicked are destroyed, they have never learnt justice;   10
    corrupt in a land of honest ways,
   they do not regard the majesty of the LORD.

   O LORD, thy hand is lifted high,   11
   but the bitter enemies of thy people do not see it;[a]
   let the fire of thy enmity destroy them.
O LORD, thou wilt bestow prosperity on us;   12
for in truth all our works are thy doing.
   O LORD our God,   13
   other lords than thou have been our masters,
   but thee alone do we invoke by name.
   The dead will not live again,   14
    those long in their graves will not rise;
to this end thou hast punished them and destroyed them,
    and made all memory of them perish.
   Thou hast enlarged the nation, O LORD,   15
   enlarged it and won thyself honour,
   thou hast extended all the frontiers of the land.
   In our distress, O LORD, we[b] sought thee out,   16
   chastened by the mere whisper of thy rebuke.
   As a woman with child, when her time is near,   17
   is in labour and cries out in her pains,
so were we in thy presence, O LORD.
    We have been with child, we have been in labour,   18
    but have brought forth wind.
    We have won no success for the land,
   and no one will be born to inhabit the world.
But thy dead live, their bodies will rise again.   19
   They that sleep in the earth will awake and shout for joy;
    for thy dew is a dew of sparkling light,
and the earth will bring those long dead to birth again.

[a] *Prob. rdg.; Heb. adds* let them see and be ashamed.   [b] *Prob. rdg.; Heb.* they.

20   Go, my people, enter your rooms
          and shut your doors behind you;
      withdraw for a brief while, until wrath has gone by.
21   For see, the LORD is coming from his place
          to punish the inhabitants of the earth for their sins;
            then the earth shall uncover her blood-stains
            and hide her slain no more.

27   On that day the LORD will punish
      with his cruel sword, his mighty and powerful sword,
          Leviathan that twisting*ᵃ* sea-serpent,
          that writhing serpent Leviathan,
          and slay the monster of the deep.

2   On that day sing to the pleasant vineyard,
3   I the LORD am its keeper,
      moment by moment I water it for fear its green leaves fail.
          Night and day I tend it,
4   but I get no wine;
      I would as soon have briars and thorns,
      then I would wage war upon it and burn it all up,
5   unless it grasps me as its refuge and makes peace with me—
          unless it makes peace with me.

6   In time to come Jacob's offspring shall take root
          and Israel shall bud and blossom,
          and they shall fill the whole earth with fruit.

7   Has God struck him down as he struck others down?
          Has the slayer been slain as he slew others?
8-10*ᵇ* This then purges Jacob's iniquity,
          this*ᶜ* has removed his sin:
      that he grinds all altar stones to powder like chalk;
          no sacred poles and incense-altars are left standing.

          The fortified city is left solitary,
          and his quarrel with her ends in brushing her away, *ᵈ*
      removing her by a cruel blast when the east wind blows;
      it is a homestead stripped bare, deserted like a wilderness;
          there the calf grazes and there lies down,
           and crops every twig.
11   Its boughs snap off when they grow dry,
      and women come and light their fires with them.
          For they are a people without sense;
          therefore their maker will show them no mercy,
          he who formed them will show them no favour.

ᵃ Or primeval.   *ᵇ Verses 8–10 re-arranged thus : 9, 10a, 8, 10b.*   *ᶜ Prob. rdg. ;*
Heb. adds all fruit.   *ᵈ Prob. rdg. ; Heb. adds* by dismissing her.

On that day the LORD will beat out the grain,   12
from the streams of the Euphrates to the Torrent of Egypt;
but you Israelites will be gleaned
one by one.

On that day   13
a blast shall be blown on a great trumpet,
and those who are lost in Assyria
and those dispersed in Egypt will come in
and worship the LORD on the holy mountain, in Jerusalem.

Assyria and Judah

Oh, the proud garlands of the drunkards of Ephraim   **28**
and the flowering sprays, so lovely in their beauty,
on the heads of revellers dripping with perfumes,
overcome with wine!
See, the Lord has one at his bidding, mighty and strong,   2
whom he sets to work with violence against the land,
like a sweeping storm of hail, like a destroying tempest,
like a torrent of water in overwhelming flood.
The proud garlands of Ephraim's drunkards   3
shall be trampled underfoot,
and the flowering sprays, so lovely in their beauty   4
on the heads dripping with perfumes,
shall be like early figs ripe before summer;
he who sees them plucks them,
and their bloom is gone while they lie in his hand.
On that day the LORD of Hosts shall be a lovely garland,   5
a beautiful diadem for the remnant of his people,
a spirit of justice for one who presides in a court of justice,   6
and of valour for*a* those who repel the enemy at the gate.

These too are addicted to wine,   7
clamouring in their cups:
priest and prophet are addicted to strong drink
and bemused with wine;
clamouring in their cups, confirmed topers,*b*
hiccuping in drunken stupor;
every table is covered with vomit,   8
filth that leaves no clean spot.
Who is it that the prophet hopes to teach,   9
to whom will what they hear make sense?

---

a for: *prob. rdg.; Heb. om.*   *b* These too . . . topers: *or* These too lose their way
through wine and are set wandering by strong drink: priest and prophet lose their way
through strong drink and are fuddled with wine; are set wandering by strong drink,
lose their way through tippling.

Are they babes newly weaned, just taken from the breast?
10 It is all harsh cries and raucous shouts,
'A little more here, a little there!'
11 So it will be with barbarous speech and strange tongue
that this people will hear God speaking,
12 this people to whom he once said,
'This is true rest; let the exhausted have rest.
This is repose', and they refused to listen.
13 Now to them the word of the LORD will be
harsh cries and raucous shouts,
'A little more here, a little there!'—
and so, as they walk, they will stumble backwards,
they will be injured, trapped and caught.
14 Listen then to the word of the LORD, you arrogant men
who rule this people in Jerusalem.
15 You say, 'We have made a treaty with Death
and signed a pact with Sheol:
so that, when the raging flood sweeps by, it shall not touch us;
for we have taken refuge in lies
and sheltered behind falsehood.'
16 These then are the words of the Lord GOD:
Look, I am laying a stone in Zion, a block of granite,
a precious corner-stone for a firm foundation;
he who has faith shall not waver.
17 I will use justice as a plumb-line
and righteousness as a plummet;
hail shall sweep away your refuge of lies,
and flood-waters carry away your shelter.
18 Then your treaty with Death shall be annulled
and your pact with Sheol shall not stand;
the raging waters will sweep by,
and you will be like land swept by the flood.
19 As often as it sweeps by, it will take you;
morning after morning it will sweep by,
day and night.
The very thought of such tidings
will bring nothing but dismay;
20 for 'The bed is too short for a man to stretch,
and the blanket too narrow to cover him.'
21 But the LORD shall arise as he rose on Mount Perazim
and storm with rage as he did in the Vale of Gibeon
to do what he must do—how strange a deed!
to perform his work—how outlandish a work!
22 But now have done with your arrogance,
lest your bonds grow tighter;
for I have heard destruction decreed
by the Lord GOD of Hosts for the whole land.

Listen and hear what I say,　　　　　　　　　　23
　　attend and hear my words.
Will the ploughman continually plough for the sowing,　24
　　breaking his ground and harrowing it?
Does he not, once he has levelled it,　　　　　　25
broadcast the dill and scatter the cummin?
　　Does he not plant the wheat in rows
　　with barley*a* and spelt along the edge?
Does not his God instruct him and train him aright?　26
Dill is not threshed with a sledge,　　　　　　　27
　　and the cartwheel is not rolled over cummin;
　　dill is beaten with a rod,
　　　and cummin with a flail.
Corn is crushed, but not to the uttermost,　　　28
　　not with a final crushing;
his cartwheels rumble over it and break it up,
　　but they do not grind it fine.
This message, too, comes from the Lord of Hosts,　29
　　whose purposes are wonderful
　　and his power great.

Alas for Ariel! Ariel,　　　　　　　　　　　**29**
　　the city where David encamped.
Add year to year,
　　let the pilgrim-feasts run their round,
　　and I will bring Ariel to sore straits,　　　2
when there shall be moaning and lamentation.
I will make her my Ariel indeed, my fiery altar.
I will throw my army round you like a wall;　　3
I will set a ring of outposts all round you
and erect siege-works against you.
　　You shall be brought low, you will speak out of the ground　4
　　and your words will issue from the earth;
your voice will come like a ghost's from the ground,
　　and your words will squeak out of the earth.
Yet the horde of your enemies shall crumble into dust,　5
　　the horde of ruthless foes shall fly like chaff.
　　Then suddenly, all in an instant,
　　punishment shall come from the Lord of Hosts　6
　　with thunder and earthquake and a great noise,
with storm and tempest and a flame of devouring fire;
and the horde of all the nations warring against Ariel,　7
　　all their baggage-trains and siege-works,
　　　and all her oppressors themselves,
　　shall fade as a dream, a vision of the night.
　　Like a starving man who dreams　　　　　　8
　　　and thinks that he is eating,

a Prob. rdg.; Heb. adds an unintelligible word.

> but wakes up to find himself empty,
>> or a thirsty man who dreams
>>> and thinks that he is drinking,
> but wakes up to find himself thirsty and dry,
>> so shall the horde of all the nations be
>>> that war against Mount Zion.

9   Loiter and be dazed, enjoy yourselves and be blinded,
>> be drunk but not with wine, reel but not with strong drink;
10 for the LORD has poured upon you a spirit of deep stupor;
>> he has closed your eyes, the prophets,
>>> and muffled your heads, the seers.

11 All prophetic vision has become for you like a sealed book. Give such a book to one who can read and say, 'Come, read this'; he will answer,
12 'I cannot', because it is sealed. Give it to one who cannot read and say, 'Come, read this'; he will answer, 'I cannot read.'
13 Then the Lord said:

> Because this people approach me with their mouths
>> and honour me with their lips
>>> while their hearts are far from me,
> and their religion is but a precept of men, learnt by rote,
14 therefore I will yet again shock this people,
>> adding shock to shock:
>>> the wisdom of their wise men shall vanish
>>> and the discernment of the discerning shall be lost.

15 Shame upon those who seek to hide their purpose
>> too deep for the LORD to see,
> and who, when their deeds are done in the dark,
>> say, 'Who sees us? Who knows of us?'
16 How you turn things upside down,
>> as if the potter ranked no higher than the clay!
> Shall the thing made say of its maker, 'He did not make me'?
> Shall the pot say of the potter, 'He has no skill'?
17 The time is but short
>> before Lebanon goes back to grassland
>>> and the grassland is no better than scrub.

18 On that day deaf men shall hear
>> when a book is read,
>>> and the eyes of the blind shall see
>>> out of impenetrable darkness.
19 The lowly shall once again rejoice in the LORD,
>> and the poorest of men exult in the Holy One of Israel.
20 The ruthless shall be no more, the arrogant shall cease to be;
>> those who are quick to see mischief,
21 those who charge others with a sin
> or lay traps for him who brings the wrongdoer into court

or by falsehood deny justice to the righteous—
all these shall be exterminated.

Therefore these are the words of the LORD the God of the house of   22
Jacob, the God who ransomed Abraham:

This is no time for Jacob to be shamed,
no time for his face to grow pale;
for his descendants will hallow my name   23
when they see what I have done in their nation.
They will hallow the Holy One of Jacob
and hold the God of Israel in awe;
those whose minds are confused will gain understanding,   24
and the obstinate will receive instruction.

Oh, rebel sons! says the LORD,   **30**
you make plans, but not of my devising,
you weave schemes, but not inspired by me,
piling sin upon sin;
you hurry down to Egypt without consulting me,   2
to seek protection under Pharaoh's shelter
and take refuge under Egypt's wing.
Pharaoh's protection will bring you disappointment   3
and refuge under Egypt's wing humiliation;
for, though his officers are at Zoan   4
and his envoys reach as far as Hanes,
all are left in sorry plight by that unprofitable nation,   5
no help they find, no profit, only disappointment and disgrace.

The Beasts of the South: an oracle.   6

Through a land of hardship and distress
the tribes of lioness and roaring lion,
sand-viper and venomous flying serpent,
carry their wealth on the backs of asses
and their treasures on camels' humps
to an unprofitable people.
Vain and worthless is the help of Egypt;   7
therefore have I given her this name,
Rahab Quelled.
Now come and write it on a tablet,   8
engrave it as an inscription before their eyes,
that it may be there in future days,
a testimony for all time.
For they are a race of rebels, disloyal sons,   9
sons who will not listen to the LORD's instruction;
they say to the seers, 'You shall not see',   10
and to the visionaries, 'You shall have no true visions;
give us smooth words and seductive visions.

11   Turn aside, leave the straight path,
     and rid us for ever of the Holy One of Israel.'

12   These are the words of the Holy One of Israel:
     Because you have rejected this warning
       and trust in devious and dishonest practices,
         resting on them for support,
13   therefore you shall find this iniquity will be
       like a crack running down
       a high wall, which bulges
    and suddenly, all in an instant, comes crashing down,
14   as an earthen jar is broken with a crash,
       mercilessly shattered,
    so that not a shard is found among the fragments
       to take fire from the glowing embers,
       or to scoop up water from a pool.

15   These are the words of the Lord GOD the Holy One of Israel:
     Come back, keep peace, and you will be safe;
    in stillness and in staying quiet, there lies your strength.
16   But you would have none of it; you said, No,
       we will take horse and flee;
       therefore you shall be put to flight:
       We will ride apace;
       therefore swift shall be the pace of your pursuers.
17   When a thousand flee at the challenge of one,
    you shall all flee at the challenge of five, until you are left
    like a pole on a mountain-top, a signal post on a hill.
18   Yet the LORD is waiting to show you his favour,
      yet he yearns to have pity on you;
       for the LORD is a God of justice.
     Happy are all who wait for him!

19   O people of Zion who dwell in Jerusalem, you shall weep no more. The
LORD will show you favour and answer you when he hears your cry for
20   help. The Lord may give you bread of adversity and water of affliction,
but he who teaches you shall no longer be hidden out of sight, but with
21   your own eyes you shall see him always. If you stray from the road to right
or left you shall hear with your own ears a voice behind you saying, This
22   is the way; follow it. You will reject, as things unclean, your silvered
images and your idols sheathed in gold; you will loathe them like a foul
23   discharge and call them ordure.*a* The Lord will give you rain for the seed
you sow, and as the produce of your soil he will give you heavy crops of
corn in plenty. When that day comes the cattle shall graze in broad pastures;
24   the oxen and asses that work your land shall be fed with well-seasoned
25   fodder, winnowed with shovel and fork. On each high mountain and each
lofty hill shall be streams of running water, on the day of massacre when the
26   highest in the land fall. The moon shall shine with a brightness like the

---

        a call them ordure: *or* say to them, Be off.

sun's, and the sun with seven times his wonted brightness, seven days'
light in one, on the day when the LORD binds up the broken limbs of his
people and heals their wounds.

See, the name of the LORD comes from afar,   27
   his anger blazing and his doom heavy.
His lips are charged with wrath
   and his tongue is a devouring fire.
His breath is like a torrent in spate,   28
   rising neck-high,
a yoke to force the nations to their ruin,
a bit in the mouth to guide the peoples astray.
But for you there shall be songs,   29
   as on a night of sacred pilgrimage,
your hearts glad, as the hearts of men who walk to the sound of the pipe
on their way to the LORD's hill, to the rock of Israel.
Then the LORD shall make his voice heard in majesty   30
and show his arm sweeping down in fierce anger
   with devouring flames of fire,
with cloudburst and tempests of rain and hailstones;
for at the voice of the LORD Assyria's heart fails her,   31
   as she feels the stroke of his rod.
Tambourines and harps and shaking sistrums   32
   shall keep time
   with every stroke of his rod,
of the chastisement which the LORD inflicts on her.
Long ago was Topheth made ready,[a]   33
   made deep and broad,
its fire-pit a blazing mass of logs,
and the breath of the LORD like a stream of brimstone
   blazing in it.

Shame upon those who go down to Egypt for help   **31**
   and rely on horses,
putting their trust in chariots many in number
and in horsemen in their thousands,
but do not look to the Holy One of Israel
   or seek guidance of the LORD!
Yet the LORD too in his wisdom can bring about trouble   2
   and he does not take back his words;
he will rise up against the league of evildoers,
   against all who help those who do wrong.
The Egyptians are men, not God,[b]   3
their horses are flesh, not spirit;
and, when the LORD stretches out his hand,
the helper will stumble and he who is helped will fall,
   and they will all vanish together.

[a] *Prob. rdg.; Heb. adds* is that prepared also for the king?   [b] *Or* gods.

4   This is what the LORD has said to me:

As a lion or a young lion growls over its prey
when the muster of shepherds is called out against it,
    and is not scared at their noise
    or cowed by their clamour,
so shall the LORD of Hosts come down to do battle
    for Mount Zion and her high summit.

5   Thus the LORD of Hosts, like a bird hovering over its young,
    will be a shield over Jerusalem;
        he will shield her and deliver her,
        standing over her and delivering her.

6   O Israel, come back to him whom you have so deeply offended,
7   for on that day when you spurn, one and all,
    the idols of silver and the idols of gold
    which your own sinful hands have made,

8   Assyria shall fall by the sword, but by no sword of man;
    a sword that no man wields shall devour him.
    He shall flee before the sword,
    and his young warriors shall be put to forced labour,
9   his officers shall be helpless from terror
    and his captains too dismayed to flee.
        This is the very word of the LORD
    whose fire blazes in Zion,
    and whose furnace is set up in Jerusalem.

32   Behold, a king shall reign in righteousness
    and his rulers rule with justice,
2   and a man shall be a refuge from the wind
    and a shelter from the tempest,
    or like runnels of water in dry ground,
like the shadow of a great rock in a thirsty land.
3   The eyes that can see will not be clouded,
    and the ears that can hear will listen;
4   the anxious heart will understand and know,
and the man who stammers will at once speak plain.
5   The scoundrel will no longer be thought noble,
    nor the villain called a prince;
6   for the scoundrel will speak like a scoundrel
    and will hatch evil in his heart;
        he is an impostor in all his actions,
    and in his words a liar even to the LORD;
        he starves the hungry of their food
        and refuses drink to the thirsty.
7   The villain's ways are villainous
    and he devises infamous plans
    to ruin the poor with his lies
    and deny justice to the needy.

But the man of noble mind forms noble designs   8
and stands firm in his nobility.

You women that live at ease, stand up   9
　　and hear what I have to say.
You young women without a care, mark my words.
You have no cares now, but when the year is out, you will tremble,   10
for the vintage will be over and no produce gathered in.
　　You who are now at ease, be anxious;   11
　　tremble, you who have no cares.
　　Strip yourselves bare;
　　put a cloth round your waists
　　and beat your breasts   12
for the pleasant fields and fruitful vines.
On the soil of my people shall spring up thorns and briars,   13
in every happy home and in the busy town,
for the palace is forsaken and the crowded streets deserted;   14
citadel*a* and watch-tower are turned into open heath,
the joy of wild asses ever after and pasture for the flocks,
until a spirit from on high is lavished upon us.   15
　　Then the wilderness will become grassland
　　and grassland will be cheap as scrub;
　　then justice shall make its home in the wilderness,   16
　　and righteousness dwell in the grassland;
　　when righteousness shall yield peace   17
and its fruit be quietness and confidence for ever.
　　Then my people shall live in a tranquil country,   18
dwelling in peace, in houses full of ease;
　　it will be cool on the slopes of the forest then,   19
　　and cities shall lie peaceful in the plain.
　　Happy shall you be, sowing every man by the water-side,   20
　　　and letting ox and ass run free.

Ah! you destroyer, yourself undestroyed,   **33**
　　betrayer still unbetrayed,
　　when you cease to destroy you will be destroyed,
　　after all your betrayals, you will be betrayed yourself.

O Lord, show us thy favour; we hope in thee.   2
　　Uphold us every morning,
　　save us when troubles come.
　　At the roar of the thunder the peoples flee,   3
　　at thy rumbling nations are scattered;
their spoil is swept up as if young locusts had swept it,   4
　　like a swarm of locusts men swarm upon it.

The Lord is supreme, for he dwells on high;   5
if you fill Zion with justice and with righteousness,

　　　　　　a Or hill; *Heb.* Ophel.

6   then he will be the mainstay of the age: *a*
         wisdom and knowledge are the assurance of salvation;
            the fear of the LORD is her *b* treasure.

7   Hark, how the valiant cry aloud for help,
            and those sent to sue for peace weep bitterly!
8   The highways are deserted, no travellers tread the roads.
         Covenants are broken, treaties are flouted;
               man is of no account.
9   The land is parched and wilting,
            Lebanon is eaten away and crumbling;
            Sharon has become a desert,
            Bashan and Carmel are stripped bare.
10   Now, says the LORD, I will rise up.
         Now I will exalt myself, now lift myself up.
11   What you conceive and bring to birth is chaff and stubble;
            a wind like fire shall devour you.
12   Whole nations shall be heaps of white ash,
         or like thorns cut down and set on fire.
13   You who dwell far away, hear what I have done;
            acknowledge my might, you who are near.
14   In Zion sinners quake with terror,
            the godless are seized with trembling and ask,
         Can any of us live with a devouring fire?
         Can any live in endless burning?
15   The man who lives an upright life and speaks the truth,
            who scorns to enrich himself by extortion,
         who snaps his fingers at a bribe,
            who stops his ears to hear nothing of bloodshed,
            who closes his eyes to the sight of evil—
16   that is the man who shall dwell on the heights,
            his refuge a fastness in the cliffs,
         his bread secure and his water never failing.

17   Your eyes shall see a king in his splendour
            and will look upon a land of far distances.
18   You will call to mind what once you feared:
         'Where then is he that counted, where is he that weighed,
            where is he that counted the treasures?'
19   You will no longer see that barbarous people,
            that people whose speech was so hard to catch,
            whose stuttering speech you could not understand.

20   Look upon Zion, city of our solemn feasts,
            let your eyes rest on Jerusalem,
         a land of comfort, a tent that shall never be shifted,
            whose pegs shall never be pulled up,
               not one of its ropes cast loose.

a the age: *prob. rdg.; Heb.* your times.   *b* *Prob. rdg.; Heb.* his.

There we have the LORD's majesty; [a]   21
    it will be a place[b] of rivers and broad streams;
    but[c] no galleys shall be rowed there,
    no stately ship sail by.
For the LORD our judge, the LORD our law-giver,   22
the LORD our king—he himself will save us.
    [Men may say, Your rigging is slack;   23
    it will not hold the mast firm in its socket,
        nor can the sails be spread.]
Then the blind man shall have a full share of the spoil
    and the lame shall take part in the pillage;
    no man who dwells there shall say, 'I am sick';   24
and the sins of the people who live there shall be pardoned.

Edom and Israel

Approach, you nations, to listen,   **34**
    and attend, you peoples;
    let the earth listen and everything in it,
    the world and all that it yields;
    for the LORD's anger is turned against all the nations   2
    and his wrath against all the host of them:
he gives them over to slaughter and destruction.
    Their slain shall be flung out,   3
the stench shall rise from their corpses,
and the mountains shall stream with their blood.
All the host of heaven shall crumble into nothing,   4
the heavens shall be rolled up like a scroll,
    and the starry host fade away,
as the leaf withers from the vine
    and the ripening fruit from the fig-tree;
    for the sword of the LORD[d] appears in heaven.   5
See how it descends in judgement on Edom,
on the people whom he dooms[e] to destruction.
The LORD has a sword steeped in blood,   6
    it is gorged with fat,
the fat of rams' kidneys, and the blood of lambs and goats;
    for he has a sacrifice in Bozrah,
    a great slaughter in Edom.
Wild oxen shall come down and buffaloes[f] with them,   7
    bull and bison together,
and the land shall drink deep of blood
and the soil be sated with fat.
    For the LORD has a day of vengeance,   8

[a] *Or* threshing-floor.   [b] it . . . place: *or* instead.   [c] *Or* and.
[d] the sword of the LORD: *prob. rdg.; Heb.* my sword.   [e] *Prob. rdg.; Heb.* I doom.
[f] and buffaloes: *prob. rdg.; Heb. om.*

the champion of Zion has a year when he will requite.

9   Edom's torrents shall be turned into pitch
           and its soil into brimstone,
and the land shall become blazing pitch,

10   which night and day shall never be quenched,
         and its smoke shall go up for ever.
        From generation to generation it shall lie waste,
         and no man shall pass through it ever again.

11   Horned owl and bustard shall make their home in it,
        screech-owl and raven shall haunt it.
        He has stretched across it a measuring-line of chaos,

12   and its frontiers shall be a jumble of stones.
        No king shall be acclaimed there,
         and all its princes shall come to nought.

13   Thorns shall sprout in its palaces;
        nettles and briars shall cover its walled towns.
It shall be rough land fit for wolves, a haunt of desert-owls.

14   Marmots shall consort with jackals,
        and he-goat shall encounter he-goat.
        There too the nightjar shall rest
        and find herself a place for repose.

15   There the sand-partridge shall make her nest,
        lay her eggs and hatch them
        and gather her brood under her wings;
        there shall the kites gather,
         one after another.

16   Consult the book of the LORD and read it:
        not one of these shall be lacking,
         not one miss its fellow,
        for with his own mouth he has ordered it
        and with his own breath he has brought them together.

17   He it is who has allotted each its place,
        and his hand has measured out their portions;
         they shall occupy it for ever
         and dwell there from generation to generation.

35   Let the wilderness and the thirsty land be glad,
        let the desert rejoice and burst into flower.

2   Let it flower with fields of asphodel,
        let it rejoice and shout for joy.
        The glory of Lebanon is given to it,
         the splendour too of Carmel and Sharon;
these shall see the glory of the LORD, the splendour of our God.

3   Strengthen the feeble arms,
        steady the tottering knees;

4   say to the anxious, Be strong and fear not.
        See, your God comes with vengeance,
with dread retribution he comes to save you.

> Then shall blind men's eyes be opened, 5
> and the ears of the deaf unstopped.
> Then shall the lame man leap like a deer, 6
> and the tongue of the dumb shout aloud;
> for water springs up in the wilderness,
> and torrents flow in dry land.
> The mirage becomes a pool, 7
> the thirsty land bubbling springs;
> instead of reeds and rushes, grass shall grow
> in the rough land where wolves now lurk.
> And there shall be a causeway there 8
> which shall be called the Way of Holiness,
> and the unclean shall not pass along it;
> it shall become a pilgrim's way, *a*
> no fool shall trespass on it.
> No lion shall come there, 9
> no savage beast climb on to it;
> not one shall be found there.
> By it those he has ransomed shall return
> and the LORD's redeemed come home; 10
> they shall enter Zion with shouts of triumph,
> crowned with everlasting gladness.
> Gladness and joy shall be their escort,
> and suffering and weariness shall flee away.

Jerusalem delivered from Sennacherib

IN THE FOURTEENTH YEAR of the reign of Hezekiah, Sennacherib king 36 1*b* of Assyria attacked and took all the fortified cities of Judah. From Lachish 2 he sent the chief officer*c* with a strong force to King Hezekiah at Jerusalem; and he halted by the conduit of the Upper Pool on the causeway which leads to the Fuller's Field. There Eliakim son of Hilkiah, the comptroller of the household, came out to him, with Shebna the adjutant-general 3 and Joah son of Asaph, the secretary of state. The chief officer said to 4 them, 'Tell Hezekiah that this is the message of the Great King, the king of Assyria: "What ground have you for this confidence of yours? Do you 5 think fine words can take the place of skill and numbers? On whom then do you rely for support in your rebellion against me? On Egypt? Egypt 6 is a splintered cane that will run into a man's hand and pierce it if he leans on it. That is what Pharaoh king of Egypt proves to all who rely on him. And if you tell me that you are relying on the LORD your God, is he not the 7 god whose hill-shrines and altars Hezekiah has suppressed, telling Judah and Jerusalem that they must prostrate themselves before this altar alone?"

'Now, make a bargain with my master the king of Assyria: I will give 8 you two thousand horses if you can find riders for them. Will you reject 9

a a pilgrim's way: *prob. rdg.; Heb. unintelligible.* *b* *Verses 1–22: cp. 2 Kgs. 18. 13–37; 2 Chr. 32. 1–19.* *c* Or sent Rab-shakeh.

10 the authority of even the least of my master's servants and rely on Egypt for chariots and horsemen? Do you think that I have come to attack this land and destroy it without the consent of the LORD? No; the LORD himself said to me, "Attack this land and destroy it." '

11 Eliakim, Shebna, and Joah said to the chief officer, 'Please speak to us in Aramaic, for we understand it; do not speak Hebrew to us within earshot

12 of the people on the city wall.' The chief officer answered, 'Is it to your master and to you that my master has sent me to say this? Is it not to the people sitting on the wall who, like you, will have to eat their own dung

13 and drink their own urine?' Then he stood and shouted in Hebrew, 'Hear

14 the message of the Great King, the king of Assyria. These are the king's

15 words: "Do not be taken in by Hezekiah. He cannot save you. Do not let him persuade you to rely on the LORD, and tell you that the LORD will save you and that this city will never be surrendered to the king of Assyria."

16 Do not listen to Hezekiah; these are the words of the king of Assyria: "Make peace with me. Come out to me, and then you shall each eat the fruit of his own vine and his own fig-tree, and drink the water of his own

17 cistern, until I come and take you to a land like your own, a land of grain

18 and new wine, of corn and vineyards. Beware lest Hezekiah mislead you by telling you that the LORD will save you. Did the god of any of these

19 nations save his land from the king of Assyria? Where are the gods of Hamath and Arpad? Where are the gods of Sepharvaim? Where are the

20 gods of Samaria? Did they save Samaria from me? Among all the gods of these nations is there one who saved his land from me? And how is the LORD to save Jerusalem?" '

21 The people were silent and answered not a word, for the king had given

22 orders that no one was to answer him. Eliakim son of Hilkiah, comptroller of the household, Shebna the adjutant-general, and Joah son of Asaph, secretary of state, came to Hezekiah with their clothes rent and reported what the chief officer had said.

37 1*a* When King Hezekiah heard their report, he rent his clothes and wrapped

2 himself in sackcloth, and went into the house of the LORD. He sent Eliakim comptroller of the household, Shebna the adjutant-general, and the senior

3 priests, all covered in sackcloth, to the prophet Isaiah son of Amoz, to give him this message from the king: 'This day is a day of trouble for us, a day of reproof and contempt. We are like a woman who has no strength

4 to bear the child that is coming to the birth. It may be that the LORD your God heard the words of the chief officer whom his master the king of Assyria sent to taunt the living God, and will confute what he, the LORD

5 your God, heard. Offer a prayer for those who still survive.' King Hezekiah's

6 servants came to Isaiah, and he told them to say this to their master: 'This is the word of the LORD: "Do not be alarmed at what you heard when the

7 lackeys of the king of Assyria blasphemed me. I will put a spirit in him, and he shall hear a rumour and withdraw to his own country; and there I will make him fall by the sword." '

8 So the chief officer withdrew. He heard that the king of Assyria had

9 left Lachish, and he found him attacking Libnah. But when the king learnt

a Verses 1–38 : cp. 2 Kgs. 19. 1–37 ; 2 Chr. 32. 20–22.

that Tirhakah king of Cush was on the way to make war on him, he sent
messengers again[a] to Hezekiah king of Judah, to say to him, 'How can   10
you be deluded by your god on whom you rely when he promises that
Jerusalem shall not fall into the hands of the king of Assyria? Surely you 11
have heard what the kings of Assyria have done to all countries, exterminating their people; can you then hope to escape? Did their gods save   12
the nations which my forefathers destroyed, Gozan, Harran, Rezeph, and
the people of Beth-eden living in Telassar? Where are the kings of Hamath, 13
of Arpad, and of Lahir, Sepharvaim, Hena, and Ivvah?'

Hezekiah took the letter from the messengers and read it; then he went   14
up into the house of the LORD, spread it out before the LORD and offered 15
this prayer: 'O LORD of Hosts, God of Israel, enthroned on the cherubim, 16
thou alone art God of all the kingdoms of the earth; thou hast made heaven
and earth. Turn thy ear to me, O LORD, and listen; open thine eyes, O LORD, 17
and see; hear the message that Sennacherib has sent to taunt the living God.
It is true, O LORD, that the kings of Assyria have laid waste every country, 18
that they have consigned their gods to the fire and destroyed them; for   19
they were no gods but the work of men's hands, mere wood and stone. But 20
now, O LORD our God, save us from his power, so that all the kingdoms of
the earth may know that thou, O LORD, alone art God.'

Isaiah son of Amoz sent to Hezekiah and said, 'This is the word of   21
the LORD the God of Israel: I have heard your prayer to me concerning
Sennacherib king of Assyria. This is the word which the LORD has spoken 22
concerning him:

> The virgin daughter of Zion disdains you,
>> she laughs you to scorn;
> the daughter of Jerusalem tosses her head
>> as you retreat.
>> Whom have you taunted and blasphemed?   23
>> Against whom have you clamoured,
> casting haughty glances at the Holy One of Israel?
>> You have sent your servants to taunt the Lord,   24
>> and said:
>> With my countless chariots I have gone up
>> high in the mountains, into the recesses of Lebanon.
>> I have cut down its tallest cedars,
>> the best of its pines,
> I have reached its highest limit of forest and meadow.[b]
>> I have dug wells   25
>> and drunk the waters of a foreign land,
> and with the soles of my feet I have dried up
>> all the streams of Egypt.
>
>> Have you not heard long ago?   26
>> I did it all.

[a] again: *prob. rdg., cp. 2 Kgs. 19. 9; Heb.* and he heard.   [b] and meadow: *prob.
rdg.; Heb.* its meadow.

> In days gone by I planned it
> and now I have brought it about,
> making fortified cities tumble down
> into heaps of rubble.

27   Their citizens, shorn of strength,
> disheartened and ashamed,
> were but as plants in the field, as green herbs,
> as grass on the roof-tops blasted before the east wind.

28   I know your rising up and your sitting down,
> your going out and your coming in.

29   The frenzy of your rage against me and your arrogance
> have come to my ears.
> I will put a ring in your nose
> and a hook in your lips,
> and I will take you back by the road
> on which you have come.

30 This shall be the sign for you: this year you shall eat shed grain and in the
31 second year what is self-sown; but in the third year sow and reap, plant
32 vineyards and eat their fruit. The survivors left in Judah shall strike fresh
root under ground and yield fruit above ground, for a remnant shall come
out of Jerusalem and survivors from Mount Zion. The zeal of the LORD
of Hosts will perform this.

33   'Therefore, this is the word of the LORD concerning the king of Assyria:

> He shall not enter this city
> nor shoot an arrow there,
> he shall not advance against it with shield
> nor cast up a siege-ramp against it.

34   By the way on which he came he shall go back;
> this city he shall not enter.
> This is the very word of the LORD.

35   I will shield this city to deliver it,
> for my own sake and for the sake of my servant David.'

36   The angel of the LORD went out and struck down a hundred and eighty-
five thousand men in the Assyrian camp; when morning dawned, they
37 all lay dead. So Sennacherib king of Assyria broke camp, went back to
38 Nineveh and stayed there. One day, while he was worshipping in the temple
of his god Nisroch, Adrammelech and Sharezer his sons murdered him
and escaped to the land of Ararat. He was succeeded by his son Esarhaddon.

38 1 *a*   At this time Hezekiah fell dangerously ill and the prophet Isaiah son
of Amoz came to him and said, 'This is the word of the LORD: Give your
last instructions to your household, for you are a dying man and will not
2 recover.' Hezekiah turned his face to the wall and offered this prayer to
3 the LORD: 'O LORD, remember how I have lived before thee, faithful and
loyal in thy service, always doing what was good in thine eyes.' And he
4 5 wept bitterly. Then the word of the LORD came to Isaiah: 'Go and say to
Hezekiah: "This is the word of the LORD the God of your father David:

a Verses 1–8, 21, 22 : cp. 2 Kgs. 20. 1–11.

I have heard your prayer and seen your tears; I will add fifteen years to
your life. I will deliver you and this city from the king of Assyria and will   6
protect this city."' Then Isaiah told them to apply a fig-plaster; so they   21*a*
made one and applied it to the boil, and he recovered. Then Hezekiah said,   22
'By what sign shall I know that I shall go up into the house of the LORD?'
And Isaiah said,*b* 'This shall be your sign from the LORD that he will do   7
what he has promised. Watch the shadow cast by the sun on the stairway   8
of Ahaz: I will bring backwards ten steps the shadow which has gone down
on the stairway.' And the sun went back ten steps on the stairway down
which it had gone.

A poem of Hezekiah king of Judah after his recovery from his illness, as   9
it was written down:

> I thought: In the prime of life I must pass away;   10
> for the rest of my years I am consigned to the gates of Sheol.
> I said: I shall no longer see the LORD   11
> in the land of the living;
> never again, like those who live in the world,
> shall I look on a man.
> My dwelling is taken from me,   12
> pulled up like a shepherd's tent;
> thou hast cut short my life like a weaver
> who severs the web from the thrum.
> From morning to night thou tormentest me,
> then I am racked with pain till the morning.   13
> All my bones are broken, as a lion would break them;
> from morning to night thou tormentest me.
> I twitter as if I were a swallow,   14
> I moan like a dove.
> My eyes falter as I look up to the heights;
> O Lord, pay heed, stand surety for me.
> How can I complain, what can I say to the LORD   15
> when he himself has done this?
> I wander to and fro all my life long
> in the bitterness of my soul.
> Yet, O Lord, my soul shall live with thee;   16
> do thou give my spirit rest.*c*
> Restore me and give me life.
> Bitterness had indeed been my lot in place of prosperity;   17
> but thou by thy love hast brought me back
> from the pit of destruction;
> for thou hast cast all my sins behind thee.
> Sheol cannot confess thee,   18
> Death cannot praise thee,
> nor can they who go down to the abyss
> hope for thy truth.

---

a *Verses 21, 22 transposed.*   *b* And Isaiah said: *prob. rdg., cp. 2 Kgs. 20. 9; Heb. om.*
c Yet . . . rest: *prob. rdg.; Heb. unintelligible.*

19   The living, the living alone can confess thee
            as I do this day,
      as a father makes thy truth known, O God, to his sons.
20   The LORD is at hand to save me;
        so let us sound the music of our praises
      all our life long in the house of the LORD.*a*

39 1*b*   At this time Merodach-baladan son of Baladan king of Babylon sent
envoys with a gift to Hezekiah; for he had heard that he had been ill and
2 was well again. Hezekiah welcomed them and showed them all his treasury,
silver and gold, spices and fragrant oil, his entire armoury and everything
to be found among his treasures; there was nothing in his house and in all
3 his realm that Hezekiah did not show them. Then the prophet Isaiah came
to King Hezekiah and asked him, 'What did these men say and where have
they come from?' 'They have come from a far-off country,' Hezekiah
4 answered, 'from Babylon.' Then Isaiah asked, 'What did they see in your
house?' 'They saw everything,' Hezekiah replied; 'there was nothing among
5 my treasures that I did not show them.' Then Isaiah said to Hezekiah,
6 'Hear the word of the LORD of Hosts: The time is coming, says the LORD,
when everything in your house, and all that your forefathers have amassed
till the present day, will be carried away to Babylon; not a thing shall be
7 left. And some of the sons who will be born to you, sons of your own
begetting, shall be taken and shall be made eunuchs in the palace of the
8 king of Babylon.' Hezekiah answered, 'The word of the LORD which you
have spoken is good'; thinking to himself that peace and security would
last out his lifetime.

News of the returning exiles

40   Comfort, comfort my people;*c*
         —it is the voice of your God;
2   speak tenderly to Jerusalem *d*
         and tell her this,
     that she has fulfilled her term of bondage,
        that her penalty is paid;
     she has received at the LORD's hand
        double*e* measure for all her sins.

3   There is a voice that cries:
     Prepare a road for the LORD through the wilderness,
    clear a highway across the desert for our God.
4   Every valley shall be lifted up,
     every mountain and hill brought down;
     rugged places shall be made smooth
        and mountain-ranges become a plain.

---

a Verses 21, 22 transposed to follow verse 6.   *b Verses 1–8: cp. 2 Kgs. 20. 12–19.*
c Comfort . . . people: *or* Comfort, O my people, comfort.   *d* speak . . . Jerusalem: *or* bid Jerusalem be of good heart.   *e* double: *or* full.

Thus shall the glory of the LORD be revealed,   5
and all mankind together shall see it;
    for the LORD himself has spoken.

A voice says, 'Cry',   6
and another asks, 'What shall I cry?'
'That all mankind is grass,
    they last no longer than a flower of the field.
The grass withers, the flower fades,   7
when the breath of *a* the LORD blows upon them; *b*
the grass withers, the flowers fade,   8
    but the word of our God endures for evermore.'

You who bring Zion good news, *c* up with you to the mountain-top; 9
    lift up your voice and shout,
    you who bring good news to Jerusalem, *d*
        lift it up fearlessly;
cry to the cities of Judah, 'Your God is here.'
Here is the Lord GOD coming in might,   10
    coming to rule with his right arm.
        His recompense comes with him,
        he carries his reward before him.
He will tend his flock like a shepherd   11
    and gather them together with his arm;
he will carry the lambs in his bosom
    and lead the ewes to water.

Israel delivered and redeemed

Who has gauged the waters in the palm of his hand,   12
or with its span set limits to the heavens?
Who has held all the soil of earth in a bushel,
or weighed the mountains on a balance
    and the hills on a pair of scales?
Who has set limits to the spirit of the LORD?   13
What counsellor stood at his side to instruct him?
With whom did he confer to gain discernment?   14
Who taught him how to do justice
    or gave him lessons in wisdom?
Why, to him nations are but drops from a bucket,   15
    no more than moisture on the scales;
coasts and islands weigh as light as specks of dust.
    All Lebanon does not yield wood enough for fuel   16
    or beasts enough for a sacrifice.

a the breath of: *or* a wind from.   *b Prob. rdg.; Heb. adds* surely the people are grass.
c You . . . news: *or* O Zion, bringer of good news.   *d* you . . . Jerusalem: *or*
O Jerusalem, bringer of good news.

17   All nations dwindle to nothing before him,
            he reckons them mere nothings, less than nought.

18   What likeness will you find for God
            or what form to resemble his?
19   Is it an image which a craftsman sets up,
            and a goldsmith covers with plate
            and fits with studs of silver as a costly gift?
20   Or is it mulberry-wood that will not rot which a man chooses,
            seeking out a skilful craftsman for it,
            to mount an image that will not fall?

[6*a*]   Each workman helps the others,
            each man encourages his fellow.
[7*a*]   The craftsman urges on the goldsmith,
            the gilder urges the man who beats the anvil,
            he declares the soldering to be sound;
            he fastens the image with nails
            so that it will not fall down.

21   Do you not know, have you not heard,
            were you not told long ago,
            have you not perceived ever since the world began,
22   that God sits throned on the vaulted roof of earth,
                whose inhabitants are like grasshoppers*b*?
            He stretches out the skies like a curtain,
            he spreads them out like a tent to live in;
23   he reduces the great to nothing
            and makes all earth's princes less than nothing.
24   Scarcely are they planted, scarcely sown,
            scarcely have they taken root in the earth,
                before he blows upon them and they wither away,
                and a whirlwind carries them off like chaff.
25   To whom then will you liken me,
                whom set up as my equal?
                asks the Holy One.
26   Lift up your eyes to the heavens;
            consider who created it all,
            led out their host one by one
            and called them all by their names;
                through his great might, his might and power,
                not one is missing.
27   Why do you complain, O Jacob,
                and you, Israel, why do you say,
            'My plight is hidden from the LORD
            and my cause has passed out of God's notice'?

a *These are verses 6 and 7 of ch. 41, transposed to this point.*   *b* Or locusts.

Do you not know, have you not heard?   28
The LORD, the everlasting God, creator of the wide world,
    grows neither weary nor faint;
      no man can fathom his understanding.
He gives vigour to the weary,   29
new strength to the exhausted.
Young men may grow weary and faint,   30
even in their prime they may stumble and fall;
but those who look to the LORD will win new strength,   31
they will grow wings like eagles;
they will run and not be weary,
they will march on and never grow faint.

Keep silence before me, all you coasts and islands;   **41**
let the peoples come to meet me.*a*
Let them come near, then let them speak;
we will meet at the place of judgement, I and they.
Tell me, who raised up that one from the east,   2
one greeted by victory wherever he goes?
Who is it that puts nations into his power
and makes kings go down before him,*b*
he scatters them with his sword like dust
and with his bow like chaff before the wind;
he puts them to flight and passes on unscathed,   3
swifter than any traveller on foot?
Whose work is this, I ask, who has brought it to pass?   4
Who has summoned the generations from the beginning?
It is I, the LORD, I am the first,
and to the last of them I am He.
Coasts and islands saw it and were afraid,   5
    the world trembled from end to end.*c*

But you, Israel my servant,   8*d*
you, Jacob whom I have chosen,
    race of Abraham my friend,
      I have taken you up,   9
have fetched you from the ends of the earth,
    and summoned you from its farthest corners,
I have called you my servant,
have chosen you and not cast you off:
fear nothing, for I am with you;   10
be not afraid, for I am your God.
I strengthen you, I help you,
I support you with my victorious right hand.

---

a come to meet me: *prob. rdg., transposing, with slight change, from end of verse 5; Heb.*
win new strength (*repeated from* 40. 31).   *b* before him: *prob. rdg.; Heb. om.*
c *See note on verse 1.*   *d* *Verses 6 and 7 transposed to follow* 40. 20.

11   Now shall all who defy you
             be disappointed and put to shame;
           all who set themselves against you
             shall be as nothing; they shall vanish.

12   You will look for your assailants but not find them;
           all who take up arms against you
             shall be as nothing, nothing at all.

13   For I, the LORD your God,
           take you by the right hand;
           I say to you, Do not fear;
           it is I who help you,

14   fear not, Jacob you worm and Israel poor louse.
           It is I who help you, says the LORD,
             your ransomer, the Holy One of Israel.

15   See, I will make of you a sharp threshing-sledge,
             new and studded with teeth;
           you shall thresh the mountains and crush them
           and reduce the hills to chaff;

16   you shall winnow them, the wind shall carry them away
           and a great gale shall scatter them.
           Then shall you rejoice in the LORD
             and glory in the Holy One of Israel.

17   The wretched and the poor look for water and find none,
             their tongues are parched with thirst;
           but I the LORD will give them an answer,
           I, the God of Israel, will not forsake them.

18   I will open rivers among the sand-dunes
             and wells in the valleys;
           I will turn the wilderness into pools
           and dry land into springs of water;

19   I will plant cedars in the wastes,
           and acacia and myrtle and wild olive;
           the pine shall grow on the barren heath
           side by side with fir and box,

20   that men may see and know,
           may once for all give heed and understand
           that the LORD himself has done this,
             that the Holy One of Israel has performed it.

21   Come, open your plea, says the LORD,
          present your case, says Jacob's King;

22   let them come forward, these idols,
           let them foretell the future.
           Let them declare the meaning of past events
             that we may give our minds to it;
           let them predict things that are to be
             that we may know their outcome.

23   Declare what will happen hereafter;

then we shall know you are gods.
Do what you can, good or ill,
anything that may grip us with fear and awe.
You cannot! You are sprung from nothing,   24
your works are rotten;
whoever chooses you is vile as you are.
I roused one from the north, and he obeyed;   25
I called one from the east, summoned him in^a my name,
he marches over viceroys as if they were mud,
like a potter treading his clay.
Tell us, who declared this from the beginning, that we might know it,   26
or told us beforehand so that we could say, 'He was right'?
Not one declared, not one foretold,
not one heard a sound from you.
Here is one who will speak first as advocate for Zion,   27
here I appoint defending counsel for Jerusalem;
but from the other side no advocate steps forward   28
and, when I look, there is no one there.
I ask a question and no one answers;
see what empty things they are!   29
      Nothing that they do has any worth,
their effigies are wind, mere nothings.

Here is my servant, whom I uphold,   **42**
my chosen one in whom I delight,
I have bestowed my spirit upon him,
and he will make justice shine on the nations.
He will not call out or lift his voice high,   2
or ^b make himself heard in the open street.
He will not break a bruised reed,   3
or snuff out a smouldering wick;
he will make justice shine on every race,^c
never faltering, never breaking down,^d   4
he will plant justice on earth,
while coasts and islands wait for his teaching.

Thus speaks the LORD who is God,   5
he who created the skies and stretched them out,
who fashioned the earth and all that grows in it,
who gave breath to its people,
the breath of life to all who walk upon it:
I, the LORD, have called you with righteous purpose   6
and taken you by the hand;
I have formed you, and appointed you
to be a light^e to all peoples,
a beacon for the nations,

---

^a summoned him in: *or* who will call on.   ^b He will not . . . *or*: *or* In very truth
he will call out and lift his voice high, and . . .   ^c on every race: *or* in truth.
^d never faltering . . . down: *or* he will neither rebuke nor wound.   ^e *Or* a covenant.

7   to open eyes that are blind,
 to bring captives out of prison,
  out of the dungeons where they lie in darkness.

8   I am the LORD; the LORD^a is my name;
 I will not give my glory to another god,
  nor my praise to any idol.

9   See how the first prophecies have come to pass,
 and now I declare new things;
before they break from the bud I announce them to you.

10   Sing a new song to the LORD,
  sing his praise throughout the earth,
   you that sail the sea, and all sea-creatures,
  and you that inhabit the coasts and islands.

11   Let the wilderness and its towns rejoice,
  and the villages of the tribe of Kedar.
Let those who live in Sela shout for joy
  and cry out from the hill-tops.

12   You coasts and islands, all uplift his praises;
 let all ascribe glory to the LORD.

13   The LORD will go forth as a warrior,
 he will rouse the frenzy of battle like a hero;
 he will shout, he will raise the battle-cry
  and triumph over his foes.

14   Long have I lain still,
 I kept silence and held myself in check;
 now I will cry like a woman in labour,
  whimpering, panting and gasping.

15   I will lay waste mountains and hills
  and shrivel all their green herbs;
 I will turn rivers into desert wastes^b
  and dry up all the pools.

16   Then will I lead blind men on their way^c
 and guide them by paths they do not know;
I will turn darkness into light before them
  and straighten their twisting roads.
All this I will do and leave nothing undone.

17   Those who trust in an image,
those who take idols for their gods
turn tail in bitter shame.

18   Hear now, you that are deaf;
 you blind men, look and see:

19   yet who is blind but my servant,
who so deaf as the messenger whom I send?
Who so blind as the one who holds my commission,
  so deaf as the servant of the LORD?

---

^a the LORD: *or* He.   ^b desert wastes: *prob. rdg.; Heb.* coasts and islands.
^c *Prob. rdg.; Heb. adds* which they do not know.

You have seen much but remembered little,   20
your ears are wide open but nothing is heard.
It pleased the LORD, for the furtherance of his justice,   21
to make his law a law of surpassing majesty;
yet here is a people plundered and taken as prey,   22
all of them ensnared, trapped in holes,
  lost to sight in dungeons,
carried off as spoil without hope of rescue,
as plunder with no one to say, 'Give it back.'
Hear this, all of you who will,   23
listen henceforward and give me a hearing:
who gave away Jacob for plunder,   24
  who gave Israel away for spoil?
Was it not the LORD? They sinned against him,
they would not follow his ways
  and refused obedience to his law;
so in his anger he poured out upon Jacob   25
his wrath and the fury of battle.
It wrapped him in flames, yet still he did not learn the lesson,
scorched him, yet he did not lay it to heart.

But now this is the word of the LORD,   **43**
the word of your creator, O Jacob,
  of him who fashioned you, Israel:
Have no fear; for I have paid your ransom;
I have called you by name and you are my own.
When you pass through deep waters, I am with you,   2
  when you pass through rivers,
  they will not sweep you away;
walk through fire and you will not be scorched,
through flames and they will not burn you.
For I am the LORD your God,   3
  the Holy One of Israel, your deliverer;
for your ransom I give Egypt,
Nubia and Seba are your price.
You are more precious to me than the Assyrians,   4
you are honoured and I have loved you,
I would give the Edomites in exchange for you,
and the Leummim for your life.

  Have no fear; for I am with you;   5
I will bring your children from the east
  and gather you all from the west.
I will say to the north, 'Give them up',   6
  and to the south, 'Do not hold them back.
Bring my sons and daughters from afar,
  bring them from the ends of the earth;
bring every one who is called by my name,   7

all whom I have created, whom I have formed,
all whom I have made for my glory.'

8   Bring out this people,
    a people who have eyes but are blind,
who have ears but are deaf.

9   All the nations are gathered together
    and the peoples assembled.
Who amongst them can expound this thing
    and interpret for us all that has gone before?
Let them produce witnesses to prove their case,
or let them listen and say, 'That is the truth.'

10   My witnesses, says the LORD, are you, my servants,
    you whom I have chosen
to know me and put your faith in me
    and understand that I am He.
Before me there was no god fashioned
    nor ever shall be after me.

11   I am the LORD, I myself,
    and none but I can deliver.

12   I myself have made it known in full, and declared it,
I and no alien god amongst you,
    and you are my witnesses, says the LORD.

13   I am God; from this very day I am He.
What my hand holds, none can snatch away;
    what I do, none can undo.

14   Thus says the LORD your ransomer, the Holy One of Israel:
    For your sakes I have sent to Babylon;
I will lay the Chaldaeans prostrate as they flee,
    and their cry of triumph will turn to groaning.

15   I am the LORD, your Holy One,
    your creator, Israel, and your King.

16   Thus says the LORD,
    who opened a way in the sea
    and a path through mighty waters,

17   who drew on chariot and horse to their destruction,
    a whole army, men of valour;
    there they lay, never to rise again;
they were crushed, snuffed out like a wick:

18   Cease to dwell on days gone by
    and to brood over past history.

19   Here and now I will do a new thing;
    this moment it will break from the bud.
    Can you not perceive it?
I will make a way even through the wilderness
    and paths in the barren desert;

20   the wild beasts shall do me honour,
    the wolf and the ostrich;

for I will provide water in the wilderness
 and rivers in the barren desert,
  where my chosen people may drink.
I have formed this people for myself   21
 and they shall proclaim my praises.
Yet you did not call upon me, O Jacob;   22
much less did you weary yourself in my service, O Israel.
You did not bring me sheep as whole-offerings 23
 or honour me with sacrifices;
  I asked you for no burdensome offerings
  and wearied you with no demands for incense.
You did not buy me sweet-cane with your money 24
 or glut me with the fat of your sacrifices;
 rather you burdened me with your sins
  and wearied me with your iniquities.
I alone, I am He,   25
who for his own sake wipes out your transgressions,
 who will remember your sins no more.
Cite me by name, let us argue it out;   26
 set forth your pleading and justify yourselves.
Your first father transgressed,   27
 your spokesmen rebelled against me,
 and your princes profaned my sanctuary;   28
so I sent Jacob to his doom
 and left Israel to execration.

Hear me now, Jacob my servant,   **44**
 hear me, my chosen Israel.
  Thus says the LORD your maker,   2
 your helper, who fashioned you from birth:
 have no fear, Jacob my servant,
 Jeshurun whom I have chosen,
 for I will pour down rain on a thirsty land,   3
  showers on the dry ground.
 I will pour out my spirit on your offspring
  and my blessing on your children.
 They shall spring up like a green tamarisk,   4
 like poplars by a flowing stream.
This man shall say, 'I am the LORD's man',   5
 that one shall call himself a son of Jacob,
another shall write the LORD's name on his hand
 and shall add the name of Israel to his own.

 Thus says the LORD, Israel's King,   6
 the LORD of Hosts, his ransomer:
I am the first and I am the last,
 and there is no god but me.
 Who is like me? Let him stand up,   7
 let him declare himself and speak and show me his evidence,

let him announce beforehand[a] things to come,
let him[b] declare what is yet to happen.

8   Take heart, do not be afraid.
Did I not foretell this long ago?
I declared it, and you are my witnesses.
Is there any god beside me,
or any creator, even one that I do not know?

9   Those who make idols are less than nothing;
all their cherished images profit nobody;
their worshippers are blind,
sheer ignorance makes fools of them.

10   If a man makes a god or casts an image,
his labour is wasted.

11   Why! its votaries show their folly;
the craftsmen too are but men.
Let them all gather together and confront me,
all will be afraid and look the fools they are.

12 The blacksmith sharpens a graving tool and hammers out his work[c] hot from the coals and shapes it with his strong arm; when he grows hungry
13 his strength fails, if he has no water to drink he tires. The woodworker draws his line taut and marks out a figure with a scriber; he planes the wood and measures it with callipers, and he carves it to the shape of a man, comely as the human form, to be set up presently in a house.[d]

14 A man plants a cedar and the rain makes it grow, so that later on he will have cedars to cut down; or he chooses an ilex or an oak to raise a stout
15 tree for himself in the forest. It becomes fuel for his fire: some of it he takes and warms himself, some he kindles and bakes bread on it, and some he makes into a god and prostrates himself, shaping it into an idol and
16 bowing down before it. The one half of it he burns in the fire and on this he roasts meat, so that he may eat his roast and be satisfied; he also warms himself at it and he says, 'Good! I can feel the heat, I am growing warm.'
17 Then what is left of the wood he makes into a god by carving it into shape; he bows down to it and prostrates himself and prays to it, saying, 'Save me;
18 for thou art my god.' Such people neither know nor understand, their eyes
19 made too blind to see, their minds too narrow to discern. Such a man will not use his reason, he has neither the wit nor the sense to say, 'Half of it I have burnt, yes, and used its embers to bake bread; I have roasted meat on them too and eaten it; but the rest of it I turn into this abominable thing
20 and so I am worshipping a log of wood.' He feeds on ashes indeed! His own deluded mind has misled him, he cannot recollect himself so far as to say, 'Why! this thing in my hand is a sham.'

21   Remember all this, Jacob,
remember, Israel, for you are my servant,
I have fashioned you, and you are to serve me;

---

[a] let him announce beforehand: *prob. rdg.; Heb.* since my appointing an ancient people and ...   [b] *Prob. rdg.; Heb.* them.   [c] his work: *prob. rdg.; Heb.* he works.
[d] *Or* a shrine.

you shall not forget me, Israel.
I have swept away your sins like a dissolving mist, 22
    and your transgressions are dispersed like clouds;
turn back to me; for I have ransomed you.
Shout in triumph, you heavens, for it is the LORD's doing; 23
    cry out for joy, you lowest depths of the earth;
    break into songs of triumph, you mountains,
    you forest and all your trees;
    for the LORD has ransomed Jacob
    and made Israel his masterpiece.

Thus says the LORD, your ransomer, 24
    who fashioned you from birth:
I am the LORD who made all things,
    by myself I stretched out the skies,
    alone I hammered out the floor of the earth.
I frustrate false prophets and their signs 25
    and make fools of diviners;
I reverse what wise men say
    and make nonsense of their wisdom.
I make my servants' prophecies come true 26
    and give effect to my messengers' designs.
    I say of Jerusalem,
    'She shall be inhabited once more',
and of the cities of Judah, 'They shall be rebuilt;
    all their ruins I will restore.'
I say to the deep waters, 'Be dried up; 27
    I will make your streams run dry.'
I say to Cyrus, 'You shall be my shepherd 28
    to carry out all my purpose,
so that Jerusalem may be rebuilt
    and the foundations of the temple may be laid.'

Thus says the LORD to Cyrus his anointed, **45**
    Cyrus whom he has taken by the hand
    to subdue nations before him
    and undo the might of kings;
    before whom gates shall be opened
    and no doors be shut:
I will go before you 2
    and level the swelling hills;
    I will break down gates of bronze
    and hack through iron bars.
I will give you treasures from dark vaults, 3
    hoarded in secret places,
that you may know that I am the LORD,
    Israel's God who calls you by name.

4   For the sake of Jacob my servant and Israel my chosen
         I have called you by name
      and given you your title, though you have not known me.
5   I am the LORD, there is no other;
            there is no god beside me.
         I will strengthen you though you have not known me,
6   so that men from the rising and the setting sun
         may know that there is none but I:
            I am the LORD, there is no other;
7   I make the light, I create darkness,
            author alike of prosperity and trouble.
      I, the LORD, do all these things.

8   Rain righteousness, you heavens,
         let the skies above pour down;
            let the earth open to receive it,
            that it may bear the fruit of salvation
         with righteousness in blossom at its side.
         All this I, the LORD, have created.

9   Will the pot contend[a] with the potter,
         or the earthenware [b] with the hand that shapes it?
      Will the clay ask the potter what he is making?
         or his [c] handiwork say to him, 'You have no skill'?
10   Will the babe say [d] to his father, 'What are you begetting?',
         or to his mother, 'What are you bringing to birth?'
11   Thus says the LORD, Israel's Holy One, his maker:
         Would you dare question me concerning my children,
         or instruct me in my handiwork?
12   I alone, I made the earth
         and created man upon it;
      I, with my own hands, stretched out the heavens
         and caused all their host to shine.
13   I alone have roused this man in righteousness,
            and I will smooth his path before him;
         he shall rebuild my city
            and let my exiles go free—
            not for a price nor for a bribe,
            says the LORD of Hosts.

14   Thus says the LORD:
         Toilers of Egypt and Nubian merchants
            and Sabaeans bearing tribute [e]
      shall come into your power and be your slaves,
      shall come and march behind you in chains;

---

[a] Will . . . contend: *prob. rdg.; Heb.* Ho! he has contended.   [b] *Or* shard.
[c] *Prob. rdg.; Heb.* your.   [d] Will . . . say: *prob. rdg.; Heb.* Ho! you that say.
[e] bearing tribute: *or* men of stature.

they shall bow down before you in supplication, saying,
'Surely God is among you and there is no other,
    no other god.
How then canst thou be a god that hidest thyself,   15
    O God of Israel, the deliverer?'

Those who defy him are confounded and brought to shame,   16
those who make idols perish in confusion.
    But Israel has been delivered by the LORD,   17
      delivered for all time to come;
they shall not be confounded or put to shame for all eternity.

Thus says the LORD, the creator of the heavens,   18
    he who is God,
  who made the earth and fashioned it
    and himself fixed it fast,
  who created it no empty void,
    but made it for a place to dwell in:
I am the LORD, there is no other.
I do not speak in secret, in realms of darkness,   19
  I do not say to the sons of Jacob,
    'Look for me in the empty void.'
I the LORD speak what is right, declare what is just.
  Gather together, come, draw near,   20
    all you survivors of the nations,
  you fools, who carry your wooden idols in procession
  and pray to a god that cannot save you.
Come forward and urge your case, consult together: 21
  who foretold this in days of old,
    who stated it long ago?
  Was it not I the LORD?
  There is no god but me;
there is no god other than I, victorious and able to save.
  Look to me and be saved,   22
    you peoples from all corners of the earth;
  for I am God, there is no other.
    By my life I have sworn,   23
  I have given a promise of victory,
    a promise that will not be broken,
  that to me every knee shall bend
    and by me every tongue shall swear.
In the LORD alone, men shall say,   24
    are victory and might;
  and all who defy him
  shall stand ashamed in his presence,
  but all the sons of Israel shall stand victorious   25
    and find their glory in the LORD.

46 Bel has crouched down, Nebo has stooped low:
their images, once carried in your processions,
   have been loaded on to beasts and cattle,
   a burden for the weary creatures;
2   they stoop and they crouch;
not for them to bring the burden to safety;
   the gods themselves go into captivity.
3   Listen to me, house of Jacob
and all the remnant of the house of Israel,
a load on me from your birth, carried by me from the womb:
4   till you grow old I am He,
and when white hairs come, I will carry you still;
I have made you and I will bear the burden,
   I will carry you and bring you to safety.
5   To whom will you liken me? Who is my equal?
With whom can you compare me? Where is my like?
6   Those who squander their bags of gold
and weigh out their silver with a balance
hire a goldsmith to fashion them into a god;
   then they worship it and fall prostrate before it;
7   they hoist it shoulder-high and carry it home;
    they set it down on its base;
there it must stand, it cannot stir from its place.
Let a man cry to it as he will, it never answers him;
   it cannot deliver him from his troubles.

8   Remember this, you rebels,
consider it well, and abandon hope,
9   remember all that happened long ago;
for I am God, there is no other,
I am God, and there is no one like me;
10   I reveal the end from the beginning,
from ancient times I reveal what is to be;
I say, 'My purpose shall take effect,
I will accomplish all that I please.'
11   I summon a bird of prey[a] from the east,
one from a distant land to fulfil my purpose.
   Mark this; I have spoken, and I will bring it about,
I have a plan to carry out, and carry it out I will.
12   Listen to me, all you stubborn hearts,
   for whom victory is far off:
13   I bring my victory near, it is not far off,
   and my deliverance shall not be delayed;
I will grant deliverance in Zion
   and give my glory to Israel.[b]

[a] a bird of prey: *or* a massed host.
[b] and give my glory to Israel: *or* for Israel my glory.

Down with you, sit in the dust,   **47**
    virgin daughter of Babylon.
Down from your throne, sit on the ground,
    daughter of the Chaldaeans;
never again shall men call you
    soft-skinned and delicate.
Take up the millstone, grind meal, uncover your tresses;   2
strip off your skirt, bare your thighs, wade through rivers,
    so that your nakedness may be plain to see   3
    and your shame exposed.
I will take vengeance, I will treat with none of you,
    says the Holy One of Israel, our ransomer,   4
      whose name is the Lord of Hosts.

    Sit silent,   5
be off into the shadows, daughter of the Chaldaeans;
for never again shall men call you
    queen of many kingdoms.
    When I was angry with my people,   6
    I dishonoured my own possession
    and gave them into your power.
You showed them no mercy,
you made your yoke weigh heavy on the aged.
You said then, 'I shall reign a queen for ever',   7
    while*a* you gave no thought to this
    and did not consider how it would end.
    Now therefore listen to this,   8
you lover of luxury, carefree on your throne.
    You say to yourself,
'I am, and who but I?
No widow's weeds for me, no deaths of children.'
    Yet suddenly, in a single day,   9
    these two things shall come upon you;
they shall both come upon you in full measure:*b*
    children's deaths and widowhood,
    for all your monstrous sorceries, your countless spells.
Secure in your wicked ways you thought, 'No one is looking.'   10
Your wisdom betrayed you, omniscient as you were,
    and you said to yourself,
'I am, and who but I?'
    Therefore evil shall come upon you,   11
    and you will not know how to master it;
disaster shall befall you,
    and you will not be able to charm it away;
    ruin all unforeseen
shall come suddenly upon you.

a for ever', while: *or* of a wide realm, for all time'; but.
b in full measure: *or* at random.

12   Persist in your spells and your monstrous sorceries,[a]
          maybe you can get help from them,
              maybe you will yet inspire awe.
13   But no! in spite of your many wiles you are powerless.
      Let your astrologers, your star-gazers
   who foretell your future month by month,
              persist, and save you!
14   But look, they are gone like chaff;
              fire burns them up;
      they cannot snatch themselves from the flames;
          this is no glowing coal to warm them,
      no fire for them to sit by.
15   So much for your magicians
      with whom you have trafficked all your life:
      they have stumbled off, each his own way,
          and there is no one to save you.

48   Hear this, you house of Jacob,
              you who are called by the name of Israel,
              you who spring from the seed of Judah;
              who swear by the name of the LORD
              and boast in the God of Israel,
              but not in honesty or sincerity,
2   although you call yourselves citizens of a holy city
              and lean for support on the God of Israel;
              his name is the LORD of Hosts.
3   Long ago I announced what would first happen,
      I revealed it with my own mouth;
      suddenly I acted and it came about.
4   I knew that you were stubborn,
              your neck stiff as iron, your brow like bronze,
5   therefore I told you of these things long ago,
      and declared them before they came about,
      so that you could not say, 'This was my idol's doing;
      my image, the god that I fashioned, he ordained them.'
6   You have heard what I said; consider it well,
      and you must admit the truth of it.
      Now I show you new things,
              hidden things which you did not know before.
7   They were not created long ago, but in this very hour;
      you had never heard of them before today.
      You cannot say, 'I know them already.'
8   You neither heard nor knew,
      long ago your ears were closed;
      for I knew that you were untrustworthy, treacherous,
      a notorious rebel from your birth.

[a] *Prob. rdg.; Heb. adds* with which you have trafficked all your life (*cp. verse 15*).

For the sake of my own name I was patient,^{*a*}   9
rather than destroy you I held myself in check.
See how I tested you, not as silver is tested,   10
  but in the furnace of affliction; there I purified you.
For my honour, for my own honour I did it;   11
let them disparage my past triumphs^{*b*} if they will:
I will not give my glory to any other god.

Hear me, Jacob,   12
  and Israel whom I called:
I am He; I am the first,
  I am the last also.
With my own hands I founded the earth,   13
with my right hand I formed the expanse of sky;
  when I summoned them,
    they sprang at once into being.
Assemble, all of you, and listen to me;   14
  which of you has declared what is coming,
that he whom I love shall wreak my^{*c*} will on Babylon
  and the Chaldaeans shall be scattered?
I, I myself, have spoken, I have called him,   15
I have made him appear, and wherever he goes he shall prosper.
Draw near to me and hear this: 16
  from the beginning I have never spoken in secret;
  from the moment of its first happening I was there.^{*d*}

Thus says the LORD your ransomer, the Holy One of Israel: 17
  I am the LORD your God:
    I teach you for your own advantage
  and lead you in the way you must go.
If only you had listened to my commands,   18
your prosperity would have rolled on like a river in flood
  and your just success like the waves of the sea;
    in number your children would have been like the sand   19
      and your descendants countless as its grains;
their name would never be erased or blotted from my sight.
Come out of Babylon, hasten away from the Chaldaeans;   20
proclaim it with loud songs of triumph,
  crying the news to the ends of the earth;
tell them, 'The LORD has ransomed his servant Jacob.'
Though he led them through desert places they suffered no thirst,   21
for them he made water run from the rock,
  for them he cleft the rock and streams gushed forth.

There is no peace for the wicked,   22
  says the LORD.

---

^{*a*} *See note on verse 11.*   ^{*b*} my past triumphs: *transposed from verse 9.*   ^{*c*} *Or* his.
^{*d*} *Prob. rdg.; Heb. adds* and now the Lord GOD has sent me, and his spirit.

Israel a light to the nations

49
Listen to me, you coasts and islands,
pay heed, you peoples far away:
from birth the LORD called me,
he named me from my mother's womb.

2
He made my tongue his sharp sword
and concealed me under cover of his hand;
he made me a polished arrow
and hid me out of sight in his quiver.

3
He said to me, 'You are my servant,
Israel through whom I shall win glory';
so I rose to honour in the LORD's sight
and my God became my strength.[a]

4
Once I said, 'I have laboured in vain;
I have spent my strength for nothing, to no purpose';
yet in truth my cause is with the LORD
and my reward is in God's hands.

5
And now the LORD who formed me in the womb to be his servant,
to bring Jacob back to him
that Israel should be gathered to him,[b]
now the LORD calls me again:[c]

6
it is too slight a task for you, as my servant,
to restore the tribes of Jacob,
to bring back the descendants of Israel:
I will make you a light to the nations,
to be my salvation[d] to earth's farthest bounds.

7
Thus says the Holy One, the LORD who ransoms Israel,
to one who thinks little of himself,
whom every nation abhors,
the slave of tyrants:
When they see you kings shall rise,
princes shall rise and bow down,
because of the LORD who is faithful,
because of the Holy One of Israel who has chosen you.

8
Thus says the LORD:
In the hour of my favour I answered you,
and I helped you on the day of deliverance,[e]
putting the land to rights
and sharing out afresh its desolate fields;

9
I said to the prisoners, 'Go free',
and to those in darkness, 'Come out and be seen.'

---

[a] so I rose . . . strength: *transposed from end of verse 5.*   [b] be gathered to him:
or not be swept away.   [c] *See note on verse 3.*   [d] to be my salvation: *or that*
my salvation may reach.   [e] *Prob. rdg.; Heb. adds* I have formed you, and
appointed you to be a light to all peoples (*cp. 42. 6*).

They shall find pasture in the desert sands^a
and grazing on all the dunes.
    They shall neither hunger nor thirst,   10
no scorching heat or sun shall distress them;
    for one who loves them shall lead them
    and take them to water at bubbling springs.
    I will make every hill a path   11
    and build embankments for my highways.
See, they come; some from far away,   12
these from the north and these from the west
    and those from the land of Syene.
Shout for joy, you heavens, rejoice, O earth,   13
    you mountains, break into songs of triumph,
    for the LORD has comforted his people
    and has had pity on his own in their distress.

    But Zion says,   14
'The LORD has forsaken me; my God has forgotten me.'
    Can a woman forget the infant at her breast,   15
    or a loving mother the child of her womb?
Even these forget, yet I will not forget you.
    Your walls are always before my eyes,   16
    I have engraved them on the palms of my hands.
    Those who are to rebuild you make better speed   17
        than those who pulled you down,
    while those who laid you waste depart.
    Raise your eyes and look around you: 18
see how they assemble, how they are flocking back to you.
    By my life I, the LORD, swear it,
    you shall wear them proudly as your jewels,
        and adorn yourself with them like a bride;
    I did indeed make you waste and desolate,   19
        I razed you to the ground,
but your boundaries^b shall now be too narrow
        for your inhabitants—
    and those who laid you in ruins are far away.
The children born in your bereavement shall yet say in your hearing, 20
'This place is too narrow; make room for me to live in.'
    Then you will say to yourself,   21
    'All these children, how did I come by them,
bereaved and barren as I was?
Who reared them
    when I was left alone, left by myself;
    where did I get them all?'

---

^a desert sands: *prob. rdg.; Heb.* ways.   ^b I did . . . boundaries: *or* your wasted
and desolate land, your ruined countryside.

22   The Lord GOD says,
Now is the time: I will beckon to the nations
    and hoist a signal to the peoples,
    and they shall bring your sons in their arms
    and carry your daughters on their shoulders;
23   kings shall be your foster-fathers
    and their princesses shall be your nurses.
They shall bow to the earth before you
    and lick the dust from your feet;
and you shall know that I am the LORD
    and that none who look to me will be disappointed.
24   Can his prey be taken from the strong man,
or the captive be rescued from the ruthless?
25   And the LORD answers,
The captive shall be taken even from the strong,
    and the prey of the ruthless shall be rescued;
I will contend with all who contend against you
    and save your children from them.
26 I will force your oppressors to feed on their own flesh
and make them drunk with their own blood as if with fresh wine,
    and all mankind shall know
    that it is I, the LORD, who save you,
        I your ransomer, the Mighty One of Jacob.

50   The LORD says,
Is there anywhere a deed of divorce
    by which I have put your mother away?
    Was there some creditor of mine
    to whom I sold you?
No; it was through your own wickedness that you were sold
and for your own misconduct that your mother was put away.
2   Why, then, did I find no one when I came?
    Why, when I called, did no one answer?
Did you think my arm too short to redeem,
    did you think I had no power to save?
Not so. By my rebuke I dried up the sea
    and turned rivers into desert;
    their fish perished for lack of water
    and died on the thirsty ground;
3   I clothed the skies in mourning
and covered them with sackcloth.

4   The Lord GOD has given me
    the tongue of a teacher
    and skill to console the weary
    with a word in the morning;
    he sharpened my hearing
that I might listen like one who is taught.

The Lord GOD opened my ears   5
and I did not disobey or turn back in defiance.
  I offered my back to the lash,   6
    and let my beard be plucked from my chin,
I did not hide my face from spitting and insult;
  but the Lord GOD stands by to help me;   7
  therefore no insult can wound me.
I have set my face like flint,
  for I know that I shall not be put to shame,
  because one who will clear my name is at my side.   8
Who dare argue against me? Let us confront one another.
Who will dispute my cause? Let him come forward.
The Lord GOD will help me;   9
  who then can prove me guilty?
They will all wear out like a garment,
  the moths will eat them up.

Which of you fears the LORD and obeys his servant's commands?   10
The man who walks in dark places with no light,
yet trusts in the name of the LORD and leans on his God.
  But you who kindle a fire and set fire-brands alight,   11
  go, walk into your own fire
  and among the fire-brands you have set ablaze.
  This is your fate at my hands:
    you shall lie down in torment.

Listen to me, all who follow the right and seek the LORD: **51**
  look to the rock from which you were hewn,
    to the quarry from which you were dug;
  look to your father Abraham   2
    and to Sarah who gave you birth:
when I called him he was but one,
  I blessed him and made him many.
The LORD has indeed comforted Zion,   3
  comforted all her ruined homes,
turning her wilderness into an Eden,
  her thirsty plains into a garden of the LORD.
Joy and gladness shall be found in her,
  thanksgiving and melody.
  Pay heed to me, my people,   4
  and hear me, O my nation;
  for my law shall shine forth
and I will flash the light of my judgement over the nations.
My victory is near, my deliverance has gone *a* forth   5
  and my arm shall rule the nations;
  for me coasts and islands shall wait
    and they shall look to me for protection.

a *Or* shone.

6   Lift your eyes to the heavens,
       look at the earth beneath:
       the heavens grow murky as smoke;
       the earth wears into tatters like a garment,
       and those who live on it die like maggots;
       but my deliverance is everlasting
           and my saving power shall never wane.

7   Listen to me, my people who know what is right,
       you who lay my law to heart:
           do not fear the taunts of men,
           let no reproaches dismay you;
8   for the grub will devour them like a garment
       and the moth as if they were wool,
       but my saving power shall last for ever
           and my deliverance to all generations.

9   Awake, awake, put on your strength, O arm of the LORD,
       awake as you did long ago, in days gone by.
           Was it not you
       who hacked the Rahab in pieces and ran the dragon through?
10   Was it not you
       who dried up the sea, the waters of the great abyss,
       and made the ocean depths a path for the ransomed?
11   So the LORD's people shall come back, set free,
       and enter Zion with shouts of triumph,
           crowned with everlasting joy;
           joy and gladness shall overtake them as they come,
           and sorrow and sighing shall flee away.
12   I, I myself, am he that comforts you.
       Why then fear man, man who must die,
           man frail as grass?
13   Why have you forgotten the LORD your maker,
       who stretched out the skies and founded the earth?
           Why are you continually afraid, all the day long,
       why dread the fury of oppressors ready to destroy you?
           Where is that fury?
14   He that cowers under it shall soon stand upright and not die,
       he shall soon reap the early crop and not lack bread.

15   I am the LORD your God, the LORD of Hosts is my name. I cleft the sea
16   and its waves roared, that I might fix the heavens in place and form the
       earth and say to Zion, 'You are my people.' I have put my words in your
       mouth and kept you safe under the shelter of my hand.

17   Awake, awake; rise up, Jerusalem.
       You have drunk from the LORD's hand
           the cup of his wrath,
           drained to its dregs the bowl of drunkenness;

of all the sons you have borne there is not one to guide you,   18
of all you have reared, not one to take you by the hand.
These two disasters have overtaken you;   19
who can console you?—
havoc and ruin, famine and the sword;
who can comfort you?
Your sons are in stupor, they lie at the head of every street,   20
like antelopes caught in the net,
glutted with the wrath of the LORD,
the rebuke of your God.
Therefore listen to this, in your affliction,   21
drunk that you are, but not with wine:
thus says the LORD, your Lord and your God,   22
who will plead his people's cause:
Look, I take from your hand
the cup of drunkenness;
you shall never again drink from the bowl of my wrath,
I will give it instead to your tormentors and oppressors,   23
those who said to you, 'Lie down and we will walk over you';
and you made your backs like the ground beneath them,
like a roadway for passers-by.

Awake, awake, put on your strength, O Zion,   **52**
put on your loveliest garments, holy city of Jerusalem;
for never shall the uncircumcised and the unclean enter you again.
Rise up, captive Jerusalem, shake off the dust;   2
loose your neck from the collar that binds it,
O captive daughter of Zion.

The LORD says, You were sold but no price was paid, and without pay-   3
ment you shall be ransomed. The Lord GOD says, At the beginning my   4
people went down into Egypt to live there, and at the end it was the
Assyrians who oppressed them; but now what do I find here? says the   5
LORD. My people carried off and no price paid, their rulers derided,
and my name reviled all day long, says the LORD. But on that day my   6
people shall know my name; they shall know that it is I who speak; here
I am.

How lovely on the mountains are the feet of the herald   7
who comes to proclaim prosperity and bring good news,
the news of deliverance,
calling to Zion, 'Your God is king.'
Hark, your watchmen raise their voices   8
and shout together in triumph;
for with their own eyes they shall see
the LORD returning in pity to Zion.
Break forth together in shouts of triumph,   9
you ruins of Jerusalem;
for the LORD has taken pity on his people
and has ransomed Jerusalem.

883

10   The LORD has bared his holy arm
            in the sight of all nations,
         and the whole world from end to end
            shall see the deliverance of our God.

11   Away from Babylon; come out, come out,
            touch nothing unclean.
         Come out from Babylon, keep yourselves pure,
            you who carry the vessels of the LORD.

12   But you shall not come out in urgent haste
            nor leave like fugitives;
         for the LORD will march at your head,
            your rearguard will be Israel's God.

13   Behold, my servant shall prosper,
         he shall be lifted up, exalted to the heights.

14   Time was when many [a] were aghast at you, my people; [b]
15   so now many nations [c] recoil at sight of him,
         and kings curl their lips in disgust.
         For they see what they had never been told
            and things unheard before fill their thoughts.

53   Who could have believed what we have heard,
         and to whom has the power of the LORD been revealed?

2   He grew up before the LORD like a young plant
            whose roots are in parched ground;
         he had no beauty, no majesty to draw our eyes,
            no grace to make us delight in him;
         his form, disfigured, lost all the likeness of a man,
            his beauty changed beyond human semblance. [d]

3   He was despised, he shrank from the sight of men,
            tormented and humbled by suffering;
         we despised him, we held him of no account,
            a thing from which men turn away their eyes.

4   Yet on himself he bore our sufferings,
            our torments he endured,
         while we counted him smitten by God,
            struck down by disease and misery;

5   but he was pierced for our transgressions,
            tortured for our iniquities;
         the chastisement he bore is health for us
         and by his scourging we are healed.

6   We had all strayed like sheep,
         each of us had gone his own way;
         but the LORD laid upon him
            the guilt of us all.

---

[a] *Or* the great.   [b] *See note on 53. 2.*   [c] *Or* great nations.   [d] his form . . .
semblance: *transposed from end of 52. 14.*

He was afflicted, he submitted to be struck down   7
    and did not open his mouth;
he was led like a sheep to the slaughter,
like a ewe that is dumb before the shearers.*a*
Without protection, without justice,*b* he was taken away;   8
    and who gave a thought to his fate,
      how he was cut off from the world of living men,
stricken to the death for my people's transgression?
He was assigned a grave with the wicked,   9
a burial-place among the refuse of mankind,
though he had done no violence
    and spoken no word of treachery.
Yet the LORD took thought for his tortured servant   10
and healed him who had made himself *c* a sacrifice for sin;
so shall he enjoy long life and see his children's children,
    and in his hand the LORD's cause shall prosper.
After all his pains he shall be bathed in light,   11
after his disgrace he shall be fully vindicated;
so shall he, my servant, vindicate many,
    himself bearing the penalty of their guilt.
Therefore I will allot him a portion with the great,   12
    and he shall share the spoil with the mighty,
because he exposed himself to face death *d*
    and was reckoned among transgressors,
because he bore the sin of many
    and interceded for their transgressions.

Sing aloud, O barren woman who never bore a child,   **54**
break into cries of joy, you who have never been in labour;
    for the deserted wife has more sons than she who lives in wedlock,
      says the LORD.
Enlarge the limits of your home,   2
    spread wide the curtains of your tent;
let out its ropes to the full
    and drive the pegs home;
for you shall break out of your confines right and left,   3
your descendants shall dispossess wide regions,*e*
and re-people cities now desolate.
Fear not; you shall not be put to shame,   4
you shall suffer no insult, have no cause to blush.
It is time to forget the shame of your younger days
and remember no more the reproach of your widowhood;
for your husband is your maker, whose name is the LORD of Hosts;   5
     your ransomer is the Holy One of Israel
    who is called God of all the earth.

a Prob. rdg.; Heb. adds and he would not open his mouth.   *b* Without protection,
without justice: *or* After arrest and sentence.   *c* healed . . . himself: *prob. rdg.;*
Heb. he made sick, if you make.   *d Or* because he poured out his life to the death.
e wide regions: *or* the nations.

6   The LORD has acknowledged you a wife again,
           once deserted and heart-broken,
           your God has called you a bride still young
              though once rejected.
7   On the impulse of a moment I forsook you,
    but with tender affection I will bring you home again.
8   In sudden anger
      I hid my face from you for a moment;
    but now have I pitied you with a love which never fails,
           says the LORD who ransoms you.
9   These days recall for me the days of Noah:
      as I swore that the waters of Noah's flood
      should never again pour over the earth,
           so now I swear to you
    never again to be angry with you or reproach you.
10   Though the mountains move and the hills shake,
      my love shall be immovable and never fail,
           and my covenant of peace shall not be shaken.
      So says the LORD who takes pity on you.

11   O storm-battered city, distressed and disconsolate,
      now I will set your stones in the finest mortar
           and your foundations in lapis lazuli;
12   I will make your battlements of red jasper[a]
           and your gates of garnet;[b]
           all your boundary-stones shall be jewels.
13   Your masons shall all be instructed by the LORD,
          and your sons shall enjoy great prosperity;
14   and in triumph[c] shall you be restored.
    You shall be free from oppression and have no fears,
    free from terror, and it shall not come near you;
15   should any attack you, it will not be my doing,
    the aggressor, whoever he be, shall perish for his attempt.
16   It was I who created the smith
      to fan the coals in the furnace
      and forge weapons each for its purpose,
    and I who created the destroyer to lay waste;
17   but now no weapon made to harm you shall prevail,
    and you shall rebut every charge brought against you.
      Such is the fortune of the servants of the LORD;
          their vindication comes from me.
      This is the very word of the LORD.

55   Come, all who are thirsty, come, fetch water;
    come, you who have no food, buy corn and eat;
    come and buy, not for money, not for a price.[d]

[a] *Or* carbuncle.   [b] *Or* firestone.   [c] *Or* in righteousness.
[d] *Prob. rdg.; Heb. adds* wine and milk.

Why spend money and get what is not bread,   2
  why give the price of your labour and go unsatisfied?
Only listen to me and you will have good food to eat,
  and you will enjoy the fat of the land.
Come to me and listen to my words,   3
  hear me, and you shall have life:
  I will make a covenant with you, this time for ever,
to love you faithfully as I loved David.
I made him a witness to all races,   4
  a prince and instructor of peoples;
and you in turn shall summon nations you do not know,   5
and nations that do not know you shall come running to you,
  because the LORD your God,
  the Holy One of Israel, has glorified you.

Inquire of the LORD while he is present,   6
call upon him when he is close at hand.
Let the wicked abandon their ways   7
  and evil men their thoughts:
let them return to the LORD, who will have pity on them,
  return to our God, for he will freely forgive.
For my thoughts are not your thoughts,   8
  and your ways are not my ways.
  This is the very word of the LORD.
For as the heavens are higher than the earth,   9
so are my ways higher than your ways
  and my thoughts than your thoughts;
and as the rain and the snow come down from heaven   10
and do not return until they have watered the earth,
  making it blossom and bear fruit,
and give seed for sowing and bread to eat,
so shall the word which comes from my mouth prevail;   11
  it shall not return to me fruitless
without accomplishing my purpose
  or succeeding in the task I gave it.
  You shall indeed go out with joy   12
  and be led forth in peace.
Before you mountains and hills shall break into cries of joy,
and all the trees of the wild shall clap their hands,
  pine-trees shall shoot up in place of camel-thorn,   13
  myrtles instead of briars;
  all this shall win the LORD a great name,
  imperishable, a sign for all time.

Warnings to keep the moral law

56 These are the words of the LORD:
Maintain justice, do the right;
for my deliverance is close at hand,
and my righteousness will show itself victorious.

2 Happy is the man who follows these precepts,
happy the mortal who holds them fast,
who keeps the sabbath undefiled,
who refrains from all wrong-doing!

3 The foreigner who has given his allegiance to the LORD must not say,
'The LORD will keep me separate from his people for ever';
and the eunuch must not say,
'I am nothing but a barren tree.'

4 For these are the words of the LORD:
The eunuchs who keep my sabbaths,
who choose to do my will and hold fast to my covenant,

5 shall receive from me something better than sons and daughters,
a memorial and a name in my own house and within my walls;
I will give them an everlasting name,
a name imperishable for all time.

6 So too with the foreigners who give their allegiance to me, the LORD,
to minister to me and love my name
and to become my servants,
all who keep the sabbath undefiled
and hold fast to my covenant:

7 them will I bring to my holy hill
and give them joy in my house of prayer.
Their offerings and sacrifices shall be acceptable on my altar;
for my house shall be called
a house of prayer for all nations.

8 This is the very word of the Lord GOD,
who brings home the outcasts of Israel:
I will yet bring home all that remain to be brought in.

9 Come, beasts of the plain, beasts of the forest,
come, eat your fill,

10 for Israel's watchmen are blind, all of them unaware.
They are all dumb dogs who cannot bark,
stretched on the ground, dreaming, lovers of sleep,

11 greedy dogs that can never have enough.
They are shepherds who understand nothing,
absent each of them on his own pursuits,
each intent on his own gain wherever he can find it.

12 'Come,' says each of them, 'let me fetch wine,
strong drink, and we will drain it down;
let us make tomorrow like today,
or greater far!'

The righteous perish,   57
   and no one takes it to heart;
men of good faith are swept away, but no one cares,
the righteous are swept away before the onset of evil,
    but they enter into peace;   2
    they have run a straight course
    and rest in their last beds.

Come, stand forth, you sons of a soothsayer.   3
You spawn of an adulterer and a harlot,
    who is the target of your jests?   4
    Against whom do you open your mouths
    and wag your tongues,
children of sin that you are, spawn of a lie,
    burning with lust under the terebinths,   5
    under every spreading tree,
   and sacrificing children in the gorges,
    under the rocky clefts?
    And you, woman,   6
   your place is with the creatures of the gorge;
    that is where you belong.
   To them you have dared to pour a libation
    and present an offering of grain.[a]
   On a high mountain-top   7
    you have made your bed;
   there too you have gone up to offer sacrifice.
   In spite of all this am I to relent?[b]
Beside door and door-post you have put up your sign.   8
   Deserting me, you have stripped and lain down
    on the wide bed which you have made,
   and you drove bargains with men
    for the pleasure of sleeping together,
   and you have committed countless acts of fornication
    in the heat of your lust.
   You drenched your tresses in oil   9
    blended with many perfumes;
   you sent out your procurers far and wide
    even down to the gates of Sheol.
   Worn out by your unending excesses,   10
    even so you never said, 'I am past hope.'
    You earned a livelihood
    and so you had no anxiety.
Whom do you fear so much, that you should be false,   11
that you never remembered me or gave me a thought?
Did I not hold my peace and seem not to see
    while you showed no fear of me?

---

[a] *See note on verse 7.*   [b] *Line transposed from end of verse 6.*

12   Now I will denounce your conduct
              that you think so righteous.

13   These idols of yours shall not help when you cry;
              no idol shall save you.
           The wind shall carry them off, one and all,
              a puff of air shall blow them away;
           but he who makes me his refuge shall possess the earth
              and inherit my holy hill.

14   Then a voice shall be heard:
          Build up a highway, build it and clear the track,
              sweep away all that blocks my people's path.

15   Thus speaks the high and exalted one,
         whose name is holy, who lives for ever:
              I dwell in a high and holy place
                 with him who is broken and humble in spirit,
                to revive the spirit of the humble,
                to revive the courage of the broken.

16   I will not be always accusing,
              I will not continually nurse my wrath.
              For a breath of life passed out from me,
              and by my own act I created living creatures.

17   For a time I was angry at the guilt of Israel;
              I smote him in my anger and withdrew my favour.
              But he ran wild and went his wilful way.

18   Then I considered his ways,
              I cured him and gave him relief,
        and I brought him comfort in full measure,

19   brought peace to those who mourned for him,
              by the words that issue from my lips,
        peace for all men, both near and far,
              and so I cured him, says the LORD.

20   But the wicked are like a troubled sea,
              a sea that cannot rest,
        whose troubled waters cast up mud and filth.

21   There is no peace for the wicked,
                says the LORD.

58   Shout aloud without restraint;
           lift up your voice like a trumpet.
           Call my people to account for their transgression
              and the house of Jacob for their sins,

2   although they ask counsel of me day by day
              and say they delight in knowing my ways,
           although, like nations which have acted rightly
              and not forsaken the just laws of their gods,
           they ask me for righteous laws
              and say they delight in approaching God.

Why do we fast, if thou dost not see it?   3
Why mortify ourselves, if thou payest no heed?
Since you serve your own interest only on your fast-day
    and make all your men work the harder,
since your fasting leads only to wrangling and strife   4
    and dealing vicious blows with the fist,
    on such a day you are keeping no fast
    that will carry your cry to heaven.
Is it a fast like this that I require,   5
    a day of mortification such as this,
    that a man should bow his head like a bulrush
    and make his bed on sackcloth and ashes?
    Is this what you call a fast,
    a day acceptable to the LORD?
Is not this what I require of you as a fast: 6
    to loose the fetters of injustice,
    to untie the knots of the yoke,
        to snap every yoke
    and set free those who have been crushed?
Is it not sharing your food with the hungry,   7
taking the homeless poor into your house,
    clothing the naked when you meet them
    and never evading a duty to your kinsfolk?
Then shall your light break forth like the dawn   8
and soon you will grow healthy like a wound newly healed;
    your own righteousness shall be your vanguard
        and the glory of the LORD your rearguard.
Then, if you call, the LORD will answer;   9
    if you cry to him, he will say, 'Here I am.'
    If you cease to pervert justice,
to point the accusing finger and lay false charges,
    if you feed the hungry from your own plenty   10
        and satisfy the needs of the wretched,
    then your light will rise like dawn out of darkness
        and your dusk be like noonday;
    the LORD will be your guide continually   11
    and will satisfy your needs in the shimmering heat;
        he will give you strength of limb;
    you will be like a well-watered garden,
like a spring whose waters never fail.
The ancient ruins will be restored by your own kindred   12
    and you will build once more on ancestral foundations;
you shall be called Rebuilder of broken walls,
    Restorer of houses in ruins.

If you cease to tread the sabbath underfoot,   13
    and keep my holy day free from your own affairs,
    if you call the sabbath a day of joy

891

and the LORD's holy day a day to be honoured,
if you honour it by not plying your trade,
not seeking your own interest
or attending to your own affairs,

14 then you shall find your joy in the LORD,
and I will set you riding on the heights of the earth,
and your father Jacob's patrimony shall be yours to enjoy;
the LORD himself has spoken it.

59 The LORD's arm is not so short that he cannot save
nor his ear too dull to hear;
2 it is your iniquities that raise a barrier
between you and your God,
because of your sins he has hidden his face
so that he does not hear you.
3 Your hands are stained with blood
and your fingers with crime;
your lips speak lies
and your tongues utter injustice.
4 No man sues with just cause,
no man goes honestly to law;
all trust in empty words, all tell lies,
conceive mischief and give birth to trouble.
5 They hatch snakes' eggs, they weave cobwebs;
eat their eggs and you will die,
for rotten eggs hatch only rottenness.
6 As for their webs, they will never make cloth,
no one can use them for clothing;
their works breed trouble
and their hands are busy with deeds of violence.
7 They rush headlong into crime
in furious haste to shed innocent blood;
their schemes are schemes of mischief
and leave a trail of ruin and devastation.
8 They do not know the way to peace,
no justice guides their steps;
all the paths they follow are crooked;
no one who walks in them enjoys true peace.

9 Therefore justice is far away from us,
right does not reach us;
we look for light but all is darkness,
for the light of dawn, but we walk in deep gloom.
10 We grope like blind men along a wall,
feeling our way like men without eyes;
we stumble at noonday as if it were twilight,
like dead men in the ghostly underworld.
11 We growl like bears,
like doves we moan incessantly,

     waiting for justice, and there is none;
     for deliverance, but it is still far away.

     Our acts of rebellion against thee are past counting   12
     and our sins bear witness against us;
we remember our many rebellions, we know well our guilt:
     we have rebelled and broken faith with the LORD,   13
     we have relapsed and forsaken our God;
we have conceived lies in our hearts and repeated them
     in slanderous and treacherous words.
     Justice is rebuffed and flouted   14
     while righteousness stands aloof;
     truth stumbles in the market-place
     and honesty is kept out of court,
     so truth is lost to sight,   15
     and whoever shuns evil is thought a madman.

The LORD saw, and in his eyes it was an evil thing,
     that there was no justice;
     he saw that there was no man to help   16
     and was outraged that no one intervened;
     so his own arm brought him victory
     and his own integrity upheld him.
     He put on integrity as a coat of mail   17
     and the helmet of salvation on his head;
     he put on garments of vengeance
     and wrapped himself in a cloak of jealous anger.
     High God of retribution that he is,   18
     he pays in full measure,
wreaking his anger on his foes, retribution on his enemies.
     So from the west men shall fear his name,   19
     fear his glory from the rising of the sun;
     for it shall come like a shining river,
     the spirit of the LORD hovering over it,
     come as the ransomer of Zion   20
     and of all in Jacob who repent of their rebellion.
     This is the very word of the LORD.

This, says the LORD, is my covenant, which I make with them: My   21
spirit which rests on you and my words which I have put into your mouth
shall never fail you from generation to generation of your descendants from
now onward for ever. The LORD has said it.

Promise of the new Jerusalem

60 Arise, Jerusalem,
    rise clothed in light; your light has come
      and the glory of the LORD shines over you.
2 For, though darkness covers the earth
      and dark night the nations,
    the LORD shall shine upon you
    and over you shall his glory appear;
3   and the nations shall march towards your light
      and their kings to your sunrise.

4 Lift up your eyes and look all around:
    they flock together, all of them, and come to you;
    your sons also shall come from afar,
    your daughters walking beside them leading the way.
5   Then shall you see, and shine with joy,
    then your heart shall thrill with pride:
    the riches of the sea shall be lavished upon you
    and you shall possess the wealth of nations.

6   Camels in droves shall cover the land,
      dromedaries of Midian and Ephah,
    all coming from Sheba
    laden with golden spice*a* and frankincense,
      heralds of the LORD's praise.
7 All Kedar's flocks shall be gathered for you,
      rams of Nebaioth shall serve your need,
    acceptable offerings on my altar,
    and glory shall be added to glory in my temple.

8   Who are these that sail along like clouds,
      that fly like doves to their dovecotes?
9 They are vessels assembling from the coasts and islands,
      ships from Tarshish leading the convoy;
    they bring your sons from afar,
    their gold and their silver with them,
      to the honour of the LORD your God,
      the Holy One of Israel;
      for he has made you glorious.

10   Foreigners shall rebuild your walls
      and their kings shall be your servants;
      for though in my wrath I struck you down,
      now I have shown you pity and favour.
11   Your gates shall be open continually,
    they shall never be shut day or night,
    that through them may be brought the wealth of nations
      and their kings under escort.

a golden spice: *or* gold.

For the nation or kingdom which refuses to serve you shall perish, and   12
wide regions shall be laid utterly waste.

       The wealth of Lebanon shall come to you,   13
pine, fir,[a] and boxwood,[b] all together,
     to bring glory to my holy sanctuary,
     to honour the place where my feet rest.
The sons of your oppressors shall come forward to do homage,   14
all who reviled you shall bow low at your feet;
     they shall call you the City of the LORD,
       the Zion of the Holy One of Israel.

       No longer will you be deserted,   15
     a wife hated and unvisited;[c]
     I will make you an eternal pride
     and a never-ending joy.
     You shall suck the milk of nations   16
     and be suckled at the breasts of kings.
So you shall know that I the LORD am your deliverer,
     your ransomer the Mighty One of Jacob.

       For bronze[d] I will bring you gold   17
     and for iron I will bring silver,
bronze[d] for timber and iron for stone;
     and I will make your government be peace
     and righteousness rule over you.
The sound of violence shall be heard no longer in your land,   18
     or ruin and devastation within your borders;
     but you shall call your walls Deliverance
     and your gates Praise.

       The sun shall no longer be your light by day,   19
nor the moon shine on you when evening falls;
     the LORD shall be your everlasting light,
       your God shall be your glory.
     Never again shall your sun set   20
       nor your moon withdraw her light;
but the LORD shall be your everlasting light
     and the days of your mourning shall be ended.

       Your people shall all be righteous   21
and shall for ever possess the land,
     a shoot of my own planting,
a work of my own hands to bring me glory.
The few shall become ten thousand,   22
     the little nation great.
     I am the LORD;
soon, in the fullness of time, I will bring this to pass.

---

[a] *Or* elm.   [b] *Or* cypress.   [c] *Or* divorced and unmated.   [d] *Or* copper.

61 The spirit of the Lord GOD is upon me
because the LORD has anointed me;
he has sent me to bring good news to the humble,
    to bind up the broken-hearted,
to proclaim liberty to captives
    and release to those in prison;

2 to proclaim a year of the LORD's favour
    and a day of the vengeance of our God;
    to comfort all who mourn, *a*

3 to give them garlands instead of ashes,
    oil of gladness instead of mourners' tears,
    a garment of splendour for the heavy heart.
They shall be called Trees of Righteousness,
    planted by the LORD for his glory.

4   Ancient ruins shall be rebuilt
    and sites long desolate restored;
    they shall repair the ruined cities
and restore what has long lain desolate.

5 Foreigners shall serve as shepherds of your flocks,
    and aliens shall till your land and tend your vines;

6 but you shall be called priests of the LORD
    and be named ministers of our God;
    you shall enjoy the wealth of other nations
    and be furnished *b* with their riches.

7 And so, because shame in double measure
and jeers and insults *c* have been my people's lot,
they shall receive in their own land a double measure of
    wealth,
    and everlasting joy shall be theirs.

8 For I, the LORD, love justice
    and hate robbery and wrong-doing;
I will grant them a sure reward
    and make an everlasting covenant with them;

9   their posterity will be renowned among the nations
    and their offspring among the peoples;
all who see them will acknowledge in them
a race whom the LORD has blessed.

10   Let me rejoice in the LORD with all my heart,
    let me exult in my God;
for he has robed me in salvation as a garment
    and clothed me in integrity as a cloak,
like a bridegroom with his priestly garland,
    or a bride decked in her jewels.

11   For, as the earth puts forth her blossom
    or bushes in the garden burst into flower,

---

a Prob. rdg.; Heb. adds to appoint to Zion's mourners.   *b* be furnished: *prob. rdg.;*
Heb. unintelligible.   *c* and insults: *prob. rdg.; Heb.* they shout in triumph.

so shall the Lord GOD make righteousness and praise
 blossom before all the nations.

  For Zion's sake I will not keep silence,   **62**
   for Jerusalem's sake I will speak out,
 until her right shines forth like the sunrise,
 her deliverance like a blazing torch,
 until the nations see the triumph of your right   2
  and all kings see your glory.
 Then you shall be called by a new name
 which the LORD shall pronounce with his own lips;
 you will be a glorious crown in the LORD's hand,   3
  a kingly diadem in the hand of your God.
No more shall men call you Forsaken,   4
no more shall your land be called Desolate,
but you shall be named Hephzi-bah*ᵃ*
 and your land Beulah;*ᵇ*
 for the LORD delights in you
  and to him your land is wedded.
  For, as a young man weds a maiden,   5
   so you shall wed him who rebuilds you,
 and your God shall rejoice over you
  as a bridegroom rejoices over the bride.
I have posted watchmen on your walls, Jerusalem,   6
who shall not keep silence day or night:
 'You who invoke the LORD's name,
take no rest, give him no rest   7
  until he makes Jerusalem
 a theme of endless praise on earth.'

The LORD has sworn with raised right hand and mighty arm: 8
Never again will I give your grain to feed your foes
 or let foreigners drink the new wine
  for which you have toiled;
but those who bring in the corn shall eat and praise the LORD, 9
and those who gather the grapes shall drink in my holy courts.

  Go out of the gates, go out,   10
  prepare a road for my people;
 build a highway, build it up,
  clear away the boulders;
 raise a signal to the peoples.
 This is the LORD's proclamation   11
  to earth's farthest bounds:
 Tell the daughter of Zion,
  Behold, your deliverance has come.
  His recompense comes with him;
  he carries his reward before him;

  ᵃ That is My delight is in her. *ᵇ That is* Wedded.

12   and they shall be called a Holy People,
      the Ransomed of the LORD,
     a People long-sought, a City not forsaken.

63   'Who is this coming from Edom,
      coming from Bozrah, his garments stained red?
     Under his clothes his muscles stand out,
      and he strides, stooping in his might.'
     It is I, who announce that right has won the day,
      I, who am strong to save.

2   'Why is your clothing all red,
     like the garments of one who treads grapes in the vat?'

3   I have trodden the winepress alone;
     no man, no nation was with me.
      I trod them down in my rage,
      I trampled them in my fury;
     and their life-blood spurted over my garments
      and stained all my clothing.

4   For I resolved on a day of vengeance;
     the year for ransoming my own had come.

5   I looked for a helper but found no one,
      I was amazed that there was no one to support me;
     yet my own arm brought me victory,
     alone my anger supported me.

6   I stamped on nations in my fury,
      I pierced them in my rage
     and let their life-blood run out upon the ground.

7   I will recount the LORD's acts of unfailing love
     and the LORD's praises as High God,
      all that the LORD has done for us
     and his great goodness to the house of Israel,
      all that he has done for them in his tenderness
      and by his many acts of love.

8   He said, 'Surely they are my people,
      my sons who will not play me false';

9   and he became their deliverer in all their troubles.
     It was no envoy, no angel, but he himself that delivered them;
     he himself ransomed them by his love and pity,
      lifted them up and carried them
      through all the years gone by.

10   Yet they rebelled and grieved his holy spirit;
     only then was he changed into their enemy
      and himself fought against them.

11   Then men remembered days long past
     and him who drew out[a] his people:

---

[a] *That is* Moses *whose name resembles the Heb. verb meaning* draw out, *cp.* Exod. 2. 10 *and the note there.*

Where is he who brought them up from the Nile
   with the shepherd*a* of his flock?
Where is he who put within him
   his holy spirit,
who made his glorious power march   12
   at the right hand of Moses,
dividing the waters before them,
to win for himself an everlasting name,
   causing them to go through the depths   13
   sure-footed as horses in the wilderness,
like cattle moving down into a valley without stumbling,   14
   guided by the spirit of the LORD?
So didst thou lead thy people
to win thyself a glorious name.

Look down from heaven and behold   15
from the heights where thou dwellest holy and glorious.
   Where is thy zeal, thy valour,
   thy burning and tender love?
Stand not aloof;*b* for thou art our father,   16
though Abraham does not know us nor Israel acknowledge us.
Thou, LORD, art our father;
   thy name is our Ransomer*c* from of old.
Why, LORD, dost thou let us wander from thy ways   17
   and harden our hearts until we cease to fear thee?
   turn again for the sake of thy servants,
     the tribes of thy patrimony.
Why have wicked men trodden down thy sanctuary,*d*   18
   why have our enemies trampled on thy shrine?
We have long been reckoned as beyond thy sway,   19
   as if we had not been named thy own.

Why didst thou not rend the heavens and come down,   **64**
   and make the mountains shudder before thee
   as when fire blazes up in brushwood   2
   or fire makes water boil?
   then would thy name be known to thy enemies
   and nations tremble at thy coming.
When thou didst terrible things that we did not look for,   3
   the mountains shuddered before thee.
Never has ear heard*e* or eye seen   4
any other god taking the part of those who wait for him.
Thou dost welcome him who rejoices to do what is right,   5
   who remembers thee in thy ways.
   Though thou wast angry, yet we sinned,
   in spite of it we have done evil from of old,

---

a Or shepherds.   *b Stand not aloof: prob. rdg.; Heb. obscure in context.*   *c Or* our
Kinsman.   *d Why . . . sanctuary: prob. rdg.; Heb.* For a little while they possessed
thy holy people. *e Never . . . heard: prob. rdg.; Heb.* They have never heard or listened.

6   we all became like a man who is unclean
and all our righteous deeds like a filthy rag;
    we have all withered[a] like leaves
    and our iniquities sweep us away like the wind.

7   There is no one who invokes thee by name
    or rouses himself to cling to thee;
    for thou hast hidden thy face from us
    and abandoned us to our iniquities.

8   But now, LORD, thou art our father;
    we are the clay, thou the potter,
      and all of us are thy handiwork.

9   Do not be angry beyond measure, O Lord,
    and do not remember iniquity for ever;
    look on us all, look on thy people.

10   Thy holy cities are a wilderness,
Zion a wilderness, Jerusalem desolate;

11   our sanctuary, holy and glorious,
    where our fathers praised thee,
      has been burnt to the ground
and all that we cherish is a ruin.

12   After this, O LORD, wilt thou hold back,
    wilt thou keep silence and punish us beyond measure?

65   I was there to be sought by a people who did not ask,
    to be found by men who did not seek me.
    I said, 'Here am I, here am I',
    to a nation that did not invoke me by name.

2   I spread out my hands all day
    appealing to an unruly people
who went their evil way,
    following their own devices,

3   a people who provoked me
    continually to my face,
offering sacrifice in gardens, burning incense on brick
    altars,

4   crouching among graves, keeping vigil all night long,
eating swine's flesh, their cauldrons full of a tainted brew.

5   'Stay where you are,' they cry,
    'do not dare touch me; for I am too sacred for you.'
    Such people are a smouldering fire,
    smoking in my nostrils all day long.

6   All is on record before me; I will not keep silence;

7   I will repay[b] your iniquities,
yours and your fathers', all at once, says the LORD,
    because they burnt incense[c] on the mountains
      and defied me on the hills;

---

[a] have all withered: *or* are all carried away.   [b] *Prob. rdg., transposing* and then pay *to follow* reward.   [c] *Or* sacrifices.

I will first measure out their reward
    and then pay them in full.

These are the words of the LORD: 8
As there is new wine in a cluster of grapes
and men say, 'Do not destroy it; there is a blessing in it',
    so will I do for my servants' sake:
    I will not destroy the whole nation.
I will give Jacob children to come after him   9
and Judah heirs who shall possess my mountains;
    my chosen shall inherit them
and my servants shall live there.
Flocks shall range over Sharon,   10
    and the Vale of Achor be a pasture for cattle;
    they shall belong to my people who seek me.
But you that forsake the LORD and forget my holy   11
        mountain,
    who spread a table for the god of Fate,
    and fill bowls of spiced wine in honour of Fortune,
I will deliver you to your fate, to execution,   12
and you shall all bend the neck to the sword,
    because I called and you did not answer,
    I spoke and you did not listen;
    and you did what was wrong in my eyes
    and you chose what was against my will.
Therefore these are the words of the Lord GOD: 13
My servants shall eat but you shall starve;
my servants shall drink but you shall go thirsty;
my servants shall rejoice but you shall be put to shame;
    my servants shall shout in triumph   14
        in the gladness of their hearts,
    but you shall cry from sorrow
    and wail from anguish of spirit;
your name shall be used as an oath by my chosen,   15
    and the Lord GOD shall give you over to death;
    but his servants he shall call by another name.
He who invokes a blessing on himself in the land   16
    shall do so by the God whose name is Amen,
    and he who utters an oath in the land
    shall do so by the God of Amen;
    the former troubles are forgotten
    and they are hidden from my sight.
    For behold, I create   17
new heavens and a new earth.
    Former things shall no more be remembered
    nor shall they be called to mind.
    Rejoice and be filled with delight,   18
    you boundless realms which I create;

for I create Jerusalem to be a delight
and her people a joy;
19 I will take delight in Jerusalem and rejoice in my people;
weeping and cries for help
shall never again be heard in her.
20 There no child shall ever again die an infant,
no old man fail to live out his life;
every boy shall live his hundred years before he dies,
whoever falls short of a hundred shall be despised. *a*
21 Men shall build houses and live to inhabit them,
plant vineyards and eat their fruit;
22 they shall not build for others to inhabit
nor plant for others to eat.
My people shall live the long life of a tree,
and my chosen shall enjoy the fruit of their labour.
23 They shall not toil in vain or raise children for misfortune.
For they are the offspring of the blessed of the LORD
and their issue after them;
24 before they call to me, I will answer,
and while they are still speaking I will listen.
25 The wolf and the lamb shall feed together
and the lion shall eat straw like cattle. *b*
They shall not hurt or destroy in all my holy mountain,
says the LORD.

66 These are the words of the LORD:
Heaven is my throne and earth my footstool.
Where will you build a house for me,
where shall my resting-place be?
2 All these are of my own making
and all these are mine.
This is the very word of the LORD.

The man I look to is a man down-trodden and distressed,
one who reveres my words.
3 But to sacrifice an ox or to *c* kill a man,
slaughter a sheep or break a dog's neck,
offer grain or offer pigs' blood,
burn incense as a token and worship an idol—
all these are the chosen practices of men
who *d* revel in their own loathsome rites.
4 I too will practise those wanton rites of theirs
and bring down on them the very things they dread;
for I called and no one answered,
I spoke and no one listened.

---

a Or cursed.　　　　　*b* *Prob. rdg.; Heb. adds* and the food of the snake shall be dust.
c to sacrifice an ox or to: *or* those who sacrifice an ox and . . .　　　*d* are the chosen
practices of men who: *or* have chosen their own devices and . . .

They did what was wrong in my eyes
and chose practices not to my liking.

Hear the word of the LORD, you who revere his word: 5
    Your fellow-countrymen who hate you,
  who spurn you because you bear my name, have said,
    'Let the LORD show his glory,
    then we shall see you rejoice';
    but they shall be put to shame.
That roar from the city, that uproar in the temple, 6
is the sound of the LORD dealing retribution to his foes.

Shall a woman bear a child without pains? 7
give birth to a son before the onset of labour?
    Who has heard of anything like this? 8
    Who has seen any such thing?
Shall a country be born after one day's labour,
shall a nation be brought to birth all in a moment?
But Zion, at the onset of her pangs, bore her sons.
    Shall I bring to the point of birth and not deliver? 9
    the LORD says;
  shall I who deliver close the womb?
    your God has spoken.

Rejoice with Jerusalem and exult in her, 10
    all you who love her;
  share her joy with all your heart,
  all you who mourn over her.
Then you may suck and be fed from the breasts that give comfort, 11
delighting in her plentiful milk.
    For thus says the LORD: 12
I will send peace flowing over her like a river,
and the wealth of nations like a stream in flood;
    it shall suckle you,
    and you shall be carried in their arms
    and dandled on their knees.
    As a mother comforts her son, 13
  so will I myself comfort you,
    and you shall find comfort in Jerusalem.
    This you shall see and be glad at heart, 14
    your limbs shall be as fresh as grass in spring;
the LORD shall make his power known among his servants
    and his indignation felt among his foes.
For see, the LORD is coming in fire, 15
    with his chariots like a whirlwind,
  to strike home with his furious anger
    and with the flaming fire of his reproof.
The LORD will judge by fire, 16
    with fire he will test all living men,

and many will be slain by the LORD;
17   those who hallow and purify themselves in garden-rites,
       one after another in a magic ring,
   those who eat the flesh of pigs and rats[a] and all vile vermin,
       shall meet their end, one and all,
       says the LORD,
18   for I know their deeds and their thoughts.

   Then I myself will come to gather all nations and races,
       and they shall come and see my glory;
19   and I will perform a sign among them.
   I will spare some of them and send them to the nations,
       to Tarshish, Put, and Lud,[b]
       to Meshek, Rosh,[c] Tubal, and Javan,[d]
   distant coasts and islands which have never yet heard of me
       and have not seen my glory;
       these shall announce that glory among the nations.
20   From every nation they shall bring your countrymen
       on horses, in chariots and wagons,
           on mules and dromedaries,
           as an offering to the LORD,
       on my holy mountain Jerusalem,
           says the LORD,
       as the Israelites bring offerings
       in pure vessels to the LORD's house;
21   and some of them I will take for priests, for Levites,
           says the LORD.
22   For, as the new heavens and the new earth
   which I am making shall endure in my sight,
           says the LORD,
   so shall your race and your name endure;
23   and month by month at the new moon,
           week by week on the sabbath,
   all mankind shall come to bow down before me,
           says the LORD;
24   and they shall come out and see
   the dead bodies of those who have rebelled against me;
       their worm shall not die nor their fire be quenched,
           and they shall be abhorred by all mankind.

---

[a] *Or* jerboas.   [b] *Or* Lydia.   [c] Meshek, Rosh: *prob. rdg.; Heb.* those who
draw the bow.   [d] *Or* Greece.

THE BOOK OF THE PROPHET
JEREMIAH

THE WORDS OF JEREMIAH son of Hilkiah, one of the priests 1
at Anathoth in Benjamin. The word of the LORD came to him in the 2
thirteenth year of the reign of Josiah son of Amon, king of Judah;
also during the reign of Jehoiakim son of Josiah, king of Judah, until the 3
eleventh year of Zedekiah son of Josiah, king of Judah, was completed.
In the fifth month the people of Jerusalem were carried away into exile.

Jeremiah's call and two visions

THE WORD OF THE LORD CAME TO ME: 'Before I formed you in the 4 5
womb I knew you for my own; before you were born I consecrated you,
I appointed you a prophet to the nations.' 'Ah! Lord GOD,' I answered, 6
'I do not know how to speak; I am only a child.' But the LORD said, 'Do 7
not call yourself a child; for you shall go to whatever people I send you
and say whatever I tell you to say. Fear none of them, for I am with you 8
and will keep you safe.' This was the very word of the LORD. Then the 9
LORD stretched out his hand and touched my mouth, and said to me, 'I
put my words into your mouth. This day I give you authority over nations 10
and over kingdoms, to pull down and to uproot, to destroy and to demolish,
to build and to plant.'

The word of the LORD came to me: 'What is it that you see, Jeremiah?' 11
'An almond in early bloom',*a* I answered. 'You are right,' said the LORD to 12
me, 'for I am early on the watch*b* to carry out my purpose.' The word of 13
the LORD came to me a second time: 'What is it that you see?' 'A cauldron',
I said, 'on a fire, fanned by the wind; it is tilted away from the north.'
The LORD said: 14

> From the north disaster shall flare up
>> against all who live in this land;
> for now I summon all peoples and kingdoms of the north, 15
>> says the LORD.
> Their kings shall come and each shall set up his throne
>> before the gates of Jerusalem,
>> against her walls on every side,
>> and against all the cities of Judah.
> I will state my case against my people 16
>> for all the wrong they have done in forsaking me,
> in burning sacrifices to other gods,
>> worshipping the work of their own hands.

a Heb. shaked.   *b Heb.* shoked.

17   Brace yourself, Jeremiah;
         stand up and speak to them.
       Tell them everything I bid you,
    do not let your spirit break at sight of them,
       or I will break you before their eyes.

18   This day I make you a fortified city,
         a pillar of iron, a wall of bronze,
         to stand fast against the whole land,
    against the kings and princes of Judah,
       its priests and its people.

19   They will make war on you but shall not overcome you,
       for I am with you and will keep you safe.
       This is the very word of the LORD.

Exhortations to Israel and Judah

2 1 2 THE WORD OF THE LORD CAME TO ME: Go, make a proclamation that all Jerusalem shall hear: These are the words of the LORD:

       I remember the unfailing devotion of your youth,
         the love of your bridal days,
     when you followed me in the wilderness,
         through a land unsown.

3   Israel then was holy to the LORD,
         the firstfruits of his harvest;
       no one who devoured her went unpunished,
       evil always overtook them.
       This is the very word of the LORD.

4   Listen to the word of the LORD, people of Jacob, families of Israel, one
5 and all. These are the words of the LORD:

       What fault did your forefathers find in me,
         that they wandered far from me,
     pursuing empty phantoms and themselves becoming empty;
6   that they did not ask, 'Where is the LORD,
         who brought us up from Egypt,
         and led us through the wilderness,
         through a country of deserts and shifting sands,
         a country barren and ill-omened, where no man ever trod,
         no man made his home?'
7   I brought you into a fruitful land
         to enjoy its fruit and the goodness of it;
         but when you entered upon it you defiled it
         and made the home I gave you loathsome.
8   The priests no longer asked, 'Where is the LORD?'
       Those who handled the law had no thought of me,
         the shepherds of the people rebelled against me;

the prophets prophesied in the name of Baal
and followed gods powerless to help.

Therefore I will bring a charge against you once more,   9
  says the LORD,
against you and against your descendants.

  Cross to the coasts and islands of Kittim and see,   10
send to Kedar and consider well,
see whether there has been anything like this:

has a nation ever changed its gods,   11
  although they were no gods?
But my people have exchanged their Glory
  for a god altogether powerless.

  Stand aghast at this, you heavens,   12
  tremble in utter despair,
    says the LORD.

Two sins have my people committed: 13
  they have forsaken me,
  a spring of living water,
and they have hewn out for themselves cisterns,
  cracked cisterns that can hold no water.

Is Israel a slave? Was he born in slavery?   14
If not, why has he been despoiled?

Why do lions roar and growl at him?   15
Why has his land been laid waste,
why are his cities razed to the ground and abandoned?

Men of Noph and Tahpanhes   16
  will break your heads.

Is it not your desertion of the LORD your God   17
  that brings all this upon you?

And now, why should you make off to Egypt   18
  to drink the waters of the Shihor?
Or why make off to Assyria
  to drink the waters of the River?

It is your own wickedness that will punish you,   19
  your own apostasy that will condemn you.

See for yourselves how bitter a thing it is and how evil,
to forsake the LORD your God and revere me no longer.
  This is the very word of the Lord GOD of Hosts.

Ages ago you broke your yoke and snapped your traces,   20
  crying, 'I will not be your slave';
  and you sprawled in promiscuous vice
  on all the hill-tops, under every spreading tree.

I planted you as a choice red vine,   21
  true stock all of you,
yet now you are turned into a vine
  debased and worthless!

The stain of your sin is still there and I see it,   22

though you wash with soda and do not stint the soap.
   This is the very word of the Lord GOD.

23 How can you say, 'I am not polluted, not I!
   I have not followed the Baalim'?
Look how you conducted yourself in the valley;
   remember what you have done.
   You have been like a she-camel,
twisting and turning as she runs,
24   rushing alone into*a* the wilderness,
snuffing the wind in her lust;
   who can restrain her in her heat?
No one need tire himself out in pursuit of her;
   she is easily found at mating time.
25 Why not save your feet from stony ground
   and your throats from thirst?
But you said, 'No; I am desperate.
   I love foreign gods and I must go after them.'
26 As a thief is ashamed when he is found out,
   so the people of Israel feel ashamed,
they, their kings, their princes,
   their priests and their prophets;
27 they say 'You are our father' to a block of wood
   and cry 'Mother' to a stone.
But on me they have turned their backs
   and averted their faces from me.
And now on the day of disaster they say,
   'Rise up and save us.'
28 Where are they, those gods you made for yourselves?
Let them come and save you in the day of disaster.
For you, Judah, have as many gods as you have towns. *b*
29   The LORD answers,
Why argue your case with me?
You are rebels, every one of you.
30 In vain I struck down your sons,
   the lesson was not learnt;
still your own sword devoured your prophets
   like a ravening lion.
31 *c* Have I shown myself inhospitable to Israel
   like some wilderness or waterless land?
Why do my people say, 'We have broken away;
   we will never come back to thee'?

32   Will a girl forget her finery
     or a bride her ribbons?
   Yet my people have forgotten me
     over and over again.

---

a rushing alone into: *prob. rdg.; Heb.* a wild-ass taught in.   *b* towns: *or* blood-spattered altars.   *c* *Prob. rdg.; Heb. prefixes* You, O generation, see the word of the LORD.

How well you pick your way in search of lovers!   33
Why! even the worst of women can learn from you.
Yes, and there is blood on the corners of your robe—   34
   the life-blood of the innocent poor.
      You did not get it by housebreaking
      but by your sacrifices under every oak.
You say, 'I am innocent;   35
   surely his anger has passed away.'
But I will challenge your claim
   to have done no sin.
Why do you so lightly change your course?   36
Egypt will fail you as Assyria did;
   you shall go out from here,   37
      each of you with his hands above his head,
   for the LORD repudiates those in whom you trusted,
   and from them you shall gain nothing.

If a man puts away his wife   **3**
   and she leaves him,
and if she then becomes another's,
   may he go back to her again?
Is not that woman defiled,
   a forbidden thing?
You have played the harlot with many lovers;
   can you come back to me?
      says the LORD.
Look up to the high bare places and see: 2
   where have you not been ravished?
You sat by the wayside to catch lovers,
   like an Arab lurking in the desert,
and defiled the land
   with your fornication and your wickedness.
Therefore the showers were withheld   3
   and the spring rain failed.
But yours was a harlot's brow,
   and you were resolved to show no shame.
Not so long since, you called me 'Father,   4
   dear friend of my youth',
thinking, 'Will he be angry for ever?   5
   Will he rage eternally?'
This is how you spoke; you have done evil
   and gone unchallenged.

In the reign of King Josiah, the LORD said to me, Do you see what 6
apostate Israel did? She went up to every hill-top and under every spreading tree, and there she played the whore. Even after she had done all this, 7
I said to her, Come back to me, but she would not. That faithless woman,
her sister Judah, saw it all; she saw too that I had put apostate Israel away 8
and given her a note of divorce because she had committed adultery. Yet

that faithless woman, her sister Judah, was not afraid; she too has gone and
9 played the whore. She defiled the land with her thoughtless harlotry and
10 her adulterous worship of stone and wood. In spite of all this that faithless
woman, her sister Judah, has not come back to me in good faith, but only
in pretence. This is the very word of the LORD.

11 The LORD said to me, Apostate Israel is less to blame than that faithless
12 woman Judah. Go and proclaim this message to the north:

> Come back to me, apostate Israel,
> says the LORD,
> I will no longer frown on you.
> For my love is unfailing, says the LORD,
> I will not be angry for ever.
13 Only you must acknowledge your wrongdoing,
> confess your rebellion against the LORD your God.
> Confess your promiscuous traffic with foreign gods
> under every spreading tree,
> confess that you have not obeyed me.
> This is the very word of the LORD.

14 Come back to me, apostate children, says the LORD, for I am patient
with you, and I will take you, one from a city and two from a clan, and bring
15 you to Zion. There will I give you shepherds after my own heart, and they
16 shall lead you with knowledge and understanding. In those days, when
you have increased and become fruitful in the land, says the LORD, men
shall speak no more of the Ark of the Covenant of the LORD; they shall not
17 think of it nor remember it nor resort to it; it will be needed no more. At
that time Jerusalem shall be called the Throne of the LORD. All nations
shall gather in Jerusalem to honour the LORD's name; never again shall
18 they follow the promptings of their evil and stubborn hearts. In those days
Judah shall join Israel, and together they shall come from a northern land
into the land I gave their fathers as their patrimony.

19 I said, How gladly would I treat you as a son,
> giving you a pleasant land,
> a patrimony fairer than that of any nation!
> I said, You shall call me Father
> and never cease to follow me.
20 But like a woman who is unfaithful to her lover,
> so you, Israel, were unfaithful to me.
> This is the very word of the LORD.
21 Hark, a sound of weeping on the bare places,
> Israel's people pleading for mercy!
> For they have taken to crooked ways
> and ignored the LORD their God.
22 Come back to me, wayward*a* sons;
> I will heal your apostasy.

a Or apostate.

O LORD, we come! We come to thee;
for thou art our God.
There is no help in worship on the hill-tops,   23
    no help from clamour on the heights;
truly in the LORD our God
    is Israel's only salvation.
From our early days   24
    Baal, god of shame, has devoured
    the fruits of our fathers' labours,
their flocks and herds, their sons and daughters.
Let us lie down in shame, wrapped round by our dishonour,   25
    for we have sinned against the LORD our God,
        both we and our fathers,
        from our early days till now,
    and we have not obeyed the LORD our God.

If you will but come back, O Israel,   **4**
if you will but come back to me, says the LORD,
if you will banish your loathsome idols from my sight,
    and stray no more,
    if you swear by the life of the LORD,   2
    in truth, in justice and uprightness,
then shall the nations pray to be blessed like you [a]
and in you [a] shall they boast.

These are the words of the LORD to the men of Judah and Jerusalem: 3
    Break up your fallow ground,
        do not sow among thorns,
    circumcise yourselves to the service of the LORD,   4
        circumcise your hearts,
        men of Judah and dwellers in Jerusalem,
    lest the fire of my fury blaze up and burn unquenched,
        because of your evil doings.
    Tell this in Judah,   5
        proclaim it in Jerusalem,
    blow the trumpet throughout the land,
        sound the muster,
    give the command, Stand to!—and let us fall back
        on the fortified cities.
    Raise the signal—To Zion!   6
        make for safety, lose no time,
    for I bring disaster out of the north,
        and dire destruction.
    A lion has come out from his lair,   7
        the destroyer of nations;
    he has struck his tents, he has broken camp,
        to harry your land
    and lay your cities waste and unpeopled.

[a] *Prob. rdg.; Heb.* him.

8   Well may you put on sackcloth,
          beat the breast and wail,
       for the anger of the Lord
          is not averted from us.

9   On that day, says the Lord,
       the hearts of the king and his officers shall fail them,
       priests shall be struck with horror and prophets dumbfounded.

10   And I said, O Lord God, thou surely didst deceive this people and Jerusalem in saying, 'You shall have peace', while the sword is at our throats.

11   At that time this people and Jerusalem shall be told:

       A scorching wind from the high bare places in the wilderness
          sweeps down upon my people,
       no breeze for winnowing or for cleansing;

12   a wind too strong for these
          will come at my bidding,
          and now I will state my case against them.

13   Like clouds the enemy advances
          with a whirlwind of chariots;
       his horses are swifter than eagles—
          alas, we are overwhelmed!

14   O Jerusalem, wash the wrongdoing from your heart
          and you may yet be saved;
       how long will you cherish
          your evil schemes?

15   Hark, a runner from Dan,
          tidings of evil from Mount Ephraim!

16   Tell all this to the nations,
          proclaim the doom of Jerusalem:
       hordes of invaders come from a distant land,
       howling against the cities of Judah.

17   Their pickets are closing in all round her,
          because she has rebelled against me.
          This is the very word of the Lord.

18   Your own ways, your own deeds
       have brought all this upon you;
       this is your punishment,
       and all this comes of your rebellion.[a]

19   Oh, the writhing of my bowels
          and the throbbing of my heart!
          I cannot keep silence.
       I hear the sound of the trumpet,
          the sound of the battle-cry.

20   Crash upon crash,
          the land goes down in ruin,

---

[a] your rebellion: *prob. rdg.; Heb. obscure.*

my tents are thrown down,
    their coverings torn to shreds.
How long must I see the standard raised   21
    and hear the trumpet call?
My people are fools, they know nothing of me;   22
silly children, with no understanding,
they are clever only in wrongdoing,
    and of doing right they know nothing.

I saw the earth, and it was without form and void;   23
    the heavens, and their light was gone.
I saw the mountains, and they reeled;   24
    all the hills rocked to and fro.
I saw, and there was no man,   25
    and the very birds had taken flight.
I saw, and the farm-land was wilderness,   26
    and the towns all razed to the ground,
before the LORD in his anger.
    These are the words of the LORD: 27
The whole land shall be desolate,
    though I will not make an end of it.
Therefore the earth will mourn   28
and the heavens above turn black.
For I have made known my purpose;
I will not relent or change my mind.

At the sound of the horsemen and archers   29
    the whole country is in flight;
they creep into caves, they hide in thickets,
    they scramble up the crags.
Every town is forsaken,
    no one dwells there.

And you, what are you doing?   30
When you dress yourself in scarlet,
    deck yourself out with golden ornaments,
and make your eyes big with antimony,
    you are beautifying yourself to no purpose.
Your lovers spurn you
    and are out for your life.
I hear a sound as of a woman in labour,   31
    the sharp cry of one bearing her first child.
It is Zion, gasping for breath,
    clenching her fists.
Ah me! I am weary,
    weary of slaughter.

Go up and down the streets of Jerusalem   5
    and see for yourselves;
search her wide squares:

can you find any man who acts justly,
   who seeks the truth,
that I may forgive that city?

2   Men may swear by the life of the LORD,
but they only perjure themselves.

3   O LORD, are thine eyes not set upon the truth?
Thou didst strike them down,
   but they took no heed;
didst pierce them to the heart,
   but they refused to learn.
They set their faces harder than flint
   and refused to come back.

4   I said, 'After all, these are the poor,
   these are stupid folk,
who do not know the way of the LORD,
   the ordinances of their God.

5   I will go to the great
   and speak with them;
for they will know the way of the LORD,
   the ordinances of their God.'
But they too have broken the yoke
   and snapped their traces.

6   Therefore a lion out of the scrub shall strike them down,
   a wolf from the plains shall ravage them;
a leopard shall prowl about their cities
and maul any who venture out.
For their rebellious deeds are many,
   their apostasies past counting.

7   How can I forgive you for all this?
Your sons have forsaken me and sworn by gods
   that are no gods.
I gave them all they needed, yet they preferred adultery,
   and haunted the brothels;

8   each neighs after another man's wife,
like a well-fed and lusty stallion.

9   Shall I not punish them for this?
   the LORD asks.
Shall I not take vengeance
   on such a people?

10   Go along her rows of vines and slash them,
   yet do not make an end of them.
Hack away her green branches,
   for they are not the LORD's.

11   Faithless are Israel and Judah,
both faithless to me.
   This is the very word of the LORD.

12   They have denied the LORD,
saying, 'He does not exist.

No evil shall come upon us;
we shall never see sword or famine.
The prophets will prove mere wind, 13
the word not in them.'

And so, because you talk in this way, these are the words of the LORD 14
the God of Hosts to me:

I will make my words a fire in your mouth;
and it shall burn up this people like brushwood.

I bring against you, Israel, a nation from afar, 15
an ancient people established long ago,
says the LORD.
A people whose language you do not know,
whose speech you will not understand;
they are all mighty warriors, 16
their jaws are a grave, wide open,
to devour your harvest and your bread, 17
to devour your sons and your daughters,
to devour your flocks and your herds,
to devour your vines and your fig-trees.
They shall batter down the cities in which you trust,*a*
walled though they are.

But in those days, the LORD declares, I will still not make an end of you. 18
When you ask, 'Why has the LORD our God done all this to us?' I shall 19
answer, 'As you have forsaken me and served alien gods in your own land,
so shall you serve foreigners*b* in a land that is not yours.'

Tell this to the people of Jacob, 20
proclaim it in Judah:
Listen, you foolish and senseless people, 21
who have eyes and see nothing,
ears and hear nothing.
Have you no fear of me? says the LORD; 22
will you not shiver before me,
before me, who made the shivering sand to bound the sea,
a barrier it never can pass?
Its waves heave and toss but they are powerless;
roar as they may, they cannot pass.
But this people has a rebellious and defiant heart, 23
rebels they have been and now they are clean gone.
They did not say to themselves, 24
'Let us fear the LORD our God,
who gives us the rains of autumn
and spring showers in their turn,
who brings us unfailingly
fixed seasons of harvest.'

a Prob. rdg.; Heb. adds with the sword. *b* Or foreign gods.

25   But your wrongdoing has upset nature's order,
      and your sins have kept from you her kindly gifts.
26   For among my people there are wicked men,
          who lay snares like a fowler's net *a*
          and set deadly traps to catch men.
27   Their houses are full of fraud,
      as a cage is full of birds.
      They grow rich and grand,
28   bloated and rancorous;
      their thoughts are all of evil,
          and they refuse to do justice,
      the claims of the orphan they do not put right
      nor do they grant justice to the poor.
29   Shall I not punish them for this?
          says the LORD;
      shall I not take vengeance
          on such a people?

30   An appalling thing, an outrage,
      has appeared in this land:
31   prophets prophesy lies and priests go hand in hand with them,
      and my people love to have it so.
          How will you fare at the end of it all?

6   Save yourselves, men of Benjamin,
          come out of Jerusalem,
      blow the trumpet in Tekoa,
      fire the beacon on Beth-hakkerem,
      for calamity looms from the north
          and great disaster.
2   Zion, delightful and lovely:
          her end is near—
3   she to whom the shepherds come
          and bring their flocks with them.
      There they pitch their tents all round her,
          each grazing his own strip of pasture.
4   Declare war solemnly against her;
      come, let us attack her at noon.
      Too late! the day declines
          and the shadows lengthen.
5   Come then, let us attack her by night
          and destroy her palaces.
6   These are the words of the LORD of Hosts:
      Cut down the trees of Jerusalem
          and raise siege-ramps against her,
      the city whose name is Licence,
      oppression is rampant in her.

a who . . . net: *prob. rdg.; Heb. unintelligible.*

> As a well keeps its water fresh,　　　　　　　　7
> so she keeps her evil fresh.
> Violence and outrage echo in her streets;
> sickness and wounds stare me in the face.
>> Learn your lesson, Jerusalem,　　　　　　　　8
> lest my love for you be torn from my heart,
>> and I leave you desolate,
>> a land where no one can live.
> These are the words of the LORD of Hosts:　　　9
>> Glean the remnant of Israel
>> like a vine,
> pass your hand like a vintager one last time
>> over the branches.
>> To whom can I address myself,　　　　　　　10
> to whom give solemn warning? Who will hear me?
> Their ears are uncircumcised;
>> they cannot listen;
> they treat the LORD's word as a reproach;
>> they show no concern with it.
> But I am full of the anger of the LORD,　　　　11
>> I cannot hold it in.
> I must pour it out on the children in the street
>> and on the young men in their gangs.
> Man and wife alike shall be caught in it,
>> the greybeard and the very old.
> Their houses shall be turned over to others,　　12
> their fields and their women alike.
>> For I will raise my hand, says the LORD,
> against the people of the country.
> For all, high and low,　　　　　　　　　　　13
>> are out for ill-gotten gain;
> prophets and priests are frauds,
>> every one of them;
> they dress my people's wound, but skin-deep only,　14
>> with their saying, 'All is well.'
>> All well? Nothing is well!
> Are they ashamed when they practise their abominations?　15
>> Ashamed? Not they!
>> They can never be put out of countenance.
> Therefore they shall fall with a great crash,[a]
> and be brought to the ground on the day of my reckoning.
>> The LORD has said it.

These are the words of the LORD: Stop at the cross-roads; look for　16
the ancient paths; ask, 'Where is the way that leads to what is good?'
Then take that way, and you will find rest for yourselves. But they said,
'We will not.' Then I will appoint watchmen to direct you; listen for their　17

---

[a] with a great crash: *or* where they fall *or* among the fallen.

18 trumpet-call. But they said, 'We will not.' Therefore hear, you nations, and
19 take note, all you who witness it, of the plight of this people. Listen, O
    earth, I bring ruin on them, the harvest of all their scheming; for they have
20 given no thought to my words and have spurned my instruction. What
    good is it to me if frankincense is brought from Sheba and fragrant spices
    from distant lands? I will not accept your whole-offerings, your sacrifices
21 do not please me. Therefore these are the words of the LORD:

>   I will set obstacles before this people
>   which shall bring them to the ground;
>   fathers and sons, friends and neighbours
>   shall all perish together.

22 These are the words of the LORD:

>   See, a people is coming from a northern land,
>   a great nation rouses itself from earth's farthest corners.
23 >   They come with bow and sabre, cruel men and pitiless,
>   bestriding their horses, they sound like the thunder of the sea,
>   they are like men arrayed for battle against you, Zion.
24 >   We have heard tell of them
>   and our hands hang limp,
>   agony grips us, the anguish of a woman in labour.
25 >   Do not go out into the country,
>   do not walk by the high road;
>   for the foe, sword in hand,
>   is a terror let loose.
26 >   Daughter of my people, wrap yourself in sackcloth,
>   sprinkle ashes over yourself, wail bitterly,
>   as one who mourns an only son;
>   in an instant shall the marauder be upon us.

27 >   I have appointed you an assayer of my people;
>   you will know how to test them and will assay their conduct;
28 >   arch-rebels all of them,
>   mischief-makers, corrupt to a man.
29 >   The bellows puff and blow, the furnace glows;
>   in vain does the refiner smelt the ore,
>   lead, copper and iron[a] are not separated out.
30 >   Call them spurious silver;
>   for the LORD has spurned them.

False religion and its punishment

7 1 2 THIS WORD CAME FROM THE LORD to Jeremiah. Stand at the gate of
    the LORD's house and there make your proclamation: Listen to the
    words of the LORD, all you men of Judah who come in through these gates
3   to worship him. These are the words of the LORD of Hosts the God of

---

[a] copper and iron: *transposed from after* mischief-makers *in verse 28.*

Israel: Mend your ways and your doings, that I may let you live in this
place. You keep saying, 'This place*a* is the temple of the LORD, the temple   4
of the LORD, the temple of the LORD!' This catchword of yours is a lie;
put no trust in it. Mend your ways and your doings, deal fairly with one   5
another, do not oppress the alien, the orphan, and the widow, shed no   6
innocent blood in this place, do not run after other gods to your own ruin.
Then will I let you live in this place, in the land which I gave long ago to   7
your forefathers for all time. You gain nothing by putting your trust in   8
this lie. You steal, you murder, you commit adultery and perjury, you   9
burn sacrifices to Baal, you run after other gods whom you have not known;
then you come and stand before me in this house, which bears my name, and   10
say, 'We are safe'; safe, you think, to indulge in all these abominations. Do   11
you think that this house, this house which bears my name, is a robbers'
cave? I myself have seen all this, says the LORD. Go to my shrine at Shiloh,   12
which once I made a dwelling for my Name, and see what I did to it because
of the wickedness of my people Israel. And now you have done all these   13
things, says the LORD; though I took pains to speak to you, you did not
listen, and though I called, you gave no answer. Therefore what I did to   14
Shiloh I will do to this house which bears my name, the house in which
you put your trust, the place I gave to you and your forefathers; I will   15
fling you away out of my sight, as I flung away all your kinsfolk, the whole
brood of Ephraim.

Offer up no prayer, Jeremiah, for this people, raise no plea or prayer on   16
their behalf, and do not intercede with me; for I will not listen to you.
Do you not see what is going on in the cities of Judah and in the streets of   17
Jerusalem? Children are gathering wood, fathers lighting fires, women   18
kneading dough to make crescent-cakes in honour of the queen of heaven;
and drink-offerings are poured out to other gods than me—all to provoke
and hurt me. But is it I, says the LORD, whom they hurt? No; it is them-   19
selves, covering their own selves with shame. Therefore, says the Lord GOD,   20
my anger and my fury shall fall on this place, on man and beast, on trees
and crops, and it shall burn unquenched.

These are the words of the LORD of Hosts the God of Israel: Add whole-   21
offerings to sacrifices and eat the flesh if you will. But when I brought your   22
forefathers out of Egypt, I gave them no commands about whole-offering
and sacrifice; I said not a word about them. What I did command them   23
was this: If you obey me, I will be your God and you shall be my people.
You must conform to all my commands, if you would prosper. But they   24
did not listen; they paid no heed, and persisted in disobedience with evil
and stubborn hearts; they looked backwards and not forwards, from the   25
day when your forefathers left Egypt until now. I took pains to send to
them all my servants the prophets; they did not listen to me, they paid no   26
heed, but were obstinate and proved even more wicked than their forefathers. When you tell them this, they will not listen to you; if you call them,   27
they will not answer. Then you shall say to them, This is the nation that   28
did not obey the LORD its God nor accept correction; truth has perished,
it is heard no more on their lips.

a This place: *prob. rdg.; Heb.* Those.

29   O Jerusalem, cut off your hair,
           the symbol of your dedication, and throw it away;
        raise up a lament on the high bare places.

For the LORD has spurned the generation which has roused his wrath, and
30 has abandoned them. For the men of Judah have done what is wrong in my
eyes, says the LORD. They have defiled with their loathsome idols the house
31 that bears my name, they have built a shrine of Topheth in the Valley of
Ben-hinnom, at which to burn their sons and daughters; that was no
32 command of mine, nor did it ever enter my thought. Therefore a time is
coming, says the LORD, when it shall no longer be called Topheth or the
Valley of Ben-hinnom, but the Valley of Slaughter; for the dead shall be
33 buried in Topheth because there is no room elsewhere. So the bodies of
this people shall become food for the birds of the air and the wild beasts,
34 and there will be no one to scare them away. From the cities of Judah and
the streets of Jerusalem I will banish all sounds of joy and gladness, the
voice of the bridegroom and the bride; for the land shall become desert.

8   At that time, says the LORD, men shall bring out from their graves the
bones of the kings of Judah, of the officers, priests, and prophets, and of
2 all who lived in Jerusalem. They shall expose them to the sun, the moon,
and all the host of heaven, whom they loved and served and adored, to
whom they resorted and bowed in worship. Those bones shall not be
3 gathered up nor buried but shall become dung on the ground. All the
survivors of this wicked race, wherever I have banished them, would rather
die than live. This is the very word of the LORD of Hosts.

4   You shall say to them, These are the words of the LORD:

        If men fall, can they not also rise?
        If a man breaks away, can he not return?
5   Then why are this people so wayward,
           incurable in their waywardness?
        Why have they clung to their treachery
           and refused to return to their obedience?
6   I have listened to them
           and heard not one word of truth,
       not one sinner crying remorsefully,
         'Oh, what have I done?'
       Each one breaks away *a* in headlong career
       as a war-horse plunges in battle.

7   The stork in the sky
           knows the time to migrate,
       the dove and the swift and the wryneck
           know the season of return;
       but my people do not know the ordinances of the LORD.
8   How can you say, 'We are wise,
           we have the law of the LORD',
       when scribes with their lying pens
           have falsified it?

           a breaks away: *or* is wayward.

The wise are put to shame, they are dismayed and have lost their wits.　9
> They have spurned the word of the LORD,
>> and what sort of wisdom is theirs?

Therefore will I give their wives to other men　10
>> and their lands to new owners.
> For all, high and low,
>> are out for ill-gotten gain;
> prophets and priests are frauds,
>> every one of them;
> they dress my people's wound, but skin-deep only,　11
>> with their saying, 'All is well.'
>> All well? Nothing is well!
> Are they ashamed when they practise their abominations?　12
>> Ashamed? Not they!
>> They can never be put out of countenance.

Therefore they shall fall with a great crash,[a]
and be brought to the ground on the day of my reckoning.
> The LORD has said it.
> I would gather their harvest, says the LORD,　13
> but there are no grapes on the vine,
> no figs on the fig-tree;
> even their leaves are withered.

Why do we sit idle? Up, all of you together,　14
let us go into our walled cities and there meet our doom.
> For the LORD our God has struck us down,
> he has given us a draught of bitter poison;
>> for we have sinned against the LORD.
> Can we hope to prosper when nothing goes well?　15
> Can we hope for respite when the terror falls suddenly?　16
> The snorting of his horses is heard from Dan;

at the neighing of his stallions the whole land trembles.
The enemy come; they devour the land and all its store,
> city and citizens alike.

Beware, I am sending snakes against you,　17
> vipers, such as no man can charm,
> and they shall bite you.
>> This is the very word of the LORD.

> How can I bear my sorrow?[b]　18
> I am sick at heart.
> Hark, the cry of my people　19
> from a distant land:
>> 'Is the LORD not in Zion?
>> Is her King no longer there?'
> Why do they provoke me with their images
> and foreign gods?

---

[a] with a great crash: *or* where they fall *or* among the fallen.　　[b] How . . . sorrow?:
prob. rdg.; Heb. unintelligible.

20   Harvest is past, summer is over,
         and we are not saved.
21   I am wounded at the sight of my people's wound;
         I go like a mourner, overcome with horror.
22   Is there no balm in Gilead,
         no physician there?
      Why has no new skin grown over their wound?

9   Would that my head were all water,
         my eyes a fountain of tears,
      that I might weep day and night
         for my people's dead!

2   Oh that I could find in the wilderness a shelter by the wayside,
      that I might leave my people and depart!
         Adulterers are they all, a mob of traitors.
3   The tongue is their weapon, a bow ready bent.
      Lying, not truth, is master in the land.
         They run from one sin to another,
         and for me they care nothing.
         This is the very word of the LORD.

4   Be on your guard, each man against his friend;
         put no trust even in a brother.
      Brother supplants brother,^a
      and friend slanders friend.
5   They make game of their friends
         but never speak the truth;
      they have trained their tongues to lies;
      deep in their sin, they cannot retrace their steps.
6   Wrong follows wrong, deceit follows deceit;
         they refuse to acknowledge me.
         This is the very word of the LORD.
7   Therefore these are the words of the LORD of Hosts:
      I am their refiner and will assay them.
      How can I disregard my people?
8   Their tongue is a cruel arrow,
      their mouths speak lies.
      One speaks amicably to another,
      while inwardly he plans a trap for him.
9   Shall I not punish them for this?
         says the LORD;
      shall I not take vengeance
         on such a people?

10   Over the mountains will I raise weeping and wailing,
         and over the desert pastures will I chant a dirge.

---

^a *Brother supplants brother: or* Every brother is a supplanter like Jacob (*cp. Gen.
27. 35 and note*).

They are scorched and untrodden,
　　they hear no lowing of cattle;
birds of the air and beasts have fled and are gone.

I will make Jerusalem a heap of ruins, a haunt of wolves, 11
and the cities of Judah an unpeopled waste.

What man is wise enough to understand this, to understand what the 12
LORD has said and to proclaim it? Why has the land become a dead land,
scorched like the desert and untrodden? The LORD said, It is because they 13
forsook my law which I set before them; they neither obeyed me nor conformed to it. They followed the promptings of their own stubborn hearts, 14
they followed the Baalim as their forefathers had taught them. Therefore 15
these are the words of the LORD of Hosts the God of Israel: I will feed this
people with wormwood and give them bitter poison to drink. I will scatter 16
them among nations whom neither they nor their forefathers have known;
I will harry them with the sword until I have made an end of them.

These are the words of the LORD of Hosts: 17

Summon the wailing women to come,
　　send for the women skilled in keening
to come quickly and raise a lament for us, 18
　　that our eyes may run with tears
　　and our eyelids be wet with weeping.
Hark, hark, lamentation is heard in Zion: 19
　　How fearful is our ruin! How great our shame!
We have left our lands, our houses have been pulled down.
　　Listen, you women, to the words of the LORD, 20
　　that your ears may catch what he says.
　　Teach your daughters the lament,
　　let them teach one another this dirge:
　　Death has climbed in through our windows, 21
　　　　it has entered our palaces,
　　it sweeps off the children in the open air
　　　　and drives young men from the streets.

This is the word of the LORD: 22
　　The corpses of men shall fall and lie like dung in the fields,
　　　　like swathes behind the reaper, but no one shall gather them.

These are the words of the LORD: 23
　　Let not the wise man boast of his wisdom
　　　　nor the valiant of his valour;
　　let not the rich man boast of his riches;
　　but if any man would boast, let him boast of this, 24
　　that he understands and knows me.
For I am the LORD, I show unfailing love,
　　I do justice and right upon the earth;
　　　　for on these I have set my heart.
　　This is the very word of the LORD.

25 The time is coming, says the LORD, when I will punish all the circum-
26 cised, Egypt and Judah, Edom and Ammon, Moab, and all who haunt the
fringes of the desert;[a] for all alike, the nations and Israel, are uncircumcised
in heart.

10 Listen, Israel, to this word that the LORD has spoken against you:

2   Do not fall into the ways of the nations,
             do not be awed by signs in the heavens;
             it is the nations who go in awe of these.

3   For the carved images of the nations are a sham,
             they are nothing but timber cut from the forest,
             worked with his chisel by a craftsman;

4   he adorns it with silver and gold,
         fastening them on with hammer and nails
           so that they do not fall apart.

5   They can no more speak than a scarecrow in a plot of cucumbers;
             they must be carried, for they cannot walk.
           Do not be afraid of them: they can do no harm,
             and they have no power to do good.

6   Where can one be found like thee, O LORD?
         Great thou art and great the might of thy name.

7   Who shall not fear thee, king of the nations?
             for fear is thy fitting tribute.
           Where among the wisest of the nations and all their royalty
             can one be found like thee?

8   They are fools and blockheads one and all,
             learning their nonsense from a log of wood.

9   The beaten silver is brought from Tarshish
             and the gold from Ophir;
           all are the work of craftsmen and goldsmiths.
           They are draped in violet and purple,
             all the work of skilled men.

10   But the LORD is God in truth,
           a living god, an eternal king.
           The earth quakes under his wrath,
           nations cannot endure his fury.

11   [You shall say this to them: The gods who did not make heaven and earth
shall perish from the earth and from under these heavens.]

12[b]   God made the earth by his power,
           fixed the world in place by his wisdom,
           unfurled the skies by his understanding.

13   At the thunder of his voice the waters in heaven are amazed;[c]
           he brings up the mist from the ends of the earth,
           he opens rifts[d] for the rain
           and brings the wind out of his storehouses.

[a] who ... desert: *or* the dwellers in the desert who clip the hair on their temples.   [b] *Verses 12-16: cp. 51. 15-19.*   [c] At the thunder ... amazed: *prob. rdg.; Heb.* At the sound of his giving tumult of waters in heaven.   [d] rifts: *prob. rdg.; Heb.* lightnings.

All men are brutish and ignorant;   14
every goldsmith is discredited by his idol;
for the figures he casts are a sham,
there is no breath in them.
They are worth nothing, mere mockeries,   15
which perish when their day of reckoning comes.
God, Jacob's creator, is not like these;   16
 for he is the maker of all.
 Israel is the people he claims as his own;
 the LORD of Hosts is his name.

Put your goods together and carry them out of the country,   17
 living as you are under siege.
For these are the words of the LORD: 18
 This time I will uproot
the whole population of the land,
and I will press them hard and squeeze them dry.

 O the pain of my wounds!   19
 Cruel are the blows I suffer.
But this is my plight, I said, and I must endure it.
My home is ruined, my tent-ropes all severed,   20
 my sons have left me and are gone,
there is no one to pitch my tent again,
 no one to put up its curtains.
 The shepherds of the people are mere brutes;   21
 they never consult the LORD,
 and so they do not prosper,
and all their flocks at pasture are scattered.

Hark, a rumour comes flying,   22
 then a mounting uproar from the land of the north,
an army to make Judah's cities desolate, a haunt of wolves.
 I know, O LORD,   23
that man's ways are not of his own choosing;
nor is it for a man to determine his course in life.
Correct us, O LORD, but with justice, not in anger,   24
 lest thou bring us almost to nothing.
Pour out thy fury on nations   25
 that have not acknowledged thee,
on tribes that have not invoked thee by name;
for they have devoured Jacob and made an end of him
 and have left his home a waste.

Warnings and punishment

11 ¹ ² T HE WORD WHICH CAME TO JEREMIAH from the LORD: Listen to
the terms of this covenant and repeat them to the men of Judah and the
3 inhabitants of Jerusalem. Tell them, These are the words of the LORD the
God of Israel: A curse on the man who does not observe the terms of this
4 covenant by which I bound your forefathers when I brought them out of
Egypt, from the smelting-furnace. I said, If you obey me and do all that I
5 tell you, you shall become my people and I will become your God. And I
will thus make good the oath I swore to your forefathers, that I would give
them a land flowing with milk and honey, the land you now possess.
6 I answered, 'Amen, LORD.' Then the LORD said: Proclaim all these terms
in the cities of Judah and in the streets of Jerusalem. Say, Listen to the
7 terms of this covenant and carry them out. I have protested to your forefathers since I brought them out of Egypt, till this day; I took pains to
8 warn them: Obey me, I said. But they did not obey; they paid no attention
to me, but each followed the promptings of his own stubborn and wicked
heart. So I brought on them all the penalties laid down in this covenant
by which I had bound them, whose terms they did not observe.

9 The LORD said to me, The men of Judah and the inhabitants of Jeru-
10 salem have entered into a conspiracy: they have gone back to the sins of
their earliest forefathers and refused to listen to me. They have followed
other gods and worshipped them; Israel and Judah have broken the
11 covenant which I made with their fathers. Therefore these are the words
of the LORD: I now bring on them disaster from which they cannot escape;
12 though they cry to me for help I will not listen. The inhabitants of the cities
of Judah and of Jerusalem may go and cry for help to the gods to whom
they have burnt sacrifices; they will not save them in the hour of disaster.
13 For you, Judah, have as many gods as you have towns; you have set up as
14 many altars to burn sacrifices to Baal as there are streets in Jerusalem. So
offer up no prayer for this people; raise no cry or prayer on their behalf,
for I will not listen when they call to me in the hour of disaster.

15   What right has my beloved in my house
              with her shameless ways?
          Can the flesh of fat offerings on the altar
              ward off the disaster that threatens you?
16   Once the LORD called you an olive-tree,
              leafy and fair;
          but now with a great roaring noise
              you will feel sharp anguish; *a*
          fire sets its leaves alight
              and consumes *b* its branches.

17   The LORD of Hosts who planted you has threatened you with disaster,
because of the harm Israel and Judah brought on themselves when they
provoked me to anger by burning sacrifices to Baal.

a you will feel sharp anguish: *transposed from end of verse 15.*   *b* consumes: *prob.*
rdg.; *Heb.* they consume.

It was the LORD who showed me, and so I knew; he opened my eyes to 18
what they were doing. I had been like a sheep led obedient to the slaughter; 19
I did not know that they were hatching plots against me and saying, 'Let
us cut down the tree while the sap is in it; let us destroy him out of the
living, so that his very name shall be forgotten.'

> O LORD of Hosts who art a righteous judge, 20
>> testing the heart and mind,
>> I have committed my cause to thee;
>> let me see thy vengeance upon them.

Therefore these are the words of the LORD about the men of Anathoth who 21
seek to take my life, and say, 'Prophesy no more in the name of the LORD
or we will kill you'—these are his words: I will punish them: their young 22
men shall die by the sword, their sons and daughters shall die by famine.
Not one of them shall survive; for in the year of their reckoning I will 23
bring ruin on the men of Anathoth.

> O LORD, I will dispute with thee, for thou art just; **12**
>> yes, I will plead my case before thee.
> Why do the wicked prosper
>> and traitors live at ease?
>> Thou hast planted them and their roots strike deep, 2
>> they grow up and bear fruit.
>> Thou art ever on their lips,
>>> yet far from their hearts.
> But thou knowest me, O LORD, thou seest me; 3
>> thou dost test my devotion to thyself.
> Drag them away like sheep to the shambles;
>> set them apart for the day of slaughter.

>> How long must the country lie parched 4
>>> and its green grass wither?
> No birds and beasts are left, because its people are so wicked,
>> because they say, 'God will not see what we are doing.'

> If you have raced with men and the runners have worn you down, 5
>>> how then can you hope to vie with horses?
>> If you fall headlong in easy country,
>>> how will you fare in Jordan's dense thickets?
> All men, your brothers and kinsmen, are traitors to you, 6
>> they are in full cry after you;
> trust them not, for all the fine words they give you.

>> I have forsaken the house of Israel, 7
>>> I have cast off my own people.
> I have given my beloved into the power of her foes.
> My own people have turned on me like a lion from the scrub, 8
> roaring against me; therefore I hate them.
>>> Is this land of mine a hyena's lair, 9
>>>> with birds of prey hovering all around it?
> Come, you wild beasts; come, all of you, flock to the feast.

10   Many shepherds have ravaged my vineyard
       and trampled down my field,
    they have made my pleasant field a desolate wilderness,
11   made it a waste land, waste and waterless, to my sorrow.
    The whole land is waste, and no one cares.

12   Plunderers have swarmed across the high bare places in the wilderness,
a sword of the LORD devouring the land from end to end; no creature can find peace.

13   Men sow wheat and reap thistles;
    they sift but get no grain.
    They are disappointed of their[a] harvest
    because of the anger of the LORD.

14   These are the words of the LORD about all those evil neighbours who are laying hands on the land which I gave to my people Israel as their patri-
16[b] mony: I will uproot them from that[c] soil. Yet, if they will learn the ways of my people, swearing by my name, 'By the life of the LORD', as they taught my people to swear by the Baal, they shall form families among my
17 people. But if they will not listen, I will uproot that people, uproot and
15 destroy them. Also I will uproot Judah from among them; but after I have uprooted them, I will have pity on them again and will bring each man back to his patrimony and his land. This is the very word of the LORD.

13   These were the words of the LORD to me: Go and buy yourself a linen
2 girdle and put it round your waist, but do not let it come near water. So
3 I bought it as the LORD had told me and put it round my waist. The LORD
4 spoke to me a second time: Take the girdle which you bought and put round your waist; go at once to Perath and hide it in a crevice among the rocks.
5 6 So I went and hid the girdle at[d] Perath, as the LORD had told me. After a long time the LORD said to me: Go at once to Perath and fetch back the
7 girdle which I told you to hide there. So I went to Perath and looked for the place where I had hidden it, but when I picked it up, I saw that it was
8 9 spoilt, and no good for anything. Again the LORD spoke to me and these were his words: Thus will I spoil the gross pride of Judah, the gross pride
10 of Jerusalem. This wicked nation has refused to listen to my words; they have followed other gods, serving them and bowing down to them. So it
11 shall be[e] like this girdle, no good for anything. For, just as a girdle is bound close to a man's waist, so I bound all Israel and all Judah to myself, says the LORD, so that they should become my people to win a name for me, and praise and glory; but they did not listen.

12   You shall say this to them: These are the words of the LORD the God of Israel: Wine-jars should be filled with wine. They will answer, 'We know
13 quite well that wine-jars should be filled with wine.' Then you shall say to them, These are the words of the LORD: I will fill all the inhabitants of this land with wine until they are drunk—kings of David's line who sit on
14 his throne, priests, prophets, and all who live in Jerusalem. I will dash them

---

[a] *Prob. rdg.; Heb.* your.   [b] *The rest of verse 14 and verse 15 transposed to follow*
destroy them in verse 17.   [c] *Prob. rdg.; Heb.* their.   [d] *Or* by.   [e] *Prob.*
rdg.; Heb. And let it be.

to pieces one against another, fathers and sons alike, says the LORD, I will show them no compassion or pity or tenderness; nor refrain from destroying them.*a*

> Hear and attend. Be not too proud to listen,   15
> for it is the LORD who speaks.
> Ascribe glory to the LORD your God   16
> before the darkness falls,
> before your feet stumble
> on the twilit hill-sides,
> before he turns the light you look for
> to deep gloom and thick darkness.
> If in those depths of gloom you will not listen,   17
> then for very anguish I can only weep and shed tears,*b*
> my eyes must stream with tears;
> for the LORD's flock is carried away into captivity.
> Say to the king and the queen mother:*c*   18
> Down, take a humble seat,
> for your proud crowns are fallen from your heads.
> Your cities in the Negeb are besieged,   19
> and no one can relieve them;
> all Judah has been swept into exile,
> swept clean away.
> Lift up your eyes and see   20
> those who are coming from the north.
> Where is the flock that was entrusted to you,
> the flock you were so proud of?
> What will you say when you suffer   21
> because your leaders*d* cannot be found,
> though it was you who trained them
> to be your head?
> Will not pangs seize you,
> like the pangs of a woman in labour,
> when you wonder,   22
> 'Why has this come upon me?'
> For your many sins your skirts are torn off you,
> your limbs uncovered.
>
> Can the Nubian change his skin,   23
> or the leopard its spots?
> And you? Can you do good,
> you who are schooled in evil?
> Therefore I will scatter you*e* like chaff   24
> driven by the desert wind.
> This is your lot, the portion of the rebel,   25
> measured out by me, says the LORD,

---

a nor refrain ... them: *or* so corrupt are they.   *b* If ... shed tears: *or* If you will not listen to this, for very anguish I must weep in secret.   *c* *Or* queen.
d leaders: *transposed from next line.*   *e* *Prob. rdg.; Heb.* them.

> because you have forsaken me
> and trusted in false gods.

26   So I myself have stripped off your skirts
> and laid bare your shame.

27   Your adulteries, your lustful neighing,
> your wanton lewdness, are an offence to me.[a]
> On the hills and in the open country
> I have seen your foul deeds.
> Alas, Jerusalem, unclean that you are!
> How long, how long will you delay?[b]

14   This came to Jeremiah as the word of the LORD concerning the drought:

2   Judah droops, her cities languish,
> her men sink to the ground;
> Jerusalem's cry goes up.

3   Their flock-masters send their boys for water;
> they come to the pools but find no water there.
> Back they go, with empty vessels;

4   the produce[c] of the land has failed,
> because there is no rain.
> The farmers' hopes are wrecked,
> they uncover their heads for grief.

5   The hind calves in the open country
> and forsakes her young
> because there is no grass;

6   for lack of herbage, wild asses stand on the high bare places
> and snuff the wind for moisture,
> as wolves do, and their eyes begin to fail.

7   Though our sins testify against us,
> yet act,[d] O LORD, for thy own name's sake.
> Our disloyalties indeed are many; we have sinned against thee.

8   O hope of Israel, their saviour in time of trouble,
> must thou be a stranger in the land,
> a traveller pitching his tent for a night?

9   Must thou be like a man suddenly overcome,
> like a man powerless to save himself?
> Thou art in our midst, O LORD,
> and thou hast named us thine; do not forsake us.

10 The LORD speaks thus of this people: They love to stray from my ways, they wander where they will. Therefore he has no more pleasure in them;
11 he remembers their guilt now, and punishes their sins. Then the LORD
12 said to me, Do not pray for the well-being of this people. When they fast, I will not listen to their cry; when they sacrifice whole-offering and grain-offering, I will not accept them. I will make an end of them with sword,
13 with famine and pestilence. But I said, O Lord GOD, the prophets tell them that they shall see no sword and suffer no famine; for thou wilt give them

---

[a] an offence to me (*Heb.* you): *transposed from verse 26.*   [b] How . . . delay?: *prob. rdg.; Heb. unintelligible.*   [c] the produce: *prob. rdg.; Heb. obscure.*   [d] Or turn away.

lasting prosperity in this place. The LORD answered me, The prophets 14
are prophesying lies in my name. I have not sent them; I have given them
no charge; I have not spoken to them. The prophets offer them false
visions, worthless augury, and their own deluding fancies. Therefore these 15
are the words of the LORD about the prophets who, though not sent by me,
prophesy in my name and say that neither sword nor famine shall touch
this land: By sword and by famine shall those prophets meet their end.
The people to whom they prophesy shall be flung out into the streets of 16
Jerusalem, victims of famine and sword; they, their wives, their sons, and
their daughters, with no one to bury them: I will pour down upon them the
evil they deserve.

So this is what you shall say to them: 17
Let my eyes stream with tears,
ceaselessly, day and night.
For the virgin daughter of my people
has been broken in pieces,
struck by a cruel blow.
If I go out into the country, 18
I see men slain by the sword;
if I enter the city, I see the ravages of famine;
prophet and priest alike
go begging round the land and are never at rest.
Hast thou spurned Judah utterly? 19
Dost thou loathe Zion?
Why hast thou wounded us, and there is no remedy;
why let us hope for better days, and we find nothing good,
for a time of healing, and all is disaster?
We acknowledge our wickedness, 20
the guilt of our forefathers;
O Lord, we have sinned against thee.
Do not despise the place where thy name dwells 21
nor bring contempt on the throne of thy glory.
Remember thy covenant with us and do not make it void.
Can any of the false gods of the nations give rain? 22
Or do the heavens send showers of themselves?
Art thou not God, O LORD,
that we may hope in thee?
It is thou only who doest*ᵃ* all these things.

The LORD said to me, Even if Moses and Samuel stood before me, I **15**
would not be moved to pity this people. Banish them from my presence;
let them be gone. When they ask where they are to go, you shall say to them, 2
These are the words of the LORD:

Those who are for death shall go to their death,
and those for the sword to the sword;
those who are for famine to famine,
and those for captivity to captivity.
ᵃ Or madest.

3   Four kinds of doom do I ordain for them, says the LORD: the sword to
kill, dogs to tear, birds of prey from the skies and beasts from their lairs
4 to devour and destroy. I will make them repugnant to all the kingdoms
of the earth, because of the crimes of Manasseh son of Hezekiah, king of
Judah, in Jerusalem.

5   Who will take pity on you, Jerusalem,
           who will offer you consolation?
        Who will turn aside to wish you well?
6   You cast me off, says the LORD,
           you turned your backs on me.
       So I stretched out my hand and ruined you;
           I was weary of relenting.
7   I winnowed them and scattered them
           through the cities of the land;
       I brought bereavement on them, I destroyed my people,
           for they would not abandon their ways.
8   I made widows among them more in number
           than the sands of the sea;
       I brought upon them a horde of raiders [a]
           to plunder at high noon.
       I made the terror of invasion fall upon them
           all in a moment.
9   The mother of seven sons grew faint,
           she sank into a swoon;
       her light was quenched while it was yet day;
           she was left humbled and shamed.
       All the remnant I gave to perish by the sword
           at the hand of their enemies.
       This is the very word of the LORD.

Confessions and addresses

10   Alas, alas, my mother, that you ever gave me birth!
       a man doomed to strife, with the whole world against me.
       I have borrowed from no one, I have lent to no one,
           yet all men abuse me.
11 The LORD answered,

       But I will greatly strengthen you;
       in time of distress and in time of disaster
       I will bring the enemy to your feet.
12   Can iron break steel from the north?[b]
15   LORD, thou knowest;
       remember me, LORD, and come to visit me,
       take vengeance for me on my persecutors.

[a] I brought . . . raiders: *prob. rdg.; Heb. obscure.*   [b] *Prob. rdg.; Heb. adds* and bronze.
Heb. also adds (13) I will give away your wealth as spoil, and your treasure for no payment,
because of your sin throughout your country. (14) I will make your enemies pass through a
land you do not know; for my anger is a blazing fire and it shall burn for ever (*cp. 17. 3, 4*).

Be patient with me and take me not away,
see what reproaches I endure for thy sake.
I have to suffer those who despise thy words,   16
but thy word is joy and happiness to me,
for thou hast named me thine,
O LORD, God of Hosts.
I have never kept company with any gang of roisterers,   17
or made merry with them;
because I felt thy hand upon me I have sat alone;
for thou hast filled me with indignation.
Why then is my pain unending,   18
my wound desperate and incurable?
Thou art to me like a brook that is not to be trusted,
whose waters fail.

This was the LORD's answer: 19
If you will turn back to me, I will take you back
and you shall stand before me.
If you choose noble utterance and reject the base,
you shall be my spokesman.
This people will turn again to you,
but you will not turn to them.
To withstand them I will make you impregnable,   20
a wall of bronze.
They will attack you but they will not prevail,
for I am with you to deliver you
and save you, says the LORD;
I will deliver you from the wicked,   21
I will rescue you from the ruthless.

The word of the LORD came to me: You shall not marry a wife; you **16** 1 2
shall have neither son nor daughter in this place. For these are the words 3
of the LORD concerning sons and daughters born in this place, the mothers
who bear them and the fathers who beget them in this land: When men 4
die, struck down by deadly ulcers, there shall be no wailing for them and
no burial; they shall be like dung lying upon the ground. When men
perish by sword or famine, their corpses shall become food for birds and
for beasts.

For these are the words of the LORD: Enter no house where there is a 5
mourning-feast; do not go in to wail or to bring comfort, for I have withdrawn my peace from this people, says the LORD, my love and affection.
High and low shall die in this land, but there shall be no burial, no wailing 6
for them; no one shall gash himself, or shave his head. No one shall give 7
the mourner a portion of bread to console him for the dead, nor give him
the cup of consolation, even for his father or mother. Nor shall you enter 8
a house where there is feasting, to sit eating and drinking there. For these 9
are the words of the LORD of Hosts, the God of Israel: In your own days,
in the sight of you all, and in this very place, I will silence all sounds of
joy and gladness, and the voice of bridegroom and bride.

10   When you tell this people all these things they will ask you, 'Why has the LORD decreed that this great disaster is to come upon us? What wrong have we done? What sin have we committed against the LORD our God?'

11   You shall answer, Because your forefathers forsook me, says the LORD, and followed other gods, serving them and bowing down to them. They forsook

12   me and did not keep my law. And you yourselves have done worse than your forefathers; for each of you follows the promptings of his wicked and

13   stubborn heart instead of obeying me. So I will fling you headlong out of this land into a country unknown to you and to your forefathers; there you

14   can serve other gods day and night, for I will show you no favour. There-fore, says the LORD, the time is coming when men shall no longer swear,

15   'By the life of the LORD who brought the Israelites up from Egypt', but, 'By the life of the LORD who brought the Israelites back from a northern land and from all the lands to which he had dispersed them'; and I will bring them back to the soil which I gave to their forefathers.

16   I will send for many fishermen, says the LORD, and they shall fish for them. After that I will send for many hunters, and they shall hunt them

17   out from every mountain and hill and from the crevices in the rocks. For my eyes are on all their ways; they are not hidden from my sight, nor is

18   their wrongdoing concealed from me. I will first make them pay in full[a] for the wrong they have done and the sin they have committed by defiling with the dead lumber of their idols the land which belongs to me, and by filling it with their abominations.

19   O LORD, my strength and my stronghold,
            my refuge in time of trouble,
        to thee shall the nations come
            from the ends of the earth and say,
        Our forefathers inherited only a sham,
            an idol vain and useless.

20   Can man make gods for himself?
            They would be no gods.

21   Therefore I am teaching them,
        once for all will I teach them
            my power and my might,
        and they shall learn that my name is the LORD.

17   The sin of Judah is recorded with an iron tool, engraved on the tablet of their heart with a point of adamant and carved on the horns of their

2   altars to bear witness against them.[b] Their altars and their sacred poles

3   stand by every spreading tree, on the heights and the hills in the mountain country. I will give away your wealth as spoil, and all your treasure for no

4   payment,[c] because of your[d] sin throughout your country. You will lose possession[e] of the patrimony which I gave you. I will make you serve your enemies as slaves in a land you do not know; for my anger is a blazing fire[f] and it shall burn for ever.

[a] in full: *or* double.   [b] to bear . . . them: *prob. rdg.; Heb.* as their sons remember.
[c] for no payment: *prob. rdg., cp. 15. 13; Heb.* your hill-shrines.   [d] your: *prob. rdg.,*
cp. 15. 13; Heb. om.   [e] You . . . possession: *prob. rdg.; Heb. obscure.*   [f] for . . .
fire: *prob. rdg., cp. 15. 14; Heb.* for you have kindled a fire in my anger.

These are the words of the LORD: 5

> A curse on the man who trusts in man
>   and leans for support on human kind,
>   while his heart is far from the LORD!
> He shall be like a juniper in the desert;   6
>   when good comes he shall not see it.
> He shall dwell among the rocks in the wilderness,
>   in a salt land where no man can live.
> Blessed is the man who trusts in the LORD,   7
>   and rests his confidence upon him.
> He shall be like a tree planted by the waterside,   8
>   that stretches its roots along the stream.
> When the heat comes it has nothing to fear;
>   its spreading foliage stays green.
> In a year of drought it feels no care,
>   and does not cease to bear fruit.

> The heart is the most deceitful of all things,   9
> desperately sick;[a] who can fathom it?
> I, the LORD, search the mind   10
>   and test the heart,
> requiting man for his conduct,
>   and as his deeds deserve.
> Like a partridge which gathers into its nest   11
>   eggs which it has not laid,
>   so is the man who amasses wealth unjustly.
> Before his days are half done he must leave it,
> and prove but a fool at the last.

> O throne of glory, exalted from the beginning,   12
>   the place of our sanctuary,
> O LORD on whom Israel's hope is fixed,   13
>   all who reject thee shall be put to shame;
> all in this land who forsake thee shall be humbled,[b]
> for they have rejected the fountain of living water.[c]
> Heal me, O LORD, and I shall be healed,   14
>   save me and I shall be saved;
>   for thou art my praise.
> They say to me, 'Where is the word of the LORD?   15
>   Let it come if it can!'
> It is not the thought of disaster that makes me press after thee;   16
>   never did I desire this day of despair.
> Thou knowest all that has passed my lips;
>   it was approved by thee.
> Do not become a terror to me;   17
>   thou art my only refuge on the day of disaster.

[a] *the most . . . sick: or too deceitful for any man.*   [b] *humbled: prob. rdg.; Heb.*
written.   [c] *Prob. rdg.; Heb. adds the* LORD.

18 May my persecutors be foiled, not I;
    may they be terrified, not I.
      Bring on them the day of disaster;
      destroy them, destroy them utterly.

19 These were the words of the LORD to me: Go and stand in the Benjamin[a]
    Gate, through which the kings of Judah go in and out, and in all the gates
20 of Jerusalem. Say, Hear the words of the LORD, you princes of Judah,
    all you men of Judah, and all you inhabitants of Jerusalem who come
21 in through these gates. These are the words of the LORD: Observe this with
    care, that you do not carry any load on the sabbath or bring it through the
22 gates of Jerusalem. You shall not bring any load out of your houses or do
    any work on the sabbath, but you shall keep the sabbath day holy as I
23 commanded your forefathers. Yet they did not obey or pay attention, but
24 obstinately refused to hear or learn their lesson. Now if you will obey me,
    says the LORD, and refrain from bringing any load through the gates of
    this city on the sabbath, and keep that day holy by doing no work on it,
25 then kings shall come through the gates of this city, kings[b] who shall sit
    on David's throne. They shall come riding in chariots or on horseback,
    escorted by their captains, by the men of Judah and the inhabitants of
26 Jerusalem; and this city shall be inhabited for ever. People shall come from
    the cities of Judah, the country round Jerusalem, the land of Benjamin,
    the Shephelah, the hill-country and the Negeb, bringing whole-offerings,
    sacrifices, grain-offerings, and frankincense, bringing also thank-offerings
27 to the house of the LORD. But if you do not obey me by keeping the sabbath
    day holy and by not carrying any load as you come through the gates of
    Jerusalem on the sabbath, then I will set fire to those gates; it shall consume
    the palaces of Jerusalem and shall not be put out.

18 1 2 These are the words which came to Jeremiah from the LORD: Go down
    at once to the potter's house, and there I will tell you what I have to say.
3 So I went down to the potter's house and found him working at the wheel.
4 Now and then a vessel he was making out of the clay would be spoilt in his
   hands, and then he would start again and mould it into another vessel to
5 6 his liking. Then the word of the LORD came to me: Can I not deal with you,
   Israel, says the LORD, as the potter deals with his clay? You are clay in my
7 hands like the clay in his, O house of Israel. At any moment I may threaten
8 to uproot a nation or a kingdom, to pull it down and destroy it. But if the
   nation which I have threatened turns back from its wicked ways, then I
9 shall think better of the evil I had in mind to bring on it. Or at any moment
10 I may decide to build or to plant a nation or a kingdom. But if it does evil
   in my sight and does not obey me, I shall think better of the good I had in
11 mind for it. Go now and tell the men of Judah and the inhabitants of Jerusalem that these are the words of the LORD: I am the potter; I am preparing
   evil for you and perfecting my designs against you. Turn back, every one
12 of you, from his evil course; mend your ways and your doings. But they
   answer, 'Things are past hope. We will do as we like, and each of us will

---

[a] Benjamin: *prob. rdg.; Heb.* sons of the people.   [b] *Prob. rdg.; Heb. adds* and
officers.

follow the promptings of his own wicked and stubborn heart.' Therefore   13
these are the words of the LORD:

> Inquire among the nations: who ever heard the like of this?
> The virgin Israel has done a thing most horrible.
> Will the snow cease to fall on the rocky slopes of Lebanon?   14
> Will the cool rain streaming in torrents ever fail?
> No, but my people have forgotten me;   15
>> they burn sacrifices to a mere idol,
>> so they stumble in their paths, the ancient ways,
>> and they take to byways and unmade roads;
>> their own land they lay waste,   16
>> and men will jeer at it for ever in contempt.
> All who go by will be horror-struck and shake their heads.
>> Like a wind from the east   17
> I will scatter them before their enemies.
>> In the hour of their downfall
> I will turn my back towards them and not my face.

'Come, let us decide what to do with Jeremiah', men say. 'There will   18
still be priests to guide us, still wise men to advise, still prophets to proclaim
the word. Come, let us invent some charges against him; let us pay no
attention to his message.'

> But do thou, O LORD, pay attention,   19
>> and hear what my opponents are saying against me.
> Is good to be repaid with evil? *a*   20
> Remember how I stood before thee,
> pleading on their behalf
> to avert thy wrath from them.
> Therefore give their sons over to famine,   21
>> leave them at the mercy of the sword.
> Let their women be childless and widowed,
>> let death carry off their men,
> let their young men be cut down in battle.
> Bring raiders upon them without warning,   22
>> and let screams of terror ring out from their houses.
> For they have dug a pit to catch me
> and have hidden snares for my feet.
> Well thou knowest, O LORD,   23
>> all their murderous plots against me.
>> Do not blot out their wrongdoing
> or annul their sin;
> when they are brought stumbling into thy presence,
> deal with them on the day of thy anger.

These are the words of the LORD: Go and buy an earthenware jar.   **19**
Then take with you some of the elders of the people and of the priests,
and go out to the Valley of Ben-hinnom, on which the Gate of the Pot-   2
sherds opens, and there proclaim what I tell you. Say, Hear the word of   3

---

a *Prob. rdg.; Heb. adds* they have dug a pit for me (*cp. verse 22*).

the LORD, you princes of Judah and inhabitants of Jerusalem. These are the words of the LORD of Hosts the God of Israel: I will bring on this place

4 a disaster which shall ring in the ears of all who hear of it. For they have forsaken me, and treated this place as if it were not mine, burning sacrifices to other gods whom neither they nor their fathers nor the kings of Judah

5 have known, and filling this place with the blood of the innocent. They have built shrines to Baal, where they burn their sons as whole-offerings to Baal. It was no command of mine; I never spoke of it; it never entered my

6 thought. Therefore, says the LORD, the time is coming when this place shall no longer be called Topheth or the Valley of Ben-hinnom, but the

7 Valley of Slaughter. In this place I will shatter the plans of Judah and Jerusalem as a jar is shattered; I will make the people fall by the sword before their enemies, at the hands of those who would kill them, and I will

8 give their corpses to the birds and beasts to devour. I will make this city a scene of horror and contempt, so that every passer-by will be horror-

9 struck and jeer in contempt at the sight of its wounds. I will compel men to eat the flesh of their sons and their daughters; they shall devour one another's flesh in the dire straits to which their enemies and those who

10 would kill them will reduce them in the siege. Then you must shatter the

11 jar before the eyes of the men who have come with you and say to them, These are the words of the LORD of Hosts: Thus will I shatter this people and this city as one shatters an earthen vessel so that it cannot be mended, and the dead shall be buried in Topheth because there is no room elsewhere

12 to bury them. This is what I will do to this place, says the LORD, and to

13 those who live there: I will make this city like Topheth. Because of their defilement, the houses of Jerusalem and those of the kings of Judah shall be like Topheth, every one of the houses on whose roofs men have burnt sacrifices to the host of heaven and poured drink-offerings to other gods.

14 Jeremiah came in from Topheth, where the LORD had sent him to pro-phesy, and stood in the court of the LORD's house. He said to all the people,

15 These are the words of the LORD of Hosts the God of Israel: I am bringing on this city and on all its blood-spattered altars every disaster with which I have threatened it, for its people have remained obstinate and refused to listen to me.

20 When Pashhur son of Immer the priest, the chief officer in the house

2 of the LORD, heard Jeremiah prophesying these things, he had him flogged*a* and put him into the stocks at the Upper Gate of Benjamin, in the house of

3 the LORD. The next morning he released him, and Jeremiah said to him,

4 The LORD has called you not Pashhur but Magor-missabib.*b* For these are the words of the LORD: I will make you a terror to yourself and to all your friends; they shall fall by the sword of the enemy before your very eyes. I will hand over all Judah to the king of Babylon, and he will deport

5 them to Babylon and put them to the sword. I will give all this city's store of wealth and riches and all the treasures of the kings of Judah to their enemies; they shall seize them as spoil and carry them off to Babylon.

6 You, Pashhur, and all your household shall go into captivity and come to Babylon. There shall you die and there shall you be buried, you and all your friends to whom you have been a false prophet.

a had him flogged: *or* struck him.　　*b* *That is* Terror let loose.

938

O LORD, thou hast duped me, and I have been thy dupe;   7
    thou hast outwitted me and hast prevailed.
I have been made a laughing-stock all the day long,
everyone mocks me.
Whenever I speak I must needs cry out   8
and proclaim violence and destruction.
I am reproached and mocked all the time
for uttering the word of the LORD.
Whenever I said, 'I will call him to mind no more,   9
    nor speak in his name again',
then his word was imprisoned in my body,
like a fire blazing in my heart,
and I was weary with holding it under,
and could endure no more.
    For I heard many whispering, *a*   10
    'Denounce him! we will denounce him.'
All my friends were on the watch for a false step,
saying, 'Perhaps he may be tricked, then we can catch him
    and take our revenge.'
But the LORD is on my side, strong and ruthless,   11
therefore my persecutors shall stumble and fall powerless.
Bitter shall be their abasement when they fail,
    and their shame shall long be remembered.
O LORD of Hosts, thou dost test the righteous   12
and search the depths of the heart;
to thee have I committed my cause,
let me see thee take vengeance on them.
Sing to the LORD, praise the LORD;   13
for he rescues the poor from those who would do them wrong.

A curse on the day when I was born!   14
    Be it for ever unblessed,
    the day when my mother bore me!
A curse on the man who brought word to my father,   15
    'A child is born to you, a son',
    and gladdened his heart!
That man shall fare like the cities   16
which the LORD overthrew without mercy.
He shall hear cries of alarm in the morning
    and uproar at noon,
because death did not claim me before birth,   17
and my mother did not become my grave,
    her womb great with me for ever.
Why did I come forth from the womb   18
to know only sorrow and toil,
to end my days in shame?

      a   *Prob. rdg.; Heb. adds* Terror let loose.

Kings and prophets denounced

21 THE WORD WHICH CAME FROM THE LORD to Jeremiah when King
Zedekiah sent to him Pashhur son of Malchiah and Zephaniah the
2 priest, son of Maaseiah, with this request: 'Nebuchadrezzar king of Babylon is making war on us; inquire of the LORD on our behalf. Perhaps
the LORD will perform a miracle as he has done in past times, so that
3 Nebuchadrezzar may raise the siege.' But Jeremiah answered them, Tell
4 Zedekiah, these are the words of the LORD the God of Israel: I will turn
back upon you your own weapons with which you are fighting the king of
Babylon and the Chaldaeans besieging you outside the wall; and I will
5 bring them into the heart of this city. I myself will fight against you in
burning rage and great fury, with an outstretched hand and a strong arm.
6 I will strike down those who live in this city, men and cattle alike; they
7 shall die of a great pestilence. After that, says the LORD, I will take Zedekiah
king of Judah, his courtiers and the people, all in this city who survive
pestilence, sword, and famine, and hand them over to Nebuchadrezzar the
king of Babylon, to their enemies and those who would kill them. He shall
put them to the sword and shall show no pity, no mercy or compassion.
8 You shall say further to this people, These are the words of the LORD:
I offer you now a choice between the way of life and the way of death.
9 Whoever remains in this city shall die by sword, by famine, or by pestilence,
but whoever goes out to surrender to the Chaldaeans, who are now besieging you, shall survive; he shall take home his life, and nothing more.
10 I have set my face against this city, meaning to do them harm, not good,
says the LORD. It shall be handed over to the king of Babylon, and he shall
burn it to the ground.

11   To the royal house of Judah.
           Listen to the word of the LORD:
12   O house of David, these are the words of the LORD:
           Administer justice betimes,
           rescue the victim from his oppressor,
     lest the fire of my fury blaze up and burn unquenched
           because of your evil doings.

13   The LORD says,
       I am against you who lie in the valley,
           you, the rock in the plain,
       you who say, 'Who can come down upon us?
       Who can penetrate our lairs?'
14   I will punish you as you deserve,
           says the LORD,
       I will kindle fire on the heathland around you,
       and it shall consume everything round about.

22   These were the words of the LORD: Go down to the house of the king of
2 Judah and say this: Listen to the words of the LORD, O king of Judah, you
who sit on David's throne, you and your courtiers and your people who

come in at these gates. These are the words of the Lord: Deal justly and　3
fairly, rescue the victim from his oppressor, do not ill-treat or do violence
to the alien, the orphan or the widow, do not shed innocent blood in this
place. If you obey, and only if you obey, kings who sit on David's throne shall　4
yet come riding through these gates in chariots and on horses, with their
retinue of courtiers and people. But if you do not listen to my words, then　5
by myself I swear, says the Lord, this house shall become a desolate ruin.
For these are the words of the Lord about the royal house of Judah:　6

> Though you are dear to me as Gilead
> 　or as the heights of Lebanon,
> I swear that I will make you a wilderness,
> 　a land of unpeopled cities.
> I will dedicate an armed host to fight against you,　7
> 　a ravening horde;
> they shall cut your choicest cedars down
> 　and fling them on the fire.

Men of many nations shall pass by this city and say to one another,　8
'Why has the Lord done this to such a great city?' The answer will be,　9
'Because they forsook their covenant with the Lord their God; they
worshipped other gods and served them.'

> Weep not for the dead nor brood over his loss.　10
> Weep rather for him who has gone away,
> 　for he shall never return,
> 　never again see the land of his birth.

For these are the words of the Lord concerning Shallum son of Josiah,　11
king of Judah, who succeeded his father on the throne and has gone away:
He shall never return; he shall die in the place of his exile and never see　12
this land again.

> Shame on the man who builds his house by unjust means　13
> 　and completes its roof-chambers by fraud,
> 　making his countrymen work without payment,
> 　giving them no wage for their labour!
> Shame on the man who says, 'I will build a spacious house　14
> 　with airy roof-chambers,
> set windows in it, panel it with cedar
> 　and paint it with vermilion'!
> If your cedar is more splendid,　15
> 　does that prove you a king?
> Think of your father: he ate and drank,
> dealt justly and fairly; all went well with him.
> He dispensed justice to the lowly and poor; [a]　16
> did not this show he knew me? says the Lord.
> But you have no eyes, no thought for anything but gain,　17
> 　set only on the innocent blood you can shed,
> 　on cruel acts of tyranny.

---

a Prob. rdg.; Heb. adds all went well (*repeated from verse 15*).

18   Therefore these are the words of the LORD concerning Jehoiakim son of Josiah, king of Judah:

> For him no mourner shall say, 'Alas, brother, dear brother!'
> no one say, 'Alas, lord and master!'

19   He shall be buried like a dead ass,
> dragged along and flung out
> beyond the gates of Jerusalem.

20   Get up into Lebanon and cry aloud,
> make your voice heard in Bashan,
> cry aloud from Abarim, for all who befriend you are broken.

21   I spoke to you in your days of prosperous ease,
> but you said, 'I will not listen.'
> This is how you behaved since your youth;
> never have you obeyed me.

22   The wind shall carry away all your friends,[a]
> your lovers shall depart into exile.
> Then you will be put to shame and abashed
> for all your evil deeds.[b]

23   You dwellers in Lebanon, who make your nests among the
> cedars,
> how you will groan when the pains come upon you,
> like the pangs of a woman in labour!

24   By my life, says the LORD, Coniah son of Jehoiakim, king of Judah, shall be the signet-ring on my right hand no longer. Yes, Coniah, I will
25 pull you off. I will hand you over to those who seek your life, to those you fear, to Nebuchadrezzar king of Babylon and to the Chaldaeans.
26 I will fling you headlong, you and the mother who gave you birth, into another land, a land where you were not born; and there shall you both
27 die. They shall never come back to their own land, the land for which they long.
28   This man, Coniah, then, is he a mere puppet, contemptible and broken, only a thing unwanted? Why else are he and his children flung out headlong and hurled into a country they do not know?
29 30 O land, land, land, hear the words of the LORD: These are the words of the LORD: Write this man down as stripped of all honour, one who in his own life shall not prosper, nor shall he leave descendants to sit in prosperity on David's throne or rule again in Judah.

23   Shame on the shepherds who let the sheep of my flock scatter and be
2 lost! says the LORD. Therefore these are the words of the LORD the God of Israel about the shepherds who tend my people: You have scattered and dispersed my flock. You have not watched over them; but I am
3 watching you to punish you for your evil doings, says the LORD. I will myself gather the remnant of my sheep from all the lands to which I have dispersed them. I will bring them back to their homes, and they
4 shall be fruitful and increase. I will appoint shepherds to tend them;

---

a Or shepherds.   *b Or* calamities.

they shall never again know fear or dismay or punishment. This is the
very word of the LORD.

> The days are now coming, says the LORD,   5
> when I will make a righteous Branch spring from David's line,
>   a king who shall rule wisely,
> maintaining law and justice in the land.
> In his days Judah shall be kept safe,   6
> and Israel shall live undisturbed.
> This is the name to be given to him:
>   The LORD is our Righteousness.

Therefore the days are coming, says the LORD, when men shall no longer   7
swear, 'By the life of the LORD who brought Israel up from Egypt', but,   8
'By the life of the LORD who brought the descendants of the Israelites back
from a northern land and from all the lands to which he had dispersed them,
to live again on their own soil.'

On the prophets.   9

> Deep within me my heart is broken,
> there is no strength in my bones;
> because of the LORD, because of his dread words
> I have become like a drunken man,
> like a man overcome with wine.
> For the land is full of adulterers,   10
> and because of them the earth lies parched,
>   the wild pastures have dried up.
> The course that they run is evil,
>   and their powers are misused.
> For prophet and priest alike are godless;   11
> I have come upon the evil they are doing even in my own house.
>   This is the very word of the LORD.

> Therefore the path shall turn slippery beneath their feet;   12
> they shall be dispersed in the dark and shall fall there.
> For I will bring disaster on them when their day of reckoning comes.
>   This is the very word of the LORD.
> I found the prophets of Samaria men of no sense: 13
> they prophesied in Baal's name and led my people Israel astray.
> In the prophets of Jerusalem I see a thing most horrible: 14
> adulterers and hypocrites that they are,
>   they encourage evildoers,
> so that no man turns back from his sin;
> to me all her inhabitants are like Sodom and Gomorrah.

These then are the words of the LORD of Hosts concerning the prophets: 15

> I will give them wormwood to eat
> and a bitter poison to drink;
>   for a godless spirit has spread over all the land
>   from the prophets of Jerusalem.

16 These are the words of the LORD of Hosts:

> Do not listen to what the prophets say,
> who buoy you up with false hopes;
> the vision they report springs from their own imagination,
> it is not from the mouth of the LORD.

17 They say to those who spurn the word of the LORD,
> 'Prosperity shall be yours';
> and to all who follow the promptings of their own stubborn heart they say,
> 'No disaster shall befall you.'

18 But which of them has stood in the council of the LORD,
> seen him and heard his word?
> Which of them has listened to his word and obeyed?

19 See what a scorching wind has gone out from the LORD,
> a furious whirlwind;
> it whirls round the heads of the wicked.

20 The LORD's anger is not to be turned aside,
> until he has accomplished and fulfilled his deep designs.
> In days to come you will fully understand.

21 I did not send these prophets, yet they went in haste;
> I did not speak to them, yet they prophesied.

22 If they have stood in my council,
> let them proclaim my words to my people
> and turn them from their evil course and their evil doings.

23 Am I a god only near at hand, not far away?
24 Can a man hide in any secret place and I not see him?
> Do I not fill heaven and earth?
> This is the very word of the LORD.

25 I have heard what the prophets say, the prophets who speak lies in my
26 name and cry, 'I have had a dream, a dream!' How long will it be till they
change their tune, these prophets who prophesy lies and give voice to
27 their own inventions? By these dreams which they tell one another these
men think they will make my people forget my name, as their fathers
28 forgot my name for the name of *a* Baal. If a prophet has a dream, let him
tell his dream; if he has my word, let him speak my word in truth. What
29 has chaff to do with grain? says the LORD. Do not my words scorch *b* like
30 fire? says the LORD. Are they not like a hammer that splinters rock? I am
against the prophets, says the LORD, who steal my words from one another
31 for their own use. I am against the prophets, says the LORD, who concoct
32 words of their own and then say, 'This is his very word.' I am against the
prophets, says the LORD, who dream lies and retail them, misleading my
people with wild and reckless falsehoods. It was not I who sent them or
commissioned them, and they will do this people no good. This is the
very word of the LORD.

33 When you are asked by this people or by a prophet or priest what the
burden of the LORD's message is, you shall answer, You are his burden,
34 and I shall throw you down, says the LORD. If prophet or priest or layman

---

a for the name of: *or* by their worship of.   *b* scorch: *prob. rdg.; Heb.* thus.

uses the term 'the LORD's burden', I will punish that man and his family. The form of words you shall use in speaking amongst yourselves is: 'What answer has the LORD given?' or, 'What has the LORD said?' You shall never again mention 'the burden of the LORD'; that is reserved for the man to whom he entrusts his message. If you do, you will make nonsense of the words of the living God, the LORD of Hosts our God. This is the form you shall use in speaking to a prophet: 'What answer has the LORD given?' or, 'What has the LORD said?' But to any of you who do say, 'the burden of the LORD', the LORD speaks thus: Because you say, 'the burden of the LORD', though I sent to tell you not to say it, therefore I myself will carry you like a burden and throw you down, casting out of my sight both you and the city which I gave to you and to your forefathers. I will inflict on you endless reproach, endless shame which shall never be forgotten.

Two visions

THIS IS WHAT THE LORD SHOWED ME: I saw two baskets of figs set out in front of the sanctuary of the LORD. This was after Nebuchadrezzar king of Babylon had deported from Jerusalem Jeconiah son of Jehoiakim, king of Judah, with the officers of Judah, the craftsmen and the smiths,[a] and taken them to Babylon. In one basket the figs were very good, like the figs that are first ripe; in the other the figs were very bad, so bad that they were not fit to eat. The LORD said to me, 'What are you looking at, Jeremiah?' 'Figs,' I answered, 'the good very good, and the bad so bad that they are not fit to eat.' Then this word came to me from the LORD: These are the words of the LORD the God of Israel: I count the exiles of Judah whom I sent away from this place to the land of the Chaldaeans as good as these good figs. I will look upon them meaning to do them good, and I will restore them to their land; I will build them up and not pull them down, plant them and not uproot them. I will give them the wit to know me, for I am the LORD; they shall become my people and I will become their God, for they will come back to me with all their heart. But Zedekiah king of Judah, his officers and the survivors of Jerusalem, whether they remain in this land or live in Egypt—all these I will treat as bad figs, says the LORD, so bad that they are not fit to eat. I will make them repugnant to all the kingdoms of the earth, a reproach, a by-word, an object-lesson and a thing of ridicule wherever I drive them. I will send against them sword, famine, and pestilence until they have vanished from the land which I gave to them and to their forefathers.

This came to Jeremiah as the word concerning all the people of Judah in the fourth year of Jehoiakim son of Josiah, king of Judah (that is the first year of Nebuchadrezzar king of Babylon). This is what the prophet Jeremiah said to all Judah and all the inhabitants of Jerusalem: For twenty-three years, from the thirteenth year of Josiah son of Amon, king of Judah, to the present day, I have been receiving the words of the LORD and taking pains to speak to you, but you have not listened. The LORD has

[a] *the smiths: or* the harem.

945

taken pains to send you his servants the prophets, but you have not listened
5 or shown any inclination to listen. If each of you will turn from his wicked
ways and evil courses, he has said, then you shall for ever live on the soil
6 which the LORD gave to you and to your forefathers. You must not follow
other gods, serving and worshipping them, nor must you provoke me to
anger with the idols your hands have made; then I will not do you harm.
7 But you did not listen to me, says the LORD; you provoked me to anger
with the idols your hands had made and so brought harm upon yourselves.
8   Therefore these are the words of the LORD of Hosts: Because you have
9 not listened to my words, I will summon all the tribes of the north, says
the LORD: I will send for my servant Nebuchadrezzar king of Babylon.
I will bring them against this land and all its inhabitants and all these
nations round it; I will exterminate them and make them a thing of horror
10 and derision, a scandal for ever. I will silence all sounds of joy and gladness among them, the voices of bridegroom and bride, and the sound of
11 the handmill; I will quench the light of every lamp. For seventy years this
whole country shall be a scandal and a horror; these nations shall be in
12 subjection to the king of Babylon. When those seventy years are completed, I will punish the king of Babylon and his people, says the LORD,
for all their misdeeds and make the land of the Chaldaeans a waste for ever.
13 I will bring upon that country all I have said, all that is written in this book,
14 all that Jeremiah has prophesied against these peoples. They will be the
victims*a* of mighty nations and great kings, and thus I will repay them for
their actions and their deeds.

15   These were the words of the LORD the God of Israel to me: Take from
my hand this cup of fiery wine and make all the nations to whom I send
16 you drink it. When they have drunk it they will vomit and go mad; such
17 is the sword which I am sending among them. Then I took the cup from
the LORD's hand, gave it to all the nations to whom he sent me and made
18 them drink it: to Jerusalem, the cities of Judah, its kings and officers,
making them a scandal, a thing of horror and derision and an object of
19 ridicule, as they still are: to Pharaoh king of Egypt, his courtiers, his
20 officers, all his people, and all his rabble of followers, all the kings of the
land of Uz, all the kings of the Philistines: to Ashkelon, Gaza, Ekron, and
21 22 the remnant of Ashdod: also to Edom, Moab, and the Ammonites, all the
kings of Tyre, all the kings of Sidon, and the kings of the coasts and islands:
23 24 to Dedan, Tema, Buz, and all who roam the fringes of the desert,*b* all the
25 kings of Arabia living in the wilderness, all the kings of Zamri, all the kings
26 of Elam, and all the kings of the Medes, all the kings of the north, neighbours or far apart, and all the kingdoms on the face of the earth. Last of all
27 the king of Sheshak*c* shall drink. You shall say to them, These are the
words of the LORD of Hosts the God of Israel: Drink this, get drunk and
be sick; fall, to rise no more, before the sword which I am sending among
28 you. If they refuse to take the cup from you and to drink, say to them, These
29 are the words of the LORD of Hosts: You must and shall drink. I will first
punish the city which bears my name; do you think that you can be exempt?

a They . . . victims: *prob. rdg.; Heb.* They were the victims.   *b* who roam . . .
desert: *or* who clip the hair on their temples.   *c* *A name for Babylon.*

No, you cannot be exempt, for I am invoking the sword against all that inhabit the earth. This is the very word of the LORD of Hosts.

Prophesy to them and tell them all I have said: 30

      The LORD roars from Zion on high
      and thunders from his holy dwelling-place.
      Yes, he roars across the heavens, his home;
an echo comes back like the shout of men treading grapes.
      The great noise reaches to the ends of the earth   31
        and all its inhabitants.
      For the LORD brings a charge against the nations,
      he goes to law with all mankind
      and has handed the wicked over to the sword.
        This is the very word of the LORD.

      These are the words of the LORD of Hosts: 32
      Ruin spreads from nation to nation,
a mighty tempest is blowing up from the ends of the earth.

In that day those whom the LORD has slain shall lie like dung on the   33
ground from one end of the earth to the other; no one shall wail for them,
they shall not be taken up and buried.

      Howl, shepherds, cry aloud,   34
      sprinkle yourselves with ashes, you masters of the flock.
      It is your turn to go to the slaughter,
        and you shall fall like fine rams.
      The shepherds shall have nowhere to flee,   35
        the flockmasters no way of escape.
Hark, the shepherds cry out, the flockmasters howl,   36
        for the LORD is ravaging their pasture,
and their peaceful homesteads lie in ruins beneath his anger.   37
      They flee like a young lion abandoning his lair,   38
      for their land has become a waste,
wasted by the cruel sword and by his anger.

Jerusalem laid under a curse

At the beginning of the reign of Jehoiakim son of Josiah, king   26
of Judah, this word came to Jeremiah from the LORD: These are the   2
words of the LORD: Stand in the court of the LORD's house and speak to
the inhabitants of all the cities of Judah who come to worship there. You
shall tell them everything that I command you to say to them, keeping
nothing back. Perhaps they may listen, and every man may turn back   3
from his evil courses. Then I will relent, and give up my purpose to bring
disaster on them for their evil deeds. You shall say to them, These are   4
the words of the LORD: If you do not obey me, if you do not follow the law I
have set before you, and listen to the words of my servants the prophets,   5
the prophets whom I have taken pains to send to you, but you have never
listened to them, then I will make this house like Shiloh and this city an   6
object of ridicule to all nations on earth.

7 The priests, the prophets, and all the people heard Jeremiah say this
8 in the LORD's house and, when he came to the end of what the LORD had
commanded him to say to them, priests, prophets, and people seized him
9 and threatened him with death. 'Why', they demanded, 'have you prophesied in the LORD's name that this house shall become like Shiloh and
this city waste and uninhabited?' The people all gathered against Jeremiah
10 in the LORD's house. The officers of Judah heard what was happening, and
they went up from the royal palace to the LORD's house and took their
11 places there at the entrance of the new gate. Then the priests and the
prophets said to the officers and all the people, 'Condemn this fellow to
death. He has prophesied against this city: you have heard it with your own
12 ears.' Then Jeremiah said to the officers and the people, 'The LORD sent me
13 to prophesy against this house and this city all that you have heard. If you
now mend your ways and your doings and obey the LORD your God, then
he may relent and revoke the disaster with which he has threatened you.
14 But I am in your hands; do with me whatever you think right and proper.
15 Only you may be certain that, if you put me to death, you and this city and
all who live in it will be guilty of murdering an innocent man; for in very
truth the LORD has sent me to you to say all this in your hearing.'
16 Then the officers and all the people said to the priests and the prophets,
'This man ought not to be condemned to death, for he has spoken to us in
17 the name of the LORD our God.' Some of the elders of the land also stood
18 up and said to the assembled people, 'In the time of Hezekiah king of
Judah, Micah of Moresheth was prophesying and said to all the people
of Judah: "These are the words of the LORD of Hosts:

> Zion shall become a ploughed field,
> Jerusalem a heap of ruins,
> and the temple-hill rough heath."

19 Did King Hezekiah and all Judah put him to death? Did not the king show
reverence for the LORD and seek to placate him? Then the LORD relented
and revoked the disaster with which he had threatened them. Are we to
bring great disaster on ourselves?'
20 There was another man who prophesied in the name of the LORD, Uriah
son of Shemaiah, from Kiriath-jearim. He also prophesied against this
21 city and this land, just as Jeremiah had done. King Jehoiakim with all his
officers and his bodyguard heard what he said and sought to put him to
22 death. When Uriah heard of it, he was afraid and fled to Egypt. King
23 Jehoiakim sent Elnathan son of Akbor with others to fetch Uriah from
Egypt, and they brought him to the king. He had him put to death by the
24 sword, and his body flung into the burial-place of the common people. But
Ahikam son of Shaphan used his influence on Jeremiah's behalf to save
him from death at the hands of the people.

A rising against Nebuchadrezzar checked

AT THE BEGINNING OF THE REIGN of Zedekiah son of Josiah, king of 27 Judah, this word came from the LORD to Jeremiah: These are the 2 words of the LORD to me: Take the cords and bars of a yoke and put them on your neck. Then send to the kings of Edom, Moab, Ammon, Tyre, and 3 Sidon by the envoys who have come from them to Zedekiah king of Judah in Jerusalem, and give them the following message for their masters: 4 These are the words of the LORD of Hosts the God of Israel: Say to your masters: I made the earth with my great strength and with outstretched 5 arm, I made man and beast on the face of the earth, and I give it to whom I see fit. I now give all these lands to my servant Nebuchadrezzar king 6 of Babylon, and I give him also all the beasts of the field to serve him. All nations shall serve him, and his son and his grandson, until the 7 destined hour of his own land comes, and then mighty nations and great kings shall use him as they please. If any nation or kingdom will 8 not serve Nebuchadrezzar king of Babylon or submit to his yoke, I will punish them with sword, famine, and pestilence, says the LORD, until I leave them entirely in his power. Therefore do not listen to your pro- 9 phets, your diviners, your wise women, your soothsayers, and your sorcerers when they tell you not to serve the king of Babylon. They are 10 prophesying falsely to you; and so you will be carried far from your own land, and I shall banish you and you will perish. But if any nation 11 submits to the yoke of the king of Babylon and serves him, I will leave them on their own soil, says the LORD; they shall cultivate it and live there.

I have said all this to Zedekiah king of Judah: If you will submit to the 12 yoke of the king of Babylon and serve him and his people, then you shall save your lives. Why should you and your people die by sword, famine, and 13 pestilence, the fate with which the LORD has threatened any nation which does not serve the king of Babylon? Do not listen to the prophets who tell 14 you not to become subject to the king of Babylon; they are prophesying falsely to you. I have not sent them, says the LORD; they are prophesying 15 falsely in my name, and so I shall banish you and you will perish, you and these prophets who prophesy to you.

I said to the priests and all the people, These are the words of the 16 LORD: Do not listen to your prophets who tell you that the vessels of the LORD's house will very soon be brought back from Babylon; they are only prophesying falsely to you. Do not listen to them; serve the 17 king of Babylon, and save your lives. Why should this city become a ruin? If they are prophets, and if they have the word of the LORD, let 18 them intercede with the LORD of Hosts to grant that the vessels still left in the LORD's house, in the royal palace, and in Jerusalem, may not be carried off to Babylon. For these are the words of the LORD of Hosts 19 concerning the pillars, the sea, the trolleys, and all the other vessels still left in this city, which Nebuchadrezzar king of Babylon did not take 20 when he deported Jeconiah son of Jehoiakim, king of Judah, from

Jerusalem to Babylon, together with all the nobles of Judah and Jerusalem.
21 These indeed are the words of the LORD of Hosts the God of Israel concerning the vessels still left in the LORD's house, in the royal palace, and
22 in Jerusalem: They shall be taken to Babylon and stay there until I recall them, says the LORD; then I will bring them back and restore them to this place.

28 That same year,[a] in the fifth month of the first[b] year of the reign of Zedekiah king of Judah, Hananiah son of Azzur, the prophet from Gibeon, said to me in the house of the LORD, in the presence of the priests and all
2 the people, 'These are the words of the LORD of Hosts the God of Israel:
3 I have broken the yoke of the king of Babylon. Within two years I will bring back to this place all the vessels of the LORD's house which Nebuchadrezzar king of Babylon took from here and carried off to Babylon.
4 I will also bring back to this place, says the LORD, Jeconiah son of Jehoiakim, king of Judah, and all the exiles of Judah who went to Babylon; for I will
5 break the yoke of the king of Babylon.' The prophet Jeremiah said to Hananiah the prophet in the presence of the priests and all the people
6 standing in the LORD's house: 'May it be so! May the LORD indeed do this: may he fulfil all that you have prophesied, by bringing back the vessels of
7 the LORD's house and all the exiles from Babylon to this place! Only hear
8 what I have to say to you and to all the people: the prophets who preceded you and me from earliest times have foretold war, famine, and pestilence
9 for many lands and for great kingdoms. If a prophet foretells prosperity, when his words come true it will be known that the LORD has sent him.'
10 Then the prophet Hananiah took the yoke from the neck of the prophet
11 Jeremiah and broke it, saying before all the people, 'These are the words of the LORD: Thus will I break the yoke of Nebuchadrezzar king of Babylon; I will break it off the necks of all nations within two years';[c] and the
12 prophet Jeremiah went his way. After Hananiah had broken the yoke which had been on Jeremiah's neck, the word of the LORD came to Jeremiah:
13 Go and say to Hananiah, These are the words of the LORD: You have
14 broken bars of wood; in their place you shall get bars of iron. For these are the words of the LORD of Hosts the God of Israel: I have put a yoke of iron on the necks of all these nations, making them serve Nebuchadrezzar king of Babylon. They shall serve him, and I have given him even the beasts of
15 the field. Then Jeremiah said to Hananiah, 'Listen, Hananiah. The LORD has not sent you, and you have led this nation to trust in false prophecies.
16 Therefore these are the words of the LORD: Beware, I will remove you from the face of the earth; you shall die within the year, because you have
17 preached rebellion against the LORD.' The prophet Hananiah died that same year, in the seventh month.

29 Jeremiah sent a letter from Jerusalem to the remaining elders among the exiles, to the priests and prophets, and to all the people whom Nebu-
2 chadrezzar had deported from Jerusalem to Babylon, after King Jeconiah had left Jerusalem with the queen mother and the eunuchs, the officers of

[a] *Prob. rdg.; Heb. adds* at the beginning of the reign.   [b] *Prob. rdg.; Heb.* fourth.
[c] *within two years: or* while there are still two full years to run.

Judah and Jerusalem, the craftsmen and the smiths.*a* The prophet en- 3
trusted the letter to Elasah son of Shaphan and Gemariah son of Hilkiah,
whom Zedekiah king of Judah had sent to Babylon to King Nebuchadrezzar. This is what he wrote: These are the words of the LORD of Hosts the 4
God of Israel: To all the exiles whom I have carried off from Jerusalem to
Babylon: Build houses and live in them; plant gardens and eat their pro- 5
duce. Marry wives and beget sons and daughters; take wives for your sons 6
and give your daughters to husbands, so that they may bear sons and
daughters and you may increase there and not dwindle away. Seek the 7
welfare of any city to which I have carried you off, and pray to the LORD
for it; on its welfare your welfare will depend. For these are the words of 8
the LORD of Hosts the God of Israel: Do not be deceived by the prophets
or the diviners among you, and do not listen to the wise women whom you
set to dream dreams. They prophesy falsely to you in my name; I did not 9
send them. This is the very word of the LORD.

These are the words of the LORD: When a full seventy years has passed 10
over Babylon, I will take up your cause and fulfil the promise of good things
I made you, by bringing you back to this place. I alone know my purpose 11
for you, says the LORD: prosperity and not misfortune, and a long line of
children after you. If you invoke me and pray to me, I will listen to you: 12
when you seek me, you shall find me; if you search with all your heart, I 13 14
will let you find me, says the LORD. I will restore your fortunes and gather
you again from all the nations and all the places to which I have banished
you, says the LORD, and bring you back to the place from which I have
carried you into exile.

You say that the LORD has raised up prophets for you in Babylon. These 15 16
are the words of the LORD concerning the king who sits on the throne of
David and all the people who live in this city, your fellow-countrymen who
have not gone into exile with you. These are the words of the LORD of 17
Hosts: I bring upon them sword, famine, and pestilence, and make them
like rotten figs, too bad to be eaten. I pursue them with sword, famine, 18
and pestilence, and make them repugnant to all the kingdoms of the earth,
an object of execration and horror, of derision and reproach, among all
the nations to which I have banished them. Just as they did not listen to 19
my words, says the LORD, when I took pains to send them my servants the
prophets, so you did not listen, says the LORD. But now, you exiles whom 20
I have sent from Jerusalem to Babylon, listen to the words of the LORD.
These are the words of the LORD of Hosts the God of Israel concerning 21
Ahab son of Kolaiah and Zedekiah son of Maaseiah, who prophesy falsely
to you in my name. I will hand them over to Nebuchadrezzar king of
Babylon, and he will put them to death before your eyes. Their names shall 22
be used by all the exiles of Judah in Babylon when they curse a man; they
shall say, May the LORD treat you like Zedekiah and Ahab, whom the king
of Babylon roasted in the fire! For their conduct in Israel was an outrage: 23
they committed adultery with other men's wives, and without my authority
prophesied in my name, and what they prophesied was false. I know; I
can testify. This is the very word of the LORD.

a the smiths: *or* the harem.

24 25 To Shemaiah the Nehelamite.*ᵃ* These are the words of the LORD of
Hosts the God of Israel: You have sent a letter in your own name to
26 Zephaniah son of Maaseiah the priest, in which you say: 'The LORD has
appointed you to be priest in place of Jehoiada the priest, and it is your
duty, as officer in charge of the LORD's house, to put every madman who
27 sets up as a prophet into the stocks and the pillory. Why, then, have you
not reprimanded Jeremiah of Anathoth, who poses as a prophet before
28 you? On the strength of this he has sent to us in Babylon and said, "Your
exile will be long; build houses and live in them, plant gardens and eat
29 their produce."' Zephaniah the priest read this letter to Jeremiah the
30 31 prophet, and the word of the LORD came to Jeremiah: Send and tell all
the exiles that these are the words of the LORD concerning Shemaiah the
Nehelamite: Because Shemaiah has prophesied to you, though I did not
send him, and has led you to trust in false prophecies, these are now the
32 words of the LORD: I will punish Shemaiah and his children. He shall have
no one to take his place in this nation and enjoy the prosperity which I will
bestow on my people, says the LORD, because he has preached rebellion
against me.

Hopes for the restoration of Jerusalem

30 1 2 THE WORD WHICH CAME TO JEREMIAH from the LORD. These are
the words of the LORD the God of Israel: Write in a book all that I
3 have said to you, for this is the very word of the LORD: The time is coming
when I will restore the fortunes of my people Israel and Judah, says the
LORD, and bring them back to the land which I gave to their forefathers;
and it shall be their possession.

4 5   This is what the LORD has said to Israel and Judah. These are the words
of the LORD:

> You shall hear a cry of terror, of fear without relief.
6   Ask and see: can a man bear a child?
>   Why then do I see every man
>   gripping his sides like a woman in labour,
> every face changed, all turned pale?
7   Awful is that day:
>   when has there been its like?
>   A time of anguish for Jacob,
>   yet he shall come through it safely.

8   In that day, says the LORD of Hosts, I will break their yoke off their
necks and snap their cords; foreigners shall no longer use them as they
9 please; they shall serve the LORD their God and David their king, whom
I will raise up for them.

10   And you, Jacob my servant, have no fear;
>   despair not, O Israel, says the LORD.

ᵃ Prob. rdg.; Heb. adds you shall say, saying.

For I will bring you back safe from afar
and your offspring from the land where they are captives;
and Jacob shall be at rest once more,
    prosperous and unafraid.
For I am with you and will save you, says the LORD.   11
    I will make an end of all the nations
    amongst whom I have scattered you,
but I will not make an end of you;
    though I punish you as you deserve,
    I will not sweep you clean away.

For these are the words of the LORD to Zion: 12
    Your injury is past healing,
        cruel was the blow you suffered.
    There can be no^a remedy for your sore,   13
        the new skin cannot grow.
    All your lovers have forgotten you;   14
        they look for you no longer.
    I have struck you down
as an enemy strikes, and punished you cruelly;
for your wickedness is great and your sins are many.
    Why complain of your injury,   15
        that your sore cannot be healed?^b
    I have done this to you,
because your wickedness is great and your sins are many.

Yet all who devoured you shall themselves be devoured,   16
all your oppressors shall go into captivity.
    Those who plunder you shall be plundered,
        and those who despoil you I will give up to be spoiled.
    I will cause the new skin to grow   17
        and heal your wounds, says the LORD,
    although men call you the Outcast,
        Zion, nobody's friend.

These are the words of the LORD: 18
    Watch; I will restore the fortunes of Jacob's clans
        and show my love for all his dwellings.
    Every city shall be rebuilt on its mound of ruins,
        every mansion shall have its familiar household.
    From them praise shall be heard   19
        and sounds of merrymaking.
    I will increase them, they shall not diminish,
    I will raise them to honour, they shall no longer be despised.
    Their sons shall be what they once were,   20
        and their community shall be established in my sight.
    I will punish all their oppressors;

---

^a *Prob. rdg.; Heb. adds* one judging your case.   ^b *Why . . . healed?: or* Cry not
for help in your injury. Your sore cannot be healed.

21   a ruler shall appear, one of themselves,
          a governor shall arise from their own number.
        I will myself bring him*a* near and so he*b* shall approach me;
        for no one ventures of himself to approach me,
              says the LORD.
22   So you shall be my people,
          and I will be your God.
23   See what a scorching wind has gone out from the LORD,
          a sweeping whirlwind.
        It whirls round the heads of the wicked;
24   the LORD's anger is not to be turned aside,
        till he has finished and achieved his heart's desire.
        In days to come you will understand.

31   At that time, says the LORD, I will become God of all the families of
  2 Israel, and they shall become my people. These are the words of the
     LORD:

          A people that survived the sword
            found favour in the wilderness;
          Israel journeyed to find rest;
  3   long ago*c* the LORD appeared to them:
        I have dearly loved you from of old,
        and still I maintain my unfailing care for you.
  4   I will build you up again, O virgin Israel,
          and you shall be rebuilt.
        Again you shall adorn yourself with jingles,
          and go forth with the merry throng of dancers.
  5   Again you shall plant vineyards on the hills of Samaria,
          vineyards which those who planted them defiled;
  6   for a day will come when the watchmen on Ephraim's hills cry out,
        Come, let us go up to Zion, to the LORD our God.

  7 For these are the words of the LORD:
          Break into shouts of joy for Jacob's sake,
            lead the nations, crying loud and clear,
          sing out your praises and say,
            The LORD has saved his people,
            and preserved a remnant of Israel.
  8   See how I bring them from the land of the north;
          I will gather them from the ends of the earth,
          their blind and lame among them,
            women with child and women in labour,
            a great company.
  9   They come home, weeping as they come,
            but I will comfort them and be their escort.
          I will lead them to flowing streams;
        they shall not stumble, their path will be so smooth.

          a Or them.   *b Or* they.   *c* long ago: *or* from afar.

For I have become a father to Israel,
and Ephraim is my eldest son.

Listen to the word of the LORD, you nations,　　　　　10
announce it, make it known to coasts and islands far away:
　　He who scattered Israel shall gather them again
　　and watch over them as a shepherd watches his flock.
For the LORD has ransomed Jacob　　　　　11
and redeemed him from a foe too strong for him.
They shall come with shouts of joy to Zion's height,　　　　　12
shining with happiness at the bounty of the LORD,
the corn, the new wine, and the oil,
　　the young of flock and herd.
They shall become like a watered garden
and they shall never want again.
Then shall the girl show her joy in the dance,　　　　　13
　　young men and old shall rejoice;
I will turn their mourning into gladness,
I will relent and give them joy to outdo their sorrow.
I will satisfy the priests with the fat of the land　　　　　14
and fill my people with my bounty.
　　This is the very word of the LORD.

These are the words of the LORD:　　　　　15
　　Hark, lamentation is heard in Ramah, and bitter weeping,
　　Rachel weeping for her sons.
　　She refuses to be comforted: they are no more.

These are the words of the LORD:　　　　　16
　　Cease your loud weeping,
　　　　shed no more tears;
　　for there shall be a reward for your toil,
　　　　they shall return from the land of the enemy.
　　You shall leave descendants after you; *a*　　　　　17
　　your sons shall return to their own land.
I listened; Ephraim was rocking in his grief:　　　　　18
'Thou hast trained me to the yoke like an unbroken calf,
　　and now I am trained;
　　　　restore me, let me return,
　　for thou, LORD, art my God.
Though I broke loose I have repented:　　　　　19
now that I am tamed I beat my breast;
　　in shame and remorse
I reproach myself for the sins of my youth.'
Is Ephraim still my dear son,　　　　　20
a child in whom I delight?
　　As often as I turn my back on him
　　I still remember him;

　a You shall . . . you: *or* There shall be hope for your posterity.

and so my heart yearns for him,
    I am filled with tenderness towards him.
      This is the very word of the LORD.

21   Build cairns to mark your way,
    set up sign-posts;
    make sure of the road,
      the path which you will tread.
      Come back, virgin Israel,
    come back to your cities.

22   How long will you twist and turn, my wayward child?
    For the LORD has created a new thing in the earth:
      a woman turned into a man.

23   These are the words of the LORD of Hosts the God of Israel: Once more shall these words be heard in the land of Judah and in her cities, when I restore their fortunes:

      The LORD bless you,
    the LORD, your true goal,[a] your holy mountain.

24   Ploughmen and shepherds who wander with their flocks
    shall live together there.[b]

25   For I have given deep draughts to the thirsty,
    and satisfied those who were faint with hunger.

26   Thereupon I woke and looked about me, and my dream[c] had been pleasant.

27   The time is coming, says the LORD, when I will sow Israel and Judah
28 with the seed of man and the seed of cattle. As I watched over them with intent to pull down and to uproot, to demolish and destroy and harm, so now will I watch over them to build and to plant. This is the very word of the LORD.

29   In those days it shall no longer be said,

      'The fathers have eaten sour grapes
      and the children's teeth are set on edge';

30 for a man shall die for his own wrongdoing; the man who eats sour grapes shall have his own teeth set on edge.

31   The time is coming, says the LORD, when I will make a new covenant
32 with Israel and Judah. It will not be like the covenant I made with their forefathers when I took them by the hand and led them out of Egypt. Although they broke my covenant, I was patient with them, says the LORD.
33 But this is the covenant which I will make with Israel after those days, says the LORD; I will set my law within them and write it on their hearts; I will
34 become their God and they shall become my people. No longer need they teach one another to know the LORD; all of them, high and low alike, shall know me, says the LORD, for I will forgive their wrongdoing and remember their sin no more.

35   These are the words of the LORD, who gave the sun for a light by day

---

[a] *the LORD . . . goal: or* O home of righteousness.   [b] *Prob. rdg.; Heb. adds* Judah and all his cities.   [c] *Or* sleep.

and the moon and stars for a light by night, who cleft the sea and its waves roared; the LORD of Hosts is his name:

> If this fixed order could vanish out of my sight,   36
>   says the LORD,
> then the race of Israel too could cease for evermore
>   to be a nation in my sight.

These are the words of the LORD: If any man could measure the heaven 37 above or fathom the depths of the earth beneath, then I could spurn the whole race of Israel because of all they have done. This is the very word of the LORD.

The time is coming, says the LORD, when the city shall be rebuilt in the 38 LORD's honour from the Tower of Hananel to the Corner Gate. The 39 measuring line shall then be laid straight out over the hill of Gareb and round Goath.[a] All the valley and every field as far as the gorge of the 40 Kidron to the corner by the Horse Gate eastwards shall be holy to the LORD. It shall never again be pulled down or demolished.

The word which came to Jeremiah from the LORD in the tenth year of **32** Zedekiah king of Judah (the eighteenth year of Nebuchadrezzar). At that 2 time the forces of the Babylonian king were besieging Jerusalem, and the prophet Jeremiah was imprisoned in the court of the guard-house attached to the royal palace. Zedekiah king of Judah had imprisoned him 3 after demanding what he meant by this prophecy: 'These are the words of the LORD: I will deliver this city into the hands of the king of Babylon, and he shall take it. Zedekiah king of Judah will not escape from the Chal- 4 daeans but will be surrendered to the king of Babylon; he will speak with him face to face and see him with his own eyes. Zedekiah will be taken to 5 Babylon and will remain there until I turn my thoughts to him, says the LORD. However much you fight against the Chaldaeans you will have no success.'

Jeremiah said, The word of the LORD came to me: Hanamel son of your 6 7 uncle Shallum is coming to see you and will say, 'Buy my field at Anathoth; you have the right of redemption, as next of kin, to buy it.' As the LORD 8 had foretold, my cousin Hanamel came to the court of the guard-house and said, 'Buy my field at Anathoth in Benjamin. You have the right of redemp- tion and possession as next of kin; buy it.' I knew that this was the LORD's message; so I bought the field at Anathoth from my cousin Hanamel and 9 weighed out the price, seventeen shekels of silver. I signed and sealed the 10 deed and had it witnessed; then I weighed out the money on the scales. I took my copies of the deed of purchase, both the sealed and the unsealed, 11 and gave them to Baruch son of Neriah, son of Mahseiah, in the presence 12 of Hanamel my cousin, of the witnesses whose names were on the deed of purchase, and of the Judaeans sitting in the court of the guard-house. In 13 the presence of them all I gave my instructions to Baruch: These are the 14 words of the LORD of Hosts the God of Israel: Take these copies of the deed of purchase, the sealed and the unsealed, and deposit them in an earthenware jar so that they may be preserved for a long time. For these 15

[a] *Or* Goah.

are the words of the LORD of Hosts the God of Israel: The time will come when houses, fields, and vineyards will again be bought and sold in this
16 land. After I had given the deed of purchase to Baruch son of Neriah, I
17 prayed to the LORD: O Lord GOD, thou hast made the heavens and the earth by thy great strength and with thy outstretched arm; nothing is
18 impossible for thee. Thou keepest faith with thousands and thou dost requite the sins of fathers on to the heads of their sons. O great and mighty
19 God whose name is the LORD of Hosts, great are thy purposes and mighty thy actions. Thine eyes watch all the ways of men, and thou rewardest
20 each according to his ways and as his deeds deserve. Thou didst work signs and portents in Egypt and hast continued them to this day, both in Israel and amongst all men, and hast won for thyself a name that lives on
21 to this day. Thou didst bring thy people Israel out of Egypt with signs and portents, with a strong hand and an outstretched arm, and with terrible
22 power. Thou didst give them this land which thou didst promise with an
23 oath to their forefathers, a land flowing with milk and honey. They came and took possession of it, but they did not obey thee or follow thy law, they disobeyed all thy commands; and so thou hast brought this disaster upon
24 them. Look at the siege-ramps, the men who are advancing to take the city, and the city given over to its assailants from Chaldaea, the victim of sword, famine, and pestilence. The word thou hast spoken is fulfilled and
25 thou dost see it. And yet thou hast bidden me buy the field, O Lord GOD, and have the deed witnessed, even though the city is given to the Chaldeans.

26 27 These are the words of the LORD to Jeremiah: I am the LORD, the God of
28 all flesh; is anything impossible for me? Therefore these are the words of the LORD: I will deliver this city into the hands of the Chaldaeans and
29 of Nebuchadrezzar king of Babylon, and he shall take it. The Chaldaeans who are fighting against this city will enter it, set it on fire and burn it down, with the houses on whose roofs sacrifices have been burnt to Baal and drink-offerings poured out to other gods, by which I was provoked to anger.

30 From their earliest days Israel and Judah have been doing what is wrong
31 in my eyes, provoking me to anger by their actions, says the LORD. For this city has so roused my anger and my fury, from the time it was built down
32 to this day, that I would rid myself of it. Israel and Judah, their kings, officers, priests, prophets, and everyone living in Jerusalem and Judah
33 have provoked me to anger by their wrongdoing. They have turned their backs on me and averted their faces; though I took pains to teach them,
34 they would not hear or learn their lesson. They set up their loathsome idols
35 in the house which bears my name and so defiled it. They built shrines to Baal in the Valley of Ben-hinnom, to surrender their sons and daughters to Molech. It was no command of mine, nor did it ever enter my thought to do this abominable thing and lead Judah into sin.

36 Now, therefore, these are the words of the LORD the God of Israel to this city of which you say, 'It is being given over to the king of Babylon,
37 with sword, famine, and pestilence': I will gather them from all the lands to which I banished them in my anger, rage, and fury, and I will bring

them back to this place and let them dwell there undisturbed. They shall 38
become my people and I will become their God. I will give them one heart 39
and one way of life so that they shall fear me at all times, for their own good
and the good of their children after them. I will enter into an eternal 40
covenant with them, to follow them unfailingly with my bounty; I will
fill their hearts with fear of me, and so they will not turn away from me.
I will rejoice over them, rejoice to do them good, and faithfully with all 41
my heart and soul I will plant them in this land. For these are the words 42
of the LORD: As I brought on this people such great disaster, so will I
bring them all the prosperity which I now promise them. Fields shall 43
again be bought and sold in this land of which you now say, 'It is desolate,
without man or beast; it is given over to the Chaldaeans.' Fields shall be 44
bought and sold, deeds signed, sealed, and witnessed, in Benjamin, in the
neighbourhood of Jerusalem, in the cities of Judah, of the hill-country, of
the Shephelah, and of the Negeb; for I will restore their fortunes. This is
the very word of the LORD.

The word of the LORD came to Jeremiah a second time while he was still **33**
imprisoned in the court of the guard-house: These are the words of the 2
LORD who made the earth, who formed it and established it; the LORD is
his name: If you call to me I will answer you, and tell you great and 3
mysterious things which you do not understand. These are the words of 4
the LORD the God of Israel concerning the houses in this city and the royal
palace, which are to be razed to the ground, concerning siege-ramp and
sword, and attackers*a* who fill the houses with the corpses of those whom 5
he struck down in his furious rage: I hid my face from this city because of
their wicked ways, but now I will bring her healing; I will heal and cure 6
Judah and Israel, and will let my people see an age of peace and security.
I will restore their fortunes and build them again as once they were. I will 7 8
cleanse them of all the wickedness and sin that they have committed; I
will forgive all the evil deeds they have done in rebellion against me. This 9
city will win me a name*b* and praise and glory before all the nations on
earth, when they hear of all the blessings I bestow on her; and they shall
be moved and filled with awe because of the blessings and the peace which
I have brought upon her.

These are the words of the LORD: You say of this place, 'It is in ruins, 10
and neither man nor beast lives in the cities of Judah or in the streets of
Jerusalem. It is all a waste, inhabited by neither man nor beast.' Yet in
this place shall be heard once again the sounds of joy and gladness, the 11
voice of the bridegroom and the bride; here too shall be heard voices
shouting, 'Praise the LORD of Hosts, for he is good, for his love endures
for ever', as they offer praise and thanksgiving in the house of the LORD.
For I will restore the fortunes of the land as once they were. This is the
word of the LORD.

These are the words of the LORD of Hosts: In this place and in all its 12
cities, now ruined and inhabited by neither man nor beast, there shall
once more be a refuge where shepherds may fold their flocks. In the cities 13
of the hill-country, of the Shephelah, of the Negeb, in Benjamin, in the

a Prob. rdg.; Heb. adds the Chaldaeans.   *b Prob. rdg.; Heb. adds of joy.*

neighbourhood of Jerusalem and the cities of Judah, flocks will once more pass under the shepherd's hand as he counts them. This is the word of the LORD.

14 Wait, says the LORD, the days are coming when I will bestow on Israel
15 and Judah all the blessings I have promised them. In those days, at that time, I will make a righteous Branch of David spring up; he shall maintain
16 law and justice in the land. In those days Judah shall be kept safe and Jerusalem shall live undisturbed; and this shall be her name: The LORD is our Righteousness.

17 For these are the words of the LORD: David will never lack a successor
18 on the throne of Israel, nor will the levitical priests lack a man who shall come before me continually to present whole-offerings, to burn grain-offerings and to make other offerings.

19 20 This word came from the LORD to Jeremiah: These are the words of the LORD: If the law that I made for the day and the night could be annulled
21 so that they fell out of their proper order, then my covenant with my servant David could be annulled so that none of his line should sit upon his throne; so also could my covenant with the levitical priests who minister
22 to me. Like the innumerable host of heaven or the countless sands of the sea, I will increase the descendants of my servant David and the Levites who minister to me.

23 24 The word of the LORD came to Jeremiah: Have you not observed how this people have said, 'It is the two families whom he chose that the LORD has spurned'? So others will despise my people and no longer regard them
25 as a nation. These are the words of the LORD: If I had not made my law
26 for day and night nor established a fixed order in heaven and earth, then I would spurn the descendants of Jacob and of my servant David, and would not take any of David's line to be rulers over the descendants of Abraham, Isaac and Jacob. But now I will restore their fortunes and have compassion upon them.

Events under Jehoiakim and Zedekiah

34 THE WORD WHICH CAME TO JEREMIAH from the LORD when Nebuchadrezzar king of Babylon and his army, with all his vassal kingdoms
2 and nations, were fighting against Jerusalem and all her towns: These are the words of the LORD the God of Israel: Go and say to Zedekiah king of Judah, These are the words of the LORD: I will give this city into the
3 hands of the king of Babylon and he will burn it down. You shall not escape, you will be captured and handed over to him. You will see him face to
4 face, and he will speak to you in person; and you shall go to Babylon. But listen to the LORD's word to you, Zedekiah king of Judah. This is his word:
5 You shall not die by the sword; you will die a peaceful death, and they will kindle fires in your honour like the fires kindled in former times for the kings your ancestors who preceded you. 'Alas, my lord!' they will say as they beat their breasts in mourning for you. This I have spoken. This
6 is the very word of the LORD. The prophet Jeremiah repeated all this to

Zedekiah king of Judah in Jerusalem when the army of the king of Babylon 7
was attacking Jerusalem and the remaining cities of Judah, namely
Lachish and Azekah. These were the only fortified cities left in Judah.

The word that came to Jeremiah from the LORD after Zedekiah had 8
made a covenant with all the people in Jerusalem to proclaim an act of
freedom for the slaves. All who had Hebrew slaves, male or female, were 9
to set them free; they were not to keep their fellow Judaeans in servitude.
All the officers and people, having made this covenant to set free their 10
slaves, both male and female, and not to keep them in servitude any longer,
fulfilled its terms and let them go. Afterwards, however, they changed their 11
minds and forced back again into slavery the men and women whom they
had freed. Then this word came from the LORD to Jeremiah: These are 12 13
the words of the LORD the God of Israel: I made a covenant with your
forefathers on the day that I brought them out of Egypt, out of the land of
slavery. These were its terms: 'Within seven years each of you shall set free 14
any Hebrew who has sold himself to you as a slave and has served you
for six years; you shall set him free.' Your forefathers did not listen to me
or obey me. You, on the contrary, recently proclaimed an act of freedom 15
for the slaves and made a covenant in my presence, in the house that bears
my name, and so have done what is right in my eyes. But you too have 16
profaned my name. You have all taken back the slaves you had set free and
you have forced them, both male and female, to be your slaves again.
Therefore these are the words of the LORD: After you had proclaimed an 17
act of freedom, a deliverance for your kinsmen and your neighbours, you
did not obey me; so I will proclaim a deliverance for you, says the LORD,
a deliverance over to sword, to pestilence, and to famine, and I will make
you repugnant to all the kingdoms of the earth. You have disregarded my 18
covenant and have not fulfilled the terms to which you yourselves had
agreed; so I will make you like the calf of the covenant when they cut it
into two and passed between the pieces. Those who passed between the 19
pieces of the calf were the officers of Judah and Jerusalem, the eunuchs
and priests and all the people of the land. I will give them up to their 20
enemies who seek their lives, and their bodies shall be food for birds of
prey and wild beasts. I will deliver Zedekiah king of Judah and his officers 21
to their enemies who seek their lives and to the army of the king of Babylon,
which is now raising the siege. I will give the command, says the LORD, 22
and will bring them back to this city. They shall attack it and take it and
burn it down, and I will make the cities of Judah desolate and unpeopled.

The word which came to Jeremiah from the LORD in the days of Jehoia- **35**
kim son of Josiah, king of Judah: Go and speak to the Rechabites, bring 2
them to one of the rooms in the house of the LORD and offer them wine to
drink. So I fetched Jaazaniah son of Jeremiah, son of Habaziniah, with his 3
brothers and all his sons and all the family of the Rechabites. I brought 4
them into the house of the LORD to the room of the sons of Hanan son
of Igdaliah, the man of God; this adjoins the officers' room above that of
Maaseiah son of Shallum, the keeper of the threshold. I set bowls full of 5
wine and drinking-cups before the Rechabites and invited them to drink
wine; but they said, 'We will not drink wine, for our forefather Jonadab 6

son of Rechab laid this command on us: "You shall never drink wine,
7 neither you nor your children. You shall not build houses or sow seed or
plant vineyards; you shall have none of these things. Instead, you shall
remain tent-dwellers all your lives, so that you may live long in the land
8 where you are sojourners." We have honoured all the commands of our
forefather Jonadab son of Rechab and have drunk no wine all our lives,
9 neither we nor our wives, nor our sons, nor our daughters. We have not
built houses to live in, nor have we possessed vineyards or sown fields.
10 We have lived in tents, obeying and observing all the commands of our
11 forefather Jonadab. But when Nebuchadrezzar king of Babylon invaded
the land we said, "Come, let us go to Jerusalem before the advancing
Chaldaean and Aramaean armies." And we have stayed in Jerusalem.'

12 13   Then the word of the LORD came to Jeremiah: These are the words of
the LORD of Hosts the God of Israel: Go and say to the men of Judah and
the inhabitants of Jerusalem, You must accept correction and obey my
14 words, says the LORD. The command of Jonadab son of Rechab to his
descendants not to drink wine has been honoured; they have not drunk
wine to this day, for they have obeyed their ancestor's command. But I
have taken especial pains to warn you and yet you have not obeyed me.
15 I sent my servants the prophets especially to say to you, 'Turn back every
one of you from his evil course, mend your ways and cease to follow other
gods and worship them; then you shall remain on the land that I have
given to you and to your forefathers.' Yet you did not obey or listen to me.
16 The sons of Jonadab son of Rechab have honoured their ancestor's com-
17 mand laid on them, but this people have not listened to me. Therefore,
these are the words of the LORD the God of Hosts, the God of Israel:
Because they did not listen when I spoke to them, nor answer when I called
them, I will bring upon Judah and upon all the inhabitants of Jerusalem
18 the disaster with which I threatened them. To the Rechabites Jeremiah
said, These are the words of the LORD of Hosts the God of Israel: Because
you have kept the command of Jonadab your ancestor and obeyed all his
19 instructions and carried out all that he told you to do, therefore these are
the words of the LORD of Hosts the God of Israel: Jonadab son of Rechab
shall not want a descendant to stand before me for all time.

36 IN THE FOURTH YEAR OF JEHOIAKIM son of Josiah, king of Judah,
2 this word came to Jeremiah from the LORD: Take a scroll and write on it
every word that I have spoken to you about Jerusalem and Judah and all
the nations, from the day that I first spoke to you in the reign of Josiah
3 down to the present day. Perhaps the house of Judah will be warned of the
calamity that I am planning to bring on them, and every man will abandon
his evil course; then I will forgive their wrongdoing and their sin. So
4 Jeremiah called Baruch son of Neriah, and he wrote on the scroll at Jere-
5 miah's dictation all the words which the LORD had spoken to him. He gave
Baruch this instruction: 'I am prevented from going to the LORD's house.
6 You must go there in my place on a fast-day and read the words of the LORD
in the hearing of the people from the scroll you have written at my dictation.
You shall read them in the hearing of all the men of Judah who come in

from their cities. Then perhaps they will present a petition to the LORD 7
and every man will abandon his evil course; for the LORD has spoken
against this people in great anger and wrath.' Baruch son of Neriah did all 8
that the prophet Jeremiah had told him to do, and read the words of the
LORD in the LORD's house out of the book.

In the ninth month of the fifth year of the reign of Jehoiakim son of 9
Josiah, king of Judah, all the people in Jerusalem and all who came there
from the cities of Judah proclaimed a fast before the LORD. Then Baruch 10
read Jeremiah's words in the house of the LORD out of the book in the
hearing of all the people; he read them from the room of Gemariah son
of the adjutant-general Shaphan in the upper court at the entrance to the
new gate of the LORD's house. Micaiah son of Gemariah, son of Shaphan, 11
heard all the words of the LORD out of the book and went down to the 12
palace, to the adjutant-general's room where all the officers were gathered
—Elishama the adjutant-general, Delaiah son of Shemaiah, Elnathan son
of Akbor, Gemariah son of Shaphan, Zedekiah son of Hananiah and all the
other officers. There Micaiah repeated all the words he had heard when 13
Baruch read out of the book in the people's hearing. Then the officers sent 14
Jehudi son of Nethaniah, son of Shelemiah, son of Cushi, to Baruch with
this message: 'Come here and bring the scroll from which you read in the
people's hearing.' So Baruch son of Neriah brought the scroll to them, and 15
they said, 'Sit down and*a* read it to us.' When they heard what he read, 16
they turned to each other trembling and said, 'We must report this to the
king.' They asked Baruch to tell them how he had come to write all this. 17
He said to them, 'Jeremiah dictated every word of it to me, and I wrote it 18
down in ink in the book.' The officers said to Baruch, 'You and Jeremiah 19
must go into hiding so that no one may know where you are.' When they 20
had deposited the scroll in the room of Elishama the adjutant-general, they
went to the court and reported everything to the king.

The king sent Jehudi to fetch the scroll. When he had fetched it from the 21
room of Elishama the adjutant-general, he read it to the king and to all the
officers in attendance. It was the ninth month of the year, and the king was 22
sitting in his winter apartments with a fire burning in a brazier in front of
him. When Jehudi had read three or four columns of the scroll, the king 23
cut them off with a penknife and threw them into the fire in the brazier.
He went on doing so until the whole scroll had been thrown on the fire.
Neither the king nor any of his courtiers who heard these words showed 24
any fear or rent their clothes; and though Elnathan, Delaiah, and Gemariah 25
begged the king not to burn the scroll, he would not listen to them. The 26
king then ordered Jerahmeel, a royal prince,*b* Seraiah son of Azriel, and
Shelemiah son of Abdeel to fetch the scribe Baruch and the prophet
Jeremiah; but the LORD had hidden them.

After the king had burnt the scroll with all that Baruch had written on 27
it at Jeremiah's dictation, the word of the LORD came to Jeremiah: Now 28
take another scroll and write on it all the words that were on the first scroll
which Jehoiakim king of Judah burnt. You shall say to Jehoiakim king of 29
Judah, These are the words of the LORD: You burnt this scroll and said,

a Sit down and: *or* This time.   *b* a royal prince: *or* the king's deputy.

Why have you written here that the king of Babylon shall come and destroy
30 this land and exterminate both men and beasts? Therefore these are the
words of the LORD about Jehoiakim king of Judah: He shall have no one to
succeed him on the throne of David, and his dead body shall be exposed
31 to scorching heat by day and frost by night. I will punish him and also
his offspring and his courtiers for their wickedness, and I will bring down
on them and on the inhabitants of Jerusalem and on the men of Judah all
the calamities with which I threatened them, and to which they turned a
32 deaf ear. Then Jeremiah took another scroll and gave it to the scribe Baruch
son of Neriah, who wrote on it at Jeremiah's dictation all the words of the
book which Jehoiakim king of Judah had burnt; and much else was added
to the same effect.

37 King Zedekiah son of Josiah was set on the throne of Judah by Nebuchadrezzar king of Babylon, in succession to Coniah son of Jehoiakim.
2 Neither he nor his courtiers nor the people of the land listened to the words
which the LORD spoke through the prophet Jeremiah.

3 King Zedekiah sent Jehucal son of Shelemiah and the priest Zephaniah
son of Maaseiah to the prophet Jeremiah to say to him, 'Pray for us to the
4 LORD our God.' At the time Jeremiah was free to come and go among the
5 people; he had not yet been thrown into prison. Meanwhile, Pharaoh's
army had marched out of Egypt, and when the Chaldaeans who were
6 besieging Jerusalem heard of it they raised the siege. Then this word came
7 from the LORD to the prophet Jeremiah: These are the words of the LORD
the God of Israel: Say to the king of Judah who sent you to consult me,
Pharaoh's army which marched out to help you is on its way back to Egypt,
8 its own land, and the Chaldaeans will return to the attack. They will cap-
9 ture this city and burn it to the ground. These are the words of the LORD:
Do not deceive yourselves, do not imagine that the Chaldaeans will go away
10 and leave you alone. They will not go; for even if you defeated the whole
Chaldaean force with which you are now fighting, and only the wounded
were left lying in their tents, they would rise and burn down the city.

11 When the Chaldaean army had raised the siege of Jerusalem because of
12 the advance of Pharaoh's army, Jeremiah was on the point of leaving
Jerusalem to go into Benjamite territory and take possession of his patri-
13 mony in the presence of the people there. Irijah son of Shelemiah, son of
Hananiah, the officer of the guard, was in the Benjamin Gate when Jeremiah reached it, and he arrested the prophet, accusing him of going over
14 to the Chaldaeans. 'It is a lie,' said Jeremiah; 'I am not going over to the
Chaldaeans.' Irijah would not listen to him but arrested him and brought
15 him before the officers. The officers were indignant with Jeremiah; they
flogged him and imprisoned him in the house of Jonathan the scribe, which
16 they had converted into a prison; for Jeremiah had been put into a vaulted
pit beneath the house, and here he remained for a long time.

17 King Zedekiah had Jeremiah brought to him and consulted him privately
in the palace, asking him if there was a word from the LORD. 'Indeed there
is,' said Jeremiah; 'you shall fall into the hands of the king of Babylon.'
18 Then Jeremiah said to King Zedekiah, 'What wrong have I done to you
or your courtiers or this people? Why have you thrown me into prison?

Where are your prophets who prophesied that the king of Babylon would   19
not attack you or your country? I pray you now, my lord king, give me a   20
hearing and let my petition be presented: do not send me back to the house
of Jonathan the scribe, or I shall die there.' Then King Zedekiah gave the   21
order and Jeremiah was committed to the court of the guard-house and
was granted a daily ration of one loaf from the Street of the Bakers, until
the bread in the city was all gone. So Jeremiah remained in the court of
the guard-house.

Shephatiah son of Mattan, Gedaliah son of Pashhur, Jucal son of   38
Shelemiah, and Pashhur son of Malchiah heard what Jeremiah was saying
to all the people: These are the words of the LORD: Whoever remains in   2
this city shall die by sword, by famine, or by pestilence, but whoever goes
out to surrender to the Chaldaeans shall survive; he shall survive, he shall
take home his life and nothing more. These are the words of the LORD: 3
This city will fall into the hands of the king of Babylon's army, and they
will capture it. Then the officers said to the king, 'The man must be put   4
to death. By talking in this way he is discouraging the soldiers and the rest
of the people left in the city. He is pursuing not the people's welfare but
their ruin.' King Zedekiah said, 'He is in your hands; the king is powerless   5
against you.' So they took Jeremiah and threw him into the pit,*a* in the   6
court of the guard-house, letting him down with ropes. There was no water
in the pit, only mud, and Jeremiah sank in the mud. Now Ebed-melech   7-8
the Cushite, a eunuch, who was in the palace, heard that they had thrown
Jeremiah into the pit and went to tell the king, who was seated in the
Benjamin Gate. 'Your majesty,' he said, 'these men have shown great   9
wickedness in their treatment of the prophet Jeremiah. They have thrown
him into the pit, and when there is no more bread in the city he will die of
hunger where he lies.' Thereupon the king told Ebed-melech the Cushite   10
to take three men with him and hoist Jeremiah out of the pit before he died.
So Ebed-melech went to the palace with the men and took some tattered,   11
cast-off clothes from the wardrobe*b* and let them down with ropes to
Jeremiah in the pit. Ebed-melech the Cushite said to Jeremiah, 'Put these   12
old clothes under your armpits to ease the ropes.' Jeremiah did this, and   13
they pulled him up out of the pit with the ropes; and he remained in the
court of the guard-house.

King Zedekiah had the prophet Jeremiah brought to him by the third   14
entrance to the LORD's house and said to him, 'I want to ask you something;
hide nothing from me.' Jeremiah answered, 'If I speak out, you will   15
certainly put me to death; if I offer you any advice, you will not take it.'
But King Zedekiah swore to Jeremiah privately, 'By the life of the LORD   16
who gave us our lives, I will not put you to death, nor will I hand you over
to these men who are seeking to take your life.' Jeremiah said to Zedekiah,   17
'These are the words of the LORD the God of Hosts, the God of Israel: If
you go out and surrender to the officers of the king of Babylon, you shall
live and this city shall not be burnt down; you and your family shall live.
But if you do not surrender to the officers of the king of Babylon, the city   18

a Prob. rdg.; Heb. adds Malchiah son (*or* deputy) of the king.   *b* the wardrobe:
prob. rdg.; Heb. underneath the treasury.

shall fall into the hands of the Chaldaeans, and they shall burn it down, and
19 you will not escape them.' King Zedekiah said to Jeremiah, 'I am afraid
of the Judaeans who have gone over to the enemy. I fear the Chaldaeans will
20 give me up to them and I shall be roughly handled.' Jeremiah answered,
'They will not give you up. If you obey the LORD in everything I tell you,
21 all will be well with you and you shall live. But if you refuse to go out and
22 surrender, this is what the LORD has shown me: all the women left in the
king of Judah's palace will be led out to the officers of the king of Babylon
and they will say:

> Your own friends have misled you
> and have been too strong for you;
> they have let your feet sink in the mud
> and have turned away and left you.

23 All your women and children will be led out to the Chaldaeans, and you
will not escape; you will be seized by the king of Babylon and this city will
24 be burnt down.' Zedekiah said to Jeremiah, 'Let no one know about this,
25 and you shall not be put to death. If the officers hear that I have been speaking with you and they come to you and say, "Tell us what you said to the
king and what he said to you; hide nothing from us, and we will not put
26 you to death", then answer, "I was presenting a petition to the king not to
27 send me back to the house of Jonathan to die there."' The officers all
came to Jeremiah and questioned him, and he said to them just what the
king had told him to say; so their talk came to an end and they were none
28 the wiser. Jeremiah remained in the court of the guard-house till the day
Jerusalem fell.

39 1ª IN THE TENTH MONTH OF THE NINTH YEAR of the reign of Zedekiah
king of Judah, Nebuchadrezzar advanced with all his army against Jeru-
2 salem, and they laid siege to it. In the fourth month of the eleventh year
3 of Zedekiah, on the ninth day of the month, the city was thrown open. All
the officers of the king of Babylon came in and took their seats in the middle
gate: Nergalsarezer of Simmagir, Nebusarsekim*ᵇ* the chief eunuch,*ᶜ*
Nergalsarezer the commander of the frontier troops,*ᵈ* and all the other
4 officers of the king of Babylon. When Zedekiah king of Judah saw them,
he and all his armed escort left the city and fled by night by way of the
king's garden through the gate called Between the Two Walls. They
5 escaped towards the Arabah, but the Chaldaean army pursued them and
overtook Zedekiah in the lowlands of Jericho. The king was seized and
brought before Nebuchadrezzar king of Babylon at Riblah in the land of
6 Hamath, and he pleaded his case before him. The king of Babylon slew
Zedekiah's sons before his eyes at Riblah; he also put to death the nobles
7 of Judah. Then Zedekiah's eyes were put out, and he was bound in fetters
8 of bronze to be brought to Babylon. The Chaldaeans burnt the royal palace
and the house of the LORD and the houses*ᵉ* of the people, and pulled down

---

ª Verses 1–10: cp. 52. 4–16 and 2 Kgs. 25. 1–12.   ᵇ Probably a different form of
Nebushazban (*verse 13*).   *ᶜ the chief eunuch: or Rab-saris.   ᵈ the commander*
. . . *troops: or Rab-mag.*   *ᵉ of the LORD and the houses: prob. rdg.; Heb. om.*

the walls of Jerusalem. Nebuzaradan captain of the bodyguard deported 9
to Babylon the rest of the people left in the city, those who had deserted to
him and any remaining artisans.[a] At the same time the captain of the guard 10
left behind the weakest class of the people, those who owned nothing at all,
and made them vine-dressers and labourers.

Nebuchadrezzar king of Babylon sent orders about Jeremiah to Nebu- 11
zaradan captain of the guard. 'Take him,' he said; 'take special care of 12
him, and do him no harm of any kind, but do for him whatever he says.'
So Nebuzaradan captain of the guard sent Nebushazban the chief eunuch, 13
Nergalsarezer the commander of the frontier troops, and all the chief
officers of the king of Babylon, and they fetched Jeremiah from the court 14
of the guard-house and handed him over to Gedaliah son of Ahikam, son
of Shaphan, to take him out to the Residence. So he stayed with his own
people.

The word of the LORD had come to Jeremiah while he was under arrest 15
in the court of the guard-house: Go and say to Ebed-melech the Cushite, 16
These are the words of the LORD of Hosts the God of Israel: I will make
good the words I have spoken against this city, foretelling ruin and not
prosperity, and when that day comes you will be there to see it. But I will 17
preserve you on that day, says the LORD, and you shall not be handed over
to the men you fear. I will keep you safe and you shall not fall a victim to 18
the sword; because you trusted in me you shall escape, you shall take home
your life and nothing more. This is the very word of the LORD.

Jeremiah after the capture of Jerusalem

THE WORD WHICH CAME FROM THE LORD concerning Jeremiah: **40**
Nebuzaradan captain of the guard had taken him in chains to Ramah
along with the other exiles from Jerusalem and Judah who were being
deported to Babylon; and there he set him free, and took it upon himself 2
to say to Jeremiah, 'The LORD your God threatened this place with disaster,
and has duly carried out his threat that this should happen to all of you 3
because you have sinned against the LORD and not obeyed him. But as 4
for you, Jeremiah, today I remove the fetters from your wrists. Come with
me to Babylon if you wish, and I will take special care of you; but if you
prefer not to come, well and good. The whole country lies before you; go
wherever you think best.' Jeremiah had not yet answered when Nebu- 5
zaradan went on,[b] 'Go back to Gedaliah son of Ahikam, son of Shaphan,
whom the king of Babylon had appointed governor of the cities of Judah,
and stay with him openly; or else go wherever you choose.' Then the captain
of the guard granted him an allowance of food, and gave him a present,
and so took leave of him. Jeremiah then came to Gedaliah son of Ahikam 6
at Mizpah and stayed with him among the people left in the land.

When all the captains of the armed bands in the country-side and their 7
men heard that the king of Babylon had appointed Gedaliah son of Ahikam

---

[a] artisans: *prob. rdg., cp. 52. 15; Heb.* people who were left.   [b] Jeremiah . . . went
on: *prob. rdg.; Heb. unintelligible in context.*

governor of the land, and had put him in charge of the weakest class of the population, men, women, and children, who had not been deported to
8 Babylon, they came to him at Mizpah; Ishmael son of Nethaniah came, and Johanan and Jonathan sons of Kareah, Seraiah son of Tanhumeth, the sons of Ephai[a] from Netophah, and Jezaniah of Beth-maacah, with their
9 men. Gedaliah son of Ahikam, son of Shaphan, gave them all this assurance: 'Have no fear of the Chaldaean officers. Settle down in the land and
10 serve the king of Babylon; and then all will be well with you. I am to stay in Mizpah and attend upon the Chaldaeans whenever they come, and you are to gather in the summer-fruits, wine, and oil, store them in jars, and
11 settle in the towns you have taken over.' The Judaeans also, in Moab, Ammon, Edom and other countries, heard that the king of Babylon had left a remnant in Judah and that he had set over them Gedaliah son of
12 Ahikam, son of Shaphan. The Judaeans, therefore, from all the places where they were scattered, came back to Judah and presented themselves before Gedaliah at Mizpah; and they gathered in a considerable store of fruit and wine.

13 Johanan son of Kareah and all the captains of the armed bands from the
14 country-side came to Gedaliah at Mizpah and said to him, 'Do you know that Baalis king of the Ammonites has sent Ishmael son of Nethaniah to
15 assassinate you?' But Gedaliah son of Ahikam did not believe them. Then Johanan son of Kareah said in private to Gedaliah, 'Let me go, unknown to anyone else, and kill Ishmael son of Nethaniah. Why allow him to assassinate you, and so let all the Judaeans who have rallied round you be
16 scattered and the remnant of Judah lost?' Gedaliah son of Ahikam answered him, 'Do no such thing. Your story about Ishmael is a lie.'

41 In the seventh month Ishmael son of Nethaniah, son of Elishama, who was a member of the royal house, came with ten men to Gedaliah son of
2 Ahikam at Mizpah. While they were at table with him there, Ishmael son of Nethaniah and the ten men with him rose to their feet and assassinated Gedaliah son of Ahikam, son of Shaphan, whom the king of Babylon had
3 appointed governor of the land. They also murdered the Judaeans with
4 him in Mizpah and the Chaldaeans who happened to be there. The second day after the murder of Gedaliah, while it was not yet common knowledge,
5 there came eighty men from Shechem, Shiloh, and Samaria. They had shaved off their beards, their clothes were rent and their bodies gashed, and they were carrying grain-offerings and frankincense to take to the
6 house of the LORD. Ishmael son of Nethaniah came out weeping from Mizpah to meet them and, when he met them, he said, 'Come to Gedaliah
7 son of Ahikam.' But as soon as they reached the centre of the town, Ishmael son of Nethaniah and his men murdered them and threw their bodies into
8 a pit, all except ten of them who said to Ishmael, 'Do not kill us, for we have a secret hoard in the country, wheat and barley, oil and honey.' So he held
9 his hand and did not kill them with the others. The pit into which he threw the bodies of those whose death he had caused by using Gedaliah's name was the pit which King Asa had made when threatened by Baasha king
10 of Israel; and the dead bodies filled it. He rounded up the rest of the

_____
[a] Or Ophai.

968

people in Mizpah, that is the king's daughters and all who remained in
Mizpah when Nebuzaradan captain of the guard appointed Gedaliah son
of Ahikam governor; and with these he set out to cross over into Ammon.
When Johanan son of Kareah and all the captains of the armed bands heard 11
of the crimes committed by Ishmael son of Nethaniah, they took all the 12
men they had and went to attack him. They found him by the great pool
in Gibeon. The people with Ishmael were glad when they saw Johanan 13
son of Kareah and the captains of the armed bands with him; and all whom 14
Ishmael had taken prisoner at Mizpah turned and joined Johanan son of
Kareah. But Ishmael son of Nethaniah escaped from Johanan with eight 15
men, and they made their way to the Ammonites.

   Johanan son of Kareah and all the captains of the armed bands took from 16
Mizpah the survivors whom he had rescued from Ishmael son of Nethaniah
after the murder of Gedaliah son of Ahikam—men, armed and unarmed,
women, children, and eunuchs, whom he had brought back from Gibeon.
They started out and broke their journey at Kimham's holding near 17
Bethlehem, on their way into Egypt to escape the Chaldaeans. They were 18
afraid because Ishmael son of Nethaniah had assassinated Gedaliah son
of Ahikam, whom the king of Babylon had appointed governor of the
country.

   All the captains of the armed bands, including Johanan son of Kareah 42
and Azariah son of Hoshaiah, together with the people, high and low,
came to the prophet Jeremiah and said to him, 'May our petition be 2
acceptable to you: Pray to the LORD your God on our behalf and on behalf
of this remnant; for, as you see for yourself, only a few of us remain out of
many. Pray that the LORD your God may tell us which way we ought to go 3
and what we ought to do.' Then the prophet Jeremiah said to them, 'I have 4
heard your request and will pray to the LORD your God as you desire, and
whatever answer the LORD gives I will tell you; I will keep nothing back.'
They said to Jeremiah, 'May the LORD be a true and faithful witness against 5
us if we do not keep our oath! We swear that we will do whatever the LORD
your God sends you to tell us. Whether we like it or not, we will obey the 6
LORD our God to whom we send you, in order that it may be well with us;
we will obey the LORD our God.'

   Within ten days the word of the LORD came to Jeremiah; so he summoned 7 8
Johanan son of Kareah, all the captains of the armed bands with him, and
all the people, both high and low. He said to them, These are the words of 9
the LORD the God of Israel, to whom you sent me to present your petition:
If you will stay in this land, then I will build you up and not pull you down, 10
I will plant you and not uproot you; I grieve for the disaster which I have
brought upon you. Do not be afraid of the king of Babylon whom you now 11
fear. Do not be afraid of him, says the LORD; for I am with you, to save you
and deliver you from his power. I will show you compassion, and he too 12
will have compassion on you; he will let you stay on your own soil. But it 13
may be that you will disobey the LORD your God and say, 'We will not stay
in this land. No, we will go to Egypt, where we shall see no sign of war, 14
never hear the sound of the trumpet, and not starve for want of bread; and
there we will live.' Then hear the word of the LORD, you remnant of Judah. 15

These are the words of the LORD of Hosts the God of Israel: If you are
16 bent on going to Egypt, if you do settle there, then the sword you fear will
overtake you in Egypt, and the famine you dread will still be with you,
17 even in Egypt, and there you will die. All the men who are bent on going
to Egypt and settling there will die by sword, by famine, or by pestilence;
not one shall escape or survive the calamity which I will bring upon them.
18 These are the words of the LORD of Hosts the God of Israel: As my anger
and my wrath were poured out upon the inhabitants of Jerusalem, so will
my wrath be poured out upon you when you go to Egypt; you will become
an object of execration and horror, of ridicule and reproach; you will
19 never see this place again. To you, then, remnant of Judah, the LORD says,
Do not go to Egypt. Make no mistake, I can bear witness against you this
20 day. You deceived yourselves when you sent me to the LORD your God and
said, 'Pray for us to the LORD our God; tell us all that the LORD our God
21 says and we will do it.' I have told you everything today; but you have not
22 obeyed the LORD your God in what he sent me to tell you. So now be sure
of this: you will die by sword, by famine, and by pestilence in the place
where you desire to go and make your home.

43 When Jeremiah had finished reciting to the people all that the LORD
2 their God had sent him to say, Azariah son of Hoshaiah and Johanan son
of Kareah and their party had the effrontery to say to*a* Jeremiah, 'You are
lying; the LORD our God has not sent you to forbid us to go and make our
3 home in Egypt. Baruch son of Neriah has incited you against us in order
to put us in the power of the Chaldaeans, so that they may kill us or deport
4 us to Babylon.' Johanan son of Kareah and the captains of the armed bands
5 and all the people refused to obey the LORD and stay in Judah. So Johanan
son of Kareah and the captains collected the remnant of Judah, all who had
returned from the countries among which they had been scattered to
6 make their home in Judah—men, women and children, including the
king's daughters, all the people whom Nebuzaradan captain of the guard
had left with Gedaliah son of Ahikam, son of Shaphan, as well as the pro-
7 phet Jeremiah and Baruch son of Neriah; these all went to Egypt and came
to Tahpanhes, disobeying the LORD.

8 9 The word of the LORD came to Jeremiah at Tahpanhes: Take some large
stones and set them in cement in the pavement at the entrance to Pharaoh's
10 palace in Tahpanhes. Let the Judaeans see you do it and say to them, These
are the words of the LORD of Hosts the God of Israel: I will send for my
servant Nebuchadrezzar king of Babylon, and he will place his throne on
11 these stones that I have set there, and spread his canopy over them. He
will then proceed to strike Egypt down, killing those doomed to death,
taking captive those who are for captivity, and putting to the sword those
12 who are for the sword. He will set fire to the temples of the Egyptian gods,
burning the buildings and carrying the gods into captivity. He will scour
the land of Egypt as a shepherd scours his clothes to rid them of lice. He
13 will leave Egypt with his purpose achieved. He will smash the sacred
pillars of Beth-shemesh in Egypt and burn down the temples of the
Egyptian gods.

a to say to: *or* to say: It is being said to.

The word that came to Jeremiah for all the Judaeans who were living in **44**
Egypt, in Migdol, Tahpanhes, Noph, and the district of Pathros: These **2**
are the words of the LORD of Hosts the God of Israel: You have seen the
calamity that I brought upon Jerusalem and all the cities of Judah: today
they are laid waste and left uninhabited, all because of the wickedness of **3**
those who provoked me to anger by going after other gods, gods unknown
to them, by burning sacrifices to them. It was you and your fathers who
did this. I took pains to send all my servants the prophets to you with this **4**
warning: 'Do not do this abominable thing which I hate.' But your fathers **5**
would not listen; they paid no heed. They did not give up their wickedness
or cease to burn sacrifices to other gods; so my anger and wrath raged like **6**
a fire through the cities of Judah and the streets of Jerusalem, and they
became the desolate ruin that they are today.

Now these are the words of the LORD the God of Hosts, the God of **7**
Israel: Why bring so great a disaster upon yourselves? Why bring destruction upon Judaeans, men and women, children and babes, and leave
yourselves without a survivor? This is what comes of your provoking me **8**
by all your idolatry in burning sacrifices to other gods in Egypt where you
have made your home. You will destroy yourselves and become an object
of ridicule and reproach to all the nations of the earth. Have you forgotten **9**
all the wickedness committed by your forefathers, by the kings of Judah
and their wives, by yourselves and your wives in the land of Judah and in
the streets of Jerusalem? To this day you have shown no remorse, no **10**
reverence; you have not conformed to the law and the statutes which I
set before you and your forefathers. These, therefore, are the words of the **11**
LORD of Hosts the God of Israel: I have made up my mind to bring calamity
upon you and exterminate the people of Judah. I will deal with the rem- **12**
nant of Judah who were bent on going to make their home in Egypt; in
Egypt they shall all meet their end. Some shall fall by the sword, others
will meet their end by famine. High and low alike will die by sword or by
famine and will be an object of execration and horror, of ridicule and reproach. I will punish those who live in Egypt as I punished those in **13**
Jerusalem, by sword, famine, and pestilence. Those who had remained in **14**
Judah came to make their home in Egypt, confident that they would
return and live once more in Judah. But they shall not return;*a* not one of
them shall survive, not one escape.

Then all the men who knew that their wives were burning sacrifices to **15**
other gods and the crowds of women standing by*b* answered Jeremiah,
'We will not listen to what you tell us in the name of the LORD. We intend **16 17**
to fulfil all the promises by which we have bound ourselves: we will burn
sacrifices to the queen of heaven and pour drink-offerings to her as we used
to do, we and our fathers, our kings and our princes, in the cities of Judah
and in the streets of Jerusalem. We then had food in plenty and were
content; no calamity touched us. But from the time we left off burning **18**
sacrifices to the queen of heaven and pouring drink-offerings to her, we
have been in great want, and in the end we have fallen victims to sword and

---

a Prob. rdg.; Heb. adds except fugitives.   *b Prob. rdg.; Heb. adds* and all the people
who lived in Egypt, in Pathros.

19 famine.' And the women said, 'When we burnt sacrifices to the queen of
heaven and poured drink-offerings to her, our husbands knew full well
that we were making crescent-cakes marked with her image and pouring
20 drink-offerings to her.' When Jeremiah received this answer from these
21 men and women and all the people, he said, 'The LORD did not forget those
sacrifices which you and your fathers, your kings and princes and the
people of the land burnt in the cities of Judah and in the streets of Jeru-
22 salem, and they mounted up in his mind until he could no longer tolerate
them, so wicked were your deeds and so abominable the things you did.
Your land became a desolate waste, an object of horror and ridicule, with
23 no inhabitants, as it still is. This calamity has come upon you because you
burnt these sacrifices and sinned against the LORD and did not obey the
LORD or conform to his laws, statutes, and teachings.'

24 Jeremiah further said to all the people and to the women, Listen to the
25 word of the LORD, all you from Judah who live in Egypt. These are the
words of the LORD of Hosts the God of Israel: You women have made your
actions match your words. 'We will carry out our vows', you said, 'to burn
sacrifices to the queen of heaven and to pour drink-offerings to her.' Well
26 then, fulfil your vows by all means, and make your words good. But listen
to the word of the LORD, all you from Judah who live in Egypt. I have sworn
by my great name, says the LORD, that my name shall never again be on the
lips of the men of Judah; they shall no longer swear in Egypt, 'By the life of
27 the Lord GOD.' I am on the watch to bring you evil and not good, and all
the men of Judah who are in Egypt shall meet their end by sword and by
28 famine until not one is left.[a] It is then that all the survivors of Judah who
have made their home in Egypt shall know whose word prevails, theirs or
mine.

29 This is the sign I give you, says the LORD, that I intend to punish you
in this place, so that you may learn that my words against you will prevail
30 to bring evil upon you: These are the words of the LORD: I will hand over
Pharaoh Hophra king of Egypt to his enemies and to those who seek his
life, just as I handed over Zedekiah king of Judah to his enemy Nebuchadrezzar king of Babylon who was seeking to take his life.

45 THE WORD WHICH THE PROPHET JEREMIAH SPOKE to Baruch son
of Neriah when he wrote these words in a book at Jeremiah's dictation in
2 the fourth year of Jehoiakim son of Josiah, king of Judah: These are the
3 words of the LORD the God of Israel concerning you, Baruch: You said,
'Woe is me, for the LORD has added grief to all my trials. I have worn my-
4 self out with my labours and have had no respite.' This is what you shall
say to Baruch, These are the words of the LORD: What I have built, I
demolish; what I have planted, I uproot. So it will be with the whole earth.
5 You seek great things for yourself. Leave off seeking them; for I will
bring disaster upon all mankind, says the LORD, and I will let you live
wherever you go, but you shall save your life and nothing more.

> [a] *Prob. rdg.; Heb. adds* Few will escape the sword in Egypt to return to Judah.

Prophecies against the nations

THIS CAME TO THE PROPHET JEREMIAH as the word of the LORD **46** concerning the nations.

Of Egypt: concerning the army of Pharaoh Necho king of Egypt at **2** Carchemish on the river Euphrates, which Nebuchadrezzar king of Babylon defeated in the fourth year of Jehoiakim son of Josiah, king of Judah.

> Hold shield and buckler ready **3**
> and advance to battle;
> harness the horses, let the riders mount; **4**
> form up, your helmets on, your lances burnished;
> on with your coats of mail!
> But now, what sight is this? **5**
> They are broken and routed,
> their warriors beaten down;
> they have turned to flight and do not look behind them.
> Terror let loose!
> This is the very word of the LORD.

> Can the swift escape, can the warrior save himself? **6**
> In the north, by the river Euphrates,
> they stumble and fall.

> Who is this rising like the Nile, **7**
> like its streams turbulent in flood?
> Egypt is rising like the Nile, **8**
> like its streams turbulent in flood.

He[a] says:

> I will rise and cover the earth,
> I will destroy both city and people.

> Charge, horsemen! On, you flashing chariots, on! **9**
> Forward, the warriors,
> Cushites and men of Put carrying shields,
> Lydians grasping their bent bows!
> This is the day of the Lord, the GOD of Hosts, **10**
> a day of vengeance, vengeance on his enemies;
> the sword shall devour and be sated,
> drunk with their blood.
> For the GOD of Hosts, the Lord, holds sacrifice
> in a northern land, by the river Euphrates.
> Go up into Gilead and fetch balm, **11**
> O virgin people of Egypt.
> You have tried many remedies, all in vain;
> no skin shall grow over your wounds.

[a] *Or* It.

12 The nations have heard your cry,
      and the earth echoes with your screams;
        warrior stumbles against warrior
        and both fall together.

13 The word which the LORD spoke to the prophet Jeremiah when Nebu-
    chadrezzar king of Babylon was coming to harry the land of Egypt:

14 Announce it in Egypt, proclaim it in Migdol,
        proclaim it in Noph and Tahpanhes.
      Say, Stand to! Be ready!
      for a sword devours all around you.

15 Why does Apis flee, why does your bull-god not *a* stand fast?
        The LORD has thrust him out.

16 The rabble of Egypt stumbles and falls,
          man against man;
        each says, 'Quick, back to our people,
      to the land of our birth, far from the cruel sword!'

17 Give Pharaoh of Egypt the title King Bombast,
        the man who missed his moment.

18 By my life, says the King
        whose name is the LORD of Hosts,
        one shall come mighty as Tabor among the hills,
          as Carmel by the sea.

19 Make ready your baggage for exile,
        you native people of Egypt;
      for Noph shall become a waste,
          ruined and unpeopled.

20 Egypt was a lovely heifer,
      but a gadfly from the north descended on her.

21 The mercenaries in her land were like stall-fed calves;
      but they too turned and fled,
          not one of them stood his ground.
        The hour of their downfall has come upon them,
          their day of reckoning.

22 Hark, she is hissing like a snake,
        for the enemy has come in all his force.
      They fall upon her with axes
        like woodcutters at their work.

23 They cut down her forest, says the LORD,
        and it flaunts itself no more;
      for they are many as locusts and past counting.

24 The Egyptians are put to shame, enslaved to a northern race.

25 The LORD of Hosts the God of Israel has spoken:
        I will punish Amon god of No, *b*
      Egypt with her gods and her princes,
      Pharaoh and all who trust in him.

---

a Why does Apis . . . not: *or* Why is your bull-god routed, why does he not . . .
b *Prob. rdg.; Heb. adds* and Pharaoh.

I will deliver them to those bent on their destruction,   26
to Nebuchadrezzar king of Babylon and his troops;
yet in after time the land shall be peopled as of old.
      This is the very word of the LORD.

But you, Jacob my servant, have no fear,   27
    despair not, O Israel;
for I will bring you back safe from afar
    and your offspring from the land where they are captives;
and Jacob shall be at rest once more,
      prosperous and unafraid.
O Jacob my servant, have no fear,   28
says the LORD; for I am with you.
    I will make an end of all the nations
      amongst whom I have banished you;
    but I will not make an end of you;
      though I punish you as you deserve,
      I will not sweep you clean away.

This came to the prophet Jeremiah as the word of the LORD concerning   **47**
the Philistines before Pharaoh's harrying of Gaza: The LORD has spoken: 2
    See how waters are rising from the north
    and swelling to a torrent in spate,
    flooding the land and all that is in it,
      cities and all who live in them.
      Men shall shriek in alarm
    and all who live in the land shall howl.
    Hark, the pounding of his chargers' hooves,   3
    the rattle of his chariots and their rumbling wheels!
    Fathers spare no thought for their children;
      their hands hang powerless,
because the day is upon them when Philistia will be despoiled,   4
and Tyre and Sidon destroyed to the last defender;
    for the LORD will despoil the Philistines,
      that remnant of the isle of Caphtor.
Gaza is shorn bare, Ashkelon ruined.   5
    Poor remnant of their strength,
    how long will you gash yourselves and cry:
    Ah, sword in the hand of the LORD,   6
      how long will it be before you rest?
Sheathe yourself, rest and be quiet.
How can it rest? for the LORD has given it work to do   7
      against Ashkelon and the plain by the sea;
      there he has assigned the sword its task.

Of Moab. The LORD of Hosts the God of Israel has spoken: **48**
      Alas for Nebo! it is laid waste;
      Kiriathaim is put to shame and captured,

Misgab reduced to shame and dismay;
2   Moab is renowned no longer.
In Heshbon they plot evil against her:
    Come, destroy her, and leave her no longer a nation.
    And you who live in Madmen shall be struck down,
    your people pursued by the sword.
3   Hark to the cries of anguish from Horonaim:
    great havoc and disaster!
4   Moab is broken.
    Their cries are heard as far as Zoar.
5   On the ascent of Luhith
      men go up weeping bitterly;
      on the descent of Horonaim
    cries of 'Disaster!' are heard.
6 Flee, flee for your lives
    like a sand-grouse in the wilderness.
7 Because you have trusted in your defences and your arsenals,
      you too will be captured,
    and Kemosh will go into exile,
    his priests and his captains with him;
8   and a spoiler shall descend on every city.
    No city shall escape,
valley and tableland will be laid waste and plundered;
    the LORD has spoken.

9   Let a warning flash to Moab,[a]
for she shall be laid in ruins[b]
and her cities shall become waste places
    with no inhabitant.
10 A curse on him who is slack in doing the LORD's work!
A curse on him who withholds his sword from bloodshed!

11   All his life long, Moab has lain undisturbed
like wine settled on its lees,
not emptied from vessel to vessel;
    he has not gone into exile.
Therefore the taste of him is unaltered,
    and the flavour stays unchanged.
12 Therefore the days are coming, says the LORD,
when I will send men to tilt the jars; they shall tilt them
and empty his vessels and smash his jars;
13   and Moab shall be betrayed by Kemosh,
    as Israel was betrayed by Bethel,
      a god in whom he trusted.

14   How can you say, 'We are warriors
      and men valiant in battle'?

---

[a] Let . . . Moab: *or* Doom Moab to become saltings.   [b] laid in ruins: *prob. rdg.*;
Heb. obscure.

The spoiler of Moab and her cities has come up,   15
and the flower of her army goes down to the slaughter.
This is the very word of the King whose name is the LORD of Hosts.

The downfall of Moab is near at hand,   16
disaster rushes swiftly upon him.
Grieve for him, all you his neighbours   17
and all you who acknowledge him,
and say, 'Alas! The commander's staff is broken,
broken is the baton of honour.'
Come down from your place of honour,   18
sit on the thirsty ground, you natives of Dibon;
for the spoiler of Moab has come upon you
and destroyed your citadels.
You that live in Aroer, stand on the roadside and watch,   19
ask the fugitives, the man running, the woman escaping,
ask them, 'What has happened?'

Moab is reduced to shame and dismay: 20
howl and shriek,
proclaim by the Arnon that Moab is despoiled,
and that judgement has come to the tableland, to Holon and Jahazah, 21
Mephaath and Dibon, Nebo and Beth-diblathaim and Kiriathaim, Beth- 22 23
gamul, Beth-meon, Kirioth and Bozrah, and to all the cities of Moab far 24
and near.

Moab's horn is hacked off   25
and his strong arm is broken,
says the LORD.

Make Moab drunk—he has defied the LORD—   26
until he overflows with his vomit
and even he becomes a butt for derision.
But was Israel ever your butt?   27
Was he ever in company with thieves,
that whenever you spoke of him you should shake your head?
Leave your cities, you inhabitants of Moab,   28
and find a home among the crags;
become like a dove which nests
in the rock-face at the mouth of a cavern.

We have heard of Moab's pride, and proud indeed he is,   29
proud, presumptuous, overbearing, insolent.
I know his arrogance, says the LORD;   30
his boasting is false, false are his deeds.
Therefore I will howl over Moab   31
and cry in anguish at the fate of every soul in Moab;
I will moan over the men of Kir-heres.
I will weep for you more than I wept for Jazer,   32
O vine of Sibmah

whose branches spread out to the sea
and stretch as far as Jazer.
The despoiler has fallen on your fruit and on your vintage,
33   gladness and joy are taken away
from the meadows of Moab,
and I have stopped the flow of wine from the vats;
nor shall shout follow shout from the harvesters—not one shout.

34 Heshbon and[a] Elealeh utter cries of anguish which are heard in Jahaz; the
sound carries from Zoar to Horonaim and Eglath-shelishiyah; for the
35 waters of Nimrim have become a desolate waste. In Moab I will stop their
sacrificing at hill-shrines and burning of offerings to their gods, says the
36 LORD. Therefore my heart wails for Moab like a reed-pipe, wails like a
pipe for the men of Kir-heres. Their hard-earned wealth has vanished.
37 Every man's head is shorn in mourning, every beard shaved, every hand
38 gashed, and every waist girded with sackcloth. On Moab's roofs and in her
broad streets nothing is heard but lamentation; for I have broken Moab
39 like a useless thing.[b] Moab in her dismay has shamefully turned to flight.
Moab has become a butt of derision and a cause of dismay to all her neighbours.
40   For the LORD has spoken:

A vulture shall swoop down
and spread out his wings over Moab.
41   The towns are captured, the strongholds taken;
on that day the spirit of Moab's warriors shall fail
like the spirit of a woman in childbirth.
42   Then Moab shall be destroyed, no more to be a nation;
for he defied the LORD.
43   The hunter's scare, the pit, and the trap
threaten all who dwell in Moab,
says the LORD.
44   If a man runs from the scare
he will fall into the pit;
if he climbs out of the pit
he will be caught in the trap.
All this will I bring on Moab in the year of their reckoning.
This is the very word of the LORD.

45   In the shadow of Heshbon the fugitives stand helpless;
for fire has blazed out from Heshbon,
flames have shot out from the palace of Sihon;
they devour the homeland of Moab
and the country of the sons of tumult.
46   Alas for you, Moab! the people of Kemosh have vanished,
for your sons are taken into captivity
and your daughters led away captive.

---

[a] and: *prob. rdg., cp. Isa. 15. 4; Heb.* as far as.   [b] *Prob. rdg.; Heb. adds* says
the LORD.

Yet in days to come I will restore Moab's fortunes.　　　　47
　　This is the very word of the LORD.
Here ends the sentence on Moab.

Of the people of Ammon. Thus says the LORD:　　　　**49**

Has Israel no sons? Has he no heir?
Why has Milcom inherited the land of Gad,
　　and why do his people live in the cities of Gad?
Look, therefore, a time is coming,　　　　2
　　　says the LORD,
when I will make Rabbath Ammon hear the battle-cry,
　　when it will become a desolate mound of ruins
　　and its villages will be burnt to ashes,
　　and Israel shall disinherit those who disinherited him,
　　　says the LORD.

Howl, Heshbon, for Ai is despoiled.　　　　3
　　Cry aloud, you villages round Rabbath Ammon,
put on sackcloth and beat your breast,
　　and score your bodies with gashes.
For Milcom will go into exile,
　　and with him his priests and officers.
Why do you boast of your resources,　　　　4
　　you whose resources are melting away,
you wayward people who trust in your arsenals,
　　and say, 'Who will dare attack me?'
Beware, I am bringing fear upon you from every side,*a*　　　　5
　　and every one of you shall be driven headlong
　　with no man to round up the stragglers.
Yet after this I will restore the fortunes of Ammon.　　　　6
　　This is the very word of the LORD.

Of Edom. The LORD of Hosts has said:　　　　7

Is wisdom no longer to be found in Teman?
Have her sages no skill in counsel?
　　Has their wisdom decayed?
The people of Dedan have turned and fled　　　　8
　　and taken refuge in remote places;
for I will bring Esau's calamity upon him
　　when his day of reckoning comes.
When the vintagers come to you　　　　9*b*
　　they will surely leave gleanings;
and if thieves raid your early crop in the night,
　　they will take only as much as they want.
But I have ransacked Esau's treasure,　　　　10
　　I have uncovered his hiding-places,
　　and he has nowhere to conceal himself;

---

a *Prob. rdg.; Heb. adds* says the Lord GOD of Hosts.　　*b* *Verses 9 and 10 : cp. Obad. 5, 6.*

his children, his kinsfolk and his neighbours are despoiled;
    there is no one to help him.
11   What! am I to save alive your fatherless children?
        Are your widows to trust in me?

12 For the LORD has spoken: Those who were not doomed to drink the
    cup shall drink it none the less. Are you alone to go unpunished? You
13 shall not go unpunished; you shall drink it. For by my life, says the LORD,
    Bozrah shall become a horror and reproach, a byword and a thing of
    ridicule; and all her towns shall be a byword for ever.

14*a*   When a herald was sent among the nations, crying,
        'Gather together and march against her,
            rouse yourselves for battle',
        I heard this message from the LORD:

15   Look, I make you the least of all nations,
            an object of all men's contempt.
16   Your overbearing arrogance and your insolent heart
                have led you astray,
            you who haunt the crannies among the rocks
            and keep your hold on the heights of the hills.
        Though you build your nest high as a vulture,
            thence I will bring you down.
        This is the very word of the LORD.
17   Edom shall become a scene of horror,
            all who pass that way shall be horror-struck
            and shall jeer in derision at the blows she has borne,
18   overthrown like Sodom and Gomorrah and their neighbours,*b*
            says the LORD.
        No man shall live there,
            no mortal make a home in her.
19   Look, like a lion coming up
            from Jordan's dense thickets to the perennial pastures,
        in a moment I will chase every one away
            and round up the choicest of*c* her rams.
        For who is like me? Who is my equal?
        What shepherd can stand his ground before me?

20 Therefore listen to the LORD's whole purpose against Edom and all his
    plans against the people of Teman:

        The young ones of the flock shall be carried off,
            and their pasture shall be horrified at their fate.
21   At the sound of their fall the land quakes;
            it cries out, and the cry is heard at the Red Sea.*d*

22   A vulture shall soar and swoop down
            and spread out his wings over Bozrah,

a *Verses 14–16: cp. Obad. 1–4.*   *b* *Or* inhabitants.   *c* the choicest of: *prob.*
rdg.; Heb. who is chosen?   *d* *Or* the Sea of Reeds.

and on that day the spirit of Edom's warriors shall fail
　like the spirit of a woman in labour.

Of Damascus.   23

　Hamath and Arpad are in confusion,
　　for they have heard news of disaster;
　they are tossed up and down in anxiety
　　like the unresting sea.
Damascus has lost heart and turns to flight;   24
　　trembling has seized her,
the pangs of childbirth have gripped her.
　How forlorn is the town of joyful song,   25
　　the city of gladness!
Therefore her young men shall fall in her streets   26
and all her warriors lie still in death that day.
　　This is the very word of the LORD of Hosts.
Then will I kindle a fire against the wall of Damascus   27
　and it shall consume the palaces of Ben-hadad.

Of Kedar and the royal princes *a* of Hazer which Nebuchadrezzar king   28
of Babylon subdued. The LORD has said:

　Come, attack Kedar,
　　despoil the Arabs of the east.
　Carry off their tents and their flocks,   29
　　their tent-hangings and all their vessels,
　　drive off their camels too,
and a cry shall go up: 'Terror let loose!'
　Flee, flee; make haste,   30
　take refuge in remote places, O people of Hazer,
　for the king of Babylon has laid his plans
　and formed a design against you,
　　says the LORD.
Come, let us attack a nation living at peace,   31
　　in fancied security,
　with neither gates nor bars,
　　sufficient to themselves.
　Their camels shall be carried off as booty,   32
　　their vast herds of cattle as plunder;
I will scatter them before the wind to roam the fringes of the desert, *b*
　and bring ruin upon them from every side.
　Hazer shall become a haunt of wolves,   33
　　for ever desolate;
　no man shall live there,
　no mortal make a home in her.
　　This is the very word of the LORD.

a royal princes: *or* kingdom.　　　　*b* them . . . desert: *or* to the wind those who clip
the hair on their temples.

34   This came to the prophet Jeremiah as the word of the LORD concerning
35 Elam, at the beginning of the reign of Zedekiah king of Judah: Thus says
the LORD of Hosts:

> Listen, I will break the bow of Elam,
>   the chief weapon of their might;

36
> I will bring four winds against Elam
>   from the four quarters of heaven;
> I will scatter them before these four winds,
>   and there shall be no nation
> to which the exiles from Elam shall not come.

37
> I will break Elam before their foes,
>   before those who are bent on their destruction;
> I will vent my anger upon them in disaster;
> I will harry them with the sword
>   until I make an end of them.

38
> Then I will set my throne in Elam,
> and there I will destroy the king and his officers.
>   This is the very word of the LORD.

39
> Yet in days to come I will restore the fortunes of Elam.
>   This is the very word of the LORD.

50   The word which the LORD spoke concerning Babylon, concerning the
land of the Chaldaeans, through the prophet Jeremiah:

2
> Declare and proclaim among the nations,
>   keep nothing back, spread the news:
>   Babylon is taken,
> Bel is put to shame, Marduk is in despair;
>   the idols of Babylon are put to shame,
>   her false gods are in despair.

3
> For a nation out of the north has fallen upon her;
>   they will make her land a desolate waste
>   where neither man nor beast shall live.

4   In those days, at that time, says the LORD, the people of Israel and the
people of Judah shall come together and go in tears to seek the LORD their
5 God; they shall ask after Zion, turning their faces towards her, and they
shall come and join themselves to the LORD in an everlasting covenant
which shall not be forgotten.

6   My people were lost sheep, whose shepherds let them stray and run
wild on the mountains; they went from mountain to hill and forgot their
7 fold. Whoever found them devoured them, and their enemies said, 'We
incur no guilt, because they have sinned against the LORD, the LORD who
is the true goal and the hope of all their fathers.'

8
> Flee from Babylon, from the land of the Chaldaeans;
>   go forth, and be like he-goats leading the flock.

9
> For I will stir up a host of mighty nations
>   and bring them against Babylon,
>   marshalled against her from a northern land;

and from the north she shall be captured.
Their arrows shall be like a practised warrior
who never comes back empty-handed;
the Chaldaeans shall be plundered,   10
and all who plunder them shall take their fill.
This is the very word of the LORD.
You ravaged my patrimony; but though you rejoice and exult,   11
though you run free like a heifer after threshing,
though you neigh like a stallion,
your mother shall be cruelly disgraced,   12
she who bore you shall be put to shame.
Look at her, the mere rump of the nations,
a wilderness, parched and desert,
unpeopled through the wrath of the LORD,   13
nothing but a desolate waste;
all who pass by Babylon shall be horror-struck
and jeer in derision at the sight of her wounds.

Marshal your forces against Babylon, on every side,   14
you whose bows are ready strung;
shoot at her, spare no arrows.
Shout in triumph over her, she has thrown up her hands,   15
her bastions are down, her walls demolished;
this is the vengeance of the LORD.
Take vengeance on her;
as she has done, so do to her.
Destroy every sower in Babylon,   16
every reaper with his sickle at harvest-time.
Before the cruel sword every man will go back to his people,
every man flee to his own land.

Israel is a scattered flock   17
harried and chased by lions:
as the king of Assyria was the first to feed on him,
so the king of Babylon was the last to gnaw his bones.
Therefore the LORD of Hosts the God of Israel says this: 18

I will punish the king of Babylon and his country
as I have punished the king of Assyria.
I will bring Israel back to his pasture,   19
and he shall graze on Carmel and Bashan;
in the hills of Ephraim and Gilead he shall eat his fill.

In those days, says the LORD, when that time comes, search shall be   20
made for the iniquity of Israel but there shall be none, and for the sin of
Judah but it shall not be found; for those whom I leave as a remnant I will
forgive.

Attack the land of Merathaim;   21
attack it and the inhabitants of Pekod;

put all to the sword and destroy them,
and do whatever I bid you.
This is the very word of the LORD.

22   Hark, the sound of war in the land
and great destruction!
23   See how the hammer of all the earth
is hacked and broken in pieces,
how Babylon has become
a horror among the nations.
24   O Babylon, you have laid a snare to be your own undoing;
you have been trapped, all unawares;
there you are, you are caught,
because you have challenged the LORD.
25   The LORD has opened his arsenal
and brought out the weapons of his wrath;
for this is work for the Lord the GOD of Hosts
in the land of the Chaldaeans.
26   Her harvest-time has come:
throw open her granaries,*a* pile her in heaps;
destroy her, let no survivor be left.
27   Put all her warriors to the sword;
let them be led to the slaughter.
Woe upon them! for their time has come,
their day of reckoning.
28   I hear the fugitives escaping from the land of Babylon
to proclaim in Zion the vengeance of the LORD our God.

29   Let your arrows be heard whistling against Babylon,
all you whose bows are ready strung.
Pitch your tents all around her
so that no one escapes.
Pay her back for all her misdeeds;
as she has done, so do to her,
for she has insulted the LORD the Holy One of Israel.
30   Therefore her young men shall fall in her streets,
and all her warriors shall lie still in death that day.
This is the very word of the LORD.

31   I am against you, insolent city;
for your time has come, your day of reckoning.
This is the very word of the Lord GOD of Hosts.
32   Insolence shall stumble and fall
and no one shall lift her up,
and I will kindle fire in the heath around her
and it shall consume everything round about.

a Or cattle-pens.

The LORD of Hosts has said this: 33

The peoples of Israel and Judah together are oppressed;
their captors hold them firmly and refuse to release them.
But they have a powerful advocate,   34
whose name is the LORD of Hosts;
he himself will plead their cause,
bringing distress on Babylon and turmoil on its people.

A sword hangs over the Chaldaeans,   35
over the people of Babylon, her officers and her wise men,
says the LORD.
A sword over the false prophets, and they are made fools,   36
a sword over her warriors, and they despair,
a sword over her horses and her chariots   37
and over all the rabble within her,
and they shall become like women;
a sword over her treasures, and they shall be plundered,
a sword over her waters, and they shall dry up;   38
for it is a land of idols
that glories in its dreaded gods.*a*

Therefore marmots and jackals shall skulk in it, desert-owls shall haunt   39
it, nevermore shall it be inhabited by men and no one shall dwell in it
through all the ages. As when God overthrew Sodom and Gomorrah and   40
their neighbours,*b* says the LORD, no man shall live there, no mortal make
a home in her.

See, a people is coming from the north, a great nation,   41
mighty*c* kings rouse themselves from earth's farthest corners;
armed with bow and sabre, they are cruel and pitiless;   42
bestriding horses, they sound like the thunder of the sea;
they are like men arrayed for battle against you, Babylon.
The king of Babylon has heard news of them   43
and his hands hang limp;
agony grips him, anguish as of a woman in labour.
Look, like a lion coming up   44
from Jordan's dense thickets to the perennial pastures,
in a moment I will chase every one away
and round up the choicest of*d* the rams.
For who is like me? Who is my equal?
What shepherd can stand his ground before me?

Therefore listen to the LORD's whole purpose against Babylon and all   45
his plans against the land of the Chaldaeans:
The young ones of the flock shall be carried off
and their pasture shall be horrified at their fate.
At the sound of the capture of Babylon   46
the land quakes and her cry is heard among the nations.

a dreaded gods: *or* dire portents.   *b* *Or* inhabitants.   *c* *Or* many.
d the choicest of: *prob. rdg.; Heb.* who is chosen?

51 For thus says the LORD:

> I will raise a destroying wind
> > against Babylon and those who live in Kambul,[a]

2
> > and I will send winnowers to Babylon,
> > who shall winnow her and empty her land;
> for they shall assail her on all sides on the day of disaster.

3
> > How shall the archer then string his bow
> > > or put on his coat of mail?

> Spare none of her young men, destroy all her host,

4
> > and let them fall dead in the land of the Chaldaeans,
> > > pierced through in her streets.

5
> Israel and Judah are not left widowed
> > by their God, by the LORD of Hosts;
> > but the land of the Chaldaeans is full of guilt,
> > > condemned by the Holy One of Israel.

6
> Flee out of Babylon, every man for himself,
> > or you will be struck down for her sin;
> > for this is the LORD's day of vengeance,
> > and he is paying her full recompense.

7
> Babylon has been a gold cup in the LORD's hand
> > to make all the earth drunk;
> > the nations have drunk of her wine,
> > and that has made them mad.

8
> Babylon falls suddenly and is broken.
> > Howl over her,
> > > fetch balm for her wound;
> > > > perhaps she will be healed.

9
> We would have healed Babylon, but she would not be[b] healed.
> Leave her and let us be off, each to his own country;
> > for her doom reaches to heaven
> > > and mounts up to the skies.

10
> > The LORD has made our innocence plain to see;
> > come, let us proclaim in Zion
> > > what the LORD our God has done.

11
> > Sharpen the arrows, fill the quivers.
> The LORD has roused the spirit of the king of the Medes;
> > for the LORD's purpose against Babylon is to destroy it,
> > and his vengeance is the avenging of his temple.

12
> > Raise the standard against Babylon's walls,
> mount a strong guard, post a watch, set an ambush;
> for the LORD has both planned and carried out
> what he threatened to do to the people of Babylon.

13
> O opulent city, standing beside great waters,
> > your end has come, your destiny is certain.

---

[a] Kambul: *prob. rdg.; Heb.* the heart of my opponents.　　[b] would not be: *or* was not.

The LORD of Hosts has sworn by himself, saying,   14
Once I filled you with men, countless as locusts,
    yet a song of triumph shall be chanted over you.

    God made the earth by his power,   15*a*
    fixed the world in place by his wisdom,
    unfurled the skies by his understanding.
At the thunder of his voice the waters in heaven are amazed;*b*   16
    he brings up the mist from the ends of the earth,
    he opens rifts*c* for the rain
    and brings the wind out of his storehouses.
All men are brutish and ignorant,   17
    every goldsmith is discredited by his idol;
    for the figures he casts are a sham,
    there is no breath in them.
They are worth nothing, mere mockeries,   18
    which perish when their day of reckoning comes.
God, Jacob's creator, is not like these;   19
      for he is the maker of all.
      Israel is the people he claims as his own;
      the LORD of Hosts is his name.

You are my battle-axe, my weapon of war;   20
with you I will break nations in pieces,
and with you I will destroy kingdoms.
With you I will break horse and rider,   21
with you I will break chariot and rider,
with you I will break man and woman,   22
with you I will break young and old,
with you I will break young man and maiden,
with you I will break shepherd and flock,   23
with you I will break ploughman and team,
with you I will break viceroys and governors.
So will I repay Babylon and the people of Chaldaea   24
for all the wrong which they did in Zion in your sight.
    This is the very word of the LORD.

    I am against you, O destroying mountain,*d*   25
      you who destroy the whole earth,
    and I will stretch out my hand against you
      and send you tumbling from your terraces
      and make you a burnt-out mountain.
No stone of yours shall be used as a corner-stone,   26
      no stone for a foundation;
    but you shall be desolate, for ever waste.
    This is the very word of the LORD.

---

a *Verses 15–19: cp. 10. 12–16.*   *b* At the thunder ... amazed: *prob. rdg.; Heb.* At the
sound of his giving tumult of waters in heaven.   *c* rifts: *prob. rdg.; Heb.* lightnings.
d Or O Mount of the Destroyer.

27   Raise a standard in the land,*a*
    blow the trumpet among the nations,
    hallow the nations for war against her,
summon the kingdoms of Ararat, Minni, and Ashkenaz,
    appoint a commander-in-chief against her,
bring up the horses like a dark swarm of locusts;*b*

28   hallow the nations for war against her,
    the king of the Medes, his viceroys and governors,
        and all the lands of his realm.

29   The earth quakes and writhes;
    for the LORD's designs against Babylon are fulfilled,
to make the land of Babylon desolate and unpeopled.

30   Babylon's warriors have given up the fight,
        they skulk in the forts;
their courage has failed, they have become like women.
Her buildings are set on fire, the bars of her gates broken.

31   Runner speeds to meet runner,
    messenger to meet messenger,
    bringing news to the king of Babylon
that every quarter of his city is taken,

32   the river-crossings are seized,
the guard-towers set on fire
    and the garrison stricken with panic.

33 For the LORD of Hosts the God of Israel has spoken:
    Babylon is like a threshing-floor when it is trodden;
    soon, very soon, harvest-time will come.

34   'Nebuchadrezzar king of Babylon has devoured me
        and sucked me dry,
    he has set me aside like an empty jar.
    Like a dragon he has gulped me down;
    he has filled his maw with my delicate flesh
        and spewed me up.

35   On Babylon be the violence done to me,
        the vengeance taken upon me!',
        Zion's people shall say.
    'My blood be upon the Chaldaeans!',
        Jerusalem shall say.

36 Therefore the LORD says:
    I will plead your cause, I will avenge you;
    I will dry up her sea*c* and make her waters fail;

37   and Babylon shall become a heap of ruins, a haunt of wolves,
    a scene of horror and derision, with no inhabitant.

38   Together they roar like young lions,
    they growl like the whelps of a lioness.

    a Or earth.   *b Or* hoppers.   *c Possibly the Euphrates.*

I will cause their drinking bouts to end in fever   39
and make them so drunk that they will writhe and toss,
then sink into unending sleep, never to wake.
     This is the very word of the LORD.
I will bring them like lambs to the slaughter,   40
    rams and he-goats together.
Sheshak*ᵃ* is captured,   41
    the pride of the whole earth taken;
Babylon has become a horror amongst the nations!
    The sea has surged over Babylon,   42
      she is covered by its roaring waves.
Her cities have become waste places,   43
    a land dried up and desert,
a land in whose cities no man lives
and through which no mortal travels.
    I will punish Bel in Babylon   44
and make him bring up what he has swallowed;
nations shall never again come streaming to him.
    The wall of Babylon has fallen;
come out of her, O my people,
and let every man save himself   45
    from the anger of the LORD.
    Then beware of losing heart,   46
fear no rumours spread abroad in the land,
    as rumour follows rumour,
    each year a new one:
violence on earth and ruler against ruler.
    Therefore a time is coming   47
      when I will punish Babylon's idols,
    and all her land shall be put to shame,
and all her slain shall lie fallen in her midst.
    Heaven and earth and all that is in them   48
      shall sing in triumph over Babylon;
for marauders from the north shall overrun her.
    This is the very word of the LORD.
Babylon must fall for the sake of *ᵇ* Israel's slain,   49
as the slain of all the world fell for the sake of Babylon.
You who have escaped from her sword, off with you, do not linger.   50
    Remember the LORD from afar
and call Jerusalem to mind.
    We are put to shame by the reproaches we have heard,   51
    and our faces are covered with confusion:
strangers have entered the sacred courts of the LORD's house.

A time is coming therefore, says the LORD,   52
    when I will punish her idols,
    and all through the land there shall be the groaning of the wounded.

ᵃ A name for Babylon.   *ᵇ for the sake of: prob. rdg.; Heb. om.*

53   Though Babylon should reach to the skies
     and make her high towers inaccessible,
     I will send marauders to overrun her.
       This is the very word of the LORD.

54   Hark, cries of agony from Babylon!
     Sounds of destruction from the land of the Chaldaeans!

55   For the LORD is despoiling Babylon
     and will silence the hum of the city,
     before the advancing wave that booms and roars
       like mighty waters.

56   For marauders march on Babylon herself,
     her warriors are captured and their bows are broken;
     for the LORD, a God of retribution, will repay in full.

57   I will make her princes and her wise men drunk,
     her viceroys and governors and warriors,
     and they shall sink into unending sleep, never to wake.
       This is the very word of the King,
       whose name is the LORD of Hosts.

58   The LORD of Hosts says:
     The walls of broad Babylon shall be razed to the ground,
       her lofty gates shall be set on fire.
     Worthless now is the thing for which the nations toiled;
       the peoples wore themselves out for a mere nothing.

59   The instructions given by the prophet Jeremiah to the quartermaster Seraiah son of Neriah and grandson of Mahseiah, when he went to Babylon with Zedekiah king of Judah in the fourth year of his reign.

60   Jeremiah, having written down in a[a] book[b] a full description of the
61 disaster which would come upon Babylon, said to Seraiah, 'When you
62 come to Babylon, look at this, read it all and then say, "Thou, O LORD, hast declared thy purpose to destroy this place and leave it with no one
63 living in it, man or beast; it shall be desolate, for ever waste." When you have finished reading the book, tie a stone to it and throw it into the
64 Euphrates, and then say, "So shall Babylon sink, never to rise again after the disaster which I shall bring upon her."'

Thus far are the collected sayings of Jeremiah.

Historical note about the fall of Jerusalem

52 1[c]   ZEDEKIAH WAS TWENTY-ONE YEARS OLD when he came to the throne, and he reigned in Jerusalem for eleven years; his mother was
2 Hamutal daughter of Jeremiah of Libnah. He did what was wrong in the
3 eyes of the LORD, as Jehoiakim had done. Jerusalem and Judah so angered

---

[a] *Or* one.   [b] *Prob. rdg.; Heb. adds* all these things which are written concerning Babylon.   [c] *Verses 1–27 : cp. 39. 1–10 and 2 Kgs. 24. 18—25. 21.*

the LORD that in the end he banished them from his sight; and Zedekiah rebelled against the king of Babylon.

In the ninth year of his reign, in the tenth month, on the tenth day of 4 the month, Nebuchadrezzar king of Babylon advanced with all his army against Jerusalem, invested it and erected watch-towers against it on every side; the siege lasted till the eleventh year of King Zedekiah. In the 5 6 fourth month of that year, on the ninth day of the month, when famine was severe in the city and there was no food for the common people, the city 7 was thrown open. When Zedekiah king of Judah saw this, he and*ᵃ* all his armed escort left the city and fled by night through the gate called Between the Two Walls, near the king's garden. They escaped towards the Arabah, although the Chaldaeans were surrounding the city. But the Chaldaean 8 army pursued the king and overtook him in the lowlands of Jericho; and all his company was dispersed. The king was seized and brought before 9 the king of Babylon at Riblah in the land of Hamath, where he pleaded his case before him. The king of Babylon slew Zedekiah's sons before his 10 eyes; he also put to death all the princes of Judah in Riblah. Then the king 11 of Babylon put Zedekiah's eyes out, bound him with fetters of bronze, brought him to Babylon and committed him to prison till the day of his death.

In the fifth month, on the tenth day of the month, in the nineteenth year 12 of Nebuchadrezzar king of Babylon, Nebuzaradan, captain of the king's bodyguard,*ᵇ* came to Jerusalem and set fire to the house of the LORD and 13 the royal palace; all the houses in the city, including the mansion of Gedaliah,*ᶜ* were burnt down. The Chaldaean forces with the captain of 14 the guard pulled down the walls all round Jerusalem. *ᵈ*Nebuzaradan 15 captain of the guard deported the rest of the people left in the city, those who had deserted to the king of Babylon and any remaining artisans. The 16 captain of the guard left only the weakest class of people to be vine-dressers and labourers.

The Chaldaeans broke up the pillars of bronze in the house of the LORD, 17 the trolleys, and the sea of bronze, and took the metal to Babylon. They 18 took also the pots, shovels, snuffers, tossing-bowls, saucers, and all the vessels of bronze used in the service of the temple. The captain of the 19 guard took away the precious metal, whether gold or silver, of which the cups, firepans, tossing-bowls, pots, lamp-stands, saucers, and flagons were made. The bronze of the two pillars, of the one sea and of the twelve 20 oxen supporting it, which King Solomon had made for the house of the LORD, was beyond weighing. The one pillar was eighteen cubits high and 21 twelve cubits in circumference; it was hollow and the metal was four fingers thick. It had a capital of bronze, five cubits high, and a decoration of net- 22 work and pomegranates ran all round it, wholly of bronze. The other pillar, with its pomegranates, was exactly like it. Ninety-six pomegranates were 23 exposed to view and there were a hundred in all on the network all round.

ᵃ When Zedekiah . . . and: *prob. rdg., cp. 39. 4; Heb. om.* *ᵇ* captain . . . body-guard: *prob. rdg., cp. 2 Kgs. 25. 8; Heb.* captain of the bodyguard stood before the king of Babylon. *ᶜ* Gedaliah: *prob. rdg.; Heb.* the great man. *ᵈ* *Prob. rdg., cp. 39. 9 and 2 Kgs. 25. 11; Heb. prefixes* The weakest class of the people (*cp. verse 16*).

24   The captain of the guard took Seraiah the chief priest and Zephaniah
25 the deputy chief priest and the three on duty at the entrance; he took also
from the city a eunuch who was in charge of the fighting men, seven of
those with right of access to the king who were still in the city, the adjutant-
general[a] whose duty was to muster the people for war, and sixty men of
26 the people who were still there. These Nebuzaradan captain of the guard
27 brought to the king of Babylon at Riblah. There, in the land of Hamath,
the king of Babylon had them flogged and put to death. So Judah went into
exile from their own land.

28   These were the people deported by Nebuchadrezzar in the seventeenth[b]
29 year: three thousand and twenty-three Judaeans. In his eighteenth year,
30 eight hundred and thirty-two people from Jerusalem; in his twenty-third
year, seven hundred and forty-five Judaeans were deported by Nebuzaradan the captain of the bodyguard: all together four thousand six
hundred people.

31[c]   In the thirty-seventh year of the exile of Jehoiachin king of Judah, on
the twenty-fifth day of the twelfth month, Evil-merodach king of Babylon
in the year of his accession showed favour to Jehoiachin king of Judah. He
32 brought him out of prison, treated him kindly and gave him a seat at table
33 above the kings with him in Babylon. So Jehoiachin discarded his prison
34 clothes and lived as a pensioner of the king for the rest of his life. For his
maintenance a regular daily allowance was given him by the king of
Babylon as long as he lived, to the day of his death.

LAMENTATIONS

Sorrows of captive Zion

1   How solitary lies the city, once so full of people!
        Once great among nations, now become a widow;
        once queen among provinces, now put to forced labour!

2   Bitterly she weeps in the night,
               tears run down her cheeks;
            she has no one to bring her comfort
               among all that love her;
            all her friends turned traitor
               and became her enemies.

3   Judah went into the misery of exile
               and endless servitude.
            Settled among the nations,
               she found no resting-place;
            all her persecutors fell upon her
               in her sore straits.

[a] *Prob. rdg.; Heb. adds* commander-in-chief.   [b] *Prob. rdg.; Heb.* seventh.
[c] *Verses 31–34: cp. 2 Kgs. 25. 27–30.*

The paths to Zion mourn,   4
   for none attend her sacred feasts;
all her gates are desolate.
   Her priests groan and sigh,
   her virgins are cruelly treated.
How bitter is her fate!
Her adversaries have become her masters,   5
   her enemies take their ease,
   for the LORD has cruelly punished her
because of misdeeds without number;
   her young children have gone,
driven away captive by the enemy.
All majesty has vanished   6
   from the daughter of Zion.
Her princes have become like deer
   that can find no pasture
and run on, their strength all spent,
   pursued by the hunter.
   Jerusalem has remembered   7
her days of misery and wandering,*a*
when her people fell into the power of the adversary
   and there was no one to help her.
The adversary saw and mocked
   at her fallen state.
Jerusalem had sinned greatly,   8
and so she was treated like a filthy rag;
all those who had honoured her held her cheap,
   for they had seen her nakedness.
What could she do but sigh
   and turn away?
   Uncleanness clung to her skirts,   9
and she gave no thought to her fate.
   Her fall was beyond belief
and there was no one to comfort her.
Look, LORD, upon her misery,
   see how the enemy has triumphed.
The adversary stretched out his hand   10
   to seize all her treasures;
then it was that she saw Gentiles
   entering her sanctuary,
Gentiles forbidden by thee to enter
   the assembly, for it was thine.
   All her people groaned,   11
   they begged for bread;
they sold their treasures for food
   to give them strength again.

---

a *Prob. rdg.; Heb. adds* all her treasures which have been from days of old.

Look, O Lord, and see
how cheap I am accounted.
12 Is it of no concern to you who pass by?
If only you would look and see:
is there any agony like mine,
like these my torments
with which the Lord has cruelly punished me
in the day of his anger?
13 He sent down fire from heaven,
it ran through my bones;
he spread out a net to catch my feet,
and turned me back;
he made me an example of desolation,
racked with sickness all day long.
14 My transgressions were bound*a* upon me,
his own hand knotted them round me;
his yoke was lifted on to my neck,
my strength failed beneath its weight;
the Lord abandoned me to its hold,*b*
and I could not stand.
15 The Lord treated with scorn
all the mighty men within my walls;
he marshalled rank on rank against me
to crush my young warriors.
The Lord trod down, like grapes in the press,
the virgin daughter of Judah.
16 For these things I weep over my plight,*c*
my eyes run with tears;
for any to comfort me and renew my strength
are far to seek;
my sons are an example of desolation,
for the enemy is victorious.

17 Zion lifted her hands in prayer,
but there was no one to comfort her;
the Lord gave Jacob's enemies the order
to beset him on every side.
Jerusalem became a filthy rag in their midst.

18 The Lord was in the right;
it was I who rebelled against his commands.
Listen, O listen, all you nations,
and look on my agony:
my virgins and my young men are gone into captivity.
19 I called to my lovers, they broke faith with me;
my priests and my elders in the city
went hungry and could find nothing,

---

a bound: *prob. rdg.; Heb. word unknown.*   *b* its hold: *prob. rdg.; Heb. obscure.*
c my plight: *prob. rdg.; Heb. my eye.*

although they sought food for themselves
    to renew their strength.
See, LORD, how sorely I am distressed.   20
    My bowels writhe in anguish
and my stomach turns within me,
    because I wantonly rebelled.
The sword makes orphans in the streets,
    as plague does within doors.
Hear me when I groan   21
    with no one to comfort me.
All my enemies, when they heard of my calamity,
rejoiced at what thou hadst done;
but hasten the day thou hast promised
    when they shall become like me.
Let all their evil deeds come before thee;   22
    torment them in their turn,
as thou hast tormented me
    for all my transgressions;
for my sighs are many and my heart is faint.

Zion's hope of relief after punishment

What darkness the Lord in his anger   2
    has brought upon the daughter of Zion!
He hurled down from heaven to earth
    the glory of Israel,
and did not remember in the day of his anger
    that Zion was his footstool.
The Lord overwhelmed without pity   2
    all the dwellings of Jacob.
    In his wrath he tore down
the strongholds of the daughter of Judah;
he levelled with the ground and desecrated
    the kingdom and its rulers.
In his anger he hacked down   3
the horn of Israel's pride,
he withdrew his helping hand
    when the enemy came on;
and he blazed in Jacob like flaming fire
    that rages far and wide.
In enmity he strung his bow;   4
    he took his stand like an adversary
    and with his strong arm he slew
all those who had been his delight;
he poured his fury out like fire
    on the tent of the daughter of Zion.
The Lord played an enemy's part   5
    and overwhelmed Israel.

He overwhelmed all their towered mansions
and brought down their strongholds in ruins;
sorrow upon sorrow he brought
to the daughter of Judah.

6 He stripped his tabernacle as a vine is stripped,
and made the place of assembly a ruin.
In Zion the LORD blotted out all memory
of festal assembly*a* and of sabbath;
king and priest alike he scorned
in the grimness of his anger.

7 The Lord spurned his own altar
and laid a curse upon his sanctuary.
He delivered the walls of her mansions
into the power of the enemy;
in the LORD's very house they raised shouts of victory
as on a day of festival.

8 The LORD was minded to bring down in ruins
the walls of the daughter of Zion;
he took their measure with his line
and did not scruple to demolish her;
he made rampart and wall lament,
and both together lay dejected.

9 Her gates are sunk into the earth,
he has shattered and broken their bars;
her king and her rulers are among the Gentiles,
and there is no law;
her prophets too have received
no vision from the LORD.

10 The elders of the daughter of Zion
sit on the ground and sigh;
they have cast dust on their heads
and clothed themselves in sackcloth;
the virgins of Jerusalem
bow their heads to the ground.

11 My eyes are blinded with tears,
my bowels writhe in anguish.
In my bitterness my bile is spilt on the earth
because of my people's wound,
when children and infants faint
in the streets of the town

12 and cry to their mothers,
'Where can we get corn and wine?'—
when they faint like wounded things
in the streets of the city,
gasping out their lives
in their mothers' bosom.

a festal assembly: *or* appointed seasons.

How can I cheer you? Whose plight is like yours,　　13
　　daughter of Jerusalem?
To what can I compare you for your comfort,
　　virgin daughter of Zion?
For your wound gapes wide as the ocean;
　　who can heal you?
The visions that your prophets saw for you　　14
　　were false and painted shams;
they did not bring home to you your guilt
　　and so reverse your fortunes.
The visions that they saw for you were delusions,
　　false and fraudulent.*a*
　　All those who pass by　　15
snap their fingers at you;
they hiss and wag their heads at you,
　　daughter of Jerusalem:
'Is this the city once called Perfect in beauty,
　　Joy of the whole earth?'
　　All your enemies　　16
make mouths and jeer at you;
they hiss and grind their teeth,
　　saying, 'Here we are,
this is the day we have waited for;
　　we have lived to see it.'

The LORD has done what he planned to do,　　17
　　he has fulfilled his threat,
all that he ordained from days of old.
　　He has demolished without pity
and let the enemy rejoice over you,
filling your adversaries with pride.
Cry with a full heart*b* to the Lord,　　18
　　O wall of the daughter of Zion;
let your tears run down like a torrent
　　by day and by night.
Give yourself not a moment's rest,
　　let your tears never cease.
Arise and cry aloud in the night;　　19
　　at the beginning of every watch
pour out your heart like water
　　in the Lord's very presence.
Lift up your hands to him
　　for the lives of your children.*c*
Look, LORD, and see:　　20
　　who is it that thou hast thus tormented?

a fraudulent: *or* causing banishment.　　　*b* Cry . . . heart: *prob. rdg.*; *Heb.* Their
heart cried.　　　*c* *Prob. rdg.*; *Heb. adds* who faint with hunger at every street-
corner.

Must women eat the fruit of their wombs,
 the children they have brought safely to birth?
Shall priest and prophet be slain
 in the sanctuary of the Lord?

21 There in the streets young men and old
 lie on the ground.
My virgins and my young men have fallen
 by sword and by famine;
thou hast slain them in the day of thy anger,
 slaughtered them without pity.

22 Thou didst summon my enemies against me from
  every side,
 like men assembling for a festival;
not a man escaped, not one survived
 in the day of the LORD's anger.
All whom I brought safely to birth and reared
 were destroyed by my enemies.

3 I am the man who has known affliction,
 I have felt the rod of his wrath.

2 It was I whom he led away and left to walk
 in darkness, where no light is.

3 Against me alone he has turned his hand,
 and so it is all day long.

4 He has wasted away my flesh and my skin
 and broken all my bones;

5 he has built up walls around me,
 behind and before,

6 and has cast me into a place of darkness
 like a man long dead.

7 He has walled me in so that I cannot escape,
 and weighed me down with fetters;

8 even when I cry out and call for help,
 he rejects my prayer.

9 He has barred my road with blocks of stone
 and tangled up my way.

10 He lies in wait for me like a bear
 or a lion lurking in a covert.

11 He has made my way refractory and lamed me
 and left me desolate.

12 He has strung his bow
and made me the target for his arrows;

13 he has pierced my kidneys with shafts
 drawn from his quiver.

14 I have become a laughing-stock to all nations,
 the target of their mocking songs all day.

15 He has given me my fill of bitter herbs
 and made me drunk with wormwood.

He has broken my teeth on gravel;   16
    fed on ashes, I am racked with pain;
peace has gone out of my life,   17
    and I have forgotten what prosperity means.
Then I cry out that my strength has gone   18
    and so has my hope in the LORD.

The memory of my distress and my wanderings   19
    is*a* wormwood and gall.
    Remember, O remember,   20
and stoop down to me.*b c*
All this I take to heart   21
    and therefore I will wait patiently:
the LORD's true love is surely not spent,*d*   22
    nor has his compassion failed;
    they are new every morning,   23
    so great is his constancy.
The LORD, I say, is all that I have;   24
    therefore I will wait for him patiently.
The LORD is good to those who look for him,   25
    to all who seek him;
it is good to wait in patience and sigh   26
    for deliverance by the LORD.
    It is good, too, for a man   27
to carry the yoke in his youth.
Let him sit alone and sigh   28
    if it is heavy upon him;
let him lay his face in the dust,   29
    and there may yet be hope.
Let him turn his cheek to the smiter   30
    and endure full measure of abuse;
for the Lord will not cast off   31
    his servants*e* for ever.
He may punish cruelly, yet he will have compassion   32
    in the fullness of his love;
he does not willingly afflict   33
    or punish any mortal man.

To trample underfoot   34
    any prisoner in the land,
to deprive a man of his rights   35
    in defiance of the Most High,
to pervert justice in the courts—   36
    such things the Lord has never approved.

---

a The memory . . . is: *or* Remember my distress and my wanderings, the . . .
b stoop down to me: *prob. original rdg., altered in Heb. to* I sink down.
c Remember . . . me: *or* I remember, I remember them and sink down.
d spent: *prob. rdg.; Heb. unintelligible.*   *e* his servants: *prob. rdg.; Heb. om.*

37 Who can command and it is done,
if the Lord has forbidden it?

38 Do not both bad and good proceed
from the mouth of the Most High?

39 Why should any man living complain,
any mortal who has sinned?

40 Let us examine our ways and put them to the test
and turn back to the LORD;

41 let us lift up our hearts, not our hands,
to God in heaven.

42 We ourselves have sinned and rebelled,
and thou hast not forgiven.

43 In anger thou hast turned*a* and pursued us
and slain without pity;

44 thou hast hidden thyself behind the clouds
beyond reach of our prayers;

45 thou hast treated us as offscouring and refuse
among the nations.

46 All our enemies make mouths
and jeer at us.

47 Before us lie hunter's scare and pit,
devastation and ruin.

48 My eyes run with streams of water
because of my people's wound.

49 My eyes stream with unceasing tears
and refuse all comfort,

50 while the LORD in heaven looks down
and watches my affliction,*b*

51 while the LORD torments*c* me
with the fate of all the daughters of my city.

52 Those who for no reason were my enemies
drove me cruelly like a bird;

53 they thrust me alive into the silent pit,
and they closed it over me with a stone;

54 the waters rose high above my head,
and I said, 'My end has come.'

55 But I called on thy name, O LORD,
from the depths of the pit;

56 thou heardest my voice; do not turn a deaf ear
when I cry, 'Come to my relief.'

57 Thou wast near when I called to thee;
thou didst say, 'Have no fear.'

58 Lord, thou didst plead my cause
and ransom my life;

a *Prob. rdg.; Heb.* hidden.
b my affliction: *prob. rdg.; Heb.* my eye.
c the LORD torments: *prob. rdg.; Heb.* tormenting.

thou sawest, Lord, the injustice done to me 59
and gavest judgement in my favour;
thou sawest their vengeance, 60
all their plots against me.
Thou didst hear their bitter taunts, O Lord, 61
their many plots against me,
the whispering, the murmurs of my enemies 62
all the day long.
See how, whether they sit or stand, 63
they taunt me bitterly.
Pay them back for their deeds, O Lord, 64
pay them back what they deserve.
Show them how hard thy heart can be, 65
how little concern thou hast for them.
Pursue them in anger and exterminate them 66
from beneath thy heavens, O Lord.

How dulled is the gold, **4**
how tarnished the fine gold!
The stones of the sanctuary[a] lie strewn
at every street-corner.
See Zion's precious sons, 2
once worth their weight in finest gold,
now counted as pitchers of earthenware
made by any potter's hand.
Even whales[b] uncover the teat 3
and suckle their young;
but the daughters of my people are cruel
as ostriches in the desert.
The sucking infant's tongue 4
cleaves to its palate from thirst;
young children beg for bread
but no one offers them a crumb.
Those who once fed delicately 5
are desolate in the streets,
and those nurtured in purple
now grovel on dunghills.
The punishment[c] of my people is worse 6
than the penalty[d] of Sodom,
which was overthrown in a moment
and no one wrung his hands.
Her crowned princes[e] were once purer than snow, 7
whiter than milk;
they were ruddier than branching coral,[f]
and their limbs were lapis lazuli.

[a] The stones of the sanctuary: *or* Bright gems.   [b] *Prob. rdg.; Heb.* jackals.
[c] *Or* iniquity.   [d] *Or* sin.   [e] crowned princes: *or* Nazirites.   [f] than . . .
coral: *prob. rdg.; Heb.* branch than coral.

8 But their faces turned blacker than soot,
    and no one knew them in the streets;
the skin was drawn tight over their bones,
    dry as touchwood.

9 Those who died by the sword were more fortunate
    than those who died of hunger;
these wasted away, deprived
    of the produce of the field.

10 Tender-hearted women with their own hands
    boiled their own children;
their children became their food
    in the day of my people's wounding.

11 The LORD glutted his rage
    and poured forth his anger;
he kindled a fire in Zion,
    and it consumed her foundations.

12 This no one believed, neither the kings of the earth
    nor anyone that dwelt in the world:
that enemy or invader would enter
    the gates of Jerusalem.

13 It was for the sins of her prophets
    and for the iniquities of her priests,
who shed within her walls
    the blood of the righteous.

14 They wandered blindly in the streets,
    so stained with blood
that men would not touch
    even their garments.

15 'Away, away; unclean!' men cried to them.
    'Away, do not come near.'
They hastened away, they wandered among the nations,[a]
    unable to find any resting-place.

16 The LORD himself scattered them,
    he thought of them no more;
he showed no favour to priests,
    no pity for elders.

17 Still we strain our eyes,
    looking in vain for help.
We have watched and watched
    for a nation powerless to save us.

18 When we go out, we take to by-ways
    to avoid the public streets;
our days are all but finished,[b]
    our end has come.

---

[a] *Prob. rdg.; Heb. adds* they said.   [b] our . . . finished: *prob. rdg.; Heb.* our end has drawn near, our days are complete.

Our pursuers have shown themselves swifter   19
    than vultures in the sky;
they are hot on our trail over the hills,
they lurk to catch us in the wilderness.
    The LORD's anointed, the breath of life to us,   20
    was caught in their machinations;
    although we had thought to live
among the nations, safe under his protection.

Rejoice and be glad, daughter of Edom,   21
    you who live in the land of Uz.
Yet the cup shall pass to you in your turn,
and when you are drunk you will expose yourself to shame.
The punishment for your sin, daughter of Zion, is now complete,   22
    and never again shall you be carried into exile.
But you, daughter of Edom, your sin shall be punished,
    and your guilt revealed.

A prayer for remembrance and restoration

Remember, O LORD, what has befallen us;   **5**
    look, and see how we are scorned.
Our patrimony is turned over to strangers   2
    and our homes to foreigners.
We are like orphans, without a father;   3
    our mothers are like widows.
We must buy our own water to drink,   4
our own wood can only be had at a price.
The yoke is on our necks, we are overdriven;   5
we are weary and are given no rest.
We came to terms, now with the Egyptians,   6
now with the Assyrians, to provide us with food.
Our fathers sinned and are no more,   7
and we bear the burden of their guilt.
Slaves have become our rulers,   8
and there is no one to rescue us from them.
We must bring in our food from the wilderness,   9
    risking our lives in the scorching heat.*a*
Our skins are blackened as in a furnace   10
by the ravages of starvation.
Women were raped in Zion,   11
    virgins raped in the cities of Judah.
Princes were hung up by their hands,   12
and elders received no honour.
Young men toil to grind corn,   13
and boys stumble under loads of wood.

    a in the scorching heat: *or* by the sword.

14   Elders have left off their sessions in the gate,
               and young men no longer pluck the strings.
15   Joy has fled from our hearts,
               and our dances are turned to mourning.
16   The garlands have fallen from our heads;
               woe betide us, sinners that we are.
17   For this we are sick at heart,
               for all this our eyes grow dim:
18   because Mount Zion is desolate
               and over it the jackals run wild.

19   O Lord, thou art enthroned for ever,
               thy throne endures from one generation to another.
20   Why wilt thou quite forget us
               and forsake us these many days?
21   O Lord, turn us back to thyself, and we will come back;
               renew our days as in times long past.
22   For if thou hast utterly rejected us,
               then great indeed has been thy anger against us.

THE BOOK OF THE PROPHET
EZEKIEL

Ezekiel's call to be a prophet

ON THE FIFTH DAY OF THE FOURTH MONTH in 1
the thirtieth year, while I was among the exiles by the river Kebar,[a]
the heavens were opened and I saw a vision of God. On the fifth 2
day of the month in the fifth year of the exile of King Jehoiachin, the word 3
of the LORD came to Ezekiel son of Buzi the priest, in Chaldaea, by the
river Kebar, and there the hand of the LORD came upon him.

I saw a storm wind coming from the north, a vast cloud with flashes of 4
fire and brilliant light about it; and within was a radiance like brass, glowing in the heart of the flames. In the fire was the semblance of four living 5
creatures in human form. Each had four faces and each four wings; their 6 7
legs were straight, and their hooves were like the hooves of a calf, glittering
like a disc of bronze. Under the wings on each of the four sides were human 8
hands; all four creatures had faces and wings, and their wings touched one 9
another. They did not turn as they moved; each creature went straight
forward. Their faces were like this: all four had the face of a man and the 10
face of a lion on the right, on the left the face of an ox and the face of an
eagle. Their wings were spread; each living creature had one pair touching 11
its neighbours',[b] while one pair covered its body. They moved straight 12
forward in whatever direction the spirit[c] would go; they never swerved
in their course. The appearance of the creatures was as if fire from burning 13
coals or torches were darting to and fro among them; the fire was radiant,
and out of the fire came lightning.[d]

As I looked at the living creatures, I saw wheels on the ground, one 15
beside each of the four.[e] The wheels sparkled like topaz, and they were 16
all alike: in form and working they were like a wheel inside a wheel, and 17
when they moved in any of the four directions they never swerved in their
course. All four had hubs and each hub had a projection which had the 18
power of sight,[f] and the rims of the wheels were full of eyes all round.
When the living creatures moved, the wheels moved beside them; when 19
the creatures rose from the ground, the wheels rose; they moved in what- 20
ever direction the spirit[c] would go; and the wheels rose together with them,
for the spirit of the living creatures was in the wheels. When the one moved, 21
the other moved; when the one halted, the other halted; when the creatures

---

[a] Or the Kebar canal.   [b] its neighbours': *prob. rdg.; Heb. unintelligible.*
[c] Or wind.   [d] *Prob. rdg., cp. Sept.; Heb. adds* (14) *and the living creatures went
out (prob. rdg.; Heb. obscure) and in like rays of light.*   [e] one ... four: *prob. rdg.;
Heb. obscure.*   [f] the power of sight: *prob. rdg.; Heb.* fear.

rose from the ground, the wheels rose together with them, for the spirit of the creatures was in the wheels.

22 Above the heads of the living creatures was, as it were, a vault glittering like a sheet of ice, awe-inspiring, stretched over their heads above them.
23 Under the vault their wings were spread straight out, touching one
24 another, while one pair covered the body of each. I heard, too, the noise of their wings; when they moved it was like the noise of a great torrent or of a cloud-burst,*a* like the noise of a crowd or of an armed camp; when they
25 halted their wings dropped. A sound was heard above the vault over their
26 heads, as they halted with drooping wings. Above the vault over their heads there appeared, as it were, a sapphire*b* in the shape of a throne, and high
27 above all, upon the throne, a form in human likeness. I saw what might have been brass glowing like fire in a furnace from the waist upwards; and from the waist downwards I saw what looked like fire with encircling
28 radiance. Like a rainbow in the clouds on a rainy day was the sight of that encircling radiance; it was like the appearance of the glory of the LORD.

When I saw this I threw myself on my face, and heard a voice speaking
2 1 2 to me: Man, he said, stand up, and let me talk with you. As he spoke, a spirit came into me and stood me on my feet, and I listened to him speak-
3 ing. He said to me, Man, I am sending you to the Israelites, a nation of rebels who have rebelled against me. Past generations of them have been
4 in revolt against me to this very day, and this generation to which I am sending you is stubborn and obstinate. When you say to them, 'These are
5 the words of the Lord GOD', they will know that they have a prophet among them, whether they listen or whether they refuse to listen, because
6 they are rebels. But you, man, must not be afraid of them or of what they say, though they are rebels against you and renegades, and you find your-self sitting on scorpions. There is nothing to fear in what they say, and
7 nothing in their looks to terrify you, rebels though they are. You must speak my words to them, whether they listen or whether they refuse to
8 listen, rebels that they are. But you, man, must listen to what I say and not be rebellious like them. Open your mouth and eat what I give you.

9 10 Then I saw a hand stretched out to me, holding a scroll. He unrolled it before me, and it was written all over on both sides with dirges and laments
3 and words of woe. Then he said to me, 'Man, eat what is in front of you,
2 eat this scroll; then go and speak to the Israelites.' So I opened my mouth
3 and he gave me the scroll to eat. Then he said, 'Man, swallow this scroll I give you, and fill yourself full.' So I ate it, and it tasted as sweet as honey.

4 Man, he said to me, go and tell the Israelites what I have to say to them.
5 You are sent not to people whose speech is thick and difficult, but to
6 Israelites. No; I am not sending you to great nations whose speech is so thick and so difficult that you cannot make out what they say; if however I
7 had sent you to them they would have listened to you. But the Israelites will refuse to listen to you, for they refuse to listen to me, so brazen are
8 they all and stubborn. But I will make you a match for them. I will make
9 you as brazen as they are and as stubborn as they are. I will make your

a Or of the Almighty.   *b* Or lapis lazuli.

brow like adamant, harder than flint. Never fear them, never be terrified
by them, rebels though they are. And he said to me, Listen carefully, man,   10
to all that I have to say to you, and take it to heart. Go to your fellow-   11
countrymen in exile and speak to them. Whether they listen or refuse to
listen, say, 'These are the words of the Lord God.'

Then a spirit *a* lifted me up, and I heard behind me a fierce rushing sound   12
as the glory of the Lord rose *b* from his place. I heard the sound of the living   13
creatures' wings brushing against one another, the sound of the wheels
beside them, and a fierce rushing sound. A spirit *a* lifted me and carried me   14
along, and I went full of exaltation, the hand of the Lord strong upon me.
So I came to the exiles at Tel-abib who were settled by the river Kebar.   15
For seven days I stayed with them, dumbfounded.

At the end of seven days the word of the Lord came to me: Man, I have   16 17
made you a watchman for the Israelites; you will take messages from me
and carry my warnings to them. It may be that I pronounce sentence of   18
death on a wicked man: *c* if you do not warn him to give up his wicked ways
and so save his life, the guilt is his; because of his wickedness he shall die,
but I will hold you answerable for his death. But if you have warned him   19
and he still continues in his wicked and evil ways, he shall die because of
his wickedness, but you will have saved yourself. Or it may be that a   20
righteous man turns away and does wrong, and I let that be the cause of
his downfall; he will die because you have not warned him. He will die
for his sin; the righteous deeds he has done will not be taken into account,
and I will hold you answerable for his death. But if you have warned the   21
righteous man not to sin and he has not sinned, then he will have saved his
life because he has been warned, and you will have saved yourself.

The impending ruin of Jerusalem

THE HAND OF THE LORD CAME UPON ME there, and he said to me,   22
Rise up; go out into the plain, and there I will speak to you. So I rose   23
and went out into the plain; the glory of the Lord was there, like the glory
which I had seen by the river Kebar, and I threw myself down on my face.
Then a spirit came into me and stood me on my feet, and spoke to me: Go,   24
he said, and shut yourself up in your house. You shall be tied and bound   25
with ropes, man, so that you cannot go out among the people. I will fasten   26
your tongue to the roof of your mouth and you will be unable to speak;
you will not be the one to rebuke them, rebels though they are. But when   27
I have something to say to you, I will give you back the power of speech.
Then you will say to them, 'These are the words of the Lord God.' If
anyone will listen, he may listen, and, if he refuses to listen, he may refuse;
for they are rebels.

Man, take a tile and set it before you. Draw a city on it, the city of   **4**
Jerusalem: lay siege to it, erect watch-towers against it, raise a siege-ramp,   2
put mantelets in position, and bring battering-rams against it all round.

---

a Or wind.   *b* rose: *prob. rdg.; Heb. obscure.*   *c* *Prob. rdg.; Heb. adds*
if you do not warn him.

3 Then take an iron griddle, and put it as a wall of iron between you and the city. Keep your face turned towards the city; it will be the besieged and you the besieger. This will be a sign to the Israelites.

4 Now lie on your left side, and I will lay Israel's iniquity on you; you shall
5 bear their iniquity for as many days as you lie on that side. Allowing one day for every year of their iniquity, I ordain that you bear it for one hundred
6 and ninety days; thus you shall bear Israel's iniquity. When you have completed all this, lie down a second time on your right side, and bear
7 Judah's iniquity for forty days; I count one day for every year. Then turn your face towards the siege of Jerusalem and bare your arm, and prophesy
8 against it. See how I tie you with ropes so that you cannot turn over from one side to the other until you complete the days of your distress.

9 Then take wheat and barley, beans and lentils, millet and spelt. Mix them all in one bowl and make your bread out of them. You are to eat it during
10 the one hundred and ninety days you spend lying on your side. And you must weigh out your food; you may eat twenty shekels' weight a day,
11 taking it from time to time. Measure out your drinking water too; you
12 may drink a sixth of a hin a day, taking it from time to time. You are to eat your bread baked like barley cakes, using human dung as fuel, and you
13 must bake it where people can see you. Then the LORD said, 'This is the kind of bread, unclean bread, that the Israelites will eat in the foreign lands
14 into which I shall drive them.' But I said, 'O Lord GOD, I have never been made unclean, never in my life have I eaten what has died naturally or been
15 killed by wild beasts; no tainted meat has ever passed my lips.' So he allowed me to use cow-dung instead of human dung to bake my bread.

16 Then he said to me, Man, I am cutting short their daily bread in Jerusalem; people will weigh out anxiously the bread they eat, and measure
17 with dismay the water they drink. So their food and their water will run short until they are dismayed at the sight of one another; they will waste away because of their iniquity.

5 Man, take a sharp sword, take it like a barber's razor and run it over your
2 head and your chin. Then take scales and divide the hair into three. When the siege comes to an end, burn one third of the hair in a fire in the centre of the city; cut up one third with the sword all round the city; scatter one
3 third to the wind, and I will follow it with drawn sword. Take a few of these
4 hairs and tie them up in a fold of your robe. Then take others of them, throw them into the fire and burn them, and out of them fire will come upon all Israel.

5 These are the words of the Lord GOD: This city of Jerusalem I have set
6 among the nations, with other countries around her, and she has rebelled against my laws and my statutes more wickedly than those nations and countries; for her people have rejected my laws and refused to conform to my statutes.

7 Therefore the Lord GOD says: Since you have been more ungrateful than the nations around you and have not conformed to my statutes and have
8 not kept my laws or even the laws of the nations around you, therefore, says the Lord GOD, I, in my turn, will be against you; I will execute judge-
9 ments in your midst for the nations to see, such judgements as I have never

executed before nor ever will again, so abominable have your offences been. Therefore, O Jerusalem, fathers will eat their children and children 10 their fathers in your midst; I will execute judgements on you, and any who are left in you I will scatter to the four winds. As I live, says the Lord GOD, 11 because you have defiled my holy place with all your vile and abominable rites, I in my turn will consume you without pity; I in my turn will not spare you. One third of your people shall die by pestilence and perish by 12 famine in your midst; one third shall fall by the sword in the country round about; and one third I will scatter to the four winds and follow with drawn sword. Then my anger will be spent, I will abate my fury against 13 them and be calm; when my fury is spent they will know that it is I, the LORD, who spoke in jealous passion. I have made you a scandal*a* and a 14 reproach to the nations around you, and all who pass by will see it. You 15 will be an object of reproach and abuse, a terrible lesson to the nations around you, when I pass sentence on you and do judgement in anger and fury. I, the LORD, have spoken. When I shoot the deadly arrows of famine 16 against you,*b* arrows of destruction, I will shoot to destroy you. I will bring famine upon you and cut short your daily bread; I will unleash 17 famine and beasts of prey upon you, and they will leave you childless. Pestilence and slaughter will sweep through you, and I will bring the sword upon you. I, the LORD, have spoken.

These were the words of the LORD to me: Man, look towards the **6** 1 2 mountains of Israel, and prophesy to them: Mountains of Israel, hear the 3 word of the Lord GOD. This is his word to mountains and hills, watercourses and valleys: I am bringing a sword against you, and I will destroy your hill-shrines. Your altars will be made desolate, your incense-altars 4 shattered, and I will fling down your slain before your idols. I will strew 5 the corpses of the Israelites before their idols, and I will scatter your bones about your altars. In all your settlements the blood-spattered altars*c* shall 6 be laid waste and the hill-shrines made desolate. Your altars will be waste and desolate and your idols shattered and useless, your incense-altars hewn down, and all your works wiped out; with the slain falling about you, 7 you shall know that I am the LORD. But when they fall,*d* I will leave you, 8 among the nations, some who survive the sword. When you are scattered in foreign lands, these survivors, in captivity among the nations, will 9 remember how I was grieved because their hearts had turned wantonly from me and their eyes had gone roving wantonly after idols. Then they will loathe themselves for all the evil they have done with their abominations. So they will know that I am the LORD, that I was uttering no vain 10 threat when I said that I would bring this evil upon them.

These are the words of the Lord GOD: Beat your hands together, stamp 11 with your foot, bemoan your vile abominations, people of Israel. Men will fall by sword, famine, and pestilence. Far away they will die by pestilence; 12 at home they will fall by the sword; any who survive or are spared will die by famine, and so at last my anger will be spent. You will know that I am 13 the LORD when their slain fall among the idols round their altars, on every

---

a Or desolation.   *b* *Prob. rdg.; Heb.* them.   *c* blood-spattered altars: *or* cities.   *d* when they fall: *prob. rdg.; Heb. obscure.*

high hill, on all mountain-tops, under every spreading tree, under every leafy terebinth, wherever they have brought offerings of soothing odour
14 for their idols one and all. So I will stretch out my hand over them and make the land a desolate waste in all their settlements, more desolate than the desert of Riblah.*a* They shall know that I am the LORD.

7 1 2   The word of the LORD came to me: Man, the Lord GOD says this to the land of Israel: An end is coming, the end is coming upon the four corners
3 of the land.*b* The end is now upon you; I will unleash my anger against you; I will call you to account for your doings and bring your abominations
4 upon your own heads. I will neither pity nor spare you: I will make you suffer for your doings and the abominations that continue in your midst. So you shall know that I am the LORD.

5   These are the words of the Lord GOD: Behold, it comes, disasters one
6 7 upon another; the end, the end, it comes, it comes.*c* Doom is coming upon you, dweller in the land; the time is coming, the day is near, with confusion
8 and the crash of thunder.*d* Now, in an instant, I will vent my rage upon you and let my anger spend itself. I will call you to account for your doings
9 and bring your abominations upon your own heads. I will neither pity nor spare; I will make you suffer for your doings and the abominations that continue in your midst. So you shall know that it is I, the LORD, who strike the blow.

10   Behold, the day! the doom is here, it has burst upon them. Injustice
11 buds, insolence blossoms, violence shoots up into injustice and wickedness. And it is all their fault, the fault of their turmoil and tumult and
12 all their restless ways. The time has come, the day has arrived; the buyer has no reason to be glad, and the seller none for regret, for I am angry
13 at all their turmoil. The seller will never go back on his bargain while either of them lives; for the bargain will never be reversed because of the turmoil, and no man will exert himself, even in his iniquity, as long
14 as he lives. The trumpet has sounded and all is ready, but no one goes out to war.

15   Outside is the sword, inside are pestilence and famine; in the country men will die by the sword, in the city famine and pestilence will carry
16 them off. If any escape and take to the mountains, like moaning doves,
17 there will I slay them, each for his iniquity, while their hands hang limp
18 and their knees run with urine. They will go in sackcloth, shuddering from
19 head to foot, with faces downcast and heads close shaved. They shall fling their silver into the streets and cast aside their gold like filth; their silver and their gold will be powerless to save them on the day of the LORD's fury. Their hunger will not be satisfied nor their bellies filled; for their
20 iniquity will be the cause of their downfall. They have fed their pride on their beautiful jewels, which they made into vile and abominable images.
21 Therefore I will treat their jewels like filth, I will hand them over as plunder to foreigners and as booty to the most evil people on earth, and these will
22 defile them. I will turn my face from them and let my treasured land be profaned; brigands will come in and defile it.

a Prob. rdg.; Heb. Diblah.   *b Or* earth.   *c Prob. rdg.; Heb. adds* it wakes up, behold it comes.   *d* and the crash of thunder: *prob. rdg.; Heb. unintelligible.*

Clench your fists, for the land is full of bloodshed*a* and the city full of   23
violence. I will let in the scum of nations to take possession of their houses;   24
I will quell the pride of the strong, and their sanctuaries shall be profaned.
Shuddering will come over them, and they will look in vain for peace.   25
Tempest shall follow upon tempest and rumour upon rumour. Men will   26
go seeking a vision from a prophet; there will be no more guidance from
a priest, no counsel from elders. The king will mourn, the prince will be   27
clothed with horror, the hands of the common people will shake with
fright. I will deal with them as they deserve, and call them to account for
their doings; and so they shall know that I am the LORD.

Jerusalem's guilt and punishment

ON THE FIFTH DAY OF THE SIXTH MONTH in the sixth year, I was   8
sitting at home and the elders of Judah were with me. Suddenly the
hand of the Lord GOD came upon me, and I saw what looked like a man.   2
He seemed to be all fire from the waist down and to shine and glitter like
brass from the waist up. He stretched out what seemed a hand and seized   3
me by the forelock. A spirit*b* lifted me up between heaven and earth,
carried me to Jerusalem in a vision of God and put me down at the entrance
to the inner gate facing north, where stands the image of Lust to rouse
lustful passion. The glory of the God of Israel was there, like the vision   4
I had seen in the plain. The LORD said to me, 'Man, look northwards.'   5
I did so, and there to the north of the altar gate, at the entrance, was that
image of Lust. 'Man,' he said, 'do you see what they are doing? The   6
monstrous abominations which the Israelites practise here are driving me
far from my sanctuary, and you will see even more such abominations.'

Then he brought me to the entrance of the court, and I looked and found   7
a hole in the wall. 'Man,' he said to me, 'dig through the wall.' I did so,   8
and it became an opening. 'Go in,' he said, 'and see the vile abominations   9
they practise here.' So I went in and saw figures of reptiles, beasts, and   10
vermin, and all the idols of the Israelites, carved round the walls. Seventy   11
elders of Israel were standing in front of them, with Jaazaniah son of
Shaphan in the middle, and each held a censer from which rose the fragrant
smoke of incense. 'Man,' he said to me, 'do you see what the elders of   12
Israel are doing in darkness, each at the shrine of his own carved image?
They think that the LORD does not see them, or that he has forsaken the
country. You will see', he said, 'yet more monstrous abominations which   13
they practise.'

Then he brought me to that gateway of the LORD's house which faces   14
north; and there I saw women sitting and wailing for Tammuz. 'Man,   15
do you see that?' he asked me. 'But you will see abominations more
monstrous than these.' So he took me to the inner court of the LORD's   16
house, and there, by the entrance to the sanctuary of the LORD, between
porch and altar, were some twenty-five men with their backs to the
sanctuary and their faces to the east, prostrating themselves to the rising

---

a bloodshed: *prob. rdg.; Heb.* the judgement of bloodshed.   *b* Or wind.

17 sun. He said to me, 'Man, do you see that? Is it because they think these
abominations a trifle, that the Jews have filled the country with violence?
They provoke me further to anger, even while they seek to appease me;
18 I will turn upon them in my rage; I will neither pity nor spare. Loudly
as they may cry to me, I will not listen.'

9 A loud voice rang in my ears: 'Here they come, those appointed to
2 punish the city, each carrying his weapon of destruction.' Then I saw six
men approaching from the road that leads to the upper northern gate,
each carrying a battle-axe, one man among them dressed in linen, with pen
3 and ink at his waist; and they halted by the altar of bronze. Then the glory
of the God of Israel rose from above the cherubim. He came to the terrace
of the temple and called to the man dressed in linen with pen and ink at
4 his waist. 'Go through the city, through Jerusalem,' said the LORD, 'and
put a mark on the foreheads of those who groan and lament over the
5 abominations practised there.' Then I heard him say to the others, 'Follow
6 him through the city and kill without pity; spare no one. Kill and destroy
them all, old men and young, girls, little children and women, but touch
no one who bears the mark. Begin at my sanctuary.' So they began with
7 the elders in front of the temple. 'Defile the temple,' he said, 'and fill the
courts with dead bodies; then go out into the city and kill.'
8 While they did their work, I was left alone; and I threw myself upon my
face, crying out, 'O Lord GOD, must thou destroy all the Israelites who are
9 left, pouring out thy anger on Jerusalem?' He answered, 'The iniquity of
Israel and Judah is great indeed; the land is full of murder, the city is filled
with injustice. They think the LORD has forsaken this country; they think
10 he sees nothing. But I will neither pity nor spare them; I will make them
11 answer for all they have done.' Then the man dressed in linen with pen
and ink at his waist came and made his report: 'I have done what thou hast
commanded.'

10 Then I saw, above the vault over the heads of the cherubim, as it were a
2 throne of sapphire*a* visible above them. The LORD said to the man dressed
in linen, 'Come in between the circling wheels under the cherubim, and
take a handful of the burning embers lying among the cherubim; then
toss them over the city.' So he went in before my eyes.
3 The cherubim stood on the right side of the temple as a man enters, and
4 a cloud filled the inner court. The glory of the LORD rose high from above
the cherubim and moved on to the terrace; and the temple was filled with
5 the cloud, while the radiance of the glory of the LORD filled the court. The
sound of the wings of the cherubim could be heard as far as the outer
6 court, as loud as if God Almighty were speaking. Then he told the man
dressed in linen to take fire from between the circling wheels and among
7 the cherubim; the man came and stood by a wheel, and a cherub from
among the cherubim put its hand into the fire that lay among them, and,
taking some fire, gave it to the man dressed in linen; and he received it and
went out.
8 Under the wings of the cherubim there appeared what seemed a human
9 hand. And I saw four wheels beside the cherubim, one wheel beside each

a Or lapis lazuli.

cherub. They had the sparkle of topaz, and all four were alike, like a wheel 10
inside a wheel. When the cherubim moved in any of the four directions, 11
they never swerved in their course; they went straight on in the direction
in which their heads were turned, never swerving in their course. Their 12
whole bodies, their backs and hands and wings, as well as the wheels,
were full of eyes all round the four of them.*a* The whirring of the wheels 13
sounded in my ears. Each had four faces: the first was that of a cherub, 14
the second that of a man, the third that of a lion, and the fourth that of
an eagle.

Then the cherubim raised themselves up, those same living creatures I 15
had seen by the river Kebar. When the cherubim moved, the wheels moved 16
beside them; when the cherubim lifted their wings and rose from the
ground, the wheels did not turn away from them. When the one halted, 17
the other halted; when the one rose, the other rose; for the spirit of the
creatures was in the wheels. Then the glory of the LORD left the temple 18
terrace and halted above the cherubim. The cherubim lifted their wings 19
and raised themselves from the ground; I watched them go with the
wheels beside them. They halted at the eastern gateway of the LORD's
house, and the glory of the God of Israel was over them.

These were the living creatures I had seen beneath the God of Israel at 20
the river Kebar; I knew that they were cherubim. Each had four faces and 21
four wings and the semblance of human hands under their wings. Their 22
faces were like those I had seen in vision by the river Kebar;*b* they moved,
each one of them, straight forward.

A spirit*c* lifted me up and brought me to the eastern gate of the LORD's **11**
house, the gate that faces east. By the doorway were twenty-five men, and
I saw among them two of high office, Jaazaniah son of Azzur and Pelatiah
son of Benaiah. The LORD said to me, Man, it is these who are planning 2
mischief and plotting trouble in this city, saying to themselves, 'There 3
will be no building of houses yet awhile; the city is a stewpot and we are
the meat in it.' Therefore, said he, prophesy against them, prophesy, O man. 4
Then the spirit of the LORD came suddenly upon me, and he told me to 5
say, These are the words of the LORD: This is what you are saying to yourselves, you men of Israel; well do I know the thoughts that rise in your
mind. You have killed and killed in this city and heaped the streets with 6
the slain. These, therefore, are the words of the Lord GOD: The bodies 7
of the slain that you have put there, it is they that are the meat. The city
is indeed the stewpot, but I will take you out of it. It is a sword that you 8
fear, and a sword I will bring upon you, says the Lord GOD. I will take you 9
out of it; I will give you over to a foreign power; I will bring you to justice.
You too shall fall by the sword when I judge you on the frontier of Israel; 10
thus you shall know that I am the LORD. So the city will not be your 11
stewpot, nor you the meat in it. On the frontier of Israel I will judge you;
thus you shall know that I am the LORD. You have not conformed to my 12
statutes nor kept my laws, but you have followed the laws of the nations
around you.

a Prob. rdg.; Heb. adds their wheels.   b Prob. rdg.; Heb. adds and them.
c Or wind.

13   While I was prophesying, Pelatiah son of Benaiah fell dead; and I threw myself upon my face, crying aloud, 'O Lord GOD, must thou make an end of all the Israelites who are left?'

14 15   The word of the LORD came to me: Man, they are your brothers, your brothers and your kinsmen, this whole people of Israel, to whom the men who now live in Jerusalem have said, 'Keep your distance from the LORD;
16 the land has been made over to us as our property.' Say therefore, These are the words of the Lord GOD: When I sent them far away among the nations and scattered them in many lands, for a while I became their
17 sanctuary in the countries to which they had gone. Say therefore, These are the words of the Lord GOD: I will gather them from among the nations and assemble them from the countries over which I have scattered them,
18 and I will give them the soil of Israel. When they come into it, they will
19 do away with all their vile and abominable practices. I will give them a different heart and put a new spirit into them; I will take the heart of stone
20 out of their bodies and give them a heart of flesh. Then they will conform to my statutes and keep my laws. They will become my people, and I will
21 become their God. But as for those whose heart is set upon*a* their vile and abominable practices, I will make them answer for all they have done. This is the very word of the Lord GOD.

22   Then the cherubim lifted their wings, with the wheels beside them and
23 the glory of the God of Israel above them. The glory of the LORD rose up
24 and left the city, and halted on the mountain to the east of it. And a spirit *b* lifted me up and brought me to the exiles in Chaldaea. All this came in a vision sent by the spirit of God, and then the vision that I had seen left me.
25 I told the exiles all that the LORD had revealed to me.

Jerusalem's downfall certain

12 1 2   THE WORD OF THE LORD CAME TO ME: Man, you live among a rebellious people. Though they have eyes they will not see, though they
3 have ears they will not hear, because they are a rebellious people. Therefore, man, pack up what you need for a journey into exile, by day before their eyes; then set off on your journey. When you leave home and go off into exile before their eyes, it may be they will see that they are rebels.
4 Bring out your belongings, packed as for exile; do it by day, before their eyes, and then at evening, still before their eyes, leave home, as if you were
5 going into exile. Next, before their eyes, break a hole through the wall, and
6 carry your belongings out through it. When dusk falls, take your pack on your shoulder, before their eyes, and carry it out, with your face covered so that you cannot see the ground. I am making you a warning sign for the Israelites.
7   I did exactly as I had been told. By day I brought out my belongings, packed as for exile, and at evening I broke through the wall with my hands. When dusk fell, I shouldered my pack and carried it out before their eyes.

a Prob. rdg.; Heb. adds the heart of.   *b Or* wind.

Next morning, the word of the LORD came to me: Man, he said, have 8 9
not the Israelites, that rebellious people, asked you what you are doing?
Tell them that these are the words of the Lord GOD: This oracle concerns 10
the prince in Jerusalem, and all the Israelites therein.*a* Tell them that you 11
are a sign to warn them; what you have done will be done to them; they
will go into exile and captivity. Their prince will shoulder his pack in the 12
dusk and go through a hole made to let him out, with his face covered so
that he cannot be seen nor himself see the ground. But I will cast my net 13
over him, and he will be caught in the meshes. I will bring him to Babylon,
the land of the Chaldaeans, though he will not see it; and there he will die.
I will scatter his bodyguard and drive all his squadrons to the four winds; 14
I will follow them with drawn sword. Then they shall know that I am the 15
LORD, when I disperse them among the nations and scatter them through
many lands. But I will leave a few of them who will escape sword, famine, 16
and pestilence, to tell the whole story of their abominations to the peoples
among whom they go; and they shall know that I am the LORD.

And the word of the LORD came to me: Man, he said, as you eat you must 17 18
tremble, and as you drink you must shudder with dread. Say to the com- 19
mon people, These are the words of the Lord GOD about those who live in
Jerusalem and about the land of Israel: They will eat with dread and be
filled with horror as they drink; the land shall be filled with horror because
it is sated with the violence of all who live there. Inhabited cities shall be 20
deserted, and the land shall become a waste. Thus you shall know that
I am the LORD.

The word of the LORD came to me: Man, he said, what is this proverb 21 22
current in the land of Israel: 'Time runs on, visions die away'? Say to 23
them, These are the words of the Lord GOD: I have put an end to this
proverb; it shall never be heard in Israel again. Say rather to them, The
time, with all the vision means, is near. There will be no more false visions, 24
no specious divination among the Israelites, for I, the LORD, will say what 25
I will, and it shall be done. It shall be put off no longer: in your lifetime,
you rebellious people, I will speak, I will act. This is the very word of the
Lord GOD.

The word of the LORD came to me: Man, he said, the Israelites say that 26 27
the vision you now see is not to be fulfilled for many years: you are prophesying of a time far off. Say to them, These are the words of the Lord 28
GOD: No word of mine shall be delayed; even as I speak it shall be done.
This is the very word of the Lord GOD.

The LORD said to me, Man, prophesy of the prophets of Israel; prophesy, 13 1 2
and say to those who prophesy out of their own hearts, Hear what the LORD
says: These are the words of the Lord GOD: Oh, the wicked folly of the 3
prophets! Their inspiration comes from themselves; they have seen no
vision. Your prophets, Israel, have been like jackals among ruins. They have 4 5
not gone up into the breach to repair the broken wall round the Israelites,
that they may stand firm in battle on the day of the LORD. Oh, false vision 6
and lying divination! Oh, those prophets who say, 'It is the very word of
the LORD', when it is not the LORD who has sent them; yet they expect their

a therein: prob. rdg.; Heb. among them.

7   words to control the event. Is it not a false vision that you prophets have seen? Is not your divination a lie? You call it the very word of the LORD, but it is not I who have spoken.

8   These, then, are the words of the Lord GOD: Because your words are
9   false and your visions a lie, I am against you, says the Lord GOD. I will raise my hand against the prophets whose visions are false, whose divinations are a lie. They shall have no place in the counsels of my people; they shall not be entered in the roll of Israel nor set foot upon its soil. Thus
10   you shall know that I am the Lord GOD. Rightly, for they have misled my people by saying that all is well when all is not well. It is as if they were
11   building a wall and used whitewash for the daubing. Tell these daubers that it will fall; rain will pour down in torrents, and I will send hailstones
12   hard as rock streaming down and I will unleash a stormy wind. When the building falls, men will ask, 'Where is the plaster you should have used?'
13   So these are the words of the Lord GOD: In my rage I will unleash a stormy wind; rain will come in torrents in my anger, hailstones hard as rock in my
14   fury, until all is destroyed. I will demolish the building which you have daubed with whitewash and level it to the ground, so that its foundations are laid bare. It shall fall, and you shall be destroyed within it; thus you
15   shall know that I am the LORD. I will spend my rage on the building and on those who daubed it with wash; and people *a* will say, 'The building is
16   gone and the men who daubed it are gone, those prophets of Israel who prophesied to Jerusalem, who saw visions of prosperity when there was no prosperity.' This is the very word of the Lord GOD.

17   Now turn, man, to the women of your people who prophesy out of their
18   own hearts, and prophesy to them. Say to them, These are the words of the Lord GOD: I loathe you, you women who hunt men's lives by sewing magic bands upon the wrists and putting veils over the heads of persons of every age; are you to hunt the lives of my people and keep your own lives
19   safe? You have violated my sanctity before my people with handfuls of barley and scraps of bread. You bring death to those who should not die, and life to those who should not live, by lying to this people of mine who
20   listen to lies. So these are the words of the Lord GOD: I am against your magic bands with which you hunt men's lives for the excitement of it. I will tear them from your arms and set those lives at liberty, lives that you
21   hunt for the excitement of it. I will tear up your long veils and save my people from you; you shall no longer have power to hunt them. Thus you
22   shall know that I am the LORD. You discouraged the righteous man with lies, when I meant him no hurt; you so strengthened the wicked that he
23   would not abandon his evil ways and be saved; and therefore you shall never see your false visions again nor practise your divination any more. I will rescue my people from your power; and thus you shall know that I am the LORD.

14   Some of the elders of Israel came to visit me, and while they sat with me
2 3   the LORD said to me, Man, these people have set their hearts on their idols and keep their eyes fixed on the sinful things that cause their downfall.
4   Am I to let such men consult me? Speak to them and tell them that these

<hr>

a Prob. rdg.; Heb. I.

are the words of the Lord GOD: If any Israelite, with his heart set on his idols and his eyes fixed on the sinful things that cause his downfall, comes to a prophet, I, the LORD, in my own person, shall be constrained to answer him, despite his many idols. My answer will grip the hearts of the Israelites, 5 estranged from me as they are, one and all, through their idols. So tell the 6 Israelites that these are the words of the Lord GOD: Turn away, turn away from your idols; turn your backs on all your abominations. If any man, 7 Israelite or alien, renounces me, sets his heart upon idols and fixes his eyes upon the vile thing that is his downfall—if such a man comes to consult me through a prophet, I, the LORD, in my own person, shall be constrained to answer him. I will set my face against that man; I will make him an 8 example and a byword; I will rid my people of him. Thus you shall know that I am the LORD. If a prophet is seduced into making a prophecy, it is 9 I the LORD who have seduced him; I will stretch out my hand and rid my people Israel of him. Both shall be punished; the prophet and the man who 10 consults him alike are guilty. And never again will the Israelites stray from 11 their allegiance, never again defy my will and bring pollution upon themselves; they will become my people, and I will become their God. This is the very word of the Lord GOD.

These were the words of the LORD to me: Man, when a country sins by 12 13 breaking faith with me, I will stretch out my hand and cut short its daily bread. I will send famine upon it and destroy both men and cattle. Even if 14 those three men were living there, Noah, Danel*a* and Job, they would save none but themselves by their righteousness. This is the very word of the Lord GOD. If I should turn wild beasts loose in a country to destroy its 15 inhabitants, until it became a waste through which no man would pass for fear of the beasts, then, if those three men were living there, as I live, says 16 the Lord GOD, they would not save even their own sons and daughters; they would save themselves alone, and the country would become a waste. Or if I should bring the sword upon that country and command it to go 17 through the land and should destroy men and cattle, then, if those three 18 men were living there, as I live, says the Lord GOD, they could save neither son nor daughter; they would save themselves alone. Or if I should send 19 pestilence on that land and pour out my fury upon it in blood, to destroy men and cattle, then, if Noah, Danel and Job were living there, as I live, 20 says the Lord GOD, they would save neither son nor daughter; they would save themselves alone by their righteousness.

These were the words of the Lord GOD: How much less hope is there for 21 Jerusalem when I inflict on her these four punishments of mine, sword and famine, wild beasts and pestilence, to destroy both men and cattle! Some 22 will be left in her, some survivors to be brought out, both sons and daughters. Look at them as they come out to you, and see how they have behaved and what they have done. This will be some comfort to you for all the harm I have done to Jerusalem and all I have inflicted upon her. It will bring you 23 comfort when you see how they have behaved and what they have done; for you will know that it was not without reason that I dealt thus with her. This is the very word of the Lord GOD.

a Or, as otherwise read, Daniel.

15 These were the words of the LORD to me:

2   Man, how is the vine better than any other tree,
       than a branch from a tree in the forest?

3   Is wood got from it
               fit to make anything useful?
           Can men make it into a peg
           and hang things on it?

4   If it is put on the fire for fuel,
               if its two ends are burnt by the fire
               and the middle is charred,
               is it fit for anything useful?

5   Nothing useful could be made of it even when whole;
       how much less, when it is burnt by the fire and charred,
           can it be made into anything useful!

6 So these are the words of the Lord GOD:

       I treat the vine, as against forest-trees,
           only as fuel for the fire,
       even so I treat the people of Jerusalem;

7   I set my face against them.
       Though they escape from the fire, fire shall burn them up.
           Thus you shall know that I am the LORD
           when I set my face against them,

8   making the land a waste
           because they have broken faith.
           This is the very word of the Lord GOD.

16 1 2   The word of the LORD came to me: Man, he said, make Jerusalem see
3 her abominable conduct. Tell her that these are the words of the Lord GOD
   to her: Canaan is the land of your ancestry and there you were born; an
4 Amorite was your father and a Hittite your mother. This is how you were
   treated at birth: when you were born, your navel-string was not tied, you
   were not bathed in water ready for the rubbing, you were not salted as you
5 should have been nor wrapped in swaddling clothes. No one cared for
   you enough to do any of these things or, indeed, to have any pity for you;
   you were thrown out on the bare ground in your own filth on the day of
6 your birth. Then I came by and saw you kicking helplessly in your own
7 blood; I spoke to you, there in your blood, and bade you live. I tended you
   like an evergreen plant, like something growing in the fields; you throve
   and grew. You came to full womanhood; your breasts became firm and
   your hair grew, but still you were naked and exposed.

8   Again I came by and saw that you were ripe for love. I spread the skirt
   of my robe over you and covered your naked body. Then I plighted my
   troth and entered into a covenant with you, says the Lord GOD, and you
9 became mine. Then I bathed you in water and washed off the blood and
10 anointed you with oil. I gave you robes of brocade and sandals of stout
11 hide; I fastened a linen girdle round you and dressed you in lawn. For
12 jewellery I put bracelets on your arms and a chain round your neck; I gave
   you a nose-ring, I put pendants in your ears and a beautiful coronet on your

head. You had ornaments of gold and silver, your dresses were of linen,   13
lawn, and brocade. You had flour and honey and olive oil for food, and you
grew very beautiful, you grew into a queen. The fame of your beauty went   14
all over the world, for the splendour with which I decked you made it
perfect. This is the very word of the Lord GOD.

But you trusted to your beauty and prostituted your fame; you com-   15
mitted fornication, offering yourself freely to any passer-by for your
beauty to become his. You took some of your clothes and decked a platform   16
for yourself in gay colours and there you committed fornication; you had
intercourse with him for your beauty to become his.*a* You took the splen-   17
did ornaments of gold and silver which I had given you, and made for
yourself male images with which you committed fornication. You covered   18
them with your robes of brocade and offered up my oil and my incense
before them. You took the food I had given you, the flour, the oil, and the   19
honey, with which I had fed you, and set it before them as an offering of
soothing odour. This is the very word of the Lord GOD.

You took the sons and daughters whom you had borne to me, and   20
sacrificed them to these images for their food. Was this of less account than
your fornication? No! you slaughtered my children and handed them over,   21
you surrendered them to your images. With all your abominable fornica-   22
tion you forgot those early days when you lay naked and exposed, kicking
helplessly in your own blood.

After all the evil you had done (Oh! the pity of it, says the Lord GOD),   23
you built yourself a couch and constructed a high-stool in every open place. 24
You built up your high-stools at the top of every street and disgraced your   25
beauty, offering your body to any passer-by in countless acts of fornication.
You committed fornication with your gross neighbours, the Egyptians,   26
and you provoked me to anger by your countless acts of fornication.

I stretched out my hand against you and cut down your portion. Then   27
I gave you up to women who hated you, Philistine women, who were so
disgusted by your lewd ways. Not content with this, you committed   28
fornication with the Assyrians, led them into fornication and still were not
content. You committed countless acts of fornication in Chaldaea, the   29
land of commerce, and even with this you were not content.

How you anger me! says the Lord GOD. You have done all this like the   30
imperious whore you are. You have built your couch at the top of every   31
street and constructed your stool in every open place, but, unlike the common prostitute, you have scorned a fee. An adulterous wife who owes   32
obedience to her husband takes a fee from*b* strangers. The prostitute also   33
takes her fee; but you give presents to all your lovers, you bribe them to
come from all quarters to commit fornication with you. You are the very   34
opposite of other women in your fornication: no one runs after you, you
do not receive a fee, you give it. You are the very opposite.

Listen to the words of the LORD, whore that you are. These are the words 35 36
of the Lord GOD: You have been prodigal in your excesses, you have
exposed your naked body in fornication with your lovers. In return for

a you had intercourse . . . his: *prob. rdg.; Heb. obscure.*   *b* a fee from: *prob. rdg.;*
Heb. om.

your abominable idols and for the slaughter of the children you have
37 given them, I will gather all those lovers to whom you made advances,[a]
all whom you loved and all whom you hated. I will gather them in from all
quarters against you; I will strip you naked before them, and they shall
38 see your whole body naked. I will put you on trial for adultery and murder,
39 and I will charge you with[b] blood shed in jealousy and fury. Then I will
hand you over to them. They will demolish your couch and pull down
your high-stool; they will strip your clothes off, take away your splendid
40 ornaments, and leave you naked and exposed. They will bring up the mob
against you and stone you, they will hack you to pieces with their swords.
41 They will burn down your houses and execute judgement on you, and
many women shall see it. I will put an end to your fornication, and you
42 shall never again give a fee to your lovers. Then I will abate my fury, and
my jealousy will turn away from you. I will be calm and will no longer be
43 provoked to anger. For you had forgotten the days of your youth and
exasperated me with all your doings: so I in my turn brought retribution
upon you for your deeds. This is the very word of the Lord GOD.

Did you not commit these obscenities, as well as all your other abomina-
44 tions? Dealers in proverbs will say of you, 'Like mother, like daughter.'
45 You are a true daughter of a mother who loathed her husband and children.
You are a true sister of your sisters who loathed their husbands and children. You are all daughters of a Hittite mother and an Amorite father.
46 Your elder sister was Samaria, who lived with her daughters to the north
of you; your younger sister, who lived with her daughters to the south of
47 you, was Sodom. Did you not behave as they did and commit the same
48 abominations? You came very near to doing even worse than they. As I
live, says the Lord GOD, your sister Sodom and her daughters never be-
49 haved as you and your daughters have done. This was the iniquity of your
sister Sodom: she and her daughters had pride of wealth and food in
plenty, comfort and ease, and yet she never helped the poor and wretched.
50 They grew haughty and did deeds abominable in my sight, and I made
51 away with them, as you have seen. Samaria was never half the sinner you
have been; you have committed more abominations than she, abominations
52 which have made your sister seem innocent. You must bear the humiliation which you thought your sisters deserved. Your sins are so much more
abominable than theirs that they appear innocent in comparison with you;
and now you must bear your shame and humiliation and make your sisters
seem innocent.

53 But I will restore the fortunes of Sodom and her daughters and of
54 Samaria and her daughters, and I will restore yours at the same time. Even
though you bring them comfort, you will bear your shame, you will be
55 disgraced for all you have done; but when your sister Sodom and her
daughters become what they were of old, and when your sister Samaria
and her daughters become what they were of old, then you and your
56 daughters will be restored. Did you not hear and talk much of your sister
57 Sodom in the days of your pride, before your wickedness was exposed, in

[a] to whom . . . advances: or whom you charmed.   [b] charge you with: prob.
mng.; Heb. give you.

the days when the daughters of Aram with those about her were disgraced,
and the daughters of the Philistines round about, who so despised you?
Now you too must bear the consequences of your lewd and abominable 58
conduct. This is the very word of the LORD.

These are the words of the Lord GOD: I will treat you as you have 59
deserved, because you violated a covenant and made light of a solemn oath.
But I will remember the covenant I made with you when you were young, 60
and I will establish with you a covenant which shall last for ever. And you 61
will remember your past ways and feel ashamed when you receive your
sisters, the elder and the younger. For I will give them to you as daughters,
and they shall not be outside your covenant.*a* Thus I will establish my 62
covenant with you, and you shall know that I am the LORD. You will 63
remember, and will be so ashamed and humiliated that you will never
open your mouth again once I have accepted expiation for all you have
done. This is the very word of the Lord GOD.

These were the words of the LORD to me: Man, speak to the Israelites 17 1 2
in allegory and parable. Tell them that these are the words of the Lord 3
GOD:

> A great eagle
> with broad wings and long pinions,
> in full plumage, richly patterned,
>   came to Lebanon.
>   He took the very top of a cedar-tree,
>   he plucked its highest twig;   4
>   he carried it off to a land of commerce,
>   and planted it in a city of merchants.
>   Then he took a native seed   5
>   and put it in nursery-ground;
>   he set it like a willow,
>   a shoot beside abundant water.
>   It sprouted and became a vine,   6
>   sprawling low along the ground
>   and bending its trailing boughs towards him*b*
>   with its roots growing beneath him.
> So it became a vine, it branched out
>   and put forth shoots.
> But there was another great eagle   7
> with broad wings and thick plumage;
> and this vine gave its roots
>   a twist towards him;*b*
>   it pushed out its trailing boughs towards him,
> seeking drink from the bed where it was planted,
>   though it had been set   8
> in good ground beside abundant water
> that it might bear shoots and be fruitful
>   and become a noble vine.

---

a and they . . . covenant: *or* though not on the ground of your covenant.   *b* *Or* inwards.

9   Tell them that these are the words of the Lord GOD:

> Can such a vine flourish?
> Will not its roots be broken off
>   and its fruit be stripped,
> and all its fresh sprouting leaves wither,
> until it is uprooted and carried away
>   with little effort and few hands?

10
> If it is transplanted, can it flourish?
> Will it not be utterly shrivelled,
>   as though by the touch of the east wind,
>   on the bed where it ought to sprout?

11 12   These were the words of the LORD to me: Say to that rebellious people, Do you not know what this means? The king of Babylon came to Jerusalem, took its king and its officers and had them brought to him at Bab-
13   ylon. He took a prince of the royal line and made a treaty with him, putting
14   him on his oath. He took away the chief men of the country, so that it should become a humble kingdom unable to raise itself but ready to
15   observe the treaty and keep it in force. But the prince rebelled against him and sent messengers to Egypt, asking for horses and men in plenty. Can such a man prosper? Can he escape destruction if he acts in this way? Can
16   he violate a covenant and escape? As I live, says the Lord GOD, I swear that he shall die in the land of the king who put him on the throne; he made light of his oath and violated the covenant he made with him. He shall die
17   in Babylon. Pharaoh will send no large army, no great host, to protect him in battle; no siege-ramp will be raised, no watch-tower put up, nor will
18   the lives of many men be lost. He has violated a covenant and has made light of his oath. He had submitted, and yet he did all these things; he shall not escape.

19   These then are the words of the Lord GOD: As I live, he has made light of the oath he took by me and has violated the covenant I made with him. I will
20   bring retribution upon him; I will cast my net over him, and he shall be caught in its meshes. I will carry him to Babylon and bring him to judge-
21   ment there, because he has broken faith with me. In all his squadrons every commander shall fall by the sword; those who are left will be scattered to the four winds. Thus you shall know that it is I, the LORD, who have spoken.

22   These are the words of the Lord GOD:

> I, too, will take a slip
>   from the lofty crown of the cedar
>   and set it in the soil;
> I will pluck a tender shoot from the topmost branch
>   and plant it.

23
> I will plant it high on a lofty mountain,
>   the highest mountain in Israel.
> It will put out branches, bear its fruit,
>   and become a noble cedar.
> Winged birds of every kind will roost under it,
>   they will roost in the shelter of its sweeping boughs.

All the trees of the country-side will know   24
    that it is I, the LORD,
who bring low the tall tree
and raise the low tree high,
who dry up the green tree
and make the dry tree put forth buds.
I, the LORD, have spoken and will do it.

THESE WERE THE WORDS OF THE LORD TO ME: What do you all mean **18** 1 2
by repeating this proverb in the land of Israel:

    'The fathers have eaten sour grapes,
      and the children's teeth are set on edge'?

As I live, says the Lord GOD, this proverb shall never again be used in 3
Israel. Every living soul belongs to me; father and son alike are mine. The 4
soul that sins shall die.

Consider the man who is righteous and does what is just and right. He 5 6
never feasts at mountain-shrines, never lifts his eyes to the idols of Israel,
never dishonours another man's wife, never approaches a woman during
her periods. He oppresses no man, he returns the debtor's pledge, he never 7
robs. He gives bread to the hungry and clothes to those who have none.
He never lends either at discount or at interest. He shuns injustice 8
and deals fairly between man and man. He conforms to my statutes and 9
loyally observes my laws. Such a man is righteous: he shall live, says the
Lord GOD.

He may have a son who is a man of violence and a cut-throat who turns 10
his back on these rules.[a] He obeys none of them, he feasts at mountain- 11
shrines, he dishonours another man's wife, he oppresses the unfortunate 12
and the poor, he is a robber, he does not return the debtor's pledge,
he lifts his eyes to idols and joins in abominable rites; he lends both at 13
discount and at interest. Such a man shall not live. Because he has committed all these abominations he shall die, and his blood will be on his
own head.

This man in turn may have a son who sees all his father's sins; he sees, 14
but he commits none of them. He never feasts at mountain-shrines, never 15
lifts his eyes to the idols of Israel, never dishonours another man's wife.
He oppresses no man, takes no pledge, does not rob. He gives bread to the 16
hungry and clothes to those who have none. He shuns injustice, he never 17
lends either at discount or at interest. He keeps my laws and conforms
to my statutes. Such a man shall not die for his father's wrongdoing; he
shall live.

His father may have been guilty of oppression and robbery and may have 18
lived an evil life among his kinsfolk, and so has died because of his iniquity.
You may ask, 'Why is the son not punished for his father's iniquity?' 19
Because he has always done what is just and right and has been careful
to obey all my laws, therefore he shall live. It is the soul that sins, and no 20
other, that shall die; a son shall not share a father's guilt, nor a father his

    [a] who turns ... rules: *prob. rdg.; Heb. unintelligible.*

son's. The righteous man shall reap the fruit of his own righteousness, and the wicked man the fruit of his own wickedness.

21   It may be that a wicked man gives up his sinful ways and keeps all my laws, doing what is just and right. That man shall live; he shall not die.
22 None of the offences he has committed shall be remembered against him;
23 he shall live because of his righteous deeds. Have I any desire, says the Lord GOD, for the death of a wicked man? Would I not rather that he should mend his ways and live?

24   It may be that a righteous man turns back from his righteous ways and commits every kind of abomination that the wicked practise; shall he do this and live? No, none of his former righteousness will be remembered in
25 his favour; he has broken his faith, he has sinned, and he shall die. You say that the Lord acts without principle? Listen, you Israelites, it is you who
26 act without principle, not I. If a righteous man turns from his righteousness, takes to evil ways and dies,*a* it is because of these evil ways that he dies.
27 Again, if a wicked man turns from his wicked ways and does what is just
28 and right, he will save his life. If he sees his offences as they are and turns his back on them all, then he shall live; he shall not die.

29   'The Lord acts without principle', say the Israelites. No, Israelites, it
30 is you who act without principle, not I. Therefore, Israelites, says the Lord GOD, I will judge every man of you on his deeds. Turn, turn from
31 your offences, or your iniquity will be your downfall. Throw off the load of your past misdeeds; get yourselves a new heart and a new spirit. Why
32 should you die, you men of Israel? I have no desire for any man's death. This is the very word of the Lord GOD.

19 1 2   Raise a lament over the princes of Israel and say:

> Your mother was a lioness
>   among the lions!
> She made her lair among the young lions
>   and many were the cubs she bore.

3
> One of her cubs she raised,
>   and he grew into a young lion.
> He learnt to tear his prey,
>   he devoured men.

4
> Then the nations shouted at*b* him
>   and he was caught in their pit,
> and they dragged him with hooks to the land of Egypt.

5
> His case, she saw, was desperate, her hope was lost;
>   so she took another of her cubs
>   and made him a young lion.

6
> He prowled among the lions
>   and acted like a young lion.
> He learnt to tear his prey,
>   he devoured men;

7
> he broke down their palaces, laid their cities in ruins.

---

a *Prob. rdg.; Heb. adds* because of them.
b shouted at: *or* heard a report about.

The land and all that was in it
was aghast at the noise of his roaring.
From the provinces all round   8
the nations raised the hue and cry;
they cast their net over him
and he was caught in their pit.
With hooks they drew him into a cage   9
and brought him to the king of Babylon,
who flung him into prison,
that his voice might never again be heard
on the mountains of Israel.

Your mother was a vine in a vineyard*a*   10
planted by the waterside.
It grew fruitful and luxuriant,
for there was water in plenty.
It had stout branches,   11
fit to make sceptres for those who bear rule.
It grew tall, finding its way through the foliage,
and conspicuous for its height and many trailing boughs.
But it was torn up in anger and thrown to the ground;   12
the east wind blighted it,
its fruit was blown off,
its strong branches were blighted,
and fire burnt it.
Now it is replanted in the wilderness,   13
in a dry and thirsty land;
and fire bursts forth from its own branches   14
and burns up its shoots.*b*
It has no strong branch any more
to make a sceptre for those who bear rule.

This is the lament and as a lament it passed into use.

ON THE TENTH DAY OF THE FIFTH MONTH in the seventh year, some   **20**
of the elders of Israel came to consult the LORD and were sitting with me.
Then this word came to me from the LORD: Man, say to the elders of   2 3
Israel, This is the word of the Lord GOD: Do you come to consult me? As
I live, I will not be consulted by you. This is the very word of the Lord GOD.
Will you judge them? Will you judge them, O man? Then tell them of   4
the abominations of their forefathers and say to them, These are the words 5
of the Lord GOD: When I chose Israel, with uplifted hand I bound myself
by oath to the race of Jacob and revealed myself to them in Egypt; I lifted
up my hand and declared: I am the LORD your God. On that day I swore   6
with hand uplifted that I would bring them out of Egypt into the land I
had sought out for them, a land flowing with milk and honey, fairest of all
lands. I told them, every one, to cast away the loathsome things on which 7

a in a vineyard: *prob. rdg.; Heb. obscure in context.*   *b* *Prob. rdg.; Heb. adds* its fruit.

they feasted their eyes and not to defile themselves with the idols of Egypt. I am the LORD your God, I said.

8 But they rebelled against me, they refused to listen to me, and not one of them cast away the loathsome things on which he feasted his eyes or forsook the idols of Egypt. I had thought to pour out my wrath and exhaust

9 my anger on them in Egypt. I acted for the honour of my name, that it might not be profaned in the sight of the nations among whom Israel was

10 living: I revealed myself to them by bringing Israel out of Egypt. I brought

11 them out of Egypt and led them into the wilderness. There I gave my statutes to them and taught them my laws, so that by keeping them men

12 might have life. Further, I gave them my sabbaths as a sign between us, so that they should know that I, the LORD, was hallowing them for myself.

13 But the Israelites rebelled against me in the wilderness; they did not conform to my statutes, they rejected my laws, though by keeping them men might have life, and they utterly desecrated my sabbaths. So again I thought to pour out my wrath on them in the wilderness to destroy them.

14 I acted for the honour of my name, that it might not be profaned in the sight of the nations who had seen me bring them out.

15 Further, I swore to them in the wilderness with uplifted hand that I would not bring them into the land I had given them, that land flowing

16 with milk and honey, fairest of all lands. For they had rejected my laws, they would not conform to my statutes and they desecrated my sabbaths,

17 because they loved to follow idols of their own. Yet I pitied them too much

18 to destroy them and did not make an end of them in the wilderness. I commanded their sons in the wilderness not to conform to their fathers' statutes, nor observe their laws, nor defile themselves with their idols.

19 I said, I am the LORD your God, you must conform to my statutes; you

20 must observe my laws and act according to them. You must keep my sabbaths holy, and they will become a sign between us; so you will know that I am the LORD your God.

21 But the sons too rebelled against me. They did not conform to my statutes or observe my laws, though any who had done so would have had life through them, and they desecrated my sabbaths. Again I thought to pour out my wrath and exhaust my anger on them in the wilderness.

22 I acted for the honour of my name, that it might not be profaned in the

23 sight of the nations who had seen me bring them out. Yes, and in the wilderness I swore to them with uplifted hand that I would disperse them

24 among the nations and scatter them abroad, because they had disobeyed my laws, rejected my statutes, desecrated my sabbaths, and turned longing

25 eyes toward the idols of their forefathers. I did more; I imposed on them statutes that were not good statutes, and laws by which they could not win

26 life. I let them defile themselves with gifts to idols; I made them surrender their eldest sons to them so that I might fill them with horror. Thus they would know that I am the LORD.

27 Speak then, O man, to the Israelites and say to them, These are the words of the Lord GOD: Once again your forefathers insulted me and broke faith

28 with me: when I brought them into the land which I had sworn with uplifted hand to give them, they marked down every hill-top and every

leafy tree, and there they offered their sacrifices, they made the gifts which roused my anger, they set out their offerings of soothing odour and poured out their drink-offerings. I asked them, What is this hill-shrine to which 29 you are going up? And 'hill-shrine' has been its name ever since.

So tell the Israelites, These are the words of the Lord GOD: Are you 30 defiling yourselves as your forefathers did? Are you wantonly giving yourselves to their loathsome gods? When you bring your gifts, when you 31 pass your sons through the fire, you are still defiling yourselves in the service of your crowd of idols. How can I let you consult me, men of Israel? As I live, says the Lord GOD, I will not be consulted by you. When you 32 say to yourselves, 'Let us become like the nations and tribes of other lands and worship wood and stone', you are thinking of something that can never be. As I live, says the Lord GOD, I will reign over you with a strong 33 hand, with arm outstretched and wrath outpoured. I will bring you out 34 from the peoples and gather you from the lands over which you have been scattered by my strong hand, my outstretched arm and outpoured wrath. I will bring you into the wilderness of the peoples; there will I confront 35 you, and there will I state my case against you. Even as I did in the wilder- 36 ness of Egypt against your forefathers, so will I state my case against you. This is the very word of the Lord GOD.

I will pass you under the rod and bring you within the bond*a* of the 37 covenant. I will rid you of those who revolt and rebel against me. I will 38 take them out of the land where they are now living, but they shall not set foot on the soil of Israel. Thus shall you know that I am the LORD.

Now, men of Israel, these are the words of the Lord GOD: Go, sweep 39 away your idols, every man of you. So in days to come you will never be disobedient to me or desecrate my holy name with your gifts and your idolatries. But on my holy hill, the lofty hill of Israel, says the Lord GOD, 40 there shall the Israelites serve me in the land, every one of them. There will I receive them with favour; there will I demand your contribution and the best of your offerings, with all your consecrated gifts. I will receive 41 your offerings of soothing odour, when I have brought you out from the peoples and gathered you from the lands where you have been scattered. I, and only I, will have your worship, for all the nations to see.

You will know that I am the LORD, when I bring you home to the soil 42 of Israel, to the land which I swore with uplifted hand to give your fore-fathers. There you will remember your past ways and all the wanton deeds 43 with which you have defiled yourselves, and will loathe yourselves for all the evils you have done. You will know that I am the LORD, when I have 44 dealt with you, O men of Israel, not as your wicked ways and your vicious deeds deserve but for the honour of my name. This is the very word of the Lord GOD.

These were the words of the LORD to me: Man, turn and face towards 45 46 Teman*b* and pour out your words to the south; prophesy to the rough country of the Negeb. Say to it, Listen to the words of the LORD. These are 47 the words of the Lord GOD: I will set fire to you, and the fire will consume all the wood, green and dry alike. Its fiery flame shall not be put out, but

a Or muster.   *b Or* face southward.

1027

48 from the Negeb northwards every face will be scorched by it. All men will
see that it is I, the LORD, who have set it ablaze; it shall not be put out.
49 'Ah no! O Lord GOD,' I cried; 'they say of me, "He deals only in parables."'

21 1 2   These were the words of the LORD to me: Man, turn and face towards
Jerusalem, and pour out your words against her sanctuary;*a* prophesy
3 against the land of Israel. Say to the land of Israel, These are the words of
the LORD: I am against you; I will draw my sword from the scabbard and
4 cut off from you both righteous and wicked. It is because I would cut off
your righteous and your wicked equally that my sword will be drawn from
5 the scabbard against all men, from the Negeb northwards. All men shall
know that I the LORD have drawn my sword; it shall never again be sheathed.
6 Groan in their presence, man, groan bitterly until your lungs are bursting.
7 When they ask you why you are groaning, say to them, 'I groan at the thing
I have heard; when it comes, all hearts melt, all courage fails, all hands fall
limp, all men's knees run with urine. It is coming. It is here.' This is the
very word of the Lord GOD.

8 9   These were the words of the LORD to me: Prophesy, man, and say, This
is the word of the Lord:

> A sword, a sword is sharpened and burnished,
10 > sharpened to kill and kill again,
> burnished to flash*b* like lightning.
> Ah! the club is brandished, my son,
> to defy all wooden idols!
11 > The sword is given to be burnished
> ready for the hand to grasp.
> The sword—it is sharpened,
> it is burnished,
> ready to be put into the slayer's hand.

12 Cry, man, and howl; for all this falls on my people, it falls on Israel's
princes who are delivered over to the sword and are slain with my people.
13 Therefore beat your breast in remorse, for it is the test—and what if it is
not in truth the club of defiance? This is the very word of the Lord GOD.

14 > But you, man, prophesy and clap your hands together;
> swing the sword twice, thrice:
> it is the sword of slaughter,
> the great sword of slaughter whirling about them.
15 > That their hearts may be troubled and many stumble and fall,
> I have set the threat of the sword at all their gates,
> the threat of the sword*c* made to flash like lightning
> and drawn to kill.
16 > Be sharpened, turn right; be unsheathed, turn left,
> wherever your point is aimed.

17 I, too, will clap my hands together and abate my anger. I, the LORD, have
spoken.

---

a her sanctuary: *prob. rdg.; Heb.* sanctuaries.   *b* to flash: *prob. rdg.; Heb.*
unintelligible.   *c* the threat of the sword: *prob. rdg.; Heb. obscure in context.*

These were the words of the LORD to me: Man, trace out two roads by 18 19
which the sword of the king of Babylon may come, starting both of them
from the same land. Then carve a signpost, carve it at the point where the
highway forks. Mark out a road for the sword to come to the Ammonite 20
city of Rabbah, to Judah, and to Jerusalem at the heart of it. For the king 21
of Babylon halts to take the omens at the parting of the ways, where the
road divides. He casts lots with arrows, consults teraphim*a* and inspects
the livers of beasts. The augur's arrow marked 'Jerusalem' falls at his right 22
hand: here, then,*b* he must raise a shout and sound the battle-cry, set
battering-rams against the gates, pile siege-ramps and build watch-towers.
It may well seem to the people that the auguries are false, whereas they 23
will put me in mind of their wrongdoing, and they will fall into the enemies'
hand. These therefore are the words of the Lord GOD: Because you have 24
kept me mindful of your wrongdoing by your open rebellion, and your
sins have been revealed in all your acts, because you have kept yourselves
in my mind, you will fall into the enemies' hand by force.

You, too, you impious and wicked prince of Israel, your fate has come 25
upon you in the hour of final punishment. These are the words of the Lord 26
GOD: Put off your diadem, lay aside your crown. All is changed; raise the
low and bring down the high. Ruin! Ruin! I will bring about such ruin as 27
never was before, until the rightful sovereign comes. Then I will give
him all.

Man, prophesy and say, These are the words of the Lord GOD to the 28
Ammonites and to their shameful god:

A sword, a sword drawn for slaughter,
burnished for destruction,*c*
to flash like lightning!
Your visions are false, your auguries a lie, 29
which bid you bring it*d* down
upon the necks of impious and wicked men,
whose fate has come upon them
in the hour of final punishment.
Sheathe it again. 30
I will judge you in the place where you were born,
the land of your origin.
I will pour out my rage upon you; 31
I will breathe out my blazing wrath over you.
I will hand you over to brutal men,
skilled in destruction.
You shall become fuel for fire, 32
your blood shall be shed within the land
and you shall leave no memory behind.
For I, the LORD, have spoken.

These were the words of the LORD to me: Man, will you judge her, will 22 1 2
you judge the murderous city and bring home to her all her abominable

a Or household gods.   *b Prob. rdg.; Heb. adds* he must set battering-rams.
c for destruction: *prob. rdg.; Heb. obscure.*   *d Prob. rdg.; Heb.* you.

3 deeds? Say to her, These are the words of the Lord GOD: Alas for the city that sheds blood within her walls and brings her fate upon herself, the city
4 that makes herself idols and is defiled thereby! The guilt is yours for the blood you have shed, the pollution is on you for the idols you have made. You have shortened your days by this and brought the end of your years nearer. This is why I exposed you to the contempt of the nations and the
5 mockery of every country. Lands far and near will taunt you with your
6 infamy and gross disorder. In you the princes of Israel, one and all, have
7 used their power to shed blood; men have treated their fathers and mothers with contempt, they have oppressed the alien and ill-treated the orphan
8 and the widow. You have disdained what is sacred to me and desecrated
9 my sabbaths. In you, Jerusalem, informers have worked to procure bloodshed; in you are men who have feasted at mountain-shrines and have
10 committed lewdness. In you men have exposed their fathers' nakedness;
11 they have violated women during their periods; they have committed an outrage with their neighbours' wives and have lewdly defiled their daughters-in-law; they have ravished their sisters, their own fathers'
12 daughters. In you men have accepted bribes to shed blood, and they have exacted discount and interest on their loans. You have oppressed your fellows for gain, and you have forgotten me. This is the very word of the Lord GOD.

13 See, I strike with my clenched fist in anger at your ill-gotten gains and
14 at the bloodshed within your walls. Will your strength or courage stand
15 when I deal with you? I, the LORD, have spoken and I will act. I will disperse you among the nations and scatter you abroad; thus will I rid you
16 altogether of your defilement. I will sift you*a* in the sight of the nations, and you will know that I am the LORD.

17 18 These were the words of the LORD to me: Man, to me all Israelites are
19 an alloy, their silver alloyed with copper, tin, iron, and lead.*b* Therefore, these are the words of the Lord GOD: Because you have all become alloyed,
20 I will gather you together into Jerusalem, as a mass of silver, copper, iron, lead, and tin is gathered into a crucible for the fire to be blown to full heat to melt them. So will I gather you in my anger and wrath, set you there and
21 melt you; I will collect you and blow up the fire of my anger until you are
22 melted within it. You will be melted as silver is melted in a crucible, and you will know that I, the LORD, have poured out my anger upon you.

23 24 These were the words of the LORD to me: Man, say to Jerusalem, You are like a land on which no rain has fallen; no shower has come down upon
25 you*c* in the days of indignation. The princes within her are like lions growling as they tear their prey. They have devoured men, and seized their treasure and all their wealth; they have widowed many women within her
26 walls. Her priests have done violence to my law*d* and profaned what is sacred to me. They make no distinction between sacred and common, and lead men to see no difference between clean and unclean. They have dis-
27 regarded my sabbaths, and I am dishonoured among them. Her officers

---

a I will sift you: *or* You will be profaned.   *b* their silver . . . lead: *prob. rdg.*; Heb. copper, tin, iron, and lead inside a crucible; they are an alloy, silver.   *c* *Prob. rdg.*; Heb. it.   *d* *Or* instruction.

within her are like wolves tearing their prey, shedding blood and destroying men's lives to acquire ill-gotten gain. Her prophets use whitewash 28
instead of plaster;[a] their vision is false and their divination a lie. They say,
'This is the word of the Lord GOD', when the LORD has not spoken. The 29
common people are bullies and robbers; they ill-treat the unfortunate
and the poor, they are unjust and cruel to the alien. I looked for a man among 30
them who could build up a barricade, who could stand before me in the
breach to defend the land from ruin; but I found no such man. I poured 31
out my indignation upon them and utterly destroyed them in the fire of my
wrath. Thus I brought on them the punishment they had deserved. This
is the very word of the Lord GOD.

The word of the LORD came to me: Man, he said, there were once two 23 12
women, daughters of the same mother. They played the whore in Egypt, 3
played the whore while they were still girls; for there they let their breasts
be fondled and their virgin bosoms pressed. The elder was named Oholah, 4
her sister Oholibah. They became mine and bore me sons and daughters.
'Oholah' is Samaria, 'Oholibah' Jerusalem. While she owed me obedience 5
Oholah played the whore and was infatuated with her Assyrian lovers,
staff officers in blue,[b] viceroys and governors, handsome young cavaliers 6
all of them, riding on horseback. She played the whore with all of them, 7
the flower of the Assyrian youth; and she let herself be defiled with all their
idols, wherever her lust led her. She never gave up the whorish ways she 8
had learnt in Egypt, where men had lain with her when young, had pressed
her virgin bosom and overwhelmed her with their fornication. So I 9
abandoned her to her lovers, the Assyrians, with whom she was infatuated.
They ravished her, they took her sons and daughters, and they killed her 10
with the sword. She became a byword among women, and judgement was
passed upon her.

Oholibah, her sister, had watched her, and she gave herself up to lust 11
and played the whore worse than her sister. She, too, was infatuated with 12
Assyrians, viceroys, governors and staff officers, all handsome young
cavaliers, in full dress, riding on horseback. I found that she too had let 13
herself be defiled; both had gone the same way; but she carried her fornica- 14
tion to greater lengths: she saw male figures carved on the wall, sculptured
forms of Chaldaeans, picked out in vermilion. Belts were round their 15
waists, and on their heads turbans with dangling ends. All seemed to be
high officers and looked like Babylonians, natives of Chaldaea. As she 16
looked she was infatuated with them, so she sent messengers to Chaldaea
for them. And the Babylonians came to her to share her bed, and defiled her 17
with fornication; she was defiled by them until she was filled with revulsion. She made no secret that she was a whore but let herself be ravished 18
until I was filled with revulsion against her as I was against her sister. She 19
played the whore again and again, remembering how in her youth she had
played the whore in Egypt. She was infatuated with their male prostitutes, 20
whose members were like those of asses and whose seed came in floods like
that of horses. So, Oholibah, you relived the lewdness of your girlhood in 21
Egypt when you let your bosom be pressed and your breasts fondled.[c]

[a] Cp. 13. 8–16.　　　[b] Or violet.　　　[c] fondled: *prob. rdg.*; *Heb. unintelligible.*

22 Therefore these are the words of the Lord God: I will rouse them against you, Oholibah, those lovers of yours who have filled you with revulsion,

23 and bring them upon you from every side, the Babylonians and all those Chaldaeans, men of Pekod, Shoa, and Koa, and all the Assyrians with them. Handsome young men they are, viceroys and governors, commanders and

24 staff officers,[a] riding on horseback. They will come against you with war-horses, with chariots and wagons, with a host drawn from the nations, armed with shield, buckler, and helmet; they will beset you on every side. I will give them authority to judge, and they will use that authority to judge

25 you. I will turn my jealous wrath loose on you, and they will make you feel their fury. They will cut off your nose and your ears, and in the end you[b]

26 will fall by the sword.[c] They will strip you of your clothes and take away

27 all your finery. So I will put a stop to your lewdness and the way in which you learnt to play the whore in Egypt. You will never cast longing eyes on such things again, never remember Egypt any more.

28 These are the words of the Lord God: I am handing you over to those

29 whom you hate, those who have filled you with revulsion; and they will make you feel their hatred. They will take all you have earned and leave you naked and exposed; that body with which you have played the whore

30 will be ravished. It is your lewdness and your fornication that have brought this upon you, it is because you have followed alien peoples and played

31 the whore and have allowed yourself to be defiled with their idols. You have followed in your sister's footsteps, and I will put her cup into your hand.

32 These are the words of the Lord God:

> You shall drink from your sister's cup,
>   a cup deep and wide,
> charged with mockery and scorn,
>   more than ever cup can hold.

33 It[d] will be full of drunkenness and grief,
>   a cup of ruin and desolation,
> the cup of your sister Samaria;

34 and you shall drink it to the dregs.
>   Then you will chew[e] it in pieces
>   and tear out your breasts.
> This is my verdict, says the Lord God.

35 Therefore, these are the words of the Lord God: Because you have forgotten me and flung me behind your back, you must bear the guilt of your lewdness and your fornication.

36 The Lord said to me, Man, will you judge Oholah and Oholibah? Then

37 tax them with their vile offences. They have committed adultery, and there is blood on their hands. They have committed adultery with their idols and offered my children to them for food, the children they had borne

38 me. This too they have done to me: they have polluted my sanctuary and

---

[a] staff officers: *prob. rdg., cp. verses 5 and 12;* Heb. obscure.   [b] in the end you: *or* your successors.   [c] *Prob. rdg.;* Heb. *adds* They will take your sons and daughters, and in the end you will be burnt.   [d] *Prob. rdg.;* Heb. You.   [e] *Or* dash.

desecrated my sabbaths. They came into my sanctuary and desecrated it 39
by slaughtering their sons as an offering to their idols; this they did in my
own house. They would send for men from a far-off country; and the men 40
came at the messenger's bidding. You bathed your body for these men, you
painted your eyes, decked yourself in your finery, you sat yourself upon a 41
bed of state and had a table put ready before it and laid my own incense
and my own oil on it. Loud were the voices of the light-hearted crowd; 42
and besides ordinary folk Sabaeans were there, brought from the wilderness; they put bracelets on the women's hands and beautiful garlands on
their heads. I thought: Ah that woman, grown old in adultery! Now they 43
will commit fornication with her—with her of all women! They resorted to 44
her as a prostitute; they resorted to Oholah and Oholibah, those lewd
women. Upright men will condemn them for their adultery and blood- 45
shed; for adulterous they are, and blood is on their hands.

These are the words of the Lord GOD: Summon the invading host; 46
abandon them to terror and rapine. Let the host stone them and hack them 47
to pieces with their swords, kill their sons and daughters and burn down
their houses. Thus I will put an end to lewdness in the land, and other 48
women shall be taught not to be as lewd as they. You shall pay the penalty 49
for your lewd conduct and be punished for your idolatries, and you will
know that I am the Lord GOD.

These were the words of the LORD, spoken to me on the tenth day of the **24**
tenth month in the ninth year: Man, write down a name for this day, this 2
very day: This is the day the king of Babylon invested Jerusalem. Sing a 3
song of derision to this people of rebels; say to them, These are the words
of the Lord GOD:

> Set a cauldron on the fire,
>> set it on and pour water into it.
> Into it collect the pieces, 4
>> all the choice pieces,
> cram it with leg and shoulder and the best of the bones;
>> take the best of the flock. 5
> Pack the logs*a* round it underneath;
>> seethe the stew
> and boil the bones in it.
>
> O city running with blood, 6
> O pot green with corrosion,
>> corrosion that will never be clean!

Therefore these are the words of the Lord GOD:

> Empty it, piece after piece,
>> though no lot is cast for any of them.
> The city had blood in her midst 7
>> and she poured it out on the gleaming rock,
> not on the ground: she did not pour it there
>> for the dust to cover it.

a Prob. rdg., cp. verse 10; Heb. bones.

8   But I too have spilt blood on the gleaming white rock
            so that it cannot be covered,
     to make anger flare up and to call down vengeance.

9 Therefore these are the words of the Lord GOD:

        O city running with blood,
        I too will make a great fire-pit.

10   Fill it with logs, light the fire;
        make an end of the meat,
     pour out all the broth*a* and the bones with it.*b*

11   Then set the pot empty on the coals
     so that its copper may be heated red-hot,
        and then the impurities in it may be melted
          and its corrosion burnt off.

12   Try as you may,*c*
     the corrosion is so deep that it will not come off;
        only fire will rid it of corrosion for you.

13   Even so, when I cleansed you in your filthy lewdness,
        you did not become clean from it,
          and therefore you shall never again be clean
        until I have satisfied my anger against you.

14   I, the LORD, have spoken; the time is coming, I will act. I will not refrain nor pity nor relent; I will judge you for your conduct and for all that you have done. This is the very word of the Lord GOD.

15 16   These were the words of the LORD to me: Man, I am taking from you at one blow the dearest thing you have, but you must not wail or weep
17 or give way to tears. Keep in good heart; be quiet, and make no mourning for the dead; cover your head as usual and put sandals on your feet. You shall not cover your upper lip in mourning nor eat the bread of despair.

18   I spoke to the people in the morning; and that very evening my wife
19 died. Next morning I did as I was told. The people asked me to say what
20 meaning my behaviour had for them. I answered, These were the words
21 of the LORD to me: Tell the Israelites, This is the word of the Lord GOD: I will desecrate my sanctuary, which has been the pride of your strength, the delight of your eyes and your heart's desire; and the sons and daughters
22 whom you have left behind shall fall by the sword. But, I said, you shall do as I have done: you shall not cover your upper lip in mourning nor eat
23 the bread of despair. You shall cover your head and put sandals on your feet; you shall not wail nor weep. Because of your wickedness you will
24 pine away and will lament to*d* one another. The LORD says, Ezekiel will be a sign to warn you, and when it happens you will do as he has done, and you will know that I am the Lord GOD.

25   And now, man, a word for you: I am taking from them that fortress whose beauty so gladdened them, the delight of their eyes, their heart's
26 desire; I am taking their sons and their daughters. Soon fugitives will come

---

a pour . . . broth: *prob. rdg.; Heb.* mix ointment.   *b* with it: *prob. rdg.; Heb.* will be scorched.   *c* Try as you may: *prob. rdg.; Heb. obscure.*   *d* Or for.

and tell you their news by word of mouth. At once you will recover the 27
power of speech and speak with the fugitives; you will no longer be
dumb. So will you be a portent to them, and they shall know that I am
the LORD.

Prophecies against foreign nations

THESE WERE THE WORDS OF THE LORD TO ME: Man, look towards 25 1 2
the Ammonites and prophesy against them. Say to the Ammonites, 3
Listen to the word of the Lord GOD. These are his words: Because you
cried 'Aha!' when you saw my holy place desecrated, the soil of Israel laid
waste and the people of Judah sent into exile, I will hand you over as a 4
possession to the tribes of the east. They shall pitch their camps and put
up their dwellings among you; they shall eat your crops; they shall drink
your milk. I will make Rabbah a camel-pasture and Ammon a sheep-walk. 5
Thus you shall know that I am the LORD. These are the words of the Lord 6
GOD: Because you clapped your hands and stamped your feet, and exulted
over the land of Israel with single-minded scorn, I will stretch out my hand 7
over you and make you the prey of the nations and cut you off from all
other peoples; in every land I will exterminate you and bring you to utter
ruin. Thus you shall know that I am the LORD.

These are the words of the Lord GOD: Because Moab said, 'Judah is 8
like all the rest', I will expose the flank of Moab and lay open its cities,*a* 9
from one end to the other—the fairest of its cities: Beth-jeshimoth, Baal-
meon and Kiriathaim. I will hand over Moab and Ammon together to the 10
tribes of the east to be their possession, so that the Ammonites shall not
be remembered among the nations, and so that I may execute judgement 11
upon Moab. Thus they shall know that I am the LORD.

These are the words of the Lord GOD: Because Edom took deliberate 12
revenge on Judah and by so doing incurred lasting guilt, I will stretch 13
my hand out over Edom, says the Lord GOD, and destroy both man and
beast in it, laying waste the land from Teman as far as Dedan; they
shall fall by the sword. I will wreak my vengeance upon Edom through 14
my people Israel. They will deal with Edom as my anger and fury
demand, and it shall feel my vengeance. This is the very word of the
Lord GOD.

These are the words of the Lord GOD: Because the Philistines have 15
taken deliberate revenge and have avenged themselves with single-minded
scorn, giving vent to their age-long enmity in destruction, I will stretch 16
out my hand over the Philistines, says the Lord GOD, I will wipe out the
Kerethites and destroy all the rest of the dwellers by the sea. I will take 17
fearful vengeance upon them and punish them in my fury. When I take
my vengeance, they shall know that I am the LORD.

a and lay . . . cities: *prob. rdg.; Heb.* from the cities, from its cities.

26 These were the words of the Lord to me on the first day of the first
2 month in the eleventh year: Man, Tyre has said of Jerusalem,

> Aha! she that was the gateway of the nations
>   is broken,
> her gates swing open to me;
> I grow rich, she lies in ruins.

3 Therefore these are the words of the Lord God:

> I am against you, Tyre,
> and will bring up many nations against you
>   as the sea brings up its waves;
4 they will destroy the walls of Tyre and pull down her towers.
>   I will scrape the soil off her
> and make her a gleaming rock,
5 she shall be an islet where men spread their nets;
>   I have spoken, says the Lord God.
> She shall become the prey of nations,
6 and her daughters*a* shall be slain by the sword in the open country.

Thus they shall know that I am the Lord.

7 These are the words of the Lord God: I am bringing against Tyre from
the north Nebuchadrezzar king of Babylon, king of kings. He will come
with horses and chariots, with cavalry and a great army.

> 8   Your daughters in the open country
>   he will put to the sword.
>   He will set up watch-towers against you,
>   pile up siege-ramps against you
>   and raise against you a screen of shields.
> 9 He will launch his battering-rams on your walls
>   and break down your towers with his axes.
> 10 He will cover you with dust from the thousands of his cavalry;
>   at the thunder of his horses
>   and of his chariot-wheels
>   your walls will quake when he enters your gates
>   as men enter a city that is breached.
> 11   He will trample all your streets
>   with the hooves of his horses
>   and put your people to the sword,
>   and your strong pillars will fall to the ground.
> 12   Your wealth will become spoil,
>   your merchandise will be plundered,
>   your walls levelled,
>   your pleasant houses pulled down,
>   your stones, your timber and your rubble
>   will be dumped into the sea.
> 13   So I will silence the clamour of your songs,
>   and the sound of your harps shall be heard no more.

a Or daughter-towns.

> I will make you a gleaming rock,   14
> a place for fishermen to spread their nets,
>   and you shall never be rebuilt.
> I, the LORD, have spoken.
>   This is the very word of the Lord GOD.

These are the words of the Lord GOD to Tyre: How the coasts and 15
islands will shake at the sound of your downfall, while the wounded groan,
and the slaughter goes on in your midst! Then all the sea-kings will come 16
down from their thrones, and lay aside their cloaks, and strip off their
brocaded robes. They will wear coarse loin-cloths; they will sit on the
ground, shuddering at every moment, horror-struck at your fate. Then 17
they will raise this dirge over you:

> How you are undone, swept from the sea,
>   O famous city!
> You whose strength lay in the sea,
>   you and your inhabitants,
> who spread their terror throughout the mainland.[a]
> Now the coast-lands tremble on the day of your downfall,   18
> and the isles of the sea are appalled at your passing.

For these are the words of the Lord GOD: When I make you a desolate 19
city, like a city where no man can live, when I bring up the primeval ocean
against you and the great waters cover you, I will thrust you down with 20
those that descend to the abyss, to the dead of all the ages. I will make you
dwell in the underworld as in places long desolate, with those that go down
to the abyss. So you will never again be inhabited or take your place in the
land of the living. I will bring you to a fearful end, and you shall be no more; 21
men may look for you but will never find you again. This is the very word
of the Lord GOD.

These were the words of the LORD to me: Man, raise a dirge over Tyre **27** 1 2
and say, Tyre, throned above your harbours, you who carry the trade of 3
the nations to many coasts and islands, these are the words of the Lord GOD:

> O Tyre, you said,
>   'I am perfect in beauty.'
> Your frontiers are on the high seas,   4
>   your builders made your beauty perfect;
> they fashioned all your timbers   5
>   of pine from Senir;
> they took a cedar from Lebanon
>   to raise up a mast over you.
> They made your oars of oaks from Bashan;   6
>   they made your deck strong[b] with box-wood
>   from the coasts of Kittim.
>   Your canvas was linen,   7
>   patterned linen from Egypt
>   to make your sails;

---

[a] the mainland: *prob. rdg.*; *Heb.* her inhabitants.   [b] strong: *prob. rdg.*; *Heb.* ivory.

      your awnings were violet and purple
        from the coasts of Elishah.
8   Men of Sidon and Arvad became your oarsmen;
        you had skilled men within you, O Tyre,
          who served as your helmsmen.
9   You had skilled veterans from Gebal
          caulking your seams.
      You had all sea-going ships and their sailors
        to market your wares;
10   men of Pharas,[a] Lud,[b] and Put, served
        as warriors in your army;
        they hung shield and helmet around you,
        and it was they who gave you your glory.
11   Men of Arvad and Cilicia manned all your walls,
        men of Gammad were posted on your towers
        and hung their shields around your battlements;
      it was they who made your beauty perfect.

12 Tarshish was a source of your commerce, from its abundant resources
13 offering silver and iron, tin and lead, as your staple wares. Javan,[c] Tubal,
and Meshech dealt with you, offering slaves and vessels of bronze as your
14 imports. Men from Togarmah offered horses, mares, and mules as
15 your staple wares. Rhodians dealt with you, great islands were a source
of your commerce, paying what was due to you in ivory and ebony.
16 Edom was a source of your commerce, so many were your undertakings,
and offered purple garnets, brocade and fine linen, black coral and
17 red jasper,[d] for your staple wares. Judah and Israel dealt with you,
offering wheat from Minnith, and meal, syrup, oil, and balsam, as your
18 imports. Damascus was a source of your commerce, so many were your
undertakings, from its abundant resources offering wine of Helbon and
19 wool of Suhar, and casks of wine from Izalla,[e] for your staple wares;
20 wrought iron, cassia, and sweet cane were among your imports. Dedan
21 dealt with you in coarse woollens for saddle-cloths. Arabia and all the
chiefs of Kedar were the source of your commerce in lambs, rams,
22 and he-goats; this was your trade with them. Dealers from Sheba and
Raamah dealt with you, offering the choicest spices, every kind of precious
23 stone and gold, as your staple wares. Harran, Kanneh, and Eden, dealers
24 from Asshur and all Media, dealt with you; they were your dealers
in gorgeous stuffs, violet cloths and brocades, in stores of coloured
fabric rolled up and tied with cords; your dealings with them were in
these.

25   Ships of Tarshish were the caravans for your imports;
        you were deeply laden with full cargoes
          on the high seas.
26   Your oarsmen brought you into many waters,
        but on the high seas an east wind wrecked you.

[a] *Or* Persia.   [b] *Or* Lydia.   [c] *Or* Ionia.   [d] *Or* and carbuncles.
[e] casks . . . Izalla: *prob. rdg.; Heb. obscure.*

Your wealth, your staple wares, your imports,   27
  your sailors and your helmsmen,
your caulkers, your merchants, and your warriors,
  all your ship's company,
    all who were with you,
were flung into the sea on the day of your disaster;
at the cries of your helmsmen the troubled waters tossed.   28

When all the rowers disembark from their ships,   29
when the sailors, the helmsmen all together, go ashore,
  they exclaim over your fate,   30
    they cry out bitterly;
  they throw dust on their heads
    and sprinkle themselves with ashes.
  They tear out their hair at your plight   31
    and put on sackcloth;
  they weep bitterly over you,
    bitterly wailing.
In their lamentation they raise a dirge over you,   32
  and this is their dirge:
  Who was like Tyre,
with her buildings piled*a* off shore?
When your wares were unloaded off the sea   33
you met the needs of many nations;
  with your vast resources and your imports
  you enriched the kings of the earth.
Now you are broken by the sea   34
  in deep water;
your wares and all your company are gone overboard.
All who dwell on the coasts and islands   35
  are aghast at your fate;
  horror is written on the faces of their kings
    and their hair stands on end.
Among the nations the merchants jeer in derision at you;   36
you have come to a fearful end and shall be no more for ever.

These were the words of the LORD to me: Man, say to the prince of **28** 1 2
Tyre, This is the word of the Lord GOD:

In your arrogance you say,
  'I am a god;
I sit throned like a god on the high seas.'
  Though you are a man and no god,
  you try to think the thoughts of a god.
What? are you wiser than Danel*b*?   3
  Is no secret too dark for you?

a with her buildings piled: *prob. rdg.; Heb. obscure.*   *b Or, as otherwise read,*
Daniel; *cp. 14. 14, 20.*

4   Clever and shrewd as you are,
           you have amassed wealth for yourself,
         you have amassed gold and silver in your treasuries;
5   by great cleverness in your trading
               you have heaped up riches,
           and with your riches your arrogance has grown.

6 Therefore these are the words of the Lord GOD:

           Because you try to think the thoughts of a god
7   I will bring strangers against you,
               the most ruthless of nations,
           who will draw their swords against your fine wisdom
               and lay your pride in the dust,
8   sending you down to the pit*a* to die
           a death of disgrace on the high seas.
9   Will you dare to say that you are a god
               when you face your assailants,
           though you are a man and no god
               in the hands of those who lay you low?
10   You will die strengthless
               at the hands of strangers.

   For I have spoken. This is the very word of the Lord GOD.
11 12   These were the words of the LORD to me: Man, raise this dirge over the
   king of Tyre, and say to him, This is the word of the Lord GOD:

           You set the seal on perfection;
           full of wisdom you were and altogether beautiful.
13   You were in an Eden, a garden of God,
           adorned with gems of every kind:
           sardin and chrysolite and jade,
           topaz, cornelian and green jasper,
           lapis lazuli,*b* purple garnet and green felspar.
           Your jingling beads were of gold,
           and the spangles you wore were made for you
               on the day of your birth.
14   I set you with a towering cherub*c* as guardian;
               you were on God's holy hill
           and you walked proudly among stones that flashed with fire.
15   You were blameless in all your ways
               from the day of your birth
           until your iniquity came to light.
16   Your commerce grew so great,
           lawlessness filled your heart and you went wrong,
           so I brought you down in disgrace from the mountain of God,
               and the guardian cherub banished you*d*
               from among the stones that flashed like fire.

a Or to destruction.   *b Or* sapphire.   *c* I set ... cherub: *prob. rdg.; Heb.*
You were a towering cherub whom I set.   *d* and the ... you: *or* and I parted
you, O guardian cherub, ...

Your beauty made you arrogant, 17
you misused your wisdom to increase your dignity.
　　I flung you to the ground,
　　I left you there, a sight for kings to see.
So great was your sin in your wicked trading 18
　　that you desecrated your sanctuaries.
　　So I kindled a fire within you,
　　and it devoured you.
　　I left you as ashes on the ground
　　for all to see.
All among the nations who knew you were aghast: 19
you came to a fearful end and shall be no more for ever.

These were the words of the LORD to me: Man, look towards Sidon and 20 21
prophesy against her. These are the words of the Lord GOD: 22

　　Sidon, I am against you
　　and I will show my glory in your midst.

　　Men will know that I am the LORD
　　when I execute judgement upon her
　　and thereby prove my holiness.
　　I will let loose pestilence upon her 23
　　and bloodshed in her streets;
　　the slain will fall in her streets,
　　beset on all sides by the sword;
　　then men will know that I am the LORD.

No longer shall the Israelites suffer from the scorn of their neighbours, 24
the pricking of briars and scratching of thorns, and they shall know that
I am the Lord GOD.

These are the words of the Lord GOD: When I gather the Israelites from 25
the peoples among whom they are scattered, I shall thereby prove my
holiness in the sight of all nations. They shall live on their native soil,
which I gave to my servant Jacob. They shall live there in peace of mind, 26
build houses and plant vineyards; they shall live there in peace of mind
when I execute judgement on all their scornful neighbours. Thus they
shall know that I am the LORD their God.

These were the words of the LORD to me on the twelfth day of the tenth **29**
month in the tenth year: Man, look towards Pharaoh king of Egypt and 2
prophesy against him and all his country. Say, These are the words of the 3
Lord GOD:

　　I am against you,
　　　Pharaoh king of Egypt,
　　　you great monster,
　　lurking in the streams of the Nile.
　　You have said, 'My Nile is my own;
　　　it was I who made it.'

4   I will put hooks in your jaws
            and make them cling *a* to your scales.
         I will hoist you out of its streams
            with all its fish clinging to your scales.

5   I will fling you into the wilderness,
            you and all the fish in your streams;
            you will fall on the bare ground
            with none to pick you up and bury you;
         I will make you food
            for beasts and for birds.

6   So all who live in Egypt will know
            that I am the LORD,
         for the support that you gave to the Israelites
            was no better than a reed,

7   which splintered in the hand when they grasped you,
            and tore their armpits;
         when they leaned upon you, you snapped
            and their limbs gave way.

8   This therefore is the word of the Lord GOD: I am bringing a sword upon
9 you to destroy both man and beast. The land of Egypt shall become a desolate waste, and they shall know that I am the LORD, because you said,
10 'The Nile is mine; it was I who made it.' I am against you therefore, you and your Nile, and I will make Egypt desolate, wasted by drought, from
11 Migdol to Syene and up to the very frontier of Cush. No foot of man shall pass through it, no foot of beast; it shall lie uninhabited for forty years.
12 I will make the land of Egypt the most desolate of desolate lands; her cities shall lie derelict among the ruined cities. For forty years shall they lie derelict, and I will scatter the Egyptians among the nations and disperse them among the lands.

13   These are the words of the Lord GOD: At the end of forty years I will gather the Egyptians from the peoples among whom they are scattered.
14 I will turn the fortunes of Egypt and bring them back to Pathros, the
15 land of their origin, where they shall become a petty kingdom. She shall be the most paltry of kingdoms and never again exalt herself over the
16 nations, for I will make the Egyptians too few to rule over them. The Israelites will never trust Egypt again; this will be a reminder to them of their sin in turning to Egypt for help. They shall know that I am the Lord GOD.

17   These were the words of the LORD to me on the first day of the first
18 month in the twenty-seventh year: Man, long did Nebuchadrezzar king of Babylon keep his army in the field against Tyre, until every head was rubbed bare and every shoulder chafed. But neither he nor his army gained
19 anything from Tyre for their long service against her. This, therefore, is the word of the Lord GOD: I am giving the land of Egypt to Nebuchadrezzar king of Babylon. He shall carry off its wealth, he shall spoil and plunder
20 it, and so his army will be paid. I have given him the land of Egypt as the

---

a make them cling: *prob. rdg.; Heb.* make the fish of your streams cling.

wages for his service because they have disregarded me. This is the very word of the Lord GOD.

At that time I will make Israel put out fresh shoots, and give you 21 back the power to speak among them, and they will know that I am the LORD.

These were the words of the LORD to me: Man, prophesy and say, These **30** 1 2 are the words of the Lord GOD:

> Woe, woe for the day!
> for a day is near,   3
> a day of the LORD is near,
> a day of cloud, a day of reckoning for the nations.
> Then a sword will come upon Egypt,   4
> and there will be anguish in Cush,
> when the slain fall in Egypt,
> when its wealth is taken and its foundations are torn up.
> Cush and Put and Lud,*a*   5
> all the Arabs and Libyans and the peoples of allied lands,
> shall fall with them by the sword.

These are the words of the LORD: 6

> All who support Egypt shall fall
> and her boasted might be brought low;
> from Migdol to Syene men shall fall by the sword.
> This is the very word of the Lord GOD.

They shall be the most desolate of desolate lands, and their cities shall 7 lie derelict among the ruined cities. When I set Egypt on fire and all her 8 helpers are broken, they will know that I am the LORD. When that time 9 comes messengers shall go out in haste from my presence to alarm Cush, still without a care, and anguish shall come upon her in Egypt's hour. Even now it is on the way.

These are the words of the Lord GOD: 10

> I will make an end of Egypt's hordes
> by the hands of Nebuchadrezzar king of Babylon.
> He and his people with him, the most ruthless of nations,   11
> will be brought to ravage the land.
> They will draw their swords against Egypt
> and fill the land with the slain.
> I will make the streams of the Nile dry land   12
> and sell Egypt to evil men;
> I will lay waste the land and everything in it by foreign hands.
> I, the LORD, have spoken.

These are the words of the Lord GOD: 13

> I will make an end of the lordlings *b*
> and wipe out the princelings *c* of Noph;
> and never again shall a prince arise in Egypt.

a Or Lydia.   *b Or* idols.   *c Or* false gods.

Then I will put fear in that land,

14   I will lay Pathros waste and set fire to Zoan
and execute judgement on No.

15   I will pour out my rage upon Sin,
the bastion of Egypt,
and destroy the horde of Noph.

16   I will set Egypt on fire,
and Syene shall writhe in anguish;
the walls of No shall be breached
and flood-waters shall burst into it.

17   The young men of On and Pi-beseth*a* shall fall by the sword
and the cities themselves go into captivity.

18   Daylight shall fail in Tahpanhes
when I break the yoke of Egypt there;
then her boasted might shall be subdued;
a cloud shall cover her,
and her daughters*b* shall go into captivity.

19   Thus I will execute judgement on Egypt,
and they shall know that I am the LORD.

20 This was the word of the LORD to me on the seventh day of the first
21 month in the eleventh year: Man, I have broken the arm of Pharaoh king
of Egypt. See, it has not been bound up with dressings and bandage to
22 give it strength to wield a sword. These, therefore, are the words of the
Lord GOD: I am against Pharaoh king of Egypt; I will break both his arms,
23 the sound and the broken, and make the sword drop from his hand. I will
scatter the Egyptians among the nations and disperse them over many
24 lands. Then I will strengthen the arms of the king of Babylon and put my
sword in his hand; but I will break Pharaoh's arms, and he shall lie wounded
25 and groaning before him. I will give strength to the arms of the king of
Babylon, but the arms of Pharaoh will fall. Men will know that I am the
LORD, when I put my sword in the hand of the king of Babylon, and he
26 stretches it out over the land of Egypt. I will scatter the Egyptians among
the nations and disperse them over many lands, and they shall know that
I am the LORD.

31 On the first day of the third month in the eleventh year this word came
2 to me from the LORD: Man, say to Pharaoh king of Egypt and all his
horde:

What are you like in your greatness?

3   Look at Assyria: it was a cedar in Lebanon,
whose fair branches overshadowed the forest,
towering high with its crown finding a way through the foliage.

4   Springs nourished it, underground waters gave it height,
their streams washed the soil all round it
and sent forth their rills to every tree in the country.

5   So it grew taller than every other tree.

a Or Bubastis.   *b Or* daughter-towns.

> Its boughs were many, its branches spread far;
>   for water was abundant in the channels.
> In its boughs all the birds of the air had their nests,   6
> under its branches all wild creatures bore their young,
> and in its shadow all great nations made their home.
>
> A splendid great tree it was, with its long spreading boughs,   7
> for its roots were beside abundant waters.
> No cedar in God's garden overshadowed it,   8
> no fir could compare with its boughs,
> and no plane-tree had such branches;
>   not a tree in God's garden
> could rival its beauty.
> I, the LORD, gave it beauty   9
>   with its mass of spreading boughs,
> the envy of all the trees in Eden,
>   the garden of God.

Therefore these are the words of the Lord GOD: Because it grew so high 10 and pushed its crown up through the foliage, and its pride mounted as it grew, therefore I handed it over to a prince of the nations to deal with it; 11 I made an example of it as its wickedness deserved. Strangers from the 12 most ruthless of nations hewed it down and flung it away. Its sweeping boughs fell on the mountains and in all the valleys, and its branches lay broken beside all the streams in the land. All nations of the earth came out from under its shade and left it. All the birds of the air settled on its fallen 13 trunk; the wild creatures all stood by its branches. Never again, therefore, 14 shall the well-watered trees grow so high or push their crowns up through the foliage. Nor shall the strongest of them, well watered though they be, stand erect in their full height; for all have been given over to death, to the world below, to share the common doom and go down to the abyss.

These are the words of the Lord GOD: When he went down to Sheol, 15 I closed the deep over him as a gate, I dammed its rivers, the great waters were held back. I put Lebanon in mourning for him, and all the trees of the country-side wilted. I made nations shake with the crash of his fall, 16 when I brought him down to Sheol with those who go down to the abyss. From this all the trees of Eden, all the choicest and best of Lebanon, all the well-watered trees, drew comfort in the world below. They too like him 17 had gone down to Sheol, to those slain with the sword; and those who had lived in his shadow were scattered among the nations. Which among the 18 trees of Eden was like you in glory and greatness? Yet you will be brought down with the trees of Eden to the world below; you will lie with those who have been slain by the sword, in the company of the strengthless dead. This stands for Pharaoh and all his horde. This is the very word of the Lord GOD.

On the first day of the twelfth month in the twelfth year the word of the **32** LORD came to me: Man, raise a dirge over Pharaoh king of Egypt and say 2 to him:

> Young lion of the nations, you are undone.
> You were like a monster in the waters of the Nile

scattering the water with its snout, *a b*
churning the water with its feet
and fouling the streams.

3　These are the words of the Lord GOD: When many nations are gathered
together I will spread my net over you, and you will be dragged up in its
4　meshes. I will fling you on land, dashing you down on the bare ground.
I will let all the birds of the air settle upon you and all the wild beasts gorge
5　themselves on your flesh. Your flesh I will lay on the mountains, and fill
6　the valleys with the worms that feed on it. I will drench the land with your
discharge, drench it with your blood to the very mountain-tops, and the
7　watercourses shall be full of you. When I put out your light I will veil
the sky and blacken its stars; I will veil the sun with a cloud, and the
8　moon shall not give its light. I will darken all the shining lights of the
sky above you and bring darkness over your land. This is the very word
of the Lord GOD.

9　I will disquiet many peoples when I bring your broken army among the
10　nations into lands you have never known. I will appal many peoples with
your fate; when I brandish my sword in the faces of their kings, their hair
shall stand on end. In the day of your downfall each shall tremble for his
11　own fate from moment to moment. For these are the words of the Lord
12　GOD: The sword of the king of Babylon shall come upon you. I will make
the whole horde of you fall by the sword of warriors who are of all men the
most ruthless. They shall make havoc of the pride of Egypt, and all its
13　horde shall be wiped out. I will destroy all their cattle beside many waters.
14　No foot of man, no hoof of beast, shall ever churn them up again. Then
will I let their waters settle and their streams run smooth as oil. This is
15　the very word of the Lord GOD. When I have laid Egypt waste, and the
whole land is devastated, when I strike down all who dwell there, they shall
know that I am the LORD.

16　This is a dirge, and the women of the nations shall sing it as a dirge. They
shall sing it as a dirge, as a dirge over Egypt and all its horde. This is the
very word of the Lord GOD.

17　On the fifteenth day of the first month in the twelfth year, the word of
the LORD came to me:

18　Man, raise a lament, you and the daughters of the nations,
　　　over the hordes of Egypt and her nobles,
　　whom I will bring down*c* to the world below
　　with those that go down to the abyss.

19　　　　Are you better favoured than others?
　　Go down and be laid to rest with the strengthless dead.

20　A sword stands ready. Those who marched with her, and all her horde,
21　shall fall into the midst of those slain by the sword. Warrior chieftains in
Sheol speak to Pharaoh and those who aided him:
　　The strengthless dead, slain by the sword, have come down and are

---

a snout: *prob. rdg.; Heb.* streams.　　*b* scattering . . . snout: *or* heaving itself up in
the streams.　　*c* her nobles . . . down: *prob. rdg.; Heb. obscure.*

laid to rest. There is Assyria with all her company, her buried around her, 22
all of them slain and fallen by the sword. Her graves are set in the recesses 23
of the abyss, with her company buried around her, all of them slain, fallen
by the sword, men who once filled the land of the living with terror. There 24
is Elam, with all her hordes buried around her, all of them slain, fallen by
the sword; they have gone down strengthless to the world below, men who
struck terror into the land of the living but now share the disgrace of those
that go down to the abyss. In the midst of the slain a resting-place has been 25
made for her, with all her hordes buried around her; all of them strengthless, slain by the sword. For they who once struck terror into the land of
the living now share the disgrace of those that go down to the abyss; they
are assigned a place in the midst of the slain. There are Meshech and Tubal 26
with all their hordes, with their buried around them, all of them strengthless and slain by the sword, men who once struck terror into the land of
the living. Do they not rest with warriors fallen strengthless,*a* who have 27
gone down to Sheol with their weapons, their swords under their heads and
their shields over their bones,*b* though the terror of their prowess once lay
on the land of the living? You also, Pharaoh, shall lie broken in the company 28
of the strengthless dead, resting with those slain by the sword. There is 29
Edom, her kings and all her princes, who, for all their prowess, have been
lodged with those slain by the sword; they shall rest with the strengthless
dead and with those that go down to the abyss. There are all the princes 30
of the North and all the Sidonians, who have gone down in shame with the
slain, for all the terror they inspired by their prowess. They rest strengthless with those slain by the sword, and they share the disgrace of those that
go down to the abyss.

Pharaoh will see them and will take comfort for his lost hordes—Pharaoh 31
who, with all his army, is slain by the sword, says the Lord GOD; though 32
he spread*c* terror throughout the land of the living, yet he with all his
horde is laid to rest with those that are slain by the sword, in the company
of the strengthless dead. This is the very word of the Lord GOD.

The remnant of Israel in the land

THESE WERE THE WORDS OF THE LORD TO ME: Man, say to your 33 1 2
fellow-countrymen, When I set armies in motion against a land, its
people choose one of themselves to be a watchman. When he sees the 3
enemy approaching and blows his trumpet to warn the people, then if 4
anyone does not heed the warning and is overtaken by the enemy, he is
responsible for his own fate. He is responsible because, when he heard the 5
alarm, he paid no heed to it; if he had heeded it, he would have escaped.
But if the watchman does not blow his trumpet or warn the people when 6
he sees the enemy approaching, then any man who is killed is caught with
all his sins upon him; but I will hold the watchman answerable for his
death.

a Prob. rdg.; Heb. from strengthless ones.   *b* and . . . bones: *prob. rdg.; Heb.*
unintelligible.   *c Prob. rdg.; Heb.* I have spread.

7   Man, I have appointed you a watchman for the Israelites. You will take
8 messages from me and carry my warnings to them. It may be that I pronounce sentence of death on a man because he is wicked; if you do not warn
him to give up his ways, the guilt is his and because of his wickedness he
9 shall die, but I will hold you answerable for his death. But if you have
warned him to give up his ways, and he has not given them up, he will die
because of his wickedness, but you will have saved yourself.

10   Man, say to the Israelites, You complain, 'We are burdened by our sins
11 and offences; we are pining away because of them; we despair of life.' So
tell them: As I live, says the Lord GOD, I have no desire for the death of
the wicked. I would rather that a wicked man should mend his ways
and live. Give up your evil ways, give them up; O Israelites, why should
you die?

12   Man, say to your fellow-countrymen, When a righteous man goes wrong,
his righteousness shall not save him. When a wicked man mends his ways,
his former wickedness shall not bring him down. When a righteous man
13 sins, all his righteousness cannot save his life. It may be that, when I tell
the righteous man that he will save his life, he presumes on his righteousness and does wrong; then none of his righteous acts will be remembered:
14 he will die for the wrong he has done. It may be that when I pronounce
sentence of death on the wicked, he mends his ways and does what is just
15 and right: if he then restores the pledges he has taken, repays what he has
stolen, and, doing no more wrong, follows the rules that ensure life, he
16 shall live and not die. None of the sins he has committed shall be remembered against him; he shall live, because he does what is just and right.

17   Your fellow-countrymen are saying, 'The Lord acts without principle',
18 but it is their ways that are unprincipled. When a righteous man gives up
19 his righteousness and does wrong, he shall die because of it; and when a
wicked man gives up his wickedness and does what is just and right, he
20 shall live. How, Israel, can you say that the Lord acts without principle,
when I judge every man of you on his deeds?

21   On the fifth day of the tenth month in the twelfth year of our captivity,
fugitives came to me from Jerusalem and told me that the city had fallen.
22 The evening before they arrived, the hand of the LORD had come upon me,
and by the time they reached me in the morning the LORD had given me
back my speech. My speech was restored and I was no longer dumb.

23 24   These were the words of the LORD to me: Man, the inhabitants of these
wastes on the soil of Israel say, 'When Abraham took possession of the
land he was but one; now we are many, and the land has been granted to
25 us in possession.' Tell them, therefore, that these are the words of the
Lord GOD: You eat meat with the blood in it, you lift up your eyes to idols,
26 you shed*a* blood; and yet you expect to possess the land! You trust to the
sword, you commit abominations, you defile one another's wives; and you
27 expect to possess the land! Tell them that these are the words of the Lord
GOD: As I live, among the ruins they shall fall by the sword; in the open
country I will give them for food to beasts; in dens and caves they shall die
28 by pestilence. I will make the land a desolate waste; her boasted might

a Or pour out.

1048

shall be brought to nothing, and the mountains of Israel shall be an untrodden desert. When I make the land a desolate waste because of all the   29
abominations they have committed, they will know that I am the LORD.

Man, your fellow-countrymen gather in groups and talk of you under   30
walls and in doorways and say to one another, 'Let us go and see what
message there is from the LORD.' So my people will come crowding in, as   31
people do, and sit down in front of you. They will hear what you have to
say, but they will not do it. 'Fine words *a*!' they will say, but their hearts
are set on selfish gain. You are no more to them than a singer of fine songs *b*   32
with a lovely voice, or a clever harpist; they will listen to what you say but
will certainly not do it. But when it comes, as come it will, they will know   33
that there has been a prophet in their midst.

These were the words of the LORD to me: Prophesy, man, against the   **34** 1 2
shepherds of Israel; prophesy and say to them, You shepherds, these are
the words of the Lord GOD: How I hate the shepherds of Israel who care
only for themselves! Should not the shepherd care for the sheep? You   3
consume the milk, wear the wool, and slaughter the fat beasts, but you do
not feed the sheep. You have not encouraged the weary, tended the sick,   4
bandaged the hurt, recovered the straggler, or searched for the lost; and
even the strong you have driven with ruthless severity. They are scattered,   5
they have no shepherd, they have become the prey of wild beasts. My   6
sheep go straying over the mountains and on every high hill, my flock is
dispersed over the whole country, with no one to ask after them or search
for them.

Therefore, you shepherds, hear the words of the LORD. As surely as I   7 8
live, says the Lord GOD, because my sheep are ravaged by wild beasts and
have become their prey for lack of a shepherd, because my shepherds have
not asked after the sheep but have cared only for themselves and not for
the sheep—therefore, you shepherds, hear the words of the LORD. These   9 10
are the words of the Lord GOD: I am against the shepherds and will demand
my sheep from them. I will dismiss those shepherds: they shall care only
for themselves no longer; I will rescue my sheep from their jaws, and they
shall feed on them no more.

For these are the words of the Lord GOD: Now I myself will ask after   11
my sheep and go in search of them. As a shepherd goes in search of his   12
sheep when his flock is dispersed all around him, so I will go in search of
my sheep and rescue them, no matter where they were scattered in dark
and cloudy days. I will bring them out from every nation, gather them in   13
from other lands, and lead them home to their own soil. I will graze them
on the mountains of Israel, by her streams and in all her green fields. I   14
will feed them on good grazing-ground, and their pasture shall be the high
mountains of Israel. There they will rest, there in good pasture, and find
rich grazing on the mountains of Israel. I myself will tend my flock, I   15
myself pen them in their fold, says the Lord GOD. I will search for the lost,   16
recover the straggler, bandage the hurt, strengthen the sick, leave the
healthy and strong to play, and give them their proper food.

As for you, my flock, these are the words of the Lord GOD: I will judge   17

a Fine words: *or* Love songs.   *b* fine songs: *or* love songs.

18 between one sheep and another. You rams and he-goats! Are you not satisfied with grazing on good herbage, that you must trample down the rest with your feet? Or with drinking clear water, that you must churn up 19 the rest with your feet? My flock has to eat what you have trampled and 20 drink what you have churned up. These, therefore, are the words of the Lord GOD to them: Now I myself will judge between the fat sheep and the 21 lean. You hustle the weary with flank and shoulder, you butt them with your horns until you have driven them away and scattered them abroad. 22 Therefore I will save my flock, and they shall be ravaged no more; I will 23 judge between one sheep and another. Then I will set over them one shepherd to take care of them, my servant David; he shall care for them 24 and become their shepherd. I, the LORD, will become their God, and my servant David shall be a prince among them. I, the LORD, have spoken. 25 I will make a covenant with them to ensure prosperity; I will rid the land of wild beasts, and men shall live in peace of mind on the open pastures and 26 sleep in the woods. I will settle them in the neighbourhood of my hill and 27 send them rain in due season, blessed rain. Trees in the country-side shall bear their fruit, the land shall yield its produce, and men shall live in peace of mind on their own soil. They shall know that I am the LORD when I break the bars of their yokes and rescue them from those who have en- 28 slaved them. They shall never be ravaged by the nations again nor shall wild beasts devour them; they shall live in peace of mind, with no one to 29 alarm them. I will give prosperity to their plantations; they shall never again be victims of famine in the land nor any longer bear the taunts of the 30 nations. They shall know that I, the LORD their God, am with them, and 31 that they are my people Israel, says the Lord GOD. You are my flock, my people, the flock I feed, and I am your God. This is the very word of the Lord GOD.

35 1 2   These were the words of the LORD to me: Man, look towards the hill- 3 country of Seir and prophesy against it. Say, These are the words of the Lord GOD:

> O hill-country of Seir, I am against you:
> I will stretch out my hand over you
> and make you a desolate waste.

4
> I will lay your cities in ruins
> and you shall be made desolate;
> thus you shall know that I am the LORD.

5
> For you have maintained an immemorial feud
> and handed over the Israelites to the sword
>   in the hour of their doom,
>   at the time of their final punishment.

6
> Therefore, as I live, says the Lord GOD,
> I make blood your destiny, and blood shall pursue you;
>   you are most surely guilty of blood,
>   and blood shall pursue you.

7
> I will make the hill-country of Seir a desolate waste
> and put an end to all in it who pass to and fro;

I will fill your hills and your valleys with its slain,   8
and those slain by the sword shall fall into your streams.
I will make you desolate for ever,   9
and your cities shall not be inhabited;
thus you shall know that I am the LORD.

You say, The two nations and the two countries shall be mine and I   10
will take possession of them, though the LORD is^a there. Therefore, as   11
I live, says the Lord GOD, your anger and jealousy shall be requited, for
I will do to you what you have done in your hatred against them. I shall be
known among you when I judge you; you shall know that I am the LORD.   12
I have heard all your blasphemies; you have said, 'The mountains of
Israel are desolate and have been given to us to devour.' You have set   13
yourselves up against me and spoken recklessly against me. I myself have
heard you. These are the words of the Lord GOD: I will make you so   14
desolate that the whole world will gloat over you. I will do to you as you   15
did to Israel my own possession when you gloated over its desolation.
O hill-country of Seir, you will be desolate, and it will be the end of all
Edom. Thus men will know that I am the LORD.

And do you, man, prophesy to the mountains of Israel and say, Moun-   **36**
tains of Israel, hear the words of the LORD. These are the words of the Lord   2
GOD: The enemy has said, 'Aha! now the everlasting highlands are ours.'
Therefore prophesy and say, These are the words of the Lord GOD: You   3
mountains of Israel, all round you men gloated over you and trampled you
down when you were seized and occupied by the rest of the nations; your
name was bandied about in the common talk of men. Therefore, listen to   4
the words of the Lord GOD when he speaks to the mountains and hills, to
the streams and valleys, to the desolate palaces and deserted cities, all
plundered and despised by the rest of the nations round you. These are   5
the words of the Lord GOD: In the fire of my jealousy I have spoken plainly
against the rest of the nations, and against Edom above all. For Edom,
swollen with triumphant scorn, seized on my land to hold it up to public
contempt. Therefore prophesy over the soil of Israel and say to the moun-   6
tains and hills, the streams and valleys, These are the words of the Lord
GOD: I have spoken my mind in jealousy and anger because you have had
to endure the taunts of all nations. Therefore, says the Lord GOD, I have   7
sworn with uplifted hand that the nations round about shall be punished
for^b their taunts. But you, mountains of Israel, you shall put forth your   8
branches and yield your fruit for my people Israel, for their home-coming
is near. See now, I am for you, I will turn to you, and you shall be tilled and   9
sown. I will plant many men upon you—the whole house of Israel. The   10
cities shall again be inhabited and the palaces rebuilt. I will plant many men   11
and beasts upon you; they shall increase and be fruitful. I will make you
populous as in days of old and more prosperous than you were at first.
Thus you will know that I am the LORD. I will make men—my people   12
Israel—tread your paths again. They shall settle in you, and you shall be
their possession; but you shall never again rob them of their children.

      a Or has been.   *b* be punished for: *or* bear.

13 These are the words of the Lord God: People say that you are a land that
14 devours men and robs your tribes of their children. But you shall never
   devour men any more nor rob your tribes of their children, says the Lord
15 God. I will never let you hear the taunts of the nations again nor shall you
   have to endure the reproaches of the peoples. This is the very word of the
   Lord God.

16 17 These were the words of the Lord to me: Man, when the Israelites lived
   on their own soil they defiled it with their ways and deeds; their ways were
18 foul and disgusting in my sight. I poured out my fury upon them because
   of the blood they had poured out upon the land, and the idols with which
19 they had defiled it. I scattered them among the nations, and they were
   dispersed among different countries; I passed on them the sentence which
20 their ways and deeds deserved. When they came among those nations,
   they caused my holy name to be profaned wherever they came: men said
   of them, 'These are the people of the Lord, and it is from his land that they
21 have come.' And I spared them for the sake of my holy name which the
   Israelites had profaned among the nations to whom they had gone.

22 Therefore tell the Israelites that these are the words of the Lord God:
   It is not for your sake, you Israelites, that I am acting, but for the sake of
   my holy name, which you have profaned among the peoples where you
23 have gone. I will hallow my great name, which has been profaned among
   those nations. When they see that I reveal my holiness through you, the
24 nations will know that I am the Lord, says the Lord God. I will take you
   out of the nations and gather you from every land and bring you to your
25 own soil. I will sprinkle clean water over you, and you shall be cleansed
   from all that defiles you; I will cleanse you from the taint of all your idols.
26 I will give you a new heart and put a new spirit within you; I will take the
27 heart of stone from your body and give you a heart of flesh. I will put my
   spirit into you and make you conform to my statutes, keep my laws and
28 live by them. You shall live in the land which I gave to your ancestors; you
29 shall become my people, and I will become your God. I will save you from
   all that defiles you; I will call to the corn and make it plentiful; I will bring
30 no more famine upon you. I will make the trees bear abundant fruit and
   the ground yield heavy crops, so that you will never again have to bear the
31 reproach of famine among the nations. You will recall your wicked ways
   and evil deeds, and you will loathe yourselves because of your wickedness
32 and your abominations. It is not for your sake that I am acting; be sure of
   that, says the Lord God. Feel, then, the shame and disgrace of your ways,
   men of Israel.

33 These are the words of the Lord God: When I cleanse you of all your
   wickedness, I will re-people the cities, and the palaces shall be rebuilt.
34 The land now desolate shall be tilled, instead of lying waste for every
35 passer-by to see. Men will say that this same land which was waste has
   become like a garden of Eden, and people will make their homes in the
36 cities once ruined, wasted, and shattered, but now well fortified. The
   nations still left around you will know that it is I, the Lord, who have
   rebuilt the shattered cities and planted anew the waste land; I, the Lord,
   have spoken and will do it.

These are the words of the Lord GOD: Yet again will I let the Israelites 37
ask me to act in their behalf. I will make their men numerous as sheep,
like the sheep offered as holy-gifts, like the sheep in Jerusalem at times of 38
festival. So shall their ruined cities be filled with human flocks, and they
shall know that I am the LORD.

The hand of the LORD came upon me, and he carried me out by his **37**
spirit and put me down in a plain full of bones. He made me go to and fro 2
across them until I had been round them all;*a* they covered the plain,
countless numbers of them, and they were very dry. He said to me, 'Man, 3
can these bones live again?' I answered, 'Only thou knowest that, Lord
GOD.' He said to me, 'Prophesy over these bones and say to them, O dry 4
bones, hear the word of the LORD. This is the word of the Lord GOD to 5
these bones: I will put breath*b* into you, and you shall live. I will fasten 6
sinews on you, bring flesh upon you, overlay you with skin, and put breath
in you, and you shall live; and you shall know that I am the LORD.' I began 7
to prophesy as he had bidden me, and as I prophesied there was a rustling
sound and the bones fitted themselves together. As I looked, sinews 8
appeared upon them, flesh covered them, and they were overlaid with
skin, but there was no breath in them. Then he said to me, 'Prophesy to 9
the wind, prophesy, man, and say to it, These are the words of the Lord
GOD: Come, O wind, come from every quarter and breathe into these
slain, that they may come to life.' I began to prophesy as he had bidden me: 10
breath came into them; they came to life and rose to their feet, a mighty
host. He said to me, 'Man, these bones are the whole people of Israel. They 11
say, "Our bones are dry, our thread of life is snapped, our web is severed
from the loom."*c* Prophesy, therefore, and say to them, These are the 12
words of the Lord GOD: O my people, I will open your graves and bring
you up from them, and restore you to the land of Israel. You shall know 13
that I am the LORD when I open your graves and bring you up from them,
O my people. Then I will put my spirit*d* into you and you shall live, and I 14
will settle you on your own soil, and you shall know that I the LORD have
spoken and will act. This is the very word of the LORD.'

These were the words of the LORD to me: Man, take one leaf of a wooden 15 16
tablet and write on it, 'Judah and his associates of Israel.' Then take another
leaf and write on it, 'Joseph, the leaf of Ephraim and all his associates of
Israel.' Now bring the two together to form one tablet; then they will be a 17
folding tablet in your hand. When your fellow-countrymen ask you to tell 18
them what you mean by this, say to them, These are the words of the Lord 19
GOD: I am taking the leaf of Joseph, which belongs to Ephraim and his
associate tribes of Israel, and joining*e* to it the leaf of Judah. Thus I shall
make them one tablet, and they shall be one in my hand. The leaves on 20
which you write shall be visible in your hand for all to see.

Then say to them, These are the words of the Lord GOD: I am gathering 21
up the Israelites from their places of exile among the nations; I will
assemble them from every quarter and restore them to their own soil.

a He made . . . all: *or* He made me pass all round them.　　*b* *Or* wind *or* spirit.
c our web . . . loom: *prob. rdg.; Heb.* we are completely cut off.　　*d* *Or* breath.
e *Prob. rdg.; Heb. adds* them.

22 I will make them one single nation in the land, on the mountains of Israel, and they shall have one king; they shall no longer be two nations or divided
23 into two kingdoms. They shall never again be defiled with their idols, their loathsome ways and all their disloyal acts; I will rescue them from all their sinful backsliding and purify them. Thus they shall become my people,
24 and I will become their God. My servant David shall become king over them, and they shall have one shepherd. They shall conform to my laws,
25 they shall observe and carry out my statutes. They shall live in the land which I gave my servant Jacob, the land where your fathers lived. They and their descendants shall live there for ever, and my servant David shall
26 for ever be their prince. I will make a covenant with them to bring them prosperity; this covenant shall be theirs for ever.*a* I will greatly increase
27 their numbers, and I will put my sanctuary for ever in their midst. They shall live under the shelter of my dwelling; I will become their God and
28 they shall become my people. The nations shall know that I the LORD am keeping Israel sacred to myself, because my sanctuary is in the midst of them for ever.

God's triumph over the world

38 1 2 THESE WERE THE WORDS OF THE LORD TO ME: Man, look towards Gog, the prince of Rosh, Meshech, and Tubal, in the land of Magog,
3 and prophesy against him. Say, These are the words of the Lord GOD:
4 I am against you, Gog, prince of Rosh, Meshech, and Tubal. I will turn you about, I will put hooks in your jaws. I will lead you out, you and your whole army, horses and horsemen, all fully equipped, a great host with
5 shield and buckler, every man wielding a sword, and with them the men
6 of Pharas, Cush, and Put, all with shield and helmet; Gomer and all its squadrons, Beth-togarmah with its squadrons from the far recesses of the
7 north—a great concourse of peoples with you. Be prepared; make ready, you and all the host which has gathered to join you, and hold yourselves
8 in reserve for me.*b* After many days you will be summoned; in years to come you will enter a land restored from ruin, whose people are gathered from many nations upon the mountains of Israel that have been desolate so long. The Israelites, brought out from the nations, will all be living
9 undisturbed; and you will come up, driving in like a hurricane; you will cover the land like a cloud, you and all your squadrons, a great concourse of peoples.
10 This is the word of the Lord GOD: At that time a thought will enter
11 your head and you will plan evil. You will say, 'I will attack a land of open villages, I will fall upon a people living quiet and undisturbed,
12 undefended by walls, with neither gates nor bars.' You will expect to come plundering, spoiling, and stripping bare the ruins where men now live again, a people gathered out of the nations, a people acquiring cattle
13 and goods, and making their home at the very centre of the world. Sheba

a Prob. rdg.; Heb. adds and I will put them.   *b* and hold . . . me: *or* and you shall be their rallying-point.

and Dedan, the traders of Tarshish and her leading merchants, will say to you, 'Is it for plunder that you have come? Have you gathered your host to get spoil, to carry off silver and gold, to seize cattle and goods, to collect rich spoil?'

Therefore, prophesy, man, and say to Gog, These are the words of the 14 Lord GOD: In that day when my people Israel is living undisturbed, will 15 you not awake and come with many nations from your home in the far recesses of the north, all riding on horses, a great host, a mighty army? You 16 will come up against my people Israel; and in those future days you will be like a cloud covering the earth. I will bring you against my land, that the nations may know me, when they see me prove my holiness at your expense, O Gog.

This is the word of the Lord GOD: When I spoke in days of old through 17 my servants the prophets, who prophesied in those days unceasingly, it was you whom I threatened to bring against Israel. On that day, when at 18 length Gog comes against the land of Israel, says the Lord GOD, my wrath will boil over. In my jealousy and in the heat of my anger I swear that on 19 that day there shall be a great earthquake throughout the land of Israel. The fish in the sea and the birds in the air, the wild animals and all reptiles 20 that move on the ground, all mankind on the face of the earth, all shall be shaken before me. Mountains shall be torn up, the terraced hills collapse, and every wall crash to the ground. I will summon universal terror against 21 Gog, says the Lord GOD, and his men shall turn their swords against one another. I will bring him to judgement with pestilence and bloodshed; I 22 will pour down teeming rain, hailstones hard as rock, and fire and brimstone, upon him, upon his squadrons, upon the whole concourse of peoples with him. Thus will I prove myself great and holy and make myself known 23 to many nations; they shall know that I am the LORD.

And you, man, prophesy against Gog and say, These are the words of **39** the Lord GOD: I am against you, Gog, prince of Rosh, Meshech, and Tubal. I will turn you about and drive you, I will fetch you up from the far recesses 2 of the north and bring you to the mountains of Israel. I will strike the bow 3 from your left hand and dash the arrows from your right hand. There on 4 the mountains of Israel you shall fall, you, all your squadrons, and your allies; I will give you as food to the birds of prey and the wild beasts. You 5 shall fall on the bare ground, for it is I who have spoken. This is the very word of the Lord GOD. I will send fire on Magog and on those who live 6 undisturbed in the coasts and islands, and they shall know that I am the LORD. My holy name I will make known in the midst of my people Israel 7 and will no longer let it be profaned; the nations shall know that in Israel I, the LORD, am holy.

Behold, it comes; it shall be, says the Lord GOD, the day of which I have 8 spoken. The dwellers in the cities of Israel shall come out and gather 9 weapons to light their fires, buckler and shield, bow and arrows, throwing-stick and lance, and they shall kindle fires with them for seven years. They 10 shall take no wood from the fields nor cut it from the forests but shall light their fires with the weapons. Thus they will plunder their plunderers and spoil their spoilers. This is the very word of the Lord GOD.

11 In that day I will give to Gog, instead of[a] a burial-ground in Israel, the valley of Abarim east of the Sea.[b] There they shall bury Gog and all his horde, and all Abarim will be blocked; and they shall call it the Valley of
12 Gog's Horde. For seven months the Israelites shall bury them and purify
13 the land; all the people shall take their share in the burying. The day that I win myself honour shall be a memorable day for them. This is the very
14 word of the Lord God. Men shall be picked for the regular duty of going through the country and searching for[c] any left above ground, to purify
15 the land; they shall begin their search at the end of the seven months. They shall go through the country, and whenever one of them sees a human bone he shall put a marker beside it, until it has been buried in the Valley of
16 Gog's Horde. So no more shall be heard of that great horde,[d] and the land will be purified.

17 Man, these are the words of the Lord God: Cry to every bird that flies and to all the wild beasts: Come, assemble, gather from every side to my sacrifice, the great sacrifice I am making for you on the mountains of
18 Israel; eat flesh and drink blood, eat the flesh of warriors and drink the blood of princes of the earth; all these are your rams and sheep, he-goats
19 and bulls, and buffaloes of Bashan. You shall cram yourselves with fat and drink yourselves drunk on blood at the sacrifice which I am preparing for
20 you. At my table you shall eat your fill of horses and riders, of warriors and all manner of fighting men. This is the very word of the Lord God.

21 I will show my glory among the nations; all shall see the judgement that
22 I execute and the heavy hand that I lay upon them. From that day for-
23 wards the Israelites shall know that I am the Lord their God. The nations shall know that the Israelites went into exile for their iniquity, because they were faithless to me. So I hid my face from them and handed them over
24 to their enemies, and they fell, every one of them, by the sword. I dealt with them as they deserved, defiled and rebellious as they were, and hid my face from them.

25 These, therefore, are the words of the Lord God: Now I will restore the fortunes of Jacob and show my affection for all Israel, and I will be jealous
26 for my holy name. They shall forget their shame and all their unfaithfulness to me, when they are at home again on their own soil, undisturbed, with
27 no one to alarm them. When I bring them home out of the nations and gather them from the lands of their enemies, I will make them an example
28 of my holiness, for many nations to see. They will know that I am the Lord their God, because I who sent them into exile among the nations will bring them together again on the soil of their own land and leave none of them
29 behind. No longer will I hide my face from them, I who have poured out my spirit upon Israel. This is the very word of the Lord God.

---

[a] *Prob. rdg.; Heb. adds* there.   [b] *That is* the Dead Sea.   [c] searching for: *prob. rdg.; Heb.* burying those who are passing through.   [d] So . . . horde: *prob. rdg.; Heb. obscure.*

The restored theocracy

A T THE BEGINNING OF THE YEAR, on the tenth day of the month, in **40**
the twenty-fifth year of our exile, that is fourteen years after the
destruction of the city, on that very day, the hand of the LORD came upon
me and he brought me there. In a vision God brought me to the land of **2**
Israel and set me on a very high mountain, where I saw what seemed the
buildings of a city facing me. He led me towards it, and I saw a man like **3**
a figure of bronze holding a cord of linen thread and a measuring-rod, and
standing at the gate. 'Man,' he said to me, 'look closely and listen care- **4**
fully; mark well all that I show you, for this is why you have been brought
here. Tell the Israelites all that you see.'

Round the outside of the temple ran a wall. The length of the rod which **5**
the man was holding was six cubits, reckoning by the long cubit which was
one cubit and a hand's breadth. He measured the thickness and the height
of the wall; each was one rod. He came to a gate which faced eastwards, **6**
went up its steps and measured the threshold of the gateway; its depth
was one rod. Each cell was one rod long and one rod wide; the space between **7**
the cells five cubits, and the threshold of the gateway at the end of the
vestibule on the side facing the temple one rod. He measured the vestibule **8**
of the gate and found it eight cubits, with pilasters two cubits thick; the **9**
vestibule of the gateway lay at the end near the temple. Now the cells of **10**
the gateway, looking back eastwards, were three in number on each side;
all three of the same size, and their pilasters on each side of the same size
also. He measured the entrance into the gateway; it was ten cubits wide, **11**
and the gateway itself throughout its length thirteen cubits wide. In front **12**
of the cells on each side lay a kerb, one cubit wide; each cell was six cubits
by six. He measured the width of the gateway through the cell doors which **13**
faced one another, from the back of one cell to the back of the opposite
cell; he made it twenty-five cubits, and the vestibule twenty cubits, across; **14**
the gateway on every side projected into*a* the court. From the front of the **15**
entrance-gate to the outer face of the vestibule of the inner gate the distance was fifty cubits. Both cells and pilasters had loopholes all round **16**
inside the gateway, and the vestibule had windows all round within and
palms carved on each pilaster.

He brought me to the outer court, and I saw rooms and a pavement all **17**
round the court: in all, thirty rooms on the pavement. The pavement ran **18**
up to the side of the gateways, as wide as they were long; this was the lower
pavement. He measured the width of the court from the front of the lower **19**
gateway to the outside of the inner gateway; it was a hundred cubits. He
led me round to the north and I saw a gateway facing northwards, belong- **20**
ing to the outer court, and he measured its length and its breadth. Its cells, **21**
three on each side, together with its pilasters and its vestibule, were the
same size as those of the first gateway, fifty cubits long by twenty-five wide.
So too its windows, and those of*b* its vestibule, and its palms were the same **22**
size as those of the gateway which faced east; it was approached by seven

a Prob. rdg., Heb. adds pilaster.   *b* those of: *prob. rdg.; Heb. om.*

23 steps with its vestibule facing them. A gate like that on the east side led to the inner court opposite the northern gateway; he measured from gateway
24 to gateway, and it was a hundred cubits. Then he led me round to the south, and I found a gateway facing southwards. He measured its cells, its pilas-
25 ters, and its vestibule, and found it the same size as the others, fifty cubits long by twenty-five wide. Both gateway and vestibule had windows all
26 round like the others. It was approached by seven steps with a vestibule
27 facing them and palms carved on each pilaster. The inner court had a gate-way facing southwards, and he measured from gateway to gateway; it was a hundred cubits.

28 He brought me into the inner court through the southern gateway,
29 measured it and found it the same size as the others. So were its cells, pilasters, and vestibule, fifty cubits long by twenty-five wide. It and its
31 vestibule had windows all round.*a* Its vestibule faced the outer court; it had palms carved on its pilasters, and eight steps led up to it.

32 Then he brought me into the inner court, towards the east, and measured
33 the gateway and found it the same size as the others. So too were its cells, pilasters, and vestibule; it and its vestibule had windows all round, and it
34 was fifty cubits long by twenty-five wide. Its vestibule faced the outer court and had a palm carved on each pilaster; eight steps led up to it.
35 Then he brought me to the north gateway and measured it and found it
36 the same size as the others. So were its cells, pilasters, and vestibule, and
37 it had windows all round; it was fifty cubits long by twenty-five wide. Its vestibule faced the outer court and had palms carved on the pilaster at each side; eight steps led up to it.

38 There was a room opening out from the vestibule of the gateway;*b* here
39 the whole-offerings were washed. In the vestibule of the gateway were two tables on each side, at which to slaughter the whole-offering, the sin-
40 offering, and the guilt-offering. At the corner on the outside, as one goes up to the opening of the northern gateway, stood two tables, and two more
41 at the other corner of the vestibule of the gateway. Another four stood on each side at the corner of the gateway, eight tables in all at which slaughter-
42 ing was done. Four tables used for the whole-offering were of hewn stone, each a cubit and a half long by a cubit and a half wide and a cubit high; and on them they put the instruments used for the whole-offering and other
43 sacrifices. The flesh of the offerings was on the tables, and ledges a hand's breadth in width were fixed all round facing inwards.

44 Then he brought me right into the inner court, and I saw two rooms in the inner court, one at the corner of the northern gateway, facing south,
45 and one at the corner of the southern gateway, facing north. This room facing south, he told me, is for the priests who have charge of the temple.
46 The room facing north is for the priests who have charge of the altar; these are the sons of Zadok, who alone of the Levites may come near to
47 serve the LORD. He measured the court; it was square, a hundred cubits each way, and the altar lay in front of the temple.

a *So some MSS.; others add* (30) It had vestibules all round, and it was twenty-five cubits long by five wide.   *b* the vestibule of the gateway: *prob. rdg.; Heb.* pilasters, the gates.

Then he brought me into the vestibule of the temple, and measured a 48
pilaster of the vestibule; it was five cubits on each side, the width of the
gateway fourteen cubits and that of the corners of the gateway three
cubits in each direction. The vestibule was twenty cubits long by twelve 49
wide; ten steps led up to it, and by the pilasters rose pillars, one on each
side.

Then he brought me into the sanctuary and measured the pilasters; **41**
they were six cubits wide on each side. The opening was ten cubits wide 2
and its corners five cubits wide in each direction. He measured its length;
it was forty cubits, and its width twenty. He went inside and measured the 3
pilasters at the opening: they were two cubits; the opening itself was six
cubits, and the corners of the opening were seven cubits in each direction.
Then he measured the room at the far end of the sanctuary; its length and 4
its breadth were each twenty cubits. He said to me, 'This is the Holy of
Holies.'

He measured the wall of the temple; it was six cubits high, and each 5
arcade all round the house was four cubits wide. The arcades were arranged 6
in three tiers, each tier in thirty sections. In the wall all round the temple
there were intakes for the arcades, so that they could be supported without
being fastened into the wall of the temple. The higher up the arcades were, 7
the broader they were all round by the addition of the intakes, one above
the other all round the temple; the temple itself had a ramp running upwards on a base, and in this way one went up from the lowest to the highest
tier by way of the middle tier.

Then I saw a raised pavement all round the temple, and the foundations 8
of the arcades were flush with it and measured a full rod, six cubits high.
The outer wall of the arcades was five cubits thick. There was an un- 9
occupied area beside the terrace*a* which was adjacent to the temple, and 11 *b*
the arcades opened on to this area, one opening facing northwards and one
southwards; the unoccupied area was five cubits wide on all sides. There 10
was a free space*c* twenty cubits wide all round the temple. On the western 12
side, at the far end of the free space, stood a building seventy cubits wide;
its wall was five cubits thick all round, and its length ninety cubits.

He measured the temple; it was a hundred cubits long; and the free 13
space, the building, and its walls, a hundred cubits in all. The eastern front 14
of the temple and the free space was a hundred cubits wide. He measured 15
the length of the building at the far end of the free space to the west of the
temple, and its corridors on each side: a hundred cubits.

The sanctuary, the inner shrine and the outer vestibule were panelled;
the embrasures all round the three of them were framed with wood all 16
round. From the ground up to the windows and above the door, both in 17
the inner and outer chambers, round all the walls, inside and out, were 18
carved figures,*d* cherubim and palm-trees, a palm between every pair of
cherubim. Each cherub had two faces: one the face of a man, looking 19
towards one palm-tree, and the other the face of a lion, looking towards

a beside the terrace: *prob. rdg.; Heb.* between the arcades.   *b Verses 10 and 11*
transposed.   *c* There . . . space: *prob. rdg.; Heb.* Between the rooms.   *d* carved
figures: *prob. rdg.; Heb.* measures and carving.

another palm-tree. Such was the carving round the whole of the temple.
20 The cherubim and the palm-trees were carved from the ground up to the
21 top of the doorway and on the wall of the sanctuary. The door-posts of
the sanctuary were square.*[a]*

22   In front of*[b]* the Holy Place was what seemed an altar of wood, three
cubits high and two cubits long; it was fitted with corner-posts, and its
base and sides also were of wood. He told me that this was the table which
23 stood before the LORD. The sanctuary had a double door, and the Holy
24 Place also had a double door: the double doors had swinging leaves, a pair
25 for each door. Cherubim and palm-trees like those on the walls were
carved on them.*[c]* Outside there was a wooden cornice over the vestibule;
26 on both sides of the vestibule were loopholes, with palm-trees carved at
the corners.*[d]*

42   Then he took me to the outer court round by the north and brought me
to the rooms facing the free space and facing the buildings to the north.
2 The length along the northern side was a hundred cubits, and the breadth
3 fifty. Facing the free space measuring twenty cubits, which adjoined the
inner court, and facing the pavement of the outer court, were corridors at
4 three levels corresponding to each other. In front of the rooms a passage, ten
cubits wide and a hundred cubits long, ran towards the inner court; their
5 entrances faced northwards. The upper rooms were shorter than the lower
and middle rooms, because the corridors took building space from them.
6 For they were all at three levels and had no pillars as the courts had, so that
7 the lower and middle levels were recessed from the ground upwards. An
outside wall, fifty cubits long, ran parallel to the rooms and in front of them,
8 on the side of the outer court. The rooms adjacent to the outer court were
9 fifty cubits long, and those facing the sanctuary a hundred cubits. Below
these rooms was an entry from the east as one entered them from the outer
10 court where the wall of the court began.*[e]* On the south side, passing by the
11 free space and the building, were other rooms with a passage in front of
them. These rooms corresponded, in length and breadth and in general
12 character, to those facing north, whose exits and entrances were the same
as those of the rooms on the south. As one*[f]* went eastwards, where the
13 passages began, there was an entrance in the face of the inner*[g]* wall. Then
he said to me, 'The northern and southern rooms facing the free space
are the consecrated rooms where the priests who approach the LORD may
eat the most sacred offerings. There they shall put these offerings as well
as the grain-offering, the sin-offering, and the guilt-offering; for the place
14 is holy. When the priests have entered the Holy Place they shall not go
into the outer court again without leaving here the garments they have
worn while performing their duties, for these are holy. They shall put on
other garments when they approach the place assigned to the people.'
15   When he had finished measuring the inner temple, he brought me out
towards the gateway which faces eastwards and measured the whole

---

[a] The door-posts . . . square: *prob. rdg.; Heb. unintelligible.*   *[b]* In front of: *prob.
rdg.; Heb. The face of.*   *[c]* *Prob. rdg.; Heb. adds* on the doors of the sanctuary.
[d] *Prob. rdg.; Heb. adds* and the arcades of the temple and the cornices.   *[e]* began:
prob. rdg.; Heb. breadth.   *[f]* *Prob. rdg.; Heb.* they.   *[g]* *Prob. rdg.; Heb. word unknown.*

area. He measured the east side with the measuring-rod, and it was five 16
hundred cubits. He turned and measured the north side with his rod, and 17
it was five hundred cubits. He turned to the south side and measured it 18
with his rod; it was five hundred cubits. He turned to the west and measured 19
it with his rod; it was five hundred cubits. So he measured all four sides; 20
in each direction the surrounding wall measured five hundred cubits.
This marked off the sacred area from the profane.

He led me to the gate, the gate facing eastwards, and I beheld the glory 43 1 2
of the God of Israel coming from the east. His voice was like the sound of
a mighty torrent, and the earth shone with his glory. The form that I saw 3
was the same as that which I had seen when he came to destroy the city,
and as that which I had seen by the river Kebar,[a] and I fell on my face.
The glory of the LORD came up to the temple towards the gate which faced 4
eastwards. A spirit[b] lifted me up and brought me into the inner court, and 5
the glory of the LORD filled the temple. Then I heard one speaking to me 6
from the temple, and the man was standing at my side. He said, Man, do 7
you see the place of my throne, the place where I set my feet, where I will
dwell among the Israelites for ever? Neither they nor their kings shall
ever defile my holy name again with their wanton disloyalty, and with the
corpses[c] of their kings when they die. They set their threshold by mine 8
and their door-post beside mine, with a wall between me and them, and
they defiled my holy name with the abominations they committed, and
I destroyed them in my anger. But now they shall abandon their wanton 9
disloyalty and remove the corpses[c] of their kings far from me, and I will
dwell among them for ever. So tell the Israelites, man, about this temple, 10
its appearance and proportions, that they may be ashamed of their iniquities. If they are ashamed of all they have done, you shall describe to 11
them the temple and its fittings, its exits and entrances, all the details and
particulars of its elevation and plan; explain them and draw them before
their eyes, so that they may keep them in mind and carry them out. This 12
is the plan of the temple to be built on the top of the mountain; all its
precincts on every side shall be most holy.

These were the dimensions of the altar in cubits (the cubit that is a cubit 13
and a hand's breadth). This was the height of the altar: the base was a
cubit high[d] and projected a cubit; on its edge was a rim one span deep.
From the base to the cubit-wide ridge of the lower pedestal-block was two 14
cubits, and from this shorter pedestal-block to the cubit-wide ridge of the
taller pedestal-block was four cubits. The altar-hearth was four cubits 15
high and was surmounted by four horns a cubit high. The hearth was twelve 16
cubits long and twelve cubits wide, being a perfect square. The upper 17
pedestal-block was fourteen cubits long and fourteen cubits wide along
its four sides, and the rim round it was half a cubit deep. The base of the
altar projected a cubit, and there were steps facing eastwards.

He said to me, Man, these are the words of the Lord GOD: These are 18
the regulations for the altar when it has been made, for sacrificing whole-
offerings on it and flinging the blood against it. The levitical priests of the 19

---

[a] *Or* the Kebar canal.   [b] *Or* wind.   [c] *Or* effigies.   [d] the base . . . high:
prob. rdg.; Heb. the base of the cubit.

family of Zadok, and they alone, may come near to me to serve me, says
20 the Lord God. You shall assign them a young bull for a sin-offering; you
shall take some of the blood and put it on the four horns of the altar, on the
four corners of the upper pedestal and all round the rim, and so purify it
21 and make expiation for it. Then take the bull assigned as the sin-offering,
and they shall destroy it by fire in the proper place within the precincts
22 but outside the Holy Place. On the second day you shall present a he-goat
without blemish as a sin-offering, and with it they shall purify the altar
23 as they did with the bull. When you have completely purified the altar,
you shall present a young bull without blemish and a ram without blemish
24 from the flock. You shall present them before the Lord; the priests shall
25 throw salt on them and sacrifice them as a whole-offering to the Lord. For
seven days you shall provide as a daily sin-offering a goat, a young bull,
and a ram from the flock; all of them shall be provided free from blemish.
26 For seven days they shall make expiation for the altar, and pronounce it
27 ritually clean, and consecrate it. At the end of that time, on the eighth day
and onwards, the priests shall sacrifice on the altar your whole-offerings
and your shared-offerings, and I will accept you. This is the very word of
the Lord God.

44 He again brought me round to the outer gate of the sanctuary facing
2 eastwards, and it was shut. The Lord said to me, This gate shall be kept
shut; it must not be opened. No man may enter by it, for the Lord the God
3 of Israel has entered by it. It shall be kept shut. The prince, however, when
he is here as prince, may sit there to eat food in the presence of the Lord;
he shall come in and go out by the vestibule of the gate.

4 He brought me round to the northern gate facing the temple, and I saw
5 the glory of the Lord filling the Lord's house, and I fell on my face. The
Lord said to me, Mark well, man, look closely, and listen carefully to all
that I say to you, to all the rules and regulations for the house of the Lord.
Mark well the entrance to the house of the Lord and all the exits from the
6 sanctuary. Say to that rebel people of Israel, These are the words of the
7 Lord God: Enough of all these abominations of yours, you Israelites! You
have added to them by bringing foreigners, uncircumcised in mind and
body, to stand in my sanctuary and defile my house when you present my
food to me, both fat and blood, and they have made my covenant void.
8 Instead of keeping charge of my holy things yourselves, you have chosen
to put these men in charge of my sanctuary.

9 These are the words of the Lord God: No foreigner, uncircumcised in
mind and body, shall enter my sanctuary, not even a foreigner living among
10 the Israelites. But the Levites, though they deserted me when the Israelites
went astray after their idols and had to bear the punishment of their in-
11 iquity, shall yet do service in my sanctuary. They shall take charge of the
gates of the temple and do service there. They shall slaughter the whole-
offering and the sacrifice for the people and shall be in attendance to serve
12 them. Because they served them in the presence of their idols and brought
Israel to the ground by their iniquity, says the Lord God, I have sworn
with uplifted hand that they shall bear the punishment of their iniquity.
13 They shall not have access to me, to serve me as priests; they shall not come

near to my holy things or to the Holy of Holies; they shall bear the shame
of the abominable deeds they have done. I will put them in charge of the 14
temple with all the service which must be performed there.

But the levitical priests of the family of Zadok remained in charge of my 15
sanctuary when the Israelites went astray from me; these shall approach
me to serve me. They shall be in attendance on me, presenting the fat and
the blood, says the Lord GOD. It is they who shall enter my sanctuary and 16
approach my table to serve me and observe my charge. When they come to 17
the gates of the inner court they shall dress in linen; they shall wear no wool
when they serve me at the gates of the inner court and within. They shall 18
wear linen turbans, and linen drawers on their loins; they shall not fasten
their clothes with a belt so that they sweat. When they go out to the people in 19
the outer court, they shall take off the clothes they have worn while serving,
leave them in the sacred rooms and put on other clothes; otherwise they
will transmit the sacred influence to the people through their clothing.

They shall neither shave their heads nor let their hair grow long; they shall 20
only clip their hair. No priest shall drink wine when he is to enter the inner 21
court. He may not marry a widow or a divorced woman; he may marry a 22
virgin of Israelite birth. He may, however, marry the widow of a priest.

They shall teach my people to distinguish the sacred from the profane, 23
and show them the difference between clean and unclean. When disputes 24
break out, they shall take their place in court, and settle the case according
to my rules. At all my appointed seasons they shall observe my laws and
statutes. They shall keep my sabbaths holy.

They shall not defile themselves by contact with any dead person, 25
except*a* father or mother, son or daughter, brother or unmarried sister.
After purification, they shall count seven days and then be clean. When 26 27
they enter the inner court to serve in the Holy Place, they shall present
their sin-offering, says the Lord GOD.

They shall own no patrimony in Israel; I am their patrimony. You shall 28
grant them no holding in Israel; I am their holding. The grain-offering, 29
the sin-offering, and the guilt-offering shall be eaten by them, and everything in Israel devoted to God shall be theirs. The first of all the first- 30
fruits and all your contributions of every kind shall belong wholly to the
priests. You shall give the first lump of your dough to the priests, that a
blessing may rest upon your home. The priests shall eat no carrion, bird 31
or beast, whether it has died naturally or been killed by a wild animal.

When you divide the land by lot among the tribes for their possession, **45**
you shall set apart from it a sacred reserve for the LORD, twenty-five
thousand cubits in length and twenty thousand in width; the whole en-
closure shall be sacred. Of this a square plot, five hundred cubits each way, 2
shall be devoted to the sanctuary, with fifty cubits of open land round it.
From this area you shall measure out a space twenty-five thousand by ten 3
thousand cubits, in which the sanctuary, the holiest place of all, shall stand.
This space is for the priests who serve in the sanctuary and who come 4
nearest in serving the LORD. It shall include space for their houses and a
sacred plot for the sanctuary. An area of twenty-five thousand by ten 5

a any . . . except: *or* anyone else's dead, but only their own . . .

thousand cubits shall belong to the Levites, the temple servants; on this
6 shall stand the towns in which they live. You shall give to each town an
area of five thousand by twenty-five thousand cubits alongside the sacred
7 reserve; this shall belong to all Israel. On either side of the sacred reserve
and of the city's holding the prince shall have a holding facing the sacred
reserve and the city's holding, running westwards on the west and eastwards
on the east. It shall run alongside one of the tribal portions, and stretch
8 to the western limit of the land and to the eastern. It shall be his holding
in Israel; the princes of Israel shall never oppress my people again but
shall give the land to Israel, tribe by tribe.

9 THESE ARE THE WORDS OF THE LORD GOD: Enough, princes of Israel!
Put an end to lawlessness and robbery; maintain law and justice; relieve
10 my people and stop your evictions, says the Lord GOD. Your scales shall
11 be honest, your bushel and your gallon shall be honest. There shall be one
standard for each, taking each as the tenth of a homer, and the homer shall
12 have its fixed standard. Your shekel weight shall contain twenty gerahs;
your mina shall contain weights of ten*a* and twenty-five and fifteen shekels.
13 These are the contributions you shall set aside: out of every homer of
14 wheat or of barley, one sixth of an ephah. For oil the rule is*b* one tenth of a
15 bath from every kor (at ten bath to the kor); one sheep in every flock of
two hundred is to be reserved by every Israelite clan. For a grain-offering,
a whole-offering, and a shared-offering, to make expiation for them, says
16 the Lord GOD, all the people of the land shall bring*c* this contribution to
17 the prince in Israel; and the prince shall be responsible for the whole-
offering, the grain-offering, and the drink-offering, at pilgrim-feasts, new
moons, sabbaths, and every sacred season observed by Israel. He himself
is to provide the sin-offering and the grain-offering, the whole-offering
and the shared-offering, needed to make expiation for Israel.
18 These are the words of the Lord GOD: On the first day of the first
month you shall take a young bull without blemish, and purify the sanctuary.
19 The priest shall take some of the blood from the sin-offering and put it on
the door-posts of the temple, on the four corners of the altar pedestal and
20 on the gate-posts of the inner court. You shall do the same on the seventh
day of the month;*d* in this way you shall make expiation for the temple.
21 On the fourteenth day of the first month you shall hold the Passover,
22 the pilgrim-feast of seven days; bread must be eaten unleavened. On that
day the prince shall provide a bull as a sin-offering for himself and for all
23 the people. During the seven days of the feast he shall offer daily as a
whole-offering to the LORD seven bulls and seven rams without blemish,
24 and a he-goat as a daily sin-offering. With every bull and ram he shall provide a grain-offering of one ephah, together with a hin of oil for each ephah.
25 He shall do the same thing also on the fifteenth day of the seventh month at
the pilgrim-feast; this also shall last seven days, and he shall provide the
same sin-offering and whole-offering and the same quantity of grain and oil.

a *Prob. rdg.; Heb.* twenty.   *b* *Prob. rdg.; Heb. adds* the bath, the oil.
c All . . . bring: *prob. rdg.; Heb. unintelligible.*   *d* *Prob. rdg.; Heb. adds* This
comes from a man who is wrong and foolish. *Cp. Lev. 23. 24; Num. 29. 1.*

These are the words of the Lord GOD: The eastern gate of the inner **46**
court shall remain closed for the six working days; it may be opened only
on the sabbath and at new moon. When the prince comes through the 2
porch of the gate from the outside, he shall halt at the door-post, and
the priests shall sacrifice his whole-offering and shared-offerings. On the
terrace he shall bow down at the gate and then go out, but the gate shall
not be shut till the evening. On sabbaths and at new moons the people 3
also shall bow down before the LORD at the entrance to that gate.

The whole-offering which the prince sacrifices to the LORD shall be as 4
follows: on the sabbath, six sheep without blemish and a ram without
blemish; the grain-offering shall be an ephah with the ram and as much 5
as he likes with the sheep, together with a hin of oil for every ephah. At 6
the new moon it shall be a young bull without blemish, six sheep and a ram,
all without blemish. He shall provide as the grain-offering to go with the 7
bull one ephah and with the ram one ephah, with the sheep as much as he
can afford, adding a hin of oil for every ephah.

When the prince comes in, he shall enter through the porch of the gate 8
and come out by the same way. But on festal days when the people come 9
before the LORD, a man who enters by the northern gate to bow down shall
leave by the southern gate, and a man who enters by the southern gate shall
leave by the northern gate. He shall not turn back and go out through the
gate by which he came in but shall go straight on. The prince shall then be 10
among them, going in when they go in and coming out when they come out.

At pilgrim-feasts and on festal days the grain-offering shall be an ephah 11
with a bull, an ephah with a ram and as much as he likes with a sheep,
together with a hin of oil for every ephah.

When the prince provides a whole-offering or shared-offerings as a 12
voluntary sacrifice to the LORD, the eastern gate shall be opened for him,*a*
and he shall make his whole-offering and his shared-offerings as he does
on the sabbath; when he goes out the gate shall be closed*b* behind him.

You shall provide a yearling sheep without blemish daily as a whole- 13
offering to the LORD; you shall provide it morning by morning. With it 14
every morning you shall provide as a grain-offering one sixth of an ephah
with a third of a hin of oil to moisten the flour; the LORD's grain-offering
is an observance prescribed for all time. Morning by morning, as a regular 15
whole-offering, they shall offer a sheep with the grain-offering and the oil.

These are the words of the Lord GOD: When the prince makes a gift 16
out of his property to any of his sons, it shall belong to his sons, since it is
part of the family property. But when he makes such a gift to one of his 17
slaves, it shall be his only till the year of manumission, when it shall revert
to the prince; it is the property of his sons and shall belong to them.

The prince shall not oppress the people by taking part of their holdings; 18
he shall give his sons an inheritance from his own holding of land, so that
my people may not be scattered and separated from their holdings.

Then he brought me through the entrance by the side of the gate to the 19
rooms which face north (the sacred rooms reserved for the priests), and,

a the eastern . . . him: *or* he shall open the gate facing east.   *b* the gate . . . closed:
or he shall close the gate.

20 pointing to a place on their western side, he said to me, 'This is the place where the priests shall boil the guilt-offering and the sin-offering and bake the grain-offering; they shall not take it into the outer court for fear they
21 transmit the sacred influence to the people.' Then he brought me into the outer court and took me across to the four corners of the court, at each of
22 which there was a further court. These four courts were vaulted and were
23 the same size, forty cubits long by thirty cubits wide. Round each of the four was a row of stones, with fire-places constructed close up against the
24 rows. He said to me, 'These are the kitchens where the attendants shall boil the people's sacrifices.'

47   He brought me back to the gate of the temple, and I saw a spring of water issuing from under the terrace of the temple towards the east; for the temple faced east. The water was running down along the right side,
2 to the south of the altar. He took me out through the northern gate and brought me round by an outside path to the eastern gate of the court, and
3 water was trickling from the right side. When the man went out eastwards he had a line in his hand. He measured a thousand cubits and made me
4 walk through the water; it came up to my ankles. He measured another thousand and made me walk through the water; it came up to my knees. He measured another thousand and made me walk through the water;
5 it was up to my waist. Another thousand, and it was a torrent I could not cross, for the water had risen and was now deep enough to swim in; it
6 had become a torrent that could not be crossed. 'Mark this, man', he said,
7 and led me back to the bank of the torrent. When we came back to the bank
8 I saw a great number of trees on each side. He said to me, 'This water flows out to the region lying east, and down to the Arabah; at last it will reach
9 that sea whose waters are foul, and they will be sweetened. When any one of the living creatures that swarm upon the earth comes where the torrent flows, it shall draw life from it. The fish shall be innumerable; for these waters come here so that the others may be sweetened, and where the tor-
10 rent flows everything shall live. From En-gedi as far as En-eglaim fisher-men shall stand on its shores, for nets shall be spread there. Every kind
11 of fish shall be there in shoals, like the fish of the Great Sea; but its swamps and pools shall not have their waters sweetened but shall be left as salt-
12 pans. Beside the torrent on either bank all trees good for food shall spring up. Their leaves shall not wither, their fruit shall not cease; they shall bear early every month. For their water comes from the sanctuary; their fruit is for food and their foliage for enjoyment.'

13   These are the words of the Lord GOD: These are the boundary lines within which the twelve tribes of Israel shall enter into possession of the
14 land, Joseph receiving two portions. The land which I swore with hand uplifted to give to your fathers you shall divide with each other; it shall be
15 assigned to you by lot as your patrimony. This is the frontier: on its northern side, from the Great Sea through Hethlon, Lebo-hamath,
16 Zedad, Berutha, and Sibraim, which are between the frontiers of Damascus
17 and Hamath, to Hazar-enan, near the frontier of Hauran. So the frontier shall run from the sea to Hazar-enan on the frontier of Damascus and
18 northwards; this is its northern side. The eastern side runs alongside the

territories of Hauran, Damascus, and Gilead, and alongside the territory of Israel; Jordan sets the boundary to the eastern sea, to Tamar. This is the eastern side. The southern side runs from Tamar to the waters of 19 Meribah-by-Kadesh; the region assigned to you reaches the Great Sea. This is the southern side towards the Negeb. The western side is the Great 20 Sea, which forms a boundary as far as a point opposite Lebo-hamath. This is the western side. You shall distribute this land among the tribes 21 of Israel and assign it by lot as a patrimony for yourselves and for any aliens 22 living in your midst who leave sons among you. They shall be treated as native-born in Israel and with you shall receive a patrimony by lot among the tribes of Israel. You shall give the alien his patrimony with the tribe 23 in which he is living. This is the very word of the Lord GOD.

These are the names of the tribes: In the extreme north, in the direction **48** of Hethlon, to Lebo-hamath and Hazar-enan, with Damascus on the northern frontier in the direction of Hamath, and so from the eastern side to the western, shall be Dan: one portion.

Bordering on Dan, from the eastern side to the western, shall be Asher: 2 one portion.

Bordering on Asher, from the eastern side to the western, shall be 3 Naphtali: one portion.

Bordering on Naphtali, from the eastern side to the western, shall be 4 Manasseh: one portion.

Bordering on Manasseh, from the eastern side to the western, shall be 5 Ephraim: one portion.

Bordering on Ephraim, from the eastern side to the western, shall be 6 Reuben: one portion.

Bordering on Reuben, from the eastern side to the western, shall be 7 Judah: one portion.

Bordering on Judah, from the eastern side to the western, shall be the 8 reserve which you shall set apart. Its breadth shall be twenty-five thousand cubits and its length the same as that of the other portions, from the eastern side to the western, and the sanctuary shall be in the middle of it.

The reserve which you shall set apart for the LORD shall measure twenty- 9 five thousand cubits by twenty*a* thousand. The reserve shall be appor- 10 tioned thus: the priests shall have an area measuring twenty-five thousand cubits on the north side, ten thousand on the west, ten thousand on the east, and twenty-five thousand on the south side; the sanctuary of the LORD shall be in the middle of it. It shall be for the consecrated priests, the sons 11 of Zadok, who kept my charge and did not follow the Israelites when they went astray, as the Levites did. The area set apart for the priests from 12 the reserved territory shall be most sacred, reaching the frontier of the Levites.

The Levites shall have a portion running parallel to the border of the 13 priests. It shall be twenty-five thousand cubits long by ten thousand wide; altogether, the length shall be twenty-five thousand cubits and the breadth ten thousand. They shall neither sell nor exchange any part of it, nor shall 14 the best of the land be alienated; for it is holy to the LORD.

a Prob. rdg.; Heb. ten.

15 The strip which is left, five thousand cubits in width by twenty-five thousand, is the city's secular land for dwellings and common land, and
16 the city shall be in the middle of it. These shall be its dimensions: on the northern side four thousand five hundred cubits, on the southern side four thousand five hundred cubits, on the eastern side four thousand five hundred cubits, on the western side four thousand five hundred cubits.
17 The common land belonging to the city shall be two hundred and fifty cubits to the north, two hundred and fifty to the south, two hundred and
18 fifty to the east, and two hundred and fifty to the west. What is left parallel to the reserve, ten thousand cubits to the east and ten thousand to the west, [a]
19 shall provide food for those who work in the city. Those who work in the city shall cultivate it; they may be drawn from any of the tribes of Israel.
20 You shall set apart the whole reserve, twenty-five thousand cubits
21 square, as sacred, as far as the holding of the city. What is left over on each side of the sacred reserve and the holding of the city shall be assigned to the prince. Eastwards, what lies over against the reserved twenty-five thousand cubits, as far as the eastern side, and westwards, what lies over against the twenty-five thousand cubits to the western side, parallel to the tribal portions, shall be assigned to the prince; the sacred reserve and the
22 sanctuary itself shall be in the centre. The [b] holding of the Levites and the [b] holding of the city shall be in the middle of that which is assigned to the prince; it shall be between the frontiers of Judah and Benjamin.
23 The rest of the tribes: from the eastern side to the western shall be Benjamin: one portion.
24 Bordering on Benjamin, from the eastern side to the western, shall be Simeon: one portion.
25 Bordering on Simeon, from the eastern side to the western, shall be Issachar: one portion.
26 Bordering on Issachar, from the eastern side to the western, shall be Zebulun: one portion.
27 Bordering on Zebulun, from the eastern side to the western, shall be Gad: one portion.
28 Bordering on Gad, on the side of the Negeb, the border on the south stretches from Tamar to the waters of Meribah-by-Kadesh, to the Brook as far as the Great Sea.
29 This is the land which you shall allot as a patrimony to the tribes of Israel, and these shall be their lots. This is the very word of the Lord GOD.
30-31 These are to be the ways out of the city, and they are to be named after the tribes of Israel. The northern side, four thousand five hundred cubits
32 long, shall have three gates, those of Reuben, Judah, and Levi; the eastern side, four thousand five hundred cubits long, three gates, those of Joseph,
33 Benjamin, and Dan; the southern side, four thousand five hundred cubits
34 long, three gates, those of Simeon, Issachar, and Zebulun; the western side, four thousand five hundred cubits long, three gates, those of Gad,
35 Asher, and Naphtali. The perimeter of the city shall be eighteen thousand cubits, and the city's name for ever after shall be Jehovah-shammah. [c]

[a] *Prob. rdg.; Heb. adds* and it shall be parallel to the sacred reserve.   [b] *Prob. rdg.;* Heb. Some of the.   [c] *That is* the LORD is there.

THE BOOK OF
DANIEL

Jews at the court of Nebuchadnezzar

IN THE THIRD YEAR OF THE REIGN OF JEHOIAKIM 1
king of Judah, Nebuchadnezzar king of Babylon came to Jerusalem
and laid siege to it. The Lord delivered Jehoiakim king of Judah into 2
his power, together with all that was left of the vessels of the house of God;
and he carried them off to the land of Shinar, to the temple of his god,
where he deposited the vessels in the treasury. Then the king ordered 3
Ashpenaz, his chief eunuch, to take certain of the Israelite exiles, of the
blood royal and of the nobility, who were to be young men of good looks 4
and bodily without fault, at home in all branches of knowledge, well-
informed, intelligent, and fit for service in the royal court; and he was to
instruct them in the literature and language of the Chaldaeans. The king 5
assigned them a daily allowance of food and wine from the royal table.
Their training was to last for three years, and at the end of that time they
would*a* enter the royal service.

Among them there were certain young men from Judah called Daniel, 6
Hananiah, Mishael and Azariah; but the master of the eunuchs gave them 7
new names: Daniel he called Belteshazzar, Hananiah Shadrach, Mishael
Meshach and Azariah Abed-nego. Now Daniel determined not to con- 8
taminate himself by touching the food and wine assigned to him by the
king, and he begged the master of the eunuchs not to make him do so.
God made the master show kindness and goodwill to Daniel, and he said 9 10
to him, 'I am afraid of my lord the king: he has assigned you your food and
drink, and if he sees you looking dejected, unlike the other young men of
your own age, it will cost me my head.' Then Daniel said to the guard 11
whom the master of the eunuchs had put in charge of Hananiah, Mishael,
Azariah and himself, 'Submit us to this test for ten days. Give us only 12
vegetables to eat and water to drink; then compare our looks with those of 13
the young men who have lived on the food assigned by the king, and be
guided in your treatment of us by what you see.'*b* The guard listened to 14
what they said and tested them for ten days. At the end of ten days they 15
looked healthier and were better nourished than all the young men who
had lived on the food assigned them by the king. So the guard took away 16
the assignment of food and the wine they were to drink, and gave them only
the vegetables.

To all four of these young men God had given knowledge and under- 17
standing of books and learning of every kind, while Daniel had a gift for

---

a at the end . . . would: *or* all of them were to.   *b* be guided . . . see: *or* treat
us as you see fit.

18 interpreting visions and dreams of every kind. The time came which the
king had fixed for introducing the young men to court, and the master of
19 the eunuchs brought them into the presence of Nebuchadnezzar. The
king talked with them and found none of them to compare with Daniel,
20 Hananiah, Mishael and Azariah; so they entered the royal service. Whenever the king consulted them on any matter calling for insight and judgement, he found them ten times better than all the magicians and exorcists
21 in his whole kingdom. Now Daniel was there till the first year of King
Cyrus.

2 In the second year of his reign Nebuchadnezzar had dreams, and his
2 mind was so troubled that he could not sleep. Then the king gave orders
to summon the magicians, exorcists, sorcerers, and Chaldaeans to tell him
3 what he had dreamt. They came in and stood in the royal presence, and
the king said to them, 'I have had a dream and my mind has been troubled
4 to know what my dream was.' The Chaldaeans, speaking in Aramaic, said,
a'Long live the king! Tell us what you dreamt and we will tell you the
5 interpretation.' The king answered, 'This is my declared intention. If you
do not tell me both dream and interpretation, you shall be torn in pieces
6 and your houses shall be forfeit.*b* But if you can tell me the dream and the
interpretation, you will be richly rewarded and loaded with honours. Tell
7 me, therefore, the dream and its interpretation.' They answered a second
time, 'Let the king tell his servants the dream, and we will tell him the
8 interpretation.' The king answered, 'It is clear to me that you are trying to
9 gain time, because you see that my intention has been declared. If you do
not make known to me the dream, there is one law that applies to you, and
one only. What is more, you have agreed among yourselves to tell me a
pack of lies to my face in the hope that with time things may alter. Tell me
the dream, therefore, and I shall know that you can give me the interpreta-
10 tion.' The Chaldaeans answered in the presence of the king, 'Nobody on
earth can tell your majesty what you wish to know; no great king or prince
11 has ever made such a demand of magician, exorcist, or Chaldaean. What
your majesty requires of us is too hard; there is no one but the gods, who
12 dwell remote from mortal men, who can give you the answer.' At this the
king lost his temper and in a great rage ordered the death of all the wise men
13 of Babylon. A decree was issued that the wise men were to be executed, and
accordingly men were sent to fetch Daniel and his companions for
execution.

14 When Arioch, the captain of the king's bodyguard, was setting out to
execute the wise men of Babylon, Daniel approached him cautiously and
15 with discretion and said, 'Sir, you represent the king; why has his majesty
16 issued such a peremptory decree?' Arioch explained everything; so Daniel
went in to the king's presence and begged for a certain time by which he
17 would give the king the interpretation. Then Daniel went home and told
18 the whole story to his companions, Hananiah, Mishael and Azariah. They
should ask the God of heaven in his mercy, he said, to disclose this secret,
so that they and he with the rest of the wise men of Babylon should not be

---

a *The Aramaic text begins here and continues to the end of ch. 7.*   *b* *Or made into
a dunghill (mng. of Aram. word uncertain).*

put to death. Then in a vision by night the secret was revealed to Daniel, 19
and he blessed the God of heaven in these words: 20

> Blessed be God's name from age to age,
> for all wisdom and power are his.
> He changes seasons and times;   21
> he deposes kings and sets them up;
> he gives wisdom to the wise
> and all their store of knowledge to the men who know;
> he reveals deep mysteries;   22
> he knows what lies in darkness,
> and light has its dwelling with him.
> To thee, God of my fathers, I give thanks and praise,   23
> for thou hast given me wisdom and power;
> thou hast now revealed to me what we asked,
> and told us what the king is concerned to know.

Daniel therefore went to Arioch who had been charged by the king to   24
put to death the wise men of Babylon and said to him, 'Do not put the wise
men of Babylon to death. Take me into the king's presence, and I will now
tell him the interpretation of the dream.' Arioch in great trepidation brought 25
Daniel before the king and said to him, 'I have found among the Jewish
exiles a man who will make known to your majesty the interpretation of your
dream.' Thereupon the king said to Daniel (who was also called Belteshaz- 26
zar), 'Can you tell me what I saw in my dream and interpret it?' Daniel   27
answered in the king's presence, 'The secret about which your majesty
inquires no wise man, exorcist, magician, or diviner can disclose to you.
But there is in heaven a god who reveals secrets, and he has told King   28
Nebuchadnezzar what is to be at the end of this age. This is the dream
and these the visions that came into your head: the thoughts that came to 29
you, O king, as you lay on your bed, were thoughts of things to come, and
the revealer of secrets has made known to you what is to be. This secret   30
has been revealed to me not because I am wise beyond all living men, but
because your majesty is to know the interpretation and understand the
thoughts which have entered your mind.

'As you watched, O king, you saw a great image. This image, huge and   31
dazzling, towered before you, fearful to behold. The head of the image was 32
of fine gold, its breast and arms of silver, its belly and thighs of bronze,^a
its legs of iron, its feet part iron and part clay. While you looked, a stone 33 34
was hewn from a mountain, not by human hands; it struck the image on
its feet of iron and clay and shattered them. Then the iron, the clay, the 35
bronze, the silver, and the gold, were all shattered to fragments and were
swept away like chaff before the wind from a threshing-floor in summer,
until no trace of them remained. But the stone which struck the image
grew into a great mountain filling the whole earth. That was the dream.   36
We shall now tell your majesty the interpretation. You, O king, king of   37
kings, to whom the God of heaven has given the kingdom with all its power,
authority, and honour; in whose hands he has placed men and beasts and   38

---

a Or copper.

birds of the air, wherever they dwell, granting you sovereignty over them
39 all—you are that head of gold. After you there shall arise another kingdom,
inferior to yours, and yet a third kingdom, of bronze, which shall have
40 sovereignty over the whole world. And there shall be a fourth kingdom,
strong as iron; as iron shatters and destroys all things, it shall break and
41 shatter the whole earth.[a] As, in your vision, the feet and toes were part
potter's clay and part iron, it shall be a divided kingdom. Its core shall be
42 partly of iron just as you saw iron mixed with the common clay; as the toes
were part iron and part clay, the kingdom shall be partly strong and partly
43 brittle. As, in your vision, the iron was mixed with common clay, so shall
men mix with each other by intermarriage, but such alliances shall not be
44 stable: iron does not mix with clay. In the period of those kings the God
of heaven will establish a kingdom which shall never be destroyed; that
kingdom shall never pass to another people; it shall shatter and make an
45 end of all these kingdoms, while it shall itself endure for ever. This is the
meaning of your vision of the stone being hewn from a mountain, not by
human hands, and then shattering the iron, the bronze, the clay, the silver,
and the gold. The mighty God has made known to your majesty what is
to be hereafter. The dream is sure and the interpretation to be trusted.'
46   Then King Nebuchadnezzar prostrated himself and worshipped Daniel,
and gave orders that sacrifices and soothing offerings should be made to
47 him. 'Truly,' he said, 'your god is indeed God of gods and Lord over kings,
48 a revealer of secrets, since you have been able to reveal this secret.' Then
the king promoted Daniel, bestowed on him many rich gifts, and made him
regent over the whole province of Babylon and chief prefect over all the
49 wise men of Babylon. Moreover at Daniel's request the king put Shadrach,
Meshach and Abed-nego in charge of the administration of the province
of Babylon. Daniel himself, however, remained at court.

3 KING NEBUCHADNEZZAR MADE AN IMAGE OF GOLD, ninety feet high
and nine feet broad. He had it set up in the plain of Dura in the province of
2 Babylon. Then he sent out a summons to assemble the satraps, prefects,
viceroys, counsellors, treasurers, judges, chief constables, and all governors of provinces to attend the dedication of the image which he had set
3 up. So they assembled—the satraps, prefects, viceroys, counsellors,
treasurers, judges, chief constables, and all governors of provinces—for
the dedication of the image which King Nebuchadnezzar had set up; and
4 they stood before the image which Nebuchadnezzar had set up. Then the
herald loudly proclaimed, 'O peoples and nations of every language, you
5 are commanded, when you hear the sound of horn, pipe, zither, triangle,
dulcimer, music, and singing of every kind, to prostrate yourselves and
6 worship the golden image which King Nebuchadnezzar has set up. Whoever does not prostrate himself and worship shall forthwith be thrown into a
7 blazing furnace.' Accordingly, no sooner did all the peoples hear the sound
of horn, pipe, zither, triangle, dulcimer, music, and singing of every kind,
than all the peoples and nations of every language prostrated themselves
and worshipped the golden image which King Nebuchadnezzar had set up.

    [a] the whole earth: *prob. rdg.; Aram.* and like iron which shatters all these.

It was then that certain Chaldaeans came forward and brought a charge 8
against the Jews. They said to King Nebuchadnezzar, 'Long live the king! 9
Your majesty has issued an order that every man who hears the sound of 10
horn, pipe, zither, triangle, dulcimer, music, and singing of every kind
shall fall down and worship the image of gold. Whoever does not do so shall 11
be thrown into a blazing furnace. There are certain Jews, Shadrach, Me- 12
shach and Abed-nego, whom you have put in charge of the administration of the province of Babylon. These men, your majesty, have taken
no notice of your command; they do not serve your god, nor do they worship the golden image which you have set up.' Then in rage and fury 13
Nebuchadnezzar ordered Shadrach, Meshach and Abed-nego to be fetched,
and they were brought into the king's presence. Nebuchadnezzar said to 14
them, 'Is it true, Shadrach, Meshach and Abed-nego, that you do not
serve my god or worship the golden image which I have set up? If you are 15
ready at once to prostrate yourselves when you hear the sound of horn,
pipe, zither, triangle, dulcimer, music, and singing of every kind, and to
worship the image that I have set up, well and good. But if you do not
worship it, you shall forthwith be thrown into the blazing furnace; and
what god is there that can save you from my power?' Shadrach, Meshach 16
and Abed-nego said to King Nebuchadnezzar, 'We have no need to answer
you on this matter. If there is a god who is able to save us from the blazing 17
furnace, it is our God whom we serve, and he will save us from your power,
O king; but if not, be it known to your majesty that we will neither serve 18
your god nor worship the golden image that you have set up.'

Then Nebuchadnezzar flew into a rage with Shadrach, Meshach and 19
Abed-nego, and his face was distorted with anger. He gave orders that the
furnace should be heated up to seven times its usual heat, and commanded 20
some of the strongest men in his army to bind Shadrach, Meshach and
Abed-nego and throw them into the blazing furnace. Then those men in 21
their trousers, their shirts, and their hats and all their other clothes, were
bound and thrown into the blazing furnace. Because the king's order was 22
urgent and the furnace exceedingly hot, the men who were carrying
Shadrach, Meshach and Abed-nego were killed by the flames that leapt out;
and those three men, Shadrach, Meshach and Abed-nego, fell bound into 23
the blazing furnace.

Then King Nebuchadnezzar was amazed and sprang to his feet in great 24
trepidation. He said to his courtiers, 'Was it not three men whom we threw
bound into the fire?' They answered the king, 'Assuredly, your majesty.'
He answered, 'Yet I see four men walking about in the fire free and un- 25
harmed; and the fourth looks like a god.' Nebuchadnezzar approached the 26
door of the blazing furnace and said to the men, 'Shadrach, Meshach and
Abed-nego, servants of the Most High God, come out, come here.' Then
Shadrach, Meshach and Abed-nego came out from the fire. And the satraps, 27
prefects, viceroys, and the king's courtiers gathered round and saw how
the fire had had no power to harm the bodies of these men; the hair of their
heads had not been singed, their trousers were untouched, and no smell of
fire lingered about them.

Then Nebuchadnezzar spoke out, 'Blessed is the God of Shadrach, 28

Meshach and Abed-nego. He has sent his angel to save his servants who put their trust in him, who disobeyed the royal command and were willing to yield themselves to the fire rather than to serve or worship any god other
29 than their own God. I therefore issue a decree that any man, to whatever people or nation he belongs, whatever his language, if he speaks blasphemy against the God of Shadrach, Meshach and Abed-nego, shall be torn to pieces and his house shall be forfeit;[a] for there is no other god who can
30 save men in this way.' Then the king advanced the fortunes of Shadrach, Meshach and Abed-nego in the province of Babylon.

4 KING NEBUCHADNEZZAR TO ALL PEOPLES AND NATIONS of every
2 language living in the whole world: May all prosperity be yours! It is my pleasure to recount the signs and marvels which the Most High God has worked for me:

3 How great are his signs,
and his marvels overwhelming!
His kingdom is an everlasting kingdom,
his sovereignty stands to all generations.

4 I, Nebuchadnezzar, was living peacefully at home in the luxury of my
5 palace. As I lay on my bed, I saw a dream which terrified me; and fantasies
6 and visions which came into my head dismayed me. So I issued an order summoning into my presence all the wise men of Babylon to make known
7 to me the interpretation of the dream. Then the magicians, exorcists, Chaldaeans, and diviners came in, and in their presence I related my dream.
8 But they could not interpret it. And yet another came into my presence, Daniel, who is called Belteshazzar after the name of my god, a man possessed by the spirit of the holy gods. To him, too, I related the dream:
9 'Belteshazzar, chief of the magicians, whom I myself know to be possessed by the spirit of the holy gods, and whom no secret baffles, listen to the vision I saw in a dream, and tell me its interpretation.
10 'Here is the vision which came into my head as I was lying upon my bed:
As I was looking,
I saw a tree of great height at the centre of the earth;
11 the tree grew and became strong,
reaching with its top to the sky
and visible to earth's farthest bounds.
12 Its foliage was lovely,
and its fruit abundant;
and it yielded food for all.
Beneath it the wild beasts found shelter,
the birds lodged in its branches,
and from it all living creatures fed.
13 'Here is another vision which came into my head as I was lying upon my bed:
As I was watching, there was a Watcher,
a Holy One coming down from heaven.

_____
[a] *Or* made into a dunghill (*mng. of Aram. word uncertain*).

He cried aloud and said,   14
"Hew down the tree, lop off the branches,
strip away the foliage, scatter the fruit.
   Let the wild beasts flee from its shelter
      and the birds from its branches,
but leave the stump with its roots in the ground.   15
   So, tethered with an iron ring,
   let him eat his fill of the lush grass;
   let him be drenched with the dew of heaven
   and share the lot of the beasts in their pasture;
   let his mind cease to be a man's mind,   16
   and let him be given the mind of a beast.
   Let seven times pass over him.
   The issue has been determined by the Watchers   17
   and the sentence pronounced by the Holy Ones.

Thereby the living will know that the Most High is sovereign in the kingdom of men: he gives the kingdom to whom he will and he may set over it the humblest of mankind."

'This is the dream which I, King Nebuchadnezzar, have dreamed; now,   18 Belteshazzar, tell me its interpretation; for, though all the wise men of my kingdom are unable to tell me what it means, you can tell me, since the spirit of the holy gods is in you.'

Daniel, who was called Belteshazzar, was dumbfounded for a moment,   19 dismayed by his thoughts; but the king said, 'Do not let the dream and its interpretation dismay you.' Belteshazzar answered, 'My lord, if only the dream were for those who hate you and its interpretation for your enemies! The tree which you saw grow and become strong, reaching with its top to   20 the sky and visible to earth's farthest bounds, its foliage lovely and its fruit   21 abundant, a tree which yielded food for all, beneath which the wild beasts dwelt and in whose branches the birds lodged, that tree, O king, is you.   22 You have grown and become strong. Your power has grown and reaches the sky; your sovereignty stretches to the ends of the earth. Also, O king,   23 you saw a Watcher, a Holy One, coming down from heaven and saying, "Hew down the tree and destroy it, but leave its stump with its roots in the ground. So, tethered with an iron ring, let him eat his fill of the lush grass; let him be drenched with the dew of heaven and share the lot of the beasts until seven times pass over him." This is the interpretation,   24 O king—it is a decree of the Most High which touches my lord the king. You will be banished from the society of men; you will have to live with   25 the wild beasts; you will feed on grass like oxen and you will be drenched with the dew of heaven. Seven times will pass over you until you have learnt that the Most High is sovereign over the kingdom of men and gives it to whom he will. The command was given to leave the stump of the tree with   26 its roots. By this you may know that from the time you acknowledge the sovereignty of heaven your rule will endure. Be advised by me, O king: 27 redeem your sins by charity and your iniquities by generosity to the wretched. So may you long enjoy peace of mind.'

28 29   All this befell King Nebuchadnezzar. At the end of twelve months
30   the king was walking on the roof of the royal palace at Babylon, and he
exclaimed, 'Is not this Babylon the great which I have built as a royal
residence by my own mighty power and for the honour of my majesty?'
31   The words were still on his lips, when a voice came down from heaven: 'To
you, King Nebuchadnezzar, the word is spoken: the kingdom has passed
32   from you. You are banished from the society of men and you shall live
with the wild beasts; you shall feed on grass like oxen, and seven times will
pass over you until you have learnt that the Most High is sovereign over
33   the kingdom of men and gives it to whom he will.' At that very moment
this judgement came upon Nebuchadnezzar. He was banished from the
society of men and ate grass like oxen; his body was drenched by the dew
of heaven, until his hair grew long like goats' hair and his nails like eagles'
talons.[a]
34   At the end of the appointed time, I, Nebuchadnezzar, raised my eyes
to heaven and I returned to my right mind. I blessed the Most High,
praising and glorifying the Ever-living One:

> His sovereignty is never-ending
> and his rule endures through all generations;
35   all dwellers upon earth count for nothing
> and he deals as he wishes with the host of heaven;[b]
> no one may lay hand upon him
> and ask him what he does.

36   At that very time I returned to my right mind and my majesty and royal
splendour were restored to me for the glory of my kingdom. My courtiers
and my nobles sought audience of me. I was established in my kingdom
37   and my power was greatly increased. Now I, Nebuchadnezzar, praise and
exalt and glorify the King of heaven; for all his acts are right and his ways
are just and those whose conduct is arrogant he can bring low.

Belshazzar's feast

5   BELSHAZZAR THE KING GAVE A BANQUET for a thousand of his
2   nobles and was drinking wine in the presence of the thousand. Warmed
by the wine, he gave orders to fetch the vessels of gold and silver which his
father Nebuchadnezzar had taken from the sanctuary at Jerusalem, that
he and his nobles, his concubines and his courtesans, might drink from
3   them. So the vessels of gold and silver from the sanctuary in the house of
God at Jerusalem were brought in, and the king and his nobles, his con-
4   cubines and his courtesans, drank from them. They drank wine and praised
the gods of gold and silver, of bronze and iron, and of wood and stone.
5   Suddenly there appeared the fingers of a human hand writing on the plaster
of the palace wall opposite the lamp, and the king could see the back of
6   the hand as it wrote. At this the king's mind was filled with dismay and he
turned pale, he became limp in every limb and his knees knocked together.

[a] goats' hair . . . eagles' talons: *prob. rdg.; Aram.* eagles' and his nails like birds'.
[b] *Prob. rdg.; Aram. adds* and the dwellers upon earth.

He called loudly for the exorcists, Chaldaeans, and diviners to be brought 7
in; then, addressing the wise men of Babylon, he said, 'Whoever can read
this writing and tell me its interpretation shall be robed in purple and
honoured with a chain of gold round his neck and shall rank as third in the
kingdom.' Then all the king's wise men came in, but they could not read 8
the writing or interpret it to the king. King Belshazzar sat there pale and 9
utterly dismayed, while his nobles were perplexed.

The king and his nobles were talking when the queen entered the 10
banqueting-hall: 'Long live the king!' she said. 'Why this dismay, and
why do you look so pale? There is a man in your kingdom who has in him 11
the spirit of the holy gods, a man who was known in your father's time to
have a clear understanding and godlike wisdom. King Nebuchadnezzar,
your father, appointed him chief of the magicians, exorcists, Chaldaeans,
and diviners. This same Daniel, whom the king named Belteshazzar, is 12
known to have a notable spirit, with knowledge and understanding, and
the gift of interpreting dreams, explaining riddles and unbinding spells;*a*
let him be summoned now and he will give the interpretation.' Daniel was 13
then brought into the king's presence and the king said to him, 'So you are
Daniel, one of the Jewish exiles whom the king my father brought from
Judah. I have heard that you possess the spirit of the holy gods and that 14
you are a man of clear understanding and peculiar wisdom. The wise men, 15
the exorcists, have just been brought into my presence to read this writing
and tell me its interpretation, and they have been unable to interpret it.
But I have heard it said of you that you are able to give interpretations and 16
to unbind spells.*b* So now, if you are able to read the words and tell me what
they mean, you shall be robed in purple and honoured with a chain of gold
round your neck and shall rank as third in the kingdom.' Then Daniel 17
answered in the king's presence, 'Your gifts you may keep for yourself;
or else give your rewards to another. Nevertheless I will read the writing
to your majesty and tell you its interpretation. My lord king, the Most 18
High God gave your father Nebuchadnezzar a kingdom and power and
glory and majesty; and, because of this power which he gave him, all 19
peoples and nations of every language trembled before him and were afraid.
He put to death whom he would and spared whom he would, he promoted
them at will and at will degraded them. But, when he became haughty, 20
stubborn and presumptuous, he was deposed from his royal throne and
his glory was taken from him. He was banished from the society of men, 21
his mind became like that of a beast, he had to live with the wild asses and
to eat grass like oxen, and his body was drenched with the dew of heaven,
until he came to know that the Most High God is sovereign over the kingdom of men and sets up over it whom he will. But you, his son Belshazzar, 22
did not humble your heart, although you knew all this. You have set your- 23
self up against the Lord of heaven. The vessels of his temple have been
brought to your table; and you, your nobles, your concubines, and your
courtesans have drunk from them. You have praised the gods of silver and
gold, of bronze and iron, of wood and stone, which neither see nor hear
nor know, and you have not given glory to God, in whose charge is your

a Or and solving problems.   *b* Or and to solve problems.

24 very breath and in whose hands are all your ways. This is why that hand
25 was sent from his very presence and why it wrote this inscription. And
these are the words of the writing which was inscribed: *Mene mene tekel*
26 *u-pharsin*. Here is the interpretation: *mene*:[a] God has numbered the days
27 of your kingdom and brought it to an end; *tekel*:[b] you have been weighed
28 in the balance and found wanting; *u-pharsin*:[c] and your kingdom has
29 been divided and given to the Medes and Persians.' Then Belshazzar gave
the order and Daniel was robed in purple and honoured with a chain of
gold round his neck, and proclamation was made that he should rank as
third in the kingdom.
30 31   That very night Belshazzar king of the Chaldaeans was slain, and Darius
the Mede took the kingdom, being then sixty-two years old.

Daniel in the lions' pit

6 IT PLEASED DARIUS TO APPOINT SATRAPS over the kingdom, a
2   hundred and twenty in number in charge of the whole kingdom, and
over them three chief ministers, to whom the satraps should send reports
so that the king's interests might not suffer; of these three, Daniel was one.
3 In the event Daniel outshone the other ministers and the satraps because
of his ability, and the king had it in mind to appoint him over the whole
4 kingdom. Then the chief ministers and the satraps began to look round for
some pretext to attack Daniel's administration of the kingdom, but they
failed to find any malpractice on his part; for he was faithful to his trust.
5 Since they could discover no neglect of duty or malpractice, they said,
'There will be no charge to bring against this Daniel unless we find one
6 in his religion.' These chief ministers and satraps watched for an oppor-
7 tunity to approach the king, and said to him, 'Long live King Darius! All
we, the ministers of the kingdom, prefects, satraps, courtiers, and viceroys, have taken counsel and agree that the king should issue a decree and
bring an ordinance into force, that whoever within the next thirty days shall
present a petition to any god or man other than the king shall be thrown
8 into the lions' pit. Now, O king, issue the ordinance and have it put in
writing, so that it may be unalterable, for the law of the Medes and Persians
9 stands for ever.' Accordingly King Darius issued the ordinance in written
form.
10   When Daniel learnt that this decree had been issued, he went into his
house. He had had windows made in his roof-chamber looking towards
Jerusalem; and there he knelt down three times a day and offered prayers
11 and praises to his God as his custom had always been. His enemies watched
for an opportunity to catch Daniel and found him at his prayers making
12 supplication to his God. Then they came into the king's presence and
reminded him of the ordinance. 'Your majesty,' they said, 'have you not
issued an ordinance that any person who, within the next thirty days, shall
present a petition to any god or man other than your majesty shall be

---

[a] *That is* numbered.   [b] *That is* shekel *or* weight.   [c] *Prob. rdg.; Aram.* pheres.
There is a play on three possible meanings halves *or* divisions *or* Persians.

thrown into the lions' pit?' The king answered, 'Yes, it is fixed. The law
of the Medes and Persians stands for ever.' So in the king's presence they 13
said, 'Daniel, one of the Jewish exiles, has ignored the ordinance issued by
your majesty, and is making petition to his god three times a day.' When 14
the king heard this, he was greatly distressed. He tried to think of a way to
save Daniel, and continued his efforts till sunset; then those same men 15
watched for an opportunity to approach the king, and said to him, 'Your
majesty must know that by the law of the Medes and Persians no ordinance
or decree issued by the king may be altered.' So the king gave orders and 16
Daniel was brought and thrown into the lions' pit; but he said to Daniel,
'Your own God, whom you serve continually, will save you.' A stone was 17
brought and put over the mouth of the pit, and the king sealed it with his
signet and with the signets of his nobles, so that no one might intervene
to rescue Daniel.

The king went back to his palace and spent the night fasting; no woman 18
was brought to him and sleep eluded him. At dawn, as soon as it was light, 19
he rose and went in fear and trembling to the pit. When the king reached 20
it, he called anxiously to Daniel, 'Daniel, servant of the living God, has
your God whom you serve continually been able to save you from the
lions?' Then Daniel answered, 'Long live the king! My God sent his angel 21 22
to shut the lions' mouths so that they have done me no injury, because in
his judgement I was found innocent;[a] and moreover, O king, I had done
you no injury.' The king was overjoyed and gave orders that Daniel should 23
be lifted out of the pit. So Daniel was lifted out and no trace of injury was
found on him, because he had put his faith in his God. By order of the king 24
Daniel's accusers were brought and thrown into the lions' pit with their
wives and children, and before they reached the floor of the pit the lions
were upon them and crunched them up, bones and all.

Then King Darius wrote to all peoples and nations of every language 25
throughout the whole world: 'May your prosperity increase! I have issued 26
a decree that in all my royal domains men shall fear and reverence the God
of Daniel;

> for he is the living God, the everlasting,
> whose kingly power shall not be weakened;
>   whose sovereignty shall have no end—
> a saviour, a deliverer, a worker of signs and wonders 27
>   in heaven and on earth,
> who has delivered Daniel from the power of the lions.'

So this Daniel prospered during the reigns of Darius and Cyrus the 28
Persian.

Daniel's visions

IN THE FIRST YEAR OF BELSHAZZAR king of Babylon, as Daniel lay 7
on his bed, dreams and visions came into his head. Then he wrote down
the dream, and here his account begins:

---

[a] *in his judgement . . . innocent: or before him success was granted me.*

2   In my visions of the night I, Daniel, was gazing intently and I saw a
3   great sea churned up by the four winds of heaven, and four huge beasts
4   coming up out of the sea, each one different from the others. The first was
    like a lion but had an eagle's wings. I watched until its wings were plucked
    off and it was lifted from the ground and made to stand on two feet like
5   a man; it was also given the mind of a man. Then I saw another, a second
    beast, like a bear. It was half crouching and had three ribs in its mouth,
    between its teeth. The command was given: 'Up, gorge yourself with
6   flesh.' After this as I gazed I saw another, a beast like a leopard with four
    bird's wings on its back; this creature had four heads, and it was invested
7   with sovereign power. Next in my visions of the night I saw a fourth beast,
    dreadful and grisly, exceedingly strong, with great iron teeth and bronze
    claws.[a] It crunched and devoured, and trampled underfoot all that was
    left. It differed from all the beasts which preceded it in having ten horns.
8   While I was considering the horns I saw another horn, a little one, spring-
    ing up among them, and three of the first horns were uprooted to make
    room for it. And in that horn were eyes like the eyes of a man, and a mouth
9   that spoke proud words. I kept looking, and then

> thrones were set in place and one ancient in years took his seat,
> his robe was white as snow and the hair of his head like cleanest
>   wool.
> Flames of fire were his throne and its wheels blazing fire;
10 > a flowing river of fire streamed out before him.[b]
> Thousands upon thousands served him
> and myriads upon myriads attended his presence.
> The court sat, and the books were opened.

11 Then because of the proud words that the horn was speaking, I went
    on watching until the beast was killed and its carcass destroyed: it was given
12 to the flames. The rest of the beasts, though deprived of their sovereignty,
13 were allowed to remain alive for a time and a season. I was still watching
    in visions of the night and I saw one like a man coming with the clouds of
    heaven; he approached the Ancient in Years and was presented to him.
14 Sovereignty and glory and kingly power were given to him, so that all
    people and nations of every language should serve him; his sovereignty
    was to be an everlasting sovereignty which should not pass away, and his
    kingly power such as should never be impaired.
15 My spirit within me was troubled, and, dismayed by the visions which
16 came into my head, I, Daniel, approached one of those who stood there
    and inquired from him what all this meant; and he told me the interpreta-
17 tion. 'These great beasts, four in number,' he said, 'are four kingdoms
18 which shall rise from the ground. But the saints[c] of the Most High shall
    receive the kingly power and shall retain it for ever, for ever and ever.'
19 Then I desired to know what the fourth beast meant, the beast that was
    different from all the others, very dreadful with its iron teeth and bronze
    claws, crunching and devouring and trampling underfoot all that was left.
20 I desired also to know about the ten horns on its head and the other horn

---

[a] and bronze claws: *prob. rdg., cp. verse 19; Aram. om.*   [b] *Or it.*   [c] *Or holy one:*

which sprang up and at whose coming three of them fell—the horn that
had eyes and a mouth speaking proud words and appeared larger than the
others. As I still watched, that horn was waging war with the saints and　21
overcoming them until the Ancient in Years came. Then judgement was　22
given in favour of the saints of the Most High, and the time came when
the saints gained possession of the kingly power. He gave me this answer:　23
'The fourth beast signifies a fourth kingdom which shall appear upon earth.
It shall differ from the other kingdoms and shall devour the whole earth,
tread it down and crush it. The ten horns signify the appearance of ten　24
kings in this kingdom, after whom another king shall arise, differing from
his predecessors; and he shall bring low three kings. He shall hurl defiance　25
at the Most High and shall wear down the saints of the Most High. He
shall plan to alter the customary times and law; and the saints shall be
delivered into his power for a time and times and half a time. Then the　26
court shall sit, and he shall be deprived of his sovereignty, so that in the
end it may be destroyed and abolished. The kingly power, sovereignty, and　27
greatness of all the kingdoms under heaven shall be given to the people of
the saints of the Most High. Their kingly power is an everlasting power and
all sovereignties shall serve them and obey them.'

　　Here the account ends. As for me, Daniel, my thoughts dismayed me　28
greatly and I turned pale; and I kept these things in my mind.

　　[a] In the third year of the reign of King Belshazzar, while I was in Susa　**8** 1-2
the capital city of the province of Elam, a vision appeared to me, Daniel,
similar to my former vision. In this vision I was watching beside the stream
of the Ulai. I raised my eyes and there I saw a ram with two horns standing　3
between me and the stream. The two horns were long, the one longer than
the other, growing up behind. I watched the ram butting west and north　4
and south. No beasts could stand before it, no one could rescue from its
power. It did what it liked, making a display of its strength. While I　5
pondered this, suddenly a he-goat came from the west skimming over the
whole earth without touching the ground; it had a prominent horn between
its eyes. It approached the two-horned ram which I had seen standing　6
between me and the stream and rushed at it with impetuous force. I saw　7
it advance on the ram, working itself into a fury against it, then strike the
ram and break its two horns; the ram had no strength to resist. The he-
goat flung it to the ground and trampled on it, and there was no one to
save the ram.

　　Then the he-goat made a great display of its strength. Powerful as it　8
was, its great horn snapped and in its place there sprang out towards the
four quarters of heaven four prominent horns. Out of one of them there　9
issued one small horn, which made a prodigious show of strength south
and east and towards the fairest of all lands. It aspired to be as great as the　10
host of heaven, and it cast down to the earth some of the host and some of
the stars and trod them underfoot. It aspired to be as great as the Prince　11
of the host, suppressed his regular offering and even threw down his
sanctuary. The heavenly hosts were delivered up, and it raised itself[b]　12

---

[a] *Here the Hebrew text resumes (see note at 2. 4).*　　　　　[b] and it raised itself: *prob.*
rdg.; Heb. om.

impiously against the regular offering and threw true religion to the ground;
13 in all that it did it succeeded. I heard a holy one speaking and another holy one answering him, whoever he was. The one said, 'For how long will the period of this vision last? How long will the regular offering be suppressed, how long will impiety cause desolation,[a] and both the Holy
14 Place and the fairest of all lands[b] be given over to be trodden down?' The answer came, 'For two thousand three hundred evenings and mornings; then the Holy Place shall emerge victorious.'

15 All the while that I, Daniel, was seeing the vision, I was trying to understand it. Suddenly I saw standing before me one with the semblance of a
16 man; at the same time I heard a human voice calling to him across the bend
17 of the Ulai, 'Gabriel, explain the vision to this man.' He came up to where I was standing; I was seized with terror at his approach and threw myself on my face. But he said to me, 'Understand, O man: the vision points to
18 the time of the end.' When he spoke to me, I fell to the ground in a trance;
19 but he grasped me and made me stand up where I was. And he said, 'I shall make known to you what is to happen at the end of the wrath; for
20 there is an end to the appointed time. The two-horned ram which you saw
21 signifies the kings of Media and Persia, the he-goat is the kingdom[c] of
22 the Greeks and the great horn on his forehead is the first king. As for the horn which was snapped off and replaced by four horns: four kingdoms shall rise out of that nation, but not with power comparable to his.

23   In the last days of those kingdoms,
      when their sin is at its height,
    a king shall appear, harsh and grim, a master of stratagem.
24   His power shall be great, he shall work havoc untold;
      he shall succeed in whatever he does.
    He shall work havoc among great nations and upon a holy people.
25   His mind shall be ever active,
    and he shall succeed in his crafty designs;
      he shall conjure up great plans
    and, when they least expect it, work havoc on many.
    He shall challenge even the Prince of princes
    and be broken, but not by human hands.
26   This revelation which has been given
    of the evenings and the mornings is true;
    but you must keep the vision secret,
      for it points to days far ahead.'

27   As for me, Daniel, my strength failed me and I lay sick for a while. Then I rose and attended to the king's business. But I was perplexed by the revelation and no one could explain it.

9 IN THE FIRST YEAR OF THE REIGN OF DARIUS son of Ahasuerus (a Mede by birth, who was appointed king over the kingdom of the Chal-
2 daeans) I, Daniel, was reading the scriptures and reflecting on the seventy

---

[a] will impiety cause desolation: *prob. rdg.; Heb. obscure.*   [b] fairest of all lands: *prob. rdg., cp. verse 9; Heb.* host.   [c] *Prob. rdg.; Heb.* king.

years which, according to the word of the LORD to the prophet Jeremiah, 3
were to pass while Jerusalem lay in ruins. Then I turned to the Lord God
in earnest prayer and supplication with fasting and sackcloth and ashes.
I prayed to the LORD my God, making confession thus: 4

'Lord, thou great and terrible God who faithfully keepest the covenant
with those who love thee and observe thy commandments, we have sinned, 5
we have done what was wrong and wicked; we have rebelled, we have
turned our backs on thy commandments and thy decrees. We have not 6
listened to thy servants the prophets, who spoke in thy name to our kings
and princes, to our forefathers and to all the people of the land. O Lord, 7
the right is on thy side; the shame, now as ever, belongs to us, the men of
Judah and the citizens of Jerusalem, and to all the Israelites near and far
in every land to which thou hast banished them for their treachery towards
thee. O LORD, the shame falls on us as on our kings, our princes and our 8
forefathers; we have all sinned against thee. Compassion and forgiveness 9
belong to the Lord our God, though we have rebelled against him. We 10
have not obeyed the LORD our God, we have not conformed to the laws
which he laid down for us through his servants the prophets. All Israel 11
has broken thy law and not obeyed thee, so that the curses set out in the
law of Moses thy servant in the adjuration and the oath have rained down
upon us; for we have sinned against him. He has fulfilled all that he said 12
about us and about our rulers, by bringing upon us and upon Jerusalem a
calamity greater than has ever happened in all the world. It was all fore- 13
shadowed in the law of Moses, this calamity which has come upon us; yet
we have done nothing to propitiate the LORD our God; we have neither
repented of our wrongful deeds nor remembered that thou art true to thy
word. The LORD has been biding his time and has now brought this calam- 14
ity upon us. In all that he has done the LORD our God has been right; yet
we have not obeyed him.

'And now, O Lord our God who didst bring thy people out of Egypt by 15
a strong hand, winning for thyself a name that lives on to this day, we have
sinned, we have done wrong. O Lord, by all thy saving deeds we beg that 16
thy wrath and anger may depart from Jerusalem, thy city, thy holy hill;
through our own sins and our fathers' guilty deeds Jerusalem and thy
people have become a byword among all our neighbours. And now, our 17
God, listen to thy servant's prayer and supplication; for thy own sake,
O Lord, make thy face shine upon thy desolate sanctuary. Lend thy 18
ear, O God, and hear, open thine eyes and look upon our desolation and
upon the city that bears thy name; it is not by virtue of our own saving
acts but by thy great mercy that we present our supplications before thee.
O Lord, hear; O Lord, forgive; O Lord, listen and act; for thy own sake 19
do not delay, O God, for thy city and thy people bear thy name.'

Thus I was speaking and praying, confessing my own sin and my people 20
Israel's sin, and presenting my supplication before the LORD my God on
behalf of his holy hill. While I was praying, the man Gabriel, whom I had 21
already seen in the vision, came close to*a* me at the hour of the evening
sacrifice, flying swiftly.*b* He spoke clearly to me and said, 'Daniel, I have 22

     a Or touched.   *b* flying swiftly: *prob. rdg.*; *Heb.* thoroughly wearied.

23 now come to enlighten your understanding. As you were beginning your
supplications a word went forth; this I have come to pass on to you, for
you are a man greatly beloved. Consider well the word, consider the vision:
24 Seventy weeks are marked out for your people and your holy city; then
rebellion shall be stopped,[a] sin brought to an end,[b] iniquity expiated,
everlasting right ushered in, vision and prophecy sealed, and the Most
25 Holy Place anointed. Know then and understand: from the time that the
word went forth that Jerusalem should be restored and rebuilt, seven
weeks shall pass till the appearance of one anointed, a prince; then for
sixty-two weeks it shall remain restored, rebuilt with streets and conduits.
26 At the critical time, after the sixty-two weeks, one who is anointed shall
be removed with no one to take his part; and the horde of an invading
prince shall work havoc on city and sanctuary. The end of it shall be a
27 deluge, inevitable war with all its horrors. He shall make a firm league with
the mighty[c] for one week; and, the week half spent, he shall put a stop to
sacrifice and offering. And in the train of these abominations shall come
an author of desolation; then, in the end, what has been decreed concerning
the desolation will be poured out.'

10 IN THE THIRD YEAR OF CYRUS king of Persia a word was revealed to
Daniel who had been given the name Belteshazzar. Though this word
was true, it cost him[d] much toil to understand it; nevertheless understanding came to him in the course of the vision.
2 3   In those days I, Daniel, mourned for three whole weeks. I refrained from
all choice food; no meat or wine passed my lips, and I did not anoint myself
4 until the three weeks had gone by. On the twenty-fourth day of the first
month, I found myself on the bank of the great river, that is the Tigris;
5 I looked up and saw a man clothed in linen with a belt of gold from Ophir
6 round his waist. His body gleamed like topaz, his face shone like lightning,
his eyes flamed like torches, his arms and feet sparkled like a disc of bronze;
7 and when he spoke his voice sounded like the voice of a multitude. I,
Daniel, alone saw the vision, while those who were near me did not see it,
8 but great fear fell upon them and they stole away, and I was left alone
gazing at this great vision. But my strength left me; I became a sorry figure
9 of a man, and retained no strength. I heard the sound of his words and,
10 when I did so, I fell prone on the ground in a trance. Suddenly a hand
11 grasped me and pulled me up on to my hands and knees. He said to me,
'Daniel, man greatly beloved, attend to the words I am speaking to you
and stand up where you are, for I am now sent to you.' When he addressed
12 me, I stood up trembling and he said, 'Do not be afraid, Daniel, for from
the very first day that you applied your mind to understand and to mortify
yourself before your God, your prayers have been heard, and I have come
13 in answer to them. But the angel prince of the kingdom of Persia resisted
me for twenty-one days, and then, seeing that I had held out there, Michael,
one of the chief princes, came to help me against the prince of the kingdom
14 of Persia. And I have come to explain to you what will happen to your
people in days to come; for this too is a vision for those days.'

[a] *Or* restrained.   [b] *Or* sealed.   [c] *Or* many.   [d] him: *prob. rdg.; Heb. om.*

While he spoke to me I hung my head and was struck dumb. Suddenly 15 16
one like a man touched my lips. Then I opened my mouth to speak and
addressed him as he stood before me: 'Sir, this has pierced me to the heart,
and I retain no strength. How can my lord's servant presume to talk with 17
such as my lord, since my strength has failed me and no breath is left in
me?' Then the figure touched me again and restored my strength. He said, 18 19
'Do not be afraid, man greatly beloved; all will be well with you. Be strong,
be strong.' When he had spoken to me, I recovered strength and said,
'Speak, sir, for you have given me strength.' He said, 'Do you know why 20
I have come to you? I am first going back to fight with the prince of Persia,
and, as soon as I have left, the prince of Greece will appear: I have no ally 21-11 1
on my side to help and support me, except Michael your prince.*a* However
I will tell you what is written in the Book of Truth. Here and now I will 2
tell you what is true:
  'Three more kings will appear in Persia, and the fourth will far surpass
all the others in wealth; and when he has extended his power through his
wealth, he will rouse the whole world against the kingdom of Greece. Then 3
there will appear a warrior king. He will rule a vast kingdom and will do
what he chooses. But as soon as he is established, his kingdom will be 4
shattered and split up north, south, east and west. It will not pass to his
descendants, nor will any of his successors have an empire like his; his
kingdom will be torn up by the roots and given to others as well as to them.
Then the king of the south will become strong; but another of the captains 5
will surpass him in strength and win a greater kingdom. In due course the 6
two will enter into a friendly alliance; to redress the balance the daughter
of the king of the south will be given in marriage to the king of the north,
but she will not maintain her influence and their line will not last. She and
her escort, her child, and also her lord and master, will all be the victims
of foul play. Then another shoot from the same stock as hers will appear 7
in his father's place, will penetrate the defences of the king of the north
and enter his fortress, and will win a decisive victory over his people. He 8
will take back as booty to Egypt even the images of their gods cast in metal
and their precious vessels of silver and gold. Then for some years he will
refrain from attacking the king of the north. After that the king of the 9
north will overrun the southern kingdom but will retreat to his own land.
  'His sons will press on to assemble a great armed horde. One of them 10
will sweep on and on like an irresistible flood. And after that he will press
on as far as his enemy's stronghold. The king of the south, his anger roused, 11
will march out to do battle with the king of the north who, in turn, will raise
a great horde, but it will be delivered into the hands of his enemy. When 12
this horde has been captured, the victor will be elated and he will slaughter
tens of thousands, yet he will not maintain his advantage. Then the king 13
of the north will once more raise a horde even greater than the last and,
when the years come round, will advance with a great army and a large
baggage-train. During these times many will resist the king of the south, 14
but some hotheads among your own people will rashly attempt to give
substance to a vision and will come to disaster. Then the king of the north 15

  a Prob. rdg.; Heb. adds and as for me, in the first year of Darius the Mede.

will come and throw up siege-ramps and capture a fortified town, and the forces of the south will not stand up to him; even the flower of their army

16 will not be able to hold their ground. And so his adversary will do as he pleases and meet with no opposition. He will establish himself in the fairest

17 of all lands and it will come wholly into his power. He will resolve to subjugate all the dominions of the king of the south; and he will come to fair terms with him,*a* and he will give him a young woman in marriage, for the destruction of the kingdom; but she will not persist nor serve his purpose.

18 Then he will turn to the coasts and islands and take many prisoners, but a foreign commander *b* will put an end to his challenge by wearing him

19 down; *c* thus he will throw back his challenge on to him. He will fall back upon his own strongholds; there he will come to disaster and be overthrown and be seen no more.

20 'He will be succeeded by one who will send out an officer with a royal escort to extort tribute; after a short time this king too will meet his end, yet neither openly nor in battle.

21 'A contemptible creature will succeed but will not be given recognition as king; yet he will seize the kingdom by dissimulation and intrigue in

22 time of peace. He will sweep away all forces of opposition as he advances,

23 and even the Prince of the Covenant will be broken. He will enter into fraudulent alliances and, although the people behind him are but few, he

24 will rise to power and establish himself in time of peace. He will overrun the richest districts of the province and succeed in doing what his fathers and forefathers failed to do, distributing spoil, booty, and property to his followers. He will lay his plans against fortresses, but only for a time.

25 'He will rouse himself in all his strength and courage and lead a great army against the king of the south, but the king of the south will press the campaign against him with a very great and numerous army; yet the king

26 of the south will not persist, for traitors will lay their plots. Those who eat at his board will be his undoing; his army will be swept away, and many

27 will fall on the field of battle. The two kings will be bent on mischief and, sitting at the same table, they will lie to each other with advantage to

28 neither. Yet there will still be an end to the appointed time. Then one will return home with a long baggage-train, and with anger in his heart against the Holy Covenant; he will work his will and return to his own land.

29 'At the appointed time he will once more overrun the south, but he will

30 not succeed as he did before. Ships from the west will sail against him, and he will receive a rebuff. He will turn and vent his fury against the Holy Covenant; on his way back he will take due note of those who have for-

31 saken it. Armed forces dispatched by him will desecrate the sanctuary and the citadel and do away with the regular offering. And there they will set

32 up "the abominable thing that causes desolation". He will win over by plausible promises those who are ready to condemn the covenant, but the

33 people who are faithful to their God will hold firm and fight back. Wise leaders of the nation will give guidance to the common people; yet for a

34 while they will fall victims to fire and sword, to captivity and pillage. But

a and he . . . with him: *prob. rdg.; Heb. obscure.*   *b* *Or* consul *or* legate.
c by wearing him down: *prob. rdg.; Heb. obscure.*

these victims will not want for help, though small, even if many who join
them are insincere. Some of these leaders will themselves fall victims for a 35
time so that they may be tested, refined and made shining white. Yet there
will still be an end*a* to the appointed time. The king will do what he chooses; 36
he will exalt and magnify himself above every god and against the God of
gods he will utter monstrous blasphemies. All will go well for him until
the time of wrath ends, for what is determined must be done. He will 37
ignore his ancestral gods, and the god beloved of women; to no god will
he pay heed but will exalt himself above them all. Instead he will honour 38
the god of the citadel, a god unknown to his ancestors, with gold and silver,
gems and costly gifts. He will garrison his strongest fortresses with aliens, 39
the people of a foreign god. Those whom he favours he will load with
honour, putting them in office over the common people and distributing
land at a price.

 'At the time of the end, he and the king of the south will make feints at 40
one another, and the king of the north will come storming against him with
chariots and cavalry and many ships. He will overrun land after land,
sweeping over them like a flood, amongst them the fairest of all lands, and 41
tens of thousands shall fall victims. Yet all these lands [including Edom
and Moab and the remnant of the Ammonites] will survive his attack. He 42
will reach out to land after land, and Egypt will not escape. He will gain 43
control of her hidden stores of gold and silver and of all her treasures;
Libyans and Cushites will follow in his train. Then rumours from east and 44
north will alarm him, and he will depart in a great rage to destroy and to
exterminate many. He will pitch his royal pavilion between the sea and 45
the holy hill, the fairest of all hills; and he will meet his end with no one
to help him.

   At that moment Michael shall appear,   **12**
    Michael the great captain,
    who stands guard over your fellow-countrymen;
    and there will be a time of distress
    such as has never been
    since they became a nation till that moment.
  But at that moment your people will be delivered,*b*
    every one who is written in the book:
  many of those who sleep in the dust of the earth will wake,   2
    some to everlasting life
  and some to the reproach of eternal abhorrence.
  The wise leaders shall shine like the bright vault of heaven,   3
    and those who have guided the people in the true path
    shall be like the stars for ever and ever.

But you, Daniel, keep the words secret and seal the book till the time of 4
the end. Many will be at their wits' end, and punishment will be heavy.'

 And I, Daniel, looked and saw two others standing, one on this bank of 5
the river and the other on the opposite bank. And I said to the man clothed 6
in linen who was above the waters of the river, 'How long will it be before

---

 a Yet . . . end: *prob. rdg.; Heb. has different word order.*   *b Or* will escape.

7 these portents cease?' The man clothed in linen above the waters lifted to heaven his right hand and his left, and I heard him swear by him who lives for ever: 'It shall be for a time, times, and a half. When the power of the holy people ceases to be dispersed, all these things shall come to an end.'
8 I heard but I did not understand, and so I said, 'Sir, what will the issue of
9 these things be?' He replied, 'Go your way, Daniel, for the words are kept
10 secret and sealed till the time of the end. Many shall purify themselves and be refined, making themselves shining white, but the wicked shall continue in wickedness and none of them shall understand; only the wise
11 leaders shall understand. From the time when the regular offering is abolished and "the abomination of desolation" is set up, there shall be
12 an interval of one thousand two hundred and ninety days. Happy the man who waits and lives to see the completion of one thousand three hundred
13 and thirty-five days! But go your way to the end and rest, and you shall arise to your destiny at the end of the age.'

HOSEA

THE WORD OF THE LORD which came to Hosea son of Beeri **1**
during the reigns of Uzziah, Jotham, Ahaz, and Hezekiah, kings
of Judah, and during the reign of Jeroboam son of Jehoash king
of Israel.

Hosea's unfaithful wife

THIS IS THE BEGINNING of the LORD's message by Hosea. He said, **2**
Go, take a wanton for your wife and get children of her wantonness;
for like a wanton this land is unfaithful to the LORD. So he went and took **3**
Gomer, a worthless woman;[a] and she conceived and bore him a son. And **4**
the LORD said to him,

> Call him Jezreel;[b] for in a little while
> I will punish the line of Jehu for the blood shed in Jezreel
>   and put an end to the kingdom of Israel.
>   On that day **5**
> I will break Israel's bow in the Vale of Jezreel.

She conceived again and bore a daughter, and the LORD said to him, **6**

> Call her Lo-ruhamah;[c]
> for I will never again show love to Israel,
>   never again forgive them.[d]

After weaning Lo-ruhamah, she conceived and bore a son; and the LORD **8 9**
said,

> Call him Lo-ammi;[e]
>   for you are not my people,
> and I will not be your God.
> The Israelites shall become countless as the sands of the sea **10**
>   which can neither be measured nor numbered;
> it shall no longer be said, 'They are not my people',
>   they shall be called Sons of the Living God.
> Then the people of Judah and of Israel shall be reunited **11**
>   and shall choose for themselves a single head,
>   and they shall become masters of the earth;
>   for great shall be the day of Jezreel.

[a] a worthless woman: or daughter of Diblaim.   [b] That is God shall sow.
[c] That is Not loved.   [d] Prob. rdg.; Heb. adds (7) Then I will love Judah and will
save them. I will save them not by bow or sword or weapon of war, by horses or by horsemen, but by the LORD their God.   [e] That is Not my people.

2   Then you will say to your brothers, 'You are my people',
and to your sisters, 'You are loved.'

2   Plead my cause with your mother;
is she not my wife and I her husband?[a]
Plead with her to forswear those wanton looks,
to banish the lovers from her bosom.

3   Or I will strip her and expose her
naked as the day she was born;
I will make her bare as the wilderness,
parched as the desert,
and leave her to die of thirst.

4   I will show no love for her children;
they are the offspring of wantonness,

5   and their mother is a wanton.
She who conceived them is shameless;
she says, 'I will go after my lovers;
they give me my food and drink,
my wool and flax, my oil and my perfumes.'

6   Therefore I will block her road with thorn-bushes
and obstruct her path with a wall,
so that she can no longer follow her old ways.

7   When she pursues her lovers she will not overtake them,
when she looks for them she will not find them;
then she will say,
'I will go back to my husband again;
I was better off with him than I am now.'

8   For she does not know that it is I who gave her
corn, new wine, and oil,
I who lavished upon her silver and gold
which they spent on the Baal.

9   Therefore I will take back
my corn at the harvest and my new wine at the vintage,
and I will take away the wool and the flax
which I gave her to cover her naked body;

10   so I will show her up for the lewd thing she is,
and no lover will want to steal her from me.

12[b]   I will ravage the vines and the fig-trees,
which she says are the fee
with which her lovers have hired her,
and turn them into jungle where wild beasts shall feed.

11   I will put a stop to her merrymaking,
her pilgrimages and new moons, her sabbaths[c] and festivals.

13   I will punish her for the holy days
when she burnt sacrifices to the Baalim,

[a] is she . . . husband?: *or* for she is no longer my wife nor I her husband.
[b] *Verses 11 and 12 transposed.*
[c] *Or* her full moons.

when she decked herself with earrings and necklaces,
ran after her lovers and forgot me.
This is the very word of the LORD.

But now listen,   14
I will woo her, I will go with her into the wilderness
and comfort her:
there I will restore her vineyards,   15
turning the Vale of Trouble into the Gate of Hope,[a]
and there she will answer as in her youth,
when she came up out of Egypt.
On that day she shall call me 'My husband'   16
and shall no more call me 'My Baal';[b]
and I will wipe from her lips the very names of the Baalim;   17
never again shall their names be heard.
This is the very word of the LORD.[c]

Then I will make a covenant on behalf of Israel with the wild beasts,   18
the birds of the air, and the things that creep on the earth, and I will break
bow and sword and weapon of war and sweep them off the earth, so that
all living creatures may lie down without fear. I will betroth you to myself 19
for ever, betroth you in lawful wedlock with unfailing devotion and love;
I will betroth you to myself to have and to hold, and you shall know the   20
LORD. At that time I will give answer, says the LORD, I will answer for the   21
heavens and they will answer for the earth, and the earth will answer for   22
the corn, the new wine, and the oil, and they will answer for Jezreel.
Israel shall be my new sowing in the land, and I will show love to Lo-   23
ruhamah and say to Lo-ammi, 'You are my people', and he will say, 'Thou
art my God.'
The LORD said to me,   3

Go again and love a woman
loved by another man, an adulteress,
and love her as I, the LORD, love the Israelites
although they resort to other gods
and love the raisin-cakes offered to their idols.

So I got her back[d] for fifteen pieces of silver, a homer of barley and a   2
measure of wine; and I said to her,   3

Many a long day you shall live in my house
and not play the wanton,
and have no intercourse with a man, nor I with you.

For the Israelites shall live many a long day   4
without king or prince,
without sacrifice or sacred pillar,
without image or household gods;

---

[a] turning . . . Hope: *or* Emek-achor to Pethah-tikvah.   [b] *Also means* My husband.
[c] This . . . LORD: *transposed from after* On that day *in verse 16.*   [d] got her back:
or bought her.

5   but after that they will again seek
       the LORD their God and David their king,
       and turn anxiously to the LORD for his bounty in days to come.

God's case against Israel

4   Hear the word of the LORD, O Israel;
       for the LORD has a charge to bring against the people of the land:
              There is no good faith or mutual trust,
              no knowledge of God in the land,
2   oaths are imposed and broken, they kill and rob;
              there is nothing but adultery and licence,[a]
              one deed of blood after another.
3   Therefore the land shall be dried up,
              and all who live in it shall pine away,
              and with them the wild beasts and the birds of the air;
              even the fish shall be swept from the sea.
4   But it is not for any man to bring a charge,
              it is not for him to prove a case;
              the quarrel with you, false priest, is mine.

5   Priest?[b] By day and by night you blunder on,
              you and the prophet with you.
6   My people are ruined for lack of knowledge;
              your own countrymen are brought to ruin.[c]
       You have rejected knowledge,
       and I will reject you from serving me as priest.
              You have forgotten the teaching of God,
       and I, your God, will forget your sons.

7   The more priests there are, the more they sin against me;
              their dignity I will turn into dishonour.
8   They feed on the sin of my people
              and batten on their iniquity.
9   But people and priest shall be treated alike.
       I will punish them for their conduct
       and repay them for their deeds:
10   they shall eat but never be satisfied,
       behave wantonly but their lust will never be overtaxed,
              for they have forsaken the LORD
11   to give themselves to sacred prostitution.
12   New wine and old steal my people's wits:[d]
              they ask advice from a block of wood
              and take their orders from a fetish;

[a] and licence: *prob. rdg.; Heb.* they exceed.   [b] the quarrel ... Priest?: *prob. rdg.;*
Heb. and your people are like those who quarrel with a priest.   [c] My people ...
ruin: *or* Your mother (Israel) is destroyed, my people destroyed for lack of knowledge.
[d] steal ... wits: *or* embolden my people.

for a spirit of wantonness has led them astray
and in their lusts they are unfaithful to their God.
　Your men sacrifice on mountain-tops　　　　　　　　　13
　　and burn offerings on the hills,
　　under oak and poplar
and the terebinth's pleasant shade.
　Therefore your daughters play the wanton
　　and your sons' brides commit adultery.
　I will not punish your daughters for playing the wanton　14
　　nor your sons' brides for their adultery,
because your men resort to wanton women
　　and sacrifice with temple-prostitutes.
　A people without understanding comes to grief;
　　they are a mother turned wanton.　　　　　　　　　15
　Bring no guilt-offering,*a* Israel;
　　do not come to Gilgal, Judah,
do not go up to Beth-aven to swear by the life of the LORD,
since Israel has run wild, wild as a heifer;　　　　　　16
　　and will the LORD now feed this people
　　like lambs in a broad meadow?
　Ephraim, keeping company with idols,　　　　　　　17
　　has held a drunken orgy,*b*　　　　　　　　　　　　18
　　they have practised sacred prostitution,
　they have preferred dishonour to glory.
The wind shall sweep them away, wrapped in its wings,　19
　　and they will find their sacrifices a delusion.

　Hear this, you priests,　　　　　　　　　　　　　**5**
and listen, all Israel; let the royal house mark my words.
　　Sentence is passed on you;
　for you have been a snare at Mizpah,
　and a net spread out on Tabor.
　The rebels! they have shown base ingratitude,　　　2
　but I will punish them all.
　I have cared for Ephraim　　　　　　　　　　　　3
　and I have not neglected Israel;
　but now Ephraim has played the wanton
　　and Israel has defiled himself.
　Their misdeeds have barred their way back to their God;　4
　　for a wanton spirit is in them,
　　and they care nothing for the LORD.
　Israel's arrogance cries out against him;　　　　　5
　*c*Ephraim's guilt is his undoing,
　and Judah no less is undone.
　They go with sacrifices of sheep and cattle　　　　6
　to seek the LORD, but do not find him.

a Bring no guilt-offering: *prob. rdg.*; *Heb.* Let him not be guilty.　　*b* a drunken
orgy: *prob. rdg.*; *Heb. unintelligible.*　　*c Prob. rdg.*; *Heb. prefixes* Israel.

He has withdrawn himself from them;
7   for they have been unfaithful to him,
and their sons are bastards.
Now an invader shall devour their fields.
8   Blow the trumpet in Gibeah,
the horn in Ramah,
raise the battle-cry in Beth-aven:
'Benjamin, we are with you!'
9 On the tribes of Israel I have proclaimed this unalterable doom:
on the day of punishment Ephraim shall be laid waste.
10 The rulers of Judah act like men who move their neighbour's boundary;
on them will I pour out my wrath like a flood.
11   Ephraim is an oppressor trampling on justice,
doggedly pursuing what is worthless.
12   But I am a festering sore to Ephraim,
a canker to the house of Judah.
13   So when Ephraim found that he was sick,
Judah that he was covered with sores,
Ephraim went to Assyria,
he went in haste to the Great King;
but he has no power to cure you
or to heal your sores.
14   Yes indeed, I will be fierce as a panther to Ephraim,
fierce as a lion to Judah—
I will maul the prey and go,
carry it off beyond hope of rescue—I, the LORD.
15   I will go away and return to my place
until in their horror they seek me,
and look earnestly for me in their distress.

6   Come, let us return to the LORD;
for he has torn us and will heal us,
he has struck us and he will bind up our wounds;
2   after two days he will revive us,
on the third day he will restore us,
that in his presence we may live.
3 Let us humble ourselves, let us strive to know the LORD,
whose justice dawns like morning light,*a*
and its dawning is as sure as the sunrise.
It will come to us like a shower,
like spring rains that water the earth.

4   O Ephraim, how shall I deal with you?
How shall I deal with you, Judah?
Your loyalty to me is like the morning mist,
like dew that vanishes early.
5   Therefore have I lashed you through the prophets
and torn you*b* to shreds with my words;

a Line transposed from end of verse 5.   *b Prob. rdg.; Heb. them.*

loyalty is my desire, not sacrifice,　　　　　　　　　　6
　　not whole-offerings but the knowledge of God.

At Admah*a* they have broken my covenant,　　　　　　7
　　there they have played me false.
Gilead is a haunt of evildoers,　　　　　　　　　　　8
　　marked by a trail of blood;
like robbers lying in wait for a man,　　　　　　　　9
　　priests are banded together
　　to do murder on the road to Shechem;
　　their deeds are outrageous.
At Israel's sanctuary I have seen a horrible thing:　　10
　　there Ephraim played the wanton
　　and Israel defiled himself.
And for you, too, Judah, comes a harvest of reckoning.　11

When I would reverse the fortunes of my people,
　　when I would heal Israel,　　　　　　　　　　　　**7**
　　then the guilt of Ephraim stands revealed,
　　and all the wickedness of Samaria;
　　they have not kept faith.
They are thieves, they break into houses;*b*
they are robbers, they strip people in the street,
little thinking that I have their wickedness ever in mind.　2
　　Now their misdeeds beset them
　　and stare me in the face.
They win over the king with their wickedness　　　　3
　　and princes with their treachery,
lecherous all of them, hot as an oven over the fire　　4
　　which the baker does not stir
　　after kneading the dough until it is proved.
On their king's festal day the officers　　　　　　　5
　　begin to be inflamed with wine,
　　and he joins in the orgies of arrogant men;
for their hearts are heated by it*c* like an oven.　　　6
　　　While they are relaxed all night long
　　　their passion slumbers,
　　but in the morning it flares up
　　　like a blazing fire;
they all grow feverish, hot as an oven,　　　　　　7
　　and devour their rulers.
King after king falls from power,
　　but not one of them calls upon me.
Ephraim and his aliens make a sorry mixture;　　　8
Ephraim has become a cake half-baked.
　　Foreigners fed on his strength,　　　　　　　　9
　　　but he was unaware;

---

a At Admah: *prob. rdg.; Heb.* Like Adam.　　　*b* houses: *prob. rdg.; Heb. om.*
c are heated by it: *prob. rdg.; Heb.* draw near.

        even his grey hairs turned white,
           but he was unaware.

10   So Israel's arrogance cries out against them;
        but they do not return to the LORD their God
           nor seek him, in spite of it all.

11   Ephraim is a silly senseless pigeon,
        now calling upon Egypt, now turning to Assyria for help.

12   Wherever they turn, I will cast my net over them
        and will bring them down like birds on the wing;
        I will take them captive as soon as I hear them flocking.

13   Woe betide them, for they have strayed from me!
    May disaster befall them for rebelling against me!
        I long to deliver them,
    but they tell lies about me.

14   There is no sincerity in their cry to me;
        for all their howling on their pallets
        and gashing of themselves over corn and new wine,
           they are turning away from me.

15   Though I support them, though I give them strength of arm,
        they plot evil against me.

16   Like a bow gone slack,
        they relapse into the worship of their high god;*a*
           their talk is all lies,*b*
    and so their princes shall fall by the sword.

8   Put the trumpet to your lips!
    A*c* vulture hovers over the sanctuary of the LORD:
        they have broken my covenant
        and rebelled against my instruction.

2   They cry to me for help:
    'We know thee, God of Israel.'*d*

3   But Israel is utterly loathsome;
        and therefore he shall run before the enemy.

4   They make kings, but not by my will;
        they set up officers, but without my knowledge;
    they have made themselves idols of their silver and gold.*e*

5   Your calf-gods stink, O Samaria;
    my anger flares up against them.
    Long will it be before they prove innocent.

6   For what sort of a god is this bull?
        It is no god,
    a craftsman made it;
    the calf of Samaria will be broken in fragments.

---

a they relapse . . . god: *prob. rdg.; Heb. obscure.*   *b Prob. rdg.; Heb. adds* that is their stammering speech in Egypt.   *c Prob. rdg.; Heb.* Like a. ·   *d* We . . . Israel: *prob. rdg.; Heb.* O my God, we know thee, Israel.   *e Prob. rdg.; Heb. adds* so that he may be cut off.

Israel sows the wind and reaps the whirlwind;   7
there are no heads on the standing corn, it yields no grain;
and, if it yielded any, strangers would swallow it up.
   Israel is now swallowed up,   8
  lost among the nations,
   a worthless nothing.
For, like a wild ass that has left the herd,   9
  they have run to Assyria.
Ephraim has bargained for lovers;
and, because they have bargained among the nations,   10
  I will now round them up,
  and then they will soon abandon
this setting up of kings and princes.
For Ephraim in his sin has multiplied altars,   11
altars have become his sin.
Though I give him countless rules in writing,   12
  they are treated as invalid.
Though they sacrifice flesh as offerings to me and eat them,   13
  I,*a* the LORD, will not accept them.
Their guilt will be remembered
  and their sins punished.
They shall go back to Egypt,
or in Assyria they shall eat unclean food.

Israel has forgotten his Maker   14
  and built palaces,
Judah has multiplied walled cities;
  but I will set fire to his cities,
   and it shall devour his castles.

Do not rejoice, Israel, do not exult like other peoples;   **9**
  for like a wanton you have forsaken your God,
   you have loved an idol*b*
on every threshing-floor heaped with corn.
Threshing-floor and winepress shall know them no more,   2
  new wine shall disown*c* them.
   They shall not dwell in the LORD's land;   3
Ephraim shall go back to Egypt,
or in Assyria they shall eat unclean food.
They shall pour out no wine to the LORD,   4
they shall not bring their sacrifices to him;
  that would be mourners' fare for them,
  and all who ate it would be polluted.
  For their food shall only stay their hunger;
  it shall not be offered in the house of the LORD.
What will you do for the festal day,   5
  the day of the LORD's pilgrim-feast?

a Prob. rdg.; Heb. he.   *b* an idol: *or* a harlot's fee.   *c Or* fail.

6   For look, they have fled from a scene of devastation:
           Egypt shall receive them,
           Memphis shall be their grave;
           the sands of Syrtes shall wreck them,
           weeds shall inherit their land,
           thorns shall grow in their dwellings.
7   The days of punishment are come,
           the days of vengeance are come
           when Israel shall be humbled.
           Then the prophet shall be made a fool
           and the inspired seer a madman
           by your great guilt.
8   With great enmity Ephraim lies in wait for God's people
       while the prophet is a fowler's trap by all their paths,
           a snare in the very temple of God.
9   They lead them deep into sin as at the time of Gibeah.
       Their guilt will be remembered and their sins punished.

10   I came upon Israel like grapes in the wilderness,
           I looked on their forefathers
           with joy like the first ripe figs;
           but they resorted to Baal-peor
           and consecrated themselves to a thing of shame,
11   and Ephraim became as loathsome as the thing he loved.
           Their honour shall fly away like a bird:
           no childbirth, no fruitful womb, no conceiving;
12   even if they rear their children,
               I will make them childless, without posterity.
       Woe to them indeed when I turn away from them!

13   As lion-cubs emerge only to be hunted,*a*
       so must Ephraim bring out his children for slaughter.
14   Give them, O LORD—what wilt thou give them?
       Give them a womb that miscarries and dry breasts.

15   All their wickedness was seen at Gilgal; there did I hate them.
       For their evil deeds I will drive them from my house,
           I will love them no more: all their princes are in revolt.
16   Ephraim is struck down:
       their root is withered, and they yield no fruit;
           if ever they give birth,
           I will slay the dearest offspring of their womb.

17   My God shall reject them,
               because they have not listened to him,
       and they shall become wanderers among the nations.

---

a As lion-cubs . . . hunted: *prob. rdg.; Heb. unintelligible.*

God's judgement on Israel

Israel is like a rank vine **10**
  ripening its fruit:
his fruit grows more and more, and more and more his altars;
the fairer his land becomes, the fairer he makes his sacred pillars.
They are crazy now, they are mad. 2
  God himself will hack down their altars
  and wreck their sacred pillars.
Well may they say, 'We have no king, 3
  for we do not fear the LORD;
  and what can the king do for us?'
    There is nothing but talk, 4
imposing of oaths and making of treaties, all to no purpose;
  and litigation spreads like a poisonous weed
    along the furrows of the fields.
The inhabitants of Samaria tremble for the calf-god of Beth-aven; 5
the people mourn over it[a] and its priestlings howl,
  distressed for their image, their glory,
    which is carried away into exile.
It shall be carried to Assyria 6
as tribute to the Great King;
  disgrace shall overtake Ephraim
and Israel shall feel the shame of their disobedience.
Samaria and her king are swept away 7
  like flotsam on the water;
    the hill-shrines of Aven are wiped out, 8
    the shrines where Israel sinned;
thorns and thistles grow over her altars.
  So they will say to the mountains, 'Cover us',
  and to the hills, 'Fall on us.'

Since the day of Gibeah Israel has sinned; 9
there they took their stand in rebellion.
Shall not war overtake them in Gibeah?
I have come against the rebels to chastise them, 10
and the peoples shall mass against them
  in hordes for their two deeds of shame.
Ephraim is like a heifer broken in, 11
  which loves to thresh corn,
across whose fair neck I have laid a yoke;[b]
  I have harnessed Ephraim to the pole that he[c] may plough,
  that Jacob may harrow his land.
Sow for yourselves in justice, 12
  and you will reap what loyalty deserves.
  Break up your fallow;

---

[a] the people mourn over it: or the high god and his people mourn. [b] a yoke:
prob. rdg.; Heb. om.   [c] he: prob. rdg.; Heb. Judah.

for it is time to seek the LORD,
  seeking him till he comes and gives you just measure of rain.

13   You have ploughed wickedness into your soil,
          and the crop is mischief;
          you have eaten the fruit of treachery.

        Because you have trusted in your chariots,
          in the number of your warriors,

14   the tumult of war shall arise against your people,
          and all your fortresses shall be razed
      as Shalman razed Beth-arbel in the day of battle,
      dashing the mother to the ground with her babes.

15   So it shall be done to you, Bethel,
          because of your evil scheming;
    as sure as day dawns, the king of Israel shall be swept away.

11   When Israel was a boy, I loved him;
        I called my son out of Egypt;

2   but the more I called, the further they went from me;
        they must needs sacrifice to the Baalim
          and burn offerings before carved images.

3   It was I who taught Ephraim to walk,
        I who had taken them in my arms;

4   but they did not know that I harnessed them in leading-strings[a]
        and led them with bonds of love[b]—
    that I had lifted them like a little child[c] to my cheek,
        that I had bent down to feed them.

5   Back they shall go to Egypt,
        the Assyrian shall be their king;
          for they have refused to return to me.

6   The sword shall be swung over their blood-spattered altars
        and put an end to their prattling priests

7   and devour my people in return for all their schemings,
        bent on rebellion as they are.
      Though they call on their high god,
        even then he will not reinstate them.

8   How can I give you up, Ephraim,
        how surrender you, Israel?
      How can I make you like Admah
        or treat you as Zeboyim?
      My heart is changed within me,
        my remorse kindles already.

9   I will not let loose my fury,
      I will not turn round and destroy Ephraim;
      for I am God and not a man,
        the Holy One in your midst;

---

[a] leading-strings: *or* cords of leather.   [b] bonds of love: *or* reins of hide.
[c] I had . . . child: *prob. rdg.*; *Heb.* like those who lift up a yoke.

I will not come with threats^a like a roaring lion.   10
    No; when I roar, I who am God,
   my sons shall come with speed out of the west.
They will come speedily, flying like birds out of Egypt,   11
    like pigeons from Assyria,
    and I will settle them in their own homes.
   This is the very word of the LORD.
Ephraim besets me with treachery,   12
    the house of Israel besets me with deceit;
   and Judah is still restive under God,
    still loyal to the idols he counts holy.
Ephraim is a shepherd whose flock is but^b wind,   **12**
a hunter chasing the east wind all day;^c
he makes a treaty with Assyria
and carries tribute of oil to Egypt.

The LORD has a charge to bring against Judah   2
and is resolved to punish Jacob for his conduct;
   he will requite him for his misdeeds.
   Even in the womb Jacob overreached his brother,   3
   and in manhood he strove with God.
   The divine angel stood firm and held his own;^d   4
   Jacob wept and begged favour for himself.
    Then God met him at Bethel
   and there spoke with him.
The LORD the God of Hosts, the LORD is his name.   5

   Turn back all of you by God's help;   6
   practise loyalty and justice
   and wait always upon your God.
   False scales are in merchants' hands,   7
    and they love to cheat;
    so Ephraim says,   8
'Surely I have become a rich man, I have made my fortune';
   but all his gains will not pay
    for the guilt^e of his sins.
Yet I have been the LORD your God since your days in Egypt;   9
I will make you live in tents yet again, as in the old days.

   I spoke to the prophets,   10
   it was I who gave vision after vision;
   I spoke through the prophets in parables.
   Was there idolatry in Gilead?   11
    Yes: they were worthless
   and sacrificed to bull-gods in Gilgal;
their altars were common as heaps of stones beside a ploughed field.

---

^a *Prob. rdg.; Heb. adds* they shall go after the LORD.   ^b is a ... but: *or* feeds on.
^c *Prob. rdg.; Heb. adds* piling up treachery and havoc.   ^d The divine ... own: *or*
He stood firm against an angel, but flagged.   ^e for the guilt: *prob. rdg.; Heb.*
for me, guilt.

12   Jacob fled to the land of Aram;
        Israel did service to win a wife,
            to win a wife he tended sheep.

13   By a prophet the LORD brought up Israel out of Egypt
            and by a prophet he was tended.

14   Ephraim has given bitter provocation;
        therefore his Lord will make him answerable
            for his own death
        and bring down upon his own head the blame
            for all that he has done.

13   When the Ephraimites mumbled their prayers,
        God himself denounced Israel;
        they were guilty of Baal-worship and died.
2   Yet now they sin more and more;
        they have made themselves an image of cast metal,
        they have fashioned their silver into idols,
            nothing but the work of craftsmen;
            men say of them,
        'Those who kiss calf-images offer human sacrifice.'

3   Therefore they shall be like the morning mist
            or like dew that vanishes early,
        like chaff blown from the threshing-floor
            or smoke from a chimney.
4   But I have been the LORD your God since your days in Egypt,
            when you knew no other saviour than me,
                no god but me.
5   I cared for you in the wilderness,
6   in a land of burning heat, as if you were in pasture.
            So they were filled,
        and, being filled, grew proud;
            and so they forgot me.
7   So now I will be like a panther to them,
        I will prowl like a leopard by the wayside;
8   I will meet them like a she-bear robbed of her cubs
            and tear their ribs apart,
        like a lioness I will devour them on the spot,
            I will rip them up like a wild beast.
9   I have destroyed you, O Israel; who is there to help you?
10   Where now is your king that he may save you,
            or the rulers in all your cities
            for whom you asked me,
        begging for king and princes?
11   I gave you a king in my anger,
            and in my fury took him away.

Ephraim's guilt is tied up in a scroll,   12
his sins are kept on record.
When the pangs of his birth came over his mother,   13
he showed himself a senseless child;
for at the proper time he could not present himself
at the mouth of the womb.
Shall I redeem him from Sheol?   14
Shall I ransom him from death?
Oh, for your plagues, O death! Oh, for your sting, Sheol!
I will put compassion out of my sight.
Though he flourishes among the reeds,^a   15
an east wind shall come, a blast from the LORD,
rising over the desert;
Ephraim's spring will fail and his fountain run dry.
It will carry away as spoil
his whole store of costly treasures.
Samaria will become desolate because she has rebelled against her God;   16
her babes will fall by the sword and be dashed to the ground,
her women with child shall be ripped up.

Repentance, forgiveness, and restoration

Return, O Israel, to the LORD your God;   **14**
for you have stumbled in your evil courses.
Come with your words ready,   2
come back to the LORD;
say to him, 'Thou dost not endure iniquity.^b
Accept our plea,
and we will pay our vows with cattle from our pens.
Assyria shall not save us, nor will we seek horses to ride;   3
what we have made with our own hands
we will never again call gods;
for in thee the fatherless find a father's love.'

I will heal their apostasy; of my own bounty will I love them;   4
for my anger is turned away from them.
I will be as dew to Israel   5
that he may flower like the lily,
strike root like the poplar^c
and put out fresh shoots,   6
that he may be as fair as the olive
and fragrant as Lebanon.
Israel shall again dwell in my^d shadow   7
and grow corn in abundance;

^a among the reeds: *prob. rdg.; Heb.* between (*or* a son of) brothers.   ^b Thou . . .
iniquity: *or* Thou wilt surely take away iniquity.   ^c *Prob. rdg.; Heb.* like Lebanon.
^d *Prob. rdg.; Heb.* its.

> they shall flourish like a vine
> and be famous as the wine of Lebanon.

8 What has Ephraim any more to do with idols?
> I have spoken and I affirm it:
> I am the pine-tree that shelters you;
> to me you owe your fruit.

9   Let the wise consider these things and let him who considers take note; for the LORD's ways are straight and the righteous walk in them, while sinners stumble.

JOEL

1 The word of the LORD which came to Joel son of Pethuel.

The day of the LORD

2 Listen, you elders;
> hear me, all you who live in the land:
> has the like of this happened in all your days
> or in your fathers' days?

3 Tell it to your sons and they may tell theirs;
> let them pass it on from generation to generation.

4 What the locust has left the swarm eats,
> what the swarm has left the hopper eats,
> and what the hopper has left the grub eats.

5 Wake up, you drunkards, and lament your fate;
> mourn for the fresh wine, all you wine-drinkers,
> because it is lost to you.

6 For a horde has overrun my land,
> mighty and past counting;
> their teeth are a lion's teeth;
> they have the fangs of a lioness.

7 They have ruined my vines
> and left my fig-trees broken and leafless,
> they have plucked them bare
> and stripped them of their bark;
> they have left the branches white.

8 Wail like a virgin wife in sackcloth,
> wailing over the bridegroom of her youth:

9 the drink-offering and grain-offering are lost
> to the house of the LORD.
> Mourn, you priests, ministers of the LORD,

10 the fields are ruined, the parched earth mourns;

for the corn is ruined, the new wine is desperate,
    the oil has failed.
Despair, you husbandmen; you vinedressers, lament,   11
    because the wheat and the barley,
      the harvest of the field, is lost.
The vintage is desperate, and the fig-tree has failed;   12
    pomegranate, palm, and apple,
    all the trees of the country-side are parched,
    and none make merry over harvest.

    Priests, put on sackcloth and beat your breasts;   13
      lament, you ministers of the altar;
come, lie in sackcloth all night long, you ministers of my God;
      for grain-offering and drink-offering
    are withheld from the house of your God.
Proclaim a solemn fast, appoint a day of abstinence.   14
    You elders, summon all that live in the land
      to come together in the house of your God,
    and cry to the LORD.
    Alas! the day is near,   15
    the day of the LORD: it comes,
    a mighty destruction from the Almighty.
    Look! it stares us in the face;   16
    the house of our God has lost its food,
      lost all its joy and gladness.
    The soil is parched,   17
      the dykes are dry,
      the granaries are deserted,
      the barns ruinous;
      for the rains have failed.
    The cattle are exhausted,   18
      the herds of oxen distressed
    because they have no pasture;
    the flocks of sheep waste away.
    To thee I cry, O LORD;   19
    for fire has devoured the open pastures
and the flames have burnt up all the trees of the country-side.
The very cattle in the field look up to thee;   20
    for the water-channels are dried up,
    and fire has devoured the open pastures.

    Blow the trumpet in Zion,   **2**
    sound the alarm upon my holy hill;
    let all that live in the land tremble,
      for the day of the LORD has come,
    surely a day of darkness and gloom is upon us,   2
      a day of cloud and dense fog;
    like a blackness spread over the mountains
    a mighty, countless host appears;

their like has never been known,
nor ever shall be in ages to come;
3   their vanguard a devouring fire,
their rearguard leaping flame;
before them the land is a garden of Eden,
behind them a wasted wilderness;
nothing survives their march.
4   On they come, like squadrons of horse,
like war-horses they charge;
5 bounding over the peaks they advance with the rattle of chariots,
like flames of fire burning up the stubble,
like a countless host in battle array.
6   Before them nations tremble,
every face turns pale.
7   Like warriors they charge,
they mount the walls like men at arms,
each marching in line,
no confusion in the ranks,
8   none jostling his neighbour,
none breaking line.
They plunge through streams without halting their advance;
9 they burst into the city, leap on to the wall,
climb into the houses,
entering like thieves through the windows.
10   Before them the earth shakes,
the heavens shudder,
sun and moon are darkened,
and the stars forbear to shine.
11   The LORD thunders before his host;
his is a mighty army,
countless are those who do his bidding.
Great is the day of the LORD and terrible,
who can endure it?
12   And yet, the LORD says, even now
turn back to me with your whole heart,
fast, and weep, and beat your breasts.
13   Rend your hearts and not your garments;
turn back to the LORD your God;
for he is gracious and compassionate,
long-suffering and ever constant,
always ready to repent of the threatened evil.
14   It may be he will turn back and repent
and leave a blessing behind him,
blessing enough for grain-offering and drink-offering
for the LORD your God.

15   Blow the trumpet in Zion,
proclaim a solemn fast, appoint a day of abstinence;

gather the people together, proclaim a solemn assembly;   16
      summon the elders,
gather the children, yes, babes at the breast;
    bid the bridegroom leave his chamber
      and the bride her bower.
    Let the priests, the ministers of the LORD,   17
      stand weeping between the porch and the altar
and say, 'Spare thy people, O LORD, thy own people,
    expose them not to reproach,
      lest other nations make them a byword
    and everywhere men ask,
      "Where is their God?"'

Israel forgiven and restored

    Then the LORD's love burned with zeal for his land,   18
      and he was moved with compassion for his people.
He answered their appeal and said,   19
I will send you corn, and new wine, and oil,
      and you shall have your fill;
    I will expose you no longer
      to the reproach of other nations.
    I will remove the northern peril far away from you   20
and banish them into a land parched and waste,
    their vanguard into the eastern sea
      and their rear into the western,
and the stench shall rise from their rotting corpses
    because of their proud deeds!
Earth, be not afraid, rejoice and be glad;   21
    for the LORD himself has done a proud deed.
    Be not afraid, you cattle in the field;   22
    for the pastures shall be green,
    the trees shall bear fruit,
the fig and the vine yield their harvest.
      O people of Zion,   23
    rejoice and be glad in the LORD your God,
who gives you good food in due measure[a]
    and sends down rain[b] as of old.
    The threshing-floors shall be heaped with grain,   24
the vats shall overflow with new wine and oil.
    So I will make good the years   25
      that the swarm has eaten,
    hopper and grub and locust,
my great army which I sent against you;

[a] *Or* gives you a sign pointing to prosperity.   [b] *Prob. rdg.; Heb. adds* spring rain and autumn rain.

26   and you shall eat, you shall eat your fill
     and praise the name of the LORD your God
      who has done wonders for you,[a]

27   and you shall know that I am present in Israel,
  that I and no other am the LORD your God;
    and my people shall not again be brought to shame.

28   Thereafter the day shall come
    when I will pour out my spirit on all mankind;
    your sons and your daughters shall prophesy,
    your old men shall dream dreams
    and your young men see visions;

29   I will pour out my spirit in those days
      even upon slaves and slave-girls.

30 I will show portents in the sky and on earth,
    blood and fire and columns of smoke;

31   the sun shall be turned into darkness
      and the moon into blood
 before the great and terrible day of the LORD comes.

32 Then everyone who invokes the LORD by name
      shall be saved:
    for when the LORD gives the word
    there shall yet be survivors on Mount Zion
      and in Jerusalem a remnant[b]
      whom the LORD will call.[c]

3   When that time comes, on that day
  when I reverse the fortunes of Judah and Jerusalem,

2   I will gather all the nations together
    and lead them down to the Valley of the LORD's Judgement
      and there bring them to judgement
  on behalf of Israel, my own possession;
    for they have scattered my people
      throughout their own countries,
      have taken each their portion of my land

3   and shared out my people by lot,
    bartered a boy for a whore,
 and sold a girl for wine and drunk it down.

4   What are you to me, Tyre and Sidon and all the districts of Philistia? Can you pay me back for anything I have done? Is there anything that you can do to me? Swiftly and speedily I will make your deeds recoil upon

5 your own heads; for you have taken my silver and my gold and carried off

6 my costly treasures into your temples; you have sold the people of Judah and Jerusalem to the Greeks, and removed them far beyond their own

7 frontiers. But I will rouse them to leave the places to which you have sold

8 them. I will make your deeds recoil upon your own heads: I will sell your

---

[a] *Prob. rdg.; Heb. adds* and my people shall not again be brought to shame (*cp. verse 27*).
[b] a remnant: *prob. rdg.; Heb.* among the remnant.   [c] *Or* when the LORD calls.

sons and your daughters to the people of Judah, and they shall sell them to
the Sabaeans, a nation far away. The LORD has spoken.

Proclaim this amongst the nations: 9–12ᵃ
Declare a holy war, call your troops to arms!
  Beat your mattocks into swords
    and your pruning-hooks into spears.ᵇ
Rally to each other's help, all you nations round about.
Let the weakling say, 'I am strong',
  and let the coward show himself brave.ᶜ
  Let all the nations hear the call to arms
    and come to the Valley of the LORD's Judgement;
let all the warriors come and draw near
    and muster there;
      for there I will take my seat
    and judge all the nations round about.

Ply the sickle, for the harvest is ripe;   13
  come, tread the grapes,
for the press is full and the vats overflow;
  great is the wickedness of the nations.
The roar of multitudes, multitudes, in the Valley of Decision!   14
  The day of the LORD is at hand
    in the Valley of Decision;
  sun and moon are darkened   15
  and the stars forbear to shine.
  The LORD roars from Zion   16
  and thunders from Jerusalem;
  heaven and earth shudder,
  but the LORD is a refuge for his people
    and the defence of Israel.

Thus you shall know that I am the LORD your God,   17
  dwelling in Zion my holy mountain;
  Jerusalem shall be holy,
and no one without the right shall pass through her again.
  When that day comes,   18
  the mountains shall run with fresh wine
  and the hills flow with milk.
All the streams of Judah shall be full of water,
  and a fountain shall spring from the LORD's house
    and water the gorge of Shittim,
  but Egypt shall become a desert   19
  and Edom a deserted waste,
    because of the violence done to Judah
    and the innocent blood shed in her land;

ᵃ *The order of lines in verses 9–12 has been re-arranged in several places.*   ᵇ Beat . . .
spears: *cp. Isa. 2. 4; Mic. 4. 3.*   ᶜ and let . . . brave: *prob. rdg.; Heb.* O LORD
bring down thy warriors.

20-21   and I will spill their blood,
        the blood I have not yet spilt.
      Then there shall be people living in Judah for ever,
      in Jerusalem generation after generation;
      and the LORD will dwell in Zion.

AMOS

1 THE WORDS OF AMOS, one of the sheep-farmers of Tekoa,
which he received in visions concerning Israel during the reigns of
Uzziah king of Judah and Jeroboam son of Jehoash king of Israel,
2 two years before the earthquake. He said,

      The LORD roars from Zion
      and thunders from Jerusalem;
      the shepherds' pastures are scorched
      and the top of Carmel*a* is dried up.

The sins of Israel and her neighbours

3 These are the words of the LORD:

      For crime after crime of Damascus
          I will grant them no reprieve,
      because they threshed Gilead under threshing-sledges spiked with iron.
4   Therefore will I send fire upon the house of Hazael,
          fire that shall eat up Ben-hadad's palaces;
5   I will crush the great men of Damascus
      and wipe out those who live in the Vale of Aven
          and the sceptred ruler of Beth-eden;
      the people of Aram shall be exiled to Kir.
      It is the word of the LORD.

6 These are the words of the LORD:

      For crime after crime of Gaza
          I will grant them no reprieve,
      because they deported a whole band of exiles
          and delivered them up to Edom.
7   Therefore will I send fire upon the walls of Gaza,
          fire that shall consume its palaces.
8   I will wipe out those who live in Ashdod
          and the sceptred ruler of Ashkelon;
      I will turn my hand against Ekron,
          and the remnant of the Philistines shall perish.
      It is the word of the Lord GOD.

a top of Carmel: *or* choicest farmland.

These are the words of the LORD: 9

> For crime after crime of Tyre
> I will grant them no reprieve,
> because, forgetting the ties of kinship,
> they delivered a whole band of exiles to Edom.
> Therefore will I send fire upon the walls of Tyre,   10
> fire that shall consume its palaces.

These are the words of the LORD: 11

> For crime after crime of Edom
> I will grant them no reprieve,
> because, sword in hand, they hunted their kinsmen down,
> stifling their natural affections.
> Their anger raged unceasing,
> their fury stormed unchecked.
> Therefore will I send fire upon Teman,   12
> fire that shall consume the palaces of Bozrah.

These are the words of the LORD: 13

> For crime after crime of the Ammonites
> I will grant them no reprieve,
> because in their greed for land
> they invaded the ploughlands of Gilead.
> Therefore will I set fire to the walls of Rabbah,   14
> fire that shall consume its palaces
> amid war-cries on the day of battle,
> with a whirlwind on the day of tempest;
> then their king shall be carried into exile,   15
> he and his officers with him.
> It is the word of the LORD.

These are the words of the LORD: 2

> For crime after crime of Moab
> I will grant them no reprieve,
> because they burnt the bones of the king of Edom to ash.*a*
> Therefore will I send fire upon Moab,   2
> fire that shall consume the palaces in their towns;
> Moab shall perish in uproar,
> with war-cries and the sound of trumpets,
> and I will cut off the ruler from among them   3
> and kill all their officers with him.
> It is the word of the LORD.

These are the words of the LORD: 4

> For crime after crime of Judah
> I will grant them no reprieve,
> because they have spurned the law of the LORD
> and have not observed his decrees,

a to ash: *or* for lime.

> and have been led astray by the false gods
>   that their fathers followed.
> 5   Therefore will I send fire upon Judah,
>   fire that shall consume the palaces of Jerusalem.

6 These are the words of the LORD:

> For crime after crime of Israel
>   I will grant them no reprieve,
> because they sell the innocent for silver
>   and the destitute for a pair of shoes.
> 7   They grind the heads of the poor into the earth
>   and thrust the humble out of their way.
> Father and son resort to the same girl,
>   to the profanation of my holy name.
> 8   Men lie down beside every altar
>   on garments seized in pledge,
> and in the house of their God*ᵃ* they drink liquor
>   got by way of fines.
>
> 9   Yet it was I who destroyed the Amorites before them,
>   though they were tall as cedars,
>   though they were sturdy as oaks,
>   I who destroyed their fruit above
>   and their roots below.
> 10 It was I who brought you up from the land of Egypt,
> I who led you in the wilderness forty years,
>   to take possession of the land of the Amorites;
> 11 I raised up prophets from your sons,
>   Nazirites from your young men.
>   Was it not so indeed, you men of Israel?
>   says the LORD.
> 12 But you made the Nazirites drink wine,
> and said to the prophets, 'You shall not prophesy.'
> 13 Listen, I groan under the burden of you,
>   as a wagon creaks under a full load.
> 14 Flight shall not save the swift,
>   the strong man shall not rally his strength.
>   The warrior shall not save himself,
> 15 the archer shall not stand his ground;
>   the swift of foot shall not be saved,
>   nor the horseman escape;
> 16 on that day the bravest of warriors
> shall be stripped of his arms and run away.
>   This is the very word of the LORD.

ᵃ Or gods.

Israel's sins and threatened punishment

LISTEN, ISRAELITES, to these words that the LORD addresses to you, **3**
to the whole nation which he brought up from Egypt:

For you alone have I cared   2
among all the nations of the world;
therefore will I punish you
for all your iniquities.
Do two men travel together   3
unless they have agreed?
Does a lion roar in the forest   4
if he has no prey?
Does a young lion growl in his den
if he has caught nothing?
Does a bird fall into a trap on the ground   5
if the striker is not set for it?
Does a trap spring from the ground
and take nothing?
If a trumpet sounds the alarm,   6
are not the people scared?
If disaster falls on a city,
has not the LORD been at work?*ª*
For the Lord GOD does nothing   7
without giving to his servants the prophets knowledge of his plans.
The lion has roared; who is not terrified?   8
The Lord GOD has spoken; who will not prophesy?

Stand upon the palaces in Ashdod   9
and upon the palaces of Egypt,
and proclaim aloud:
'Assemble on the hills of Samaria,
look at the tumult seething among her people
and at the oppression in her midst;
what do they care for honesty   10
who hoard in their palaces the gains of crime and violence?'
This is the very word of the LORD.
Therefore these are the words of the Lord GOD: 11

An enemy shall surround*ᵇ* the land;
your stronghold shall be thrown down
and your palaces sacked.
These are the words of the LORD: 12

As a shepherd rescues out of the jaws of a lion
two shin bones or the tip of an ear,
so shall the Israelites who live in Samaria be rescued
like a corner of a couch or a chip from the leg of a bed.*ᶜ*

ª If disaster ... work?: *or* If there is evil in a city, will not the LORD act?   *ᵇ* shall
surround: *prob. rdg.; Heb. and round.*   *ᶜ* or a chip ... bed: *prob. rdg.; Heb. obscure.*

13   Listen and testify against the family of Jacob.
This is the very word of the Lord GOD, the God of Hosts.

14   On the day when I deal with Israel
         for all their crimes,
     I will most surely deal with the altars of Bethel:
     the horns of the altar shall be hacked off
         and shall fall to the ground.

15   I will break down both winter-house and summer-house;
         houses of ivory shall perish,
     and great houses be demolished.
         This is the very word of the LORD.

4   Listen to this,
you cows of Bashan who live on the hill of Samaria,
you who oppress the poor and crush the destitute,
who say to your lords, 'Bring us drink':

2   the Lord GOD has sworn by his holiness
that your time is coming
     when men shall carry you away on their shields[a]
     and your children in fish-baskets.

3   You shall each be carried straight out
         through the breaches in the walls
         and pitched on a dunghill.[b]
         This is the very word of the LORD.

4   Come to Bethel—and rebel!
Come to Gilgal—and rebel the more!
Bring your sacrifices for the morning,
your tithes within three days.

5   Burn your thank-offering without leaven;
announce, proclaim your freewill offerings;
for you love to do what is proper, you men of Israel!
         This is the very word of the Lord GOD.

6   It was I who kept teeth idle
         in all your cities,
who brought famine on all your settlements;
         yet you did not come back to me.
         This is the very word of the LORD.

7   It was I who withheld the showers from you
while there were still three months to harvest.
     I would send rain on one city
     and no rain on another;
     rain would fall on one field,
and another would be parched for lack of it.

8   From this city and that, men would stagger to another
for water to drink, but would not find enough;

[a] *Or* baskets.   [b] a dunghill: *prob. rdg.; Heb.* the Harmon.

        yet you did not come back to me.
        This is the very word of the Lord.

I blasted you with black blight and red;   9
    I laid waste^a your gardens and vineyards;
the locust devoured your fig-trees and your olives;
        yet you did not come back to me.
        This is the very word of the Lord.

I sent plague upon you like the plagues of Egypt;   10
    I killed with the sword
        your young men and your troops of horses.
    I made your camps stink in your nostrils;
        yet you did not come back to me.
        This is the very word of the Lord.

    I brought destruction amongst you   11
as God destroyed Sodom and Gomorrah;
you were like a brand snatched from the fire;
        yet you did not come back to me.
        This is the very word of the Lord.

Therefore, Israel, this is what I will do to you;   12
and, because this is what I will do to you,
    Israel, prepare to meet your God.
It is he who forges the thunder and creates the wind,   13
    who showers abundant rain on the earth,^b
    who darkens the dawn with thick clouds
    and marches over the heights of the earth—
    his name is the Lord the God of Hosts.

Listen to these words; I raise a dirge over you, O Israel: **5**
    She has fallen to rise no more,   2
        the virgin Israel,
    prostrate on her own soil, with no one to lift her up.

These are the words of the Lord God: 3
        The city that marched out to war a thousand strong
            shall have but a hundred left,
            that which marched out a hundred strong
        shall have but ten men of Israel left.

These are the words of the Lord to the people of Israel: 4
    Resort to me, if you would live, not to Bethel;   5
    go not to Gilgal, nor pass on to Beersheba;
        for Gilgal shall be swept away
        and Bethel brought to nothing.
    If you would live, resort to the Lord,   6
    or he will break out against Joseph like fire,
    fire which will devour Israel with no one to quench it;

<hr>

^a I laid waste: prob. rdg.; Heb. to increase.   ^b who showers ... earth: prob. rdg.;
Heb. who tells his thoughts to mankind.

8 *a*   he who made the Pleiades and Orion,
who turned darkness into morning
and darkened day into night,
  who summoned the waters of the sea
and poured them over the earth,

9   who makes Taurus rise after Capella
and Taurus set hard on the rising of the Vintager *b*—
  he who does this, his name is the LORD. *c*

7   You that turn justice upside down *d*
and bring righteousness to the ground,

10   you that hate a man who brings the wrongdoer to court
and loathe him who speaks the whole truth:

11   for all this, because you levy taxes on the poor
and extort a tribute of grain from them,
though you have built houses of hewn stone,
  you shall not live in them,
though you have planted pleasant vineyards,
  you shall not drink wine from them.

12   For I know how many your crimes are
and how countless your sins,
you who persecute the guiltless, hold men to ransom
and thrust the destitute out of court.

13   At that time, therefore, a prudent man will stay quiet,
  for it will be an evil time.

14   Seek good and not evil,
  that you may live,
that the LORD the God of Hosts may be firmly on your side,
  as you say he is.

15   Hate evil and love good;
  enthrone justice in the courts;
it may be that the LORD the God of Hosts
will be gracious to the survivors of Joseph.

16   Therefore these are the words of the LORD the God of Hosts:

    There shall be wailing in every street,
and in all open places cries of woe.
The farmer shall be called to mourning,
and those skilled in the dirge to *e* wailing;

17   there shall be lamentation in every vineyard;
for I will pass through the midst of you,
  says the LORD.

18   Fools who long for the day of the LORD,
what will the day of the LORD mean to you?
It will be darkness, not light.

a Verse 7 transposed to follow verse 9.   *b* who makes . . . Vintager: *prob. rdg.; Heb.*
who smiles destruction on the strong, and destruction comes on the fortified city.
c his . . . LORD: *transposed from end of verse 8.*   *d* upside down: *prob. rdg.; Heb.*
poison.   *e Prob. rdg.; Heb. places* to before *those skilled.*

It will be as when a man runs from a lion, 19
 and a bear meets him,
or turns into a house and leans his hand on the wall,
 and a snake bites him.
The day of the LORD is indeed darkness, not light, 20
 a day of gloom with no dawn.

I hate, I spurn your pilgrim-feasts; 21
 I will not delight in your sacred ceremonies.
When you present your sacrifices and offerings 22
 I will not accept them,
nor look on the buffaloes of your shared-offerings.
Spare me the sound of your songs; 23
I cannot endure the music of your lutes.
Let justice roll on like a river 24
and righteousness like an ever-flowing stream.
Did you bring me sacrifices and gifts, 25
you people of Israel, those forty years in the wilderness?
 No! but now you shall take up 26
 the shrine of your idol king
 and the pedestals of your images,*a*
which you have made for yourselves,
and I will drive you into exile beyond Damascus. 27

So says the LORD; the God of Hosts is his name.

Shame on you who live at ease in Zion, **6**
and you, untroubled on the hill of Samaria,
 men of mark in the first of nations,
you to whom the people of Israel resort!
Go, look at Calneh, 2
travel on to Hamath the great,
 then go down to Gath of the Philistines—
are you better than these kingdoms?
Or is your *b* territory greater than theirs*c*?
You who thrust the evil day aside 3
and make haste to establish violence. *d*
You who loll on beds inlaid with ivory 4
 and sprawl over your couches,
feasting on lambs from the flock
 and fatted calves,
you who pluck the strings of the lute 5
and invent musical instruments like David,
 you who drink wine by the bowlful 6
 and lard yourselves with the richest of oils,
but are not grieved at the ruin of Joseph—

---

a Prob. rdg.; Heb. adds the star of your gods. *b Prob. rdg.; Heb.* their. *c Prob. rdg.; Heb.* yours. *d* You . . . violence: *or* You who invoke the day of wrong-doing and bring near the sabbath of violence.

7   now, therefore,
         you shall head the column of exiles;
           that will be the end of sprawling and revelry.

8   The Lord GOD has sworn by himself:
         I loathe the arrogance of Jacob,
           I loathe his palaces;
         city and all in it I will abandon to their fate.

9   If ten men are left in one house,
           they shall die,
10   and a man's uncle and the embalmer shall take him up
         to carry his body out of the house for burial,
     and they shall call to someone in a corner of the house,
     'Any more there?', and he shall answer, 'No.'
           Then he will add, 'Hush!'—
     for the name of the LORD must not be mentioned.
11   For the LORD will command,
         and at the shock the great house will be rubble
           and the cottage matchwood.

12   Can horses gallop over rocks?
         Can the sea be ploughed with oxen?
         Yet you have turned into venom the process of law
           and justice itself into poison,
13   you who are jubilant over a nothing*a* and boast,
     'Have we not won power *a* by our own strength?'
14   O Israel, I am raising a nation against you,
           and they shall harry your land
         from Lebo-hamath to the gorge of the Arabah.
     This is the very word of the LORD the God of Hosts.

Visions foretelling doom upon Israel

7   THIS WAS WHAT THE LORD GOD SHOWED ME: a swarm of locusts
     hatched out when the late corn, which comes after the king's early
2   crop, was beginning to sprout. As they were devouring the last of the
     herbage in the land, I said, 'O Lord GOD, forgive; what will Jacob be after
3   this? He is so small.' Then the LORD relented and said, 'This shall not
     happen.'
4   This was what the Lord GOD showed me: the Lord GOD was summon-
     ing a flame of fire *b* to devour the great abyss, and to devour all creation.
5   I said, 'O Lord GOD, I pray thee, cease; what will Jacob be after this? He
6   is so small.' The LORD relented and said, 'This also shall not happen.'

---

a a nothing *and* power: *Heb.* Lo-debar *and* Karnaim, *making a word-play on the two
place-names.*   *b* a flame of fire: *prob. rdg.; Heb.* to contend with fire.

This was what the LORD showed me: there was a man standing by a 7
wall^a with a plumb-line in his hand. The LORD said to me, 'What do you 8
see, Amos?' 'A plumb-line', I answered, and the Lord said, 'I am setting
a plumb-line to the heart of my people Israel; never again will I pass them
by. The hill-shrines of Isaac shall be desolated and the sanctuaries of 9
Israel laid waste; I will rise, sword in hand, against the house of Jeroboam.'

Amaziah, the priest of Bethel, reported to Jeroboam king of Israel: 10
'Amos is conspiring against you in Israel; the country cannot tolerate what
he is saying. He says, "Jeroboam shall die by the sword, and Israel shall 11
be deported far from their native land."' To Amos himself Amaziah said, 12
'Be off, you seer! Off with you to Judah! You can earn your living and do
your prophesying there. But never prophesy again at Bethel, for this is 13
the king's sanctuary, a royal palace.' 'I am^b no prophet,' Amos replied to 14
Amaziah, 'nor am I a prophet's son; I am^b a herdsman and a dresser of
sycomore-figs. But the LORD took me as I followed the flock and said to 15
me, "Go and prophesy to my people Israel." So now listen to the word of 16
the LORD. You tell me I am not to prophesy against Israel or go drivelling
on against the people of Isaac. Now these are the words of the LORD: Your 17
wife shall become a city strumpet^c and your sons and daughters shall fall
by the sword. Your land shall be divided up with a measuring-line, you
yourself shall die in a heathen country, and Israel shall be deported far
from their native land and go into exile.'

This was what the Lord GOD showed me: there was a basket of summer 8
fruit, and he said, 'What are you looking at, Amos?' I answered, 'A basket 2
of ripe summer^d fruit.' Then the LORD said to me, 'The time is ripe^d for
my people Israel. Never again will I pass them by. In that day, says the 3
Lord GOD, the singing women in the palace shall howl, "So many dead men,
flung out everywhere! Silence!"'

Listen to this, you who grind the destitute and plunder^e the humble, 4
you who say, 'When will the new moon be over so that we may sell corn? 5
When will the sabbath be past so that we may open our wheat again, giving
short measure in the bushel and taking overweight in the silver, tilting the
scales fraudulently, and selling the dust of the wheat; that we may buy the 6
poor for silver and the destitute for a pair of shoes?' The LORD has sworn 7
by the pride of Jacob: I will never forget any of their doings.

> Shall not the earth shake for this? 8
> Shall not all who live on it grieve?
> All earth shall surge and seethe like the Nile
> and subside like the river of Egypt.

> On that day, says the Lord GOD, 9
> I will make the sun go down at noon
> and darken the earth in broad daylight.
> I will turn your pilgrim-feasts into mourning 10
> and all your songs into lamentation.

---

^a *Prob. rdg.; Heb. adds* of a plumb-line. ^b *Or* was. ^c become...strumpet: *or*
be carried off as a prostitute in a raid. ^d ripe summer *and* ripe: *a play on the Heb.*
qais (summer) *and* qes (end). ^e and plunder: *prob. rdg.; Heb.* to destroy.

I will make you all put sackcloth round your waists
and have all your heads shaved.
I will make it like mourning for an only son
and the end of it a bitter day.

11   The time is coming, says the Lord GOD,
            when I will send famine on the land,
not hunger for bread or thirst for water,
            but for hearing the word of the LORD.
12   Men shall stagger from north to south,[a]
they shall range from east to west,
seeking the word of the LORD,
            but they shall not find it.
13   On that day fair maidens and young men
            shall faint from thirst;
14   all who take their oath by Ashimah, goddess of Samaria,
all who swear, 'By the life of your god, O Dan',
and, 'By the sacred way to Beersheba',
shall fall to rise no more.

9   I saw the LORD standing by the altar, and he said:

Strike the capitals so that the whole porch is shaken;
            I will smash them all into pieces[b]
and I will kill them to the last man[c] with the sword.
No fugitive shall escape,
no survivor find safety;
2   if they dig down to Sheol,
thence shall my hand take them;
            if they climb up to heaven,
            thence will I bring them down.
3   If they hide on the top of Carmel,
there will I search out and take them;
if they conceal themselves from me in the depths of the sea,
there will I bid the sea-serpent bite them.
4   If they are herded into captivity by their enemies,
there will I bid the sword slay them,
and I will fix my eye on them
            for evil and not for good.

5   The Lord the GOD of Hosts,
at whose touch the earth heaves,
            and all who dwell on it wither,[d]
it surges like the Nile,
            and subsides like the river of Egypt,
6   who builds his stair up to the heavens
and arches his ceiling over the earth,

---

[a] south: *prob. rdg.; Heb.* west.   [b] I will . . . pieces: *prob. rdg.; Heb.* I will hack them
on the heads of them all.   [c] them to the last man: *or* their children.   [d] *Or* mourn.

who summons the waters of the sea
and pours them over the land—
his name is the LORD.

Are not you Israelites like Cushites to me?　　　　7
says the LORD.
Did I not bring Israel up from Egypt,
the Philistines from Caphtor, the Aramaeans from Kir?
Behold, I, the Lord GOD,　　　　8
have my eyes on this sinful kingdom,
and I will wipe it off the face of the earth.

A remnant spared and restored

Yet I will not wipe out the family of Jacob root and branch,
says the LORD.
No; I will give my orders,　　　　9
I will shake Israel to and fro through all the nations
as a sieve is shaken to and fro
and not one pebble falls to the ground.
They shall die by the sword, all the sinners of my people,　　　　10
who say, 'Thou wilt not let disaster come near us
or overtake us.'
On that day I will restore　　　　11
David's fallen house;
I will repair its gaping walls and restore its ruins;
I will rebuild it as it was long ago,
that they may possess what is left of Edom　　　　12
and all the nations who were once named mine.

This is the very word of the LORD, who will do this.

A time is coming, says the LORD,　　　　13
when the ploughman shall follow hard on the vintager,*a*
and he who treads the grapes after him who sows the seed.
The mountains shall run with fresh wine,
and every hill shall wave with corn.
I will restore the fortunes of my people Israel;　　　　14
they shall rebuild deserted cities and live in them,
they shall plant vineyards and drink their wine,
make gardens and eat the fruit.
Once more I will plant them on their own soil,　　　　15
and they shall never again be uprooted
from the soil I have given them.
It is the word of the LORD your God.

a Or reaper.

OBADIAH

Edom's pride and downfall

1^a The vision of Obadiah: what the Lord GOD has said concerning Edom.

When a herald was sent out among the nations, crying,
'Rouse yourselves;
let us rouse ourselves to battle against Edom',
I heard this message from the LORD:

2   Look, I make you the least of all nations,
an object of contempt.

3   Your proud, insolent heart has led you astray;
you who haunt the crannies among the rocks,
making your home on the heights,
you say to yourself, 'Who can bring me to the ground?'

4   Though you soar as high as a vulture
and your nest is set among the stars,
thence I will bring you down.
This is the very word of the LORD.

5^b   If thieves or robbers come to you by night,
though your loss be heavy,
they will steal only what they want;
if vintagers come to you,
will they not leave gleanings?

6   But see how Esau's treasure is ransacked,
his secret wealth hunted out!

7   All your former allies march you to the frontier,
your confederates mislead you and bring you low,
your own kith and kin lay a snare for your feet,
a snare that works blindly, without wisdom.

8   And on that very day
I will destroy all the sages of Edom
and leave no wisdom on the mount of Esau.
This is the very word of the LORD.

9   Then shall your warriors, O Teman, be so enfeebled,
that every man shall be cut down on the mount of Esau.

10   For the murderous violence done to your brother Jacob
you shall be covered with shame and cut off for ever.

---

^a *Verses 1–4: cp. Jer. 49. 14–16.*   ^b *Verses 5 and 6: cp. Jer. 49. 9, 10.*

On the day when you stood aloof,   11
on the day when strangers carried off his wealth,
when foreigners trooped in by his gates
and parcelled out Jerusalem by lot,
you yourselves were of one mind with them.
Do not gloat over your brother on the day of his misfortune,   12
nor rejoice over Judah on his day of ruin;
do not boast on the day of distress,
nor enter my people's gates on the day of his downfall.   13
Do not gloat over his fall on the day of his downfall
nor seize his treasure on the day of his downfall.
Do not wait at the cross-roads to cut off his fugitives   14
nor betray the survivors on the day of distress.

For soon the day of the LORD will come on all the nations: 15
you shall be treated as you have treated others,
and your deeds will recoil on your own head.
The draught that you have drunk on my holy mountain   16
all the nations shall drink continually;
they shall drink and gulp down
and shall be as though they had never been;
but on Mount Zion there shall be those that escape,   17
and it shall be holy,
and Jacob shall dispossess those that dispossessed them.
Then shall the house of Jacob be fire,   18
the house of Joseph flame,
and the house of Esau shall be chaff;
they shall blaze through it and consume it,
and the house of Esau shall have no survivor.
The LORD has spoken.
Then they shall possess the Negeb, the mount of Esau,   19
and the Shephelah of the Philistines;
they shall possess the country-side of Ephraim and Samaria,
and Benjamin shall possess Gilead.
Exiles of Israel*a* shall possess*b* Canaan as far as Zarephath,   20
exiles of Jerusalem*c* shall possess the cities of the Negeb.
Those who find safety on Mount Zion shall go up   21
to hold sway over the mount of Esau,
and dominion shall belong to the LORD.

---

a *Prob. rdg.; Heb. adds* this army.   *b* shall possess: *prob. rdg.; Heb.* which.
c *Prob. rdg.; Heb. adds* who are in Sepharad.

JONAH

Jonah's mission to Nineveh

1 THE WORD OF THE LORD CAME TO JONAH son of
2 Amittai: 'Go to the great city of Nineveh, go now and denounce it,
3 for its wickedness stares me in the face.' But Jonah set out for Tarshish to escape from the LORD. He went down to Joppa, where he found a ship bound for Tarshish. He paid his fare and went on board, meaning
4 to travel by it to Tarshish out of reach of the LORD. But the LORD let loose a hurricane, and the sea ran so high in the storm that the ship threatened
5 to break up. The sailors were afraid, and each cried out to his god for help. Then they threw things overboard to lighten the ship. Jonah had gone
6 down into a corner of the ship and was lying sound asleep when the captain came upon him. 'What, sound asleep?' he said. 'Get up, and call on your god; perhaps he will spare us a thought and we shall not perish.'
7 At last the sailors said to each other, 'Come and let us cast lots to find out who is to blame for this bad luck.' So they cast lots, and the lot fell on
8 Jonah. 'Now then,' they said to him, 'what is your business? Where do
9 you come from? What is your country? Of what nation are you?' 'I am a Hebrew,' he answered, 'and I worship the LORD the God of heaven, who
10 made both sea and land.' At this the sailors were even more afraid. 'What can you have done wrong?' they asked. They already knew that he was
11 trying to escape from the LORD, for he had told them so. 'What shall we do with you', they asked, 'to make the sea go down?' For the storm grew
12 worse and worse. 'Take me and throw me overboard,' he said, 'and the sea will go down. I know it is my fault that this great storm has struck
13 you.' The crew rowed hard to put back to land but in vain, for the sea ran
14 higher and higher. At last they called on the LORD and said, 'O LORD, do not let us perish at the price of this man's life; do not charge us with the
15 death of an innocent man. All this, O LORD, is thy set purpose.' Then they took Jonah and threw him overboard, and the sea stopped raging.
16 So the crew were filled with the fear of the LORD and offered sacrifice
17 and made vows to him. But the LORD ordained that a great fish should swallow Jonah, and for three days and three nights he remained in its belly.

2 Jonah prayed to the LORD his God from the belly of the fish:

2   I called to the LORD in my distress,
            and he answered me;
        out of the belly of Sheol I cried for help,
            and thou hast heard my cry.
3   Thou didst cast me into the depths, far out at sea,
            and the flood closed round me;
        all thy waves, all thy billows, passed over me.

I thought I was banished from thy sight   4
and should never see thy holy temple again.

The water about me rose up to my neck;   5
the ocean was closing over me.

Weeds twined about my head
in the troughs of the mountains;   6

I was sinking into a world
whose bars would hold me fast for ever.

But thou didst bring me up alive from the pit, O LORD my God.

As my senses failed me I remembered the LORD,   7
and my prayer reached thee in thy holy temple.

Men who worship false gods may abandon their loyalty,   8
but I will offer thee sacrifice with words of praise;   9
I will pay my vows; victory is the LORD's.

Then the LORD spoke to the fish and it spewed Jonah out on to the dry land. 10
The word of the LORD came to Jonah a second time: 'Go to the great   **3** 1 2
city of Nineveh, go now and denounce it in the words I give you.' Jonah 3-4
obeyed at once and went to Nineveh. He began by going a day's journey
into the city, a vast city, three days' journey across, and then proclaimed:
'In forty days Nineveh shall be overthrown!' The people of Nineveh 5
believed God's word. They ordered a public fast and put on sackcloth,
high and low alike. When the news reached the king of Nineveh he rose 6
from his throne, stripped off his robes of state, put on sackcloth and sat
in ashes. Then he had a proclamation made in Nineveh: 'This is a decree 7
of the king and his nobles. No man or beast, herd or flock, is to taste food,
to graze or to drink water. They are to clothe themselves in sackcloth and 8
call on God with all their might. Let every man abandon his wicked ways
and his habitual violence. It may be that God will repent and turn away 9
from his anger: and so we shall not perish.' God saw what they did, and 10
how they abandoned their wicked ways, and he repented and did not bring
upon them the disaster he had threatened.

Jonah was greatly displeased and angry, and he prayed to the LORD: **4** 1 2
'This, O LORD, is what I feared when I was in my own country, and to
forestall it I tried to escape to Tarshish; I knew that thou art "a god
gracious and compassionate, long-suffering and ever constant, and always
willing to repent of the disaster".*a* And now, LORD, take my life: I should 3
be better dead than alive.' 'Are you so angry?' said the LORD. Jonah went 4 5
out and sat down on the east of the city. There he made himself a shelter
and sat in its shade, waiting to see what would happen in the city. Then the 6
LORD God ordained that a climbing gourd*b* should grow up over his head
to throw its shade over him and relieve his distress, and Jonah was grateful
for the gourd. But at dawn the next day God ordained that a worm should 7
attack the gourd, and it withered; and at sunrise God ordained that a scorch- 8
ing wind should blow up from the east. The sun beat down on Jonah's head
till he grew faint. Then he prayed for death and said, 'I should be better
dead than alive.' At this God said to Jonah, 'Are you so angry over the 9

---

a a god . . . disaster: *cp. Exod. 34. 6.*   *b* a climbing gourd: *or a castor-oil plant.*

10 gourd?' 'Yes,' he answered, 'mortally angry.' The LORD said, 'You are sorry
    for the gourd, though you did not have the trouble of growing it, a plant
11 which came up in a night and withered in a night. And should not I be sorry
    for the great city of Nineveh, with its hundred and twenty thousand who
    cannot tell their right hand from their left, and cattle without number?'

MICAH

1 THIS IS THE WORD OF THE LORD which came to Micah
   of Moresheth during the reigns of Jotham, Ahaz, and Hezekiah, kings
   of Judah; which he received in visions concerning Samaria and
Jerusalem.

The rulers of Israel and Judah denounced

2   Listen, you peoples, all together;
       attend, O earth and all who are in it,
    that the Lord GOD, the Lord from his holy temple,
          may bear witness against you.
3   For look, the LORD is leaving his dwelling-place;
       down he comes and walks on the heights of the earth.
4   Beneath him mountains dissolve
          like wax before the fire,
          valleys are torn open,
       as when torrents pour down the hill-side—
5   and all for the crime of Jacob and the sin of Israel.
    What is the crime of Jacob? Is it not Samaria?
    What is the hill-shrine of Judah? Is it not Jerusalem?
6   So I will make Samaria
    a heap of ruins in open country,
          a place for planting vines;
       I will pour her stones down into the valley
          and lay her foundations bare.
7   All her carved figures shall be shattered,
       her images burnt one and all;
       I will make a waste heap of all her idols.
          She amassed them out of fees for harlotry,
          and a harlot's fee shall they become once more.
8   Therefore I must howl and wail,
          go naked and distraught;
       I must howl like a wolf, mourn like a desert-owl.
9   Her wound cannot be healed;
          for the stroke has bitten deep into Judah,
          it has fallen on the gate of my people,
          upon Jerusalem itself.

Will you not weep your fill, weep your eyes out in Gath?   10
In Beth-aphrah sprinkle yourselves with dust;
    take the road, you that dwell in Shaphir;   11
have not the people of Zaanan gone out in shame from their city?
    Beth-ezel is a place of lamentation,
  she can lend you support no longer.
The people of Maroth are greatly alarmed,   12
for disaster has come down from the LORD
  to the very gate of Jerusalem.
Harness the steeds to the chariot, O people of Lachish,   13
for you first led the daughter of Zion into sin;
  to you must the crimes of Israel be traced.
Let Moresheth-gath be given her dismissal.   14
  Beth-achzib has^a disappointed^b the kings of Israel.
And you too, O people of Mareshah,   15
  I will send others to take your place;
and the glory of Israel shall hide in the cave of Adullam.
  Shave the hair from your head in mourning   16
    for the children of your delight;
  make yourself bald as a vulture,
    for they have left you and gone into exile.

Shame on those who lie in bed planning evil and wicked deeds   **2**
  and rise at daybreak to do them,
    knowing that they have the power!
They covet land and take it by force;   2
  if they want a house they seize it;
they rob a man of his home
  and steal every man's inheritance.

Therefore these are the words of the LORD: 3

Listen, for this whole brood I am planning disaster,
  whose yoke you cannot shake from your necks
and walk upright; it shall be your hour of disaster.

    On that day   4
  they shall take up a poem about you
  and raise a lament thrice told,
  saying, 'We are utterly despoiled:
the land of the LORD's^c people changes hands.
  How shall a man have power^d
to restore our fields, now parcelled out^e?'
  Therefore there shall be no one to assign to you   5
    any portion by lot in the LORD's assembly.

---

^{a} Beth-achzib has: *prob. rdg.; Heb.* The houses of Achzib have. ^{b} *Heb.* achzab.
^{c} the LORD's: *prob. rdg.; Heb.* my. ^{d} have power: *prob. rdg.; Heb.* remove from me.
^{e} now parcelled out: *prob. rdg.; Heb.* he will parcel out.

6   How they rant! They may say, 'Do not rant';
              but this ranting is all their own,
              these insults are their *a* own invention.

7   Can one ask, O house of Jacob,
              'Is the LORD's patience truly at an end?
                  Are these his deeds?
              Does not good come of the LORD's words?
                  He is the upright man's best friend.'
8   But you are no *b* people for me,
              rising up as my enemy to my *c* face,
              to strip the cloak from him that was safe *d*
              and take away the confidence of returning warriors,
9   to drive the women of my people from their pleasant homes
        and rob the children of my glory for ever.
10   Up and be gone; this is no resting-place for you,
        you that to defile yourselves would commit any mischief,
              mischief however cruel.

11   If anyone had gone about in a spirit of falsehood and lies, saying, 'I will
rant to you of wine and strong drink', his ranting would be what this people
like.

12   I will assemble you, the whole house of Jacob;
              I will gather together those that are left in Israel.
       I will herd them like sheep in a fold,
              like a grazing flock which stampedes at the sight of a man.
13   So their leader breaks out before them,
        and they all break through the gate and escape,
           and their king goes before them,
              and the LORD leads the way.

3 And I said:

        Listen, you leaders of Jacob, rulers of Israel,
           should you not know what is right?
2   You hate good and love evil,
       you flay men alive and tear the very flesh from their bones;
3   you devour the flesh of my people,
            strip off their skin,
               splinter their bones;
          you shred them like flesh into a pot,
               like meat into a cauldron.

4   Then they will call to the LORD, and he will give them no answer;
       when that time comes he will hide his face from them,
          so wicked are their deeds.

5   These are the words of the LORD concerning the prophets who lead

---

a *Prob. rdg.; Heb.* his.   *b* But . . . no: *prob. rdg.; Heb.* But yesterday.   *c* my: *prob.*
rdg.; Heb. om.   *d* the cloak . . . safe: *prob. rdg.; Heb.* mantle, cloak.

my people astray, who promise prosperity in return for a morsel of food,
who proclaim a holy war against them if they put nothing into their
mouths:

> Therefore night shall bring you no vision,   6
>> darkness no divination;
>> the sun shall go down on the prophets,
>> the day itself shall be black above them.
> Seers and diviners alike shall blush for shame;   7
>> they shall all put their hands over their mouths,
>> because there is no answer from God.

> But I am full of strength,*a* of justice and power,   8
>> to denounce his crime to Jacob
>>> and his sin to Israel.
> Listen to this, leaders of Jacob,   9
>> rulers of Israel,
> you who make justice hateful
> and wrest it from its straight course,
>> building Zion in bloodshed   10
>>> and Jerusalem in iniquity.
> Her rulers sell justice,   11
> her priests give direction in return for a bribe,
> her prophets take money for their divination,
>> and yet men rely on the LORD.
> 'Is not the LORD among us?' they say;
> 'then no disaster can befall us.'
>> Therefore, on your account   12
> Zion shall become a ploughed field,
> Jerusalem a heap of ruins,
> and the temple hill rough heath.

A remnant restored in an age of peace

> In days to come   4 1*b*
> the mountain of the LORD's house
> shall be set over all other mountains,
> lifted high above the hills.
> Peoples shall come streaming to it,
> and many nations shall come and say,   2
> 'Come, let us climb up on to the mountain of the LORD,
>> to the house of the God of Jacob,
>>> that he may teach us his ways
>>> and we may walk in his paths.'
> For instruction issues from Zion,
>> and out of Jerusalem comes the word of the LORD;

a Prob. rdg.; Heb. adds the spirit of the LORD.   *b Verses 1–3: cp. Isa. 2. 2–4.*

3   he will be judge between many peoples
and arbiter among mighty nations afar.
          They shall beat their swords into mattocks
            and their spears into pruning-knives;
nation shall not lift sword against nation
          nor ever again be trained for war,

4   and each man shall dwell under his own vine,
            under his own fig-tree, undisturbed.
          For the LORD of Hosts himself has spoken.

5   All peoples may walk, each in the name of his god,
          but we will walk in the name of the LORD our God
            for ever and ever.

6   On that day, says the LORD,
            I will gather those who are lost;
I will assemble the exiles and I will strengthen the weaklings.

7   I will preserve the lost as a remnant
            and turn the derelict into a mighty nation.
The LORD shall be their king on Mount Zion
          now and for ever.

8   And you, rocky bastion, hill of Zion's daughter,
            the promises to you shall be fulfilled;
            and your former sovereignty shall come again,
            the dominion of the daughter of Jerusalem.

9   Why are you now filled with alarm?
            Have you no king?
            Have you no counsellor left,
          that you are seized with writhing like a woman in labour?

10   Lie writhing on the ground like a woman in childbirth,
            O daughter of Zion;
          for now you must leave the city
            and camp in the open country;
            and so you will come to Babylon.
            There you shall be saved,
there the LORD will deliver you from your enemies.

11   But now many nations are massed against you;
          they say, 'Let her suffer outrage,
            let us gloat over Zion.'

12   But they do not know the LORD's thoughts
            nor understand his purpose;
          for he has gathered them like sheaves to the threshing-floor.

13   Start your threshing, daughter of Zion;
          for I will make your horns of iron,
          your hooves will I make of bronze,
          and you shall crush many peoples.
         You shall devote their ill-gotten gain to the LORD,
          their wealth to the Lord of all the earth.

Get you behind your walls, you people of a walled city;   5
     the siege is pressed home against you:
Israel's ruler shall be struck on the cheek with a rod.
     But you, Bethlehem in Ephrathah,   2
     small as you are to be among Judah's clans,
out of you shall come forth a governor for Israel,
     one whose roots are far back in the past, in days gone by.
     Therefore only so long as a woman is in labour   3
          shall he give up Israel;
          and then those that survive of his race
          shall rejoin their brethren.
     He shall appear and be their shepherd   4
          in the strength of the LORD,
     in the majesty of the name of the LORD his God.
And they shall continue, for now his greatness shall reach
          to the ends of the earth;
     and he shall be a man of peace.   5

     When the Assyrian comes into our land,
          when he tramples our castles,
we will raise against him seven men or eight
          to be shepherds and princes.
     They shall shepherd Assyria with the sword   6
     and the land of Nimrod with bare blades;
they shall deliver us from the Assyrians
     when they come into our land,
          when they trample our frontiers.

All that are left of Jacob, surrounded by many peoples,   7
          shall be like dew from the LORD,
          like copious showers on the grass,
          which do not wait for man's command
          or linger for any man's bidding.
All that are left of Jacob among the nations,   8
          surrounded by many peoples,
shall be like a lion among the beasts of the forest,
          like a young lion loose in a flock of sheep;
as he prowls he will trample and tear them,
          with no rescuer in sight.
Your hand shall be raised high over your foes,   9
and all who hate you shall be destroyed.

On that day, says the LORD,   10
I will destroy all your horses among you
          and make away with your chariots.
I will destroy the cities of your land   11
          and raze your fortresses.
I will destroy all your sorcerers,   12
and there shall be no more soothsayers among you.

13 I will destroy your images and all the sacred pillars in your land;
    you shall no longer bow in reverence before things your own hands made.

14 I will pull down the sacred poles in your land,
    and demolish your blood-spattered altars.

15 In anger and fury will I take vengeance
    on all nations who disobey me.

Israel denounced for her people's sins

6 Hear now what the LORD is saying:

    Up, state your case to the mountains;
    let the hills hear your plea.

2 Hear the LORD's case, you mountains,
    you everlasting pillars that bear up the earth;
    for the LORD has a case against his people,
    and will argue it with Israel.

3 O my people, what have I done to you?
    Tell me how I have wearied you; answer me this.

4 I brought you up from Egypt,
    I ransomed you from the land of slavery,
    I sent Moses and Aaron and Miriam to lead you.

5 Remember, my people,
    what Balak king of Moab schemed against you,
    and how Balaam son of Beor answered him;
    consider the journey[a] from Shittim to Gilgal,
    in order that you may know the triumph of the LORD.

6 What shall I bring when I approach the LORD?
    How shall I stoop before God on high?
    Am I to approach him with whole-offerings or yearling calves?

7 Will the LORD accept thousands of rams
    or ten thousand rivers of oil?
    Shall I offer my eldest son for my own wrongdoing,
    my children for my own sin?

8 God[b] has told you what is good;
    and what is it that the LORD asks of you?
    Only to act justly, to love loyalty,
    to walk wisely before your God.

9 Hark, the LORD, the fear of whose name brings success,
    the LORD calls to the city.

10 Listen, O tribe of Judah and citizens in assembly,[c]
    can I overlook[d] the infamous false measure,[e]
    the accursed short bushel?

---

[a] consider the journey: *prob. rdg.; Heb. om.*   [b] God: *prob. rdg.; Heb. obscure.*
[c] citizens in assembly: *prob. rdg.; Heb. unintelligible.*   [d] can I overlook: *prob. rdg.; Heb. obscure.*   [e] *Prob. rdg.; Heb. adds* infamous treasures.

Can I connive at false scales or a bag of light weights?   11
    Your rich men are steeped in violence,   12
        your townsmen are all liars,
  and their tongues frame deceit.
    But now I will inflict a signal punishment on you   13
        to lay you waste for your sins:
  you shall eat but not be satisfied,   14
        your food shall lie heavy on your stomach;
        you shall come to labour but not bring forth,
        and even if you bear a child
        I will give it to the sword;
  you shall sow but not reap,   15
you shall press the olives but not use the oil,
        you shall tread the grapes but not drink the wine.
    You have kept the precepts of Omri;   16
        what the house of Ahab did, you have done;
        you have followed all their ways.
  So I will lay you utterly waste;
        the nations shall jeer at your citizens,
        and their insults you shall bear.

Disappointment turned to hope

Alas! I am now like the last gatherings of summer fruit,   **7**
        the last gleanings of the vintage,
        when there are no grapes left to eat,
  none of those early figs that I love.
    Loyal men have vanished from the earth,   2
    there is not one upright man.
    All lie in wait to do murder,
each man drives his own kinsman like a hunter into the net.
    They are bent eagerly on wrongdoing,   3
    the officer who presents the requests,*a*
    the judge who gives judgement *b* for reward,
    and the nobleman who harps on his desires.
    Thus their goodness is twisted *c* like rank weeds   4
    and their honesty like briars. *d*
    As soon as thine eye sees, thy punishment falls;
    at that moment bewilderment seizes them.
Trust no neighbour, put no confidence in your closest friend;   5
  seal your lips even from the wife of your bosom.
    For son maligns father,   6
        daughter rebels against mother,
        daughter-in-law against mother-in-law,
        and a man's enemies are his own household.

---

a the requests: *prob. rdg.; Heb. om.*   *b* who gives judgement: *prob. rdg.; Heb. om.*
c twisted: *prob. rdg.; Heb. obscure.*   *d* their honesty like briars: *prob. rdg.;*
Heb. obscure.

7   But I will look for the LORD,
       I will wait for God my saviour; my God will hear me.
8   O my enemies, do not exult over me;
          I have fallen, but shall rise again;
       though I dwell in darkness, the LORD is my light.
9   I will bear the anger of the LORD, for I have sinned against him,
       until he takes up my cause and gives judgement for me,
       until he brings me out into light, and I see his justice.
10   Then may my enemies see and be abashed,
       those who said to me, 'Where is he, the LORD your God?'
       Then shall they be trampled like mud in the streets;
          I shall gloat over them;
11   that will be a day for rebuilding your walls,
          a day when your frontiers will be extended,
12   a day when men will come seeking you
            from Assyria to Egypt
          and from Egypt to the Euphrates,
          from every sea and every mountain;
13   and the earth with its inhabitants shall be waste.
          This shall be the fruit of their deeds.

14   Shepherd thy people with thy crook,
            the flock that is thy very own,
       that dwells by itself on the heath and in the meadows;
       let them graze in Bashan and Gilead, as in days gone by.
15   Show us *a* miracles as in the days when thou camest out of Egypt;
16   let the nations see and be taken aback for all their might,
          let them keep their mouths shut,
            make their ears deaf,
17   let them lick the dust like snakes,
            like creatures that crawl upon the ground.
       Let them come trembling and fearful from their strongholds,
          let them fear thee, O LORD our God.

18   Who is a god like thee? Thou takest away guilt,
       thou passest over the sin of the remnant of thy own people,
          thou dost not let thy anger rage for ever
          but delightest in love that will not change.
19   Once more thou wilt show us tender affection
            and wash out our guilt,
          casting all our sins into the depths of the sea.
20   Thou wilt show good faith to Jacob,
            unchanging love to Abraham,
       as thou didst swear to our fathers in days gone by.

          a *Prob. rdg.; Heb.* I will show him.

NAHUM

An oracle about Nineveh: the book of the vision of Nahum the Elkoshite. **1**

The vengeance of the LORD on his enemies

The LORD is a jealous god, a god of vengeance; 2*a*
the LORD takes vengeance and is quick to anger.*b*
c In whirlwind and storm he goes on his way, 3
   and the clouds are the dust beneath his feet.
He rebukes the sea and dries it up 4
   and makes all the streams fail.
Bashan and Carmel languish,
   and on Lebanon the young shoots wither.
The mountains quake before him, 5
   the hills heave and swell,
and the earth, the world and all that lives in it,
   are in tumult at his presence.
Who can stand before his wrath? 6
   Who can resist his fury?
His anger pours out*d* like a stream of fire,
and the rocks melt*e* before him.
The LORD is a sure refuge 7
for those who look to him in time of distress;
he cares for all who seek his protection
and brings them safely*f* through the sweeping flood; 8
he makes a final end of all who oppose him
and pursues his enemies into darkness.
No adversaries dare oppose him twice; 9–11
all are burnt up*g* like tangled briars.
Why do you make plots against the LORD?
He himself will make an end of you all.
From you has come forth a wicked counsellor,
plotting evil against the LORD.
The LORD takes vengeance on his adversaries,
against his enemies he directs his wrath;
with skin scorched black, they are consumed
like stubble that is parched and dry.

*a Verses 2–14 are an incomplete alphabetic acrostic poem; some parts have been re-arranged
accordingly.* *b The rest of verse 2, The LORD takes . . . wrath, transposed to verse 11.*
*c Prob. rdg.; Heb. inserts two lines The LORD is long-suffering and of great might, but the
LORD does not sweep clean away.* *d pours out: or fuses or melts.* *e Prob. rdg.;
Heb. are torn down.* *f brings them safely: prob. rdg.; Heb. om.* *g all are burnt
up: prob. rdg.; Heb. for until.*

Israel and Judah rid of the invaders

These are the words of the LORD:

13 Now I will break his yoke from your necks
      and snap the cords that bind you.
14 Image and idol will I hew down in the house of your God.
      This is what the LORD has ordained for you:
      never again shall your offspring be scattered;
      and I will grant you burial, fickle though you have been.
12   Has the punishment been so great?
      Yes, but it has passed away and is gone.
      I have afflicted you, but I will not afflict you again.

15 See on the mountains the feet of the herald
      who brings good news.
      Make your pilgrimages, O Judah,
      and pay your vows.
      For wicked men shall never again overrun you;
      they are totally destroyed.
2 2*ᵃ* The LORD will restore the pride of Jacob and Israel alike,
      although plundering hordes have stripped them bare
      and pillaged their vines.

Nineveh's enemies triumphant

1   The battering-ram is mounted against your bastions,
      the siege is closing in.
    Watch the road and brace yourselves;
      put forth all your strength.
3   The shields of their warriors are gleaming red,
      their soldiers are all in scarlet;
      their chariots, when the line is formed,
      are like flickering*ᵇ* fire;
4   squadrons of horse advance on the city in mad frenzy;*ᶜ*
    they jostle one another in the outskirts, like waving torches;
5   the leaders display their prowess*ᵈ*
      as they dash to and fro like lightning,
      rushing*ᵉ* in headlong career;
    they hasten to the wall, and mantelets are set in position.
6   The sluices of the rivers are opened, the palace topples down;
7   the train of captives goes into exile,
      their slave-girls are carried off,
      moaning like doves and beating their breasts;

ᵃ Verses 1 and 2 transposed.   *ᵇ flickering: prob. rdg.; Heb. obscure.*
ᶜ Prob. rdg.; Heb. adds chariots.   *ᵈ display their prowess: or shout their own names.*
ᵉ Prob. rdg.; Heb. stumbling.

and Nineveh has become like a pool of water,   8
like the waters round her, which are ebbing away.
'Stop! Stop!' they cry; but none turns back.

Spoil is taken, spoil of silver and gold;   9
        there is no end to the store,
    treasure beyond the costliest that man can desire.
    Plundered, pillaged, stripped bare!   10
Courage melting and knees giving way,
writhing limbs, and faces drained of colour!
        Where now is the lions' den,   11
    the cave *a* where the lion cubs lurked,
    where the lion and *b* lioness and young cubs
            went unafraid,
    the lion which killed to satisfy its whelps   12
    and for its mate broke the neck of the kill,
    mauling its prey to fill its lair,
        filling its den with the mauled prey?

I am against you, says the LORD of Hosts,   13
    I will smoke out your pride, *c*
    and a sword shall devour your cubs.
    I will leave you no more prey on the earth,
    and the sound of your feeding *d* shall no more be heard.

Ah! blood-stained city, steeped in deceit,   **3**
full of pillage, never empty of prey!
        Hark to the crack of the whip,   2
    the rattle of wheels and stamping of horses,
    bounding chariots, chargers rearing,   3
        swords gleaming, flash of spears!
    The dead are past counting, their bodies lie in heaps,
    corpses innumerable, men stumbling over corpses—
all for a wanton's monstrous wantonness,   4
        fair-seeming, a mistress of sorcery,
        who beguiled nations and tribes
        by her wantonness and her sorceries.
I am against you, says the LORD of Hosts,   5
    I will uncover your breasts to your disgrace
    and expose your naked body to every nation,
        to every kingdom your shame.
    I will cast loathsome filth over you,   6
    I will count you obscene and treat you like excrement.

Then all who see you will shrink from you and say,   7
'Nineveh is laid waste; who will console her?'
Where shall I look for anyone to comfort you?

---

a Prob. rdg.; Heb. pasture.   *b* and: *prob. rdg.; Heb. om.*   *c* your pride: *prob.*
rdg.; Heb. her chariot.   *d* your feeding: *prob. rdg.; Heb.* your messenger.

8 Will you fare better than No-amon?—
  she that lay by the streams of the Nile,
   surrounded by water,
 whose rampart was the Nile, waters her wall;

9 Cush and Egypt were her strength, and it was boundless,
 Put and the Libyans brought her help.

10 She too became an exile and went into captivity,
 her infants too were dashed to the ground at every street-corner,
  her nobles were shared out by lot,
  all her great men were thrown into chains.

11 You too shall hire yourself out, flaunting your sex;
 you too shall seek refuge from the enemy.

12 Your fortifications are like figs when they ripen:
 if they are shaken, they fall into the mouth of the eater.

13 The troops*a* in your midst are a pack of women,
 the gates of your country stand open to the enemy,
 and fire consumes their bars.

14 Draw yourselves water for the siege,
  strengthen your fortifications;
 down into the clay, trample the mortar,
  repair the brickwork.

15 Even then the fire will consume you,
  and the sword will cut you down.*b*
  Make yourselves many as the locusts,
  make yourselves many as the hoppers,

16 a swarm which spreads out and then flies away.
 You have spies as numerous as the stars in the sky;

17 your secret agents are like locusts,
  your commanders like the hoppers
 which lie dormant in the walls on a cold day;
 but when the sun rises, they scurry off,
 and no one knows where they have gone.

18 Your shepherds slumber, O king of Assyria,
  your flock-masters lie down to rest;
 your troops*a* are scattered over the hills,
  and no one rounds them up.

19 Your wounds cannot be assuaged, your injury is mortal;
 all who have heard of your fate clap their hands in joy.
 Are there any whom your ceaseless cruelty has not borne down?

a Or people. *b Prob. rdg.; Heb. adds* and consume you like the locust (*or* hopper).

HABAKKUK

An oracle which the prophet Habakkuk received in a vision. 1

Divine justice

How long, O LORD, have I cried to thee, unanswered? 2
I cry, 'Violence!', but thou dost not save.
  Why dost thou let me see such misery, 3
  why countenance *a* wrongdoing?

Devastation and violence confront me;
strife breaks out, discord raises its head,
  and so law grows effete; 4
  justice does not come forth victorious;
  for the wicked outwit the righteous,
  and so justice comes out perverted.

Look, you treacherous people, look: 5
  here is what will astonish you and stun you,
for there is work afoot in your days
which you will not believe when it is told you.
It is this: I am raising up the Chaldaeans, 6
that savage and impetuous nation,
  who cross the wide tracts of the earth
to take possession of homes not theirs.
  Terror and awe go with them; 7
their justice and judgement are of their own making.
Their horses are swifter than hunting-leopards, 8
  keener than wolves of the plain; *b*
  their cavalry wait ready, they spring forward,
  they come flying from afar
  like vultures swooping to devour the prey.
Their whole army advances, violence in their hearts; 9
  a sea of faces rolls on;
  they bring in captives countless as the sand.
  Kings they hold in derision, 10
  rulers they despise;
  they despise every fortress,
  they raise siege-works and capture it.
  Then they pass on like the wind and are gone; 11
and dismayed are all those whose strength was their god.

a Or dost thou let me see.   *b* Or evening.

12   Art thou not from of old, O Lord?—
        my God, the holy, the immortal.*a*
     O Lord, it is thou who hast appointed them to execute judgement;
     O mighty God, thou who hast destined them to chastise,
13   thou whose eyes are too pure to look upon evil,
        and who canst not countenance wrongdoing,
        why dost thou countenance the treachery of the wicked?
     Why keep silent when they devour men more righteous than they?
14   Why dost thou make men like the fish of the sea,
        like gliding creatures that obey no ruler?
15   They haul them up with hooks, one and all,
            they catch them in nets
            and drag them in their trawls;
        then they make merry and rejoice,
16   sacrificing to their nets
            and burning offerings*b* to their trawls;
        for by these they live sumptuously
            and enjoy rich fare.
17   Are they then to unsheathe the sword every day,
        to slaughter the nations without pity?

2   I will stand at my post,
        I will take up my position on the watch-tower,
        I will watch to learn what he will say through me,
            and what I shall reply when I am challenged.*c*
2   Then the Lord made answer:
     Write down the vision, inscribe it on tablets,
        ready for a herald to carry it with speed;*d*
3   for there is still a vision for the appointed time.
        At the destined hour it will come in breathless haste,
            it will not fail.
        If it delays, wait for it;
            for when it comes will be no time to linger.

4   The reckless will be unsure of himself,
        while the righteous man will live by being faithful;*e*
5   as for the traitor in his over-confidence,
        still less will he ride out the storm, for all his bragging.
        Though he opens his mouth as wide as Sheol
        and is insatiable as Death,
            gathering in all the nations,
            making all peoples his own harvest,
6   surely they will all turn upon him
        with insults and abuse, and say,

---

a the immortal: *prob. original rdg., altered in Heb. to* we shall not die.   *b Or* incense.
c when I am challenged: *or* concerning my complaint.   *d* ready . . . speed:
or so that a man may read it easily.   *e Or* by his faithfulness (*cp. Romans 1. 17;
Galatians 3. 11*).

'Woe betide you who heap up wealth that is not yours ^a
and enrich yourself with goods taken in pledge!'
Will not your creditors suddenly start up,   7
   will not all awake who would shake you till you are empty,
and will you not fall a victim to them?
Because you yourself have plundered mighty ^b nations,   8
   all the rest of the world will plunder you,
      because of bloodshed and violence done in the land,
      to the city and all its inhabitants.

Woe betide you who seek unjust gain for your house,   9
   to build your nest on a height,
to save yourself from the grasp of wicked men!
Your schemes to overthrow mighty ^b nations   10
   will bring dishonour to your house
   and put your own life in jeopardy.
The very stones will cry out from the wall,   11
and from the timbers a beam will answer them.

Woe betide you who have built a town with bloodshed   12
   and founded a city on fraud,
   so that nations toil for a pittance,   13
   and peoples weary themselves for a mere nothing!
Is not all this the doing of the LORD of Hosts?
For the earth shall be full of the knowledge of the glory of the LORD   14
   as the waters fill the sea.

Woe betide you who make your ^c companions drink the outpouring of 15
     your wrath,
   making them drunk, that you may watch their naked orgies!
Drink deep draughts of shame, not of glory;   16
you too shall drink until you stagger.
The cup in the LORD's right hand is passed to you,
and your shame will exceed ^d your glory.
   The violence done to Lebanon shall sweep over you,   17
   the havoc done to its beasts shall break your own spirit,
     because of bloodshed and violence done in the land,
     to the city and all its inhabitants.

What use is an idol when its maker has shaped it?—   18
   it is only an image, a source of lies;
or when the maker trusts what he has made?—
   he is only making dumb idols.
   Woe betide him who says to the wood, 'Wake up',   19
   to the dead stone, 'Bestir yourself'!^e

---

^a *Prob. rdg.; Heb. adds* till when.   ^b *Or* many.   ^c *Prob. rdg.; Heb.* his.
^d will exceed: *prob. rdg.; Heb. unintelligible.*   ^e *Prob. rdg.; Heb. adds* he will
teach.

Why, it is firmly encased in gold and silver
and has no breath in it.

20   But the LORD is in his holy temple;
let all the earth be hushed in his presence.

A prayer for mercy

3 A prayer of the prophet Habakkuk.

2   O LORD, I have heard tell of thy deeds;
I have seen, O LORD, thy work.*a*
In the midst of the years thou didst make thyself known,
and in thy wrath thou didst remember mercy.

3   God comes from Teman,
the Holy One from Mount Paran;
his radiance overspreads the skies,
and his splendour fills the earth.

4   He rises like the dawn,
with twin rays starting forth at his side;
the skies are*b* the hiding-place of his majesty,
and the everlasting *c* ways are for*d* his swift flight.*e*

5   Pestilence stalks before him,
and plague comes forth behind.

6   He stands still and shakes the earth,
he looks and makes the nations tremble;
the eternal mountains are riven,
the everlasting*c* hills subside,

7   the tents of Cushan are snatched away,*f*
the tent-curtains of Midian flutter.

8   Art thou angry with the streams?
Is thy wrath against the sea, O LORD?
When thou dost mount thy horses,
thy riding is to victory.

9   Thou dost draw thy bow from its case *g*
and charge thy quiver with shafts.
Thou cleavest the earth with rivers;

10–11   the mountains see thee and writhe with fear.
The torrent of water rushes by,
and the deep sea thunders aloud.
The sun forgets to turn in his course,*h*
and the moon stands still at her zenith,
at the gleam of thy speeding arrows
and the glance of thy flashing spear.

---

a Prob. rdg.; Heb. adds in the midst of the years quicken it.   *b* the skies are:
prob. rdg.; Heb. there is.   *c Or* ancient.   *d* and . . . are for: *transposed from
end of verse 6.*   *e* his swift flight: *transposed, with slight change, from verse 7.*
f are snatched away: *prob. rdg.; Heb.* under wickedness.   *g* Thou . . . case:
prob. rdg.; Heb. Thy bow was quite bared.   *h* The sun . . . course: *prob. rdg.;
Heb.* The sun raised the height of his hands.

With threats thou dost bestride the earth   12
and trample down the nations in anger.
   Thou goest forth to save thy people,   13
   thou comest to save thy anointed;
thou dost shatter the wicked man's house from the roof down,*a*
uncovering its foundations to the bare rock.*b*
Thou piercest their*c* chiefs with thy*d* shafts,   14
and their leaders are torn from them by the whirlwind,
   as they open*e* their jaws
to devour their wretched victims in secret.

When thou dost tread the sea with thy horses   15
   the mighty waters boil.
I hear, and my belly quakes;   16
my lips quiver at the sound;
trembling comes over my bones,
and my feet totter in their tracks;
   I sigh for the day of distress
to dawn over my assailants.
   Although the fig-tree does not burgeon,   17
   the vines bear no fruit,
   the olive-crop fails,
the orchards yield no food,
the fold is bereft of its flock
   and there are no cattle in the stalls,
yet I will exult in the LORD   18
   and rejoice in the God of my deliverance.
The LORD God is my strength,   19
who makes my feet nimble as a hind's
   and sets me to range the heights.

ZEPHANIAH

THIS IS THE WORD OF THE LORD which came to 1
Zephaniah son of Cushi, son of Gedaliah, son of Amariah, son of
Hezekiah, in the time of Josiah son of Amon king of Judah.

Doom on Judah and her neighbours

I will sweep the earth clean of all that is on it,   2
   says the LORD.
I will sweep away both man and beast,   3
   I will sweep the birds from the air and the fish from the sea,

---

a the wicked ... down: *prob. rdg.; Heb.* a head from the house of the wicked.   *b* bare
rock: *prob. rdg.; Heb.* neck.   *c* their: *prob. rdg.; Heb. om.*   *d Prob. rdg.;
Heb.* his.   *e* from them ... open: *prob. rdg.; Heb. obscure.*

and I will bring the wicked to their knees [a]
and wipe out mankind from the earth.
This is the very word of the LORD.

4 I will stretch my hand over Judah
and all who live in Jerusalem;
I will wipe out from this place the last remnant of Baal
and the very name of the heathen priests,

5 those who bow down upon the house-tops
to worship the host of heaven
and who swear by Milcom,

6 those who have turned their backs on the LORD,
who have not sought the LORD or consulted him.

7 Silence before the Lord GOD!
for the day of the LORD is near.
The LORD has prepared a sacrifice
and has hallowed his guests.

8 On the day of the LORD's sacrifice
I will punish the royal house and its chief officers
and all who ape outlandish fashions.

9 On that day
I will punish all who dance on the temple terrace,
who fill their master's [b] house with crimes of violence and fraud.

10 On that day, says the LORD,
an outcry shall be heard from the Fish Gate,
wailing from the second quarter of the city,
a loud crash from the hills;

11 and [c] those who live in the Lower Town shall wail.
For it is all over with the merchants,
and all the dealers in silver are wiped out.

12 At that time
I will search Jerusalem with a lantern
and punish all who sit in stupor over the dregs of their wine,
who say to themselves,
'The LORD will do nothing, good or bad.'

13 Their wealth shall be plundered,
their houses laid waste;
they shall build houses but not live in them,
they shall plant vineyards but not drink the wine from them.

14 The great day of the LORD is near,
it comes with speed;
no runner so fast as that day,
no raiding band so swift. [d]

---

[a] *I will bring . . . knees: prob. rdg.; Heb.* the ruins with the wicked. [b] *Or* their Lord's.
[c] *and: prob. rdg.; Heb. om.* [d] *no runner . . . swift: prob. rdg.; Heb.* hark, the
day of the LORD is bitter, there the warrior cries aloud.

That day is a day of wrath,   15
a day of anguish and affliction,
a day of destruction and devastation,
a day of murk and gloom,
a day of cloud and dense fog,
a day of trumpet and battle-cry   16
over fortified cities and lofty battlements.
I will bring dire distress upon men;   17
they shall walk like blind men for their sin against the LORD.
Their blood shall be spilt like dust
and their bowels like dung;
neither their silver nor their gold   18
shall avail to save them.
On the day of the LORD's wrath, by the fire of his jealousy
the whole land shall be consumed;
for he will make an end, a swift end,
of all who live in the land.

Gather together, you unruly nation, gather together,   **2**
before you are sent far away and vanish*a* like chaff,   2
before the burning anger of the LORD comes upon you,
before the day of the LORD's anger comes upon you.
Seek the LORD,   3
all in the land who live humbly by his laws,
seek righteousness, seek a humble heart;
it may be that you will find shelter
in the day of the LORD's anger.
For Gaza shall be deserted,   4
Ashkelon left desolate,
the people of Ashdod shall be driven out*b* at noonday
and Ekron uprooted.

Listen, you who live by the coast, you Kerethite settlers.   5
The word of the LORD is spoken against you;
I will subdue you,*c* land of the Philistines,
I will lay you waste and leave you without inhabitants,
and you, Kereth, shall be all shepherds' huts*d* and sheepfolds;   6
and the coastland shall belong to the survivors of Judah.   7
They shall pasture their flocks by the sea*e*
and lie down at evening in the houses of Ashkelon,
for the LORD their God will turn to them
and restore their fortunes.

I have heard the insults of Moab, the taunts of Ammon,   8
how they have insulted my people
and encroached on their frontiers.

---

a you are . . . vanish: *prob. rdg.; Heb.* obscure.   *b* the people . . . out: *or* Ashdod
shall be made an example.   *c* I . . . you: *prob. rdg.; Heb.* Canaan.   *d* you . . .
huts: *Heb. has these words in a different order.*   *e* by the sea: *prob. rdg.; Heb.* upon them.

9   Therefore, by my life,
        says the LORD of Hosts, the God of Israel,
        Moab shall be like Sodom,
            Ammon like Gomorrah,
        a pile of weeds, a rotting heap of saltwort,
            waste land for evermore.
        The survivors of my people shall plunder them,
        the remnant of my nation shall possess their land.

10 This will be retribution for their pride, because they have insulted the
11 people of the LORD of Hosts and encroached upon their rights. The LORD
will appear against them with all his terrors; for he will reduce to beggary
all the gods of the earth, and all the coasts and islands of the nations will
worship him, every man in his own home.

12   You Cushites also shall be killed
            by the sword of the LORD.*a*
13   So let him stretch out his hand over the north
            and destroy Assyria,
        make Nineveh desolate,
            arid as the wilderness.
14   Flocks shall couch there,
            and all the beasts of the wild.
        Horned owl and ruffed bustard shall roost on her capitals;
            the tawny owl shall hoot in the window,
            and the bustard stand in the porch.*b*
15   This is the city that exulted in fancied security,
        saying to herself, 'I am, and I alone.'
        And what is she now? A waste, a haunt for wild beasts,
        at which every passer-by shall hiss and shake his fist.

3   Shame on the tyrant city, filthy and foul!
2   No warning voice did she heed, she took no rebuke to heart,
        she did not trust in the LORD or come near to her God.
3   Her officers were lions roaring in her midst,
            her rulers wolves of the plain*c*
            that did not wait*d* till morning,
4   her prophets were reckless, no true prophets.
        Her priests profaned the sanctuary
            and did violence to the law.
5   But the LORD in her midst is just;
            he does no wrong;
        morning by morning he gives judgement,
            without fail at daybreak.*e*

6   I have wiped out the proud;
            their battlements are laid in ruin.

a the sword of the LORD: *prob. rdg.; Heb.* my sword.   *b Prob. rdg.; Heb. adds an
unintelligible phrase.*   *c Or* evening.   *d Or* carry off.   *e Prob. rdg.; Heb.
adds* but the wrongdoer knows no shame.

I have made their streets a desert where no one passes.
Their cities are laid waste, deserted, unpeopled.
In the hope that she would remember all my instructions,   7
  I said, 'Do but fear me
    and take my rebuke to heart';
but they were up betimes and went about their evil deeds.

  Wait for me, therefore, says the LORD,   8
  wait for the day when I stand up to accuse you;
  for mine it is to gather nations
    and assemble kingdoms,
to pour out on them my indignation,
    all the heat of my anger;
the whole earth shall be consumed by the fire of my jealousy.
  I will give all peoples once again pure lips,   9
  that they may invoke the LORD by name
  and serve him with one consent.
  From beyond the rivers of Cush   10
my suppliants of the Dispersion shall bring me tribute.

A remnant preserved

  On that day, Jerusalem,   11
you shall not be put to shame for all your deeds
  by which you have rebelled against me;
for then I will rid you
  of your proud and arrogant citizens,
and never again shall you flaunt your pride
  on my holy hill.
But I will leave in you a people   12
  afflicted and poor.
The survivors in Israel shall find refuge in the name of the LORD; 13
they shall no longer do wrong or speak lies,
  no words of deceit shall pass their lips;
for they shall feed and lie down
  with no one to terrify them.

  Zion, cry out for joy;   14
  raise the shout of triumph, Israel;
  be glad, rejoice with all your heart,
    daughter of Jerusalem.
The LORD has rid you of your adversaries,   15
  he has swept away your foes;
the LORD is among you as king, O Israel;
  never again shall you fear disaster.

On that day this shall be the message to Jerusalem: 16
Fear not, O Zion; let not your hands fall slack.

17   The LORD your God is in your midst,
      like a warrior, to keep you safe;
    he will rejoice over you and be glad;
      he will show you his love once more;
    he will exult over you with a shout of joy
18   as in days long ago.*a*

    I will take your cries of woe *b* away from you;
    and you shall no longer endure reproach for her.
19   When that time comes, see,
    I will deal with all your oppressors.
    I will rescue the lost and gather the dispersed;
    I will win my people praise and renown
      in all the world where once they were despised.
20   When the time comes for me to gather you, *c*
      I will bring you home.
  I will win you renown and praise
    among all the peoples of the earth,
  when I bring back your prosperity; and you shall see it.
    It is the LORD who speaks.

HAGGAI

Zerubbabel restorer of the temple

1 IN THE SECOND YEAR OF KING DARIUS, on the first
day of the sixth month, the word of the LORD came through the prophet
Haggai to Zerubbabel son of Shealtiel, governor of Judah, and to
2 Joshua son of Jehozadak, the high priest: These are the words of the LORD
of Hosts: This nation says to itself that it is not yet time for the house of
3 the LORD to be rebuilt. Then this word came through Haggai the prophet:
4 Is it a time for you to live in your own well-roofed houses, while this house
5 lies in ruins? Now these are the words of the LORD of Hosts: Consider your
6 way of life. You have sown much but reaped little; you eat but never as
much as you wish, you drink but never more than you need, you are clothed
but never warm, and the labourer puts his wages into a purse with a hole in
7 it. These are the words of the LORD of Hosts: Consider your way of life.
8 Go up into the hills, fetch timber, and build a house acceptable to me,
9 where I can show my glory,*d* says the LORD. You look for much and get
little. At the moment when you would bring home the harvest, I blast it.
Why? says the LORD of Hosts. Because my house lies in ruins, while
10 each of you has a house that he can run to. It is your fault that the heavens

---

a as . . . ago: *prob. rdg.; Heb. obscure.*   *b* cries of woe: *prob. rdg.; Heb. obscure.*
c When . . . you: *prob. rdg.; Heb.* and in the time, my gathering you.   *d* show my
glory: *or* be honoured.

withhold their dew and the earth its produce. So I have proclaimed a 11
drought against land and mountain, against corn, new wine, and oil, and
all that the ground yields, against man and cattle and all the products of
man's labour.

Zerubbabel son of Shealtiel, Joshua son of Jehozadak, the high priest, 12
and the rest of the people listened to what the LORD their God had said
and what the prophet Haggai said when the LORD their God sent him, and
they were filled with fear because of the LORD. So Haggai the LORD's 13
messenger, as the LORD had commissioned him, said to the people: I am
with you, says the LORD. Then the LORD stirred up the spirit of Zerubbabel 14
son of Shealtiel, governor of Judah, of Joshua son of Jehozadak, the high
priest, and of the rest of the people; they came and began work on the
house of the LORD of Hosts their God on the twenty-fourth day of the sixth 15
month.

In the second year of King Darius, on the twenty-first day of the seventh **2**
month, these words came from the LORD through the prophet Haggai:
Say to Zerubbabel son of Shealtiel, governor of Judah, to Joshua son of 2
Jehozadak, the high priest, and to the rest of the people: Is there anyone 3
still among you who saw this house in its former glory? How does it appear
to you now? Does it not seem to you as if it were not there? But now, 4
Zerubbabel, take heart, says the LORD; take heart, Joshua son of Jehozadak,
high priest. Take heart, all you people, says the LORD. Begin the work, for
I am with you, says the LORD of Hosts, and my spirit is present among you. 5
Have no fear. For these are the words of the LORD of Hosts: One thing 6
more: I will shake heaven and earth, sea and land, I will shake all nations; 7
the treasure of all nations shall come hither, and I will fill this house with
glory;*a* so says the LORD of Hosts. Mine is the silver and mine the gold, 8
says the LORD of Hosts, and the glory*a* of this latter house shall surpass 9
the glory*a* of the former, says the LORD of Hosts. In this place will I grant
prosperity and peace. This is the very word of the LORD of Hosts.

In the second year of Darius, on the twenty-fourth day of the ninth 10
month, this word came from the LORD to the prophet Haggai: These are 11
the words of the LORD of Hosts: Ask the priests to give their ruling: If a 12
man is carrying consecrated flesh in a fold of his robe, and he lets the fold
touch bread or broth or wine or oil or any other kind of food, will that also
become consecrated? And the priests answered, 'No.' Haggai went on, 13
But if a person defiled by contact with a corpse touches any one of these
things, will that also become defiled? 'It will', answered the priests. Haggai 14
replied, So it is with this people and nation and all that they do, says the
LORD; whatever offering they make here is defiled in my sight. And now 15
look back over recent times down to this day: before one stone was laid
on another in the LORD's temple, what was your plight? If a man came to a 16
heap of corn expecting twenty measures, he found but ten; if he came to
a wine-vat to draw fifty measures, he found but twenty. I blasted you 17
and all your harvest with black blight and red and with hail, and yet you
had no mind to return to me, says the LORD. Consider, from this day 18
onwards, from this twenty-fourth day of the ninth month, the day when the

a Or wealth.

19 foundations of the temple of the LORD are laid, consider: will the seed still be diminished*a* in the barn? Will the vine and the fig, the pomegranate and the olive, still bear no fruit? Not so, from this day I will bless you.

20   On that day, the twenty-fourth day of the month, the word of the LORD
21 came to Haggai a second time: Tell Zerubbabel, governor of Judah, I will
22 shake heaven and earth; I will overthrow the thrones of kings, break the power of heathen realms, overturn chariots and their riders; horses and
23 riders shall fall by the sword of their comrades. On that day, says the LORD of Hosts, I will take you, Zerubbabel son of Shealtiel, my servant, and will wear you as a signet-ring; for you it is that I have chosen. This is the very word of the LORD of Hosts.

ZECHARIAH

Zechariah's commission

1 IN THE EIGHTH MONTH of the second year of Darius, the word of the LORD came to the prophet Zechariah son of Berechiah,
2 3 son of Iddo: The LORD was very angry with your forefathers. Say to the people, These are the words of the LORD of Hosts: Come back to me,
4 and I will come back to you, says the LORD of Hosts. Do not be like your forefathers. They heard the prophets of old proclaim, 'These are the words of the LORD of Hosts: Turn back from your evil ways and your evil deeds.'
5 But they did not listen or pay heed to me, says the LORD. And where are
6 your forefathers now? And the prophets, do they live for ever? But the warnings and the decrees with which I charged my servants the prophets —did not these overtake your forefathers? Did they not then repent and say, 'The LORD of Hosts has treated us as he purposed; as our lives and as our deeds deserved, so has he treated us'?

Eight visions with their interpretations

7 ON THE TWENTY-FOURTH DAY of the eleventh month, the month Shebat, in the second year of Darius, the word of the LORD came to the prophet Zechariah son of Berechiah, son of Iddo.
8   Last night I had a vision. I saw a man on a bay horse standing among the myrtles in a hollow; and behind him were other horses, black, dappled,
9 and white. 'What are these, sir?' I asked, and the angel who talked with me
10 answered, 'I will show you what they are.' Then the man standing among the myrtles said, 'They are those whom the LORD has sent to range through
11 the world.' They reported to the angel of the LORD as he stood among the myrtles: 'We have ranged through the world; the whole world is still and
12 at peace.' Thereupon the angel of the LORD said, 'How long, O LORD of Hosts, wilt thou withhold thy compassion from Jerusalem and the cities

a diminished: *prob. rdg.; Heb. om.*

of Judah, upon whom thou hast vented thy wrath these seventy years?'
Then the LORD spoke kind and comforting words to the angel who talked 13
with me, and the angel said to me, Proclaim, These are the words of the 14
LORD of Hosts: I am very jealous for Jerusalem and Zion. I am full of 15
anger against the nations that enjoy their ease, because, while my anger
was but mild, they heaped evil on evil. Therefore these are the words of 16
the LORD: I have come back to Jerusalem with compassion, and my house
shall be rebuilt in her, says the LORD of Hosts, and the measuring-line shall
be stretched over Jerusalem. Proclaim once more, These are the words of 17
the LORD of Hosts: My cities shall again overflow with good things; once
again the LORD will comfort Zion, once again he will make Jerusalem the
city of his choice.

I lifted my eyes and there I saw four horns. I asked the angel who talked 18 19
with me what they were, and he answered, 'These are the horns which
scattered Judah*a* and Jerusalem.' Then the LORD showed me four smiths. 20
I asked what they were coming to do, and he said, 'Those horns scattered 21
Judah and Jerusalem so completely that no man could lift his head. But
these smiths have come to reunite them and to throw down the horns of
the nations which had raised them against the land of Judah and scattered
its people.'

I lifted my eyes and there I saw a man carrying a measuring-line. I 2 1 2
asked him where he was going, and he said, 'To measure Jerusalem and
see what should be its breadth and length.' Then, as the angel who talked 3
with me was going away, another angel came out to meet him and said 4
to him, Run to the young man there and tell him that Jerusalem shall
be a city without walls, so numerous shall be the men and cattle within
it. I will be a wall of fire round her, says the LORD, and a glory in the midst 5
of her.

Away, away; flee from the land of the north, says the LORD, for I will 6
make you spread your wings like the four winds of heaven, says the LORD.
Away, escape, you people of Zion who live in Babylon. 7

For these are the words of the LORD of Hosts, spoken when he sent me 8
on a glorious mission*b* to the nations who have plundered you, for whoever
touches you touches the apple of his eye: I raise*c* my hand against them; 9
they shall be plunder for their own slaves. So you shall know that the LORD
of Hosts has sent me. Shout aloud and rejoice, daughter of Zion; I am 10
coming, I will make my dwelling among you, says the LORD. Many nations 11
shall come over to the LORD on that day and become his people, and he will
make his dwelling with you. Then you shall know that the LORD of Hosts
has sent me to you. The LORD will once again claim Judah as his own 12
possession in the holy land, and make Jerusalem the city of his choice.

Silence, all mankind, in the presence of the LORD! For he has bestirred 13
himself out of his holy dwelling-place.

The angel who talked with me came back and roused me as a man is 4 1*d*
roused from sleep. He asked me what I saw, and I answered, 'A lamp-
stand all of gold with a bowl on it; it holds seven lamps, and there are seven

a *Prob. rdg.; Heb. adds* Israel.   *b* on a glorious mission: *prob. rdg.; Heb.* after glory.
c *Or* wave.   *d* *3. 1–10 transposed to follow 4. 14.*

3 pipes for the lamps on top of it, with two olive-trees standing by it, one on
11ᵃ the right of the bowl and another on the left.' I asked him, 'What are these
two olive-trees, the one on the right and the other on the left of the lamp-
12 stand?' I asked also another question, 'What are the two sprays of olive
beside the golden pipes which discharge the golden oil from their bowls?'
13 14 He said, 'Do you not know what these mean?' 'No, sir', I answered. 'These
two', he said, 'are the two consecrated with oil who attend the Lord of all
the earth.'

3 1   Then he showed me Joshua the high priest standing before the angel of
the LORD, with the Adversary ᵇ standing at his right hand to accuse him.
2 The LORD said to the Adversary, 'The LORD rebuke you, Satan, the LORD
rebuke you who are venting your spite on Jerusalem.ᶜ Is not this man a
3 brand snatched from the fire?' Now Joshua was wearing filthy clothes as
4 he stood before the angel; and the angel turned and said to those in attendance on him, 'Take off his filthy clothes.' Then he turned to him and said,
'See how I have taken away your guilt from you; I will clothe you in fine
5 vestments'; and he added, 'Let a clean turban be put on his head.' So they
put a clean turban on his head and clothed him in clean garments, while
6 the angel of the LORD stood by. Then the angel of the LORD gave Joshua
7 this solemn charge: These are the words of the LORD of Hosts: If you will
conform to my ways and carry out your duties, you shall administer my
house and be in control of my courts, and I grant you the right to come and
8 go amongst these in attendance here. Listen, Joshua the high priest, you
and your colleagues seated here before you, all you who are an omen of
9-10 things to come: I will now bring my servant, the Branch. In one day I will
wipe away the guilt of the land. On that day, says the LORD of Hosts, you
shall all of you invite one another to come and sit each under his vine and
his fig-tree.

Here is the stone that I set before Joshua, a stone in which are seven
4 4ᵈ eyes. I will reveal its meaning to you, says the LORD of Hosts. Then I
asked the angel of the LORD who talked with me, 'Sir, what are these?'
5 And he answered, 'Do you not know what these mean?' 'No, sir', I
answered. 'These seven', he said, 'are the eyes of the LORD ranging over the
whole earth.' ᵉ

6   Then he turned and said to me, This is the word of the LORD concerning
Zerubbabel: Neither by force of arms nor by brute strength, but by my
7 spirit! says the LORD of Hosts. How does a mountain, the greatest mountain, compare with Zerubbabel? It is no higher than a plain. He shall bring
8 out the stone called Possession ᶠ while men acclaim its beauty. This word
9 came to me from the LORD: Zerubbabel with his own hands laid the foundation of this house and with his own hands he shall finish it. So shall you
10 know that the LORD of Hosts has sent me to you. Who has despised the
day of small things? He shall rejoice when he sees Zerubbabel holding the
stone called Separation. ᶠ

ᵃ *4. 4–10 transposed to follow 3. 10.*   ᵇ *Heb.* the Satan.   ᶜ the
LORD . . . Jerusalem: *or the* LORD who has chosen Jerusalem rebuke you.   ᵈ *See note*
on 4. 11 above.   ᵉ These seven . . . earth: *transposed from verse 10.*
ᶠ *Cp. Lev. 20. 24–26.*

I looked up again and saw a flying scroll. He asked me what I saw, and **5** 1 2
I answered, 'A flying scroll, twenty cubits long and ten cubits wide.' This, 3
he told me, is the curse which goes out over the whole land; for by the
writing on one side every thief shall be swept clean away, and by the writing
on the other every perjurer shall be swept clean away. I have sent it out, 4
the LORD of Hosts has said, and it shall enter the house of the thief and the
house of the man who has perjured himself in my name; it shall stay inside
that house and demolish it, timbers and stones and all.

The angel who talked with me came out and said to me, 'Raise your 5
eyes and look at this thing that comes forth.' I asked what it was, and he 6
said, 'It is a great barrel coming forth,' and he added, 'so great is their guilt
in all the land.' Then a round slab of lead was lifted, and a woman was 7
sitting there inside the barrel. He said, 'This is Wickedness', and he thrust 8
her down into the barrel and rammed the leaden weight upon its mouth.
I looked up again and saw two women coming forth with the wind in their 9
wings (for they had wings like a stork's), and they carried the barrel between earth and sky. I asked the angel who talked with me where they 10
were taking the barrel, and he answered, 'To build a house for it [a] in the 11
land of Shinar; when the house is ready, it [b] shall be set on the place prepared for it [a] there.'

I looked up again and saw four chariots coming out between two moun- **6**
tains, and the mountains were made of copper. [c] The first chariot had bay 2
horses, the second black, the third white, and the fourth dappled. I asked 3 4
the angel who talked with me, 'Sir, what are these?' He answered, 'These 5
are the four winds of heaven which have been attending the Lord of the
whole earth, and they are now going forth. The chariot with the black 6
horses is going to the land of the north, that with the white to the far west, [d]
that with the dappled to the south, and that with the roan to the land of the 7
east.' [e] They were eager to go and range over the whole earth; so he said,
'Go and range over the earth', and the chariots did so. Then he called me 8
to look and said, 'Those going to the land of the north have given my spirit
rest in the land of the north.'

The word of the LORD came to me: Take silver and gold from the exiles, 9 10
from Heldai, Tobiah, Jedaiah, and [f] Josiah son of Zephaniah, who have
come back from Babylon. Take it and make a crown; put the crown on the 11
head of Joshua son of Jehozadak, the high priest, [g] and say to him, These 12
are the words of the LORD of Hosts: Here is a man named the Branch;
he will shoot up from the ground where he is and will build the temple of
the LORD. It is he who will build the temple of the LORD, he who will 13
assume royal dignity, will be seated on his throne and govern, with a priest
at his right side, and concord shall prevail between them. The crown shall 14
be in the charge of Heldai, Tobiah, Jedaiah, and Josiah son of Zephaniah,
as a memorial in the temple of the LORD.

[a] *Or* her.　　[b] *Or* she.　　[c] *Or* bronze.　　[d] to the far west: *prob.
rdg.; Heb.* behind them.　　[e] to the land of the east: *prob. rdg.;
Heb. om.*　　[f] and: *prob. rdg.; Heb.* and go on that day yourself and go to
the house of . . .　　[g] Joshua . . . priest: *possibly an error for* Zerubbabel son of
Shealtiel, *cp. 3. 5; 4. 9.*

15 Men from far away shall come and work on the building of the temple of the LORD; so shall you know that the LORD of Hosts has sent me to you. If only you will obey the LORD your God!

Joy and gladness in the coming age

7 THE WORD OF THE LORD CAME TO ZECHARIAH in the fourth year of the reign of King Darius, on the fourth day of Kislev, the ninth month.
2 Bethel-sharezer sent Regem-melech with his men to seek the favour of
3 the LORD. They were to say to the priests in the house of the LORD of Hosts and to the prophets, 'Am I to lament and abstain in the fifth month as I
4 have done for so many years?' Then the word of the LORD of Hosts came
5 to me: Say to all the people of the land and to the priests, When you fasted and lamented in the fifth and seventh months these seventy years, was it
6 indeed in my honour that you fasted? And when you ate and drank, was
7 it not to please yourselves? Was it not this that the LORD proclaimed through the prophets of old, while Jerusalem was populous and peaceful, as were the cities round her, and the Negeb and the Shephelah?

8 9 The word of the LORD came to Zechariah: These are the words of the LORD of Hosts: Administer true justice, show loyalty and compassion to
10 one another, do not oppress the orphan and the widow, the alien and the
11 poor, do not contrive any evil one against another. But they refused to listen, they turned their backs on me in defiance, they stopped their ears
12 and would not hear. Their hearts were adamant; they refused to accept instruction and all that the LORD of Hosts had taught them by his spirit through the prophets of old; and they suffered under the anger of the LORD
13 of Hosts. As they did not listen when I *a* called, so I did not listen when
14 they called, says the LORD of Hosts, and I drove them out among all the nations to whom they were strangers, leaving their land a waste behind them, so that no one came and went. Thus they made their pleasant land a waste.

8 1 2 The word of the LORD of Hosts came to me: These are the words of the LORD of Hosts: I have been very jealous for Zion, fiercely jealous for her.
3 Now, says the LORD, I have come back to Zion and I will dwell in Jerusalem. Jerusalem shall be called the City of Truth, and the mountain of the LORD
4 of Hosts shall be called the Holy Mountain. These are the words of the LORD of Hosts: Once again shall old men and old women sit in the streets
5 of Jerusalem, each leaning on a stick because of their great age; and the streets of the city shall be full of boys and girls, playing in the streets.
6 These are the words of the LORD of Hosts: Even if it may seem impossible *b* to the survivors of this nation on that day, will it also seem impossible to
7 me? *c* This is the very word of the LORD of Hosts. These are the words of the LORD of Hosts: See, I will rescue my people from the countries of the
8 east and the west, and bring them back to live in Jerusalem. They shall be my people, and I will be their God, in truth and justice.

---

a Prob. rdg.; Heb. he.   *b* Or wonderful.   *c* will . . . me?: or it will seem wonderful also to me.

These are the words of the LORD of Hosts: Take courage, you who in 9
these days hear, from the prophets who were present when the foundations were laid for the house of the LORD of Hosts, their promise that the
temple is to be rebuilt. Till that time there was no hiring either of man or 10
of beast, no one could safely go about his business because of his enemies,
and I set all men one against another. But now I am not the same towards 11
the survivors of this people as I was in former days, says the LORD of Hosts.
For they shall sow in safety; the vine shall yield its fruit and the soil its 12
produce, the heavens shall give their dew; with all these things I will
endow the survivors of this people. You, house of Judah and house of 13
Israel, have been the very symbol of a curse to all the nations; and now I
will save you, and you shall become the symbol of a blessing. Courage!
Do not be afraid.

For these are the words of the LORD of Hosts: Whereas I resolved to 14
ruin you because your ancestors roused me to anger, says the LORD of
Hosts, and I did not relent, so in these days I have once more[a] resolved to 15
do good to Jerusalem and to the house of Judah; do not be afraid. This is 16
what you shall do: speak the truth to each other, administer true and sound
justice in the city gate. Do not contrive any evil one against another, and 17
do not love perjury, for all this I hate. This is the very word of the LORD.

The word of the LORD of Hosts came to me: These are the words of the 18 19
LORD of Hosts: The fasts of the fourth month and of the fifth, the seventh,
and the tenth, shall become festivals of joy and gladness for the house of
Judah. Love truth and peace.

These are the words of the LORD of Hosts: Nations and dwellers in great 20
cities shall yet come; people of one city shall come to those of another and 21
say, 'Let us go and entreat the favour of the LORD, and resort to the LORD
of Hosts; and I will come too.' So great nations and mighty peoples shall 22
resort to the LORD of Hosts in Jerusalem and entreat his favour. These are 23
the words of the LORD of Hosts: In those days, when ten men from nations
of every language pluck up courage, they shall pluck the robe of a Jew and
say, 'We will go with you because we have heard that God is with you.'

Judah's triumph over her enemies

An oracle: the word of the LORD.   9

> He has come to the land of Hadrach
>   and[b] established himself in Damascus;
>   for the capital city[c] of Aram is the LORD's,
>   as are all the tribes of Israel.
> [d]Sidon has closed her frontier against Hamath,   2
>   for she is very wary.
> Tyre has built herself a rampart;   3
>   she has heaped up silver like dust
>   and gold like mud in the streets.

[a] once more: *or* changed my mind and.   [b] He has come ... and: *prob. rdg.*;
Heb. In the land of Hadrach he has ...   [c] capital city: *or* chief part.   [d] *Prob.*
rdg.; Heb. prefixes Tyre and.

4   But wait, the Lord will dispossess her
and strike down the power of her ships,
and the city itself will be destroyed by fire.

5   Let Ashkelon see it and be afraid;
Gaza shall writhe in terror,
and Ekron's hope shall be extinguished;
kings shall vanish from Gaza,
    and Ashkelon shall be unpeopled;

6   half-breeds shall settle in Ashdod,
and I will uproot the pride of the Philistine.

7   I will dash the blood of sacrifices from his mouth
and his loathsome offerings from his teeth;
and his survivors shall belong[a] to our God
and become like a clan in Judah,
    and Ekron like a Jebusite.

8   And I will post a garrison for my house
    so that no one may pass in or out,
and no oppressor shall ever overrun them.
[This I have lived to see with my own eyes.]

9   Rejoice, rejoice, daughter of Zion,
shout aloud, daughter of Jerusalem;
for see, your king is coming to you,
his cause won, his victory gained,
humble and mounted on an ass,
on a foal, the young of a she-ass.

10   He shall banish chariots from Ephraim
    and war-horses from Jerusalem;
the warrior's bow shall be banished.
He shall speak peaceably to every nation,
and his rule shall extend from sea to sea,
from the River to the ends of the earth.

11   And as for you, by your covenant with me sealed in blood
I release your prisoners from the dungeon.[b]

12   (Come back to the stronghold, you prisoners who wait in hope.)
Now is the day announced
when I will grant you twofold[c] reparation.

13   For my bow is strung, O Judah;
I have laid the arrow to it, O Ephraim;
I have roused your sons, O Zion,[d]
and made you into the sword of a warrior.

14   The LORD shall appear above them,
and his arrow shall flash like lightning;
the Lord GOD shall blow a blast on the horn
and march with the storm-winds of the south.

---

[a] his survivors shall belong: *or* he shall become kin.   [b] *Prob. rdg.; Heb. adds* no water in it.   [c] *Or* equal.   [d] *Prob. rdg.; Heb. adds* against your sons, O Javan (*or* Greece).

The LORD of Hosts will be their shield;   15
they shall prevail, they shall trample on the sling-stones;
they shall be roaring drunk as if with wine,
brimful as a bowl, drenched like the corners of the altar.
So on that day the LORD their God   16
will save them, his own people, like sheep,
  setting them all about his land,
    like^a jewels set to sparkle in a crown.

What wealth, what beauty, is theirs: 17
corn to strengthen young men,
  and new wine for maidens!
Ask of the LORD rain in the autumn,   **10**
ask him for rain in the spring,
the LORD who makes the storm-clouds,
and he will give you showers of rain
and to every man grass in his field;
for the household gods make mischievous promises;   2
diviners see false signs,
they tell lying dreams^b
  and talk raving nonsense.
Men wander about like sheep
in distress for lack of a shepherd.
My anger is turned against the shepherds,   3
  and I will visit with punishment the leaders of the flock;
but the LORD of Hosts will visit his flock,
  the house of Judah,
and make them his royal war-horses.
They shall be corner-stone and tent-peg,   4
they shall be the bow ready for battle,
and from them shall come every commander.
Together they shall be like warriors   5
who tramp the muddy ways in battle,
and they will fight because the LORD is with them;
they will put horsemen shamefully to rout.
And I will give strength to the house of Judah   6
and grant victory to^c the house of Joseph;
I will restore them, for I have pitied them,
and they shall be as though I had never cast them off;
for I am the LORD their God and I will answer them.
So Ephraim shall be like warriors,   7
glad like men cheerful with wine,
and their sons shall see and be glad;
so let their hearts exult in the LORD.
I will whistle to call them in, for I have redeemed them;   8
and they shall be as many as once they were.

---

^a like: *prob. rdg.; Heb.* for.   ^b they ... dreams: *or* dreaming women make empty
promises.   ^c grant victory to: *or* expand.

9   If I disperse them*a* among the nations,
          in far-off lands they will remember me
          and will rear their sons and then return.
10   Then will I fetch them home from Egypt
          and gather them in from Assyria;
          I will lead them into Gilead and Lebanon
          until there is no more room for them.
11   Dire distress*b* shall come upon the Euphrates
          and shall beat down its turbulent waters;
          all the depths of the Nile shall run dry.
        The pride of Assyria shall be brought down,
          and the sceptre of Egypt shall pass away;
12   but Israel's strength shall be in the Lord,
          and they shall march proudly in his name.
        This is the very word of the Lord.

11   Throw open your gates, O Lebanon,
        that fire may feed on your cedars.
2   Howl, every pine-tree; for the cedars have fallen,
        mighty trees are ravaged.
        Howl, every oak of Bashan;
        for the impenetrable forest is laid low.
3   Hark to the howling of the shepherds,
        for their rich pastures are ravaged.
        Hark to the roar of the young lions,
        for Jordan's dense thickets are ravaged.

4 These were the words of the Lord my God: Fatten the flock for slaughter.
5 Those who buy will slaughter it and incur no guilt; those who sell will say, 'Blessed be the Lord, I am rich!' Its shepherds will have no pity for it.
6 For I will never again pity the inhabitants of the earth, says the Lord. I will put every man in the power of his neighbour and his king, and as each country is crushed I will not rescue him from their hands.
7 So I fattened the flock for slaughter for the dealers. I took two staves: one
8 I called Favour and the other Union, and so I fattened the flock. In one month I got rid of the three shepherds, for I had lost patience with them
9 and they had come to abhor me. Then I said to the flock, 'I will not fatten you any more. Any that are to die, let them die; any that stray, let them
10 stray; and the rest can devour one another.' I took my staff called Favour and snapped it in two, annulling the covenant which the Lord*c* had made
11 with all nations. So it was annulled that day, and the dealers who were
12 watching me knew that all this was the word of the Lord. I said to them, 'If it suits you, give me my wages; otherwise keep them.' Then
13 they weighed out my wages, thirty pieces of silver. The Lord said to me, 'Throw it into the treasury.' I took the thirty pieces of silver—that noble sum at which I was valued and rejected by them!—and threw them into
14 the house of the Lord, into the treasury. Then I snapped in two my

a Or scatter them like seed.   *b* Dire distress: or An enemy.   *c* the Lord: *prob. rdg.; Heb.* I.

second staff called Union, annulling the brotherhood between Judah and Israel.

Then the LORD said to me, Equip yourself again as a shepherd, a worth- 15
less one; for I am about to install a shepherd in the land who will neither 16
miss any that are lost nor search for those that have gone astray nor heal
the injured nor nurse the sickly, but will eat the flesh of the fat beasts and
throw away their broken bones.

> Alas for the worthless shepherd who abandons the sheep!   17
> A sword shall fall on his arm and on his right eye;
>   his arm shall be shrivelled
>   and his right eye blinded.
> This is the very word of the LORD of Hosts: 13 7 *a*
> O sword, awake against my shepherd
>   and against him who works with me.
> Strike the shepherd, and the sheep will be scattered,
>   and I will turn my hand against the shepherd boys.
> This also is the very word of the LORD: 8
>   It shall happen throughout the land
> that two thirds of the people shall be struck down and die,
>   while one third of them shall be left there.
> Then I will pass this third through the fire   9
>   and I will refine them as silver is refined,
>   and assay them as gold is assayed.
> Then they will invoke me by my name,
>   and I myself will answer them;
>   I will say, 'They are my people',
> and they shall say, 'The LORD is our God.'

Jerusalem a centre of worship for all men

AN ORACLE. This is the word of the LORD concerning Israel, the very 12
word of the LORD who stretched out the heavens and founded the
earth, and who formed the spirit of man within him: I am making the 2
steep approaches to Jerusalem slippery for all the nations pressing round
her; and Judah will be caught up in the siege of Jerusalem. On that day, 3
when all the nations of the earth will be gathered against her, I will make
Jerusalem a rock too heavy for any people to remove, and all who try to
lift it shall injure themselves. On that day, says the LORD, I will strike 4
every horse with panic and its rider with madness; I will keep watch over
Judah, but I will strike all the horses of the other nations with blindness.
Then the clans of Judah shall say to themselves, 'The inhabitants of 5
Jerusalem find their strength*b* in the LORD of Hosts their God.'

On that day I will make the clans of Judah like a brazier in woodland, 6
like a torch blazing among sheaves of corn. They shall devour all the nations
round them, right and left, while the people of Jerusalem remain safe in

---

a 13. 7–9 *transposed to this point.*   *b* The . . . strength: *prob. rdg.; Heb.* O inhabitants of Jerusalem, I am strong.

7 their city. The Lord will first set free all the families *a* of Judah, so that the glory of David's line and of the inhabitants of Jerusalem may not surpass that of Judah.

8   On that day the Lord will shield the inhabitants of Jerusalem; on that day the very weakest of them shall be like David, and the line of David like God, like the angel of the Lord going before them.

9   On that day I will set about destroying all the nations that come against
10 Jerusalem, but I will pour a spirit of pity and compassion into the line of David and the inhabitants of Jerusalem. Then

> They shall look on me, on him whom they have pierced,

and shall wail over him as over an only child, and shall grieve for him bitterly as for a first-born son.

11   On that day the mourning in Jerusalem shall be as great as the mourning
12 over Hadad-rimmon in the vale of Megiddo. The land shall wail, each family by itself: the family of David by itself and its women by themselves;
13 the family of Nathan by itself and its women by themselves; the family of Levi by itself and its women by themselves; the family of Shimei by itself
14 and its women by themselves; all the remaining families by themselves and their women by themselves.

13   On that day a fountain shall be opened for the line of David and for the inhabitants of Jerusalem, to remove all sin and impurity.

2   On that day, says the Lord of Hosts, I will erase the names of the idols from the land, and they shall be remembered no longer; I will also remove
3 the prophets and the spirit of uncleanness from the land. Thereafter, if a man continues to prophesy, his parents, his own father and mother, will say to him, 'You shall live no longer, for you have spoken falsely in the name of the Lord.' His own father and mother will pierce him through
4 because he has prophesied. On that day every prophet shall be ashamed of his vision when he prophesies, nor shall he wear a robe of coarse hair in
5 order to deceive. He will say, 'I am no prophet, I am a tiller of the soil who
6 has been schooled in lust from boyhood.' 'What', someone will ask, 'are these scars on your chest?' And he will answer, 'I got them in the house of my lovers.' *b*

14   A day is coming for the Lord to act, and the plunder taken from you
2 shall be shared out while you stand by. I will gather all the peoples to fight against Jerusalem; the city shall be taken, the houses plundered and the women raped. Half the city shall go into exile, but the rest of the nation in
3 the city shall not be wiped out. The Lord will come out and fight against
4 those peoples, as in the days of his prowess on the field of battle. On that day his feet will stand on the Mount of Olives, which is opposite Jerusalem to the east, and the mountain shall be cleft in two by an immense valley running east and west; half the mountain shall move northwards
5 and half southwards. The valley between the hills *c* shall be blocked, for the new valley between them will reach as far as Asal. Blocked it shall be as it was blocked by the earthquake in the time of Uzziah king of Judah, and the Lord my God will appear with all the holy ones.

---

a Or tents.   b Verses 7-9 transposed to follow 11. 17.   c Prob. rdg.; Heb. my hills.

On that day there shall be neither heat nor cold nor frost. It shall be all 6 7
one day, whose coming is known only to the LORD, without distinction of
day or night, and at evening-time there shall be light.

On that day living water shall issue from Jerusalem, half flowing to the 8
eastern sea and half to the western, in summer and winter alike. Then the 9
LORD shall become king over all the earth; on that day the LORD shall be
one LORD and his name the one name. The whole land shall be levelled, 10
flat as the Arabah from Geba to Rimmon southwards; but Jerusalem shall
stand high in her place, and shall be full of people from the Benjamin
Gate [to the point where the former gate stood,] to the Corner Gate, and
from the Tower of Hananel to the king's wine-vats. Men shall live in 11
Jerusalem, and never again shall a solemn ban be laid upon her; men shall
live there in peace. The LORD will strike down all the nations who warred 12
against Jerusalem, and the plague shall be this: their flesh shall rot while
they stand on their feet, their eyes shall rot in their sockets, and their
tongues shall rot in their mouths.

On that day a great panic, sent by the LORD, shall fall on them. At the 13
very moment when a man would encourage his comrade his hand shall be
raised to strike him down. Judah too shall join in the fray in Jerusalem, and 14
the wealth of the surrounding nations will be swept away—gold and silver
and apparel in great abundance. And slaughter shall be the fate of horse and 15
mule, camel and ass, the fate of every beast in those armies.

All who survive of the nations which attacked Jerusalem shall come up 16
year by year to worship the King, the LORD of Hosts, and to keep the
pilgrim-feast of Tabernacles. If any of the families of the earth do not go 17
up to Jerusalem to worship the King, the LORD of Hosts, no rain shall fall
upon them. If any family of Egypt does not go up and enter the city, then 18
the same disaster shall overtake it as that which the LORD will inflict on
any nation which does not go up to keep the feast. This shall be the punish- 19
ment of Egypt and of any nation which does not go up to keep the feast of
Tabernacles.

On that day, not a bell on a war-horse but shall be inscribed 'Holy to 20
the LORD', and the pots in the house of the LORD shall be like the bowls
before the altar. Every pot in Jerusalem and Judah shall be holy to the 21
LORD of Hosts, and all who sacrifice shall come and shall take some of ·
them and boil the flesh in them. So when that time comes, no trader shall
again be seen in the house of the LORD of Hosts.

MALACHI

1 An oracle. The word of the LORD to Israel through Malachi.ᵃ

Religious decline and hope of recovery

2 I LOVE YOU, says the LORD. You ask, 'How hast thou shown love to us?'
3 Is not Esau Jacob's brother? the LORD answers. I love Jacob, but I hate Esau; I have turned his mountains into a waste and his ancestral home
4 into a lodging in the wilderness. When Edom says, 'We are beaten down; let us rebuild our ruined homes', these are the words of the LORD of Hosts: If they rebuild, I will pull down. They shall be called a realm of wicked-
5 ness, a people whom the LORD has cursed for ever. You yourselves will see it with your own eyes; you yourselves will say, 'The LORD's greatness reaches beyond the realm of Israel.'

6 A son honours his father, and a slave goes in fear of his master. If I am a father, where is the honour due to me? If I am a master, where is the fear due to me? So says the LORD of Hosts to you, you priests who despise my
7 name. You ask, 'How have we despised thy name?' Because you have offered defiled food on my altar. You ask, 'How have we defiled thee?' Because you have thought that the table of the LORD may be despised,
8 that if you offer a blind victim, there is nothing wrong, and if you offer a victim lame or diseased, there is nothing wrong. If you brought such a gift to the governor, would he receive you or show you favour? says the
9 LORD of Hosts. But now, if you placate God, he may show you mercy; if you do this, will he withhold his favour from you? So the LORD of Hosts
10 has spoken. Better far that one of you should close the great door altogether, so that the light might not fall thus all in vain upon my altar! I have no pleasure in you, says the LORD of Hosts; I will accept no offering from you.
11 From furthest east to furthest west my name is great among the nations. Everywhere fragrant sacrifice and pure gifts are offered in my name; for
12 my name is great among the nations, says the LORD of Hosts. But you profane it by thinking that the table of the LORD may be defiled, and that
13 you can offer on it food you yourselves despise. You sniff at it, says the LORD of Hosts, and say, 'How irksome!' If you bring as your offering victims that are mutilated, lame, or diseased, shall I accept them from you? says the
14 LORD. A curse on the cheat who pays his vows by sacrificing a damaged victim to the Lord, though he has a sound ram in his flock! I am the great king, says the LORD of Hosts, and my name is held in awe among the nations.

2 1 2 And now, you priests, this decree is for you: if you will not listen to me and pay heed to the honouring of my name, says the LORD of Hosts, then I will lay a curse upon you. I will turn your blessings into a curse; yes, into

ᵃ Malachi: *or* my messenger.

a curse, because you pay no heed. I will cut off your arm,[a] fling offal in   3
your faces, the offal of your pilgrim-feasts, and I will banish you from my
presence. Then you will know that I have issued this decree against you: 4
my covenant with Levi falls to the ground, says the LORD of Hosts. My   5
covenant was with him: I bestowed life and prosperity on him; I laid on
him the duty of reverence, he revered me and lived in awe of my name.
The instruction he gave was true, and no word of injustice fell from his   6
lips; he walked in harmony with me and in uprightness, and he turned
many back from sin. For men hang upon the words of the priest and seek   7
knowledge and instruction from him, because he is the messenger of the
LORD of Hosts. But you have turned away from that course; you have made   8
many stumble with your instruction; you have set at nought the covenant
with the Levites, says the LORD of Hosts. So I, in my turn, have made you   9
despicable and mean in the eyes of the people, in so far as you disregard
my ways and show partiality in your instruction.

Have we not all one father? Did not one God create us? Why do we   10
violate the covenant of our forefathers by being faithless to one another?
Judah is faithless, and abominable things are done in Israel and in Jeru-   11
salem; Judah has violated the holiness of the LORD by loving and marrying
daughters of a foreign god. May the LORD banish any who do this from the   12
dwellings of Jacob, nomads or settlers, even though they bring offerings
to the LORD of Hosts.

Here is another thing that you do: you weep and moan, and you drown   13
the altar of the LORD with tears, but he still refuses to look at the offering
or receive an acceptable gift from you. You ask why. It is because the LORD   14
has borne witness against you on behalf of the wife of your youth. You have
been unfaithful to her, though she is your partner and your wife by solemn
covenant. Did not the one God make her, both flesh and spirit? And what   15
does the one God require but godly children? Keep watch on your spirit,
and do not be unfaithful to the wife of your youth. If a man divorces   16
or puts away his spouse, he overwhelms her with cruelty, says the LORD
of Hosts the God of Israel. Keep watch on your spirit, and do not be
unfaithful.

You have wearied the LORD with your talk. You ask, 'How have we   17
wearied him?' By saying that all evildoers are good in the eyes of the LORD,
that he is pleased with them, or by asking, 'Where is the God of justice?'
Look, I am sending my messenger[b] who will clear a path before me.   3
Suddenly the Lord whom you seek will come to his temple; the messenger
of the covenant in whom you delight is here, here already, says the LORD
of Hosts. Who can endure the day of his coming? Who can stand firm when   2
he appears? He is like a refiner's fire, like fuller's soap; he will take his seat,   3
refining and purifying;[c] he will purify the Levites and cleanse them like
gold and silver, and so they shall be fit to bring offerings to the LORD. Thus   4
the offerings of Judah and Jerusalem shall be pleasing to the LORD as they
were in days of old, in years long past. I will appear before you in court,   5
prompt to testify against sorcerers, adulterers, and perjurers, against those

---

[a] *Or* posterity.   [b] my messenger: *Heb.* Malachi.   [c] *Prob. rdg.; Heb. adds*
silver.

who wrong*a* the hired labourer, the widow, and the orphan, who thrust the alien aside and have no fear of me, says the LORD of Hosts.

6   I am the LORD, unchanging; and you, too, have not ceased to be sons of
7   Jacob. From the days of your forefathers you have been wayward and have not kept my laws. If you will return to me, I will return to you, says the
8   LORD of Hosts. You ask, 'How can we return?' May man defraud God, that you defraud me? You ask, 'How have we defrauded thee?' Why, in
9   tithes and contributions. There is a curse, a curse on you all, the whole
10 nation of you, because you defraud me. Bring the tithes into the treasury, all of them; let there be food in my house. Put me to the proof, says the LORD of Hosts, and see if I do not open windows in the sky and pour a
11 blessing on you as long as there is need. I will forbid pests to destroy the produce of your soil or make your vines barren, says the LORD of Hosts.
12 All nations shall count you happy, for yours shall be a favoured land, says the LORD of Hosts.

Murmurers warned, the righteous triumphant

13 YOU HAVE USED HARD WORDS ABOUT ME, says the LORD, and then
14 you ask, 'How have we spoken against thee?' You have said, 'It is useless to serve God; what do we gain from the LORD of Hosts by observing
15 his rules and behaving with deference? We ourselves count the arrogant happy; it is evildoers who are successful; they have put God to the proof and come to no harm.'
16 Then those who feared the LORD talked together, and the LORD paid heed and listened. A record was written before him of those who feared
17 him and kept his name in mind. They shall be mine, says the LORD of Hosts, my own possession against the day that I appoint, and I will spare
18 them as a man spares the son who serves him. You will again tell good men from bad, the servant of God from the man who does not serve him.

4   The day comes, glowing like a furnace; all the arrogant and the evildoers shall be chaff, and that day when it comes shall set them ablaze, says
2   the LORD of Hosts, it shall leave them neither root nor branch. But for you who fear my name, the sun of righteousness shall rise with healing in
3   his wings, and you shall break loose like calves released from the stall. On the day that I act, you shall trample down the wicked, for they will be ashes under the soles of your feet, says the LORD of Hosts.
4   Remember the law of Moses my servant, the rules and precepts which I bade him deliver to all Israel at Horeb.
5   Look, I will send you the prophet Elijah before the great and terrible
6   day of the LORD comes. He will reconcile fathers to sons and sons to fathers, lest I come and put the land under a ban to destroy it.

a *Prob. rdg.; Heb. adds* the wages of.

APPENDIX

MEASURES OF LENGTH

	span	cubit	rod[a]
span	1	..	..
cubit	2	1	..
rod[a]	12	6	1

The 'short cubit' was traditionally the measure from the elbow to the knuckles of the closed fist; and what seems to be intended as a 'long cubit' measured a 'cubit and a hand-breadth', i.e. 7 instead of 6 hand-breadths (Ezek. 40. 5). What is meant by cubits 'according to the old standard of measurement' (2 Chr. 3. 3) is presumably this pre-exilic cubit of 7 hand-breadths. Modern estimates of the Hebrew cubit range from 12 to 25·2 inches, without allowing for varying local standards.

MEASURES OF CAPACITY

liquid measures	equivalences	dry measures
'log'	1 'log'	..
..	4 'log'	'kab'
..	7⅕ 'log'	'omer'
'hin'	12 'log'	..
'bath'	72 'log'	'ephah'
'kor'	720 'log'	'homer' or 'kor'

According to ancient authorities the Hebrew 'log' was of the same capacity as the Roman *sextarius*; this according to the best available evidence was equivalent to 0·99 pint of the English standard.

WEIGHTS AND COINS

	heavy (Phoenician) standard			light (Babylonian) standard		
	shekel	mina	talent	shekel	mina	talent
shekel	1	..	..	1	..	..
mina	50	1	..	60	1	..
talent	3,000	60	1	3,600	60	1

The 'gerah' was 1/20 of the sacred or heavy shekel and probably 1/24 of the light shekel.

The 'sacred shekel' according to tradition was identical with the heavy shekel;

[a] Hebrew literally 'reed', the length of Ezekiel's measuring-rod.

1165

APPENDIX

while the 'shekel of the standard recognized by merchants' (Gen. 23. 16) was perhaps a weight stamped with its value as distinct from one not so stamped and requiring to be weighed on the spot.

The weight and value of the shekel varied so greatly according to the district and with the passing centuries that its evaluation in modern terms is impossible. Recent discoveries suggest that it may have weighed approximately 11·5 grammes.

Coins are not mentioned before the Exile. Only the 'daric' (1 Chr. 29. 7) and the 'drachma' (Ezra 2. 69; Neh. 7. 70–72), if this is a distinct coin, are found in the Old Testament; the former is said to have been a month's pay for a soldier in the Persian army, while the latter will have been the Greek silver drachma, estimated at approximately 4·4 grammes. The 'shekel' of this period (Neh. 5. 15) as a coin was probably the Graeco-Persian *siglos* weighing 5·6 grammes.

THE NEW
ENGLISH BIBLE

THE NEW TESTAMENT

CONTENTS

INTRODUCTION
TO THE NEW TESTAMENT

THIS TRANSLATION of the New Testament was undertaken with the object of providing English readers, whether familiar with the Bible or not, with a faithful rendering of the best available Greek text into the current speech of our own time, and a rendering which should harvest the gains of recent biblical scholarship.

It is now some three centuries and a half since King James's men put out what we have come to know as the Authorized Version. Two hundred and seventy years later the New Testament was revised. The Revised Version of the New Testament, which appeared in 1881, marked a new departure especially in that it abandoned the so-called Received Text, which had reigned ever since printed editions of the New Testament began, but which the advance of textual criticism had antiquated. The Revisers no longer followed (as their predecessors had done) the text of the majority of manuscripts, which, being for the most part of late date, had been exposed not only to the accidental corruptions of long-continued copying, but also in part to deliberate correction and 'improvement'. Instead, they followed a very small group of manuscripts, the earliest, and in their judgement the best, of those which had survived. During the years which have passed since their time, textual criticism has not stood still. Manuscripts have been discovered of substantially earlier date than any which the Revisers knew. Other important sources of evidence have been either freshly discovered or made more fully available. Meanwhile the methods of textual criticism have themselves been refined and estimates of the value of particular manuscripts have sometimes been reconsidered. The problem of restoring a form of text as near as possible to the vanished autographs now appears less simple than it did to our predecessors. There is not at the present time any critical text which would command the same degree of general acceptance as the Revisers' text did in its day. Nor has the time come, in the judgement of most scholars, to construct such a text, since new material constantly comes to light, and the debate continues. The present translators therefore could do no other than consider variant readings on their merits, and, having weighed the evidence for themselves, select for translation in each passage the reading which to the best of their judgement seemed most likely to represent what the author wrote. Where other readings seemed to deserve serious consideration they have been recorded in footnotes. In assessing the evidence, the translators have taken into account (*a*) ancient manuscripts of the New Testament in Greek, (*b*) manuscripts of early translations into other languages, and (*c*) quotations from the New Testament by early Christian writers. These three sources of evidence are collectively referred to as 'witnesses'. A large number of variants, however, are such as could make no appreciable difference to the meaning so far as it could be represented in translation, and these have been passed over in silence. The translators are well aware that their judgement is at best provisional, but they believe the text they have followed to be an improvement on that underlying the earlier translations. This text can now be read in *The Greek New Testament*, edited by R. V. G. Tasker (Oxford and Cambridge University Presses, 1964).

So much for the text. The next step was the effort to understand the original as accurately as possible, as a preliminary to turning it into English. The Revisers of 1881 believed that a better knowledge of the Greek language made it possible to correct a number of mistranslations in the older version, though in doing so they were somewhat limited by the instruction 'to introduce as few alterations as possible . . . consistently with faithfulness'. Since their time the study of the Greek language has no more stood still than has textual criticism. In particular, our knowledge of the kind of Greek used by most of the New Testament writers has been greatly enriched since 1881 by the discovery of many thousands of papyrus documents in popular or non-literary Greek of about the same period as the New Testament. It would be wrong to suggest that they lead to any far-reaching change in our understanding of the Greek of the New Testament period, but they have often made possible a better appreciation of the finer shades of idiom, which sometimes clarifies the meaning of passages in the New Testament. Its language is indeed in many respects more flexible and easy-going than the Revisers were ready to allow, and invites the translator to use a larger freedom.

Our task, however, differed in an important respect from that of the Revisers of 1881. They were instructed not only to introduce as few alterations as possible, but also 'to limit, as far as possible, the expression of such alterations to the language of the Authorised and earlier English Versions'. The present translators were subject to no such limitation. In accordance with the original decision of the Joint Committee they were to make the attempt to use consistently the idiom of contemporary English to convey the meaning of the Greek.

The older translators, on the whole, considered that fidelity to the original demanded that they should reproduce, as far as possible, characteristic features of the language in which it was written, such as the syntactical order of words, the structure and division of sentences, and even such irregularities of grammar as were indeed natural enough to authors writing in the easy idiom of popular Hellenistic Greek, but less natural when turned into English. The present translators were enjoined to replace Greek constructions and idioms by those of contemporary English.

This meant a different theory and practice of translation, and one which laid a heavier burden on the translators. Fidelity in translation was not to mean keeping the general framework of the original intact while replacing Greek words by English words more or less equivalent. A word, indeed, in one language is seldom the exact equivalent of a word in a different language. Each word is the centre of a whole cluster of meanings and associations, and in different languages these clusters overlap but do not often coincide. The place of a word in the clause or sentence, or even in a larger unit of thought, will determine what aspect of its total meaning is in the foreground. The translator can hardly hope to convey in another language every shade of meaning that attaches to the word in the original, but if he is free to exploit a wide range of English words covering a similar area of meaning and association he may hope to carry over the meaning of the sentence as a whole. Thus we have not felt obliged (as did the Revisers of 1881) to make an effort to render the same Greek word everywhere by the same English word. We have in this respect returned to the wholesome practice of King James's men, who (as they expressly state in their preface) recognized no such obligation.

We have conceived our task to be that of understanding the original as precisely as we could (using all available aids), and then saying again in our own native idiom what we believed the author to be saying in his. We have found that in practice this frequently compelled us to make decisions where the older method of translation allowed a comfortable ambiguity. In such places we have been aware that we take a risk, but we have thought it our duty to take the risk rather than remain on the fence.

In doing our work, we have constantly striven to follow our instructions and render the Greek, as we understood it, into the English of the present day, that is, into the natural vocabulary, constructions, and rhythms of contemporary speech. We have sought to avoid archaism, jargon, and all that is either stilted or slipshod.

It should be said that our intention has been to offer a translation in the strict sense, and not a paraphrase, and we have not wished to encroach on the field of the commentator. But if the best commentary is a good translation, it is also true that every intelligent translation is in a sense a paraphrase. The line between translation and paraphrase is a fine one. But we have had recourse to deliberate paraphrase with great caution, and only in a few passages where without it we could see no way to attain our aim of making the meaning as clear as it could be made. Taken as a whole, our version claims to be a translation, free, it may be, rather than literal, but a faithful translation nevertheless, so far as we could compass it.

For this edition, the translation of the New Testament has been given a careful revision, in which account has been taken of numerous criticisms and suggestions which have come in from various quarters. It is hoped that the modifications introduced, mostly in minor details and seldom reflecting any substantial change of view about the meaning of a passage, will be found to be in the direction of improvement.

In the course of revision, consideration has been given to passages from the Old Testament quoted in the New. These have now been harmonized with the present version of the Old Testament, where this seemed desirable, and practicable. But the quotations are in Greek, and the Greek is by no means always an exact equivalent of the Hebrew. Where it is not, we have deemed it our duty to render the Greek as it lay before us, and not to attempt to reproduce the underlying Hebrew. On this point there has been consultation between representatives of the Old and the New Testament panels.

The translators are as conscious as anyone can be of the limitations and imperfections of their work. No one who has not tried it can know how impossible an art translation is. Only those who have meditated long upon the Greek original are aware of the richness and subtlety of meaning that may lie even within the most apparently simple sentence, or know the despair that attends all efforts to bring it out through the medium of a different language. Yet we may hope that we have been able to convey to our readers something at least of what the New Testament has said to us during these years of work, and trust that under the providence of Almighty God this translation may open the truth of the Scriptures to many who have been hindered in their approach to it by barriers of language.

C. H. D.

MARGINAL NUMBERS

THE conventional verse divisions in the New Testament date only from 1551 and have no basis in the manuscripts. Any system of division into numbered verses is foreign to the spirit of this translation, which is intended to convey the meaning in continuous natural English rather than to correspond sentence by sentence with the Greek.

For purposes of reference, and of comparison with other translations, verse numbers are placed in the margin opposite the line in which the first word belonging to the verse in question appears. Sometimes, however, successive verses are combined in a continuous English sentence, so that the precise point where a new verse begins cannot be fixed; occasionally in the interests of clarity the order of successive verses is reversed (e.g. at John 4. 7, 8).

THE GOSPEL

THE GOSPEL ACCORDING TO
MATTHEW

The coming of Christ

A TABLE OF THE DESCENT of Jesus Christ, son of David, 1
son of Abraham.
 Abraham was the father of Isaac, Isaac of Jacob, Jacob of Judah 2
and his brothers, Judah of Perez and Zarah (their mother was Tamar), 3
Perez of Hezron, Hezron of Ram, Ram of Amminadab, Amminadab of 4
Nahshon, Nahshon of Salma, Salma of Boaz (his mother was Rahab), 5
Boaz of Obed (his mother was Ruth), Obed of Jesse; and Jesse was the 6
father of King David.

David was the father of Solomon (his mother had been the wife of
Uriah), Solomon of Rehoboam, Rehoboam of Abijah, Abijah of Asa, 7
Asa of Jehoshaphat, Jehoshaphat of Joram, Joram of Azariah, Azariah of 8 9
Jotham, Jotham of Ahaz, Ahaz of Hezekiah, Hezekiah of Manasseh, 10
Manasseh of Amon, Amon of Josiah; and Josiah was the father of Jeconiah 11
and his brothers at the time of the deportation to Babylon.

After the deportation Jeconiah was the father of Shealtiel, Shealtiel of 12
Zerubbabel, Zerubbabel of Abiud, Abiud of Eliakim, Eliakim of Azor, 13
Azor of Zadok, Zadok of Achim, Achim of Eliud, Eliud of Eleazar, Eleazar 14 15
of Matthan, Matthan of Jacob, Jacob of Joseph, the husband of Mary, who 16
gave birth to[a] Jesus called Messiah.

There were thus fourteen generations in all from Abraham to David, 17
fourteen from David until the deportation to Babylon, and fourteen from
the deportation until the Messiah.

THIS IS THE STORY of the birth of the Messiah. Mary his mother was 18
betrothed to Joseph; before their marriage she found that she was with
child by the Holy Spirit. Being a man of principle, and at the same time 19
wanting to save her from exposure, Joseph desired to have the marriage
contract set aside quietly. He had resolved on this, when an angel of the 20
Lord appeared to him in a dream. 'Joseph son of David,' said the angel,
'do not be afraid to take Mary home with you as your wife. It is by the
Holy Spirit that she has conceived this child. She will bear a son; and you 21
shall give him the name Jesus (Saviour), for he will save his people from
their sins.' All this happened in order to fulfil what the Lord declared 22
through the prophet: 'The virgin will conceive and bear a son, and he 23

[a] *Some witnesses read* Joseph, to whom was betrothed Mary, a virgin, who gave birth
to . . .; *one witness has* Joseph, and Joseph, to whom Mary, a virgin, was betrothed, was
the father of . . .

24 shall be called Emmanuel', a name which means 'God is with us'. Rising from sleep Joseph did as the angel had directed him; he took Mary home
25 to be his wife, but had no intercourse with her until her son was born. And he named the child Jesus.

2 JESUS WAS BORN at Bethlehem in Judaea during the reign of Herod.
2 After his birth astrologers from the east arrived in Jerusalem, asking, 'Where is the child who is born to be king of the Jews?*a* We observed the rising of
3 his star, and we have come to pay him homage.' King Herod was greatly
4 perturbed when he heard this; and so was the whole of Jerusalem. He called a meeting of the chief priests and lawyers of the Jewish people, and put before them the question: 'Where is it that the Messiah is to be born?'
5 'At Bethlehem in Judaea', they replied; and they referred him to the
6 prophecy which reads: 'Bethlehem in the land of Judah, you are far from least in the eyes of*b* the rulers of Judah; for out of you shall come a leader to be the shepherd of my people Israel.'
7 Herod next called the astrologers to meet him in private, and ascertained
8 from them the time when the star had appeared. He then sent them on to Bethlehem, and said, 'Go and make a careful inquiry for the child. When you have found him, report to me, so that I may go myself and pay him homage.'
9 They set out at the king's bidding; and the star which they had seen at its rising went ahead of them until it stopped above the place where the
10 11 child lay. At the sight of the star they were overjoyed. Entering the house, they saw the child with Mary his mother, and bowed to the ground in homage to him; then they opened their treasures and offered him gifts:
12 gold, frankincense, and myrrh. And being warned in a dream not to go back to Herod, they returned home another way.
13 After they had gone, an angel of the Lord appeared to Joseph in a dream, and said to him, 'Rise up, take the child and his mother and escape with them to Egypt, and stay there until I tell you; for Herod
14 is going to search for the child to do away with him.' So Joseph rose from sleep, and taking mother and child by night he went away with
15 them to Egypt, and there he stayed till Herod's death. This was to fulfil what the Lord had declared through the prophet: 'I called my son out of Egypt.'
16 When Herod saw how the astrologers had tricked him he fell into a passion, and gave orders for the massacre of all children in Bethlehem and its neighbourhood, of the age of two years or less, corresponding with
17 the time he had ascertained from the astrologers. So the words spoken
18 through Jeremiah the prophet were fulfilled: 'A voice was heard in Rama, wailing and loud laments; it was Rachel weeping for her children, and refusing all consolation, because they were no more.'
19 The time came that Herod died; and an angel of the Lord appeared in
20 a dream to Joseph in Egypt and said to him, 'Rise up, take the child and his mother, and go with them to the land of Israel, for the men who threatened
21 the child's life are dead.' So he rose, took mother and child with him, and

a Or Where is the king of the Jews who has just been born?   *b Or* least among.

came to the land of Israel. Hearing, however, that Archelaus had succeeded 22 his father Herod as king of Judaea, he was afraid to go there. And being warned by a dream, he withdrew to the region of Galilee; there he settled in 23 a town called Nazareth. This was to fulfil the words spoken through the prophets: 'He shall be called a Nazarene.'

ABOUT THAT TIME John the Baptist appeared as a preacher in the **3** Judaean wilderness; his theme was: 'Repent; for the kingdom of Heaven 2 is upon you!' It is of him that the prophet Isaiah spoke when he said, 3 'A voice crying aloud in the wilderness, "Prepare a way for the Lord; clear a straight path for him."'

John's clothing was a rough coat of camel's hair, with a leather belt 4 round his waist, and his food was locusts and wild honey. They flocked to 5 him from Jerusalem, from all Judaea, and the whole Jordan valley, and 6 were baptized by him in the River Jordan, confessing their sins.

When he saw many of the Pharisees and Sadducees coming for baptism 7 he said to them: 'You vipers' brood! Who warned you to escape from the coming retribution? Then prove your repentance by the fruit it bears; 8 and do not presume to say to yourselves, "We have Abraham for our 9 father." I tell you that God can make children for Abraham out of these stones here. Already the axe is laid to the roots of the trees; and every tree 10 that fails to produce good fruit is cut down and thrown on the fire. I baptize 11 you with water, for repentance; but the one who comes after me is mightier than I. I am not fit to take off his shoes. He will baptize you with the Holy Spirit and with fire. His shovel is ready in his hand and he will winnow his 12 threshing-floor; the wheat he will gather into his granary, but he will burn the chaff on a fire that can never go out.'

Then Jesus arrived at the Jordan from Galilee, and came to John to be 13 baptized by him. John tried to dissuade him. 'Do you come to me?' he 14 said; 'I need rather to be baptized by you.' Jesus replied, 'Let it be so for the 15 present; we do well to conform in this way with all that God requires.' John then allowed him to come. After baptism Jesus came up out of the 16 water at once, and at that moment heaven opened; he saw the Spirit of God descending like a dove to alight upon him; and a voice from heaven 17 was heard saying, 'This is my Son, my Beloved,*a* on whom my favour rests.'

JESUS WAS THEN LED AWAY by the Spirit into the wilderness, to be **4** tempted by the devil.

For forty days and nights he fasted, and at the end of them he was 2 famished. The tempter approached him and said, 'If you are the Son of 3 God, tell these stones to become bread.' Jesus answered, 'Scripture says, 4 "Man cannot live on bread alone; he lives on every word that God utters."'

The devil then took him to the Holy City and set him on the parapet of 5 the temple. 'If you are the Son of God,' he said, 'throw yourself down; for 6 Scripture says, "He will put his angels in charge of you, and they will support you in their arms, for fear you should strike your foot against

a Or This is my only Son.

5

7 a stone."' Jesus answered him, 'Scripture says again, "You are not to put the Lord your God to the test."'

8 Once again, the devil took him to a very high mountain, and showed him 9 all the kingdoms of the world in their glory. 'All these', he said, 'I will give 10 you, if you will only fall down and do me homage.' But Jesus said, 'Begone, Satan! Scripture says, "You shall do homage to the Lord your God and worship him alone."'

11 Then the devil left him; and angels appeared and waited on him.

12 When he heard that John had been arrested, Jesus withdrew to Galilee; 13 and leaving Nazareth he went and settled at Capernaum on the Sea of 14 Galilee, in the district of Zebulun and Naphtali. This was to fulfil the pas- 15 sage in the prophet Isaiah which tells of 'the land of Zebulun, the land of Naphtali, the Way of the Sea, the land beyond Jordan, heathen Galilee', and says:

16   'The people that lived in darkness saw a great light;
    light dawned on the dwellers in the land of death's dark shadow.'

17 From that day Jesus began to proclaim the message: 'Repent; for [a] the kingdom of Heaven is upon you.'

18 JESUS WAS WALKING by the Sea of Galilee when he saw two brothers, Simon called Peter and his brother Andrew, casting a net into the lake; 19 for they were fishermen. Jesus said to them, 'Come with me, and I will 20 make you fishers of men.' And at once they left their nets and followed him.

21 He went on, and saw another pair of brothers, James son of Zebedee and his brother John; they were in the boat with their father Zebedee, 22 overhauling their nets. He called them, and at once they left the boat and their father, and followed him.

23 He went round the whole of Galilee, teaching in the synagogues, preach- ing the gospel of the Kingdom, and curing whatever illness or infirmity 24 there was among the people. His fame reached the whole of Syria; and sufferers from every kind of illness, racked with pain, possessed by devils, 25 epileptic, or paralysed, were all brought to him, and he cured them. Great crowds also followed him, from Galilee and the Ten Towns, [b] from Jerusalem and Judaea, and from Transjordan.

The Sermon on the Mount

5 WHEN HE SAW the crowds he went up the hill. There he took his seat, 2 and when his disciples had gathered round him he began to address them. And this is the teaching he gave:

3   'How blest are those who know their need of God;
    the kingdom of Heaven is theirs.

4   How blest are the sorrowful;
    they shall find consolation.

[a] *Some witnesses omit* Repent; for.   [b] *Greek* Decapolis.

How blest are those of a gentle spirit;   5
    they shall have the earth for their possession.

How blest are those who hunger and thirst to see right prevail; [a]   6
    they shall be satisfied.

How blest are those who show mercy;   7
    mercy shall be shown to them.

How blest are those whose hearts are pure;   8
    they shall see God.

How blest are the peacemakers;   9
    God shall call them his sons.

How blest are those who have suffered persecution for the cause of right;   10
    the kingdom of Heaven is theirs.

'How blest you are, when you suffer insults and persecution and every   11
kind of calumny for my sake. Accept it with gladness and exultation, for   12
you have a rich reward in heaven; in the same way they persecuted the
prophets before you.

'You are salt to the world. And if salt becomes tasteless, how is its salt-   13
ness to be restored? It is now good for nothing but to be thrown away and
trodden underfoot.

'You are light for all the world. A town that stands on a hill cannot be   14
hidden. When a lamp is lit, it is not put under the meal-tub, but on the   15
lamp-stand, where it gives light to everyone in the house. And you, like   16
the lamp, must shed light among your fellows, so that, when they see the
good you do, they may give praise to your Father in heaven.

'DO NOT SUPPOSE that I have come to abolish the Law and the prophets;   17
I did not come to abolish, but to complete. I tell you this: so long as heaven   18
and earth endure, not a letter, not a stroke, will disappear from the Law
until all that must happen has happened.[b] If any man therefore sets aside   19
even the least of the Law's demands, and teaches others to do the same, he
will have the lowest place in the kingdom of Heaven, whereas anyone who
keeps the Law, and teaches others so, will stand high in the kingdom of
Heaven. I tell you, unless you show yourselves far better men than the   20
Pharisees and the doctors of the law, you can never enter the kingdom of
Heaven.

'You have learned that our forefathers were told, "Do not commit   21
murder; anyone who commits murder must be brought to judgement."
But what I tell you is this: Anyone who nurses anger against his brother [c]   22
must be brought to judgement. If he abuses his brother he must answer
for it to the court; if he sneers at him he will have to answer for it in the
fires of hell.

'If, when you are bringing your gift to the altar, you suddenly remember   23
that your brother has a grievance against you, leave your gift where it is   24
before the altar. First go and make your peace with your brother, and only
then come back and offer your gift.

[a] *Or* to do what is right.   [b] *Or* before all that it stands for is achieved.   [c] *Some witnesses insert* without good cause.

25 'If someone sues you, come to terms with him promptly while you are both on your way to court; otherwise he may hand you over to the judge,
26 and the judge to the constable, and you will be put in jail. I tell you, once you are there you will not be let out till you have paid the last farthing.
27 'You have learned that they were told, "Do not commit adultery."
28 But what I tell you is this: If a man looks on a woman with a lustful eye, he has already committed adultery with her in his heart.
29 'If your right eye is your undoing, tear it out and fling it away; it is better for you to lose one part of your body than for the whole of it to be thrown
30 into hell. And if your right hand is your undoing, cut it off and fling it away; it is better for you to lose one part of your body than for the whole of it to go to hell.
31 'They were told, "A man who divorces his wife must give her a note of
32 dismissal." But what I tell you is this: If a man divorces his wife for any cause other than unchastity he involves her in adultery; and anyone who marries a divorced woman commits adultery.
33 'Again, you have learned that our forefathers were told, "Do not break
34 your oath", and, "Oaths sworn to the Lord must be kept." But what I tell you is this: You are not to swear at all—not by heaven, for it is God's
35 throne, nor by earth, for it is his footstool, nor by Jerusalem, for it is the
36 city of the great King, nor by your own head, because you cannot turn
37 one hair of it white or black. Plain "Yes" or "No" is all you need to say; anything beyond that comes from the devil.
38 'You have learned that they were told, "Eye for eye, tooth for tooth."
39 But what I tell you is this: Do not set yourself against the man who wrongs you. If someone slaps you on the right cheek, turn and offer him your left.
40 If a man wants to sue you for your shirt, let him have your coat as well.
41 42 If a man in authority makes you go one mile, go with him two. Give when you are asked to give; and do not turn your back on a man who wants to borrow.
43 'You have learned that they were told, "Love your neighbour, hate your
44 enemy." But what I tell you is this: Love your enemies[a] and pray for your
45 persecutors;[b] only so can you be children of your heavenly Father, who makes his sun rise on good and bad alike, and sends the rain on the honest
46 and the dishonest. If you love only those who love you, what reward can
47 you expect? Surely the tax-gatherers do as much as that. And if you greet only your brothers, what is there extraordinary about that? Even the
48 heathen do as much. There must be no limit to your goodness, as your heavenly Father's goodness knows no bounds.

6 'BE CAREFUL not to make a show of your religion before men; if you do, no reward awaits you in your Father's house in heaven.
2 'Thus, when you do some act of charity, do not announce it with a flourish of trumpets, as the hypocrites do in synagogue and in the streets to win
3 admiration from men. I tell you this: they have their reward already. No; when you do some act of charity, do not let your left hand know what your

---

[a] *Some witnesses insert* bless those who curse you, do good to those who hate you.
[b] *Some witnesses insert* and those who treat you spitefully.

right is doing; your good deed must be secret, and your Father who sees 4
what is done in secret will reward you. *a*

'Again, when you pray, do not be like the hypocrites; they love to say 5
their prayers standing up in synagogue and at the street-corners, for
everyone to see them. I tell you this: they have their reward already. But 6
when you pray, go into a room by yourself, shut the door, and pray to your
Father who is there in the secret place; and your Father who sees what is
secret will reward you.*a*

'In your prayers do not go babbling on like the heathen, who imagine 7
that the more they say the more likely they are to be heard. Do not imitate 8
them. Your Father knows what your needs are before you ask him.

'This is how you should pray: 9

> "Our Father in heaven,
> thy name be hallowed;
> thy kingdom come, 10
> thy will be done,
> on earth as in heaven.
> Give us today our daily bread.*b* 11
> Forgive us the wrong we have done, 12
> as we have forgiven those who have wronged us.
> And do not bring us to the test, 13
> but save us from the evil one." *c d*

For if you forgive others the wrongs they have done, your heavenly Father 14
will also forgive you; but if you do not forgive others, then the wrongs you 15
have done will not be forgiven by your Father.

'So too when you fast, do not look gloomy like the hypocrites: they make 16
their faces unsightly so that other people may see that they are fasting.
I tell you this: they have their reward already. But when you fast, anoint 17
your head and wash your face, so that men may not see that you are fasting, 18
but only your Father who is in the secret place; and your Father who sees
what is secret will give you your reward.

'DO NOT STORE UP for yourselves treasure on earth, where it grows rusty 19
and moth-eaten, and thieves break in to steal it. Store up treasure in 20
heaven, where there is no moth and no rust to spoil it, no thieves to break
in and steal. For where your treasure is, there will your heart be also. 21

'The lamp of the body is the eye. If your eyes are sound, you will have 22
light for your whole body; if the eyes are bad, your whole body will be in 23
darkness. If then the only light you have is darkness, the darkness is
doubly dark.

'No servant can be the slave of two masters; for either he will hate the 24
first and love the second, or he will be devoted to the first and think
nothing of the second. You cannot serve God and Money.

'Therefore I bid you put away anxious thoughts about food and drink 25

---

a   Some witnesses add openly.   *b   Or* our bread for the morrow.   *c   Or* from evil.
d   Some witnesses add For thine is the kingdom and the power and the glory, for ever.
Amen.

to keep you alive, and clothes to cover your body. Surely life is more than
26 food, the body more than clothes. Look at the birds of the air; they do not
sow and reap and store in barns, yet your heavenly Father feeds them. You
27 are worth more than the birds! Is there a man of you who by anxious
28 thought can add a foot to his height*a*? And why be anxious about clothes?
Consider how the lilies grow in the fields; they do not work, they do not
29 spin;*b* and yet, I tell you, even Solomon in all his splendour was not
30 attired like one of these. But if that is how God clothes the grass in the
fields, which is there today, and tomorrow is thrown on the stove, will he
31 not all the more clothe you? How little faith you have! No, do not ask
anxiously, "What are we to eat? What are we to drink? What shall we
32 wear?" All these are things for the heathen to run after, not for you,
33 because your heavenly Father knows that you need them all. Set your
mind on God's kingdom and his justice before everything else, and all the
34 rest will come to you as well. So do not be anxious about tomorrow;
tomorrow will look after itself. Each day has troubles enough of its own.

7 1 2 'PASS NO JUDGEMENT, and you will not be judged. For as you judge
others, so you will yourselves be judged, and whatever measure you deal
3 out to others will be dealt back to you. Why do you look at the speck of
sawdust in your brother's eye, with never a thought for the great plank in
4 your own? Or how can you say to your brother, "Let me take the speck out
5 of your eye", when all the time there is that plank in your own? You hypocrite! First take the plank out of your own eye, and then you will see clearly
to take the speck out of your brother's.

6 'Do not give dogs what is holy; do not throw your pearls to the pigs:
they will only trample on them, and turn and tear you to pieces.

7 'Ask, and you will receive; seek, and you will find; knock, and the door
8 will be opened. For everyone who asks receives, he who seeks finds, and
to him who knocks, the door will be opened.

9 'Is there a man among you who will offer his son a stone when he asks
10 11 for bread, or a snake when he asks for fish? If you, then, bad as you are,
know how to give your children what is good for them, how much more will
your heavenly Father give good things to those who ask him!

12 'Always treat others as you would like them to treat you: that is the Law
and the prophets.

13 'Enter by the narrow gate. The gate is wide that leads to perdition,
14 there is plenty of room on the road,*c* and many go that way; but the gate
that leads to life is small and the road is narrow,*d* and those who find it
are few.

15 'Beware of false prophets, men who come to you dressed up as sheep
16 while underneath they are savage wolves. You will recognize them by the
fruits they bear. Can grapes be picked from briars, or figs from thistles?
17 In the same way, a good tree always yields good fruit, and a poor tree bad

a Or a day to his life.
b One witness reads Consider the lilies: they neither card nor spin, nor labour.
c Some witnesses read The road that leads to perdition is wide with plenty of room.
d Some witnesses read but the road that leads to life is small and narrow.

fruit. A good tree cannot bear bad fruit, or a poor tree good fruit. And when 18 19
a tree does not yield good fruit it is cut down and burnt. That is why I say 20
you will recognize them by their fruits.

'Not everyone who calls me "Lord, Lord" will enter the kingdom of 21
Heaven, but only those who do the will of my heavenly Father. When that 22
day comes, many will say to me, "Lord, Lord, did we not prophesy in your
name, cast out devils in your name, and in your name perform many
miracles?" Then I will tell them to their face, "I never knew you; out of my 23
sight, you and your wicked ways!"

'What then of the man who hears these words of mine and acts upon 24
them? He is like a man who had the sense to build his house on rock. The 25
rain came down, the floods rose, the wind blew, and beat upon that house;
but it did not fall, because its foundations were on rock. But what of the 26
man who hears these words of mine and does not act upon them? He is
like a man who was foolish enough to build his house on sand. The rain 27
came down, the floods rose, the wind blew, and beat upon that house;
down it fell with a great crash.'

When Jesus had finished this discourse the people were astounded at 28
his teaching; unlike their own teachers he taught with a note of authority. 29

Teaching and healing

AFTER HE HAD COME DOWN from the hill he was followed by a great 8
crowd. And now a leper[a] approached him, bowed low, and said, 2
'Sir, if only you will, you can cleanse me.' Jesus stretched out his hand, 3
touched him, and said, 'Indeed I will; be clean again.' And his leprosy
was cured immediately. Then Jesus said to him, 'Be sure you tell nobody; 4
but go and show yourself to the priest, and make the offering laid down
by Moses for your cleansing; that will certify the cure.'

When he had entered Capernaum a centurion came up to ask his help. 5
'Sir,' he said, 'a boy of mine lies at home paralysed and racked with pain.' 6
Jesus said, 'I will come and cure him.'[b] But the centurion replied, 'Sir, 7 8
who am I to have you under my roof? You need only say the word and the
boy will be cured. I know, for I am myself under orders, with soldiers under 9
me. I say to one, "Go", and he goes; to another, "Come here", and he
comes; and to my servant, "Do this", and he does it.' Jesus heard him with 10
astonishment, and said to the people who were following him, 'I tell you
this: nowhere, even in Israel, have I found such faith.

'Many, I tell you, will come from east and west to feast with Abraham, 11
Isaac, and Jacob in the kingdom of Heaven. But those who were born to 12
the kingdom will be driven out into the dark, the place of wailing and
grinding of teeth.'

Then Jesus said to the centurion, 'Go home now; because of your faith, 13
so let it be.' At that moment the boy recovered.

a The words leper, leprosy, *as used in this translation, refer to some disfiguring skin disease*
which entailed ceremonial defilement. It is different from what is now called leprosy.
b Or Am I to come and cure him?

14 Jesus then went to Peter's house and found Peter's mother-in-law in bed
15 with fever. So he took her by the hand; the fever left her, and she got up and waited on him.

16 When evening fell, they brought to him many who were possessed by devils; and he drove the spirits out with a word and healed all who were
17 sick, to fulfil the prophecy of Isaiah: 'He took away our illnesses and lifted our diseases from us.' *a*

18 AT THE SIGHT of the crowds surrounding him Jesus gave word to cross
19 to the other shore. A doctor of the law came up, and said, 'Master, I will
20 follow you wherever you go.' Jesus replied, 'Foxes have their holes, the birds their roosts; but the Son of Man has nowhere to lay his head.'
21 Another man, one of his disciples, said to him, 'Lord, let me go and bury
22 my father first.' Jesus replied, 'Follow me, and leave the dead to bury their dead.'

23 24 Jesus then got into the boat, and his disciples followed. All at once a great storm arose on the lake, till the waves were breaking right over the
25 boat; but he went on sleeping. So they came and woke him up, crying:
26 'Save us, Lord; we are sinking!' 'Why are you such cowards?' he said; 'how little faith you have!' Then he stood up and rebuked the wind and the
27 sea, and there was a dead calm. The men were astonished at what had happened, and exclaimed, 'What sort of man is this? Even the wind and the sea obey him.'

28 When he reached the other side, in the country of the Gadarenes, he was met by two men who came out from the tombs; they were possessed
29 by devils, and so violent that no one dared pass that way. 'You son of God,' they shouted, 'what do you want with us? Have you come here to torment
30 us before our time?' In the distance a large herd of pigs was feeding;
31 and the devils begged him: 'If you drive us out, send us into that herd
32 of pigs.' 'Begone!' he said. Then they came out and went into the pigs; the whole herd rushed over the edge into the lake, and perished in the water.

33 The men in charge of them took to their heels, and made for the town, where they told the whole story, and what had happened to the madmen.
34 Thereupon all the town came out to meet Jesus; and when they saw him
9 they begged him to leave the district and go. So he got into the boat and crossed over, and came to his own town.

2 And now some men brought him a paralysed man lying on a bed. Seeing their faith Jesus said to the man, 'Take heart, my son; your sins are for-
3 given.' At this some of the lawyers said to themselves, 'This is blasphemous
4 talk.' Jesus knew what they were thinking, and said, 'Why do you harbour
5 these evil thoughts? Is it easier to say, "Your sins are forgiven", or to say,
6 "Stand up and walk"? But to convince you that the Son of Man has the right on earth to forgive sins'—he turned to the paralysed man—'stand up, take
7 your bed, and go home.' Thereupon the man got up, and went off home.
8 The people were filled with awe at the sight, and praised God for granting such authority to men.

a Or and bore the burden of our diseases.

AS HE PASSED ON from there Jesus saw a man named Matthew at his seat 9 in the custom-house, and said to him, 'Follow me'; and Matthew rose and followed him.

When Jesus was at table in the house, many bad characters—tax- 10 gatherers and others—were seated with him and his disciples. The 11 Pharisees noticed this, and said to his disciples, 'Why is it that your master eats with tax-gatherers and sinners?' Jesus heard it and said, 'It is not the 12 healthy that need a doctor, but the sick. Go and learn what that text means, 13 "I require mercy, not sacrifice." I did not come to invite virtuous people, but sinners.'

Then John's disciples came to him with the question: 'Why do we and 14 the Pharisees fast, but your disciples do not?' Jesus replied, 'Can you 15 expect the bridegroom's friends to go mourning while the bridegroom is with them? The time will come when the bridegroom will be taken away from them; that will be the time for them to fast.

'No one sews a patch of unshrunk cloth on to an old coat; for then the 16 patch tears away from the coat, and leaves a bigger hole. Neither do you 17 put new wine into old wine-skins; if you do, the skins burst, and then the wine runs out and the skins are spoilt. No, you put new wine into fresh skins; then both are preserved.'

EVEN AS HE SPOKE, there came a president of the synagogue, who bowed 18 low before him and said, 'My daughter has just died; but come and lay your hand on her, and she will live.' Jesus rose and went with him, and so 19 did his disciples.

Then a woman who had suffered from haemorrhages for twelve years 20 came up from behind, and touched the edge of his cloak; for she said to 21 herself, 'If I can only touch his cloak, I shall be cured.' But Jesus turned and 22 saw her, and said, 'Take heart, my daughter; your faith has cured you.' And from that moment she recovered.

When Jesus arrived at the president's house and saw the flute-players 23 and the general commotion, he said, 'Be off! The girl is not dead: she is 24 asleep'; and they only laughed at him. But, when everyone had been turned 25 out, he went into the room and took the girl by the hand, and she got up. This story became the talk of all the country round. 26

As he passed on Jesus was followed by two blind men, who cried out, 27 'Son of David, have pity on us!' And when he had gone indoors they came 28 to him. Jesus asked, 'Do you believe that I have the power to do what you want?' 'Yes, sir', they said. Then he touched their eyes, and said, 'As you 29 have believed, so let it be'; and their sight was restored. Jesus said to them 30 sternly, 'See that no one hears about this.' But as soon as they had gone out 31 they talked about him all over the country-side.

They were on their way out when a man was brought to him, who was 32 dumb and possessed by a devil; the devil was cast out and the patient 33 recovered his speech. Filled with amazement the onlookers said, 'Nothing like this has ever been seen in Israel.' [a]

[a] *Some witnesses add* (34) But the Pharisees said, 'He casts out devils by the prince of devils.'

35 SO JESUS WENT ROUND all the towns and villages teaching in their synagogues, announcing the good news of the Kingdom, and curing every kind
36 of ailment and disease. The sight of the people moved him to pity: they
37 were like sheep without a shepherd, harassed and helpless; and he said to
38 his disciples, 'The crop is heavy, but labourers are scarce; you must therefore beg the owner to send labourers to harvest his crop.'

10 Then he called his twelve disciples to him and gave them authority to
cast out unclean spirits and to cure every kind of ailment and disease.
2 These are the names of the twelve apostles: first Simon, also called
Peter, and his brother Andrew; James son of Zebedee, and his brother
3 John; Philip and Bartholomew, Thomas and Matthew the tax-gatherer,
4 James son of Alphaeus, Lebbaeus,*a* Simon, a member of the Zealot party,
and Judas Iscariot, the man who betrayed him.

5 These twelve Jesus sent out with the following instructions: 'Do not
6 take the road to gentile lands, and do not enter any Samaritan town; but
7 go rather to the lost sheep of the house of Israel. And as you go proclaim
8 the message: "The kingdom of Heaven is upon you." Heal the sick, raise
the dead, cleanse lepers, cast out devils. You received without cost; give
without charge.

9 10 'Provide no gold, silver, or copper to fill your purse, no pack for the road,
no second coat, no shoes, no stick; the worker earns his keep.

11 'When you come to any town or village, look for some worthy person in it,
12 and make your home there until you leave. Wish the house peace as you
13 enter it, so that, if it is worthy, your peace may descend on it; if it is not
14 worthy, your peace can come back to you. If anyone will not receive you
or listen to what you say, then as you leave that house or that town shake
15 the dust of it off your feet. I tell you this: on the day of judgement it will
be more bearable for the land of Sodom and Gomorrah than for that town.

16 'Look, I send you out like sheep among wolves; be wary as serpents,
innocent as doves.

17 'And be on your guard, for men will hand you over to their courts, they
18 will flog you in the synagogues, and you will be brought before governors
19 and kings, for my sake, to testify before them and the heathen. But when
you are arrested, do not worry about what you are to say; when the time
20 comes, the words you need will be given you; for it is not you who will be
speaking: it will be the Spirit of your Father speaking in you.

21 'Brother will betray brother to death, and the father his child; children
22 will turn against their parents and send them to their death. All will hate
you for your allegiance to me; but the man who holds out to the end will be
23 saved. When you are persecuted in one town, take refuge in another; I tell
you this: before you have gone through all the towns of Israel the Son of
Man will have come.

24 'A pupil does not rank above his teacher, or a servant above his master.
25 The pupil should be content to share his teacher's lot, the servant to share
his master's. If the master has been called Beelzebub, how much more his
household!

26 'So do not be afraid of them. There is nothing covered up that will not

a Some witnesses read Thaddaeus.

be uncovered, nothing hidden that will not be made known. What I say 27
to you in the dark you must repeat in broad daylight; what you hear
whispered you must shout from the house-tops. Do not fear those who kill 28
the body, but cannot kill the soul. Fear him rather who is able to destroy
both soul and body in hell.

'Are not sparrows two a penny? Yet without your Father's leave not 29
one of them can fall to the ground. As for you, even the hairs of your head 30
have all been counted. So have no fear; you are worth more than any 31
number of sparrows.

'Whoever then will acknowledge me before men, I will acknowledge 32
him before my Father in heaven; and whoever disowns me before men, 33
I will disown him before my Father in heaven.

'You must not think that I have come to bring peace to the earth; I have 34
not come to bring peace, but a sword. I have come to set a man against his 35
father, a daughter against her mother, a son's wife against her mother-in-
law; and a man will find his enemies under his own roof. 36

'No man is worthy of me who cares more for father or mother than for 37
me; no man is worthy of me who cares more for son or daughter; no man 38
is worthy of me who does not take up his cross and walk in my footsteps.
By gaining his life a man will lose it; by losing his life for my sake, he will 39
gain it.

'To receive you is to receive me, and to receive me is to receive the One 40
who sent me. Whoever receives a prophet as a prophet will be given a 41
prophet's reward, and whoever receives a good man because he is a good
man will be given a good man's reward. And if anyone gives so much as a cup 42
of cold water to one of these little ones, because he is a disciple of mine,
I tell you this: that man will assuredly not go unrewarded.'

When Jesus had finished giving his twelve disciples their instructions, **11**
he left that place and went to teach and preach in the neighbouring
towns.

JOHN, WHO WAS IN PRISON, heard what Christ was doing, and sent his 2
own disciples to him with this message: 'Are you the one who is to come, or 3
are we to expect some other?' Jesus answered, 'Go and tell John what you 4
hear and see: the blind recover their sight, the lame walk, the lepers are 5
made clean, the deaf hear, the dead are raised to life, the poor are hearing
the good news—and happy is the man who does not find me a stumbling- 6
block.'

When the messengers were on their way back, Jesus began to speak to 7
the people about John: 'What was the spectacle that drew you to the
wilderness? A reed-bed swept by the wind? No? Then what did you go 8
out to see? A man dressed in silks and satins? Surely you must look in
palaces for that. But why did you go out? To see a prophet? Yes indeed, 9
and far more than a prophet. He is the man of whom Scripture says, 10

　　"Here is my herald, whom I send on ahead of you,
　　　and he will prepare your way before you."

I tell you this: never has there appeared on earth a mother's son greater 11 than John the Baptist, and yet the least in the kingdom of Heaven is greater than he.

12 'Ever since the coming of John the Baptist the kingdom of Heaven has
13 been subjected to violence and violent men *a* are seizing it. For all the
14 prophets and the Law foretold things to come until John appeared, and
15 John is the destined Elijah, if you will but accept it. If you have ears, then hear.

16 'How can I describe this generation? They are like children sitting in the market-place and shouting at each other,

17   "We piped for you and you would not dance."
     "We wept and wailed, and you would not mourn."

18 For John came, neither eating nor drinking, and they say, "He is pos-
19 sessed." The Son of Man came eating and drinking, and they say, "Look at him! a glutton and a drinker, a friend of tax-gatherers and sinners!" And yet God's wisdom is proved right by its results.'

20 THEN HE SPOKE of the towns in which most of his miracles had been
21 performed, and denounced them for their impenitence. 'Alas for you, Chorazin!' he said; 'alas for you, Bethsaida! If the miracles that were performed in you had been performed in Tyre and Sidon, they would have
22 repented long ago in sackcloth and ashes. But it will be more bearable,
23 I tell you, for Tyre and Sidon on the day of judgement than for you. And as for you, Capernaum, will you be exalted to the skies? No, brought down to the depths! For if the miracles had been performed in Sodom which
24 were performed in you, Sodom would be standing to this day. But it will be more bearable, I tell you, for the land of Sodom on the day of judgement than for you.'

25 At that time Jesus spoke these words: 'I thank thee, Father, Lord of heaven and earth, for hiding these things from the learned and wise, and
26 27 revealing them to the simple. Yes, Father, such *b* was thy choice. Everything is entrusted to me by my Father; and no one knows the Son but the Father, and no one knows the Father but the Son and those to whom the Son may choose to reveal him.

28 'Come to me, all whose work is hard, whose load is heavy; and I will give
29 you relief. Bend your necks to my yoke, and learn from me, for I am gentle
30 and humble-hearted; and your souls will find relief. For my yoke is good to bear, my load is light.'

Controversy

12 ONCE ABOUT THAT TIME Jesus went through the cornfields on the Sabbath; and his disciples, feeling hungry, began to pluck some ears
2 of corn and eat them. The Pharisees noticed this, and said to him, 'Look, your disciples are doing something which is forbidden on the Sabbath.'

---

a Or has been forcing its way forward, and men of force . . .   *b* Or Yes, I thank thee, Father, that such . . .

He answered, 'Have you not read what David did when he and his men   3
were hungry? He went into the House of God and ate the sacred bread,   4
though neither he nor his men had a right to eat it, but only the priests.
Or have you not read in the Law that on the Sabbath the priests in the   5
temple break the Sabbath and it is not held against them? I tell you, there   6
is something greater than the temple here. If you had known what that text   7
means, "I require mercy, not sacrifice", you would not have condemned
the innocent. For the Son of Man is sovereign over the Sabbath.'   8

He went on to another place, and entered their synagogue. A man was   9 10
there with a withered arm, and they asked Jesus, 'Is it permitted to heal on
the Sabbath?' (They wanted to frame a charge against him.) But he said to   11
them, 'Suppose you had one sheep, which fell into a ditch on the Sabbath;
is there one of you who would not catch hold of it and lift it out? And surely   12
a man is worth far more than a sheep! It is therefore permitted to do good
on the Sabbath.' Turning to the man he said, 'Stretch out your arm.' He   13
stretched it out, and it was made sound again like the other. But the   14
Pharisees, on leaving the synagogue, laid a plot to do away with him.

Jesus was aware of it and withdrew. Many followed, and he cured all   15
who were ill; and he gave strict injunctions that they were not to make   16
him known. This was to fulfil Isaiah's prophecy: 17

'Here is my servant, whom I have chosen,   18
    my beloved, on whom my favour rests;
I will put my Spirit upon him,
    and he will proclaim judgement among the nations.
He will not strive, he will not shout,   19
    nor will his voice be heard in the streets.
He will not snap off the broken reed,   20
    nor snuff out the smouldering wick,
    until he leads justice on to victory.
In him the nations shall place their hope.'   21

THEN THEY BROUGHT HIM a man who was possessed; he was blind and   22
dumb; and Jesus cured him, restoring both speech and sight. The by-   23
standers were all amazed, and the word went round: 'Can this be the Son of
David?' But when the Pharisees heard it they said, 'It is only by Beelzebub   24
prince of devils that this man drives the devils out.'

He knew what was in their minds; so he said to them, 'Every kingdom   25
divided against itself goes to ruin; and no town, no household, that is
divided against itself can stand. And if it is Satan who casts out Satan, Satan   26
is divided against himself; how then can his kingdom stand? And if it is   27
by Beelzebub that I cast out devils, by whom do your own people drive
them out? If this is your argument, they themselves will refute you. But   28
if it is by the Spirit of God that I drive out the devils, then be sure the
kingdom of God has already come upon you.

'Or again, how can anyone break into a strong man's house and make off   29
with his goods, unless he has first tied the strong man up before ransacking
the house?

30   'He who is not with me is against me, and he who does not gather with
me scatters.

31   'And so I tell you this: no sin, no slander, is beyond forgiveness for men,
except slander spoken against the Spirit, and that will not be forgiven.
32   Any man who speaks a word against the Son of Man will be forgiven; but if
anyone speaks against the Holy Spirit, for him there is no forgiveness,
either in this age or in the age to come.

33   'Either make the tree good and its fruit good, or make the tree bad and
34   its fruit bad; you can tell a tree by its fruit. You vipers' brood! How can
your words be good when you yourselves are evil? For the words that the
35   mouth utters come from the overflowing of the heart. A good man produces
good from the store of good within himself; and an evil man from evil
within produces evil.

36   'I tell you this: there is not a thoughtless word that comes from men's
37   lips but they will have to account for it on the day of judgement. For out
of your own mouth you will be acquitted; out of your own mouth you will
be condemned.'

38   At this some of the doctors of the law and the Pharisees said, 'Master,
39   we should like you to show us a sign.' He answered: 'It is a wicked, godless
generation that asks for a sign; and the only sign that will be given it is
40   the sign of the prophet Jonah. Jonah was in the sea-monster's belly for
three days and three nights, and in the same way the Son of Man will be
41   three days and three nights in the bowels of the earth. At the Judgement,
when this generation is on trial, the men of Nineveh will appear against it [a]
and ensure its condemnation, for they repented at the preaching of Jonah;
42   and what is here is greater than Jonah. The Queen of the South will appear
at the Judgement when this generation is on trial, [b] and ensure its condemnation, for she came from the ends of the earth to hear the wisdom of
Solomon; and what is here is greater than Solomon.

43   'When an unclean spirit comes out of a man it wanders over the deserts
44   seeking a resting-place, and finds none. Then it says, "I will go back to the
home I left." So it returns and finds the house unoccupied, swept clean,
45   and tidy. Off it goes and collects seven other spirits more wicked than
itself, and they all come in and settle down; and in the end the man's
plight is worse than before. That is how it will be with this wicked
generation.'

46   He was still speaking to the crowd when his mother and brothers
47   appeared; they stood outside, wanting to speak to him. Someone said,
'Your mother and your brothers are here outside; they want to speak to
48   you.' Jesus turned to the man who brought the message, and said, 'Who
49   is my mother? Who are my brothers?'; and pointing to the disciples, he
50   said, 'Here are my mother and my brothers. Whoever does the will of my
heavenly Father is my brother, my sister, my mother.'

13 1 2   THAT SAME DAY Jesus went out and sat by the lake-side, where so many
people gathered round him that he had to get into a boat. He sat there, and

---

[a] *Or* will rise again together with it.   [b] *Or* At the Judgement the Queen of the
South will be raised to life together with this generation.

all the people stood on the shore. He spoke to them in parables, at some 3
length.

He said: 'A sower went out to sow. And as he sowed, some seed fell along 4
the footpath; and the birds came and ate it up. Some seed fell on rocky 5
ground, where it had little soil, and it sprouted quickly because it had no
depth of earth; but when the sun rose the young corn was scorched, and 6
as it had no root it withered away. Some seed fell among thistles; and the 7
thistles shot up, and choked the corn. And some of the seed fell into good 8
soil, where it bore fruit, yielding a hundredfold or, it might be, sixtyfold
or thirtyfold. If you have ears, then hear.' 9

The disciples went up to him and asked, 'Why do you speak to them in 10
parables?' He replied, 'It has been granted to you to know the secrets of 11
the kingdom of Heaven; but to those others it has not been granted. For 12
the man who has will be given more, till he has enough and to spare; and the
man who has not will forfeit even what he has. That is why I speak to 13
them in parables; for they look without seeing, and listen without hearing
or understanding. There is a prophecy of Isaiah which is being fulfilled 14
for them: "You may hear and hear, but you will never understand; you
may look and look, but you will never see. For this people's mind has 15
become gross; their ears are dulled, and their eyes are closed. Otherwise,
their eyes might see, their ears hear, and their mind understand, and then
they might turn again, and I would heal them."

'But happy are your eyes because they see, and your ears because they 16
hear! Many prophets and saints, I tell you, desired to see what you now see, 17
yet never saw it; to hear what you hear, yet never heard it.

'You, then, may hear the parable of the sower. When a man hears the 18 19
word that tells of the Kingdom but fails to understand it, the evil one comes
and carries off what has been sown in his heart. There you have the seed
sown along the footpath. The seed sown on rocky ground stands for the 20
man who, on hearing the word, accepts it at once with joy; but as it strikes 21
no root in him he has no staying-power, and when there is trouble or
persecution on account of the word he falls away at once. The seed sown 22
among thistles represents the man who hears the word, but worldly cares
and the false glamour of wealth choke it, and it proves barren. But the seed 23
that fell into good soil is the man who hears the word and understands it,
who accordingly bears fruit, and yields a hundredfold or, it may be, sixtyfold or thirtyfold.'

Here is another parable that he put before them: 'The kingdom of 24
Heaven is like this. A man sowed his field with good seed; but while every- 25
one was asleep his enemy came, sowed darnel among the wheat, and made
off. When the corn sprouted and began to fill out, the darnel could be seen 26
among it. The farmer's men went to their master and said, "Sir, was it not 27
good seed that you sowed in your field? Then where has the darnel come
from?" "This is an enemy's doing", he replied. "Well then," they said, 28
"shall we go and gather the darnel?" "No," he answered; "in gathering it you 29
might pull up the wheat at the same time. Let them both grow together till 30
harvest; and at harvest-time I will tell the reapers, 'Gather the darnel first,
and tie it in bundles for burning; then collect the wheat into my barn.' "'

31 And this is another parable that he put before them: 'The kingdom of Heaven is like a mustard-seed, which a man took and sowed in his field.
32 As a seed, mustard is smaller than any other; but when it has grown it is bigger than any garden-plant; it becomes a tree, big enough for the birds to come and roost among its branches.'

33 He told them also this parable: 'The kingdom of Heaven is like yeast, which a woman took and mixed with half a hundredweight of flour till it was all leavened.'

34 In all this teaching to the crowds Jesus spoke in parables; in fact he never
35 spoke to them without a parable. This was to fulfil the prophecy of Isaiah: [a]

'I will open my mouth in parables;
I will utter things kept secret since the world was made.'

36 He then dismissed the people, and went into the house, where his disciples came to him and said, 'Explain to us the parable of the darnel in
37 the field.' And this was his answer: 'The sower of the good seed is the Son
38 of Man. The field is the world; the good seed stands for the children of the
39 Kingdom, the darnel for the children of the evil one. The enemy who sowed the darnel is the devil. The harvest is the end of time. The reapers are
40 angels. As the darnel, then, is gathered up and burnt, so at the end of time
41 the Son of Man will send out his angels, who will gather out of his kingdom
42 whatever makes men stumble, and all whose deeds are evil, and these will be thrown into the blazing furnace, the place of wailing and grinding of
43 teeth. And then the righteous will shine as brightly as the sun in the kingdom of their Father. If you have ears, then hear.

44 'The kingdom of Heaven is like treasure lying buried in a field. The man who found it, buried it again; and for sheer joy went and sold everything he had, and bought that field.

45 'Here is another picture of the kingdom of Heaven. A merchant looking
46 out for fine pearls found one of very special value; so he went and sold everything he had, and bought it.

47 'Again the kingdom of Heaven is like a net let down into the sea, where
48 fish of every kind were caught in it. When it was full, it was dragged ashore. Then the men sat down and collected the good fish into pails and threw the
49 worthless away. That is how it will be at the end of time. The angels will
50 go forth, and they will separate the wicked from the good, and throw them into the blazing furnace, the place of wailing and grinding of teeth.

51 'Have you understood all this?' he asked; and they answered, 'Yes.'
52 He said to them, 'When, therefore, a teacher of the law has become a learner in the kingdom of Heaven, he is like a householder who can produce from his store both the new and the old.'

53 54 WHEN HE HAD FINISHED these parables Jesus left that place, and came to his home town, where he taught the people in their synagogue. In amazement they asked, 'Where does he get this wisdom from, and these
55 miraculous powers? Is he not the carpenter's son? Is not his mother called
56 Mary, his brothers James, Joseph, Simon, and Judas? And are not all his

---

a Some witnesses omit of Isaiah.

sisters here with us? Where then has he got all this from?' So they fell 57
foul of him, and this led him to say, 'A prophet will always be held in
honour, except in his home town, and in his own family.' And he did not 58
work many miracles there: such was their want of faith.

It was at that time that reports about Jesus reached the ears of Prince 14
Herod. 'This is John the Baptist,' he said to his attendants; 'John has been 2
raised to life, and that is why these miraculous powers are at work in him.'

Now HEROD had arrested John, put him in chains, and thrown him into 3
prison, on account of Herodias, his brother Philip's wife; for John had told 4
him: 'You have no right to her.' Herod would have liked to put him to 5
death, but he was afraid of the people, in whose eyes John was a prophet.
But at his birthday celebrations the daughter of Herodias danced before the 6
guests, and Herod was so delighted that he took an oath to give her any- 7
thing she cared to ask. Prompted by her mother, she said, 'Give me here 8
on a dish the head of John the Baptist.' The king was distressed when he 9
heard it; but out of regard for his oath and for his guests, he ordered the
request to be granted, and had John beheaded in prison. The head was 10 11
brought in on a dish and given to the girl; and she carried it to her mother.
Then John's disciples came and took away the body, and buried it; and 12
they went and told Jesus.

WHEN HE HEARD what had happened Jesus withdrew privately by boat 13
to a lonely place; but people heard of it, and came after him in crowds by
land from the towns. When he came ashore, he saw a great crowd; his 14
heart went out to them, and he cured those of them who were sick. When 15
it grew late the disciples came up to him and said, 'This is a lonely place,
and the day has gone; send the people off to the villages to buy themselves
food.' He answered, 'There is no need for them to go; give them something 16
to eat yourselves.' 'All we have here', they said, 'is five loaves and two 17
fishes.' 'Let me have them', he replied. So he told the people to sit down on 18 19
the grass; then, taking the five loaves and the two fishes, he looked up to
heaven, said the blessing, broke the loaves, and gave them to the disciples;
and the disciples gave them to the people. They all ate to their hearts' 20
content; and the scraps left over, which they picked up, were enough to
fill twelve great baskets. Some five thousand men shared in this meal, to 21
say nothing of women and children.

Then he made the disciples embark and go on ahead to the other side, 22
while he sent the people away; after doing that, he went up the hill-side to 23
pray alone. It grew late, and he was there by himself. The boat was already 24
some furlongs from the shore,*a* battling with a head-wind and a rough sea.
Between three and six in the morning he came to them, walking over the 25
lake. When the disciples saw him walking on the lake they were so shaken 26
that they cried out in terror: 'It is a ghost!' But at once he spoke to them: 27
'Take heart! It is I; do not be afraid.'

Peter called to him: 'Lord, if it is you, tell me to come to you over the 28
water.' 'Come', said Jesus. Peter stepped down from the boat, and walked 29

---

a Some witnesses read already well out on the water.

30 over the water towards Jesus. But when he saw the strength of the gale he was seized with fear; and beginning to sink, he cried, 'Save me, Lord.'
31 Jesus at once reached out and caught hold of him, and said, 'Why did you
32 hesitate? How little faith you have!' They then climbed into the boat;
33 and the wind dropped. And the men in the boat fell at his feet, exclaiming, 'Truly you are the Son of God.'

34 35   So they finished the crossing and came to land at Gennesaret. There Jesus was recognized by the people of the place, who sent out word to all
36 the country round. And all who were ill were brought to him, and he was begged to allow them simply to touch the edge of his cloak. And everyone who touched it was completely cured.

15 THEN JESUS WAS APPROACHED by a group of Pharisees and lawyers
2 from Jerusalem, with the question: 'Why do your disciples break the
3 ancient tradition? They do not wash their hands before meals.' He answered them: 'And what of you? Why do you break God's commandment in the
4 interest of your tradition? For God said, "Honour your father and mother",
5 and, "The man who curses his father or mother must suffer death." But you say, "If a man says to his father or mother, 'Anything of mine which might
6 have been used for your benefit is set apart for God', then he must not honour his father or his mother." You have made God's law null and void
7 out of respect for your tradition. What hypocrisy! Isaiah was right when he
8 prophesied about you: "This people pays me lip-service, but their heart
9 is far from me; their worship of me is in vain, for they teach as doctrines the commandments of men." '
10   He called the crowd and said to them, 'Listen to me, and understand
11 this: a man is not defiled by what goes into his mouth, but by what comes out of it.'
12   Then the disciples came to him and said, 'Do you know that the Phari-
13 sees have taken great offence at what you have been saying?' His answer was: 'Any plant that is not of my heavenly Father's planting will be rooted
14 up. Leave them alone; they are blind guides,*a* and if one blind man guides another they will both fall into the ditch.'

15 16   Then Peter said, 'Tell us what that parable means.' Jesus answered,
17 'Are you still as dull as the rest? Do you not see that whatever goes in by the mouth passes into the stomach and so is discharged into the drain?
18 But what comes out of the mouth has its origins in the heart; and that is
19 what defiles a man. Wicked thoughts, murder, adultery, fornication, theft,
20 perjury, slander—these all proceed from the heart; and these are the things that defile a man; but to eat without first washing his hands, that cannot defile him.'

a Some witnesses insert of blind men.

Jesus and his disciples

J ESUS THEN LEFT that place and withdrew to the region of Tyre and   21
Sidon. And a Canaanite woman from those parts came crying out, 'Sir!   22
have pity on me, Son of David; my daughter is tormented by a devil.' But   23
he said not a word in reply. His disciples came and urged him: 'Send her
away; see how she comes shouting after us.' Jesus replied, 'I was sent to the   24
lost sheep of the house of Israel, and to them alone.' But the woman came   25
and fell at his feet and cried, 'Help me, sir.' To this Jesus replied, 'It is not   26
right to take the children's bread and throw it to the dogs.' 'True, sir,' she   27
answered; 'and yet the dogs eat the scraps that fall from their masters'
table.' Hearing this Jesus replied, 'Woman, what faith you have! Be it   28
as you wish!' And from that moment her daughter was restored to health.

After leaving that region Jesus took the road by the Sea of Galilee and   29
went up to the hills. When he was seated there, crowds flocked to him,   30
bringing with them the lame, blind, dumb, and crippled, and many other
sufferers; they threw them down at his feet, and he healed them. Great   31
was the amazement of the people when they saw the dumb speaking, the
crippled strong, the lame walking, and sight restored to the blind; and they
gave praise to the God of Israel.

Jesus called his disciples and said to them, 'I feel sorry for all these   32
people; they have been with me now for three days and have nothing to eat.
I do not want to send them away unfed; they might turn faint on the way.'
The disciples replied, 'Where in this lonely place can we find bread enough   33
to feed such a crowd?' 'How many loaves have you?' Jesus asked. 'Seven,'   34
they replied; 'and there are a few small fishes.' So he ordered the people   35
to sit down on the ground; then he took the seven loaves and the fishes,   36
and after giving thanks to God he broke them and gave to the disciples,
and the disciples gave to the people. They all ate to their hearts' content; and   37
the scraps left over, which they picked up, were enough to fill seven
baskets. Four thousand men shared in this meal, to say nothing of women   38
and children. He then dismissed the crowds, got into a boat, and went to   39
the neighbourhood of Magadan.

The Pharisees and Sadducees came, and to test him they asked him to   **16**
show them a sign from heaven. His answer was: *a* 'It is a wicked generation   2 4
that asks for a sign; and the only sign that will be given it is the sign of
Jonah.' So he went off and left them.

In crossing to the other side the disciples had forgotten to take bread   5
with them. So, when Jesus said to them, 'Beware, be on your guard against   6
the leaven of the Pharisees and Sadducees', they began to say among them-   7
selves, 'It is because we have brought no bread!' Knowing what was in their   8
minds, Jesus said to them: 'Why do you talk about bringing no bread?
Where is your faith? Do you not understand even yet? Do you not remem-   9
ber the five loaves for the five thousand, and how many basketfuls you

a Some witnesses here insert 'In the evening you say, "It will be fine weather, for the sky
is red"; (3) and in the morning you say, "It will be stormy today; the sky is red and lowering." You know how to interpret the appearance of the sky; can you not interpret the signs
of the times?'

10 picked up? Or the seven loaves for the four thousand, and how many
11 basketfuls you picked up? How can you fail to see that I was not speaking
about bread? Be on your guard, I said, against the leaven of the Pharisees
12 and Sadducees.' Then they understood: they were to be on their guard,
not against baker's leaven, but against the teaching of the Pharisees and
Sadducees.

13 WHEN HE CAME to the territory of Caesarea Philippi, Jesus asked his
14 disciples, 'Who do men say that the Son of Man is*a*?' They answered,
'Some say John the Baptist, others Elijah, others Jeremiah, or one of the
15 16 prophets.' 'And you,' he asked, 'who do you say I am?' Simon Peter
17 answered: 'You are the Messiah, the Son of the living God.' Then Jesus
said: 'Simon son of Jonah, you are favoured indeed! You did not learn
18 that from mortal man; it was revealed to you by my heavenly Father. And
I say this to you: You are Peter, the Rock; and on this rock I will build my
19 church, and the powers of death shall never conquer it.*b* I will give you
the keys of the kingdom of Heaven; what you forbid on earth shall be forbidden in heaven, and what you allow on earth shall be allowed in heaven.'
20 He then gave his disciples strict orders not to tell anyone that he was the
Messiah.

21 From that time Jesus began to make it clear to his disciples that he had
to go to Jerusalem, and there to suffer much from the elders, chief priests,
and doctors of the law; to be put to death and to be raised again on the third
22 day. At this Peter took him by the arm and began to rebuke him: 'Heaven
23 forbid!' he said. 'No, Lord, this shall never happen to you.' Then Jesus
turned and said to Peter, 'Away with you, Satan; you are a stumbling-
block to me. You think as men think, not as God thinks.'

24 Jesus then said to his disciples, 'If anyone wishes to be a follower of mine,
he must leave self behind; he must take up his cross and come with me.
25 Whoever cares for his own safety is lost; but if a man will let himself be lost
26 for my sake, he will find his true self. What will a man gain by winning
the whole world, at the cost of his true self? Or what can he give that will
27 buy that self back? For the Son of Man is to come in the glory of his Father
with his angels, and then he will give each man the due reward for what
28 he has done. I tell you this: there are some of those standing here who
will not taste death before they have seen the Son of Man coming in his
kingdom.'

17 SIX DAYS LATER Jesus took Peter, James, and John the brother of James,
2 and led them up a high mountain where they were alone; and in their
presence he was transfigured; his face shone like the sun, and his clothes
3 became white as the light. And they saw Moses and Elijah appear, con-
4 versing with him. Then Peter spoke: 'Lord,' he said, 'how good it is that
we are here! If you wish it, I will make three shelters here, one for you,
5 one for Moses, and one for Elijah.' While he was still speaking, a bright
cloud suddenly overshadowed them, and a voice called from the cloud:

a Some witnesses read that I, the Son of Man, am.   *b Or* the gates of death shall
never close upon it.

'This is my Son, my Beloved,^a on whom my favour rests; listen to him.'
At the sound of the voice the disciples fell on their faces in terror. Jesus then 6 7
came up to them, touched them, and said, 'Stand up; do not be afraid.'
And when they raised their eyes they saw no one, but only Jesus.   8

On their way down the mountain, Jesus enjoined them not to tell anyone 9
of the vision until the Son of Man had been raised from the dead. The 10
disciples put a question to him: 'Why then do our teachers say that Elijah
must come first?' He replied, 'Yes, Elijah will come and set everything 11
right. But I tell you that Elijah has already come, and they failed to recog- 12
nize him, and worked their will upon him; and in the same way the Son of
Man is to suffer at their hands.' Then the disciples understood that he 13
meant John the Baptist.

When they returned to the crowd, a man came up to Jesus, fell on his 14
knees before him, and said, 'Have pity, sir, on my son: he is an epileptic 15
and has bad fits, and he keeps falling about, often into the fire, often into
water. I brought him to your disciples, but they could not cure him.' Jesus 16 17
answered, 'What an unbelieving and perverse generation! How long shall
I be with you? How long must I endure you? Bring him here to me.' Jesus 18
then spoke sternly to the boy; the devil left him, and from that moment he
was cured.

Afterwards the disciples came to Jesus and asked him privately, 'Why 19
could not we cast it out?' He answered, 'Your faith is too small. I tell you 20
this: if you have faith no bigger even than a mustard-seed, you will say to
this mountain, "Move from here to there!", and it will move; nothing will
prove impossible for you.'^b

THEY WERE GOING about together in Galilee when Jesus said to them, 22
'The Son of Man is to be given up into the power of men, and they will kill 23
him; then on the third day he will be raised again.' And they were filled
with grief.

On their arrival at Capernaum the collectors of the temple-tax came up 24
to Peter and asked, 'Does your master not pay temple-tax?' 'He does', 25
said Peter. When he went indoors Jesus forestalled him by asking, 'What
do you think about this, Simon? From whom do earthly monarchs collect
tax or toll? From their own people, or from aliens?' 'From aliens', said 26
Peter. 'Why then,' said Jesus, 'their own people are exempt! But as we do 27
not want to cause offence, go and cast a line in the lake; take the first fish
that comes to the hook, open its mouth, and you will find a silver coin;
take that and pay it in; it will meet the tax for us both.'

At that time the disciples came to Jesus and asked, 'Who is the greatest **18**
in the kingdom of Heaven?' He called a child, set him in front of them, 2
and said, 'I tell you this: unless you turn round and become like children, 3
you will never enter the kingdom of Heaven. Let a man humble himself 4
till he is like this child, and he will be the greatest in the kingdom of Heaven.
Whoever receives one such child in my name receives me. But if a man is 5 6
a cause of stumbling to one of these little ones who have faith in me, it

---

^a *Or* This is my only Son.   ^b *Some witnesses add* (21) But there is no means of
casting out this sort but prayer and fasting.

would be better for him to have a millstone hung round his neck and be
7 drowned in the depths of the sea. Alas for the world that such causes of
stumbling arise! Come they must, but woe betide the man through whom
they come!

8   'If your hand or your foot is your undoing, cut it off and fling it away;
it is better for you to enter into life maimed or lame, than to keep two hands
9 or two feet and be thrown into the eternal fire. If it is your eye that is your
undoing, tear it out and fling it away; it is better to enter into life with one
eye than to keep both eyes and be thrown into the fires of hell.

10   'Never despise one of these little ones; I tell you, they have their guardian
angels in heaven, who look continually on the face of my heavenly Father. *a*
12   'What do you think? Suppose a man has a hundred sheep. If one of them
strays, does he not leave the other ninety-nine on the hillside and go in
13 search of the one that strayed? And if he should find it, I tell you this: he
is more delighted over that sheep than over the ninety-nine that never
14 strayed. In the same way, it is not your heavenly Father's will that one of
these little ones should be lost.

15   'If your brother commits a sin, *b* go and take the matter up with him,
strictly between yourselves, and if he listens to you, you have won your
16 brother over. If he will not listen, take one or two others with you, so that
all facts may be duly established on the evidence of two or three witnesses.
17 If he refuses to listen to them, report the matter to the congregation; and
if he will not listen even to the congregation, you must then treat him as you
would a pagan or a tax-gatherer.

18   'I tell you this: whatever you forbid on earth shall be forbidden in heaven,
and whatever you allow on earth shall be allowed in heaven.

19   'Again I tell you this: if two of you agree on earth about any request you
20 have to make, that request will be granted by my heavenly Father. For
where two or three have met together in my name, I am there among them.'

21   Then Peter came up and asked him, 'Lord, how often am I to forgive
22 my brother if he goes on wronging me? As many as seven times?' Jesus
replied, 'I do not say seven times; I say seventy times seven. *c*

23   'The kingdom of Heaven, therefore, should be thought of in this way:
There was once a king who decided to settle accounts with the men who
24 served him. At the outset there appeared before him a man whose debt
25 ran into millions. *d* Since he had no means of paying, his master ordered him
to be sold to meet the debt, with his wife, his children, and everything he
26 had. The man fell prostrate at his master's feet. "Be patient with me," he
27 said, "and I will pay in full"; and the master was so moved with pity that
28 he let the man go and remitted the debt. But no sooner had the man gone
out than he met a fellow-servant who owed him a few pounds; *e* and catching
hold of him he gripped him by the throat and said, "Pay me what you owe."
29 The man fell at his fellow-servant's feet, and begged him, "Be patient with
30 me, and I will pay you"; but he refused, and had him jailed until he should
31 pay the debt. The other servants were deeply distressed when they saw

---

a Some witnesses add (11) For the Son of Man came to save the lost.   *b Some witnesses insert* against you.   *c Or* seventy-seven times.   *d Literally* who owed
10,000 talents.   *e Literally* owed him 100 denarii.

what had happened, and they went to their master and told him the whole
story. He accordingly sent for the man. "You scoundrel!" he said to him; 32
"I remitted the whole of your debt when you appealed to me; were you 33
not bound to show your fellow-servant the same pity as I showed you?"
And so angry was the master that he condemned the man to torture until 34
he should pay the debt in full. And that is how my heavenly Father will 35
deal with you, unless you each forgive your brother from your hearts.'

W HEN JESUS HAD FINISHED this discourse he left Galilee and came into **19**
the region of Judaea across Jordan. Great crowds followed him, and he 2
healed them there.

Some Pharisees came and tested him by asking, 'Is it lawful for a man to 3
divorce his wife on any and every ground?'*a* He asked in return, 'Have you 4
never read that the Creator made them from the beginning male and
female?'; and he added, 'For this reason a man shall leave his father and 5
mother, and be made one with his wife; and the two shall become one flesh.
It follows that they are no longer two individuals: they are one flesh. What 6
God has joined together, man must not separate.' 'Why then', they ob- 7
jected, 'did Moses lay it down that a man might divorce his wife by note of
dismissal?' He answered, 'It was because your minds were closed that 8
Moses gave you permission to divorce your wives; but it was not like that
when all began. I tell you, if a man divorces his wife for any cause other 9
than unchastity, and marries another, he commits adultery.'*b*

The disciples said to him, 'If that is the position with husband and wife, 10
it is better not to marry.' To this he replied, 'That is something which not 11
everyone can accept, but only those for whom God has appointed it. For 12
while some are incapable of marriage because they were born so, or were
made so by men, there are others who have themselves renounced marriage
for the sake of the kingdom of Heaven. Let those accept it who can.'

They brought children for him to lay his hands on them with prayer. 13
The disciples rebuked them, but Jesus said to them, 'Let the children come 14
to me; do not try to stop them; for the kingdom of Heaven belongs to such
as these.' And he laid his hands on the children, and went his way. 15

And now a man came up and asked him, 'Master, what good must I do 16
to gain eternal life?' 'Good?' said Jesus. 'Why do you ask me about that? 17
One alone is good. But if you wish to enter into life, keep the commandments.' 'Which commandments?' he asked. Jesus answered, 'Do not 18
murder; do not commit adultery; do not steal; do not give false evidence;
honour your father and mother; and love your neighbour as yourself.' 19
The young man answered, 'I have kept all these. Where do I still fall short?' 20
Jesus said to him, 'If you wish to go the whole way, go, sell your possessions, 21
and give to the poor, and then you will have riches in heaven; and come,
follow me.' When the young man heard this, he went away with a heavy 22
heart; for he was a man of great wealth.

Jesus said to his disciples, 'I tell you this: a rich man will find it hard to 23
enter the kingdom of Heaven. I repeat, it is easier for a camel to pass through 24

a Or Is there any ground on which it is lawful for a man to divorce his wife?
b Some witnesses add And the man who marries a woman so divorced commits adultery.

the eye of a needle than for a rich man to enter the kingdom of God.'
25 The disciples were amazed to hear this. 'Then who can be saved?' they
26 asked. Jesus looked at them, and said, 'For men this is impossible; but
everything is possible for God.'

27   At this Peter said, 'We here have left everything to become your fol-
28 lowers. What will there be for us?' Jesus replied, 'I tell you this: in the world
that is to be, when the Son of Man is seated on his throne in heavenly splendour, you my followers will have thrones of your own, where you will sit
29 as judges of the twelve tribes of Israel. And anyone who has left brothers
or sisters, father, mother, or children, land or houses for the sake of my
30 name will be repaid many times over, and gain eternal life. But many who
are first will be last, and the last first.

20   'The kingdom of Heaven is like this. There was once a landowner who
2 went out early one morning to hire labourers for his vineyard; and after
3 agreeing to pay them the usual day's wage*a* he sent them off to work. Going
out three hours later he saw some more men standing idle in the market-
4 place. "Go and join the others in the vineyard," he said, "and I will pay
5 you a fair wage"; so off they went. At midday he went out again, and at
6 three in the afternoon, and made the same arrangement as before. An hour
before sunset he went out and found another group standing there; so he
said to them, "Why are you standing about like this all day with nothing
7 to do?" "Because no one has hired us", they replied; so he told them, "Go
8 and join the others in the vineyard." When evening fell, the owner of the
vineyard said to his steward, "Call the labourers and give them their pay,
9 beginning with those who came last and ending with the first." Those who
had started work an hour before sunset came forward, and were paid the
10 full day's wage.*b* When it was the turn of the men who had come first,
they expected something extra, but were paid the same amount as the
11 12 others. As they took it, they grumbled at their employer: "These late-
comers have done only one hour's work, yet you have put them on a level
13 with us, who have sweated the whole day long in the blazing sun!" The
owner turned to one of them and said, "My friend, I am not being unfair
14 to you. You agreed on the usual wage for the day,*c* did you not? Take your
15 pay and go home. I choose to pay the last man the same as you. Surely I am
free to do what I like with my own money. Why be jealous because I am
16 kind?" Thus will the last be first, and the first last.'

Challenge to Jerusalem

17 JESUS WAS JOURNEYING towards Jerusalem, and on the way he took
18 the Twelve aside, and said to them, 'We are now going to Jerusalem, and
the Son of Man will be given up to the chief priests and the doctors of the
19 law; they will condemn him to death and hand him over to the foreign
power, to be mocked and flogged and crucified, and on the third day he
will be raised to life again.'

a *Literally* one denarius for the day.   *b* *Literally* one denarius each.
c *Literally* You agreed on a denarius.

The mother of Zebedee's sons then came before him, with her sons. She 20
bowed low and begged a favour. 'What is it you wish?' asked Jesus. 'I want 21
you', she said, 'to give orders that in your kingdom my two sons here may
sit next to you, one at your right, and the other at your left.' Jesus turned 22
to the brothers and said, 'You do not understand what you are asking.
Can you drink the cup that I am to drink?' 'We can', they replied. Then he 23
said to them, 'You shall indeed share my cup; but to sit at my right or left
is not for me to grant; it is for those to whom it has already been assigned
by my Father.'

When the other ten heard this, they were indignant with the two 24
brothers. So Jesus called them to him and said, 'You know that in the world, 25
rulers lord it over their subjects, and their great men make them feel the
weight of authority; but it shall not be so with you. Among you, whoever 26
wants to be great must be your servant, and whoever wants to be first must 27
be the willing slave of all—like the Son of Man; he did not come to be 28
served, but to serve, and to give up his life as a ransom for many.'

As they were leaving Jericho he was followed by a great crowd of people. 29
At the roadside sat two blind men. When they heard it said that Jesus was 30
passing they shouted, 'Have pity on us, Son of David.' The people told 31
them sharply to be quiet. But they shouted all the more, 'Sir, have pity on
us; have pity on us, Son of David.' Jesus stopped and called the men. 32
'What do you want me to do for you?' he asked. 'Sir,' they answered, 'we 33
want our sight.' Jesus was deeply moved, and touched their eyes. At once 34
their sight came back, and they followed him.

THEY WERE NOW nearing Jerusalem; and when they reached Bethphage **21**
at the Mount of Olives, Jesus sent two disciples with these instructions: 2
'Go to the village opposite, where you will at once find a donkey tethered
with her foal beside her; untie them, and bring them to me. If anyone speaks 3
to you, say, "Our Master needs them"; and he will let you take them at
once.'[a] This was to fulfil the prophecy which says, 'Tell the daughter of 4 5
Zion, "Here is your king, who comes to you in gentleness, riding on an ass,
riding on the foal of a beast of burden."'

The disciples went and did as Jesus had directed, and brought the donkey 6 7
and her foal; they laid their cloaks on them and Jesus mounted. Crowds of 8
people carpeted the road with their cloaks, and some cut branches from the
trees to spread in his path. Then the crowd that went ahead and the others 9
that came behind raised the shout: 'Hosanna to the Son of David! Blessings
on him who comes in the name of the Lord! Hosanna in the heavens!'

When he entered Jerusalem the whole city went wild with excitement. 10
'Who is this?' people asked, and the crowd replied, 'This is the prophet 11
Jesus, from Nazareth in Galilee.'

Jesus then went into the temple and drove out all who were buying and 12
selling in the temple precincts; he upset the tables of the money-changers
and the seats of the dealers in pigeons; and said to them, 'Scripture says, 13
"My house shall be called a house of prayer"; but you are making it a
robbers' cave.'

　　a Or "Our Master needs them and will send them back straight away."

14 In the temple blind men and cripples came to him, and he healed them.
15 The chief priests and doctors of the law saw the wonderful things he did, and heard the boys in the temple shouting, 'Hosanna to the Son of David!',
16 and they asked him indignantly, 'Do you hear what they are saying?' Jesus answered, 'I do; have you never read that text, "Thou hast made
17 children and babes at the breast sound aloud thy praise"?' Then he left them and went out of the city to Bethany, where he spent the night.

18 19 Next morning on his way to the city he felt hungry; and seeing a fig-tree at the roadside he went up to it, but found nothing on it but leaves. He said to the tree, 'You shall never bear fruit any more!'; and the tree withered
20 away at once. The disciples were amazed at the sight. 'How is it', they asked,
21 'that the tree has withered so suddenly?' Jesus answered them, 'I tell you this: if only you have faith and have no doubts, you will do what has been done to the fig-tree; and more than that, you need only say to this mountain, "Be lifted from your place and hurled into the sea", and what you
22 say will be done. And whatever you pray for in faith you will receive.'

23 He entered the temple, and the chief priests and elders of the nation came to him with the question: 'By what authority are you acting like this?
24 Who gave you this authority?' Jesus replied, 'I have a question to ask you
25 too; answer it, and I will tell you by what authority I act. The baptism of John: was it from God, or from men?' This set them arguing among themselves: 'If we say, "from God", he will say, "Then why did you not
26 believe him?" But if we say, "from men", we are afraid of the people, for
27 they all take John for a prophet.' So they answered, 'We do not know.' And Jesus said: 'Then neither will I tell you by what authority I act.

28 'But what do you think about this? A man had two sons. He went to the
29 first, and said, "My boy, go and work today in the vineyard." "I will, sir",
30 the boy replied; but he never went. The father came to the second and said the same. "I will not", he replied, but afterwards he changed his mind
31 and went. Which of these two did as his father wished?' 'The second', they said. Then Jesus answered, 'I tell you this: tax-gatherers and prostitutes
32 are entering the kingdom of God ahead of you. For when John came to show you the right way to live, you did not believe him, but the tax-gatherers and prostitutes did; and even when you had seen that, you did not change your minds and believe him.

33 'Listen to another parable. There was a landowner who planted a vine-yard: he put a wall round it, hewed out a winepress, and built a watch-
34 tower; then he let it out to vine-growers and went abroad. When the vintage season approached, he sent his servants to the tenants to collect
35 the produce due to him. But they took his servants and thrashed one,
36 killed another, and stoned a third. Again, he sent other servants, this time
37 a larger number; and they did the same to them. At last he sent to them his
38 son. "They will respect my son", he said. But when they saw the son the tenants said to one another, "This is the heir; come on, let us kill him, and
39 get his inheritance." And they took him, flung him out of the vineyard,
40 and killed him. When the owner of the vineyard comes, how do you think
41 he will deal with those tenants?' 'He will bring those bad men to a bad end', they answered, 'and hand the vineyard over to other tenants, who will let

him have his share of the crop when the season comes.' Then Jesus said 42
to them, 'Have you never read in the scriptures: "The stone which the
builders rejected has become the main corner-stone. This is the Lord's
doing, and it is wonderful in our eyes"? Therefore, I tell you, the kingdom 43
of God will be taken away from you, and given to a nation that yields the
proper fruit.'ᵃ

When the chief priests and Pharisees heard his parables, they saw that 45
he was referring to them; they wanted to arrest him, but they were afraid 46
of the people, who looked on Jesus as a prophet.

THEN JESUS SPOKE to them again in parables: 'The kingdom of Heaven 22 1 2
is like this. There was a king who prepared a feast for his son's wedding;
but when he sent his servants to summon the guests he had invited, they 3
would not come. He sent others again, telling them to say to the guests, 4
"See now! I have prepared this feast for you. I have had my bullocks and
fatted beasts slaughtered; everything is ready; come to the wedding at
once." But they took no notice; one went off to his farm, another to his 5
business, and the others seized the servants, attacked them brutally, and 6
killed them. The king was furious; he sent troops to kill those murderers 7
and set their town on fire. Then he said to his servants, "The wedding-feast 8
is ready; but the guests I invited did not deserve the honour. Go out to the 9
main thoroughfares, and invite everyone you can find to the wedding."
The servants went out into the streets, and collected all they could find, 10
good and bad alike. So the hall was packed with guests.

'When the king came in to see the company at table, he observed one 11
man who was not dressed for a wedding. "My friend," said the king, "how 12
do you come to be here without your wedding clothes?" He had nothing
to say. The king then said to his attendants, "Bind him hand and foot; 13
turn him out into the dark, the place of wailing and grinding of teeth." For 14
though many are invited, few are chosen.'

THEN THE PHARISEES went away and agreed on a plan to trap him in his 15
own words. Some of their followers were sent to him in company with men 16
of Herod's party. They said, 'Master, you are an honest man, we know; you
teach in all honesty the way of life that God requires, truckling to no man,
whoever he may be. Give us your ruling on this: are we or are we not per- 17
mitted to pay taxes to the Roman Emperor?' Jesus was aware of their 18
malicious intention and said to them, 'You hypocrites! Why are you
trying to catch me out? Show me the money in which the tax is paid.' They 19
handed him a silver piece. Jesus asked, 'Whose head is this, and whose 20
inscription?' 'Caesar's', they replied. He said to them, 'Then pay Caesar 21
what is due to Caesar, and pay God what is due to God.' This answer took 22
them by surprise, and they went away and left him alone.

The same day Sadducees came to him, maintaining that there is no 23
resurrection. Their question was this: 'Master, Moses said, "If a man 24
should die childless, his brother shall marry the widow and carry on his

ᵃ *Some witnesses add* (44) Any man who falls on this stone will be dashed to pieces; and
if it falls on a man he will be crushed by it.

25 brother's family." Now we knew of seven brothers. The first married and
26 died, and as he was without issue his wife was left to his brother. The same
thing happened with the second, and the third, and so on with all seven.
27 28 Last of all the woman died. At the resurrection, then, whose wife will she
29 be, for they had all married her?' Jesus answered: 'You are mistaken,
30 because you know neither the scriptures nor the power of God. At the
resurrection men and women do not marry; they are like angels in heaven.
31 'But about the resurrection of the dead, have you never read what God
32 himself said to you: "I am the God of Abraham, the God of Isaac, and the
33 God of Jacob"? He is not God of the dead but of the living.' The people
heard what he said, and were astounded at his teaching.
34 Hearing that he had silenced the Sadducees, the Pharisees met together;
35 36 and one of their number *a* tested him with this question: 'Master, which is
37 the greatest commandment in the Law?' He answered, ' "Love the Lord
38 your God with all your heart, with all your soul, with all your mind." That
39 is the greatest commandment. It comes first. The second is like it: "Love
40 your neighbour as yourself." Everything in the Law and the prophets
hangs on these two commandments.'
41 42 Turning to the assembled Pharisees Jesus asked them, 'What is your
opinion about the Messiah? Whose son is he?' 'The son of David', they
43 replied. 'How then is it', he asked, 'that David by inspiration calls him
44 "Lord"? For he says, "The Lord said to my Lord, 'Sit at my right hand
45 until I put your enemies under your feet.' " If David calls him "Lord",
46 how can he be David's son?' Not a man could say a word in reply; and from
that day forward no one dared ask him another question.

23 1 2 JESUS THEN ADDRESSED the people and his disciples in these words:
3 'The doctors of the law and the Pharisees sit in the chair of Moses; therefore
do what they tell you; pay attention to their words. But do not follow their
4 practice; for they say one thing and do another. They make up heavy packs
and pile them on men's shoulders, but will not raise a finger to lift the load
5 themselves. Whatever they do is done for show. They go about with broad
6 phylacteries *b* and with large tassels on their robes; they like to have places
7 of honour at feasts and the chief seats in synagogues, to be greeted respect-
fully in the street, and to be addressed as "rabbi".
8 'But you must not be called "rabbi"; for you have one Rabbi, and you are
9 all brothers. Do not call any man on earth "father"; for you have one Father,
10 and he is in heaven. Nor must you be called "teacher"; you have one
11 12 Teacher, the Messiah. The greatest among you must be your servant. For
whoever exalts himself will be humbled; and whoever humbles himself
will be exalted.
13 'Alas, alas for you, lawyers and Pharisees, hypocrites that you are! You
shut the door of the kingdom of Heaven in men's faces; you do not enter
yourselves, and when others are entering, you stop them. *c*

---

a *Some witnesses insert* a lawyer.   *b* *See Deuteronomy 6. 8–9 and Exodus 13. 9.*
c *Some witnesses add* (14) Alas for you, lawyers and Pharisees, hypocrites! You eat up
the property of widows, while you say long prayers for appearance' sake. You will receive
the severest sentence.

'Alas for you, lawyers and Pharisees, hypocrites! You travel over sea 15
and land to win one convert; and when you have won him you make him
twice as fit for hell as you are yourselves.

'Alas for you, blind guides! You say, "If a man swears by the sanctuary, 16
that is nothing; but if he swears by the gold in the sanctuary, he is bound
by his oath." Blind fools! Which is the more important, the gold, or the 17
sanctuary which sanctifies the gold? Or you say, "If a man swears by the 18
altar, that is nothing; but if he swears by the offering that lies on the altar,
he is bound by his oath." What blindness! Which is the more important, the 19
offering, or the altar which sanctifies it? To swear by the altar, then, is to 20
swear both by the altar and by whatever lies on it; to swear by the sanctuary 21
is to swear both by the sanctuary and by him who dwells there; and to swear 22
by heaven is to swear both by the throne of God and by him who sits
upon it.

'Alas for you, lawyers and Pharisees, hypocrites! You pay tithes of mint 23
and dill and cummin; but you have overlooked the weightier demands of
the Law, justice, mercy, and good faith. It is these you should have practised, without neglecting the others. Blind guides! You strain off a midge, 24
yet gulp down a camel!

'Alas for you, lawyers and Pharisees, hypocrites! You clean the outside of 25
cup and dish, which you have filled inside by robbery and self-indulgence!
Blind Pharisee! Clean the inside of the cup first; then the outside will be 26
clean also.

'Alas for you, lawyers and Pharisees, hypocrites! You are like tombs 27
covered with whitewash; they look well from outside, but inside they are
full of dead men's bones and all kinds of filth. So it is with you: outside you 28
look like honest men, but inside you are brim-full of hypocrisy and crime.

'Alas for you, lawyers and Pharisees, hypocrites! You build up the tombs 29
of the prophets and embellish the monuments of the saints, and you say, 30
"If we had been alive in our fathers' time, we should never have taken part
with them in the murder of the prophets." So you acknowledge that you 31
are the sons of the men who killed the prophets. Go on then, finish off what 32
your fathers began! *a*

'You snakes, you vipers' brood, how can you escape being condemned 33
to hell? I send you therefore prophets, sages, and teachers; some of them 34
you will kill and crucify, others you will flog in your synagogues and hound
from city to city. And so, on you will fall the guilt of all the innocent blood 35
spilt on the ground, from innocent Abel to Zechariah son of Berachiah,
whom you murdered between the sanctuary and the altar. Believe me, this 36
generation will bear the guilt of it all.

'O Jerusalem, Jerusalem, the city that murders the prophets and stones 37
the messengers sent to her! How often have I longed to gather your
children, as a hen gathers her brood under her wings; but you would not
let me. Look, look! there is your temple, forsaken by God.*b c* And I tell 38 39
you, you shall never see me until the time when you say, "Blessings on him
who comes in the name of the Lord." '

a Or You too must come up to your fathers' standards.   *b Or* Look, your home is
desolate.   *c Some witnesses add* and laid waste.

Prophecies and warnings

24 JESUS WAS LEAVING the temple when his disciples came and pointed to
2 the temple buildings. He answered, 'Yes, look at it all. I tell you this:
not one stone will be left upon another; all will be thrown down.'

3 When he was sitting on the Mount of Olives the disciples came to speak
to him privately. 'Tell us,' they said, 'when will this happen? And what will
be the signal for your coming and the end of the age?'

4 5 Jesus replied: 'Take care that no one misleads you. For many will come
claiming my name and saying, "I am the Messiah"; and many will be
6 misled by them. The time is coming when you will hear the noise of battle
near at hand and the news of battles far away; see that you are not alarmed.
7 Such things are bound to happen; but the end is still to come. For nation
will make war upon nation, kingdom upon kingdom; there will be famines
8 and earthquakes in many places. With all these things the birth-pangs of
the new age begin.

9 'You will then be handed over for punishment and execution; and men
10 of all nations will hate you for your allegiance to me. Many will fall from
11 their faith; they will betray one another and hate one another. Many false
12 prophets will arise, and will mislead many; and as lawlessness spreads,
13 men's love for one another will grow cold. But the man who holds out to the
14 end will be saved. And this gospel of the Kingdom will be proclaimed
throughout the earth as a testimony to all nations; and then the end will
come.

15 'So when you see "the abomination of desolation", of which the prophet
16 Daniel spoke, standing in the holy place (let the reader understand), then
17 those who are in Judaea must take to the hills. If a man is on the roof, he
18 must not come down to fetch his goods from the house; if in the field, he
19 must not turn back for his coat. Alas for women with child in those days,
20 and for those who have children at the breast! Pray that it may not be
21 winter when you have to make your escape, or Sabbath. It will be a time of
great distress; there has never been such a time from the beginning of the
22 world until now, and will never be again. If that time of troubles were not
cut short, no living thing could survive; but for the sake of God's chosen it
will be cut short.

23 'Then, if anyone says to you, "Look, here is the Messiah", or, "There he
24 is", do not believe it. Impostors will come claiming to be messiahs or
prophets, and they will produce great signs and wonders to mislead even
25 God's chosen, if such a thing were possible. See, I have forewarned you.
26 If they tell you, "He is there in the wilderness", do not go out; or if they
27 say, "He is there in the inner room", do not believe it. Like lightning
from the east, flashing as far as the west, will be the coming of the Son
of Man.

28 'Wherever the corpse is, there the vultures will gather.

29 'As soon as the distress of those days has passed, the sun will be darkened,
the moon will not give her light, the stars will fall from the sky, the celestial
30 powers will be shaken. Then will appear in heaven the sign that heralds

the Son of Man. All the peoples of the world will make lamentation, and they will see the Son of Man coming on the clouds of heaven with great power and glory. With a trumpet blast he will send out his angels, and they 31 will gather his chosen from the four winds, from the farthest bounds of heaven on every side.

'Learn a lesson from the fig-tree. When its tender shoots appear and 32 are breaking into leaf, you know that summer is near. In the same way, 33 when you see all these things, you may know that the end is near,[a] at the very door. I tell you this: the present generation will live to see it all. Heaven 34 35 and earth will pass away; my words will never pass away.

'But about that day and hour no one knows, not even the angels in 36 heaven, not even the Son; only the Father.

'As things were in Noah's days, so will they be when the Son of Man 37 comes. In the days before the flood they ate and drank and married, until 38 the day that Noah went into the ark, and they knew nothing until the flood 39 came and swept them all away. That is how it will be when the Son of Man comes. Then there will be two men in the field; one will be taken, the other 40 left; two women grinding at the mill; one will be taken, the other left. 41

'Keep awake, then; for you do not know on what day your Lord is to 42 come. Remember, if the householder had known at what time of night the 43 burglar was coming, he would have kept awake and not have let his house be broken into. Hold yourselves ready, therefore, because the Son of Man 44 will come at the time you least expect him.

'Who is the trusty servant, the sensible man charged by his master to 45 manage his household staff and issue their rations at the proper time? Happy that servant who is found at his task when his master comes! I tell 46 47 you this: he will be put in charge of all his master's property. But if he is 48 a bad servant and says to himself, "The master is a long time coming", and 49 begins to bully the other servants and to eat and drink with his drunken friends, then the master will arrive on a day that servant does not expect, 50 at a time he does not know, and will cut him in pieces. Thus he will find his 51 place among the hypocrites, where there is wailing and grinding of teeth.

'When that day comes, the kingdom of Heaven will be like this. There 25 were ten girls, who took their lamps and went out to meet the bridegroom. Five of them were foolish, and five prudent; when the foolish ones took 2 3 their lamps, they took no oil with them, but the others took flasks of oil 4 with their lamps. As the bridegroom was late in coming they all dozed off 5 to sleep. But at midnight a cry was heard: "Here is the bridegroom! Come 6 out to meet him." With that the girls all got up and trimmed their lamps. 7 The foolish said to the prudent, "Our lamps are going out; give us some of 8 your oil." "No," they said; "there will never be enough for all of us. You 9 had better go to the shop and buy some for yourselves." While they were 10 away the bridegroom arrived; those who were ready went in with him to the wedding; and the door was shut. And then the other five came back. 11 "Sir, sir," they cried, "open the door for us." But he answered, "I declare, 12 I do not know you." Keep awake then; for you never know the day or the 13 hour.

a Or that he is near.

14 'It is like a man going abroad, who called his servants and put his capital
15 in their hands; to one he gave five bags of gold, to another two, to another
16 one, each according to his capacity. Then he left the country. The man who
    had the five bags went at once and employed them in business, and made
17 18 a profit of five bags, and the man who had the two bags made two. But the
    man who had been given one bag of gold went off and dug a hole in the
19 ground, and hid his master's money. A long time afterwards their master
20 returned, and proceeded to settle accounts with them. The man who had
    been given the five bags of gold came and produced the five he had made:
    "Master," he said, "you left five bags with me; look, I have made five more."
21 "Well done, my good and trusty servant!" said the master. "You have
    proved trustworthy in a small way; I will now put you in charge of some-
22 thing big. Come and share your master's delight." The man with the two
    bags then came and said, "Master, you left two bags with me; look, I have
23 made two more." "Well done, my good and trusty servant!" said the
    master. "You have proved trustworthy in a small way; I will now put you
24 in charge of something big. Come and share your master's delight." Then
    the man who had been given one bag came and said, "Master, I knew you
    to be a hard man: you reap where you have not sown, you gather where you
25 have not scattered; so I was afraid, and I went and hid your gold in the
26 ground. Here it is—you have what belongs to you." "You lazy rascal!"
    said the master. "You knew that I reap where I have not sown, and gather
27 where I have not scattered? Then you ought to have put my money on
28 deposit, and on my return I should have got it back with interest. Take the
29 bag of gold from him, and give it to the one with the ten bags. For the man
    who has will always be given more, till he has enough and to spare; and
30 the man who has not will forfeit even what he has. Fling the useless servant
    out into the dark, the place of wailing and grinding of teeth!"
31   'When the Son of Man comes in his glory and all the angels with him,
32 he will sit in state on his throne, with all the nations gathered before him.
    He will separate men into two groups, as a shepherd separates the sheep
33 from the goats, and he will place the sheep on his right hand and the goats
34 on his left. Then the king will say to those on his right hand, "You have my
    Father's blessing; come, enter and possess the kingdom that has been
35 ready for you since the world was made. For when I was hungry, you gave
    me food; when thirsty, you gave me drink; when I was a stranger you took
36 me into your home, when naked you clothed me; when I was ill you came
37 to my help, when in prison you visited me." Then the righteous will reply,
    "Lord, when was it that we saw you hungry and fed you, or thirsty and
38 gave you drink, a stranger and took you home, or naked and clothed you?
39 40 When did we see you ill or in prison, and come to visit you?" And the king
    will answer, "I tell you this: anything you did for one of my brothers here,
41 however humble, you did for me." Then he will say to those on his left
    hand, "The curse is upon you; go from my sight to the eternal fire that is
42 ready for the devil and his angels. For when I was hungry you gave me
43 nothing to eat, when thirsty nothing to drink; when I was a stranger you
    gave me no home, when naked you did not clothe me; when I was ill and in
44 prison you did not come to my help." And they too will reply, "Lord, when

was it that we saw you hungry or thirsty or a stranger or naked or ill or in prison, and did nothing for you?" And he will answer, "I tell you this: 45 anything you did not do for one of these, however humble, you did not do for me." And they will go away to eternal punishment, but the righteous 46 will enter eternal life.'

The final conflict

WHEN JESUS HAD FINISHED this discourse he said to his disciples, **26** 'You know that in two days' time it will be Passover, and the Son 2 of Man is to be handed over for crucifixion.'

Then the chief priests and the elders of the nation met in the palace of the 3 High Priest, Caiaphas; and there they conferred together on a scheme to 4 have Jesus arrested by some trick and put to death. 'It must not be during 5 the festival,' they said, 'or there may be rioting among the people.'

JESUS WAS AT BETHANY in the house of Simon the leper, when a woman 6 7 came to him with a small bottle of fragrant oil, very costly; and as he sat at table she began to pour it over his head. The disciples were indignant 8 when they saw it. 'Why this waste?' they said; 'it could have been sold for 9 a good sum and the money given to the poor.' Jesus was aware of this, and 10 said to them, 'Why must you make trouble for the woman? It is a fine thing she has done for me. You have the poor among you always; but you will 11 not always have me. When she poured this oil on my body it was her way of 12 preparing me for burial. I tell you this: wherever in all the world this gospel 13 is proclaimed, what she has done will be told as her memorial.'

THEN ONE OF THE TWELVE, the man called Judas Iscariot, went to the 14 chief priests and said, 'What will you give me to betray him to you?' 15 They weighed him out*a* thirty silver pieces. From that moment he began 16 to look out for an opportunity to betray him.

On the first day of Unleavened Bread the disciples came to ask Jesus, 17 'Where would you like us to prepare for your Passover supper?' He 18 answered, 'Go to a certain man in the city, and tell him, "The Master says, 'My appointed time is near; I am to keep Passover with my disciples at your house.'"' The disciples did as Jesus directed them and prepared for 19 Passover.

In the evening he sat down with the twelve disciples; and during supper 20 21 he said, 'I tell you this: one of you will betray me.' In great distress they 22 exclaimed one after the other, 'Can you mean me, Lord?' He answered, 23 'One who has dipped his hand into this bowl with me will betray me. The 24 Son of Man is going the way appointed for him in the scriptures; but alas for that man by whom the Son of Man is betrayed! It would be better for that man if he had never been born.' Then Judas spoke, the one who was 25 to betray him: 'Rabbi, can you mean me?' Jesus replied, 'The words are yours.'*b*

a Or agreed to pay him . . .   *b Or* It is as you say.

26 During supper Jesus took bread, and having said the blessing he broke it
and gave it to the disciples with the words: 'Take this and eat; this is my
27 body.' Then he took a cup, and having offered thanks to God he gave it to
28 them with the words: 'Drink from it, all of you. For this is my blood, the
29 blood of the covenant, shed for many for the forgiveness of sins. I tell you,
never again shall I drink from the fruit of the vine until that day when I
drink it new with you in the kingdom of my Father.'

30 After singing the Passover Hymn, they went out to the Mount of Olives.
31 Then Jesus said to them, 'Tonight you will all fall from your faith on my
account; for it stands written: "I will strike the shepherd down and the
32 sheep of his flock will be scattered." But after I am raised again, I will go on
33 before you into Galilee.' Peter replied, 'Everyone else may fall away on
34 your account, but I never will.' Jesus said to him, 'I tell you, tonight before
35 the cock crows you will disown me three times.' Peter said, 'Even if I must
die with you, I will never disown you.' And all the disciples said the same.

36 JESUS THEN CAME with his disciples to a place called Gethsemane. He
37 said to them, 'Sit here while I go over there to pray.' He took with him
Peter and the two sons of Zebedee. Anguish and dismay came over him,
38 and he said to them, 'My heart is ready to break with grief. Stop here, and
39 stay awake with me.' He went on a little, fell on his face in prayer, and said,
'My Father, if it is possible, let this cup pass me by. Yet not as I will, but
as thou wilt.'

40 He came to the disciples and found them asleep; and he said to Peter,
41 'What! Could none of you stay awake with me one hour? Stay awake, and
pray that you may be spared the test. The spirit is willing, but the flesh is
weak.'

42 He went away a second time, and prayed: 'My Father, if it is not possible
43 for this cup to pass me by without my drinking it, thy will be done.' He came
44 again and found them asleep, for their eyes were heavy. So he left them
and went away again; and he prayed the third time, using the same words
as before.

45 Then he came to the disciples and said to them, 'Still sleeping? Still
taking your ease? The hour has come! The Son of Man is betrayed to
46 sinful men. Up, let us go forward; the traitor is upon us.'

47 While he was still speaking, Judas, one of the Twelve, appeared; with
him was a great crowd armed with swords and cudgels, sent by the chief
48 priests and the elders of the nation. The traitor gave them this sign: 'The
49 one I kiss is your man; seize him'; and stepping forward at once, he said,
50 'Hail, Rabbi!', and kissed him. Jesus replied, 'Friend, do what you are here
to do.'[a] They then came forward, seized Jesus, and held him fast.

51 At that moment one of those with Jesus reached for his sword and drew
52 it, and he struck at the High Priest's servant and cut off his ear. But Jesus
said to him, 'Put up your sword. All who take the sword die by the sword.
53 Do you suppose that I cannot appeal to my Father, who would at once
54 send to my aid more than twelve legions of angels? But how then could the
scriptures be fulfilled, which say that this must be?'

[a] *Or* Friend, what are you here for?

At the same time Jesus spoke to the crowd: 'Do you take me for a bandit, 55
that you have come out with swords and cudgels to arrest me? Day after
day I sat teaching in the temple, and you did not lay hands on me. But this 56
has all happened to fulfil what the prophets wrote.'

Then the disciples all deserted him and ran away.

JESUS WAS LED OFF under arrest to the house of Caiaphas the High Priest, 57
where the lawyers and elders were assembled. Peter followed him at a 58
distance till he came to the High Priest's courtyard, and going in he sat
down there among the attendants, meaning to see the end of it all.

The chief priests and the whole Council tried to find some allegation 59
against Jesus on which a death-sentence could be based; but they failed 60
to find one, though many came forward with false evidence. Finally two
men alleged that he had said, 'I can pull down the temple of God, and 61
rebuild it in three days.' At this the High Priest rose and said to him, 'Have 62
you no answer to the charge that these witnesses bring against you?' But 63
Jesus kept silence. The High Priest then said, 'By the living God I charge
you to tell us: Are you the Messiah, the Son of God?' Jesus replied, 'The 64
words are yours.*a* But I tell you this: from now on, you will see the Son of
Man seated at the right hand of God*b* and coming on the clouds of heaven.'
At these words the High Priest tore his robes and exclaimed, 'Blasphemy! 65
Need we call further witnesses? You have heard the blasphemy. What is 66
your opinion?' 'He is guilty,' they answered; 'he should die.'

Then they spat in his face and struck him with their fists; and others 67
said, as they beat him, 'Now, Messiah, if you are a prophet, tell us who 68
hit you.'

Meanwhile Peter was sitting outside in the courtyard when a serving- 69
maid accosted him and said, 'You were there too with Jesus the Galilean.'
Peter denied it in face of them all. 'I do not know what you mean', he said. 70
He then went out to the gateway, where another girl, seeing him, said to 71
the people there, 'This fellow was with Jesus of Nazareth.' Once again he 72
denied it, saying with an oath, 'I do not know the man.' Shortly afterwards 73
the bystanders came up and said to Peter, 'Surely you are another of them;
your accent gives you away!' At this he broke into curses and declared 74
with an oath: 'I do not know the man.' At that moment a cock crew; and 75
Peter remembered how Jesus had said, 'Before the cock crows you will
disown me three times.' He went outside, and wept bitterly.

WHEN MORNING CAME, the chief priests and the elders of the nation met **27**
in conference to plan the death of Jesus. They then put him in chains and 2
led him away, to hand him over to Pilate, the Roman Governor.

When Judas the traitor saw that Jesus had been condemned, he was 3
seized with remorse, and returned the thirty silver pieces to the chief
priests and elders. 'I have sinned,' he said; 'I have brought an innocent 4
man to his death.' But they said, 'What is that to us? See to that yourself.'
So he threw the money down in the temple and left them, and went and 5
hanged himself.

a Or It is as you say.   *b Literally* of the Power.

6 Taking up the money, the chief priests argued: 'This cannot be put into
7 the temple fund; it is blood-money.' So after conferring they used it to
8 buy the Potter's Field, as a burial-place for foreigners. This explains the
9 name 'Blood Acre', by which that field has been known ever since; and in
   this way fulfilment was given to the prophetic utterance of Jeremiah:
   'They took*a* the thirty silver pieces, the price set on a man's head (for that
10 was his price among the Israelites), and gave the money for the potter's field,
   as the Lord directed me.'

11 Jesus was now brought before the Governor; and as he stood there the
   Governor asked him, 'Are you the king of the Jews?' 'The words are
12 yours',*b* said Jesus; and to the charges laid against him by the chief priests
13 and elders he made no reply. Then Pilate said to him, 'Do you not hear all
14 this evidence that is brought against you?'; but he still refused to answer
   one word, to the Governor's great astonishment.

15 At the festival season it was the Governor's custom to release one
16 prisoner chosen by the people. There was then in custody a man of some
17 notoriety, called Jesus*c* Bar-Abbas. When they were assembled Pilate
   said to them, 'Which would you like me to release to you—Jesus*c* Bar-
18 Abbas, or Jesus called Messiah?' For he knew that it was out of malice
   that they had brought Jesus before him.

19 While Pilate was sitting in court a message came to him from his wife:
   'Have nothing to do with that innocent man; I was much troubled on his
   account in my dreams last night.'

20 Meanwhile the chief priests and elders had persuaded the crowd to ask
21 for the release of Bar-Abbas and to have Jesus put to death. So when the
   Governor asked, 'Which of the two do you wish me to release to you?',
22 they said, 'Bar-Abbas.' 'Then what am I to do with Jesus called Messiah?'
23 asked Pilate; and with one voice they answered, 'Crucify him!' 'Why,
   what harm has he done?' Pilate asked; but they shouted all the louder,
   'Crucify him!'

24 Pilate could see that nothing was being gained, and a riot was starting;
   so he took water and washed his hands in full view of the people, saying,
25 'My hands are clean of this man's blood; see to that yourselves.' And with
26 one voice the people cried, 'His blood be on us, and on our children.' He
   then released Bar-Abbas to them; but he had Jesus flogged, and handed
   him over to be crucified.

27 PILATE'S SOLDIERS then took Jesus into the Governor's headquarters,
28 where they collected the whole company round him. They stripped him
29 and dressed him in a scarlet mantle; and plaiting a crown of thorns they
   placed it on his head, with a cane in his right hand. Falling on their knees
30 before him they jeered at him: 'Hail, King of the Jews!' They spat on him,
31 and used the cane to beat him about the head. When they had finished their
   mockery, they took off the mantle and dressed him in his own clothes.

32 Then they led him away to be crucified. On their way out they met a man
   from Cyrene, Simon by name, and pressed him into service to carry his
   cross.

a Or I took.   *b Or* It is as you say.   *c Some witnesses omit* Jesus.

So they came to a place called Golgotha (which means 'Place of a skull') 33
and there he was offered a draught of wine mixed with gall; but when he 34
had tasted it he would not drink.

After fastening him to the cross they divided his clothes among them by 35
casting lots, and then sat down there to keep watch. Over his head was 36 37
placed the inscription giving the charge: 'This is Jesus the king of the Jews.'

Two bandits were crucified with him, one on his right and the other on 38
his left.

The passers-by hurled abuse at him: they wagged their heads and cried, 39 40
'You would pull the temple down, would you, and build it in three days?
Come down from the cross and save yourself, if you are indeed the Son of
God.' So too the chief priests with the lawyers and elders mocked at him: 41
'He saved others,' they said, 'but he cannot save himself. King of Israel, 42
indeed! Let him come down now from the cross, and then we will believe
him. Did he trust in God? Let God rescue him, if he wants him—for he 43
said he was God's Son.' Even the bandits who were crucified with him 44
taunted him in the same way.

From midday a darkness fell over the whole land, which lasted until 45
three in the afternoon; and about three Jesus cried aloud, '*Eli, Eli, lema* 46
sabachthani?', which means, 'My God, my God, why hast thou forsaken
me?' Some of the bystanders, on hearing this, said, 'He is calling Elijah.' 47
One of them ran at once and fetched a sponge, which he soaked in sour 48
wine, and held it to his lips on the end of a cane. But the others said, 49
'Let us see if Elijah will come to save him.'

Jesus again gave a loud cry, and breathed his last. At that moment the 50 51
curtain of the temple was torn in two from top to bottom. There was an
earthquake, the rocks split and the graves opened, and many of God's 52
saints were raised from sleep; and coming out of their graves after his 53
resurrection they entered the Holy City, where many saw them. And when 54
the centurion and his men who were keeping watch over Jesus saw the
earthquake and all that was happening, they were filled with awe, and they
said, 'Truly this man was a son of God.'*a*

A NUMBER OF WOMEN were also present, watching from a distance; they 55
had followed Jesus from Galilee and waited on him. Among them were 56
Mary of Magdala, Mary the mother of James and Joseph, and the mother
of the sons of Zebedee.

When evening fell, there came a man of Arimathaea, Joseph by name, 57
who was a man of means, and had himself become a disciple of Jesus. He 58
approached Pilate, and asked for the body of Jesus; and Pilate gave orders
that he should have it. Joseph took the body, wrapped it in a clean linen 59
sheet, and laid it in his own unused tomb, which he had cut out of the rock; 60
he then rolled a large stone against the entrance, and went away. Mary of 61
Magdala was there, and the other Mary, sitting opposite the grave.

Next day, the morning after that Friday, the chief priests and the 62
Pharisees came in a body to Pilate. 'Your Excellency,' they said, 'we recall 63
how that impostor said while he was still alive, "I am to be raised again

a Or the Son of God.

64 after three days." So will you give orders for the grave to be made secure
until the third day? Otherwise his disciples may come, steal the body,
and then tell the people that he has been raised from the dead; and the final
65 deception will be worse than the first.' 'You may have your guard,' said
66 Pilate; 'go and make it secure as best you can.' So they went and made the
grave secure; they sealed the stone, and left the guard in charge.

28 THE SABBATH WAS OVER, and it was about daybreak on Sunday, when
2 Mary of Magdala and the other Mary came to look at the grave. Suddenly
there was a violent earthquake; an angel of the Lord descended from
heaven; he came to the stone and rolled it away, and sat himself down on it.
3 4 His face shone like lightning; his garments were white as snow. At the sight
of him the guards shook with fear and lay like the dead.
5 The angel then addressed the women: 'You', he said, 'have nothing to
6 fear. I know you are looking for Jesus who was crucified. He is not here; he
has been raised again, as he said he would be. Come and see the place where
7 he was laid, and then go quickly and tell his disciples: "He has been raised
from the dead and is going on before you into Galilee; there you will see
him." That is what I had to tell you.'
8 They hurried away from the tomb in awe and great joy, and ran to tell
9 the disciples. Suddenly Jesus was there in their path. He gave them his
greeting, and they came up and clasped his feet, falling prostrate before
10 him. Then Jesus said to them, 'Do not be afraid. Go and take word to my
brothers that they are to leave for Galilee. They will see me there.'
11 The women had started on their way when some of the guard went into
the city and reported to the chief priests everything that had happened.
12 After meeting with the elders and conferring together, the chief priests
13 offered the soldiers a substantial bribe and told them to say, 'His disciples
14 came by night and stole the body while we were asleep.' They added, 'If
this should reach the Governor's ears, we will put matters right with him
15 and see that you do not suffer.' So they took the money and did as they were
told. This story became widely known, and is current in Jewish circles to
this day.
16 The eleven disciples made their way to Galilee, to the mountain where
17 Jesus had told them to meet him. When they saw him, they fell prostrate
18 before him, though some were doubtful. Jesus then came up and spoke to
them. He said: 'Full authority in heaven and on earth has been committed
19 to me. Go forth therefore and make all nations my disciples; baptize men
everywhere in the name of the Father and the Son and the Holy Spirit,
20 and teach them to observe all that I have commanded you. And be assured,
I am with you always, to the end of time.'

THE GOSPEL ACCORDING TO
MARK

The coming of Christ

1 HERE BEGINS THE GOSPEL of Jesus Christ the Son of God.[a]
2 In the prophet Isaiah it stands written: 'Here is my herald whom I send on ahead of you, and he will prepare your way. 3 A voice crying aloud in the wilderness, "Prepare a way for the Lord; clear a straight path for him."' 4 And so it was that John the Baptist appeared in the wilderness proclaiming a baptism in token of repentance, for the forgiveness of sins; 5 and they flocked to him from the whole Judaean country-side and the city of Jerusalem, and were baptized by him in the River Jordan, confessing their sins.

6 John was dressed in a rough coat of camel's hair, with a leather belt round his waist, and he fed on locusts and wild honey. 7 His proclamation ran: 'After me comes one who is mightier than I. I am not fit to unfasten his shoes. 8 I have baptized you with water; he will baptize you with the Holy Spirit.'

9 It happened at this time that Jesus came from Nazareth in Galilee and was baptized in the Jordan by John. 10 At the moment when he came up out of the water, he saw the heavens torn open and the Spirit, like a dove, descending upon him. 11 And a voice spoke from heaven: 'Thou art my Son, my Beloved;[b] on thee my favour rests.'

12 13 Thereupon the Spirit sent him away into the wilderness, and there he remained for forty days tempted by Satan. He was among the wild beasts; and the angels waited on him.

In Galilee: success and opposition

14 AFTER JOHN HAD BEEN ARRESTED, Jesus came into Galilee proclaiming the Gospel of God: 15 'The time has come; the kingdom of God is upon you; repent, and believe the Gospel.'

16 Jesus was walking by the Sea of Galilee when he saw Simon and his brother Andrew on the lake at work with a casting-net; for they were fishermen. 17 Jesus said to them, 'Come with me, and I will make you fishers of men.' 18 And at once they left their nets and followed him.

19 When he had gone a little further he saw James son of Zebedee and his brother John, who were in the boat overhauling their nets. 20 He called them;

---

[a] *Some witnesses omit* the Son of God.   [b] *Or* Thou art my only Son.

and, leaving their father Zebedee in the boat with the hired men, they went
off to follow him.

21 They came to Capernaum, and on the Sabbath he went to synagogue and
22 began to teach. The people were astounded at his teaching, for, unlike the
23 doctors of the law, he taught with a note of authority. Now there was a man
24 in the synagogue possessed by an unclean spirit. He shrieked: 'What do
you want with us, Jesus of Nazareth? Have you[a] come to destroy us?
25 I know who you are—the Holy One of God.' Jesus rebuked him: 'Be silent',
26 he said, 'and come out of him.' And the unclean spirit threw the man into
27 convulsions and with a loud cry left him. They were all dumbfounded and
began to ask one another, 'What is this? A new kind of teaching! He speaks
with authority. When he gives orders, even the unclean spirits submit.'
28 The news spread rapidly, and he was soon spoken of all over the district of
Galilee.

29 On leaving the synagogue they went straight to the house of Simon and
30 Andrew; and James and John went with them. Simon's mother-in-law
31 was ill in bed with fever. They told him about her at once. He came
forward, took her by the hand, and helped her to her feet. The fever left
her and she waited upon them.

32 That evening after sunset they brought to him all who were ill or pos-
33 34 sessed by devils; and the whole town was there, gathered at the door. He
healed many who suffered from various diseases, and drove out many
devils. He would not let the devils speak, because they knew who he was.

35 Very early next morning he got up and went out. He went away to a lonely
36 spot and remained there in prayer. But Simon and his companions searched
37 38 him out, found him, and said, 'They are all looking for you.' He answered,
'Let us move on to the country towns in the neighbourhood; I have to
39 proclaim my message there also; that is what I came out to do.' So all
through Galilee he went, preaching in the synagogues and casting out the
devils.

40 Once he was approached by a leper, who knelt before him begging his
41 help. 'If only you will,' said the man, 'you can cleanse me.' In warm
indignation Jesus stretched out his hand,[b] touched him, and said, 'Indeed
42 I will; be clean again.' The leprosy left him immediately, and he was clean.
43 44 Then he dismissed him with this stern warning: 'Be sure you say nothing
to anybody. Go and show yourself to the priest, and make the offering
45 laid down by Moses for your cleansing; that will certify the cure.' But the
man went out and made the whole story public; he spread it far and wide,
until Jesus could no longer show himself in any town, but stayed outside in
the open country. Even so, people kept coming to him from all quarters.

2 When after some days he returned to Capernaum, the news went round
2 that he was at home; and such a crowd collected that the space in front of
the door was not big enough to hold them. And while he was proclaiming
3 the message to them, a man was brought who was paralysed. Four men
4 were carrying him, but because of the crowd they could not get him near.
So they opened up the roof over the place where Jesus was, and when they

[a] *Or* You have.   [b] *Some witnesses read* Jesus was sorry for him and stretched out
his hand; *one witness has simply* He stretched out his hand.

had broken through they lowered the stretcher on which the paralysed man was lying. When Jesus saw their faith, he said to the paralysed man, 'My 5 son, your sins are forgiven.'

Now there were some lawyers sitting there and they thought to them- 6 selves, 'Why does the fellow talk like that? This is blasphemy! Who but 7 God alone can forgive sins?' Jesus knew in his own mind that this was 8 what they were thinking, and said to them: 'Why do you harbour thoughts like these? Is it easier to say to this paralysed man, "Your sins are forgiven", 9 or to say, "Stand up, take your bed, and walk"? But to convince you that 10 the Son of Man has the right on earth to forgive sins'—he turned to the paralysed man—'I say to you, stand up, take your bed, and go home.' 11 And he got up, and at once took his stretcher and went out in full view of 12 them all, so that they were astounded and praised God. 'Never before', they said, 'have we seen the like.'

Once more he went away to the lake-side. All the crowd came to him, 13 and he taught them there. As he went along, he saw Levi son of Alphaeus 14 at his seat in the custom-house, and said to him, 'Follow me'; and Levi rose and followed him.

When Jesus was at table in his house, many bad characters—tax- 15 gatherers and others—were seated with him and his disciples; for there were many who followed him. Some doctors of the law who were Pharisees 16 noticed him eating in this bad company, and said to his disciples, 'He eats with tax-gatherers and sinners!' Jesus heard it and said to them, 'It is not 17 the healthy that need a doctor, but the sick; I did not come to invite virtuous people, but sinners.'

Once, when John's disciples and the Pharisees were keeping a fast, some 18 people came to him and said, 'Why is it that John's disciples and the disciples of the Pharisees are fasting, but yours are not?' Jesus said to them, 19 'Can you expect the bridegroom's friends to fast while the bridegroom is with them? As long as they have the bridegroom with them, there can be no fasting. But the time will come when the bridegroom will be taken 20 away from them, and on that day they will fast.

'No one sews a patch of unshrunk cloth on to an old coat; if he does, the 21 patch tears away from it, the new from the old, and leaves a bigger hole. No one puts new wine into old wine-skins; if he does, the wine will burst 22 the skins, and then wine and skins are both lost. Fresh skins for new wine!'

One Sabbath he was going through the cornfields; and his disciples, as 23 they went, began to pluck ears of corn. The Pharisees said to him, 'Look, 24 why are they doing what is forbidden on the Sabbath?' He answered, 'Have 25 you never read what David did when he and his men were hungry and had nothing to eat? He went into the House of God, in the time of Abiathar 26 the High Priest, and ate the sacred bread, though no one but a priest is allowed to eat it, and even gave it to his men.'

He also said to them, 'The Sabbath was made for the sake of man and 27 not man for the Sabbath: therefore the Son of Man is sovereign even over 28 the Sabbath.'

On another occasion when he went to synagogue, there was a man in the 3 congregation who had a withered arm; and they were watching to see 2

3
4
whether Jesus would cure him on the Sabbath, so that they could bring a charge against him. He said to the man with the withered arm, 'Come and stand out here.' Then he turned to them: 'Is it permitted to do good or to do evil on the Sabbath, to save life or to kill?' They had nothing to say;

5
and, looking round at them with anger and sorrow at their obstinate stupidity, he said to the man, 'Stretch out your arm.' He stretched it out

6
and his arm was restored. But the Pharisees, on leaving the synagogue, began plotting against him with the partisans of Herod to see how they could make away with him.

7
8
JESUS WENT AWAY to the lake-side with his disciples. Great numbers from Galilee, Judaea and Jerusalem, Idumaea and Transjordan, and the neighbourhood of Tyre and Sidon, heard what he was doing and came to

9
10
see him. So he told his disciples to have a boat ready for him, to save him from being crushed by the crowd. For he cured so many that sick people of

11
all kinds came crowding in upon him to touch him. The unclean spirits too, when they saw him, would fall at his feet and cry aloud, 'You are the Son of

12
God'; but he insisted that they should not make him known.

13
14
He then went up into the hill-country and called the men he wanted; and they went and joined him. He appointed twelve as his companions,

15
16
whom he would send out to proclaim the Gospel, with a commission to drive out devils. So he appointed the Twelve: to Simon he gave the name

17
Peter; then came the sons of Zebedee, James and his brother John, to whom

18
he gave the name Boanerges, Sons of Thunder; then Andrew and Philip and Bartholomew and Matthew and Thomas and James the son of Alphaeus

19
and Thaddaeus and Simon, a member of the Zealot party, and Judas Iscariot, the man who betrayed him.

20
21
He entered a house; and once more such a crowd collected round them that they had no chance to eat. When his family heard of this, they set out to take charge of him; for people were saying that he was out of his mind.*ª*

22
The doctors of the law, too, who had come down from Jerusalem, said, 'He is possessed by Beelzebub', and, 'He drives out devils by the prince of

23
24
devils.' So he called them to come forward, and spoke to them in parables: 'How can Satan drive out Satan? If a kingdom is divided against itself,

25
26
that kingdom cannot stand; if a household is divided against itself, that house will never stand; and if Satan is in rebellion against himself, he is divided and cannot stand; and that is the end of him.

27
'On the other hand, no one can break into a strong man's house and make off with his goods unless he has first tied the strong man up; then he can ransack the house.

28 29
'I tell you this: no sin, no slander, is beyond forgiveness for men; but whoever slanders the Holy Spirit can never be forgiven; he is guilty of

30
eternal sin.' He said this because they had declared that he was possessed by an unclean spirit.

31
32
Then his mother and his brothers arrived, and remaining outside sent in a message asking him to come out to them. A crowd was sitting round and word was brought to him: 'Your mother and your brothers are outside

ª Or of him. 'He is out of his mind', they said.

asking for you.' He replied, 'Who is my mother? Who are my brothers?' 33
And looking round at those who were sitting in the circle about him he said, 34
'Here are my mother and my brothers. Whoever does the will of God is 35
my brother, my sister, my mother.'

ON ANOTHER OCCASION he began to teach by the lake-side. The crowd **4**
that gathered round him was so large that he had to get into a boat on the
lake, and there he sat, with the whole crowd on the beach right down
to the water's edge. And he taught them many things by parables. 2
As he taught he said:
'Listen! A sower went out to sow. And it happened that as he sowed, 3 4
some seed fell along the footpath; and the birds came and ate it up. Some 5
seed fell on rocky ground, where it had little soil, and it sprouted quickly
because it had no depth of earth; but when the sun rose the young corn was 6
scorched, and as it had no root it withered away. Some seed fell among 7
thistles; and the thistles shot up and choked the corn, and it yielded no
crop. And some of the seed fell into good soil, where it came up and grew, 8
and bore fruit; and the yield was thirtyfold, sixtyfold, even a hundredfold.'
He added, 'If you have ears to hear, then hear.' 9
When he was alone, the Twelve and others who were round him ques- 10
tioned him about the parables. He replied, 'To you the secret of the 11
kingdom of God has been given; but to those who are outside everything
comes by way of parables, so that (as Scripture says) they may look and 12
look, but see nothing; they may hear and hear, but understand nothing;
otherwise they might turn to God and be forgiven.'
So he said, 'You do not understand this parable? How then are you to 13
understand any parable? The sower sows the word. Those along the foot- 14 15
path are people in whom the word is sown, but no sooner have they heard
it than Satan comes and carries off the word which has been sown in them.
It is the same with those who receive the seed on rocky ground; as soon as 16
they hear the word, they accept it with joy, but it strikes no root in them; 17
they have no staying-power; then, when there is trouble or persecution on
account of the word, they fall away at once. Others again receive the seed 18
among thistles; they hear the word, but worldly cares and the false glamour 19
of wealth and all kinds of evil desire come in and choke the word, and it
proves barren. And there are those who receive the seed in good soil; they 20
hear the word and welcome it; and they bear fruit thirtyfold, sixtyfold,
or a hundredfold.'
He said to them, 'Do you bring in the lamp to put it under the meal-tub, 21
or under the bed? Surely it is brought to be set on the lamp-stand. For 22
nothing is hidden unless it is to be disclosed, and nothing put under cover
unless it is to come into the open. If you have ears to hear, then hear.' 23
He also said, 'Take note of what you hear; the measure you give is the 24
measure you will receive, with something more besides. For the man who 25
has will be given more, and the man who has not will forfeit even what
he has.'
He said, 'The kingdom of God is like this. A man scatters seed on the land; 26
he goes to bed at night and gets up in the morning, and the seed sprouts 27

28 and grows—how, he does not know. The ground produces a crop by itself,
29 first the blade, then the ear, then full-grown corn in the ear; but as soon
as the crop is ripe, he plies the sickle, because harvest-time has come.'

30   He said also, 'How shall we picture the kingdom of God, or by what
31 parable shall we describe it? It is like the mustard-seed, which is smaller
32 than any seed in the ground at its sowing. But once sown, it springs up
and grows taller than any other plant, and forms branches so large that the
birds can settle in its shade.'

33   With many such parables he would give them his message, so far as they
34 were able to receive it. He never spoke to them except in parables; but
privately to his disciples he explained everything.

Miracles of Christ

35 THAT DAY, in the evening, he said to them, 'Let us cross over to the other
36   side of the lake.' So they left the crowd and took him with them in the
boat where he had been sitting; and there were other boats accompanying
37 him. A heavy squall came on and the waves broke over the boat until it
38 was all but swamped. Now he was in the stern asleep on a cushion; they
39 roused him and said, 'Master, we are sinking! Do you not care?' He awoke,
rebuked the wind, and said to the sea, 'Hush! Be still!' The wind dropped
40 and there was a dead calm. He said to them, 'Why are you such cowards?
41 Have you no faith even now?' They were awestruck and said to one
another, 'Who can this be? Even the wind and the sea obey him.'

5   So they came to the other side of the lake, into the country of the Gera-
2 senes. As he stepped ashore, a man possessed by an unclean spirit came up
3 to him from among the tombs where he had his dwelling. He could no
4 longer be controlled; even chains were useless; he had often been fettered
and chained up, but he had snapped his chains and broken the fetters. No
5 one was strong enough to master him. And so, unceasingly, night and day,
he would cry aloud among the tombs and on the hill-sides and cut himself
6 with stones. When he saw Jesus in the distance, he ran and flung himself
7 down before him, shouting loudly, 'What do you want with me, Jesus, son
8 of the Most High God? In God's name do not torment me.' (For Jesus was
9 already saying to him, 'Out, unclean spirit, come out of this man!') Jesus
asked him, 'What is your name?' 'My name is Legion,' he said, 'there are
10 so many of us.' And he begged hard that Jesus would not send them out
of the country.

11   Now there happened to be a large herd of pigs feeding on the hill-side,
12 and the spirits begged him, 'Send us among the pigs and let us go into
13 them.' He gave them leave; and the unclean spirits came out and went
into the pigs; and the herd, of about two thousand, rushed over the edge into
the lake and were drowned.

14   The men in charge of them took to their heels and carried the news to the
town and country-side; and the people came out to see what had happened.
15 They came to Jesus and saw the madman who had been possessed by the
legion of devils, sitting there clothed and in his right mind; and they were

afraid. The spectators told them how the madman had been cured and 16
what had happened to the pigs. Then they begged Jesus to leave the district. 17

As he was stepping into the boat, the man who had been possessed begged 18
to go with him. Jesus would not allow it, but said to him, 'Go home to 19
your own folk and tell them what the Lord in his mercy has done for you.'
The man went off and spread the news in the Ten Towns *a* of all that Jesus 20
had done for him; and they were all amazed.

As soon as Jesus had returned by boat to the other shore, a great crowd 21
once more gathered round him. While he was by the lake-side, the president 22
of one of the synagogues came up, Jairus by name, and, when he saw him,
threw himself down at his feet and pleaded with him. 'My little daughter', 23
he said, 'is at death's door. I beg you to come and lay your hands on her to
cure her and save her life.' So Jesus went with him, accompanied by a great 24
crowd which pressed upon him.

Among them was a woman who had suffered from haemorrhages for 25
twelve years; and in spite of long treatment by many doctors, on which 26
she had spent all she had, there had been no improvement; on the contrary,
she had grown worse. She had heard what people were saying about Jesus, 27
so she came up from behind in the crowd and touched his cloak; for she said 28
to herself, 'If I touch even his clothes, I shall be cured.' And there and then 29
the source of her haemorrhages dried up and she knew in herself that she
was cured of her trouble. At the same time Jesus, aware that power had gone 30
out of him, turned round in the crowd and asked, 'Who touched my
clothes?' His disciples said to him, 'You see the crowd pressing upon you 31
and yet you ask, "Who touched me?"' Meanwhile he was looking round 32
to see who had done it. And the woman, trembling with fear when she 33
grasped what had happened to her, came and fell at his feet and told him
the whole truth. He said to her, 'My daughter, your faith has cured you. 34
Go in peace, free for ever from this trouble.'

While he was still speaking, a message came from the president's house, 35
'Your daughter is dead; why trouble the Rabbi further?' But Jesus, over- 36
hearing the message as it was delivered, said to the president of the synagogue, 'Do not be afraid; only have faith.' After this he allowed no one to 37
accompany him except Peter and James and James's brother John. They 38
came to the president's house, where he found a great commotion, with
loud crying and wailing. So he went in and said to them, 'Why this crying 39
and commotion? The child is not dead: she is asleep'; and they only 40
laughed at him. But after turning all the others out, he took the child's
father and mother and his own companions and went in where the child was
lying. Then, taking hold of her hand, he said to her, '*Talitha cum*', which 41
means, 'Get up, my child.' Immediately the girl got up and walked about— 42
she was twelve years old. At that they were beside themselves with amazement. He gave them strict orders to let no one hear about it, and told them 43
to give her something to eat.

He left that place and went to his home town accompanied by his **6**
disciples. When the Sabbath came he began to teach in the synagogue; 2
and the large congregation who heard him were amazed and said, 'Where

a Greek Decapolis.

does he get it from?', and, 'What wisdom is this that has been given him?',
3 and, 'How does he work such miracles? Is not this the carpenter, the son
of Mary,*a* the brother of James and Joseph and Judas and Simon? And
4 are not his sisters here with us?' So they fell foul of him. Jesus said to them,
'A prophet will always be held in honour except in his home town, and
5 among his kinsmen and family.' He could work no miracle there, except
6 that he put his hands on a few sick people and healed them; and he was
taken aback by their want of faith.

7 ON ONE OF HIS TEACHING JOURNEYS round the villages he summoned
the Twelve and sent them out in pairs on a mission. He gave them authority
8 over unclean spirits, and instructed them to take nothing for the journey
9 beyond a stick: no bread, no pack, no money in their belts. They might wear
10 sandals, but not a second coat. 'When you are admitted to a house', he
11 added, 'stay there until you leave those parts. At any place where they will
not receive you or listen to you, shake the dust off your feet as you leave,
12 as a warning to them.' So they set out and called publicly for repentance.
13 They drove out many devils, and many sick people they anointed with
oil and cured.

14 Now King Herod heard of it, for the fame of Jesus had spread; and
people were saying,*b* 'John the Baptist has been raised to life, and that is
15 why these miraculous powers are at work in him.' Others said, 'It is Elijah.'
16 Others again, 'He is a prophet like one of the old prophets.' But Herod,
when he heard of it, said, 'This is John, whom I beheaded, raised from
the dead.'

17 For this same Herod had sent and arrested John and put him in prison
on account of his brother Philip's wife, Herodias, whom he had married.
18 19 John had told Herod, 'You have no right to your brother's wife.' Thus
Herodias nursed a grudge against him and would willingly have killed him,
20 but she could not; for Herod went in awe of John, knowing him to be a good
and holy man; so he kept him in custody. He liked to listen to him, although
the listening left him greatly perplexed.

21 Herodias found her opportunity when Herod on his birthday gave a
banquet to his chief officials and commanders and the leading men of
22 Galilee. Her daughter came in*c* and danced, and so delighted Herod and
his guests that the king said to the girl, 'Ask what you like and I will give it
23 you.' And he swore an oath to her: 'Whatever you ask I will give you, up
24 to half my kingdom.' She went out and said to her mother, 'What shall I ask
25 for?' She replied, 'The head of John the Baptist.' The girl hastened back
at once to the king with her request: 'I want you to give me here and now, on
26 a dish, the head of John the Baptist.' The king was greatly distressed, but
out of regard for his oath and for his guests he could not bring himself to
27 refuse her. So the king sent a soldier of the guard with orders to bring
28 John's head. The soldier went off and beheaded him in the prison, brought
the head on a dish, and gave it to the girl; and she gave it to her mother.

a Some witnesses read Is not this the son of the carpenter and Mary . . .   *b Some
witnesses read* and he said . . .   *c Or* A festive occasion came when Herod on his
birthday gave . . . of Galilee. The daughter of Herodias came in . . .

When John's disciples heard the news, they came and took his body 29
away and laid it in a tomb.

The apostles now rejoined Jesus and reported to him all that they had 30
done and taught. He said to them, 'Come with me, by yourselves, to some 31
lonely place where you can rest quietly.' (For they had no leisure even to
eat, so many were coming and going.) Accordingly, they set off privately by 32
boat for a lonely place. But many saw them leave and recognized them, 33
and came round by land, hurrying from all the towns towards the place,
and arrived there first. When he came ashore, he saw a great crowd; and his 34
heart went out to them, because they were like sheep without a shepherd;
and he had much to teach them. As the day wore on, his disciples came up to 35
him and said, 'This is a lonely place and it is getting very late; send the 36
people off to the farms and villages round about, to buy themselves something to eat.' 'Give them something to eat yourselves', he answered. They 37
replied, 'Are we to go and spend twenty pounds*ᵃ* on bread to give them a
meal?' 'How many loaves have you?' he asked; 'go and see.' They found 38
out and told him, 'Five, and two fishes also.' He ordered them to make the 39
people sit down in groups on the green grass, and they sat down in rows, 40
a hundred rows of fifty each. Then, taking the five loaves and the two fishes, 41
he looked up to heaven, said the blessing, broke the loaves, and gave them
to the disciples to distribute. He also divided the two fishes among them.
They all ate to their hearts' content; and twelve great basketfuls of scraps 42 43
were picked up, with what was left of the fish. Those who ate the loaves 44
numbered five thousand men.

As soon as it was over he made his disciples embark and cross to Bethsaida 45
ahead of him, while he himself sent the people away. After taking leave of 46
them, he went up the hill-side to pray. It grew late and the boat was already 47
well out on the water, while he was alone on the land. Somewhere between 48
three and six in the morning, seeing them labouring at the oars against a
head-wind, he came towards them, walking on the lake. He was going to
pass them by; but when they saw him walking on the lake, they thought 49
it was a ghost and cried out; for they all saw him and were terrified. But 50
at once he spoke to them: 'Take heart! It is I; do not be afraid.' Then he 51
climbed into the boat beside them, and the wind dropped. At this they were
completely dumbfounded, for they had not understood the incident of 52
the loaves; their minds were closed.

So they finished the crossing and came to land at Gennesaret, where they 53
made fast. When they came ashore, he was immediately recognized; and 54 55
the people scoured that whole country-side and brought the sick on
stretchers to any place where he was reported to be. Wherever he went, to 56
farmsteads, villages, or towns, they laid out the sick in the market-places
and begged him to let them simply touch the edge of his cloak; and all who
touched him were cured.

ᵃ Literally 200 denarii.

Growing tension

7 A GROUP OF PHARISEES, with some doctors of the law who had come
2 from Jerusalem, met him and noticed that some of his disciples were
eating their food with 'defiled' hands—in other words, without washing
3 them. (For the Pharisees and the Jews in general never eat without washing
4 the hands,[a] in obedience to an old-established tradition; and on coming
from the market-place they never eat without first washing. And there are
many other points on which they have a traditional rule to maintain, for
5 example, washing of cups and jugs and copper bowls.) Accordingly, these
Pharisees and the lawyers asked him, 'Why do your disciples not conform
6 to the ancient tradition, but eat their food with defiled hands?' He answered,
'Isaiah was right when he prophesied about you hypocrites in these words:
7 "This people pays me lip-service, but their heart is far from me: their
worship of me is in vain, for they teach as doctrines the commandments of
8 men." You neglect the commandment of God, in order to maintain the
tradition of men.'
9 He also said to them, 'How well you set aside the commandment of God
10 in order to maintain[b] your tradition! Moses said, "Honour your father
and your mother", and, "The man who curses his father or mother must
11 suffer death." But you hold that if a man says to his father or mother,
"Anything of mine which might have been used for your benefit is Cor-
12 ban"' (meaning, set apart for God), 'he is no longer permitted to do any-
13 thing for his father or mother. Thus by your own tradition, handed down
among you, you make God's word null and void. And many other things
that you do are just like that.'
14 On another occasion he called the people and said to them, 'Listen to
15 me, all of you, and understand this: nothing that goes into a man from
outside can defile him; no, it is the things that come out of him that defile
a man.'[c]
17 When he had left the people and gone indoors, his disciples questioned
18 him about the parable. He said to them, 'Are you as dull as the rest? Do you
not see that nothing that goes from outside into a man can defile him,
19 because it does not enter into his heart but into his stomach, and so passes
20 out into the drain?' Thus he declared all foods clean. He went on, 'It is
21 what comes out of a man that defiles him. For from inside, out of a man's
22 heart, come evil thoughts, acts of fornication, of theft, murder, adultery,
ruthless greed, and malice; fraud, indecency, envy, slander, arrogance, and
23 folly; these evil things all come from inside, and they defile the man.'
24 Then he left that place and went away into the territory of Tyre. He
found a house to stay in, and he would have liked to remain unrecognized,
25 but this was impossible. Almost at once a woman whose young daughter
was possessed by an unclean spirit heard of him, came in, and fell at his
26 feet. (She was a Gentile, a Phoenician of Syria by nationality.) She begged
27 him to drive the spirit out of her daughter. He said to her, 'Let the children

---

[a] *Some witnesses insert* with the fist; *others insert* frequently, *or* thoroughly.   [b] *Some*
witnesses read establish.   [c] *Some witnesses here add* (16) If you have ears to hear,
then hear.

be satisfied first; it is not fair to take the children's bread and throw it to the
dogs.' 'Sir,' she answered, 'even the dogs under the table eat the children's 28
scraps.' He said to her, 'For saying that, you may go home content; the 29
unclean spirit has gone out of your daughter.' And when she returned 30
home, she found the child lying in bed; the spirit had left her.

On his return journey from Tyrian territory he went by way of Sidon to 31
the Sea of Galilee through the territory of the Ten Towns.*ᵃ* They brought 32
to him a man who was deaf and had an impediment in his speech, with the
request that he would lay his hand on him. He took the man aside, away 33
from the crowd, put his fingers into his ears, spat, and touched his tongue.
Then, looking up to heaven, he sighed, and said to him, '*Ephphatha*', 34
which means 'Be opened.' With that his ears were opened, and at the same 35
time the impediment was removed and he spoke plainly. Jesus forbade them 36
to tell anyone; but the more he forbade them, the more they published it.
Their astonishment knew no bounds: 'All that he does, he does well,' they 37
said; 'he even makes the deaf hear and the dumb speak.'

THERE WAS ANOTHER OCCASION about this time when a huge crowd 8
had collected, and, as they had no food, Jesus called his disciples and
said to them, 'I feel sorry for all these people; they have been with me now 2
for three days and have nothing to eat. If I send them home unfed, they 3
will turn faint on the way; some of them have come from a distance.' The 4
disciples answered, 'How can anyone provide all these people with bread
in this lonely place?' 'How many loaves have you?' he asked; and they 5
answered, 'Seven.' So he ordered the people to sit down on the ground; 6
then he took the seven loaves, and, after giving thanks to God, he broke the
bread and gave it to his disciples to distribute; and they served it out to the
people. They had also a few small fishes, which he blessed and ordered 7
them to distribute. They all ate to their hearts' content, and seven baskets 8
were filled with the scraps that were left. The people numbered about four 9
thousand. Then he dismissed them; and, without delay, got into the boat 10
with his disciples and went to the district of Dalmanutha.*ᵇ*

Then the Pharisees came out and engaged him in discussion. To test 11
him they asked him for a sign from heaven. He sighed deeply to himself 12
and said, 'Why does this generation ask for a sign? I tell you this: no sign
shall be given to this generation.' With that he left them, re-embarked, and 13
went off to the other side of the lake.

Now they had forgotten to take bread with them; they had no more than 14
one loaf in the boat. He began to warn them: 'Beware,' he said, 'be on your 15
guard against the leaven of the Pharisees and the leaven of Herod.' They 16
said among themselves, 'It is because we have no bread.' Knowing what 17
was in their minds, he asked them, 'Why do you talk about having no
bread? Have you no inkling yet? Do you still not understand? Are your
minds closed? You have eyes: can you not see? You have ears: can you 18
not hear? Have you forgotten? When I broke the five loaves among five 19
thousand, how many basketfuls of scraps did you pick up?' 'Twelve',
they said. 'And how many when I broke the seven loaves among four 20

ᵃ Greek Decapolis.   *ᵇ Some witnesses give* Magedan; *others give* Magdala.

21 thousand?' They answered, 'Seven.' He said, 'Do you still not understand?'

22   They arrived at Bethsaida. There the people brought a blind man to
23 Jesus and begged him to touch him. He took the blind man by the hand
and led him away out of the village. Then he spat on his eyes, laid his
24 hands upon him, and asked whether he could see anything. The man's
sight began to come back, and he said, 'I see men; they look like trees, but
25 they are walking about.' Jesus laid his hands on his eyes again; he looked
26 hard, and now he was cured so that he saw everything clearly. Then Jesus
sent him home, saying, 'Do not tell anyone in the village.' *a*

27 JESUS AND HIS DISCIPLES set out for the villages of Caesarea Philippi.
28 On the way he asked his disciples, 'Who do men say I am?' They answered,
'Some say John the Baptist, others Elijah, others one of the prophets.'
29 'And you,' he asked, 'who do you say I am?' Peter replied: 'You are the
30 Messiah.' Then he gave them strict orders not to tell anyone about him;
31 and he began to teach them that the Son of Man had to undergo great
sufferings, and to be rejected by the elders, chief priests, and doctors of
32 the law; to be put to death, and to rise again three days afterwards. He spoke
about it plainly. At this Peter took him by the arm and began to rebuke him.
33 But Jesus turned round, and, looking at his disciples, rebuked Peter. 'Away
with you, Satan,' he said; 'you think as men think, not as God thinks.'

34   Then he called the people to him, as well as his disciples, and said to
them, 'Anyone who wishes to be a follower of mine must leave self behind;
35 he must take up his cross, and come with me. Whoever cares for his own
safety is lost; but if a man will let himself be lost for my sake and for the
36 Gospel, that man is safe. What does a man gain by winning the whole world
37 38 at the cost of his true self? What can he give to buy that self back? If anyone
is ashamed of me and mine *b* in this wicked and godless age, the Son of Man
will be ashamed of him, when he comes in the glory of his Father and of the
holy angels.' *c*

9   He also said, 'I tell you this: there are some of those standing here who
will not taste death before they have seen the kingdom of God already
come in power.'

2   Six days later Jesus took Peter, James, and John with him and led them
up a high mountain where they were alone; and in their presence he was
3 transfigured; his clothes became dazzling white, with a whiteness no
4 bleacher on earth could equal. They saw Elijah appear, and Moses with
5 him, and there they were, conversing with Jesus. Then Peter spoke:
'Rabbi,' he said, 'how good it is that we are here! Shall we make three
6 shelters, one for you, one for Moses, and one for Elijah?' (For he did not
7 know what to say; they were so terrified.) Then a cloud appeared, casting
its shadow over them, and out of the cloud came a voice: 'This is my Son,
8 my Beloved; *d* listen to him.' And now suddenly, when they looked around,
there was nobody to be seen but Jesus alone with themselves.

a Some witnesses read Do not go into the village.   *b Some witnesses read* me and my
words.   *c Some witnesses read* Father with the holy angels.   *d Or* This is my
only Son.

On their way down the mountain, he enjoined them not to tell anyone 9
what they had seen until the Son of Man had risen from the dead. They 10
seized upon those words, and discussed among themselves what this
'rising from the dead' could mean. And they put a question to him: 'Why 11
do our teachers say that Elijah must come first?' He replied, 'Yes, Elijah 12
does come first to set everything right. Yet how is it *a* that the scriptures
say of the Son of Man that he is to endure great sufferings and to be treated
with contempt? However, I tell you, Elijah has already come and they have 13
worked their will upon him, as the scriptures say of him.'

When they came back to the disciples they saw a large crowd surrounding 14
them and lawyers arguing with them. As soon as they saw Jesus the whole 15
crowd were overcome with awe, and they ran forward to welcome him.
He asked them, 'What is this argument about?' A man in the crowd spoke 16 17
up: 'Master, I brought my son to you. He is possessed by a spirit which
makes him speechless. Whenever it attacks him, it dashes him to the 18
ground, and he foams at the mouth, grinds his teeth, and goes rigid. I asked
your disciples to cast it out, but they failed.' Jesus answered: 'What an 19
unbelieving and perverse generation! How long shall I be with you? How
long must I endure you? Bring him to me.' So they brought the boy to him; 20
and as soon as the spirit saw him it threw the boy into convulsions, and he
fell on the ground and rolled about foaming at the mouth. Jesus asked his 21
father, 'How long has he been like this?' 'From childhood,' he replied;
'often it has tried to make an end of him by throwing him into the fire or 22
into water. But if it is at all possible for you, take pity upon us and help us.'
'If it is possible!' said Jesus. 'Everything is possible to one who has 23
faith.' 'I have faith,' cried the boy's father; 'help me where faith falls 24
short.' Jesus saw then that the crowd was closing in upon them, so he 25
rebuked the unclean spirit. 'Deaf and dumb spirit,' he said, 'I command
you, come out of him and never go back!' After crying aloud and racking 26
him fiercely, it came out; and the boy looked like a corpse; in fact, many
said, 'He is dead.' But Jesus took his hand and raised him to his feet, and 27
he stood up.

Then Jesus went indoors, and his disciples asked him privately, 'Why 28
could not we cast it out?' He said, 'There is no means of casting out this 29
sort but prayer.' *b*

THEY NOW LEFT that district and made a journey through Galilee. Jesus 30
wished it to be kept secret; for he was teaching his disciples, and telling 31
them, 'The Son of Man is now to be given up into the power of men, and
they will kill him, and three days after being killed, he will rise again.'
But they did not understand what he said, and were afraid to ask. 32

So they came to Capernaum; and when he was indoors, he asked them, 33
'What were you arguing about on the way?' They were silent, because on 34
the way they had been discussing who was the greatest. He sat down, 35
called the Twelve, and said to them, 'If anyone wants to be first, he must
make himself last of all and servant of all.' Then he took a child, set him 36

a Or Elijah, you say, comes first to set everything right: then how is it ...   *b Some*
witnesses add and fasting.

37 in front of them, and put his arm round him. 'Whoever receives one of these children in my name', he said, 'receives me; and whoever receives me, receives not me but the One who sent me.'

38   John said to him, 'Master, we saw a man driving out devils in your name,
39 and as he was not one of us, we tried to stop him.' Jesus said, 'Do not stop him; no one who does a work of divine power in my name will be able the
40 next moment to speak evil of me. For he who is not against us is on our side.
41 I tell you this: if anyone gives you a cup of water to drink because you are followers of the Messiah, that man assuredly will not go unrewarded.

42   'As for the man who is a cause of stumbling to one of these little ones who have faith, it would be better for him to be thrown into the sea with
43 a millstone round his neck. If your hand is your undoing, cut it off; it is better for you to enter into life maimed than to keep both hands and
45 go to hell and the unquenchable fire.*a* And if your foot is your undoing, cut it off; it is better to enter into life a cripple than to keep both your feet
47 and be thrown into hell.*b* And if it is your eye, tear it out; it is better to enter into the kingdom of God with one eye than to keep both eyes and be thrown
48 into hell, where the devouring worm never dies and the fire is not quenched.
49   'For everyone will be salted with fire.
50   'Salt is a good thing; but if the salt loses its saltness, what will you season it with?

'Have salt in yourselves; and be*c* at peace with one another.'

10 ON LEAVING THOSE PARTS he came into the regions of Judaea and Trans-jordan; and when a crowd gathered round him once again, he followed his
2 usual practice and taught them. The question was put to him:*d* 'Is it
3 lawful for a man to divorce his wife?' This was to test him. He asked in
4 return, 'What did Moses command you?' They answered, 'Moses per-
5 mitted a man to divorce his wife by note of dismissal.' Jesus said to them, 'It was because your minds were closed that he made this rule for you;
6 but in the beginning, at the creation, God made them male and female.
7 For this reason a man shall leave his father and mother, and be made one
8 with his wife;*e* and the two shall become one flesh. It follows that they
9 are no longer two individuals: they are one flesh. What God has joined together, man must not separate.'

10   When they were indoors again the disciples questioned him about this
11 matter; he said to them, 'Whoever divorces his wife and marries another
12 commits adultery against her: so too, if she divorces her husband and marries another, she commits adultery.'

13   They brought children for him to touch. The disciples rebuked them,
14 but when Jesus saw this he was indignant, and said to them, 'Let the children come to me; do not try to stop them; for the kingdom of God

a Some witnesses add (44) where the devouring worm never dies and the fire is not quenched.   *b Some witnesses add* (46) where the devouring worm never dies and the fire is not quenched.   *c Or* Have the salt of fellowship and be . . .; *or* You have the salt of fellowship between you; then be . . .   *d Some witnesses read* The Phari-sees came forward and asked him the question . . .   *e Some witnesses omit* and be made . . . wife.

belongs to such as these. I tell you, whoever does not accept the kingdom 15
of God like a child will never enter it.' And he put his arms round them, 16
laid his hands upon them, and blessed them.

As he was starting out on a journey, a stranger ran up, and, kneeling 17
before him, asked, 'Good Master, what must I do to win eternal life?'
Jesus said to him, 'Why do you call me good? No one is good except God 18
alone. You know the commandments: "Do not murder; do not commit 19
adultery; do not steal; do not give false evidence; do not defraud; honour
your father and mother." ' 'But, Master,' he replied, 'I have kept all these 20
since I was a boy.' Jesus looked straight at him; his heart warmed to him, 21
and he said, 'One thing you lack: go, sell everything you have, and give to
the poor, and you will have riches in heaven; and come, follow me.' At 22
these words his face fell and he went away with a heavy heart; for he was a
man of great wealth.

Jesus looked round at his disciples and said to them, 'How hard it will 23
be for the wealthy to enter the kingdom of God!' They were amazed that 24
he should say this, but Jesus insisted, 'Children, how hard it is *a* to enter
the kingdom of God! It is easier for a camel to pass through the eye of 25
a needle than for a rich man to enter the kingdom of God.' They were more 26
astonished than ever, and said to one another, 'Then who can be saved?'
Jesus looked at them and said, 'For men it is impossible, but not for God; 27
everything is possible for God.'

At this Peter spoke. 'We here', he said, 'have left everything to become 28
your followers.' Jesus said, 'I tell you this: there is no one who has given 29
up home, brothers or sisters, mother, father or children, or land, for my
sake and for the Gospel, who will not receive in this age a hundred times as 30
much—houses, brothers and sisters, mothers and children, and land—
and persecutions besides; and in the age to come eternal life. But many 31
who are first will be last and the last first.'

Challenge to Jerusalem

THEY WERE ON THE ROAD, going up to Jerusalem, Jesus leading the 32
way; and the disciples were filled with awe, while those who followed
behind were afraid. He took the Twelve aside and began to tell them
what was to happen to him. 'We are now going to Jerusalem,' he said; 33
'and the Son of Man will be given up to the chief priests and the doctors
of the law; they will condemn him to death and hand him over to the foreign
power. He will be mocked and spat upon, flogged and killed; and three days 34
afterwards, he will rise again.'

James and John, the sons of Zebedee, approached him and said, 'Master, 35
we should like you to do us a favour.' 'What is it you want me to do?' he 36
asked. They answered, 'Grant us the right to sit in state with you, one at 37
your right and the other at your left.' Jesus said to them, 'You do not under- 38
stand what you are asking. Can you drink the cup that I drink, or be baptized with the baptism I am baptized with?' 'We can', they answered. Jesus 39

a Some witnesses insert for those who trust in riches.

40 said, 'The cup that I drink you shall drink, and the baptism I am baptized with shall be your baptism; but to sit at my right or left is not for me to grant; it is for those to whom it has already been assigned.' *a*

41 When the other ten heard this, they were indignant with James and
42 John. Jesus called them to him and said, 'You know that in the world the recognized rulers lord it over their subjects, and their great men make
43 them feel the weight of authority. That is not the way with you; among you,
44 whoever wants to be great must be your servant, and whoever wants to be
45 first must be the willing slave of all. For even the Son of Man did not come to be served but to serve, and to give up his life as a ransom for many.'

46 They came to Jericho; and as he was leaving the town, with his disciples and a large crowd, Bartimaeus son of Timaeus, a blind beggar, was seated
47 at the roadside. Hearing that it was Jesus of Nazareth, he began to shout,
48 'Son of David, Jesus, have pity on me!' Many of the people told him to hold his tongue; but he shouted all the more, 'Son of David, have pity on me.'
49 Jesus stopped and said, 'Call him'; so they called the blind man and said,
50 'Take heart; stand up; he is calling you.' At that he threw off his cloak,
51 sprang up, and came to Jesus. Jesus said to him, 'What do you want me to do for you?' 'Master,' the blind man answered, 'I want my sight back.'
52 Jesus said to him, 'Go; your faith has cured you.' And at once he recovered his sight and followed him on the road.

11 THEY WERE NOW APPROACHING Jerusalem, and when they reached Bethphage and Bethany, at the Mount of Olives, he sent two of his disciples
2 with these instructions: 'Go to the village opposite, and, just as you enter, you will find tethered there a colt which no one has yet ridden. Untie it
3 and bring it here. If anyone asks, "Why are you doing that?", say, "Our
4 Master *b* needs it, and will send it back here without delay."' So they went off, and found the colt tethered at a door outside in the street. They were
5 untying it when some of the bystanders asked, 'What are you doing, un-
6 tying that colt?' They answered as Jesus had told them, and were then
7 allowed to take it. So they brought the colt to Jesus and spread their cloaks
8 on it, and he mounted. And people carpeted the road with their cloaks,
9 while others spread brushwood which they had cut in the fields; and those who went ahead and the others who came behind shouted, 'Hosanna!
10 Blessings on him who comes in the name of the Lord! Blessings on the coming kingdom of our father David! Hosanna in the heavens!'

11 He entered Jerusalem and went into the temple, where he looked at the whole scene; but, as it was now late, he went out to Bethany with the Twelve.

12 13 On the following day, after they had left Bethany, he felt hungry, and, noticing in the distance a fig-tree in leaf, he went to see if he could find anything on it. But when he came there he found nothing but leaves; for
14 it was not the season for figs. He said to the tree, 'May no one ever again eat fruit from you!' And his disciples were listening.
15 So they came to Jerusalem, and he went into the temple and began driving out those who bought and sold in the temple. He upset the tables

a Some witnesses add by my Father.　　　　*b Or* Its owner.

of the money-changers and the seats of the dealers in pigeons; and he   16
would not allow anyone to use the temple court as a thoroughfare for
carrying goods. Then he began to teach them, and said, 'Does not Scripture   17
say, "My house shall be called a house of prayer for all the nations"? But
you have made it a robbers' cave.' The chief priests and the doctors of the   18
law heard of this and sought some means of making away with him; for
they were afraid of him, because the whole crowd was spellbound by his
teaching. And when evening came he went out of the city.   19

Early next morning, as they passed by, they saw that the fig-tree had   20
withered from the roots up; and Peter, recalling what had happened, said   21
to him, 'Rabbi, look, the fig-tree which you cursed has withered.' Jesus   22
answered them, 'Have faith in God. I tell you this: if anyone says to this   23
mountain, "Be lifted from your place and hurled into the sea", and has no
inward doubts, but believes that what he says is happening, it will be done
for him. I tell you, then, whatever you ask for in prayer, believe that you   24
have received it and it will be yours.

'And when you stand praying, if you have a grievance against anyone,   25
forgive him, so that your Father in heaven may forgive you the wrongs
you have done.' *a*

THEY CAME ONCE MORE to Jerusalem. And as he was walking in the   27
temple court the chief priests, lawyers, and elders came to him and said,   28
'By what authority are you acting like this? Who gave you authority to
act in this way?' Jesus said to them, 'I have a question to ask you too;   29
and if you give me an answer, I will tell you by what authority I act. The   30
baptism of John: was it from God, or from men? Answer me.' This set   31
them arguing among themselves: 'What shall we say? If we say, "from
God", he will say, "Then why did you not believe him?" Shall we say,   32
"from men"?'—but they were afraid of the people, for all held that John
was in fact a prophet. So they answered, 'We do not know.' And Jesus said   33
to them, 'Then neither will I tell you by what authority I act.'

He went on to speak to them in parables: 'A man planted a vineyard   **12**
and put a wall round it, hewed out a winepress, and built a watch-tower;
then he let it out to vine-growers and went abroad. When the season came,   2
he sent a servant to the tenants to collect from them his share of the produce.
But they took him, thrashed him, and sent him away empty-handed. Again,   3 4
he sent them another servant, whom they beat about the head and treated
outrageously. So he sent another, and that one they killed; and many more   5
besides, of whom they beat some, and killed others. He had now only one   6
left to send, his own dear son. *b* In the end he sent him. "They will respect
my son", he said. But the tenants said to one another, "This is the heir;   7
come on, let us kill him, and the property will be ours." So they seized him   8
and killed him, and flung his body out of the vineyard. What will the owner   9
of the vineyard do? He will come and put the tenants to death and give the
vineyard to others.

'Can it be that you have never read this text: "The stone which the   10

---

a Some witnesses add (26) But if you do not forgive others, then the wrongs you have
done will not be forgiven by your Father in heaven.   *b Or his only son.*

11 builders rejected has become the main corner-stone. This is the Lord's doing, and it is wonderful in our eyes"?'

12   Then they began to look for a way to arrest him, for they saw that the parable was aimed at them; but they were afraid of the people, so they left him alone and went away.

13 A NUMBER OF PHARISEES and men of Herod's party were sent to trap
14 him with a question. They came and said, 'Master, you are an honest man, we know, and truckle to no one, whoever he may be; you teach in all honesty the way of life that God requires. Are we or are we not permitted
15 to pay taxes to the Roman Emperor? Shall we pay or not?' He saw how crafty their question was, and said, 'Why are you trying to catch me out?
16 Fetch me a silver piece, and let me look at it.' They brought one, and he said to them, 'Whose head is this, and whose inscription?' 'Caesar's', they
17 replied. Then Jesus said, 'Pay Caesar what is due to Caesar, and pay God what is due to God.' And they heard him with astonishment.

18   Next Sadducees came to him. (It is they who say that there is no resur-
19 rection.) Their question was this: 'Master, Moses laid it down for us that if there are brothers, and one dies leaving a wife but no child, then the next
20 should marry the widow and carry on his brother's family. Now there were
21 seven brothers. The first took a wife and died without issue. Then the second married her, and he too died without issue. So did the third.
22 Eventually the seven of them died, all without issue. Finally the woman
23 died. At the resurrection, when they come back to life, whose wife will she
24 be, since all seven had married her?' Jesus said to them, 'You are mistaken, and surely this is the reason: you do not know either the scriptures or the
25 power of God. When they rise from the dead, men and women do not marry; they are like angels in heaven.

26   'But about the resurrection of the dead, have you never read in the Book of Moses, in the story of the burning bush, how God spoke to him and said, "I am the God of Abraham, the God of Isaac, and the God of Jacob"?
27 God is not God of the dead but of the living. You are greatly mistaken.'

28   Then one of the lawyers, who had been listening to these discussions and had noted how well he answered, came forward and asked him, 'Which
29 commandment is first of all?' Jesus answered, 'The first is, "Hear, O
30 Israel: the Lord our God is the only Lord; love the Lord your God with all your heart, with all your soul, with all your mind, and with all your
31 strength." The second is this: "Love your neighbour as yourself." There is
32 no other commandment greater than these.' The lawyer said to him, 'Well said, Master. You are right in saying that God is one and beside him there
33 is no other. And to love him with all your heart, all your understanding, and all your strength, and to love your neighbour as yourself—that is far
34 more than any burnt offerings or sacrifices.' When Jesus saw how sensibly he answered, he said to him, 'You are not far from the kingdom of God.'

35   After that nobody ventured to put any more questions to him; and Jesus went on to say, as he taught in the temple, 'How can the teachers of the law
36 maintain that the Messiah is "Son of David"? David himself said, when inspired by the Holy Spirit, "The Lord said to my Lord, 'Sit at my right

hand until I put your enemies under your feet.' " David himself calls him 37
"Lord"; how can he also be David's son?'

   There was a great crowd and they listened eagerly.^a He said as he taught 38
them, 'Beware of the doctors of the law, who love to walk up and down in
long robes, receiving respectful greetings in the street; and to have the 39
chief seats in synagogues, and places of honour at feasts. These are the men 40
who eat up the property of widows, while they say long prayers for appearance' sake, and they will receive the severest sentence.'^b

   Once he was standing opposite the temple treasury, watching as people 41
dropped their money into the chest. Many rich people were giving large
sums. Presently there came a poor widow who dropped in two tiny coins, 42
together worth a farthing. He called his disciples to him. 'I tell you this,' 43
he said: 'this poor widow has given more than any of the others; for those 44
others who have given had more than enough, but she, with less than
enough, has given all that she had to live on.'

AS HE WAS LEAVING the temple, one of his disciples exclaimed, 'Look, **13**
Master, what huge stones! What fine buildings!' Jesus said to him, 'You 2
see these great buildings? Not one stone will be left upon another; all will
be thrown down.'

   When he was sitting on the Mount of Olives facing the temple he was 3
questioned privately by Peter, James, John, and Andrew. 'Tell us,' they 4
said, 'when will this happen? What will be the sign when the fulfilment of
all this is at hand?'

   Jesus began: 'Take care that no one misleads you. Many will come 5 6
claiming my name, and saying, "I am he"; and many will be misled by
them.

   'When you hear the noise of battle near at hand and the news of battles 7
far away, do not be alarmed. Such things are bound to happen; but the end
is still to come. For nation will make war upon nation, kingdom upon 8
kingdom; there will be earthquakes in many places; there will be famines.
With these things the birth-pangs of the new age begin.

   'As for you, be on your guard. You will be handed over to the courts. 9
You will be flogged in synagogues. You will be summoned to appear before
governors and kings on my account to testify in their presence. But before 10
the end the Gospel must be proclaimed to all nations. So when you are 11
arrested and taken away, do not worry beforehand about what you will say,
but when the time comes say whatever is given you to say; for it is not you
who will be speaking, but the Holy Spirit. Brother will betray brother to 12
death, and the father his child; children will turn against their parents
and send them to their death. All will hate you for your allegiance to me; 13
but the man who holds out to the end will be saved.

   'But when you see "the abomination of desolation" usurping a place 14
which is not his (let the reader understand), then those who are in Judaea
must take to the hills. If a man is on the roof, he must not come down into 15

^a *Or* The mass of the people listened eagerly.   ^b *Or* As for those who eat up the
property of widows, while they say long prayers for appearance' sake, they will have an
even sterner judgement to face.

16 the house to fetch anything out; if in the field, he must not turn back for his
17 coat. Alas for women with child in those days, and for those who have
18 19 children at the breast! Pray that it may not come in winter. For those days
will bring distress such as never has been until now since the beginning
20 of the world which God created—and will never be again. If the Lord had
not cut short that time of troubles, no living thing could survive. However,
for the sake of his own, whom he has chosen, he has cut short the time.

21 'Then, if anyone says to you, "Look, here is the Messiah", or, "Look,
22 there he is", do not believe it. Impostors will come claiming to be messiahs
or prophets, and they will produce signs and wonders to mislead God's
23 chosen, if such a thing were possible. But you be on your guard; I have
forewarned you of it all.

24 'But in those days, after that distress, the sun will be darkened, the moon
25 will not give her light; the stars will come falling from the sky, the celestial
26 powers will be shaken. Then they will see the Son of Man coming in the
27 clouds with great power and glory, and he will send out the angels and
gather his chosen from the four winds, from the farthest bounds of earth
to the farthest bounds of heaven.

28 'Learn a lesson from the fig-tree. When its tender shoots appear and are
29 breaking into leaf, you know that summer is near. In the same way, when
you see all this happening, you may know that the end is near,*a* at the very
30 31 door. I tell you this: the present generation will live to see it all. Heaven
and earth will pass away; my words will never pass away.

32 'But about that day or that hour no one knows, not even the angels in
heaven, not even the Son; only the Father.

33 34 'Be alert, be wakeful.*b* You do not know when the moment comes. It is
like a man away from home: he has left his house and put his servants in
charge, each with his own work to do, and he has ordered the door-keeper
35 to stay awake. Keep awake, then, for you do not know when the master
of the house is coming. Evening or midnight, cock-crow or early dawn—
36 37 if he comes suddenly, he must not find you asleep. And what I say to you,
I say to everyone: Keep awake.'

The final conflict

14 NOW THE FESTIVAL of Passover and Unleavened Bread was only two
days off; and the chief priests and the doctors of the law were trying
2 to devise some cunning plan to seize him and put him to death. 'It must not
be during the festival,' they said, 'or we should have rioting among the
people.'

3 Jesus was at Bethany, in the house of Simon the leper. As he sat at table,
a woman came in carrying a small bottle of very costly perfume, pure oil
4 of nard. She broke it open and poured the oil over his head. Some of those
5 present said to one another angrily, 'Why this waste? The perfume might
have been sold for thirty pounds*c* and the money given to the poor'; and

---

a Or that he is near.   *b* *Some witnesses add* and pray.   *c* *Literally* 300 denarii;
some witnesses read more than 300 denarii.

they turned upon her with fury. But Jesus said, 'Let her alone. Why must 6
you make trouble for her? It is a fine thing she has done for me. You have 7
the poor among you always, and you can help them whenever you like;
but you will not always have me. She has done what lay in her power; she 8
is beforehand with anointing my body for burial. I tell you this: wherever 9
in all the world the Gospel is proclaimed, what she has done will be told as
her memorial.'

Then Judas Iscariot, one of the Twelve, went to the chief priests to 10
betray him to them. When they heard what he had come for, they were 11
greatly pleased, and promised him money; and he began to look for a good
opportunity to betray him.

NOW ON THE FIRST DAY of Unleavened Bread, when the Passover lambs 12
were being slaughtered, his disciples said to him, 'Where would you like
us to go and prepare for your Passover supper?' So he sent out two of his 13
disciples with these instructions: 'Go into the city, and a man will meet
you carrying a jar of water. Follow him, and when he enters a house give 14
this message to the householder: "The Master says, 'Where is the room
reserved for me to eat the Passover with my disciples?'" He will show you 15
a large room upstairs, set out in readiness. Make the preparations for us
there.' Then the disciples went off, and when they came into the city 16
they found everything just as he had told them. So they prepared for
Passover.

In the evening he came to the house with the Twelve. As they sat at 17 18
supper Jesus said, 'I tell you this: one of you will betray me—one who is
eating with me.' At this they were dismayed; and one by one they said to 19
him, 'Not I, surely?' 'It is one of the Twelve', he said, 'who is dipping into 20
the same bowl with me. The Son of Man is going the way appointed for him 21
in the scriptures; but alas for that man by whom the Son of Man is betrayed!
It would be better for that man if he had never been born.'

During supper he took bread, and having said the blessing he broke it 22
and gave it to them, with the words: 'Take this; this is my body.' Then he 23
took a cup, and having offered thanks to God he gave it to them; and they
all drank from it. And he said, 'This is my blood, the blood of the covenant, 24
shed for many. I tell you this: never again shall I drink from the fruit of 25
the vine until that day when I drink it new in the kingdom of God.'

After singing the Passover Hymn, they went out to the Mount of Olives. 26
And Jesus said, 'You will all fall from your faith; for it stands written: 27
"I will strike the shepherd down and the sheep will be scattered." Never- 28
theless, after I am raised again I will go on before you into Galilee.' Peter 29
answered, 'Everyone else may fall away, but I will not.' Jesus said, 'I tell 30
you this: today, this very night, before the cock crows twice, you yourself
will disown me three times.' But he insisted and repeated: 'Even if I must 31
die with you, I will never disown you.' And they all said the same.

WHEN THEY REACHED a place called Gethsemane, he said to his disciples, 32
'Sit here while I pray.' And he took Peter and James and John with him. 33
Horror and dismay came over him, and he said to them, 'My heart is ready 34

35 to break with grief; stop here, and stay awake.' Then he went forward a
little, threw himself on the ground, and prayed that, if it were possible,
36 this hour might pass him by. 'Abba, Father,' he said, 'all things are possible to thee; take this cup away from me. Yet not what I will, but what
thou wilt.'

37   He came back and found them asleep; and he said to Peter, 'Asleep,
38 Simon? Were you not able to stay awake for one hour? Stay awake, all of
you; and pray that you may be spared the test. The spirit is willing, but the
39 40 flesh is weak.' Once more he went away and prayed. *a* On his return he
found them asleep again, for their eyes were heavy; and they did not know
how to answer him.

41   The third time he came and said to them, 'Still sleeping? Still taking your
ease? Enough!*b* The hour has come. The Son of Man is betrayed to sinful
42 men. Up, let us go forward! My betrayer is upon us.'

43   Suddenly, while he was still speaking, Judas, one of the Twelve, appeared,
and with him was a crowd armed with swords and cudgels, sent by the
44 chief priests, lawyers, and elders. Now the traitor had agreed with them
upon a signal: 'The one I kiss is your man; seize him and get him safely
45 away.' When he reached the spot, he stepped forward at once and said to
46 Jesus, 'Rabbi', and kissed him. Then they seized him and held him fast.
47   One of the party *c* drew his sword, and struck at the High Priest's servant,
48 cutting off his ear. Then Jesus spoke: 'Do you take me for a bandit, that
49 you have come out with swords and cudgels to arrest me? Day after day
I was within your reach as I taught in the temple, and you did not lay hands
50 on me. But let the scriptures be fulfilled.' Then the disciples all deserted
him and ran away.

51   Among those following was a young man with nothing on but a linen
52 cloth. They tried to seize him; but he slipped out of the linen cloth and ran
away naked.

53 THEN THEY LED Jesus away to the High Priest's house, where the chief
54 priests, elders, and doctors of the law were all assembling. Peter followed
him at a distance right into the High Priest's courtyard; and there he
remained, sitting among the attendants, warming himself at the fire.

55   The chief priests and the whole Council tried to find some evidence
56 against Jesus to warrant a death-sentence, but failed to find any. Many
57 gave false evidence against him, but their statements did not tally. Some
58 stood up and gave false evidence against him to this effect: 'We heard him
say, "I will pull down this temple, made with human hands, and in three
59 days I will build another, not made with hands."' But even on this point
their evidence did not agree.

60   Then the High Priest stood up in his place and questioned Jesus: 'Have
61 you no answer to the charges that these witnesses bring against you?' But
he kept silence; he made no reply.

     Again the High Priest questioned him: 'Are you the Messiah, the Son
62 of the Blessed One?' Jesus said, 'I am; and you will see the Son of Man

a *Some witnesses add* using the same words.   *b* *The Greek is obscure; a possible mean-*
ing is 'The money has been paid', 'The account is settled.'   *c* *Or of the bystanders.*

seated at the right hand of God *a* and coming with the clouds of heaven.'
Then the High Priest tore his robes and said, 'Need we call further wit- 63
nesses? You have heard the blasphemy. What is your opinion?' Their 64
judgement was unanimous: that he was guilty and should be put to death.

Some began to spit on him, blindfolded him, and struck him with their 65
fists, crying out, 'Prophesy!'*b* And the High Priest's men set upon him
with blows.

Meanwhile Peter was still below in the courtyard. One of the High 66
Priest's serving-maids came by and saw him there warming himself. She 67
looked into his face and said, 'You were there too, with this man from
Nazareth, this Jesus.' But he denied it: 'I know nothing,' he said; 'I do 68
not understand what you mean.' Then he went outside into the porch;*c*
and the maid saw him there again and began to say to the bystanders, 'He 69
is one of them'; and again he denied it. 70

Again, a little later, the bystanders said to Peter, 'Surely you are one of
them. You must be; you are a Galilean.' At this he broke out into curses, 71
and with an oath he said, 'I do not know this man you speak of.' Then the 72
cock crew a second time; and Peter remembered how Jesus had said to
him, 'Before the cock crows twice you will disown me three times.' And he
burst into tears.

AS SOON AS MORNING CAME, the chief priests, having made their plan 15
with the elders and lawyers in full council, put Jesus in chains; then they
led him away and handed him over to Pilate. Pilate asked him, 'Are you the 2
king of the Jews?' He replied, 'The words are yours.'*d* And the chief priests 3
brought many charges against him. Pilate questioned him again: 'Have you 4
nothing to say in your defence? You see how many charges they are
bringing against you.' But, to Pilate's astonishment, Jesus made no 5
further reply.

At the festival season the Governor used to release one prisoner at the 6
people's request. As it happened, the man known as Barabbas was then in 7
custody with the rebels who had committed murder in the rising. When 8
the crowd appeared *e* asking for the usual favour, Pilate replied, 'Do you 9
wish me to release for you the king of the Jews?' For he knew it was out of 10
malice that they had brought Jesus before him. But the chief priests incited 11
the crowd to ask him to release Barabbas rather than Jesus. Pilate spoke 12
to them again: 'Then what shall I do with the man you call king of the
Jews?' They shouted back, 'Crucify him!' 'Why, what harm has he done?' 13 14
Pilate asked; but they shouted all the louder, 'Crucify him!' So Pilate, in 15
his desire to satisfy the mob, released Barabbas to them; and he had Jesus
flogged and handed him over to be crucified.

Then the soldiers took him inside the courtyard (the Governor's head- 16
quarters*f*) and called together the whole company. They dressed him in 17
purple, and plaiting a crown of thorns, placed it on his head. Then they 18
began to salute him with, 'Hail, King of the Jews!' They beat him about the 19

a Literally of the Power.   *b Some witnesses add* Who hit you? *as in Matthew and*
Luke.   *c Some witnesses insert* and a cock crew.   *d Or* It is as you say.
e Some witnesses read shouted.   *f Greek* praetorium.

head with a cane and spat upon him, and then knelt and paid mock homage
20 to him. When they had finished their mockery, they stripped him of the
purple and dressed him in his own clothes.

21 THEN THEY TOOK HIM OUT to crucify him. A man called Simon, from
Cyrene, the father of Alexander and Rufus, was passing by on his way in
from the country, and they pressed him into service to carry his cross.

22   They brought him to the place called Golgotha, which means 'Place
23 24 of a skull'. He was offered drugged wine, but he would not take it. Then
they fastened him to the cross. They divided his clothes among them,
casting lots to decide what each should have.

25 26   The hour of the crucifixion was nine in the morning, and the inscription
27 giving the charge against him read, 'The king of the Jews.' Two bandits
were crucified with him, one on his right and the other on his left. [a]

29   The passers-by hurled abuse at him: 'Aha!' they cried, wagging their
heads, 'you would pull the temple down, would you, and build it in three
30 31 days? Come down from the cross and save yourself!' So too the chief
priests and lawyers jested with one another: 'He saved others,' they said,
32 'but he cannot save himself. Let the Messiah, the king of Israel, come down
now from the cross. If we see that, we shall believe.' Even those who were
crucified with him taunted him.

33   At midday a darkness fell over the whole land, which lasted till three in
34 the afternoon; and at three Jesus cried aloud, '*Eli, Eli, lema sabachthani?*',
35 which means, 'My God, my God, why hast thou forsaken me?' [b] Some of
36 the bystanders, on hearing this, said, 'Hark, he is calling Elijah.' A man
ran and soaked a sponge in sour wine and held it to his lips on the end of
37 a cane. 'Let us see', he said, 'if Elijah will come to take him down.' Then
38 Jesus gave a loud cry and died. And the curtain of the temple was torn in
39 two from top to bottom. And when the centurion who was standing opposite
him saw how he died, [c] he said, 'Truly this man was a son of God.' [d]

40 A NUMBER OF WOMEN were also present, watching from a distance.
Among them were Mary of Magdala, Mary the mother of James the
41 younger and of Joseph, and Salome, who had all followed him and waited
on him when he was in Galilee, and there were several others who had come
up to Jerusalem with him.

42   By this time evening had come; and as it was Preparation-day (that is,
43 the day before the Sabbath), Joseph of Arimathaea, a respected member of
the Council, a man who looked forward to the kingdom of God, bravely
44 went in to Pilate and asked for the body of Jesus. Pilate was surprised to
hear that he was already dead; so he sent for the centurion and asked him
45 whether it was long since he died. And when he heard the centurion's
46 report, he gave Joseph leave to take the dead body. So Joseph bought a
linen sheet, took him down from the cross, and wrapped him in the sheet.

[a] *Some witnesses add* (28) Thus that text of Scripture came true which says, 'He was
reckoned among criminals.'   [b] *Some witnesses read* My God, my God, why hast thou
shamed me?   [c] *Some witnesses read* saw that he died with a cry.   [d] *Or* the
Son of God.

Then he laid him in a tomb cut out of the rock, and rolled a stone against the
entrance. And Mary of Magdala and Mary the mother of Joseph were 47
watching and saw where he was laid.

When the Sabbath was over, Mary of Magdala, Mary the mother of **16**
James, and Salome bought *a* aromatic oils intending to go and anoint him;
and very early on the Sunday morning, just after sunrise, they came to the 2
tomb. They were wondering among themselves who would roll away the 3
stone for them from the entrance to the tomb, when they looked up and 4
saw that the stone, huge as it was, had been rolled back already. They 5
went into the tomb, where they saw a youth sitting on the right-hand side,
wearing a white robe; and they were dumbfounded. But he said to them, 6
'Fear nothing; you are looking for Jesus of Nazareth, who was crucified.
He has been raised again; he is not here; look, there is the place where they
laid him. But go and give this message to his disciples and Peter: "He is 7
going on before you into Galilee; there you will see him, as he told you."'
Then they went out and ran away from the tomb, beside themselves with 8
terror. They said nothing to anybody, for they were afraid. *b*

When he had risen from the dead early on Sunday morning he appeared 9
first to Mary of Magdala, from whom he had formerly cast out seven
devils. She went and carried the news to his mourning and sorrowful 10
followers, but when they were told that he was alive and that she had seen 11
him they did not believe it.

Later he appeared in a different guise to two of them as they were 12
walking, on their way into the country. These also went and took the news 13
to the others, but again no one believed them.

Afterwards while the Eleven were at table he appeared to them and 14
reproached them for their incredulity and dullness, because they had not
believed those who had seen him after he was raised from the dead. Then he 15
said to them: 'Go forth to every part of the world, and proclaim the Good
News to the whole creation. Those who believe it and receive baptism will 16
find salvation; those who do not believe will be condemned. Faith will bring 17
with it these miracles: believers will cast out devils in my name and speak in
strange tongues; if they handle snakes or drink any deadly poison, they will 18
come to no harm; and the sick on whom they lay their hands will recover.'

So after talking with them the Lord Jesus was taken up into heaven, and 19
he took his seat at the right hand of God; but they went out to make their 20
proclamation everywhere, and the Lord worked with them and confirmed
their words by the miracles that followed.

And they delivered all these instructions briefly to Peter and his companions. Afterwards Jesus himself sent out by them from east to west the
sacred and imperishable message of eternal salvation. *c*

a Some witnesses omit When the Sabbath ... Salome, *reading* And they went and bought ...
*b At this point some of the most ancient witnesses bring the book to a close; others continue
with verses 9–20, as printed here, or in some cases expanded with additional matter; yet
others insert here the paragraph* And they delivered ... eternal salvation (*here printed
below verse 20*), *and in one of them this is the conclusion of the book; in the remainder, verses
9–20 follow it.   c See note b.*

THE GOSPEL ACCORDING TO
LUKE

1 THE AUTHOR TO THEOPHILUS: Many writers have undertaken to draw up an account of the events that have hap-
2 pened among us, following the traditions handed down to us by
3 the original eyewitnesses and servants of the Gospel. And so I in my turn, your Excellency, as one who has gone over the whole course of these events
4 in detail, have decided to write a connected narrative for you, so as to give you authentic knowledge about the matters of which you have been informed.

The coming of Christ

5 IN THE DAYS of Herod king of Judaea there was a priest named Zechariah, of the division of the priesthood called after Abijah. His wife also was of
6 priestly descent; her name was Elizabeth. Both of them were upright and devout, blamelessly observing all the commandments and ordinances of
7 the Lord. But they had no children, for Elizabeth was barren, and both were well on in years.

8 Once, when it was the turn of his division and he was there to take part
9 in divine service, it fell to his lot, by priestly custom, to enter the sanctuary
10 of the Lord and offer the incense; and the whole congregation was at
11 prayer outside. It was the hour of the incense-offering. There appeared to
12 him an angel of the Lord, standing on the right of the altar of incense. At
13 this sight, Zechariah was startled, and fear overcame him. But the angel said to him, 'Do not be afraid, Zechariah; your prayer has been heard:
14 your wife Elizabeth will bear you a son, and you shall name him John. Your
15 heart will thrill with joy and many will be glad that he was born; for he will be great in the eyes of the Lord. He shall never touch wine or strong drink.
16 From his very birth he will be filled with the Holy Spirit; and he will bring
17 back many Israelites to the Lord their God. He will go before him as forerunner,*a* possessed by the spirit and power of Elijah, to reconcile father and child, to convert the rebellious to the ways of the righteous, to prepare a people that shall be fit for the Lord.'
18 Zechariah said to the angel, 'How can I be sure of this? I am an old man and my wife is well on in years.'
19 The angel replied, 'I am Gabriel; I stand in attendance upon God, and
20 I have been sent to speak to you and bring you this good news. But now listen: you will lose your power of speech, and remain silent until the day

a Or In his sight he will go forth.

when these things happen to you, because you have not believed me, though at their proper time my words will be proved true.'

Meanwhile the people were waiting for Zechariah, surprised that he was 21 staying so long inside. When he did come out he could not speak to them, 22 and they realized that he had had a vision in the sanctuary. He stood there making signs to them, and remained dumb.

When his period of duty was completed Zechariah returned home. After 23 24 this his wife Elizabeth conceived, and for five months she lived in seclusion, thinking, 'This is the Lord's doing; now at last he has deigned to take away 25 my reproach among men.'

In the sixth month the angel Gabriel was sent from God to a town in 26 Galilee called Nazareth, with a message for a girl betrothed to a man named 27 Joseph, a descendant of David; the girl's name was Mary. The angel went 28 in and said to her, 'Greetings, most favoured one! The Lord is with you.' But she was deeply troubled by what he said and wondered what this greet- 29 ing might mean. Then the angel said to her, 'Do not be afraid, Mary, for 30 God has been gracious to you; you shall conceive and bear a son, and you 31 shall give him the name Jesus. He will be great; he will bear the title "Son of 32 the Most High"; the Lord God will give him the throne of his ancestor David, and he will be king over Israel[a] for ever; his reign shall never end.' 33 'How can this be?' said Mary; 'I am still a virgin.' The angel answered, 'The 34 35 Holy Spirit will come upon you, and the power of the Most High will over- shadow you; and for that reason the holy child to be born will be called "Son of God".[b] Moreover your kinswoman Elizabeth has herself conceived a son 36 in her old age; and she who is reputed barren is now in her sixth month, for 37 God's promises can never fail.'[c] 'Here am I,' said Mary; 'I am the Lord's 38 servant; as you have spoken, so be it.' Then the angel left her.

About this time Mary set out and went straight to a town in the uplands 39 of Judah. She went into Zechariah's house and greeted Elizabeth. And 40 41 when Elizabeth heard Mary's greeting, the baby stirred in her womb. Then Elizabeth was filled with the Holy Spirit and cried aloud, 'God's blessing 42 is on you above all women, and his blessing is on the fruit of your womb. Who am I, that the mother of my Lord should visit me? I tell you, when 43 44 your greeting sounded in my ears, the baby in my womb leapt for joy. How 45 happy is she who has had faith that the Lord's promise would be fulfilled!'

And Mary[d] said: 46

'Tell out, my soul, the greatness of the Lord,
        rejoice, rejoice, my spirit, in God my saviour;   47
        so tenderly has he looked upon his servant,   48
                humble as she is.
        For, from this day forth,
        all generations will count me blessed,
        so wonderfully has he dealt with me,   49
                the Lord, the Mighty One.

---

a Literally the house of Jacob.   *b Or* the child to be born will be called holy, "Son of God".   *c Some witnesses read* for with God nothing will prove impossible.
d So the majority of witnesses; some read Elizabeth; *the original may have had no name.*

His name is Holy;
50   his mercy sure from generation to generation
toward those who fear him;
51   the deeds his own right arm has done
disclose his might:
the arrogant of heart and mind he has put to rout,
52   he has brought down monarchs from their thrones,
but the humble have been lifted high.
53   The hungry he has satisfied with good things,
the rich sent empty away.

54   He has ranged himself at the side of Israel his servant;
55   firm in his promise to our forefathers,
he has not forgotten to show mercy to Abraham
and his children's children, for ever.'

56   Mary stayed with her about three months and then returned home.

57 NOW THE TIME CAME for Elizabeth's child to be born, and she gave birth
58 to a son. When her neighbours and relatives heard what great favour the
59 Lord had shown her, they were as delighted as she was. Then on the eighth
day they came to circumcise the child; and they were going to name him
60 Zechariah after his father. But his mother spoke up and said, 'No! he is to
61 be called John.' 'But', they said, 'there is nobody in your family who has
62 that name.' They inquired of his father by signs what he would like him to
63 be called. He asked for a writing-tablet and to the astonishment of all wrote
64 down, 'His name is John.' Immediately his lips and tongue were freed and
65 he began to speak, praising God. All the neighbours were struck with awe,
and everywhere in the uplands of Judaea the whole story became common
66 talk. All who heard it were deeply impressed and said, 'What will this child
become?' For indeed the hand of the Lord was upon him. *a*
67   And Zechariah his father was filled with the Holy Spirit and uttered this
prophecy:

68   'Praise to the God of Israel!
For he has turned to his people, saved them and set them free,
69   and has raised up a deliverer of victorious power
from the house of his servant David.

70   So he promised: age after age he proclaimed
by the lips of his holy prophets,
71   that he would deliver us from our enemies,
out of the hands of all who hate us;
72   that he would deal mercifully with our fathers,
calling to mind his solemn covenant.

73   Such was the oath he swore to our father Abraham,
74   to rescue us from enemy hands,

a Some witnesses read 'What will this child become, for indeed the hand of the Lord is upon him?'

and grant us, free from fear, to worship him
with a holy worship, with uprightness of heart, 75
in his presence, our whole life long.

And you, my child, you shall be called Prophet of the Highest, 76
for you will be the Lord's forerunner, to prepare his way
and lead his people to salvation through knowledge of him, 77
by the forgiveness of their sins:
for in the tender compassion of our God 78
the morning sun from heaven will rise *a* upon us,
to shine on those who live in darkness, under the cloud of death, 79
and to guide our feet into the way of peace.'

As the child grew up he became strong in spirit; he lived out in the wilds 80
until the day when he appeared publicly before Israel.

IN THOSE DAYS a decree was issued by the Emperor Augustus for a **2**
registration to be made throughout the Roman world. This was the first 2
registration of its kind; it took place when Quirinius *b* was governor of
Syria. For this purpose everyone made his way to his own town; and so 3 4
Joseph went up to Judaea from the town of Nazareth in Galilee, to register 5
at the city of David, called Bethlehem, because he was of the house of
David by descent; and with him went Mary who was betrothed to him.
She was expecting a child, and while they were there the time came for her 6
baby to be born, and she gave birth to a son, her first-born. She wrapped 7
him in his swaddling clothes, and laid him in a manger, because there was
no room for them to lodge in the house.

Now in this same district there were shepherds out in the fields, keeping 8
watch through the night over their flock, when suddenly there stood before 9
them an angel of the Lord, and the splendour of the Lord shone round
them. They were terror-stricken, but the angel said, 'Do not be afraid; 10
I have good news for you: there is great joy coming to the whole people.
Today in the city of David a deliverer has been born to you—the Messiah, 11
the Lord. *c* And this is your sign: you will find a baby lying wrapped in 12
his swaddling clothes, in a manger.' All at once there was with the angel 13
a great company of the heavenly host, singing the praises of God:

'Glory to God in highest heaven, 14
and on earth his peace for men on whom his favour rests.' *d*

After the angels had left them and gone into heaven the shepherds said 15
to one another, 'Come, we must go straight to Bethlehem and see this thing
that has happened, which the Lord has made known to us.' So they went 16
with all speed and found their way to Mary and Joseph; and the baby was
lying in the manger. When they saw him, they recounted what they had 17
been told about this child; and all who heard were astonished at what the 18
shepherds said. But Mary treasured up all these things and pondered over 19

a Some witnesses read has risen. *b Or* This was the first registration carried out
while Quirinius . . . *c Some witnesses read* to you—the Lord's Messiah. *d Some
witnesses read* and on earth his peace, his favour towards men.

20 them. Meanwhile the shepherds returned glorifying and praising God for what they had heard and seen; it had all happened as they had been told.

21   Eight days later the time came to circumcise him, and he was given the name Jesus, the name given by the angel before he was conceived.

22   Then, after their purification had been completed in accordance with the Law of Moses, they brought him up to Jerusalem to present him to the
23 Lord (as prescribed in the law of the Lord: 'Every first-born male shall be
24 deemed to belong to the Lord'), and also to make the offering as stated in the law: 'A pair of turtle doves or two young pigeons.'

25   There was at that time in Jerusalem a man called Simeon. This man was upright and devout, one who watched and waited for the restoration of
26 Israel, and the Holy Spirit was upon him. It had been disclosed to him by the Holy Spirit that he would not see death until he had seen the Lord's
27 Messiah. Guided by the Spirit he came into the temple; and when the parents brought in the child Jesus to do for him what was customary under
28 the Law, he took him in his arms, praised God, and said:

29   'This day, Master, thou givest thy servant his discharge in peace;
        now thy promise is fulfilled.
30 For I have seen with my own eyes
31 the deliverance which thou hast made ready in full view of all the nations:
32 a light that will be a revelation to the heathen,
        and glory to thy people Israel.'

33   The child's father and mother were full of wonder at what was being
34 said about him. Simeon blessed them and said to Mary his mother, 'This
35 child is destined to be a sign which men reject; and you too shall be pierced to the heart. Many in Israel will stand or fall*a* because of him, and thus the secret thoughts of many will be laid bare.'

36   There was also a prophetess, Anna the daughter of Phanuel, of the tribe of Asher. She was a very old woman, who had lived seven years with her
37 husband after she was first married, and then alone as a widow to the age of eighty-four.*b* She never left the temple, but worshipped day and night,
38 fasting and praying. Coming up at that very moment, she returned thanks to God; and she talked about the child to all who were looking for the liberation of Jerusalem.

39   When they had done everything prescribed in the law of the Lord, they
40 returned to Galilee to their own town of Nazareth. The child grew big and strong and full of wisdom; and God's favour was upon him.

41   Now it was the practice of his parents to go to Jerusalem every year for
42 the Passover festival; and when he was twelve, they made the pilgrimage
43 as usual. When the festive season was over and they started for home, the boy Jesus stayed behind in Jerusalem. His parents did not know of this;
44 but thinking that he was with the party they journeyed on for a whole day, and only then did they begin looking for him among their friends and
45 relations. As they could not find him they returned to Jerusalem to look for
46 him; and after three days they found him sitting in the temple surrounded

---

a Or Many in Israel will fall and rise again . . .
b Or widow for another eighty-four years.

by the teachers, listening to them and putting questions; and all who heard 47
him were amazed at his intelligence and the answers he gave. His parents 48
were astonished to see him there, and his mother said to him, 'My son, why
have you treated us like this? Your father and I have been searching for you
in great anxiety.' 'What made you search?' he said. 'Did you not know that 49
I was bound to be in my Father's house?' But they did not understand what 50
he meant. Then he went back with them to Nazareth, and continued to be 51
under their authority; his mother treasured up all these things in her heart.
As Jesus grew up he advanced in wisdom and in favour with God and men. 52

IN THE FIFTEENTH YEAR of the Emperor Tiberius, when Pontius Pilate **3**
was governor of Judaea, when Herod was prince of Galilee, his brother
Philip prince of Ituraea and Trachonitis, and Lysanias prince of Abilene,
during the high-priesthood of Annas and Caiaphas, the word of God came 2
to John son of Zechariah in the wilderness. And he went all over the Jordan 3
valley proclaiming a baptism in token of repentance for the forgiveness of
sins, as it is written in the book of the prophecies of Isaiah: 4

'A voice crying aloud in the wilderness,
"Prepare a way for the Lord;
clear a straight path for him.
Every ravine shall be filled in, 5
and every mountain and hill levelled;
the corners shall be straightened,
and the rugged ways made smooth;
and all mankind shall see God's deliverance."' 6

Crowds of people came out to be baptized by him, and he said to them: 7
'You vipers' brood! Who warned you to escape from the coming retribution? Then prove your repentance by the fruit it bears; and do not begin 8
saying to yourselves, "We have Abraham for our father." I tell you that
God can make children for Abraham out of these stones here. Already the 9
axe is laid to the roots of the trees; and every tree that fails to produce good
fruit is cut down and thrown on the fire.'

The people asked him, 'Then what are we to do?' He replied, 'The man 10 11
with two shirts must share with him who has none, and anyone who has food
must do the same.' Among those who came to be baptized were tax- 12
gatherers, and they said to him, 'Master, what are we to do?' He told them, 13
'Exact no more than the assessment.' Soldiers on service also asked him, 14
'And what of us?' To them he said, 'No bullying; no blackmail; make do
with your pay!'

The people were on the tiptoe of expectation, all wondering about John, 15
whether perhaps he was the Messiah, but he spoke out and said to them 16
all: 'I baptize you with water; but there is one to come who is mightier
than I. I am not fit to unfasten his shoes. He will baptize you with the Holy
Spirit and with fire. His shovel is ready in his hand, to winnow his threshing- 17
floor and gather the wheat into his granary; but he will burn the chaff on
a fire that can never go out.'

In this and many other ways he made his appeal to the people and 18

19 announced the good news. But Prince Herod, when he was rebuked by
    him over the affair of his brother's wife Herodias and for his other misdeeds,
20 crowned them all by shutting John up in prison.

21 DURING A GENERAL BAPTISM of the people, when Jesus too had been
22 baptized and was praying, heaven opened and the Holy Spirit descended
    on him in bodily form like a dove; and there came a voice from heaven,
    'Thou art my Son, my Beloved;*a* on thee my favour rests.'*b*
23   When Jesus began his work he was about thirty years old, the son, as
24 people thought, of Joseph, son of Heli, son of Matthat, son of Levi, son of
25 Melchi, son of Jannai, son of Joseph, son of Mattathiah, son of Amos,
26 son of Nahum, son of Esli, son of Naggai, son of Maath, son of Mattathiah,
27 son of Semein, son of Josech, son of Joda, son of Johanan, son of Rhesa, son
28 of Zerubbabel, son of Shealtiel, son of Neri, son of Melchi, son of Addi,
29 son of Cosam, son of Elmadam, son of Er, son of Joshua, son of Eliezer, son
30 of Jorim, son of Matthat, son of Levi, son of Symeon, son of Judah, son of
31 Joseph, son of Jonam, son of Eliakim, son of Melea, son of Menna, son
32 of Mattatha, son of Nathan, son of David, son of Jesse, son of Obed, son of
33 Boaz, son of Salmon, son of Nahshon, son of Amminadab,*c* son of Arni,*d*
34 son of Hezron, son of Perez, son of Judah, son of Jacob, son of Isaac, son of
35 Abraham, son of Terah, son of Nahor, son of Serug, son of Reu, son of
36 Peleg, son of Eber, son of Shelah, son of Cainan, son of Arpachshad, son
37 of Shem, son of Noah, son of Lamech, son of Methuselah, son of Enoch,
38 son of Jared, son of Mahalaleel, son of Cainan, son of Enosh, son of Seth,
    son of Adam, son of God.

4 1 2   Full of the Holy Spirit, Jesus returned from the Jordan, and for forty days
    was led by the Spirit up and down the wilderness and tempted by the devil.
        All that time he had nothing to eat, and at the end of it he was famished.
3   The devil said to him, 'If you are the Son of God, tell this stone to become
4   bread.' Jesus answered, 'Scripture says, "Man cannot live on bread
    alone."'
5   Next the devil led him up and showed him in a flash all the kingdoms of
6   the world. 'All this dominion will I give to you,' he said, 'and the glory
    that goes with it; for it has been put in my hands and I can give it to anyone
7 8 I choose. You have only to do homage to me and it shall all be yours.' Jesus
    answered him, 'Scripture says, "You shall do homage to the Lord your
    God and worship him alone."'
9   The devil took him to Jerusalem and set him on the parapet of the temple.
10 'If you are the Son of God,' he said, 'throw yourself down; for Scripture
11 says, "He will give his angels orders to take care of you", and again, "They
    will support you in their arms for fear you should strike your foot against
12 a stone."' Jesus answered him, 'It has been said, "You are not to put the
    Lord your God to the test."'
13   So, having come to the end of all his temptations, the devil departed,
    biding his time.

a Or Thou art my only Son.   *b* Some witnesses read My Son art thou; this day I
have begotten thee.   *c* Some witnesses add son of Admin.   *d* Some witnesses
read Aram; Ruth 4. 19 and 1 Chronicles 2. 9 have Ram.

In Galilee : success and opposition

THEN JESUS, armed with the power of the Spirit, returned to Galilee; 14
and reports about him spread through the whole country-side. He 15
taught in their synagogues and all men sang his praises.

So he came to Nazareth, where he had been brought up, and went to 16
synagogue on the Sabbath day as he regularly did. He stood up to read the
lesson and was handed the scroll of the prophet Isaiah. He opened the scroll 17
and found the passage which says,

'The spirit of the Lord is upon me because he has anointed me; 18
he has sent me to announce good news to the poor,
to proclaim release for prisoners and recovery of sight for the blind;
to let the broken victims go free,
to proclaim the year of the Lord's favour.' 19

He rolled up the scroll, gave it back to the attendant, and sat down; and all 20
eyes in the synagogue were fixed on him.

He began to speak: 'Today', he said, 'in your very hearing this text has 21
come true.'[a] There was a general stir of admiration; they were surprised 22
that words of such grace should fall from his lips. 'Is not this Joseph's
son?' they asked. Then Jesus said, 'No doubt you will quote the proverb 23
to me, "Physician, heal yourself!", and say, "We have heard of all your
doings at Capernaum; do the same here in your own home town." I tell 24
you this,' he went on: 'no prophet is recognized in his own country. There 25
were many widows in Israel, you may be sure, in Elijah's time, when for
three years and six months the skies never opened, and famine lay hard
over the whole country; yet it was to none of those that Elijah was sent, 26
but to a widow at Sarepta in the territory of Sidon. Again, in the time 27
of the prophet Elisha there were many lepers in Israel, and not one of
them was healed, but only Naaman, the Syrian.' At these words the whole 28
congregation were infuriated. They leapt up, threw him out of the town, 29
and took him to the brow of the hill on which it was built, meaning to
hurl him over the edge. But he walked straight through them all, and went 30
away.

Coming down to Capernaum, a town in Galilee, he taught the people on 31
the Sabbath, and they were astounded at his teaching, for what he said had 32
the note of authority. Now there was a man in the synagogue possessed by 33
a devil, an unclean spirit. He shrieked at the top of his voice, 'What do you 34
want with us, Jesus of Nazareth? Have you[b] come to destroy us? I know
who you are—the Holy One of God.' Jesus rebuked him: 'Be silent', he 35
said, 'and come out of him.' Then the devil, after throwing the man down
in front of the people, left him without doing him any injury. Amazement 36
fell on them all and they said to one another: 'What is there in this man's
words? He gives orders to the unclean spirits with authority and power,
and out they go.' So the news spread, and he was the talk of the whole 37
district.

[a] Or 'Today', he said, 'this text which you have just heard has come true.'
[b] Or You have.

38 On leaving the synagogue he went to Simon's house. Simon's mother-
39 in-law was in the grip of a high fever; and they asked him to help her. He
came and stood over her and rebuked the fever. It left her, and she got up
at once and waited on them.

40 At sunset all who had friends suffering from one disease or another
brought them to him; and he laid his hands on them one by one and cured
41 them. Devils also came out of many of them, shouting, 'You are the Son of
God.' But he rebuked them and forbade them to speak, because they knew
that he was the Messiah.

42 When day broke he went out and made his way to a lonely spot. But the
people went in search of him, and when they came to where he was they
43 pressed him not to leave them. But he said, 'I must give the good news
of the kingdom of God to the other towns also, for that is what I was sent
44 to do.' So he proclaimed the Gospel in the synagogues of Judaea.*a*

5 One day as he stood by the Lake of Gennesaret, and the people crowded
2 upon him to listen to the word of God, he noticed two boats lying at the
water's edge; the fishermen had come ashore and were washing their nets.
3 He got into one of the boats, which belonged to Simon, and asked him to
put out a little way from the shore; then he went on teaching the crowds
4 from his seat in the boat. When he had finished speaking, he said to Simon,
5 'Put out into deep water and let down your nets for a catch.' Simon
answered, 'Master, we were hard at work all night and caught nothing at all;
6 but if you say so, I will let down the nets.' They did so and made a big haul
7 of fish; and their nets began to split. So they signalled to their partners in
the other boat to come and help them. This they did, and loaded both boats
8 to the point of sinking. When Simon saw what had happened he fell at
9 Jesus's knees and said, 'Go, Lord, leave me, sinner that I am!' For he and
10 all his companions were amazed at the catch they had made; so too were his
partners James and John, Zebedee's sons. 'Do not be afraid,' said Jesus to
11 Simon; 'from now on you will be catching men.' As soon as they had
brought the boats to land, they left everything and followed him.

12 He was once in a certain town where there happened to be a man covered
with leprosy; seeing Jesus, he bowed to the ground and begged his help.
13 'Sir,' he said, 'if only you will, you can cleanse me.' Jesus stretched out his
hand, touched him, and said, 'Indeed I will; be clean again.' The leprosy
14 left him immediately. Jesus then ordered him not to tell anybody. 'But go,'
he said, 'show yourself to the priest, and make the offering laid down by
15 Moses for your cleansing; that will certify the cure.' But the talk about him
spread all the more; great crowds gathered to hear him and to be cured of
16 their ailments. And from time to time he would withdraw to lonely places
for prayer.

17 One day he was teaching, and Pharisees and teachers of the law were
sitting round. People had come from every village of Galilee and from
Judaea and Jerusalem,*b* and the power of the Lord was with him to heal the
18 sick. Some men appeared carrying a paralysed man on a bed. They tried

a Or the Jewish synagogues; *some witnesses read* the synagogues of Galilee.
b *Some witnesses read* and Pharisees and teachers of the law, who had come from every
village of Galilee and from Judaea and Jerusalem, were sitting round.

to bring him in and set him down in front of Jesus, but finding no way to 19
do so because of the crowd, they went up on to the roof and let him down
through the tiling, bed and all, into the middle of the company in front of
Jesus. When Jesus saw their faith, he said, 'Man, your sins are forgiven you.' 20

The lawyers and the Pharisees began saying to themselves, 'Who is this 21
fellow with his blasphemous talk? Who but God alone can forgive sins?'
But Jesus knew what they were thinking and answered them: 'Why do you 22
harbour thoughts like these? Is it easier to say, "Your sins are forgiven 23
you", or to say, "Stand up and walk"? But to convince you that the Son of 24
Man has the right on earth to forgive sins'—he turned to the paralysed
man—'I say to you, stand up, take your bed, and go home.' And at once 25
he rose to his feet before their eyes, took up the bed he had been lying on,
and went home praising God. They were all lost in amazement and praised 26
God; filled with awe they said, 'You would never believe the things we
have seen today.'

Later, when he went out, he saw a tax-gatherer, Levi by name, at his seat 27
in the custom-house, and said to him, 'Follow me'; and he rose to his feet, 28
left everything behind, and followed him.

Afterwards Levi held a big reception in his house for Jesus; among the 29
guests was a large party of tax-gatherers and others. The Pharisees and the 30
lawyers of their sect complained to his disciples: 'Why do you eat and
drink', they said, 'with tax-gatherers and sinners?' Jesus answered them: 31
'It is not the healthy that need a doctor, but the sick; I have not come to 32
invite virtuous people, but to call sinners to repentance.'

Then they said to him, 'John's disciples are much given to fasting and the 33
practice of prayer, and so are the disciples of the Pharisees; but yours eat
and drink.' Jesus replied, 'Can you make the bridegroom's friends fast 34
while the bridegroom is with them? But a time will come: the bridegroom 35
will be taken away from them, and that will be the time for them to fast.'

He told them this parable also: 'No one tears a piece from a new cloak 36
to patch an old one; if he does, he will have made a hole in the new cloak,
and the patch from the new will not match the old. Nor does anyone put 37
new wine into old wine-skins; if he does, the new wine will burst the skins,
the wine will be wasted, and the skins ruined. Fresh skins for new wine! 38
And no one after drinking old wine wants new; for he says, "The old wine 39
is good."'

One Sabbath he was going through the cornfields, and his disciples were **6**
plucking the ears of corn, rubbing them in their hands, and eating them.
Some of the Pharisees said, 'Why are you doing what is forbidden on the 2
Sabbath?' Jesus answered, 'So you have not read what David did when he 3
and his men were hungry? He went into the House of God and took the 4
sacred bread to eat and gave it to his men, though priests alone are allowed
to eat it, and no one else.' He also said, 'The Son of Man is sovereign even 5
over the Sabbath.'

On another Sabbath he had gone to synagogue and was teaching. There 6
happened to be a man in the congregation whose right arm was withered;
and the lawyers and the Pharisees were on the watch to see whether Jesus 7
would cure him on the Sabbath, so that they could find a charge to bring

8 against him. But he knew what was in their minds and said to the man with
the withered arm, 'Get up and stand out here.' So he got up and stood there.
9 Then Jesus said to them, 'I put the question to you: is it permitted to do
10 good or to do evil on the Sabbath, to save life or to destroy it?' He looked
round at them all and then said to the man, 'Stretch out your arm.' He
11 did so, and his arm was restored. But they were beside themselves with
anger, and began to discuss among themselves what they could do to
Jesus.

12   During this time he went out one day into the hills to pray, and spent the
13 night in prayer to God. When day broke he called his disciples to him, and
14 from among them he chose twelve and named them Apostles: Simon, to
whom he gave the name of Peter, and Andrew his brother, James and
15 John, Philip and Bartholomew, Matthew and Thomas, James son of
16 Alphaeus, and Simon who was called the Zealot, Judas son of James, and
Judas Iscariot who turned traitor.

17   He came down the hill with them and took his stand on level ground.
There was a large concourse of his disciples and great numbers of people
from Jerusalem and Judaea and from the seaboard of Tyre and Sidon,
18 who had come to listen to him, and to be cured of their diseases. Those who
19 were troubled with unclean spirits were cured; and everyone in the crowd
was trying to touch him, because power went out from him and cured
them all.

20 THEN TURNING TO HIS DISCIPLES he began to speak:
'How blest are you who are in need; the kingdom of God is yours.
21   'How blest are you who now go hungry; your hunger shall be satisfied.
'How blest are you who weep now; you shall laugh.
22   'How blest you are when men hate you, when they outlaw you and insult
you, and ban your very name as infamous, because of the Son of Man.
23 On that day be glad and dance for joy; for assuredly you have a rich reward
in heaven; in just the same way did their fathers treat the prophets.
24   'But alas for you who are rich; you have had your time of happiness.
25 'Alas for you who are well-fed now; you shall go hungry.
'Alas for you who laugh now; you shall mourn and weep.
26 'Alas for you when all speak well of you; just so did their fathers treat
the false prophets.
27   'But to you who hear me I say:
28   'Love your enemies; do good to those who hate you; bless those who
29 curse you; pray for those who treat you spitefully. When a man hits you on
the cheek, offer him the other cheek too; when a man takes your coat, let
30 him have your shirt as well. Give to everyone who asks you; when a man
31 takes what is yours, do not demand it back. Treat others as you would
like them to treat you.
32   'If you love only those who love you, what credit is that to you? Even
33 sinners love those who love them. Again, if you do good only to those who
34 do good to you, what credit is that to you? Even sinners do as much. And
if you lend only where you expect to be repaid, what credit is that to you?
35 Even sinners lend to each other to be repaid in full. But you must love your

enemies and do good; and lend without expecting any return;*ᵃ* and you will have a rich reward: you will be sons of the Most High, because he himself is kind to the ungrateful and wicked. Be compassionate as your 36 Father is compassionate.

'Pass no judgement, and you will not be judged; do not condemn, and 37 you will not be condemned; acquit, and you will be acquitted; give, and 38 gifts will be given you. Good measure, pressed down, shaken together, and running over, will be poured into your lap; for whatever measure you deal out to others will be dealt to you in return.'

He also offered them a parable: 'Can one blind man be guide to another? 39 Will they not both fall into the ditch? A pupil is not superior to his teacher; 40 but everyone, when his training is complete, will reach his teacher's level.

'Why do you look at the speck of sawdust in your brother's eye, with 41 never a thought for the great plank in your own? How can you say to your 42 brother, "My dear brother, let me take the speck out of your eye", when you are blind to the plank in your own? You hypocrite! First take the plank out of your own eye, and then you will see clearly to take the speck out of your brother's.

'There is no such thing as a good tree producing worthless fruit, nor 43 yet a worthless tree producing good fruit. For each tree is known by its own 44 fruit: you do not gather figs from thistles, and you do not pick grapes from brambles. A good man produces good from the store of good within 45 himself; and an evil man from evil within produces evil. For the words that the mouth utters come from the overflowing of the heart.

'Why do you keep calling me "Lord, Lord"—and never do what I tell 46 you? Everyone who comes to me and hears what I say, and acts upon it— 47 I will show you what he is like. He is like a man who, in building his house, 48 dug deep and laid the foundations on rock. When the flood came, the river burst upon that house, but could not shift it, because it had been soundly built. But he who hears and does not act is like a man who built his house 49 on the soil without foundations. As soon as the river burst upon it, the house collapsed, and fell with a great crash.'

WHEN HE HAD FINISHED addressing the people, he went to Capernaum. 7 A centurion there had a servant whom he valued highly; this servant was 2 ill and near to death. Hearing about Jesus, he sent some Jewish elders with 3 the request that he would come and save his servant's life. They approached 4 Jesus and pressed their petition earnestly: 'He deserves this favour from you,' they said, 'for he is a friend of our nation and it is he who built us our 5 synagogue.' Jesus went with them; but when he was not far from the 6 house, the centurion sent friends with this message: 'Do not trouble further, sir; it is not for me to have you under my roof, and that is why I 7 did not presume to approach you in person. But say the word and my servant will be cured. I know, for in my position I am myself under orders, 8 with soldiers under me. I say to one, "Go", and he goes; to another, "Come here", and he comes; and to my servant, "Do this", and he does it.' When 9 Jesus heard this, he admired the man, and, turning to the crowd that was

---

ᵃ Or without ever giving up hope; some witnesses read without giving up hope of anyone.

following him, he said, 'I tell you, nowhere, even in Israel, have I found
10 faith like this.' And the messengers returned to the house and found the
servant in good health.

11   Afterwards[a] Jesus went to a town called Nain, accompanied by his
12 disciples and a large crowd. As he approached the gate of the town he met
a funeral. The dead man was the only son of his widowed mother; and
13 many of the townspeople were there with her. When the Lord saw her his
14 heart went out to her, and he said, 'Weep no more.' With that he stepped
forward and laid his hand on the bier; and the bearers halted. Then he
15 spoke: 'Young man, rise up!' The dead man sat up and began to speak;
16 and Jesus gave him back to his mother. Deep awe fell upon them all, and
they praised God. 'A great prophet has arisen among us', they said, and
17 again, 'God has shown his care for his people.' The story of what he had
done ran through all parts of Judaea and the whole neighbourhood.

18 19   John too was informed of all this by his disciples. Summoning two of
their number he sent them to the Lord with this message: 'Are you the one
20 who is to come, or are we to expect some other?' The messengers made
their way to Jesus and said, 'John the Baptist has sent us to you: he asks,
21 "Are you the one who is to come, or are we to expect some other?"' There
and then he cured many sufferers from diseases, plagues, and evil spirits;
22 and on many blind people he bestowed sight. Then he gave them his answer:
'Go', he said, 'and tell John what you have seen and heard: how the blind
recover their sight, the lame walk, the lepers are made clean, the deaf hear,
23 the dead are raised to life, the poor are hearing the good news—and happy
is the man who does not find me a stumbling-block.'

24   After John's messengers had left, Jesus began to speak about him to the
crowds: 'What was the spectacle that drew you to the wilderness? A reed-
25 bed swept by the wind? No? Then what did you go out to see? A man
dressed in silks and satins? Surely you must look in palaces for grand
26 clothes and luxury. But what did you go out to see? A prophet? Yes indeed,
27 and far more than a prophet. He is the man of whom Scripture says,

> "Here is my herald, whom I send on ahead of you,
>   and he will prepare your way before you."

28 I tell you, there is not a mother's son greater than John, and yet the least
in the kingdom of God is greater than he.'
29   When they heard him, all the people, including the tax-gatherers,
30 praised God, for they had accepted John's baptism; but the Pharisees and
lawyers, who refused his baptism, had rejected[b] God's purpose for
themselves.

31   'How can I describe the people of this generation? What are they like?
32 They are like children sitting in the market-place and shouting at each other,

> "We piped for you and you would not dance."
> "We wept and wailed, and you would not mourn."

---

[a] *Some witnesses read* On the next day.   [b] *Or* '. . . greater than he. And all the
people, including the tax-gatherers, when they heard him, accepted John's baptism and
acknowledged the righteous dealing of God; but the Pharisees and lawyers, by refusing
his baptism, rejected . . .'

For John the Baptist came neither eating bread nor drinking wine, and 33
you say, "He is possessed." The Son of Man came eating and drinking, 34
and you say, "Look at him! a glutton and a drinker, a friend of tax-gatherers
and sinners!" And yet God's wisdom is proved right by all who are her 35
children.'

One of the Pharisees invited him to eat with him; he went to the Pharisee's 36
house and took his place at table. A woman who was living an immoral life 37
in the town had learned that Jesus was at table in the Pharisee's house and
had brought oil of myrrh in a small flask. She took her place behind him, 38
by his feet, weeping. His feet were wetted with her tears and she wiped
them with her hair, kissing them and anointing them with the myrrh.
When his host the Pharisee saw this he said to himself, 'If this fellow were 39
a real prophet, he would know who this woman is that touches him, and
what sort of woman she is, a sinner.' Jesus took him up and said, 'Simon, 40
I have something to say to you.' 'Speak on, Master', said he. 'Two men were 41
in debt to a money-lender: one owed him five hundred silver pieces, the
other fifty. As neither had anything to pay with he let them both off. Now, 42
which will love him most?' Simon replied, 'I should think the one that was 43
let off most.' 'You are right', said Jesus. Then turning to the woman, he 44
said to Simon, 'You see this woman? I came to your house: you provided
no water for my feet; but this woman has made my feet wet with her tears
and wiped them with her hair. You gave me no kiss; but she has been kissing 45
my feet ever since I came in. You did not anoint my head with oil; but she 46
has anointed my feet with myrrh. And so, I tell you, her great love proves 47
that her many sins have been forgiven; where little has been forgiven, little
love is shown.' Then he said to her, 'Your sins are forgiven.' The other 48 49
guests began to ask themselves, 'Who is this, that he can forgive sins?' But 50
he said to the woman, 'Your faith has saved you; go in peace.'

AFTER THIS he went journeying from town to town and village to village, 8
proclaiming the good news of the kingdom of God. With him were the
Twelve and a number of women who had been set free from evil spirits 2
and infirmities: Mary, known as Mary of Magdala, from whom seven
devils had come out, Joanna, the wife of Chuza a steward of Herod's, 3
Susanna, and many others. These women provided for them out of their
own resources.

People were now gathering in large numbers, and as they made their 4
way to him from one town after another, he said in a parable: 'A sower 5
went out to sow his seed. And as he sowed, some seed fell along the footpath, where it was trampled on, and the birds ate it up. Some seed fell on 6
rock and, after coming up, withered for lack of moisture. Some seed fell 7
in among thistles, and the thistles grew up with it and choked it. And some 8
of the seed fell into good soil, and grew, and yielded a hundredfold.' As
he said this he called out, 'If you have ears to hear, then hear.'

His disciples asked him what this parable meant, and he said, 'It has been 9 10
granted to you to know the secrets of the kingdom of God; but the others
have only parables, so that they may look but see nothing, hear but understand nothing.

11 12 'This is what the parable means. The seed is the word of God. Those along the footpath are the men who hear it, and then the devil comes and carries off the word from their hearts for fear they should believe and be
13 saved. The seed sown on rock stands for those who receive the word with joy when they hear it, but have no root; they are believers for a while, but
14 in the time of testing they desert. That which fell among thistles represents those who hear, but their further growth is choked by cares and wealth
15 and the pleasures of life, and they bring nothing to maturity. But the seed in good soil represents those who bring a good and honest heart to the hearing of the word, hold it fast, and by their perseverance yield a harvest.

16 'Nobody lights a lamp and then covers it with a basin or puts it under the bed. On the contrary, he puts it on a lamp-stand so that those who come in
17 may see the light. For there is nothing hidden that will not become public, nothing under cover that will not be made known and brought into the open.

18 'Take care, then, how you listen; for the man who has will be given more, and the man who has not will forfeit even what he thinks he has.'

19 His mother and his brothers arrived but could not get to him for the
20 crowd. He was told, 'Your mother and brothers are standing outside, and
21 they want to see you.' He replied, 'My mother and my brothers—they are those who hear the word of God and act upon it.'

22 One day he got into a boat with his disciples and said to them, 'Let us
23 cross over to the other side of the lake.' So they put out; and as they sailed along he went to sleep. Then a heavy squall struck the lake; they began to
24 ship water and were in grave danger. They went to him, and roused him, crying, 'Master, Master, we are sinking!' He awoke, and rebuked the wind and the turbulent waters. The storm subsided and all was calm.
25 'Where is your faith?' he asked. In fear and astonishment they said to one another, 'Who can this be? He gives his orders to wind and waves, and they obey him.'

26 So they landed in the country of the Gergesenes,*a* which is opposite
27 Galilee. As he stepped ashore he was met by a man from the town who was possessed by devils. For a long time he had neither worn clothes nor lived
28 in a house, but stayed among the tombs. When he saw Jesus he cried out, and fell at his feet shouting, 'What do you want with me, Jesus, son of the Most High God? I implore you, do not torment me.'

29 For Jesus was already ordering the unclean spirit to come out of the man. Many a time it had seized him, and then, for safety's sake, they would secure him with chains and fetters; but each time he broke loose, and with the devil in charge made off to the solitary places.

30 Jesus asked him, 'What is your name?' 'Legion', he replied. This was
31 because so many devils had taken possession of him. And they begged him not to banish them to the Abyss.

32 There happened to be a large herd of pigs nearby, feeding on the hill; and the spirits begged him to let them go into these pigs. He gave them
33 leave; the devils came out of the man and went into the pigs, and the herd rushed over the edge into the lake and were drowned.

a Some witnesses read Gerasenes; *others read* Gadarenes.

The men in charge of them saw what had happened, and, taking to their 34
heels, they carried the news to the town and country-side; and the people 35
came out to see for themselves. When they came to Jesus, and found the
man from whom the devils had gone out sitting at his feet clothed and in
his right mind, they were afraid. The spectators told them how the madman 36
had been cured. Then the whole population of the Gergesene *a* district 37
asked him to go, for they were in the grip of a great fear. So he got into the
boat and returned. The man from whom the devils had gone out begged 38
leave to go with him; but Jesus sent him away: 'Go back home,' he said, 39
'and tell them everything that God has done for you.' The man went all over
the town spreading the news of what Jesus had done for him.

When Jesus returned, the people welcomed him, for they were all 40
expecting him. Then a man appeared—Jairus was his name and he was 41
president of the synagogue. Throwing himself down at Jesus's feet he
begged him to come to his house, because he had an only daughter, about 42
twelve years old, who was dying. And while Jesus was on his way he could
hardly breathe for the crowds.

Among them was a woman who had suffered from haemorrhages for 43
twelve years; and *b* nobody had been able to cure her. She came up from 44
behind and touched the edge of *c* his cloak, and at once her haemorrhage
stopped. Jesus said, 'Who was it that touched me?' All disclaimed it, and 45
Peter and his companions said, 'Master, the crowds are hemming you in
and pressing upon you!' But Jesus said, 'Someone did touch me, for I felt 46
that power had gone out from me.' Then the woman, seeing that she was 47
detected, came trembling and fell at his feet. Before all the people she
explained why she had touched him and how she had been instantly cured.
He said to her, 'My daughter, your faith has cured you. Go in peace.' 48

While he was still speaking, a man came from the president's house with 49
the message, 'Your daughter is dead; trouble the Rabbi no further.' But 50
Jesus heard, and interposed. 'Do not be afraid,' he said; 'only show faith
and she will be well again.' On arrival at the house he allowed no one to go 51
in with him except Peter, John, and James, and the child's father and
mother. And all were weeping and lamenting for her. He said, 'Weep no 52
more; she is not dead: she is asleep'; and they only laughed at him, well 53
knowing that she was dead. But Jesus took hold of her hand and called her: 54
'Get up, my child.' Her spirit returned, she stood up immediately, and 55
he told them to give her something to eat. Her parents were astounded; 56
but he forbade them to tell anyone what had happened.

HE NOW CALLED the Twelve together and gave them power and authority 9
to overcome all the devils and to cure diseases, and sent them to proclaim 2
the kingdom of God and to heal. 'Take nothing for the journey,' he told 3
them, 'neither stick nor pack, neither bread nor money; nor are you each
to have a second coat. When you are admitted to a house, stay there, 4
and go on from there. As for those who will not receive you, when you leave 5
their town shake the dust off your feet as a warning to them.' So they set 6

---

a Some witnesses read Gerasene; *others read* Gadarene.   *b Some witnesses add*
though she had spent all she had on doctors.   *c Some witnesses omit* the edge of.

out and travelled from village to village, and everywhere they told the good news and healed the sick.

7 Now Prince Herod heard of all that was happening, and did not know what to make of it; for some were saying that John had been raised from
8 the dead, others that Elijah had appeared, others again that one of the old
9 prophets had come back to life. Herod said, 'As for John, I beheaded him myself; but who is this I hear such talk about?' And he was anxious to see him.

10 On their return the apostles told Jesus all they had done; and he took
11 them with him and withdrew privately to a town called Bethsaida. But the crowds found out and followed him. He welcomed them, and spoke to them about the kingdom of God, and cured those who were in need of
12 healing. When evening was drawing on, the Twelve came up to him and said, 'Send these people away; then they can go into the villages and farms round about to find food and lodging; for we are in a lonely place here.'
13 'Give them something to eat yourselves', he replied. But they said, 'All we have is five loaves and two fishes, nothing more—unless perhaps we
14 ourselves are to go and buy provisions for all this company.' (There were about five thousand men.) He said to his disciples, 'Make them sit down
15 16 in groups of fifty or so.' They did so and got them all seated. Then, taking the five loaves and the two fishes, he looked up to heaven, said the blessing over them, broke them, and gave them to the disciples to distribute to the
17 people. They all ate to their hearts' content; and when the scraps they left were picked up, they filled twelve great baskets.

18 One day when he was praying alone in the presence of his disciples, he
19 asked them, 'Who do the people say I am?' They answered, 'Some say John the Baptist, others Elijah, others that one of the old prophets has come
20 back to life.' 'And you,' he said, 'who do you say I am?' Peter answered,
21 'God's Messiah.' Then he gave them strict orders not to tell this to anyone.
22 And he said, 'The Son of Man has to undergo great sufferings, and to be rejected by the elders, chief priests, and doctors of the law, to be put to death and to be raised again on the third day.'

23 And to all he said, 'If anyone wishes to be a follower of mine, he must leave self behind; day after day he must take up his cross, and come with me.
24 Whoever cares for his own safety is lost; but if a man will let himself be lost
25 for my sake, that man is safe. What will a man gain by winning the whole
26 world, at the cost of his true self? For whoever is ashamed of me and mine, *a* the Son of Man will be ashamed of him, when he comes in his glory and
27 the glory of the Father and the holy angels. And I tell you this: there are some of those standing here who will not taste death before they have seen the kingdom of God.'

28 About eight days after this conversation he took Peter, John, and James
29 with him and went up into the hills to pray. And while he was praying the appearance of his face changed and his clothes became dazzling white.
30 Suddenly there were two men talking with him; these were Moses and
31 Elijah, who appeared in glory and spoke of his departure, the destiny he
32 was to fulfil in Jerusalem. Meanwhile Peter and his companions had been

a Some witnesses read me and my words.

in a deep sleep; but when they awoke, they saw his glory and the two men
who stood beside him. And as these were moving away from Jesus, Peter 33
said to him, 'Master, how good it is that we are here! Shall we make three
shelters, one for you, one for Moses, and one for Elijah?'; but he spoke
without knowing what he was saying. The words were still on his lips, 34
when there came a cloud which cast a shadow over them; they were afraid
as they entered the cloud, and from it came a voice: 'This is my Son, my 35
Chosen; listen to him.' When the voice had spoken, Jesus was seen to be 36
alone. The disciples kept silence and at that time told nobody anything of
what they had seen.

Next day when they came down from the hills he was met by a large 37
crowd. All at once there was a shout from a man in the crowd: 'Master, look 38
at my son, I implore you, my only child. From time to time a spirit seizes 39
him, gives a sudden scream, and throws him into convulsions with foaming
at the mouth, and it keeps on mauling him and will hardly let him go. I 40
asked your disciples to cast it out, but they could not.' Jesus answered, 41
'What an unbelieving and perverse generation! How long shall I be with
you and endure you all? Bring your son here.' But before the boy could 42
reach him the devil dashed him to the ground and threw him into convulsions. Jesus rebuked the unclean spirit, cured the boy, and gave him
back to his father. And they were all struck with awe at the majesty of God. 43

Amid the general wonder and admiration at all he was doing, Jesus said to
his disciples, 'What I now say is for you: ponder my words. The Son of 44
Man is to be given up into the power of men.' But they did not understand 45
this saying; it had been hidden from them, so that they should not *a* grasp
its meaning, and they were afraid to ask him about it.

A dispute arose among them: which of them was the greatest? Jesus 46 47
knew what was passing in their minds, so he took a child by the hand and
stood him at his side, and said, 'Whoever receives this child in my name 48
receives me; and whoever receives me receives the One who sent me. For
the least among you all—he is the greatest.'

'Master,' said John, 'we saw a man driving out devils in your name, but 49
as he is not one of us we tried to stop him.' Jesus said to him, 'Do not stop 50
him, for he who is not against you is on your side.'

Journeys and encounters

A S THE TIME APPROACHED when he was to be taken up to heaven, he 51
set his face resolutely towards Jerusalem, and sent messengers ahead. 52
They set out and went into a Samaritan village to make arrangements for
him; but the villagers would not have him because he was making for 53
Jerusalem. When the disciples James and John saw this they said, 'Lord, 54
may we call down fire from heaven to burn them up *b* ?' But he turned and 55
rebuked them, *c* and they went on to another village. 56

a Or it was so obscure to them that they could not . . .   *b Some witnesses add* as
Elijah did.   *c Some witnesses insert* 'You do not know', he said, 'to what spirit you
belong; (56) for the Son of Man did not come to destroy men's lives but to save them.'

57 As they were going along the road a man said to him, 'I will follow you
58 wherever you go.' Jesus answered, 'Foxes have their holes, the birds their
59 roosts; but the Son of Man has nowhere to lay his head.' To another he
said, 'Follow me', but the man replied, 'Let me go and bury my father
60 first.' Jesus said, 'Leave the dead to bury their dead; you must go and
announce the kingdom of God.'

61 Yet another said, 'I will follow you, sir; but let me first say good-bye to my
62 people at home.' To him Jesus said, 'No one who sets his hand to the plough
and then keeps looking back *a* is fit for the kingdom of God.'

10 After this the Lord appointed a further seventy-two *b* and sent them on
2 ahead in pairs to every town and place he was going to visit himself. He
said to them: 'The crop is heavy, but labourers are scarce; you must there-
3 fore beg the owner to send labourers to harvest his crop. Be on your way.
4 And look, I am sending you like lambs among wolves. Carry no purse or
5 pack, and travel barefoot. Exchange no greetings on the road. When you
6 go into a house, let your first words be, "Peace to this house." If there is a
man of peace there, your peace will rest upon him; if not, it will return and
7 rest upon you. Stay in that one house, sharing their food and drink; for the
8 worker earns his pay. Do not move from house to house. When you come
into a town and they make you welcome, eat the food provided for you;
9 heal the sick there, and say, "The kingdom of God has come close to you."
10 When you enter a town and they do not make you welcome, go out into its
11 streets and say, "The very dust of your town that clings to our feet we wipe
off to your shame. Only take note of this: the kingdom of God has come
12 close." I tell you, it will be more bearable for Sodom on the great Day than
for that town.

13 'Alas for you, Chorazin! Alas for you, Bethsaida! If the miracles that
were performed in you had been performed in Tyre and Sidon, they would
14 have repented long ago, sitting in sackcloth and ashes. But it will be more
15 bearable for Tyre and Sidon at the Judgement than for you. And as for you,
Capernaum, will you be exalted to the skies? No, brought down to the
depths!

16 'Whoever listens to you listens to me; whoever rejects you rejects me.
And whoever rejects me rejects the One who sent me.'

17 The seventy-two *b* came back jubilant. 'In your name, Lord,' they said,
18 'even the devils submit to us.' He replied, 'I watched how Satan fell, like
19 lightning, out of the sky. And now you see that I have given you the power
to tread underfoot snakes and scorpions and all the forces of the enemy,
20 and nothing will ever harm you. *c* Nevertheless, what you should rejoice
over is not that the spirits submit to you, but that your names are enrolled
in heaven.'

21 At that moment Jesus exulted in the Holy *d* Spirit and said, 'I thank thee,
Father, Lord of heaven and earth, for hiding these things from the learned
and wise, and revealing them to the simple. Yes, Father, such *e* was thy

a Some witnesses read No one who looks back as he sets hand to the plough . . .
b Some witnesses read seventy. *c Or* and he will have no way at all to harm
you. *d Some witnesses omit* Holy. *e Or* Yes, I thank thee, Father,
that such . . .

choice.' Then turning to his disciples he said,*a* 'Everything is entrusted to   22
me by my Father; and no one knows who the Son is but the Father, or who
the Father is but the Son, and those to whom the Son may choose to
reveal him.'

Turning to his disciples in private he said, 'Happy the eyes that see what   23
you are seeing! I tell you, many prophets and kings wished to see what you   24
now see, yet never saw it; to hear what you hear, yet never heard it.'

ON ONE OCCASION a lawyer came forward to put this test question to   25
him: 'Master, what must I do to inherit eternal life?' Jesus said, 'What is   26
written in the Law? What is your reading of it?' He replied, 'Love the   27
Lord your God with all your heart, with all your soul, with all your strength,
and with all your mind; and your neighbour as yourself.' 'That is the right   28
answer,' said Jesus; 'do that and you will live.'

But he wanted to vindicate himself, so he said to Jesus, 'And who is my   29
neighbour?' Jesus replied, 'A man was on his way from Jerusalem down to   30
Jericho when he fell in with robbers, who stripped him, beat him, and
went off leaving him half dead. It so happened that a priest was going down   31
by the same road; but when he saw him, he went past on the other side.
So too a Levite came to the place, and when he saw him went past on the   32
other side. But a Samaritan who was making the journey came upon him,   33
and when he saw him was moved to pity. He went up and bandaged his   34
wounds, bathing them with oil and wine. Then he lifted him on to his own
beast, brought him to an inn, and looked after him there. Next day he pro-   35
duced two silver pieces and gave them to the innkeeper, and said, "Look
after him; and if you spend any more, I will repay you on my way back."
Which of these three do you think was neighbour to the man who fell into   36
the hands of the robbers?' He answered, 'The one who showed him kind-   37
ness.' Jesus said, 'Go and do as he did.'

While they were on their way Jesus came to a village where a woman   38
named Martha made him welcome in her home. She had a sister, Mary,   39
who seated herself at the Lord's feet and stayed there listening to his words.
Now Martha was distracted by her many tasks, so she came to him and said,   40
'Lord, do you not care that my sister has left me to get on with the work by
myself? Tell her to come and lend a hand.' But the Lord answered,   41
'Martha, Martha, you are fretting and fussing about so many things; but   42
one thing is necessary.*b* The part that Mary has chosen is best; and it shall
not be taken away from her.'

Once, in a certain place, Jesus was at prayer. When he ceased, one of his   **11**
disciples said, 'Lord, teach us to pray, as John taught his disciples.' He   2
answered, 'When you pray, say,

> "Father,*c* thy name be hallowed;
> thy kingdom come.*d*

---

a Some witnesses omit Then ... he said.   *b Some witnesses read* but few things are
necessary, or rather, one alone; *others omit* you are fretting ... necessary.   *c Some
witnesses read* Our Father in heaven.   *d One witness reads* thy kingdom come upon us;
some others have thy Holy Spirit come upon us and cleanse us; *some insert* thy will be
done, on earth as in heaven.

3   Give us each day our daily bread. *a*
4   And forgive us our sins,
     for we too forgive all who have done us wrong.
     And do not bring us to the test." ' *b*

5   Then he said to them, 'Suppose one of you has a friend who comes to
     him in the middle of the night and says, "My friend, lend me three loaves,
6   for a friend of mine on a journey has turned up at my house, and I have
7   nothing to offer him"; and he replies from inside, "Do not bother me. The
     door is shut for the night; my children and I have gone to bed; and I can-
8   not get up and give you what you want." I tell you that even if he will not
     provide for him out of friendship, the very shamelessness of the request
9   will make him get up and give him all he needs. And so I say to you, ask,
     and you will receive; seek, and you will find; knock, and the door will be
10   opened. For everyone who asks receives, he who seeks finds, and to him
     who knocks, the door will be opened.

11   'Is there a father among you who will offer his son *c* a snake when he asks
12 13 for fish, or a scorpion when he asks for an egg? If you, then, bad as you are,
     know how to give your children what is good for them, how much more will
     the heavenly Father give the Holy Spirit *d* to those who ask him!'

14   HE WAS DRIVING OUT a devil which was dumb; and when the devil had
     come out, the dumb man began to speak. The people were astonished,
15   but some of them said, 'It is by Beelzebub prince of devils that he drives
16   the devils out.' Others, by way of a test, demanded of him a sign from
17   heaven. But he knew what was in their minds, and said, 'Every kingdom
18   divided against itself goes to ruin, and a divided household falls. Equally
     if Satan is divided against himself, how can his kingdom stand?—since,
19   as you would have it, I drive out the devils by Beelzebub. If it is by Beelze-
     bub that I cast out devils, by whom do your own people drive them out?
20   If this is your argument, they themselves will refute you. But if it is by the
     finger of God that I drive out the devils, then be sure the kingdom of God
     has already come upon you.

21   'When a strong man fully armed is on guard over his castle his posses-
22   sions are safe. But when someone stronger comes upon him and over-
     powers him, he carries off the arms and armour on which the man had
     relied and divides the plunder.

23   'He who is not with me is against me, and he who does not gather with
     me scatters. *e*

24   'When an unclean spirit comes out of a man it wanders over the deserts
     seeking a resting-place; and if it finds none, it says, "I will go back to the
25 26 home I left." So it returns and finds the house *f* swept clean, and tidy. Off
     it goes and collects seven other spirits more wicked than itself, and they all
     come in and settle down; and in the end the man's plight is worse than
     before.'

---

a *Or* our bread for the morrow.   *b* *Some witnesses add* but save us from the evil
one (*or* from evil).   *c* *Some witnesses insert* a stone when he asks for bread,
or . . .   *d* *Some witnesses read* a good gift; *some others read* good things.
e *Some witnesses add* me.   *f* *Some witnesses insert* unoccupied.

While he was speaking thus, a woman in the crowd called out, 'Happy 27
the womb that carried you and the breasts that suckled you!' He rejoined, 28
'No, happy are those who hear the word of God and keep it.'

With the crowds swarming round him he went on to say: 'This is a 29
wicked generation. It demands a sign, and the only sign that will be given
it is the sign of Jonah. For just as Jonah was a sign to the Ninevites, so will 30
the Son of Man be to this generation. At the Judgement, when the men of 31
this generation are on trial, the Queen of the South will appear against*a*
them and ensure their condemnation, for she came from the ends of the
earth to hear the wisdom of Solomon; and what is here is greater than
Solomon. The men of Nineveh will appear at the Judgement when this 32
generation is on trial, and ensure *b* its condemnation, for they repented at
the preaching of Jonah; and what is here is greater than Jonah.

'No one lights a lamp and puts it in a cellar,*c* but rather on the lamp- 33
stand so that those who enter may see the light. The lamp of your body is 34
the eye. When your eyes are sound, you have light for your whole body;
but when the eyes are bad, you are in darkness. See to it then that the light 35
you have is not darkness. If you have light for your whole body with no 36
trace of darkness, it will all be as bright as when a lamp flashes its rays
upon you.'

WHEN HE HAD FINISHED SPEAKING, a Pharisee invited him to a meal. 37
He came in and sat down. The Pharisee noticed with surprise that he had 38
not begun by washing before the meal. But the Lord said to him, 'You 39
Pharisees! You clean the outside of cup and plate; but inside you there is
nothing but greed and wickedness. You fools! Did not he who made the 40
outside make the inside too? But let what is in the cup *d* be given in charity, 41
and all is clean.

'Alas for you Pharisees! You pay tithes of mint and rue and every 42
garden-herb, but have no care for justice and the love of God. It is these
you should have practised, without neglecting the others.*e*

'Alas for you Pharisees! You love the seats of honour in synagogues, and 43
salutations in the market-places.

'Alas, alas, you are like unmarked graves over which men may walk with- 44
out knowing it.'

In reply to this one of the lawyers said, 'Master, when you say things 45
like this you are insulting us too.' Jesus rejoined: 'Yes, you lawyers, it is 46
no better with you! For you load men with intolerable burdens, and will
not put a single finger to the load.

'Alas, you build the tombs of the prophets whom your fathers murdered, 47
and so testify that you approve of the deeds your fathers did; they com- 48
mitted the murders and you provide the tombs.

'This is why the Wisdom of God said, "I will send them prophets and 49
messengers; and some of these they will persecute and kill"; so that this 50

---

a Or will be raised to life together with . . . *b Or* At the Judgement the men of
Nineveh will rise again together with this generation and will ensure . . . *c Some
witnesses insert* or under the meal-tub. *d Or* what you can afford. *e Some witnesses omit* It is . . . others.

generation will have to answer for the blood of all the prophets shed since
51 the foundation of the world; from the blood of Abel to the blood of Zechariah who perished between the altar and the sanctuary. I tell you, this
generation will have to answer for it all.

52   'Alas for you lawyers! You have taken away the key of knowledge. You
did not go in yourselves, and those who were on their way in, you stopped.'

53   After he had left the house, the lawyers and Pharisees began to assail
54 him fiercely and to ply him with a host of questions, laying snares to catch
him with his own words.

12 MEANWHILE, WHEN A CROWD of many thousands had gathered,
packed so close that they were treading on one another, he began to speak
first to his disciples: 'Beware of the leaven of the Pharisees; I mean their
2 hypocrisy. There is nothing covered up that will not be uncovered,
3 nothing hidden that will not be made known. You may take it, then, that
everything you have said in the dark will be heard in broad daylight, and
what you have whispered behind closed doors will be shouted from the
house-tops.

4   'To you who are my friends I say: Do not fear those who kill the body and
5 after that have nothing more they can do. I will warn you whom to fear:
fear him who, after he has killed, has authority to cast into hell. Believe me,
he is the one to fear.

6   'Are not sparrows five for twopence? And yet not one of them is over-
7 looked by God. More than that, even the hairs of your head have all been
counted. Have no fear; you are worth more than any number of sparrows.

8   'I tell you this: everyone who acknowledges me before men, the Son of
9 Man will acknowledge before the angels of God; but he who disowns me
before men will be disowned before the angels of God.

10   'Anyone who speaks a word against the Son of Man will receive forgiveness; but for him who slanders the Holy Spirit there will be no forgiveness.

11   'When you are brought before synagogues and state authorities, do
not begin worrying about how you will conduct your defence or what you
12 will say. For when the time comes the Holy Spirit will instruct you what
to say.'

13   A man in the crowd said to him, 'Master, tell my brother to divide the
14 family property with me.' He replied, 'My good man, who set me over you
15 to judge or arbitrate?'[a] Then he said to the people, 'Beware! Be on your
guard against greed of every kind, for even when a man has more than
16 enough, his wealth does not give him life.' And he told them this parable:
17 'There was a rich man whose land yielded heavy crops. He debated with
18 himself: "What am I to do? I have not the space to store my produce. This
is what I will do," said he: "I will pull down my storehouses and build them
19 bigger. I will collect in them all my corn and other goods, and then say to
myself, 'Man, you have plenty of good things laid by, enough for many
20 years: take life easy, eat, drink, and enjoy yourself.'" But God said to
him, "You fool, this very night you must surrender your life; you have
21 made your money—who will get it now?" That is how it is with the

----

^a *Some witnesses omit* or arbitrate.

man who amasses wealth for himself and remains a pauper in the sight of God.[a]

'Therefore', he said to his disciples, 'I bid you put away anxious thoughts about food to keep you alive and clothes to cover your body. Life is more than food, the body more than clothes. Think of the ravens: they neither sow nor reap; they have no storehouse or barn; yet God feeds them. You are worth far more than the birds! Is there a man among you who by anxious thought can add a foot to his height[b]? If, then, you cannot do even a very little thing, why are you anxious about the rest? 22 23 24 25 26

'Think of the lilies: they neither spin nor weave;[c] yet I tell you, even Solomon in all his splendour was not attired like one of these. But if that is how God clothes the grass, which is growing in the field today, and tomorrow is thrown on the stove, how much more will he clothe you! How little faith you have! And so you are not to set your mind on food and drink; you are not to worry. For all these are things for the heathen to run after; but you have a Father who knows that you need them. No, set your mind upon his kingdom, and all the rest will come to you as well. 27 28 29 30 31

'Have no fear, little flock; for your Father has chosen to give you the Kingdom. Sell your possessions and give in charity. Provide for yourselves purses that do not wear out, and never-failing treasure in heaven, where no thief can get near it, no moth destroy it. For where your treasure is, there will your heart be also. 32 33 34

'Be ready for action, with belts fastened and lamps alight. Be like men who wait for their master's return from a wedding-party, ready to let him in the moment he arrives and knocks. Happy are those servants whom the master finds on the alert when he comes. I tell you this: he will fasten his belt, seat them at table, and come and wait on them. Even if it is the middle of the night or before dawn when he comes, happy they if he finds them alert. And remember, if the householder had known what time the burglar was coming he would not have let his house be broken into. Hold yourselves ready, then, because the Son of Man will come at the time you least expect him.' 35 36 37 38 39 40

Peter said, 'Lord, do you intend this parable specially for us or is it for everyone?' The Lord said, 'Well, who is the trusty and sensible man whom his master will appoint as his steward, to manage his servants and issue their rations at the proper time? Happy that servant who is found at his task when his master comes! I tell you this: he will be put in charge of all his master's property. But if that servant says to himself, "The master is a long time coming", and begins to bully the menservants and maids, and eat and drink and get drunk; then the master will arrive on a day that servant does not expect, at a time he does not know, and will cut him in pieces. Thus he will find his place among the faithless. 41 42 43 44 45 46

'The servant who knew his master's wishes, yet made no attempt to carry them out, will be flogged severely. But one who did not know them and earned a beating will be flogged less severely. Where a man has been given 47 48

---

[a] *Some witnesses omit* That . . . God; *others add at the end* When he said this he cried out, 'If you have ears to hear, then hear.'   [b] *Or* a day to his life.   [c] *Some witnesses read* they grow, they do not toil or spin.

much, much will be expected of him; and the more a man has had entrusted
to him the more he will be required to repay.

49   'I have come to set fire to the earth, and how I wish it were already
50   kindled! I have a baptism to undergo, and what constraint I am under until
51   the ordeal is over! Do you suppose I came to establish peace on earth? No
52   indeed, I have come to bring division. For from now on, five members of a
53   family will be divided, three against two and two against three; father
against son and son against father, mother against daughter and daughter
against mother, mother against son's wife and son's wife against her
mother-in-law.'

54   He also said to the people, 'When you see cloud banking up in the west,
55   you say at once, "It is going to rain", and rain it does. And when the wind is
56   from the south, you say, "There will be a heat-wave", and there is. What
hypocrites you are! You know how to interpret the appearance of earth and
sky; how is it you cannot interpret this fateful hour?

57   'And why can you not judge for yourselves what is the right course?
58   When you are going with your opponent to court, make an effort to settle
with him while you are still on the way; otherwise he may drag you before
the judge, and the judge hand you over to the constable, and the constable
59   put you in jail. I tell you, you will not come out till you have paid the last
farthing.'

13   AT THAT VERY TIME there were some people present who told him about
2   the Galileans whose blood Pilate had mixed with their sacrifices. He
answered them: 'Do you imagine that, because these Galileans suffered
this fate, they must have been greater sinners than anyone else in Galilee?
3   I tell you they were not; but unless you repent, you will all of you come to
4   the same end. Or the eighteen people who were killed when the tower fell
on them at Siloam—do you imagine they were more guilty than all the
5   other people living in Jerusalem? I tell you they were not; but unless you
repent, you will all of you come to the same end.'

6   He told them this parable: 'A man had a fig-tree growing in his vineyard;
7   and he came looking for fruit on it, but found none. So he said to the vine-
dresser, "Look here! For the last three years I have come looking for fruit
on this fig-tree without finding any. Cut it down. Why should it go on
8   using up the soil?" But he replied, "Leave it, sir, this one year while I dig
9   round it and manure it. And if it bears next season, well and good; if not,
you shall have it down."'

10 11   One Sabbath he was teaching in a synagogue, and there was a woman
there possessed by a spirit that had crippled her for eighteen years. She
12   was bent double and quite unable to stand up straight. When Jesus saw her
13   he called her and said, 'You are rid of your trouble.' Then he laid his hands
14   on her, and at once she straightened up and began to praise God. But the
president of the synagogue, indignant with Jesus for healing on the
Sabbath, intervened and said to the congregation, 'There are six working-
15   days: come and be cured on one of them, and not on the Sabbath.' The
Lord gave him his answer: 'What hypocrites you are!' he said. 'Is there a
single one of you who does not loose his ox or his donkey from the manger

and take it out to water on the Sabbath? And here is this woman, a daughter 16
of Abraham, who has been kept prisoner by Satan for eighteen long years:
was it wrong for her to be freed from her bonds on the Sabbath?' At these 17
words all his opponents were covered with confusion, while the mass of
the people were delighted at all the wonderful things he was doing.

'What is the kingdom of God like?' he continued. 'What shall I compare 18
it with? It is like a mustard-seed which a man took and sowed in his 19
garden; and it grew to be a tree and the birds came to roost among its
branches.'

Again he said, 'The kingdom of God, what shall I compare it with? It is 20 21
like yeast which a woman took and mixed with half a hundredweight of
flour till it was all leavened.'

HE CONTINUED HIS JOURNEY through towns and villages, teaching as 22
he made his way towards Jerusalem. Someone asked him, 'Sir, are only a 23
few to be saved?' His answer was: 'Struggle to get in through the narrow 24
door; for I tell you that many will try to enter and not be able.

'When once the master of the house has got up and locked the door, you 25
may stand outside and knock, and say, "Sir, let us in!", but he will only
answer, "I do not know where you come from." Then you will begin to say, 26
"We sat at table with you and you taught in our streets." But he will repeat, 27
"I tell you, I do not know where you come from. Out of my sight, all of
you, you and your wicked ways!" There will be wailing and grinding of 28
teeth there, when you see Abraham, Isaac, and Jacob, and all the prophets,
in the kingdom of God, and yourselves thrown out. From east and west 29
people will come, from north and south, for the feast in the kingdom of
God. Yes, and some who are now last will be first, and some who are first 30
will be last.'

At that time a number of Pharisees came to him and said, 'You should 31
leave this place and go on your way; Herod is out to kill you.' He replied, 32
'Go and tell that fox, "Listen: today and tomorrow I shall be casting out
devils and working cures; on the third day I reach my goal." However, 33
I must be on my way today and tomorrow and the next day, because it is
unthinkable for a prophet to meet his death anywhere but in Jerusalem.

'O Jerusalem, Jerusalem, the city that murders the prophets and stones 34
the messengers sent to her! How often have I longed to gather your children, as a hen gathers her brood under her wings; but you would not let
me. Look, look! there is your temple, forsaken by God. And I tell you, 35
you shall never see me until the time comes when you say, "Blessings on
him who comes in the name of the Lord!"'

ONE SABBATH he went to have a meal in the house of a leading Pharisee; 14
and they were watching him closely. There, in front of him, was a man 2
suffering from dropsy. Jesus asked the lawyers and the Pharisees: 'Is it 3
permitted to cure people on the Sabbath or not?' They said nothing. So 4
he took the man, cured him, and sent him away. Then he turned to them 5
and said, 'If one of you has a donkey *a* or an ox and it falls into a well, will

a Some witnesses read son.

6   he hesitate to haul it up on the Sabbath day?' To this they could find no
     reply.
7   When he noticed how the guests were trying to secure the places of
8   honour, he spoke to them in a parable: 'When you are asked by someone to
     a wedding-feast, do not sit down in the place of honour. It may be that some
9   person more distinguished than yourself has been invited; and the host
     will come and say to you, "Give this man your seat." Then you will look
10   foolish as you begin to take the lowest place. No, when you receive an
     invitation, go and sit down in the lowest place, so that when your host
     comes he will say, "Come up higher, my friend." Then all your fellow-
11   guests will see the respect in which you are held. For everyone who exalts
     himself will be humbled; and whoever humbles himself will be exalted.'
12   Then he said to his host, 'When you are having a party for lunch or
     supper, do not invite your friends, your brothers or other relations, or
     your rich neighbours; they will only ask you back again and so you will
13   be repaid. But when you give a party, ask the poor, the crippled, the lame,
14   and the blind; and so find happiness. For they have no means of repaying
     you; but you will be repaid on the day when good men rise from the dead.'
15   One of the company, after hearing all this, said to him, 'Happy the man
16   who shall sit at the feast in the kingdom of God!' Jesus answered, 'A man
17   was giving a big dinner party and had sent out many invitations. At dinner-
     time he sent his servant with a message for his guests, "Please come, every-
18   thing is now ready." They began one and all to excuse themselves. The first
     said, "I have bought a piece of land, and I must go and look over it; please
19   accept my apologies." The second said, "I have bought five yoke of oxen,
20   and I am on my way to try them out; please accept my apologies." The
     next said, "I have just got married and for that reason I cannot come."
21   When the servant came back he reported this to his master. The master of the
     house was angry and said to him, "Go out quickly into the streets and alleys
     of the town, and bring me in the poor, the crippled, the blind, and the
22   lame." The servant said, "Sir, your orders have been carried out and there
23   is still room." The master replied, "Go out on to the highways and along
24   the hedgerows and make them come in; I want my house to be full. I tell
     you that not one of those who were invited shall taste my banquet."'
25   Once when great crowds were accompanying him, he turned to them
26   and said: 'If anyone comes to me and does not hate his father and mother,
     wife and children, brothers and sisters, even his own life, he cannot be a
27   disciple of mine. No one who does not carry his cross and come with me
28   can be a disciple of mine. Would any of you think of building a tower with-
     out first sitting down and calculating the cost, to see whether he could
29   afford to finish it? Otherwise, if he has laid its foundation and then is not
30   able to complete it, all the onlookers will laugh at him. "There is the man",
31   they will say, "who started to build and could not finish." Or what king
     will march to battle against another king, without first sitting down to con-
     sider whether with ten thousand men he can face an enemy coming to meet
32   him with twenty thousand? If he cannot, then, long before the enemy
33   approaches, he sends envoys, and asks for terms. So also none of you can
     be a disciple of mine without parting with all his possessions.

'Salt is a good thing; but if salt itself becomes tasteless, what will you 34
use to season it? It is useless either on the land or on the dung-heap: it can 35
only be thrown away. If you have ears to hear, then hear.'

ANOTHER TIME, the tax-gatherers and other bad characters were all **15**
crowding in to listen to him; and the Pharisees and the doctors of the law 2
began grumbling among themselves: 'This fellow', they said, 'welcomes
sinners and eats with them.' He answered them with this parable: 'If one 3 4
of you has a hundred sheep and loses one of them, does he not leave the
ninety-nine in the open pasture and go after the missing one until he has
found it? How delighted he is then! He lifts it on to his shoulders, and home 5 6
he goes to call his friends and neighbours together. "Rejoice with me!"
he cries. "I have found my lost sheep." In the same way, I tell you, there 7
will be greater joy in heaven over one sinner who repents than over ninety-
nine righteous people who do not need to repent.

'Or again, if a woman has ten silver pieces and loses one of them, does 8
she not light the lamp, sweep out the house, and look in every corner till
she has found it? And when she has, she calls her friends and neighbours 9
together, and says, "Rejoice with me! I have found the piece that I lost."
In the same way, I tell you, there is joy among the angels of God over one 10
sinner who repents.'

Again he said: 'There was once a man who had two sons; and the 11 12
younger said to his father, "Father, give me my share of the property." So
he divided his estate between them. A few days later the younger son 13
turned the whole of his share into cash and left home for a distant country,
where he squandered it in reckless living. He had spent it all, when a severe 14
famine fell upon that country and he began to feel the pinch. So he went 15
and attached himself to one of the local landowners, who sent him on to his
farm to mind the pigs. He would have been glad to fill his belly with[a] the 16
pods that the pigs were eating; and no one gave him anything. Then he 17
came to his senses and said, "How many of my father's paid servants have
more food than they can eat, and here am I, starving to death! I will set 18
off and go to my father, and say to him, 'Father, I have sinned, against
God and against you; I am no longer fit to be called your son; treat me as 19
one of your paid servants.'" So he set out for his father's house. But while 20
he was still a long way off his father saw him, and his heart went out to him.
He ran to meet him, flung his arms round him, and kissed him. The son 21
said, "Father, I have sinned, against God and against you; I am no longer
fit to be called your son."[b] But the father said to his servants, "Quick! 22
fetch a robe, my best one, and put it on him; put a ring on his finger and
shoes on his feet. Bring the fatted calf and kill it, and let us have a feast to 23
celebrate the day. For this son of mine was dead and has come back to life; 24
he was lost and is found." And the festivities began.

'Now the elder son was out on the farm; and on his way back, as he 25
approached the house, he heard music and dancing. He called one of the 26
servants and asked what it meant. The servant told him, "Your brother 27

---

[a] *Some witnesses read* to have his fill of . . .   [b] *Some witnesses add* treat me as one of
your paid servants.

28 has come home, and your father has killed the fatted calf because he has
29 him back safe and sound." But he was angry and refused to go in. His
father came out and pleaded with him; but he retorted, "You know how
I have slaved for you all these years; I never once disobeyed your orders;
30 and you never gave me so much as a kid, for a feast with my friends. But
now that this son of yours turns up, after running through your money
31 with his women, you kill the fatted calf for him." "My boy," said the father,
32 "you are always with me, and everything I have is yours. How could we
help celebrating this happy day? Your brother here was dead and has come
back to life, was lost and is found." '

16 He said to his disciples, 'There was a rich man who had a steward, and he
2 received complaints that this man was squandering the property. So he
sent for him, and said, "What is this that I hear? Produce your accounts,
3 for you cannot be manager here any longer." The steward said to himself,
"What am I to do now that my employer is dismissing me? I am not strong
4 enough to dig, and too proud to beg. I know what I must do, to make sure
that, when I have to leave, there will be people to give me house and home."
5 He summoned his master's debtors one by one. To the first he said, "How
6 much do you owe my master?" He replied, "A thousand gallons of olive
oil." He said, "Here is your account. Sit down and make it five hundred;
7 and be quick about it." Then he said to another, "And you, how much do
you owe?" He said, "A thousand bushels of wheat", and was told, "Take
8 your account and make it eight hundred." And the master applauded the
dishonest steward for acting so astutely. For the worldly are more astute
than the other-worldly in dealing with their own kind.

9 'So I say to you, use your worldly wealth to win friends for yourselves,
so that when money is a thing of the past you may be received into an
eternal home.

10 'The man who can be trusted in little things can be trusted also in great;
and the man who is dishonest in little things is dishonest also in great
11 things. If, then, you have not proved trustworthy with the wealth of this
12 world, who will trust you with the wealth that is real? And if you have
proved untrustworthy with what belongs to another, who will give you
what is your own?

13 'No servant can be the slave of two masters; for either he will hate the
first and love the second, or he will be devoted to the first and think nothing
of the second. You cannot serve God and Money.'

14 15 The Pharisees, who loved money, heard all this and scoffed at him. He
said to them, 'You are the people who impress your fellow-men with your
righteousness; but God sees through you; for what sets itself up to be
admired by men is detestable in the sight of God.

16 'Until John, it was the Law and the prophets: since then, there is the
good news of the kingdom of God, and everyone forces his way in.

17 'It is easier for heaven and earth to come to an end than for one dot or
stroke of the Law to lose its force.

18 'A man who divorces his wife and marries another commits adultery;
and anyone who marries a woman divorced from her husband commits
adultery.

'There was once a rich man, who dressed in purple and the finest linen, 19
and feasted in great magnificence every day. At his gate, covered with sores, 20
lay a poor man named Lazarus, who would have been glad to satisfy his 21
hunger with the scraps from the rich man's table. Even the dogs used to
come and lick his sores. One day the poor man died and was carried away 22
by the angels to be with Abraham. The rich man also died and was buried,
and in Hades, where he was in torment, he looked up; and there, far away, 23
was Abraham with Lazarus close beside him. "Abraham, my father," he 24
called out, "take pity on me! Send Lazarus to dip the tip of his finger in
water, to cool my tongue, for I am in agony in this fire." But Abraham said, 25
"Remember, my child, that all the good things fell to you while you were
alive, and all the bad to Lazarus; now he has his consolation here and it is
you who are in agony. But that is not all: there is a great chasm fixed be- 26
tween us; no one from our side who wants to reach you can cross it, and
none may pass from your side to us." "Then, father," he replied, "will 27
you send him to my father's house, where I have five brothers, to warn 28
them, so that they too may not come to this place of torment?" But Abraham 29
said, "They have Moses and the prophets; let them listen to them." "No, 30
father Abraham," he replied, "but if someone from the dead visits them,
they will repent." Abraham answered, "If they do not listen to Moses and 31
the prophets they will pay no heed even if someone should rise from the
dead."'

HE SAID TO HIS DISCIPLES, 'Causes of stumbling are bound to arise; **17**
but woe betide the man through whom they come. It would be better for 2
him to be thrown into the sea with a millstone round his neck than to cause
one of these little ones to stumble. Keep watch on yourselves. 3

'If your brother wrongs you, reprove him; and if he repents, forgive
him. Even if he wrongs you seven times in a day and comes back to you 4
seven times saying, "I am sorry", you are to forgive him.'

The apostles said to the Lord, 'Increase our faith'; and the Lord 5 6
replied, 'If you had faith no bigger even than a mustard-seed, you could
say to this mulberry-tree, "Be rooted up and replanted in the sea"; and it
would at once obey you.

'Suppose one of you has a servant ploughing or minding sheep. When 7
he comes back from the fields, will the master say, "Come along at once
and sit down"? Will he not rather say, "Prepare my supper, fasten your 8
belt, and then wait on me while I have my meal; you can have yours afterwards"? Is he grateful to the servant for carrying out his orders? So with 9 10
you: when you have carried out all your orders, you should say, "We are
servants and deserve no credit; we have only done our duty."'

In the course of his journey to Jerusalem he was travelling through the 11
borderlands of Samaria and Galilee. As he was entering a village he was 12
met by ten men with leprosy. They stood some way off and called out to 13
him, 'Jesus, Master, take pity on us.' When he saw them he said, 'Go and 14
show yourselves to the priests'; and while they were on their way, they
were made clean. One of them, finding himself cured, turned back praising 15
God aloud. He threw himself down at Jesus's feet and thanked him. And 16

17 he was a Samaritan. At this Jesus said: 'Were not all ten cleansed? The
18 other nine, where are they? Could none be found to come back and give
19 praise to God except this foreigner?' And he said to the man, 'Stand up
and go on your way; your faith has cured you.'

20 THE PHARISEES ASKED HIM, 'When will the kingdom of God come?'
He said, 'You cannot tell by observation when the kingdom of God comes.
21 There will be no saying, "Look, here it is!" or "there it is!"; for in fact the
kingdom of God is among you.' *a*
22 He said to the disciples, 'The time will come when you will long to see
23 one of the days of the Son of Man, but you will not see it. They will say to
you, "Look! There!" and "Look! Here!" Do not go running off in pursuit.
24 For like the lightning-flash that lights up the earth from end to end, will
25 the Son of Man be when his day comes. But first he must endure much
suffering and be repudiated by this generation.
26 'As things were in Noah's days, so will they be in the days of the Son of
27 Man. They ate and drank and married, until the day that Noah went into
28 the ark and the flood came and made an end of them all. As things were in
Lot's days, also: they ate and drank; they bought and sold; they planted
29 and built; but the day that Lot went out from Sodom, it rained fire and
30 sulphur from the sky and made an end of them all—it will be like that on the
day when the Son of Man is revealed.
31 'On that day the man who is on the roof and his belongings in the house
must not come down to pick them up; he, too, who is in the fields must not
32 33 go back. Remember Lot's wife. Whoever seeks to save his life will lose it;
and whoever loses it will save it, and live.
34 'I tell you, on that night there will be two men in one bed: one will be
35 taken, the other left. There will be two women together grinding corn: one
37 will be taken, the other left.' *b* When they heard this they asked, 'Where,
Lord?' He said, 'Where the corpse is, there the vultures will gather.'

18 HE SPOKE TO THEM in a parable to show that they should keep on praying
2 and never lose heart: 'There was once a judge who cared nothing for God
3 or man, and in the same town there was a widow who constantly came
4 before him demanding justice against her opponent. For a long time he
refused; but in the end he said to himself, "True, I care nothing for God
5 or man; but this widow is so great a nuisance that I will see her righted
6 before she wears me out with her persistence."' The Lord said, 'You
7 hear what the unjust judge says; and will not God vindicate his chosen,
who cry out to him day and night, while he listens patiently to them *c*?
8 I tell you, he will vindicate them soon enough. But when the Son of Man
comes, will he find faith on earth?'
9 And here is another parable that he told. It was aimed at those who were
10 sure of their own goodness and looked down on everyone else. 'Two men

---

a *Or* for in fact the kingdom of God is within you, *or* for in fact the kingdom of God is
within your grasp, *or* for suddenly the kingdom of God will be among you.
b *Some witnesses add* (36) two men in the fields: one will be taken, the other left.
c *Or* delays to help them.

went up to the temple to pray, one a Pharisee and the other a tax-gatherer. The Pharisee stood up and prayed thus:ᵃ "I thank thee, O God, that I am 11 not like the rest of men, greedy, dishonest, adulterous; or, for that matter, like this tax-gatherer. I fast twice a week; I pay tithes on all that I get." 12 But the other kept his distance and would not even raise his eyes to heaven, 13 but beat upon his breast, saying, "O God, have mercy on me, sinner that I am." It was this man, I tell you, and not the other, who went home 14 acquitted of his sins. For everyone who exalts himself will be humbled; and whoever humbles himself will be exalted.'

They even brought babies for him to touch. When the disciples saw 15 them they rebuked them, but Jesus called for the children and said, 'Let 16 the little ones come to me; do not try to stop them; for the kingdom of God belongs to such as these. I tell you that whoever does not accept the king- 17 dom of God like a child will never enter it.'

A man of the ruling class put this question to him: 'Good Master, what 18 must I do to win eternal life?' Jesus said to him, 'Why do you call me good? 19 No one is good except God alone. You know the commandments: "Do not 20 commit adultery; do not murder; do not steal; do not give false evidence; honour your father and mother."' The man answered, 'I have kept all 21 these since I was a boy.' On hearing this Jesus said, 'There is still one 22 thing lacking: sell everything you have and distribute to the poor, and you will have riches in heaven; and come, follow me.' At these words his heart 23 sank; for he was a very rich man. When Jesus saw it he said, 'How hard it 24 is for the wealthy to enter the kingdom of God! It is easier for a camel to go 25 through the eye of a needle than for a rich man to enter the kingdom of God.' Those who heard asked, 'Then who can be saved?' He answered, 26 27 'What is impossible for men is possible for God.'

Peter said, 'We here have left our belongings to become your followers.' 28 Jesus said, 'I tell you this: there is no one who has given up home, or wife, 29 brothers, parents, or children, for the sake of the kingdom of God, who 30 will not be repaid many times over in this age, and in the age to come have eternal life.'

Challenge to Jerusalem

H E TOOK THE TWELVE ASIDE and said, 'We are now going up to 31 Jerusalem; and all that was written by the prophets will come true for the Son of Man. He will be handed over to the foreign power. He will be 32 mocked, maltreated, and spat upon. They will flog him and kill him. And 33 on the third day he will rise again.' But they understood nothing of all this; 34 they did not grasp what he was talking about; its meaning was concealed from them.

As he approached Jericho a blind man sat at the roadside begging. Hear- 35 36 ing a crowd going past, he asked what was happening. They told him, 37 'Jesus of Nazareth is passing by.' Then he shouted out, 'Jesus, Son of 38

ᵃ *Some witnesses read* stood up by himself and prayed thus; *others read* stood up and prayed thus privately.

39 David, have pity on me.' The people in front told him to hold his tongue;
40 but he called out all the more, 'Son of David, have pity on me.' Jesus
stopped and ordered the man to be brought to him. When he came up he
41 asked him, 'What do you want me to do for you?' 'Sir, I want my sight
42 back', he answered. Jesus said to him, 'Have back your sight; your faith
43 has cured you.' He recovered his sight instantly; and he followed Jesus,
praising God. And all the people gave praise to God for what they had
seen.

19 1 2   Entering Jericho he made his way through the city. There was a man
3 there named Zacchaeus; he was superintendent of taxes and very rich. He
was eager to see what Jesus looked like; but, being a little man, he could
4 not see him for the crowd. So he ran on ahead and climbed a sycomore-
5 tree in order to see him, for he was to pass that way. When Jesus came to the
place, he looked up and said, 'Zacchaeus, be quick and come down; I
6 must come and stay with you today.' He climbed down as fast as he could
7 and welcomed him gladly. At this there was a general murmur of dis-
8 approval. 'He has gone in', they said, 'to be the guest of a sinner.' But
Zacchaeus stood there and said to the Lord, 'Here and now, sir, I give half
my possessions to charity; and if I have cheated anyone, I am ready to
9 repay him four times over.' Jesus said to him, 'Salvation has come to this
10 house today!—for this man too is a son of Abraham, and the Son of Man
has come to seek and save what is lost.'

11   While they were listening to this, he went on to tell them a parable,
because he was now close to Jerusalem and they thought the reign of God
12 might dawn at any moment. He said, 'A man of noble birth went on a long
13 journey abroad, to be appointed king and then return. But first he called
ten of his servants and gave them a pound each, saying, "Trade with this
14 while I am away." His fellow-citizens hated him, and they sent a delega-
15 tion on his heels to say, "We do not want this man as our king." However,
back he came as king, and sent for the servants to whom he had given the
16 money, to see what profit each had made. The first came and said, "Your
17 pound, sir, has made ten more." "Well done," he replied; "you are a good
servant. You have shown yourself trustworthy in a very small matter, and
18 you shall have charge of ten cities." The second came and said, "Your
19 pound, sir, has made five more"; and he also was told, "You too, take
20 charge of five cities." The third came and said, "Here is your pound, sir;
21 I kept it put away in a handkerchief. I was afraid of you, because you are a
hard man: you draw out what you never put in and reap what you did not
22 sow." "You rascal!" he replied; "I will judge you by your own words.
You knew, did you, that I am a hard man, that I draw out what I never put
23 in, and reap what I did not sow? Then why did you not put my money on
deposit, and I could have claimed it with interest when I came back?"
24 Turning to his attendants he said, "Take the pound from him and give it
25 26 to the man with ten." "But, sir," they replied, "he has ten already." "I tell
you," he went on, "the man who has will always be given more; but the
27 man who has not will forfeit even what he has. But as for those enemies of
mine who did not want me for their king, bring them here and slaughter
them in my presence."'

WITH THAT JESUS WENT FORWARD and began the ascent to Jerusalem. 28
As he approached Bethphage and Bethany at the hill called Olivet, he sent 29
two of the disciples with these instructions: 'Go to the village opposite; 30
as you enter it you will find tethered there a colt which no one has yet
ridden. Untie it and bring it here. If anyone asks why you are untying it, 31
say, "Our Master needs it."' The two went on their errand and found it 32
as he had told them; and while they were untying the colt, its owners asked, 33
'Why are you untying that colt?' They answered, 'Our Master needs it.' 34
So they brought the colt to Jesus. 35

Then they threw their cloaks on the colt, for Jesus to mount, and 36
they carpeted the road with them as he went on his way. And now, as he 37
approached the descent from the Mount of Olives, the whole company
of his disciples in their joy began to sing aloud the praises of God for all
the great things they had seen:

'Blessings on him who comes as king in the name of the Lord! 38
Peace in heaven, glory in highest heaven!'

Some Pharisees who were in the crowd said to him, 'Master, reprimand 39
your disciples.' He answered, 'I tell you, if my disciples keep silence the 40
stones will shout aloud.'

When he came in sight of the city, he wept over it and said, 'If only you 41 42
had known, on this great day, the way that leads to peace! But no; it is
hidden from your sight. For a time will come upon you, when your enemies 43
will set up siege-works against you; they will encircle you and hem you in
at every point; they will bring you to the ground, you and your children 44
within your walls, and not leave you one stone standing on another,
because you did not recognize God's moment when it came.'

Then he went into the temple and began driving out the traders, with 45 46
these words: 'Scripture says, "My house shall be a house of prayer"; but
you have made it a robbers' cave.'

Day by day he taught in the temple. And the chief priests and lawyers 47
were bent on making an end of him, with the support of the leading
citizens, but found they were helpless, because the people all hung upon 48
his words.

ONE DAY, as he was teaching the people in the temple and telling them **20**
the good news, the priests and lawyers, and the elders with them, came
upon him and accosted him. 'Tell us', they said, 'by what authority you are 2
acting like this; who gave you this authority?' He answered them, 'I have 3
a question to ask you too: tell me, was the baptism of John from God or 4
from men?' This set them arguing among themselves: 'If we say, "from 5
God", he will say, "Why did you not believe him?" And if we say, "from 6
men", the people will all stone us, for they are convinced that John was a
prophet.' So they replied that they could not tell. And Jesus said to them, 7 8
'Then neither will I tell you by what authority I act.'

He went on to tell the people this parable: 'A man planted a vineyard, 9
let it out to vine-growers, and went abroad for a long time. When the 10
season came, he sent a servant to the tenants to collect from them his share

of the produce; but the tenants thrashed him and sent him away empty-
11 handed. He tried again and sent a second servant; but he also was thrashed,
12 outrageously treated, and sent away empty-handed. He tried once more
13 with a third; this one too they wounded and flung out. Then the owner of
the vineyard said, "What am I to do? I will send my own dear son;*a*
14 perhaps they will respect him." But when the tenants saw him they talked
it over together. "This is the heir," they said; "let us kill him so that the
15 property may come to us." So they flung him out of the vineyard and killed
16 him. What then will the owner of the vineyard do to them? He will come
and put these tenants to death and let the vineyard to others.'

17   When they heard this, they said, 'God forbid!' But he looked straight
at them and said, 'Then what does this text of Scripture mean: "The stone
18 which the builders rejected has become the main corner-stone"? Any
man who falls on that stone will be dashed to pieces; and if it falls on a man
he will be crushed by it.'

19   The lawyers and chief priests wanted to lay hands on him there and then,
for they saw that this parable was aimed at them; but they were afraid of
20 the people. So they watched their opportunity and sent secret agents in the
guise of honest men, to seize upon some word of his as a pretext for hand-
21 ing him over to the authority and jurisdiction of the Governor. They put
a question to him: 'Master,' they said, 'we know that what you speak and
teach is sound; you pay deference to no one, but teach in all honesty the
22 way of life that God requires. Are we or are we not permitted to pay taxes
23 24 to the Roman Emperor?' He saw through their trick and said, 'Show me a
silver piece. Whose head does it bear, and whose inscription?' 'Caesar's',
25 they replied. 'Very well then,' he said, 'pay Caesar what is due to Caesar,
26 and pay God what is due to God.' Thus their attempt to catch him out in
public failed, and, astonished by his reply, they fell silent.

27   Then some Sadducees came forward. They are the people who deny
28 that there is a resurrection. Their question was this: 'Master, Moses laid
it down for us that if there are brothers, and one dies leaving a wife but no
child, then the next should marry the widow and carry on his brother's
29 family. Now, there were seven brothers: the first took a wife and died child-
30 31 less; then the second married her, then the third. In this way the seven of
32 33 them died leaving no children. Afterwards the woman also died. At the
resurrection whose wife is she to be, since all seven had married her?'
34 35 Jesus said to them, 'The men and women of this world marry; but those
who have been judged worthy of a place in the other world and of the
36 resurrection from the dead, do not marry, for they are not subject to death
any longer. They are like angels; they are sons of God, because they share
37 in the resurrection. That the dead are raised to life again is shown by Moses
himself in the story of the burning bush, when he calls the Lord, "the God
38 of Abraham, Isaac, and Jacob". God is not God of the dead but of the living;
for him all are *b* alive.'

39 40   At this some of the lawyers said, 'Well spoken, Master.' For there was
no further question that they ventured to put to him.

41   He said to them, 'How can they say that the Messiah is son of David?

a Or my only son.   *b Or* they are all.

For David himself says in the Book of Psalms: "The Lord said to my   42
Lord, 'Sit at my right hand until I make your enemies your footstool.'"   43
Thus David calls him "Lord"; how then can he be David's son?'   44

   In the hearing of all the people Jesus said to his disciples: 'Beware of the   45 46
doctors of the law who love to walk up and down in long robes, and have
a great liking for respectful greetings in the street, the chief seats in our
synagogues, and places of honour at feasts. These are the men who eat up   47
the property of widows, while they say long prayers for appearance' sake;
and they will receive the severest sentence.'

He looked up and saw the rich people dropping their gifts into the chest   **21**
of the temple treasury; and he noticed a poor widow putting in two tiny   2
coins. 'I tell you this,' he said: 'this poor widow has given more than any   3
of them; for those others who have given had more than enough, but she,   4
with less than enough, has given all she had to live on.'

SOME PEOPLE WERE TALKING about the temple and the fine stones   5
and votive offerings with which it was adorned. He said, 'These things   6
which you are gazing at—the time will come when not one stone of them
will be left upon another; all will be thrown down.' 'Master,' they asked,   7
'when will it all come about? What will be the sign when it is due to
happen?'

   He said, 'Take care that you are not misled. For many will come claim-   8
ing my name and saying, "I am he", and, "The Day is upon us." Do not
follow them. And when you hear of wars and insurrections, do not fall into   9
a panic. These things are bound to happen first; but the end does not follow
immediately.' Then he added, 'Nation will make war upon nation, kingdom   10
upon kingdom; there will be great earthquakes, and famines and plagues   11
in many places; in the sky terrors and great portents.

   'But before all this happens they will set upon you and persecute you.   12
You will be brought before synagogues and put in prison; you will be haled
before kings and governors for your allegiance to me. This will be your   13
opportunity to testify; so make up your minds not to prepare your defence   14
beforehand, because I myself will give you power of utterance and a   15
wisdom which no opponent will be able to resist or refute. Even your   16
parents and brothers, your relations and friends, will betray you. Some of
you will be put to death; and all will hate you for your allegiance to me.   17
But not a hair of your head shall be lost. By standing firm you will win true   18 19
life for yourselves.

   'But when you see Jerusalem encircled by armies, then you may be sure   20
that her destruction is near. Then those who are in Judaea must take to the   21
hills; those who are in the city itself must leave it, and those who are out
in the country must not enter; because this is the time of retribution, when   22
all that stands written is to be fulfilled. Alas for women who are with child   23
in those days, or have children at the breast! For there will be great distress
in the land and a terrible judgement upon this people. They will fall at the   24
sword's point; they will be carried captive into all countries; and Jerusalem will be trampled down by foreigners until their day has run its
course.

25 'Portents will appear in sun, moon, and stars. On earth nations will
stand helpless, not knowing which way to turn from the roar and surge of
26 the sea; men will faint with terror at the thought of all that is coming
27 upon the world; for the celestial powers will be shaken. And then they
will see the Son of Man coming on a cloud with great power and glory.
28 When all this begins to happen, stand upright and hold your heads high,
because your liberation is near.'

29 30 He told them this parable: 'Look at the fig-tree, or any other tree. As
31 soon as it buds, you can see for yourselves that summer is near. In the
same way, when you see all this happening, you may know that the kingdom
of God is near.

32 33 'I tell you this: the present generation will live to see it all. Heaven and
earth will pass away; my words will never pass away.

34 'Keep a watch on yourselves; do not let your minds be dulled by dissipation and drunkenness and worldly cares so that the great Day closes upon
35 you suddenly like a trap; for that day will come on all men, wherever they
36 are, the whole world over. Be on the alert, praying at all times for strength
to pass safely through all these imminent troubles and to stand in the presence of the Son of Man.'

37 His days were given to teaching in the temple; and then he would leave
38 the city and spend the night on the hill called Olivet. And in the early
morning the people flocked to listen to him in the temple. *a*

The final conflict

22 NOW THE FESTIVAL of Unleavened Bread, known as Passover, was
2 approaching, and the chief priests and the doctors of the law were
trying to devise some means of doing away with him; for they were afraid
of the people.

3 Then Satan entered into Judas Iscariot, who was one of the Twelve;
4 and Judas went to the chief priests and officers of the temple police to
5 discuss ways and means of putting Jesus into their power. They were
6 greatly pleased and undertook to pay him a sum of money. He agreed, and
began to look out for an opportunity to betray him to them without
collecting a crowd.

7 Then came the day of Unleavened Bread, on which the Passover victim
8 had to be slaughtered, and Jesus sent Peter and John with these instruc-
9 tions: 'Go and prepare for our Passover supper.' 'Where would you like
10 us to make the preparations?' they asked. He replied, 'As soon as you set
foot in the city a man will meet you carrying a jar of water. Follow him into
11 the house that he enters and give this message to the householder: "The
Master says, 'Where is the room in which I may eat the Passover with my
12 disciples?'" He will show you a large room upstairs all set out: make the
13 preparations there.' They went and found everything as he had said. So
they prepared for Passover.

14 When the time came he took his place at table, and the apostles with him;

a Some witnesses here insert the passage printed on p. 143.

and he said to them, 'How I have longed[a] to eat this Passover with you 15
before my death! For I tell you, never again shall I[b] eat it until the time 16
when it finds its fulfilment in the kingdom of God.'

Then he took a cup, and after giving thanks he said, 'Take this and share 17
it among yourselves; for I tell you, from this moment I shall drink from the 18
fruit of the vine no more until the time when the kingdom of God comes.'
And he took bread, gave thanks, and broke it; and he gave it to them, with 19
the words: 'This is my body.'[c]

'But mark this—my betrayer is here, his hand with mine on the table. 21
For the Son of Man is going his appointed way; but alas for that man by 22
whom he is betrayed!' At this they began to ask among themselves which of 23
them it could possibly be who was to do this thing.

Then a jealous dispute broke out: who among them should rank highest? 24
But he said, 'In the world, kings lord it over their subjects; and those in 25
authority are called their country's "Benefactors". Not so with you: on the 26
contrary, the highest among you must bear himself like the youngest,
chief of you like a servant. For who is greater—the one who sits at table or 27
the servant who waits on him? Surely the one who sits at table. Yet here
am I among you like a servant.

'You are the men who have stood firmly by me in my times of trial; and 28 29
now I vest in you the kingship which my Father vested in me; you shall eat 30
and drink at my table in my kingdom and sit[d] on thrones as judges of the
twelve tribes of Israel.

'Simon, Simon, take heed: Satan has been given leave to sift all of you 31
like wheat; but for you I have prayed that your faith may not fail; and when 32
you have come to yourself, you must lend strength to your brothers.'
'Lord,' he replied, 'I am ready to go with you to prison and death.' Jesus 33 34
said, 'I tell you, Peter, the cock will not crow tonight until you have three
times over denied that you know me.'

He said to them, 'When I sent you out barefoot without purse or pack, 35
were you ever short of anything?' 'No', they answered. 'It is different now,' 36
he said; 'whoever has a purse had better take it with him, and his pack too;
and if he has no sword, let him sell his cloak to buy one. For Scripture says, 37
"And he was counted among the outlaws", and these words, I tell you,
must find fulfilment in me; indeed, all that is written of me is being fulfilled.' 'Look, Lord,' they said, 'we have two swords here.' 'Enough, 38
enough!' he replied.

THEN HE WENT OUT and made his way as usual to the Mount of Olives, 39
accompanied by the disciples. When he reached the place he said to them, 40
'Pray that you may be spared the hour of testing.' He himself withdrew 41
from them about a stone's throw, knelt down, and began to pray: 'Father, 42

---

[a] *Or* said to them, 'I longed . . .'   [b] *Some witnesses read* For I tell you, I shall not . . .
[c] *Some witnesses add, in whole or in part, and with various arrangements, the following:*
'which is given for you; do this as a memorial of me.' (20) In the same way he took the
cup after supper, and said, 'This cup, poured out for you, is the new covenant sealed by
my blood.'   [d] *Or* trial; and as my Father gave me the right to reign, so I give you
the right to eat and to drink . . . and to sit . . .

if it be thy will, take this cup away from me. Yet not my will but thine be done.'

43 And now there appeared to him an angel from heaven bringing him
44 strength, and in anguish of spirit he prayed the more urgently; and his sweat was like clots of blood falling to the ground. *a*

45 When he rose from prayer and came to the disciples he found them
46 asleep, worn out by grief. 'Why are you sleeping?' he said. 'Rise and pray that you may be spared the test.'

47 WHILE HE WAS STILL SPEAKING a crowd appeared with the man called Judas, one of the Twelve, at their head. He came up to Jesus to
48 kiss him; but Jesus said, 'Judas, would you betray the Son of Man with a kiss?'

49 When his followers saw what was coming, they said, 'Lord, shall we use
50 our swords?' And one of them struck at the High Priest's servant, cutting
51 off his right ear. But Jesus answered, 'Let them have their way.' Then he touched the man's ear and healed him. *b*

52 Turning to the chief priests, the officers of the temple police, and the elders, who had come to seize him, he said, 'Do you take me for a bandit,
53 that you have come out with swords and cudgels to arrest me? Day after day, when I was in the temple with you, you kept your hands off me. But this is your moment—the hour when darkness reigns.'

54 Then they arrested him and led him away. They brought him to the
55 High Priest's house, and Peter followed at a distance. They lit a fire in the
56 middle of the courtyard and sat round it, and Peter sat among them. A serving-maid who saw him sitting in the firelight stared at him and said,
57 'This man was with him too.' But he denied it: 'Woman,' he said, 'I do
58 not know him.' A little later someone else noticed him and said, 'You also
59 are one of them.' But Peter said to him, 'No, I am not.' About an hour passed and another spoke more strongly still: 'Of course this fellow was
60 with him. He must have been; he is a Galilean.' But Peter said, 'Man, I do not know what you are talking about.' At that moment, while he was still
61 speaking, a cock crew; and the Lord turned and looked at Peter. And Peter remembered the Lord's words, 'Tonight before the cock crows you will disown me three times.' *c*

63 64 The men who were guarding Jesus mocked at him. They beat him, they blindfolded him, and they kept asking him, 'Now, prophet, who hit you?
65 Tell us that.' And so they went on heaping insults upon him.

66 WHEN DAY BROKE, the elders of the nation, chief priests, and doctors
67 of the law assembled, and he was brought before their Council. 'Tell us,' they said, 'are you the Messiah?' 'If I tell you,' he replied, 'you will not
68 69 believe me; and if I ask questions, you will not answer. But from now on,
70 the Son of Man will be seated at the right hand of Almighty God.' *d* 'You are the Son of God, then?' they all said, and he replied, 'It is you who say I

---

a Some witnesses omit And now . . . ground.   *b Or* 'Let me do as much as this', *and*
touching the man's ear, he healed him.   *c Some witnesses add* (62) He went outside,
and wept bitterly, *as in Matthew 26. 75.*   *d Literally* of the Power of God.

am.'*a* They said, 'Need we call further witnesses? We have heard it our- 71
selves from his own lips.'

With that the whole assembly rose, and they brought him before Pilate. **23**
They opened the case against him by saying, 'We found this man subvert- 2
ing our nation, opposing the payment of taxes to Caesar, and claiming to be
Messiah, a king.'*b* Pilate asked him, 'Are you the king of the Jews?' He 3
replied, 'The words are yours.'*c* Pilate then said to the chief priests and 4
the crowd, 'I find no case for this man to answer.' But they insisted: 'His 5
teaching is causing disaffection among the people all through Judaea. It
started from Galilee and has spread as far as this city.'

When Pilate heard this, he asked if the man was a Galilean, and on 6 7
learning that he belonged to Herod's jurisdiction he remitted the case to
him, for Herod was also in Jerusalem at that time. When Herod saw Jesus 8
he was greatly pleased; having heard about him, he had long been wanting
to see him, and had been hoping to see some miracle performed by him.
He questioned him at some length without getting any reply; but the chief 9 10
priests and lawyers appeared and pressed the case against him vigorously.
Then Herod and his troops treated him with contempt and ridicule, and 11
sent him back to Pilate dressed in a gorgeous robe. That same day Herod 12
and Pilate became friends; till then there had been a standing feud between
them.

Pilate now called together the chief priests, councillors, and people, and 13 14
said to them, 'You brought this man before me on a charge of subversion.
But, as you see, I have myself examined him in your presence and found
nothing in him to support your charges. No more did Herod, for he has 15
referred him back to us. Clearly he has done nothing to deserve death. I 16
therefore propose to let him off with a flogging.' But*d* there was a general 18
outcry, 'Away with him! Give us Barabbas.' (This man had been put in 19
prison for a rising that had taken place in the city, and for murder.) Pilate 20
addressed them again, in his desire to release Jesus, but they shouted back, 21
'Crucify him, crucify him!' For the third time he spoke to them: 'Why, 22
what wrong has he done? I have not found him guilty of any capital offence.
I will therefore let him off with a flogging.' But they insisted on their 23
demand, shouting that Jesus should be crucified. Their shouts prevailed
and Pilate decided that they should have their way. He released the man 24 25
they asked for, the man who had been put in prison for insurrection and
murder, and gave Jesus up to their will.

AS THEY LED HIM AWAY to execution they seized upon a man called 26
Simon, from Cyrene, on his way in from the country, put the cross on his
back, and made him walk behind Jesus carrying it.

Great numbers of people followed, many women among them, who 27
mourned and lamented over him. Jesus turned to them and said, 'Daugh- 28
ters of Jerusalem, do not weep for me; no, weep for yourselves and your
children. For the days are surely coming when they will say, "Happy are 29

a Or You are right, for I am.   *b Or* to be an anointed king.   *c Or* It is as
you say.   *d Some witnesses read* (17) At festival time he was obliged to release one
person for them; (18) and now . . .

the barren, the wombs that never bore a child, the breasts that never fed
30 one." Then they will start saying to the mountains, "Fall on us", and to the
31 hills, "Cover us." For if these things are done when the wood is green,
what will happen when it is dry?'

32 There were two others with him, criminals who were being led away to
33 execution; and when they reached the place called The Skull, they crucified
him there, and the criminals with him, one on his right and the other on his
34 left. Jesus said, 'Father, forgive them; they do not know what they are
doing.'ᵃ

35 They divided his clothes among them by casting lots. The people stood
looking on, and their rulers jeered at him: 'He saved others: now let him
36 save himself, if this is God's Messiah, his Chosen.' The soldiers joined in
37 the mockery and came forward offering him their sour wine. 'If you are
38 the king of the Jews,' they said, 'save yourself.' There was an inscription
above his head which ran: 'This is the king of the Jews.'

39 One of the criminals who hung there with him taunted him: 'Are not
40 you the Messiah? Save yourself, and us.' But the other rebuked him:
41 'Have you no fear of God? You are under the same sentence as he. For us
it is plain justice; we are paying the price for our misdeeds; but this man has
42 done nothing wrong.' And he said, 'Jesus, remember me when you come
43 to your throne.'ᵇ He answered, 'I tell you this: today you shall be with me
in Paradise.'

44 By now it was about midday and a darkness fell over the whole land,
45 which lasted until three in the afternoon; the sun's light failed. And the
46 curtain of the temple was torn in two. Then Jesus gave a loud cry and
said, 'Father, into thy hands I commit my spirit'; and with these words he
47 died. The centurion saw it all, and gave praise to God. 'Beyond all doubt',
he said, 'this man was innocent.'

48 The crowd who had assembled for the spectacle, when they saw what
had happened, went home beating their breasts.

49 HIS FRIENDS had all been standing at a distance; the women who had
accompanied him from Galilee stood with them and watched it all.

50 Now there was a man called Joseph, a member of the Council, a good,
51 upright man, who had dissented from their policy and the action they had
taken. He came from the Judaean town of Arimathaea, and he was one
52 who looked forward to the kingdom of God. This man now approached
53 Pilate and asked for the body of Jesus. Taking it down from the cross, he
wrapped it in a linen sheet, and laid it in a tomb cut out of the rock, in which
54 no one had been laid before. It was Friday, and the Sabbath was about to
begin.

55 The women who had accompanied him from Galilee followed; they took
56 note of the tomb and observed how his body was laid. Then they went home
and prepared spices and perfumes; and on the Sabbath they rested in
24 obedience to the commandment. But on the Sunday morning very early
2 they came to the tomb bringing the spices they had prepared. Finding that

---

ᵃ *Some witnesses omit* Jesus said, 'Father . . . doing.'   ᵇ *Some witnesses read* come
in royal power.

the stone had been rolled away from the tomb, they went inside; but the 3
body was not to be found. While they stood utterly at a loss, all of a sudden 4
two men in dazzling garments were at their side. They were terrified, and 5
stood with eyes cast down, but the men said, 'Why search among the dead
for one who lives?*a* Remember what he told you while he was still in 6
Galilee, about the Son of Man: how he must be given up into the power of 7
sinful men and be crucified, and must rise again on the third day.' Then 8
they recalled his words and, returning from the tomb, they reported all this 9
to the Eleven and all the others.

The women were Mary of Magdala, Joanna, and Mary the mother*b* of 10
James, and they, with the other women, told the apostles. But the story 11
appeared to them to be nonsense, and they would not believe them.*c*

THAT SAME DAY two of them were on their way to a village called Emmaus, 13
which lay about seven miles from Jerusalem, and they were talking 14
together about all these happenings. As they talked and discussed it with 15
one another, Jesus himself came up and walked along with them; but 16
something kept them from seeing who it was. He asked them, 'What is it 17
you are debating as you walk?' They halted, their faces full of gloom, and 18
one, called Cleopas, answered, 'Are you the only person staying in Jerusalem not to know*d* what has happened there in the last few days?' 'What 19
do you mean?' he said. 'All this about Jesus of Nazareth,' they replied,
'a prophet powerful in speech and action before God and the whole people;
how our chief priests and rulers handed him over to be sentenced to death, 20
and crucified him. But we had been hoping that he was the man to liberate 21
Israel. What is more, this is the third day since it happened, and now some 22
women of our company have astounded us: they went early to the tomb,
but failed to find his body, and returned with a story that they had seen a 23
vision of angels who told them he was alive. So some of our people went to 24
the tomb and found things just as the women had said; but him they did
not see.'

'How dull you are!' he answered. 'How slow to believe all that the 25
prophets said! Was the Messiah not bound to suffer thus before entering 26
upon his glory?' Then he began with Moses and all the prophets, and 27
explained to them the passages which referred to himself in every part of
the scriptures.

By this time they had reached the village to which they were going, and 28
he made as if to continue his journey, but they pressed him: 'Stay with us, 29
for evening draws on, and the day is almost over.' So he went in to stay with
them. And when he had sat down with them at table, he took bread and 30
said the blessing; he broke the bread, and offered it to them. Then their 31
eyes were opened, and they recognized him; and he vanished from their
sight. They said to one another, 'Did we not feel our hearts on fire as he 32
talked with us on the road and explained the scriptures to us?'

a Some witnesses insert He is not here: he has been raised.   *b Or* wife, *or* daughter.
c Some witnesses add (12) Peter, however, got up and ran to the tomb, and, peering in, saw
the wrappings and nothing more; and he went home amazed at what had happened.
d Or Have you been staying by yourself in Jerusalem, that you do not know . . .

33 Without a moment's delay they set out and returned to Jerusalem. There
34 they found that the Eleven and the rest of the company had assembled, and
were saying, 'It is true: the Lord has risen; he has appeared to Simon.'
35 Then they gave their account of the events of their journey and told how
he had been recognized by them at the breaking of the bread.

36   As they were talking about all this, there he was, standing among them. *a*
37 38 Startled and terrified, they thought they were seeing a ghost. But he said,
'Why are you so perturbed? Why do questionings arise in your minds?
39 Look at my hands and feet. It is I myself. Touch me and see; no ghost has
41 flesh and bones as you can see that I have.'*b* They were still unconvinced,
still wondering, for it seemed too good to be true. So he asked them, 'Have
42 you anything here to eat?' They offered him a piece of fish they had cooked,
43 which he took and ate before their eyes.

44   And he said to them, 'This is what I meant by saying, while I was still
with you, that everything written about me in the Law of Moses and in the
45 prophets and psalms was bound to be fulfilled.' Then he opened their
46 minds to understand the scriptures. 'This', he said, 'is what is written:
that the Messiah is to suffer death and to rise from the dead on the third
47 day, and that in his name repentance bringing the forgiveness of sins is to
48 be proclaimed to all nations. Begin from Jerusalem; it is you who are the
49 witnesses to it all. And mark this: I am sending upon you my Father's
promised gift; so stay here in this city until you are armed with the power
from above.'

50   Then he led them out as far as Bethany, and blessed them with uplifted
51 52 hands; and in the act of blessing he parted from them.*c* And they*d* returned
53 to Jerusalem with great joy, and spent all their time in the temple praising God.

THE GOSPEL ACCORDING TO

JOHN

The coming of Christ

1 WHEN ALL THINGS BEGAN, the Word already was.*e*
The Word dwelt with God, and what God was, the Word was.
2 3   The Word, then, was with God at the beginning, and through
him all things came to be; no single thing was created without him. All
4 that came to be was alive with his life,*f* and that life was the light of men.
5 The light shines on in the dark, and the darkness has never mastered it.

---

a Some witnesses insert And he said to them, 'Peace be with you!'   *b Some witnesses*
insert (40) After saying this he showed them his hands and feet.   *c Some witnesses*
add and was carried up into heaven.   *d Some witnesses insert* worshipped
him and . . .   *e Or* The Word was at the creation.   *f Or* no single created
thing came into being without him. There was life in him . . .

There appeared a man named John, sent from God; he came as a wit- 6 7
ness to testify to the light, that all might become believers through him.
He was not himself the light; he came to bear witness to the light. The real 8 9
light which enlightens every man was even then coming into the world.*a*

He was in the world;*b* but the world, though it owed its being to him, 10
did not recognize him. He entered his own realm, and his own would not 11
receive him. But to all who did receive him, to those who have yielded him 12
their allegiance, he gave the right to become children of God, not born of 13
any human stock, or by the fleshly desire of a human father, but the offspring of God himself. So the Word became flesh; he came to dwell 14
among us, and we saw his glory, such glory as befits the Father's only Son,
full of grace and truth.

Here is John's testimony to him: he cried aloud, 'This is the man I 15
meant when I said, "He comes after me, but takes rank before me"; for
before I was born, he already was.'

Out of his full store we have all received grace upon grace; for while the 16 17
Law was given through Moses, grace and truth came through Jesus Christ.
No one has ever seen God; but God's only Son, he who is nearest to the 18
Father's heart, he has made him known.*c*

THIS IS THE TESTIMONY which John gave when the Jews of Jerusalem 19
sent a deputation of priests and Levites to ask him who he was. He con- 20
fessed without reserve and avowed, 'I am not the Messiah.' 'What then? 21
Are you Elijah?' 'No', he replied. 'Are you the prophet we await?' He
answered 'No.' 'Then who are you?' they asked. 'We must give an answer 22
to those who sent us. What account do you give of yourself?' He answered 23
in the words of the prophet Isaiah: 'I am a voice crying aloud in the wilderness, "Make the Lord's highway straight."'

Some Pharisees who were in the deputation asked him, 'If you are not 24 25
the Messiah, nor Elijah, nor the prophet, why then are you baptizing?'
'I baptize in water,' John replied, 'but among you, though you do not know 26
him, stands the one who is to come after me. I am not good enough to un- 27
fasten his shoes.' This took place at Bethany beyond Jordan, where John 28
was baptizing.

The next day he saw Jesus coming towards him. 'Look,' he said, 'there 29
is the Lamb of God; it is he who takes away the sin of the world. This is he 30
of whom I spoke when I said, "After me a man is coming who takes rank
before me"; for before I was born, he already was. I myself did not know 31
who he was; but the very reason why I came, baptizing in water, was that
he might be revealed to Israel.'

John testified further: 'I saw the Spirit coming down from heaven like 32
a dove and resting upon him. I did not know him, but he who sent me to 33
baptize in water had told me, "When you see the Spirit coming down upon
someone and resting upon him, you will know that this is he who is to

---

a Or The light was in being, light absolute, enlightening every man born into the world.
b Or The Word, then, was in the world.   *c Some witnesses read* but the only one,
the one nearest to the Father's heart, has made him known; *others read* but the only one,
himself God, the nearest to the Father's heart, has made him known.

34 baptize in Holy Spirit." I saw it myself, and I have borne witness. This is God's Chosen One.' *a*

35 36 The next day again John was standing with two of his disciples when Jesus passed by. John looked towards him and said, 'There is the Lamb 37 38 of God.' The two disciples heard him say this, and followed Jesus. When he turned and saw them following him, he asked, 'What are you looking for?' They said, 'Rabbi' (which means a teacher), 'where are you staying?' 39 'Come and see', he replied. So they went and saw where he was staying, and spent the rest of the day with him. It was then about four in the afternoon.

40 One of the two who followed Jesus after hearing what John said was 41 Andrew, Simon Peter's brother. The first thing he did was to find *b* his brother Simon. He said to him, 'We have found the Messiah' (which is the 42 Hebrew for 'Christ'). He brought Simon to Jesus, who looked at him and said, 'You are Simon son of John. You shall be called Cephas' (that is, Peter, the Rock).

43 44 The next day Jesus decided to leave for Galilee. He met Philip, who, like Andrew and Peter, came from Bethsaida, and said to him, 'Follow me.' 45 Philip went to find Nathanael, and told him, 'We have met the man spoken of by Moses in the Law, and by the prophets: it is Jesus son of Joseph, from 46 Nazareth.' 'Nazareth!' Nathanael exclaimed; 'can anything good come 47 from Nazareth?' Philip said, 'Come and see.' When Jesus saw Nathanael coming, he said, 'Here is an Israelite worthy of the name; there is nothing 48 false in him.' Nathanael asked him, 'How do you come to know me?' Jesus 49 replied, 'I saw you under the fig-tree before Philip spoke to you.' 'Rabbi,' 50 said Nathanael, 'you are the Son of God; you are king of Israel.' Jesus answered, 'Is this the ground of your faith, that I told you I saw you under 51 the fig-tree? You shall see greater things than that.' Then he added, 'In truth, in very truth I tell you all, you shall see heaven wide open, and God's angels ascending and descending upon the Son of Man.'

Christ the giver of life

2 ON THE THIRD DAY there was a wedding at Cana-in-Galilee. The 2 mother of Jesus was there, and Jesus and his disciples were guests 3 also. The wine gave out, so Jesus's mother said to him, 'They have no wine 4 left.' He answered, 'Your concern, mother, is not mine. My hour has not 5 yet come.' His mother said to the servants, 'Do whatever he tells you.' 6 There were six stone water-jars standing near, of the kind used for Jewish 7 rites of purification; each held from twenty to thirty gallons. Jesus said to the servants, 'Fill the jars with water', and they filled them to the brim. 8 'Now draw some off', he ordered, 'and take it to the steward of the feast'; 9 and they did so. The steward tasted the water now turned into wine, not knowing its source; though the servants who had drawn the water knew. 10 He hailed the bridegroom and said, 'Everyone serves the best wine first,

a Some witnesses read This is the Son of God.   *b Some witnesses read* In the morning he found . . .

and waits until the guests have drunk freely before serving the poorer sort; but you have kept the best wine till now.'

This deed at Cana-in-Galilee is the first of the signs by which Jesus 11 revealed his glory and led his disciples to believe in him.

AFTER THIS he went down to Capernaum in company with his mother, 12 his brothers, and his disciples, but they did not stay there long. As it was 13 near the time of the Jewish Passover, Jesus went up to Jerusalem. There 14 he found in the temple the dealers in cattle, sheep, and pigeons, and the money-changers seated at their tables. Jesus made a whip of cords and 15 drove them out of the temple, sheep, cattle, and all. He upset the tables of the money-changers, scattering their coins. Then he turned on the dealers 16 in pigeons: 'Take them out,' he said; 'you must not turn my Father's house into a market.' His disciples recalled the words of Scripture, 'Zeal for thy 17 house will destroy me.' The Jews challenged Jesus: 'What sign', they 18 asked, 'can you show as authority for your action?' 'Destroy this temple,' 19 Jesus replied, 'and in three days I will raise it again.' They said, 'It has 20 taken forty-six years to build this temple. Are you going to raise it again in three days?' But the temple he was speaking of was his body. After his 21 22 resurrection his disciples recalled what he had said, and they believed the Scripture and the words that Jesus had spoken.

WHILE HE WAS in Jerusalem for Passover many gave their allegiance to 23 him when they saw the signs that he performed. But Jesus for his part 24 would not trust himself to them. He knew men so well, all of them, that he 25 needed no evidence from others about a man, for he himself could tell what was in a man.

THERE WAS ONE of the Pharisees named Nicodemus, a member of the 3 Jewish Council, who came to Jesus by night. 'Rabbi,' he said, 'we know 2 that you are a teacher sent by God; no one could perform these signs of yours unless God were with him.' Jesus answered, 'In truth, in very truth 3 I tell you, unless a man has been born over again he cannot see the kingdom of God.' 'But how is it possible', said Nicodemus, 'for a man to be born 4 when he is old? Can he enter his mother's womb a second time and be born?' Jesus answered, 'In truth I tell you, no one can enter the kingdom 5 of God without being born from water and spirit. Flesh can give birth only 6 to flesh; it is spirit that gives birth to spirit. You ought not to be astonished, 7 then, when I tell you that you must be born over again. The wind*a* blows 8 where it wills; you hear the sound of it, but you do not know where it comes from, or where it is going. So with everyone who is born from spirit*a*.'

Nicodemus replied, 'How is this possible?' 'What!' said Jesus. 'Is this 9 10 famous teacher of Israel ignorant of such things? In very truth I tell you, 11 we speak of what we know, and testify to what we have seen, and yet you all reject our testimony. If you disbelieve me when I talk to you about 12 things on earth, how are you to believe if I should talk about the things of heaven?

a wind *and* spirit *are translations of the same Greek word, which has both meanings.*

13 'No one ever went up into heaven except the one who came down from
14 heaven, the Son of Man whose home is in heaven. *a* This Son of Man must
15 be lifted up as the serpent was lifted up by Moses in the wilderness, so that
everyone who has faith in him may in him possess eternal life.

16 'God loved the world so much that he gave his only Son, that everyone
17 who has faith in him may not die but have eternal life. It was not to judge
the world that God sent his Son into the world, but that through him the
world might be saved.

18 'The man who puts his faith in him does not come under judgement;
but the unbeliever has already been judged in that he has not given his
19 allegiance to God's only Son. Here lies the test: the light has come into the
world, but men preferred darkness to light because their deeds were evil.
20 Bad men all hate the light and avoid it, for fear their practices should be
21 shown up. The honest man comes to the light so that it may be clearly seen
that God is in all he does.'

22 AFTER THIS, Jesus went into Judaea with his disciples, stayed there with
23 them, and baptized. John too was baptizing at Aenon, near to Salim,
because water was plentiful in that region; and people were constantly
24 coming for baptism. This was before John's imprisonment.
25 Some of John's disciples had fallen into a dispute with Jews about puri-
26 fication; so they came to him and said, 'Rabbi, there was a man with you
on the other side of the Jordan, to whom you bore your witness. Here he is,
27 baptizing, and crowds are flocking to him.' John's answer was: 'A man
28 can have only what God gives him. You yourselves can testify that I said,
29 "I am not the Messiah; I have been sent as his forerunner." It is the bridegroom to whom the bride belongs. The bridegroom's friend, who stands
by and listens to him, is overjoyed at hearing the bridegroom's voice. This
30 joy, this perfect joy, is now mine. As he grows greater, I must grow less.'
31 He who comes from above is above all others; he who is from the earth
belongs to the earth and uses earthly speech. He who comes from heaven *b*
32 bears witness to what he has seen and heard, yet no one accepts his witness.
33 34 To accept his witness is to attest that God speaks the truth; for he whom
God sent utters the words of God, so measureless is God's gift of the Spirit.
35 36 The Father loves the Son and has entrusted him with all authority. He who
puts his faith in the Son has hold of eternal life, but he who disobeys the
Son shall not see that life; God's wrath rests upon him.

4 A REPORT NOW REACHED the Pharisees: 'Jesus is winning and baptizing
2 more disciples than John'; although, in fact, it was only the disciples who
3 were baptizing and not Jesus himself. When Jesus learned this, he left
4 Judaea and set out once more for Galilee. He had to pass through Samaria,
5 and on his way came to a Samaritan town called Sychar, near the plot of
6 ground which Jacob gave to his son Joseph and the spring called Jacob's
well. It was about noon, and Jesus, tired after his journey, sat down by
the well.

---

a Some witnesses omit whose home is in heaven.   *b Some witnesses insert* is above
all and . . .

The disciples had gone away to the town to buy food. Meanwhile a 8 7
Samaritan woman came to draw water. Jesus said to her, 'Give me a drink.'
The Samaritan woman said, 'What! You, a Jew, ask a drink of me, a 9
Samaritan woman?' (Jews and Samaritans, it should be noted, do not use
vessels in common.*a*) Jesus answered her, 'If only you knew what God 10
gives, and who it is that is asking you for a drink, you would have asked
him and he would have given you living water.' 'Sir,' the woman said, 11
'you have no bucket and this well is deep. How can you give me "living
water"? Are you a greater man than Jacob our ancestor, who gave us the 12
well, and drank from it himself, he and his sons, and his cattle too?' Jesus 13
said, 'Everyone who drinks this water will be thirsty again, but whoever 14
drinks the water that I shall give him will never suffer thirst any more.
The water that I shall give him will be an inner spring always welling up
for eternal life.' 'Sir,' said the woman, 'give me that water, and then I shall 15
not be thirsty, nor have to come all this way to draw.'

Jesus replied, 'Go home, call your husband and come back.' She 16 17
answered, 'I have no husband.' 'You are right', said Jesus, 'in saying that
you have no husband, for, although you have had five husbands, the man 18
with whom you are now living is not your husband; you told me the truth
there.' 'Sir,' she replied, 'I can see that you are a prophet. Our fathers 19 20
worshipped on this mountain, but you Jews say that the temple where God
should be worshipped is in Jerusalem.' 'Believe me,' said Jesus, 'the time 21
is coming when you will worship the Father neither on this mountain, nor
in Jerusalem. You Samaritans worship without knowing what you worship, 22
while we worship what we know. It is from the Jews that salvation comes.
But the time approaches, indeed it is already here, when those who are 23
real worshippers will worship the Father in spirit and in truth. Such are the
worshippers whom the Father wants. God is spirit, and those who worship 24
him must worship in spirit and in truth.' The woman answered, 'I know 25
that Messiah' (that is Christ) 'is coming. When he comes he will tell us
everything.' Jesus said, 'I am he, I who am speaking to you now.' 26

At that moment his disciples returned, and were astonished to find him 27
talking with a woman; but none of them said, 'What do you want?' or,
'Why are you talking with her?' The woman put down her water-jar and 28
went away to the town, where she said to the people, 'Come and see a man 29
who has told me everything I ever did. Could this be the Messiah?' They 30
came out of the town and made their way towards him.

Meanwhile the disciples were urging him, 'Rabbi, have something to 31
eat.' But he said, 'I have food to eat of which you know nothing.' At this 32 33
the disciples said to one another, 'Can someone have brought him food?'
But Jesus said, 'It is meat and drink for me to do the will of him who sent 34
me until I have finished his work.

'Do you not say, "Four months more and then comes harvest"? But 35
look, I tell you, look round on the fields; they are already white, ripe for
harvest. The reaper is drawing his pay and gathering a crop for eternal life, 36
so that sower and reaper may rejoice together. That is how the saying comes 37

---

a Or Jews, it should be noted, are not on familiar terms with Samaritans; *some witnesses
omit these words.*

38 true: "One sows, and another reaps." I sent you to reap a crop for which you have not toiled. Others toiled and you have come in for the harvest of their toil.'

39 Many Samaritans of that town came to believe in him because of the
40 woman's testimony: 'He told me everything I ever did.' So when these Samaritans had come to him they pressed him to stay with them; and he
41 stayed there two days. Many more became believers because of what they
42 heard from his own lips. They told the woman, 'It is no longer because of what you said that we believe, for we have heard him ourselves; and we know that this is in truth the Saviour of the world.'

43 44 WHEN THE TWO DAYS were over he set out for Galilee; for Jesus himself
45 declared that a prophet is without honour in his own country. On his arrival in Galilee the Galileans gave him a welcome, because they had seen all that he did at the festival in Jerusalem; they had been at the festival themselves.

46 Once again he visited Cana-in-Galilee, where he had turned the water into wine. An officer in the royal service was there, whose son was lying ill
47 at Capernaum. When he heard that Jesus had come from Judaea into Galilee, he came to him and begged him to go down and cure his son, who
48 was at the point of death. Jesus said to him, 'Will none of you ever believe
49 without seeing signs and portents?' The officer pleaded with him, 'Sir,
50 come down before my boy dies.' Then Jesus said, 'Return home; your son
51 will live.' The man believed what Jesus said and started for home. When he was on his way down his servants met him with the news, 'Your boy is
52 going to live.' So he asked them what time it was when he began to recover.
53 They said, 'Yesterday at one in the afternoon the fever left him.' The father noted that this was the exact time when Jesus had said to him, 'Your son will live', and he and all his household became believers.

54 This was now the second sign which Jesus performed after coming down from Judaea into Galilee.

5 LATER ON Jesus went up to Jerusalem for one of the Jewish festivals. *a*
2 Now at the Sheep-Pool in Jerusalem there is a place with five colonnades.
3 Its name in the language of the Jews is Bethesda. In these colonnades there
5 lay a crowd of sick people, blind, lame, and paralysed. *b* Among them was
6 a man who had been crippled for thirty-eight years. When Jesus saw him lying there and was aware that he had been ill a long time, he asked him,
7 'Do you want to recover?' 'Sir,' he replied, 'I have no one to put me in the pool when the water is disturbed, but while I am moving, someone else
8 is in the pool before me.' Jesus answered, 'Rise to your feet, take up your
9 bed and walk.' The man recovered instantly, took up his stretcher, and began to walk.

10 That day was a Sabbath. So the Jews said to the man who had been

---

a Some witnesses read for the Jewish festival.   *b Some witnesses add* waiting for the disturbance of the water; *some further insert* (4) for from time to time an angel came down into the pool and stirred up the water. The first to plunge in after this disturbance recovered from whatever disease had afflicted him.

cured, 'It is the Sabbath. You are not allowed to carry your bed on the
Sabbath.' He answered, 'The man who cured me said, "Take up your bed 11
and walk." ' They asked him, 'Who is the man who told you to take up 12
your bed and walk?' But the cripple who had been cured did not know; for 13
the place was crowded and Jesus had slipped away. A little later Jesus found 14
him in the temple and said to him, 'Now that you are well again, leave your
sinful ways, or you may suffer something worse.' The man went away and 15
told the Jews that it was Jesus who had cured him.

It was works of this kind done on the Sabbath that stirred the Jews to 16
persecute Jesus. He defended himself by saying, 'My Father has never 17
yet ceased his work, and I am working too.' This made the Jews still more 18
determined to kill him, because he was not only breaking the Sabbath, but,
by calling God his own Father, he claimed equality with God.

To this charge Jesus replied, 'In truth, in very truth I tell you, the Son 19
can do nothing by himself; he does only what he sees the Father doing:
what the Father does, the Son does. For the Father loves the Son and shows 20
him all his works, and will show greater yet, to fill you with wonder. As 21
the Father raises the dead and gives them life, so the Son gives life to men,
as he determines. And again, the Father does not judge anyone, but has 22
given full jurisdiction to the Son; it is his will that all should pay the same 23
honour to the Son as to the Father. To deny honour to the Son is to deny
it to the Father who sent him.

'In very truth, anyone who gives heed to what I say and puts his trust in 24
him who sent me has hold of eternal life, and does not come up for judgement, but has already passed from death to life. In truth, in very truth I 25
tell you, a time is coming, indeed it is already here, when the dead shall
hear the voice of the Son of God, and all who hear shall come to life. For 26
as the Father has life-giving power in himself, so has the Son, by the
Father's gift.

'As Son of Man, he has also been given the right to pass judgement. Do 27 28
not wonder at this, because the time is coming when all who are in the
grave shall hear his voice and come out: those who have done right will rise 29
to life; those who have done wrong will rise to hear their doom. I cannot 30
act by myself; I judge as I am bidden, and my sentence is just, because my
aim is not my own will, but the will of him who sent me.

'If I testify on my own behalf, that testimony does not hold good. There 31 32
is another who bears witness for me, and I know that his testimony holds.
Your messengers have been to John; you have his testimony to the truth. 33
Not that I rely on human testimony, but I remind you of it for your own 34
salvation. John was a lamp, burning brightly, and for a time you were 35
ready to exult in his light. But I rely on a testimony higher than John's. 36
There is enough to testify that the Father has sent me, in the works my
Father gave me to do and to finish—the very works I have in hand. This 37
testimony to me was given by the Father who sent me, although you never
heard his voice, or saw his form. But his word has found no home in you, 38
for you do not believe the one whom he sent. You study the scriptures 39
diligently, supposing that in having them you have eternal life; yet, although their testimony points to me, you refuse to come to me for that life. 40

41 42   'I do not look to men for honour. But with you it is different, as I know
43   well, for you have no love for God in you. I have come accredited by my
Father, and you have no welcome for me; if another comes self-accredited
44   you will welcome him. How can you have faith so long as you receive
honour from one another, and care nothing for the honour that comes from
45   him who alone is God? Do not imagine that I shall be your accuser at the
Father's tribunal. Your accuser is Moses, the very Moses on whom you
46   have set your hope. If you believed Moses you would believe what I tell
47   you, for it was about me that he wrote. But if you do not believe what he
wrote, how are you to believe what I say?'

6   SOME TIME LATER Jesus withdrew to the farther shore of the Sea of
2   Galilee (or Tiberias), and a large crowd of people followed who had seen
3   the signs he performed in healing the sick. Then Jesus went up the hill-
4   side and sat down with his disciples. It was near the time of Passover, the
5   great Jewish festival. Raising his eyes and seeing a large crowd coming
towards him, Jesus said to Philip, 'Where are we to buy bread to feed these
6   people?' This he said to test him; Jesus himself knew what he meant to do.
7   Philip replied, 'Twenty pounds *a* would not buy enough bread for every
8   one of them to have a little.' One of his disciples, Andrew, the brother of
9   Simon Peter, said to him, 'There is a boy here who has five barley loaves
10   and two fishes; but what is that among so many?' Jesus said, 'Make the
people sit down.' There was plenty of grass there, so the men sat down,
11   about five thousand of them. Then Jesus took the loaves, gave thanks, and
distributed them to the people as they sat there. He did the same with the
12   fishes, and they had as much as they wanted. When everyone had had
enough, he said to his disciples, 'Collect the pieces left over, so that nothing
13   may be lost.' This they did, and filled twelve baskets with the pieces left
uneaten of the five barley loaves.
14   When the people saw the sign Jesus had performed, the word went
round, 'Surely this must be the prophet that was to come into the world.'
15   Jesus, aware that they meant to come and seize him to proclaim him king,
withdrew again to the hills by himself.
16 17   At nightfall his disciples went down to the sea, got into their boat, and
pushed off to cross the water to Capernaum. Darkness had already fallen,
18   and Jesus had not yet joined them. By now a strong wind was blowing and
19   the sea grew rough. When they had rowed about three or four miles they saw
20   Jesus walking on the sea and approaching the boat. They were terrified, but
21   he called out, 'It is I; do not be afraid.' Then they were ready to take him
aboard, and immediately the boat reached the land they were making for.

22   NEXT MORNING the crowd was standing on the opposite shore. They
had seen only one boat there, and Jesus, they knew, had not embarked
23   with his disciples, who had gone away without him. Boats from Tiberias,
however, came ashore *b* near the place where the people had eaten the
24   bread over which the Lord gave thanks. *c* When the people saw that neither

a Literally 200 denarii.   *b* Some witnesses read Other boats from Tiberias came
ashore . . .   *c* Some witnesses omit over which . . . thanks.

Jesus nor his disciples were any longer there, they themselves went aboard these boats and made for Capernaum in search of Jesus. They found him 25 on the other side. 'Rabbi,' they said, 'when did you come here?' Jesus 26 replied, 'In very truth I know that you have not come looking for me because you saw signs, but because you ate the bread and your hunger was satisfied. You must work, not for this perishable food, but for the food that 27 lasts, the food of eternal life.

'This food the Son of Man will give you, for he it is upon whom God the Father has set the seal of his authority.' 'Then what must we do', they 28 asked him, 'if we are to work as God would have us work?' Jesus replied, 29 'This is the work that God requires: believe in the one whom he has sent.'

They said, 'What sign can you give us to see, so that we may believe you? 30 What is the work you do? Our ancestors had manna to eat in the desert; as 31 Scripture says, "He gave them bread from heaven to eat." ' Jesus answered, 32 'I tell you this: the truth is, not that Moses gave you the bread from heaven, but that my Father gives you the real bread from heaven. The bread that 33 God gives comes down *a* from heaven and brings life to the world.' They 34 said to him, 'Sir, give us this bread now and always.' Jesus said to them, 35 'I am the bread of life. Whoever comes to me shall never be hungry, and whoever believes in me shall never be thirsty. But you, as I said, do not 36 believe although you have seen. *b* All that the Father gives me will come to 37 me, and the man who comes to me I will never turn away. I have come down 38 from heaven, not to do my own will, but the will of him who sent me. It is 39 his will that I should not lose even one of all that he has given me, but raise them all up on the last day. For it is my Father's will that everyone who 40 looks upon the Son and puts his faith in him shall possess eternal life; and I will raise him up on the last day.'

At this the Jews began to murmur disapprovingly because he said, 'I am 41 the bread which came down from heaven.' They said, 'Surely this is Jesus 42 son of Joseph; we know his father and mother. How can he now say, "I have come down from heaven"?' Jesus answered, 'Stop murmuring among 43 yourselves. No man can come to me unless he is drawn by the Father who 44 sent me; and I will raise him up on the last day. It is written in the prophets: 45 "And they shall all be taught by God." Everyone who has listened to the Father and learned from him comes to me.

'I do not mean that anyone has seen the Father. He who has come from 46 God has seen the Father, and he alone. In truth, in very truth I tell you, the 47 believer possesses eternal life. I am the bread of life. Your forefathers ate 48 49 the manna in the desert and they are dead. I am speaking of the bread that 50 comes down from heaven, which a man may eat, and never die. I am that 51 living bread which has come down from heaven; if anyone eats this bread he shall live for ever. Moreover, the bread which I will give is my own flesh; I give it for the life of the world.'

This led to a fierce dispute among the Jews. 'How can this man give us 52 his flesh to eat?' they said. Jesus replied, 'In truth, in very truth I tell you, 53 unless you eat the flesh of the Son of Man and drink his blood you can have no life in you. Whoever eats my flesh and drinks my blood possesses eternal 54

     a Or is he who comes down . . .   *b Some witnesses add* me.

55 life, and I will raise him up on the last day. My flesh is real food; my blood
56 is real drink. Whoever eats my flesh and drinks my blood dwells continually
57 in me and I dwell in him. As the living Father sent me, and I live because
58 of the Father, so he who eats me shall live because of me. This is the
bread which came down from heaven; and it is not like the bread which
our fathers ate: they are dead, but whoever eats this bread shall live for
ever.'

59 THIS WAS SPOKEN in synagogue when Jesus was teaching in Capernaum.
60 Many of his disciples on hearing it exclaimed, 'This is more than we can
61 stomach! Why listen to such talk?' Jesus was aware that his disciples were
62 murmuring about it and asked them, 'Does this shock you? What if you
63 see the Son of Man ascending to the place where he was before? The spirit
alone gives life; the flesh is of no avail; the words which I have spoken to
64 you are both spirit and life. And yet there are some of you who have no
faith.' For Jesus knew all along who were without faith and who was to
65 betray him. So he said, 'This is why I told you that no one can come to me
unless it has been granted to him by the Father.'

66   From that time on, many of his disciples withdrew and no longer went
67 about with him. So Jesus asked the Twelve, 'Do you also want to leave me?'
68 Simon Peter answered him, 'Lord, to whom shall we go? Your words are
69 words of eternal life. We have faith, and we know that you are the Holy
70 One of God.' Jesus answered, 'Have I not chosen you, all twelve? Yet one
71 of you is a devil.' He meant Judas, son of Simon Iscariot. He it was who
would betray him, and he was one of the Twelve.

The great controversy

7 AFTERWARDS JESUS went about in Galilee. He wished to avoid Judaea
2 because the Jews were looking for a chance to kill him. As the Jewish
3 Feast of Tabernacles was close at hand, his brothers said to him, 'You
should leave this district and go into Judaea, so that your disciples there
4 may see the great things you are doing. Surely no one can hope to be in the
public eye if he works in seclusion. If you really are doing such things as
5 these, show yourself to the world.' For even his brothers had no faith in
6 him. Jesus said to them, 'The right time for me has not yet come, but any
7 time is right for you. The world cannot hate you; but it hates me for
8 exposing the wickedness of its ways. Go to the festival yourselves. I am
not*a* going up to this festival because the right time for me has not yet
9 come.' With this answer he stayed behind in Galilee.
10   Later, when his brothers had gone to the festival, he went up himself,
11 not publicly, but almost in secret. The Jews were looking for him at the
12 festival and asking, 'Where is he?', and there was much whispering about
him in the crowds. 'He is a good man', said some. 'No,' said others, 'he is
13 leading the people astray.' However, no one talked about him openly, for
fear of the Jews.

a Some witnesses read not yet.

WHEN THE FESTIVAL was already half over, Jesus went up to the temple 14
and began to teach. The Jews were astonished: 'How is it', they said, 'that 15
this untrained man has such learning?' Jesus replied, 'The teaching that I 16
give is not my own; it is the teaching of him who sent me. Whoever has the 17
will to do the will of God shall know whether my teaching comes from him
or is merely my own. Anyone whose teaching is merely his own, aims at 18
honour for himself. But if a man aims at the honour of him who sent him
he is sincere, and there is nothing false in him.

'Did not Moses give you the Law? Yet you all break it. Why are you try- 19
ing to kill me?' The crowd answered, 'You are possessed! Who wants to 20
kill you?' Jesus replied, 'Once only have I done work on the Sabbath, and 21
you are all taken aback. But consider: Moses gave you the law of cir- 22
cumcision (not that it originated with Moses but with the patriarchs) and
you circumcise on the Sabbath. Well then, if a child is circumcised on the 23
Sabbath to avoid breaking the Law of Moses, why are you indignant with
me for giving health on the Sabbath to the whole of a man's body? Do not 24
judge superficially, but be just in your judgements.'

At this some of the people of Jerusalem began to say, 'Is not this the man 25
they want to put to death? And here he is, speaking openly, and they have 26
not a word to say to him. Can it be that our rulers have actually decided
that this is the Messiah? And yet we know where this man comes from, 27
but when the Messiah appears no one is to know where he comes from.'
Thereupon Jesus cried aloud as he taught in the temple, 'No doubt you 28
know me; no doubt you know where I come from.*a* Yet I have not come of
my own accord. I was sent by the One who truly is, and him you do not
know. I know him because I come from him and he it is who sent me.' At 29 30
this they tried to seize him, but no one laid a hand on him because his
appointed hour had not yet come. Yet among the people many believed in 31
him. 'When the Messiah comes,' they said, 'is it likely that he will perform
more signs than this man?'

The Pharisees overheard these mutterings of the people about him, so 32
the chief priests and the Pharisees sent temple police to arrest him. Then 33
Jesus said, 'For a little longer I shall be with you; then I am going away to
him who sent me. You will look for me, but you will not find me. Where 34
I am, you cannot come.' So the Jews said to one another, 'Where does he 35
intend to go, that we should not be able to find him? Will he go to the
Dispersion among the Greeks, and teach the Greeks? What did he mean 36
by saying, "You will look for me, but you will not find me. Where I am,
you cannot come"?'*b*

ON THE LAST and greatest day of the festival Jesus stood and cried aloud, 37
'If anyone is thirsty let him come to me; whoever believes in me, let him 38
drink.' As Scripture says, 'Streams of living water shall flow out from
within him.'*c* He was speaking of the Spirit which believers in him would 39

a Or Do you know me? And do you know where I come from?   *b Some witnesses
here insert the passage printed on p. 143.*   *c Or* 'If any man is thirsty let him come
to me and drink. He who believes in me, as Scripture says, streams of living water shall
flow out from within him.'

receive later; for the Spirit had not yet been given, because Jesus had not yet been glorified.

40   On hearing this some of the people said, 'This must certainly be the
41 expected prophet.' Others said, 'This is the Messiah.' Others again, 'Surely
42 the Messiah is not to come from Galilee? Does not Scripture say that the
Messiah is to be of the family of David, from David's village of Bethlehem?'
43 44 Thus he caused a split among the people. Some were for seizing him, but
no one laid hands on him.

45   The temple police came back to the chief priests and Pharisees, who
46 asked, 'Why have you not brought him?' 'No man', they answered, 'ever
47 spoke as this man speaks.' The Pharisees retorted, 'Have you too been
48 misled? Is there a single one of our rulers who has believed in him, or of
49 the Pharisees? As for this rabble, which cares nothing for the Law, a curse
50 is on them.' Then one of their number, Nicodemus (the man who had
51 once visited Jesus), intervened. 'Does our law', he asked them, 'permit us
to pass judgement on a man unless we have first given him a hearing and
52 learned the facts?' 'Are you a Galilean too?' they retorted. 'Study the
scriptures and you will find that prophets do not come from Galilee.' *a*

8 12 ONCE AGAIN JESUS addressed the people: 'I am the light of the world.
No follower of mine shall wander in the dark; he shall have the light of life.'
13   The Pharisees said to him, 'You are witness in your own cause; your
14 testimony is not valid.' Jesus replied, 'My testimony is valid, even though
I do bear witness about myself; because I know where I come from, and
where I am going. You do not know either where I come from or where I
15 am going. You judge by worldly standards. I pass judgement on no man,
16 but if I do judge, my judgement is valid because it is not I alone who
17 judge, but I and he who sent me. In your own law it is written that the
18 testimony of two witnesses is valid. Here am I, a witness in my own cause,
19 and my other witness is the Father who sent me.' They asked, 'Where is
your father?' Jesus replied, 'You know neither me nor my Father; if you
knew me you would know my Father as well.'

20   These words were spoken by Jesus in the treasury as he taught in the
temple. Yet no one arrested him, because his hour had not yet come.

21   Again he said to them, 'I am going away. You will look for me, but you
22 will die in your sin; where I am going you cannot come.' The Jews then
said, 'Perhaps he will kill himself: is that what he means when he says,
23 "Where I am going you cannot come"?' So Jesus continued, 'You belong
to this world below, I to the world above. Your home is in this world, mine
24 is not. That is why I told you that you would die in your sins. If you do not
25 believe that I am what I am, you will die in your sins.' They asked him,
26 'Who are you?' Jesus answered, 'Why should I speak to you at all? *b* I have
much to say about you—and in judgement. But he who sent me speaks the
truth, and what I heard from him I report to the world.'
27   They did not understand that he was speaking to them about the Father.
28 So Jesus said to them, 'When you have lifted up the Son of Man you will

a *Some witnesses here insert the passage 7. 53–8. 11, which is printed on p. 143.*
b Or What I have told you all along.

know that I am what I am. I do nothing on my own authority, but in all
that I say, I have been taught by my Father. He who sent me is present 29
with me, and has not left me alone; for I always do what is acceptable to
him.' As he said this, many put their faith in him. 30

Turning to the Jews who had believed him, Jesus said, 'If you dwell 31
within the revelation I have brought, you are indeed my disciples; you 32
shall know the truth, and the truth will set you free.' They replied, 'We 33
are Abraham's descendants; we have never been in slavery to any man.
What do you mean by saying, "You will become free men"?' 'In very truth 34
I tell you', said Jesus, 'that everyone who commits sin is a slave. The slave 35
has no permanent standing in the household, but the son belongs to it for
ever. If then the Son sets you free, you will indeed be free. 36

'I know that you are descended from Abraham, but you are bent on 37
killing me because my teaching makes no headway with you. I am revealing 38
in words what I saw in my Father's presence; and you are revealing in
action what you learned from your father.' They retorted, 'Abraham is our 39
father.' 'If you were Abraham's children', Jesus replied, 'you would do as
Abraham did. *a* As it is, you are bent on killing me, a man who told you the 40
truth, as I heard it from God. That is not how Abraham acted. You are 41
doing your own father's work.'

They said, 'We are not base-born; God is our father, and God alone.'
Jesus said, 'If God were your father, you would love me, for God is the 42
source of my being, and from him I come. I have not come of my own
accord; he sent me. Why do you not understand my language? It is 43
because my revelation is beyond your grasp.

'Your father is the devil and you choose to carry out your father's desires. 44
He was a murderer from the beginning, and is not rooted in the truth;
there is no truth in him. When he tells a lie he is speaking his own language,
for he is a liar and the father of lies. But I speak the truth and therefore you 45
do not believe me. Which of you can prove me in the wrong? *b* If what I say 46
is true, why do you not believe me? He who has God for his father listens 47
to the words of God. You are not God's children; that is why you do not
listen.'

The Jews answered, 'Are we not right in saying that you are a Samaritan, 48
and that you are possessed?' 'I am not possessed,' said Jesus; 'I am honour- 49
ing my Father, but you dishonour me. I do not care about my own glory; 50
there is one who does care, and he is judge. In very truth I tell you, if any- 51
one obeys my teaching he shall never know what it is to die.'

The Jews said, 'Now we are certain that you are possessed. Abraham is 52
dead; the prophets are dead; and yet you say, "If anyone obeys my teaching he shall not know what it is to die." Are you greater than our father 53
Abraham, who is dead? The prophets are dead too. What do you claim
to be?'

Jesus replied, 'If I glorify myself, that glory of mine is worthless. It is 54
the Father who glorifies me, he of whom you say, "He is our God",
though you do not know him. But I know him; if I said that I did not 55

---

a *Some witnesses read* 'If you are Abraham's children', Jesus replied, 'do as Abraham did.'
b *Or* Which of you convicts me of sin?

know him I should be a liar like you. But in truth I know him and obey his
word.

56   'Your father Abraham was overjoyed to see my day; he saw it and was
57 glad.' The Jews protested, 'You are not yet fifty years old. How can you
58 have seen Abraham?'*a* Jesus said, 'In very truth I tell you, before Abraham
was born, I am.'

59   They picked up stones to throw at him, but Jesus was not to be seen;
and he left the temple.*b*

9 1 2   AS HE WENT on his way Jesus saw a man blind from his birth. His disciples
put the question, 'Rabbi, who sinned, this man or his parents? Why was
3 he born blind?' 'It is not that this man or his parents sinned,' Jesus
answered; 'he was born blind so that God's power might be displayed in
4 curing him. While daylight lasts we*c* must carry on the work of him who
5 sent me; night comes, when no one can work. While I am in the world I
am the light of the world.'

6   With these words he spat on the ground and made a paste with the
7 spittle; he spread it on the man's eyes, and said to him, 'Go and wash in
the pool of Siloam.' (The name means 'sent'.) The man went away and
washed, and when he returned he could see.

8   His neighbours and those who were accustomed to see him begging said,
9 'Is not this the man who used to sit and beg?' Others said, 'Yes, this is the
man.' Others again said, 'No, but it is someone like him.' The man himself
10 11 said, 'I am the man.' They asked him, 'How were your eyes opened?' He
replied, 'The man called Jesus made a paste and smeared my eyes with it,
and told me to go to Siloam and wash. I went and washed, and gained my
12 sight.' 'Where is he?' they asked. He answered, 'I do not know.'

13 14   THE MAN who had been blind was brought before the Pharisees. As it was
15 a Sabbath day when Jesus made the paste and opened his eyes, the Pharisees
now asked him by what means he had gained his sight. The man told them,
16 'He spread a paste on my eyes; then I washed, and now I can see.' Some of
the Pharisees said, 'This fellow is no man of God; he does not keep the
Sabbath.' Others said, 'How could such signs come from a sinful man?'
17 So they took different sides. Then they continued to question him: 'What
have you to say about him? It was your eyes he opened.' He answered,
'He is a prophet.'

18   The Jews would not believe that the man had been blind and had gained
19 his sight, until they had summoned his parents and questioned them: 'Is
this man your son? Do you say that he was born blind? How is it that he
20 can see now?' The parents replied, 'We know that he is our son, and that
21 he was born blind. But how it is that he can now see, or who opened his
eyes, we do not know. Ask him; he is of age; he will speak for himself.'
22 His parents gave this answer because they were afraid of the Jews; for the
Jewish authorities had already agreed that anyone who acknowledged Jesus

a Some witnesses read How can Abraham have seen you?   *b Or the division may be
made after the words* was not to be seen; *the paragraph following would then begin* Then
Jesus left the temple, and as he went . . .   *c Some witnesses read* I.

as Messiah should be banned from the synagogue. That is why the parents 23
said, 'He is of age; ask him.'

So for the second time they summoned the man who had been blind, 24
and said, 'Speak the truth before God. We know that this fellow is a sinner.'
'Whether or not he is a sinner, I do not know', the man replied. 'All I know 25
is this: once I was blind, now I can see.' 'What did he do to you?' they asked. 26
'How did he open your eyes?' 'I have told you already,' he retorted, 'but 27
you took no notice. Why do you want to hear it again? Do you also want to
become his disciples?' Then they became abusive. 'You are that man's 28
disciple,' they said, 'but we are disciples of Moses. We know that God 29
spoke to Moses, but as for this fellow, we do not know where he comes
from.'

The man replied, 'What an extraordinary thing! Here is a man who has 30
opened my eyes, yet you do not know where he comes from! It is common 31
knowledge that God does not listen to sinners; he listens to anyone who is
devout and obeys his will. To open the eyes of a man born blind—it is un- 32
heard of since time began. If that man had not come from God he could 33
have done nothing.' 'Who are you to give us lessons,' they retorted, 'born 34
and bred in sin as you are?' Then they expelled him from the synagogue.

Jesus heard that they had expelled him. When he found him he asked, 35
'Have you faith in the Son of Man *a*?' The man answered, 'Tell me who he 36
is, sir, that I should put my faith in him.' 'You have seen him,' said Jesus; 37
'indeed, it is he who is speaking to you.' 'Lord, I believe', he said, and 38
bowed before him.

Jesus said, 'It is for judgement that I have come into this world—to give 39
sight to the sightless and to make blind those who see.' Some Pharisees in 40
his company asked, 'Do you mean that we are blind?' 'If you were blind,' 41
said Jesus, 'you would not be guilty, but because you say "We see", your
guilt remains.

'In truth I tell you, in very truth, the man who does not enter the sheep- **10**
fold by the door, but climbs in some other way, is nothing but a thief or a
robber. The man who enters by the door is the shepherd in charge of the 2
sheep. The door-keeper admits him, and the sheep hear his voice; he calls 3
his own sheep by name, and leads them out. When he has brought them all 4
out, he goes ahead and the sheep follow, because they know his voice. They 5
will not follow a stranger; they will run away from him, because they do not
recognize the voice of strangers.'

This was a parable that Jesus told them, but they did not understand 6
what he meant by it.

So Jesus spoke again: 'In truth, in very truth I tell you, I am the door of 7
the sheepfold. The sheep paid no heed to any who came before me, for 8
these were all thieves and robbers. I am the door; anyone who comes into 9
the fold through me shall be safe. He shall go in and out and shall find
pasturage.

'The thief comes only to steal, to kill, to destroy; I have come that men 10
may have life, and may have it in all its fullness. I am the good shepherd; 11

a Some witnesses read Son of God.

12 the good shepherd lays down his life for the sheep. The hireling, when he sees the wolf coming, abandons the sheep and runs away, because he is no shepherd and the sheep are not his. Then the wolf harries the flock and
13 scatters the sheep. The man runs away because he is a hireling and cares nothing for the sheep.

14 'I am the good shepherd; I know my own sheep and my sheep know me—
15 as the Father knows me and I know the Father—and I lay down my life for
16 the sheep. But there are other sheep of mine, not belonging to this fold, whom I must bring in; and they too will listen to my voice. There will then
17 be one flock, one shepherd. The Father loves me because I lay down my
18 life, to receive it back again. No one has robbed me of it; I am laying it down of my own free will. I have the right to lay it down, and I have the right to receive it back again; this charge I have received from my Father.'

19 20 These words once again caused a split among the Jews. Many of them
21 said, 'He is possessed, he is raving. Why listen to him?' Others said, 'No one possessed by an evil spirit could speak like this. Could an evil spirit open blind men's eyes?'

22 IT WAS WINTER, and the festival of the Dedication was being held in
23 Jerusalem. Jesus was walking in the temple precincts, in Solomon's
24 Portico. The Jews gathered round him and asked: 'How long must you
25 keep us in suspense? If you are the Messiah say so plainly.' 'I have told you,' said Jesus, 'but you do not believe. My deeds done in my Father's
26 name are my credentials, but because you are not sheep of my flock you
27 do not believe. My own sheep listen to my voice; I know them and they
28 follow me. I give them eternal life and they shall never perish; no one shall
29 snatch them from my care. My Father who has given them to me is greater
30 than all, and no one can snatch them *a* out of the Father's care. My Father and I are one.'

31 32 Once again the Jews picked up stones to stone him. At this Jesus said to them, 'I have set before you many good deeds, done by my Father's
33 power; for which of these would you stone me?' The Jews replied, 'We are not going to stone you for any good deed, but for your blasphemy. You,
34 a mere man, claim to be a god.' *b* Jesus answered, 'Is it not written in your
35 own Law, "I said: You are gods"? Those are called gods to whom the word
36 of God was delivered—and Scripture cannot be set aside. Then why do you charge me with blasphemy because I, consecrated and sent into the world by the Father, said, "I am God's son"?

37 38 'If I am not acting as my Father would, do not believe me. But if I am, accept the evidence of my deeds, even if you do not believe me, so that you may recognize and know that the Father is in me, and I in the Father.'

39 This provoked them to one more attempt to seize him. But he escaped from their clutches.

a Some witnesses read My Father is greater than all, and that which he has given me no one can snatch . . .; *others read* That which my Father has given me is greater than all, and no one can snatch it . . .   *b Or* claim to be God.

Victory over death

JESUS WITHDREW AGAIN across the Jordan, to the place where John 40
had been baptizing earlier. There he stayed, while crowds came to him. 41
They said, 'John gave us no miraculous sign, but all that he said about this
man was true.' Many came to believe in him there. 42

There was a man named Lazarus who had fallen ill. His home was at **11**
Bethany, the village of Mary and her sister Martha. (This Mary, whose 2
brother Lazarus had fallen ill, was the woman who anointed the Lord with
ointment and wiped his feet with her hair.) The sisters sent a message to 3
him: 'Sir, you should know that your friend lies ill.' When Jesus heard 4
this he said, 'This illness will not end in death; it has come for the glory of
God, to bring glory to the Son of God.' And therefore, though he loved 5
Martha and her sister and Lazarus, after hearing of his illness Jesus waited 6
for two days in the place where he was.

After this, he said to his disciples, 'Let us go back to Judaea.' 'Rabbi,' 7 8
his disciples said, 'it is not long since the Jews there were wanting to stone
you. Are you going there again?' Jesus replied, 'Are there not twelve hours 9
of daylight? Anyone can walk in day-time without stumbling, because he
sees the light of this world. But if he walks after nightfall he stumbles, 10
because the light fails him.'

After saying this he added, 'Our friend Lazarus has fallen asleep, but I 11
shall go and wake him.' The disciples said, 'Master, if he has fallen asleep 12
he will recover.' Jesus, however, had been speaking of his death, but they 13
thought that he meant natural sleep. Then Jesus spoke out plainly: 14
'Lazarus is dead. I am glad not to have been there; it will be for your good 15
and for the good of your faith. But let us go to him.' Thomas, called 'the 16
Twin', said to his fellow-disciples, 'Let us also go, that we may die with
him.'

ON HIS ARRIVAL Jesus found that Lazarus had already been four days 17
in the tomb. Bethany was just under two miles from Jerusalem, and many 18 19
of the people had come from the city to Martha and Mary to condole with
them on their brother's death. As soon as she heard that Jesus was on his 20
way, Martha went to meet him, while Mary stayed at home.

Martha said to Jesus, 'If you had been here, sir, my brother would not 21
have died. Even now I know that whatever you ask of God, God will grant 22
you.' Jesus said, 'Your brother will rise again.' 'I know that he will rise 23 24
again', said Martha, 'at the resurrection on the last day.' Jesus said, 'I am 25
the resurrection and I am life.*a* If a man has faith in me, even though he die,
he shall come to life; and no one who is alive and has faith shall ever die. 26
Do you believe this?' 'Lord, I do,' she answered; 'I now believe that you 27
are the Messiah, the Son of God who was to come into the world.'

With these words she went to call her sister Mary, and taking her aside, 28
she said, 'The Master is here; he is asking for you.' When Mary heard this 29
she rose up quickly and went to him. Jesus had not yet reached the village, 30
but was still at the place where Martha had met him. The Jews who were in 31

a Some witnesses omit and I am life.

the house condoling with Mary, when they saw her start up and leave the house, went after her, for they supposed that she was going to the tomb to weep there.

32 So Mary came to the place where Jesus was. As soon as she caught sight of him she fell at his feet and said, 'O sir, if you had only been here my
33 brother would not have died.' When Jesus saw her weeping and the Jews
34 her companions weeping, he sighed heavily and was deeply moved. 'Where
35 have you laid him?' he asked. They replied, 'Come and see, sir.' Jesus wept.
36 37 The Jews said, 'How dearly he must have loved him!' But some of them said, 'Could not this man, who opened the blind man's eyes, have done something to keep Lazarus from dying?'

38 Jesus again sighed deeply; then he went over to the tomb. It was a cave,
39 with a stone placed against it. Jesus said, 'Take away the stone.' Martha, the dead man's sister, said to him, 'Sir, by now there will be a stench; he
40 has been there four days.' Jesus said, 'Did I not tell you that if you have
41 faith you will see the glory of God?' So they removed the stone.

Then Jesus looked upwards and said, 'Father, I thank thee; thou hast
42 heard me. I knew already that thou always hearest me, but I spoke for the sake of the people standing round, that they might believe that thou didst send me.'

43 44 Then he raised his voice in a great cry: 'Lazarus, come forth.' The dead man came out, his hands and feet swathed in linen bands, his face wrapped in a cloth. Jesus said, 'Loose him; let him go.'

45 NOW MANY of the Jews who had come to visit Mary and had seen what
46 Jesus did, put their faith in him. But some of them went off to the Pharisees and reported what he had done.

47 Thereupon the chief priests and the Pharisees convened a meeting of the Council. 'What action are we taking?' they said. 'This man is performing
48 many signs. If we leave him alone like this the whole populace will believe in him. Then the Romans will come and sweep away our temple and our
49 nation.' But one of them, Caiaphas, who was High Priest that year, said,
50 'You know nothing whatever; you do not use your judgement; it is more to your interest that one man should die for the people, than that the whole
51 nation should be destroyed.' He did not say this of his own accord, but as the High Priest in office that year, he was prophesying that Jesus would
52 die for the nation—would die not for the nation alone but to gather
53 together the scattered children of God. So from that day on they plotted his death.

54 Accordingly Jesus no longer went about publicly in Judaea, but left that region for the country bordering on the desert, and came to a town called Ephraim, where he stayed with his disciples.

55 THE JEWISH PASSOVER was now at hand, and many people went up from the country to Jerusalem to purify themselves before the festival.
56 They looked out for Jesus, and as they stood in the temple they asked one another, 'What do you think? Perhaps he is not coming to the festival.'
57 Now the chief priests and the Pharisees had given orders that anyone

who knew where he was should give information, so that they might
arrest him.

SIX DAYS BEFORE the Passover festival Jesus came to Bethany, where **12**
Lazarus lived whom he had raised from the dead. There a supper was ₂
given in his honour, at which Martha served, and Lazarus sat among the
guests with Jesus. Then Mary brought a pound of very costly perfume, ₃
pure oil of nard, and anointed the feet of Jesus and wiped them with her
hair, till the house was filled with the fragrance. At this, Judas Iscariot, a ₄
disciple of his—the one who was to betray him—said, 'Why was this per- ₅
fume not sold for thirty pounds *a* and given to the poor?' He said this, not ₆
out of any care for the poor, but because he was a thief; he used to pilfer
the money put into the common purse, which was in his charge. 'Leave her ₇
alone', said Jesus. 'Let her keep it till the day when she prepares for my
burial; for you have the poor among you always, but you will not always ₈
have me.' *b*
    A great number of the Jews heard that he was there, and came not only ₉
to see Jesus but also Lazarus whom he had raised from the dead. The chief ₁₀
priests then resolved to do away with Lazarus as well, since on his account ₁₁
many Jews were going over to Jesus and putting their faith in him.

THE NEXT DAY the great body of pilgrims who had come to the festival, ₁₂
hearing that Jesus was on the way to Jerusalem, took palm branches and ₁₃
went out to meet him, shouting, 'Hosanna! Blessings on him who comes
in the name of the Lord! God bless the king of Israel!' Jesus found a ₁₄
donkey and mounted it, in accordance with the text of Scripture: 'Fear no ₁₅
more, daughter of Zion; see, your king is coming, mounted on an ass's colt.'
    At the time his disciples did not understand this, but after Jesus had ₁₆
been glorified they remembered that this had been written about him, and
that this had happened to him. The people who were present when he ₁₇
called Lazarus out of the tomb and raised him from the dead told what they
had seen and heard. That is why the crowd went to meet him; they had ₁₈
heard of this sign that he had performed. The Pharisees said to one ₁₉
another, 'You see you are doing no good at all; why, all the world has gone
after him!'

AMONG THOSE who went up to worship at the festival were some Greeks. ₂₀
They came to Philip, who was from Bethsaida in Galilee, and said to him, ₂₁
'Sir, we should like to see Jesus.' So Philip went and told Andrew, and the ₂₂
two of them went to tell Jesus. Then Jesus replied: 'The hour has come for ₂₃
the Son of Man to be glorified. In truth, in very truth I tell you, a grain of ₂₄
wheat remains a solitary grain unless it falls into the ground and dies; but
if it dies, it bears a rich harvest. The man who loves himself is lost, but he ₂₅
who hates himself in this world will be kept safe for eternal life. If anyone ₂₆
serves me, he must follow me; where I am, my servant will be. Whoever
serves me will be honoured by my Father.
    'Now my soul is in turmoil, and what am I to say? Father, save me from ₂₇

a Literally for 300 denarii.   *b Some witnesses omit* for you have . . . have me.

28 this hour.*ª* No, it was for this that I came to this hour. Father, glorify thy
name.' A voice sounded from heaven: 'I have glorified it, and I will glorify
29 it again.' The crowd standing by said it was thunder, while others said,
30 'An angel has spoken to him.' Jesus replied, 'This voice spoke for your sake,
31 not mine. Now is the hour of judgement for this world; now shall the Prince
32 of this world be driven out. And I shall draw all men to myself, when I am
33 lifted up from the earth.' This he said to indicate the kind of death he was
to die.

34   The people answered, 'Our Law teaches us that the Messiah continues
for ever. What do you mean by saying that the Son of Man must be lifted
35 up? What Son of Man is this?' Jesus answered them: 'The light is among
you still, but not for long. Go on your way while you have the light, so that
darkness may not overtake you. He who journeys in the dark does not know
36 where he is going. While you have the light, trust to the light, so that you
may become men of light.' After these words Jesus went away from them
into hiding.

37 IN SPITE OF the many signs which Jesus had performed in their presence
38 they would not believe in him, for the prophet Isaiah's utterance had to be
fulfilled: 'Lord, who has believed what we reported, and to whom has the
39 Lord's power been revealed?' So it was that they could not believe, for
40 there is another saying of Isaiah's: 'He has blinded their eyes and dulled
their minds, lest they should see with their eyes, and perceive with their
41 minds, and turn to me to heal them.' Isaiah said this because *ᵇ* he saw his
glory and spoke about him.

42   For all that, even among those in authority a number believed in him,
but would not acknowledge him on account of the Pharisees, for fear of
43 being banned from the synagogue. For they valued their reputation with
men rather than the honour which comes from God.

44 SO JESUS CRIED ALOUD: 'When a man believes in me, he believes in him
45 46 who sent me rather than in me; seeing me, he sees him who sent me. I have
come into the world as light, so that no one who has faith in me should
47 remain in darkness. But if anyone hears my words and pays no regard to
them, I am not his judge; I have not come to judge the world, but to save the
48 world. There is a judge for the man who rejects me and does not accept my
49 words; the word that I spoke will be his judge on the last day. I do not speak
on my own authority, but the Father who sent me has himself commanded
50 me what to say and how to speak. I know that his commands are eternal life.
What the Father has said to me, therefore—that is what I speak.'

ª Or . . . turmoil. Shall I say, "Father, save me from this hour"?   *ᵇ Some witnesses
read* when.

Farewell discourses

IT WAS BEFORE the Passover festival. Jesus knew that his hour had come **13** and he must leave this world and go to the Father. He had always loved his own who were in the world, and now he was to show the full extent of his love.

The devil had already put it into the mind of Judas son of Simon Iscariot 2 to betray him. During supper, Jesus, well aware that the Father had 3 entrusted everything to him, and that he had come from God and was going back to God, rose from table, laid aside his garments, and taking a 4 towel, tied it round him. Then he poured water into a basin, and began to 5 wash his disciples' feet and to wipe them with the towel.

When it was Simon Peter's turn, Peter said to him, 'You, Lord, washing 6 my feet?' Jesus replied, 'You do not understand now what I am doing, but 7 one day you will.' Peter said, 'I will never let you wash my feet.' 'If I do 8 not wash you,' Jesus replied, 'you are not in fellowship with me.' 'Then, 9 Lord,' said Simon Peter, 'not my feet only; wash my hands and head as well!'

Jesus said, 'A man who has bathed needs no further washing;*a* he is 10 altogether clean; and you are clean, though not every one of you.' He 11 added the words 'not every one of you' because he knew who was going to betray him.

After washing their feet and taking his garments again, he sat down. 12 'Do you understand what I have done for you?' he asked. 'You call me 13 "Master" and "Lord", and rightly so, for that is what I am. Then if I, 14 your Lord and Master, have washed your feet, you also ought to wash one another's feet. I have set you an example: you are to do as I have done for 15 you. In very truth I tell you, a servant is not greater than his master, nor 16 a messenger than the one who sent him. If you know this, happy are you 17 if you act upon it.

'I am not speaking about all of you; I know whom I have chosen. But 18 there is a text of Scripture to be fulfilled: "He who eats bread with me has turned against me."*b* I tell you this now, before the event, so that when it 19 happens you may believe that I am what I am. In very truth I tell you, he 20 who receives any messenger of mine receives me; receiving me, he receives the One who sent me.'

After saying this, Jesus exclaimed in deep agitation of spirit, 'In truth, 21 in very truth I tell you, one of you is going to betray me.' The disciples 22 looked at one another in bewilderment: whom could he be speaking of? One of them, the disciple he loved, was reclining close beside Jesus. So 23 24 Simon Peter nodded to him and said, 'Ask who it is he means.' That 25 disciple, as he reclined, leaned back close to Jesus and asked, 'Lord, who is it?' Jesus replied, 'It is the man to whom I give this piece of bread when 26 I have dipped it in the dish.' Then, after dipping it in the dish, he took it out and gave it to Judas son of Simon Iscariot. As soon as Judas had received 27 it Satan entered him. Jesus said to him, 'Do quickly what you have to do.'

---

a Some witnesses read needs only to wash his feet.   *b Literally* has lifted his heel against me.

28 29 No one at the table understood what he meant by this. Some supposed that, as Judas was in charge of the common purse, Jesus was telling him to buy what was needed for the festival, or to make some gift to the poor.
30 As soon as Judas had received the bread he went out. It was night.

31 WHEN HE HAD GONE OUT Jesus said, 'Now the Son of Man is glorified,
32 and in him God is glorified. If God is glorified in him,[a] God will also
33 glorify him in himself; and he will glorify him now. My children, for a little longer I am with you; then you will look for me, and, as I told the
34 Jews, I tell you now, where I am going you cannot come. I give you a new commandment: love one another; as I have loved you, so you are to love
35 one another. If there is this love among you, then all will know that you are my disciples.'
36   Simon Peter said to him, 'Lord, where are you going?' Jesus replied, 'Where I am going you cannot follow me now, but one day you will.'
37 Peter said, 'Lord, why cannot I follow you now? I will lay down my life
38 for you.' Jesus answered, 'Will you indeed lay down your life for me? I tell you in very truth, before the cock crows you will have denied me three times.

14   'Set your troubled hearts at rest. Trust in God always; trust also in me.
2 There are many dwelling-places in my Father's house; if it were not so I should have told you; for I am going there on purpose to prepare a place
3 for you.[b] And if I go and prepare a place for you, I shall come again and
4 receive you to myself, so that where I am you may be also; and my way
5 there is known to you.'[c] Thomas said, 'Lord, we do not know where you
6 are going, so how can we know the way?' Jesus replied, 'I am the way; I am the truth and I am life; no one comes to the Father except by me.
7   'If you knew me you would know my Father too.[d] From now on you do
8 know him; you have seen him.' Philip said to him, 'Lord, show us the
9 Father and we ask no more.' Jesus answered, 'Have I been all this time with you, Philip, and you still do not know me? Anyone who has seen me
10 has seen the Father. Then how can you say, "Show us the Father"? Do you not believe that I am in the Father, and the Father in me? I am not myself the source of the words I speak to you: it is the Father who dwells
11 in me doing his own work. Believe me when I say that I am in the Father and the Father in me; or else accept the evidence of the deeds themselves.
12 In truth, in very truth I tell you, he who has faith in me will do what I am doing; and he will do greater things still because I am going to the Father.
13 Indeed anything you ask in my name I will do, so that the Father may be
14 glorified in the Son. If you ask[e] anything in my name I will do it.
15 16   'If you love me you will obey my commands; and I will ask the Father, and he will give you another to be your Advocate, who will be with you for
17 ever—the Spirit of truth. The world cannot receive him, because the world neither sees nor knows him; but you know him, because he dwells with you

[a] *Some witnesses omit* If God . . . in him.   [b] *Or if it were not so, should I have told you that I am going to prepare a place for you?*   [c] *Some witnesses read* also. You know where I am going and you know the way.   [d] *Some witnesses read* If you know me you will know my Father too.   [e] *Some witnesses insert* me.

and is*a* in you. I will not leave you bereft; I am coming back to you. In a 18 19
little while the world will see me no longer, but you will see me; because
I live, you too will live; then you will know that I am in my Father, and you 20
in me and I in you. The man who has received my commands and obeys 21
them—he it is who loves me; and he who loves me will be loved by my
Father; and I will love him and disclose myself to him.'

Judas asked him—the other Judas, not Iscariot—'Lord, what can have 22
happened, that you mean to disclose yourself to us alone and not to the
world?' Jesus replied, 'Anyone who loves me will heed what I say; then 23
my Father will love him, and we will come to him and make our dwelling
with him; but he who does not love me does not heed what I say. And the 24
word you hear is not mine: it is the word of the Father who sent me. I have 25
told you all this while I am still here with you; but your Advocate, the Holy 26
Spirit whom the Father will send in my name, will teach you everything,
and will call to mind all that I have told you.

'Peace is my parting gift to you, my own peace, such as the world cannot 27
give. Set your troubled hearts at rest, and banish your fears. You heard me 28
say, "I am going away, and coming back to you." If you loved me you would
have been glad to hear that I was going to the Father; for the Father is
greater than I. I have told you now, beforehand, so that when it happens you 29
may have faith.

'I shall not talk much longer with you, for the Prince of this world 30
approaches. He has no rights over me; but the world must be shown that 31
I love the Father, and do exactly as he commands; so up, let us go forward!*b*

'I AM THE REAL VINE, and my Father is the gardener. Every barren branch **15** 1 2
of mine he cuts away; and every fruiting branch he cleans, to make it more
fruitful still. You have already been cleansed by the word that I spoke to 3
you. Dwell in me, as I in you. No branch can bear fruit by itself, but only 4
if it remains united with the vine; no more can you bear fruit, unless you
remain united with me.

'I am the vine, and you the branches. He who dwells in me, as I dwell in 5
him, bears much fruit; for apart from me you can do nothing. He who does 6
not dwell in me is thrown away like a withered branch. The withered
branches are heaped together, thrown on the fire, and burnt.

'If you dwell in me, and my words dwell in you, ask what you will, and 7
you shall have it. This is my Father's glory, that you may bear fruit in 8
plenty and so be my disciples.*c* As the Father has loved me, so I have loved 9
you. Dwell in my love. If you heed my commands, you will dwell in my 10
love, as I have heeded my Father's commands and dwell in his love.

'I have spoken thus to you, so that my joy may be in you, and your joy 11
complete.*d* This is my commandment: love one another, as I have loved 12
you. There is no greater love than this, that a man should lay down his life 13

a *Some witnesses read* shall be.   *b* *Or* for the Prince of this world is coming, though he
has nothing in common with me. But he is coming so that the world may recognize that
I love the Father, and do exactly as he commands. Up, and let us go forward to meet
him!   *c* *Some witnesses read* that you may bear fruit in plenty. Thus you will be my
disciples.   *d* *Or* so that I may have joy in you and your joy may be complete.

14 15 for his friends. You are my friends, if you do what I command you. I call you servants no longer; a servant does not know what his master is about. I have called you friends, because I have disclosed to you everything that I
16 heard from my Father. You did not choose me: I chose you. I appointed you to go on and bear fruit, fruit that shall last; so that the Father may give
17 you all that you ask in my name. This is my commandment to you: love one another.

18 19 'If the world hates you, it hated me first, as you know well. *a* If you belonged to the world, the world would love its own; but because you do not belong to the world, because I have chosen you out of the world, for that
20 reason the world hates you. Remember what I said: "A servant is not greater than his master." As they persecuted me, they will persecute you;
21 they will follow your teaching as little as they have followed mine. It is on my account that they will treat you thus, because they do not know the One who sent me.

22 'If I had not come and spoken to them, they would not be guilty of sin;
23 but now they have no excuse for their sin: he who hates me, hates my
24 Father. If I had not worked among them and accomplished what no other man has done, they would not be guilty of sin; but now they have both
25 seen and hated both me and my Father. *b* However, this text in their Law had to come true: *c* "They hated me without reason."

26 'But when your Advocate has come, whom I will send you from the Father—the Spirit of truth that issues from the Father—he will bear
27 witness to me. And you also are my witnesses, because you have been with me from the first.

16 'I have told you all this to guard you against the breakdown of your
2 faith. They will ban you from the synagogue; indeed, the time is coming when anyone who kills you will suppose that he is performing a religious
3 duty. They will do these things because they do not know either the Father
4 or me. I have told you all this so that when the time comes for it to happen you may remember my warning. I did not tell you this at first, because
5 then I was with you; but now I am going away to him who sent me. None
6 of you asks me "Where are you going?" Yet you are plunged into grief
7 because of what I have told you. Nevertheless I tell you the truth: it is for your good that I am leaving you. If I do not go, your Advocate will not
8 come, whereas if I go, I will send him to you. When he comes, he will con-
9 fute the world, and show where wrong and right and judgement lie. He will
10 convict them of wrong, by their refusal to believe in me; he will convince them that right is on my side, by showing that I go to the Father when I
11 pass from your sight; and he will convince them of divine judgement, by showing that the Prince of this world stands condemned.

12 'There is still much that I could say to you, but the burden would be too
13 great for you now. However, when he comes who is the Spirit of truth, he will guide you into all the truth; for he will not speak on his own authority, but will tell only what he hears; and he will make known to you the things

a Or bear in mind that it hated me first.   *b* Or but now they have indeed seen my work and yet have hated both me and my Father.   *c* Or let this text in their Law come true.

that are coming. He will glorify me, for everything that he makes known to 14
you he will draw from what is mine. All that the Father has is mine, and that 15
is why I said, "Everything that he makes known to you he will draw from
what is mine."

'A LITTLE WHILE, and you see me no more; again a little while, and you 16
will see me.' Some of his disciples said to one another, 'What does he mean 17
by this: "A little while, and you will not see me, and again a little while,
and you will see me", and by this: "Because I am going to my Father"?'
So they asked, 'What is this "little while" that he speaks of? We do not 18
know what he means.'

Jesus knew that they were wanting to question him, and said, 'Are you 19
discussing what I said: "A little while, and you will not see me, and again
a little while, and you will see me"? In very truth I tell you, you will weep 20
and mourn, but the world will be glad. But though you will be plunged in
grief, your grief will be turned to joy. A woman in labour is in pain because 21
her time has come; but when the child is born she forgets the anguish in
her joy that a man has been born into the world. So it is with you: for the 22
moment you are sad at heart; but I shall see you again, and then you will be
joyful, and no one shall rob you of your joy. When that day comes you will 23
ask nothing of me. In very truth I tell you, if you ask the Father for anything in my name, he will give it you.*a* So far you have asked nothing in my 24
name. Ask and you will receive, that your joy may be complete.

'Till now I have been using figures of speech; a time is coming when I 25
shall no longer use figures, but tell you of the Father in plain words. When 26
that day comes you will make your request in my name, and I do not say
that I shall pray to the Father for you, for the Father loves you himself, 27
because you have loved me and believed that I came from God. I came from 28
the Father and have come into the world. Now I am leaving the world
again and going to the Father.' His disciples said, 'Why, this is plain speak- 29
ing; this is no figure of speech. We are certain now that you know every- 30
thing, and do not need to be questioned; because of this we believe that you
have come from God.'

Jesus answered, 'Do you now believe? Look,*b* the hour is coming, has 31 32
indeed already come, when you are all to be scattered, each to his home,
leaving me alone. Yet I am not alone, because the Father is with me. I have 33
told you all this so that in me you may find peace. In the world you will
have trouble. But courage! The victory is mine; I have conquered the
world.'

AFTER THESE WORDS Jesus looked up to heaven and said: **17**
'Father, the hour has come. Glorify thy Son, that the Son may glorify
thee. For thou hast made him sovereign over all mankind, to give eternal 2
life to all whom thou hast given him. This is eternal life: to know thee who 3
alone art truly God, and Jesus Christ whom thou hast sent.

'I have glorified thee on earth by completing the work which thou gavest 4

---

a Some witnesses read if you ask the Father for anything, he will give it you in my name.
b Or At the moment you believe; but look . . .

5 me to do; and now, Father, glorify me in thy own presence with the glory which I had with thee before the world began.

6 'I have made thy name known to the men whom thou didst give me out of the world. They were thine, thou gavest them to me, and they have 7 obeyed thy command. Now they know that all thy gifts have come to me 8 from thee; for I have taught them all that I learned from thee, and they have received it: they know with certainty that I came from thee; they have had faith to believe that thou didst send me.

9 'I pray for them; I am not praying for the world but for those whom 10 thou hast given me, because they belong to thee. All that is mine is thine, and what is thine is mine; and through them has my glory shone.

11 'I am to stay no longer in the world, but they are still in the world, and I am on my way to thee. Holy Father, protect by the power of thy name those 12 whom thou hast given me,*a* that they may be one, as we are one. When I was with them, I protected by the power of thy name those whom thou hast given me,*b* and kept them safe. Not one of them is lost except the man who must be lost, for Scripture has to be fulfilled.

13 'And now I am coming to thee; but while I am still in the world I speak these words, so that they may have my joy within them in full measure. 14 I have delivered thy word to them, and the world hates them because they 15 are strangers in the world, as I am. I pray thee, not to take them out of the 16 world, but to keep them from the evil one. They are strangers in the world, 17 18 as I am. Consecrate them by the truth;*c* thy word is truth. As thou hast 19 sent me into the world, I have sent them into the world, and for their sake I now consecrate myself, that they too may be consecrated by the truth.*c*

20 'But it is not for these alone that I pray, but for those also who through 21 their words put their faith in me; may they all be one: as thou, Father, art in me, and I in thee, so also may they be in us, that the world may believe 22 that thou didst send me. The glory which thou gavest me I have given to 23 them, that they may be one, as we are one; I in them and thou in me, may they be perfectly one. Then the world will learn that thou didst send me, that thou didst love them as thou didst me.

24 'Father, I desire that these men, who are thy gift to me, may be with me where I am, so that they may look upon my glory, which thou hast given me 25 because thou didst love me before the world began. O righteous Father, although the world does not know thee, I know thee, and these men know 26 that thou didst send me. I made thy name known to them, and will make it known, so that the love thou hadst for me may be in them, and I may be in them.'

---

a Or keep in loyalty to thee those whom thou hast given me; *some witnesses read* protect them by the power of thy name which thou hast given me.   *b* Or kept in loyalty to thee those whom thou hast given me; *some witnesses read* protected them by the power of thy name which thou hast given me.   *c* Or in truth.

The final conflict

AFTER THESE WORDS, Jesus went out with his disciples, and crossed **18** the Kedron ravine. There was a garden there, and he and his disciples went into it. The place was known to Judas, his betrayer, because Jesus 2 had often met there with his disciples. So Judas took a detachment of 3 soldiers, and police provided by the chief priests and the Pharisees, equipped with lanterns, torches, and weapons, and made his way to the garden. Jesus, knowing all that was coming upon him, went out to them 4 and asked, 'Who is it you want?' 'Jesus of Nazareth', they answered. Jesus 5 said, 'I am he.' And there stood Judas the traitor with them. When he said, 6 'I am he', they drew back and fell to the ground. Again Jesus asked, 'Who 7 is it you want?' 'Jesus of Nazareth', they answered. Then Jesus said, 'I have 8 told you that I am he. If I am the man you want, let these others go.' (This 9 was to make good his words, 'I have not lost one of those whom thou gavest me.') Thereupon Simon Peter drew the sword he was wearing and struck 10 at the High Priest's servant, cutting off his right ear. (The servant's name was Malchus.) Jesus said to Peter, 'Sheathe your sword. This is the cup 11 the Father has given me; shall I not drink it?'

THE TROOPS with their commander, and the Jewish police, now arrested 12 Jesus and secured him. They took him first to Annas.[a] Annas was father- 13 in-law of Caiaphas, the High Priest for that year[a]—the same Caiaphas 14 who had advised the Jews that it would be to their interest if one man died for the whole people. Jesus was followed by Simon Peter and an- 15 other disciple. This disciple, who was acquainted with the High Priest, went with Jesus into the High Priest's courtyard, but Peter halted at 16 the door outside. So the other disciple, the High Priest's acquaintance, went out again and spoke to the woman at the door, and brought Peter in. The maid on duty at the door said to Peter, 'Are you another of this 17 man's disciples?' 'I am not', he said. The servants and the police had 18 made a charcoal fire, because it was cold, and were standing round it warming themselves. And Peter too was standing with them, sharing the warmth.

The High Priest questioned Jesus about his disciples and about what 19 he taught. Jesus replied, 'I have spoken openly to all the world; I have 20 always taught in synagogue and in the temple, where all Jews congregate; I have said nothing in secret. Why question me? Ask my hearers what I 21 told them; they know what I said.' When he said this, one of the police 22 who was standing next to him struck him on the face, exclaiming, 'Is that the way to answer the High Priest?' Jesus replied, 'If I spoke amiss, state 23 it in evidence; if I spoke well, why strike me?'

So Annas sent him bound to Caiaphas the High Priest.[b] 24

Meanwhile Simon Peter stood warming himself. The others asked, 'Are 25 you another of his disciples?' But he denied it: 'I am not', he said. One of 26 the High Priest's servants, a relation of the man whose ear Peter had cut

---

[a] *See note on verse 24.*   [b] *Some witnesses give this verse after* first to Annas *in verse 13; others at the end of verse 13.*

27 off, insisted, 'Did I not see you with him in the garden?' Peter denied
again; and just then a cock crew.

28 FROM CAIAPHAS Jesus was led into the Governor's headquarters. It was
now early morning, and the Jews themselves stayed outside the head-
29 quarters to avoid defilement, so that they could eat the Passover meal.^a So
Pilate went out to them and asked, 'What charge do you bring against this
30 man?' 'If he were not a criminal,' they replied, 'we should not have brought
31 him before you.' Pilate said, 'Take him away and try him by your own law.'
32 The Jews answered, 'We are not allowed to put any man to death.' Thus
they ensured the fulfilment of the words by which Jesus had indicated the
manner of his death.

33   Pilate then went back into his headquarters and summoned Jesus. 'Are
34 you the king of the Jews?' he asked.^b Jesus said, 'Is that your own idea, or
35 have others suggested it to you?' 'What! am I a Jew?' said Pilate. 'Your
own nation and their chief priests have brought you before me. What have
36 you done?' Jesus replied, 'My kingdom does not belong to this world. If
it did, my followers would be fighting to save me from arrest by the Jews.
37 My kingly authority comes from elsewhere.' 'You are a king, then?' said
Pilate. Jesus answered, ' "King" is your word. My task is to bear witness
to the truth. For this was I born; for this I came into the world, and all
38 who are not deaf to truth listen to my voice.' Pilate said, 'What is truth?',
and with those words went out again to the Jews. 'For my part,' he said,
39 'I find no case against him. But you have a custom that I release one
prisoner for you at Passover. Would you like me to release the king of the
40 Jews?' Again the clamour rose: 'Not him; we want Barabbas!' (Barabbas
was a bandit.)

19 1 2 Pilate now took Jesus and had him flogged; and the soldiers plaited a
crown of thorns and placed it on his head, and robed him in a purple cloak.
3 Then time after time they came up to him, crying, 'Hail, King of the Jews!',
and struck him on the face.

4   Once more Pilate came out and said to the Jews, 'Here he is; I am bring-
5 ing him out to let you know that I find no case against him'; and Jesus
came out, wearing the crown of thorns and the purple cloak. 'Behold the
6 Man!' said Pilate. The chief priests and their henchmen saw him and
shouted, 'Crucify! crucify!' 'Take him and crucify him yourselves,' said
7 Pilate; 'for my part I find no case against him.' The Jews answered, 'We
have a law; and by that law he ought to die, because he has claimed to be
Son of God.'

8 9   When Pilate heard that, he was more afraid than ever, and going back
into his headquarters he asked Jesus, 'Where have you come from?' But
10 Jesus gave him no answer. 'Do you refuse to speak to me?' said Pilate.
'Surely you know that I have authority to release you, and I have authority
11 to crucify you?' 'You would have no authority at all over me', Jesus replied,
'if it had not been granted you from above; and therefore the deeper guilt
lies with the man who handed me over to you.'

^a *Or* could share in the offerings of the Passover season.   ^b *Or* 'You are king of
the Jews, I take it', he said.

From that moment Pilate tried hard to release him; but the Jews kept 12
shouting, 'If you let this man go, you are no friend to Caesar; any man who
claims to be a king is defying Caesar.' When Pilate heard what they were 13
saying, he brought Jesus out and took his seat on the tribunal at the place
known as 'The Pavement' ('Gabbatha' in the language of the Jews). It was 14
the eve of Passover,ᵃ about noon. Pilate said to the Jews, 'Here is your king.'
They shouted, 'Away with him! Away with him! Crucify him!' 'Crucify 15
your king?' said Pilate. 'We have no king but Caesar', the Jews replied.
Then at last, to satisfy them, he handed Jesus over to be crucified. 16

JESUS WAS NOW TAKEN in charge and, carrying his own cross, went out 17
to the Place of the Skull, as it is called (or, in the Jews' language, 'Golgotha'),
where they crucified him, and with him two others, one on the right, one 18
on the left, and Jesus between them.

And Pilate wrote an inscription to be fastened to the cross; it read, 'Jesus 19
of Nazareth King of the Jews.' This inscription was read by many Jews, 20
because the place where Jesus was crucified was not far from the city, and
the inscription was in Hebrew, Latin, and Greek. Then the Jewish chief 21
priests said to Pilate, 'You should not write "King of the Jews"; write, "He
claimed to be king of the Jews."' Pilate replied, 'What I have written, I 22
have written.'

The soldiers, having crucified Jesus, took possession of his clothes, and 23
divided them into four parts, one for each soldier, leaving out the tunic.
The tunic was seamless, woven in one piece throughout; so they said to 24
one another, 'We must not tear this; let us toss for it'; and thus the text of
Scripture came true: 'They shared my garments among them, and cast
lots for my clothing.'

That is what the soldiers did. But meanwhile near the cross where Jesus 25
hung stood his mother, with her sister, Mary wife of Clopas, and Mary of
Magdala. Jesus saw his mother, with the disciple whom he loved standing 26
beside her. He said to her, 'Mother, there is your son'; and to the disciple, 27
'There is your mother'; and from that moment the disciple took her into
his home.

After that, Jesus, aware that all had now come to its appointed end, said 28
in fulfilment of Scripture, 'I thirst.' A jar stood there full of sour wine; so 29
they soaked a sponge with the wine, fixed it on a javelin,ᵇ and held it up to
his lips. Having received the wine, he said, 'It is accomplished!' He bowed 30
his head and gave up his spirit. ᶜ

Because it was the eve of Passover,ᵈ the Jews were anxious that the 31
bodies should not remain on the cross for the coming Sabbath, since that
Sabbath was a day of great solemnity; so they requested Pilate to have
the legs broken and the bodies taken down. The soldiers accordingly came 32
to the first of his fellow-victims and to the second, and broke their legs;
but when they came to Jesus, they found that he was already dead, so they 33
did not break his legs. But one of the soldiers stabbed his side with a lance, 34
and at once there was a flow of blood and water. This is vouched for by an 35

ᵃ *Or* It was Friday in Passover.   ᵇ *So one witness; the others read* on marjoram.
ᶜ *Or* breathed out his life.   ᵈ *Or* Because it was Friday in Passover . . .

eyewitness, whose evidence is to be trusted. He knows that he speaks the
36 truth, so that you too may believe; for this happened in fulfilment of the
37 text of Scripture: 'No bone of his shall be broken.' And another text says,
'They shall look on him whom they pierced.'

38 AFTER THAT, PILATE was approached by Joseph of Arimathaea, a disciple
of Jesus, but a secret disciple for fear of the Jews, who *a* asked to be allowed
to remove the body of Jesus. Pilate gave the permission; so Joseph came
39 and took the body away. He was joined by Nicodemus (the man who had
first visited Jesus by night), who brought with him a mixture of myrrh
40 and aloes, more than half a hundredweight. They took the body of Jesus
and wrapped it, with the spices, in strips of linen cloth according to Jewish
41 burial-customs. Now at the place where he had been crucified there was a
42 garden, and in the garden a new tomb, not yet used for burial. There,
because the tomb was near at hand and it was the eve of the Jewish Sabbath,
they laid Jesus.

20 EARLY ON THE SUNDAY MORNING, while it was still dark, Mary of
Magdala came to the tomb. She saw that the stone had been moved away
2 from the entrance, and ran to Simon Peter and the other disciple, the one
whom Jesus loved. 'They have taken the Lord out of his tomb,' she cried,
3 'and we do not know where they have laid him.' So Peter and the other set
4 out and made their way to the tomb. They were running side by side, but
5 the other disciple outran Peter and reached the tomb first. He peered in
6 and saw the linen wrappings lying there, but did not enter. Then Simon
Peter came up, following him, and he went into the tomb. He saw the linen
7 wrappings lying, and the napkin which had been over his head, not lying
8 with the wrappings but rolled together in a place by itself. Then the
disciple who had reached the tomb first went in too, and he saw and
9 believed; until then they had not understood the scriptures, which showed
that he must rise from the dead.

10 11 So the disciples went home again; but Mary stood at the tomb outside,
12 weeping. As she wept, she peered into the tomb; and she saw two angels in
white sitting there, one at the head, and one at the feet, where the body of
13 Jesus had lain. They said to her, 'Why are you weeping?' She answered,
'They have taken my Lord away, and I do not know where they have laid
14 him.' With these words she turned round and saw Jesus standing there,
15 but did not recognize him. Jesus said to her, 'Why are you weeping? Who
is it you are looking for?' Thinking it was the gardener, she said, 'If it is
you, sir, who removed him, tell me where you have laid him, and I will
16 take him away.' Jesus said, 'Mary!' She turned to him and said, 'Rabbuni!'
17 (which is Hebrew for 'My Master'). Jesus said, 'Do not cling to me, *b* for
I have not yet ascended to the Father. But go to my brothers, and tell them
that I am now ascending *c* to my Father and your Father, my God and your
18 God.' Mary of Magdala went to the disciples with her news: 'I have seen
the Lord!' she said, and gave them his message.

a Or of Arimathaea. He was a disciple of Jesus, but had gone into hiding for fear of the
Jews. He now . . .   *b* Or Touch me no more.   *c* Or I am going to ascend . . .

Late that Sunday evening, when the disciples were together behind 19
locked doors, for fear of the Jews, Jesus came and stood among them. 'Peace
be with you!' he said, and then showed them his hands and his side. So 20
when the disciples saw the Lord, they were filled with joy. Jesus repeated, 21
'Peace be with you!', and said, 'As the Father sent me, so I send you.'
Then he breathed on them, saying, 'Receive the Holy Spirit! If you 22 23
forgive any man's sins, they stand forgiven; if you pronounce them
unforgiven, unforgiven they remain.'

One of the Twelve, Thomas, that is 'the Twin', was not with the rest 24
when Jesus came. So the disciples told him, 'We have seen the Lord.' 25
He said, 'Unless I see the mark of the nails on his hands, unless I put my
finger into the place where the nails were, and my hand into his side, I will
not believe it.'

A week later his disciples were again in the room, and Thomas was with 26
them. Although the doors were locked, Jesus came and stood among them,
saying, 'Peace be with you!' Then he said to Thomas, 'Reach your finger 27
here; see my hands. Reach your hand here and put it into my side. Be
unbelieving no longer, but believe.' Thomas said, 'My Lord and my 28
God!' Jesus said, 'Because you have seen me you have found faith. Happy 29
are they who never saw me and yet have found faith.'

There were indeed many other signs that Jesus performed in the pre- 30
sence of his disciples, which are not recorded in this book. Those here 31
written have been recorded in order that you may hold the faith*a* that Jesus
is the Christ, the Son of God, and that through this faith you may possess
life by his name.

SOME TIME LATER, Jesus showed himself to his disciples once again, by **21**
the Sea of Tiberias; and in this way. Simon Peter and Thomas 'the Twin' 2
were together with Nathanael of Cana-in-Galilee. The sons of Zebedee
and two other disciples were also there. Simon Peter said, 'I am going out 3
fishing.' 'We will go with you', said the others. So they started and got into
the boat. But that night they caught nothing.

Morning came, and there stood Jesus on the beach, but the disciples 4
did not know that it was Jesus. He called out to them, 'Friends, have you 5
caught anything?' They answered 'No.' He said, 'Shoot the net to star- 6
board, and you will make a catch.' They did so, and found they could
not haul the net aboard, there were so many fish in it. Then the disciple 7
whom Jesus loved said to Peter, 'It is the Lord!' When Simon Peter
heard that, he wrapped his coat about him (for he had stripped) and
plunged into the sea. The rest of them came on in the boat, towing the 8
net full of fish; for they were not far from land, only about a hundred
yards.

When they came ashore, they saw a charcoal fire there, with fish laid on 9
it, and some bread. Jesus said, 'Bring some of your catch.' Simon Peter 10 11
went aboard and dragged the net to land, full of big fish, a hundred and
fifty-three of them; and yet, many as they were, the net was not torn. Jesus 12
said, 'Come and have breakfast.' None of the disciples dared to ask 'Who

a *Some witnesses read* that you may come to believe . . .

13 are you?' They knew it was the Lord. Jesus now came up, took the bread, and gave it to them, and the fish in the same way.

14 This makes the third time that Jesus appeared to his disciples after his resurrection from the dead.

15 After breakfast, Jesus said to Simon Peter, 'Simon son of John, do you love me more than all else*a*?' 'Yes, Lord,' he answered, 'you know that I

16 love you.'*b* 'Then feed my lambs', he said. A second time he asked, 'Simon son of John, do you love me?' 'Yes, Lord, you know I love you.'*b* 'Then

17 tend my sheep.' A third time he said, 'Simon son of John, do you love me*c*?' Peter was hurt that he asked him a third time, 'Do you love me?'*d* 'Lord,' he said, 'you know everything; you know I love you.'*b* Jesus said, 'Feed my sheep.

18 'And further, I tell you this in very truth: when you were young you fastened your belt about you and walked where you chose; but when you are old you will stretch out your arms, and a stranger will bind you fast,

19 and carry you where you have no wish to go.' He said this to indicate the manner of death by which Peter was to glorify God. Then he added, 'Follow me.'

20 Peter looked round, and saw the disciple whom Jesus loved following— the one who at supper had leaned back close to him to ask the question,

21 'Lord, who is it that will betray you?' When he caught sight of him, Peter

22 asked, 'Lord, what will happen to him?' Jesus said, 'If it should be my will that he wait until I come, what is it to you? Follow me.'

23 That saying of Jesus became current in the brotherhood, and was taken to mean that that disciple would not die. But in fact Jesus did not say that he would not die; he only said, 'If it should be my will that he wait until I come, what is it to you?'

24. It is this same disciple who attests what has here been written. It is in fact he who wrote it, and we know that his testimony is true.*e*

25 There is much else that Jesus did. If it were all to be recorded in detail, I suppose the whole world could not hold the books that would be written.

---

a Or more than they do.   *b Or* that I am your friend.   *c Or* are you my friend?
d Or that at the third asking he should have said, 'Are you my friend?'   *e Some witnesses here insert the passage printed on p. 143.*

An incident in the temple*

AND THEY WENT each to his home, and Jesus to the Mount of Olives. 53 1*
At daybreak he appeared again in the temple, and all the people 2
gathered round him. He had taken his seat and was engaged in teaching
them when the doctors of the law and the Pharisees brought in a woman 3
caught committing adultery. Making her stand out in the middle they said 4
to him, 'Master, this woman was caught in the very act of adultery. In the 5
Law Moses has laid down that such women are to be stoned. What do you
say about it?' They put the question as a test, hoping to frame a charge 6
against him. Jesus bent down and wrote with his finger on the ground.
When they continued to press their question he sat up straight and said, 7
'That one of you who is faultless shall throw the first stone.' Then once 8
again he bent down and wrote on the ground. When they heard what he 9
said, one by one they went away,*a* the eldest first; and Jesus was left alone,
with the woman still standing there. Jesus again sat up and *b* said to the 10
woman, 'Where are they? Has no one condemned you?' She answered, 'No 11
one, sir.' Jesus said, 'Nor do I condemn you. You may go; do not sin
again.'

* *This passage, which in the most widely received editions of the New Testament is printed
in the text of John, 7. 53—8. 11, has no fixed place in our witnesses. Some of them do not
contain it at all. Some place it after Luke 21. 38, others after John 7. 36, or 7. 52, or 21. 24.*

a *Some witnesses insert* convicted by their conscience. *b* *Some witnesses insert*
seeing no one but the woman.

ACTS OF THE APOSTLES

ACTS OF THE APOSTLES

The beginnings of the church

IN THE FIRST PART of my work, Theophilus, I wrote of all that 1 Jesus did and taught from the beginning until the day when, after 2 giving instructions through the Holy Spirit to the apostles whom he had chosen, he was taken up to heaven. He showed himself to these men 3 after his death, and gave ample proof that he was alive: over a period of forty days he appeared to them and taught them about the kingdom of God. While he was in their company he told them not to leave Jerusalem. 4 'You must wait', he said, 'for the promise made by my Father, about which you have heard me speak: John, as you know, baptized with water, but you 5 will be baptized with the Holy Spirit, and within the next few days.'

So, when they were all together, they asked him, 'Lord, is this the time 6 when you are to establish once again the sovereignty of Israel?' He 7 answered, 'It is not for you to know about dates or times, which the Father has set within his own control. But you will receive power when the Holy 8 Spirit comes upon you; and you will bear witness for me in Jerusalem, and all over Judaea and Samaria, and away to the ends of the earth.'

When he had said this, as they watched, he was lifted up, and a cloud 9 removed him from their sight. As he was going, and as they were gazing 10 intently into the sky, all at once there stood beside them two men in white who said, 'Men of Galilee, why stand there looking up into the sky? This 11 Jesus, who has been taken away from you up to heaven, will come in the same way as you have seen him go.'

Then they returned to Jerusalem from the hill called Olivet, which is 12 near Jerusalem, no farther than a Sabbath day's journey. Entering the city 13 they went to the room upstairs where they were lodging: Peter and John and James and Andrew, Philip and Thomas, Bartholomew and Matthew, James son of Alphaeus and Simon the Zealot, and Judas son of James. All 14 these were constantly at prayer together, and with them a group of women, including Mary the mother of Jesus, and his brothers.

It was during this time that Peter stood up before the assembled brother- 15 hood, about one hundred and twenty in all, and said: 'My friends, the 16 prophecy in Scripture was bound to come true, which the Holy Spirit, through the mouth of David, uttered about Judas who acted as guide to those who arrested Jesus. For he was one of our number and had his place 17 in this ministry.' (This Judas, be it noted, after buying a plot of land with 18 the price of his villainy, fell forward on the ground, and burst open, so that his entrails poured out. This became known to everyone in Jerusalem, and 19

they named the property in their own language Akeldama, which means
20 'Blood Acre'.) 'The text I have in mind', Peter continued, 'is in the Book of
Psalms: "Let his homestead fall desolate; let there be none to inhabit it";
21 and again, "Let another take over his charge." Therefore one of those
who bore us company all the while we had the Lord Jesus with us, coming
22 and going, from John's ministry of baptism until the day when he was
taken up from us—one of those must now join us as a witness to his
resurrection.'
23　Two names were put forward: Joseph, who was known as Barsabbas,
24 and bore the added name of Justus; and Matthias. Then they prayed and
said, 'Thou, Lord, who knowest the hearts of all men, declare which of
25 these two thou hast chosen to receive this office of ministry and apostleship
26 which Judas abandoned to go where he belonged.' They drew lots and the
lot fell on Matthias, who was then assigned a place among the twelve
apostles.*a*

2　WHILE THE DAY of Pentecost was running its course they were all
2 together in one place, when suddenly there came from the sky a noise like
that of a strong driving wind, which filled the whole house where they were
3 sitting. And there appeared to them tongues like flames of fire, dispersed
4 among them and resting on each one. And they were all filled with the Holy
Spirit and began to talk in other tongues, as the Spirit gave them power of
utterance.
5　Now there were living in Jerusalem devout Jews*b* drawn from every
6 nation under heaven; and at this sound the crowd gathered, all bewildered
7 because each one heard his own language spoken. They were amazed and
in their astonishment exclaimed, 'Why, they are all Galileans, are they not,
8 these men who are speaking? How is it then that we hear them, each of us
9 in his own native language? Parthians, Medes, Elamites; inhabitants of
10 Mesopotamia, of Judaea and Cappadocia, of Pontus and Asia, of Phrygia
and Pamphylia, of Egypt and the districts of Libya around Cyrene; visitors
11 from Rome, both Jews and proselytes, Cretans and Arabs, we hear them
12 telling in our own tongues the great things God has done.' And they were
all amazed and perplexed, saying to one another, 'What can this mean?'
13 Others said contemptuously, 'They have been drinking!'
14　But Peter stood up with the Eleven, raised his voice, and addressed them:
'Fellow Jews, and all you who live in Jerusalem, mark this and give me a
15 hearing. These men are not drunk, as you imagine; for it is only nine in the
16 17 morning. No, this is what the prophet spoke of: "God says, 'This will
happen in the last days: I will pour out upon everyone a portion of my
spirit; and your sons and daughters shall prophesy; your young men shall
18 see visions, and your old men shall dream dreams. Yes, I will endue even
my slaves, both men and women, with a portion of my spirit, and they shall
19 prophesy. And I will show portents in the sky above, and signs on the earth
20 below—blood and fire and drifting smoke. The sun shall be turned to darkness, and the moon to blood, before that great, resplendent day, the day of

a Some witnesses read was then appointed a colleague of the eleven apostles.
b Some witnesses read devout men.

the Lord, shall come. And then, everyone who invokes the name of the 21
Lord shall be saved.' "

'Men of Israel, listen to me: I speak of Jesus of Nazareth, a man singled 22
out by God and made known to you through miracles, portents, and signs,
which God worked among you through him, as you well know. When he 23
had been given up to you, by the deliberate will and plan of God, you used
heathen men to crucify and kill him. But God raised him to life again, 24
setting him free from the pangs of death, because it could not be that death
should keep him in its grip.

'For David says of him: 25

"I foresaw that the presence of the Lord would be with me always,
      for he is at my right hand so that I may not be shaken;
therefore my heart was glad and my tongue spoke my joy; 26
      moreover, my flesh shall dwell in hope,
for thou wilt not abandon my soul to death, 27
      nor let thy loyal servant suffer corruption.
Thou hast shown me the ways of life, 28
      thou wilt fill me with gladness by thy presence."

'Let me tell you plainly, my friends, that the patriarch David died and 29
was buried, and his tomb is here to this very day. It is clear therefore that 30
he spoke as a prophet, who knew that God had sworn to him that one of
his own direct descendants should sit on his throne; and when he said he 31
was not abandoned to death, and his flesh never suffered corruption, he
spoke with foreknowledge of the resurrection of the Messiah. The Jesus we 32
speak of has been raised by God, as we can all bear witness. Exalted thus 33
with *a* God's right hand, he received the Holy Spirit from the Father, as
was promised, and all that you now see and hear flows from him. For it was 34
not David who went up to heaven; his own words are: "The Lord said to
my Lord, 'Sit at my right hand until I make your enemies your footstool.' " 35
Let all Israel then accept as certain that God has made this Jesus, whom 36
you crucified, both Lord and Messiah.'

When they heard this they were cut to the heart, and said to Peter and 37
the apostles, *b* 'Friends, what are we to do?' 'Repent,' said Peter, 'repent 38
and be baptized, every one of you, in the name of Jesus the Messiah for the
forgiveness of your sins; and you will receive the gift of the Holy Spirit.
For the promise is to you, and to your children, and to all who are far away, 39
everyone whom the Lord our God may call.'

In these and many other words he pressed his case and pleaded with 40
them: 'Save yourselves', he said, 'from this crooked age.' Then those who 41
accepted his word were baptized, and some three thousand were added to
their number that day.

They met constantly to hear the apostles teach, and to share the common 42
life, to break bread, and to pray. A sense of awe was everywhere, and many 43
marvels and signs were brought about through the apostles. All whose 44
faith had drawn them together held everything in common: *c* they would 45

---

a Or at.   *b* Some witnesses read the rest of the apostles.   *c* Or All who had
become believers held everything together in common.

sell their property and possessions and make a general distribution as the
46 need of each required. With one mind they kept up their daily attendance
at the temple, and, breaking bread in private houses, shared their meals
47 with unaffected joy, as they praised God and enjoyed the favour of the
whole people. And day by day the Lord added to their number those
whom he was saving.

3 ONE DAY at three in the afternoon, the hour of prayer, Peter and John
2 were on their way up to the temple. Now a man who had been a cripple
from birth used to be carried there and laid every day by the gate of the
3 temple called 'Beautiful Gate', to beg from people as they went in. When
he saw Peter and John on their way into the temple he asked for charity.
4 But Peter fixed his eyes on him, as John did also, and said, 'Look at us.'
5 6 Expecting a gift from them, the man was all attention. And Peter said, 'I
have no silver or gold; but what I have I give you: in the name of Jesus
7 Christ of Nazareth, walk.' Then he grasped him by the right hand and
8 pulled him up; and at once his feet and ankles grew strong; he sprang up,
stood on his feet, and started to walk. He entered the temple with them,
9 leaping and praising God as he went. Everyone saw him walking and
10 praising God, and when they recognized him as the man who used to sit
begging at Beautiful Gate, they were filled with wonder and amazement at
what had happened to him.

11 And as he was clutching Peter and John all the people came running in
12 astonishment towards them in Solomon's Portico, as it is called. Peter saw
them coming and met them with these words: 'Men of Israel, why be
surprised at this? Why stare at us as if we had made this man walk by some
13 power or godliness of our own? The God of Abraham, Isaac, and Jacob,
the God of our fathers, has given the highest honour to his servant Jesus,
14 whom you committed for trial and repudiated in Pilate's court—repudiated
the one who was holy and righteous when Pilate had decided to release him.
15 You begged as a favour the release of a murderer, and killed him who has
led the way to life. But God raised him from the dead; of that we are
16 witnesses. And the name of Jesus, by awakening faith, has strengthened
this man, whom you see and know, and this faith has made him completely
well, as you can all see for yourselves.

17 'And now, my friends, I know quite well that you acted in ignorance,
18 and so did your rulers; but this is how God fulfilled what he had foretold
in the utterances of all the prophets: that his Messiah should suffer.
19 Repent then and turn to God, so that your sins may be wiped out. Then
20 the Lord may grant you a time of recovery and send you the Messiah he
21 has already appointed, that is, Jesus. He must be received into heaven until
the time of universal restoration comes, of which God spoke by his holy
22 prophets.*a* Moses said, "The Lord God will raise up a prophet for you
from among yourselves as he raised me;*b* you shall listen to everything
23 he says to you, and anyone who refuses to listen to that prophet must
24 be extirpated from Israel." And so said all the prophets, from Samuel
onwards; with one voice they all predicted this present time.

a Some witnesses add from the beginning of the world.   *b Or* like me.

'You are the heirs of the prophets; you are within the covenant which 25
God made with your fathers, when he said to Abraham, "And in your offspring all the families on earth shall find blessing." When God raised up 26
his Servant, he sent him to you first, to bring you blessing by turning
every one of you from your wicked ways.'

They were still addressing the people when the chief^a priests came upon **4**
them, together with the Controller of the Temple and the Sadducees,
exasperated at their teaching the people and proclaiming the resurrection 2
from the dead—the resurrection of Jesus. They were arrested and put in 3
prison for the night, as it was already evening. But many of those who had 4
heard the message became believers. The number of men now reached
about five thousand.

Next day the Jewish rulers, elders, and doctors of the law met in Jeru- 5
salem. There were present Annas the High Priest, Caiaphas, Jonathan, ^b 6
Alexander, and all who were of the high-priestly family. They brought the 7
apostles before the court and began the examination. 'By what power',
they asked, 'or by what name have such men as you done this?' Then 8
Peter, filled with the Holy Spirit, answered, 'Rulers of the people and
elders, if the question put to us today is about help given to a sick man, and 9
we are asked by what means he was cured, here is the answer, for all of you 10
and for all the people of Israel: it was by the name of Jesus Christ of
Nazareth, whom you crucified, whom God raised from the dead; it is by
his name ^c that this man stands here before you fit and well. This Jesus is 11
the stone rejected by the builders which has become the keystone—and
you are the builders. There is no salvation in anyone else at all,^d for there 12
is no other name under heaven granted to men, by which we may receive
salvation.'

Now as they observed the boldness of Peter and John, and noted that 13
they were untrained laymen, they began to wonder, then recognized them
as former companions of Jesus. And when they saw the man who had been 14
cured standing with them, they had nothing to say in reply. So they ordered 15
them to leave the court, and then discussed the matter among themselves.
'What are we to do with these men?' they said; 'for it is common knowledge 16
in Jerusalem that a notable miracle has come about through them; and we
cannot deny it. But to stop this from spreading further among the people, 17
we had better caution them never again to speak to anyone in this name.'
They then called them in and ordered them to refrain from all public 18
speaking and teaching in the name of Jesus.

But Peter and John said to them in reply: 'Is it right in God's eyes for us 19
to obey you rather than God? Judge for yourselves. We cannot possibly 20
give up speaking of things we have seen and heard.'

The court repeated the caution and discharged them. They could not 21
see how they were to punish them, because the people were all giving glory
to God for what had happened. The man upon whom this miracle of heal- 22
ing had been performed was over forty years old.

As soon as they were discharged they went back to their friends and 23

---

^a *Some witnesses omit* chief.   ^b *Some witnesses read* John.   ^c *Some witnesses*
insert and no other.   ^d *Some witnesses omit* There is no . . . at all.

24 told them everything that the chief priests and elders had said. When they heard it, they raised their voices as one man and called upon God:

'Sovereign Lord, maker of heaven and earth and sea and of everything
25 in them, who by the Holy Spirit,[a] through the mouth of David thy servant, didst say,

> "Why did the Gentiles rage and the peoples lay their plots in vain?
26 The kings of the earth took their stand and the rulers made common cause
> against the Lord and against his Messiah."

27 They did indeed make common cause in this very city against thy holy servant Jesus whom thou didst anoint as Messiah. Herod and Pontius
28 Pilate conspired with the Gentiles and peoples of Israel to do all the things
29 which, under thy hand and by thy decree, were foreordained. And now, O Lord, mark their threats, and enable thy servants to speak thy word with
30 all boldness. Stretch out thy hand to heal and cause signs and wonders to be done through the name of thy holy servant Jesus.'
31 When they had ended their prayer, the building where they were assembled rocked, and all were filled with the Holy Spirit and spoke the word of God with boldness.

32 THE WHOLE BODY of believers was united in heart and soul. Not a man of them claimed any of his possessions as his own, but everything was held
33 in common, while the apostles bore witness with great power to the resur-
34 rection of the Lord Jesus. They were all held in high esteem; for they had never a needy person among them, because all who had property in land
35 or houses sold it, brought the proceeds of the sale, and laid the money at the feet of the apostles; it was then distributed to any who stood in need.
36 For instance, Joseph, surnamed by the apostles Barnabas (which means
37 'Son of Exhortation'), a Levite, by birth a Cypriot, owned an estate, which he sold; he brought the money, and laid it at the apostles' feet.

5 But there was another man, called Ananias, with his wife Sapphira, who
2 sold a property. With the full knowledge of his wife he kept back part of the
3 purchase-money, and part he brought and laid at the apostles' feet. But Peter said, 'Ananias, how was it that Satan so possessed your mind that you
4 lied to the Holy Spirit, and kept back part of the price of the land? While it remained, did it not remain yours? When it was turned into money, was it not still at your own disposal? What made you think of doing this thing?
5 You have lied not to men but to God.' When Ananias heard these words he
6 dropped dead; and all the others who heard were awestruck. The younger men rose and covered his body, then carried him out and buried him.
7 About three hours passed, and then his wife came in, unaware of what
8 had happened. Peter turned to her and said, 'Tell me, were you paid such
9 and such a price for the land?' 'Yes,' she said, 'that was the price.' Then Peter said, 'Why did you both conspire to put the Spirit of the Lord to the test? Hark! there at the door are the footsteps of those who buried your
10 husband; and they will carry you away.' And suddenly she dropped dead

a Some witnesses omit by the Holy Spirit.

at his feet. When the young men came in, they found her dead; and they
carried her out and buried her beside her husband. And a great awe fell 11
upon the whole church, and upon all who heard of these events; and many 12
remarkable and wonderful things took place among the people at the hands
of the apostles.

THEY USED TO MEET by common consent in Solomon's Portico, no one 13
from outside their number venturing to join with them. But people in
general spoke highly of them,[a] and more than that, numbers of men and 14
women were added to their ranks as believers in the Lord.[b] In the end the 15
sick were actually carried out into the streets and laid there on beds and
stretchers, so that even the shadow of Peter might fall on one or another as
he passed by; and the people from the towns round Jerusalem flocked in, 16
bringing those who were ill or harassed by unclean spirits, and all of them
were cured.

Then the High Priest and his colleagues, the Sadducean party as it then 17
was, were goaded into action by jealousy. They proceeded to arrest the 18
apostles, and put them in official custody. But an angel of the Lord opened 19
the prison doors during the night, brought them out, and said, 'Go, take 20
your place in the temple and speak to the people, and tell them about this
new life and all it means.' Accordingly they entered the temple at day- 21
break and went on with their teaching.

When the High Priest arrived with his colleagues they summoned the
'Sanhedrin', that is, the full senate of the Israelite nation, and sent to the
jail to fetch the prisoners. But the police who went to the prison failed to 22
find them there, so they returned and reported, 'We found the jail securely 23
locked at every point, with the warders at their posts by the doors, but when
we opened them we found no one inside.' When they heard this, the Con- 24
troller of the Temple and the chief priests were wondering what could have
become of them,[c] and then a man arrived with the report, 'Look! the men 25
you put in prison are there in the temple teaching the people.' At that the 26
Controller went off with the police and fetched them, but without using
force for fear of being stoned by the people.

So they brought them and stood them before the Council; and the High 27
Priest began his examination. 'We expressly ordered you', he said, 'to 28
desist from teaching in that name; and what has happened? You have filled
Jerusalem with your teaching, and you are trying to make us responsible
for that man's death.' Peter replied for himself and the apostles: 'We must 29
obey God rather than men. The God of our fathers raised up Jesus whom 30
you had done to death[d] by hanging him on a gibbet. He it is whom God has 31
exalted with his own right hand[e] as leader and saviour, to grant Israel
repentance and forgiveness of sins. And we are witnesses to all this, and so 32
is the Holy Spirit given by God to those who are obedient to him.'

[a] *Or* . . . Portico. Although others did not venture to join them, the common people
spoke highly of them.   [b] *Or* and an ever-increasing number of believers, both
men and women, were added to the Lord.   [c] *Or* wondering about them, what
this could possibly mean.   [d] *Or* . . . Jesus, and you did him to death . . .
[e] *Or* at his right hand.

33 This touched them on the raw, and they wanted to put them to death.
34 But a member of the Council rose to his feet, a Pharisee called Gamaliel, a
teacher of the law held in high regard by all the people. He moved that the
35 men be put outside for a while. Then he said, 'Men of Israel, be cautious in
36 deciding what to do with these men. Some time ago Theudas came forward, claiming to be somebody, and a number of men, about four hundred,
joined him. But he was killed and his whole following was broken up and
37 disappeared. After him came Judas the Galilean at the time of the census;
he induced some people to revolt under his leadership, but he too perished
38 and his whole following was scattered. And so now: keep clear of these men,
I tell you; leave them alone. For if this idea of theirs or its execution is of
39 human origin, it will collapse; but if it is from God, you will never be able
to put them down, and you risk finding yourselves at war with God.'
40 They took his advice. They sent for the apostles and had them flogged;
then they ordered them to give up speaking in the name of Jesus, and dis-
41 charged them. So the apostles went out from the Council rejoicing that they
42 had been found worthy to suffer indignity for the sake of the Name. And
every day they went steadily on with their teaching in the temple and in
private houses, telling the good news of Jesus the Messiah.[a]

The church moves outwards

6 DURING THIS PERIOD, when disciples were growing in number,
there was disagreement between those of them who spoke Greek[b]
and those who spoke the language of the Jews.[c] The former party complained that their widows were being overlooked in the daily distribution.
2 So the Twelve called the whole body of disciples together and said, 'It
would be a grave mistake for us to neglect the word of God in order to wait
3 at table. Therefore, friends, look out seven men of good reputation from
your number, men full of the Spirit and of wisdom, and we will appoint
4 them to deal with these matters, while we devote ourselves to prayer and
5 to the ministry of the Word.' This proposal proved acceptable to the whole
body. They elected Stephen, a man full of faith and of the Holy Spirit,
Philip, Prochorus, Nicanor, Timon, Parmenas, and Nicolas of Antioch,
6 a former convert to Judaism. These they presented to the apostles, who
prayed and laid their hands on them.
7 The word of God now spread more and more widely; the number of
disciples in Jerusalem went on increasing rapidly, and very many of the
priests adhered to the Faith.
8 Stephen, who was full of grace and power, began to work great miracles
9 and signs among the people. But some members of the synagogue called
the Synagogue of Freedmen, comprising Cyrenians and Alexandrians
and people from Cilicia and Asia, came forward and argued with Stephen,
10 but could not hold their own against the inspired wisdom with which he
11 spoke. They then put up men who alleged that they had heard him make

[a] *Or* the good news that the Messiah was Jesus.   [b] *Literally* the Hellenists.
[c] *Literally* the Hebrews.

blasphemous statements against Moses and against God. They stirred up 12
the people and the elders and doctors of the law, set upon him and seized
him, and brought him before the Council. They produced false witnesses 13
who said, 'This man is for ever saying things against this holy place and
against the Law. For we have heard him say that Jesus of Nazareth will 14
destroy this place and alter the customs handed down to us by Moses.' And 15
all who were sitting in the Council fixed their eyes on him, and his face
appeared to them like the face of an angel.

Then the High Priest asked, 'Is this so?' And he said, 'My brothers, 7 1 2
fathers of this nation, listen to me. The God of glory appeared to Abraham
our ancestor while he was in Mesopotamia, before he had settled in Harran,
and said: "Leave your country and your kinsfolk and come away to a land 3
that I will show you." Thereupon he left the land of the Chaldaeans and 4
settled in Harran. From there, after his father's death, God led him to
migrate to this land where you now live. He gave him nothing in it to call 5
his own, not one yard; but promised to give it in possession to him and his
descendants after him, though he was then childless. God spoke in these 6
terms: "Abraham's descendants shall live as aliens in a foreign land, held
in slavery and oppression for four hundred years. And I will pass judge- 7
ment", said God, "on the nation whose slaves they are; and after that they
shall come out free, and worship me in this place." He then gave him the 8
covenant of circumcision, and so, after Isaac was born, he circumcised him
on the eighth day; and Isaac begot Jacob, and Jacob the twelve patriarchs.

'The patriarchs out of jealousy sold Joseph into slavery in Egypt, but 9
God was with him and rescued him from all his troubles. He also gave him 10
a presence and powers of mind which so commended him to Pharaoh king
of Egypt, that he appointed him chief administrator for Egypt and the whole
of the royal household.

'But famine struck all Egypt and Canaan, and caused great hardship; 11
and our ancestors could find nothing to eat. But Jacob heard that there was 12
food in Egypt and sent our fathers there. This was their first visit. On the 13
second visit Joseph was recognized by his brothers, and his family con-
nections were disclosed to Pharaoh. So Joseph sent an invitation to his father 14
Jacob and all his relatives, seventy-five persons altogether; and Jacob went 15
down into Egypt. There he ended his days, as also our forefathers did.
Their remains were later removed to Shechem and buried in the tomb 16
which Abraham had bought and paid for from the clan of Emmor at
Shechem.

'Now as the time approached for God to fulfil the promise he had made 17
to Abraham, our nation in Egypt grew and increased in numbers. At length 18
another king, who knew nothing of Joseph, ascended the throne of Egypt.
He made a crafty attack on our race, and cruelly forced our ancestors to 19
expose their children so that they should not survive. At this time Moses 20
was born. He was a fine child, and pleasing to God. For three months he
was nursed in his father's house, and when he was exposed, Pharaoh's 21
daughter herself adopted him and brought him up as her own son. So 22
Moses was trained in all the wisdom of the Egyptians, a powerful speaker
and a man of action.

23 'He was approaching the age of forty, when it occurred to him to look
24 into the conditions of his fellow-countrymen the Israelites. He saw one of
them being ill-treated, so he went to his aid, and avenged the victim by
25 striking down the Egyptian. He thought his fellow-countrymen would
understand that God was offering them deliverance through him, but they
26 did not understand. The next day he came upon two of them fighting, and
tried to bring them to make up their quarrel. "My men," he said, "you are
27 brothers; why are you ill-treating one another?" But the man who was at
fault pushed him away. "Who set you up as a ruler and judge over us?"
28 he said. "Are you going to kill me as you killed the Egyptian yesterday?"
29 At this Moses fled the country and settled in Midianite territory. There
two sons were born to him.
30 'After forty years had passed, an angel appeared to him in the flame of a
31 burning bush in the desert near Mount Sinai. Moses was amazed at the
sight. But as he approached to look closely, the voice of the Lord was heard:
32 "I am the God of your fathers, the God of Abraham, Isaac, and Jacob."
33 Moses was terrified and dared not look. Then the Lord said to him, "Take
34 off your shoes; the place where you are standing is holy ground. I have
indeed seen how my people are oppressed in Egypt and have heard their
groans; and I have come down to rescue them. Up, then; let me send you
to Egypt."
35 'This Moses, whom they had rejected with the words, "Who made you
ruler and judge?"—this very man was commissioned as ruler and liberator
by God himself, speaking through the angel who appeared to him in the
36 bush. It was Moses who led them out, working miracles and signs in Egypt,
37 at the Red Sea, and for forty years in the desert. It was he again who said to
the Israelites, "God will raise up a prophet for you from among yourselves
38 as he raised me."*a* He it was who, when they were assembled there in the
desert, conversed with the angel who spoke to him on Mount Sinai, and
with our forefathers; he received the living utterances of God, to pass
on to us.
39 'But our forefathers would not accept his leadership. They thrust him
40 aside. They wished themselves back in Egypt, and said to Aaron, "Make
us gods to go before us. As for that Moses, who brought us out of Egypt,
41 we do not know what has become of him." That was when they made the
bull-calf, and offered sacrifice to the idol, and held a feast in honour of the
42 thing their hands had made. But God turned away from them and gave
them over to the worship of the host of heaven, as it stands written in the
book of the prophets: "Did you bring me victims and offerings those forty
43 years in the desert, you house of Israel? No, you carried aloft the shrine of
Moloch and the star of the god Rephan, the images which you had made
for your adoration. I will banish you beyond Babylon."
44 'Our forefathers had the Tent of the Testimony in the desert, as God
commanded when he told Moses to make it after the pattern which he had
45 seen. Our fathers of the next generation, with Joshua, brought it with them
when they dispossessed the nations whom God drove out before them, and
46 there it was until the time of David. David found favour with God and

a Or like me.

asked to be allowed to provide a dwelling-place for the God of Jacob;[a] but it was Solomon who built him a house. However, the Most High does 47 48 not live in houses made by men: as the prophet says, "Heaven is my throne 49 and earth my footstool. What kind of house will you build for me, says the Lord; where is my resting-place? Are not all these things of my own 50 making?"

'How stubborn you are, heathen still at heart and deaf to the truth! You 51 always fight against the Holy Spirit. Like fathers, like sons. Was there ever 52 a prophet whom your fathers did not persecute? They killed those who foretold the coming of the Righteous One; and now you have betrayed him and murdered him, you who received the Law as God's angels gave it to 53 you, and yet have not kept it.'

This touched them on the raw and they ground their teeth with fury. 54 But Stephen, filled with the Holy Spirit, and gazing intently up to heaven, 55 saw the glory of God, and Jesus standing at God's right hand. 'Look,' he 56 said, 'there is a rift in the sky; I can see the Son of Man standing at God's right hand!' At this they gave a great shout and stopped their ears. Then 57 they made one rush at him and, flinging him out of the city, set about 58 stoning him. The witnesses laid their coats at the feet of a young man named Saul. So they stoned Stephen, and as they did so, he called out, 'Lord Jesus, 59 receive my spirit.' Then he fell on his knees and cried aloud, 'Lord, do not 60 hold this sin against them', and with that he died. And Saul was among 8 those who approved of his murder.

THIS WAS THE BEGINNING of a time of violent persecution for the church in Jerusalem; and all except the apostles were scattered over the country districts of Judaea and Samaria. Stephen was given burial by 2 certain devout men, who made a great lamentation for him. Saul, mean- 3 while, was harrying the church; he entered house after house, seizing men and women, and sending them to prison.

As for those who had been scattered, they went through the country 4 preaching the Word. Philip came down to a city in Samaria and began pro- 5 claiming the Messiah to them. The crowds, to a man, listened eagerly to 6 what Philip said, when they heard him and saw the miracles that he per- formed. For in many cases of possession the unclean spirits came out with 7 a loud cry; and many paralysed and crippled folk were cured; and there was 8 great joy in that city.

A man named Simon had been in the city for some time, and had swept 9 the Samaritans off their feet with his magical arts, claiming to be someone great. All of them, high and low, listened eagerly to him. 'This man', they 10 said, 'is that power of God which is called "The Great Power".' They 11 listened because they had for so long been carried away by his magic. But 12 when they came to believe Philip with his good news about the kingdom of God and the name of Jesus Christ, they were baptized, men and women alike. Even Simon himself believed, and was baptized, and thereupon was 13 constantly in Philip's company. He was carried away when he saw the powerful signs and miracles that were taking place.

[a] *Some witnesses read* for the house of Jacob.

14 The apostles in Jerusalem now heard that Samaria had accepted the
15 word of God. They sent off Peter and John, who went down there and
prayed for the converts, asking that they might receive the Holy Spirit.
16 For until then the Spirit had not come upon any of them. They had been
17 baptized into the name of the Lord Jesus, that and nothing more. So Peter
and John laid their hands on them and they received the Holy Spirit.

18 When Simon saw that the Spirit was bestowed through the laying on of
19 the apostles' hands, he offered them money and said, 'Give me the same
power too, so that when I lay my hands on anyone, he will receive the Holy
20 Spirit.' Peter replied, 'Your money go with you to damnation, because you
21 thought God's gift was for sale! You have no part nor lot in this, for you
22 are dishonest with God. Repent of this wickedness and pray the Lord to
23 forgive you for imagining such a thing. I can see that you are doomed to
24 taste the bitter fruit and wear the fetters of sin.'*a* Simon answered, 'Pray
to the Lord for me yourselves and ask that none of the things you have
spoken of may fall upon me.'

25 So, after giving their testimony and speaking the word of the Lord, they
took the road back to Jerusalem, bringing the good news to many Samaritan
villages on the way.

26 Then the angel of the Lord said to Philip, 'Start out and go south to the
road that leads down from Jerusalem to Gaza.' (This is the desert road.)
27 So he set out and was on his way when he caught sight of an Ethiopian.
This man was a eunuch, a high official of the Kandake, or Queen, of
Ethiopia, in charge of all her treasure. He had been to Jerusalem on a
28 pilgrimage and was now on his way home, sitting in his carriage and read-
29 ing aloud the prophet Isaiah. The Spirit said to Philip, 'Go and join the
30 carriage.' When Philip ran up he heard him reading the prophet Isaiah
31 and said, 'Do you understand what you are reading?' He said, 'How can I
understand unless someone will give me the clue?' So he asked Philip to
get in and sit beside him.
32 The passage he was reading was this: 'He was led like a sheep to be
slaughtered; and like a lamb that is dumb before the shearer, he does
33 not open his mouth. He has been humiliated and has no redress. Who
will be able to speak of his posterity? For he is cut off from the world of
living men.'

34 'Now', said the eunuch to Philip, 'tell me, please, who it is that the
35 prophet is speaking about here: himself or someone else?' Then Philip
36 began. Starting from this passage, he told him the good news of Jesus. As
they were going along the road, they came to some water. 'Look,' said the
eunuch, 'here is water: what is there to prevent my being baptized?';*b*
38 and he ordered the carriage to stop. Then they both went down into the
39 water, Philip and the eunuch; and he baptized him. When they came up
out of the water the Spirit snatched Philip away, and the eunuch saw no
40 more of him, but went happily on his way. Philip appeared at Azotus, and
toured the country, preaching in all the towns till he reached Caesarea.

a Literally you are for gall of bitterness and a fetter of unrighteousness.
b Some witnesses insert (37) Philip said, 'If you whole-heartedly believe, it is permitted.'
He replied, 'I believe that Jesus Christ is the Son of God.'

MEANWHILE SAUL was still breathing murderous threats against the 9
disciples of the Lord. He went to the High Priest and applied for letters to 2
the synagogues at Damascus authorizing him to arrest anyone he found,
men or women, who followed the new way, and bring them to Jerusalem.
While he was still on the road and nearing Damascus, suddenly a light 3
flashed from the sky all around him. He fell to the ground and heard a voice 4
saying, 'Saul, Saul, why do you persecute me?' 'Tell me, Lord,' he said, 5
'who you are.' The voice answered, 'I am Jesus, whom you are persecuting.
But get up and go into the city, and you will be told what you have to do.' 6
Meanwhile the men who were travelling with him stood speechless; they 7
heard the voice but could see no one. Saul got up from the ground, but 8
when he opened his eyes he could not see; so they led him by the hand and
brought him into Damascus. He was blind for three days, and took no 9
food or drink.

There was a disciple in Damascus named Ananias. He had a vision in 10
which he heard the voice of the Lord: 'Ananias!' 'Here I am, Lord', he
answered. The Lord said to him, 'Go at once to Straight Street, to the 11
house of Judas, and ask for a man from Tarsus named Saul. You will find
him at prayer; he has had a vision of a man named Ananias coming in and 12
laying his hands on him to restore his sight.' Ananias answered, 'Lord, I 13
have often heard about this man and all the harm he has done to thy people
in Jerusalem. And he is here with authority from the chief priests to arrest 14
all who invoke thy name.' But the Lord said to him, 'You must go, for this 15
man is my chosen instrument to bring my name before the nations and
their kings, and before the people of Israel. I myself will show him all that 16
he must go through for my name's sake.'

So Ananias went. He entered the house, laid his hands on him and said, 17
'Saul, my brother, the Lord Jesus, who appeared to you on your way here,
has sent me to you so that you may recover your sight, and be filled with the
Holy Spirit.' And immediately it seemed that scales fell from his eyes, and 18
he regained his sight. Thereupon he was baptized, and afterwards he took 19
food and his strength returned.

He stayed some time with the disciples in Damascus. Soon he was pro- 20
claiming Jesus publicly in the synagogues: 'This', he said, 'is the Son of
God.' All who heard were astounded. 'Is not this the man', they said, 'who 21
was in Jerusalem trying to destroy those who invoke this name? Did he not
come here for the sole purpose of arresting them and taking them to the
chief priests?' But Saul grew more and more forceful, and silenced the 22
Jews of Damascus with his cogent proofs that Jesus was the Messiah.

As the days mounted up, the Jews hatched a plot against his life; but 23 24
their plans became known to Saul. They kept watch on the city gates day
and night so that they might murder him; but his converts took him one 25
night and let him down by the wall, lowering him in a basket.

When he reached Jerusalem he tried to join the body of disciples there; 26
but they were all afraid of him, because they did not believe that he was
really a convert. Barnabas, however, took him by the hand and introduced 27
him to the apostles. He described to them how Saul had seen the Lord on
his journey, and heard his voice, and how he had spoken out boldly in the

28 name of Jesus at Damascus. Saul now stayed with them, moving about
29 freely in Jerusalem. He spoke out boldly and openly in the name of the
    Lord, talking and debating with the Greek-speaking Jews.[a] But they
30 planned to murder him, and when the brethren learned of this they
    escorted him to Caesarea and saw him off to Tarsus.

31 MEANWHILE THE CHURCH, throughout Judaea, Galilee, and Samaria,
    was left in peace to build up its strength. In the fear of the Lord, upheld by
    the Holy Spirit, it held on its way and grew in numbers.
32   Peter was making a general tour, in the course of which he went down to
33 visit God's people at Lydda. There he found a man named Aeneas who had
34 been bed-ridden with paralysis for eight years. Peter said to him, 'Aeneas,
    Jesus Christ cures you; get up and make your bed', and immediately he
35 stood up. All who lived in Lydda and Sharon saw him; and they turned
    to the Lord.
36   In Joppa there was a disciple named Tabitha (in Greek, Dorcas, mean-
37 ing a gazelle), who filled her days with acts of kindness and charity. At that
    time she fell ill and died; and they washed her body and laid it in a room
38 upstairs. As Lydda was near Joppa, the disciples, who had heard that Peter
    was there, sent two men to him with the urgent request, 'Please come over
39 to us without delay.' Peter thereupon went off with them. When he arrived
    they took him upstairs to the room, where all the widows came and stood
    round him in tears, showing him the shirts and coats that Dorcas used to
40 make while she was with them. Peter sent them all outside, and knelt down
    and prayed. Then, turning towards the body, he said, 'Get up, Tabitha.'
41 She opened her eyes, saw Peter, and sat up. He gave her his hand and
    helped her to her feet. Then he called the members of the congregation
42 and the widows and showed her to them alive. The news spread all over
43 Joppa, and many came to believe in the Lord. Peter stayed on in Joppa for
    some time with one Simon, a tanner.
10   At Caesarea there was a man named Cornelius, a centurion in the Italian
2   Cohort, as it was called. He was a religious man, and he and his whole
    family joined in the worship of God. He gave generously to help the Jewish
3   people, and was regular in his prayers to God. One day about three in the
    afternoon he had a vision in which he clearly saw an angel of God, who
4   came into his room and said, 'Cornelius!' He stared at him in terror. 'What
    is it, my lord?' he asked. The angel said, 'Your prayers and acts of charity
5   have gone up to heaven to speak for you before God. And now send to
6   Joppa for a man named Simon, also called Peter: he is lodging with another
7   Simon, a tanner, whose house is by the sea.' So when the angel who was
    speaking to him had gone, he summoned two of his servants and a military
8   orderly who was a religious man, told them the whole story, and sent them
    to Joppa.
9   Next day, while they were still on their way and approaching the city,
10 about noon Peter went up on the roof to pray. He grew hungry and wanted
    something to eat. While they were getting it ready, he fell into a trance.
11 He saw a rift in the sky, and a thing coming down that looked like a great

[a] *Literally* the Hellenists.

sheet of sail-cloth. It was slung by the four corners, and was being lowered
to the ground. In it he saw creatures of every kind, whatever walks or 12
crawls or flies. Then there was a voice which said to him, 'Up, Peter, kill 13
and eat.' But Peter said, 'No, Lord, no: I have never eaten anything pro- 14
fane or unclean.' The voice came again a second time: 'It is not for you to 15
call profane what God counts clean.' This happened three times; and then 16
the thing was taken up again into the sky.

While Peter was still puzzling over the meaning of the vision he had 17
seen, the messengers of Cornelius had been asking the way to Simon's
house, and now arrived at the entrance. They called out and asked if 18
Simon Peter was lodging there. But Peter was thinking over the vision, 19
when the Spirit said to him, 'Some *a* men are here looking for you; make 20
haste and go downstairs. You may go with them without any misgiving,
for it was I who sent them.' Peter came down to the men and said, 'You 21
are looking for me? Here I am. What brings you here?' 'We are from the 22
centurion Cornelius,' they replied, 'a good and religious man, acknowledged as such by the whole Jewish nation. He was directed by a holy angel
to send for you to his house and to listen to what you have to say.' So Peter 23
asked them in and gave them a night's lodging. Next day he set out with
them, accompanied by some members of the congregation at Joppa.

The day after that, he arrived at Caesarea. Cornelius was expecting them 24
and had called together his relatives and close friends. When Peter arrived, 25
Cornelius came to meet him, and bowed to the ground in deep reverence.
But Peter raised him to his feet and said, 'Stand up; I am a man like any- 26
one else.' Still talking with him he went in and found a large gathering. 27
He said to them, 'I need not tell you that a Jew is forbidden by his religion 28
to visit or associate with a man of another race; yet God has shown me
clearly that I must not call any man profane or unclean. That is why I 29
came here without demur when you sent for me. May I ask what was your
reason for sending?'

Cornelius said, 'Four days ago, just about this time, I was in the house 30
here saying the afternoon prayers, when suddenly a man in shining robes
stood before me. He said: "Cornelius, your prayer has been heard and your 31
acts of charity remembered before God. Send to Joppa, then, to Simon 32
Peter, and ask him to come. He is lodging in the house of Simon the tanner,
by the sea." So I sent to you there and then; it was kind of you to come. 33
And now we are all met here before God, to hear all that the Lord has
ordered you to say.'

Peter began: 'I now see how true it is that God has no favourites, but 34 35
that in every nation the man who is godfearing and does what is right is
acceptable to him. He sent his word to the Israelites and gave the good 36
news of peace through Jesus Christ, who is Lord of all. I need not tell you 37
what happened lately all over the land of the Jews, starting from Galilee
after the baptism proclaimed by John. You know about Jesus of Nazareth, 38
how God anointed him with the Holy Spirit and with power. He went
about doing good and healing all who were oppressed by the devil, for God
was with him. And we can bear witness to all that he did in the Jewish 39

a One witness reads Two; *others read* Three.

country-side and in Jerusalem. He was put to death by hanging on a
40 gibbet; but God raised him to life on the third day, and allowed him to
41 appear, not to the whole people, but to witnesses whom God had chosen
in advance—to us, who ate and drank with him after he rose from the dead.
42 He commanded us to proclaim him to the people, and affirm that he is the
one who has been designated by God as judge of the living and the dead.
43 It is to him that all the prophets testify, declaring that everyone who trusts
in him receives forgiveness of sins through his name.'
44 Peter was still speaking when the Holy Spirit came upon all who were
45 listening to the message. The believers who had come with Peter, men of
Jewish birth, were astonished that the gift of the Holy Spirit should have
46 been poured out even on Gentiles. For they could hear them speaking in
tongues of ecstasy and acclaiming the greatness of God. Then Peter spoke:
47 'Is anyone prepared to withhold the water for baptism from these persons,
48 who have received the Holy Spirit just as we did ourselves?' Then he
ordered them to be baptized in the name of Jesus Christ. After that they
asked him to stay on with them for a time.

11 News came to the apostles and the members of the church in Judaea
2 that Gentiles too had accepted the word of God; and when Peter came up
to Jerusalem those who were of Jewish birth raised the question with him.
3 'You have been visiting men who are uncircumcised,' they said, 'and sitting
4 at table with them!' Peter began by laying before them the facts as they had
happened.
5 'I was in the city of Joppa', he said, 'at prayer; and while in a trance I
had a vision: a thing was coming down that looked like a great sheet of sail-
cloth, slung by the four corners and lowered from the sky till it reached me.
6 I looked intently to make out what was in it and I saw four-footed creatures
7 of the earth, wild beasts, and things that crawl or fly. Then I heard a voice
8 saying to me, "Up, Peter, kill and eat." But I said, "No, Lord, no: nothing
9 profane or unclean has ever entered my mouth." A voice from heaven
answered a second time, "It is not for you to call profane what God counts
10 clean." This happened three times, and then they were all drawn up again
11 into the sky. At that moment three men, who had been sent to me from
12 Caesarea, arrived at the house where I was*a* staying; and the Spirit told
me to go with them.*b* My six companions here came with me and we went
13 into the man's house. He told us how he had seen an angel standing in his
14 house who said, "Send to Joppa for Simon also called Peter. He will speak
15 words that will bring salvation to you and all your household." Hardly had
I begun speaking, when the Holy Spirit came upon them, just as upon us
16 at the beginning. Then I recalled what the Lord had said: "John baptized
17 with water, but you will be baptized with the Holy Spirit." God gave them
no less a gift than he gave us when we put our trust in the Lord Jesus
Christ; then how could I possibly stand in God's way?'
18 When they heard this their doubts were silenced. They gave praise to
God and said, 'This means that God has granted life-giving repentance to
the Gentiles also.'

a Some witnesses read we were.   *b Some witnesses add* making no distinctions;
others add without any misgiving, *as in 10. 20.*

MEANWHILE THOSE who had been scattered after the persecution that 19
arose over Stephen made their way to Phoenicia, Cyprus, and Antioch,
bringing the message to Jews only and to no others. But there were some 20
natives of Cyprus and Cyrene among them, and these, when they arrived
at Antioch, began to speak to Gentiles as well, telling them the good news
of the Lord Jesus. The power of the Lord was with them, and a great many 21
became believers, and turned to the Lord.

The news reached the ears of the church in Jerusalem; and they sent 22
Barnabas to Antioch. When he arrived and saw the divine grace at work, 23
he rejoiced, and encouraged them all to hold fast to the Lord with resolute
hearts; for he was a good man, full of the Holy Spirit and of faith. And 24
large numbers were won over to the Lord.

He then went off to Tarsus to look for Saul; and when he had found 25 26
him, he brought him to Antioch. For a whole year the two of them lived
in fellowship with the congregation there, and gave instruction to large
numbers. It was in Antioch that the disciples first got the name of
Christians.

During this period some prophets came down from Jerusalem to Antioch. 27
One of them, Agabus by name, was inspired to stand up and predict a 28
severe and world-wide famine, which in fact occurred in the reign of
Claudius. So the disciples agreed to make a contribution, each according 29
to his means, for the relief of their fellow-Christians in Judaea. This they 30
did, and sent it off to the elders, in the charge of Barnabas and Saul.

IT WAS ABOUT THIS TIME that King Herod attacked certain members **12**
of the church. He beheaded James, the brother of John, and then, when 2 3
he saw that the Jews approved, proceeded to arrest Peter also. This
happened during the festival of Unleavened Bread. Having secured him, 4
he put him in prison under a military guard, four squads of four men each,
meaning to produce him in public after Passover. So Peter was kept in 5
prison under constant watch, while the church kept praying fervently for
him to God.

On the very night before Herod had planned to bring him forward, 6
Peter was asleep between two soldiers, secured by two chains, while outside the doors sentries kept guard over the prison. All at once an angel of 7
the Lord stood there, and the cell was ablaze with light. He tapped Peter
on the shoulder and woke him. 'Quick! Get up', he said, and the chains fell
away from his wrists. The angel then said to him, 'Do up your belt and put 8
your sandals on.' He did so. 'Now wrap your cloak round you and follow
me.' He followed him out, with no idea that the angel's intervention was 9
real: he thought it was just a vision. But they passed the first guard-post, 10
then the second, and reached the iron gate leading out into the city, which
opened for them of its own accord. And so they came out and walked the
length of one street; and the angel left him.

Then Peter came to himself. 'Now I know it is true,' he said; 'the Lord 11
has sent his angel and rescued me from Herod's clutches and from all that
the Jewish people were expecting.' When he realized how things stood, 12
he made for the house of Mary, the mother of John Mark, where a large

13 company was at prayer. He knocked at the outer door and a maid called
14 Rhoda came to answer it. She recognized Peter's voice and was so overjoyed
that instead of opening the door she ran in and announced that Peter was
15 standing outside. 'You are crazy', they told her; but she insisted that it was
so. Then they said, 'It must be his guardian angel.'

16 Meanwhile Peter went on knocking, and when they opened the door and
17 saw him, they were astounded. With a movement of the hand he signed to
them to keep quiet, and told them how the Lord had brought him out of
prison. 'Report this to James and the members of the church', he said.
Then he left the house and went off elsewhere.

18 When morning came, there was consternation among the soldiers: what
19 could have become of Peter? Herod made close search, but failed to find
him, so he interrogated the guards and ordered their execution.

20 Afterwards he left Judaea to reside for a time at Caesarea. He had for some
time been furiously angry with the people of Tyre and Sidon, who now by
common agreement presented themselves at his court. There they won
over Blastus the royal chamberlain, and sued for peace, because their
21 country drew its supplies from the king's territory. So, on an appointed
day, attired in his royal robes and seated on the rostrum, Herod harangued
22 them; and the populace shouted back, 'It is a god speaking, not a man!'
23 Instantly an angel of the Lord struck him down, because he had usurped
the honour due to God; he was eaten up with worms and died.

24 Meanwhile the word of God continued to grow and spread.

25 Barnabas and Saul, their task fulfilled, returned from Jerusalem,*a* taking
John Mark with them.

The church breaks barriers

13 THERE WERE AT ANTIOCH, in the congregation there, certain prophets
and teachers: Barnabas, Simeon called Niger, Lucius of Cyrene,
2 Manaen, who had been at the court of Prince Herod, and Saul. While they
were keeping a fast and offering worship to the Lord, the Holy Spirit said,
'Set Barnabas and Saul apart for me, to do the work to which I have called
3 them.' Then, after further fasting and prayer, they laid their hands on
them and let them go.

4 So these two, sent out on their mission by the Holy Spirit, came down to
5 Seleucia, and from there sailed to Cyprus. Arriving at Salamis, they
declared the word of God in the Jewish synagogues. They had John with
6 them as their assistant. They went through the whole island as far as
Paphos, and there they came upon a sorcerer, a Jew who posed as a prophet,
7 Bar-Jesus by name. He was in the retinue of the Governor, Sergius Paulus,
an intelligent man, who had sent for Barnabas and Saul and wanted to
8 hear the word of God. This Elymas the sorcerer (so his name may be
translated) opposed them, trying to turn the Governor away from the
9 Faith. But Saul, also known as Paul, filled with the Holy Spirit, fixed his

a Some witnesses read their task fulfilled, returned to Jerusalem; *or, as it might be rendered,*
their task at Jerusalem fulfilled, returned.

eyes on him and said, 'You swindler, you rascal, son of the devil and enemy 10
of all goodness, will you never stop falsifying the straight ways of the Lord?
Look now, the hand of the Lord strikes: you shall be blind, and for a time 11
you shall not see the sunlight.' Instantly mist and darkness came over him
and he groped about for someone to lead him by the hand. When the 12
Governor saw what had happened he became a believer, deeply impressed
by what he learned about the Lord.

Leaving Paphos, Paul and his companions went by sea to Perga in Pam- 13
phylia; John, however, left them and returned to Jerusalem. From Perga 14
they continued their journey as far as Pisidian Antioch. On the Sabbath
they went to synagogue and took their seats; and after the readings from 15
the Law and the prophets, the officials of the synagogue sent this message to
them: 'Friends, if you have anything to say to the people by way of exhortation, let us hear it.' Paul rose, made a gesture with his hand, and began: 16

'Men of Israel and you who worship our God, listen to me! The God 17
of this people of Israel chose our fathers. When they were still living as
aliens in Egypt he made them into a nation and brought them out of that
country with arm outstretched. For some forty years he bore with their 18
conduct[a] in the desert. Then in the Canaanite country he overthrew seven 19
nations, whose lands he gave them to be their heritage for some four 20
hundred and fifty years, and afterwards appointed judges for them until
the time of the prophet Samuel.

'Then they asked for a king and God gave them Saul the son of Kish, 21
a man of the tribe of Benjamin, who reigned for forty years. Then he 22
removed him and set up David as their king, giving him his approval in
these words: "I have found David son of Jesse to be a man after my own
heart, who will carry out all my purposes." This is the man from whose 23
posterity God, as he promised, has brought Israel a saviour, Jesus. John 24
made ready for his coming by proclaiming baptism as a token of repentance to the whole people of Israel. And when John was nearing the end of 25
his course, he said, "I am not what you think I am. No, after me comes one
whose shoes I am not fit to unfasten."

'My brothers, you who come of the stock of Abraham, and others 26
among you who revere our God, we are the people to whom the message
of this salvation has been sent. The people of Jerusalem and their rulers 27
did not recognize him, or understand the words of the prophets which are
read Sabbath by Sabbath; indeed they fulfilled them by condemning him.
Though they failed to find grounds for the sentence of death, they asked 28
Pilate to have him executed. And when they had carried out all that the 29
scriptures said about him, they took him down from the gibbet and laid
him in a tomb. But God raised him from the dead; and there was a period 30 31
of many days during which he appeared to those who had come up with
him from Galilee to Jerusalem.

'They are now his witnesses before our nation; and we are here to give 32
you the good news that God, who made the promise to the fathers, has
fulfilled it for the children[b] by raising Jesus from the dead, as indeed it 33

---

a Some witnesses read he sustained them.   *b Some witnesses read* our children; *others*
read us their children.

stands written, in the second *a* Psalm: "You are my son; this day I have
34 begotten you." Again, that he raised him from the dead, never again to
revert to corruption, he declares in these words: "I will give you the bless-
35 ings promised to David, holy and sure." This is borne out by another
36 passage: "Thou wilt not let thy loyal servant suffer corruption." As for
David, when he had served the purpose of God in his own generation, he
37 died, and was gathered to his fathers, and suffered corruption; but the one
38 whom God raised up did not suffer corruption; and you must understand,
my brothers, that it is through him that forgiveness of sins is now being
39 proclaimed to you. It is through him that everyone who has faith is acquitted
of everything for which there was no acquittal under the Law of Moses.
40 Beware, then, lest you bring down upon yourselves the doom proclaimed
41 by the prophets: "See this, you scoffers, wonder, and begone; for I am
doing a deed in your days, a deed which you will never believe when you
are told of it." '

42   As they were leaving the synagogue they were asked to come again and
43 speak on these subjects next Sabbath; and after the congregation had dispersed, many Jews and gentile worshippers went along with Paul and
Barnabas, who spoke to them and urged them to hold fast to the grace
of God.

44   On the following Sabbath almost the whole city gathered to hear the
45 word of God. When the Jews saw the crowds, they were filled with jealous
46 resentment, and contradicted what Paul said, with violent abuse. But Paul
and Barnabas were outspoken in their reply. 'It was necessary', they said,
'that the word of God should be declared to you first. But since you reject
it and thus condemn yourselves as unworthy of eternal life, we now turn
47 to the Gentiles. For these are our instructions from the Lord: "I have
appointed you to be a light for the Gentiles, and a means of salvation to
48 earth's farthest bounds." ' When the Gentiles heard this, they were overjoyed and thankfully acclaimed the word of the Lord, and those who were
49 marked out for eternal life became believers. So the word of the Lord
50 spread far and wide through the region. But the Jews stirred up feeling
among the women of standing who were worshippers, and among the
leading men of the city; a persecution was started against Paul and
51 Barnabas, and they were expelled from the district. So they shook the dust
52 off their feet in protest against them and went to Iconium. And the converts were filled with joy and with the Holy Spirit.

14   At Iconium similarly they went *b* into the Jewish synagogue and spoke to
such purpose that a large body both of Jews and Gentiles became believers.
2 But the unconverted Jews stirred up the Gentiles and poisoned their minds
3 against the Christians. For some time Paul and Barnabas stayed on and
spoke boldly and openly in reliance on the Lord; and he confirmed the
message of his grace by causing signs and miracles to be worked at their
4 hands. The mass of the townspeople were divided, some siding with the
5 Jews, others with the apostles. But when a move was made by Gentiles and
Jews together, with the connivance of the city authorities, to maltreat
6 them and stone them, they got wind of it and made their escape to the

---

a Some witnesses read first.   *b Or* At Iconium they went together . . .

Lycaonian cities of Lystra and Derbe and the surrounding country, where 7 they continued to spread the good news.

At Lystra sat a crippled man, lame from birth, who had never walked in 8 his life. This man listened while Paul was speaking. Paul fixed his eyes on 9 him and saw that he had the faith to be cured, so he said to him in a loud 10 voice, 'Stand up straight on your feet'; and he sprang up and started to walk. When the crowds saw what Paul had done, they shouted, in their 11 native Lycaonian, 'The gods have come down to us in human form.' And 12 they called Barnabas Jupiter, and Paul they called Mercury, because he was the spokesman. And the priest of Jupiter, whose temple was just out- 13 side the city, brought oxen and garlands to the gates, and he and all the people were about to offer sacrifice.

But when the apostles Barnabas and Paul heard of it, they tore their 14 clothes and rushed into the crowd shouting, 'Men, what is this that you 15 are doing? We are only human beings, no less mortal than you. The good news we bring tells you to turn from these follies to the living God, who made heaven and earth and sea and everything in them. In past ages he 16 allowed all nations to go their own way; and yet he has not left you without 17 some clue to his nature, in the kindness he shows: he sends you rain from heaven and crops in their seasons, and gives you food and good cheer in plenty.'

With these words they barely managed to prevent the crowd from offer- 18 ing sacrifice to them.

Then Jews from Antioch and Iconium came on the scene and won over 19 the crowds. They stoned Paul, and dragged him out of the city, thinking him dead. The converts formed a ring round him, and he got to his feet 20 and went into the city. Next day he left with Barnabas for Derbe.

After bringing the good news to that town, where they gained many 21 converts, they returned to Lystra, then to Iconium, and then to Antioch, heartening the converts and encouraging them to be true to their religion. 22 They warned them that to enter the kingdom of God we must pass through many hardships. They also appointed elders for them in each congrega- 23 tion, and with prayer and fasting committed them to the Lord in whom they had put their faith.

Then they passed through Pisidia and came into Pamphylia. When they 24 25 had given the message at Perga, they went down to Attalia, and from there 26 set sail for Antioch, where they had originally been commended to the grace of God for the task which they had now completed. When they arrived 27 and had called the congregation together, they reported all that God had done through them, and how he had thrown open the gates of faith to the Gentiles. And they stayed for some time with the disciples there. 28

NOW CERTAIN PERSONS who had come down from Judaea began to 15 teach the brotherhood that those who were not circumcised in accordance with Mosaic practice could not be saved. That brought them into fierce 2 dissension and controversy with Paul and Barnabas. And so it was arranged that these two and some others from Antioch should go up to Jerusalem to see the apostles and elders about this question.

3   They were sent on their way by the congregation, and travelled through Phoenicia and Samaria, telling the full story of the conversion of the Gentiles. The news caused great rejoicing among all the Christians there.

4   When they reached Jerusalem they were welcomed by the church and the apostles and elders, and reported all that God had done through them.

5 Then some of the Pharisaic party who had become believers came forward and said, 'They must be circumcised and told to keep the Law of Moses.'

6 7   The apostles and elders held a meeting to look into this matter; and, after a long debate, Peter rose and addressed them. 'My friends,' he said, 'in the early days, as you yourselves know, God made his choice among you and ordained that from my lips the Gentiles should hear and believe

8 the message of the Gospel. And God, who can read men's minds, showed his approval of them by giving the Holy Spirit to them, as he did to us.

9 He made no difference between them and us; for he purified their hearts

10 by faith. Then why do you now provoke God by laying on the shoulders of these converts a yoke which neither we nor our fathers were able to

11 bear? No, we believe that it is by the grace of the Lord Jesus that we are saved, and so are they.'

12   At that the whole company fell silent and listened to Barnabas and Paul as they told of all the signs and miracles that God had worked among the Gentiles through them.

13   When they had finished speaking, James summed up: 'My friends,' he

14 said, 'listen to me. Simeon has told how it first happened that God took notice of the Gentiles, to choose from among them a people to bear his

15 name; and this agrees with the words of the prophets, as Scripture has it:

16   "Thereafter I will return and rebuild the fallen house of David;
      even from its ruins I will rebuild it, and set it up again,

17   that they may seek the Lord—all the rest of mankind,
    and the Gentiles, whom I have claimed for my own.
    Thus says the Lord, whose work it is,

18   made known long ago."

19   'My judgement therefore is that we should impose no irksome restric-

20 tions on those of the Gentiles who are turning to God, but instruct them by letter to abstain from things polluted by contact with idols, from fornica-

21 tion, from anything that has been strangled, and from blood.*a* Moses, after all, has never lacked spokesmen in every town for generations past; he is read in the synagogues Sabbath by Sabbath.'

22   Then the apostles and elders, with the agreement of the whole church, resolved to choose representatives and send them to Antioch with Paul and Barnabas. They chose two leading men in the community, Judas Barsabbas

23 and Silas, and gave them this letter to deliver:
    'We, the apostles and elders, send greetings as brothers to our brothers

24 of gentile origin in Antioch, Syria, and Cilicia. Forasmuch as we have heard that some of our number, without any instructions from us, have *b*

---

a Some witnesses omit from fornication; *others omit* from anything that has been strangled; *some add (after* blood) and to refrain from doing to others what they would not like done to themselves.   *b Some witnesses read* have gone out and . . .

disturbed you with their talk and unsettled your minds, we have resolved 25
unanimously to send to you our chosen representatives with our well-
beloved Barnabas and Paul, who have devoted themselves to the cause of 26
our Lord Jesus Christ. We are therefore sending Judas and Silas, who will 27
themselves confirm this by word of mouth. It is the decision of the Holy 28
Spirit, and our decision, to lay no further burden upon you beyond these
essentials: you are to abstain from meat that has been offered to idols, from 29
blood, from anything that has been strangled,*a* and from fornication.*b* If
you keep yourselves free from these things you will be doing right.
Farewell.'

So they were sent off on their journey and travelled down to Antioch, 30
where they called the congregation together, and delivered the letter.
When it was read, they all rejoiced at the encouragement it brought. Judas 31 32
and Silas, who were prophets themselves, said much to encourage and
strengthen the members, and, after spending some time there, were dis- 33
missed with the good wishes of the brethren, to return to those who had
sent them.*c* But Paul and Barnabas stayed on at Antioch, and there, along 35
with many others, they taught and preached the word of the Lord.

Paul leads the advance

AFTER A WHILE Paul said to Barnabas, 'Ought we not to go back now 36
to see how our brothers are faring in the various towns where we
proclaimed the word of the Lord?' Barnabas wanted to take John Mark 37
with them; but Paul judged that the man who had deserted them in 38
Pamphylia and had not gone on to share in their work was not the man to
take with them now. The dispute was so sharp that they parted company. 39
Barnabas took Mark with him and sailed for Cyprus, while Paul chose Silas. 40
He started on his journey, commended by the brothers to the grace of the
Lord, and travelled through Syria and Cilicia bringing new strength to the 41
congregations.

He went on to Derbe and to Lystra, and there he found a disciple named **16**
Timothy, the son of a Jewish Christian mother and a Gentile father. He 2
was well spoken of by the Christians at Lystra and Iconium, and Paul 3
wanted to have him in his company when he left the place. So he took him
and circumcised him, out of consideration for the Jews who lived in those
parts; for they all knew that his father was a Gentile. As they made their 4
way from town to town they handed on the decisions taken by the apostles
and elders in Jerusalem and enjoined their observance. And so, day by day, 5
the congregations grew stronger in faith and increased in numbers.

They travelled through the Phrygian and Galatian region,*d* because 6
they were prevented by the Holy Spirit from delivering the message in
the province of Asia; and when they approached the Mysian border they 7

a Some witnesses omit from anything that has been strangled.   *b Some witnesses*
omit and from fornication; *and some add* and refrain from doing to others what you would
not like done to yourselves.   *c Some witnesses add* (34) But Silas decided to
remain there.   *d Or* through Phrygia and the Galatian region.

8 tried to enter Bithynia; but the Spirit of Jesus would not allow them, so
9 they skirted*ᵃ* Mysia and reached the coast at Troas. During the night a
   vision came to Paul: a Macedonian stood there appealing to him and say-
10 ing, 'Come across to Macedonia and help us.' After he had seen this vision
   we at once set about getting a passage to Macedonia, concluding that God
   had called us to bring them the good news.

11   So we sailed from Troas and made a straight run to Samothrace, the
12 next day to Neapolis, and from there to Philippi, a city of the first rank in
   that district of Macedonia, and a Roman colony. Here we stayed for some
13 days, and on the Sabbath day we went outside the city gate by the riverside, where we thought there would be a place of prayer,*ᵇ* and sat down and
14 talked to the women who had gathered there. One of them named Lydia,
   a dealer in purple fabric from the city of Thyatira, who was a worshipper
   of God, was listening, and the Lord opened her heart to respond to what
15 Paul said. She was baptized, and her household with her, and then she said
   to us, 'If you have judged me to be a believer in the Lord, I beg you to come
   and stay in my house.' And she insisted on our going.

16   Once, when we were on our way to the place of prayer, we met a slave-
   girl who was possessed by an oracular spirit and brought large profits to
17 her owners by telling fortunes. She followed Paul and the rest of us, shouting, 'These men are servants of the Supreme God, and are declaring to you
18 a way of salvation.' She did this day after day, until Paul could bear it no
   longer. Rounding on the spirit he said, 'I command you in the name of
   Jesus Christ to come out of her', and it went out there and then.

19   When the girl's owners saw that their hope of gain had gone, they seized
   Paul and Silas and dragged them to the city authorities in the main square;
20 and bringing them before the magistrates, they said, 'These men are
21 causing a disturbance in our city; they are Jews; they are advocating
22 customs which it is illegal for us Romans to adopt and follow.' The mob
   joined in the attack; and the magistrates tore off the prisoners' clothes and
23 ordered them to be flogged. After giving them a severe beating they flung
   them into prison and ordered the jailer to keep them under close guard.
24 In view of these orders, he put them in the inner prison and secured their
   feet in the stocks.

25   About midnight Paul and Silas, at their prayers, were singing praises to
26 God, and the other prisoners were listening, when suddenly there was such
   a violent earthquake that the foundations of the jail were shaken; all the
27 doors burst open and all the prisoners found their fetters unfastened. The
   jailer woke up to see the prison doors wide open, and assuming that the
28 prisoners had escaped, drew his sword intending to kill himself. But Paul
29 shouted, 'Do yourself no harm; we are all here.' The jailer called for lights,
   rushed in and threw himself down before Paul and Silas, trembling with
30 fear. He then escorted them out and said, 'Masters, what must I do to be
31 saved?' They said, 'Put your trust in the Lord Jesus, and you will be saved,
32 you and your household.' Then they spoke the word of the Lord*ᶜ* to him
33 and to everyone in his house. At that late hour of the night he took them

---

ᵃ Possibly traversed.   *ᵇ Some witnesses read* where there was a recognized place
of prayer.   *ᶜ Some witnesses read* of God.

and washed their wounds; and immediately afterwards he and his whole
family were baptized. He brought them into his house, set out a meal, and   34
rejoiced with his whole household in his new-found faith in God.

When daylight came the magistrates sent their officers with instructions   35
to release the men. The jailer reported the message to Paul: 'The magistrates   36
have sent word that you are to be released. So now you may go free, and
blessings on your journey.'ᵃ But Paul said to the officers: 'They gave us a   37
public flogging, though we are Roman citizens and have not been found
guilty; they threw us into prison, and are they now to smuggle us out
privately? No indeed! Let them come in person and escort us out.' The   38
officers reported his words. The magistrates were alarmed to hear that they
were Roman citizens, and came and apologized to them. Then they   39
escorted them out and requested them to go away from the city. On leaving   40
the prison, they went to Lydia's house, where they met their fellow-
Christians, and spoke words of encouragement to them; then they departed.

THEY NOW TRAVELLED by way of Amphipolis and Apollonia and   **17**
came to Thessalonica, where there was a Jewish synagogue. Following his   2
usual practice Paul went to their meetings; and for the next three Sabbaths
he argued with them, quoting texts of Scripture which he expounded and   3
applied to show that the Messiah had to suffer and rise from the dead.
'And this Jesus,' he said, 'whom I am proclaiming to you, is the Messiah.'
Some of them were convinced and joined Paul and Silas; so did a great   4
number of godfearing Gentiles and a good many influential women.ᵇ

But the Jews in their jealousy recruited some low fellows from the dregs   5
of the populace, roused the rabble, and had the city in an uproar. They
mobbed Jason's house, with the intention of bringing Paul and Silas before
the town assembly. Failing to find them, they dragged Jason himself and   6
some members of the congregation before the magistrates, shouting, 'The
men who have made trouble all over the world have now come here; and   7
Jason has harboured them. They all flout the Emperor's laws, and assert
that there is a rival king, Jesus.' These words caused a great commotion in   8
the mob, which affected the magistrates also. They bound over Jason and   9
the others, and let them go.

As soon as darkness fell, the members of the congregation sent Paul and   10
Silas off to Beroea. On arrival, they made their way to the synagogue. The   11
Jews here were more civil than those at Thessalonica: they received the
message with great eagerness, studying the scriptures every day to see
whether it was as they said. Many of them therefore became believers,   12
and so did a fair number of Gentiles, women of standing as well as men.
But when the Thessalonian Jews learned that the word of God had now   13
been proclaimed by Paul in Beroea, they came on there to stir up trouble
and rouse the rabble. Thereupon the members of the congregation sent   14
Paul off at once to go down to the coast, while Silas and Timothy both
stayed behind. Paul's escort brought him as far as Athens, and came away   15
with instructions for Silas and Timothy to rejoin him with all speed.

a Some witnesses read . . . free and take your journey.   *b Some witnesses read* a good
many wives of leading men.

16 Now while Paul was waiting for them at Athens he was exasperated to see
17 how the city was full of idols. So he argued in the synagogue with the Jews
and gentile worshippers, and also in the city square every day with casual
18 passers-by. And some of the Epicurean and Stoic philosophers joined
issue with him. Some said, 'What can this charlatan be trying to say?';
others, 'He would appear to be a propagandist for foreign deities'—this
19 because he was preaching about Jesus and Resurrection. So they took him
and brought him before the Court of Areopagus*a* and said, 'May we know
20 what this new doctrine is that you propound? You are introducing ideas
that sound strange to us, and we should like to know what they mean.'
21 (Now the Athenians in general and the foreigners there had no time for
anything but talking or hearing about the latest novelty.)

22   Then Paul stood up before the Court of Areopagus*b* and said: 'Men of
Athens, I see that in everything that concerns religion you are uncommonly
23 scrupulous. For as I was going round looking at the objects of your worship,
I noticed among other things an altar bearing the inscription "To an Unknown God". What you worship but do not know—this is what I now
proclaim.

24   'The God who created the world and everything in it, and who is Lord
25 of heaven and earth, does not live in shrines made by men. It is not because
he lacks anything that he accepts service at men's hands, for he is himself
26 the universal giver of life and breath and all else. He created every race of
men of one stock, to inhabit the whole earth's surface. He fixed the epochs
27 of their history*c* and the limits of their territory. They were to seek God,
and, it might be, touch and find him; though indeed he is not far from each
28 one of us, for in him we live and move, in him we exist; as some of your own
29 poets*d* have said, "We are also his offspring." As God's offspring, then,
we ought not to suppose that the deity is like an image in gold or silver or
30 stone, shaped by human craftsmanship and design. As for the times of
ignorance, God has overlooked them; but now he commands mankind, all
31 men everywhere, to repent, because he has fixed the day on which he will
have the world judged, and justly judged, by a man of his choosing; of this
he has given assurance to all by raising him from the dead.'

32   When they heard about the raising of the dead, some scoffed; and others
33 said, 'We will hear you on this subject some other time.' And so Paul left
34 the assembly. However, some men joined him and became believers,
including Dionysius, a member of the Court of Areopagus; also a woman
named Damaris, and others besides.

18 1 2   After this he left Athens and went to Corinth. There he fell in with a Jew
named Aquila, a native of Pontus, and his wife Priscilla; he had recently
arrived from Italy because Claudius had issued an edict that all Jews should
3 leave Rome. Paul approached them and, because he was of the same trade,
he made his home with them, and they carried on business together; they
4 were tent-makers. He also held discussions in the synagogue Sabbath by
Sabbath, trying to convince both Jews and Gentiles.

5   Then Silas and Timothy came down from Macedonia, and Paul devoted

---

a Or brought him to Mars' Hill.   *b Or* in the middle of Mars' Hill.   *c Or* fixed
the ordered seasons . . .   *d Some witnesses read* some among you.

himself entirely to preaching, affirming before the Jews that the Messiah
was Jesus. But when they opposed him and resorted to abuse, he shook out 6
the skirts of his cloak and said to them, 'Your blood be on your own heads!
My conscience is clear; now I shall go to the Gentiles.' With that he left, 7
and went to the house of a worshipper of God named Titius Justus, who
lived next door to the synagogue. Crispus, who held office in the synagogue, 8
now became a believer in the Lord, with all his household; and a number
of Corinthians listened and believed, and were baptized. One night in a 9
vision the Lord said to Paul, 'Have no fear: go on with your preaching and
do not be silenced, for I am with you and no one shall attempt to do you 10
harm;*a* and there are many in this city who are my people.' So he settled 11
down for eighteen months, teaching the word of God among them.

But when Gallio was proconsul of Achaia, the Jews set upon Paul in a 12
body and brought him into court. 'This man', they said, 'is inducing people 13
to worship God in ways that are against the law.' Paul was just about to 14
speak when Gallio said to them, 'If it had been a question of crime or grave
misdemeanour, I should, of course, have given you Jews a patient hearing,
but if it is some bickering about words and names and your Jewish law, 15
you may see to it yourselves; I have no mind to be a judge of these matters.'
And he had them ejected from the court. Then there was a general attack 16 17
on Sosthenes, who held office in the synagogue, and they gave him a beating in full view of the bench. But all this left Gallio quite unconcerned.

Paul stayed on for some time, and then took leave of the brotherhood 18
and set sail for Syria, accompanied by Priscilla and Aquila. At Cenchreae
he had his hair cut off, because he was under a vow. When they reached 19
Ephesus he parted from them and went himself into the synagogue, where
he held a discussion with the Jews. He was asked to stay longer, but declined 20
and set out from Ephesus, saying, as he took leave of them, 'I shall come 21
back to you if it is God's will.' On landing at Caesarea, he went up and 22
paid his respects to the church, and then went down to Antioch. After 23
spending some time there, he set out again and made a journey through the
Galatian country and on through Phrygia, bringing new strength to all
the converts.

NOW THERE ARRIVED at Ephesus a Jew named Apollos, an Alexandrian 24
by birth, an eloquent man,*b* powerful in his use of the scriptures. He had 25
been instructed in the way of the Lord and was full of spiritual fervour;
and in his discourses he taught accurately the facts about Jesus,*c* though
he knew only John's baptism. He now began to speak boldly in the syna- 26
gogue, where Priscilla and Aquila heard him; they took him in hand and
expounded the new way*d* to him in greater detail. Finding that he wished 27
to go across to Achaia, the brotherhood gave him their support, and wrote
to the congregation there to make him welcome. From the time of his
arrival, he was very helpful to those who had by God's grace become
believers; for he strenuously confuted the Jews, demonstrating publicly 28
from the scriptures that the Messiah is Jesus.

a Or and you will not be harmed by anyone's attacks.   *b Or a learned man.*
c Some witnesses read about the Lord.   *d Some witnesses read the way of God.*

19 While Apollos was at Corinth, Paul travelled through the inland regions
2 till he came to Ephesus. There he found a number of converts, to whom he
said, 'Did you receive the Holy Spirit when you became believers?' 'No,'
3 they replied, 'we have not even heard that there is a Holy Spirit.' He said,
'Then what baptism were you given?' 'John's baptism', they answered.
4 Paul then said, 'The baptism that John gave was a baptism in token of
repentance, and he told the people to put their trust in one who was to
5 come after him, that is, in Jesus.' On hearing this they were baptized into
6 the name of the Lord Jesus; and when Paul had laid his hands on them, the
Holy Spirit came upon them and they spoke in tongues of ecstasy and
7 prophesied. Altogether they were about a dozen men.
8 During the next three months he attended the synagogue and, using
argument and persuasion, spoke boldly and freely about the kingdom of
9 God. But when some proved obdurate and would not believe, speaking
evil of the new way before the whole congregation, he left them, withdrew
his converts, and continued to hold discussions daily in the lecture-hall
10 of Tyrannus. This went on for two years, with the result that the whole
population of the province of Asia, both Jews and Gentiles, heard the word
11 12 of the Lord. And through Paul God worked singular miracles: when
handkerchiefs and scarves which had been in contact with his skin were
carried to the sick, they were rid of their diseases and the evil spirits came
out of them.
13 But some strolling Jewish exorcists tried their hand at using the name
of the Lord Jesus on those possessed by evil spirits; they would say, 'I
14 adjure you by Jesus whom Paul proclaims.' There were seven sons of
15 Sceva, a Jewish chief priest, who were using this method, when the evil
spirit answered back and said, 'Jesus I acknowledge, and I know about
16 Paul, but who are you?' And the man with the evil spirit flew at them, overpowered them all, and handled them with such violence that they ran out
17 of the house stripped and battered. This became known to everybody in
Ephesus, whether Jew or Gentile; they were all awestruck, and the name
18 of the Lord Jesus gained in honour. Moreover many of those who had
become believers came and openly confessed that they had been using
19 magical spells. And a good many of those who formerly practised magic
collected their books and burnt them publicly. The total value was reckoned
20 up and it came to fifty thousand pieces of silver. In such ways the word of
the Lord showed its power, spreading more and more widely and effec-
tively.
21 When things had reached this stage, Paul made up his mind[a] to visit
Macedonia and Achaia and then go on to Jerusalem; and he said, 'After I
22 have been there, I must see Rome also.' So he sent two of his assistants,
Timothy and Erastus, to Macedonia, while he himself stayed some time
longer in the province of Asia.
23 Now about that time, the Christian movement gave rise to a serious dis-
24 turbance. There was a man named Demetrius, a silversmith who made
silver shrines of Diana and provided a great deal of employment for the
25 craftsmen. He called a meeting of these men and the workers in allied

---

a Or Paul, led by the Spirit, resolved . . .

trades, and addressed them. 'Men,' he said, 'you know that our high standard of living depends on this industry. And you see and hear how this 26 fellow Paul with his propaganda has perverted crowds of people, not only at Ephesus but also in practically the whole of the province of Asia. He is telling them that gods made by human hands are not gods at all. There is 27 danger for us here; it is not only that our line of business will be discredited, but also that the sanctuary of the great goddess Diana will cease to command respect; and then it will not be long before she who is worshipped by all Asia and the civilized world is brought down from her divine pre-eminence.'

When they heard this they were roused to fury and shouted, 'Great is 28 Diana of the Ephesians!' The whole city was in confusion; they seized 29 Paul's travelling-companions, the Macedonians Gaius and Aristarchus, and made a concerted rush with them into the theatre. Paul wanted to 30 appear before the assembly but the other Christians would not let him. Even some of the dignitaries of the province, who were friendly towards 31 him, sent and urged him not to venture into the theatre. Meanwhile some 32 were shouting one thing, some another; for the assembly was in confusion and most of them did not know what they had all come for. But some of the 33 crowd explained the trouble to Alexander, whom the Jews had pushed to the front, and he, motioning for silence, attempted to make a defence before the assembly. But when they recognized that he was a Jew, a single 34 cry arose from them all: for about two hours they kept on shouting, 'Great is Diana of the Ephesians!'

The town clerk, however, quieted the crowd. 'Men of Ephesus,' he said, 35 'all the world knows that our city of Ephesus is temple-warden of the great Diana and of that symbol of her which fell from heaven. Since these facts 36 are beyond dispute, your proper course is to keep quiet and do nothing rash. These men whom you have brought here as culprits have committed 37 no sacrilege and uttered no blasphemy against our goddess. If therefore 38 Demetrius and his craftsmen have a case against anyone, assizes are held and there are such people as proconsuls; let the parties bring their charges and countercharges. If, on the other hand, you have some further question 39 to raise, it will be dealt with in the statutory assembly. We certainly run the 40 risk of being charged with riot for this day's work. There is no justification for it, and if the issue is raised we shall be unable to give any explanation of this uproar.' With that he dismissed the assembly.   41

WHEN THE DISTURBANCE had ceased, Paul sent for the disciples and, **20** after encouraging them, said good-bye and set out on his journey to Macedonia. He travelled through those parts of the country, often speaking 2 words of encouragement to the Christians there, and so came into Greece. When he had spent three months there and was on the point of embarking 3 for Syria, a plot was laid against him by the Jews, so he decided to return by way of Macedonia. He was accompanied by Sopater son of Pyrrhus, 4 from Beroea, the Thessalonians Aristarchus and Secundus, Gaius the Doberian*a* and Timothy, and the Asians Tychicus and Trophimus. These 5

***

a Some witnesses read the Derbaean.

6   went ahead and waited for us at Troas; we ourselves set sail from Philippi after the Passover season,[a] and in five days reached them at Troas, where we spent a week.

7   On the Saturday night, in our assembly for the breaking of bread, Paul, who was to leave next day, addressed them, and went on speaking until mid-
8   night. Now there were many lamps in the upper room where we were
9   assembled; and a youth named Eutychus, who was sitting on the window-ledge, grew more and more sleepy as Paul went on talking. At last he was completely overcome by sleep, fell from the third storey to the ground,
10 and was picked up for dead. Paul went down, threw himself upon him, seizing him in his arms, and said to them, 'Stop this commotion; there is
11 still life in him.' He then went upstairs, broke bread and ate, and after
12 much conversation, which lasted until dawn, he departed. And they took the boy away alive and were immensely comforted.

13 We went ahead to the ship and sailed for Assos, where we were to take Paul aboard. He had made this arrangement, as he was going to travel by
14 road. When he met us at Assos, we took him aboard and went on to Mity-
15 lene. Next day we sailed from there and arrived opposite Chios, and on the second day we made Samos. On the following day[b] we reached Miletus.
16 For Paul had decided to pass by Ephesus and so avoid having to spend time in the province of Asia; he was eager to be in Jerusalem, if he possibly
17 could, on the day of Pentecost. He did, however, send from Miletus to
18 Ephesus and summon the elders of the congregation; and when they joined him, he spoke as follows:

'You know how, from the day that I first set foot in the province of Asia,
19 for the whole time that I was with you, I served the Lord in all humility amid the sorrows and trials that came upon me through the machinations
20 of the Jews. You know that I kept back nothing that was for your good: I delivered the message to you; I taught you, in public and in your homes;
21 with Jews and Gentiles alike I insisted on repentance before God and
22 trust in our Lord Jesus. And now, as you see, I am on my way to Jerusalem, under the constraint of the Spirit.[c] Of what will befall me there I know
23 nothing, except that in city after city the Holy Spirit assures me that
24 imprisonment and hardships await me. For myself, I set no store by life; I only want to finish the race, and complete the task which the Lord Jesus assigned to me, of bearing my testimony to the gospel of God's grace.

25 'One word more: I have gone about among you proclaiming the King-
26 dom, but now I know that none of you will see my face again. That being
27 so, I here and now declare that no man's fate can be laid at my door; for I have kept back nothing; I have disclosed to you the whole purpose of
28 God. Keep watch over yourselves and over all the flock of which the Holy Spirit has given you charge, as shepherds of the church of the Lord,[d]
29 which he won for himself by his own blood.[e] I know that when I am gone,
30 savage wolves will come in among you and will not spare the flock. Even

---

[a] *Literally* after the days of Unleavened Bread.   [b] *Some witnesses read* . . . Samos, and, after stopping at Trogyllium, on the following day . . .   [c] *Or* under an inner compulsion.   [d] *Some witnesses read* of God.   [e] *Or, according to some witnesses,* by the blood of his Own.

from your own body there will be men coming forward who will distort the truth to induce the disciples to break away and follow them. So be on 31 the alert; remember how for three years, night and day, I never ceased to counsel each of you, and how I wept over you.

'And now I commend you to God and to his gracious word, which has 32 power to build you up and give you your heritage among all who are dedicated to him. I have not wanted anyone's money or clothes for myself; 33 you all know that these hands of mine earned enough for the needs of my- 34 self and my companions. I showed you that it is our duty to help the weak 35 in this way, by hard work, and that we should keep in mind the words of the Lord Jesus, who himself said, "Happiness lies more in giving than in receiving." '

As he finished speaking, he knelt down with them all and prayed. Then 36 37 there were loud cries of sorrow from them all, as they folded Paul in their arms and kissed him. What distressed them most was his saying that they 38 would never see his face again. So they escorted him to his ship.

When we had parted from them and set sail, we made a straight run and **21** came to Cos; next day to Rhodes, and thence to Patara.[a] There we found 2 a ship bound for Phoenicia, so we went aboard and sailed in her. We came 3 in sight of Cyprus, and leaving it to port, we continued our voyage to Syria, and put in at Tyre, for there the ship was to unload her cargo. We went and 4 found the disciples and stayed there a week; and they, warned by the Spirit, urged Paul to abandon his visit to Jerusalem. But when our time 5 ashore was ended, we left and continued our journey; and they and their wives and children all escorted us out of the city. We knelt down on the beach and prayed, then bade each other good-bye; we went aboard, and 6 they returned home.

We made the passage from Tyre and reached Ptolemais, where we 7 greeted the brotherhood and spent one day with them. Next day we left 8 and came to Caesarea. We went to the home of Philip the evangelist, who was one of the Seven, and stayed with him. He had four unmarried 9 daughters, who possessed the gift of prophecy. When we had been there 10 several days, a prophet named Agabus arrived from Judaea. He came to us, 11 took Paul's belt, bound his own feet and hands with it, and said, 'These are the words of the Holy Spirit: Thus will the Jews in Jerusalem bind the man to whom this belt belongs, and hand him over to the Gentiles.' When 12 we heard this, we and the local people begged and implored Paul to abandon his visit to Jerusalem. Then Paul gave his answer: 'Why all these 13 tears? Why are you trying to weaken my resolution? For my part I am ready not merely to be bound but even to die at Jerusalem for the name of the Lord Jesus.' So, as he would not be persuaded, we gave up and said, 14 'The Lord's will be done.'

At the end of our stay we packed our baggage and took the road up to 15 Jerusalem. Some of the disciples from Caesarea came along with us, bring- 16 ing a certain Mnason of Cyprus, a Christian from the early days, with whom we were to lodge. So we reached Jerusalem, where the brotherhood 17 welcomed us gladly.

---

[a] *Some witnesses add* and Myra.

18   Next day Paul paid a visit to James; we were with him, and all the elders
19 attended. He greeted them, and then described in detail all that God had
20 done among the Gentiles through his ministry. When they heard this,
they gave praise to God. Then they said to Paul: 'You see, brother, how
many thousands of converts we have among the Jews, all of them staunch
21 upholders of the Law. Now they have been given certain information
about you: it is said that you teach all the Jews in the gentile world to turn
their backs on Moses, telling them to give up circumcising their children
22 and following our way of life. What is the position, then? They are sure to
23 hear that you have arrived. You must therefore do as we tell you. We have
24 four men here who are under a vow; take them with you and go through the
ritual of purification with them, paying their expenses, after which they
may shave their heads. Then everyone will know that there is nothing in
the stories they were told about you, but that you are a practising Jew
25 and keep the Law yourself. As for the gentile converts, we sent them our
decision that they must abstain from meat that has been offered to idols,
from blood, from anything that has been strangled,[a] and from fornication.'
26 So Paul took the four men, and next day, after going through the ritual of
purification with them, he went into the temple to give notice of the date
when the period of purification would end and the offering be made for
each one of them.

From Jerusalem to Rome

27   BUT JUST BEFORE the seven days were up, the Jews from the province
of Asia saw him in the temple. They stirred up the whole crowd, and
28 seized him, shouting, 'Men of Israel, help, help! This is the fellow who
spreads his doctrine all over the world, attacking our people, our law, and
this sanctuary. On top of all this he has brought Gentiles into the temple
29 and profaned this holy place.' For they had previously seen Trophimus
the Ephesian with him in the city, and assumed that Paul had brought him
into the temple.
30   The whole city was in a turmoil, and people came running from all
directions. They seized Paul and dragged him out of the temple; and at
31 once the doors were shut. While they were clamouring for his death, a
report reached the officer commanding the cohort, that all Jerusalem was in
32 an uproar. He immediately took a force of soldiers with their centurions
and came down on the rioters at the double. As soon as they saw the
33 commandant and his troops, they stopped beating Paul. The commandant
stepped forward, arrested him, and ordered him to be shackled with two
34 chains; he then asked who the man was and what he had been doing. Some
in the crowd shouted one thing, some another. As he could not get at the
truth because of the hubbub, he ordered him to be taken into barracks.
35 When Paul reached the steps, he had to be carried by the soldiers because
36 of the violence of the mob. For the whole crowd were at their heels yelling,
'Kill him!'

[a] *Some witnesses omit* from anything that has been strangled.

Just before Paul was taken into the barracks he said to the commandant, 37
'May I have a word with you?' The commandant said, 'So you speak
Greek, do you? Then you are not the Egyptian who started a revolt some 38
time ago and led a force of four thousand terrorists out into the wilds?'
Paul replied, 'I am a Jew, a Tarsian from Cilicia, a citizen of no mean city. 39
I ask your permission to speak to the people.' When permission had been 40
given, Paul stood on the steps and with a gesture called for the attention of
the people. As soon as quiet was restored, he addressed them in the Jewish
language:

'Brothers and fathers, give me a hearing while I make my defence before **22**
you.' When they heard him speaking to them in their own language, they 2
listened the more quietly. 'I am a true-born Jew,' he said, 'a native of 3
Tarsus in Cilicia. I was brought up in this city, and as a pupil of Gamaliel
I was thoroughly trained in every point of our ancestral law. I have always
been ardent in God's service, as you all are today. And so I began to per- 4
secute this movement to the death, arresting its followers, men and
women alike, and putting them in chains. For this I have as witnesses the 5
High Priest and the whole Council of Elders. I was given letters from them
to our fellow-Jews at Damascus, and had started out to bring the Christians
there to Jerusalem as prisoners for punishment; and this is what happened. 6
I was on the road and nearing Damascus, when suddenly about midday a
great light flashed from the sky all around me, and I fell to the ground. 7
Then I heard a voice saying to me, "Saul, Saul, why do you persecute me?"
I answered, "Tell me, Lord, who you are." "I am Jesus of Nazareth," he 8
said, "whom you are persecuting." My companions saw the light, but did 9
not hear the voice that spoke to me. "What shall I do, Lord?" I said, and 10
the Lord replied, "Get up and continue your journey to Damascus; there
you will be told of all the tasks that are laid upon you." As I had been 11
blinded by the brilliance of that light, my companions led me by the hand,
and so I came to Damascus.

'There, a man called Ananias, a devout observer of the Law and well 12
spoken of by all the Jews of that place, came and stood beside me and said, 13
"Saul, my brother, recover your sight." Instantly I recovered my sight and
saw him. He went on: "The God of our fathers appointed you to know his 14
will and to see the Righteous One and to hear his very voice, because you 15
are to be his witness before the world, and testify to what you have seen
and heard. And now why delay? Be baptized at once, with invocation of 16
his name, and wash away your sins."

'After my return to Jerusalem, I was praying in the temple when I fell 17
into a trance and saw him there, speaking to me. "Make haste", he said, 18
"and leave Jerusalem without delay, for they will not accept your testimony
about me." "Lord," I said, "they know that I imprisoned those who believe 19
in thee, and flogged them in every synagogue; and when the blood of 20
Stephen thy witness was shed I stood by, approving, and I looked after
the clothes of those who killed him." But he said to me, "Go, for I am send- 21
ing you far away to the Gentiles."'

Up to this point they had given him a hearing; but now they began 22
shouting, 'Down with him! A scoundrel like that is better dead!' And as 23

24 they were yelling and waving their cloaks and flinging dust in the air, the commandant ordered him to be brought into the barracks and gave instructions to examine him by flogging, and find out what reason there
25 was for such an outcry against him. But when they tied him up for the lash,*a* Paul said to the centurion who was standing there, 'Can you legally flog a man who is a Roman citizen, and moreover has not been found
26 guilty?' When the centurion heard this, he went and reported it to the commandant. 'What do you mean to do?' he said. 'This man is a Roman
27 citizen.' The commandant came to Paul. 'Tell me, are you a Roman
28 citizen?' he asked. 'Yes', said he. The commandant rejoined, 'It cost me a large sum to acquire this citizenship.' Paul said, 'But it was mine by birth.'
29 Then those who were about to examine him withdrew hastily, and the commandant himself was alarmed when he realized that Paul was a Roman citizen and that he had put him in irons.

30 THE FOLLOWING DAY, wishing to be quite sure what charge the Jews were bringing against Paul, he released him and ordered the chief priests and the entire Council to assemble. He then took Paul down and stood him before them.

23 Paul fixed his eyes on the Council and said, 'My brothers, I have lived all my life, and still live today, with a perfectly clear conscience before God.'
2 At this the High Priest Ananias ordered his attendants to strike him on the
3 mouth. Paul retorted, 'God will strike you, you whitewashed wall! You sit there to judge me in accordance with the Law; and then in defiance of
4 the Law you order me to be struck!' The attendants said, 'Would you insult
5 God's High Priest?' 'My brothers,' said Paul, 'I had no idea that he was High Priest; Scripture, I know, says: "You must not abuse the ruler of your people."'
6 Now Paul was well aware that one section of them were Sadducees and the other Pharisees, so he called out in the Council, 'My brothers, I am a Pharisee, a Pharisee born and bred; and the true issue in this trial is our
7 hope of the resurrection of the dead.' At these words the Pharisees and Sadducees fell out among themselves, and the assembly was divided.
8 (The Sadducees deny that there is any resurrection, or angel, or spirit, but
9 the Pharisees accept them.) So a great uproar broke out; and some of the doctors of the law belonging to the Pharisaic party openly took sides and declared, 'We can find no fault with this man; perhaps an angel or spirit
10 has spoken to him.' The dissension was mounting, and the commandant was afraid that Paul would be torn in pieces, so he ordered the troops to go down, pull him out of the crowd, and bring him into the barracks.
11 The following night the Lord appeared to him and said, 'Keep up your courage; you have affirmed the truth about me in Jerusalem, and you must do the same in Rome.'
12 When day broke, the Jews banded together and took an oath not to eat
13 or drink until they had killed Paul. There were more than forty in this
14 conspiracy. They came to the chief priests and elders and said, 'We have bound ourselves by a solemn oath not to taste food until we have killed

a Or tied him up with thongs.

Paul. It is now for you, acting with the Council, to apply to the com- 15
mandant to bring him down to you, on the pretext of a closer investigation
of his case; and we have arranged to do away with him before he arrives.'

But the son of Paul's sister heard of the ambush; he went to the barracks, 16
obtained entry, and reported it to Paul. Paul called one of the centurions 17
and said, 'Take this young man to the commandant; he has something to
report.' The centurion took him and brought him to the commandant. 18
'The prisoner Paul', he said, 'sent for me and asked me to bring this young
man to you; he has something to tell you.' The commandant took him by 19
the arm, drew him aside, and asked him, 'What is it you have to report?'
He said, 'The Jews have made a plan among themselves and will request 20
you to bring Paul down to the Council tomorrow, on the pretext of obtain-
ing more precise information about him. Do not listen to them; for a party 21
more than forty strong are lying in wait for him. They have sworn not to
eat or drink until they have done away with him; they are now ready, and
wait only for your consent.' So the commandant dismissed the young man, 22
with orders not to let anyone know that he had given him this information.

Then he called a couple of his centurions and issued these orders: 'Get 23
ready two hundred infantry to proceed to Caesarea, together with seventy
cavalrymen and two hundred light-armed troops;^a parade three hours
after sunset. Provide also mounts for Paul so that he may ride through under 24
safe escort to Felix the Governor.' And he wrote a letter to this effect: 25
'Claudius Lysias to His Excellency the Governor Felix. Your Excel- 26
lency: This man was seized by the Jews and was on the point of being 27
murdered when I intervened with the troops and removed him, because
I discovered that he was a Roman citizen. As I wished to ascertain the 28
charge on which they were accusing him, I took him down to their Council.
I found that the accusation had to do with controversial matters in their 29
law, but there was no charge against him meriting death or imprisonment.
However, I have now been informed of an attempt to be made on the man's 30
life, so I am sending him to you at once, and have also instructed his
accusers to state their case against him before you.'^b

Acting on their orders, the infantry took Paul and brought him by night 31
to Antipatris. Next day they returned to their barracks, leaving the cavalry 32
to escort him the rest of the way. The cavalry entered Caesarea, delivered 33
the letter to the Governor, and handed Paul over to him. He read the letter, 34
asked him what province he was from, and learned that he was from Cilicia.
'I will hear your case', he said, 'when your accusers arrive.' He then 35
ordered him to be held in custody at his headquarters in Herod's palace.

FIVE DAYS LATER the High Priest Ananias came down, accompanied by 24
some of the elders and an advocate named Tertullus, and they laid an
information against Paul before the Governor. When the prisoner was 2
called, Tertullus opened the case.

'Your Excellency,' he said, 'we owe it to you that we enjoy unbroken
peace. It is due to your provident care that, in all kinds of ways and in all

^a Or two hundred spearmen (*the meaning of the Greek word is uncertain*).
^b *Some witnesses read* '. . . before you. Farewell.'

sorts of places, improvements are being made for the good of this province.
3 4 We welcome this, sir, most gratefully. And now, not to take up too much
5 of your time, I crave your indulgence for a brief statement of our case. We
have found this man to be a perfect pest, a fomenter of discord among the
6 Jews all over the world, a ringleader of the sect of the Nazarenes. He even
8 made an attempt to profane the temple; and then we arrested him. *a* If you
will examine him yourself you can ascertain from him the truth of all the
9 charges we bring.' The Jews supported the attack, alleging that the facts
were as he stated.

10   Then the Governor motioned to Paul to speak, and he began his reply:
'Knowing as I do that for many years you have administered justice in this
11 province, I make my defence with confidence. You can ascertain the facts
for yourself. It is not more than twelve days since I went up to Jerusalem
12 on a pilgrimage. They did not find me arguing with anyone, or collecting
a crowd, either in the temple or in the synagogues or up and down the city;
13 14 and they cannot make good the charges they bring against me. But this
much I will admit: I am a follower of the new way (the "sect" they speak of),
and it is in that manner that I worship the God of our fathers; for I believe
15 all that is written in the Law and the prophets, and in reliance on God I
hold the hope, which my accusers too accept, that there is to be a resur-
16 rection of good and wicked alike. Accordingly I, no less than they, train
myself to keep at all times a clear conscience before God and man.

17   'After an absence of several years I came to bring charitable gifts to my
18 nation and to offer sacrifices. They found me in the temple ritually purified
and engaged in this service. I had no crowd with me, and there was no
19 disturbance. But some Jews from the province of Asia were there, and if
they had any charge against me it is they who ought to have been in court
20 to state it. Failing that, it is for these persons here present to say what
21 crime they discovered when I was brought before the Council, apart from
this one open assertion which I made as I stood there: "The true issue in
my trial before you today is the resurrection of the dead."'

22   Then Felix, who happened to be well informed about the Christian
movement, adjourned the hearing. 'When Lysias the commanding officer
23 comes down', he said, 'I will go into your case.' He gave orders to the
centurion to keep Paul under open arrest and not to prevent any of his
friends from making themselves useful to him.

24   Some days later Felix came with his wife Drusilla, who was a Jewess,
and sending for Paul he let him talk to him about faith in Christ Jesus.
25 But when the discourse turned to questions of morals, self-control, and
the coming judgement, Felix became alarmed and exclaimed, 'That will
do for the present; when I find it convenient I will send for you again.'
26 At the same time he had hopes of a bribe from Paul; and for this reason he
27 sent for him very often and talked with him. When two years had passed,
Felix was succeeded by Porcius Festus. Wishing to curry favour with the
Jews, Felix left Paul in custody.

a Some witnesses insert It was our intention to try him under our law; (7) but Lysias the
commandant intervened and took him by force out of our hands, (8) ordering his accusers
to come before you.

THREE DAYS AFTER taking up his appointment Festus went up from **25**
Caesarea to Jerusalem, where the chief priests and the Jewish leaders **2**
brought before him the case against Paul. They asked Festus to favour **3**
them against him, and pressed for him to be brought up to Jerusalem, for
they were planning an ambush to kill him on the way. Festus, however, **4**
replied, 'Paul is in safe custody at Caesarea, and I shall be leaving Jerusalem shortly myself; so let your leading men come down with me, and if **5**
there is anything wrong, let them prosecute him.'

After spending eight or ten days at most in Jerusalem, he went down to **6**
Caesarea, and next day he took his seat in court and ordered Paul to be
brought up. When he appeared, the Jews who had come down from **7**
Jerusalem stood round bringing many grave charges, which they were
unable to prove. Paul's plea was: 'I have committed no offence, either **8**
against the Jewish law, or against the temple, or against the Emperor.'
Festus, anxious to ingratiate himself with the Jews, turned to Paul and **9**
asked, 'Are you willing to go up to Jerusalem and stand trial on these
charges before me there?' But Paul said, 'I am now standing before the **10**
Emperor's tribunal, and that is where I must be tried. Against the Jews I
have committed no offence, as you very well know. If I am guilty of any **11**
capital crime, I do not ask to escape the death penalty; but if there is no
substance in the charges which these men bring against me, it is not open
to anyone to hand me over as a sop to them. I appeal to Caesar!' Then **12**
Festus, after conferring with his advisers, replied, 'You have appealed to
Caesar: to Caesar you shall go.'

After an interval of some days King Agrippa and Bernice arrived at **13**
Caesarea on a courtesy visit to Festus. They spent several days there, and **14**
during this time Festus laid Paul's case before the king. 'We have a man',
he said, 'left in custody by Felix; and when I was in Jerusalem the chief **15**
priests and elders of the Jews laid an information against him, demanding
his condemnation. I answered them, "It is not Roman practice to hand over **16**
any accused man before he is confronted with his accusers and given an
opportunity of answering the charge." So when they had come here with **17**
me I lost no time; the very next day I took my seat in court and ordered the
man to be brought up. But when his accusers rose to speak, they brought **18**
none of the charges I was expecting; they merely had certain points of dis- **19**
agreement with him about their peculiar religion, and about someone
called Jesus, a dead man whom Paul alleged to be alive. Finding myself **20**
out of my depth in such discussions, I asked if he was willing to go to
Jerusalem and stand his trial there on these issues. But Paul appealed to be **21**
remanded in custody for His Imperial Majesty's decision, and I ordered
him to be detained until I could send him to the Emperor.' Agrippa said to **22**
Festus, 'I should rather like to hear the man myself.' 'Tomorrow', he
answered, 'you shall hear him.'

So next day Agrippa and Bernice came in full state and entered the **23**
audience-chamber accompanied by high-ranking officers and prominent
citizens; and on the orders of Festus Paul was brought up. Then Festus **24**
said, 'King Agrippa, and all you gentlemen here present with us, you see
this man: the whole body of the Jews approached me both in Jerusalem

25 and here, loudly insisting that he had no right to remain alive. But it was clear to me that he had committed no capital crime, and when he himself
26 appealed to His Imperial Majesty, I decided to send him. But I have nothing definite about him to put in writing for our Sovereign. Accordingly I have brought him up before you all and particularly before you, King Agrippa, so that as a result of this preliminary inquiry I may have
27 something to report. There is no sense, it seems to me, in sending on a prisoner without indicating the charges against him.'

26 Agrippa said to Paul, 'You have our permission to speak for yourself.' Then Paul stretched out his hand and began his defence:

2 'I consider myself fortunate, King Agrippa, that it is before you that I am to make my defence today upon all the charges brought against me by
3 the Jews, particularly as you are expert in all Jewish matters, both our customs and our disputes. And therefore I beg you to give me a patient hearing.

4 'My life from my youth up, the life I led from the beginning among my
5 people and in Jerusalem, is familiar to all Jews. Indeed they have known me long enough and could testify, if they only would, that I belonged to the
6 strictest group in our religion: I lived as a Pharisee. And it is for a hope kindled by God's promise to our forefathers that I stand in the dock today.
7 Our twelve tribes hope to see the fulfilment of that promise, worshipping with intense devotion day and night; and for this very hope I am im-
8 peached, and impeached by Jews, Your Majesty. Why is it considered incredible among you that God should raise dead men to life?

9 'I myself once thought it my duty to work actively against the name of
10 Jesus of Nazareth; and I did so in Jerusalem. It was I who imprisoned many of God's people by authority obtained from the chief priests; and when they
11 were condemned to death, my vote was cast against them. In all the synagogues I tried by repeated punishment to make them renounce their faith; indeed my fury rose to such a pitch that I extended my persecution to foreign cities.

12 'On one such occasion I was travelling to Damascus with authority and
13 commission from the chief priests; and as I was on my way, Your Majesty, in the middle of the day I saw a light from the sky, more brilliant than the
14 sun, shining all around me and my travelling-companions. We all fell to the ground, and then I heard a voice saying to me in the Jewish language, "Saul, Saul, why do you persecute me? It is hard for you, this kicking
15 against the goad." I said, "Tell me, Lord, who you are"; and the Lord
16 replied, "I am Jesus, whom you are persecuting. But now, rise to your feet and stand upright. I have appeared to you for a purpose: to appoint you my servant and witness, to testify both to what you have seen and to what
17 you shall yet see of me. I will rescue you from this people and from the
18 Gentiles to whom I am sending you. I send you to open their eyes and turn them from darkness to light, from the dominion of Satan to God, so that, by trust in me, they may obtain forgiveness of sins, and a place with those whom God has made his own."

19 20 'And so, King Agrippa, I did not disobey the heavenly vision. I turned first to the inhabitants of Damascus, and then to Jerusalem and all the

country of Judaea, and to the Gentiles, and sounded the call to repent
and turn to God, and to prove their repentance by deeds. That is why the   21
Jews seized me in the temple and tried to do away with me. But I had God's   22
help, and so to this very day I stand and testify to great and small alike. I
assert nothing beyond what was foretold by the prophets and by Moses:
that the Messiah must suffer, and that he, the first to rise from the dead,   23
would announce the dawn to Israel and to the Gentiles.'

While Paul was thus making his defence, Festus shouted at the top of his   24
voice, 'Paul, you are raving; too much study is driving you mad.' 'I am   25
not mad, Your Excellency,' said Paul; 'what I am saying is sober truth.
The king is well versed in these matters, and to him I can speak freely.   26
I do not believe that he can be unaware of any of these facts, for this has
been no hole-and-corner business. King Agrippa, do you believe the   27
prophets? I know you do.' Agrippa said to Paul, 'You think it will not take   28
much to win me over and make a Christian of me.' 'Much or little,' said   29
Paul, 'I wish to God that not only you, but all those also who are listening
to me today, might become what I am, apart from these chains.'

With that the king rose, and with him the Governor, Bernice, and the   30
rest of the company, and after they had withdrawn they talked it over.   31
'This man', they said, 'is doing nothing that deserves death or imprisonment.' Agrippa said to Festus, 'The fellow could have been discharged, if   32
he had not appealed to the Emperor.'

WHEN IT WAS DECIDED that we should sail for Italy, Paul and some   **27**
other prisoners were handed over to a centurion named Julius, of the
Augustan Cohort. We embarked in a ship of Adramyttium, bound for   2
ports in the province of Asia, and put out to sea. In our party was Aristarchus, a Macedonian from Thessalonica. Next day we landed at Sidon;   3
and Julius very considerately allowed Paul to go to his friends to be cared
for. Leaving Sidon we sailed under the lee of Cyprus because of the head-   4
winds, then across the open sea off the coast of Cilicia and Pamphylia, and   5
so reached Myra in Lycia.

There the centurion found an Alexandrian vessel bound for Italy and   6
put us aboard. For a good many days we made little headway, and we were   7
hard put to it to reach Cnidus. Then, as the wind continued against us, off
Salmone we began to sail under the lee of Crete, and, hugging the coast,   8
struggled on to a place called Fair Havens, not far from the town of Lasea.

By now much time had been lost, the Fast was already over, and it was   9
risky to go on with the voyage. Paul therefore gave them this advice: 'I can   10
see, gentlemen,' he said, 'that this voyage will be disastrous: it will mean
grave loss, loss not only of ship and cargo but also of life.' But the centurion   11
paid more attention to the captain and to the owner of the ship than to
what Paul said; and as the harbour was unsuitable for wintering, the   12
majority were in favour of putting out to sea, hoping, if they could get so
far, to winter at Phoenix, a Cretan harbour exposed south-west and north-
west. So when a southerly breeze sprang up, they thought that their pur-   13
pose was as good as achieved, and, weighing anchor, they sailed along the
coast of Crete hugging the land. But before very long a fierce wind, the   14

15 'North-easter' as they call it, tore down from the landward side. It caught
the ship and, as it was impossible to keep head to wind, we had to give way
16 and run before it. We ran under the lee of a small island called Cauda, and
17 with a struggle managed to get the ship's boat under control. When they
had hoisted it aboard, they made use of tackle and undergirded the ship.
Then, because they were afraid of running on to the shallows of Syrtis,
18 they lowered the mainsail and let her drive. Next day, as we were making
19 very heavy weather, they began to lighten the ship; and on the third day
20 they jettisoned the ship's gear with their own hands. For days on end there
was no sign of either sun or stars, a great storm was raging, and our last
hopes of coming through alive began to fade.

21   When they had gone for a long time without food, Paul stood up among
them and said, 'You should have taken my advice, gentlemen, not to sail
22 from Crete; then you would have avoided this damage and loss. But now
23 I urge you not to lose heart; not a single life will be lost, only the ship. For
last night there stood by me an angel of the God whose I am and whom I
24 worship. "Do not be afraid, Paul," he said; "it is ordained that you shall
appear before the Emperor; and, be assured, God has granted you the
25 lives of all who are sailing with you." So keep up your courage: I trust in
26 God that it will turn out as I have been told; though we have to be cast
ashore on some island.'

27   The fourteenth night came and we were still drifting in the Sea of Adria.
In the middle of the night the sailors felt that land was getting nearer.
28 They sounded and found twenty fathoms. Sounding again after a short
29 interval they found fifteen fathoms; and fearing that we might be cast
ashore on a rugged coast they dropped four anchors from the stern and
30 prayed for daylight to come. The sailors tried to abandon ship; they had
already lowered the ship's boat, pretending they were going to lay out
31 anchors from the bows, when Paul said to the centurion and the soldiers,
32 'Unless these men stay on board you can none of you come off safely.' So
the soldiers cut the ropes of the boat and let her drop away.

33   Shortly before daybreak Paul urged them all to take some food. 'For
the last fourteen days', he said, 'you have lived in suspense and gone
34 hungry; you have eaten nothing whatever. So I beg you to have something
to eat; your lives depend on it. Remember, not a hair of your heads will be
35 lost.' With these words, he took bread, gave thanks to God in front of them
36 all, broke it, and began eating. Then they all plucked up courage, and took
37 food themselves. There were on board two hundred and seventy-six of us
38 in all. When they had eaten as much as they wanted they lightened the ship
by dumping the corn in the sea.

39   When day broke they could not recognize the land, but they noticed
a bay with a sandy beach, on which they planned, if possible, to run the
40 ship ashore. So they slipped the anchors and let them go; at the same time
they loosened the lashings of the steering-paddles, set the foresail to the
41 wind, and let her drive to the beach. But they found themselves caught
between cross-currents and ran the ship aground, so that the bow stuck
fast and remained immovable, while the stern was being pounded to pieces
42 by the breakers. The soldiers thought they had better kill the prisoners for

fear that any should swim away and escape; but the centurion wanted to   43
bring Paul safely through and prevented them from carrying out their plan.
He gave orders that those who could swim should jump overboard first
and get to land; the rest were to follow, some on planks, some on parts of   44
the ship. And thus it was that all came safely to land.

Once we had made our way to safety we identified the island as Malta.   **28**
The rough islanders treated us with uncommon kindness: because it was   2
cold and had started to rain, they lit a bonfire and made us all welcome.
Paul had got together an armful of sticks and put them on the fire, when a   3
viper, driven out by the heat, fastened on his hand. The islanders, seeing   4
the snake hanging on to his hand, said to one another, 'The man must be
a murderer; he may have escaped from the sea, but divine justice has not
let him live.' Paul, however, shook off the snake into the fire and was none   5
the worse. They still expected that any moment he would swell up or drop   6
down dead, but after waiting a long time without seeing anything extraordinary happen to him, they changed their minds and now said, 'He is
a god.'

In the neighbourhood of that place there were lands belonging to the   7
chief magistrate of the island, whose name was Publius. He took us in and
entertained us hospitably for three days. It so happened that this man's   8
father was in bed suffering from recurrent bouts of fever and dysentery.
Paul visited him and, after prayer, laid his hands upon him and healed
him; whereupon the other sick people on the island came also and were   9
cured. They honoured us with many marks of respect, and when we were   10
leaving they put on board provision for our needs.

Three months had passed when we set sail in a ship which had wintered   11
in the island; she was the *Castor and Pollux* of Alexandria. We put in at   12
Syracuse and spent three days there; then we sailed round and arrived at   13
Rhegium. After one day a south wind sprang up and we reached Puteoli
in two days. There we found fellow-Christians and were invited to stay a   14
week with them. And so to Rome. The Christians there had had news of   15
us and came out to meet us as far as Appii Forum and Tres Tabernae, and
when Paul saw them, he gave thanks to God and took courage.

WHEN WE ENTERED ROME Paul was allowed to lodge by himself with a   16
soldier in charge of him. Three days later he called together the local   17
Jewish leaders; and when they were assembled, he said to them: 'My
brothers, I, who never did anything against our people or the customs of
our forefathers, am here as a prisoner; I was handed over to the Romans
at Jerusalem. They examined me and would have liked to release me be-   18
cause there was no capital charge against me; but the Jews objected, and   19
I had no option but to appeal to the Emperor; not that I had any accusation to bring against my own people. That is why I have asked to see you   20
and talk to you, because it is for the sake of the hope of Israel that I am in
chains, as you see.' They replied, 'We have had no communication from   21
Judaea, nor has any countryman of ours arrived with any report or gossip
to your discredit. We should like to hear from you what your views are;   22
all we know about this sect is that no one has a good word to say for it.'

23   So they fixed a day, and came in large numbers as his guests. He dealt
at length with the whole matter; he spoke urgently of the kingdom of God
and sought to convince them about Jesus by appealing to the Law of Moses
24 and the prophets. This went on from dawn to dusk. Some were won over
25 by his arguments; others remained sceptical. Without reaching any agreement among themselves they began to disperse, but not before Paul had
said one thing more: 'How well the Holy Spirit spoke to your fathers
26 through the prophet Isaiah when he said, "Go to this people and say: You
may hear and hear, but you will never understand; you may look and look,
27 but you will never see. For this people's mind has become gross; their ears
are dulled, and their eyes are closed. Otherwise, their eyes might see, their
ears hear, and their mind understand, and then they might turn again, and
28 I would heal them." Therefore take notice that this salvation of God has
been sent to the Gentiles; the Gentiles will listen.'*a*

30   He stayed there two full years at his own expense, with a welcome for all
31 who came to him, proclaiming the kingdom of God and teaching the facts
about the Lord Jesus Christ quite openly and without hindrance.

a Some witnesses add (29) After he had spoken, the Jews went away, arguing vigorously
among themselves.

LETTERS

THE LETTER OF PAUL
TO THE
ROMANS

The Gospel according to Paul

FROM PAUL, SERVANT of Christ Jesus, apostle by God's call, 1
set apart for the service of the Gospel.

This gospel God announced beforehand in sacred scriptures 2
through his prophets. It is about his Son: on the human level he was born 3
of David's stock, but on the level of the spirit—the Holy Spirit—he was 4
declared Son of God by a mighty act in that he rose from the dead:*a* it is
about Jesus Christ our Lord. Through him I received the privilege of a 5
commission in his name to lead to faith and obedience men in all nations,
yourselves among them, you who have heard the call and belong to Jesus 6
Christ.

I send greetings to all of you in Rome whom God loves and has called 7
to be his dedicated people. Grace and peace to you from God our Father
and the Lord Jesus Christ.

Let me begin by thanking my God, through Jesus Christ, for you all, 8
because all over the world they are telling the story of your faith. God is 9
my witness, the God to whom I offer the humble service of my spirit by
preaching the gospel of his Son: God knows how continually I make
mention of you in my prayers, and am always asking that by his will I may, 10
somehow or other, succeed at long last in coming to visit you. For I long to 11
see you; I want to bring you some spiritual gift to make you strong; or 12
rather, I want to be among you to be myself encouraged by your faith as
well as you by mine.

But I should like you to know,*b* my brothers, that I have often planned 13
to come, though so far without success, in the hope of achieving something
among you, as I have in other parts of the world. I am under obligation to 14
Greek and non-Greek, to learned and simple; hence my eagerness to 15
declare the Gospel to you in Rome as well as to others. For I am not 16
ashamed of the Gospel. It is the saving power of God for everyone who
has faith—the Jew first, but the Greek also—because here is revealed 17
God's way of righting wrong, a way that starts from faith and ends
in faith;*c* as Scripture says, 'he shall gain life who is justified through
faith'.

---

a Or declared Son of God with full powers from the time when he rose from the dead.
b Some witnesses read I believe you know.   *c Or* . . . wrong. It is based on faith
and addressed to faith.

18 FOR WE SEE divine retribution revealed from heaven and falling upon all the godless wickedness of men. In their wickedness they are stifling the
19 truth. For all that may be known of God by men lies plain before their eyes;
20 indeed God himself has disclosed it to them. His invisible attributes, that is to say his everlasting power and deity, have been visible, ever since the world began, to the eye of reason, in the things he has made. There is
21 therefore no possible defence for their conduct; knowing God, they have refused to honour him as God, or to render him thanks. Hence all their thinking has ended in futility, and their misguided minds are plunged in
22 darkness. They boast of their wisdom, but they have made fools of them-
23 selves, exchanging the splendour of immortal God for an image shaped like mortal man, even for images like birds, beasts, and creeping things.
24 For this reason God has given them up to the vileness of their own
25 desires, and the consequent degradation of their bodies, because they have bartered away the true God for a false one,^a and have offered reverence and worship to created things instead of to the Creator, who is blessed for ever; amen.
26 In consequence, I say, God has given them up to shameful passions.
27 Their women have exchanged natural intercourse for unnatural, and their men in turn, giving up natural relations with women, burn with lust for one another; males behave indecently with males, and are paid in their own persons the fitting wage of such perversion.
28 Thus, because they have not seen fit to acknowledge God, he has given them up to their own depraved reason. This leads them to break all rules
29 of conduct. They are filled with every kind of injustice, mischief, rapacity, and malice; they are one mass of envy, murder, rivalry, treachery, and
30 malevolence; whisperers and scandal-mongers, hateful to God, insolent, arrogant, and boastful; they invent new kinds of mischief, they show no
31 loyalty to parents, no conscience, no fidelity to their plighted word; they
32 are without natural affection and without pity. They know well enough the just decree of God, that those who behave like this deserve to die, and yet they do it; not only so, they actually applaud such practices.

2 You therefore have no defence—you who sit in judgement, whoever you may be—for in judging your fellow-man you condemn yourself, since
2 you, the judge, are equally guilty. It is admitted that God's judgement is
3 rightly passed upon all who commit such crimes as these; and do you imagine—you who pass judgement on the guilty while committing the same crimes yourself—do you imagine that you, any more than they, will
4 escape the judgement of God? Or do you think lightly of his wealth of kindness, of tolerance, and of patience, without recognizing that God's
5 kindness is meant to lead you to a change of heart? In the rigid obstinacy of your heart you are laying up for yourself a store of retribution for the
6 day of retribution, when God's just judgement will be revealed, and he will
7 pay every man for what he has done. To those who pursue glory, honour, and immortality by steady persistence in well-doing, he will give eternal
8 life; but for those who are governed by selfish ambition, who refuse obedience to the truth and take the wrong for their guide, there will be

^a *Or* the truth of God for the lie.

the fury of retribution. There will be trouble and distress for every human 9
being who is an evil-doer, for the Jew first and for the Greek also; and for 10
every well-doer there will be glory, honour, and peace, for the Jew first
and also for the Greek.

For God has no favourites: those who have sinned outside the pale of 11 12
the Law of Moses will perish outside its pale, and all who have sinned
under that law will be judged by the law. It is not by hearing the law, but 13
by doing it, that men will be justified before God. When Gentiles who do 14
not possess the law carry out its precepts by the light of nature, then,
although they have no law, they are their own law, for they display the 15
effect of the law inscribed on their hearts. Their conscience is called as
witness, and their own thoughts argue the case on either side, against them
or even for them, on the day when God judges the secrets of human hearts 16
through Christ Jésus. So my gospel declares.

But as for you—you may bear the name of Jew; you rely upon the law 17
and are proud of your God; you know his will; instructed by the law, you 18
know right from wrong; you are confident that you are the one to guide 19
the blind, to enlighten the benighted, to train the stupid, and to teach the 20
immature, because in the law you see the very shape of knowledge and
truth. You, then, who teach your fellow-man, do you fail to teach your- 21
self? You proclaim, 'Do not steal'; but are you yourself a thief? You say, 22
'Do not commit adultery'; but are you an adulterer? You abominate false
gods; but do you rob their shrines? While you take pride in the law, you 23
dishonour God by breaking it. For, as Scripture says, 'Because of you the 24
name of God is dishonoured among the Gentiles.'

Circumcision has value, provided you keep the law; but if you break the 25
law, then your circumcision is as if it had never been. Equally, if an un- 26
circumcised man keeps the precepts of the law, will he not count as circumcised? He may be uncircumcised in his natural state, but by fulfilling 27
the law he will pass judgement on you who break it, for all your written
code and your circumcision. The true Jew is not he who is such in externals, 28
neither is the true circumcision the external mark in the flesh. The true 29
Jew is he who is such inwardly, and the true circumcision is of the heart,
directed not by written precepts but by the Spirit; such a man receives his
commendation not from men but from God.

Then what advantage has the Jew? What is the value of circumcision? **3**
Great, in every way. In the first place, the Jews were entrusted with the 2
oracles of God. What if some of them were unfaithful? Will their faithless- 3
ness cancel the faithfulness of God? Certainly not! God must be true 4
though every man living were a liar; for we read in Scripture, 'When thou
speakest thou shalt be vindicated, and win the verdict when thou art
on trial.'

Another question: if our injustice serves to bring out God's justice, what 5
are we to say? Is it unjust of God (I speak of him in human terms) to bring
retribution upon us? Certainly not! If God were unjust, how could he 6
judge the world?

Again, if the truth of God brings him all the greater honour because of 7
my falsehood, why should I any longer be condemned as a sinner? Why 8

not indeed 'do evil that good may come', as some libellously report me as saying? To condemn such men as these is surely no injustice.

9 What then? Are we Jews any better off?[a] No, not at all![b] For we have already drawn up the accusation that Jews and Greeks alike are all under 10 the power of sin. This has scriptural warrant:

> 'There is no just man, not one;
11 no one who understands, no one who seeks God.
12 All have swerved aside, all alike have become debased;
> there is no one to show kindness; no, not one.

13 Their throat is an open grave,
> they use their tongues for treachery,
> adders' venom is on their lips,
14 and their mouth is full of bitter curses.

15 Their feet hasten to shed blood,
16 ruin and misery lie along their paths,
17 they are strangers to the high-road of peace,
18 and reverence for God does not enter their thoughts.'

19 Now all the words of the law are addressed, as we know, to those who are within the pale of the law, so that no one may have anything to say in self-defence, but the whole world may be exposed to the judgement of 20 God. For (again from Scripture) 'no human being can be justified in the sight of God' for having kept the law: law brings only the consciousness of sin.

21 BUT NOW, quite independently of law, God's justice has been brought to 22 light. The Law and the prophets both bear witness to it: it is God's way of righting wrong, effective through faith in Christ for all who have such 23 faith—all, without distinction. For all alike have sinned, and are deprived 24 of the divine splendour, and all are justified by God's free grace alone, 25 through his act of liberation in the person of Christ Jesus. For God designed him to be the means of expiating sin by his sacrificial death, effective through faith. God meant by this to demonstrate his justice, 26 because in his forbearance he had overlooked the sins of the past—to demonstrate his justice now in the present, showing that he is himself just and also justifies any man who puts his faith in Jesus.

27 What room then is left for human pride? It is excluded. And on what principle? The keeping of the law would not exclude it, but faith does. 28 For our argument is that a man is justified by faith quite apart from success in keeping the law.

29 Do you suppose God is the God of the Jews alone? Is he not the God of 30 Gentiles also? Certainly, of Gentiles also, if it be true that God is one. And he will therefore justify both the circumcised in virtue of their faith, and 31 the uncircumcised through their faith. Does this mean that we are using faith to undermine law? By no means: we are placing law itself on a firmer footing.

> [a] *Or* Are we Jews any worse off?   [b] *Or* Not in all respects.

WHAT, THEN, are we to say about Abraham, our ancestor in the natural **4**
line? If Abraham was justified by anything he had done, then he has a 2
ground for pride. But he has no such ground before God; for what does 3
Scripture say? 'Abraham put his faith in God, and that faith was counted
to him as righteousness.' Now if a man does a piece of work, his wages are 4
not 'counted' as a favour; they are paid as debt. But if without any work to 5
his credit he simply puts his faith in him who acquits the guilty, then his
faith is indeed 'counted as righteousness'. In the same sense David speaks 6
of the happiness of the man whom God 'counts' as just, apart from any
specific acts of justice: 'Happy are they', he says, 'whose lawless deeds are 7
forgiven, whose sins are buried away; happy is the man whose sins the 8
Lord does not count against him.' Is this happiness confined to the 9
circumcised, or is it for the uncircumcised also? Consider: we say, 'Abraham's faith was counted as righteousness'; in what circumstances was it so 10
counted? Was he circumcised at the time, or not? He was not yet circumcised, but uncircumcised; and he later received the symbolic rite of 11
circumcision as the hall-mark of the righteousness which faith had given
him when he was still uncircumcised. Consequently, he is the father of all
who have faith when uncircumcised, so that righteousness is 'counted' to
them; and at the same time he is the father of such of the circumcised as 12
do not rely upon their circumcision alone, but also walk in the footprints
of the faith which our father Abraham had while he was yet uncircumcised.

For it was not through law that Abraham, or his posterity, was given the 13
promise that the world should be his inheritance, but through the righteousness that came from faith. For if those who hold by the law, and they alone, 14
are heirs, then faith is empty and the promise goes for nothing, because 15
law can bring only retribution; but where there is no law there can be no
breach of law. The promise was made on the ground of faith, in order that 16
it might be a matter of sheer grace, and that it might be valid for all Abraham's posterity, not only for those who hold by the law, but for those also
who have the faith of Abraham. For he is the father of us all, as Scripture 17
says: 'I have appointed you to be father of many nations.' This promise,
then, was valid before God, the God in whom he put his faith, the God
who makes the dead live and summons things that are not yet in existence
as if they already were. When hope seemed hopeless, his faith was such 18
that he became 'father of many nations', in agreement with the words
which had been spoken to him: 'Thus shall your descendants be.' With- 19
out any weakening of faith he contemplated his own body, as good as dead
(for he was about a hundred years old), and the deadness of Sarah's womb,
and never doubted God's promise in unbelief, but, strong in faith, gave 20
honour to God, in the firm conviction of his power to do what he had 21
promised. And that is why Abraham's faith was 'counted to him as 22
righteousness'.

Those words were written, not for Abraham's sake alone, but for our 23 24
sake too: it is to be 'counted' in the same way to us who have faith in the
God who raised Jesus our Lord from the dead; for he was given up to 25
death for our misdeeds, and raised to life to justify us. *a*

a Or raised to life because we were now justified.

5 THEREFORE, NOW THAT we have been justified through faith, let us
2 continue at peace *a* with God through our Lord Jesus Christ, through
whom we have been allowed to enter the sphere of God's grace, where we
now stand. Let us exult *b* in the hope of the divine splendour that is to be
3 ours. More than this: let us even exult *c* in our present sufferings, because
4 we know that suffering trains us to endure, and endurance brings proof
5 that we have stood the test, and this proof is the ground of hope. Such a
hope is no mockery, because God's love has flooded our inmost heart
through the Holy Spirit he has given us.

6   For at the very time when we were still powerless, then Christ died for
7 the wicked. Even for a just man one of us would hardly die, though perhaps
8 for a good man one might actually brave death; but Christ died for us while
we were yet sinners, and that is God's own proof of his love towards us.
9 And so, since we have now been justified by Christ's sacrificial death, we
shall all the more certainly be saved through him from final retribution.
10 For if, when we were God's enemies, we were reconciled to him through
the death of his Son, how much more, now that we are reconciled, shall
11 we be saved by his life! But that is not all: we also exult in God through our
Lord Jesus, through whom we have now been granted reconciliation.

12   Mark what follows. It was through one man that sin entered the world,
and through sin death, and thus death pervaded the whole human race,
13 inasmuch as all men have sinned. For sin was already in the world before
there was law, though in the absence of law no reckoning is kept of sin.
14 But death held sway from Adam to Moses, even over those who had not
sinned as Adam did, by disobeying a direct command—and Adam fore-
shadows the Man who was to come.

15   But God's act of grace is out of all proportion to Adam's wrongdoing.
For if the wrongdoing of that one man brought death upon so many, its
effect is vastly exceeded by the grace of God and the gift that came to so
16 many by the grace of the one man, Jesus Christ. And again, the gift of God
is not to be compared in its effect with that one man's sin; for the judicial
action, following upon the one offence, issued in a verdict of condemnation, but the act of grace, following upon so many misdeeds, issued in a
17 verdict of acquittal. For if by the wrongdoing of that one man death
established its reign, through a single sinner, much more shall those who
receive in far greater measure God's grace, and his gift of righteousness,
live and reign through the one man, Jesus Christ.

18   It follows, then, that as the issue of one misdeed was condemnation for
19 all men, so the issue of one just act is acquittal and life for all men. For as
through the disobedience of the one man the many were made sinners, so
through the obedience of the one man the many will be made righteous.

20   Law intruded into this process to multiply law-breaking. But where sin
21 was thus multiplied, grace immeasurably exceeded it, in order that, as sin
established its reign by way of death, so God's grace might establish its
reign in righteousness, and issue in eternal life through Jesus Christ
our Lord.

a Some witnesses read we are at peace.   *b Or* We exult.   *c Or* we even
exult.

What are we to say, then? Shall we persist in sin, so that there may be 6
all the more grace? No, no! We died to sin: how can we live in it any 2
longer? Have you forgotten that when we were baptized into union with 3
Christ Jesus we were baptized into his death? By baptism we were buried 4
with him, and lay dead, in order that, as Christ was raised from the dead
in the splendour of the Father, so also we might set our feet upon the new
path of life.

For if we have become incorporate with him in a death like his, we shall 5
also be one with him in a resurrection like his. We know that the man we 6
once were has been crucified with Christ, for the destruction of the sinful
self, so that we may no longer be the slaves of sin, since a dead man is no 7
longer answerable for his sin. But if we thus died with Christ, we believe 8
that we shall also come to life with him. We know that Christ, once raised 9
from the dead, is never to die again: he is no longer under the dominion of
death. For in dying as he died, he died to sin, once for all, and in living as 10
he lives, he lives to God. In the same way you must regard yourselves as 11
dead to sin and alive to God, in union with Christ Jesus.

So sin must no longer reign in your mortal body, exacting obedience to 12
the body's desires. You must no longer put its several parts at sin's disposal, 13
as implements for doing wrong. No: put yourselves at the disposal of God,
as dead men raised to life; yield your bodies to him as implements for doing
right; for sin shall no longer be your master, because you are no longer 14
under law, but under the grace of God.

What then? Are we to sin, because we are not under law but under 15
grace? Of course not. You know well enough that if you put yourselves at 16
the disposal of a master, to obey him, you are slaves of the master whom
you obey; and this is true whether you serve sin, with death as its result;
or obedience, with righteousness as its result. But God be thanked, you, 17
who once were slaves of sin, have yielded whole-hearted obedience to the
pattern of teaching to which you were made subject,*a* and, emancipated 18
from sin, have become slaves of righteousness (to use words that suit your 19
human weakness)—I mean, as you once yielded your bodies to the service
of impurity and lawlessness, making for moral anarchy, so now you must
yield them to the service of righteousness, making for a holy life.

When you were slaves of sin, you were free from the control of righteous- 20
ness; and what was the gain? Nothing but what now makes you ashamed, 21
for the end of that is death. But now, freed from the commands of sin, and 22
bound to the service of God, your gains are such as make for holiness, and
the end is eternal life. For sin pays a wage, and the wage is death, but God 23
gives freely, and his gift is eternal life, in union with Christ Jesus our
Lord.

You cannot be unaware, my friends—I am speaking to those who have 7
some knowledge of law—that a person is subject to the law so long as he is
alive, and no longer. For example, a married woman is by law bound to her 2
husband while he lives; but if her husband dies, she is discharged from the
obligations of the marriage-law. If, therefore, in her husband's lifetime 3
she consorts with another man, she will incur the charge of adultery; but

a Or which was handed on to you.

if her husband dies she is free of the law, and she does not commit adultery
4 by consorting with another man. So you, my friends, have died to the law
by becoming identified with the body of Christ, and accordingly you have
found another husband in him who rose from the dead, so that we may
5 bear fruit for God. While we lived on the level of our lower nature, the sinful passions evoked by the law worked in our bodies, to bear fruit for death.
6 But now, having died to that which held us bound, we are discharged from
the law, to serve God in a new way, the way of the spirit, in contrast to the
old way, the way of a written code.

7   What follows? Is the law identical with sin? Of course not. But except
through law I should never have become acquainted with sin. For example,
I should never have known what it was to covet, if the law had not said,
8 'Thou shalt not covet.' Through that commandment sin found its opportunity, and produced in me all kinds of wrong desires. In the absence of
9 law, sin is a dead thing. There was a time when, in the absence of law, I
was fully alive; but when the commandment came, sin sprang to life and
10 I died. The commandment which should have led to life proved in my
11 experience to lead to death, because sin found its opportunity in the commandment, seduced me, and through the commandment killed me.

12   Therefore the law is in itself holy, and the commandment is holy and
13 just and good. Are we to say then that this good thing was the death of me?
By no means. It was sin that killed me, and thereby sin exposed its true
character: it used a good thing to bring about my death, and so, through the
commandment, sin became more sinful than ever.

14   We know that the law is spiritual; but I am not: I am unspiritual, the
15 purchased slave of sin. I do not even acknowledge my own actions as mine,
16 for what I do is not what I want to do, but what I detest. But if what I do
is against my will, it means that I agree with the law and hold it to be
17 admirable. But as things are, it is no longer I who perform the action, but
18 sin that lodges in me. For I know that nothing good lodges in me—in my
unspiritual nature, I mean—for though the will to do good is there, the
19 deed is not. The good which I want to do, I fail to do; but what I do is the
20 wrong which is against my will; and if what I do is against my will, clearly
it is no longer I who am the agent, but sin that has its lodging in me.

21   I discover this principle, then: that when I want to do the right, only
22 the wrong is within my reach. In my inmost self I delight in the law of God,
23 but I perceive that there is in my bodily members a different law, fighting
against the law that my reason approves and making me a prisoner under
24 the law *a* that is in my members, the law of sin. Miserable creature that I
25 am, who is there to rescue me out of this body doomed to death *b*? God
alone, through Jesus Christ our Lord! Thanks be to God! In a word then,
I myself, subject to God's law as a rational being, am yet, *c* in my unspiritual nature, a slave to the law of sin.

8   The conclusion of the matter is this: there is no condemnation for those
2 who are united with Christ Jesus, because in Christ Jesus the life-giving
3 law of the Spirit has set you free from the law of sin and death. What the

---

a Or by means of the law.   *b Or* out of the body doomed to this death.
c Or Thus, left to myself, while subject . . . rational being, I am yet . . .

law could never do, because our lower nature robbed it of all potency, God has done: by sending his own Son in a form like that of our own sinful nature, and as a sacrifice for sin,[a] he has passed judgement against sin within that very nature, so that the commandment of the law may find 4 fulfilment in us, whose conduct, no longer under the control of our lower nature, is directed by the Spirit.

Those who live on the level of our lower nature have their outlook 5 formed by it, and that spells death; but those who live on the level of the 6 spirit have the spiritual outlook, and that is life and peace. For the outlook 7 of the lower nature is enmity with God; it is not subject to the law of God; indeed it cannot be: those who live on such a level cannot possibly please 8 God.

But that is not how you live. You are on the spiritual level, if only God's 9 Spirit dwells within you; and if a man does not possess the Spirit of Christ, he is no Christian. But if Christ is dwelling within you, then although the 10 body is a dead thing because you sinned, yet the spirit is life itself because you have been justified.[b] Moreover, if the Spirit of him who raised Jesus 11 from the dead dwells within you, then the God who raised Christ Jesus from the dead will also give new life to your mortal bodies through his indwelling Spirit.

It follows, my friends, that our lower nature has no claim upon us; 12 we are not obliged to live on that level. If you do so, you must die. But 13 if by the Spirit you put to death all the base pursuits of the body, then you will live.

For all who are moved by the Spirit of God are sons of God. The Spirit 14 15 you have received is not a spirit of slavery leading you back into a life of fear, but a Spirit that makes us sons, enabling us to cry 'Abba! Father!' In that cry the Spirit of God joins with our spirit in testifying that we are 16 God's children; and if children, then heirs. We are God's heirs and Christ's 17 fellow-heirs, if we share his sufferings now in order to share his splendour hereafter.

For I reckon that the sufferings we now endure bear no comparison with 18 the splendour, as yet unrevealed, which is in store for us. For the created 19 universe waits with eager expectation for God's sons to be revealed. It was 20 made the victim of frustration, not by its own choice, but because of him who made it so;[c] yet always there was hope, because[d] the universe itself 21 is to be freed from the shackles of mortality and enter upon the liberty and splendour of the children of God. Up to the present, we know, the whole 22 created universe groans in all its parts as if in the pangs of childbirth. Not 23 only so, but even we, to whom the Spirit is given as firstfruits of the harvest to come, are groaning inwardly while we wait for God to make us his sons and[e] set our whole body free. For we have been saved, though only in 24 hope. Now to see is no longer to hope: why should a man endure and wait[f] for what he already sees? But if we hope for something we do not yet 25 see, then, in waiting for it, we show our endurance.

[a] *Or* and to deal with sin.   [b] *Or* so that you may live rightly.   [c] *Or* because God subjected it.   [d] *Or* with the hope that . . .   [e] *Some witnesses omit* make us his sons and.   [f] *Some witnesses read* why should a man hope . . .

26   In the same way the Spirit comes to the aid of our weakness. We do not
even know how we ought to pray,[a] but through our inarticulate groans the
27 Spirit himself is pleading for us, and God who searches our inmost being
knows what the Spirit means, because he pleads for God's people in God's
28 own way; and in everything, as we know, he co-operates for good with those
29 who love God[b] and are called according to his purpose. For God knew his
own before ever they were, and also ordained that they should be shaped
to the likeness of his Son, that he might be the eldest among a large family
30 of brothers; and it is these, so fore-ordained, whom he has also called. And
those whom he called he has justified, and to those whom he justified he
has also given his splendour.
31   With all this in mind, what are we to say? If God is on our side, who is
32 against us? He did not spare his own Son, but gave him up for us all; and
33 with this gift how can he fail to lavish upon us all he has to give? Who will
be the accuser of God's chosen ones? It is God who pronounces acquittal;
34 then who can condemn? It is Christ—Christ who died, and, more than that,
was raised from the dead—who is at God's right hand, and indeed pleads
35 our cause.[c] Then what can separate us from the love of Christ? Can
affliction or hardship? Can persecution, hunger, nakedness, peril, or the
36 sword? 'We are being done to death for thy sake all day long,' as Scripture
37 says; 'we have been treated like sheep for slaughter'—and yet, in spite of
38 all, overwhelming victory is ours through him who loved us. For I am
convinced that there is nothing in death or life, in the realm of spirits or
superhuman powers, in the world as it is or the world as it shall be, in the
39 forces of the universe, in heights or depths—nothing in all creation that can
separate us from the love of God in Christ Jesus our Lord.

The purpose of God in history

9   I AM SPEAKING the truth as a Christian, and my own conscience,
2   enlightened by the Holy Spirit, assures me it is no lie: in my heart there
3 is great grief and unceasing sorrow. For I could even pray to be outcast
4 from Christ myself for the sake of my brothers, my natural kinsfolk. They
are Israelites: they were made God's sons; theirs is the splendour of the
divine presence, theirs the covenants, the law, the temple worship, and the
5 promises. Theirs are the patriarchs, and from them, in natural descent,
sprang the Messiah.[d] May God, supreme above all, be blessed for ever![e]
Amen.
6   It is impossible that the word of God should have proved false. For not
7 all descendants of Israel are truly Israel, nor, because they are Abraham's

---

[a] *Or* what it is right to pray for.   [b] *Or* and, as we know, all things work together
for good for those who love God; *some witnesses read* and we know God himself co-
operates for good with those who love God.   [c] *Or* Who will be the accuser
of God's chosen ones? Will it be God himself? No, he it is who pronounces acquittal.
Who will be the judge to condemn? Will it be Christ—he who died, and, more than
that, . . . right hand? No, he it is who pleads our cause.   [d] *Greek* Christ.
[e] *Or* sprang the Messiah, supreme above all, God blessed for ever; *or* sprang the Messiah,
who is supreme above all. Blessed be God for ever!

offspring, are they all his true children;[a] but, in the words of Scripture, 'Through the line of Isaac your descendants shall be traced.'[b] That is to 8 say, it is not those born in the course of nature who are children of God; it is the children born through God's promise who are reckoned as Abraham's descendants. For the promise runs: 'At the time fixed I will come, 9 and Sarah shall have a son.'

But that is not all, for Rebekah's children had one and the same father, 10 our ancestor Isaac; and yet, in order that God's selective purpose might 11 stand, based not upon men's deeds but upon the call of God, she was told, 12 even before they were born, when they had as yet done nothing, good or ill, 'The elder shall be servant to the younger'; and that accords with the 13 text of Scripture, 'Jacob I loved and Esau I hated.'

What shall we say to that? Is God to be charged with injustice? By no 14 means. For he says to Moses, 'Where I show mercy, I will show mercy, 15 and where I pity, I will pity.' Thus it does not depend on man's will or 16 effort, but on God's mercy. For Scripture says to Pharaoh, 'I have raised 17 you up for this very purpose, to exhibit my power in my dealings with you, and to spread my fame over all the world.' Thus he not only shows mercy 18 as he chooses, but also makes men stubborn as he chooses.

You will say, 'Then why does God blame a man? For who can resist his 19 will?' Who are you, sir, to answer God back? Can the pot speak to the 20 potter and say, 'Why did you make me like this?'? Surely the potter can 21 do what he likes with the clay. Is he not free to make out of the same lump two vessels, one to be treasured, the other for common use?

But what if God, desiring to exhibit[c] his retribution at work and to make 22 his power known, tolerated very patiently those vessels which were objects of retribution due for destruction, and did so in order to make known the 23 full wealth of his splendour upon vessels which were objects of mercy, and which from the first had been prepared for this splendour?

Such vessels are we, whom he has called from among Gentiles as well 24 as Jews, as it says in the Book of Hosea: 'Those who were not my people 25 I will call My People, and the unloved nation I will call My Beloved. For 26 in the very place where they were told "you are no people of mine", they shall be called Sons of the living God.' But Isaiah makes this proclamation 27 about Israel: 'Though the Israelites be countless as the sands of the sea, only a remnant shall be saved; for the Lord's sentence on the land will be 28 summary and final'; as also he said previously, 'If the Lord of Hosts had 29 not left us the mere germ of a nation, we should have become like Sodom, and no better than Gomorrah.'

Then what are we to say? That Gentiles, who made no effort after 30 righteousness, nevertheless achieved it, a righteousness based on faith; whereas Israel made great efforts after a law of righteousness, but never 31 attained to it. Why was this? Because their efforts were not based on faith, 32 but (as they supposed) on deeds. They fell over the 'stone' mentioned in 33 Scripture: 'Here I lay in Zion a stone to trip over, a rock to stumble against; but he who has faith in him will not be put to shame.'

a Or all children of God.   *b* Or God's call shall be for your descendants in the line of Isaac.   *c* Or although he had the will to exhibit . . .

10 Brothers, my deepest desire and my prayer to God is for their
2 salvation. To their zeal for God I can testify; but it is an ill-informed zeal.
3 For they ignore God's way of righteousness, and try to set up their own, and
4 therefore they have not submitted themselves to God's righteousness. For
   Christ ends the law and brings righteousness for everyone who has faith. *a*
5   Of legal righteousness Moses writes, 'The man who does this shall gain
6 life by it.' But the righteousness that comes by faith says, 'Do not say to
   yourself, "Who can go up to heaven?" ' (that is to bring Christ down),
7 'or, "Who can go down to the abyss?" ' (to bring Christ up from the dead).
8 But what does it say? 'The word is near you: it is upon your lips and in your
9 heart.' This means the word of faith which we proclaim. If on your lips is
   the confession, 'Jesus is Lord', and in your heart the faith that God raised
10 him from the dead, then you will find salvation. For the faith that leads to
   righteousness is in the heart, and the confession that leads to salvation is
   upon the lips.
11   Scripture says, 'Everyone who has faith in him will be saved from shame'
12 —everyone: there is no distinction between Jew and Greek, because the
   same Lord is Lord of all, and is rich enough for the need of all who invoke
13 him. For everyone, as it says again—'everyone who invokes the name of the
14 Lord will be saved'. How could they invoke one in whom they had no faith?
   And how could they have faith in one they had never heard of? And how
15 hear without someone to spread the news? And how could anyone spread
   the news without a commission to do so? And that is what Scripture
   affirms: 'How welcome are the feet of the messengers of good news!'
16   But not all have responded to the good news. For Isaiah says, 'Lord,
17 who has believed our message?' We conclude that faith is awakened by the
   message, and the message that awakens it comes through the word of
   Christ.
18   But, I ask, can it be that they never heard it? Of course they did: 'Their
   voice has sounded all over the earth, and their words to the bounds of the
19 inhabited world.' But, I ask again, can it be that Israel failed to recognize
   the message? In reply, I first cite Moses, who says, 'I will use a nation that
   is no nation to stir your envy, and a foolish nation to rouse your anger.'
20 But Isaiah is still more daring: 'I was found', he says, 'by those who were
   not looking for me; I was clearly shown to those who never asked about me';
21 while to Israel he says, 'All day long I have stretched out my hands to an
   unruly and defiant people.'

11 I ask then, has God rejected his people? I cannot believe it! I am an
2 Israelite myself, of the stock of Abraham, of the tribe of Benjamin. No!
   God has not rejected the people which he acknowledged of old as his own.
   You know (do you not?) what Scripture says in the story of Elijah—how
3 Elijah pleads with God against Israel: 'Lord, they have killed thy prophets,
   they have torn down thine altars, and I alone am left, and they are seeking
4 my life.' But what does the divine voice say to him? 'I have left myself
5 seven thousand men who have not knelt to Baal.' In just the same way at
   the present time a 'remnant' has come into being, selected by the grace of

   a Or Christ is the end of the law as a way to righteousness for everyone who has faith.

God. But if it is by grace, then it does not rest on deeds done, or grace 6 would cease to be grace.

What follows? What Israel sought, Israel has not achieved, but the 7 selected few have achieved it. The rest were made blind to the truth, exactly as it stands written: 'God brought upon them a numbness of 8 spirit; he gave them blind eyes and deaf ears, and so it is still.' Similarly 9 David says:

> 'May their table be a snare and a trap,
> both stumbling-block and retribution!
> May their eyes become so dim that they lose their sight! 10
> Bow down their backs unceasingly!'

I now ask, did their failure mean complete downfall? Far from it! 11 Because they offended, salvation has come to the Gentiles, to stir Israel to emulation. But if their offence means the enrichment of the world, and 12 if their falling-off means the enrichment of the Gentiles, how much more their coming to full strength!

But I have something to say to you Gentiles. I am a missionary to the 13 Gentiles, and as such I give all honour to that ministry when I try to stir 14 emulation in the men of my own race, and so to save some of them. For if 15 their rejection has meant the reconciliation of the world, what will their acceptance mean? Nothing less than life from the dead! If the first portion 16 of dough is consecrated, so is the whole lump. If the root is consecrated, so are the branches. But if some of the branches have been lopped off, and 17 you, a wild olive, have been grafted in among them, and have come to share the same root and sap as the olive, do not make yourself superior to 18 the branches. If you do so, remember that it is not you who sustain the root: the root sustains you.

You will say, 'Branches were lopped off so that I might be grafted in.' 19 Very well: they were lopped off for lack of faith, and by faith you hold your 20 place. Put away your pride, and be on your guard; for if God did not spare 21 the native branches, no more will he spare you. Observe the kindness and 22 the severity of God—severity to those who fell away, divine kindness to you, if only you remain within its scope; otherwise you too will be cut off, whereas they, if they do not continue faithless, will be grafted in; for it is 23 in God's power to graft them in again. For if you were cut from your native 24 wild olive and against all nature grafted into the cultivated olive, how much more readily will they, the natural olive-branches, be grafted into their native stock!

For there is a deep truth here, my brothers, of which I want you to take 25 account, so that you may not be complacent about your own discernment: this partial blindness has come upon Israel only until the Gentiles have been admitted in full strength; when that has happened, the whole of 26 Israel will be saved, in agreement with the text of Scripture:

> 'From Zion shall come the Deliverer;
> he shall remove wickedness from Jacob.
> And this is the covenant I will grant them, 27
> when I take away their sins.'

28 In the spreading of the Gospel they are treated as God's enemies for your
sake; but God's choice stands, and they are his friends for the sake of the
29 patriarchs. For the gracious gifts of God and his calling are irrevocable.
30 Just as formerly you were disobedient to God, but now have received mercy
31 in the time of their disobedience, so now, when you receive mercy, they
have proved disobedient, but only in order that they too may receive mercy.
32 For in making all mankind prisoners to disobedience, God's purpose was
to show mercy to all mankind.

33   O depth of wealth, wisdom, and knowledge in God! How unsearchable
34 his judgements, how untraceable his ways! Who knows the mind of the
35 Lord? Who has been his counsellor? Who has ever made a gift to him, to
36 receive a gift in return? Source, Guide, and Goal of all that is—to him be
glory for ever! Amen.

Christian behaviour

12 THEREFORE, MY BROTHERS, I implore you by God's mercy to offer
your very selves to him: a living sacrifice, dedicated and fit for his
2 acceptance, the worship offered by mind and heart.[a] Adapt yourselves no
longer to the pattern of this present world, but let your minds be remade
and your whole nature thus transformed. Then you will be able to discern
the will of God, and to know what is good, acceptable, and perfect.
3   In virtue of the gift that God in his grace has given me I say to everyone
among you: do not be conceited or think too highly of yourself; but think
your way to a sober estimate based on the measure of faith that God has dealt
4 to each of you. For just as in a single human body there are many limbs and
5 organs, all with different functions, so all of us, united with Christ, form
one body, serving individually as limbs and organs to one another.
6   The gifts we possess differ as they are allotted to us by God's grace,
and must be exercised accordingly: the gift of inspired utterance, for
7 example, in proportion to a man's faith; or the gift of administration, in
8 administration. A teacher should employ his gift in teaching, and one who
has the gift of stirring speech should use it to stir his hearers. If you give to
charity, give with all your heart; if you are a leader, exert yourself to lead;
if you are helping others in distress, do it cheerfully.
9 10   Love in all sincerity, loathing evil and clinging to the good. Let love for
our brotherhood breed warmth of mutual affection. Give pride of place
to one another in esteem.
11   With unflagging energy, in ardour of spirit, serve the Lord.[b]
12   Let hope keep you joyful; in trouble stand firm; persist in prayer.
13   Contribute to the needs of God's people, and practise hospitality.
14   Call down blessings on your persecutors—blessings, not curses.
15   With the joyful be joyful, and mourn with the mourners.
16   Care as much about each other as about yourselves. Do not be haughty,
but go about with humble folk. Do not keep thinking how wise you are.

[a] Or ... acceptance, for such is the worship which you, as rational creatures, should offer.
[b] *Some witnesses read* meet the demands of the hour.

Never pay back evil for evil. Let your aims be such as all men count 17 honourable. If possible, so far as it lies with you, live at peace with all men. 18 My dear friends, do not seek revenge, but leave a place for divine retribu- 19 tion; for there is a text which reads, 'Justice is mine, says the Lord, I will repay.' But there is another text: 'If your enemy is hungry, feed him; if he 20 is thirsty, give him a drink; by doing this you will heap live coals on his head.' Do not let evil conquer you, but use good to defeat evil. 21

Every person must submit to the supreme authorities. There is no **13** authority but by act of God, and the existing authorities are instituted by him; consequently anyone who rebels against authority is resisting a divine 2 institution, and those who so resist have themselves to thank for the punishment they will receive. For government, a terror to crime, has no 3 terrors for good behaviour. You wish to have no fear of the authorities? Then continue to do right and you will have their approval, for they are 4 God's agents working for your good. But if you are doing wrong, then you will have cause to fear them; it is not for nothing that they hold the power of the sword, for they are God's agents of punishment, for retribution on the offender. That is why you are obliged to submit. It is an obligation 5 imposed not merely by fear of retribution but by conscience. That is also 6 why you pay taxes. The authorities are in God's service and to these duties they devote their energies.

Discharge your obligations to all men; pay tax and toll, reverence and 7 respect, to those to whom they are due. Leave no claim outstanding against 8 you, except that of mutual love. He who loves his neighbour has satisfied every claim of the law. For the commandments, 'Thou shalt not commit 9 adultery, thou shalt not kill, thou shalt not steal, thou shalt not covet', and any other commandment there may be, are all summed up in the one rule, 'Love your neighbour as yourself.' Love cannot wrong a neighbour; 10 therefore the whole law is summed up in love. *a*

In all this, remember how critical the moment is. It is time for you to 11 wake out of sleep, for deliverance is nearer to us now than it was when first we believed. It is far on in the night; day is near. Let us therefore throw off 12 the deeds of darkness and put on our armour as soldiers of the light. Let us 13 behave with decency as befits the day: no revelling or drunkenness, no debauchery or vice, no quarrels or jealousies! Let Christ Jesus himself be 14 the armour that you wear; give no more thought to satisfying the bodily appetites.

IF A MAN IS WEAK in his faith you must accept him without attempting **14** to settle doubtful points. For instance, one man will have faith enough to 2 eat all kinds of food, while a weaker man eats only vegetables. The man who 3 eats must not hold in contempt the man who does not, and he who does not eat must not pass judgement on the one who does; for God has accepted him. Who are you to pass judgement on someone else's servant? Whether 4 he stands or falls is his own Master's business; and stand he will, because his Master has power to enable him to stand.

Again, this man regards one day more highly than another, while that 5

a Or the whole law is fulfilled by love.

man regards all days alike. On such a point everyone should have reached
6 conviction in his own mind. He who respects the day has the Lord in mind
in doing so, and he who eats meat has the Lord in mind when he eats, since
he gives thanks to God; and he who abstains has the Lord in mind no less,
since he too gives thanks to God.

7 For no one of us lives, and equally no one of us dies, for himself alone.
8 If we live, we live for the Lord; and if we die, we die for the Lord. Whether
9 therefore we live or die, we belong to the Lord. This is why Christ died
10 and came to life again, to establish his lordship over dead and living. You,
sir, why do you pass judgement on your brother? And you, sir, why do you
hold your brother in contempt? We shall all stand before God's tribunal.
11 For Scripture says, 'As I live, says the Lord, to me every knee shall bow and
12 every tongue acknowledge God.' So, you see, each of us will have to answer
for himself.

13 Let us therefore cease judging one another, but rather make this simple
judgement: that no obstacle or stumbling-block be placed in a brother's
14 way. I am absolutely convinced, as a Christian,*a* that nothing is impure in
itself; only, if a man considers a particular thing impure, then to him it is
15 impure. If your brother is outraged by what you eat, then your conduct is
no longer guided by love. Do not by your eating bring disaster to a man for
16 whom Christ died! What for you is a good thing must not become an occa-
17 sion for slanderous talk; for the kingdom of God is not eating and drink-
18 ing, but justice, peace, and joy, inspired by the Holy Spirit. He who thus
shows himself a servant of Christ is acceptable to God and approved
by men.

19 Let us then pursue the things that make for peace and build up the
20 common life. Do not ruin the work of God for the sake of food. Everything
is pure in itself, but anything is bad for the man who by his eating causes
21 another to fall. It is a fine thing to abstain from eating meat or drinking
22 wine, or doing anything which causes your brother's downfall. If you have
a clear conviction, apply it to yourself in the sight of God. Happy is the
23 man who can make his decision with a clear conscience!*b* But a man who
has doubts is guilty if he eats, because his action does not arise from his
conviction, and anything which does not arise from conviction is sin.*c*

15 Those of us who have a robust conscience must accept as our own burden
2 the tender scruples of weaker men, and not consider ourselves. Each of us
must consider his neighbour and think what is for his good and will build
3 up the common life. For Christ too did not consider himself, but might
have said, in the words of Scripture, 'The reproaches of those who re-
4 proached thee fell upon me.' For all the ancient scriptures were written
for our own instruction, in order that through the encouragement they give
5 us we may maintain our hope with fortitude. And may God, the source of
all fortitude and all encouragement, grant that you may agree with one
6 another after the manner of Christ Jesus, so that with one mind and one
voice you may praise the God and Father of our Lord Jesus Christ.

7 In a word, accept one another as Christ accepted us, to the glory of God.

a Or on the authority of the Lord Jesus.   *b Or* who does not bring judgement
upon himself by what he approves!   *c See p. 209, note c.*

I mean that Christ became a servant of the Jewish people to maintain the 8
truth of God by making good his promises to the patriarchs, and at the 9
same time to give the Gentiles cause to glorify God for his mercy. As
Scripture says, 'Therefore I will praise thee among the Gentiles and sing
hymns to thy name'; and again, 'Gentiles, make merry together with his 10
own people'; and yet again, 'All Gentiles, praise the Lord; let all peoples 11
praise him.' Once again, Isaiah says, 'There shall be the Scion of Jesse, 12
the one raised up to govern the Gentiles; on him the Gentiles shall set their
hope.' And may the God of hope fill you with all joy and peace by your 13
faith in him, until, by the power of the Holy Spirit, you overflow with hope.

MY FRIENDS, I have no doubt in my own mind that you yourselves are 14
quite full of goodness and equipped with knowledge of every kind, well
able to give advice to one another; nevertheless I have written to refresh 15
your memory, and written somewhat boldly at times, in virtue of the gift
I have from God. His grace has made me a minister of Christ Jesus to the 16
Gentiles; my priestly service is the preaching of the gospel of God, and
it falls to me to offer the Gentiles to him as *a* an acceptable sacrifice, consecrated by the Holy Spirit.

Thus in the fellowship of Christ Jesus I have ground for pride in the 17
service of God. I will venture to speak of those things alone in which I have 18
been Christ's instrument to bring the Gentiles into his allegiance, by word
and deed, by the force of miraculous signs and by the power of the Holy 19
Spirit. As a result I have completed the preaching of the gospel of Christ
from Jerusalem as far round as Illyricum. It is my ambition to bring the 20
Gospel to places where the very name of Christ has not been heard, for I
do not want to build on another man's foundation; but, as Scripture says, 21

> 'They who had no news of him shall see,
> and they who never heard of him shall understand.'

That is why I have been prevented all this time from coming to you. 22
But now I have no further scope in these parts, and I have been longing for 23
many years to visit you on my way to Spain; for I hope to see you as I 24
travel through, and to be sent there with your support after having enjoyed
your company for a while. But at the moment I am on my way to Jerusalem, 25
on an errand to God's people there. For Macedonia and Achaia have 26
resolved to raise a common fund for the benefit of the poor among God's
people at Jerusalem. They have resolved to do so, and indeed they are under 27
an obligation to them. For if the Jewish Christians shared their spiritual
treasures with the Gentiles, the Gentiles have a clear duty to contribute to
their material needs. So when I have finished this business and delivered 28
the proceeds under my own seal, I shall set out for Spain by way of your
city, and I am sure that when I arrive I shall come to you with a full 29
measure of the blessing of Christ.

I implore you by our Lord Jesus Christ and by the love that the Spirit 30
inspires, be my allies in the fight; pray to God for me that I may be saved 31
from unbelievers in Judaea and that my errand to Jerusalem may find

---

a Or . . . of God, so that the worship which the Gentiles offer may be . . .

32 acceptance with God's people, so that by his will I may come to you in a
33 happy frame of mind and enjoy a time of rest with you. The God of peace
be with you all. Amen. *a*

16 I COMMEND TO YOU PHOEBE, a fellow-Christian who holds office in the
2 congregation at Cenchreae. Give her, in the fellowship of the Lord, a
welcome worthy of God's people, and stand by her in any business in
which she may need your help, for she has herself been a good friend to
many, including myself.

3   Give my greetings to Prisca and Aquila, my fellow-workers in Christ
4 Jesus. They risked their necks to save my life, and not I alone but all the
5 gentile congregations are grateful to them. Greet also the congregation at
their house.

     Give my greetings to my dear friend Epaenetus, the first convert to
6 7 Christ in Asia, and to Mary, who toiled hard for you. Greet Andronicus
and Junias*b* my fellow-countrymen and comrades in captivity. They are
eminent among the apostles, and they were Christians before I was.

8 9   Greetings to Ampliatus, my dear friend in the fellowship of the Lord, to
10 Urban my comrade in Christ, and to my dear Stachys. My greetings to
Apelles, well proved in Christ's service, to the household of Aristobulus,
11 and my countryman Herodion, and to those of the household of Narcissus
12 who are in the Lord's fellowship. Greet Tryphaena and Tryphosa, who
toil in the Lord's service, and dear Persis who has toiled in his service so
13 long. Give my greetings to Rufus, an outstanding follower of the Lord,
14 and to his mother, whom I call mother too. Greet Asyncritus, Phlegon,
15 Hermes, Patrobas, Hermas, and all friends in their company. Greet
Philologus and Julia,*c* Nereus and his sister, and Olympas, and all God's
people associated with them.

16   Greet one another with the kiss of peace. All Christ's congregations
send you their greetings.

17   I implore you, my friends, keep your eye on those who stir up quarrels
and lead others astray, contrary to the teaching you received. Avoid them,
18 for such people are servants not of Christ our Lord but of their own
appetites, and they seduce the minds of innocent people with smooth and
19 specious words. The fame of your obedience has spread everywhere. This
makes me happy about you; yet I should wish you to be experts in goodness
20 but simpletons in evil; and the God of peace will soon crush Satan beneath
your feet. The grace of our Lord Jesus be with you! *d*

21   Greetings to you from my colleague Timothy, and from Lucius, Jason,
22 and Sosipater my fellow-countrymen. (I Tertius, who took this letter
23 down, add my Christian greetings.) Greetings also from Gaius, my host
and host of the whole congregation, and from Erastus, treasurer of this
city, and our brother Quartus. *e*

---

a *See p. 209, note c.*   *b* *Or* Junia; *some witnesses read* Julia, *or* Julias.
c *Or* Julias; *some witnesses read* Junia, *or* Junias.   *d* *The words* The grace . . . with
you *are omitted at this point in some witnesses; in some, these or similar words are given as
verse 24, and in some others after verse 27 (see note on verse 23).*   *e* *Some witnesses
add* (24) The grace of our Lord Jesus Christ be with you all! Amen.

To HIM who has power to make your standing sure, according to the   25
Gospel I brought you and the proclamation of Jesus Christ, according to
the revelation of that divine secret kept in silence for long ages but now   26
disclosed, and through prophetic scriptures by eternal God's command
made known to all nations, to bring them to faith and obedience—to God   27
who alone is wise, through Jesus Christ,*a* be glory for endless ages! Amen.*b c*

THE FIRST LETTER OF PAUL
TO THE
CORINTHIANS

Unity and order in the church

FROM PAUL, APOSTLE of Jesus Christ at God's call and by   1
God's will, together with our colleague Sosthenes, to the congrega-   2
tion of God's people at Corinth, dedicated to him in Christ Jesus,
claimed by him as his own, along with all men everywhere who invoke the
name of our Lord Jesus Christ—their Lord as well as ours.

Grace and peace to you from God our Father and the Lord Jesus Christ.   3
I am always thanking God for you. I thank him for his grace given to   4
you in Christ Jesus. I thank him for all the enrichment that has come to   5
you in Christ. You possess full knowledge and you can give full expression
to it, because in you the evidence for the truth of Christ has found con-   6
firmation. There is indeed no single gift you lack, while you wait expec-   7
tantly for our Lord Jesus Christ to reveal himself. He will keep you firm   8
to the end, without reproach on the Day of our Lord Jesus. It is God him-   9
self who called you to share in the life of his Son Jesus Christ our Lord;
and God keeps faith.

I appeal to you, my brothers, in the name of our Lord Jesus Christ: 10
agree among yourselves, and avoid divisions; be firmly joined in unity of
mind and thought. I have been told, my brothers, by Chloe's people that   11
there are quarrels among you. What I mean is this: each of you is saying,   12
'I am Paul's man', or 'I am for Apollos'; 'I follow Cephas', or 'I am
Christ's.' Surely Christ has not been divided among you! Was it Paul who   13
was crucified for you? Was it in the name of Paul that you were baptized?
Thank God, I never baptized one of you—except Crispus and Gaius. So   14 15
no one can say you were baptized in my name.—Yes, I did baptize the   16

a Some witnesses insert to whom.   *b Here some witnesses add* The grace of our
Lord Jesus Christ be with you!   *c Some witnesses place verses 25–27 at
the end of chapter 14, one other places them at the end of chapter 15, and others omit them
altogether.*

17 household of Stephanas; I cannot think of anyone else. Christ did not send me to baptize, but to proclaim the Gospel; and to do it without relying on the language of worldly wisdom, so that the fact of Christ on his cross might have its full weight.

18 This doctrine of the cross is sheer folly to those on their way to ruin,
19 but to us who are on the way to salvation it is the power of God. Scripture says, 'I will destroy the wisdom of the wise, and bring to nothing the
20 cleverness of the clever.' Where is your wise man now, your man of learning, or your subtle debater—limited, all of them, to this passing age?
21 God has made the wisdom of this world look foolish. As God in his wisdom ordained, the world failed to find him by its wisdom, and he chose to save
22 those who have faith by the folly of the Gospel. Jews call for miracles,
23 Greeks look for wisdom; but we proclaim Christ—yes, Christ nailed to the cross; and though this is a stumbling-block to Jews and folly to Greeks,
24 yet to those who have heard his call, Jews and Greeks alike, he is the power of God and the wisdom of God.

25 Divine folly is wiser than the wisdom of man, and divine weakness
26 stronger than man's strength. My brothers, think what sort of people you are, whom God has called. Few of you are men of wisdom, by any human
27 standard; few are powerful or highly born. Yet, to shame the wise, God has chosen what the world counts folly, and to shame what is strong, God
28 has chosen what the world counts weakness. He has chosen things low and
29 contemptible, mere nothings, to overthrow the existing order. And so
30 there is no place for human pride in the presence of God. You are in Christ Jesus by God's act, for God has made him our wisdom; he is our righteous-
31 ness; in him we are consecrated and set free. And so (in the words of Scripture), 'If a man must boast, let him boast of the Lord.'

2 As for me, brothers, when I came to you, I declared the attested truth of
2 God *a* without display of fine words or wisdom. I resolved that while I was with you I would think of nothing but Jesus Christ—Christ nailed to the
3 4 cross. I came before you weak, nervous, and shaking with fear. The word I spoke, the gospel I proclaimed, did not sway you with subtle arguments;
5 it carried conviction by spiritual power, so that your faith might be built not upon human wisdom but upon the power of God.

6 And yet I do speak words of wisdom to those who are ripe for it, not a wisdom belonging to this passing age, nor to any of its governing powers,
7 which are declining to their end; I speak God's hidden wisdom, his secret
8 purpose framed from the very beginning to bring us to our full glory. The powers that rule the world have never known it; if they had, they would
9 not have crucified the Lord of glory. But, in the words of Scripture, 'Things beyond our seeing, things beyond our hearing, things beyond our
10 imagining, all prepared by God for those who love him', these it is that God has revealed to us through the Spirit.

For the Spirit explores everything, even the depths of God's own
11 nature. Among men, who knows what a man is but the man's own spirit within him? In the same way, only the Spirit of God knows what God is.
12 This is the Spirit that we have received from God, and not the spirit of

a Some witnesses read I declared God's secret purpose . . .

the world, so that we may know all that God of his own grace has given us; and, because we are interpreting spiritual truths to those who have the 13 Spirit, we speak of these gifts of God in words found for us not by our human wisdom but by the Spirit. A man who is unspiritual refuses what 14 belongs to the Spirit of God; it is folly to him; he cannot grasp it, because it needs to be judged in the light of the Spirit. A man gifted with the Spirit 15 can judge the worth of everything, but is not himself subject to judgement by his fellow-men. For (in the words of Scripture) 'who knows the mind of 16 the Lord? Who can advise him?' We, however, possess the mind of Christ.

FOR MY PART, my brothers, I could not speak to you as I should speak 3 to people who have the Spirit. I had to deal with you on the merely natural plane, as infants in Christ. And so I gave you milk to drink, instead of solid 2 food, for which you were not yet ready. Indeed, you are still not ready for it, for you are still on the merely natural plane. Can you not see that while 3 there is jealousy and strife among you, you are living on the purely human level of your lower nature? When one says, 'I am Paul's man', and another, 4 'I am for Apollos', are you not all too human?

After all, what is Apollos? What is Paul? We are simply God's agents 5 in bringing you to the faith. Each of us performed the task which the Lord allotted to him: I planted the seed, and Apollos watered it; but God made 6 it grow. Thus it is not the gardeners with their planting and watering who 7 count, but God, who makes it grow. Whether they plant or water, they work 8 as a team,*ᵃ* though each will get his own pay for his own labour. We are 9 God's fellow-workers;*ᵇ* and you are God's garden.

Or again, you are God's building. I am like a skilled master-builder 10 who by God's grace laid the foundation, and someone else is putting up the building. Let each take care how he builds. There can be no other 11 foundation beyond that which is already laid; I mean Jesus Christ himself. If anyone builds on that foundation with gold, silver, and fine stone, or 12 with wood, hay, and straw, the work that each man does will at last be 13 brought to light; the day of judgement will expose it. For that day dawns in fire, and the fire will test the worth of each man's work. If a man's build- 14 ing stands, he will be rewarded; if it burns, he will have to bear the loss; 15 and yet he will escape with his life, as one might from a fire. Surely you 16 know that you are God's temple, where the Spirit of God dwells. Anyone 17 who destroys God's temple will himself be destroyed*ᶜ* by God, because the temple of God is holy; and that temple you are.

Make no mistake about this: if there is anyone among you who fancies 18 himself wise—wise, I mean, by the standards of this passing age—he must become a fool to gain true wisdom. For the wisdom of this world is folly in 19 God's sight. Scripture says, 'He traps the wise in their own cunning', and 20 again, 'The Lord knows that the arguments of the wise are futile.' So never 21 make mere men a cause for pride. For though everything belongs to you— Paul, Apollos, and Cephas, the world, life, and death, the present and the 22

ᵃ Or Whether they plant or water, it is all the same.　　　*ᵇ Or* We are fellow-workers in God's service.　　　*ᶜ Some witnesses read* is himself destroyed.

23 future, all of them belong to you—yet you belong to Christ, and Christ to God.

4 We must be regarded as Christ's subordinates and as stewards of the
2 secrets of God. Well then, stewards are expected to show themselves trust-
3 worthy. For my part, if I am called to account by you or by any human court of judgement, it does not matter to me in the least. Why, I do not even pass
4 judgement on myself, for I have nothing on my conscience; but that does
5 not mean I stand acquitted. My judge is the Lord. So pass no premature judgement; wait until the Lord comes. For he will bring to light what darkness hides, and disclose men's inward motives; then will be the time for each to receive from God such praise as he deserves.

6 Into this general picture, my friends, I have brought Apollos and myself on your account, so that you may take our case as an example, and learn to 'keep within the rules', as they say, and may not be inflated with pride
7 as you patronize one and flout the other. Who makes you, my friend, so important? What do you possess that was not given you? If then you really received it all as a gift, why take the credit to yourself?

8 All of you, no doubt, have everything you could desire. You have come into your fortune already. You have come into your kingdom—and left us out. How I wish you had indeed won your kingdom; then you might
9 share it with us! For it seems to me God has made us apostles the most abject of mankind. We are like men condemned to death in the arena, a
10 spectacle to the whole universe—angels as well as men. We are fools for Christ's sake, while you are such sensible Christians. We are weak; you
11 are so powerful. We are in disgrace; you are honoured. To this day we go hungry and thirsty and in rags; we are roughly handled; we wander from
12 place to place; we wear ourselves out working with our own hands. They
13 curse us, and we bless; they persecute us, and we submit to it; they slander us, and we humbly make our appeal. We are treated as the scum of the earth, the dregs of humanity, to this very day.

14 I am not writing thus to shame you, but to bring you to reason; for you
15 are my dear children. You may have ten thousand tutors in Christ, but you have only one father. For in Christ Jesus you are my offspring, and
16 mine alone, through the preaching of the Gospel. I appeal to you there-
17 fore to follow my example. That is the very reason why I have sent Timothy, who is a dear son to me and a most trustworthy Christian; he will remind you of the way of life in Christ which I follow, and which I teach every-
18 where in all our congregations. There are certain persons who are filled
19 with self-importance because they think I am not coming to Corinth. I shall come very soon, if the Lord will; and then I shall take the measure of these self-important people, not by what they say, but by what power is in them.
20 21 The kingdom of God is not a matter of talk, but of power. Choose, then: am I to come to you with a rod in my hand, or in love and a gentle spirit?

5 I ACTUALLY HEAR REPORTS of sexual immorality among you, immorality such as even pagans do not tolerate: the union of a man with his
2 father's wife. And you can still be proud of yourselves! You ought to have gone into mourning; a man who has done such a deed should have been

rooted out of your company. For my part, though I am absent in body, I 3
am present in spirit, and my judgement upon the man who did this thing is
already given, as if I were indeed present: you all being assembled in the 4
name of our Lord Jesus, and I with you in spirit, with the power of our
Lord Jesus over us, this man is to be consigned to Satan for the destruction 5
of the body, so that his spirit may be saved on the Day of the Lord.

Your self-satisfaction ill becomes you. Have you never heard the saying, 6
'A little leaven leavens all the dough'? The old leaven of corruption is work- 7
ing among you. Purge it out, and then you will be bread of a new baking.
As Christians you are unleavened Passover bread; for indeed our Passover
has begun; the sacrifice is offered—Christ himself. So we who observe the 8
festival must not use the old leaven, the leaven of corruption and wickedness, but only the unleavened bread which is sincerity and truth.

In my letter I wrote that you must have nothing to do with loose livers. 9
I was not, of course, referring to pagans who lead loose lives or are grabbers 10
and swindlers or idolaters. To avoid them you would have to get out of the
world altogether. I now write that you must have nothing to do with any 11
so-called Christian who leads a loose life, or is grasping, or idolatrous, a
slanderer, a drunkard, or a swindler. You should not even eat with any
such person. What business of mine is it to judge outsiders? God is their 12 13
judge. You are judges within the fellowship. Root out the evil-doer from
your community.

IF ONE OF YOUR NUMBER has a dispute with another, has he the face to 6
take it to pagan law-courts instead of to the community of God's people?
It is God's people who are to judge the world; surely you know that. And 2
if the world is to come before you for judgement, are you incompetent to
deal with these trifling cases? Are you not aware that we are to judge angels? 3
How much more, mere matters of business! If therefore you have such 4
business disputes, how can you entrust jurisdiction to outsiders, men
who count for nothing in our community? I write this to shame you. Can 5
it be that there is not a single wise man among you able to give a decision
in a brother-Christian's cause? Must brother go to law with brother—and 6
before unbelievers? Indeed, you already fall below your standard in going 7
to law with one another at all. Why not rather suffer injury? Why not
rather let yourself be robbed? So far from this, you actually injure and 8
rob—injure and rob your brothers! Surely you know that the unjust will 9
never come into possession of the kingdom of God. Make no mistake: no
fornicator or idolater, none who are guilty either of adultery or of homo-
sexual perversion, no thieves or grabbers or drunkards or slanderers or 10
swindlers, will possess the kingdom of God. Such were some of you. But 11
you have been through the purifying waters; you have been dedicated to
God and justified through the name of the Lord Jesus and the Spirit of
our God.

'I am free to do anything', you say. Yes, but not everything is for my 12
good. No doubt I am free to do anything, but I for one will not let anything
make free with me. 'Food is for the belly and the belly for food', you say. 13
True; and one day God will put an end to both. But it is not true that the

14 body is for lust; it is for the Lord—and the Lord for the body. God not
15 only raised our Lord from the dead; he will also raise us by his power. Do you not know that your bodies are limbs and organs of Christ? Shall I then take from Christ his bodily parts and make them over to a harlot? Never!
16 You surely know that anyone who links himself with a harlot becomes physically one with her (for Scripture says, 'The pair shall become one
17 flesh'); but he who links himself with Christ is one with him, spiritually.
18 Shun fornication. Every other sin that a man can commit is outside the
19 body; but the fornicator sins against his own body. Do you not know that your body is a shrine of the indwelling Holy Spirit, and the Spirit is God's
20 gift to you? You do not belong to yourselves; you were bought at a price. Then honour God in your body.

The Christian in a pagan society

7 AND NOW for the matters you wrote about.
It is a good thing for a man to have nothing to do with women;*a*
2 but because there is so much immorality, let each man have his own wife
3 and each woman her own husband. The husband must give the wife what
4 is due to her, and the wife equally must give the husband his due. The wife cannot claim her body as her own; it is her husband's. Equally, the husband
5 cannot claim his body as his own; it is his wife's. Do not deny yourselves to one another, except when you agree upon a temporary abstinence in order to devote yourselves to prayer; afterwards you may come together again; otherwise, for lack of self-control, you may be tempted by Satan.
6 7 All this I say by way of concession, not command. I should like you all to be as I am myself; but everyone has the gift God has granted him, one this gift and another that.
8 To the unmarried and to widows I say this: it is a good thing if they stay
9 as I am myself; but if they cannot control themselves, they should marry. Better be married than burn with vain desire.
10 To the married I give this ruling, which is not mine but the Lord's: a
11 wife must not separate herself from her husband; if she does, she must either remain unmarried or be reconciled to her husband; and the husband must not divorce his wife.
12 To the rest I say this, as my own word, not as the Lord's: if a Christian has a heathen wife, and she is willing to live with him, he must not divorce
13 her; and a woman who has a heathen husband willing to live with her must
14 not divorce her husband. For the heathen husband now belongs to God through his Christian wife, and the heathen wife through her Christian husband. Otherwise your children would not belong to God, whereas in
15 fact they do. If on the other hand the heathen partner wishes for a separation, let him have it. In such cases the Christian husband or wife is under
16 no compulsion; but God's call is a call to live in peace. Think of it: as a wife you may be your husband's salvation; as a husband you may be your wife's salvation.

a Or You say, 'It is a good thing . . . women'; . . .

However that may be, each one must order his life according to the gift 17
the Lord has granted him and his condition when God called him. That is
what I teach in all our congregations. Was a man called with the marks of 18
circumcision on him? Let him not remove them. Was he uncircumcised
when he was called? Let him not be circumcised. Circumcision or un- 19
circumcision is neither here nor there; what matters is to keep God's commands. Every man should remain in the condition in which he was called. 20
Were you a slave when you were called? Do not let that trouble you; but if 21
a chance of liberty should come, take it.*ᵃ* For the man who as a slave 22
received the call to be a Christian is the Lord's freedman, and, equally,
the free man who received the call is a slave in the service of Christ. You 23
were bought at a price; do not become slaves of men. Thus each one, my 24
friends, is to remain before God in the condition in which he received
his call.

On the question of celibacy, I have no instructions from the Lord, but 25
I give my judgement as one who by God's mercy is fit to be trusted.

It is my opinion, then, that in a time of stress like the present this is the 26
best way for a man to live—it is best for a man to be as he is. Are you bound 27
in marriage? Do not seek a dissolution. Has your marriage been dissolved?
Do not seek a wife. If, however, you do marry, there is nothing wrong in 28
it; and if a virgin marries, she has done no wrong. But those who marry
will have pain and grief in this bodily life, and my aim is to spare you.

What I mean, my friends, is this. The time we live in will not last long. 29
While it lasts, married men should be as if they had no wives; mourners 30
should be as if they had nothing to grieve them, the joyful as if they did not
rejoice; buyers must not count on keeping what they buy, nor those who 31
use the world's wealth on using it to the full. For the whole frame of this
world is passing away.

I want you to be free from anxious care. The unmarried man cares for 32
the Lord's business; his aim is to please the Lord. But the married man 33
cares for worldly things; his aim is to please his wife; and he has a divided 34
mind. The unmarried or celibate woman cares*ᵇ* for the Lord's business;
her aim is to be dedicated to him in body as in spirit; but the married
woman cares for worldly things; her aim is to please her husband.

In saying this I have no wish to keep you on a tight rein. I am thinking 35
simply of your own good, of what is seemly, and of your freedom to wait
upon the Lord without distraction.

But if a man has a partner in celibacy*ᶜ* and feels that he is not behaving 36
properly towards her, if, that is, his instincts are too strong for him,*ᵈ* and
something must be done, he may do as he pleases; there is nothing wrong
in it; let them marry.*ᵉ* But if a man is steadfast in his purpose, being under 37
no compulsion, and has complete control of his own choice; and if he has
decided in his own mind to preserve his partner*ᶠ* in her virginity, he will

---

ᵃ Or but even if a chance of liberty should come, choose rather to make good use of your
servitude.   *ᵇ Some witnesses read* . . . his wife. And there is a difference between
the wife and the virgin. The unmarried woman cares . . .   *ᶜ Or* a virgin daughter
(*or* ward).   *ᵈ Or* if she is ripe for marriage.   *ᵉ Or* let the girl and her
lover marry.   *ᶠ Or* his daughter.

38 do well. Thus, he who marries his partner *a* does well, and he who does not will do better.

39   A wife is bound to her husband as long as he lives. But if the husband die, she is free to marry whom she will, provided the marriage is within the
40 Lord's fellowship. But she is better off as she is; that is my opinion, and I believe that I too have the Spirit of God.

8 Now about food consecrated to heathen deities.

    Of course we all 'have knowledge', as you say. This 'knowledge' breeds
2 conceit; it is love that builds. If anyone fancies that he knows, he knows
3 nothing yet, in the true sense of knowing. But if a man loves, *b* he is acknowledged by God. *c*

4   Well then, about eating this consecrated food: of course, as you say, 'a false god has no existence in the real world. There is no god but one.'
5 For indeed, if there be so-called gods, whether in heaven or on earth—as
6 indeed there are many 'gods' and many 'lords'—yet for us there is one God, the Father, from whom all being comes, towards whom we move; and there is one Lord, Jesus Christ, through whom all things came to be, and we through him.

7   But not everyone knows this. There are some who have been so accustomed to idolatry *d* that even now they eat this food with a sense of its heathen consecration, and their conscience, being weak, is polluted by the
8 eating. Certainly food will not bring us into God's presence: if we do not
9 eat, we are none the worse, and if we eat, we are none the better. But be
10 careful that this liberty of yours does not become a pitfall for the weak. If a weak character sees you sitting down to a meal in a heathen temple—you, who 'have knowledge'—will not his conscience be emboldened to eat food
11 consecrated to the heathen deity? This 'knowledge' of yours is utter
12 disaster to the weak, the brother for whom Christ died. In thus sinning against your brothers and wounding their conscience, *e* you sin against
13 Christ. And therefore, if food be the downfall of my brother, I will never eat meat any more, for I will not be the cause of my brother's downfall.

9 Am i not a free man? Am I not an apostle? Did I not see Jesus our
2 Lord? Are not you my own handiwork, in the Lord? If others do not accept me as an apostle, you at least are bound to do so, for you are yourselves the very seal of my apostolate, in the Lord.

3 4   To those who put me in the dock this is my answer: Have I no right to
5 eat and drink? Have I no right to take a Christian wife about with me, like
6 the rest of the apostles and the Lord's brothers, and Cephas? Or are
7 Barnabas and I alone bound to work for our living? Did you ever hear of a man serving in the army at his own expense? or planting a vineyard with-
8 out eating the fruit of it? or tending a flock without using its milk? Do not
9 suppose I rely on these human analogies, for the law says the same; in the

---

a *Or* gives his daughter in marriage.   *b* *Some witnesses read* loves God.
c *Or* he is recognized.   *d* *Some witnesses read* in whom the consciousness of the false god is so persistent . . .   *e* *Some witnesses insert* weak as it is.

Law of Moses we read, 'You shall not muzzle a threshing ox.' Do you suppose God's concern is with oxen? Or is the reference clearly to ourselves? 10 Of course it refers to us, in the sense that the ploughman should plough and the thresher thresh in the hope of getting some of the produce. If we 11 have sown a spiritual crop for you, is it too much to expect from you a material harvest? If you allow others these rights, have not we a stronger 12 claim?

But I have availed myself of no such right. On the contrary, I put up with all that comes my way rather than offer any hindrance to the gospel of Christ. You know (do you not?) that those who perform the temple service 13 eat the temple offerings, and those who wait upon the altar claim their share of the sacrifice. In the same way the Lord gave instructions that those 14 who preach the Gospel should earn their living by the Gospel. But I have 15 never taken advantage of any such right, nor do I intend to claim it in this letter. I had rather die! No one shall make my boast an empty boast. Even 16 if I preach the Gospel, I can claim no credit for it; I cannot help myself; it would be misery to me not to preach. If I did it of my own choice, I should 17 be earning my pay; but since I do it apart from my own choice, I am simply discharging a trust.*a* Then what is my pay? The satisfaction of preaching 18 the Gospel without expense to anyone; in other words, of waiving the rights which my preaching gives me.

I am a free man and own no master; but I have made myself every man's 19 servant, to win over as many as possible. To Jews I became like a Jew, to 20 win Jews; as they are subject to the Law of Moses, I put myself under that law to win them, although I am not myself subject to it. To win Gentiles, 21 who are outside the Law, I made myself like one of them, although I am not in truth outside God's law, being under the law of Christ. To the weak 22 I became weak, to win the weak. Indeed, I have become everything in turn to men of every sort, so that in one way or another I may save some. All this I do for the sake of the Gospel, to bear my part in proclaiming it. 23

You know (do you not?) that at the sports all the runners run the race, 24 though only one wins the prize. Like them, run to win! But every athlete 25 goes into strict training. They do it to win a fading wreath; we, a wreath that never fades. For my part, I run with a clear goal before me; I am like 26 a boxer who does not beat the air; I bruise my own body and make it know 27 its master, for fear that after preaching to others I should find myself rejected.

You should understand, my brothers, that our ancestors were all under **10** the pillar of cloud, and all of them passed through the Red Sea; and so they 2 all received baptism into the fellowship of Moses in cloud and sea. They 3 all ate the same supernatural food, and all drank the same supernatural 4 drink; I mean, they all drank from the supernatural rock that accompanied their travels—and that rock was Christ. And yet, most of them were not 5 accepted by God, for the desert was strewn with their corpses.

These events happened as symbols to warn us not to set our desires on 6 evil things, as they did. Do not be idolaters, like some of them; as Scripture 7

a *Or* If I do it willingly I am earning my pay; if I did it unwillingly I should still have a trust laid upon me.

8 has it, 'the people sat down to feast and rose up to revel'. Let us not commit fornication, as some of them did—and twenty-three thousand died in
9 one day. Let us not put the power of the Lord [a] to the test, as some of them
10 did—and were destroyed by serpents. Do not grumble against God, as
some of them did—and were destroyed by the Destroyer.

11   All these things that happened to them were symbolic, and were recorded
for our benefit as a warning. For upon us the fulfilment of the ages has
12 come. If you feel sure that you are standing firm, beware! You may fall.
13 So far you have faced no trial beyond what man can bear. God keeps faith,
and he will not allow you to be tested above your powers, but when the
test comes he will at the same time provide a way out, by enabling you to
sustain it.

14 15 SO THEN, DEAR FRIENDS, shun idolatry. I speak to you as men of sense.
16 Form your own judgement on what I say. When we bless 'the cup of blessing', is it not a means of sharing in the blood of Christ? When we break
17 the bread, is it not a means of sharing in the body of Christ? Because there
is one loaf, we, many as we are, are one body; [b] for it is one loaf of which we
all partake.

18   Look at the Jewish people. Are not those who partake in the sacrificial
19 meal sharers in the altar? What do I imply by this? that an idol is anything
20 but an idol? or food offered to it anything more than food? No; but the
sacrifices the heathen offer are offered (in the words of Scripture) 'to
demons and to that which is not God'; and I will not have you become
21 partners with demons. You cannot drink the cup of the Lord and the cup
of demons. You cannot partake of the Lord's table and the table of demons.
22 Can we defy the Lord? Are we stronger than he?

23   'We are free to do anything', you say. Yes, but is everything good for us?
'We are free to do anything', but does everything help the building of the
24 community? Each of you must regard, not his own interests, but the other
man's.

25   You may eat anything sold in the meat-market without raising questions
26 of conscience; for the earth is the Lord's and everything in it.

27   If an unbeliever invites you to a meal and you care to go, eat whatever is
28 put before you, without raising questions of conscience. But if somebody
says to you, 'This food has been offered in sacrifice', then, out of con-
29 sideration for him, and for conscience' sake, do not eat it—not your conscience, I mean, but the other man's.

'What?' you say, 'is my freedom to be called in question by another
30 man's conscience? If I partake with thankfulness, why am I blamed for
31 eating food over which I have said grace?' Well, whether you eat or drink,
32 or whatever you are doing, do all for the honour of God: give no offence
33 to Jews, or Greeks, or to the church of God. For my part I always try
to meet everyone half-way, regarding not my own good but the good
11 of the many, so that they may be saved. Follow my example as I follow
Christ's.

---

[a] *Some witnesses read* of Christ.
[b] *Or* For we, many as we are, are one loaf, one body.

I COMMEND YOU for always keeping me in mind, and maintaining the 2
tradition I handed on to you. But I wish you to understand that, while 3
every man has Christ for his Head, woman's head is man,*a* as Christ's
Head is God. A man who keeps his head covered when he prays or pro- 4
phesies brings shame on his head; a woman, on the contrary, brings shame 5
on her head if she prays or prophesies bare-headed; it is as bad as if her head
were shaved. If a woman is not to wear a veil she might as well have her 6
hair cut off; but if it is a disgrace for her to be cropped and shaved, then
she should wear a veil. A man has no need to cover his head, because man 7
is the image of God, and the mirror of his glory, whereas woman reflects
the glory of man.*b* For man did not originally spring from woman, but 8
woman was made out of man; and man was not created for woman's sake, 9
but woman for the sake of man; and therefore it is woman's duty to have a 10
sign of authority*c* on her head, out of regard for the angels.*d* And yet, in 11
Christ's fellowship woman is as essential to man as man to woman. If 12
woman was made out of man, it is through woman that man now comes to
be; and God is the source of all.

Judge for yourselves: is it fitting for a woman to pray to God bare- 13
headed? Does not Nature herself teach you that while flowing locks dis- 14
grace a man, they are a woman's glory? For her locks were given for 15
covering.

However, if you insist on arguing, let me tell you, there is no such 16
custom among us, or in any of the congregations of God's people.

In giving you these injunctions I must mention a practice which I can- 17
not commend: your meetings tend to do more harm than good. To begin 18
with, I am told that when you meet as a congregation you fall into sharply
divided groups; and I believe there is some truth in it (for dissensions are 19
necessary if only to show which of your members are sound). The result 20
is that when you meet as a congregation, it is impossible for you to eat the
Lord's Supper, because each of you is in such a hurry to eat his own, and 21
while one goes hungry another has too much to drink. Have you no homes 22
of your own to eat and drink in? Or are you so contemptuous of the church
of God that you shame its poorer members? What am I to say? Can I
commend you? On this point, certainly not!

For the tradition which I handed on to you came to me from the Lord 23
himself: that the Lord Jesus, on the night of his arrest, took bread and, 24
after giving thanks to God, broke it and said: 'This is my body, which is
for you; do this as a memorial of me.' In the same way, he took the cup 25
after supper, and said: 'This cup is the new covenant sealed by my blood.
Whenever you drink it, do this as a memorial of me.' For every time you 26
eat this bread and drink the cup, you proclaim the death of the Lord, until
he comes.

It follows that anyone who eats the bread or drinks the cup of the Lord 27
unworthily will be guilty of desecrating the body and blood of the Lord.
A man must test himself before eating his share of the bread and drinking 28

a Or a woman's head is her husband.   *b* Or a woman reflects her husband's glory.
c *Some witnesses read* to have a veil.   *d* Or and therefore a woman should keep
her dignity on her head, for fear of the angels.

29 from the cup. For he who eats and drinks eats and drinks judgement on
30 himself if he does not discern the Body. That is why many of you are feeble
31 and sick, and a number have died. But if we examined ourselves, we should
32 not thus fall under judgement. When, however, we do fall under the
    Lord's judgement, he is disciplining us, to save us from being condemned
    with the rest of the world.

33   Therefore, my brothers, when you meet for a meal, wait for one another.
34 If you are hungry, eat at home, so that in meeting together you may not
    fall under judgement. The other matters I will arrange when I come.

Spiritual gifts

12 ABOUT GIFTS OF THE SPIRIT, there are some things of which I do
    not wish you to remain ignorant.

2   You know how, in the days when you were still pagan, you were swept
3   off to those dumb heathen gods, however you happened to be led.[a] For
    this reason I must impress upon you that no one who says 'A curse on
    Jesus!' can be speaking under the influence of the Spirit of God. And no
    one can say 'Jesus is Lord!' except under the influence of the Holy Spirit.

5   There are varieties of gifts, but the same Spirit. There are varieties of
6   service, but the same Lord. There are many forms of work, but all of them,
7   in all men, are the work of the same God. In each of us the Spirit is mani-
8   fested in one particular way, for some useful purpose. One man, through
    the Spirit, has the gift of wise speech, while another, by the power of the
9   same Spirit, can put the deepest knowledge into words. Another, by the
    same Spirit, is granted faith; another, by the one Spirit, gifts of healing,
10 and another miraculous powers; another has the gift of prophecy, and
    another ability to distinguish true spirits from false; yet another has the
    gift of ecstatic utterance of different kinds, and another the ability to
11 interpret it. But all these gifts are the work of one and the same Spirit,
    distributing them separately to each individual at will.

12   For Christ is like a single body with its many limbs and organs, which,
13 many as they are, together make up one body. For indeed we were all
    brought into one body by baptism, in the one Spirit, whether we are Jews
    or Greeks, whether slaves or free men, and that one Holy Spirit was poured
    out for all of us to drink.

14 15   A body is not one single organ, but many. Suppose the foot should say,
    'Because I am not a hand, I do not belong to the body', it does belong to the
16 body none the less. Suppose the ear were to say, 'Because I am not an eye,
17 I do not belong to the body', it does still belong to the body. If the body were
    all eye, how could it hear? If the body were all ear, how could it smell?
18 But, in fact, God appointed each limb and organ to its own place in the
19 body, as he chose. If the whole were one single organ, there would not be
20 a body at all; in fact, however, there are many different organs, but one
21 body. The eye cannot say to the hand, 'I do not need you'; nor the head to

---

[a] *Or* . . . pagan, you would be seized by some power which drove you to those dumb
heathen gods.

the feet, 'I do not need you.' Quite the contrary: those organs of the body 22
which seem to be more frail than others are indispensable, and those parts 23
of the body which we regard as less honourable are treated with special
honour. To our unseemly parts is given a more than ordinary seemliness,
whereas our seemly parts need no adorning. But God has combined the 24
various parts of the body, giving special honour to the humbler parts, so 25
that there might be no sense of division in the body, but that all its organs
might feel the same concern for one another. If one organ suffers, they all 26
suffer together. If one flourishes, they all rejoice together.

Now you are Christ's body, and each of you a limb or organ of it. Within 27 28
our community God has appointed, in the first place apostles, in the second
place prophets, thirdly teachers; then miracle-workers, then those who
have gifts of healing, or ability to help others or power to guide them, or
the gift of ecstatic utterance of various kinds. Are all apostles? all prophets? 29
all teachers? Do all work miracles? Have all gifts of healing? Do all speak 30
in tongues of ecstasy? Can all interpret them? The higher gifts are those 31
you should aim at.

And now I will show you the best way of all.

I may speak in tongues of men or of angels, but if I am without love, I **13**
am a sounding gong or a clanging cymbal. I may have the gift of prophecy, 2
and know every hidden truth; I may have faith strong enough to move
mountains; but if I have no love, I am nothing. I may dole out all I possess, 3
or even give my body to be burnt,*a* but if I have no love, I am none the
better.

Love is patient; love is kind and envies no one. Love is never boastful, 4
nor conceited, nor rude; never selfish, not quick to take offence. Love keeps 5
no score of wrongs; does not gloat over other men's sins, but delights in the 6
truth. There is nothing love cannot face; there is no limit to its faith, its 7
hope, and its endurance.

Love will never come to an end. Are there prophets? their work will be 8
over. Are there tongues of ecstasy? they will cease. Is there knowledge?
it will vanish away; for our knowledge and our prophecy alike are partial, 9
and the partial vanishes when wholeness comes. When I was a child, my 10 11
speech, my outlook, and my thoughts were all childish. When I grew up,
I had finished with childish things. Now we see only puzzling reflections 12
in a mirror, but then we shall see face to face. My knowledge now is partial;
then it will be whole, like God's knowledge of me. In a word, there are three 13
things that last for ever: faith, hope, and love; but the greatest of them all
is love.

Put love first; but there are other gifts of the Spirit at which you should **14**
aim also, and above all prophecy. When a man is using the language of 2
ecstasy he is talking with God, not with men, for no man understands him;
he is no doubt inspired, but he speaks mysteries. On the other hand, when 3
a man prophesies, he is talking to men, and his words have power to build;
they stimulate and they encourage. The language of ecstasy is good for the 4
speaker himself, but it is prophecy that builds up a Christian community.
I should be pleased for you all to use the tongues of ecstasy, but better 5

a Some witnesses read even seek glory by self-sacrifice.

pleased for you to prophesy. The prophet is worth more than the man of ecstatic speech—unless indeed he can explain its meaning, and so help to
6 build up the community. Suppose, my friends, that when I come to you I use ecstatic language: what good shall I do you, unless what I say contains something by way of revelation, or enlightenment, or prophecy, or instruction?
7 Even with inanimate things that produce sounds—a flute, say, or a lyre —unless their notes mark definite intervals, how can you tell what tune is
8 being played? Or again, if the trumpet-call is not clear, who will prepare
9 for battle? In the same way if your ecstatic utterance yields no precise meaning, how can anyone tell what you are saying? You will be talking into
10 the air. How many different kinds of sound there are, or may be, in the
11 world! Nothing is altogether soundless. Well then, if I do not know the meaning of the sound the speaker makes, his words will be gibberish to me,
12 and mine to him. You are, I know, eager for gifts of the Spirit; then aspire above all to excel in those which build up the church.
13 I say, then, that the man who falls into ecstatic utterance should pray
14 for the ability to interpret. If I use such language in my prayer, the Spirit
15 in me prays, but my intellect lies fallow. What then? I will pray as I am inspired to pray, but I will also pray intelligently. I will sing hymns as
16 I am inspired to sing, but I will sing intelligently too. Suppose you are praising God in the language of inspiration: how will the plain man who is present be able to say 'Amen' to your thanksgiving, when he does not know
17 what you are saying? Your prayer of thanksgiving may be all that could be
18 desired, but it is no help to the other man. Thank God, I am more gifted in
19 ecstatic utterance than any of you,[a] but in the congregation I would rather speak five intelligible words, for the benefit of others as well as myself, than thousands of words in the language of ecstasy.
20 Do not be childish, my friends. Be as innocent of evil as babes, but at
21 least be grown-up in your thinking. We read in the Law: 'I will speak to this nation through men of strange tongues, and by the lips of foreigners;
22 and even so they will not heed me, says the Lord.' Clearly then these 'strange tongues' are not intended as a sign for believers, but for un-believers, whereas prophecy is designed not for unbelievers but for those
23 who hold the faith. So if the whole congregation is assembled and all are using the 'strange tongues' of ecstasy, and some uninstructed persons or
24 unbelievers should enter, will they not think you are mad? But if all are uttering prophecies, the visitor, when he enters, hears from everyone
25 something that searches his conscience and brings conviction, and the secrets of his heart are laid bare. So he will fall down and worship God, crying, 'God is certainly among you!'
26 To sum up, my friends: when you meet for worship, each of you con-tributes a hymn, some instruction, a revelation, an ecstatic utterance, or the interpretation of such an utterance. All of these must aim at one thing:
27 to build up the church. If it is a matter of ecstatic utterance, only two should
28 speak, or at most three, one at a time, and someone must interpret. If there is no interpreter, the speaker had better not address the meeting at

[a] Or . . . man. I say the thanksgiving; I use ecstatic speech more than any of you.

all, but speak to himself and to God. Of the prophets, two or three may 29
speak, while the rest exercise their judgement upon what is said. If some- 30
one else, sitting in his place, receives a revelation, let the first speaker stop.
You can all prophesy, one at a time, so that the whole congregation may 31
receive instruction and encouragement. It is for prophets to control pro- 32
phetic inspiration, for the God who inspires them is not a God of disorder 33
but of peace.

As in all congregations of God's people, women*a* should not address the 34
meeting. They have no licence to speak, but should keep their place as the
law directs. If there is something they want to know, they can ask their 35
own husbands at home. It is a shocking thing that a woman should address
the congregation.

Did the word of God originate with you? Or are you the only people to 36
whom it came? If anyone claims to be inspired or a prophet, let him recog- 37
nize that what I write has the Lord's authority. If he does not acknowledge 38
this, God does not acknowledge him.*b*

In short, my friends, be eager to prophesy; do not forbid ecstatic utter- 39
ance; but let all be done decently and in order. 40

Life after death

A ND NOW, MY BROTHERS, I must remind you of the gospel that I **15**
preached to you; the gospel which you received, on which you have
taken your stand, and which is now bringing you salvation. Do you still 2
hold fast the Gospel as I preached it to you? If not, your conversion was
in vain. *c*

First and foremost, I handed on to you the facts which had been im- 3
parted to me: that Christ died for our sins, in accordance with the scriptures; that he was buried; that he was raised to life on the third day, 4
according to the scriptures; and that he appeared to Cephas, and after- 5
wards to the Twelve. Then he appeared to over five hundred of our brothers 6
at once, most of whom are still alive, though some have died. Then he 7
appeared to James, and afterwards to all the apostles.

In the end he appeared even to me. It was like an abnormal birth; I had 8 9
persecuted the church of God and am therefore inferior to all other
apostles—indeed not fit to be called an apostle. However, by God's grace 10
I am what I am, nor has his grace been given to me in vain; on the contrary,
in my labours I have outdone them all—not I, indeed, but the grace of
God working with me. But what matter, I or they? This is what we all 11
proclaim, and this is what you believed.

Now if this is what we proclaim, that Christ was raised from the dead, 12
how can some of you say there is no resurrection of the dead? If there be 13
no resurrection, then Christ was not raised; and if Christ was not raised, 14

a Or of peace, as in all communities of God's people. Women . . .   *b Some
witnesses read* If he refuses to recognize this, let him refuse!   *c Or* Do you
remember the terms in which I preached the Gospel to you?—for I assume you did not
accept it thoughtlessly.

15 then our gospel is null and void, and so is your faith; and we turn out to be lying witnesses for God, because we bore witness that he raised Christ to 16 life, whereas, if the dead are not raised, he did not raise him. For if the dead 17 are not raised, it follows that Christ was not raised; and if Christ was not raised, your faith has nothing in it and you are still in your old state of sin. 18 It follows also that those who have died within Christ's fellowship are 19 utterly lost. If it is for this life only that Christ has given us hope,*a* we of all men are most to be pitied.

20 But the truth is, Christ was raised to life—the firstfruits of the harvest 21 of the dead. For since it was a man who brought death into the world, a 22 man also brought resurrection of the dead. As in Adam all men die, so in 23 Christ all will be brought to life; but each in his own proper place: Christ the firstfruits, and afterwards, at his coming, those who belong to Christ. 24 Then comes the end, when he delivers up the kingdom to God the Father, 25 after abolishing every kind of domination, authority, and power. For he is 26 destined to reign until God has put all enemies under his feet; and the last 27 enemy to be abolished is death.*b* Scripture says, 'He has put all things in subjection under his feet.' But in saying 'all things', it clearly means to 28 exclude God who subordinates them; and when all things are thus subject to him, then the Son himself will also be made subordinate to God who made all things subject to him, and thus God will be all in all.

29 Again, there are those who receive baptism on behalf of the dead. Why should they do this? If the dead are not raised to life at all, what do they mean by being baptized on their behalf?

30 31 And we ourselves—why do we face these dangers hour by hour? Every day I die: I swear it by my pride in you, my brothers—for in Christ Jesus 32 our Lord I am proud of you. If, as the saying is, I 'fought wild beasts' at Ephesus, what have I gained by it?*c* If the dead are never raised to life, 'let us eat and drink, for tomorrow we die'.

33 34 Make no mistake: 'Bad company is the ruin of a good character.' Come back to a sober and upright life and leave your sinful ways. There are some who know nothing of God; to your shame I say it.

35 But, you may ask, how are the dead raised? In what kind of body? 36 How foolish! The seed you sow does not come to life unless it has first 37 died; and what you sow is not the body that shall be, but a naked grain, 38 perhaps of wheat, or of some other kind; and God clothes it with the body of 39 his choice, each seed with its own particular body. All flesh is not the same flesh: there is flesh of men, flesh of beasts, of birds, and of fishes—all dif- 40 ferent. There are heavenly bodies and earthly bodies; and the splendour of 41 the heavenly bodies is one thing, the splendour of the earthly, another. The sun has a splendour of its own, the moon another splendour, and the stars 42 another, for star differs from star in brightness. So it is with the resurrection of the dead. What is sown in the earth as a perishable thing is raised

---

a Or If it is only an uncertain hope that our life in Christ has given us . . . *b* Or Then at the end, when . . . power (for he . . . feet), the last enemy, death, will be abolished. *c* Or If, as men do, I had fought wild beasts at Ephesus, what good would it be to me? or If I had been in no better case than one fighting beasts in the arena at Ephesus, what good would it be to me?

imperishable. Sown in humiliation, it is raised in glory; sown in weakness, 43
it is raised in power; sown as an animal body, it is raised as a spiritual body. 44
    If there is such a thing as an animal body, there is also a spiritual body.
It is in this sense that Scripture says, 'The first man, Adam, became an 45
animate being', whereas the last Adam has become a life-giving spirit.
Observe, the spiritual does not come first; the animal body comes first, and 46
then the spiritual. The first man was made 'of the dust of the earth': the 47
second man is from heaven. The man made of dust is the pattern of all 48
men of dust, and the heavenly man is the pattern of all the heavenly. As 49
we have worn the likeness of the man made of dust, so we shall wear the
likeness of the heavenly man.
    What I mean, my brothers, is this: flesh and blood can never possess 50
the kingdom of God, and the perishable cannot possess immortality.
Listen! I will unfold a mystery: we shall not all die, but we shall all be 51
changed in a flash, in the twinkling of an eye, at the last trumpet-call. For 52
the trumpet will sound, and the dead will rise immortal, and we shall be
changed. This perishable being must be clothed with the imperishable, 53
and what is mortal must be clothed with immortality. And when *a* our 54
mortality has been clothed with immortality, then the saying of Scripture
will come true: 'Death is swallowed up; victory is won!' 'O Death, where 55
is your victory? O Death, where is your sting?' The sting of death is sin, 56
and sin gains its power from the law; but, God be praised, he gives us the 57
victory through our Lord Jesus Christ.
    Therefore, my beloved brothers, stand firm and immovable, and work for 58
the Lord always, work without limit, since you know that in the Lord your
labour cannot be lost.

Christian giving

AND NOW about the collection in aid of God's people: you should 16
follow my directions to our congregations in Galatia. Every Sunday 2
each of you is to put aside and keep by him a sum in proportion to his gains,
so that there may be no collecting when I come. When I arrive, I will give 3
letters of introduction to persons approved by you, and send them to carry
your gift to Jerusalem. If it should seem worth while for me to go as well, 4
they shall go with me.
    I shall come to Corinth after passing through Macedonia—for I am 5
travelling by way of Macedonia—and I may stay with you, perhaps even 6
for the whole winter, and then you can help me on my way wherever I go
next. I do not want this to be a flying visit; I hope to spend some time with 7
you, if the Lord permits. But I shall remain at Ephesus until Whitsuntide, 8
for a great opportunity has opened for effective work, and there is much 9
opposition.
    If Timothy comes, see that you put him at his ease; for it is the Lord's 10
work that he is engaged upon, as I am myself; so no one must slight him. 11

a Some witnesses insert our perishable nature has been clothed with the imperishable,
and . . .

Send him happily on his way to join me, since I am waiting for him with
12   our friends. As for our friend Apollos, I urged him strongly to go to
Corinth with the others, but he was quite determined not to go*ᵃ* at present;
he will go when opportunity offers.

13 14   Be alert; stand firm in the faith; be valiant and strong. Let all you do be
done in love.

15   I have a request to make of you, my brothers. You know that the
Stephanas family were the first converts in Achaia, and have laid themselves
16   out to serve God's people. I wish you to give their due position to such
persons, and indeed to everyone who labours hard at our common task.
17   It is a great pleasure to me that Stephanas, Fortunatus, and Achaicus have
18   arrived, because they have done what you had no chance to do; they have
relieved my mind—and no doubt yours too. Such men deserve recognition.

19   Greetings from the congregations in Asia. Many greetings in the Lord
20   from Aquila and Prisca and the congregation at their house. Greetings from
all the brothers. Greet one another with the kiss of peace.

21   This greeting is in my own hand—Paul.

22   If anyone does not love the Lord, let him be outcast.
Marana tha—Come, O Lord!
23   The grace of the Lord Jesus Christ be with you.
24   My love to you all in Christ Jesus. Amen.

THE SECOND LETTER OF PAUL
TO THE
CORINTHIANS

Personal religion and the ministry

1   From Paul, apostle of Christ Jesus by God's will, and
our colleague Timothy, to the congregation of God's people at
Corinth, together with all who are dedicated to him throughout the
whole of Achaia.

2   Grace and peace to you from God our Father and the Lord Jesus Christ.
3   Praise be to the God and Father of our Lord Jesus Christ, the all-
4   merciful Father, the God whose consolation never fails us! He comforts
us in all our troubles, so that we in turn may be able to comfort others in
any trouble of theirs and to share with them the consolation we ourselves
5   receive from God. As Christ's cup of suffering overflows, and we suffer
6   with him, so also through Christ our consolation overflows. If distress be
our lot, it is the price we pay for your consolation, for your salvation; if our

ᵃ Or but it was by no means the will of God that he should go ...

226

lot be consolation, it is to help us to bring you comfort, and strength to face
with fortitude the same sufferings we now endure. And our hope for you is   7
firmly grounded;[a] for we know that if you have part in the suffering, you
have part also in the divine consolation.

In saying this, we should like you to know, dear friends, how serious   8
was the trouble that came upon us in the province of Asia. The burden of
it was far too heavy for us to bear, so heavy that we even despaired of life.
Indeed, we felt in our hearts that we had received a death-sentence. This   9
was meant to teach us not to place reliance on ourselves, but on God who
raises the dead. From such mortal peril God delivered us; and he will   10
deliver us again,[b] he on whom our hope is fixed. Yes, he will continue to
deliver us, if you will co-operate by praying for us. Then, with so many   11
people praying for our deliverance, there will be many to give thanks on
our behalf for the gracious favour God has shown towards us.

There is one thing we are proud of: our conscience assures us that in our   12
dealings with our fellow-men, and above all in our dealings with you, our
conduct has been governed by a devout and godly sincerity,[c] by the grace
of God and not by worldly wisdom. There is nothing in our letters to you   13
but what you can read for yourselves, and understand too. Partial as your   14
present knowledge of us is, you will I hope come to understand fully that
you have as much reason to be proud of us, as we of you, on the Day of our
Lord Jesus.

It was because I felt so confident about all this that I had intended to   15
come first of all to you[d] and give you the benefit of a double visit: I meant to   16
visit you on my way to Macedonia, and after leaving Macedonia, to return
to you, and you would then send me on my way to Judaea. That was my   17
intention; did I lightly change my mind?[e] Or do I, when I frame my plans,
frame them as a worldly man might, so that it should rest with me to say
'yes' and 'yes', or 'no' and 'no'? As God is true, the language in which we   18
address you is not an ambiguous blend of Yes and No. The Son of God,   19
Christ Jesus, proclaimed among you by us (by Silvanus and Timothy, I
mean, as well as myself), was never a blend of Yes and No. With him it
was, and is, Yes. He is the Yes pronounced upon God's promises, every one   20
of them. That is why, when we give glory to God, it is through Christ Jesus
that we say 'Amen'. And if you and we belong to Christ, guaranteed as his   21
and anointed, it is all God's doing; it is God also who has set his seal upon us,   22
and as a pledge of what is to come has given the Spirit to dwell in our hearts.

I appeal to God to witness what I am going to say; I stake my life upon it: 23
it was out of consideration for you that I did not after all come to Corinth.
Do not think we are dictating the terms of your faith; your hold on the   24
faith is secure enough. We are working with you for your own happiness.
So I made up my mind that my next visit to you must not be another pain-   2
ful one. If I cause pain to you, who is left to cheer me up, except you, whom   2
I have offended? This is precisely the point I made in my letter: I did not   3

---

[a] *Some witnesses give these clauses* If distress . . . firmly grounded *in different sequence.*
[b] *Some witnesses read* and he still delivers us.   [c] *Some witnesses read* by sincere
and godly singleness of mind.   [d] *Or* had originally intended to come to you . . .
[e] *Or* In forming this intention, did I act irresponsibly?

want, I said, to come and be made miserable by the very people who ought to have made me happy; and I had sufficient confidence in you all to know
4 that for me to be happy is for all of you to be happy. That letter I sent you came out of great distress and anxiety; how many tears I shed as I wrote it! But I never meant to cause you pain; I wanted you rather to know the love, the more than ordinary love, that I have for you.

5 Any injury that has been done, has not been done to me; to some extent,
6 not to labour the point, it has been done to you all. The penalty on which
7 the general meeting has agreed has met the offence well enough. Something very different is called for now: you must forgive the offender and put heart into him; the man's sorrow must not be made so severe as to
8 overwhelm him. I urge you therefore to assure him of your love for him
9 by a formal act. I wrote, I may say, to see how you stood the test, whether
10 you fully accepted my authority. But anyone who has your forgiveness has mine too; and when I speak of forgiving (so far as there is anything for me to forgive), I mean that as the representative of Christ I have forgiven him
11 for your sake.*a* For Satan must not be allowed to get the better of us; we know his wiles all too well.

12 Then when I came to Troas, where I was to preach the gospel of Christ,
13 and where an opening awaited me for the Lord's work, I still found no relief of mind, for my colleague Titus was not there to meet me; so I took
14 leave of the people there and went off to Macedonia. But thanks be to God, who continually leads us about, captives in Christ's triumphal procession, and everywhere uses us to reveal and spread abroad the fragrance of the
15 knowledge of himself! We are indeed the incense offered by Christ to God, both for those who are on the way to salvation, and for those who are on the
16 way to perdition: to the latter it is a deadly fume that kills, to the former a
17 vital fragrance that brings life. Who is equal to such a calling? At least we do not go hawking the word of God about, as so many do; when we declare the word we do it in sincerity, as from God and in God's sight, as members of Christ.

3 ARE WE BEGINNING all over again to produce our credentials? Do we,
2 like some people, need letters of introduction to you, or from you? No, you are all the letter we need, a letter written on our heart; any man can
3 see it for what it is and read it for himself. And as for you, it is plain that you are a letter that has come from Christ, given to us to deliver: a letter written not with ink but with the Spirit of the living God, written not on stone tablets but on the pages of the human heart.
4 It is in full reliance upon God, through Christ, that we make such claims.
5 There is no question of our being qualified in ourselves: we cannot claim
6 anything as our own. The qualification we have comes from God; it is he who has qualified us to dispense his new covenant—a covenant expressed not in a written document, but in a spiritual bond; for the written law condemns to death, but the Spirit gives life.
7 The law, then, engraved letter by letter upon stone, dispensed death, and yet it was inaugurated with divine splendour. That splendour, though

---

a Or that I have forgiven him for your sake, in the presence of Christ.

it was soon to fade, made the face of Moses so bright that the Israelites could not gaze steadily at him. But if so, must not even greater splendour 8 rest upon the divine dispensation of the Spirit? If splendour accompanied 9 the dispensation under which we are condemned, how much richer in splendour must that one be under which we are acquitted! Indeed, the splendour 10 that once was is now no splendour at all; it is outshone by a splendour greater still. For if that which was soon to fade had its moment of splendour, how much greater is the splendour of that which endures! 11

With such a hope as this we speak out boldly; it is not for us to do as 12 13 Moses did: he put a veil over his face to keep the Israelites from gazing on that fading splendour until it was gone. But in any case their minds had 14 been made insensitive, for that same veil is there to this very day when the lesson is read from the old covenant; and it is never lifted, because only in Christ is the old covenant abrogated.[a] But to this very day, every time the 15 Law of Moses is read, a veil lies over the minds of the hearers. However, 16 as Scripture says of Moses, 'whenever he turns to the Lord the veil is removed'.[b] Now the Lord of whom this passage speaks is the Spirit; and 17 where the Spirit of the Lord is, there is liberty. And because for us there is 18 no veil over the face, we all reflect as in a mirror the splendour of the Lord; thus we are transfigured into his likeness, from splendour to splendour; such is the influence of the Lord who is Spirit.

SEEING THEN THAT WE have been entrusted with this commission, which 4 we owe entirely to God's mercy, we never lose heart. We have renounced 2 the deeds that men hide for very shame; we neither practise cunning nor distort the word of God; only by declaring the truth openly do we recommend ourselves, and then it is to the common conscience of our fellow-men and in the sight of God. And if indeed our gospel be found veiled, 3 the only people who find it so are those on the way to perdition. Their 4 unbelieving minds are so blinded by the god of this passing age, that the gospel of the glory of Christ, who is the very image of God, cannot dawn upon them and bring them light. It is not ourselves that we proclaim; we 5 proclaim Christ Jesus as Lord, and ourselves as your servants, for Jesus' sake. For the same God who said, 'Out of darkness let light shine', has 6 caused his light to shine within us, to give the light of revelation—the revelation of the glory of God in the face of Jesus Christ.

We are no better than pots of earthenware to contain this treasure, and 7 this proves that such transcendent power does not come from us, but is God's alone. Hard-pressed on every side, we are never hemmed in; 8 bewildered, we are never at our wits' end; hunted, we are never abandoned 9 to our fate; struck down, we are not left to die. Wherever we go we carry 10 death with us in our body, the death that Jesus died, that in this body also life may reveal itself, the life that Jesus lives. For continually, while still 11 alive, we are being surrendered into the hands of death, for Jesus' sake, so that the life of Jesus also may be revealed in this mortal body of ours. Thus 12 death is at work in us, and life in you.

[a] *Or* in Christ is it abolished.
[b] *Or* as Scripture says, when one turns to the Lord the veil is removed.

13 But Scripture says, 'I believed, and therefore I spoke out', and we too,
14 in the same spirit of faith, believe and therefore speak out; for we know that he who raised the Lord Jesus to life will with Jesus raise us too, and
15 bring us to his presence, and you with us. Indeed, it is for your sake that all things are ordered, so that, as the abounding grace of God is shared by more and more, the greater may be the chorus of thanksgiving that ascends to the glory of God.

16 No wonder we do not lose heart! Though our outward humanity is in
17 decay, yet day by day we are inwardly renewed. Our troubles are slight and short-lived; and their outcome an eternal glory which outweighs them
18 far. Meanwhile our eyes are fixed, not on the things that are seen, but on the things that are unseen: for what is seen passes away; what is unseen is
5 eternal. For we know that if the earthly frame that houses us today should be demolished, we possess a building which God has provided—a house
2 not made by human hands, eternal, and in heaven. In this present body we do indeed groan; we yearn to have our heavenly habitation put on over this
3 one—in the hope that, being thus clothed, we shall not find ourselves naked.
4 We groan indeed, we who are enclosed within this earthly frame; we are oppressed because we do not want to have the old body stripped off. Rather our desire is to have the new body put on over it, so that our mortal part
5 may be absorbed into life immortal. God himself has shaped us for this very end; and as a pledge of it he has given us the Spirit.

6 Therefore we never cease to be confident. We know that so long as we
7 are at home in the body we are exiles from the Lord; faith is our guide, we
8 do not see him. *a* We are confident, I repeat, and would rather leave our
9 home in the body and go to live with the Lord. We therefore make it our
10 ambition, wherever we are, here or there, to be acceptable to him. For we must all have our lives laid open before the tribunal of Christ, where each must receive what is due to him for his conduct in the body, good or bad.

11 WITH THIS FEAR of the Lord before our eyes we address our appeal to men. To God our lives lie open, as I hope they also lie open to you in your
12 heart of hearts. This is not another attempt to recommend ourselves to you: we are rather giving you a chance to show yourselves proud of us; then you will have something to say to those whose pride is all in outward show and
13 not in inward worth. It may be we are beside ourselves, but it is for God;
14 if we are in our right mind, it is for you. For the love of Christ leaves us no choice, when once we have reached the conclusion that one man died for
15 all and therefore all mankind has died. His purpose in dying for all was that men, while still in life, should cease to live for themselves, and should
16 live for him who for their sake died and was raised to life. With us therefore worldly standards have ceased to count in our estimate of any man; even if once they counted in our understanding of Christ, they do so now no
17 longer. When anyone is united to Christ, there is a new world;*b* the old order has gone, and a new order has already begun. *c*

---

a Or faith is our guide and not the things we see.   *b* Or a new act of creation.
c Or When anyone is united to Christ he is a new creature: his old life is over; a new life has already begun.

From first to last this has been the work of God. He has reconciled us men 18
to himself through Christ, and he has enlisted us in this service of reconciliation. What I mean is, that God was in Christ reconciling the world to 19
himself, [a] no longer holding men's misdeeds against them, and that he has
entrusted us with the message of reconciliation. We come therefore as 20
Christ's ambassadors. It is as if God were appealing to you through us: in
Christ's name, we implore you, be reconciled to God! Christ was innocent 21
of sin, and yet for our sake God made him one with the sinfulness of men, [b]
so that in him we might be made one with the goodness of God himself.
Sharing in God's work, we urge this appeal upon you: you have received **6**
the grace of God; do not let it go for nothing. God's own words are: 2

'In the hour of my favour I gave heed to you;
on the day of deliverance I came to your aid.'

The hour of favour has now come; now, I say, has the day of deliverance
dawned.

In order that our service may not be brought into discredit, we avoid giving 3
offence in anything. As God's servants, we try to recommend ourselves 4
in all circumstances by our steadfast endurance: in distress, hardships,
and dire straits; flogged, imprisoned, mobbed; overworked, sleepless, 5
starving. We recommend ourselves by the innocence of our behaviour, 6
our grasp of truth, our patience and kindliness; by gifts of the Holy Spirit,
by sincere love, by declaring the truth, by the power of God. We wield the 7
weapons of righteousness in right hand and left. Honour and dishonour, 8
praise and blame, are alike our lot: we are the impostors who speak the
truth, the unknown men whom all men know; dying we still live on; 9
disciplined by suffering, we are not done to death; in our sorrows we 10
have always cause for joy; poor ourselves, we bring wealth to many;
penniless, we own the world.

Men of Corinth, we have spoken very frankly to you; we have opened 11
our heart wide to you all. On our part there is no constraint; any constraint 12
there may be is in yourselves. In fair exchange then (may a father speak so 13
to his children?) open wide your hearts to us.

Problems of church life and discipline

DO NOT UNITE yourselves with unbelievers; they are no fit mates 14
for you. What has righteousness to do with wickedness? Can light
consort with darkness? Can Christ agree with Belial, or a believer join 15
hands with an unbeliever? Can there be a compact between the temple of 16
God and the idols of the heathen? And the temple of the living God is
what we are. God's own words are: 'I will live and move about among
them; I will be their God, and they shall be my people.' And therefore, 17
'come away and leave them, separate yourselves, says the Lord; touch
nothing unclean. Then I will accept you, says the Lord, the Ruler of all 18

[a] *Or* God was reconciling the world to himself by Christ.   [b] *Or* and yet God
made him a sin-offering for us.

being; I will be a father to you, and you shall be my sons and daughters.'
7 Such are the promises that have been made to us, dear friends. Let us therefore cleanse ourselves from all that can defile flesh or spirit, and in the fear of God complete our consecration.

2 DO MAKE A PLACE for us in your hearts! We have wronged no one, ruined
3 no one, taken advantage of no one. I do not want to blame you. Why, as I have told you before, the place you have in our heart is such that, come
4 death, come life, we meet it together. I am perfectly frank with you. I have great pride in you. In all our many troubles my cup is full of consolation, and overflows with joy.

5   Even when we reached Macedonia there was still no relief for this poor body of ours; instead, there was trouble at every turn, quarrels all round
6 us, forebodings in our heart. But God, who brings comfort to the downcast,
7 has comforted us by the arrival of Titus, and not merely by his arrival, but by his being so greatly comforted about you. He has told us how you long for me, how sorry you are, and how eager to take my side; and that has made me happier still.

8   Even if I did wound you by the letter I sent, I do not now regret it. I may have been sorry for it when I saw that the letter had caused you pain,
9 even if only for a time; but now I am happy, not that your feelings were wounded but that the wound led to a change of heart. You bore the smart as God would have you bear it, and so you are no losers by what we did.
10 For the wound which is borne in God's way brings a change of heart too salutary to regret; but the hurt which is borne in the world's way brings
11 death. You bore your hurt in God's way, and see what its results have been! It made you take the matter seriously and vindicate yourselves. How angered you were, how apprehensive! How your longing for me awoke, yes, and your devotion and your eagerness to see justice done! At every
12 point you have cleared yourselves of blame in this trouble. And so, although I did send you that letter, it was not the offender or his victim that most concerned me. My aim in writing was to help to make plain to you, in the
13 sight of God, how truly you are devoted to us. That is why we have been so encouraged.

    But besides being encouraged ourselves we have also been delighted beyond everything by seeing how happy Titus is: you have all helped to
14 set his mind completely at rest. Anything I may have said to him to show my pride in you has been justified. Every word we ever addressed to you bore the mark of truth; and the same holds of the proud boast we made in
15 the presence of Titus: that also has proved true. His heart warms all the more to you as he recalls how ready you all were to do what he asked, meet-
16 ing him as you did in fear and trembling. How happy I am now to have complete confidence in you!

8 WE MUST TELL YOU, friends, about the grace of generosity which God
2 has imparted to *ᵃ* our congregations in Macedonia. The troubles they have been through have tried them hard, yet in all this they have been so

    ᵃ Or how gracious God has been to . . .

exuberantly happy that from the depths of their poverty they have shown themselves lavishly open-handed. Going to the limit of their resources, as 3 I can testify, and even beyond that limit, they begged us most insistently, 4 and on their own initiative, to be allowed to share in this generous service to their fellow-Christians. And their giving surpassed our expectations; 5 for they gave their very selves, offering them in the first instance to the Lord, but also, under God, to us. The upshot is that we have asked Titus, 6 who began it all, to visit you and bring this work of generosity also to completion. You are so rich in everything—in faith, speech, knowledge, and 7 zeal of every kind, as well as in the loving regard you have for us*a*—surely you should show yourselves equally lavish in this generous service! This 8 is not meant as an order; by telling you how keen others are I am putting your love to the test. For you know how generous our Lord Jesus Christ 9 has been: he was rich, yet for your sake he became poor, so that through his poverty you might become rich.

Here is my considered opinion on the matter. What I ask you to do is in 10 your own interests. You made a good beginning last year both in the work you did and in your willingness to undertake it. Now I want you to go on 11 and finish it: be as eager to complete the scheme as you were to adopt it, and give according to your means. Provided there is an eager desire to give, 12 God accepts what a man has; he does not ask for what he has not. There is 13 no question of relieving others at the cost of hardship to yourselves; it is a 14 question of equality. At the moment your surplus meets their need, but one day your need may be met from their surplus. The aim is equality; as Scripture has it, 'The man who got much had no more than enough, and 15 the man who got little did not go short.'

I thank God that he has made Titus as keen on your behalf as we are! 16 For Titus not only welcomed our request; he is so eager that by his own 17 desire he is now leaving to come to you. With him we are sending one of 18 our company whose reputation is high among our congregations everywhere for his services to the Gospel. Moreover they have duly appointed 19 him to travel with us and help in this beneficent work, by which we do honour to the Lord himself and show our own eagerness to serve. We want 20 to guard against any criticism of our handling of this generous gift; for 21 our aims are entirely honourable, not only in the Lord's eyes, but also in the eyes of men.

With these men we are sending another of our company whose enthu- 22 siasm we have had many opportunities of testing, and who is now all the more earnest because of the great confidence he has in you. If there is any 23 question about Titus, he is my partner and my associate in dealings with you; as for the others, they are delegates of our congregations, an honour to Christ.*b* Then give them clear expression of your love and justify our 24 pride in you; justify it to them, and through them to the congregations.

About the provision of aid for God's people, it is superfluous for me to 9 write to you. I know how eager you are to help; I speak of it with pride to 2 the Macedonians: I tell them that Achaia had everything ready last year;

---

a Some witnesses read the love we have for you, *or* the love which we have kindled in your hearts.   *b Or* they are ... congregations; they reflect Christ.

3 and most of them have been fired by your zeal. My purpose in sending these friends is to ensure that what we have said about you in this matter should not prove to be an empty boast. By that I mean, I want you to be
4 prepared, as I told them you were; for if I bring with me men from Macedonia and they find you are not prepared, what a disgrace it will be to us,
5 let alone to you, after all the confidence we have shown! I have accordingly thought it necessary to ask these friends to go on ahead to Corinth, to see that your promised bounty is in order before I come; it will then be awaiting me as a bounty indeed, and not as an extortion.
6 Remember: sparse sowing, sparse reaping; sow bountifully, and you will
7 reap bountifully. Each person should give as he has decided for himself; there should be no reluctance, no sense of compulsion; God loves a cheer-
8 ful giver. And it is in God's power to provide you richly with every good gift; thus you will have ample means in yourselves to meet each and every
9 situation, with enough and to spare for every good cause. Scripture says of such a man: 'He has lavished his gifts on the needy, his benevolence stands
10 fast for ever.' Now he who provides seed for sowing and bread for food will provide the seed for you to sow; he will multiply it and swell the harvest of
11 your benevolence, and you will always be rich enough to be generous.
12 Through our action such generosity will issue in thanksgiving to God, for as a piece of willing service this is not only a contribution towards the needs of God's people; more than that, it overflows in a flood of thanksgiving to
13 God. For through the proof which this affords, many will give honour to God when they see how humbly you obey him and how faithfully you confess the gospel of Christ; and will thank him for your liberal contribu-
14 tion to their need and to the general good. And as they join in prayer on your behalf, their hearts will go out to you because of the richness of the
15 grace which God has imparted to you. Thanks be to God for his gift beyond words!

Trials of a Christian missionary

10 BUT I, PAUL, appeal to you by the gentleness and magnanimity of Christ—I, so feeble (you say) when I am face to face with you, so
2 brave when I am away. Spare me, I beg you, the necessity of such bravery when I come, for I reckon I could put on as bold a face as you please against
3 those who charge us with moral weakness. Weak men we may be, but it is
4 not as such that we fight our battles. The weapons we wield are not merely
5 human,*a* but divinely potent to demolish strongholds; we demolish sophistries and all that rears its proud head against the knowledge of God;
6 we compel every human thought to surrender in obedience to Christ; and we are prepared to punish all rebellion when once you have put yourselves in our hands.
7 Look facts in the face. *b* Someone is convinced, is he, that he belongs to

a Or charge us with worldly standards. We live, no doubt, in the world; but it is not on that level that we fight our battles. The weapons we wield are not those of the world . . .
b Or You are looking only at what catches the eye.

Christ? Let him think again, and reflect that we belong to Christ as much as he does. Indeed, if I am somewhat over-boastful about our authority— 8 an authority given by the Lord to build you up, not pull you down—I shall make my boast good. So you must not think of me as one who scares you 9 by the letters he writes. 'His letters', so it is said, 'are weighty and powerful; 10 but when he appears he has no presence, and as a speaker he is beneath contempt.' People who talk in that way should reckon with this: when I 11 come, my actions will show the same man as my letters showed in my absence.

We should not dare to class ourselves or compare ourselves with any of 12 those who put forward their own claims. What fools they are to measure themselves by themselves, to find in themselves their own standard of comparison!ᵃ With us there will be no attempt to boast beyond our proper 13 sphere; and our sphere is determined by the limit God laid down for us, which permitted us to come as far as Corinth. We are not overstretching 14 our commission, as we should be if it did not extend to you, for we were the first to reach Corinth in preaching the gospel of Christ. And we do not 15 boast of work done where others have laboured, work beyond our proper sphere. Our hope is rather that, as your faith grows, we may attain a position among you greater than ever before, but still within the limits of our sphere. Then we can carry the Gospel to lands that lie beyond you, never 16 priding ourselves on work already done in another man's sphere. If a man 17 must boast, let him boast of the Lord. Not the man who recommends him- 18 self, but the man whom the Lord recommends—he and he alone is to be accepted.

I wish you would bear with me in a little of my folly; please do bear with **11** me. I am jealous for you, with a divine jealousy; for I betrothed you to 2 Christ, thinking to present you as a chaste virgin to her true and only husband. But as the serpent in his cunning seduced Eve, I am afraid that 3 your thoughts may be corrupted and you may lose yourᵇ single-hearted devotion to Christ. For if someone comes who proclaims another Jesus, 4 not the Jesus whom we proclaimed, or if you then receive a spirit different from the Spirit already given to you, or a gospel different from the gospel you have already accepted, you manage to put up with that well enough. Have I in any way come short of those superlative apostles? I think not. 5 I may be no speaker, but knowledge I have; at all times we have made 6 known to you the full truth.

Or was this my offence, that I made no charge for preaching the gospel 7 of God, lowering myself to help in raising you? It is true that I took toll of 8 other congregations, acceptingᶜ support from them to serve you. Then, 9 while I was with you, if I ran short I sponged on no one; anything I needed was fully met by our friends who came from Macedonia; I made it a rule, as I always shall, never to be a burden to you. As surely as the truth of Christ 10 is in me, I will preserve my pride in this matter throughout Achaia, and nothing shall stop me. Why? Is it that I do not love you? God knows I do. 11

ᵃ *Some witnesses read* On the contrary we measure ourselves by ourselves, by our own standard of comparison. ᵇ *Some witnesses insert* purity and . . . ᶜ *Or* Did I take toll of other congregations by accepting . . .?

12   And I shall go on doing as I am doing now, to cut the ground from under those who would seize any chance to put their vaunted apostleship on the
13 same level as ours. Such men are sham-apostles, crooked in all their
14 practices, masquerading as apostles of Christ. There is nothing surprising
15 about that; Satan himself masquerades as an angel of light. It is therefore a simple thing for his agents to masquerade as agents of good. But they will meet the end their deeds deserve.

16   I repeat: let no one take me for a fool; but if you must, then give me the
17 privilege of a fool, and let me have my little boast like others. I am not
18 speaking here as a Christian, but like a fool, if it comes to bragging. So
19 many people brag of their earthly distinctions that I shall do so too. How
20 gladly you bear with fools, being yourselves so wise! If a man tyrannizes over you, exploits you, gets you in his clutches, puts on airs, and hits you
21 in the face, you put up with it. And we, you say, have been weak! I admit the reproach.

   But if there is to be bravado (and here I speak as a fool), I can indulge in
22 it too. Are they Hebrews? So am I. Israelites? So am I. Abraham's descen-
23 dants? So am I. Are they servants of Christ? I am mad to speak like this, but I can outdo them. More overworked than they, scourged more severely,
24 more often imprisoned, many a time face to face with death. Five times the
25 Jews have given me the thirty-nine strokes; three times I have been beaten with rods; once I was stoned; three times I have been shipwrecked, and for
26 twenty-four hours I was adrift on the open sea. I have been constantly on the road; I have met dangers from rivers, dangers from robbers, dangers from my fellow-countrymen, dangers from foreigners, dangers in towns,
27 dangers in the country, dangers at sea, dangers from false friends. I have toiled and drudged, I have often gone without sleep; hungry and thirsty, I have often gone fasting; and I have suffered from cold and exposure.
28   Apart from these external things,*a* there is the responsibility that weighs
29 on me every day, my anxious concern for all our congregations. If anyone is weak, do I not share his weakness? If anyone is made to stumble, does
30 my heart not blaze with indignation? If boasting there must be, I will boast
31 of the things that show up my weakness. The God and Father of the Lord
32 Jesus (blessed be his name for ever!) knows that what I say is true. When I was in Damascus, the commissioner of King Aretas kept the city under
33 observation so as to have me arrested; and I was let down in a basket, through a window in the wall, and so escaped his clutches.

12 I AM OBLIGED TO BOAST. It does no good; but I shall go on to tell of
2 visions and revelations granted by the Lord. I know a Christian man who fourteen years ago (whether in the body or out of it, I do not know—God
3 knows) was caught up as far as the third heaven. And I know that this same
4 man (whether in the body or out of it, I do not know—God knows) was caught up into paradise, and heard words so secret that human lips may not
5 repeat them. About such a man as that I am ready to boast; but I will not
6 boast on my own account, except of my weaknesses. If I should choose to boast, it would not be the boast of a fool, for I should be speaking the

a Or Apart from things which I omit.

truth. But I refrain, because I should not like anyone to form an estimate of me which goes beyond the evidence of his own eyes and ears. And so, 7 to keep me from being unduly elated by the magnificence of such revelations, I was given *a* a sharp physical pain *b* which came as Satan's messenger to bruise me; this was to save me from being unduly elated. Three 8 times I begged the Lord to rid me of it, but his answer was: 'My grace is 9 all you need; power comes to its full strength in weakness.' I shall therefore prefer to find my joy and pride in the very things that are my weakness; and then the power of Christ will come and rest upon me. Hence I am well 10 content, for Christ's sake, with weakness, contempt, persecution, hardship, and frustration; for when I am weak, then I am strong.

I AM BEING VERY FOOLISH, but it was you who drove me to it; my 11 credentials should have come from you. In no respect did I fall short of these superlative apostles, even if I am a nobody. The marks of a true 12 apostle were there, in the work I did among you, which called for such constant fortitude, and was attended by signs, marvels, and miracles. Is 13 there anything in which you were treated worse than the other congregations—except this, that I never sponged upon you? How unfair of me! I crave forgiveness.

Here am I preparing to pay you a third visit; and I am not going to 14 sponge upon you. It is you I want, not your money; parents should make provision for their children, not children for their parents. As for me, I 15 will gladly spend what I have for you—yes, and spend myself to the limit. If I love you overmuch, am I to be loved the less? But, granted that I did 16 not prove a burden to you, still I was unscrupulous enough, you say, to use a trick to catch you. Who, of the men I have sent to you, was used by me to 17 defraud you? I begged Titus to visit you, and I sent our friend with him. 18 Did Titus defraud you? Have we not both been guided by the same Spirit, and followed the same course?

Perhaps you think that all this time we have been addressing our defence 19 to you. No; we are speaking in God's sight, and as Christian men. Our whole aim, my own dear people, is to build you up. I fear that when I come 20 I may perhaps find you different from what I wish you to be, and that you may find me also different from what you wish. I fear I may find quarrelling and jealousy, angry tempers and personal rivalries, backbiting and gossip, arrogance and general disorder. I am afraid that, when I come again, my 21 God may humiliate me in your presence, that I may have tears to shed over many of those who have sinned in the past and have not repented of their unclean lives, their fornication and sensuality.

This will be my third visit to you; and all facts must be established by the **13** evidence of two or three witnesses. To those who have sinned in the past, 2 and to everyone else, I repeat the warning I gave before; I gave it in person on my second visit, and I give it now in absence. It is that when I come this time, I will show no leniency. Then you will have the proof you seek of the 3

a Some witnesses read . . . ears, and because of the magnificence of the revelations themselves. Therefore to keep me from being unduly elated I was given . . .   *b Or a* painful wound to my pride (*literally* a stake, *or* thorn, for the flesh).

Christ who speaks through me, the Christ who, far from being weak with
4 you, makes his power felt among you. True, he died on the cross in weakness, but he lives by the power of God; and we who share his weakness shall
by the power of God live with him in your service.

5 Examine yourselves: are you living the life of faith? Put yourselves to the
test. Surely you recognize that Jesus Christ is among you?—unless of
6 course you prove unequal to the test. I hope you will come to see that we
7 are not unequal to it. Our prayer to God is that you may do no wrong; we
are not concerned to be vindicated ourselves; we want you to do what is
8 right, even if we should seem to be discredited. For we have no power to
9 act against the truth, but only for it. We are well content to be weak at any
time if only you are strong. Indeed, my whole prayer is that all may be put
10 right with you. My purpose in writing this letter before I come, is to spare
myself, when I come, any sharp exercise of authority—authority which the
Lord gave me for building up and not for pulling down.

11 And now, my friends, farewell. Mend your ways; take our appeal to
heart; agree with one another; live in peace; and the God of love and peace
12 13 will be with you. Greet one another with the kiss of peace. All God's
people send you greetings.
14 The grace of the Lord Jesus Christ, and the love of God, and fellowship
in the Holy Spirit, be with you all.

THE LETTER OF PAUL
TO THE
GALATIANS

Faith and freedom

1 FROM PAUL, AN APOSTLE, not by human appointment or
human commission, but by commission from Jesus Christ and
2 from God the Father who raised him from the dead. I and the group
of friends now with me send greetings to the Christian congregations of
Galatia.
3 Grace and peace to you from God the Father and our Lord Jesus Christ, *a*
4 who sacrificed himself for our sins, to rescue us out of this present age of
5 wickedness, as our God and Father willed; to whom be glory for ever and
ever. Amen.
6 I am astonished to find you turning so quickly away from him who
7 called you by grace, *b* and following a different gospel. Not that it is in fact

a Some witnesses read God our Father and the Lord Jesus Christ. *b Some
witnesses read* from Christ who called you by grace, *or* from him who called you by grace
of Christ.

another gospel; only there are persons who unsettle your minds by trying to distort the gospel of Christ. But if anyone, if we ourselves or an angel 8 from heaven, should preach a gospel at variance with the gospel we preached to you, he shall be held outcast. I now repeat what I have said 9 before: if anyone preaches a gospel at variance with the gospel which you received, let him be outcast!

Does my language now sound as if I were canvassing for men's support? 10 Whose support do I want but God's alone? Do you think I am currying favour with men? If I still sought men's favour, I should be no servant of Christ.

I must make it clear to you, my friends, that the gospel you heard me 11 preach is no human invention. I did not take it over from any man; no man 12 taught it me; I received it through a revelation of Jesus Christ.

You have heard what my manner of life was when I was still a practising 13 Jew: how savagely I persecuted the church of God, and tried to destroy it; and how in the practice of our national religion I was outstripping many of 14 my Jewish contemporaries in my boundless devotion to the traditions of my ancestors. But then in his good pleasure God, who had set me apart from 15 birth and called me through his grace, chose to reveal his Son to me and 16 through me, in order that I might proclaim him among the Gentiles. When that happened, without consulting any human being, without going up to 17 Jerusalem to see those who were apostles before me, I went off at once to Arabia, and afterwards returned to Damascus.

Three years later I did go up to Jerusalem to get to know Cephas. I 18 stayed with him for a fortnight, without seeing any other of the apostles, 19 except *a* James the Lord's brother. What I write is plain truth; before God 20 I am not lying.

Next I went to the regions of Syria and Cilicia, and remained unknown 21 22 by sight *b* to Christ's congregations in Judaea. They only heard it said, 'Our 23 former persecutor is preaching the good news of the faith which once he tried to destroy'; and they praised God for me. 24

Next, fourteen years later, I went again *c* to Jerusalem with Barnabas, **2** taking Titus with us. I went up because it had been revealed by God that 2 I should do so. I laid before them—but at a private interview with the men of repute—the gospel which I am accustomed to preach to the Gentiles, to make sure that the race I had run, and was running, should not be run in vain. Yet even my companion Titus, Greek though he is, was not compelled 3 to be circumcised. That course was urged only as a concession to certain *d* 4 sham-Christians, interlopers who had stolen in to spy upon the liberty we enjoy in the fellowship of Christ Jesus. These men wanted to bring us into bondage, but not for one moment did I yield to their dictation; I was deter- 5 mined that the full truth of the Gospel should be maintained for you. *e*

---

a Or but only.   *b Or* unknown personally.   *c Some witnesses omit* again.
d Or The question was later raised because of certain . . .   *e Or, following the reading of some witnesses,* Yet even . . . is, was under no absolute compulsion to be circumcised, but for the sake of certain . . . of Christ Jesus, with the intention of bringing us into bondage, I yielded to their demand for the moment, to ensure that gospel truth should not be prevented from reaching you.

6 But as for the men of high reputation (not that their importance matters to me: God does not recognize these personal distinctions)—these men of

7 repute, I say, did not prolong the consultation,[a] but on the contrary acknowledged that I had been entrusted with the Gospel for Gentiles as

8 surely as Peter had been entrusted with the Gospel for Jews. For God whose action made Peter an apostle to the Jews, also made me an apostle to the Gentiles.

9 Recognizing, then, the favour thus bestowed upon me, those reputed pillars of our society, James, Cephas, and John, accepted Barnabas and myself as partners, and shook hands upon it, agreeing that we should go

10 to the Gentiles while they went to the Jews. All they asked was that we should keep their poor in mind, which was the very thing I made[b] it my business to do.

11 But when Cephas came to Antioch, I opposed him to his face, because

12 he was clearly in the wrong. For until certain persons[c] came from James he was taking his meals with gentile Christians; but when they[d] came he drew back and began to hold aloof, because he was afraid of the advocates

13 of circumcision. The other Jewish Christians showed the same lack of principle; even Barnabas was carried away and played false like the rest.

14 But when I saw that their conduct did not square with[e] the truth of the Gospel, I said to Cephas, before the whole congregation, 'If you, a Jew born and bred, live like a Gentile, and not like a Jew, how can you insist that Gentiles must live like Jews?'

15 16 We ourselves are Jews by birth, not Gentiles and sinners. But we know that no man is ever justified by doing what the law demands, but only through faith in Christ Jesus; so we too have put our faith in Jesus Christ, in order that we might be justified through this faith, and not through deeds dictated by law; for by such deeds, Scripture says, no mortal man shall be justified.

17 If now, in seeking to be justified in Christ, we ourselves no less than the Gentiles turn out to be sinners against the law,[f] does that mean that Christ

18 is an abettor of sin? No, never! No, if I start building up again a system which I have pulled down, then it is that I show myself up as a transgressor

19 20 of the law. For through the law I died to law—to live for God. I have been crucified with Christ: the life I now live is not my life, but the life which Christ lives in me; and my present bodily life is lived by faith in the Son of

21 God, who loved me and gave himself up for me. I will not nullify the grace of God; if righteousness comes by law, then Christ died for nothing.

3 YOU STUPID GALATIANS! You must have been bewitched—you before

2 whose eyes Jesus Christ was openly displayed upon his cross! Answer me one question: did you receive the Spirit by keeping the law or by believing

3 the gospel message[g]? Can it be that you are so stupid? You started with the

---

a Or gave me no further instructions.   *b Or had made, or have made.*   *c Some witnesses read a certain person.*   *d Some witnesses read he.*   *e Or I saw that they were not making progress towards . . .*   *f Or no less than the Gentiles have accepted the position of sinners against the law.*   *g Or or by the message of faith, or or by hearing and believing.*

spiritual; do you now look to the material to make you perfect? Have all   4
your great experiences been in vain—if vain indeed they should be? I ask   5
then: when God gives you the Spirit and works miracles among you, why
is this? Is it because you keep the law, or is it because you have faith in the
gospel message? Look at Abraham: he put his faith in God, and that faith   6
was counted to him as righteousness.

You may take it, then, that it is the men of faith who are Abraham's sons.   7
And Scripture, foreseeing that God would justify the Gentiles through   8
faith, declared the Gospel to Abraham beforehand: 'In you all nations shall
find blessing.' Thus it is the men of faith who share the blessing with faith-   9
ful Abraham.

On the other hand those who rely on obedience to the law are under a   10
curse; for Scripture says, 'A curse is on all who do not persevere in doing
everything that is written in the Book of the Law.' It is evident that no one   11
is ever justified before God in terms of law; because we read, 'he shall gain
life who is justified through faith'. Now law is not at all a matter of having   12
faith: we read, 'he who does this shall gain life by what he does'.

Christ bought us freedom from the curse of the law by becoming for our   13
sake an accursed thing; for Scripture says, 'A curse is on everyone who is
hanged on a gibbet.' And the purpose of it all was that the blessing of   14
Abraham should in Jesus Christ be extended to the Gentiles, so that we
might receive the promised Spirit through faith.

My brothers, let me give you an illustration. Even in ordinary life, when   15
a man's will and testament has been duly executed, no one else can set it
aside or add a codicil. Now the promises were pronounced to Abraham and   16
to his 'issue'. It does not say 'issues' in the plural, but in the singular, 'and
to your issue'; and the 'issue' intended is Christ. What I am saying is this: 17
a testament, or covenant, had already been validated by God; it cannot be
invalidated, and its promises rendered ineffective, by a law made four
hundred and thirty years later. If the inheritance is by legal right, then it is   18
not by promise; but it was by promise that God bestowed it as a free gift
on Abraham.

Then what of the law? It was added to make wrongdoing a legal offence.[a]   19
It was a temporary measure pending the arrival of the 'issue' to whom the
promise was made. It was promulgated through angels, and there was an
intermediary; but an intermediary is not needed for one party acting alone,   20
and God is one.

Does the law, then, contradict the promises? No, never! If a law had   21
been given which had power to bestow life, then indeed righteousness
would have come from keeping the law. But Scripture has declared the   22
whole world to be prisoners in subjection to sin, so that faith in Jesus Christ
may be the ground on which the promised blessing is given, and given to
those who have such faith.

Before this faith came, we were close prisoners in the custody of law,   23
pending the revelation of faith. Thus the law was a kind of tutor in charge   24
of us until Christ should come,[b] when we should be justified through faith;
and now that faith has come, the tutor's charge is at an end.   25

    [a] Or added because of offences.   [b] Or a kind of tutor to conduct us to Christ.

26 For through faith you are all sons of God in union with Christ Jesus.
27 Baptized into union with him, you have all put on Christ as a garment.
28 There is no such thing as Jew and Greek, slave and freeman, male and
29 female; for you are all one person in Christ Jesus. But if you thus belong to
Christ, you are the 'issue' of Abraham, and so heirs by promise.

4 This is what I mean: so long as the heir is a minor, he is no better off
2 than a slave, even though the whole estate is his; he is under guardians and
3 trustees until the date fixed by his father. And so it was with us. During
4 our minority we were slaves to the elemental spirits of the universe,*a* but
when the term was completed, God sent his own Son, born of a woman,
5 born under the law, to purchase freedom for the subjects of the law, in
order that we might attain the status of sons.

6 To prove that you are sons, God has sent into our hearts the Spirit of his
7 Son, crying 'Abba! Father!' You are therefore no longer a slave but a son,
and if a son, then also by God's own act an heir.

8 Formerly, when you did not acknowledge God, you were the slaves of
9 beings which in their nature are no gods.*b* But now that you do acknowledge God—or rather, now that he has acknowledged you—how can you
turn back to the mean and beggarly spirits of the elements?*c* Why do you
10 propose to enter their service all over again? You keep special days and
11 months and seasons and years. You make me fear that all the pains I spent
on you may prove to be labour lost.

12 PUT YOURSELVES in my place, my brothers, I beg you, for I have put
13 myself in yours. It is not that you did me any wrong. As you know, it was
14 bodily illness that originally*d* led to my bringing you the Gospel, and you
resisted any temptation to show scorn or disgust at the state of my poor
body;*e* you welcomed me as if I were an angel of God, as you might have
15 welcomed Christ Jesus himself. Have you forgotten how happy you thought
yourselves in having me with you? I can say this for you: you would have
16 torn out your very eyes, and given them to me, had that been possible! And
have I now made myself your enemy by being frank with you?

17 The persons I have referred to are envious of you, but not with an
honest envy:*f* what they really want is to bar the door to you so that you
18 may come to envy*g* them. It is always a fine thing to deserve an honest
19 envy*h*—always, and not only when I am present with you, dear children.
For my children you are, and I am in travail with you over again until you
20 take the shape of Christ. I wish I could be with you now; then I could
modify my tone;*i* as it is, I am at my wits' end about you.

21 TELL ME NOW, you who are so anxious to be under law, will you not listen
22 to what the Law says? It is written there that Abraham had two sons, one

---

a Or the elements of the natural world, *or* elementary ideas belonging to this world.
b Or were slaves to 'gods' which in reality do not exist.   *c* See note on 4. 3.
d Or formerly, *or* on the first of my two visits.   *e* Or you showed neither
scorn nor disgust at the trial my poor body was enduring.   *f* Or paying
court to you, but not with honest intentions.   *g* Or pay court to.   *h* Or to be
honourably wooed.   *i* Or now, and could exchange words with you.

by his slave and the other by his free-born wife. The slave-woman's son 23
was born in the course of nature, the free woman's through God's promise.
This is an allegory. The two women stand for two covenants. The one 24
bearing children into slavery is the covenant that comes from Mount Sinai:
that is Hagar. Sinai is a mountain in Arabia and it represents the Jerusalem 25
of today, for she and her children are in slavery. But the heavenly Jeru- 26
salem is the free woman; she is our mother. For Scripture says, 'Rejoice, 27
O barren woman who never bore child; break into a shout of joy, you who
never knew a mother's pangs; for the deserted wife shall have more children than she who lives with the husband.'

And you, my brothers, like Isaac, are children of God's promise. But 28 29
just as in those days the natural-born son persecuted the spiritual son, so
it is today. But what does Scripture say? 'Drive out the slave-woman and 30
her son, for the son of the slave shall not share the inheritance with the free
woman's son.' You see, then, my brothers, we are no slave-woman's 31
children; our mother is the free woman. Christ set us free, to be free men.* **5**
Stand firm, then, and refuse to be tied to the yoke of slavery again.

Mark my words: I, Paul, say to you that if you receive circumcision 2
Christ will do you no good at all. Once again, you can take it from me that 3
every man who receives circumcision is under obligation to keep the entire
law. When you seek to be justified by way of law, your relation with Christ 4
is completely severed: you have fallen out of the domain of God's grace.
For to us, our hope of attaining that righteousness which we eagerly await 5
is the work of the Spirit through faith. If we are in union with Christ Jesus 6
circumcision makes no difference at all, nor does the want of it; the only
thing that counts is faith active in love.*b*

You were running well; who was it hindered you from following the 7
truth? Whatever persuasion he used, it did not come from God who is call- 8
ing you; 'a little leaven', remember, 'leavens all the dough'. United with 9 10
you in the Lord, I am confident that you will not take the wrong view; but
the man who is unsettling your minds, whoever he may be, must bear
God's judgement. And I, my friends, if I am still advocating circumcision, 11
why is it I am still persecuted? In that case, my preaching of the cross is a
stumbling-block no more. As for these agitators, they had better go the 12
whole way and make eunuchs of themselves!

You, MY FRIENDS, were called to be free men; only do not turn your 13
freedom into licence for your lower nature, but be servants to one another in
love. For the whole law can be summed up in a single commandment: 14
'Love your neighbour as yourself.' But if you go on fighting one another, 15
tooth and nail, all you can expect is mutual destruction.

I mean this: if you are guided by the Spirit you will not fulfil the desires 16
of your lower nature. That nature sets its desires against the Spirit, while 17
the Spirit fights against it. They are in conflict with one another so that
what you will to do you cannot do. But if you are led by the Spirit, you are 18
not under law.

Anyone can see the kind of behaviour that belongs to the lower nature: 19

a Or What Christ has done is to set us free.   *b Or* inspired by love.

20 fornication, impurity, and indecency; idolatry and sorcery; quarrels, a contentious temper, envy, fits of rage, selfish ambitions, dissensions, party
21 intrigues, and jealousies; drinking bouts, orgies, and the like. I warn you, as I warned you before, that those who behave in such ways will never inherit the kingdom of God.

22 But the harvest of the Spirit is love, joy, peace, patience, kindness, good-
23 ness, fidelity, gentleness, and self-control. There is no law dealing with such
24 things as these. And those who belong to Christ Jesus have crucified the
25 lower nature with its passions and desires. If the Spirit is the source of our life, let the Spirit also direct our course.
26 We must not be conceited, challenging one another to rivalry, jealous
6 of one another. If a man should do something wrong, my brothers, on a sudden impulse,[a] you who are endowed with the Spirit must set him right again very gently. Look to yourself, each one of you: you may be tempted
2 too. Help one another to carry these heavy loads, and in this way you will fulfil the law of Christ.
3 For if a man imagines himself to be somebody, when he is nothing, he is
4 deluding himself. Each man should examine his own conduct for himself; then he can measure his achievement by comparing himself with himself
5 and not with anyone else. For everyone has his own proper burden to bear.
6 When anyone is under instruction in the faith, he should give his teacher a share of all good things he has.
7 Make no mistake about this: God is not to be fooled; a man reaps what
8 he sows. If he sows seed in the field of his lower nature, he will reap from it a harvest of corruption, but if he sows in the field of the Spirit, the Spirit
9 will bring him a harvest of eternal life. So let us never tire of doing good, for if we do not slacken our efforts we shall in due time reap our harvest.
10 Therefore, as opportunity offers, let us work for the good of all, especially members of the household of the faith.

11 12 YOU SEE these big letters? I am now writing to you in my own hand. It is all those who want to make a fair outward and bodily show who are trying to force circumcision upon you; their sole object is to escape persecution
13 for the cross of Christ. For even those who do receive circumcision are not thoroughgoing observers of the law; they only want you to be circumcised
14 in order to boast of your having submitted to that outward rite. But God forbid that I should boast of anything but the cross of our Lord Jesus Christ, through which[b] the world is crucified to me and I to the world!
15 Circumcision is nothing; uncircumcision is nothing; the only thing that
16 counts is new creation! Whoever they are who take this principle for their guide, peace and mercy be upon them, and upon the whole Israel of God!
17 In future let no one make trouble for me, for I bear the marks of Jesus branded on my body.
18 The grace of our Lord Jesus Christ be with your spirit, my brothers. Amen.

[a] *Or* If a man is caught doing something wrong, my brothers, . . .   [b] *Or* whom.

THE LETTER OF PAUL
TO THE
EPHESIANS

The glory of Christ in the church

FROM PAUL, APOSTLE of Christ Jesus, commissioned by the 1
will of God, to God's people at Ephesus,*a* believers incorporate in
Christ Jesus.

Grace to you and peace from God our Father and the Lord Jesus Christ. 2

Praise be to the God and Father of our Lord Jesus Christ, who has 3
bestowed on us in Christ every spiritual blessing in the heavenly realms.
In Christ he chose us before the world was founded, to be dedicated, to be 4
without blemish in his sight, to be full of love; and he*b* destined us—such 5
was his will and pleasure—to be accepted as his sons through Jesus Christ,
in order that the glory of his gracious gift, so graciously bestowed on us in 6
his Beloved, might redound to his praise. For in Christ our release is 7
secured and our sins are forgiven through the shedding of his blood.
Therein lies the richness of God's free grace lavished upon us, imparting 8
full wisdom and insight. He has made known to us his hidden purpose— 9
such was his will and pleasure determined beforehand in Christ—to be 10
put into effect when the time was ripe: namely, that the universe, all in
heaven and on earth, might be brought into a unity in Christ.

In Christ indeed we have been given our share in the heritage, as was 11
decreed in his design whose purpose is everywhere at work. For it was his
will that we, who were the first to set our hope on Christ,*c* should cause his 12
glory to be praised. And you too, when you had heard the message of the 13
truth, the good news of your salvation, and had believed it, became incorporate in Christ and received the seal of the promised Holy Spirit; and 14
that Spirit is the pledge that we shall enter upon our heritage, when God
has redeemed what is his own, to his praise and glory.

Because of all this, now that I have heard of the faith you have in the 15
Lord Jesus and of the love you bear towards all God's people, I never 16
cease to give thanks for you when I mention you in my prayers. I pray that 17
the God of our Lord Jesus Christ, the all-glorious Father, may give you the
spiritual powers of wisdom and vision, by which there comes the knowledge of him. I pray that your inward eyes may be illumined, so that you 18
may know what is the hope to which he calls you, what the wealth and

---

a Some witnesses omit at Ephesus.　　　　　　*b Or* . . . sight. In his love he . . .
c Or who already enjoyed the hope of Christ, *or* whose expectation and hope are in
Christ.

19 glory of the share he offers you among his people in their heritage, and how
vast the resources of his power open to us who trust in him. They are
20 measured by his strength and the might which he exerted in Christ when
he raised him from the dead, when he enthroned him at his right hand in
21 the heavenly realms, far above all government and authority, all power and
dominion, and any title of sovereignty that can be named, not only in this
22 age but in the age to come. He put everything in subjection beneath his feet,
23 and appointed him as supreme head to the church, which is his body and
as such holds within it the fullness of him who himself receives the entire
fullness of God. *a*

2 1 2 TIME WAS when you were dead in your sins and wickedness, when you
followed the evil ways of this present age, when you obeyed the commander of the spiritual powers of the air, the spirit now at work among
3 God's rebel subjects. We too were once of their number: we all lived our
lives in sensuality, and obeyed the promptings of our own instincts and
notions. In our natural condition we, like the rest, lay under the dreadful
4 judgement of God. But God, rich in mercy, for the great love he bore us,
5 brought us to life with Christ even when we were dead in our sins; it is by
6 his grace you are saved. And in union with Christ Jesus he raised us up and
7 enthroned us with him in the heavenly realms, so that he might display in
the ages to come how immense are the resources of his grace, and how great
8 his kindness to us in Christ Jesus. For it is by his grace you are saved,
9 through trusting him; it is not your own doing. It is God's gift, not a
10 reward for work done. There is nothing for anyone to boast of. For we are
God's handiwork, created in Christ Jesus to devote ourselves to the good
deeds for which God has designed us.

11   Remember then your former condition: you, Gentiles as you are out-
wardly, *b* you, 'the uncircumcised' so called by those who are called 'the
12 circumcised' (but only with reference to an outward rite)—you were at that
time separate from Christ, strangers to the community of Israel, outside
God's covenants and the promise that goes with them. Your world was a
13 world without hope and without God. But now in union with Christ Jesus
you who once were far off have been brought near through the shedding of
14 Christ's blood. For he is himself our peace. Gentiles and Jews, he has made
the two one, and in his own body of flesh and blood has broken down the
15 enmity which stood like a dividing wall between them; for he annulled the
law with its rules and regulations, so as to create out of the two a single new
16 humanity in himself, thereby making peace. This was his purpose, to
reconcile the two in a single body to God through the cross, on which he
killed the enmity. *c*

17   So he came and proclaimed the good news: peace to you who were far
18 off, and peace to those who were near by; for through him we both alike
19 have access to the Father in the one Spirit. Thus you are no longer aliens in

a Or as supreme head to the church, which is his body and as such holds within it the
fullness of him who fills the universe in all its parts; *or* as supreme head to the church
which is his body, and to be all that he himself is who fills the universe in all its parts.
b Or by birth.   *c Or* . . . cross. Thus in his own person he put the enmity to death.

a foreign land, but fellow-citizens with God's people, members of God's household. You are built upon the foundation laid by the apostles and prophets, and Christ Jesus himself is the foundation-stone.[a] In him the whole building[b] is bonded together and grows into a holy temple in the Lord. In him you too are being built with all the rest into a spiritual dwelling for God. 20 21 22

WITH THIS IN MIND I make my prayer, I, Paul, who in the cause of you Gentiles am now the prisoner of Christ Jesus—for surely you have heard how God has assigned the gift of his grace to me for your benefit. It was by a revelation that his secret was made known to me. I have already written a brief account of this, and by reading it you may perceive that I understand the secret of Christ. In former generations this was not disclosed to the human race; but now it has been revealed by inspiration to his dedicated apostles and prophets, that through the Gospel the Gentiles are joint heirs with the Jews, part of the same body, sharers together in the promise made in Christ Jesus. Such is the gospel of which I was made a minister, by God's gift, bestowed unmerited on me in the working of his power. To me, who am less than the least of all God's people, he has granted of his grace the privilege of proclaiming to the Gentiles the good news of the unfathomable riches of Christ, and of bringing to light how this hidden purpose was to be put into effect. It was hidden for long ages in God the creator of the universe, in order that now, through the church, the wisdom of God in all its varied forms might be made known to the rulers and authorities in the realms of heaven. This is in accord with his age-long purpose, which he achieved in Christ Jesus our Lord. In him we have access to God with freedom, in the confidence born of trust in him. I beg you, then, not to lose heart over my sufferings for you; indeed, they are your glory. 3 2 3 4 5 6 7 8 9 10 11 12 13

With this in mind, then, I kneel in prayer to the Father, from whom every family[c] in heaven and on earth takes its name, that out of the treasures of his glory he may grant you strength and power through his Spirit in your inner being, that through faith Christ may dwell in your hearts in love. With deep roots and firm foundations, may you be strong to grasp, with all God's people, what is the breadth and length and height and depth of the love of Christ, and to know it, though it is beyond knowledge. So may you attain to fullness of being, the fullness of God himself.[d] 14 15 16 17 18 19

Now to him who is able to do immeasurably more than all we can ask or conceive, by the power which is at work among us, to him be glory in the church and in Christ Jesus from generation to generation evermore! Amen. 20 21

I ENTREAT YOU, THEN—I, a prisoner for the Lord's sake: as God has called you, live up to your calling. Be humble always and gentle, and patient too. Be forbearing with one another and charitable. Spare no effort to make fast with bonds of peace the unity which the Spirit gives. There is one 4 2 3 4

[a] *Or* built upon the foundation of the apostles and prophets, and Christ Jesus himself is the keystone.   [b] *Or* every structure.   [c] *Or* his whole family.
[d] *Or* the fullness which God requires.

body and one Spirit, as there is also one hope held out in God's call to you;
5 6 one Lord, one faith, one baptism; one God and Father of all, who is over all and through all and in all.

7 But each of us has been given his gift, his due portion of Christ's bounty.
8 Therefore Scripture says:

> 'He ascended into the heights
> with captives in his train;
> he gave gifts to men.'

9 Now, the word 'ascended' implies that he also descended to the lowest
10 level, down to the very earth.[a] He who descended is no other than he who
11 ascended far above all heavens, so that he might fill the universe. And these were his gifts: some to be apostles, some prophets, some evangelists,
12 some pastors and teachers, to equip God's people for work in his service,
13 to the building up of the body of Christ. So shall we all at last attain to the unity inherent in our faith and our knowledge of the Son of God—to mature manhood, measured by nothing less than the full stature of Christ.
14 We are no longer to be children, tossed by the waves and whirled about by every fresh gust of teaching, dupes of crafty rogues and their deceitful
15 schemes. No, let us speak the truth in love; so shall we fully grow up into
16 Christ. He is the head, and on him the whole body depends. Bonded and knit together by every constituent joint, the whole frame grows through the due activity of each part, and builds itself up in love.

17 This then is my word to you, and I urge it upon you in the Lord's name.
18 Give up living like pagans with their good-for-nothing notions. Their wits are beclouded, they are strangers to the life that is in God, because ignor-
19 ance prevails among them and their minds have grown hard as stone. Dead to all feeling, they have abandoned themselves to vice, and stop at nothing
20 21 to satisfy their foul desires. But that is not how you learned Christ. For were you not told of him, were you not as Christians taught the truth as it
22 is in Jesus?—that, leaving your former way of life, you must lay aside that old human nature which, deluded by its lusts, is sinking towards death.
23 24 You must be made new in mind and spirit, and put on the new nature of God's creating, which shows itself in the just and devout life called for by the truth.

25 Then throw off falsehood; speak the truth to each other, for all of us are the parts of one body.
26 If you are angry, do not let anger lead you into sin; do not let sunset find
27 you still nursing it; leave no loop-hole for the devil.
28 The thief must give up stealing, and instead work hard and honestly with his own hands, so that he may have something to share with the needy.
29 No bad language must pass your lips, but only what is good and helpful
30 to the occasion, so that it brings a blessing to those who hear it. And do not grieve the Holy Spirit of God, for that Spirit is the seal with which you
31 were marked for the day of our final liberation. Have done with spite and passion, all angry shouting and cursing, and bad feeling of every kind.

---

[a] *Or* descended to the regions beneath the earth.

Be generous to one another, tender-hearted, forgiving one another as 32
God in Christ forgave you.

In a word, as God's dear children, try to be like him, and live in love as **5** 1 2
Christ loved you, and gave himself up on your behalf as an offering and
sacrifice whose fragrance is pleasing to God.

Fornication and indecency of any kind, or ruthless greed, must not be so 3
much as mentioned among you, as befits the people of God. No coarse, 4
stupid, or flippant talk; these things are out of place; you should rather be
thanking God. For be very sure of this: no one given to fornication or 5
indecency, or the greed which makes an idol of gain, has any share in the
kingdom of Christ and of God.

Let no one deceive you with shallow arguments; it is for all these things 6
that God's dreadful judgement is coming upon his rebel subjects. Have no 7
part or lot with them. For though you were once all darkness, now as 8
Christians you are light. Live like men who are at home in daylight, for 9
where light is, there all goodness springs up, all justice and truth. Try to 10
find out what would please the Lord; take no part in the barren deeds of 11
darkness, but show them up for what they are. The things they do in secret 12
it would be shameful even to mention. But everything, when once the light 13
has shown it up, is illumined, and everything thus illumined is all light.
And so the hymn says: 14

> 'Awake, sleeper,
> rise from the dead,
> and Christ will shine upon you.'

Be most careful then how you conduct yourselves: like sensible men, 15
not like simpletons. Use the present opportunity to the full, for these are 16
evil days. So do not be fools, but try to understand what the will of the 17
Lord is. Do not give way to drunkenness and the dissipation that goes with 18
it, but let the Holy Spirit fill you: speak to one another in psalms, hymns, 19
and *a* songs; sing and make music in your hearts to the Lord; and in the 20
name of our Lord Jesus Christ give thanks every day for everything to our
God and Father.

Be subject to one another out of reverence for Christ. 21

Wives, be subject to your husbands as to the Lord; for the man is the 22 23
head of the woman, just as Christ also is the head of the church. Christ is,
indeed, the Saviour of the body; but just as the church is subject to Christ, 24
so must women be to their husbands in everything.

Husbands, love your wives, as Christ also loved the church and gave 25
himself up for it, to consecrate it, cleansing it by water and word, so that 26 27
he might present the church to himself all glorious, with no stain or wrinkle
or anything of the sort, but holy and without blemish. In the same way men 28
also are bound to love their wives, as they love their own bodies. In loving
his wife a man loves himself. For no one ever hated his own body: on the 29
contrary, he provides and cares for it; and that is how Christ treats the
church, because it is his body, of which we are living parts. Thus it is that 30 31
(in the words of Scripture) 'a man shall leave his father and mother and

a Some witnesses insert spiritual, *as in Colossians 3. 16.*

32 shall be joined to his wife, and the two shall become one flesh'. It is a great truth that is hidden here. I for my part refer it to Christ and to the church,

33 but it applies also individually: each of you must love his wife as his very self; and the woman must see to it that she pays her husband all respect.

6 1 2 Children, obey your parents, for it is right that you should. 'Honour your father and mother' is the first commandment with a promise attached,

3 in the words: 'that it may be well with you and that you may live long in the land'.

4 You fathers, again, must not goad your children to resentment, but give them the instruction, and the correction, which belong to a Christian upbringing.

5 Slaves, obey your earthly masters with fear and trembling, single-

6 mindedly, as serving Christ. Do not offer merely the outward show of service, to curry favour with men, but, as slaves of Christ, do whole-

7 heartedly the will of God. Give the cheerful service of those who serve the

8 Lord, not men. For you know that whatever good each man may do, slave or free, will be repaid him by the Lord.

9 You masters, also, must do the same by them. Give up using threats; remember you both have the same Master in heaven, and he has no favourites.

10 11 Finally then, find your strength in the Lord, in his mighty power. Put on all the armour which God provides, so that you may be able to stand

12 firm against the devices of the devil. For our fight is not against human foes, but against cosmic powers, against the authorities and potentates of this

13 dark world, against the superhuman forces of evil in the heavens. Therefore, take up God's armour; then you will be able to stand your ground when things are at their worst, to complete every task and still to stand.

14 Stand firm, I say. Fasten on the belt of truth; for coat of mail put on

15 integrity; let the shoes on your feet be the gospel of peace, to give you firm

16 footing; and, with all these, take up the great shield of faith, with which you

17 will be able to quench all the flaming arrows of the evil one. Take salvation for helmet; for sword, take that which the Spirit gives you—the words that

18 come from God. Give yourselves wholly to prayer and entreaty; pray on every occasion in the power of the Spirit. To this end keep watch and per-

19 severe, always interceding for all God's people; and pray for me, that I may be granted the right words when I open my mouth, and may boldly and

20 freely make known his hidden purpose, for which I am an ambassador— in chains. Pray that I may speak of it boldly, as it is my duty to speak.

21 You will want to know about my affairs, and how I am; Tychicus will give you all the news. He is our dear brother and trustworthy helper in the

22 Lord's work. I am sending him to you on purpose to let you know all about us, and to put fresh heart into you.

23 Peace to the brotherhood and love, with faith, from God the Father

24 and the Lord Jesus Christ. God's grace be with all who love our Lord Jesus Christ, grace and immortality. *a*

a Or who love . . . Christ with love imperishable.

THE LETTER OF PAUL
TO THE
PHILIPPIANS

The apostle and his friends

FROM PAUL AND TIMOTHY, servants of Christ Jesus, to all 1
those of God's people, incorporate in Christ Jesus, who live at
Philippi, including their bishops and deacons.

Grace to you and peace from God our Father and the Lord Jesus Christ. 2
I thank my God whenever I think of you; and when I pray for you all, 3 4
my prayers are always joyful, because of the part you have taken in the 5
work of the Gospel from the first day until now. Of one thing I am certain: 6
the One who started the good work in you will bring it to completion by
the Day of Christ Jesus. It is indeed only right that I should feel like this 7
about you all, because you hold me in such affection, and because, when I
lie in prison or appear in the dock to vouch for the truth of the Gospel, you
all share in the privilege that is mine.*a* God knows how I long for you all, 8
with the deep yearning of Christ Jesus himself. And this is my prayer, that 9
your love may grow ever richer and richer in knowledge and insight of
every kind, and may thus bring you the gift of true discrimination.*b* Then 10
on the Day of Christ you will be flawless and without blame, reaping the 11
full harvest of righteousness that comes through Jesus Christ, to the glory
and praise of God.

Friends, I want you to understand that the work of the Gospel has 12
been helped on, rather than hindered, by this business of mine. My im- 13
prisonment in Christ's cause has become common knowledge to all at
headquarters*c* here, and indeed among the public at large; and it has given 14
confidence to most of our fellow-Christians to speak the word of God fearlessly and with extraordinary courage.

Some, indeed, proclaim Christ in a jealous and quarrelsome spirit; 15
others proclaim him in true goodwill, and these are moved by love for me; 16
they know that it is to defend the Gospel that I am where I am. But the 17
others, moved by personal rivalry, present Christ from mixed motives,
meaning to stir up fresh trouble for me as I lie in prison.*d* What does it 18
matter? One way or another, in pretence or sincerity, Christ is set forth,
and for that I rejoice.

a Or I am justified in taking this view about you all, because I hold you in closest union,
as those who, when I lie . . . of the Gospel, all share in the privilege that is mine.
b Or may teach you by experience what things are most worth while.   *c Or* to
all the imperial guard, *or* to all at the Residency (*Greek* Praetorium).   *d Or* meaning
to make use of my imprisonment to stir up fresh trouble.

19   Yes, and rejoice I will, knowing well that the issue of it all will be my
deliverance, because you are praying for me and the Spirit of Jesus Christ
20   is given me for support.[a] For, as I passionately hope, I shall have no cause
to be ashamed, but shall speak so boldly that now as always the greatness
of Christ will shine out clearly in my person, whether through my life or
21 22 through my death. For to me life is Christ, and death gain; but what if my
living on in the body may serve some good purpose? Which then am I to
23   choose? I cannot tell. I am torn two ways: what I should like is to depart
24   and be with Christ; that is better by far; but for your sake there is greater
25   need for me to stay on in the body. This indeed I know for certain: I shall
stay, and stand by you all to help you forward and to add joy to your faith,
26   so that when I am with you again, your pride in me may be unbounded in
Christ Jesus.

27   Only, let your conduct be worthy of the gospel of Christ, so that whether
I come and see you for myself or hear about you from a distance, I may
know that you are standing firm, one in spirit, one in mind, contending as
28   one man for the gospel faith, meeting your opponents without so much as
a tremor. This is a sure sign to them that their doom is sealed, but a sign
29   of your salvation, and one afforded by God himself; for you have been
granted the privilege not only of believing in Christ but also of suffering
30   for him. You and I are engaged in the same contest; you saw me in it once,
and, as you hear, I am in it still.

2   IF THEN our common life in Christ yields anything to stir the heart, any
loving consolation, any sharing of the Spirit, any warmth of affection or
2   compassion, fill up my cup of happiness by thinking and feeling alike,
with the same love for one another, the same turn of mind, and a common
3   care for unity. There must be no room for rivalry and personal vanity
among you, but you must humbly reckon others better than yourselves.
4   Look to each other's interest and not merely to your own.

5   Let your bearing towards one another arise out of your life in Christ
6   Jesus.[b] For the divine nature was his from the first; yet he did not think
7   to snatch at equality with God,[c] but made himself nothing, assuming the
8   nature of a slave. Bearing the human likeness, revealed in human shape,
he humbled himself, and in obedience accepted even death—death on a
9   cross. Therefore God raised him to the heights and bestowed on him the
10   name above all names, that at the name of Jesus every knee should bow—
11   in heaven, on earth, and in the depths—and every tongue confess, 'Jesus
Christ is Lord', to the glory of God the Father.

12   So you too, my friends, must be obedient, as always; even more, now
that I am away, than when I was with you. You must work out your own
13   salvation in fear and trembling; for it is God who works in you, inspiring
both the will and the deed, for his own chosen purpose.

14 15 Do all you have to do without complaint or wrangling. Show yourselves
guileless and above reproach, faultless children of God in a warped and

---

[a] *Or* supplies me with all I need.   [b] *Or* Have that bearing towards one another
which was also found in Christ Jesus.   [c] *Or* yet he did not prize his equality
with God.

crooked generation, in which you shine^a like stars in a dark world^b and 16
proffer the word of life.^c Thus you will be my pride on the Day of Christ,
proof that I did not run my race in vain, or work in vain. But if my life- 17
blood is to crown that sacrifice which is the offering up of your faith, I am
glad of it, and I share my gladness with you all. Rejoice, you no less than 18
I, and let us share our joy.

I HOPE (under the Lord Jesus) to send Timothy to you soon; it will 19
cheer me to hear news of you. There is no one else here who sees things as 20
I do, and takes^d a genuine interest in your concerns; they are all bent on 21
their own ends, not on the cause of Christ Jesus. But Timothy's record is 22
known to you: you know that he has been at my side in the service of the
Gospel like a son working under his father. Timothy, then, I hope to send 23
as soon as ever I can see how things are going with me; and I am confident, 24
under the Lord, that I shall myself be coming before long.

I feel also I must send our brother Epaphroditus, my fellow-worker and 25
comrade, whom you commissioned to minister to my needs. He has been 26
missing all of you sadly, and has been distressed that you heard he was ill.
(He was indeed dangerously ill, but God was merciful to him, and merciful 27
no less to me, to spare me sorrow upon sorrow.) For this reason I am all 28
the more eager to send him, to give you the happiness of seeing him again,
and to relieve my sorrow. Welcome him then in the fellowship of the Lord 29
with whole-hearted delight. You should honour men like him; in Christ's 30
cause he came near to death, risking his life to render me the service you
could not give.

And now, friends, farewell; I wish you joy in the Lord. 3

TO REPEAT what I have written to you before is no trouble to me, and it
is a safeguard for you. Beware of those dogs and their malpractices. Beware 2
of those who insist on mutilation—'circumcision' I will not call it; we are 3
the circumcised, we whose worship is spiritual,^e whose pride is in Christ
Jesus, and who put no confidence in anything external. Not that I am with- 4
out grounds myself even for confidence of that kind. If anyone thinks to
base his claims on externals, I could make a stronger case for myself:
circumcised on my eighth day, Israelite by race, of the tribe of Benjamin, 5
a Hebrew born and bred;^f in my attitude to the law, a Pharisee; in pious 6
zeal, a persecutor of the church; in legal rectitude, faultless. But all such 7
assets I have written off because of Christ. I would say more: I count 8
everything sheer loss, because all is far outweighed by the gain of knowing
Christ Jesus my Lord, for whose sake I did in fact lose everything. I count
it so much garbage,^g for the sake of gaining Christ and finding myself 9
incorporate in him, with no righteousness of my own, no legal rectitude,

^a *Or* . . . generation. Shine out among them . . .   ^b *Or* in the firmament.
^c *Or* as the very principle of its life.   ^d *Or* no one else here like him, who
takes . . .   ^e *Some witnesses read* who worship God in the spirit; *others read* who
worship by the Spirit of God.   ^f *Or* a Hebrew-speaking Jew of a Hebrew-speaking
family.   ^g *Or* dung.

but the righteousness which comes *a* from faith in Christ, given by God in
10 response to faith. All I care for is to know Christ, to experience the power
of his resurrection, and to share his sufferings, in growing confor-
11 mity with his death, if only I may finally arrive at the resurrection from
the dead.

12   It is not to be thought that I have already achieved all this. I have not yet
reached perfection, but I press on, hoping to take hold of that for which
13 Christ once took hold of me. My friends, I do not reckon myself to have got
hold of it yet. All I can say is this: forgetting what is behind me, and reach-
14 ing out for that which lies ahead, I press towards the goal to win the prize
which is God's call to the life above, in Christ Jesus.

15   Let us then keep to this way of thinking, those of us who are mature. If
there is any point on which you think differently, this also God will make
16 plain to you. Only let our conduct be consistent with the level we have
already reached.

17   Agree together, my friends, to follow my example. You have us for a
18 model; watch those whose way of life conforms to it. For, as I have often
told you, and now tell you with tears in my eyes, there are many whose
19 way of life makes them enemies of the cross of Christ. They are heading for
destruction, appetite is their god, and they glory in their shame. Their
20 minds are set on earthly things. We, by contrast, are citizens of heaven,
and from heaven we expect our deliverer to come, the Lord Jesus Christ.
21 He will transfigure the body belonging to our humble state, and give it a
form like that of his own resplendent body, by the very power which
4 enables him to make all things subject to himself. Therefore, my friends,
beloved friends whom I long for, my joy, my crown, stand thus firm in the
Lord, my beloved!

2   I beg Euodia, and I beg Syntyche, to agree together in the Lord's fellow-
3 ship. Yes, and you too, my loyal comrade, I ask you to help these women,
who shared my struggles in the cause of the Gospel, with Clement and my
other fellow-workers, whose *b* names are in the roll of the living.

4   Farewell; I wish you all joy in the Lord. I will say it again: all joy be
yours.

5   Let your magnanimity be manifest to all.

6   The Lord is near; have no anxiety, but in everything make your requests
7 known to God in prayer and petition with thanksgiving. Then the peace of
God, which is beyond our utmost understanding, *c* will keep guard over
your hearts and your thoughts, in Christ Jesus.

8   And now, my friends, all that is true, all that is noble, all that is just and
pure, all that is lovable and gracious, *d* whatever is excellent and admirable
—fill all your thoughts with these things.

9   The lessons I taught you, the tradition I have passed on, all that you
heard me say or saw me do, put into practice; and the God of peace will
be with you.

a Or and in him finding that, though I have no righteousness of my own, no legal rectitude, I have the righteousness which comes . . .   *b Some witnesses read* my
fellow-workers, and the others whose . . .   *c Or* of far more worth than
human reasoning.   *d Or* of good repute.

IT IS A GREAT JOY to me, in the Lord, that after so long your care for me 10
has now blossomed afresh. You did care about me before for that matter;
it was opportunity that you lacked. Not that I am alluding to want, for I 11
have learned to find resources in myself whatever my circumstances. I 12
know what it is to be brought low, and I know what it is to have plenty.
I have been very thoroughly initiated into the human lot with all its ups
and downs—fullness and hunger, plenty and want. I have strength for any- 13
thing through him who gives me power. But it was kind of you to share the 14
burden of my troubles.

As you know yourselves, Philippians, in the early days of my mission, 15
when I set out from Macedonia, you alone of all our congregations were
my partners in payments and receipts; for even at Thessalonica you con- 16
tributed to my needs, not once but twice over. Do not think I set my heart 17
upon the gift; all I care for is the profit accruing to you. However, here I 18
give you my receipt for everything—for more than everything; I am paid
in full, now that I have received from Epaphroditus what you sent. It is a
fragrant offering, an acceptable sacrifice, pleasing to God. And my God 19
will supply all your wants out of the magnificence of his riches in Christ
Jesus. To our God and Father be glory for endless ages! Amen. 20

Give my greetings, in the fellowship of Christ Jesus, to each one of God's 21
people. The brothers who are now with me send their greetings to you,
and so do all God's people here, particularly those who belong to the 22
imperial establishment.

The grace of our Lord Jesus Christ be with your spirit. 23

THE LETTER OF PAUL
TO THE
COLOSSIANS

The centre of Christian belief

FROM PAUL, APOSTLE of Christ Jesus commissioned by the 1
will of God, and our colleague Timothy, to God's people at Colossae, 2
brothers in the faith, incorporate in Christ.

Grace to you and peace from God our Father.

In all our prayers to God, the Father of our Lord Jesus Christ, we 3
thank him for you, because we have heard of the faith you hold in Christ 4
Jesus, and the love you bear towards all God's people. Both spring from the 5
hope stored up for you in heaven—that hope of which you learned when the
message of the true Gospel first came to you. In the same way it is coming 6
to men the whole world over; everywhere it is growing and bearing fruit

7 as it does among you, and has done since the day when you heard of the graciousness of God and recognized it for what in truth it is. You were taught this by Epaphras, our dear fellow-servant, a trusted worker for
8 Christ on our^a behalf, and it is he who has brought us the news of your God-given love.^b

9 For this reason, ever since the day we heard of it, we have not ceased to pray for you. We ask God that you may receive from him all wisdom and
10 spiritual understanding for full insight into his will, so that your manner of life may be worthy of the Lord and entirely pleasing to him. We pray that you may bear fruit in active goodness of every kind, and grow in the
11 knowledge of God. May he strengthen you, in his glorious might, with ample power to meet whatever comes with fortitude, patience, and joy;
12 and to give thanks^c to the Father who has made you fit to share the heritage of God's people in the realm of light.

13 He rescued us from the domain of darkness and brought us away into
14 the kingdom of his dear Son, in whom our release is secured and our sins
15 forgiven. He is the image of the invisible God; his is the primacy over^d all
16 created things. In him everything in heaven and on earth was created, not only things visible but also the invisible orders of thrones, sovereignties, authorities, and powers: the whole universe has been created through him
17 and for him. And he exists before everything, and all things are held to-
18 gether in him. He is, moreover, the head of the body, the church. He is its origin, the first to return from the dead, to be in all things alone supreme.
19 For in him the complete being of God, by God's own choice, came to dwell.
20 Through him God chose to reconcile the whole universe to himself, making peace through the shedding of his blood upon the cross—to reconcile all things, whether on earth or in heaven, through him alone.

21 Formerly you were yourselves estranged from God; you were his enemies
22 in heart and mind, and your deeds were evil. But now by Christ's death in his body of flesh and blood God has reconciled you to himself, so that he may present you before himself as dedicated men, without blemish and
23 innocent in his sight. Only you must continue in your faith, firm on your foundations, never to be dislodged from the hope offered in the gospel which you heard. This is the gospel which has been proclaimed in the whole creation under heaven; and I, Paul, have become its minister.

24 It is now my happiness to suffer for you. This is my way of helping to complete, in my poor human flesh, the full tale of Christ's afflictions still
25 to be endured, for the sake of his body which is the church. I became its servant by virtue of the task assigned to me by God for your benefit: to
26 deliver his message in full; to announce the secret hidden for long ages and
27 through many generations, but now disclosed to God's people, to whom it was his will to make it known—to make known how rich and glorious it is among all nations. The secret is this: Christ in^e you, the hope of a glory to come.

28 He it is whom we proclaim. We admonish everyone without distinction,

---

^a *Some witnesses read* your.   ^b *Or* your love within the fellowship of the Spirit.
^c *Or* with fortitude and patience, and to give joyful thanks . . .   ^d *Or* image of the invisible God, born before . . .   ^e *Or* among.

we instruct everyone in all the ways of wisdom, so as to present each one of you as a mature member of Christ's body. To this end I am toiling 29 strenuously with all the energy and power of Christ at work in me. For I 2 want you to know how strenuous are my exertions for you and the Laodiceans and all who have never set eyes on me. I want them to continue in 2 good heart and in the unity of love, and to come to the full wealth of conviction which understanding brings, and grasp God's secret. That secret is Christ himself; in him lie hidden all God's treasures of wisdom and know-3 ledge. I tell you this to save you from being talked *a* into error by specious 4 arguments. For though absent in body, I am with you in spirit, and rejoice 5 to see your orderly array and the firm front which your faith in Christ presents.

THEREFORE, SINCE JESUS was delivered to you as Christ and Lord, 6 live your lives in union with him. Be rooted in him; be built in him; be con-7 solidated in the faith you were taught; *b* let your hearts overflow with thankfulness. Be on your guard; do not let your minds be captured by 8 hollow and delusive speculations, based on traditions of man-made teaching and centred on the elemental spirits of the universe *c* and not on Christ.

For it is in Christ that the complete being of the Godhead dwells 9 embodied, *d* and in him you have been brought to completion. Every power 10 and authority in the universe is subject to him as Head. In him also you were 11 circumcised, not in a physical sense, but by being divested of the lower nature; this is Christ's way of circumcision. For in baptism *e* you were 12 buried with him, in baptism also you were raised to life with him through your faith in the active power of God who raised him from the dead. And 13 although you were dead because of your sins and because you were morally uncircumcised, he has made you alive with Christ. For he has forgiven us all our sins; he has cancelled the bond which pledged us to the decrees of 14 the law. It stood against us, but he has set it aside, nailing it to the cross. On that cross he discarded the cosmic powers and authorities like a gar-15 ment; he made a public spectacle of them and led them *f* as captives in his triumphal procession.

ALLOW NO ONE therefore to take you to task about what you eat or drink, 16 or over the observance of festival, new moon, or sabbath. These are no 17 more than a shadow of what was to come; the solid reality is Christ's. You 18 are not to be disqualified by the decision of people who go in for self-mortification and angel-worship, and try to enter into some vision of their own. Such people, bursting with the futile conceit of worldly minds, lose 19 hold upon the Head; yet it is from the Head that the whole body, with all

a Or What I mean is this: no one must talk you . . .   *b Or* by your faith, as you were taught.   *c Or* the elements of the natural world, *or* elementary ideas belonging to this world.   *d Or* corporately.   *e Or* . . . nature, in the very circumcision of Christ himself; for in baptism . . .   *f Or* he stripped himself of his physical body, and thereby boldly made a spectacle of the cosmic powers and authorities, and led them . . .; *or* he despoiled the cosmic powers and authorities, and boldly made a spectacle of them, leading them . . .

its joints and ligaments, receives its supplies, and thus knit together grows according to God's design.

20   Did you not die with Christ and pass beyond reach of the elemental spirits of the universe*a*? Then why behave as though you were still living
21 the life of the world? Why let people dictate to you: 'Do not handle this,
22 do not taste that, do not touch the other'—all of them things that must perish as soon as they are used? That is to follow merely human injunctions
23 and teaching. True, it has an air of wisdom, with its forced piety, its self-mortification, and its severity to the body; but it is of no use at all in combating sensuality.

3   Were you not raised to life with Christ? Then aspire to the realm above,
2 where Christ is, seated at the right hand of God, and let your thoughts
3 dwell on that higher realm, not on this earthly life. I repeat, you died; and
4 now your life lies hidden with Christ in God. When Christ, who is our life, is manifested, then you too will be manifested with him in glory.

5   Then put to death those parts of you which belong to the earth—fornication, indecency, lust, foul cravings, and the ruthless greed which is
6 nothing less than idolatry. Because of these, God's dreadful judgement is
7 impending; and in the life you once lived these are the ways you yourselves
8 followed. But now you must yourselves lay aside all anger, passion, malice,
9 cursing, filthy talk—have done with them! Stop lying to one another, now
10 that you have discarded the old nature with its deeds and have put on the new nature, which is being constantly renewed in the image of its Creator
11 and brought to know God. There is no question here of Greek and Jew, circumcised and uncircumcised, barbarian, Scythian, slave and freeman; but Christ is all, and is in all.

12   Then put on the garments that suit God's chosen people, his own, his
13 beloved: compassion, kindness, humility, gentleness, patience. Be forbearing with one another, and forgiving, where any of you has cause for
14 complaint: you must forgive as the Lord forgave you. To crown all, there
15 must be love, to bind all together and complete the whole. Let Christ's peace be arbiter in your hearts; to this peace you were called as members of
16 a single body. And be filled with gratitude. Let the message of Christ dwell among you in all its richness. Instruct and admonish each other with the utmost wisdom. Sing thankfully in your hearts to God,*b* with psalms and
17 hymns and spiritual songs. Whatever you are doing, whether you speak or act, do everything in the name of the Lord Jesus, giving thanks to God the Father through him.

18 WIVES, BE SUBJECT to your husbands; that is your Christian duty.
19 20 Husbands, love your wives and do not be harsh with them. Children, obey your parents in everything, for that is pleasing to God and is the Christian
21 way. Fathers, do not exasperate your children, for fear they grow dis-
22 heartened. Slaves, give entire obedience to your earthly masters, not merely with an outward show of service, to curry favour with men, but with single-
23 mindedness, out of reverence for the Lord. Whatever you are doing, put

---

a Or the elements of the natural world, *or* elementary ideas belonging to this world.
b *Some witnesses read* the Lord.

your whole heart into it, as if you were doing it for the Lord and not for men, knowing that there is a Master who will give you your heritage as a 24 reward for your service. Christ is the Master whose slaves you must be. Dishonesty will be requited, and he has no favourites. Masters, be just and 25 **4** 1 fair to your slaves, knowing that you too have a Master in heaven.

Persevere in prayer, with mind awake and thankful heart; and include a 2 3 prayer for us, that God may give us an opening for preaching, to tell the secret of Christ; that indeed is why I am now in prison. Pray that I may 4 make the secret plain, as it is my duty to do.

Behave wisely towards those outside your own number; use the present 5 opportunity to the full. Let your conversation be always gracious, and 6 never insipid; study how best to talk with each person you meet.

YOU WILL HEAR all about my affairs from Tychicus, our dear brother 7 and trustworthy helper and fellow-servant in the Lord's work. I am send- 8 ing him to you on purpose to let you know all about us and to put fresh heart into you. With him comes Onesimus, our trustworthy and dear 9 brother, who is one of yourselves. They will tell you all the news here.

Aristarchus, Christ's captive like myself, sends his greetings; so does 10 Mark, the cousin of Barnabas (you have had instructions about him; if he comes, make him welcome), and Jesus Justus. Of the Jewish Christians, 11 these are the only ones who work with me for the kingdom of God, and they have been a great comfort to me. Greetings from Epaphras, servant of 12 Christ, who is one of yourselves. He prays hard for you all the time, that you may stand fast, ripe in conviction*a* and wholly devoted to doing God's will. For I can vouch for him, that he works tirelessly for you and the people 13 at Laodicea and Hierapolis. Greetings to you from our dear friend Luke, 14 the doctor, and from Demas. Give our greetings to the brothers at Laodicea, 15 and Nympha and the congregation at her house.*b* And when this letter is 16 read among you, see that it is also read to the congregation at Laodicea, and that you in return read the one from Laodicea. This special word to 17 Archippus: 'Attend to the duty entrusted to you in the Lord's service, and discharge it to the full.'

This greeting is in my own hand—PAUL. Remember I am in prison. 18 God's grace be with you.

a Or stand fast, mature and complete . . .   *b Some witnesses read* Nymphas and the congregation at his house.

THE FIRST LETTER OF PAUL
TO THE
THESSALONIANS

Hope and discipline

1 FROM PAUL, Silvanus, and Timothy to the congregation of Thessalonians who belong to God the Father and the Lord Jesus Christ.
Grace to you and peace.

2 We always thank God for you all, and mention you in our prayers con-
3 tinually. We call to mind, before our God and Father, how your faith has
shown itself in action, your love in labour, and your hope of our Lord Jesus
4 Christ in fortitude. We are certain, brothers beloved by God, that he has
5 chosen you and that *a* when we brought you the Gospel, we brought it not
in mere words but in the power of the Holy Spirit, and with strong conviction, as you know well. That is the kind of men we were at Thessalonica,
and it was for your sake.

6 And you, in your turn, followed the example set by us and by the Lord;
the welcome you gave the message meant grave suffering for you, yet you
7 rejoiced in the Holy Spirit; thus you have become a model for all believers
8 in Macedonia and in Achaia. From Thessalonica the word of the Lord
rang out; and not in Macedonia and Achaia alone, but everywhere your
9 faith in God has reached men's ears. No words of ours are needed, for they
themselves spread the news of our visit to you and its effect: how you turned
10 from idols, to be servants of the living and true God, and to wait expectantly for the appearance from heaven of his Son Jesus, whom he raised
from the dead, Jesus our deliverer from the terrors of judgement to come.

2 You know for yourselves, brothers, that our visit to you was not fruitless.
2 Far from it; after all the injury and outrage which to your knowledge we
had suffered at Philippi, we declared the gospel of God to you frankly and
3 fearlessly, by the help of our God. A hard struggle it was. Indeed, the appeal
we make never springs from error or base motive; there is no attempt to
4 deceive; but God has approved us as fit to be entrusted with the Gospel,
and on those terms we speak. We do not curry favour with men; we seek
5 only the favour of God, who is continually testing our hearts. Our words
have never been flattering words, as you have cause to know; nor, as God
6 is our witness, have they ever been a cloak for greed. We have never sought
honour from men, from you or from anyone else, although as Christ's own
7 envoys we might have made our weight felt; but we were as gentle with you
8 as a nurse caring fondly for her children. With such yearning love we chose

a Or . . . chosen you, because . . .

260

to impart to you not only the gospel of God but our very selves, so dear had
you become to us. Remember, brothers, how we toiled and drudged. We 9
worked for a living night and day, rather than be a burden to anyone, while
we proclaimed before you the good news of God.

We call you to witness, yes and God himself, how devout and just and 10
blameless was our behaviour towards you who are believers. As you well 11
know, we dealt with you one by one, as a father deals with his children,
appealing to you by encouragement, as well as by solemn injunctions, to 12
live lives worthy of the God who calls you into his kingdom and glory.

This is why we thank God continually, because when we handed on 13
God's message, you received it, not as the word of men, but as what it truly
is, the very word of God at *a* work in you who hold the faith. You have 14
fared like the congregations in Judaea, God's people in Christ Jesus. You
have been treated by your countrymen as they are treated by the Jews,
who killed the Lord Jesus and the prophets *b* and drove us out, the Jews 15
who are heedless of God's will and enemies of their fellow-men, hindering 16
us from speaking to the Gentiles to lead them to salvation. All this time
they have been making up the full measure of their guilt, and now retribution has overtaken them for good and all. *c*

MY FRIENDS, when for a short spell you were lost to us—lost to sight, not 17
to our hearts—we were exceedingly anxious to see you again. So we did 18
propose to come to Thessalonica—I, Paul, more than once—but Satan
thwarted us. For after all, what hope or joy or crown of pride is there for 19
us, what indeed but you, when we stand before our Lord Jesus at his
coming? It is you who are indeed our glory and our joy. 20

So when we could bear it no longer, we decided to remain alone at 3
Athens, and sent Timothy, our brother and God's fellow-worker *d* in the 2
service of the gospel of Christ, to encourage you to stand firm for the faith
and, under all these hardships, not to be shaken; *e* for you know that this 3
is our appointed lot. When we were with you we warned you that we were 4
bound to suffer hardship; and so it has turned out, as you know. And thus 5
it was that when I could bear it no longer, I sent to find out about your faith,
fearing that the tempter might have tempted you and my labour might
be lost.

But now Timothy has just arrived from Thessalonica, bringing good 6
news of your faith and love. He tells us that you always think kindly of us,
and are as anxious to see us as we are to see you. And so in all our diffi- 7
culties and hardships your faith reassures us about you. It is the breath of 8
life to us that you stand firm in the Lord. What thanks can we return to 9
God for you? What thanks for all the joy you have brought us, making us
rejoice before our God while we pray most earnestly night and day to be 10
allowed to see you again and to mend your faith where it falls short?

May our God and Father himself, and our Lord Jesus, bring us direct to 11
you; and may the Lord make your love mount and overflow towards one 12

---

a Or word of God who is at . . .   *b* *Some witnesses read* their own prophets.
c Or now at last retribution has overtaken them.   *d* Or and fellow-worker for
God; *one witness has simply* and fellow-worker.   *e* Or beguiled away.

13 another and towards all, as our love does towards you. May he make your hearts firm, so that you may stand before our God and Father holy and faultless when our Lord Jesus comes with all those who are his own.

4 AND NOW, MY FRIENDS, we have one thing to beg and pray of you, by our fellowship with the Lord Jesus. We passed on to you the tradition of the way we must live to please God; you are indeed already following it, but we beg you to do so yet more thoroughly.

2 For you know what orders we gave you, in the name of the Lord Jesus.
3 This is the will of God, that you should be holy: you must abstain from
4 fornication; each one of you must learn to gain mastery over his body, to
5 hallow and honour it, not giving way to lust like the pagans who are
6 ignorant of God; and no man must do his brother wrong in this matter,[a] or invade his rights, because, as we told you before with all emphasis, the
7 Lord punishes all such offences. For God called us to holiness, not to
8 impurity. Anyone therefore who flouts these rules is flouting, not man, but God who bestows upon you his Holy Spirit.

9 About love for our brotherhood you need no words of mine, for you are
10 yourselves taught by God to love one another, and you are in fact practising this rule of love towards all your fellow-Christians throughout Mace-
11 donia. Yet we appeal to you, brothers, to do better still. Let it be your ambition to keep calm and look after your own business, and to work with
12 your hands, as we ordered you, so that you may command the respect of those outside your own number, and at the same time may never be in want.

13 WE WISH YOU not to remain in ignorance, brothers, about those who sleep in death; you should not grieve like the rest of men, who have no
14 hope. We believe that Jesus died and rose again; and so it will be for those who died as Christians; God will bring them to life with Jesus.[b]
15 For this we tell you as the Lord's word: we who are left alive until the
16 Lord comes shall not forestall those who have died; because at the word of command, at the sound of the archangel's voice and God's trumpet-call, the Lord himself will descend from heaven; first the Christian dead will
17 rise, then we who are left alive shall join them, caught up in clouds to meet
18 the Lord in the air. Thus we shall always be with the Lord. Console one another, then, with these words.

5 1 2 About dates and times, my friends, we need not write to you, for you know perfectly well that the Day of the Lord comes like a thief in the night.
3 While they are talking of peace and security, all at once calamity is upon them, sudden as the pangs that come upon a woman with child; and there
4 will be no escape. But you, my friends, are not in the dark, that the day
5 should overtake you like a thief.[c] You are all children of light, children of
6 day. We do not belong to night or darkness, and we must not sleep like
7 the rest, but keep awake and sober. Sleepers sleep at night, and drunkards
8 are drunk at night, but we, who belong to daylight, must keep sober, armed with faith and love for coat of mail, and the hope of salvation for

---

[a] *Or* must overreach his brother in his business (*or* in lawsuits). [b] *Or* will bring them in company with Jesus. [c] *Some witnesses read* thieves.

helmet. For God has not destined us to the terrors of judgement, but to the 9
full attainment of salvation through our Lord Jesus Christ. He died for us 10
so that we, awake or asleep, might live in company with him. Therefore 11
hearten one another, fortify one another—as indeed you do.

WE BEG YOU, BROTHERS, to acknowledge those who are working so hard 12
among you, and in the Lord's fellowship are your leaders and counsellors.
Hold them in the highest possible esteem and affection for the work they do. 13
    You must live at peace among yourselves. And we would urge you, 14
brothers, to admonish the careless, encourage the faint-hearted, support
the weak, and to be very patient with them all.
    See to it that no one pays back wrong for wrong, but always aim at doing 15
the best you can for each other and for all men.
    Be always joyful; pray continually; give thanks whatever happens; for 16 17 18
this is what God in Christ wills for you.
    Do not stifle inspiration, and do not despise prophetic utterances, but 19 20 21
bring them all to the test and then keep what is good in them and avoid the 22
bad of whatever kind. *a*
    May God himself, the God of peace, make you holy in every part, and 23
keep you sound in spirit, soul, and body, without fault when our Lord
Jesus Christ comes. He who calls you is to be trusted; he will do it. 24
    Brothers, pray for us also. 25
    Greet all our brothers with the kiss of peace. 26
    I adjure you by the Lord to have this letter read to the whole brother- 27
hood.
    The grace of our Lord Jesus Christ be with you! 28

THE SECOND LETTER OF PAUL
TO THE
THESSALONIANS

Hope and discipline

FROM PAUL, Silvanus, and Timothy to the congregation of Thes- 1
salonians who belong to God our Father and the Lord Jesus Christ.
    Grace to you and peace from God the Father and the Lord Jesus 2
Christ.
    Our thanks are always due to God for you, brothers. It is right that we 3
should thank him, because your faith increases mightily, and the love you

*a Or . . . utterances. Put everything to the test; keep hold of what is good and avoid every
kind of evil.*

4 have, each for all and all for each, grows ever greater. Indeed we boast about you ourselves among the congregations of God's people, because your faith remains so steadfast under all your persecutions, and all the
5 troubles you endure. See how this brings out the justice of God's judgement. It will prove you worthy of the kingdom of God, for which indeed you are suffering.

6 It is surely just that God should balance the account by sending trouble
7 to those who trouble you, and relief to you who are troubled, and to us as well, when our Lord Jesus Christ is revealed from heaven with his
8 mighty angels in blazing fire. Then he will do justice upon those who refuse to acknowledge God and upon those who will not obey *a* the
9 gospel of our Lord Jesus. They will suffer the punishment of eternal ruin, cut off from the presence of the Lord and the splendour of his might,
10 when on that great Day he comes to be glorified among his own and adored among all believers; for you did indeed believe the testimony we brought you.

11 With this in mind we pray for you always, that our God may count you worthy of his calling, and mightily bring to fulfilment every good pur-
12 pose and every act inspired by faith, so that the name of our Lord Jesus may be glorified in you, and you in him, according to the grace of our God and the Lord Jesus Christ.

2 AND NOW, BROTHERS, about the coming of our Lord Jesus Christ and
2 his gathering of us to himself: I beg you, do not suddenly lose your heads or alarm yourselves, whether at some oracular utterance, or pronouncement, or some letter purporting to come from us, alleging that the Day of
3 the Lord is already here. Let no one deceive you in any way whatever. That day cannot come before the final rebellion against God, when wickedness
4 will be revealed in human form, the man doomed to perdition. He is the Enemy. He rises in his pride against every god, so called, every object of men's worship, and even takes his seat in the temple of God claiming to be a god himself.

5 You cannot but remember that I told you this while I was still with you;
6 you must now be aware of the restraining hand which ensures that he shall
7 be revealed only at the proper time. For already the secret power of wickedness is at work, secret only for the present until the Restrainer disappears
8 from the scene. And then he will be revealed, that wicked man whom the Lord Jesus will destroy with the breath of his mouth, and annihilate by the
9 radiance of his coming. But the coming of that wicked man is the work of Satan. It will be attended by all the powerful signs and miracles of the Lie,
10 and all the deception that sinfulness can impose on those doomed to destruction. Destroyed they shall be, because they did not open their
11 minds to love of the truth, so as to find salvation. Therefore God puts them
12 under a delusion, which works upon them to believe the lie, so that they may all be brought to judgement, all who do not believe the truth but make sinfulness their deliberate choice.

a Or justice upon those who refuse . . . and will not obey . . .

BUT WE ARE BOUND to thank God always for you, brothers beloved by 13
the Lord, because from the beginning of time God chose you *a* to find
salvation in the Spirit that consecrates you, and in the truth that you
believe. It was for this that he called you through the gospel we brought, 14
so that you might possess for your own the splendour of our Lord Jesus
Christ.

Stand firm, then, brothers, and hold fast to the traditions which you have 15
learned from us by word or by letter. And may our Lord Jesus Christ him- 16
self and God our Father, who has shown us such love, and in his grace has
given us such unfailing encouragement and such bright hopes, still 17
encourage and fortify you in every good deed and word!

And now, brothers, pray for us, that the word of the Lord may have **3**
everywhere the swift and glorious course that it has had among you, and 2
that we may be rescued from wrong-headed and wicked men; for it is not
all who have faith. But the Lord is to be trusted, and he will fortify you and 3
guard you from the evil one. We feel perfect confidence about you, in the 4
Lord, that you are doing and will continue to do what we order. May the 5
Lord direct your hearts towards God's love and the steadfastness of Christ!

These are our orders to you, brothers, in the name of our Lord Jesus 6
Christ: hold aloof from every Christian brother who falls into idle habits,
and does not follow the tradition you received from us. You know your- 7
selves how you ought to copy our example: we were no idlers among you;
we did not accept board and lodging from anyone without paying for it; 8
we toiled and drudged, we worked for a living night and day, rather than
be a burden to any of you—not because we have not the right to main- 9
tenance, but to set an example for you to imitate. For even during our stay 10
with you we laid down the rule: the man who will not work shall not eat.
We mention this because we hear that some of your number are idling 11
their time away, minding everybody's business but their own. To all such 12
we give these orders, and we appeal to them in the name of the Lord Jesus
Christ to work quietly for their living.

But you, my friends, must never tire of doing right. If anyone disobeys 13 14
our instructions given by letter, mark him well, and have no dealings with
him until he is ashamed of himself. I do not mean treat him as an enemy, 15
but give him friendly advice, as one of the family. May the Lord of peace 16
himself give you peace at all times and in all ways. *b* The Lord be with
you all.

The greeting is in my own hand, signed with my name, PAUL; this 17
authenticates all my letters; this is how I write. The grace *c* of our Lord 18
Jesus Christ be with you all.

---

a *Some witnesses read* because God chose you as his firstfruits . . . *b* *Some*
witnesses read at all times, wherever you may be. *c* *Or* . . . letters. My message is
this: the grace . . .

THE FIRST LETTER OF PAUL
TO
TIMOTHY

Church order

1 FROM PAUL, APOSTLE of Christ Jesus by command of God
2 our Saviour and Christ Jesus our hope, to Timothy his true-born
son in the faith.

Grace, mercy, and peace to you from God the Father and Christ Jesus
our Lord.

3 When I was starting for Macedonia, I urged you to stay on at Ephesus.
You were to command certain persons to give up teaching erroneous
4 doctrines and studying those interminable myths and genealogies, which
issue in mere speculation and cannot make known God's plan for us,
which works through faith.*a*

5 The aim and object of this command is the love which springs from a
clean heart, from a good conscience, and from faith that is genuine.
6 Through falling short of these, some people have gone astray into a wilder-
7 ness of words. They set out to be teachers of the moral law, without understanding either the words they use or the subjects about which they are so
dogmatic.

8 We all know that the law is an excellent thing, provided we treat it as
9 law, recognizing that it is not aimed at good citizens, but at the lawless
and unruly, the impious and sinful, the irreligious and worldly; at parricides
10 and matricides, murderers and fornicators, perverts, kidnappers, liars,
11 perjurers—in fact all whose behaviour flouts the wholesome teaching which
conforms with the gospel entrusted to me, the gospel which tells of the
glory of God in his eternal felicity.

12 I thank him who has made me equal to the task, Christ Jesus our Lord;
I thank him for judging me worthy of this trust and appointing me to his
13 service—although in the past I had met him with abuse and persecution
and outrage. But because I acted ignorantly in unbelief I was dealt with
14 mercifully; the grace of our Lord was lavished upon me, with the faith and
love which are ours in Christ Jesus.

15 Here are words you may trust, words that merit full acceptance: 'Christ
Jesus came into the world to save sinners'; and among them I stand first.
16 But I was mercifully dealt with for this very purpose, that Jesus Christ
might find in me the first occasion for displaying all his patience, and that I
might be typical of all who were in future to have faith in him and gain

a Or cannot promote the faithful discharge of God's stewardship.

eternal life. Now to the King of all worlds, immortal, invisible, the only 17 God, be honour and glory for ever and ever! Amen.

This charge, son Timothy, I lay upon you, following that prophetic 18 utterance which first pointed you out to me. So fight gallantly, armed with 19 faith and a good conscience. It was through spurning conscience that certain persons made shipwreck of their faith, among them Hymenaeus and 20 Alexander, whom I consigned to Satan, in the hope that through this discipline they might learn not to be blasphemous.

FIRST OF ALL, then, I urge that petitions, prayers, intercessions, and **2** thanksgivings be offered for all men; for sovereigns and all in high office, 2 that we may lead a tranquil and quiet life in full observance of religion and high standards of morality. Such prayer is right, and approved by God our 3 Saviour, whose will it is that all men should find salvation and come to 4 know the truth. For there is one God, and also one mediator between God 5 and men, Christ Jesus, himself man, who sacrificed himself to win freedom 6 for all mankind, so providing, at the fitting time, proof of the divine purpose; of this I was appointed herald and apostle (this is no lie, but the truth), 7 to instruct the nations in the true faith.

It is my desire, therefore, that everywhere prayers be said by the men 8 of the congregation, who shall lift up their hands with a pure intention, excluding angry or quarrelsome thoughts. Women again must dress in 9 becoming manner, modestly and soberly, not with elaborate hair-styles, not decked out with gold or pearls, or expensive clothes, but with good 10 deeds, as befits women who claim to be religious. A woman must be a 11 learner, listening quietly and with due submission. I do not permit a woman 12 to be a teacher, nor must woman domineer over man; she should be quiet. For Adam was created first, and Eve afterwards; and it was not Adam who 13 14 was deceived; it was the woman who, yielding to deception, fell into sin. Yet she will be saved through motherhood*a*—if only women continue in 15 faith,*b* love, and holiness, with a sober mind.

There is a popular saying:*c* 'To aspire to leadership is an honourable **3** ambition.' Our leader, therefore, or bishop, must be above reproach, faith- 2 ful to his one wife,*d* sober, temperate, courteous, hospitable, and a good teacher; he must not be given to drink, or a brawler, but of a forbearing 3 disposition, avoiding quarrels, and no lover of money. He must be one who 4 manages his own household well and wins obedience from his children, and a man of the highest principles. If a man does not know how to control 5 his own family, how can he look after a congregation of God's people? He 6 must not be a convert newly baptized, for fear the sin of conceit should bring upon him a judgement contrived by the devil.*e* He must moreover 7 have a good reputation with the non-Christian public, so that he may not be exposed to scandal and get caught in the devil's snare.

a Or saved through the Birth of the Child, *or* brought safely through childbirth. *b Or* if only husband and wife continue in mutual fidelity . . .   *c Some witnesses* read Here are words you may trust, *which some interpreters attach to the end of the preceding paragraph.*   *d Or* married to one wife, *or* married only once.   *e Or* the judgement once passed on the devil.

8 Deacons, likewise, must be men of high principle, not indulging in double talk, given neither to excessive drinking nor to money-grubbing.
9 They must be men who combine a clear conscience with a firm hold on the
10 deep truths of our faith. No less than bishops, they must first undergo a
11 scrutiny, and if there is no mark against them, they may serve. Their wives, *a* equally, must be women of high principle, who will not talk scandal, sober
12 and trustworthy in every way. A deacon must be faithful to his one wife, *b*
13 and good at managing his children and his own household. For deacons with a good record of service may claim a high standing and the right to speak openly on matters of the Christian faith.

14 15 I am hoping to come to you before long, but I write this in case I am delayed, to let you know how men ought to conduct themselves in God's household, that is, the church of the living God, the pillar and bulwark of
16 the truth. And great beyond all question is the mystery of our religion:

> 'He who was manifested in the body,
>   vindicated in the spirit,
>   seen by angels;
>   who was proclaimed among the nations,
>   believed in throughout the world,
>   glorified in high heaven.'

4 THE SPIRIT SAYS expressly that in after times some will desert from the faith and give their minds to subversive doctrines inspired by devils,
2 through the specious falsehoods of men whose own conscience is branded
3 with the devil's sign. They forbid marriage and inculcate abstinence from certain foods, though God created them to be enjoyed with thanksgiving
4 by believers who have inward knowledge of the truth. For everything that God created is good, and nothing is to be rejected when it is taken with
5 thanksgiving, since it is hallowed by God's own word and by prayer.
6 By offering such advice as this to the brotherhood you will prove a good servant of Christ Jesus, bred in the precepts of our faith and of the sound
7 instruction which you have followed. Have nothing to do with those godless myths, fit only for old women. Keep yourself in training for the practice
8 of religion. The training of the body does bring limited benefit, but the benefits of religion are without limit, since it holds promise not only for
9 this life but for the life to come. Here are words you may trust, words that
10 merit full acceptance: 'With this before us we labour and struggle, *c* because *d* we have set our hope on the living God, who is the Saviour of all men'—the Saviour, above all, of believers.

11 12 Pass on these orders and these teachings. Let no one slight you because you are young, but make yourself an example to believers in speech and
13 behaviour, in love, fidelity, and purity. Until I arrive devote your attention to the public reading of the scriptures, to exhortation, and to teaching.

a Or . . . serve. Deaconesses . . .   *b* Or married to one wife, *or* married only once.
c *Some witnesses read* suffer reproach.   *d* Or since 'It holds promise . . . to come.'
These are words . . . acceptance. For this is the aim of all our labour and struggle, since . . .

Do not neglect the spiritual endowment you possess, which was given you, 14
under the guidance of prophecy, through the laying on of the hands of the
elders as a body. *a*

Make these matters your business and your absorbing interest, so that 15
your progress may be plain to all. Persevere in them, keeping close watch 16
on yourself and your teaching; by doing so you will further the salvation
of yourself and your hearers.

Never be harsh with an elder; appeal to him as if he were your father. 5
Treat the younger men as brothers, the older women as mothers, and the 2
younger as your sisters, in all purity.

The status of widow is to be granted only to widows who are such in the 3
full sense. But if a widow has children or grandchildren, then they should 4
learn as their first duty to show loyalty to the family and to repay what they
owe to their parents and grandparents; for this God approves. A widow, 5
however, in the full sense, one who is alone in the world, has all her hope
set on God, and regularly attends the meetings for prayer and worship
night and day. But a widow given over to self-indulgence is as good as 6
dead. Add these orders to the rest, so that the widows may be above 7
reproach. But if anyone does not make provision for his relations, and 8
especially for members of his own household, he has denied the faith and
is worse than an unbeliever.

A widow should not be put on the roll under sixty years of age. She must 9
have been faithful in marriage to one man, and must produce evidence of 10
good deeds performed, showing whether she has had the care of children,
or given hospitality, or washed the feet of God's people, or supported those
in distress—in short, whether she has taken every opportunity of doing
good.

Younger widows may not be placed on the roll. For when their passions 11
draw them away from Christ, they hanker after marriage and stand con- 12
demned for breaking their troth with him. Moreover, in going round from 13
house to house they learn to be idle, and worse than idle, gossips and busy-
bodies, speaking of things better left unspoken. It is my wish, therefore, 14
that young widows shall marry again, have children, and preside over a
home; then they will give no opponent occasion for slander. For there have 15
in fact been some who have taken the wrong turning and gone to the devil.

If a Christian man or woman has widows in the family, he must sup- 16
port them himself; *b* the congregation must be relieved of the burden, so
that it may be free to support those who are widows in the full sense of
the term.

Elders who do well as leaders should be reckoned worthy of a double 17
stipend, in particular those who labour at preaching and teaching. For 18
Scripture says, 'You shall not muzzle a threshing ox'; and besides, 'the
worker earns his pay'.

Do not entertain a charge against an elder unless it is supported by two 19
or three witnesses. Those who commit sins you must expose publicly, to 20
put fear into the others. Before God and Christ Jesus and the angels who 21

a Or through your ordination as an elder.   *b Some witnesses read* If a Christian
woman has widows in her family, she must support them herself.

are his chosen, I solemnly charge you, maintain these rules, and never
22 pre-judge the issue, but act with strict impartiality. Do not be over-hasty
in laying on hands in ordination,[a] or you may find yourself responsible for
other people's misdeeds; keep your own hands clean.

23   Stop drinking nothing but water; take a little wine for your digestion,
for your frequent ailments.

24   While there are people whose offences are so obvious that they run
before them into court, there are others whose offences have not yet over-
25 taken them. Similarly, good deeds are obvious, or even if they are not, they
cannot be concealed for ever.

6   All who wear the yoke of slavery must count their own masters worthy
of all respect, so that the name of God and the Christian teaching are not
2 brought into disrepute. If the masters are believers, the slaves must not
respect them any less for being their Christian brothers. Quite the contrary; they must be all the better servants because those who receive the
benefit of their service are one with them in faith and love.

3   THIS IS WHAT you are to teach and preach. If anyone is teaching otherwise, and will not give his mind to wholesome precepts—I mean those of
4 our Lord Jesus Christ—and to good religious teaching, I call him a
pompous ignoramus. He is morbidly keen on mere verbal questions and
quibbles, which give rise to jealousy, quarrelling, slander, base suspicions,
5 and endless wrangles: all typical of men who have let their reasoning
powers become atrophied and have lost grip of the truth. They think
6 religion should yield dividends; and of course religion does yield high
7 dividends, but only to the man whose resources are within him. We
brought nothing into the world; for that matter we cannot take anything
8 with us when we leave, but if we have food and covering we may rest
9 content. Those who want to be rich fall into temptations and snares and
many foolish harmful desires which plunge men into ruin and perdition.
10 The love of money is the root of all evil things, and there are some who in
reaching for it have wandered from the faith and spiked themselves on
many thorny griefs.

11   But you, man of God, must shun all this, and pursue justice, piety,
12 fidelity, love, fortitude, and gentleness. Run the great race of faith and take
hold of eternal life. For to this you were called; and you confessed your
13 faith nobly before many witnesses. Now in the presence of God, who gives
life to all things, and of Jesus Christ, who himself made the same noble
confession and gave his testimony to it before Pontius Pilate, I charge you
14 to obey your orders irreproachably and without fault until our Lord Jesus
15 Christ appears. That appearance God will bring to pass in his own good
time—God who in eternal felicity alone holds sway. He is King of kings and
16 Lord of lords; he alone possesses immortality, dwelling in unapproachable
light. No man has ever seen or ever can see him. To him be honour and
might for ever! Amen.

17   Instruct those who are rich in this world's goods not to be proud, and
not to fix their hopes on so uncertain a thing as money, but upon God, who

[a] *Or* in restoring an offender by the laying on of hands.

endows us richly with all things to enjoy. Tell them to do good and to grow 18
rich in noble actions, to be ready to give away and to share, and so acquire 19
a treasure which will form a good foundation for the future. Thus they will
grasp the life which is life indeed.

Timothy, keep safe that which has been entrusted to you. Turn a deaf 20
ear to empty and worldly chatter, and the contradictions of so-called
'knowledge', for many who lay claim to it have shot far wide of the faith. 21
Grace be with you all!

THE SECOND LETTER OF PAUL
TO
TIMOTHY

Character of a Christian minister

FROM PAUL, APOSTLE of Jesus Christ by the will of God, 1
whose promise of life is fulfilled in Christ Jesus, to Timothy his 2
dear son.

Grace, mercy, and peace to you from God the Father and our Lord
Jesus Christ.

I thank God—whom I, like my forefathers, worship with a pure inten- 3
tion—when I mention you in my prayers; this I do constantly night and
day. And when I remember the tears you shed, I long to see you again to 4
make my happiness complete. I am reminded of the sincerity of your faith, 5
a faith which was alive in Lois your grandmother and Eunice your mother
before you, and which, I am confident, lives in you also.

That is why I now remind you to stir into flame the gift of God which is 6
within you through the laying on of my hands. For the spirit that God gave 7
us is no craven spirit, but one to inspire strength, love, and self-discipline.
So never be ashamed of your testimony to our Lord, nor of me his prisoner, 8
but take your share of suffering for the sake of the Gospel, in the strength
that comes from God. It is he who brought us salvation and called us to a 9
dedicated life, not for any merit of ours but of his own purpose and his own
grace, which was granted to us in Christ Jesus from all eternity, but has 10
now at length been brought fully into view by the appearance on earth of
our Saviour Jesus Christ. For he has broken the power of death and
brought life and immortality to light through the Gospel.

Of this Gospel I, by his appointment, am herald, apostle, and teacher. 11
That is the reason for my present plight; but I am not ashamed of it, 12
because I know who it is in whom*a* I have trusted, and am confident of his

a Or I know the one whom . . .

power to keep safe what he has put into my charge,[a] until the great Day.
13 Keep before you an outline of the sound teaching which[b] you heard from
14 me, living by the faith and love which are ours in Christ Jesus. Guard the
treasure put into our charge, with the help of the Holy Spirit dwelling
within us.

15 As you know, everyone in the province of Asia deserted me, including
16 Phygelus and Hermogenes. But may the Lord's mercy rest on the house
of Onesiphorus! He has often relieved me in my troubles. He was not
17 ashamed to visit a prisoner, but took pains to search me out when he came
18 to Rome, and found me. I pray that the Lord may grant him to find mercy
from the Lord on the great Day. The many services he rendered at Ephesus
you know better than I could tell you.

2 Now therefore, my son, take strength from the grace of God which is ours
2 in Christ Jesus. You heard my teaching in the presence of many witnesses;
put that teaching into the charge of men you can trust, such men as will be
competent to teach others.

3 4 Take your share of hardship, like a good soldier of Christ Jesus. A
soldier on active service will not let himself be involved in civilian affairs;
5 he must be wholly at his commanding officer's disposal. Again, no athlete
6 can win a prize unless he has kept the rules. The farmer who gives his
7 labour has first claim on the crop. Reflect on what I say, for the Lord will
help you to full understanding.

8 Remember Jesus Christ, risen from the dead, born of David's line. This
9 is the theme of my gospel, in whose service I am exposed to hardship, even
to the point of being shut up like a common criminal; but the word of God
10 is not shut up. And I endure it all for the sake of God's chosen ones, with
this end in view, that they too may attain the glorious and eternal salvation
which is in Christ Jesus.

11 Here are words you may trust:

'If we died with him, we shall live with him;
12 if we endure, we shall reign with him.
If we deny him, he will deny us.
13 If we are faithless, he keeps faith,
for he cannot deny himself.'

14 GO ON REMINDING people of this, and charge them solemnly before
God to stop disputing about mere words; it does no good, and is the ruin
15 of those who listen. Try hard to show yourself worthy of God's approval,
as a labourer who need not be ashamed; be straightforward in your pro-
16 clamation of the truth. Avoid empty and worldly chatter; those who
17 indulge in it will stray further and further into godless courses, and the
infection of their teaching will spread like a gangrene. Such are Hymenaeus
18 and Philetus; they have shot wide of the truth in saying that our resurrection
19 has already taken place, and are upsetting people's faith. But God has laid
a foundation, and it stands firm, with this inscription: 'The Lord knows his

[a] *Or* what I have put into his charge.   [b] *Or* Keep before you as a model of sound
teaching that which . . .

own', and, 'Everyone who takes the Lord's name upon his lips must for- 20
sake wickedness.' Now in any great house there are not only utensils of
gold and silver, but also others of wood or earthenware; the former are
valued, the latter held cheap. To be among those which are valued and 21
dedicated, a thing of use to the Master of the house, a man must cleanse
himself from all those evil things;*a* then he will be fit for any honourable
purpose.

Turn from the wayward impulses of youth, and pursue justice, integrity, 22
love, and peace with all who invoke the Lord in singleness of mind. Have 23
nothing to do with foolish and ignorant speculations. You know they breed
quarrels, and the servant of the Lord must not be quarrelsome, but kindly 24
towards all. He should be a good teacher, tolerant, and gentle when 25
discipline is needed for the refractory. The Lord may grant them a change
of heart and show them the truth, and thus they may come to their senses 26
and escape from the devil's snare, in which they have been caught and held
at his will. *b*

You must face the fact: the final age of this world is to be a time of 3
troubles. Men will love nothing but money and self; they will be arrogant, 2
boastful, and abusive; with no respect for parents, no gratitude, no piety,
no natural affection; they will be implacable in their hatreds, scandal- 3
mongers, intemperate and fierce, strangers to all goodness, traitors, 4
adventurers, swollen with self-importance. They will be men who put
pleasure in the place of God, men who preserve the outward form of 5
religion, but are a standing denial of its reality. Keep clear of men like these.
They are the sort that insinuate themselves into private houses and there 6
get miserable women into their clutches, women burdened with a sinful
past, and led on by all kinds of desires, who are always wanting to be taught, 7
but are incapable of reaching a knowledge of the truth. As Jannes and 8
Jambres defied Moses, so these men defy the truth; they have lost the
power to reason, and they cannot pass the tests of faith. But their successes 9
will be short-lived, for, like those opponents of Moses, they will come to
be recognized by everyone for the fools they are.

But you, my son, have followed, step by step, my teaching and my 10
manner of life, my resolution, my faith, patience, and spirit of love, and my
fortitude under persecutions and sufferings—all that I went through at 11
Antioch, at Iconium, at Lystra, all the persecutions I endured; and the
Lord rescued me out of them all. Yes, persecution will come to all who want 12
to live a godly life as Christians, whereas wicked men and charlatans will 13
make progress from bad to worse, deceiving and deceived. But for your 14
part, stand by the truths you have learned and are assured of. Remember
from whom you learned them; remember that from early childhood you 15
have been familiar with the sacred writings which have power to make you
wise and lead you to salvation through faith in Christ Jesus. Every inspired 16
scripture has its use for teaching the truth and refuting error, or for
reformation of manners and discipline in right living, so that the man who 17
belongs to God may be efficient and equipped for good work of every kind.

a Or must separate himself from these persons.   *b Or* escape from the devil's
snare, caught now by God and made subject to his will.

4 Before God, and before Christ Jesus who is to judge men living and
2 dead, I charge you solemnly by his coming appearance and his reign, proclaim the message, press it home on all occasions,[a] convenient or in-
convenient, use argument, reproof, and appeal, with all the patience that
3 the work of teaching requires. For the time will come when they will not
stand wholesome teaching, but will follow their own fancy and gather a
4 crowd of teachers to tickle their ears. They will stop their ears to the truth
5 and turn to mythology. But you yourself must keep calm and sane at all
times; face hardship, work to spread the Gospel, and do all the duties of
your calling.

6 AS FOR ME, already my life is being poured out on the altar, and the hour
7 for my departure is upon me. I have run the great race, I have finished the
8 course, I have kept faith. And now the prize awaits me, the garland of
righteousness which the Lord, the all-just Judge, will award me on that
great Day; and it is not for me alone, but for all who have set their hearts
on his coming appearance.

9 10 Do your best to join me soon; for Demas has deserted me because his
heart was set on this world; he has gone to Thessalonica, Crescens to
11 Galatia,[b] Titus to Dalmatia; I have no one with me but Luke. Pick up
12 Mark and bring him with you, for I find him a useful assistant. Tychicus
13 I have sent to Ephesus. When you come, bring the cloak I left with Carpus
at Troas, and the books, above all my notebooks.
14 Alexander the copper-smith did me a great deal of harm. Retribution
15 will fall upon him from the Lord. You had better be on your guard against
16 him too, for he violently opposed everything I said. At the first hearing of
my case no one came into court to support me; they all left me in the lurch;
17 I pray that it may not be held against them. But the Lord stood by me and
lent me strength, so that I might be his instrument in making the full
proclamation of the Gospel for the whole pagan world to hear; and thus I
18 was rescued out of the lion's jaws. And the Lord will rescue me from every
attempt to do me harm, and keep me safe until his heavenly reign begins.[c]
Glory to him for ever and ever! Amen.
19 Greetings to Prisca and Aquila, and the household of Onesiphorus.
20 Erastus stayed behind at Corinth, and I left Trophimus ill at Miletus.
21 Do try to get here before winter.
Greetings from Eubulus, Pudens, Linus, and Claudia, and from all the
brotherhood here.
22 The Lord be with your spirit. Grace be with you all!

[a] *Or* be on duty at all times.   [b] *Or* Gaul; *some witnesses read* Gallia.
[c] *Or* from all that evil can do, and bring me safely into his heavenly kingdom.

THE LETTER OF PAUL TO
TITUS

Training for the Christian life

FROM PAUL, SERVANT of God and apostle of Jesus Christ, 1
marked as such by faith and knowledge and hope—the faith of
God's chosen people, knowledge of the truth as our religion has it,
and the hope of eternal life.ᵃ Yes, it is eternal life that God, who cannot lie, 2
promised long ages ago, and now in his own good time he has openly 3
declared himself in the proclamation which was entrusted to me by
ordinance of God our Saviour.

To Titus, my true-born son in the faith which we share, grace and peace 4
from God our Father and Christ Jesus our Saviour.

My intention in leaving you behind in Crete was that you should set in 5
order what was left over, and in particular should institute elders in each
town. In doing so, observe the tests I prescribed: is he a man of un- 6
impeachable character, faithful to his one wife,ᵇ the father of children who
are believers, who are under no imputation of loose living, and are not out
of control? For as God's steward a bishop must be a man of unimpeachable 7
character. He must not be overbearing or short-tempered; he must be no
drinker, no brawler, no money-grubber, but hospitable, right-minded, 8
temperate, just, devout, and self-controlled. He must adhere to the true 9
doctrine, so that he may be well able both to move his hearers with wholesome teaching and to confute objectors.

There are all too many, especially among Jewish converts, who are out 10
of all control; they talk wildly and lead men's minds astray. Such men must 11
be curbed, because they are ruining whole families by teaching things they
should not, and all for sordid gain. It was a Cretan prophet, one of their 12
own countrymen, who said, 'Cretans were always liars, vicious brutes,
lazy gluttons'—and he told the truth! All the more reason why you should 13
pull them up sharply, so that they may come to a sane belief, instead of 14
lending their ears to Jewish myths and commandments of merely human
origin, the work of men who turn their backs upon the truth.

To the pure all things are pure; but nothing is pure to the tainted minds 15
of disbelievers, tainted alike in reason and conscience. They profess to 16
acknowledge God, but deny him by their actions. Their detestable obstinacy
disqualifies them for any good work.

For your own part, what you say must be in keeping with wholesome 2

ᵃ *Or* apostle of Jesus Christ, to bring God's chosen people to faith and to a knowledge of
the truth as our religion has it, with its hope for eternal life.   ᵇ *See note on*
1 Timothy 3. 2.

2 doctrine. Let the older men know that they should be sober, high-principled,
3 and temperate, sound in faith, in love, and in endurance. The older
women, similarly, should be reverent in their bearing, not scandal-
4 mongers or slaves to strong drink; they must set a high standard, and school
5 the younger women to be loving wives and mothers, temperate, chaste, and
kind, busy at home, respecting the authority of their own husbands. Thus
the Gospel will not be brought into disrepute.

6 7 Urge the younger men, similarly, to be temperate in all things, and set
them a good example yourself. In your teaching, you must show integrity
8 and high principle, and use wholesome speech to which none can take
exception. This will shame any opponent, when he finds not a word to say
to our discredit.

9 Tell slaves to respect their masters' authority in everything, and to
10 comply with their demands without answering back; not to pilfer, but to
show themselves strictly honest and trustworthy; for in all such ways they
will add lustre to the doctrine of God our Saviour.

11 For the grace of God has dawned upon the world with healing for all
12 mankind; and by it we are disciplined to renounce godless ways and
worldly desires, and to live a life of temperance, honesty, and godliness in
13 the present age, looking forward to the happy fulfilment of our hope when
14 the splendour of our great God and Saviour *a* Christ Jesus will appear. He
it is who sacrificed himself for us, to set us free from all wickedness and to
make us a pure people marked out for his own, eager to do good.

15 These, then, are your themes; urge them and argue them. And speak
with authority: let no one slight you.

3 Remind them to be submissive to the government and the authorities,
2 to obey them, and to be ready for any honourable form of work; *b* to
slander no one, not to pick quarrels, to show forbearance and a consistently gentle disposition towards all men.
3 For at one time we ourselves in our folly and obstinacy were all astray.
We were slaves to passions and pleasures of every kind. Our days were
passed in malice and envy; we were odious ourselves and we hated one
4 another. But when the kindness and generosity of God our Saviour dawned
5 upon the world, then, not for any good deeds of our own, but because he
was merciful, he saved us through the water of rebirth and the renewing
6 power of *c* the Holy Spirit. For he sent down the Spirit upon us plentifully
7 through Jesus Christ our Saviour, so that, justified by his grace, we might
8 in hope become heirs to eternal life. These are words you may trust.

Such are the points I should wish you to insist on. Those who have
come to believe in God should see that they engage in honourable occupa-
tions, which are not only honourable in themselves, but also useful to their
9 fellow-men. *d* But steer clear of foolish speculations, genealogies, quarrels,
and controversies over the Law; they are unprofitable and pointless.
10 A heretic should be warned once, and once again; after that, have done

---

a Or of the great God and our Saviour . . .   *b* Or ready always to do good.
c Or the water of rebirth and of renewal by . . .   *d* Or should make it their
business to practise virtue. These precepts are good in themselves and useful to
society.

with him, recognizing that a man of that sort has a distorted mind and 11
stands self-condemned in his sin.

When I send Artemas to you, or Tychicus, make haste to join me at 12
Nicopolis, for that is where I have determined to spend the winter. Do 13
your utmost to help Zenas the lawyer and Apollos on their travels, and see
that they are not short of anything. And our own people must be taught to 14
engage in honest employment to produce the necessities of life; they must
not be unproductive.

All who are with me send you greetings. My greetings to those who are 15
our friends in truth.*a* Grace be with you all!

a Or our friends in the faith.

THE LETTER OF PAUL TO
PHILEMON

A runaway slave

1 FROM PAUL, a prisoner of Christ Jesus, and our colleague
2 Timothy, to Philemon our dear friend and fellow-worker, and
Apphia our sister, and Archippus our comrade-in-arms, and the
congregation at your house.

3 Grace to you and peace from God our Father and the Lord Jesus Christ.
4 5 I thank my God always when I mention you in my prayers, for I hear
of your love and faith towards the Lord Jesus and towards all God's
6 people. My prayer is that your fellowship with us in our common faith may
deepen the understanding of all the blessings that our union with Christ
7 brings us.*a* For I am delighted and encouraged by your love; through you,
my brother, God's people have been much refreshed.

8 Accordingly, although in Christ I might make bold to point out your
9 duty, yet, because of that same love, I would rather appeal to you. Yes, I,
10 Paul, ambassador as I am of Christ Jesus—and now his prisoner—appeal
to you about my child, whose father I have become in this prison.
11 I mean Onesimus, once so little use to you, but now useful indeed, both
12 to you and to me. I am sending him back to you, and in doing so I am send-
13 ing a part of myself. I should have liked to keep him with me, to look after
14 me as you would wish, here in prison for the Gospel. But I would rather do
nothing without your consent, so that your kindness may be a matter not
15 of compulsion, but of your own free will. For perhaps this is why you lost
16 him for a time, that you might have him back for good, no longer as a slave,
but as more than a slave—as a dear brother, very dear indeed to me and
how much dearer to you, both as man and as Christian.

17 If, then, you count me partner in the faith, welcome him as you would
18 welcome me. And if he has done you any wrong or is in your debt, put that
19 down to my account. Here is my signature, PAUL; I undertake to repay—
20 not to mention that you owe your very self to me as well. Now brother, as a
Christian, be generous with me, and relieve my anxiety; we are both in
Christ!

21 I write to you confident that you will meet my wishes; I know that you
22 will in fact do better than I ask. And one thing more: have a room ready
for me, for I hope that, in answer to your prayers, God will grant me to you.
23 24 Epaphras, Christ's captive like myself, sends you greetings. So do Mark,
Aristarchus, Demas, and Luke, my fellow-workers.
25 The grace of the Lord Jesus Christ be with your spirit!

a Or that bring us to Christ.

A LETTER TO
HEBREWS

Christ divine and human

WHEN IN FORMER TIMES God spoke to our forefathers, 1
he spoke in fragmentary and varied fashion through the prophets.
But in this the final age he has spoken to us in the Son whom 2
he has made heir to the whole universe, and through whom he created all
orders of existence: the Son who is the effulgence of God's splendour and 3
the stamp of God's very being, and sustains^a the universe by his word of
power. When he had brought about the purgation of sins, he took his seat
at the right hand of Majesty on high, raised as far above the angels, as the 4
title he has inherited is superior to theirs.

For God never said to any angel, 'Thou art my Son; today I have be- 5
gotten thee', or again, 'I will be father to him, and he shall be my son.'
Again, when he presents the first-born to the world, he says, 'Let all the 6
angels of God pay him homage.' Of the angels he says, 7

> 'He who makes his angels winds,
> and his ministers a fiery flame';

but of the Son, 8

> 'Thy throne, O God, is for ever and ever,
> and the sceptre ^b of justice is the sceptre of his kingdom.
> Thou hast loved right and hated wrong; 9
> therefore, O God, thy God^c has set thee above thy fellows,
> by anointing with the oil of exultation.'

And again, 10

> 'By thee, Lord, were earth's foundations laid of old,
> and the heavens are the work of thy hands.
> They shall pass away, but thou endurest; 11
> like clothes they shall all grow old;
> thou shalt fold them up like a cloak; 12
> yes, they shall be changed like any garment.
> But thou art the same, and thy years shall have no end.'

To which of the angels has he ever said, 'Sit at my right hand until I 13
make thy enemies thy footstool'? What are they all but ministrant 14
spirits, sent out to serve, for the sake of those who are to inherit salvation?

---

^a Or bears along.　　　^b Or God is thy throne for ever and ever, and thy sceptre ...
^c Or therefore God who is thy God ...

2 Thus we are bound to pay all the more heed to what we have been told,
2 for fear of drifting from our course. For if the word spoken through angels
had such force that any transgression or disobedience met with due retribu-
3 tion, what escape can there be for us if we ignore a deliverance so great?
For this deliverance was first announced through the lips of the Lord him-
4 self; those who heard him confirmed it to us, and God added his testimony
by signs, by miracles, by manifold works of power, and by distributing the
gifts of the Holy Spirit at his own will.

5 For it is not to angels that he has subjected the world to come, which is
6 our theme. But there is somewhere a solemn assurance which runs:

'What is man, that thou rememberest him,
or the son of man, that thou hast regard to him?
7 Thou didst make him for a short while lower than the angels;
thou didst crown him with glory and honour;
8 thou didst put all things in subjection beneath his feet.'

For in subjecting all things to him, he left nothing that is not subject. But
9 in fact we do not yet see all things in subjection to man. In Jesus, however,
we do see one who[a] for a short while was made lower than the angels,
crowned now with glory and honour because he suffered death, so that,
by God's gracious will, in tasting death he should stand[b] for us all.

10 It was clearly fitting that God for whom and through whom all things
exist should, in bringing many sons to glory, make the leader who delivers
11 them perfect through sufferings. For a consecrating priest and those
whom he consecrates are all of one stock; and that is why the Son does not
12 shrink from calling men his brothers, when he says, 'I will proclaim thy
13 name to my brothers; in full assembly I will sing thy praise'; and again,
'I will keep my trust fixed on him'; and again, 'Here am I, and the children
14 whom God has given me.' The children of a family share the same flesh
and blood; and so he too shared ours, so that through death he might break
15 the power of him who had death at his command, that is, the devil; and
might liberate those who, through fear of death, had all their lifetime been
16 in servitude. It is not angels, mark you, that he takes to himself, but the
17 sons of Abraham. And therefore he had to be made like these brothers of
his in every way, so that he might be merciful and faithful as their high
18 priest before God, to expiate the sins of the people. For since he himself has
passed through the test of suffering, he is able to help those who are meeting their test now.

3 Therefore, brothers in the family of God, who share a heavenly calling,
2 think of the Apostle and High Priest of the religion we profess,[c] who was
faithful to God who appointed him. Moses also was faithful in God's
3 household; and Jesus, of whom I speak, has been deemed worthy of greater
honour than Moses, as the founder of a house enjoys more honour than
4 his household. For every house has its founder; and the founder of all is
5 God. Moses, then, was faithful as a servitor in God's whole household;

---

[a] *Or* in subjection to him. But we see Jesus, who . . .   [b] *Some witnesses read* so that
apart from God he should taste death . . .   [c] *Or* of him whom we confess as God's
Envoy and High Priest.

his task was to bear witness to the words that God would speak; but Christ   6
is faithful as a son, set over his household. And we are that household of his,
if only we are fearless and keep our hope high.

'TODAY', THEREFORE, as the Holy Spirit says—   7

> 'Today if you hear his voice,
>   do not grow stubborn as in those days of rebellion,   8
> at that time of testing in the desert,
> where your forefathers tried me and tested me,   9
> and saw^a the things I did for forty years.
> And so, I was indignant with that generation   10
> and I said, Their hearts are for ever astray;
> they would not discern my ways;
> as I vowed in my anger, they shall never enter my rest.'   11

See to it, brothers, that no one among you has the wicked, faithless   12
heart of a deserter from the living God; but day by day, while that word   13
'Today' still sounds in your ears, encourage one another, so that no one
of you is made stubborn by the wiles of sin. For we have become Christ's   14
partners^b if only we keep our original confidence firm to the end.

When Scripture says, 'Today if you hear his voice, do not grow stubborn   15
as in those days of rebellion', who, I ask, were those who heard and rebelled?   16
All those, surely, whom Moses had led out of Egypt. And with whom was   17
God indignant for forty years? With those, surely, who had sinned, whose
bodies lay where they fell in the desert. And to whom did he vow that they   18
should not enter his rest, if not to those who had refused to believe? We   19
perceive that it was unbelief which prevented their entering.

Therefore we must have before us the fear that while the promise of   **4**
entering his rest remains open, one or another among you should be found
to have missed his chance. For indeed we have heard the good news, as   2
they did. But in them the message they heard did no good, because it met
with no faith in those who heard it. It is we, we who have become believers,   3
who enter the rest referred to in the words, 'As I vowed in my anger, they
shall never enter my rest.' Yet God's work has been finished ever since the
world was created; for does not Scripture somewhere speak thus of the   4
seventh day: 'God rested from all his work on the seventh day'?—and   5
once again in the passage above we read, 'They shall never enter my rest.'
The fact remains that someone must enter it, and since those who first   6
heard the good news failed to enter through unbelief, God fixes another   7
day. Speaking through the lips of David after many long years, he uses the
words already quoted: 'Today if you hear his voice, do not grow stubborn.'
If Joshua had given them rest, God would not thus have spoken of another   8
day after that. Therefore, a sabbath rest still awaits the people of God; for   9 10
anyone who enters God's rest, rests from his own work as God did from
his. Let us then make every effort to enter that rest, so that no one may fall   11
by following this evil example of unbelief.

> ^a *Or* though they saw . . .   ^b *Or* have been given a share in Christ.

12 For the word of God is alive and active. It cuts more keenly than any
two-edged sword, piercing as far as the place where life and spirit, joints
13 and marrow, divide. It sifts the purposes and thoughts of the heart. There
is nothing in creation that can hide from him; everything lies naked and
exposed to the eyes of the One with whom we have to reckon.

14 Since therefore we have a great high priest who has passed through the
heavens, Jesus the Son of God, let us hold fast to the religion we profess.
15 For ours is not a high priest unable to sympathize with our weaknesses,
but one who, because of his likeness to us, has been tested every way,[a]
16 only without sin. Let us therefore boldly approach the throne of our
gracious God, where we may receive mercy and in his grace find timely help

The shadow and the real

5   FOR EVERY HIGH PRIEST is taken from among men and appointed
    their representative before God, to offer gifts and sacrifices for sins.
2   He is able to bear patiently with the ignorant and erring, since he too is
3   beset by weakness; and because of this he is bound to make sin-offerings
4   for himself no less than for the people. And nobody arrogates the honour
5   to himself: he is called by God, as indeed Aaron was. So it is with Christ:
he did not confer upon himself the glory of becoming high priest; it was
granted by God, who said to him, 'Thou art my Son; today I have begotten
6   thee'; as also in another place he says, 'Thou art a priest for ever, in the
7   succession of Melchizedek.' In the days of his earthly life he offered
up prayers and petitions, with loud cries and tears, to God who was able to
deliver him from the grave. Because of his humble submission his prayer
8   was heard: son though he was, he learned obedience in the school of
9   suffering, and, once perfected, became the source of eternal salvation for
10 all who obey him, named by God high priest in the succession of Melchizedek.

11 About Melchizedek we have much to say, much that is difficult to
12 explain, now that you have grown so dull of hearing. For indeed, though
by this time you ought to be teachers, you need someone to teach you the
ABC of God's oracles over again; it has come to this, that you need milk
13 instead of solid food. Anyone who lives on milk, being an infant, does not
14 know[b] what is right. But grown men can take solid food; their perceptions
are trained by long use to discriminate between good and evil.

6   Let us then stop discussing the rudiments of Christianity. We ought
not to be laying over again the foundations of faith in God and of repen-
2   tance from the deadness of our former ways, by instruction[c] about cleansing rites and the laying-on-of-hands, about the resurrection of the dead
3   and eternal judgement. Instead, let us advance towards maturity; and so
we shall, if God permits.
4   For when men have once been enlightened, when they have had a taste

---

[a] Or who has been tested every way, as we are.   [b] Or is incompetent to speak of . . .
[c] Or, according to some witnesses, laying the foundations over again: repentance from the
deadness of our former ways and faith in God, instruction . . .

of the heavenly gift and a share in the Holy Spirit, when they have experi- 5
enced the goodness of God's word and the spiritual energies of the age to
come, and after all this have fallen away, it is impossible to bring them 6
again to repentance; for with their own hands they are crucifying[a] the
Son of God and making mock of his death. When the earth drinks in the 7
rain that falls upon it from time to time, and yields a useful crop to those
for whom it is cultivated, it is receiving its share of blessing from God; but 8
if it bears thorns and thistles, it is worthless and God's curse hangs over it;
the end of that is burning. But although we speak as we do, we are convinced 9
that you, my friends, are in the better case, and this makes for your salvation. For God would not be so unjust as to forget all that you did for love 10
of his name, when you rendered service to his people, as you still do. But 11
we long for every one of you to show the same eager concern, until your hope
is finally realized. We want you not to become lazy, but to imitate those 12
who, through faith and patience, are inheriting the promises.

When God made his promise to Abraham, he swore by himself, because 13
he had no one greater to swear by: 'I vow that I will bless you abundantly 14
and multiply your descendants.' Thus it was that Abraham, after patient 15
waiting, attained the promise. Men swear by a greater than themselves, 16
and the oath provides a confirmation to end all dispute; and so God, desir- 17
ing to show even more clearly to the heirs of his promise how unchanging
was his purpose, guaranteed it by oath. Here, then, are two irrevocable 18
acts in which God could not possibly play us false, to give powerful
encouragement to us, who have claimed his protection by grasping[b] the
hope set before us. That hope we hold. It is like an anchor for our lives, an 19
anchor safe and sure. It enters in through the veil, where Jesus has entered 20
on our behalf as forerunner, having become a high priest for ever in the
succession of Melchizedek.

This melchizedek, king of Salem, priest of God Most High, met 7
Abraham returning from the rout of the kings and blessed him; and Abra- 2
ham gave him a tithe of everything as his portion. His name, in the first place,
means 'king of righteousness'; next he is king of Salem, that is, 'king of
peace'. He has no father, no mother, no lineage; his years have no beginning, 3
his life no end. He is like the Son of God: he remains a priest for all time.

Consider now how great he must be for Abraham the patriarch to give 4
him a tithe of the finest of the spoil. The descendants of Levi who take the 5
priestly office are commanded by the Law to tithe the people, that is, their
kinsmen, although they too are descendants of Abraham. But Melchizedek, 6
though he does not trace his descent from them, has tithed Abraham himself, and given his blessing to the man who received the promises; and 7
beyond all dispute the lesser is always blessed by the greater. Again, in the 8
one instance tithes are received by men who must die; but in the other, by
one whom Scripture affirms to be alive. It might even be said that Levi, 9
who receives tithes, has himself been tithed through Abraham; for he was 10
still in his ancestor's loins when Melchizedek met him.

a Or crucifying again.　　*b Or* to give to us, who have claimed his protection, a powerful incentive to grasp . . .

11 Now if perfection had been attainable through the Levitical priesthood (for it is on this basis that the people were given the Law), what further need would there have been to speak of another priest arising, in the suc-
12 cession of Melchizedek, instead of the succession of Aaron? For a change of
13 priesthood must mean a change of law. And the one here spoken of belongs to a different tribe, no member of which has ever had anything to do with
14 the altar. For it is very evident that our Lord is sprung from Judah, a tribe to which Moses made no reference in speaking of priests.

15 The argument becomes still clearer, if the new priest who arises is one
16 like Melchizedek, owing his priesthood not to a system of earth-bound
17 rules but to the power of a life that cannot be destroyed. For here is the testimony: 'Thou art a priest for ever, in the succession of Melchizedek.'
18 19 The earlier rules are cancelled as impotent and useless, since the Law brought nothing to perfection; and a better hope is introduced, through which we draw near to God.

20 21 How great a difference it makes that an oath was sworn! There was no oath sworn when those others were made priests; but for this priest an oath was sworn, as Scripture says of him: 'The Lord has sworn and will
22 not go back on his word, "Thou art a priest for ever."' How far superior
23 must the covenant also be of which Jesus is the guarantor! Those other priests are appointed in numerous succession, because they are prevented
24 by death from continuing in office; but the priesthood which Jesus holds
25 is perpetual, because he remains for ever. That is why he is also able to save absolutely those who approach God through him; he is always living to plead on their behalf.

26 Such a high priest does indeed fit our condition—devout, guileless, un-
27 defiled, separated from sinners, raised high above the heavens. He has no need to offer sacrifices daily, as the high priests do, first for his own sins and then for those of the people; for this he did once and for all when he
28 offered up himself. The high priests made by the Law are men in all their frailty; but the priest appointed by the words of the oath which supersedes the Law is the Son, made perfect now for ever.

8 NOW THIS IS my main point: just such a high priest we have, and he has
2 taken his seat at the right hand of the throne of Majesty in the heavens, a ministrant in the real sanctuary, the tent pitched by the Lord and not by
3 man. Every high priest is appointed to offer gifts and sacrifices; hence, this
4 one too must have*a* something to offer. Now if he had been on earth, he would not even have been a priest, since there are already priests who offer
5 the gifts which the Law prescribes, though they minister in a sanctuary which is only a copy and shadow of the heavenly. This is implied when Moses, about to erect the tent, is instructed by God: 'See to it that you make everything according to the pattern shown you on the mountain.'
6 But in fact the ministry which has fallen to Jesus is as far superior to theirs as are the covenant he mediates and the promises upon which it is legally secured.
7 Had that first covenant been faultless, there would have been no need

a Or must have had.

to look for a second in its place. But God, finding fault with them, says, 8 'The days are coming, says the Lord, when I will conclude a new covenant with the house of Israel and the house of Judah. It will not be like the 9 covenant I made with their forefathers when I took them by the hand to lead them out of Egypt; because they did not abide by the terms of that covenant, and I abandoned them, says the Lord. For the covenant I will 10 make with the house of Israel after those days, says the Lord, is this: I will set my laws in their understanding and write them on their hearts; and I will be their God, and they shall be my people. And they shall not 11 teach one another, saying to brother and fellow-citizen,*a* "Know the Lord!" For all of them, high and low, shall know me; I will be merciful 12 to their wicked deeds, and I will remember their sins no more.' By speak- 13 ing of a new covenant, he has pronounced the first one old; and anything that is growing old and ageing will shortly disappear.

THE FIRST COVENANT indeed had its ordinances of divine service and **9** its sanctuary, but a material sanctuary. For a tent was prepared—the first 2 tent—in which was the lamp-stand, and the table with the bread of the Presence; this is called the Holy Place. Beyond the second curtain was the 3 tent called the Most Holy Place. Here was a golden altar of incense, and 4 the ark of the covenant plated all over with gold, in which were a golden jar containing the manna, and Aaron's staff which once budded, and the tablets of the covenant; and above it the cherubim of God's glory, over- 5 shadowing the place of expiation. On these we cannot now enlarge.

Under this arrangement, the priests are always entering the first tent 6 in the discharge of their duties; but the second is entered only once a year, 7 and by the high priest alone, and even then he must take with him the blood which he offers on his own behalf and for the people's sins of ignor- ance. By this the Holy Spirit signifies that so long as the earlier tent still 8 stands, the way into the sanctuary remains unrevealed. All this is symbolic, 9 pointing to the present time. The offerings and sacrifices there prescribed cannot give the worshipper inward perfection. It is only a matter of food 10 and drink and various rites of cleansing—outward ordinances in force until the time of reformation.

But now Christ has come, high priest of good things already in being.*b* 11 The tent of his priesthood is a greater and more perfect one, not made by men's hands, that is, not belonging to this created world; the blood of his 12 sacrifice is his own blood, not the blood of goats and calves; and thus he has entered the sanctuary once and for all and secured an eternal deliver- ance. For if the blood of goats and bulls and the sprinkled ashes of a heifer 13 have power to hallow those who have been defiled and restore their external purity, how much greater is the power of the blood of Christ; he offered 14 himself without blemish to God, a spiritual and eternal sacrifice; and his blood will cleanse our conscience from the deadness of our former ways and fit us for the service of the living God.

And therefore he is the mediator of a new covenant, or testament, under 15

a Some witnesses read brother and neighbour.   *b Some witnesses read* good things which were (*or are*) to be.

which, now that there has been a death to bring deliverance from sins committed under the former covenant, those whom God has called may receive
16 the promise of the eternal inheritance. For where there is a testament it is
17 necessary for the death of the testator to be established. A testament is
operative only after a death: it cannot possibly have force while the testator
18 is alive. Thus we find that the former covenant itself was not inaugurated
19 without blood. For when, as the Law directed, Moses had recited all the
commandments to the people, he took the blood of the calves, with water,
scarlet wool, and marjoram, and sprinkled the law-book itself and all the
20 people, saying, 'This is the blood of the covenant which God has enjoined
21 upon you.' In the same way he also sprinkled the tent and all the vessels of
22 divine service with blood. Indeed, according to the Law, it might almost be
said, everything is cleansed by blood and without the shedding of blood
there is no forgiveness.

23   If, then, these sacrifices cleanse the copies of heavenly things, those
24 heavenly things themselves require better sacrifices to cleanse them. For
Christ has entered, not that sanctuary made by men's hands which is only
a symbol of the reality, but heaven itself, to appear now before God on our
25 behalf. Nor is he there to offer himself again and again, as the high priest
26 enters the sanctuary year by year with blood not his own. If that were so,
he would have had to suffer many times since the world was made. But as
it is, he has appeared once and for all at the climax of history to abolish sin
27 by the sacrifice of himself. And as it is the lot of men to die once, and after
28 death comes judgement, so Christ was offered once to bear the burden of
men's sins,[a] and will appear a second time, sin done away, to bring salvation to those who are watching for him.

10 FOR THE LAW contains but a shadow, and no true image,[b] of the good
things which were to come; it provides for the same sacrifices year after
year, and with these it can never bring the worshippers to perfection for all
2 time.[c] If it could, these sacrifices would surely have ceased to be offered,
because the worshippers, cleansed once for all, would no longer have any
3 sense of sin. But instead, in these sacrifices year after year sins are brought
4 to mind, because sins can never be removed by the blood of bulls and goats.
5   That is why, at his coming into the world, he says:

'Sacrifice and offering thou didst not desire,
but thou hast prepared a body for me.
6   Whole-offerings and sin-offerings thou didst not delight in.
7   Then I said, "Here am I: as it is written of me in the scroll,
I have come, O God, to do thy will."'

8 First he says, 'Sacrifices and offerings, whole-offerings and sin-offerings,
thou didst not desire nor delight in'—although the Law prescribes them—
9 and then he says, 'I have come to do thy will.' He thus annuls the former
10 to establish the latter. And it is by the will of God that we have been

---

a *Or* to remove men's sins.   b *One witness reads* a shadow and likeness . . .
c *Or* bring to perfection the worshippers who come continually.

consecrated, through the offering of the body of Jesus Christ once and for all.

Every priest stands performing his service daily and offering time after 11 time the same sacrifices, which can never remove sins. But Christ offered 12 for all time one sacrifice for sins, and took his seat at the right hand of God, where he waits henceforth until his enemies are made his footstool. For 13 14 by one offering he has perfected for all time those who are thus consecrated. Here we have also the testimony of the Holy Spirit: he first says, 'This is 15 16 the covenant which I will make with them after those days, says the Lord: I will set my laws in their hearts and write them on their understanding'; then he adds, 'and their sins and wicked deeds I will remember no more 17 at all.' And where these have been forgiven, there are offerings for sin no 18 longer.

SO NOW, MY FRIENDS, the blood of Jesus makes us free to enter boldly 19 into the sanctuary by the new, living way which he has opened for us 20 through the curtain, the way of his flesh.*ᵃ* We have, moreover, a great 21 priest set over the household of God; so let us make our approach in 22 sincerity of heart and full assurance of faith, our guilty hearts sprinkled clean, our bodies washed with pure water. Let us be firm and unswerving 23 in the confession of our hope, for the Giver of the promise may be trusted. We ought to see how each of us may best arouse others to love and active 24 goodness, not staying away from our meetings, as some do, but rather 25 encouraging one another, all the more because you see the Day drawing near.

For if we wilfully persist in sin after receiving the knowledge of the 26 truth, no sacrifice for sins remains: only a terrifying expectation of judge- 27 ment and a fierce fire which will consume God's enemies. If a man dis- 28 regards the Law of Moses, he is put to death without pity on the evidence of two or three witnesses. Think how much more severe a penalty that man 29 will deserve who has trampled under foot the Son of God, profaned the blood of the covenant by which he was consecrated, and affronted God's gracious Spirit! For we know who it is that has said, 'Justice is mine: I will 30 repay'; and again, 'The Lord will judge his people.' It is a terrible thing to 31 fall into the hands of the living God.

Remember the days gone by, when, newly enlightened, you met the 32 challenge of great sufferings and held firm. Some of you were abused and 33 tormented to make a public show, while others stood loyally by those who were so treated. For indeed you shared the sufferings of the prisoners, and 34 you cheerfully accepted the seizure of your possessions, knowing that you possessed something better and more lasting. Do not then throw away 35 your confidence, for it carries a great reward. You need endurance, if you 36 are to do God's will and win what he has promised. For 'soon, very soon' 37 (in the words of Scripture), 'he who is to come will come; he will not delay; and by faith my righteous servant shall find life; but if a man shrinks back, 38 I take no pleasure in him.' But we are not among those who shrink back 39 and are lost; we have the faith to make life our own.

ᵃ Or through the curtain of his flesh.

A call to faith

11 AND WHAT IS FAITH? Faith gives substance*a* to our hopes, and makes us certain of realities we do not see.

2 It is for their faith that the men of old stand on record.

3 By faith we perceive that the universe was fashioned by the word of God, so that the visible came forth from the invisible.

4 By faith Abel offered a sacrifice greater than Cain's, and through faith his goodness was attested, for his offerings had God's approval; and through faith he continued to speak after his death.

5 By faith Enoch was carried away to another life without passing through death; he was not to be found, because God had taken him. For it is the testimony of Scripture that before he was taken he had pleased God, 6 and without faith it is impossible to please him; for anyone who comes to God must believe that he exists and that he rewards those who search for him.

7 By faith Noah, divinely warned about the unseen future, took good heed and built an ark to save his household. Through his faith he put the whole world in the wrong, and made good his own claim to the righteousness which comes of faith.

8 By faith Abraham obeyed the call to go out to a land destined for him-9 self and his heirs, and left home without knowing where he was to go. By faith he settled as an alien in the land promised him, living in tents, as did 10 Isaac and Jacob, who were heirs to the same promise. For he was looking forward to the city with firm foundations, whose architect and builder is God.

11 By faith even Sarah herself received strength to conceive, though she was past the age, because she judged that he who had promised would keep 12 faith; and therefore from one man, and one as good as dead, there sprang descendants numerous as the stars or as the countless grains of sand on the sea-shore.

13 All these persons died in faith. They were not yet in possession of the things promised, but had seen them far ahead and hailed them, and confessed themselves no more than strangers or passing travellers on earth. 14 Those who use such language show plainly that they are looking for a 15 country of their own. If their hearts had been in the country they had left, 16 they could have found opportunity to return. Instead, we find them longing for a better country—I mean, the heavenly one. That is why God is not ashamed to be called their God; for he has a city ready for them.

17 By faith Abraham, when the test came, offered up Isaac: he had received 18 the promises, and yet he was on the point of offering his only son, of whom he had been told, 'Through the line of Isaac your descendants shall be 19 traced.'*b* For he reckoned that God had power even to raise from the dead —and from the dead, he did, in a sense, receive him back.

20 21 By faith Isaac blessed Jacob and Esau and spoke of things to come. By faith Jacob, as he was dying, blessed each of Joseph's sons, and worshipped

a Or assurance.　　*b Or* God's call shall be for your descendants in the line of Isaac.

God, leaning on the top of his staff. By faith Joseph, at the end of his life, 22 spoke of the departure of Israel from Egypt, and instructed them what to do with his bones.

By faith, when Moses was born, his parents hid him for three months, 23 because they saw what a fine child he was; they were not afraid of the king's edict. By faith Moses, when he grew up, refused to be called the son of 24 Pharaoh's daughter, preferring to suffer hardship with the people of God 25 rather than enjoy the transient pleasures of sin. He considered the stigma 26 that rests on God's Anointed greater wealth than the treasures of Egypt, for his eyes were fixed upon the coming day of recompense. By faith he left 27 Egypt, and not because he feared the king's anger; for he was resolute, as one who saw the invisible God.

By faith he celebrated the Passover and sprinkled the blood, so that the 28 destroying angel might not touch the first-born of Israel. By faith they 29 crossed the Red Sea as though it were dry land, whereas the Egyptians, when they attempted the crossing, were drowned.

By faith the walls of Jericho fell down after they had been encircled on 30 seven successive days. By faith the prostitute Rahab escaped the doom of 31 the unbelievers, because she had given the spies a kindly welcome.

Need I say more? Time is too short for me to tell the stories of Gideon, 32 Barak, Samson, and Jephthah, of David and Samuel and the prophets. Through faith they overthrew kingdoms, established justice, saw God's 33 promises fulfilled. They muzzled ravening lions, quenched the fury of 34 fire, escaped death by the sword. Their weakness was turned to strength, they grew powerful in war, they put foreign armies to rout. Women 35 received back their dead raised to life. Others were tortured to death, disdaining release, to win a better resurrection. Others, again, had to face jeers 36 and flogging, even fetters and prison bars. They were stoned,*a* they were 37 sawn in two, they were put to the sword, they went about dressed in skins of sheep or goats, in poverty, distress, and misery. They were too good for 38 a world like this. They were refugees in deserts and on the hills, hiding in caves and holes in the ground. These also, one and all, are commemorated 39 for their faith; and yet they did not enter upon the promised inheritance, because, with us in mind, God had made a better plan, that only in com- 40 pany with us should they reach their perfection.

AND WHAT OF OURSELVES? With all these witnesses to faith around **12** us like a cloud, we must throw off every encumbrance, every sin to which we cling,*b* and run with resolution the race for which we are entered, our 2 eyes fixed on Jesus, on whom faith depends from start to finish: Jesus who, for the sake of the joy that lay ahead of him,*c* endured the cross, making light of its disgrace, and has taken his seat at the right hand of the throne of God.

Think of him who submitted to such opposition from sinners: that will 3 help you not to lose heart and grow faint. In your struggle against sin, you 4

---

a Some witnesses insert they were put to the question. *one witness reads* the sin which all too readily distracts us.

b Or every clinging sin; *c Or* who, in place of the joy that was open to him, . . .

5 have not yet resisted to the point of shedding your blood. You have forgotten the text of Scripture which addresses you as sons and appeals to you in these words:

'My son, do not think lightly of the Lord's discipline,
nor lose heart when he corrects you;
6   for the Lord disciplines those whom he loves;
he lays the rod on every son whom he acknowledges.'

7 You must endure it as discipline: God is treating you as sons. Can anyone
8 be a son, who is not disciplined by his father? If you escape the discipline
9 in which all sons share, you must be bastards and no true sons. Again, we paid due respect to the earthly fathers who disciplined us; should we not
10 submit even more readily to our spiritual Father, and so attain life? They disciplined us for this short life according to their lights; but he does so for
11 our true welfare, so that we may share his holiness. Discipline, no doubt, is never pleasant; at the time it seems painful, but in the end it yields for those who have been trained by it the peaceful harvest of an honest life.
12 13 Come, then, stiffen your drooping arms and shaking knees, and keep your steps from wavering. Then the disabled limb will not be put out of joint, but regain its former powers.
14   Aim at peace with all men, and a holy life, for without that no one will
15 see the Lord. Look to it that there is no one among you who forfeits the grace
16 of God, no bitter, noxious weed growing up to poison the whole, no immoral person, no one worldly-minded like Esau. He sold his birthright
17 for a single meal, and you know that although he wanted afterwards to claim the blessing, he was rejected; though he begged for it to the point of tears, he found no way open for second thoughts.

18 REMEMBER WHERE YOU STAND: not before the palpable, blazing fire of
19 Sinai, with the darkness, gloom, and whirlwind, the trumpet-blast and the
20 oracular voice, which they heard, and begged to hear no more; for they could not bear the command, 'If even an animal touches the mountain, it must be
21 stoned.' So appalling was the sight, that Moses said, 'I shudder with fear.'
22   No, you stand before Mount Zion and the city of the living God,
23 heavenly Jerusalem, before myriads of angels, the full concourse and assembly of the first-born citizens of heaven, and God the judge of all,
24 and the spirits of good men made perfect, and Jesus the mediator of a new covenant, whose sprinkled blood has better things to tell than the blood
25 of Abel. See that you do not refuse to hear the voice that speaks. Those who refused to hear the oracle speaking on earth found no escape; still less shall
26 we escape if we refuse to hear the One who speaks from heaven. Then indeed his voice shook the earth, but now he has promised, 'Yet once again
27 I will shake not earth alone, but the heavens also.' The words 'once again'—and only once—imply that the shaking of these created things means their
28 removal, and then what is not shaken will remain. The kingdom we are given is unshakable; let us therefore give thanks to God, and so worship
29 him as he would be worshipped, with reverence and awe; for our God is a devouring fire.

NEVER CEASE TO LOVE your fellow-Christians. **13**

Remember to show hospitality. There are some who, by so doing, have 2 entertained angels without knowing it.

Remember those in prison as if you were there with them; and those who 3 are being maltreated, for you like them are still in the world.

Marriage is honourable; let us all keep it so, and the marriage-bond 4 inviolate; for God's judgement will fall on fornicators and adulterers.

Do not live for money; be content with what you have; for God him- 5 self has said, 'I will never leave you or desert you'; and so we can take 6 courage and say, 'The Lord is my helper, I will not fear; what can man do to me?'

Remember your leaders, those who first spoke God's message to you; 7 and reflecting upon the outcome of their life and work, follow the example of their faith.

Jesus Christ is the same yesterday, today, and for ever. So do not be 8 9 swept off your course by all sorts of outlandish teachings; it is good that our souls should gain their strength from the grace of God, and not from scruples about what we eat, which have never done any good to those who were governed by them.

Our altar is one from which *a* the priests of the sacred tent have no right 10 to eat. As you know, those animals whose blood is brought as a sin-offering 11 by the high priest into the sanctuary, have their bodies burnt outside the camp, and therefore Jesus also suffered outside the gate, to consecrate the 12 people by his own blood. Let us then go to him outside the camp, bearing 13 the stigma that he bore. For here we have no permanent home, but we are 14 seekers after the city which is to come. Through Jesus, then, let us con- 15 tinually offer up to God the sacrifice of praise, that is, the tribute of lips which acknowledge his name, and never forget to show kindness and to 16 share what you have with others; for such are the sacrifices which God approves.

Obey your leaders and defer to them; for they are tireless in their con- 17 cern for you, as men who must render an account. Let it be a happy task for them, and not pain and grief, for that would bring you no advantage.

Pray for us; for we are convinced that our conscience is clear; our one 18 desire is always to do what is right. All the more earnestly I ask for your 19 prayers, that I may be restored to you the sooner.

May the God of peace, who brought up from the dead our Lord Jesus, 20 the great Shepherd of the sheep, by the blood of the eternal covenant, make 21 you perfect in all goodness so that you may do his will; and may he make of us what he would have us be through Jesus Christ, to whom be glory for ever and ever! Amen.

I beg you, brothers, bear with this exhortation; for it is after all a short 22 letter. I have news for you: our friend Timothy has been released; and if 23 he comes in time he will be with me when I see you.

Greet all your leaders and all God's people. Greetings to you from our 24 Italian friends.

God's grace be with you all! 25

a Or one like that from which . . .

A LETTER OF
JAMES

Practical religion

1 FROM JAMES, a servant of God and the Lord Jesus Christ.
Greetings to the Twelve Tribes dispersed throughout the world.
2 My brothers, whenever you have to face trials of many kinds,
3 count yourselves supremely happy, in the knowledge that such testing of
4 your faith breeds fortitude, and if you give fortitude full play you will go
5 on to complete a balanced character that will fall short in nothing. If any
of you falls short in wisdom, he should ask God for it and it will be given
him, for God is a generous giver who neither refuses nor reproaches any-
6 one. But he must ask in faith, without a doubt in his mind; for the doubter
7 is like a heaving sea ruffled by the wind. A man of that kind must not expect
8 the Lord to give him anything; he is double-minded, and never can keep *a*
a steady course.

9 The brother in humble circumstances may well be proud that God lifts
10 him up; and the wealthy brother must find his pride in being brought low.
11 For the rich man will disappear like the flower of the field; once the sun is
up with its scorching heat the flower withers, its petals fall, and what was
lovely to look at is lost for ever. So shall the rich man wither away as he
goes about his business.

12 Happy the man who remains steadfast under trial, for having passed that
test he will receive for his prize the gift of life promised to those who love
13 God. No one under trial or temptation should say, 'I am being tempted by
God'; for God is untouched by evil, *b* and does not himself tempt anyone.
14 Temptation arises when a man is enticed and lured away by his own lust;
15 then lust conceives, and gives birth to sin; and sin full-grown breeds
death.

16 17 Make no mistake, my friends. All good giving, every perfect gift, comes *c*
from above, from the Father of the lights of heaven. With him there is no
18 variation, no play of passing shadows.*d* Of his set purpose, by declaring the
truth, he gave us birth to be a kind of firstfruits of his creatures.

19 Of that you may be certain, my friends. But each of you must be quick
20 to listen, slow to speak, and slow to be angry. For a man's anger cannot
21 promote the justice of God. Away then with all that is sordid, and the malice
that hurries to excess, and quietly accept the message planted in your hearts,
which can bring you salvation.

---

a Or anything; a double-minded man never keeps . . .   *b* Or God cannot be
tempted by evil.   *c* Or All giving is good, and every perfect gift comes . . .
d Some witnesses read no variation, or shadow caused by change.

Only be sure that you act on the message and do not merely listen; for 22
that would be to mislead yourselves. A man who listens to the message but 23
never acts upon it is like one who looks in a mirror at the face nature gave
him. He glances at himself and goes away, and at once forgets what he 24
looked like. But the man who looks closely into the perfect law, the law 25
that makes us free, and who lives in its company, does not forget what he
hears, but acts upon it; and that is the man who by acting will find
happiness.

A man may think he is religious, but if he has no control over his tongue, 26
he is deceiving himself; that man's religion is futile. The kind of religion 27
which is without stain or fault in the sight of God our Father is this: to
go to the help of orphans and widows in their distress and keep oneself
untarnished by the world.

MY BROTHERS, believing as you do in our Lord Jesus Christ, who reigns **2**
in glory, you must never show snobbery. For instance, two visitors may 2
enter your place of worship, one a well-dressed man with gold rings, and
the other a poor man in shabby clothes. Suppose you pay special attention 3
to the well-dressed man and say to him, 'Please take this seat', while to the
poor man you say, 'You can stand; or you may sit here*a* on the floor by my
footstool', do you not see that you are inconsistent and judge by false 4
standards?

Listen, my friends. Has not God chosen those who are poor in the eyes 5
of the world to be rich in faith and to inherit the kingdom he has promised
to those who love him? And yet you have insulted the poor man. More- 6
over, are not the rich your oppressors? Is it not they who drag you into
court and pour contempt on the honoured name by which God has 7
claimed you?

If, however, you are observing the sovereign law laid down in Scripture, 8
'Love your neighbour as yourself', that is excellent. But if you show snob- 9
bery, you are committing a sin and you stand convicted by that law as
transgressors. For if a man keeps the whole law apart from one single 10
point, he is guilty of breaking all of it. For the One who said, 'Thou shalt 11
not commit adultery', said also, 'Thou shalt not commit murder.' You may
not be an adulterer, but if you commit murder you are a law-breaker all the
same. Always speak and act as men who are to be judged under a law of 12
freedom. In that judgement there will be no mercy for the man who has 13
shown no mercy. Mercy triumphs over judgement.

MY BROTHERS, what use is it for a man to say he has faith when he does 14
nothing to show it? Can that faith save him? Suppose a brother or a sister 15
is in rags with not enough food for the day, and one of you says, 'Good luck 16
to you, keep yourselves warm, and have plenty to eat', but does nothing to
supply their bodily needs, what is the good of that? So with faith; if it does 17
not lead to action, it is in itself a lifeless thing.

But someone may object: 'Here is one who claims to have faith and 18

a Some witnesses read Stand where you are or sit here . . .; *others read* Stand where you
are or sit . . .

another who points to his deeds.' To which I reply: 'Prove to me that this faith you speak of is real though not accompanied by deeds, and by my
19 deeds I will prove to you my faith.' You have faith enough to believe that there is one God. Excellent! The devils have faith like that, and it makes
20 them tremble. But can you not see, you quibbler, that faith divorced from
21 deeds is barren? Was it not by his action, in offering his son Isaac upon the
22 altar, that our father Abraham was justified? Surely you can see that faith was at work in his actions, and that by these actions the integrity of his
23 faith was fully proved. Here was fulfilment of the words of Scripture: 'Abraham put his faith in God, and that faith was counted to him as
24 righteousness'; and elsewhere he is called 'God's friend'. You see then that
25 a man is justified by deeds and not by faith in itself. The same is true of the prostitute Rahab also. Was not she justified by her action in welcoming the messengers into her house and sending them away by a different route?
26 As the body is dead when there is no breath left in it, so faith divorced from deeds is lifeless as a corpse.

3 MY BROTHERS, not many of you should become teachers, for you may be certain that we who teach shall ourselves be judged with greater strict-
2 ness. All of us often go wrong; the man who never says a wrong thing is a
3 perfect character, able to bridle his whole being. If we put bits into horses'
4 mouths to make them obey our will, we can direct their whole body. Or think of ships: large they may be, yet even when driven by strong gales they can be directed by a tiny rudder on whatever course the helmsman
5 chooses. So with the tongue. It is a small member but it can make huge claims.*a*

What an immense stack of timber*b* can be set ablaze by the tiniest spark!
6 And the tongue is in effect a fire. It represents among our members the world with all its wickedness; it pollutes our whole being; it keeps the
7 wheel of our existence red-hot, and its flames are fed by hell. Beasts and birds of every kind, creatures that crawl on the ground or swim in the sea,
8 can be subdued and have been subdued by mankind; but no man can sub-
9 due the tongue. It is an intractable evil, charged with deadly venom. We use it to sing the praises of our Lord and Father, and we use it to invoke
10 curses upon our fellow-men who are made in God's likeness. Out of the same mouth come praises and curses. My brothers, this should not be so.
11 Does a fountain gush with both fresh and brackish water from the same
12 opening? Can a fig-tree, my brothers, yield olives, or a vine figs? No more does salt water yield fresh.

13 WHO AMONG YOU is wise or clever? Let his right conduct give practical
14 proof of it, with the modesty that comes of wisdom. But if you are harbour-ing bitter jealousy and selfish ambition in your hearts, consider whether
15 your claims are not false, and a defiance of the truth. This is not the
16 wisdom that comes from above; it is earth-bound, sensual, demonic. For
17 with jealousy and ambition come disorder and evil of every kind. But the wisdom from above is in the first place pure; and then peace-loving,

a Or it is a great boaster.   *b Or* What a huge forest . . .

considerate, and open to reason; it is straightforward and sincere, rich in mercy and in the kindly deeds that are its fruit. True justice is the harvest 18 reaped by peacemakers from seeds sown in a spirit of peace.

What causes conflicts and quarrels among you? Do they not spring from 4 the aggressiveness of your bodily desires? You want something which you 2 cannot have, and so you are bent on murder; you are envious, and cannot attain your ambition, and so you quarrel and fight. You do not get what you want, because you do not pray for it. Or, if you do, your requests are not 3 granted because you pray from wrong motives, to spend what you get on your pleasures. You false, unfaithful creatures! Have you never learned 4 that love of the world is enmity to God? Whoever chooses to be the world's friend makes himself God's enemy. Or do you suppose that Scripture has 5 no meaning when it says that the spirit which God implanted in man turns towards envious desires? And yet the grace he gives is stronger. Thus 6 Scripture says, 'God opposes the arrogant and gives grace to the humble.' Be submissive then to God. Stand up to the devil and he will turn and run. 7 Come close to God, and he will come close to you. Sinners, make your 8 hands clean; you who are double-minded, see that your motives are pure. Be sorrowful, mourn and weep. Turn your laughter into mourning and 9 your gaiety into gloom. Humble yourselves before God and he will lift 10 you high.

Brothers, you must never disparage one another. He who disparages a 11 brother or passes judgement on his brother disparages the law and judges the law. But if you judge the law, you are not keeping it but sitting in judgement upon it. There is only one lawgiver and judge, the One who is 12 able to save life and destroy it. So who are you to judge your neighbour?

A WORD WITH YOU, you who say, 'Today or tomorrow we will go off 13 to such and such a town and spend a year there trading and making money.' Yet you have no idea what tomorrow will bring. Your life, what is it? You 14 are no more than a mist, seen for a little while and then dispersing. What 15 you ought to say is: 'If it be the Lord's will, we shall live to do this or that.' But instead, you boast and brag, and all such boasting is wrong. Well then, 16 17 the man who knows the good he ought to do and does not do it is a sinner.

Next a word to you who have great possessions. Weep and wail over the 5 miserable fate descending on you. Your riches have rotted; your fine clothes 2 are moth-eaten; your silver and gold have rusted away, and their very rust 3 will be evidence against you and consume your flesh like fire. You have piled up wealth in an age that is near its close. The wages you never paid to the 4 men who mowed your fields are loud against you, and the outcry of the reapers has reached the ears of the Lord of Hosts. You have lived on earth 5 in wanton luxury, fattening yourselves like cattle—and the day for slaughter has come. You have condemned the innocent and murdered him; he offers 6 no resistance.

Be patient, my brothers, until the Lord comes. The farmer looking for 7 the precious crop his land may yield can only wait in patience, until the autumn and spring rains have fallen. You too must be patient and stout- 8 hearted, for the coming of the Lord is near. My brothers, do not blame 9

your troubles on one another, or you will fall under judgement; and there
10 stands the Judge, at the door. If you want a pattern of patience under ill-
11 treatment, take the prophets who spoke in the name of the Lord; remember: 'We count those happy who stood firm.' You have all heard how Job
stood firm, and you have seen how the Lord treated him in the end. For
the Lord is full of pity and compassion.

12 ABOVE ALL THINGS, my brothers, do not use oaths, whether 'by
heaven' or 'by earth' or by anything else. When you say yes or no, let it be
plain 'Yes' or 'No', for fear that you expose yourselves to judgement.
13   Is anyone among you in trouble? He should turn to prayer. Is anyone
14 in good heart? He should sing praises. Is one of you ill? He should send
for the elders of the congregation to pray over him and anoint him with oil
15 in the name of the Lord. The prayer offered in faith will save the sick man,
the Lord will raise him from his bed, and any sins he may have committed
16 will be forgiven. Therefore confess your sins to one another, and pray for
one another, and then you will be healed. A good man's prayer is powerful
17 and effective. Elijah was a man with human frailties like our own; and when
he prayed earnestly that there should be no rain, not a drop fell on the land
18 for three years and a half; then he prayed again, and down came the rain
and the land bore crops once more.
19   My brothers, if one of your number should stray from the truth and
20 another succeed in bringing him back, be sure of this: any man who brings
a sinner back from his crooked ways will be rescuing his soul from death
and cancelling innumerable sins.

THE FIRST LETTER OF
PETER

The calling of a Christian

1 FROM PETER, APOSTLE of Jesus Christ, to those of God's
scattered people who lodge for a while in Pontus, Galatia, Cappa-
2 docia, Asia, and Bithynia—chosen of old in the purpose of God the
Father, hallowed to his service by the Spirit, and consecrated with the
sprinkled blood of Jesus Christ.
    Grace and peace to you in fullest measure.
3   Praise be to the God and Father of our Lord Jesus Christ, who in his
great mercy gave us new birth into a living hope by the resurrection of
4 Jesus Christ from the dead! The inheritance to which we are born is one
5 that nothing can destroy or spoil or wither. It is kept for you in heaven, and
you, because you put your faith in God, are under the protection of his

power until salvation comes—the salvation which is even now in readiness and will be revealed at the end of time.

6 This is cause for great joy, even though now you smart for a little while, 7 if need be, under trials of many kinds. Even gold passes through the assayer's fire, and more precious than perishable gold is faith which has stood the test. These trials come so that your faith may prove itself worthy of all praise, glory, and honour when Jesus Christ is revealed.

8 You have not seen him, yet you love him; and trusting in him now with-9 out seeing him, you are transported with a joy too great for words, while 10 you reap the harvest of your faith, that is, salvation for your souls. This salvation was the theme which the prophets pondered and explored, those 11 who prophesied about the grace of God awaiting you. They tried to find out what was the time,*a* and what the circumstances, to which the spirit of Christ in them pointed, foretelling the sufferings in store for Christ and 12 the splendours to follow; and it was disclosed to them that the matter they treated of was not for their time but for yours. And now it has been openly announced to you through preachers who brought you the Gospel in the power of the Holy Spirit sent from heaven. These are things that angels long to see into.

13 You must therefore be mentally stripped for action, perfectly self-controlled. Fix your hopes on the gift of grace which is to be yours when 14 Jesus Christ is revealed. As obedient children, do not let your characters be shaped any longer by the desires you cherished in your days of ignorance. 15 The One who called you is holy; like him, be holy in all your behaviour, 16 because Scripture says, 'You shall be holy, for I am holy.'

17 If you say 'our Father' to the One who judges every man impartially on the record of his deeds, you must stand in awe of him while you live out 18 your time on earth. Well you know that it was no perishable stuff, like gold or silver, that bought your freedom from the empty folly of your tradi-19 tional ways. The price was paid in precious blood, as it were of a lamb 20 without mark or blemish—the blood of Christ. Predestined before the foundation of the world, he was made manifest in this last period of time 21 for your sake. Through him you have come to trust in God who raised him from the dead and gave him glory, and so your faith and hope are fixed on God.

22 Now that by obedience to the truth you have purified your souls until you feel sincere affection towards your brother Christians, love one another 23 whole-heartedly with all your strength. You have been born anew, not of mortal parentage but of immortal, through the living and enduring word 24 of God.*b* For (as Scripture says)

> 'All mortals are like grass;
> all their splendour like the flower of the field;
> the grass withers, the flower falls;
> 25 but the word of the Lord endures for evermore.'

And this 'word' is the word of the Gospel preached to you.

a Or who was the person . . .   *b Or* through the word of the living and enduring God.

2 Then away with all malice and deceit, away with all pretence and
2 jealousy and recrimination of every kind! Like the new-born infants you
are, you must crave for pure milk (spiritual milk, I mean), so that you may
3 thrive upon it to your souls' health. Surely you have tasted that the Lord
is good.

4 So come to him, our living Stone—the stone rejected by men but
5 choice and precious in the sight of God. Come, and let yourselves be built,
as living stones, into a spiritual temple; become a holy priesthood,*a* to offer
6 spiritual sacrifices acceptable to God through Jesus Christ. For it stands
written:

> 'I lay in Zion a choice corner-stone of great worth.
> The man who has faith in it will not be put to shame.'

7 The great worth of which it speaks is for you who have faith. For those
who have no faith, the stone which the builders rejected has become
8 not only the corner-stone,*b* but also 'a stone to trip over, a rock to
stumble against'. They fall when they disbelieve the Word. Such was their
appointed lot!

9 But you are a chosen race, a royal priesthood, a dedicated nation, and a
people claimed by God for his own, to proclaim the triumphs of him who
10 has called you out of darkness into his marvellous light. You are now the
people of God, who once were not his people; outside his mercy once, you
have now received his mercy.

11 DEAR FRIENDS, I beg you, as aliens in a foreign land, to abstain from
12 the lusts of the flesh which are at war with the soul. Let all your behaviour
be such as even pagans can recognize as good, and then, whereas they
malign you as criminals now, they will come to see for themselves that you
live good lives, and will give glory to God on the day when he comes to
hold assize.

13 Submit yourselves to every human institution for the sake of the Lord,
14 whether to the sovereign as supreme, or to the governor as his deputy for
the punishment of criminals and the commendation of those who do right.
15 For it is the will of God that by your good conduct you should put ignorance and stupidity to silence.

16 Live as free men; not however as though your freedom were there to
17 provide a screen for wrongdoing, but as slaves in God's service. Give due
honour to everyone: love to the brotherhood, reverence to God, honour to
the sovereign.

18 Servants, accept the authority of your masters with all due submission,
not only when they are kind and considerate, but even when they are per-
19 verse. For it is a fine*c* thing if a man endure the pain of undeserved suffer-
20 ing because God is in his thoughts. What credit is there in fortitude when
you have done wrong and are beaten for it? But when you have behaved
21 well and suffer for it, your fortitude is a fine thing*d* in the sight of God. To

---

a Or a spiritual temple for the holy work of priesthood.   *b Or* the apex of the
building.   *c Or* creditable.   *d Or* is creditable.

that you were called, because Christ suffered[a] on your behalf, and thereby
left you an example; it is for you to follow in his steps. He committed no sin, 22
he was convicted of no falsehood; when he was abused he did not retort 23
with abuse, when he suffered he uttered no threats, but committed his
cause to the One who judges justly. In his own person he carried our sins 24
to[b] the gibbet, so that we might cease to live for sin and begin to live for
righteousness. By his wounds you have been healed. You were straying like 25
sheep, but now you have turned towards the Shepherd and Guardian of
your souls.

In the same way you women must accept the authority of your husbands, 3
so that if there are any of them who disbelieve the Gospel they may be won
over, without a word being said, by observing the chaste and reverent be- 2
haviour of their wives. Your beauty should reside, not in outward adorn- 3
ment—the braiding of the hair, or jewellery, or dress—but in the inmost 4
centre of your being, with its imperishable ornament, a gentle, quiet spirit,
which is of high value in the sight of God. Thus it was among God's 5
people in days of old: the women who fixed their hopes on him adorned
themselves by submission to their husbands. Such was Sarah, who obeyed 6
Abraham and called him 'my master'. Her children you have now become,
if you do good and show no fear.

In the same way, you husbands must conduct your married life with 7
understanding: pay honour to the woman's body, not only because it is
weaker, but also because you share together in the grace of God which
gives you life. Then your prayers will not be hindered.

To sum up: be one in thought and feeling, all of you; be full of brotherly 8
affection, kindly and humble-minded. Do not repay wrong with wrong, or 9
abuse with abuse; on the contrary, retaliate with blessing, for a blessing is
the inheritance to which you yourselves have been called.

> 'Whoever loves life and would see good days 10
> must restrain his tongue from evil
> and his lips from deceit;
> must turn from wrong and do good, 11
> seek peace and pursue it.
> For the Lord's eyes are turned towards the righteous, 12
> his ears are open to their prayers;
> but the Lord's face is set against wrong-doers.'

WHO IS GOING to do you wrong if you are devoted to what is good? 13
And yet if you should suffer for your virtues, you may count yourselves 14
happy. Have no fear of them:[c] do not be perturbed, but hold the Lord 15
Christ in reverence in your hearts.[d] Be always ready with your defence
whenever you are called to account for the hope that is in you, but make that
defence with modesty and respect. Keep your conscience clear, so that 16
when you are abused, those who malign your Christian conduct may be
put to shame. It is better to suffer for well-doing, if such should be the will 17

---

[a] *Some witnesses read* died.   [b] *Or* on.   [c] *Or* Do not fear what they fear.
[d] *Or* hold Christ in reverence in your hearts, as Lord.

18 of God, than for doing wrong. For Christ also died[a] for our sins[b] once and for all. He, the just, suffered for the unjust, to bring us to God.

19   In the body he was put to death; in the spirit he was brought to life. And in the spirit he went and made his proclamation to the imprisoned spirits.

20 They had refused obedience long ago, while God waited patiently in the days of Noah and the building of the ark, and in the ark a few persons, eight

21 in all, were brought to safety through the water. This water prefigured the water of baptism through which you are now brought to safety. Baptism is not the washing away of bodily pollution, but the appeal made to God by a good conscience; and it brings salvation through the resurrection of

22 Jesus Christ, who entered heaven after receiving the submission of angelic authorities and powers, and is now at the right hand of God.

4   Remembering that Christ endured bodily suffering, you must arm your-selves with a temper of mind like his. When a man has thus endured bodily

2 suffering he has finished with sin, and for the rest of his days on earth he

3 may live, not for the things that men desire, but for what God wills. You had time enough in the past to do all the things that men want to do in the pagan world. Then you lived in licence and debauchery, drunkenness,

4 revelry, and tippling, and the forbidden worship of idols. Now, when you no longer plunge with them into all this reckless dissipation, they cannot

5 understand it, and they vilify you accordingly; but they shall answer for it to him who stands ready to pass judgement on the living and the dead.

6 Why was the Gospel preached to those who are dead? In order that, although in the body they received the sentence common to men, they might in the spirit be alive with the life of God.

7   The end of all things is upon us, so you must lead an ordered and sober

8 life, given to prayer. Above all, keep your love for one another at full

9 strength, because love cancels innumerable sins. Be hospitable to one

10 another without complaining. Whatever gift each of you may have received, use it in service to one another, like good stewards dispensing the grace of

11 God in its varied forms. Are you a speaker? Speak as if you uttered oracles of God. Do you give service? Give it as in the strength which God supplies. In all things so act that the glory may be God's through Jesus Christ; to him belong glory and power for ever and ever. Amen.

12 MY DEAR FRIENDS, do not be bewildered by the fiery ordeal that is

13 upon you, as though it were something extraordinary. It gives you a share in Christ's sufferings, and that is cause for joy; and when his glory is

14 revealed, your joy will be triumphant. If Christ's name is flung in your teeth as an insult, count yourselves happy, because then that glorious Spirit

15 which is the Spirit of God is resting upon you. If you suffer, it must not be

16 for murder, theft, or sorcery,[c] nor for infringing the rights of others. But if anyone suffers as a Christian, he should feel it no disgrace, but confess that name to the honour of God.

17   The time has come for the judgement to begin; it is beginning with God's own household. And if it is starting with you, how will it end for those who

---

[a] *Some witnesses read* suffered.   [b] *Some witnesses read* for sins; *others read* for sins on our behalf.   [c] *Or* other crime.

refuse to obey the gospel of God? It is hard enough for the righteous to be 18
saved; what then will become of the impious and sinful? So even those who 19
suffer, if it be according to God's will, should commit their souls to him—
by doing good; their Maker will not fail them.

And now I appeal to the elders of your community, as a fellow-elder and 5
a witness of Christ's sufferings, and also a partaker in the splendour that is
to be revealed. Tend that flock of God whose shepherds you are, and do it, 2
not under compulsion, but of your own free will, as God would have it;
not for gain but out of sheer devotion; not tyrannizing over those who are 3
allotted to your care, but setting an example to the flock. And then, when 4
the Head Shepherd appears, you will receive for your own the unfading
garland of glory.

In the same way you younger men must be subordinate to your elders. 5
Indeed, all of you should wrap yourselves in the garment of humility
towards each other, because God sets his face against the arrogant but
favours the humble. Humble yourselves then under God's mighty hand, 6
and he will lift you up in due time. Cast all your cares on him, for you are 7
his charge.

Awake! be on the alert! Your enemy the devil, like a roaring lion, prowls 8
round looking for someone to devour. Stand up to him, firm in faith, and 9
remember that your brother Christians are going through the same kinds
of suffering while they are in the world. And the God of all grace, who called 10
you into his eternal glory in Christ, will himself, after your brief suffering,
restore, establish, and strengthen you on a firm foundation. He holds 11
dominion for ever and ever. Amen.

I write you this brief appeal through Silvanus, our trusty brother as I 12
hold him, adding my testimony that this is the true grace of God. In this
stand fast.

Greetings from her who dwells in Babylon, chosen by God like you, 13
and from my son Mark. Greet one another with the kiss of love. 14
Peace to you all who belong to Christ!

THE SECOND LETTER OF
PETER

The remedy for doubt

1 FROM SIMEON PETER, servant and apostle of Jesus Christ, to those who through the justice of our God and Saviour Jesus Christ share our faith and enjoy equal privilege with ourselves.

2 Grace and peace be yours in fullest measure, through the knowledge of God and Jesus our Lord.

3 His divine power has bestowed on us everything that makes for life and true religion, enabling us to know the One who called us by his own 4 splendour and might. Through this might and splendour he has given us his promises, great beyond all price, and through them you may escape the corruption with which lust has infected the world, and come to share in the very being of God.

5 With all this in view, you should try your hardest to supplement your 6 faith with virtue, virtue with knowledge, knowledge with self-control, 7 self-control with fortitude, fortitude with piety, piety with brotherly kindness, and brotherly kindness with love.

8 These are gifts which, if you possess and foster them, will keep you from being either useless or barren in the knowledge of our Lord Jesus Christ. 9 The man who lacks them is short-sighted and blind; he has forgotten how 10 he was cleansed from his former sins. All the more then, my friends, exert yourselves to clinch God's choice and calling of you. If you behave so, you 11 will never come to grief. Thus you will be afforded full and free admission into the eternal kingdom of our Lord and Saviour Jesus Christ.

12 And so I will not hesitate to remind you of this again and again, although you know it and are well grounded in the truth that has already reached 13 you. Yet I think it right to keep refreshing your memory so long as I still 14 lodge in this body. I know that very soon I must leave it; indeed our Lord 15 Jesus Christ has told me so.[a] But I will see to it that after I am gone you will have means of remembering these things at all times.

16 It was not on tales artfully spun that we relied when we told you of the power of our Lord Jesus Christ and his coming; we saw him with our own 17 eyes in majesty, when at the hands of God the Father he was invested with honour and glory, and there came to him from the sublime Presence a voice which said: 'This is my Son, my Beloved,[b] on whom my favour rests.' 18 This voice from heaven we ourselves heard; when it came, we were with him on the sacred mountain.

---

[a] *Or* I must leave it, as our Lord Jesus Christ told me.   [b] *Or* This is my only Son.

All this only confirms for us the message of the prophets,[a] to which you 19
will do well to attend, because it is like a lamp shining in a murky place,
until the day breaks and the morning star rises to illuminate your minds.

BUT FIRST NOTE THIS: no one can interpret any prophecy of Scrip- 20
ture by himself. For it was not through any human whim that men pro- 21
phesied of old; men they were, but, impelled by the Holy Spirit, they
spoke the words of God.

But Israel had false prophets as well as true; and you likewise will have 2
false teachers among you. They will import disastrous heresies, disowning
the very Master who bought them, and bringing swift disaster on their own
heads. They will gain many adherents to their dissolute practices, through 2
whom the true way will be brought into disrepute. In their greed for money 3
they will trade on your credulity with sheer fabrications.

But the judgement long decreed for them has not been idle; perdition
waits for them with unsleeping eyes. God did not spare the angels who 4
sinned, but consigned them to the dark pits of hell,[b] where they are
reserved for judgement. He did not spare the world of old (except for 5
Noah, preacher of righteousness, whom he preserved with seven others),
but brought the deluge upon that world of godless men. The cities of Sodom 6
and Gomorrah God burned to ashes, and condemned them to total destruction, making them an object-lesson for godless men in future days. But he 7
rescued Lot, who was a good man, shocked by the dissolute habits of the
lawless society in which he lived; day after day every sight, every sound, 8
of their evil courses tortured that good man's heart. Thus the Lord is well 9
able to rescue the godly out of trials, and to reserve the wicked under
punishment until the day of judgement.

Above all he will punish those who follow their abominable lusts. They 10
flout authority; reckless and headstrong, they are not afraid to insult
celestial beings, whereas angels, for all their superior strength and might, 11
employ no insults in seeking judgement against them before the Lord.

These men are like brute beasts, born in the course of nature to be 12
caught and killed. They pour abuse upon things they do not understand;
like the beasts they will perish, suffering hurt for the hurt they have 13
inflicted. To carouse in broad daylight is their idea of pleasure; while they
sit with you at table they are an ugly blot on your company, because they
revel in their own deceptions.[c]

They have eyes for nothing but women, eyes never at rest from sin. 14
They lure the unstable to their ruin; past masters in mercenary greed,
God's curse is on them! They have abandoned the straight road and lost 15
their way. They have followed in the steps of Balaam son of Beor, who
consented to take pay for doing wrong, but had his offence brought home 16
to him when the dumb beast spoke with a human voice and put a stop to
the prophet's madness.

These men are springs that give no water, mists driven by a storm; the 17

---

a *Or* And in the message of the prophets we have something still more certain.
b *Some witnesses read* consigned them to darkness and chains in hell.   c *Some
witnesses read* in their love-feasts.

18 place reserved for them is blackest darkness. They utter big, empty words, and make of sensual lusts and debauchery a bait to catch those who have
19 barely begun to escape from their heathen environment. They promise them freedom, but are themselves slaves of corruption; for a man is the
20 slave of whatever has mastered him. They had once escaped the world's defilements through the knowledge of our Lord and Saviour Jesus Christ; yet if they have entangled themselves in these all over again, and are
21 mastered by them, their plight in the end is worse than before. How much better never to have known the right way, than, having known it, to turn
22 back and abandon the sacred commandments delivered to them! For them the proverb has proved true: 'The dog returns to its own vomit', and, 'The sow after a wash rolls in the mud again.'

3 THIS IS NOW my second letter to you, my friends. In both of them I have been recalling to you what you already know, to rouse you to honest
2 thought. Remember the predictions made by God's own prophets, and the commands given by the Lord and Saviour through your apostles.
3   Note this first: in the last days there will come men who scoff at religion
4 and live self-indulgent lives, and they will say: 'Where now is the promise of his coming? Our fathers have been laid to their rest, but still everything continues exactly as it has always been since the world began.'
5   In taking this view they lose sight of the fact *a* that there were heavens and earth long ago, created by God's word out of water and with water;
6 7 and by water that first world was destroyed, the water of the deluge. And the present heavens and earth, again by God's word, have been kept in store for burning; they are being reserved until the day of judgement when the godless will be destroyed.
8   And here is one point, my friends, which you must not lose sight of: with the Lord one day is like a thousand years and a thousand years like
9 one day. It is not that the Lord is slow in fulfilling his promise, as some suppose, but that he is very patient with you, because it is not his will for any to be lost, but for all to come to repentance.
10   But the Day of the Lord will come; it will come, unexpected as a thief. On that day the heavens will disappear with a great rushing sound, the elements will disintegrate in flames, and the earth with all that is in it will be laid bare. *b*
11   Since the whole universe is to break up in this way, think what sort of people you ought to be, what devout and dedicated lives you should live!
12 Look eagerly for the coming of the Day of God and work to hasten it on; that day will set the heavens ablaze until they fall apart, and will melt the
13 elements in flames. But we have his promise, and look forward to new heavens and a new earth, the home of justice.
14   With this to look forward to, do your utmost to be found at peace with
15 him, unblemished and above reproach in his sight. Bear in mind that our Lord's patience with us is our salvation, as Paul, our friend and brother,
16 said when he wrote to you with his inspired wisdom. And so he does in all his other letters, wherever he speaks of this subject, though they contain

a Or They choose to overlook the fact . . .   *b Some witnesses read* will be burnt up.

some obscure passages, which the ignorant and unstable misinterpret to their own ruin, as they do the other scriptures.[a]

But you, my friends, are forewarned. Take care, then, not to let these 17 unprincipled men seduce you with their errors; do not lose your own safe foothold. But grow in the grace and in the knowledge of our Lord and 18 Saviour Jesus Christ.[b] To him be glory now and for all eternity!

THE FIRST LETTER OF
JOHN

Recall to fundamentals

IT WAS THERE from the beginning; we have heard it; we have 1 seen it with our own eyes; we looked upon it, and felt it with our own hands; and it is of this we tell. Our theme is the word of life. This life 2 was made visible; we have seen it and bear our testimony; we here declare to you the eternal life which dwelt with the Father and was made visible to us. What we have seen and heard we declare to you, so that you and we 3 together may share in a common life, that life which we share with the Father and his Son Jesus Christ. And we write this in order that the joy of 4 us all may be complete.

Here is the message we heard from him and pass on to you: that God is 5 light, and in him there is no darkness at all. If we claim to be sharing in his 6 life while we walk in the dark, our words and our lives are a lie; but if we 7 walk in the light as he himself is in the light, then we share together a common life, and we are being cleansed from every sin by the blood of Jesus his Son.

If we claim to be sinless, we are self-deceived and strangers to the truth. 8 If we confess our sins, he is just, and may be trusted to forgive our sins and 9 cleanse us from every kind of wrong; but if we say we have committed no 10 sin, we make him out to be a liar, and then his word has no place in us.

My children, in writing thus to you my purpose is that you should not 2 commit sin. But should anyone commit a sin, we have one to plead our cause[c] with the Father, Jesus Christ, and he is just. He is himself the 2 remedy for the defilement of our sins, not our sins only but the sins of all the world.

Here is the test by which we can make sure that we know him: do we 3 keep his commands? The man who says, 'I know him', while he disobeys 4 his commands, is a liar and a stranger to the truth; but in the man who is 5 obedient to his word, the divine love has indeed come to its perfection.

---

[a] *Or* his other writings.   [b] *Or* But grow up, by the grace of our Lord and Saviour Jesus Christ, and by knowing him.   [c] *Literally* we have an advocate . . .

6   Here is the test by which we can make sure that we are in him: whoever claims to be dwelling in him, binds himself to live as Christ himself lived.
7   Dear friends, I give you no new command. It is the old command which you always had before you; the old command is the message which you
8   heard at the beginning. And yet again it is a new command that I am giving you—new in the sense that the darkness is passing and the real light already shines. Christ has made this true, and it is true in your own experience.

9   A man may say, 'I am in the light'; but if he hates his brother, he is still
10 in the dark. Only the man who loves his brother dwells in light: there is
11 nothing to make him stumble. But one who hates his brother is in darkness; he walks in the dark and has no idea where he is going, because the darkness has made him blind.

12 I write to you, my children, because your sins have been forgiven for his sake.*a*
13 I write to you, fathers, because you know him who is and has been from the beginning. *b*
    I write to you, young men, because you have mastered the evil one.

14 To you, children, I have written because you know the Father.
    To you, fathers, I have written because you know him who is and has been from the beginning.*b*
    To you, young men, I have written because you are strong; God's word remains in you, and you have mastered the evil one.

15 Do not set your hearts on the godless world or anything in it. Anyone
16 who loves the world is a stranger to the Father's love. Everything the world affords, all that panders to the appetites or entices the eyes, all the glamour of its life, springs not from the Father but from the godless world.
17 And that world is passing away with all its allurements, but he who does God's will stands for evermore.

18 MY CHILDREN, this is the last hour! You were told that Antichrist was to come, and now many antichrists have appeared; which proves to us
19 that this is indeed the last hour. They went out from our company, but never really belonged to us; if they had, they would have stayed with us. They went out, so that it might be clear that not all in our company truly belong to it.*c*
20 You, no less than they, are among the initiated;*d* this is the gift of the
21 Holy One, and by it you all have knowledge.*e* It is not because you are ignorant of the truth that I have written to you, but because you know it, and because lies, one and all, are alien to the truth.
22 Who is the liar? Who but he that denies that Jesus is the Christ? He is
23 Antichrist, for he denies both the Father and the Son: to deny the Son is to be without the Father; to acknowledge the Son is to have the Father too.

a Or forgiven, since you bear his name.   *b Or* him whom we have known from the beginning.   *c Or* that none of them truly belong to us.
d Literally have an anointing (*Greek* chrism).   *e Some witnesses read* you have all knowledge.

You therefore must keep in your hearts that which you heard at the begin- 24
ning; if what you heard then still dwells in you, you will yourselves dwell
in the Son and also in the Father. And this is the promise that he himself 25
gave us, the promise of eternal life.

So much for those who would mislead you. But as for you, the initiation *a* 26 27
which you received from him stays with you; you need no other teacher,
but learn all you need to know from his initiation, which is real and no
illusion. As he taught you, then, dwell in him.

Even now, my children, dwell in him, so that when he appears we may 28
be confident and unashamed before him at his coming. If you know that he 29
is righteous, you must recognize that every man who does right is his child.
How great is the love that the Father has shown to us! We were called God's **3**
children, and such we are; *b* and the reason why the godless world does not
recognize us is that it has not known him. Here and now, dear friends, we 2
are God's children; what we shall be has not yet been disclosed, but we
know that when it is disclosed *c* we shall be like him, *d* because we shall see
him as he is. Everyone who has this hope before him purifies himself, as 3
Christ is pure.

To commit sin is to break God's law: sin, in fact, is lawlessness. Christ 4 5
appeared, as you know, to do away with sins, and there is no sin in him.
No man therefore who dwells in him is a sinner; the sinner has not seen 6
him and does not know him.

My children, do not be misled: it is the man who does right who is 7
righteous, as God is righteous; the man who sins is a child of the devil, 8
for the devil has been a sinner from the first; and the Son of God appeared
for the very purpose of undoing the devil's work.

A child of God does not commit sin, because the divine seed remains 9
in him; he cannot be a sinner, because he is God's child. That is the dis- 10
tinction between the children of God and the children of the devil: no one
who does not do right is God's child, nor is anyone who does not love his
brother. For the message you have heard from the beginning is this: that 11
we should love one another; unlike Cain, who was a child of the evil one 12
and murdered his brother. And why did he murder him? Because his own
actions were wrong, and his brother's were right.

My brothers, do not be surprised if the world hates you. We for our part 13 14
have crossed over from death to life; this we know, because we love our
brothers. The man who does not love is still in the realm of death, for 15
everyone who hates his brother is a murderer, and no murderer, as you
know, has eternal life dwelling within him. It is by this that we know what 16
love is: that Christ laid down his life for us. And we in our turn are bound
to lay down our lives for our brothers. But if a man has enough to live on, 17
and yet when he sees his brother in need shuts up his heart against him,
how can it be said that the divine love *e* dwells in him?

My children, love must not be a matter of words or talk; it must be 18

a Literally the anointing.   *b Or* We are called children of God! Not only
called, we really are his children.   *c Or* when he appears.   *d Or* we
are God's children, though he has not yet appeared; what we shall be we know, for when
he does appear we shall be like him.   *e Or* that love for God . . .

19 genuine, and show itself in action. This is how we may know that we belong
20 to the realm of truth, and convince ourselves in his sight that even if our
conscience condemns us, God is greater than our conscience [a] and knows all.

21 Dear friends, if our conscience does not condemn us, then we can ap-
22 proach God with confidence, and obtain from him whatever we ask, because
23 we are keeping his commands and doing what he approves. This is his
command: to give our allegiance to his Son Jesus Christ and love one
24 another as he commanded. When we keep his commands we dwell in him
and he dwells in us. And this is how we can make sure that he dwells within
us: we know it from the Spirit he has given us.

4 BUT DO NOT TRUST any and every spirit, my friends; test the spirits,
to see whether they are from God, for among those who have gone out into
2 the world there are many prophets falsely inspired. This is how we may
recognize the Spirit of God: every spirit which acknowledges that Jesus
3 Christ has come in the flesh is from God, and every spirit which does not
thus acknowledge Jesus is not from God. This is what is meant by 'Antichrist';[b] you have been told that he was to come, and here he is, in the
world already!

4 But you, my children, are of God's family, and you have the mastery
over these false prophets, because he who inspires you is greater than he
5 who inspires the godless world. They are of that world, and so therefore is
6 their teaching; that is why the world listens to them. But we belong to
God, and a man who knows God listens to us, while he who does not belong
to God refuses us a hearing. That is how we distinguish the spirit of truth
from the spirit of error.

7 Dear friends, let us love one another, because love is from God. Every-
8 one who loves is a child of God and knows God, but the unloving know
9 nothing of God. For God is love; and his love was disclosed to us in this,
10 that he sent his only Son into the world to bring us life. The love I speak
of is not our love for God, but the love he showed to us in sending his Son
11 as the remedy for the defilement of our sins. If God thus loved us, dear
12 friends, we in turn are bound to love one another. Though God has never
been seen by any man, God himself dwells in us if we love one another; his
love is brought to perfection within us.

13 Here is the proof that we dwell in him and he dwells in us: he has im-
14 parted his Spirit to us. Moreover, we have seen for ourselves, and we attest,
15 that the Father sent the Son to be the saviour of the world, and if a man
acknowledges that Jesus is the Son of God, God dwells in him and he dwells
16 in God. Thus we have come to know and believe the love which God
has for us.

God is love; he who dwells in love is dwelling in God, and God in him.
17 This is for us the perfection of love, to have confidence on the day of judgement, and this we can have, because even in this world we are as he is.

---

[a] *Or* and reassure ourselves in his sight in matters where our conscience condemns us,
because God is greater than our conscience . . .; *or* and yet we shall do well to convince
ourselves that if even our own conscience condemns us, still more will God who is greater
than conscience . . . [b] *Or* This is the spirit of Antichrist.

There is no room for fear in love; perfect love banishes fear. For fear brings 18
with it the pains of judgement, and anyone who is afraid has not attained
to love in its perfection. We love because he loved us first. But if a man says, 19 20
'I love God', while hating his brother, he is a liar. If he does not love the
brother whom he has seen, it cannot be that he loves God whom he has not
seen. And indeed this command comes to us from Christ himself: that 21
he who loves God must also love his brother.

Everyone who believes that Jesus is the Christ is a child of God, and to 5
love the parent means to love his child; it follows that when we love God 2
and obey his commands we love his children too. For to love God is to 3
keep his commands; and they are not burdensome, because every child of 4
God is victor over the godless world. The victory that defeats the world is
our faith, for who is victor over the world but he who believes that Jesus 5
is the Son of God?

This is he who came with water and blood: Jesus Christ. He came, not 6
by water alone, but by water and blood; and there is the Spirit to bear
witness, because the Spirit is truth. For there are three witnesses, the Spirit, 7 8
the water, and the blood, and these three are in agreement. We accept 9
human testimony, but surely divine testimony is stronger, and this three-
fold testimony is indeed that of God himself, the witness he has borne to his
Son. He who believes in the Son of God has this testimony in his own 10
heart, but he who disbelieves God, makes him out to be a liar, by refusing
to accept God's own witness to his Son. The witness is this: that God has 11
given us eternal life, and that this life is found in his Son. He who possesses 12
the Son has life indeed; he who does not possess the Son of God has not
that life.

THIS LETTER is to assure you that you have eternal life. It is addressed 13
to those who give their allegiance to the Son of God.

We can approach God with confidence for this reason: if we make 14
requests which accord with his will he listens to us; and if we know that 15
our requests are heard, we know also that the things we ask for are ours.

If a man sees his brother committing a sin which is not a deadly sin, he 16
should pray to God for him, and he will grant him life—that is, when men
are not guilty of deadly sin. There is such a thing as deadly sin, and I do
not suggest that he should pray about that; but although all wrongdoing is 17
sin, not all sin is deadly sin.

We know that no child of God is a sinner; it is the Son of God who keeps 18
him safe, and the evil one cannot touch him.

We know that we are of God's family, while the whole godless world lies 19
in the power of the evil one.

We know that the Son of God has come and given us understanding to 20
know him who is real; indeed we are in him who is real, since we are in his
Son Jesus Christ. This is the true God, this is eternal life. My children, be 21
on the watch against false gods.

309

THE SECOND LETTER OF
JOHN

Truth and love

1 THE ELDER to the Lady chosen by God, and her children, whom
2 I love in truth—and not I alone but all who know the truth—for
the sake of the truth that dwells among us and will be with us for ever.
3 Grace, mercy, and peace shall be with us from God the Father and from
Jesus Christ the Son of the Father, in truth and love.

4 I was delighted to find that some of your children are living by the truth,
5 as we were commanded by the Father. And now I have a request to make of
you. Do not think I am giving a new command; I am recalling the one we
6 have had before us from the beginning: let us love one another. And love
means following the commands of God. This is the command which was
given you from the beginning, to be your rule of life.

7 Many deceivers have gone out into the world, who do not acknowledge
Jesus Christ as coming in the flesh. These are the persons described as the
8 Antichrist, the arch-deceiver. Beware of them, so that you may not lose
all that we worked for, but receive your reward in full.

9 Anyone who runs ahead too far, and does not stand by the doctrine of
the Christ, is without God; he who stands by that doctrine possesses both
10 the Father and the Son. If anyone comes to you who does not bring this
11 doctrine, do not welcome him into your house or give him a greeting; for
anyone who gives him a greeting is an accomplice in his wicked deeds.

12 I have much to write to you, but I do not care to put it down in black and
white. But I hope to visit you and talk with you face to face, so that our joy
13 may be complete. The children of your Sister, chosen by God, send their
greetings.

THE THIRD LETTER OF
JOHN

Trouble in the church

THE ELDER to dear Gaius, whom I love in truth.   1
My dear Gaius, I pray that you may enjoy good health, and that   2
all may go well with you, as I know it goes well with your soul. I was   3
delighted when friends came and told me how true you have been; indeed
you are true in your whole life. Nothing gives me greater joy than to hear   4
that my children are living by the truth.

My dear friend, you show a fine loyalty in everything that you do for these   5
our fellow-Christians, strangers though they are to you. They have spoken   6
of your kindness before the congregation here. Please help them on their
journey in a manner worthy of the God we serve. It was on Christ's work   7
that they went out; and they would accept nothing from pagans. We are   8
bound to support such men, and so play our part in spreading the truth.

I sent a letter to the congregation, but Diotrephes, their would-be   9
leader,*a* will have nothing to do with us. If I come, I will bring up the   10
things he is doing. He lays baseless and spiteful charges against us; not
satisfied with that, he refuses to receive our friends, and he interferes with
those who would do so, and tries to expel them from the congregation.

My dear friend, do not imitate bad examples, but good ones. The well-   11
doer is a child of God; the evil-doer has never seen God.

Demetrius gets a good testimonial from everybody—yes, and from the   12
truth itself. I add my testimony, and you know that my testimony is true.

I have much to write to you, but I do not care to set it down with pen   13
and ink. I hope to see you very soon, and we will talk face to face. Peace   14
be with you. Our friends send their greetings. Greet our friends one by one.

a *Or* who enjoys being their leader.

A LETTER OF
JUDE

The danger of false belief

1 FROM JUDE, servant of Jesus Christ and brother of James, to those whom God has called, who live in the love of God the Father and in the safe keeping of Jesus Christ.

2 Mercy, peace, and love be yours in fullest measure.

3 My friends, I was fully engaged in writing to you about our salvation—which is yours no less than ours—when it became urgently necessary to write at once and appeal to you to join the struggle in defence of the faith,

4 the faith which God entrusted to his people once and for all. It is in danger from certain persons who have wormed their way in, the very men whom Scripture long ago marked down for the doom they have incurred. They are the enemies of religion; they pervert the free favour of our God into licentiousness, disowning Jesus Christ, our only Master and Lord.*a*

5 You already know it all, but let me remind you how the Lord,*b* having once delivered the people of Israel out of Egypt, next time destroyed those

6 who were guilty of unbelief. Remember too the angels, how some of them were not content to keep the dominion given to them but abandoned their proper home; and God has reserved them for judgement on the great Day,

7 bound beneath the darkness in everlasting chains. Remember Sodom and Gomorrah and the neighbouring towns; like the angels, they committed fornication and followed unnatural lusts; and they paid the penalty in eternal fire, an example for all to see.

8 So too with these men today. Their dreams lead them to defile the body,

9 to flout authority, and to insult celestial beings. In contrast, when the archangel Michael was in debate with the devil, disputing the possession of Moses's body, he did not presume to condemn him in insulting words,*c* but said, 'May the Lord rebuke you!'

10 But these men pour abuse upon things they do not understand; the things they do understand, by instinct like brute beasts, prove their un-

11 doing. Alas for them! They have gone the way of Cain; they have plunged into Balaam's error for pay; they have rebelled like Korah, and they share his doom.

12 These men are a blot on your love-feasts, where they eat and drink without reverence. They are shepherds who take care only of themselves. They are clouds carried away by the wind without giving rain, trees that in

---

a Or disowning our one and only Master, and Jesus Christ our Lord. *b* Some witnesses read Jesus (*which might be understood as* Joshua). *c* Or to charge him with blasphemy.

season bear no fruit, dead twice over and pulled up by the roots. They are 13
fierce waves of the sea, foaming shameful deeds; they are stars that have
wandered from their course, and the place for ever reserved for them is
blackest darkness.

It was to them that Enoch, the seventh in descent from Adam, directed 14
his prophecy when he said: 'I saw the Lord come with his myriads of
angels, to bring all men to judgement and to convict all the godless of all 15
the godless deeds they had committed, and of all the defiant words which
godless sinners had spoken against him.'

They are a set of grumblers and malcontents. They follow their lusts. 16
Big words come rolling from their lips, and they court favour to gain their
ends. But you, my friends, should remember the predictions made by the 17
apostles of our Lord Jesus Christ. This was the warning they gave you: 18
'In the final age there will be men who pour scorn on religion, and follow
their own godless lusts.'

These men draw a line between spiritual and unspiritual persons, 19
although they are themselves*a* wholly unspiritual. But you, my friends, 20
must fortify yourselves in your most sacred faith. Continue to pray in the
power of the Holy Spirit. Keep yourselves in the love of God, and look 21
forward to the day when our Lord Jesus Christ in his mercy will give
eternal life.

There are some doubting souls who need your pity;*b* snatch them from 22 23
the flames and save them.*c* There are others for whom your pity must be
mixed with fear; hate the very clothing that is contaminated with sensuality.

Now to the One who can keep you from falling and set you in the presence 24
of his glory, jubilant and above reproach, to the only God our Saviour, be 25
glory and majesty, might and authority, through Jesus Christ our Lord,
before all time, now, and for evermore. Amen.

a Or These men create divisions; they are . . .   *b Some witnesses read* There
are some who raise disputes; these you should refute.   *c So one witness; the rest*
read some you should snatch from the flames and save.

THE REVELATION
OF JOHN

THE REVELATION
OF JOHN

THIS IS THE REVELATION given by God to Jesus Christ. 1
It was given to him so that he might show his servants what must
shortly happen. He made it known by sending his angel to his servant
John, who, in telling all that he saw, has borne witness to the word of God 2
and to the testimony of Jesus Christ.[a]

Happy is the man who reads, and happy those who listen to the words of 3
this prophecy and heed what is written in it. For the hour of fulfilment
is near.

A message from Christ to the churches

JOHN TO THE SEVEN CHURCHES in the province of Asia. 4
Grace be to you and peace, from him who is and who was and who is
to come, from the seven spirits before his throne, and from Jesus Christ, 5
the faithful witness, the first-born from the dead and ruler of the kings of
the earth.

To him who loves us and freed us from our sins with his life's blood,
who made of us a royal house, to serve as the priests of his God and Father 6
—to him be glory and dominion for ever and ever! Amen.

Behold, he is coming with the clouds! Every eye shall see him, and 7
among them those who pierced him; and all the peoples of the world shall
lament in remorse. So it shall be. Amen.

'I am the Alpha and the Omega', says the Lord God, who is and who 8
was and who is to come, the sovereign Lord of all.

I, John, your brother, who share with you in the suffering and the 9
sovereignty and the endurance which is ours in Jesus—I was on the island
called Patmos because I had preached God's word and borne my testimony
to Jesus. It was on the Lord's day, and I was caught up by the Spirit; and 10
behind me I heard a loud voice, like the sound of a trumpet, which said to 11
me, 'Write down what you see on a scroll and send it to the seven churches:
to Ephesus, Smyrna, Pergamum, Thyatira, Sardis, Philadelphia, and
Laodicea.' I turned to see whose voice it was that spoke to me; and when I 12
turned I saw seven standing lamps of gold, and among the lamps one like 13
a son of man, robed down to his feet, with a golden girdle round his breast.
The hair of his head was white as snow-white wool, and his eyes flamed like 14
fire; his feet gleamed like burnished brass refined in a furnace, and his 15
voice was like the sound of rushing waters. In his right hand he held seven 16

[a] Or has borne his testimony to the word of God and to Jesus Christ.

stars, and out of his mouth came a sharp two-edged sword; and his face
shone like the sun in full strength.

17   When I saw him, I fell at his feet as though dead. But he laid his right
18 hand upon me and said, 'Do not be afraid. I am the first and the last, and
I am the living one; for I was dead and now I am alive for evermore, and
19 I hold the keys of Death and Death's domain. Write down therefore what
you have seen, what is now, and what will be hereafter.
20   'Here is the secret meaning of the seven stars which you saw in my right
hand, and of the seven lamps of gold: the seven stars are the angels of the
seven churches, and the seven lamps are the seven churches.

2 'To the angel of the church at Ephesus write:
    ' "These are the words of the One who holds the seven stars in his right
2 hand and walks among the seven lamps of gold: I know all your ways,
your toil and your fortitude. I know you cannot endure evil men; you have
put to the proof those who claim to be apostles but are not, and have found
3 them false. Fortitude you have; you have borne up in my cause and never
4 5 flagged. But I have this against you: you have lost your early love. Think
from what a height you have fallen; repent, and do as you once did. Otherwise, if you do not repent, I shall come to you and remove your lamp from
6 its place. Yet you have this in your favour: you hate the practices of the
7 Nicolaitans, as I do. Hear, you who have ears to hear, what the Spirit says
to the churches! To him who is victorious I will give the right to eat from
the tree of life that stands in the Garden of God."
8   'To the angel of the church at Smyrna write:
    ' "These are the words of the First and the Last, who was dead and
9 came to life again: I know how hard pressed you are, and poor—and yet
you are rich; I know how you are slandered by those who claim to be Jews
10 but are not—they are Satan's synagogue. Do not be afraid of the suffering
to come. The Devil will throw some of you into prison, to put you to the
test; and for ten days you will suffer cruelly. Only be faithful till death,
11 and I will give you the crown of life. Hear, you who have ears to hear, what
the Spirit says to the churches! He who is victorious cannot be harmed by
the second death."
12   'To the angel of the church at Pergamum write:
    ' "These are the words of the One who has the sharp two-edged sword:
13 I know where you live; it is the place where Satan has his throne. And yet
you are holding fast to my cause. You did not deny your faith in me even
at the time when Antipas, my faithful witness, was killed in your city, the
14 home of Satan. But I have a few matters to bring against you: you have in
Pergamum some that hold to the teaching of Balaam, who taught Balak
to put temptation in the way of the Israelites. He encouraged them to eat
15 food sacrificed to idols and to commit fornication, and in the same way you
16 also have some who hold the doctrine of the Nicolaitans. So repent! If
you do not, I shall come to you soon and make war upon them with the
17 sword that comes out of my mouth. Hear, you who have ears to hear,
what the Spirit says to the churches! To him who is victorious I will
give some of the hidden manna; I will give him also a white stone, and

on the stone will be written a new name, known to none but him that receives it."

'To the angel of the church at Thyatira write: 18

' "These are the words of the Son of God, whose eyes flame like fire and whose feet gleam like burnished brass: I know all your ways, your love and 19 faithfulness, your good service and your fortitude; and of late you have done even better than at first. Yet I have this against you: you tolerate that 20 Jezebel, the woman who claims to be a prophetess, who by her teaching lures my servants into fornication and into eating food sacrificed to idols. I have given her time to repent, but she refuses to repent of her fornication. 21 So I will throw her on to a bed of pain,*a* and plunge her lovers into terrible 22 suffering, unless they forswear what she is doing; and her children I will 23 strike dead. This will teach all the churches that I am the searcher of men's hearts and thoughts, and that I will reward each one of you according to his deeds. And now I speak to you others in Thyatira, who do not accept 24 this teaching and have had no experience of what they like to call the deep secrets of Satan; on you I will impose no further burden. Only hold fast to 25 what you have, until I come. To him who is victorious, to him who per- 26 severes in doing my will to the end, I will give authority over the nations— that same authority which I received from my Father—and he shall rule 27 them with an iron rod, smashing them to bits like earthenware; and I will 28 give him also the star of dawn. Hear, you who have ears to hear, what the 29 Spirit says to the churches!"

'To the angel of the church at Sardis write: 3

' "These are the words of the One who holds the seven spirits of God, the seven stars: I know all your ways; that though you have a name for being alive, you are dead. Wake up, and put some strength into what is left, 2 which must otherwise die! For I have not found any work of yours com- pleted in the eyes of my God. So remember the teaching you received; 3 observe it, and repent. If you do not wake up, I shall come upon you like a thief, and you will not know the moment of my coming. Yet you have a few 4 persons in Sardis who have not polluted their clothing. They shall walk with me in white, for so they deserve. He who is victorious shall thus be 5 robed all in white; his name I will never strike off the roll of the living, for in the presence of my Father and his angels I will acknowledge him as mine. Hear, you who have ears to hear, what the Spirit says to the churches!"' 6

'To the angel of the church at Philadelphia write: 7

' "These are the words of the holy one, the true one, who holds the key of David; when he opens none may shut, when he shuts none may open: I know all your ways; and look, I have set before you an open door, which 8 no one can shut. Your strength, I know, is small, yet you have observed my commands and have not disowned my name. So this is what I will do: 9 I will make those of Satan's synagogue, who claim to be Jews but are lying frauds, come and fall down at your feet; and they shall know that you are my beloved people. Because you have kept my command and stood fast, I will 10 also keep you from the ordeal that is to fall upon the whole world and test its inhabitants. I am coming soon; hold fast what you have, and let no one 11

---

a One witness reads into a furnace.

12 rob you of your crown. He who is victorious—I will make him a pillar in
the temple of my God; he shall never leave it. And I will write the name of
my God upon him, and the name of the city of my God, that new Jerusalem which is coming down out of heaven from my God, and my own new

13 name. Hear, you who have ears to hear, what the Spirit says to the
churches!"

14   'To the angel of the church at Laodicea write:
       ' "These are the words of the Amen, the faithful and true witness, the

15 prime source of all God's creation: I know all your ways; you are neither

16 hot nor cold. How I wish you were either hot or cold! But because you are

17 lukewarm, neither hot nor cold, I will spit you out of my mouth. You say,
'How rich I am! And how well I have done! I have everything I want.'
In fact, though you do not know it, you are the most pitiful wretch, poor,

18 blind, and naked. So I advise you to buy from me gold refined in the fire, to
make you truly rich, and white clothes to put on to hide the shame of your

19 nakedness, and ointment for your eyes so that you may see. All whom I
love I reprove and discipline. Be on your mettle therefore and repent.

20 Here I stand knocking at the door; if anyone hears my voice and opens the

21 door, I will come in and sit down to supper with him and he with me. To
him who is victorious I will grant a place on my throne, as I myself was

22 victorious and sat down with my Father on his throne. Hear, you who have
ears to hear, what the Spirit says to the churches!" '

The opening of the sealed book

4 AFTER THIS I LOOKED, and there before my eyes was a door opened
in heaven; and the voice that I had first heard speaking to me like a
trumpet said, 'Come up here, and I will show you what must happen here-

2 after.' At once I was caught up by the Spirit. There in heaven stood a

3 throne, and on the throne sat one whose appearance was like the gleam of
jasper and cornelian; and round the throne was a rainbow, bright as an

4 emerald. In a circle about this throne were twenty-four other thrones, and
on them sat twenty-four elders, robed in white and wearing crowns of gold.

5 From the throne went out flashes of lightning and peals of thunder. Burning before the throne were seven flaming torches, the seven spirits of God,

6 and in front of it stretched what seemed a sea of glass, like a sheet of ice.
In the centre, round the throne itself, were four living creatures, covered

7 with eyes, in front and behind. The first creature was like a lion, the second
like an ox, the third had a human face, the fourth was like an eagle in flight.

8 The four living creatures, each of them with six wings, had eyes all over,
inside and out; and by day and by night without a pause they sang:

'Holy, holy, holy is God the sovereign Lord of all, who was, and is, and
is to come!'

9   As often as the living creatures give glory and honour and thanks to the

10 One who sits on the throne, who lives for ever and ever, the twenty-four
elders fall down before the One who sits on the throne and worship him

who lives for ever and ever; and as they lay their crowns before the throne
they cry:

> 'Thou art worthy, O Lord our God, to receive glory and honour and 11
> power, because thou didst create all things; by thy will they were
> created, and have their being!'

Then I saw in the right hand of the One who sat on the throne a scroll, 5
with writing inside and out, and it was sealed up with seven seals. And I 2
saw a mighty angel proclaiming in a loud voice, 'Who is worthy to open the
scroll and to break its seals?' There was no one in heaven or on earth or 3
under the earth able to open the scroll or to look inside it. I was in tears 4
because no one was found who was worthy to open the scroll or to look
inside it. But one of the elders said to me: 'Do not weep; for the Lion from 5
the tribe of Judah, the Scion of David, has won the right to open the scroll
and break its seven seals.'

Then I saw standing in the very middle of the throne, inside the circle 6
of living creatures and the circle of elders,*a* a Lamb with the marks of
slaughter upon him. He had seven horns and seven eyes, the eyes which are
the seven spirits of God sent out over all the world. And the Lamb went 7
up and took the scroll from the right hand of the One who sat on the throne.
When he took it, the four living creatures and the twenty-four elders fell 8
down before the Lamb. Each of the elders had a harp, and they held golden
bowls full of incense, the prayers of God's people, and they were singing a 9
new song:

> 'Thou art worthy to take the scroll and to break its seals, for thou wast
> slain and by thy blood didst purchase for God men of every tribe and
> language, people and nation; thou hast made of them a royal house, to 10
> serve our God as priests; and they shall reign upon earth.'

Then as I looked I heard the voices of countless angels. These were all 11
round the throne and the living creatures and the elders. Myriads upon
myriads there were, thousands upon thousands, and they cried aloud: 12

> 'Worthy is the Lamb, the Lamb that was slain, to receive all power and
> wealth, wisdom and might, honour and glory and praise!'

Then I heard every created thing in heaven and on earth and under the 13
earth and in the sea, all that is in them, crying:

> 'Praise and honour, glory and might, to him who sits on the throne and
> to the Lamb for ever and ever!'

And the four living creatures said, 'Amen', and the elders fell down and 14
worshipped.

THEN I WATCHED as the Lamb broke the first of the seven seals; and I 6
heard one of the four living creatures say in a voice like thunder, 'Come!'
And there before my eyes was a white horse, and its rider held a bow. He 2
was given a crown, and he rode forth, conquering and to conquer.

a Or standing between the throne, with the four living creatures, and the elders . . .

3 When the Lamb broke the second seal, I heard the second creature say,
4 'Come!' And out came another horse, all red. To its rider was given power to take peace from the earth and make men slaughter one another; and he was given a great sword.

5 When he broke the third seal, I heard the third creature say, 'Come!' And there, as I looked, was a black horse; and its rider held in his hand a
6 pair of scales. And I heard what sounded like a voice from the midst of the living creatures, which said, 'A whole day's wage for a quart of flour, a whole day's wage for three quarts of barley-meal! But spare the olive and the vine.'

7 When he broke the fourth seal, I heard the voice of the fourth creature
8 say, 'Come!' And there, as I looked, was another horse, sickly pale; and its rider's name was Death, and Hades came close behind. To him was given power over a quarter of the earth, with the right to kill by sword and by famine, by pestilence and wild beasts.

9 When he broke the fifth seal, I saw underneath[a] the altar the souls of those who had been slaughtered for God's word and for the testimony they
10 bore. They gave a great cry: 'How long, sovereign Lord, holy and true, must it be before thou wilt vindicate us and avenge our blood on the
11 inhabitants of the earth?' Each of them was given a white robe; and they were told to rest a little while longer, until the tally should be complete of all their brothers in Christ's service who were to be killed as they had been.

12 Then I watched as he broke the sixth seal. And there was a violent earthquake; the sun turned black as a funeral pall and the moon all red as blood;
13 14 the stars in the sky fell to the earth, like figs shaken down by a gale; the sky vanished, as a scroll is rolled up, and every mountain and island was moved
15 from its place. Then the kings of the earth, magnates and marshals, the rich and the powerful, and all men, slave or free, hid themselves in caves and
16 mountain crags; and they called out to the mountains and the crags, 'Fall on us and hide us from the face of the One who sits on the throne and from
17 the vengeance of the Lamb.' For the great day of their vengeance has come, and who will be able to stand?

7 After this I saw four angels stationed at the four corners of the earth, holding back the four winds so that no wind should blow on sea or land
2 or on any tree. Then I saw another angel rising out of the east, carrying the seal of the living God; and he called aloud to the four angels who had been
3 given the power to ravage land and sea: 'Do no damage to sea or land or trees until we have set the seal of our God upon the foreheads of his
4 servants.' And I heard the number of those who had received the seal. From all the tribes of Israel there were a hundred and forty-four thousand:
5 twelve thousand from the tribe of Judah, twelve thousand from the tribe
6 of Reuben, twelve thousand from the tribe of Gad, twelve thousand from the tribe of Asher, twelve thousand from the tribe of Naphtali, twelve
7 thousand from the tribe of Manasseh, twelve thousand from the tribe of Simeon, twelve thousand from the tribe of Levi, twelve thousand from
8 the tribe of Issachar, twelve thousand from the tribe of Zebulun, twelve

---

[a] *Or* at the foot of . . .

thousand from the tribe of Joseph, and twelve thousand from the tribe of
Benjamin.

After this I looked and saw a vast throng, which no one could count, 9
from every nation, of all tribes, peoples, and languages, standing in front
of the throne and before the Lamb. They were robed in white and had
palms in their hands, and they shouted together: 10

'Victory to our God who sits on the throne, and to the Lamb!'

And all the angels stood round the throne and the elders and the four 11
living creatures, and they fell on their faces before the throne and worshipped God, crying: 12

'Amen! Praise and glory and wisdom, thanksgiving and honour, power
and might, be to our God for ever and ever! Amen.'

Then one of the elders turned to me and said, 'These men that are robed 13
in white—who are they and from where do they come?' But I answered, 14
'My lord, you know, not I.' Then he said to me, 'These are the men who
have passed through the great ordeal; they have washed their robes and
made them white in the blood of the Lamb. That is why they stand before 15
the throne of God and minister to him day and night in his temple; and he
who sits on the throne will dwell with them. They shall never again feel 16
hunger or thirst, the sun shall not beat on them nor any scorching heat,
because the Lamb who is at the heart of the throne will be their shepherd 17
and will guide them to the springs of the water of life; and God will wipe all
tears from their eyes.'

Now when the Lamb broke the seventh seal, there was silence in heaven 8
for what seemed half an hour. Then I looked, and the seven angels that 2
stand in the presence of God were given seven trumpets.

Then another angel came and stood at the altar, holding a golden censer; 3
and he was given a great quantity of incense to offer with the prayers of all
God's people upon the golden altar in front of the throne. And from the 4
angel's hand the smoke of the incense went up before God with the prayers
of his people. Then the angel took the censer, filled it from the altar fire, 5
and threw it down upon the earth; and there were peals of thunder, lightning, and an earthquake.

The powers of darkness conquered

THEN THE SEVEN ANGELS that held the seven trumpets prepared to 6
blow them.

The first blew his trumpet; and there came hail and fire mingled with 7
blood, and this was hurled upon the earth. A third of the earth was burnt,
a third of the trees were burnt, all the green grass was burnt.

The second angel blew his trumpet; and what looked like a great blazing 8
mountain was hurled into the sea. A third of the sea was turned to blood,
a third of the living creatures in it died, and a third of the ships on it 9
foundered.

10 The third angel blew his trumpet; and a great star shot from the sky,
11 flaming like a torch; and it fell on a third of the rivers and springs. The name of the star was Wormwood; and a third of the water turned to wormwood, and men in great numbers died of the water because it had been poisoned.

12 The fourth angel blew his trumpet; and a third part of the sun was struck, a third of the moon, and a third of the stars, so that the third part went dark and a third of the light of the day failed, and of the night.

13 Then I looked, and I heard an eagle calling with a loud cry as it flew in mid-heaven: 'Woe, woe, woe to the inhabitants of the earth when the trumpets sound which the three last angels must now blow!'

9 Then the fifth angel blew his trumpet; and I saw a star that had fallen from heaven to earth, and the star was given the key of the shaft of the
2 abyss. With this he opened the shaft of the abyss; and from the shaft smoke rose like smoke from a great furnace, and the sun and the air were darkened
3 by the smoke from the shaft. Then over the earth, out of the smoke, came
4 locusts, and they were given the powers that earthly scorpions have. They were told to do no injury to the grass or to any plant or tree, but only to
5 those men who had not received the seal of God on their foreheads. These they were allowed to torment for five months, with torment like a scorpion's
6 sting; but they were not to kill them. During that time these men will seek death, but they will not find it; they will long to die, but death will elude them.

7 In appearance the locusts were like horses equipped for battle. On their heads were what looked like golden crowns; their faces were like human
8 9 faces and their hair like women's hair; they had teeth like lions' teeth, and wore breastplates like iron; the sound of their wings was like the noise of
10 horses and chariots rushing to battle; they had tails like scorpions, with stings in them, and in their tails lay their power to plague mankind for five
11 months. They had for their king the angel of the abyss, whose name, in Hebrew, is Abaddon, and in Greek, Apollyon, or the Destroyer.

12 The first woe has now passed. But there are still two more to come.

13 The sixth angel then blew his trumpet; and I heard a voice coming from between the horns of the golden altar that stood in the presence of God.
14 It said to the sixth angel, who held the trumpet: 'Release the four angels
15 held bound at the great river Euphrates!' So the four angels were let loose, to kill a third of mankind. They had been held ready for this moment, for
16 this very year and month, day and hour. And their squadrons of cavalry, whose count I heard, numbered two hundred million.

17 This was how I saw the horses and their riders in my vision: They wore breastplates, fiery red, blue, and sulphur-yellow; the horses had heads like lions' heads, and out of their mouths came fire, smoke, and sulphur.
18 By these three plagues, that is, by the fire, the smoke, and the sulphur that
19 came from their mouths, a third of mankind was killed. The power of the horses lay in their mouths, and in their tails also; for their tails were like snakes, with heads, and with them too they dealt injuries.

20 The rest of mankind who survived these plagues still did not abjure the gods their hands had fashioned, nor cease their worship of devils and of

idols made from gold, silver, bronze, stone, and wood, which cannot see or hear or walk. Nor did they repent of their murders, their sorcery, their 21 fornication, or their robberies.

THEN I SAW another mighty angel coming down from heaven. He was 10 wrapped in cloud, with the rainbow round his head; his face shone like the sun and his legs were like pillars of fire. In his hand he held a little scroll 2 unrolled. His right foot he planted on the sea, and his left on the land. Then 3 he gave a great shout, like the roar of a lion; and when he shouted, the seven thunders spoke. I was about to write down what the seven thunders had 4 said; but I heard a voice from heaven saying, 'Seal up what the seven thunders have said; do not write it down.' Then the angel that I saw stand- 5 ing on the sea and the land raised his right hand to heaven and swore by him 6 who lives for ever and ever, who created heaven and earth and the sea and everything in them: 'There shall be no more delay; but when the time 7 comes for the seventh angel to sound his trumpet, the hidden purpose of God will have been fulfilled, as he promised to his servants the prophets.'

Then the voice which I heard from heaven was speaking to me again, 8 and it said, 'Go and take the open scroll in the hand of the angel that stands on the sea and the land.' So I went to the angel and asked him to give me the 9 little scroll. He said to me, 'Take it, and eat it. It will turn your stomach sour, although in your mouth it will taste sweet as honey.' So I took the little 10 scroll from the angel's hand and ate it, and in my mouth it did taste sweet as honey; but when I swallowed it my stomach turned sour.

Then they said to me, 'Once again you must utter prophecies over 11 peoples and nations and languages and many kings.'

I was given a long cane, a kind of measuring-rod, and told: 'Now go and 11 measure the temple of God, the altar, and the number of the worshippers. But have nothing to do with the outer court of the temple; do not measure 2 that; for it has been given over to the Gentiles, and they will trample the Holy City underfoot for forty-two months. And I have two witnesses, 3 whom I will appoint to prophesy, dressed in sackcloth, all through those twelve hundred and sixty days.' These are the two olive-trees and the two 4 lamps that stand in the presence of the Lord of the earth. If anyone seeks 5 to do them harm, fire pours from their mouths and consumes their enemies; and thus shall the man die who seeks to do them harm. These two have the 6 power to shut up the sky, so that no rain may fall during the time of their prophesying; and they have the power to turn water to blood and to strike the earth at will with every kind of plague. But when they have completed 7 their testimony, the beast that comes up from the abyss will wage war upon them and will defeat and kill them. Their corpses will lie in the street of the 8 great city, whose name in allegory is Sodom, or Egypt, where also their Lord was crucified. For three days and a half men from every people and 9 tribe, of every language and nation, gaze upon their corpses and refuse them burial. All men on earth gloat over them, make merry, and exchange pre- 10 sents; for these two prophets were a torment to the whole earth. But at the 11 end of the three days and a half the breath of life from God came into them; and they stood up on their feet to the terror of all who saw it. Then a loud 12 voice was heard speaking to them from heaven, which said, 'Come up here!' And they went up to heaven in a cloud, in full view of their enemies.

13 At that same moment there was a violent earthquake, and a tenth of the city fell. Seven thousand people were killed in the earthquake; the rest in terror did homage to the God of heaven.

14 The second woe has now passed. But the third is soon to come.

15 Then the seventh angel blew his trumpet; and voices were heard in heaven shouting:

'The sovereignty of the world has passed to our Lord and his Christ, and he shall reign for ever and ever!'

16 And the twenty-four elders, seated on their thrones before God, fell on
17 their faces and worshipped God, saying:

'We give thee thanks, O Lord God, sovereign over all, who art and who wast, because thou hast taken thy great power into thy hands and
18 entered upon thy reign. The nations raged, but thy day of retribution has come. Now is the time for the dead to be judged; now is the time for recompense to thy servants the prophets, to thy dedicated people, and all who honour thy name, both great and small, the time to destroy those who destroy the earth.'

19 Then God's temple in heaven was laid open, and within the temple was seen the ark of his covenant. There came flashes of lightning and peals of thunder, an earthquake, and a storm of hail.

12 NEXT APPEARED a great portent in heaven, a woman robed with the sun, beneath her feet the moon, and on her head a crown of twelve stars.
2 She was pregnant, and in the anguish of her labour she cried out to be
3 delivered. Then a second portent appeared in heaven: a great red dragon
4 with seven heads and ten horns; on his heads were seven diadems, and with his tail he swept down a third of the stars in the sky and flung them to the earth. The dragon stood in front of the woman who was about to give
5 birth, so that when her child was born he might devour it. She gave birth to a male child, who is destined to rule all nations with an iron rod. But her
6 child was snatched up to God and his throne; and the woman herself fled into the wilds, where she had a place prepared for her by God, there to be sustained for twelve hundred and sixty days.

7 Then war broke out in heaven. Michael and his angels waged war upon
8 the dragon. The dragon and his angels fought, but they had not the
9 strength to win, and no foothold was left them in heaven. So the great dragon was thrown down, that serpent of old that led the whole world astray, whose name is Satan, or the Devil—thrown down to the earth, and his angels with him.

10 Then I heard a voice in heaven proclaiming aloud: 'This is the hour of victory for our God, the hour of his sovereignty and power, when his Christ comes to his rightful rule! For the accuser of our brothers is overthrown,
11 who day and night accused them before our God. By the sacrifice of the

Lamb they have conquered him, and by the testimony which they uttered;[a] for they did not hold their lives too dear to lay them down. Rejoice then, 12 you heavens and you that dwell in them! But woe to you, earth and sea, for the Devil has come down to you in great fury, knowing that his time is short!'

When the dragon found that he had been thrown down to the earth, he 13 went in pursuit of the woman who had given birth to the male child. But 14 the woman was given two great eagle's wings, to fly to the place in the wilds where for three years and a half she was to be sustained, out of reach of the serpent. From his mouth the serpent spewed a flood of water after the 15 woman to sweep her away with its spate. But the earth came to her rescue 16 and opened its mouth and swallowed the river which the dragon spewed from his mouth. At this the dragon grew furious with the woman, and went 17 off to wage war on the rest of her offspring, that is, on those who keep God's commandments and maintain their testimony to Jesus. He took his stand **13** on the sea-shore.

Then[b] out of the sea I saw a beast rising. It had ten horns and seven heads. On its horns were ten diadems, and on each head a blasphemous name. The beast I saw was like a leopard, but its feet were like a bear's and 2 its mouth like a lion's mouth. The dragon conferred upon it his power and rule, and great authority. One of its heads appeared to have received a 3 death-blow; but the mortal wound was healed. The whole world went after the beast in wondering admiration. Men worshipped the dragon because 4 he had conferred his authority upon the beast; they worshipped the beast also, and chanted, 'Who is like the Beast? Who can fight against it?'

The beast was allowed to mouth bombast and blasphemy, and was given 5 the right to reign for forty-two months. It opened its mouth in blasphemy 6 against God, reviling his name and his heavenly dwelling.[c] It was also 7 allowed to wage war on God's people and to defeat them, and was granted[d] authority over every tribe and people, language and nation. All on earth 8 will worship it, except those whose names the Lamb that was slain keeps in his roll of the living, written there since the world was made.

Hear, you who have ears to hear! Whoever is to be made prisoner, a 9 10 prisoner he shall be. Whoever takes the sword to kill, by the sword he is bound to be killed. This is where the fortitude and faithfulness of God's people have their place.

Then I saw another beast, which came up out of the earth; it had two 11 horns like a lamb's, but spoke like a dragon. It wielded all the authority of 12 the first beast in its presence, and made the earth and its inhabitants worship this first beast, whose mortal wound had been healed. It worked 13 great miracles, even making fire come down from heaven to earth before men's eyes. By the miracles it was allowed to perform in the presence of 14 the beast it deluded the inhabitants of the earth, and made them erect an image in honour of the beast that had been wounded by the sword and yet

---

[a] *Or* the word of God to which they bore witness.   [b] *Some witnesses read* . . . testimony to Jesus. Then I stood by the sea-shore and . . .   [c] *Some witnesses read* reviling his name and his dwelling-place, that is, those that live in heaven. [d] *Some witnesses read* It was granted . . . (*omitting the words* was also . . . them, and).

15 lived. It was allowed to give breath to the image of the beast, so that it could
speak, and could cause all who would not worship the image to be put to
16 death. Moreover, it caused everyone, great and small, rich and poor, slave
17 and free, to be branded with a mark on his right hand or forehead, and no
one was allowed to buy or sell unless he bore this beast's mark, either name
18 or number. (Here is the key; and anyone who has intelligence may work out
the number of the beast. The number represents a man's name, and the
numerical value of its letters is six hundred and sixty-six.)

Visions of the end

14 THEN I LOOKED, and on Mount Zion stood the Lamb, and with him
were a hundred and forty-four thousand who had his name and the
2 name of his Father written on their foreheads. I heard a sound from heaven
like the noise of rushing water and the deep roar of thunder; it was the
3 sound of harpers playing on their harps. There before the throne, and the
four living creatures and the elders, they were singing a new song. That
song no one could learn except the hundred and forty-four thousand, who
4 alone from the whole world had been ransomed. These are men who did
not defile themselves with women, for they have kept themselves chaste,
and they follow the Lamb wherever he goes. They have been ransomed as
5 the firstfruits of humanity for God and the Lamb. No lie was found in their
lips; they are faultless.
6   Then I saw an angel flying in mid-heaven, with an eternal gospel to
proclaim to those on earth, to every nation and tribe, language and people.
7 He cried in a loud voice, 'Fear God and pay him homage; for the hour of
his judgement has come! Worship him who made heaven and earth, the
sea and the water-springs!'
8   Then another angel, a second, followed, and he cried, 'Fallen, fallen is
Babylon the great, she who has made all nations drink the fierce wine of*a*
her fornication!'
9   Yet a third angel followed, crying out loud, 'Whoever worships the
10 beast and its image and receives its mark on his forehead or hand, he shall
drink the wine of God's wrath, poured undiluted into the cup of his
vengeance. He shall be tormented in sulphurous flames before the holy
11 angels and before the Lamb. The smoke of their torment will rise for ever
and ever, and there will be no respite day or night for those who worship
12 the beast and its image or receive the mark of its name.' This is where the
fortitude of God's people has its place—in keeping God's commands and
remaining loyal to Jesus.
13   Moreover, I heard a voice from heaven, saying, 'Write this: "Happy
are the dead who die in the faith of Christ! Henceforth",*b* says the Spirit,*c*
"they may rest from their labours; for they take with them the record of
their deeds."'

---

a Or drink the wine of God's wrath upon . . .   *b Or* Assuredly.   *c Some
witnesses read* ". . . the dead who henceforth die in the faith of Christ!" "Yes," *says the*
Spirit . . .

Then as I looked there appeared a white cloud, and on the cloud sat one 14
like a son of man. He had on his head a crown of gold and in his hand a
sharp sickle. Another angel came out of the temple and called in a loud 15
voice to him who sat on the cloud: 'Stretch out your sickle and reap; for
harvest-time has come, and earth's crop is over-ripe.' So he who sat on the 16
cloud put his sickle to the earth and its harvest was reaped.

Then another angel came out of the heavenly temple, and he also had a 17
sharp sickle. Then from the altar came yet another, the angel who has 18
authority over fire, and he shouted to the one with the sharp sickle:
'Stretch out your sickle, and gather in earth's grape-harvest, for its clusters
are ripe.' So the angel put his sickle to the earth and gathered in its grapes, 19
and threw them into the great winepress of God's wrath. The winepress 20
was trodden outside the city, and for two hundred miles around blood
flowed from the press to the height of the horses' bridles.

Then I saw another great and astonishing portent in heaven: seven angels **15**
with seven plagues, the last plagues of all, for with them the wrath of God
is consummated.

I saw what seemed a sea of glass shot with fire, and beside the sea of 2
glass, holding the harps which God had given them, were those who had
won the victory over the beast and its image and the number of its name.
They were singing the song of Moses, the servant of God, and the song 3
of the Lamb, as they chanted:

'Great and marvellous are thy deeds, O Lord God, sovereign over all;
just and true are thy ways, thou king of the ages.*a* Who shall not revere 4
thee, Lord, and do homage to thy name? For thou alone art holy. All
nations shall come and worship in thy presence, for thy just dealings
stand revealed.'

After this, as I looked, the sanctuary of the heavenly Tent of Testimony 5
was thrown open, and out of it came the seven angels with the seven plagues. 6
They were robed in fine linen, clean and shining, and had golden girdles
round their breasts. Then one of the four living creatures gave the seven 7
angels seven golden bowls full of the wrath of God who lives for ever and
ever; and the sanctuary was filled with smoke from the glory of God and 8
his power, so that no one could enter it until the seven plagues of the seven
angels were completed.

Then from the sanctuary I heard a loud voice, and it said to the seven **16**
angels, 'Go and pour out the seven bowls of God's wrath on the earth.'

So the first angel went and poured his bowl on the earth; and foul 2
malignant sores appeared on those men that wore the mark of the beast
and worshipped its image.

The second angel poured his bowl on the sea, and it turned to blood like 3
the blood from a corpse; and every living thing in the sea died.

The third angel poured his bowl on the rivers and springs, and they 4
turned to blood.

Then I heard the angel of the waters say, 'Just art thou in these thy 5
judgements, thou Holy One who art and wast; for they shed the blood of 6

a Some witnesses read king of the nations.

thy people and of thy prophets, and thou hast given them blood to drink.
7 They have their deserts!' And I heard the altar cry, 'Yes, Lord God, sovereign over all, true and just are thy judgements!'
8   The fourth angel poured his bowl on the sun; and it was allowed to burn
9 men with its flames. They were fearfully burned; but they only cursed the name of God who had the power to inflict such plagues, and they refused to repent or do him homage.
10 The fifth angel poured his bowl on the throne of the beast; and its kingdom was plunged in darkness. Men gnawed their tongues in agony,
11 but they only cursed the God of heaven for their sores and pains, and would not repent of what they had done.
12 The sixth angel poured his bowl on the great river Euphrates; and its water was dried up, to prepare the way for the kings from the east.
13 Then I saw coming from the mouth of the dragon, the mouth of the beast, and the mouth of the false prophet, three foul spirits like frogs.
14 These spirits were devils, with power to work miracles. They were sent out to muster all the kings of the world for the great day of battle of God
15 the sovereign Lord. ('That is the day when I come like a thief! Happy the man who stays awake and keeps on his clothes, so that he will not have to go
16 naked and ashamed for all to see!') So they assembled the kings at the place called in Hebrew Armageddon.
17 Then the seventh angel poured his bowl on the air; and out of the
18 sanctuary came a loud voice from the throne, which said, 'It is over!' And there followed flashes of lightning and peals of thunder, and a violent
19 earthquake, like none before it in human history, so violent it was. The great city was split in three; the cities of the world fell in ruin; and God did not forget Babylon the great, but made her drink the cup which was
20 filled with the fierce wine of his vengeance. Every island vanished; there
21 was not a mountain to be seen. Huge hailstones, weighing perhaps a hundredweight, fell on men from the sky; and they cursed God for the plague of hail, because that plague was so severe.

17 THEN ONE OF THE SEVEN ANGELS that held the seven bowls came and spoke to me and said, 'Come, and I will show you the judgement on the
2 great whore, enthroned above the ocean. The kings of the earth have committed fornication with her, and on the wine of her fornication men all over
3 the world have made themselves drunk.' In the Spirit he carried me away into the wilds, and there I saw a woman mounted on a scarlet beast which was covered with blasphemous names and had seven heads and ten horns.
4 The woman was clothed in purple and scarlet and bedizened with gold and jewels and pearls. In her hand she held a gold cup, full of obscenities and
5 the foulness of her fornication; and written on her forehead was a name with a secret meaning: 'Babylon the great, the mother of whores and of
6 every obscenity on earth.' The woman, I saw, was drunk with the blood of God's people and with the blood of those who had borne their testimony to Jesus.
7   As I looked at her I was greatly astonished. But the angel said to me, 'Why are you so astonished? I will tell you the secret of the woman and

of the beast she rides, with the seven heads and the ten horns. The beast 8
you have seen is he who once was alive, and is alive no longer, but has yet
to ascend out of the abyss before going to perdition. Those on earth whose
names have not been inscribed in the roll of the living ever since the world
was made will all be astonished to see the beast; for he once was alive, and
is alive no longer, and has still to appear.

'But here is the clue for those who can interpret it. The seven heads are 9
seven hills on which the woman sits. They represent also seven kings,*a* of 10
whom five have already fallen, one is now reigning, and the other has yet
to come; and when he does come he is only to last for a little while. As for 11
the beast that once was alive and is alive no longer, he is an eighth—and
yet he is one of the seven, and he is going to perdition. The ten horns you 12
saw are ten kings who have not yet begun to reign, but who for one hour are
to share with the beast the exercise of royal authority; for they have but a 13
single purpose among them and will confer their power and authority upon
the beast. They will wage war upon the Lamb, but the Lamb will defeat 14
them, for he is Lord of lords and King of kings, and his victory will be
shared by his followers, called and chosen and faithful.'*b*

Then he said to me, 'The ocean you saw, where the great whore sat, is 15
an ocean of peoples and populations, nations and languages. As for the ten 16
horns you saw, they together with the beast will come to hate the whore;
they will strip her naked and leave her desolate, they will batten on her
flesh and burn her to ashes. For God has put it into their heads to carry out 17
his purpose, by making common cause and conferring their sovereignty
upon the beast until all that God has spoken is fulfilled. The woman you 18
saw is the great city that holds sway over the kings of the earth.'

After this I saw another angel coming down from heaven; he came with **18**
great authority and the earth was lit up with his splendour. Then in a 2
mighty voice he proclaimed, 'Fallen, fallen is Babylon the great! She has
become a dwelling for demons, a haunt for every unclean spirit, for every
vile and loathsome bird. For all nations have drunk deep of*c* the fierce 3
wine of her fornication; the kings of the earth have committed fornication
with her, and merchants the world over have grown rich on her bloated
wealth.'

Then I heard another voice from heaven that said: 'Come out of her, 4
my people, lest you take part in her sins and share in her plagues. For her 5
sins are piled high as heaven, and God has not forgotten her crimes. Pay 6
her back in her own coin, repay her twice over for her deeds! Double for
her the strength of the potion she mixed! Mete out grief and torment to 7
match her voluptuous pomp! She says in her heart, "I am a queen on my
throne! No mourning for me, no widow's weeds!" Because of this her 8
plagues shall strike her in a single day—pestilence, bereavement, famine,
and burning—for mighty is the Lord God who has pronounced her
doom!'

The kings of the earth who committed fornication with her and wallowed 9
in her luxury will weep and wail over her, as they see the smoke of her

---

a Or emperors.   *b* Or ... kings, and his followers are faithful men, called
and selected for service.   *c* *Other witnesses read* have been ruined by ...

10   conflagration. They will stand at a distance, for horror at her torment, and
will say, 'Alas, alas for the great city, the mighty city of Babylon! In a single
hour your doom has struck!'

11   The merchants of the earth also will weep and mourn for her, because
12   no one any longer buys their cargoes, cargoes of gold and silver, jewels
and pearls, cloths of purple and scarlet, silks and fine linens; all kinds of
scented woods, ivories, and every sort of thing made of costly woods,
13   bronze, iron, or marble; cinnamon and spice, incense, perfumes and
frankincense; wine, oil, flour and wheat, sheep and cattle, horses, chariots,
14   slaves, and the lives of men. 'The fruit you longed for', they will say, 'is
gone from you; all the glitter and the glamour are lost, never to be yours
15   again!' The traders in all these wares, who gained their wealth from her,
will stand at a distance for horror at her torment, weeping and mourning
16   and saying, 'Alas, alas for the great city, that was clothed in fine linen and
17   purple and scarlet, bedizened with gold and jewels and pearls! Alas that
in one hour so much wealth should be laid waste!'

        Then all the sea-captains and voyagers, the sailors and those who traded
18   by sea, stood at a distance and cried out as they saw the smoke of her con-
19   flagration: 'Was there ever a city like the great city?' They threw dust on
their heads, weeping and mourning and saying, 'Alas, alas for the great
city, where all who had ships at sea grew rich on her wealth! Alas that in a
single hour she should be laid waste!'

20   But let heaven exult over her; exult, apostles and prophets and people
of God; for in the judgement against her he has vindicated your cause!

21   Then a mighty angel took up a stone like a great millstone and hurled
it into the sea and said, 'Thus shall Babylon, the great city, be sent hurtling
22   down, never to be seen again! No more shall the sound of harpers and
minstrels, of flute-players and trumpeters, be heard in you; no more shall
craftsmen of any trade be found in you; no more shall the sound of the mill
23   be heard in you; no more shall the light of the lamp be seen in you; no
more shall the voice of the bride and bridegroom be heard in you! Your
traders were once the merchant princes of the world, and with your sorcery
you deceived all the nations.'

24   For the blood of the prophets and of God's people was found in her, the
blood of all who had been done to death on earth.

19   After this I heard what sounded like the roar of a vast throng in heaven;
and they were shouting:

2   'Alleluia! Victory and glory and power belong to our God, for true and
just are his judgements! He has condemned the great whore who corrupted the earth with her fornication, and has avenged upon her the
blood of his servants.'

3   Then once more they shouted:

        'Alleluia! The smoke goes up from her for ever and ever!'

4   And the twenty-four elders and the four living creatures fell down and
worshipped God as he sat on the throne, and they too cried:

        'Amen! Alleluia!'

Then a voice came from the throne which said: 'Praise our God, all you 5
his servants, you that fear him, both great and small!'

Again I heard what sounded like a vast crowd, like the noise of rushing 6
water and deep roars of thunder, and they cried:

'Alleluia! The Lord our God, sovereign over all, has entered on his
reign! Exult and shout for joy and do him homage, for the wedding-day 7
of the Lamb has come! His bride has made herself ready, and for her 8
dress she has been given fine linen, clean and shining.'

(Now the fine linen signifies the righteous deeds of God's people.)

Then the angel said to me, 'Write this: "Happy are those who are 9
invited to the wedding-supper of the Lamb!"' And he added, 'These are
the very words of God.' At this I fell at his feet to worship him. But he said 10
to me, 'No, not that! I am but a fellow-servant with you and your brothers
who bear their testimony to Jesus. It is God you must worship. Those who
bear testimony to Jesus are inspired like the prophets.' [a]

THEN I SAW heaven wide open, and there before me was a white horse; 11
and its rider's name was Faithful and True, for he is just in judgement and
just in war. His eyes flamed like fire, and on his head were many diadems. 12
Written upon him was a name known to none but himself, and he was 13
robed in a garment drenched in blood. [b] He was called the Word of God,
and the armies of heaven followed him on white horses, clothed in fine 14
linen, clean and shining. From his mouth there went a sharp sword with 15
which to smite the nations; for he it is who shall rule them with an iron
rod, and tread the winepress of the wrath and retribution of God the
sovereign Lord. And on his robe and on his thigh there was written the 16
name: 'King of kings and Lord of lords.'

Then I saw an angel standing in the sun, and he cried aloud to all the 17
birds flying in mid-heaven: 'Come and gather for God's great supper, to 18
eat the flesh of kings and commanders and fighting men, the flesh of horses
and their riders, the flesh of all men, slave and free, great and small!' Then 19
I saw the beast and the kings of the earth and their armies mustered to do
battle with the Rider and his army. The beast was taken prisoner, and so 20
was the false prophet who had worked miracles in its presence and deluded
those that had received the mark of the beast and worshipped its image.
The two of them were thrown alive into the lake of fire with its sulphurous
flames. The rest were killed by the sword which went out of the Rider's 21
mouth; and all the birds gorged themselves on their flesh.

Then I saw an angel coming down from heaven with the key of the abyss **20**
and a great chain in his hands. He seized the dragon, that serpent of old, 2
the Devil or Satan, and chained him up for a thousand years; he threw 3
him into the abyss, shutting and sealing it over him, so that he might seduce
the nations no more till the thousand years were over. After that he must
be let loose for a short while.

[a] *Or* . . . worship. For testimony to Jesus is the spirit that inspires prophets.
[b] *Some witnesses read* spattered with blood.

4 Then I saw thrones, and upon them sat those to whom judgement was committed. I could see the souls of those who had been beheaded for the sake of God's word and their testimony to Jesus, those who had not worshipped the beast and its image or received its mark on forehead or hand. These came to life again and reigned with Christ for a thousand years,
5 though the rest of the dead did not come to life until the thousand years
6 were over. This is the first resurrection. Happy indeed, and one of God's own people, is the man who shares in this first resurrection! Upon such the second death has no claim; but they shall be priests of God and of Christ, and shall reign with him for the thousand years.

7 When the thousand years are over, Satan will be let loose from his
8 dungeon; and he will come out to seduce the nations in the four quarters of the earth and to muster them for battle, yes, the hosts of Gog and Magog,
9 countless as the sands of the sea. So they marched over the breadth of the land and laid siege to the camp of God's people and the city that he loves.
10 But fire came down on them from heaven and consumed them; and the Devil, their seducer, was flung into the lake of fire and sulphur, where the beast and the false prophet had been flung, there to be tormented day and night for ever.

11 Then I saw a great white throne, and the One who sat upon it; from his presence earth and heaven vanished away, and no place was left for them.
12 I could see the dead, great and small, standing before the throne; and books were opened. Then another book was opened, the roll of the living. From what was written in these books the dead were judged upon the
13 record of their deeds. The sea gave up its dead, and Death and Hades gave up the dead in their keeping; they were judged, each man on the record of
14 his deeds. Then Death and Hades were flung into the lake of fire. This lake
15 of fire is the second death; and into it were flung any whose names were not to be found in the roll of the living.

21 THEN I SAW a new heaven and a new earth, for the first heaven and
2 the first earth had vanished, and there was no longer any sea. I saw the holy city, new Jerusalem, coming down out of heaven from God, made ready like
3 a bride adorned for her husband. I heard a loud voice proclaiming from the throne: 'Now at last God has his dwelling among men! He will dwell among them and they shall be his people, and God himself will be with them. *a*
4 He will wipe every tear from their eyes; there shall be an end to death, and to mourning and crying and pain; for the old order has passed away!'
5 Then he who sat on the throne said, 'Behold! I am making all things new!' (And he said to me, 'Write this down; for these words are trustworthy
6 and true. Indeed they are already fulfilled.') 'I am the Alpha and the Omega, the beginning and the end. A draught from the water-springs of life will be
7 my free gift to the thirsty. All this is the victor's heritage; and I will be his
8 God and he shall be my son. But as for the cowardly, the faithless, and the vile, murderers, fornicators, sorcerers, idolaters, and liars of every kind, their lot will be the second death, in the lake that burns with sulphurous flames.'

a Some witnesses read God-with-them shall himself be their God (*see Isaiah* 7. 14; 8. 8).

Then one of the seven angels that held the seven bowls full of the seven 9
last plagues came and spoke to me and said, 'Come, and I will show you the
bride, the wife of the Lamb.' So in the Spirit he carried me away to a great 10
high mountain, and showed me the holy city of Jerusalem coming down out
of heaven from God. It shone with the glory of God; it had the radiance 11
of some priceless jewel, like a jasper, clear as crystal. It had a great high 12
wall, with twelve gates, at which were twelve angels; and on the gates were
inscribed the names of the twelve tribes of Israel. There were three gates 13
to the east, three to the north, three to the south, and three to the west.
The city wall had twelve foundation-stones, and on them were the names 14
of the twelve apostles of the Lamb.

The angel who spoke with me carried a gold measuring-rod, to measure 15
the city, its wall, and its gates. The city was built as a square, and was as 16
wide as it was long. It measured by his rod twelve thousand furlongs, its
length and breadth and height being equal. Its wall was one hundred and 17
forty-four cubits high, that is, by human measurements, which the angel
was using. The wall was built of jasper, while the city itself was of pure gold, 18
bright as clear glass. The foundations of the city wall were adorned with 19
jewels of every kind, the first of the foundation-stones being jasper, the
second lapis lazuli, the third chalcedony, the fourth emerald, the fifth 20
sardonyx, the sixth cornelian, the seventh chrysolite, the eighth beryl,
the ninth topaz, the tenth chrysoprase, the eleventh turquoise, and the
twelfth amethyst. The twelve gates were twelve pearls, each gate being 21
made from a single pearl. The streets of the city were of pure gold, like
translucent glass.

I saw no temple in the city; for its temple was the sovereign Lord God 22
and the Lamb. And the city had no need of sun or moon to shine upon it; 23
for the glory of God gave it light, and its lamp was the Lamb. By its light 24
shall the nations walk, and the kings of the earth shall bring into it all their
splendour. The gates of the city shall never be shut by day—and there will 25
be no night. The wealth and splendour of the nations shall be brought into 26
it; but nothing unclean shall enter, nor anyone whose ways are false or 27
foul, but only those who are inscribed in the Lamb's roll of the living.

Then he showed me the river of the water of life, sparkling like crystal, **22**
flowing from the throne of God and of the Lamb down the middle of the 2
city's street. On either side of the river stood a tree of life, which yields
twelve crops of fruit, one for each month of the year; the leaves of the trees
serve for the healing of the nations. Every accursed thing shall disappear. 3
The throne of God and of the Lamb will be there, and his servants shall
worship him; they shall see him face to face, and bear his name on their 4
foreheads. There shall be no more night, nor will they need the light of 5
lamp or sun, for the Lord God will give them light; and they shall reign
for evermore.

THEN HE SAID to me, 'These words are trustworthy and true. The Lord 6
God who inspires the prophets has sent his angel to show his servants what
must shortly happen. And, remember, I am coming soon!' 7
Happy is the man who heeds the words of prophecy contained in this

8   book! It is I, John, who heard and saw these things. And when I had heard
    and seen them, I fell in worship at the feet of the angel who had shown
9   them to me. But he said to me, 'No, not that! I am but a fellow-servant
    with you and your brothers the prophets and those who heed the words of
10 this book. It is God you must worship.' Then he told me, 'Do not seal up
11 the words of prophecy in this book, for the hour of fulfilment is near. Mean-
    while, let the evil-doer go on doing evil and the filthy-minded wallow in his
    filth, but let the good man persevere in his goodness and the dedicated
    man be true to his dedication.'

12 'Yes, I am coming soon, and bringing my recompense with me, to
13 requite everyone according to his deeds! I am the Alpha and the Omega,
    the first and the last, the beginning and the end.'

14 Happy are those who wash their robes clean! They will have the right
15 to the tree of life and will enter by the gates of the city. Outside are dogs,
    sorcerers and fornicators, murderers and idolaters, and all who love and
    practise deceit.

16 'I, Jesus, have sent my angel to you with this testimony for the churches.
    I am the scion and offspring of David, the bright star of dawn.'

17 'Come!' say the Spirit and the bride.
    'Come!' let each hearer reply.
    Come forward, you who are thirsty; accept the water of life, a free gift
    to all who desire it.

18 For my part, I give this warning to everyone who is listening to the
    words of prophecy in this book: should anyone add to them, God will add
19 to him the plagues described in this book; should anyone take away from the
    words in this book of prophecy, God will take away from him his share in
    the tree of life and the Holy City, described in this book.

20 He who gives this testimony speaks: 'Yes, I am coming soon!'
    Amen. Come, Lord Jesus!

21 The grace of the Lord Jesus be with you all.*a*

   a Some witnesses read with all; *others read* with all God's people; *others read* with God's
   people; *some add* Amen.